For Lord Mackay of Clashfern,
from the authors, with many
thanks for his generous
assistance.

Alexander Layton

Stephen O'Malley

20 Nov. 1989.

European Civil Practice

AUSTRALIA AND NEW ZEALAND
The Law Book Company Ltd.
Sydney : Melbourne : Perth

CANADA AND U.S.A.
The Carswell Company Ltd.
Agincourt, Ontario

INDIA
N.M. Tripathi Private Ltd.
Bombay
and
Eastern Law House Private Ltd.
Calcutta and Delhi
M.P.P. House Bangalore

ISRAEL
Steimatzky's Agency Ltd.
Jerusalem : Tel Aviv : Haifa

PAKISTAN
Pakistan Law House,
Karachi

European Civil Practice

by

Stephen O'Malley, M.A.,

of the Inner Temple, Barrister,
Recorder of the Crown Court

and

Alexander Layton, M.A.,

of the Middle Temple, Barrister

London
Sweet & Maxwell
1989

Published in 1989 by
Sweet & Maxwell Limited of
South Quay Plaza, 183 Marsh Wall,
London E14
Computerset by Promenade Graphics
Cheltenham.

Printed and Bound in Great Britain by
Hartnolls Limited, Bodmin, Cornwall.

British Library Cataloguing in Publication Data

O'Malley, Stephen
European Civil Practice
1. European Community. Law
I. Title   II. Layton, Alexander
341'.094

ISBN 0–421–26290–7

Foreword

Stephen O'Malley first told me about this book when we met in Luxembourg when I was appearing as an advocate before the European Court of Justice. I am delighted now to accept the authors' invitation to contribute this foreword and to see the book in print.

This is an extremely important and useful book for practitioners both in England and Wales and elsewhere in Europe. Lawyers in this country are becoming more and more aware of the important international dimensions of their work.

This book will be an invaluable addition to the literature on this vital subject, and by their work too in preparing it, the authors have put the profession very much in their debt.

Mackay of Clashfern

Preface

The idea of writing this book first came to us in the late 1970s. At that time one of us, through the kindness of Mr. J. Th. Vermeulen, then Dean of the Bar of the Hague, had been able with others to establish an English barristers' practice in The Hague. Chambers in Brussels had followed. The other one of us had been active in the European Movement at the time of Britain's entry into the EEC and during the 1975 referendum, and had studied law as a post graduate in Munich and Strasbourg. We observed in most of our colleagues in England a lack of interest in European legal matters born, in part, of a lack of knowledge and a lack of an easy means to acquire knowledge. It seemed to us that there was a need for a practical text book for English lawyers which discussed the English legal system in a wider European context.

The Brussels Convention of 1968 on Jurisdiction and the Enforcement of Judgments in Civil and Commercial Matters, to which the United Kingdom had acceded in 1978, was the obvious vehicle for such a book. It struck us that by contrast with much of EEC law, which is concerned with more specialised matters, the 1968 Convention was of practical importance for the conduct of ordinary civil and commercial litigation. We watched the progress of the Civil Jurisdiction and Judgments Bill towards its enactment in 1982, while we attempted to equip ourselves for the task of writing the book. The long period which it eventually took to write the book was due partly to the time which the Contracting States took to ratify the 1978 Accession Convention. However, we must admit that it was due as well to the size of the task which we had set ourselves. In the event, publication of this book now is opportune, as it coincides with the impending completion of the internal market of the European Communities.

What has evolved is a book in three parts. The first part is designed to guide the ordinary English practitioner through the difficulties which may arise in proceedings in England and Wales which have a foreign, notably a European, element. In drawing together the many aspects of English practice and procedure and in considering them in the light of the Civil Jurisdiction and Judgments Act 1982, we have come to two important conclusions. First, it seems to us that the 1982 Act has fundamentally altered the basis of the civil jurisdiction of the English courts. In all cases covered by the Act, *whether or not the 1968 Convention applies,* jurisdiction is no longer based on the plaintiff being able to serve a writ on the defendant. Jurisdiction is now based on the rules set out in the Act and its Schedules, which have their origins in continental legal

vii

systems. Secondly, we noted that the 1968 Convention creates a single European area for jurisdictional purposes. We concluded that there was no reason in principle why the English courts should not, in cases to which the 1968 Convention applies, exercise an extended jurisdiction to make orders such as Mareva injunctions which affected assets outside the territorial limits of England and Wales. As it happened, in the summer of 1988, the Court of Appeal held that, even apart from the Convention, there were exceptional cases in which the court might grant a Mareva injunction with extraterritorial effect. We predict that as the English courts become more familiar with the 1968 Convention and with continental legal systems, such orders will become more commonplace.

The second part of the book is a commentary on the 1968 Convention and on the 1982 Act. In preparing it, we have constantly been aware that continental modes of legal thought often differ from our own. A purposive approach to interpretation and the absence of any doctrine of *forum non conveniens* or other general discretionary powers in matters of international jurisdiction, are, to an English lawyer, the two most striking differences. We have been much assisted by the several other major commentaries on the Convention published in Germany, France and elsewhere. As a text in the English language, we hope that this part of the book will make accessible to a wider readership the jurisprudence on the Convention as it has developed on the continent since 1973. We have sought to analyse the case law of the European Court of Justice in interpreting the Convention, and to draw on the decisions of national courts in other Contracting States, in a way that will be readily familiar to English lawyers. As European integration proceeds, English courts and practitioners will need to become increasingly familiar with continental legal concepts and procedures. The role of the European Court in ruling on the interpretation of the Convention will reinforce this process. At the time of writing, the Court of Appeal, in *The Atlantic Emperor*, has made the first English reference to the European Court for an interpretative ruling on the Convention.

The third part of the book contains comparative descriptions of the legal systems, the rules of jurisdiction, and the civil procedures of the various Contracting States to the 1968 Convention. It is intended as a starting point for lawyers familiar with one system of law and procedure who find themselves having to advise clients whose disputes are to be litigated in another Contracting State. It may help in narrowing the available options open to litigants who may choose in which of several jurisdictions to issue proceedings; it may assist in following the various steps which are being taken once proceedings have been issued elsewhere; and it may ease the task of identifying and understanding unfamiliar foreign legal documents.

It is not intended as a substitute for the expert advice of foreign lawyers. The comparative exercise which we have undertaken in this part of the book has proved exceptionally difficult, as anyone who has attempted it will know. We had not only to ask the right questions, but we had also to try to understand the answers without being falsely influenced by comparisons with our own legal system. We have tried to convey our understanding without lapsing into potentially misleading legal jargon. Others will judge how successful we have been. We are very grateful to our national contributors for their painstaking efforts and their very substantial patience, as we acknowledge below.

We will welcome all criticism, in the hope that we may improve the form and content of the book in the future.

S. O'M.
A. L.

The Temple,
June 1989

The law in Part I and the case law of the European Court of Justice in Part II is stated as at April 1, 1989; the decisions of national courts of other Contracting States are as reported in the English language version of the Digest of Case Law of the European Communities (Part D) and various other published sources as at January 1, 1989; the law in Part III is stated as at June 1, 1989. In each case, we have been able to include some later updating material.

While we have made every effort to ensure the accuracy of the law stated in this book, errors and omissions are bound to have occurred and it seems necessary to say that we can accept no responsibility for the consequences of reliance on any statements contained herein.

Contents

PART 1 Proceedings in England and Wales

PART 2 The 1968 Convention on Jurisdiction and Judgments and the Civil Jurisdiction and Judgments Act 1982

Contents

Contents

Acknowledgments

Many people have given us assistance or support or encouragement in the years which it has taken to write this book. We wish to express our gratitude to them, even though it is not possible to mention them all. Our foremost thanks are due to our families and our closest friends for their support and their patience; they know the extent of our gratitude. Our special thanks are also due to our national contributors, whose names also appear at the start of Chapters 48 to 58, to those others who have also helped us understand the legal systems of other European countries, and to those who have helped us with research, with encouragement, and with practical assistance: Ferdinando Albinese (Strasbourg), Monya Anyadike-Danes, Master John Bickford-Smith, John Bosnak (Arnhem), Elisabeth Brand (Strasbourg), Geoffrey Brice Q.C., Hugo Callens (Antwerp), Michael Carpenter, Yannis Chrysospathis (Athens), Michael Collon, Andrew Colvin (Paris), Martin Cook, Robin Cooper, Andrew Donaldson Q.C. (Belfast), Adair Dyer (The Hague), Ulrich Feldman (Köln), Harry Ferment (The Hague), Thomas Försterling (Düsseldorf), Nicholas Forwood Q.C. (Brussels), Leslie Galsworthy, Lynette Gill, Avery Glize-Kane (Cannes), John Gold, Guy Harles (Luxembourg), Thea Walch (Luxembourg), Emmanuel Hayaux du Tilly (Paris), Carsten Iversen (Copenhagen), Thomas Jestaedt (Munich), John Kahlke (Copenhagen), Alfred Kellerman (The Hague), Sabine Kolkmann, Christian Kohler (European Court of Justice), Professor Jean Laemens (Antwerp), Shelley Lane, Professor Paul Lemmens (Leuven), Hartmut Linke (Hamm), Petria McDonnell (Dublin), Anthony McLellan (European Commission), Paul and Parvin Mahoney (Strasbourg), Rolf Meurs-Gerken (Copenhagen), Stewart Newcombe (Lyon), Karl Newman, Clemens van Nispen tot Sevenaer (The Hague), Dermod O'Brien Q.C. (Askerswell), Prof. Allan Philip (Copenhagen), Nicoletta Portalupi (Milan), Randi Bach Poulson (Copenhagen), Etienne Rocher (Paris), Elizabeth Rylands, Walter Semple (Glasgow), Richard and Anne Swetenham (Luxembourg), Harry Tebbens (European Court of Justice), Master Keith Topley, Volker Triebel (Düsseldorf), Paul Verguts (Antwerp), J. Th. Vermeulen (The Hague), Master Ian Warren, Reinhard Welter (Mainz), Richard White, and Christopher Willans.

We would like also to thank those at Sweet and Maxwell who gave us the opportunity to write the book in the first place, whom we forced to give the concept of "deadline" a wholly new dimension of flexibility, and who have patiently helped to bring the book to

Acknowledgments

fruition. Our thanks are also due to Jenny Bough, for her work in preparing the index.

We wish to make special acknowledgment of our thanks to Lord Mackay of Clashfern who, as Lord Advocate, encouraged us in this venture some years ago and who now, as Lord Chancellor, has kindly contributed the foreword.

S. O'M.
A. L.

Bibliography

Aalders, C.A.V. et al.	Branches and Subsidiaries in the European Common Market (2nd ed., 1976)
Anton, A.E.	Civil Jurisdiction in Scotland (1984); with supplement (1987)
Anton, A.E.	Private International Law (1967)
Bennion, F.	Statutory Interpretation
Black, R.	Civil Jurisdiction: The New Rules (1983)
Borrie, G., Lowe N.	The Law of Contempt (1973)
Brown, L.N., Garner, J.F.	French Administrative Law (3rd ed., 1973)
Bülow, A. and Böckstiegel, K.-H.	*Der Internationaler Rechtsverkehr in Zivil– und Handelssachen*
Buzzard, J. H., May, R., Howard, M. N. (ed.)	Phipson on Evidence (13th ed., 1982)
Cappelletti, M. (ed.)	International Encyclopaedia of Comparative Law, vol. XVI: Civil Procedure
Cappelletti M., Perillo, J.M.	Civil Procedure in Italy (1965)
Cohn, E.J. (ed.)	Manual of German Law (2nd ed., 1971)
College of Law	Jurisdiction and Enforcement of Judgments in Europe (1985)
Collins, L.	The Civil Jurisdiction and Judgments Act 1982 (1983)
Collins L. (ed.)	Dicey and Morris on the Conflict of Laws (11th ed., 1987)
Commonwealth Secretariat	The Hague Conventions on the Service of Process, the Taking of Evidence and Legalisation—Explanatory Documentation (2nd ed.)
Council of Europe	The Practical Guide to the Recognition and Enforcement of foreign judicial decisions in civil and commercial law (1975)
Council of Europe	Judicial Organisation in Europe (1975)
Council of Europe	Replies made by Governments to the Questionnaire on Legal Aid and Advice (1978)
Cross, Sir R.	Cross on Evidence (6th ed. 1985)

Dashwood, A., Halcon, R.J., White, R.C.A.	A Guide to the Civil Jurisdiction and Judgments Convention (1987)
David, R.	English Law and French Law (1980)
David, R., Brierley, J.E.C.	Major Legal Systems in the World Today (3rd ed. 1985)
David R., de Vries, H.P.	The French Legal System (1958)
Denza, E.	Diplomatic Law (1976)
Dickson, B.	The Legal System in Northern Ireland (1984)
Droz, G.A.L.	*Compétence Judiciaire et Effets des Jugements dans le Marché Commun* (1972)
Droz, G. A. L.	*Pratique de la Convention de Bruxelles du 27 Septembre 1968* (1973)
Ehrenzweig, A. A., Jayme, E.	Private International Law (1973)
Engelmann, A., et al. (Millar, R.W., transl.)	A History of Continental Civil Procedure (1927)
Gee, S.M.A., Andrews, G. M.	Mareva Injunctions (1987)
Geimer, R., Schütze, R.A.	*Internationale Urteilsannerkennung (Band I, 1. Halbband: Das EWG-Übereinkommen über die gerichtliche Zuständigkeit und die Vollstreckung gerichtlicher Entscheidungen in Zivil und Handelssachen)* (1983)
Giuliano, M., Lagarde, P.	Report on the Convention on the Law Applicable to Contractual Obligations (1980)
Goff of Chieveley, Lord, Jones, G.	The Law of Restitution (3rd ed. 1986)
Goldrein, P., Wilkinson, K. H. P.,	Commercial Litigation: Pre-emptive Remedies (1987)
Gothot, P., Holleaux, D.	*La Convention de Bruxelles du 27.9.1968* (1985)
Graulich, P., Guillitte, P., et al.	Guide to Foreign Legal Materials: Belgium, Luxembourg, Netherlands (1968)
Grimes, R., Horgan P.	Introduction to Law in the Republic of Ireland (1981)
Gutteridge, H.C.	Comparative Law (2nd ed. 1949)
Guy, D., Leigh, G.	The EEC and Intellectual Property (1981)
Hague Conference on Private International Law	Practical Handbook on the Operation of The Hague Convention of 15 November 1965 on the Service Abroad

	of Judicial and Extra Judicial Documents in Civil or Commercial Matters (1983); with updating supplements
Hague Conference on Private International Law	Practical Handbook on the Operation of the Hague Convention of 18 March 1970 on the Taking of Evidence Abroad in Civil or Commercial Matters (1984); with updating supplements
Hague Conference on Private International Law	*Actes et Documents de la dixième session* (1964)
Hague Conference on Private International Law	*Actes et Documents de la onzième session* (1968)
Hague Conference on Private International Law	Acts and Documents of the fourteenth session
Hartley, T.C.	Civil Jurisdiction and Judgments (1984)
Hinton, H.	Evidence and Service Abroad (1930)
Holdsworth, Sir W. S.	History of English Law (1903-72)
Horn, N., Kötz, H., Leser, H.G. (Weir, A., transl.)	German Private and Commercial Law: An Introduction (1982)
House of Lords Select Committee on the European Communities	International Access to Justice (Session 1987–88, Second Report)
Hoyle, M.	The Mareva Injunction 'and Related Orders (1985)
Ivamy, E.R.H.	General Principles of Insurance Law (5th ed. 1986)
Jackson, D.	Civil Jurisdiction and Judgments—Maritime Claims (1987)
Jackson, J., Davies, D. J. A.	Matrimonial Finance and Taxation (4th ed. 1986)
Jacob, Sir J.I.H.	Chitty and Jacob's Queen's Bench Forms (21st ed., 1986); with supplement (1988)
Jacob, Sir J.I.H.	The Reform of Civil Procedural Law (1982)
Jacob, Sir J.I.H. (ed.)	Bullen & Leake & Jacob's Precedents of Pleading (12th ed. 1975)
Jacob, Sir J.I.H. (ed.)	Private International Litigation (1988)
Jacobs, F.G., Roberts, S. (ed.)	The Effect of Treaties in Domestic Law (1987)
Jenard, P.	Report on the Convention on jurisdiction and the enforcement of judgments in civil and commercial matters (1979)

Jenard, P. — Report on the Protocols on the interpretation by the Court of Justice of the Convention of 29 February 1968 on the mutual recognition of companies and legal persons and of the Convention of 27 September 1968 on jurisdiction and the enforcement of judgments in civil and commercial matters (1979)

Kahn-Freund, Sir O., Lévy, C., Rudden, B. — A Source-book on French Law (1979)

Kaye, P. — Civil Jurisdiction and Enforcement of Foreign Judgments (1987)

Kerr, W.W. — The Law and Practice as to Receivers and Administrators (16th ed., 1983)

Kropholler, J. — *Europäisches Zivilprozessrecht* (2nd ed., 1987)

Lasok, D., Stone, P.A. — Conflict of Laws in the European Community (1987)

Lasok, K.P.E. — The European Court of Justice: Practice and Procedure (1984)

Law Commission — Classification of Limitation in Private International Law (Working Paper No. 75, 1980)

Legal Aid Board — Legal Aid Handbook 1989 (1989)

Lewis, C. — State and Diplomatic Immunity (2nd ed., 1985)

McNair, Lord, Watts, A. D. — Legal Effects of War (4th ed.)

Mann, F.A. — Foreign Affairs in English Courts (1986)

Markesinis, B.S. — The German Law of Torts (1986)

Maxwell, Lord — Report of the Scottish Committee on Jurisdiction and Enforcement (1980)

Morris, J.H.C. — The Conflict of Laws (2nd ed., 1980)

Mustill, M., Boyd, S. — Commercial Arbitration (2nd ed., 1989)

Nadelmann, K. H. — Conflict of Laws: International and Interstate (1972)

National Association of Credit Management — Digest of Commercial Laws of the World

Nedjatigil, Z.M., Trice, J.E. — English and Continental Systems of Administrative Law (1978)

North, P.M. — Cheshire and North's Private International Law (11th ed., 1987)

North, P.M. (ed.) — Contract Conflicts (1982)

Patchett, K.W. — Recognition of Commercial Judgments

and Awards in the Commonwealth (1984)

Philip, A.   *Værneting—Tvangsfuldbyrdelse af fremmede retsafgørelser* (1986)

Picarda, H. A. P.   The Law Relating to Receivers and Managers (1984)

Picard-Besson   *Les Assurances Terrestres en Droit Français* (3rd ed., 1972)

Piggott, F.T.   Service out of the Jurisdiction (1892)

Pocar, F.   *Codice delle Convenzioni sulla Giurisdizione e L'Esecuzione delle Sentenze Straniere nella C.E.E.* (1980); with supplement (1983)

Rabel, E.   The Conflict of Laws: A Comparative Study (2nd ed., 1960)

Read, H.E.   Recognition and Enforcement of Foreign Judgments in the Common Law Units of the British Commonwealth (1938)

Ready, N.P.   Brooke's Treatise on the office of a notary in England (10th ed.)

Robinson, O.F., Fergus, T.D., Gordon, W.M.   An Introduction to European Legal History (1985)

Schlesinger, R.B.   Comparative Law (4th ed. 1980)

Schlosser, P.   Report on the Convention on the Association of the Kingdom of Denmark, Ireland and the United Kingdom of Great Britain and Northern Ireland to the Convention on jurisdiction and the enforcement of judgments in civil and commercial matters and to the protocol on its interpretation by the Court of Justice (1979)

Schmitthof, C. (ed.)   The Harmonisation of European Company Law (1973)

Schiut, S.R., van der Beek, J.M., Raap, B.K.   Dutch Business Law (1979)

Sinclair, Sir I.   The Vienna Convention on the Law of Treaties (2nd ed., 1986)

Smit, H. (ed.)   International Co-operation in Litigation: Europe (1965)

Spencer Bower, G., Turner, Sir A.K.   The Doctrine of Res Judicata (2nd ed., 1969)

Spry, I. C. F.   Principles of Equitable Remedies (3rd. ed. 1984.)

Steiner, H. J., Vaghts, D. F.   Transnational Legal Problems (2nd ed., 1976)

Strobl, Killius & Vobrugg   Business Law Guide to Germany (1986)

Summerskill, M. B.   Oil Rigs: Law and insurance (1979)

Tidd, W.   Practice of the Courts of King's Bench (2nd ed., 1824)

Thomas, D.   Maritime Liens (1980)

Trott, R.W.   Germany: Practical Legal Guide (1977)

Usher, J.   European Court Practice (1983)

Walker, D.M.   The Scottish Legal System, an Introduction (5th ed., 1981)

Welter, R.   *Zwangsvollstreckung und Arrest in Forderungen—insbesondere Kontenpfändung—in Fällen mit Auslandsberührung* (1988)

Weser, M.   *Convention communautaire sur la compétence judiciaire et l'éxécution des décisions* (1975)

Zweigert, K., Kötz, H. (Weir, A., transl.)   An Introduction to Comparative Law (2nd ed, 1987)

List of books referred to by
author alone

Anton

Civil Jurisdiction in Scotland (1984), by A. E. Anton; with supplement (1987)

Bülow/Böckstiegel

Erläuterungen zu dem Übereinkommen über die gerichtiliche Zuständigkeit und die Vollstreckung gerichtilicher Entscheidungen in Zivil- und Handelssachen (1977) by Arthur Bülow and Karl-Heinz Böckstiegel, in collaboration with Hartmut Linke, Gerd Müller and Dieter Schlafen, in *Der Internationaler Rechtsverkehr in Zivil- und Handelssachen*

Cheshire and North

Private International Law (11th ed., 1987)

Chitty and Jacob

Queen's Bench Forms (21st ed., 1986); with supplement (1988)

Collins

The Civil Jurisdiction and Judgments Act 1982 (1983), by Lawrence Collins

Court Forms

Atkin's Encyclopaedia of Court Forms in Civil Proceedings (2nd ed.)

Dashwood/Halcon/White

A Guide to the Civil Jurisdiction and Judgments Convention (1987), by Alan Dashwood, Richard J. Halcon and Robin C. A. White

Dicey and Morris

The Conflict of Laws (11th ed., 1987)

Droz

Compétence Judiciaire et Effets des Jugements dans le Marché Commun (1972), by Georges A. L. Droz

Geimer/Schütze

Internationale Urteilsannerkennung (Band I, 1. Halbband: Das EWG-Übereinkommen über die gerichtliche Zuständigkeit und die Vollstreckung gerichtlicher Entschidungen in Zivil- und Handelssachen) (1983), by Reinhold Gemier anf Rolf A. Schütze

Gothot/Holleaux

La Convention de Bruxelles du 27.9.1968 (1985), by Pierre Gothot and Dominique Holleaux

Halsbury's Laws

Halsbury's Laws of England (4th ed.)

xxiii

Halsbury's Statutes	Halsbury's Statutes (4th ed.)
Hartley	Civil Jurisdiction and Judgments (1984), by T. C. Hartley
Jenard	Report on the Convention on jurisdiction and the enforcement of judgments in civil and commercial matters, by P. Jenard, (1979) O.J. No. C59/1 (see paras. A1.01 *et seq.* below)
Jenard (Protocols)	Report on the Protocols on the interpretation by the Court of Justice of the Convention of 29 February 1968 on the mutual recognition of companies and legal persons and of the Convention of 27 September 1968 on jurisdiction and the enforcement of judgments in civil and commercial matters, by P. Jenard, (1979) O.J. No. C59/66 (see paras. A1.269 *et seq.* below)
Kaye	Civil Jurisdiction and Enforcement of Foreign Judgments (1987), by Peter Kaye
Kropholler	*Europäisches Zivilprozessrecht* (2nd ed., 1987)
Maxwell	Report of the Scottish Committee on Jurisdiction and Enforcement (H.M.S.O., 1980)
Pocar	*Codice delle Convenzioni sulla Giurisdizione e L'Esecuzione delle Sentenze Straniere nella C.E.E.* (1980), by Fausto Pocar; with supplement (1983)
Schlosser	Report on the Convention on the Association of the Kingdom of Denmark, Ireland and the United Kingdom of Great Britain and Northern Ireland to the Convention on jurisdiction and the enforcement of judgments in civil and commercial matters and to the protocol on its interpretation by the Court of Justice, by Peter Schlosser, (1979) O.J. No. C.59/71 (see paras. A1.287 *et seq.* below)
Weser	*Convention communautaire sur la compétence judiciaire et l'exécution des décisions* (1975), by Martha Weser

Table of Abbreviations

Cox C.C.	Cox's Criminal Cases (Criminal Cases Series)
D.L.R.	Dominion Law Reports
De G.F. & J.	De Gex, Fisher & Jones, temp. Campbell (Chancery Series)
De G. & Sm.	De Gex & Smale, temp. Knight-Bruce & Parker (Vice-Chancellor's Court Series)
Dick	Dickens (Chancery Series)
Dir.com.scambiint.	Il diritto comunitario e degli scambi internazionali
Dir.Mar.	Il diritto marittimo
Doug.	Douglas (King's Bench Series)
Dow & Ry.N.P.	Dowling & Ryland (Nisi Prius Series)
Dr. & Sm.	Drewry & Smale (Vice-Chancellor's Court Series)
E.B. & E.	Ellis, Blackburn & Ellis (Queen's Bench Series)
E.C.C.	European Commercial Cases
E.C.R.	European Court Reports
E.F.T.A.	European Free Trade Association
E.L.Rev.	European Law Review
Ent.BGH	Ent scheidungen der Bundesgerichtshofes
Eur.L.Dig.	European Law Digest
F.L.R.	Family Law Reports
F.L.R.	Financial Law Reports
F.S.R.	Fleet Street Reports
Fam.	Family Division (Law Reports Third Series)
Foro it.	Il foro italiano
Foro.pad	Il foro padano
Gaz.Palais	Gazette du Palais
Giff.	Giffard (Vice-Chancellor's Court Series)
Giur.it.	Giurisprudenza italiana
Giust.Civ.	Giustizia civile
H.Bl.	H. Blackstone (Common Pleas series)
H.L.Cas.	House of Lords Cases
H.L.Deb.	House of Lords Debates

H. & N.	Hurlstone & Norman (Exchequer Series)
I.C.L.Q.	International and Comparative Law Quarterly
I.C.R.	Industrial Cases Reports
I.Prax	Praxis des Internationalen Privat-und Verfahrensrechts
I.P.Rspr.	Die deutsche Rechtsprechung auf dem Gebiete des Internationalen Priva-trechts
J.P.L.	Journal of Planning and Environment Law
Journal dr.int.	Journal du droit international
Journal trib.	Journal des tribunaux
Jur.	Jurist Reports
Jur.comm.Belg.	Jurisprudence commerciale de Belgique
Jur.N.S.	Jurist Reports, New Series
Jur.Port Anvers	Jurisprudence du Port d'Anvers
K.B.	King's Bench (Law Reports Third Series)
Keb.	Keble (King's Bench Series)
L.G.R.	Local Government Reports
L.J.C.P.	Law Journal Reports (New Series) Common Pleas
L.J.Ch.	Law Journal Reports (New Series) Chancery
L.J.P.	Law Journal Reports (New Series) Probate, Divorce and Admiralty
L.J.Q.B.	Law Journal Reports (New Series) Queen's Bench
L.M.C.L.Q.	Lloyd's Maritime and Commercial Law Quarterly
L.R.Eq.	Equity Cases (Law Reports First Series)
L.R.H.L.	English and Irish Appeals, House of Lords (Law Reports First Series)
L.R.P.D.	Probate Division (Law Reports Second Series)
L.R.Q.B.	Queen's Bench (Law Reports First Series)
L.S.Gaz.	Law Society's Gazette

Table of Abbreviations

L.T.	Law Times Reports
L.T.O.S.	Law Times, Old Series
Ld.Raym.	Lord Raymond (King's Bench Series)
Lev.	Levinz (King's Bench Series)
Ll.L.R.	Lloyd's List Law Reports (1919–1950)
Lloyd's Rep.	Lloyd's List Law Reports (1951–date)
M.C.R.	Matrimonial Causes Rules 1977
M. & W.	Meeson & Welsby (Exchequer Series)
Madd.	Maddock (Vice-Chancellor's Court Series)
Mans.	Manson's Bankruptcy and Company Cases 1893–1914
Mar. L.C.	Maritime Law Cases
Mod.L.R.	Modern Law Review
Moo.P.C.	Moore, E.F. (Privy Council Series)
N.J.W.	Neue Juristische Wochenschrift
N.L.J.	New Law Journal
Ned.Jur.	Nederlandse Jurisprudentie
O.J.	Official Journal (of the European Communities)
P.	Probate Division (Law Reports Third Series)
P.C.	Privy Council
P.D.	Probate Division (Law Reports Second Series)
Pas.Lux.	Pasicrisie Luxembourgeoise
Q.B.	Queen's Bench (Law Reports Third Series)
R.	The Reports, 1893–1895
R. & I.T.	Rating and Income Tax
R.I.W.	Recht der Internationalen Wirschaft
R.P.C.	Reports of Patent Cases
R.S.C.	Rules of the Supreme Court
R.T.R.	Road Traffic Reports
Rev.critique	Revue critique de droit international privé
Rev.soc.	Revue des societés-Journal des societés
Riv.dir.int.priv.proc.	Rivista di diritto internazionale privato e processuale

xxviii

S.I.	Statutory Instrument
S.J.	Solicitors' Journal
S.R. & O.	Statutory Rules and Orders
S.T.C.	Simon's Tax Cases
Sem.jur.(Ed.Gén)	La semaine juridique—Juris-Classeur Périodique (Edition Générale)
Show.	Shower (King's Bench Series)
Sid.	Siderfin (King's Bench Series)
Sol.Jo.	Solicitors' Journal
Somm.	Sommaires
Stark.	Starkie (Nisi Prius Series)
Str.	Strange J. (King's Bench Series)
T.C.	Tax Cases
T.L.R.	Times Law Reports
T.R.	Taxation Reports
T.R.	Term Reports (King's Bench Series)
Term Rep.	Term Reports (King's Bench Series)
V.-C.	Vice-Chancellor (Chancery Series)
Vent.	Ventris (King's Bench Series)
Vern.	Vernon (Chancery Series)
Ves.	Vesey Junior (Chancery Series)
Ves.Sen	Vesey Senior (Chancery Series)
W.L.R.	Weekly Law Reports
W.N.	Weekly Notes (Reports)
W.R.	Weekly Reporter
W.W.R.	Western Weekly Reports
Yb.Eur.Law	Yearbook of European Law

Table of Cases: United Kingdom

xliii

Table of Cases: European Court of Justice

Numerical order

Alphabetical order

Table of Foreign Cases

Belgium

Table of Foreign Cases

Table of Foreign Cases

lxvii

Germany (date order)

Table of Foreign Cases

Italy

Table of Foreign Cases

Table of Foreign Cases

Table of Foreign Cases

Table of Foreign Cases

Table of Foreign Cases

Luxembourg

Table of Foreign Cases

United States of America

Central Commission for the Navigation of the Rhine

Table of Statutes

Table of Statutory Instruments

Table of Statutory Instruments

Rules of the Supreme Court

County Court Rules
(S.I. 1981 No. 1687)

Table of Foreign Legislation

Table of Principle Conventions

Table of Principle Conventions

Table of Principle Conventions

Table of International Treaties and Conventions

Table of International Treaties and Conventions

Table of International Treaties and Conventions

Table of International Treaties and Conventions

Table of Official Reports on the Conventions

Table of Official Reports on the Conventions

PART 1

Proceedings in England and Wales

PART 1 deals with various aspects of procedure and practice as they apply to private international litigation in the English courts in the light of the 1968 Convention on Jurisdiction and the Enforcement of Judgments and the Civil Jurisdiction and Judgments Act 1982.

Chapter 1 deals with the jurisdiction of the English courts, and in particular with territorial and adjudicatory jurisdiction, with the allocation of jurisdiction internationally, within the United Kingdom and locally, with jurisdiction *in personam* and *in rem*, with the role of discretion in the exercise of jurisdiction and with the extra-territorial effects of the exercise of jurisdiction by the English courts.

Chapter 2 deals with the capacity to sue and be sued of various kinds of parties, and with parties' immunities from suit.

Chapter 3 deals with the commencement of proceedings, and in particular with the basis on which jurisdiction may be exercised under the 1968 Convention and the 1982 Act, with choice of venue and with the preparation and issue of proceedings.

Chapter 4 deals with the service of process both within and outside the jurisdiction and examines the various international conventions which govern the service of English process in other European countries.

Chapter 5 deals with challenges to the assumption or exercise of jurisdiction by the English courts or to the regularity of service of their process.

Chapter 6 deals with security for costs.

Chapter 7 deals with interim relief, including Mareva injunctions and Anton Piller orders, both in English proceedings and in aid of proceedings in other countries.

Chapter 8 deals with evidence (and in particular with those aspects of English law and practice most likely to arise in litigation containing international elements), with the various international conventions which govern the taking of evidence in other European countries and with the taking of evidence in England for use in proceedings abroad.

Chapter 9 deals with the proof of foreign law in English proceedings.

1

Chapter 10 deals with the recognition and enforcement of judgments in England and Wales, especially under the 1968 Convention and the 1982 Act, with the bases on which the recognition or enforcement of such judgments may be disputed, with the enforcement of foreign non-money judgments, with protective measures in aid of execution, with methods of execution and with the enforcement of judgments as between the different parts of the United Kingdom.

Chapter 11 deals with maintenance orders, in particular with the jurisdictional effects of the 1968 Convention and the 1982 Act, with recognition and enforcement under the 1982 Act and under other schemes, and with the enforcement abroad of English maintenance orders.

Chapter 12 deals with legal aid.

THE JURISDICTION OF THE ENGLISH COURTS

A. INTRODUCTION

An examination of what is meant by jurisdiction is the necessary **1.01** starting point for a book on the practice of civil and commercial litigation in Europe. The aim of this chapter is to consider what is meant by the term jurisdiction, the circumstances in which English courts are required to accept or decline jurisdiction and, where they have a discretion, the basis on which they exercise it.

At the outset, it must be stressed that the Civil Jurisdiction and Judgments Act 1982 has brought about fundamental changes to the basis upon which courts in the United Kingdom exercise jurisdiction in civil and commercial matters.[1] These changes take effect at three levels. First at the level of international jurisdiction,[1a] the Act incorporates into the law of the United Kingdom the 1968 Brussels Convention on Jurisdiction and Enforcement of Judgments in Civil and Commercial Matters, as amended by the Accession Convention

---

[1] The meaning of the term "civil and commercial" is discussed at paras. 1.09 and 14.08 *et seq.* below.

[1a] The term "international jurisdiction" is described at para. 1.05 below.

of 1978. Together with their associated Protocols, these conventions are referred to compendiously in this book as the 1968 Convention. The 1968 Convention lays down a set of unified rules which regulate the international jurisdiction, and sometimes the local jurisdiction,[2] of the courts of the Contracting States[3] in cases to which the Convention applies. Secondly, the 1982 Act adopts these rules, with minor modifications, so as to allocate jurisdiction as between the three law areas of the United Kingdom, that is to say, England and Wales, Scotland and Northern Ireland.[4] Thirdly, the Act provides the basis of jurisdiction in each of the three parts of the United Kingdom, in a very large number of ordinary civil and commercial cases, even though they may be entirely internal to that part of the United Kingdom.[5]

When jurisdiction is determined in accordance with the Convention or the Act, it may still be necessary to refer to one or more aspects of English law which lie beyond the boundaries of those schemes.[6] In cases to which the Act and the Convention do not apply, the jurisdiction of the English courts continues to be founded in much the same manner as before the Act came into effect.[7]

B. TERMINOLOGY

1. The meaning of "jurisdiction"

1.02   The word "jurisdiction" is used in relation to courts in a number of different senses.[8] It may mean the geographical area within which the courts of a given legal system primarily exert their authority. The word is commonly used in this sense in the Rules of the

---

[2] The term "local jurisdiction" is described at para. 3.19 below.
[3] The Contracting States are Belgium, Denmark, France, the Federal Republic of Germany, Ireland, Italy, Luxembourg, Netherlands and the U.K.; see para. 13.01 below.
[4] s.16 and Sched. 4: see para. 1.23 below. The Act also provides that matters of local jurisdiction within Scotland are to be determined in accordance with rules which follow the scheme of the 1968 Convention: s.20 and Sched. 8.
[5] The proposition that the Act has this third effect is discussed at para. 1.24 below.
[6] *e.g.* the requirement that the jurisdiction of the court must be properly invoked by due service on the defendant is discussed at para. 1.15 below.
[7] See paras. 1.25 *et seq.* below.
[8] Gutteridge, "Le Conflit des Lois de Compétence judiciaire dans les Actions personnelles" (1933) 44 Hague Recueil 125; Mann, "The Doctrine of Jurisdiction in International Law" (1964) 1 Hague Recueil 9; Smit, "The terms jurisdiction and competence in comparative law" (1961) 10 Am.Jo.Comp.L. 164; Steiner, *Transnational Legal Problems*, p. 729 *et seq.*; Pryles, "The basis of adjudicatory competence in Private International Law" (1972) 21 I.C.L.Q. 61; Ehrensweig and Jayme, *Private International Law* (1973) vol. 2, p. 5.

Supreme Court, in particular in Order 11.[9] The geographical extent of the territorial jurisdiction of the English courts is discussed below.[10] The word "jurisdiction" may also be used to refer to the powers of a court,[11] either generally,[12] or in the context of some specific power,[13] or by reference to some particular factor such as the subject-matter of the claim,[14] or its value, or the person over whom the powers are exercised.[15] Specifically, the term "jurisdiction" may be used to mean the power or ability of a court to adjudicate in any particular matter.[16] Its use in this sense is equivalent to the French "*compétence*," the Italian "*competenza*," and the German "*Zuständigkeit*"; the terms "adjudicatory jurisdiction," or "competence" are sometimes used to distinguish this meaning of the word.

The "jurisdiction" in the geographical sense. In the geographical sense **1.03** the limits of the jurisdiction of the English courts, known as the territorial limits, extend to England and Wales,[17] and the territorial waters[18]

---

[9] For example, " . . . service of a writ out of the jurisdiction is permissible with the leave of the Court . . . ": R.S.C. Ord. 11, r. 1(1); see *Supreme Court Practice* para. 11/1/4.

[10] Paras. 1.03 *et seq.*

[11] See *Guaranty Trust Company of New York* v. *Hannay & Co.* [1915] 2 K.B. 536, at p. 563; *Garthwaite* v. *Garthwaite* [1964] P. 365, at p. 387.

[12] As in "court of summary jurisdiction."

[13] For example, " . . . the Court has an inherent jurisdiction to stay all proceedings before it which are obviously frivolous . . . ": *Supreme Court Practice*, para. 18/19/18.

[14] "Admiralty jurisdiction"; "Divorce jurisdiction," etc. See n. 24 below.

[15] "The Court has no jurisdiction inherent or otherwise over any person other than those properly brought before it . . . ": *Brydges* v. *Brydges and Wood* [1909] P. 187; see *Supreme Court Practice*, para. [4605].

[16] *Re Smith* (1876) L.R. 1 P.D. 300; *The Fagernes* [1926] P. 185; [1927] P. 311 C.A.; *Anisminic Ltd.* v. *Foreign Compensation Commission* [1969] 2 A.C. 47, where the problem of terminology is discussed.

[17] Under the Wales and Berwick Act 1746, s.3, "England" included Wales and Berwick-on-Tweed; see also *R.* v. *Cowle* (1759) 2 Burr 834; but by the Welsh Language Act 1967, s.4, in future Acts "England" does not include Wales. By the Interpretation Act 1978, ss.5 and 22(1), Scheds. 1 and 2, "England" means the area consisting of the counties established by s.1 of the Local Government Act 1972, Greater London, and the Isles of Scilly.

[18] Territorial Sea Act 1987, s.1. By a legal fiction, ships of the Royal Navy are deemed to be in the parish of Stepney, in London, and in consequence they are treated as being within the jurisdiciton of the High Court whether they are on the high seas or in a foreign port, see *Seagrove* v. *Parkes* [1891] 1 Q.B. 551. Oil rigs are generally treated as if they were ships, unless they are in defined areas of the continental shelf, see Summerskill, *Oil Rigs: Law and Insurance.* For civil jurisdiction over activities on oil rigs and similar installations, or connected with the exploration or exploitation of the sea bed, in defined areas of the continental shelf, see Oil and Gas (Enterprise) Act 1982, s.23 and Civil Jurisdiction (Offshore Activities) Order, (S.I. 1987 No. 2197) see also Dicey and Morris, p. 1410.

5

up to the 12-mile limit.[19] Scotland and Northern Ireland form, with England and Wales, the United Kingdom,[20] but they are outside the territorial jurisdiction of the English courts. The Isle of Man and the Channel Islands are not part of the United Kingdom and they also are outside the jurisdiction of the English courts.[21] The extent of the territorial limits is to be determined by the Crown, through the Home Secretary, and communicated to the court by the Attorney-General.[22] The judgment of any court outside England and Wales is a foreign judgment for the purposes of enforcement in the English courts.[23]

1.04   *Adjudicatory jurisdiction or competence.* The adjudicatory jurisdiction or competence of a court to hear and determine a particular case will depend on one or more of a number of factors defined by the national law of the state of the court. There may be provisions requiring cases concerning a particular subject-matter to be brought before particular kinds of court.[24] For example, in the English legal system many employment cases can only be heard by an industrial tribunal. Generally, however, and particularly in the international context, the factors which most decisively determine a court's competence are usually territorial in character.[25] Thus a court's powers will often be defined by reference to the location of the subject-matter of the dispute, or of the events giving rise to it, or the location of the defendant's domicile. The concept of local territorial jurisdiction, or venue, is relatively unfamiliar to English lawyers because the jurisdiction of the High Court extends over the whole territory of England and Wales. Wherever the High Court is sitting, it is competent to determine cases connected with any part of England and Wales. The place of trial is determined principally to suit the convenience of the parties.[26] By contrast, in many conti-

---

[19] *Seagrove* v. *Parkes* [1891] 1 Q.B. 551; *Fraser* v. *Ackers* (1891) 35 Sol.J. 477. The 12-mile limit was substituted for a 3-mile limit by the Territorial Sea Act 1987.

[20] Interpretation Act 1978, s.5, Sched. 1; Union with Scotland Act 1706, Preamble, Art. 1; Interpretation Act 1978, s.22(1), Sched. 2, para. 5(*a*).

[21] *Ewing* v. *Orr-Ewing* (1885) 10 App.Cas. 453 at p. 473; also *Supreme Court Practice*, para. [5165]. *cf. Chloride Industrial Batteries* v. *F. & W. Freight* [1989] 1 W.L.R. 45.

[22] Dicey and Morris, p. 28. See, *The Fagernes* [1927] P. 311, *R.* v. *Kent Justices (ex p. Lye)* [1967] 2 Q.B. 153, *Post Office* v. *Estuary Radio Ltd.* [1968] 2 Q.B. 740.

[23] See chap. 10 below.

[24] Subject-matter competence is known as jurisdiction *"ratione materiae."*

[25] Territorial competence is known as jurisdiction *"ratione loci."* See also *Sirdar Gurdyal Singh* v. *The Rajah of Faridkote* [1894] A.C. 670.

[26] R.S.C. Ord. 33, r. 4; the jurisdiction of the county court is statutory and it has hitherto been regarded as general, in the territorial sense (see *Sharma* v. *Knight* [1986] 1 W.L.R. 757.) but subject to rules of venue which are similar to those of continental courts, see paras. 1.24 and 3.21 below.

nental systems the competence of courts is in principle limited to a particular geographical area.[27]

The meaning of "international jurisdiction." Because a state has no **1.05** power by itself to give effect to its judgments outside its international boundaries, it is necessary, if a judgment is to have international effect in this sense, for it to be recognised and enforced by the courts of the state in which it is sought to be made effective. However, as the competence of national courts is determined by national law it follows that, in any particular case, the courts of another state may not necessarily accept that the court of the first state was competent to try the case. If it is accepted by the court of the second state that the court of the first state was competent to adjudicate in the case, then (at least in the view of the second court) the first court is said to have had international jurisdiction. Whether it has international jurisdiction is principally relevant for the purposes of recognition and enforcement of the first court's judgments. There are numerous circumstances, generally accepted as a matter of public international law, in which courts will recognise and give effect to judgments given by the courts of other states, and by virtue of which courts may be said to have international jurisdiction.[28] As will be seen, the 1968 Convention, by laying down a common rule for the exercise of jurisdiction, establishes the international jurisdiction of any court which decides a case under the Convention.

Jurisdiction in personam. A court exercises jurisdiction *in personam* **1.06** in respect of a claim which is brought against an individual or entity, in an action *in personam*. The resulting judgment establishes the rights of the parties *inter se* and generally requires the defendant, if unsuccessful, to pay money or to do (or not to do) some specified act.

Jurisidiction in rem. A court exercises jurisdiction *in rem* when its judgment determines the status of a person or a thing, as distinct from the particular interest in it of a party to the litigation, and such a judgment is evidence of the matter decided which is conclusive as against the whole world.[29] Jurisdiction *in rem* is commonly exercised in actions *in rem*,[30] but there are some proceedings *in*

---

[27] See para. 1.17 below and chaps. 48 to 58 below, at para. 27.
[28] *Turnbull* v. *Walker* (1892) 67 L.T.R. 767.
[29] See *Fracis, Times & Co.* v. *Carr* (1900) 82 L.T.R. 698; *Lazarus-Barlow* v. *Regent Estates Co. Ltd.* [1949] 2 K.B. 465, *per* Evershed L.J. at p. 475.
[30] See paras. 1.31 *et seq.* below.

personam, involving questions of status, which may result in a judgment *in rem*.

2. Classification of proceedings

1.07   *Actions.* Similarly the English legal system adopts a classification of actions in which they are described as being either *in personam* or *in rem*.[31] As will be seen, actions *in rem* are restricted in practice to claims against ships in Admiralty proceedings.[32] The vast majority of civil actions are *in personam*. They are none the less so if the subject-matter of the proceedings is an object or thing. As Mr. Justice Holmes said:

> "If the technical object of the suit is to establish a claim against some particular person . . . or to bar some individual claim or objection, so that only certain persons are entitled to be heard in defence, the action is *in personam*, although it may concern the right to, or possession of, a tangible thing."[33]

Other proceedings. Probate actions and administration actions do not comfortably fit within the above classification as proceedings either *in personam* or *in rem* and they can be regarded for present purposes as *sui generis*. Other kinds of proceedings including proceedings for divorce or judicial separation, for wardship, adoption and legitimation, for bankruptcy, winding-up, and the administration of estates, cannot properly be regarded as actions at all.[34] The bases on which courts assume jurisdiction in respect of these latter types of proceedings fall outside the scope of the 1968 Convention[35] and the scope of this work.

3. The meaning of "domicile"

1.08   The 1982 Act has introduced a new concept of "domicile" into English law, which should not be confused with the traditional common law concept of domicile. The new concept of "domicile" is of central importance in the determination of jurisdiction. The primary jurisdictional rule under the 1968 Convention and the 1982 Act is that a defendant must be sued in the appropriate court for the place in which he is domiciled and for this purpose the "seat" of a

---

[31] See 37 *Halsbury's Laws* (4th ed.), para. 85.
[32] See paras. 1.31 *et seq.* below.
[33] *Tyler* v. *Judges of the Court of Registration* (1900) 175 Mass 71; see also *Castrique* v. *Imrie* (1870) 4 H.L. 414, at p. 428.
[34] Dicey and Morris, p. 265; 37 *Halsbury's Laws* (4th ed.), para. 17.
[35] See paras. 14.04 *et seq.* below.

corporation or association is equated with its domicile.[36] The Convention leaves the definition of "domicile" and "seat" to national law, but it contains provisions for identifying what law is to be applied in determining a person's domicile or seat.[37] The 1982 Act contains definitions of the terms domicile and seat.[38]

4. The meaning of "civil and commercial"

The expression "civil and commercial matters" appears in the 1.09 title to the 1968 Convention and in Article 1. Its meaning is discussed comprehensively in the commentary to the Convention, to which reference should be made.[39] Generally, it covers those areas of law which in England are regarded as subject to civil, as distinct from criminal, law, but which exclude matters of public law.

C. JURISDICTION IN ACTIONS *IN PERSONAM*

1. Introduction

The source of the courts' jurisdiction

Although the Supreme Court is of statutory origin, having been 1.10 established by the Supreme Court of Judicature Act 1873, its jurisdiction has never been comprehensively defined by statute. The 1873 Act abolished the old courts of common law and equity and transferred to the High Court, subject to minor exceptions, the jurisdiction which had formerly been vested in, or had been exercised by, the old courts and the powers which they had exercised "in pursuance of statute, law, or custom."[40] The modern general jurisdiction of the High Court is founded on section 19 of the Supreme Court Act 1981 which provides that the High Court shall exercise "all such jurisdiction . . . as is conferred by this or any other Act and all such other jurisdiction as was exercisable by it immediately before the commencement of this Act."[41] The modern county court

---

[36] 1968 Convention, Art. 53, first para.: para. 31.23 below; 1982 Act, s.42(1): para. 44.11 below.
[37] Arts. 52 and 53; see chap. 31.
[38] ss.41 to 46; paras. 44.01 *et seq.* below.
[39] See para. 14.08 below.
[40] Supreme Court of Judicature Act, 1873, s.16.
[41] The High Court has an inherent jurisdiction to regulate its own procedure: see *Supreme Court Practice*, para. 18/19/18; see also *Bremer Vulcan Schiffbau und Maschinenfabrik* v. *South India Shipping Corp.* [1981] A.C. 909, *per* Lord Diplock; Jacob, "The Inherent Jurisdiction of the Court" in *The Reform of Civil Procedural Law*, pp. 221 *et seq.*

is entirely a creature of statute and most of its powers are expressly defined by legislation.[42]

The constituent elements of adjudicatory jurisdiction

1.11   The English courts have the power to determine whether or not they have jurisdiction to adjudicate upon the merits of the particular case which is before them.[43] The question ordinarily only arises for active consideration in cases involving some foreign element, in the form of the foreign domicile of the defendant, or the foreign location of property, or the location abroad of events material to the litigation. Historically the courts themselves have had to decide in which cases they have had jurisdiction according to the common law. They have approached the task of defining their own jurisdiction by the development of rules, some mandatory, others discretionary, which lead them to assume or to decline jurisdiction. These rules relate to the three main elements of any proceedings, the plaintiff, the defendant, and the subject-matter of the proceedings. Accordingly, when determining whether or not to exercise jurisdiction in any particular case, an English court has required that it be satisfied as to the following, each of which is discussed below: first, that the subject-matter of the case is one in respect of which it is prepared to exercise jurisdiction[44]; secondly, that the plaintiff is a person at whose instance it is prepared to exercise jurisdiction[45]; and thirdly, that the defendant is a person over whom it is able or is prepared to exercise jurisdiction.[46]

1.12   *The relevance of the subject-matter of the proceedings.* The court must have jurisdiction over the subject-matter of the proceedings. It is well established that the court will not entertain proceedings which are principally concerned with questions of the title to, or the right to possession of immovable property outside the jurisdiction[47] unless the issue is raised incidentally,[48] or unless there exists between the parties some personal obligation arising out of a con-

---

[42] See 11 *Halsbury's Statutes* (4th ed.) pp. 395 *et seq.*
[43] *Wilkinson* v. *Barking Corp.* [1948] 1 K.B. 721, *Williams and Glynn's Bank p.l.c.* v. *Astro Dinamico Compania Naviera S.A.* [1984] 1. W.L.R. 438.
[44] See para. 1.12 below.
[45] See para. 1.13 below.
[46] *Ibid.* In proceedings *in rem*, it is the thing, rather than the person, over which the court must be prepared to exercise jurisdiction. See para. 1.31 below.
[47] *British South Africa Co.* v. *Compania de Moçambique* [1893] A.C. 602; 1982 Act, s.30(1), para. 43.20 below; Dicey and Morris, pp. 293 *et seq.*; Cheshire and North, pp. 255 *et seq.*
[48] *British South Africa Co.* v. *Companhia de Moçambique* [1893] A.C. 602, *per* Lord Herschell at p. 626, but *cf. St. Pierre* v. *South American Stores* [1936] 1 K.B. 382, *Tito* v. *Waddell* [1977] Ch. 106, *Buttes Gas and Oil Co.* v. *Hammer* [1982] A.C. 888.

tract or a fiduciary relationship or fraud, which does not depend for its existence on the law of the *locus* of the immovable property.[49] Nor will the English courts entertain an action for the enforcement of a foreign penal, revenue or other public law obligation, or one which is founded on a foreign act of state,[50] or an obligation arising under foreign law which is repugnant to English public policy.[51] Strictly, as regards jurisdiction, these rules are subject to the 1968 Convention.[52]

The recognition and enforcement of foreign judgments may be refused under the 1968 Convention on a number of grounds, including public policy. The circumstances in which, in cases falling within the 1982 Act and the 1968 Convention, jurisdiction must be declined on account of the subject-matter of the proceedings are discussed below.[53]

Plaintiff. Questions relating to the identity of the plaintiff or his **1.13** capacity to sue are discussed in detail in Chapter 2. They rarely cause any problems in practice as only an alien enemy in time of war is absolutely barred from bringing proceedings.[54]

Defendant. The question whether the defendant is a person over whom the court is either able or prepared to exercise jurisdiction has two aspects. First, there must exist a basis for the court's jurisdiction over him and, secondly, he must have been properly brought before the court following service of its originating process. The basis on which a defendant is subject to the court's jurisdiction may affect the particular rules which govern the propriety of service on him.[55] Whatever the potential basis for the court's jurisdiction, the defendant must be a person who is not immune from being

---

[49] *Deschamps* v. *Miller* [1908] 1 Ch. 856, at p. 863; *Bank of Africa* v. *Cohen* [1909] 2 Ch. 129.
[50] Dicey and Morris, pp. 100–110; Cheshire and North, pp. 112–130; *Huntington* v. *Attrill* [1893] A.C. 150; *Government of India* v. *Taylor* [1955] A.C. 491; *Att.-Gen. of New Zealand* v. *Ortiz* [1984] A.C. 1; *Williams & Humbert Ltd.* v. *W. & H. Trade Marks (Jersey) Ltd.* [1986] A.C. 368.
[51] Dicey and Morris, pp. 92–99; Cheshire and North, pp. 130–140.
[52] The scope of the 1968 Convention is discussed in chap. 14. Some provisions of the 1968 Convention and Sched. 4 to the 1982 Act have the effect of excluding the jurisdiction of the English courts on the basis of the subject-matter of the dispute: see Art. 16 (paras. 20.01 *et seq.* and 45.19 below) and Art. 19 (paras. 22.01 *et seq.* and 45.25 below). Note also that most actions concerning foreign penal, revenue and other public laws will fall outside the scope of the Convention.
[53] See chap. 27, especially at paras. 27.13 *et seq.* below.
[54] See para. 2.03, n. 4 below.
[55] See para. 4.02 below.

sued. The immunity of certain parties from suit is examined further in Chapter 2.[56]

Different bases of jurisdiction in personam

1.14   There are four different bases of jurisdiction *in personam*: first jurisdiction may be founded on the presence of the defendant within the territorial limits[57] at the commencement of the proceedings[58]; secondly, a party who is physically outside the territorial limits may submit to the jurisdiction of the court[59]; thirdly, the court may assume jurisdiction over persons outside the territorial jurisdiction in certain classes of case[60]; and fourthly, various statutes provide that the court is to have jurisdiction in particular cases, usually in accordance with international conventions.[61]

The 1982 Act, implementing the 1968 Convention, is the principal example of this last category. However, as will be seen, the 1982 Act does more than simply extend the provisions of the 1968 Convention to the United Kingdom. It contains rules which allocate jurisdiction as between England and Wales, Scotland and Northern Ireland,[62] and, in many cases, it even provides the foundation of the jurisdiction of the courts in each part of the United Kingdom.[63] So far-reaching are the effects of the 1982 Act that it is proposed to divide the present treatment of the jurisdiction of the English courts into two main parts, dealing first with cases in which jurisdiction is founded on the 1982 Act, and secondly, with cases in which jurisdiction is founded on other bases. These other bases are discussed later in this chapter under the four categories mentioned above.

The role of service

1.15   Historically, the court's jurisdiction has been regarded as being based on the service of a writ or other originating process. This came about through the thoroughly practical notion that a person who could be physically subjected to the court's processes was the proper object of the exercise of its jurisdiction.[64] Physical subjection to the court's processes was naturally dependent on the pres-

---

[56] Paras. 2.13 *et seq.* below.
[57] The territorial limits are described at para. 1.03 above.
[58] See para. 1.26 below.
[59] See para. 1.27 below.
[60] See para. 1.28 below.
[61] See para. 1.29 below.
[62] See para. 1.23 below.
[63] See para. 1.24 below.
[64] See *McDonald* v. *Mabee* (1917) 243 U.S. 90, *per* Holmes J.: "The foundation of jurisdiction is power."; *Sirdar Gurdyal Singh* v. *The Rajah of Faridkote* [1894] A.C. 670; *Turnbull* v. *Walker* (1892) 67 L.T. 767; *Tallack* v. *Tallack* [1927] P. 211.

ence of the defendant within the territorial limits of the court's jurisdiction. Over the years, however, the court extended its jurisdiction to beyond the territorial limits of the realm by the adoption of rules of court which permitted the service of proceedings on persons outside the jurisdiction in a number of specified circumstances, subject to the court's discretion. In all the permitted circumstances it was considered that there was or might be a sufficient connection between the proceedings themselves and the territory of England and Wales to justify the assumption of jurisdiction.

It is suggested that to regard jurisdiction as being *based* on service is misleading. The function of service was, and remains, to summon the defendant to court to answer the claim made against him. Service may therefore be regarded as a prerequisite to the *exercise* of the adjudicatory jurisdiction of the court, but the court's jurisdiction is itself based on the rules of law giving effect to one or more of the four bases of jurisdiction mentioned above.[65]

The role of discretion

Cases to which the 1968 Convention does not apply. As is discussed later in this chapter,[65a] English courts have long exercised an overriding discretion in deciding whether or not to assume jurisdiction over a particular matter, especially if it contains international elements. In cases to which the 1968 Convention does not apply, the court may exercise its discretion, depending on the circumstances, either to allow the plaintiff to invoke the court's jurisdiction or to stay proceedings in which the jurisdiction has been invoked. **1.16**

As a safeguard against abuse, the court has controlled the exercise of its jurisdiction over persons situated outside its territorial limits, by making service of a writ out of the jurisdiction dependent on leave.[66] In this way the court has been able to examine every case and to decide whether, in the exercise of its discretion, it was proper to extend its jurisdiction to persons beyond the territorial limits of the realm. On the other hand, if the plaintiff has invoked the court's jurisdiction as of right by serving a writ on a defendant within the court's territorial jurisdiction, the court may nonetheless be prepared, in its discretion, to exercise its power to stay the pro-

---

[65] It may be that service is necessary to *invoke* the jurisdiction: *The Banco* [1971] P. 137 (C.A.); *The Berny* [1979] Q.B. 80; but note that these cases arose under the Administration of Justice Act 1956, s.3, which has since been replaced by the Supreme Court Act 1981, s.21, the wording of which is materially different.

[65a] See paras. 1.36 *et seq.* below.

[66] In addition to the cases to which the 1968 Convention applies, there are some other types of case under other statutory regimes in which leave is not required to serve a writ out of the jurisdiction: see para. 1.29 below.

ceedings.[67] The principles on which the court acts in exercising its discretion on jurisdictional matters in cases to which the 1968 Convention does not apply are discussed below.[68]

Cases to which the 1968 Convention applies. In cases to which the 1968 Convention applies, the circumstances in which the court retains a discretion to assume jurisdiction, or to stay its proceedings on jurisdictional grounds, are severely curtailed.[69]

Continental systems contrasted

1.17   The rules of jurisdiction in continental legal systems are more clear-cut and less dependent on discretion than in the English legal system.[70] They are founded on the general principle derived from Roman law, *actor sequitur forum rei*,[71] that every person is entitled to be sued in the local courts of his own domicile.[72] Accordingly, the competence of courts is often limited to a particular geographical area and the court system usually has a decentralised structure.[73] In addition to the general rule of jurisdiction based on domicile, further rules may determine, according to the subject-matter and value of the claim, the level or type of court in which the defendant is to be sued, or alternatively provide that he may exceptionally be sued in some court other than his local court. Differences exist between particular continental legal systems as to the rules applied by those courts to determine whether they have competence to entertain particular proceedings.[74] Most countries, too, have their own types of exorbitant jurisdiction.[75]

2. Jurisdiction of the English courts under the Civil Jurisdiction and Judgments Act 1982

1.18   As was observed at the start of this chapter, the Civil Jurisdiction and Judgments Act 1982 takes effect certainly at two, and probably at three, levels.[76] First, at the level of international jurisdiction, the

---

[67] Supreme Court Act 1981, s.49(3). A stay of proceedings by reason of an arbitration clause is outside the scope of this book.

[68] Paras. 1.41 *et seq.*

[69] The exercise of discretion in cases to which the 1968 Convention applies is discussed at paras. 1.36 *et seq.* below.

[70] See Schlosser, paras. 76 *et seq.* (paras. A1.363 *et seq.* below); de Vries and Lowenfeld, "Jurisdiction in personal actions—A comparison of civil law views" (1959) 44 Iowa L.Rev. 306.

[71] "The plaintiff shall follow the court of the defendant." The word *rei* is the genitive both of *res* (thing) and of *reus* (defendant).

[72] See Jenard, para. A1.80 below.

[73] See chaps. 48 to 55 below, at paras. 18 to 23.

[74] See chaps. 48 to 55 below, at paras. 24 to 31.

[75] See para. 16.12 below; M. Weser "Bases of Judicial Jurisdiction in the Common Market Countries" (1961) 10 Am.Jo.Comp. Law 323.

[76] Paras. 1.01 and 1.05 above.

Act incorporates the 1968 Convention into United Kingdom law.[77] Secondly, it applies the majority of the Convention's jurisdictional rules, with minor modifications, for the purpose of allocating jurisdiction as between England and Wales, Scotland and Northern Ireland.[78] Thirdly, as is contended below,[78a] the Act provides the basis of jurisdiction in each of the three parts of the United Kingdom, in a very large number of ordinary civil and commercial cases, even though they may be entirely internal to that particular part of the United Kingdom.

The 1968 Convention

The purpose of the 1968 Convention was to unify the jurisdictional rules of the Contracting States, at least as regards cases with the requisite international element, and to abolish the exercise of exorbitant jurisdiction in cases coming within its scope, so as to bring about a common system for the enforcement of judgments within the European Community.[79] In applying the Convention's rules to the United Kingdom, the 1982 Act has introduced into English law fundamental changes in the bases of adjudicatory jurisdiction. In cases to which the Convention applies it has removed the courts' power to exercise jurisdiction over persons temporarily in England and Wales by the mere service upon them of the writ, and over persons abroad by the giving of leave to serve proceedings on them out of the jurisdiction. It has substituted the Convention's obligatory rules of jurisdiction.[80] The 1982 Act has extended to the entire world the geographical area within which an English writ may be served without leave on a person over whom the court has jurisdiction pursuant to the Convention or the Act. The inherent power of the English High Court to stay proceedings remains, but it must not be exercised where to do so would be inconsistent with the 1968 Convention.[81]

Outline of the jurisdictional rules of the 1968 Convention. Chapters **1.20** 13 to 38 of this book contain a detailed analysis of the provisions of the Convention, its protocols, and the two Accession Conventions. The following paragraphs are intended to serve as the briefest outline of their jurisdictional rules. It is generally necessary to take account of the Convention only when the defendant is domiciled[82]

---

[77] 1982 Act, s.2(1).
[78] s.16 and Sched. 4; the Act also provides that matters of local jurisdiction within Scotland are to be determined in accordance with rules which follow the scheme of the 1968 Convention, s.20 and Sched. 8.
[78a] See para. 1.24 below.
[79] See paras. 13.09 *et seq.* below.
[80] See paras. 1.37 *et seq.* and 15.02 below.
[81] 1982 Act, s.49, see paras. 1.46 and 44.40 below.
[82] Arts. 52 and 53. See also ss.41–46 of the 1982 Act, paras. 44.01 *et seq.* below.

15

in a Contracting State[83] and the case contains international features.[84] The application of the Convention is confined to "civil and commercial matters" within the meaning of that phrase given to it by the European Court of Justice.[85] Certain matters are, by Article 1 of the Convention, excluded from its ambit. These are revenue,[86] customs[87] and administrative[88] matters, cases which concern the status or legal capacity of natural persons,[89] rights in property arising out of a matrimonial relationship,[90] wills,[91] succession,[92] bankruptcy,[93] proceedings relating to the winding-up of insolvent companies or other legal persons,[94] judicial arrangements, compositions and analogous proceedings,[95] social security[96] and arbitration.[97] Matters falling within the scope of certain specialised international conventions are subject to the jurisdictional rules of those conventions which override conflicting provisions of the 1968 Convention.[98]

1.21   The Convention's jurisdictional rules constitute a uniform code directly applicable in all the Contracting States.[99] The general jurisdictional rule is that when a defendant is domiciled in a Contracting State any proceedings against him must be brought there unless one of the Convention's other jurisdictional rules permits the proceedings to be brought in some other Contracting State.[1] None of the national rules of exorbitant jurisdiction may be applied to a defendant who is domiciled in a Contracting State.[2] In addition to its general rule of jurisdiction, the Convention contains special rules which provide that proceedings may be brought in cases of contract in the courts for the place of performance of the obligation in ques-

---

[83] See para. 13.01 below.
[84] See para. 13.10 below.
[85] Art. 1, first para.; paras. 14.08 *et seq.* below.
[86] Art. 1, first para.; para. 14.17 below.
[87] *Ibid.*
[88] *Ibid.*
[89] Art. 1, second para., sub-para. (1); para. 14.19 below.
[90] Art. 1, second para., sub-para. (1); para. 14.20 below.
[91] Art. 1, second para., sub-para. (1); para. 14.25 below.
[92] *Ibid.*
[93] Art. 1, second para., sub-para. (2); para. 14.26 below.
[94] *Ibid.*
[95] *Ibid.*
[96] Art. 1, second para., sub-para. (3); para. 14.30 below.
[97] Art. 1, second para., sub-para. (4); para. 14.31 below.
[98] See Art. 57 and para. 1.29 below.
[99] See para. 13.14 below.
[1] Art. 2; para. 16.01 below.
[2] Art. 3; para. 16.09 below. they may, however, be applied as against a defendant domiciled in a non-Contracting State: Art. 4; see para. 16.15 below.

tion,[3] and in cases of tort, in the courts for the place where the harmful event occurred.[4] Further special rules make provision for cases relating to maintenance,[5] civil compensation in criminal proceedings,[6] disputes arising out of the operation of branches and agencies,[7] and for cases concerning trusts,[8] salvage claims,[9] and Admiralty limitation claims.[10] Special rules also apply to cases with multiple defendants,[11] third parties,[12] and counterclaims.[13] Further special rules apply to consumer cases,[14] and to cases relating to insurance.[15] Certain classes of proceedings are allocated to the exclusive jurisdiction of the Contracting State which is, in effect, most closely connected with the matter in dispute. These include proceedings which have as their object certain rights in immovable property[16] matters of company law,[17] entries in public registers,[18] the registration and validity of intellectual property rights[19] and the enforcement of judgments.[20] The Convention's rules as to jurisdiction may in certain circumstances be excluded by agreement between the parties,[21] and, except where the Convention gives the courts of one Contracting State exclusive jurisdiction, it permits jurisdiction to be founded on the entry of an appearance.[22]

The consequences of the application of the 1968 Convention. The **1.22** courts of all Contracting States, including the English courts, are bound by the jurisdictional rules of the 1968 Convention.[23] Some of these rules simply provide that, in a given case, the courts of a Contracting State as a whole are to have jurisdiction.[24] In such cases it is left to the domestic law of the state concerned to determine the par-

---

[3] Art. 5(1); para. 17.02 below.
[4] Art. 5(3); para. 17.44 below.
[5] Art. 5(2); para. 17.31 below.
[6] Art. 5(4); para. 17.53 below.
[7] Art. 5(5); para. 17.55 below.
[8] Art. 5(6); para. 17.65 below.
[9] Art. 5(7); para. 17.70 below.
[10] Art. 6A; para. 17.96 below.
[11] Art. 6(1); para. 17.74 below.
[12] Art. 6(2); para. 17.82 below.
[13] Art. 6(3); para. 17.90 below.
[14] Arts. 13–15; chap. 19 below.
[15] Art. 7–12A; chap. 18 below.
[16] Art. 16(1); para. 20.11 below.
[17] Art. 16(2); para. 20.26 below.
[18] Art. 16(3); para. 20.30 below.
[19] Art. 16(4); para. 20.32 below.
[20] Art. 16(5); para. 20.40 below.
[21] Art. 17; para. 21.01 below.
[22] Art. 18; para. 21.83 below.
[23] See paras. 15.02 *et seq.* The Act and Convention are subject to special rules of interpretation, see paras. 13.22 *et seq.* below.
[24] *e.g.* Arts. 2, 5(6), 8 first para., and 14.

ticular part of that state in which the courts are to have jurisdiction. Accordingly, where the Convention allocates jurisdiction to the courts of the United Kingdom generally, Schedule 4 to the 1982 Act determines which part of the United Kingdom is to have jurisdiction. Some of the Convention's rules confer jurisdiction on courts within a particular locality within a Contracting State.[25] In such cases Schedule 4 has no application, as the Act states that its provisions are subject to the Convention.[26]

The jurisdictional scheme within the United Kingdom: Schedule 4 of the 1982 Act

1.23   In some instances[27] the 1968 Convention allocates jurisdiction to the courts of the United Kingdom generally, without specifying in which of the three parts of the United Kingdom proceedings should be brought. It was accordingly necessary for rules to be devised to allocate jurisdiction in such cases as between the three parts of the United Kingdom. This has largely been achieved by section 16 and Schedule 4 of the 1982 Act.[28] The opportunity was taken to introduce rules which, save in limited respects,[29] mirror and follow the numbering of the Articles of the Convention, and which apply in all proceedings, whether or not the Convention itself applies. The allocation of jurisdiction may depend on the subject-matter of the proceedings,[30] on the domicile of the defendant or on a combination of both of these. If the subject-matter of the proceedings falls within Article 16, jurisdiction is allocated exclusively to the part of the United Kingdom which has the closest connection with that subject-matter.[31] Apart from these cases, a defendant who is domiciled in the United Kingdom may be sued either in the part of the United Kingdom in which he is domiciled or, if the special rules in Articles 5 to 18 of Schedule 4 provide a basis for the court's jurisdiction, in another part of the United Kingdom.

1.24   *Application of Schedule 4 to cases internal to England and Wales.* It is clear that the jurisdictional rules in Schedule 4 allocate jurisdiction within the United Kingdom in those cases in which the Con-

---

[25] *e.g.* Arts. 5(1), 5(2), 5(3), 5(5), 6(1), 8 second para., and 9.
[26] 1982 Act, s.16(4).
[27] *e.g.* Arts. 2, 5(6), 8 first para., and 14.
[28] The detailed application of s.16 and Sched. 4 is discussed at paras. 41.02 *et seq.* below. The allocation of jurisdiction in certain cases concerning trusts and consumer contracts is effected by s.10 of the 1982 Act: para. 40.30 below.
[29] The principle differences concern jurisdiction agreements (see para. 45.42 below), and matters relating to insurance (see para. 45.14 below).
[30] The subject-matter of the proceedings must fall within the scope of the Convention. See paras. 14.04 *et seq.* below. Certain proceedings, listed in Sched. 5, are excluded from Sched. 4; see para. 45.30 below.
[31] See Sched. 4, Art. 16, para. 45.19 below.

vention allocates jurisdiction to the courts of the United Kingdom generally, without also identifying which court, or the courts of which part of the United Kingdom, are to have jurisdiction. It is clear that these rules also allocate jurisdiction in those cases which have connections with more than one part of the United Kingdom but not with any other state, and the subject-matter of which falls within the scope of the Convention.

The question arises, however, as to whether section 16 and Schedule 4 apply to those cases which fall within the scope of the Convention as regards their subject-matter, but in which the elements connecting the case to the United Kingdom relate only to one particular part of the United Kingdom, whether it is England and Wales, Scotland or Northern Ireland. In other words, for example, if an action is brought in the English courts, between parties both of whom are domiciled in England, in respect of a contract to be performed in England, is the undoubted jurisdiction of the English courts based on Schedule 4 of the 1982 Act? For the reasons discussed below, it is suggested that section 16 and Schedule 4 do have this effect.[32] If this is right, then leave to serve the English defendant out of the jurisdiction (assuming he has gone away temporarily) is not required.[33] The question may be of practical importance in certain cases.[34]

Section 16(1) of the 1982 Act provides that,

> "The provisions set out in Schedule 4 . . . shall have effect for determining, for each part of the United Kingdom, whether the courts of law of that part, or any particular court of law in that part, have or has jurisdiction. . . ."

These words are quite general and do not purport to be limited to cases in which there are connections with more than one part of the United Kingdom. The subsection refers to determining the jurisdiction of "any particular court" within a particular part of the United Kingdom and this suggests that the section is capable of being concerned with questions of jurisdiction *within* a part of the United Kingdom without jurisdiction in any other part of the United Kingdom necessarily being in question. It is to be noted,

---

[32] This effect of s.16 and Sched. 4 is not acknowledged by other authors, who appear to regard its effect as being limited to allocating jurisdiction as between the three parts of the U.K. in cases which have connections with more than one of those parts.

[33] R.S.C., Ord. 11, r. 1(2). Note that Ord. 11, r. 1(1)(*a*) (which enables leave to be granted for service of a writ out of the jurisdiction if relief is sought against a person domiciled within the jurisdiction) still has a residual function for cases which fall outside the scope of the 1968 Convention.

[34] Leave may be necessary to enter a default judgment: see paras. 4.53 *et seq.* below.

moreover, that the wording of the jurisdictional rules in Schedule 4 closely follows that of Schedule 1 (the Convention).

3. Jurisdiction in cases which fall outside the scope of the 1982 Act

Introduction

1.25 It has been observed that the 1982 Act defines the jurisdiction of the English courts both as regards cases to which the Convention itself applies, and as regards cases to which Schedule 4 applies.[35] Schedule 4 is expressed to apply only to cases in which both the subject-matter is within the scope of the Convention[36] and *either* the defendant is domiciled in the United Kingdom *or* the proceedings are within the exclusive jurisdiction of the court (as provided for by Article 16 of Schedule 4) regardless of domicile. In cases to which neither the Convention nor Schedule 4 applies the jurisdiction of the English court is founded on the rules which applied before the coming into effect of the 1982 Act.[37] As has been seen,[38] these rules provide for four possible bases of jurisdiction *in personam*: first, jurisdiction may be founded on the presence of the defendant within the territorial limits at the commencement of the proceedings; secondly, a party who is physically outside the territorial limits may submit to the jurisdiction of the court; thirdly, the court may assume jurisdiction over persons outside the territorial jurisdiction in certain classes of case; and fourthly, various statutes provide that the court is to have jurisdiction in particular cases, usually in accordance with international conventions. These rules are discussed more fully below.

Bases of jurisdiction

1.26 *Jurisdiction based on presence.* Subject to a number of statutory exceptions, the most important of which are the jurisdictional rules in the 1982 Act,[39] the civil courts have jurisdiction *in personam* over a defendant who is properly served with the proceedings while he is within[40] England and Wales.[41] This is the original common law basis for jurisdiction. As Lord Haldane said:

"The root principle of English law about jurisdiction is that the judges stand in the place of the Sovereign in whose name they admin-

---

[35] See para. 1.18 above.
[36] The scope of the Convention is discussed at para. 14.04 *et seq.*
[37] The relevant parts of the 1982 Act came into effect on January 1, 1987; see para. 47.23 below.
[38] See para. 1.14 above.
[39] The other statutory exceptions are discussed at para. 1.29 below.
[40] *Myerson* v. *Martin* [1979] 1 W.L.R. 1390.
[41] Modes of service on various parties are described at paras. 404 *et seq.* below.

ister justice, and that therefore whoever is served with the King's writ, and can be compelled consequently to submit to the decree made, is a person over whom the Courts have jurisdiction."[42]

According to this rule any presence, however temporary, is sufficient to found jurisdiction,[43] unless the defendant has been induced by deception to come into the jurisdiction for the purpose of being served with process.[44] Once the defendant has been properly served within the jurisdiction the court will retain jurisdiction over him after he has left.[45] The questions which arise, particularly in cases involving corporations and partnerships, as to what constitutes presence within the jurisdiction for these purposes are dealt with elsewhere,[46] as are the circumstances in which the court may permit substituted service of a defendant who is outside the jurisdiction.[47]

The exercise of jurisdiction by the above means over transient foreigners[48] is based on the notion that a person visiting a foreign state owes temporary allegiance to the sovereign of that state and is therefore amenable to that sovereign's jurisdiction during his presence there. As has been said:

> "When an alien in amity cometh into England, because so long as he is within England he is within the King's protection; therefore so long as he is here he oweth unto the King a local obedience or legiance."[49]

Temporary presence is nonetheless regarded internationally as an exorbitant basis for jurisdiction, at least in continental systems.[50] It will be seen[51] that by Article 3 of the 1968 Convention it may not, in

---

[42] *John Russell & Co. v. Cayzer, Irvine & Co. Ltd.* [1916] 2 A.C. 298 at p. 302; see also *Employers' Liability Assurance Corporation v. Sedgwick, Collins & Co.* [1927] A.C. 95, at p. 114.

[43] *Maharanee of Baroda v. Wildenstein* [1972] 2 Q.B. 283; *Colt Industries Inc. v. Sarlie* [1966] 1 W.L.R. 440.

[44] *Watkins v. North American Land & Timber Co. Ltd.* (1904) 20 T.L.R. 534. and *Stein v. Valkenhuysen* (1858) E.B. & E. 65.

[45] *Razelos v. Razelos (No. 2)* [1970] 1 W.L.R. 392, *per* Baker J. at p. 403. In exceptional cases a defendant may be restrained from leaving the jurisdiction. See para. 7.10, n. 71 below.

[46] See paras. 4.09 *et seq.* below

[47] See para. 4.15 below.

[48] As in *Maharanee of Baroda v. Wildenstein* [1972] 2 Q.B. 285.

[49] *Calvin's Case* (1608) 7 Co.Rep. 1a; see also *Carrick v. Hancock* (1895) 12 T.L.R. 59, *per* Lord Russell of Killowen.

[50] Supplementary Protocol to the Hague Convention on the Recognition and Enforcement of Foreign Judgments in Civil and Commercial Matters, 1968; see also De Winter, "Excessive Jurisdiction in Private International Law" (1968) 17 I.C.L.Q. 706, (1969) 18 I.C.L.Q. 618; Schlosser, para. 86 (para. A1.374 below).

[51] Para. 16.13 below.

cases which fall within the scope of the Convention, found jurisdiction against persons domiciled in other Contracting States.[52]

1.27   *Jurisdiction based on consent.* Subject to the 1982 Act, the civil courts have jurisdiction *in personam* over a defendant who is outside the territorial limits of the court's jurisdiction if he submits or can be taken to have submitted to the jurisdiction. Submission to the jurisdiction may come about in a variety of ways. A common case is that in which a contract contains a choice of jurisdiction clause whereby the parties consent to the resolution of all disputes arising in respect of the contract by the English courts. A choice of jurisdiction in favour of the English courts may also arise by implication when the contract provides that it is to be governed by English law.[53] If a person resident outside the jurisdiction appoints a person within the jurisdiction to accept service he will be taken to have submitted to the jurisdiction.[54] It should be noted that any foreign company with a place of business established in Great Britain is under a statutory obligation to appoint such a person.[55] However it should be noted that in cases which are subject to the jurisdictional rules of the 1982 Act, whether under the Convention or under Schedule 4, the appointment of a person to accept service will not found the jurisdiction of the English courts. This is because in such cases jurisdiction is not founded on service but on the rules of the Convention or of Schedule 4, as the case may be.[56] It will be necessary to have regard to the provisions of Article 17 of the Convention or of Schedule 4.

A defendant who is not otherwise subject to the English court's jurisdiction submits to it if he acknowledges service of the writ (even if it was not duly served[57]) and does not contest the jurisdiction.[58] Similarly, a foreign plaintiff who brings proceedings in an

---

[52] Nor may it be employed against defendants domiciled in Scotland or Northern Ireland; see 1982 Act, Sched. 4, Art. 3, para. 45.04 below.

[53] This basis of jurisdiction is not now favoured, see *Amin Rasheed Shipping Corporation* v. *Kuwait Insurance Co.* [1984] A.C. 50. Contrast the position under Art. 17 of the 1968 Convention (para. 21.01 below), qualified by Art. 35 of the 1978 Accession Convention (para. 37.11 below) in respect of written agreements made before the coming into effect of the 1982 Act.

[54] *Tharsis Sulphur Co.* v. *Société des Métaux* (1889) 58 L.J.Q.B. 435; *Montgomery, Jones & Co.* v. *Liebenthal & Co.* [1898] 1 Q.B. 487.

[55] Companies Act 1985, s.691(1)(*b*)(iii). See para. 4.13 below.

[56] See para. 1.19 above.

[57] R.S.C. Ord. 10, r. 1(5); see para. 4.51 below.

[58] *Derby & Co.* v. *Larsson* [1976] 1 W.L.R. 202 H.L.; *South African Republic* v. *Compagnie Franco-Belge du Chemin de Fer du Nord* [1897] 2 Ch. 487; [1898] 1 Ch. 190. *Factories Insurance Co.* v. *Anglo-Scottish Insurance Co.* (1913) 29 T.L.R. 312; *High Commission for India* v. *Ghosh* [1960] 1 Q.B. 134; see para. 5.11.

English court will be taken to have impliedly consented to its juris-diction in respect of any counterclaim concerning related matters.[59] If the counterclaim does concern some matter that is related to the subject-matter of the claim it is immaterial that leave to serve process outside the jurisdiction would not have been given in respect of it.[60]

Jurisdiction assumed over persons outside the territorial limits. Since   **1.28** about the mid-nineteenth century the courts have had the dis-cretionary power to assume jurisdiction over persons, regardless of their nationality, who are outside the territorial limits of the juris-diction, by authorising the service of proceedings on them. This is known as the "assumed" or "extended" jurisdiction of the English courts. Its basis is entirely statutory, and has, for many years, been contained in Order 11 of the Rules of the Supreme Court.[61] This Order specifies a number of instances in which the court, on the application of the plaintiff, may, in its discretion,[62] grant leave for service of a writ, or other process[63] outside the jurisdiction. With the coming into effect of the 1982 Act the scope for application of this assumed jurisdiction has been limited to those cases which do not fall within the 1968 Convention, or Schedule 4[64] of the 1982 Act.[65]

Jurisdiction as of right over persons outside the territorial limits. In   **1.29** addition to the cases in which jurisdiction is assumed by the court in the exercise of its discretion, there is a range of cases in which the plaintiff may invoke the jurisdiction of the court as of right over persons outside the territorial jurisdiction. In these cases, the leave of the court is not required for the issue or service of the writ.[66] By far the most important and far-reaching of these are, of course, the rules contained in the 1968 Convention, implemented in the United Kingdom by the 1982 Act. The Convention and the Act have been

---

[59] *Union Bank of the Middle East* v. *Clapham* (1981) 125 Sol.Jo. 862. *cf.* Art. 6(3) of the 1968 Convention, para. 17.94 below.

[60] *Derby & Co.* v. *Larsson* [1976] 1 W.L.R. 202, at p. 205. *cf.* Art. 18 of the 1968 Convention, para. 21.83 below.

[61] Certain Admiralty writs *in personam* may also be served out of the jurisdiction: R.S.C., Ord. 75, r. 4. See also para. 4.16 below.

[62] The exercise of discretion is discussed at para. 1.45 below.

[63] R.S.C. Ord. 11, r. 9. Formerly, as a concession to foreign sovereignty, notice of the writ, as opposed to the writ itself, was served out of the jurisdiction.

[64] Sched. 4, of the 1982 Act contains the intra-U.K. jurisdictional rules: see para. 45.01 below.

[65] R.S.C., Ord. 11, r. 1(1).

[66] R.S.C., Ord. 6, r. 7(1); Ord. 11, r. 1(2).

described above and they form the main subject-matter of this book.

In addition, there are various other cases in which the court's jurisdiction may be invoked as of right, notwithstanding that the person against whom the claim is made is not within the jurisdiction or that the wrongful act or omission giving rise to the claim did not take place within the jurisdiction.[67] In each of these cases, the jurisdiction is conferred by an enactment of English law, most of which[68] implement specialised multilateral international conventions.[69]

1.30   The jurisdictional regimes under those specialised conventions are of narrow application, but their effect is preserved within the framework of the 1968 Convention by Article 57, although the precise extent to which the specialised jurisdictional rules interlock with the rules in the 1968 Convention may sometimes be a matter of considerable difficulty.[70] It should be noted that the 1982 Act and Article 57 may have the radical effect of implementing in English law the full jurisdictional regimes in the specialised conventions,[71] irrespective of whether or not that is also the effect of the legislation specifically devoted to implementing them, although the latter remains effective for their detailed implementation.

The more important conventions to which the United Kingdom is a party and which contain jurisdictional rules for civil and commercial matters are listed in Appendix 2.[72] They have mostly been given effect by specific implementing legislation and they concern such matters as carriage by air,[73] carriage by rail,[74] carriage by

---

[67] R.S.C., Ord. 6, r. 7(1)(*a*)(ii); Ord. 11, r. 1(2)(*b*).
[68] But see the reference below to the Protection of Trading Interests Act 1980, s.6(5).
[69] Conversely, the jurisdictional regimes implemented by the 1982 Act and by these other enactments may have the effect of depriving English courts of jurisdiction which they would otherwise have on the basis of the defendant's presence within the territorial limits: *Rothmans of Pall Mall (Overseas) Ltd.* v. *Saudi Arabian Airlines Corp.* [1981] Q.B. 368 (C.A.).
[70] See paras. 33.06 *et seq.* below.
[71] *The Nordglimt* [1987] 2 Lloyds Rep. 470, at p. 479, *per* Hobhouse J., quoted at para. 33.19 below.
[72] Paras. A2.31 *et seq.* below; see also Dicey and Morris, pp. 509 *et seq.*
[73] Warsaw Convention 1929, as amended at the Hague in 1955 and at Montreal in 1975, implemented by the Carriage by Air Act 1961, by the Carriage by Air (Application of Provisions) Order 1967 and by the Carriage by Air and Road Act 1979 (not yet in force); Guadalajara Convention 1961, implemented by the Carriage by Air (Supplementary Provisions) Act 1962.
[74] Berne Convention 1980 ("COTIF"), implemented by the International Transport Conventions Act 1983.

road,[75] various maritime matters,[76] air navigation services,[77] employment of crew of aircraft and ships[78] and oil pollution by ships.[79] In at least one case, jurisdiction may be founded as of right against a person outside the jurisdiction, despite the absence of a convention to that effect.[80]

D. JURISDICTION IN ACTIONS *IN REM*

An action *in rem* is an action which is brought, in effect, against a *res*   **1.31** or thing,[81] and in which the court has the power to direct the arrest of the property concerned. An action *in rem* can only be brought in respect of certain kinds of claim in Admiralty proceedings. The basis of the action is the presence of the property within the jurisdiction[82] and the service on it of the writ.

A detailed description of the Admiralty jurisdiction of the English courts is beyond the scope of this work. It is sufficient for present purposes to state that the Admiralty jurisdiction of the High Court is based mainly on statute, and is contained principally in

---

[75] Geneva Convention on the Contract for the International Carriage of Goods by Road 1956 ("CMR"), implemented by the Carriage of Goods by Road Act 1965; Geneva Convention on the Contract for the International Carriage of Passengers and Luggage 1973, implemented by the Carriage of Passengers by Road Act 1974 (not yet in force).

[76] Brussels Conventions on Collision and on Arrest of Sea-going Ships, implemented by ss.21 and 22 of the Supreme Court Act 1981 and s.26 of the Civil Jurisdiction and Judgments Act 1982; Athens Convention relating to the Carriage of Passengers and their Luggage by Sea 1974, implemented by the Merchant Shipping Act 1979; Geneva Convention on a Code of Conduct for Liner Conferences 1974, implemented by the Merchant Shipping (Liner Conferences) Act 1982.

[77] Chicago Convention on International Civil Aviation 1944, Brussels Convention relating to Co-operation for the Safety of Air Navigation 1960 and Protocol 1981, and Multilateral Agreement relating to Route Charges 1981, variously implemented by the Civil Aviation Act 1982 and Civil Aviation (Eurocontrol) Act 1983.

[78] *e.g.*, European Convention on Consular Functions 1967, implemented by the Consular Relations Act 1968.

[79] Brussels Convention on Civil Liability for Oil Pollution Damage 1969, implemented by the Merchant Shipping (Oil Pollution) Act 1971.

[80] Protection of Trading Interests Act 1980, s.6(5), under which the English courts have jurisdiction to entertain proceedings for the recovery of excess amounts payable under a judgment for multiple damages. Jurisdiction under this subsection does not fall within Art. 57 of the 1968 Convention; in the case of conflict, therefore, the Convention's jurisdictional provisions take priority.

[81] See *The Burns* [1907] P. 137, *per* Fletcher Moulton L.J. at p. 149.

[82] *Castrique* v. *Imrie* (1870) L.R. 4 H.L. 427, and see para. 1.33 below.

sections 20 to 27 of the Supreme Court Act 1981.[83] Section 20 lists a wide range of maritime claims and matters which may form the subject of Admiralty proceedings.[84] An Admiralty action *in personam* may be brought against a named defendant, or *in rem* against a ship, cargo, freight or other property[85] in connection with which an Admiralty claim is made.[86] Claimants generally prefer the procedure *in rem* to that *in personam* because it enables them to secure the arrest and detention of the property in question and because it does not involve tracing and serving an identified defendant. The arrest of the property usually has the effect of forcing the defendant to come forward.

1.32   The action *in rem* is commenced by the issue of a writ out of the Admiralty Registry. The writ is directed to "the owners and other persons interested in . . . [the property in question]" and it is served by being physically attached to the property.[87] This may only be done within the limits of the territorial jurisdiction of the English courts. At any time after issue of the writ, application may be made to the court for a warrant for the arrest of the property. The warrant is served by the Admiralty Marshal or his substitute, usually when the writ is served, by physical attachment to the property. Its effect is to place the property in the custody of the court until the action has been determined or the release of the property has been ordered.[88] The owner or other person interested in the property can only secure its release by acknowledging service of the writ and by providing bail, or other security, or paying the amount claimed into court. A person who appears to defend the proceedings, if he does not successfully apply to set the writ aside, is taken to have submitted to the jurisdiction and the proceedings continue against him as an action *in personam*.[89] If no person appears in the action to prevent the arrest of the property or to provide security for

---

[83] The Admiralty jurisdiction of the county court is closely modelled on that of the High Court, see County Courts Act 1984, ss.26–31; the upper limit to the county court's Admiralty jurisdiction is generally £5,000, save in respect of salvage claims when it is £15,000.

[84] s.20 gives substantial effect to the International Convention Relating to the Arrest of Sea-going Ships, and the International Convention on Certain Rules concerning Civil Jurisdiction in Matters of Collision, both signed at Brussels on May 10, 1952, (Cmnd. 8954).

[85] An action *in rem* may be brought against an aircraft or a hovercraft, or a "sister" ship in the same ownership as that in respect of which the claim is made.

[86] Supreme Court Act 1981, s.21.

[87] Service is dispensed with when the defendant's solicitor agrees to accept service and undertakes to provide security or to pay money into court.

[88] Shipowners will commonly forestall the arrest of their vessels by entering a *caveat* against arrest and by agreeing to enter an appearance and to provide bail or other security.

[89] *The Lloydiana* [1983] 2 Lloyd's Rep. 313.

its release, judgment in default will follow, upon proof of the claim, and the property will be sold to satisfy the plaintiff's claim, subject to other claims ranking in priority to or *in pari passu* with the plaintiff's claim.

1. The basis of jurisdiction *in rem*

Historically the basis of the Admiralty Court's jurisdiction *in rem*   **1.33**
was the arrest of the ship or other property within the jurisdiction,[90] but this is no longer the case. The court's jurisdiction is said to be invoked by the service of the writ.[91] The writ may be issued wherever the ship may be but it can only be served, and the court is only able to exercise jurisdiction *in rem* over the ship, when it comes within the court's territorial jurisdiction. It may be said therefore that jurisdiction *in rem* is based on the presence of the property in question within the jurisdiction. Where a writ *in rem* is issued against a ship which is still outside the jurisdiction of the court, and the defendant or his representatives agree to accept service and to put up security to prevent it from being arrested, the action becomes an action *in personam* in respect of which jurisdiction is based on the acknowledgment of service by or on behalf of the defendant.[92]

2. Effect of 1968 Convention on jurisdiction *in rem*[93]

Admiralty matters are usually "civil and commercial" and as   **1.34**
such fall within the material scope of the 1968 Convention. The Convention lays down special jurisdictional rules applicable to certain claims for remuneration in respect of salvage of cargo or freight,[94] and claims for limitation of liability.[95] Apart from these cases, no special provision is made in the Convention for Admiralty matters, and, subject to the major qualification introduced by Article 57, the Convention's ordinary rules of jurisdiction apply to Admiralty cases as they apply to any other cases.[96]
The effect of the Convention on the Admiralty action *in rem* is

---

[90] See *The Dictator* [1892] P. 304, at p. 313.
[91] Thomas, *Maritime Liens*, para. 97. See also *The Banco* [1971] P. 137, at p. 153 (C.A.); *The Good Herald* [1987] 1 Lloyd's Rep. 236.
[92] *The Monica S.* [1968] P. 471, at p. 763; *The Berny* [1978] 1 All E.R. 1065. See also *The August 8* [1983] 2 A.C. 450, at p. 456 (H.L.).
[93] See generally, Jackson, *Civil Jurisdiction and Judgments—Maritime Claims*; Brice, "Maritime Claims: The European Judgments Convention," [1987] L.M.C.L.Q. 281.
[94] Art. 5(7), see para. 17.70 below.
[95] Art. 6A, see para. 17.96 below.
[96] The negotiators of the Accession Convention decided, after some deliberation, not to include a section dealing specifically with Admiralty jurisdiction: see Schlosser para. 121, para. A1.404 below.

uncertain and it gives rise to a number of problems. Actions *in rem* are not mentioned as such in the Convention, but Article 3 provides that the rules in the United Kingdom which enable jurisdiction to be founded on the presence or seizure of property "shall not be applicable as against" persons domiciled in other Contracting States.[97] In the Schlosser Report it is stated that these provisions of Article 3 refer to "some characteristic features of Scottish law."[98] It is hard, however, to avoid the conclusion that they also exclude the bringing of an English action *in rem* against the property of a defendant domiciled in another Contracting State.[99] It might be argued that, as an action *in rem* is brought not against an identified defendant but against a *res*,[1] it falls outside the ambit of the 1968 Convention, which regulates the circumstances in which defendants domiciled in Contracting States may be sued.[2] In reality, however, the plaintiff's claim is against an identifiable party, but the *res* is subjected to the court's procedures as a matter of practical convenience, until the defendant appears in the action. It is submitted that the exercise of *in rem* jurisdiction against a defendant's property is, in the language of the second paragraph of Article 3, the application, "as against" that defendant, of the particular jurisdictional rule.[3] The basis of the jurisdiction of English courts *in rem* is, as was concluded above,[4] the presence of the defendant's property within the territorial jurisdiction. Although the writ may be issued against a ship or other property wherever it is, jurisdiction may only be exercised, whether by service of the writ or arrest of the ship, when the ship comes within the court's territorial jurisdiction. Accordingly it would seem that this type of English jurisdiction is caught by the prohibition contained in Article 3.[5]

---

[97] See para. 16.09 below.
[98] Schlosser, para. 86, see para. A1.374.
[99] As to defendants in Scotland or Northern Ireland, see the 1982 Act, s.17 and Sched. 5, para. 6, which is apparently intended to exclude maritime claims from Sched. 4; but *quaere* whether it only excludes those claims covered by the Arrest Convention 1952, see further para. 1.35 below.
[1] See *The Burns* [1907] P. 137, *per* Fletcher Moulton L.J. at p. 149.
[2] In *The Nordglimt* [1987] 2 Lloyd's Rep. 470 at p. 482, Hobhouse J. held that an action *in rem* only acquires the character of an action between a plaintiff and a shipowner when the latter enters an appearance and the action becomes *in personam*. That decision was made in the context of Art. 21 of the 1968 Convention (*lis alibi pendens*) and it has since been distinguished and explained in *The Linda* [1988] 1 Lloyd's Rep. 175.
[3] See *The Cristina* [1938] A.C. 485, at p. 492, where Lord Atkin regarded the issue of a writ *in rem* as directly impleading the defendant.
[4] Para. 1.33.
[5] To similar effect, see Jackson, *Civil Jurisdiction and Judgments—Maritime Claims*, p. 151.

The effect of Article 57 of the 1968 Convention. The drastic conse- **1.35**
quences of the above conclusion on the exercise of Admiralty jurisdiction *in rem* are, however, to a large extent mitigated by the
operation of Article 57 of the Convention.[6] The general effect of
this Article is to preserve the rules of jurisdiction established by
existing international conventions governing particular matters[7]
where they conflict with the 1968 Convention. The Brussels Arrest
Convention and the Brussels Collision Jurisdiction Convention,
both of 1952,[8] are such conventions. The Arrest Convention provides for the arrest of ships as security for maritime claims, as
defined, and it confers international jurisdiction on the courts of its
contracting states in respect of such claims. The Collision Jurisdiction Convention contains rules for the allocation of jurisdiction in
cases arising out of maritime collisions. The Conventions have not
been directly implemented into English law, although many of their
provisions have been put into effect by sections 20 and 22 of the
Supreme Court Act 1981.[9] In so far as the exercise of jurisdiction *in
rem* by the English courts is founded on these conventions, or other
conventions saved by Article 57, the prohibition which Article 3
would impose in a case falling within the 1968 Convention is overridden.

E. Discretion in Matters Affecting Jurisdiction

The court's power to exercise discretion is one of the principal **1.36**
characteristics of English jurisdictional rules, but like much else in
this field the United Kingdom's accession to the 1968 Convention
has brought about far-reaching changes in the scope of the court's
discretionary powers in matters of jurisdiction.[10] In cases to which
the 1968 Convention and 1982 Act do not apply, the court's discretionary powers remain unaltered, but where the court's jurisdiction derives from the Convention those powers are severely
curtailed. There is also an intermediate class of cases in which the
jurisdiction of the court is founded both on the Convention and on
other provisions of the 1982 Act, in which the court retains a wider

---

[6] This mitigating effect applies only as regards ships, because their arrest is governed by the Brussels Arrest Convention (see n. 8 below). That convention does
not apply to the arrest of cargo, freight or other property.
[7] See paras. 33.07 and Appendix 2 below.
[8] International Convention relating to the Arrest of Sea-going Ships, and the
International Convention on Certain Rules concerning Civil Jurisdiction in
Matters of Collision, both signed at Brussels on May 10, 1952, (Cmd. 8954).
[9] See *The Nordglimt* [1987] 2 Lloyd's Rep. 470, in which Hobhouse J. held that
the conventions referred to in Article 57 had been indirectly incorporated into
English municipal law by the 1982 Act.
[10] The 1968 Convention does not affect the court's discretion to stay or strike out
proceedings on procedural grounds: see para. 44.42 below.

discretion than if the jurisdiction were founded on the Convention alone.

1. Discretion in cases to which the 1968 Convention applies

1.37   The jurisdictional rules in the 1968 Convention are generally compulsory in nature[11] and if a court's jurisdiction is properly invoked under these rules the court is normally bound to exercise that jurisdiction. Correspondingly, English courts are required by the Convention to examine their own jurisdiction and to decline jurisdiction of their own motion[12] either if the case is one in respect of which the courts of another Contracting State have exclusive jurisdiction under Article 16[13] or if the defendant is domiciled in another Contracting State and does not enter an appearance, unless the court's jurisdiction is derived from the Convention.[14]

It follows that there is generally no place in the Convention's scheme of rules for a court to exercise discretion either in deciding whether or not to accept jurisdiction, or in deciding whether or not to stay proceedings on jurisdictional grounds.[15] There are, however, two classes of exception, under which the court may stay proceedings commenced before it in accordance with the Convention.

Discretion conferred by the Convention

1.38   First, the Convention itself confers discretionary powers on a court to stay or dismiss proceedings in certain circumstances if the same or a related dispute is the subject of earlier proceedings in the courts of another Contracting State.[16] Because these powers form part of the Convention's own scheme of rules, they are probably to be exercised on the same principles in each of the Contracting States.

Conflicts of jurisdiction with non-Contracting States

1.39   The second class of exceptions to the otherwise compulsory nature of the Convention's rules arises because the Convention is generally silent as to conflicts of jurisdiction between the courts of a Contracting State and those of non-Contracting States. If proceedings are properly brought before a court which has jurisdiction

---

[11] Para. 15.02 below.

[12] See para. 22.09 below.

[13] Art. 19, para. 22.01 below.

[14] Art. 20, para. 22.11 below. The court is required to stay its proceedings instead of dismissing them in certain circumstances: Art. 20, second and third paras.

[15] See para. 15.02, n. 8a below. The extent to which the 1968 Convention is incompatible with a discretion to stay proceedings is discussed at paras. 44.42 to 44.44 below.

[16] Art. 21, second para. (para. 23.10 below); and Art. 22 (paras. 23.11 *et seq.* below).

under the Convention, may the court decline to exercise that juris-diction on the ground that a court in a non-Contracting State also has jurisdiction? It seems that a discretion to do so may arise in the three types of case mentioned below.

Jurisdiction agreements. First, if the parties have concluded a valid jurisdiction agreement in favour of the courts of a non-Contracting State, it seems that an English court may decide to give effect to it[17] according to its normal criteria,[18] provided that the case is not gov-erned by one of the rules in the Convention which take precedence over Article 17.[19]

Lis alibi pendens. Secondly, an English court may probably stay proceedings which have been properly commenced before it, if pro-ceedings involving the same cause of action and between the same parties have already been commenced in a non-Contracting State, and provided the judgment given in those proceedings would fulfil the criteria necessary for its recognition in England.[20] The principal criteria for recognition of such a judgment are that it be final and conclusive on the merits and be given by a court of competent juris-diction.[21]

Exclusive jurisdiction. Thirdly, if the proceedings are principally concerned with one of the matters mentioned in Article 16 of the Convention, but the subject-matter is based in, or connected with, a non-Contracting State rather than a Contracting State, it is prob-able that an English court would be permitted to stay proceedings in favour of the courts of the non-Contracting State.[22]

Discretion otherwise excluded. The discretion to stay proceedings **1.40** in favour of the courts of a non-Contracting State probably extends only to those three classes of case. Each of them involves a conflict of jurisdiction which, if it arose as between different Contracting States, the Convention would resolve by requiring that jurisdiction be declined in favour of the foreign court. In this respect they are exceptional: in most cases, the fact that the courts of another Con-tracting State also had jurisdiction over the proceedings would not enable the court first seised to decline jurisdiction. There is no

---

[17] See para. 21.13 below.
[18] The exercise of discretion to stay proceedings under English law is discussed at paras. 1.41 *et seq.* below.
[19] The provisions which may take precedence over Art. 17 are Arts. 12, 15, 16, 18 and 57: see para. 21.04 below.
[20] See para. 23.06 below. See also Art. 27(5) of the Convention, para. 27.59 below.
[21] See Dicey and Morris, p. 426, rule 36(2). It is not a condition for the recog-nition, as distinct from the enforcement, of such a judgment that it should be a money judgment.
[22] See paras. 20.06 *et seq.* below.

reason, it is suggested, to suppose that a court with jurisdiction under the Convention may stay its proceedings in equivalent circumstances in favour of a court of a non-Contracting State, even if the latter is a more appropriate forum.

2. Discretion in cases to which the 1968 Convention does not apply

1.41 In cases to which the 1968 Convention does not apply, English courts continue to enjoy discretionary powers in matters affecting jurisdiction. On one hand, the court has a discretion to stay or strike out proceedings on jurisdictional grounds[23] and, on the other hand, it has a discretion to accept jurisdiction over persons outside its territorial jurisdiction, by permitting the service of a writ on such a person.[24]

Staying or striking out proceedings

The power to stay or strike out proceedings is not confined to any particular class of case and it may be exercised whenever it is necessary to prevent injustice,[25] but in practice there are three types of case in which it is normally exercised, namely where there is another court which is more appropriate for the resolution of the dispute (*forum non conveniens*), where the same dispute is being litigated before another court (*lis alibi pendens*) and where a jurisdiction agreement has been concluded in favour of another court.[26]

1.42 *Forum non conveniens.* The term "*forum non conveniens,*" which is derived from Scottish law, refers to the principles on which the court generally exercises its discretion in deciding whether or not to stay proceedings[27] in favour of a foreign court. These principles were comprehensively reviewed by the House of Lords in *Spiliada Maritime Corporation* v. *Cansulex Ltd.*[28] The court must be satisfied that "there is some other available forum, having competent jurisdiction, which is the appropriate forum for the trial of the action, *i.e.* in which the case may be tried more suitably for the interests of all the parties and the ends of justice."[29] If the plaintiff has invoked

---

[23] See Dicey and Morris, Chap. 13; Cheshire and North, pp. 221 *et seq.*

[24] See Dicey and Morris, pp. 304 *et seq.*; Cheshire and North, pp. 193 *et seq.*

[25] The court's powers to stay or strike out proceedings, where to do so is not inconsistent with the 1968 Convention, are expressly reserved by the 1982 Act, s.49 (paras. 44.41 *et seq.* below).

[26] A stay of proceedings because the parties have agreed to arbitration is not considered, arbitration being outside the scope of this book.

[27] *Supreme Court Practice*, paras. [5215–5218]; Dicey and Morris, pp. 389–395; Cheshire and North, pp. 222 *et seq.*

[28] [1987] A.C. 460.

[29] *Ibid.* at p. 476. The term "*conveniens*" means "appropriate" and not "convenient": *ibid.*, p. 475.

the jurisdiction as of right, usually by service on the defendant within the territorial limits, the burden on the defendant is to show that there is another available forum which is "clearly or distinctly more appropriate than the English forum."[30] The court will consider first those factors which point in the direction of another forum, including the availability of witnesses, the law governing the transaction and the residence or place of business of the parties; if it concludes that there is no other more appropriate forum, it will ordinarily refuse a stay.[31] If there is a forum which is *prima facie* more appropriate, the burden shifts to the plaintiff to show that there are circumstances by reason of which justice requires that a stay should nevertheless not be granted.[32] The fact that a plaintiff might be deprived of some advantage by reason of differences in the applicable systems of civil procedure is not normally a sufficient reason for refusing a stay.[33]

Lis alibi pendens. A stay of proceedings may be granted if the **1.43** same or similar issues are being litigated between the same parties both in England and in another country.[34] The foreign proceedings are referred to as a *lis alibi pendens* and although it is mentioned separately here, the fact that there are different proceedings in different countries is treated in English law as a specific factor to be taken into account by the court in applying the principles of *forum non conveniens* outlined above, rather than as a separate class of case. In general, the courts prefer to prevent a multiplicity of proceedings, although the factors weighing against the grant of a stay may outweigh those in favour of staying the proceedings.[35] In an appropriate case, the court may be willing to restrain the continuance of the foreign proceedings rather than stay the English proceedings.[36] The fact that one set of proceedings has been commenced before the other set of proceedings is not a decisive factor in the exercise of the discretion.

Jurisdiction agreements. The court will usually grant a stay of Eng- **1.44** lish proceedings on the application of the defendant, if the proceedings have been brought in breach of an agreement between the

---

[30] *Ibid.*, at p. 477.
[31] *Ibid.*, at p. 478.
[32] *Ibid.* at p. 478.
[33] *Ibid.*, at pp. 482 *et seq.*
[34] *Société Nationale Industrielle Aerospatiale* v. *Lee Kui Jak* [1987] A.C. 871; *Supreme Court Practice*, para. [5228]; Dicey and Morris pp. 395–396; Cheshire and North, pp. 234–237.
[35] *Hawke Bay Shipping Co. Ltd.* v. *The First National Bank of Chicago (The Efthimis)* [1986] 1 Lloyd's Rep. 244.
[36] See para. 1.51 below. Dicey and Morris, pp. 396–398; Cheshire and North, pp. 244–252.

parties to refer their disputes to the exclusive jurisdiction of a foreign court.[37] The validity of the jurisdiction agreement is determined by its proper law.[38] The grant or refusal of a stay, however, remains a matter for the court's discretion. The principles on which the court proceeds are not the same as those which apply in the case of *forum non conveniens*, not least because considerable importance is attached in this context to the principle that parties should abide by their agreement. In exercising its discretion, the court considers all the circumstances of the case.[39]

Permitting service out of the jurisdiction

1.45   The court has a discretion to permit the service of a writ out of the jurisdiction if the case falls within one or more of the categories set out in Order 11, rule 1(1) of the Rules of the Supreme Court.[40] The discretion is necessarily exercised in the first instance on the plaintiff's *ex parte* application, but it may be reviewed *inter partes* on the defendant's application, without the defendant thereby submitting to the jurisdiction.[41] As with an application for a stay of proceedings on the ground of *forum non conveniens*, the question which the court has to consider is whether England is the appropriate forum, in the sense that the case can be suitably tried there for the interests of all the parties and the ends of justice.[42] The burden is on the plaintiff to show not only that England is the appropriate forum but also that this is clearly so.[43] The discretion to allow service of a writ outside the jurisdiction is considered further in Chapter 3.[44]

3. Discretion in cases in which the 1968 Convention regulates only the court's international jurisdiction

1.46   In those cases in which the 1968 Convention allocates jurisdiction to the courts of the United Kingdom generally, without specifying in which part of the United Kingdom the proceedings should be

---

[37] Dicey and Morris, pp. 402 *et seq.*; Cheshire and North, pp. 237–242.
[38] *Mackender* v. *Feldia A.G.* [1967] 2 Q.B. 590.
[39] A statement of the important factors to be taken into account has been formulated by Brandon J., and approved by him in the Court of Appeal and House of Lords: *The Eleftheria* [1970] P. 94, at p. 110; *Aratra Potato Co. Ltd.* v. *Egyptian Navigation Co. (The El Almira)* [1981] 2 Lloyds Rep. 119, at pp. 123–124 (C.A.); *The Sennar (No. 2)* [1985] 1 W.L.R. 490, at p. 500 (H.L.).
[40] *Supreme Court Practice*, paras. 11/1/1–11/1/28; Dicey and Morris, pp. 304–308; Cheshire and North, pp. 205–212. The court may also permit service out of the jurisdiction of an Admiralty writ *in personam* in similar cases: R.S.C. Ord. 75, r. 4.
[41] R.S.C., Ord. 12, r. 8(6).
[42] *Spiliada Maritime Corporation* v. *Cansulex Ltd.* [1987] A.C. 460, at p. 480.
[43] *Ibid.*, at p. 481.
[44] Para. 3.29 below.

brought, the jurisdiction of the English court is governed by section 16 and Schedule 4 of the 1982 Act.[45] The discretionary powers of the English court as regards jurisdiction in these cases are a combination of the two sets of rules described above. The only discretion retained by the court to stay its proceedings in favour of a court outside the United Kingdom is the limited discretion described above in connection with cases to which the 1968 Convention applies. On the other hand, it retains a discretion to stay its proceedings in favour of the courts in another part of the United Kingdom,[46] which it exercises on the principles described above in connection with cases to which the 1968 Convention does not apply.

F. EXTRATERRITORIAL EFFECTS OF THE EXERCISE OF JURISDICTION

So far this chapter has been concerned with the circumstances in which the English courts will entertain jurisdiction *in personam* or *in rem* in cases which contain foreign elements. It is necessary also to examine the extent to which the English courts will make orders to enjoin or compel the performance of acts within the territory of another state and to consider the effect of the 1968 Convention upon this exercise of jurisdiction.   1.47

The English courts have taken the view that their power to enjoin or compel the performance of an act is not restricted to the territorial limits, nor is it dependent on the defendant being resident within the territorial limits.[47] A defendant who is resident in another state is in precisely the same position as one who is resident in England and Wales, so far as concerns the orders which the court can make against him, provided he has properly been made subject to the court's jurisdiction, and has a sufficient connection with England and Wales.[48] However, given that the granting of injunctive relief is discretionary, the willingness of the courts to make orders with extraterritorial effect has been limited in the past by two factors in particular: first, the risk of infringing the sovereignty of the other state and, secondly, the practical difficulty of enforcing com-

---

[45] See para. 1.23 above; as regards trust and consumer contracts, see also s.10, para. 40.30 below.
[46] See para. 44.44 below.
[47] See n. 48 below. Note also the jurisdiction asserted by the Admiralty Court over acts on the high seas: *The Tubantia* [1924] P. 78.
[48] *Carron Iron Co.* v. *Maclaren* (1855) 5 H.L.Cas. 416; *Re Liddell's Settlement Trusts* [1936] Ch. 365; *Royal Exchange Assurance Co.* v. *Compania Naviera Santi S.A. (The Tropaioforos)* [1962] 1 Lloyd's Rep. 410. Where the order concerns conduct within England and Wales the fact that the defendant is outside the jurisdiction is unlikely to be an inhibiting factor, see, *e.g. Tozier* v. *Hawkins* (1885) 15 Q.B.D. 680 (action to restrain an Irish defendant from publishing a libel in England).

pliance with an English order by a defendant who is outside the jurisdiction.[48a]

1.48   The implementation of the 1968 Convention has substantially affected the questions both of sovereignty and of enforceability. It has created a new jurisdictional area within which these considerations have considerably diminished force. The national sovereignty of all the Contracting States has been qualified by the adoption of common rules as to jurisdiction and as to recognition and enforcement of judgments. Moreover, whereas formerly it was not possible to enforce non-money judgments in other jurisdictions, the Convention now provides, as between Contracting States, a means whereby they can readily be enforced. In consequence the Convention has greatly extended the possible scope for the making of orders with extraterritorial effect.

1.49   *Sovereignty.* In principle, any exercise of authority by one state in the territory of another state is forbidden as an infringement of the sovereignty of the latter state. This prohibition includes peaceable measures such as the service of documents, the taking of evidence,[49] the carrying out of police or tax investigations, or the performance of notarial acts.[50] In practice the majority of states either have agreed by treaty to limited activities of this kind taking place on a reciprocal basis or they are prepared to tolerate them. However no state will tolerate an attempt by a foreign court to secure the performance of an act which is illegal by the law of that state or which interferes with the established rights of non-parties in that state.[51] The adoption of the 1968 Convention by the Contracting States involves a partial surrender of sovereignty. As has been seen, exorbitant grounds of jurisdiction may no longer be relied upon, and national courts are bound to observe the Convention's rules and to

---

[48a] The extraterritorial effects of English Mareva injunctions were extensively reviewed by the Court of Appeal in *Babanaft International Co. S.A.* v. *Bassatne* [1989] 2 W.L.R. 232; *Republic of Haiti* v. *Duvalier* [1989] 2 W.L.R. 261; *Derby & Co. Ltd.* v. *Weldon* [1989] 2 W.L.R. 276; and *Derby & Co. Ltd.* v. *Weldon (Nos. 3 & 4)* [1989] 2 W.L.R. 412. See paras. 7.23 *et seq.* below.
[49] See para. 8.42 below.
[50] See the Aide Memoire of Her Majesty's Government to the EEC Commission (October 20, 1969): Brit.Pract.Int.L. 1967 p. 58, and the statement of principles of international law in anti-trust cases, as understood by Her Majesty's Government; F. A. Mann, "The Doctrine of Justification in International Law" (1964) 1 Hague Recueil 9.
[51] *British Nylon Spinners Ltd.* v. *I.C.I.* [1953] Ch. 19, *per* Evershed M.R. at p. 25; *X. A.G.* v. *A. Bank* [1983] 2 All E.R. 464.

enforce the judgments of the courts of the other Contracting States. As the Convention has established the mechanism in each Contracting State for enforcing mandatory orders made by the courts of other Contracting States, and as courts are bound to enforce such orders, subject to very narrow exceptions,[52] considerations based on respect for foreign sovereignty must, it is submitted, now have diminished force.

Enforceability. The enforceability of its order is an important con- **1.50** sideration which the English court takes into account when deciding whether or not to make the order. The presence overseas of the defendant or his assets presents obvious difficulties in the way of enforcement and this has, in the past, frequently led the courts to decline jurisdiction or to refuse injunctive relief.[53] That is not to say that the courts have always refused to make orders required to be complied with in another jurisdiction. The court may be prepared to make the order despite there being no immediate prospect of it being enforced.[54] The provisions for enforcement established under Title III of the 1968 Convention now provide the machinery which was hitherto lacking to compel compliance with English injunctions in other Contracting States. The fact that the English court will not itself be supervising the enforcement of the order will still be an important factor in its deciding whether or not to make the order.

Restrictions imposed by the 1968 Convention. Although the general **1.51** effect of the Convention is greatly to extend the scope for the making of orders intended to take effect in other Contracting States, there are certain respects in which it restricts the power of the English courts to make such orders. The English courts have long exercised the power to restrain persons subject to its jurisdiction from instituting or prosecuting suits in foreign courts.[55] The principles upon which this jurisdiction is exercised were reviewed and restated by Lord Goff of Chieveley in the *Aerospatiale* case.[56] Although the exercise of such jurisdiction might seem to be a gross infringement

---

[52] Arts. 27 and 28, paras. 27.12 *et seq.* below.
[53] For example, *Norris* v. *Chambres* (1861) 3 De G.F. & J. 583; *Marshall* v. *Marshall* (1888) 38 Ch.D. 330; *Tallack* v. *Tallack & Broekma* [1927] P. 211; *Goff* v. *Goff* [1934] P. 107; *Wyler* v. *Lyons* [1963] P. 274.
[54] *Hospital for Sick Children* v. *Walt Disney Productions Inc.* [1967] 1 All E.R. 1005, (injunction against a foreign corporation with no assets in the jurisdiction).
[55] *Carron Iron Co.* v. *Maclaren* (1855) 5 H.L.Cas. 416; see Dicey and Morris, pp. 396–398, Cheshire and North, pp. 224–252.
[56] *Société Nationale Industrielle Aerospatiale* v. *Lee Kui Jak* [1987] A.C. 871; *Du Pont de Nemours* v. *Agnew (No.2)* [1988] 2 Lloyd's Rep. 240 (C.A.).

of foreign judicial sovereignty, the English courts have asserted that the order operates *in personam* and that it "does not pretend to interference with the other court."[57]

As between the Contracting States to the 1968 Convention, questions of multiplicity of proceedings and competing jurisdictions are now exclusively regulated by Articles 21 and 23 of the Convention and accordingly the English court is unable to restrain the bringing or prosecution of proceedings in other Contracting States on the ground that they should be brought before the English courts. Only at the stage of recognition or enforcement might the English court possibly be able to refuse to recognise the resultant foreign judgment on public policy grounds. It could not do so if this involved a review of the jurisdiction of the foreign court or if the public policy objections related to the jurisdiction of the foreign court.[58]

1.52   Even if the English court had jurisdiction under the Convention to entertain an application for an injunction to restrain proceedings before the courts of another Contracting State, it is suggested that such an injunction should not be granted, as being inconsistent with the scheme and purpose of the Convention.[59] Given that the English courts are bound, in most cases, to recognise and enforce the judgments given by the courts of other Contracting States, they should not be able to deny parties access to those courts.

So, for example, an injunction should probably not now be granted to restrain the commencement or prosecution of proceedings in another Contracting State in breach of an agreement conferring exclusive jurisdiction on the English courts.[60]

Jurisdiction over proceedings concerned with the enforcement of judgments is exclusively assigned to the courts of the Contracting State in which the judgment has been or is to be enforced[61] and the English court would therefore have no jurisdiction to grant an injunction restraining the enforcement of a judgment in another Contracting State.[62] Similarly, if the courts of another Contracting

---

[57] *Bushby* v. *Munday* (1821) 5 Madd. 279, at p. 307, *per* Sir John Leach V.-C.
[58] See paras. 27.62 and 27.73 below.
[59] See Cheshire and North, p. 253.
[60] It may also be inconsistent with the 1968 Convention for an injunction to be granted restraining proceedings from being commenced or prosecuted in another Contracting State in breach of an arbitration agreement: see paras. 14.32 and 43.29 below.
[61] Art. 16(5), see paras. 20.40 *et seq.* below.
[62] *C.f. Ellerman Lines* v. *Read* [1928] 2 K.B. 144; *Mike Trading and Transport Ltd.* v. *Pagnan & Fratelli, The Lisboa,* [1980] 2 Lloyd's Rep. 546, (injunction to discontinue arrest proceedings in Italy.)

State had exclusive jurisdiction under one of the other provisions of Article 16,[63] the English court should probably not grant an injunction restraining those proceedings[64]; such an injunction would deprive the plaintiff of a forum altogether.

---

[63] Chap. 20 below. See, for example, Art. 16(1), relating to rights *in rem* in, or tenancies of, immovable property. Compare the former position in such cases as *Penn* v. *Lord Baltimore* (1750) 1 Ves.Se. 444, *Duder* v. *Amsterdamsch Trustees Kantoor* [1902] 2 Ch. 132, *Deschamps* v. *Miller* [1908] 1 Ch. 856; *Richard West & Partners (Inverness) Ltd.* v. *Dick* [1969] 2 Ch. 424; *Cook Industries* v. *Galliher* [1979] Ch. 439.

[64] If the application for an injunction were proceedings which had "as their object" the specified subject-matter, the English court would not even have jurisdiction to entertain the application.

CHAPTER 2

PARTIES: CAPACITY AND IMMUNITY

A. INTRODUCTION

2.01 As was seen in Chapter 1, the identity and attributes of a party[1] may affect the court's ability to entertain any particular proceedings, irrespective of any matter concerning service of process or the subject matter of the proceedings. The plaintiff and the defendant must both be persons, natural or legal, whom the court accepts as capable of taking part in proceedings in their own names, and at the instance of whom, or over whom, the court is prepared to exercise its jurisdiction. In English law, as in all legal systems, the capacity of parties is a matter of procedure and is governed by the *lex fori*. This chapter examines those factors relating to foreign parties which may affect their capacity to sue or be sued in the English courts.

B. THE CAPACITY TO SUE AND TO BE SUED

2.02 An individual or a legal person may have the capacity in general terms to sue or be sued without necessarily being entitled under substantive law, or for reasons of jurisdiction, to bring or defend any particular proceedings. A distinction may also be drawn between a person's capacity to be a party to proceedings and his capacity to conduct them: thus, as in most legal systems, a minor is capable of being a party to proceedings but he may only conduct them in the name of a person of full capacity.

---

[1] A party is defined by the Supreme Court Act, 1981, s.151(1); see also 37 *Halsbury's Laws* (4th ed.), para. 23.

40

English procedural law generally adopts a flexible approach to the subject of parties and once proceedings have been started the High Court has extensive powers to bring before it as parties all those persons whose presence is necessary for the effectual adjudications of the matters in dispute and any connected matters.[2]

1. Foreign individuals

Any adult individual of sound mind has capacity to sue or be sued in the English courts in his or her own name,[3] and that capacity is not in any way affected by matters of foreign nationality or domicile[4]; but the fact that a party is resident outside the court's territorial jurisdiction may give rise to certain procedural consequences, apart from questions of the court's jurisdiction to entertain the proceedings. For example, foreign residence might render him liable to provide security for costs[5] and he will be subject to various requirements concerning the giving of an address for service within the jurisdiction.[6] An applicant for an injunction who is resident outside the jurisdiction may be required to deposit security to underwrite an undertaking in damages.[7]

2.03

2. Persons under a disability

A person under a disability, being a minor[8] or a mental patient[9] may not bring any proceedings except by his next friend and may not acknowledge service, defend, counterclaim or intervene in any proceedings except by his *guardian ad litem*,[10] appointed in accord-

2.04

---

[2] R.S.C., Ord. 15, r. 6.
[3] An individual carrying on business within the jurisdiction in a name or style other than his own name may be sued in that name as if it were the name of a firm. This applies whether or not he is within the jurisdiction: R.S.C., Ord. 81, r. 9.
[4] An alien enemy is an exception. A person who is voluntarily resident in, or who is carrying on business in, an enemy's country is classed as an alien enemy, regardless of his nationality. As such he cannot bring proceedings in the English courts, but he may be sued. If sued he may appeal any decision that is given against him: *Porter v. Freudenberg* [1915] 1 K.B. 857; see the cases cited in the *Supreme Court Practice* at para. [4669] and also McNair and Watts: *Legal Effects of War* (4th ed.), chap. 3.
[5] See para. 6.07 below.
[6] See para. 3.31 below.
[7] See para. 7.06 below.
[8] *I.e.* under 18 years of age: Family Law Reform Act 1969, s.1(2).
[9] *I.e.* a person who, by reason of mental disorder is incapable of managing and administering his property and affairs: Mental Health Act 1983, s.94.
[10] R.S.C., Ord. 80, r. 2.

ance with English procedural rules.[11] There is no requirement that the next friend or guardian so appointed should be resident within the jurisdiction, but if as a plaintiff he is not, he may be ordered to provide security for costs.[12] As the capacity to sue and be sued is a matter of procedural law for the *lex fori*, the question whether a foreign person is a minor is to be determined by English law, even if he has attained his majority under the law of his domicile.

3. Foreign representative parties

2.05   A person who has a representative capacity arising by virtue of foreign law may wish to bring or to defend proceedings in England and in such circumstances the English court is confronted by two conflicting principles.[13] It can either give effect to the representative party's right under foreign law to act in the proceedings in his own name, or it can insist that English procedure for his appointment to the representative capacity should be complied with. Both solutions have been variously adopted. The English court has recognised the right of a foreign curator of a foreign mental patient to act in English proceedings in his own name,[14] even when the patient was a domiciled Englishman resident abroad.[15] Where foreign personal representatives of deceased persons had failed to obtain a grant of representation in England, English courts have refused to recognise their capacity to bring claims on behalf of the estates[16]; and the entitlement of a foreign administrator of absentee's property to bring a claim on behalf of the absentee has also not been recognised.[17] Foreign receivers or assignees in bankruptcy who have a right, according to the law of the country in which they were appointed, to sue in their own names for a chose in action due to a person in respect of whose property they were appointed, have

---

[11] R.S.C., Ord. 80, r. 3.

[12] *Didisheim* v. *London and Westminster Bank* [1900] 2 Ch. 15; *New York Security & Trust Co.* v. *Keyser* [1901] Ch. 666; *Supreme Court Practice*, para. 80/3/1; see para. 6.06 below.

[13] *Kamouh* v. *Associated Electrical Industries International Ltd.* [1980] Q.B. 199, *per* Parker J. at p. 206.

[14] *Didisheim* v. *London and Westminster Bank* [1900] 2 Ch. 15; *Pélégrin* v. *Coutts and Co.* [1915] 1 Ch. 696. Dicey and Morris, Rule 112.

[15] *In re Garnier* (1872) L.R. 13 Eq. 532.

[16] *New York Breweries Co. Ltd.* v. *Att.-Gen.* [1899] A.C. 62; *Finnegan* v. *Cementation Co. Ltd.* [1953] 1 Q.B. 688. See Revenue Act 1884 s.11, and Dicey and Morris, rule 132. Note that by the Administration of Estates Act 1971, there is provision for reciprocal recognition of grants of representation as between England and Wales, Scotland, and Northern Ireland.

[17] *Kamouh* v. *Associated Electrical Industries International Ltd.*, above.

been held to have a similar right before the English courts.[18] However, before an English court will recognise a foreign receiver's title to assets located in England and Wales, or direct the setting up of an auxilliary receivership, it will examine the basis upon which the foreign court assumed jurisdiction. It will consider the connection between the defendant in the foreign proceedings and the jurisdiction of the foreign court which appointed the receiver, and will only recognise that court's order as having effect outside the territorial jurisdiction of that court if it finds the connection to be sufficiently close to justify such recognition according to English principles of private international law.[19]

4. Foreign corporations

A foreign corporation duly created according to the laws of a **2.06** foreign state is, for reasons of comity,[20] recognised by English law as having legal personality and may, so long as it continues in existence under the law of its incorporation, sue and be sued by its corporate name in the English courts.[21] A company which has ceased to exist in the country of its incorporation cannot sue[22] or be sued[23] in England. As in the case of English corporate bodies a foreign corporation can only act in English proceedings through a solicitor.[24] The fact of incorporation in accordance with foreign law should be pleaded in the statement of claim or defence, and, if not admitted, should be proved.[25]

---

[18] *Macaulay* v. *Guaranty Trust Co. of New York* (1927) 44 T.L.R. 99; Dicey and Morris, Rule 166. The liquidator of a foreign company is in the same position, see *Bank of Ethiopia* v. *National Bank of Egypt* [1937] Ch. 513, and Dicey and Morris, Rule 178.

[19] *Schemmer* v. *Property Resources Ltd.* [1975] Ch. 273, at p. 278; Dicey and Morris, Rule 179(2); Picarda, *The Law Relating to Receivers and Managers*, p. 358.

[20] The United Kingdom has not yet ratified the EEC Convention on the Mutual Recognition of Companies and Legal Persons, of February 29, 1968; See the detailed analysis of the Convention by Goldman (1969) 6 C.M.L.Rev. 1045; note also the Hague Convention of June 1, 1956 concerning the Recognition of the Legal Personality of Foreign Companies Associations and Foundations which has not come into force having had insufficient ratifications.

[21] *National Bank of St. Charles* v. *de Bernales* (1825) 1 C. & P. 569; *General Steamship Navigation Co.* v. *Guillon* (1843) 11 M. & W. 877; *Russian Commercial Bank* v. *Comptoir d'Escompte de Mulhouse* [1925] A.C. 112, at p. 149; *Lazard Brothers & Co.* v. *Midland Bank Ltd.* [1933] A.C. 289, *per* Lord Wright at p. 297.

[22] *Russian and English Bank* v. *Baring Bros. & Co. Ltd.* [1932] 1 Ch. 435.

[23] *Lazard Bros.* v. *Bank Industrielle de Moscou* [1932] 1 K.B. 617.

[24] See R.S.C., Ord. 5, r. 6 and the notes thereto.

[25] See *Bullen and Leake and Jacob's Precedents of Pleading* (12th ed.) p. 333; para. 3.32 below.

5. Foreign partnerships[26]

2.07   As a matter of English law, a partnership arises when two or more persons carry on business in common with a view to profit.[27] A partnership has no legal existence distinct from its members and therefore cannot sue or be sued in its own right in the English courts. If partners carry on business within the jurisdiction of the English court, though, they may sue or be sued in the firm's name.[28] This rule of procedural law, discussed in greater detail below, does not alter the principle that it is the individual partners who sue and who are sued,[29] a principle which applies wherever they are resident or domiciled.

The term "foreign partnership" is inexact and two meanings should be distinguished. First, it may refer to a partnership formally constituted according to foreign law, which may or may not possess a legal personality distinct from its members; and, secondly, it may refer to persons whom English law would regard as carrying on business in partnership, but who are "foreign" in the sense that the partners are resident or domiciled outside the jurisdiction, or carry on business as partners principally or wholly outside the jurisdiction, or both.

2.08   If a partnership constituted according to foreign law has its own legal personality,[30] it may sue or be sued in its own right, using its own name. The question of whether such a partnership has legal personality will be determined by the law of the country in which it was formed, and its status according to that law will be recognised by English courts.[31] If it does not have legal personality, it has no existence distinct from its members capable of recognition by English law. Whether it can sue and be sued in its own name will, as in

---

[26] See Dicey and Morris, p. 293; for a historical treatment of this topic see Campbell, "Jurisdiction over the non-resident doing business in England," (1961) 10 I.C.L.Q. 401.

[27] Partnership Act 1890, s.1. A limited partnership created under the Limited Partnerships Act 1907 is not a legal entity: see *Re Barnard* [1932] 1 Ch. 272.

[28] R.S.C., Ord. 81, r. 1; C.C.R. Ord. 5, r. 9.

[29] *Western National Bank* v. *Perez Triana & Co.* [1891] 1 Q.B. 304, *per* Lindley L.J. at p. 314.

[30] Legal personality is accorded by certain legal systems to bodies which are not incorporated. The principal forms of company and other entity capable of existing under the law of the other Contracting States to the 1968 Convention are set out in chaps. 48 to 55 at para. 73. See also the commentary on Art. 53, para. 31.25 below.

[31] *Von Hellfeld* v. *Rechnitzer and Mayer Frères & Co.* [1914] 1 Ch. 748 (C.A.); *Dreyfus* v. *Commissioner of Inland Revenue* (1929) 14 T.C. 560, at p. 577 (C.A.); *Skyline Associates* v. *Small* (1974) 50 D.L.R. (3rd) 217; Cheshire and North, p. 901.

the case of an English partnership, depend upon whether it carries on business within the territorial jurisdiction of the English court.

Where two or more persons claim to be entitled, or are alleged to be liable, as partners in respect of a cause of action, English procedural law permits them to sue or be sued in the name of the firm if they carry on business within the jurisdiction.[32] A firm carries on business within the jurisdiction if it has a place of business there,[33] whether or not it has another place of business or its principal place of business outside the jurisdiction.[34] Employment of an agent within the jurisdiction may not be sufficient for these purposes.[35] When the Central Office is requested to issue a writ in which a foreign partnership is named as plaintiff or defendant it refuses, as a matter of practice, to issue the writ, unless the individual partners are named.[36]

Where partners sue or are sued in the firm's name, the court has **2.09** power, on the application of the other party, to order the disclosure of the names and residential addresses of the partners in the firm as at the date when the cause of action accrued.[37] Acknowledgment of service may not be given in the firm's name but only in the names of the individual partners[38] and special provisions apply to partners who deny having been partners, or liable as such, at any material time. The rules provide for service on partnerships sued in the firm's name,[39] including a provision for service on the partnership at its principal place of business within the jurisdiction, whether or not any member of the firm is out of the jurisdiction.[40] Where judgment is obtained against a partnership in the firm's name, the rules also contain restrictions on its execution against any partner who was not subject to the jurisdiction of the court.[41]

---

[32] R.S.C., Ord. 81, r. 1; C.C.R. Ord. 5, r. 9. This rule avoids the inconvenience of using the names of individual partners in an action by or against a firm.

[33] See para. 4.10 below; *Lysaght Ltd.* v. *Clark & Co.* [1891] 1 Q.B. 552; *Worcester City Banking Co.* v. *Firbank & Co.* [1894] 1 Q.B. 784.

[34] *South India Shipping Corporation Ltd.* v. *Export-Import Bank of Korea* [1985] 1 W.L.R. 585.

[35] *Singleton* v. *Roberts & Co.* (1894) 70 L.T. 687, a purchasing agent who sent goods abroad; See *Konstantinidis* v. *World Tankers Corporation*, *("The World Harmony")*, [1967] p. 341, where the meaning of "place of business" is discussed and the authorities reviewed.

[36] *Supreme Court Practice*, para. 81/1/13.

[37] R.S.C., Ord. 81, r. 2. *cf.* the court's power to order the disclosure of the identity of persons suing in Admiralty proceedings as "the owners and other persons interested in [a ship or cargo]": see 1 *Halsbury's Laws* (4th ed.) para. 362.

[38] R.S.C., Ord. 81, r. 4. The action continues in the name of the firm.

[39] See para. 4.10 below.

[40] R.S.C., Ord. 81, r. 3(1); *Meyer* v. *Louis Dreyfus* [1940] 4 All E.R. 157.

[41] R.S.C., Ord. 81, r. 5. The rule fails to take account of the compulsory nature of jurisdiction under the 1968 Convention and the provisions of R.S.C., Ord. 11,

In some legal systems an individual partner cannot be sued until the partnership has been sued and its assets exhausted. Such rules do not affect the partner's capacity, as a matter of English law, to be sued; but they may afford a good defence to the action, depending on whether they are characterised by English conflicts rules as substantive or procedural.[42]

6. Foreign states

2.10   A foreign state which is recognised as such by Her Majesty's Government may sue, and subject to the question of immunity,[43] may be sued in the English courts.[44] By suing, it submits to the jurisdiction of the English courts in respect of the subject matter of the proceedings.[45] Problems may arise in relation to the purported governmental acts of a state which is not recognised by Her Majesty's Government, particularly if they directly affect family or property rights of individuals.[46] However, a foreign governmental body not recognised by Her Majesty's Government may still have *locus standi* before the English courts if it was set up by an independent state which has been so recognised.[47]

7. Foreign sovereigns and heads of state

2.11   A foreign sovereign or head of state has the capacity to sue in the English courts.[48] His capacity to be sued is discussed below under the topic of immunity.[49]

---

r. 1(2), whereby a writ may be served out of the jurisdiction without the leave of the court. The restriction may make it advisable to join as a separately-named defendant any partner whom it is suspected may have been out of the jurisdiction when the writ was issued. Such a defendant would be "a necessary or proper party" within the meaning of Ord. 11, r. 1(1)(c). See *West of England Steamship Owners' Protection and Indemnity Association, Ltd.* v. *John Holman and Sons.* [1957] 1 W.L.R. 1164.

[42] Dicey and Morris, p. 178; Cheshire and North, pp. 86–87.

[43] See paras. 2.13 to 2.21 below.

[44] *United States of America* v. *Wagner* (1867) 2 Ch.App. 582 (C.A.); *Republic of Peru* v. *Peruvian Guano Co.* (1887) 36 Ch.D. 489.

[45] State Immunity Act 1978, s.2(3)(a). See para. 2.15 below.

[46] See *Aksionairnoye Obschestvo A.M. Luther* v. *James Sagor and Co.* [1921] 1 K.B. 456. See *Carl Zeiss Stiftung* v. *Rayner & Keeler Ltd.* [1967] 1 A.C. 853, *per* Lord Wilberforce at p. 954.

[47] *Carl Zeiss Stiftung* v. *Rayner & Keeler Ltd.* [1967] 1 A.C. 853; *Gur Corporation* v. *Trust Bank of Africa* [1987] Q.B. 599 (C.A.).

[48] *The Emperor of Austria* v. *Day and Kossuth* (1861) 2 Giff. 628.

[49] See paras. 2.17 and 2.18 below.

8. International organisations

Under the International Organisations Acts 1968 and 1981 the **2.12** legal capacities of a corporate body have been conferred by Orders in Council on a number of international organisations.[50] As such they are able to bring proceedings in the English courts. Their capacity to be sued is subject to the privileges and immunities which those Acts confer on them.[51]

C. STATE IMMUNITY AND DIPLOMATIC PRIVILEGE

1. State Immunity

Immunity, whether it is enjoyed by a state, a sovereign, a diplo- **2.13** matic agent or other person, exempts the holder from the jurisdiction of the local courts. It does not relieve the state or person of legal liability.[52]

2. Foreign states

It has been a long established rule of public international law that **2.14** the courts of one sovereign state do not have jurisdiction over another sovereign state. According to the "absolute" theory of state immunity, a state enjoyed immunity in respect of all its activities even when they were of a commercial character.[53] This was regarded as being the common law as late as the mid 1970's although other countries were increasingly turning to the "restrictive" theory, under which immunity was only accorded in respect of the sovereign or public acts of a state.[54] Judicial and academic opinion in England was also moving towards the adoption of the restrictive theory. In 1972 the United Kingdom became a signatory to the European Convention on State Immunity which sought to deprive states and government bodies of immunity in respect of non-governmental activities.[55] In 1977 the Privy Council[56] and the Court of Appeal[57] in turn rejected the concept of absolute immunity. Ultimately the provisions of the European Convention on State Immunity were introduced into English law by the State

---

[50] See 10 *Halsbury's Statutes* (4th ed.), p. 597 n.; *J.H. Rayner (Mincing Lane) Ltd. v. Dept. of Trade and Industry* [1988] 3 W.L.R. 1033.
[51] See para. 2.21 below.
[52] *Dickinson v. Del Solar* [1930] 1 K.B. 376.
[53] *The Porto Alexandre* [1920] P. 30; *The Cristina* [1938] A.C. 485.
[54] See the *Tate Letter*, 26 Dept. State Bull. 984; Steiner and Vaghts, *Transnational Legal Problems*, (2nd ed.) p. 647.
[55] Cmnd. 5081; see Sinclair, "The European Convention on State Immunity" (1973) 22 I.C.L.Q. 254.
[56] *Philippine Admiral (Owners) v. Wallem Shipping (Hong Kong) Ltd.* [1977] A.C. 373.
[57] *Trendtex Trading Corporation v. Central Bank of Nigeria* [1977] Q.B. 529.

Immunity Act 1978,[58] and the House of Lords took the opportunity of affirming the acceptance of the restrictive theory (in respect of matters arising before the coming into force of the State Immunity Act) in the case of *I Congresso del Partido*.[59]

2.15   *State Immunity Act 1978*.[60] This Act now regulates the extent to which foreign states are immune from the jurisdiction of the English courts. Immunity extends to the sovereign or other head of state in his public capacity, to the government of the foreign state, and to any department of government of that state.[61] It does not, generally,[62] extend to any separate entity[63] which is distinct from the executive organs of the government of the state and which is capable of suing and being sued.[64] It does not affect any immunity or privilege conferred by the Diplomatic Privileges Act 1964 or the Consular Relations Act 1968.[65]

The Act, while retaining the general principle of immunity, specifies in some detail a number of exceptions to that principle. The court must give effect to the Act even if the defendant state does not appear.[66] The exceptions cover a variety of situations in which a state might be sued in respect of commercial activities. They include the following categories of proceedings:

(i) proceedings in which the state has submitted to the jurisdiction either by prior agreement in writing, or by bringing the proceedings or by intervening in them, or by taking a step in the proceedings, other than to claim

---

[58] The Act also gives effect to the Brussels Convention on the Unification of Certain Rules concerning the Immunity of State–owned Ships (1926) Cmnd. 5672 and Protocol (1934) Cmnd. 5673. Under this convention immunity for government owned vessels is waived.

[59] *The Playa Largo (Owners of Cargo)* v. *I Congresso del Partido (Owners)* [1983] 1 A.C. 244.

[60] See the discussion of the State Immunity Act 1978 and the conventions in the *Supreme Court Practice* at para. [4671].

[61] Section 14(1). A provincial Government may be a department of state, see *Swiss-Israel Trade Bank* v. *Government of Salta and Banco Provinciale de Salta* [1972] 1 Lloyd's Rep. 497.

[62] A separate entity enjoys immunity if the proceedings relate to acts done in the exercise of sovereign authority if they would have enjoyed exemption if they had been performed by the state; see State Immunity Act 1978, s.14(2).

[63] As to what constitutes a separate entity see *Krojina* v. *Tass Agency* [1949] 2 All E.R. 274; *Baccus S.L.R.* v. *Servicio Nacional del Trigo* [1957] 1 Q.B. 438; *Trendtex Trading Corporation* v. *Central Bank of Nigeria* [1977] Q.B. 529; *C. Czarnicow Ltd.* v. *Centrala Handlu Zagranicznego Rolimpex* [1979] A.C. 351. *Mellinger* v. *New Brunswick Development Board* [1971] 1 W.L.R. 604. Note the procedural privileges afforded to central banks by virtue of s.14(4).

[64] State Immunity Act 1978, s.14.

[65] *Ibid.*, s.16.

[66] *Ibid.*, s.2(1).

immunity.[67] The making of a counterclaim only amounts
to submission to the jurisdiction in respect of the claim if
it arises out of the same legal relationship or facts as the
claim.[68]

(ii) proceedings arising out of commercial transactions, as
defined.[69]

(iii) proceedings relating to contracts of employment of individuals made in the United Kingdom when the work is to
be performed wholly or partly in the United Kingdom.[70]
Immunity is retained if at the time when the proceedings
are brought the employee is a national of the state concerned, or if he was neither a national of, nor resident in,
the United Kingdom when the contract was made, or if
the parties otherwise agreed in writing.[71] The provisions
of the Act do not apply to employment in diplomatic
missions or consular posts.[72]

(iv) proceedings in respect of death or personal injury or
damage or loss of tangible property caused by an act or
omission in the United Kingdom.[73]

(v) proceedings relating to any interest of the state in immovable property in the United Kingdom or its use or possession of such property.[74] This provision does not apply
to proceedings concerning a state's title to or possession of
property used for the purpose of its diplomatic mission.[75]

(vi) proceedings relating to patents or trademarks and similar
rights registered in the United Kingdom.[76]

(vii) proceedings which arise out of the state's membership of a
body corporate, unincorporated body or partnership,
which has members other than states and which is established in the United Kingdom.[77]

---

[67] *Ibid.*, s.2(1).
[68] *Ibid.*, s.2(6). A counterclaim unconnected with the subject matter of the claim,
if established, can only operate as a set-off: see *Mighell* v. *Sultan of Johore* [1894]
1 Q.B. 149; *Supreme Court Practice*, para. 15/2/8.
[69] By s.3(3), "commercial transaction" means any contract for the supply of goods
and services, any loan or guarantee, and any other transaction of a commercial,
industrial, financial, professional or other similar character in which the state
engages other than in the exercise of its sovereign authority.
[70] State Immunity Act 1978, s.4.
[71] *Ibid.*, s.4(2).
[72] *Ibid.*, s.16(1)(*a*).
[73] *Ibid.*, s.5.
[74] *Ibid.*, s.6(1); see *Intpro Properties* v. *Sauvel and the French Government* [1983]
Q.B. 1019.
[75] State Immunity Act 1978, s.16(1)(*b*).
[76] *Ibid.*, s.7.
[77] *Ibid.*, s.8.

(viii) proceedings in the United Kingdom relating to arbitration to which the state has agreed in writing.[78]

(ix) admiralty proceedings relating to ships belonging to the state if they are being used for commercial purposes.[79]

2.16 *Procedural privileges.* The State Immunity Act 1978 and the Rules of the Supreme Court contain a number of provisions which are designed to ensure that the objectives of the Act are attained. Service of proceedings on a foreign state must be effected through the Foreign and Commonwealth Office of the United Kingdom government to the ministry of foreign affairs of the state concerned.[80] Service is deemed to take place on the date of such service, but the foreign state has two months thereafter within which to file notice of intention to defend.[81] A judgment in default of filing notice of intention to defend may not be entered against a foreign state without the leave of the court,[82] and if such judgment is entered the state has two months in which to apply for the judgment to be set aside. This period of two months runs from the date of service of a copy of the judgment on its ministry of foreign affairs, as above. There are also restrictions upon the giving of injunctions and other orders against a foreign state, and upon the enforcement of judgments against the property of a foreign state.[83]

3. Sovereign immunity

2.17 By section 20 of the State Immunity Act 1978 the provisions of the Diplomatic Privileges Act 1964[84] are extended to a sovereign or other head of state, members of his family forming part of his household, and his private servants, regardless of the nationality or place of residence of the person in respect of whom immunity is claimed.[85]

---

[78] *Ibid.*, s.9.

[79] *Ibid.*, s.10.

[80] *Ibid.*, s.12(1); see paras. 4.28 and 4.29 below. Where leave to serve out of the jurisdiction is required under R.S.C., Ord. 11, this too must be obtained: see s.12(7).

[81] State Immunity Act 1978, s.12(2).

[82] *Ibid.*, s.12(4), R.S.C., Ord. 13, r. 7(A), R.S.C., Ord. 42, r. 3(A).

[83] State Immunity Act 1978, s.13; the European Convention on State Immunity is a convention within the ambit of Art. 57 of the 1968 Convention. See, generally, pára. 33.06 below; Kaye, p. 1556–9. As to the enforcement in the U.K. of foreign judgments against other states, see the 1982 Act, s.31, para. 43.21 below.

[84] See next para.

[85] See also *Duff Development Co.* v. *Government of Kelantan* [1923] 1 Ch. 385; *Supreme Court Practice*, para. 45/1/16.

4. Diplomatic privilege

The law relating to diplomatic privilege is contained in the Diplomatic Privileges Act 1964, which is expressed to take effect in substitution for any previous enactment or rule of law.[86] The Act brought into effect in the United Kingdom the Vienna Convention on Diplomatic Relations 1961.[87] In outline it provides that the premises of the mission,[88] the private residences of the head of the mission[89] and all staff of diplomatic status, and the official correspondence,[90] archives and documents of the mission[91] are to be "inviolable." The head of mission, all staff of diplomatic status, and all administrative and technical staff of the mission, together with members of their families forming part of their households, not being nationals of the receiving state, are also to be "inviolable" and exempt from any form of arrest or detention.[92] The above persons are also immune from the criminal jurisdiction of the receiving state and from its civil and administrative jurisdiction except in actions involving real property, succession, or professional or commercial activity in which they are concerned as a private individuals.[93] None of the above persons are obliged to give evidence as a witness,[94] nor may any measures of execution be taken against them, save in respect of the above limited classes of action.[95] Such measures may not in any event be taken if they infringe the inviolability of the person or residence of the party protected by immunity. Immunity from criminal and civil jurisdiction of the receiving state may be expressly waived by the sending state or by the head of mission.[96] There must be a separate express waiver of immunity from execution of any judgment.[97]

2.18

---

[86] Diplomatic Privileges Act 1964, s.1. Consequently the cases referred to in the *Supreme Court Practice*, para. 65/2/3 should, it is submitted, be treated with caution.

[87] Cmnd. 1368.

[88] Art. 22(1) and Art. 1(i); as long as they are being currently so used: see *Westminster City Council* v. *Government of the Islamic Republic of Iran* [1986] 1 W.L.R. 979.

[89] Art. 22(1) and Art. 1(i).

[90] Art. 27(2).

[91] Art. 24.

[92] Art. 29 and Art. 37. It should be noted that national rules as to domicile sometimes contain special provisions relating to diplomats who are serving abroad.

[93] Art. 31.

[94] Art. 31(2); see *Supreme Court Practice*, para. 57/2/2.

[95] Art. 31(3).

[96] Art. 32(1), *R.* v. *Madan* [1961] 2 Q.B. 1; *Empson* v. *Smith* [1966] 1 Q.B. 426; *Shaw* v. *Shaw* [1979] Fam. 62.

[97] Art. 32(4).

2.19   *Proof of diplomatic status.* Section 4 of the Diplomatic Privileges Act 1964 provides that a certificate issued by or under the authority of the Secretary of State stating any fact relating to any question of entitlement to any privilege or immunity under the Act shall be conclusive evidence of that fact.

5. Consular privilege

2.20   The Consular Relations Act 1968 applies various provisions of the Vienna Convention on Consular Relations 1963.[98] This distinguishes between consular offices headed by career consular officers and those headed by honorary consular officers[99] and extends more far reaching privileges to the former. Where a consular office is headed by a career official the convention provides that the consular premises, the official correspondence and the archives and documents of the consular post are to be "inviolable."[1] The head of the consular post and other consular officers are immune from arrest or detention save in the case of grave crime.[2] However these persons, together with administrative and technical staff of the consular post, are not immune from civil jurisdiction in the receiving state save in respect of acts performed in the exercise of consular functions.[3] Even in respect of such acts there is no immunity where the proceedings arise out of a contract concluded by the consular officer in which he did not contract expressly or impliedly as agent of the sending state, or where the proceedings are brought by a third party arising out of an accident in the receiving state caused by a vehicle, vessel, or aircraft.[4] There is a qualified obligation on the part of members of a consular post to give evidence. If called as a witness they may only decline to give evidence concerning matters connected with their official functions, or to produce official correspondence or other documents, or to give expert evidence concerning the law of the sending state.[5] Any of the above immunities from jurisdiction may be waived in writing on behalf of the sending state[6] but there must be a separate express waiver of immunity from execution of any judgment.[7]

---

[98] Cmnd. 2113. The convention is set out in Sched. 1 of the Act.
[99] Art. 1(2). As to the immunities enjoyed by an honorary consular officer see Arts. 58 to 67 of the convention.
[1] Art. 31, 33, and 35.
[2] Art. 41(1).
[3] Art. 43(1).
[4] Art. 43(2).
[5] Art. 44.
[6] Art. 45.
[7] Art. 45(4).

6. International organisations

Under the International Organisations Act 1968 and 1981 certain **2.21** privileges, immunities and facilities are accorded to a number of international organisations and to their representatives, officers and employees. The organisations, of which there are currently over 50,[8] and the extent of the privileges and immunities conferred are specified by Order in Council. Broadly speaking they are put in a position which is comparable to that enjoyed by diplomatic missions.[9]

---

[8] For example the United Nations, the International Monetary Fund, the International Court of Justice, and the European Patent Organisation. They are listed in 10 *Halsbury's Statutes* (4th ed.) p. 597.

[9] See *J.H. Rayner (Mincing Lane) Ltd.* v. *Dept. of Trade and Industry* [1988] 3 W.L.R. 1033 and *Maclaine Watson & Co. Ltd.* v. *International Tin Council* [1988] 3 W.L.R. 1169.

CHAPTER 3

THE COMMENCEMENT OF PROCEEDINGS

A. INTRODUCTION

3.01   Before the commencement of the Civil Jurisdiction and Judgments Act 1982, the effect of the English rules of jurisdiction was that proceedings could be brought in England and Wales if the defendant could be served with the process of the court.[1] As a general rule service on a defendant who was physically present within the territorial jurisdiction of the High Court (the whole of England and Wales)[2] was good service, as was service within the jurisdiction on the place of business or agent of a foreign individual or entity.[3] The rules of court also enabled service to be effected on defendants who were outside the jurisdiction in a considerable number of specified circumstances, provided that the leave of the court was obtained.[4]

---

[1] This did not apply if jurisdiction was excluded under a specialised convention, see para. 3.17 below.

[2] In a territorial context, the term "jurisdiction" is used to refer to England and Wales, the territorial jurisdiction of the High Court: see para. 1.03 above. The general territorial jurisdiction of county courts and other lower courts is probably limited to their districts (see paras. 3.19 and 3.21 below), but service of their process may normally be effected anywhere in England and Wales.

[3] See paras. 1.26 above and 4.07, 4.12 and 4.13 below.

[4] R.S.C., Ord. 11; C.C.R., Ord. 8: see paras. 1.28 to 1.30 above and 4.16 et seq. below. In cases in which the defendant did not acknowledge service, the enforcement abroad of the resulting judgement frequently presented problems.

For practical purposes if a defendant could be served, the English court would have jurisdiction, irrespective of where service had taken place, although the court might, in its discretion, decide not to exercise its jurisdiction and might instead stay the proceedings on the ground that the English court was a *forum non conveniens*.

The 1982 Act, with the implementation of the 1968 Convention, has introduced new rules of jurisdiction which must be taken into account by all those contemplating or involved in litigation with European transnational elements. If proceedings to which the Convention applies are brought before an English court when it does not have jurisdiction under the Convention, not only may they be open to challenge by the defendant but there are various circumstances in which the court itself must declare of its own motion that it has no jurisdiction.[5] It is a significant feature of the new scheme of rules that the court has little if any discretion in their application; if its jurisdiction has been validly invoked, it may not decline to exercise it on the grounds that it is a *forum non conveniens*.

The procedural steps to be taken by parties initiating and defend- **3.02** ing proceedings in the English courts will differ according to the basis upon which the court has, or is alleged to have, jurisdiction. In particular, in cases to which the Convention or Schedule 4 of the 1982 Act apply,[6] the proceedings may now be issued without the leave of the court and served out of the jurisdiction anywhere in the world without leave,[7] but the Plaintiff's solicitor must indorse the writ with a statement in the form required by the rules of court.[8] In cases to which the 1968 Convention and Schedule 4 do not apply, (and which do not fall within one of the specialised statutory regimes)[9], it remains necessary, if it is intended to serve the writ or other originating document out of the jurisdiction, to obtain leave to issue it.[10] In proceedings to which the Convention does not apply which are not intended to be served out of the jurisdiction, the writ or other originating document will be marked "Not for service out of the jurisdiction."[11]

---

[5] Arts. 19, 20 and 21; see chaps. 22 and 23 below.
[6] As regards cases which have connections with Scotland or Northern Ireland, it is sufficient if the subject-matter of the case falls within the Convention, even if the Convention does not apply to it: 1982 Act, s.16(1)(a): para. 41.07 below.
[7] The note in the *Supreme Court Practice* at para. 11/4/1 which seemingly suggests that leave is required to serve a writ on a defendant who is outside the Contracting States is incorrect in this respect.
[8] R.S.C., Ord. 6, r. 7(1)(b); C.C.R., Ord. 3, r. 3(7): see para. 3.25 below.
[9] See paras. 3.17 and 3.23 below.
[10] R.S.C., Ord. 6, r. 7(1); C.C.R., Ord. 3, r. 3(5).
[11] *Practice Note (Writ: Service Abroad)* [1987] 1 W.L.R. 86.

B. The Basis for the Jurisdiction of English Courts

3.03 A prospective plaintiff may be concerned to determine whether the
English courts have jurisdiction to hear and determine his case
under the Convention. In cases to which the 1968 Convention
applies, the English court may acquire jurisdiction either by the
application of the Convention alone or by the combined application
of the Convention and the internal United Kingdom rules in Schedule 4 of the 1982 Act.[12] This is because, where the Convention does
no more than to provide that the courts of the United Kingdom
generally are to have jurisdiction, the rules in Schedule 4 allocate
jurisdiction to particular parts or courts within the United Kingdom. If the 1968 Convention does not apply, the English court may
still have jurisdiction under the 1982 Act.[13] Whether or not the
1968 Convention or 1982 Act would otherwise apply, if the English
court has jurisdiction under statutory rules which give effect to certain specialised conventions, those rules take priority.[14] If neither
the 1968 Convention nor the 1982 Act applies, then the English
court will have jurisdiction if the defendant can be "properly"
served with the proceedings in accordance with the pre-existing
rules which continue to apply in this class of case.

1. Jurisdiction under the 1968 Convention and 1982 Act

Initial questions

3.04 For the Convention to apply to any particular case, the following
three questions must, subject to certain exceptions which are
referred to below, be answered affirmatively. For the scheme of
rules in Schedule 4 to the 1982 Act to apply, the first two of these
questions, in modified form, must also be answered affirmatively.

(i) *Does the subject matter of the case come within the general scope of
the Convention?* In order to do so, two requirements must be fulfilled: First, the case must concern a "civil or commercial matter"
within the meaning of Article 1 of the Convention[15]; secondly it
must not concern a subject matter which is excluded from the Convention by Article 1,[16] or which falls within the scope of certain of
the specialised conventions contemplated by Article 57.[17] If the

---

[12] 1982 Act, ss.16 and 17 (chap. 41 below), Scheds. 4 and 5 (chap. 45 below).
[13] See para. 3.04 below.
[14] See para. 3.17 below.
[15] See paras. 14.03 *et seq.* below.
[16] See paras. 14.18 *et seq.* below.
[17] For example the Convention on the Contract for the International Carriage of
Goods by Road (CMR) (1956), given effect in English law as the Schedule to the
Carriage of Goods by Road Act 1965: see paras. 1.29 to 1.30 above, and
paras. 33.06 *et seq.* and 45.36 below.

case partly concerns subject-matter which falls outside the Convention then, unless that part can be, and is, severed, the Convention does not apply to the case and the English court's jurisdiction is determined in accordance with the former rules.[18]

The same question applies, subject to minor modification,[19] in respect of Schedule 4. It is a condition of the application of Schedule 4 for the subject-matter of the case to fall within the Convention, and it is immaterial that the Convention does not apply to it.[20]

(ii) *Is the defendant domiciled in one of the Contracting States?*[21] To **3.05** determine whether a defendant is domiciled in the United Kingdom, and if so, in which part,[22] it is necessary to apply the tests set out in Part V of the 1982 Act.[23] In order to determine whether the defendant is domiciled in another Contracting State, it is necessary to apply the law of that state in the case of an individual[24] or English private international law in the case of a corporation or association.[25] Where there are two or more defendants, one of whom is domiciled in a Contracting State, the Convention is not prevented from applying to the proceedings in respect of that defendant by reason only that the other defendant is not so domiciled.[26] It should be noted that the Convention may still apply to limited classes of cases in which the defendant is not domiciled in a Contracting State.[27]

The equivalent question for the application of Schedule 4 is whether the defendant is domiciled in the United Kingdom.[28]

(iii) *Does the case contain a sufficient international element?* In most **3.06** cases it should be clear whether or not this condition is satisfied. This requirement is discussed below in the introduction to the commentary on the Convention.[29] International elements will be clearly

---

[18] See paras. 1.25 *et seq.* above and 3.27 to 3.30 below.
[19] The matters listed in Sched. 5 to the 1982 Act are also excluded: paras. 45.30 *et seq.* below.
[20] 1982 Act, s.16(1)(a): para. 41.07 below.
[21] The Contracting States are listed at para. 13.01 below.
[22] The part of the U.K. in which the defendant is domiciled is relevant in applying the special rules of jurisdiction in the Convention and Sched. 4, referred to at paras. 3.10 to 3.13 below.
[23] 1982 Act, ss.41 to 46; see paras. 44.01 to 44.35 below.
[24] Art. 52, para. 31.01 below. The law of domicile in the other Contracting States is summarised at paras. 25 and 26 of chaps. 48 to 58 below.
[25] Art. 53, para. 31.23 below. The relevant rules of English private international law are ss.42(6) and 42(7) of the 1982 Act, para. 44.11 below.
[26] Jurisdiction over the other defendant will be determined according to whatever rules apply apart from the Convention.
[27] See para. 3.14 below.
[28] 1982 Act, s.16(1)(b) para. 41.08 below.
[29] See paras. 13.10 to 13.11 below.

be present if the parties are domiciled in different Contracting States or if the events giving rise to the proceedings took place in a Contracting State different from that of the domicile of one or other of the parties.

Jurisdiction based on domicile

3.07   Having concluded that, in accordance with the rules set out above, the Convention does apply to a particular case, the courts of the state in which the defendant is domiciled will have jurisdiction,[30] unless this jurisdiction is excluded or its exercise prevented in one of a limited number of ways.[31] Subject to the exceptions mentioned below, the particular court which has jurisdiction is to be determined by national law.

If the defendant is domiciled in the United Kingdom, the Convention provides that the courts of the United Kingdom are normally to have jurisdiction over him but, subject to the exceptions mentioned below, the Convention *itself* does not determine in which of the three parts of the United Kingdom[32] the courts are to have jurisdiction, leaving that to be determined by United Kingdom law. The 1982 Act has accordingly provided rules in Schedule 4 of the Act for that purpose, which largely reproduce the scheme contained in the Convention. So, if England and Wales is the part of the United Kingdom in which the defendant is domiciled, the English courts have jurisdiction in proceedings against him, unless that jurisdiction is excluded or its exercise is prevented in one of a limited number of ways.[33] Here again, subject to the exceptions mentioned below, the rules in Schedule 4 do not determine which particular court is to have jurisdiction and this is to be determined by other rules of English law.[34] However, because the High Court has jurisdiction over the whole of England and Wales, the omission is of little significance in cases at the level of the High Court.[35]

3.08   *Exceptions.* In general, the Convention does not specify the particular locality or the particular court in which a defendant may be sued in the state of his own domicile, although it does often specify this if he is being sued in a Contracting State other than that of his domicile.[36] Similarly, Schedule 4 does not normally specify the par-

---

[30] See para. 3.05 above.
[31] 1968 Convention, Art. 2: para. 16.00 below. The ways in which the jurisdiction may be excluded, or its exercise may be prevented, are discussed at paras. 3.15 to 3.16 below.
[32] England and Wales, Scotland and Northern Ireland.
[33] 1982 Act, Sched. 4, Art. 2; but see para. 3.15 below.
[34] See para. 3.19 below.
[35] As regards the competence of courts according to the subject-matter of the case, see para. 1.04 above.
[36] See the special rules of jurisdiction referred to below.

ticular locality or court in which a defendant may be sued in the part of the United Kingdom where he is domiciled. In a number of cases, though, the Convention specifies that a person may be sued in the courts for a particular place, or in a particular court, and does so in such a way that the rule applies whether or not that person is domiciled in the Contracting State where that place or that court is located. Schedule 4 contains equivalent rules, which apply whether or not the defendant is domiciled in the part of the United Kingdom where that place or that court is located. These rules, which feature below in the list of special rules of jurisdiction, apply in the following cases:

(i) in the case of a co-defendant, third party, or defendant to a counterclaim;[37]
(ii) in the case of limitation actions in Admiralty;[38]
(iii) in the case of certain actions against insurers;[39]
(iv) in the case of choice of jurisdiction agreements.[40]

In addition, unless the defendant challenges the jurisdiction or another court has exclusive jurisdiction under Article 16, a court in which a defendant enters an appearance has jurisdiction.[41]

Domicile is not an exclusive basis for jurisdiction. The fact that the **3.09** courts of the Contracting State where he is domiciled have jurisdiction over a defendant does not mean that the courts of another Contracting State may not also, in a given case, have jurisdiction over him on a ground other than domicile, on the basis of one of the special rules referred to below.[42] Similarly, the courts of Scotland or Northern Ireland may have jurisdiction over a defendant domiciled in England in such a case.

Jurisdiction based on special rules

In addition to the general rule enabling a person to be sued in the **3.10** courts of the Contracting State where he is domiciled, the Convention contains special rules of jurisdiction in Articles 5 to 18 and

---

[37] 1968 Convention, Art. 6 (paras. 17.73 *et seq.* below); Sched. 4 Art. 6 (para. 45.11 below).
[38] 1968 Convention, Art. 6A (paras. 17.96 *et seq.* below); Sched. 4, Art. 6A (para. 45.13 below).
[39] 1968 Convention, Arts. 9 and 10 (paras. 18.23 *et seq.* below); there are no equivalent rules in Sched. 4: see para. 45.14 below.
[40] 1968 Convention, Art. 17 (paras. 21.01 *et seq.* below); Sched. 4, Art. 17 (para. 45.21 below); As regards jurisdiction agreements in insurance and consumer matters, see 1968 Convention, Arts. 12 and 15 (paras. 18.45 *et seq.* and 19.44 below) and Sched. 4, Art. 15 (para. 45.18 below).
[41] 1968 Convention, Art. 18 (paras. 21.83 *et seq.* below); Sched. 4, Art. 18 (para. 45.24 below).
[42] See next para.

Article 24. Under some of these rules, the jurisdiction of the court in the United Kingdom arises only if the defendant is *not* domiciled in the United Kingdom but is domiciled in another Contracting State[43]; in others it arises if the defendant is domiciled in any Contracting State, including the United Kingdom; and in yet others it applies irrespective of where the defendant is domiciled.

Where the Convention allocates jurisdiction to the courts of the United Kingdom generally, without specifying which particular court or courts are to have jurisdiction, an English court may have jurisdiction under the equivalent special rules in Articles 5 to 18 and Article 24 of Schedule 4. These rules also apply if the defendant is domiciled in the United Kingdom but the Convention does not apply to the case.[44]

These special rules of jurisdiction are summarised below. Reference should thereafter be made to the text of the Convention and of Schedule 4 to the 1982 Act and to the commentary in Part II of this book. It should be noted that, below the level of the High Court, jurisdiction in certain types of case may be local in character. Resulting questions of choice of venue are discussed below.[45]

3.11 The English courts will normally have jurisdiction in the following cases over a person domiciled in another Contracting State or in another part of the United Kingdom,[46] but, unless otherwise stated, only over such a person. In considering whether the English court has jurisdiction under these rules, however, it should be remembered that the jurisdiction may be excluded or its exercise prevented in one of a limited number of ways:[47]

(i) In a matter relating to a contract, where the place of performance of the obligation in question is in England and Wales,[48] the High Court or, if appropriate, the county court (local to the place of performance) will have jurisdiction.[49]

(ii) In a matter relating to maintenance, the English court will have jurisdiction either if the maintenance creditor is

---

[43] Jurisdiction under the Convention over a person not domiciled in a Contracting State is discussed at para. 3.14 below.

[44] 1982 Act, s.16(1)(a): para. 41.07 below.

[45] See paras. 3.14 *et seq.* below.

[46] If the jurisdiction arises pursuant to the Convention in any of these cases, the English court may not decline to exercise it on the grounds of *forum non conveniens*; but if the jurisdiction arises *solely* under Sched. 4, the court still has that discretion: 1982 Act, s.49, see paras. 1.41 *et seq.* above and 44.40 below.

[47] See para. 3.15 below.

[48] The place of performance is to be determined according to English choise of law rules, that is, according to the proper law of the contract: see paras. 17.12 *et seq.*

[49] 1968 Convention, Art. 5(1) (para. 17.02 below); Sched. 4, Art. 5(1) (para. 45.06 below).

domiciled or habitually resident in England and Wales, or if the matter is ancillary to proceedings concerning the status of a person in respect of which the English court already has jurisdiction.[50]

(iii) In a matter relating to tort, when the place where the harmful event occurred is in England and Wales the High Court, or, if appropriate, the county court (local to the place where the harmful event occurred), will have jurisdiction.[51]

(iv) As regards a civil claim for compensation or restitution based on an act giving rise to criminal proceedings, the Crown Court or magistrates court seized of the criminal proceedings will have jurisdiction.[52]

(v) As regards a dispute arising out of the operations of a branch, agency or other establishment in England and Wales, the High Court, or, if appropriate, the county court (local to the place where the branch, agency or other establishment is situated), will have jurisdiction.[53]

(vi) In a case brought against the settlor, trustee or beneficiary of a trust which is domiciled in England, the English courts will have jurisdiction.[54]   **3.12**

(vii) The English courts will have jurisdiction in respect of certain salvage claims.[55]

(viii) In proceedings concerning debts secured on immovable property in England and Wales, or in certain proceedings relating to movable property in England and Wales, persons domiciled in Scotland or Northern Ireland (but not those domiciled in another Contracting State) may be sued in the High Court or, if appropriate, in the county court.[56]

---

[50] 1968 Convention, Art. 5(2) (para. 17.31 below); Sched. 4, Art. 5(2) (para. 45.06 below). As regards allocation of local jurisdiction in England and Wales, see para. 3.14 below.

[51] 1968 Convention, Art. 5(3) (para. 17.44 below); Sched. 4, Art. 5(3) (para. 45.06 below).

[52] 1968 Convention, Art. 5(4) (para. 17.53 below); Sched. 4, Art. 5(4) (para. 45.06 below). It is probable, but not certain, that the English court's powers to make a compensation or restitution order fall within this provision.

[53] 1968 Convention, Art. 5(5) (para. 17.55 below); Sched. 4, Art. 5(5) (para. 45.06 below).

[54] 1968 Convention, Art. 5(6) (para. 17.65 below); Sched. 4, Art. 5(6) (para. 45.06 below).

[55] 1968 Convention, Art. 5(7) (para. 17.70 below); Sched. 4, Art. 5(7) (para. 45.06 below).

[56] Sched. 4, Art. 5(8) (para. 45.08 below). The Convention itself does not contain an equivalent provision.

(ix) The English courts will have jurisdiction in proceedings which have as their object the decision of an organ of a corporation or association with its seat in England and Wales, irrespective of the defendant's domicile.[57]

(x) A person domiciled in any Contracting State, or in any part of the United Kingdom, may be joined as a co-defendant in proceedings brought before an English court against a defendant domiciled in England and Wales.[58]

(xi) A third party domiciled in any Contracting State, or in any part of the United Kingdom, may be joined in proceedings before an English court unless it can be shown that they were instituted solely with the object of removing the third party from the jurisdiction of the court which would be competent in his case.[59]

(xii) A person domiciled in any Contracting State, or in any part of the United Kingdom, who brings proceedings in an English court may have a counterclaim brought against him in that court, if it arises from the same contract or facts on which his original claim is based.[60]

(xiii) Claims for limitation of liability arising from the use or operation of a ship may, irrespective of where the defendant is domiciled, be brought in an English court, where that court would have had jurisdiction under the Convention in respect of the use and operation of the ship.[61]

3.13 (xiv) Special rules are applied by the Convention in matters relating to insurance, some of which are not dependent on the domicile of the parties.[62] Among other provisions, an insured person who is domiciled in England and Wales may bring proceedings in the High Court or, if appropriate, the county court (local to the place of his domicile)

---

[57] 1968 Convention, Art. 16(2) (para. 20.26 below); Sched. 4, para. 5A (para. 45.09 below). The Convention allocates jurisdiction over these cases on an exclusive basis to the courts of the U.K.; Sched. 4 allocates it to a part of the U.K. on a non-exclusive basis. For the special definition of "seat" for the purposes of these cases, see the 1982 Act, s.43 (para. 44.20 below).

[58] 1968 Convention, Art. 6(1) (para. 17.74 below); Sched. 4, Art. 6(1) (para. 45.11 below).

[59] 1968 Convention, Art. 6(2) (para. 17.82 below); Sched. 4, Art. 6(2) (para. 45.11 below).

[60] 1968 Convention, Art. 6(3) (para. 17.90 below); Sched. 4, Art. 6(3) (para. 45.11 below).

[61] 1968 Convention, Art. 6A (para. 17.96 below); Sched. 4, Art. 6A (para. 45.13 below).

[62] 1968 Convention, Arts. 7 to 12A (chap. 18 below). Sched. 4 does not contain equivalent provisions.

against an insurer who is, or who may be deemed to be, domiciled in another Contracting State.[63]

(xv) Special rules are applied to cases concerning consumer contracts.[64] In particular a person who supplies goods or services or credit to a consumer and who is, or who may be deemed to be, domiciled in any Contracting State, may be sued in the English courts in respect of the consumer contract by a consumer domiciled in England and Wales.[65]

(xvi) The English courts have exclusive jurisdiction, regardless of the defendant's domicile, over proceedings which have as their object certain rights in real property in England and Wales,[66] the dissolution of a corporation or association which has its seat in England and Wales, or the validity or nullity of its constitution,[67] the validity of entries in public registers kept in England and Wales,[68] or the enforcement of judgments in England and Wales.[69] The courts of the United Kingdom have exclusive jurisdiction, irrespective of the defendant's domicile, over proceedings which have as their object the registration or validity of certain intellectual property rights registered there.[70]

(xvii) The English courts have jurisdiction where there has been agreement to that effect between the parties (at least one of whom is domiciled in a Contracting State), provided the agreement was in proper form.[71]

(xviii) An English court may acquire jurisdiction over a case if the defendant enters an appearance to the proceedings and does not contest the jurisdiction, even if the court would

---

[63] 1968 Convention, Art. 8, first para., sub-para. (2): para. 18.14 below.

[64] 1968 Convention, Arts. 13 to 15 (chap. 19 below); Sched. 4, Arts. 13 to 15 (paras. 45.15 to 45.18 below).

[65] 1968 Convention, Art. 14, first para. (para. 19.35 below); Sched. 4, Art. 14, first para. (para. 45.17 below).

[66] 1968 Convention, Art. 16(1) (paras. 20.11 *et seq.* below); Sched. 4, Art. 16(1) (para. 45.19 below).

[67] 1968 Convention, Art. 16(2) (paras. 20.26 *et seq.* below); Sched. 4, Art. 16(2) (para. 45.19 below). As regards proceedings which have as their object the decision of an organ of such a corporation or association, see sub-para. (ix) above. "Seat" is given a special definition for the purposes of these cases: 1982 Act, s.43 (para. 44.20 below).

[68] 1968 Convention, Art. 16(3) (paras. 20.30 *et seq.* below); Sched. 4, Art. 16(3) (para. 45.19 below).

[69] 1968 Convention, Art. 16(5) (paras. 20.40 *et seq.* below); Sched. 4, Art. 16(5) (para. 45.19 below).

[70] 1968 Convention, Art. 16(4) (paras. 20.32 *et seq.* below). These matters are excluded from the scope of Sched. 4 by para. 2 of Sched. 5 (para. 45.32 below).

[71] 1968 Convention, Art. 17 (paras. 21.01 *et seq.* below); Sched. 4, Art. 17 (para. 45.21 below).

not have jurisdiction under any other provision of the Convention or Schedule 4, and irrespective of the defendant's domicile.[72] However, the English court cannot acquire jurisdiction by virtue of a voluntary submission if the courts of another Contracting State have exclusive jurisdiction under Article 16 of the Convention, or the courts of another part of the United Kingdom have jurisdiction under Article 16 of Schedule 4.

(xix) The English courts have jurisdiction to grant provisional and protective measures even if the courts of another Contracting State or another part of the United Kingdom have jurisdiction as to the substance of the matter in dispute.[73]

Jurisdiction over a defendant not domiciled in a Contracting State

3.14 In the circumstances mentioned below, the effect of the Convention may be to give the courts of the United Kingdom jurisdiction over a defendant who is not domiciled in the United Kingdom or in any other Contracting State. Except in these cases, the question whether the English court has jurisdiction over such a defendant is to be determined not by the Convention, but by the other rules of English law.[74]

Exclusive jurisdiction (Article 16). The United Kingdom courts may have jurisdiction by reason of the fact that the subject-matter of the proceedings is such as to bring them within the exclusive jurisdiction provisions of Article 16 of the Convention.[75] If, as will usually be the case, the subject-matter of the proceedings is such as also to bring them within Article 16 of Schedule 4, that Article will determine whether the English court has jurisdiction.[76]

Jurisdiction agreements (Article 17). Courts in the United Kingdom will have jurisdiction if the plaintiff is domiciled in any Contracting State and if he and the defendant are parties to a jurisdiction

---

[72] 1968 Convention, Art. 18 (paras. 21.83 *et seq.* below); Sched. 4, Art. 18 (para. 45.24 below). If the defendant is domiciled in a non-Contracting State, it is not certain that this confers jurisdiction: para. 21.87 below.

[73] 1968 Convention, Art. 24 (chap. 24 below); Sched. 4, Art. 24 (para. 45.29 below).

[74] 1968 Convention, Art. 4, first para. (para. 16.15 below).

[75] Chap. 20 below.

[76] If proceedings have as their object the decision of an organ of a corporation or association with its seat in the U.K. (Art. 16(2) of the Convention), the English court has jurisdiction if the seat is in England and Wales (Sched. 4, Art. 5A) or if any other provision of Sched. 4 gives it jurisdiction: 1982 Act, s.16(1)(*b*). If the proceedings concern the registration or validity of certain intellectual property rights, the jurisdiction is determined by other provisions of English law: Sched. 5, para. 2 (para. 45.32 below).

agreement which complies with the requirements of form in Article 17 of the Convention and which confers jurisdiction on those courts.[77] If a particular court in England has been chosen, that court has jurisdiction.[78]

Insurance or consumer cases (Article 15). If the claim is against an insurer or against a supplier of goods, services or credit to a consumer, and if the claim arises out of the operations of the insurer's or supplier's branch, agency or other establishment situated in the United Kingdom, the insurer or supplier is deemed by the Convention to be domiciled in the United Kingdom,[79] and deemed by English law to be domiciled in the part of the United Kingdom where the branch, agency or other establishment is situated.[80] The question whether the English court has jurisdiction is to be decided accordingly.

Limitation claims (Article 6A). If a court in the United Kingdom has jurisdiction to entertain a claim relating to liability arising from the use or operation of a ship, that court, or another court substituted for the purpose, also has jurisdiction to entertain a claim for the limitation of that liability.[81] The question whether the English court has jurisdiction is to be decided by other provisions of English law.[82]

Entry of appearance (Article 18). English courts can acquire jurisdiction by reason of the defendant entering an appearance without contesting the jurisdiction.[83] In this case, however, the fact that the defendant is not domiciled in a Contracting State may mean that the jurisdiction arises under English law, rather than under the Convention.[84]

---

[77] Paras. 21.01 *et seq.* below.

[78] 1968 Convention, Art. 17. For the same reason, if a court in another part of the U.K. has been chosen, that court has jurisdiction. If the courts of the U.K. generally have been chosen, without any further choice having been expressed, the question whether English courts have jurisdiction, rather than courts in Scotland or Northern Ireland, is to be decided by the general rules of English law. Note that Art. 17 of Sched. 4 does not apply, because the defendant is not domiciled in the U.K.: 1982 Act, s.16(1)(*b*) (para. 41.08 below).

[79] 1968 Convention, Art. 8, second para. (para. 18.11 below) and Art. 13, second para. (para. 19.01 below).

[80] 1982 Act, s.44 (para. 44.27 below).

[81] 1968 Convention, Art. 6A (para. 17.96 below).

[82] Note that Art. 6A of Sched. 4 does not apply, because the person against whom the claim is made for limitation of liability is not domiciled in the U.K.: 1982 Act, s.16(1)(*b*) (para. 41.08 below).

[83] 1968 Convention, Art. 18: para. 21.83 below.

[84] See para. 21.87 below.

Exclusion of the jurisdiction of the English court

3.15   In a limited number of cases, notwithstanding the fact that the defendant is domiciled in England and Wales, or that the English court may appear to have jurisdiction under one of the special rules of jurisdiction listed above, the jurisdiction of the English court is excluded, or the court is prevented from exercising it. These are cases in respect of which exclusive jurisdiction or priority of jurisdiction is vested by the Convention in the courts of another Contracting State. This situation arises principally in the cases listed below.

Where the case before the English court is principally concerned with a matter over which the courts of another Contracting State have exclusive jurisdiction by virtue of Article 16 of the Convention, then the English court must, of its own motion, declare that it has no jurisdiction.[85] The same applies if the jurisdiction of the English court is excluded in favour of the courts of another part of the United Kingdom by Article 16 of Schedule 4 to the 1982 Act.[86] If the matter is within the exclusive jurisdiction of both the English court and the court of another Contracting State, any court other than the court first seised must decline jurisdiction.[87]

3.16   (i) Where the case before the English court concerns a dispute which is the subject of a valid agreement conferring exclusive jurisdiction on the courts of another Contracting State, or on a competent court of another part of the United Kingdom, the English court must decline jurisdiction unless the defendant submits to the English jurisdiction by entering an appearance without contesting the court's jurisdiction.[88]

(ii) Where there are proceedings already pending in the courts of another Contracting State, which involve the same cause of action and the same parties as in proceedings before the English court, the latter is required to decline

---

[85] 1968 Convention, Art. 19 (para. 22.01 below).
[86] Sched. 4, Art. 19 (para. 45.25 below).
[87] 1968 Convention, Art. 23 (para. 23.24 below). Conflicts of exclusive jurisdiction between different parts of the U.K. may be resolved by the court's general powers to stay its proceedings, which are preserved in this context by the 1982 Act, s.49 (para. 44.40 below).
[88] 1968 Convention, Art. 17 (para. 21.01 below). As regards the effect of non-exclusive choices of jurisdiction, see paras. 21.46 *et seq.* below. If the choice of jurisdiction clause falls within Art. 17 of Sched. 4 (para. 45.21 below), but not within Art. 17 of the 1968 Convention, the English court nonetheless retains its power to stay the proceedings on the ground that it is not a *forum non conveniens*: 1982 Act, s.49 (para. 44.40 below). See *Spiliada Maritime Corp.* v. *Cansulex Ltd.* [1987] A.C. 460; *Supreme Court Practice*, paras. [5215–5218]; para. 1.42 above.

jurisdiction in favour of the foreign court, except that if the jurisdiction of the foreign court is being contested, the English court may stay its proceedings instead.[89] If the earlier proceedings are pending in another part of the United Kingdom, the English court may exercise its discretionary powers under the general provisions of English law.[90]

(iii) Where an action has been commenced in the courts of another Contracting State, and a related action is then brought in the English court, the latter may stay its proceedings while the action is pending at first instance in the other court. If the action before it can be consolidated with the action proceeding in the foreign court the English court should decline jurisdiction.[91] If the related action is in another part of the United Kingdom, the English court again retains its discretionary powers.[92]

2. Jurisdiction under statutory rules giving effect to certain conventions

The United Kingdom is party to a number of international con- **3.17**
ventions, concerned principally with maritime claims,[93] international transport, and pollution, which contain rules relating to jurisdiction.[94] Where, in a particular case, the English courts have jurisdiction under enactments giving effect to such a convention and the 1968 Convention also applies, the 1968 Convention does not deprive the English courts of that jurisdiction even where the defendant is domiciled in a Contracting State which is not a party to the special convention.[95] In such a case, however, Article 20 of the 1968 Convention requires the English court to take certain steps to ensure that it has jurisdiction and that the defendant has been adequately notified as to the proceedings.[96] Similarly, if an English court would have jurisdiction under a statutory provision or rule of

---

[89] 1968 Convention, Art. 21 (para. 23.01 below).
[90] 1982 Act, s.49 (para. 44.40 below); *Supreme Court Practice*, paras. [5228–5230]; para. 1.43 above.
[91] 1968 Convention, Art. 22 (para. 23.11 below).
[92] 1982 Act, s.49 (para. 44.40 below); *Supreme Court Practice*, paras. [5228–5230]; para. 1.43 above.
[93] R.S.C., Ord. 75, r. 2(1); leave is not required for the issue or service of a writ *in personam* out of the jurisdiction if it falls within that rule, see Ord. 11, r. 1(1). A writ *in rem* may not be served out of the jurisdiction; see paras. 1.31 to 1.35 above.
[94] See paras. 1.29 to 1.30 above.
[95] See Art. 57 of the 1968 Convention, paras. 33.06 *et seq.* below.
[96] Art. 25(2) of the 1978 Convention, para. 33.07 below.

law implementing any such convention, Schedule 4 to the 1982 Act does not operate to deprive it of that jurisdiction.[97]

3. Jurisdiction under common law rules

3.18   If the English court does not have jurisdiction by virtue of the provisions either of the Convention, or Schedule 4 of the 1982 Act, or any of the other statutory jurisdictional regimes referred to above, then jurisdiction can be founded only by serving proceedings on the defendant, either within the jurisdiction or, if the leave of the court can be obtained,[98] out of the jurisdiction.

C. CHOICE OF VENUE IN ENGLAND AND WALES

1. Local jurisdiction

3.19   A number of the Articles in the Convention are worded so as to allocate jurisdiction not only to a particular Contracting State but also to the courts in a particular locality within that state.[99] This reflects the fact that, in many continental legal systems, courts exercise jurisdiction over their particular locality. Thus, for example, the Convention allocates jurisdiction in matters of contract to the courts for the *place* of performance of the obligation in question, in matters of tort to the courts for the *place* where the harmful event occurred, and in respect of disputes arising out of the operation of a branch, agency, or other establishment, to the courts for the *place* where the branch, agency or establishment is situated.

If the place referred to in any such rule is in the United Kingdom, the rule operates not only on the international level, but also within the United Kingdom to determine which particular courts have jurisdiction over the case. At the level of the High Court, if the place referred to is in England and Wales, the operation of these rules presents no problem, because that court has jurisdiction over the entire territory of England and Wales. At the level of the lower courts, however, the position is less clear. As regards maintenance cases, the local jurisdiction of magistrates' courts is relevant under Article 5(2), and that of industrial tribunals may be relevant in some employment cases under Articles 5(1) and 5(5). The local jurisdiction of county courts is of more general importance and is examined below.

---

[97] 1982 Act, Sched. 5, para. 6 (para. 45.36 below).
[98] R.S.C., Ord. 11, r. 1(1); C.C.R., Ord. 8, r. 2(1).
[99] Arts. 5(1), 5(2), 5(3), 5(5), 6(1), 8 and 9.

2. Proceedings in the High Court

Any proceedings in the High Court may be issued either in Lon- **3.20** don out of the Central Office of the High Court or in any district registry. It is suggested that the provisions of the Convention conferring jurisdiction on the courts of a specific place c*a*n, in relation to proceedings at the level of the High Court, only be construed as referring to the whole of England and Wales as one place. It follows from this that the established rules of venue in High Court matters are not affected. If a writ is issued in a district registry it may be indorsed with a statement that the cause of action arose within the district. If it is not so endorsed a defendant who does not reside or carry on business within that district or, if the defendant is a company, does not have its registered office there, may apply for the transfer of the proceedings the Royal Courts of Justice in London or to another district registry.[1]

3. Proceedings in the county court

The wording of the County Courts Act 1984, which consolidates **3.21** earlier legislation, suggests that the jurisdiction of any particular county court is limited to the district in which it is situated.[2] If this were the case then reference in the Convention to the courts for a specific place would clearly refer, in proceedings at the level of the county court, to the local county court for the place in question. However it has been held by the Court of Appeal that the jurisdiction of the county court is general,[3] and that, even where a statute appears to confer jurisdiction in respect of a specific matter on a particular county court,[4] proceedings in respect of such matter which have been commenced in the wrong county court are not a nullity but may, under the county court rules,[5] be transferred to the correct court, or may be continued in the same court, or may be struck out, at the discretion of the court.[6] It is nonetheless considered that the provisions of the Convention referring to the courts of a particular place should still be construed as referring, at the

---

[1] R.S.C., Ord. 4, rr. 5(4) and 5(5).
[2] The County Courts Act, 1984, s.1(1) provides: "For the purposes of this Act, England and Wales shall be divided into districts, and a court shall be held under this Act for each district at one or more places in it; and throughout the whole of each district the court so held for the district shall have such jurisdiction and powers as are conferred by this Act and any other enactment for the time being in force."
[3] *Sharma* v. *Knight* [1986] 1 W.L.R. 757.
[4] There are many instances of English statutes allocating jurisdiction in specific cases to a particular county court; see 13 *Court Forms* (1987 issue) p. 324.
[5] C.C.R. Ord. 16, r. 2.
[6] *R.* v. *Judge Lailey, ex parte Koffman* [1932] 1 K.B. 568, p. 577; *Faulkner* v. *Love* [1977] Q.B. 937.

level of the county court, to the county court for the district in which relevant place is situated. Proceedings commenced in the "wrong" court will, if the objection as to venue is taken, simply be transferred to the correct court.[6a] If the defendant does not take the point but participates in the proceedings then the court seized will, in most cases, acquire jurisdiction pursuant to Article 18 of the Convention.[7]

D. PREPARATION AND ISSUE OF THE WRIT

3.22 This section is confined to a description of those aspects of the practice and procedure of the High Court which affect the preparation and issue of a writ in a civil or commercial matter and which are of particular relevance in proceedings involving an international element. It does not attempt to describe the many procedural requirements relating generally to the form and issue of originating process. Such differences of practice and procedure as exist in this connection between different divisions of the High Court, between different sections of those divisions, and between different types of originating process, are minor. Where such differences occur, the practice and procedure described is that which obtains in a normal action *in personam* begun by writ in the Queen's Bench Division.

1. Issue of writ for service out of the jurisdiction

Issue without leave; indorsement as to jurisdiction

3.23 If a writ is to be served out of the jurisdiction, leave to issue it is required unless it fulfils two conditions. First, the jurisdiction of the court must be founded solely on the Civil Jurisdiction and Judgments Act 1982 or on one of the other statutory regimes giving effect to certain international conventions[8]; and secondly, if jurisdiction is founded on solely on the 1982 Act, the writ must be indorsed with a statement confirming the court's jurisdiction.[9]

3.24 *The first condition: jurisdiction.* The first condition requires that *each* claim in the writ be either
    (i) one which by virtue of the Civil Jurisdiction and Judgments Act 1982 the court has power to hear and determine, or
    (ii) one which by virtue of any other enactment the court has

---

[6a] See Schlosser, para. 80 (para. A1.367 below); see also para. 44.44, n. 57 below.
[7] See para. 21.83 below.
[8] R.S.C., Ord. 6, r. 7(1)(a). The special statutory regimes are referred to at paras. 1.29 to 1.30 above. In one case, jurisdiction can arise under such a statutory regime in the absence of a specialised convention: Protection of Trading Interests Act 1981, s.6(5).
[9] In the county court, a statement to the same effect must be included in the particulars of claim: C.C.R., Ord. 3, r. 3(7).

power to hear and determine notwithstanding that the person against whom the claim is made is not within the jurisdiction of the court, or that the wrongful act, neglect, or default, giving rise to the claim did not take place within the court's territorial jurisdiction.

The occasions on which a claim arises under the second limb of that rule will be fairly rare; but the first limb of the rule affects a substantial number of cases. It involves those claims in which the court's jurisdiction is founded on the 1968 Convention alone,[10] those in which it is founded wholly on Schedule 4 to the 1982 Act,[11] and those in which it is founded on a combination of both of them. It should be noted that the great majority of all claims of a civil or commercial nature fulfil this condition. It is no bar to the issue of the writ without leave that some claims arise under one limb of that rule and some under the other,[12] although such a case is likely to be rare.

The second condition: indorsement as to jurisdiction. If jurisdiction **3.25** over each of the claims in the writ[13] is founded on the 1968 Convention or Schedule 4 to the 1982 Act, the writ must bear an indorsement confirming the court's jurisdiction over those claims before it may be issued without the leave of the court for service out of the jurisdiction.[14] The matters to be stated in the indorsement are prescribed, and the following may be used as a form of indorsement, which should be signed by or on behalf of the plaintiff's solicitor, or by the plaintiff if he is acting in person:

> The court has power under the Civil Jurisdiction and Judgments Act 1982 to hear and determine each claim made herein. No proceedings involving the same cause(s) of action are pending between the parties [or any of them] in Scotland, Northern Ireland, or the territory of any Contracting State to which the Conventions mentioned in section 1 of that Act apply.
> Dated the   day of   19
>
> > Signed:
> > (Solicitor for the Plaintiff)

The indorsement is not required in a case to which the Convention

---

[10] 1982 Act, s.2, para. 40.03 below.
[11] 1982 Act, s.16, para. 41.01 below.
[12] See the discussion of mixed claims below.
[13] The indorsement is not required if the court's power to hear and determine each claim arises under the enactments referred to in R.S.C., Ord. 6, r. 7(1)(a)(ii). In the rare case in which some claims fall under the 1982 Act and some under one of those other enactments, an indorsement is still required, and its terms would need to be adapted as appropriate.
[14] R.S.C., Ord. 6, r. 7(1)(b).

or Schedule 4 of the 1982 Act applies if service is to take place in England and Wales.[15] Any writ which is not so indorsed and from which it appears that one or more of the defendants are outside the jurisdiction, must be marked "Not for service out of the jurisdiction."[16]

Mixed claims

3.26   If a writ contains various claims, only some of which the court has power to hear and determine under the statutory regimes,[17] the writ may not be issued for service out of the jurisdiction without the leave of the court.[18] Various situations may arise. For example, the other claims may be ones in which the court may grant leave to serve the writ out of the jurisdiction under Order 11, rule 1(1). In this case, an application should be made for leave to serve the writ out of the jurisdiction, and the affidavit should distinguish between those claims which the court has power to hear and determine under the statutory regimes and those claims which it does not. Other situations may be more complex and it may be that the court will refuse leave to serve a writ out of the jurisdiction, even if it has jurisdiction over part of the claim under the statutory regimes. In other cases it may give leave to serve the writ on some but not other defendants.

Issue with the leave of the court

3.27   If a writ is to be served out of the jurisdiction, the leave of the court is required before the writ may be issued,[19] except in those cases, considered above, in which the court's power to hear and determine the case is founded on the 1982 Act or a specialised statutory regime. The claim must be of a kind in which the court may grant leave for the writ to be served out of the jurisdiction,[20] and

---

[15] See the terms of R.S.C., Ord. 6, r. 7(1), which applies only to writs "to be served out of the jurisdiction."

[16] *Practice Note (Writ: Service Abroad)* [1987] 1 W.L.R. 86; Queen's Bench Masters' Practice Direction No. 11, *Supreme Court Practice* para. [730].

[17] The statutory regimes are the 1968 Convention, Sched. 4 to the 1982 Act and the "other enactments" referred to in R.S.C., Ord. 6, r. 7(1)(a)(ii) and Ord. 11, r. 1(2)(b); see paras. 1.29 and 1.30 above.

[18] The conditions under which a writ may be issued for service, and served, out of the jurisdiction are that *each* claim is one which the court has power to hear and determine pursuant to the statutory regimes: R.S.C., Ord. 6, r. 7(1)(a) and Ord. 11, r. 1(2).

[19] The cases in which the leave of the court is required under certain statutes before a writ may be issued even for service within the jurisdiction, are not considered here: see *Supreme Court Practice*, para. 6/7/2.

[20] R.S.C., Ord. 11, r. 1(1).

the decision whether to grant such leave is a matter for the court's discretion.

Application for leave. Application for leave to issue a writ for ser-   **3.28**
vice out of the jurisdiction is combined with the application for
leave to serve the writ there. It is made *ex parte* to the master[21] with
an affidavit in support. This must set out the grounds for the application, it must identify the country in which service is likely to be
carried out, and it must state the deponent's belief that the plaintiff
has a good cause of action.

Exercise of the court's discretion. The manner in which the court   **3.29**
approaches the exercise of its discretion to grant leave for the issue
and service of a writ out of the jurisdiction, is discussed in detail in
the Supreme Court Practice,[22] to which reference should be made.
In summary, it is for the applicant for leave, normally the plaintiff,
to satisfy the court that his case comes within one of the heads set
out in Order 11, rule 1(1), and that the case is a proper one for service out of the jurisdiction. The case must come within both the
letter and the spirit of the rules.[23] Any doubt as to the construction
of the rules will be resolved in favour of the defendant.[24] As the
application for leave is *ex parte* there must be full and fair disclosure
of all relevant facts. The applicant must have a good arguable case
both that the claim comes within the rules, and that it is proper for
the court to exercise its discretion in favour of granting leave.[25] The
court must exercise its discretion "with extreme caution and with
full regard in every case to the circumstances."[26] The court will
consider whether it constitutes a *forum conveniens* for the trial of the
action, taking account of whether foreign proceedings are pending,
where the witnesses and evidence are located, the governing law,
and the real object of the English proceedings.[27] A choice of juris-

---

[21] R.S.C., Ord. 11, r. 4. In the Queen's Bench Division the affidavit is left with
the masters' secretary for consideration by the master. In the Chancery Division
it is left with the masters' appointments clerk for consideration by the master or
the judge: see *Supreme Court Practice* para. 11/4/2. In cases in the Commercial
Court, the application for leave is made to the judge, see R.S.C., Ord. 72, r. 4.
[22] *Supreme Court Practice*, paras. 11/1/1–11/1/28.
[23] *Johnson v. Taylor Brothers* [1920] A.C. 144.
[24] *The Hagen* [1908] P. 189.
[25] *Maroux v. Sociedade Comercial Abel Pereira de Fonseca S.A.R.L.* [1972] 1
W.L.R. 962; *Diamond v. Bank of London and Montreal Ltd.* [1979] 2 W.L.R.
228. See also R.S.C., Ord. 11, r. 4(2).
[26] *Cordova Land Co. Ltd. v. Victor Brothers Inc.* [1966] 1 W.L.R. 793.
[27] *Spilidada Maritime Corp. v. Cansulex Ltd.* [1987] A.C. 460; *Société Général de
Paris v. Dreyfus Brothers* (1885) 29 Ch.D. 239 *per* Pearson J. at p. 242 (reversed
on different grounds (1887) 37 Ch.D. 215). See also *Kroch v. Rossell et cie.*
[1937] 1 All E.R. 725; *Carvahlo v. Hull, Blyth (Angola) Ltd.* [1979] 1 W.L.R.
1228. See also para. 1.45 above.

diction clause in favour of a foreign court will normally be respected by the English court.[28]

3.30 *The order for leave.* The order will specify the country in which the writ is to be served,[29] and the time for acknowledgment of service, taken from the extra jurisdiction tables,[30] unless the court otherwise orders.

2. Other procedural requirements

The parties' addresses

3.31 *Plaintiff.* The address of every plaintiff must be given in the writ.[31] A plaintiff who is resident outside the jurisdiction must also give an address for service within the jurisdiction, that is to say an address at which subsequent pleadings and other documents can be served in the course of the proceedings.[32] This will, if he is acting through a solicitor, be that solicitor's address.[33] If a plaintiff in person who is resident outside the jurisdiction cannot give an address for service within the jurisdiction the proceedings may be stayed.[34] A foreign company which is registered under section 691 of the Companies Act 1985 must give its registered address within the jurisdiction.[35] As a foreign company can only act in English proceedings through a solicitor, that solicitor's address within the jurisdiction will be the company's address for service for the purposes of the proceedings.

Defendant. The defendant's address must be stated in the writ as accurately as possible.[36]

---

[28] *Mackender v. Feldia A.G.* [1967] 2 Q.B. 590; *Unterweser Reederei G.m.b.H. v. Zapata Off-Shore Co., The Chaparral,* [1968] 2 Lloyd's Rep. 158. Note that if *either* party is domiciled in a Contracting State, a choice of jurisdiction in favour of an English court which complies with Art. 17 of the 1968 Convention (para. 21.01 below), brings the case within Ord. 11, r. 1(2), and that if *neither* party is domiciled in a Contracting State, a choice of jurisdiction in favour of another Contracting State must be respected unless the chosen court has declined jurisdiction: para. 21.71 below.

[29] See Queen's Bench Masters' Practice Direction No. 11, *Supreme Court Practice,* para. [730] and Queen's Bench Masters' Practice Form No. PF6, *Supreme Court Practice,* para. [207]; 35 *Court Forms* 235.

[30] *Supreme Court Practice,* para. [901].

[31] R.S.C., Ord. 6, r. 1, and Appendix A, Form No. 1.

[32] R.S.C., Ord. 6, r. 5(1)(b).

[33] R.S.C., Ord. 6, r. 5(2)(a).

[34] *Supreme Court Practice,* para. 6/5/3.

[35] See para. 4.13 below.

[36] *Supreme Court Practice,* para. 6/1/6.

Description of the parties

The full names of all natural persons who are parties should be **3.32** stated in the title to the proceedings. A foreign corporate body[37] should be also named and, strictly, its name and title should be set out in full, although a practice has developed whereby foreign entities are described in the style in which they enjoy legal rights and liabilities in their own country[38] and are named using normal appropriate abbreviations.[39] It is good practice, whether or not the parties titles have been abbreviated, for the legal nature of the foreign corporate entity to be pleaded in the statement of claim. In any event, if the true legal description of a party does not sufficiently appear from its name, it must be more fully described in the writ.[40]

Claims expressed in a foreign currency

Since the decision of the House of Lords in *Miliangos* v. *George* **3.33** *Frank (Textiles) Ltd.*[41] it has been permissible for an English court to give a judgment for a sum of money expressed in a foreign currency. It is immaterial whether the claim is for debt or for damages. The court has a discretion to select the currency which best expresses the plaintiff's loss.[42] The practice relating to the making of claims and the enforcement of judgments in a foreign currency is the subject of a Queen's Bench Masters' Practice Direction.[43] One of the requirements which this lays down is for the writ to be indorsed with a certificate as to the sterling rate of exchange for the particular currency at or about the date of its issue. The following is the form of the indorsement, which should be signed by or on

---

[37] As to the capacity of foreign corporations to sue and be sued see para. 2.06 above.

[38] *Supreme Court Practice*, paras. 6/5/6, 11/5/3.

[39] The normal forms of corporate entity under the laws of the other Contracting States are referred to with their normal abbreviations at para. 73 in chaps. 48 to 58 below.

[40] *Practice Direction (Central Office: Description of Parties)* [1969] 1 W.L.R. 1259; Queen's Bench Masters' Practice Direction 13(1), *Supreme Court Practice*, para. [735].

[41] [1976] A.C. 443. *Supreme Court Practice*, para. 42/1/5.

[42] *Services Europe Atlantique Sud SEAS* v. *Stockholms Rederiaktiebolag SVEA (The Folias)* [1979] A.C. 685; see *Hoffman* v. *Soaffer* [1982] 1 W.L.R. 1350, in which damages for pain, suffering and loss of amenity awarded to a foreign national who had been injured on a visit to England, were expressed in sterling while damages for the remainder of his losses were expressed in the currency of his country.

[43] *Practice Direction (Judgment: Foreign Currency)* [1976] 1 W.L.R. 83; [1976] 1 All E.R. 669, as amended by *Practice Direction (Judgment: Foreign Currency)* [1977] 1 W.L.R. 197; [1977] 1 All E.R. 554; Queen's Bench Masters' Practice Direction No. 8B, *Supreme Court Practice*, para. [724].

behalf of the plaintiff's solicitor, or by the plaintiff if he is acting in person:

"Sterling equivalent of amount claimed
I/We certify that the rate current in London for the purchase of [*state the unit of the foreign currency claimed*] at the close of business on the-day of   19   [*being the date next to or most nearly preceding the date of issue of the Writ*] was   to the £ Sterling and at this rate the debt or liquidated demand claimed herein, namely [*state the sum of the foreign currency claimed*] amounts to   or exceeds £5000 [*as the case may be*].
Dated the   day of   19

Signed:
(Solicitor for the Plaintiff)."

If the grounds for claiming a judgment expressed in foreign currency are not apparent from the nature of the case, the facts relied upon in support of the claim should be pleaded in the statement of claim. Foreign currency may only be lodged in court if it is paid into court in satisfaction of all or part of a plaintiff's claim or if the court so permits.[44]

Indorsement of time for acknowledgment of service

3.34   When the writ is served it must be accompanied by a copy of the prescribed form of acknowledgment of service in which the title and number of the action have been entered.[45] The writ itself must state the time within which the defendant must acknowledge service. This is inserted by the party issuing the writ.[46] In the case of a writ to be served within the jurisdiction the period is 14 days or such longer period as the court may direct.[47] Where the writ is to be served out of the jurisdiction without leave[48] the periods within which the acknowledgment of service must be returned depend on where it is to be served. For service in Scotland, Northern Ireland or the European territory of another Contracting State,[49] in a case to which the 1982 Act applies, the period is 21 days from and

---

[44] Court Funds Rules 1987, r. 38; *Supreme Court Practice*, para. [1161]; see also para. 22/1/8.
[45] R.S.C., Ord. 10, r. 1(6); Appendix A, Form No. 14, *Supreme Court Practice*, para. [9]. *See Practice Direction (Commencement of Proceedings)* issued June 12, 1980; *Practice Direction (Writ: New Forms of Service)* [1980] 3 All E.R. 822, Queen's Bench Masters' Practice Direction No. 12, *Supreme Court Practice*, para. [725].
[46] *Practice Note (Writ: Service Abroad)* [1987] 1 W.L.R. 86.
[47] R.S.C., Ord. 12, r. 5; A longer period might be proper where the court grants leave under Ord. 10, r. 2 for service on the agent within the jurisdiction of an overseas principal. See para. 4.14 below.
[48] *I.e.* in the cases defined in R.S.C., Ord. 11, r. 1(2).
[49] The European territories of the Contracting States are described at paras. 34.01 *et seq.* below.

including the day of service.[50] For service in any non-European territory of a Contracting State the period is 31 days from and including the day of service.[51] For service elsewhere in the world where the court has jurisdiction under the 1982 Act[52] the period is determined in accordance with the extra jurisdiction table.[53] This table also determines the period which applies in all cases in which the court has jurisdiction under one of the specialised statutory regimes.[54] Where the leave of the court is required for service of the writ out of the jurisdiction[55] the master will specify the period within which the acknowledgment of service must be returned in accordance with the extra jurisdiction table.[56] Where service is to be effected on a foreign state the time for returning the acknowledgment of service begins to run two months after receipt by the ministry for foreign affairs of the defendant state.[57]

Indorsement as to costs

Where the plaintiff's claim is for a debt or liquidated demand **3.35** only it must be indorsed with a statement of the amount claimed and the costs, together with a statement that the proceedings will be stayed if the defendant pays the full amount claimed within the time limited for acknowledging service.[58] The costs recoverable, which are fixed in accordance with a scale,[59] are known as "14 day costs." Where service is to be effected out of the jurisdiction an additional fixed amount is recoverable in respect of the costs of service.[60] This will frequently be inadequate to cover the actual costs of service out of the jurisdiction. If a greater amount is sought to be specified in the writ application should be made to the master for leave to claim an appropriate amount.[61] Now that service itself may take place out of the jurisdiction without leave in cases where the court has jurisdiction under the 1982 Act, the application should be made to the practice master.

---

[50] R.S.C., Ord. 11, r. 1(3)(a). In the county court, see C.C.R, Ord. 8, rr. 2(3) and 2(4).
[51] R.S.C., Ord. 11, r. 1(3)(b).
[52] See paras. 3.02 and 3.14 above.
[53] R.S.C., Ord. 11, r. 1(3)(c); *Supreme Court Practice*, para. [901].
[54] R.S.C., Ord. 11, r. 1(3)(c). See paras. 1.29 and 1.30 above.
[55] That is, in cases to which R.S.C., Ord. 11, r. 1(1) applies.
[56] R.S.C., Ord. 11, r. 4(4), and the Queen's Bench Master's Practice Direction No. 11, *Supreme Court Practice*, para. [730]; see also para. [901].
[57] State Immunity Act 1978, s.12(2). See para. 4.39 below.
[58] R.S.C., Ord. 6, r. 2(1)(b).
[59] R.S.C., Ord. 62, App. 3. Where the claim is in a foreign currency, the scale is applied by taking the exchange rate indorsed on the writ: see para. 3.33 above.
[60] *Supreme Court Practice*, para. 62/A3/2.
[61] *Supreme Court Practice*, para. 6/2/23.

Concurrent writs

3.36   The court has power to issue a concurrent writ, on the application of the plaintiff, at any time during the validity of the original writ.[62] This may be desirable if attempts to serve the writ are made in more than one place or if the original has been lost. A concurrent writ is simply a duplicate of the original writ marked with the word "concurrent" with an official stamp. Its contents will differ only as regards the purpose for which it was issued. Thus a writ to be served within the jurisdiction in a Convention case will not need the indorsement as to jurisdiction required by Order 6, rule 7.[63] If a defendant leaves the jurisdiction after the issue of a writ issued for service within the jurisdiction a concurrent writ for service out of the jurisdiction may be issued. In a Convention case it would need to be indorsed in accordance with Order 6, rule 7. In a non-Convention case, to which Order 11, rule 1(1) applied, leave to issue the concurrent writ would be required.[64]

Duration of the writ

3.37   Once the writ has been issued, it is valid for the purposes of service, in the first instance, for 12 months from the date of its issue.[65] The validity may be extended for up to 12 months at a time, by order of the court, and such extension may even be granted after the expiry of the writ's initial period of validity, if the court so allows.[66] The extension must be marked on the writ.[67] The writ must be served within the period of its validity; if it is not, this is an irregularity which the defendant may challenge.[68] A person named as a defendant in a writ which has not been served on him may require the plaintiff to serve the writ or discontinue the action against him.[69]

---

[62] R.S.C., Ord. 6, r. 6.
[63] See para. 3.25 above.
[64] *Supreme Court Practice*, para. 65/4/10.
[65] R.S.C., Ord. 6, r. 8(1). The validity of a concurrent writ expires on the same date as the validity of the original writ.
[66] R.S.C., Ord. 6, r. 8(2); see *Kleinwort Benson Ltd.* v. *Barbral Ltd.* [1987] A.C. 597; *Waddon* v. *Whitecroft Scovill Ltd.* [1988] 1 W.L.R. 309 (H.L); *Goldenglow Nut Food Co.* v. *Commodin (Produce) and others* [1987] 2 Lloyd's Rep. 569 (C.A.).
[67] R.S.C., Ord. 6, r. 8(3).
[68] See para. 5.02 below.
[69] R.S.C., Ord. 12, r. 8A.

CHAPTER 4

SERVICE OF PROCESS

A. INTRODUCTION

A defendant is brought into proceedings *in personam* by the service **4.01** upon him of the court's originating process. In English law, the responsibility for effecting service on the defendant is usually placed on the plaintiff or his agent.[1] Most continental legal systems, on the other hand, give this responsibility to the court or to publicly appointed officials.[2] The law of each country contains detailed rules regulating the service of the process of its courts within its own territory, and English law on this topic is examined in part B of this chapter.

---

[1] R.S.C., Ord. 10, r. 1(1). In the county court, the responsibility for serving a defendant often lies with the court: C.C.R., Ord. 7, r. 10.
[2] See paras. 13 and 38 of chaps. 48 to 58 below.

If the jurisidiction of the courts of one country is invoked against a defendant who is located outside the territory of that country, the regularity of service upon him becomes subject not only to any rules which that country may apply to those circumstances, but also to the law of the country where he is located and to any international conventions which may exist between the two countries. The framework of additional English rules and international conventions is discussed in part C of this chapter, and the particular means of serving defendants located in other European countries is discussed in part D. Acknowledgment of service, the effects of failure to acknowledge service and the entry of default judgments are discussed in part E of this chapter. In part F, the service in England of the process of foreign courts is described.

4.02 *Service and jurisdiction.* Before the 1982 Act, the jurisdiction of the High Court was generally regarded as well-founded if the defendant could legitimately be served with the court's process, either within the court's territorial jurisdiction or, with the leave of the court, outside it.[3] In this sense, jurisdiction was based on service.[3a] Now, however, in most civil and commercial cases, the jurisdiction of the English court is based on the 1968 Convention and the 1982 Act.[4] It follows that, in any case to which the Convention or Act applies, if the English court does not have jurisdiction according to the rules of the Convention, it cannot acquire jurisdiction simply through service of the proceedings upon the defendant. This applies irrespective of where the defendant is,[5] even if he is within the court's territorial jurisdiction, and even where the rules of court expressly provide for a particular method of service within the jurisdiction on a defendant who is outside the jurisdiction. The acknowledgment of service by a defendant is not regarded in the first instance as a submission to the jurisdiction,[6] nor as a waiver of irregularity in the writ or service thereof or in any order giving leave to serve it out of the jurisdiction.[7]

---

[3] See paras. 1.25 *et seq.* above.
[3a] See para. 1.15 above.
[4] The 1968 Convention and Sched. 4 to the 1982 Act generally apply to all civil and commercial cases in which the defendant is domiciled in a Contracting State (including the U.K.), as well as to various other cases: see paras. 3.04 *et seq.* above.
[5] *Cf. Rothmans of Pall Mall (Overseas) Ltd.* v. *Saudi Arabian Airlines Corporation* [1981] Q.B. 368, decided under the Warsaw Convention 1929; see *Supreme Court Practice* para. 65/3/12.
[6] See para. 5.11 below.
[7] R.S.C., Ord. 12, r. 7. See para. 4.51 below.

Terminology. In this chapter the term jurisdiction is ordinarily **4.03** used in its territorial sense to refer to the territory of England and Wales.[8] The rules and practices described in this chapter are ordinarily those which apply to a normal action *in personam* begun by writ in the Queen's Bench Division. The differences between the rules and practices of the different divisions of the High Court, between different sections of those divisions, and between different forms of originating process, are minor.

B. SERVICE WITHIN THE JURISDICTION

The various methods available under the rules for serving a writ **4.04** or other originating process on a defendant within the jurisdiction are discussed below. Different rules apply to different types of defendant.

Documents other than originating process. Once the originating process has been served, subsequent pleadings and other documents which require to be served on a defendant may generally be served within the jurisdiction on his proper address for service,[9] which, if he is acting by a solicitor on the record, will be the solicitor's address[10] and, if he is acting in person, on the address for service given in the acknowledgment of service.[11] Pleadings and other documents to be served on the plaintiff must generally be served at the address within the jurisdiction given by him for this purpose.[12] Certain documents, however, must normally be served personally on the party to whom they are directed.[13]

1. Accepting or agreeing service

Acceptance by the defendant's solicitor. Even if service is carried out **4.05** otherwise than in accordance with the rules, the defect is generally capable of being cured if the defendant accepts, or can be taken to have accepted, service. Where a defendant's solicitor indorses on the writ a statement that he accepts service on behalf of the defend-

---

[8] See para. 1.03 above.
[9] R.S.C., Ord. 65, r. 5. The documents may be served by leaving them at that address, by post, by document exchange, or in such other manner as the court may direct.
[10] *Supreme Court Practice*, paras. 65/5/2, 65/5/7.
[11] R.S.C., Ord. 12, r. 3(2).
[12] R.S.C., Ord. 6, r. 5(2); see para. 3.31 above.
[13] *Supreme Court Practice*, para. 65/1/2.

ant the writ is deemed to have been duly served on the defendant.[14] If the writ is not duly served, but the defendant acknowledges service of it, it is deemed to have been duly served unless the contrary is shown.[15] The parties may agree on a method of service if it is not prohibited by the rules[16]; and this applies also to foreign defendants who can appoint a particular person to accept service.[17]

4.06   *Service of process in pursuance of a contract.* Where the High Court has jurisdiction, whether by agreement between the parties or otherwise, to hear and determine any action in respect of a contract, and the parties have agreed on the manner in which, the place at which, or the person upon whom service is to be effected, service in accordance with that agreement is deemed to be good service.[18] Thus a contract between parties one or more of whom are outside the jurisdiction may provide for service within the jurisdiction on a person appointed to accept service on behalf of a foreign party. The rule covers service both within and out of the jurisdiction but in cases in which leave to serve out of the jurisdiction is required[19] such leave must be obtained.[20]

2. Service on individuals

4.07   The general rules which regulate service on any defendant apply in particular to service on individuals, whereas in their application to corporate bodies and other types of defendant they may be modified or qualified.

The primary rule for service on a defendant to proceedings in the High Court[21] is that he must be served personally with the writ,[22] or other document by which the proceedings are commenced. This applies unless under any particular rule or enactment an alternative method of service is authorised.[23] As will be seen below, this

---

[14] R.S.C., Ord. 10, r. 1(4); *Manta Line Inc.* v. *Seraphim Sofianites* [1984] 1 Lloyd's Rep. 14; see *Supreme Court Practice*, para. 10/1/12. Such an indorsement does not constitute notice of intention to defend the action, and does not preclude the entry of a default judgment: see para. 4.54 below.

[15] R.S.C., Ord. 10, r. 1(5); see also para. 4.54 below.

[16] *Supreme Court Practice*, para. 65/4/3.

[17] *Montgomery & Co.* v. *Liebenthal & Co.* [1898] 1 Q.B. 487; *Supreme Court Practice*, para. 65/3/14.

[18] R.S.C., Ord. 10, r. 3.

[19] R.S.C., Ord. 11, r. 1(1).

[20] R.S.C., Ord. 10, r. 3(2). The text of this sub-rule is incorrectly printed in the *Supreme Court Practice*: see para. 4.23 n. 5 below. Ord. 10, r. 3(3) applies to service of a writ relating to a contract subject to a choice of jurisdiction agreement: see para. 4.23 n. 6 below.

[21] In the county court, proceedings may be served personally or by post by the court: C.C.R., Ord. 7, r. 10.

[22] R.S.C., Ord. 10, r. 1(1).

[23] R.S.C., Ord. 10, r. 1(7).

general rule applies not only to service within the jurisdiction, but also service outside it, subject to the law of the country where service is effected.[24] The responsibility for effecting personal service within the jurisdiction rests with the plaintiff or his agent. Personal service on an individual is effected by leaving the document with that individual, and the courts have developed strict guidelines as to what constitutes personal service within this rule.[25]

The rules provide, as an alternative which is usually used in practice, that service on a defendant may be effected within the jurisdiction by sending a copy of the writ by first-class post to his usual or last known address or by inserting it, in a sealed enveloped addressed to the defendant, through the letter box at that address.[26]

Particular individuals

Sole trader. It should be noted that if a person is carrying on business in the jurisdiction under a name or style other than his own name, he may be served within the jurisdiction in accordance with the rules relating to partnerships,[27] whether or not he is personally within the jurisdiction.[28] **4.08**

Diplomats and consuls. If a person benefits from diplomatic or consular privilege,[29] service upon him may be disallowed.[30]

Members of H.M. Forces; foreign armed forces. Special arrangements exist to assist in the service of proceedings on members of the armed forces[31] and of the United States Air Force.[32]

---

[24] R.S.C., Ord. 11, r. 5(2): see paras. 4.24 and 4.25 below.
[25] R.S.C., Ord. 65, r. 2; *Supreme Court Practice*, para. 65/2/1. Personal service may not be effected on a Sunday except, in cases of urgency, with the leave of the court.
[26] R.S.C., Ord. 10, r. 1(2). Service is deemed to be effected on the seventh day after the writ was posted or put through the letter box, and there are prescribed particulars which must be included in any affidavit of service by this method: Ord. 10, r. 1(3). For additional precautions which may be taken if service is effected in this way, see Chitty and Jacob, pp. 50–51. The defendant need not be physically within the jurisdiction at the time of service: *Barclays Bank of Swaziland Ltd.* v. *Hahn* [1989] 1 W.L.R. 13.
[27] R.S.C., Ord. 81, r. 9. The rules relating to partnerships are discussed at para. 4.10 below.
[28] The amended version of R.S.C., Ord. 81, r. 9 has the effect of revoking in this respect the decision in *St. Gobain* v. *Hoyermann's Agency* [1893] 2 Q.B. 96; the note in the *Supreme Court Practice* at para. 81/9/4 is seemingly incorrect on this point.
[29] Diplomatic Privileges Act 1964; Consular Relations Act 1969.
[30] See *Supreme Court Practice*, para. 65/2/3.
[31] Memorandum issued by Lord Chancellor's Office, July 26, 1979: see *Supreme Court Practice*, paras. 65/2/8–10.
[32] See *Supreme Court Practice*, para. 65/2/11.

3. Service on English companies and on partnerships

4.09   *English companies.* A company formed and registered under the Companies Acts may be served by leaving the document at, or by sending it by post to, its registered office.[33] If it is served by post, the writ is deemed to be served, subject to proof to the contrary, in the ordinary course of post.[34] This is taken to mean, unless the contrary is shown, that service is effected on the second working day after it was posted in the case of first class post, and on the fourth working day after it was posted in the case of second class post.[35]

4.10   *Partnerships carrying on business within the jurisdiction.* If two or more persons are alleged to be liable as partners in respect of a cause of action and if they are carrying on business within the jurisdiction, they may be sued in the firm name[36] and the writ may be served in any of three ways. First, it may be served on any one or more of the partners as individuals in the manner described above.[37] Secondly, it may be served at the principal place of business of the partnership within the jurisdiction on any person having at the time of service the control or management of the partnership business there.[38] In this case, service can only be personal service on that person. Thirdly, the writ may be served by sending a copy of it by ordinary first class post to the firm at its principal place of business within the jurisdiction.[39]

Every person who is served whether as a partner or as a person having the control or management of the firm must at the same time be given a written notice stating the capacity in which he is served.[40] There is no provision for service on a partnership by inserting a copy of the writ through the letter box at the principal place of business of the firm.[41] The fact that any or all of the partners may be resident outside the jurisdiction does not affect the validity of service. However a partner who was resident outside

---

[33] Companies Act 1985, s.725; R.S.C., Ord. 65, r. 3(2).
[34] Interpretation Act 1978, s.7.
[35] *Practice Direction (Q.B.D.: Postal Service)* [1985] 1 W.L.R. 489; Queen's Bench Masters' Practice Direction 26A, *Supreme Court Practice*, para. [763]. This does not affect the provisions of R.S.C., Ord. 10, r. 1(3) (para. 4.07 above) concerning service of proceedings on an individual.
[36] R.S.C., Ord. 81, r. 1; see para. 2.08 above. The same rules apply also to any person carrying on business within the jurisdiction under a name or style other than his own name: Ord. 81, r. 9: see para. 4.08 above.
[37] R.S.C., Ord. 81, r. 3(1)(a). As to service of the writ on a person out of the jurisdiction, see paras. 4.23 *et seq.* below.
[38] R.S.C., Ord. 81, r. 3(1)(b).
[39] R.S.C., Ord. 81, r. 3(1)(c): see *Austin Rover Group Ltd.* v. *Crouch Butler Savage Association* [1986] 1 W.L.R. 1102.
[40] R.S.C., Ord. 81, r. 3(4).
[41] *Cf.* R.S.C., Ord. 10, r. 1(2).

the jurisdiction at the time of issue of the proceedings will not be personally affected by any judgment unless he was served as a partner[42] or unless he acknowledged service as a partner.[43]

4. Service on other corporate bodies

A corporate body may be served, unless provision is made other- **4.11** wise by any enactment, by serving the document personally on an officer in a position of authority, such as its chairman or president, principal officer, secretary, or treasurer.[44] As an alternative to personal service on an officer of the body corporate, a writ may be served on a body corporate by first class post within the jurisdiction at its registered office or principal office, or by insertion through the letter box there.[45] Unless the contrary is shown, the writ will be deemed to be served on the seventh day after it was posted or put through the letter box.

It is important to note that other provision is made, for example, for English registered companies[46] and for foreign companies with a place of business in Great Britain,[47] and that this rule does not apply to such companies. It applies to such bodies as local authorities, building societies, and bodies incorporated by royal charter.

5. Service on foreign companies and other bodies

Scottish companies. A company formed and registered under the **4.12** Companies Acts may be served by leaving the document at, or by sending it by post to, its registered office in Scotland.[48] If it is carrying on business in England and Wales it may be served by leaving the court's process at, or by sending it by post to, the company's principal place of business in England and Wales, addressed to the manager or other head officer in England and Wales of the com-

---

[42] R.S.C., Ord. 81, r. 5.
[43] R.S.C., Ord. 81, r. 4: acknowledgment of service may not be given in the firm's name but only in the names of the individual partners. Similarly, execution of any judgment given against the firm will be limited to the property within the jurisdiction, being the property of the firm, or that of any person who acknowledged service as a partner, or who admitted to being a partner, or who was adjudged to be a partner, or who, having been served as a partner, failed to acknowledge service: R.S.C., Ord. 81, r. 5.
[44] R.S.C., Ord. 65, r. 3(1).
[45] R.S.C., Ord. 65, r. 3(2); Ord. 10, r. 1(2).
[46] Companies Act 1985, s.725, para. 4.09 above.
[47] *Ibid.*, s.695, para. 4.13 below.
[48] *Ibid.*, s.725(1).

Proceedings in England and Wales

pany[49]; but in this case a copy of the process must be sent by post to the company's registered office.[50]

4.13   *Foreign companies established in Great Britain.*[51] The Companies Act 1985 imposes a duty on any company incorporated outside Great Britain[52] which establishes a place of business in Great Britain, to register the names and addresses of one or more persons resident in Great Britain who are authorised to accept service of process on behalf of the company.[53] Service of process on a foreign company may be effected by addressing it to any such person and leaving it at, or sending it by post to, such address.[54] If the company has failed to register the name and address of such person, or if the person registered refuses to accept service or for any reason cannot be served, any document to be served may be left at or sent by post to any place of business established by the company in Great Britain.[55] The place of business established by the company must be fixed and definite[56] and it must be established at the time of service.[57] Older cases at common law, under which a foreign company carrying on business in England was treated as having a presence within the jurisdiction sufficient to enable it to be served there,[58] may be a guide to the meaning of "establishes a place of business" in the Companies Act. It has been held sufficient if the place of business was only established for a short period[59]; and even if the action is in respect of business not carried on there.[60]

Although under the law as it stood before the passing of the 1982

---

[49] *Ibid.*, s.725(2); this provision is permissive and other forms of service may be used instead: *Stylo Shoes Ltd.* v. *Prices Tailors* [1960] Ch. 386; see *Supreme Court Practice*, para. 65/3/19.
[50] Companies Act 1985, s.725(3).
[51] See *Supreme Court Practice*, para. 65/3/11. Such companies are called "oversea" companies by the Companies Act.
[52] Great Britain means England and Wales and Scotland; a company registered in Northern Ireland is a foreign company, see *Supreme Court Practice*, para. 65/3/17. Oversea companies incorporated in the Channel Islands or the Isle of Man which establish a place of business in Great Britain are under more extensive obligations: Companies Act 1985, s.699.
[53] Companies Act 1985, s.691. The register is kept by the registrar of companies. See Dicey and Morris, p. 296.
[54] Companies Act 1985, s.695(1). As to service by post, see para. 4.09 above.
[55] *Ibid.*, s.695(2). By s.744, a place of business includes a share transfer or share registration office. See *South Indian Shipping Corporation Ltd.* v. *Export-Import Bank of Korea* [1985] 1 W.L.R. 585, where the fact that no banking transactions were carried out at the office in question did not prevent it from being the bank's "place of business."
[56] *The Theodohus* [1977] 2 Lloyd's Rep. 428.
[57] *Deverall* v. *Grant Advertising Inc.* [1955] Ch. 111.
[58] Cheshire and North, p. 190; *Supreme Court Practice*, para. 65/3/12.
[59] *Dunlop Pneumatic Tyre Co. Ltd.* v *A/G Cudell & Co.* [1902] 1 K.B. 342.
[60] *Haggin* v. *Comptior d'Escompte de Paris* (1889) 23 Q.B.D. 519.

Act the delivery of the name and address for registration normally amounted to a submission to the jurisdiction of the court,[61] such would not now be the effect in any case covered by the 1968 Convention or that Act, because the English court acquires its jurisdiction not by reason of the defendant's presence, nor by service of the proceedings, but solely by virtue of the Convention and the Act.[62]

6. Service on agent of overseas principal

In an action relating to a contract, the court may grant leave for **4.14** the service of the writ within the jurisdiction on the agent of a foreign principal, subject to certain conditions.[63] Application for leave is made *ex parte* to the master supported by an affidavit. The granting of leave is subject to the following formal requirements and to discretionary considerations referred to below:

(a) the contract must have been entered into within the jurisdiction with or through an agent who is either an individual residing or carrying on business within the jurisdiction or a body corporate having a registered office or a place of business within the jurisdiction;

(b) the principal for whom the agent was acting must have been at the time of the contract, and must be at the time of the application for leave, neither a person residing or carrying on business within the jurisdiction, nor a body corporate with a registered office or a place of business within the jurisdiction; and

(c) at the time of the application for leave the agent's authority must not have been terminated, or he must still be in business relations with the principal.[64]

When leave is given for service of the proceedings on the agent, a time for acknowledgment of service must be specified in the order,[65]

---

[61] See *Employers Liability Assurance Corporation Ltd.* v. *Sedgwick Collins & Co. Ltd.* [1927] A.C. 95; *The Madrid* [1937] P., *per* Bucknill J., at p. 45. *Cf. Rothmans of Pall Mall (Overseas) Ltd.* v. *Saudi Arabian Airlines Corp.* [1981] Q.B. 368, C.A., where jurisdiction was held not to be founded despite service on the defendant at its place of business within the jurisdiction, because the English courts did not have jurisdiction under the statutory scheme in the Carriage by Air Act 1961 giving effect to the Warsaw Convention.

[62] Under Art. 5(5) of the 1968 Convention (para. 17.55 below) and Art. 5(5) of Sched. 4 to the 1982 Act (para. 45.06 below), for example, the High Court has jurisdiction over a defendant domiciled in another Contracting State or in another part of the U.K., as regards a dispute arising out of the operations of a branch, agency or other establishment situated in England and Wales.

[63] R.S.C., Ord. 10, r. 2; *Supreme Court Practice*, para. 65/3/13; Chitty and Jacob, pp. 59 *et seq.*

[64] R.S.C., Ord. 10, r. 2(1).

[65] R.S.C., Ord. 10, r. 2(2).

and a copy of the order and of the writ must be sent to the defendant at his address out of the jurisdiction.[66]

The granting of leave is discretionary[67] and it will only be granted when there are difficulties in serving the overseas principal. The mere fact that the principal is resident outside the jurisdiction is not a sufficient reason for authorising service on the agent. It must be remembered that, in cases to which the 1968 Convention applies, if the court does not have jurisdiction according to the rules of the Convention, it cannot acquire jurisdiction simply by service on an agent,[68] even though the rules of court provide for this method of service.

7. Substituted service

4.15 Substituted service is any method of service which the court authorises to take the place either of personal service or of service by one or other of the alternative methods prescribed by Order 10, rule 1(2).[69] The court is empowered to order substituted service if service by normal methods is shown to be "impracticable".[70] Application is made *ex parte* to the practice master or to the district registrar with an affidavit in support.[71] Substituted service may take whatever form may be appropriate to bring the existence of the proceedings to the defendant's notice,[72] for example, by service on some person shown to be in communication with the defendant, or by advertisement. The method ordered must be one which in all reasonable probability, if not certainty, will be effective to bring knowledge of the writ to the defendant.[73]

However, substituted service may only be ordered in respect of proceedings which at the time of their issue could lawfully be served. Thus, if the writ is to be served out of the jurisdiction, it must have been issued in conformity with Order 6, rule 7, whether by being duly indorsed or by being issued pursuant to the leave of

---

[66] R.S.C., Ord. 10, r. 2(3).

[67] *Supreme Court Practice*, para. 10/2/2.

[68] An agent for the purposes of the present rule does not necessarily constitute an "branch agency or other establishment" for the purposes of Art. 5(5) of the 1968 Convention and Sched. 4 to the 1982 Act: see paras. 17.61 *et seq.* below.

[69] There cannot be substituted service of a writ *in rem*: *The Good Herald* [1987] 1 Lloyd's Rep. 236.

[70] R.S.C., Ord. 65, r. 4; See *Re Conan Doyle's Will Trusts* [1971] Ch. 982; See the detailed notes in the *Supreme Court Practice* at paras. 65/4/1 *et seq.*; see 35 *Court Forms* (1983 Issue) pp. 93 *et seq.*

[71] For a form of affidavit, see *Chitty and Jacob*, p. 54; see also *Supreme Court Practice*, para. 65/4/9.

[72] *Re McLaughlin* [1950] A.C. 343.

[73] *Porter* v. *Freudenberg* [1915] 1 K.B. 857.

the court.[74] Subject to that point, the court may, in an appropriate case, give leave for steps to be taken within the jurisdiction by way of substituted service on a defendant who is outside the jurisdiction.[75] If it is shown that the defendant has left the jurisdiction to evade service, or after knowledge of the writ has come to his notice, the court may order substituted service if, on the facts, it would be just.[76]

Substituted service effected with the leave of the court is generally good service, but in a case to which the 1968 Convention or Schedule 4 of the 1982 Act applies, substituted service on a defendant domiciled in another Contracting State or in another part of the United Kingdom must be such as to satisfy certain further requirements designed to ensure that the defendant is given adequate notice of the proceedings.[77]

C. SERVICE OUT OF THE JURISDICTION: THE FRAMEWORK

Background. It has already been observed[78] that from about the **4.16** middle of the last century the English courts extended their jurisdiction over defendants who were outside the territorial jurisdiction by allowing the writ or originating summons to be served outside the jurisdiction, with the leave of the court, in a number of specified cases.[79] These cases, which are now listed in Order 11 of the Rules of the Supreme Court, were all cases in which there was a clear connection between the subject matter of the proceedings and the territory of England and Wales. At the same time, to prevent the undue infringement of foreign sovereignty, the court retained

---

[74] See *Supreme Court Practice*, paras. 6/7/2, and 65/4/11; *Myerson* v. *Martin* [1979] 1 W.L.R. 1390. On the other hand, if the defendant is out of the jurisdiction but the court has power to hear and determine the case under the 1968 Convention and 1982 Act, the fact that the writ was not indorsed in accordance with R.S.C., Ord. 6, r. 7(1)(b) at the time of its issue should not preclude the court from ordering substituted service within the jurisdiction in a proper case. It would be otherwise if the substituted service were itself to take place outside the jurisdiction.

[75] *Western Suburban Building Society* v. *Rucklidge* [1905] 2 Ch. 472.

[76] *Porter* v. *Freudenberg* [1915] 1 K.B. 857, but see Dicey and Morris, p. 292. See also the authorities cited in the *Supreme Court Practice* at para. 65/4/5. The master may give leave for any increased costs of substituted service to be indorsed on the writ, see *Supreme Court Practice*, para. 6/2/23.

[77] 1968 Convention, Art. 20 (para. 22.11 below); Hague Service Convention, Art. 15 (para. A2.09 below); 1982 Act, Sched. 4, Art. 20 (para. 45.26 below). See the discussion at paras. 22.17 *et seq.* below. Enforcement in other Contracting States of a default judgment entered after substituted service may also prove difficult by reason of Art. 27(2) of the 1968 Convention: see para. 27.24 below.

[78] See paras. 1.15 and 1.28 above.

[79] See Holdsworth, *History of English Law*, (vol. 9), p. 254; *Lenders* v. *Anderson* (1883) 12 Q.B.D. 56.

the discretion to grant or refuse leave to serve the proceedings out of the jurisdiction. In certain other cases the English courts latterly acquired jurisdiction pursuant to specialised international conventions, notwithstanding that the defendant was outside the jurisdiction or that the wrongful act, neglect, or default, took place outside the jurisdiction.[80] In such cases leave to serve the proceedings outside the jurisdiction was not, and is not, required, because the court's international jurisdiction arises by international agreement and there can consequently be no question of infringing foreign sovereignty. The 1968 Convention, supplemented by Schedule 4 to the 1982 Act, creates an international jurisdictional regime similar to that created by the specialised conventions, albeit of far wider application,[80a] and it follows that where the jurisdiction of the English court arises under these new rules, no infringement of the sovereignty of the other Contracting States can be said to occur.

4.17 *New jurisdictional rules.* In any case in which the English court has jurisdiction under the Convention or Schedule 4 to the 1982 Act, the plaintiff may invoke that jurisdiction as of right, regardless of the whereabouts of the defendant. Accordingly, the need for the court to control the service of proceedings out of the jurisdiction by the granting of leave no longer exists in such cases, and the proceedings may be served on the defendant without leave, not only in all of the Contracting States, but anywhere in the world.[81] Leave to serve a writ out of the jurisdiction is still required, however, in cases to which the new jurisdictional regime does not apply.

1. The requirement of leave for service out of the jurisdiction

4.18 If a writ or other originating process is to be served out of the jurisdiction, it may be necessary for the leave of the court to be obtained.

Service out of the jurisdiction without leave

The cases in which leave to serve proceedings out of the jurisdiction is not required are set out in Order 11, rule 1(2) of the Rules of the Supreme Court,[82] which refers to two different categories of claim in which the English courts have statutory jurisdiction. The

---

[80] See paras. 1.29 and 1.30 above.
[80a] *Cf. Babanaft International Co. S.A.* v. *Bassatne*, [1989] 2 W.L.R. 232, at p. 246, where Kerr L.J. stated the object of the 1968 Convention as being to create something analogous to a single law district for the whole of the EEC.
[81] The note in the *Supreme Court Practice* at para. 11/4/1 which seemingly suggests that leave is still required in a Convention case for service in a non-Contracting State is incorrect in this respect.
[82] C.C.R., Ord. 8, r. 2(2) is in equivalent terms.

first category contains those writs in which every claim is one which, by virtue of the 1982 Act, the court has power to hear and determine, and to which certain further conditions apply.[83] The conditions which must be met for a writ to be issued and served without leave have already been considered in detail.[84] The second category contains those claims which "by virtue of any other enactment," the court has power to hear and determine notwithstanding that the defendant is not within the jurisdiction or that the wrongful act, neglect or default giving rise to the claim did not take place within the jurisdiction.[85] With one exception,[85a] these other enactments are those which give effect in English law to jurisdictional regimes in certain specified international conventions.[86] In cases to which they apply, they take priority over the 1968 Convention and 1982 Act.[87] Care must be exercised before a writ is served out of the jurisdiction without leave, because if leave is required, such service is an irregularity which the court may be unwilling to correct.[88]

Service out of the jurisdiction with leave

The cases in which leave is required to serve proceedings out of **4.19** the jurisdiction are set out in R.S.C., Order 11, rule 1(1).[89] These form a statutory code for all those types of case, (other than Admiralty proceedings),[90] in which the court assumes jurisdiction over persons outside the jurisdiction by means of service of proceedings on them. The code does not of course apply to cases in which the court has statutory jurisdiction under the 1982 Act, or otherwise, as

---

[83] R.S.C., Ord. 11, r. 1(2)(a). Leave may nonetheless be required if only some of the claims in the writ fall within the jurisdictional regime of the 1968 Convention and 1982 Act: see para. 4.20 below.

[84] See paras. 3.23 *et seq.* above.

[85] R.S.C., Ord. 11, r. 1(2)(b).

[85a] Protection of Trading Interests Act 1980, s.6(5): see para. 1.30, n. 80 above.

[86] See paras. 1.29, 1.30 and 3.17 above.

[87] 1968 Convention, Art. 57 (para. 33.06 below); 1982 Act, Sched. 5, para. 6 (para. 45.36 below). The inter-relationship between the specialised conventions and the 1968 Convention is less than straightforward: see paras. 33.10 *et seq.* below.

[88] *Dalal v. Dalal*, (1983) L.S.Gaz. 2140; *Camera Care Ltd. v. Victor Hasselblad AB*, [1986] E.C.C. 373, (C.A.); *Leal v. Dunlop Bio-Processors International Ltd.* [1984] 1 W.L.R. 874, (C.A.)

[89] The County Court Rules contain equivalent provisions: C.C.R. Ord. 8, r. 2(1).

[90] Service of a writ out of the jurisdiction in an Admiralty action *in personam* is subject to additional requirements: R.S.C., Ord. 75, r. 4 and Supreme Court Act 1981, s.22; as to the compatibility of these requirements with the Convention, see Jackson, *Civil Jurisdiction and Judgments—Maritime Claims*, p.151. Service of a writ in an action *in rem* is not permitted out of the jurisdiction: Ord. 75, rr. 8 and 11.

discussed in the preceding paragraph, except in respect of a writ containing some claims which fall within the statutory rules of jurisdiction and some which fall outside them, as discussed in the next paragraph. The application for leave, the exercise of the court's discretion and the order made on the application have already been examined.[91] The jurisdiction of the English courts is dependent, in these cases, on the validity of the issue and service of the court's originating process. Consequently, in these cases, any irregularity affecting these matters can call into question the jurisdiction of the court.

Mixed claims

4.20   A writ may only be served out of the jurisdiction without leave if *each* claim in it is one which the court has power to hear and determine under the statutory regimes contained in the 1968 Convention, Schedule 4 to the 1982 Act and the "other enactments" referred to in the rules of court.[92] As has already been observed, a writ may contain various claims, some of which fall within those regimes and some of which do not. Leave is required for the service of such a writ out of the jurisdiction.[93]

Service of process in Scotland and Northern Ireland

4.21   In cases in which leave is sought to serve proceedings in Scotland or Northern Ireland, the court is required to consider the comparative cost and convenience of proceeding there instead of in England.[94] This requirement is now of only minimal application, in view of the fact that in most cases leave is no longer required for the service of English process in either of those jurisdictions.[95]

Service of subsequent summonses, pleadings and orders

4.22   As has already been observed, the defendant is required to give notice in his acknowledgment of service of an address within the jurisdiction for service on him of subsequent summonses, notices and orders in the action.[96] However, some such documents may still need to be served out of the jurisdiction, either because the defendant has failed to comply with that requirement, or because the document is one which must be served personally, or because

---

[91] See paras. 3.27 to 3.30 above.
[92] R.S.C., Ord. 6, r. 7(1)(a)(ii) and Ord. 11, r. 1(2)(b).
[93] See para. 3.26 above.
[94] R.S.C., Ord. 11, r. 4(3); C.C.R., Ord. 8, r. 5(1).
[95] 1982 Act, s.16 and Sched. 4.
[96] See para. 4.04 above.

the person to be served is not a party, or for some other reason. The service outside the jurisdiction of a summons, notice or order given or made in any proceedings requires the leave of the court unless the originating process in those proceedings could have been served out of the jurisdiction without leave.[97]

2. Methods of service outside the jurisdiction

The methods by which a writ may be served outside the jurisdic- **4.23**
tion do not vary according to whether or not leave is required for its issue and service, but they do vary somewhat according to the country where service is to be effected. As a matter of English law, service may be effected either, on one hand, by the plaintiff or his agent, or, on the other hand, through official channels. The requirements of English law, however, may be qualified by requirements of bilateral or multilateral conventions and by the law of the foreign country in question. In some countries, official channels are not available for service,[98] while in others service by the plaintiff or his agent is not allowed or is subject to restrictions. The particular methods which are available for service in each of the Contracting States to the 1968 Convention are discussed below.[99]

In any case in which a writ is to be served outside the jurisdiction, it must be accompanied by a form of acknowledgment of service, which may need to be modified "as may be appropriate."[1] Apart from the various methods of service described below, a writ will be deemed to have been regularly served if the defendant's solicitor indorses on it a statement that he accepts service[2] or, unless the contrary is shown, if the defendant acknowledges service of it.[3] Similarly, if in an action relating to a contract, the writ is served out of the jurisdiction in accordance with a manner of service specified in the contract, it will be deemed to have been duly served,[4] provided that, if leave for its service is required, such leave had been

---

[97] R.S.C., Ord. 11, r. 9(4).
[98] Under R.S.C., Ord. 11, r. 6, official channels are not available in respect of other parts of the U.K. and are only available in respect of independent Commonwealth countries, colonies and certain other territories under the provisions of the Hague Service Convention, discussed at paras. 4.30 to 4.33 below: see para. 4.27 below.
[99] Paras. 4.40 to 4.50 below.
[1] R.S.C., Ord. 10, r. 1(6); Ord. 11, r. 5(1).
[2] R.S.C., Ord. 10, r. 1(4); Ord. 11, r. 5(1). See para. 4.05 above.
[3] R.S.C., Ord. 10, r. 1(5); Ord. 11, r. 5(1). See para. 4.05 above. A challenge to the regularity of service in these circumstances is discussed at paras. 5.11 *et seq.* below.
[4] R.S.C., Ord. 10, r. 3(1). See para. 4.06 above.

granted.[5] A further rule makes special provision in connection with the service of a writ in a claim relating to a contract subject to a jurisdiction agreement.[6] Moreover, substituted service is permitted out of the jurisdiction in certain circumstances,[7] and it should be noted that although service by post out of the jurisdiction is not normally permitted under English law,[8] it may be available by way of substituted service.

Service by the plaintiff or his agent

4.24   The plaintiff or his agent may serve the writ out of the jurisdiction either in the English manner or in the foreign manner, but in neither case may anything be done which is contrary to the law of the country where service is to be effected.[9] Usually, the plaintiff's solicitor instructs some person such as a lawyer or process server in the foreign country concerned to arrange for the service of the proceedings. In most European countries, service in the English manner is not permitted or is subject to substantial restrictions.

4.25   *Service in the English manner.* If service in the English manner is permitted in the country where the writ is to be served, it should be effected by one of the methods envisaged by English law, unless the method is one which applies solely to service within the jurisdiction. Thus, for example, while an individual defendant may be served by post within the jurisdiction, this method is not available as a matter of English law for service out of the jurisdiction.[10] Similarly, the rule enabling a partnership carrying on business within the jurisdiction to be served at its place of business does not apply to a place of business outside the jurisdiction.[11] On the other hand, a foreign registered company is a body corporate for which no other provision is made by an enactment under English law and if it is to be served out of the jurisdiction in the English manner this may be

---

[5] R.S.C., Ord. 10, r. 3(2). The text of this sub-rule is incorrectly printed in the *Supreme Court Practice*. The words from "has been granted" to the end should read "has been granted under Ord. 11, r. 1(1) or service of the writ permitted without leave under Ord. 11, r. 1(2).": see The Rules of the Supreme Court (Amendment No. 2) 1983, (S.I. 1983 No. 1181.), rule 5

[6] R.S.C., Ord. 10, r. 3(3). The purpose and meaning of this sub-rule is problematic. It appears to have the potentially prejudicial effect of regularising service of a writ which has been effected irregularly in any respect, in cases where a contract contains a choice of jurisdiction clause. It makes no reference to a chosen mode of service and it appears to add nothing else to Ord. 11, r. 1(2)(a).

[7] R.S.C., Ord. 65, r. (4); Ord. 11, r. 5(1); *Supreme Court Practice*, para. 65/4/11.

[8] See para. 4.25 below.

[9] R.S.C., Ord. 11, r. 5(2).

[10] R.S.C., Ord. 10, r. 1(2): see para. 4.07 above.

[11] R.S.C., Ord. 81, r. 3(1)(b): see para. 4.10 above.

done by the same method as would be employed for a corporate body other than a limited company[12] within the jurisdiction.[13]

Service in the foreign manner. If the writ is to be served by the **4.26** plaintiff or his agent in the foreign manner, it must be served by a method which is in accordance with the law of the country where service is effected. Thus, for example, if the foreign country permits service to be effected by post, it is not necessary to serve the writ personally,[14] even though postal service would not be permitted out of the jurisdiction under English law. In some European countries, service may be effected by an official process-server such as a *huissier* acting directly as the agent for the English plaintiff.[15]

Service through official channels

There are four different types of official channels through which **4.27** a writ may be served out of the jurisdiction, namely:

(*a*) through the British consular authorities of the foreign country,[16]

(*b*) through the judicial authorities of the foreign country,[17]

(*c*) through the Central Authority or other authority designated under the Hague Service Convention,[18] and

(*d*) through the government of the foreign country.[19]

Which of these channels is available in respect of each country depends on:

(i) whether the United Kingdom has a relevant bilateral convention with the foreign country in question and if so what its terms are,

(ii) whether the foreign country is a party to the Hague Service Convention and if so what declarations have been made by it thereunder, and

(iii) the law and practice of the foreign country.

---

[12] See para. 4.11 above. As regards Scottish companies and foreign companies established in Great Britain, see paras. 4.12 and 4.13 above.

[13] R.S.C., Ord. 65, r. 3: *Supreme Court Practice*, para. 11/5/2.

[14] R.S.C., Ord. 11, r. 5(3)(a).

[15] See paras. 4.41 (Belgium); 4.43 (France); 4.48 (Luxembourg); and 4.49 (Netherlands) below.

[16] R.S.C., Ord. 11, rr. 6(2)(b), 6(2A)(b)(ii), 6(3)(b).

[17] R.S.C., Ord. 11, rr. 6(2)(b) 6(2A)(b)(i). Transmission through judicial officers is also permitted under Art. IV of the 1968 Protocol (para. 35.17 below), although adjustments have not been made to the rules of court to accommodate this means of transmission: see para. 4.38 below. For the present purposes, service through foreign judicial officers is not treated as an official means of transmission if they are instructed direct by the plaintiff or his agent: see the preceding paragraph.

[18] R.S.C., Ord. 11, r. 6(2A)(a).

[19] R.S.C., Ord. 11, r. 6(3)(a).

4.28 *Procedure for using official channels.*[20] If official channels are to be used in England and Wales to effect service out of the jurisdiction, the applicant or his solicitor must lodge a request for service in the Central Office[21] and attend personally in the master's secretary's department[22] to lodge the necessary documents. The request should follow the recommended form,[23] specifying which of the official channels is to be used, the method of service chosen,[24] and undertaking to discharge any expenses that might be incurred in effecting service.[25] It must be accompanied by a copy of the writ for each person to be served and one further copy.[26] Every copy of the writ must be accompanied by a translation into the official language of the country where service is to take place, unless the official language or one of the official languages of that country is English or unless the writ is to be served by a British consular authority on a British subject.[27] The translation must be certified by the person making it to be a correct translation and the certificate must state that person's full name and address and his qualifications for making the translation.[28]

4.29 *Transmission of documents and return of certificate.* The documents are then sent by the masters' secretary to the Parliamentary Under-Secretary of the Foreign and Commonwealth Office at the Treaty and Nationality Department of the Foreign Office with a request that he arrange for the writ to be served by the method indicated by in the request.[29] The request is then forwarded, usually through

---

[20] The procedure described is that of the High Court. In the county court, the procedure is similar: C.C.R., Ord. 8, r. 10. The documents to be served out of the jurisdiction are forwarded by the county court registrar to the Senior Master of the Queen's Bench Division for onward transmission.

[21] R.S.C., Ord. 11, r. 6(4).

[22] Room No. 47

[23] Queen's Bench Masters' Practice Form No. 7, *Supreme Court Practice,* para. [208]; Chitty and Jacob, p. 73; 35 *Court Forms* (1983 issue) 211.

[24] R.S.C., Ord. 11, r. 6(4).

[25] R.S.C., Ord. 11, r. 8.

[26] R.S.C., Ord. 11, r. 6(4).

[27] R.S.C., Ord. 11, r. 6(5). If there is more than one official language of the country where service is to take place the translation must be into the language which is appropriate to the place in that country where service is to be effected. Some countries have declared themselves willing under the Hague Convention to accept documents in, or translated into, one or more languages other than their official language. Although providing a translation into one of those other languages would not satisfy the requirements of the rules, it is suggested that a liberal attitude can be taken in those circumstances, and the irregularity should usually be treated as immaterial.

[28] R.S.C., Ord. 11, r. 6(6). As to translations generally, see para. 8.16 below.

[29] R.S.C., Ord. 11, r. 6(7).

consular channels, to the appropriate authorities in the foreign country. Alternatively, under the Hague Service Convention, the documents are sent by the master's secretary direct to the relevant authorities of the foreign country, with a request that the documents be served in the appropriate manner.[30] In due course the British consular authority in the country of service or the governmental, judicial or other authority in that country will return to the Central Office an official certificate to the effect that service has, or as the case may be, has not, taken place. This official certificate is evidence of the facts stated therein.[31] The master's secretary then writes to the applicant's solicitor to notify him of the receipt of the certificate, and of the amount of the expenses to pay.[32] If the certificate is in a foreign language, the applicant's solicitor should instruct a translator to translate it.[33]

3. The Hague Convention on service of documents abroad

Many of the other Contracting States of the 1968 Convention **4.30** were parties to the multilateral Hague Civil Procedure Conventions of 1905 and 1954, which provided for, among other things, the service of judicial documents. These earlier conventions were largely replaced in 1965 and 1970 by two new conventions, one on the service of documents and one on the taking of evidence.[34] The first of these, the Convention on the Service Abroad of Judicial and Extra-judicial Documents in Civil and Commercial Matters, signed at the Hague on November 15, 1965[35] (to give it its full title) has been ratified or acceded to by some 27 countries including most of those with which this book is concerned.[36] It applies to the service abroad

---

[30] See para. 4.31 below. The requirement in Ord. 11, r. 6(7) that the documents "shall" be sent to the Foreign Office is, sensibly, ignored in practice.

[31] R.S.C., Ord. 11, r. 5(5). A document purporting to be such a certificate is deemed, until the contrary is proved, to be such a certificate: Ord. 11, r. 5(7).

[32] Any expenses are payable to the Foreign Office.

[33] *Supreme Court Practice*, para. 11/6/4.

[34] The Hague Evidence Convention is described in Chap. 8, paras. 8.26 *et seq.* below.

[35] Cmnd. 3986; T.S. 50 (1969); the text of the Convention is set out at paras. A2.03 *et seq.* below. See also Graveson, The Tenth Session of the Hague Conference on Private International Law (1965) I.C.L.Q. 539; *Practical Handbook on the operation of the Hague Convention of 15 November 1965 on the Service Abroad of Judicial and Extra-Judicial Documents in Civil and Commercial Matters*, (Hague Conference on Private International Law, 1983); *The Hague Conventions on the Service of Process, the Taking of Evidence and Legalisation, Explanatory Documentation prepared for Commonwealth Jurisdictions* (Commonwealth Secretariat, revised edition, 1985).

[36] The countries which have ratified or acceded to the Hague Service Convention are listed at para. A2.03 below. They include all the Contracting States to the 1968 Convention, except Ireland.

of judicial or extrajudicial documents[37] in all civil and commercial matters.[38]

The Hague "Service" Convention, as it is commonly called, provides a system of channels by which courts and other competent authorities in one country can request the assistance of authorities in other countries in serving judicial and extrajudicial documents, provided the address of the person to be served is known.[39] These formal means of transmission and execution of requests for service are discussed below. The provisions of the convention are, however, permissive and parties are not obliged to use the procedures which it lays down. It envisages that parties may use other methods of service, whether available under the internal law of the state where service is to take place,[40] or under other conventions,[41] but it does not authorise service by such means if they are not otherwise lawful.

The convention envisages that, provided the state of destination does not object, judicial documents may be sent by post,[42] or service may be effected by the judicial officers, officials or other competent persons of the state of destination, at the request of such persons in the state of origin[43] or of "any person interested" in the proceedings in that state.[44] Similarly, it is permissible for diplomatic or consular agents to serve the addressee directly, provided that no compulsion is used and provided that the state of destination has not declared its objection to such service within its territory on persons other than the nationals of the state of origin.[45] Alternatively, consular agents, and, in exceptional circumstances, diplomatic agents, may effect service indirectly on an addressee by using some officially designated channel in the receiving state.[46]

---

[37] "Extrajudicial" documents are various forms of formal document not formally connected with legal proceedings: see para. 35.18, n. 33 below.

[38] The meaning of "civil and commercial matters" is not the same in the context of the Hague Conventions as under the 1968 Convention: see *Re State of Norway's Application (Nos. 1 & 2)* [1989] 2 W.L.R. 458 (H.L.). In practice the Central Authorities of most countries will accept all judicial documents other than those relating to criminal and, sometimes, tax matters.

[39] If the address is not known or is inaccurate, the authorities still often use the convention's channels in practice: see n. 56 below.

[40] Art. 19.

[41] Arts. 24 and 25.

[42] Art. 10(a). Service by post is not permitted, for example, in Germany: see para. 4.44 below.

[43] Art. 10(b). Competent persons include official process servers.

[44] Art. 10(c).

[45] Art. 8.

[46] Art. 9.

Transmission through formal channels. The principal formal chan- **4.31** nel of transmission under the Hague Service Convention is for requests to carry out service to be sent by a competent authority or judicial officer in the state of origin[47] to the Central Authority designated by each signatory state.[48] The request must be in a prescribed form and it must be accompanied by the document to be served in duplicate[49] and by a summary of the document to be served, also in a prescribed form.[50]

The convention envisages three types of service through the channel of the Central Authority: formal service,[51] informal delivery[52] and any "particular method" of service requested by the applicant.[53] With formal service the Central Authority will arrange for the document to be served by an "appropriate agency" in accordance with its normal rules for service under its municipal law. In such cases the request and the document to be served must usually be translated into the language of the state addressed.[54]

Formal service may involve the applicant in having to pay the **4.32** costs of the process server, but it has the advantage of minimising the opportunity for the defendant to dispute that he has been served. This may be particularly important if the judgment is to be enforced in due course in the state addressed. Instead of being formally served, the document may always be informally delivered to

---

[47] The designation of persons as competent authorities for the purpose of forwarding requests for service is a matter for the law of the state of origin. It was apparently envisaged that English solicitors might address such requests direct to the Central Authority of the state of destination: *Practical Handbook*, above, p. 30; *Actes et documents de la dixième session* (1964), vol. III, pp. 184–188. In practice, requests for service are transmitted in accordance with R.S.C., Ord. 11, r. 6: para. 4.27 above.

[48] Each signatory state is required by Art. 2 to designate a Central Authority which acts as a receiving authority. Federal states may designate more than one Central Authority, and Germany has done so. The contracting states may also designate other authorities which are competent to receive requests, and the U.K. has done so: see para. 4.60, n. 16 below.

[49] Art. 3. The prescribed form of request, set out at para. A4.04 below, is drawn up in the masters' secretary's department and forwarded in the name of the senior master to the Central Authority or other competent authority of the other country.

[50] The prescribed form of summary is set out at para. A4.06 below. It too is drawn up in the masters' secretary's department. The 14th Session of the Hague Conference on Private International Law recommended a revised form for this summary, set out at para. A4.07 below, which it urged the contracting states to adopt. It is not yet in use in England.

[51] Art. 5, first para., sub-para. (a).

[52] Art. 5, second para.

[53] Art. 5, first para., sub-para. (b).

[54] Art. 5, third para. Documents forwarded by the senior master must be translated: see para. 4.28 above.

an addressee who accepts it voluntarily.[55] The Central Authority in the state addressed usually arranges for the document to be delivered by a police officer or collected by the addressee from a police station. The documents to be served need not be translated and the costs of a process server are avoided. The third type of service envisaged by the convention, any "particular method" requested by the applicant, is rarely employed. The state addressed is bound to comply with the applicant's request unless it is incompatible with local law.

The Central Authority may reject a request which does not conform with the provisions of the convention, but if it does so it must promptly inform the applicant and specify the objections to the request.[56] A contracting state may only refuse to comply with a request which complies with the convention if compliance would, in view of the state addressed, infringe its sovereignty or security.[57] The applicant is absolved from liability to pay any fee or charge to the state addressed for its services, but must pay the costs of any judicial officer or other person competent under the law of the state addressed, and the costs arising from any special method of service that is requested.[58]

4.33   *Certificate of service.* The Hague Service Convention requires the Central Authority, or some other designated authority, which has arranged for service to take place, to complete a certificate in a prescribed form[59] stating the method, date and place of service, and identifying the person to whom the document was delivered.[60] If the document has not been served the certificate must set out the reasons why attempts were unsuccessful. The certificate is then returned to the person who sent the request. The second copy of the document which has been served often accompanies the certificate, thereby making it quite clear exactly what has been served.

Article 15 of the Hague Service Convention, which contains important provisions relating to the giving and setting aside of judg-

---

[55] This method is commonly used in Belgium, France and the Netherlands: see paras. 4.41, 4.43 and 4.49 below.

[56] Art. 4. The Central Authorities are often willing in practice to accept requests which do not comply with the convention. For example, if the defendant's address is not known accurately, they may be willing to seek him out.

[57] Art. 13. A request may not be refused on the ground that the state addressed claims exclusive jurisdiction over the subject-matter of the claim or that its law would not permit the action. *Cf.*, Art. 12 of the Hague Evidence Convention, discussed at para. 8.28 below.

[58] Art. 12.

[59] The certificate is on the back of the request: see para. A4.05 below.

[60] Art. 6.

ments in default of appearance in cases in which service has been carried out under its terms, is discussed below.[61]

4. The United Kingdom's bilateral conventions

The United Kingdom did not become a party to either of the **4.34** Hague conventions on civil procedure of 1905 or 1954,[62] because it considered that bilateral conventions were a more appropriate means of achieving compatability between English civil procedure and that of the individual contracting states. During the inter-war years the United Kingdom concluded a number of bilateral civil procedure conventions not limited to the service of proceedings but covering also, variously, matters such as the taking of evidence, security for costs and legal aid.[63] They generally provide a procedure for the transmission of documents to be served through consular channels and judicial officers. The Hague Service Convention does not derogate from the earlier bilateral conventions,[64] although, for practical purposes, it does often supercede them if service is required in any country which is party to that convention.[65] The following discussion is concerned only with the conventions with Belgium, Denmark, France, Germany, Greece, Italy and the Netherlands, although much of it also applies to the other bilateral conventions. Costs and fees are not generally payable under these conventions, except in respect of the services of process-servers or in respect of any special means of service requested.

Transmission through formal channels. The bilateral conventions **4.35** provide for the transmission of a request for service to the competent authority in the state where service is to be effected by the local consular authority of the state of origin. The precise requirements as to the contents of the request vary from country to country, but they normally require a statement of the names and descriptions of the parties, the name and address of the person to be served and the nature of the document. The request must normally be drawn up in the language of the country where service is to take place and be accompanied by the writ or other document to be served in duplicate.[66] The writ or other document must be drawn up in or translated into the language of the state addressed and the translation

---

[61] Para. 4.59 below.
[62] See para. 4.30 above.
[63] The bilateral conventions concluded with states which are Contracting States to the 1968 Convention are listed with references at para. A2.01 below.
[64] Art. 25.
[65] All the Contracting States to the 1968 Convention on Jurisdiction and the Enforcement of Judgments, except Ireland, are parties to the Hague Service Convention. See para. A2.03 below.
[66] The convention with France requires the original document and two copies.

must be certified by the consular officer of the requesting state or, in the case of Belgium, Germany and Italy, by an official or sworn translator of either country.[67] The service will be effected by the competent authority in accordance with its local procedures or by any special means requested[68] provided that such means is not incompatible with the local law. In the case of Belgium and Germany, the document may alternatively be served by the competent authority by simple delivery to a willing recipient. Proof of the fact, manner and date of service, or a statement of the reasons why service could not be effected, is provided by the competent authority indorsing a certificate on one of the copies of the document to be served, and returning it to the requesting consular authority.

4.36 *Other methods of service.* The bilateral conventions also permit service to be effected in their territory by the consular authorities of the state of origin, directly on the recipient of the writ or other document, except, in the case of Denmark and Germany, on nationals of the state where service is to be effected. With the exception of the convention with France (which is silent on the point), the conventions also permit service to be effected by a person appointed by the judicial authorities of the state of origin or by the party at whose instigation service is being effected, but this option is subject to various restrictions. The convention with Belgium requires that the agent be appointed by a tribunal of the state of origin, those with Denmark and Germany do not permit service by this means on nationals of the state where service is effected, and the convention with Italy requires that the agent be an Italian notary or advocate, who instructs an official process server. Documents served by one of these means must often be translated into the language of the country where service is to take place, unless the recipient is a national of the state of origin. Several of the conventions[69] permit service by post, but the validity of such service remains a question for the law of the state of origin.[70] Several of the conventions[71] permit service by the competent officials of the state where service is to be effected, on the direct instructions of the party concerned, and some conventions[72] also permit service by any other method, subject to a test of its legality by the law of the state where it takes place.

---

[67] As to who is qualified to act as a translator, see para. 71 of chaps. 48 to 55 below.
[68] This is not available under the convention with France.
[69] Those with Belgium, Denmark, Germany, Greece and the Netherlands.
[70] Postal service out of the jurisdiction is not generally valid in English law, but it may be valid by way of substituted service: see para. 4.15 above.
[71] Those with Belgium, Germany, Italy and the Netherlands.
[72] Those with Denmark, Italy and the Netherlands.

5. Service out of the jurisdiction in the absence of an applicable convention

Service may also be effected through official channels on an *ad* **4.37**
hoc basis in countries with which there is no convention, with the
exception of independent Commonwealth countries and the Republic of Ireland.[73] When a writ is to be served on a defendant in such a
country, the writ may be served through the foreign government, if
it is willing to effect service, or through the British consular authority in that country, provided that this is not contrary to the law of
that country.[74]

6. Service under Article IV of the 1968 Protocol

The Annexed Protocol of the 1968 Convention contains an **4.38**
additional provision for the transmission of judicial and extrajudicial documents between Contracting States for the purposes of service.[75] Unless the Contracting State in which service is to take place
declares otherwise (and only Germany has done so), such documents may be sent by the appropriate public officers of the state of
origin directly to the appropriate public officers of the state where
service is to be effected, who forward it to the addressee in the manner specified by the law of the latter state. This is equivalent to one
of the provisions in the Hague Service Convention.[76]

7. Service on a foreign state

Under the State Immunity Act 1978, any writ or other document **4.39**
required to be served on a foreign state[77] must, unless the state
agrees otherwise, be served by being transmitted through the
Foreign and Commonwealth Office to the ministry of foreign affairs
of that state.[78] A request for such service is lodged with the senior
master who then sends the writ to the Foreign and Commonwealth
Office for onward transmission.[79] Leave to issue the writ and to

---

[73] The exclusion also applies to Scotland, Northern Ireland, the Channel Islands,
the Isle of Man, any associated state and any colony: see R.S.C., Ord. 11,
r. 6(1).
[74] R.S.C., Ord. 11, r. 6(3); see the list of countries in the *Supreme Court Practice*,
para. 11/6/3. The European countries (not being parties to the Hague Service
Convention) which permit service by British consular authorities are: Andorra,
Iceland, and Monaco (upon British subjects only).
[75] 1968 Protocol, Art. IV, para. 35.17 below.
[76] Art. 10(b).
[77] Note that the definition of state includes the head of state, the government of the
state, and any government department: State Immunity Act 1978, s.14; see
para. 2.15 above.
[78] State Immunity Act 1978, s.12.
[79] R.S.C., Ord. 11, r. 7. See also *Supreme Court Practice*, paras. 10/1/10, 11/1/9
and 65/2/4.

serve it out of the jurisdiction must also have been obtained unless the court's jurisdiction is founded on the Convention or the other statutory schemes.[80] The service is deemed to have been effected when the writ or document is received at the ministry of foreign affairs of the state concerned.[81]

D. SERVICE OUT OF THE JURISDICTION: PARTICULAR COUNTRIES

4.40 This section is designed to summarise the various means which are available for the purpose of serving the process of English courts in each of the Contracting States to the 1968 Convention (including Greece), whether under the Hague Service Convention,[82] under the United Kingdom's bilateral conventions, or otherwise.[83] It should be remembered, though, that writs and other originating process which may be served out of the jurisdiction without the leave of the court may be served anywhere in the world.[84] It should also be noted that, while a particular method of service may be permitted in various countries, (for example service by post), it does not necessarily follow that that method of service is "in accordance with" the law of that country for the purposes of the English rules of court.[85]

Belgium

4.41 Belgium is a party to the Hague Convention and has a bilateral convention with the United Kingdom.[86] Documents may be transmitted through official channels by the senior master,[87] either direct or through consular channels to the Belgian Ministry of Justice under the Hague Convention or through the local British consul to the *Procureur du Roi* for the place of service under the bilateral convention. The document may then be served formally

---

[80] See para. 4.18 above. It may be that such leave is anyway required, because Ord. 11, r. 7 only expressly contemplates service on a foreign state if leave has been granted under Ord. 11, r. 1.

[81] State Immunity Act, 1978, s.12(1). There are restrictions on the entry of a default judgment against a state: s.12(4) and 12(5). As to proof of such service, see para. 4.54 below.

[82] Paras. 4.30 to 4.33 above.

[83] Where the available methods of service are limited by the law or practice of the other country, the current position should be checked in cases of doubt with a lawyer of the country in question or with its embassy.

[84] See para. 4.17 above.

[85] R.S.C., Ord. 11, r. 5(3)(a): see para. 4.26 above.

[86] The Hague Convention is described at paras. 4.30 to 4.33 above and set out at paras. A2.04 *et seq.* below. The bilateral conventions are described at paras. 4.34 to 4.36 above; references to the bilateral convention with Belgium appear at para. A2.01 below.

[87] R.S.C., Ord. 11, r. 6. The procedure for transmission through official channels is described at para. 4.28 above.

by a *huissier*[88] whose charges will be payable by the applicant,[89] but informal delivery by police officers is often effected on a willing recipient. The document to be served should be accompanied by a translation into whichever is the appropriate language for the place of service.[90]

Service may also be effected directly on a recipient, regardless of his nationality, by the local British consul[91] or by some other person appointed by the English court[92]; documents to be served in this way must be drawn up in, or accompanied by a translation into, the language appropriate for the part of Belgium where the document is to be served,[93] unless the recipient is a British subject. Belgium also permits a *huissier* to be instructed directly by the judicial authorities in England[94] or by the plaintiff.[95] Documents may be sent by post if this is permissible under English law.[96] Where official channels have been used, service may be proved by a certificate issued by the

---

[88] See para. 48.13 below.

[89] Service may be effected by some special means if this is requested by the requesting authority, and a charge may be made for doing so.

[90] French, Flemish or German: see para. 48.01 below. As to translations generally, see para. 8.16 below. The requirement to provide translations is imposed by R.S.C., Ord. 11, r. 6(5). Under the bilateral convention, the request for service must be translated, but the document for service need only be translated if the applicant wishes to ensure that it is served formally by a *huissier*, and the translation must be certified by the British consular authority or an official or sworn translator. This is so regardless of the nationality of the recipient.

[91] Bilateral convention, Art. IV(a). Documents for service by the consul are lodged with the senior master under R.S.C., Ord. 11, r. 6(2)(b).

[92] Bilateral convention, Art. IV(b). If a person other than the British consul is to effect service, the document to be served is endorsed as follows:

> "Pursuant to Article 4(b) of the Convention between Great Britain and Belgium, I hereby appoint [*name*] to be the agent for the purposes of service of this document.
> Dated this   day of   , 19 .
> Senior Master of the Supreme Court in England."

The applicant nominates the agent and the indorsement is signed by the senior master: Hinton, *Evidence and Service Abroad*, p. 69. The former practice was for the indorsement to be placed on the document by the master's secretary's department on production of the order granting leave for service out of the jurisdiction, but this may no longer be necessary in cases in which leave for service is not required.

[93] French, Flemish or German: see para. 48.01 below. This translation need not be certified by the consul.

[94] This does not happen in practice.

[95] Hague Convention, Art. 10(b) and (c); bilateral convention, Art. VI; 1968 Protocol, Art. IV. The document may be sent to the *huissier* either direct or through the national chamber of *huissiers*: *Chambre Nationale de Huissiers de Justice, Avenue de Waterloo 6, 1000 Brussels*; (tel: 512.15.12).

[96] Postal service out of the jurisdiction is not generally available under English law: see para. 4.25 above.

105

Procureur du Roi or by the *huissier* or, if service has been effected by the British consul directly, by his certificate. In other cases, it is to be proved by affidavit, even if the service was actually effected by a *huissier*.

Denmark

4.42   Denmark is a party to the Hague Convention and has a bilateral convention with the United Kingdom.[97] Documents may be transmitted through official channels by the senior master,[98] either direct through the Danish Ministry of Justice under the Hague Convention or through the local British consul to the *byret*[99] for the place of service. The document is served formally by post by the local court or by personal delivery by the official process-server, free of charge to the applicant.[1] There is no separate system of informal delivery. The document to be served should be accompanied by a translation into Danish.[2]

Service may also be effected directly on a recipient regardless of his nationality, by the local British consul[3] or, unless the recipient is a Danish national, by some other person appointed by the party on whose application the document was issued.[4] Documents to be served by a party's agent must be drawn up in, or accompanied by a translation into, Danish,[5] unless the recipient is a British subject. There are no independent process-servers in Denmark who may be

---

[97] The Hague Convention is described at paras. 4.30 to 4.33 above and set out at paras. A2.04 *et seq.* below. The bilateral conventions are described at paras. 4.34 to 4.36 above; references to the bilateral convention with Denmark appear at para. A2.01 below.
[98] R.S.C., Ord. 11, r. 6. The procedure for transmission through official channels is described at para. 4.28 above.
[99] The byret is the local court: see para. 49.19 below.
[1] Service may be effected by some special means if this is requested by the requesting authority, but a charge may be made for doing so.
[2] The requirement to provide translations is imposed by R.S.C., Ord. 11, r. 6(5). Under the bilateral convention, the request for service and the document to be served must be translated, irrespective of the nationality of the recipient, and the translation of the document to be served must be certified by the British consular authority. As to translations generally, see para. 8.16 below.
[3] Hague Convention, Art. 8. Documents for service by the consul are lodged with the senior master under R.S.C., Ord. 11, r. 6(2)(b). A translation of the document to be served is required, but it need not be certified by the consul.
[4] Bilateral convention, Art. 4(a). Although theoretically possible, the English court will not itself appoint a person under this Article to carry out service.
[5] A disadvantage of this option is that the translation must be certified by a British consul: bilateral convention: Art. 4(b). As to translations generally, see para. 8.16 below.

instructed directly by the parties.[6] Documents may be sent by post if this is permissible under English law.[7] Where official channels have been used, service may be proved by a certificate issued by the Danish court responsible for service or, if service has been effected by the British consul directly, by his certificate. In other cases, it is to be proved by affidavit.

France

France is a party to the Hague Convention and has a bilateral **4.43** convention with the United Kingdom.[8] Documents may be transmitted through official channels by the senior master,[9] either direct through the French Ministry of Justice under the Hague Convention or through the local British consul to the *Procureur de la République* for the place of service. If formal service is requested, the document may be served formally by a *huissier*[10] and a nominal charge is payable in advance by the applicant, but informal delivery by police officers or *gendarmes* may be effected instead on a willing recipient. The document to be served should be accompanied by a translation into French.[11]

Service may also be effected directly on a recipient, regardless of his nationality, by the local British consul.[12] France also permits a *huissier* to be instructed directly by the judicial authorities in Eng-

---

[6] In theory, the official process-servers (para. 49.38 below) may be instructed direct by the judicial authorities in England (Hague Convention, Art. 10(b) and (c); bilateral convention, Art. 5(a); 1968 Protocol, Art. IV), but this does not happen in practice and it would seem to have no advantage over the use of official channels.

[7] Postal service out of the jurisdiction is not generally available under English law: see para. 4.25 above.

[8] The Hague Convention is described at paras. 4.30 to 4.33 above and set out at paras. A2.04 *et seq.* below. The bilateral conventions are described at paras. 4.34 to 4.36 above; references to the bilateral convention with France appear at para. A2.01 below.

[9] R.S.C., Ord. 11, r. 6. The procedure for transmission through official channels is described at para. 4.28 above.

[10] See para. 50.13 below.

[11] The requirement to provide translations is imposed by R.S.C., Ord. 11, r. 6(5). Under the bilateral convention, the request for service and the document to be served must be translated, irrespective of the nationality of the recipient, and the translation of the document to be served must be certified by the British consular authority. An extra copy of the translation of the document to be served must be supplied. As to translations generally, see para. 8.16 below.

[12] Bilateral convention, Art. IV. Documents for service by the consul are lodged with the senior master under R.S.C., Ord. 11, r. 6(2)(b). A translation of the document to be served is required, unless the recipient is a British subject.

land.[13] Documents may be sent by post if this is permissible under English law.[14] Where official channels have been used, service may be proved by a certificate issued by the *Procureur de la République* or, if service has been effected by the British consul directly, by his certificate. In other cases, it is to be proved by affidavit.

Germany

4.44 Germany is a party to the Hague Convention and the bilateral convention concluded in 1928 by the German Reich with the United Kingdom is still in force in relation to the Federal Republic.[15] Documents may be transmitted through official channels by the senior master,[16] either directly or through consular channels to the Central Authorities designated for each *Land* under the Hague Convention (usually the *Land* Ministry of Justice) or through the local British consul to the president of the *Landgericht*[17] for the place of service. If formal service is requested, the document is formally served by post by the relevant Central Authority, free of charge to the applicant.[18] If service by informal delivery is to be effected, the document is sent by the Central Authority to the local court (*Amtsgericht*) and it is then delivered by a judicial officer to the recipient, who is allowed to inspect it before deciding whether to accept it; this procedure is also free of charge to the applicant. The document to be served should be accompanied by a translation into German.[19]

---

[13] Hague Convention, Art. 10(b); 1968 Protocol, Art. IV. It may be that a *huissier* can be instructed direct by an English solicitor: see para. 4.30, n. 43 above. Enquiries may be made to the national chamber of *huissiers*: *Chambre Nationale des Huissiers, 44 rue de Douai, 75009 Paris.*

[14] Postal service out of the jurisdiction is not generally available under English law: see para. 4.25 above.

[15] The Hague Convention is described at paras. 4.30 to 4.33 above and set out at paras. A2.04 *et seq.* below. The bilateral conventions are described at paras. 4.34 to 4.36 above; references to the bilateral convention with Germany appear at para. A2.01 below. In practice, the bilateral convention is normally only used for serving British soldiers in Germany.

[16] R.S.C., Ord. 11, r. 6. The procedure for transmission through official channels is described at para. 4.28 above.

[17] See para. 52.20 below.

[18] Service may also be effected by some special means requested by the requesting authority, but a charge may be made for doing so.

[19] The requirement to provide translations is imposed by R.S.C., Ord. 11, r. 6(5). Under the bilateral convention, the request for service must be translated, but the document for service need only be translated if the applicant wishes to ensure that it is served formally in accordance with German law. The translation must be certified by the British consular authority or an official or sworn translator. This is so regardless of the nationality of the recipient. Service by informal delivery may be effected under either the bilateral or Hague Convention without

Service may also be effected directly on a recipient, unless he is a German national, by the local British consul[20] or by some other person appointed by the party on whose application the document was issued.[21] Documents to be served by a party's agent need not be drawn up in, or accompanied by a translation into, German. Germany also permits its judicial officers to be instructed directly by the judicial authorities in England.[22] Documents may be sent by post if this is permissible under English law.[23] Where official channels have been used, service may be proved by a certificate issued by the German Central Authority or court responsible for service or, if service has been effected by the British consul directly, by his certificate. In other cases, it is to be proved by affidavit.

Greece

Greece is a party to the Hague Convention and has a bilateral **4.45** convention with the United Kingdom.[24] Documents may be transmitted through official channels by the senior master,[25] either directly through the Greek Ministry of Foreign Affairs under the Hague Convention or through the local British consul to the *Procureur* for the district court for the place of service, under the bilateral convention. The document may be served formally by a judicial

---

a translation of the document to be served, although Ord. 11, r. 6(5) still requires a translation if the recipient is not a British subject. As to translations generally, see para. 8.16 below.

[20] Bilateral convention, Art. 5(a). Under the Hague Convention (Art. 8), service by the consul may only be effected on a British national. Documents for service by the consul are lodged with the senior master under R.S.C., Ord. 11, r. 6(2)(b), and must be accompanied by a translation into German unless the recipient is a British subject.

[21] Bilateral convention, Art. 5(b). This is subject to a test of validity in the German courts. Although theoretically possible, the English court will not itself appoint a person under this Article to carry out service.

[22] Bilateral convention, Art. 7. Such a request is unlikely to be well received, in view of Germany's declaration under both the Hague Convention (Art. 10(b)) and the Annexed Protocol to the 1968 Convention (Art. IV) that it objects to this method of service.

[23] Bilateral convention, Art. 6. Germany has objected to this method of service under the Hague Convention. Postal service out of the jurisdiction is not generally available under English law: see para. 4.25 above.

[24] The Hague Convention is described at paras. 4.30 to 4.33 above and set out at paras. A2.04 *et seq.* below. The bilateral conventions are described at paras. 4.34 to 4.36 above; references to the bilateral convention with Greece appear at para. A2.01 below.

[25] R.S.C., Ord. 11, r. 6. The procedure for transmission through official channels is described at para. 4.28 above.

marshall.[26] The document to be served should be accompanied by a translation into Greek.[27]

Service may also be effected directly on a recipient, regardless of his nationality, by the local British consul[28] or by some other person appointed by the party on whose application the document was issued.[29] Documents to be served by the British consul must be drawn up in, or accompanied by a translation into, Greek,[30] unless the recipient is a British subject. The judicial marshals may be instructed directly by the parties.[31] Documents may be sent by post if this is permissible under English law.[32] Where official channels have been used, service may be proved by a certificate issued by the competent Greek authorities responsible for service or, if service has been effected by the British consul directly, by his certificate. In other cases, it is to be proved by affidavit.

Ireland

4.46   Ireland is a party neither to the Hague Convention nor to a bilateral convention with the United Kingdom. Service cannot be effected through official channels[33] and can therefore only be effected by the plaintiff or his agent directly, either in the English

---

[26] Service may be effected by some special means if this is requested by the requesting authority, and a charge may be made for doing so.

[27] The requirement to provide translations is imposed by R.S.C., Ord. 11, r. 6(5). Under the bilateral convention, the request for service and the document to be served must be translated, irrespective of the nationality of the recipient, and the translation of the document to be served must be certified by the British consular authority. As to translations generally, see para. 8.16 below.

[28] Hague Convention, Art. 8; bilateral convention, Art. 4(a)(1). Documents for service by the consul are lodged with the senior master under R.S.C., Ord. 11, r. 6(2)(b).

[29] Bilateral convention, Art. 4(a)(2). Although theoretically possible, the English court will not itself appoint a person under this Article to carry out service.

[30] The translation must be certified by a British consul: bilateral convention: Art. 4(b). As to translations generally, see para. 8.16 below. A translation is not, apparently, required in respect of a document served by a party's agent, but if the recipient is not a British subject, it is desirable: bilateral convention, Art. 4(c).

[31] The judicial marshals may also be instructed by a Greek lawyer on behalf of a party. In theory, they may as an alternative be instructed direct by the judicial authorities in England (Hague Convention, Art. 10(b); bilateral convention, Art. 4(a)(2)), but this does not happen in practice and it would seem to have no advantage over the use of official channels.

[32] Postal service out of the jurisdiction is not generally available under English law: see para. 4.25 above.

[33] R.S.C., Ord. 11, r. 6(1)(e). The mechanism provided by Art. IV of the 1968 Protocol (para. 4.38 above) is also theoretically available, but it is as yet unclear how this would work in practice.

manner or in the Irish manner.[34] Service on an individual must normally be effected personally, but it seems that a limited company may be served by post.

Italy

Italy is a party to the Hague Convention and has a bilateral convention with the United Kingdom.[35] Documents may be transmitted through official channels by the senior master,[36] either direct through the appropriate office of the *corte d'appello* in Rome under the Hague Convention or through the local British consul to the *procuratore generale* for the *corte d'appello* for the place of service, under the bilateral convention, or to the appropriate judicial authorities for the place of service, under the Hague Convention.[37] The document may be served formally by an official process server,[38] whose charges will be payable (in a nominal sum) by the applicant in advance.[39] The document to be served should be accompanied by a translation into Italian.[40]   **4.47**

Service may also be effected directly on a recipient, regardless of his nationality, by the local British consul[41] or by some other person appointed by the party on whose application the document was issued.[42] Documents to be served by this method must be drawn up

---

[34] Para. 4.26 above. See also para. 52.38 below.
[35] The Hague Convention is described at paras. 4.30 to 4.33 above and set out at paras. A2.04 *et seq.* below. The bilateral conventions are described at paras. 4.34 to 4.36 above; references to the bilateral convention with Italy appear at para. A2.01 below.
[36] R.S.C., Ord. 11, r. 6. The procedure for transmission through official channels is described at para. 4.28 above.
[37] Art. 9, first para.
[38] *Ufficiale guidiziario*: see para. 53.38 below.
[39] Service may be effected by some special means if this is requested by the requesting authority, and a charge may be made for doing so.
[40] The requirement to provide translations is imposed by R.S.C., Ord. 11, r. 6(5). Under the bilateral convention, the request for service and the document to be served must be translated, irrespective of the nationality of the recipient, and the translation of the document to be served must be certified by the British consular authority, or by an official or sworn translator. As to translations generally, see para. 8.16 below.
[41] Hague Convention, Art. 8; bilateral convention, Art. 4(a). Documents for service by the consul are lodged with the senior master under R.S.C., Ord. 11, r. 6(2)(b).
[42] Hague Convention, Art. 10(c); bilateral convention, Art. 4(b). Although theoretically possible, the English court will not itself appoint a person under these Articles to carry out service. The bilateral convention requires (for historical reasons which no longer apply) that the agent be an Italian advocate or notary who acts through a competent Italian official. No such restriction applies under the Hague Convention.

in, or accompanied by a translation into, Italian,[43] unless the recipient is a British subject.[44] The official process servers may be instructed directly by the parties.[45] Documents may be sent by post if this is permissible under English law.[46] Where official channels have been used, service may be proved by a certificate issued by the Italian courts or process-servers responsible for service or, if service has been effected by the British consul directly, by his certificate. In other cases, it is to be proved by affidavit.

Luxembourg

4.48 Luxembourg is a party to the Hague Convention but does not have a bilateral convention with the United Kingdom.[47] Under the Hague Convention, documents may be transmitted through official channels by the senior master[48] to the *Parquet général* of the *Cour Supérieure de Justice* either directly or through the British consul. The document may be served formally by a *huissier*[49] whose charges will be payable by the applicant,[50] but informal delivery by police officers is often effected on a willing recipient. The document to be served should be accompanied by a translation into French or German.[51]

Service may also be effected by the local British consul on a recipient of British nationality, but not otherwise.[52] Luxembourg also permits a *huissier* to be instructed directly by the judicial auth-

---

[43] Bilateral convention, Art. 4. As to translations generally, see para. 8.16 below.

[44] If the recipient is a British subject, and no translation is provided, service through consular channels may involve extra charges to cover the consular officer's travelling expenses.

[45] In theory, the official process servers may also be instructed direct by the judicial authorities in England (Hague Convention, Art. 10(b); 1968 Protocol, Art. IV), but this does not happen in practice.

[46] Hague Convention, Art. 10(a). Postal service out of the jurisdiction is not generally available under English law: see para. 4.25 above.

[47] The Hague Convention is described at paras. 4.30 to 4.33 above and set out at paras. A2.04 *et seq.* below.

[48] R.S.C., Ord. 11, r. 6. The procedure for transmission through official channels is described at para. 4.28 above.

[49] See para. 54.13 below.

[50] Service may be effected by some special means if this is requested by the requesting authority, and a charge may be made for doing so.

[51] French is the official language, and the requirement to provide translations imposed by R.S.C., Ord. 11, r. 6(5) refers to the official language. However, translations into German are accepted as an alternative in Luxembourg under the Hague Convention, and it is suggested that translations in that language should also be accepted for the purposes of the rules: see para. 54.01 below.

[52] Documents for service by the consul are lodged with the senior master under R.S.C., Ord. 11, r. 6(2)(b). No translation is required.

orities in England[53] or by the plaintiff[54] and documents to be served by a *huissier* should be drawn up in French or German or accompanied by a translation into one of those languages. Documents may be sent by post if this is permissible under English law.[55] Where official channels have been used, service may be proved by a certificate issued by the *Parquet général* or, if service has been effected by the British consul directly, by his certificate. In other cases, it is to be proved by affidavit, even if the service was actually effected by a *huissier*.

The Netherlands

The Netherlands is a party to the Hague Convention and has a **4.49** bilateral convention with the United Kingdom.[56] Documents may be transmitted through official channels by the senior master,[57] either through the local British consul to the *Officier van Justitie* (public prosecutor) of the *Arrondissementsrechtbank* for the place of service, or under the Hague Convention direct to the same officer or to his counterpart in the Hague. The local public prosecutor will be responsible for the service of the document; he may cause it to be served formally by an official process server,[58] whose charges may be payable by the applicant.[59] However, informal delivery by police officers will normally be attempted on the instructions of the public prosecutor. If the recipient refuses to accept delivery, formal service will be undertaken. The document to be served should be accompanied by a translation into Dutch.[60]

---

[53] This does not happen in practice.

[54] Hague Convention, Art. 10(b) and (c); 1968 Protocol, Art. IV. The document may be sent to the *huissier* either direct or through the national chamber of *huissiers*: *Chambre des Huissiers de Justice, 57 route de Thionville, Luxembourg*; (tel: 48.73.18).

[55] Postal service out of the jurisdiction is not generally available under English law: see para. 4.25 above.

[56] The Hague Convention is described at paras. 4.30 to 4.33 above and set out at paras. A2.04 *et seq.* below. The bilateral conventions are described at paras. 4.34 to 4.36 above; references to the bilateral convention with the Netherlands appear at para. A2.01 below.

[57] R.S.C., Ord. 11, r. 6. The procedure for transmission through official channels is described at para. 4.28 above.

[58] *Gerechtsdeurwaarder*: see para. 55.13 below.

[59] Service may be effected by some special means if this is requested by the requesting authority, and a charge may be made for doing so.

[60] The requirement to provide translations is imposed by R.S.C., Ord. 11, r. 6(5). If the recipient is a British subject and service is under the Hague Convention, a translation seems not to be required. Under the bilateral convention, the request for service and the document to be served must be translated, irrespective of the nationality of the recipient, and the translation of the document to be served must be certified by the British consular authority. As to translations generally, see para. 8.16 below.

Service may also be effected directly on a recipient, regardless of his nationality, by the local British consul[61] or by some other person appointed by the party on whose application the document was issued.[62] Documents to be served by this method need not be drawn up in, or accompanied by a translation into, Dutch.[63] An official process server may be instructed directly by a party.[64] Documents may be sent by post if this is permissible under English law.[65] Where official channels have been used, service may be proved by a certificate issued by the public prosecutor responsible for service or, if service has been effected by the British consul directly, by his certificate. In other cases, it is to be proved by affidavit, even service has been effected by an official process server.

Scotland and Northern Ireland

4.50   Service in Scotland and Northern Ireland is normally effected by the plaintiff or his agent directly, either in the English manner or in the Scottish or Northern Irish manner as appropriate.[66] Service on a company registered in Scotland and not carrying on business in England and Wales may be effected by posting the writ to its registered office.[67] Companies registered in Northern Ireland are not covered by this provision and accordingly may be served in the same way as other foreign companies.

Service by the plaintiff or his agent are probably the only means available for serving the process of English courts on a defendant in other parts of the United Kingdom.[68] However, the Hague Con-

---

[61] Hague Convention, Art. 8; bilateral convention, Art. 4(a)(1). Documents for service by the consul are lodged with the senior master under R.S.C., Ord. 11, r. 6(2)(b).

[62] Hague Convention, Art. 10(c); bilateral convention, Art. 4(a)(2). Although theoretically possible, the English court will not itself appoint a person under these Articles to carry out service.

[63] Bilateral convention, Art. 4(c). As to translations generally, see para. 8.16 below.

[64] Hague Convention, Art. 10(c); bilateral convention, Art. 4(a)(3). The document may be sent to the *deurwaarder* either direct or through the national chamber of process-servers: *Koninklijke Vereniging van Gerechtsdeurwaarders, van Switenstraat 2, Gouda, Netherlands.* In theory, the official process servers may also be instructed direct by the judicial authorities in England (Hague Convention, Art. 10(b); 1968 Protocol, Art. IV), but this does not happen in practice.

[65] Hague Convention, Art. 10(a); bilateral convention, Art. 4(a)(4). Postal service out of the jurisdiction is not generally available under English law: see para. 4.25 above.

[66] R.S.C., Ord. 11, r. 5(3)(a); see paras. 4.24 to 4.26 above. See also paras. 57.38 and 58.38 below.

[67] Companies Act 1985, s.725; see para. 4.12 above.

[68] R.S.C., Ord. 11, r. 6(1)(a). The same applies to service in the Channel Islands and the Isle of Man.

vention applies also to the other parts of the United Kingdom[69] and, although the rules do not seem to envisage its use for purposes internal to the United Kingdom, this possibility is not excluded by the rules and it may be that its procedures could be used in practice in an appropriate case.

E. ACKNOWLEDGMENT OF SERVICE AND DEFAULT JUDGMENTS

1. Acknowledgment of service

Every writ or originating summons must, when it is served, be **4.51** accompanied by the appropriate form of acknowledgment of service in accordance with by the Rules of the Supreme Court.[70] The writ itself directs the defendant to satisfy the plaintiff's claim, or to return the acknowledgment of service within a given number of days, stating whether or not he intends to contest the proceedings. The period for returning the acknowledgment of service is ordinarily 14 days, but a longer period is specified on the writ if service is outside the jurisdiction.[71] The prescribed forms of acknowledgment of service contain detailed "Directions for Acknowledgment of Service." together with "Notes for Guidance." There are boxes for the defendant to tick to indicate whether he intends to contest the proceedings. The acknowledgment of service must be signed by the defendant's solicitor, or, if he is acting in person, by the party himself. If the defendant is out of the jurisdiction his address for service will be that of his solicitor within the jurisdiction. If he is acting in person he must give an address for service within the jurisdiction.[72]

There are no instructions as to what the defendant should do if he wishes to challenge the court's jurisdiction or to apply to set aside service on account of an irregularity. In such a case he must indicate that he intends to contest the proceedings, and then make an appropriate application as described below.[73] The return of the acknowl-

---

[69] The Hague Service Convention applies to the three parts of the United Kingdom, and it has also been extended, on terms which vary somewhat from territory to territory, to Anguilla, Bermuda, Cayman Islands, Falkland Islands and dependencies, Gibraltar, Guernsey, Hong Kong, Isle of Man, Jersey, Montserrat, Pitcairn, St. Christopher and Nevis, St. Helena and dependencies, Turks and Caicos Islands, and the British Virgin Islands. It seems that it may be used for service outside the U.K. in these territories.

[70] R.S.C., Ord. 10, r. 1(6) (writs—Form 14, Appendix A); Ord. 10, r. 5(1) (originating summonses—Form 15, Appendix A). The requirement does not apply to *ex parte* originating summonses or those under Ord. 113. An acknowledgment of service is also required in respect of a counterclaim and in third party proceedings.

[71] See para. 3.34 above.

[72] R.S.C., Ord. 12, r. 3(2).

[73] See paras. 5.11 *et seq.* below.

edgment of service does not constitute a waiver on the part of the defendant of any irregularity as to the writ or its service.[74] However if he thereafter fails, within the time limited for serving the defence, to contest jurisdiction or the regularity of the writ or its service, he will be taken to have submitted to the jurisdiction.[75]

4.52   If the defendant fails to return the acknowledgment of service within the time allowed he runs the risk of the plaintiff obtaining judgment against him in default of giving notice of intention to defend.[76] He may return the acknowledgment of service and give notice of his intention to defend out of time, as long as judgment has not been entered against him,[77] but he does not thereby gain any longer period for contesting the jurisdiction or serving his defence.[78]

Where a defendant intends not to defend a claim for a liquidated sum but wishes to have time to pay he may state in the acknowledgment of service that he intends to apply for a stay of execution of any judgment entered against him. If he then issues a summons for a stay within 14 days, supported by an affidavit of means, execution of the judgment by writ of *fieri facies* will be stayed until after the application has been heard, unless the court otherwise directs.[79]

2. Default judgments

4.53   In most civil and commercial cases, if the defendant fails to give notice of intention to defend, the plaintiff may enter a default judgment against him, although leave is sometimes required. The cases in which a judgment in default of notice of intention to defend may be obtained are those in which the proceedings have been begun by writ and in which the plaintiff's claim is for a liquidated sum,[80] for unliquidated damages,[81] for detention of goods,[82] or for possession of land.[83] In respect of all other claims it is necessary for the plaintiff to proceed with the action as if notice of intention to defend had been given, and to serve a statement of claim if this has not been indorsed on the writ. If the defendant thereafter fails to

---

[74] R.S.C., Ord. 12, r. 7; C.C.R., Ord. 9, r. 13.
[75] R.S.C., Ord. 12, r. 8(7).
[76] R.S.C., Ord. 13; see paras. 4.53 *et seq.* below.
[77] R.S.C., Ord. 12, r. 6(1).
[78] R.S.C., Ord. 12, r. 6(2).
[79] R.S.C., Ord. 13, r. 8; Ord. 47, r. 1.
[80] R.S.C., Ord. 13, r. 1.
[81] R.S.C., Ord. 13, r. 2; here there is an interlocutory judgment for damages to be assessed.
[82] R.S.C., Ord. 13, r. 3.
[83] R.S.C., Ord. 13, r. 4; As to proceedings begun by originating summons see R.S.C., Ord. 28, r. 6.

serve his defence within the time allowed the plaintiff may apply for final judgment against him in default of defence.[84]

In order to obtain a judgment in default, the plaintiff must demonstrate that the writ was, or is deemed to have been, served on the defendant and that the defendant has failed to give notice of intention to defend or to serve a defence, as the case may be. The judgment is obtained by the administrative procedure of "entering" it in the Central Office of the High Court or in the district registry out of which the writ was issued.[85] In a substantial number of cases, the plaintiff requires leave to enter a default judgment, which he may only obtain on proof of the court's jurisdiction and related matters.[86] The application for leave is considered below in more detail after proof of service.

Proof of service of the writ

In order to ensure that the writ has been served on the defendant, **4.54** the rules provide[87] that a judgment in default of notice of intention to defend shall not be entered unless either the defendant has acknowledged service,[88] or an affidavit proving service is filed on behalf of the plaintiff, or the plaintiff produces a copy of the writ endorsed with a statement by the defendant's solicitor that he accepts service on the defendant's behalf.[89] An affidavit of service must state by whom, where, and how the writ was served, giving the day of the week[90] and date on which it was served.[91] Where service has taken place out of the jurisdiction through official channels,[92] proof of service may be by official certificate.[93] The writ must be endorsed with a statement that the time for service of the

---

[84] R.S.C., Ord. 13, r. 5; *Supreme Court Practice*, para. 13/6/1.
[85] R.S.C., Ord. 42; App. A, Forms 39–42; *Supreme Court Practice*, paras. 13/1/4, and [34–37]. If the defendant has issued a summons to set aside the service of the writ, it is an abuse of the process of the court to enter a default judgment: *Bankers Trust Co.* v. *Galadari* (1986) 130 Sol.Jo. 986.
[86] See para. 4.55 below.
[87] R.S.C., Ord. 13, r. 7(1).
[88] The defendant must have stated in the acknowledgment of service that he does not intend to defend the proceedings. The court must be asked to search for an acknowledgment of service and if none is found a certificate to this effect will be provided.
[89] See R.S.C., Ord. 10, r. 1(4) and para. 4.05 above.
[90] Service within the jurisdiction is not permitted on a Sunday without the leave of the court, see R.S.C., Ord. 65, r. 10; this rule does not apply to service out of the jurisdiction which is governed by local law, see *Supreme Court Practice*, para. 65/10/1.
[91] R.S.C., Ord. 65, r. 8; specimen forms of affidavit are set out in the Queen's Bench Masters' Practice Forms, Nos. 122–131; *Supreme Court Practice*, paras. [327–341]; Chitty and Jacob, pp. 89 *et seq.*
[92] R.S.C., Ord. 11, r. 6: see para. 4.27 above.
[93] R.S.C., Ord. 11, r. 5(5).

117

defence has expired and that the defendant is in default of serving his defence.[94] Service on a foreign state is proved by a certificate to that effect by the Secretary of State for Foreign and Commonwealth Affairs.[95]

Proof of jurisdiction and related matters

4.55   *Leave to enter judgment.* In addition to proving service, the plaintiff must obtain leave to enter a default judgment if both of two conditions are fulfilled:[96] first, if the court's jurisdiction is founded on the 1982 Act and, secondly, if *either* the writ has been served out of the jurisdiction under Order 11, rule 1(2)(a)[97] *or* the writ has been served within the jurisdiction on a person domiciled in Scotland or Northern Ireland or any other Convention territory.[98]

4.56   *The application for leave.* An affidavit is required in support of an application for leave to enter a default judgment, and it should be emphasised that drafting such an affidavit may be a matter of some complexity and require a detailed appreciation of the manner in which the court's jurisdiction arises under the 1968 Convention and 1982 Act. Order 13, rule 7B(2) of the Rules of the Supreme Court[99] states:

> "An application for leave to enter judgment may be made *ex parte* and shall be supported by an affidavit stating that in the deponent's belief—
> (a) each claim made by the writ is one which by virtue of the Civil Jurisdiction and Judgments Act 1982 the Court has power to hear and determine,
> (b) no other court has exclusive jurisdiction within the meaning of Schedule 1 or under Schedule 4 to the Act to hear and determine such claim, and
> (c) where the writ is served out of the jurisdiction under Order 11, r. 1(2)(a) such service satisfied the requirements of Sched-

---

[94] See *Supreme Court Practice*, para. 10/1/3; *Practice Direction (Judgment by Default)* [1979] 1 W.L.R 851; Queen's Bench Masters' Practice Direction No. 14A, *Supreme Court Practice*, para. [760].

[95] R.S.C., Ord. 11, r. 5(6).

[96] R.S.C., Ord. 13, r. 7B(1).

[97] Service out of the jurisdiction under that provision is permitted without leave, provided the writ is duly indorsed with a statement as to the court's jurisdiction: see para. 4.18 above.

[98] "Convention territory" means the territory of any of the Contracting States: R.S.C., Ord. 13, r. 7B(3), 1982 Act, s.1(3); 1968 Convention, Art. 60 (paras. 34.01 to 34.09 below). On a strict construction, "any other Convention territory" would seem to include England and Wales; but it is submitted that that constructon was not intended, and that leave is not necessary to enter a default judgment against a defendant domiciled within the jurisdiction.

[99] These provisions apply also in the county court: C.C.R. Ord. 9, r. 6(4).

ule 1 or, as the case may require, of Article 20 of Schedule 4 to
that Act,
and giving in each case the sources and grounds of such belief.''

Each of these requirements is considered below in turn, but it
should be noted that this affidavit is of central importance in
enabling the court to exercise its duties, under the 1968 Convention
and Schedule 4 to the 1982 Act, to examine its own jurisdiction of
its own motion, and to ensure the defendant's procedural rights
have been observed, before entering a default judgment against a
person domiciled in another Contracting State or another part of
the United Kingdom.[1] The court has an equivalent duty to decline
jurisdiction in a case which, by virtue of Article 16,[2] falls within the
exclusive jurisdiction of the courts of another Contracting State or
of another part of the United Kingdom.[3] This latter duty arises
regardless of the domicile of the defendant, and it is not clear how,
if the writ has been served within the jurisdiction, the court complies with this duty before entering a default judgment against a
person who is domiciled in England and Wales or who is not domiciled in any Contracting State. The same problem arises where the
writ is served within the jurisdiction on such a person in a case over
which the courts of another Contracting State have jurisdiction by
virtue of Article 17.[4]

Proving the court's jurisdiction: sub-paragraphs (a) and (b). A writ **4.57**
which has been served out of the jurisdiction without the leave of
the court should have been duly indorsed with a statement of the
court's jurisdiction,[5] but this is not a requirement which applies to
service within the jurisdiction. In either case, the affidavit should
state the basis on which the court's jurisdiction arises under the
1982 Act, preferably citing by number the Articles of the Convention and Schedule 4 which are relevant to each claim in the writ.
The facts on which the jurisdiction is based must be set out in sufficient detail to enable the court to be satisfied, by making its own
assessment of them, that it has power to hear and determine the
case. The sources of the deponent's belief must also be stated. In

---

[1] These duties arise under the first paragraph of Art. 20 of the 1968 Convention
(para. 22.11 below) and its counterpart in Sched. 4 (para. 45.26 below).
[2] 1968 Convention, Art. 16: para. 20.01 below; Sched. 4, Art. 16, para. 45.19
below.
[3] 1968 Convention, Art. 19: para. 22.01 below; Sched. 4, Art. 19, para. 45.25
below.
[4] See paras. 21.43 and 21.72 below. The equivalent problem does not arise within
the U.K., because Art. 17 of Sched. 4 (para. 45.21 below) does not confer
exclusive jurisdiction on the chosen court and does not confer priority of jurisdiction if neither party is domiciled in any part of the U.K.
[5] R.S.C., Ord. 11, r. 1(2)(a), see para. 3.25 above.

stating his grounds for believing that no other court has exclusive jurisdiction within the meaning of Schedule 1 or under Schedule 4,[6] the deponent should recall that exclusive jurisdiction may arise either, by reference to the principal subject-matter of the claim, under Article 16 of the Convention or of Schedule 4, or by virtue of a choice of jurisdiction agreement under Article 17 of the Convention.[7]

4.58   *Protection of the defendant: sub-paragraph (c).* If service has been effected outside the jurisdiction without the court's leave, the deponent must not only prove the court's jurisdiction, but also that the defendant has had adequate notice of the proceedings. He must do this by stating his belief that the requirements of Schedule 1 or of Article 20 of Schedule 4 have been complied with. The requirements referred to are principally those of the second paragraph of Article 20 of the Convention or Schedule 4, or the alternative requirements of Article 15 of the Hague Service Convention.[8]

The second paragraph of Article 20 applies in all cases other than those in which the defendant has been served out of the jurisdiction, either under the Hague Service Convention[9] or, possibly, by another method permitted by that convention.[10] However, if the defendant has been served within the jurisdiction, the affidavit in support of an application for leave to enter a default judgment need not deal with the question of service.[11] The second paragraph of Article 20 provides as follows:

> "The court shall stay the proceedings so long as it is not shown that the defendant has been able to receive the document instituting the proceedings . . . in sufficient time to enable him to arrange for his defence, or that all necessary steps have been taken to this end."

The deponent must state the grounds for his belief that the service out of the jurisdiction complied with the relevant provisions. In practice he will be able to do this from the information necessary for

---

[6] The reason for referring to jurisdiction "within the meaning" of Sched. 1, but "under" Sched. 4 is because Sched. 1 is for convenience of reference only: see para. 40.04 below.

[7] See n. 4 above.

[8] See paras. 22.21 *et seq.* below; Ireland is not a party to this convention.

[9] The Hague Service Convention is discussed at paras. 4.30 to 4.33 above.

[10] Art. 19 of the Hague Service Convention permits other methods of service not specifically provided for by its terms. It is not clear whether Art. 15 applies to such other methods.

[11] R.S.C., Ord. 13, r. 7B(2)(c) only applies if the writ has been served out of the jurisdiction. It is not clear how the court is to satisfy itself that the requirements of the second paragraph of Art. 20 have been complied with if the defendant has been served within the jurisdiction, except by a general assumption that the 14 days allowed by the rules for returning the acknowledgment of service is sufficient for the defendant to prepare his defence.

the affidavit of service required by the rules for the entry of a default judgment,[12] which will prove (or at least raise a strong presumption) that the defendant has indeed received it. The requirement that the defendant has had sufficient time to arrange for his defence is likely to be regarded as having been fulfilled as, necessarily, the time allowed for acknowledgment of service will have expired.[13] Only if the defendant applies to set the judgment aside is it likely that arguments will become apparent as to why, on the facts of the particular case, he did not have sufficient time to arrange his defence.

Where there has been service out of the jurisdiction in accord- **4.59** ance with the Hague Service Convention,[14] and the defendant has not acknowledged service, Article 15 of that Convention provides that judgment in default may not be given until it is established that either:

(i) the writ was served by a method prescribed by the internal law of the State addressed for the service of documents in domestic actions upon persons who are within its territory, or

(ii) the document was actually delivered to the defendant or to his residence by another method provided for by that Convention. It must also be shown, in either case, that the service or delivery was effected in sufficient time to enable the defendant to defend.

If the procedure for transmission of the writ through official channels has been employed in accordance with the Hague Service Convention, and no certificate of any kind has been received back through official channels, it may still be permissible, so far as the terms of Article 20 the Convention are concerned, for the English court to give a default judgment. This is because the United Kingdom has made a declaration under the second part of Article 15 of the Hague Service Convention which permits a court to give judgment in these circumstances if a period of not less than six months has elapsed since the transmission of the document, and if every reasonable effort has been made to obtain the certificate through the competent authorities of the state addressed. Notwithstanding this provision, the English court might still be reluctant to give leave for a default judgment to be entered in such circumstances.

---

[12] R.S.C., Ord. 13, r. 7(1)(b): see para. 4.54 above.
[13] See para. 4.54 at n. 94 above.
[14] See paras. 4.30 to 4.33 above.

F. SERVICE OF FOREIGN PROCESS IN ENGLAND AND WALES

4.60 English law permits any person to serve on any other person the originating process of a foreign court or any other document connected with foreign litigation, whether it is compulsory in nature or not. There are in England no official process servers equivalent to the French *huissier* and there are no English legal requirements that have to be complied with for the service of foreign documents.[15]

The Rules of Supreme Court do, however, provide a procedure to be followed when requests are received by the senior master for the service of foreign process in civil or commercial matters.[16] This procedure applies whether the request is received from a consular or other authority of a foreign country pursuant to the Hague Service Convention or a bilateral convention, or whether it is received from the Secretary of State for Foreign and Commonwealth Affairs with a recommendation that service should be effected.[17] The rules provide for the request to be accompanied by two copies of the document to be served, which must be translated into English unless the foreign court certifies that the recipient understands the foreign language of the document. The senior master arranges for the service of the document, usually by county court clerks or bailiffs, whose services are usually provided free of charge.

4.61 The document may be served either personally or by insertion through the letter box of the person to be served.[18] The process server returns the copy of the document with an appropriate affidavit, or a certificate, or a report as evidence of service. If he is unable to carry out service he returns the copy of the document, giving the reason why service could not be effected either in an affidavit, or a certificate, or a report. The senior master returns the copy of the document served to the requesting authority, together with a certificate, bearing the seal of the Supreme Court, stating when and how service was effected or the reason why service could not be effected, as the case may be, with a notification of the costs to be paid, if any, certified by the taxing master. In practice the costs of service are usually waived, particularly in the case of countries which themselves charge no fee, unless there are exceptional circumstances.

---

[15] See Jacob, *Private International Litigation*, para. 16.20.
[16] R.S.C., Ord. 69. In the U.K. the Central Authority designated for the purposes of the Hague Service Convention is the Secretary of State for Foreign and Commonwealth Affairs, but the Senior Master of the Supreme Court, Queen's Bench Division, has been designated for England and Wales as an "other authority" under Art. 18 of the Hague Convention.
[17] This could arise when there was no convention with the country concerned and the request came through diplomatic channels.
[18] R.S.C., Ord. 69, rr. 3(2) and 3(3); Ord. 10(2)(b).

CHAPTER 5

CONTESTING JURISDICTION AND SERVICE

A. INTRODUCTION

This chapter examines the circumstances in which, and the pro-   **5.01**
cedure by which, a person may contest the jurisdiction of the court,
or the regularity of the writ[1] or its service.[2] In part B of the chapter
there is a discussion of the grounds which might support such challenges, with particular reference to the grounds which must be considered in the new context of the 1968 Convention. An account of
the procedure to be adopted follows in part C of the chapter and
part D deals with applications to set aside judgments given in
default of notice of intention to defend, or in default of defence, in
which questions of jurisdiction and service arise. The circumstances in which the court may, in non-Convention cases, decline to
continue to entertain proceedings by ordering a stay are dealt with
principally in Chapter 1.[3] Challenges to the jurisdiction of the English court to grant interim relief in aid of proceedings in other Contracting States are dealt with in Chapter 7.

It was seen in Chapters 1 and 3 that the jurisdiction of the English courts can be founded on one of a number of bases, which
may be divided into four categories: jurisdiction under the 1968
Convention, jurisdiction under Schedule 4 to the 1982 Act (*i.e.*

---

[1] References to proceedings begun by writ apply, with necessary modifications, to
proceedings begun by originating summons, see R.S.C., Ord. 10, r. 5.
[2] A challenge to the regularity of a writ or its service is treated by the Rules of the
Supreme Court as a challenge to the jurisdiction of the court: see R.S.C.,
Ord. 12, r. 8.
[3] At paras. 1.41 *et seq.* above. The limited cases in which, under the Convention,
the court has power to stay its proceedings on jurisdictional grounds are discussed at para. 5.06 below.

123

intra-United Kingdom cases), jurisdiction under certain statutory rules implementing the schemes of specialised international conventions, and jurisdiction based on traditional rules involving service of the writ.[3a] The first three categories are not mutually exclusive and the rules of jurisdiction in the 1968 Convention, in particular, may be supplemented in some cases by those in Schedule four to the 1982 Act. It was seen in Chapters 3 and 4 that the procedure for the issue and service of writs differs substantially depending on the basis on which the court's jurisdiction is founded. Any defendant must therefore consider, first, whether the English court has jurisdiction over the case which has been brought against him and if so on what basis, and secondly, whether the appropriate procedural requirements regarding the form and service of the writ have been complied with. Dependent on these considerations, grounds may exist upon which to challenge the jurisdiction of the court, the regularity of the issue of the writ, or the regularity of its service. In those cases in which the court's jurisdiction is based on traditional rules, a challenge to the regularity of the issue or service of the writ on certain grounds may amount to a challenge to the court's jurisdiction.

B. GROUNDS FOR CONTESTING SERVICE OR JURISDICTION

5.02   Whatever the basis for the court's jurisdiction a writ may only be served while it is still valid, that is to say within one year of its issue, subject to any extension which may have been granted.[4] Service of a writ after the expiry of its validity is an irregularity which will render service liable to be set aside. So too, regardless of the basis of the court's jurisdiction, an irregularity in the manner of service may give grounds for setting aside service. It has been seen that English process may be served in a foreign country either in the English manner or in accordance with methods available for the service of local process in the country of service.[5] Whatever method of service is employed it must not be contrary to the law of the country in which service is effected.[6] It follows that any breach of the law of that country will give grounds for setting it aside. If the defendant can satisfy the court that he never received the writ, although this assertion is more likely to be made after a default judgment has been entered, the court may be prepared to declare that he has not been duly served.

[3a] See paras. 1.14 and 1.15 above.
[4] R.S.C., Ord. 6, r. 8; see para. 3.37 above.
[5] See paras. 4.25 and 4.26 above.
[6] R.S.C., Ord. 11, r. 5(2).

1. Cases under the 1968 Convention

Whether or not the 1968 Convention applies in any particular **5.03** case depends upon the Convention's jurisdictional rules. These rules are summarised in Chapter 3 and appear in their full text with commentaries in Chapters 13 to 38 of this book. In very general terms the subject matter of the case must come within the scope of the Convention, the defendant must be domiciled in a Contracting State (subject to certain exceptions), and the proceedings must have a sufficient international element.[7] The rules themselves are compulsory in the sense that if the court has jurisdiction under the Convention then it may not decline to exercise it on the ground that the English court is not a *forum conveniens*.[8] Conversely, if the court does not have jurisdiction, the fact that the defendant has been duly served with the writ, whether within or out of the jurisdiction, will not give it jurisdiction.[9] In certain rare instances, where there are related proceedings pending before a court in another Contracting State, the court is permitted to stay the English proceedings.[10] However if the defendant acknowledges service and does not contest the jurisdiction, the effect of Article 18 of the Convention is to give the English court jurisdiction, the defendant having thereby submitted to the jurisdiction.[11] This will always be the case except where the subject matter of the proceedings is of a kind reserved to the exclusive jurisdiction of another Contracting State by virtue of Article 16 of the Convention.[12] If the English court decides that it does not have jurisdiction under the Convention, but that the courts of another Contracting State have, then an order for interim relief already granted might be permitted to continue as a protective measure under Article 24.[13]

Grounds for challenging jurisdiction. Reference may be made here **5.04** to a number of the more general rules of jurisdiction of the 1968 Convention to indicate the kind of situations in which the jurisdic-

---

[7] If the case involves parties or matters connected with Scotland or Northern Ireland, but not extending to any other Contracting State, then although it will be governed by the jurisdictional rules contained in Sched. 4 to the Act, it may not be subject to the Convention, see paras. 13.10 and 21.06 below.

[8] Schlosser, paras. 76–81, (paras. A1.363–A1.369, below).

[9] *Rothmans of Pall Mall (Overseas) Ltd.* v. *Saudi Arabian Airlines Corporation* [1981] Q.B. 368.

[10] Arts. 21 and 22; see paras. 5.06 and 23.01 *et seq.* below.

[11] See para. 21.84 below. R.S.C., Ord. 12, r. 7 contains a provides similar provision but must be qualified by the provisions of the Convention or Sched. 4 where they give exclusive jurisdiction to other courts; see para. 5.11 below.

[12] See para. 21.35 below.

[13] See para. 7.31 below.

tion of the English court might be open to challenge. At the outset it should be apparent that in any case in which the defendant is domiciled in England and Wales the English court is likely to have jurisdiction under Article 2 of the Convention and of Schedule 4. The only provisions of the Convention which derogate from this rule are those in Articles 16,[14] 17,[15] and 21 to 23[16] which are of relatively narrow application. If the defendant is not domiciled in England and Wales but in another Contracting State, then that other Contracting State will have jurisdiction over the case by reason of Article 2 of the 1968 Convention, subject, as above, to Articles 16, 17, and 21 to 23. The English court will only then have jurisdiction if it can be founded on one of the other rules of the Convention.[17] If the defendant is domiciled in Scotland or Northern Ireland the English courts will only have jurisdiction (in a case to which the Convention applies)[18] where the provisions of Schedule 4 allocate jurisdiction to the English courts.

5.05   It should be apparent from the nature of the case which jurisdictional rule the plaintiff is seeking to rely upon. The defendant should however be alert to a number of possible pitfalls for the plaintiff which might have effect, in cases in which the defendant is not domiciled in England and Wales, of depriving the English court of jurisdiction. In a case arising out of a contract the English court will have jurisdiction over a defendant domiciled in another part of the United Kingdom[19] or in another Contracting State[20] under Article 5(1), if the place of performance of the obligation in question is England and Wales. Where this place is will be decided by the proper law of the contract as determined by English private

---

[14] Art. 16 of the 1968 Convention grants to national courts exclusive jurisdiction over proceedings principally concerned with certain rights in immovable property, company matters, entries in public registers, the registration of various intellectual property rights, and the enforcement of judgments. Art. 16 of Sched. 4 is in equivalent, but not identical terms. See generally paras. 20.01 *et seq.* and 45.01 *et seq.* below.

[15] Art. 17 of the 1968 Convention enables parties, at least one of whom is domiciled in a Contracting State, to choose which courts are to have jurisdiction over their dispute. See generally paras. 21.01 *et seq.* below. A similar, but not identical, provision appears in Sched. 4: para. 45.21 below.

[16] Arts. 21 to 23 contain rules relating to *lis alibi pendens*. In some situations the English court is obliged to decline jurisdiction, in others it has a discretion to stay the proceedings; see paras. 5.06 and, generally, 23.01 *et seq.* below.

[17] Arts. 5(1), 5(2), 5(3), 5(5), 6(1), 8, 9, 16 and 17; see para. 3.11 above.

[18] Intra-U.K. cases within Sched. 4 but outside the Convention are discussed at para. 5.08 below.

[19] Under Art. 5(1) of Sched. 4.

[20] Under Art. 5(1) of the Convention.

international law. If the proper law is foreign law the place of performance may differ from that which it would have been under English law.[21] In a case arising in tort the English court will have jurisdiction over a defendant domiciled in another part of the United Kingdom[22] or in another Contracting State under Article 5(3) if the harmful event occurred in England and Wales. Some losses suffered in England and Wales, particularly economic losses, might be regarded as being too remote to found jurisdiction under Article 5(3).

Similarly, in a case brought under Article 5(5), arising out of the operations of a branch, agency or other establishment of a person or entity domiciled in another part of the United Kingdom or another Contracting State there might be argument as to whether the dispute did arise out of the operations of the branch. Furthermore the European Court has interpreted the phrase "branch, agency or other establishment" somewhat narrowly.[23] A distinction, in some cases, is capable of being drawn between a branch, agency or other establishment, and a subsidiary of a foreign parent company.[24] In a case in which the jurisdiction of the English court is purportedly based on a choice of jurisdiction clause, the defendant should consider whether the clause complies with the provisions of Article 17 of the Convention.[25] At least one of the parties must be domiciled in a Contracting State, and formal requirements must be satisfied. The agreement conferring jurisdiction on the English court must be in writing, or evidenced in writing, save in a dispute arising out of international trade or commerce, in which case it may be in a form which accords with practices in that trade or commerce of which the parties were or ought to have been aware.

Staying proceedings under the Convention. The High Court has **5.06** inherent power to order a stay of proceedings so as to prevent the abuse of its process.[26] This power has been exercised in the past to exclude cases on the grounds of *forum non conveniens, lis alibi pendens* and where there has been a foreign jurisdiction clause.[27] The

---

[21] In some continental systems it is for the creditor to seek out the debtor and the obligation to pay is at the debtor's domicile; see chaps. 48 to 58, at para. 28.
[22] See para. 17.45 below.
[23] See para. 17.61 below.
[24] See paras. 17.61 to 17.63 below; see Fawcett: "Methods of carrying on business and Art. 5(5) of the Brussels Convention": (1984) 9 E.L.Rev. 326; Kaye, p. 606 and n. 1301 (p. 775).
[25] See paras. 21.01 *et seq.* below.
[26] Supreme Court Act 1981, s.49(3). The power is exercisable by the county court by virtue of the County Court's Act 1984, s.38.
[27] See paras. 1.41 *et seq.* above.

limiting effect of the Convention on the power to grant a stay is recognised in section 49 of the 1982 Act, which provides that

> "Nothing in this Act shall prevent any court in the United Kingdom from staying, sisting, striking out or dismissing any proceedings before it, on the ground of *forum non conveniens* or otherwise, where to do so is not inconsistent with the 1968 Convention."[28]

Having regard to the compulsory nature of the Convention's jurisdictional rules,[29] the English court may only stay proceedings on jurisdictional grounds in the limited cases provided for under the Convention. By Article 21, where the proceedings before the English court involve the same parties and the same cause of action as proceedings already pending before a court in another Contracting State, the English court must decline jurisdiction in favour of the other court. Where the jurisdiction of the other court is being contested, the proceedings before the English court may be stayed.[30] When the proceedings before the foreign court are merely related to the English proceedings, the English court has a discretion whether or not to order a stay.[31] The power of the English court to order a stay in the above cases may, it is suggested, be exercised at any stage prior to judgment.

5.07 If, according to the rules in the 1968 Convention and Schedule 4 to the 1982 Act, the English court has jurisdiction, the writ, if it was served out of the jurisdiction, must have been indorsed, before it was issued, with a statement confirming the court's jurisdiction.[32] If the indorsement is omitted from the writ both its issue and service on a defendant out of the jurisdiction will be irregular and may be challenged by an application made in accordance with the procedure described below.[33] The court will then have to decide whether or not to exercise its powers under Order 2 of the Rules of the Supreme Court to cure the irregularity by giving leave to amend the writ by adding the necessary indorsement. It will refuse to allow an irregularity to be cured where the defendant would be deprived of a defence of limitation.[34] Where the writ is served within the jurisdiction in a case to which the Convention applies it need bear no special indorsement as to the applicability of the Convention. The defendant should nonetheless be alert to consider whether the English court does indeed have jurisdiction under the Convention.

---

[28] See para. 44.40 below.
[29] See para. 15.02 below.
[30] See para. 23.10 below.
[31] Art. 22; see para. 23.15 below.
[32] R.S.C., Ord. 6, r. 7(1); see para. 3.25 above.
[33] See para. 5.12 below.
[34] *Leal* v. *Dunlop Bio-Processes Ltd.* [1984] 1 W.L.R. 874.

2. Cases under Schedule 4 to the 1982 Act

Section 16 and Schedule 4 to the 1982 Act contain jurisdictional **5.08**
rules which apply in two different types of case. In cases in which
the Convention gives jurisdiction to the courts of the United Kingdom as a whole, without greater particularity, they allocate jurisdiction as between England and Wales, Scotland and Northern
Ireland. In cases to which the Convention does not apply but in
which either the defendant is domiciled in the United Kingdom, or
United Kingdom courts have jurisdiction regardless of domicile,
they attribute jurisdiction to the courts of particular parts of the
United Kingdom, or to particular courts there.[35] The rules in
Schedule 4 are, as has been seen, modelled on the Convention, and
therefore objections to the jurisdiction similar to those discussed in
relation to the Convention will be available.[36] Similarly, a writ in a
case in which the English court has jurisdiction under Schedule 4
must, if it is to be served outside the jurisdiction, bear an indorsement confirming the court's jurisdiction.[37]

3. Cases under the special conventions

Where the English court has jurisdiction under statutory pro- **5.09**
visions in accordance with a specialised international convention,
the writ may be served out of the jurisdiction without leave notwithstanding that the person against whom the claim is made is outside the jurisdiction, or that the matters giving rise to the claim took
place outside the jurisdiction.[38] In such cases no indorsement as to
the court's jurisdiction is required.[39] A challenge to the court's jurisdiction will depend on the provisions of the jurisdictional rules
applicable.

4. Cases in which jurisdiction is based on traditional rules

In cases to which the neither the Convention nor Schedule 4 of the **5.10**
1982 Act, nor any special statutory rules apply, the jurisdiction of
the English court is based on traditional rules. Service of the writ can
be effected within the jurisdiction on the defendant if he is physically present, or by one of the alternative means of service within the
jurisdiction permitted by the Rules of the Supreme Court on defend-

---

[35] 1982 Act, s.16.
[36] The scheme of Sched. 4, by omitting articles comparable to Arts. 21 and 22 of
the Convention, retains the principle of *forum non conveniens* and the power of
the English courts to grant a stay in favour of courts of another part of the U.K.
in purely intra-U.K. cases; see paras. 1.46 above and 44.44 below.
[37] R.S.C., Ord. 6, r. 7(1); see para. 3.25 above.
[38] See para. 1.29 above.
[39] See para. 3.27 above.

ants who are outside the jurisdiction.[40] Any challenge to the writ or to the regularity of service will depend upon whether the requirements of the relevant rules have been complied with. It is open to the defendant in an appropriate case to ask that the proceedings be stayed on the ground of *forum non conveniens*, or *lis alibi pendens*, or to give effect to a foreign jurisdiction clause.[41] Service out of the jurisdiction can only take place in accordance with the provisions of Order 11, rule 1(1). As has been seen in Chapter 3, the case must fall within one or more of the categories specified in that rule, and the leave of the court for service outside the jurisdiction must be obtained. The possible grounds of challenge may relate to questions as to whether the case properly falls within the specified categories or as to whether the court exercised its discretion rightly in granting leave. In addition the regularity of the service itself may be called into question. A writ which has been served outside the jurisdiction without leave on the erroneous assumption that the Convention applied will be liable to be set aside by reason of the absence of leave.[42]

C. Procedure for Contesting Jurisdiction and Service

5.11   It is a feature common to many systems of civil procedure that a challenge to the jurisdiction must be made at the first possible moment in the proceedings and that any participation in them other than to challenge the jurisdiction is liable to be regarded as a submission to the jurisdiction. Thus, under the procedure which existed before 1979, a defendant who entered an ordinary or unconditional appearance to proceedings in the English courts was held to have waived any right to object to the writ on the ground of lack of jurisdiction or any other irregularity and to have submitted to the court's jurisdiction. Although the current Rules of the Supreme Court require the lodging of an acknowledgment of service which contains a "notice to defend,"[43] it is expressly provided that this is not to be treated as a waiver of any irregularity in the writ, its service, or in any order giving leave to serve the writ out of the jurisdiction.[44] So long as the defendant makes an appropriate

---

[40] See paras. 4.04 *et seq.* above.

[41] See paras. 1.41 *et seq.* above; *Supreme Court Practice*, paras. [5204 *et seq.*; 5215 *et seq.*; 5228 *et seq.*].

[42] *Dalal* v. *Dalal* (1983) *The Times* May 20; *Camera Care Ltd.* v. *Victor Hasselblad AB* [1986] E.C.C. 373, (1986) *The Times* June 6, (C.A.); *Leal* v. *Dunlop Bio-Processors International Ltd.* [1984] 1 W.L.R. 874 (C.A.)

[43] As defined in R.S.C., Ord. 1, r. 4(1). The acknowledgment of service gives no instructions as to how the jurisdiction of the court may be challenged: see para. 4.51 above.

[44] R.S.C., Ord. 12, r. 7; C.C.R., Ord. 9, r. 13, see para. 4.51 above.

application to dispute the jurisdiction of the court, as described below, he will not be taken to have submitted to the English jurisdiction.[45] The defendant should nonetheless be careful not to take any step in the action which could arguably be construed as constituting a submission to the jurisdiction.[46]

The procedure for contesting service or jurisdiction in the High Court is contained in Order 12, rule 8,[47] which provides a uniform procedure for raising a variety of objections to jurisdiction and service, and enables a variety of orders to be made in consequence. The possible objections may be that the court has no jurisdiction over the defendant, or over the subject matter of the case, or that there is some irregularity concerning the writ or its service. The procedure may also be employed if it is intended to apply for a stay of the proceedings.[48] The procedure is only available to the defendant if he has returned the acknowledgment of service and has given notice of intention to defend the proceedings.[49] Thereafter he must apply to the court, within the time limited for service of the defence,[50] for such of the orders or relief set out in Order 12, rule 8(1)(a) to (h), as is appropriate to the case, namely: **5.12**

   (a) an order setting aside the writ or service of the writ on him, or

   (b) an order declaring that the writ has not been duly served on him, or

   (c) the discharge of any order giving leave to serve the writ on him out of the jurisdiction, or

   (d) the discharge of any order extending the validity of the writ for the purpose of service, or

---

[45] R.S.C., Ord. 12, r. 8(6). This gives effect to the second sentence of Art. 18. Note the corresponding provision relating to foreign judgments in s.33 of the 1982 Act, para. 43.30 below.

[46] See *Supreme Court Practice*, para. [5718] "taking a step in the action"; *Re Dulles' Settlements No. 2* [1951] Ch. 842; *Williams and Glynn's Bank* v. *Astro Dinamico* [1984] 1 W.L.R. 439.

[47] In the county court an application to set aside the service of process, or to discharge the order giving leave to serve it out of the jurisdiction may be made under C.C.R., Ord. 8, r. 12. Other applications may be made under C.C.R., Ord. 13, r. 1.

[48] *Supreme Court Practice*, para. [5207].

[49] If judgment (*e.g.* a default judgment) has been given, leave is required to give an acknowledgment of service and notice of intention to defend; see para. 5.14 below.

[50] See R.S.C., Ord. 18, r. 2. This will be 14 days after the time limited for acknowledging service of the writ or 14 days after the statement of claim is served on him (whichever is the later), or such longer period as may be allowed by the court or agreed by the parties.

     (e) the protection or release of any property of the defendant seized or threatened with seizure in the proceedings, or

     (f) the discharge of any order made to prevent any dealing with any property of the defendant, or

     (g) a declaration that in the circumstances of the case the court has no jurisdiction over the subject matter of the claim to the relief or remedy claimed in the action, or

     (h) such other relief as may be appropriate.

5.13   The application is made by way of summons in the Queen's Bench Division, by way of motion in Admiralty proceedings *in rem*, or by way of summons or motion in any other action.[51] It is important to note that the grounds of the application must be stated in the summons or notice of motion, and must be supported by evidence on affidavit served with the summons or notice of motion.[52] The time limited for making the application[53] may be extended on an application[54] which may be made even after the time has expired. While the application disputing the jurisdiction of the court is pending the plaintiff should not enter judgment in default of defence.[55] The application will normally be determined by the master on the application but it may be adjourned for trial as a preliminary issue.[56]

    If the court makes no order on the application or dismisses it, the notice of intention to defend the proceedings ceases to have effect and the defendant may file a further acknowledgment of service giving notice of intention to defend. If, as will normally be the case, the original period for returning the acknowledgment of service has expired, the leave of the court will be required.[57] The master should conveniently be asked to give such leave when he dismisses the application disputing the jurisdiction of the court. If the defendant does not file a further acknowledgment of service giving notice of intention to defend (on the merits) the plaintiff may apply for judgment in default of appearance.[58]

---

[51] R.S.C., Ord. 12, r. 8(3).

[52] R.S.C., Ord. 12, r. 8(4).

[53] As to whether the time limit applies to the issue of the summons (or notice of motion) or to its service see: *Carmel Exporters (Sales) Ltd.* v. *Sea-Land Services* [1981] 1 W.L.R. 1068; *The Broken Hill Proprietary Co.* v. *Xerakis* [1982] 2 Lloyd's Rep. 304.

[54] R.S.C., Ord. 3, r. 5.

[55] *Supreme Court Practice*, para. 12/7–8/3.

[56] R.S.C., Ord. 12, r. 8(5); but see *Supreme Court Practice*, para. 12/7–8/5.

[57] R.S.C., Ord. 12, r. 6.

[58] R.S.C., Ord. 13; see paras. 4.53 *et seq.* above.

D. SETTING ASIDE DEFAULT JUDGMENTS

The court has power to set aside judgments given either in default **5.14** of notice of intention to defend, or in default of defence.[59] A distinction exists between regular and irregular default judgments. A regular default judgment is one given when the defendant has been duly served but when, for some reason, he has failed, within the times allowed, to give notice of intention to defend, or, having given such notice, has failed to serve his defence.[60] Application must be made to set the judgment aside, supported by an affidavit showing that the defendant has a defence on the merits[61] and explaining why no notice of intention to defend was given, or why no defence was served. The power to set aside a regular judgment is discretionary[62] and the court may impose terms such as ordering the defendant to bring money into court. In a case to which the Convention or Schedule 4 to the 1982 Act applies, if a default judgment is set aside on the ground that the English court lacks jurisdiction, a provisional or protective measure may be able to continue in force under Article 24 of the Convention or the Schedule.[63]

An irregular judgment is one which has been obtained following some irregularity, usually relating to jurisdiction or to service. The rules provide that a defendant who wishes to dispute matters of jurisdiction and service must first give notice of intention to defend,[64] but it is also provided that save with the leave of the court, such notice may not be given after judgment has been given.[65] Accordingly, where a judgment has been entered in default of notice of intention to defend, the defendant must include in the summons to set aside the judgment a request for leave to give notice of intention to defend.[66] The application to set aside the judgment must be made within a reasonable time from when the defendant became aware that the judgment had been given.[67]

---

[59] R.S.C., Ord. 19, r. 9.

[60] The court must, of course, have jurisdiction in respect of the proceedings.

[61] The defendant need only show that there is an arguable or triable issue: *Drayton Giftware Ltd.* v. *Varyland Ltd.* (1982) 132 N.L.J. 558; see *Supreme Court Practice*, para. 13/9/5; *Alpine Bulk Transport Co.* v. *Saudi Eagle Shipping Co.* [1986] 2 Lloyd's Rep. 221. In a proper case the application may be made by a stranger to the proceedings, see *Jaques* v. *Harrison* (1883) 12 Q.B.D. 165.

[62] See *Evans* v. *Bartlam* [1937] A.C. 473, 480, *per* Lord Atkin.

[63] See para. 7.31, below.

[64] R.S.C., Ord. 12, r. 8.

[65] R.S.C., Ord. 12, r. 6.

[66] *Reynolds* v. *Coleman* (1887) 36 Ch.D. 453; *Hewitson* v. *Fabre* (1889) 21 Q.B.D. 6.

[67] *Vann* v. *Awford* (1986) 83 L.S.Gaz. 1725, [1986] *The Times* April 23. *cf.* Art. 16 of the Hague Service Convention, para. 42.10 below.

5.15   Although the court has a wide discretionary power under the rules to correct irregularities,[68] that power should not be exercised so as to circumvent the requirements of other rules.[69] Where leave to serve out of the jurisdiction is required, failure to obtain such leave is an irregularity which is capable of being cured.[70] Where, as could well happen in a case to which the 1968 Convention applies, the court lacks jurisdiction over the proceedings, the judgment should be treated as a nullity and should be set aside, regardless of whether service was within or out of the jurisdiction. The irregularities of service which entitle a defendant to apply to have service set aside will also entitle him to apply for the judgment to be set aside. They have been discussed above.[71]

In a case to which the Convention applies, the effect of Article 20 of the Convention and (where it applies) Article 15 of the Hague Service Convention is to strenghen the position of the defendant. The limitations which these provisions impose on the giving of default judgments are outlined in Chapter 4.[72] In a case in which, for example, the defendant can show that the method of service adopted allowed him insufficient time to enter an appearance, the judgment might be set aside as being irregular.

---

[68] R.S.C., Ord. 2, r. 2.
[69] *Supreme Court Practice*, para. 2/1/1; an accidental slip or omission may be corrected: *Armitage* v. *Parsons* [1908] 2 K.B. 410.
[70] *Leal* v. *Dunlop Bio-Processes International Ltd.* [1984] 1 W.L.R. 874, in which, as the limitation period had expired, the court refused to cure the irregularity.
[71] See para. 5.02 *et seq.* above.
[72] See paras. 4.58 and 4.59 above.

CHAPTER 6

SECURITY FOR COSTS

A. INTRODUCTION

This chapter discusses the topic of security for costs[1] principally in **6.01** relation to actions and other proceedings brought by persons who are resident outside the jurisdiction. The security for costs which may be required of a foreign judgment creditor who is seeking to enforce a foreign judgment in the English courts is discussed in Chapter 10.

Security for costs may be defined as the sum of money required to be deposited, or other security required to be given, by a plaintiff for the purpose of guaranteeing to the defendant the trouble free recovery of his costs in the event of the plaintiff being ordered to pay those costs. In English civil procedure the ordering of security for costs is not restricted to cases in which the plaintiff is resident outside the jurisdiction.[2] Under the Rules of the Supreme Court security may also be ordered in three other types of case in which the successful recovery by the defendant of his costs might be in some doubt. Thus the court has power to order security when the plaintiff is a nominal plaintiff and there is reason to believe that he will be unable to pay the defendant's costs if so ordered,[3] or if the plaintiff's address is either not given in the writ, or is incorrectly

---

[1] Security for costs is known in many continental jurisdictions as "*cautio judicatum solvi.*" Practice in other Contracting States is described at para. 48 of chaps. 48 to 55 below.

[2] In addition to security for costs ordered under the R.S.C., security for costs may also be ordered under various enactments. See 37 *Halsbury's Laws* (4th ed.), para. 298.

[3] R.S.C., Ord. 23, r. 1(1)(b); see n. 26 below.

stated,[4] or if it is changed in the course of the litigation in order to evade its consequences.[5] Furthermore, although the impecuniosity of a plaintiff who is a natural person is not a ground for ordering security,[6] section 726 of the Companies Act 1985 enables the court to order a plaintiff which is a limited company to provide security for costs when it appears that it may be unable to meet a successful defendant's costs.

6.02   The exercise of the power to order a non-resident plaintiff to provide security is discretionary.[7] The justification for the power is the minimising of any difficulty which might be encountered by the defendant in enforcing an award of costs made against the plaintiff, in the event of his losing the action. The Civil Jurisdiction and Judgments Act 1982, by facilitating the enforcement of such awards, has introduced an important new element into the exercise by the court of its discretion whether or not to order security for costs.[8] In order to assess how the court ought now to exercise its discretion in Convention cases it is necessary to examine both the history of the practice of ordering security and the modern principles of its exercise.

B. The History of the Practice of Ordering Security for Costs

6.03   The practice of the courts in ordering foreign plaintiffs to provide security for costs has a curious history.[9] Up to the mid-eighteenth century the courts, though prepared to order security for costs on various grounds[10] against plaintiffs within the jurisdiction, refused to order security against foreign plaintiffs. It was feared that it would affect trade because a foreigner might not be able to find security "in a strange country."[11] In *Boswell* v. *Irish* (1767)[12] it was stated that such an application was "altogether contrary to rule" . . . (and) . . . "the fashion for such applications was clogging the course of justice." Yet 20 years later Buller J. justified the making of an order for security against a plaintiff resident in North

---

[4] R.S.C., Ord. 23, r. 1(1)(c); *ibid.*
[5] R.S.C., Ord. 23, r. 1(1)(d); *ibid.*
[6] Save in respect of proceedings in the Court of Appeal: see R.S.C., Ord. 59, r. 10(5), and the *Supreme Court Practice* para. 59/10/18.
[7] R.S.C., Ord. 23, r. 1(1); The principles upon which discretion is exercised are discussed at paras. 6.09 *et seq.* below.
[8] See para. 6.13 below.
[9] See the account by Millet J. in *D.S.Q. Property Ltd.* v. *Lotus Ltd.* [1987] 1 W.L.R. 127.
[10] Tidd, *Practice of the Courts of Kings Bench* (2nd ed., 1824), p. 446.
[11] *Real et al.* v. *Macky* (1744) 2 Str. 1206.
[12] 4 Burr. 2105; and see *Maxwell* v. *Mayer* (1760) 2 Burr. 1026.

America, saying "if a verdict be given against the plaintiff he is not within the reach of our law so as to have process served on him for the costs."[13] Thereafter it became the settled practice of the courts to order security to be provided by plaintiffs who were resident abroad. The Rules of the Supreme Court 1883 made no express reference to plaintiffs outside the jurisdiction but merely provided that whenever security was required it should be given "at such times and in such manner and form" as the court or judge should direct.[14] By the end of the nineteenth century the settled practice had, in the view of Lopes L.J., become the inflexible rule.[15] Only in respect of plaintiffs resident in Scotland or Ireland was an exception made.[16] This was because, as was held in *Raeburn* v. *Andrews*,[17] an English defendant, if successful, had an effective means of enforcing an order for costs against the such a plaintiff under the provisions of the Judgments Extension Act 1868. The Act provided for the registration of a certificate of the English order for costs which enabled it to be readily enforced in the other two jurisdictions. In 1920 an amendment to the Rules of the Supreme Court expressly declared that in an action brought by a non-resident plaintiff founded on a judgment or a negotiable instrument the ordering of security was to be in the discretion of the court.[18] Otherwise orders for security were made against non-resident plaintiffs as a matter of course.[19]

The passing of the Administration of Justice Act 1920 and the **6.04** Foreign Judgments (Reciprocal Enforcement) Act 1933 introduced statutory schemes for the mutual recognition and enforcement of judgments as between the United Kingdom and certain foreign countries.[20] In *Kohn* v. *Rinson & Stafford (Brod.) Ltd.*[21] it was argued that the principle in *Raeburn* v. *Andrews*[22] could be extended by analogy to cases covered by these statutory schemes. The argument was rejected by Denning J. who distinguished the

---

[13] *Pray* v. *Edie* (1786) 1 T.R. 267.
[14] R.S.C., 1883, Ord. 65, r. 6.
[15] *Crozat* v. *Brogden* (1894) 2 Q.B. 30.
[16] As to the present position relating to parties in Scotland and Northern Ireland see para. 6.08 below.
[17] *Raeburn* v. *Andrews* (1874) L.R. 9 Q.B. 118; the Judgments Extension Act 1868 also applied to Ireland but it ceased to have effect in the Republic of Ireland in 1922. It has been repealed by the s.54 and Sched. 14 of the 1982 Act, see para. 6.08 below.
[18] R.S.C, 1920 Ord. 65, r. 6b.
[19] *Wakely* v. *Triumph Cycle Co. Ltd.* [1924] 1 K.B. 214.
[20] See para. 10.04 below.
[21] [1948] 1 K.B. 327, followed in *Hudson Strumpffabrik GmbH* v. *Bentley Engineering Co. Ltd.* [1962] 2 Q.B. 587.
[22] (1874) L.R. 9 Q.B. 118.

method of enforcement under the Acts of 1920 and 1933 from that under the Judgments Extension Act 1868. He found that under the latter Act the process of registering a judgment was automatic, whereas under the Acts of 1920 and 1933 it was not. The Acts of 1920 and 1933 involved "a judicial officer being put in motion" and the process could be "the subject of dispute and even in some cases of trial between the parties."[23]

C. THE MODERN EXERCISE OF THE POWER TO ORDER SECURITY

1. The Rules of the Supreme Court: Order 23

6.05   The power of the High Court to order security for costs against a plaintiff who is resident outside the jurisdiction is now derived from Order 23 of the Rules of the Supreme Court,[24] which provides as follows:

> "1. (1) Where, on the application of a defendant to an action or other proceeding in the High Court, it appears to the Court:
>
>> (a) that the plaintiff is ordinarily resident out of the jurisdiction, . . .
>> (b), (c), and (d),[25]
>
> then if, having regard to all the circumstances of the case, the Court thinks it just to do so, it may order the plaintiff to give such security for the defendant's costs of the action or other proceeding as it thinks just.
> (2) . . .[26]
> (3) The references in the foregoing paragraphs to a plaintiff and a

---

[23] Whether an order for costs awarded in favour of a defendant against an unsuccessful plaintiff is within the scheme of the Acts is in any event doubtful, see *Koven* v. *Toole* (1954) 13 W.W.R. (N.S.) 444, but *contra*, *Cavanagh* v. *Lisogar* (1956) 19 W.W.R. 230 (Alta) (Canada).

[24] Ord. 23 originates from R.S.C., (Rev) 1962. It replaces the former Ord. 65, rr. 6, 6A, 6B and 7, and it embodies earlier case law. It does not affect the power of the court under any other enactment to require security to be given for the costs of any proceedings, see Ord. 23, r. 3 and the enactments listed 37 *Halsbury's Laws* (4th ed.) para. 298. In the county court the power to order security for costs is contained in C.C.R., Ord. 13, r. 8.

[25] "(b) that the plaintiff (not being a plaintiff who is suing in a representative capacity) is a nominal plaintiff who is suing for the benefit of some other person and that there is reason to believe that he will be unable to pay the costs of the defendant if ordered to do so,
(c) subject to para. (2) that the plaintiff's address is not stated in the writ or other originating process or is incorrectly stated therein, or
(d) that the plaintiff has changed his address during the course of the proceedings with a view to evading the consequence of the litigation,".

[26] "(2) The Court shall not require the plaintiff to give security by reason only of paragraph (1)(c) if he satisfies the Court that the failure to state the address or the mis-statement thereof was made innocently and without intention to deceive."

138

defendant shall be construed as references to the person (howsoever described on the record) who is in the position of plaintiff or defendant, as the case may be, in the proceeding in question, including a proceeding on a counterclaim.

2. Where an order is made requiring any party to give security for costs, the security shall be given in such manner, at such time, and on such terms (if any) as the Court may direct."

2. Persons who can be ordered to provide security

Plaintiffs and those in the position of plaintiffs. It is to be noted that **6.06** the definition of persons who can be ordered to provide security extends not only to plaintiffs in the formal sense but also to any person who is in the position of plaintiff in relation to any claim.[27] A defendant who introduces a counterclaim is prima facie in the position of a plaintiff in relation to that counterclaim. If the counterclaim is in respect of matters unconnected with the claim and is in the nature of a cross action the defendant will normally be ordered to provide security.[28] Conversely, he will not be ordered to provide security if the counterclaim arises out of the same subject matter as the claim and is in substance, if not technically, in the nature of a defence to the action.[29] However, for the purposes of determining which party is the true plaintiff, the court will not conduct an examination of each issue in the case to see upon which party the burden of proof may lie.[30] In some interpleader proceedings both the plaintiff and the defendant may each be in the position of claimants. In such situations either party, if resident outside the jurisdiction, may be ordered to give security.[31] Ordinarily, however, a defendant who is resident outside the jurisdiction will not be ordered to give security.[32] The fact that a party, though technically a plaintiff, has been compelled to take defensive proceedings may lead the court, in its discretion, not to order that party to give security.[33] A third party cannot apply for security against the plaintiff unless and until he obtains leave to defend the main action.[34]

[27] R.S.C., Ord. 23, r. 1(3); see *Hitachi Shipbuilding and Engineering Co. Ltd.* v. *Viafiel Compania Naviera SA* [1981] 2 Lloyd's Rep. 498.
[28] *Sykes* v. *Sacerdoti* (1885) 15 Q.B.D. 423.
[29] *Neck* v. *Taylor* [1893] 1 Q.B. 560.
[30] *Hitachi Shipbuilding and Engineering Co. Ltd.* v. *Viafiel Compania Naviera S.A.* [1981] 2 Lloyd's Rep. 498; *Banque du Rhone S.A.* v. *Fuerst Day Lawson Ltd.* [1968] 2 Lloyd's Rep. 153.
[31] *Tomlinson* v. *Land Finance Corporation* (1884) 14 Q.B.D. 539; *Tudor Furnishers Ltd.* v. *Montaque and Co.* [1950] Ch. 113.
[32] *N.V. Beleggings Compagnie "Uranus"* v. *Bank of England* [1948] 1 All E.R. 465.
[33] *Visco* v. *Minter* [1969] P. 82.
[34] *Taly N.D.C. International N.V.* v. *Terra Nova Insurance Co. Ltd. and others and Chandler Hargreaves Whittall & Co. Ltd.* [1986] 1 All E.R. 69.

6.07   *Ordinary residence out of the jurisdiction.* The party ordered to give security on this ground must be ordinarily resident[35] outside the jurisdiction. Such residence does not compel the court to order security, as the exercise of the power is discretionary.[36] Examples are discussed below which show that the ordering of security against a plaintiff who is ordinarily resident out of the jurisdiction is by no means automatic. When both parties are ordinarily resident outside the jurisdiction the court may nonetheless make an order in favour of the defendant.[37] A plaintiff who is only temporarily out of the jurisdiction will not be ordered to provide security, but a plaintiff who goes abroad permanently after the commencement of the proceedings may be ordered to provide security.[38] The mere fact that the plaintiff within the jurisdiction has no fixed address is not a ground for ordering security.[39]

6.08   *Plaintiffs in Scotland and Northern Ireland.* Before the commencement of the Civil Jurisdiction and Judgments Act 1982 it was settled that plaintiffs resident in Scotland or Northern Ireland would not, by reason of that residence, be ordered to provide security for costs.[40] This was because the scheme for enforcement of English judgments under the Judgments Extension Act 1868 was considered to be a sufficient protection for defendants resident in England. The Judgments Extension Act has now been repealed by the Civil Jurisdiction and Judgments Act 1982.[41] The scheme for enforcement under the 1868 Act has been replaced by the provisions of sections 18 and 19, and Schedules 6 and 7 of the 1982 Act[42] and is discussed more fully in Chapters 10 and 46 below. As the scheme under the 1982 Act is, in respect of money provisions at least, comparable to that under the 1868 Act, the principle in *Raeburn* v. *Andrews* will, it is suggested, continue to apply to money claims.

3. Principles of exercise of discretion

6.09   The purposes of ordering security for costs is to guarantee the defendant the trouble free recovery of his costs should he be awarded them. The court has complete discretion in determining

---

[35] As to the meaning of ordinarily resident, see Dicey and Morris, p. 164.
[36] R.S.C., Ord. 23, r. 1. See paras. 6.09 *et seq.* below for the principles upon which discretion is exercised.
[37] *The Silver Fir* [1980] 1 Lloyd's Rep. 371.
[38] *Massey* v. *Allen* (1879) 12 Ch.D. 807; *Appah* v. *Monseu* [1967] 1 W.L.R. 893.
[39] *Chellow* v. *Brown* [1923] 2 K.B. 844; *Knight* v. *Ponsonby* [1925] 1 K.B. 545; *Brooks* v. *Wilkins* [1927] W.N. 136.
[40] *Raeburn* v. *Andrews* (1874) L.R. 9 Q.B. 118.
[41] s.54 and Sched. 14 of the 1982 Act.
[42] See paras. 10.63 *et seq.*, and 46.01 *et seq.* below.

whether or not to make the order. The following considerations may be derived from the decided cases. If there is adequate security for the defendant's costs already located within the jurisdiction the court may refrain from making an order.[43] This may be the plaintiff's own property, provided it is sufficiently substantial and of a fixed and permanent nature,[44] or it may be the property of a co-plaintiff who is resident within the jurisdiction.[45] The defendant may also be sufficiently protected if there is a substantial payment into court or an open offer of a substantial amount in settlement of the plaintiff's claim.[46] Security was refused in respect of a counter-claim by a foreign defendant whose assets within the jurisdiction had been seized by the plaintiff in Mareva injunction proceedings on the claim.[47] If there is a high degree of probability that the plaintiff will succeed in his claim that is a factor to be taken into account against the ordering of security, and conversely, if there is a high degree of probability that he will fail.[48] But when the likely outcome of the proceedings is less obvious the court should not attempt an evaluation of the merits of the respective cases.[49] In practice a non-resident plaintiff suing on a bill of exchange is unlikely to be ordered to provide security unless the bill is challenged on grounds of fraud.[50]

Certain considerations have in the past been rejected by the **6.10** courts as being immaterial to the exercise of the discretion in the matter of security for costs. Thus a plaintiff who is legally aided cannot on that ground alone escape an order for security. However the quantum of the order might well be set at a level which reflects the fact that the costs recoverable against him will be limited in accordance with the Legal Aid Act 1988[51] and that the court would be anxious not to shut out his claim altogether.[52] The courts have

---

[43] *Kevorkian v. Burney (No. 2)* [1937] 4 All E.R. 468.
[44] *Ebrard v. Grassier* (1884) 28 Ch.D. 232.
[45] *D'Hormusgee v. Grey* (1882) 10 Q.B.D. 13.
[46] *Demolition and Construction Co. Ltd. v. Kent River Board* [1963] 2 Lloyd's Rep. 7.
[47] *Hitachi Shipbuilding and Engineering Co. Ltd. v. Viafiel Compania Naviera S.A.* [1981] 2 Lloyd's Rep. 498.
[48] See the *Supreme Court Practice*, para. 23/1–3/2.
[49] *Porzelack K.G. v. Porzelack (U.K.) Ltd.* [1987] 1 W.L.R. 420.
[50] *Banque du Rhone S.A. v. Fuerst Day Lawson Ltd.* [1968] 2 Lloyd's Rep. 153.
[51] Legal Aid Act 1988, s.17(1); The Civil Legal Aid (General) Regulations 1989, (S.I. No. 339), reg. 123.
[52] *Jackson v. John Dickinson & Co. (Bolton) Ltd.* [1952] 1 All E.R. 104; *Friedmann v. Austay (London) Ltd.* [1954] 1 W.L.R. 466; *Caldwell v. Sunters* [1972] Ch. 478.

also rejected the argument that the plaintiff has been compelled to sue in the English courts by a jurisdiction clause.[53]

6.11   *Effect of international conventions.* Certain multilateral conventions, listed below, expressly forbid the imposition of security for costs in proceedings which come within their ambit.[54] The bilateral conventions listed in the Supreme Court Practice[55] are generally not material for the present purposes because, insofar as they preclude the ordering of security for costs, they do so only in respect of the nationals of one Contracting State who bring proceedings in another Contracting State when they are resident in that latter state.[56] It should be noted that Article 17 of the Hague Convention on Civil Procedure of March 1, 1954 prohibits the ordering of security for costs against nationals of, who are resident in, the contracting states, on the ground of foreign residence or domicile. Whereas a number of European States, including the original Contracting States to the 1968 Convention and Denmark, have ratified the Hague Civil Procedure Convention, the United Kingdom has not. Its provisions therefore have no legal effect in England and Wales. The Hague Convention on International Access to Justice of October 25th, 1980 contains a similar prohibition against the ordering of security for costs.[57] The United Kingdom participated in the drawing up of this convention but has not yet ratified it.[58]

6.12   *Effect of membership of the European Communities.* The accession of the United Kingdom to the European Communities in 1973 has added, in cases in which the plaintiff is resident in another Member State, a further factor to be considered by the court in deciding, in its discretion, whether or not to order security. As is stated in the *Supreme Court Practice*[59] "It ought not to be presumed that fellow

---

[53] *Hudson Strumpffabrik GmbH* v. *Bentley Engineering Co. Ltd.* [1962] 2 Q.B. 587, *per* Môcatta J.; *Aeronave S.P.A.* v. *Westland Charters Ltd.* [1971] 1 W.L.R. 1445.

[54] Carriage of Goods by Rail (Berne, 1952), Art. 55(4): Carriage of Passengers by Rail Act 1965, s.1(1) and Sched. Art. 56(4); Carriage of Goods by Road (Geneva, May 19, 1956), Art. 31(5): see Carriage of Goods by Road Act 1965, Carriage of Passengers by Road Act 1974, s.1(1) and Sched. 3, Art. 41(6).

[55] *Supreme Court Practice*, para. 23/1–3/17; see para. A2.01 below.

[56] Security for costs cannot be awarded against French nationals if they possess immovable property in the jurisdiction or other property not readily transferable which is sufficient to cover the costs: see Art. 3 of the Supplementary Convention between the U.K. and France to facilitate the conduct of legal proceedings, April 15, 1936, Cmnd. 6206 (1940).

[57] Cmnd. 8281, Art. 14; see Acts and Documents of the 14th Session of the Hague Conference on Private International Law, p. 235.

[58] See *Report of the House of Lords Select Committee on the European Communities: International Access to Justice*. (Session 1987–88, Second Report).

[59] *Supreme Court Practice*, para. 23/1–3/2.

members of (the) Community will not honour orders made by the courts of England." In practice the Queen's Bench masters frequently exercise their discretion in favour of plaintiffs resident in other community countries.[60] Order 23 has been held not to infringe Article 7 of the Treaty of Rome, which forbids discrimination on the grounds of *nationality*, as the material criterion is foreign *residence*.[61]

Effect of the 1982 Act. The Civil Jurisdiction and Judgments Act **6.13** 1982 and the 1968 Convention have introduced an effective means whereby a successful defendant resident in the United Kingdom can enforce an order for costs against the unsuccessful plaintiff in another Contracting State. The term judgment is defined widely in Article 25 of the Convention and it expressly includes "a determination of costs or expenses by an officer of the court." The procedure for enforcing such orders is laid down in Articles 31 to 49 of the Convention. Given that the justification for ordering security for costs is to reduce the difficulty in recovering costs against an unsuccessful foreign plaintiff, the improved methods of enforcement under the Convention constitute an important factor to be taken into account by the Court.[62] But the existence of the improved methods of enforcement is not decisive against the making of an order for security.[63] In addition to the fact that the Convention provides improved machinery for enforcing orders for costs, there are wider considerations which may, in appropriate cases, influence the court against ordering the provision of security by plaintiffs resident in other Contracting States. It might be said to be counter to the spirit of the Convention for the English courts to impose a financial disincentive on a plaintiff who brings his proceedings in the English court either because it is the sole forum available under the Convention,[64] or, if there is a choice of jurisdic-

---

[60] Following *Landi den Hertog BV* v. *Stopps* [1976] F.S.R. 497; but *cf. Meijer* v. *John H. Taylor Ltd.* [1981] F.S.R. 279, *Compagnie Francaise de Television* v. *Thorn Consumer Electronics Ltd.* [1981] F.S.R. 497, and *C. van der Lely NV* v. *Watveare Overseas Ltd.* [1982] F.S.R. 122.

[61] *Landi den Hertog BV* v. *Stopps* [1976] F.S.R. 497. This view has been adopted by the House of Lords Select Committee on the European Communities, see *Report of the House of Lords Select Committee on the European Communities: International Access to Justice.* (Session 1987–88, Second Report); see also *Boussac* v. *Gerstenmeier* [1980] E.C.R. 3427.

[62] *De Bry* v. *Fitzgerald, The Independent,* November 14, 1988 (C.A.).

[63] *Porzelack K.G.* v. *Porzelack (U.K.) Ltd.* [1987] 1 W.L.R. 420, *per* Sir Nicholas Browne-Wilkinson, V.-C.

[64] As where the English courts have exclusive jurisdiction under Art. 16 of the Convention. Where the English courts have jurisdiction under Art. 17 it might be said that the defendant had himself chosen the English forum: see *Hudson Strumpffabrik GmbH* v. *Bentley Engineering Co. Ltd.* [1962] 2 Q.B. 587, *per* Mocatta J.; *Aeronave S.P.A.* v. *Westland Charters Ltd.* [1971] 1 W.L.R. 1445.

tion, because he has chosen England by reason of it being the defendant's domicile. It should be noted that Article 45 of the Convention prohibits the ordering of security for costs on the grounds of foreign nationality, domicile or residence in applications for enforcement of judgments.[65]

D. PROCEDURE FOR OBTAINING SECURITY FOR COSTS

1. Application for security for costs[66]

6.14 Before applying to the court for an order for security, a written request for reasonable security should first be made to the plaintiff. It may be that an undertaking by the plaintiff's solicitor in lieu of security for costs will be acceptable to the defendant.[67] If an acceptable sum of money by way of security is offered it may be paid in to court without an order being made.[68] If the matter cannot be agreed an application for an order for security for costs must be made to the court. The application may be made at any time but it is normal to postpone making it until after service of the defence.[69] It is made by ordinary summons (before the summons for directions), or on the hearing of the summons for directions, by notice under the summons for directions. There should be an affidavit in support, setting out the amount of security sought, specifying the stage up to which the security is sought, and exhibiting a skeleton bill of costs.[70]

2. The order for security for costs

6.15 The Rules of the Supreme Court provide that where an order is made requiring any party to give security for costs, the security should be given in such manner, at such time, and on such terms (if any) as the court shall direct.[71] The security generally takes the form of a sum of money deposited with the court, but sometimes the court will accept the guarantee of some credit-worthy third party[72] or a bond given with or without sureties.[73] The amount of

---

[65] See para. 28.85 below.
[66] See 13 *Court Forms* (1983 Issue), the Procedural Table p. 151. For applications for security to the Court of Appeal see 5 *Court Forms* (1984 Issue), p. 266, and R.S.C., Ord. 59, r. 10(5) and the notes thereto.
[67] See *Supreme Court Practice*, para. 23/1–3/24.
[68] See *Supreme Court Practice*, para. 23/1–3/25.
[69] *Stevens* v. *Walker* [1936] 2 K.B. 215.
[70] See *T. Sloyan & Sons (Builders) Ltd.* v. *Brothers of Christian Instruction* [1974] 3 All E.R. 715 (where the court complained of the absence of figures), and *Bennett* v. *Digby* [1982] 7 L.S.Gaz. 75: see the observations of Lawton L.J.
[71] R.S.C., Ord. 23, r. 2.
[72] *Supreme Court Practice*, para. 23/1–3/27.
[73] See, *e.g.*, *C. van der Lely N.V.* v. *Watveare Overseas Ltd.* [1982] F.S.R. 122.

the security is fixed by the master. This used to be a conventional amount of two thirds of the estimated party and party costs up to the stage to which security was ordered,[74] thereby taking into account the possibility that the action might be settled.[75] However the Court of Appeal has now disapproved of this "rule."[76] When the stage up to which security has been ordered is passed a further application for security may be made.[77] The order will normally direct that proceedings be stayed until security has been given. If security is then not given the proceedings may be dismissed.[78]

---

[74] See *Sir Lindsay Parkinson & Co. Ltd.* v. *Triplan Ltd.* [1973] Q.B. 609.
[75] See *Dominion Brewery Ltd.* v. *Foster* (1897) 77 L.T. 507.
[76] *Procon (Great Britain) Ltd.* v. *Provincial Building Co.* [1984] 1 W.L.R. 557.
[77] There is no rule that the court will not grant more than two applications for security: *Merton* v. *Times Publishing Co.* (1931) 48 T.L.R. 34.
[78] *La Grange* v. *McAndrew* (1879) 4 Q.B.D. 210.

CHAPTER 7

INTERIM RELIEF

A. INTRODUCTION

1. Scope of the chapter

7.01 This chapter examines the various forms of interim relief available in the English courts and the circumstances in which orders for interim relief may be made, either in aid of English proceedings or in aid of proceedings in other Contracting States.

English law in this field is evolving rapidly and the discussion in this chapter examines, in particular, the effects of the 1968 Convention and the 1982 Act, both on the jurisdiction of English courts to grant interim relief in proceedings involving international elements, and on the exercise of the court's discretion in granting such relief.

Interim relief in cases involving Scotland or Northern Ireland is also considered in this chapter.[1] The various types of relief available in the other Contracting States in aid of English proceedings are summarised in Chapters 48 to 55.[2] The enforcement in England

---

[1] See paras. 7.32 et seq. below.
[2] See chaps. 48 to 55 at paras. 58 et seq.

and Wales of provisional or protective measures ordered by the courts of other Contracting States is discussed in Chapter 10.[3]

2. Meaning of interim relief

The term "interim relief" is used in this chapter because it is more familiar to English practitioners than the term "provisional measures" which is used in the 1968 Convention. For practical purposes the two terms are synonymous and, together with the term "protective measures," they are used to describe the wide range of orders which courts may make in the course of proceedings with a view to achieving one or more of the following purposes pending trial:[4] **7.02**

(i) to restrain the conduct complained of in the proceedings;
(ii) to enforce an obligation sought to be enforced in the proceedings, including the making of an interim payment;
(iii) to prevent the disposal by the defendant of his assets so as to frustrate the enforcement of any judgment which might be obtained;
(iv) to preserve the subject-matter of the dispute;
(v) to dispose of the subject-matter of the dispute;
(vi) to preserve evidence;
(vii) to obtain the disclosure by one party to the other of documentary and other evidence;[5]
(viii) to obtain a report relating to the matters in dispute from an expert appointed by the court.[6]

Although provisional and protective measures are ordinarily granted pending trial they may also, in some instances, be granted pending an appeal or pending the execution of a judgment.[7]

Courts in each of the Contracting States have a variety of powers at their disposal for the purpose of achieving objectives of the kind listed above. In England, although the injunction has long been an effective remedy for the protection of a party's legal or equitable rights, it was not until the 1970's that the courts were prepared to grant protective measures in respect of the assets in the hands of the

---

[3] See para. 10.61 below.
[4] As to orders for security for costs see para. 7.27, n. 72 below.
[5] The extent to which procedures for the obtaining of evidence may properly be regarded as interim relief or provisional measures is discussed at para. 25.29 below, as is their non-availability in aid of proceedings in other Contracting States.
[6] See the preceding footnote.
[7] See the 1982 Act, s.24 (para. 43.01 below); the 1968 Convention, Arts. 24 and 39 (paras. 24.01 and 28.55 below); and Schlosser para. 221 (para. A1.521 below). See also the discussion of Mareva injunctions in aid of execution at para. 10.21 below.

defendant from which any judgment in the plaintiff's favour might need to be satisfied.[8] In this respect the English procedures have lagged far behind those available in continental systems.[9]

3. Effect of the 1968 Convention

7.03   There are two main respects in which the 1968 Convention extends the range of interim relief available to litigants in Contracting States. First, Article 24 enables an application for interim relief to be made in the courts of one Contracting State in a case in which, under the Convention, the courts of another Contracting State have jurisdiction as to the substance of the matter.[10] Secondly, the effect of the wide definition of "judgment" in Article 25 is that an order for interim relief made in one Contracting State is, in principle, enforceable in the other Contracting States (provided that it has been made in adversarial proceedings[11]). It follows that the Convention permits the English courts to grant interim relief in aid of proceedings contemplated or pending in the courts of another Contracting State.[12] It also obliges English courts to recognise and enforce provisional and protective measures granted by the courts of other Contracting States.[13]

Accordingly, if in the course of proceedings in the English courts it becomes necessary to obtain some form of interim relief to take effect in another Contracting State, a number of options may be open to the applicant. For example, he may be able to obtain from the English court an order requiring the other party to perform or to refrain from some act in the other Contracting State.[14] Such an order could only be directly enforced by the English court by some appropriate method of enforcement *in personam* in England and Wales. Alternatively the order of the English court could be taken to the courts of the other Contracting State for enforcement in that state in accordance with Title III of the Convention. As a further alternative, the applicant could go directly to the courts of the other Contracting State and, taking advantage of Article 24 of the Con-

---

[8] See para. 7.07 below (Mareva injunctions). As to the power of arrest in Admiralty proceedings see para. 7.22 below.

[9] Nonetheless the flexibility of injunctive relief led Professor Schlosser to remark on "the wide variety of provisional measures available in the law of Ireland and of the U.K.": para. 183 (para. A1.479 below).

[10] See chap. 24 below, especially at paras. 24.06 *et seq.*; also para. 25.25 below.

[11] See paras. 10.61, 25.25 and 27.27 below.

[12] The power to do so arises under s.25 of the 1982 Act; see paras. 7.26 and 43.03 below.

[13] Title III of the Convention; see para. 10.07 and chap. 20 below.

[14] See para. 7.23 below.

vention, apply for whatever form of relief against the other party may be available in that state.

Despite the apparent extent of the remedies which Article 24   **7.04** makes available to the litigant, it must be emphasised that it does not itself confer on the court any new power to grant interim relief nor does it create any new type of relief.[15] The 1982 Act, however, confers powers on United Kingdom courts to grant interim relief in the circumstances envisaged by Article 24, namely in those cases in which the main proceedings have been or are to be commenced either in the courts of another Contracting State[16] or, to a limited extent, in the courts of another part of the United Kingdom.[17]

Discretion. The limited extent to which English courts retain a discretion in deciding whether to accept or decline jurisdiction in a case to which the 1968 Convention applies has been discussed in Chapter 1.[18] Once the English court has accepted jurisdiction, whether under the 1968 Convention or (as is permissible in the context of Article 24)[19] under other English rules, it still retains a discretion as to how it will exercise that jurisdiction if the relief sought is itself discretionary. It remains to be seen how far the English courts will be encouraged by the Convention to extend the exercise of that discretion, especially in cases where the interim order may have extraterritorial effect. This question is discussed below.[20]

B. INTERIM RELIEF IN ENGLISH PROCEEDINGS

This section examines the various forms of interim relief available   **7.05** in aid of proceedings before the English courts, including the extent to which the court may be prepared or able to make orders which are intended to take effect outside the jurisdiction. Most of the principal types of interim relief are set out in Order 29 of the Rules of the Supreme Court.

---

[15] See Jenard Report, para. A1.185 below; see also para. 24.03 below.
[16] See para. 7.26 below. This power may also be exercised in relation to proceedings in non-Contracting States, or which fall outside the scope of the Convention, or to arbitration proceedings if so provided by Order in Council, see 1982 Act ss.25(3) (para. 43.03 below) and 27(3) (Scotland). No such Order in Council has yet been made.
[17] See para. 7.32 below.
[18] Para. 1.37 above.
[19] Para. 24.01 below.
[20] Para. 7.23 below.

1. Interlocutory injunctions (generally)

An injunction is an order of the court requiring a party to do, or to refrain from doing, some particular act.[21] Section 37(1) of the Supreme Court Act 1981 provides that:

> "The High Court may by order (whether interlocutory or final) grant an injunction or appoint a receiver[22] in all cases in which it appears to the court to be just and convenient to do so."

It should be observed that the section makes no distinction between an interlocutory and a final, or perpetual, injunction. The court's powers to grant either are the same.[23] In most cases in which a final injunction is being sought there will have been an application for an interlocutory injunction pending the trial of the action. Indeed the jurisdiction of the court to grant an interlocutory injunction depends, in most cases,[24] upon the existence of a claim over which the court has jurisdiction.[25] The court grants an interlocutory injunction to mitigate the risk of injustice to the plaintiff during the period before the merits of the dispute can be resolved, without itself closely investigating those merits. In practice, however, the decision reached may often determine the issue between the parties, either because the matters giving rise to the dispute are transitory, or because neither side can afford to wait for a final decision and accordingly they accept the view of the court or settle the case on some similar basis.[26]

---

[21] The remedy of an injunction originates from the inherent equitable jurisdiction of the Court of Chancery, and the Court of Exchequer, to protect the rights of the parties, and was made available to the courts of common law by the Common Law Procedure Act 1854. By the Judicature Act 1873, s.16, the power to grant injunctions was vested in every branch of the High Court; see Spry, *Equitable Remedies* (3rd ed.) p. 317; *The North London Railway Co.* v. *The Great Northern Railway Co.* (1883) 11 Q.B.D. 30.

[22] For the appointment of receivers, see para. 7.16 below.

[23] Note that by s.12(6) of the Arbitration Act 1950 the High Court has the same power to grant interim relief in relation to an arbitration as in High Court proceedings; see, generally, Mustill & Boyd: *Commercial Arbitration* (2nd ed.) pp. 328 *et seq.* Arbitration is outside the scope of this work.

[24] See *The Siskina* [1979] A.C. 210, *The Steamship Mutual Underwriting Association (Bermuda) Ltd.* v. *Thakur Shipping Co. Ltd.* [1986] 2 Lloyd's Rep. 439, *Siporex Trading* v. *Comdel Commodities* [1986] 2 Lloyd's Rep. 428. The excepted cases are those arising under ss.24, 25 and 27 of the 1982 Act: see paras. 7.26 *et seq.* below.

[25] *Siskina (Cargo owners)* v. *Distos Cia Naviera S.A. (The Siskina)* [1979] A.C. 210; *Bremer Vulkan Schiffbau und Maschinenfabrik* v. *South India Shipping Corp. Ltd.* [1981] A.C. 909; *Lonrho Ltd.* v. *Shell Petroleum Ltd. (No. 2)* [1982] A.C. 173; *Associated Newspapers Group P.L.C.* v. *Insert Media Ltd.* [1988] 1 W.L.R. 509.

[26] *Fellows and Sons* v. *Fisher* [1976] Q.B. 122, at p. 129, *per* Lord Denning M.R.

An application for an injunction may be made at any time before **7.06** or after trial and whether or not an injunction has been claimed in the party's originating process or pleadings.[27] In urgent cases the application may be made before any proceedings have been commenced.[28] Initially an interlocutory injunction may be granted on an interim basis. Where the application has been made *ex parte* it will ordinarily be granted to take effect only until there can be an *inter partes* hearing. The principles upon which the discretion of the court is exercised were laid down by the House of Lords in *American Cyanamid Co. v. Ethicon Ltd.*[29] The court will normally grant an injunction to preserve the original *status quo* between the parties in any situation in which there is a serious question to be tried, where damages will not adequately compensate the plaintiff for the alleged infringement of his rights, and where the balance of convenience, or the "balance of justice,"[30] supports the granting of an injunction. The order may be made either unconditionally or on such terms and conditions as the court thinks just.[31] The plaintiff will usually be required to give an undertaking to pay damages to the defendant for any loss sustained by reason of the injunction should it be held at the trial that the injunction was wrongly granted. A plaintiff who is outside the jurisdiction may be ordered to bring a sum of money into court, or to provide other security, to fortify the undertaking.[32] The defendant may consent to being bound in the manner sought by the plaintiff and may be prepared to enter into an undertaking to be so bound. This has the same effect as an injunction[33] and the plaintiff may be ordered to give a cross-undertaking as to damages. Regardless of whether an interlocutory

---

[27] R.S.C., Ord. 29, r. 1; *Practice Direction (Judge in Chambers: Procedure)* [1983] 1 W.L.R. 433, which specifies the documents to be lodged and the matters to be contained in the affidavit.

[28] R.S.C., Ord. 29, r. 1(3). The plaintiff will have to give an undertaking to issue a writ as soon as practicable. In *Allen v. Jambo Holdings Ltd.* [1980] 1 W.L.R. 1252, the initial injunction was granted by Drake J. on the telephone.

[29] [1975] A.C. 396; see also *Garden Cottage Foods Ltd. v. Milk Marketing Board* [1984] 1 A.C. 130.

[30] *per* Sir John Donaldson M.R. in *Francombe v. Mirror Group Newspapers Ltd.* [1984] 1 W.L.R. 892. See also *Birmingham Corporation v. Perry Barr Stadium Ltd.* [1972] 1 All E.R. 725; *Hubbard v. Vosper* [1972] Q.B. 84.

[31] s.37(2) Supreme Court Act 1981. The Court of Appeal should not substitute its own discretion for that of the judge: *Hadmor Productions Ltd. v. Hamilton* [1983] A.C. 191.

[32] *Harman Pictures N.V. v. Osborne* [1967] 1 W.L.R. 723, *Vapormatic Co. Ltd. v. Sparex Ltd.* [1976] 1 W.L.R. 939.

[33] Provided that it is embodied in the written order of the court, see *Millburn v. Newton Colliery Ltd.* (1908) 52 S.J. 317; *Biba Ltd. v. Stratford Investments Ltd.* [1973] Ch. 281.

injunction is granted, the judge may consider that the early trial of the action should be ordered.[34]

The county court has jurisdiction to grant an injunction, whether interlocutory or final, but only if it is ancillary to a claim for money or other relief within the substantive jurisdiction of the court.[35]

2. Mareva injunctions[36]

7.07   An interlocutory injunction will be granted to prevent the defendant from removing his assets from the jurisdiction, or from otherwise disposing of or dealing with them within the jurisdiction so as to frustrate the enforcement of any judgment obtained in due course. This type of relief is of particular importance in international litigation where the risk of a defendant removing his assets from the jurisdiction is much increased. It is remarkable that it was not until 1975 that the power of the court to grant injunctions of this kind was first defined and used, in the cases of *Nippon Yusen Kaisha* v. *Karageorgis*[37] and of *Mareva Compania Naviera S.A.* v. *International Bulkcarriers S.A.*[38] It had formerly been settled law that a creditor could do nothing until judgment to prevent the debtor from dealing with his assets as he wished.[39] Initially Mareva injunctions were used to prevent foreign defendants from removing their assets from the jurisdiction but from 1980 they were extended to defendants residing within the jurisdiction.[40] The remedy has not been restricted to commercial cases but has been used in the fields of intellectual property,[41] personal injuries,[42] nuisance[43] and

---

[34] R.S.C., Ord. 29, r. 5. See *Practice Direction* [1981] 1 W.L.R. 1296, para. 8(a) and (b).
[35] County Courts Act 1984, s.38. C.C.R., Ord. 13, r. 6; Ord. 29, r. 1 and see *R.* v. *Cheshire County Court Judge and National Society of Boilermakers, ex p. Malone* [1921] 2 K.B. 694. The county court has no power to award interim relief in aid of foreign proceedings, see s.25 of the 1982 Act; para. 43.03 below.
[36] See generally the *Supreme Court Practice* para. 29/1/20; Hoyle, *The Mareva Injunction and Related Orders* (1985); Goldrein and Wilkinson: *Commercial Litigation, Pre-emptive Remedies* (1987). Gee and Andrews: *Mareva Injunctions* (1987).
[37] [1975] 1 W.L.R. 1093.
[38] [1975] 2 Lloyd's Rep. 509.
[39] *Mills* v. *Northern Railway of Buenos Aires Co.* (1870) L.R. 5 Ch.App. 621; *Lister & Co.* v. *Stubbs* (1890) 45 Ch.D. 1.
[40] *Barclay-Johnson* v. *Yuill* [1980] 3 All E.R. 190; *Prince Abdul Rahman Bin Turki Al Sudiary* v. *Abu-Taha* [1980] 3 All E.R. 409.
[41] *House of Spring Gardens Ltd.* v. *Waite* [1985] F.S.R. 173.
[42] *Allen* v. *Jambo Holdings Ltd.* [1980] 1 W.L.R. 1252.
[43] *Dellborg* v. *Corix Properties* (1980) (unreported) Court of Appeal Transcripts No. 541.

matrimonial causes,[44] in aid of arbitration,[45] in aid of execution[46] and to restrain the disposal of suspected proceeds of crime.[47] The power of the court to grant a Mareva injunction received statutory recognition in section 37(3) of the Supreme Court Act 1981 which provides that:

> "The power of the court under subsection (1) to grant an interlocutory injunction restraining a party to any proceedings from removing from the jurisdiction of the High Court, or otherwise dealing with,[48] assets located within that jurisdiction shall be exercisable in cases where that party is, as well as in cases where he is not, domiciled resident or present within that jurisdiction."[49]

Application for a Mareva injunction. In order to preserve the   **7.08** element of surprise the initial application for a Mareva injunction is usually made *ex parte*.[50] In a particularly urgent case it may be made before the issue of the writ, on the plaintiff's undertaking to issue the writ. If the case is one in which leave to serve the writ out of the jurisdiction is required the appropriate leave must also be obtained.[51] The plaintiff must show that he has a good arguable case[52] and that there is a probability that, if the injunction is not granted, execution of the ultimate judgment will be frustrated.[53] The assets to be the subject of the order may be tangible or intang-

---

[44] *Emanuel* v. *Emanuel* [1982] 1 W.L.R. 669; *K.* v. *K.* (1982) 13 Fam. Law 46.

[45] See Arbitration Act 1950, s.12(6)(*h*), Mustill and Boyd, *Commercial Arbitration* (2nd ed.), p. 341.

[46] *Orwell Steel (Erection and Fabrication Ltd.)* v. *Asphalt and Tarmac (U.K.) Ltd.* [1984] 1 W.L.R. 1097, *Hill Samuel & Co. Ltd.* v. *Littaur* (1985) 135 NLJ 556, *Babanaft International Co. S.A.* v. *Bassatne*; [1989] 2 W.L.R. 232 and see para. 10.21 below.

[47] *Chief Constable of Kent* v. *V.* [1983] Q.B. 34; but see *Chief Constable of Hampshire* v. *A.* [1985] Q.B. 132. The court also has power to make restraint and charging orders under the Drug Trafficking Offences Act 1986.

[48] In *Z Ltd.* v. *A-Z and AA-LL* [1982] Q.B. 558 it was held that the words "otherwise dealing with" were not restricted to the removal of assets from the jurisdiction.

[49] The section is declaratory of the court's inherent jurisdiction: *C.B.S. United Kingdom Ltd.* v. *Lambert* [1983] Ch. 37. For an example of a Mareva injunction granted by a county court see *Naz* v. *Kaleem* [1980] C.L.Y. 409.

[50] In the Queen's Bench Division it is made to the judge in chambers and in the Chancery Division it is made on motion to the judge: *Supreme Court Practice*, para. 29/1/7; see *Practice Direction (Judge in Chambers; Procedure)* [1983] 1 W.L.R. 433, which specifies the documents to be lodged and the matters to be contained in the affidavit.

[51] See para. 3.27 above.

[52] *Intraco Ltd.* v. *Notis Shipping Corporation of Liberia* [1981] 2 Lloyd's Rep. 256; *Third Chandris Shipping Corporation* v. *Unimarine S.A.* [1979] 1 Q.B. 645; *Cybil Inc. of Panama* v. *Tinpuship* (unreported) August 4, 1978 (C.A.), "reasonable evidence of future assets may be sufficient"; *Nimemia Maritime Corporation* v. *Trave Schiffahrtsgesellschaft m.b.H. und Co. K.G.* [1983] 1 W.L.R. 1412.

[53] *Third Chandris Shipping Corporation* v. *Unimarine S.A.* [1979] 1 Q.B. 645.

ible and it was previously thought that they must be in the jurisdiction.[54] They should be identified to the court as precisely as possible.[55] If it is sought to freeze a bank account, the branch of the bank and, if possible, the number of the account should be identified.[56] The plaintiff must make full and frank disclosure of all matters within his knowledge that might affect the granting of the injunction.[57] If it is discovered that the applicant has not been frank with the court the injunction will normally be discharged.[58] The plaintiff will be required to give an undertaking in damages and further terms may be imposed to avoid or minimise the prejudice to the defendant or third parties.[59]

7.09 *The order and its effect.* The injunction is normally granted *ex parte* in the first instance for a short interim period pending an *inter partes* hearing.[60] However the practice of expressing the duration of the order as being "until judgment or further order" has the advantage to the plaintiff of putting the onus on the defendant to apply to the court for the variation or discharge of the order. The order will usually be expressed to apply to the assets in question up to a speci-

---

[54] *Intraco Ltd.* v. *Notis Shipping Corporation of Liberia* [1981] 2 Lloyd's Rep. 256. It is now clear that in an appropriate case an order may be made relating to assets outside the jurisdiction either at an interlocutory stage (*Republic of Haiti* v. *Duvalier* [1989] 2 W.L.R. 261; *Derby & Co. Ltd.* v. *Weldon* [1989] 2 W.L.R. 276; *Derby & Co. Ltd.* v. *Weldon (Nos. 3 & 4)* [1989] 2 W.L.R. 412) or in aid of execution (*Babanaft International Co. S.A.* v. *Bassatne* [1989] 2 W.L.R. 232) although the cases in which such an order is appropriate may be rare. See para. 7.24 below as to the disclosure of assets outside the jurisdiction and the extraterritorial effect of interim orders generally.

[55] Where they cannot be identified it is sufficient that there are grounds for believing that there are assets in the jurisdiction: *Third Chandris Shipping Corporation* v. *Unimarine S.A.* [1979] 1 Q.B. 645.

[56] *Z Ltd.* v. *A-Z and AA-LL* [1982] Q.B. 558; *SCF Finance Co.* v. *Masri* [1985] 1 W.L.R. 876 (order freezing a *joint* bank account).

[57] *Third Chandris Shipping Corporation* v. *Unimarine S.A.* [1979] 1 Q.B. 645; see also *R.* v. *Kensington Income Tax Commissioners* [1917] 1 K.B. 486.

[58] *Negocios del Mar S.A.* v. *Doric Shipping Corporation S.A.* [1979] 1 Lloyd's Rep. 331; *Bank Mellat* v. *Nikpour* [1982] Com L.R. 158; *Yardley* v. *Higson* [1984] F.S.R. 304; *Lloyd's Bowmakers Ltd.* v. *Arrow Holdings Plc* [1988] 1 W.L.R. 1337 (C.A.); but *cf. Brink's-Mat* v. *Elcombe* (1987) [1988] 1 W.L.R. 1350; *Dormeuil Frères S.A.* v. *Nicolian International (Textiles) Ltd.* [1988] 1 W.L.R. 1362.

[59] *Searose Ltd.* v. *Seatrain U.K. Ltd.* [1981] 1 W.L.R. 894; *Clipper Marine Co. Ltd. of Monrovia* v. *Mineralimportexport* [1981] 1 W.L.R. 1262. This applies even if the plaintiff is legally aided when the value of such an undertaking is negligible: see *Allen* v. *Jambo Holdings Ltd.* [1980] 1 W.L.R. 1252; *Z Ltd.* v. *A-Z and AA-LL* [1982] Q.B. 558.

[60] See the observations of Kerr L.J. in support of this practice in *Z Ltd.* v. *A-Z and AA-LL* [1982] Q.B. 558. If it is intended to seek enforcement of the order under the 1968 Convention in another Contracting State there must have been an *inter partes hearing*, see paras. 7.29 and 24.09 below.

fied maximum amount. In the case of funds in a bank account there is sometimes provision for drawings of an appropriate weekly amount for living expenses.[61] The order takes effect from the moment it is pronounced. It operates on the defendant *in personam*[62] and it is capable of binding assets which are acquired subsequently to the date of the order.[63] Any person with knowledge of the order, who does any act which assists in the disposal of the assets is guilty of contempt.[64] The plaintiff will usually be required to give an undertaking to notify the defendant and any affected third party of the terms of the injunction and to inform third parties of their right to apply to the court for a variation or for directions. A bank with notice of the order will be bound by it and may have to refuse to act on its client's instructions.[65] The order does not give the plaintiff priority over other creditors but any disposal of the assets in question will have to be the subject of an application to the court for a variation of the order.[66]

Orders in aid of a Mareva injunction. Apart from the primary **7.10** order against the defendant restraining him from disposing of or otherwise dealing with the assets affected, the court may make such subsidiary orders as may be necessary to secure the effectiveness of the injunction. He may be ordered to identify his assets[67] or to dis-

[61] *P.C.W. (Underwriting Agencies) Ltd.* v. *Dixon* [1983] 2 All E.R. 158 and 697 (C.A.); *House of Spring Gardens Ltd.* v. *Waite* [1985] F.S.R. 173.
[62] *Cretanor Maritime Co. Ltd.* v. *Irish Marine Management Ltd.* [1978] 1 W.L.R. 966; *Ashtiani* v. *Kashi* [1986] Q.B. 888, at p. 404, *per* Neill L.J. A Mareva injunction nevertheless has certain effects *in rem*: *Z Ltd.* v. *A-Z and AA-LL*, above, at p. 573, *per* Lord Denning M.R. and *Babanaft International S.A.* v. *Bassatne* [1989] 2 W.L.R. 232, 249, *per* Kerr L.J.
[63] *T.D.K. Tape Distributors (U.K.) Ltd.* v. *Videochoice Ltd.* [1986] 1 W.L.R. 141.
[64] See para. 7.25 below. But if such persons are outside the jurisdiction, they may be protected by a proviso to the order: *Babanaft International S.A.* v. *Bassatne*, above; *Republic of Haiti* v. *Duvalier* [1989] 2 W.L.R. 261; *Derby & Co. Ltd.* v. *Weldon* [1989] 2 W.L.R. 276; *Derby & Co. Ltd.* v. *Weldon (Nos. 3 & 4)* [1989] 2 W.L.R. 412; see paras. 7.23 and 7.24 below.
[65] *Z Ltd.* v. *A-Z and AA-LL* [1982] Q.B. 558, where the Court of Appeal gave detailed consideration to the position of banks in relation to *Mareva* injunctions. See also *The Theotokos* [1983] 2 All E.R. 65 and *Babanaft International S.A.* v. *Bassatne*, above, *per* Kerr L.J.
[66] *Cretanor Maritime Co. Ltd.* v. *Irish Marine Management Ltd.* [1978] 1 W.L.R. 966; *Iraqi Ministry of Defence* v. *Arcepey Shipping Co. S.A.* [1981] Q.B. 65. The difficulty that the order may have the effect of giving security in a foreign jurisdiction should be obviated by suitable undertakings, *Derby & Co. Ltd.* v. *Weldon*, above.
[67] *R.C.A. Corporation* v. *Reddingtons Rare Records* [1974] 1 W.L.R. 1445; *A and another* v. *C and others* [1981] 1 Q.B. 956; *A. J. Bekhor & Co. Ltd.* v. *Bilton* [1981] 1 Q.B. 923; *C.B.S. United Kingdom Ltd.* v. *Lambert and another* [1983] 1 Ch. 37; *House of Spring Gardens Ltd.* v. *Waite* [1985] F.S.R. 173; *Interpool* v. *Galani* [1987] 3 W.L.R. 1042; *Maclaine Watson & Co. Ltd.* v. *International Tin*

close their whereabouts, or to deliver them up.[68] A tracing order[69] may be made, or an Anton Piller order.[70] He may even be restrained from leaving the jurisdiction.[71]

7.11   *Application for discharge or variation.* The defendant may apply to the court for the discharge of the injunction on the ground that it was not properly obtained or for its variation if, for example, its effect is unduly oppressive or if it restricts his legitimate business activities.[72] If the defendant seeks the variation of the order so that he can discharge other liabilities, he may be required to give information as to any other assets which may be available for this purpose,[73] both within and outside the jurisdiction.[74] If the defendant can provide security which is acceptable to the plaintiff the order may be discharged by consent. Any person who has a better claim than the defendant to the assets in question may apply for the discharge of the order,[75] as may any person whose business rights are substantially interfered with by the order.[76] On the discharge of the order, the defendant may apply for an enquiry as to damages, pur-

---

Council (No. 2) [1988] 3 W.L.R. 1190 (C.A.). The defendant will not normally be ordered *ex parte* to disclose assets outside the jurisdiction (except in the case of a proprietory claim or a tracing action): see *Ashtiani* v. *Kashi* [1987] Q.B. 888, *Reilly* v. *Fryer* [1988] 2 F.T.L.R. 69 (C.A.); *cf. Republic of Haiti* v. *Duvalier (No. 1), The Independent,* June 13, 1988 (C.A.). A disclosure order will however normally be granted in respect of assets outside the jurisdiction if the Mareva injunction extends to those assets, although the use of disclosed information may be limited by proviso or undertaking: *Derby & Co. Ltd.* v. *Weldon,* above; *Derby & Co. Ltd.* v. *Weldon (Nos. 3 & 4),* above. See also para. 7.24 below.

[68] *C.B.S. United Kingdom Ltd.* v. *Lambert and another* [1983] 1 Ch. 37, where guidelines for this type of order were laid down; *Republic of Haiti* v. *Duvalier (No. 1), The Independent,* June 13, 1988.

[69] *Mediteranea Raffineria Siciliana Petroli SpA* v. *Mabanaft GmbH*; *Bankers Trust Co.* v. *Shapira and others* [1980] 1 W.L.R. 1274; *Chase Manhatten Bank NA* v. *Israel-British Bank (London) Ltd.* [1981] Ch. 105. A tracing order may be appropriate where the defendant has received moneys belonging or due to the plaintiff in breach of a fiduciary duty.

[70] *A. J. Bekhor & Co. Ltd.* v. *Bilton* [1981] 1 Q.B. 923.

[71] *Bayer A.G.* v. *Winter* [1986] 1 W.L.R. 497, *Re Oriental Credit Ltd.* [1988] 2 W.L.R. 172. Compare the writ *ne exeat regno*, para. 7.19 below.

[72] *Iraqi Ministry of Defence* v. *Arcepey Shipping Co. S.A.* [1981] Q.B. 65; *Avant Petroleum Inc.* v. *Gatoil Overseas Inc.* [1986] 2 Lloyd's Rep. 236; *Siporex Trading* v. *Comdel Commodities* [1986] 2 Lloyd's Rep. 428. The operation of the discharge may be stayed pending appeal.

[73] *A.J. Bekhor & Co. Ltd.* v. *Bilton* [1981] 1 Q.B. 923.

[74] *Ashtiani* v. *Kashi* [1987] Q.B. 888 at p. 905.

[75] *Cretanor Maritime Co. Ltd.* v. *Irish Marine Management Ltd.* [1978] 1 W.L.R. 966; *cf. Felixstowe Dock and Railway Co.* v. *United States Lines Inc.* [1987] 2 Lloyd's Rep. 76.

[76] *Galaxia Maritime S.A.* v. *Mineralimportexport* [1982] 1 W.L.R. 539.

suant to the undertaking given by the plaintiff on the grant of the order.[77]

3. Anton Piller orders

An Anton Piller[78] order is a form of mandatory injunction[79] **7.12** which requires the defendant to permit the plaintiff's representatives to enter the defendant's property to search for and seize certain documents and property, so that they may be preserved until the trial. The power to make such orders exists under the inherent jurisdiction of the court to order the detention and preservation of the subject-matter of the proceedings and of any related documents.[80] The relief is mainly sought in cases in which intellectual property rights are alleged to have been infringed but it is not restricted to such cases.[81]

The criteria for the granting of this type of relief were laid down by the Court of Appeal in *Anton Piller KG* v. *Manufacturing Processes Ltd.*[82] The applicant must have a very strong prima facie case. The potential or actual damage to his interests must be very serious. There must be clear evidence that the defendant has in his possession incriminating documents or objects, and that there is a real possibility that he may dispose of or destroy them before any application *inter partes* can be made.[83] If there is evidence that the defendant has been engaging in "nefarious activity" or has acted dishonestly the risk of disposal or destruction may be inferred.[84] The order can only be made against a person against whom the plaintiff has a cause of action.[85]

---

[77] See para. 7.25 below.

[78] *Anton Piller KG* v. *Manufacturing Processes Ltd.* [1976] Ch. 55. See generally the *Supreme Court Practice* para. 29/2–3/6; Hoyle, *The Mareva Injunction and Related Orders* (1985); Goldrein and Wilkinson, *Commercial Litigation, Pre-emptive Remedies* (1987), pp. 201 *et seq.*

[79] *E.M.I.* v. *Pandit* [1975] 1 W.L.R. 302, *per* Templeman J.

[80] This power has been held to extend to the preservation of evidential documents not themselves forming the subject-matter of the proceedings: *Yousif* v. *Salama* [1980] 1 W.L.R. 1540. It exists independently of R.S.C., Ord. 29, r. 2(2).

[81] See, *e.g.*, *Yousif* v. *Salama* [1980] 1 W.L.R. 1540 (claim for commission under an agency agreement); *Emanuel* v. *Emanuel* [1982] 1 W.L.R. 669, (claim for ancillary relief in divorce proceedings); *Distributori Automatici Italia SpA* v. *Holford General Trading Co. Ltd.* [1985] 1 W.L.R. 1066 (in aid of execution).

[82] [1976] Ch. 55.

[83] See *Dunlop Holdings Ltd.* v. *Staravia Ltd.* [1982] Com.L.R. 3, *per* Oliver L.J.; *Yousif* v. *Salama* [1980] 1 W.L.R. 1540.

[84] *A.B.* v. *C.D.E.* [1982] R.P.C. 509.

[85] See para. 7.05 above.

7.13   *Application for an Anton Piller order.* As with the Mareva injunction, the element of surprise is essential and the application is made *ex parte.*[86] The application must be supported by appropriate affidavit evidence. Full and frank disclosure must be made of all matters which might affect the granting of the order or it will be discharged.[87] The plaintiff will be required to give a cross-undertaking in damages and there should be evidence that he is good for the damages.[88] A plaintiff who is outside the jurisdiction may be ordered to bring a sum of money into court to fortify the undertaking.[89] He may also be required to undertake not to allow any person to have access to the documents without the leave of the court.[90]

7.14   *The order and its effect.*[91] The order should identify the premises to be searched[92] and the persons authorised to carry out the search.[93] It should be served by or in the presence of a qualified solicitor who must supervise the search as an officer of the court.[94] The order should be read to the defendant or to the person in charge of the premises in question and its effect should be explained to him. A copy of the evidence given in support of the application should also be served with the order,[95] and the defendant or the recipient should be informed of his right to consult his solicitor before complying with the order.[96] The order does not entitle the plaintiff to enter the premises by means of force. The sanction for disobedience is that the plaintiff may move to commit the defend-

---

[86] In the Queen's Bench Division it is made to the judge in chambers and in the Chancery Division it is made on motion to the judge: *Supreme Court Practice*, para. 29/1/7; see *Practice Direction (Judge in Chambers; Procedure)* [1983] 1 W.L.R. 433, which specifies the documents to be lodged and the matters to be contained in the affidavit. As to the hearing of appeals *in camera*, see *Practice Note (Court of Appeal: Anton Piller Orders)* [1982] 1 W.L.R. 1420, (C.A.)

[87] *Thermax v. Schott Industrial Glass* [1981] F.S.R. 289; *Digital Equipment Corporation v. Darkcrest Ltd.* [1984] Ch. 512; *cf. Gallery Cosmetics Ltd. v. Number 1* [1981] F.S.R. 556; *Dormeuil Frères S.A. v. Nicolian International (Textiles) Ltd.* [1988] 1 W.L.R. 1362.

[88] *Vapormatic Co. Ltd. v. Sparex Ltd.* [1976] 1 W.L.R. 939; *Columbia Picture Industries Inc. v. Robinson* [1986] 3 W.L.R. 542.

[89] *Harman Pictures N.V. v. Osborne* [1967] 1 W.L.R. 723.

[90] *Customs and Excise Commissioners v. A. E. Hamlin & Co.* [1984] 1 W.L.R. 509; *cf. E.M.I. Records Ltd. v. Spillane* [1986] 1 W.L.R. 967.

[91] See *Pall Europe Ltd. v. Microfiltrex Ltd.* [1976] R.P.C. 326; *E.M.I. Ltd. v. Pandit* [1976] R.P.C. 333.

[92] *Protector Alarms v. Maxim Alarms Ltd.* [1978] F.S.R. 442.

[93] *Vapormatic Co. Ltd. v. Sparex Ltd.* [1976] 1 W.L.R.939.

[94] *Universal City Studios Inc. v. Mukhtar & Sons Ltd.* [1976] 2 All E.R. 330. Sometimes the order allows this role to be performed by a fellow of the Institute of Legal Executives.

[95] *International Electronics Ltd. v. Weigh Data Ltd.* [1980] F.S.R. 423.

[96] *A.B. v. C.D.E.* [1982] R.P.C. 509.

ant for contempt.[97] There may be appropriate supplementary
orders to ensure the effectiveness of the primary order, for
example, requiring the defendant to disclose the names and
addresses of his suppliers and customers,[98] or restraining him from
communicating the terms of the order to a third party, other than
for the purpose of obtaining legal advice.

Application to discharge the order. The order requires immediate
compliance, subject to allowing the defendant sufficient time to
take legal advice. The defendant can apply to the court for the order
to be discharged but he runs the risk of being held to have been in
contempt for his refusal if his application fails.[99] Save in respect of
certain proceedings concerning intellectual property rights and
passing off,[1] a person may refuse to answer questions or disclose
documents on the ground of privilege against self-incrimination.[2]
As with any other injunction given upon the plaintiff's undertaking
in damages, the defendant may apply on its discharge for an
enquiry as to damages.[3]

7.15

4. The appointment of a receiver

The appointment of a receiver as a form of interim relief is to be
distinguished from an appointment of a receiver by way of
execution of a judgment.[4] The power to appoint a receiver derives
from section 37 of the Supreme Court Act 1981, and it may be exercised whenever the court considers it to be "just and convenient" to
do so.[4a] The type of case in which the appointment of a receiver by
the court is most appropriate is where the court considers that disputed property is at risk and should be kept out of the possession of
both parties until the issues between them have been resolved, as,

7.16

---

[97] *W.E.A. Records* v. *Visions Channel 4* [1983] 1 W.L.R. 721; see para. 7.25 below.
[98] *Norwich Pharmacal Co.* v. *Commissioners of Customs and Excise* [1974] A.C. 133; *E.M.I. Ltd.* v. *Sarwar* [1977] F.S.R. 146; but such an order should not be made on an *ex parte* application: *Wilmot Breedon Ltd.* v. *Visions Channel 4 Ltd.* [1981] F.S.R. 115.
[99] *W.E.A. Records Ltd.* v. *Visions Channel 4 Ltd.* [1983] 1 W.L.R. 721; *Hallmark Cards Inc.* v. *Image Artists Ltd.* [1977] F.S.R. 150.
[1] Supreme Court Act 1981, s.72.
[2] *Rank Film Distributors Ltd.* v. *Video Information Centre* [1982] A.C. 380; *Universal City Studios Inc.* v. *Hubbard* [1984] Ch. 225, C.A.; *Charles of the Ritz Group* v. *Jory* [1986] F.S.R. 14.
[3] See para. 7.25 below.
[4] See R.S.C., Ord. 30 (receivers in general), Ord. 51 (receivers by way of equit-able execution), Kerr, *Receivers* (16th ed., 1983), and Picarda, *Receivers and Managers* (1984).
[4a] In *Derby & Co. Ltd.* v. *Weldon (Nos. 3 & 4)* [1989] 2 W.L.R. 412, a receiver was appointed over assets situated outside the jurisdiction: see para. 7.24 below.

for example, in a partnership action. Application is made by summons or motion.[5]

5. Orders for the preservation, inspection or delivery up of property

7.17   The High Court has extensive statutory powers,[6] in addition to its inherent power, to make orders relating to physical property[7] which is the subject-matter of the dispute or in relation to which any question may arise in the proceedings. It may make an order for the detention, custody, preservation or inspection of any such property[8] and it may order the taking of samples[9] and the conducting of observations and experiments.[10] Orders relating to these matters may be made before the proceedings have commenced[11] or while they are in progress,[12] and they may be directed at non-parties[13] as well as at parties. The court may authorise any person to enter upon any land or building in the possession of a party to enable the order to be carried out.[14] It may order the delivery up of goods under section 4 of the Torts (Interference with Goods) Act 1977.[15] In a dispute concerning a specific fund the court may order the fund to be paid into court or otherwise secured.[16] In a dispute which concerns any property (other than land), the early sale of which would be desirable (usually because it is perishable), the court may order a sale in such manner as it considers appropriate.[17] The court also has power to order the recovery of property which the defendant claims to be entitled to retain because it is subject to a lien or it constitutes security for a claim, provided a sum in respect of the claim, with

---

[5] See *Supreme Court Practice*, paras. 30/1/5 and 30/1/6.
[6] See Supreme Court Act, ss.33 and 34; R.S.C., Ord. 29.
[7] It will not, under Ord. 29, order the inspection of a manufacturing and packaging process: *Tudor Accumulator Co. Ltd.* v. *China Mutual Steam Navigation Co. Ltd.* [1930] W.N. 200; but in patent actions see R.S.C., Ord. 104, r. 10(2)(g). Documents may be "property," see *Re Saxton (dec'd)* [1962] 1 W.L.R. 859.
[8] R.S.C., Ord. 29, r. 2(1); where an order for the custody of property is made it is usually entrusted to a third person, such as a bank.
[9] R.S.C., Ord. 29, r. 3.
[10] R.S.C., Ord. 29, r. 3.
[11] Supreme Court Act 1981, s.33(1), R.S.C., Ord. 29, r. 7A(1).
[12] R.S.C., Ord. 29, rr. 2–4.
[13] The power can only be exercised against non-parties when the proceedings are in respect of personal injury or death; see Supreme Court Act 1981, s.34(3), R.S.C., Ord. 29, r. 7A(2).
[14] R.S.C., Ord. 29, rr. 2(2) & 3(2).
[15] R.S.C., Ord. 29, r. 2A. In a proper case it may order the defendant to allow the plaintiff to collect his property, see *Howard E. Perry & Co. Ltd.* v. *British Railways Board* [1980] 1 W.L.R. 1375.
[16] R.S.C., Ord. 29, r. 2(3).
[17] R.S.C., Ord. 29, r. 4.

costs and interest, is brought into court.[18] Application for any of
the above orders is made to the master by a summons supported
by an affidavit, in accordance with the particular rule relied upon.
Unless the court otherwise directs, an application by a defendant
may only be made after he has returned the acknowledgment of
service.[19]

6. Orders for the interim payment of money

The High Court has a general power to order a party to proceed- **7.18**
ings to make an interim payment to another party or to the court on
account of any damages, debt or other sum (other than costs),
claimed in the proceedings.[20] The Rules of the Supreme Court lay
down the procedure to be followed and the criteria to be applied by
the court. The amount ordered will be such sum as appears to the
court to be just, not exceeding a reasonable proportion of the probable amount of any final judgment.[21] At the conclusion of the proceedings any necessary adjustments in the amount due to (or from)
the defendant will be made. An application for an interim payment
is often combined with an application for summary judgment.[22]

7. Arrest of debtors and writs *ne exeat regno*

The arrest of debtors was an ancient practice which had been **7.19**
severely curtailed by the latter part of the nineteenth century, but
which still survives in a limited form.[23] At common law, the power
of arrest was confined to those cases falling within section 6 of the
Debtors Act 1869. Equity had been willing to follow the common
law in giving effect to that power of arrest by a limited use of the
ancient writ *ne exeat regno*, in respect of equitable claims. Strictly,
the powers under the Debtors Act and in equity are separate, and
each may only be exercised where the other does not apply,
although since the fusion of the courts of common law and equity in
1875 they have both been exercised by the High Court.

Under section 6 of the Debtors Act 1869, a judge of the High
Court may order that a defendant be arrested and imprisoned for up

---

[18] R.S.C., Ord. 29, r. 6.
[19] R.S.C., Ord. 29, r. 2(6).
[20] Supreme Court Act 1981, s.32; County Courts Act 1984, s.50. The power to award
provisional damages for personal injuries under Supreme Court Act 1981, s.32A,
and County Courts Act 1984, s.51 should not be regarded as a form of interim
relief. Note also the powers under R.S.C., Ord. 29, r. 8 to order the payment of
income *pendente lite* and under Ord. 43 to make a summary order for account.
[21] R.S.C., Ord. 29, rr. 11–18.
[22] R.S.C., Ord. 29, r. 10(2).
[23] See Mitchell, "Powers of Arrest in Civil Law," (1987) L.S.Gaz. 2345; Chitty
and Jacob, pp. 600 *et seq. Cf.* the protective measure under German law of *persönlicher Arrest*, see para. 51.59 below.

to six months unless and until he gives the prescribed security, not exceeding the amount claimed in the action, that he will not go out of England without the leave of the court. Four conditions must be satisfied before the order may be made, summarised by Megarry J. as follows:

> "(1) The action is one in which the defendant would formerly have been liable to arrest at law. (2) A good cause of action for at least £50 is established. (3) There is 'probable cause' that the defendant is 'about to quit' England unless he is arrested. (4) 'the absence of the defendant from England will materially prejudice the plaintiff in the prosecution of his action.' "[24]

The ancient writ *ne exeat regno* may be issued by the High Court in those cases in which, though the debt is not a legal debt, these four conditions are satisfied.[25]

As regards the first condition, a defendant was only liable for arrest at common law for a debt certain and a claim for damages will not therefore support an arrest.[26] The second and third conditions are straightforward, but as regards the fourth condition, it should be noted that it is the prosecution to judgment of the cause of action in debt which must be prejudiced by the defendant's absence from England.[27] It is not sufficient if it is merely the execution of a judgment that will be prejudiced.[28] The second, third and fourth conditions must be established by evidence on oath.[29]

8. Orders for obtaining evidence

7.20   Provisions for the obtaining of evidence are excluded from the definition of interim relief in section 25(7) of the 1982 Act[30] and that Act does not therefore permit them to be made in aid of proceedings in other Contracting States.[31] The term "provision for obtaining evidence" covers orders for the examination of witnesses

---

[24] *Felton* v. *Callis* [1969] 1 Q.B. 200, at p. 211.

[25] *Allied Arab Bank* v. *Hajjar* [1988] 2 W.L.R. 942, 947.

[26] As regards the writ *ne exeat regno*, equity follows the law in this respect: *Colverson* v. *Bloomfield* (1885) 29 Ch.D. 341; *Allied Arab Bank* v. *Hajjar*, above, at p. 948. A writ *ne exeat regno* has been issued in respect of arrears of periodical payments in a matrimonial case: *Clark* v. *Clark* (1988) 138 N.L.J., p. P 101.

[27] *Allied Arab Bank* v. *Hajjar*, at p. 947.

[28] This is the function of a *Mareva* injunction, which may be supported by an order restraining the defendant from leaving the jurisdiction: see para. 7.10 above.

[29] In *Al Nahkel for Contracting and Trading Ltd.* v. *Lowe* [1986] Q.B. 235, Tudor Price J. accepted counsel's undertaking to have affidavits sworn.

[30] Para. 43.11 below.

[31] See para. 7.26 below. The scope of this exclusion is discussed in greater detail at para. 7.28 below.

or for the production of real evidence, including certain evidential documents, and it probably also extends to orders for discovery and orders for appointing a court expert. Orders for the examination of witnesses, or for obtaining evidence in other ways, may nonetheless be made in aid of foreign proceedings under the Evidence (Proceedings in Other Jurisdictions) Act 1975.[32]

Discovery. Orders for discovery of documents are normally made after the close of pleadings,[33] requiring the parties mutually to disclose to each other the existence of documents which are or have been in their possession, custody or power, and which relate to the matters in question in the proceedings.[34] Thereafter documents not protected by privilege may be mutually inspected. In certain types of case, discovery and inspection take place without the order of the court,[35] but in all cases the court has power to order such discovery and inspection as may be appropriate.

The appointment of a court expert. The civil procedure of many of **7.21** the other Contracting States makes considerable use of experts appointed by the court to investigate the matters in dispute and to report to the court.[36] In these other Contracting States experts are only rarely instructed by the parties themselves to present evidence for consideration by the court. In English civil procedure the reverse is the case. Experts are commonly called to give evidence by one or both parties on matters of scientific or technical complexity. The power of the High Court, on the application of a party, to appoint a "court expert" to inquire and to report on a question of fact or opinion is only very rarely exercised.[37] While an order appointing a court expert might possibly be regarded as a protective measure if its purpose was to investigate and report on a transient set of facts, it would probably, as has already been observed, be a provision for obtaining evidence and as such could not be made under the 1982 Act in aid of proceedings in another Contracting State.

---

[32] See paras. 8.63 *et seq.* below.
[33] Note the power to order discovery before proceedings: Supreme Court Act 1981, s.33(2), R.S.C., Ord. 29, r. 7A; and the power, exceptionally, to order discovery before pleadings in aid of interlocutory relief: *R.H.M. Foods* v. *Bovril* [1982] 1 All E.R. 673, C.A.
[34] See, generally, R.S.C., Ord. 24.
[35] This is the case for most actions for personal injuries: R.S.C., Ord. 25, r. 8.
[36] See chaps. 48 to 55, at para. 53.
[37] See R.S.C., Ord. 40 and R.S.C., Ord. 32, r. 16 (Chancery Division). The wider power under Ord. 104, r. 15, in patent cases, to appoint a scientific adviser, is also rarely used.

9. Arrest in maritime claims

7.22   The High Court has power, in an Admiralty action *in rem*, to issue a warrant for the arrest of the property, usually a ship, against which the proceedings are brought.[38] The warrant is executed by the Admiralty Marshal or his substitute fixing the warrant to the property while it is within the limits of the territorial jurisdiction. The arrest may be prevented or the property may be released by the provision of bail or other security by the person affected by the arrest. Other claimants may lodge *caveats* with the court to prevent the release. As proceedings *in rem* are brought against property, as distinct from a person,[39] the seizure of that property for the purposes of satisfying any ultimate judgment is a clear example of a provisional or protective measures as contemplated by Article 24 of the 1968 Convention.[40] Warrants for arrest of property are expressly excluded from the definition of "interim relief" in section 25 of the 1982 Act,[41] but there is specific provision relating to them in section 26. This enables proceedings *in rem* to be used for the purpose of obtaining security to satisfy a judgment in foreign proceedings or an arbitration award.[42] The arrest of property in proceedings *in rem* should be distinguished from the Mareva injunction. Whereas the warrant of arrest creates, or protects, a right in the property seized, the Mareva injunction merely restrains the defendant *in personam* from disposing of the property affected by the order.[43] A Mareva injunction could, in an appropriate case, be used in an Admiralty claim *in personam* to supplement the arrest of property in proceedings *in rem*.[44]

10. Extraterritorial effect of English interim orders

7.23   As has been mentioned, whether or not the court has a discretion to accept jurisdiction over an application for interim relief, the decision whether or not to grant an interim order is itself discretion-

---

[38] R.S.C., Ord. 75, r. 5. The county court has similar power: C.C.R., Ord. 40, r. 4. The power is exercisable at any time after the issue of the writ and before final judgment: see *The Alletta* [1974] 1 Lloyd's Rep. 40.

[39] *The Burns* [1907] P. 137, at p. 149. See para. 1.31 above.

[40] The Admiralty jurisdiction *in rem* of the English courts may be excluded by Art. 3 of the 1968 Convention except in cases to which the Brussels Arrest Convention applies: para. 1.34 above. But, the courts' powers to order the arrest of a ship or other property may nonetheless be relied on in aid of proceedings in another Contracting State, pursuant to Art. 24 of the 1968 Convention: see para. 24.01 below.

[41] See para. 43.03.

[42] See *The Jalamatsya* [1987] 2 Lloyd's Rep. 164.

[43] See *Cretanor Maritime Co.* v. *Irish Marine Management Ltd.*, *The Cretan Harmony*, [1978] 1 Lloyd's Rep. 425, at p. 429, *per* Buckley, L.J.

[44] See *The Rena K* [1979] Q.B. 377 at p. 410.

ary.[45] In cases in which the court's orders can only be put into effect outside the limits of its territorial jurisdiction, the exercise of discretion has been much influenced in the past by considerations of respect for foreign sovereignty and difficulties of enforcement.[46] However, as has been seen, the strength of these considerations is much reduced in the context of the 1968 Convention,[47] and it remains to be seen how far English courts will now more readily grant interim orders having effect in other Contracting States.

Until recently, a Mareva injunction would not be granted in respect of assets outside the jurisdiction.[48] This area of the law is developing rapidly. As Kerr L.J. has pointed out, "some situations, which are nowadays by no means uncommon, cry out—as a matter of justice to plaintiffs—for disclosure orders and Mareva type injunctions covering foreign assets of defendants even before judgment."[49] Accordingly, in an appropriate case, a Mareva injunction will be granted in respect of assets outside the jurisdiction, provided effect is given to certain safeguards by means of a proviso added to the order or by undertakings given by the plaintiff.[50] In particular, the court seeks to protect the position of third parties outside the jurisdiction, so that such persons are not to be affected by the terms of the order,[51] but this proviso may be qualified in such a way as to enable a foreign court to give effect to the order within its own jurisdiction.[52] It remains to be seen how the terms of such provisos develop in practice, and whether a distinction comes to be drawn between, on one hand, persons subject to the jurisdiction of the courts of Contracting States to the 1968 Convention and

7.24

---

[45] Para. 7.04 above.
[46] See paras. 1.47 *et seq.* above.
[47] Para. 1.48 above.
[48] *Third Chandris Shipping Corp.* v. *Unimarine S.A.* [1979] Q.B. 645, at pp. 668–669; *Intraco Ltd.* v. *Notios Shipping Corp. (The Bhoja Trader)* [1981] 2 Lloyd's Rep. 256; but different considerations applied if the claim concerned ownership of the assets in question, by tracing or otherwise: *Ashtiani* v. *Kashi* [1987] Q.B. 888, 890, *per* Dillon L.J.
[49] *Babanaft International Co. S.A.* v. *Bassatne* [1989] 2 W.L.R. 232, 247.
[50] *Babanaft International Co. S.A.* v. *Bassatne*, above; *Republic of Haiti* v. *Duvalier* [1981] 2 W.L.R. 261; *Derby & Co. Ltd.* v. *Weldon* [1989] 2 W.L.R. 276; *Derby & Co. Ltd.* v. *Weldon (Nos. 3 & 4)* [1989] 2 W.L.R. 412; see para. 7.08 above.
[51] *Babanaft International Co. S.A.* v. *Bassatne*, above; *Derby & Co. Ltd.* v. *Weldon (Nos. 3 & 4)*, above; but *cf. Derby & Co. Ltd.* v. *Weldon*, where a similar result was achieved by an untertaking: see p. 284, *per* Nicholls L.J. If the order applied to third parties outside the jurisdiction, they would be exposed to the risk of proceedings for contempt if they knowingly assisted in a breach of the order (see para. 10.58 below). This would be regarded as an unwarranted extra-territorial exercise of sovereignty.
[52] *Babanaft International Co. S.A.* v. *Bassatne*, above, at p. 243, *per* Kerr L.J.; *Derby & Co. Ltd.* v. *Weldon (Nos. 3 & 4)*, above, at p. 425. This qualification overcomes the difficulty referred to in the previous note.

assets located in those States and, on the other hand, persons and assets outside the jurisdiction of the Contracting States.[53]

If a Mareva injunction is granted in respect of assets outside the jurisdiction, an ancillary order for the defendant to disclose those assets may also be granted, whether the injunction is granted as an interim measure before judgment[54] or in aid of execution[55]; but the plaintiff may be restrained by his own undertaking or by a proviso to the order from using such information in other proceedings abroad, unless he first obtains the permission of the English court.[56] If the injunction is granted in respect only of assets within the jurisdiction, an order for disclosure of assets outside the jurisdiction was formerly rarely granted,[57] but it remains to be seen how the practice will now develop.

The court has been willing to grant Anton Piller orders in respect of premises located outside the jurisdiction, provided the defendant is, or can properly be made, subject to the *in personam* jurisdiction of the court.[58]

11. Enforcement of interim orders

7.25   A breach of an interim order may render the person in breach liable to penalties for contempt of court. This topic is discussed in Chapter 10,[59] but it should be noted here that contemnors have been imprisoned for breach of Mareva injunctions.[60]

An undertaking in damages is nearly always required of a plaintiff as a condition for the grant of a Mareva injunction, an Anton Piller order, other interlocutory injunctions and most other types of interim order. If and when the order is discharged, either because the plaintiff fails at trial or because it is established before trial that the order should not have been granted in the first instance, the

---

[53] It is suggested that such a distinction can properly be drawn in principle, because of the extent to which sovereignty has been qualified by the 1968 convention: see para. 1.48 above; but see *Derby & Co. Ltd. v. Weldon (Nos. 3 & 4)* [1989] 2 W.L.R. 412, 428.

[54] *Republic of Haiti* v. *Duvalier*, above; *Derby & Co. Ltd.* v. *Weldon*, above.

[55] *Maclaine Watson & Co. Ltd.* v. *International Tin Council (No. 2)* [1988] 3 W.L.R. 1190; *Babanaft International Co. S.A.* v. *Bassatne*, above.

[56] *Derby & Co. Ltd.* v. *Weldon*, above.

[57] *Ashtiani* v. *Kashi* [1987] Q.B. 888; *Reilly* v. *Fryer* [1988] 2 F.T.L.R. 69.

[58] *Cook Industries* v. *Galliher* [1979] Ch. 438; *Altertext Inc.* v. *Advanced Data Communications Ltd.* [1985] 1 W.L.R. 457. There must be some concern, it is suggested, as to whether these orders took sufficient account of the judicial sovereignty of the countries in which they were effected: see para. 8.42 below.

[59] Para. 10.58 below.

[60] *Enfield London Borough Council* v. *Mahoney* [1983] 1 W.L.R. 749; *Popinschal* v. *Phillips, The Times*, January 20, 1988; *cf. Danchevsky* v. *Danchevsky* (1975) Fam. L. 17.

defendant may apply for an inquiry as to damages.[61] The inquiry will usually be carried out by a master. The defendant is not entitled to damages as of right and has no cause of action independent of the plaintiff's undertaking.[62] In special circumstances an inquiry as to damages may therefore be refused[63] and the defendant would anyway be well advised to apply for the inquiry when the order is discharged, even if the inquiry is then adjourned until after the trial of the action.

C. Interim Relief in Aid of Proceedings in Other Contracting States

1. Introduction

The basis for the grant of interim relief by the English court is its 7.26 concern that, pending the final determination of the dispute between the parties, the interests of either party should not be prejudiced. The court's interim order normally presupposes that, unless the dispute is settled amicably, it will be the subject of a substantive hearing in due course, leading to a final judgment on the merits. A plaintiff in proceedings before a foreign court against a defendant with assets in England might wish those assets to be preserved for the satisfaction of his judgment. Before the passing of the 1982 Act the only way in which he could secure those assets was by starting parallel proceedings before the English court. He could then have sought a Mareva injunction, ostensibly in aid of the English proceedings.[64] If it was not possible to start parallel proceedings in England because the English court lacked jurisdiction over the substance of the dispute, there was no power to grant interim relief.[65]

Article 24 of the 1968 Convention complements the Convention's jurisdictional rules by permitting the courts of a Contracting State to grant such provisional and protective measures as are available under national law even if the jurisdiction over the substance of the case is allocated by the Convention to another Contracting State.[66] Accordingly, under section 25 of the 1982 Act,[67] the High Court is now able to take advantage of Article 24 and grant interim relief where there are actual or contemplated proceedings in the courts of

---

[61] *Ushers Brewery Ltd.* v. *P.S. King & Co. Ltd.* [1972] Ch. 148; see *Supreme Court Practice*, para. 29/1/12.

[62] *Fletcher Sutcliffe Wild Ltd.* v. *Burch* [1982] F.S.R. 64.

[63] *Smith* v. *Day* (1882) 21 Ch.D. 421; *Griffiths* v. *Blake* (1884) 27 Ch.D. 474.

[64] *e.g.*, see *House of Spring Gardens* v. *Waite* [1985] F.S.R. 173.

[65] *The Siskina* [1979] A.C. 210.

[66] Para. 24.01 below.

[67] Para. 43.01 below; see also *Republic of Haiti* v. *Duvalier (No. 1), The Independent*, June 13, 1988 (C.A.).

Proceedings in England and Wales

another Contracting State, the subject-matter of which is within the scope of the Convention.[68] It is not relevant for this purpose whether the jurisdiction of the courts of the other Contracting State in respect of the main proceedings arises under the Convention's own rules or (under Article 4 of the Convention) in some other way. Thus an application can be made to the High Court for interim relief in aid of civil or commercial proceedings in another Contracting State which are based on the exercise of exorbitant jurisdiction over a defendant domiciled in a non-Contracting State.[69]

The Act also empowers the High Court to grant interim relief pending trial or pending an appeal, either when the issue before the court is the court's own jurisdiction in respect of the substantive proceedings (or, seemingly, in respect of the application for interim relief itself)[70] or when there is a reference to the European Court of Justice.[71]

2. Types of interim relief available

7.27   The question as to what types of interim relief can be obtained in aid of proceedings in other Contracting States is difficult to answer with certainty. Section 25 of the 1982 Act provides that the court may grant any form of interim relief which it can ordinarily grant in proceedings relating to matters within its jurisdiction,[72] except a warrant for the arrest of property[73] or a provision for obtaining evidence.[74] It might be said that certain forms of interim relief could only be available in respect of the English proceedings in which they are granted, because that is the true construction of the relevant statutory provisions (such as Order 29 of the Rules of the Supreme Court). It is suggested, however, that the definition of "interim relief" in section 25(7) of the 1982 Act is wide enough to make these forms of interim relief available in aid of proceedings in

---

[68] As to Scotland and Northern Ireland see para. 7.32 below; Extensions may be made by Order in Council to enable interim relief to be granted in aid of foreign proceedings in non-Contracting States, other foreign proceedings which fall outside the scope of the Convention, or foreign arbitration proceedings. No such Order in Council has yet been made. The scope of the Convention is discussed in chap. 14 below.
[69] The principal types of exorbitant jurisdiction are listed in Art. 3, see para. 16.09 below.
[70] See Kaye, p. 1163.
[71] s.24, para. 43.01 below.
[72] In *Bank Mellat* v. *Heliniki Techniki S.A.* [1984] Q.B. 291, Kerr J. doubted whether an order for security for costs was "interim relief" within the meaning of s.25.
[73] s.25(7)(a), para. 43.11 below. This relates to the power in Admiralty cases to order the arrest of ships and cargo: see para. 7.22 above.
[74] s.25(7)(b), para. 43.11 below. The scope of this exclusion is considered below.

168

other Contracting States.[75] In any event, the particular categories of relief provided by Order 29 are merely the formal expression of the court's wide power to grant interlocutory relief. As has been said,

" . . . there is no limitation to the practice of the court with regard to interlocutory applications so far as they are necessary and reasonable applications ancillary to the due performance of its functions, namely the administration of justice at the hearing of the cause."[76]

Provisions for obtaining evidence. The exclusion of provisions for   **7.28** the obtaining of evidence from the categories of interim relief referred to in section 25 is consistent with the view expressed in the Schlosser Report that the Convention is not concerned with those interlocutory decisions which are not intended to govern the legal relationship of the parties, but which arrange the further conduct of the proceedings.[77] Orders concerned with the taking of evidence are seen as procedural and as being appropriately catered for by the Hague civil procedure and evidence conventions[78] and the words "provision for obtaining evidence" in section 25 of the 1982 Act have been held to mean provision for obtaining evidence in the substantive action.[79] Some types of interim relief, such as Mareva injunctions or orders for the preservation or custody of the subject-matter of foreign proceedings, are clearly not in any way connected with the obtaining of evidence.[80] On the other hand, orders for discovery of documents or for interrogatories clearly are provisions for the obtaining of evidence. Problems arise with the classification of orders of which the object or effect may be the protection or preservation of property for evidential purposes, such as Anton Piller orders[81] or other orders for the inspection of property.[82] It is suggested that the solution lies in seeing whether the relief sought is of a kind which is obtainable under the Hague Evidence Convention 1970.[83] If it is, and if the object of the order is the obtaining of evi-

---

[75] See para. 24.07 above.

[76] *Smith* v. *Peters* (1875) L.R. 20 Eq. 511, at pp. 512–513, *per* Sir George Jessel M.R. That was a case in which a mandatory interlocutory injunction was granted. The passage quoted was cited with approval in *Astro Exito Navegacion S.A.* v. *Southland Enterprise Co. Ltd. (No. 2)* [1982] Q.B. 1248 (C.A.).

[77] Schlosser, para. 187 (para. A1.483 below). Note the power of the Secretary of State under the Protection of Trading Interests Act 1980, s.4, to forbid the production of a document to a foreign court, see para. 8.69 below.

[78] Schlosser, paras. 184, 185, (paras. A1.480–A1.481 below).

[79] *Republic of Haiti* v. *Duvalier (No. 1)*, *The Independent*, June 13, 1988 (C.A.).

[80] An order for disclosure of the location of the defendant's assets in England, made as part of a Mareva injunction, is not a provision for obtaining evidence: *Republic of Haiti* v. *Duvalier (No. 1)*, *The Independent*, June 13, 1988 (C.A.).

[81] See para. 7.12 above.

[82] *e.g.* under R.S.C., Ord. 29, rr. 2 and 7A.

[83] See paras. 8.26 *et seq.* below.

dence, then it will not be a type of interim relief available in aid of proceedings in another Contracting State. Arguably a distinction might be drawn between a measure for "obtaining" evidence and one for "protecting and preserving" evidence.[84]

3. Method of application

7.29   The application for interim relief under section 25 of the 1982 Act is made either to the judge or to the master depending on the nature of the relief sought.[85] If the foreign proceedings have not yet been commenced it is necessary to show that the intended court will have jurisdiction[86] and that there is a genuine intention of bringing them.[87] A foreign applicant may have to provide security for his undertaking in damages.[88] If the initial application is made *ex parte*, the initial order is not capable of recognition or enforcement in another Contracting State until the respondent has had notice of it and has had an opportunity to challenge it in adversarial proceedings.[89]

4. The discretion of the court

7.30   The granting of interim relief in purely English proceedings is always a matter for the discretion of the court. Article 24 does not put the applicant for relief in aid of foreign proceedings in any different position from that of an applicant for interim relief in purely English proceedings. The court retains its normal discretion to do what seems right and just between the parties and to impose whatever terms and conditions it thinks just.[90] However it is expressly provided that the court may refuse to grant relief if, in its opinion, the fact that it has no jurisdiction over the subject-matter of the main proceedings makes it inexpedient for the court to grant the relief.[91] It is suggested that the court should no more undertake a detailed review of the prospects of success in the foreign proceed-

---

[84] Kaye, p. 1152.
[85] A suggested form of proceedings appears at para. A4.02 below.
[86] As was seen at para. 7.26 above, this may be jurisdiction arising either under the Convention or under the private international law of the Contracting State concerned.
[87] The English court might impose a time limit for the bringing of the foreign proceedings. As to the effect of the foreign court having exclusive jurisdiction, see paras. 7.31 and 24.08 below.
[88] See 22 *Court Forms* 110; *cf. Vapormatic Co. Ltd.* v. *Sparex Ltd.* [1976] 1 W.L.R. 939.
[89] *Denilauler* v. *Snc. Couchet Frères* [1980] E.C.R. 1553, discussed at paras. 24.10, 25.26 and 27.26 below.
[90] See, *e.g.* Supreme Court Act 1981, s.37(2).
[91] 1982 Act, s.25(2), see para. 43.07 below.

ings than it would if the interim relief were sought in English proceedings.[92]

5. Effect of foreign jurisdiction clause

The question arises as to whether the English court can entertain **7.31**
an application for interim relief when the jurisdiction of the foreign
court is founded on an exclusive jurisdiction clause. It has been
seen that, so far as the Convention is concerned, Article 24 permits
an application for provisional or protective measures to be made to
the courts of one Contracting State even if the courts of another
Contracting State have jurisdiction under the Convention. This
includes the situation in which the other Contracting State has
exclusive jurisdiction under an agreement which satisfies the
requirements of Article 17.[93] The power of the High Court under
section 25 of the 1982 Act to grant interim relief in aid of proceedings in other Contracting States and other parts of the United Kingdom is expressed to exist "where proceedings have been or are to be
commenced" in the other jurisdiction.

It follows that, in cases where the courts of another Contracting
State have exclusive jurisdiction over the substance of a dispute,
there is no objection in principle to the English court granting
interim relief in aid of foreign proceedings. What is less clear is
whether the English court would be willing to grant such relief if
the jurisdiction agreement applied not only to the substance of the
dispute but also, either expressly or by necessary implication, to
proceedings for interim relief themselves.[94]

D. Interim Relief in Aid of Proceedings in Scotland or Northern Ireland

The High Court has power under the 1982 Act to grant interim **7.32**
relief in aid of proceedings which have been or which are to be commenced in Scotland or Northern Ireland, provided that their subject-matter falls within the scope of the Convention.[95] This power

---

[92] In English proceedings, the court considers the prospects of success only to
satisfy itself that there is a serious question to be tried, that damages are not an
adequate remedy and that the balance of convenience is in favour of the injunction being granted: *American Cyanamid Co.* v. *Ethicon Ltd.* [1975] A.C. 396;
Derby & Co. Ltd. v. *Weldon* [1989] 2 W.L.R. 276, 283: see para. 7.06 above.
[93] Collins, "Provisional Measures, the Conflict of Laws and the Brussels Convention" (1981) Yb.E.L. 249, at p. 258; see paras. 21.01 *et seq.* If the agreement
does not satisfy the requirements of Art. 17 it is of no effect and the other rules
of the Convention apply to determine jurisdiction.
[94] *cf. Mike Trading and Transport Ltd.* v. *R. Pagnan & Fratelli (The Lisboa)* [1980]
2 Lloyds Rep. 546, especially, *per* Lord Denning M.R. at pp. 548–549.
[95] s.16, Sched. 4, Art. 24: para. 45.29 below.

exists even if, under the rules of Schedule 4 of the Act, jurisdiction over the substance of the case is allocated to the Scottish or Northern Ireland courts. Although the English court might, in an appropriate case,[96] grant relief which took effect in Scotland or Northern Ireland,[97] the only form of relief which is enforceable in Scotland or Northern Ireland under the registration procedures in Schedules 6 and 7 of the Act is an order for the making of an interim payment.[98]

---

[96] See para. 7.23 above.
[97] See *Protector Alarms* v. *Maxim Alarms* [1978] F.S.R. 442, in which the High Court refused to make an Anton Piller order in respect of premises in Scotland.
[98] s.18(5)(*d*), para. 41.25 below. See also para. 7.18 above.

CHAPTER 8

EVIDENCE

A. INTRODUCTION

In English law, by contrast with many continental legal systems,[1] it **8.01** is generally the responsibility of the parties to obtain the evidence to support their contentions; the court will not undertake this task itself, although it will assist the parties by making orders for discovery of documents, admission of interrogatories, disclosures of witnesses' statements and experts reports and the attendance of witnesses. Furthermore, the admissibility of evidence in English civil proceedings is governed by detailed rules.[2] Part B of this chapter examines some of the rules of English law, concerning both the obtaining of evidence and its admissibility, which are of particular significance in the context of international litigation.

---

[1] In many continental systems, the parties may identify the evidence which they say supports their contentions, but court chooses what (if any) of that evidence it wishes to have brought before it; and the courts also frequently order their own investigations. The evidence is then "freely evaluated" by the court: see chaps. 48 to 58, at paras. 49 to 53 below.

[2] Consideration of the general law of evidence is beyond the scope of this book. Reference should be made to specialist works such as *Phipson on Evidence* (13th ed.), *Cross on Evidence* (6th ed.), and 17 *Halsbury's Laws* (4th edn.).

The courts of different countries have long been willing to assist each other, in the interests of international comity, to obtain evidence located in their jurisdiction for use in other jurisdictions. This system of co-operation is now largely regulated in Europe by international conventions, and its framework is described in part C of this chapter. The details of how English courts obtain the assistance of courts in other countries (particularly in the other Contracting States to the 1968 Convention) are described in part D, and the means by which the English courts give such assistance to other countries is described in part E.

B. EVIDENCE IN ENGLISH PROCEEDINGS

1. Oral evidence

8.02   The primary method for giving evidence at trial in English proceedings is by the direct oral evidence of witnesses examined in person.[3] Provided the attendance of a witness can be obtained,[4] the rules as to what evidence he may give are not affected by the fact that he may be resident outside England and Wales, or of foreign nationality, or would not (but for his presence in England or Wales) be subject to the personal jurisdiction of the court. If a witness will not attend voluntarily, he may be summoned to attend by a writ of *subpoena*[5] served anywhere in the United Kingdom.[6] If the witness is outside the United Kingdom, he cannot be summoned to attend in person.

Interpreters. If a party or witness is unable to speak or understand English[7] he may be permitted to give evidence through an inter-

---

[3] R.S.C., Ord. 38, r. 1. The court has power to order that evidence of a particular fact shall be given at the trial in such manner as may be specified in the order: R.S.C., Ord. 38, r. 3.

[4] Methods of obtaining the evidence of witnesses who are outside the jurisdiction are discussed at paras. 8.40 *et seq.* below. As regards witnesses who are in the jurisdiction, but unable to attend the trial, see para. 8.03 below.

[5] R.S.C., Ord. 38, rr. 14–19. A *subpoena* to attend for the purpose of giving evidence in person is called a *subpoena ad testificandum*; one to produce documents or other things of an evidential nature is called a *subpoena duces tecum*. Similar provisions apply in the county court: C.C.R., Ord. 20, r. 12. See further, as to the attendance of witnesses, R.S.C., Ord. 32, r. 7; Ord. 54, r. 9; Chitty and Jacob, pp. 536–547; 18 *Court Forms* (1985 issue) 335–339, 377–378, 395–406, 462–466; and, as to the production of documents, R.S.C., Ord. 38, r. 13; C.C.R., Ord. 20, r. 3, Ord. 20, r. 11; 18 *Court Forms* (1985 issue) 367, 386, 448–451, 474–476.

[6] Supreme Court Act 1981, s.36. See para. 8.58 below.

[7] In practice, a witness who speaks or understands some English, but is not fluent, will often be permitted the assistance of an interpreter. As to the use of Welsh in courts in Wales, see Welsh Language Act 1967, ss.1, 5; Welsh Courts Act 1942, *passim*; 10 *Halsbury's Laws* (4th ed.), para. 707.

Evidence

preter. The use of an interpreter is entirely a matter within the discretion of the judge, but the discretion must be exercised judicially.[8] An interpreter need not have any specific qualifications beyond the capacity to speak the foreign language,[9] but must be a person who cannot have any bias.[10] The interpreter will take an oath or make an affirmation before embarking on the interpretation.[11]

2. Evidence taken before an examiner

If a witness is unlikely to be able to attend the trial, his evidence **8.03** may be taken at some convenient place by an examiner appointed for the purpose.[12] This procedure may be used where the witness is likely to leave the country before the trial takes place. It may also be used where the witness is ill or infirm or if, being a woman, she is pregnant and likely to give birth at about the time of the trial, or in any other case where it appears necessary for the purposes of justice.[13] Its use for the purpose of examining witnesses in other countries is discussed separately below.[14]

The application and order. The party who wishes the evidence of a **8.04** witness to be taken before an examiner applies to the court[15] for an order[16] to that effect. The person appointed as examiner may be

---

[8] *Re Fuld, Hartley* v. *Fuld* [1965] 1 W.L.R. 1336; *Re Trepca Mines* [1960] 1 W.L.R. 24. (reversed on another point [1960] 1 W.L.R. 1273).
[9] Qualified interpreters who are accredited with the Metropolitan Police are available through the Association of Police and Court Interpeters, 9 Farmer St., London W8 7SN (tel: 01–727 6982).
[10] *R.* v. *Mitchell* (1969) 114 Sol.Jo. 86; *Singh* v. *Singh* [1971] P. 226.
[11] The oath must comply with the Oaths Act 1978. Its usual form is: "*I swear by Almighty God [or I, (name), do solemnly, sincerely and truly declare and affirm] that I will well and faithfully interpret and true explanation make of all such matters and things as shall be required of me according to the best of my skill and understanding.*"
[12] R.S.C., Ord. 39; C.C.R., Ord. 20, r. 13; see Chitty and Jacob, pp. 537 ff; 18 *Court Forms* (1985 issue) 341–344, 380–381, 409–419. The examiner is paid a fixed fee and his expenses: R.S.C., Ord. 39, r. 19.
[13] R.S.C., Ord. 39, r. 1. A specialised use of this procedure is available in some circumstances in an action commenced for the purpose of perpetuating a witness's testimony in support of the plaintiff's claim that he would become entitled, upon the happening of a future event, to certain property or other rights: R.S.C., Ord. 39, r. 15.
[14] Para. 8.44. The examination of a witness for the purpose of foreign proceedings is also governed in part by this procedure: R.S.C., Ord. 70, r. 4: see paras. 8.63 and 8.74 *et seq.* below.
[15] The application in the High Court is made by summons in the prescribed form: *Supreme Court Practice*, para. 39/1/5; R.S.C., App. A, Form No. 31, *Supreme Court Practice*, para. [26]; Chitty and Jacob, p. 559; 18 *Court Forms* (1985 issue) 409.
[16] R.S.C., App. A, Form No. 32, *Supreme Court Practice*, para. [27]; Chitty and Jacob, p. 560; 18 *Court Forms* (1985 issue) 410.

175

agreed by the parties, and a junior barrister is usually appointed for this purpose. Alternatively, the order may appoint an examiner of the court, in which case one of the barristers on the court's rota will be appointed[17] or, if the examination is to take place outside London, the local District Registrar may be appointed. There is power, which is rarely exercised, to order the examination to take place before a judge.[18] Unless the order is made by consent, the application should be supported by an affidavit setting out the circumstances relied upon.[19] The order may be made on such terms or subject to such conditions as the court may think fit.

8.05   *The examination and deposition.* The examination is conducted at the time and place specified in the order or fixed by the examiner. The witness is sworn[20] and is generally examined, cross-examined and re-examined in the same manner as at the trial of an action. The attendance of the witness may be secured by *subpoena* and he may be ordered to be sworn and to answer lawful questions.[21] The examiner may be assisted by an interpreter.[22] The evidence is noted by the examiner or (more usually) by a shorthand writer[23] in the form of a deposition. The deposition is then read back to the witness and he is asked to sign it, although these requirements may be dispensed with by the written agreement of the parties, and this is the usual practice if a shorthand writer has been employed.[24] The deposition is authenticated by the examiner's signature and sent by him to the court.[25] If the witness objects to answer any question, or if objection is taken to any question, the objection and the grounds for it must be set out in the deposition, together with the witness's answer to the question and a statement of the examiner's views on the objection; although the propriety of the question and the

---

[17] R.S.C, Ord. 39, r. 17.
[18] This will only be ordered in exceptional circumstances: *Supreme Court Practice*, para. 39/1/4; *Re Brickman's Settlement, Brickman* v. *Goddard Trustees (Jersey)* [1982] 1 All E.R. 336; *Practice Note (Chancery: Deposition)* [1981] 1 W.L.R. 1560; (1981) 125 Sol.Jo. 862. The power to appoint a master as an examiner is never exercised.
[19] For forms of Affidavit, see Chitty and Jacob, pp. 559–560; 18 *Court Forms* (1985 issue) 409.
[20] The examiner is empowered to administer the oath: Evidence Act 1851, s.16. For a form of oath to be administered to the witness, see Chitty and Jacob, p. 563.
[21] Supreme Court Act 1981, s.36(6); R.S.C., Ord. 39, r. 5.
[22] *Marquis of Bute* v. *James* (1886) 33 Ch.D. 157.
[23] For forms of oath to be taken by the shorthand writer, see Chitty and Jacob, p. 566; 18 *Court Forms* (1985 issue) 408.
[24] R.S.C., Ord. 39, r. 11; *Supreme Court Practice*, para. 39/11/2.
[25] R.S.C., Ord. 39, r. 11; *Supreme Court Practice*, paras. 39/11/3–39/11/5. The examiner is not obliged to send his deposition until his fees and expenses have been paid: R.S.C., Ord. 39, r. 19(3).

admissibility of the answer remain matters solely for the court to decide.[26]

Admission of deposition in evidence. The deposition is placed on **8.06** the court file and may be inspected there by any party to the proceedings but not, except with the leave of the court, by any other person.[27] It does not automatically form part of the evidence in the case.[28] It may only be put in evidence if the other party consents or if it is proved to the satisfaction of the court that the witness is dead, or beyond the jurisdiction of the court, or unable from sickness or other infirmity to attend the trial.[29] The party wishing to adduce the evidence must give reasonable notice to the other party.[30] An office copy of the deposition should be obtained, which will be admissible without further proof.[31]

3. Affidavits

The presentation of a witness's evidence to the court in a written **8.07** form is usually done by affidavit, which is a formal statement bearing the title of the proceedings to which it relates[32] and which the witness (called the deponent) swears or affirms to be true before a person authorised to take affidavits.[33] Affidavits are of very great practical importance in the conduct of litigation, especially at the interlocutory stages.[34] Documents, usually in bundles, referred to in the affidavit may be exhibited to it.[35] Affidavits, but not usually the exhibits, are filed in the court office and form part of the court record. The rules and practice relating to the form, use and contents of affidavits are detailed and beyond the scope of this book;

---

[26] R.S.C., Ord. 39, r. 10.
[27] R.S.C., Ord. 63, r. 4.
[28] *Fisher* v. *C.H.T. Ltd.* [1965] 1 W.L.R. 1093.
[29] R.S.C., Ord. 38, r. 9(1). Evidence on this point may usually be given by affidavit. If the contents of the affidavit used in support of the original application still hold good, it may be used; but otherwise an up-to-date affidavit should be sworn. Forms of affidavit for this purpose appear at Chitty and Jacob, p. 570 and 18 *Court Forms* (1985 issue) 409.
[30] R.S.C., Ord. 38, r. 9(2).
[31] R.S.C., Ord. 38, rr. 9(3), 10.
[32] R.S.C., Ord. 41, r. 1.
[33] The persons authorised to take affidavits are described below. For the form and use of affidavits, see 17 *Halsbury's Laws* (4th ed.), paras. 307–321; 3 *Court Forms* (1979 issue), pp. 343 *et seq.*
[34] See, for example, the forms of affidavit prescribed or recommended for various purposes, in the *Supreme Court Practice*, vol. 2, listed at pp. xi–xii.
[35] R.S.C., Ord. 41, r. 11; *Practice Direction (Evidence: Documents)* [1983] 1 W.L.R. 922; *Supreme Court Practice*, para. 41/11/1.

the discussion below is confined to those aspects which are of particular relevance in litigation containing an international element.

8.08 *Affidavits: foreign language.* Where the deponent to an affidavit does not understand English, either the affidavit may be sworn in a foreign language and then translated, or it may be sworn in English through an interpreter.[36] Each course involves certain formalities.[37] If the affidavit is sworn in the foreign language,[38] a translation must be filed with it and the translation must be verified.[39] This verification may either be by an affidavit of the translator (usually a qualified translator) annexing both the original affidavit and the translation,[40] or by a sworn indorsement of verification[41] on the translation, which is itself annexed to the original. If the affidavit is to be sworn in England, it (and the oath) must first be interpreted to the deponent and the interpreter must swear to the accuracy of the translation.[42] If documents exhibited to an affidavit are themselves in a foreign language, translations of the documents should be provided.[43]

8.09 *Who may take affidavits.* English law permits the following persons to take affidavits anywhere for the purposes of proceedings in England: commissioners for oaths,[44] solicitors who have a practising certificate in force,[45] notaries public,[46] officers of the court authorised to do so by the judge or by rules or orders, for purposes

---

[36] The former course was thought to be preferable by Vaisey J. in *Re Sarazin's Letters Patent* (1947) 64 R.P.C. 51.

[37] See 3 *Court Forms* (1979 issue) 363. The costs of translation are recoverable on taxation: *Supreme Court Practice*, para. 62/12/6.

[38] The oath must be translated: for a form of jurat, see 3 *Court Forms* (1979 issue) 395.

[39] For a form of indorsement verifying the translation, see 3 *Court Forms* (1979 issue) 396.

[40] *Re Sarazin's Letters Patent*, above; *Supreme Court Practice*, para. 41/12/7; 17 *Halsbury's Laws* (4th ed.), para. 321.

[41] For a form of verification, see 3 *Court Forms* (1979 issue) 396. Where the signature of the deponent is in foreign characters, transliteration of the signature should likewise be verified.

[42] For forms of jurat for an affidavit sworn through an interpreter, see Chitty and Jacob, p. 529; 3 *Court Forms* (1979 issue) 395. It is important that the interpreter's identity and qualification be clearly stated: *Re Sarazin's Letters Patent*, above, at p. 54.

[43] See para. 8.16 below.

[44] Commissioners for Oaths Act 1889, s.1(2); Commissioners for Oaths Act 1891, s.1.

[45] Solicitors Act 1974, s.81(1).

[46] Statute only extends the powers of commissioners for oaths to those notaries who are admitted to practice within the jurisdiction of the Company of Scriveners (*i.e.*, in parts of central London): Administration of Justice Act 1985,

connected with their duties[47] and, in connection with county court proceedings, any judge or registrar of a county court or justice of the peace.[48] Judicial notice will be taken of the seal or signature of these persons, and the affidavit need not be separately proved.

In addition, English law permits a number of persons to take affidavits abroad for the purposes of English proceedings. Officers in H.M. Forces not below the rank of lieutenant-commander (Royal Navy), major (Army), or squadron-leader (Royal Air Force) may take affidavits outside the United Kingdom from serving members of the armed forces, from certain other employees, and from certain members of their families.[49] British ambassadors and certain other diplomatic and consular officers may take affidavits in the country or place where they exercise their diplomatic or consular functions.[50] Any other person who is authorised to administer an oath in any place outside England may do so for the purposes of English proceedings.[51] As a matter of English law, a person's authority to administer oaths in a place outside England need not be authority to adminster the oath for the purposes of English proceedings; but the authority under foreign law is not sufficient if it is limited to a particular matter, as in the case of an arbitrator.[52]

The exercise of these powers to administer oaths outside England is of limited practical use however, unless the affidavit is admitted in evidence without the necessity of proving the seal or signature of the person taking the affidavit. It will be so admitted, provided one of two conditions is fulfilled. First, if that authority is derived otherwise than from the law of a foreign country, proof of the seal or sig-

---

s.65. In practice, most notaries are also practising solicitors. In their notarial capacity, they normally administer oaths for use abroad, but not for the purpose of English litigation.

[47] Commissioners for Oaths Act 1889, s.2; County Courts Act 1984, s.58; R.S.C., Ord. 32, r. 8. The power to administer oaths to witnesses legally called before them extends also to all persons having by law or by consent of the parties authority to hear, receive and examine evidence: Evidence Act 1851, s.16; see also, as to arbitrators and umpires, Arbitration Act 1950, s.12(3).

[48] County Courts Act 1984, s.58.

[49] Emergency Laws (Miscellaneous Provisions) Act 1953, s.10; Army Act 1955, s.204, Sched. 5; Air Force Act 1955, s.204, Sched. 5; Armed Forces Act 1981, s.1(1). The full names and rank of the officer, and the place where the affidavit was taken, must be stated in the jurat if the affidavit is to be admitted in evidence without further proof. For forms of jurat, see 3 *Court Forms* (1979 issue) 394.

[50] Commissioners for Oaths Act 1889, s.6; Oaths and Evidence (Overseas Authorities and Countries) Act 1963, s.3. This power may be extended to the diplomats of other countries representing the interests of the U.K.: Oaths & Evidence (Overseas Countries & Authorities) Act 1963, s.2.

[51] Commissioners for Oaths Act 1889, s.3(1).

[52] *Kevan v. Crawford* (1876) 32 L.J.Ch. 658, *per* James L.J.

nature is not necessary.[53] Secondly, if the seal or signature purports to be that of a court, judge, notary public or person having authority to administer oaths in a part of the Commonwealth outside England and Wales, then the affidavit taken in that part of the Commonwealth will be admitted without proof of that seal or signature.[54] On the other hand, if the affidavit is sworn before a person not authorised by English law, or by the law of another part of the Commonwealth or Ireland,[55] the seal or signature of the person taking the affidavit and his authority to administer an oath must generally be proved.[56] It is the practice to require the authority to be proved by a certificate of the local court[57]; but it may also be proved by the affidavit of a person who can depose to that authority.[58] It has been held that the authority can be proved by the certificate of a British consular officer,[59] but it is no longer the practice of those officers to issue such certificates.[60] Instead, under the Hague Convention Abolishing the Requirement of Legalisation for Foreign Public Documents,[61] application may be made to the competent authority[62] of the foreign country for the grant of a certificate (called an "apostille") which certifies "the authenticity of the signature, the capacity in which the person signing the document has acted and, where appropriate, the identity of the seal or stamp which the document bears." It is considered that such a certificate would now be regarded as sufficient proof of the foreign official's

---

[53] Commissioners for Oaths Act 1889, s.3(2). Ireland is not a foreign country: Ireland Act 1949, s.2(1).

[54] R.S.C., Ord. 41, r. 12. For a form of jurat for an affidavit sworn before a commissioner in Scotland or Northern Ireland, see Chitty and Jacob, p. 528; 3 *Court Forms* (1979 issue) 394.

[55] It has been held not to be necessary to prove the authority of a commissioner for oaths in Ireland: *Hume Pipe and Concrete Construction Co. Ltd.* v. *Moracrete Ltd.* [1942] 1 K.B. 189.

[56] 17 *Halsbury's Laws* (4th ed.), para. 320.

[57] *Supreme Court Practice*, para. 41/12/4; *Cooper* v. *Moon* [1884] W.N. 78 ("In the present case the affidavit purports to have been sworn before a foreign local magistrate, and I think that the seal and attestation of the local court may from comity of nations be taken as authenticating his authority to administer an oath.").

[58] *Warren* v. *Swinburne* (1845) 9 Jur. 910.

[59] *Brittlebank* v. *Smith* (1884) 50 L.T. 491.

[60] See *Supreme Court Practice*, para. 41/12/4.

[61] Signed on October 5, 1961. The following European countries had ratified or acceded to the Convention (as at March 22, 1989): Austria, Belgium, Cyprus, Finland, France, Germany (Federal Republic), Greece, Hungary, Italy, Liechtenstein, Luxembourg, Malta, Netherlands, Norway, Portugal, Spain, Switzerland, Turkey, U.K., and Yugoslavia. The U.S. and many other countries have also ratified or acceded to it.

[62] The competent authority in the U.K. is the Foreign and Commonwealth Office: see para. 8.62, n. 22 below.

authority. Proof of the official's signature without proof of his authority to administer oaths may sometimes by sufficient.[63]

Affidavits for use abroad. English law is liberal in allowing oaths to **8.10** be administered in the United Kingdom for the purposes of taking evidence for use in foreign civil proceedings. Such oaths may be administered in the United Kingdom by any person appointed for that purpose by a court or other judicial authority of the country under whose law the proceedings are carried on.[64] In addition, diplomatic agents and consular officers may administer oaths and take affidavits required by a person for a use in the state which they represent or under its laws, or required by a national of that state (but not for use in the United Kingdom, except under the laws of some other country).[65] Notaries public have long exercised the right to administer oaths and take affidavits for use in countries abroad where notarial acts are recognised.[66] If the law or practice of the foreign country requires the authentication of the seal or signature of the person signing the document or administering the oath[67] a certificate may be obtained from the Foreign and Commonwealth Office.[68]

4. Civil Evidence Act 1968

Written hearsay. It is a general rule of evidence that hearsay state- **8.11** ments are not admissible. The rule is notoriously difficult to define,[69] but it is clear that a statement in a document is regarded for these purposes as a hearsay statement, even if the person drawing up the document had personal knowledge of the matters in the statement. The rule against hearsay is subject, however, to a number of exceptions of which the most important, in the context of civil proceedings, arise under the Civil Evidence Act 1968. That

---

[63] In *Re London Asphalte Co. Ltd.* (1907) 23 T.L.R. 406, the court was willing to assume, without proof or verification, that a German notary had authority to administer oaths; and in *Kevan v. Crawford* (1876) L.J.Ch. 658, the limited authority of a Belgian *juge de paix* to administer an oath was regarded as sufficient. Similarly, proof of the foreign official's authority has been waived where the value of the case was small: *Mayne v. Butler* (1864) 11 L.T. 410; 13 W.R. 128. See also *Re Davis's Trusts* (1869) L.R. 8 Eq. 98; *Supreme Court Practice*, para. 41/12/2; 17 *Halsbury's Laws* (4th ed.), para. 320.
[64] Oaths and Evidence (Overseas Authorities and Countries) Act 1963, s.1. The section confers no power to compel a person to take an oath.
[65] Consular Relations Act 1968, s.10.
[66] *Brooke's Notary* (9th ed.), p. 18.
[67] But see the Hague Convention referred to at para. 8.09 above.
[68] See para. 8.62, n.22 below.
[69] See, for example, *Cross on Evidence* (6th ed.), pp. 453 *et seq.*

Act allows hearsay statements,[70] including a witness's written statement of facts known to him, to be admitted in evidence in certain circumstances, including where the witness is "beyond the seas."[71]

8.12 *Scheme of the Act.* The scheme of the Act is to permit out-of-court statements, whether made orally or in a document,[72] to be *admissible* as evidence of facts stated therein if direct oral evidence of those facts would be admissible.[73] Whether the statements are actually *admitted* as evidence depends on whether a number of procedural requirements have been fulfilled.[74] First, notice of a party's intention that the statement should be given in evidence should be served on the other party within the time limits provided by the rules.[75] If the party who wishes to put the statement in evidence contends that the witness cannot or should not be called as a witness for any of a number of specified reasons, he must say so in the notice and set out the reason relied upon.[76] The specified reasons include the fact that the witness is "beyond the seas."[77] If the other party wishes to require the party giving the original notice to call the witness at the trial or hearing, that other party must serve a counter-notice.[78] If the original statement had contained a statement that the witness could not or should not be called to give evidence because, for example, he was beyond the seas, then the other party may only serve a counter-notice if he contends that the wit-

---

[70] As to the operation of the Act in connection with foreign public documents, see para. 8.20 below.

[71] The term "beyond the seas" means outside England and Wales, Scotland and Northern Ireland: *Rover International Ltd.* v. *Cannon Films Sales Ltd.* [1987] 1 W.L.R. 1597.

[72] There is some doubt as to whether affidavits (and experts' reports) are "documents" for the purposes of the Civil Evidence Act 1968: *Rover International Ltd.* v. *Cannon Films Sales Ltd.* [1987] 1 W.L.R. 1597, 1604.

[73] Civil Evidence Act 1968, s.2. Similar rules apply to certain records and to certain statements produced by computer: *ibid.*, ss.4 and 5. If a statement of non-expert opinion would be admissible, hearsay evidence of that opinion may also be admitted: Civil Evidence Act 1972, s.1(1), R.S.C., Ord. 38, r. 34; C.C.R., Ord. 20, r. 26.

[74] R.S.C., Ord. 38, rr. 20–34; C.C.R., Ord. 20, rr. 14–26.

[75] R.S.C., Ord. 38, r. 21; C.C.R., Ord. 20, r. 15. For forms of notice, see *Supreme Court Practice*, paras. [601] *et seq.*; Chitty and Jacob, pp. 502 *et seq.*; 18 *Court Forms* (1985) issue), 432 *et seq.*

[76] R.S.C., Ord. 38, r. 22(3); C.C.R., Ord. 20, r. 16.

[77] Civil Evidence Act 1968, s.8(2)(b); R.S.C., Ord. 38, r. 25; C.C.R., Ord. 20, r. 16. There are five specified reasons, the other reasons being that the person in question is dead, or unfit by reason of his bodily or mental condition to attend as a witness or that despite the exercise of reasonable diligence it has not been possible to identify or find him or that he cannot reasonably be expected to have any recollection of matters relevant to the accuracy or otherwise of the statement to which the notice relates.

[78] R.S.C., Ord. 38, r. 26; C.C.R., Ord. 20, r. 17.

ness can or should be called, in which case the counter-notice must contain a statement to that effect.[79]

The service of a counter-notice stating that a witness, who was **8.13** said in the original notice to be beyond the seas, could or should be called as a witness at the trial or hearing does not have the effect of preventing the hearsay statement being admitted in evidence. What it may do, though, is to raise the question whether the witness is in fact beyond the seas, a question which the court can order to be determined before the trial.[80] If it is established or accepted that the witness is beyond the seas, the hearsay statement may be admitted as of right and the court has no discretion to exclude it, even if it is not shown that reasonable efforts have been made to secure the attendance of the witness.[81] On the other hand, if the procedural requirements have not been complied with, the court may still permit the statement to be admitted, but this is a matter for the court's discretion.[82] The weight (if any) to be attached to the evidence admitted under the provisions of the Civil Evidence Act is a matter which the court may estimate having regard to all the circumstances from which any inference can reasonably be drawn as to the statement's accuracy.[83]

5. Documentary evidence

There are three aspects of the law and practice relating to docu- **8.14** mentary evidence which may give rise to particular problems in proceedings containing an international element, namely the discovery of documents located abroad, the treatment of documents in a foreign language, and proof of entries in foreign registers and other foreign documents.

Discovery of documents located abroad. Because most continental **8.15** systems of civil procedure do not normally require a party to disclose documents[84] in his possession which are adverse to his case,[85] it is frequently difficult in practice for English solicitors to impress sufficiently strongly on their foreign clients the extent of their obligations under English discovery procedures. They must nevertheless attempt to do so, because the requirements of the rules as to

---

[79] R.S.C., Ord. 38, r. 26(2); C.C.R., Ord. 20, r. 17(2).
[80] R.S.C., Ord. 38, r. 27; C.C.R., Ord. 20, r. 18.
[81] *Rasool* v. *West Midlands Passenger Transport Executive* [1974] 3 All E.R. 638; *Piermay Shipping Co. S.A.* v. *Chester* [1978] 1 W.L.R. 411.
[82] R.S.C., Ord. 38, r. 29; C.C.R., Ord. 20, r. 20; *Supreme Court Practice,* para. 38/29/1 and the cases cited there. See, for example, *Rover International Ltd.* v. *Cannon Film Sales Ltd.* [1987] 1 W.L.R. 1597, 1604.
[83] Civil Evidence Act 1968, s.6(3).
[84] The disclosure of documents by non-parties is considered at para. 8.72 below.
[85] See chaps. 48 to 58, at paras. 51 and 52 below.

discovery are not relaxed in the case of foreign parties, even when the documents are located outside the jurisdiction of the court. If a solicitor knows that his client has documents in his possession custody or power which he has not disclosed, or if the client fails to give the solicitor the information to which he is entitled, it is the solicitor's duty to withdraw from the case.[86]

The rules of court provide for the inspection of disclosed documents at a place notified by the disclosing party,[87] but if the court considers that the place specified is unreasonable, it has power to specify the place at which the documents are to be produced for inspection.[88] It is not necessarily unreasonable to make disclosed documents available for inspection at a place located abroad[89]; but different considerations apply if the order is an order against a non-party to produce documents outside the jurisdiction.[90]

8.16   *Documents in a foreign language.* The meaning in English of a document in a foreign language is treated as a question of fact to be proved by a person competent to do so.[91] The factual translation of the document in this sense may involve translating scientific, technical or legal expressions in the document but, it is suggested, the evidence remains of a factual nature, rather than expert evidence.[92] The translation of a document is to be distinguished from the question of its construction, which remains a question of law for the court,[93] although for this purpose the court may require additional evidence (of an expert nature) as to any foreign law applicable to the case, and particularly of foreign rules of construction applicable to the document in question.[94] The cumbersome results of having to prove individual translations can be avoided in practice if the parties are able to prepare and agree translations in advance of a trial or hearing. The translations may then conveniently be interleaved into

---

[86] *Myers* v. *Elman* [1940] A.C. 282.

[87] R.S.C., Ord. 24, r. 9; C.C.R., Ord. 14, r. 3.

[88] R.S.C., Ord. 24, r. 11(1)(c); C.C.R., Ord. 14, r. (1)(c). The same power applies as regards the time and manner of inspection.

[89] *Whyte & Co.* v. *Ahrens & Co.* (1884) 50 L.T. 344 (where production of documents was ordered in Japan).

[90] *Mackinnon* v. *Donaldson, Lufkin and Jenrette Securities Corp.* [1986] Ch. 482: see paras. 8.43 *et seq.* below.

[91] *Shore* v. *Wilson* (1842) 9 Cl. & Fin. 355, 511 (*per* Erskine J.), 555 (*per* Parke B.), 566 (*per* Tindall C.J.).

[92] If it were expert evidence, it would not generally be admissible (except with the leave of the court), unless all parties agreed or a direction for its admission had been made under R.S.C., Ord. 38, rr. 35 *et seq.*

[93] 12 *Halsbury's Laws* (4th ed.), para. 1461.

[94] *Ascherberg, Hopwood & Crewe Ltd.* v. *Casa Musicale Sonzogno di Pietro Ostali S.N.C.* [1971] 1 W.L.R. 1128; *A/S Tallinna Laevauhisus* v. *Estonian State Steamship Line* (1947) 80 Ll.L.R. 99 at p. 108. As to proof of foreign law generally, see chap. 9.

any agreed bundle of documents. Similarly, translations of documents exhibited to affidavits can be interleaved in the exhibit, although if the deponent to the affidavit is not himself competent to swear to the accuracy of the translations, a separate affidavit will be required for that purpose.

If an issue in any proceedings depends on a particular meaning or construction of a document in a foreign language, the party contending for that particular meaning or construction should include that contention in his pleadings, in order not to take the other party by surprise.[95]

Foreign judgments, registers and other documents

General rules relating to foreign documents.[96] As a matter of common law, certain public documents and certain records were admissible as evidence of the facts stated in them.[97] The admissibility of such documents and records has been preserved by the Civil Evidence Act 1968.[98] Provided that certain conditions were fulfilled,[99] foreign and colonial registers were regarded as public documents for the purposes of this rule.[1] Other foreign documents, either of a public or of a private nature, may be admissible as evidence of the facts stated in them under the general provisions of the Civil Evidence Act 1968 regarding statements made out of court, or in certain records, or produced by computer.[2] Certificates relating to the service of English process abroad may be admissible under the Rules of the Supreme Court.[3] Special provisions apply to the proof and admissibility of certain judgments and other documents for the purposes of the 1968 Convention.[3a]

8.17

---

[95] *Ibid.*

[96] There are various rules of law which facilitate the proof of foreign judgments, foreign registers and other foreign public and private documents. Many such documents are susceptible of proof in more than one way. This section discusses first the general rules which relate to the admissibility of foreign documents (especially public docments); separate sections below discuss foreign judgments, entries in foreign official registers and official certificates, and authentic instruments.

[97] 17 *Halsbury's Laws*, paras. 76 and 77.

[98] Civil Evidence Act 1968, s.9(1), (2)(c), (2)(d).

[99] The register must have been required by the local law to be kept, for the purpose of public use, and the entries must have been promptly made by the proper official: see *Sturla* v. *Freccia* (1880) 5 App.Cas. 623, 643; *Ioannou* v. *Demetriou* [1952] A.C. 84; *R.* v. *Halpin* [1975] Q.B. 907.

[1] 17 *Halsbury's Laws*, paras. 169, 178; see para. 8.20 below.

[2] Civil Evidence Act 1968, ss.2, 4 and 5. See para. 8.11 above.

[3] See R.S.C., Ord. 11, rr. 5(5)–(7) and para. 4.33 above.

[3a] 1982 Act, s.11, see paras. 8–19 and 40.32 *et seq.* below.

8.18   *Foreign documents: copies and secondary evidence.* If a public document is admissible in evidence, it may be proved instead by a copy which satisfies certain criteria which depend on the nature of the document.[4] As regards foreign public documents, copies of these may be admitted under the various statutory schemes referred to below. One of the types of copy permitted by those schemes (now rarely used) is an "examined copy," that is, a copy which a witness, who has read and been able to understand the whole of the original document, swears to be a true copy.[5] As regards private documents, secondary evidence of these (by copies or other adequate means) may be admitted if the original is shown not to be available.[6] This may be the case, for example, where the original is abroad in the custody of a person who is not willing to produce it voluntarily.[7] Enquiry should be made of the person having custody of the document[8] and the purpose of the enquiry should be made known to him.[9] In addition, if a statement in a document is admissible under sections 2 to 5 of the Civil Evidence Act 1968, the statement may be proved by producing that document, or (whether or not that document is still in existence) a copy of it or of the material part thereof, authenticated in such manner as the court may approve.[10] Documents which are admissible in evidence in Northern Ireland[11] or the British Colonies[12] are likewise admissible in England.[13]

8.19   *Foreign acts of state, judgments and other judicial documents.* Foreign acts of state, judgments and certain other official and

---

[4] 17 *Halsbury's Laws*, paras. 145 to 149.
[5] *Ibid.*, para. 147.
[6] *Ibid.*, paras. 9, 10, 138–144. It may be that the rules which relate to public documents apply also to certain categories of private documents, namely documents which, although private in one sense, are intended to be made public, such as commercial instruments, bills of exchange, charterparties, etc. "which are the indicia of property throughout the world": *Boyle* v. *Wiseman* (1855) 156 E.R. 598, at p. 601 (*per* Pollock C.B.).
[7] *Re Lemme* [1892] P. 89; *Re von Linden* [1896] P. 148; *Permanent Trustee Co. of New South Wales* v. *Fels* [1918] A.C. 879.
[8] The application should be made to the person having legal custody of the document, not mere possession: *Crispin* v. *Doglioni* (1863) 32 L.J.P.M. & A. 109.
[9] *Boyle* v. *Wiseman* (1855) 156 E.R. 598.
[10] Civil Evidence Act 1968, s.6(1). An application for directions as to the manner of authentication is made to the master: R.S.C., Ord. 38, r. 33, Ord. 32, rr. 11, 14. For forms of summons for this purpose, see *Supreme Court Practice*, para. [613]; Chitty and Jacob, p. 510. In the county court, the application is made to the judge or registrar: C.C.R., Ord. 1, r. 8; Ord. 20, r. 24.
[11] The provision is one which formerly applied to Ireland: see the enactments listed at 17 *Halsbury's Statutes* (4th ed.) 86.
[12] "British colony" is defined as including the Channel Islands and the Isle of Man and "all other possessions of the British Crown, wheresoever and whatsoever": see Evidence Act 1851, s.19.
[13] Evidence Act 1851, ss. 9, 11.

judicial documents may be proved in accordance with the provisions of section 7 of the Evidence Act 1851.[14] That section enables the documents to which it applies to be proved by the production of an examined copy[15] or an authenticated copy. For the purpose of specifying what constitutes an authenticated copy, the section divides the documents to which it applies into two separate categories. The first category is "all proclamations, treaties and other acts of state of any foreign state or of any British colony."[16] In the case of these documents, the authenticated copy must purport to be sealed with the seal of the foreign state or British colony to which the original document belongs. The second category is "all judgments, decrees, orders and other judicial proceedings of any court of justice in any foreign state or any British colony, and all affidavits, pleadings, and other legal documents filed or deposited in any such court." The authenticated copy of any of these documents must purport either to be sealed with the seal of the foreign or colonial court to which the original document belongs or, if that court has no seal, by purporting to be signed by the judge or one of the judges of that court, who must attach a statement in writing that the court has no seal. Copies of documents to which the section applies which have been duly authenticated are to be admitted in evidence in every case in which the original document could have been received in evidence without any proof of the seal or signature or of the truth of the statement that the court has no seal, or of the judicial character of the signatory.

A somewhat simpler method of proof is available in respect of judgments to which the 1968 Convention applies. For the purposes of that Convention, section 11 of the 1982 Act provides that a document which purports to be a copy of a judgment given by a court of a Contracting State other than the United Kingdom is deemed without further proof to be a true copy if it is duly authenticated.[17] It is regarded as being duly authenticated if it purports to bear the seal of that court or to be certified by any person in his capacity as a judge or officer of that court to be a true copy of a judgment of that court.[18] These provisions do not apply to the other documents, such as affidavits and pleadings, which fall within the ambit of the 1851 Act, but they do not prejudice the admissibility of any document which is otherwise admissible.[19]

---

[14] See further, 17 *Halsbury's Laws* (4th ed.), para. 160; *Phipson on Evidence* (13th ed.), para. 36–64.
[15] As to the meaning of "examined copy," see para. 8.18 above.
[16] As to meaning of "British colony," see Evidence Act 1851, s.19, noted at n. 12 above.
[17] 1982 Act, s.11(1)(a), para. 40.32 below.
[18] 1982 Act, s.11(2), para. 40.32 below.
[19] 1982 Act, s.11(3), para. 40.32 below.

8.20   *Foreign official registers and certificates.* It has already been noted that at common law certain public documents were admitted as evidence of the matters stated in them, and that this rule has been preserved by the Civil Evidence Act 1968.[20] This rule extended to foreign registers which were required to be kept by the law of the country where they were located or by English law.[21] If the registers were admissible in evidence, certified and examined copies of entries in them were also admissible,[22] provided the certificate or other official extract was in a form required by the relevant foreign law.[23]

As regards the European countries with which this work is concerned, and various other countries, this rule is now of somewhat reduced importance, because entries in some foreign public registers are now admissible as evidence pursuant to specific statutory provisions. Under the Evidence (Foreign Dominion and Colonial Documents) Act 1933, and section 5 of the Oaths and Evidence (Overseas Authorities and Countries) Act 1963, Orders in Council may be made which have the effect of enabling specified foreign registers and certain official books of record to be admissible as evidence of the matters recorded in them and facilitating the admission in evidence of official certificates and official documents issued as proof of matters covered by the Order.[24] Such Orders in Council have been made in respect of all the other Contracting States to the 1968 Convention (except Greece).[25] These provisions have generally only been applied to the registers relating to matters of personal status (births, marriages, deaths, adoption and so forth), and not to registers of companies and other legal persons. Their usefulness in ordinary civil and commercial litigation is consequently much reduced.

---

[20] Para. 8.17 above.
[21] See 17 *Halsbury's Laws* (4th ed.), para. 178 and the cases cited there.
[22] *Lyell* v. *Kennedy* (1889) 14 App.Cas. 437, at p. 448.
[23] 17 *Halsbury's Laws* (4th ed.), para. 178.
[24] The matters for which the Orders in Council may provide are set out in the Evidence (Foreign, Dominion and Colonial Documents) Act 1933, s.1(2).
[25] Evidence (Belgium) Order 1933, S.R. & O. 1933 No. 383; Evidence (Denmark) Order 1969 (S.I. 1969 No. 144); Evidence (France) Order in Council 1937, S.R. & O. 1937 No. 515; Evidence (Federal Republic of Germany) Order 1970 (S.I. 1970 No. 819); Evidence (Republic of Ireland) Order 1969 (S.I. 1969 No. 1059); Evidence (Italy) Order 1969 (S.I. 1969 No. 145); Evidence (Luxembourg) Order 1972 (S.I. 1972 No. 116); Evidence (the Netherlands) Order 1970 (S.I. 1970 No. 284). The orders in respect of other countries are listed in the *Supreme Court Practice*, para. 38/10/5. Conventions providing reciprocity in this connection were concluded with Belgium (Brussels, December 21, 1928, Treaty Series No. 3 (1929) Cmnd. 3260, 128 State Papers 281) and France (Paris, April 3, 1937, Treaty Series No. 24 (1937) Cmnd. 5476, 141 State Papers 301).

Authentic instruments. Article 50 of the 1968 Convention[26] enables **8.21**
documents which have been formally drawn up or registered as
authentic instruments in another Contracting State to be enforced
in the United Kingdom in the same manner as judgments.[27] The
enforceability of such documents depends *inter alia* upon their satisfying the conditions necessary to establish their authenticity in their
state of origin.[28] Two questions are to be distinguished, namely,
first, what conditions must be satisfied for the authenticity of the
instrument to be established and, secondly, how the English court
is to be satisfied that the instrument satisfies these conditions. The
first question is to be decided by the law of the state of origin, but
the second is to be decided in accordance with the rules of procedure under the Convention,[29] supplemented as necessary by English rules of evidence.

Unless and until any different provision is made by Order in
Council under section 13 of the 1982 Act[30] or otherwise, it seems
that the only rule of English law which will be relevant in this connection is that which requires foreign law to be proved as a matter
of fact.[31] Evidence will need to be adduced as to the requirements
of foreign law which regulate the authenticity of the instrument.
Once it is acquainted with those conditions, the English court
should consider as a matter of fact whether the instrument which
has been produced to it satisfies them.[32]

C. INTERNATIONAL JUDICIAL ASSISTANCE: THE FRAMEWORK

1. Introduction

International judicial assistance. Most countries are willing to give **8.22**
assistance to the courts or other judicial authorities of other countries in obtaining evidence in their territory, in serving documents
there and in various other ways.[33] The term "judicial assistance" or
"judicial co-operation" is used to refer to these activities. As
regards the obtaining of evidence, this assistance may be of an
active kind, involving the authorities or courts of the foreign

---

[26] Paras. 10.49 below and 30.01 below.
[27] Similar provisions apply to court settlements: Art. 51 of the 1968 Convention,
para. 30.14 below.
[28] Para. 30.09 below.
[29] *Ibid.*
[30] Para. 40.38 below.
[31] Para. 9.03 below.
[32] See para. 30.12 as to the matters which it may be possible to raise in objecting to
the validity of the instrument.
[33] Service of documents is discussed separately in chap. 4. Supplying extracts from
a country's official registers (para. 8.20 above) or information on its law
(paras. 9.09 *et seq.* below) are other forms of judicial assistance.

country in seeking out the evidence required; or it may be of a passive kind, in permitting the parties or foreign authorities to seek out the evidence themselves. Each country has its own rules governing the means by which evidence may be gathered for use abroad, and the conditions which apply. These rules may vary depending on which country is seeking the assistance, the nationality of the witness and, in particular, whether there is a convention on judicial co-operation between the countries involved.

8.23   *Obtaining evidence abroad.* There are three principal methods by which evidence may be obtained in one country for use in another country. First, it may be obtained without the involvement of official channels, by the voluntary co-operation of the witness in making a statement or deposing to an affidavit, although in some countries this may be prohibited to a greater or lesser extent as a breach of judicial sovereignty.[34] Secondly, the evidence may be taken before a diplomatic or consular officer of the state in which the evidence is required, or before some other commissioner or examiner appointed by that state or by its courts. Thirdly, the evidence may be taken by the courts or other judicial authorities of the state where the witness is located, pursuant to "letters of request" or "letters rogatory" issued by the court or judicial authority of the state where the evidence is to be used. The second and third methods are often regulated by bilateral or multilateral conventions. Each of these methods is considered in more detail below.[35]

8.24   *Conventions.* The United Kingdom is a party to a number of conventions on the taking of evidence abroad which are examined in more detail below. Most importantly, it is a party to the Hague Convention of March 18, 1970 on the Taking of Evidence Abroad in Civil or Commercial Matters. This convention now provides the principal official means for obtaining evidence in each of the countries which are parties to it for use in any of the others. In addition, the United Kingdom also has bilateral conventions on judicial co-operation with some 24 countries, including many of the Contracting States to the 1968 Convention.

If evidence is required in a country which is a party to the Hague Convention and which also has a bilateral convention with the United Kingdom, the party seeking the evidence may choose which procedure to invoke.[36] The procedure for invoking the assistance of the foreign courts or other judicial authorities under the Hague Convention is usually cheaper and, because it avoids diplomatic

---

[34] Para. 8.42 below.
[35] Paras. 8.40 *et seq.* below (obtaining evidence abroad for use in England); paras. 8.59 *et seq.* below (obtaining evidence in England for use abroad).
[36] See further, para. 8.48 below.

channels, it may often be faster, especially as regards other European countries. In some cases though, there may be an advantage in invoking the procedure under the bilateral conventions, either to obtain the assistance of the diplomatic service or because the terms of the bilateral conventions are better suited in some respect to the particular circumstances of the case.

Effect of conventions in English law. In order for an international **8.25** convention to be given effect in English law, it must first be incorporated by or pursuant to an Act of Parliament, except that where English law and practices do not need to be adjusted in order to secure compliance with the convention, such incorporation may be dispensed with. There are various means which are employed to give effect to conventions in English law[37] and in some of them the fact that the enactment gives effect to the treaty may not be expressly mentioned.

Neither the Hague Convention of 1970 nor any of the bilateral civil procedure conventions has been expressly incorporated into English law, although effect is given to some of their provisions for the taking of evidence in the United Kingdom by the Evidence (Proceedings in other Jurisdictions) Act 1975.[38] They do, however, affect the exercise of the court's powers to issue letters of request addressed to the authorities of foreign countries and the liability to pay the costs of the judicial assistance requested. They also affect the practices adopted by the High Court and by the diplomatic service in connection with the transmission of letters of request and depositions. It will therefore be necessary to consider their provisions in a little detail.

2. The Hague Convention on the taking of evidence abroad

As has already been observed,[39] many continental countries were **8.26** parties to the Hague Conventions on civil procedure of 1905 and 1954. These earlier conventions were largely replaced in 1965 and 1970 by two new conventions, one on the service of documents abroad (which has already been described)[40] and one on the taking of evidence abroad, both of which have been ratified by the United

---

[37] See the section by Professor R. Higgins Q.C. in Jacobs and Roberts (ed.), *The Effect of Treaties in Domestic Law*, at pp. 123 *et seq.*; also Mann, *Foreign Affairs in English Courts*, at pp. 97 *et seq.*

[38] See paras. 8.63 *et seq.* below. They are also referred to in R.S.C., Ord. 39, r. 2(2), in connection with the court's powers to make an order appointing a special examiner to take evidence in a foreign country: see para. 8.44 below, and in R.S.C., Ord. 11, rr. 5 and 6, in connection with service of documents: see paras. 4.30 and 4.34 above.

[39] Para. 4.30 above.

[40] The Hague Convention of November 15, 1965 on the Service Abroad of Judicial and Extrajudicial Documents in Civil or Commercial Matters: para. 4.30 above.

Kingdom. The second of these, the Convention on the Taking of
Evidence Abroad in Civil or Commercial Matters signed at the
Hague on March 18, 1970 (to give it its full title),[41] has been ratified
or acceded to by some 19 countries, including most of those with
which this book is concerned.[42] It was principally designed to provide a relatively simple and uniform system for the obtaining of evidence pursuant to letters of request through the judicial authorities
of the contracting states and to streamline the various procedures
for obtaining evidence by diplomatic and consular officials. The
convention permits signatory states to make declarations at the time
of signature or subsequently which have the effect of varying its
precise application from state to state. It applies to "civil or commercial matters," a term which it does not define.[43]

Letters of request

8.27   Chapter I of the Hague Convention (Articles 1 to 14) is concerned
with the taking of evidence by the courts of the country where the
witness or other evidence is located, pursuant to letters of request
(*commissions rogatoires*). These may be issued by the judicial authorities of one state and addressed to the competent authorities of
another state requesting the latter to obtain evidence or perform
some other judicial act.[44] An important feature of the Hague Convention is that it requires each of the contracting states to designate
a central authority for the purpose of receiving incoming letters of
request from abroad and transmitting them to the authorities competent to put them into effect.[45] The information to be included in

---

[41] Cmnd. 6727, Treaty Series No. 20 (1977). The text of the convention is set out
in App. 2, at paras. A2.17 *et seq.* below.
[42] The countries which have ratified or acceded to the convention are as follows (as at
March 22, 1989): Argentina, Barbados, Cyprus, Czechoslovakia, Denmark, Fin-
land, France, Germany (Federal Republic), Israel, Italy, Luxembourg, Monaco,
Netherlands (extended also to Aruba), Norway, Portugal, Singapore, Spain,
Sweden, U.K. (extended also to Akrotiri and Dhekelia, Anguilla, Cayman Islands,
Falkland Islands and Dependencies, Gibraltar, Guernsey, Hong Kong, Isle of
Man and Jersey), and the U.S. (extended also to Guam, Puerto Rico and the Virgin
Islands). Switzerland has signed but not yet ratified the convention. Note that
Belgium, Greece and Ireland have not signed the convention. (Note also that the list
of countries in the *Supreme Court Practice* at para. 39/2–3/4 is incomplete).
[43] As a matter of English law, the term "civil or commercial matters" is to be construed more widely in this context than under the 1968 Convention: *Re State of
Norway's Application (Nos. 1 & 2)* [1989] 2 W.L.R. 458 (H.L.); see para. 14.13
below.
[44] Art. 1. *Cf.* Evidence (Proceedings in Other Jurisdictions) Act 1975, s.2(3): see
para. 8.63 below.
[45] Art. 2. Federal states may designate more than one central authority and Germany, for example, has done so. The contracting states may also designate
further competent authorities: Art. 24. The U.K. has done so: see para. 8.64,
n. 32 below.

the letter of request is specified in the convention[46] and there are provisions regulating the language in which the letter may be drawn up.[47] The scope of a letter of request may sometimes create problems, especially in connection with pre-trial discovery.[48]

Execution of letter of request. The authority which sends the letter **8.28** of request, if it so requests, will be informed of the time and place of the examination in order that the parties or their representatives may be present. This information will be sent direct to the parties or their representatives if that authority so requests.[49] The letter of request is primarily to be executed in accordance with the laws and procedures of the state to which it is addressed, but the requesting state may ask for some special procedure to be followed and such a request will be respected unless it is incompatible with the internal law of the state of execution or is impossible of performance by reason of that state's internal practice or procedure or by reason of practical difficulties.[50] The Explanatory Report on the Hague Convention stressed the narrowness of the grounds on which the requested authorities can decline to follow the special procedure requested. It states, "To be 'incompatible' with the internal law of the State of execution does not mean 'different' from the internal law. It means that there must be some constitutional inhibition or some absolute statutory prohibition."[51] Similarly, the use of the words "impossible of performance" rather than "impracticable" was deliberate, with a view to maximising international co-operation. As the Explanatory Report notes, "It is not sufficient for the foreign practice to be 'difficult' to administer or 'inconvenient'; compliance must be truly 'impossible.'"[52]

A witness may be compelled to give evidence in the execution of letters of request,[53] but may refuse to answer questions on the grounds that he has a privilege or a duty not to do so under the law either of the state of execution or of the state from which the request emanated.[54] The only grounds on which the execution of a

---

[46] Art. 3. A model form of letter of request, in a revised version, was recommended by the Special Commission of the Hague Conference on Private International Law in May 1985. It appears para. A4.09 below.

[47] Art. 4.

[48] There is a specific provision concerning discovery of documents in Art. 23, discussed at para. 8.32 below. The approach of the English courts in considering the permissible scope of letters of request is discussed at paras. 8.67 *et seq.* below.

[49] Art. 7. The revised model letter of request (para. A4.09 below) includes provision for the parties to be informed of the time and place of the examination.

[50] Art. 9.

[51] *Actes et documents de la onzième session* (1968), vol. IV, p. 208.

[52] *Ibid.*

[53] Art. 10.

[54] Art. 11.

letter of request which complies with the convention[55] may be refused are that the execution of the letter of request does not fall within the functions of the judiciary in the state of execution or that the state addressed considers that its sovereignty or security would be prejudiced thereby.[56] Once the letter of request has been executed, the depositions or other evidence is transmitted back to the authority which sent the letter of request, by the same channel which was used for the letter.[57]

8.29 *Costs.* The only costs which the state of execution may generally recover from the requesting state are the fees paid to experts and interpreters, or the cost occasioned by the use of any special procedure requested in the letters of request.[58] However, if the letter of request can only be executed by the appointment of an examiner, the costs incurred in doing so (the examiner's fees and disbursements) may also be recovered if the requesting authority gave its consent to the appointment of an examiner.[59]

Evidence taken by consuls or commissioners

8.30 Chapter II of the Hague Convention (Articles 15 to 22) concerns the taking of evidence by consuls[60] for use in proceedings which have been commenced in the state which they represent. It also contains similar provisions in respect of commissioners appointed by a court in another contracting state for the purpose of taking evidence for such proceedings. Unless the state in which the evidence is to be taken (the host state) declares that its prior permission is required, a consul may take the evidence of a person who has the nationality of the state which he represents.[61] He may also take the evidence of nationals of the host state or of a third state, if the competent authority has given its permission generally or in the particular case and if he complies with any condition specified in the

---

[55] If the central authority receiving the letter of request considers that it does not comply with the convention, it is required promptly to notify the authority which sent the letter of request, specifying its objection: Art. 5.

[56] Art. 12. The fact the requested authority considers the letters of request to infringe the public policy (*ordre public*) of that state in some way is not expressly a ground for refusing to execute it, but the grounds of rejection of a letter of request which is prejudicial to the sovereignty or security may be expressed in this way in practice. As to the incorporation of Art. 12 into English law, see paras. 8.69 and 8.79 below.

[57] Art. 13.

[58] Art. 14, first and second paras. Special provisions apply under Art. 26 where, as in the U.S., constitutional difficulties are created by the prohibition on a claim for costs being made.

[59] Art. 14, third para.

[60] The convention uses the fuller description "diplomatic officer or consular agent."

[61] Art. 15.

permission.[62] These latter provisions also apply to a commissioner appointed for the purpose of taking evidence, whatever the nationality of the witness.[63]

A witness may not be compelled to give evidence by the consul or commissioner but, if the host state so declares, the consul or commissioner may apply to the competent authority of that state for appropriate assistance to obtain the evidence by such measures of compulsion as are available under its law.[64] The consul or commissioner may, subject to the terms of any permission by the authorities of the host state, take all kinds of evidence which are not incompatible with the law of that state and administer an oath.[65] Similarly, the evidence may be taken in the manner provided by the law applicable to the court in which the action is pending, provided that such manner is not forbidden by the law of the state where the evidence is taken.[66] A witness may invoke privilege to the same extent as if he were giving evidence pursuant to a letter of request[67] and he may be legally represented.[68]

General provisions

Chapter III of the Hague Convention contains general clauses for putting the Convention into effect and defining the circumstances in which declarations may be made by signatory states and the scope of those declarations. It states that the acts provided for by the convention may be performed on less restrictive conditions pursuant to national law[69] and it preserves the operation of bilateral conventions on the taking of evidence.[70] It also contains an important provision on discovery of documents. **8.31**

Discovery of documents. Article 23 of the convention provides that "A Contracting State may at the time of signature, ratification or accession, declare that it will not execute Letters of Request issued for the purpose of obtaining pre-trial discovery of documents as known in Common Law countries."[71] This is a difficult provision, because it does not mention pre-trial discovery of witnesses' evidence as known in the United States, nor does it distinguish **8.32**

---

[62] Art. 16.
[63] Art. 17.
[64] Art. 18.
[65] Art. 21(a). As to the meaning of "incompatible," see para. 8.28 above.
[66] Art. 21(d).
[67] Arts. 11, 21(e).
[68] Art. 20.
[69] Art. 27(b).
[70] Art. 32.
[71] This Article was included in the convention at the request of the U.K. delegation to the negotiations at which the convention was drafted: *Actes et documents,* above, p. 204.

between the systems of discovery of documents known in different common law countries. Most European countries have made declarations under this Article.[72]

3. The United Kingdom's bilateral conventions

8.33   The taking of evidence abroad by means of letters of request (*commissions rogatoires*), or by diplomatic or consular officials or by other persons appointed as examiners, was one of the subjects covered by the United Kingdom's bilateral conventions on civil procedure concluded in the 1920's and 1930's.[73] These conventions are still in force[74] and they can provide an alternative to the Hague Convention as a means for taking evidence abroad.[75] The following discussion is concerned only with the conventions with Belgium, Denmark, France, Germany, Greece, Italy and the Netherlands, although much of it also applies to the other bilateral conventions. The individual requirements of each of the other Contracting States to the 1968 Convention are set out later in this chapter.[75a]

8.34   *Letters of request.* The bilateral conventions provide for the evidence to be taken by the courts or judicial authorities of the state addressed for use in proceedings in the requesting state, pursuant to letters of request transmitted through diplomatic channels.[76] With the exception of the convention with France, the conventions require the letter of request is to be drawn up in the language of the state addressed,[77] or to be accompanied by a translation into that language, which must be certified as correct by a diplomatic or consular officer of the requesting state or (except for Denmark and Greece) by an official or sworn translator of either country.[78] In the case of the convention with France, the letter of request is to be drawn up in the language of the requesting state and accompanied by a translation into the language of the state addressed.[79]

---

[72] As regards the U.K., see para. 8.72 below. As regards other European countries, see paras. 8.48 *et seq.* below.

[73] The countries with which the U.K. has bilateral conventions are listed in the *Supreme Court Practice*, at para. 39/2–3/3, and at paras. 11/6/2 and 23/1/17 (which give more detailed information). The conventions with Belgium, Denmark, France, Germany, Greece, Italy and the Netherlands are listed with references at para. A2.01 below.

[74] The conventions with Estonia, Latvia and Lithuania are, *de facto*, no longer operative.

[75] In the case of Belgium and Greece, which are not parties to the Hague Convention, the bilateral conventions are particularly significant.

[75a] See paras. 8.48 *et seq.* below.

[76] See para. 8.47 below and *Supreme Court Practice*, para. 39/2–3/9.

[77] The Belgian convention refers to "one of the languages" of the authority applied to.

[78] As to who is qualified to act as a translator, see chaps. 48 to 55 at para. 71 below.

[79] Certification of the translation is not required by the French convention.

The consul transmitting the request will be informed (if he so desires) of when and where the letter of request will be executed, so that the parties or their representatives may be present. The procedure which the requested authority follows in taking the evidence will generally be that provided by its own law or practice, but it will accede to a special request for a particular procedure to be followed, provided that that procedure is not incompatible with its law. The conventions with Denmark, Greece and the Netherlands specify the contents of the letter of request and provide expressly that it may request the court addressed to allow such questions to be put *viva voce* as the parties may desire. In each case, the convention makes it incumbent on the authorities of the state addressed to give effect to the letter of request using the same measures of compulsion as it would use if the request emanated from its own country. The only grounds on which the state addressed may refuse to execute a letter of request are if the authenticity of the letter of request is not established,[80] if the execution of the letter of request does not fall within the functions of the judiciary in the state addressed[81] or if the state addressed considers that the request affects or compromises its sovereignty or safety.

Evidence taken by a consul or other suitable person. The courts of **8.35** the country where the evidence is required may appoint a diplomatic or consular officer (hereafter referred to as a consul) of that country to take the evidence of a witness in another country. This does not involve the intervention of the foreign court or authorities. Except in the case of France and Germany, any other suitable person may also be appointed as examiner. The witness may be requested to attend but, unless he is a national of the state where the evidence is to be used, the document making the request must be in the language of the state where the evidence is to be taken. The consul or other examiner may administer an oath to the witness, but no measures of compulsion may be used to require the witness to attend or to give evidence. The evidence may be taken in accordance with the procedure of the country where it is to be used; but the conventions with Denmark, Greece, Italy and the Netherlands state that the evidence should not be contrary to the law of the state where it is being taken. The parties may be present or they may be represented by persons entitled to appear before the courts of the state where the evidence is to be used or (except as regards Belgium and France) of the state where the evidence is being taken.

The conventions with France, Germany and Italy also contain **8.36** provisions enabling compulsory powers to be used to compel wit-

---

[80] This is not expressed as a ground of refusal in the Netherlands convention.
[81] This is not expressed as a ground of refusal in the French convention.

nesses to give evidence before an examiner in certain circumstances. The conventions with France and Italy make it clear that it is the court of the state applied to which is to appoint the examiner in these circumstances,[82] but that the person appointed may be the consul of the requesting state or any other person proposed by that state. It seems that the appointment would be made pursuant to letters of request issued for that purpose.[83] The procedure is similar to that where the examiner is appointed by the court of the requesting state, but the witness can be compelled to attend the examination, to give evidence and to produce documents, under the compulsory powers of the court addressed, and he may be liable for perjury under the law of that state.[84] Under the convention with Germany, on the other hand, only a diplomatic or consular officer of the requesting state may be appointed as the examiner, and it seems that the appointment is to be made by the court of that state; but the compulsory powers of the state applied to are available against witnesses who are nationals of the requesting state, to compel them to attend, give evidence and produce documents.[85]

4. The American dimension

8.37   A substantial proportion of requests for international judicial assistance received in the United Kingdom and other European countries emanate from the United States, often in connection with pre-trial discovery. American courts may make orders for pre-trial discovery of witnesses' evidence or of documents under the Federal Rules of Civil Procedure, which they enforce by sanctions in the litigation. Alternatively, they make an order under the procedures provided for by the Hague Convention, requesting the production of evidence in another country, either from a party to the litigation or from a third party witness. European courts and governments have sometimes regarded such orders as unduly burdensome or intrusive,[86] especially where trading interests are involved. In addition to making declarations under Article 23 of the Hague Convention,[87] a number of European countries have enacted so-called "blocking statutes" to restrict the effect which may be given to

---

[82] Under the convention with France, the procedure is only available if the law of the state applied to authorises it, and it seems that French law does not do so. In England, this aspect of the convention adds nothing to the general powers of the English court (see para. 8.77 below).

[83] As to English practice, see para. 8.65 below.

[84] As to liability for perjury under English law, see para. 8.59, n. 9 below.

[85] It seems that a letter of request should be issued by the requesting state in order to invoke these powers: see para. 8.52, n. 63 below.

[86] The extent to which English courts will execute letters of request issued in connection with pre-trial discovery of evidence is discussed at para. 8.72 below.

[87] Para. 8.32 above.

Evidence

United States orders for discovery or evidence. The United States Supreme Court has also considered the international effect of such orders, especially in the context of the Hague Convention.

Blocking statutes. The purpose of a blocking statute is to prevent a   **8.38**
party or witness from complying with an order by a foreign (usually American) court for the production of evidence, usually by the imposition of criminal sanctions. It may apply automatically in specified circumstances,[88] or it may apply by order of the government;[89] and it may apply to restrict compliance with an order made in the foreign proceedings which does not invoke procedures for international judicial assistance (such as the Hague Convention) or it may restrict the extent to which effect will be given to letters of request.[90]

The Aerospatiale decision. The role of the Hague Convention in   **8.39**
assisting American courts trying international litigation has been the subject of an important decision of the United States' Supreme Court in the so-called *Aerospatiale* case.[91] Passengers injured in an aviation accident in the United States sued the French manufacturers of the aircraft for negligence and manufacturing a defective product. The defendants objected to giving discovery pursuant to the Federal Rules of Civil Procedure, on the grounds that the evidence required was situated in France and that under French penal law they could not give discovery except in compliance with the Hague Convention. One of the questions raised was whether international comity required that American litigants should use the procedures under the Hague Convention as a "first resort" for obtaining evidence abroad, and should only resort to alternative procedures available under national law if the foreign court refused to comply with the request.

By a majority of five to four, the Supreme Court held that there was no such general rule, but that in determining whether to have resort to the Hague Convention's procedures American courts should conduct a scrutiny in each case of the particular facts, sovereign interests and likelihood that such resort would prove effective. Especially as regards pre-trial discovery procedures, the Supreme

---

[88] See, for example, the French "Law relating to the Communication of Economic, Commercial, Industrial, Financial or Technical Documents or Information to Foreign Nationals or Legal Persons," Law 80/538 of July 16, 1980.
[89] See, for example, Protection of Trading Interests Act 1980, s.2, para. 8.69 below.
[90] In this connection, the blocking statute should comply with Art. 12 of the Hague Convention, discussed at para. 8.28 above. See Protection of Trading Interests Act 1980, s.4, para. 8.69 below.
[91] *Société Nationale Industrielle Aerospatiale et al. v. United States District Court for the Southern District of Iowa* (1987) 107 S.Ct. 2542.

199

Court urged lower courts to exercise special vigilance to protect foreign parties from unnecessary or burdensome orders. There was a powerful dissenting opinion on this question. The view of the majority was that respect for the civil law concept of judicial sovereignty (under which the gathering of evidence is a public judicial act, rather than a private matter for the parties)[92] and wider considerations of comity supported a general presumption in favour of using the Hague Convention.[93]

D. OBTAINING EVIDENCE ABROAD FOR USE IN ENGLISH PROCEEDINGS

1. Obtaining evidence without the intervention of the English court

8.40 *Attendance of witnesses.* It has already been observed that the primary method of adducing evidence at the trial of an action in England is by the examination of witnesses orally in open court. If the witness is outside the United Kingdom, his attendance before an English court can only be voluntary and he cannot be compelled to attend, by *subpoena* or otherwise.[94] His evidence may be given in written form under the provisions of the Civil Evidence Act[95] or by affidavit,[96] or it may be recorded in a deposition taken abroad by one of the official means referred to below.

8.41 *Gathering evidence abroad.* If a witness's evidence is to be submitted in the form of an unsworn statement or affidavit, the statement or affidavit may have to be prepared abroad. Similarly, other steps may need to be taken in other countries to obtain documents or other evidential material. The manner in which a party obtains the evidence to support his case is generally of no concern to the English court, although he may be assisted by the rules relating to discovery, interrogatories and attendance of witnesses. The court will not generally restrain a party to an action from using the means lawfully available to him in other countries for obtaining evidence. It will only do so if his conduct invades or threatens to invade a legal or equitable right of the other party, for the enforcement of which

---

[92] See further para. 8.42 below.
[93] In its *amicus curiae* brief, the U.K. had also argued that "where a state signatory to the Convention has signified by domestic law or practice . . . that information located in that state should be obtained from foreign litigants exclusively under the Hague Evidence Convention or some other international agreement, due regard for foreign sovereign interests counsels that the Convention machinery should be employed in the first instance."
[94] As regards witnesses in Scotland or Northern Ireland, see para. 8.61 below.
[95] See para. 8.11 above.
[96] See para. 8.07 above. Affidavits are also the normal means of giving evidence at interlocutory stages.

he is amenable to the jurisdiction of the English court, or if he behaves or threatens to behave in an unconscionable manner.[97] Conduct which is oppressive or vexatious or which interferes with the due process of the English court would be regarded as unconscionable.[98]

Foreign judicial sovereignty. An examination in any detail of the **8.42** means which are lawfully available in other countries for the gathering of evidence there is beyond the scope of this work, but it should be noted that the taking of a statement from even a willing and co-operative witness in other European countries may be complicated by questions concerning the judicial sovereignty of those countries.[99] This is a matter for which lawyers trained in common law systems, who would regard the taking of statements as entirely routine, are likely to be unprepared. In some continental systems of law, the questioning of a witness is regarded as a matter within the prerogative of the judiciary and, if it is performed by an unauthorised person, it would be regarded as a usurpation of those functions; it may even amount to a breach of the criminal law.[1] That, at least, is the theoretical position, although it seems that there may be a divergence between theory and practice in these matters. If the person asking the questions or taking the evidence is authorised to do so generally (by national law or international convention) or in the particular case, there is no difficulty. In the countries which adhere to these concepts of judicial sovereignty,[2] though, the strength of objection in practice may vary.[3]

In general, if the taking of evidence is not authorised, or the more formal or extensive the procedure involved, the more likely it is that the theoretical objections will have practical application. So, the formal taking of depositions by *viva voce* questioning of a witness

---

[97] *South Carolina Insurance Co.* v. *Assurantie Maatschappij "De Zeven Provincien" N.V.* [1987] A.C. 24.
[98] *Ibid.*, at p. 41.
[99] Dicey and Morris, p. 201.
[1] See, for example, the Report of the U.S. delegation to the Eleventh Session of the Hague Conference on Private International Law, (1969) 8 International Legal Materials 785, at p. 806, quoted by Blackmun J. in *Société Nationale Industrielle Aerospatiale et al.* v. *United States District Court for the Southern District of Iowa*, above.
[2] The governments of, *inter alia*, France, Germany, Italy, Luxembourg, Norway and Switzerland reported to the Hague Conference that they objected to the voluntary taking of evidence without intervention of their courts: *Actes de documents de la onzième session* (1968), vol. IV, pp. 21 *et seq.* There may also be objection in Austria and Spain: see Smit (ed.), *International Co-operation in Litigation: Europe*, at pp. 26 and 329.
[3] Of major European countries, Germany seems to take the most restrictive attitude. The foreign country's attitude may also depend on the nationality of the witness: see paras. 8.43 *et seq.* below.

by or before an examiner is more likely to be regarded as contravening the sovereignty of the state where it occurs than the informal questioning of a witness for the purpose of preparing a proof of evidence or draft affidavit.[4] If the statement is prepared by means of questions put in writing by correspondence, it is likely not to be regarded as a breach of sovereignty at all. In any case of doubt, though, the practitioner should seek the advice of a lawyer in the country in which he wishes to take the statement.

2. Obtaining evidence abroad under an order of the English court

8.43   The international framework for taking evidence abroad has been described above. Of the Contracting States to the 1968 Convention, only Ireland has no convention with the United Kingdom regulating the taking of evidence.[5] If evidence is to be taken in another country, the High Court will either order the appointment of a special examiner or order the issue of letters of request.[6] The particular procedures which are appropriate in the case of each of the other Contracting States to the 1968 Convention are described below. An order made and served in England against a person who is not a party to proceedings, to produce evidence which is located abroad, is likely to be an infringement of the sovereignty of the foreign country and such an order will accordingly be made only in exceptional circumstances.[7]

8.44   *Appointment of a special examiner.* An order may be made for the appointment of a special examiner to take the evidence of a witness abroad, provided the law of the foreign state permits it.[8] A British

---

[4] It seems that, in most or all of the Contracting States to the 1968 Convention, objection has rarely if ever been taken in modern times to the unauthorised but informal questioning of a willing witness. In practice, any objections raised are likely to relate to formal taking of depositions for evidence or pre-trial discovery in American litigation.

[5] The only other West European countries which have no convention with the U.K. on the topic are Andorra, Iceland, Liechtenstein, San Marino and the Vatican.

[6] R.S.C., Ord. 39, r. 2. The High Court also exercises this power in connection with county court proceedings, pursuant to an originating summons to a Queen's Bench master or district registrar: County Courts Act 1984, s.56; R.S.C, Ord. 107, r. 3; Ord. 32, r. 23. For forms of summonses, see R.S.C., App. A, Form No. 10; *Supreme Court Practice*, para. [4]; Chitty and Jacob, p. 584; 18 *Court Forms* (1985 issue), p. 470.

[7] *Mackinnon v. Donaldson Lufkin and Jenrette Securities Corp.* [1986] Ch. 482, where Hoffman J. discharged an order under the Banker's Books Evidence Act 1879 and a *subpoena duces tecum* served on the London branch of an American bank, requiring them to produce documents which were located in the U.S.

[8] R.S.C., Ord. 39, r. 2(1)(b).

consul may be appointed as the examiner, if this is allowed under a convention with the country in question or (if there is no convention) with the leave of the Secretary of State.[9] The application is made by summons[10] to the master.[11] Unless the order is made by consent, the application should be supported by an affidavit setting out all the circumstances relied upon.[12] The practice is the same as that for the appointment of an examiner to take the evidence of a witness in England,[13] but the form of the order is different.[14] The order will normally provide for the examination to take place in accordance with English procedure, including the administration of an oath or affirmation,[15] and with examination, cross-examination, and re-examination; but particular directions may be included in the order, including a requirement that particular questions or interrogatories be put to particular witnesses.[16]

The order is then sent by the applicant's solicitor to the examiner[17] who arranges the time and place of the examination. The applicant's agent then notifies the other parties.[18] Each party is generally responsible for securing the attendance of his witnesses before the examiner, but the examiner himself may request their attendance under the terms of the relevant conventions.[19] The

---

[9] R.S.C., Ord. 39, r. 2(2).

[10] For forms of summonses, see R.S.C., App. A, Form No. 36; *Supreme Court Practice*, para. [31]; Chitty and Jacob, pp. 572, 580; 18 *Court Forms* (1985 issue), p. 419.

[11] References to the master should be taken as referring also to district registrars (R.S.C., Ord. 32, r. 23) and the Admiralty registrar (*Supreme Court Practice*, para. 39/2/–3/8).

[12] *Supreme Court Practice*, para. 39/1/5. For forms of affidavit, see Chitty and Jacob, p. 573; 18 *Court Forms* (1985 issue), pp. 419, 420.

[13] See para. 8.03 above.

[14] The form of order is prescribed: R.S.C., App. A, Form No. 37; see *Supreme Court Practice*, para. [32]; Chitty and Jacob, pp. 574, 580; 18 *Court Forms* (1985 issue), p. 421. If it is proposed to invoke the assistance of the courts of the foreign country to secure the attendance of witnesses before the consul or other examiner, the order will need to be adapted to provide also for the issue of letters of request for that purpose. Appropriate forms of order and letter of request are set out at paras. A4.10 to A4.13 below.

[15] See para. 8.45 above.

[16] R.S.C., Ord. 39, r. 8; *Supreme Court Practice*, para. 39/8/1.

[17] It is the practice to require the applicant's solicitor to give the solicitor for the other party seven days notice of his intention to send the order to the examiner and then or subsequently to give him notice of the name and address of the applicant's agent in the country where the examination is to take place: see Chitty and Jacob, p. 575; 18 *Court Forms* (1985 issue) p. 423.

[18] See Chitty and Jacob, p. 575.

[19] As to any special requirements as to the language and contents of the summons or request, see paras. 8.48 *et seq.* below.

examination is conducted in the same manner as an examination taking place in England[20] except that in most cases compulsory powers are not available to secure the attendance of witnesses or to order them to give evidence. An oath may be administered.[21] Once the examination has been completed, it is the examiner's responsibility to send the depositions to the senior master.

8.45 *Issue of letters of request.* If it is proposed to invoke the assistance of the authorities of the foreign country, either to take the evidence themselves or to appoint a person to do so, then an application[22] may be made to the High Court for an order[23] for the issue of a letter of request. The party who obtains the order must then draw up the letter of request. There is a prescribed form for the letter of request[24] which may be varied if the order so provides. Where the letter of request is to be executed in a state signatory to the Hague Convention, though, it may be appropriate for the letter of request to be in the revised model form recommended by the Special Commission of the Hague Conference on Private International Law,[25] and if so the order should be appropriately worded.

Whatever the precise form of the letter of request, it must contain (or have annexed) a fully detailed statement of the matters on which the witness is to be examined, or a list of questions to be put to the witness. If the evidence of the witness is to be obtained by means of written questions, a list of interrogatories and cross-interrogatories to be put to him on the examination must be lodged with the letter of request.[26] Especially if the letter of request is addressed to the judicial authorities of a continental country, without a request that the witness be examined in the English style by examination, cross-examination and re-examination by the parties or their representatives, it is desirable that the questions should be set

---

[20] See para. 8.03 above.
[21] See para. 8.09 above. Unless the examiner is a "British tribunal or British officer," the witness will probably not be liable in English law for perjury committed abroad: see Perjury Act 1911, ss.1(3) and 1(5).
[22] The application is by summons to the master (or district registrar or Admiralty registrar). for the form of the summons, see R.S.C., App. A, Form No. 33; *Supreme Court Practice*, para. [28]; Chitty and Jacob, p. 576; 18 *Court Forms* (1985 issue), p. 423.
[23] R.S.C., Ord. 39, r. 2(1)(a). The form of order is prescribed: R.S.C., App. A, Form No. 34; *Supreme Court Practice*, para. [29]; Chitty and Jacob, p. 576; 18 *Court Forms* (1985 issue), p. 423.
[24] R.S.C., App. A, Form No. 35; *Supreme Court Practice*, para. [30]; Chitty and Jacob, p. 577; 18 *Court Forms* (1985 issue), p. 424.
[25] The revised model form is set out in App. 4 at para. A4.09 below.
[26] R.S.C., Ord. 39, r. 3(3). For a form of interrogatories, see Chitty and Jacob, p. 578; 18 *Court Forms* (1985 issue) p. 425.

out in some detail. If the description of the evidence to be taken is formulated by way of written questions, the prescribed form does not require a separate statement of the matters on which the witness is to be examined; but it may nonetheless be helpful to the foreign judicial authorities if such a statement is included and if the letter of request is worded in such a way as to authorise those authorities to ask supplementary questions arising from the witness's answers.

Once it has been prepared the letter of request is lodged at the **8.46** Central Office of the High Court.[27] It must be accompanied by a translation into the official language of the country where it is to be executed unless either the senior master has given a general direction in relation to that country that no translation need be provided[28] or the official language or one of the official languages of that country is English.[29] The translation must be certified by the person making it to be a correct translation and the certificate must state that person's full name and address and his qualifications for making the translation.[30] When the letter of request is lodged, the party obtaining the order must also file an undertaking signed by him or his solicitor[31] to be responsible for all the expenses incurred by the Secretary of State in respect of the letter of request.[32]

Transmission and execution of request; return of deposition. The **8.47** letters of request are forwarded to the competent authority of the state where they are to be executed, either directly by the senior master (under the Hague Convention) or by diplomatic channels through the Foreign Office. The foreign authorities will fix the time and place for the examination, summon the witnesses and (if so requested) notify the parties or their agents specified in the request. When the letter of request has been executed, the evidence will be transmitted back to the High Court through the same channels as were used to transmit the letter of request and the party who obtained the order, or his solicitor, will be informed. If the witness's evidence has been recorded in a language other than English,

---

[27] R.S.C., Ord. 39, r. 3(2).
[28] The senior master has not made any such general direction.
[29] R.S.C., Ord. 39, r. 3(4). Several countries where English is not an official language are nonetheless willing to accept letters of request in English: see paras. 8.48 *et seq.* below.
[30] R.S.C., Ord. 39, r. 3(5). As to translations, see para. 8.16 above.
[31] Queen's Bench Masters' Practice Form No. PF 79; *Supreme Court Practice*, para. [283]; Chitty and Jacob, p. 579; 18 *Court Forms* (1985 issue), p. 426.
[32] R.S.C., Ord. 39, r. 3(6). Once he has been duly notified of the amount of the expenses, he must pay them to the finance officer of the Foreign and Commonwealth Office and produce a receipt to the proper officer of the High Court.

that party or his solicitor should instruct a translator to translate the deposition. The translation should be verified by the oath of the translator[33] and it is then filed with the deposition. The deposition may then be used in evidence in the same way as a deposition taken in England.[34]

3. Procedures in respect of particular countries

8.48   This section is designed to summarise the principal requirements which apply to the taking of evidence for the purpose of proceedings in England in each of the other Contracting States to the 1968 Convention (including Greece), whether under the Hague Convention (including the various declarations made under it by the different countries)[35] or under the United Kingdom's bilateral conventions. The bilateral or other multilateral agreements between these states and states other than the United Kingdom are not considered.

Belgium

8.49   Belgium is not a party to the Hague Convention; but witnesses may be examined there under the bilateral convention.[36] The letter of request should be addressed to the *tribunal de première instance* for the place where it is to be executed and it must be translated into French or Flemish as appropriate.[36a] Although the convention does not say so, the choice of appropriate language will depend on where the letter of request is to be executed.[37] It will be transmitted through the local British consul to the *Procureur du Roi* for the place of execution, who will request the president of the *tribunal de première instance*[38] to appoint a judge to take the examination.

Alternatively, witnesses may be examined by or before an examiner (including a British consul) appointed by the English court. The witness is under no compulsion to appear before the examiner, and this fact must be expressly stated in the summons requesting

---

[33] *Supreme Court Practice*, para. 39/2–3/7.
[34] R.S.C., Ord. 38, r. 9. See para. 8.06 above.
[35] For further information on the Hague Evidence Convention, see the *Practical Handbook* on its operation, published by the Hague Conference on Private International Law.
[36] The bilateral conventions are described at para. 8.33 above. References to the bilateral convention with Belgium appear at para. A2.01 below.
[36a] In respect of a small part of eastern Belgium, German is the appropriate language.
[37] As to the official languages in different parts of Belgium, see para. 48.01 below.
[38] See para. 48.20 below.

the witness to attend.[39] Unless the witness has British nationality, the summons must be in French or Flemish as appropriate.[39a]

Denmark

Denmark is a party to the Hague Convention and has a bilateral **8.50** convention with the United Kingdom.[40] Letters of request must be translated into Danish.[41] They will be transmitted by the senior master to the Danish Ministry of Justice, or by the local British consul to that Ministry or (if the witness lives outside Copenhagen) to the local court for the place of execution. The examination will take place before the appropriate local court (*byret*).[42] The Danish authorities may permit English judicial personnel to be present at the examination.[43] A letter of request will not be executed in Denmark under the Hague Convention[44] if it was "issued for the purpose of obtaining pre-trial discovery of documents," which the Danish government has declared to apply to any letter of request which requires a person,

"(a) to state what documents relevant to the proceedings to which the Letter of Request relates are, or have been, in his possession, other than particular documents specified in the Letter of Request; or

(b) to produce any documents other than particular documents which are specified in the Letter of Request, and which are likely to be in his possession."

Witnesses may also be examined by or before an examiner (including a British consul) appointed by the English court.[45] The witness is under no compulsion to appear before the examiner.

---

[39] Art. XI(c) of the bilateral convention.
[39a] See n. 36a above.
[40] The Hague Convention is described at para. 8.26 above and set out at paras. A2.17 *et seq.* below. The bilateral conventions are described at para. 8.33 above; references to the bilateral convention with Denmark appear at para. A2.01 below.
[41] Denmark will also accept letters of request in English (or Norwegian or Swedish); but this is not provided for in the English rules of court.
[42] See para. 49.19 below.
[43] Hague Convention, Art. 8. There is no equivalent provision under the bilateral convention.
[44] Art. 23: see para. 8.32 above. The same restriction probably applies in practice to letters of request issued under the bilateral convention.
[45] This is under the bilateral convention, Art. 9. Under the Hague Convention, examination before a consul requires the permission of the Danish Ministry of Justice, and examination before other examiners is not permissible.

Unless the witness has British nationality, the summons must be in Danish or be accompanied by a translation into Danish.

France

8.51 France is a party to the Hague Convention and has a bilateral convention with the United Kingdom.[46] Letters of request should be addressed to the *tribunal de grande instance*[47] for the place where they are to be executed and they must be translated into French. They will be transmitted by the senior master to the French Ministry of Justice, or by the local British consul to the *Procureur de la République* for the place of execution. The examination will take place before a judge appointed for the purpose by the president of the local *tribunal de grande instance*. English judicial personnel may be present at the examination.[48] A letter of request will not be executed in France under the Hague Convention[49] if it was "issued for the purpose of obtaining pre-trial discovery of documents," but the French Government has declared that this does not apply "when the requested documents are enumerated limitatively in the Letter of Request and have a direct and precise link with the object of the procedure."

Witnesses may also be examined in France by or before an examiner appointed by the English court, but without the use of compulsory powers.[50] If it is proposed to appoint a British consul, this may be done by the English court without the intervention of the French authorities, pursuant to the bilateral convention.[51] Unless the witness has British nationality, the summons must be in French or accompanied by a translation into French.[52] If it is proposed to appoint a person other than a British consul, the permission of the

---

[46] The Hague Convention is described at para. 8.26 above and set out at paras. A2.17 *et seq.* below. The bilateral conventions are described at para. 8.33 above; references to the bilateral convention with France appear at para. A2.01 below. See also Platto (ed.), *Obtaining Evidence in Another Jurisdiction*, p. 27.

[47] See para. 50.20 below.

[48] Hague Convention, Art. 8. There is no equivalent provision in the bilateral convention.

[49] Art. 23: see para. 8.32 above. The same restriction probably applies in practice to letters of request issue under the bilateral convention.

[50] The powers under the bilateral convention with France for the appointment of an examiner by the court addressed, including the use of compulsory powers, do not seem to apply to an examination in France: see para. 8.36, n. 82 above.

[51] Art. VII. Under the Hague Convention, by contrast, except where the witness in question is a British national, prior permission is required from the French Ministry of Justice, which will be given subject to certain general conditions: see the *Practical Handbook* on the Hague Evidence Convention at p. 57, and the text following n. 54 below

[52] This requirement is express under the Hague Convention, but not under the bilateral convention.

French Ministry of Justice must first be obtained in each case.[53] The French government has declared that permission will be granted, subject to certain general conditions.[54] These conditions include the requirements that the evidence should be taken exclusively within the premises of embassies or consulates but which are accessible to the public, that witnesses should be regularly summoned by an official document in French or accompanied by a French translation, giving certain specified particulars, including statements that appearance is voluntary, that the witness is entitled to the assistance of a lawyer, and that the witnesses may invoke privilege. The relevant department of the Ministry of Justice must be sent copies of the witness summonses and must be notified of the time and place of the hearing so that it can be represented should the occasion arise.

Germany

The Federal Republic of Germany is a party to the Hague Convention and the bilateral convention concluded in 1928 by the German Reich with the United Kingdom is still in force for the Federal Republic.[55] Letters of request should be addressed to the *Landgericht*[55a] and must be translated into German. They will be transmitted by the senior master to the competent authority for the *Land* where they are to be executed,[56] or by the local British consul to president of the *Landgericht* for the place of execution. If the *Landgericht* finds that the letter of request is in order, it will transfer it to the *Amtsgericht*[57] for the district where the witness resides, and a judge of that court will conduct the examination. The German authorities may permit English judicial personnel to be present at the examination.[58] A letter of request will not be executed in Ger-

8.52

---

[53] The request for permission must be sent by the senior master, stating "(1) the reasons which have led to choosing this method of investigation rather than that of the Letters of Request, having regard to the costs occasioned by the proceedings; and (2) the criteria for designations of commissioners in cases where that commissioner does not reside in France."

[54] See the *Practical Handbook* on the Hague Evidence Convention, at p. 58.

[55] The Hague Convention is described at para. 8.26 above and set out at paras. A2.17 *et seq.* below. The bilateral conventions are described at para. 8.33 above; references to the bilateral convention with Germany appear at para. A2.01 below. See also Platto (ed.) *Obtaining Evidence in Another Jurisdiction*, p. 41.

[55a] See paras. 51.19–51.20 below.

[56] The Ministry of Justice for each *Land* is usually the Central Authority under the Hague Convention.

[57] See paras. 51.19–51.20 below.

[58] Hague Convention, Art. 8. Permission may be granted by the relevant Central Authority for the *Land* in question. There is no equivalent provision in the bilateral convention.

many under the Hague Convention[59] if it was "issued for the purpose of obtaining pre-trial discovery of documents as known in common law countries," but regulations are in the course of preparation which are expected to relax this restriction.

Witnesses may also be examined by or before a British consul or other examiner appointed by the English court, but the conditions under which this may occur vary according to the person appointed and the nationality of the witness. German nationals may be examined only by a British consul, and only if they consent,[60] but the intervention of the German authorities is not necessary. British nationals may be examined by a British consul, and this too does not involve the intervention of the German authorities, provided no compulsory powers are to be used.[61] However, the German courts must, if duly requested, take the necessary steps to secure the attendance of British nationals before the British consul and their giving evidence and production of documents.[62] For this purpose it seems that a letter of request should be issued by the English court.[63] Witnesses who are neither German nationals nor British nationals may be examined by or before a British consul without the intervention of the German authorities[64] and it may be that the German authorities have a discretion to use compulsory powers against such witnesses in the same manner as applies to British nationals.[65] Examiners other than British consuls may be appointed to take the evidence of persons who do not have German nationality, but prior permission of the German authorities is required and it may be that the permission will be granted only on condition that the preparation and actual taking of the evidence is subject to the control of the local court and a member of that court may be present during the examination.[66]

---

[59] Art. 23: see para. 8.32 above. The same restriction probably applies in practice to letters of request issued under the bilateral convention.

[60] Bilateral convention, Art. 11. The notification referred to in that Article was made by the German Ambassador in London on February 15, 1929: see 128 BSP 306. German nationals cannot be examined under Chapter II of the Hague Convention.

[61] *Ibid.*; Hague Convention, Art. 15.

[62] Bilateral convention, Art. 12.

[63] Para. 8.36 above. For an appropriate form of order and letter of request, see paras. A4.10–A4.11 below.

[64] Bilateral convention, Art. 11. Under Art. 16 of the Hague Convention, such witnesses may only be examined by a consul if permission is obtained from the German authorities.

[65] It may be that the first sentence of Art. 12(a) of the bilateral convention should be so construed.

[66] Hague Convention, Art. 17.

Evidence

Greece

Greece is not a party to the Hague Convention, but witnesses **8.53**
may be examined there under the bilateral convention.[67] The letter
of request, which must be translated into Greek[68] will be transmitted through the local British consul to the *procureur* for the district
court for the place where the witness resides, or in case of doubt, to
the Ministry of Justice. The examination will take place before the
full court or, more usually, one of its judges appointed for the
purpose.

Witnesses of any nationality may also be examined by or before
an examiner (including a British consul) appointed by the English
court, but without the use of any compulsory powers.[69] Unless the
witness has British nationality, the summons must be in Greek.

Ireland

Ireland is a party neither to the Hague Convention nor to a **8.54**
bilateral convention with the United Kingdom. A letter of request
(in English) may nonetheless be issued for execution in Ireland. It
may then be sent by diplomatic channels to the Minister of Justice
who transmits it to the Master of the High Court.[70] If it is found to
be in order, an examiner (usually the District Justice[71] for the place
where the witness lives) is appointed to execute the letters of
request. Alternatively, with the leave of the Secretary of State, an
order may be made appointing a British consul or other suitable
person to take the evidence.

Italy

Italy is a party to the Hague Convention and has a bilateral con- **8.55**
vention with the United Kingdom.[72] Letters of request may be
addressed to the *corte d'appello*[73] for the place where they are to be
executed and they must be translated into Italian.[74] They will be
transmitted by the senior master to the Italian Ministry of Foreign
Affairs for onward transmission to the *corte d'appello* for the dis-

---

[67] The bilateral conventions are described at para. 8.33 above. References to the
bilateral convention with Greece appear at para. A2.01 below.
[68] The translation must be certified as correct by the British consul: bilateral convention, Art. 7(b).
[69] Bilateral convention, Art. 8.
[70] See para. 52.23 below.
[71] See para. 52.19 below.
[72] The Hague Convention is described at para. 8.26 above and set out at
paras. A2.17 *et seq.* below. The bilateral conventions are described at para. 8.33
above; references to the bilateral convention with Italy appear at para. A2.01
below.
[73] See para. 53.21 below.
[74] Italy will also accept letters of request in English or in French; but this is not
provided for under English rules of court.

211

trict where they are to be executed, or by the local British consul to the *procuratore generale* at that court. If the *corte d'appello* finds that the letter of request is in order, it will transfer it to the *pretura* for the district where the witness resides, and a judge of that court will conduct the examination.[75] The local *corte d'appello* may permit English judicial personnel to be present at the examination.[76] A letter of request will not be executed in Italy under the Hague Convention[77] if it was issued for the purpose of obtaining pre-trial discovery of documents.

Witnesses of any nationality may also be examined in Italy by or before a British consul or other examiner appointed by the English court, without the intervention of the Italian authorities, provided no compulsory powers are used.[78] Unless the witness has British nationality, the summons must be in Italian or accompanied by a translation into Italian. However, if it is intended that compulsory powers should be used, the British consul or any other person proposed by the British court may first be appointed by the Italian court pursuant to letters of request[79] to take the evidence according to English procedure. In this case, the Italian court must take the necessary steps to secure the attendance of and giving evidence of witnesses and other persons to be examined and the production of documents, making use, if necessary, of its compulsory powers.[80] Alternatively, the examiner may himself apply to the Italian court for appropriate assistance to obtain the evidence by compulsion,[81] probably even if the Italian authorities have not been involved in his appointment as examiner.[82]

---

[75] See para. 53.19 below.

[76] Hague Convention, Art. 8. Permission may be granted by the relevant corte d'appello. There is no equivalent provision in the bilateral convention.

[77] Art. 23: see para. 8.32 above. The same restriction probably applies in practice to letters of request issued under the bilateral convention.

[78] Bilateral convention, Art. 11.

[79] Bilateral convention, Art. 12. See para. 8.36 above. For appropriate forms of English order and letter of request, see paras. A4.12–A4.13 below.

[80] Bilateral convention, Art. 12(b).

[81] Hague Convention, Art. 18. In this case the Italian court is not bound to grant the application for appropriate assistance, but it avoids the rather cumbersome procedure of letters of request for the Italian court to appoint the English court's nominee as examiner.

[82] Art. 18 of the Hague Convention, and the Italian declaration under it, refer to a consul or commissioner taking evidence under Arts. 15, 16 or 17. Under Arts. 16 and 17, the permission of the appropriate corte d'appello is to be obtained before a non-British witness can be examined before a consul or any witness can be examined before a commissioner (*i.e.*, any other examiner); although this permission is not required under the bilateral convention. It is probable that the bilateral convention derogates from the requirement for prior permission to be obtained, without derogating from the examiner's right to apply for the assistance of the Italian court: see Arts. 27(b), 28(g) and 32.

Luxembourg

Luxembourg is a party to the Hague Convention but has no bila-   **8.56**
teral convention with the United Kingdom.[83] Letters of request
must be translated into French.[84] They will be transmitted by the
senior master to the *Parquet général* at the *Cour supérieure de Justice*,[85]
who will present them for execution. English judicial personnel may
be present at the examination.[86] A letter of request will not be
executed in Luxembourg under the Hague Convention[87] if it was
issued for the purpose of obtaining pre-trial discovery of documents.

Witnesses may also be examined in Luxembourg before a British
consul or other examiner appointed by the English court; but no
compulsory powers are available. Moreover, where the witness to
be examined does not have British nationality, or where the examination is to be conducted before an examiner other than a consul,
prior permission of the Luxembourg *Parquet général* is required.[88]
This permission is given in each particular case on the same terms
as are imposed by the French authorities.[89]

Netherlands

The Netherlands is a party to the Hague Convention and has a   **8.57**
bilateral convention with the United Kingdom.[90] Letters of request
must be translated into Dutch.[91] They will be transmitted by the
senior master or local British consul to the *Officier van Justitie* at the
arrondissementsrechtbank[92] of the Hague or (in the case of the consul)
of the area where they are to be executed for onward transmission
to the *kantongerecht*[93] for the district where the witness resides.
The judge of that court then carries out the examination. The
court which executes the letter of request may permit English

---

[83] The Hague Convention is described at para. 8.26 above and set out at paras.
   A2.17 *et seq.* below.
[84] Luxembourg will also accept letters of request in English or in German; but this
   is not provided for under English rules of court.
[85] See para. 54.21 below.
[86] Hague Convention, Art. 8.
[87] Art. 23: see para. 8.32 above.
[88] Hague Convention, Arts. 16 and 17.
[89] See para. 8.51, nn. 51 and 54 above; *Practical Handbook*, pp. 75, 76.
[90] The Hague Convention is described at para. 8.26 above and set out at paras.
   A2.17 *et seq.* below. It has been extended by the Netherlands to Aruba, but
   under some different conditions from those described here. The bilateral conventions are described at para. 8.33 above; references to the bilateral convention
   with the Netherlands appear at para. A2.01 below. See also Platto (ed.), *Obtaining Evidence in Another Jurisdiction*, p. 91.
[91] See para. 55.20 below.
[92] The Netherlands will also accept letters of request in English, in French or in
   German; but this is not provided for under English rules of court.
[93] See para. 55.19 below.

213

judicial personnel to be present at the examination.[94] Letters of request will not be executed in the Netherlands under the Hague Convention[95] if they were "issued for the purpose of obtaining pre-trial discovery of documents as known in common law countries," which the Dutch government has declared as being defined as any letters of request which require a person:

> "(a) to state which of the documents which are relevant to the proceedings in which the Letter of Request relates have been in his possession, custody or power; or
> (b) to produce any documents specified in the Letter of Request as being documents which the court which is conducting the proceedings believes to be in his possession, custody or power."

Witnesses of any nationality may also be examined in the Netherlands by or before a British consul or other examiner appointed by the English court, without the intervention of the Dutch authorities, but without the use of any compulsory powers.[96] Unless the witness has British nationality, the summons must be in Dutch or accompanied by a translation into Dutch.

Scotland and Northern Ireland

8.58   Unlike witnesses in foreign countries, witnesses in Scotland or Northern Ireland can be summoned to give evidence or produce documents to a court in England by a writ of *subpoena*. The leave of the court is required, however, for the issue of the *subpoena*, which must be in a special form.[97] The application for leave is ordinarily made *ex parte*[98] on affidavit[99] and will only be granted if it appears to the court to be proper to compel the witness's personal attend-

---

[94] Hague Convention, Art. 8. There is no equivalent provision in the bilateral convention.
[95] Art. 23: see para. 8.32 above. The same restriction probably applies in practice to letters of request issued under the bilateral convention.
[96] Bilateral convention, Art. 8. As regards examiners other than consuls, this is more liberal than the Hague Convention, under which prior permission is required from the president of the arrondissementsrechtbank for the district where the examination is to take place, which is likely only to be granted on fairly restrictive conditions: see *Practical Handbook*, p. 79.
[97] Supreme Court Act 1981, s.36; R.S.C., Ord. 38, r. 14. For forms of *subpoena*, see R.S.C., App. A, Form Nos. 28–30: *Supreme Court Practice*, paras. [23]–[25]; Chitty and Jacob, p. 545 and *passim*; 18 *Court Forms* (1985 issue), p. 397.
[98] *Supreme Court Practice*, para. 28/14–19/8. In the Chancery Division, an *ex parte* summons may be required: see 18 *Court Forms* (1985 issue), p. 397.
[99] For forms of affidavit, see Chitty and Jacob, p. 554; 18 *Court Forms* (1985 issue), p. 396.

ance.[1] Alternatively, a special examiner may be appointed to take the evidence.[2]

E. OBTAINING EVIDENCE IN ENGLAND AND WALES FOR USE ABROAD

1. Obtaining evidence without intervention of the English court

Evidence given voluntarily. A witness in England may make a 8.59 statement or give evidence voluntarily to any person, including a foreign consul or other person appointed by a foreign court or tribunal,[3] and for whatever purposes the statement is being made or the evidence taken. The witness may, however, be restrained from giving evidence if, by doing so, he would infringe the rights of third parties[4] or if the Secretary of State makes a direction to protect commercial information or documents being disclosed for the purposes of foreign proceedings.[5] As regards evidence being taken for the purposes of civil proceedings in a foreign court, compulsory measures to require the witness to attend or give evidence are only available from the High Court, and only in limited circumstances.[6] An oath may be administered to the witness by any person agreed upon by the parties or empowered by English law to do so[7]; this includes any person appointed by a court or other judicial authority in any other country for the purpose of taking evidence for use in

---

[1] Supreme Court Act 1981, s.36(1).
[2] Evidence (Proceedings in Other Jurisdictions) Act 1975, s.1; R.S.C., Ord. 39: see para. 8.04 above; *Supreme Court Practice*, para. 39/2–3/2; *Campbell* v. *Attorney-General* (1867) L.R. 2 Ch.App. 571.
[3] *Supreme Court Practice*, para. 70/1–6/2. *South Carolina Insurance Co.* v. *Assurantie Maatschappij "De Zeven Provincien" N.V.* [1987] A.C. 24, at pp. 41–42.
[4] *X. AG* v. *A Bank* [1983] 2 All E.R. 464; *cf. Re State of Norway's Application* [1987] Q.B. 433 (C.A.), affm'd. [1989] 2 W.L.R. 458 (H.L.).
[5] Protection of Trading Interests Act 1980, s.2. The Secretary of State may make a direction to prohibit compliance with a requirement imposed by a court, tribunal or authority of an overseas country (or certain requests to the same effect) for the production of commercial documents located outside that country or to furnish any commercial information to such court, tribunal or authority, or to publish any such document or information. The direction may be made if the requirement infringes the U.K.'s jurisdiction or is otherwise prejudicial to its sovereignty, or if compliance with the requirement would be prejudicial to the U.K.'s security or its relations with any other country. He may also make the direction if the requirement is made otherwise than for the purpose of proceedings which have already been instituted in the overseas country, or if it seeks general discovery of documents. See, for example, *British Airways Board* v. *Laker Airways Ltd.* [1985] A.C. 58. Breach of the direction is an offence: s.3.
[6] See para. 8.77 below.
[7] Evidence Act 1851, s.16; see para. 8.05 above.

proceedings, not being criminal proceedings, carried on under the law of that country.[8] If the witness takes such an oath, he will then be liable under English law if he commits perjury.[9]

8.60 *Evidence given under conventions.* The general rules outlined above apply whether the evidence is being taken pursuant to Chapter II of the Hague Evidence Convention,[10] by a foreign consul or other examiner under a bilateral convention on civil procedure[11] or in the absence of any convention. As has been observed, these conventions have not been expressly incorporated into English law,[12] but they are given effect by existing law[13] and they may affect the practice of the courts. Accordingly, although the United Kingdom government has stipulated under the Hague Convention[14] that permission is required from the Foreign and Commonwealth Office in certain circumstances,[15] before foreign consuls or commissioners appointed by foreign courts may carry out examinations, such stipulations are probably of no legal effect in the internal law of the England and Wales.[16] The same applies to the restrictions imposed on the examination of witnesses under some of the bilateral conventions.[17]

---

[8] Oaths and Evidence (Overseas Authorities and Countries) Act 1963, s.1.
[9] Perjury Act 1911, ss.1(1) and 1(4).
[10] The Hague Evidence Convention is described at para. 8.26 above and set out at paras. A2.17 *et seq.* below. It has been extended by the U.K. to apply also to the sovereign base areas of Akrotiri and Dhekelia, to Anguilla, the Cayman Islands, the Falkland Islands and Dependencies, Gibraltar, Hong Kong, the Isle of Man, Guernsey (including Alderney and Sark) and Jersey. Its application in these territories is frequently different in detail from that in the U.K., but only the latter is described here.
[11] The bilateral conventions are described at para. 8.33 above and references to them appear at para. A2.01 below.
[12] See para. 8.25 above.
[13] The courts have recognised that the Evidence (Proceedings in Other Jurisdictions) Act 1975 was passed to enable the U.K. to ratify the Hague Convention: *e.g., Rio Tinto Zinc Corp.* v. *Westinghouse Electric Corp.*, [1978] A.C. 547, *passim*; *Re State of Norway's Application (Nos. 1 & 2)* [1989] 2 W.L.R. 458, 464 (H.L.).
[14] Arts. 16 and 17.
[15] No declaration has been made under Art. 15, and consuls may accordingly examine their own nationals without permission. Under Art. 16, the U.K. has declared that permission is not required for the examination of witnesses of other nationalities by a consul of a state which does not itself require permission to be obtained for the purpose of obtaining evidence under that Article. A similar declaration has been made under Art. 17 in respect of commissioners examining witnesses of any nationality.
[16] It may be that breach of these conditions would be a factor which should weigh with the court in deciding whether to comply with a request for assistance under Art. 18: see para. 8.68 below.
[17] See paras. 8.48 *et seq.* above.

Evidence

Scotland and Northern Ireland. A witness in England may be com- **8.61**
pelled to attend a court in Scotland or Northern Ireland (or to
attend before an examiner appointed by those courts)[18] by warrant
of citation or *subpoena* in special form, issued by the Court of
Session or the High Court of Northern Ireland.[19]

Legalisation and certification of documents. The seals or signatures **8.62**
on certain documents, usually of a public or official nature, may
need to be authenticated for the purposes of being used in other
countries. Formerly this was done by a process of "legalisation,"[20]
but many countries no longer require this formal procedure.
Instead, many countries will now accept documents which have
merely been certified by having an "apostille" attached to them.[21]
The relevant authority in the United Kingdom, as regards both
legalisation and certification, is the Foreign and Commonwealth
Office.[22] Judgments of English courts may be certified by the High
Court[23]; and similar provisions apply to the certification of other
orders or documents filed in the High Court which are required for
use in a foreign court.[24]

2. Obtaining evidence for use abroad under an order of the English court

The High Court will execute letters of request[25] issued by foreign **8.63**
courts in order to obtain evidence for the purpose of civil proceedings[26] before them. The whole procedure is regulated by the Evidence (Proceedings in Other Jurisdictions) Act 1975[27] and in taking
evidence for these purposes no distinction is drawn between letters
of request issued by foreign courts under the Hague Evidence Convention, those issued under the bilateral civil procedure conventions and those issued in the absence of any convention. If the

---

[18] Evidence (Proceedings in other Jurisdictions) Act 1975, s.4.
[19] Attendance of Witnesses Act 1854.
[20] See para. 29.31 below.
[21] See para. 8.09 above.
[22] Legalisation Office, Foreign and Commonwealth Office, Clive House, 70 Petty
France, London SW1H 9HD. Application may be made in person or by post.
[23] 1982 Act, s.12 (para. 40.36 *et seq.* below); R.S.C., Ord. 71, r. 36 (see
para. 10.70 below); R.S.C., Ord. 71, r. 13.
[24] *Practice Directions (Documents for Use Abroad: Q.B.D. and Ch.D.)* [1971] 1
W.L.R. 604; *Supreme Court Practice*, paras. [747] and [806].
[25] As to the sufficiency of a letter of request, see *Simpson* v. *Hazard* [1887] W.N.
115.
[26] "Civil proceedings" means proceedings in a civil or commercial matter: Evidence (Proceedings in Other Jurisdictions) Act 1975, s.9(1); see also *Re State of
Norway's Application (Nos. 1 & 2)* [1989] 2 W.L.R. 458 (H.L.).
[27] *Rio Tinto Zinc Corp.* v. *Westinghouse Electric Corp.* [1978] A.C. 547, *per* Lord
Diplock, at p. 632; see also n. 13 above. The 1975 Act is supplemented by
R.S.C., Ord. 70.

request is for the examination of witnesses, the procedure involves the appointment of an examiner to take the evidence and in most respects it is the same as that which applies where the evidence is being taken by an examiner for the purposes of proceedings in England.[28] There are detailed restrictions on the English court's power to execute a letter of request which is issued to obtain pre-trial discovery, especially of documents, and the drafting of a letter of request in this field requires special care. This aspect is discussed in more detail below.[29]

8.64 *Transmission of letters of request.* Letters of request issued by foreign courts may be presented to the High Court on an application by an interested party,[30] or they may be transmitted to the senior master, either through the Foreign and Commonwealth Office,[31] or direct from the foreign court or judicial authorities,[32] or by the diplomatic or consular authorities in England of the foreign country in question.[33]

The application

8.65 An application for an order to give effect to letters of request is made *ex parte* on affidavit to a master of the Queen's Bench Division.[34] The application may be made by a party to the foreign proceedings (usually the party for whose purposes the letter of request was issued by the foreign court)[35] or by the Treasury Solicitor acting, in effect, on behalf of the foreign court.[36] The affidavit in support of the application must exhibit the letter of request and, if it is not in English, a translation of it into English.[37] The affidavit

---

[28] Para. 8.03 above; R.S.C., Ord. 39.
[29] Paras. 8.70 *et seq.*
[30] See paras. 8.65 *et seq.* below.
[31] The Foreign and Commonwealth Office has been designated as the Central Authority under Art. 2 of the Hague Convention, in respect of the whole of the U.K. and the territories to which the convention has been extended (except the Channel Islands): see para. 8.60, n. 10 above. This route will probably also have been employed in the case of letters of request from countries with which the U.K. does not have a civil procedure convention.
[32] The senior master of the Supreme Court of Judicature (Queen's Bench Division) has been designated as an "other authority" for England and Wales under Art. 24 of the Hague Convention. Separate "other authorities" have been designated for Scotland, Northern Ireland and the other territories.
[33] This is the means specified by the bilateral conventions.
[34] R.S.C., Ord. 70, rr. 1(2) and 2(1).
[35] This is the more normal procedure where the request emanates from a country (usually the U.S.) in which the parties are themselves responsible for gathering the evidence.
[36] The Treasury Solicitor may be involved if the letter of request has been sent to the senior master, either by the Foreign and Commonwealth Office or direct under a civil procedure convention: R.S.C., Ord. 70, r. 3.
[37] R.S.C., Ord. 70, r. 2(2). As to translations, see para. 8.16 above.

should state such details as are necessary to establish that the letter of request was issued by or on behalf of a court or tribunal ("the requesting court") exercising jurisdiction in any other part of the United Kingdom or in any country or territory outside the United Kingdom; and that the evidence to which the application relates is to be obtained for the purposes of civil proceedings which either have been instituted before the requesting court or whose institution before that court is contemplated.[38] In practice, it should also set out the names (and preferably the addresses) of the witnesses to be examined, or details of the acts to be performed,[39] together with the identity of any examiner proposed, and details of any special procedure which the letter of request asks for, and such other matters as the applicant wishes to have included in the order.[40]

The order

The court's powers. The court has power to make such provision **8.66** for obtaining evidence in England as may appear to it to be appropriate for giving effect to the foreign court's request, including the power to require a person specified in the order to take such steps as the court may consider appropriate for that purpose.[41] This general power is subject to a number of qualifications and exceptions. Most frequently, such orders will be for the examination of witnesses, either orally or in writing, or for the production of documents.[42] But the order may also, for example, be for the inspection, photographing, preservation, custody or detention of any property, for the taking of samples of any property and carrying out of any experiments on or with any property, for the medical examination of any person, or for the taking and testing of blood samples.[43] In family law cases, orders are sometimes made for a report by the court welfare officer. Because the order is made on an *ex parte* application, the witness or other person against whom it is made may apply to

---

[38] Evidence (Proceedings in Other Jurisdictions) Act 1975, s.1.

[39] The other types of order which can be made are discussed at para. 8.66 below.

[40] For forms of affidavit, see Queen's Bench Masters' Practice Form No. PF 152, *Supreme Court Practice*, para. [363]; Chitty and Jacob, p. 587; 18 *Court Forms* (1985 issue), p. 426.

[41] Evidence (Proceedings in Other Jurisdictions) Act 1975, s.2(1).

[42] *Ibid.* s.2(2)(a) and (b). The form of order is prescribed, but may be adapted to suit the circumstances of the case: R.S.C., App. A, Form No. 93; *Supreme Court Practice*, para. [92]; Chitty and Jacob, p. 592; 18 *Court Forms* (1985 issue), p. 428. A limited company cannot be ordered to attend to give evidence on oath, although it may be required to attend and produce specified documents by its proper officer: *Penn-Texas Corp.* v. *Murat Anstalt* [1964] 1 Q.B. 40; *Penn-Texas Corp.* v. *Murat Anstalt (No. 2)* [1964] 2 Q.B. 647; *Panthalu* v. *Ramnord Research Laboratories Ltd.* [1966] 2 Q.B. 173. For forms of summons and order, see Chitty and Jacob, pp. 594–595.

[43] Evidence (Proceedings in Other Jurisdictions) Act 1975, s.2(2)(c) to (f).

the court for the order to be set aside or varied.[44] The application should be by summons, supported by an affidavit.[45]

8.67 *Qualification of the court's powers.* The general power of the English High Court to make an order giving effect to a foreign court's request for obtaining evidence is qualified in a number of respects, which are discussed below. First, the exercise of the court's power is discretionary. Secondly, the power may not be exercised if the request infringes the jurisdiction of the United Kingdom or is otherwise prejudicial to its sovereignty. Thirdly, the court does not have an unfettered choice in the steps which it can order to be taken; and its powers are anyway confined to giving effect to letters of request issued for obtaining "evidence" for use in "civil proceedings."[46] Fourthly, there are specific limitations on the making of orders to disclose or produce documents.

8.68 *Discretion.* As a matter of internal English law, it appears from the language of both the Evidence (Proceedings in Other Jurisdictions) Act 1975 and the rules of court made under it, that the court has a discretion whether or not to give effect to letters of request emanating from foreign countries. The Hague Convention[47] and the bilateral conventions, however, use mandatory language, and, as a matter of international comity, the courts will so exercise their discretion as to give effect to a letter of request unless they are driven to the clear conclusion that they cannot do so.[48] It may be driven to that conclusion if the application for assistance is frivolous, vexatious or an abuse of the process of the court.[49] Also, if the request is for evidence which the witness would be permitted not to give on the grounds of privilege, the court may decline to make the order if the witness asserts the privilege in opposing the order.[50]

---

[44] R.S.C., Ord. 32, r. 6; *Supreme Court Practice*, para. 32/1–6/14. For forms of summonses, see Chitty and Jacob, p. 594.

[45] *Supreme Court Practice*, para. 70/1–6/19.

[46] The court's powers are extended to obtaining evidence for criminal proceedings in an overseas court by s.5 of the Evidence (Proceedings in Other Jurisdictions) Act 1975: for a form of order, see Chitty and Jacob, p. 598. They have also been extended to enable evidence to be taken for the purposes of proceedings in the European Court of Justice: s.6 of the 1975 Act.

[47] Art. 9, last sentence.

[48] *Re State of Norway's Application* [1987] Q.B. 433, 470 (C.A.), affm'd [1989] 2 W.L.R. 458 (H.L.). As Lord Denning M.R. said in *Rio Tinto Zinc Corp.* v. *Westinghouse Electric Corp.* [1978] A.C. 547, at p. 560, "Such is the request made by the United States Federal Court. It is our duty and our pleasure to do all we can to assist that court, just as we would expect the United States court to help us in like circumstances. 'Do unto others as you would have done by.' "; see also *ibid.*, at p. 612, *per* Lord Wilberforce.

[49] *Ibid.*, at p. 634, *per* Lord Diplock.

[50] The normal method of asserting a duty or privilege not to give evidence would be at the examination: see para. 8.75 below.

Evidence

Infringement of the United Kingdom's jurisdiction or sovereignty. **8.69**
Section 4 of the Protection of Trading Interests Act 1980 provides:

"A court in the United Kingdom shall not make an order under section 2 of the Evidence (Proceedings in Other Jurisdictions) Act 1975 for giving effect to a request issued by or on behalf of a court or tribunal of an overseas country if it is shown that the request infringes the jurisdiction of the United Kingdom or is otherwise prejudicial to the sovereignty of the United Kingdom; and a certificate signed by the Secretary of State to the effect that it infringes that jurisdiction or is so prejudicial shall be conclusive evidence of that fact."[51]

It will be noted that letters of request may be found to infringe the United Kingdom's jurisdiction or sovereignty even without the Secretary of State issuing a certificate to that effect.[52]

Steps for obtaining evidence: direct and indirect testimony. The **8.70**
court's powers to give effect to a letter of request only arise if it is satisfied that the evidence is to be "obtained for the purposes of civil proceedings" in the requesting court,[53] and it may only order particular steps to be taken for those purposes if it could require such steps to be taken by way of obtaining evidence for the purpose of civil proceedings in the High Court.[54] These limitations have both a procedural aspect and a substantive aspect. From the procedural point of view, they limit the steps which may be taken in execution of the letter of request.[55] From the substantive point of

---

[51] This section gives effect to part of the second ground in Art. 12 of the Hague Convention (para. 8.28 above) on which execution of a letter of request may be refused. See also para. 8.79 below.

[52] Considered in isolation, the meaning of the terms "infringes the jurisdiction" and "prejudicial to the sovereignty" is not clear. The fact that the foreign court seeks evidence by means of a letter of request to be executed under the direction of the High Court would normally mean that due regard had been paid to U.K. sovereignty and the exercise of its jurisdiction. However, the context in which the Act was enacted was that of hostility to the extra-territorial assertion by the U.S. of *its* sovereignty by the exercise of *its* jurisdiction of an investigatory character in penal anti-trust proceedings: see the submissions of the Attorney-General, summarised by Lord Wilberforce in *Rio Tinto Zinc Corp.* v. *Westinghouse Electric Corp.* [1978] A.C. 547, at p. 616. See also *Re State of Norway's Application* [1987] Q.B. 433, 481 (C.A.), affm'd. [1989] 2 W.L.R. 458 (H.L.).

[53] Evidence (Proceedings in Other Jurisdictions) Act 1975, s.1(b).

[54] *Ibid.*, s.2(3). The court is not precluded from ordering the taking of evidence otherwise than on oath, when this is asked for by the requesting court.

[55] The first ground stated in Art. 12 of the Hague Convention (para. 8.28 above) on which the court may refuse to execute a letter of request is that its execution does not fall within the functions of the judiciary. Because the gathering of evidence is not a judicial function under English law, a strict application of that ground of refusal might result in the rejection of requests which the court has power to order to be performed, such as the inspection or preservation of property, or the conduct of a medical examination. This subsection enables practical effect to be given in English law to that part of Art. 12.

221

view, they prevent effect being given to letters of request which are not directed to "obtaining evidence for the purpose of civil proceedings."

In the ordinary way, in the absence of evidence to the contrary, the courts will accept the statement by the requesting court that the evidence requested is for use in civil proceedings[56] and the fact that evidence may also be used for some other purpose is not a reason for refusing to give effect to the letters of request.[57] Before the 1975 Act was passed, though, it had become established, particularly in the context of requests from American courts, that English courts would not assist in obtaining testimony other than direct material immediately relevant to the issue in dispute, and that indirect material by way of discovery or of a "fishing" nature could not be obtained.[58]

8.71   Since the 1975 Act, it has been held, as regards oral evidence, that where letters of request ask for the examination of a witness on behalf of the applicant it is inappropriate for the English court to consider in detail whether his evidence would be relevant and admissible so far as the requesting court is concerned.[59] Nevertheless it seems that English courts continue to maintain a suspicious attitude to American pre-trial discovery procedure, although evidence taken at that stage is not necessarily to be excluded. Similarly, they remain reluctant to permit evidence, even if it is required for the purposes of the trial itself, to be sought by way of "fishing."[59a] In this sense, "fishing" has been described as "a roving inquiry, by means of the examination and cross-examination of witnesses, which is not designed to establish by means of their evidence allegations of fact which have been raised bona fide with adequate particulars, but to obtain information which may lead to obtaining evidence in general support of a party's case."[60]

In the present state of development of the law, it is not easy to identify a test which will be applied by the courts. It seems that the English courts would prefer to be reassured that the evidence would

---

[56] *Rio Tinto Zinc Corp.* v. *Westinghouse Electric Corp.* [1978] A.C. 547, at p. 634, *per* Lord Diplock.

[57] *Ibid.*, p. 611, *per* Lord Wilberforce.

[58] *Radio Corporation of America* v. *Rauland Corporation* [1956] 1 Q.B. 618, at pp. 643–644; *Rio Tinto Zinc Corp.* v. *Westinghouse Electric Corp.*, above, at pp. 608, 619, 642.

[59] *Asbestos Insurance Coverage Cases* [1985] 1 W.L.R. 331.

[59a] It may be that different considerations apply, depending on whether or not the evidence is required for the purposes of trial: see the various dicta in *State of Norway's Application* [1987] Q.B. 433, at p. 482 *per* Kerr L.J., p. 490 *per* Glidewell L.J., p. 496 *et seq. per* Ralph Gibson L.J. and in *State of Norway's Application (No. 2)* [1988] 3 W.L.R. 603 at p. 659, *per* Woolf L.J.; these questions were left open by the House of Lords: [1989] 2 W.L.R. 458, 479.

[60] *State of Norway's Application* [1987] Q.B. 433, 482, *per* Kerr L.J.

be admissible for the purpose of determining the issue in the foreign proceedings, but in the last analysis it will leave that question to the requesting court. If it regards the request as too wide-ranging, though, it may impose some limitations on the terms of the order.

Disclosure and production of documents. A further limitation on the **8.72** orders which may be made is imposed in the case of documentary evidence by section 2(4) of the 1975 Act, which provides that an order to give effect to a letter of request shall not require a person:

"(a) to state what documents relevant to the proceedings to which the application for the order relates are or have been in his possession, custody or power; or

(b) to produce any documents other than particular documents specified in the order as being documents appearing to the court making the order to be, or to be likely to be, in his possession, custody or power."[61]

The interpretation of this subsection has had to be considered by English courts on a number of occasions, and it is clear that they take a strict attitude to the production of documents by non-party witnesses. Although for the purpose of English proceedings a witness may be required to produce documents under a *subpoena duces tecum* which are identified as members of a specific class,[62] the test under the 1975 Act is stricter.[63] Although several documents may be described compendiously, the exact document in each case must be clearly indicated; and the court must be satisfied by evidence that the documents are actual documents which exist (or did exist) and that they are likely to be in the respondent's possession.[64]

"Blue-pencilling." If part of a request from a foreign court is such **8.73** that the English court is not willing to execute it, the court is willing to cut out inappropriate parts of the request, rather than reject it in its entirety; but it will only do so if it can thereby make an order

---

[61] The U.K. has made a declaration under Art. 23 of the Hague Convention (para. 8.32 above), to the effect that it will not execute letters of request issued for the purpose of obtaining pre-trial discovery of documents, and in doing so it defined the types of letters of request which it would not execute in the terms used in this subsection.

[62] *Rio Tinto Zinc Corp.* v. *Westinghouse Electric Corp.* [1978] A.C. 547, 562, *per* Lord Denning M.R.

[63] *Ibid.*, at p. 635, *per* Lord Diplock.

[64] *Asbestos Insurance Coverage Cases* [1985] 1 W.L.R. 331, 337–338. Actual documents are to be contrasted with conjectural documents, which may or may not exist.

which is acceptable and proper, and it will not otherwise re-draft the request.[65]

The examination

8.74 *The examiner.* The applicant may nominate a suitable person to act as the examiner.[66] It is normal to nominate a barrister to take the evidence, but any other suitable person may be appointed and, especially if the evidence is to be taken in accordance with the practices of the requesting court, foreign consuls or foreign lawyers may be suitable persons to appoint. If the applicant does not nominate a suitable person, the court will appoint one of the examiners on its rota of examiners, or a district registrar or some other suitable and qualified person.[67]

8.75 *The conduct of the examination.* The arrangements for the examination are made by the applicant's solicitor (or the Treasury Solicitor if he is acting). In liason with the examiner, the witnesses and any other parties whom he knows will be attending, he will arrange for the attendance of any short-hand writer or interpreter who may be necessary.[68] Except for the purpose of invoking privilege,[69] and subject to any specific directions contained in the order, the examination will take place in the English mode, with examination, cross-examination and re-examination by the parties or their representatives.[70] Where the Treasury Solicitor is acting on behalf of the foreign court, especially if the parties do not attend or are not represented, his representatives will attend the examination and put questions to the witnesses.[71]

The court may make directions in its order as to the conduct of the examination. It will strive to comply with any particular request which the foreign court may make as to the procedure to be adopted, even if the procedure would not be permissible in an English court. An order for the examination of witnesses to be recorded

---

[65] *State of Norway's Application* [1987] Q.B. 433, 484, *per* Glidewell L.J., affm'd [1989] 2 W.L.R. 458; *J. Barber & Sons* v. *Lloyd's Underwriters* [1987] Q.B. 103.
[66] R.S.C., Ord. 70, r. 4(1).
[67] *Ibid.*
[68] *Supreme Court Practice*, para. 70/1–6/22.
[69] See para. 8.79 below.
[70] R.S.C., Ord. 70, r. 4(2). Counsel, solicitors and solicitors' clerks may act as representatives: *Supreme Court Practice*, paras. 39/8/1 and [3882]. Foreign lawyers may also be able to act as representatives: see European Communities (Service of Lawyers) Order 1978, (S.I. No. 1910) (para. A2.51 below).
[71] If the foreign court has submitted written questions to be put to the witness, the court could order them to be answered as if they were interrogatories made under R.S.C., Ord. 26; but the usual practice would be to require the witness to attend an examination and answer the questions orally.

on video-tape has been made in this way.[72] The court will give as much help to the foreign court as it can,[73] and will have regard to the procedural law of the foreign court in ruling on an objection to any question.[74] As has been seen, the examiner himself has no power to rule on the objection.[75] Subject to any directions contained in the order, the parties, their representatives and the witnesses may be present at the examination, but the examiner has a discretion as to who else he permits to be present.[76]

Legal representation. The extent, if at all, to which a witness is entitled to have a legal representative with him when he gives his evidence, and what that representative may do, are less than clear.[77] Under the Hague Convention, he has such a right,[78] but under English law it may be that the limit of his entitlement is, if he is incapable of an informed judgment on whether to object to questions put to him, and in the discretion of the examiner, to be granted the "indulgence" of having an adviser who could object on his behalf and formulate the grounds of objection as required by the rules.[79] **8.76**

Attendance of witnesses. The order of the court giving effect to the letters of request is an order that the witnesses must attend. If a copy of the order is indorsed with a penal notice and duly served on the witness, it is equivalent to a *subpoena*.[80] The court's powers to order evidence to be taken in aid of foreign proceedings are exclusively statutory[81] and it follows that these measures of compulsion **8.77**

---

[72] *J. Barber & Sons* v. *Lloyds Underwriters* [1987] Q.B. 103.
[73] *Desilla* v. *Fells* (1879) 40 L.T. 423, *per* Cockburn L.J.
[74] *Ibid.*; *R.* v. *Rathbone; ex p. Dikko* [1985] Q.B. 630, 648, where the court's approach to such an objection is discussed.
[75] Para. 8.05 above.
[76] *Supreme Court Practice*, para. 39/8/1. The U.K. has declared under Art. 8 of the Hague Convention that judicial personnel of the requesting state may be present without prior permission. If it is intended to invoke this privilege, it would be advisable for the foreign court to say so in the letters of request and for a direction to be included in the order.
[77] See *Rio Tinto Zinc Corp.* v. *Westinghouse Electric Corp.* [1978] A.C. 547, 563, *per* Lord Denning M.R., distinguished by Forbes J. in *R.* v. *Rathbone; ex p. Dikko* [1985] Q.B. 630, 651–652.
[78] Art. 20, para. A2.25 below. The term "persons concerned" in that Article is said by the Explanatory Report certainly to include witnesses: *Actes et documents de la onzième session* (1968), vol. IV, p. 214.
[79] *R.* v. *Rathbone; ex p. Dikko* (above), at p. 653. Art. 20 of the Hague Convention appears not to have been cited to the court.
[80] R.S.C., Ord. 70, r. 4(2); Ord. 39, r. 5; Ord. 45, r. 7.
[81] *Rio Tinto Zinc Corp.* v. *Westinghouse Electric Corp.* [1978] A.C. 547, at p. 633, *per* Lord Diplock; *Re State of Norway's Application (Nos. 1 & 2)* [1989] 2 W.L.R. 458, 466, *per* Lord Goff.

are only available where the court makes an order for the examination of a witness in pursuance of a request issued by or on behalf of a requesting court.[82] Where, therefore, a foreign consul or commissioner has been appointed by a foreign court to take a witness's evidence and he is entitled under the terms of a convention to apply to the English court for assistance is securing the attendance of the witness by the use of compulsory powers,[83] an application made by him is probably to be regarded as an application made "on behalf of" the foreign court. The order made by the High Court would not need to appoint the applicant as an examiner,[84] merely to order the witness to attend before him and give evidence.[85]

Privilege

8.78   A witness giving evidence in execution of a letter of request is entitled to claim privilege both under English law[86] and under the law of the requesting court.[87] To claim privilege under English law, the witness should object to giving the evidence.[88] If the claim to privilege is not conceded, the examiner files at the Central Office a certificate of the witness's refusal to give the evidence[89] and the party by whom the evidence is required may then apply to the court for an order that the witness should give the evidence.[90]

---

[82] Evidence (Proceedings in Other Jurisdictions) Act 1975, ss.1 and 2(1); R.S.C., Ord. 70.

[83] The U.K. has made a declaration under Art. 18 of the Hague Convention (see para. 8.30 above) stipulating that a diplomatic officer, consular agent or commissioner authorised to take evidence under Arts. 15, 16 and 17 may apply to the senior master to obtain such evidence by compulsion, provided that the contracting state whose diplomatic officer, consular agent or commissioner makes the application has made a declaration reciprocal under Art. 18. The declarations of other European signatory states are referred to at paras. 8.48 *et seq.* above. A similar situation may arise under the bilateral conventions with France, Germany and Italy: see para. 8.36 above. As to the effect of this declaration in internal English law, see para. 8.25 above.

[84] Under the bilateral conventions with France and Italy the appointment of the foreign consul or commissioner may be made by the English court: see para. 8.36 above.

[85] The terms of the individual conventions should be consulted to see what, if any, restrictions they place on the evidence which may be given: *e.g.*, Hague Convention, Art. 21(a), para. 8.30 above.

[86] Evidence (Proceedings in Other Jurisdictions) Act 1975, s.3(1)(a).

[87] *Ibid.*, s.3(1)(b).

[88] References to "giving evidence" include references to answering questions and producing documents: *ibid.*, s.3(4).

[89] For a form of certificate, see Chitty and Jacob, p. 595.

[90] R.S.C., Ord. 39, r. 5. Unless the master orders a summons to be issued, the order may be made on an *ex parte* application; but if it is, the witness may apply to set it aside under Ord. 32, r. 6.

Privilege under English law. There is a range of grounds on which   **8.79**
a person may claim privilege from giving evidence in English civil
proceedings.[91] The principal categories of such privilege extend to
protect a person from having to give evidence which would tend to
expose him or his spouse to proceedings for an offence or for the
recovery of a penalty[92]; or, generally, from having to disclose
matters communicated between a legal adviser and his client, or
communicated between parties to a dispute with a view to settlement and expressed to be "without prejudice." In addition, in the
present context, a person cannot be compelled to give evidence if
his doing so would prejudice the security of the United Kingdom.[93]
A certificate signed by or on behalf of the Secretary of State to the
effect that it would be so prejudicial for that person to do so is conclusive evidence of that fact; but such a certificate is not a necessary
condition of this ground of privilege.

English law recognises the importance of a duty of confidentiality
in respect of commercial and professional confidences; but confidentiality is not itself a ground of privilege. Where confidentiality is
asserted, the court weighs the benefit of having the confidential evidence against the disadvantage of breaching the confidentiality, and
it may decline to order the witness to breach the confidence.[94]

Privilege under foreign law. There are two different procedures for   **8.80**
giving effect to a claim for privilege under the law of the requesting
court. First, if the letter of request contains a statement of the privilege or duty under which the witness may refuse to give the evidence, the procedure is the same as that for giving effect to a claim
for privilege under English law. If the statement in the letter of
request supports the claim to privilege, the witness will not be compelled to give the evidence.[95] Secondly, if the witness's claim to
privilege is not supported by a statement in the letter of request, he

---

[91] See 17 *Halsbury's Laws* (4th ed.), paras. 235 *et seq.*; *Phipson on Evidence* (13th
ed.), chap. 15; *Cross on Evidence* (6th ed.), chap. XII.
[92] Civil Evidence Act 1968, s.14. The privilege only applies to proceedings for an
offence or a penalty under the law of any part of the U.K. but this includes
penalties under EEC law: *Rio Tinto Zinc Corp.* v. *Westinghouse Electric Corp.*
[1978] A.C. 547.
[93] Evidence (Proceedings in Other Jurisdictions) Act 1975, s.3(3). This subsection gives effect to part of the second ground in Art. 12 of the Hague Convention (para. 8.28 above) on which execution of a letter of request may be
refused. See also para. 8.69 above.
[94] *Re State of Norway's Application* [1987] Q.B. 433, at pp. 484 *et seq.*, *per* Kerr
L.J.; pp. 489 *et seq.*, *per* Glidewell L.J.; and pp. 499 *et seq.*, *per* Ralph Gibson
L.J.; *Re State of Norway's Application (No. 2)* [1988] 3 W.L.R. 603, at p. 660
per Woolf L.J.; affm'd [1989] 2 W.L.R. 458, 479 (H.L.).
[95] Evidence (Proceedings in Other Jurisdictions) Act 1975, s.3(2). See also the
Hague Convention, Arts. 3 and 11, paras. A2.05 and A2.08 below.

may be compelled to give the evidence, but the evidence will not be transmitted to the requesting court if that court, on the matter being referred to it, upholds the claim to privilege.[96] Effect is given to this procedure by the examiner causing the evidence in respect of which privilege is claimed to be kept separate from the rest of the evidence. The senior master initially retains the separate deposition or document and refers the claim for privilege to the requesting court. If that court rejects the claim, he then transmits the separate deposition or document to that court.[97]

Transmission of the evidence

8.81   Once the evidence has been taken, and subject to any other provision in the court's order giving effect to the letter of request, the deposition or other evidence is sent to the senior master, who causes a certificate bearing the court's seal to be attached to it.[98] It is then transmitted to the requesting court either through the Foreign and Commonwealth Office, or directly to the requesting authority.[99]

---

[96] *Ibid.* The witness may be compelled either by the examiner or, if he does not do so, by the court under the procedure outlined above: R.S.C., Ord. 70, r. 6(2).
[97] R.S.C., Ord. 70, r. 6(3); Chitty and Jacob, p. 596.
[98] Queen's Bench Masters' Practice Form No. PF 153; *Supreme Court Practice*, para. [364]; Chitty and Jacob, p. 599.
[99] R.S.C., Ord. 70, r. 5.

CHAPTER 9

FOREIGN LAW

1. Introduction

In the course of litigation it is sometimes necessary to apply rules **9.01** of foreign law. The law of any country or territory other than England and Wales is foreign law,[1] including the laws of Scotland, Northern Ireland, British colonies and protectorates, Commonwealth and politically foreign countries. European Community law, on the other hand, is regarded as part of English law, as are the rules of customary public international law[2] and any conventions which have been enacted into English law.[3] This chapter is concerned with the status of foreign legal rules as a matter of English law and the manner in which they are determined and applied.

Choice of law rules. The question whether a particular issue is **9.02** governed by English law or by the law of some other country is determined by English choice of law rules. These rules make up the bulk of that branch of English law known as private international law (or "conflict of laws"),[4] which is to be distinguished from English domestic or internal law. The function of choice of law rules is not to determine the substance of the right or duty in question, but to determine which system of law, or the law of which country, applies to that right or duty. Its substance is then to be described according to the rules of that system of law. The law of different

---

[1] *The Torni* [1932] P. 27, at p. 37.

[2] *Trendtex Trading Corporation* v. *Central Bank of Nigeria* [1977] Q.B. 529, at pp. 554, and 579; *Planmount* v. *Republic of Zaire* [1981] 1 All E.R. 1110; *I Congresso di Partido* [1983] 1 A.C. 244, at p. 265.

[3] See Jacobs and Roberts (ed.), *The Effect of Treaties in Domestic Law*, chap. 7 by Prof. R. Higgins Q.C.

[4] For discussion of the definition and scope of this branch of the law, see Dicey and Morris, pp. 3 *et seq.*; Cheshire and North, pp. 3 *et seq.* The details of English choice of law rules are generally beyond the scope of this book, and reference should be made to those and other specialist works. In addition to choice of law rules, private international law also concerns choice of jurisdiction and the recognition and enforcement of foreign judgments.

countries may apply to different issues in the same proceedings. Like any other rule of English law, choice of law rules are to be applied by the court of its own motion and without the need for proof of their contents. If the application of these rules indicates that foreign law governs a particular issue, the content of the foreign rules is not generally a matter of which the court may take judicial notice.

2. Status of foreign law

9.03   *Foreign law: fact or law?* A party to proceedings who wishes to rely on foreign law must generally plead the foreign rule and, if it is not admitted,[5] establish it by evidence.[6] If it is admitted, it need not be proved.[7] In this respect, a foreign law is treated as a question of fact but, as the courts have recognised, it is "a question of fact of a peculiar kind."[8] In some respects, its treatment by English law is closer to that of a question of law and to regard it merely as a question of fact may therefore be misleading. For example, questions of foreign law are questions for the judge alone, even when he is sitting with a jury,[9] and an appellate court will substitute its own findings of foreign law for those of the lower court more readily than in respect of ordinary questions of fact.[10] In certain circumstances the previous decisions of other courts may be relied upon to establish the foreign law.[11] Moreover, the House of Lords sitting on appeal from English courts treats the law of Scotland and Northern Ireland as matters of law rather than as matters of fact[12] and the Judicial Com-

---

[5] It may be admitted expressly or by implication: R.S.C., Ord. 18, r. 13; Ord. 27, r. 2.
[6] Other methods of establishing foreign law are discussed at paras. 9.09 *et seq.* below. If foreign law is not proved, the court generally applies English law: see para. 9.05 below.
[7] *Prowse* v. *European and American Steamship Co.* (1860) 13 Moo.P.C. 484; *Moulis* v. *Owen* [1907] 1 K.B. 746. There may be an exception if the admission is wholly fictitious: *Royston* v. *Cavey* [1947] K.B. 204.
[8] *Parkasho* v. *Singh* [1968] P. 233, 250; *Dalmia Dairy Industries Ltd.* v. *National Bank of Pakistan* [1978] 2 Lloyds Rep. 223, at p. 286. In some respects it may be better understood as a question of opinion rather than fact: see para. 9.07 below.
[9] Supreme Court Act 1981, s.69(5), replacing earlier provisions dating from 1920. The rule applies also in criminal trials: *R.* v. *Hammer* [1923] 2 K.B. 786.
[10] *Parkasho* v. *Singh*, above; *Dalmia Dairy Industries Ltd.* v. *National Bank of Pakistan*, above.
[11] Civil Evidence Act 1972, s.4(2): see para. 9.10 below.
[12] *De Thoren* v. *Attorney-General* (1876) App.Cas. 686; *Elliott* v. *Lord Joicey* [1935] A.C. 209, at p. 236; *MacShannon* v. *Rockware Glass Ltd.* [1978] A.C. 795, at pp. 815 and 821.

mittee of the Privy Council does the same in respect of those territories from which it may entertain appeals.[13]

A distinction should also be drawn between two different purposes for which an English court has to consider foreign law. On one hand, where English choice of law rules require the application of foreign law to determine some issue in the proceedings, the foreign law must generally be established by evidence. On the other hand the English court may refer to the decisions of foreign courts and other sources of foreign law without their having to be proved, in order to gain assistance in the ascertainment and interpretation of English law.[14]

Pleading foreign law. If a party contends that a rule of foreign law **9.04** gives rise to or defines a right or duty upon which he wishes to rely in English proceedings, in addition to pleading the factual basis of his claim, he must plead the foreign law.[15] In other words, he must identify in his pleadings the system of law which he says applies, as well as the particular issues to which it applies, and he must give particulars of the contents of the foreign rule.[16] It is also good practice for him to identify any particular legislative provision or other source of law upon which he will rely and, in an appropriate case, he may be ordered to give these particulars.[17]

Failure to establish foreign law. If the content of a relevant foreign **9.05** rule is not established, either by evidence or by one of the other means discussed below, the court normally applies English law[18]; but it does not always do so[19] and in a suitable case it may re-open the matter to allow foreign law to be proved.[20] In a number of

---

[13] *Cf.* British Law Ascertainment Act 1859, s.4.
[14] Scottish and Commonwealth decisions are cited fairly often in English courts. The citation of foreign decisions is of particular significance in the context of the 1968 Convention: see paras. 13.26 *et seq.* below; and other conventions: see 17 *Halsbury's Laws* (4th edn.), para. 103.
[15] This is subject to an exception under the British Law Ascertainment Act 1859: see para. 9.12 below.
[16] *Ascherberg Hopwood & Crew Ltd.* v. *Casa Musicale Sonzogno di Pietro Ostali S.N.C.* [1971] 1 W.L.R. 173, 1128. In an appropriate case, the pleading may incorporate an expert's report or affidavit by reference: *ibid.*, p. 1131.
[17] *Supreme Court Practice*, para. 18/8/7.
[18] *Lloyd* v. *Guibert* (1865) L.R. 1 Q.B. 115, at p. 129; *Nouvelle Banque de l'Union* v. *Ayton* (1891) 7 T.L.R. 377; *Re A/S Tank of Oslo and Agence Strauss* [1940] 1 All E.R. 40, at p. 42; *Re Parana Plantations Ltd.* [1946] 2 All E.R. 214, at pp. 217–218; *Szechter* v. *Szechter* [1971] p. 286, at p. 296. This rule or practice is frequently described as a presumption that foreign law is the same as English law, but this is not satisfactory: see Dicey and Morris, p. 228.
[19] *Guepratt* v. *Young* (1854) 4 De G. & Sm. 217; *R.* v. *Governor of Brixton Prison, ex p. Caldough* [1961] 2 All E.R. 606.
[20] *De Reneville* v. *De Reneville* [1948] P. 100.

respects this rule is unsatisfactory in modern conditions,[21] especially in the context of increasingly close co-operation between European countries in the civil and commercial field,[22] and it remains to be seen whether it will be modified. It is anyway questionable whether it applies to proceedings for summary judgment.[23]

3. Proving foreign law

9.06   The principal means of establishing a rule of foreign law is by the evidence of a suitably qualified witness.[24] There are certain other means of doing so, both at common law and under statute,[25] but these other methods are of limited application and, in the case of the common law rules, they are perhaps uncertain in their scope. It is therefore generally advisable to obtain the evidence of a suitable witness. It is not sufficient to cite foreign decisions or books of authority for the purpose of proving foreign law,[26] nor, except in accordance with the Civil Evidence Act 1972,[27] to cite previous English decisions in which the same point of foreign law has been decided.[28] The burden of proving foreign law lies on the party who relies on the rule in question.[29]

9.07   *Who is suitably qualified?* Any statement of law made by a person other than a competent court or legislative authority is essentially a statement of opinion rather than fact.[30] In order that a witness's opinion may be admissible as credible evidence, therefore, he must be able to speak as an expert, and accordingly he must state the

---

[21] For example, its strict application seems hard to reconcile with the Foreign Limitation Periods Act 1974: see para. 9.14 below, or with the requirement that the legal personality of a legal person should be determined by the law of the place of its incorporation: see paras. 2.07–2.08 above. In connection with Art. 52 of the 1968 Convention, see para. 31.14 below.

[22] The rule would be particularly unsatisfactory in the context of the EEC Convention on the Law Applicable to Contractual Obligations, when it comes into force.

[23] *Western National Bank of New York* v. *Perez, Triana & Co.* (1890) 6 T.L.R. 366; *National Shipping Corporation* v. *Arab* [1971] 2 Lloyd's Rep. 363.

[24] *Lazard Bros. & Co.* v. *Midland Bank* [1933] A.C. 289.

[25] See paras. 9.09 *et seq.* below.

[26] *Buerger* v. *New York Life Assurance Company* (1927) 96 L.J.K.B. 930, at p. 940; *Beatty* v. *Beatty* [1924] 1 K.B. 807, 814–815; *Guaranty Trust of New York* v. *Hannay & Co.* [1918] 2 K.B. 623, at pp. 638, 667; *cf. Callwood* v. *Callwood* [1960] A.C. 659, where evidence by way of the decision of a court in a third country was deprecated.

[27] See para. 9.10 below.

[28] *Lazard Bros. & Co.* v. *Midland Bank*, above.

[29] *Dynamit A.C.* v. *Rio Tinto Co.* [1918] A.C. 260, at p. 301; *Guaranty Trust Co. of New York* v. *Hannay & Co.* [1918] 2 K.B. 623, at p. 655.

[30] *Cf.* Cheshire and North, p. 108. It is a statement of what, in the speaker's opinion, a competent court *would* hold the law to be in the actual or hypothetical circumstances stipulated.

qualifications or experience which enable him to do so. It is then a matter for the court to decide in each case whether the witness's credentials as an expert on the particular issue of foreign law are sufficient.[31] The Civil Evidence Act 1972, s.4(1), provides:

> "It is hereby declared that in civil proceedings a person who is suitably qualified to do so on account of his knowledge or experience is competent to give expert evidence as to the law of any county or territory outside the United Kingdom, or of any part of the United Kingdom other than England and Wales, irrespective of whether he has acted or is entitled to act as a legal practitioner there."

This subsection, which was probably declaratory of the existing law, makes it clear that it is not necessary for the witness to be a qualified legal practitioner; practical experience or specialist study will suffice. Most commonly, expert evidence of foreign law is given by qualified legal practitioners of the foreign country in question, even if they do not practice there,[32] or by academic lawyers who have specialised in the foreign legal system.[33] Other persons may be competent to give the relevant evidence, even if they are not lawyers at all,[34] if their knowledge or experience enables them to do so.[35] Thus, bankers,[36] a former stock broker,[37] a former colonial governor,[38] a bishop[39] and diplomats[40] have all been accepted as competent witnesses in respect of aspects of foreign law with which they were familiar.

---

[31] It is submitted that this is a question of fact for the court; the decisions cited below, as to persons who have been held to be suitably qualified, may therefore be helpful as analogies, but should probably not be regarded as decisive as a matter of law.

[32] Foreign qualified lawyers practising in London are often used as experts in High Court litigation.

[33] *Brailey* v. *Rhodesia Consolidated Ltd.* [1910] 2 Ch. 95; see, *e.g. X A.G.* v. *A Bank* [1983] 2 All E.R. 464, at p. 473.

[34] A lawyer qualified in one jurisdiction may be competent to give evidence on the law of another jurisdiction, by reason of his knowledge or experience: *In the goods of Whitelegg* [1899] P. 267; *Wilson* v. *Wilson* [1903] P. 157; *Rossano* v. *Manufacturer's Life Insurance Co.* [1963] 2 Q.B. 352, at p. 373.

[35] It is sometimes said that the knowledge or experience must necesarily have been acquired in the course of the witness's profession or calling: see Cheshire and North, p. 108; *cf.* Dicey and Morris, pp. 221–222. It is submitted that, in the light of s.4(1) of the Civil Evidence Act 1972, that is not now a condition.

[36] *De Beéche* v. *South American Stores Ltd.* [1935] A.C. 148; *Ajami* v. *Comptroller of Customs* [1954] 1 W.L.R. 1405.

[37] *Vander Donckt* v. *Thellusson* (1849) 8 C.B. 812.

[38] *Cooper-King* v. *Cooper-King* [1900] P. 65.

[39] *The Sussex Peerage Case* (1844) 11 Cl. & Fin. 85.

[40] *In the goods of Dost Aly Khan* (1880) 6 P.D. 6; *In the goods of Oldenburg* (1884) 9 P.D. 234; *Lacon* v. *Higgins* (1822) Dow & Ry.N.P. 38.

9.08   *The evidence of foreign law.* At trial, evidence of foreign law is normally given by an expert witness orally, although in a suitable case it may be given by affidavit[41] or in other written form.[42] Affidavit evidence of foreign law is often given at the interlocutory stages of proceedings, but the court may decline to try disputed questions of foreign law on affidavit.[43] An order may be made for the evidence of a foreign lawyer to be taken abroad by an examiner if such evidence is not readily available in England.[44] As with any expert evidence, there are restrictions on the circumstances in which it may be adduced at a trial or hearing. Except with the leave of the court or where all the parties agree or where the evidence is given by affidavit, the expert evidence may only be given if the party seeking to adduce it has applied to the court to determine whether directions should be given for its prior disclosure.[45]

In giving evidence, the expert may refer to the sources of the foreign law, including texts of legislation, decisions of the courts and the writings of learned commentators;[46] but the court is entitled to examine any such material, especially if conflicting evidence has been given. The court must weigh the conflicting opinions of the experts and make its own assessment of the soure material produced by them, in order to arrive at its own conclusions as to the meaning of the law.[47] The court gives particular weight to the decisions of foreign courts as evidence of their own foreign law,[48] but such decisions are not regarded as decisive.[49] English courts should not overlook the fact that such decisions may be

---

[41] R.S.C., Ord. 38, r. 2.

[42] As to various forms of written evidence, see paras. 8.11 *et seq.* above; and, regarding admission of a hearsay statement of expert evidence, see also R.S.C., Ord. 38, r. 41.

[43] *National Shipping Corporation* v. *Arab* [1971] 2 Lloyd's Rep. 363.

[44] *Armour* v. *Walker* (1883) 25 Ch.D. 673; see *Supreme Court Practice*, para. 39/1/4; see para. 8.44 above.

[45] R.S.C., Ord. 38, r. 36; C.C.R., Ord. 20, r. 27; as regards personal injury actions, see also R.S.C., Ord. 25, r. 8(1)(b). If the foreign law has been fully pleaded, the disclosure of expert evidence may merely duplicate the pleading.

[46] *Nelson* v. *Bridport* (1845) 8 Beav. 527; *Concha* v. *Murietta* (1889) 40 Ch.D. 543; *Lazard Bros. & Co.* v. *Midland Bank* [1935] A.C. 289, at p. 298.

[47] *Concha* v. *Murietta,* above; *Russian Commercial and Industrial Bank* v. *Comptoir d'Escompete de Mulhouse* [1923] 2 K.B. 630, at p. 643; *Princess Paley Olga* v. *Weisz* [1929] 1 K.B. 718; *De Beéch* v. *South American Stores Ltd.* [1935] A.C. 148; *Royer Guillet & Cie.* v. *Rouyer Guillet & Co. Ltd.* [1949] 1 All E.R. 244; *Parkasho* v. *Singh* [1968] P. 233, at p. 250.

[48] *Bremer* v. *Freeman* (1857) 10 Moo.P.C. 306; *Beatty* v. *Beatty* [1924] 1 K.B. 807; *Re Annersley* [1926] Ch. 692; at pp. 707–708; *Bankers and Shippers Co. of New York* v. *Liverpool Marine and General Insurance Co. Ltd.* (1926) 24 Ll.L.R. 85; *In the Estate of Fuld (No. 3)* [1968] P. 675, at pp. 701–702.

[49] *Guaranty Trust of New York* v. *Hannay* [1918] 2 K.B. 623, at p. 638, 667; *Callwood* v. *Callwood* [1960] A.C. 659.

accorded less respect in civil law systems than in systems of law based on the doctrine of precedent.[50] If the witness's evidence is uncontradicted, the court should be reluctant to reject it,[51] but it may do so in an exceptional case.[52] Where the construction of foreign legal texts is material, evidence as to the methods of their construction should also be adduced;[53] if it is not, the court will put its own construction on the text, using English principles of construction.[54] The construction of documents governed by foreign law is a matter for the English court to perform, using such foreign rules of construction as may have been proved.[55]

Although no practice to this effect has developed, there is no apparent reason why, in an appropriate case, the court should not itself appoint an expert to consider and report on questions of foreign law.[56] Similarly, if complex questions of foreign law arise, the court might exercise its power to call in the aid of a suitably qualified assessor.[57]

4. Other means establishing foreign law

At common law

The court will not normally conduct its own researches into **9.09** foreign law,[58] but, in some cases, the court may be willing to investigate foreign law without the evidence of witnesses to assist it, although it will normally only do so with the agreement of the parties.[59] It seems that, although the court may be willing to construe and apply foreign law in this way, it is under no obligation to do so

---

[50] See, *e.g. Fothergill* v. *Monarch Airlines* [1981] A.C. 251; see also para. 13.27 below.

[51] *Sharif* v. *Azad* [1967] 1 Q.B. 603, at p. 616.

[52] *e.g. Buerger* v. *New York Life Assurance Co.* (1927) 96 L.J.K.B. 930, at p. 941; *A/S Tallinna Laevauhisus* v. *Estonian State Steamship Line* (1947) 80 Ll.L.R. 99, at p. 108.

[53] *e.g. Castrique* v. *Imrie* (1870) L.R. 4 H.L. 414, at p. 430.

[54] *Hartmann* v. *Kønig* (1933) 50 T.L.R. 114, at p. 117; *Re Parana Plantations Ltd.* [1946] 2 All E.R. 214, at pp. 217–218; *Jabbour* v. *Custodian of Israeli Absentee Property* [1954] 1 W.L.R. 139, at pp. 147–148.

[55] *Ibid.*, *Royer Guillet & Cie* v. *Rouyer Guillet & Co. Ltd.* [1949] 1 All E.R. 244.

[56] R.S.C., Ord. 40. The exclusion from that Order (by r. 1(1)) of "questions of law or construction" does not, it is submitted, exclude questions of foreign law from its ambit: see *Supreme Court Practice*, para. 40/1–6/1.

[57] Supreme Court Act 1981, s.70; R.S.C., Ord. 33, r. 6.

[58] *Di Sora* v. *Phillips* (1863) 10 H.L.C. 624, 640.

[59] *Lacon* v. *Higgins* (1822) Dowl. & Ry.N.P. 38, 42; *Jabbour* v. *Custodian of Israeli Absentee Property* [1954] 1 W.L.R. 139, at pp. 147–148; *Re Marshall* [1957] Ch. 507; *Dalmia Dairy Industries* v. *National Bank of Pakistan* [1978] 2 Lloyd's Rep. 223, at p. 236. *Cf. Re Sebba* [1959] Ch. 166; *Wilson, Smithett & Cope Ltd.* v. *Terruzzi* [1976] Q.B. 683. See also *Beatty* v. *Beatty* [1924] 1 K.B. 807, at pp. 814–815, where the Court of Appeal determined foreign law as arbitrators on the material before it, some of which was not in evidence.

and, except for the purpose of construing foreign statutes,[60] it is hesitant to do so. Judicial notice may be taken of a rule of foreign law if it amounts to a notorious fact[61] and certain rules of colonial law may be judicially noticed if these are themselves determined by English law.[62]

Pursuant to statute

9.10 *Civil Evidence Act 1972, section 4(2).* This sub-section enables evidence on a point of foreign law to be adduced in certain circumstances by citing a previous finding or decision made on the point by certain courts in England. The finding or decision must have been "reported or recorded in citable form," which means a report, transcript or other document which, if the decision had been one of English law, could have been cited as authority in English proceedings.[63] The finding or decision must have been made in proceedings at first instance in the High Court or Crown Court (or in certain obsolete courts)[64] or on appeal arising out of any of those proceedings,[65] or by the Judicial Committee of the Privy Council on appeal from any court outside the United Kingdom.[66] This sub-section does not, apparently, cover decisions of the High Court made on appeal (for example from the Crown Court or a magistrates' court), or of the Court of Appeal or House of Lords in proceedings heard at first instance in the county court, or of the House of Lords on appeal from the courts of Scotland or Northern Ireland.

If a finding or decision on a point of foreign law is adduced as evidence under this sub-section, the foreign law is to be taken to be in accordance with the finding or decision, unless the contrary is proved; but this presumption does not apply if the finding or decision conflicts with another finding or decision on the same point

---

[60] In some cases, the court appears to have considered foreign law without it having been proved in evidence: *Re Cohn* [1945] Ch. 5; see Dicey and Morris, pp. 219–220.

[61] *Saxby* v. *Fulton* [1909] 2 K.B. 208, at p. 211, where the legality of roulette in Monte Carlo was judicially noticed; and *Re Turner* [1906] W.N. 27, where the fact that the law of different German states varied considerably was judicially noticed. But in *Harmann* v. *Konig* (1933) 50 T.L.R. 114, at p. 117, the court declined to take judicial notice of the fact that the construction of documents is more liberal in continental legal systems than under English law, because the fact was not notorious.

[62] See Dicey and Morris, pp. 218–219; see also Evidence (Colonial Statutes) Act 1907, para. 9.11 below.

[63] s.4(5).

[64] s.4(4)(a). The other courts are courts of quarter session (now replaced by the Crown Court) and the Courts of Chancery of the counties palantine of Durham and Lancaster (now merged into the High Court).

[65] s.4(4)(b).

[66] s.4(4)(c).

also adduced under this sub-section in the same proceedings.[67] However, except with the leave of the court, the finding or decision is only admissible if certain requirements of the rules of court have been complied with.[68]

In High Court proceedings,[69] a party who intends to adduce such a finding or decision on a question of foreign law must serve a notice of his intention to do so on every other party to the proceedings.[70] The notice must be served within 14 days after the close of pleadings in most actions begun by writ[71] and, in any other cause or matter, within 21 days after the date on which an appointment for a first hearing of the cause or matter is obtained,[72] or, in each case, within such other period as the court may specify. The notice must specify the question on which the finding or decision was made and must specify the document in which it is reported or recorded in citable form,[73] although an affidavit containing these particulars is sufficient notice in proceedings in which affidavit evidence may be given, if it is served within the above time limits.[74] An affidavit served for the purpose of interlocutory proceedings, such as a challenge to the jurisdiction or an application for summary judgment, may be sufficient notice for the purpose of subsequent hearings, including the trial of the action.[75]

Express provision for judicial notice. Judicial notice may be taken **9.11** of foreign law in accordance with an express statutory provision to this effect.[76]

Evidence (Colonial Statutes) Act 1907. Copies of the legislation[77] of any "British possession" are admissible as evidence if they pur-

---

[67] s.4(2)(b) and proviso.
[68] s.4(3).
[69] Similar provisions apply in the county court: C.C.R., Ord. 20, r. 25.
[70] R.S.C., Ord. 38, r. 7(1).
[71] R.S.C., Ord. 38, r. 7(1)(a). The proceedings are those to which Ord. 25, r. 1 applies. Note that this does *not* include, *inter alia*, proceedings in which the plaintiff has applied for judgment under Ords. 14 or 86 and in which directions have been given under the relevant order, most personal injury actions, actions to be tried as official referees' business, or actions in which an application to transfer to the commercial list is pending: Ord. 25, r. 1(2).
[72] R.S.C., Ord. 38, r. 7(1)(b).
[73] R.S.C., Ord. 38, r. 7(2) For a form of notice, see *Supreme Court Practice*, Form EF 15, para. [615]; Chitty and Jacob, p. 498.
[74] R.S.C., Ord. 38, r. 7(3).
[75] *Supreme Court Practice*, para. 38/7/1.
[76] *e.g.* judicial notice may be taken of the law of another part of the U.K. under the Maintenance Orders Act 1950, s.22(2).
[77] The documents referred to are "Copies of Acts, ordinances, and statutes passed . . . by the Legislature of any British possession, and of orders, regulations and other instruments issued or made . . . under the authority of any such Act, ordinance, or statute . . . ": s.1(1).

port to be printed by the Government printer. The expression "British possession" means any part of "Her Majesty's dominions,"[78] but the Act also still applies to many former colonies by reason of the terms of the United Kingdom legislation which conferred or recognised the independent or republican status of these countries.[79]

9.12   *British Law Ascertainment Act 1859.* This Act provides a mechanism by which the law of any part of "His Majesty's dominions"[80] may be ascertained for the purpose of proceedings in an English court, by asking the opinion of a superior court of that dominion.[81] This procedure may be invoked in any case in which the English court considers it necessary or expedient for the proper disposal of an action, especially where complex questions of law arise; but it is a matter for the court's discretion whether it does so.[82] It may be invoked of the court's own motion, even if foreign law has not been pleaded.[83] The English court directs that a case be prepared setting forth the facts. The order for settlement of a case is obtained on a motion or summons and the case is then brought into Chambers and settled there.[84] The court or a judge thereof then settles the questions of law arising out of the facts on which the opinion of the

---

[78] s.1(3). As to the meaning of "Her Majesty's dominions," see 6 *Halsbury's Laws* (4th ed.), para. 803; 7 *Halsbury's Statutes* (4th edn.), p. 4. The expression includes the Channel Islands and the Isle of Man, British colonies and protectorates, and independent Commonwealth countries of which the Queen is head of state.

[79] Such legislation usually provides that the existing law of the U.K. shall continue to apply to these countries as if they had not become republics. See, *e.g.* Bangladesh Act 1973, s.1; Belize Act 1981, s.4; Botswana Independence Act 1966, s.2; Cyprus Act 1960, s.3; Republic of the Gambia Act 1970, s.1; Ghana (Consequential Provisions) Act 1960, s.1; Guyana Republic Act 1970, s.1; India (Consequential Provisions) Act 1949, s.1; Ireland Act 1949, s.3(2); Kenya Republic Act 1965, s.1; Lesotho Independence Act 1966, s.2; Nigeria Republic Act 1963, s.1; Malaysia Act 1963, s.3; Malawi Republic Act 1966, s.1; Malta Republic Act 1975, s.1; Seychelles Act 1976, s.5; Sierra Leone Republic Act 1972, s.1; Singapore Act 1966, s.1; Sri Lanka Republic Act 1972, s.1; Swaziland Independence Act 1968, s.3; Tanganyika Republic Act 1962, s.1 and Zanzibar Act 1963, s.1; Tonga Act 1970, s.1; Trinidad and Tobago Republic Act 1976, s.1; Uganda Act 1964, s.1; West Indies Act 1967, s.14 (and Orders made thereunder); Zambia Independence Act 1964, s.2; and Zimbabwe Independence Act 1979, ss.4 and 5 (and Orders made thereunder). See also Isle of Man Act 1979, s.12.

[80] See n. 78 above.

[81] The Act also applies to many former dominions: see the provisions cited at n. 79 above; but it will only be of practical application in relation to a country in which the Act remains in force or which is otherwise willing to co-operate in answering a request from an English court.

[82] *Lord* v. *Colvin* (1860) 1 Dr. & Sm. 24.

[83] *Topham* v. *Duke of Portland* (1863) 1 De G.J. & S. 517; *Eglinton* v. *Lamb* (1867) 15 L.T. 657.

[84] *Supreme Court Practice*, para. 39/2–3/10.

foreign court is required, and the case and questions of law are then remitted to the foreign court for its opinion. The Act provides that the parties may present a petition to the foreign court asking it to pronounce its opinion, with or without hearing argument, and the foreign court then provides its opinion.[85] A certified copy of the opinion is provided to any of the parties who may require it[86] which may then be lodged with the English court with a notice of motion for that court to apply the opinion to the facts of the case. The opinion is binding on the English court.[87]

European Convention on Information on Foreign Law (1968).[88]   **9.13**
This Convention is designed to facilitate the task of judicial authorities in obtaining information on foreign law in civil and commercial matters.[89] It is in force as between most European countries, including the United Kingdom,[90] but no legislation has been passed to enact it into English law. Nonetheless, it is submitted that in an appropriate case an English court may be able to take advantage of its provisions for mutual judicial assistance, either under its powers to issue a letter of request for the taking of evidence abroad[91] or under the court's inherent jurisdiction.[92]

The Convention provides that a request for information may be made by a judicial authority in a Contracting State,[93] stating as exactly as possible the questions on which information concerning the law of the requested state is desired[94] and the facts necessary for a proper understanding of the request and the formulation of an exact and precise reply.[95] Copies of documents may be attached if

---

[85] s.1.
[86] s.2.
[87] s.3. Foreign law is no longer a question for the jury: Supreme Court Act 1981, s.69(5).
[88] Cmnd. 4229, T.S. No. 117 (1969), European Treaty Series, No. 62. It was signed in London on June 7, 1968 and came into force on December 17, 1969. There is also a Protocol: see below.
[89] But see the Protocol, mentioned below.
[90] The following countries have ratified the Convention: Austria, Belgium, Costa Rica, Cyprus, Denmark, France, Germany, Greece, Iceland, Italy, Liechtenstein, Luxembourg, Malta, Netherlands, Norway, Portugal, Spain, Sweden, Switzerland, Turkey and the U.K.
[91] R.S.C., Ord. 39, rr. 13; see para. 8.45 above.
[92] It is submitted that an analogy can properly be drawn with the court's inherent power to invoke the assistance of an expert: see *Supreme Court Practice*, para. 40/1–6/1 and the cases cited there.
[93] Art. 3(1).
[94] Art. 4(1). The request must relate to questions in the civil and commercial fields, but it may include questions in other fields which are incidental to the principal questions in the request: Art. 4(3).
[95] Art. 4(2).

necessary.[96] The request is transmitted through national liaison bodies designated for the purpose,[97] and the receiving authority may answer the request itself or may transmit the request to some other body, either of an official or private character, or to a private lawyer, to draw up the answer.[98] The request must be in the language of the state addressed or accompanied by a translation into that language and the reply will also be in that language.[99] The object of the reply is to give information in an objective and impartial manner on the law of the requested state to the judicial authority from which the request emanated. It will contain, as appropriate, relevant legal texts and relevant judicial decisions, and it may also be accompanied by extracts from relevant doctrinal works, *travaux préparatoires* and explanatory commentaries.[1] The information given in the reply does not bind the judicial authority from which it emanates.[2]

A Protocol to the Convention has also been signed[3] which extends its operation in two respects. First, it provides for information to be supplied in the criminal field[4] and, secondly, it enables requests for information in civil and commercial matters to emanate from persons acting for legally aided parties in actual or contemplated proceedings.[5] This latter extension, however, has not been acceded to by the United Kingdom.[6]

5. Limitation periods

9.14   One aspect of English private international law of particular practical significance is the choice of law rules relating to limitation. Formerly, the question of whether English or foreign law applied to determine matters of limitation and prescription depended on whether the foreign law was characterised as procedural or substan-

---

[96] *Ibid.*

[97] Arts. 2 and 5. The U.K. has designated the Legal and Executive Branch of the Foreign and Commonwealth Office, from whom further information may be obtained.

[98] Art. 6.

[99] Art. 14. *cf.* para. 8.47 above for appropriate arrangements for translating a reply in a foreign language.

[1] Art. 7.

[2] Art. 8.

[3] Cmnd. 8431, T.S. No. 88 (1981), European Treaty Series, No. 97, signed in Strasbourg, March 15, 1978, which entered into force as regards the U.K. on December 3, 1981. Of the states which have ratified the Convention, only the following have not also ratified the Protocol: Costa Rica, Iceland, Liechentstein, Malta and Turkey.

[4] Protocol, chap. 1.

[5] Protocol, chap. 2.

[6] In ratifying the Protocol, the following states have declared that they are not bound by chap. 2: Cyprus, the Netherlands, Switzerland and the U.K.

tive. The Foreign Limitation Periods Act 1984,[7] however, has clarified the law in this area, linking questions of limitation and prescription with the substantive law applicable to the case.

Under the Act, which applies to any action or proceedings in a court in England and Wales,[8] English choice of law rules are applied to determine the system of law which applies to an issue in the proceedings.[9] If that is foreign law, then subject to one exception, the foreign law of limitation applies to the issue. This is so irrespective of whether the foreign law is procedural or substantive, either according to its own classification or according to English classification.[10] Only if both English law and foreign law apply to the substantive issue (as in the case of a tort committed outside England and Wales)[11] does English law of limitation apply, and then it applies in addition to the foreign law,[12] so that, in general the shorter limitation period is effective.

The exception to this principle is that if the application of a foreign limitation period would be contrary to public policy, it is to be disregarded.[13] Public policy is not defined, but the application of a limitation period is expressly stated to be contrary to public policy to the extent that its application would cause undue hardship to a person who is, or who might be made, a party to the action or proceedings.[14]

For the purpose of determining what the law of any country is on **9.15** questions of limitation, the rules of private international law of that country are to be ignored.[15] A country's law of limitation includes the rules relating to, and to the effect of, the application, extension, reduction or interruption of limitation periods;[16] but any rule of foreign law is to be ignored if and to the extent that it provides for a limitation period to be interrupted or extended by virtue of a party's absence from a jurisdiction or country.[17] The English court must attempt to exercise any discretion provided by the foreign law

---

[7] The Act came into force on October 1, 1985 (S.I. 1985 No. 1276.)
[8] s.1(1). The Act also applies to arbitration: s.5.
[9] s.1(1).
[10] s.4(2). Limitation, for the purposes of the Act, includes foreign rules of prescription which extinguish the right as well as rules of limitation which merely bar the remedy.
[11] *Phillips* v. *Eyre* (1870) L.R. 6 Q.B. 1; *Boys* v. *Chaplin* [1971] A.C. 356.
[12] s.1(1)(b); s.1(2).
[13] s.2(1). This enables the English court to temper the effects of unduly long or unduly short limitation periods.
[14] s.2(2).
[15] *i.e.* the doctrine of *renvoi* is excluded: s.1(5). Accordingly, the 1984 Act itself is, for this purpose, not regarded as part of the English law of limitation.
[16] s.4(1)(a).
[17] s.2(3).

in the same manner as it would be exercised by the courts of the country concerned.[18] English law applies to determine whether, and if so when, proceedings have been commenced,[19] including questions relating to new claims in pending proceedings.[20]

A country's law of limitation also includes any rule by which proceedings may be brought within an indefinite period.[21] The English law of limitation does not include rules by virtue of which the court may refuse equitable relief on the grounds of acquiescence or otherwise;[22] but in the application of these rules to cases governed by foreign substantive law, an English court must have regard to the provisions of that law.[23]

---

[18] s.1(4).
[19] s.1(3).
[20] Limitation Act 1980, s.35.
[21] 1984 Act, s.4(1)(b).
[22] s.4(3); the doctrine of *laches* is therefore not affected.
[23] s.4(3).

CHAPTER 10

RECOGNITION AND ENFORCEMENT

A. INTRODUCTION

It is a corollary of the territorial nature of the concepts of sover- **10.01**
eignty and jurisdiction that a judgment of a court should have effect
only within the state in which it is given. However the broader
interests of justice obviously require the development of some system by which judgments can be recognised and, when necessary,
enforced in other states. National sovereignty still requires that it
should be the laws and the courts of the state in which enforcement
is sought that should determine the circumstances in which foreign
judgments are to be recognised or enforced and should govern the
processes of enforcement. Each of the legal systems in Western
Europe has developed its own rules and procedures for the recognition and enforcement of foreign judgments, subject to modifications brought about by bilateral and multilateral conventions.[1]

---

[1] See *The practical guide to the recognition and enforcement of foreign judicial decisions
in civil and commercial law*: Council of Europe (1975).

Before proceeding to discuss recognition and enforcement under English law, the distinction should be noted between the recognition of a foreign judgment and its enforcement. Whenever a court sanctions the enforcement of a foreign judgment it necessarily also recognises its legal validity. Conceptually, recognition precedes and is distinct from enforcement. In some circumstances a court may be called upon to recognise the legal validity of a foreign judgment and to give effect to the judgment in some way other than by sanctioning its enforcement. It may be that a foreign judgment, for instance a judgment in favour of a defendant, is not capable of enforcement, but the defendant may nonetheless seek to rely upon such a judgment in proceedings in England or elsewhere.

10.02   Under English law, foreign judgments[2] may be recognised and enforced in accordance with rules developed by the common law or in accordance with one of a number of statutory schemes which may apply to the judgment in question. Only if a foreign judgment is not so enforceable or entitled to recognition may fresh proceedings be brought on the original cause of action.[3] Judgments in civil and commercial matters given in one of the other Contracting States to the 1968 Convention will usually be enforceable in England under the Civil Jurisdiction and Judgments Act 1982.[4] Judgments given in the courts of a number of Commonwealth and colonial countries, and of certain European countries not parties to the 1968 Convention, will be enforceable under either the Administration of Justice Act 1920, or the Reciprocal Enforcement of Judgments Act 1933.[5] However, the starting point of an examination of English rules and procedures for recognition and enforcement of foreign judgments is the common law, both from the historical point of view and because, if a foreign judgment is not enforceable under any of the statutory schemes, it may still be enforceable by a common law action on the judgment.[6]

1. Enforcement at common law by action on the judgment

10.03   The English courts have recognised and enforced foreign judgments at least since the seventeenth century.[7] Initially the basis of

---

[2] The enforcement of foreign arbitral awards is outside the scope of this work. See Arbitration Act 1950, Part II; Mustill and Boyd, *Commercial Arbitration* (2nd ed.), pp. 421 *et seq.*

[3] 1982 Act, s.34, para. 43.36 below.

[4] See para. 10.05 below.

[5] See para. 10.04 below; Patchett. *Recognition of Commercial Judgments and Awards in the Commonwealth.*

[6] But, see para 10.03, n. 24a below.

[7] Sack, *Law, A Century of Progress, 1853–1935* (1937), Vol. 3, pp. 388 *et seq.*; Holdsworth, *History of English Law*, Vol. 11, pp. 270 *et seq.*; *Wier's Case* (1607) 1 Rolle, Abridgment 530, p. 12; *Jurado* v. *Gregory* (1670) 1 Vent. 32; *Hughes* v. *Cornelius* (1683) 2 Show. 232; *Ewer* v. *Jones* (1704) 2 Ld.Raym. 934.

such recognition was regarded to be the comity of nations and the need to ensure that English judgments would be recognised abroad.[8] Later it was considered that the foreign judgment gave rise to a simple contract debt based on an implied promise on the part of the judgment debtor to satisfy the judgment,[9] and the enforcing creditor brought an action at common law "on the judgment." It has now been long established that the English courts will recognise and enforce at common law a judgment *in personam*[10] given by a foreign court for a sum of money,[11] provided that it is final and conclusive[12] and that the court which gave it was a court which had jurisdiction according to rules which corresponded to the English rules of private international law. Thus, the defendant must have been resident or present in the foreign country when the proceedings were commenced[13] or he must have submitted to the jurisdiction by express prior agreement[14] or by appearing voluntarily and defending himself.[15] For this latter purpose appearing solely to contest the jurisdiction is not regarded as submitting to the jurisdiction.[16] Additionally the foreign judgment will not be recognised or enforced if to do so would be contrary to public policy,[17] if it would give effect to the penal or revenue laws of a foreign country,[18] or in certain other instances.[19] Provided the foreign judgment satisfies the above conditions, the English court will not investigate the

---

[8] *Roach* v. *Garvan* (1748) 1 Ves.Sen. 157, 159; *Geyer* v. *Aquilar* (1798) 7 Term Rep. 681; *Wright* v. *Simpson* (1802) 6 Ves. 714 at p. 730, *per* Lord Eldon; *Alves* v. *Bunbury* (1814) 4 Camp. 28, *per* Lord Ellenborough.

[9] *Dupleix* v. *De Roven* (1705) 2 Vern. 540; *Walker* v. *Witter* (1778) 1 Dougl. K.B. 1; *Russell* v. *Smyth* (1842) 9 M. & W. 810, 819; *Williams* v. *Jones* (1845) 13 M. & W. 628, 633; *Godard* v. *Gray* (1870) L.R. 6 Q.B. 139, 149–150; *Schibsby* v. *Westenholz* (1870) L.R. 6 Q.B. 155; *Grant* v. *Easton* (1883) 13 Q.B.D. 302.

[10] As to foreign judgments *in rem*, see Cheshire and North, pp. 354 *et seq.*

[11] Explained by Read, *Recognition and Enforcement of Foreign Judgments in the Common Law Units of the British Commonwealth* (1938), p. 113. The sum must be fixed: *Sadler* v. *Robins* (1808) 1 Camp. 253.

[12] *Nouvion* v. *Freeman* (1889) 15 App.Cas. 1; 8 *Halsbury's Laws* (4th ed.) para. 734.

[13] *Gurdyal Singh* v. *Rajah of Faridkote* (1894) A.C. 670.

[14] *Copin* v. *Adamson* (1874) L.R. 9 Ex. 345, affirmed (1875) L.R. 1 Ex.D. 17; *Vogel* v. *R & A Kohnstamm Ltd.* [1973] 1 Q.B. 133; Cohn "The Enforcement of Foreign Judgments against Partnerships" (1962) 11 I.C.L.Q. 583.

[15] *De Cosse Brissac* v. *Rathbone* (1861) 6 H. & N. 301; as explained in *Schibsby* v. *Westenholz* (1870) L.R. 6 Q.B. 155, 162; see Cheshire and North, p. 345.

[16] 1982 Act s.33(1), and see chap. 5.

[17] See para. 10.28 below.

[18] *Folliot* v. *Ogden* (1789) 1 H.Bl. 135; *Huntingdon* v. *Attrill* [1893] A.C. 156; *Banco de Vizcaya* v. *Don Alfonso de Borbon y Austria* [1935] 1 K.B. 140; *Government of India* v. *Taylor* [1955] A.C. 491; *Att.-Gen. of New Zealand* v. *Ortiz* [1984] A.C. 1.; *U.S.A.* v. *Inkley* [1988] 3 W.L.R. 304 (C.A.).

[19] See Cheshire and North, pp. 370 *et seq.*

merits of the foreign judgment, even where it is alleged that there is fresh evidence,[20] or that the evidence before the foreign court was insufficient or defective,[21] or that the judgment was based on a mistake of law.[22] If an appeal is pending before the foreign court, the English court will only grant a stay of the action pending the outcome of the appeal.[23]

The common law action on a foreign judgment described above has remained a useful, and in many cases the only, method of enforcing some foreign judgments,[24] although, if the judgment is enforceable under the 1933 Act or the 1982 Act, it may not be enforced in this way.[24a] The creditor brings an action in the normal way by serving a writ on the defendant in which the foreign judgment is pleaded as the basis for the claim.[25] If the defendant does not return the acknowledgment of service, the plaintiff can sign judgment in default without even having to produce the judgment, let alone having to have it translated or certified or authenticated. If the defendant returns the acknowledgment of service, whether or not he also serves a defence, the plaintiff can apply for summary judgment under Order 14[26] and exhibit the foreign judgment, or a copy of it, to his affidavit.

2. Recognition and enforcement under the Administration of Justice Act 1920 and the Foreign Judgments (Reciprocal Enforcement) Act 1933

10.04   It is not intended to make more than a passing reference to the schemes for recognition and enforcement under the 1920 and 1933 Acts. The 1920 Act does not apply to any of the Contracting States of the 1968 Convention and the application of the 1933 Act to any of these is now extremely limited. The Contracting States to which the 1933 Act formerly applied are Belgium, France, the Federal

---

[20] *Henderson* v. *Henderson* (1844) 6 Q.B. 297.
[21] *De Cosse Brissac* v. *Rathbone* (1861) 6 H. & N. 301; *Scott* v. *Pilkington* (1862) 2 B. & S. 11.
[22] *Bank of Australia* v. *Nias* (1851) 16 Q.B. 717.
[23] *Nouvion* v. *Freeman* (1889) 15 App.Cas. 1; *Colt Industries Inc.* v. *Sarlie (No. 2)* [1966] 1. W.L.R. 1287.
[24] As *e.g.* in *Colt Industries Inc.* v. *Sarlie (No. 2)* [1966] 1 W.L.R. 1287. The only method of enforcement in the county court is by the common law action as, save in respect of certain Canadian decisions, enforcement under the 1920 and 1933 Acts must be by registration in the High Court.
[24a] 1933 Act, s. 6; as to the 1982 Act, see *De Wolf* v. *Cox B.V.* [1976] E.C.R. 1759, para. 25.35 below. A judgment which is enforceable under the 1920 Act can form the basis of a common law action, subject to costs penalties.
[25] A precedent for the statement of claim is given in *Bullen and Leake and Jacob's Precedents of Pleading* (12th ed.) p. 587.
[26] See Goldrein and Wilkinson, *Commercial Litigation: Pre-emptive Remedies*, p. 286.

Republic of Germany, Italy and the Netherlands.[27] By Article 55 of the 1968 Convention, the conventions between the United Kingdom and those countries are superseded, except in respect of matters which fall outside the scope of the 1968 Convention and in respect of judgments given in those Contracting States before January 1, 1987.[28] The 1933 Act does, of course, continue to apply to certain other European non-Contracting States,[29] the Channel Islands and the Isle of Man,[30] to judgments given under certain specialised conventions in non-Contracting States,[31] as well as to various Commonwealth and other non-European states.[32]

B. RECOGNITION AND ENFORCEMENT OF FOREIGN JUDGMENTS UNDER THE CIVIL JURISDICTION AND JUDGMENTS ACT 1982 AND THE 1968 CONVENTION

1. Introduction

The Civil Jurisdiction and Judgments Act 1982 has, by giving effect to the 1968 Convention,[33] established in the United Kingdom a new system for the recognition and enforcement of judgments given in other Contracting States. In respect of matters to which the 1968 Convention applies,[34] its provisions relating to recognition and enforcement entirely replace the provisions of Part II of the Administration of Justice Act 1920 and the Foreign Judgments (Reciprocal Enforcement) Act 1933. Those Acts, however, still apply in respect of countries[35] and matters[36] which are outside the ambit of the Convention. Foreign judgments which come within the scope of the Convention can only be enforced by means of the procedure laid

10.05

---

[27] Belgium—S.R. & O. 1936 No. 1169; France—S.R. & O. 1936 No. 609; Federal Republic of Germany—(S.I. 1961 No. 1199); Italy—(S.I. 1973 No. 1894); Netherlands—(S.I. 1969 No. 1063) as amended by (S.I. 1977 No. 2149).

[28] See Art. 56, see para. 33.03 below.

[29] Austria—(S.I. 1962 No. 1339); Norway—(S.I. 1962 No. 636).

[30] Bailiwick of Jersey—(S.I. 1973 No. 612); Island of Guernsey—(S.I. 1973 No. 610); Isle of Man—(S.I. 1973 No. 611). By s.39 of the 1982 Act, that Act may, by Order in Council, be extended to the Isle of Man, the Channel Islands and certain other territories.

[31] See Patchett, *Recognition of Commercial Judgments and Awards in the Commonwealth*, p. 98 and Dicey and Morris, pp. 525 *et seq.*

[32] See, generally, Patchett *op. cit.*

[33] 1982 Act, s.2(1), para 40.03 below.

[34] The scope of application of the Convention is described in chap. 14 below. In general the enforcement provisions of the Convention apply in England and Wales to judgments given in a Contracting State after January 1, 1987.

[35] *e.g.*, Austria and Norway.

[36] *e.g.*, the enforcement of certain arbitration awards, by virtue of s.10A of the 1933 Act (added by s.35(1) and Sched. 10 of the 1982 Act), or judgments thereon given in the countries listed at n. 27 above.

down in Title III of the Convention. Following the abolition of the non-merger rule, it is no longer possible for a person to bring proceedings in England and Wales on a cause of action in respect of which a judgment has been given in his favour in proceedings between the same parties, or their privies, in a court of another part of the United Kingdom or in an overseas country, unless that judgment is not enforceable or entitled to recognition in England and Wales or, as the case may be, in Northern Ireland.[37] Nor is it possible to bring an action at common law on the foreign judgment.[38] The recognition and enforcement of foreign maintenance orders is subject to a special scheme which is described in Chapter 11. The 1982 Act also establishes a new scheme, described separately below,[39] for the recognition and enforcement of judgments as between the three law areas of the United Kingdom.

10.06   The main objective of the 1968 Convention was to establish a simple and speedy system for the recognition and enforcement of judgments. This objective is achieved by the laying down of common rules of jurisdiction as between the Contracting States and by the adoption of common conditions for recognition and enforcement in accordance with a simple standard procedure. The opportunity for courts addressed for enforcement to review the bases upon which jurisdiction was assumed is kept to a minimum[40] and in no circumstances may a foreign judgment be reviewed as to its substance.[41] There are limited specific grounds upon which recognition and enforcement may be refused.[42] Recognition may be accorded to a foreign judgment either in accordance with the same procedure applicable to enforcement or without any special procedure being required.[43] The procedure for enforcement entails, initially, the making of an application, *ex parte*, for an order for enforcement of the judgment.[44] In England the order for enforcement is constituted by the registration of the judgment in the High Court in accordance with a procedure similar to that employed under the pre-existing statutory schemes. The application must be supported by certain documentary evidence.[45] No applicant is required to provide security for costs solely on the ground that he is not domiciled

---

[37] 1982 Act, s.34, which abolishes the non-merger rule, see para. 43.36 below.
[38] *De Wolf* v. *Cox BV* [1976] E.C.R. 1759. See para. 25.35 below.
[39] See paras. 10.63 *et seq.* below.
[40] See paras. 10.26 and 27.62 below.
[41] See paras. 27.75 and 28.27 below.
[42] See para. 10.27 below.
[43] See paras. 10.10 and 27.01 below.
[44] See para. 10.11 below.
[45] See para. 10.14 below.

or resident within the jurisdiction.[46] An applicant who was in receipt of legal aid in the Contracting State of origin is entitled to full legal aid in England and Wales.[47] Notice of the order for enforcement must be served on the judgment debtor who has a set period within which he may appeal to have the registration set aside or stayed.[48] During this period, and until any appeal against registration has been determined, no measures of enforcement, other than protective measures, may be taken against the judgment debtor's property.[49] If an appeal is, or is to be, lodged against the foreign judgment itself in the state of origin, the English court may stay the proceedings for enforcement until determination of the foreign appeal.[50] If there is no appeal, or no successful appeal, against the registration of the judgment, it may be enforced in England and Wales as it if were a judgment of the High Court.[51]

2. Judgments capable of recognition and enforcement under the 1968 Convention

The most far-reaching of the changes that the 1982 Act and the Convention have brought to the enforcement of judgments in the English courts is the extension of the types of judgment which may be enforced. As has been observed, at common law and under the various statutory schemes prior to the 1982 Act, the English courts would only enforce a foreign judgment if it was for a fixed or ascertainable sum of money and if it was final and conclusive as between the parties. The statutory schemes were further limited to the judgments of superior courts.[52] Article 25 defines the types of judgment which may be recognised and enforced as:

10.07

> "any judgment given by a court or tribunal of a Contracting State,[53] whatever the judgment may be called, including a decree, order, decision or writ of execution, as well as the determination of costs or expenses by an officer of the court."

It follows from this wide definition of "judgment" that, subject

---

[46] Art. 45; see para. 28.85 below.
[47] See paras. 12.13 and 28.81 below.
[48] See para. 10.25 below.
[49] *Ibid.*
[50] See para. 10.45 below.
[51] See para. 10.19 below.
[52] Note s.35(1) and Sched. 10 of the 1982 Act, permitting the extension of the scheme of the 1933 Act to inferior courts and to judgments for interim payments; see para. 43.39 below.
[53] The European Court of Justice is not a court *of* a Contracting State but its money judgments are enforceable in England by registration in the High Court pursuant to the European Community (Enforcement of Community Judgments) Order 1972 (S.I. No. 1590) R.S.C., Ord. 71. rr. 15.–24. See Cheshire and North, p. 398.

to the transitional provisions of the Convention,[54] the classes of judgment enforceable under the 1982 Act and the Convention extend to the following types of judgments and orders given in other Contracting States, by judicial tribunals of all levels, whether or not they can strictly be regarded as courts, so long as they are enforceable in the state of origin:[55]

   (i) money judgments and orders;

   (ii) non-money judgments and orders, for example foreign orders equivalent to injunctions, decrees for specific performance or for specific delivery of chattels;

   (iii) interim and interlocutory orders, so long as they govern the legal relations of the parties and do not merely arrange the further conduct of the proceedings;[56]

   (iv) various forms of summary order to pay debts, for example the French *injonction de payer*,[57] the German *Mahnbeschied*,[58] and the Dutch *betalingsbevel*;[59]

   (v) orders for the payment of penalties imposed by the foreign court for non-compliance with court orders,[60] for example the Dutch *dwangsom*[61] and the French *astreinte*;[62]

   (vi) compensation awarded by a criminal court exercising civil jurisdiction;[63]

   (vii) orders for costs;

10.08 The Convention further provides that the partial enforcement of a judgment may be obtained and that a judgment part of which is enforceable under the Convention may be enforced as to that part.[64] A judgment given in a Contracting State on an earlier judgment which is foreign to that state is probably not enforceable in England and

---

[54] The transitional provisions are described in outline at para. 10.09 below, and are discussed in detail at paras. 32.01 *et seq.* below.

[55] Art. 31, para. 10.37 below; the subject-matter of the proceedings must also fall within the scope of the Convention; see Art. 1, para. 14.03 below. The recognition and enforcement of Scottish and Northern Irish judgments are discussed at para. 10.63 below.

[56] See Schlosser, paras. 184–187 (paras. A1.480–A1.483 below); thus orders for discovery or the taking of evidence are not enforceable in other Contracting States under the Convention: see paras. 25.29 *et seq.* below; *cf.* para. 7.28 above.

[57] See para. 50.62 below.

[58] See para. 51.61 below.

[59] See para. 55.62 below.

[60] Art. 43, as explained by Jenard, para. A1.232 below; the sum must be fixed, see para. 28.80 below.

[61] See *Klomps* v. *Michel* [1981] E.C.R. 1593.

[62] As at common law, see *Raulin* v. *Fischer* [1911] 2 K.B. 93.

[63] See para. 17.53 below.

[64] Art. 42; see para. 28.71 below.

Wales, but the reverse may not necessarily be the case.[65] The recognition and enforcement of a judgment given against a foreign state or other party entitled to state immunity is subject to certain restrictions.[66]

The recognition and enforcement provisions of the Convention apply to all judgments given in proceedings the subject-matter of which falls within its scope.[67] The jurisdictional rules, in particular those which forbid the exercise of exorbitant jurisdiction,[68] only apply in favour of persons who are domiciled in the Contracting States. In consequence a judgment obtained in a Contracting State against a person not domiciled in the Contracting States may be founded on an exorbitant basis of jurisdiction, but it must nonetheless be recognised and enforced under the Convention. Relief from this effect of the Convention may only be obtained if the Contracting state in which enforcement is sought has concluded a convention with the State in which the defendant is domiciled, as provided in Article 59 of the Convention.[69] It should also be noted that the Convention's enforcement procedures are available in respect of judgments given under certain specialised conventions, such as the Geneva Convention on the Carriage of Goods by Road (C.M.R.).[70]

Transitional provisions. As between the United Kingdom and the **10.09** other Contracting States the recognition and enforcement provisions of the 1968 Convention apply not only to judgments given in proceedings commenced after January 1, 1987,[71] but also, in two types of case, to judgments given after that date in proceedings which were commenced before that date. The two types of case are those in which jurisdiction was founded on rules which accorded with the jurisdictional rules of the Convention and those in which jurisdiction was founded on rules which accorded with the provisions of a convention between the United Kingdom and the state

---

[65] See paras. 25.32 *et seq.* below. Note also s.18(7) of the 1982 Act, para. 41.26 below.

[66] See 1982 Act, s.31, para. 43.21 below; State Immunity Act 1978, s.13; see also paras. 2.16 and 2.18 above.

[67] See para. 10.34 below.

[68] Art. 3; see para. 16.09 below; See Jenard, para. A1.186 below; Pryles and Trindade "The Common Market (E.E.C.) Convention on Jurisdiction and Enforcement of Judgments in Civil and Commercial Matters—Possible Impact upon Australian Citizens" (1974) 48 Australian L.J. 185.

[69] See para. 33.24 below. The countries which have concluded conventions under Art. 59 are noted at para. 33.29 below.

[70] The specialised conventions are those within the contemplation of Art. 57, as interpreted by Art. 25(2) of the 1978 Accession Convention. See para. 33.06 below.

[71] The date of the commencement of the main provisions of the Civil Jurisdiction and Judgments Act 1982. The transitional provisions are described more fully at paras. 32.01 *et seq.* below.

of origin which was in force when the proceedings were instituted.[72]

3. Recognition of foreign judgments under the 1968 Convention

10.10   It has been noted above that although a foreign judgment which is to be enforced by order of the English court must necessarily be recognised by the English court, there are some circumstances in which recognition without enforcement may be required by a party.[73] Articles 26 to 30 of the 1968 Convention contain provisions relating to the recognition, as opposed to the enforcement, of judgments.[74] Article 26 of the Convention provides that a judgment given in a Contracting State shall be recognised in the other Contracting States without any special procedure being required. The Article then identifies two types of situation in which the need for recognition may arise. First, if recognition is the principal issue in a dispute, application may be made to the High Court for a declaration of recognition of the foreign judgment by following the same procedure as is provided under the Convention for the enforcement of a foreign judgment.[75] Secondly, if the question of recognition arises incidentally in proceedings the outcome of which will be determined by the decision on recognition, the court hearing those proceedings will have jurisdiction over that question.[76] The circumstances in which it is open to the English courts to refuse to recognise a foreign judgment to which the Convention applies are the same as those for appealing an order for registration for enforcement and they are discussed in detail below.[77] Obligatory grounds for refusal are set out in Articles 27 and 28.[78] The provision of Article 29, in relation to recognition, that in no circumstances may a foreign judgment be reviewed as to its substance, also applies to enforcement and is discussed below.[79] If a judgment has been registered in England for recognition and if, within the time allowed for appealing against the registration, an "ordinary" appeal is brought in the state of origin, the registration continues to be valid,[80] but

---

[72] 1978 Convention, Art. 34, paras. 37.06 *et seq.* below; 1982 Act, s.2(2), para. 43.03 below.
[73] See para. 10.01 above.
[74] See para. 25.02 below.
[75] Art. 26, second para., para. 27.04 below. Although s.4 of the 1982 Act (para. 40.08 below) is limited to applications for enforcement, effect is given to the second para. of Art. 26 by R.S.C., Ord. 71, r. 35.
[76] Art. 26, third para.; see para. 27.01 below.
[77] Art. 34, second para.; see para. 10.27 below.
[78] See para. 25.12 below.
[79] Art. 34, third para.; see para. 28.27 below.
[80] *cf. Re a Debtor (No. 11 of 1939)* [1939] 2 All E.R. 400.

the party bringing the appeal in the state of origin may apply to the English court for a stay of the proceedings.[81]

4. Procedure for recognition and enforcement under the 1968 Convention

Except in the situation referred to above when a court of trial **10.11** determines a question of recognition arising incidentally in proceedings, recognition of a foreign judgment is obtained by the same procedure as is laid down for enforcement. The general form of this procedure is set out in Articles 31 to 49 of the Convention. Whereas in the other Contracting States a specific order for enforcement must be obtained from a designated court, in the United Kingdom enforcement is by means of registration of the foreign judgment in the appropriate court.[82] It follows that references in the Convention to "decision authorising enforcement" refer, in respect of judgments to be enforced in the United Kingdom, to the registration of such judgments, following the court's order for registration. The effect of registration of such a judgment in an appropriate United Kingdom court is to give the judgment the same force and effect, for the purposes of enforcement, as it would have had if it had been an original judgment of that court. In England and Wales the appropriate court is the High Court.[83] The register, which corresponds to the registers kept under the Acts of 1920 and 1933,[84] is kept in the Central Office under the direction of the senior master of the Queen's Bench Division.[85] The procedure is set out in Order 71 of the Rules of the Supreme Court and is described in detail in the following paragraphs.

The application for registration

The application for registration will normally be made by the **10.12** judgment creditor but the Convention allows it to be made by "any interested party."[86] The Rules of the Supreme Court provide[87] that applications for registration under section 4 of the 1982 Act are to be assigned to Queen's Bench Division and that the powers con-

---

[81] Art. 30, see paras. 10.45 and 27.78 below.
[82] Art. 32 (see para. 28.09 below); 1982 Act, s.4 (see para. 40.08 below). In Scotland the appropriate court is the Court of Session (see para. 58.71 below), and in Northern Ireland it is the High Court of Northern Ireland (see para. 57.71 below).
[83] This is, in the case of a money claim, regardless of the amount of the judgment debt.
[84] The Administration of Justice Act 1920 and the Foreign Judgments (Reciprocal Enforcement) Act, 1933.
[85] R.S.C, Ord. 71, r. 31.
[86] Art. 31; see paras. 10.39 and 28.07 below.
[87] R.S.C., Ord. 71, r. 26.

ferred on the court by the Act shall be exercised by the master or the judge in accordance with the provisions of Order 32, rule 11. This provides that the masters of the Queen's Bench Division shall have power to transact all such business and exercise all such authority as may be exercised by a judge in chambers, subject to certain exceptions. The registration of foreign judgments has hitherto only been possible in respect of money judgments and has been within the usual jurisdiction of the masters. However, some types of judgment that can now be registered under the 1982 Act fall within the jurisdiction reserved to a High Court judge, for instance, proceedings under section 37 of the Supreme Court Act 1981 for the grant of an injunction or for the appointment of a receiver. In any such case it is probable that the application for registration should be made *ex parte* to the judge in chambers. Furthermore Article 39 provides that "the decision authorising enforcement" (being in the United Kingdom the act of registration) "shall carry with it the power to proceed to any . . . protective measures." It may therefore be necessary, when it is intended to apply both for registration and for protective measures of a kind falling exclusively within the competence of a judge,[88] for the application for registration to be heard by the judge in chambers. However, other forms of protective measure may be obtained from the master, and in such cases the appropriate application may be joined with the application for registration.[89]

10.13   The registration of a judgment for enforcement normally presupposes the prospect of proceeding to execution as soon as possible, but in an appropriate case the judgment creditor may wish to register a judgment on a speculative basis.[90] This could arise, for example when it was expected that assets would be brought within the jurisdiction at a future date. With a registered judgment the judgment creditor would have a firm foundation for an application for a Mareva injunction in respect of them.

Article 34 requires that at the registration stage of the proceedings the party against whom enforcement is sought should not be entitled to make any submissions on the application.[91] Accordingly, it is provided that the application is to be *ex parte*.[92] The application is made by presenting the affidavit and its accompanying docu-

---

[88] *e.g.* a Mareva injunction; see para. 10.21 below.
[89] See paras. 10.20 *et seq.* below.
[90] See para. 28.13 below.
[91] See para. 28.25 below.
[92] Art. 34 (see para. 28.22 below) and R.S.C., Ord. 71, r. 27. Contrast the power which the master has under the rules relating to the Acts of 1920 and 1933 to direct that the application for registration should be on an *inter partes* summons.

ments to the master. As the procedure is *ex parte* there must be full and frank disclosure to the master of all material facts.[93]

Evidence in support of the application for registration. The appli-   **10.14**
cation must be supported by an affidavit which exhibits the documents and provides the information required under the evidential provisions of the Convention. The detailed requirements are set out in Order 71, rule 28 of the Rules of the Supreme Court.[94] The affidavit must accordingly:

(a) exhibit the following documents, (as to the proof and admissibility of which see section 11 of the 1982 Act)[95]—

    (i) the judgment or a verified or certified or otherwise duly authenticated copy thereof[96] together with such other document or documents as may be requisite to show that, according to the law of the state in which it has been given, the judgment is enforceable[97] and has been served[98];

    (ii) in the case of a judgment given in default, the original or a certified true copy of the document which establishes that the party in default was served with the document instituting the proceedings or with an equivalent document[99];

    (iii) where it is the case, a document showing that the party making the application is in receipt of legal aid in the state in which the judgment was given[1];

---

[93] See the cases cited at para. 7.08 n. 58 above.

[94] These requirements are mainly derived from the provisions of Arts. 33, 46 and 47 of the Convention.

[95] See paras. 29.01 *et seq.* and 40.32 below.

[96] See Art. 46(1) and the commentary thereon at para. 29.01 below.

[97] There may sometimes be no such document but English courts will be permitted to conclude from the judgment itself or from the procedural law of the Contracting State of origin that it is enforceable there. See the commentary on Art. 47(1) at para. 29.07 below. If the application is for registration for the purposes of recognition, as distinct from enforcement, such document is "requisite" for the purposes of R.S.C., Ord. 71, r.28(1)(a)(i).

[98] See Art. 47(1). The requirement for the judgment to have been served derives from this Article, but see the commentary at para. 29.15 below in which it is questioned whether it is always obligatory for the judgment to have been served.

[99] By R.S.C., Ord. 71, r. 28(2) where these documents are not produced the court may fix a time within which they are to be produced, or may accept equivalent documents, or may dispense with the production of the documents. This discretion is derived from Art. 48. See the discussion at para. 29.22 where it is suggested that the court's discretion may be more far-reaching. However, by Art. 27(2) the court is obliged to examine the question whether the document was "*duly*" served *in sufficient time* to enable the defendant to prepare his defence (although the rule of the R.S.C. is silent as to this).

[1] The requirement for documentation concerning legal aid arises under Art. 47(2) at para. 29.18 below.

(iv) where the judgment or document is not in the English language, a translation thereof into English certified by a notary public or a person qualified for the purpose in one of the Contracting States or authenticated by affidavit[2];

(b) state—

(i) whether the judgment provides for the payment of a sum or sums of money;
(ii) whether interest is recoverable on the judgment or part thereof in accordance with the law of the state in which the judgment was given, and if such be the case, the rate of interest, the date from which interest is recoverable, and the date on which interest ceases to accrue[3];

(c) give an address within the jurisdiction of the court for service of process on the party making the application[4] and state, so far as is known to the deponent, the name and the usual or last known address or place of business of the person against whom judgment was given[5];

(d) state to the best of the information or belief of the deponent—

(i) the grounds on which the right to enforce the judgment is vested in the party making the application[6];
(ii) as the case may require, either that at the date of the application the judgment has not been satisfied, or the part or amount in respect of which it remains unsatisfied.[7]

---

[2] See Art. 48 and para. 29.29 below. The persons qualified to certify translations in most Contracting States are mentioned in a footnote to para. 48.71 in Chaps. 48 to 58 below. As to translations generally, see para. 8.16 above.

[3] This information enables the court to award interest on the judgment in accordance with s.7 of the 1982 Act. See para. 40.20 below.

[4] This is required by Art. 33; see para. 28.16 below.

[5] The judgment debtor's address is required so that the court can be satisfied as to the judgment debtor's identity and to verify, if necessary, that he has been served with the notice of registration.

[6] Art. 31, however, permits an application for enforcement to be made by "any interested party." See the discussion at paras. 10.39, 27.05 and 28.07 below. In most cases in which the applicant is not the original judgment creditor the rights in the judgment have become vested in him by succession or assignment. However, as it is not for the Rules of the Supreme Court to seek to interpret the Convention by defining the class of person to whom Art. 31 relates, the rule requires the applicant to inform the court of his entitlement to enforce the judgment. Yet the applicant for registration will not always be a person who is entitled to *enforce* the judgment, see Art. 26, second para., para. 27.01 below.

[7] This requirement corresponds with that under R.S.C., Ord. 71, r. 3(1)(c)(ii) and it assists the court in ascertaining the precise amount in respect of which enforcement is sought.

Article 34 requires the decision on the application to be given **10.15**
without delay. As the application is *ex parte*, the existence of
grounds of objection will not normally become apparent until the
debtor appeals. However, should it appear from the face of the
documents accompanying the application that grounds for refusal
under Articles 27 to 28 exist, the master should refuse to register
the judgment.[8] Provided the application appears to be in order,
registration will be granted.

The order for registration

The order giving leave to register a judgment is drawn up by or **10.16**
on behalf of the party making the application for registration. The
effect of registration is that the foreign judgment thenceforth has
the same force and effect, for the purposes of its enforcement, as if
it had been originally given in the High Court.[9] The judgment is
registered in its original currency.[10] The order must state the period
within which an appeal may be made against registration and must
contain a notification that execution on the judgment will not issue
until after the expiration of that period.[11] The period within which an
appeal may be brought is one month from the date of service of the
notice of registration if the judgment debtor is domiciled in the
United Kingdom and two months if he is domiciled in another Contracting State or elsewhere.[12] The order may be conditional on the
provision of such security as the court may determine other than
security for costs.[13] The reasonable costs and expenses of and
incidental to registration are recoverable as if they were sums recoverable under the judgment.[14] Article 35 of the Convention imposes the
requirement that the decision given on the application to register is to
be brought to the notice of the judgment creditor without delay. It
states that this should be done by the "appropriate officer of the
court," but allows the precise procedure to be determined by the

---

[8] See, by analogy, Schlosser, para. 190(a) (para. A1.486 below).
[9] 1982 Act, s.4(3). Note, however, that an actual or prospective appeal in the state
of origin may give grounds for a stay of the English enforcement proceedings.
See para. 10.45 below.
[10] Although there is no express provision to this effect in the Act or the rules,
Collins (p. 116) suggests that it would be consistent with the practice under the
Act of 1933. Following the decision of the House of Lords in *Miliangos* v. *George
Frank (Textiles) Ltd.* (1976) A.C. 443, the Administration of Justice Act 1977,
s.4 repealed s.2(3) of the Act of 1933. See also *Practice Direction* [1976] 1
W.L.R. 83; Law Com. Rep. No. 124, Cmnd. 9064 (1983), para. 3.15.
[11] R.S.C., Ord. 71, r. 30. This corresponds with R.S.C., Ord. 71, r. 5.
[12] R.S.C., Ord. 71, r. 32(3)(d). The time limits must be strictly observed: see
para. 28.34 below. "Month" means a calendar month, see R.S.C., Ord. 3, r. 1.
[13] Art. 38, third para., para. 28.43 below. This is not specifically provided for in
the Rules of the Supreme Court. See para. 28.51 below.
[14] 1982 Act, s.4(2). See the next para.

law of the state in which enforcement is sought. If the application is made in person to the master, his decision is communicated in person.

10.17   *Interest and costs.* The affidavit in support of an application for registration under the Convention of a judgment for a sum of money must state whether interest is recoverable on the judgment or part thereof in accordance with the law of the state in which the judgment was given, and if such be the case, it must specify the rate of interest, the date from which it is recoverable, and the date on which it ceases to accrue.[15] Particulars of such interest are then registered and the judgment debt then carries interest in accordance with those particulars.[16] The costs and expenses of registration are recoverable as if they were sums recoverable under the foreign judgment itself.[17] Interest on the costs and expenses of registration is recoverable under the ordinary rules applicable to interest on English judgments.[18]

10.18   *Renewal of application to register.* If registration of the judgment has been refused for some reason which can be cured by the applicant, such as incomplete supporting documentation,[19] there is nothing to prevent the renewal of the application after the defect has been cured. As the applicant must make full and frank disclosure of all matters relevant to the application[20] the master should be told of the earlier unsuccessful application.

Effect of registration

10.19   A judgment registered under the 1968 Convention is, for the purposes of enforcement, of the same force and effect as if it had originally been given by the High Court and had been entered.[21] The assimilation of the registered judgment to a judgment of the High Court extends only to "the purposes of enforcement." It follows that all the methods of execution available in respect of a judgment of the High Court are available to enforce the registered judgment in so far as they are appropriate to the particular form of judg-

---

[15] R.S.C., Ord. 71, r. 28(1)(b)(ii).
[16] 1982 Act, s.7(1).
[17] 1982 Act, s.4(3).
[18] 1982 Act, s.7(3); Judgments Act 1838, s.17.
[19] When the documentation is incomplete the court should be urged not to refuse the application but to exercise its powers under R.S.C., Ord. 71, r. 28(2) to fix a time for the production of the documents, or to accept equivalent documents, or to dispense with their production as allowed by Art. 48; see para. 29.20 below.
[20] As the application is *ex parte* the court must be told of any facts known to the applicant which might lead the court not to grant relief *ex parte*. See para. 10.13, n. 93 above.
[21] 1982 Act, s.4(3); see para. 40.08 below.

ment.[22] Execution is however stayed until after the expiry of the time for appealing and the determination of any appeal.[23] It is possible to found a bankruptcy notice on a judgment registered under the 1982 Act.[24]

Application for protective measures

Article 39 of the Convention provides that "the decision authorising enforcement" (being, in the United Kingdom, the act of registration) "*shall carry with it* the power to proceed to . . . protective measures." This ensures that the interests of the judgment creditor will be protected during the period allowed by the Convention for appealing against the order for registration, during which no final enforcement measures are permitted. The Jenard Report states: **10.20**

> "The power arises automatically. Even in those states whose law requires proof that the case calls for prompt action or that there is any risk in delay the applicant will not have to establish that either of those elements is present; the power to proceed to protective measures is not a matter for the discretion of the court."[25]

The European Court of Justice has confirmed that Article 39 confers on the judgment creditor the right to proceed to take such measures and it has held that that right is not to be restricted by any requirements of national procedural law which frustrate the objective of Article 39. It went so far as to hold, in the case of the Italian procedural requirement to obtain authorisation of protective measures in confirmatory proceedings, that there is no obligation to obtain such specific authorisation.[26]

The Convention leaves it to the procedural law of each Contracting State to determine the kinds of protective measure that are available. Article 39 is reflected in the Rules of the Supreme Court which provide that, during the period for appeal against registration and pending the determination of any appeal, execution may not issue, but that that is not to prevent the court from granting protective measures.[27] It is settled that under English law the protection of a party who is proceeding to execution of a judgment may be secured by means of a Mareva injunction[28] or an Anton Piller **10.21**

---

[22] For the execution of registered judgments see para. 10.55 below.

[23] R.S.C., Ord. 71, r. 34.

[24] *Re a Judgment Debtor* [1939] Ch. 601. A bankruptcy notice may not be founded on an unregistered foreign judgment: *Re a Bankruptcy Notice* [1898] 1 Q.B. 383.

[25] Jenard, para. A1.226 below.

[26] *Capelloni and Aquilini v. Pelkmans* [1985] E.C.R. 31.47; see para. 28.58 below.

[27] R.S.C., Ord. 71, r. 34.

[28] *Steward Chartering Ltd. v. C. & O. Managements S.A.* [1980] 1 W.L.R. 460; *Faith Panton Property Plan Ltd. v. Hodgetts* [1981] 1 W.L.R. 927; *Orwell Steel (Erection and Fabrication) Ltd. v. Asphalt and Tarmac (U.K.) Ltd.* [1984] 1 W.L.R. 1097; *Hill Samuel & Co. Ltd. v. Littaur* [1985] N.L.J. 57; the court will

order.[29] The judgment debtor can be restrained from disposing of his assets and a third party, such as a bank, is bound by the order of the court. The remedy of an injunction is essentially discretionary and the proposition that Article 39 gives an execution creditor the right to a Mareva injunction is one that may startle English courts. The court may conclude that, while it is obliged to grant protective measures, the nature and extent of those measures, given the breadth and flexibility of protective measures under English law, must remain a matter for the court's discretion, at least where the measure sought is injunctive.

It is suggested that the ability of the court to grant protection to a judgment creditor is not limited to the potent remedy of the Mareva injunction, and that far simpler methods of protection exist. In English procedure there are various methods of execution by which, in one way or another, a judgment debtor's assets are attached or secured for execution. Under the writ of *fieri facias* the sheriff seizes the debtor's goods, frequently taking "walking possession" as a first step.[30] In garnishee proceedings the debt due to the judgment debtor is bound in the hands of the garnishee on service of the garnishee order *nisi*. A charging order *nisi* provides the judgment creditor with security in the form of the charge over the property to which the order relates. The initial stage of each of these procedures is protective in nature and there is no reason in principle why they should not be employed in appropriate circumstances to secure the objectives of Article 39.[31] It is to be noted that in many continental systems there is a close parallel between those procedures by which assets are seized by way of execution and those measures of a protective nature by which a party's assets are provisionally attached prior to judgment and execution.[32] Moreover, provisional attachments are frequently converted to final attachments at the stage of execution.

---

also restrain a defendant from disposing of his assets outside the jurisdiction, see *Babanaft International Co. S.A.* v. *Basatne* [1989] 2 W.L.R. 232 (C.A.): see para. 7.24 above.

[29] *Distributori Automatici Italia SpA* v. *Holford General Trading Co. Ltd.* [1985] 1 W.L.R. 1066.

[30] *National Commercial Bank of Scotland* v. *Arcam Demolition* [1966] 2 Q.B. 593.

[31] It is to be noted that the Schlosser Report, written in 1978, stated (para. 221, see para. A1.521 below) that the new member states would have to introduce protective measures, in so far as this did not arise as an automatic result of the entry into force of the Convention. A similar point is made in relation to Scotland in the Maxwell Report, para. 6.95(b).

[32] See *e.g.* France—*saisie conservatoire* (para. 50.59 below) and *saisie execution* (para. 50.68 below); Italy—*sequestro conservativo* (para. 53.59 below) and *execution* (para. 53.68 below); Netherlands—*conservatoir beslag* (para. 55.59 below) and *executoriaal beslag* (para. 55.68 below).

The employment of existing methods of execution as protective **10.22** measures would enable the master to make an appropriate order at the same time as the order for registration itself. It would be possible for the application for the appropriate measure to be joined with that for registration and the master could make whatever directions are necessary to limit the effects of the measure to those which are purely protective. In the case of a money judgment to be enforced by a writ of *fieri facias*, leave to issue the writ would be given but the sheriff might be directed to enter only into walking possession and not to proceed further without the leave of the court. Garnishee orders *nisi* and charging orders *nisi* could be returnable at a date which is subsequent to the time limit for appealing the registration and, in the event of an appeal against registration, the hearing would be further adjourned so as to coincide with the hearing of the appeal.

Notice of registration to the judgment debtor

Having obtained, by registering the judgment, an order for its **10.23** enforcement, it is incumbent on the applicant to serve notice of registration on the person against whom the judgment is to be enforced. In the present text he is referred to as the judgment debtor, on the assumption that the judgment to be enforced is for payment of a sum of money, although other types of judgment are also enforceable under the Convention.[33] Until the notice has been served, the period for appealing, at the expiry of which the judgment may be enforced (if there has been no appeal), does not start to run.[34] The notice must be served on the person against whom the judgment is to be enforced. This may be done by delivering it to him personally or by sending it to him at his usual or last known address or place of business or in such other manner as the court may direct.[35] If service out of the jurisdiction is necessary this may be done without leave and the methods of service used for writs may likewise be used for the service of the notice of registration.[36]

The notice must[37] give full particulars of the registered judgment and of the order for registration, and it must give the name and address for service within the jurisdiction of the party who made the application. It must inform the person against whom judgment

---

[33] See the wide definition of "judgment," discussed at paras. 10.07 above and 26.01 below.

[34] See para. 28.33 below.

[35] R.S.C., Ord. 71, r. 32. This rule closely follows the provisions of Ord. 71, r. 5, the comparable rule relating to the notification procedure under the Acts of 1920 and 1933.

[36] R.S.C., Ord. 71, r. 32(2).

[37] The following requirements are laid down by R.S.C., Ord. 71, r. 32.

was given of his right to appeal[38] against the order for registration, stating the period within which an appeal may be made.[39] During the time allowed for issuing the summons and pending the disposal of the appeal, the enforcement of the judgment is automatically stayed, and no execution may issue, although the creditor has a right to take protective measures.[40]

5. Appeals—introduction

10.24   *Appeal by the judgment creditor against refusal to register.* Under Article 40, the judgment creditor may appeal against a refusal to order the registration of a judgment.[41] The appeal is by way of summons *inter partes*[42] to the judge in chambers.[43] Although the Convention specifies no time limit for the bringing of an appeal against the refusal to register a judgment, the Rules of the Supreme Court require such an appeal to be brought within a month of the refusal of the application for registration.[44] Further appeal by the judgment creditor is limited, as is further appeal by the judgment debtor, to a single point of law. This final appeal is discussed below.[45]

10.25   *Appeal by the judgment debtor against an order for registration.* An appeal by the judgment debtor[46] is brought by way of summons to the judge in chambers.[47] This appeal[48] is comparable to the application to set aside registration under the 1933 Act. The instituting of an appeal operates automatically to stay the execution of

---

[38] Under Art. 36.
[39] R.S.C., Ord. 71, r. 32(3)(d). The period within which appeal may be made is one month from the date of service of the notice of registration if the judgment debtor is domiciled in the U.K. and two months if he is domiciled in another Contracting State or elsewhere; see R.S.C., Ord. 71, r. 33, and paras. 28.33 and 28.34 below. "Month" means a calendar month, see R.S.C., Ord. 3, r. 1.
[40] Art. 39 and 1982 Act, s.4(4); R.S.C., Ord. 71, r. 30(3) and r. 34; see paras. 10.20 above and 28.55 below.
[41] Appeals in maintenance cases are discussed separately at para. 11.17 below.
[42] *Firma P.* v. *Firma K.* [1984] E.C.R. 3033; see para. 28.65 below.
[43] R.S.C., Ord. 71, r. 33(1). Where the refusal of the order for registration is made by a judge, the appeal is to the High Court (see Art. 40) and, because the order appealed from was made *ex parte*, this is still to a single judge in chambers (see R.S.C., Ord. 55, rr. (1) and (2)).
[44] R.S.C., Ord. 71, r. 33(2)(b).
[45] Art. 41, see paras. 10.41 and 28.69 below.
[46] Art. 37, first para., para. 28.38 below. It is only the judgment debtor who may appeal against the registration of the judgment: *Deutsche Genossenschaftsbank* v. *Brasserie du Pêcheur S.A.* [1985] E.C.R. 1981; see para. 28.32 below.
[47] As the order for registration is always made *ex parte*, the appeal is still to the judge in chambers even if the order for registration was made by a judge; *cf.* n.43 above.
[48] R.S.C., Ord. 71, r. 33(1).

the registered judgment until the determination of the appeal.[49] The summons must be served within one month of service of notice of registration of the judgment, or within two months of service of the notice if it was served on a party not domiciled within the jurisdiction.[50] If the party against whom judgment was given is not domiciled in a Contracting State and an application for an extension of time is made within two months of service of a notice of registration, the Rules of the Supreme Court provide that the court may extend the period within which an appeal may be made against an order for registration.[51] However, the European Court has since emphasised the strictness of the time limits in Article 36 and there is a chance that such an extension would be contrary to the Convention.[52]

The summons should set out the grounds relied upon for appealing the order for registration and should be supported by an appropriate affidavit. Unless, at the hearing of the appeal, the judgment debtor can put forward sufficient grounds[53] to challenge the registration, the judgment creditor may proceed to whatever method of execution may be appropriate as if the judgment were an original English judgment.[54] If there are valid grounds for setting aside the registration of the judgment the court may not impose terms, such as the payment of money into court, as a condition of setting aside the registration.[55]

Summary of grounds of appeal. One of the fundamental principles **10.26** of the Convention is that, subject to limited exceptions, the enforcing court ("the court addressed") is not entitled to examine the merits of the case or the basis upon which jurisdiction was exercised by the court which gave the judgment ("the court of origin").[56] It is provided both in Article 29, in respect of recognition, and in Article 34, in respect of enforcement, that in no circumstances may the foreign judgment be reviewed as to its substance.[57] The principal grounds upon which under the Convention registration can be

---

[49] Art. 39 and 1982 Act, s.4(4); R.S.C., Ord. 71, r. 34.
[50] R.S.C., Ord. 71, r. 33(2). These time limits are strict: see para. 28.34 below.
[51] R.S.C., Ord. 71, r. 33(3); see para. 28.37 below. "Month" means a calendar month, see R.S.C., Ord. 3, r. 1.
[52] *Hoffmann* v. *Krieg*, case 145/86, decision of February 4, 1988, *The Times*, March 26, 1988; see the commentary to Art. 36 (paras. 28.33 *et seq.* below).
[53] The possible grounds of appeal are discussed at para. 10.27. As to the effect of an intended or pending appeal in the Contracting State of origin, see para. 10.45 below.
[54] 1982 Act, s.4(3). As to execution of registered judgments see para. 10.50 below.
[55] See, by analogy with the 1933 Act, *Syal* v. *Heyward* [1948] 2 K.B. 443.
[56] See para. 25.01 below.
[57] See paras. 27.75 and 28.27 below.

appealed are those contained in Articles 27 and 28.[58] There are additional grounds upon which an appeal against the registration may be allowed, for instance if the subject-matter of the judgment is outside the scope of the Convention, if the judgment is incapable of enforcement in the country of origin or if certain procedural formalities have not been complied with. The grounds of appeal are summarised below and are then discussed more fully in this chapter, with cross-references to the detailed treatment of the Convention and of the 1982 Act in Part II of this work.

10.27   The grounds of appeal may be summarised as follows:

(i) that recognition or enforcement would be contrary to public policy in the United Kingdom;[59]

(ii) that, where the foreign judgment was given in default of appearance, the defendant was not duly served with the proceedings in sufficient time to enable him to arrange for his defence;[60]

(iii) that the foreign judgment is irreconcilable with a judgment given in the United Kingdom in a dispute between the same parties;[61]

(iv) that the court of origin has, in order to arrive at its judgment, decided a preliminary question concerning the status or legal capacity of natural persons, rights in property arising out of a matrimonial relationship, wills or succession in a way which conflicts with a rule of English private international law, unless the same result would have been reached by the application of English private international law;[62]

(v) that the judgment is irreconcilable with an earlier judgment given in a non-Contracting State involving the same cause of action between the same parties, provided that the earlier judgment fulfils the conditions necessary for recognition in the United Kingdom;[63]

(vi) that the judgment conflicts with the Convention's rules relating to insurance matters and consumer contracts or the rules relating to exclusive jurisdiction;[64]

(vii) that the judgment is not a judgment to which the Conven-

---

[58] Arts. 27 and 28 are applied to applications for enforcement by Art. 34.
[59] Art. 27(1); see paras. 10.28 and 27.13 below.
[60] Art. 27(2); see paras. 10.29 and 27.21 below.
[61] Art. 27(3); see paras. 10.30 and 27.43 below.
[62] Art. 27(4); see paras. 10.31 and 27.52 below.
[63] Art. 27(5); see paras. 10.32 and 27.59 below.
[64] Art. 28 first para.; see paras. 10.33 and 27.62 below.

tion applies, in that its subject-matter falls outside the scope of the Convention;[65]

(viii) that the judgment is not one to which the simplified enforcement procedure of the Convention applies because it orders the taking of provisional and protective measures, it was made without the party against whom it was directed having been summoned to appear, and it was intended to be enforced without prior service of the judgment on that party;[65a]

(ix) that the judgment is not a judgment to which the Convention applies, by reason of the operation of the Convention's transitional provisions;[66]

(x) that the judgment is not enforceable in the state of origin;[67]

(xi) that the judgment was not served on the person against whom it is to be enforced;[68]

(xii) that the party who registered the judgment was not entitled to do so, being neither the judgment creditor nor any other interested party;[69]

(xiii) that the procedural formalities laid down in the Convention or the Rules of the Supreme Court have not been complied with;[70]

(xiv) that the judgment was given in respect of a civil claim in, or dependent upon, criminal proceedings in which the defendant did not appear and did not have the opportunity of arranging his defence in his absence;[71]

(xv) that (in a case in which the court of origin had jurisdiction only by virtue of a specialised convention) the requisite conditions for recognition and enforcement under that convention have not been fulfilled;[71a]

(xvi) that the court of origin assumed jurisdiction on an exorbitant basis over a person who was domiciled or habitually resident in a non-Contracting State with which the United Kingdom has a convention pursuant to Article 59 of the 1968 Convention.[71b]

---

[65] See para. 10.34 below.
[65a] See para. 10.35 below.
[66] See para. 10.36 below.
[67] See para. 10.37 below.
[68] See para. 10.38 below.
[69] See para. 10.39 below.
[70] See para. 10.40 below.
[71] Art. II, 1968 Protocol; see para. 10.41 below.
[71a] See para. 10.42 below.
[71b] See para. 10.43 below.

6. The grounds of appeal discussed

10.28 (i) *that recognition or enforcement would be contrary to public policy in the United Kingdom*

It is a feature common to all schemes for recognition and enforcement that a court addressed is entitled to refuse to recognise or enforce a foreign judgment on the ground of domestic public policy. "Public policy" is aptly defined in the Maxwell Report[72] as "those mandatory rules of law which a state considers so fundamental to its moral, social or economic order that they should prevent the application of foreign laws and judgments which conflict with them." Thus courts would refuse to recognise and enforce judgments based on laws which were considered to be fundamentally immoral.[73]

The statutory schemes established under the Acts of 1920 and 1933 both contained provisions to this effect.[74] The 1968 Convention is no exception to this general rule although, as will be seen, the circumstances in which recognition or enforcement of a judgment can be refused under the Convention for reasons of public policy are considerably narrower than under pre-existing law. Article 27(1) provides that a judgment shall not be recognised "if such recognition is contrary to public policy in the state in which recognition is sought." Although it is for the courts of each Contracting State to apply national notions of public policy, the Convention does not permit the English courts to apply considerations of public policy in precisely the same way as they did hitherto. First, the third paragraph of Article 28 expressly states that the test of public policy may not be applied to the rules relating to jurisdiction. It follows that even if it was quite apparent that a court in another Contracting State purported to take jurisdiction under the Convention on an entirely misconceived basis, the English court could not refuse to recognise the judgment on public policy grounds. Equally an objection could not be raised on the ground of public policy to a judgment based on the exercise of exorbitant jurisdiction over a defendant domiciled in a non-Contracting State.[75] Secondly, it is provided by Article 29 that a judgment may not, in any circum-

---

[72] Report of the Scottish Committee on Jurisdiction and Enforcement (1980), para. 6.26.
[73] For the position at common law, see Dicey and Morris, pp. 92 *et seq.*; Cheshire and North, pp. 112 *et seq.*
[74] Administration of Justice Act 1920, s.9(2)(f); Foreign Judgments (Reciprocal Enforcement) Act, 1933, s.4(1)(a)(v).
[75] Jenard, para. A1.190 below; but see Art. 59, para. 33.24 below.

stances, be reviewed as to its substance. Accordingly an error of law or fact leading to the decision in the court of trial could not give rise to a question of public policy in relation to its enforcement. Thirdly, the very concept of public policy is one to which a uniform interpretation would probably be applied by the European Court of Justice, although its detailed content would be left to national courts to determine. The scope of public policy in particular matters is considered in detail in the commentary to Article 27(1).[76]

It is suggested that reliance upon the existence of fraud[77] or the breach of the rules of natural justice as grounds for refusal to recognise a foreign judgment are merely particular examples of public policy objections. The Schlosser Report[78] recognises that in principle fraud can constitute "an offence against the public policy of the state addressed" but it suggests however that in every case there will be adequate means of challenging the judgment in question in the courts of the state of origin. Where the issue of fraud has been raised unsuccessfully in the court of trial it cannot be relied upon, on the same evidence, as a ground of appeal before the English courts, as this would involve reviewing the judgment as to its substance, which is forbidden by Article 29.

(ii) that, where the foreign judgment was given in default of **10.29**
appearance, the defendant was not duly served with the proceedings in
sufficient time to enable him to arrange for his defence

The Convention contains a number of procedural safeguards which are designed to prevent judgments in default of appearance being made or enforced against defendants who have not had any or any sufficient notice of the proceedings. It has been seen that where a defendant is domiciled in one Contracting State and is sued in a court in another Contracting State and does not enter an appearance, the court of trial must examine its jurisdiction of its own motion and must decline jurisdiction unless it is satisfied that it has jurisdiction under the Convention. Even then it must stay the proceedings unless it can be shown that the defendant "was able to receive the document instituting the proceedings . . . in sufficient time to enable him to arrange his defence or that all necessary steps have been taken to this end."[79] If, the above precautions having been taken, a judgment in default is nonetheless given, the Conven-

---

[76] See para. 27.13 below.
[77] See para. 27.20 below.
[78] At para. 192, (para. A1.488 below).
[79] Art. 20; see para. 22.11 below.

tion lays down further safeguards to be observed by any court that is called upon to enforce the default judgment. Article 27(2), which is extended to enforcement by virtue of Article 34, provides that a judgment in default of appearance shall not be recognised "if the defendant was not duly served[80] with the document which instituted the proceedings or with an equivalent document in sufficient time to enable him to arrange his defence;" that is to say in sufficient time to enable him to take whatever procedural steps were necessary under local law to prevent judgment in default being obtained against him.[81] Article 27(2) is wider in the protection which it affords, in that it applies to defendants domiciled in the Contracting State of the court of trial, and it requires proof of due service on the non-appearing defendant. Articles 46(2) and 48 contain evidential requirements concerning proof of service.

It is not necessary to show that the defendant had actual knowledge of the proceedings. Under the procedural laws of many Contracting States, service on a defendant abroad may be deemed to take place when the document instituting the proceedings is delivered to the local official responsible for transmitting it in accordance with the Hague Service Convention.[82] The English court is justified in assuming that, following "due" service in accordance with the procedural law of the state of origin,[83] the document came to the defendant's knowledge. The court is then to decide whether the time thereafter available to the defendant was sufficient in his particular circumstances. It should be noted that the periods allowed by the Extra Jurisdiction Tables for returning the acknowledgment of service in corresponding English proceedings are considerably shorter than those allowed by the procedural rules of other Contracting States. The English court is not bound by the time limits provided by the domestic law of the trial court or by the fact that the trial court may be taken to have observed its obligations under Article 20 of the Convention and to have con-

---

[80] The words "duly served" mean served in accordance with the law of the state in which the judgment was given; see para. 27.31 below and Jenard, para. A1.191 below. The sufficiency of time is a question of fact not to be determined by the procedural law of either the trial court or the enforcing court: *Debaeker & Plouvier* v. *Bouwman* [1985] E.C.R. 1779; para. 27.38 below.

[81] See the discussion of the parallel topic under the Administration of Justice Act 1920 in Patchett, *Recognition of Commercial Judgments and Awards in the Commonwealth*, pp. 149–150.

[82] *e.g.* in France (see para. 50.38 below) and the Netherlands (see para. 55.38 below); see Schlesinger, *Comparative Law* (4th ed.), p. 385.

[83] *Klomps* v. *Michel* [1981] E.C.R. 1593, discussed at para. 27.37 below. The English court is not bound by the trial court's findings: *Pendy Plastic Products* v. *Pluspunkt* [1982] E.C.R. 2723 discussed at para. 27.41 below.

cluded that the defendant had had sufficient time to arrange his defence.[84]

(iii) that the foreign judgment is irreconcilable with a judgment given in   **10.30**
the United Kingdom in a dispute between the same parties

This ground of appeal is provided by Article 27(3). As is observed in the commentary to that Article[85] the conflicting judgments need not necessarily be in respect of the same cause of action as long as the respective proceedings were between the same parties. If the United Kingdom is the state addressed, the effect of Article 27(3) is ordinarily to give priority to the United Kingdom judgment.[86] However it should be noted that if both judgments concern the same cause of action and the judgment in the United Kingdom was given *after* that which is being sought to be enforced, arguably it is the earlier judgment that should be recognised.[87] Where the judgment sought to be enforced in England conflicts with a judgment given in another Contracting State the Convention is silent as to what should be done. It is suggested[88] that priority should be accorded to that which was given in the proceedings which started first. The United Kingdom judgment need not itself fall within the scope of the Convention.[88a]

(iv) that the court of origin has, in order to arrive at its judgment,   **10.31**
decided a preliminary question concerning the status or legal capacity of
natural persons, rights in property arising out of a matrimonial
relationship, wills or succession in a way which conflicts with a rule of
English private international law, unless the same result would have
been reached by the application of English private international law

This ground is provided by Article 27(4) which provides a limited exception to the general principle that recognition may not be refused on the ground that the court of origin erred in law. Reference should be made to the commentary on that Article[89] for a discussion of this ground of objection.

---

[84] See para. 27.41 below. Examples of the approach of the courts of other Contracting States are given at para. 27.38, n. 27.
[85] See para. 27.44 below.
[86] *Vervaeke* v. *Smith (Messina and Att.-Gen. intervening)* [1981] A.C. 145. Conflicts between judgments being enforced under the intra-U.K. scheme for enforcement are discussed at paras. 46.12 and 46.22 below.
[87] See para. 27.48 below.
[88] See para. 27.50 below.
[88a] See para. 27.47 below,
[89] See para. 27.53 below.

10.32 *(v) that the judgment is irreconcilable with an earlier judgment given in a non-Contracting State involving the same cause of action between the same parties, provided that the earlier judgment fulfils the conditions necessary for recognition in the United Kingdom*

This ground, which is somewhat narrower than the comparable ground provided under the 1933 Act,[90] is afforded by Article 27(5) and is discussed further in the commentary below.[91]

10.33 *(vi) that the judgment conflicts with the Convention's rules relating to insurance matters and consumer contracts or the rules relating to exclusive jurisdiction*

This ground of appeal is afforded by Article 28.[92] It is one of the few instances in which it is permissible to review the assumption of jurisdiction by the court of origin, but it is subject to the condition that the English court is bound by any findings of fact on which the original court based its jurisdiction.

The Convention's rules relating to insurance matters are contained in Articles 7 to 12A. These provide that whereas an insured may sue an insurer in the courts of the insured's domicile or (in the case of liability or real property insurance) in the courts of the place in which the harmful event occurred, the insurer may generally only sue the insured in the courts of the latter's domicile. The Convention's rules relating to consumer contracts are contained in Articles 13 to 15. These provide that whereas a consumer may sue the other party to a "consumer contract" in the courts of the consumer's domicile, he may generally only be sued by the other party in the courts of his (the consumer's) domicile. In practice this ground of objection will only be raised where the insured or the consumer, having been sued in the wrong court, has suffered a judgment in default of appearance, because if the defendant has appeared and participated voluntarily in the proceedings the court will have acquired jurisdiction under Article 18.

The Convention's rules relating to exclusive jurisdiction are contained in Article 16, and are discussed more fully in the commentary to that Article.[93] The ground of appeal will arise where the judgment to be enforced concerns a matter in respect of which, under Article 16, the English courts have exclusive jurisdiction. However, as in the case of consumer contracts and insurance matters, the English court is bound by any findings of fact on which the original court based its jurisdiction.

---

[90] Foreign Judgments (Reciprocal Enforcement) Act 1933, s.4(1)(b).
[91] See para. 27.59 below.
[92] See para. 27.62 below.
[93] See paras. 20.01 *et seq.* below.

(vii) that the judgment is not a judgment to which the Convention   **10.34**
applies, in that its subject-matter falls outside the scope of the
Convention

For the enforcement provisions of the Convention to apply, the subject-matter of the claim must come within the scope of the Convention itself.[94] Thus a judgment in a matter which was not civil or commercial within the meaning of Article 1 of the Convention would not be enforceable under it.[95] Included under this head of objection would be judgments in respect of fines in criminal proceedings[96] or in respect of tax liabilities in another Contracting State. The fact that the court of origin has assumed jurisdiction contrary to an arbitration agreement may not be a sufficient reason to refuse recognition.[97] A judgment which falls partly within and partly outside the Convention may be enforced as to the part which falls within the Convention.[98]

A judgment given in a Contracting State, the subject-matter of which falls within the scope of the Convention, is enforceable in other Contracting States even where the defendant is domiciled in a non-Contracting State and jurisdiction has been assumed over such a defendant on an exorbitant basis. This is because Article 31 of the Convention applies the enforcement provisions of the Convention to judgments given in a Contracting State which are enforceable in that Contracting State, regardless of the basis upon which jurisdiction has been assumed. The prohibition against the use of exorbitant jurisdictions contained in Article 3 is limited to actions against persons domiciled in the Contracting States.

(viii) that the judgment is not one to which the simplified enforcement   **10.35**
procedure of the Convention applies because it orders the taking of
provisional and protective measures, it was made without the party
against whom it was directed having been summoned to appear, and it
was intended to be enforced without prior service of the judgment on that
party

This ground of objection is applicable to the attempted enforcement of orders for provisional and protective measures which have been made *ex parte*.[99] It was decided by the Court of Justice in *Denilauler* v. *Couchet Frères*[1] that this type of order was not enforceable

---

[94] See Art. 1, para. 14.03 below.
[95] *Cf.*, for example, *Berliner Industriebank AG* v. *Jost* [1971] 2 Q.B. 463; *Peter Buchanan Ltd. and MacHarg* v. *McVey* [1955] A.C. 516.
[96] Note the circumstances in which civil fines may be enforced. See Art. 43, para. 28.76 below.
[97] See para. 14.32 below.
[98] Art. 42, see para. 28.71 below.
[99] See para. 24.09 below.
[1] [1980] E.C.R. 1553.; see para. 25.19 below.

under the Convention. An order for provisional or protective measures made in one Contracting State is enforceable in another only if it is made in adversarial proceedings, though it may be made in default in such proceedings.

10.36 *(ix) that the judgment is not a judgment to which the Convention applies, by reason of the operation of the Convention's transitional provisions*

A judgment given in another Contracting State on or after January 1, 1987[2] in proceedings which commenced before that date is only enforceable in the United Kingdom under the Convention if jurisdiction was founded on rules which accorded either with the jurisdictional rules of the Convention or with the provisions of a convention between the United Kingdom and the state of origin which was in force when the proceedings were instituted.[3] The Contracting States with which the United Kingdom has bilateral enforcement conventions are Belgium, the Federal Republic of Germany, France, Italy, and the Netherlands.[4]

10.37 *(x) that the judgment is not enforceable in the state of origin*[5]

The enforceability of the foreign judgment under the law of the Contracting State of origin is an express precondition to its registration in England and Wales.[6] The procedural laws of the Contracting States differ substantially as to the moment at which a judgment becomes enforceable, as to whether the judgment must first be formally drawn up, as to whether it must be served on the losing party, and as to the effect on enforceability of the bringing of an appeal.[7]

A provisionally enforceable judgment is enforceable under the Convention. It is common in many of the Contracting States for a judgment to be expressed to be provisionally enforceable. This merely means that it is to be enforceable at the risk of the enforcing party, so that, in the event of a successful appeal, he has to compensate the other party for losses caused by the enforcement.[8] Some judgments may, as a matter of procedural law, always be provisionally enforceable, others may only be so if so declared by the court. Generally a judgment which is provisionally enforceable remains so

---

[2] The date of the commencement of the main provisions of the Civil Jurisdiction and Judgments Act 1982, see para. 47.23 below.

[3] Art. 34(3) of the 1978 Convention, para. 37.06 below; see also Art. 12(2) of the 1982 Convention, para. 38.04 (not yet in force).

[4] These conventions with their references are listed at para. A2.02 below.

[5] See Art. 31; Schlosser, para. 220 (para. A1.520 below).

[6] See chaps. 48 to 55 as to enforceability in the state of origin.

[7] See para. 66 of chaps. 48 to 55.

[8] See para. 25.21 below. If the judgment is later set aside on appeal the enforcing party is liable to compensate the other party for losses caused as a result of the enforcement of the judgment.

despite the bringing of an appeal. In such a case the judgment creditor can apply to the English court for a stay of execution under Article 38.[9] If enforcement has been stayed in the country of origin, the judgment is of necessity not enforceable there and accordingly it cannot be registered in England. A judgment which has already been satisfied is not enforceable in the state of origin and accordingly should not be registered.[10]

(xi) that the judgment was not served on the person against whom it is to be enforced **10.38**

In some of the Contracting States a copy of the judgment, in an official form, has to be served on the losing party before it becomes enforceable against him in the state of origin.[11] Failure to comply with such a requirement would clearly found a valid ground for appealing the registration of a judgment. It is however to be observed in addition that Article 47(1) requires an application for registration to be supported by evidence that the judgment to be enforced "is enforceable and has been served."[12] This requirement is repeated in the Rules of the Supreme Court.[13] Although Article 47(1) appears on its face to require service of the judgment to have taken place, whether or not that was required by the national law of the court of origin, it is questionable whether this is in fact the case.[14]

(xii) that the person by whom the application for registration was made is not an "interested party" **10.39**

Articles 26 and 31 enable an application for recognition or enforcement to be made by "any interested party."[15] It is for the national law of the state of origin to determine what interest the applicant has in the judgment, but it is a question for interpretation under the Convention whether that interest is sufficient to give rise to the right to apply for enforcement in another Contracting State. The equivalent provision under the 1933 Act (which is limited to the enforcement of money judgments) is "that the rights in the judgment are not vested in the person by whom the application for registration was made."[16] The definition of an "interested party" in the 1982 Act could well be wider and might include a person, other

---

[9] See para. 10.45 below.
[10] See Jenard, para. A1.222 below; Schlosser, para. 220 (para. A1.520 below).
[11] See chaps. 48 to 55. In some states time for appealing runs from the date of such service.
[12] See the commentary to Art. 47(1) at para. 29.07 below.
[13] R.S.C., Ord. 71, r. 28(1)(a)(i).
[14] See para. 29.16 below.
[15] Art. 26, second para. and Art. 31, first para.; see paras. 27.05 and 28.07 below.
[16] Foreign Judgments (Reciprocal Enforcement) Act 1933, s.4(1)(a)(vi).

than a direct party to the original proceedings, who had an interest in the defendant obeying a court order to perform some non-money obligation.

10.40 *(xiii) that the procedural formalities laid down in the Convention or the Rules of the Supreme Court have not been complied with*

The procedural requirements of the Convention concerning the making of the application for enforcement are set out in Articles 32, 33, 46 and 47. Although Article 34 provides that the application may be refused "only for one of the reasons specified in Articles 27 and 28," a challenge on procedural grounds may still be made. Furthermore, as Article 33 expressly provides that the procedure for making the application shall be governed by the law of the state in which enforcement is sought, a failure to comply with the requirements of the Rules of the Supreme Court could equally be fatal to an application. Thus, a registration would probably be set aside on appeal if there were substantial defects or inconsistencies in the supporting documentation.[17] The copy of the judgment must satisfy the conditions necessary to establish its authenticity in accordance with the law of the Contracting State of origin.[18] In the case of a judgment given in default there must be a document which establishes that the judgment debtor was served with the "document instituting the proceedings or with an equivalent document."[19] If it appeared from the documentation that the judgment debt had been registered in an incorrect amount or that interest had been incorrectly calculated,[20] or that the defendant's name had been incorrectly given in the judgment, there would also be strong grounds for setting aside the registration on appeal. If such matters became evident to the court when it was considering registration it might refuse to register the judgment, or, in some cases, as is suggested in the Jenard Report,[21] it might adjourn the application to enable the documentation to be put in order, or it might refuse to entertain the application.

10.41 *(xiv) that the judgment was given in respect of a civil claim in, or dependent upon, criminal proceedings in which the defendant did not appear and did not have the opportunity of arranging his defence in his absence*

Article II of the 1968 Annexed Protocol provides that the courts of a Contracting State need not recognise or enforce a civil judg-

---

[17] See Arts. 46 to 49, chap. 29 below.
[18] Art. 46(1), para. 29.01 below; see also s.11 of the 1982 Act, para. 40.32 below.
[19] Art. 46(2), subject to the court's power under Art. 48 to dispense with this; see para. 29.20 below.
[20] *Cf.* Oberlandsgericht Stuttgart, Order of June 16, 1978, Digest I–36–B2.
[21] Jenard, para. A1.216 below.

ment given in criminal proceedings[22] in another Contracting State of which the defendant was not a national, for an offence which was not intentionally committed, if the defendant did not appear and did not have the opportunity to arrange his defence. This provision is discussed below in the commentary to the 1968 Protocol.[23]

(xv) that (in a case in which the court of origin had jurisdiction only by virtue of a specialised convention) the requisite conditions for recognition and enforcement under that convention have not been fulfilled   **10.42**

Article 57 of the 1968 Convention[24] provides, in effect, that where jurisdiction is exercised in one Contracting State pursuant to a specialised convention[25] the resulting judgment may be recognised and enforced in accordance with the procedure of the 1968 Convention but subject to any additional conditions which may be required by the specialised convention. If, in any particular case, the United Kingdom is not party to the convention involved, the judgment may be recognised and enforced in accordance with the 1968 Convention.[26]

(xvi) that the court of the Contracting State of origin assumed jurisdiction on an exorbitant basis over a person who was domiciled or habitually resident in a non-Contracting State with which the United Kingdom has a convention pursuant to Article 59 of the 1968 Convention   **10.43**

The prohibition against the courts of the Contracting States assuming jurisdiction on exorbitant bases is expressed to apply only in respect of defendants who are domiciled in a Contracting State.[27] The Contracting States are permitted by Article 59 of the Convention to enter into conventions for recognition and enforcement of judgments with non-Contracting States in which they assume an obligation not to recognise or enforce such judgments given in other Contracting States against persons who are domiciled or habitually

---

[22] The same applies in civil proceedings the result of which is determined by the result of the criminal proceedings; see *Re Rinkau* [1981] E.C.R. 1391 and para. 35.07 below.
[23] See para. 35.05 below.
[24] This Article is to be interpreted in accordance with Art. 25(2) of the 1978 Convention; see Schlosser, para. 238 (para. A1.543 below) and the commentary to Art. 57 at para. 33.06 below.
[25] Many of these were listed at Annex II to the Schlosser Report. A selected list appears at paras. A2.31 *et seq.* below. Selected texts are set out in the *The practical guide to the recognition and enforcement of foreign judicial decisions*, Council of Europe; see also para. 1.30 above.
[26] Schlosser, para. 245 (para. A1.553 below).
[27] See Art. 3, which sets out the principal exorbitant bases of jurisdiction, para. 16.09 below.

resident in the relevant non-Contracting State.[28] Article 28 expressly states that a judgment shall not be recognised in a case provided for in Article 59. The only convention so far entered into by the United Kingdom in which such an obligation is assumed is that with Canada.[29]

7. Appeals—further aspects

10.44   *Powers of the court on the hearing of the appeal.* The registration of the foreign judgment pursuant to the Convention constitutes the issue of an order for its enforcement,[30] but no measures of enforcement, other than protective measures, may be taken until the expiry of the prescribed period and the determination of any appeal.[31] In the majority of cases, due to the *ex parte* nature of the registration procedure, the court will be unaware of any possible objections to the registration until the hearing of the appeal to the judge in chambers. It will generally be for the appellant, the judgment debtor, to show cause why the registration should be set aside or the proceedings stayed.[32] The appeal is by way of rehearing and the court should be satisfied that the requirements necessary for the registration of the judgment were satisfied at the date of registration. It may not, save in the limited instances already discussed,[33] review the substance of the original judgment even if new matters have arisen since the date of the registration.[34] If a ground for setting aside the registration is established, then the court has no discretion in the matter and must direct accordingly. If no ground for setting aside is established then the appeal must be dismissed. The judgment may then be executed subject to the court's general powers to order a stay of execution in certain cases.[35] The court also has power under the Convention to make execution conditional on the provision of security by the judgment creditor.[36] The Convention makes it clear[37] that there must be no delay in dealing with the application for registration and appeal.

---

[28] See para. 33.24 below.
[29] The Reciprocal Enforcement of Judgments (Canada) Order 1987, (S.I. 1987 No. 468); see para. 33.31 below.
[30] See para. 28.01 below.
[31] Art. 39, see para. 28.55 below.
[32] See Jenard, para. A1.222 below.
[33] See paras. 10.30 to 10.34 above.
[34] This is the view expressed in the Schlosser Report, para. 220, (para. A1.520 below); but see para. 28.41 below. As to the position if the appeal has been (or is to be) lodged in the state of origin, see the next para.
[35] *e.g.* R.S.C., Ord. 47, r. 1. See the distinction drawn in the next paragraph between a stay of appeal proceedings and a stay of execution, and see para. 10.36 below.
[36] Art. 38, third para. The power can only be exercised when the court gives its decision on the appeal, not pending that decision: see para. 28.51 below.
[37] Arts. 34 and 35, see paras. 28.22 and 28.28 below.

The hearing of appeals to the judge against orders for registration are treated as vacation business.[38]

Effect of an appeal in the Contracting State of origin. The bring- **10.45**
ing of an appeal in respect of the original judgment before the
courts of the Contracting State of origin may have a number of
effects on its registration and enforcement in England. In most
Contracting States, a judgment is not enforceable until the expiry
of the time for appeal and the disposal of any appeal, unless the
judgment has been declared to be, or is by law, provisionally
enforceable.[39] A judgment which is not enforceable in the state of
origin may not be registered in England. If a judgment has been
properly registered in England and if an "ordinary" appeal[40] is
brought in the state of origin, the registration continues to be
valid,[41] but the judgment debtor may apply to the English court
for a stay of the proceedings.[42] He may also generally do this
where he merely intends to bring such an appeal,[43] the time for so
doing not having expired, but in this case the English court may
impose a time limit for the bringing of the foreign appeal. The
power to grant a stay is discretionary and it has been suggested by
the European Court of Justice that a stay should be granted "whenever reasonable doubt arises with regard to the fate of the decision
in the state in which it was given."[44] If the effect of the appeal
before the court of origin is to suspend the enforceability of the
judgment in the state of origin[45] or if enforceability is suspended by
order of the courts of the state of origin, then it is suggested that the
English court should always grant the stay. The stay will normally
be expressed to be until the determination of the appeal or until

---

[38] See the *Supreme Court Practice* para. 64/4/2 and *Practice Note* [1983] 1 W.L.R. 432.

[39] See para. 10.37 above and chaps. 48 to 55 below, paras. 59 and 60.

[40] See para. 27.82 below; Schlosser, paras. 195–204 (paras. A1.490 to A1.500 below).

[41] *Re a Debtor (No. 11 of 1939)* [1939] 2 All E.R. 400, decided in relation to the comparable situation under the 1933 Act.

[42] The Rules of the Supreme Court do not expressly provide for a stay in these cir- cumstances. Apart from its power under the Convention, the court has an inher- ent power to stay any proceedings where it thinks fit to do so; see Supreme Court Act, 1981, s.49(3). The application for a stay should be made on sum- mons to a master: *Supreme Court Practice* para. [5207].

[43] Art. 38, first para. But if the application for registration was merely to obtain a declaration of *recognition*, the application for a stay of proceedings may only be made if the appeal has been lodged in the country of origin: see Art. 30 para. 27.78 below.

[44] See *Industrial Diamond Supplies* v. *Riva* [1977] E.C.R. 2175. See para. 27.83 below.

[45] As in the Netherlands, save where the judgment is provisionally enforceable, see para. 55.66 below.

further order. If an appellant fails to prosecute the foreign appeal with sufficient diligence the judgment creditor will doubtless apply to the court for the stay to be removed. However, even if the order for the registration is eventually upheld, the court retains various powers to order a stay of execution.[46]

10.46 *Further appeals.* As has been seen, the judgment debtor's appeal against an order for registration[47] or the judgment creditor's appeal against its refusal[48] are heard in England by a judge in chambers.[49] The rights of recourse against the decision made on such an appeal are limited by the Convention to a single appeal on a point of law.[50] This appeal may either be to the Court of Appeal or, under the leap-frog procedure, to the House of Lords.[51] The appellate courts may also refer points of interpretation to the European Court of Justice in limited circumstances.[52]

8. Enforcement of authentic instruments and court settlements

10.47 *Authentic instruments.* Article 50 of the Convention provides for the enforcement as between Contracting States of authentic instruments.[53] These are formal documents, authenticated either by a notary or other public officer or by registration in special registers, which are capable of enforcement as if they were judgments. Authentic instruments exist in some form or other under the laws of all Contracting States except Ireland. They have no equivalent in England and Wales or Northern Ireland, but in Scotland documents registered in the Books of Council and Session or in sheriff court books are enforceable as authentic instruments.[54] Article 50 provides for their enforceability as between Contracting States by the same methods as exist for judgments. The instrument must satisfy the conditions necessary to establish its authenticity in its state of

---

[46] See para. 10.54 below.
[47] Art. 37, first para.; see para. 28.38 below.
[48] Art. 40; see para. 28.63 below.
[49] See paras. 10.24 and 10.25 above.
[50] Art. 37, second para., see para. 28.42 below; Art. 41, see para. 28.69 below.
[51] 1982 Act, s.6, para. 40.18 below. Further appeals in maintenance cases are considered separately at para. 11.17 below.
[52] 1971 Protocol, Art. 2, para. 36.03 below.
[53] See para. 30.01 below.
[54] See para. 58.70 below. Scottish authentic instruments are enforceable in England under the intra-U.K. scheme for enforcement, see 1982 Act, s.18(2)(c), para. 41.18 below.

origin and it must be enforceable there. The evidential requirements of Articles 46 to 49 apply as appropriate. Enforcement can only be refused on the ground of public policy.

Court settlements. Article 51 provides that a settlement which has **10.48** been approved by a court in the course of proceedings in a Contracting State, and which is enforceable in that state, shall be enforceable in other Contracting States under the same conditions as authentic instruments.[55]

Enforcement in England and Wales. Authentic instruments and **10.49** court settlements originating in other Contracting States may be enforced in England and Wales by registration pursuant to the Convention itself. Although the 1982 Act envisages the making of an Order in Council to make specific provisions for the enforcement of authentic instruments and court settlements,[56] no such Order has yet been made. Until the making of this Order in Council it will be necessary for a party seeking enforcement of an authentic instrument or of a court settlement to follow the procedure in the Convention, adapting the procedure laid down for judgments under the 1982 Act by the Rules of the Supreme Court.

C. THE EXECUTION OF JUDGMENTS FROM OTHER CONTRACTING STATES

1. Introduction

Execution and the effect of the Convention. The execution[57] in Eng- **10.50** land and Wales, of judgments given in other Contracting States, gives rise to a number of practical problems, particularly in relation to non-money judgments. Questions arise both as to the time at which and manner in which a party may be said to be bound by the terms of a foreign judgment, and as to how English enforcement procedures are to be employed so as to give effect to it.

It may be helpful at the outset to note the distinction which may be said to exist between, on the one hand, the authority of any judgment or order and, on the other hand, its effect.[58] A judgment has authority as a determination of the parties' rights and duties and is binding on them from the time it is pronounced, unless and until it is successfully appealed or set aside. It also has effect as an instru-

---

[55] See para. 30.14 below.
[56] 1982 Act, s.13; para. 40.38 below.
[57] As to the meaning of "execution" see 17 *Halsbury's Laws* (4th ed.), para. 401.
[58] See paras . 25.06 *et seq.* below.

ment for asserting those rights and enforcing those duties. This effect is secured not by the mere fact that it is authoritative, but by sanctions which, in consequence of the judgment, may lawfully be applied in the event of non-compliance. The threat of those sanctions may itself be sufficient to secure compliance. Most systems of law postpone the judgment creditor's opportunity to take measures to enforce the judgment, so as to allow the judgment debtor time either to comply voluntarily with the judgment or order, or to seek to have it overturned or varied. In order to prevent this period of postponement being abused, the judgment creditor is often permitted to enforce the judgment on a provisional basis or to take protective measures.

10.51   The system of rules for recognition and enforcement of judgments under the Convention adopts this same mechanism. If a judgment or order is given in any Contracting State in a matter which falls within the Convention, its authority is immediately and automatically extended into the other Contracting States without any special procedure being required.[59] The point at which the judgment becomes effective in other Contracting States by allowing the judgment creditor to proceed with measures of enforcement there, is postponed until an order for its enforcement has been issued[60] and the time has expired for appealing against that order or any such appeal has been determined.[61] In the meantime, the Convention gives the judgment creditor the right to take protective measures.[62]

10.52   *Execution in England.* The effect of this scheme in England under the 1982 Act and the Convention is that once a foreign judgment is registered, it has the same force and effect, for the purposes of its enforcement, as if it had originally been given by the High Court.[63] However, except as regards protective measures,[64] it cannot be enforced until the expiry of the period allowed for the bringing of, and the determination of, any appeal against the registration.[65] This period commences on the date of service of notice of registration and runs for one or two months,[66] subject to any extension,[67] or

---

[59] Art. 26, first para., para. 27.03 below.
[60] Art. 31, para. 28.01 below.
[61] Art. 39, para. 28.55 below.
[62] *Ibid.*
[63] 1982 Act, s.4(3), para. 40.08 below.
[64] See para. 10.20 above.
[65] Art. 39; R.S.C., Ord. 71, r. 34.
[66] See para. 10.25 above.
[67] See paras. 28.33 *et seq.* below.

until the determination of any appeal.[68] Once that period has expired and the judgment creditor may take measures of enforcement, those measures are available not only to enforce future compliance with the judgment, but also to punish earlier breaches of the judgment, including those which occurred before the judgment became registered.

The assimilation of a foreign judgment to an English judgment to the same effect applies even if the judgment is in terms in which an English judgment would not have been given.[69] The 1982 Act contains a provision for the making of rules of court to regulate the manner in which and the conditions subject to which registered judgments may be enforced,[70] but no such rules have been made. The existing methods of enforcement must presumably be considered to be sufficiently flexible to deal with the wide variety of foreign orders now capable of enforcement under the 1982 Act, at least until more experience of them is gained. The English court must do its best to enforce the judgment according to its terms.[71] Its enforcement in England should generally give it no greater effect there than it was capable of having in its Contracting State of origin, and its enforcement should be subject to any conditions and limitations to which it would be subject in that other state.

Supervision of execution by the High Court. The High Court super- **10.53** vises and controls the processes of execution in a variety of ways. By issuing a writ of execution or by making some order by way of execution, the court exercises control over the inception of the enforcement process.[72] It may make ancillary orders in aid of execution for the freezing of a judgment debtor's assets,[73] the discovery of documents relevant to the execution,[74] or the examination

---

[68] In addition to expressly prohibiting the issue of execution at any earlier time, the rules impose a practical impediment to earlier execution by providing that any party wishing to issue execution must produce to the proper officer of the court an affidavit of service of the notice of registration and of any order made by the court in relation to the judgment: R.S.C., Ord. 71, r. 34(3).

[69] 1982 Act, s.4(3), para. 40.08 below. See also *Deutsche Genossenschaftsbank* v. *Brasserie du Pêcheur* [1985] E.C.R. 1981, discussed at para. 28.32 below.

[70] 1982 Act, s.4(4).

[71] See para. 25.10 below.

[72] There are restrictions on execution by virtue of state immunity: State Immunity Act, 1978, ss.13, 18 and 19; see para. 2.16, n.83 above; and diplomatic privilege: Diplomatic Privileges Act 1964, Sched. 1, Art. 31(3); see para. 2.18, n.97 above.

[73] *Steward Chartering Ltd.* v. *C & O Managements S.A.* [1980] 1 W.L.R. 460; *Faith Panton Property Plan Ltd.* v. *Hodgetts* [1981] 1 W.L.R. 927; *Orwell Steel (Erection and Fabrication) Ltd.* v. *Asphalt and Tarmac (U.K.) Ltd.* [1984] 1 W.L.R. 1097; *Hill Samuel & Co. Ltd.* v. *Littaur* [1985] N.L.J. 57.

[74] *Distributori Automatici Italia SpA* v. *Holford General Trading Co. Ltd.* [1985] 1 W.L.R. 106; R.S.C., Ord. 48, r. 1.

of any person, liable to satisfy the judgment, as to his means[75] or as to any difficulty arising in connection with the enforcement of the judgment.[76] Furthermore the court has powers to grant a stay of execution.

10.54   *Stay of execution.* Under English law, the court has a general power to order a stay of *proceedings* if the justice of the case so demands,[77] but its powers to order a stay of *execution* are more limited.[78] A party may apply for a stay by reason of matters which have occurred since the date of the judgment[79] or, in the case of execution by writ of *fieri facias*, if the court is satisfied that there are special circumstances which render it inexpedient to enforce the judgment.[80] These powers under English law to grant a stay are, however, subject to the Convention. They are not affected by the fact that the Convention requires a judgment to be enforced when an order for its enforcement has been issued,[81] nor generally by the fact that the Convention itself regulates the circumstances in which a stay of the proceedings for an order for recognition or enforcement may be granted in the event of an ordinary appeal in the state of origin.[82] This is because the Convention provides a uniform means of obtaining an order for enforcement, but leaves matters of execution largely to the internal law of the state where the judgment is being enforced.[83] The European Court has held, however, that a stay of execution may not be granted to a judgment debtor on a ground which he could have relied on in an appeal against the order

---

[75] R.S.C., Ord. 48, r. 1. The examination is not limited to assets within the jurisdiction: *Interpool Ltd.* v. *Galani* [1988] Q.B. 738 (C.A.). See also *Maclaine Watson & Co. Ltd.* v. *International Tin Council (No. 2)* [1989] 3 W.L.R. 1190 (C.A.), a case to which Ord. 48 did not apply.

[76] R.S.C., Ord. 48, r. 2.

[77] The court has inherent power to grant a stay of any proceedings where it thinks fit to do so; see Supreme Court Act, 1981, s.49(3), and *Supreme Court Practice*, paras. [5204] *et seq.* A stay of execution of a final judgment is a stay of proceedings for these purposes: *Wright* v. *Redgrave* (1879) 11 Ch.D. 24; *Re Artistic Colour Print Co.* (1880) 14 Ch.D. 502, at p. 505.

[78] *London Permanent Benefit Building Society* v. *de Baer* [1969] 1 Ch. 321; *Jones* v. *Savery* [1951] 1 All E.R. 820; *T.C. Trustees Ltd.* v. *J.S. Darwen (Successors) Ltd.* [1969] 2 Q.B. 295.

[79] R.S.C., Ord. 45, r. 11.

[80] R.S.C., Ord. 47, r. 1; *Ferdinand Wagner* v. *Laubscher Bros. & Co.* [1970] 2 Q.B. 313, decided under the 1933 Act. As to execution of registered judgments see further at para. 10.55 below. A stay of *fi. fa.* does not prevent the creditor from proceeding with other measures of execution.

[81] Art. 31, para. 28.06 below.

[82] Arts. 30 and 38, paras. 27.78 and 28.43 below; see para. 10.45 above.

[83] *Deutsche Genossenschaftsbank* v. *Brasserie du Pêcheur* [1985] E.C.R. 1981, discussed at para. 28.32 below.

for enforcement, the time limits in Article 36 would otherwise be rendered ineffective.[83a]

2. Methods of execution

The choice of the means of enforcing the judgment is left to the **10.55** party who is to enforce it, although, as has been seen, the court exercises varying degrees of supervision and control over its implementation. The choice will depend initially on whether the foreign judgment contains money provisions or non-money provisions. The former present far fewer practical problems than the latter.[84] It is proposed to deal separately with these two types of provision, although in some instances the registered judgment will contain both types of provision and will require, on occasions, a combination of more than one method of execution. The execution of foreign provisional and protective measures and of financial penalties is also discussed below.[85]

Money provisions

A money provision in a judgment is one that provides for the **10.56** payment of one or more sums of money.[86] A money provision is enforceable by all the methods of enforcement available in respect of English money judgments,[87] namely: a writ of *fieri facias*,[88] garnishee proceedings,[89] a charging order,[90] the appointment of a receiver,[91] an attachment of earnings order,[92] and, in certain

---

[83a] *Hoffmann* v. *Krieg* case 145/86, decision of February 4, 1988, *The Times*, March 26, 1988; see para. 28.33 below.

[84] This distinction is reflected in the differing registration procedures for intra-U.K. enforcement; see 1982 Act s.18(1) and Scheds. 6 and 7.

[85] See para. 10.61 below.

[86] A judgment for unquantified damages might be recognised but could not be enforced. As to interest and costs see para. 10.17 above. As to the enforcement of foreign civil monetary penalties, see para. 10.62 below.

[87] The means of enforcement available in the High Court are enumerated in R.S.C., Ord. 45, r. 1. Money judgments of the High Court may also be enforced in the county court: County Courts Act 1984, s.105; C.C.R., Ord. 25, r. 11. This power is particularly significant as regards attachment of earnings orders.

[88] R.S.C., Ord. 47.

[89] R.S.C., Ord. 49. The garnishee must be within the jurisdiction but the debt need not be recoverable within the jurisdiction, *S.C.F. Finance Co. Ltd.* v. *Masri (No. 3)* [1987] Q.B. 1028 (C.A.); *cf. Deutsche Schatbau-und Tiefbohrgesellschaft m.b.H.* v. *Shell International Petroleum Co. Ltd.* [1988] 3 W.L.R. 230 (H.L.).

[90] R.S.C., Ord. 50; a charging order is a type of execution: see *Re Overseas Aviation Engineering (G.B.) Ltd.* [1963] Ch. 24, 40.

[91] R.S.C., Ord. 51.

[92] C.C.R., Ord. 27.

cases,[93] an order for committal[94] and a writ of sequestration.[95] Where, as will ordinarily be the case,[96] the registered judgment is expressed in a foreign currency the enforcing party must comply with certain requirements so as to inform the court of the current sterling value of the judgment debt, and the judgment debtor will normally have the option of paying the sterling equivalent.[97]

Non-money provisions

10.57   *Effect of registration.* In the context of non-money provisions, it is important to recall that when a foreign order is registered in England the court does not make a fresh order in the terms of the foreign order. The effect of the registration is to extend the effect of the foreign order, in its original terms, into England and to make English means of enforcement available to secure compliance with it or to punish its breach.[98]

10.58   *Types of provisions.* Non-money provisions, apart from those which are merely declaratory, may be of two kinds, those which order a party to do an act and those which order a party to refrain from doing an act. Such orders, when made by an English court, usually take the form of injunctions, unless they are of a purely procedural nature.[99] If a person disobeys an injunction[1] he is, provided his disobedience may be regarded as contumacious,[2] and provided certain procedural requirements have been complied with, liable to be punished for civil contempt of court.[3] This punishment may take the form of committal to prison of the contemnor, the seques-

---

[93] R.S.C., Ord. 45, r. 5.
[94] R.S.C., Ord. 52.
[95] R.S.C., Ord. 46, r. 5.
[96] See para. 10.16, n.10 above.
[97] *Practice Direction (Judgments, Foreign Currency)* [1976] 1 W.L.R. 83, [1977] 1 W.L.R. 197, para. 11. (writ of *fi. fa.*), para. 12 (garnishee proceedings), para. 13 (other modes of enforcement); Queen's Bench Masters' Practice Direction 8B, *Supreme Court Practice*, para. [724].
[98] See Collins, p. 116; Schlosser, para. 212 (para. A1.510) seems to suggest that there should be parity between the type of sanction imposed by the enforcing court and that available before the court of origin. This would be consistent with the principle that the judgment should have no greater effect than in the state of origin.
[99] Procedural orders probably do not fall within the Convention's enforcement scheme: see para. 25.29 below.
[1] Breach of an undertaking to the court is for these purposes equivalent to breach of an injunction if it has been recorded in court: see *Neath Canal Co.* v. *Ynisarwed Resalven Colliery Co.* (1875) 10 Ch.App. 450; *Millburn* v. *Newton Colliery Ltd.* (1908) 52 S.J. 317; *Gandolfo* v. *Gandolfo* [1981] Q.B. 359; *Biba Ltd.* v. *Stratford Investments Ltd.* [1973] Ch. 281.
[2] *Steiner Products* v. *Willy Steiner* [1966] 1 W.L.R. 986; *Greek City Co. Ltd.* v. *Demetriou* [1983] 2 All E.R. 921.
[3] Borrie and Lowe, *Law of Contempt.*

tration of his property[4] or a fine.[5] Where a corporate body is in contempt of court a director or officer of that body may be liable to committal or sequestration of his property. Any person who knowingly assists a contempt of court will himself be in contempt and liable to be punished.[6] The procedural requirements referred to above concern the service of the original order, endorsed with a "penal notice," on the person against whom, or the body against which, it is to be enforced, and the service of any further order extending or limiting the time within which a required act must be carried out.[7] Service of these orders may be dispensed with if the person concerned was present when the order was made or if he has been notified of the terms of the order whether by telephone, telegram or otherwise.[8] It is suggested that a non-party who has notice of the terms of a registered judgment for a non-money provision in the nature of an injunction is bound by those terms and would be guilty of contempt if he knowingly assisted in its breach.[9]

Non-money provisions which order a party to abstain from doing an **10.59** *act.* This type of order will be treated by the court, for the purposes of enforcement, as being the equivalent to a restraining injunction. Upon registration it acquires, for the purposes of enforcement, the same force and effect as if it had *originally*[10] been made by the English court. Subject to possible objections on the ground of public policy,[11] it is immaterial that the English court would not have made the particular order. Orders to refrain from doing an act are enforced under English procedure by committal or fining for contempt or by sequestration. The question of enforcement does not arise until there has been a breach of the order. If the party against whom the order was made has already acted in breach of it before it has been registered in England, enforcement measures can be taken only after registration and, unless protective measures are appropriate,[12] after the time for appealing registration has expired. However,

---

[4] R.S.C., Ord. 45, r. 5. See the notes on Ord. 45 in the *Supreme Court Practice.* See *Board of Governors of Hospital for Sick Children* v. *Walt Disney Productions Inc.* [1968] Ch. 52, for an example of enforcement of an injunction against a foreign corporation's assets within the jurisdiction by sequestration.

[5] *Phonographic Performance Ltd.* v. *Amusement Centres (Peckham) Ltd.* [1964] Ch. 195; see R.S.C., Ord. 52, r. 9; Chitty and Jacob, p. 823.

[6] *Seaward* v. *Paterson* [1897] 1 Ch. 545; *Elliott* v. *Klinger* [1967] 1 W.L.R. 1165.

[7] R.S.C., Ord. 45, r. 7. See Pettitt, "Injunction, Service and Committal" (1977) 40 Mod.L.R. 220.

[8] R.S.C., Ord. 45, r. 7(6). See *Att.-Gen.* v. *Newspaper Publishing Plc* [1988] Ch. 333.

[9] *Supreme Court Practice*, para. 29/1/18.

[10] 1982 Act, s.4(3).

[11] See para. 10.28 above.

[12] See para. 10.20 above.

if the breach is continuing, or is threatened, then those enforcement measures might, in a proper case, be taken as protective measures.

10.60 *Non-money provisions which order a party to perform an act.* This type of order will in most cases[13] be treated by the court, for the purposes of enforcement, as being the equivalent to a mandatory injunction. As with a restraining order it acquires upon registration the same force and effect for the purposes of enforcement, as if it had *originally*[14] been made by the English court. Subject to possible objections on the ground of public policy,[15] it is immaterial that the English court would not have made the particular order. The registration of the foreign judgment presupposes that performance of the act required to be performed has not yet been completed, and that English enforcement procedures are being invoked so that their coercive effect will secure obedience to the order.[16] Unless it is a case in which the taking of protective measures is justified,[17] an order for committal or sequestration cannot be made until the expiry of the period for appealing the registration and the disposal of any appeal.

10.61 *Foreign provisional and protective orders.* It should be noted that foreign judgments registrable under the Act include interim judgments for provisonal or protective measures, provided that they have been given in adversarial proceedings.[18] Such orders will often contain non-money provisions and there is a wide variety of forms in which they may be made.[19] The English court must enforce them by the most appropriate means available.[20] Apart from an interim order for the payment of money by one party to another, which is enforced as a money provision, provisional and protective measures

---

[13] A judgment for the delivery of goods may be enforced in some circumstances by a writ of specific delivery; see R.S.C., Ord. 45, r. 4.

[14] 1982 Act, s.4(3).

[15] See para. 10.28 above.

[16] It is suggested that the court's powers under R.S.C., Ord. 45, r. 6 are exercisable in relation to a registered judgment and that the English court can specify a time for compliance with the order, at least in so far as it does not make the judgment more onerous than it was in the state of origin. Additionally, the High Court has power to order the performance of the act by another person at the expense of the disobedient party, see R.S.C., Ord. 45, r. 8.

[17] See para. 10.20 above.

[18] See para. 24.09 below. Orders of the foreign court which do not govern the legal relation of the parties, for instance those for the further conduct of the proceedings, are not enforceable under the Convention: see Schlosser, paras. 184–187 (paras. A1.480–A1.483 below), and para. 25.29 below; *cf.* paras. 7.27 *et seq.* above.

[19] See chaps. 48 to 58, at paras. 58 *et seq.* below.

[20] Schlosser refers to the greater problems of continental courts enforcing U.K. orders for provisional measures: Schlosser para. 183 (para. A1.479 below).

are likely to take effect as non-money provisions enforceable as though they were injunctions.

Financial penalties. In many continental countries, as the **10.62** Schlosser Report points out,[21] orders containing non-money provisions are normally coupled with a daily penalty to be recovered in default of compliance with the order. Article 43 of the Convention allows the enforcing court to secure the recovery of this penalty if its amount has been specified by the original court. It is recoverable in England as a money provision.[22]

D. The Enforcement of Judgments Between Different Parts of the United Kingdom

1. Introduction

Background. The three parts of the United Kingdom constitute **10.63** separate law areas which, for jurisdictional purposes, are treated as though they were separate states.[23] Before the 1982 Act came into effect a judgment given in one part of the United Kingdom would ordinarily be enforced in another part by means of registration pursuant to the Judgments Extension Act 1868 or the Inferior Courts Judgments Extension Act 1882. The former Act applied to judgments or decrees for debts, damages or costs of the superior courts of England, Scotland and Ireland.[24] The judgment was "extended" by entering a certificate in respect of it, issued by the trial court, in a register in the country in which enforcement was sought, and the judgment thereupon became enforceable as though it were a judgment of the court in which it was registered. The latter Act provided a similar, but more limited, scheme for the registration and enforcement of judgments given by inferior courts. The accession of the United Kingdom to the 1968 Convention necessitated the wholesale reform of these arrangements for enforcement within the United Kingdom to bring them into line with the Convention. Accordingly Part II of the 1982 Act establishes an entirely new scheme for the recognition and enforcement of judgments as between the three parts of the United Kingdom.[25]

---

[21] Schlosser, paras. 211 *et seq.* (paras. A1.509 *et seq.* below), referring to Belgium, France and Luxembourg; see further, chaps. 48 to 58 below, at para. 69.

[22] See para. 28.79 below as to the question whether the recoverability of the fine depends on its being payable to a party rather than to the state.

[23] See Maxwell Report, paras. 15.15 *et seq.*

[24] From 1922 it applied as between England, Scotland and Northern Ireland; see *Banfield* v. *Chester* (1925) 94 L.J.K.B. 805.

[25] The 1868 and 1882 Acts are repealed; see the 1982 Act, s.54 and Sched. 14.

10.64   *Division of jurisdiction within the United Kingdom.* New jurisdictional rules, modelled on those of the Convention, now allocate jurisdiction as between the three parts of the United Kingdom.[26] These rules apply when the subject-matter of the proceedings is within the scope of the Convention (whether or not the Convention itself applies to the proceedings), and when either the defendant is domiciled in the United Kingdom or the proceedings are, by virtue of the Convention, within the exclusive jurisdiction of the courts of the United Kingdom. Certain classes of proceedings are expressly excluded from the application of the rules of jurisdiction.[27] As in the Convention, the basic rule of jurisdiction is that a person domiciled in the United Kingdom is to be sued in the part in which he is domiciled.[28] There are rules of special jurisdiction which in most respects follow the rules of the Convention.[29]

2. Enforcement of judgments within the United Kingdom

10.65   The judgments which are capable of recognition and enforcement under Part II of the 1982 Act are, in general terms, the same as those to which the Convention's enforcement procedures apply.[30] Notably, however, they do not include judgments or orders for provisional or protective measures, other than orders for the making of interim payments,[31] or judgments of foreign courts registered pursuant to the 1920 or 1933 Acts or the Convention.[32] A common law "judgment on a foreign judgment" could, seemingly, be enforced under Part II of the Act.[33] The definition of "judgment" also includes "any document which in Scotland has been registered for execution in the Books of Council and Session or in the sheriff court books kept for any sheriffdom."[34] If a judgment is enforceable under the registration procedure provided for in Part II of the Act it is not enforceable in England by any other method.[35] The Act assumes that judgments given in one part of the United Kingdom will be automatically recognised (as distinct from enforced) in other parts of the United Kingdom, but it does provide that, subject to minor exceptions, recognition is not to be refused solely on the ground that the court of trial was not, according to the

---

[26] See paras. 1.18 to 1.24 above. The rules are set out in Sched. 4 of the 1982 Act; see the commentary at para. 45.01 *et seq.* below.
[27] 1982 Act, s.17 and Sched. 5.
[28] 1982 Act, Sched. 4, Art. 2.
[29] See para. 1.23 above.
[30] 1982 Act, s.18; see the commentary on this section at para. 41.13 below.
[31] 1982 Act, s.18(5)(d), para. 41.25 below.
[32] 1982 Act, s.18(7), para. 41.26 below.
[33] See Collins, p. 132.
[34] 1982 Act, s.18(2)(c), para. 41.18 below; see para. 58.70 below.
[35] 1982 Act, s.18(8), para. 41.26 below; note the saving for arbitration awards.

private international law of the court addressed, a court of competent jurisdiction.[36]

The 1982 Act provides two types of procedure for the enforcement of judgments given elsewhere in the United Kingdom, dependent upon whether the provision to be enforced is a "money provision" or a "non-money provision".

Enforcement of money provisions. The procedure for the enforcement of money provisions is set out in Schedule 6 to the Act and in the Rules of the Supreme Court.[37] It is modelled on the system which existed previously under the Judgments Extension Act 1868 and it provides for the obtaining of a certificate of the judgment from the court of origin,[38] and the registration of the certificate in the High Court.[39] The court of origin may not issue a certificate of the judgment until the time for appeal has expired and any appeal has been disposed of, or if execution on the judgment has been stayed in its court of origin.[40] Upon registration of the certificate, the judgment becomes enforceable as if it had been a judgment of the High Court.[41] There are no provisions for the judgment debtor to be notified of the registration but he may apply for a stay of execution on the ground that he intends to apply to the court of origin for the judgment to be set aside or quashed.[42] He may also apply to the High Court for the registration to be set aside on the grounds that the registration was contrary to the provisions of Schedule 6 of the Act,[43] or that the judgment was in respect of a matter which had previously been the subject of a judgment given by another court or tribunal which had jurisdiction in the matter.[44]

10.66

Enforcement of non-money provisions. The procedure for the enforcement of non-money provisions is set out in Schedule 7 of the Act[45] and in the Rules of the Supreme Court.[46] The party seeking the enforcement of the judgment registers the judgment itself in the

10.67

---

[36] 1982 Act, s.19, para. 41.27 below.
[37] See para. 46.01 below; see R.S.C., Ord. 71, r. 37.
[38] See para. 46.03 below.
[39] The registration is effected by producing the certificate and a certified true copy of the judgment at the Central Office within six months of its issue: R.S.C., Ord. 71, r. 37(1).
[40] Sched. 6, para. 3, see para. 46.04 below.
[41] Sched. 6, para. 6, see para. 46.07 below.
[42] Sched. 6, para. 9, see para. 46.11 below.
[43] Sched. 6, para. 10(a), see para. 46.12 below. If this ground is established the registration must be set aside.
[44] Sched. 6, para. 10(b), see para. 46.12 below. If this ground is established the registration may be set aside.
[45] See the commentary on Sched. 7 at para. 46.13 below.
[46] R.S.C., Ord. 71, r. 38.

High Court together with a certificate from the court of origin to the effect that the time for appeal has expired and no appeal has been brought or that an appeal has been disposed of. The application for registration may be *ex parte* or, on the direction of the court, *inter partes*.[47] The order for registration is made in the same manner as under the Convention[48] except that no affidavit is required on an *ex parte* application. The party against whom enforcement is sought must be notified of the registration and is allowed a period during which he may make an application to set aside the registration. This application is made by summons on affidavit, and the court may order any issue to be tried.[49] The registered judgment is enforceable as if it were a judgment of the High Court[50] but no enforcement measures, other than protective measures,[51] may be taken during the period for applying to set the registration aside or until determination of any such application.[52] As with the enforcement of money provisions, the court has express power to grant a stay of execution on the application of the party against whom execution is sought if he satisfies the court that he intends to apply to the court of origin for the judgment to be set aside or quashed.[53] He may also apply to the High Court for the registration to be set aside on the grounds that the registration was contrary to the provisions of Schedule 7 of the Act,[54] or that the judgment was in respect of a matter which had previously been the subject of a judgment by another court or tribunal which had jurisdiction in the matter.[55]

10.68   *Obtaining a certificate of a judgment for enforcement in other parts of the United Kingdom.* The procedure for obtaining the certificate of the judgment is set out in Schedule 6 of the 1982 Act, for money provisions, and in Schedule 7, for non-money provisions, and is described in the commentary to the 1982 Act below.[56]

---

[47] R.S.C., Ord. 71, r. 38(1).
[48] R.S.C., Ord. 71, r. 38(3) applies the procedure under R.S.C., Ord. 71, rr. 30 and 32. An affidavit under R.S.C., Ord. 71, r. 3 is required if the master directs the issue of a summons under Ord. 71, r. 38(1).
[49] R.S.C., Ord. 71, r. 38(4) applies the procedure under R.S.C., Ord. 71, r. 9(1) and (2).
[50] Sched. 7, para. 6, see para. 46.19 below.
[51] R.S.C., Ord. 71, r. 30(3).
[52] It seems that this should be inferred from the wording of R.S.C., Ord. 71, r. 30(2) (applied by R.S.C., Ord. 71, r. 38(3)).
[53] Sched. 7, para. 8, see para. 46.21 below.
[54] Sched. 7, para. 9(a). If this ground is established the registration must be set aside.
[55] Sched. 7, para. 9(b). If this ground is established the registration may be set aside.
[56] See paras. 46.03 *et seq.* and 46.15 *et seq.* below.

Execution in England of judgments from Scotland or Northern Ire- **10.69**
land. It has been seen that the procedure for registration of judgments from Scotland or Northern Ireland differs depending upon
whether the order to be enforced is a money provision or a non-
money provision.[57] The effect of registration, in either case, is to
give the judgment the same force and effect for the purposes of
enforcement, as if it were a judgment of the High Court and the
methods of execution are the same as for such judgments.[58]

E. CERTIFIED COPIES OF ENGLISH JUDGMENTS FOR ENFORCEMENT IN OTHER CONTRACTING STATES

A party who has obtained a judgment in the High Court which he **10.70**
wishes to have enforced in another Contracting State will in due
course have to make an application for an order for enforcement to
the appropriate foreign court designated in Article 32. The application has to be supported by the documents specified in Articles 46
and 47, which include a copy of the judgment "which satisfies the
conditions necessary to establish its authenticity." The Rules of the
Supreme Court contain provisions to enable such a copy of the
judgment to be obtained, together with a certificate giving particulars relating to the judgment and to other requisite matters.[59] An *ex
parte* application must be made to the master supported by an affidavit setting out a number of specific matters relating to the proceedings. A certified office copy of the judgment is then prepared
together with a certificate in Form 110 giving the requisite information concerning the proceedings.

---

[57] Para. 10.65 above.
[58] See paras. 10.55 *et seq.* above.
[59] 1982 Act, s.12, para. 40.36 below; R.S.C., Ord. 71, r. 36; for the county court,
see C.C.R., Ord. 35, r. 3.

CHAPTER 11

MAINTENANCE ORDERS

A. INTRODUCTION

11.01 The 1968 Convention does not generally apply to matters of family law,[1] but maintenance is an exception.[2] As regards jurisdiction in maintenance cases, the effects of the Convention and the 1982 Act are not far-reaching and may be described briefly. As regards the recognition and enforcement of maintenance orders, on the other hand, the provisions of the 1968 Convention and the 1982 Act form a new part of a rather complex international framework of conventions and other arrangements and they need to be considered in that context.

1. Jurisdictional effects of the 1982 Act

11.02 Subject to one exception, the 1968 Convention provides an exclusive basis for the international jurisdiction of the courts in those cases to which it applies.[3] The exception to this principle, discussed below,[4] arises where jurisdiction is founded on the rules of another

---

[1] Art. 1, second para.; see para. 14.20 below.
[2] The meaning of "maintenance" in the context of the Convention is discussed at paras. 17.34 et seq. below; see also para. 40.13 below.
[3] See paras. 13.00, 13.09, 13.10 et seq. and 15.01 et seq. below.
[4] Para. 11.09.

international convention. English courts have a variety of powers to make orders for the maintenance either of a present or former spouse, or of children, and either as orders ancillary to proceedings concerning a person's status or independently of such proceedings. A consideration of those powers is beyond the scope of this work, but the effects of the 1968 Convention and the 1982 Act are now described.[5]

Respondent domiciled in England and Wales. If the respondent is **11.03** domiciled in England and Wales, English courts which have powers under English law to make maintenance orders may exercise these powers whether or not the application is ancillary to status proceedings.[6] This is merely an example of the Convention's general rule of jurisdiction, under which a defendant may be sued in the courts of the state where he is domiciled. For this purpose, "domicile" is defined by section 41 of the 1982 Act[7] and in practical terms the 1968 Convention and 1982 Act add little to the other jurisdictional rules of English law in matters relating to maintenance.

Respondent domiciled in another Convention territory. If the respon- **11.04** dent is domiciled in another part of the United Kingdom or in another Contracting State, the jurisdiction of the English courts may arise under Article 5(2) of the 1968 Convention or of Schedule 4 to the 1982 Act.[8] Under these provisions, the English courts may have jurisdiction on either or both of two different grounds.

First, whether or not the application is ancillary to status proceedings, a maintenance creditor who is domiciled or habitually resident in England and Wales may make an application for a maintenance order in the English courts for the place where she is domiciled or habitually resident, against a person who is domiciled in another part of the United Kingdom or in another Contracting State. If this jurisdiction is exercised by a magistrates' court against a person domiciled in another Contracting State, rules of court

---

[5] The circumstances in which English courts have jurisdiction to make maintenance orders are summarised by Dicey and Morris, at pp. 745–765, 811–817 and 819–822. See also the Family Law Act 1986 and the Family Law Reform Act 1987. As to whether an application under the Inheritance (Provision for Family and Dependants) Act 1975 can be an application for maintenance, see para. 17.37 below.

[6] 1968 Convention, Art. 2, para. 16.01 below; 1982 Act, Sched. 4, Art. 2, para. 45.02 below. But see the reference to jurisdiction agreements below.

[7] Para. 44.01 below.

[8] 1968 Convention, Art. 5(2), see para. 17.31 below; 1982 Act, Sched. 4, Art. 5(2), see para. 45.06 below; but see the reference to jurisdiction agreements below. As regards the magistrates' court, see Magistrates' Courts (Civil Jurisdiction and Judgments Act 1982) Rules 1986, S.I. 1986 No. 1962, r. 10.

require the justices' clerk to send to the Secretary of State certain information about the proceedings.[9]

11.05   Secondly, if the application for a maintenance order is ancillary to proceedings before an English court concerning a person's status, and if that court has powers to make ancillary maintenance orders, it may exercise those powers against a person who is domiciled in another part of the United Kingdom or in another Contracting State. This is so, irrespective of whether that person was the respondent in the status proceedings and irrespective of the domicile of the maintenance creditor. As a matter of English law, ancillary maintenance orders may be made in proceedings for divorce, nullity of marriage, or judicial separation,[10] in custody proceedings[11] and in certain guardianship proceedings.[12] In this connection it should be noted that English courts have power to make maintenance orders after the grant by a foreign court of a divorce, annulment of marriage or judicial separation, provided that certain conditions are fulfilled,[13] but that such an application is not treated as ancillary to status proceedings for the purpose of the 1968 Convention, because it is necessarily made to a court other than that seised of the status proceedings. As has been seen, jurisdiction to make a maintenance order in these circumstances may nonetheless arise on the basis of the domicile in England and Wales of either the respondent or the maintenance creditor.

11.06   *Other grounds of jurisdiction.* Courts in England which have power to make maintenance orders also have jurisdiction over a person who submits to the jurisdiction by entering an appearance otherwise than solely to contest the jurisdiction of the court[14] or pursuant to a jurisdiction agreement.[15] A jurisdiction agreement is unlikely to arise in this context, but if it does, it may exclude the jurisdiction

---

[9] Magistrates' Courts (Civil Jurisdiction and Judgments Act 1982) Rules 1986, rr. 10(2), 11(2). The information enables the Home Office to assist the maintenance creditor in enforcing the order in another Contracting State: see para. 11.29 below.

[10] Matrimonial Causes Act 1973.

[11] Guardianship of Minors Act 1971.

[12] Guardianship of Minors Act 1971, s.11C. Affiliation proceedings were abolished with effect from April 1, 1989, and replaced by a system of declarations of parentage and orders for financial relief: Family Law Reform Act 1987, ss.12, 17 and 22.

[13] Matrimonial and Family Proceedings Act 1984, Part III.

[14] 1968 Convention, Art. 18, para. 21.83 below; 1982 Act, Sched. 4, Art. 18, para. 45.24 below.

[15] 1968 Convention, Art. 17, para. 21.01 below; 1982 Act, Sched. 4, Art. 17, para. 45.21 below.

of otherwise competent courts.[16] In certain circumstances, English courts may have jurisdiction over a trustee or beneficiary if the trust is domiciled in England.[17]

Variation and revocation. Applications for the variation or revocation of a maintenance order are subject to the provisions of the 1968 Convention, as if they were fresh proceedings. It follows that courts which were competent under the Convention to make the maintenance order may not necessarily be competent to vary or revoke it.[18]

2. Reciprocal enforcement of maintenance orders

English law contains seven[19] different sets of rules for the enforcement of maintenance orders made by foreign courts.[20] Depending on the country where the maintenance order was made, one or more of these sets of rules may apply:

    (i) Orders made in other Contracting States to the 1968 Convention may be enforced under the 1982 Act;

    (ii) Orders which are made in countries which are parties to the Hague Convention of October 2, 1973 on the Recognition and Enforcement of Decisions Relating to Maintenance Obligations[21] ("Hague Convention countries") may be enforced under a modified version of Part I of the Maintenance Orders (Reciprocal Enforcement) Act 1972 (the "1972 Act").[22] With the exception of Belgium, Denmark, Greece and Ireland, all the Contracting States to the 1968 Convention are also Hague Convention countries for this purpose;

11.07

---

[16] See paras. 21.02 *et seq.* below. It would exclude the jurisdiction of an otherwise competent court in Scotland or Northern Ireland: see para. 45.22 below.

[17] 1968 Convention, Art. 5(6), para. 17.65 below; 1982 Act, Sched. 4, Art. 5(6), para. 45.06 below. This would seem only to be relevant if an application for maintenance under the Inheritance (Provision for Families and Dependents) Act 1975 falls within the Convention, as to which, see para. 17.37 below.

[18] See para. 17.43 below. See the Magistrates' Courts (Civil Jurisdiction and Judgments Act 1982) Rules 1986 (S.I. 1986 No. 1962), r. 11.

[19] An eighth set of rules applied in respect of certain ancillary maintenance orders made in some colonial territories: Colonial and Other Territories (Divorce Jurisdiction) Acts 1926 to 1950. The system had become practically redundant and these Acts were repealed in their entirety by the Family Law Act 1986, Sched. 2.

[20] See Dicey and Morris, pp. 770–779.

[21] Cmnd. 7939.

[22] Reciprocal Enforcement of Maintenance Orders (Hague Convention Countries) Order 1979, (S.I. 1979 No. 1317), amended by (S.I. 1981 Nos. 837, 1545 and 1674), (S.I. 1983 Nos. 885 and 1523) and (S.I. 1987 No. 1282.) See para. 11.25 below.

(iii) Orders made in Ireland may be enforced under a different modified version of Part I of the 1972 Act, although the continued validity of these rules may now be in doubt;[23]

(iv) Orders made in other designated reciprocating countries[24] may be enforced under Part I of the 1972 Act; these are mainly Commonwealth countries;

(v) Orders made in certain other Commonwealth countries may be enforced under the Maintenance Orders (Facilities for Enforcement) Act 1920;[25]

(vi) Orders made in Scotland or Northern Ireland may be enforced under the Maintenance Orders Act 1950;

(vii) At common law a foreign maintenance order which is final and conclusive can be enforced by an action in England;[26] but maintenance orders to which the 1968 Convention applies cannot be enforced by this method.[27]

The first of these regimes, under the 1968 Convention, is discussed in greater detail in part B of this chapter and part C contains a summary of the system of enforcement under the Hague Convention, under the bilateral arrangements with Ireland, and as between the different parts of the United Kingdom.

11.08   *United Nations convention.* An alternative system for the recovery of maintenance abroad is provided by Part II of the Maintenance Orders (Reciprocal Enforcement) Act 1972, which gives effect to the United Nations Convention on the Recovery Abroad of Maintenance done at New York on June 20, 1956.[28] This system, which applies in relation to the so-called Convention countries,[29] provides for the transmission of an application for maintenance to the country in which the respondent is residing (or to the jurisdiction of which he is otherwise subject). The application is then entertained by the courts of the latter country in accordance with its own law.

---

[23] Reciprocal Enforcement of Maintenance Orders (Republic of Ireland) Order 1974, (S.I. 1974 No. 2140.) See paras. 11.09 and 11.26 below.

[24] Reciprocal Enforcement of Maintenance Orders (Designation of Reciprocating Countries) Orders 1974, 1975, 1979 and 1983, (S.I. 1974 No. 556), (S.I. 1975 No. 2187), (S.I. 1979 No. 115, and S.I. 1983 No. 1125).

[25] Maintenance Orders (Facilities for Enforcement) Order 1959, (S.I. 1959 No. 377), amended by (S.I. 1975 No. 2188), (S.I. 1979 No. 116), (S.I. 1983, No. 1124) and by the Pakistan Act 1974, s.4(4).

[26] See Dicey and Morris, pp. 771–773.

[27] *De Wolf* v. *Cox* [1976] E.C.R. 1759; see para. 25.36 below.

[28] Cmnd. 4485.

[29] Recovery Abroad of Maintenance (Convention Countries) Order 1975, (S.I. 1975 No. 423), amended by (S.I. 1978 No. 279 and S.I. 1982 No. 1530). Part II of the 1972 Act also applies in a modified form to certain states of the U.S.A.: Recovery Abroad of Maintenance (United States of America) Order 1979, (S.I. 1979 No. 1314), amended by (S.I. 1981 No. 606 and S.I. 1984 No. 1824).

With the exception of Ireland, all the Contracting States to the 1968 Convention are also "Convention countries" for the purposes of Part II of the 1972 Act.

3. Relationship between the 1982 Act and other rules

The 1968 Convention and 1982 Act form the principal legislative **11.09** basis for the international jurisdiction of the English courts to make maintenance orders and for the enforcement of such orders made in other Contracting States. They do not, however, provide the only such basis. This is because Article 57 of the 1968 Convention preserves the operation of conventions which, in relation to particular matters, govern jurisdiction or the recognition of enforcement of judgments.[30]

Jurisdiction. An English court may exercise jurisdiction pursuant to the provisions of Part II of the Maintenance Orders (Reciprocal Enforcement) Act 1972 over a person domiciled in another Contracting State to the 1968 Convention, if that state is also a "Convention country" for the purposes of the 1972 Act, even if the English court would not have jurisdiction under the 1982 Act. This is because the United Nations convention,[31] to which Part II of the 1972 Act gives effect, is one which governs jurisdiction in relation to maintenance.[32] On the other hand, the Hague Convention[33] does *not* govern jurisdiction,[34] despite the fact that the English implementing legislation in the modified version of Part I of the 1972 Act[35] contains provisions conferring jurisdiction on English courts.[36]

The bilateral arrangements with Ireland do govern jurisdiction and it may be, therefore, that the modified version of Part I of the 1972 Act[37] which gives effect to them forms an alternative basis for jurisdiction as against a person residing in the Republic of Ireland. But this depends upon the bilateral arrangements being a "convention" for the purposes of Article 57 of the 1968 Convention, a matter which is not clear.[38] If they are not a convention, it would seem to be inconsistent with the European Court's decision in *De*

---

[30] Para. 33.06 below; see also s.9(1) of the 1982 Act, para. 40.27 below.
[31] See n. 28 above.
[32] Dicey and Morris, p. 762.
[33] See n. 21 above.
[34] The provisions relating to jurisdiction in Arts. 7 and 8 of the Hague Convention do so only as conditions for recognition and enforcement; they do not themselves confer international jurisdiction.
[35] See n. 22 above.
[36] Dicey and Morris, p. 763.
[37] See n. 23 above.
[38] Kaye, p. 1432, n. 5.

Wolf v. *Cox*[39] for these bilateral arrangements to remain in effect. The better view is probably that they are a "convention" for these purposes.[40]

11.10   *Recognition and enforcement.* Where a maintenance order has been made in another country which is both a Contracting State to the 1968 Convention and a Hague Convention country for the purposes of Part I of the Maintenance Orders (Reciprocal Enforcement) Act 1972,[41] the maintenance creditor has a choice, preserved by Article 57 of the 1968 Convention,[42] as to which system to use for the enforcement of the order in England. Similarly, an order made in Ireland may be enforced in England under the 1982 Act or, if this remains in force,[43] under the modified version of Part I of the 1972 Act. The 1982 Act does not affect the provisions for enforcement of maintenance orders as between different parts of the United Kingdom, which continue to be governed by the Maintenance Orders Act 1950.[44]

B. Enforcement under the 1982 Act

1. Registration in the magistrates' court

11.11   The provisions of Title III of the 1968 Convention apply to the recognition and enforcement of maintenance orders as well as to other judgments.[45] As regards the United Kingdom, the Convention contains certain provisions which relate exclusively to maintenance orders, which are dealt with separately from other judgments. In England, enforcement is carried out after registration of the maintenance order in a magistrates' court, although, as will be seen, the order may then be re-registered in the High Court.

Transmission. Article 32 of the 1968 Convention provides that an application for the enforcement of a maintenance order in England is to be made to a magistrates' court on the transmission by the Secretary of State.[46] This provision is duplicated in the 1982 Act[47] and reflects the existing practice under Part I of the Maintenance

---

[39] [1976] E.C.R. 1759, discussed at para. 25.36 below.
[40] Dicey and Morris, p. 763; Collins, p. 123. See Vienna Convention on the Law of Treaties, Cmnd. 7964, Art. XX.
[41] See para. 11.25 below.
[42] The precise extent to which the 1968 Convention leaves the Hague Convention unaffected may be a question of some difficulty: see paras. 33.16 *et seq.* below, particularly the cases cited at n. 37.
[43] See para. 11.09 above.
[44] 1982 Act, ss.18(3)(*a*) and 18(5)(*a*), paras. 41.20 and 41.23 below.
[45] See chap. 10 above and chaps. 25 to 29 below.
[46] Para. 28.09 below.
[47] s.5(1), para. 40.12 below.

Orders (Reciprocal Enforcement) Act 1972.[48] It has the considerable advantage of avoiding the necessity for a maintenance creditor
in another Contracting State to instruct a solicitor in England to
make the application on her behalf for the registration of the maintenance order. If, however, such a solicitor is instructed, it seems
that he cannot submit the application to the magistrates' court himself, but must submit it to the Secretary of State for transmission to
the magistrates' court. The Secretary of State for this purpose is the
Home Secretary.[49]

Local jurisdiction. Which particular local court has jurisdiction to   **11.12**
entertain an application for the enforcement of a maintenance order
is governed by the second paragraph of Article 32.[50] This provides
that jurisdiction is to be determined by reference to the place of
domicile of the party against whom enforcement is sought, or, if
that person is not domiciled in the Contracting State in which
enforcement is sought, by reference to the place of enforcement.[51]
In its application to England, this provision is supplemented by
rules of court,[52] which require the justices' clerk[53] to take such
steps as he thinks fit for the purpose of ascertaining whether the
payer under the order to which the application relates is residing
within the jurisdiction of the court and to consider any information
he possesses as to the nature and location of the payer's assets.[54]
If he is satisfied that the payer is not resident within the jurisdiction
of the court, he must do one of two things. Either he must return
the application to the Secretary of State, with a statement of such
information as he possesses as to the whereabouts of the payer and
the nature and location of his assets,[55] or, if the payer is not resident
within the jurisdiction of the court but has assets there, he may
register the order.[56] In the latter case, however, if he is of the
opinion that the payer is resident in the jurisdiction of another

---

[48] 1972 Act, s.6(2).
[49] The department which handles questions of reciprocal enforcement of maintenance orders is C(2) Division, Home Office, Queen Anne's Gate, London SW1H
9AT; telephone 01–273 3000.
[50] Para. 28.09 below.
[51] See the commentary on this provision at para. 28.12 below. See also 1982 Act,
s. 15(3), para. 40.42 below, which enables anything which is to be done by a
particular magistrates' court to be done by another magistrates' court for the
same petty sessions area.
[52] The Magistrates' Courts (Civil Jurisdiction and Judgments Act 1982) Rules
1986, (S.I. 1986 No. 1982), referred to hereafter as the "1986 Rules."
[53] The justices' clerk is the "prescribed officer" referred to in s.5(2) of the 1982
Act: 1986 Rules, r. 3.
[54] 1986 Rules, r. 4(2).
[55] 1986 Rules, r. 4(3).
[56] 1986 Rules, r. 4(4).

magistrates' court in England and Wales, he may return the application to the Secretary of State instead of registering the order.[57] The rules of court also enable the justices' clerk to transfer a registered maintenance order to another magistrates' court with jurisdiction over the payer,[58] or, if the court no longer has jurisdiction over the payer, to cancel the registration and refer the matter back to the Secretary of State.[59]

11.13 *Registration.* On receiving an application for registration of a maintenance order under Article 31 of the 1968 Convention, the justices' clerk is required to consider it and, unless he refuses it for one of the reasons referred to below, to register it for the purposes of enforcement.[60] In considering the application, he must take into account the documents sent to him which are mentioned in Articles 46 and 47 of the 1968 Convention[61] and he has the powers conferred by Article 48[62] to dispense with the production of these documents, to specify a time for their production, to accept equivalent documents or to call for translations.

11.14 *Refusal to register.* The justices' clerk may refuse to register a maintenance order on the basis that the court lacks local jurisdiction[63] or on one of the grounds specified in Articles 27 and 28 of the 1968 Convention. These grounds are discussed in detail elsewhere,[64] but it should be noted that the ground under Article 27(4) is particularly relevant in the context of maintenance orders ancillary to status proceedings. An order may be refused recognition and enforcement on this ground if, in order to arrive at its judgment, the court of origin decided a preliminary question concerning the status or legal capacity of natural persons, rights in property arising out of a matrimonial relationship, wills or succession, in a way that conflicts with a rule of English private international law, unless the same result would have been reached if English rules of private international law had been applied. In addition to the grounds

---

[57] 1986 Rules, r. 4(4), proviso. In order strictly to comply with the terms of the second paragraph of Art. 32, it may be that he should be required to do this if the payer is domiciled elsewhere in the U.K. as a whole; but this is not provided for in the Rules.

[58] 1986 Rules, r. 8.

[59] 1986 Rules, r. 9.

[60] 1968 Convention, Art. 34, para. 28.22 below; 1982 Act, ss.5(2) and 5(3) para. 40.12 below; 1986 Rules, r. 4(1). He may also register only part of the order: Art. 42 para. 28.71 below.

[61] Paras. 29.01 *et seq.* below. The rules of evidence in the 1982 Act, s.11 (para. 40.32 below) and in the 1986 Rules, r. 13, apply for this purpose.

[62] Para. 29.20 below.

[63] The mechanism for determining local jurisdiction under the 1986 Rules, rr. 4(2) to 4(4) is described above.

[64] See paras. 10.26–10.43 above and the passages referred to therein.

under Articles 27 and 28, the application may also be refused on certain other subsidiary grounds.[65]

2. Notifications

Applicant's address. Article 33 of the 1968 Convention[66] requires **11.15** the applicant to give an address for the service of process within the jurisdiction of the court applied to, or, if national law does not provide for the furnishing of such an address, to appoint a representative *ad litem*. In relation to maintenance orders, English law apparently makes no provision for the applicant to furnish an address for service within the court's jurisdiction[67] and, although the Schlosser Report envisaged that the justices' clerk would be appointed as the representative *ad litem*,[68] no provision to that effect has been made in the implementing legislation.

Decision on the application. Once the justices' clerk has decided **11.16** whether or not to register the maintenance order, he must give notice of his decision to the applicant.[69] If his decision is to register the order, he must also give notice to the payer[70] and to the Secretary of State.[71] If the order is registered, and the justices' clerk is of the opinion that the order, or part of it, is one which would be appropriate for enforcement in the High Court, he is required to notify the applicant accordingly and to notify him of the possibility of making an application for the order to be re-registered in the High Court.[72] The clerk is also required to take reasonable steps to notify the maintenance creditor of the available means of enforcement of the order.[73]

Change of payer's address. The payer under a registered order is obliged to notify the justices' clerk of any change of address, and he is guilty of an offence if, without reasonable excuse, he fails to do so.[74]

---

[65] *Ibid.* These grounds are not referred to in the 1986 Rules, r. 4(1), but arise by operation of the Convention itself.

[66] Para. 28.16 below; see also *Carron* v. *Federal Republic of Germany* [1987] 1 C.M.L.R. 838, discussed at para. 28.20 below.

[67] The 1986 Rules, rr. 4(5) and 4(6), refer to "the address provided by the applicant," but do not require that any such address should be within the court's jurisdiction.

[68] Schlosser, para. 218 (para. A1.518 below).

[69] 1968 Convention, Art. 35, para. 28.28 below; 1986 Rules, rr. 4(5), 4(6)(c).

[70] 1968 Convention, Art. 36, para. 28.30 below; 1986 Rules, r. 4(6)(b).

[71] 1986 Rules, r. 4(6)(a).

[72] 1986 Rules, r. 4(7). Re-registration in the High Court is carried out under the Maintenance Orders Act 1958: see para. 11.20 below.

[73] 1986 Rules, r. 6(3).

[74] 1982 Act, s.5(7): see para. 40.12 below.

3. Appeals

11.17   If the justices' clerk registers the order, the payer may appeal against that decision. His time for doing so is one month from the service on him of the notice of the clerk's decision or, if he is domiciled in another Contracting State, two months from that date.[75] Similarly, if the justices' clerk refuses to register the order, the applicant may appeal[76] and it seems that the time for doing so is six months from the date of the clerk's decision.[77] The appeal is made by way of a complaint to the court in which the order is registered, or in which the application for its registration has been refused.[78] A summons is issued addressed to the respondent[79] and the complaint is determined after an *inter partes* hearing before the court. The decision made by the court may itself be appealed on a point of law by way of case stated to the High Court,[80] and the application for the justices to state a case must be made within 21 days from the day the decision was made.[81] There is no appeal from the decision of the High Court.[82]

4. Effect of registration

11.18   *Order equated with English order.* Subject to four matters, a maintenance order which is registered in the magistrates' court under the 1982 Act is to be treated for the purposes of its enforcement as if it had been originally made by that court.[83] The order may be enforced by the methods available for the enforcement of a magis-

---

[75] 1968 Convention, Art. 36: see para. 28.30 below.
[76] 1968 Convention, Art. 40, para. 28.63 below.
[77] Magistrates' Courts Act 1980, s.127.
[78] 1986 Rules, r. 5. The appeal may be made to another magistrates' court for the same petty sessions area: 1982 Act, s. 15(3), para. 40.42 below.
[79] Magistrates' Courts Act 1980, s.51. The procedure on the complaint is that prescribed by Part II of that Act. In the absence of an address for service within the jurisdiction of the court (see above) it seems that the summons must be served on the applicant (the respondent to the appeal) at the address provided by him. If this address is overseas, attention should be paid to the means of service permitted: see chap. 4 above.
[80] 1982 Act, s.6(3), para. 40.18 below. The appeal is under s.111 of the Magistrates' Courts Act 1980. This appeal is to be heard by a single judge or a Divisional Court of the Family Division, under R.S.C., Ord. 56, r. 5(2)(b). Note that the relevant amendment introduced by R.S.C. (Amendment) (No. 2) 1988 (S.I. 1988 No. 1340), has been omitted from the supplement to the *Supreme Court Practice*.
[81] Magistrates' Courts Act 1980, s.111(2).
[82] 1968 Convention, Art. 37, second para., and Art. 41, paras. 28.38 and 28.69 below.
[83] 1982 Act, s.5(4), para. 40.12 below.

trates' court maintenance order[84] and it may be re-registered in the
High Court for the purposes of its enforcement.[85] The assimilation
of the registered order to the status of an order made by the magistrates' court also means that arrears due under the order are
recoverable not only back to the date of registration, but also, if
necessary, back to the date of the original order. It is questionable,
however, whether the court's general powers to remit arrears[86] may
be exercised in respect of a maintenance order registered under the
1982 Act; this may well be inconsistent with Article 31 of the 1968
Convention.[87]

The four respects in which the position of a maintenance order **11.19**
registered under the 1982 Act is not treated as if it were an order
made originally by the magistrates' court are as follows:

(i) The order cannot be re-registered in another part of the
United Kingdom by virtue of its registration in England.[88]
Instead, the original foreign order may be registered
directly in Scotland or Northern Ireland.

(ii) A maintenance order registered under the 1982 Act is subject to the provisions of Article 39 of the 1968 Convention,[89] which imposes restrictions on the enforcement of
the order if an appeal is pending or if the time for appeal is
still running.[90] This important provision is discussed
further below.

(iii) Whatever the currency of the original order, it is payable
in England in sterling;[91] and even if interest is payable
under the original order, it is not payable under the registered order, unless it is re-registered in the High Court.[92]

(iv) Restrictions may be imposed by rules of court on the man-

---

[84] 1982 Act, s.5(5A), which as regards England and Wales, replaces s.5(6) with
effect from April 1, 1989: see para. 40.12 below. The means of enforcement
available in respect of the order are summarised at para. 11.28 below.
[85] Maintenance Orders Act 1958, s.1. By s.1(4) of that Act, maintenance orders
registered under the 1982 Act are expressly brought within the scheme of re-
registration.
[86] Magistrates' Courts Act 1980, s.95.
[87] See para. 28.01 below.
[88] Orders registered under the 1982 Act are excluded from the scope of its intra-
U.K. scheme of enforcement, by s.18(7) (para. 41.13 below); and they are not
included in the list of orders to which Part II of the Maintenance Orders Act
1950 applies: s.16(2) of that Act.
[89] 1982 Act, s.5(5); para. 40.12 below.
[90] Para. 28.55 below.
[91] 1982 Act, s.8, para. 40.24 below; see para. 11.22 below.
[92] 1982 Act, ss.5(5) and 7(4), paras. 40.12 and 40.20 below; see para. 11.22 below.

ner in which and the conditions subject to which an order may be enforced.[93] Notably, the rules provide that the sums payable under the registered order must be paid through the clerk of the court, leaving no discretion for the sums to be made payable direct from the payer to the creditor.[94]

11.20 *Re-registration in the High Court.* An order which has been registered in a magistrates' court under the 1982 Act may be re-registered in the High Court under the Maintenance Orders Act 1958 and enforced as if it were an order of the High Court. This procedure is particularly relevant where it is intended to enforce a maintenance order against the payer's assets, whether or not the payer is domiciled in England, or where the order requires the payment of a lump sum in the nature of maintenance or the charging of property.[95]

The application for re-registration is made to the magistrates' court in which the order is registered by any person entitled to receive the payments under the order[96] "either directly or through another person or for transmission to another person."[97] In effect, therefore, the application may be made either by the justices' clerk, who is entitled to receive the payments directly,[98] or by the maintenance creditor.[99] The justices' clerk may not make an application unless he is requested to do so in writing by the maintenance creditor, but he must comply with any such request unless it appears unreasonable to him to do so.[1] If the justices clerk makes an application in compliance with such a request, the risk as to costs is borne by the maintenance creditor.[2]

The court has a discretion whether or not to grant the application.[3] If the application is granted, it has the effect of preventing

---

[93] 1982 Act, s.5(5), para. 40.12 below. The rule-making power is in ss.48(2) and 48(3), para. 44.38 below.

[94] 1986 Rules, r. 6.

[95] See para. 17.35 below; *cf.* Maintenance Orders Act 1958, ss.2(3A) and 2(3B), Maintenance Orders (Reciprocal Enforcement) Act 1972, ss.9(1A) and 21(1) and 21(2).

[96] Maintenance Orders Act 1958, s.2(3); Magistrates' Courts (Maintenance Orders Act 1958) Rules 1959: (S.I. 1959 No. 3), amended by (S.I. 1971 No. 809), (S.I. 1977 No. 1890), (S.I. 1980 No. 1896) and (S.I. 1986 No. 1962). As to the time when the application may be made, see the discussion of Art. 39 of the 1968 Convention, below.

[97] Maintenance Orders Act 1958, s.21(2).

[98] 1986 Rules, r. 6.

[99] The justices' clerk is under certain duties to notify a maintenance creditor of her rights to make such an application: 1986 Rules, rr. 4(7) and 6(3).

[1] Maintenance Orders Act 1958, s.20(1).

[2] *Ibid.*

[3] Maintenance Orders Act 1958, s.2(3).

any further steps being taken to enforce the order in the magistrates' court.[4] A certified copy of the order is sent to the High Court[5] for registration.[6] Once the order has been registered in the High Court it is enforceable in all respects as if it had been made in the High Court, but not by any other means.[7]

Article 39 of the 1968 Convention. In the context of maintenance **11.21** orders, this Article[8] precludes the taking of "measures of enforcement," other than protective measures against the payer's property, during the time specified for an appeal against the registration of the order and until any such appeal has been determined. It follows that, until the expiry of that period, no warrant of commitment, attachment of earnings order or other means of finally enforcing the maintenance order may be issued, whether in the magistrates' court or, after re-registration there, in the High Court. The effect of this Article is discussed in some detail in Chapter 10,[9] to which reference should be made.

During the time for appealing or pending the determination of an appeal, however, the power to take such protective measures as may be available arises automatically by reason of the initial registration by the justices' clerk. Such protective measures are only generally available in aid of the enforcement of a maintenance order if it is registered in the High Court.[10] The question arises whether an application for re-registration of the order amounts to a measure of enforcement for the purposes of Article 39. If it does, an application for re-registration could not be made until after the time for appealing had expired or an appeal had been determined. It is suggested, though, that this is not the case and that an application for re-registration may be made during this period.[11] In appropriate circumstances, the registration of the order in the magistrates' court, followed by its immediate re-registration in the High Court, would enable the maintenance creditor to have the benefit of the protective measures available in the High Court to prevent the dis-

---

[4] *Ibid.*, s.2(4).

[5] *Ibid.*, s.2(4)(c). The order may be sent to the Principal Registry or to a district registry: R.S.C., Ord. 105, r. 7(2)(b).

[6] *Ibid.*, s.2(5); R.S.C., Ord. 105, r. 9. See para. 11.22 below as to the recovery of interest under an order registered in the High Court.

[7] *Ibid.*, ss.3(1) and 3(4).

[8] Para. 28.55 below.

[9] Paras. 10.20 *et seq.* above.

[10] It may be, though, that a Mareva injunction could be obtained under s.25 of the 1982 Act (para. 43.03 below) in the High Court to protect the execution of a maintenance order which had not been registered there.

[11] *Contra*, Home Office Circular 83/1986, Notes for Guidance, para. 6.

sipation or removal of the payer's assets pending an appeal against the registration of the order or the determination of that appeal.

11.22   *Currency.* A foreign maintenance order registered under the 1982 Act is payable only in sterling, the amounts payable being converted at the date of registration. This is the effect of section 8 of the 1982 Act and reference should be made to the commentary on that section.[12]

Interest. Interest is not recoverable on maintenance orders registered in the magistrates' court,[13] even if interest is recoverable on the sums payable under the maintenance order pursuant to the law of its country of origin, and even if the order itself stipulates that the payer is required to pay interest. Interest may, however, be recovered if the order is re-registered in the High Court. If, on a successful application to the magistrates' court for the order to be re-registered in the High Court, the applicant shows that interest is payable under the order in its country of origin at a particular rate, and from a particular date or time, the court issues a certificate to that effect and sends it with the certified copy of the order to the High Court.[14] The certificate is then registered with the order and interest is payable in accordance with it.[15]

11.23   *Payment.* Payment under an order registered in the magistrates' court is made to the justices' clerk as directed by him. He sends the payment by post to the court of origin or to such other person or authority as that court or the Secretary of State may from time to time direct.[16] As already observed, he has no power to order the payer to make payment direct to the creditor. If the sums payable under the order are in arrears, the justices clerk may (and in some cases must) proceed in his own name to recover them.[17] The means of enforcement of a registered maintenance order are discussed below.

Variation and revocation. If an order which is registered in a magistrates' court is varied or revoked by a court which is competent to do so in a Contracting State,[18] the registration is altered accordingly.[19]

---

[12] Para. 40.25 below.
[13] 1982 Act, s.7(4), para. 40.20 below.
[14] Maintenance Orders Act 1958, s.2A (see para. 47.14 below). See para. 11.20 above.
[15] *Ibid.*, ss.2A(3)–2A(5).
[16] 1986 Rules, r. 6(1).
[17] 1986 Rules, r. 6(2).
[18] The court which is competent to vary the order may be different from that which made the order originally: see para. 11.06 above.
[19] 1986 Rules, r. 7.

C. Enforcement under other Statutory Schemes

The enforcement of maintenance orders made in other Contracting **11.24**
States to the 1968 Convention is only permissible under a scheme
other than that provided by that Convention and the 1982 Act if
that scheme gives effect to an international convention. It is not
therefore proposed to consider the systems of enforcement at common law, under the Maintenance (Facilities Enforcement) Act
1920[20] or, as regards reciprocating countries,[21] under Part I of the
Maintenance Orders (Reciprocal Enforcement) Act 1972. Similarly, the United Nations convention, given effect by Part II of that
Act,[22] does not provide for the enforcement of foreign maintenance
orders and is not considered further here.

1. Hague Convention[23]

Maintenance orders made in other Hague Convention countries[24] **11.25**
may be enforced in England and Wales under that Convention by a
procedure similar to that which has been adopted for the purpose of
the 1968 Convention and 1982 Act. Such orders are governed by a
modified version of Part I of the Maintenance Orders Act 1972.[25] If
the Secretary of State receives a maintenance order from abroad, he
forwards it to the justices' clerk for registration.[26] The grounds on
which registration of the order may or must be refused are, however, rather different from those which apply under the 1968 Convention;[27] notably, the extent to which the English court is able to
review the jurisdiction of the court of origin is wider under the
Hague Convention.[28] An appeal against the registration or the refusal to register the order may be brought by either party within one
month. The order may be re-registered in the High Court for
enforcement there.[29]

---

[20] See para. 11.07 above.
[21] These are mainly Commonwealth countries: see para. 11.07 above.
[22] See para. 11.08 above.
[23] Hague Convention of October 2, 1973 on the Recognition and Enforcement of
Decisions Relating to Maintenance Obligations, Cmnd. 7939.
[24] Czechoslovakia, Denmark, Federal Republic of Germany, Finland, France,
Italy, Luxembourg, Netherlands, Norway, Portugal, Spain, Sweden, Switzerland and Turkey.
[25] Reciprocal Enforcement of Maintenance Orders (Hague Convention Countries)
Order 1979, (S.I. 1979 No. 1317), amended by (S.I. 1981 Nos. 837, 1545 and
1674), (S.I. 1983 Nos. 885 and 1523) and (S.I. 1987 No. 1282), (the "1979
Order"), Sched. 3. Effect has not been given to Danish and Spanish ratification.
[26] 1979 Order, Sched. 3, s.6(2).
[27] 1979 Order, Sched. 3, ss.6(5) to 6(7).
[28] 1979 Order, Sched. 3, s.6(7); *cf.* 1968 Convention, Art. 28, third para.,
para. 27.62 below.
[29] Maintenance Orders Act 1958: *cf.* para. 11.20 above.

In view of the similarities between the systems available under the 1968 Convention and the 1982 Act on one hand, and the Hague Convention and 1972 Act on the other, the matters which are likely to be most relevant in deciding which system to choose are the different grounds on which registration may be refused, the fact that jurisdiction under the 1982 Act to register the order may in some circumstances be based on the presence of assets rather than the payer's residence within the territorial jurisdiction of the court,[30] and the fact that the maintenance creditor has the right under the 1968 Convention to take protective measures during the pendency of an appeal.[31]

2. Republic of Ireland

11.26   A different modified version of Part I of the Maintenance Orders (Reciprocal Enforcement) Act 1972[32] gives effect to bilateral arrangements between the United Kingdom and the Republic of Ireland. It has already been observed that there may be some doubt as to whether those arrangements survive the accession of Ireland to the 1968 Convention.[33] The grounds on which registration of a maintenance order may be refused under these arrangements are narrower than under either the Hague Convention or the 1968 Convention.[34] As with the arrangements implementing the Hague Convention, jurisdiction to register the order may not be founded on the presence of the payer's assets.[35]

3. Scotland and Northern Ireland

11.27   Maintenance orders made in other parts of the United Kingdom are enforceable in England under the Maintenance Orders Act 1950. The maintenance creditor applies to the court which made the maintenance order for a certified copy of the order to be sent to the appropriate court in the other part of the United Kingdom.[36] As regards orders to be enforced in England, if the order was made by

---

[30] The presence of assets within the territorial jurisdiction of the court now enables a maintenance order made in a reciprocating country to be registered in a magistrates' court under Part I of the 1972 Act, by reason of the amendments made by Part III of Sched. 11 to the 1982 Act, para. 47.16 below. Those amendments, however, have not been carried over into the 1979 Order and do not, therefore, apply to orders made in Hague Convention countries.
[31] See para. 11.21 above.
[32] Reciprocal Enforcement of Maintenance Orders (Republic of Ireland) Order 1974, (S.I. 1974 No. 2140), (the "1974 Order"), Sched. 2.
[33] See para. 11.09 above.
[34] 1974 Order, Sched. 2, s.6(5).
[35] The amendments referred to in n. 30 above have also not been carried over into the 1974 Order.
[36] Maintenance Orders Act 1950 (the "1950 Act"), ss.17(1) and 17(2).

the Court of Session or the Supreme Court of Judicature of Northern Ireland, it is sent to the High Court, and if it was made by any other court, it is sent to the magistrates' court for the district in which the defendant appears to be.[37] The copy order is then registered in that court[38] and notice sent to the court in Scotland or Northern Ireland which made the order.[39] An order registered in a magistrates' court may be re-registered in the High Court under the Maintenance Orders Act 1958.[40] A registered order may be enforced in all respects as if it had been made by the court in which it is registered.[41] Interest is not recoverable in respect of an order registered in the magistrates' court[42]; but interest may be recoverable under an order which is registered in the High Court under the 1950 Act[43] or which has been registered in the magistrates' court and then re-registered in the High Court under the 1958 Act.[44]

D. Means of Enforcement

A maintenance order registered in the magistrates' court may be enforced by means of an attachment of earnings order.[45] Alternatively, it may be enforced by means of a warrant of distress on the payer's goods or a warrant of commitment committing the defaulter to prison,[46] but these warrants may only be issued on a complaint to the magistrates' court,[47] and subject to certain further restrictions. As has been seen, if the means of enforcement in the magistrates' court are inadequate, the order may be re-registered in the High Court.[48] **11.28**

If the maintenance order is re-registered in the High Court, it may be enforced as if it were an order made by that court. Some of the means of enforcing orders in the Family Division are subject not only to the Rules of the Supreme Court, but also the Matrimonial Causes Rules. A payer under a maintenance order may be summoned to appear on a judgment summons to be examined as to his means[49] and he may be committed to prison for failure to make

---

[37] 1950 Act, s.17(3).
[38] 1950 Act, s.17(4); R.S.C., Ord. 105, r. 5(1); Maintenance Orders Act (Summary Jurisdiction) Rules 1950 (the "1950 Rules"), r. 7.
[39] 1950 Act, s.17(5); R.S.C., Ord. 105, r. 5(3); 1950 Rules, r. 7.
[40] *Cf.* para. 11.20 above.
[41] 1950 Act, s.18(1).
[42] 1950 Act, s.18(1A).
[43] 1950 Act, s.18(1B).
[44] 1950 Act, s.18(1A), 1958 Act, s.2A.
[45] Attachment of Earnings Act 1971.
[46] Magistrates' Courts Act 1980, s.76(1).
[47] Magistrates' Courts Act 1980, s.93.
[48] Para. 11.20 above.
[49] Matrimonial Causes Rules 1977 ("M.C.R."), rr. 87–89.

payment.[50] Orders may also be enforced by the following means: attachment of earnings;[51] charging order;[52] garnishment;[53] writ of *fieri facias*;[54] or the appointment of a receiver.[55] The payer may also be orally examined and ordered to produce books and documents. A debt by way of arrears under a maintenance order probably may not support a bankruptcy claim,[56] but a lump sum is a sum provable in a bankruptcy.[57]

E. Enforcing English Maintenance Orders Abroad

1. Enforcement under the 1968 Convention

11.29   A maintenance order made by a court in England may be enforced in the other Contracting States to the 1968 Convention, whether or not the English court's jurisdiction to make the order arose under the 1968 Convention. The order may be enforced under the 1968 Convention not only in the Contracting State where the payer is domiciled, but also in any such state in which he has assets.[58] No provision is made in the 1968 Convention for any central authority in the Contracting States to assist in the transmission of the order to the court by which it is to be enforced, but, as regards a maintenance order made in the magistrates' court, the Home Office is willing to assist maintenance creditors on an informal basis.[59] Alternatively, the maintenance creditor may instruct a lawyer in the foreign country to act for her in the enforcement of the order. If she is legally aided in England, she is entitled to legal aid in the other Contracting States to the 1968 Convention, at least for the initial stages of the enforcement procedure.[60]

If the maintenance order has been made in England, a person wishing to obtain a copy of the order for the purposes of its recognition or enforcement in another Contracting State may do so on

---

[50] Debtors Act 1869, s.5; Administration of Justice Act 1970, s.11; R.S.C., Ord. 45; M.C.R., r. 90.
[51] Attachment of Earnings Act 1971; M.C.R., r. 86(5).
[52] Charging Orders Act 1979; R.S.C., Ord. 50.
[53] R.S.C., Ord. 49.
[54] R.S.C., Ords. 30 and 51.
[55] R.S.C., Ord. 48.
[56] See Insolvency Rules 1986, (S.I. 1986 No. 1925), rule 6.9.6.
[57] *Curtis* v. *Curtis* [1969] 1 W.L.R. 422.
[58] 1968 Convention, Art. 32, second para.: para. 28.09 below.
[59] Home Office Circular 83/1986, para. 6. See para. 11.11, n. 49 above. If the order has been made or varied in the exercise of jurisdiction under Art. 5(2) of the 1968 Convention, the Home Office should already have been sent information concerning the application for the order: see para. 11.05 above.
[60] 1968 Convention, Art. 44: para. 28.81 below. See also para. 12.13 below.

application to the court which made the order.[61] Additionally, if the order was made in the magistrates' court, the applicant may obtain a certificate giving particulars of payments made and arrears accrued under the order.[62] If the order was made pursuant to the exercise of a magistrates' court's jurisdiction under Article 5(2) of the 1968 Convention,[63] the justices' clerk is under a duty to provide a certified copy of the order and other relevant documentation to the complainant, whether or not she makes an application for that purpose.[64]

2. Enforcement under the Hague Convention

Instead of using the system of enforcement under the 1968 Con- **11.30** vention, a maintenance creditor under a maintenance order made in England who wishes to enforce it in another Hague Convention country may use the system of enforcement under that convention.[65] Here too there is no requirement in the convention for the states which are parties to it to provide a central authority to assist the maintenance creditor, but the assistance given by the Home Office in such a case is more formal in character. The order is sent to the Home Office with other prescribed information, with a view to its onward transmission to the appropriate authorities in the other Hague Convention country.[66] Other factors which are relevant in deciding which system to use have already been discussed.[67]

3. Enforcement in other parts of the United Kingdom

The system of re-registration of maintenance orders in other **11.31** parts of the United Kingdom under the Maintenance Orders Act 1950 has already been described.[68]

---

[61] 1982 Act, s.12, para. 40.36 below; 1986 Rules, r. 12; R.S.C., Ord. 71, r. 36; C.C.R., Ord. 35, r. 3.
[62] 1986 Rules, r. 12(5).
[63] See paras. 11.04–11.05 above.
[64] 1986 Rules, r. 10(6). Similar provisions apply as regards an order for the variation or revocation of a maintenance order: 1986 Rules, r. 11(5). The documents provided are those required for the purposes of Arts. 46 and 47 of the 1968 Convention: paras. 29.01 *et seq.* below.
[65] See para. 11.25 above.
[66] See Reciprocal Enforcement of Maintenance Orders (Hague Convention Countries) Order 1979, Sched. 3, s.2.
[67] Para. 11.25 above.
[68] Para. 11.27 above.

CHAPTER 12

LEGAL AID

1. Introduction

12.01　Three types of publicly-funded assistance are available in England and Wales[1] in connection with civil disputes. Each is subject to detailed conditions governing the persons who are eligible and the scope of assistance offered. First, *legal advice and assistance* may be provided on matters of English law and its application, under the so-called "Green Form scheme." Secondly, *assistance by way of representation* (ABWOR) may be provided in connection with certain proceedings before courts and tribunals. Thirdly, *legal aid* may be granted in connection with most civil proceedings.

The Legal Aid Act 1988, which came into force on April 1, 1989, made a number of changes in this area of the law and transferred the administration of legal aid from the Law Society to a new statutory body, the Legal Aid Board. This chapter is confined to a brief summary of the three systems and a discussion of those aspects of legal aid which are of particular relevance to litigation with a European dimension.[2]

2. Legal advice and assistance; Assistance by way of representation

12.02　*Green Form scheme.* Under this scheme, a person who is financially eligible may be given preliminary advice and assistance on the application of English law to any particular circumstances which

---

[1] The systems of legal aid available in other Contracting States to the 1968 Convention are summarised in chaps. 48 to 58 below, at para. 74. See also *Replies made by governments to the questionnaire on legal aid and advice* (Council of Europe, 1978).

[2] The legislation concerning all three systems, as well as legal aid in criminal proceedings and juvenile courts and under the duty solicitor scheme, is to be collected in the *Legal Aid Handbook 1989*, to be published by the Legal Aid Board. As regards civil proceedings, further information may also be obtained from Area Legal Aid offices.

have arisen in relation to that person and as to the steps which that person might appropriately take in those circumstances.[3] The scheme does not cover the giving of advice in connection with proceedings outside England and Wales, nor on the application of foreign law, nor does it extend to representation before a court or tribunal. The cost of the advice which may be given in the first instance is limited and may be exceeded only with the approval of the legal aid authorities.[4] A person resident outside England and Wales may make a postal application to a solicitor for advice and assistance, provided that this has been authorised in the particular instance by the legal aid authorities, who must be satisfied that it is reasonable in the circumstances.[5]

Assistance by way of representation. This scheme enables a person **12.03** who is financially eligible to receive assistance in the conduct of certain proceedings. Assistance is only available with the approval of the legal aid authorities and the proceedings to which it applies are domestic proceedings in the magistrates' court, proceedings before a Mental Health Review Tribunal and proceedings before a board of prison visitors.[6]

Financial eligibility. A person is financially eligible to receive **12.04** assistance under the Green Form scheme if his disposable capital does not exceed £850 and if either his disposable income does not exceed £122 per week or he is in receipt of certain social security benefits.[7] The calculation of disposable capital and disposable income is carried out by the solicitor to whom the person has applied, in accordance with detailed regulations.[8] The client may be required to make a contribution to the cost of assistance provided to him, depending again on his resources. Similar financial conditions apply in the case of assistance under the ABWOR scheme.[9]

3. Legal Aid

The most important form of publicly-funded assistance, **12.05** especially in the context of litigation with a European dimension, is legal aid. This system enables a person of limited financial means to

---

[3] Legal Aid Act 1988, s.8(1). See also the Legal Advice and Assistance Regulations 1989, (S.I. 1989 No. 340).
[4] Legal Aid Act 1988, s.10.
[5] Legal Advice and Assistance Regulations 1989, above, reg. 15.
[6] Legal Advice and Assistance (Scope) Regulations 1989 (S.I. 1989 No. 550).
[7] Legal Aid Act 1988, s.9. The benefits referred to are those by way of income support or family credit.
[8] Legal Advice and Assistance Regulations 1989, above, reg. 9 and Sched. 2.
[9] *Ibid.*

prosecute or defend civil proceedings in England and Wales at little or no cost to himself. The legal aid fund, which is financed by central government, meets the fees of solicitors and counsel, although a litigant may be required to contribute the costs either directly or by deduction from sums recovered by him in the proceedings. Legal aid is not automatically available; in addition to being financially eligible, the applicant must have a reasonable case on the merits.

Proceedings covered by legal aid

12.06   Although legal aid is available in respect of most civil proceedings in courts, and some tribunals, in England and Wales,[10] it is not available in connection with proceedings before courts in other countries, even if those courts have exclusive jurisdiction over the proceedings. If a question is referred to the European Court of Justice for a preliminary ruling in connection with proceedings in which a party is legally aided, legal aid may be extended to cover those proceedings.[11]

Application for legal aid

12.07   An application for legal aid must be made in writing to the Legal Aid Board.[12] The application should normally be in the prescribed form[13] and it must state the name of the solicitor selected by the applicant to act for him. It must also give information sufficient to enable the legal aid authorities to know the nature of the proceedings and the merits of the case, and to enable the applicant's resources to be assessed.

12.08   *Applicants resident outside the United Kingdom.* If the applicant is resident outside the United Kingdom, the application for legal aid must be made to the legal aid authorities in London.[14] If he cannot be present in the United Kingdom when his application is considered, special provisions apply as follows. These special provisions may be waived by the legal aid authorities if compliance with them would

---

[10] Legal Aid Act 1988, s. 14(1), Sched. 2. The proceedings for which legal aid may be granted are exhaustively defined.

[11] Civil Legal Aid (General) Regulations 1989, reg. 51(b)(vi); see para. 12.11. The European Court itself is able to offer some financial assistance to parties to proceedings before it: further information may be obtained from The Registry, European Court of Justice, L–2926 Luxembourg.

[12] The administration of civil legal aid was transferred from the Law Society to a new Legal Aid Board under the Legal Aid Act 1988.

[13] Civil Legal Aid (General) Regulations 1989, regs. 11–13. Forms are available from the legal aid offices; different forms are provided for different purposes.

[14] Civil Legal Aid (General) Regulations 1989, reg. 13. The application should be made to the Area Director, No. 14 (London West) Legal Aid Area, 29–37 Red Lion St., London WC1R 4PP; (tel: 01–405 6991).

cause serious difficulty, inconvenience or delay and if the application is otherwise in order.[15]

The application may be in English or French and it must be sworn by the applicant. If the applicant is resident in the Commonwealth or the Republic of Ireland, the swearing must take place before a justice of the peace or magistrate or any person for the time being authorised by law in the place where he is to administer an oath for any judicial or other legal purpose; or if the applicant is resident elsewhere, the swearing must take place before a consular officer in the service of the United Kingdom government, or any other person for the time being authorised to exercise the functions of such an officer or having authority to administer an oath in that place.[16]

Unless the application is made solely for certain purposes in connection with enforcing a foreign judgment or in connection with the abduction of children,[17] it must be accompanied by a statement in writing, signed by some responsible person who has knowledge of the facts, certifying that part of the application which relates to the applicant's disposable income and disposable capital.[18] These details should normally be stated in a special form which is available for that purpose.[19]

Conditions for grant of legal aid

Financial eligibility. A person is eligible for legal aid if his disposable income does not exceed £6035 per year, but, unless he is in receipt of certain social security benefits, a person may be refused legal aid if his disposable capital exceeds £6000 and it appears that he could afford to proceed without legal aid.[20] If the applicant's disposable income exceeds £2515 per year or his disposable capital exceeds £3000, he will ordinarily be required to make a contribution.[21] The applicant's resources will be assessed by an assessment officer of the Department of Social Security and the applicant may be required to attend for an interview. In assessing the applicant's disposable income and capital, the assessment officer will make certain allowances, notably to take account of the number and ages of the applicant's dependents.[22] The criteria for financial eligibility do not

12.09

---

[15] Civil Legal Aid (General) Regulations 1989, reg. 13(2).
[16] Civil Legal Aid (General) Regulations 1989, reg. 13(1)(b). As to taking oaths abroad generally, see para. 8.09 above.
[17] Civil Legal Aid (General) Regulations 1989, regs. 14 and 15; see para. 12.13 below.
[18] Civil Legal Aid (General) Regulations 1989, reg. 13(1)(c).
[19] Form L.1 (A). Other special forms apply to members of H.M. Forces.
[20] Civil Legal Aid (Assessment of Resources) Regulations 1989 (S.I. 1989 No. 338), reg. 4.
[21] *Ibid.*
[22] *Ibid.*, Sched. 2.

apply in respect of applicants for legal aid in connection with certain proceedings relating to the enforcement of foreign judgments or the abduction of children.[23]

Personal eligibility. Individuals are eligible for legal aid, regardless of their nationality, domicile or residence, but legal aid is not generally available to companies or other bodies of persons, whether incorporated or not.[24]

12.10 *Eligibility on the merits.* A person will not be granted legal aid in connection with any proceedings (except some proceedings for the enforcement of foreign judgments or in connection with the abduction of children)[25] unless he shows that he has reasonable grounds for taking, defending or being a party to the proceedings, and he may be refused legal aid if, in the particular circumstances of the case, it appears unreasonable that he should receive it or if it is more appropriate that he should receive assistance by way of representation.[26] In deciding whether it is reasonable for a person to be legally aided, the authorities will consider, among other matters, whether the benefit to be achieved by the successful pursuit of the matter would justify the cost of proceeding, although it is recognised that that test is not necessarily decisive.[27]

Grant of legal aid

12.11 If legal aid is granted, the legal aid authorities issue a certificiate in respect of the proceedings and the applicant becomes an "assisted person." The solicitor named in the certificate may then act for the assisted person in the knowledge that the legal aid fund will meet his reasonable fees and expenses in connection with the proceedings. The certificate will often contain a limitation on the steps which may be taken, in order that the legal aid authorities may review the case as it proceeds. Such limitations may be removed and certificates may be amended to cover aspects of the proceedings which would not normally be covered by legal aid.[28] An amendment to the certificate is required if legal aid is to be

---

[23] Civil Legal Aid (General) Regulations 1989, regs. 14 and 15; see para. 12.13 below.

[24] Legal Aid Act 1988, s. 2(10).

[25] Civil Legal Aid (General) Regulations 1989, regs. 14 and 15; see para. 12.13 below.

[26] Legal Aid Act 1988, s. 15(3). These criteria are further refined by the Civil Legal Aid (General) Regulations 1989, regs. 29 to 31 and 33. As regards ABWOR, see para. 12.03 above.

[27] See Notes for Guidance issued by the Legal Aid Board, in *Legal Aid Handbook 1989*.

[28] Civil Legal Aid (General) Regulations 1989, reg. 51.

extended to cover proceedings in the European Court of Justice on a reference for a preliminary ruling,[29] or for representation by an EEC lawyer.[30]

Obtaining authority for certain expenditure. If the conduct of the **12.12** proceedings requires the instruction of an expert or certain other steps of an unusual (or unusually expensive) nature, the solicitor may apply to the legal aid authorities to sanction the expenditure involved.[31] The decision whether to give prior authorisation in respect of such items of expenditure lies within the discretion of the legal aid authorities and each application is considered on its merits.

Obtaining prior authorisation to incur the cost of instructing an expert or taking other steps of an unusual or unusually expensive nature is likely to be particularly important in the context of litigation involving a European dimension. It would be wise, for example, for a solicitor acting for a legally aided party to obtain prior authorisation from the legal aid authorities for steps such as the obtaining of an expert opinion on foreign law,[32] the service of process outside the jurisdiction, especially if it is effected by a foreign lawyer or judicial officer instructed by the legally aided party,[33] or the taking of evidence outside the jurisdiction or before a special examiner.[34] Similarly, it may often be advisable to obtain prior authorisation for any unusual expenditure on the services of an interpreter or in obtaining translations.

Enforcement of foreign judgments; child abduction

Special rules apply to the grant of legal aid in connection with **12.13** three specific classes of proceedings. First, as regards an application for the registration of a judgment under section 4 of the Civil Juris-

---

[29] Civil Legal Aid (General) Regulations 1989, reg. 51(b)(vi). References for a preliminary ruling may be made under Art. 177 of the EEC Treaty or under the 1971 Protocol on Interpretation of the 1968 Convention: see chap. 36 below.

[30] Civil Legal Aid (General) Regulations 1989, reg. 51(b)(vii). An EEC lawyer is a person entitled to practice as an advocate, or the equivalent, in the other EEC countries (except, yet, Spain or Portugal). The term is defined by the European Communities (Services of Lawyers) Order 1978, Art. 2, (S.I. 1978 No. 1910), para. A2.51 below. Because legal aid only extends to proceedings in England and Wales, legally aided representation by such a lawyer is likely to occur very rarely in practice. The advice of a foreign lawyer does not involve "representation" by that lawyer.

[31] Civil Legal Aid (General) Regulations 1989, regs. 60 and 61. If the expenditure is not sanctioned in advance, the solicitor runs the risk that it will not be recoverable on taxation: reg. 63.

[32] See chap. 9 above on Foreign Law.

[33] See chap. 4 above on Service.

[34] See chap. 8 above on Evidence.

diction and Judgments Act 1982,[35] the applicant is entitled to legal aid without making any contribution and regardless of his financial resources, if he benefitted from complete or partial legal aid or exemption from costs or expenses in the country where the judgment was given.[36] Legal aid may not be refused on the grounds referred to in section 15(2) or 15(3) of the Legal Aid Act 1988.[37] The legal aid granted under this special provision does not extend to appealing against a refusal to register the judgment, nor to resisting an appeal against an order for registration, for which the applicant may apply for legal aid in the normal way.[38] Secondly, the same rules apply as regards appeals to a magistrates' court against the registration of, or the refusal to register, a maintenance order made in a Hague Convention country pursuant to the Maintenance Orders (Reciprocal Enforcement) Act 1972.[39] Thirdly, similar rules apply in connection with certain proceedings under the Child Abduction and Custody Act 1985.[40]

4. Transmission abroad of applications for legal aid

12.14   It has already been observed that legal aid is not available for proceedings in other countries. Nevertheless, a person may be eligible for legal aid under the schemes which are operated in other countries.[41] The United Kingdom is a party to the European Agreement on the Transmission of Applications for Legal Aid.[42] Under that convention, a person may submit his application in the state where he is habitually resident and it is then sent through the designated transmitting authority to the state in which legal aid is sought. The transmitting and receiving authority for the United Kingdom is the

---

[35] Para. 40.08 below. This section concerns judgments other than maintenance orders, which, under s. 5 of the 1982 Act, are to be enforced on transmission by the Secretary of State. Maintenance orders nonetheless fall within the terms of Art. 44 of the 1968 Convention: see next note.

[36] 1968 Convention, Art. 44, para. 28.81 below; Civil Legal Aid (General) Regulations 1989, reg. 15. See also paras. 10.14 above and 29.07 below as regards the documents proving the applicant's entitlement to legal aid in the country of origin.

[37] See para. 12.10 above.

[38] See para. 28.83 below.

[39] Civil Legal Aid (General) Regulations 1989, reg. 15(1)(a); the enforcement of maintenance orders under the Hague Convention is described at para. 11.30 above.

[40] Civil Legal Aid (General) Regulations 1989, reg. 14.

[41] If and when the Hague Convention on International Access to Justice of October 25, 1980 (Cmnd. 8281) comes into force in the U.K. legal aid will be available to U.K. nationals in other states which have ratified that convention, without regard to their nationality. See *Report of the House of Lords Select Committee on the European Communities: International Access to Justice* (Session 1987–88, Second Report). See also para. 12.01, n. 1 above.

[42] Cmnd. 7179, T.S. No. 39 (1978).

Legal Aid Board. The other signatory states to the Agreement are Austria, Belgium, Denmark, Finland, France, Greece, Italy, Luxembourg, Norway, Portugal, Spain, Sweden, and Turkey.[43]

Applications for transmission to other countries should be prepared on the same forms as are used for an application for legal aid by a person resident in the United Kingdom.[44] They should be submitted to the Legal Aid Head Office,[45] from which more detailed information may be obtained. The application may normally be in English, but a translation may be required, either of the application itself or of statements which accompany it. Notably, this is so as regards applications for transmission to France or Austria. Advice and assistance under the Green Form scheme is available, subject to financial eligibility, for the preparation of applications for transmission abroad under the European Agreement, including obtaining any necessary translations.

---

[43] It should be noted that of the countries with which this book is particularly concerned, the Federal Republic of Germany, the Netherlands and Ireland are not parties to this Agreement.

[44] See para. 12.07 above. Financial details should be included on Form L1 (Rev). See Notes for Guidance issued by the Legal Aid Board, in *Legal Aid Handbook 1989.*

[45] The Director, Legal Aid, Legal Aid Head Office, Newspaper House, 8–16 Great New Street, London EC4 3BN; (tel: 01–353 7411).

PART 2

The 1968 Convention on Jurisdiction and Judgments and the Civil Jurisdiction and Judgments Act 1982

PART 2 contains an article-by-article commentary on the 1968 Convention on Jurisdiction and the Enforcement of Judgments in Civil and Commercial Matters and on its associated conventions, including discussion of all the decisions on its interpretation made by the European Court of Justice. This part also contains a section-by-section commentary on the Civil Jurisdiction and Judgments Act 1982.

Chapter 13 is an introduction to the Conventions, their history, their scheme and purpose and their interpretation.

Chapter 14 deals with the scope of the 1968 Convention, as determined by the Preamble and Article 1.

Chapter 15 is an introduction to Title II of the 1968 Convention, which concerns jurisdiction.

Chapters 16 to 24 contain commentary on the jurisdictional provisions of the 1968 Convention, contained in Articles 2 to 24.

Chapter 25 is an introduction to Title III of the 1968 Convention, which concerns the recognition and enforcement of judgments.

Chapters 26 to 29 contain commentary on Articles 25 to 49 of the 1968 Convention, which govern the recognition and enforcement of judgments.

Chapters 30 to 34 contain commentary on the remaining Articles of the 1968 Convention, which deal with authentic instruments and court settlements, domicile and seat, transitional provisions, the relationship of the 1968 Convention with other conventions, and final provisions.

Chapters 35 to 38 contain commentary on the 1968 Annexed Protocol, the 1971 Protocol on Interpretation and the 1978 and 1982 Accession Conventions.

Chapter 39 contains a general introduction to the Civil Jurisdiction and Judgments Act 1982.

Chapter 40 contains commentary on sections 1 to 15 of the 1982 Act, which govern the implementation of the Conventions in the United Kingdom.

Chapter 41 contains commentary on sections 16 to 19 of the 1982 Act, which are concerned with jurisdiction, and with the recognition and enforcement of judgments, as between the different parts of the United Kingdom.

Chapters 42 to 44 contain commentary on the remaining sections of the 1982 Act.

Chapters 45 to 47 contain commentary on the Schedules to the 1982 Act (other than the Coventions).

CHAPTER 13

INTRODUCTION TO THE CONVENTION

A. BACKGROUND TO THE 1968 CONVENTION

The Convention on Jurisdiction and Enforcement of Judgments in 13.01
Civil and Commercial Matters was signed at Brussels on September
23, 1968 on behalf of the original six Member States of the European Community. The states which are now parties to it, as
amended by the subsequent Accession Conventions, are the first 10
of the 12 Member States of the European Community: Belgium,
Denmark, France, the Federal Republic of Germany, Greece, Ireland, Italy, Luxembourg, the Netherlands and the United Kingdom. It is not yet in force in Greece.[1]

1. The original contracting states

In its original form, the 1968 Convention came into force 13.02
between the original six Member States of the European Community on February 1, 1973.[2] Until then, judgments given by the
courts of Member States of the Community could be recognised in
the other Member States and enforced by their courts only in a

---

[1] See the rest of this section, and paras. 34.11, 37.18 and 38.08 below. The precise territorial limits of the Convention's application are defined in Art. 60 (para. 34.01 below). It extends to West Berlin but not, unless and until the U.K. declares otherwise, the Channel Islands or the Isle of Man: see also ss.39 and 52 of the 1982 Act, paras. 43.48 and 44.49 below.

[2] Belgium, France, the Federal Republic of Germany, Italy, Luxembourg and the Netherlands.

323

piecemeal fashion. There was a network of bilateral conventions on the recognition and enforcement of judgments in civil and commercial matters, but this network was far from comprehensive.[3] France, for example, had no bilateral convention with Germany or with the Netherlands and only Belgium had signed conventions with all the other Member States. In addition to the bilateral conventions, there were various multilateral conventions concerned with subjects of a more specialised nature, but here too the coverage was not complete, either as regards the signatory states or as regards the subject-matter concerned.[4]

13.03   When the EEC Treaty was signed in 1957, the six original Member States agreed by Article 220 that they would enter into negotiations with each other:

> "with a view to securing for the benefit of their nationals . . . the simplification of formalities governing the reciprocal recognition and enforcement of judgments of courts or tribunals and of arbitration awards."

For this purpose, a Committee of Experts was set up by the Member States in 1960 to conduct the negotiations. It adopted a radical approach to its task and in 1964 it produced a draft convention not only dealing with the recognition and enforcement of judgments,[5] but setting out direct rules of jurisdiction applicable in all the Contracting States.[6] It is this feature which makes the 1968 Convention distinctive and which is the key to its far-reaching influence on the national rules of civil procedure in the Contracting States.[7] The Committee noted that Article 220 of the EEC Treaty referred to the "nationals" of the Member States, but concluded

---

[3] A list of the bilateral conventions in force between the Contracting States before the 1968 Convention came into effect is set out in Art. 55, para. 33.01 below. They continue to have effect in relation to matters to which the 1968 Convention does not apply: Art. 56, para. 33.03 below. The texts of the bilateral conventions and a summary of the law of each of the Contracting States on the recognition and enforcement of judgments are contained in *The Practical Guide to the Recognition and Enforcement of Judicial Decisions in Civil and Commercial Law*, Council of Europe, 1975.

[4] These multilateral conventions continue to have effect: Art. 57, para. 33.06 below.

[5] Arbitral awards were not included, in view of the fact that the Council of Europe had prepared a draft European convention on arbitration and the fact that the New York Convention on the recognition and enforcement of foreign arbitral awards had been signed on June 10, 1958. (See Jenard, para. A1.54 below). That convention is given effect in the U.K. by the Arbitration Act 1975.

[6] Jenard, paras. A1.28, A1.60–A1.61 below. See also para. 14.34 below.

[7] The nature and effect of the Convention's direct rules of jurisdiction are discussed in chap. 15 below.

that nationality was not a satisfactory basis upon which to construct the new rules.[8] It noted that the connecting factor in international procedure is usually the domicile or residence of the parties[9] and it proposed that that should be the principal basis for the Convention's jurisdictional rules.[10]

The draft convention was generally accepted by the Contracting States and, after some modification, it was signed in 1968. It was ratified by the various Contracting States during 1970 to 1972 and it came into effect on February 1, 1973.[11] In 1971, the Contracting States concluded a Protocol on the Interpretation of the 1968 Convention by the European Court of Justice and this came into force on September 1, 1975.[12]

2. Accession of new Contracting States

1978 Convention. When the United Kingdom, Denmark and Ireland joined the European Community, they undertook to accede to the conventions provided for by Article 220 of the EEC Treaty and, **13.04**

> "to enter into negotiations with the original Member States in order to make the necessary adjustments thereto."[13]

In the event, the negotiations went further than merely to make the adjustments necessary to accommodate the legal systems of the three new Contracting States and included certain revisions of substance, especially in relation to jurisdiction over insurance and consumer disputes and commercial usages concerning choice of jurisdiction. The negotiations for these adjustments were conducted in a working party of representatives from the then nine members of the European Communities and resulted in a Convention signed by these nine states on October 9, 1978.[14] This amended the 1968 Convention and the 1971 Protocol and provided

---

[8] Jenard, paras. A1.64–A1.65 below; Droz, p. 9.
[9] The concept of domicile for these purposes is entirely distinct from the concept of domicile as it is generally known in common law systems. It is discussed in the commentary on Art. 52, para. 31.05 below, and in the context of English law in the commentary on s.41 of the 1982 Act, para. 44.04 below. The "seat" of a company is equated with its domicile by Art. 53: para. 31.23 below. The seat of a company for the purposes of English law is determined by ss.42 and 43 of the 1982 Act, paras. 44.11 *et seq.* below.
[10] Jenard, paras. A1.66 *et seq.*; Art. 2, para. 16.01 below.
[11] See para. 34.12 below.
[12] Chap. 36 below.
[13] Act concerning the Conditions of Accession and the Adjustments to the Treaties, Art. 3(2).
[14] O.J. 1978 L 304, October 30, 1978, Cmnd. 7395. See chap. 37 below.

for the accession to them of the United Kingdom, Denmark and Ireland.[15]

Due to prolonged delay, latterly on the part of Belgium, in ratifying the 1978 Convention, the amended version of the 1968 Convention and the 1971 Protocol did not come into force between each of the original six Contracting States and Denmark until November 1, 1986 and between each of those states and the United Kingdom until January 1, 1987. It came into force as between Ireland and the eight other Contracting States on June 1, 1988.[16]

13.05   *Greek Accession, 1982 Convention.* When Greece joined the EEC, it too undertook to accede to the 1968 Convention and the 1971 Protocol (as amended by the 1978 Convention)[17] and a further convention was concluded for that purpose on October 25, 1982.[18] That convention made certain formal amendments to the text of the 1968 Convention and Protocols, and these have been incorporated in the texts discussed below, although they are not yet in force.[19] The amendments do not produce any substantive changes affecting the operation of the Convention in the other Contracting States.

Spain and Portugal. Article 3 of the Act of Accession of Spain and Portugal to the European Communities is to similar effect and their accession to the 1968 Convention and the 1971 Protocol may be expected in due course.

3. Official reports

13.06   The original Committee of Experts set up in 1960 was chaired by Professor Bülow, of the German Federal Ministry of Justice, and had as its *rapporteur* Mr. P. Jenard, of the Belgian Ministry of Foreign Affairs. This committee produced two official reports, on the 1968 Convention and the 1971 Protocol respectively. The working party which drafted the 1978 Convention was chaired by Mr. Jenard and had Professor Peter Schlosser of Munich University as its *rapporteur*. It, too, produced an official report. All three official reports (in this work referred to as "Jenard," "Jenard, *Protocols*"

---

[15] The history of the negotiations is mentioned in the Jenard and Schlosser Reports (discussed below) and also in many of the standard works on the Conventions referred to in the bibliography. Also, see K. M. Newman, "Background and Scheme of the Civil Jurisdiction and Judgments Act 1982" in *Jurisdiction and Enforcement of Judgments in Europe* (College of Law, 1985) and Kerr L.J. (1978) 75 L.S.Gaz. 1190.

[16] See para. 37.19 below.

[17] Art. 3 of the Act of Greek Accession to the European Communities.

[18] O.J. 1982 L 388, December 31, 1982. See chap. 38 below.

[19] The 1982 Convention will come into force in accordance with its Art. 15, para. 38.08 below.

and "Schlosser," respectively) are reproduced in Appendix 1 below.[20] A similar official report, by Professors D. I. Evirgenis and K. D. Kerameus has also been produced in respect of Greek accession to the 1968 Convention.[20a]

4. EFTA countries, Lugano Convention

A convention closely modelled on the 1968 Convention has been concluded between the EEC countries and other European countries, which are members of the European Free Trade Association (EFTA).[20b] This convention, which was opened for signature at Lugano on September 16, 1988,[20c] will come into force as between the states which have ratified it from time to time.[20d] Additional states may be invited to accede.[20e] Although the Lugano Convention is largely identical with the 1968 Convention there are some differences of substance[20f] and there is no provision for its interpretation by the European Court of Justice.[20g] It provides a regime separate from, but parallel to, that established by the 1968 Convention and it is not discussed in this book.

13.07

B. THE SCHEME OF THE 1968 CONVENTION

The general scheme of the 1968 Convention is to provide uniform and directly applicable rules of jurisdiction which form part of the law of each of the Contracting States. The courts of those states are bound to consider their jurisdiction in the light of those rules in any case to which the Convention applies. The Convention then provides that judgments given by the courts of the Contracting States are to be accorded virtually automatic recognition and enforcement in the other Contracting States, and lays down a uniform procedure

13.08

---

[20] The Reports are given a special status in the law of the U.K. as aids to the interpretation of the Conventions: see 1982 Act, s.3, para. 40.05 below.

[20a] O.J. 1986 C 298, November 24, 1986.

[20b] The convention was drawn up at a diplomatic conference in which the representatives of all twelve EEC countries and the representatives of Austria, Finland, Iceland, Norway, Sweden and Switzerland participated. Not all those states have yet signed the convention.

[20c] O.J. 1988 L 319, November 25, 1988.

[20d] Lugano Convention, Art. 61(3). It must first be ratified by at least one EEC member and by one EFTA member.

[20e] Lugano Convention, Art. 62(1)(b).

[20f] These concern, notably, contracts of employment (Art. 5(1)), actions concerning contractual matters as well as rights *in rem* in immovable property (Art. 6(4)), short-hold tenancies (Art. 16(1)), jurisdiction agreements (Art. 17), *lis alibi pendens* (Art. 21) and the grounds on which recognition may be refused (Art. 28).

[20g] Protocol 2 provides for an exchange of information on the convention's interpretation. An Official Report by Mr. Jenard is being prepared.

to be followed for that purpose. It provides that the jurisdiction of the court of origin may only be reviewed in a few exceptional cases and permits recognition and enforcement to be refused only in limited and tightly defined circumstances. The Convention is sometimes referred to as the "EEC Judgments Convention", or simply as the "Brussels Convention", or, in a phrase borrowed from the United States, as the "Full Faith and Credit Convention."

The Convention is made up of a Preamble and 68 Articles, which are grouped into eight "Titles." Two of the Titles are sub-divided into "Sections." Title I defines the material scope of the Convention.[21] Title II and Title III together make up the bulk of the Convention and are concerned, respectively, with jurisdiction and with recognition and enforcement. Each of these Titles is described below in greater detail in a general introduction.[22] Title IV concerns the enforcement of authentic instruments and court settlements[23] and Title V provides choice of law rules for determining the domicile of an individual and the seat of a corporation.[24] Title VI contains transitional provisions.[25] Title VII regulates the relationship between the 1968 Convention and other conventions. It applies both to conventions between the different Contracting States and to those between Contracting States and non-Contracting States.[26] Title VIII contains final provisions concerning such matters as ratification, commencement and authenticity of texts.[27]

C. The 1968 Convention: Its Principles and Interpretation

1. The purposes of the Convention

13.09   An understanding of the Convention's purposes is essential for its proper interpretation. At its core is a unifying purpose. The Convention operates internationally in the context of the European Community, in a juridically and territorially confined area. It forms part of the legal order of the Community and provides a single set of rules, directly effective in each Contracting State and forming part

---

[21] Art. 1, para. 40.01 below.
[22] Title II contains Arts. 2 to 24; its general introduction is in chap. 15. Title III contains Arts. 25 to 49; its general introduction is in chap. 25.
[23] Arts. 50 and 51, chap. 30 below.
[24] Arts. 52 and 53, chap. 31 below.
[25] Art. 54, chap. 32 below. Transitional provisions for the accession of the new Contracting States under the 1978 Convention are contained in Arts. 34 to 36 of that Convention, paras. 37.06–37.14 below.
[26] Arts. 55 to 59, chap. 33 below.
[27] Arts. 60 to 68, chap. 34 below.

of its municipal law of jurisdiction and civil procedure.[27a] The Convention's rules take precedence over those of national law,[28] which cannot affect the scope or objectives of the Convention in its application to any particular case.[29] Like European Community law, it is to be given a uniform interpretation in all the Contracting States.

The uniform application of the Convention is assisted and supervised by the European Court, which has jurisdiction to make definitive rulings on its interpretation when questions are referred by national courts.[30] The European Court has considered the Convention's purposes on numerous occasions. In doing so, it has identified a number of principles in the Convention and it has laid down certain criteria to be borne in mind in the interpretation of the Convention.

International character of dispute. The Convention determines the **13.10** *international* jurisdiction of the courts in the Community,[31] as is made clear by the wording of the Preamble.[32] It is therefore necessary, for the Convention to apply, that the particular case should have some international element. This question is of particular practical importance in relation to choice of jurisdiction agreements, and it is discussed in more detail in the commentary on Article 17.[33]

The international element may be fairly limited, but the Convention does not apply to disputes which are purely internal to a single Contracting State.[34] The Convention's jurisdictional rules are generally founded on the domicile of a party (usually the defendant) within the territory of a Contracting State,[35] but the fact that he is domiciled there may not always be enough to bring those rules into operation. So, where both parties are domiciled in the same Contracting State the dispute may not be international and the Conven-

---

[27a] " . . . the object of the Judgments Convention was to create something analogous to a single law district for the whole of the EEC", *per* Kerr L.J., *Babanaft International Co. S.A.* v. *Bassatne* [1989] 2 W.L.R. 232.

[28] *Sanicentral G.m.b.H.* v. *Collin* [1979] E.C.R. 3423, at p. 3492 (para. 5); *Duijnstee* v. *Goderbauer* [1983] E.C.R. 3663, at pp. 3674–3675 (para. 13).

[29] *Capelloni and Aquilini* v. *Pelkmans* [1985] E.C.R. 3147 (para. 21).

[30] 1971 Protocol on Interpretation, chap. 36 below.

[31] Jenard, para. A1.33 below; Droz, paras. 26–32; Bülow/Böckstiegel, p. 11, Weser, paras. 188*bis*–188*quinquies*. As to the meaning of "international jurisdiction", see para. 1.05 above.

[32] Para. 14.01 below.

[33] Para. 21.06 below.

[34] As a matter of the law of the U.K., the question whether a case falls within the *scope* of the Convention is relevant even for cases purely internal to the U.K.: s.16(1)(a) of the 1982 Act, para. 41.01 below.

[35] The territorial scope of the Convention is governed by Art. 60, para. 34.01 below.

tion may not apply, even if one of the parties would be regarded by the law of another Contracting State as being domiciled in that state.[36] The fact that a party does not have the nationality of the state where the dispute is being litigated is also not enough to give the dispute an international character. Nationality of the parties, as distinct from their domicile, it not relevant for the purposes of the Convention, save that the second paragraph of Article 2 requires that persons who are not nationals of the Contracting State where they are domiciled should be governed by the rules of jurisdiction applicable to nationals of that state.

13.11   The Convention provides no definition of the international character necessary for it to apply, but this may be deduced from the provisions of Title II, which contains the rules which lay down the international jurisdiction of national courts. In the end, the question of whether an international element is present will depend upon the circumstances of each individual case. The recognition and enforcement of judgments given in other Contracting States— the subject of Title III—automatically involves an international element.

Perhaps the most obvious examples of an international element sufficient to bring the Convention into play are provided by the rules of special jurisdiction. Even where both parties are domiciled in the same Contracting State, if the dispute concerns a contract to be performed, or a tort committed, in another Contracting State, the dispute will be international in character and a court in the other state will have jurisdiction under Article 5(1) or 5(3) of the Convention. The international character is not removed merely because the parties choose the jurisdiction of the courts of their own state.[37] The effects of the Convention applying are even more marked where the exclusive jurisdiction provisions of Article 16 apply. For example, a dispute between two parties domiciled in the United Kingdom concerning the letting of a holiday home in France may only be adjudicated upon by the courts of France.[38]

Less obviously, an international element is involved if a court of another Contracting State is seised of the same dispute between the same parties or of another dispute, whether or not it involves the

---

[36] Art. 52 determines which law applies to decide domicile: see paras. 31.01 *et seq.* below.
[37] Para. 21.06 below.
[38] Art. 16(1), para. 20.11 below; *Rösler* v. *Rottwinkel* [1985] E.C.R. 99, discussed at para. 20.18 below.

same parties, which is closely enough related to raise the risk of irreconcilable judgments.[39]

The Convention and the Community. The Convention's unifying **13.12** purpose in a European Community context is expressly referred to in the Preamble[40] and is borne out by a number of important characteristics of the Convention. For example, the Convention contains direct rules of jurisdiction, applicable in all the Contracting States, of which the starting point is the defendant's domicile or seat within the Community, regardless of his nationality.[41] The rules sometimes deprive courts of jurisdiction[42] and sometimes regulate even the local jurisdiction of the courts,[43] while national courts are generally prohibited from reviewing the jurisdiction of the courts of other Contracting States[44] and are prevented from reviewing the substance of their decisions.[45] The rules of the Convention take precedence over those of national procedural law[46] and the meaning of many of the concepts in the Convention is independent of the meaning of equivalent concepts in national law.[47] These factors all emphasise the *communautaire* nature of the Convention.

Community legal order. The European Court of Justice has **13.13** stressed that the Convention was established pursuant to Article 220 of the EEC Treaty and forms part of the Community legal order.[48] It does not strictly form part of European Community law and, from the point of view of public international law, it has a separate existence. But its connection with the European Community

---

[39] Bülow/Böckstiegel, p. 20; the rules for *lis alibi pendens* and related actions are in Arts. 21 to 23, chap. 23 below.
[40] Para. 14.01 below.
[41] Art. 2, para. 16.01 below; see Jenard, para. A1.55 below.
[42] The exclusive jurisdiction rules in Art. 16 are the best examples of this.
[43] Art. 5 provides the most important examples of local jurisdiction being regulated by the Convention. This aspect is discussed in greater detail in the general introduction to Title II, at para. 15.06 below.
[44] Art. 28, third para., para. 27.62 below.
[45] Art. 29, para. 27.75 below.
[46] Para. 13.09, n.28 above.
[47] Para. 13.16 below.
[48] *Industrie Tessili Italiana Como v. Dunlop AG* [1976] E.C.R. 1473, at p. 1484 (para. 9); *Bavaria & Co. KG and Germanair GmbH & Co. KG v. Eurocontrol* [1977] E.C.R. 1517, at p. 1525 (para. 4); *Société Bertrand v. Paul Ott KG* [1978] E.C.R. 1431, at p. 1445 (paras. 14 and 16); *Etablissements Somafer SA v. Saar-Ferngas AG* [1978] E.C.R. 2183, at p. 2190 (para. 4); *Sanicentral GmbH v. Collin* [1979] E.C.R. 3423, at p. 3429 (para. 5); *Peters v. Zuid Nederlandse Aannemers Vereniging* [1983] E.C.R. 987, at p. 1002 (para. 17); *Duijnstee v. Goderbauer* [1983] E.C.R. 3663, at pp. 3674–3675 (paras. 13–14); *Gubish Maschinenfabrik v. Palumbo*, case 144/86, decision of December 8, 1987 (paras. 7 and 8), *The Times*, January 12, 1988.

is self-evident and is strengthened by the jurisdiction given to the European Court of Justice to interpret its provisions.[49] In addition, the European Court has expressly stated that the Convention must be interpreted with regard to its relationship with the EEC Treaty.[50]

Member States of the European Community have been permitted by the European Court to intervene under Article 20 of the Protocol on the Statute of the European Court of Justice in references made to that Court under the 1971 Protocol on Interpretation, even when they were not parties to the 1968 Convention[51] or had not brought it into effect (and the United Kingdom frequently did so). This serves further to emphasise the connection between the Convention and the European Community.

13.14   *Effect on national law.* Unlike the EEC Treaty and Community law, the Convention does not affect the substantive law of the Contracting States,[52] but it does strike deep into the structure of rules governing the jurisdiction of courts in the Contracting States. This is particularly apparent in England, where the jurisdiction of the courts has been characterised by discretion and the loosely-defined concept of "inherent jurisdiction" and where now, by contrast, jurisdictional rules, compulsory in nature and inspired by the traditions of continental law,[53] take effect across a wide range of civil and commercial cases containing some international element. The Convention's code of jurisdictional rules has even been adopted, in a slightly modified form, for the allocation of jurisdiction between the different parts of the United Kingdom, although here a measure of discretion has been preserved.[54]

13.15   *Objectives.* In addition to stressing the Community nature of the Convention, the European Court has laid emphasis on a number of its characteristics. In some cases, the Court has referred to the Preamble for this purpose, in others it has drawn on the structure and contents of the Convention, and it has frequently stated that

---

[49] Kohler, "Practical Experience of the Brussels Jurisdiction and Judgments Convention in the Six Original Contracting States" (1985) 34 I.C.L.Q. 563, 565.
[50] *Industrie Tessili Italiana Como* v. *Dunlop AG* [1976] E.C.R. 1473.
[51] *Industrie Tesilli* v. *Dunlop AG*, above, at p. 1484 (para. 8).
[52] *Sanicentral GmbH* v. *Collin* [1979] E.C.R. 3423, at p. 3492 (para. 5).
[53] Schlosser, para. 76 (para. A1.363 below).
[54] 1982 Act, s.49, para. 44.40 below.

the interpretation of the Convention must have regard to its principles and objectives, its structure and scheme.[55] The principal objectives of the Convention referred to by the European Court are the determination of the international jurisdiction[56] of the courts in the Community[57] and the simplification of formalities governing the reciprocal enforcement of judgments,[58] including the provision of rapid and effective procedures for these purposes.[59] Particular attention may also be attached to the strengthening of legal protection of persons established in the Community,[60] for example by protecting the rights of defendants,[61] or

---

[55] *Industrie Tessili Italiana Como* v. *Dunlop AG* [1976] E.C.R. 1473, at p. 1484 (para. 9); *Etablissements Somafer SA* v. *Saar-Ferngas AG* [1978] E.C.R. 2183, at p. 2190 (para. 4); *Ivenel* v. *Schwab* [1982] E.C.R. 1891, at p. 1899 (para. 10); *Gerling Konzern AG* v. *Amministrazione del Tesoro dello Stato* [1983] E.C.R. 2503, at p. 2515 (para. 11); *Duijnstee* v. *Goderbauer* [1983] E.C.R. 3663, at p. 3674 (para. 10); *A-S Autoteile Service GmbH* v. *Malhé* [1985] E.C.R. 2267, at p. 2277, (para. 14); *Berghoefer GmbH & Co. KG* v. *A.S.A. SA* [1985] E.C.R. 2699, at p. 2708 (para. 12) *Kalfelis* v. *Schröder, Münchmeyer, Hengst & Co.*, case 189/87, decision of September 27, 1988 (para. 16), *The Times*, October 5, 1988.

[56] Para. 13.10 above.

[57] *De Bloos* v. *Bouyer* [1976] E.C.R. 1497, at p. 1508 (para. 8); *Sanicentral GmbH* v. *Collin* [1979] E.C.R. 3423, at p. 3492 (para. 5); *Duijnstee* v. *Goderbauer* [1983] E.C.R. 3663, at p. 3674 (para. 11).

[58] *Industrie Tessili Italiana Como* v. *Dunlop AG* [1976] E.C.R. 1473, at p. 1484 (para. 9); *De Bloos* v. *Bouyer, loc. cit.*; *De Wolf* v. *Cox B.V.* [1976] E.C.R. 1759, at p. 1768 (para. 15); *Société Bertrand* v. *Paul Ott KG* [1978] E.C.R. 1431, at p. 1445 (para. 14); *Etablissements Somafer SA* v. *Saar-Ferngas AG* [1978] E.C.R. 2183, at p. 2190 (para. 4); *Gourdain* v. *Nadler* [1979] E.C.R. 733, at p. 743 (para. 3); *Duijnstee* v. *Goderbauer, loc. cit.*; *Calzaturificio Brennero SAS* v. *Wendel GmbH Schuhproduktion International* [1984] E.C.R. 3971, at p. 3981 (paras. 7 and 10); *Debaecker and Plouvier* v. *Bouwman* [1985] E.C.R. 1779, at p. 1796 (para. 10); *Deutsche Genossenschaftsbank* v. *Brasserie du Pêcheur SA* [1985] E.C.R. 1981, at p. 1992 (para. 16); *Capelloni and Aquilini* v. *Pelkmans* [1985] E.C.R. 3147, at p. 3158 (para. 15); *Gubisch Maschinenfabrik* v. *Palumbo*, case 144/86, decision of December 8, 1987 (para. 8), *The Times*, January 12, 1988.

[59] *De Bloos* v. *Bouyer loc. cit.*; *Meeth* v. *Glacetal S.à.r.l.* [1978] E.C.R. 2133, at p. 2142 (para. 8); *Duijnstee* v. *Goderbauer, loc. cit.*; *Calzaturificio Brennero SAS* v. *Wendel GmbH Schuhproduktion International, loc. cit.* (para. 10); *Spitzley* v. *Sommer Exploitation SA* [1985] E.C.R. 787, at p. 799 (para. 21); *Hoffman* v. *Krieg*, case 145/86, decision of February 4, 1988 (para. 10), *The Times*, March 26, 1988; Jenard, para. A1.186 below; see also para. 25.06 below.

[60] *Industrie Tessili Italiana Como* v. *Dunlop AG loc. cit.*; *Etablissements Somafer SA* v. *Saar-Ferngas AG loc. cit.*; *Gourdain* v. *Nadler loc. cit.*; *Effer SPA* v. *Kantner* [1982] E.C.R. 825, at p. 834 (para. 6); *Duijnstee* v. *Goderbauer, loc. cit.*; *Debaecker and Plouvier* v. *Bouwman, loc. cit. Gubisch Maschinenfabrik* v. *Palumbo, loc. cit.*; see also Jenard, para. A1.3 below.

[61] *Denilauler* v. *Couchet Frères* [1980] E.C.R. 1553, at p. 1569 (para. 13); *Elefanten Schuh Gmbh* v. *Jacqmain* [1981] E.C.R. 1671, at p. 1685 (para. 14); *Rohr SA* v. *Ossberger* [1981] E.C.R. 2431, at p. 2439 (para. 7); *Pendy Plastic Products* v. *Pluspunkt* [1982] E.C.R. 2723, at p. 2736 (para. 13); *Debaecker and Plouvier* v. *Bouwman* [1985] E.C.R. 1779, at p. 1799 (para. 20).

of socially or economically weaker parties.[62] The Convention also seeks to avoid a multiplicity of jurisdictions,[63] with a view to promoting uniformity, legal certainty and the protection of litigants.[64] The European Court has regarded the special jurisdictions[65] as a derogation from the general rule in Article 2, but one justified by some close connecting factor between the court in question and the parties or subject-matter of the dispute[66] (particularly in the case of exclusive jurisdictions).[67] It has also stated that the freedom is given to a plaintiff to choose a special jurisdiction under Article 5, "with a view to the efficacious conduct of the proceedings."[68]

2. Classification of concepts: national and independent interpretations

13.16   From the outset, the European Court has recognised that for the Convention to be effective as part of the legal order of the Community and to achieve its objectives of promoting legal certainty and securing equal treatment for litigants throughout the Community, it cannot be used merely as a code of conflicts rules. Many of the provisions of the Convention itself must be given the same meaning in all the Contracting States, although others are to be interpreted according to the relevant national law.[69]

---

[62] *Société Bertrand* v. *Paul Ott KG* [1978] E.C.R. 1431, at p. 1446 (para. 21); *Ivenel* v. *Schwab* [1982] E.C.R. 1891, at p. 1901 (para. 16); *Gerling Konzern AG* v. *Amministrazione del Tesoro dello Stato* [1983] E.C.R. 2503, at p. 2516 (para. 17).

[63] *De Bloos* v. *Bouyer* [1976] E.C.R. 1497, at p. 1508 (para. 9); *Effer SPA* v. *Kantner, loc. cit.; Peters* v. *Zuid Nederlandse Aannemers Vereniging* [1983] E.C.R. 987, at p. 1002 (para. 17).

[64] *Effer SPA* v. *Kantner, loc. cit.; Peters* v. *Zuid Nederlandse Aannemers Vereniging, loc. cit.; Rösler* v. *Rottwinkel* [1985] E.C.R. 99, at p. 127 (para. 23); *Kalfelis* v. *Schröder, Münchmeyer, Hengst & Co.*, case 189/87, decision of September 27, 1988 (paras. 10 and 15), *The Times*, October 5, 1988.

[65] The special rules of jurisdiction are those in Arts. 5 to 6A, but the principle applies also to the rules in Arts. 7 to 16.

[66] *Handelswekerij G.J.Bier B.V.* v. *Mines de Potasse d'Alsace S.A.* [1976] E.C.R. 1735, at p. 1746 (para. 11); *Etablissements Somafer SA* v. *Saar-Ferngas AG* [1978] E.C.R. 2183, at p. 2191 (para. 7); *Zelger* v. *Salinitri (No. 1)* [1980] E.C.R. 89, at p. 96 (para. 3); *Effer SPA* v. *Kantner, loc. cit.; Ivenel* v. *Schwab* [1982] E.C.R. 1891, at p. 1899 (para. 10); *Peters* v. *Zuid Nederlandse Aannemers Vereniging* [1983] E.C.R. 987, at p. 1002 (para. 12); *Rösler* v. *Rottwinkel* [1985] E.C.R. 99, at p. 126 (para. 19); *Kalfelis* v. *Schröder, Münchmeyer, Hengst & Co.*, above (paras. 8 and 19).

[67] Chap. 20 below; *Sanders* v. *Van der Putte* [1977] E.C.R. 2383, at p. 2391 (paras. 17 and 18); *Rösler* v. *Rottwinkel* [1985] E.C.R. 99, at p. 126 (para. 20).

[68] *Handelswekerij G.J.Bier B.V.* v. *Mines de Potasse d'Alsace S.A., loc. cit.*

[69] Kohler, "The Case Law of the European Court on the Judgments Convention" (1982) 7 E.L.R. 3 and 103; Kohler, "Practical Experience of the Brussels Jurisdiction and Judgments Convention in the Six Original Contracting States" (1985) 34 I.C.L.Q. 563; Tebbens, "L'Interpretation dynamique, par la Cour de

National interpretation. Only in a small number of cases is a con-   **13.17**
cept employed by the Convention to be interpreted according to the
relevant national law. The clearest example of this concerns the
concepts of "domicile" and "seat," for which Articles 52 and 53
provide choice of law rules expressly referring to national law.

An interpretation according to national law has also been preferred in a number of decisions of the European Court. In its first
decision on the Convention, the Court ruled that the "place of performance" of a contract for the purposes of Article 5(1) was to be
determined according to the proper law of the obligation in question as determined by the conflicts rules of the *lex fori*.[70] In its
second decision, the Court held that the "obligation in question"
was that which corresponded to the contractual right on which the
plaintiff's claim was based. It also held that the question of charac-
terising that obligation in a claim for compensation by way of
damages, either as one which replaced an unperformed obligation
or as an independent obligation, was a question to be determined by
the proper law of the contract.[71]

In *Industrie Tessili* v. *Dunlop*, the European Court referred to the   **13.18**
choice between national and independent interpretation and said
that the choice of appropriate option had to be made in respect of
each of the provisions of the Convention.[72] It is noticeable, though,
that the choice of the national option has only since been made by
the European Court in relation to procedural matters,[73] although
national courts have, understandably enough, tended to interpret
the Convention according to the concepts current in their own legal
system.[74]

Justice Européenne, de la compétence en matière contractuelle", in *Unification and Comparative Law in Theory and Practice—Contributions in honour of Jean Georges Sauveplanne*, p. 75.

[70] *Industrie Tessili Italiana Como* v. *Dunlop AG* [1976] E.C.R. 1473.

[71] *De Bloos* v. *Bouyer* [1976] E.C.R. 1497.

[72] [1976] E.C.R. 1473, at pp. 1484–1485 (paras. 8–10). Reference to the choice between national and international interpretation also appears in *Industrial Diamond Supplies* v. *Riva* [1977] E.C.R. 2175, at pp. 2187–2188 (para. 22); *Etablissements Somafer SA* v. *Saar-Ferngas AG* [1978] E.C.R. 2183, at p. 2190 (para. 10); *Zelger* v. *Salinitri (No. 2)* [1984] E.C.R. 2397, at pp. 2407–2408 (paras. 10–13) and *Kalfelis* v. *Schröder, Münchmeyer, Hengst & Co.*, case 189/87, decision of September 27, 1988 (para. 15), *The Times*, October 5, 1988.

[73] *Elefanten Schuh GmbH* v. *Jacqmain* [1981] E.C.R. 1671 (submissions considered by national law to be the first defence addressed to the court): see para. 21.94 below; *Zelger* v. *Salinitri (No. 2)* [1984] E.C.R. 2397 (the point at which national law regards an action as becoming definitively pending): see para. 23.05 below.

[74] Kohler, *op. cit.*, (1985) 34 I.C.L.Q. 563, at p. 565.

On the other hand, it is well-established that national procedural law applies to determine detailed questions on which the Convention is silent. In respect of some of these matters the Convention itself refers to national law, such as the procedure for making an application for enforcement of a judgment given in another Contracting State,[75] or the types of provisional order which can be made in the absence of jurisdiction over the substance of the matter,[76] and the European Court has stated that the Convention leaves the resolution of any question not covered by its specific provisions to the procedural law of the court hearing the proceedings.[77]

13.19   *Independent interpretation.* As the case law of the European Court has developed, it has become apparent that many of the concepts in the Convention are to be given an independent interpretation. While some of these are defined in the Convention itself ("judgment" is defined in Article 25 and "related actions" in Article 23), in most of the cases where the European Court has held that a given concept in the Convention is to be interpreted on an independent basis, it has reached that conclusion by a process of purposive interpretation, examining the scheme and objectives of the Convention.

Among the objectives of the Convention are the need to ensure that the rights and obligations of persons to whom it applies are equal and uniform[78] and the need to promote legal certainty within the Community legal order.[79] The European Court has referred to these objectives and has proceeded to deduce that the Convention's

---

[75] Art. 33, first para., para. 28.16 below.
[76] Art. 24, para. 24.01 below.
[77] *Capelloni and Aquilini v. Pelkmans* [1985] E.C.R. 3147, at p. 3159 (para. 20). See also *Deutsche Genossenschaftsbank v. Brasserie du Pêcheur* [1985] E.C.R. 1981, at p. 1992 (para. 18) (the procedure for enforcing enforceable instruments) and *Carron v. Federal Republic of Germany* [1986] E.C.R. 2437, at p. 2444 (paras. 8 and 13) (the time at which and manner in which an applicant must give an address for service within the state addressed, pursuant to Art. 33, and the sanction for failure to do so.)
[78] *LTU Lufttransport v. Eurocontrol* [1976] E.C.R. 1541, at p. 1551 (para. 3); *Bavaria & Co. KG and Germanair GmbH & Co. KG v. Eurocontrol* [1977] E.C.R. 1517, at p. 1525 (para. 4); *Etablissements Somafer SA v. Saar-Ferngas AG* [1978] E.C.R. 2183, at p. 2191 (para. 8); *Netherlands State v. Rüffer* [1980] E.C.R. 3807, at p. 3821 (para. 14); *Duijnstee v. Goderbauer* [1983] E.C.R. 3663, at p. 3675 (para. 17); *Arcado v. Haviland*, case 9/87, decision of March 8, 1988, [1989] E.C.C. 1; *Kalfelis v. Schröder, Münchmeyer, Hengst & Co.*, case 189/87, decision of September 27, 1988 (paras. 10 and 15), *The Times*, October 5, 1988.
[79] *Bavaria & Co. and Germanair GmbH & Co. KG v. Eurocontrol, loc. cit.; Etablissements Somafer SA v. Saar-Ferngas AG, loc. cit.; Duijnstee v. Goderbauer, loc. cit.*, (para. 14).

concepts should be classified or interpreted in a uniform manner,[80] or according to an independent interpretation.[81] A uniform or independent interpretation should be conducted in accordance with the Convention's objectives and its scheme or structure[82] and in accordance with general principles which stem from the corpus of national legal systems.[83] For this purpose, the European Court has compared concepts in the laws of Contracting States, on some occasions identifying "core" concepts, common to the laws of all or most Contracting States[84] and on other occasions pointing to the divergences between the concepts found in the different national legal systems.[85] It has also referred to EEC law and the EEC Contractual Obligations Convention.[85a]

The European Court had adopted such processes of reasoning in deciding that an independent interpretation should be given to a number of concepts in the Convention and it has provided interpretations, some of which are exhaustive. For example, concepts relating to the scope of the Convention have been given an indepen- **13.20**

[80] *Bavaria & Co. KG and Germanair GmbH & Co. KG* v. *Eurocontrol, loc. cit.*; *Industrial Diamond Supplies* v. *Riva* [1977] E.C.R. 2175, at pp. 2187–2188 (para. 22); *Société Bertrand* v. *Paul Ott KG* [1978] E.C.R. 1431, at p. 1445 (para. 15); *Gourdain* v. *Nadler* [1979] E.C.R. 733, at p. 743 (para. 3).
[81] *LTU Lufttransport* v. *Eurocontrol loc. cit.*; *Gourdain* v. *Nadler, loc. cit.*; *Netherlands State* v. *Rüffer* [1980] E.C.R. 3807, at p. 3819 (paras. 7 and 8); *Rinkau* [1981] E.C.R. 1391, at p. 1400 (para. 11); *Peters* v. *Zuid Nederlandse Aannemers Vereniging* [1983] E.C.R. 987, at p. 1002 (paras. 9 and 10); *Duijnstee* v. *Goderbauer* [1983] E.C.R. 3663, at p. 3675 (para. 17); *Arcado* v. *Haviland*, case 9/87, decision of March 8, 1988, (paras. 10 and 11), [1989] E.C.C. 1; *Kalfelis* v. *Schröder, Münchmeyer, Hengst & Co.*, case 189/87, decision of September 27, 1988 (para. 16), *The Times*, October 5, 1988.
[82] *LTU Lufttransport* v. *Eurocontrol, loc. cit.*; *Industrial Diamond Supplies* v. *Riva, loc. cit.*; *Gourdain* v. *Nadler, loc. cit.*; *Netherlands State* v. *Rüffer, loc. cit.*; *Rinkau, loc. cit*; *Peters* v. *Zuid Nederlandse Aannemers Vereniging, loc. cit.*; *Duijnstee* v. *Goderbauer, loc. cit.*; *Arcado* v. *Haviland*, loc. cit.; *Kalfelis* v. *Schröder Münchmeyer Hengst & Co.*, above (paras. 15 and 16).
[83] *LTU Lufttransport* v. *Eurocontrol, loc. cit.*; *Gourdain* v. *Nadler, loc. cit.*; *Netherlands State* v. *Rüffer, loc. cit.*; *Rinkau, loc. cit*; *Duijnstee* v. *Goderbauer, loc. cit.*
[84] *Handelswekerij G.J.Bier B.V.* v. *Mines de Potasse d'Alsace S.A.* [1976] E.C.R. 1735, at p. 1747 (para. 22); *Industrial Diamond Supplies* v. *Riva, loc. cit.*; *Société Bertrand* v. *Paul Ott KG* [1978] E.C.R. 1431, at p. 1446 (para. 19); *Rinkau, loc. cit.*; *Zelger* v. *Salinitri (No. 2)* [1984] E.C.R. 2397, at pp. 2407–2408 (paras. 10–13); *Six Constructions* v. *Humbert* case 32/88, decision of February 15, 1989 (para 21), not yet reported.
[85] Divergences have been used to justify both an independent interpretation (*Industrial Diamond Supplies* v. *Riva, loc. cit.*; *Duijnstee* v. *Goderbauer* [1983] E.C.R. 3663, at p. 3676 (para. 18) *Gubisch* v. *Palumbo*, case 144/86, decision of December 8, 1987 (para. 10), *The Times*, January 12, 1988) and a reference to national law (*Zelger* v. *Salinitri (No. 2), loc. cit.*).
[85a] *Arcado* v. *Haviland*, case 9/87, decision of March 8, 1988 (paras. 14 and 15), not yet reported; *Ivenel* v. *Schwab* [1982] E.C.R. 1891, at p. 1900 (paras. 13 and 14).

dent meaning, such as "civil and commercial matters,"[86] "rights in property arising out of a matrimonial relationship"[87] and "bankruptcy, proceedings relating to the winding-up of insolvent companies or other legal persons, judicial arrangements, compositions and analogous proceedings."[88]

More frequently, an independent interpretation has been given to concepts relating to jurisdiction: "matters relating to a contract";[89] "tort, *delict* or *quasi-delict*";[89a] "place where the harmful event occurred";[90] "branch, agency or other establishment";[91] "sale of goods on instalment credit terms";[92] "tenancies of immovable property";[93] "proceedings concerned with the registration or validity of patents";[94] "proceedings concerned with the enforcement of judgments";[95] "agreement in writing"[96] and "oral agreement evidenced in writing";[97] "concluded for the benefit of only one of the parties";[98] and "offence which was not intentionally committed."[99]

13.21   Certain concepts relating to the procedures for recognition and enforcement laid down by the Convention have also been given an

---

[86] Art. 1, first para.: *LTU Lufttransport* v. *Eurocontrol* [1976] E.C.R. 1541; *Netherlands State* v. *Rüffer* [1980] E.C.R. 3807.

[87] Art. 1, second para., sub-para. (1): *De Cavel* v. *De Cavel (No. 1)* [1979] E.C.R. 1055; *De Cavel* v. *De Cavel (No. 2)* [1980] E.C.R. 731 (where "matters relating to maintenance" in Art. 5(2) was also considered); *W. (C.H.)* v. *H. (G.J.)* [1982] E.C.R. 1189.

[88] Art. 1, second para., sub-para. (2): *Gourdain* v. *Nadler* [1979] E.C.R. 733.

[89] Art. 5(1): *Peters* v. *Zuid Nederlandse Aannemers Vereniging* [1983] E.C.R. 987 (members of an association having contractual relations *inter se*); *Arcado* v. *Haviland*, case 9/87, decision of March 8, 1988, [1989] E.C.C. 1 (wrongful repudiation of a commercial agency agreement).

[89a] Art. 5(3): *Kalfelis* v. *Schröder, Münchmeyer, Hengst & Co*, case 189/87, decision of September 27, 1988, *The Times*, October 5, 1988.

[90] Art. 5(3): *Handelswekerij G.J.Bier B.V.* v. *Mines de Potasse d'Alsace S.A.* [1976] E.C.R. 1735.

[91] Art. 5(5): *De Bloos* v. *Bouyer* [1976] E.C.R. 1497, at pp. 1509–1510; *Etablissements Somafer SA* v. *Saar-Ferngas AG* [1978] E.C.R. 2183; *Blankaert and Willems PVBA* v. *Trost* [1981] E.C.R. 819; *S.A.R. Schotte G.m.b.H.* v. *Parfums Rothschild S.à.r.l.* case 218/86, decision of December 9, 1987, *The Times*, January 12, 1988.

[92] Art. 13: *Société Bertrand* v. *Paul Ott KG* [1978] E.C.R. 1431.

[93] Art. 16(1): *Sanders* v. *Van der Putte* [1977] E.C.R. 2383; *Rösler* v. *Rottwinkel* [1985] E.C.R. 99.

[94] Art. 16(4): *Duijnstee* v. *Goderbauer* [1983] E.C.R. 3663.

[95] Art. 16(5): *A-S Autoteile Service GmbH* v. *Malhé* [1985] E.C.R. 2267.

[96] Art. 17, first para.: *Estasis Salotti* v. *RÜWA GmbH* [1976] E.C.R. 1831.

[97] Art. 17, first para.: *Galeries Segoura SPRL* v. *Bonakdarian* [1976] E.C.R. 1851; *Berghoefer GmbH & Co. KG* v. *A.S.A. SA* [1985] E.C.R. 2699.

[98] Art. 17, fourth para. (as it now is): *Anterist* v. *Crédit Lyonnais* [1986] E.C.R. 1951.

[99] Art. II of the 1968 Protocol: *Rinkau* [1981] E.C.R. 1391.

independent interpretation: "document which instituted the proceedings" and "in sufficient time";[1] "ordinary appeal";[2] and "address for service of process."[3]

D. INTERPRETING THE 1968 CONVENTION—THE APPROACH OF ENGLISH COURTS

1. The Conventions as English law

The 1968 Convention, the 1971 Protocol and the 1978 Convention are all enacted into English law by the Civil Jurisdiction and Judgments Act 1982.[4] The manner in which the Act gives effect to the Conventions in English law and the schemes it adopts for the allocation of jurisdiction, and for the recognition and enforcement of judgments, as between different parts of the United Kingdom are all discussed in further detail in the commentary on the Act.[5] It should be noted here, though, that the manner in which the Conventions are given the force of law in the United Kingdom is by their direct incorporation. It is the Conventions themselves (in each of their equally authentic language versions) which are given the force of law. The English texts are set out in Schedules 1 to 3 to the Act merely for convenience of reference.

13.22

The principles of English law which govern the interpretation of international conventions generally as a matter of municipal law[6] recognise that such conventions cannot be equated directly with an English statute. They may not easily be susceptible of interpretation according to normal English canons of literal construction and they often require, rather, to be interpreted in the light of the purpose of the convention. This is sometimes called the "teleological" approach.[7] In approaching the interpretation of the 1968 Convention, English courts may find it helpful to have regard to these principles, which are considered in outline below; but regard must also be paid to the case law and principles developed by the European Court. The status of this particular convention as uniform law directly applicable in all the Contracting States and the involvement

13.23

---

[1] Art. 27(2): *Klomps* v. *Michel* [1981] E.C.R. 1593.
[2] Arts. 30 and 38: *Industrial Diamond Supplies* v. *Riva* [1977] E.C.R. 2175.
[3] Art. 33: *Carron* v. *Federal Republic of Germany* [1986] E.C.R. 2437.
[4] They are also enacted into the laws of Scotland and Northern Ireland: s.2 of the Act (para. 40.03 below).
[5] Chaps. 39 to 47 below.
[6] See Dicey and Morris, pp. 8–15.
[7] This topic is discussed in detail in Mann, *Foreign Affairs in English Courts*, pp. 102 *et seq.*; Higgins, in Jacobs and Roberts (ed.), *The Effect of Treaties in Domestic Law*, pp. 131 *et seq.*; and in Bennion, *Statutory Interpretation*, pp. 534–541, 657 *et seq.*

of the European Court in its interpretation and application, mean that the 1968 Convention is in many respects more akin to European Community law than to a normal convention on private law.

2. Aids to interpretation envisaged by the 1982 Act

13.24   *Decisions of the European Court.* English courts are required by section 3(1) of the 1982 Act to interpret the Conventions in accordance with the decisions of, and any relevant principles laid down by, the European Court of Justice (unless the question of interpretation is referred to the European Court under the 1971 Protocol). This case law of the European Court has already been considered in outline, and is considered below in detail in the commentary on the individual Articles of the Conventions. Although the doctrine of precedent is not strictly applicable to the decisions of the European Court, its rulings are definitive on the questions actually referred to it and its *obiter dicta* are of foremost importance in the interpretation of the Convention.

13.25   *Official Reports.* If it were not for section 3(3) of the Act, English law would permit reference to preparatory works such as the Official Reports only in those cases where a literal construction of the Conventions would have produced an ambiguous result or a result in apparent conflict with their purpose.[8] As it is, section 3(3) specifically sanctions reference by English courts to the Official Reports as an aid to the interpretation of the Conventions;[9] but it cannot be assumed that the European Court will always adopt the interpretation suggested by the Jenard and Schlosser Reports. They are of substantial persuasive authority, but their use as an aid to interpretation should never be uncritical.

3. Other aids to interpretation

13.26   In addition to the Official Reports and the case law of the European Court, English courts may wish to use other permissible aids in interpreting the Convention. Four such aids should be mentioned, namely the decisions of foreign courts, learned commentar-

---

[8] *Fothergill* v. *Monarch Airlines Limited* [1981] A.C. 251, at pp. 278, 283, 287, 294–295.

[9] See para. 13.06 above. The European Court also refers to the Reports as an aid to interpretation: *Rinkau* [1981] E.C.R. 1391, at p. 1399; *Elefanten Schuh Gmbh* v. *Jacqmain* [1981] E.C.R. 1671, at p. 1687; *Ivenel* v. *Schwab* [1982] E.C.R. 1891, at p. 1899; *Gerling Konzern AG* v. *Amministrazione del Tesoro dello Stato* [1983] E.C.R. 2503, at p. 2516; *Duijnstee* v. *Goderbauer* [1983] E.C.R. 3663, at p. 3677; *Hoffman* v. *Krieg*, case 145/86, decision of February 4, 1988, (paras. 10 and 21), *The Times*, March 26, 1988; *Kalfelis* v. *Schröder, Münchmeyer, Hengst & Co.*, case 189/87, decision of September 27, 1988 (para. 9), *The Times*, October 5, 1988.

ies, the other language versions of the Conventions, and the Vienna Convention on the Law of Treaties.

Decisions of foreign courts. The case law of the other Contracting States in interpreting the Convention may provide a most useful guide. English law regards this as a legitimate aid to construction, if treated with caution and especially if the decisions referred to are of higher courts or contain cogent reasoning.[10] In the context of the Conventions, moreover, reference to the decisions of the courts of other Contracting States is further justified for an additional reason.

It has already been observed that the 1968 Convention has a unifying purpose and that this is expressly alluded to in the Preamble.[11] This purpose also appears from the Joint Declaration annexed to the 1968 Convention[12] and in the Preamble to the 1971 Protocol on Interpretation.[13] It has often been stressed by the European Court of Justice and it appears plainly from the Jenard and Schlosser Reports.[14] Moreover, the Joint Declaration annexed to the 1971 Protocol envisaged an exchange of information between Contracting States on the decisions of the higher national courts[15] in the application of the 1968 Convention. Such an exchange of information was expressly intended for the purpose of securing the effective and uniform application of the Protocol on Interpretation and, by implication, of the 1968 Convention.[16]

It has been an objection to the citation of decisions of foreign **13.27** courts that the decisions themselves may not have been made within the framework of a doctrine of precedent and may well not be followed by other courts of the same country.[17] That objection is less formidable in the context of the Convention. The courts of all Contracting States are applying a uniform set of rules which are subject to the ultimate adjudication of the European Court of Justice. Nonetheless, it should be remembered that it is only the

---

[10] *Fothergill* v. *Monarch Airlines Limited*, above, at pp. 276–277, 284, 294, 301.
[11] Para. 13.09 above.
[12] Para. 35.32 below.
[13] Para. 36.01 below.
[14] Jenard, paras. A1.26–A1.34 below; Schlosser, paras. 4 and 20–22 (paras. A1.293 and A1.309–A1.312 below).
[15] Para. 36.28 below. The courts referred to are those mentioned in Art. 2(1) of the 1971 Protocol—*i.e.* the courts which may refer questions of interpretation to the European Court.
[16] The exchange now takes the form of the D Series of the Digest of Case Law relating to the European Communities, published by the European Court of Justice.
[17] *e.g.*, *Fothergill* v. *Monarch Airlines Limited* [1981] A.C. 251, *per* Lord Diplock at p. 284.

decisions of that court which are binding on English courts in this context, and that the degree of authority to be accorded to decisions of foreign courts will depend upon a whole series of factors including the status of the court, the cogency of its reasoning and the extent to which the decision forms part of a wider and consistent body of decisions.

While many decisions of national courts are referred to in the commentary on the 1968 Convention, they should be read in the light of these considerations and English courts, like their continental counterparts, should not feel obliged to follow them.

13.28 *Commentaries.* English courts have been willing to admit the importance of academic commentaries in the interpretation of conventions[18] and in doing so have recognised that such writings play a far more important role in the law and practice of continental countries than in the adversarial systems of the common law. The 1968 Convention has attracted the detailed commentary of a number of jurists, some of whom also, incidentally, were involved in its original preparation.[19] The works of these writers, in particular, are extensively cited in the commentary below on the 1968 Convention.

13.29 *Foreign language texts.* All the language versions of the 1968 Convention and 1971 Protocol are equally authentic and no one of them is to prevail over the others. In certain instances, the commentary below on the 1968 Convention draws attention to one or more of the other language versions where the English text is ambiguous or out of accord with other versions.[20] The fact that the Convention is authentic in seven different language versions[21] necessarily rules out a literal construction of the words of the Convention according to their ordinary and natural meaning in English. Where a divergence of meaning between different language versions has appeared, the European Court has adopted a construction best suited to the context of the provision and the purpose of the Convention[22] and this approach is the same as that adopted in relation to European Community law proper:

"The different language versions of a Community text must be given

---

[18] *Ibid.*, at pp. 274–275, 283–284, 286–287, 294–295.
[19] *e.g.*, the works cited in the bibliography by Droz, Weser and Bülow.
[20] For practical purposes, reference has been made to the French, German, Italian and Dutch texts more frequently than to those in Danish, Irish or Greek.
[21] Eight, when Greek accession takes effect: see para. 34.20 below.
[22] *Rinkau* [1981] E.C.R. 1391, at p. 1400 (para. 11); *Elefanten Schuh* v. *Jacqmain* [1981] E.C.R. 1671, at p. 1685 (para. 14); *Effer* v. *Kantner* [1982] E.C.R. 825, at p. 834 (para. 5); *Gubisch Maschinenfabrik* v. *Palumbo*, case 144/86, decision of December 8, 1987 (paras. 14 and 15), *The Times*, January 12, 1988.

a uniform interpretation and hence in the case of divergence between the versions the provision in question must be interpreted by reference to the purpose and general scheme of the rules of which it forms a part."[23]

Vienna Convention on the Law of Treaties. This convention,[24] by Articles 31 to 33, regulates the interpretation of those treaties concluded after it came into effect and is admitted for this purpose by English law. It probably also codifies existing public international law and may therefore be taken to apply to the interpretation of international treaties and conventions generally,[25] including the 1968 Convention in its unamended form. Articles 31 to 33 are set out in Appendix 2.[26]

13.30

---

[23] *R.* v. *Bouchereau* [1977] E.C.R. 1999, at p. 2010.
[24] May 23, 1969, Cmnd. 7964, in force in the U.K. since 1980. See, generally, Sinclair, *The Vienna Convention on the Law of Treaties* (2nd ed.).
[25] Bennion, *op. cit.*, p. 539; *Fothergill* v. *Monarch Airlines Ltd.*, above, *per* Lord Diplock at p. 282; *cf.* Lord Scarman at p. 293; *dubitante*, Lord Fraser of Tullybelton at p. 289.
[26] Paras. A2.39 to A2.40 below.

SCOPE OF THE CONVENTION
(Preamble and Article 1)

14.01

CONVENTION
on jurisdiction and the enforcement of judgments in civil and commercial matters (as amended by the Conventions of Accession)

PREAMBLE

The High Contracting Parties to the Treaty establishing the European Economic Community,

Desiring to implement the provisions of Article 220 of that Treaty by virtue of which they undertook to secure the simplification of formalities governing the reciprocal recognition and enforcement of judgments of courts or tribunals;

Anxious to strengthen in the Community the legal protection of persons therein established;

Considering that it is necessary for this purpose to determine the international jurisdiction of their courts, to facilitate recognition and to introduce an expeditious procedure for securing the enforcement of judgments, authentic instruments and court settlements;

Have decided to conclude this Convention and to this end have designated as their Plenipotentiaries:* . . .

GENERAL NOTE

The Preamble forms an integral part of the Convention and, together with Article 1, plays an important role in determining its scope.[1] It sets the 1968 Convention in the context of the European Community and refers expressly to Article 220 of the EEC Treaty,[2] which formed the basis for its original negotiation and adoption.   **14.02**

The background to the 1968 Convention and the principles by which it is to be interpreted have already been considered.[3] The strengthening of the legal protection of persons established in the Community,[4] referred to in the second paragraph of the Preamble, has been one of the factors relied upon by the European Court of Justice in identifying a unifying purpose in the Convention and prompting the independent interpretation of its concepts.[5] Similarly, the Preamble points to the necessity, referred to in the Jenard Report,[6] of defining the international jurisdiction of the courts[7] for the purposes of providing that legal protection. The references to simplifying formalities, facilitating recognition and introducing an expeditious procedure have also been mentioned by the European Court.[8]

---

* Jenard, paras. A1.3–A1.8, A1.26–A1.33 below; Schlosser, paras. 20–22 (paras. A1.309–A1.312 below); Collins, pp. 15, 17; Dashwood/Halcon/White, pp. 9, 65–66; Kaye, pp. 216–225; Anton, para. 3.05; Droz, paras. 26–32; Weser, paras. 176–188 *quinquies*; Bülow/Böckstiegel, pp. 11–17, 18a–30.

[1] Jenard, para. A1.32 below. The Preamble is a primary source for the interpretation of the 1968 Convention: see Art. 31 of the Vienna Convention on the law of Treaties, para. A2.39 below. English courts should be careful not to treat the Preamble as equivalent to the long title of an Act of Parliament, which may normally only be used as a secondary source, in cases of ambiguity.

[2] See para. 13.03 above.

[3] Chap. 13 above.

[4] Para. 13.15, n.60 above.

[5] Paras. 13.19 *et seq.* above.

[6] Jenard, paras. A1.28–A1.30 below.

[7] Paras. 1.05 and 13.10 above. In some language versions, the fourth paragraph is clearer in indicating the idea of an international legal order: *e.g.*, French, *"la compétence de leurs juridictions dans l'ordre international . . . "*; and Italian, *"la competenza dei rispettivi organi giuridizionali nell' ordinamento internazionale . . . "* See Bülow/Böckstiegel, p. 11.

[8] Para. 13.15 above.

TITLE

Article 1

14.03   **This Convention shall apply in civil and commercial matters whatever the nature of the court or tribunal. It shall not extend, in particular, to revenue, customs or administrative matters.†**

The Convention shall not apply to:

1. **the status or legal capacity of natural persons, rights in property arising out of a matrimonial relationship, wills and succession;**
2. **bankruptcy, proceedings relating to the winding–up of insolvent companies or other legal persons, judicial arrangements, compositions and analogous proceedings;†**
3. **social security;**
4. **arbitration.***

GENERAL NOTE

1. Scope of the Convention

14.04   The 1968 Convention applies in general to civil and commercial matters (a concept discussed in more detail below), subject to certain specified exceptions. The precise limits of its scope of application are nowhere defined, but the European Court of Justice, which can give definitive rulings on the interpretation of the Convention,[9] has shown that it will have regard to this Article, to the Preamble, to the terms of Article 220 of the EEC Treaty and to other factors[10] in deciding the circumstances in which the Convention applies. In particular, a case which on its face appears to come within the 1968 Convention may in fact not do so if there is no suf-

---

† The second sentence of the first para. was added by Art. 3 of the 1978 Convention. The wording of sub-para. (2) of the second para. is discussed below, para. 14.26.

* Jenard, paras. A1.32–A1.54 below; Schlosser, paras. 20–68 (paras. A1.309–A1.354 below); Collins, pp. 17–31; Dashwood, pp. 9–15, 69–79; Hartley, pp. 10–22, 96–97; Kaye, pp. 62–156; Maxwell, paras. 4.1–4.17; Anton, paras. 3.01–3.36; Droz, paras. 33–49 *bis*; Weser, paras. 189–203; Bülow/Böckstiegel, pp. 18a–30; Geimer/Schütze, pp. 113–181, 184, 988–989; Kropholler, pp. 36–55; Gothot/Holleaux, paras. 6–31; Pocar, pp. 25–45.

[9] 1971 Protocol on Interpretation, chap. 36 below. See also the discussion of the Convention's interpretation, at paras. 13.09–13.30 above.

[10] The factors which the European Court will take into account are discussed at para. 13.15 above.

ficient international element.[11] The approach of the European Court of Justice in determining the scope of the Convention has been to refer to its purpose and scheme as well as to its actual wording.[12]

The scope of the Convention is also limited by Article 57 (conventions on particular matters and secondary legislation of the European Communities),[13] by the transitional provisions in Article 54 and the second paragraph of Article 56[14] and in Articles 34 to 36 of the 1978 Convention,[15] and by Article Vb of the 1968 Annexed Protocol (employment of mariners).[16] Court settlements[17] of proceedings excluded from the scope of the Convention are themselves excluded.[18]

2. Cases partly outside the Convention's scope

Difficulties may arise if the principal subject-matter of a case falls **14.05** partly within the Convention and partly outside it.[19] In such a case, if the court would have jurisdiction over both aspects of the case, partly pursuant to the Convention and partly pursuant to its own jurisdictional law, no problem need arise. The court can accept jurisdiction and its judgment can be accorded partial recognition in the other Contracting States, pursuant to Article 42.[20] The European Court has emphasised that, so far as its field of application is concerned, nothing in the Convention links ancillary claims and principal claims.[21] If, on the other hand, the court would have jurisdiction over the part of the case within the Convention, but not over the rest, it is faced with the question of whether the various

---

[11] Paras. 13.10–13.11 above. This aspect is of particular significance in connection with choice of jurisdiction agreements: para. 21.06 below.
[12] Para. 13.15 above.
[13] Para. 33.06 below.
[14] Paras. 32.01 and 33.03 below.
[15] Paras. 37.06–37.14 below.
[16] Para. 35.24 below.
[17] Art. 51, para. 30.14 below.
[18] Bülow/Böckstiegel/Schlafen p. 304; but *cf. ibid.*, p. 26.
[19] Different considerations apply where only a preliminary or incidental question falls outside the Convention: see para. 14.18 below.
[20] Para. 28.71 below.
[21] *De Cavel* v. *De Cavel (No. 2)* [1980] E.C.R. 731, at pp. 740–741 (paras. 7–9): see para. 14.24 below (applicability of Convention to maintenance order in divorce proceedings). Two cases before national courts where a maintenance order has been severed from a decision concerning status (para. 14.19 below) are the decision of the Oberlandesgericht Karlsruhe of June 4, 1976, case 2 W 7/76, Digest D I–1.2—B1, and *Bälon* v. *Mottet*, Digest D I–1.2—B4.

issues can be severed.[22] If they can, the court must assume jurisdiction over those aspects of the case falling within the Convention. This is because the Convention's jurisdictional rules are compulsory[23] and national courts do not have discretion whether to accept or decline the jurisdiction given to them by its provisions.

14.06 If the issues are not severable, the court will have to do the best it can (in the absence of guidance from the European Court of Justice)[24] in deciding whether to accept jurisdiction over the case.[25] In doing so, it should not only consider the letter of the Convention, but it should also weigh the consequences of accepting and declining jurisdiction, in the light of the Convention's objectives and scheme[26] and it should have regard to the reasons (described in the Jenard and Schlosser Reports) why the particular subject matter has been excluded from the scope of the Convention. It should also take into account any particular jurisdictional rules which apply to those aspects of the case falling outside the scope of the Convention and the interests of other Contracting States which might have jurisdiction or where the judgment might be enforced.[27]

14.07 *Stating the basis for jurisdiction.* Where a national court has assumed jurisdiction over a case falling partly within and partly outside the Convention, either because it has jurisdiction over both parts pursuant to different rules or because the issues are not severable, it is most desirable that the court should state in its judgment the factual and legal basis upon which it has accepted jurisdiction in respect of each part of the case. This is because, in respect of those

---

[22] The principles to be applied in deciding this issue should be determined by reference to the court's own procedural law and, if necessary, the *lex causae*; although the test provided for related actions in Art. 22 (para. 23.11 below) may prove helpful, and has been used by the Italian Court of Cassation: *Bianco* v. *Andreas Kufferath*, Giust. Civ. 1980, I, p. 103; Digest D I–1.1—B6, where a dispute concerning a contract of employment was severed from one concerning social security.

[23] Para. 15.02.

[24] A national court may seek a ruling from the European Court of Justice under the 1971 Protocol on Interpretation only if the proceedings are already being heard on appeal: Arts. 2 and 3 of the 1971 Protocol, paras. 36.05–36.11 below.

[25] *P.* v. *H.*, Journal trib. 1978, p. 119, where the Cour d'Appel, Brussels, declined to sever a wife's application in divorce proceedings for an interim order for non-cohabitation and custody, from her application for maintenance pending suit, but held the Convention applicable to both.

[26] The Convention's scheme and purpose are discussed at paras. 13.08–13.15 above.

[27] Bülow/Böckstiegel pp. 25–26. The Convention does not affect national jurisdictional rules in respect of matters outside the scope of the Convention: *Hoffman* v. *Krieg*, case 145/86, decision of February 4, 1988, *The Times*, March 26, 1988, discussed at para. 27.47 below.

parts of the judgment falling within the Convention, the courts of other Contracting States may not review the substance of the decision[28] nor (subject to certain exceptions, notably Article 27(4) in this context) its assumption of jurisdiction.[29]

A. First Paragraph: Applicability of Convention

1. "civil and commercial matters"

There is no definition in the Convention of the term "civil and commercial matters," but the European Court of Justice has ruled that it is to be given an independent interpretation.[30] The concept is known to the domestic legal systems of many of the Contracting States and appears in most of the bilateral conventions between Contracting States on recognition and enforcement of judgments. The legal systems of the civil law Contracting States generally recognise a distinction between public and private law and it is clear that it is private law which includes "civil and commercial" matters.[31] The fact that matters of public law are generally excluded from the scope of the Convention is made clear by the second sentence of the Article (added by the 1978 Convention). The distinction between public and private law, though, is not the same in each Contracting State[32] and matters which the domestic law of a Contracting State would regard as matters of public law might not be so regarded by the European Court of Justice for the purposes of the Convention.[33]   **14.08**

The first Eurocontrol decision. Certain of these points are well illustrated by the case of *LTU* v. *Eurocontrol*,[34] where the European Court had to consider the term "civil and commercial matters." Eurocontrol, which is responsible for regulating the movement of civil aviation traffic, is a creature of public law. It obtained judgment in Belgium against LTU, a German concern, for the payment of certain route charges in connection with the use of air navigation equipment. In those proceedings, LTU had unsuccessfully challenged the jurisdiction of the *Tribunal de Commerce* in Brussels on   **14.09**

---

[28] Paras. 27.75 and 28.22 below.
[29] Para. 27.62 below.
[30] *LTU Lufttransportunternehmen GmbH & Co. K.G.* v. *Eurocontrol* [1976] E.C.R. 1541; *Netherlands State* v. *Rüffer* [1980] E.C.R. 3807, discussed below.
[31] Schlosser, para. 23 (para. A1.313 below), cited by Advocate General Warner in *Netherlands State* v. *Rüffer*, above, at p. 3831.
[32] Schlosser, paras. 26–28 (paras. A1.317–A1.319 below).
[33] An example might be the French law of public works contracts: *ibid.*
[34] [1976] E.C.R. 1541.

the ground that the charges claimed were governed by public law, but that court held that it had material jurisdiction because the liability to pay the charges arose out of LTU's commercial activities. LTU's appeal against that decision was dismissed as being out of time and Eurocontrol sought to enforce its judgment in Germany, pursuant to the 1968 Convention. In the course of the enforcement proceedings, the German court referred to the European Court the question whether German or Belgian law was to be applied in deciding whether the case concerned a "civil or commercial matter."

14.10   The European Court held that neither law applied for defining that term for the purposes of the 1968 Convention and observed that the terms of Article 1 "should not be interpreted as a mere reference to the internal law of one or other of the States concerned," and that "civil and commercial matters" could not be interpreted "solely in the light of the division of jurisdiction between various types of courts existing in certain States." Instead, it ruled, the concept was to be given an independent interpretation,

> "by reference, first, to the objectives and scheme of the Convention and, secondly, to the general principles which stem from the corpus of the national legal systems."[35]

The Court went on to say that, approached in that way, certain types of judicial decision should be excluded from the Convention's scope, "either by reason of the legal relationships between the parties to the action or of the subject-matter of the action," and continued:

> "Although certain judgments given in actions between a public authority and a person governed by private law may well fall within the area of application of the Convention, this is not so where the public authority acts in the exercise of its powers.
>
> Such is the case in a dispute which, like that between the parties to the main action, concerns the recovery of charges payable by a person governed by private law to a national or international body governed by public law for the use of equipment and services provided by such body, in particular where such use is obligatory and exclusive.
>
> This applies in particular where the rate of charges, the methods of calculation and the procedures for collection are fixed unilaterally in relation to the users, as is the position in the present case where the body in question unilaterally fixed the place of performance of the obligation at its registered office and selected the national courts with jurisdiction to adjudicate upon the performance of the obligation."[36]

---

[35] *Ibid.*, at p. 1551 (para. 3).
[36] *Ibid.* (para. 4).

The Rüffer decision. The words "civil and commercial matters" **14.11** were again considered by the European Court in *Netherlands State v. Rüffer*,[37] where it was held that the Convention would not apply to an action by a public body to recover the costs of removing a wreck, which it had done in exercise of its public law powers. A motor vessel belonging to Mr. Rüffer, who was domiciled in Germany, sank in the Bight of Watum, a public waterway for the administration of which the Netherlands and Germany had agreed (despite sovereignty being disputed) that the Netherlands should be responsible. That agreement extended to the removal of wrecks and the Netherlands duly removed Mr. Rüffer's vessel and sold it, but the proceeds of sale did not meet the costs of removal. The Netherlands therefore brought an action (of a kind not known to the laws of the other five Contracting States)[38] to recover the balance of those costs. Mr. Rüffer disputed the jurisdiction of the Dutch court, and the question was referred to the European Court as to whether the concept "civil and commercial matters" included a claim such as that brought by the Netherlands against Mr. Rüffer.

The European Court reiterated that an action between a public authority and a person governed by private law might come within the Convention, but that "that is not the case if the public authority is acting in the exercise of its public law powers."[39] As the Netherlands had been acting in the exercise of public law powers in removing the wreck, its action for the recovery of costs of doing so was not a civil or commercial matter:

> "The fact that in recovering those costs the administering agent acts pursuant to a debt which arises from an act of public authority is sufficient for its action, whatever the nature of the proceedings afforded by national law for that purpose, to be treated as being outside the ambit of the Brussels Convention."[40]

The second Eurocontrol decision. The fact that there might be **14.12** divergences between the meaning of "civil and commercial matters" in the 1968 Convention on one hand, and bilateral conventions and national law on the other, was recognised by the European Court of Justice in two joined cases, again involving Eurocontrol.[41] In the course of its judgment, which decided that bilateral conventions between Contracting States continue to have

---

[37] [1980] E.C.R. 3807.
[38] *Ibid., per* Advocate General Warner, at p. 3830.
[39] *Ibid.*, at p. 3819 (para. 8).
[40] *Ibid.*, at p. 3821 (para. 15).
[41] *Bavaria Fluggesellschaft Schwabe & Co. K.G. and Germanair Bedarfsluftfahrt GmbH & Co. K.G.* v. *Eurocontrol* [1977] E.C.R. 1517.

effect in relation to matters falling outside the scope of the 1968 Convention,[42] the Court said:

> "Although this result may lead to the same expression in the Brussels Convention and in a bilateral agreement being interpreted differently, this is due to the different systems in which the concept "civil and commercial matters" is used. In relation to a bilateral agreement the acceptance of a classification, made by the court first giving judgment, by the courts of another State could lead to an appropriate result having regard to the fact that the courts of the various States are independent of one another. On the other hand if this occurred in a system such as the Brussels Convention, the interpretation of which is entrusted to a court common to all parties, it would lead to undesirable divergences."[43]

14.13   *The State of Norway decisions.* The concept "civil or commercial matters" was the subject of a series of English decisions in the context of the Hague Evidence Convention. The Court of Appeal considered whether the phrase could be given the same meaning in the context of the Hague Convention as in the 1968 Convention, but the House of Lords, after reviewing a range of comparative law material, concluded that it could not. It held that the words "civil or commercial matter" were not to be construed for the purposes of the Hague Convention in accordance with a generally acceptable international interpretation.[44]

14.14   *Criminal and penal matters.* Certain matters are clearly not within the meaning of "civil and commercial," even if in some cases they may be regarded as matters of private law. Criminal proceedings and judgments are excluded,[45] although orders as to parties' civil rights made in criminal proceedings are not. Awards of civil damages in criminal proceedings (*e.g.* in traffic accident cases) are not uncommon on the continent and fall within the scope of the Convention.[46]

The Schlosser Report says that "other proceedings imposing sanctions for breaches of orders or prohibitions intended to safeguard the public interest also fall outside the scope of civil law."[47]

---

[42] Art. 56, para. 33.03 below.

[43] [1977] E.C.R. 1517, at p. 1526 (para. 7).

[44] *In re State of Norway's Application* [1987] Q.B. 433 C.A.; *In re State of Norway's Application (No. 2)* [1988] 3 W.L.R. 603, C.A.; *In re State of Norway's Application (Nos. 1 & 2)* [1989] 2 W.L.R. 458, H.L.

[45] Schlosser, para. 29 (para. A1.320 below).

[46] *Cf.* Art. 5(4) (para. 17.03 below) and Art. II of the 1968 Protocol (para. 35.05 below). A Dutch court has declined to enforce a German court's order for costs, made in criminal proceedings in favour of a victim of a traffic accident: *Sperber v. Pfeiffer*, Ned.Jur. 1980 No. 514; Digest D I–1.1—B7.

[47] Schlosser, para. 29 (para. A1.320 below).

Exemplary damages and contractual penalties, though, probably fall within civil law. The decisive factor, according to the Schlosser Report, is "whether the penalty is for the benefit of the private plaintiff or some other private individual."[48] If it is, then the matter probably falls within the Convention.

In England, it is suggested, restitution orders under section 28 of the Theft Act 1968 and compensation orders under section 35 of the Powers of Criminal Courts Act 1973 ought probably to be regarded as civil and commercial matters for the purposes of the 1968 Convention.[49]

Employment law. In some legal systems, employment law is 14.15
regarded as separate from private law. It nonetheless falls within the scope of the Convention.[50]

2. " . . . whatever the nature of the court or tribunal . . . "

The identity of the particular court or tribunal in question is not 14.16
a decisive factor in deciding whether the case is a civil or commercial matter, but the court or tribunal must be one which exercises the juridical functions of the state,[51] although the particular national rules governing its jurisdiction do not affect the applicability of the Convention. That is determined solely by the subject-matter of the case. So, for example, proceedings before the French *Conseil d'Etat* or a German administrative court (*Verwaltungsgericht*) might be in a matter which is civil or commercial within the mean-

---

[48] *Ibid.*
[49] It would seem likely that confiscation orders under the Drug Trafficking Offences Act 1986 do not fall within the Convention, being in the nature of a fine and transferring rights of ownership to the state. A more difficult question perhaps, is whether restraint and charging orders under ss.7 and 9 of that Act are "civil and commercial" matters.
[50] Jenard, paras. A1.36, A1.102–A1.106 below. Early doubts on this point have now been decisively settled: *Sanicentral GmbH* v. *Collin* [1979] E.C.R. 3423; *Ivenel* v. *Schwab* [1982] E.C.R. 1891. See also the following national cases: France: *Naturana* v. *Varenne* Receuil D.S. 1974, Jur., p. 760, Digest D I–1.1—B1; *Laforge* v. *Naturana-Miederfabriken* Receuil D.S. 1976, Jur., p. 203, Digest D I–1.1—B4; Italy: *Bianco* v. *Andreas Kufferath* Giust.Civ. 1980, I, p. 103; Digest D I–1.1—B6 (followed in *Quelle Italia s.r.l.* v. *De Cillia* Riv.dir.int.-priv.proc. 1982, p. 377; Digest D I–1.1—B6 (note) and *Rapid Plastic Productionsgesellschaft m.b.H. & Co.* v. *Romeo*, Digest D I–1.1—B6 (note)); Belgium: *D.* v. *Société de droit allemand E.* Journal trib. 1980, p. 174, Digest D I–1.1—B5; Luxembourg; *Saarfürst-Brauerei A.G., Osiris S.à.r.l.* v. *Engels* Questions Sociales 1974/75, part 2, p. 97, Digest D I–1.1—B2.
[51] Para. 26.05 below, where the meaning of "a court or tribunal of a Contracting State" is discussed in the context of Art. 25. For the U.K., see s.50 of the 1982 Act, para. 44.45 below.

ing of the Convention, despite the exclusion of administrative matters from the scope of the Convention.[52]

The nature of the proceedings is also not relevant, as the European Court has made clear[53] and it makes no difference whether the proceedings are contentious or non-contentious.[54] Maintenance orders made by the Danish administrative authorities are expressly included.[55]

3. " . . . revenue, customs or administrative matters"

14.17   These words were added by the 1978 Convention to make clear that matters of public law are excluded from the scope of the Convention.[56] It remains to be seen how they will be interpreted by the courts, although "revenue" and "customs" are perhaps easier to define than "administrative" matters.

C. SECOND PARAGRAPH: NON-APPLICABILITY OF CONVENTION

General Note

14.18   The principal reason for exclusion of the matters listed in the second paragraph, and particularly those in sub-paragraph (1), was the considerable divergence in the domestic and private international law rules of the original six Contracting States. These differences are even more marked with the accession of the new Contracting States. So far as sub-paragraphs (2) to (4) are concerned, a further reason for their exclusion was the fact that they were the subject of existing or proposed special conventions.[57]

It is probable that the enumerated exclusions apply only if the principal subject-matter of the proceedings falls within them. This seems to be the implication of Article 27(4),[58] which requires a court to refuse to recognise a judgment if, in order to arrive at its judgment, the court of the state in which the judgment was given had decided a preliminary question concerning one of the matters listed in sub-paragraph (1) of this paragraph, in a way that conflicts

---

[52] Confirmation of this point may be found in the fact that the French Conseil d'Etat expressly, and the German Bundesverwaltungsgericht by implication, are each referred to in Art. 2(1) of the 1971 Protocol on Interpretation (para. 36.05 below) as courts which may refer questions of interpretation of the Convention to the European Court of Justice.

[53] *Netherlands State* v. *Rüffer* [1980] E.C.R. 3807: see para. 14.11 above; *De Cavel* v. *De Cavel (No. 2)* [1980] E.C.R. 731, at pp. 740–741 (paras. 7–9); see paras. 14.24 and 17.41 *et seq.* below.

[54] Jenard, para. A1.36 below.

[55] Art. Va of the 1968 Annexed Protocol, para. 35.22 below.

[56] Schlosser, para. 23 (para. A1.314 below).

[57] Jenard, paras. A1.40–A1.41 below.

[58] Para. 27.52 below.

with a rule of the private international law of the state in which recognition is sought, unless the same result would have been reached by the application of the rules of private international law of that state. In other words, the Convention permits a court to recognise a judgment in certain circumstances, notwithstanding that a preliminary question on an excluded matter had had to be decided.[59]

The precise categorisation of the excluded matters is a matter for an independent interpretation of the Convention.[60]   ·

D. SECOND PARAGRAPH, SUB-PARAGRAPH (1)

1. "the status or legal capacity of natural persons . . . "

The Schlosser Report lists the principal topics covered by this exclusion,[61] namely: **14.19**

(1) the voidability and nullity of marriages, and judicial separation;
(2) the dissolution of marriages;
(3) the death of a person;
(4) the status and legal capacity of a minor (including the right to custody after divorce or legal separation of the parents) and the legal representation of a person who is mentally ill;
(5) the nationality or domicile of a person;
(6) the care custody and control of children, irrespective of whether these are in issue in divorce, guardianship, or other proceedings;
(7) the adoption of children.

In its unamended form, the Convention's wording gave rise to considerable difficulties in relation to maintenance proceedings ancillary to proceedings concerned with the status or capacity of natural persons (notably divorce and affiliation). It was recognised that such proceedings should fall within the scope of the Convention and an amendment was therefore made to Article 5(2).[62] Questions concerning access to children almost certainly fall outside the scope of the Convention.[63]

---

[59] Schlosser, para. 51 (para. A1.338 below). See also para. 17.42 below.
[60] Para. 13.19 above; *Gourdain* v. *Nadler* [1979] E.C.R. 733, discussed at para. 14.27 below.
[61] Schlosser, para. 51 (para. A1.338 below).
[62] Para. 17.31 below; see Schlosser, paras. 32–42 (paras. A1.323–A1.329 below).
[63] *e.g.*, the decision of the Arrondissementsrechtbank, 's-Hertogenbosch of June 16, 1978, Ned. Jur.—Uitspraken in Burgerlijke en Strafzaken, 1979, No. 164; Digest D I–1.2—B7; but there is at least one reported decision to the contrary: *Denisse* v. *Von Frederici*, Gaz. Palais 1979, Somm., p. 68; Digest D I–1.2—B9.

2. " . . . rights in property arising out of a matrimonial relationship . . . "

14.20   These words are a translation of the French *"les régimes matrimoniaux,"* a particular concept of French law which has analogies in the laws of the other original Contracting States. In English law, subject to certain statutory provisions, proprietary relationships between spouses are largely based on the general law, usually of trusts, and have the same status in law as proprietary relationships with third parties. The problem is discussed at some length in the Schlosser Report,[64] where the agreed statement of the negotiators is recorded:

> "The Convention does not apply to the assumption of jurisdiction by United Kingdom and Irish courts, nor to the recognition and enforcement of foreign judgments by those courts, if the subject matter of the proceedings concerns issues which have arisen between spouses, or exceptionally between a spouse and a third party, during or after the dissolution of their marriage, and which affect rights in property arising out of the matrimonial relationship. The expression "rights in property" includes all rights of administration and disposal—whether by marriage contract or by statute—of property belonging to the spouses."

14.21   *The first De Cavel decision.* The European Court of Justice has considered the scope of this exclusion in *De Cavel* v. *De Cavel (No. 1).*[65] In that case, in divorce proceedings pending in Paris, the husband obtained a protective order freezing the wife's bank account and safe in Frankfurt and placing the couple's furniture and other assets in their flat there under seal. He then applied to the court in Frankfurt for an order for the enforcement of those protective measures. He failed at first instance (because of his failure to produce certain documents) and, on appeal, because the court held that the case fell outside the Convention. He appealed to the *Bundesgerichtshof*, which referred to the European Court the question whether the 1968 Convention applied to protective measures putting under seal and freezing assets, made in proceedings concerning personal status or rights in property arising out of a matrimonial relationship. The European Court said this:

> "The enforced settlement on a provisional basis of proprietary legal relationships between spouses in the course of proceedings for divorce is closely linked to the grounds for divorce and the personal situation of the spouses or any children of the marriage and is, for that reason, inseparable from questions relating to the status of persons raised by the dissolution of the matrimonial relationship and from th

---

[64] Schlosser, paras. 43–50 (paras. A1.330–A1.337 below).
[65] [1979] E.C.R. 1055.

settlement of rights in property arising out of the matrimonial relationship.

Consequently, the term "rights in property arising out of a matrimonial relationship" includes not only property arrangements specifically and exclusively envisaged by certain national legal systems in the case of marriage but also any proprietary relationships resulting directly from the matrimonial relationship or the dissolution thereof.

Disputes relating to the assets of spouses in the course of proceedings for divorce may therefore, depending on the circumstances, concern or be closely connected with:

(1) questions relating to the status of persons; or
(2) proprietary legal relationships between spouses resulting directly from the matrimonial relationship or the dissolution thereof; or
(3) proprietary legal relationships existing between them which had no connection with the marriage.

Whereas disputes of the latter category fall within the scope of the Convention, those relating to the first two categories must be excluded therefrom.

The foregoing considerations are applicable to measures relating to the property of spouses whether they are provisional or definitive in nature."[66]

In the light of that decision, it remains to be seen what rights in **14.22** property will be regarded by the courts as "arising out of" (or, in the words of the judgment, "resulting directly from") the matrimonial relationship.[67] This problem of categorisation is one which the enforcement procedure in Title III is not well-suited to resolving.[68]

Rights in real property, if they fall within the Convention at all in

---

[66] *Ibid.*, at p. 1066 (para. 7).
[67] Little help is derived from the case of *W. (C.H.)* v. *H. (G.J.)* [1982] E.C.R. 1189, where the European Court was asked by the Hoge Raad of the Netherlands whether the exclusion in this sub-paragraph extended to an application by a husband for provisional measures to secure the delivery up of a document in his wife's possession to prevent her using it as evidence in her action against him. The action related to the husband's management of the wife's separate property, but the reference to the European Court was upon the basis that the management "must be regarded as closely connected with proprietary relationships flowing directly from the marriage bond." In the light of the terms of the reference, the European Court apparently had no difficulty in saying that the matter fell outside the Convention. The European Court therefore found no need to answer another question, as to whether the husband's application was excluded by reference to "wills and succession." A question concerning provisional measures was also submitted to the Court, and this is discussed under Art. 24 (para. 24.14 below).
[68] The enforcing court is not likely to be well equipped to determine the sources of the rights to which the judgment was intended to give effect, especially if it is an interim order: see Advocate General Warner in *De Cavel* v. *De Cavel (No. 1)* [1979] E.C.R. 1055, at p. 1074.

the context of matrimonial property, are subject to the exclusive jurisdiction provisions of Article 16(1).[69]

14.23   *Maintenance.* It is clear from Article 5(2) that maintenance obligations are not excluded from the scope of the Convention, but the borderline between maintenance and rights in property arising from a matrimonial relationship is sometimes less than clear. The nature of maintenance obligations is considered in more detail in connection with Article 5(2),[70] but it is the nature of the obligation which is important, rather than the frequency or method of payment. So, lump sum orders are probably covered if they are in lieu of periodical payment orders in the nature of maintenance, but not if they are property adjustment orders; conversely, property adjustment orders (or agreements) payable by instalments are probably not covered.[71]

14.24   *The second De Cavel decision.* In *De Cavel v. De Cavel (No. 2),*[72] the European Court of Justice ruled that both an interim order for maintenance pending suit and an order made at the time of the divorce decree awarding the wife an "interim compensatory allowance," fell within the scope of the Convention. The court emphasised that, so far as its field of application was concerned, no provision in the Convention linked the treatment of ancillary claims to the treatment of principal claims, and that the interim or final nature of a judgment is not relevant to whether it comes within the scope of the Convention.[73]

3. " . . . wills and succession"

14.25   It is usually a straightforward matter to determine whether the principal subject-matter of a case concerns wills and succession. If it does, it is excluded from the scope of the Convention, although there may be a grey area between law relating to wills and succession on one hand and the general law of trusts on the other: for example, disputes concerning the relations of trustee and persons other than beneficiaries may come within the scope of the Convention.[74] The fact that the proceedings would fall within the exclusive jurisdiction provisions of Article 16, as would be the case in relation

---

[69] Para. 20.11 below. *e.g., X* v. *Y*, Ned.Jur. 1981, No. 555; Digest D I–16.1—B5.
[70] Paras. 17.34 *et seq.* below.
[71] An order made in Belgium attaching a wife's earnings to enforce her obligations to contribute to the expenses of the family has been held by a court in the Netherlands to fall outside the Convention: *H.B.* v. *A.K.* Digest D I–1.2—B17. The correctness of the decision may be doubted.
[72] [1980] E.C.R. 731, discussed at para. 17.34 below.
[73] *Ibid.*, at pp. 740–741 (paras. 7–10).
[74] Collins, p. 27. See Art. 5(6), para. 17.65 below.

to rights *in rem* in immovable property,[75] does not affect the exclusion of the case from the scope of the Convention if it concerns wills and succession.[76]

On the other hand, the fact that an order for payment in the nature of maintenance arises under the law of succession does not automatically exclude it from the Convention.[77] Similarly, gifts are not excluded from the scope of the Convention, save to the extent that they are governed by the law on wills and succession.[78]

E. SECOND PARAGRAPH, SUB-PARAGRAPH (2)

"bankruptcy, *proceedings relating to the winding-up of insolvent companies or other legal persons, judicial arrangements, compositions and analogous proceedings*"

The words in bold italics[79] do not appear in the other language **14.26** versions. They are not an amendment, merely a broad translation. The words were inserted because the concept of bankruptcy of incorporated companies is not known to English law.[80]

It was the intention that the 1968 Convention and the EEC Convention on Bankruptcy should dovetail, so that proceedings should fall within one but not the other. But the Bankruptcy Convention has been long delayed, is still only in draft and in the meantime should preferably not be referred to for the purposes of interpreting the scope of the Brussels Convention.[81]

The proceedings contemplated by this sub-paragraph are described in the Jenard Report as follows:

> "those proceedings which, depending on the system of law involved, are based on the suspension of payments, the insolvency of the debtor or his inability to raise credit, and which involve the judicial authorities for the purpose either of compulsory and collective liquidation of the assets or simply of supervision."[82]

Gourdain v. *Nadler.* The European Court of Justice had occasion **14.27** to consider the interpretation of the exclusion in sub-paragraph (2) in *Gourdain* v. *Nadler*.[83] The liquidator (*"syndic"*) of a French company had obtained an order against the *de facto* manager of the com-

---

[75] Art. 16(1), para. 20.11 below.
[76] For example, *J.J. Wellen c.s.* v. *W. J. H. G. Wellen* Ned.Jur. 1980, No. 609; Digest D I–1.2—B11.
[77] Para. 17.37 below.
[78] Jenard, para. A1.47 below.
[79] The italics themselves do not appear in the text of the Convention.
[80] Schlosser, paras. 53 and 55–59 (paras. A1.340 and A1.343–A1.347 below).
[81] See the Opinion of Advocate General Reischl in *Gourdain* v. *Nadler* [1979] E.C.R. 733 at p. 751 and Schlosser, para. 54 (para. A1.341 below).
[82] Jenard, para. A1.48 below.
[83] [1979] E.C.R. 733.

pany and he sought to enforce it in Germany. The judgment had
been obtained under a French law which provided that the debts of
a company in liquidation could be ordered, on the application of the
liquidator or of the court's own motion, to be paid by the manager
personally if the company did not have sufficient assets to satisfy
the creditors. The *Oberlandesgericht* in Frankfurt had declined to
grant an order for enforcement[84] and on the liquidator's appeal the
Bundesgerichtshof referred to the European Court the question
whether the Convention was applicable to an order of the sort
which he had obtained.

The European Court ruled that the concepts covered by this sub-
paragraph were to be given an independent interpretation and that
if decisions relating to bankruptcy and winding-up were to be
excluded from the scope of the Convention, it was necessary that
they should:

> "derive directly from the bankruptcy or winding-up and be closely
> connected with the proceedings for the *'liquidation des biens'* or the
> *'règlement judiciaire.'* "[85]

The court examined the particular provision of French law under
which the order had been made, concluded that it was based solely
on the provisions of the law on bankruptcy and winding-up as interpreted for the purposes of the Convention, and held that the order
obtained by the liquidator was outside the scope of the Convention.[86]

---

[84] Order of September 7, 1977, case 20 W 466/77, Entscheidungen der Oberlandesgerichte in Zivilsachen 1978, p. 220.

[85] [1979] E.C.R. 733, at p. 744 (para. 4).

[86] It is of interest to note the factors which the European Court relied upon in
reaching that conclusion, namely that:

> (i) the application could only be made to the court which had made the
> winding-up order;
> (ii) only the liquidator was permitted to apply for such an order, on behalf
> of the general body of creditors;
> (iii) the managers of the company were presumed to be liable, unless they
> proved that they had managed the company with all requisite energy
> and diligence;
> (iv) the time within which the application had to be made was calculated by
> reference to the date when the final list of claims was drawn up and the
> duration of any scheme of arrangement;
> (v) if the application succeeded, it was the general body of creditors which
> benefited;
> (vi) the court could make the order against the manager, without having to
> investigate whether he was a business man able to meet his liabilities.

The decision of the Bundesgerichtshof following that ruling upheld the refusal to grant an order for enforcement: May 16, 1979, case VIII ZB 41/77, [1979]
3 C.M.L.R. 202, N.J.W. 1979, p. 2477, Digest D I-1.2—B13.

Incidental proceedings. It follows from that decision that an **14.28**
important distinction is to be drawn between, on one hand, proceedings based on the bankruptcy, winding-up or insolvency and
which derive directly from it and, on the other hand, proceedings
which are incidental to it. Only the former are excluded from the
scope of the Convention. Although the applicability of the Convention in this context is to be tested according to the independent
interpretation laid down by the European Court, a factor which
national courts have often considered is whether the outcome of the
proceedings depends upon insolvency law, or whether the insolvent
person would, but for his insolvency, have been able to pursue that
claim.[87]

Solvent companies. Because the exclusion in sub-paragraph (2) **14.29**
relates to insolvency, proceedings based on the winding-up of solvent companies fall within the Convention (and this is particularly
relevant to the exclusive jurisdiction provisions of Article 16(2)).[88]
If a company is being wound up for a reason other than its insolvency, the application of the Convention will nonetheless be
excluded if the company was in fact insolvent. It may be necessary,
therefore, for a court in one Contracting State, asked to order the
enforcement of a judgment given in another Contracting State

---

[87] *e.g.*, in a Belgian case the Convention has been held inapplicable to a liquidator's
claim for the purchase price of goods of which the defendant (who had been a
creditor of the company) had taken possession during the "*periode suspecte*"
before the commencement of the liquidation, with a view to setting off the company's trading debts: *S. A. Jaczon-Frigo* v. *B. V. Rodenburg*, Digest D I–1.2—
B5. On the other hand, for example, the Convention has been held applicable in
the following cases before national courts. Belgium: *Van Rolleghem* v. *Roth*,
Digest D I–1.2—B5 n.1 (claim by a trustee in bankruptcy for the purchase price
of goods supplied by the bankrupt before the commencement of the bankruptcy
proceedings); *Cie. Française des Transports Drouin* v. *Curator Faillissement
P.V.B.A. Intertrucking*, Digest D I–1.2—B5 n.2 (appeal against default judgment which had been obtained by company before it went into liquidation continued against liquidator); *Laick Jean* v. *Curateur à la faillite de la S.P.R.L.
Pauwels et Cie*, Digest D I–1.2—B14 (claim by liquidator of agent company for
commission and damages against principal, where the outcome of the proceedings did not depend on insolvency law); Netherlands: *Drettmann* v. *Curator in
het faillissement van Miedema's Jachtbouw B.V.*, Digest D I–1.2—B15 (liquidator's counterclaim for money and delivery of a yacht); France: *Société Forges de
Vulcain* v. *Société Index Verkaufs GmbH*, Rev. Soc. 1980, p. 557, Digest D
I–1.2—B16 (action by receiver and manager of a company undergoing a judicial
arrangement for recission of a dealership contract due to its unilateral termination by the defendant before the commencement of insolvency proceedings);
Société F.I.R. v. *Hértiers Baas*, Rev. Critique 1980, p. 121, Digest D I–27.2—
B12 (application, after the conclusion of the insolvency proceedings, by the
liquidator's assignee, for the enforcement of a judgment for payment for goods
supplied).
[88] Para. 20.26 below.

based upon the winding-up of a company for some reason other than insolvency, to examine whether the company was in fact insolvent.[89] The Schlosser Report says that legal disputes consequent upon voluntary windings-up under United Kingdom law cannot be equated with court proceedings and as such are not excluded from the scope of the Convention, and that this also applies in the case of a winding-up subject to the supervision of the court, where the court's powers "are not sufficiently clearly defined for the proceedings to be classed as judicial."[90]

F. SECOND PARAGRAPH, SUB-PARAGRAPH (3)

"social security"

14.30   Social security is not defined, but is likely to be interpreted in the light of European Community law generally.[91] The fact that social security is mentioned in the second paragraph of Article 1 illustrates that in some national legal systems certain aspects of it may be regarded as a matter of private law[92] and hence a civil or commercial matter.[93]

It is clear that not all litigation which relates to social security is excluded from the scope of the Convention. The Jenard Report states that:

" . . . the litigation on social security which is excluded from the scope of the Convention is confined to disputes arising from relationships between the administrative authorities concerned and employers or employees. On the other hand, the Convention is applicable when the authority concerned relies on a right of direct recourse against a third party responsible for injury or damage, or is subrogated as against a third party to the rights of an injured party insured

---

[89] Collins, p. 27, notes that the compulsory winding-up of solvent companies also falls within the draft Bankruptcy Convention.

[90] Schlosser, para. 57 (para. A1.345 below).

[91] See, *e.g.* Arts. 51 and 118 of the EEC Treaty and EEC Reg. 1408/71.

[92] Jenard, para. A1.50 below.

[93] *e.g.*, a court in the Netherlands has held that Belgian proceedings were outside the Convention because they related to payments in the nature of social security (employer's contributions payable under a collective agreement between employers and employees to a fund for payment to building workers laid off due to bad weather): *Nationale Patroonskas voor het betaaldverlof in de bouwbedrijven en openbare werken* v. *Janssen*, Ned.Jur. 1982, No. 99, Digest D I–1.2—B18. By contrast, in third party proceedings by an Italian company against a German company claiming indemnity against an obligation to pay employer's sickness insurance contributions, it does not seem to have been suggested that the case concerned obligations in the nature of social security: *Karl Presser u. Co. GmbH* v. *Eurosped S.R.L.*, Il Massimario del Foro Italiano 1979, Col. 1064; Digest D I–5.1.2—B28.

by it, since in doing so, it is acting in accordance with ordinary legal rules."[94]

It is suggested that this statement is not comprehensive as to the scope of the exclusion. For example, litigation between the administrative authorities concerned and persons other than employers and employees (such as self-employed persons) is also excluded if it is concerned to enforce rights which can properly be regarded as social security rights. Equally, though, the Convention applies to a wider range of rights of direct recourse or subrogated rights than those within the field of injury or damage. Rights of recovery by the administrative authorities against a maintenance debtor, where the maintenance creditor is in receipt of social security benefits, would fall within the Convention.[95]

G. SECOND PARAGRAPH, SUB-PARAGRAPH (4)

"arbitration"

The scope of this exclusion is the subject of some dispute. It is **14.31** clear that the Convention does not extend to the recognition and enforcement of arbitral awards as such, nor to judgments which incorporate such awards,[96] notwithstanding that arbitration is one of the matters referred to in Article 220 of the EEC Treaty which forms the basis for the 1968 Convention.[97] It is generally accepted, too, that the Convention does not apply to court proceedings which are really part of the arbitration process, whether that process is yet to be started, is in progress or has concluded. So, for example, proceedings are excluded from the scope of the Convention if they are for the principal purpose of appointing an arbitrator, fixing the place for the arbitration, setting aside an arbitral award, or ruling on points of law arising during the course of the arbitration.[98]

---

[94] Jenard, para. A1.53 below.
[95] Schlosser, para. 97 (para. A1.385 below).
[96] Schlosser, para. 65 (para. A1.351 below); Decision of Landgericht Hamburg of April 24, 1979, Case No. 5 O 112/79, RIW/AWD—1979, p. 493; Digest D I–1.2—B12. In England, an order may be made by the court for the enforcement of an arbitration award and a judgment may be entered in the terms of the award: Arbitration Act 1950, s.26. Both are excluded from the Convention, as is an action to enforce the award at common law. On the enforcement of arbitration awards generally, see Mustill & Boyd, *Commercial Arbitration* (2nd ed.), chap. 28.
[97] Para. 13.03 above.
[98] See Jenard, para. A1.54 below and Schlosser, paras. 64–65 (para. A1.351 below); Collins, p. 29; Geimer/Schütze, p. 180. Orders made in aid of arbitration under the Arbitration Act 1950, s.12(6), would be excluded from the scope of the Convention.

14.32   *A wider interpretation?* The disputed question is whether the scope of sub-paragraph (4) extends further, so as to exclude all disputes which the parties had agreed should be resolved by way of arbitration. That view was urged by the government of the United Kingdom during the course of the negotiations for the United Kingdom's accession to the Convention, but found little favour with the representatives of the other Contracting States and consequently no amendment was made to the Convention to accommodate this wider reading of the exclusion.[99]

The classic case will be where a court assumes jurisdiction over a dispute, despite a valid arbitration clause, and the successful party then seeks to enforce his judgment in another Contracting State pursuant to the Convention. At the recognition and enforcement stage, the court addressed has only very limited power to review the jurisdiction of the original court[1] and is not entitled to refuse to recognise and enforce such a judgment if it falls within the Convention.[2] If the argument advanced by the United Kingdom negotiators is correct, the court of the state addressed would be free to hold that the decision fell within sub-paragraph (4) and was therefore outside the scope of the Convention.[3] Its recognition and enforcement in that state would accordingly be a matter for national law and applicable international conventions.

14.33   The argument that that is the correct interpretation of the Convention, as recorded in the Schlosser Report, is that:

> "since a court in the state addressed is free, contrary to the view of the court in the state of origin, to regard a dispute as affecting the status

---

[99] Schlosser, paras. 61–62 (paras. A1.349–A1.351 below), where the respective arguments are recited. The Working Party agreed that the new Contracting States could deal with the question in their implementing legislation and the U.K. did so by section 32 of the 1982 Act (para. 43.25 below). That section requires courts in the U.K. not to recognise or enforce foreign judgments if the proceedings were (*inter alia*) brought contrary to "an agreement under which the dispute in question was to be settled otherwise than by proceedings in the courts of that country." But by subs. 32(4), that provision is expressly stated not to affect the recognition or enforcement of a judgment which is required to be recognised or enforced under the Convention, and the Act does not therefore prejudge the disputed question discussed in the next para.

[1] Paras. 27.62 *et seq.* below.

[2] The ground on which recognition and enforcement of a judgment may be refused are strictly limited: see paras. 10.27 above and 25.11 *et seq.* below.

[3] In *Marc Rich & Co. AG* v. *Società Italiana Impianti PA (The Atlantic Emperor)* [1989] E.C.C. 198, leave was given by the High Court for an originating summons to be served out of the jurisdiction in Italy, claiming the appointment of an arbitrator under the Arbitration Act 1950, s.10, despite the fact that proceedings were already on foot between the parties in Genoa. The question whether that is permissible under the Convention has since been referrred by the Court of Appeal to the European Court of Justice.

of an individual, or the law of succession, or as falling outside the scope of civil law, and therefore as being outside the scope of the 1968 Convention, it must in the same way be free to take the opposite view to that taken by the court of origin and to reject the applicability of the 1968 Convention because arbitration is involved."[4]

That argument does not mean that the court addressed may treat a judgment as falling outside the Convention if arbitration is only incidentally involved in the decision, any more than it can treat a case only incidentally involving any of the other excluded matters as being outside the Convention. The Convention specifically allows judgments to be refused recognition in certain circumstances where a preliminary question concerning personal status, matrimonial property or succession has arisen: Article 27(4); but it does not do so where a preliminary question concerning an arbitration clause has arisen.[5] It is not easy to see how, in the absence of special circumstances, arbitration can be said to form the principal subject-matter of a dispute which has been resolved by a judgment ignoring or overruling an arbitration clause.

The European Court has held that the scope of the 1968 Convention is to be determined by means of its independent interpretation[6] and the question whether the assumption of jurisdiction by a court in a Contracting State contrary to the terms of an arbitration agreement, or after holding the arbitration agreement invalid, will ultimately have to await the decision of that court.

The New York Convention. All the Contracting States are parties to **14.34** the New York Convention on the Recognition and Enforcement of Foreign Arbitral Awards of June 10, 1958,[7] Article II(3) of which requires courts of its Contracting States to respect written arbitration agreements and, at the request of one of the parties, to refer a dispute to arbitration unless it finds the agreement null and void, inoperative or incapable of being performed. It is at least arguable that the New York Convention is a "convention on a particular matter" within Article 57 of this Convention and that Article II(3) of the New York Convention "lays down conditions for the recognition and enforcement of judgments" for the purposes of that Article.[8]

---

[4] Schlosser, para. 62 (para. A1.351 below).
[5] The German Bundesgerichtshof has declined to review the decision of an Italian court which had held an arbitration clause invalid: Order of March 28, 1979, case VIII Z B 1/78, RIW/AWD—1979, p. 710, Digest DI—17.1.1—B10.
[6] *Gourdain* v. *Nadler* [1979] E.C.R. 733.
[7] U.N. Treaty Series (1959) 330 The text is set out in Mustill and Boyd, *Commercial Arbitration* (2nd ed.), pp. 725 *et seq.* In the U.K., see the Arbitration Act 1975 and the Arbitration (Foreign Awards) Order 1984, (S.I. 1984 No. 1168) and the Arbitration (Foreign Awards) (Amendment) Order 1985, (S.I. 1985 No. 455.)
[8] See Art. 25(2)(b) of the 1978 Convention, discussed at para. 33.07 below.

The interpretation of Article 57 poses particular difficulties but, if that is correct, courts in one Contracting State would have considerable scope to refuse recognition to a judgment given in defiance of a written arbitration agreement by the courts of another Contracting State.

14.35   *Freedom to arbitrate.* However wide the exclusion of arbitration from the scope of the Convention may eventually prove to be, it is clear that the Convention does not affect the right of parties to submit their dispute to arbitration if they wish, even if the dispute is one for which the Convention provides exclusive jurisdiction.[9]

---

[9] Schlosser, para. 63 (para. A1.351 below).

CHAPTER 15

JURISDICTION—GENERAL INTRODUCTION TO TITLE II

	PARA. NO.			PARA. NO.
1. Scheme of Title II	15.01	3.	Concurrent Jurisdiction	15.16
2. Summary of Provisions in				
Title II	15.04			

1. Scheme of Title II

Title II (Articles 2 to 24) governs jurisdiction and is the first of **15.01** the two substantial parts of the Convention.[1] Its provisions form part of the laws of each of the Contracting States and they constitute a comprehensive code of rules defining the jurisdiction of national courts in respect of cases which fall within the scope of the Convention.[2] They are called "direct" rules of jurisdiction,[3] because they confer jurisdiction on national courts even in circumstances where the Contracting States' other rules of jurisdiction would not do so.[4]

No discretion. The rules are compulsory.[5] The courts of the **15.02** Contracting States must examine their own jurisdiction in any case to which the Convention applies[6] and accept or decline juris-

---

[1] The jurisdiction of the English courts in the light of the Convention is discussed in chap. 1 above.

[2] The scope of the Convention is governed by Art. 1, para. 14.03 above.

[3] Jenard, paras. A1.28–A1.29 below.

[4] *e.g.*, if the national law of a given Contracting State did not recognise the jurisdiction of the court for the place of performance of a contractual obligation, the plaintiff could nonetheless sue a defendant domiciled in another Contracting State before that court in reliance on Art. 5(1), because the Convention confers jurisdiction upon that court. By ratifying the Convention, the Contracting State has conferred that jurisdiction on the court in question: Jenard, paras. A1.95–A1.96 below. Arts. I, V and Vb of the 1968 Protocol (paras. 35.01, 35.20 and 35.24 below) are exceptions, where the Convention does contain supplementary jurisdictional rules.

[5] See, *e.g.*, Schlosser, para. 22 (paras. A1.311–A1.312 below); Collins, p. 84; Droz, para. 206; Geimer/Schütze, pp. 208, 507, 918. See para. 16.06 below. In the context of exclusive jurisdiction under Art. 16, see paras. 20.07 and 20.08 below; and in the context of jurisdiction agreements under Art. 17, see paras. 21.15 and 21.16 below. See, further, n.8a below.

[6] Art. 20, para. 22.11 below. Strictly, that provision only applies where the defendant is domiciled in *another* Contracting State; but the court will usually have international jurisdiction under Art. 2 if the defendant is domiciled in the

diction accordingly.[7] It makes no difference whether or not another court has jurisdiction; if a court has jurisdiction under the Convention, it is required to exercise it if called upon to do so, except in the limited circumstances allowed by the Convention— notably the *lis pendens* and related action provisions of Articles 21 to 23.[8] National courts have no discretion in the matter and they cannot decline jurisdiction on the grounds of *forum non conveniens*.[8a]

15.03 *International and local jurisdiction.* Some provisions of the Convention allocate jurisdiction to the courts of a particular state or states.[9] In such cases, the Convention regulates only the *international* jurisdiction of the courts, and it is for national law in each state to determine which particular court may hear the matter. National laws may apply various criteria in allocating jurisdiction between different courts. They may do so by reference to the locality of the defendant's domicile or some other connecting factor, or by reference to the value or the subject-matter of the claim. Other provisions of the Convention allocate jurisdiction to a particular court[10] or the courts of a particular place,[11] and in such instances the Convention regulates both the international and the *local* jurisdiction of the courts.

---

same state as the court, and the question of whether the court also has local jurisdiction is not regulated by the Convention. If Art. 16 applies, giving the courts of another Contracting State exclusive jurisdiction over the case, the duty of the court seised to examine its own jurisdiction arises under Art. 19, para. 22.01 below.

[7] There are also limited powers for the court to stay its proceedings instead of declining jurisdiction where the same or a related issue is the subject of proceedings before the court of another Contracting State: Arts. 21 and 22, paras. 23.01 and 23.11 below. The court may also have to stay its proceedings where there is inadequate proof of service of the writ or other originating process: Art. 20, para. 22.11 below.

[8] Chap. 23 below.

[8a] *Industrie Tessili* v. *Dunlop* [1976] E.C.R. 1473. at p. 1490, *per* Advocate General Mayras; *De Wolf* v. *Cox* [1976] E.C.R. 1759, at 1759, at p. 1779, *per* Advocate General Mayras; *The Linda* [1988] 1 Lloyd's Rep. 175, at p. 180; Schlosser, paras 76–78 (paras. A1.363–A1.365 below); Maxwell Report, para. 1.26; Collins, p. 45; Jacob (ed.) *Private International Litigation*, p. 49; Cheshire and North, pp. 326–329; Lasok and Stone, *Conflict of Laws in the European Community*, pp. 280 *et seq.*; Anton, pp. 66, 180; Droz, paras. 51–52 and 206; Bülow/Böckstiegel/Schlafen, p. 33; Kropholfer, p. 62. *Cf.* Dicey and Morris, p. 388; *contra*, Kaye, pp. 1224 *et seq.*; Hartley, pp. 78 *et seq.* The extent to which English courts retain discretionary powers to stay proceedings is discussed at paras. 1.36 to 1.40 above and 44.40 to 44.44 below.

[9] *e.g.*, Arts. 2, 5(6), 8 (first para., sub-paras. (1) and (3)) and 14.

[10] *e.g.*, Arts. 6(2), 6(3), 6A and 10 (first and third paras.).

[11] *e.g.*, Arts. 5 (except 5(6)), 6(1), 8 (first para., sub-para. (2)) and 9.

2. Summary of provisions in Title II

General provisions. Title II consists of nine sections.[12] **Section 1** (Articles 2 to 4) contains general provisions relating to jurisdiction. If a defendant is domiciled[13] in a Contracting State, Article 2 confers international jurisdiction on the courts of that state, leaving national law to determine questions of local jurisdiction, and Article 3 prevents the exorbitant bases of jurisdiction available as a matter of national law from being exercised against him. Where the defendant is not domiciled in a Contracting State, though, the operation of the various national rules of jurisdiction is preserved by Article 4. As between persons domiciled in Contracting States, Articles 2 and 4 also prohibit discrimination on the grounds of nationality in the exercise of jurisdictional rules.

15.04

Special jurisdiction. The provisions contained in **section 2** (Articles 5 to 6A) are termed rules of "special jurisdiction" by the Convention. They provide additional bases for jurisdiction over a defendant domiciled in a Contracting State as an alternative to the general rule in Article 2. The special jurisdictions in Article 5 only apply if the court to which they give jurisdiction in any particular case is in one Contracting State and the defendant is domiciled in a different Contracting State. If the defendant is to be sued in the state in which he is domiciled, the general rule of jurisdiction under Article 2 applies and national law will determine the particular court with jurisdiction over the proceedings.[14] Articles 6 and 6A contain no equivalent restriction.

15.05

With one exception,[15] these rules not only determine the international jurisdiction of the courts, they also assign jurisdiction to the courts for a particular place or to a particular court. The reasoning behind this more particular assignment of jurisdiction is that the inclusion of the special rules as an alternative to the general rules is justified in each case by the existence of some special factor or close link which connects the court to which they give jurisdiction with the subject-matter of the dispute or the nature of the pro-

15.06

---

[12] The following summary of the provisions of Title II is necessarily simplified and many of the provisions are subject to certain qualifications and exceptions. These are discussed in the detailed commentary on the Convention.

[13] "Domicile" for these purposes is quite different from a common law concept of domicile: paras. 3.05 and 3.07 above and 31.05 *et seq.* below.

[14] Droz, para. 61.

[15] Art. 5(6), which relates to trusts: see para. 15.07 below.

ceedings,[16] regardless of the place where the defendant is domiciled.

Specifically, a connection with a particular place is the connecting factor in Article 5(1) (contracts), Article 5(3) (torts) and Article 5(5) (branches, agencies or other establishments); Article 5(2) (maintenance) is concerned to protect the weaker party (which in this case is conceived to be the maintenance creditor); and, with a view to avoiding conflicting decisions, Article 5(4) (civil claims before criminal courts), Article 6 (joint defendants, counterclaims and third-party proceedings) and Article 6A (limitation claims in Admiralty) cover cases where a particular court is, or (in the case of Article 6A) may be, concerned with a related matter.

15.07   Article 5(6) is included not primarily because of the connection of trusts with a particular place, but because the concept of a trust is unknown to the laws of any of the Contracting States except the United Kingdom and Ireland.[17] It is not strictly a "special" jurisdiction, because it does not confer jurisdiction on a particular court, although for the sake of convenience it has been categorised as such.[18] Article 6A is unusual in permitting the internal law of the Contracting States to vary the court which has jurisdiction under the Convention.

15.08   The connecting factors referred to above are ones which, it is suggested, the courts should bear in mind in interpreting the terms of the rules of special jurisdiction. The rules are uniform and applicable throughout the Community, irrespective of the court in which they are being applied. The European Court has held that they should be interpreted as narrowly as is consistent with giving effect to their objectives.[19] Generally, the rules of special jurisdiction have been interpreted as containing concepts common to the Community as a whole and independent from any particular national con-

---

[16] *Industrie Tessili Italiana Como* v. *Dunlop AG* [1976] E.C.R. 1473, at p. 1485 (para. 12); *Handelswekerij G. J. Bier B.V.* v. *Mines de Potasse d'Alsace S.A.* [1976] E.C.R. 1735, at p. 1746 (para. 11); *S.A.R. Schotte GmbH* v. *Parfums Rothschild S.à.r.l.*, case 218/86, decision of December 9, 1987 (para. 9), *The Times*, January 12, 1988.

[17] Paras. 17.65 *et seq.* below.

[18] Schlosser, para. 114 (para. A1.399 below).

[19] Art. 5(3): *Handelswekerij G. J. Bier B.V.* v. *Mines de Potasse d'Alsace S.A.* [1976] E.C.R. 1735, at p. 1746 (para. 11); Art. 5(5): *Etablissements Somafer SA* v. *Saar-Ferngas AG* [1978] E.C.R. 2183, at p. 2191 (para. 7); Art. 5(1): *Zelger* v. *Salinitri* [1980] E.C.R. 89, at p. 96 (para. 3); *Effer SPA* v. *Kantner* [1982] E.C.R. 825, at p. 834 (para. 6); *Ivenel* v. *Schwab* [1982] E.C.R. 1891, at p. 1899 (para. 10); *Martin Peters* v. *Zuid Nederlandse Aannemers Vereniging* [1983] E.C.R. 907, at p. 1002 (para. 12); *Kalfelis* v. *Schroeder, Münchmeyer, Hengst & Co.*, case 189/87, decision of September 27, 1988 (para. 19), *The Times*, October 5, 1988.

cepts.[20] The courts may not apply national jurisdictional rules which allow special grounds of jurisdiction in addition to those stated in Articles 5 to 6A,[21] or which purport to limit the application of those Articles.[22]

Insurance and consumer cases. **Section 3** (Articles 7 to 12A) and **15.09** **Section 4** (Articles 13 to 15) contain special codes of rules governing, respectively, matters relating to insurance[23] and consumer cases.[24] They are designed to afford special protection to the party regarded as socially or economically the weaker, namely the consumer or, in insurance cases, the policy-holder, the insured or the beneficiary. These rules apply to the exclusion of most of the Convention's other jurisdictional rules. Generally, they allow the protected party to be sued only in the courts of his own domicile,[25] but provide him with a choice of jurisdictions when he is plaintiff. The protected party may sue the insurer or supplier either in the courts of his own domicile[26] or in the courts of the defendant's domicile.[27]

Articles 12 and 15 place tight restrictions on the circumstances in which the provisions of Sections 3 and 4 may be departed from by agreement. A jurisdiction agreement entered into before the dispute has arisen will normally only be effective in cases of certain large marine and aviation risks referred to in Article 12A, or where the policy-holder is not domiciled in a Contracting State.[28]

These Sections also contain rules relating to a number of other detailed matters, such as the operations of branches, agencies or

---

[20] See para. 13.20 above. The suggestion has been made that the provisions of Arts. 5 to 6A should be interpreted in such a way as to ensure, as far as possible, that the courts of each Contracting State, in considering the question of jurisdiction in relation to any given set of facts, would reach the same conclusion as to which court or courts had jurisdiction: Bülow/Böckstiegel/Linke, p. 51. See also *Kalfelis* v. *Schröder, Münchmeyer, Hengst & Co*, above, (para. 17).

[21] Art. 3, first para.: para. 16.09 below.

[22] Droz, para. 61; Weser, para. 233; Bülow/Böckstiegel/Linke, p. 52. See also *Re M/s The Hoop*, Bundesgerichtshof, case II ZR 198/80, October 26, 1981, [1982] E.C.C. 533, Ent. BGH in Zivilsachen, vol. 82, p. 110, Digest D I–5.1.1—B15. The Convention itself, though, allows departure from the special jurisdictional rules in Articles 5 to 6A, by the rules set out in sections 3 to 6 of Title II (discussed below) and for the limited purposes envisaged by Arts. 24 and 57.

[23] Art. 7: para. 18.01 below.

[24] Art. 13, first para.: para. 19.01 below.

[25] Art. 11, first para. (para. 18.42 below); Arts. 14, second para. (para. 19.35 below).

[26] Art. 8, first para., sub-para. (1) (para. 18.11 below); Art. 14, first para. (para. 19.35 below).

[27] Art. 8, first para., sub-para. (2) (para. 18.11 below); Art. 14, first para. (para. 19.35 below).

[28] Art. 12(4).

other establishments, co-insurers, liability insurers and direct actions against insurers by injured parties.

15.10 *Exclusive jurisdiction.* **Section 5** (Article 16)[29] grants exclusive jurisdiction to the courts of the Contracting State which has the closest connection with five specific types of proceedings. The connecting factor in each case is regarded as so strong that it outweighs all other jurisdictional considerations. These rules take precedence over all the other jurisdictional provisions in Title II, they cannot be departed from by agreement, nor waived by the entry of an unconditional appearance and they apply wherever in the world the parties are domiciled. The types of proceedings covered by Article 16 are those which are principally concerned with certain rights in immovable property or tenancies (Article 16(1)), the validity of a company's constitution or the decisions of its organs, or its dissolution (Article 16(2)), the validity of entries in public registers (Article 16(3)), the registration or validity of certain intellectual property rights (Article 16(4)) and the enforcement of judgments (Article 16(5)).

15.11 *Prorogation of jurisdiction.* **Section 6** (Articles 17 and 18) governs "prorogation of jurisdiction," that is to say jurisdiction conferred by agreement (Article 17) or by the entry of an appearance without contesting the jurisdiction (Article 18).

Jurisdiction agreements. Article 17 enables parties to confer jurisdiction by agreement on the court or courts of a Contracting State, provided that their agreement is in writing, or evidenced in writing, or, in international trade or commerce, in a form which accords with certain commercial practices of which the parties are or should have been aware.[30] The provision applies when *either* party is domiciled in a Contracting State; when *neither* party is domiciled in a Contracting State, the court or courts chosen are given priority of jurisdiction.[31] The Article contains special provisions relating to jurisdiction agreements concluded for the benefit of only one of the parties[32] and relating to jurisdiction clauses in trust instruments.[33] Article 17 takes priority over most of the other jurisdictional provisions of Title II, but not over Articles 12, 15 or 16 (insurance, consumer and exclusive jurisdiction cases), nor over Article 18.[34]

---

[29] Chap 20. below.
[30] Art. 17, first para., second sentence: para. 21.01 below.
[31] Art. 17, first para., third sentence.
[32] Art. 17, fourth para.
[33] Art. 17, second para.
[34] Art. 17, third para.

Submission to the jurisdiction. Article 18 confers jurisdiction on a   **15.12**
court where the defendant enters an appearance, but it does allow
him to contest the jurisdiction if he does so at the same time as, or
before, contesting the merits. It does not confer jurisdiction,
though, where the case falls within the exclusive jurisdiction provisions of Article 16.

Court's duty to examine its jurisdiction. **Section 7** (Articles 19 and   **15.13**
20) requires courts to examine their jurisdiction of their own
motion and to decline jurisdiction if necessary. Article 20 also
requires courts to consider whether the defendant received
adequate notice of the proceedings; if he did not, the proceedings
are to be stayed and a default judgment may not be entered.[35]

Lis pendens and related actions. **Section 8** (Articles 21 to 23)[36] con-   **15.14**
tains rules for resolving conflicts of jurisdiction which arise where
the same cause of action or related actions are being litigated concurrently in different Contracting States. The court first seised is
given priority and, generally, any other court must decline jurisdiction or, in certain circumstances, stay its proceedings.

Interim relief. **Section 9** (Article 24) relates to provisional, includ-   **15.15**
ing protective, measures. It enables measures which are available
under the national law of each Contracting State to be granted, even
where the courts of another Contracting State have jurisdiction as to
the substance of the matter. A court's jurisdiction to grant interim
measures under this provision is not limited, therefore, to cases
where it has jurisdiction over the main proceedings. Accordingly, it
may rely upon its exorbitant rules of jurisdiction for the purposes of
granting interim relief. Article 24 is of particular importance for the
purpose of preserving a defendant's assets in one Contracting State
in order to satisfy an eventual judgment given in another Contracting State. The provision does not prevent the grant of an interim
order on an *ex parte* basis, but such an order may not be enforced in
the other Contracting States unless the respondent has had notice
of it.[37]

3. Concurrent jurisdiction

Where more than one court has jurisdiction in respect of any   **15.16**
given cause of action, whether under the rules of general or special
jurisdiction, the plaintiff may be able to choose his forum. In some
cases, the Convention itself allocates priority as between the differ-

---

[35] Art. 20, second and third paras.: para. 22.11 below.
[36] Chap. 23 below.
[37] *Denilauler* v. *Couchet Frères* [1980] E.C.R. 1553, discussed at paras. 25.19 and
27.26 below.

ent rules, restricting or removing the plaintiff's choice in the matter. For example, in a contract case, a jurisdiction clause under Article 17 may prevent a plaintiff from invoking the jurisdiction of the place of performance of the obligation in question under Article 5(1), but if the contract concerned a tenancy of immovable property, Article 16(1) would take priority over the jurisdiction clause. In other cases, though, the plaintiff will have concurrent jurisdictions available to him. Most obviously, he will be able to bring proceedings against a defendant in the courts of the state where the latter is domiciled and he may well also be able to sue him in the courts of another Contracting State under one or more of the provisions of Article 5.

15.17   There is no reason why the general rule of jurisdiction in Article 2 and the various special jurisdictions in Article 5 should be regarded as mutually exclusive. As between the general rule on one hand and the special rules on the other, the plaintiff may make a free choice. Problems of classification and severability may arise, though, where more than one of the special jurisdictions may be available. For example, a claim may be based on several causes of action, only one or some of which will found jurisdiction under Article 5.[38] There are two separate problems, either or both of which may arise.

First, a single claim may be capable of formulation in different ways—in contract or in tort, for example.[39] Neither the choice of substantive law which applies to the case, nor the characterisation of the cause of action according to the applicable law, is a matter for the Convention. For jurisdictional purposes, though, uniform concepts are to be derived from the Convention such that any given claim can be classified as falling under one or more of the jurisdictional rules in the Convention.[40] Irrespective of the method by which such classification should be carried out, it seems that where a claim falls under more than one of the jurisdictional rules, the plaintiff may invoke whichever of them he chooses.[41] "Matters relating to a contract" in Article 5(1) and "matters relating to tort delict and quasi-delict" in Article 5(3) are, however, mutually exclu-

---

[38] Schlosser observes, *e.g.*, that Art. 5(6) is not exclusive: para. 118 (para. A1.402 below).

[39] *S.A. Jouets Eisenmann* v. *Geobra Brandstatter G.m.b.H. & Co. K.G. and Big Spielwaren Fabrik Dipl. Ing. Ernst A. Bettag*, Tribunal de Commerce, Liège, January 4, 1983, [1985] E.C.C. 246.

[40] *Kalfelis* v. *Schröder, Münchmeyer Hengst & Co.*, case 189/87, decision of September 27, 1988 (paras. 14–18), *The Times*, October 5, 1988. See Bülow/Böckstiegel/Linke, pp. 51–52.

[41] Collins, pp. 60–61; Geimer/Schütze, pp. 289, 536.

sive, but, between them, they cover all claims seeking to establish the liability of the defendant.[42]

Secondly, a plaintiff may seek to pursue distinct claims based on **15.18** separate causes of action in the same proceedings. The Convention does not permit him to litigate matters in a court which has no jurisdiction[43] and the court will usually be required to decline jurisdiction over any such matter of its own motion.[44] But where the court has jurisdiction under more than one rule, it does not matter which rule of jurisdiction he relies upon. If the Convention gives the court jurisdiction over some but not all of the claims in the proceedings, the question of whether the court may hear and determine those parts over which it has jurisdiction depends upon the severability of the claims according to the *lex fori*.[45] As the European Court has observed, the inconvenience involved in having different issues decided by different courts can always be avoided if the plaintiff brings the proceedings in the courts of the Contracting State where the defendant is domiciled, under Article 2.[46]

---

[42] *Kalfelis* v. *Schröder Münchmeyer Hengst & Co.*, above (para 15–18); see also paras 17.45 *et seq.* below.

[43] Collins, p. 61. National courts have been prepared, though, to accept jurisdiction over related claims by analogy with the definition of "related actions" in Art. 22 (para. 23.11 below), even though strictly they do not have power to do so under the Convention: For example, *De Bloos* v. *Bouyer*, Cour d'Appel, Mons, May 3, 1977, Digest D I–5.1.1—B6; *Maschinenfabrik Moenus AG* v. *Barenghi*, foro it. 1980, I, Col. 1108, Digest D I–5.1.1—B11.

[44] See Arts. 19 and 20, chap. 22 below.

[45] See Bülow/Böckstiegel, p. 69, para. 2(d).

[46] *Kalfelis* v. *Schröder, Münchmeyer, Hengst & Co.*, above (paras 19–21).

CHAPTER 16

JURISDICTION—GENERAL PROVISIONS
(Articles 2–4)

TITLE II

SECTION 1

Article 2

16.01   Subject to the provisions of this Convention, persons domiciled in a Contracting State shall, whatever their nationality, be sued in the courts of that State.

Persons who are not nationals of the State in which they are domiciled shall be governed by the rules of jurisdiction applicable to nationals of that State.*

---

* Jenard, paras. A1.62–A1.65, A1.80–A1.81 below; Schlosser, paras. 82–86 (paras. A1.370–A1.374 below); Collins, pp. 45–47; Dashwood/Halcon/White, pp. 21–22, 84–86; Hartley, pp. 23–31, 42–43; Kaye, pp. 253–265; Maxwell, paras. 5.20–5.23, 5.28–5.33; Anton, paras. 5.04–5.08; Droz, paras. 57–60; Weser, paras. 205–218; Bülow/Böckstiegel/Schlafen, pp. 36–40; Geimer/Schütze, pp. 38, 185–192, 255, 350–372; Kropholler, pp. 64–68; Gothot/Holleaux, paras. 37–46; Pocar, pp. 46–59.

A. GENERAL NOTE

Article 2 provides the Convention's principal rule as to jurisdic-   **16.02**
tion, namely that a person domiciled in a Contracting State is to be
sued in the courts of that state.[1] This rule applies whether or not the
Convention allows a defendant to be sued before other courts in certain circumstances, and irrespective of his nationality. The other
rules of jurisdiction in Title II are by way of exception to this central principle.[2] Some of the exceptions, mentioned below, enable
another basis of jurisdiction to be invoked to the exclusion of this
general rule of jurisdiction, while others merely provide an optional
alternative forum.

Domicile. The concept of "domicile" is clearly of central import-   **16.03**
ance and while the Convention does not define the term, it provides
uniform choice of law rules in Article 52[3] which refer the question of
definition back to the national legal systems. Article 53 provides that
the "seat" of a company or other body is to be treated as its domicile,
and it is to be defined according to the private international law of
the court seised of the issue. Both concepts, therefore, may differ
depending upon the law applied in interpreting them.[4] In most of
the Contracting States, a concept of domicile is known which is akin
to the concept of habitual residence and which, it must be emphasised, is quite different from the concept of domicile as it is traditionally known to the common law. If that common law concept had
been retained for the purposes of the Convention, it would have
resulted in considerable distortions in the workings of the Convention. The United Kingdom has therefore adopted a new series of
definitions for these jurisdictional purposes.[5]

B. FIRST PARAGRAPH: PERSONS TO BE SUED IN COUNTRY OF DOMICILE

1. "Subject to the provisions of this Convention . . . "

In addition to the general rule of jurisdiction provided by this   **16.04**
Article, the Convention contains a number of jurisdictional rules
which enable a defendant to be sued in courts other than those pro-

---

[1] This rule is derived from the maxim *actor sequitur forum rei*, which is widely known
to the civil law: see Jenard, para. A1.80 below. See also para. 1.17 above.
[2] *Industrie Tessili Italiana Como* v. *Dunlop A.G.* [1976] E.C.R. 1473, at p. 1485
(para. 12).
[3] Para. 31.01 below.
[4] The terms of Arts. 52 and 53 are such that a court may have to determine a person's domicile or seat by applying the law of another Contracting State. The relevant provisions of the law of the other Contracting States are summarised in
chaps. 48 to 58, at paras. 25 and 26.
[5] ss.41–46 of the 1982 Act (paras. 44.01–44.35 below) provide a code of definitions of the concepts of "domicile" and "seat" both for the purposes of the
Convention and for the allocation of jurisdiction within the U.K.

vided by the national law of the state of his domicile. Of these, the following operate to the exclusion of the general rule contained in this Article, enabling a defendant to object if he is sued in the courts of the state of his domicile, unless the court in question also has jurisdiction under the exceptional rule:

(i) Articles 7 to 12A, which contain jurisdictional rules for matters relating to insurance, but in which Article 12 permits a choice of jurisdiction agreement to derogate from these other jurisdictional provisions in certain limited circumstances;[6]

(ii) Articles 13 to 15, which contain similar rules for consumer contracts, including (in Article 15) limited circumstances where the other jurisdictional provisions can be departed from by a choice of jurisdiction agreement;[7]

(iii) Article 16, which provides rules of exclusive jurisdiction by reference to the principal subject-matter of the dispute, irrespective of the domicile of the parties;[8]

(iv) Article 17, which enables parties, at least one of whom is domiciled in a Contracting State, to choose which courts are to have jurisdiction to determine their dispute (and which contains similar provisions in relation to trust instruments);[9]

(v) Articles 21 to 23, which contain rules for resolving problems of *lis pendens* and related actions;[10]

(vi) Article 57, which enables jurisdictional provisions to have effect if they are contained in certain conventions relating to particular matters or in secondary legislation of the European Communities.[11]

The jurisdictional rules which apply to matters relating to insurance and consumer contracts enable an action to be brought against a defendant in the courts of the state where he is domiciled, but in those cases the jurisdiction arises not by virtue of Article 2, but by virtue of Articles 8 or 14, as the case may be.

2. " . . . persons domiciled in a Contracting State shall . . . be sued in the courts of that State"

16.05   It is the *defendant's* domicile which is relevant for the purposes of this rule, and jurisdictional rules of the Convention generally apply

---

[6] Chap. 18 below.
[7] Chap. 19 below.
[8] Chap. 20 below.
[9] Paras. 21.01 *et seq.* below.
[10] Chap. 23 below.
[11] Para. 33.06 below.

irrespective of the plaintiff's domicile.[12] Only in the case of the exclusive jurisdiction provisions of Article 16 is the domicile of the parties wholly without relevance.

Article 2 gives jurisdiction generally to the courts of the state where the defendant is domiciled, and does not regulate the local jurisdiction of the courts within that state. In other words, it does not specify the particular court in which the defendant may be sued, either by reference to locality or in any other way. It leaves that matter entirely to the internal law of the state in question and in this respect, it differs from most of the rules of special jurisdiction, especially in Articles 5 to 6A.[13]

Compulsory rules. The use of the word "shall" denotes the compulsory nature of the jurisdictional rules, which is an important feature of the Convention's scheme.[14] It also emphasises that this is the primary rule of jurisdiction and that the other jurisdictional rules are exceptions to it, a fact reflected in the more restrictive interpretation given to the other jurisdictional rules.[15] **16.06**

3. " . . . whatever their nationality . . . " **16.07**

See the next paragraph.

C. SECOND PARAGRAPH: NON-NATIONALS TO BE TREATED AS NATIONALS

The Convention prohibits discrimination in jurisdictional matters on the grounds of the defendant's nationality, even if the defendant is a national of a non-Contracting State. Such a provision is of less significance in the United Kingdom[16] than in those countries where preferential treatment in some jurisdictional matters is given to nationals of that country,[17] or less advantageous treatment is given to foreigners.[18] **16.08**

---

[12] Jurisdictional rules in the Convention based on the plaintiff's domicile are confined to Art. 5(2) (maintenance creditor); Art. 8, first para., sub-para. (2) (policy-holder's domicile); and Art. 14, first para. (consumer's domicile); and in each case the jurisdictional rule requires that the defendant also be domiciled in a Contracting State. In addition, a choice-of-jurisdiction agreement can be valid under Art. 17 where only the plaintiff is domiciled in a Contracting State.

[13] Chap. 17 below.

[14] See para. 15.02 above. The compulsory nature of the rules may need in exceptional circumstances to be relaxed, if that can be done on a basis consistent with the purposes of the Convention as a whole: see paras. 1.37 *et seq.* above.

[15] Para. 15.08 above.

[16] In English law, nationality is not material to jurisdiction, at least so far as cases falling within the Convention are concerned: see Dicey and Morris, p. 31.

[17] *e.g.*, under Arts. 14 and 15 of the French *Code civil*: see paras. 16.19 and 50.30 below.

[18] *e.g.*, arguably, under Art. 23 of the German *Zivilprozessordnung*: See para. 51.30 below, and Jenard, para. A1.84 below.

Because the Convention provides a code of direct jurisdictional rules[19] it was necessary for domicile, rather than nationality, to be adopted as the basis for jurisdiction,[20] thereby departing from the terms of Article 220 of the EEC Treaty, which refers to the "nationals" of the Member States.[21] The solution adopted, when read together with the second paragraph of Article 2 and the second paragraph of Article 4, ensures that parties are accorded equality of treatment as required by Article 7 of the EEC Treaty.[22]

The nationality of a corporation, according to English law, is determined by the country of its incorporation,[23] at least if its central management and control is carried out in that country.[24] Most continental systems determine the nationality of a company or other legal person or association of natural or legal persons by reference to the location of its seat, which Article 53 equates with its domicile[25] and in such a case the second paragraph can have no application.[26]

Article 3

16.09   **Persons domiciled in a Contracting State may be sued in the Courts of another Contracting State only by virtue of the rules set out in Sections 2 to 6 of this Title.**

In particular the following provisions shall not be applicable as against them:

— **in Belgium: Article 15 of the civil code (*Code civil—Burgerlijk Wetboek*) and Article 638 of the judicial code (*Code judiciaire—Gerechtelijk Wetboek*),**

— **in Denmark: Article 248(2) of the law on civil procedure (*Lov om rettens pleje*) and Chapter 3, Article 3 of the Greenland law on civil procedure (*Lov for Grønland om rettens pleje*),**

— **in the Federal Republic of Germany: Article 23 of the code of civil procedure (*Zivilprozessordnung*),**

[— **in Greece, Article 40 of the code of civil procedure (*Κώδικας Πολιτικῆς Δικονομίας*),]†**

— **in France: Articles 14 and 15 of the civil code (*Code civil*),**

---

[19] Para. 15.01 above.
[20] Droz, para. 12.
[21] Jenard, paras. A1.61–A1.65 below.
[22] Jenard, para. A1.79 below.
[23] See Cheshire and North, p. 192 and the cases cited there.
[24] *The Pamia* [1943] 1 All E.R. 269.
[25] Para. 31.23 below.
[26] Bülow/Böckstiegel/Schlafen, pp. 317–318.

— in Ireland: the rules which enable jurisdiction to be founded on the document instituting the proceedings having been served on the defendant during his temporary presence in Ireland,

— in Italy: Articles 2 and 4, Nos. 1 and 2 of the code of civil procedure (*Codice di procedura civile*),

— in Luxembourg: Articles 14 and 15 of the civil code (*Code civil*),

— in the Netherlands: Articles 126(3) and 127 of the code of civil procedure (*Wetboek van Burgerlijke Rechtsvordering*),

— in the United Kingdom: the rules which enable jurisdiction to be founded on:

(a) the document instituting the proceedings having been served on the defendant during his temporary presence in the United Kingdom; or

(b) the presence within the United Kingdom of property belonging to the defendant; or

(c) the seizure by the plaintiff of property situated in the United Kingdom.*†

D. First Paragraph: When Persons may be Sued

1. General note

The effect of the first paragraph of this Article is to establish the **16.10** conditions under which a defendant domiciled in one Contracting State may be sued in the courts of another Contracting State, namely where, and only where, the court in question has jurisdiction under Articles 5 to 18 of the Convention. It is the counterpart of the first paragraph of Article 2, which is concerned with jurisdiction over such a defendant in the state of his domicile, and together the two provisions establish the Convention as a comprehensive code of jurisdictional rules for cases falling within its scope where the defendant is domiciled in a Contracting State.

---

*† Jenard, paras. A1.82–A1.88 below; Schlosser, paras. 83–88 (paras. A1.371–A1.376 below); Collins, pp. 47–59; Dashwood, pp. 86–87; Hartley, p. 8; Kaye, pp. 265–269; Maxwell, paras. 5.24–5.33; Anton, paras. 1.24–12.6; Droz, para. 54; Weser, paras. 234–240; Bülow/Böckstiegel/Schlafen, pp. 40–42; Geimer/Schütze, pp. 300–307, 375; Kropholler, pp. 65–68; Gothot/Holleaux, para. 53; Pocar, pp. 59–68.

† The words in square brackets were added by Art. 3 of the 1982 Convention and are not yet in force, see para. 13.05 above. The whole of the rest of the second para. was substituted for the 1968 version by Art. 4 of the 1978 Convention.

Sections 2 to 6 of Title II (Articles 5 to 18) contain all the grounds of jurisdiction laid down by the Convention, beyond the general ground in Article 2 and, with certain exceptions (notably Articles 16 and 17),[27] those grounds do not derogate from Article 2 but are additional bases of jurisdiction. Section 2 (Articles 5 to 6A) covers a variety of specific bases of jurisdiction, some of them of great practical importance; Section 3 (Articles 7 to 12A) covers insurance cases; Section 4 (Articles 13 to 15) covers consumer contracts; Section 5 (Article 16) provides rules of exclusive jurisdiction; and Section 6 (Articles 17 and 18) covers what the Convention calls "prorogation of jurisdiction," namely jurisdiction agreements and jurisdiction based on submission by the unconditional entry of an appearance.

2. Excluded bases of jurisdiction

16.11   The terms of the first paragraph are effective to exclude reliance, as against a defendant domiciled in a Contracting State, on any basis of jurisdiction not provided for by the Convention. The paragraph is not confined to the so-called "exorbitant" jurisdictions set out in the second paragraph and its interpretation is not to be limited by reference to that paragraph.[28] On the other hand, the jurisdiction of a national court may still be invoked on an exorbitant basis against a defendant domiciled in another Contracting State, for the purpose of obtaining provisional or protective measures pursuant to Article 24.[29] The availability of such provisional or protective measures as a matter of national law, though, does not affect the application of Article 3 in defining the extent of the national courts' jurisdiction over the substance of a matter falling within the material scope of the Convention.

E. Second Paragraph: Inapplicable National Provisions

1. General note

16.12   The second paragraph of Article 3 is a helpful guide to the principal exorbitant jurisdictions in the various Contracting States, although it does not purport to be an exhaustive list. The paragraph

---

[27] The exceptions are listed at para. 16.04 above.

[28] Schlosser, para. 87 (para. A1.375 below); *e.g.* the English courts will no longer be permitted to accept jurisdiction against a defendant domiciled in another Contracting State on the ground that the claim concerns a contract which was concluded in England or is governed by English law and the extensive amendments which have been made to Ord. 11 of the Rules of the Supreme Court take account of this change.

[29] Para. 24.04 below; see Collins, "Provisional Measures, the Conflict of Laws and the Brussels Convention" (1981) 1 Yb.Eur.Law 249.

is not necessary for the purposes of the first paragraph of Article 3, nor for the purposes of the second paragraph of Article 4, which permits reliance on any of the bases of jurisdiction permitted by the *lex fori* (including the "exorbitant" jurisdictions referred to in this paragraph), against persons not domiciled in a Contracting State. It is, however, necessary for the purposes of Article 59, which permits Contracting States in certain circumstances to conclude conventions with third countries in which they agree not to recognise judgments given in other Contracting States against persons domiciled or habitually resident in the third country, if the judgment could only have been founded on a basis of jurisdiction specified in this paragraph. The provisions referred to in respect of each of the Contracting States (except Greece) are summarised in the Jenard Report,[30] in the Schlosser Report[31] and in Part 3 of this book.[32]

2. "—in the United Kingdom: . . . "

Sub-paragraph (a) relates principally to England and Northern **16.13** Ireland, sub-paragraphs (b) and (c) to Scotland.[33] Service of the court's process on a defendant within the court's territorial jurisdiction (or, in certain circumstances and with the leave of the court, out of the territorial jurisdiction) has been regarded as the basis on which English courts have founded their jurisdiction and, at present, remains so for those cases in which the court's jurisdiction is not derived from the Convention or from the jurisdictional provisions of the 1982 Act.[34] It should be noted, though, that service on a foreign company's place of business within the United Kingdom[35] is not expressly referred to. Nevertheless, it would be regarded as an exorbitant basis of jurisdiction for the purposes of the first paragraph of Article 3, but it might not found an objection to recognition or enforcement under Article 59. While English courts have been prepared to exercise jurisdiction *in personam* over a defendant outside the territorial jurisdiction of the court where the subject-matter of the action has concerned property within the jurisdiction, such jurisdiction has still been invoked by the service of the process

---

[30] Jenard, paras. A1.83–A1.88 below.
[31] Schlosser, paras. 83–86 (paras. A1.371–A1.374 below).
[32] Chaps 48 to 58, at para. 30.
[33] The Scottish jurisdictions foregone are discussed in the Maxwell Report, paras. 5.25, 14.28 *et seq.* and Annex II, paras. 1(b), 2 and 3; and by Anton, para. 5.09.
[34] ss.16 and 17 (paras. 41.01 to 41.12 below) and Scheds. 4 and 5 (chap. 45 below). The role of service in relation to jurisdiction is discussed at para. 1.15 above.
[35] Companies Act 1985, s.695; see para. 4.13 above.

on the defendant.[36] This topic is discussed in greater detail in Chapter 1.[37]

16.14   The Schlosser Report suggests that the exclusion of jurisdiction based on the presence or seizure of property in the United Kingdom will mean in England that interpleader actions are no longer permissible in respect of persons domiciled in another Contracting State, in so far as the international jurisdiction of the United Kingdom courts does not result from the other provisions of the Convention.[38] It is suggested, though, that the court's jurisdiction in such a case does not depend upon the subject-matter of the interpleader summons being present or seized within the jurisdiction. It is the first paragraph, rather than the second paragraph, of Article 3 which would prevent the English court having jurisdiction in such a case, in the absence of a ground for jurisdiction in Title II.

The exclusion of jurisdiction based on the presence or seizure of property may also affect the Admiralty jurisdiction of the English courts; this topic is also discussed in greater detail in Chapter 1.[38a]

Article 4

16.15   **If the defendant is not domiciled in a Contracting State, the jurisdiction of the courts of each Contracting State shall, subject to the provisions of Article 16, be determined by the law of that State.**

As against such a defendant, any person domiciled in a Contracting State may, whatever his nationality, avail himself in that State of the rules of jurisdiction there in force, and in particular those specified in the second paragraph of Article 3, in the same way as the nationals of that State.*

F. GENERAL NOTE

16.16   The Convention provides, for cases falling within its material scope, a comprehensive code of rules governing the international jurisdiction of the courts of the Contracting States. This Article is

---

[36] *e.g.* in the case of land, under R.S.C. Ord. 11, r. 1(1)(g) (formerly r. 1(1)(a)). Where such a case concerns rights *in rem* in, or a tenancy of, immovable property within the territorial jurisdiction, Art. 16(1) (para. 20.11 below) gives the English court exclusive jurisdiction over the case.

[37] Para. 1.15 above.

[38] Schlosser, para. 88 (para. A1.376 below).

[38a] Paras. 1.34 *et seq.* above.

* Jenard, paras. A1.89–A1.94 below; Collins, pp. 49–51; Dashwood, pp. 87–88; Hartley, pp. 7–8; Kaye, pp. 677–680; Maxwell, paras. 5.34–5.37; Anton, paras. 5.10–5.11; Droz, paras. 225–241; Weser, paras. 241–243; Bülow/Böckstiegel/Schlafen, pp. 43–47; Geimer/Schütze, pp. 54, 236, 310; Kropholler, pp. 68–69; Gothot/Holleaux, para. 35; Pocar, pp. 68–69.

therefore necessary to bring within the Convention those cases which would otherwise fall outside its scope by reason of the defendant's domicile being outside the Contracting States.

G. First Paragraph: National Law Applied to Non-Domiciliaries

The effect of the first paragraph of Article 4 is twofold. First, it ensures the applicability of the rules on *lis pendens* and related actions (Articles 21 to 23)[39] in cases even where the defendant is not domiciled in a Contracting State; and, secondly, it prevents a court of a Contracting State from relying on its national rules of jurisdiction to refuse recognition and enforcement to a judgment given in another Contracting State in respect of a matter falling within the Convention's material scope. **16.17**

Exceptions. The text of the first paragraph of Article 4 tends to suggest that Article 16 is the only exception to its terms, but there are also others. One such is the second paragraph of Article 8,[40] concerned with jurisdiction over insurers who are not domiciled in a Contracting State, but who have a branch or agency there.[41] **16.18**

Also, it seems to be generally accepted[42] that where there is a jurisdiction agreement falling within Articles 12, 15 or 17,[43] giving jurisdiction over a defendant domiciled outside the Community to a court of a Contracting State, the plaintiff should not be deprived of the right to pursue his action by some national rule more restrictive than the rules of the Convention. An illustration of the type of problem which might otherwise arise is given by *Elefanten Schuh GmbH* v. *Jacqmain*,[44] where a requirement of national law as to the language of the contract was ruled to be incompatible with Article 17 and of no effect.[45] The application of national law is restricted in cases where neither party is domiciled in a Contracting State, but where they have agreed that a court or courts of a Contracting State should have jurisdiction.[46] The same arguments apply to voluntary appearance founding jurisdiction under Article 18.

[39] Chap. 23 below.
[40] Para. 18.11 below. This para. was formerly the third para. of Art. 8, until amended by the 1978 Convention.
[41] Jenard, para. A1.90n. below.
[42] Droz, paras. 228 *et seq.*; Bülow/Böckstiegel/Schlafen, p. 44; Collins, p. 51.
[43] The omission of a reference to these provisions in Art. 4 appears to have been an error: Droz. *loc. cit.*
[44] [1981] E.C.R. 1671. The case is discussed at paras. 21.27 *et seq.* below.
[45] *Ibid.*
[46] Art. 17, first para., third sentence, para. 21.71 below.

H. SECOND PARAGRAPH: EXTENSION OF EXORBITANT JURISDICTIONS

16.19   The second paragraph of Article 4 supplements the first paragraph in respect of those Contracting States where national law provides an exorbitant basis of jurisdiction by reference to the plaintiff's nationality. For example, Article 14 of the French civil code accords to French nationals the right to sue in the French courts, on the basis of their nationality alone.[47] The privilege given by that provision to persons with French nationality may not be invoked against persons domiciled in a Contracting State. On the other hand, this Article has the effect of enabling a plaintiff domiciled in France, but of some other nationality, to take advantage of Article 14 of the French civil code in the same manner as a French national as against persons domiciled outside the Contracting States.[48]

The wording of the second paragraph makes it clear, first, that the plaintiff must be domiciled in the Contracting State in which the law provides for the particular exorbitant jurisdiction, and, secondly, that that exorbitant basis of jurisdiction is not available to plaintiffs domiciled in other Contracting States.

16.20   The extension of the exorbitant jurisdictions by the second paragraph of Article 4 provoked much criticism when it was first drafted,[49] which led to the inclusion in the Convention of Article 59.[50] The extension, though, is explained by Jenard[51] on a number of grounds, notably that it brought the practice in France and Luxembourg into line with the other Contracting States, which allowed their exorbitant jurisdictions to be used by non-nationals, and that it was justified on economic grounds and grounds of Community principle.

---

[47] Art. 14 of the Luxembourg civil code is to the same effect and, in theory at least, Art. 127 of the Netherlands code of civil procedure makes similar provision: See para. 55.30 below.

[48] Special rules apply in respect of Swiss nationals: see Art. 58 (para. 33.22 below).

[49] Collins, p. 50; Hartley, p. 8, n. 9; Hay, (1968) 17; Am.Jo.Comp. L. 160 *et seq.*; Nadelmann, (1967) 67 Columbia Law Review 995, (1968) 5 C.M.L.Rev. 409 *et seq.*, *Conflict of Laws: International and Interstate* (1972) p. 245.

[50] Para. 33.24 below.

[51] Jenard, paras. A1.90–A1.94 below.

SPECIAL JURISDICTION
(Articles 5–6A)

SECTION 2

Article 5

17.01   A person domiciled in a Contracting State may, in another Contracting State, be sued:

1. in matters relating to a contract, in the courts for the place of performance of the obligation in question;
2. in matters relating to maintenance, in the courts for the place where the maintenance creditor is domiciled or habitually resident or, if the matter is ancillary to proceedings concerning the status of a person, in the court which, according to its own law, has jurisdiction to entertain those proceedings, unless that jurisdiction is based solely on the nationality of one of the parties;
3. in matters relating to tort, delict or quasi-delict, in the courts for the place where the harmful event occurred;
4. as regards a civil claim for damages or restitution which is based on an act giving rise to criminal proceedings, in the court seised of those proceedings, to the extent that that court has jurisdiction under its own law to entertain civil proceedings;
5. as regards a dispute arising out of the operations of a branch, agency or other establishment, in the courts for the place in which the branch, agency or other establishment is situated;
6. in his capacity as settlor, trustee or beneficiary of a trust created by the operation of a statute, or by a written instrument, or created orally and evidenced in writing, in the courts of the Contracting State in which the trust is domiciled;
7. as regards a dispute concerning the payment of remuneration claimed in respect of the salvage of a cargo or freight, in the court under the authority of which the cargo or freight in question:

    (a) has been arrested to secure such payment, or

(b) could have been so arrested, but bail or other security has been given;

provided that this provision shall apply only if it is claimed that the defendant has an interest in the cargo or freight or had such an interest at the time of salvage.

Article 5(1)

A person domiciled in a Contracting State may, in another   **17.02** Contracting State, be sued:

1. in matters relating to a contract, in the courts for the place of performance of the obligation in question;*†

A. Sub-Paragraph (1): Contract

1. General note

For a national court to decide whether there is jurisdiction under   **17.03** this paragraph it must answer a particularly complex series of questions.[1] In summary, and subject to the qualifications discussed in the commentary, the questions are as follows. First the court must decide whether the dispute concerns a matter relating to a contract, according to an independent interpretation of that concept.[2] Secondly, it must decide what the obligation in question is, again according to an independent interpretation.[3] Thirdly, it must apply its own conflicts of law rules to find the law applicable to that obligation.[4] Fourthly, it must apply that law to decide whether the place of performance is within its territorial jurisdiction.[5] If it is,

---

* Jenard, paras. A1.97–A1.106, A1.262 below; Schlosser, para. 133 (para. A1.416 below); Collins, pp. 51–56; Dashwood/Halcon/White, pp. 22–23, 90–95; Hartley, pp. 43–48; Kaye, pp. 489–527; Maxwell, paras. 5.38–5.41, 5.42; Anton, paras. 5.12–5.16, 5.17–5.25; Droz, paras. 62–68; Weser, paras. 221–223*ter*; Bülow/Böckstiegel/Linke, pp. 55–63; Geimer/Schütze, pp. 551–603; Kropholler, pp. 71–82; Gothot/Holleaux, paras. 54–79; Pocar, pp. 69–125.

† Arts. 5(1) and 5(2) of the 1978 Convention amended the French and Dutch texts of this para., in order to bring their meaning into line with the texts in the other languages. In its unamended form, the French text formerly referred only to *"l'obligation,"* whereas in its amended form it refers to *"l'obligation qui sert de base à la demand."* Similarly, the Dutch text, as amended, refers to *"de verbintenis, die aan de eis ten grondslag ligt."* See further, para. 17.18 below.

[1] Bülow/Böckstiegel/Linke, p. 57.
[2] Paras. 17.05 *et seq.* below.
[3] Paras. 17.18 *et seq.* below.
[4] Para. 17.13 below.
[5] Paras. 17.12 *et seq.* below.

the court must decide, fifthly, whether any of a number of other, relatively unimportant, provisions (summarised below) affect its applicability. If not, and only then, it must accept jurisdiction.

17.04   The provisions referred to in the last paragraph which may affect the applicability of Article 5(1) are as follows. First, a choice of jurisdiction clause may be effective under Article 17.[6] Secondly, as a transitional measure, if the parties expressly agreed in writing, before the 1978 Convention came into force,[7] that a contract was to be governed by English law,[8] the English courts[9] retain the right to exercise jurisdiction in the dispute.[10] Thirdly, Luxembourg domiciliaries sued under this paragraph need not submit to the jurisdiction and if they do not, the court must declare of its own motion that it has no jurisdiction.[11] Fourthly, there are special provisions relating to employment disputes between the master and a crew member of a ship registered in Denmark or Ireland.[12] These provisions are discussed in more detail in the commentary to each of those Articles.

2. "in matters relating to a contract . . . "

17.05   In most cases it will be clear whether a claim is in a "matter relating to a contract,"[13] despite differences between the legal systems of the Contracting States as to what constitutes a contract. The European Court has interpreted these words in an independent manner[14] and has held that the question whether a matter is one "relating to a contract" is to be determined by reference to an independent interpretation of that concept.[15] So, for example, it seems likely that the absence of consideration (a concept not generally known to continental legal systems) will not prevent an obligation from being contractual for the purposes of Article 5(1). By contrast with Article 5(3), which refers to quasi-delict as well as to tort and delict, Article 5(1) does not refer to quasi-contract. That is not to say that quasi-

---

[6] Paras. 21.01 *et seq.* below.

[7] January 1, 1987 in the United Kingdom: see para. 37.19 below.

[8] The same applies to the law of Scotland, Northern Ireland or Ireland.

[9] Similarly, the courts of Scotland, Northern Ireland or Ireland.

[10] 1978 Convention, Art. 35, para. 37.11 below. See also para. 21.17 below.

[11] 1968 Protocol, Art. I, para. 35.01 below.

[12] 1968 Protocol, Art. Vb, para. 35.24 below.

[13] French: "*en matière contractuelle*"; German: "*wenn ein Vertrag oder Ansprüche aus einem Vertrag den Gegenstand des Verfahrens bildet*"; Italian: "*in materia contrattuale*"; Dutch: "*ten aanzien van verbintenissen uit overeenkomst.*"

[14] *Martin Peters Bauunternehmung GmbH* v. *Zuid Nederlandse Aannemers Vereniging* [1983] E.C.R. 987, at p. 1002 (para. 13). *Arcado* v. *Haviland*, case 9/87, decision of March 8, 1988 (para. 11), [1989] E.C.C. 1.

[15] *Arcado* v. *Haviland*, *loc. cit.* The topic of independent interpretation is discussed at paras. 13.19 *et seq.* above.

contractual claims are necessarily excluded from its scope.[16] It is suggested that an independent interpretation of Article 5(1) would involve an analysis of obligations from the point of view of a number of contractual characteristics, regardless of whether the obligation in question can also bear a quasi-contractual character according to the national law of one or more of the Contracting States.

Quasi-contract. An independent interpretation of "matters relat-   **17.06**
ing to a contract" would almost certainly include within the scope of Article 5(1) some matters which English law might regard as quasi-contractual; and the connecting factor justifying the inclusion of the special jurisdiction in Article 5 is as strong in the case of many quasi-contractual claims as it is in the case of contractual matters. So, for example, a claim for reasonable remuneration on a *quantum meruit* might be based on a contract or on the principle of unjust enrichment.[17] In the former case it clearly falls within the paragraph. The German language version, for example, includes express reference to claims "based on a contract" (*Ansprüche aus einem Vertrag*).[17a] If the claim is based not on what English law would recognise as a contract, but on the principle of unjust enrichment, the question whether it falls within the independent concept of a matter relating to a contract for the purposes of Article 5(1) should turn upon the extent to which the obligation in question bears contractual characteristics.[18] A claim on a *quantum meruit* for

---

[16] As a matter of English procedural law, quasi-contractual claims fall within the scope of the contractual provisions of R.S.C., Ord. 11: see Dicey and Morris, p. 316, n. 25.

[17] Goff and Jones, *The Law of Restitution* (2nd ed.) pp. 377–380; *Craven-Ellis* v. *Canons Ltd.* [1936] 2 K.B. 403.

[17a] The fact that the claim is based on a contract brings it within Art. 5(1): *Arcado* v. *Haviland*, above (para. 13).

[18] See *Kalfelis* v. *Schröder, Münchmeyer, Hengst & Co.*, case 189/87, decision of September 27, 1988, *The Times*, October 5, 1988, discussed at paras. 17.46 and 17.77 below, which was a claim based in part on unjust enrichment.
  Pre-contractual negotiations, where no contract was concluded, have been held to fall within Art. 5(1) by the Landgericht Hamburg: case 5 O 13/75, October 29, 1975, Digest D I–5.1.1—B2. So too, in Belgium, has a claim by a sub-distributor against a supplier with whom he was not in direct contractual relationship: *S.p.r.l. André Ransy* v. *Volvo Cars B.V.*, Tribunal de Commerce, Verviers, May 31, 1976, Digest D I–5.1.1—B3; and, in Germany, a claim on the basis of unjust enrichment, for part of the purchase price of goods delivered but not ordered: Oberlandesgericht Frankfurt-am-Main, case 5 U 109/78, January 9, 1979, RIW/AWD—1979, p. 204, Digest D I–5.1.2—B19. Also, in Germany, a claim by a tiler who had not been paid for his services, for a declaration that he was entitled to place a charge on land, where that entitlement arose as a matter of statute, but was based on his contract for services: Oberlandesgericht Köln, case 9 U 221/82, March 22, 1983, [1986] E.C.C. 363. On the other hand,

payment for services rendered would be within Article 5(1) if they were performed pursuant to the defendant's request, but a claim against a fiduciary to account for a secret commission would probably be outside it.[19]

17.07 *The Peters and Arcado decisions.* Two decisions of the European Court also illustrates the requirement that the relationships in dispute should bear contractual characteristics in order to fall within Article 5(1). The first of them, *Martin Peters Bauunternehming GmbH* v. *Zuid Nederlandse Aannemers Vereniging*[20] was a claim brought in the Netherlands by the South Netherlands Contractors Association (ZNAV), an association formed with legal personality under Netherlands law, against one of its members, Peters, which was a building company with its registered office at Aachen in Germany. The claim was for certain sums by way of compensation for other members, payable under the rules of the association and fixed in amount by a meeting of members (at which Peters could have been, but was not, present). Netherlands law does not characterise the relationship between an association and its members as purely contractual but rather as a matter of "institutional" law.[21] On the reference by the *Hoge Raad*, the European Court was willing to give an independent interpretation to the term "matters relating to a contract" and held that obligations to pay money, having their basis in the relationship existing between an association and its members by virtue of membership are "matters relating to a contract," and that it makes no difference whether the obligations in question arise simply

---

where a plaintiff was the *indirect* economic beneficiary of the plaintiff's services, the claim has been by the Italian Court of Cassation to fall outside Art. 5(1): *Ernst Müller K.G.* v. *Muni*, Foro it. 1980, I, Col. 1108, Digest D I–5.1.2—B23. Similarly, an action by a holder of a bill of exchange against the drawee/acceptor, with whom he was in no direct contractual relationship as a matter of German law, was held to fall outside Art. 5(1) by the Landgericht Göttingen: case 3 O 19/76, November 9, 1976, RIW/AWD—1977, p. 235, Digest D I–5.1.1—B4; and a decision to the same effect, in an action by the holder of a cheque against a foreign bank for failure to inform the holder that it was dishonouring the cheque, where there was no direct contractual relationship between the holder and the bank, was made by the Landgericht Köln: case 30 O 12/79, March 23, 1979, RIW/AWD—1980, p. 215.

[19] Such a claim would also be outside Art. 5(6): Goff and Jones, *op. cit.*, p. 459; *Lister & Co.* v. *Stubbs* (1890) 45 Ch.D. 1 but it would probably be within Art. 5(3): see para. 17.46 below. *Cf.* Collins, p. 53, for further examples of claims inside and outside Art. 5(1).

[20] [1983] E.C.R. 987.

[21] Tebbens, "L'Interprétation dynamique, par la Cour de Justice Européenne, de la compétence en matière contractuelle", in *Unification and comparative law in theory and practice. Contributions in honour of Jean Georges Sauveplanne*, at p. 75.

from the act of becoming a member or from that act in conjunction with one or more decisions made by organs of the association.[22]

The second of these decisions, *Arcado S.A.* v. *Haviland S.A.*[22a] was a claim by an agent for compensation for wrongful repudiation of its commercial agency agreement and for the balance of commission due. The claim was brought in Belgium by the Belgian agent against the French principal, on the basis of Article 5(1). The French principal disputed the jurisdiction of the Belgian Court on the ground that the claim for compensation was of a quasi-delictual nature. On a reference by the *Cour d'Appel* in Brussels, the European Court of Justice again held that the words "matter relating to a contract" were to be given an independent interpretation. it drew attention to the fact that the entitlement to compensation was based on the failure to respect a contractual obligation[22b] and went on to hold that:

" . . . proceedings relating to the wrongful repudiation of an (independent) commercial agency agreement and the payment of commission due under such an agreement are proceedings in matters relating to a contract within the meaning of Article 5(1) . . . "

In reaching that conclusion, the European Court referred to the provisions of the EEC Directive on the co-ordination of laws of Member States relating to self-employed commercial agents[22c] and to the EEC Contractual Obligations Convention.[22d]

The way in which the plaintiff formulates his claim, especially where it is questionable whether the case is one concerning a matter relating to a contract, or where the claim can be expressed in one of a number of ways, may affect the question of whether there is jurisdiction under Article 5(1).[23] The court will decide the question of jurisdiction on the basis of the plaintiff's allegations, if they are supported by evidence,[24] by reference to the particular obligation

---

[22] [1983] E.C.R. 987, 1004.
[22a] Case 9/87, decision of March 8, 1988, [1989] E.C.C. 1.
[22b] The fact that the claims arose out of a contract has been held by the Oberlandesgericht Köln to found jurisdiction under Art. 5(1) in a building worker's claim for registration of a statutory charge on land: case 9 U 221/82, March 22, 1983, [1986] E.C.C. 363.
[22c] Council Directive 86/653, of December 18, 1986, Arts. 15 and 17: O.J. 1986 L382, p. 17.
[22d] Convention on the Law Applicable to Contractual Obligations, opened for signature in Rome on June 19, 1980 O.J. L266. See para. A2.41 below.
[23] Hartley, pp. 47–48. See also para. 15.17 above.
[24] *Effer S.p.A.* v. *Kantner* [1982] E.C.R. 825. The Convention's jurisdictional rules are compulsory (para. 15.02 above) and if the plaintiff's allegations are such as to bring the case within Art. 5(1), the court must accept jurisdiction: *Convectio S.p.A.* v. *Rummler ed altri*, Foro pad. 1979, I, Col. 419, Digest D I–5.1.2—B29.

which forms the basis of the claim[25] or, exceptionally, by reference to the "characteristic" obligation.[26]

17.08 *Examining the plaintiff's assertions.* The European Court of Justice has considered in *Effer S.p.A.* v. *Kantner*[27] whether Article 5(1) applies to a case where the defendant disputes the assertions upon which the plaintiff's claim is based. Kantner was a patent agent in Germany who was engaged by the German distributor of cranes manufactured by Effer S.p.A., an Italian undertaking, to investigate whether a particular design of folding crane jib was protected by patent in the Federal Republic. He brought an action against Effer S.p.A. in Germany, claiming payment of his fee, contending that he had been engaged by the distributor in the name of Effer and that the court had jurisdiction under Article 5(1) as the court for the place of performance of the obligation to pay the fee. Effer disputed that they had contracted with him, saying that the distributor (which had since become bankrupt) had contracted with Kantner in its own name.

Kantner was successful at first instance and on appeal and Effer then appealed to the *Bundesgerichtshof*, which referred the following question to the European Court of Justice:

> "May the plaintiff invoke the jurisdiction of the courts of the place of performance in according with Article 5(1) of the Convention even when the existence of the contract on which the claim is based is in dispute between the parties?"

17.09 In its observations, the United Kingdom argued[28] that if the claim was brought bona fide and was based on a relationship which was prima facie contractual, then a defence putting in issue the existence of the contract should not deprive the court of jurisdiction under Article 5(1). Advocate General Reischl pointed out in his Opinion that:

> "the view that jurisdiction under the Convention could not be recognised if the examination of the question of jurisdiction wholly or partly overlapped with the examination of the facts founding the claim would not be compatible with the principle, clearly expressed in the Jenard Report, that the Convention should be given a wide application.
> It is clear, however, that the judicial practice . . . of requiring no evidence of the facts founding jurisdiction if they are at the same time ingredients of the substantive claim would be incompatible with the

---

[25] *De Bloos S.p.r.l.* v. *Bouyer* [1976] E.C.R. 1497. The court may have to analyse the plaintiff's allegations to see whether they relate to matters of a contractual nature: *Omrom-Europe GmbH* v. *S.A. Office Equipment*, Bull. Cass., Chambres Civiles, 1977, Première partie, No. 230, p. 181, Digest D I–5.1.1—B7.

[26] *Ivenel* v. *Schwab* [1982] E.C.R. 1891. See paras. 17.18 to 17.30 below, on the meaning of "the obligation in question."

[27] [1982] E.C.R. 825.

[28] *Ibid.*, at p. 830.

rules of the Convention, precisely because those rules require an examination as to jurisdiction by the court *of its own motion* and with it, if necessary, the hearing of evidence limited to the determination of jurisdiction."[29]

In its judgment, the European Court dealt with the question in this way:

" . . . the national court's jurisdiction to determine questions relating to a contract includes the power to consider the existence of the constituent parts of the contract itself, since that is indispensable in order to enable the national court in which proceedings are brought to examine whether it has jurisdiction under the Convention . . . [R]espect for the aims and spirit of the Convention demands that the provision should be construed as meaning that the court called upon to decide a dispute arising out of a contract may examine, of its own motion even, the essential preconditions for its jurisdiction, having regard to conclusive and relevant evidence adduced by the party concerned, establishing the existence or inexistence of the contract."[30]

The European Court therefore answered the question put by the **17.10** *Bundesgerichtshof* in the affirmative.[31] It is suggested that the European Court's ruling does not require the existence of the contract to be tried as a preliminary issue, but does require the plaintiff to adduce sufficient evidence to establish the existence of the contract. What standard of proof is required is not entirely clear. The Court referred to "conclusive" and relevant evidence, and although it referred to the United Kingdom's submission that a prima facie case should be established, it stopped short of endorsing that submission.[32]

3. " . . . the courts for the place . . . "

It is for national procedural law to supplement the rule of local **17.11** jurisdiction laid down by Article 5(1), by determining which particular court has jurisdiction in respect of the place in question.

---

[29] *Ibid.*, at pp. 839–840.
[30] [1982] E.C.R. 825, at p. 834 (para. 7).
[31] As a result of that decision, the Bundesgerichtshof held that the place of performance according to German law (which was the applicable law) was in Germany, and that the German court had jurisdiction: case III ZR 1/80, May 13, 1982, [1983] E.C.C. 1.
[32] It is suggested that, if the issue is not to be tried, a proper test to be applied would be one akin to that applied as a matter of English procedural law under R.S.C., Ord. 11, namely whether the plaintiff is able to show a good arguable case: *Diamond* v. *Bank of London & Montreal Ltd.* [1979] Q.B. 333. Also, see Dicey and Morris, p. 307 and the cases cited there. Collins (p. 53) suggests that prima facie proof of the existence of the contract is sufficient, but also equates the position with that under Ord. 11. See also *Algemene Industrieele Mineraalen-en Ertmaatschapij* v. *Macina Minerale S.p.a.*, Arrondissementsrechtbank Rotterdam [1978] E.C.C. 382.

4. " . . . the place of performance . . . "

17.12 Some care is required in determining the "place of performance" for the purposes of Article 5(1). It is apparent from other language versions[33] that the "place of performance" covers the place where the obligation in question has been, or is to be,[34] performed pursuant to the contract, and to that extent the term must be interpreted as a rule of the Convention, rather than merely as a reference to national law. On the other hand, the European Court has decided[35] that the term is not to be given the sort of independent and autonomous interpretation which that Court has given to other concepts in the Convention.[36] Instead, in the absence of an effective agreement as to the place of performance,[37] it is to be determined by applying whichever law is held to be applicable, according to the conflicts rules of the *lex fori*, to the legal relationship in question (that is to say, in effect, the proper law of the obligation). In order to do so, of course, the court must first identify the "obligation in question."[38]

17.13 *The Tessili v. Dunlop decision.* The European Court ruled on this topic in the first case to come before it under the Convention: *Industrie Tessili Italiana Como* v. *Dunlop A.G.*[39] Tessili was an Italian undertaking which had agreed with Dunlop A.G., a German company, to manufacture ski suits to Dunlop's specification and deliver them to a carrier in Italy appointed by Dunlop. Dunlop alleged that the suits were defective and brought an action against Tessili in its local court in Germany. Tessili disputed the jurisdiction of that court and, on appeal, the question of the interpretation of "the place of performance" was referred to the European Court, which stated in its judgment:

> "It is for the court before which the matter is brought to establish under the Convention whether the place of performance is situated within its territorial jurisdiction. For this purpose it must determine in accordance with its own rules of conflict of laws what is the law applicable to the legal relationship in question and define in accordance with that law the place of performance of the contractual obligation in question.

---

[33] French: " . . . *a été ou doit être exécutée*"; German: "*erfüllt worden ist oder zu erfüllen wäre*"; Italian: "*è stata o deve essere eseguita*"; Dutch: "*is uitgevoerd of moet worden uitgevoerd.*"

[34] *Per* Advocate General Mayras, in *Industrie Tessili Italiana Como* v. *Dunlop A.G.* [1976] E.C.R. 1473, at p. 1490.

[35] *Industrie Tessili Italiana Como* v. *Dunlop A.G.* [1976] E.C.R. 1473, discussed below.

[36] Para. 13.19 above.

[37] Paras. 17.15 to 17.17 below.

[38] Determination of the "obligation in question" can be an even more tricky exercise: see paras. 17.18 *et seq.* below.

[39] [1976] E.C.R. 1473.

Having regard to the differences between national laws of contract and to the absence at this stage of legal development of any unification in the law applicable, it does not appear possible to give any more substantial guidance to the interpretation of the reference made by Article 5(1) to the "place of performance" of contractual obligations. This is all the more true since the determination of the place of performance of obligations depends on the contractual context to which these obligations belong."[40]

The purpose of Article 5(1) is to confer jurisdiction on the courts for the place where the obligation is to be performed and, the obligations in the contract being creatures of their proper law, that is the law to be applied in determining the place of performance for the purposes of jurisdiction.[41] It should be emphasised that the private international law of the *lex fori* should be used to determine the proper law[42] and not, unless it happens also to be the proper law,[43] to determine the place of performance.[44]

---

[40] *Ibid.*, at p. 1485 (paras. 13–14).

[41] As a matter of English private international law, the place of performance of a contract is generally determined by the proper law of the contract. For a more detailed treatment of English conflicts rules, reference should be made to specialist works: Dicey and Morris, chaps. 32–34 (especially, as regards the place of performance of contractual obligations, pp. 1194–1195) and Cheshire and North, chap. 18, especially pp. 492 *et seq.*

[42] Examples of cases where courts have correctly applied a foreign proper law to determine the place of performance are: Oberlandesgericht Frankfurt-am-Main, case 5 U 109/78, January 9, 1979, RIW/AWD—1979, p. 204, Digest D I–5.1.2—B19 (a case based on unjust enrichment); *Het Huis met de Groene Lantaarn B.V.* v. *Delmod International Bekleidungs-Industrie GmbH & Co.* Ned. Jur. 1979, No. 147, Digest D I–5.1.2—B16; *Bombardieri* v. *Esta Trust Reg.*, Ned. Jur. 1980, No. 512, Digest D I–5.1.2—B24; and *Theunissen* v. *Luz*, Riv.-dir.int.priv.proc. 1981, p. 928, Digest D I–5.1.2—B32 (where Italian conflicts law regarded the German *lex situs* as the proper law in a contract for the transfer of land).

[43] Examples of cases where courts have found their own law to be the proper law and then applied that to determine the place of performance are: Oberlandesgericht Düsseldorf, case 18 U 44/75, November 20, 1975, RIW/AWD—1976, p. 297, Digest D I–17.1.2—B3; *Curatrice in het faillissement van Theo Aben B.V.* v. *F. Raedemaeker*, Ned.Jur. 1980, No. 313, Digest D I–5.1.2—B20; *Allpac Holdings B.V.* v. *Carl Friederich Maier am Tor*, Gerechtshof, Amsterdam, January 31, 1979, [1982] E.C.C. 200; *Italmare Shipping Co.* v. *Verenigde Pharmaceutische Fabrieken B.V.*, Hoge Raad, June 12, 1981, Digest D I–5.1.2—B36; *Machinale Glasfabriek de Maas B.V.* v. *Emaillerie Alsacienne S.A.*, Arrondissementsrechtbank, Arnhem, July 30, 1981, [1984] E.C.C. 123; *Effer* v. *Kantner*, Bundesgerichtshof, above (note 27); Decision of the Bundesgerichtshof, case I ZR 130/82 [1985] E.C.C. 331; Oberlandesgericht Köln, case 9 U 221/82, March 22, 1983, [1986] E.C.C. 363 (where the headnote is misleading on this point).

[44] This mistake was made by the Oberlandesgericht Frankfurt-am-Main in the very case which it had referred to the European Court: *Industrie Tessili Italiana Como* v. *Dunlop A.G.*, case 21 U 158/74, March 23, 1977, Digest D

17.14   The decision has been the subject of some criticism,[45] to the effect that it will encourage forum-shopping and that its operation in conjunction with an independent concept of the "obligation in question"[46] is unnecessarily complex. The experience of national courts in applying the Uniform Law on the International Sale of Goods[47] has shown that the application of the proper law in determining the place of performance is considerably eased where the choice of law is governed by uniform rules.[48] The EEC Contractual Obligations Convention,[49] when it comes into effect, will go some way to resolving the practical difficulties which courts may encounter in applying foreign substantive law to determine the place of performance for the purposes of jurisdiction, especially if the concept of characteristic performance[50] develops in such a way as to reduce the frequency with which the debtor's payment obligation[51] is regarded as the "obligation in

---

I–5.1.2—B9. See Kohler, "Practical Experience of the Brussels Jurisdiction and Judgments Convention in the Six Original Contracting States" (1985) 34 I.C.L.Q. 563, at p. 569.

[45] Bülow/Böckstiegel/Linke, pp. 59–60.

[46] Para. 17.18 below.

[47] Cmnd. 5029; Uniform Law on International Sales Act 1967, Sched. 1. See also now the United Nations Convention on Contracts for the International Sale of Goods, signed in Vienna on April 11, 1980.

[48] For example, the Uniform Law has been applied to determine the place of performance of a seller's obligation to deliver goods: *Van den Berg Envellopen B.V.* v. *Bernard Ghesquières S.A.*, Arrondissmentsrechtbank Arnhem, July 22, 1982, Digest D I–5.1.2—B38. Much more frequently though, it has been used to determine the place of performance of a purchaser's payment obligations, especially under Art. 59 of the Uniform Law: Oberlandesgericht Bamberg, case 3 U 46/76, November 5, 1976, N.J.W. 1977, p. 505, Digest D I–5.1.2—B6; *Gottfried Kellermann GmbH* v. *P. B. A. Dura*, Hof van Beroep, Antwerp, November 30, 1977, Digest D I–17.1.2—B12; Bundesgerichtshof, case VIII ZR 199/78, April 4, 1979, Ent. BGH in Zivilsachen, Bd. 74, p. 136, Digest D I–5.1.2—B26; Oberlandesgericht Hamm, case 20 U 98/79, October 3, 1979, RIW/AWD—1980, p. 662, Digest D I–5.1.2—B26n; *Convectio S.p.A.* v. *Rummler ed altri*, Foro pad. 1979, I, Col. 419, Digest D I–5.1.2—B29 (see also Digest D I–5.1.2—B29n); *Möbus GmbH* v. *Winderickx*, Hof van Beroep, Antwerp, December 26, 1979, Digest D I–5.1.2—B30; *Allpac Holdings B.V.* v. *Carl Friederich Maier am Tor*, Gerechtshof, Amsterdam, January 31, 1979, [1982] E.C.C. 200.

[49] Convention on the Law Applicable to Contractual Obligations, opened for signature in Rome on June 19, 1980, O.J. 1980 L266. See also the Official Report by Professors Giuliano and Lagarde, O.J. 1980 C282; North, [1980] J.B.L. 382; and North (ed.), *Contract Conflicts* (in which both the Convention and the Report are reproduced). Arts. 3–6 of that Convention are set out at paras. A2.41 *et seq.* below.

[50] See para. 17.26 below.

[51] As a general rule, English law requires a debtor to seek out his creditor: *The Eider* [1983] P. 119; *Vitkovice Horni* v. *Korner* [1951] A.C. 869, at p. 885 *et seq.*; *Pick* v. *Manufacturers' Life Insurance Co.* [1958] 2 Lloyd's Rep. 93; see Dicey and

question" for the purposes of Article 5(1) of the present Convention.[52]

Choice of place of performance

The parties will often have agreed the place of performance of a   **17.15**
given obligation, either expressly or by implication and national law
usually gives effect to such a choice, although usually subject to
overriding provisions of law in the case of particular kinds of contract.[53]

The first Zelger v. Salinitri decision. A case concerning an oral
choice of place of performance came before the European Court of
Justice in *Zelger v. Salinitri (No. 1).*[54] Zelger was a businessman in
Munich and Salinitri was a businessman in Sicily.[55] The parties had

---

Morris, p. 323, p. 1195 n. 14 and p. 1196, n. 23. This is also the rule in most
continental systems, except in sales of goods, where the place of performance of
the payment obligation is generally at the place of delivery of the goods, which,
in the absence of agreement, is often the place of consignment. See chaps. 48 to
58 below, at para. 28, and the provisions cited at n. 53 below.

[52] Examples of cases where national courts have determined the place of performance of the debtor's payments obligations in accordance with the proper law of
that obligation are: *Arsidi v. Magrini*, Giust.civ. 1978, I, p. 44, Digest D
I–17.1.1—B6; *Gondert v. Pultz*, Pas.lux. 1979, p. 168, Digest D I–5.1.2—B17;
Oberlandesgericht Stuttgart, case 10 U 195/80, February 12, 1981, N.J.W.
1982, p. 529, Digest D I–5.1.2—B35; Oberlandesgericht Köln, case 16 U 136/
82, February 23, 1983, RIW/AWD—1984, p. 314, Digest D I–5.1.2—B35n.;
and, *obiter*, Landgericht Göttingen, case 3 O 19/76, November 9, 1976, RIW/
AWD—1977, p. 235, Digest D I–5.1.1—B4; *Machinale Glasfabriek de Maas
B.V. v. Emaillerie Alsacienne S.A.*, Arrondissementsrechtbank, Arnhem, July
30, 1981, [1984] E.C.C. 123.

[53] For example, Belgium: Art. 1247 of the civil code; *S.p.r.l. Créations Davos v.
Katag Gruppe top Textil A.G.*, Tribunal de Commerce, Brussels, June 13, 1977,
Digest D I–5.1.2—B12; Germany: paras. 29(2) and 38 of the code of civil procedure; see *Zelger v. Salinitri* below; France: Art. 1247 of the civil code; *Société
Gola Werke German Gotz K.G. v. André Barseghian*, Sem.jur., Edition Générale
1981, Jurisprudence, No. 19519, Digest D I–5.1.2—B25; Italy: Art. 1182 of
the civil code; *Daudray van Cauwenberghe S.A. v. Sbragi*, Foro pad. 1981, I,
col. 332; Digest D I–5.1.2—B5 n. 2; Netherlands: Art. 1429 of the civil code;
Cartonnagefabriek N.V. v. Les Editions René Touret, Ned.Jur. 1977, No. 304,
Digest D I–5.1.2—B2; England: see Dicey and Morris, pp. 1194–1195, *Zivnostenska Banka v. Frankman* [1950] A.C. 57.
   On the other hand, a Belgian court has held an agreed place of performance to
be invalid under Belgian law, where it conflicted with the "geographical reality"
of the contract, which could only be performed elsewhere; and this was despite
the fact that the parties had chosen German law (also invalidly): *Audi-NSU Auto
Union A.G. v. S.A. Adelin Petit et Cie.*, Journal trib. 1977, p. 710, Digest D
I–5.1.2—B11, upheld on appeal, Journal trib. 1979, p. 625, [1980] E.C.C. 235.

[54] [1980] E.C.R. 89. The decision of the Bundesgerichtshof in the light of this
judgment is reported at [1981] E.C.C. 191.

[55] The parties' status as businessmen (*Vollkaufleute*) was relevant to the applicability of para. 29(2) of the German code of civil procedure.

carried on business over a number of years and a dispute arose when Zelger claimed repayment of an alleged loan. He started an action in Munich, claiming that the parties had made an express oral agreement that Munich was to be the place of performance of the repayment. At first instance and on appeal,[56] the courts declined jurisdiction, on the grounds that such an agreement was not effective to found international jurisdiction because it did not comply with the requirements of form laid down in Article 17 for choice of jurisdiction agreements. The agreement would have been effective under German law to specify the place of performance and to found local jurisdiction in Munich. In the absence of valid agreement, German law provides that the place of performance of a contractual obligation to pay money is the residence of the debtor.[57] The plaintiff appealed and the German Federal Supreme Court referred to the European Court of Justice the question whether such an informal agreement was sufficient to found international jurisdiction under Article 5(1).[58]

17.16   Advocate General Capotorti argued in his Opinion[59] that Article 5(1) contained nothing to suggest that it was limited to a place of performance fixed by law, and that the parties were free to agree the place of performance. *Industrie Tessili* v. *Dunlop A.G.* had established that it was for the national court to determine the law applicable to the obligation in question and to decide the place of performance according to that law. If that law permitted the parties to agree a place of performance without imposing any special requirements of form, he said, then the agreement should be valid not only for the purpose of the law governing the substantive elements of the contract, but also for the purposes of Article 5(1). Were it otherwise, although the contract was to be performed in a particular place, the courts of that place would not have jurisdiction under Article 5(1), which would be contrary to the letter and the spirit of the provision.

17.17   The Court accepted this view. It found a distinction between the provisions of Article 5(1) and those of Article 17,[60] pointing out that the special jurisdiction provided by Article 5(1), at the option of the plaintiff, was justified by the existence of a direct link between the

---

[56] Oberlandesgericht München, case 7 U 2924/77, November 9, 1977, RIW/AWD—1978, p. 119, Digest D I–5.1.2—B15.

[57] Art. 269 of the German Civil Code; see para. 51.28 below.

[58] On the facts of *Zelger* v. *Salinitri*, if English law was the proper law of the contract, the English courts would probably have had jurisdiction even in the absence of a valid agreement as to the place of jurisdiction, because of the rule of English law that the debtor must seek out his creditor: see n. 51 above.

[59] [1980] E.C.R. 89, at pp. 98 *et seq.*

[60] Para. 21.01 below.

dispute and the court called upon to take cognizance of it; whereas Article 17 provided an exclusive jurisdiction which dispensed with the need for any objective connection between the dispute and the court designated by the parties. The European Court's ruling was in these terms:

> "If the place of performance of a contractual obligation has been specified by the parties in a clause which is valid according to the national law applicable to the contract, the court for that place has jurisdiction to take cognizance of disputes relating to that obligation under Article 5(1) of the Convention . . . , irrespective of whether the formal conditions provided for under Article 17 have been observed."[61]

The danger that an agreement on the place of performance might be used to circumvent the requirements of Article 17 as to the form of a choice of jurisdiction agreement[62] was recognised by the Advocate General, but that is a matter for national law to resolve.[63]

5. " . . . the obligation in question . . . "

The meaning of these words has been the subject of some dispute **17.18** and the European Court has had to consider their interpretation on several occasions. The Jenard Report said that "only the jurisdiction of the *forum solutionis* has been retained, that is to say the jurisdiction of the courts for the place of performance of the obligation on which the claim is based,"[64] but the original text of the French and Dutch versions left some doubt as to the identity of the obligation referred to[65] and a line of jurisprudence developed to the effect that the relevant obligation for the purposes of Article 5(1) was the principle obligation in the contract.[66-67] The European Court of Justice followed the view in the Jenard Report in *De Bloos* v. *Bouyer*,[68] but, despite the amendments to the French and Dutch

---

[61] [1980] E.C.R. 89, at p. 98.
[62] Paras. 21.52 to 21.70 below.
[63] In its decision of October 17, 1984 (Case No. I ZR 130/83), the Bundesgerichtshof showed itself willing to give effect to jurisdiction based on an agreed place of performance, where the agreement was merely by tacit incorporation of the standard German Road Haulage Conditions: [1985] RIW 148; [1985] E.C.C. 331.
[64] Para. A1.99 below.
[65] Para. 17.02 n.† above.
[66-67] *e.g., per* Advocate General Mayras, in *Industrie Tessili Italiana Como* v. *Dunlop A.G.* [1976] E.C.R. 1473, at pp. 1490 *et seq.*; Oberlandesgericht Frankfurt-am-Main, case 20 W 185/75, December 9, 1975, RIW/AWD—1976, p. 107, Digest D I–5.1.2—B4; Oberlandesgericht Düsseldorf, case 18 U 44/75, November 20, 1975, RIW/AWD—1976, p. 297, Digest D I–17.1.2—B3. See Bülow/Böckstiegel/Linke, pp. 58–60.
[68] *Etablissements A. De Bloos S.p.r.l.* v. *Société en commandite par actions Bouyer*, [1976] E.C.R. 1497, discussed at para. 17.20 below.

texts, adopted a new and quite different approach in *Ivenel* v. *Schwab*.[69] The apparent inconsistencies between these two decisions, though, have largely been resolved by the European Court's third decision on the interpretation of "the obligation in question," in *Shenavai* v. *Kreischer*.[70]

17.19   *Summary.* In summary, the effect of the European Court's decisions is that, as a general rule, the obligation which the court should consider in determining whether it has jurisdiction under Article 5(1) is the obligation which forms the basis of the plaintiff's claim. It may be an obligation which he alleges that the defendant has broken or failed to perform or it may be an obligation corresponding to the right which the plaintiff seeks to assert. Where the plaintiff relies on various obligations, the court must decide which of them is the principal obligation for the purposes of the claim and regard it as the "obligation in question" for the purposes of Article 5(1). There is an exception to the general rule, though, where certain special features of the contract require that the courts should consider, instead of the obligation which forms the basis of the claim, the obligation which is characteristic of the contract as a whole. This exception extends notably to contracts of employment, and it may be that it is confined to such cases.

Because of the importance of Article 5(1) and the very varied factual circumstances which it covers, each of the European Court's decisions is considered below in some detail.

17.20   *The first case: De Bloos v. Bouyer.* The first case to come before the European Court on the meaning of "the obligation in question" was *Etablissements A. De Bloos S.p.r.l.* v. *Société en commandite par actions Bouyer*.[71-72] Bouyer, a Belgian limited partnership, had contracted with De Bloos, a French manufacturer of agricultural machinery, to act as the exclusive distributor of De Bloos's products in Belgium. The parties fell out and Bouyer brought an action in Belgium seeking the dissolution of the contract and damages, on the grounds of De Bloos's wrongful conduct. It alleged that the defendant had unilaterally repudiated the contract without notice, by supplying goods to another distributor. The court of first instance held that the place where De Bloos's obligations arose and were to be performed was at its registered office in France. It therefore declined jurisdiction and De Bloos appealed to the *Cour d'Appel* at Mons. That court analysed the claim with a view to determining which obligation was relevant for the purposes of juris-

---

[69] [1982] E.C.R. 1891, discussed at para. 17.24 below.
[70] [1987] 3 C.M.L.R. 782, discussed at para. 17.28 below.
[71-72] [1976] E.C.R. 1497.

diction under Article 5(1) and sought a ruling from the European Court of Justice on a number of questions.

The first question asked by the national court was whether the word "obligation" in Article 5(1) might refer, "without distinction to any obligation arising out of the outline contract granting an exclusive sales concession or even arising out of the successive sales concluded in performance of the said contract, or as referring exclusively to the obligation forming the basis of the legal proceedings."[73] In considering that question, the European Court stressed the need to interpret the Convention in such a way as to avoid, as far as possible, creating a situation in which a number of courts had jurisdiction over the same contract, and continued:

> "Because of this Article 5(1) cannot be interpreted as referring to any obligation whatsoever arising under the contract in question."[74]

On the contrary, the Court said, the "obligation" referred to was "the contractual obligation forming the basis of the legal proceedings," or "that which corresponds to the contractual right on which the plaintiff's action is based"[75-76] and it is this ruling which the European Court subsequently called the "general rule."[77]

The second part of the national court's question therefore arose **17.21** (and referred to distinctions which arise in some legal systems, but may be unfamiliar to common lawyers), namely whether the contractual obligation forming the basis of the legal proceedings in a case such as this was (a) "the original obligation," (b) "the obligation to provide the equivalent of the original obligation," (c) "the obligation to pay damages where the effect of the dissolution or termination of the contract is to render void the original obligation" or, (d) the obligation to pay "fair compensation" or even "additional compensation" under certain provisions of Belgian law.[78]

Article 5(1) does not refer in terms to contractual rights, but only to the "obligation" in question. In its answer to this part of the national court's question, though, the European Court drew a distinction between a claim alleging a breach of a contractual right and a claim alleging a failure to perform a contractual obligation. In the former case, the "obligation in question" was the obligation which corresponded with the right relied upon by the plaintiff, namely in a case such as this the right of the grantee to exclusivity in the sales

---

[73] *Ibid.*, at p. 1507 (para. 5).
[74] *Ibid.*, at p. 1508 (paras. 9 and 10).
[75-76] *Ibid.*, at p. 1508 (paras. 11 and 13).
[77] *Shenavai* v. *Kreischer*, [1987] 3 C.M.L.R. 782 (para. 10).
[78] [1976] E.C.R. 1497, at p. 1507 (para. 6).

concession. By implication therefore, it was not the right to have the contract dissolved nor the right to compensation or damages. Similarly, in the latter case, the "obligation in question" was the obligation allegedly broken, rather than the consequential obligation to pay compensation or damages.[79]

17.22   It follows that the European Court considered that the obligation referred to in Article 5(1) was of a substantive rather than a consequential kind. The European Court did not find it necessary for the interpretation of the Convention to draw a distinction between the different types of substantive obligation which might arise as a matter of national law and went on to rule that,

> "in the case of actions for the payment of compensation by way of damages, it is for the national court to ascertain whether, under the law applicable to the contract, an independent contractual obligation or an obligation replacing the unperformed contractual obligation is involved."[80–81]

The case also concerned the provisions of the Convention relating to branches and agencies and this aspect is discussed under Article 5(5).[82]

17.23   *De Bloos* v. *Bouyer* is an example of a type of case in which problems have very frequently arisen before national courts in the application of the Convention, frequently in cases where a dealer is complaining before the courts of his own country about the wrongful termination of the agency by his foreign supplier. The identification of the "obligation in question," and the place of its performance, according to the different national rules has shown a range of obli-

---

[79] *Ibid.*, at pp. 1508–1509 (paras. 14 to 16).

[80–81] *Ibid.*, at p. 1509 (para. 17). By its subsequent judgment of May 3, 1977 (Journal trib. 1977, p. 637; Digest D I–5.1.1—B6), the Cour d'Appel, Mons, decided that the obligation in question for the purposes of the claim for dissolution of the contract was the obligation to give notice to terminate the contract, and that that obligation corresponded with the grantee's right to continue to make use of the exclusive concession during the period of notice within the territory to which it related. The grantor's disputed obligation was therefore to be performed in Belgium, and the Belgian courts had jurisdiction under Art. 5(1). But the court said that the claim for damages should have been brought in France, because, as a matter of Belgian law, it was based on an independent contractual obligation, which took account of goodwill, expenditure by the distributor and other factors and which gave rise to a debt payable at the debtor's offices in France. Because of the related nature of the claims, though, the Belgian courts accepted jurisdiction (although it is not clear that they had power to do so: see para. 15.18 above).

[82] Para. 17.61 below. In the event, jurisdiction could not be founded on this basis.

gations which the courts have fastened upon for the purposes of jurisdiction, such as the supplier's obligation to give notice to terminate the dealership agreement,[83] or to supply the dealer[84] or to maintain exclusivity in doing so,[85] or his obligation to pay commission,[86] or to continue the relationship until it is properly terminated.[87] They have also relied upon the principal obligations in the contract[88] and upon the obligation which was characteristic of the contract.[89]

Multiple obligations. One of the principal effects of the European   **17.24** Court's decisions in *De Bloos* v. *Bouyer* and *Industrie Tessili* v. *Dunlop* was that a court might apparently have jurisdiction over part only of a contract, where national law had the effect that different obligations in issue were to be performed in different places.[90] This problem, to which the European Court later returned in *Shenavai*

---

[83] *S.p.r.l. Arfa* v. *Erso Adrion Co.*, Jur.comm.Belg. 1977, p. 167, Digest D I–5.1.1—B1; *S.p.r.l. André Ransy* v. *Volvo Cars B.V.* Tribunal de Commerce, Verviers (Belgium), May 31, 1976, Digest D I–5.1.1—B3; *Ets. A. De Bloos S.p.r.l.* v. *Bouyer* (see n. 80–81 above); *Knauer und Co. Maschinenfabrik* v. *Callens*, Journal trib. 1978, p. 618, Digest D I–5.1.1—B8; *Sonobel* v. *Musidisc-Europe*, Journal trib. 1978, p. 685; *Laick Jean* v. *Curateur à la faillite de la S.p.r.l. Pauwels et Cie*, Cour d'Appel, Mons (Belgium) May 21, 1979, Digest D I–1.2—B14.

[84] *Brehmer* v. *Baudoin*, Cour de Cassation (France), January 23, 1979, Rev. critique 1979, p. 817, Digest D I–5.1.1—B9.

[85] *Dellinger* v. *V.K.G. Wilhelm Leppak GmbH*, Journal dr.int. 1980, p. 334; Digest D I–5.1.2—B18; *Société Forges de Vulcain* v. *Société Index Verkaufs GmbH*, Rev.soc. 1980, p. 557, Digest D I–1.2—B16.

[86] *Société Gola Werke German Gotz K.G.* v. *André Barseghian*, sem.jur., Ed.Gén. 1981, Jur., No. 19519, Digest D I–5.1.2—B25; Oberlandesgericht Frankfurt-am-Main, case 21 U 58/79, November 28, 1979, Digest D I–5.1.1—B13.

[87] *Maschinenfabrik Moenus A.G.* v. *Barenghi*, Corte di Cassazione (Italy), April 9, 1979, Foro it. 1980 I, Col. 1108, Digest D I–5.1.1—B11; *Carl Freudenberg K.G.* v. *Bureau R.C. van Oppens S.à.r.l.*, Cour de Cassation (Belgium) [1986] E.C.C. 366, Journal trib. 1984, p. 637.

[88] *Felten & Guilleaume Calswerk* v. *Grout*, Gaz. Palais 1981, Sommaires, p. 105, Digest D I–5.1.1—B14; *Aluminiumwerke Wutoschingen GmbH* v. *Soc. Landowski Samis*, Bull.Cass., Chambres Civiles 1982, Pt. I, No. 106, p. 92, Digest D I–5.1.1—B16; Landgericht München I, case 3 HKO 4714/81, I Prax 1983, p. 44, Digest D I–5.1.1—B13n. See also the cases cited at Digest D I–5.1.1—B16n.

[89] *Wittels Albert Maschinen GmbH* v. *Seal*, Bull.Cass., Chambres Civiles 1982, Pt. 5, No. 585, p. 430; Rev. critique 1983, p. 661; Digest D I–5.1.1—B17. This case is particularly interesting in adopting the "characteristic obligation" approach in the light of *Ivenel* v. *Schwab*: see next para.

[90] The difficulty is illustrated by the decision of the Belgian Cour de Cassation of January 19, 1984 in *Carl Freudenberg K.G.* v. *Bureau R.C. van Oppens S.à.r.l.*, above.

v. *Kreischer*[91] arose in *Ivenel* v. *Schwab*,[92] where the European Court of Justice adopted an approach which showed some radical departures from its earlier decisions on Article 5(1).

The second case: Ivenel v. *Schwab.* Roger Ivenel, domiciled in Strasbourg, had been engaged as a commercial representative by Schwab, who carried on business in Bavaria as a manufacturer of machines, to sell the latter's products in France.[93] He was to be paid commission and was entitled to other benefits, including allowances for clients and paid holidays. Schwab terminated the contract and Ivenel brought an action in France (in the *Conseil de prud'hommes*, Strasbourg)[94] claiming commission, compensation for loss of goodwill in lieu of notice and various other sums, including allowances. Under both French and German law, the commission was payable in Germany, and Schwab argued that the French court did not, therefore, have jurisdiction under Article 5(1). Ivenel argued that the relevant obligations were the obligation to work and the obligation to provide work, both of which were to be performed in France. The allowances were payable according to the way in which the work was performed.

The court accepted Ivenel's argument that the case concerned an individual contract of employment and that it therefore had jurisdiction over the subject-matter of the case. It also accepted his argument that it had territorial jurisdiction under Article 5(1), but this latter finding was overturned on Schwab's appeal to the *Cour d'Appel* in Colmar. Ivenel then appealed to the Social Chamber of the *Cour de Cassation*, which considered that as the proceedings concerned a contract of agency involving mutual obligations, some of which were to be performed in France and some of which were to be performed in Germany, the question of where the "obligation" within the meaning of Article 5(1) had to be performed gave rise to a problem of interpretation, which it duly referred to the European Court.

17.25   The European Court reiterated that the rules of special jurisdiction in Articles 5 and 6 seek to grant jurisdiction to the courts which have a close connection with the dispute, and referred to the com-

---

[91] [1987] 3 C.M.L.R. 782 discussed at para. 17.28 below.

[92] [1982] E.C.R. 1891. See Collins, p. 55; Hartley, pp. 45–47; Hartley, (Note) (1982) 7 Eur.L.Rev. 328; Verheul, (Note) (1982) 30 N.I.L.R. 240; Tebbens, "L'Interprétation dynamique, par la Cour de Justice Européenne, de la compétence en matière contractuelle", in *Unification and comparative law in theory and practice. Contributions in honour of Jean Georges Sauveplanne.*

[93] The status of this contract as a contract of employment, or at least as a contract falling short of a contract for services by an independent contractor, was later stressed by the European Court in *Shenavai* v. *Kreischer*: see para. 17.29 below.

[94] The court with jurisdiction in employment cases.

ment in the Jenard Report[95] that Article 5(1) would be useful in proceedings for the recovery of fees, because it provided a choice of jurisdictions,[96] and to the reasons set out in the Report for not including a special section on employment contracts.[97] It drew attention to the rule in the Contractual Obligations Convention[98] whereby the law applicable to a contract of employment, in the absence of choice (and sometimes despite it), is usually the law of the country in which the employee habitually carries out his work in performance of the contract,[99] and referred to the reason for that rule, as recorded in the experts' report on that Convention,[1] namely:

> "to provide an appropriate arrangement for matters in which the interests of one of the contracting parties were not the same as those of the other and to secure thereby adequate protection for the party who from the socio-economic point of view was to be regarded as the weaker in the contractual relationship."[2]

The European Court went on to say:

> "It follows from the foregoing account that in the matter of contracts Article 5(1) of the Convention is particularly concerned to attribute jurisdiction to the court of the country which has a close connection with the case; that in the case of a contract of employment the connection lies particularly in the law applicable to the contract; and that according to the trend in the conflict rules in regard to this matter that law is determined by the obligation characterizing the contract in question and is normally the obligation to carry out work."[3]

Further support for that ruling was drawn by the Court from a number of other matters, such as the Convention's protective purpose[4] as evidenced in the case of jurisdiction in contractual matters by the rules relating to insurance, consumer contracts and tenancies of immovable property,[5] and the need to interpret the provisions of

---

[95] Jenard, para. A1.101 below.
[96] [1982] E.C.R. 1891, at p. 1899 (para. 11).
[97] Jenard, paras. A1.102–A1.106 below.
[98] Convention on the Law Applicable to Contractual Obligations. See para. 17.14, n. 49 above. Arts. 3–6 of that Convention are set out at paras. A2.41 *et seq.* below.
[99] [1982] E.C.R. 1891, at p. 1900 (para. 13); Art. 6 of that Convention, para. A2.45 below.
[1] Report by Professors Guiliano & Lagarde O.J. 1980 C282 at pp. 25–26 see para. 17.14, n. 49 above.
[2] [1982] E.C.R. 1891, at p. 1900 (para. 14).
[3] *Ibid.,* at p. 1900 (para. 15).
[4] As to the Convention's protective purpose generally, see para. 13.15 above.
[5] In the amended version of the Convention, Arts. 7–12A, 13–15 and 16(1) respectively.

the Convention in such a way that the national court is not compelled to find that it has jurisdiction to adjudicate upon certain claims but not on others.[6]

17.26   *Characteristic performance.* The decision in *Ivenel* v. *Schwab* adopted a wholly new and different approach from that adopted previously in relation to Article 5(1) and, while it is now apparent that the decision applies only to exceptional cases, notably those concerning contracts of employment, it seemed for a time that the European Court intended it to have a wider application,[7] perhaps applying to contract cases generally.[8] The decision was based on the concept of "characteristic obligation" or "characteristic performance," which was one which adopted by the Contracting States for the purposes of the Contractual Obligations Convention.[9] For those cases exceptional enough to fall outside the general rule in *De Bloos* v. *Bouyer*,[10] the concept continues to be of practical importance in the context of Article 5(1) of the 1968 Convention.

17.27   The doctrine of characteristic performance proceeds on the assumption that most contracts involve the performance by one

---

[6] [1982] E.C.R. 1891, at p. 1901 (paras. 16–19). This latter factor is mentioned first generally (para. 18) and then specifically in relation to employment contracts (para. 19). More recently, however, the European Court has discounted this factor — see *Kalfelis* v. *Schröder, Münchmeyer, Hengst & Co.*, case 189/87, decision of September 27, 1988 (paras. 19–21), *The Times*, October 5, 1988; see para. 15.18 above.

[7] A decision of the French Cour de Cassation, for example, in a case involving a commercial representative of a foreign supplier, followed the reasoning of *Ivenel* v. *Schwab*, and suggested that that court regarded the decision in *De Bloos* v. *Bouyer* to be of limited application: *Wittels Albert Maschinen GmbH* v. *Seal*, Bull.Cass., Chambres Civiles 1982, Pt. 5, No. 585, p. 430; Rev. critique, p. 661; Digest D I–5.1.1—B17. *Ivenel* v. *Schwab* was also followed in a case involving a contract of sale between businesses, by the Arrondissementsrechtbank Alkmaar (Netherlands), July 22, 1982: Ned.Int.Priv. 1983, No. 230. See also the decision of the German Bundesarbeitsgericht (Federal Labour Court), case 2 AZR 398/85, June 17, 1986, [1988] E.C.C. 273.

[8] This apparent intention, now probably of historical interest only, might be deduced from the manner in which the *De Bloos* decision was treated in *Ivenel* v. *Schwab*. While not expressly disavowing the earlier decision, the Court stressed the fact that it had been concerned with exclusive sales concessions and introduced the words "between two commercial undertakings": see Verheul, (note) (1982) 30 N.I.L.R. 240, at p. 249. Also, the fact that the decision drew on the Contractual Obligations Convention to introduce the doctrine of characteristic performance suggests a wider intention on the part of the European Court, notably because that doctrine does not apply in that Convention to contracts of employment.

[9] See para. 17.14, n. 49 above. The Convention is not yet in force. The doctrine has a parallel in Art. 46 of the new French code of civil procedure. Arts. 3–6 of that Convention provide are set out at para. A2.41 *et seq.* below.

[10] As to the exceptional nature of *Ivenel* v. *Schwab*, see para. 17.30 below.

party of some obligation in return for payment by the other party. The former obligation, rather than the obligation to pay, is the "characteristic" obligation.[11] The contract is deemed, in most circumstances, to have its closest connection with the country where the party who is to perform the characteristic obligation has his habitual residence or its central administration,[12] although, in the case of individual contracts of employment, as already observed, different rules apply.[13]

Ivenel v. *Schwab* was open to the criticism that it detracted from the apparent legal certainty that existed in the light of the decision in *De Bloos* v. *Bouyer*, and that it appeared to be contrary to the clear wording of the amended text of the various language versions of Article 5(1). But in the light of *Shenavai* v. *Kreischer*, it is now apparent that the European Court's approach in *Ivenel* v. *Schwab* is to be confined to cases which are exceptional in character. It may even be that it applies only to contracts of employment and those of a closely similar nature.[13a]

The third case: Shenavai v. *Kreischer.* The principal decision on **17.28** the meaning of the words "the obligation in question" is *Shenavai* v. *Kreischer*.[14] Shenavai was an architect domiciled at Rockenhausen in Germany, where he also had his offices. He was engaged by Kreischer, who was domiciled in the Netherlands, to prepare plans for the construction of three holiday homes near Rockenhausen. Shenavai brought an action in his local German court for payment of his fees for that work and Kreischer disputed its jurisdiction. As a matter of German law, it was held that the place where the debt was payable was at the debtor's residence in the Netherlands, but that the place of performance of the contract as a whole was at the place of the architect's offices or the site of the proposed building. The question arose as to which of those places was the "place of performance of the obligation in question" for the purposes of Article 5(1) and that was the question which was referred to the European Court by the *Landgericht* Kaiserslautern.[15]

The European Court referred first to its observation in *Tessili* v. **17.29** *Dunlop*[16] that the special jurisdictions available under Article 5 were

---

[11] Guiliano and Lagarde Report, O.J. 1980 C282 at pp. 20–21; Hartley, p. 45; Hartley, (Note) (1982) 7 Eur.L.Rev. 328.
[12] Contractual Obligations Convention, Art. 4(2).
[13] Arts. 3–6 of the Contractual Obligations Convention are set out at paras. A2.41 *et seq.* below.
[13a] Its application to contracts of employment was confirmed in *Six Constructions Ltd.* v. *Humbert*, case 32/88, decision of February 15, 1989, not yet reported.
[14] [1987] 3 C.M.L.R. 782.
[15] *Ibid.*, para. 5.
[16] [1976] E.C.R. 1473, at p. 1485 (para. 13), discussed at para. 17.13 above.

introduced because of the existence of a particularly close relationship in certain circumstances between a dispute and the court which could be called upon to entertain it.[17] It then went on to refer[18] to the passage in its judgment in *De Bloos* v. *Bouyer* where it had said that the Convention could not be interpreted as referring to any obligation whatsoever arising under the contract in question, but that the relevant obligation was that forming the basis of the plaintiff's claim.[19] The judgment continued:

> "The general rule thereby defined admits, however, of certain exceptions, on the ground that 'matters relating to a contract' cover relationships of widely differing kinds both from the view point of their social importance and from that of the obligations entered into . . . "[20]

The Court cited as an example the exclusive jurisdiction provided by Article 16(1) for claims having as their object tenancies of immovable property. It went on to say that the decision in *Ivenel* v. *Schwab*[21] had been based on considerations of that kind, and drew attention to the fact that that case had involved a contract of representation which the national court had treated as an employment contract.[22]

> " . . . it should first be observed that contracts of employment, like other contracts for work other than on a self-employed basis, differ from other contracts — even those for the provision of services — by virtue of certain particularities: they create a lasting bond which brings the worker to some extent within the organisational framework of the business of the undertaking or employer, and they are linked to the place where the activities are pursued, which determines the application of mandatory rules and collective agreements. It is on account of those particularities that the court of the place in which the characteristic obligation of such contracts is to be performed is considered best suited to resolving the disputes to which one or more obligations under such contracts may give rise.
>
> When no such particularities exist, it is neither necessary nor appropriate to identify the obligation which characterizes the contract and to centralize at the place of performance thereof jurisdiction, based on place of performance, over disputes concerning all the obligations under the contract. The variety and multiplicity of

---

[17] *Shenavai*, above, para. 6.
[18] *Ibid.*, paras. 8 and 9.
[19] [1976] E.C.R. 1497, at p. 1508 (paras. 8–14), discussed at paras. 17.20–17.23 above.
[20] *Shenavai*, above, para. 10.
[21] [1982] E.C.R. 1891, discussed at paras. 17.24 to 17.25 above.
[22] *Shenavai*, above, para. 11.

contracts as a whole are such that the above criterion might in those other cases create uncertainty as to jurisdiction, whereas it is precisely such uncertainty which the Convention is designed to reduce.

On the other hand, no such uncertainty exists for most contracts if regard is had solely to the contractual obligation whose performance is sought in the judicial proceedings. The place in which that obligation is to be performed usually constitues the closest connecting factor between the dispute and the court having jurisdiction over it, and it is this connecting factor which explains why, in contractual matters, it is the court of the place of performance of the obligation which has jurisdiction."[23]

It is apparent from this passage in the European Court's judgment that it regards the decision in *Ivenel* v. *Schwab* as having been exceptional, and that the indications in that decision which suggested that Article 5(1) should be interpreted as applying generally to the characteristic obligation in contracts, and not just in the field of employment, should not to be followed. It remains to be seen, though, whether the approach adopted in *Ivenel* v. *Schwab* is strictly confined to cases of employment contracts, or whether other categories of contract are to be regarded as having characteristics so closely connected with a particular place that they, too, are exceptions to the general rule so that jurisdiction under Article 5(1) is to be determined by reference to their characteristic obligation. Any such exception, though, is likely to arise only in a field subject to mandatory rules of law and, perhaps, only where one party is typically the weaker from a social or economic point of view.[23a]   **17.30**

Although it did not arise in the question referred by the national court, the European Court was clearly conscious that the general rule might give rise to problems of application where the plaintiff based his claim on various obligations in the same contract and might lead to a multiplicity of jurisdictions, the very problem which the decision in *Ivenel* v. *Schwab* had avoided. It dealt with the question in its judgment by saying that secondary matters should follow the principal matter and that in such a case the principal obligation among the several obligations in issue is the one to which the court should have regard in determining its jurisdiction.[24]

---

[23] *Ibid.*, paras. 16–18.

[23a] See also *Six Constructions* v. *Paul Humbert*, case 32/88, decision of February 15, 1989, not yet reported. An employee's work was to be performed outside the Contracting States, and therefore no court had jurisdiction under Art. 5(1).

[24] *Ibid.*, para. 19. It remains to be seen whether this ruling will overcome the problems which may arise where national law provides for the performance of different obligations in different places: see para. 17.24 n. 90 above.

Article 5(2)

17.31 **[A person domiciled in a Contracting State may, in another Contracting State, be sued:]**

> 2. **in matters relating to maintenance, in the courts for the place where the maintenance creditor is domiciled or habitually resident or, if the matter is ancillary to proceedings concerning the status of a person, in the court which, according to its own law, has jurisdiction to entertain those proceedings, unless that jurisdiction is based solely on the nationality of one of the parties;*†**

B. Sub-Paragraph (2): Maintenance

1. General note

17.32   The 1968 Convention applies to maintenance proceedings[25] and provides a method for recovering maintenance from a defendant[26] domiciled in another Contracting State in addition to those provided by the United Nations Convention on the Recovery Abroad of Maintenance, done at New York on June 20, 1956 (the New York Convention, to which all the Contracting States except Ireland are parties)[27] and the Convention on the Recognition and Enforcement of Maintenance Obligations done at the Hague on October 2, 1973 (the Hague Maintenance Obligations Convention, to which Denmark, France, Germany, Italy, Luxembourg, the Netherlands and the

---

* Jenard, paras. A1.107–A1.110 below; Schlosser, paras. 36–42, 90–108 (paras. A1.326–A1.329, A1.378–A1.394 below); Collins, pp. 57–58; Dashwood/Halcon/White, pp. 24–26, 95–96; Hartley, pp. 18–19, 48–50; Kaye, pp. 527–561; Maxwell, paras. 5.43–5.58; Anton, paras. 5.26–5.34; Droz, paras. 69–72; Weser, paras. 224–225; Bülow/Böckstiegel/Linke, pp. 64–66; Geimer/Schütze, pp. 433–459, 820–821, 826; Kropholler, pp. 82–88; Gothot/Holleaux, paras. 80–84; Pocar, pp. 125–128.

† The wording of this para. was amended by Art. 5(3) of the 1978 Convention. Its original version provided only, "in matters relating to maintenance, in the courts for the place where the maintenance creditor is domiciled or habitually resident."

[25] Jenard, para. A1.107 below. See, generally, chap. 11 above.

[26] Although not always technically correct as a matter of English law, the terms "plaintiff" and "defendant" will be used in the commentary on this paragraph, rather than "applicant," "complainant," "petitioner" or "respondent."

[27] In the U.K., the New York Convention is given effect by Pt. II of the Maintenance Orders (Reciprocal Enforcement) Act 1972.

United Kingdom are parties.[28] The procedure under both those Conventions is nonetheless available in those Contracting States which are parties to them, because each is a convention to which Article 57 applies.[29]

Plaintiff maintenance creditor. Under the 1968 Convention, a plaintiff maintenance creditor has a choice of jurisdictions. She may bring her proceedings either, pursuant to Article 2, in the courts of the state where the defendant is domiciled, or, provided the defendant is domiciled in another Contracting State, in one of the courts provided for by Article 5(2).[30] This Article confers jurisdiction, first, upon the courts for the place where the maintenance creditor is domiciled or habitually resident[31] and, secondly, where the maintenance issues are ancillary to status proceedings, on the court which has jurisdiction under its own law to entertain those proceedings (unless that jurisdiction is based solely on the nationality of one of the parties).

Defendant maintenance creditor. Where the maintenance creditor is the defendant (for example, in an application for variation of a maintenance order)[32], Article 5(2) does not apply and the plaintiff maintenance debtor's application would have to be made under Article 2 to the courts of the state of the defendant creditor's domicile.[33] This is because Article 5 provides exceptions to the rule of general jurisdiction in Article 2 and confers jurisdiction only on courts other than those of the state where the defendant is domi-

---

[28] In the U.K., the Hague Maintenance Obligations Convention is given effect by Part I of the Maintenance Orders (Reciprocal Enforcement) Act 1972, as modified by the Reciprocal Enforcement of Maintenance Orders (Hague Convention Countries) Order 1979, (S.I. 1979 No. 1317). Pt. I of the 1972 Act also gives effect generally to reciprocal arrangements for the recognition and enforcement of maintenance orders reached with other designated countries. The only other Contracting State so designated is Ireland, to which special provisions apply, in that Pt. I of the 1972 Act is modified in its application to Ireland by the Reciprocal Enforcement of Maintenance Orders (Republic of Ireland) Order 1974, (S.I. 1974 No. 2140). See paras. 11.25–11.26 above.

[29] Para. 33.06 below. Art. 57 presents certain particular difficulties of interpretation, but in the light of Art. 25(2) of the 1978 Convention (para. 33.07 below) it seems that both these other conventions can co-exist with the 1968 Convention in reasonable harmony.

[30] In order for the Convention to apply at all, the case must have certain international characteristics: para. 13.10 above.

[31] Habitual residence is used as well as domicile in this paragraph as a basis of jurisdiction, for reasons discussed below.

[32] Para. 17.43 below.

[33] Schlosser, para. 107 (para. A1.393 below).

ciled.[34] If the court of the creditor defendant's domicile had jurisdiction, Article 5(2) would not be providing an exception to Article 2, but merely a more detailed expression of it.[35]

17.33 *Court to examine its jurisdiction.* The rules under Articles 21 to 23 relating to *lis pendens* and related actions apply to maintenance cases.[36] As a general rule, Article 28(3) prohibits a review, at the recognition and enforcement stage, of the jurisdiction of the court of origin[37] and for this reason, the court of origin must be especially careful to ensure that it has jurisdiction under the Convention.[38] The court should also be astute to ensure that it does not accept jurisdiction under the Convention over matters which fall outside its scope, particularly matters concerning rights in property arising out of a matrimonial relationship.[39] For example, an order for the payment of a lump sum, made in English divorce proceedings, may or may not be in the nature of maintenance and accordingly may or may not fall within the Convention.

2. "in matters relating to maintenance . . ."[40]

17.34 A maintenance payment is perhaps easier to recognise than to define and "maintenance" is not defined in the Convention. The question of whether a matter relates to "maintenance" is not likely to give rise to many problems in practice, but if the problem arises, it is suggested, the term should be given an independent interpretation so as to ensure consistency of application of the Convention. The Schlosser report notes a distinction between payments of compensation for material or non-material damage on one hand and

---

[34] Para. 15.05 above.
[35] Exceptionally, though, if the maintenance creditor were domiciled in one country but habitually resident in another, a plaintiff maintenance debtor could invoke jurisdiction under Art. 5(2) in support of an application before the courts for the place of the maintenance creditor's habitual residence. This theoretical possibility is most unlikely to occur in practice, because the Contracting States' national laws of domicile, which apply for the purposes of the Convention (see Art. 52, para. 31.01 below) treat domicile and habitual residence very similarly. As concerns the U.K., see s.41 of the 1982 Act (para. 44.01 below).
[36] Schlosser, para. 39 (para. A1.327 below).
[37] A review of jurisdiction is permitted in the limited circumstances referred to at paras. 25.11 *et seq.* below. Art. 27(4), which is particularly relevant to maintenance cases, presents certain problems in the context of Art. 5(2): see para. 17.42 below.
[38] Schlosser, para. 38 (para. A1.327 below); see also Art. 20, para. 22.11 below.
[39] See Art. 1, especially at paras. 14.20 *et seq.* above.
[40] Schlosser, paras. 91–97 (paras. A1.379–A1.385 below).

payments in the nature of maintenance on the other, but notes that the two overlap in practice.[41]

The second De Cavel decision. Two types of maintenance order came before the European Court of Justice in *De Cavel* v. *De Cavel (No. 2)*.[42] In the course of divorce proceedings in France, Mme. de Cavel had been awarded maintenance pending suit, which she sought to enforce in Germany. Subsequently, the divorce was granted and an interim award made in her favour for a "compensatory allowance" under Articles 270 *et seq.* of the French Civil Code. The German Federal Supreme Court referred to the European Court of Justice the question whether each of those orders fell within the Convention. The judgment of the European Court concentrated principally on the ancillary nature of the relief[43] and there seems to have been no dispute that the first of the two orders was a matter relating to maintenance. As to the second order, the European Court held that:

> "the 'compensatory payments' provided for in Article 270 *et seq.* of the French Civil Code and referred to in the second question are concerned with any financial obligations between former spouses after divorce which are fixed on the basis of their respective needs and resources and are equally in the nature of maintenace."[44]

It followed that they fell within the scope of the Convention. Despite the absence of a definition of "maintenance," it seems that it is the nature of the payment as maintenance that is important, not the legal basis of the obligation, nor the method or frequency of payments.

Nature of the payments. The claim need not be for periodic payments and, depending on their nature, lump sum payments, charges on property and property transfer orders may be in the nature of maintenance.[45] The laws of some Contracting States do not draw a distinction as to whether lump sum payments ordered by the Court are intended as damages or as maintenance;[46] but only   **17.35**

---

[41] Schlosser, paras. 94–95 (paras. A1.382–A1.383 below).
[42] [1980] E.C.R. 731. For discussion of *De Cavel* v. *De Cavel (No. 1)* [1979] E.C.R. 1055, an earlier reference in the same proceedings, and the factual background to the case, see para. 14.21 above.
[43] [1980] E.C.R. 731, at pp. 740–741 (paras. 6–10), discussed at para. 17.41 below. The question of ancillary relief is now largely resolved by the amendment made to the text of Art. 5(2).
[44] *Ibid.*, at p. 740 (para. 5).
[45] Schlosser, para. 93 (para. A1.381 below).
[46] English law, for example, does not draw such a distinction: Schlosser, para. 95 (para. A1.383 below).

if they are in the nature of maintenance do they fall within the scope of Article 5(2).[47]

The Schlosser Report draws attention to the absence of any mention of the legal basis for the maintenance claim and notes the marked difference in this respect from the wording of the Hague Maintenance Obligations Convention, but says that, nonetheless, there is no significant difference regarding the concept of maintenance as used in the two conventions.[48] The suggestion in the Report is that "maintenance" for the purposes of the Convention does not extend beyond the field of family law.[49] "Maintenance" obligations arising from the law of tort, it suggests, are to be treated as claims for damages, even if the amount of compensation depends on the needs of the injured party. Similarly, the suggestion is that where a "maintenance" obligation which did not previously exist is created by a contract, it is to be treated, according to its form, as a contract or gift, rather than as "matters relating to maintenance," and that accordingly it should be regarded as falling within Article 5(1) rather than Article 5(2).[50]

17.36   It remains to be seen precisely how wide an independent interpretation of the term "maintenance" is drawn, but it is suggested that the connecting factor, justifying a special jurisdiction in favour of the court for the place where the maintenance creditor is domiciled, can apply to any obligation or payment in the nature of maintenance, whatever its legal foundation, and that the nature of the obligation or payment should be the only decisive factor in determining whether a matter is one "relating to maintenance" for the purposes of Article 5(2).[51] There is no reason, it is suggested, why the various provisions of Articles 5 need be mutually exclusive.[52]

---

[47] Schlosser, para. 96 (para. A1.384 below). If there is any prospect that the order may have to be enforced abroad, it would greatly facilitate the operation of the Convention if the court making the order were to make clear in its judgment or order whether, and if so to what extent, the payments ordered represent payments in the nature of maintenance.

[48] Schlosser, para. 92 (para. A1.380 below). Art. 1 of the Hague Maintenance Obligations Convention refers to "a maintenance obligation arising from a family relationship, parentage, marriage or affinity, including a maintenance obligation towards an infant who is not legitimate."

[49] Weser, para. 224 and Droz, para. 69, also refer to maintenance only in the context of family law.

[50] Schlosser, *loc. cit.*

[51] *Semble*, Bülow/Böckstiegel/Linke, p. 64.

[52] See paras. 15.16 *et seq.* above; *e.g.* a maintenance obligation may arise in the context of a trust and fall under both Art. 5(2) and Art. 5(6). So far as contracts are concerned, it does not seem helpful to consider whether a maintenance obligation in a contract is an obligation which did not previously exist. To adopt such a criterion is likely to lead to divergent results according to the applicable law. For example, a father's obligation under English law to support his child is

Wills and succession. Because matters relating to wills and suc-   **17.37**
cession are expressly excluded from the scope of the Convention by
Article 1, the Schlosser Report says that maintenance claims arising
under the law of succession are also excluded from the scope of the
Convention.[53] The mere fact that the law of succession forms the
legal basis for the maintenance obligation, however, ought not
necessarily to exclude the obligation itself from the scope of the
Convention. So, for example, an application by a widow for an
order for maintenance by way of periodical payments out of the net
estate of her late husband[54] might fall within the scope of the Convention.[55] The principal characteristic of such an order is arguably
that it gives rise to rights of maintenance (which unquestionably fall
within the Convention), rather than that it interferes with the terms
of the will or adjusts the effects of the law on intestacy.

If an application for maintenance were made in proceedings which
were principally concerned with aspects of the will or intestacy
which clearly fell outside the Convention, the order might be severable and enforceable under the partial enforcement provisions of
Article 42.[56] If such a maintenance order were made on the basis of a
preliminary decision on the law of wills or succession, recognition of
the order might in certain circumstances be refused under Article
27(4).[57] The clear implication of that provision is that the Convention envisages an order coming within its scope despite being
founded on the law of wills or succession, and there is no apparent
reason why that should not apply as much to maintenance claims as
to any other civil and commercial matters.[58] If the widow's main-

---

an obligation which exists irrespective of whether it is incorporated in a contract
or made the subject of an order of the court. But the common law presumption
that a husband should maintain his wife is rebutted if a husband and wife part
without any agreement that the husband should maintain the wife: *Stringer* v.
Stringer [1952] P. 171, [1952] 1 All E.R. 373; Jackson, *Matrimonial Finance and
Taxation* (3rd ed.), p. 250. The laws of other Contracting States might well
adopt different approaches.

[53] Schlosser, para. 92 (para. A1.380 below).
[54] Such an order could be made in England under s.2 of the Inheritance (Provision
for Families and Dependants) Act 1975.
[55] *Semble*, in relation to para. 844(2) of the German Civil Code, Bülow/Böck-
stiegel/Linke, pp. 64–65.
[56] Para. 28.71 below. Severability at the stage of jurisdiction is discussed at
para. 14.05 above. The severance of a maintenance claim from issues falling
outside the scope of the Convention in such circumstances would be consistent
with the reasoning of Advocate General Warner in *De Cavel (No. 1)* [1979]
E.C.R. 1055 at p. 1068–1076, which in the result was adopted by the European
Court of Justice in *De Cavel (No. 2)* [1980] E.C.R. 731.
[57] Para. 27.52 below.
[58] If the matters set out in the second para. of Art. 1 (paras. 14.18 *et seq.* above) are
only of a preliminary nature, they do not prevent proceedings from falling
within the scope of the Convention: para. 14.18 above.

tenance claim stood on its own, and were not dependent on any court decision as to the law of wills or succession, the argument for the proceedings being "matters relating to maintenance" is even stronger. Again, the decisive question, it is suggested, is whether the payments are in the nature of maintenance.

17.38   *Third parties' claims for reimbursement.* Whether rights of recourse or subrogated rights against maintenance debtors[59] are "matters relating to maintenance" is a subject of some debate. Where a maintenance debtor defaults, leaving the maintenance creditor in need, a third party (such as the public social security authorities) may have to step in to meet those needs and then seek reimbursement from the maintenance debtor. Where the national laws of Contracting States provide rights of recourse in such circumstances, they are designed to achieve the same general result, but do not necessarily adopt the same means. According to both the Jenard Report[60] and the Schlosser Report,[61] such claims fall within the Convention; but it is not clear that they fall within Article 5(2). It seems that the answer to that question may depend on whether the applicable national law transfers the maintenance creditor's rights to the third party (in which case the rights themselves should still be the nature of maintenance) or gives rise to new rights in the third party.[62] English law, for example adopts the latter approach and contribution orders[63] would not be "matters relating to maintenance" under that test.[64]

There must be some doubt as to whether the European Court of Justice will approach the problem in this way. First, the Court is perhaps unlikely to favour an approach which, according to the particular legal formulae adopted by the various national laws, produces inconsistent results as between different Contracting States. Secondly, if the rights of public authorities to seek reimbursement from maintenance creditors are rights which *arise* as a matter of public law, and not merely by the transfer of private law rights, it is hard to see how the rights can fall within the Convention at all, in the light of the exclusion of social security by Article 1 and the interpretation given by the European Court of Justice to the term

---

[59] See para. 14.30 above.

[60] Para. A1.53 below.

[61] Para. 97 (para. A1.385 below).

[62] Schlosser seems to suggest that a claim by a third party for contribution or reimbursement of payments in the nature of maintenance falls outside Art. 5(2) in either event: para. 97 (para. A1.385 below). Hartley (p. 50, n. 2) disagrees, and takes the view that such orders must either be maintenance and fall within Art. 5(2) or be social security and fall outside the Convention.

[63] *e.g.* under the Child Care Act 1980.

[64] Collins, p. 57, following Schlosser (*loc. cit.*).

"civil and commercial matters."[65] But to exclude such rights would be contrary to intention of the authors of the Convention as expressed in the Jenard and Schlosser Reports.

3. " . . . the courts . . . "

The amount of maintenance payments are fixed in Denmark by the administrative authorities, not by the courts. In order to provide consistency of application of the Convention, the Danish administrative authorities are to be regarded as courts for this purpose[66]: Article Va of the Protocol.[67]   **17.39**

4. " . . . domiciled or habitually resident . . . "

The term "domicile" is not defined by the 1968 Convention, but Article 52 provides a uniform set of choice of law rules for determining which national law is to be applied in deciding whether a person is domiciled in any given Contracting State.[68]   **17.40**

The "habitual residence" of the maintenance creditor is included in this paragraph, as an alternative basis for jurisdiction, and forms an exception to the normal approach of the Convention. It was included in order to bring Article 5(2) into line with Hague Conventions on maintenance.[69] The expression is nowhere defined,[70] and there are no choice of law rules in this Convention or the Hague Conventions to assist in its interpretation.[71]

When the 1968 Convention was first drafted, the laws of several Contracting States still provided a domicile of dependence for married women[72] and there was therefore a particular need for habitual residence as an additional basis of jurisdiction in maintenance cases.

---

[65] Paras. 14.08 *et seq.* above.

[66] Schlosser, paras. 66–68 (paras. A1.352–A1.354 below).

[67] Para. 35.22 below.

[68] Para. 31.01 below. The law of the U.K. defines domicile for the purposes of the Convention in s.41 of the 1982 Act: para. 44.01 below. The law of domicile in the other Contracting States is summarised in chaps. 48 to 58 below, at para. 25.

[69] Jenard, para. A1.109 below.

[70] See Dicey and Morris, pp. 166–167; Cheshire and North, pp. 187–188.

[71] Under Art. 52, "domicile" is generally to be interpreted according to the *lex fori* (including its rules of private international law) and it is suggested that this is the proper approach also in relation to "habitual residence": see para. 31.07 below; Bülow/Böckstiegel/Linke, p. 66.

[72] The domicile of dependence was abolished in English law by the Domicile and Matrimonial Proceedings Act 1973.

5. " . . . if the matter is ancillary to proceedings concerning the status of a person, in the court which, according to its own law, has jurisdiction to entertain those proceedings, unless that jurisdiction is based solely on the nationality of one of the parties"

17.41   These words were added by the 1978 Convention to accommodate the provisions of United Kingdom law whereby maintenance issues can be dealt with by way of ancillary relief in divorce proceedings, and also because the laws of a number of the Contracting States had been amended since the Convention was originally drafted, to include similar provisions.[73] The principal topics concerning "the status of a person" are listed in the Schlosser Report.[74] In the context of Article 5(2), they include divorce, judicial separation, nullity of marriages, adoption, guardianship, affiliation[75] and care, custody and control of children.

Even before the amended text of Article 5(2) came into force, the European Court of Justice had held, in *De Cavel* v. *De Cavel (No. 2)*,[76] that the Convention applied to maintenance claims ancillary to divorce proceedings. Having noted that maintenance clearly fell within the Convention, and divorce outside it, the Court went on to say:

> "In so far as its field of application is concerned, no provision of the Convention links the treatment of ancillary claims to the treatment of principal claims. On the contrary, various provisions confirm that the Convention does not link the treatment of claims classified as 'ancillary' to the treatment of the principal claim . . .
>
> Ancillary claims . . . come within the scope of the Convention according to the subject-matter with which they are concerned and not according to the subject-matter involved in the principal claim. It was by way of applying that rule that the Court held in its judgment of March 27, 1979 in Case 143/78 *de Cavel* [1979] E.C.R. 1055, involving the same parties, that an application in the course of divorce proceedings for placing assets under seal did not come within the scope of the Convention, not on account of its ancillary nature, but because it appeared that, having regard to its true function, it concerned, in that case, rights in property arising out of the spouses' matrimonial relationship."[77]

17.42   What the amended text of Article 5(2) does is to provide an additional special jurisdiction for ancillary claims for maintenance,

---

[73] Schlosser, paras. 32–42 (paras. A1.323–A1.329 below).
[74] Para. 51 (para. A1.338 below). The list, which is not exhaustive, is reproduced at para. 14.19 above.
[75] Collins, pp. 57–58; Maxwell Report, para. 5.48. Affiliation has now been abolished in England: Family Law Reform Act 1987.
[76] [1980] E.C.R. 731. See para. 17.34 above as to other questions in the case.
[77] [1980] E.C.R. 731, at pp. 740–741 (paras. 7–9).

if such a jurisdiction is provided by the *lex fori* (including its procedural rules and private international law).[78] But that jurisdiction is
not available if the jurisdiction provided by the *lex fori* is based
solely on the nationality[79] of *one* of the parties. These words are to
be construed strictly. If the jurisdiction is based on something in
addition to the nationality of one of the parties, the exclusion does
not apply. Similarly, if the jurisdiction is based on the nationality of
both parties it would normally, in the case of ordinary civil and
commercial matters, be excluded by Article 3(2); but it seems that
that would not be sufficient to exclude it in the case of combined
maintenance and status proceedings, because in such a case it cannot be considered exorbitant.[80]

Preliminary questions of status. As a general rule, the third paragraph of Article 28[81] prohibits a review at the stage of recognition
and enforcement of the jurisdiction of the court of origin, but
Article 27(4)[82] provides an exception, permitting the court
addressed to refuse recognition, *inter alia*, if the court of origin, "in
order to arrive at its judgment, has decided a preliminary question
concerning the status or legal capacity of natural persons . . . in a
way that conflicts with the private international law of the State in
which recognition is sought, unless the same result would have
been reached by the application of the rules of private international
law of that State." On its face, that would seem to apply to ancillary
maintenance orders (or, indeed, non-ancillary ones), but if so, it
might render the amended text of Article 5(2) largely useless in
some cases. Article 5(2) makes specific reference to the jurisdiction
of the court of origin according to its own law (including, as
explained above, its private international law) and there is therefore
an argument that Article 27(4), being more general, should not be
construed so as to prevent the enforcement of an ancillary maintenance order. Although the problem is not specifically considered in
the Schlosser Report, its reference to the amended text of Article
5(2) in the context of the prohibition on a review of jurisdiction[83]

---

[78] Schlosser, para. 40 (para. A1.327 below).
[79] The exclusion is aimed principally at the exorbitant jurisdictions provided by
Art. 15 of the Belgian Civil Code and Arts. 14 and 15 of the French and Luxembourg Civil Codes: Schlosser, para. 41 (para. A1.328 below). See Art. 3,
para. 16.09 above. The jurisdiction of courts in the U.K. in matrimonial or
other relevant proceedings is not normally based on nationality: Collins, p. 58,
n. 6. An exception, to a limited extent, is guardianship proceedings: see Dicey
and Morris, pp. 424–425 and 431.
[80] Schlosser, *loc. cit.*
[81] Para. 27.63 below.
[82] Para. 27.52 below.
[83] Schlosser, para. 38 (para. A1.327 below).

suggests that that may have been the view of the negotiators of the 1978 Convention.[84]

6. Applications to vary a maintenance order

17.43 Applications to vary a maintenance order come within Article 5(2).[85] Such applications are subject to the provisions of the Convention as if they were fresh proceedings, rather than applications in the original proceedings. The consequence is that if a court, in a Contracting State other than that in which the original order was made, is asked to vary the original order, it may do so only if it has jurisdiction under the Convention.[85a] Conversely, the courts of the Contracting State where the original order was made may only vary the original order if they still have jurisdiction under the Convention.

The following example may be helpful in illustrating various applications of these rules. A maintenance order is made in German divorce proceedings against a husband domiciled in Germany, in favour of his wife who is domiciled in England:

(1) The ex-husband seeks to vary the order. The application would have to be made in England, because:
    (a) the ex-husband is not the maintenance creditor, and so does not fall within the first limb of Article 5(2);
    (b) the variation proceedings are no longer to be regarded as ancillary to the original divorce proceedings and so do not fall within the second limb of Article 5(2);
    (c) the English courts have jurisdiction as the courts of the ex-wife's domicile, pursuant to Article 2 (but not pursuant to Article 5(2)).[86]

(2) If it is the ex-wife who seeks to vary the original order, she can bring proceedings in England pursuant to the first limb of Article 5(2) or in Germany, pursuant to Article 2.

(3) If since the original order was made, the ex-husband had moved his domicile to Belgium, the ex-wife could apply in Belgium for a variation, pursuant to Article 2, but not in Germany. She could still apply in England pursuant to Article 5(2).

---

[84] In relation to the unamended text, see Droz (para. 72) and Weser (para. 225); *Onnen* v. *Nielen*, Gerechtshof, Amsterdam, February 19, 1976, Ned.Jur. 1977, No. 132; Digest D I–27.4—B1.

[85] Schlosser, paras. 98–108 (paras. A1.386–A1.394 below).

[85a] Jurisdiction may be founded on the entry of an appearance, pursuant to Art. 18: see *Re M.*, Arrondissementsrechtbank, Maastricht, January 21, 1986; (1986) Ned.Jur. 1956; [1987] Eur.L.Dig. 195.

[86] See para. 17.32 above.

The same would be true if the original order had been made in English divorce proceedings, and any other Contracting States could be substituted in the example for England, Germany and Belgium. Equally, it would make no difference if both parties had been domiciled in the same country at the date of the original order.

Article 5(3)

[A person domiciled in a Contracting State may, in another Con- 17.44 tracting State, be sued:]

> **3. in matters relating to tort, delict or quasi-delict, in the courts for the place where the harmful event occurred;***

C. Sub-Paragraph (3): Tort, Delict and Quasi-Delict

1. General note

Jurisdiction based on the place of the tort (the *forum delicti com- 17.45 missi*) is known to the legal systems of most of the Contracting States and is of particular practical application in the case of road accidents.[87] The rule of special jurisdiction provided by Article 5(3) can cover a wide range of different factual and legal circumstances and the European Court of Justice has given a liberal interpretation to its terms. It was held that a claim does not fall within Article 5(3) if it is connected with a matter "relating to a contract" within the meaning of Article 5(1); and that, between them, those two subparagraphs cover all claims which seek to establish the liability of the defendant.[87a] It may therefore frequently happen that a noncontractual claim falls within one of the other provisions of Article 5 and within this provision. There is no reason in principle, provided the claim does not also fall within the rules of exclusive jurisdiction in Article 16, why such a claim should not be brought under Article 5(3) in the courts for the place where the harmful event occurred.[88]

---

* Jenard, para. A1.111 below; Schlosser, para. 134 (para. A1.417 below); Collins, pp. 58–61; Dashwood/Halcon/White, pp. 23, 96–97; Hartley, pp. 50–52; Kaye, pp. 561–588; Maxwell, para. 5.59; Anton, paras. 5.35–5.39; Droz, paras. 73–80; Weser, paras. 225*bis*–226; Bülow/Böckstiegel/Linke, pp. 66–72; Geimer/Schütze, pp. 604–647; Kropholler, pp. 88–93; Gothot/Holleaux, paras. 85–90; Pocar, pp. 128–141.
[87] Jenard, para. A1.111 below.
[87a] See para. 17.46 below. Some proceedings may not seek to establish the liability of the defendant, and so not fall within Art. 5(3); *e.g.* it may be that the decision of the French Cour de Cassation, that proceedings for the enforcement of an earlier judgment itself based on tort did not fall within Art. 5(3), would survive the European Court's decision: *La Boissière Beauchamps S.A.* v. *Messerschmidt-Bolkow-Blohm G.m.b.H.* [1988] E.C.C. 287.
[88] See paras. 15.16 *et seq.* above.

2. "tort, delict or quasi-delict"

17.46   The European Court has held that the words "matters relating to tort, delict or quasi-delict"[89] are to be given an independent interpretation and that they include all claims which seek to put in issue a defendant's liability and which are not connected with "matters relating to a contract"[90] within the meaning of Article 5(1).

The Kalfelis decision. This ruling was made in *Kalfelis* v. *Schröder, Münchmeyer, Hengst & Co.*[91] The first defendant was a German bank which had since gone into liquidation but which in 1980 and 1981 had acted as intermediary in various spot and forward stock exchange transactions carried out by the plaintiff with the second defendant, a Luxembourg bank wholly owned by the first defendant. The forward transactions resulted in a total loss and the plaintiff brought proceedings in Germany based on contract, on tort and on the principle of unjust enrichment, all pursuant to German law. The second defendant, domiciled in Luxembourg, disputed the jurisdiction of the German courts and the *Bundesgerichtshof* referred to the European Court, *inter alia*,[92] the question whether "tort, delict or quasi-delict" was to be interpreted independently, on the basis of the Convention, or according to the *lex causae* as determined by the private international law of the forum.

As it had done in its decisions interpreting "matters relating to a contract" in Article 5(1),[93] the European Court referred to the need to ensure, so far as possible, "the equality and uniformity of the rights and obligations derived from the Convention for the Contracting States and for interested persons". It therefore held that "tort, delict or quasi-delict" could not be interpreted as a renvoi to national law, but that those words must be given an independent interpretation. Although not asked to do so by the German court, it went on to define them in the way described above.

A second part of the question referred by the *Bundesgerichtshof* was also answered by the European Court in holding that Article 5 was to be restrictively interpreted and that therefore a court which

---

[89] Where a distinction is drawn between delict and quasi-delict, it is generally based on the presence or absence of an element of intention. So far as the U.K. is concerned, "tort" is known to the laws of England and Northern Ireland, while "delict" and "quasi-delict" are known to the law of Scotland.

[90] See paras. 17.05 *et seq.* above.

[91] Case 189/87, decision of September 27, 1988, *The Times*, October 5, 1988.

[92] A question concerning the interpretation of Art. 6(1) was also referred to the European Court and is discussed at para. 17.76 below.

[93] *Peters* v. *Z.N.A.V.* [1983] E.C.R. 987, 1002; *Arcado* v. *Haviland*, case 9/87, decision of March 8, 1988 (para.10), [1989] E.C.C. 1.

had jurisdiction under Article 5(3) over that part of a claim which was based on tort did not thereby acquire jurisidiction over other parts of the claim which were based on non-tortious grounds.[93a]

3. " . . . place where the harmful event occurred"

This concept was left deliberately vague by the authors of the **17.47** Convention[94] and is open to several interpretations.[95] For example, the "place where the harmful event occurred" could be the place where the principal tortious act occurred, where the last of a series of tortious acts occurred, where the damage was suffered, where the tort had its closest connection, or various combinations of these.[96]

The Bier case. The problem of interpreting this concept was presented to the European Court of Justice in *Handelskwekerij G. J. Bier B.V.* v. *Mines de Potasse d'Alsace S.A.*[97] The allegation was that the French mine-owners were discharging chlorides into the Rhine, so polluting it that Bier's horticulture business in Holland was put to considerable expense to limit the damage to its crops. The horticulturalists, supported by the Reinwater Foundation (whose sisyphean task is to promote the purity of the waters of the Rhine), brought an action against the French mine-owners in the court at Rotterdam. The defendants objected to the jurisdiction of the Dutch court and were successful at first instance on the grounds that the event that had caused the damage could only be the discharge of the polluting salts into the Rhine, and that that had taken place within the territorial jurisdiction of the French courts. Relying on Article 5(3), the plaintiffs appealed to the *Gerechtshof* in the Hague, which referred the question of the interpretation of "the place where the harmful event occurred" to the European Court of Justice.

Advocate General Capotorti's Opinion[98] contains a careful and **17.48** detailed analysis of the various different possible interpretations, and reviews the law in each of the Contracting States (including the

---

[93a] See paras. 15.16 *et seq.* above.

[94] Jenard, para. A1.111 below.

[95] See the observations of the Commission in *Handelskwekerij G. J. Bier B.V.* v. *Mines de Potasse d'Alsace S.A.* [1976] E.C.R. 1735, at pp. 1741–1743; and Hartley, p. 51.

[96] For the position at common law, see Dicey and Morris, pp. 1382–1387; Cheshire and North, pp. 538–544; *Castree* v. *E.R. Squibb & Sons* [1981] 1 W.L.R. 1248; *Multinational Gas and Petrochemical Co.* v. *Multinational Gas and Petrochemical Services Ltd.* [1983] Ch. 258. See also *Dumez Bâtiment* v. *Hessiche Landesbank*, case 220/88 (pending).

[97] [1976] E.C.R. 1735.

[98] [1976] E.C.R. 1735, at p. 1749.

United Kingdom and Denmark). Of the interpretation which was subsequently adopted by the Court, he said:

> "we should accept that the cumulative solution, which would leave the plaintiff free to choose between the court of the place where the act was committed and the court of the place where the event occurred, may appear by its very liberality fairer and better able to accommodate the characteristics of the various types of unlawful act. Indeed we have seen that within the national legal systems this solution has now been broadly adopted."[99]

Despite that view, he thought that that solution was not in keeping with the letter and spirit of the Convention. The Court disagreed with him, and, having implicitly decided that "the place where the harmful event occurred" was to be given an independent interpretation ruled as follows:

> "Where the place of the happening of the event which may give rise to liability in tort, delict or quasi-delict and the place where that event results in damage are not identical, the expression 'place where the harmful event occurred,' in Article 5(3) . . . must be understood as being intended to cover both the place where the damage occurred and the place of the event giving rise to it.
>
> The result is that the defendant may be sued, at the option of the plaintiff, either in the courts for the place where the damage occurred or in the courts for the place of the event which gives rise to and is at the origin of that damage."[1]

In reaching its decision, the European Court referred to the place of the tortious act and the place where the damage was suffered as significant connecting factors and said that it was not appropriate to opt for one of those factors to the exclusion of the other, since each of them could, depending on the circumstances, be particularly helpful from the point of view of the evidence and of the conduct of the proceedings and pointed out that Article 5(3) covers a wide diversity of kinds of liability.

17.49   *Multiple jurisdictions.* Where a multiplicity of jurisdictions is available, the rules on *lis pendens* and related actions[2] will go some way to resolve conflicts of jurisdiction and reduce the likelihood of conflicting decisions. Where a plaintiff has sued to judgment in one jurisdiction, he will not be permitted to start a fresh action on the same cause of action in another jurisdiction;[3] but it may be that the

---

[99] *Ibid.*, at p. 1755.

[1] *Ibid.*, at pp. 1748–1749. On the basis of that decision, the Gerechtshof held that the court in Rotterdam had jurisdiction: April 22, 1977, Digest D I–5.3—B4.

[2] Arts. 21–23, chap. 23 below.

[3] *De Wolf* v. *Cox B.V.* [1976] E.C.R. 1759; para. 25.36 below. In the U.K., see also s.34 of the 1982 Act, para. 43.36 below.

effect of the *Bier* decision, in cases involving a choice of places where the harmful event can be said to have occurred, is that even by starting an action for tort delict or quasi-delict in the courts for one such place, a plaintiff will be taken to have elected that forum to the exclusion of others,[4] although, it is submitted, that would probably be too narrow an application of the European Court's decision in the case of continuing wrongs.

Remaining problems. The *Bier* case leaves a number of difficult **17.50** jurisdictional problems unanswered. For example, problems may arise where damage is suffered in a number of countries, by reason of a single act of negligence, a problem that is particularly likely to occur in product liability litigation. Similarly, the place where the harmful event occurred may be hard to identify where direct damage is suffered in one country and indirect damage in another,[5] as would be the case where a person is killed in France as the result of a car negligently manufactured in Germany, leaving a widow domiciled in England. It seems in such a case that the economic consequences of the damage should be distinguished from the damage itself (not necessarily an easy task in economic torts) and the location of the estate or person suffering damage by reason of the harmful event is not necessarily the location of the damage.[6] As Advocate General Warner has pointed out,[7] to hold that the place where the harmful event occurred was the place where the plaintiff had its seat would be tantamount to holding that, under the Convention, a plaintiff in tort had the option of suing in the courts of his own domicile, which would be quite inconsistent with the scheme of the Convention. The *Bundesgerichtshof* has held, applying the *Bier* decision, that,

> "apart from the place where the act was committed, the only

---

[4] A Dutch court has held that by choosing to sue in one place, a plaintiff had elected that forum for the purposes of Art. 5(3) and, quite apart from any question of *lis pendens* under Art. 21 (para. 23.01 below), he was precluded from bringing later proceedings on the same basis in the courts of another Contracting State: *Geobra Brandstätter GmbH & Co. K.G.* v. *Big Spielwarenfabrik Dipl.Ing. Ernst A. Bettag*, Arrondissementsrechtbank, Amsterdam, June 15, 1977, Digest D I–5.3—B5.

[5] See Droz, para. 76, written before the Convention came into effect in the original six Contracting States. See also *Dumez Bâtiment* v. *Hessische Landesbank*, case 220/88 (pending).

[6] *AGIP S.p.A.* v. *British Petroleum Co. Ltd. and Oil Chemical and Transport Finance Corporation S.A.*, Riv.dir.int.priv.proc. 1979, p. 96, Digest D I–5.3—B6; *Mecoma B.V.* v. *Stahlhandel GmbH*, Ned.Jur. 1979, No. 368, Digest D I–5.3—B7; Oberlandesgericht Hamm, case 9 U 278/77, October 3, 1978, Digest D I–5.3—B9; *Candy S.p.A.* v. *Schell e Stoecker Reinshagen GmbH*, Foro pad. 1979, I p. 225, Digest D I–5.3—B11.

[7] See his Opinion in *Netherlands* v. *Rüffer* [1980] E.C.R. 3807, at p. 3836.

other place which may be regarded as that of the harmful event is the place where the final element constituting the tort materialised"[7a]

17.51   *National courts' decisions.* The following are among the places which national courts have held to fall within the term "the place where the harmful event occurred": the place of spontaneous combustion of defective material,[8] the place of delivery of defective goods,[9] the place where imitation goods were marketed,[10] place of display for sale of goods alleged to infringe the plaintiffs' protected design,[11] the place where the plaintiff retailer's business was injured by his supplier's breach of design rights,[11a] the place of death in France of the victim of an accident which had taken place seven months earlier off the coast of Spain,[12] the place where a wrongful transfer of shares was effected,[13] the place where a plaintiff's bank guarantee had been wrongfully called upon by his customer's bank,[14] the place where negligent misstatements were relied on,[14a] the place where milk was found to contain poison allegedly emanating from the defendants' factory[15] and the place (in Corsica) where fishing, public health and tourism were adversely affected by the discharge of industrial waste into the sea off Italy.[16] On the other hand, where an artist domiciled in Paris lent paintings to Italians domiciled in Italy and the paintings were returned badly damaged, the discovery of the damage in Paris was held not to be

---

[7a] Bundesgerichtshof, case VIII ZR 320/85, September 24, 1986, [1988] E.C.C. 159.

[8] *N.V. Verzekeringsmaatschappij De Oude Zwolsche van 1895* v. *B.V. G. Beens & Zn. and another*, Arrondissementsrechtbank, Zwolle, Digest D I–5.3—B2.

[9] *Bombardieri* v. *Esta Trust Reg.*, Ned.Jur. 1980 No. 512, Digest D I–5.1.2—B24.

[10] *Forge et Coutellerie Dubois N.V.* v. *Fantu Food B.V.*, Arrondissementsrechtbank, Arnhem, Digest D I–5.3—B1.

[11] *Ideal Clima S.p.A. and others* v. *S.A. Ideal Standard*, Gaz. Palais 1982, Sommaires, p. 378, Digest D I–5.3—B13.

[11a] *S.A. Jouets Eisenmann* v. *Geobra Brandstätter G.m.b.H. & Co. K.G. and Big Spielwaren Fabrik*, Tribunal de Commerce, Liège (Belgium) [1985] E.C.C. 246.

[12] *L'Host and others* v. *Doll and others*, Bull.Cass., Chambres Civiles, 1981, Pt. I, No. 303, p. 255, Digest D I–5.3—B12.

[13] *AGIP S.p.A.* v. *British Petroleum Co. Ltd. and Oil Chemical and Transport Finance Corporation S.A.*, Riv.dir.int.priv.proc. 1979, p. 96, Digest D I–5.3—B6.

[14] Bundesgerichtshof, case VI ZR 14/83, October 16, 1984, [1987] E.C.C. 26, (1985) RIW/AWD, p. 72.

[14a] *Minster Investments Ltd.* v. *Hyundai Precision and Industry Co. Ltd.*, The Times, January 26, 1988, Q.B.D.

[15] Oberlandesgericht Karlsruhe, case 4 U 187/75, August 4, 1977, RIW/AWD 1977, p. 718, Digest D I–5.3—B8.

[16] *Société Montedison* v. *Département de la Haute Corse and others*, Cour d'Appel, Bastia, February 28, 1977, Digest D I–5.3—B3.

enough to give the French court jurisdiction under Article 5(3);[17] and where a German purchaser of Italian wine discovered that the wine was of inferior quality and sent it back, the fact that he had paid transport charges in Germany was not sufficient damage to found jurisdiction.[18]

4. Threatened wrongs

The use of the word "occurred" seems to presuppose that the **17.52** tort must already have taken place in order for jurisdiction to arise under Article 5(3),[19] and it is not clear, therefore whether there is jurisdiction under this provision to grant relief against threatened wrongs. If the wrong has already occurred, it seems that the jurisdiction extends to granting an injunction to prevent its repetition[20] and where the relief sought is of an interim nature, the court will have jurisdiction under Article 24[21] (provided it can grant such relief under its national law),[22] even if the result is likely to be decisive in practice. Between them, these provisions will cover most cases likely to arise in practice, but whether Article 5(3) will cover those cases where final relief is sought in an international context against a solely threatened wrong must await the decision of the European Court of Justice. It would seem sensible that it should.[23]

Article 5(4)

[A person domiciled in a Contracting State may, in another Con-   17.53 tracting State, be sued:]

4. as regards a civil claim for damages or restitution which is based on an act giving rise to criminal proceedings, in the court seised of those proceedings, to the extent that

---

[17] *Vasarely dit Yvaral* v. *Caramel et Ratti*, Journal dr.int. 1980, p. 892, Digest D I–5.3—B10.

[18] Bundesgerichtshof, case no. VIII ZR 320/85, September 24, 1986, [1988] E.C.C. 159, (1987) Wirtschafts- und Bankrecht, 413.

[19] Schlosser, para. 134 (para. A1.417 below).

[20] *Forge et Coutellerie Dubois N.V.* v. *Fantu Foods B.V.*, Arrondissementsrecht-bank, Arnhem, July 3, 1975, Digest D I–5.3—B1; Collins, p. 60.

[21] Para. 24.01 below. See ss.24 and 25 of the 1982 Act, paras. 43.01 *et seq.* below and chap. 7 above.

[22] For the powers of courts in England to grant provisional relief against threatened wrongs, see chap. 7, paras. 7.05–7.06 above and s.25 of the 1982 Act, para. 43.03 below. So far as the allocation of jurisdiction as between the different parts of the U.K. is concerned, the version of Art. 5(3) in Sched. 4 to the 1982 Act (para. 45.06 below) expressly provides for such jurisdiction.

[23] *Semble*, Collins, p. 60.

that court has jurisdiction under its own law to entertain civil proceedings;*

D. SUB-PARAGRAPH (4): CIVIL CLAIMS IN CRIMINAL PROCEEDINGS

17.54   Whether, and if so to what extent, a criminal court can exercise civil jurisdiction is to be decided solely according to its own law. All Article 5(4) does is to provide that if the court has that jurisdiction for the purposes of its national law, it has it also for the purposes of the Convention, so long as it is a claim for damages or restitution. It will be most relevant in traffic accident cases,[24] where, in several Contracting States, it is a common way of disposing of issues of civil liability. The fact that criminal proceedings are outside the scope of the Convention[25] self-evidently does not prevent civil claims ancillary to criminal proceedings from being within the Convention.[26]

In England, notwithstanding that a person who suffers damage is not normally a party to criminal proceedings, orders for compensation under section 35 of the Powers of Criminal Courts Act 1973 and for restitution under section 28 of the Theft Act 1968 and section 6 of the Criminal Justice Act 1972 are probably orders for "damages or restitution" for the purposes of Article 5(4),[27] although it is possible that an application for such an order would not be a civil claim. Orders for forfeiture,[28] on the other hand, are probably outside the scope of Article 5(4).

Article II of the Protocol makes special provision limiting the effect of civil orders made in default of appearance in criminal proceedings, where the proceedings are for an offence "not intentionally committed," *i.e.* not only for offences of strict liability, but also for offences involving negligence or recklessness.[29]

---

* Jenard, paras. A1.38 and A1.114 below; Collins, p. 61; Dashwood/Halcon/White, pp. 23, 97; Hartley, pp. 52–53; Kaye, pp. 588–589; Maxwell, para. 5.60; Anton, paras. 5.40–5.43; Droz, paras. 36–37, 78–80; Weser, paras. 199, 226; Bülow/Böckstiegel/Linke, pp. 72–74; Geimer/Schütze, pp. 638, 827–843; Kropholler, pp. 93–96; Gothot/Holleaux, paras. 91–92; Pocar, pp. 142–144.

[24] Droz, para. 36; Weser, para. 199; Bülow/Böckstiegel/Linke, p. 72; Collins, p. 61. See also Kaye, "Civil claims in criminal proceedings in courts of the Common Market: risks to English defendants," (1988) 7 Lit. 13.

[25] Para. 14.14 above.

[26] See *De Cavel* v. *De Cavel (No. 2)* [1980] E.C.R. 731, at p. 741.

[27] Collins, p. 61, (who cites similar provisions in a number of the United Kingdom's bilateral conventions); Hartley, p. 52. As to restraint and charging orders under ss.7 and 9 of the Drug Trafficking Offences Act 1986, see para. 14.14, n. 41 above. *Cf.*, in Scotland, Criminal Justice (Scotland) Act 1980, ss.58–67.

[28] *e.g.* under s.43 of the powers of Criminal Courts Act 1973.

[29] *Rinkau* [1981] E.C.R. 1391. See, further, the commentary on Art. II of the Protocol, para. 35.05 below.

Article 5(5)

**[A person domiciled in a Contracting State may, in another Con-   17.55
tracting State, be sued:]**

    **5. as regards a dispute arising out of the operations of a
branch, agency or other establishment, in the courts for
the place in which the branch, agency or other establishment is situated;***

E. Sub-Paragraph (5): Branches, Agencies and Other Establishments

1. General note

The purpose of this head of special jurisdiction is to prevent preju-   17.56
dice to a plaintiff whose dispute with the defendant arises out of the
operations of the latter's branch, agency or other establishment. It is
the location (and appearance of permanence)[30] of the branch, agency
or other establishment, and the fact that its operations gave rise to
the claim, which form the connecting factors justifying the jurisdiction of the court for that place.[31] It is irrelevant whether or not the
subject-matter of the dispute has any direct connection with the
court. In this respect Article 5(5) is akin to the general jurisdiction of
the defendant's domicile provided by Article 2,[32] although under
this provision the defendant is not deemed to be domiciled in the
state of the court. The jurisdiction is equivalent to that which has
been developed in France and which is also contained in rules of
German and Italian law. A number of bilateral conventions between
Contracting States[33] contain similar rules, but the terms of Article
5(5) are to be given an independent interpretation.[34] The precise
extent of the jurisdiction is a matter of some uncertainty and various
aspects of this problem are considered below.

---

* Jenard, para. A1.115 below; Collins, pp. 61–64; Dashwood/Halcon/White,
pp. 23–24, 97–100; Hartley, pp. 53–54; Kaye, pp. 589–610; Maxwell,
para. 5.61; Anton, paras. 5.44–5.49; Droz, paras. 81–82; Weser, para.227;
Bülow/Böckstiegel/Linke, pp. 74–78; Geimer/Schütze, pp. 541–551; Kropholler, pp. 96–99; Gothot/Holleaux, paras. 100–102; Pocar, pp. 144–149.
[30] See paras. 17.61 to 17.63 below.
[31] *Etablissements Somafer S.A.* v. *Saar-Ferngas A.G.* [1978] E.C.R. 2183, at
p. 2192 (para. 11).
[32] Geimer/Schütze, pp. 541–542.
[33] Jenard, para. A1.115 below, Droz para. 81, Geimer/Schütze, pp. 543–544.
Among these conventions are those entered into by the U.K. with France (January 18, 1934, Art. 4(1)(e)) and with Germany (July 14, 1960, Art. IV(1)(v)): see
para. A2.02 below.
[34] *Etablissements Somafer S.A.* v. *Saar-Ferngas A.G.* [1978] E.C.R. 2183, at
p. 2191 (para. 8).

17.57   *Defendant's domicile.* As with the other heads of jurisdiction under Article 5, the defendant must be domiciled in another Contracting State. In this respect, Article 5(5) differs from the second paragraphs of Articles 8 and 13,[35] which make similar provision in relation to contracts of insurance and consumer contracts respectively. Those latter provisions create a deemed domicile for the defendant at the place where the branch, agency or other establishment is situated. Article 5(5) does not do so and the rules as to, for example, service are consequently not affected by its terms. It would seem to follow that Article 5(5) is not applicable if the branch, agency or other establishment is itself capable of being sued as a party distinct from its principal, at least if it is intended that it should actually be joined as a defendant.[36] If the defendant is not domiciled in a Contracting State, a national court may accept jurisdiction on the basis of its own national rules, pursuant to Article 4, even if the defendant has a branch agency or other establishment in that or any other Contracting State. In order to determine where the defendant is domiciled, the national court must apply the choice of law rules set out in Articles 52 and 53.[37]

17.58   *Actions by the agent.* It seems that Article 5(5) is not effective to enable the branch, agency or other establishment itself to bring proceedings against its principal in the courts for the place where it is situated. This proposition was advanced by Advocate General Reischl in *De Bloos* v. *Bouyer* in these terms:

> "Clearly Article 5(5) . . . has the sole purpose of facilitating proceedings for *third parties* who are involved with a subsidiary establishment in that they are not obliged to lodge their application where the parent company is situate."[38]

He repeated that view in *Blankaert and Willems PVBA* v. *Trost* and went on to point out that such proceedings were anyway unlikely in practice, because the branch, agency or other establishment would probably not have its own legal personality and it would anyway probably be under the *de facto* control of its parent body.[39] On the other hand, if it has the capacity to bring proceedings at all, the branch, agency or other establishment will often be able to sue its principal in the place where it is situated on the basis of Articles

---

[35] Paras. 18.11 and 19.01 below.

[36] Bülow/Böckstiegel/Linke, p. 75. The absence of legal personality is relevant in determining whether Article 5(5) applies: see para. 17.62 below.

[37] Chap. 31 below.

[38] *Etablissements A. De Bloos S.p.r.l.* v. *Société en commandite par actions Bouyer* [1976] E.C.R. 1497, Opinion, at p. 1519. See also Collins, p. 64.

[39] *Blankaert and Willems P.V.B.A.* v. *Trost* [1981] E.C.R. 819, Opinion, at p. 838.

5(1)[40] or 5(3).[41] The *Blankaert* case involved an action by an agent against her principal, but the basis on which she sought to found jurisdiction under Article 5(5) was that the contract had been negotiated by an intermediary who was the principal's agent.[42] The European Court therefore did not need to decide whether this head of jurisdiction is available to an agent against its principal, but the likelihood is that the view expressed by Advocate General Reischl would find favour with the Court.[43]

2. " . . . a dispute arising out of the operations . . . "

The European Court of Justice has held, in *Etablissements Somafer S.A.* v. *Saar-Ferngas A.G.*, that one of the two factors linking the court with the claim, and justifying the special jurisdiction, is the fact that the dispute arose out of the operations of the branch, agency or other establishment.[44] The Court gave the concept of "operations" in this context a narrow construction. Somafer was a French company which carried out blasting work on behalf of the regional government of Saarland, in the immediate vicinity of gasmains belonging to Saar-Ferngas, a German company. Saar-Ferngas carried out measures to protect its mains and sought reimbursement of the cost from Somafer, by way of an action in the *Landgericht* at Saarbrücken. Somafer's objection to the jurisdiction was dismissed and it appealed to the *Oberlandesgericht*, which submitted a number of questions to the European Court on the interpretation of Article 5(5).[45] The Court said of these words, that: **17.59**

> "This concept of operations comprises on the one hand actions relating to rights and contractual or non-contractual obligations concerning the management properly so-called of the agency, branch or other establishment itself, such as those concerning the situation of the building where such entity is established or the local engagement of staff to work there. Further it also comprises those relating to undertakings which have been entered into at the above-mentioned place of business in the name of the parent body and which must be performed in the Contracting State where the place of business is established and also actions concerning non-contractual obligations arising from the activities in which the branch agency or other estab-

---

[40] Para. 17.02 above.
[41] Para. 17.44 above.
[42] The case is discussed in more detail at para. 17.62 below.
[43] See the passage from the judgment in *Somafer* v. *Saar-Ferngas* quoted at para. 17.61 below.
[44] [1978] E.C.R. 2183, at p. 2192 (para. 11).
[45] The principal questions related to the interpretation of "branch, agency or other establishment," and are discussed below.

lishment . . . has engaged at the place in which it is established on behalf of the parent body."[46]

17.60   It remains to be seen how closely the European Court of Justice will adhere to this definition, but the second limb does give rise to a number of problems.[46a] First, it seems unduly restrictive to confine Article 5(5) to undertakings entered into at the place of business of the branch, agency or other establishment. Contracts entered into by, say, the manager of the branch while away from his place of business ought to be included, so long as they were entered into in his capacity as branch manager rather than purely as a representative of the parent body. It is hard to believe that the European Court would not regard such contracts as falling within Article 5(5).

Secondly, the requirement that undertakings should have been entered into "in the name of the parent body" may give rise to problems where a contract has been entered into in the name of the agent, albeit clearly on behalf of his identified principal. The problem is not as serious as it might appear, in view of the fairly narrow meaning (discussed below) of "branch, agency or other establishment," but it is suggested that it is a direct legal link between the parent body and the third party that is necessary, rather than any formal requirement as to the name in which a party contracts.[47]

Thirdly, the European Court seems to have confined the meaning of "operations" to those which take place in the Contracting State where the branch, agency or other establishment is situated. As Collins observes,[48] if this is right Article 5(5) adds little in contract

---

[46] [1978] E.C.R. 2183, at pp. 2192–2193 (para. 13).

[46a] *Semble, per* Advocate General Sir Gordon Slynn, *S.A.R. Schotte G.m.b.H.* v. *Parfums Rothschild S.à.r.l.*, Case 218/86, Opinion of October 28, 1987 (not yet reported).

[47] A contract entered into in anticipation of a branch being established has been held by the Italian Corte di Cassazione not to arise out of the operations of the branch: *Ernst Müller K.G.* v. *Muni*, Foro it. 1980, I, Col. 1108, Digest D I–5.1.2—B23; but an action by a payee domiciled in Germany of a cheque drawn on a Belgian bank against a German branch of the bank has been held to fall within Art. 5(5): Landgericht Köln, case 30 O 12/79, March 23, 1979, RIW/AWD—1980, p. 215, Digest D I–5.1.1—B10.

An example of non-contractual "operations" is given by a decision of the Tribunal d'Arrondissement, Tournai: *R. Willocq* v. *Compagnie Française d'Assurance et de Réassurance, Incendie, Accidents et Risques Divers*, Digest D I–8—B2, where the plaintiff, injured in France by the defendant company's insured person, brought a direct action in Belgium. The claim was handled by the insurance company's Brussels office and was therefore held to arise out of the operations of that branch. The decision itself was based on what is now the second para. of Art. 8 (which could not have applied, the defendant company having its seat in France: see para. 18.11 below) and the action was brought in Tournai, not Brussels, but the decision is of interest as an application of the principles in *Somafer* v. *Saar-Ferngas*.

[48] Collins, p. 64.

matters to Article 5(1). It also seems to be inconsistent with the purposes of the second paragraphs of Articles 8 and 13,[49] which in this respect are identically worded.

3. " . . . branch, agency or other establishment . . . "

These words too are to be given an independent interpretation,[50] **17.61** and European Court has had to consider their meaning in four cases, two of which concerned exclusive distributors or sales representatives. Initially, the European Court adopted a narrow approach to their interpretation, but in the most recent case its approach is rather more liberal. In the first case, *De Bloos S.p.r.l.* v. *Bouyer,*[51] the question arose whether Bouyer, who claimed to have exclusive rights to sell De Bloos's goods in Belgium, was the latter's "branch, agency or other establishment" for the purposes of Article 5(5). The European Court held that one of the essential characteristics of the concepts of a branch or agency within the meaning of this paragraph was the fact of being subject to the direction and control of the parent body[52] and that the concept of "establishment" was based on the same essential characteristics.[53] Bouyer was an independent undertaking and was held in that case not to come within the definition; although in the light of *S.A.R. Schotte G.m.b.H.* v. *Parfums Rothschild S.a.r.l.* (discussed below) it is clear that an establishment's legal independence is not decisive.

The European Court again considered the meaning of "branch, agency or other establishment" in the *Somafer* case (discussed above) where the principal question was whether Somafer had a branch in Germany. Its principal place of business was undoubtedly in France, but it did have an address in Saarbrücken, with its own printed notepaper and bank account. The Court identified a number of factors which would help to identify a branch, agency or other establishment:

> "The concept of branch, agency or other establishment implies a
> place of business which has the appearance of permanency, such as
> the extension of the parent body, has a management and is materially
> equipped to negotiate business with third parties so that the latter,
> although knowing that there will if necessary be a legal link with the

---

[49] Paras. 18.11 and 19.01 below.
[50] *Etablissements Somafer S.A.* v. *Saar-Ferngas A.G.* [1978] E.C.R. 2183, at p. 2191 (para. 8). See, generally, Fawcett, "Methods of carrying on business and Article 5(5) of the Brussels Convention" (1984) 9 E.L. Rev. 325
[51] *Etablissements A. De Bloos S.p.r.l.* v. *Société en commandite par actions Bouyer* [1976] E.C.R. 1497, discussed at para. 17.20 above, in relation to Art. 5(1).
[52] At p. 1510 (para. 20).
[53] At p. 1510 (para. 21).

parent body, the head office of which is abroad, do not have to deal directly with such parent body but may transact business at the place of business constituting the extension."[54]

The Court went on to hold that the national court should find as a matter of fact whether there is an effective place of business such as to bring the dispute within the words of Article 5(5).[55]

17.62   *Direction and control.* The test of direction and control was further refined in *Blankaert and Willems PVBA* v. *Trost*.[56] Blankaert and Willems was a furniture manufacturer in Belgium which had a long-standing business relationship with Hermann Bey, an independent commercial agent in Germany, and had made Bey responsible for establishing on its behalf a sales network in Germany. Bey recruited Frau Trost as a commercial agent for Blankaert and Willems, with whom she then entered into direct contractual relations. When Blankaert and Willems terminated its contract with Frau Trost, she brought an action against them in the court for the place where Bey was established in Aachen, saying that Bey was an agency or branch of Blankaert and Willems and relying on Article 5(5). That contention was rejected at first instance but accepted on appeal and Blankaert and Willems appealed to the *Bundesgerichtshof*, which held that both Bey and Frau Trost had worked for Blankaert and Willems as commercial agents and business negotiators,[57] being, as a matter of German law,[58] independent representatives of their principal. The *Bundesgerichtshof* referred to the European Court the question whether such representatives fell within the concept of "branch, agency or other establishment" for the purposes of Article 5(5).

The European Court approached the question of interpretation narrowly. It referred to the test of direction and control laid down in the *De Bloos* decision and to the requirement laid down in the *Somafer* decision, that the branch, agency or other establishment should have the appearance of permanency, and then went on to provide an interpretation of "branch, agency or other establishment" in tightly-drawn negative terms:

---

[54] *Etablissements Somafer S.A.* v. *Saar-Ferngas A.G.* [1978] E.C.R. 2183, at p. 2192 (para. 12).

[55] In the light of the European Court's decision, the Oberlandesgericht Saarbrücken decided that there was a branch for the purposes of Art. 5(5) and accepted jurisdiction on that basis: case 2 U 185/76, April 3, 1979, RIW/AWD—1980, p. 796, Digest D I–5.5—B2.

[56] [1981] E.C.R. 819.

[57] *Handlungsvertreter* and *Vermittlungsvertreter*.

[58] Para. 84 HGB (Commercial Code): See Horn, Kötz and Leser, *German Private and Commercial Law*, pp. 227 et seq.

"it is clear that the dependency on the direction and control of that parent body is not established when the representative of that parent body is 'basically free to organise his own work and hours of work' (Article 84(1), last sentence, of the German Commercial Code) without being subject to instructions from the parent body in that regard; when he is free to represent at the same time several rival firms producing or marketing identical or similar products and, lastly, when he does not effectively participate in the completion and execution of transactions, but is restricted in principle to transmitting orders to the undertaking he represents. Those three factors preclude a concern having all those characteristics from being considered as the place of business having the appearance of permanency as an extension of the parent body."[59]

Appearance. In the *Somafer* case, the European Court referred to the "appearance" of permanency, and had described the special link justifying the existence of the jurisdiction under Article 5(5) as being, in part, "the material signs enabling the existence of the branch, agency or other establishment to be easily recognised."[60] By contrast with the rather narrow test of direction and control, which it had adopted in the *De Bloos* case and developed in the *Blankaert and Willems* case, the European Court returned in *S.A.R. Schotte G.m.b.H.* v. *Parfums Rothschild S.à.r.l.*[61] to the role played by the appearance of the branch agency or other establishment, and emphasised its importance. **17.63**

S.A.R. Schotte G.m.b.H., a German company, sold various consignments of atomizers and other accessories for the perfume business to Parfums Rothschild S.à.r.l., a French company. For this purpose, Schotte corresponded with Rothschild G.m.b.H., the German parent company of the French purchaser, both in the negotiations which preceded the contract and in the dispute which later arose as to the quality of the products. The dispute was not resolved by correspondence and Schotte started proceedings in Germany against the French company, relying on Article 5(5). The French company disputed the jurisdiction and the *Oberlandesgericht* Düsseldorf referred the question to the European Court whether Article 5(5) was satisfied where the French legal entity maintained no dependent establishment in Germany but where there was in Germany an independent legal entity which had the same name and identical management, which negotiated and conducted business in the name of the French legal entity and which was used by the latter as an extension of itself.

---

[59] [1981] E.C.R. 819, at p. 829 (para. 12).
[60] [1978] E.C.R. 2183, at p. 2192 (para. 11).
[61] Case 218/86, decision of December 9, 1987, *The Times*, January 12, 1988.

The European Court recited the passage quoted above from the *Somafer* case and went on to say that the question posed by the national court,

> " . . . envisages a case in which two companies have the same name and a common management and in which one of them, without being a dependent agency or branch of the other, transacts business for the account of the other and so acts as its extension in commercial relations. . . .
>
> In such a case, third parties who conduct business with the establishment which acts as an extension of another company must be able to rely on the appearance so created and regard that establishment as an establishment of the other company even if both companies from the point of view of company law are independent of each other.
>
> The narrow connection between the claim and the court called upon to decide it depends not only on the legal relations between the legal persons having their seats in different Contracting States but also on the way in which the two undertakings conduct themselves in public and how they present themselves *vis-à-vis* third parties in their commercial relations as against third parties."[61a]

17.64 *Conflicting seats.* One question which may give rise to problems is whether Article 5(5) may be relied upon to found jurisdiction against the principal establishment in country A of a company whose seat is in country B. Such a problem may arise where the private international law of country A (which, by Article 53, has to be applied for determining the seat of a company) provides that the seat of the company is determined by the law of the country where it is incorporated, country B, and that latter law recognises only the statutory seat of a company.[62] A similar problem might arise where the defendant was an individual domiciled in one country, but carrying on business in another. In such cases, it could be argued that the principal place of business is an "other establishment," within the meaning of Article 5(5), giving a basis for jurisdiction at the principal place of business. If the dispute arose out of the operations of that establishment, it would seem to accord with the purpose of Article 5(5) that there should be jurisdiction,[63] but the requirement of direction and control referred to in the *De Bloos* case would seem to suggest that there should be a geographical split in the running of the business.

[61a] *Ibid.* (paras. 13, 15 and 16).
[62] That is the position under Dutch law: see para. 55.26 below.
[63] Bülow/Böckstiegel/Linke, pp. 76–77.

Article 5(6)

[A person domiciled in a Contracting State may, in another Con- **17.65**
tracting State, be sued:]

> **6. in his capacity as settlor, trustee or beneficiary of a trust
> created by the operation of a statute, or by a written
> instrument, or created orally and evidenced in writing,
> in the courts of the Contracting State in which the trust
> is domiciled;*†**

F. SUB-PARAGRAPH (6): TRUSTS

1. General note

A distinction is to be drawn between, on the one hand, the inter-   **17.66**
nal relationships of a trust, which are the respective rights and
duties *inter se* of the settlor, trustees and beneficiaries and, on the
other, the external relationships of the trust, such as the trustees'
rights and duties as against third parties.[64] The Convention as originally drafted was adequate to deal with the external relationships of
a trust but not, it was felt, with the internal relationships.[65] The
Schlosser Report gives as an example the case of a trustee leaving
the United Kingdom and going to live in Corsica. It was felt that
the beneficiaries and other trustees could not be expected to seek
redress in a Corsican court.

Accordingly, Article 5(6) was included in the Convention and
provides an additional jurisdiction for actions concerning trusts.[66]
It is not exclusive and in the above example the beneficiaries or
other trustees would remain free to sue in Corsica on the basis of
Article 2, if they wished.[67] But where the subject matter of the trust
falls within one of the exclusive jurisdictional provisions of Article
16, those provisions take priority, although (as the Schlosser Report
observes)[68] the precise extent of that priority may not always be
easy to establish.

The wording of Article 5(6) does not confine its use to proceed-   **17.67**
ings concerned with the internal relationships of trusts. Despite the

---

* Schlosser, paras. 109–120 (paras. A1.395–A1.403 below); Collins, pp. 64–65;
Dashwood/Halcon/White, pp. 26, 100; Hartley, p. 55; Kaye, pp. 610–632;
Maxwell, para. 5.62; Anton, paras. 5.44–5.49; Geimer/Schütze, pp. 763–770;
Kropholler, pp. 99–102; Gothot/Holleaux, paras. 103–106.
† This para. was added to the text by Art. 5(4) of the 1978 Convention.
[64] Schlosser, paras. 109–111 (paras. A1.395–A1.397 below).
[65] Schlosser, para. 113 (para. A1.398 below).
[66] See also paras. 15.16 *et seq.* above.
[67] Schlosser, para. 118 (para. A1.402 below).
[68] Schlosser, para. 120, (para. A1.403 below).

reason for its inclusion set out in the Schlosser Report, it probably also enables proceedings to be brought at the instance of strangers to the trust in the courts of the Contracting State where the trust is domiciled.

The inclusion of a special jurisdiction in relation to trusts does not have the effect of widening the material scope of the Convention. Trusts which have as their subject matter wills, rights in property arising out of a matrimonial relationship, or bankruptcy, for example, are all excluded from the scope of the Convention by Article 1 and this paragraph would therefore have no application to an action against a settlor, trustee or beneficiary in connection with such a trust. The concept of a trust is unknown to Continental legal systems.[68a]

2. " . . . a trust created by the operation of a statute, or by a written instrument, or created orally and evidenced in writing . . . "

17.68 The effect of these words is to exclude from the scope of the rules of special jurisdiction constructive or resulting trusts, except such as arise by the operation of a statute.[69] Although it would seem that the concept of a "trust" should be given an independent meaning in the context of this paragraph,[70] there can be no doubt that such an independent concept would be drawn principally from English, Scottish and Irish law.[70a]

3. " . . . the Contracting State in which the trust is domiciled"

17.69 This paragraph, alone among the provisions of Article 5, does not regulate the local jurisdiction of the courts. The Schlosser Report explains the amended text thus:

> "The solution proposed in the new paragraph (6) of Article 5 is based on the argument that trusts, even though they have no legal personality, may be said to have a geographical centre of operation. This would fulfil functions similar to those fulfilled by the 'seat' of business associations without legal personality."[71]

[68a] Common conflicts of law principles are established, even for states in which the law does not know the concept of a trust, by the Hague Convention of July 1, 1985 on the Law Applicable to Trusts and on their Recognition. Effect is given to this convention in the U.K. by the Recognition of Trusts Act 1987 to which it is scheduled. See, generally, Hayton, "The Hague Convention on the Law Applicable to Trusts and on their Recognition" (1987) 36 I.C.L.Q. 260.

[69] Schlosser, para. 117, (para. A1.401 below).

[70] Geimer/Schütze, pp. 767–768.

[70a] See the description of a trust in the Hague Trusts Convention (n. 68a above), Art. 2., quoted by Hayton, *op. cit.* at p. 261.

[71] Schlosser, para. 114, (para. A1.399 below).

The domicile of a trust is to be determined according to the private international law of the court seised of the case.[72] As a matter of United Kingdom law, a trust is domiciled in the United Kingdom if and only if it is domiciled in a part of the United Kingdom and it is domiciled in a part of the United Kingdom if and only if the system of law of that part is the system of law with which the trust has its closest and most real connection.[73]

Article 5(7)

[A person domiciled in a Contracting State may, in another Contracting State, be sued:]   17.70

> 7. **as regards a dispute concerning the payment of remuneration claimed in respect of the salvage of a cargo or freight, in the court under the authority of which the cargo or freight in question:**
>
> (a) **has been arrested to secure such payment, or**
> (b) **could have been so arrested, but bail or other security has been given;**
>
> **provided that this provision shall apply only if it is claimed that the defendant has an interest in the cargo or freight or had such an interest at the time of salvage.*†**

G. Sub-Paragraph (7): Salvage

Article 5(7) contains a very specialised rule of jurisdiction which   17.71
was included to accommodate a particular basis on which English courts had exercised jurisdiction in claims for remuneration for salvage of cargo or freight, namely jurisdiction *in rem* based on the arrest of the cargo or the freight in question.[74] The Schlosser Report says that the object of the provision:

> "is to confer jurisdiction only with regard to those claims which are secured by a maritime lien. If the owner of a ship in difficulties has

---

[72] Art. 53, second para., para. 31.23 below.
[73] Ss.45(2) and 45(3) of the 1982 Act, para. 44.30 below. Read together with s.10, those provisions also serve for the division of jurisdiction within the United Kingdom.
* Schlosser, paras. 121–123 (paras. A1.404–A1.407 below); Collins, p. 65; Dashwood/Halcon/White, pp. 26–27, 100; Hartley, pp. 55–56; Kaye, pp. 632–634; Maxwell, para. 5.66; Geimer/Schütze, pp. 843–860; Kropholler, pp. 102–104; Gothot/Holleaux, paras. 107–108.
† This paragraph was added to the text by Art. 5(4) of the 1978 Convention.
[74] For the jurisdiction of the English courts in Admiralty matters generally, see 1 *Halsbury's Laws* (4th ed.), paras. 205 *et seq.* See also paras. 1.31 *et seq.* above.

concluded a contract for its salvage, as his contract with the cargo owner frequently obliges him to do, any disputes arising from the former contract will not be governed by this provision."[75]

The wording of the paragraph makes it clear, though, that it is not every case where the claim is secured by a maritime lien that is envisaged, but only salvage claims and only then if the defendant has (or had at the time of salvage) an interest in the cargo or freight.[76] The reason why the jurisdiction covers freight as well as cargo is to cater for the case in which the freight is payable conditionally upon the safe arrival of the cargo at its destination. If it had not been salved, no freight would have been payable and it is appropriate that the salvor should have a prior right to be satisfied out of the freight.[77]

Such jurisdiction in the case of ships is covered by Article 7 of the Brussels Convention of May 10, 1952 of the Arrest of Sea-going Ships,[78] which continues to have effect under Article 57 of the 1968 Convention.[79] That Convention does not refer to the arrest of cargo or freight and, but for Article 5(7), the 1968 Convention would have deprived the English courts of that basis of jurisdiction as against defendants domiciled in other Contracting States. The Brussels Convention of 1952 also does not provide for jurisdiction in cases where the ship has been released against bail or other security. This omission is not repaired in respect of ships by the 1968 Convention, but the problem is avoided in respect of cargo and freight by Article 5(7)(b).

17.72   The terms of the paragraph ought probably to be given an independent interpretation, but the European Court of Justice is almost certain, it is suggested, to follow the meanings given to its various expressions in international maritime law generally.

If the jurisdiction of a court in England and Wales or Northern Ireland is invoked under this paragraph, and the court then stays or dismisses the proceedings on the ground that the dispute should be submitted to arbitration or to the determination of a court elsewhere, the court has power to preserve the security under section 26 of the 1982 Act, in addition to its general powers under Article 24 to grant interim relief in the absence of substantive jurisdiction.

---

[75] Schlosser, para. 123 (para. A1.407 below).

[76] In this respect, it seems that the jurisdiction is narrower than that permitted by English law, which permits an action *in rem* against cargo or freight irrespective of its ownership: Supreme Court Act 1981, s.21(3).

[77] Schlosser, para. 122 (para. A1.406 below).

[78] This Convention is given effect in English law by ss.20–22 of the Supreme Court Act 1981, and s.26 of the Civil Jurisdiction and Judgments Act 1982, para. 43.12 below. See also *The Nordglimt* [1987] 2 Lloyd's Rep. 470.

[79] Para. 33.06 below.

But where the action falls within the 1968 Convention, the court has only limited powers to stay or dismiss the proceedings, notably under the provisions in Articles 21 to 23[80] relating to *lis pendens* and related actions.

Article 6

A person domiciled in a Contracting State may also be sued: 17.73

1. where he is one of a number of defendants, in the courts for the place where anyone of them is domiciled;
2. as a third party in an action on a warranty or guarantee or in any other third party proceedings, in the court seised of the original proceedings, unless these were instituted solely with the object of removing him from the jurisdiction of the court which would be competent in his case;
3. on a counter-claim arising from the same contract or facts on which the original claim was based, in the court in which the original claim is pending.

H. GENERAL NOTE

Article 6 provides rules of special jurisdiction based on a connec-   17.74
tion between the dispute and a particular court, where the connection is the litigation of another related dispute before that court.[81] The circumstances in which the Convention permits the litigation of one dispute to form the basis for jurisdiction over another dispute are listed in Article 6.[82] The only other examples of such circumstances are those in the rules relating to insurance and consumer contracts.[83] Where another court has exclusive jurisdiction under Article 16, that provision is to take precedence and the provisions of Article 6 do not apply to deprive that court of jurisdiction.[84] On the other hand, if the claim, third party proceedings or counterclaim are brought in a court which anyway has jurisdiction under the Convention, it is immaterial if the requirements of Article 6 are not fulfilled.

---

[80] Chap. 23 below.
[81] See paras. 15.05 *et seq.* above.
[82] *AGIP S.p.A.* v. *British Petroleum Co. Ltd. and another*, Riv.dir.int.priv.proc. 1979, p. 96, Digest D I–5.3—B6.
[83] Art. 8, first para., sub-para. (3) (para. 18.11 below); Art. 10, first and third paras. (para. 18.32 below); and Art. 14, third para. (para. 19.35 below).
[84] Art. 19, para. 22.01 below.

Article 6(1)

17.75 **A person domiciled in a Contracting State may also be sued:**

1. where he is one of a number of defendants, in the courts for the place where any one of them is domiciled;*

I. SUB-PARAGRAPH (1): CO-DEFENDANTS

1. General note

17.76 Article 6(1) enables a person to be sued as a co-defendant in the courts where another defendant is domiciled. Unlike Article 5, it does not require that the person (called here the "secondary defendant") to whom it applies should be domiciled in *another* Contracting State, and it may be used to invoke jurisdiction against the secondary defendant in the Contracting State of his own domicile, even if the particular court where the primary defendant is being sued would not otherwise have had jurisdiction over him.[85]

Article 6(1) does not state expressly whether the rule should only apply if the claim against the secondary defendant is related to that against the primary defendant[86] and, if so, what criteria are to be applied in determining whether such a relationship exists. However, in *Kalfelis* v. *Schröder, Münchmeyer, Hengst & Co.*, both these questions were referred to the European Court by the *Bundesgerichtshof*.[87] Citing the Jenard Report,[88] the European Court held that there must be a link between the claims made against each of the defendants, in order to avoid the possibility that a plaintiff might sue several defendants solely with the object of ousting the jurisdiction of the courts of the state in which the defendant is domiciled.[89]

Once the jurisdiction is founded under this provision, it seems

---

* Jenard, para. A1.116 below; Collins, pp. 65–66; Dashwood/Halcon/White, p. 101; Hartley, p. 57; Kaye, pp. 634–644; Maxwell, paras. 5.67, 5.68–5.80; Anton, paras. 5.59, 5.60–5.64; Droz, paras. 83–93; Weser, paras. 228–228*bis*; Bülow/Böckstiegel/Linke, pp. 79–82; Geimer/Schütze, pp. 209–211, 376–385, 825–825; Kropholler, pp. 105–109; Gothot/Holleaux, paras. 111, 114–119; Pocar, pp. 149–158.

[85] See, further, para. 17.78 below.

[86] *Cf.* Art. 6(2), para. 17.86 below.

[87] Case 189/87, decision of September 27, 1988, *The Times*, October 5, 1988; for other aspects of the case, see para. 17.46, where the facts are summarised.

[88] Jenard, para. A1.116 below. See also *Société Leybold-Heraeus Sogev S.I.* v. *Seima*, Cour d'Appel, Paris, January 19, 1978, RIW/AWD—1978, p. 271 (German translation), Digest D I–6—B3; *Banque Nationale de Paris* v. *Soc. Carl Felk and Soc. Serifit*, Rev. critique, 1979, p. 444, Digest D I–6—B4; and see Droz, para. 88; Weser, para. 228 *bis*; Bülow/Böckstiegel/Linke, p. 80; *cf.* Collins, p. 66.

[89] *Kalfelis* v. *Schröder, Münchmeyer, Hengst & Co.*, above (para. 9).

that it continues, even if the proceedings against the primary defendant are later dropped.[90]

The criteria to be applied in deciding whether there is a sufficient connection between the claims to enable jurisdiction over a secondary defendant to be founded on Article 6(1) have been established by the European Court on the basis of an independent interpretation of the Convention. The test to be applied by the national court in each case is whether there is such a connection between the claims at the time when they are instituted that it is expedient to hear and determine them together to avoid the risk of irreconcilable judgments resulting from separate proceedings.[91] This test, it will be noted, is the same as that applicable in the case of related actions for the purposes of Article 22. This has particular advantages in cases where one of the defendants has an agreement as to jurisdiction with the plaintiff.[92]   **17.77**

2. "the courts for the place where any one of them is domiciled"

It is important to note that this provision gives jurisdiction only where the primary defendant is being sued in the courts for the place where he is domiciled. It does *not* give a court jurisdiction over a secondary defendant merely because it is the court where the primary defendant is being sued. Consequently, because the special jurisdictions under Article 5 may not be relied on to invoke jurisdiction against a defendant in the state of his own domicile,[93] Article 6(1) will not apply to permit a secondary defendant to be joined in an action where jurisdiction against the primary defendant is based on one of the rules in Article 5.   **17.78**

If the primary defendant is not domiciled in any Contracting State, the Convention will not apply to the action against the primary defendant[94] unless it falls within the exclusive jurisdiction provisions of Article 16,[95] or unless he has concluded a jurisdiction

---

[90] *B.V. Handel- en Exploitatie Maatschappij "selene"* v. *Philips S.p.A. and others,* above; *Llambes S.A.* v. *Curator of Briza N.V.,* Ned. Jur. 1981, No. 540, Digest D I–6—B8; *Ruffini* v. *Fornano* [1981] E.C.C. 541; but *cf. Société Sait Electronics* v. *Scientific Radio Systems Inc.,* Gaz. Palais 1980, Sommaires, p. 85, Digest D I–6—B5.

[91] *Kalfelis* v. *Schröder, Münchmeyer, Hengst & Co.,* above (para. 12).

[92] *Kalfelis* v. *Schröder, Münchmeyer, Hengst & Co.,* above, *per* Advocate General Darmon, Opinion of June 15, 1988; see also para. 17.80.

[93] See para. 15.05 above.

[94] Art. 4, first para., para. 16.15 above.

[95] Chap. 20 below. If the principal subject-matter of the dispute with either defendant fell within Art. 16, that provision would anyway take precedence. If the principal subject-matter of the dispute with the other defendant did not then fall within Art. 16, it is difficult to see that the proceedings could be closely enough related to fall within Art. 6(1).

agreement with the plaintiff, falling within Article 17,[96] or has submitted to the jurisdiction under Article 18.[97] Again, the same principle applies and the plaintiff may not rely on Article 6(1) in such a case against the secondary defendant.

17.79 Because Article 6(1) refers to the courts for the *place* of the domicile of any one of the defendants, the particular court which has jurisdiction under Article 6 may not be the same as that which, under the national rules as to jurisdiction, would be competent under Article 2. It makes no difference where the plaintiff is domiciled. Nonetheless, it is only if the primary defendant has had jurisdiction against him invoked under Article 2, in the courts not only of the state of his domicile but also for the place of his domicile, that the secondary defendant may be subject to Article 6(1).

The position may be illustrated by the following example given by Droz:

> A contract is made in Milan by three parties, domiciled in France, Rome and Belgium respectively. If the party domiciled in France wishes to sue the other two, he may bring his action in Rome at the domicile of one defendant and may rely on Article 6(1) to join the Belgian domiciliary as the secondary defendant. By Italian law of civil procedure, which permits an action to be brought in the place where the contract was concluded, he may bring his action instead in Milan. But if he does so, he will not be permitted to join the Belgian as a co-defendant, because the primary defendant is not domiciled in Milan.[98]

3. Jurisdiction agreements

17.80 Problems may arise where the plaintiff has an agreement as to jurisdiction with one or other of the defendants. If the plaintiff has sued the primary defendant on the basis of a jurisdiction agreement, the principle discussed above will apply and he may only rely on Article 6(1) against the secondary defendant if the court where the primary defendant is being sued is coincidentally also the court for the place where he is domiciled.

On the other hand, if the plaintiff and the secondary defendant have entered into a jurisdiction agreement falling within Article 17, the plaintiff ought not to be permitted to depart from the agreement by relying on Article 6(1).[99] This is because the Convention generally regards jurisdiction agreements under Article 17 as conferring

---

[96] Para. 21.01 below.
[97] Para. 21.83 below.
[98] Droz, para. 86, recited in Maxwell, para. 5.69.
[99] Droz, para. 92, Bülow/Böckstiegel/Linke, p. 82.

exclusive jurisdiction on the elected forum.[1] It might appear that this interpretation would lead to a potential conflict of decisions, but such conflicts will be avoided in most cases by the application of Article 22, which provides for the staying of a later action, if it is related to another action already under way.

17.81 The position is more difficult if the jurisdiction agreement between the plaintiff and the secondary defendant does not fall within Article 17 or if, exceptionally, it is within Article 17 but provides for the non-exclusive jurisdiction of the elected forum.[2] For example, an agreement conferring exclusive jurisdiction on the courts of a non-contracting State does not fall within Article 17, but the courts of the Contracting States might well be reluctant to ignore it.[3] On the other hand, reliance by the secondary defendant upon the agreed jurisdiction of a court in a non-Contracting State might prejudice the plaintiff in the pursuit of his action against the primary defendant within the Contracting States, contrary to the purpose and spirit of the Convention. The court will have to decide in each such case whether to give effect to the jurisdiction agreement between the plaintiff and the secondary defendant. In doing so, the court should have regard to the independent test of irreconcilability set out by the European Court in *Kalfelis* v. *Schröder, Münchmeyer, Hengst & Co.*[4-5]

Article 6(2)

17.82 [A person domiciled in a Contracting State may also be sued:]

2. as a third party in an action on a warranty or guarantee or in any other third party proceedings, in the court seised of the original proceedings, unless these were instituted solely with the object of removing him from the jurisdiction of the court which would be competent in his case;*

---

[1] Paras. 21.43 *et seq.* below.
[2] Paras. 21.46 *et seq.* below.
[3] Droz, para. 93 and Bülow/Böckstiegel/Linke, p. 82, both stress the need to maintain good legal and commercial relations with third countries. See para. 1.39 above.
[4-5] See paras. 17.76 to 17.77 above.
* Jenard, paras. A1.118–A1.124 below; Schlosser, para. 135 (para. A1.418 below); Collins, pp. 66–67; Dashwood/Halcon/White, pp. 101–102; Hartley, p. 57; Kaye, pp. 645–651; Maxwell, paras. 5.81–5.89; Anton, paras. 5.65–5.68; Droz, paras. 94–102; Weser, paras. 229–231; Bülow/Böckstiegel/Linke, p. 82–85; Geimer/Schütze, pp. 385–392, 825; Kropholler, pp. 109–112; Gothot/Holleaux, paras. 112–119; Pocar, pp. 149–158.

J. SUB-PARAGRAPH (2): THIRD PARTIES[6]

1. General note

17.83   This provision may not be relied upon in Germany.[7]

The special jurisdiction provided by Article 6(2) for third party proceedings is wider than that provided by Article 6(1), in that the court may accept jurisdiction over a third party, even if its jurisdiction over the defendant is not based upon the defendant's domicile. But the jurisdiction is not unlimited. Various specific limitations are discussed below, but a number of general observations can be made.

For Article 6(2) to be invoked, jurisdiction over the defendant must, it is suggested, itself be based on the Convention (including a jurisdiction agreement under Article 17)[8], or at least not be inconsistent with it.[9] Otherwise a judgment against a third party would have to be recognised under Article 26, even if it had been obtained by the exercise of one of the exorbitant jurisdictions prohibited by Article 3.[10]

17.84   The laws of each of the Contracting States include criteria for determining when a third party may be brought into proceedings.[11] Clearly such criteria are needed for the purpose of Article 6(2) and it is probable (as the Schlosser Report suggests)[12] that each court should apply its own law in deciding whether a third party may be joined. This approach is consistent with Article 10, which deals with third party proceedings against liability insurers, and which refers expressly to the law of the court seised of the main action. On the other hand, the European Court of Justice might decide that independent criteria should be applied in order to secure the uniform application of the Convention.

The Jenard Report[13] quotes the Belgian definition of third party proceedings.[14] The definition includes reference to the voluntary intervention by a third party to protect his own interests. It has been suggested,[15] though, that Article 6(2) applies only to the case where a third party is involuntarily joined in the proceedings by

---

[6] See also the General note on Art. 6 at para. 17.74 above.
[7] See para. 17.89 below.
[8] Droz, para. 100; see para. 17.87 below.
[9] So, for example, if the main proceedings were purely internal to one Contracting State, the court's jurisdiction would not be *based* on the Convention (see paras. 13.10 *et seq.* above), but would not normally be inconsistent with it.
[10] Bülow/Böckstiegel/Linke, p. 84.
[11] In England, R.S.C., Ord. 16, r. 1(1).
[12] Schlosser, para. 135 (para. A1.418 below).
[13] Jenard, para. A1.124 below.
[14] Arts. 15 and 16 of the *Code judiciaire*.
[15] Droz, para. 98; Weser, para. 231n.; Bülow/Böckstiegel/Linke, p. 82.

another party, and not to a case of voluntary intervention, because in the latter case the court would have jurisdiction under Article 18.[16] It is not likely that the distinction would make any practical difference in England.

2. " . . . an action on a warranty or guarantee or in any other third party proceedings . . . "

These words describe the different types of third party proceedings known to the systems of civil procedure of the original Contracting States[17] (except Germany, to which Article 6(2) does not apply).[18] The Jenard Report states that it "seemed preferable" to make separate provision for guarantors or warrantors (*demande en garantie*) and for other third parties (*demande en intervention*)[19] and it may be that an independent construction of these words would limit the term "an action on a warranty or guarantee" to cases where the relief sought is from a third party by way of indemnity against or contribution to the judgment in the main action.[20] So far as proceedings in England are concerned, it seems safe to assume that third party proceedings generally are envisaged. Article 6(2) is not to be read as applying to actions on a warranty or guarantee by way of main proceedings, nor does the reference to such actions limit the general applicability of Article 6(2) to third party proceedings. Third party proceedings against insurers are treated separately by Article 10.[21] **17.85**

3. " . . . unless these were instituted solely with the object of removing him from the jurisdiction which would be competent in his case"

This proviso, while laudable, may be hard to apply in practice, not least because it is formulated as a subjective test. An example of **17.86**

---

[16] Whether the suggestion is well-founded, it seems, depends on the correct interpretation of the introductory words of Art. 18: ("Apart from jurisdiction derived from other provisions of this Convention . . . "), in which there is some ambiguity: see para. 21.90 below.
[17] *Cf.* other language versions: *"une demande en garantie ou . . . une demande en intervention," "eine Klage auf Gewährleistung oder . . . eine Interventionsklage", "un' azione di garanzia o . . . chiamata di un terzo nel processo," "een vordering tot vrijwaring of . . . een vordering tot voeging of tussenkomst."* See Geimer/Schütze, pp. 385–389.
[18] See para. 17.89 below.
[19] Jenard, para. A1.124 below.
[20] *N.V. De Jong Verenigde* v. *Coöperatieve Melkprodukten Bedrijven 'Domo-Bedum', Heinrich K.G. (Third Party),* Ned.Jur. 1981, No. 499, Digest D I–6—B7. (The main issue in the case was referred to the European Court: [1985] E.C.R. 2061).
[21] Para. 18.32 below.

sham proceedings might be where the only issue in the main action is the defendant's right of recourse against the third party,[22] or where there is no issue between the plaintiff and the defendant.[23]

4. Jurisdiction agreements

17.87   The court to which Article 6(2) gives jurisdiction is the court in which the main action is proceeding, whether or not it is the court of the defendant's domicile. Unlike Article 6(1), therefore, a jurisdiction agreement between the plaintiff and the defendant will not affect the application of Article 6(2) to a third party, unless the court has accepted jurisdiction against the defendant solely on a basis not provided for by the Convention, for example, under a jurisdiction agreement which does not fall within Article 17.

On the other hand, if the jurisdiction agreement is between the defendant and the third party, and applies to third party proceedings, the question arises whether it takes priority over the terms of Article 6(2). If the jurisdiction agreement complies with the terms of Article 17 and provides for exclusive jurisdiction, it will exclude the jurisdiction under Article 6(2), unless it does not apply to third party proceedings.[24] If on the other hand the jurisdiction agreement does not comply with Article 17 or provides only for non-exclusive jurisdiction, the court will have to decide in each case, in accordance with the principles discussed above in relation to Article 6(1),[25] whether the agreement or Article 6(2) takes priority.

5. Insurance and consumer cases

17.88   Article 6(2) does not apply in matters relating to insurance or consumer contracts.[26] This is because, by Articles 7 and 13, those matters are to be dealt with exclusively by Articles 7 to 15. Third party proceedings against liability insurers fall within the terms of Article 10.

---

[22] Bülow/Böckstiegel/Linke, p. 84.
[23] *Cf. Foglia* v. *Novello* [1980] E.C.R. 745; [1981] E.C.R. 3045.
[24] See para. 21.05 below. *Islanders Canning Corporation Ltd.* v. *Hoekstra, Hoekstra* v. *Schmalbach-Lubeca-Werke A.G.*, Arrondissementsrechtbank, Leeuwarden, September 2, 1976, Digest, D I–17.1.1—B4; *Soc. Fusion Rubbermaid* v. *S.à.r.l. Devianne Duquesnoy*, Receuil Dalloz-Sirey 1975, Jurisprudence, p. 341; *Soc. des Etablissements Voith* v. *Soc. des Chantiers et Ateliers de la Perrière and others*, Rev. critique 1983, p. 658, Digest D I–17.1.1—B19; *Technisch Handelsbureau P.J. van Louden B.V.* v. *N.V. Gieterijn Technomet*, Arrondissementsrechtbank, Arnhem, December 23, 1982, Digest D I–17.1.2—B24; *Soc. Karl Schaeff* v. *Soc Patrymat*, Recueil Dalloz-Sirey, February 23, 1989, I.R., p. 52.
[25] Para. 17.81 above.
[26] Droz, para. 94; Bülow/Böckstiegel/Linke, p. 84.

6. Germany

Article 6(2) may not be relied on in Germany. This is expressly   **17.89**
provided by Article V of the 1968 Protocol.[27] Instead, Articles 68,
72, 73 and 74 of the German Code of Civil Procedure (*Zivilprozessordnung*, ZPO)[28] may be relied upon as against any person domiciled in another Contracting State and judgments given in other
Contracting States under Article 6(2) of the Convention are to be
recognised and enforced in Germany. Similarly, the effects of a
judgment given in Germany under those Articles of the ZPO are to
be recognised in the other Contracting States. They do not provide
for a judgment to be given against the third party, but they afford
the third party an opportunity to be heard in the main action and
the judgment in that action cannot be challenged by the third party
in subsequent proceedings brought against him by the defendant.

Article 6(3)

[A person domiciled in a Contracting State may also be sued:]   **17.90**

    **3. on a counter-claim arising from the same contract or
facts on which the original claim was based, in the court
in which the original claim is pending.***

K. SUB-PARAGRAPH (3): COUNTERCLAIMS[29]

1. General note

The counterclaim must be brought in the same court as that   **17.91**
seised of the main action, even if it is by way of a separate action[30]
but, as with third party proceedings under Article 6(2), it is not
necessary that the main action should have been brought in the
court for the place of the defendant's domicile. It is a requirement
of Article 6(3), though, that the counterclaim should arise from the
same contract or facts as form the basis of the principal claim.

It is not clear whether Article 6(3) only applies if jurisdiction in   **17.92**
the main action has been assumed on a basis provided for by the

---

[27] Para. 35.20 below.
[28] Jenard, paras. A1.119–A1.123 below; see also para. 51.35 below.
* Jenard, para. A1.125 below; Collins, p. 67; Hartley, p. 57; Kaye, pp. 652–664;
Maxwell, paras. 5.90–5.91; Anton, para. 5.69; Droz, para. 103; Weser,
para. 232; Bülow/Böckstiegel/Linke, p. 86; Geimer/Schütze, pp. 211,
520–529; Kropholler, pp. 112–114; Gothot/Holleaux, paras. 112–119; Pocar,
pp. 149–158.
[29] See also the General note on Art. 6 at para. 17.24 above.
[30] See para. 17.93 below.

Convention.[31] If, for example, a plaintiff domiciled in a Contracting State invokes an exorbitant jurisdiction against a defendant not domiciled in a Contracting State, in a court which would not have jurisdiction under the Convention, has he submitted to the jurisdiction of that court for the purposes of the defendant's counterclaim?

It is suggested that the correct approach would be to say that the plaintiff should be taken to have submitted to the jurisdiction in respect of any counterclaim "arising from the same contract or facts on which the original claim was based." It is only in respect of such counterclaims that jurisdiction arises under Article 6(3) and the plaintiff has already invoked the court's jurisdiction over that particular legal relationship. This reasoning is in keeping with the decision in the European Court of Justice in *Meeth* v. *Glacetal*,[32] where it was held that the court was not precluded by a valid jurisdiction agreement from entertaining a set-off "connected with the legal relationship in dispute."[33] But it would not be in keeping with the general approach of the Convention to say that the plaintiff had submitted to the jurisdiction generally, giving the court jurisdiction under Article 18, because that would mean that the defendant could wholly circumvent the provisions of the Convention in relation to matters quite unconnected with the dispute which the plaintiff was litigating.

2. "on a counterclaim . . . "

17.93   It seems that it is not necessary for the counterclaim to be brought in the same proceedings, although a clear answer to that question will have to await the decision of the European Court. The French text refers to *"une demande reconventionnelle,"* which, under French law, need not be made in the same proceedings. The term "a counterclaim" is probably to be given an independent interpretation,[34] but national law would still apply to determine the means by which the counterclaim was instituted and pursued. It also remains unclear whether Article 6(3) would found jurisdiction against a co-defendant to a counterclaim if he was not also a plaintiff.[35]

---

[31] Bülow/Böckstiegel/Linke, p. 86, suggest that it does. But compare Arts. 11(2) and 14(3), where this is expressly provided.

[32] [1978] E.C.R. 2133, discussed in more detail at paras. 21.44 *et seq.* below.

[33] This is also the approach of English law: see Dicey and Morris, pp. 299–300.

[34] Kropholler, p. 112; Geimer/Schütze, p. 523.

[35] It may be, for example, that if the plaintiff had brought the principle proceedings in the court for the place where he was domiciled (perhaps under one of the provisions of Art. 5) he could be sued as the primary defendant on a counterclaim under this Article and the court would then have jurisdiction under Art. 6(1) against a secondary defendant to the counterclaim.

3. " . . . arising from the same contract or facts on which the original claim was based . . . "

It is generally agreed that a closer connection is required by this **17.94** provision between the main claim and the counterclaim than is required by Article 22[36] in the case of related actions.[37] The purpose of including this qualification on the circumstances in which a counterclaim may be brought was to ensure uniformity of approach between the Contracting States[38] and consequently it should be given an independent interpretation.[39]

4. Jurisdiction agreements

It will be rare for the plaintiff and the defendant to have a juris- **17.95** diction agreement which is valid under Article 17,[40] and which gives exclusive jurisdiction over the counterclaim to a court other than the court seised of the main action. In such a case, though, a clause which is valid under Article 17 may have that effect, if that is its true construction according to the applicable national law.[41]

Article 6A

Where by virtue of this Convention a court of a Contracting State **17.96** **has jurisdiction in actions relating to liability arising from the use or operation of a ship, that court, or any other court substituted**

---

[36] Para. 23.11 below.
[37] Collins, p. 67; Weser, para. 232; Bülow/Böckstiegel/Linke, p. 86; Kropholler, p. 112; Geimer/Schütze, p. 522; and, by implication, Droz, para. 103. Where a claim was based on one contract and the defendant sought to raise a counterclaim on another contract, the Hoge Raad has held that the fact that the two contracts were closely connected was not enough to give jurisdiction over the counterclaim under Art. 6(3): *Deutscher Ring Lebensversicherungsaktiengesellschaft* v. *Computer Hardware Corporation C.V.*, February 4, 1983, Ned.Jur. 1983, p. 1738; [1985] Eur.L.Dig. 118.
[38] Droz, para. 103.
[39] Bülow/Böckstiegel/Linke, p. 86.
[40] Paras. 21.01 *et seq.* below.
[41] That is what occurred in *Meeth* v. *Glacetal* [1978] E.C.R. 2133, discussed at paras. 21.44 *et seq.* below. The European Court held that Art. 17 did not preclude a court from taking account of a set-off connected with the legal relationship in dispute, if that was compatible with the clause conferring jurisdiction. The national court then ruled that the parties' intention was that each could only be sued in the courts of its own state, that the jurisdiction agreement therefore took effect and the national court could not entertain the set-off: Bundesgerichtshof, case VIII ZR 228/76, June 20, 1979, N.J.W. 1979, p. 2477, [1979] E.C.C. 457, Digest D I–17.1.1—B13.

for this purpose by the internal law of that State, shall also have jurisdiction over claims for limitation of such liability.*†

MARITIME LIMITATION CLAIMS

17.97   The Schlosser Report describes the nature and purpose of claims for limitation of liability in maritime matters and the different types of procedure commonly adopted by the Contracting States in respect of such claims.[42] Proceedings for the limitation of liability are those by which a shipowner or other person who is a potential defendant to a maritime claim can take the initiative in seeking to limit his liability. Such proceedings, which take different forms in different Contracting States, do not necessarily involve proceedings against a claimant, but where they take the form of an action by (typically) a shipowner, Article 6A provides an additional jurisdiction.

The rule of jurisdiction provided by this Article is in addition to those which would otherwise be available to a shipowner or other potential defendant under Articles 2 to 6 or, pursuant to Article 57, under a specialised convention.[43] Jurisdiction under Articles 17 and 18, on the other hand, would take priorty over this Article.[44] Article 6A enables him as plaintiff to bring the limitation proceedings in any court which would have jurisdiction over him as defendant if the proceedings concerned the use or operation of a ship, or in any other court substituted for this purpose by national law. It is irrelevant whether or not that court would have had jurisdiction over the defendant (*i.e.* the claimant) apart from this Article.

---

* Schlosser, paras. 124–130 (paras. A1.408–A1.413 below); Collins, pp. 67–68; Dashwood/Halcon/White, p. 102; Hartley, pp. 55–56; Kaye, pp. 799–803; Anton, para. 5.70; Geimer/Schütze, pp. 861–873; Kropholler, pp. 114–115; Gothot/Holleaux, paras. 107, 109.

† This Article was added to the text by Art. 6 of the 1978 Convention. In the French, Italian and Dutch texts it is called Article "6 *bis.*"

[42] Schlosser, paras. 124–130 (paras. A1.408–A1.413 below). A description of such proceedings is beyond the scope of this work. In English law, they may be brought under the Merchant Shipping Acts 1894 to 1981. See also, R.S.C., Ord. 75, rr. 37 to 40; 1 *Halsbury's Laws* (4th ed.), paras. 353–355, 461–472; *British Shipping Laws*, Vols. 1, 4, 11.

[43] International convention of October 10, 1957 relating to the limitation of the liability of owners of sea-going ships (Cmnd. 353), Merchant Shipping (Liability of Shipowners and Others) Act 1958; Athens Convention on the Carriage of Passengers and their luggage by Sea 1974 (Cmnd. 6326), Sched. 3 of the Merchant Shipping Act 1979; London convention on limitation of liability for maritime claims, of November 19, 1976 (Cmnd. 7035), Sched. 4 of the Merchant Shipping Act 1979; Brussels Convention of May 10, 1952 on the arrest of sea-going ships (Cmd. 8954). See Gaskell, "The Zeebrugge Disaster: Application of the Athens Convention 1974" (1987) 137 N.L.J. 285, 322, 383.

[44] Paras. 21.04 *et seq.* and 21.85 *et seq.* below.

If the proceedings concern the validity of a claim against a ship- **17.98**
owner, rather than the size of the claim, they do not fall within
Article 6A, but only within Articles 2 to 6[45] (or, if they are relevant,
Articles 16 to 18). Article 6A does not affect the question of what
law is applicable to the claim,[46] so if the applicable law does not
provide for limitation actions, the jurisdiction under this Article
cannot be successfully invoked. Also, Article 6A does not affect
Article 22,[47] which may be applied to stay the limitation action if
the claimant's action is started first.

---

[45] Schlosser, para. 129 (para. A1.412 below).
[46] Schlosser, para. 130 (para. A1.413 below).
[47] Para. 23.11 below.

CHAPTER 18

JURISDICTION IN MATTERS RELATING TO INSURANCE
(Articles 7–12A)

456

SECTION 3

Article 7

In matters relating to insurance, jurisdiction shall be determined by this Section, without prejudice to the provisions of Articles 4 and 5(5).* — **18.01**

A. GENERAL NOTE

Insurance is a pre-eminent example of inequality of bargaining power and the original authors of the Convention were concerned to — **18.02**

---

* Jenard, paras. A1.133–A1.136 below; Schlosser, para. 136 (paras. A1.419–A1.420 below); Collins, pp. 68–74; Dashwood/Halcon/White, p. 103; Hartley, pp. 58–63; Kaye, pp. 807–811; Maxwell, paras. 5.92–5.96, 5.112; Anton, para. 6.10; Droz, paras. 105–130; Weser, paras. 244.1–244.18; Bülow/Böckstiegel/Linke, pp. 87–94; Geimer/Schütze, pp. 212, 392–407, 495–505, 508–511, 821, 898, 959; Kropholler, pp. 116–119; Gothot/Holleaux, paras. 120–131; Pocar, pp. 158–159.

make special provision for the protection of insured persons. The European Court has said of the provisions of Section 3 of Title II (Articles 7 to 12A) that:

> "It is apparent from a consideration of the provisions of that section in the light of the documents leading to their enactment that in affording the insured a wider range of jurisdiction than that available to the insurer and in excluding any possibility of a clause conferring jurisdiction for the benefit of the insurer their purpose was to protect the insured who is most frequently faced with a predetermined contract the clauses of which are no longer negotiable and who is in a weaker economic position."[1]

The provisions of the Convention relating specifically to insurance were originally designed to afford this protection, but they were ill-suited to the particular nature and international importance of much of the non-domestic British insurance market and they were therefore amended by the Accession Convention.[2]

If a matter is one "relating to insurance," jurisdiction is to be determined by the rules in Articles 7 to 12A. The provisions of these Articles (*i.e.* Section 3 of Title II) are separate from, and not subordinate to, the normal rules of general and special jurisdiction in Articles 2 to 6A. They constitute a set of rules which, with four exceptions, are exclusively applicable to cases falling within their scope. Their scope, like that of the Convention generally, is limited to cases which have the requisite international character,[3] which are concerned with civil and commercial matters,[4] and which do not concern excluded matters.[5]

18.03   The four exceptions are:

(1) where the insurer is domiciled outside the Community and the dispute does not arise out of the operations of a branch, agency or other establishment in any of the Contracting States. This exception arises by reason of the reference to Article 4 and the terms of the second paragraph of Article 8.

(2) where the insurer is domiciled within the Community, but the dispute arises out of the operations of a branch, agency

---

[1] *Gerling Konzern A.G.* v. *Amministrazione del Tesoro dello Stato* [1983] E.C.R. 2503, at p. 2516 (para. 17). The same reasoning was applied to consumer credit for the sale of goods, covered by Arts. 13 to 15, now amended to cover consumer contracts generally: see chap. 19 below. See also para. 13.15 above.

[2] See Schlosser, paras. 136 *et seq.* (paras. A1.419 *et seq.* below). There has been some feeling that the amendments do not go far enough—see Collins, p. 68; Kerr, (1978) 75 Law Soc.Gaz. 1190.

[3] Paras. 13.10 *et seq.* above.

[4] Paras. 14.08 *et seq.* above.

[5] Paras. 14.18 *et seq.* above.

or other establishment in a different Contracting State. This exception arises by reason of the reference to Article 5(5).

(3) where the defendant enters an appearance. This exception is not specified in the Convention, but arises by way of the operation of Article 18. That Article takes precedence over all the other jurisdictional rules of the Convention, except the exclusive jurisdiction provisions of Article 16.[6]

(4) where there is a jurisdiction agreement falling within Article 12.

The importance attached by the Convention to compliance with the exhaustive provisions of Articles 7 to 12A is illustrated by the fact that, if the provisions are not complied with, recognition and enforcement of the resulting judgment is to be refused.[7]

Article 4. The effect of the reference to Article 4 is to limit the **18.04** scope of Articles 7 to 12A to cases where the defendant is domiciled in a Contracting State, whether the defendant is the insurer, the insured, the policy-holder or beneficiary.[8] If the defendant is not domiciled in a Contracting State, the court may apply its own juris-dictional rules to the case. The second paragraph of Article 8[9] extends the circumstances in which an insurer is to be regarded as domiciled in a Contracting State. It does so by way of a deeming provision, which applies where an insurer not domiciled in a Con-tracting State has a branch, agency or other establishment in one of the Contracting States.[10] In order for the second paragraph of Article 8 to be of any effect, it must take precedence over Article 4, notwithstanding the terms of this Article.[11]

Article 5(5). The effect of the reference to Article 5(5), which also **18.05** relates to branches, agencies and other establishments, is to provide a basis of jurisdiction under that provision in addition to those pro-vided by Articles 7 to 12A. By contrast with the second paragraph of Article 8, Article 5(5) is not restricted to defendants who are insurers, but founds jurisdiction only against a defendant domiciled in another Contracting State.[12] For a discussion of the particular effect of the terms of Article 5(5) in the context of insurance matters, see also the commentary on the second paragraph of

---

[6] Para. 21.85 below; Jenard, para. A1.131 below, at sub–para. (2); Maxwell, para. 5.93.
[7] Arts. 28, first para. and 34, second para. paras. 27.62 and 28.22 below.
[8] See para. 18.08 below.
[9] Para. 18.11 below.
[10] Jenard, para. A1.136 below.
[11] Para. 18.20 below; Jenard, para. A1.136 below; Schlosser, para. 150 (para. A1.442 below); Weser, para. 244.13; Bülow/Böckstiegel/Linke, p. 98.
[12] Paras. 17.55 *et seq.*

Article 8.[13] It is suggested that a Lloyd's agent—who has no authority on behalf of Lloyd's—would probably not be regarded as an agent for the purposes of Article 5(5).

" . . . matters relating to insurance . . . "

18.06   Difficulties may arise in borderline cases in deciding whether a matter relates to insurance. It seems clear that the words are to be given an independent interpretation.[14] The question whether a contract is a contract of insurance, therefore, cannot be answered by reference either to the proper law of the contract or to the *lex fori*, but by reference only to the Convention itself, according to the principles of interpretation developed by the European Court of Justice.[15]

Private law relationships. The provisions of Articles 7 to 12A are probably confined to legal relations wholly or principally of a private law character,[16] not only because of the fact that the Convention as a whole is confined to civil and commercial matters, but also because where these Articles deal with specific types of insurance, it seems that only private law relationships are envisaged. Although social security is excluded from the scope of the Convention generally,[17] the extent to which, for example, sickness insurance can be regarded not as social security but, even if it is compulsory, as a private law insurance matter, must await clarification by the courts.[18] The regulation of insurance companies as a matter of public law seems certain to fall outside the scope of the Convention.

18.07   *Direct or subrogated rights.* The exercise of direct or subrogated rights by an insurer against a third party who is responsible for a loss should not be regarded as a matter relating to insurance, first, because it is not likely to be relevant that it is an insurer rather than a private person who is exercising the rights and, secondly, because the protection afforded by Articles 7 to 12A is not necessary where it is the insurer who is the plaintiff in the action.

---

[13] Paras. 18.20 *et seq.* below.

[14] Collins, pp. 70–71, Bülow/Böckstiegel/Linke, p. 90; Geimer/Schütze, p. 401; Kropholler, p. 117.

[15] Paras. 13.09 *et seq.* above.

[16] Bülow/Böckstiegel/Linke, p. 90.

[17] Para. 14.30 above.

[18] The Italian Corte di Cassazione has rejected an argument that third party proceedings, claiming indemnity against the defendant's liability to pay sickness insurance premiums, was a "matter relating to insurance": *Karl Presser und Co. GmbH* v. *Eurosped S.R.L.*, Foro it. Mass 1979, Col. 1064, Digest D I–5.1.2—B28.

Re-insurance. The Schlosser Report[19] suggests that contracts of re-insurance are not to be equated with insurance contracts and are not covered by Articles 7 to 12A. This interpretation cannot be derived from the express words of the Convention, but it is sensible and accords with the overall purpose of this section of the Convention, not least because considerations of inequality of bargaining power generally have no place in re-insurance.

B. DEFINITIONS

The term "policy-holder" is used in the Convention, without definition.[20] The Jenard Report[21] and Schlosser Report[22] make it clear that the term is to be interpreted as referring to the person who originally contracted with the insurer. Although some other person might become the "policy-holder" by acquiring the whole legal status of the original policy-holder (by inheritance, for example) the term does not extend to a normal assignee of the policy, nor to a beneficiary under the policy. It is apparent from Article 11(1) that "policy-holder," "insured" and "beneficiary" have separate meanings.[23] **18.08**

C. CONSUMER CONTRACTS

There seems to be no reason why an insurance contract cannot also be a consumer contract within the meaning of Article 13,[24] provided that the conditions of that Article are complied with. But because the provisions of Articles 13 to 15 are more general than those of Articles 7 to 12A, the latter are to take precedence.[25] The distinction is unlikely to be of any practical importance, because the provisions dealing with consumer contracts are substantially the same as those dealing with insurance. **18.09**

---

[19] Schlosser, para. 151 (para. A1.443 below); see also Collins, p. 71; Maxwell, para. 5.93.

[20] Other language versions assist in determining its meaning: French, *preneur d'assurance*, German, *Versicherungsnehmer*, Italian, *il contraente dell'assicurazione*.

[21] Jenard, para. A1.138 below.

[22] Schlosser, para. 152 (para. A1.444 below).

[23] See, further, para. 18.45 below. For an example of a case where the insured person was not a party to the contract of insurance, see *Gerling Konzern A.G.* v. *Amministrazione del Tesoro dello Stato* [1983] E.C.R. 2503 (discussed at para. 21.19 below).

[24] The position is different in respect of jurisdiction within the United Kingdom: see next para.

[25] Schlosser, para. 156 (para. A1.449 below).

D. Intra-United Kingdom Jurisdiction

18.10   Schedule 4 to the 1982 Act, which together with section 16, governs the allocation of jurisdiction within the United Kingdom, has no equivalent of Articles 7 to 12A. Contracts of insurance are therefore treated in the same way as any other contracts. Section 44 of the 1982 Act contains provisions equivalent to the second paragraph of Article 8. Within the United Kingdom, contracts of insurance are excluded from the provisions governing consumer contracts.[26]

Article 8

18.11   **An insurer domiciled in a Contracting State may be sued:**

1.   **in the courts of the State where he is domiciled, or**
2.   **in another Contracting State, in the courts for the place where the policy-holder is domiciled, or**
3.   **if he is a co-insurer, in the courts of a Contracting State in which proceedings are brought against the leading insurer.**

An insurer who is not domiciled in a Contracting State but has a branch, agency or other establishment in one of the Contracting States shall, in disputes arising out of the operations of the branch, agency or establishment, be deemed to be domiciled in that State.*†

E. General Note

18.12   The rules of jurisdiction provided by this Article are of general application to matters relating to insurance, where the action is brought against an insurer domiciled in a Contracting State. If the insurer is not domiciled[27] in a Contracting State, or does not have a deemed domicile by virtue of the second paragraph of Article 8, the court has to decide according to its own law (including its conflicts

---

[26] Art. 13 of Sched. 4 to the 1982 Act: para. 45.15 below.

* Jenard, paras. A1.137–A1.140 below; Schlosser, paras. 149–152 (paras. A1.441–A1.444 below); Collins, pp. 64, 71; Dashwood/Halcon/White, pp. 27–28, 104; Hartley, pp. 60–61; Kaye, pp. 809–812; Maxwell, paras. 5.97–5.101, 5.112; Anton, paras. 6.11; Droz, paras. 108–115; Weser, paras. 244.4–244.9; Bülow/Böckstiegel/Linke, pp. 94–99; Geimer/Schütze, pp. 411–428; Kropholler, pp. 119–121; Gothot/Holleaux, paras. 120–126; Pocar, pp. 159–161.

† This Art. has been substituted for its predecessor by Art. 7 of the 1978 Convention and care should be taken in referring to commentaries on the unamended Convention. The substantive changes are in relation to co-insurers and former references to intermediaries are excluded. What is now the second paragraph was formerly the third paragraph.

[27] For the provisions on domicile generally, see Arts. 52 and 53 (chap. 31 below).

rules) whether it has jurisdiction.[28] If the defendant is an insurer domiciled in a Contracting State, the provisions of this Article will apply, unless there is a valid jurisdiction agreement within Article 12, or unless the case falls within one or more of the special jurisdiction provisions of Articles 5(5), 9, 10 and the second paragraph of Article 11.

F. First Paragraph

1. "in the courts of the State where he is domiciled"

This sub-paragraph gives jurisdiction over proceedings against an insurer to the courts of the state where the insurer is domiciled or, if the second paragraph of this Article applies,[29] of the state where the insurer is deemed to be domiciled. It is the equivalent of the rule of general jurisdiction in Article 2[30] and, as with that Article, local jurisdiction is determined by the national law.[31]   **18.13**

2. "in another Contracting State, in the courts for the place where the policy-holder is domiciled"

This sub-paragraph, included as one of mechanisms for the protection of the insured party, not only founds international jurisdiction against an insurer, but also determines local jurisdiction against him. It does not apply against an insurer in the state of his domicile and it is a rule of special jurisdiction equivalent to those in Article 5.[32]   **18.14**

It is the domicile of the policy-holder[33] which determines jurisdiction under this sub-paragraph. The domicile of the insured or the beneficiary of the insurance policy (if that is a different person) is not relevant.[34] But the fact that it is the policy-holder's domicile which founds jurisdiction under this sub-paragraph does not mean that only policy-holders may take advantage of the jurisdiction and it seems that any plaintiff may use it to bring an action against an insurer.[35] The time at which the domicile of the policy-holder is to be judged is the time when the proceedings are commenced.[36]

---

[28] Art. 4 (para. 16.15 above), applied in matters relating to insurance by Art. 7 (para. 18.01 above).

[29] Para. 18.20 below: insurers not domiciled in a Contracting State, but with a branch agency or other establishment in a Contracting State.

[30] Para. 16.01 above.

[31] Droz (para. 108) makes the point that it would be contrary to the Convention for the national law not to provide a forum.

[32] See paras. 15.05 *et seq.* above.

[33] For the meaning of "policy-holder," see para. 18.08 above.

[34] Jenard, para. A1.138 below.

[35] Bülow/Böckstiegel/Linke, p. 95.

[36] Jenard, para. A1.138 below.

3. "if he is a co-insurer, in the courts of a Contracting State in which proceedings are brought against the leading insurer"

18.15   This sub-paragraph provides an additional basis of jurisdiction against an insurer, where he is one of a number of co-insurers being sued, but (by contrast with Article 6(1)) it extends the jurisdiction only by reference to the courts where "proceedings are brought against the leading insurer" and not to those where any of the defendant's co-insurers are being sued. As the Schlosser Report explains,[37] an additional jurisdiction based on the leading insurer's circumstances is justifiable only if it leads to a concentration of actions arising out of an insured event. The purpose of the provision is to enable co-insurers to be sued for their share of the insurance in the court where proceedings are brought against the leading insurer, at the same time or subsequently. But a concentration of actions is not compulsory, and a co-insurer may still be sued under sub-paragraphs (1) or (2) of this paragraph or under the other provisions of Section 3 of Title II.

The proceedings against the leading insurer need not have been brought on the basis of one of the other provisions of Article 8. It is sufficient that the jurisdiction over the leading insurer be based on the Convention. Although such jurisdiction will usually be based on the provisions of Articles 7 to 12A, it may also be based on Articles 4 or 5(5).[38]

4. " . . . co-insurer . . . leading insurer . . . "

18.16   Although the terms "co-insurer" and "leading insurer" are probably to be given an independent interpretation, it is suggested that they ought not to be regarded as terms of art. Whether a person falls into one or other of those categories should be a question of fact in each case, although the courts should be slow, where there is more than one insuring party to a contract of insurance, to find that there is no leading insurer. In broad terms, a leading insurer is one who first accepts a share or line of insurance which is then also underwritten by other co-insurers, and a co-insurer is either one of a number of insurers participating in the underwriting of a single policy of insurance or one whose policy requires him to bear part of the loss. It is necessary to distinguish between co-insurers on one hand and re-insurers on the other, because Articles 7 to 12A do not apply to the latter.[39]

---

[37] Schlosser, para. 149 (para. A1.441 below).
[38] See paras. 18.04 and 18.05 above.
[39] Para. 18.07 above.

5. " . . . the courts of the Contracting State . . . "

It is not clear whether sub-paragraph (3) provides a rule of local   **18.17**
jurisdiction as well as a rule of international jurisdiction. The English text is ambiguous, referring as it does to the "*courts* of the Contracting State in which proceedings are brought against the leading insurer." The question is whether the proceedings must be brought in *the same* court. The Schlosser Report, as noted above, refers to the concentration of actions in the same court and other language versions[40] also suggest that that is the correct interpretation.[41] Unlike Article 6(1), which permits jurisdiction on the basis of the domicile of a co-defendant, this sub-paragraph does not refer to the domicile of the leading insurer, and does not need therefore to refer to a particular place. The reference to a particular court is sufficient to found local jurisdiction. It is not necessary, though, that the co-insurer and leading insurer should be sued in the same action.

6. " . . . proceedings are brought . . . "

In order to found jurisdiction under this sub-paragraph, it is   **18.18**
probably necessary that proceedings should have been commenced against the leading insurer.[42] If the leading insurer has settled with

---

[40] *e.g.*, French: "*le tribunal . . . saisi . . .* "; German: "*vor dem Gericht . . . bei dem der federführende Versicherer verklagt wird.*"

[41] Maxwell, para. 5.101.

[42] If the existence of an action against the leading insurer is strictly a condition precedent to the jurisdiction over the co-insurer under this sub-paragraph, the position in England would appear to be that a co-insurer may not, at least in the first instance, be joined as a co-defendant with the leading insurer in a writ for service out of the territorial jurisdiction, unless the English court had jurisdiction over the co-insurer on some other basis envisaged by Arts. 7 to 12A: see paras. 18.02 *et seq.* above. In such a case, if the writ were issued against both the leading insurer and the co-insurer, each claim in the writ would not be one which, by virtue of the 1982 Act, the English court would have power to hear and determine. Accordingly, leave would be required for the issue of the writ for service out of the jurisdiction (see paras. 3.23 *et seq.* above) and such leave should be refused. Similarly, such a writ issued without leave for service within the jurisdiction should be set aside.

It may be that the English courts will be able to avoid this unnecessary complication by saying that it is the fact of proceedings against the leading insurer, rather than their earlier commencement, which forms the basis of the jurisdiction, and that an action against the leading insurer started at the same time as an action against the co-insurer is sufficient to satisfy the requirements of sub-para. (3). That interpretation would seem to accord with the purpose of the provision (see Schlosser, para. 149, para. A1.441 below). On the other hand, the English courts may treat the provision as analogous to the "necessary and proper party" provisions of R.S.C., Ord. 11, r. 1(1)(c) and require that the jurisdiction actually be invoked against the leading insurer.

the plaintiff without proceedings having been commenced, the sub-paragraph has no application.[43]

It is not clear whether the jurisdiction under this sub-paragraph remains available against a co-insurer after proceedings against the leading insurer have been concluded. If the action against the co-insurer is started before the conclusion of the action against the leading insurer, the court has jurisdiction over the co-insurer at the outset of the proceedings and the jurisdiction will not be lost by the subsequent conclusion of the action against the leading insurer.[44] The proceedings are, for a time at least, concurrent and, if the procedural *lex fori* permits it, they may be consolidated. If the action against the leading insurer has been concluded before the action against the co-insurer is commenced, the principle of concentration of actions[45] does not apply to the same extent, if at all. The wording of the sub-paragraph[46] also tends to suggest that the proceedings against the leading insurer should still be under way in order for the court to have jurisdiction over the co-insurer.

G. Jurisdiction Agreements

18.19   If the plaintiff has a jurisdiction agreement with one of a number of insurers whom he proposes to sue, problems may arise similar to those in relation to Article 6(1).[47] Such a case is likely to be rare in matters relating to insurance, because the terms of Article 12 are much more restrictive than those of Article 17. Jurisdiction agreements are discussed in more detail under Article 12.[48]

H. Second Paragraph: Branch, Agency or Other Establishment

1. Deemed domicile

18.20   The second paragraph is a deeming provision. If it had not been included, Article 4 would have applied to insurers domiciled outside the Community, and the question of whether they could be sued in any given court would have been a question for the *lex fori* alone. In order to have any effect, this paragraph must take precedence over Article 4, despite the wording of Article 7.[49]

---

[43] Schlosser, para. 149 (para. A1.441 below).
[44] *Cf.* the position of co-defendants under Art. 6(1): para. 17.77 above.
[45] Schlosser, para. 149 (para. A1.441 below).
[46] The present tense is used: "the proceedings *are* brought." The other language versions are to the same effect.
[47] See paras. 17.80 *et seq.* above.
[48] Para. 18.49 below.
[49] Jenard, para. A1.136 below; Schlosser, para. 150 (para. A1.442 below); Weser, para. 244.13; Bülow/Böckstiegel/Linke, p. 98.

The provision is applicable not only to the jurisdictional rules under the first paragraph of Article 8, but to the whole of Section 3.[50] Clearly, in matters relating to insurance, it also applies to Articles 4 and 5(5). Whether, in matters other than those relating to insurance, it applies generally to the Convention as a whole, is an open question.[51] It probably does not, because the insurer's character as an *insurer* is relevant only in the context of insurance matters. Any other interpretation would create an unnecessary and artificial distinction between insurance companies and other companies, which would not be justified by the purposes for which insurers are treated exceptionally by Articles 7 to 12A.

The effect of this paragraph is to assimilate the position of an insurer who falls within its terms to the position of an insurer domiciled in the Contracting State where the branch, agency or other establishment is situated.[52] In this respect, it does more than just to extend the provisions of Article 5(5)[53] from persons domiciled within the Community to insurers domiciled outside it. It opens up against such an insurer all the jurisdictions which would be available against an insurer domiciled in that Contracting State. A plaintiff relying on Article 5(5) against an insurer domiciled in another Contracting State is constrained by the terms of that Article to sue in the courts for the *place* where the branch, agency or other establishment is situated. But if the insurer is not domiciled in a Contracting State, the plaintiff may sue him at any place permitted by the national law of the state where the branch, agency or other establishment is situated.

2. " . . . branch, agency or other establishment . . . "

The meaning of these words is discussed in the commentary on Article 5(5).[54] In relation to insurance, the Jenard Report describes the provision as applying only "when the foreign company is represented by a person able to conclude contracts with third parties on behalf of the company."[55] It remains to be seen how the courts will

18.21

---

[50] Maxwell, para. 5.97.
[51] If the second para. of Art. 8 applies to proceedings outside Arts. 7 to 12A, there is no equivalent allocation of jurisdiction as between the different parts of the U.K.: see para. 44.29 below.
[52] As a matter of U.K. law, s. 44 of the 1982 Act (para. 44.27) provides that an insurer who is deemed by this paragraph to be domiciled in the U.K. is to be treated for the purposes of the Act as domiciled in the part of the U.K. in which the branch, agency or other establishment is situated.
[53] See para. 18.05 above.
[54] Paras. 17.61 *et seq.* above.
[55] Jenard, para. A1.136 below.

approach the question of insurance brokers of the type commonly found in the United Kingdom. If the test suggested by the Jenard Report is applied, many insurance brokers would fall within the scope of the provision. On the other hand, insurance brokers do not easily pass the test of direction and control formulated by the European Court of Justice in the cases under Article 5(5).

3. " . . . disputes arising out of the operations . . . "

18.22   The meaning of these words, too, is discussed in the commentary on Article 5(5).[56] The difficulties noted there arising from the narrow construction of these words by the European Court of Justice in the *Somafer* case[57] are likely to be particularly acute in the context of the deemed domicile provisions of the second paragraph of Article 8.

If "operations" were to be restricted in this context to undertakings entered into *at the place* of business of the branch, agency or other establishment and which had to be performed there, much of the purpose of the second paragraph of Article 8 would be defeated.[58] Even if, in the context of that paragraph (which contains no reference to the place of the branch, agency or other establishment), the concept of "operations" were wider, and extended to undertakings which were entered into and had to be performed in the *Contracting State* where the branch, agency or other establishment is situated, the position would hardly be much better.[59] It

---

[56] Paras. 17.59 and 17.60 above.

[57] *Etablissements Somafer S.A.* v. *Saar-Ferngas A.G.* [1978] E.C.R. 2183.

[58] The "operations" of a branch office of an insurance company have been held at first instance to include the settlement of claims made by third parties: *Bedrijfsvereniging voor de textielindustrie* v. *General Accident Fire and Life Corporation Ltd.*, Arrondissementsrechtbank, Amsterdam, September 13, 1977, Digest D I–8—B1; *R. Willocq* v. *Compagnie Française d'Assurance et de Réassurances, Incendie, Accidents et Risques Divers*, Tribunal d'Arrondissement, Tournai (Belgium), February 18, 1980, Digest D I–8—B2. (The latter case appears to ignore the fact that the insurer was domiciled in another Contracting State: see para. 17.60, n. 47 above).

[59] The following example illustrates the difficulty. The London office of a Swiss insurance company enters into a term policy of life insurance with a person domiciled in the Republic of Ireland, with the profits payable in Ireland. On maturity of the policy, the insurers refuse to pay. Upon a strict application of the dicta in the *Somafer* case, the writing of the policy would not constitute an "operation" of the London office, because even if, on a true analysis, the contract was entered into in London, the obligation would be one which had to be performed in Ireland. If the contract was actually made in Ireland, the plaintiff would fail under both limbs of the test. In either case, the plaintiff could not enforce the policy in Ireland under sub-para. (2), nor in England under sub-para. (1) of the first para. of Art. 8. He would have to rely on any jurisdictional remedies which might be available to him under Irish law. If, instead of being Swiss, the insurance company had been French, the plaintiff could have sued in

seems most unlikely that the European Court of Justice would attribute a different meaning to the same words in the Articles 5(5) and 8. It also seems most unlikely that they would afford greater protection to an insurance company domiciled outside the Contracting States than to one domiciled in a Contracting State, although were the Court's existing dicta to be applied, that could be the effect.[60]

Article 9

In respect of liability insurance or insurance of immovable property, the insurer may in addition be sued in the courts for the place where the harmful event occured. The same applies if movable and immovable property are covered by the same insurance policy and both are adversely affected by the same contingency.*   18.23

I. GENERAL NOTE

This Article provides bases of jurisdiction against an insurer in addition to those provided by Article 8. The Jenard Report suggests that the effect of the Article is to allow an insurer to be sued in a State other than that in which he is domiciled, in the courts for the place where the harmful event occurred.[61] It is a difficult question, discussed below[62] whether Article 9 also has the wider effect of allowing an insurer to be sued in the state of his domicile[63] in the courts for the place where the harmful event occurred.   18.24

Ireland under sub-para. (2), or in France under sub-para. (1), of the first para. of Art. 8, but not in London under Art. 5(5). On the other hand, if in the context of both Art. 5(5) and the second para. of Art. 8, a wider interpretation were given to "operations," the plaintiff in the above example could have sued the Swiss company in Ireland or England, and the French company in London.

[60] In the above example, greater protection would be given to the Swiss company than to the French company.

* Jenard, para. A1.141 below; Schlosser, paras. 136–139, 148 (paras. A1.419–A1.430, A1.440 below); Collins, p. 71; Dashwood/Halcon/White, pp. 104–105; Hartley, pp. 61; Kaye, p. 812; Maxwell, paras. 5.102–5.104, 5.112; Anton, para. 6.12; Droz, paras. 116–117; Weser, para. 244.9; Bülow/Böckstiegel/Linke , pp. 100–101; Geimer/Schütze, pp. 411–428; Kropholler, pp. 121–122; Gothot/Holleaux, paras. 120–126; Pocar, pp. 161–162.

[61] Jenard, para. A1.141 below.

[62] Paras. 18.26 *et seq.*

[63] For this purpose, the state of his domicile is to be taken as including the state where a branch, agency or other establishment of the insurer is situated, if the insurer is not domiciled in a Contracting State: second paragraph of Art. 8, para. 18.20 above.

J. JURISDICTION AGAINST AN INSURER

1. " . . . liability insurance or insurance of immovable property . . . "

18.25   These expressions are to be given an independent interpretation on the basis of the Convention.[64] Although liability insurance will often not cover liability for the insured's breach of contract[65] and despite the reference to "the harmful event,"[66] it is suggested that, for the purposes of this Article and Article 10, the term "liability insurance" ought not to be limited to insurance against liability in tort.[67] Many claims which are capable of formulation both in contract and in tort, may be covered by a liability insurance policy. It would be unduly artificial to allow the applicability of Article 9 (or, even more so, Article 10) to depend upon the way in which an injured third party had formulated his claim.

Some types of insurance may be borderline. Sickness insurance, for example, may involve liability for doctors' fees, but the event insured against is the illness, rather than the liability, and is therefore probably not liability insurance. Legal expenses insurance (more common on the Continent than in the United Kingdom) may involve liability for lawyers' fees in connection with litigation or in respect of some other matter. The event insured against, giving rise to the need for a lawyer's services, may or may not be liability to a third party. It would be unfortunate if the question whether a given insuring clause fell inside or outside Article 9 were to depend on the answer to the question whether the insurer was liable under the clause.

The words "insurance of immovable property" are less likely to give rise to difficulty and they cover insurance against an event damaging the immovable property. It is suggested that it is physical damage that is envisaged, and not damage to the value of the property caused by some non-physical event. So, for example, title insurance would not fall within the scope of Article 9.

2. " . . . in addition . . . "

International and local jurisdiction under Articles 8 and 9

18.26   The use of the words "in addition" indicates that the jurisdiction under Article 9 is an additional ground to those under the first para-

---

[64] The interpretation of "liability insurance" will have to be wider than the definition of "liability insurance business" in s.83(3) of the Insurance Companies Act 1974, which excludes insurance business in respect of certain categories of liability.

[65] Ivamy, *General Principles of Insurance Law* (5th ed.), pp. 12–13.

[66] See para. 18.29 below.

[67] For a discussion of the classification of different types of insurance, see Ivamy, *op. cit.*, chap. 3.

graph of Article 8, but it is not clear whether the two Articles are mutually exclusive. If they are not mutually exclusive, the effect is as follows: the international jurisdiction of a court seised of an action against an insurer in the state where he is domiciled will be based on sub-paragraph (1) of the first paragraph of Article 8; in the normal case, local jurisdiction will then be regulated by the national law of that state; but if the case also falls within the scope of Article 9, the local jurisdiction of the court, may, as an alternative to the provisions of the national law, be founded upon this Article.

The commentaries on the unamended text of the Convention suggest that the two Articles are mutually exclusive.[68] It was said that the effect of the wording and intent of Article 9 was to present the plaintiff with a choice between relying on the first paragraph of Article 8 (as it now is) and relying on Article 9. But even if the arguments in those commentaries were correct for the purposes of the unamended text, there are arguments to the effect that Article 9 now has a wider application and allows an insurer to be sued in the state of his domicile (or deemed domicile),[69] in the courts for the place where the harmful event occurred.[70]

It will be necessary to examine the arguments in a little detail. On **18.27** the unamended text of Article 8, the only jurisdiction over an insurer in the state of his domicile was the general rule of international jurisdiction provided by what is now sub-paragraph (1) of the first paragraph of that Article. The other jurisdictional rules only permitted the insurer to be sued in a Contracting State other than that of his domicile. It was argued that the effect of Article 9 was to permit an insurer to be sued in the courts for the place where the harmful event occurred, so long as that place was not in the state of his domicile.

Two arguments were advanced. First, reliance was placed on the words "in addition"[71] as signifying that the jurisdiction under Article 9 was separate from that under Article 8. Secondly, it was said that the spirit and mechanism of the Convention required that Articles 8 and 9 be interpreted as alternatives. The argument was that the rule in Article 9 was a material rule,[72] imposing itself as a

---

[68] Jenard, para. A1.141 below; Droz, para. 116; Bülow/Böckstiegel/Linke, pp. 100–101; Kropholler, p. 121.

[69] See the second para. of Art. 8, paras. 18.20 *et seq.* above.

[70] Geimer's view is that local jurisdiction is still determined solely by national law in the state of the insurer's domicile or deemed domicile: Geimer/Schütze, p. 412, n. 193.

[71] French: "*en outre*"; German: "*ausserdem*". Reliance was also placed upon the word "also" in Art. 10.

[72] A "material" rule of jurisdiction is one where jurisdiction is based on the subject-matter of the dispute, rather than on some procedural consideration.

rule of local jurisdiction within the Contracting States, notwith-standing the provisions of their domestic law. As the Convention sought only to regulate international legal relations (and some inter-national element must, *ex hypothesi*, be present[73]) such material rules of local jurisdiction only ever applied where the defendant was sued in a state other than that of his domicile.

18.28   The following may be argued to the contrary effect. Firstly, sub-paragraph (3) of the first paragraph of Article 8 now permits a co-insurer to be sued in the courts where proceedings are brought against the leading insurer, without reference to the domicile of either of them.[74] That is a (non-material) rule of local jurisdiction, applying within the Contracting States.

Secondly, there seems to be no reason why, as a matter of textual interpretation, the words "in addition" should be read as providing that only an alternative, rather than an additional, jurisdiction is being made available by Article 9.

Thirdly, it is not necessary that the requisite international element (which undoubtedly must be present)[75] should consist in the defendant being sued in a state other than that of his domicile. Were it otherwise, Article 2 would be of little, if any, effect. The special rules of jurisdiction in Article 5 do, expressly, require that the defendant be domiciled in another Contracting State and as an observation, therefore, it is correct to say that the other material rules of local jurisdiction are subject to that requirement. On the other hand, Article 9 contains no such express requirement and the connection between the place where the harmful event occurred and the courts for that place would seem to be no less cogent a reason for giving those courts jurisdiction, merely because that place happens to be in the state of the insurer's domicile. The Con-vention contains other examples of rules of local jurisdiction which do not require that the defendant be domiciled in a state other than that in which he is being sued,[76] even though these other examples are not material rules of jurisdiction.

It is only if a valid distinction can be drawn, as a matter of the policy of the Convention, between material and non-material rules of local jurisdiction, that Articles 8 and 9 should be read as alternatives.

---

[73] See paras. 13.10 *et seq*. above.

[74] For the reasons for avoiding a reference to domicile, see Schlosser, para. 149 (para. A1.441 below).

[75] See paras. 13.10 *et seq*. above.

[76] The example of sub-para. (3) of the first para. of Art. 8 has already been cited. Other examples are Art. 6 and, to a lesser extent, Art. 6A.

3. " . . . in the courts for the place where the harmful event occurred . . . "

These words are the same as those in Article 5(3), and are fully **18.29** discussed in that context.[77] In that Article, they are qualified by the words "in matters relating to tort, delict or quasi-delict." Here, the qualification is "in respect of liability insurance or insurance of immovable property." As has already been suggested, it would not necessarily be correct to limit the application of Article 9 to tortious risks, and the fact that these words are used in relation to tort in Article 5(3) does not mean that they need be limited in this context to cases of tort. A liability arising, for example, by way of a breach of contract may also be covered. In the context of tort, the European Court of Justice has ruled in the case of *Handelswekerij G.J. Bier BV* v. *Mines de Potasse d'Alsace S.A.*[78] that the words must be understood as being intended to cover both the place where the damage occurred and the place of the event giving rise to it, where those places are not identical, and that the plaintiff may sue in either, at his option. That test may be equally applicable in relation to harmful events other than tortious acts. The problem may arise particularly in product liability insurance.

4. " . . . if movable and immovable property are covered by the same insurance policy and both are adversely affected by the same contingency"

An example of the situation envisaged by these words would be **18.30** where a building and its contents were covered by the same policy.[79] "The same contingency" will be given an independent interpretation, and it remains to be seen how widely it is construed. For example, it may be that, in the case of a burglary, the theft of the goods would be regarded as a different contingency from the damage caused by the burglar in breaking in.[80]

K. JURISDICTION AGREEMENTS

If jurisdiction is, prima facie, founded upon this Article, its terms **18.31** may be departed from only by an agreement which complies with Article 12. This aspect is discussed more fully in connection with that Article[81] but two points should be noted. First, if the policy-holder and the insurer are both domiciled in the same Contracting State, they may provide for the jurisdiction of the courts of that

---

[77] Paras. 17.47 to 17.51 above.
[78] [1976] E.C.R. 1735, discussed at paras. 17.47 *et seq.* above.
[79] Jenard, para. A1.141 below.
[80] Bülow/Böckstiegel/Linke, p. 101.
[81] Paras. 18.49 *et seq.* below.

state, so long as such an agreement is lawful according to the law of that state.[82] Secondly, a policy-holder not domiciled in a Contracting State may make a jurisdiction agreement, except in so far as the insurance is compulsory or relates to immovable property.[83] In neither case, unless the injured third party is a party to the jurisdiction agreement, will it bind him. Article 10 makes provision for insurers to be sued either directly at the instance of such an injured party or in proceedings brought against the insured.[84]

Article 10

18.32   **In respect of liability insurance, the insurer may also, if the law of the court permits it, be joined in proceedings which the injured party has brought against the insured.**

   The provisions of Articles 7, 8 and 9 shall apply to actions brought by the injured party directly against the insurer, where such direct actions are permitted.

   If the law governing such direct actions provides that the policy-holder or the insured may be joined as a party to the action, the same court shall have jurisdiction over them.*

L. GENERAL NOTE

18.33   This Article provides rules of special jurisdiction for cases of liability insurance disputes. Like the provisions of Article 6 and subparagraphs (1) and (2) of the first paragraph of Article 8, these rules of special jurisdiction are based not on the subject-matter of the dispute, but on procedural considerations. They will be particularly applicable in road accident cases.

M. FIRST PARAGRAPH: THIRD PARTY PROCEEDINGS
AGAINST INSURERS

18.34   The purpose of the first paragraph is to enable an insured defendant to have his insurer joined in the proceedings which have been instituted against him by the injured party. It is third party proceedings which are envisaged.[85] Actions brought by the injured party against

---

[82] Art. 12(3), paras. 18.57 *et seq.* below.
[83] Art. 12(4), paras. 18.60 *et seq.* below.
[84] See para. 18.32 below.
* Jenard, paras. A1.142–A1.146 below; Schlosser, para. 148 (para. A1.440 below); Collins, pp. 71–72; Dashwood/Halcon/White, pp. 27, 105; Hartley, pp. 61; Kaye, pp. 809–813; Maxwell, paras. 5.105–5.112; Anton, paras. 6.13–6.14; Droz, paras. 116, 118–126; Weser, paras. 244.11–244.12; Bülow/Böckstiegel/Linke, pp. 101–106; Geimer/Schütze, pp. 411–428; Kropholler, pp. 122–124; Gothot/Holleaux, paras. 120–126; Pocar, pp. 162–164.
[85] For a more detailed discussion of third party proceedings in the context of the Convention, see the commentary to Art. 6(2), at paras. 17.82 *et seq.* above.

the insurer are governed by the second paragraph. The provision operates as a rule of local jurisdiction, enabling the insured to sue the insurer in third party proceedings, even where they are both domiciled in the same Contracting State.

1. "In respect of liability insurance . . . may also . . . "

For a discussion of what is meant by "liability insurance," see the commentary on Article 9.[86] The words "may also" indicate that the jurisdiction under this paragraph is a further alternative to the rules in the first paragraph of Article 8.[87]   **18.35**

2. " . . . if the law of the court permits it . . . "

The words "law of the court" contain a hidden difficulty. The court is clearly the court seised of the proceedings against the insured, but the law referred to is not only the procedural law of that court. There must also be a substantive legal right capable of being asserted by the insured against the insurer, and the existence of such a right is a matter for the appropriate substantive law, as determined by the conflicts rules of the *lex fori*. This may be of particular relevance where the insured is a different person from the policy-holder.[88]   **18.36**

Third party proceedings, as understood in the other Contracting States, are not permitted in Germany, and special provision is made for that anomaly by Article V of the Protocol to the Convention.[89]

3. " . . . joined in proceedings which the injured party has brought against the insured . . . "

In order for the insurer to be joined in the proceedings as a third party, a number of conditions must be fulfilled: **18.37**

(1) The defendant must be the insured, but need not necessarily be the policy-holder.[90] For example, a named driver on a policy of motor insurance would fall within the condition. In such a case, though, the law of the court would have to permit an action by the insured against the insurer.[91]

(2) The case must have been brought in a court which has jurisdiction under the Convention.[92] Apart from the Conven-

---

[86] Para. 18.25 above.
[87] *Cf.* the commentary on the words "in addition" in Art. 9, paras. 18.26 *et seq.* above.
[88] See paras. 18.37 (at n. 91) and 18.39 below.
[89] Para. 35.20 below.
[90] For the meaning of "policy-holder," see para. 18.08 above.
[91] See para. 18.38 below.
[92] Bülow/Böckstiegel/Linke, p. 102.

tion's other provisions, the court will have jurisdiction by virtue of Article 18 if the defendant has entered an appearance otherwise than to contest the jurisdiction (provided the case does not fall within the exclusive jurisdiction provisions of Article 16).[93] The defendant's submission to the jurisdiction in those circumstances is sufficient to enable the insurer to be joined as third party. This is so, even though submission to the jurisdiction is treated by the Convention in many ways as if it were jurisdiction by agreement[94] and the insurer is not a party to that agreement.

(3) The proceedings against the insured must already have been started and not have been concluded when the third party proceedings are commenced.[95]

(4) As noted above, the *lex fori* must permit third party proceedings.

N. Second Paragraph: Victims' Direct Actions against Insurers

18.38   This rule is included for the benefit of victims, especially, but not exclusively, victims of road traffic accidents. It enables them to take advantage of each of the bases of jurisdiction set out in Articles 8 and 9 (and Article 5(5))[96] by way of a direct action against the insurer of the person who injured them, so long as such a direct action is permitted by the applicable law. It does not allow the victim to base jurisdiction upon his own domicile[97] or on the domicile of the insured.[98] Where the Convention regulates only international jurisdiction, based on the insurer's domicile,[99] some national rules of local jurisdiction will permit the action to be brought in the court for the place of the victim's domicile.[1]

" . . . where such direct actions are permitted . . . "

18.39   These words have been used specifically to include the rules of conflicts of law of the court seised of the matter.[2] The reference to the conflicts rules is necessary, because the Convention provides no

---

[93] Art. 16 is unlikely to be relevant to the sort of litigation envisaged in Art. 10.

[94] See para. 21.84 below.

[95] *Cf.* the position under sub-para. (3) of the first para. of Art. 8: see para. 18.18 above.

[96] Art. 7 applies Art. 5(5) in the context of insurance: see para. 18.05 above.

[97] Droz, para. 125.

[98] Geimer/Schütze, p. 426.

[99] Art. 8, first para., sub-para. (1): para. 18.13 above.

[1] Bülow/Böckstiegel/Linke, p. 103.

[2] Jenard, para. A1.145 below.

uniform material rule[3] of jurisdiction for direct actions against insurers.[4] The Jenard Report suggests that "the rules of conflict must be used to decide whether the law to be applied is the law of the place where the harmful event occurred, the law governing the contract of insurance or the *lex fori*."[5] It is suggested that, in practical terms, what the court will have to do is to look at the obligation in question (*i.e.* the obligation of the insurer to meet the liability), decide according to its own conflicts rules what law is applicable to that obligation,[6] and then see whether, according to that law, the obligation is one which can be enforced directly by the victim. If it is, the victim may avail himself of any of the jurisdictions in Articles 8 and 9.

Direct actions against insurers are permitted in some countries generally,[7] while in others they are permitted only in a limited class of case—usually where compulsory motor insurance is involved.[8] English law permits direct actions against liability insurers in limited circumstances only.[9]

O. THIRD PARAGRAPH: DIRECT ACTIONS; SUPPLEMENTARY PROVISIONS

Where an insurer is a defendant to a direct action brought under the second paragraph of Article 10, then, provided that the applicable law permits it, he may join the policy holder (or the insured, if they are different) as a party to the action. As noted above, the applicable law is the substantive *lex causae*, and not the procedural *lex fori*. The provision is designed to reduce the risk of irreconcilable judgments and to protect insurers from fraud.[10]   **18.40**

---

[3] For the meaning of a material rule, see para. 18.27, n. 72 above.
[4] Droz, para. 122.
[5] Jenard, para. A1.145, n. 4 below.
[6] Bülow/Böckstiegel/Linke, p. 104; Geimer/Schütze, p. 426. The solution probably adopted by English private international law is for the court to apply the choice of law rule of the country whose law governs the contract of insurance, but the point is not free from doubt: Dicey and Morris, pp. 1399–1400; Collins, p. 72.
[7] *e.g.* France, Belgium and Luxembourg.
[8] *e.g.* Germany and the Netherlands.
[9] Under the Third Parties (Rights Against Insurers) Act 1930 and under s.151 of the Road Traffic Act 1988; see 25 *Halsbury's Laws* (4th ed.), paras. 704 *et seq.*, and paras. 774, *et seq.* An action against the Motor Insurers' Bureau, under the Agreement dated November 22, 1972 between the Secretary of State for the Environment and the Motor Insurers' Bureau (Compensation of Victims of Uninsured Drivers), would probably also fall within the second para. of Art. 10: *Hardy* v. *M.I.B.* [1964] 2 Q.B. 745; *Albert* v. *M.I.B.* [1972] A.C. 301, at p. 320.
[10] Jenard, para. A1.146 below.

P. JURISDICTION AGREEMENTS

18.41   The provisions of the first paragraph of Article 10 can be derogated from by an agreement which complies with Article 12, that is to say, an agreement which fulfils one of a number of specific criteria designed to protect the policy-holder, insured or beneficiary. This aspect is discussed more fully in connection with that Article,[11] but it may be pointed out here that Article 12(3) is particularly relevant in the context of the first paragraph of Article 10, as the example given by the Jenard Report illustrates:

> An accident is caused in France by a German domiciliary insured by a German-domiciled insurer. If the German driver is sued in France, he may join the insurer in those proceedings (which is permitted by French law) unless he has entered a valid agreement with the insurer under Article 12(3) that the German courts are to have jurisdiction. The jurisdiction of the French court is not affected by the fact that the insurance contract is subject to German law.[12]

A jurisdiction agreement between the insurer and the policy-holder will not bind the injured party (unless, exceptionally, he is a party to it).[13] The provisions of the second paragraph of Article 10 can therefore rarely be departed from.

Article 11

18.42   **Without prejudice to the provisions of the third paragraph of Article 10, an insurer may bring proceedings only in the courts of the Contracting State in which the Defendant is domiciled, irrespective of whether he is the policy-holder, the insured or a beneficiary.**

The provisions of this Section shall not affect the right to bring a counterclaim in the court in which, in accordance with this Section, the original claim is pending.*

Q. GENERAL NOTE

18.43   As already observed,[14] Section 3 of Title II of the Convention is designed to lend particular protection to the weaker party in insurance transactions. Articles 8 to 10 do so by extending the bases

---

[11] Paras. 18.50 *et seq.* below.

[12] Jenard, para. A1.143 below.

[13] Schlosser, para. 148 (para. A1.440 below).

* Jenard, para. A1.147 below; Collins, p. 72; Dashwood/Halcon/White, pp. 27, 106; Hartley, p. 61; Kaye, pp. 814–816; Maxwell, paras. 5.113–5.116; Anton, para. 6.15; Droz, para. 127; Weser, paras. 244.14–244.15; Bülow/Böckstiegel/Linke, pp. 106–108; Geimer/Schütze, pp. 408–411; Kropholler, pp. 124–125; Gothot/Holleaux, paras. 120–126; Pocar, p. 164.

[14] Para. 18.02 above.

upon which jurisdiction may be invoked against an insurer. Article 11 concerns the complimentary situation, where the insurer is the plaintiff, by limiting the courts in which an insurer may bring proceedings. As with the other provisions of section 3, the case must concern a matter "relating to insurance."[15]

R. First Paragraph: The Insurer as Plaintiff

Where an insurer is the plaintiff in a case concerning a matter **18.44** "relating to insurance," the general rule of jurisdiction is equivalent to that in Article 2, namely that the insurer may bring his action in the courts of the Contracting State where the defendant is domiciled. It is the defendant's domicile at the time when the proceedings are commenced that is relevant.[16] The rule regulates international jurisdiction only, and local jurisdiction is regulated by national law.[17] If the defendant is not domiciled in a Contracting State, Article 11 does not apply, and the insurer may make use of national rules of jurisdiction in bringing his action.[18]

The general rule is essentially exclusive in character and this is emphasised by the use of the word "only." Nonetheless, it does admit of some exceptions:

(1) Where the insurer is the defendant in a direct action brought by a third party, he may join his policy-holder or insured as a party to that action by virtue of the third paragraph of Article 10. This exception is expressly provided for in the first paragraph of Article 11.

(2) The insurer may counterclaim under the second paragraph of Article 11: see below.

(3) If the insurer has a jurisdiction agreement with the defendant, he may bring the action in the agreed forum, provided the agreement complies with Article 12.

(4) Where the defendant is domiciled in one Contracting State and has a branch, agency or other establishment in another Contracting State, he may be sued in the courts for the place where the branch, agency or other establishment is situated if the dispute arises out of the operations of the branch agency or other establishment. This jurisdiction, provided by Article 5(5),[19] is expressly reserved by Article 7.[20] The corresponding rule for insurers in the second paragraph of Article 8 does not apply, because the

---

[15] Paras. 18.06 to 18.07 above.
[16] Jenard, para. A1.147 below.
[17] *Ibid.*
[18] Art. 4, applied by Art. 7: see para. 18.04 above.
[19] Para. 17.55 above.
[20] Para. 18.05 above.

domicile of the insurer is irrelevant in the context of the first paragraph of Article 11.

" . . . irrespective of whether he is the policy-holder, the insured or a beneficiary . . . "

18.45   An independent interpretation of the words "policy-holder," "insured" and "beneficiary" ought, it is submitted, to be such as to make the list of potential defendants an exhaustive one. If that is not correct, though, the list should be read as elaborating, rather than qualifying, the word "defendant." Any person whom the insurer may sue in a matter relating to insurance should be covered by Article 11. For example, if in a given case, the words "policy-holder," "insured" and "beneficiary" do not cover an assignee of the policy, the assignee should nonetheless be covered by Article 11 if sued by the insurer. The same applies to a mortgagee of insured property, a person whose interest is noted on the policy, a person whose life is insured and any other potential defendant.[21]

S. SECOND PARAGRAPH: COUNTERCLAIMS

18.46   For discussion of counterclaims generally, see the commentary on Article 6(3),[22] the wording of which differs in two material respects, discussed below, from the wording of the second paragraph of Article 11.

The constraints imposed on an insurer by the first paragraph of Article 11 do not apply to a counterclaim brought by the insurer, provided that the following conditions are fulfilled:

(1) the action against the insurer must still be pending—*i.e.* it must have commenced and not have been concluded; and

(2) the court in which the action against the insurer is pending must have jurisdiction over that action not only under the Convention generally, but specifically under Section 3 of Title II.

18.47   The Jenard Report[23] equates the second paragraph of Article 11 with Article 6(3), but a comparison of the two provisions shows two points of distinction and raises a question as to the circumstances in which an insurer can bring a counterclaim under this paragraph.

First, the second paragraph of Article 11 contains the requirement that the court seised of the original action should have jurisdiction under section 3, whereas Article 6(3) contains no equivalent provision. Its inclusion here may be explained by the policy of the

---

[21] Bülow/Böckstiegel/Linke, p. 92.

[22] Paras. 17.90 *et seq.* above.

[23] Jenard, para. A1.147 below.

Convention, which is to protect the weaker party in insurance transactions. Secondly, Article 6(3) contains the qualification that the counterclaim should arise "from the same contract or facts upon which the original claim was based," but the present provision contains no such requirement.

If the two Articles are to be read disjunctively, the absence of a reference to the contractual or factual basis for the counterclaim seems peculiar. It is submitted, therefore, that the better interpretation of the second paragraph of Article 11 is for the words "the right to bring a counterclaim" to be read as a reference to the right conferred by Article 6(3), as further circumscribed in this Article. This interpretation would explain the two points of contrast between the respective provisions and would have the merit of consistency in the application of the Convention. If this interpretation is correct, an insurer would only be entitled to bring a counterclaim under this paragraph if it arose from the same contract or facts upon which the original claim was based.

Submission to the jurisdiction. It remains to be seen how the courts will resolve the important question of whether the submission by the insurer to the jurisdiction[24] in the main action gives the court jurisdiction "in accordance with this Section." It is suggested that the correct approach would be to consider such a submission as an agreement on jurisdiction within Article 12(1), but, as with Article 6(3), perhaps only where the counterclaim arises "from the same contract or facts on which the original claim was based."[25] **18.48**

Article 12

The provisions of this section may be departed from only by an agreement on jurisdiction: 18.49

1. **which is entered into after the dispute has arisen, or**
2. **which allows the policy-holder, the insured or a beneficiary to bring proceedings in courts other than those indicated in this section, or**
3. **which is concluded between a policy-holder and an insurer, both of whom are at the time of the conclusion of the contract domiciled or habitually resident in the same Contracting State, and which has the effect of conferring jurisdiction on the courts of that State even if the harmful event were to occur abroad, provided that**

---

[24] See para. 18.03 above, the third exception.
[25] See para. 17.94 above.

such an agreement is not contrary to the law of that State, or

4. which is concluded with a policy-holder who is not domiciled in a Contracting State, except insofar as the insurance is compulsory or relates to immovable property in a Contracting State, or

5. which relates to a contract of insurance in so far as it covers one or more of the risks set out in Article 12A.*†

T. GENERAL NOTE

18.50   The purpose of Article 12, as recorded in the Jenard Report,[26] is to prevent the parties from limiting the choice offered by the Convention to the policy-holder and to prevent the insurer from avoiding the restrictions imposed under Article 11. Like the other provisions of Section 3 of Title II, it is designed to protect the weaker party to insurance transactions—the policy-holder, insured or beneficiary.[27] The nature of the British insurance market, though, where many policy-holders are not domiciled in Contracting States and where substantial sections of the market are not, in practice, subject to the sort of inequality of bargaining power the effects of which Section 3 of Title II was designed alleviate, meant that Article 12 had to be substantially amended with the United Kingdom's accession to the Convention. The Schlosser Report discusses the particular problems which faced the negotiators of the 1978 Convention, and the solutions adopted.[28]

The case must have an international character[29] and Article 12 expressly only applies when there would otherwise be jurisdiction under Articles 7 to 11—*i.e.* when one or more of the jurisdictions in Section 3 is being derogated from.

---

* Jenard, para. A1.148–A1.149 below; Schlosser, paras. 137–140 (paras. A1.421–A1.433 below); Collins, pp. 72–74; Dashwood/Halcon/White, pp. 28, 106–108; Hartley, pp. 61–62; Kaye, pp. 817–821; Maxwell, paras. 5.117–5.124; Anton, paras. 6.16–6.17; Droz, paras. 128–130; Weser, para. 244.18; Bülow/Böckstiegel/Linke, pp. 108–113; Geimer/Schütze, pp. 495–505, 508–511, 911–914; Kropholler, pp. 125–129; Gothot/Holleaux, paras. 127–131; Pocar, p. 165.

† This Art. was substituted for its predecessor by Art. 8 of the 1978 Convention. Paras. 4 and 5 are new, as are the references in para. 3 to the habitual residence of the insurer and the policy-holder and to the time of conclusion of the contract.

[26] Jenard, para. A1.148 below.

[27] See para. 18.02 above.

[28] Schlosser, paras. 136–152 (paras. A1.419–A1.444 below).

[29] See paras. 13.10 *et seq.* above.

Formal requirements. Article 12 does not contain any particular   **18.51**
requirements of form for jurisdiction agreements, and in this
respect it is quite different from the equivalent provisions of Article
17. Nevertheless, it seems clear that the requirements of form set
out in Article 17 do apply to jurisdiction agreements in Article 12.[30]
The Schlosser Report makes clear that the requirements apply to
jurisdiction agreements within Article 15[31] (which contains provisions equivalent to Article 12 for cases of consumer contracts) and
there seems to be no distinction in this respect between the two
Articles.[32] The requirements of form include those set out in the
second paragraph of Article I of the Protocol,[33] concerning persons
domiciled in Luxembourg.

If the entry of an appearance under Article 18 is to be regarded as
founding jurisdiction by agreement,[34] the formal requirements of
Article 17 will not, of course, apply in that case.

Court chosen. One of the requirements of Article 17 is that the   **18.52**
court chosen should be a court of a Contracting State. The same
almost certainly applies to jurisdiction agreements under Article
12.[35] It would be contrary to the spirit of the Convention (and particularly this Section) for jurisdiction agreements to be more readily
valid in the special case of matters relating to insurance than in
other cases. Furthermore, if confirmation is needed, it is to be
found in the Preamble, where it is made clear that the Convention
determines the international jurisdiction of the courts *of the Contracting States.* For a more detailed discussion of the choice of a
court outside the Community, see the commentary on Article 17.[36]

Parties to the jurisdiction agreement. Clearly the insurer and the   **18.53**
policy-holder would normally be parties to the jurisdiction agreement and able to rely on its terms. But an agreement may have
wider effect. For example, the European Court of Justice has held
that the insured (if different from the policy-holder) may rely on a
jurisdiction agreement if (as in Article 12(2)) it was concluded for
his benefit.[37] As a matter of logic, the same should apply to a beneficiary.

So far as an assignee of an insurance policy is concerned (a situ-

---

[30] Maxwell, para. 5.93; Collins, pp. 72–3; Droz, para. 119n.; Bülow/Böckstiegel/
Linke, p. 110; Geimer/Schütze, p. 495, n. 100.
[31] Schlosser, para. 161a (para. A1.455 below).
[32] Maxwell, para. 5.118.
[33] Para. 35.01 below.
[34] See para. 18.03 above and para. 21.84 below.
[35] Bülow/Böckstiegel/Linke, p. 100.
[36] Paras. 21.13 *et seq.* below.
[37] *Gerling Konzern A.G.* v. *Amministrazione del Tesoro dello Stato* [1983] E.C.R.
2503 (discussed at para. 21.19 below).

ation common in the transport industry)[38] it is probable that the same approach would be adopted as the European Court of Justice has adopted in the case of bills of lading.[39] If the applicable law provides that the assignee acquires the rights and obligations of the policy-holder, then the assignee will be treated as a party to the jurisdiction clause.

18.54   *Arbitration.* The Convention does not apply to arbitration. Whereas the circumstances are very limited in which a jurisdiction clause in an insurance contract will be enforced in favour of an insurer, the scope for the enforcement of an arbitration clause is much wider. An English Lord of Appeal has suggested extrajudicially,[40] that the following clause might find favour with insurers:

> "Insurers are willing that any dispute shall be litigated in England, but if the assured is not so willing, the dispute shall be referred to the exclusive jurisdiction of arbitrators in London."

As has been observed,[41] there is some dispute concerning the extent to which arbitration is excluded from the scope of the Convention. If the exclusion does not necessarily extend to all disputes which the parties had agreed would be the subject of arbitration, it is respectfully suggested that the clause might not achieve its intended effect.

B. Paragraph 1

"which is entered into after the dispute has arisen"

18.55   Except in the case of jurisdiction being based on the entry of an appearance under Article 18 (if that is properly to be regarded as jurisdiction by agreement),[42] a jurisdiction agreement entered into after the dispute has arisen will be rare.[43] Where it does arise, though, there may be some difficulty in deciding the point at which the "dispute" has "arisen." The Jenard Report says that it is "as soon as the parties disagree on a specific point and legal proceedings are imminent or contemplated."[44] Commentators, though, have

---

[38] See Schlosser, para. 140 (para. A1.431 below).

[39] *Partenreederei m.s. "Tilly Russ"* v. *Haven und Vervoerbedrijf Nova N.V. & Goeminne Hout N.V.* [1984] E.C.R. 2417 (discussed at para. 21.21 below).

[40] Lord Brandon of Oakbrook, speaking to the Bar European Group on January 13, 1983 on "Maritime and other aspects of the law as affected by the Civil Jurisdiction and Judgments Act 1982."

[41] Paras. 14.31 *et seq.* above.

[42] See para. 21.84 below.

[43] Collins, p. 73.

[44] Jenard, para. A1.148 below, citing Belgian doctrine to support the view.

adopted a range of different views on the point[45] and, as the Maxwell Report points out,[46] the test proposed in the Jenard Report may prove difficult to apply in particular cases. This is perhaps inevitable, given that the question is one of fact and degree in each case. It is suggested that the test proposed by Jenard should be modified slightly, so that proceedings should be *both* imminent *and* contemplated. This is because the practical need for an agreement on jurisdiction ought not to arise until the dispute becomes one which will apparently need litigation to resolve it. A jurisdiction agreement entered into at any earlier stage would be a precautionary measure only and would be contrary to the same policy objections as support the existence of Article 12(1) in the first place.

C. Paragraph 2

"which allows the policy-holder, the insured or a beneficiary to bring proceedings in courts other than those indicated in this section"

The effect of this paragraph is to enable a jurisdiction agreement **18.56** to be applied in favour of a policy-holder, insured or beneficiary. It may also apply in favour of other interested parties[47] in dispute with an insurer.[48] The agreement may either elect a particular court or the courts of a particular Contracting State. The court chosen must, for this paragraph to apply, be a court which would not otherwise have had jurisdiction under Articles 7 to 11. The clause must widen the choice available to the plaintiff, and this paragraph should not be read as limiting the choice.[49]

The provision imposes no limitation as to when the jurisdiction clause should have been entered into. By contrast with paragraph 1,

---

[45] Both Droz (para. 128) and Weser (para. 244.18 and Table 244.18) refer interchangeably to *"la naissance du différend"* (*"différend"* is the word used in the French text of the Convention) and *"la naissance du litige."* Bülow/Böckstiegel/Linke (pp. 111–112) suggest that the position should have been reached where the dispute (*"Streitigkeit"*) has developed to such an extent that the idea of an imminent forensic dispute must intrude and that it is not sufficient that the parties have merely established a difference of opinion on the basis of differing statements. They cite, *inter alia*, French doctrine (Picard-Besson, *Les assurances terrestres en droit français* (3rd ed., 1972), Vol. II, p. 438, *"à l'occasion d'un litige déterminé, né et actuel"*). Geimer/Schütze (p. 496) say that a dispute has arisen if a difference of opinion has arisen between the parties as to the interpretation, handling or performance of the contract and that it is not necessary for there to be specific dispute imminently involving court proceedings (*"konkret drohende gerichtliche Auseinandersetzung"*).
[46] Maxwell, para. 5.120.
[47] See para. 18.45 above.
[48] Bülow/Böckstiegel/Linke, p. 112.
[49] *Ibid.*

the agreement may,[50] but need not,[51] be made before the dispute arises.

Article 12 affects only the applicability of a jurisdiction agreement, not its validity. So, even if the clause is not expressed to be for the benefit only of the policy-holder, insured or beneficiary and is not severable, it makes no difference. But it may only be relied on to the extent that it complies with Article 12.

D. PARAGRAPH 3

1. "which is concluded between a policy-holder and an insurer, both of whom are at the time of the conclusion of the contract domiciled or habitually resident in the same Contracting State, and which has the effect of conferring jurisdiction on the courts of that State . . . "

18.57   The effect of this paragraph is to allow an insurer and a policy-holder to agree on the jurisdiction of the courts of their own state, if the law of that state allows them to do so. On its face, the paragraph would appear to state the obvious, but it should be remembered that the paragraph will only apply to derogate from the jurisdiction of courts which would otherwise have jurisdiction under Articles 7 to 11. This will usually be the case where an attempt is made to bring an insurer into proceedings which have been brought against the insured, under the first paragraph of Article 10. The present paragraph has the effect of enabling the scope of that provision to be limited.[52] Also, the Convention, including this provision, will only apply where the case has an international element.[53] Such an international element may arise where, for example, the policy-holder has moved his domicile to another Contracting State between the time when the contract was concluded and the time when the action is commenced. But for this paragraph, the policy holder in such a case would be able to bring an action against the insurer in the state of his new domicile under sub-paragraph (2) of the first paragraph of Article 8.

18.58   The new reference to the time of the conclusion of the contract is merely a clarification of the former position.[54] The inclusion of a reference to habitual residence is exceptional in the Convention. It was included to bring Article 12(3) into line with Article 15(3)[55] and

---

[50] Droz, para. 128.
[51] Bülow/Böckstiegel/Linke, p. 112, n. 26.
[52] See the example at para. 18.41 above.
[53] See paras. 13.10 *et seq.* above.
[54] Jenard, para. A1.151 below; Schlosser, para. 161a (para. A1.455 below); *contra* Collins, p. 73.
[55] Schlosser, para. 161a (para. A1.455 below).

in that context is justified by the Jenard Report[56] on grounds of equity and to cater for the case where a person has his domicile and habitual residence in different Contracting States.[57] It is not clear whether habitual residence is to be decided according to the same conflicts rules as apply to domicile[58] or whether habitual residence is to be given an independent interpretation; but it seems that Article 52 ought to apply by analogy.[59]

The same considerations apply to Article 12(3) as apply to Article 15(3), which is in very similar terms. Some of the points which arise under both provisions are discussed more fully under the latter provision.[60]

2. " . . . even if the harmful event were to occur abroad . . . "

The inclusion of these words makes it clear that paragraph 3 is intended to apply especially in relation to liability insurance and, in a suitable case, to allow derogation from the provisions of Articles 9 and the first paragraph of Article 10. They do not limit the application of paragraph 3 to cases of liability insurance. The term "harmful event" in an insurance context is discussed under Article 9.[61]   **18.59**

3. " . . . provided that such an agreement is not contrary to the law of that State"

These words do not require elaboration.

E. PARAGRAPH 4

1. "which is concluded with a policy-holder who is not domiciled in a Contracting State . . . "

Subject to the two exceptions discussed below, the effect of this paragraph is to enable the parties to an insurance policy to agree on the exclusive jurisdiction of the courts of a Contracting State which either would not otherwise have it under Articles 7 to 11, or whose jurisdiction under those Articles would not otherwise be exclusive. The paragraph only applies if the policy-holder is not domiciled in a   **18.60**

---

[56] Jenard, para. A1.151 below.
[57] In view of the definition of domicile adopted in the U.K. for the purposes of the Convention (s.41 of the 1982 Act, paras. 44.01 *et seq.* below) the distinction between habitual residence and domicile is likely to be of little if any relevance when the law of a part of the U.K. is to be applied to determine domicile.
[58] Art. 52, para. 31.01 below. That Article does not expressly refer to habitual residence.
[59] See para. 31.07 below; Bülow/Böckstiegel/Linke, pp. 66 and 129.
[60] Paras. 19.41 to 19.42 below.
[61] Para. 18.29 above.

Contracting State but, as the Schlosser Report notes, this is often the case in the British insurance market.[62]

In the absence of an exclusive jurisdiction agreement, Article 4 will apply[63] to a defendant domiciled outside the Community, enabling the courts of Contracting States to decide their jurisdiction according to their own law.

Were it not for this paragraph, jurisdiction over contracts of insurance with policy-holders domiciled outside the Community would be equally subject to the rules of jurisdiction under Articles 7 to 11. An insurer would not normally object to the courts of the state where he is domiciled having jurisdiction[64] but might prefer to exclude the jurisdiction of other courts having jurisdiction under Articles 7 to 11, such as, in the case of liability insurance (but not insurance of immovable property),[65] the courts for the place where the harmful event occurred (under Article 9) or where the insured is being sued by the injured party (under the first paragraph of Article 10). If the policy-holder is not domiciled in a Contracting State, the insurer can enter into such an exclusive jurisdiction agreement, and Article 12(4) will ensure its effectiveness.

An agreement valid under this paragraph may be applicable to an insured or beneficiary[66] as it would be to a policy-holder.[67]

2. " . . . except insofar as the insurance is compulsory . . . "

18.61   A jurisdiction agreement with a policy-holder not domiciled in a Contracting State will not be valid under Article 12(4) if the insurance is compulsory.[68] The Schlosser Report suggests that no departure from the provisions of Articles 8 to 11 is permissible where the insurance is compulsory,[69] but it is not clear how far the exclusion extends beyond the scope of paragraph 4 to jurisdiction agreements falling within the other paragraphs of Article 12.

The word "compulsory" is probably to be given an independent interpretation. The Schlosser Report[70] refers to a "statutory obligation" to insure, and it may be that insurance which is not statutorily compulsory, but which is required, for example, as a condition of a right to practice a profession, will not be regarded as

---

[62] Schlosser, para. 137 (para. A1.421 below).
[63] Art. 7, para. 18.04 above.
[64] Art. 8, first para., sub-para. (2), para. 18.14 above.
[65] See para. 18.62 below.
[66] Collins, p. 73.
[67] See para. 18.53 above.
[68] Schlosser, at para. 138 (paras. A1.423–A1.429 below), sets out some of the categories of insurance that are compulsory in various Contracting States. See also Geimer/Schütze, pp. 502–503, n. 126.
[69] Schlosser, para. 138 (para. A1.422 below).
[70] Schlosser, para. 138 (para. A1.422 below).

compulsory. Insurance required merely as a matter of contract will almost certainly not be regarded as compulsory.

3. " . . . relates to immovable property in a Contracting State"

This exception means that the jurisdiction under Article 9, to sue   **18.62** an insurer of immovable property in the courts for the place where the harmful event occurred, cannot be excluded even if the policy-holder is not domiciled in a Contracting State and even if the national law of the place where the property is situated allows juris-diction by agreement in such a case.[71] In this connection, it should be noted that Article 16(1) allocates jurisdiction over proceedings which have as their object right *in rem* in, or tenancies of, immov-able property, exclusively to the courts of the Contracting State where the property is situated.[72]

F. Paragraph 5

"which relates to a contract of insurance insofar as it covers one or more of the risks set out in Article 12A"

See the commentary on Article 12A.

Article 12A

The following are the risks referred to in Article 12(5):   **18.63**

    1. Any loss of or damage to

      (a) sea-going ships, installations situated off-shore or on the high seas, or aircraft, arising from perils which relate to their use for commercial purposes,

      (b) goods in transit other than passengers' baggage where the transit consists of or includes carriage by such ships or aircraft;

    2. Any liability, other than for bodily injury to passengers or loss of or damage to their baggage,

      (a) arising out of the use or operation of ships, instal-lations or aircraft as referred to in (1)(a) above in so far as the law of the Contracting State in which such aircraft are registered does not prohibit agreements on jurisdiction regarding insurance of such risks,

      (b) for loss or damage caused by goods in transit as des-cribed in (1)(b) above;

---

[71] Schlosser, para. 139 (Para. A1.430 below).
[72] Para. 20.11 below.

3. **Any financial loss connected with the use or operation of ships, installations or aircraft as referred to in (1)(a) above, in particular loss of freight or charter-hire;**
4. **Any risk or interest connected with any of those referred to in (1) to (3) above.*†**

A. GENERAL NOTE

18.64   This Article is to be read in connection with Article 12, and reference should be made to the commentary on that Article. These new provisions are discussed in detail in the Schlosser Report.[73] Their effect is to liberalize the Convention in matters relating to the insurance of certain marine and aviation risks by allowing parties to enter into jurisdiction agreements under Article 12(5).[74] The justifications of social protection, which are applicable to insurance generally, clearly had little or no application where the policy-holders were themselves powerful undertakings.

The provisions, read in conjunction with the commentary in the Schlosser Report, are largely self-explanatory, but one or two points may usefully be elaborated.

It is particularly relevant in this context to remember that the Convention does not affect other conventions between Contracting States relating to particular matters. This is provided by Article 57, to which reference should be made.

The terms used in Article 12A are not to be regarded as terms of art, but are to be given an independent interpretation. They constitute an exhaustive list of the risks referred to in Article 12(5). In particular, insurance of transport by land alone does not come within the terms of the Article.[75]

B. PARAGRAPH 1

1. Nature of loss or damage

18.65   This paragraph covers only damage to the vessel or aircraft or to goods. It does not cover liability insurance, which comes within paragraph 2. Certain categories of consequential financial loss are

---

* Schlosser, paras. 140–147 (paras. A1.431–A1.439 below); Collins, pp. 72–74; Dashwood/Halcon/White, pp. 108–110; Hartley, p. 62; Kaye, pp. 821–823; Maxwell, para. 5.125; Anton, paras. 6.18–6.24; Geimer/Schütze, pp. 495–505; Kropholler, pp. 129–132; Gothot/Holleaux, paras. 127–131.

† This Art. was added to the text by Art. 9 of the 1978 Convention. In the French, Italian and Dutch texts it is called Art. "12 *bis*".

[73] Schlosser, paras. 140–147 (paras. A1.431–A1.439 below).

[74] The jurisdiction agreements must comply with the requirements of Art. 17: see para. 18.51 above.

[75] Schlosser, para. 140 (para. A1.432 below).

expressly covered in paragraph 3, and it would seem, therefore, that paragraph 1 has no application to consequential loss, whether or not it falls within paragraph 3. It may be that consequential loss will fall within paragraph 4, despite the express reference to some consequential loss in paragraph 3. See the commentary on those paragraphs.

2. "(a) sea-going ships, installations situated off-shore or on the high seas, or aircraft . . . "

The Schlosser Report suggests that the term "sea-going ships"   **18.66** covers all vessels intended to travel on the sea, including hovercraft and hydrofoils and vessels which cannot move under their own power, as well as ships in the course of construction, where the damage is the result of a maritime risk—*i.e.* caused by the fact that the ship is on the water.[76]

3. " . . . arising from perils which relate to their use for commercial purposes"

These words are likely to be widely interpreted, in keeping with   **18.67** the intent of Article 12A to liberalise the rules relating to the insurance of large risks and to balance private insurance interests.[77]

4. "(b) . . . consists of or includes . . . ":

Even if the damage is caused while the goods are being carried on   **18.68** land, if part of the transit has been by sea or air, a jurisdiction clause in the insurance policy can be effective.

C. PARAGRAPH 2

1. "Any liability, other than for bodily injury to passengers or loss of or damage to their baggage, . . . "

This paragraph covers liability insurance in respect of the matters   **18.69** set out in sub-paragraphs (a) and (b), except in respect of the risks to passengers or their baggage referred to in the introductory words to the paragraph. The reason for the exception is the principle of social protection for persons in a weaker economic or bargaining position[78] and its effect is to make a jurisdiction agreement in respect of such insurance subject to the normal constraints imposed by Article 12.

---

[76] Schlosser, para. 141 (para. A1.434 below).
[77] Schlosser, para. 140 (paras. A1.431–A1.433 below).
[78] Schlosser, para. 143 (para. A1.435 below). See para. 18.02 above.

2. "(a) arising out of the use or operation . . . ":

18.70   The Schlosser Report[79] expressly avoids any suggestion as to how widely these words should be construed in relation to the construction, modification or repair of a ship. It is hard to see why "use or operation" in this sub-paragraph should be construed more narrowly than "use for commercial purposes" in sub-paragraph 1(a).

D. Paragraph 3

Financial loss

18.71   Directive 73/239/EEC is referred to in the Schlosser Report[80] as containing the same notion of financial loss. It relates to the taking-up and pursuit of the business of direct insurance, other than life insurance.[81]

E. Paragraph 4

Connected risk or interest

18.72   The risks and interests referred to in the Schlosser Report are "ancillary" risks, although that expression was deliberately not used, in order to avoid any confusion with Directive 73/239/EEC[82] and because, for the purposes of Article 12A(4), the ancillary risk need not be covered by the same policy as the principal risk. It remains to be seen how close a connection will be required with the risks referred to in paragraphs 1 to 3.

---

[79] Schlosser, para. 144 (para. A1.436 below).
[80] Schlosser, para. 146 (para. A1.438 below). See also para. 140 (para. A1.433 below).
[81] First Council Directive of July 24, 1973, on the Co-ordination of Laws, Regulations and Administrative Provisions relating to the Taking-up and Pursuit of the Business of Direct Insurance, other than Life Insurance. In the Annex, Part A, Class 16, "Miscellaneous financial loss" is defined as comprising " – employment risks, – insufficiency of income (general), – bad weather, – loss of benefits, – continuing general expenses, – unforeseen trading expenses, – loss of market value, – loss of rent or revenue, – indirect trading losses other than those mentioned above, – other financial loss (non-trading), – other forms of financial loss."
[82] *Ibid.* In the Annex, Part C, under the heading "Ancillary risks," the Directive states, "An undertaking obtaining an authorisation for a principal risk belonging to one class or a group of classes may also insure risks included in another class without an authorisation being necessary for them if they: – are connected with the principal risk, – concern the object which is covered against the principal risk, and – are covered by the contract insuring the principal risk."

CHAPTER 19

JURISDICTION OVER CONSUMER CONTRACTS
(Articles 13–15)

SECTION 4

Article 13

19.01   In proceedings concerning a contract concluded by a person for a purpose which can be regarded as being outside his trade or profession, hereinafter called 'the consumer,' jurisdiction shall be determined by this section, without prejudice to the provisions of Articles 4 and 5(5), if it is:

1. a contract for the sale of goods on instalment credit terms, or

2. a contract for a loan repayable by instalments, or for any other form of credit, made to finance the sale of goods, or

3. any other contract for the supply of goods or a contract for the supply of services, and

    (a) in the State of the consumer's domicile the conclusion of the contract was preceded by a specific invitation addressed to him or by advertising, and

    (b) the consumer took in that State the steps necessary for the conclusion of the contract.

Where a consumer enters into a contract with a party who is not domiciled in a Contracting State but has a branch, agency or other establishment in one of the Contracting States, that party shall, in disputes arising out of the operations of the branch, agency or establishment, be deemed to be domiciled in that State.

This section shall not apply to contracts of transport.*†

---

* Jenard, para. A1.150 below; Schlosser, paras. 153–161a (paras. A1.446–A1.455 below); Collins, pp. 74–77; Dashwood/Halcon/White, pp. 110–112; Hartley, pp. 58–60; Kaye, pp. 824–845; Maxwell, paras. 5.126–5.138; Anton, paras. 6.24–6.32; Droz, paras. 131–6; Weser, paras. 244.19–244.27; Bülow/Böckstiegel/Linke, pp. 113–123; Geimer/Schütze, pp. 212, 397–398, 404–407, 429–433, 495–505, 821–824, 898, 959; Kropholler, pp. 133–139; Gothot/Holleaux, paras. 120–122, 132–139; Pocar, pp. 165–8.

† This Article, together with Arts. 14 and 15, was substituted by Art. 10 of the 1978 Convention. The former provisions related only to the sale of goods on instalment credit terms and to loans, repayable by instalments, expressly made to finance such sales. The effect of the amendments is to widen the scope of the provisions to cover most consumer contracts (excluding contracts of transport). The new version also contains a paragraph (the second paragraph of Art. 13) providing for a deemed domicile for a supplier or lender not domiciled in a Contracting State, but who has a branch, agency or other establishment in a Contracting State. In a number of material respects discussed below, the meaning of the English version of the three numbered sub-paragraphs in the first paragraph

A. GENERAL NOTE

In recent years, consumer legislation has increasingly found   **19.02**
favour in all the Contracting States and it was felt that the consumer
needed to be afforded much the same protection in transfrontier
contracts as he received under national legislation.[1] The Convention is not concerned with the substance of consumer protection
laws in each of the Contracting States,[2] but with providing uniform
and compulsory rules of jurisdiction.[3] National consumer protection legislation may be based not only on the protection of the economically weaker party, but also on considerations of economic,
monetary or savings policy.[4] The objectives of Articles 13 to 15, by
contrast, were said by the European Court of Justice to be "inspired
solely by a desire to protect" certain categories of person.[5] It is in
this light that these Articles are to be interpreted.

Jurisdiction over consumer contracts is determined by Article 13
to 15 in the same way as jurisdiction over matters relating to insurance is determined by Articles 7 to 12A. Many of the same principles apply. The meaning of "consumer" is considered in more
detail below. For present purposes, the person who contracts with

---

requires a comparison with other language versions. For ease of reference, part
of the French, German and Italian texts are set out here:

French: *"1. lorsqu'il s'agit d'une vente à tempérament d'objects mobiliers corporels;*

*2. lorsqu'il s'agit d'un prêt à tempérament ou d'une autre opération de crédit liés
au financement d'une vente de tels objects;*

*3. pour tout autre contrat ayant pour objet une fourniture de services ou d'objets
mobiliers corporels . . . "*

German: *"1. wenn es sich um den Kauf beweglicher Sachen auf Teilzahlung
handelt,*

*2. wenn es sich um ein in Raten zurückzahlendes Darlehen oder um ein anderes
Kreditgeschäft handelt, die zur Finanzierung eines Kaufs derartiger Sachen bes-
timmt sind, oder*

*3. für andere Verträge, wenn sie die Erbringung einer Dienstleistung oder die
Lieferung beweglicher Sachen zum Gegenstand haben . . . "*

Italian: *"1. qualora si tratti di una vendita a rate di beni mobili materiali,*

*2. qualora si tratti di un prestito con rimborso rateizzato o di un altra operazione
di credito, connessi con il finanziamento di una vendita di tali beni,*

*3. qualora si tratti di un altro contratto che abbia per oggetto una fornitura di
servizio o di beni mobili materiali . . . "*

[1] Schlosser, para. 153 (para. A1.466 below).
[2] For a discussion of consumer protection in the context of the EEC Convention
on the Law Applicable to Contractual Obligations, see Hartley, in North (ed.),
Contract Conflicts (1982) at p. 111.
[3] *Société Bertrand* v. *Paul Ott K.G.* [1978] E.C.R. 1431 at p. 1444–1445 (paras. 12
and 13), discussed at para. 19.11 below.
[4] *Ibid.*, para. 18.
[5] See also Jenard, para. A1.150 below and Weser, para. 244.19, cited with approval by Advocate General Capotorti at [1978] E.C.R. p. 1449.

the consumer, the supplier of goods or services, or the lender, is referred to as the supplier.

19.03   The provisions of Articles 13 to 15 (Section 4 of Title II) are separate from, and not subordinate to, the normal rules of general and special jurisdiction in Articles 2 to 6A. They are a set of rules which, with four exceptions, are exclusively applicable to cases falling within their scope. Their scope, like that of the Convention generally, is limited to cases which have the requisite international character,[6] which are concerned with civil and commercial matters,[7] and which do not concern excluded matters.[8]

The four exceptions are:

(1) where the supplier is domiciled outside the Community and the dispute does not arise out of the operations of a branch, agency or other establishment in any of the Contracting States.[9] This exception arises by reason of the reference to Article 4 and the terms of the second paragraph of Article 13.

(2) where the supplier is domiciled within the Community, but the dispute arises out of the operations of a branch agency or other establishment in a different Contracting State.[10] This exception arises by reason of the reference to Article 5(5).

(3) where the defendant enters an appearance. This exception is not specified in the Convention, but arises by way of the operation of Article 18. That Article takes precedence over all the other jurisdictional rules of the Convention, except the exclusive jurisdiction provisions of Article 16.[11]

(4) where there is a jurisdiction agreement falling within Article 15.

19.04   The importance attached by the Convention to compliance with the exhaustive provisions of Articles 13 to 15 is illustrated by the fact that if the provisions are not complied with, recognition and enforcement of the resulting judgment is to be refused.[12]

19.05   *Article 4.* The effect of the reference to Article 4 is to limit the scope of Articles 13 to 15 to cases where the defendant is domiciled in a Contracting State, whether the defendant is the consumer or the supplier. If the defendant is not domiciled in a Contracting

---

[6] Paras. 13.10 *et seq.* above.
[7] Paras. 14.08 *et seq.* above.
[8] Paras. 14.18 *et seq.* above.
[9] Maxwell, paras. 5.94, 5.135.
[10] Maxwell, paras. 5.95, 5.135.
[11] Jenard, para. A1.131 below, at sub-para. (2); Maxwell, paras. 5.93, 5.135.
[12] Art. 28, first para. and Art. 34, second para., paras. 27.62 and 28.22 below.

State, the court may apply its own jurisdictional rules to the case. The second paragraph of Article 13[13] extends the circumstances in which a non-consumer party is to be regarded as being domiciled in a Contracting State. It does do by way of a deeming provision which applies where a non-consumer party not domiciled in a Contracting State has a branch, agency or other establishment in one of the Contracting States.[14] In order for the second paragraph of Article 13 to be of any effect, it must take precedence over Article 4, notwithstanding the terms of this Article.[15]

Article 5(5). The effect of the reference to Article 5(5), which also **19.06** relates to branches, agencies and other establishments, is to provide a basis of jurisdiction under that provision in addition to those in Articles 13 to 15. By contrast with the second paragraph of Article 13, Article 5(5) is not restricted to suppliers, but founds jurisdiction only against a defendant domiciled in another Contracting State.[16] In practice, though, a person is most unlikely to have a branch, agency or other establishment in another Contracting State, the operations of which can be regarded as outside his trade or profession. It follows that a consumer will rarely, if ever, come within Article 5(5). For a discussion of the particular effect of the terms of Article 5(5) in the context of consumer contracts, see also the commentary on the second paragraph of Article 13.[17]

Precedence of overlapping provisions. It has already been observed **19.07** that insurance contracts are to be dealt with under Section 3 of Title II, even if they are also consumer contracts.[18] Similarly, the provisions in sub-paragraphs (1) and (2) of the first paragraph of Article 13, relating to the sale of goods on instalment credit terms and credit for financing such sales, are more specific than the provisions in sub-paragraph (3) relating to other consumer contracts. Consequently, the former provisions have precedence[19] and the conditions in provisions (a) and (b) of sub-paragraph (3), (which require links with the state of the consumer's domicile in the case of other consumer contracts) do not apply in the case of instalment credit sales.

---

[13] Paras. 19.19 *et seq.* below.
[14] *Cf.* Jenard, para. A1.136 below.
[15] Para. 19.19 below; Schlosser, para. 159 (para. A1.452 below). For references to reasoning in relation to the equivalent provision in the second para. of Art. 8, see para. 18.04, n.11 above.
[16] Paras. 17.55 *et seq* above.
[17] Paras. 19.19 *et seq* below.
[18] Para. 18.09 above.
[19] Schlosser, para. 156 (para. A1.444 below).

B. FIRST PARAGRAPH: THE CONCEPT OF CONSUMER

" . . . a contract concluded by a person for a purpose which can be regarded as being outside his trade or profession, hereinafter called 'the consumer' . . . "

19.08   The intention of the first paragraph of Article 13 is that "only final consumers acting in a private capacity should be given special protection and not those contracting in the course of their business to pay by instalments for goods and services used."[20]

The definition of the consumer is the same[21] as that used in Article 5(1) of the EEC Convention on the Law Applicable to Contractual Obligations (the "Obligations Convention")[22] and is certain to be given an independent interpretation by the European Court of Justice.[23] Neither Article 5 of the Obligations Convention nor the present Article expressly states that the supplier need know the purpose for which the goods or services were required, nor that he should himself have contracted in the course of his business;[24] but the courts may be expected to interpolate both these requirements. The Report on the Obligations Convention, by Professors Giuliano and Lagarde[25] expressly envisages such an interpretation. The suggestion comes in an important gloss on the scope of the definition, which the European Court of Justice may be expected to follow:

> "The definition of consumer contracts corresponds to that contained in Article 13 of the Convention on jurisdiction and enforcement of judgments. It should be interpreted in the light of its purpose which is to protect the weaker party . . . Thus, in the opinion of the majority of the delegations it will, normally, only apply where the person who supplies goods or services or provides credit acts in the course of his trade or profession. Similarly, the rule does not apply to contracts made by traders, manufacturers or persons in the exercise of a profession (doctors, for example) who buy equipment or obtain services for that trade or profession. If such a person acts partly within, partly outside his trade or profession the situation only falls within the scope of Article 5 if he acts primarily outside his trade or profession. Where the receiver of goods or services or credit in fact acted primarily out-

---

[20] Schlosser, para. 153 (para. A1.446 below).
[21] Schlosser, para. 155 (para. A1.448 below).
[22] O.J. 1980 L266. Arts. 3 to 6 are reproduced at paras. A2.41 *et seq.* The Convention, which is not yet in force, provides uniform conflicts rules for contractual obligations. For a study of the Convention, see North (ed.) *Contract Conflicts* (1982).
[23] Maxwell, para. 5.133.
[24] Hartley, in North, *op. cit.*, at p. 125. For contracts falling within sub-para. (3) of the first para. see para. 19.16 below.
[25] O.J. 1980 C 282/4, reproduced in North, *op. cit.*, at p. 355.

side his trade or profession but the other person did not know this and, taking all the circumstances into account should not reasonably have known it, the situation falls outside the scope of Article 5. Thus if the receiver of goods or services holds himself out as a professional, *e.g.* by ordering goods which might well be used in his trade or profession on his professional paper, the good faith of the other party is protected and the case will not be governed by Article 5."[26]

In view of the independent interpretation to be given to the concept of a consumer, as well as to the various categories of contract set out in the first paragraph,[27] national courts will need to take care, in deciding whether a contract falls within Article 13, not to be influenced by the fact that a given person or a given contract is or is not afforded protection by its national law.[28]   **19.09**

C. First Paragraph, Sub-Paragraph (1)

"a contract for the sale of goods on instalment credit terms"

These words will be construed sufficiently widely to cover the various legal formulae used for consumer sales of goods on instalment credit terms. For example, hire purchase agreements are clearly covered, notwithstanding the fact that English law, for example, regards them principally as a contracts of bailment.[29]   **19.10**

"Goods" is probably to be given an independent interpretation. It is clear from the other language versions[30] that personal property such as choses in action or other incorporeal things are not included, but the limits of the concept are otherwise less clear.[31]

The Bertrand v. *Ott decision.* The European Court of Justice considered the meaning of "a contract for the sale of goods on instalment credit terms" in *Société Bertrand* v. *Paul Ott K.G.*[32] Bertrand, a company with its seat in France, had ordered a machine tool from   **19.11**

---

[26] The commentary on Art. 5, para. 2 of the Obligations Convention, at p. 26, reproduced in North, *op. cit.*, at p. 377.

[27] Paras. 19.10 to 19.28 below.

[28] *e.g.*, in England, a contract may not fall within the protection of the Consumer Credit Act 1974 because the credit exceeds £15,000 (s.8(2) of that Act and S.I. 1983 No. 1571), but may nonetheless be within Art. 13 of the Convention.

[29] Schlosser, para. 157 (para. A1.450 below).

[30] Para. 19.01 n. † above.

[31] For example, in English law, "goods" is defined by s.61(1) of the Sale of Goods Act 1979 as including "all personal chattels other than things in action and money . . . and in particular "goods" includes emblements, industrial growing crops and things attached to or forming part of the land, which are agreed to be severed before sale or under the contract of sale." Whether all such things are "goods" for the purposes of the Convention remains to be seen. It may be that some fall within the exclusive jurisdiction provisions of Art. 16(1), (paras. 20.11 *et seq.* below).

[32] [1978] E.C.R. 1431.

Paul Ott, a German company, and agreed to pay by two bills of exchange payable at 60 and 90 days. Bertrand defaulted on part of the first payment and the whole of the second payment and the German company obtained a default judgment in Germany, which it sought to enforce in France. In the enforcement proceedings, the judgment was held at first instance and on appeal to be enforceable. On a further appeal to the *Cour de Cassation*, Bertrand argued that the contract was a contract for the sale of goods on instalment credit terms and that, pursuant to Article 14, it could only be sued upon in the courts of the buyer's domicile. The *Cour de Cassation* referred to the European Court of Justice the question whether the contract was one which fell within Article 13.

19.12   It should be noted that, on the new wording of Article 13, which requires that the purchaser be a consumer, the point could not have been taken. Nonetheless, some of the points decided by the European Court are still relevant to the revised wording of Section 4.

First, having noted that different policy considerations had led different Contracting States to adopt a variety of different rules on the subject in their national laws, the Court held that the concept of the sale of goods on instalment credit terms was to be considered as "being independent and therefore common to all the Member States."[33] Secondly, it held that the jurisdiction provided by the second paragraph of Article 13[34] must be strictly limited to the objectives proper to Section 4, which it described as being "inspired solely by a desire to protect certain categories of buyers."

Applying those principles, the Court said that:

> " . . . an attempt must be made to elaborate an independent concept of the contract of sale on instalment credit terms in view of the general principles which are apparent in this field from the body of laws of the Member States and bearing in mind the objective of the protection of a certain category of buyers.
>
> It is clear from the rules common to the laws of the Member States that the sale of goods on instalment credit terms is to be understood as a transaction in which the price is discharged by way of several payments or which is linked to a financing contract."[35]

It concluded that the jurisdictional advantage given to buyers was restricted to buyers who were:

> "in need of protection, their economic position being one of weakness in comparison with sellers by reason of the fact that they are private final consumers and are not engaged, when buying the product

---

[33] [1978] E.C.R. 1431, at p. 1445 (para. 14). See paras. 13.19 *et seq.* above.
[34] Paras. 19.19 *et seq.* below.
[35] [1978] E.C.R. 1431, at p. 1446 (paras. 19–20).

acquired on instalment credit terms, in trade or professional activities."[36]

The European Court's ruling was in these terms:

> "The concept of the sale of goods on instalment credit terms within the meaning of Article 13 . . . is not to be understood to extend to the sale of a machine which one company agrees to make to another company on the basis of a price to be paid by way of bills of exchange spread over a period."[37]

Instalments. The number and size of instalments and the period **19.13** over which they are to be paid seems not to be a relevant consideration.[38] In addition to the passage quoted above, some assistance may be derived from a passage in the Opinion of Advocate General Capotorti:

> " . . . we must move towards a concept of sale on instalment credit terms which is characterized *typically* by the economic inferiority of the buyer, such that it may be said that the latter was induced to purchase by the system of payment of instalments, in so far as payment in a lump sum would have been the cause of economic difficulties for him."[39]

The passage must be treated with some caution, though, because the amended version of sub-paragraph (2) is not confined to loans repayable by instalments.

D. First Paragraph, Sub-Paragraph (2)

"a contract for a loan repayable by instalments, or for any other form of credit, made to finance the sale of goods"

According to the Schlosser Report credit contracts are not **19.14** contracts for the supply of services, so that, apart from this sub-paragraph, the whole of Section 4 does not apply to such contracts.[40]

It does not matter, for the purposes of this sub-paragraph,

---

[36] *Ibid.*, at para. 21.

[37] *Ibid.*, at p. 1447. On the basis of that decision, the Cour de Cassation refused to uphold Bertrand's objection to the German court's jurisdiction: judgment of January 23, 1979, Journal dr.int. 1979, p. 374; Digest D I–13.0—A1n.

[38] National courts have held that a contract does not become one for sale on instalment credit terms merely because the purchaser has paid a sum on account (Oberlandesgericht Oldenburg, case 6 U 74/75, November 14, 1975, N.J.W. 1976, p. 1043, Digest D I–5.1.2—B3), even if the balance is payable in several instalments (*Firma Wilhelm Wiest Maschinen- und Werkzeugfabrik* v. *Manufattura Ceramica Pozzi S.p.A.*, Corte di Cassazione, Riv.dir.int.priv.proc. 1976, p. 812).

[39] [1978] E.C.R. 1431, at p. 1450.

[40] Schlosser, para. 157 (para. A1.450 below).

whether the loan is repayable by instalments or by a single deferred payment. The loan must be "made to finance the sale of goods," but the former requirement that it should be "expressly" for that purpose has been removed. It would seem that the purpose of the loan will therefore have to be a question of fact in each case and may need to be decided by reference to the circumstances surrounding the making of the loan. It will probably not be sufficient that the loan was made without restrictions as to its use but was in fact used for the purpose of purchasing goods.

It follows that transactions effected by credit card will not normally be within Section 4, even if the card is used for the purchase of goods, but the position might be otherwise where, for example, a department store issues its own credit card which can be used only for the purchase of goods in that store.

19.15   This sub-paragraph is intended to be linked to sub-paragraph (1), so that what constitutes a contract for the sale of goods will have the same meaning in both sub-paragraphs.[41] This is less than clear in the English text, but in other language versions[42] the use of words which can be translated as "such" would seem to leave little doubt on the point. If it were not anyway obvious from the scheme and purpose of Section 4, a comparison of the various language versions would also confirm that "sale" is to be interpreted in this sub-paragraph as encompassing "purchase"—*i.e.* that it is the purchaser who is given credit.

E. First Paragraph, Sub-Paragraph (3)

1. "any other contract for the supply of goods or a contract for the supply of services"

19.16   For the wider class of consumer contracts envisaged by sub-paragraph (3) to fall within the scope of Article 13, certain requirements (set out in the sub-paragraph at (a) and (b)) have to be fulfilled in connection with the state of the consumer's domicile.[43] Subject to those requirements and to the conditions which apply to the first paragraph generally, this sub-paragraph covers a wide range of consumer contracts. As has been observed, insurance contracts[44] and contracts of loan[45] do not come within it, but the use of the word "supply" makes it clear that contracts other than those of sale are envisaged.

By contrast with sub-paragraphs (1) and (2), it is probably not

---

[41] *Ibid.*
[42] See para. 19.01, n. † above.
[43] *Cf.* Hartley, pp. 59–60.
[44] Paras. 18.09 and 19.07 above.
[45] Para. 19.24 above.

sufficient if the supply of goods or services is incidental to the main object of the contract. In other language versions,[46] the wording of sub-paragraph (3) differs materially in this respect from the wording of the other sub-paragraphs and requires that the *object* of the contract be the supply of goods or services. In this respect it mirrors the wording of Article 5(1) of the Obligations Conventions.[47] The English version of that Convention[48] does refer to "a contract the object of which is the supply of goods or services." In view of the fact that sub-paragraph (3) was formulated with Article 5 of the Obligations Convention in mind,[49] it seems likely that the European Court of Justice will attempt to achieve consistency between the interpretation of the two provisions. It might choose to follow the approach which it adopted in *Ivenel* v. *Schwab*[50] and apply the concept of characteristic obligation,[51] even though Article 5 of the Obligations Convention is not subject to that concept. If it is applied, a contract will fall within sub-paragraph (3) (provided the other conditions are fulfilled) if the obligation which characterises the contract is the supply of goods or services, whatever its other provisions.

2. "(a) in the State of the consumer's domicile the conclusion of the contract was preceded by a specific invitation addressed to him or by advertising, and (b) the consumer took in that State the steps necessary for the conclusion of the contract"

Consumer contracts other than those falling within sub-paragraphs (1) and (2) only come within the special provisions of Section 4 if there is a sufficiently strong connection with the state of the consumer's domicile.[52] That connection is provided for by these conditions. Like the definition of a consumer, they are drawn from Article 5 of the Obligations Convention[53] and in that Convention form the first indent of Article 5(2).[54] The Schlosser Report[55] expressly refers to the Report on the Obligations Convention for an explanation of the provisions. The relevant passage states:

     19.17

> "The first indent relates to situations where the trader has taken steps to market his goods or services in the country where the con-

---

[46] See para. 19.01, n. † above.
[47] Para. 19.08 above.
[48] The text of Arts. 3 to 6 is set out at paras. A2.41 *et seq.* below.
[49] Schlosser, para. 153 (para. A1.446 below).
[50] [1982] E.C.R. 1891, discussed at para. 17.24 above.
[51] The concept is discussed at paras. 17.26 *et seq.* above.
[52] Schlosser, para. 158 (para. A1.451 below).
[53] See para. 19.08 above.
[54] Para. A2.44 below.
[55] Schlosser, para. 158 (para. A1.451 below).

sumer resides.[56] It is intended to cover *inter alia* mail-order and door-step selling. Thus the trader must have done certain acts such as advertising in the press, or on radio or television, or in the cinema or by catalogues aimed specifically at that country, or he must have made business proposals individually through a middleman or by canvassing. If, for example, a German makes a contract in response to an advertisement published by a French company in a German publication, the contract is covered by the special rule. If, on the other hand, the German replies to an advertisement in American publications, even if they are sold in Germany, the rule does not apply unless the advertisement appeared in special editions of the publication intended for European countries. In the latter case the seller will have made a special advertisement intended for the country of the purchaser.

The Group expressly adopted the words 'steps necessary on his part'[57] in order to avoid the classic problem of determining the place where the contract was concluded. This is a particularly delicate matter in the situations referred to, because it involves international contracts normally concluded by correspondence. The word 'steps' includes *inter alia* writing or any action taken in consequence of an offer or advertisement."[58]

If the supplier is acting outside his trade or profession, the trans-frontier advertising requirement is most unlikely to have been met and the chance of the contract falling within sub-paragraph (3) will be correspondingly reduced.

Clearly, the application of the conditions (which will undoubtedly have to be uniformly interpreted) will not always be easy.[59] So far as the United Kingdom is concerned, the amount of international consumer trade is likely to be relatively small, except perhaps with Ireland.[60]

3. " . . . the State of the consumer's domicile . . . that State . . . "

19.18   The time at which the consumer's domicile is to be judged appears to be the time when proceedings are commenced.[61] This is the position generally in the Convention, except where the contrary

---

[56] The Obligations Convention refers to the habitual residence of the consumer, whereas the Brussels Convention refers to the consumer's domicile: see Schlosser, para. 153 (para. A1.446 below).
[57] The 1968 Convention is worded slightly, but not materially, differently.
[58] Report on the Obligations Convention, by Professors Giuliano and Lagarde O.J. 1980 C. 282/4, reproduced in North, *op. cit.*, at p. 355: passage on Art. 5, para. 3.
[59] Maxwell, paras. 5.129–5.133.
[60] So far as intra-U.K. cases are concerned, condition (a) is omitted from the jurisdictional provisions: 1982 Act, Sched. 4, Art. 13: para. 45.16 below.
[61] Schlosser, para. 160 (para. A1.454 below).

is stated (as, for example, in Articles 12(3) and 15(3)). In the present context, this means that if the consumer takes the steps necessary for the conclusion of a contract in the state where he was domiciled, but then moves his domicile to another state, not only will he not be able to bring an action under the second limb of the first paragraph of Article 14[62] in that new state, but also that the contract does not fall within sub-paragraph (3) at all.[63]

F. Second Paragraph: Branch, Agency or other Establishment

1. Deemed domicile

This provision, which is new in the amended version of Article 13, is the equivalent in the field of consumer contracts of the second paragraph of Article 8 in matters relating to insurance. Much of the commentary that follows duplicates the commentary on that provision, but is repeated for ease of reference. **19.19**

If this deeming provision had not been included, Article 4 would have applied to a person dealing with a consumer (a supplier) domiciled outside the Community, and the question of whether he could be sued in any given court would have been a question for the *lex fori* alone. In order to have any effect, this paragraph must take precedence over Article 4, despite the wording of the introductory section of the first paragraph.[64]

The first paragraph of Article 13 makes no reference to the domicile of the supplier and the second paragraph must have a wider application. It is suggested that, by analogy with Article 8, the provision is applicable to the whole of Section 4.[65] Clearly, in the case of consumer contracts falling within Article 13, it also applies to Articles 4 and 5(5). It is an open question whether it applies to consumer contracts not falling within the first paragraph of Article 13, but it probably does not,[66] because it is the fact that the supplier is dealing with a consumer which is relevant. The Convention affords special protection to consumers only to the extent that they and their contracts fall within the first paragraph of Article 13. If the second paragraph of Article 13 were to have a wider effect, it would create a distinction between consumer contracts not falling within Section 4 and non-consumer contracts. Such a distinction does not **19.20**

---

[62] Para. 19.29 below.
[63] Schlosser, para. 160 (para. A1.454 below); Hartley, p. 61.
[64] Schlosser, para. 159 (para. A1.452 below); Maxwell, para. 5.136; *cf.* Jenard, para. A1.136 below; Schlosser, para. 150 (para. A1.442 below); Weser, para. 244/13; Bülow/Böckstiegel Müller, p. 98.
[65] Maxwell, para. 5.136.
[66] Maxwell, para. 5.137.

seem to have been envisaged by the Convention and would not be justified by the purposes for which consumers are treated exceptionally by Section 4.

19.21   The effect of this paragraph is to assimilate the position of a party who falls within its terms to the position of a supplier domiciled in the Contracting State where the branch, agency or other establishment is situated.[67] In this respect, it does more than just to extend the provisions of Article 5(5)[68] from persons domiciled within the Community to suppliers domiciled outside it. It opens up against such a supplier all the jurisdictions which would be available against him if he were domiciled in that Contracting State. A plaintiff relying on Article 5(5) against a supplier domiciled in another Contracting State is constrained by the terms of that Article to sue in the courts for the *place* where the branch, agency or other establishment is situated. But if the supplier is not domiciled in a Contracting State, the second paragraph of Article 13 allows the plaintiff to sue him at any place permitted by the national law of the state where the branch, agency or other establishment is situated. The exorbitant jurisdictions are, however, excluded.

2. " . . . branch, agency or other establishment . . . "

19.22   For a general discussion of the meaning of these words, see the commentary on Article 5(5)[69] and, in relation to insurance, the commentary on the second paragraph of Article 8.[70]

3. " . . . disputes arising out of the operations . . . "

19.23   For a general discussion of the meaning of these words, see the commentary on Article 5(5).[71] The difficulties noted there arising from the narrow construction of these words by the European Court of Justice in the *Somafer* case[72] are discussed in the context of the second paragraph of Article 8[73] and are likely to be just as acute in the context of the second paragraph of Article 13.

To apply the *Somafer* interpretation of "operations" would be to defeat much of the purpose of the second paragraph of Article 13. This is particularly so in the case of contracts falling within sub-

---

[67] As a matter of U.K. law, s.44 of the 1982 Act (para. 44.27 below) provides that a supplier who is deemed by this paragraph to be domiciled in the U.K. is to be treated for the purposes of the Act as domiciled in the part of the U.K. in which the branch, agency or other establishment is situated.

[68] Para. 19.06 above.

[69] Paras. 17.61 *et seq.* above.

[70] Para. 18.21 above.

[71] Paras. 17.59 and 17.60 above.

[72] *Etablissements Somafer S.A.* v. *Saar-Ferngas A.G.* [1978] E.C.R. 2183.

[73] Para. 18.22 above.

paragraph (3) of the first paragraph, where a local connecting factor is required, not with the place where the branch, agency or other establishment is situated, but with the *consumer*'s domicile. If "operations" were to be restricted in the context of the second paragraph of Article 13 to undertakings entered into at the place of business of the branch, agency or other establishment and which had to be performed there, it would mean that the court would have to enquire into the question of where the contract was concluded. The passage quoted above[74] from the Report on the Obligations Convention expressly eschews such an enquiry. Even if, in the context of the second paragraph of Article 13, which contains no reference to the *place* of the branch, agency or other establishment, the concept of "operations" extended to undertakings which were entered into and had to be performed in the Contracting State where the branch, agency or other establishment is situated, the position would hardly be much better, because an enquiry into where the contract was concluded would still have to be made.

It seems unlikely that the European Court of Justice would attribute a different meaning to the same words in the contexts of Articles 5(5) and 13. But the Court's existing dicta on the interpretation of Article 5(5) would seem to lead to some most undesirable results in the context of the deemed domicile provisions.

G. THIRD PARAGRAPH: CONTRACTS OF TRANSPORT

"This section shall not apply to contracts of transport"

The scope of sub-paragraph (3) of the first paragraph of this Article is wide enough to include contracts of transport, but they have been expressly excluded from the special provisions of Section 4. As the Schlosser Report explains, they are subject under international agreements to special sets of rules and to bring them within the 1968 Convention would merely complicate the legal position.[75] It appears that this paragraph too was drawn from Article 5 of the preliminary draft of the Obligations Convention,[76] but in its final version the latter excludes contracts of carriage, unless they form part of a contract which, for an inclusive price, provides for a combination of travel and accommodation.[77] It was intended that package tours should be subject to Article 5[78] of the Obligations Convention, but it remains to be seen how they will be treated for the purposes of the Brussels Convention.

19.24

---

[74] Para. 19.17.
[75] Schlosser, para. 160 (para. A1.453 below).
[76] *Ibid.*
[77] Obligations Convention, Art. 5(4) and (5), para. A2.44 below.
[78] Giuliano & Lagarde, O.J. 1980 C 282/4, in North, *op. cit.*, at pp. 378 *et seq.*

The exclusion of contracts of transport from Section 4 means that Articles 2 to 6A (and especially Article 5(1)) remain applicable to them.[79]

Article 14

19.25   **A consumer may bring proceedings against the other party to a contract either in the courts of the Contracting State in which that party is domiciled or in the courts of the Contracting State in which he is himself domiciled.**

Proceedings may be brought against a consumer by the other party to the contract only in the courts of the Contracting State in which the consumer is domiciled.

These provisions shall not affect the right to bring a counterclaim in the court in which, in accordance with this Section, the original claim is pending.*†

H. General Note

19.26   The scope of Section 4 is established by Article 13, and this Article provides the substantive rules of jurisdiction for cases falling within that scope. The first paragraph determines where the consumer can bring his action, the second paragraph determines where the supplier or creditor can sue the consumer and the third paragraph provides for counterclaims in existing actions falling within Section 4. For the Convention to apply at all, the case must have the requisite international character.[80] The provisions of this Article are equivalent in many respects to the provisions relating to insurance and much of the following commentary duplicates the commentary on Section 3, but is repeated for ease of reference.[81]

The rules of jurisdiction provided by this Article may be departed from in a number of circumstances which are discussed under the separate paragraphs. If there is a jurisdiction agreement

---

[79] Schlosser, para. 160 (para. A1.453).

* Jenard, para. A1.151–A1.152 below; Schlosser, para. 161 (para. A1.454 below); Collins, p. 76; Dashwood/Halcon/White, p. 113; Hartley, pp. 60–61; Kaye, pp. 845–850; Maxwell, paras. 5.139–5.142; Anton, para. 6.32; Droz, paras. 132–133; Weser, paras. 244.21–244.27; Bülow/Böckstiegel/Linke, pp. 123–126; Geimer/Schütze, pp. 429–433; Kropholler, p. 139–140; Gothot/Holleaux, paras. 137–138; Pocar, pp. 168–172

† This Article was substituted, with the rest of s.4, by Art. 10 of the 1978 Convention. It closely follows its predecessor, the changes reflecting the new wider scope of Art. 13 and the adoption of the term "consumer" to describe the party protected by the section. See Schlosser, para. 161 (para. A1.454 below).

[80] Paras. 13.10 *et seq.* above.

[81] The equivalent provisions of s.3, in relation to insurance, are: for the first para. of Art. 14, subparas. (1) and (2) of the first para. of Art. 8; for the second para., the first para. of Art. 11; and for the third para., the second para. of Art. 11.

between the parties, it will be effective to derogate from the provisions of this Article only if it complies with Article 15. The entry of an appearance by the defendant under Article 18 will be effective to found jurisdiction.[82]

I. FIRST PARAGRAPH: THE CONSUMER AS PLAINTIFF

The rules of jurisdiction provided by this paragraph are of general application to consumer contracts, where the action is brought by a consumer against a supplier or creditor domiciled in a Contracting State. If the supplier or creditor is not domiciled[83] in a Contracting State, or does not have a deemed domicile by virtue of the second paragraph of Article 13, the court has to decide according to its own law (including its conflict rules) whether it has jurisdiction.[84] If the defendant is a supplier or creditor domiciled in a Contracting State and the plaintiff is a consumer, the provisions of this Article will apply, unless there is a valid jurisdiction agreement within Article 15, or unless the case falls within one or more of the special jurisdiction provisions of Articles 5(5) and the third paragraph of this Article. **19.27**

1. " . . . in the courts of the Contracting State in which that party is domiciled . . . "

This paragraph gives jurisdiction over a consumer's proceedings against a supplier or creditor to the courts of the state where the supplier or creditor is domiciled or, if the second paragraph of Article 13 applies,[85] of the state where he is deemed to be domiciled. It is the equivalent of jurisdiction under Article 2[86] and, as with that Article, local jurisdiction is determined by the national law[87] and it is irrelevant whether or not the consumer plaintiff is domiciled in a Contracting State.[88] **19.28**

2. " . . . in the courts of the Contracting State in which he is himself domiciled"

This provision, which is one of the principal mechanisms for the protection of the consumer, again founds only international jurisdiction against a supplier or creditor and local jurisdiction is deter- **19.29**

---

[82] Para. 19.03 above.
[83] For the provisions on domicile generally, see Arts. 52 and 53, chap. 31 below.
[84] Art. 4, applied by the first para. of Art. 13 (para. 19.05 above).
[85] Paras. 19.19 *et seq.* above (Suppliers or creditors not domiciled in a Contracting State, but with a branch, agency or other establishment in a Contracting State).
[86] Para. 16.01 above.
[87] Droz (para. 132) makes the point that it would be contrary to the Convention for the national law not to provide a forum.
[88] Bülow/Böckstiegel/Linke, p. 124.

mined by national law.[89] In this respect, it differs from its counter-part in matters relating to insurance,[90] where local jurisdiction is regulated by the Convention. The peculiarity is not mentioned in either the Jenard[91] or Schlosser Reports and does not seem to be readily explicable. It appears[92] that the local jurisdiction in matters relating to insurance is based on a provision found in French and Belgian law, which has no parallel in relation to consumer contracts generally. As noted above, the provision will only apply if the sup-plier or creditor defendant is domiciled (or deemed to be domiciled) in another Contracting State.

Time of domicile. The time at which the domicile of the consumer is to be judged is the time when the proceedings are commenced.[93] Consequently, if the consumer moves to a new Contracting State before the action is commenced, he may sue in the courts of his new state of domicile. In practice, he will only be able to do so where the contract is one falling within sub-paragraphs (1) and (2) of the first paragraph of Article 13. If it falls within sub-paragraph (3), he will face the difficulty that he took the steps necessary for the conclusion of the contract[94] in the state of his old domicile and that state is not the state of his domicile within the meaning of the Convention.[95] On this aspect, see further the commentary on sub-paragraph (3) of the first paragraph of Article 13.[96]

J. Second Paragraph: The Consumer as Defendant

19.30   This paragraph protects the consumer by limiting the courts in which he may be sued. As with the other provisions of Section 4, the case must be a consumer contract falling within Article 13.[97]

General rule. The general rule is that the consumer may only be sued in the courts of the Contracting State where he is domiciled. It is his domicile at the time when the proceedings are commenced which is relevant.[98] The rule regulates international jurisdiction only, and local jurisdiction is regulated by national law. Because this paragraph derogates from the general rules applicable to con-tracts, especially those in Articles 2 and 5(1), the European Court

---

[89] In the U.K. see s.10(3) of the 1982 Act, para. 40.30 below.

[90] Art. 8, first para., sub-para. (2), para. 18.14 above.

[91] Jenard, para. A1.151 below, actually suggests that the seller or lender may be sued in the *place* of the consumer's domicile.

[92] Jenard, paras. A1.137–A1.140 below; Droz, paras. 110, 132.

[93] Jenard, para. A1.152 below; Schlosser, para. 160 (para. A1.454 below).

[94] Art. 13, first para., sub-para. (3)(b), para. 19.01 above.

[95] Schlosser, para. 160 (para. A1.454 below).

[96] Para. 19.17 above.

[97] Paras. 19.01 *et seq.* above.

[98] Jenard, para. A1.152 below.

has held that this jurisdiction is to be strictly limited to the objectives of protecting consumers.[99]

Exceptions. The general rule is essentially exclusive in character **19.31** and this is emphasised by the use of the word "only." Nonetheless, it does admit of some exceptions:

(1) The defendant may counterclaim under the third paragraph of Article 14: see below.

(2) If the supplier or lender has a jurisdiction agreement with the consumer, he may bring the action in the agreed forum, provided the agreement complies with Article 15.

(3) Where the defendant (in this case the consumer) is not domiciled in a Contracting State, the plaintiff may make use of national rules of jurisdiction in bringing his action.[1]

(4) Where the defendant is domiciled in one Contracting State and has a branch, agency or other establishment in another Contracting State, he may be sued in the courts for the place where the branch, agency or other establishment is situated if the dispute arises out of the operations of the branch agency or other establishment. This rule of jurisdiction is most unlikely to be of any practical application in the present context[2] but is provided by Article 5(5),[3] and expressly reserved by the first paragraph of Article 13. The corresponding rule for suppliers and lenders in the second paragraph of Article 13 does not apply, because the domicile of the plaintiff supplier or lender is irrelevant in the context of the second paragraph of Article 14.

K. THIRD PARAGRAPH: COUNTERCLAIMS

For discussion of counterclaims generally, see the commentary on **19.32** Article 6(3).[4] The wording of that provision differs in two material respects from the wording of the third paragraph of Article 14.

The constraints imposed by the second paragraph of Article 14 on a supplier or lender suing a consumer do not apply to a counterclaim brought by the supplier or lender, provided that the following conditions are fulfilled:

(1) the action against the supplier or lender must still be

---

[99] *Société Bertrand* v. *Paul Ott K.G.* [1978] E.C.R. 1431 at p. 1445. This case is discussed at paras. 19.11 *et seq.* above.
[1] Art. 4 applied by the first para. of Art. 13, see para. 19.05 above.
[2] Para. 19.06 above.
[3] Para. 17.55 above.
[4] Paras. 17.90 *et seq.* above.

pending—*i.e.* it must have commenced and not have been concluded; and

(2) the court in which the action against the supplier or lender is pending must have jurisdiction over that action not only under the Convention generally, but specifically under Section 4 of Title II.

19.33   The Jenard Report[5] equates the third paragraph of Article 14 with Article 6(3), but a comparison of the two provisions shows the same points of distinction as exist between Article 6(3) and the second paragraph of Article 11. For the reasons discussed in relation to that latter provision,[6] it is submitted that the words "the right to bring a counterclaim" should be read as a reference to the right conferred by Article 6(3), as further circumscribed in this Article.

Article 15

19.34   **The provisions of this Section may be departed from only by an agreement:**

1. **which is entered into after the dispute has arisen, or**
2. **which allows the consumer to bring proceedings in courts other than those indicated in this Section, or**
3. **which is entered into by the consumer and the other party to the contract, both of whom are at the time of the conclusion of the contract domiciled or habitually resident in the same Contracting State, and which confers jurisdiction on the courts of that State, provided that such an agreement is not contrary to the law of that State.*†**

L. General Note

19.35   This Article is similar in its terms to paragraphs 1 to 3 of Article 12, and much of the commentary that follows duplicates the commentary on that provision, but is repeated for ease of reference.

---

[5] Jenard, para. A1.151 below.
[6] Paras. 18.46 *et seq.* above.
* Jenard, paras. A1.150, A1.152 below; Schlosser, para. 161a (para. A1.455 below); Collins, pp. 76–77; Dashwood/Halcon/White, pp. 29, 113–114; Hartley, pp. 61–62; Kaye, pp. 850–856; Maxwell, paras. 5.143–5.145; Anton, para. 6.32; Droz, paras. 134–136; Weser, para. 244.27; Bülow/Böckstiegel/Linke, pp. 126–129; Geimer/Schütze, pp. 495–505, 508–511, 911–914; Kropholler, pp. 140–141; Gothot/Holleaux, para. 139; Pocar, pp. 172–173.
† This Article, with the rest of s.6, was substituted by Art. 10 of the 1978 Convention. It is substantially the same as its predecessor, the changes reflecting the use of the term "consumer." The reference in para. 3 to the time of the conclusion of the contract is new.

The purpose of Article 15[7] is to prevent the parties from limiting the choice offered by the Convention to the consumer and to prevent the supplier or creditor from avoiding the restrictions imposed under the first paragraph of Article 14. Like the other provisions of Section 4 of Title II, it is designed to protect the consumer. The case must, of course, have an international character[8] and Article 15 only applies when there would otherwise be jurisdiction under Articles 13 and 14—*i.e.* when one or more of the jurisdictions in Section 4 is being derogated from.

Formal requirements. Article 15 does not contain any particular requirements of form for jurisdiction agreements, and in this respect is quite different from the equivalent provisions of Article 17. Nevertheless, it seems clear that the requirements of form set out in Article 17 do apply to jurisdiction agreements in Article 15.[9] The requirements of form include those set out in paragraph 2 of Article I of the Protocol,[10] concerning persons domiciled in Luxembourg.   **19.36**

If the entry of an appearance under Article 18 is to be regarded as founding jurisdiction by agreement,[11] the formal requirements of Article 17 will not, of course, apply in that case.

Court chosen. One of the requirements of Article 17 is that the court chosen should be a court of a Contracting State. The same almost certainly applies to jurisdiction agreements under Article 15.[12] It would be contrary to the spirit of the Convention (and particularly this Section) for jurisdiction agreements to be more readily valid in the special case of consumer contracts than in other cases. Furthermore, if confirmation is needed, it is to be found in the Preamble, where it is made clear that the Convention determines the international jurisdiction of the courts *of the Contracting States*. For a more detailed discussion of the choice of a court outside the Community, see the commentary on Article 17.[13]   **19.37**

Parties to the jurisdiction agreement. An agreement between a consumer and a supplier or lender may in certain circumstances have a wider effect. For example, a second consumer may, with the agreement of the lender, become an assignee of a hire-purchase contract. The assignment itself might not be in a form which satisfies the   **19.38**

---

[7] *Cf.* Jenard, para. A1.148 below.
[8] See paras. 13.10 *et seq.* above.
[9] Schlosser, para. 161a (para. A1.455 below); *cf.* Maxwell, paras. 5.93, 5.135; Collins, p. 76n; Droz, paras. 119n., 134; Bülow/Böckstiegel/Linke, pp. 110, 126.
[10] Para. 35.01 below.
[11] See paras. 19.03 above and 21.84 below.
[12] Bülow/Böckstiegel/Linke, pp. 110, 126.
[13] Paras. 21.13 *et seq.* below.

requirements of Article 17 so far as the assignee is concerned and, if so, the question would arise whether a jurisdiction agreement entered into by the first consumer with the lender could be relied on by or against the second consumer. In such a case, the same approach might be adopted as the European Court of Justice has adopted in the case of bills of lading.[14] If the applicable law provides that the assignee acquires the rights and obligations of the first consumer, then the assignee would be treated as a party to the jurisdiction clause. The approach might have to be modified in the case of agreements falling within paragraph 3, where the assignee had no connection with the state of domicile or habitual residence of the first consumer and the lender.

M. PARAGRAPHS 1–3: DEROGATION BY AGREEMENT FROM SECTION 4

1. "which is entered into after the dispute has arisen"

19.39   The commentary on the identically worded provision in Article 12(1) is equally applicable to this paragraph.[15]

Before the dispute has arisen, the consumer is protected against agreeing on the jurisdiction of courts which may not be to his liking. At such a time he is unlikely to be contemplating litigation[16] and the provision helps to redress the effects of inequality of bargaining power.

2. "which allows the consumer to bring proceedings in courts other than those indicated in this Section"

19.40   The effect of this clause is to enable a jurisdiction clause to be applied in favour of a consumer. The clause may either elect a particular court or, more usually, the courts of a particular Contracting State. The court chosen must, for this paragraph to apply, be a court which would not otherwise have had jurisdiction under Articles 13 and 14. The clause must widen the choice available to the plaintiff, and this paragraph is not to be read as limiting the choice.[17] The provision imposes no limitation as to when the jurisdiction clause should have been entered into. By contrast with para-

---

[14] *Partenreederei m.s. "Tilly Russ"* v. *Haven und Vervoerbedrijf Nova N.V. & Goeminne Hout N.V.* [1984] E.C.R. 2417, discussed at para. 21.21 below.
[15] See para. 18.55 above.
[16] Bülow/Böckstiegel/Linke, p. 127.
[17] Bülow/Böckstiegel/Linke, pp. 112, 128.

graph 1, the agreement may,[18] but need not,[19] be made before the dispute arises.

Article 15 affects only the applicability of a jurisdiction agreement, not its validity. So, even if the clause is not expressed to be for the benefit only of the consumer and is not severable, it makes no difference. But it may only be relied on to the extent that it complies with Article 15.

3. "which is entered into by the consumer and the other party to the contract, both of whom are at the time of the conclusion of the contract domiciled or habitually resident in the same Contracting State, and which confers jurisdiction on the courts of that State . . . "

The effect of this paragraph is to allow a consumer and a supplier or lender to agree on the jurisdiction of the courts of their own state, if the law of that state allows them to do so. On its face, the paragraph would appear to state the obvious, but it should be remembered that the paragraph will only apply to derogate from the jurisdiction of courts which would otherwise have jurisdiction under Article 13 and 14, and that the Convention, including this provision will only apply where the case has an international element.[20]

19.41

Full protection of a consumer who moves his domicile to another Contracting State after the conclusion of the contract should enable the consumer to sue in the courts of the state of his new domicile. But it was obviously felt[21] that that was unduly harsh on suppliers and lenders and so, in the interests of economy[22] this provision was included to enable the parties to agree on the courts of a state with which they both had a close connection, whether by domicile or by habitual residence, at the time the contract was made.

If the contract is one which initially fell within sub-paragraph (3) of the first paragraph of Article 13 and the consumer then moves his domicile, the contract will no longer fall within Section 4[23] but the jurisdiction agreement will still be applicable under Article 17. A move by the supplier or lender after the contract is made will not be relevant, because his domicile does not affect the status of a contract under sub-paragraph (3) of the first paragraph of Article 13,

---

[18] *Cf.* Droz, para. 128.
[19] *Cf.* Bülow/Böckstiegel/Linke, p. 112 n. 26.
[20] See paras. 13.10 *et seq.* above.
[21] Jenard, para. A1.152 below.
[22] Bülow/Böckstiegel/Linke, p. 128.
[23] Para. 19.18 above.

nor the court in which the consumer can sue under the first paragraph of Article 14.[24]

19.42   The new reference to the time of the conclusion of the contract is merely a clarification of the former position.[25] The inclusion of a reference to habitual residence is exceptional in the Convention, but is justified in the Jenard Report[26] on grounds of equity and to cater for the case where a person has his domicile and habitual residence in different Contracting States.[27] It also means that where a supplier and consumer have a close connection with a court by way of habitual residence short of domicile, they may still take advantage of this provision. In the context of consumer contracts, it has the additional advantage that it enables jurisdiction, at the option of the parties in a suitable case, to be based on the same criterion as will usually apply to the choice of law once Article 5 of the Obligations Convention[28] comes into effect.

It is not clear whether habitual residence is to be decided according to the same conflicts rules as apply to domicile[29] or whether habitual residence is to be given an independent interpretation. It seems, though, that Article 52 should apply by analogy.[30] Because domicile is to be determined according to Article 52, the reference to habitual residence in Article 15(3) will be particularly relevant in those cases where a fictitious legal domicile applies.[31]

4. " . . . provided that such an agreement is not contrary to the law of that States"

19.43   These words do not require elaboration.

---

[24] Bülow/Böckstiegel/Linke, p. 128.

[25] Jenard, para. A1.152 below; Schlosser, para. 161a (para. A1.455 below); *cf. contra*, Collins, p. 73. Droz's view (para. 135) was that the relevant time was the time when the *jurisdiction* agreement was entered into—usually the time of the contract.

[26] Jenard, para. A1.152 below.

[27] In view of the definition of domicile adopted in the U.K. for the purposes of the Convention (s.41 of the 1982 Act, paras. 44.01 *et seq.* below), the distinction between habitual residence and domicile is likely to be of little if any relevance when the law of a part of the U.K. is to be applied to determine domicile.

[28] Para. A2.44 below. See para. 19.08 above.

[29] Art. 52, para. 31.01 *et seq.* below. That Art. does not expressly refer to habitual residence.

[30] Para. 31.07 below. See also Bülow/Böckstiegel/Linke, pp. 66, 129.

[31] Bülow/Böckstiegel/Linke, p. 128.

EXCLUSIVE JURISDICTION
(Article 16)

SECTION 5

Article 16

The following courts shall have exclusive jurisdiction regardless   20.01
of domicile:

> **1. in proceedings which have as their object rights *in rem***
> **in, or tenancies of, immovable property, the courts of**
> **the Contracting State in which the property is situated;**

2. in proceedings which have as their object the validity of the constitution, the nullity or the dissolution of companies or other legal persons or associations of natural or legal persons, or the decisions of their organs, the courts of the Contracting State in which the company, legal person or association has its seat;
3. in proceedings which have as their object the validity of entries in public registers, the courts of the Contracting State in which the register is kept;
4. in proceedings concerned with the registration or validity of patents, trade marks, designs, or other similar rights required to be deposited or registered, the courts of the Contracting State in which the deposit or registration has been applied for, has taken place or is under the terms of an international convention deemed to have taken place;
5. in proceedings concerned with the enforcement of judgments, the courts of the Contracting State in which the judgment has been or is to be enforced.*

A. INTRODUCTION

1. General note

20.02   The matters referred to in Article 16 are likely to be distinctively and closely connected with particular Contracting States. They are therefore given exceptional treatment and the normal rules of the Convention do not apply to them. The precise nature of that connection is discussed separately in relation to each of the sub-paragraphs, but in each case the connection is sufficiently close to justify giving exclusive jurisdiction to the courts of the particular Contracting State in question.

The interpretation of Article 16 is dependent on the reasons for making jurisdiction exclusive in any given category of case. The European Court of Justice has held that:

" . . . the assignment in the interests of the proper administration of justice, of exclusive jurisdiction to the courts of one Contracting State in accordance with Article 16 of the Convention results in depriving

---

* Jenard, paras. A1.131, A1.153 below; Schlosser, paras. 162–165 (A1.456–A1.458 below); Collins, pp. 77–78; Dashwood/Halcon/White, pp. 29–30, 115–121; Hartley, pp. 63–64; Kaye, pp. 871–883, 892–975, 998–1002; Maxwell, paras. 5.154–5.161; Anton, paras. 7.02–7.06; Droz, paras. 137–146; Weser, paras. 245–249 bis; Bülow/Böckstiegel/Müller, pp. 129–132; Geimer/Schütze, pp. 192–195, 258–259, 307–309, 315–323, 324, 343–345, 1035–1044, 1047; Kropholler, pp. 142–159; Gothot/Holleaux, paras. 140–143; Pocar, pp. 173–180.

the parties of the choice of the forum which would otherwise be theirs and, in certain cases, results in their being brought before a court which is not that of the domicile of any of them. Having regard to that consideration the provisions of Article 16 must not be given a wider interpretation than is required by their objective."[1]

Domicile and nationality not relevant. Article 16 applies regardless of the nationality or domicile of the parties[2] and neither submission to another jurisdiction by the entry of an appearance (Article 18),[3] nor a jurisdiction agreement (Article 17, third paragraph)[4] can found jurisdiction contrary to its terms.[5] If a court accepts jurisdiction in breach of Article 16, its judgment "shall not" be recognised or enforced in another Contracting State: Articles 28 and 34.[6]

Exhaustive nature of the list. Article 16 is an exhaustive catalogue **20.03** of the exclusive jurisdiction provisions in the Convention[7] and it takes precedence over any contrary provisions of national law.[8] If a court is seised of a case which is principally concerned with a matter over which the courts of another Contracting State have exclusive jurisdiction under Article 16, it must decline jurisdiction *of its own motion—i.e.* even if the point is not taken by the defendant, or even if he agrees that the court should have jurisdiction.[9] If, for example, an English court has jurisdiction (even exclusive jurisdiction) over a case as a matter of English law, it must still decline jurisdiction of its own motion if the courts of another Contracting State have exclusive jurisdiction under Article 16. The only circumstances in which that will not apply are where the case *also* comes within the exclusive jurisdiction of the court seised *and* that court is the court first seised.[10]

---

[1] *Sanders* v. *van der Putte* [1977] E.C.R. 2383, at p. 2391, discussed at para. 20.16 below. The exceptional nature of jurisdiction under Art. 16 was also referred to in the European Court's judgment in *A-S Autoteile Service GmbH* v. *Malhé* [1985] E.C.R. 2267, at p. 2277, discussed at para. 20.42 below.
[2] Jenard, paras. A1.131 and A1.153 below; Bülow/Böckstiegel/Müller, p. 130.
[3] Para. 21.83 below.
[4] See para. 21.79 below.
[5] Jenard, para. A1.131 below.
[6] Paras. 27.62 and 28.22 below.
[7] The authors of the Convention considered, but decided against, including two other topics within Art. 16, namely contracts of employment and the exercise of their functions by lawyers and judicial officers (such as bailiffs): Droz, para. 163.
[8] *Duijnstee* v. *Goderbauer*, [1983] E.C.R. 3663, at p. 3675, discussed at para. 20.34 below. See also Droz, para. 137; Bülow/Böckstiegel/Müller, p. 130; *cf. Sanicentral GmbH* v. *Collin* [1979] E.C.R. 3423, discussed at para. 21.29 below.
[9] Art. 19, para. 22.01 below.
[10] Art. 23, para. 23.24 below.

Priority of Article 16. Similarly, if and to the extent that the subject-matter of an action falls both within one of the paragraphs of Article 16 and within one of the other rules of jurisdiction, the provisions of Article 16 are to have priority.[11] This will be of particular relevance where trusts are concerned.[12]

20.04   *Principal and incidental issues.* Proceedings will be subject to the exclusive jurisdiction provisions of Article 16 if their principal subject-matter falls within the Article.[13] In this respect, the wording of the English text should be approached with caution. Paragraphs 1 to 3 refer to proceedings which "have as their object" the subject-matter in question, while paragraphs 4 and 5 refer to proceedings "concerned with" that subject-matter.[14] Other language versions use the same wording for all five paragraphs and make it clear that it is the subject-matter, rather than the purpose, of the proceedings to which reference is made.[15] Even in the English version, the wording does not refer to proceedings which have as their *sole* object, or which are concerned *only* with the topic in question.

If one of the specified topics forms the subject of a preliminary or incidental issue in the proceedings, Article 16 will not apply to make the jurisdiction of the court exclusive. The considerations which require the assignment of exclusive jurisdiction to the courts of the state with which the subject matter of the dispute is connected do not apply where the principal aim of the rights which the action is brought to enforce are of a different nature from those referred to in Article 16.[16] Furthermore, Article 19 requires a court to decline jurisdiction only if the proceedings are "principally" concerned with a matter falling within the exclusive jurisdiction of the courts of another Contracting State.

20.05   *International jurisdiction.* Article 16 is concerned only with international jurisdiction. National law, including its rules of exclusive jurisdiction, will determine local jurisdiction.[17] National law is required to provide a forum for disputes falling within the exclusive

---

[11] Schlosser, para. 120 (para. A1.403 below).

[12] See para. 17.66 above.

[13] Jenard, paras. A1.153 and A1.172 below; Droz, para. 146; Bülow/Böckstiegel/ Müller, p. 131.

[14] See also para. 20.34 below.

[15] French: " . . . *en matière de* . . . "; German: " . . . *zum Gegenstand haben* . . . "; Italian: " . . . *in materia di* . . . ". See also the observation of Advocate General Sir Gordon Slynn in *Rösler* v. *Rottwinkel* [1985] E.C.R. 99 at p. 104.

[16] *Sanders* v. *van der Putte* [1977] E.C.R. 2383, at p. 2391, discussed at para. 20.16 below.

[17] Droz, paras. 144–145.

jurisdiction of its courts. It may do so on a basis different from that
provided by Article 16 (*e.g.* by reference to domicile).[18]

The effect of a jurisdiction agreement on the exclusive jurisdiction provisions is discussed in connection with Article 17.[19]

2. Subject-matter connected with a non-Contracting State

The wording of each of the paragraphs of Article 16 presupposes   **20.06**
that the principal subject-matter of the proceedings is based in, or
connected with, a Contracting State. It does not address the question of what happens if the subject-matter is connected only with a
non-Contracting State.[20] Take, for example, a case in which a person domiciled in England is sued in an English court in proceedings
concerning title to land abroad. If the land is in, say, France, the
English court must decline jurisdiction. But if the land is in, say,
Spain, the case would not appear to fall within Article 16 and the
English court would seem to be obliged to accept jurisdiction under
Article 2. The question is undoubtedly a difficult one, but, for a
number of reasons, it is suggested that to require the English court
to accept jurisdiction in such a case is unsatisfactory in practice and
may be unsound in principle.

If in the above example, the defendant were not domiciled in a
Contracting State, but the jurisdiction of the English court had
been invoked by, say, service in England, the English court would
still decline jurisdiction because the land was situated abroad.[21]
Similar rules exist in the national law of most of the Contracting
States.[22] If the English court were required to accept jurisdiction
over a defendant domiciled in England in such a case, it would
mean that it was affording less protection to a defendant domiciled
in England than it would to a defendant domiciled outside the Con-

---

[18] If by any chance national law should not provide a forum, it has been suggested
(Bülow/Böckstiegel/Müller, p. 131) that Art. 16 should also apply to found local
jurisdiction. *Cf.* the position in the U.K., under Sched. 4 to the 1982 Act,
para. 45.19 below.

[19] Para. 21.79 below.

[20] The question is raised and discussed in some detail by Droz, paras. 165–169.

[21] Dicey and Morris, p. 918; s.30 of the 1982 Act, para. 43.18 below.

[22] Jenard, para. A1.154 below; see para. 20.12 below. A court in the Netherlands
has declined jurisdiction over a case concerning a contract for the sale of land in
Spain, despite a jurisdiction clause giving it jurisdiction: *Mesch Vermögensanlage
GmbH-Emissions K.G.* v. *Orspan S.A.* Ned.Jur. 1978, No. 621, Digest D
I–17.2.—B1 but another court in the Netherlands has accepted jurisdiction over
a case concerning a contract for the sale of land in Portugal, despite a jurisdiction clause (which was not invoked at the outset) in favour of the Portuguese
court: *Scholten* v. *Empresa Turistica Vale do Lobo do Algarve L.d.A.*, Gerechtshof Leeuwarden, Ned.Jur. 1987, p. 3521, [1988] Eur.L.Dig. 163.

tracting States. That is contrary to the intention of the Convention as a whole.[23]

20.07   *Importance of connecting factor.* The purpose of Article 16 is to ensure that courts which have the closest and most real connection with a dispute are alone competent to decide it.[24] It is for that purpose alone that the courts of other Contracting States are required to decline jurisdiction in their favour. No wider or additional purpose is served by excluding the jurisdiction of the other courts. The exclusion of jurisdiction from those other courts is the necessary consequence of giving it to the courts with the closest and most real connection with the dispute. In those circumstances, the purposes of the Convention are not served by requiring other courts to accept jurisdiction over a case with which they have no connection. The use of the word "shall" in Article 2 can be seen as no more than a reflection of the principle that the Convention provides uniform rules of jurisdiction applicable throughout the Community and the fact that the courts of the State of a defendant's domicile are courts with a sufficiently close connection (the domicile) with the dispute to justify their having jurisdiction. While the jurisdiction of those courts is generally compulsory, it can only be compulsory to the extent that that serves the purposes of the Convention as a whole.[25] The same reasoning applies to courts which would have jurisdiction under one or more of the other ordinary rules.[26] In exceptional cases, it is suggested, the compulsory nature of the jurisdictional rules may be departed from, but the exceptions must be ones which are uniformly applicable across the Contracting States as a whole.

20.08   It is submitted that such an exception arises,[27] and courts of Contracting States which would have jurisdiction under one of the ordinary rules of jurisdiction may decline to exercise it, if the following conditions are fulfilled:

(1) if the subject-matter of the case is one falling with Article 16;

(2) if the connection envisaged by Article 16 exists, and exists only, with a non-Contracting State; and

---

[23] Droz, para. 168; see Jenard, para. A1.3 below, and paras. 13.12 and 13.15 above.

[24] See *Sanders* v. *van der Putte* [1977] E.C.R. 2383 at p. 2390, para. 20.16 below.

[25] As to the compulsory nature of the Convention's rules, see paras. 1.37 *et seq.*, 15.02 and 16.06 above.

[26] Arts. 5 to 15, 17 and 18.

[27] Droz, para. 168; *semble*, Bülow/Böckstiegel/Müller, pp. 131–132; *dubitante*, Collins, p. 80; Hartley, pp. 66, 78–80; Weser, para. 264. For a further limited exception, see para. 20.23 below.

(3) if the law of that court permits it to decline jurisdiction over the case.[28]

3. Interpretation

The Convention provides no definition of the various concepts referred to in Article 16 and there is some debate as to whether they are to be the subject of an independent interpretation.[29] The European Court of Justice has ruled that:

> "the term 'proceedings concerned with the registration or validity of patents' contained in Article 16(4) must be regarded as an independent concept intended to have uniform application in all the Contracting States."[30]

While that decision is confined to the terms of Article 16(4), there is no reason to suppose that the same approach will not be adopted in relation to the various other concepts in Article 16. In relation to Article 16(5), without expressly referring to the fact that it was doing so, the European Court has given an independent interpretation to "proceedings concerned with the enforcement of judgments."[31] There remains the possibility, though, that the European Court will still permit an interpretation of some of the concepts in Article 16 (especially, perhaps, in relation to immovable property) otherwise than by a purely uniform approach. The question at least remains open for argument in relation to the other concepts in Article 16 and it may well be that different considerations apply in respect of each of the separate categories of subject-matter listed in Article 16.

Application of lex situs; function of European Court. Both Droz[32] and, in the context of immovable property, the Schlosser Report[33] suggest that the various concepts in Article 16 should be decided by reference to the *lex situs*.[34] The application of the *lex situs* in the con-

20.09

20.10

---

[28] *Cf.* Maxwell, para. 5.160: "We think it would be reasonable to proceed on the basis that it is competent for us to adopt such rules of jurisdiction as we think fit in all cases where the matter to which the action relates is situated outside the Contracting States."

[29] The debate is summarised below. As to an "independent interpretation", see paras. 13.19 *et seq.* above.

[30] *Duijnstee* v. *Goderbauer* [1983] E.C.R. 3663, at p. 3679, discussed at para. 20.34 below.

[31] *A-S Autoteile Service GmbH* v. *Malhé* [1985] E.C.R. 2267, discussed at para. 20.42 below.

[32] Droz, para. 168.

[33] Schlosser, para. 168, para. A1.461 below.

[34] The question whether the term "tenancy" should be interpreted according to the *lex situs* or should be given an independent interpretation was considered by Advocate General Sir Gordon Slynn in *Rösler* v. *Rottwinkel* [1985] E.C.R. 99 at p. 104 (discussed at para. 20.18 below), but without expressing a preference.

text of Article 16 would be just as effective in avoiding conflicts of jurisdiction as the application of uniform interpretations where there is a choice of jurisdiction. It would, admittedly, involve reading Article 16 as providing not only uniform jurisdictional rules, but also a uniform conflicts rule (for the purposes of deciding jurisdiction, not on the substance of the dispute). That is something which is not beyond the function of the Convention, as Articles 52 and 53 illustrate. The view expressed in Bülow/Böckstiegel[35] also favours the application of the *lex situs*, but would retain for the European Court questions which might arise in this context concerning the overall scope of the Convention and of Article 16. On the other hand, a more recent view expressed by Collins[36] is in favour of a uniform interpretation. Many of the above views were expressed before the European Court of Justice had so strongly developed its jurisprudence on the Convention in favour of uniform interpretation.

Whether or not an independent interpretation is to be given to some or all of the concepts in Article 16, it is nonetheless clearly sensible and in accordance with the purposes of the Convention that the European Court should retain control over the interpretation of the broad limits of the concepts in Article 16. It would then be able to maintain consistency of approach between the Contracting States, to see that the scope of the Convention was not exceeded and to ensure that national courts were not arrogating to themselves exclusive jurisdictions not justified by the scope and purpose of the Convention.

Article 16(1)

20.11 **The following courts shall have exclusive jurisdiction, regardless of domicile:**

1. **in proceedings which have as their object rights *in rem* in, or tenancies of, immovable property, the courts of the Contracting State in which the property is situated;***

---

[35] Bülow/Böckstiegel/Müller, pp. 132–133.

[36] Collins, pp. 79, 82n.

* Jenard, paras. A1.154–A1.157 below; Schlosser, paras. 162–172 (paras. A1.456–A1.466 below); Collins, pp. 78–80; Dashwood/Halcon/White, pp. 29–30, 115–118; Hartley, pp. 64–66; Kaye, pp. 871–883, 892–933, 964–965, 969–971, 973, 998–999; Maxwell, paras. 5.162–5.165; Anton, paras. 7.07–7.11; Droz, paras. 137–153; Weser, paras. 245–251; Bülow/Böckstiegel/Müller, pp. 132–134; Geimer/Schütze, pp. 648–694; Kropholler, pp. 142–150; Gothot/Holleaux, paras. 144–150; Pocar, pp. 173–180.

B. Paragraph (1): Immovable Property

1. General note

The reasons for this head of exclusive jurisdiction are threefold:[37] **20.12**

(1) Actions concerning rights *in rem* in land frequently require checks, assessments and expert investigations which must be carried out on the spot.[38] Questions of both fact and law may turn on local customs, which can only properly be determined locally and it may be necessary to interpret or make entries in land registers,[39] thereby overlapping with Article 16(3).[40]

(2) Where the action concerns a tenancy of immovable property, the applicable law is likely to be particularly specialised and to contain provisions, generally of a mandatory character, governing the use of the property, such as legislation controlling the level of rents and protecting the rights of tenants.[41] Moreover, the jurisdiction may be assigned, as a matter of national law, to a general tribunal with specialist expertise.[42]

(3) Under the law of some Contracting States, local jurisdiction is not only exclusively assigned to the courts for the place where the land is situated, but this assignment is regarded as a matter of public policy. If the courts of other Contracting States had been able to exercise jurisdiction, the judgment would have been refused recognition and enforcement[43] in the State where the land was situated, which would have been contrary to the principle of free movement of judgments.[44]

The question whether "rights *in rem*," "tenancies" and "immovable property" are independent concepts for the purposes of the Convention remains to be decided by the European Court of Justice. It is suggested that they probably are.[45]

---

[37] As noted at para. 20.02 above, these reasons are relevant to the scope of Art. 16(1).

[38] *Sanders* v. *van der Putte* [1977] E.C.R. 2383, at pp. 2390–2391, discussed at para. 20.16 below; *Rösler* v. *Rottwinkel* [1985] E.C.R. 99, at p. 126, discussed at para. 20.18 below; *Scherrens* v. *Maenhout*, case 158/87, decision of July 6, 1988 (para. 10), *The Times*, September 5, 1988, discussed at para. 20.23 below; Jenard, para. A1.157 below.

[39] Jenard, *loc. cit.*

[40] Para. 20.30 below.

[41] *Rösler* v. *Rottwinkel, loc. cit.*; *Scherrens* v. *Maenhout, loc. cit.* (para. 9).

[42] *Sanders* v. *van der Putte, loc. cit.*; Bülow/Böckstiegel/Müller, p. 134.

[43] Arts. 27(1) and 34, second para., paras. 27.13 and 28.22 below.

[44] Jenard, para. A1.156.

[45] See paras. 20.09 to 20.10 above.

2. " . . . rights *in rem* . . . "

20.13   What constitutes a right *in rem* is more readily apparent in civil law than in common law systems, but equitable rights in land may also be rights *in rem*,[46] although the extent to which rights *in rem* held on trust are the "object" of proceedings concerning the trust may sometimes prove difficult to determine.[47] An action brought to enforce contractual rights of a personal nature affecting immovable property may well fall outside Article 16(1), unless the contract in question is a contract of tenancy. Contracts of tenancy give rise to special problems which are discussed below. Even outside the context of tenancies, though, the purpose of Article 16(1) in assigning jurisdiction to the courts of the state where the property is situated may sometimes be so predominant as to intrude into the field of personal rights. It would seem by analogy with the European Court's reasoning in *Rösler* v. *Rottwinkel*[48] that the answer may depend on how directly or indirectly the personal rights in question relate to the ownership of property.

20.14   *Personal rights.* Nonetheless, an action to enforce purely personal rights will probably fall outside the scope of Article 16(1), even in countries where the law does not readily distinguish between a contract and a conveyance.[49] So, for example, an action against a French domiciliary for specific performance of a contract to sell land in England, or for damages for breach of such a contract, would probably be regarded in the context of the Convention as an action to enforce personal rights and as not falling within Article 16.[50] In the absence of a jurisdiction agreement, the action could be brought in England under Article 5(1) (as the place of performance of the "obligation in question")[51] or in France under Article 2.

20.15   *Rights in movables.* A right *in rem* is not necessarily a right in immovable property.[52] For example, rights to arrest a ship,[53] unpaid vendors' liens or rights to trace money may be rights *in rem* quite unrelated to immovable property. Less obviously, rights in respect of immovable property are not necessarily rights *in rem*. For

---

[46] Schlosser, para. 172 (paras. A1.465–A1.466 below); Geimer/Schütze, p. 671.
[47] See para. 17.06 above.
[48] [1985] E.C.R. 99, at pp. 127–128 (paras. 28 and 29), discussed at para. 20.18 below.
[49] *e.g.*, France, Belgium and Italy: Schlosser, para. 171 (para. A1.464 below).
[50] Schlosser, para. 172 (para. A1.466 below); Collins, p. 79; Bülow/Böckstiegel/ Müller, p. 133.
[51] See paras. 17.18 *et seq.* above.
[52] Geimer/Schütze, pp. 608 *et seq.*
[53] See para. 20.23, n. 70 below.

example, a right to rent may be a right *in personam* and may not fall within Article 16(1).[53a]

3. " . . . tenancies . . . "

The Sanders case. The term "tenancies of immovable property" **20.16** has been considered by the European Court of Justice in two cases. The first, *Sanders* v. *van der Putte*[54] concerned a flower shop in Wuppertal in Germany run by van der Putte in premises which he leased from an insurance company. His case was that he entered into an agreement with Sanders, whereby Sanders agreed to take over the running of the business, to pay to van der Putte a sum in respect of goodwill and a monthly rent and, further, to pay the rent for the premises to the insurance company. Both Sanders and van der Putte were domiciled in Arnhem in Holland. Sanders refused to start running the business and denied the existence of the agreement, so van der Putte started proceedings against him in the Netherlands. On appeal, Sanders took the point that the Dutch court had no jurisdiction, because the proceedings related to a tenancy of immovable property in Germany. The argument was rejected on the ground that in the agreement in question the emphasis fell less on the rent or lease of immovable property than on the business as such. Sanders appealed again and the *Hoge Raad* referred (*inter alia*) the following question to the European Court:

> "Must 'tenancies of immovable property' within the meaning of Article 16 down to the end of sub-paragraph (1) of the Convention also include an agreement to rent under a usufructuary lease a retail business carried on in immovable property rented from a third party by the lessor?"

The European Court answered the question by ruling[55] that it **20.17** must not be interpreted as including such an agreement, and said this:

> "As regards the matters listed under sub-paragraphs (2), (3), (4) and (5) of [Article 16] it is clear that the courts which are given exclusive jurisdiction are those which are best placed to deal with the disputes in question.
> The same applies to the assignment of exclusive jurisdiction to the courts of the Contracting State in which the property is situated in matters relating to right *in rem* in, or tenancies of, immovable property.
> In fact, actions concerning rights *in rem* in immovable property are

---

[53a] See, further, paras. 20.20 and 20.22 below.
[54] [1977] E.C.R. 2383.
[55] [1977] E.C.R. 2383, at p. 2392.

to be judged according to the rules of the State in which the immovable property is situated since the disputes which arise result frequently in checks, inquiries and expert assessments which must be carried out on the spot, with the result that the assignment of exclusive jurisdiction satisfies the need for the proper administration of justice.

Tenancies of immovable property are generally covered by special rules and it is preferable, in the light of their complexity, that they be applied only by the courts of the States in which they are in force.

The foregoing considerations explain the assignment of exclusive jurisdiction to the courts of the State in which the immovable property is situated in the case of disputes relating to tenancies of immovable property properly so-called, that is to say, in particular, disputes between lessors and tenants as to the existence or interpretation of leases or to compensation for damage caused by the tenant and to giving up possession of the premises.

The same considerations do not apply where the principal aim of the agreement is of a different nature, in particular, where it concerns the operation of a business . . . "[56]

A further question referred by the *Hoge Raad* was whether the fact that Sanders disputed the existence of the agreement made any difference to the Court's answer. The Court ruled that it did not.[57] In the light of the European Court's ruling, the *Hoge Raad* decided that the Dutch court had jurisdiction over the proceedings.[58]

20.18   *The Rösler case.* The second case was *Rösler* v. *Rottwinkel*[59] which concerned an agreement whereby Mr. Rottwinkel agreed to let part of his holiday villa in Italy to Mr. Rösler for three weeks. Both parties were domiciled in Germany and the agreement provided for the payment of rent and certain charges, including the costs of cleaning, gas, water, electricity and heating, and provided that no more than four people were to stay overnight. The agreement stipulated that it was subject to German law. Disputes arose between the parties and Mr. Rottwinkel brought an action against Mr. Rösler in the *Landgericht* Berlin, which declined jurisdiction on the basis of Article 16(1). That decision was reversed on appeal and, following Mr. Rösler's further appeal to the *Bundesgerichtshof*, two questions were referred to the European Court of Justice.

---

[56] [1977] E.C.R. 2383, at p. 2390–2391 (paras. 11–16). The Court followed the Jenard Report, para. A1.157 below, in a number of respects in this judgment.
[57] See also *Effer S.p.A.* v. *Kantner* [1982] E.C.R. 825, discussed at para. 17.08 above.
[58] Digest D I–16.1—B3.
[59] [1985] E.C.R. 99. For a highly critical assessment of this decision, see Goudie, "Spoilt Holidays—Where to sue" (1985) 135 N.L.J. 852.

The first question concerned the applicability of Article 16(1) to short-term holiday lettings and drew attention to the agreement that German law was to apply. The Schlosser Report[60] had suggested that the underlying principle of Article 16 did not require its application to short-term agreements for the use and occupation of holiday accommodation. Nonetheless, the European Court was clearly concerned that if exceptions were to be allowed in the interpretation of Article 16(1), the Convention's purpose in assigning jurisdiction in a certain and predictable way would be endangered. It therefore held that the provision applied to all tenancies of immovable property irrespective of their special characteristics.[61] Its ruling was in these terms:

> "Article 16(1) of the Convention applies to all lettings of immovable property, even for a short term and even where they relate only to the use and occupation of a holiday home."[62]

The second question referred to the European Court was **20.19** whether, if Article 16(1) were applicable, it applied to actions for damages for breach of the lease, particularly for loss of holiday enjoyment and for the recovery of incidental charges payable under the lease. In answering the question, though, the European Court considered a wider range of topics which might be covered by Article 16(1) and, noting that the judgment in *Sanders* v. *van der Putte* had said that "proceedings which have as their object . . . tenancies of immovable property" covered disputes between landlords and tenants as to the existence or the interpretation of leases or to compensation for damage caused by the tenant, the Court went on to say that that list was not exhaustive.[63]

Rent. One particular point which should be noted is that the **20.20** European Court dealt in the *Rösler* decision with the question of rent, which had remained unclear in the light of *Sanders* v. *van der Putte*,[64] and which had been a topic of some controversy; national courts had reached different and conflicting decisions, and com-

---

[60] Schlosser, para. 164 (para. A1.457 below).
[61] [1985] E.C.R. 99, at p. 127 (para. 24).
[62] The Opinion of Advocate General Sir Gordon Slynn was to the same effect. He recognised the force of the arguments that short holiday lettings of furnished property should not be the exclusive province of the courts of the *situs*, but observed that the question was not what the Contracting States could have agreed, but what they did agree. He went on to consider whether a number of distinctions between different types of lettings could be drawn, but rejected them all: [1985] E.C.R. 99, at pp. 103–104.
[63] [1985] E.C.R. 99, at p. 127 (para. 26).
[64] Collins, p. 80.

mentators differed on the interpretation of Article 16(1).[65] It held that disputes concerning the payment of rent do fall within the exclusive jurisdiction:

> "It would in fact be contrary to one of the aims of the provision in question, namely the correct application of national legislation on tenancies, to exclude from that exclusive jurisdiction disputes which are, in some Member States at least, governed by special legislation, such as the Italian "fair rent" legislation."[66]

The Court went on briefly to consider a number of other matters which might fall within Article 16(1), before ruling on the second question in these terms:

> "All disputes concerning the obligations of the landlord or of the tenant under a tenancy, in particular those concerning the existence of tenancies or the interpretation of the terms thereof, their duration, the giving up of possession to the landlord, the repairing of damage caused by the tenant or the recovery of rent or incidental charges payable by the tenant, such as charges for the consumption of water, gas and electricity, fall within the exclusive jurisdiction conferred by Article 16(1) of the Convention on the courts of the State in which the property is situated. On the other hand, disputes which are only indirectly related to the use of the property let, such as those concerning the loss of holiday enjoyment and travel expenses, do not fall within the exclusive jurisdiction conferred by that Article."[67]

20.21 *Relationship of landlord and tenant.* It seems, therefore, that the question of whether particular rights and obligations fall within the scope of Article 16(1), where they arise in the context of a tenancy, depends not on whether they are rights *in rem* or personal rights,

---

[65] The original authors of the Convention thought that it did not cover actions to recover rent (Jenard, para. A1.157 below), but the committee which negotiated the 1978 Accession Convention could not agree (Schlosser, para. 164, para. A1.457 below). The preponderance of opinion had been in favour of such actions being included within Art. 16(1). In both cases to come before the European Court under this Article, the Advocates General have taken the view that such actions did fall within Art. 16(1) and had cited with approval the view taken by Droz to that effect (paras. 150–153): Advocate General Mayras in *Sanders* v. *van der Putte*, [1977] E.C.R. 2383, at pp. 2397–2400 and Advocate General Sir Gordon Slynn in *Rösler* v. *Rottwinkel*, [1985] E.C.R. 99, at p. 107. The same view was taken by Bülow/Böckstiegel/Müller, p. 134 and several decisions of German courts were to the same effect: Landgericht Aachen, October 24, 1975, case 5 S 339/75, N.J.W. 1976, p. 487, Digest D I–16.1—B1; Oberlandesgericht Frankfurt-am-Main, case 13 U 104/83, May 9, 1984, N.J.W. 1984, p. 2045, Digest D I–16.1—B8; Amtsgericht Offenbach, December 16, 1981, N.J.W. 1982, p. 2735, Digest D I–16.1—B8n. A decision the other way was *Société Civile Immobilière de Bourgogne* v. *Raat*, Arrondissementsrechtbank Amsterdam, November 25, 1975, Digest D I–16.1—B2.

[66] [1985] E.C.R. 99, at p. 127 (para. 26).

[67] [1985] E.C.R. 99 at p. 129.

but on the extent to which they arise directly from the relationship of landlord and tenant.[68] So for example, it may be that an action by a travel agent against a holiday-maker for payment for use and occupation of a holiday home would not be regarded as an action for rent if the holiday-maker's contract was not directly with the owner of the home.[69]

4. " . . . immovable property . . . "

The distinction between movables and immovables is familiar to continental lawyers and is known to English private international law, but it must be stressed that the distinction is different from the common law distinction between realty and personalty.[70] For discussion of this important topic, reference should be made to specialist works.[71]

20.22

5. " . . . the Contracting State in which the property is situated"

The Scherrens case. It will normally be entirely clear in which Contracting State the property is situated and these words will rarely present any problem. Cases may arise, however, in which the dispute concerns immovable property in more than one Contracting State. The European Court considered such a dispute in *Scherrens* v. *Maenhout*.[71a] Mr. Scherrens claimed to be the tenant, under a single lease, of farming land situated, as to twelve hectares, in the Netherlands and, as to five hectares, some seven kilometers away in Belgium. His claim was disputed by his mother-in-law, Mrs. Maenhout, and others, the lessors. Mr. Scherrens brought separate proceedings in Belgium and in the Netherlands in respect of the separate parcels of land; and the Dutch court, the *Gerechtshof* in Arnhem, referred to the European Court the question whether in such a case the courts of each state had exclusive jurisdiction over the land situated in that state. The European Court ruled that that was so.

20.23

The Court's judgment, however, did admit the possibility that a case might display special features such as to require an exception

---

[68] In *Sanders* v. *van der Putte*, Advocate General Mayras had urged that the wording of the Convention was wide enough to cover rights *in personam* if they related to tenancies: [1977] E.C.R. 2383, at p. 2396, but in that case the Court had not referred to the point.

[69] Landgericht Frankfurt-am-Main, case 2/24 S 28/82, May 10, 1982, N.J.W. 1982, p. 1949, Digest D I–16.1—B7n.

[70] Geimer suggests that publicly-registered ships and aircraft (although anything but "immovable") should be included in an independent interpretation of "immovable property" for the purposes of Art. 16(1): Geimer/Schütze, p. 667.

[71] Dicey and Morris, pp. 899–907; Cheshire and North, pp. 771–776.

[71a] Case 158/87, decision of July 6, 1988, *The Times*, September 5, 1988.

to the strict application of that general rule of exclusive jurisdiction. The Court said that this might occur where, for example, immovable property in one Contracting State was adjacent to land in another Contracting State, but where the property was almost entirely situated in one of those states. In such circumstances, it held, it might be appropriate to treat the property as a single unit and regard it for jurisdictional purposes as being entirely situated in one of those states.[71b] In the case before it, the Court did not consider that such special features were present.

6. Actions for Damages

20.24   The Working Party which negotiated the 1978 Convention found no difficulty in saying that actions for damages based on infringements of rights *in rem*, or damage to property in which rights *in rem* exist, did not fall within Article 16(1). They took that view because the existence and content of rights *in rem* in such actions, they said, were of marginal significance.[72] It is suggested that the view is an oversimplification. If the action concerns trespass or some other tort to land by a stranger, the view is probably correct.[73] But if the action concerns such matters as damage caused by a tenant, that is clearly within Article 16(1).[74] It remains to be seen where the line is drawn.

7. Trusts and rights in property arising out of a matrimonial relationship

20.25   *Trusts.* As the Schlosser Report points out,[75] the provisions of Article 16 take priority over the provisions of Article 5(6)[76] (which enables a settlor, trustee or beneficiary of certain trusts to be sued in the courts of the Contracting State where the trust is domiciled, if that is different from the state of the defendant's domicile)[77], but

---

[71b] *Ibid.*, para. 14.

[72] Schlosser, para. 163 (para. A1.456 below).

[73] The former rule of English law (*British South Africa Co.* v. *Companhia de Moçambique* [1893] A.C. 602; *Hesperides Hotels Ltd.* v. *Aegean Turkish Holidays Ltd.* [1979] A.C. 508) that an English court had no jurisdiction over actions for trespass to foreign land has been abrogated by s.30 of the 1982 Act: see para. 43.18 below.

[74] *Sanders* v. *van der Putte* [1977] E.C.R. 2383, at p. 2391 (para. 15), discussed at para. 20.16 above; *Rösler* v. *Rottwinkel* [1985] E.C.R. 99, 129, discussed at para. 20.20 above.

[75] Schlosser, para. 120 (para. A1.403 below).

[76] Para. 17.65 above.

[77] See further, para. 31.32 below.

there may be cases which concern trust property, which do not fall within Article 16.

Matrimonial property. Article 1, by sub-paragraph (1) of the second paragraph, excludes rights in property arising out of a matrimonial relationship altogether from the scope of the Convention and the extent of the exclusion is discussed in the commentary to that Article.[78] To the extent that such rights are not excluded, and are rights *in rem* in immovable property, they fall within this paragraph.

Article 16(2)

[The following courts shall have exclusive jurisdiction, regard- 20.26
less of domicile:]

2. **in proceedings which have as their object the validity of the constitution, the nullity or the dissolution of companies or other legal persons or associations of natural or legal persons, or the decisions of their organs, the courts of the Contracting State in which the company, legal person or association has its seat*;**

C. Paragraph (2): Corporations and Associations

1. General note

The reason for giving exclusive jurisdiction over these matters to 20.27 the courts of the state where the company or association has its seat is to avoid conflicting judgments being given as regards the existence of a company or association or as regards the validity of the decisions of its organs. It is in that state that information about the company or association will have been notified and made public.[79]

The dissolution of insolvent companies is expressly excluded from the scope of the Convention by sub-paragraph (2) of the

---

[78] Paras. 14.20 *et seq.* above.
* Jenard, paras. A1.153, A1.158 below; Schlosser, paras. 55–59; 162–165 (paras. A1.343–A1.347, A1.456–A1.458 below); Collins, pp. 42, 77–78, 80–82; Dashwood/Halcon/White, pp. 29–30, 118–119; Hartley, pp. 37–38, 66–67; Kaye, pp. 871–883, 933–949, 965–968, 972, 974, 999; Maxwell, paras. 5.166–5.170; Anton, paras. 7.12–7.17; Droz, paras. 137–146, 154–155; Weser, paras. 245–249, 252; Bülow/Böckstiegel/Müller, pp. 130–132, 135–136; Geimer/Schütze, pp. 695–763; Kropholler, pp. 142–145, 151–153; Gothot/Holleaux, paras. 151–153; Pocar, pp. 173–180.
[79] Jenard, para. A1.158 below.

second paragraph of Article 1,[80] whether or not the insolvency forms the formal basis of the dissolution. Article 16(2) does cover, though, the dissolution of solvent companies.

2. " . . . companies or other legal persons or associations of natural or legal persons . . . "

20.28   In English law, companies are always legal persons, but this is not necessarily the case in the laws of other Contracting States.[81] It is perhaps for this reason that the French, German, Italian, Dutch and Danish language versions do not refer to "companies or *other* legal persons" and do not include reference to "associations of natural or legal persons," but merely refer to "companies or legal persons." For example, the German *offene Handelsgesellschaft* is a company without legal personality[82] and is closely akin to a partnership in English law.[83] The Schlosser Report[84] says that partnerships are envisaged by Article 16(2) and this should present no difficulty in the case of formally constituted partnerships.[85] The question is perhaps more difficult where the partnership arises incidentally as a matter of law, where there is no formal partnership agreement.[86] This may be beyond the intended scope of Article 16(2).

Similarly, associations[87] may be more or less formal in character. The less formally they are constituted, the less likely they are to fall within Article 16(2). Legal persons which are the creation of public, rather than private, law seem to fall within the definition,[88] but it is hard to see how any of the questions referred to in Article 16(2)

---

[80] Paras. 14.26 *et seq.* above.

[81] Various forms of company, partnership and association capable of existing under the law of each of the Contracting States are described below in chaps. 48 to 58, at para. 73.

[82] Jenard, para. A1.246 below; Bülow/Böckstiegel/Müller, p. 135.

[83] Schlosser, para. 55 (para. A1.343 below), n. 14; Scottish partnerships are corporations within the meaning of the 1982 Act: s.50, para. 44.45 below.

[84] Schlosser, para. 162 (para. A1.456 below).

[85] *Cf.* Collins, pp. 42, 81.

[86] *e.g.*, as a matter of English law, a partnership arises by reason of persons "carrying on business in common with a view to profit": Partnership Act 1890, s.1(1).

[87] As a matter of U.K. law, s.50 of the 1982 Act (para. 44.45 below) defines "association," unless the context otherwise requires, as "an unincorporated body of persons"—a definition which may be wide enough to cover a partnership.

[88] *Cf.* Art. 58 of the EEC Treaty, which expressly refers to legal persons governed by public law. That provision excludes legal persons which are non-profit making, but that exclusion would not be apt for the purposes of the 1968 Convention.

could, in relation to public law legal persons, be "civil and commercial matters."[89]

3. " . . . the courts of the Contracting state where the company, legal person or association has its seat"

Article 53[90] provides rules for determining which law is to apply **20.29** in deciding where a company has its seat.[91] The application of those rules is capable of giving rise to a situation in which the courts of more than one Contracting State can legitimately claim that a company's seat is within its territory. If that happens, it seems that the plaintiff may choose where to bring his action.[92] Once he has chosen and started proceedings in one Contracting State, Article 23 will apply to keep him to his election,[93] although the recognition of judgments in these circumstances may give rise to difficulties.[94]

Article 16(3)

[The following courts shall have exclusive jurisdiction, regard- **20.30** less of domicile:]

    3. in proceedings which have as their object the validity of entries in public registers, the courts of the Contracting State in which the register is kept*;

D. PARAGRAPH (3): PUBLIC REGISTERS

The reasons for this head of exclusive jurisdiction appear to be to **20.31** ensure that the court having jurisdiction is familiar with the formal legal requirements for the validity of an entry and to secure ease of access to the register.

---

[89] See paras. 14.08 *et seq.* above.
[90] Para. 31.23 below.
[91] In the U.K., s.43 of the 1982 Act (para. 44.20 below) makes special provision for the purposes of Art. 16(2) for determining the seat of a corporation or association.
[92] Schlosser, para. 162 (para. A1.456 below).
[93] Para. 23.24 below. Conflicts of exclusive jurisdiction are discussed more fully in the commentary on Arts. 19, 23 and 28.
[94] See paras. 31.29 *et seq.* below.
* Jenard, paras. A1.153, A1.159 below; Schlosser, paras. 162–165 (paras. A1.456–A1.458 below); Collins, pp. 77–78, 82; Dashwood/Halcon/ White, p. 29; Hartley, p. 67; Kaye, pp. 871–883, 949–951, 968–969, 972–974, 1002; Maxwell, para. 5.171; Anton, para. 7.18; Droz, paras. 137–146, 156; Weser, paras. 245–249, 253; Bülow/Böckstiegel/Müller, pp. 130–132, 136; Geimer/Schütze, pp. 771–772; Kropholler, pp. 142–145, 153; Gothot/Holleaux, para. 154; Pocar, pp. 173–180.

The provision covers entries in any public register.[95] The paragraph refers to the *validity* of entries in the register. The comment in the Jenard Report[96] that it also applies to the effects of such entries is not supported by the wording and, it is submitted, is too wide.[97] The formal legal requirements necessary for an entry's validity justify an exclusive jurisdiction, but the effects of the entry may equally well be judged by other courts.[98] For example, the liability of an individual member of a German *Kommanditgesellschaft* might be dependant upon an entry in a German commercial register, and might be the only substantial issue in third-party proceedings,[99] where an action has been brought in a normal contractual dispute against another member, in the courts for the place of the obligation in question.[1]

Article 16(4)

20.32   [The following courts shall have exclusive jurisdiction, regardless of domicile:]

4. in proceedings concerned with the registration or validity of patents, trade marks, designs, or other similar rights required to be deposited or registered, the courts of the Contracting State in which the deposit or registration has been applied for, has taken place or is under the terms of an international convention deemed to have taken place*;

---

[95] Maxwell, para. 5.171 regards the meaning of this term as far from clear. Jenard, para. A1.159 below, refers to land registers, land charges registers and commercial registers. In England, the most obvious application of Art. 16(3) will be in relation to the various land registers, but as questions of the validity of entries in them usually concern rights *in rem* in immovable property, they would anyway usually fall within Art. 16(1) (Collins, p. 82). Art. 16(3) would seem also to apply to the companies register (which might well come within Art. 16(2) as well) and to various other registers.

[96] Jenard, para. A1.159 below.

[97] Bülow/Böckstiegel/Müller, p. 136.

[98] *Ibid.*

[99] Art. 6(2), para. 17.82 above.

[1] Art. 5(1), para. 17.02 above.

* Jenard, paras. A.153, A1.160–A1.161 below; Schlosser, paras. 162–5, 173 (paras. A1.456–A1.458, A1.467 below); Collins, pp. 77–78, 82–83; Dashwood/Halcon/White, pp. 29–30, 119–120; Hartley, pp. 67–68; Kaye, pp. 871–883, 951–955, 969, 973, 975, 1002; Droz, paras. 137–146, 157–161; Weser, paras. 245–9, 254–255; Bülow/Böckstiegel/Müller, pp. 130–132, 137–139; Geimer/Schütze, pp. 773–812; Kropholler, pp. 142–145, 154–159; Gothot/Holleaux, paras. 155–157; Pocar, pp. 173–180.

E. Paragraph (4): Intellectual Property

1. General note

Exclusive jurisdiction is assigned by this paragraph in respect of   **20.33**
certain actions concerned with intellectual property rights. Jenard[2]
explains the reasons for this head of exclusive jurisdiction as being
that the grant of a national patent is an exercise of national sovereignty. The same reasoning presumably applies to the other rights
covered by the paragraph. In practice, many cases falling within
this paragraph will also fall within Article 16(3).

The only actions covered by this paragraph are those concerned
with the registration or validity of the rights[3] and, in order to fall
within Article 16(4) at all, the question concerning registration or
validity must probably be sufficiently important for the proceedings
to have that question "as their object."[4] Other actions, such as
those for infringement, or passing off, or actions concerned with
licence agreements,[5] do not fall within Article 16(4),[6] but will normally be governed by the other provisions of the Convention. But
where, for example, a question of validity arises in an action for
infringement of a foreign patent or similar right, the court will have
to decide whether the action is "principally" concerned with the
validity of the patent or other right in deciding whether to decline
jurisdiction.[7]

**2. " . . . proceedings concerned with the registration or validity
of patents . . . "**

As has been observed, the English language version of Article   **20.34**
16(4)[8] refers to "proceedings *concerned with,* . . . " rather than "proceedings which have as their object . . . " the particular subject-
matter, but the two different wordings have the same meaning.

---

[2] Jenard, para. A1.160 below.

[3] It is not clear whether the term "registration or validity" extends to a question of
jurisdiction to determine the right to a patent, to the extent that it does not come
within an international convention: Maxwell, para. 5.172.

[4] Bülow/Böckstiegel/Müller, p. 137; see the next para.

[5] *S.A. des Etablissements Salik et S.A. Diffusal* v. *S.A. J. Esterel,* Cour d'Appel,
Paris, Rev. critique 1982, p. 135; Digest D I–16.4—B2.

[6] Jenard, para. A1.160 below (cited with approval by the European Court in
Duijnstee v. *Goderbauer* [1983] E.C.R. 3663 at p. 3679: see below); Collins,
p. 83; Maxwell, para. 5.173; Bülow/Böckstiegel/Müller, p. 138.

[7] See para. 20.04 above and Art. 19, para. 22.01 below. See also *Frigomat S.a.s.*
v. *Carpigiani,* Corte d'Appello, Milan, Foro pad. 1979, I, Col. 213, Digest D
I–16.4—B1; and *J. A. Motte* v. *Tecno S.p.A.,* Riv.dir.int.priv.proc. 1981,
p. 913, Digest D I–16.4—B3. (The latter case became principally concerned
with the validity of a patent by reason of the *defendant's* allegations).

[8] The same applies to Art. 16(5).

Duijnstee v. *Goderbauer*. The European Court has considered Article 16(4) in *Duijnstee* v. *Goderbauer*.[9] The case arose in the winding-up of a Dutch company, by way of cross-summonses between the liquidator, Mr. Duijnstee, and a former director, Mr. Goderbauer. It concerned a dispute between them as to their respective rights to patent applications in 22 countries (including certain Contracting States) in connection with an invention made by Mr. Goderbauer when he was an employee of the company. Mr. Duijnstee's claim was for an injunction ordering the transfer of patents to him by Mr. Goderbauer and the latter's claim was that he had a lien over any patents which were the property of the insolvent company. At first instance, both claims were dismissed and Mr. Duijnstee appealed to the *Hoge Raad*, which expressed doubts about its jurisdiction in the light of Article 16(4) and referred a number of questions to the European Court.[10]

20.35   As has already been observed,[11] the European Court held that the term "proceedings concerned with the registration or validity of patents" must be given an independent interpretation.[12] As a result of that ruling, the Court had to define those words, but did so in very confined terms. It drew attention to the reason for granting exclusive jurisdiction in proceedings concerned with the registration or validity of patents to the courts of the Contracting State in which the deposit or registration had been applied for, which it said was "the fact that those courts are best placed to adjudicate upon cases in which the dispute itself concerns the validity of the patent or the existence of the deposit or registration." The Court went on to say:

> "It follows that proceedings 'concerned with the registration or validity of patents' must be regarded as proceedings in which the conferring of exclusive jurisdiction of the courts of the place[13] in which the patent was granted is justified in the light of the factors mentioned above, such as proceedings relating to the validity, existence or lapse of a patent or an alleged right of priority by reason of an earlier deposit."[14]

The Court contrasted those proceedings with others in which, even though concerned with patents, the dispute itself did not concern the validity of the patent or the existence of the deposit or registra-

---

[9] [1983] E.C.R. 3663, at p. 3679.
[10] The first question, concerning the court's duty to decline jurisdiction under Art. 19, is discussed at para. 22.07 below.
[11] Para. 20.09 above.
[12] [1983] E.C.R. 3663 at p. 3679.
[13] The use of the word "place" should not be taken to imply that Art. 16(4) regulates local jurisdiction within a Contracting State. Geimer/Schütze, p. 777.
[14] [1983] E.C.R. 3663, at p. 3677 (para. 24).

tion, which it held did not fall within Article 16(4).[15] It noted that
the same distinction was drawn in both the Munich and Luxembourg Conventions,[16] especially where the dispute as to the right to
a patent concerned the invention of an employee, and went on to
rule that *Duijnstee* v. *Goderbauer* fell into that category and therefore was not covered by the Article.

3. European Patents Conventions

A detailed consideration of patent law within the context of the
European Community is beyond the scope of this work. Mention
should be made, though, of the Convention on the Grant of European Patents (Munich, 1973),[17] which is in force, and the Convention for the European Patent for the Common Market
(Luxembourg, 1975),[18] which has not yet been brought into
force.[19] Both conventions contain various provisions on jurisdiction
which take priority over the provisions of the 1968 Convention.[20]

20.36

Munich Convention. The Munich Convention provides a uniform
system for the grant of patents, but once a European patent has
been granted it has a status in the Member States equivalent to a
national patent and is national in its extent. In principle, it is subject to the same rules as a national patent, including the provisions
of the present convention. But Article 11(1) of the Recognition Protocol to the Munich Convention provides that certain specific jurisdictional rules in that protocol are to have priority over the
provisions of other conventions, of which the most important is the
present convention.[21] Where those special rules do not apply and
the action nonetheless concerns the validity or registration of a
European patent under the Munich Convention, then the courts for
the Contracting State for which the patent is granted are given
exclusive jurisdiction over the proceedings by Article Vd of the
1968 Protocol to the present convention.[22] This does not apply,
though, if the patent is a Community patent by virtue of Article 86
of the Luxembourg Convention.

---

[15] *Ibid.*, (para. 25).
[16] See the next para.
[17] Cmnd. 7090; see the Patents Act 1977, s.130(7).
[18] O.J. 1976 L 17/1; Cmnd. 6553.
[19] See Schlosser, para. 173; Bülow/Böckstiegel/Müller, p. 139; Geimer/Schütze,
pp. 801–812 see also Guy and Leigh, *The EEC and Intellectual Property*, pp. 237
et seq.
[20] Art. 57, para. 33.06 below.
[21] The precedence of those special rules is also established by Art. 57 of the present convention.
[22] Para. 35.29 below.

20.37   *Luxembourg Convention.* Under the Luxembourg Convention (when it comes into force), application may be made by means of the procedure laid down in the Munich Convention, for the grant of a Community patent, valid in all the Member States. It is one of the principles of the Luxembourg Convention that the Community patent has equal validity throughout the Community and it follows that it is not appropriate for the courts of any one Contracting State to have exclusive jurisdiction over an action concerning its validity or registration. Jurisdictional rules are provided by the Luxembourg Convention[23] which, again, have priority over those in the present convention,[24] but, where they do not apply, Article 68 of the Luxembourg Convention expressly provides that the present convention is to apply to proceedings and decisions concerning Community patents. The present convention applies to an action for infringement of a Community patent, subject to the special rules contained in the Luxembourg Convention.[25]

As a transitional arrangement under the Luxembourg Convention, the validity of the patent may be limited to one or some only of the Member States,[26] in which case it is not a Community patent, but a patent valid only for certain States. If that is so, it will not fall within the special jurisdictional rules of the Luxembourg Convention nor within the exception to Article Vd of the 1968 Protocol. If an action is concerned with the validity or registration of such a patent, then, unless it falls within the special rules in the Munich Convention, it will be subject to the exclusive jurisdiction provisions of Article 16(4) and Article Vd of the 1968 Protocol. In such a case, the action may fall within the exclusive jurisdiction of the courts of more than one Contracting State. If so, Article 23[27] will apply to grant jurisdiction to the court first seised of the matter.

4. " . . . patents, trade marks, designs, or other similar rights required to be deposited or registered . . . "

20.38   The scope of these words will almost certainly, in the light of *Duijnstee* v. *Goderbauer*[28] be subject to an independent interpretation. It would seem, though, that for intellectual property rights to come within Article 16(4) they must be ones which are required to be registered or to be the subject of the deposit (presumably with a public authority) of some sort of instrument or other means by which they can be identified and defined. That requirement can

---

[23] Luxembourg Convention, Arts. 68–72.
[24] Art. 57 of the 1968 Convention, para. 33.06 below.
[25] Maxwell, para. 5.175.
[26] Luxembourg Convention, Art. 86.
[27] Para. 23.24 below.
[28] Para. 20.34 above.

only arise as a matter of national law (or under some other international convention), and so it would seem that an independent interpretation may have to concentrate on defining how far beyond patents and trade marks the provisions of Article 16(4) are to apply and the extent to which intellectual property rights need to be afforded legal protection.[29] As an example of "other similar rights," the Jenard Report[30] cites rights such as those which protect fruit and vegetable varieties.

5. " . . . has been applied for, has taken place or is under the terms of an international convention deemed to have taken place"

As the Schlosser Report[31] observes, Article 16(4) and Article Vd **20.39** of the 1968 Protocol cover actions which may, as a matter of national law, be brought at the patent application stage. It appears that the application must have been made, and not merely be contemplated, for the provision to apply.

The international conventions under which the deposit or registration may be deemed to have taken place are the Madrid Convention of April 14, 1891, concerning the international registration of trade marks, revised at Brussels on December 14, 1900, at Washington on June 2, 1911, at The Hague on November 6, 1925 and at London on June 2, 1934, and the Hague Arrangement of November 6, 1925 on the international deposit of industrial designs, also revised at London on June 2, 1934.[32]

Article 16(5)

[The following courts shall have exclusive jurisdiction, regard- 20.40 less of domicile:]

    5. in proceedings concerned with the enforcement of judgments, the courts of the Contracting State in which the judgment has been or is to be enforced.*

---

[29] Bülow/Böckstiegel/Müller, p. 137.
[30] Jenard, para. A1.160 below.
[31] Schlosser, para. 173 (para. A1.468 below).
[32] Jenard, para. A1.161 below.
* Jenard, paras. A1.153, A1.162 below; Schlosser, paras. 162–165 (paras. A1.456–A1.458 below); Collins, pp. 77–78, 83; Dashwood/Halcon/ White, pp. 29, 120–121; Hartley, p. 68, Kaye, pp. 871–883, 956–964, 969, 973, 975, 1002; Maxwell, para. 5.178; Anton, para. 7.22; Droz, paras. 137–146, 162; Weser, paras. 245–249, 256; Bülow/Böckstiegel/Müller, pp. 130–132, 139–140; Geimer/Schütze, pp. 812–818; Kropholler, pp. 142–145, 159–160; Gothot/Holleaux, para. 158; Pocar, pp. 173–180.

F. PARAGRAPH (5): ENFORCEMENT OF JUDGMENTS

1. General note

20.41   The enforcement of judgments is an exercise of sovereign power by a state.[33] It is clearly right that the courts of that state should have exclusive jurisdiction over proceedings giving rise to, or arising out of, such enforcement. For Article 16(5) to apply, it is not necessary for the judgment to have been enforced in the state in question. It is sufficient that it is to be enforced there.

Systems of enforcement. The purpose of this head of exclusive jurisdiction can be better understood in relation to the continental systems of enforcement,[34] which are less dependent on the courts than common law systems of enforcement. Separate proceedings in respect of enforcement are therefore more common and can include, for example, proceedings for the purpose of restraining the enforcement of a judgment.[35] Such proceedings might be brought by the judgment debtor, on the grounds that the judgment had been satisfied or by a third party on the grounds that the goods on which execution was, or was to be, levied belonged to him and not to the judgment debtor.[36] Nonetheless, the Article has some practical application in the common law Contracting States, especially for the purpose of Article 19, if proceedings are brought there in breach of the exclusive jurisdiction of the courts of another Contracting State.

20.42   *The Malhé decision.* The European Court of Justice has had to consider the scope of Article 16(5) in *A-S Autoteile Service GmbH* v. *Malhé*.[37] A-S Autoteile, a German company, was owed substantial sums by another German company, PAT GmbH, which had become insolvent and of which the defendant, Mr. Malhé was a shareholder. A-S Autoteile contended that PAT had unjustly enriched Malhé by payment of fictitious profits and, as assignee of PAT's rights of action against Malhé, brought proceedings against him in Germany. Malhé disputed the jurisdiction of the German court and, after it had been contested as far as the *Bundesgerichtshof*, the issue was resolved in Malhé's favour. An order for costs in those proceedings was made against A-S Autoteile, which then brought

---

[33] Bülow/Böckstiegel/Müller, p. 139; Geimer/Schütze, p. 813. See also chap. 10 above.

[34] Measures of enforcement available in each of the Contracting States are noted in chaps. 48 to 58 below, at para. 68. See also paras. 25.16 and 25.32 below.

[35] *e.g.*, under para. 767 of the German Code of Civil Procedure: see *A-S Autoteile Service GmbH* v. *Malhé*, [1985] E.C.R. 2267, discussed below.

[36] *Cf.* an action in replevin in English law: 13 *Halsbury's Laws* (4th ed.), paras. 373 *et seq.*

[37] [1985] E.C.R. 2267.

proceedings under paragraph 767 of the German Code of Civil Procedure to restrain Malhé from enforcing the order for costs. A-S Autoteile sought in those proceedings to raise its substantive claim against Malhé by way of a set-off against the latter's order for costs.

The issue of jurisdiction over these latter proceedings was also contested up to the *Bundesgerichtshof*, which referred a number of questions to the European Court of Justice. The first question was whether proceedings such as those under paragraph 767 of the German Code of Civil Procedure fell within Article 16(5). The European Court ruled that they did,[38] citing "their close link with the enforcement procedure."[39] The second question raised the issue of what objections a party might raise in such proceedings without going beyond the limits of Article 16(5). The Court reiterated that the jurisdictional rules in Article 16 were exceptional in nature[40] and continued:

> "It follows from the specificity of the connexion required by Article 16 that a party cannot make use of the jurisdiction conferred by Article 16(5) on the courts of the place of enforcement in order to bring before those courts a dispute which falls within the jurisdiction of the courts of another Contracting State under Article 2. The use for such a purpose of the application to oppose enforcement is contrary to the division of jurisdiction which the Convention intended to establish between the court of the defendant's domicile and the court of the place of enforcement.
>
> In this case, since the German courts have already held that they have no jurisdiction over the claim relied on as a set-off, the use of that claim in order to oppose the enforcement of an order for the costs incurred in the same proceedings amounts to a clear abuse of the process on the part of the plaintiff for the purpose of obtaining indirectly from the German courts a decision regarding a claim over which those courts have no jurisdiction under the Convention."[41]

The Court therefore went on to rule in more general terms, that Article 16(5) does not make it possible:

> "in an application to oppose enforcement made to the courts of the Contracting State in which enforcement is to take place, to plead a set-off between the right whose enforcement is being sought and a claim over which the courts of that State would have no jurisdiction if it were raised independently."

---

[38] This was contrary to the Opinion of Advocate General Lenz, who urged that no decision was necessary on the point: *ibid*, at p. 2271.
[39] *Ibid.*, at p. 2277 (para. 12).
[40] *Ibid.*, (para. 16).
[41] *Ibid.*, at p. 2278 (paras. 17 and 18).

2. " . . . proceedings concerned with the enforcement of judgments . . . "

20.43   "Judgment" is widely defined by Article 25[42] and includes a wide variety of orders and decisions made by the courts and tribunals of the Contracting States. The definition in Article 25 does not extend to the judgments of non-Contracting States and it seems that proceedings concerned with the enforcement of those judgments do not fall within the provision.[43] The words "proceedings concerned with" are to be equated with the words, "proceedings which have as their object," in Articles 16(1) to (3).[44] It is not all proceedings relating to execution which fall within Article 16(5), and proceedings concerned with recognition as distinct from enforcement[45] are not covered by the provision. In cases of doubt as to whether proceedings are "concerned with the enforcement of judgments," the concept is to be given an independent interpretation.[46]

If the proceedings are capable of deciding the enforceability of the judgment or order, they probably fall within the paragraph, as do proceedings by which the type of enforcement may be decided, or by which enforcement may be stayed or limited or have conditions imposed on it.[47] Similarly, English interpleader,[48] garnishee,[49] and committal[50] proceedings will usually, if not always, fall within the exclusive jurisdiction provisions of this Article where enforcement is to take place in England. It does not matter whether

---

[42] Para. 26.01 below. The definition expressly includes a "writ of execution."

[43] So, for example, an action at common law on a judgment obtained in a non-Contracting State (para. 10.03 above) would probably not be "proceedings concerned with the enforcement of judgments" for the purposes of Art. 16(5), and it would not therefore matter whether or not the judgment was to be enforced in the U.K. The jurisdiction of an English court over such an action against a person domiciled in a Contracting State would depend on the Convention's other rules of jurisdiction. If the defendant were not domiciled in a Contracting State, the English court's jurisdiction would depend on English law: Art. 4, para. 16.15 above. In either case, though, there is some doubt whether the judgment of the English court would be recognised and enforced in the other Contracting States, despite the terms of Title III: see paras. 25.35 *et seq.* below.

[44] See para. 20.04 above.

[45] Geimer/Schütze, p. 814, note that the borderline between proceedings concerning recognition and those concerning enforcement differs according to different systems of national law, and cite French and German law. In English law, there is also a distinction to be drawn between recognition and enforcement: see Dicey and Morris, pp. 418–421. See also chap. 25 below.

[46] *A-S Autoteile Service GmbH* v. *Malhé*, above; see para. 20.42 above; Geimer/Schütze, p. 814.

[47] *e.g.*, in England, under R.S.C., Ord. 47; see para. 10.54 above.

[48] R.S.C., Ord. 17.

[49] R.S.C., Ord. 49.

[50] R.S.C., Ord. 52.

the judgment which has been or is to be enforced is a judgment given in that Contracting State or one which has had an order for its enforcement granted under Title III of the Convention.[51]

Incidental issue. Proceedings which are only incidentally con-   **20.44**
cerned with enforcement or which are not capable of deciding the enforceability of a judgment or order, or the circumstances or means of its enforcement, will usually not fall within Article 16(5). For example, proceedings to rectify the consequences of excessive or unjustified enforcement may not fall within its terms.[52] Similarly, the English procedure whereby a person against whom a judgment has been given may be examined as to his assets[53] may probably be invoked in England in aid or in anticipation of the enforcement of the judgment in another Contracting State.[54]

3. " . . . the Contracting State in which the judgment has been or is to be enforced"

If measures of enforcement have already been undertaken, it will   **20.45**
be clear where they have been undertaken and these words should pose no difficulty. If, on the other hand, no measures of enforcement have been undertaken, the jurisdiction of the court will depend on the intentions of the person in whose favour the judgment to be enforced was given (here called the "judgment creditor," even though the judgment need not be for the payment of money). If the judgment creditor intends the judgment to be enforced in a given Contracting State, he confers exclusive jurisdiction on the courts of that state in respect of any proceedings which are concerned with enforcement there, and it is probably not open to the court to consider the objective prospects of execution being successful.[55]

Some difficulty may arise where the judgment or order in question not only requires the defendant to do or refrain from doing something, but concerns also the means by which that is to occur. If those means are, in truth, measures of enforcement, it may be that the court can only make an order detailing those means of enforcement if they are to take place within that Contracting State. If measures of enforcement which are to take effect in another Contracting State form the subject-matter of proceedings, then the pro-

---

[51] Geimer/Schütze, p. 817. Title III is discussed in chaps. 25 to 29 below.
[52] Bülow/Böckstiegel/Müller, p. 140; Geimer/Schütze, pp. 815–816.
[53] R.S.C., Ord. 48; see para. 10.53 above.
[54] Collins, p. 83.
[55] There is no "*executio non conveniens*:" Geimer/Schütze, p. 817.

ceedings fall within the exclusive jurisdiction of that other state.[56] The court seised of the proceedings must decline jurisdiction in those circumstances,[57] unless the measures of enforcement are *also* to take effect in the state of the court *and* no other court has been seised of the issue first.[58] If nonetheless a court makes an order containing such provisions, then that part of the judgment may be denied recognition and enforcement in that other state.[59]

20.46   On the other hand, Article 16(5) should not be interpreted as preventing a court in one Contracting State from making an order against a defendant in another Contracting State, which is to be enforced in that other state according to the latter's laws and practices, pursuant to an order for the judgment's enforcement granted there under Title III of the Convention.[60] Equally the imposition by the courts of one Contracting State of sanctions or penalties on a defendant domiciled in another Contracting State does not infringe the sovereignty of the latter state and is not hindered by Article 16(5).[61] Only if the measures of enforcement are designed to take effect in another Contracting State without the further intervention of the courts of that state under Title III can they be regarded as falling under Article 16(5).

---

[56] So, for example, Art. 16(5) has been held to prevent a court in one Contracting State from making an order that an auditor should take extracts from the debtor's books in another Contracting State: Oberlandesgericht Nürnberg, Case No. 9 W 31/74, April 5, 1974, Digest D I–16.5—B1. English courts are probably not now permitted to restrain the enforcement in another Contracting State of a foreign judgment: see paras. 1.51 to 1.52 above; Collins, p. 83; *cf. Ellerman Lines Ltd.* v. *Read* [1928] 2 K.B. 144.

[57] Art. 19, para. 22.01 below.

[58] Art. 23, para. 23.24 below. Such a case is likely to be extremely rare in practice.

[59] Art. 28, first para. (para. 27.62 below) and Art. 42 (para. 28.71 below).

[60] Oberlandesgericht Nürnberg, case 9 U 167/75, February 25, 1976, Digest D I–16.5—B2. The jurisdiction of English courts to make orders intended to be enforced in other Contracting States, which is particularly relevant in the context of provisional and protective measures, is discussed at paras. 1.47 *et seq.* and 7.23 *et seq.* above.

[61] Oberlandesgericht Nürnberg, case 9 W 31/74, April 5, 1974, Digest D I–16.5—B1. See also Art. 43, para. 28.76 below.

CHAPTER 21

PROROGATION OF JURISDICTION
(Articles 17 and 18)

SECTION 6

Article 17

21.01   If the parties, one or more of whom is domiciled in a Contracting State, have agreed that a court or the courts of a Contracting State are to have jurisdiction to settle any disputes which have arisen or which may arise in connection with a particular legal relationship, that court or those courts shall have exclusive jurisdiction. Such an agreement conferring jurisdiction shall be either in writing or evidenced in writing or, in international trade or commerce, in a form which accords with practices in that trade or commerce of which the parties are or ought to have been aware. Where such an agreement is concluded by parties, none of whom is domiciled in a Contracting State, the courts of other Contracting States shall have no jurisdiction over their dispute unless the court or courts chosen have declined jurisdiction.

The court or courts of a Contracting State on which a trust instrument has conferred jurisdiction shall have exclusive jurisdiction in any proceedings brought against a settlor, trustee or beneficiary, if relations between these persons or their rights or obligations under the trust are involved.

Agreements or provisions of a trust instrument conferring jurisdiction shall have no legal force if they are contrary to the provisions of Article 12 or 15, or if the courts whose jurisdiction they purport to exclude have exclusive jurisdiction by virtue of Article 16.

If an agreement conferring jurisdiction was concluded for the benefit of only one of the parties, that party shall retain the right

548

**to bring proceedings in any other court which has jurisdiction by
virtue of this Convention.*†**

A. ARTICLE 17: GENERAL NOTE

Introduction. Choice of jurisdiction agreements are of great practi-   **21.02**
cal importance and Article 17 has given rise to more case law than
any other Article. The Article applies to both commercial and non-
commercial transactions and is designed to ensure that effect is
given to agreements on jurisdiction which are genuinely and con-
sciously concluded. At the same time, it seeks not to impede commercial practice by an excess of formality,[1] while affording some
protection to contracting parties—particularly those in a weaker
bargaining position—from the effects of jurisdiction clauses of
which they were not aware. It is a complex and difficult provision
which requires exceptionally detailed examination.

A number of conditions must be met for a jurisdiction clause to
be effective under Article 17. If they are not met, the court seised
may nonetheless have jurisdiction under other provisions of the
Convention or, if it applies, pursuant to its own law. In summary,
the main conditions for the application of Article 17 (each of which
is discussed more fully below) are as follows:

(1) The transaction must be within the general scope of the
    Convention;[2]
(2) The courts chosen must be the courts of a Contracting
    State;[3]

---

* Jenard, paras. A1.164–A1.170 below: Schlosser, paras. 174–179 (paras.
A1.469–A1.474 below); Collins, pp. 83–90; Dashwood/Halcon/White, pp. 31,
121–130; Hartley, pp. 68–75; Kaye, pp. 1031–1103; Maxwell, paras.
5.179–5.190; Anton, paras. 7.26–7.27; Droz, paras. 170–219; Weser, paras.
265.1–265.8; Bülow/Böckstiegel/Müller, pp. 140–153; Geimer/Schütze,
pp. 195–207, 237–249, 473–508, 874–946; Kropholler, pp. 160–200; Gothot/
Holleaux, paras. 159–187; Pocar, pp. 180–225.
† This Article was substituted for its predecessor by Art. 11 of the 1978 Convention. The former text referred to an "agreement in writing or an oral agreement
evidenced in writing." Although the English text no longer refers to an "oral"
agreement, the texts in other languages do so, and it is apparent that no change
of meaning was intended in this respect. The new wording does, however, introduce a special provision for international trade or commerce. The provisions in
the amended version relating to agreements between parties, none of whom is
domiciled in a Contracting State, and those relating to trust instruments, are
also new.
[1] Jenard, paras. A1.164–A1.166 below. The formalities have been further eased
in the amended version in relation to commercial practices.
[2] Para. 21.06 below.
[3] Paras. 21.39 *et seq.* below.

(3) At least one of the parties must be domiciled in a Contracting State;[4]

(4) The jurisdiction agreement must relate to the "particular legal relationship" in issue;[5]

(5) *Either* (a) the jurisdiction agreement must be in writing or evidenced in writing,[6] *or*, (b) if the case arises in the context of international trade or commerce, it must be "in a form which accords with practices in that trade or commerce of which the parties are or ought to have been aware";[7]

(6) The agreement must not be contrary to the special jurisdictional provisions of Article 12 (insurance cases), Article 15 (consumer cases) or Article 16 (exclusive jurisdiction);[8]

(7) An agreement concluded for the benefit of one party only will have only limited effect.[9]

1. Terminology—prorogation and derogation

21.03   Section 3 of Title II (Articles 17 and 18) is headed "Prorogation of jurisdiction."[10] It is important to recognise that the effect of Article 17 is to *confer* jurisdiction on the court or courts chosen, and that this is the meaning, in the context of the Convention, of the term "prorogation." It is a term known to continental and Scots law.[11] It is to be distinguished from a mere recognition of the jurisdiction which would otherwise apply pursuant to the Convention,[12] as is illustrated by the fact that Article 17 takes precedence over most of the Convention's other jurisdictional provisions.[13] Where an agreement prorogates the jurisdiction of a court, it may also have the effect of derogating the jurisdiction which another court would have under the Convention. From an analytical point of view, the concepts of prorogation and derogation take on particular significance in considering the effect of a jurisdiction agreement where

---

[4] Paras. 21.34 *et seq.* below.

[5] Paras. 21.41 *et seq.* below.

[6] Paras. 21.52 *et seq.* below.

[7] Para. 21.70 below.

[8] Paras. 21.77 *et seq.* below.

[9] Paras. 21.80 *et seq.* below.

[10] The unconditional entry of an appearance is an implied prorogation of jurisdiction under Art. 18: see para. 21.84 below.

[11] See Anton, *Private International Law*, p. 127.

[12] The verb "prorogate" is defined by the Shorter Oxford English Dictionary in this sense as follows: "To extend (the jurisdiction of a judge or court) to a cause in which it would otherwise be incompetent." It is not necessary in the context of the Convention, though, that the chosen court or courts should not otherwise have jurisdiction: see para. 21.06 below.

[13] See the next para.

one of the parties is domiciled outside the Contracting States[14] or where the agreement is non-exclusive in character.[15]

2. Precedence of Article 17

In common with the other provisions of the Convention, the jur- **21.04** isdictional rules in Article 17 take precedence over contrary provisions of national law, even if the latter are mandatory in character.[16] Similarly, they take precedence over all the other jurisdictional rules in the Convention, except:

(1) where the jurisdiction agreement is contrary to Articles 12 or 15; or

(2) where the courts of another Contracting State have exclusive jurisdiction under Article 16; or

(3) where the defendant enters an appearance under Article 18 and does not contest the jurisdiction;[17] or

(4) where the jurisdiction agreement is contrary to the provisions of another convention falling within Article 57.[18]

This precedence includes precedence over Article 4[19] and it fol- **21.05** lows that the exorbitant jurisdictions peculiar to the various Contracting States (such as those listed in Article 3)[20] can therefore be excluded by an agreement falling within Article 17. The precedence of Article 17 over Article 4 merits some explanation, in view of the fact that Article 4 is expressed to be subordinate to Article 16, but makes no mention of Article 17.[21] First, Article 17 enables an agreement to take effect if either of the parties is domiciled in a Contracting State—it need not be the defendant.[22] Even if neither party is domiciled in a Contracting State, the last sentence of the

---

[14] Paras. 21.34 *et seq.* below.

[15] Paras. 21.46 *et seq.* below.

[16] *S. A. Agecobel* v. *S.A. Flaminaire* Journal trib. 1976, p. 210, Digest D I–17.1.1—B2; Bundesgerichtshof, case VIII ZR 251/74, March 3, 1976, RIW/AWD 1976, p. 447, Digest D I–17.1.1—B3; *De Cuyper* v. *S.A. Kayser France*, Gaz. Palais 1978, Somm. p. 227, Digest D I–17.1.1—B7; *Huybrechts* v. *B.V. Simon-Heesen*, Arbeidsrechtbank Brussels, October 2, 1979, Digest D I–17.1.1—B7n. See paras. 21.25 *et seq.* below.

[17] See para. 21.85 below.

[18] Anton, p. 116.

[19] Under Art. 4, the *lex fori*, including the exorbitant jurisdictions mentioned in Art. 3, determines jurisdiction over defendants not domiciled in a Contracting State. See also Maxwell, para. 5.189; Droz, paras. 213, 228–232; Bülow/Böckstiegel/Müller, p. 143; Geimer/Schütze, pp. 196, 898.

[20] Para. 16.09 above.

[21] This omission appears to have been accidental: Droz, para. 229; Geimer/Schütze, p. 898, n. 103.

[22] Para. 21.34 below.

first paragraph of Article 17[23] takes effect: no other court in a Contracting State has jurisdiction over the case unless the chosen court or courts have declined jurisdiction. These provisions would be largely devoid of meaning if Article 4 were to have priority. Secondly, as a matter of general construction, Article 17 can be regarded as a particular rule of jurisdiction which should take priority over the more general provisions of Article 4.[24]

Article 17 also takes precedence over Article 6. This has been discussed above,[25] but the importance of jurisdiction agreements should be stressed in relation to third-party proceedings, especially in cases concerning the sale of goods.[26] It should also be stressed that a jurisdiction agreement may need to be carefully construed (probably in accordance with the law indicated by the conflicts rules of the *lex fori*)[27] to determine whether it envisages jurisdiction over third-party proceedings such as, for example, claims for an indemnity.[28]

3. International character

21.06 For the jurisdictional rules of the Convention to apply to a case, it must fall within the Convention's general scope.[29] There is one aspect of this apparently simple proposition which is particularly important in relation to Article 17, namely that the Convention only applies to a case if it is international in character.[30] Usually, this will present no difficulty. For example, even if two parties domiciled in the same Contracting State confer jurisdiction by agreement on the courts of another Contracting State, that is sufficient to establish

---

[23] Para. 21.71 below. This provision prevents courts in one Contracting State from accepting jurisdiction where the parties, both of whom are domiciled in non-Contracting States, have chosen the exclusive jurisdiction of the court or courts of another Contracting State, unless and until the latter has declined jurisdiction.

[24] Geimer/Schütze, p. 196.

[25] Paras. 17.80, 17.87 and 17.95.

[26] *Soc. des Etablissements Voith* v. *Soc. Chantiers et Ateliers de la Perrière and others*, Rev. critique 1983, p. 658, Digest D I–17.1.1—B19; *Technisch Handelsbureau P.J. van Louden B.V.* v. *N.V. Gieterijn Technomet*, Arrondissementsrechtbank Arnhem, December 23, 1982, Digest D I–17.1.2—B24. Collins, pp. 66–7, gives the following example: A in England sells goods to B in France who sells them to C in Italy under a contract providing for the exclusive jurisdiction of the Italian courts. C sues B in Italy and B can join A in the Italian proceedings unless the contract between A and B includes a jurisdiction agreement providing for the exclusive jurisdiction of some other court.

[27] See para. 21.33 below.

[28] *Soc. des Etablissements Voith* v. *Soc. Chantiers et Ateliers de la Perrière and others*, above.

[29] Chap. 14 above.

[30] Schlosser, para. 174 (para. A1.469 below); Droz, para. 32; but *cf.* Geimer/Schütze, p. 891; see paras. 13.10 *et seq.* above.

the international character of the case and, provided the other requirements are fulfilled, to bring it within Article 17.[31] The position might be complicated if the Convention requires an objective link between the legal relationship giving rise to the dispute and the court chosen.[32]

But what is the position where two parties domiciled in the same Contracting State enter into an agreement conferring jurisdiction on the courts of that state? The Jenard Report[33] says that the Convention would not apply to such a case because it would not have the necessary international element. That view is not necessarily correct for all cases.[34] If, but for the jurisdiction agreement, the courts of one or more other Contracting States would have had jurisdiction over the case, the effect of the jurisdiction agreement will be to deprive them of that jurisdiction. That is an effect at the international level and is sufficient to bring the case within Article 17.[35]

As a general proposition, it can be said that where a jurisdiction agreement *either* designates ("prorogates") a court or the courts of a Contracting State which would not otherwise have jurisdiction under the Convention, *or* expressly or by implication excludes ("derogates") the jurisdiction of a court or the courts of a Contracting State which would otherwise have jurisdiction under the Convention, it is to be considered international in character for the purpose of Article 17.[36]

4. No other court with jurisdiction under the Convention

Problems may arise in the following two situations: first, where,   **21.07** but for the jurisdiction agreement, no court in a Contracting State would have jurisdiction; and secondly, where the parties prorogate the jurisdiction of the only court or courts which would anyway have jurisdiction under the Convention. In each case, the agreement prorogates the jurisdiction of a court or the courts of a Con-

---

[31] Jenard, para. A1.168 below; Droz, para. 207.
[32] See para. 21.16 below.
[33] Jenard, para. A1.168 below.
[34] See Droz, paras. 186 *et seq.*
[35] Collins, p. 84; Maxwell, para. 5.183; Droz, para. 189; Bülow/Böckstiegel/Müller, pp. 143–4; Geimer/Schütze, pp. 889–891.
[36] This proposition differs from that advanced by Droz, namely that: "For the purposes of Art. 17, every agreement which designates the court or courts of a Contracting State and which excludes the normal jurisdiction which a court or the courts of another Contracting State would otherwise have under the Convention, is to be considered international in character" (Droz, para. 191). Droz's formula is not adequate to cater for some cases where the court chosen is the only court with jurisdiction under the Convention (see paras. 21.07 *et seq.* below) nor where the agreement merely excludes the jurisdiction of an otherwise competent court (see para. 21.46 below).

tracting State, without derogating from the jurisdiction of any other court in a Contracting State. These questions might appear to be of purely theoretical interest, because in either case the court chosen would have jurisdiction in any event and other courts would be required to decline jurisdiction of their own motion.[37] They may nonetheless be of practical importance if the plaintiff's domicile is (or was, at the date of the jurisdiction agreement)[38] in a Contracting State, but that of the defendant is not. In such a case, if Article 17 did not apply, the court would be free to decide whether it had jurisdiction according to its own law, by virtue of Article 4.[39]

21.08   *An illustrative example.* The following discussion illustrates the point:

(1) An example of the first situation is where a seller domiciled in Hamburg enters into a contract for the sale of goods with a buyer domiciled in the United States and the parties agree that delivery and payment are both to take place in Hamburg. If a dispute arises and the seller wishes to sue the buyer, no court has jurisdiction under the normal rules of the Convention, and the national courts would be free to apply their own law in the absence of a jurisdiction agreement. But the situation may be different if the contract contains a jurisdiction clause which complies with the formal requirements of Article 17. Assume that such a clause gives jurisdiction to the commercial court in Hamburg,[40] but is ignored by the seller who brings his action instead in England, on an exorbitant basis.[41] The question then arises whether the English court is required by the Convention to decline jurisdiction in favour of the court in Hamburg, pursuant to Article 17. The necessary elements would seem to be present: one party is domiciled in a Contracting State, a court of a Contracting State has been chosen, the formal requirements have been complied with and the case bears an international character.

21.09   There are three arguments: one against Article 17 applying and two in favour of it applying.

(i) The *first* argument, which is against Article 17 applying,

---

[37] Arts. 19 and 20, chap. 22 below.

[38] See para. 21.35 below.

[39] This assumes that Art. 16 does not apply to the case.

[40] It is necessary to assume for the purposes of the example that the agreement was not concluded solely for the benefit of the German, because of the terms of the fourth para. of Art. 17: see para. 21.80 below.

[41] English law would permit the buyer to be served with a writ within the jurisdiction, for example. This is one of the exorbitant rules of jurisdiction listed in the second para. of Art. 3, para. 16.09 above. Alternatively, if the contract is expressly subject to English law, the plaintiff might obtain leave to serve the defendant out of the jurisdiction: R.S.C. Ord. 11, r. 1(1)(d)(iii).

is that the Convention regulates jurisdiction merely *between Contracting States*, that the case must therefore have features which connect it with more than one Contracting State and that, consequently, in order to fall within Article 17 the agreement must derogate from the jurisdiction which another Contracting State would have *under the Convention*.[42] This agreement does not derogate from the jurisdiction of the English court because, under the Convention, it had no jurisdiction anyway and the only Contracting State with which the case is connected is Germany. If that is right, the English court would be free to apply its own rules as to jurisdiction.[43]

(ii) The *second* argument, which is to the effect that Article 17 should apply, is that the jurisdictional rules provided by the Convention are compulsory in character, the conditions specified in Article 17 for the Hamburg court to have exclusive jurisdiction are all fulfilled and there is nothing in the wording of Article 17 to justify a departure from that principle. Moreover, the Convention requires the courts of Contracting States each to show mutual respect for the jurisdiction of the courts of other Contracting States and the jurisdiction agreement expressly gives jurisdiction to the court in Hamburg.

(iii) The *third* argument, which is also to the effect that Article 17 should apply, is that, even if the first argument is right and it is necessary for the jurisdiction clause not only to prorogate the jurisdiction of a court or the courts of a Contracting State, but also to derogate from the jurisdiction which a court in another Contracting State would have under the Convention, that condition is actually fulfilled. This is so, the argument runs, because (a) the exorbitant jurisdiction invoked by the German plaintiff is a jurisdiction foreseen by the Convention in Article 3, (b) the jurisdiction clause, by necessary implication, excludes the English courts and, therefore, (c) it does affect the international jurisdiction of the English courts as between Contracting States. Accordingly, Article 17 applies and takes precedence over Article 4.[44] The English court must therefore decline jurisdiction in favour of the court in Hamburg.

---

[42] Para. 21.06 above; Bülow/Böckstiegel/Müller, pp. 144–5.
[43] As a matter of English law, it would not be *required* to decline jurisdiction, but could exercise its discretion: s.49 of the 1982 Act, para. 44.40 below.
[44] See para. 21.05 above.

It is submitted that the third argument is flawed. The exorbitant jurisdiction of the English court, relied on by the plaintiff, is a jurisdiction which exists *despite* the Convention, not *by virtue of* it.

21.10   (2) If, on the other hand, the American buyer were the plaintiff and sought to invoke the jurisdiction of the English court, the same three arguments would apply, except that the second argument would be strenghtened by the fact that the court in Hamburg would have jurisdiction under Article 2 and it would not be relevant to the third argument that Article 17 takes precedence over Article 4, because the defendant is not domiciled outside the Contracting States. The third argument, in favour of the English court having jurisdiction, is even less attractive when it is advanced by the American plaintiff. He would have to base his argument on the proposition that the English court has a jurisdiction foreseen by the Convention (an argument which, as has been observed, is flawed). The only jurisdiction foreseen by the Convention to which he could point is that referred to in Article 3, but he would have to do so in precisely the circumstances where Article 3 says that it may not be invoked, namely against a defendant domiciled in a Contracting State.

21.11   (3) It has already been suggested that the third argument is flawed in its reasoning and, if advanced by a plaintiff not domiciled in a Contracting State, unattractive. The question arises, then, as to which (if either) of the first two arguments is to be preferred. A definite answer must await the determination of the courts, but it is suggested that the second argument is much the stronger. It enables effect to be given to the contract entered into by the parties, it enables the parties to predict the outcome of jurisdictional issues on the basis of the Convention alone without having to consider the effect of national law (including, in the case of England, how the court's discretion is likely to be exercised) and it is in accord both with the wording of Article 17 and the wider manner in which the Convention takes effect within the legal systems of the Contracting States.

21.12   The exclusion of exorbitant jurisdictions is one of the main principles on which the Convention is founded, and one of its main features; but if the first argument is valid, it could have the incidental effect of allowing a plaintiff not domiciled in a Contracting State to have the benefit of exorbitant jurisdictions against a defendant domiciled in a Contracting State, directly contrary to Articles 2 and 3. A solution to this problem would mean that the arguments for the precedence of Article 17[45] would need to be modified, but it is

---

[45] *Ibid.*

hard to see how this could be done without creating a great deal of uncertainty. The first argument also appears to be contrary to the decision of the European Court of Justice in *Meeth* v. *Glacetal*,[46] in which the parties had elected that each could be sued in the courts of their own state of domicile.

5. Choice of court in a non-contracting State

There is nothing in the Convention to prevent parties from enter- **21.13** ing into an agreement conferring jurisdiction on a court or courts outside the Contracting States.[47] This situation is not contemplated by the Convention. In general, a court of a Contracting State faced with such a jurisdiction agreement will be free to decide whether to give effect to the agreement, and to make that decision according to its own law including its conflicts rules.[48] Article 17 does not apply to determine whether the jurisdiction agreement is effective to derogate from the jurisdiction of a court or the courts of a Contracting State in such circumstances, but the Convention is not altogether excluded, because certain jurisdictional rules take precedence over Article 17[49] and also take precedence over a jurisdiction agreement prorogating the jurisdiction of the courts of a non-Contracting State.[50]

If the court of a Contracting State, applying its own conflicts **21.14** rules, finds that foreign law applies to the question of the validity of the clause, it must apply that foreign law and see whether the clause is valid. If it is not valid according to the applicable law, the clause should be ignored and the jurisdictional rules of the Convention should be applied.[51] The reason why the court must go this far and why the Convention has an effect in this area of conflicts of law is both because the court has no discretion in the matter of its jurisdiction under Article 17[52] and because the existence of a jurisdiction agreement depriving the court of jurisdiction is a matter which the court must take into account *of its own motion.*[53]

It may, of course, be easier for the court to determine first whether it would, but for the jurisdiction agreement, have jurisdiction under the Convention. If it would not, it can decline jurisdiction without having to decide the validity of the clause, because, if

---

[46] [1978] E.C.R. 2133, discussed at paras. 21.44 *et seq.* below.
[47] Schlosser, para. 176 (para. A1.471 below).
[48] Schlosser, *loc. cit.*; Droz, paras. 216–8; Weser, para. 265.8; Bülow/Böckstiegel/ Müller, p. 143, Maxwell, para. 5.186, Kropholler, p. 167.
[49] Para. 21.04 above.
[50] Geimer/Schütze, pp. 892–893.
[51] See paras. 21.25 *et seq.* below.
[52] Para. 21.15 below.
[53] Schlosser, paras. 22 and 174 (paras. A1.311–A1.312 and A1.469 below).

the clause is not valid the court would have to apply the Convention rules anyway, and if it is valid the court would either give effect to it and decline jurisdiction or not give effect to it and again be driven back to the Convention.

6. Discretion and *forum non conveniens*

21.15   The rules of jurisdiction in the Convention are compulsory[54] and the court must examine its jurisdiction of its own motion.[55] Consequently, courts are not permitted to exercise discretion in matters of jurisdiction, nor to apply principles of *forum non conveniens*.[56] This is particularly relevant to English law, where courts are no longer able to exercise discretion as to:

> (a) whether to accept jurisdiction contrary to a valid agreement giving jurisdiction to a court or the courts of another Contracting State, even if the plaintiff proves that it is just and proper to allow the action to continue, or
>
> (b) whether to decline jurisdiction despite a valid agreement giving the English court jurisdiction.[57]

If the agreement is valid, effect must be given to it.

21.16   One question which has given rise to some doubt[58] is whether the parties' choice of jurisdiction, in order to be valid, needs to be objectively justifiable, especially where the parties are both domiciled in one state, but choose the courts of another state. Such a requirement would discourage forum shopping, but might tend towards the application of the doctrine of *forum non conveniens*. That doctrine has no place in the Convention's scheme of rules and, it is submitted, Article 17 contains no such hidden requirement. As Droz observes,[59] the parties may have been motivated by a desire to ensure complete neutrality on the part of the court which might be called upon to resolve any dispute. They may also have made the choice deliberately in view of the rules of conflicts of law obtaining in the chosen country. Not only are the principles of *forum non conveniens* contrary to the spirit, and usually the letter, of the Convention, but the closer integration of the Contracting States, both economically within the European Community and jurisdictionally by virtue of the Convention, is likely to weigh heavily with the

---

[54] Para. 15.02 above.
[55] Paras. 22.06 and 22.15 below.
[56] Collins, p. 84; Droz, para. 206; Geimer/Schütze, pp. 288, 507, 918.
[57] Dicey and Morris, pp. 410–411; see *Spiliada Maritime Corporation* v. *Cansulex Ltd.* [1987] A.C. 460 (H.L.) and paras. 1.36 *et seq.* above.
[58] Collins, p. 85.
[59] Droz, para. 212.

European Court of Justice against an interpretation of Article 17 that imposes such a requirement.[60]

7. Choice of law clauses

An agreement by the parties as to the law which is to govern their legal relationship is not generally to be regarded as a choice by them of the courts which are to have jurisdiction over their disputes,[61] although a choice of law clause may be effective to choose the applicable substantive law, even where an associated choice of jurisdiction clause fails to fulfil the requirements of Article 17.[62] A limited exception arises, though, purely as a transitional provision: Article 35 of the 1978 Convention[63] provides that if the parties to a dispute concerning a contract had agreed in writing before that Convention came into force that the contract was to be governed by the law of Ireland or of a part of the United Kingdom,[64] the courts of Ireland or that part of the United Kingdom should retain the right to exercise jurisdiction in the dispute.

21.17

So far as England is concerned, this preserves in a restricted form the jurisdiction under Order 11, rule 1(d)(iii).[65] The jurisdiction will remain discretionary,[66] and will only apply where the agreement was made before the Convention came into force and where there was an express agreement in writing. It will no longer be sufficient to found jurisdiction, even as a transitional measure, for English law to be by implication the proper law of the contract.

8. Place of performance

Instead of entering into a jurisdiction agreement, the parties may be able to achieve the same object, without having to meet the various requirements of Article 17, by agreeing upon the place of performance of a contract. By doing so, they will enable the dissatisfied party to bring his action in the courts for that place, pursuant to Article 5(1). The European Court of Justice has considered such an

21.18

---

[60] *Cf. Zelger* v. *Salinitri (No. 1)* [1980] E.C.R. 89, at p. 97; Advocate-General Capotorti in *Sanicentral* v. *Collin* [1979] E.C.R. 3423, at p. 3434; Droz, paras. 205–6; Bülow/Böckstiegel/Müller, p. 151; Geimer/Schütze, pp. 891, 917.

[61] Schlosser, para. 175 (para. A1.470 below).

[62] *Allpac Holdings B.V.* v. *Carl Friederich Maier am Tor*, Gerechtshof (Netherlands), January 31, 1979, [1982] E.C.C. 200.

[63] Para. 37.11 below; Sched. 3 of the 1982 Act.

[64] In practice, the U.K. for these purposes will not include Scotland, where jurisdiction is not accepted on this basis.

[65] Formerly Ord. 11, rule 1(f)(iii).

[66] Collins, p. 52.

agreement in *Zelger* v. *Salinitri (No. 1)*[67] and held that if the clause is valid according to the national law applicable to the contract, the court for the agreed place of performance has jurisdiction, irrespective of whether the formal conditions provided for by Article 17 have been observed. It may be, though, that such a clause would only be effective if there were an objective link between the dispute and the court called upon to resolve it. In other words, the agreement may need not to be a sham.

9. Strangers to the agreement

21.19   In certain cases, a person who was not a direct party to a jurisdiction agreement at its inception may become bound by it if his consent is clearly stated or may be clearly deduced.[68] Two cases before the European Court of Justice have concerned the applicability of a jurisdiction agreement to a person who was not a party to it.

(a) *Beneficiary under an insurance policy.* The first case was *Gerling Konzern AG* v. *Amministrazione del Tesoro dello Stato.*[69] In that case the Italian Treasury was the successor to the interests of the Bureau for the Motor Transport of Goods (the "Bureau") who were the beneficiaries under an agreement between a syndicate of insurers (represented by Gerling) and the International Road Transport Union (the "Union"). The Union had entered into the agreement with the insurers for its own benefit and for the benefit of a number of national associations of which the Bureau was one. The Union and the insurers had signed the agreement, which included a jurisdiction clause. That clause expressly provided that in the event of a dispute between one of the national associations and the insurers, the national association should be entitled to insist on proceedings before the court having jurisdiction in the country where it had its registered office.

The Treasury sought to recover from the insurers reimbursement of its outlay in respect of certain sums which were due from the Bureau to the Italian customs. For that purpose, the Treasury

---

[67] [1980] E.C.R. 89, discussed at para. 17.15 above.
[68] But a jurisdiction clause in a main contract has been held not to apply to a subcontractor with a separate legal personality: *Stadtwerke Essen A.G.* v. *Société Trailigaz and Canaguie Générale des Eaux,* Cour d'Appel, Paris, March 19, 1987 [1988] E.C.C. 291. *Cf. Poly Roermond B.V.* v. *Tisos Belgium N.V.,* Arrondissementsrechtbank Maastricht, January 31, 1980, Ned.Jur.1981, p. 622, Digest D I–17.1.1—B15 (where a successor to a person's rights and obligations under a contract was held not to have become bound by the jurisdiction clause in the contract).
[69] [1983] E.C.R. 2503.

started an action in Rome. The insurers contested the jurisdiction[70] on the grounds that neither the Bureau nor the Treasury had signed the jurisdiction agreement, and that there was therefore no written confirmation that they agreed to it, contrary to Article 17 of the Convention.

The *Corte di Cassazione* referred to the European Court the ques- **21.20** tion whether the Treasury could rely on the jurisdiction clause. The European Court did not approach the case on the basis of agency, but considered the jurisdiction agreement as *res inter alios acta*, treating the Bureau and the Treasury as beneficiaries of the agreement, rather than as principals. It observed that the requirement of writing was in order to ensure that the consent of the parties was clearly and precisely demonstrated and actually established, and that its purpose was not to impose the same requirements on a third party for whose benefit the jurisdiction clause was concluded.[71] The Court went on to rule that such third parties:

> "even if they have not expressly signed the . . . clause, may rely upon it, provided that, as between the insurer and the policy-holder, the condition as to writing laid down by Article 17 of the Convention has been satisfied and provided that the consent of the insurer in that respect has been clearly manifested."[72]

(b) Holder of a bill of lading. The second case concerning the **21.21** application of a jurisdiction agreement to a person not a party to it was *Partenreederei m.s. "Tilly Russ" v. Haven und Vervoerbedrijf Nova N.V. and Goeminne Hout N.V.*,[73] which concerned a jurisdiction clause printed on the back of each of two bills of lading.

N.V. Goeminne Hout was a Belgian company which purchased a quantity of timber from an American company. The timber was carried by *Tilly Russ*, which was owned by a German company, from a Canadian port to Antwerp. The carrier's American agents had issued bills of lading to the American shippers, which had then been transferred in the ordinary way to the Belgian purchasers. On the arrival of the cargo in Antwerp, some of the packaging was found to be damaged and some 10 planks were missing. The Belgian purchasers therefore brought an action for damages (in the sum of U.S. $ 304) against the carriers in the Antwerp Commercial Court. The carriers objected to the jurisdiction of the Belgian court,

---

[70] They also put in a defence on the merits: see para. 21.95, n. 56 below.
[71] [1983] E.C.R. 2503, at p. 2515.
[72] *Ibid.*, at p. 2518.
[73] [1984] E.C.R. 2417 (often referred to simply as *"Tilly Russ"*). At the request of the U.K. government, which stressed the importance of the case for international commerce, the decision was made by a plenary session of the Court.

pointing to the jurisdiction clause on the bills of lading, which stipulated that disputes were to be decided by the court in Hamburg.

The court of first instance held that the jurisdiction clause did not fall within Article 17 and accepted jurisdiction over the dispute, and that decision was upheld on appeal. The carriers then appealed to the Belgian *Cour de Cassation*, which referred to the European Court of Justice a question which fell into two parts. The first part concerned the validity of the jurisdiction clause as between the shipper and the carrier—the original parties to the bill of lading.[74]

21.22   The second part of the question concerned the validity of the jurisdiction clause in dealings between the carrier and a third-party holder of the bill of lading. On this part of the question, the Court said:

> "In so far as a jurisdiction clause in a bill of lading is valid under Article 17 of the Convention as between the shipper and the carrier, and in so far as a third party, by acquiring the bill of lading, has succeeded to the shipper's rights and obligations under the relevant national law, the fact of allowing the third party to remove himself from the compulsory jurisdiction provided for in the bill of lading, on the ground that he did not signify his consent thereto, would be alien to the purpose of Article 17, which is to neutralise the effect of jurisdiction clauses that might pass unnoticed in contracts.
>
> In fact, in the circumstances outlined above, acquisition of the bill of lading could not confer upon the third party more rights than those attaching to the shipper under it. The third party holding the bill of lading thus becomes vested with all the rights, and at the same time becomes subject to all the obligations mentioned in the bill of lading, including those relating to the agreement on jurisdiction."[75]

The Court therefore went on to rule that:

> "As regards the relationship between the carrier and a third party holding the bill of lading, the conditions laid down by Article 17 of the Convention are satisfied if the jurisdiction clause has been adjudged valid as between the carrier and the shipper and if, by virtue of the relevant national law, the third party, upon acquiring the bill of lading, succeeded to the shipper's rights and obligations."[76]

Earlier decisions under the Convention concerning the position of a

---

[74] This aspect is discussed at para. 21.63 below.
[75] [1984] E.C.R. 2417, at p. 2435 (paras. 24 and 25).
[76] *Ibid.*, at p. 2436. In the light of this ruling, the Belgian Court of Cassation remitted the case to the court at Ghent to determine whether the holder of the bill of lading had succeeded to the shipper's rights and obligations: Hof van Cassatie, January 25, 1985, Rechtskundig Weekbl. 1985–86, col. 994, [1986] E.C.C. 493.

third party in relation to a bill of lading must now be read subject to this decision.[77]

It should be emphasised that the question whether or not the **21.23** third party holder of the bill of lading has succeeded to the shipper's rights and obligations is to be determined by the relevant national law and that the Convention plays no role in determining which national law is applicable. As was pointed out by Advocate General Sir Gordon Slynn in his Opinion:

> "If the holder does not stand in the shoes of the original shipper under the applicable national law, then a new agreement has to be found between the holder and the carrier, either in writing or evidenced by writing, on a choice of jurisdiction clause. It does not seem to me that the mere presentation by the holder of the bill, who has already purchased the goods, to the carrier would in itself constitute such an agreement or evidence of an agreement for the purposes of Article 17 . . . "[78]

10. Luxembourg domiciliaries

By Article I of the 1968 Protocol[79] special provision is made con- **21.24** cerning the formalities necessary for a jurisdiction agreement to be binding on a Luxembourg domiciliary. The provision is discussed below.[80]

11. Interpretation, conflicts and the applicability of national law

Article 17 is concerned to establish uniform rules for the validity **21.25** of jurisdiction agreements. As with the other jurisdictional rules in the Convention, its provisions apply directly within the framework of the national legal systems, and are subject to uniform interpretation.[81] The European Court has repeatedly stressed that the

---

[77] Earlier decisions to the same effect include *Basso Legnami S.p.A.* v. *The Licenses Insurance Company Ltd. and others*, Riv.dir.int.priv.proc. 1977, p. 613; Digest D I–17.1.2—B7; *Agenzia Marittima SAGITAL S.p.A.* v. *Bangkok International Motors Ltd.*, Corte d'Appello Genoa, May 25, 1979, Digest D I–17.1.2—B17 and *Gottardo Ruffoni S.p.A.* v. *Lloyd Triestino S.p.A.*, [1984] Dir.Mar. 321 (third party's endorsement held to be sufficient acknowledgment). Other cases on the point include *Poseidon Schiffahrt GmbH* v. *N.V. Delta Lloyd* Rechtskundig Weekbl. 1978, col. 1630, Digest D I–17.1.1—B5; *Somatra N.V.* v. *Koninklijke Nederlandse Lloyd B.V.*, Hof van Beroep Antwerp, December 20, 1978, Digest D I–17.1.1—B9; *Atlas Insurance Co. Ltd.* v. *Rederij Rhenania Shipping Corp. and others*, Rechtbank van Koophandel Antwerp, May 21, 1980, Digest D I–17.1.1—B16. See also the cases cited in the notes at Digest D I–17.1.1—B5n. and B9n.
[78] [1984] E.C.R. 2417, at p. 2444.
[79] Para. 35.01 below.
[80] Para. 21.69.
[81] Paras. 13.91 *et seq.* above.

Article must be strictly construed because its purpose is to ensure that the parties have actually consented to the choice of jurisdiction and that their consent is clearly and precisely demonstrated.[82]

It is important for an understanding of Article 17 to recognise the distinction between the validity of the choice of jurisdiction as a matter of form and its validity as a matter of substantive law. The Convention is concerned only with the formal validity of the agreement, while the substantive validity is a matter for national law.[83] Defining the borderline, though, between the proper field of application of the Convention and the applicability of national law may sometimes be difficult. The question may arise in relation to any one or more of three aspects of a case, namely the form of the agreement, the procedural law of the court seised of the case, and the substantive law of the agreement.[84]

21.26   (a) *Form of the agreement.* One of the principal features of Article 17 is the series of requirements as to the form of the agreement.[85] These requirements are not only necessary but also sufficient conditions for the formal validity of the agreement. National law may not validly impose any further formal requirements. If an agreement otherwise falling within Article 17 is affected by any requirements imposed by national law as to the form of the agreement, those requirements are invalid if and to the extent that they contradict or go beyond Article 17.

That, at least, seems to be the position in the light of the European Court's decision in *Elefanten Schuh GmbH* v. *Jacqmain*,[86] but the Court adopted cautious language in that case and confined its decision closely to the question submitted.

21.27   Mr. Jacqmain was employed by Elefanten Schuh GmbH, a German company, to work in the Flemish region of Belgium and his work was performed for the company's Belgian subsidiary, Elefan SA. His contract of employment was in German and included a clause giving jurisdiction to the court at Kleve, the town in Germany where the company had its registered office. Differences arose between the parties, which led to Jacqmain's dismissal. He

---

[82] Para. 21.37 below.

[83] The choice of the relevant national law may not be easy: see Dicey and Morris pp. 405–406.

[84] The applicability of Art. 17 has proved particularly troublesome in employment cases, a field which is not expressly affored any special treatment by the Convention, but in which national law typically contains restrictions on contracting out of the jurisdictional provisions of national law.

[85] Paras. 21.52 to 21.70 below.

[86] [1981] E.C.R. 1671. See also *Estasis Salotti* v. *RÜWA GmbH* and *Galerie Segoura* v. *Bonakdarian*, discussed at para. 21.73 below.

brought an action in the *Arbeidsrechtbank*, Antwerp,[87] claiming damages from both the parent company and the subsidiary for breach of his employment contract. According to Belgian law, the relevant contract of employment should have been in the Dutch language. As it was not, the *Arbeidshof*, Antwerp,[88] held on appeal that the contract was void, and that in consequence the jurisdiction clause was invalid and Article 17 could not apply. The case went on further appeal to the *Hof van Cassatie*, which referred various questions to the European Court. One of the questions was:

> "Does it conflict with Article 17 of the Convention to rule that an agreement conferring jurisdiction on a court is void if the document in which the agreement is contained is not drawn up in the language which is prescribed by the law of a Contracting State upon penalty of nullity and if the court of the State before which the agreement is relied upon is bound by that law to declare the document to be void of its own motion?"[89]

Advocate General Sir Gordon Slynn took the view that the validity of the agreement should be decided according to the law of the chosen forum.[90] The United Kingdom government argued that a jurisdiction agreement which was severable from the contract (if there was one) should be considered in the light of Article 17 alone, but that if it were not severable, its validity should depend upon the validity of the contract itself, which would be decided pursuant to the law applicable according to the conflict rules of the forum.[91] The Commission submitted that national law only applied to the validity of the jurisdiction agreement after Article 17 had been applied.[92]

The Court, citing the Jenard Report's observations on the purpose of Article 17,[93] observed that: **21.28**

> "Article 17 is . . . intended to lay down itself the formal requirements which agreements conferring jurisdiction must meet; the purpose is to ensure legal certainty and that the parties have given their consent . . . Contracting States are not free to lay down formal requirements other than those contained in the Convention."[94]

In its ruling, the Court stated:

---

[87] The Arbeidsrechtbank is the labour court of first instance and the Arbeidshof is the labour court of appeal: see paras. 48.20 and 48.21 below.
[88] *Ibid.*
[89] Other questions referred by the Belgian Court are discussed at paras. 21.86 and 21.94 below.
[90] [1981] E.C.R. 1671, at pp. 1697–1699.
[91] *Ibid.*, at pp. 1680–1681.
[92] *Ibid.*, at p. 1681.
[93] Jenard, para. A1.165 below.
[94] [1981] E.C.R. 1671, at p. 1688.

"Article 17 . . . must be interpreted as meaning that the legislation of a Contracting State may not allow the validity of an agreement conferring jurisdiction to be called in question solely on the ground that the language used is not that prescribed by the legislation."[95]

21.29   *(b) Procedural law of the court seised.* It is worth restating that the Convention's purpose is to provide uniform jurisdictional rules which apply throughout the Community and for this purpose it takes precedence over conflicting provisions of national law. As with questions of the form of the agreement, it may sometimes be hard to distinguish between the procedural and substantive law which applies to a particular case concerned with a choice of jurisdiction agreement under Article 17.

Sanicentral GmbH v. *Collin*[96] illustrates the point, but does little to resolve the difficulty. It too was a trans-border employment case. Mr. Collin was of French nationality, domiciled in France, but he was employed by a German company, Sanicentral GmbH, to work "independently of any establishment" across the border in Germany. His contract contained a clause conferring jurisdiction over any dispute on the local German court. A dispute arose and Mr. Collin took his case before the French *Tribunal d'Instance*, which held that it had jurisdiction under French law.[97]

In the early stages of the proceedings, the question of the Convention's applicability was argued solely on the basis of the transitional provisions, because the contract had been entered into, and the dispute had arisen, before the Convention had come into force. The question referred to the European Court of Justice by the *Cour de Cassation* was largely formulated by reference to the issue arising on the transitional provisions,[98] but, as Advocate General Capotorti observed, the case afforded the opportunity for the Court to consider:

"whether clauses conferring jurisdiction which the parties to a contract of employment have agreed upon are in every case effective in accordance with Article 17 of the Convention, notwithstanding the contrary provisions of some statutory legislation in regard to the exclusion of the jurisdiction of the national courts dealing with labour relations."[99]

The Court observed:

"on the one hand, that the Convention does not affect rules of sub-

---

[95] *Ibid.*, at p. 1690.
[96] [1979] E.C.R. 3423.
[97] Art. 14 of the Civil Code, on the basis of the plaintiff's French nationality, and Art. 517–1 of the Labour Code under which, in the circumstances, the court for the district of the employee's residence had jurisdiction.
[98] This aspect of the case is discussed at paras. 32.10 *et seq.* below.
[99] [1979] E.C.R. 3423, at p. 3431.

stantive law and, on the other hand, that, as the Convention seeks to determine the jurisdiction of the courts of the Contracting States in the intra-Community legal order in regard to matters of civil jurisdiction, the national procedural laws applicable to the cases concerned are set aside in the matters governed by the Convention in favour of the provisions thereof."[1]

In its ruling, the Court stated that:

" . . . clauses conferring jurisdiction included in contracts of employment concluded [before the Convention came into force] must be considered valid even in cases in which they would have been regarded as void under the national law in force at the time when the contract was entered into."[2]

It would seem then, that any provision of national law whereby **21.30** the jurisdiction of the courts may not be ousted will only be valid to the extent that it does not conflict with the provisions of the Convention. In some cases, the particular subject-matter of the dispute may preserve the effect of national law,[3] but in other fields, such as in employment cases,[4] national law may be rendered wholly ineffective.[5]

Especially in the field of employment law, the exent to which Article 17 can override anti-ouster provisions introduced, no doubt, for sound reasons of social policy, may work considerable injustices. It may tempt unscrupulous employers to include jurisdiction clauses in their contracts of employment, specifying inconvenient fora, in the hope that such clauses will be effective to oust the jurisdiction of the court which would normally have jurisdiction, and hence discourage employees from pursuing their complaints. But the European Court of Justice has sometimes been willing to adopt a radical approach in this field[6] and it is doubtful whether it would adopt an interpretation of the Convention which permitted such an abuse.

---

[1] *Ibid.*, at p. 3429.
[2] *Ibid.*, at p. 3431.
[3] *e.g.* a dispute to which s.141 of the Rent Act 1977 applies will usually or always fall within Art. 16(1) and will not be affected by Art. 17. On the other hand, where a county court's jurisdiction in the case of a consumer contract is protected by ss.141 and 173 of the Consumer Credit Act 1974, it may find that its jurisdiction is ousted by a jurisdiction agreement, but only if the agreement complies with the narrow requirements of Art. 15.
[4] s.140 of the Employment Protection (Consolidation) Act 1978 makes an agreement purporting to oust the jurisdiction of an industrial tribunal void.
[5] For a jurisdiction clause held valid, despite the contrary provisions of French procedural law, see *Mosbacher et Société Uniputz* v. *Banque Nationale de Paris,* Journal dr. int. 1980, p. 252, Digest D I–17.1.1—B12.
[6] *Cf.* Hartley, p. 72; *Ivenel* v. *Schwab* [1982] E.C.R. 1891, discussed at para. 17.24 above.

21.31   It may be that *Sanicentral* v. *Collin* does not provide a blanket condemnation of such procedural anti-avoidance provisions. Despite the apparently wide terms of the judgment, there are three particular aspects of the case which may tend to restrict its application. First, the French court would not have had jurisdiction under the other provisions of the Convention;[7] secondly, the national rules relied upon as contradicting the jurisdiction agreement were rules which conferred jurisdiction on the French court,[8] rather than anti-ouster rules; and thirdly, only the Commission made submissions to the European Court and the case was argued principally on the question of the transitional applicability of the Convention.

21.32   *(c) Substantive law.* In principle, the Convention does not affect substantive law,[9] but where the applicable substantive law has jurisdictional effects, the law may be contrary to the Convention. The extent to which the Convention reaches into the field of substantive law is very far from clear and a question which the law of one country regards as substantive may be regarded by the law of another country as procedural. The point arises particularly clearly when the validity of a jurisdiction clause is in issue. For example, the law of one country may provide that a clause may not be relied upon, while that of another may provide that it is void. As has been observed, if a provision of national law contravenes, or goes beyond, the terms of Article 17, it will not take effect and that is so even if the provision purports to make the jurisdiction agreement void,[10] rather than merely inoperative.[11]

It appears that where a court has to consider whether it has jurisdiction (which it may have to do of its own motion),[12] the fact that the existence or validity of the agreement is in dispute makes no dif-

---

[7] See the observations of the Commission at [1979] E.C.R. 3423, at p. 3427. By allowing the French court to retain jurisdiction the Court in fact gave effect to the social considerations which later caused it to apply the doctrine of characteristic performance in employment cases: see its decision in *Ivenel* v. *Schwab*, above.

[8] In the case of Art. 14 of the Civil Code, the rule was also an exorbitant jurisdiction expressly excluded by the second para. of Art. 3: para. 16.09 above.

[9] *Sanicentral* v. *Collin*, para. 21.29 above.

[10] That was the case in *Elefanten Schuh*, para. 21.27 above.

[11] The validity of a jurisdiction clause was upheld, despite being contrary to national law in *Mosbacher et Société Uniputz* v. *Banque Nationale de Paris*, Journal dr. int. 1980, p. 252, Digest D I–17.1.1—B12. The question whether Art. 17 overrides provisions of national law which invalidate a jurisdiction clause was expressly left open by the Oberlandesgericht Frankfurt-am-Main (judgment of April 3, 1979, case 5 U 150/78) and the Bundesgerichtshof (judgment of March 20, 1980, case III ZR 151/79), RIW/AWD 1980, p. 432, [1981] E.C.C. 83, Digest D I–17.1.1—B11 and B11n.

[12] Arts. 19 and 20, paras. 22.01 and 22.11 below.

ference.[13] The court cannot decline to answer the question[14] and it will therefore have to decide the validity of the jurisdiction agreement, if necessary by deciding the validity of the wider contract in which the jurisdiction agreement is contained. What law should it apply in so doing?

It may frequently be the case that each of the parties to a contract **21.33** will argue that its own standard terms and conditions are incorporated into the contract. These terms may well contain jurisdiction clauses which are in direct conflict. Unless the court first seised of the dispute[15] knows which law to apply to resolve that issue, it cannot begin to unravel the question of whether it has jurisdiction or is required to decline it. Because the Convention does not affect substantive law, it ought not to affect the way in which national courts approach that question. It is submitted that the closest the Convention can come to providing a uniform rule is to require national courts to apply their own law, including their own conflicts rules, to determine which law governs the contract, or at least the jurisdiction agreement, and then apply that law to determine the validity of the jurisdiction agreement.[16] Once it has done that, the court will be able to determine the contents of the jurisdiction agreement and will then be able to consider it in the light of Article 17.

The application by each court of its own conflicts rules may lead to the courts of different Contracting States finding that different laws are applicable, but the theoretical possibility of a plaintiff being denied a forum altogether is avoided by the obligation on courts to recognise the decisions of the courts of the other Contracting States,[17] and the problem of conflicting decisions on the applicable law will be further eased when the Contractual Obligations Convention[18] comes into force.

Allied to the question of the validity of a jurisdiction agreement, is the question of its very existence. In considering whether the par-

---

[13] *Sanders* v. *van der Putte* [1977] E.C.R. 2383, discussed at para. 20.16 above; *Effer* v. *Kantner* [1982] E.C.R. 825, discussed at para. 17.08 above.

[14] See para. 21.15 above.

[15] Other courts will have to stay or dismiss their proceedings: Arts. 21–23, chap. 23 below.

[16] Droz, para. 214; Bülow/Böckstiegel/Müller, p. 146; Collins, p. 88; Dicey and Morris, p. 406; *contra*, Advocate General Sir Gordon Slynn, in *Elefanten Schuh* v. *Jacqmain* [1981] E.C.R. 1671, at pp. 1697–9, who observes that this solution might lead to different laws being chosen by the courts of different Contracting States, because of their different conflicts rules; *dubitante*, Geimer/Schütze, pp. 933–934.

[17] Art. 26, para. 27.01 below.

[18] EEC Convention on the Law Applicable to Contractual Obligations, opened for signature in Rome on June 19, 1980, O.J. 1980 L266. Arts. 3 to 6 are set out at paras. A2.41 *et seq.* below.

ties have entered into a jurisdiction agreement at all, within the meaning of Article 17, the court has to consider whether there was actually a consensus between the parties. This test is required by an independent interpretation of Article 17 and is perhaps the point at which the Article penetrates furthest into the field of substantive law.[19] It is considered further below.[20]

B. ARTICLE 17, FIRST PARAGRAPH: JURISDICTION AGREEMENTS

1. "If the parties, one or more of whom is domiciled in a Contracting State . . . "

21.34   One of the notable features of Article 17 is that, unlike many of the provisions of the Convention which depend on the defendant being domiciled in a Contracting State, it is sufficient for the purposes of this Article if the plaintiff is domiciled in a Contracting State. The position which arises where both parties are domiciled in the same Contracting State has already been discussed.[21]

The requirement that one or more of the parties should be domiciled in a Contracting State is a requirement which has to be met for Article 17 to apply and hence to found exclusive jurisdiction, but it should not affect the validity of the jurisdiction agreement itself.[22] It follows that Article 17 should not invalidate a jurisdiction agreement between parties, neither of whom is domiciled in a Contracting State.[22a] Such an agreement may be effective as a matter of national law to confer jurisdiction apart from the Convention, and indeed Article 17 provides a rule of priority of jurisdiction for such a case.[23]

21.35   At what point in time must the requirement be fulfilled? It seems clear that if one of the parties was domiciled in a Contracting State at the time when the jurisdiction agreement was entered into, Article 17 will apply to it even if neither party is domiciled in a Contracting State when proceedings are commenced.[24] What is less clear is whether a jurisdiction agreement entered into by parties, neither of whom is domiciled in a Contracting State, becomes subject to the requirements of Article 17, if one of the parties has

---

[19] See, for example, Oberlandesgericht Karlsruhe, December 30, 1981, case 14 U 4/81, N.J.W. 1982, p. 1950, Digest D I–17.1.1—B17.

[20] Para. 21.37.

[21] Para. 21.06 above.

[22] Droz, para. 183.

[22a] But the Hoge Raad has declined to give effect to such a jurisdiction clause in the absence of an objective connection with the chosen court: *Transocean Towage Co. Ltd.* v. *Hyundai Construction Co. Ltd.* [1987] E.C.C. 282.

[23] Para. 21.71 below.

[24] Droz, para. 184; Bülow/Böckstiegel/Müller, p. 142; Geimer/Schütze, p. 205.

become domiciled in a Contracting State by the time proceedings are commenced.

The argument in favour of making such a case subject to Article 17 is twofold. First, the purpose of the Convention is to afford protection to those domiciled within the Contracting States, and, in the context of Article 17, particularly to protect them from jurisdiction clauses of which they may not have been aware. They are no less in need of that protection by virtue of having formerly been domiciled outside the Contracting States.[25] Secondly, a court which has to decide, of its own motion if need be,[26] whether to give effect to such a jurisdiction agreement, will probably find it easier to determine the domicile of the parties at the time the proceedings commence than at the time of the agreement.

On the other hand, considerations of legal certainty would favour   **21.36**
an interpretation which did not permit the effectiveness of a jurisdiction agreement to depend upon whether one or other of the parties had moved his domicile into a Contracting State at some time after the agreement was concluded.[27] This latter argument applied in reverse permits Article 17 to apply to a jurisdiction agreement concluded at a time when at least one of the parties was domiciled in a Contracting State, even if neither party was domiciled in a Contracting State when proceedings were commenced.[28] That proposition, as already observed, is generally accepted as correct.

It is suggested that an interpretation is to be preferred which allows only the date of the agreement to be relevant in deciding whether the requirement is fulfilled, a solution which is consistent with the terms of Articles 12(3) and 15(3). A definitive answer, however, must await determination by the courts.

2. " . . . have agreed . . . "

The European Court of Justice made it clear at an early stage that   **21.37**
the question of *whether* the parties have reached agreement on a choice of jurisdiction is to be decided according to an independent test derived from the Convention itself.[29] Both *Estasis Salotti* v. *RÜWA*[30] and *Galeries Segoura SPRL* v. *Rahim Bonakdarian*,[31] referred to the European Court together by the German Federal Supreme Court, raised detailed questions on the requirements of

---

[25] Droz, para. 185.
[26] Arts. 19 and 20, paras. 22.01 and 22.11 below.
[27] Bülow/Böckstiegel/Müller, p 142, Geimer/Schütze, p. 206.
[28] Bülow/Böckstiegel/Müller, p. 142.
[29] See also para. 21.32 above.
[30] *Estasis Salotti di Colzani Aimo e Gianmario Colzani* v. *RÜWA Polstereimaschinen GmbH* [1976] E.C.R. 1831.
[31] [1976] E.C.R. 1851.

Article 17 as to the form of a jurisdiction agreement.[32] In identically worded passages in its decisions, the European Court quoted the opening passage of Article 17, and continued:

> "The way in which that provision is to be applied must be interpreted in the light of the effect of the conferment of jurisdiction by consent, which is to exclude both the jurisdiction determined by the general principle laid down in Article 2 and the special jurisdictions provided for in Articles 5 and 6 of the Convention.
>
> In view of the consequences that such an option may have on the position of the parties to the action, the requirements set out in Article 17 governing the validity of clauses conferring jurisdiction must be strictly construed.
>
> By making such validity subject to the existence of an 'agreement' between the parties, Article 17 imposes upon the court before which the matter is brought the duty of examining, first, whether the clause conferring jurisdiction upon it was in fact the subject of a consensus between the parties, which must be clearly and precisely demonstrated.
>
> The purpose of the formal requirements imposed by Article 17 is to ensure that the consensus between the parties is in fact established."[33]

21.38   That passage has been confirmed, both expressly and impliedly, by the European Court on a number of occasions[34] and may be taken as settled law. The need for consensus to be clearly and precisely demonstrated is the key to deciding whether the form of a given agreement, and the circumstances of its conclusion, are such as to bring it within Article 17. The European Court of Justice has laid down certain detailed criteria for the formal requirements, and these are discussed below,[35] but the following examples, drawn from the decisions of national courts, may be mentioned here.

Where a draft contract remained unsigned, despite the defendant having later referred to it as "the contract," the jurisdiction clause in it was held not to satisfy Article 17.[36] Similarly, it has been held

---

[32] This aspect is discussed at paras. 21.52 *et seq.* below.

[33] [1976] E.C.R. 1831 and 1851, at pp. 1841 and 1860.

[34] *Porta-Leasing* v. *Prestige International* [1980] E.C.R. 1517, at p. 1523; *Elefanten Schuh* v. *Jacqmain* [1981] E.C.R. 1671, at p. 1688; *Gerling Konzern* v. *Amministrazione del Tesoro dello Stato* [1983] E.C.R. 2503; *Partenreederei m.s. "Tilly Russ"* v. *Haven und Vervoerbedrijf Nova N.V. and Goeminne Hout N.V.* [1984] E.C.R. 2417, at p. 2432; *Berghoefer GmbH & Co KG* v. *A.S.A. SA* [1985] E.C.R. 2699, at p. 2708; *Iveco Fiat S.p.A.* v. *N.V. van Hool* [1986] E.C.R. 3337, at para. 5.

[35] Paras. 21.52 *et seq.*

[36] *Ernst Müller K.G.* v. *Muni*, Riv.dir.int.priv.proc. 1980, p. 245; Digest D I–5.1.2—B23.

that a jurisdiction clause could not be inferred from conduct,[37] nor from the mere absence of objection to a clause printed on an invoice.[38] Where competing jurisdiction clauses conflict, it is clear that there is no consensus. But the fact that a jurisdiction clause is in a foreign language (so far as the party against whom it is invoked is concerned) does not itself invalidate the agreement.[39]

3. " . . . a court or the courts of a Contracting State . . . "

Article 17 requires the courts of each Contracting State to decline **21.39** jurisdiction if the courts of another Contracting State have been validly chosen by the parties,[40] but it leaves the parties free either to choose the particular court or merely to specify in general terms the courts of a given Contracting State. The distinction is of greater importance in continental countries, where the jurisdiction of most courts is geographically limited.[41]

If the jurisdiction agreement merely makes a general reference to the *courts* of a Contracting State, how is it to be decided whether a particular court has jurisdiction? As has been observed,[42] an objective link between the subject-matter of the dispute and the chosen court is probably not required. Article 17 is quite clear in providing that the jurisdiction of the court or courts chosen is compulsory[43] and if the internal law of the state whose courts have been chosen provides for a particular court to have jurisdiction, there should be no problem.[44] If national law does not provide an answer to the

---

[37] Oberlandesgericht Frankfurt-am-Main; April 27, 1976, case 5 U 173/75, RIW/AWD 1976, p. 532 Digest D I–17.1.2—B4.

[38] *PVBA M.I.* v. *K.*, Rechtbank van Koophandel, Kortrijk (Belgium), October 7, 1975, Rechtskundig Weekbl. 1976, Col. 2030, Digest D I–17.1.2—B1.

[39] *Cotonfil s.r.l.* v. *Chemitex s.p.r.l.*, [1983] E.C.C. 8, Riv.dir.int.priv.proc. 1981, p. 920, Digest D I–17.1.2—B19.

[40] For the case where the parties have chosen a court or courts outside the Contracting States, see para. 21.13 above. A clause in a bill of lading conferring jurisdiction on the courts of the sea-carrier's principal place of business, but which did not identify the vessel's owner or operator, or the place of business, has been rejected for lack of particularity: *Spedag Scheepvaart en Expeditiebedriff B.V.* v. *Andra Reederei GmbH & Co. K.G.*, Arrondissementsrechtbank Rotterdam, November 23, 1984 [1985] Sch. en Sch. 257, [1986] Eur.L.Dig. 206.

[41] It is also limited in the U.K.—on the one hand between England and Wales, Scotland and Northern Ireland and, on the other hand, more locally at the lower levels, *e.g.* county courts, sheriff courts, magistrates' courts and industrial tribunals. See para. 3.21 above.

[42] Para. 21.16 above.

[43] Para. 21.15 above; para. 21.43 below.

[44] As between the different parts of the U.K., ss.10 and 16 and Sched. 4 of the Act (paras. 40.30, 41.01 and 45.01 *et seq.* below) will cover most cases. For any case not covered by those provisions, the court probably still has a residual *forum conveniens* discretion, purely as a matter of internal U.K. law (see para. 41.04 below).

question of which court can or should decide the case, it may be either that the agreement is without legal effect,[45] or that the national law is contrary to the Convention in not providing a forum.[46]

21.40 It is suggested that, even in those few cases where national law does not appear to provide an answer, the preferable interpretation of the Convention would be one which leaves the parties free to bring their dispute before some court in the chosen state. The plaintiff should be free to choose the court,[47] and if the defendant cannot point to another court in that state which has jurisdiction, the court chosen by the plaintiff should be required to accept jurisdiction.

A number of problems may arise in connection with a variety of non-exclusive jurisdiction agreements which do not simply choose a single court in a Contracting State or the courts of one Contracting State. These problems are discussed below.[48]

4. " . . . any disputes which have arisen or which may arise in connection with a particular legal relationship . . . "

21.41 The same two parties may have different legal relationships between them and accordingly the consensus required of the parties by Article 17 (which the formal requirements are designed to ensure)[49] needs to be consensus not only as to the court which should have jurisdiction, but also as to the "particular legal relationship" over which it should have jurisdiction. This further refinement is another example of the Convention including provisions designed to protect weaker parties from the comprehensive jurisdiction clauses of their stronger trading partners—especially those contained in written standard terms and conditions.[50]

The requirement that the agreement should relate to a "particular legal relationship" is most likely to be relevant where the parties are in a continuing business relationship[51] and a jurisdiction agree-

---

[45] It seems, at least, that this is the case if there is no "connecting factor between the contractual situation and the State whose courts have been agreed on as having jurisdiction." This is the suggestion of Professor Batiffol, in his comments on the Hague Convention on the jurisdiction of the contractual forum in disputes relating to the international sale of goods, April 15, 1958, cited in the Jenard Report (para. A1.167 below). See also Bülow/Böckstiegel/Müller, p. 152.

[46] Droz, para. 212.

[47] *Ibid.*

[48] Paras. 21.44 *et seq.*

[49] Para. 21.37 above; para. 21.53 below.

[50] Bülow/Böckstiegel/Müller, p. 150.

[51] Droz, para. 200.

ment is carried forward from one transaction to the next.[52] If, then, a different contractual relationship arises, the jurisdiction clause will only be held to apply if the court is satisfied that the parties had agreed that it should apply to the new relationship.

It will be a question of fact or mixed fact and law in each case, **21.42** whether a new legal relationship not governed by an existing jurisdiction clause has arisen. For example, company A regularly supplies company B with office furniture, under terms and conditions containing a jurisdiction clause. If A then starts to supply B with a different kind of office furniture, the legal relationship is probably the same, but if it starts to supply goods of a quite different kind, not envisaged by the parties at the time of the original jurisdiction agreement—computer software, say—it could well be that a new legal relationship had arisen.

A jurisdiction agreement can be entered into after a dispute has arisen,[53] but much more frequently will be entered into at a time when there is no dispute, as part of an overall contractual relationship. This is perfectly permissible for the purposes of Article 17.[54] Similarly, the parties can make provision in their jurisdiction agreement for future legal relationships, provided always that the consensus is defined sufficiently precisely.

5. " . . . shall have exclusive jurisdiction . . . "

(a) *Exclusive jurisdiction.* The mechanism provided by Article 17 **21.43** is designed to ensure that the parties really have agreed that a particular court is to have jurisdiction, and then to make sure (in the absence of waiver of the jurisdiction agreement, under Article 18 or otherwise) that effect is given to that agreement. If the agreement complies with the other provisions of Article 17, any court other than the court chosen is required by Articles 19 and 20 to decline jurisdiction, *of its own motion*, in favour of the chosen court or courts. Principles of *forum non conveniens* have no place in the Convention's scheme of jurisdiction,[55] the rules of which are compulsory. The use of the word "shall" confirms that the court chosen has no discretion not to accept jurisdiction and the use of the word "exclusive" confirms that courts other than the court chosen have no discretion to accept jurisdiction. If it were otherwise, Article 17

---

[52] Paras. 21.57(4) and 21.66(3)(a) below.
[53] *Quelle Italia s.r.l.* v. *De Cillia*, Riv.dir.int.priv.proc. 1982, p. 377, Digest D I–1.1—B6n.
[54] The position is different under Arts. 12 and 15, paras. 18.55 and 19.39 above.
[55] Collins, p. 84; Droz, para. 206; Geimer/Schütze, pp. 288, 507, 918. See para. 21.15 above.

would not be adequate to ensure that effect was given to the parties' express agreement.[56]

It should be stressed, though, that the effect of Article 17 is not confined to agreements conferring exclusive jurisdiction on a single court or the courts of a single place or country. Agreements conferring non-exclusive jurisdiction on a court or the courts of a Contracting State are also subject to Article 17. On one hand, parties may confer exclusive jurisdiction for different purposes on different courts or the courts of different Contracting States (multiple exclusive jurisdictions), while on the other hand, the parties may confer non-exclusive jurisdiction on one or more such court or courts.

21.44   *(b) Multiple exclusive jurisdictions.* A case in which the parties chose more than one jurisdiction, each on an exclusive basis, became before the European Court of Justice in *Meeth* v. *Glacetal S.à.r.l.*[57] In interpreting Article 17 in its application to such a case, the Court adopted a pragmatic approach and drew particular attention to the Convention's concern both with the need to respect parties' rights of independence and with the need to avoid superfluous procedure.[58]

Glacetal, a glass manufacturer based in France, agreed to supply glass to Meeth, an undertaking based in Germany. The contract provided that if Meeth sued Glacetal, the French courts alone should have jurisdiction; and if Glacetal sued Meeth, the German courts alone should have jurisdiction. Meeth failed to pay for certain deliveries and Glacetal brought an action in the German courts. Meeth raised a set-off, alleging damage caused by Glacetal's late or defective performance of its contractual obligations. At first instance, Glacetal obtained judgment and the defence of set-off was rejected on the merits. Meeth appealed and the *Oberlandesgericht* dismissed the appeal, *inter alia* on the ground that the jurisdiction agreement prevented Meeth from raising the set-off in the German courts. Meeth appealed again, and the *Bundesgerichtshof* referred two questions to the European Court.

21.45   The first question was whether Article 17 permitted a jurisdiction agreement such as that entered into by these parties. The Court ruled that it did. It pointed out that the wording of Article 17 refers

---

[56] The Jenard Report (para. A1.167 below) states that the reason for giving the chosen court exclusive jurisdiction was that that was essential to avoid different courts from being properly seised of the matter and giving conflicting, or at least, differing, judgments. This is not an adequate explanation. The solution to potential conflicts of jurisdiction in relation to Art. 17 lies in the *lis pendens* and related actions rules in Arts. 21 to 23, just as it does in relation to the many other instances where the Convention provides concurrent jurisdictions.

[57] [1978] E.C.R. 2133.

[58] *Ibid.*, at p. 2142 (para. 8).

to the choice by the parties to the contract of a single court or the courts of a single state, and continued:

> "That wording, which is based on the most widespread business practice, cannot, however, be interpreted as intending to exclude the right of the parties to agree on two or more courts for the purpose of settling any disputes which may arise . . .
>
> This applies particularly where the parties have by such an agreement reciprocally conferred jurisdiction on the courts specified in the general rule laid down by Article 2 of the Convention."[59]

The second question was whether such a jurisdiction agreement prevented the defendant from raising a set-off based on the same agreement, in answer to the plaintiff's claim. The European Court referred to the principles of the parties' rights of independence and the need to avoid superfluous procedure and continued,

> "In the light of both those objectives, Article 17 cannot be interpreted as preventing a court before which proceedings have been instituted pursuant to a clause conferring jurisdiction of the type described above from taking into account a set-off connected with the legal relationship in dispute if such court considers that course to be compatible with the letter and spirit of the clause conferring jurisdiction."[60]

(c) Non-exclusive jurisdiction agreements. Jurisdiction agreements **21.46** concluded for the benefit of one of the parties may be only partly effective by reason of the fourth paragraph of Article 17.[61] Apart from those agreements, and in addition to agreements giving exclusive jurisdiction to more than one court (discussed above) three other possible forms of non-exclusive jurisdiction agreements should be mentioned.

    (1) The first category of agreement is where the parties do not choose a particular court, or even the courts of a particular

---

[59] *Ibid.*, at pp. 2141–2142 (para. 5).

[60] *Ibid.*, at p. 2143 (para. 8). In the light of the European Court's decision, the Bundesgerichtshof held that the parties had clearly expressed their intention that each might only be sued before the courts of its own state and the set-off could not, therefore, be maintained: Judgment of June 20, 1979, case VIII ZR 228/76, N.J.W. 1979, p. 2477, [1979] E.C.C. 455, Digest D I–17.1.1—B13. The European Court's decision was followed by the French Cour de Cassation in upholding the validity of a jurisdiction clause under which the parties could be sued only in the courts of their respective domiciles: *Schumacher Maschinenbau* v. *Technic Equipment*, Rev. critique 1981, p. 134, Digest D I–17.1.1—B13n. A decision of the Oberlandesgericht Frankfurt-am-Main, to the effect that an agreement conferring jurisdiction on the court of the plaintiff's domicile was invalid, probably could not stand in the light of *Meeth* v. *Glacetal*: decision of September 20, 1978, case 18 W 38/78, Digest D I–17.1.1—B8.

[61] Para. 21.80 below. See Kohler, "Pathologisches im EVGU: Hinkende Gerichtsstandsvereinbarungen nach Art. 17 Abs. 3", I Prax 1986, p. 340.

Contracting State, but, by an agreement which otherwise complies with Article 17, expressly exclude the jurisdiction of a court which would otherwise have jurisdiction under the Convention. This case is not mentioned by Article 17, but it would seem that it should apply by analogy,[62] at least if one or more other courts had jurisdiction under the Convention. Just as a positive choice of jurisdiction is, by necessary implication, an agreement to exclude the jurisdiction of otherwise competent courts,[63] an agreement which excludes the jurisdiction of an otherwise competent court is, by necessary implication, a choice of the otherwise competent court or courts. If there is no other competent court or courts under the Convention, the agreement would take on a wholly different character, namely that of a clause which sought to oust the jurisdictional rules of the Convention altogether, including the rules in Article 17. It is submitted that an agreement of this latter character would be invalid, as being contrary to the Convention, unless it was an arbitration agreement, which is expressly outside the Convention's scope.[64]

The effect of an agreement which excluded a competent jurisdiction, but left other competent jurisdictions undisturbed, would seem to be as follows. All the other courts which had jurisdiction under the Convention would have "exclusive" jurisdiction[65] within the meaning of Article 17 and any court other than the court first seised of the case would have to decline jurisdiction under Article 23[66] (or, possibly, stay its proceedings under Article 21).[67]

21.47   (2) The second category of case is where the parties choose the courts of more than one Contracting State, by adopting some formula such as "the courts of England and France shall have exclusive jurisdiction" or "the parties agree to the jurisdiction of the courts of England and France."[68] In each case the agreement is, by necessary implication, excluding the jurisdiction of any other court which would have jurisdiction under the Convention. The interpretation of such an agreement is, in principle, the

---

[62] Bülow/Böckstiegel/Müller, p. 142.
[63] See paras. 21.03 and 21.06 above.
[64] Art. 1, second para, sub-para. (4), para. 14.31 above.
[65] See sub-para. (2) below.
[66] Para. 23.24 below.
[67] Para. 23.01 below.
[68] Collins, p. 85. A similar problem may arise within the U.K. where the "courts of the United Kingdom" are specified: see para. 41.04 below.

same as that to be applied to an agreement merely to exclude the jurisdiction of an otherwise competent court (the first category discussed above) but with the added characteristic that it goes on in addition to make a positive choice of court. In other words, in the terminology of the Convention, it is both a prorogation of the jurisdiction of the chosen court and a derogation from that of otherwise competent courts.[69] Again Article 17 should apply to the case. The courts of both England and France, in the above example, would have "exclusive jurisdiction" within the meaning of the Article and any courts other than those chosen would have to decline jurisdiction. A court in England or France would be required to accept jurisdiction (provided it had jurisdiction under national law),[70] if it was the first court seised, but would otherwise have to decline jurisdiction under Article 23[71] (or, possibly, stay its proceedings under Article 21).[72]

(3) The third category of case is where the parties make a positive choice of a particular court or the courts of a particular Contracting State, but state that the court or courts shall have "non-exclusive jurisdiction".[73] The effect of such an agreement will depend on the circumstances. Four situations can be envisaged: **21.48**

  (i) where the court or courts chosen would not otherwise have jurisdiction, and no other court in a Contracting State would otherwise have jurisdiction;

 (ii) where the court or courts chosen is or are in any event the only courts which would have jurisdiction under the Convention anyway;

(iii) where the court or courts chosen would not otherwise have jurisdiction under the Convention, but another court or other courts in the Contracting States would have jurisdiction under the Convention; and

(iv) where the court or courts chosen would anyway have jurisdiction under the Convention in any event, but another court or other courts in the Contracting States would also have jurisdiction under the Convention.

---

[69] Para. 21.03 above.
[70] See para. 21.39 above.
[71] Para. 23.24 below.
[72] Para. 23.01 below.
[73] *Cf.* Collins, p. 85. Such clauses are common in international financial transactions.

21.49   The first situation is analogous to the case already discussed[74] where parties have chosen the exclusive jurisdiction of a court which would not otherwise be competent under the Convention, the only difference being that here the choice is expressed to be "non-exclusive." For the reasons advanced in relation to an exclusive choice of jurisdiction of this type,[75] it is submitted that the jurisdiction agreement would be effective to grant jurisdiction to the chosen court, and the characterisation of the choice as "non-exclusive" makes no difference.

The same considerations apply to the second situation, which is analogous to the case, also discussed above,[76] of the exclusive choice of the court which is anyway the only court with jurisdiction under the Convention. Again, it is submitted that the choice of jurisdiction agreement would not affect the jurisdiction of the chosen court.

21.50   In both the third and fourth situations, the Convention grants jurisdiction to other courts within the Contracting States. The question in each case is whether the effect of the "non-exclusive" jurisdiction agreement is to oust the jurisdiction of those courts. If it is, it would seem that the Convention overrules the expressed wishes of the parties, without any of the Convention's purposes being advanced. The reason why courts which would otherwise be competent under the Convention to decide a dispute are required to relinquish that jurisdiction where the parties have agreed to give jurisdiction to a court or the courts of another Contracting State, is that such an agreement is not only a positive election of a forum, it is also, by necessary implication, an exclusion of the jurisdiction of the courts which would otherwise be competent.[77] On the other hand, where the parties express their choice of court to be "non-exclusive", not only is the exclusion of otherwise competent courts no longer necessary, it is actually contrary to their agreement.[78]

So, in a case in either the third or fourth category, it is submitted, the chosen court or courts should be permitted to exercise jurisdiction over the dispute, but any other court or courts with jurisdiction

---

[74] See the first example discussed at para. 21.08 above.

[75] Paras. 21.11 and 21.12 above.

[76] See the second example discussed at paras. 21.08 and 21.10 above.

[77] See paras. 21.03 and 21.06 above.

[78] As has been observed (para. 21.01, n. 56 above), the explanation for the words "shall have exclusive jurisdiction" given in the Jenard Report is not wholly convincing and it must anyway be read in the light of the judgment in *Meeth* v. *Glacetal* (discussed at paras. 21.44 *et seq.* above). Any potential conflicts of jurisdiction can be resolved by the rules in Arts. 21 to 23 on related actions and *lis pendens*.

under the Convention should also be permitted to exercise jurisdiction.

(d) Conclusion. It is suggested that the following formula accords **21.51** with the wording and intention of Article 17, as interpreted by the European Court of Justice, and covers the various different types of exclusive and non-exclusive jurisdiction agreements which may arise:

Subject to Articles 16 and 21 to 23, where a court of a Contracting State is seised of a dispute connected with a particular legal relationship and the court is satisfied—from the form, circumstances, letter and spirit of a jurisdiction agreement which applies to the dispute and which otherwise complies with Article 17—that the parties intended that court to have jurisdiction over it, that court must accept jurisdiction, whether or not another court or other courts within the Contracting States would also have jurisdiction over the dispute.

6. " . . . either in writing or evidenced in writing . . . "

(a) Generally. The words "evidenced in writing" refer to oral **21.52** agreements.[79] It is not clear whether, for the purposes of Article 17, an agreement may be valid if it was made in a manner other than (i) in writing or (ii) orally and confirmed in writing—*e.g.* where a jurisdiction agreement is subsequently incorporated in a manner falling within Article 17[80] into a contract made partly orally and partly by conduct. There would seem to be no reason in principle why such an agreement should not be valid, despite the wording of Article 17.

The European Court has held that:

> "In order to decide whether the conditions laid down in Article 17 are satisfied, it is necessary to consider separately whether the agreement of the parties to the choice of jurisdiction was expressed in the form of a written agreement or in the form of an oral agreement evidenced in writing."[81]

In the light of the amended text it is now necessary also to consider whether in international trade or commerce, the choice of jurisdiction was made in a form which accords with practices in that trade or commerce of which the parties are or ought to have been aware.[82]

---

[79] See para. 21.01, n. † above; Maxwell, para. 5.187.
[80] See paras. 21.60 *et seq.* below.
[81] *Partenreederei m.s. "Tilly Russ"* v. *Haven und Vervoerbedrijf Nova N.V. and Goeminne Hout N.V.* [1984] E.C.R. 2417, at p. 2432 (para. 15), discussed at para. 21.21 above.
[82] See para. 21.70 below.

21.53   It has already been observed[83] that the purpose of the requirements of form laid down in Article 17 is to ensure that the necessary consensus between the parties is in fact established. The Jenard Report[84] says that in some countries "a document in writing will be required only as evidence of the existence of the agreement; in others, however, it will go to the validity of the agreement." It now seems clear, though, that the formal requirements of Article 17 are to be the subject of uniform interpretation[85] and, with one exception, that writing probably does go to the validity of the agreement[86] (or, at least, its effectiveness for the purposes of Article 17). The exception arises in international trade and commerce, which is covered by the new wording of Article 17.[87] The requirements are stricter in the case of Luxembourg domiciliaries, and this special case is discussed below.[88]

The formalities required by Article 17 have been considered by the European Court of Justice on a number of occasions. For cases of international trade or commerce, the decisions must now be read in the light of the amended text of Article 17, but they remain authoritative in relation to those cases where the special provisions on international trade or commerce do not apply. The first two cases on Article 17 to come before the European Court were both concerned with standard terms and conditions of business and the decisions require consideration in some detail. The first case concerns written agreements; the second, agreements evidenced in writing. If the jurisdiction agreement has been concluded for the benefit of only one party, the position is further complicated by the terms of the fourth paragraph of Article 17.[89]

21.54   *(b) Written agreements.* The first case to come before the European Court on Article 17 was *Estasis Salotti* v. *RÜWA*,[90] which concerned the incorporation of standard conditions into a written contract.

RÜWA, a company based in Cologne, sent Colzani, an undertak-

---

[83] Para. 21.37 above.

[84] Jenard, para. A1.166 below.

[85] Where the borderline lies between uniform application of Art. 17 and the legitimate application of national law is not always easy to determine. See paras. 21.25 *et seq.* above.

[86] Geimer/Schütze, p. 479; Droz, para. 199; Weser, para. 265–6; Bülow/Böckstiegel/Müller, p. 146.

[87] Para. 21.70 below.

[88] Para. 21.69.

[89] Para. 21.80 below.

[90] *Estasis Salotti di Colzani Aimo e Gianmario Colzani* v. *RÜWA Polstereimaschinen GmbH*, [1976] E.C.R. 1831, sometimes referred to as *Colzani* v. *RÜWA*. See Collins, in Lipstein (ed.), *Harmonisation of Private International Law by the EEC*, p. 91, at p. 98.

ing based in Milan, written offers for the supply of machines for the manufacture of upholstered furniture, which started " . . . subject to the general conditions of sale . . . overleaf . . . I offer to supply you as follows. . . . " Those written conditions contained a jurisdiction clause which, *inter alia*, conferred jurisdiction on the court in Cologne. A contract was entered into in Milan, written on RÜWA's business stationery, bearing their letterhead and with their standard conditions on the back. It did not expressly refer to the conditions, but it did expressly refer to the written offers.

Colzani refused to take delivery and RÜWA sued for damages in the *Landgericht* in Cologne, which declined jurisdiction on the grounds that the parties had not validly agreed on the jurisdiction of the court. That decision was overturned on appeal and, on a further appeal, the *Bundesgerichtshof* referred two questions to the European Court of Justice, which ruled on them in these terms:

> "Where a clause conferring jurisdiction is included among the general conditions of sale of one of the parties, printed on the back of a contract, the requirement of a writing under the first paragraph of Article 17 . . . is fulfilled only if the contract signed by both parties contains an express reference to those general conditions.
>
> In the case of a contract concluded by reference to earlier offers, which were themselves made with reference to the general conditions of one of the parties including a clause conferring jurisdiction, the requirement of a writing under the first paragraph of Article 17 . . . is satisfied only if the reference is express and can therefore be checked by a party exercising reasonable care."[91]

In explaining its rulings, the European Court made a number of important observations,[92] which may be regarded as definitive in relation to written agreements: **21.55**

> " . . . the mere fact that a clause conferring jurisdiction is printed among the general conditions of one of the parties on the reverse of a contract drawn up on the commercial paper of that party does not of itself satisfy the requirements of Article 17, since no guarantee is thereby given that the other party has really consented to the clause waiving the normal rules of jurisdiction."[93]
>
> . . .
>
> "In principle, the requirement of a writing under the first paragraph of Article 17 is fulfilled if the parties have referred in the text of their contract to an offer in which reference was expressly made to general conditions including a clause conferring jurisdiction.
>
> This view of the matter, however, is valid only in the case of an express reference which can be checked by a party exercising reason-

---

[91] [1976] E.C.R. 1831, at p. 1843.
[92] An extract from the decision dealing with the interpretation of Art. 17 in general is set out at para. 21.37 above.
[93] [1976] E.C.R. 1831, at p. 1841 (para. 9).

able care, and only if it is established that the general conditions including the clause conferring jurisdiction have in fact been communicated to the other contracting party with the offer to which reference is made.

But the requirement of a writing in Article 17 would not be fulfilled in the case of indirect or implied references to earlier correspondence, for that would not yield any certainty that the clause conferring jurisdiction was in fact part of the subject-matter of the contract properly so-called."[94]

In the event, the *Bundesgerichtshof*, applying the European Court's ruling, held that the *Landgericht* Cologne did have jurisdiction.[95]

21.56   The European Court has elaborated on these observations in the later case of the *Tilly Russ*,[96] in the context of printed conditions on a bill of lading:

" . . . where a jurisdiction clause appears in the conditions printed on a bill of lading signed by the carrier, the requirement of 'an agreement in writing' within the meaning of Article 17 of the Convention is satisfied only if the shipper has expressed in writing his consent to the conditions containing that clause, either in the document in question itself or in a separate document. It must be added that the mere printing of a jurisdiction clause on the reverse of the bill of lading does not satisfy the requirements of Article 17 of the Convention, since such a procedure gives no guarantee that the other party has actually consented to the clause derogating from the ordinary jurisdiction rules of the Convention."[97]

The passage is a further example of the general principle that the consensus of the parties must be clearly and precisely demonstrated.

21.57   *(c) Written agreements summary.* In summary, the formal requirements for jurisdiction agreements made in writing (except where the international trade provisions apply)[98] seem to be as follows:

(1) Both parties must agree in writing on the choice of jurisdiction.

(2) They may do so in a single document signed by both of

---

[94] *Ibid.*, at p. 1842 (para. 12).

[95] Decision of May 4, 1977; Case VIII ZR 14/75; RIW/AWD 1977, p. 649, Digest D I–17.1.2—B9.

[96] *Partenreederei m.s. "Tilly Russ"* v. *Haven und Vervoerbedrijf Nova N.V. and Goeminne Hout N.V.* [1984] E.C.R. 2417. The case is discussed in greater detail at paras. 21.21 *et seq.* above.

[97] *Ibid.*, at p. 2432 (para. 16).

[98] Para. 21.70 below.

them or by separate documents: an exchange of letters or telexes will suffice.[99]

(3) Express reference to the jurisdiction clause is not necessary (except in the case of Luxembourg domiciliaries).[1] Reference to general conditions containing the jurisdiction clauses will suffice, but the incorporation of the general conditions must be express.[2]

(4) The express reference to the general conditions need not be direct: express reference to the terms of an earlier offer or contract will suffice, provided that that contract or offer itself contained the jurisdiction clause within the meaning of Article 17.[3] Indirect or implied reference to earlier con-

---

[99] *Firma Wilhelm Wiest Maaschinen- und Werkzeugfabrik* v. *Manufattura Ceramica Pozzi S.p.A.*, Riv.dir.int.priv.proc. 1976, p. 812, Digest D I–17.1.2—B2; *Bludau* v. *Ditta Imitalia s.n.c.* and *Ebeling* v. *Ditta Imitalia s.n.c.*, for.it., col. 1012, Digest D I–17.1.2–B19n.

[1] Para. 21.69 below.

[2] *Basso Legnami S.p.A.* v. *The Licenses Insurance Co. Ltd. and others*, Riv.dir.int. priv.proc. 1977, p. 613, Digest D I–17.1.2—B7; *S.p.r.l. Société Nouvelle Artifil Europar* v. *S.A. Dunil France*, Tribunal de Commerce, Verviers (Belgium), March 31, 1977, Digest D I–17.1.2—B8; *Cotonfil S.r.l.* v. *Chemitex s.p.r.l.*, Riv.dir.int.priv.proc. 1981, p. 920, [1983] E.C.C. 8, Digest D I–17.1.2—B19; *Luis Marburg & Söhne GmbH* v. *Ori Martin SpA* Corte di Cassazione [1985] Il Diritto Maritimo 395 [1987] Eur.L.Dig. 240; but *cf. S.A. Imprimerie-Heliogravure van Cortenbergh* v. *S.A. Dargaud Editeur*, Cour d'Appel, Brussels, March 3, 1981, Digest D I–17.1.2—B23, (jurisdiction clause was contained in conditions printed on the back of a document, but the express reference was merely to the document: clause upheld, but borderline case). A signature *above* a notice incorporating general conditions has been held insufficient to satisfy the formal requirements of Art. 17: Oberlandesgericht Hamm, January 20, 1977, case 2 U 120/76, Digest D I–5.1.2—B8; but where the signature was above the jurisdiction clause itself it has been held sufficient: Landgericht Hamburg, August 18, 1976, case 26 O 122/75, Digest D I–17.1.2—B5.

A failure to object to the other party's standard terms and conditions is not sufficient to incorporate them for the purposes of Article 17: Bundesgerichtshof, May 16, 1977, case VIII ZR 225/75, Digest D I–17.1.2—B10; *Gottfried Kellermann GmbH* v. *P.B.A. Dura*, Hof van Beroep, Antwerp (Belgium), November 30, 1977, Digest D I–17.1.2—B12; *S.A. Utexbel* v. *S.à.r.l. M.F. Mason*, Tribunal de Commerce Tournai (Belgium), January 16, 1979, Digest D I–17.1.2—B15; Oberlandesgericht Karlsruhe, December 30, 1981, case 14 U 4/81, N.J.W. 1982, p. 1950, Digest D I–17.1.1—B17; *Plaumann* v. *Machinefabrik A. van der Linden B.V.* Arrondissementsrechtbank Middleburg, July 4, 1984, [1987] E.C.C. 20; also a number of Belgian cases, cited at Digest D I–17.1.2—B15n.1 (including some decisions *contra*). These cases must be distinguished, though, from cases where oral agreement has been reached and there is then a failure to object to the other party's written evidence of the agreement: see paras. 21.64 *et seq.* below.

[3] An agreement in writing forming part of a continuing trading relationship may contain a jurisdiction clause which is valid for the purposes of Art. 17, by analogy with the circumstances in which such a clause validly forms part of an oral

tracts, offers or correspondence will not suffice. Where a written agreement has been renewed or extended after its expiry in a manner recognised by the applicable national law, a jurisdiction clause in the contract, if originally valid, will continue to be so.[4]

(5) Whether the express reference to general conditions is direct or indirect, the general terms must probably have been produced to the other party before the jurisdiction agreement was entered into.[5] It remains to be seen, though, whether it will be sufficient if the general conditions were available to the other party, even if they were not actually produced.[6]

(6) In each case, it is necessary that the other party could, by the exercise of reasonable care, have checked the general conditions referred to.[7]

21.58   (d) *Agreements evidenced in writing.* The second case to come before the European Court was *Galeries Segoura SPRL* v. *Bonakdarian*,[8] which was concerned with the incorporation of standard terms into an oral contract.

Galeries Segoura was a Belgian limited partnership. It entered into an oral contract with Bonakdarian in the free port of Hamburg for the purchase of Persian carpets. On the same day, Segoura made part payment and was handed two documents, described as "confirmation of order and invoice," which stated: "Subject to the following conditions, we have sold and delivered to you . . . [the carpets]." Printed on the back were Bonakdarian's standard conditions, which included a clause which purported to confer exclusive jurisdiction on the Hamburg courts.

Segoura defaulted on payment of the balance of the price and Bonakdarian brought an action in the *Landgericht* in Hamburg. He obtained a default judgment, which Segoura then sought successfully to have set aside, the court ruling that it had no jurisdiction because the parties had not concluded a valid jurisdiction agree-

---

agreement evidenced in writing (see para. 21.66(3)(a) below); Oberlandesgericht Stuttgart, July 24, 1979, case 6 U 31/79, RIW/AWD 1980, p. 365, Digest D I–17.1.2—B18; Oberlandesgericht Koblenz, July 4, 1980, case 2 U 52/80, Digest D I–17.1.2—B21.

[4] *Iveco Fiat SpA* v. *NV van Hool*, [1986] E.C.R. 3337. The case is discussed at para. 21.67 below.

[5] *Allpac Holdings B.V.* v. *Erich Bauer K.G.* Ned.Jur. 1978, No. 473, Digest D I–17.1.2—B13; *Argentox GmbH & Co. K.G.* v. *Dosa S.p.A.*, Corte di Cassazione, November 18, 1982 (No. 6189), Digest D I–17.1.2—B19n.2.

[6] Oberlandesgericht Koblenz, July 4, 1980, above; *cf. Argentox GmbH & Co. K.G.* v. *Dosa S.p.A.*, above.

[7] *Allpac Holdings B.V.* v. *Erich Bauer K.G.*, above.

[8] [1976] E.C.R. 1851.

ment within Article 17. Bonakdarian appealed and the decision was quashed. Segoura then appealed to the *Bundesgerichtshof*, which referred two questions to the European Court, putting two hypothetical situations.

The first question asked whether the requirements of Article 17 **21.59** were satisfied:

> "if, at the oral conclusion of a contract of sale, a vendor has stated that he wishes to rely on his general conditions of sale and if he subsequently confirms the contract in writing to the purchaser and annexes to this confirmation his general conditions of sale which contain a clause conferring jurisdiction."[9]

The second question was similar, but was concerned with the situation where, until after the conclusion of the contract, no reference was made at all to the existence of general conditions of sale. It asked whether Article 17 applied,

> "if, in dealings between merchants, a vendor, after the oral conclusion of a contract of sale, confirms in writing to the purchaser the conclusion of the contract subject to his general conditions of sale and annexes to this document his conditions of sale which include a clause conferring jurisdiction and if the purchaser does not challenge this written confirmation."[10]

Again, the European Court made a number of important observations. Dealing with the first question, it said: **21.60**

> "Even if, in an orally concluded contract, the purchaser agrees to abide by the vendor's general conditions, he is not for that reason to be deemed to have agreed to any clause conferring jurisdiction which might appear in those general conditions.
>
> It follows that a confirmation in writing of the contract by the vendor, accompanied by the text of his general conditions, is without effect, as regards any clause conferring jurisdiction which it might contain, unless the purchaser agrees to it in writing."[11]

Turning to the second question, the Court said:

> "it is patent that a clause conferring jurisdiction which might be included in those general conditions did not form part of the subject-matter of the contract concluded orally between the parties. Therefore subsequent notification of general conditions containing such a clause is not capable of altering the terms agreed between the parties, except if those conditions are expressly accepted in writing by the purchaser."[12]

It then went on to consider the two questions together, and said:

---

[9] *Ibid.*, at p. 1861 (para. 7).
[10] *Ibid.*, at p. 1861 (para. 9).
[11] *Ibid.*, at p. 1861 (para. 8).
[12] *Ibid.*, at pp. 1861–1862 (para. 10).

"It follows . . . that a unilateral declaration in writing such as the one in the present case is not sufficient to constitute an agreement on jurisdiction by consent.

However, it would be otherwise where an oral agreement forms part of a continuing trading relationship between the parties, provided also that it is established that the dealings taken as a whole are governed by the general conditions of the party giving the confirmation, and these conditions contain a clause conferring jurisdiction.

Indeed, in such a context, it would be contrary to good faith for the recipient of the confirmation to deny the existence of a jurisdiction conferred by consent, even if he had given no acceptance in writing."[13]

The Court's ruling was:

"In the case of an orally concluded contract, the requirements of the first paragraph of Article 17 . . . as to form are satisfied only if the vendor's confirmation in writing accompanied by notification of the general conditions of sale has been accepted in writing by the purchaser.

The fact that the purchaser does not raise any objections against a confirmation issued unilaterally by the other party does not amount to acceptance on his part of the clause conferring jurisdiction unless the oral agreement comes within the framework of a continuing trading relationship between the parties which is based on the general conditions of one of them, and those conditions contain a clause conferring jurisdiction."[14]

21.61   This decision raises a difficult question. From the way in which the decision is formulated, it appears that if general conditions containing a jurisdiction clause are notified by one party to the other after the conclusion of the oral contract, even if they were not referred to at the time of the contract, they can become binding if the latter party accepts them in writing. If that is right as a matter of uniform interpretation of the Convention, it raises a difficulty in relation to the validity of the jurisdiction agreement as a matter of substantive law. In many such cases, there would be no fresh consideration to support the jurisdiction clause.

It is suggested, though, that the question whether general conditions can validly be incorporated into a contract after its original conclusion is not a question of the uniform interpretation of the Convention, but a matter for the substantive law of the contract to determine.[15] Although the European Court has expressly stated that national law may not add to the formal requirements of Article

---

[13] *Ibid.*, at p. 1862 (para. 11).
[14] *Ibid.*, at p. 1863.
[15] The relationship between national law and Art. 17 is discussed at paras. 21.25 *et seq.* above.

17,[16] what is less clear is the extent to which national law can affect the validity of a jurisdiction agreement by conditions other than conditions of form.

It is submitted that, notwithstanding the wording of the Euro-   **21.62**
pean Court's decision in *Galeries Segoura* v. *Bonakdarian*, the better view is that the validity of a jurisdiction agreement on grounds other than those of form is to be decided by the substantive law of the contract, as determined by the law of the court seised of the case, including its conflict rules.[17]

However, if that view is wrong and a uniform interpretation of the Convention applies in deciding the validity of post-contract incorporation of a jurisdiction clause contained in general conditions, considerable difficulty may arise. For example, if the proper law of the contract is English law or some other law which requires consideration as a condition of validity of the contract, one may find that a jurisdiction clause in general conditions has been incorporated into an oral contract, but the other terms in the general conditions have not, even though Article 17 is designed to impose tighter requirements on a jurisdiction clause than on other clauses.

If there is an objection to the jurisdiction clause, after the contract has been entered into orally, it will not automatically take the agreement outside Article 17; but will weigh in the evidential balance in deciding whether there was in fact consensus on the choice of jurisdiction.[18]

The question whether or not an oral agreement has actually been   **21.63**
confirmed in writing, so as to satisfy the requirements of Article 17, is a question of fact in each case, but the actual agreement of the parties as to the choice of jurisdiction must always be established. In the context of printed conditions on a bill of lading, handed by the shipper to the carrier after conclusion of the contract of carriage, the European Court has said, in the *Tilly Russ* case:[19]

> "if it was established that the jurisdiction clause contained in the conditions printed on a bill of lading was the subject of a prior oral agreement between the parties expressly relating to the jurisdiction clause and that the bill of lading, signed by the carrier, was to be regarded as the written confirmation of that oral agreement, such a clause would

---

[16] *Elefanten Schuh* v. *Jacqmain* [1981] E.C.R. 1671, at p. 1688. The case is discussed at para. 21.27 above.

[17] The European Court's decision in *Iveco Fiat SpA* v. *NV van Hool*, discussed at para. 21.67 below, would seem by analogy to support this view.

[18] Bülow/Böckstiegel/Müller, p. 149.

[19] *Partenreederei m.s. "Tilly Russ"* v. *Haven und Vervoerbedrijf Nova N.V. and Goeminne Hout N.V.* [1984] E.C.R. 2417. The case is discussed at para. 21.21 above, where the facts are summarised.

satisfy the conditions laid down in Article 17 of the Convention, even if it was not signed by the shipper and therefore bore only the signature of the carrier. In fact, not only is the letter of Article 17, which expressly provides for the possibility of an oral agreement evidenced in writing, thereby observed but in addition its function, which is to ensure that the agreement of the parties is clearly established, is also fulfilled."[20]

In that case, the European Court again considered the circumstances in which a choice of jurisdiction agreement could be valid in the context of a continuing business relationship between the parties. In a further reference to the principles of good faith, the Court stated:

"such a jurisdiction clause not signed by the shipper may still satisfy the requirements laid down in Article 17 of the Convention, even in the absence of a prior oral agreement relating to that clause, provided that the bill of lading comes within the framework of a continuing business relationship between the shipper and the carrier, in so far as it is thereby established that the relationship is governed as a whole by general conditions containing the jurisdiction clause drawn up by the author of the written confirmation, in this case the carrier (see the *Segoura* judgment . . .), and provided that the bills of lading are all issued on pre-printed forms systematically containing such a jurisdiction clause. In those circumstances, it would be contrary to good faith to deny the existence of a jurisdiction agreement."[21]

21.64 The principle of good faith in this context is equivalent to the doctrine of estoppel in English law. In his Opinion in *Berghoefer GmbH & Co KG* v. *A.S.A. SA*,[22] Advocate General Sir Gordon Slynn referred to this point:

"It seems to me from the existing case law that the recipient of a document purporting to confirm an oral agreement is estopped from contesting its contents unless he does so within a reasonable time. The Court has held that, where there is a continuous course of dealing between the parties and a jurisdiction agreement forms part of the general conditions of trading of one of them, then it would be contrary to good faith for the other party to deny the existence of the jurisdiction agreement: paragraph 11 of the judgment in *Segoura*,[23] paragraph 18 of the judgment in *Tilly Russ*.[24] *A fortiori* the same principle must apply to an oral agreement relating solely to a choice of jurisdiction."

Berghoefer v. *A.S.A.* concerned a contract of commercial agency whereby Berghoefer, a German company, acted as agent in Ger-

---

[20] *Ibid.*, at p. 2433 (para. 17).
[21] *Ibid.*, at p. 2433 (para. 18).
[22] [1985] E.C.R. 2699, at p. 2702.
[23] Quoted at para. 21.60 above.
[24] Quoted at para. 21.63 above.

many for A.S.A., a French company. After the termination of the agency by A.S.A., Berghoefer brought proceedings in Germany for compensation. The written agreement between the parties had specified the exclusive jurisdiction of the *Tribunal de Commerce* at Roanne in France, but Berghoefer alleged that by a subsequent oral agreement the parties had varied that arrangement and had agreed on the exclusive jurisdiction of the *Landgericht* Moenchengladbach in Germany. They also alleged that they had written to A.S.A. confirming the variation, and that A.S.A. had raised no objection. A.S.A. disputed Berghoefer's allegations and challenged the jurisdiction of the German court. The issue reached the *Bundesgerichtshof* which, on the assumption that Berghoefer's allegations were correct, referred to the European Court the question whether the requirements of Article 17 were satisfied where an oral jurisdiction agreement had been confirmed in writing by the party for whose benefit it had been concluded.

In its judgment, the European Court again emphasised that **21.65** Article 17 must be strictly construed[25] and pointed out that, by contrast with the provisions applying to persons domiciled in Luxembourg, in the normal case it was not necessary for the written confirmation to be given by the party for whose benefit the jurisdiction agreement was concluded.[26] The Court went on to say that if it is actually established that jurisdiction has been conferred by express oral agreement and that agreement has been confirmed by one party in writing, received by the other party, the requirements of Article 17 are satisfied if that other party raises no objection to it within a reasonable time thereafter:

> "It would be a breach of good faith for a party who did not raise any objection subsequently to contest the application of the oral agreement."[27]

(e) Agreements evidenced in writing: summary. In summary, the for- **21.66** mal requirements for jurisdiction agreements made orally and evidenced in writing (except where the international trade provisions apply)[28] seem to be as follows:

(1) Both parties must agree on the choice of jurisdiction.
(2) The evidence in writing may, depending on the circumstances, be in a single document signed by both of them or by separate documents: an exchange of letters or telexes

---

[25] [1985] E.C.R. 2699, at p. 2708 (para. 13).
[26] *Ibid.*, at p. 2708 (para. 14).
[27] *Ibid.*, (para. 15).
[28] Para. 21.70 below.

will suffice.[29] Written confirmation by either party of an express oral agreement on jurisdiction[30] will also suffice if the other party fails to raise an objection within a reasonable time.

(3) The jurisdiction agreement may be entered into by the parties agreeing orally that the general conditions of one of them are to apply, provided that *either*:

    (a) the oral agreement is made in the context of a continuing trading relationship and it is established that the dealings taken as a whole are governed by those conditions, in a manner falling within Article 17, and the oral agreement is confirmed in writing by either party;[31] *or*

    (b) the conditions have been supplied to the other party before the oral agreement[32] and the oral agreement is confirmed in writing by the other party.[33]

Indirect or implied reference to earlier contracts or offers will not suffice.[34]

(4) Whether or not there is oral agreement that the general

---

[29] *E.g.*: *Firma Wilhelm Wiest Maschinen- und Werkzeugfabrik* v. *Manufattura Ceramica Pozzi S.p.A.*, Riv.dir.int.priv.proc. 1976, p. 812, Digest D I–17.1.2—B2.

[30] The same applies where the jurisdiction agreement is concluded in writing and, after the expiry of the written agreement, continues as part of a tacit contractual relationship between the parties: *Iveco Fiat SpA* v. *NV van Hool*, [1988] 1 C.M.L.R. 57, discussed at para. 21.67 below.

[31] Oberlandesgericht Stuttgart, July 24, 1979, case 6 U 31/79, RIW/AWD 1980, p. 365, Digest D I–17.1.2—B18; *Technisch Handelsbureau P.J. van Louden B.V.* v. *N.V. Gieterijn Technomet*, Arrondissementsrechtbank Arnhem, December 23, 1982, Digest D I–17.1.2—B24. *Cf.* Bundesgerichtshof, May 16, 1977, Case No. VIII ZR 225/75, Digest D I–17.1.2—B10; *Allpac Holdings B.V.* v. *Carl Friedrich Maier am Tor*, Ned.Jur. 1980, No. 46, [1982] E.C.C. 200, Digest D I–17.1.2—B16 (see n. 39 below). But it has been held not to be enough if the written confirmation does not refer to the legal context of the agreement, but merely to the goods in question, the price, delivery arrangements, etc.: Hanseatisches Oberlandesgericht Hamburg, September 19, 1984, Case No. 5 U 56/84, [1986] E.C.C. 37.

[32] As in the case of a written agreement, it remains to be seen, though, whether it is sufficient for the terms to have been available to the other party, even if they were not actually produced.

[33] But in a Belgian case where the printed conditions appear not to have been confirmed in writing, a jurisdiction clause has still been held to be validly incorporated: *S.A. Soc. Nouvelle des Paveurs Réunis* v. *S.P.R.L. Joseph Maillien et Fils*, Cour d'Appel Mons, October 17, 1977, Digest D I–17.1.2—B11. It is submitted that this decision is doubtful.

[34] *Cf. Iveco Fiat SpA* v. *NV van Hool*, [1988] 1 C.M.L.R. 57, discussed at para. 21.67 below. See also *Enna Nederland Aerosols B.V.* v. *Deutsche Prävisionsventil GmbH*, Ned.Jur. 1977, No. 576, Digest D I–17.1.2—B6.

conditions of one party are to apply, the jurisdiction agreement may also be validly entered into *either*:

(a) (if Article 17 alone governs the validity of post-contract incorporation of a jurisdiction agreement) where the general conditions are sent to the other party together with written confirmation of the oral contract and the other party expressly accepts those conditions in writing;[35] *or*

(b) (if the validity of post-contract incorporation of a jurisdiction agreement is subject both to Article 17 and to the substantive law of the contract)[36] where condition (a) is fulfilled and the jurisdiction agreement is valid according to the law of the contract.[37]

(5) Express reference to the jurisdiction clause is not necessary (except in the case of Luxembourg domiciliaries)[38] either in the oral agreement or in the written evidence. Reference to general conditions containing the jurisdiction clause will suffice.[39]

(6) In each case, it is necessary that the other party could, by the exercise of reasonable care, have checked the general conditions referred to.

(f) Expired agreements. A situation similar to that obtaining in **21.67** relation to a continuing business relationship is the case where the parties have previously entered into a written agreement containing a valid choice of jurisdiction clause, but that agreement has expired. The European Court considered such a case in *Iveco Fiat S.p.A.* v. *N.V. van Hool.*[40] The contracts in question were exclusive distribu-

---

[35] Where the oral contract was not confirmed in writing, jurisdiction has been declined: Hanseatisches Oberlandesgericht Hamburg, September 19, 1984, above. Where the confirmation contained only a general reference to an auctioneer's standard conditions, without further reference to their content, the jurisdiction clause has also been overridden: *Kunstveiligen Erasmus B.V.* v. *Salaman,* Gerechtshof, Amsterdam, Ned. Jur. 1986, 2110, [1988] Eur.L.Dig. 46.

[36] This is probably the better view: see para. 21.62 above.

[37] Hanseatisches Oberlandesgericht Hamburg, September 19, 1984, above, where it was held that the requirements of s.346 of the German Commercial Code (Handelsgesetzbuch, HGB) must be fulfilled if the document is to be a written confirmation of an oral contract. It must refer to the terms of the contract, not merely to accounting matters.

[38] See para. 21.69 below.

[39] *Allpac Holdings B.V.* v. *Carl Friedrich Maier am Tor,* above, where the Gerechtshof, Amsterdam, having held that there was no written agreement as to jurisdiction, said that where general conditions containing the clause were sent to the defendants at an early stage in negotiations and no express mention was made of the forum clause, that clause did not apply.

[40] [1986] E.C.R. 3337.

torship agreements under which van Hool, a Belgian company, had been granted certain exclusive sales rights for the Benelux countries in respect of Fiat buses, coaches and industrial vehicles. The agreements were concluded for a limited period and contained a provision whereby they could only be renewed by express written confirmation given by Fiat. In the event, no such written renewal occurred, but the parties continued the same contractual relationship for 20 years.

In 1981, differences arose between the parties, Fiat terminated the relationship, and van Hool brought proceedings against them in Belgium. Fiat objected to the jurisdiction, relying on jurisdiction clauses in the expired written contracts in favour of Italian courts. The Belgian court of first instance dismissed that objection and accepted jurisdiction, a decision that was upheld on appeal. Fiat pursued a further appeal to the Belgian *Cour de Cassation*, which referred the question of the continued validity of the jurisdiction clauses to the European Court.

21.68   The European Court pointed out that a distinction was to be drawn between two types of case, depending on the effect of the national law which applied to the agreement. On one hand, that law might permit the original written agreement to be renewed or continued otherwise than by written renewal, despite its express term to the contrary. On the other hand, the national law might give effect to the express provision that the agreements could only be renewed in writing, with the consequence that the continued contractual relationship of the parties was on the basis of an unwritten agreement. In the former case, the written contract would continue to have effect and the jurisdiction clause would therefore also continue to be valid. In the latter case, on the basis of the Court's decision in the *Berghoefer* case,[41] it would be necessary for there to be written confirmation of the jurisdiction agreement, emanating from one party to the other and not objected to by the other within a reasonable time.[42]

21.69   *(g) Luxembourg domiciliaries.* The second paragraph of Article I of the 1968 Protocol[43] provides:

> "An agreement conferring jurisdiction, within the meaning of Article 17, shall be valid with respect to a person domiciled in Luxembourg only if that person has expressly and specifically so agreed."

The rationale behind this provision is to protect persons domiciled in Luxembourg from being denied the benefit of the jurisdic-

---

[41] See para. 21.64 above.
[42] Paras. 7–9 of the judgment.
[43] Para. 35.01 below.

tion of the courts of Luxembourg by a clause conferring jurisdiction on the courts of another Contracting State. The Jenard Report says that the provision is justified by the particular nature of economic relations between Belgium and Luxembourg and by the large number of international contracts entered into by persons domiciled in Luxembourg.[44]

The effect of the provision is that a jurisdiction agreement entered into with a Luxembourg domiciliary will only be effective against such person if the conditions of Article 17 generally are fulfilled and if two further conditions are fulfilled, namely that the choice of jurisdiction should have been (a) expressly agreed and (b) specifically agreed.[45]

In *Porta-Leasing GmbH* v. *Prestige International SA*,[46] the European Court of Justice held that the first requirement (express agreement) is only fulfilled if the jurisdiction agreement is contained in a provision which is "specially and exclusively devoted to it." The second condition is only fulfilled if the Luxembourg party specifically signs the clause conferring jurisdiction "as an indication of his agreement." It is not sufficient merely to sign the contract, but the jurisdiction provision need not be in a separate document.

It seems that if these conditions are not fulfilled, but Article 17 is otherwise complied with, the jurisdiction agreement can still be relied on at the instance of the Luxembourg domiciliary.

In *Porta-Leasing*, the court was concerned with a series of written contracts. How far its observations extend to an oral contract evidenced in writing remains to be seen, but it would seem to be consistent with the decision in that case, that the written evidence should have to emanate from the Luxembourg domiciliary and relate both expressly and specifically to the jurisdiction agreement.

7. " . . . in international trade or commerce, in a form which accords with practices in that trade or commerce of which the parties are or ought to have been aware . . . "

This provision is new[47] and it is intended to relax the formal requirements of Article 17, which were thought to be inappropriate to the requirements of international trade and commerce.[48] As the Schlosser Report emphasises, though, the relaxation relates only to

21.70

---

[44] Jenard, para. A1.262 below.
[45] *S.A. Nashua Belgium* v. *S.à.r.l. Mamer (Luxembourg)*, Jurisprudence Commerciale de Belgique 1980, p. 51, Digest D II–1—B2.
[46] [1980] E.C.R. 1517.
[47] See para. 21.01, n. † above.
[48] Schlosser, para. 179 (para. A1.474 below).

the formal requirements,[49] and it is not intended to detract at all from the need for consensus as to the choice of jurisdiction to be proved, nor from the other requirements of Article 17. Its effect is likely to be greatest in connection with printed standard terms and conditions.[50] It was undoubtedly the intention of the United Kingdom members of the Working Party which negotiated the 1978 Accession Convention that these words should enable the exchange of printed standard conditions to be effective in incorporating jurisdiction agreements. It remains to be seen whether that view is correct, but some doubt must remain on the point, especially where competing sets of conditions have been exchanged which choose different jurisdictions.

If and in so far as these words are capable of importing any concepts beyond pure questions of fact, they are probably to be given an independent interpretation. It is submitted that no significance is to be attached to the different tenses in the phrase, "*are* or ought to *have been* aware." Other language versions do not contain the same distinction of tenses. The time at which the parties are to be aware of the relevant practices should be the time of the conclusion of the jurisdiction agreement.

8. "Where such an agreement is concluded by parties, none of whom is domiciled in a Contracting State, the courts of other Contracting States shall have no jurisdiction over their dispute unless the court or courts chosen have declined jurisdiction"[51]

21.71   It is no part of the Convention's function, where both parties are domiciled outside the Community, to determine whether and in what circumstances the courts of a Contracting State should or should not give effect to a jurisdiction agreement. National law applies in such a case.[52] But there is a Community interest in ensuring that the effect of such an agreement is recognised in all the Contracting States.[53] This provision therefore gives the chosen court priority of jurisdiction[54] instead of exclusive jurisdiction in such a

---

[49] *Ibid.*

[50] *Cf.* Dicey and Morris, p. 416, Illustration 9.

[51] The German text of this sentence differs from the English text in providing that the courts of other Contracting States may "not decide" ("*nicht entscheiden*") the case, rather than that they have no jurisdiction over it. The French, Italian and Dutch texts are to the same effect as the English text: "*ne peuvent connaître du differend,*" "*non possono conoscere della controversia,*" "*kunnen . . . van het geschil geen kennis nemen*").

[52] Art. 4, para. 16.15 above; Geimer/Schütze, p. 246.

[53] Schlosser, para. 177 (para. A1.472 below).

[54] Maxwell, para. 5.185.

case. If the agreement is in truth a non-exclusive jurisdiction agreement, the courts of other Contracting States should consider whether the agreement derogates from their jurisdiction in favour of the court chosen.[55] If so, this provision should prevent them from accepting jurisdiction over the dispute unless the court or courts chosen have declined jurisdiction. The provision is particularly relevant to the United Kingdom, because of the frequency with which English courts are chosen in contracts concerning international trade.[56]

For the reasons set out in relation to jurisdiction agreements falling within the other provisions of Article 17,[57] it is suggested that the point in time at which the conditions must be fulfilled should be at the time when the agreement is concluded. If that is right, the effect of the provision is to prevent courts which, if the defendant has since moved his domicile into a Contracting State, would otherwise have jurisdiction under the Convention[58] from accepting jurisdiction unless and until the chosen court has declined jurisdiction. If in such a case the chosen court was competent under the other provisions of the Convention, it would be required to accept jurisdiction. **21.72**

As has been suggested in the context of cases falling within the other provisions of Article 17,[59] the chosen court should decide whether to give effect to the jurisdiction agreement in the light of its own substantive law, including its conflicts rules.[60] If it accepts jurisdiction, the courts of other Contracting States must decline jurisdiction over the dispute, even if they would have jurisdiction under their own law. This provisions takes priority in this respect over Article 4.[61] If the chosen court declines jurisdiction on the basis that the choice of forum agreement is invalid, that decision is one which must be recognised by the courts of other Contracting States.[62] They would probably even be bound by a decision of the original court on a point of conflicts of law.[63]

---

[55] *Cf.* paras. 21.46 to 21.51 above.
[56] Schlosser, *loc. cit.*
[57] Para. 21.35 above.
[58] *e.g.* under Arts. 2 or 5(1).
[59] Paras. 21.25 *et seq.* The problems referred to there in relation to the applicability of national law do not arise in the same way in the present context, because the other requirements of Art. 17 (such as those as to the form of the agreement) do not apply to cases falling within this provision.
[60] Droz, para. 183; Bülow/Böckstiegel/Müller, p. 142; Geimer/Schütze, p. 246.
[61] Para. 16.18 above.
[62] Art. 29, para. 27.75 below; *cf.* Geimer/Schütze, p. 241.
[63] Para. 27.77 below.

C. ARTICLE 17, SECOND PARAGRAPH: TRUST INSTRUMENTS

1. "The court or courts of a Contracting State in which a trust instrument has conferred jurisdiction shall have exclusive jurisdiction in any proceedings brought against a settlor, trustee or beneficiary, if relations between these persons or their rights or obligations under the trust are involved"

Generally

21.73   The concept of the trust is not known to continental law, and the accession of the United Kingdom and Ireland necessitated a provision such as the present paragraph.[64] The extent to which the Convention applies to trusts is considered above,[65] but it should be reiterated that trusts concerned with matters excluded by Article 1[66]—such as wills, bankruptcy and rights in property arising out of a matrimonial relationship—are themselves probably excluded, whether or not the particular dispute relates to an excluded matter. The observations above as to the dispute falling within the general scope of the Convention[67] and as to interpretation, conflicts of law and national law[68] apply as much to trust instruments as to jurisdiction agreements.

21.74   The second paragraph of Article 17 does not seem to require that either the plaintiff or the settlor, trustee or beneficiary defendant should be domiciled in a Contracting State, either at the date of the trust instrument or when proceedings are commenced. In this respect, the second paragraph is much more far-reaching in its effect than the first paragraph of Article 17. Under the other rules of the Convention, if such a defendant is domiciled in a Contracting State, he may either be sued in that Contracting State under Article 2, or in the Contracting State (if different) where the trust has its seat, under Article 5(6).

Similarly, there are no express requirements of form for a choice of jurisdiction provision in a trust instrument. This may be explained by reason of the fact that a trust instrument is, at its inception, a unilateral act and there is therefore no need for proof of a consensus. The question whether a jurisdiction provision is valid is to be determined by the substantive law of the trust, as decided by the application of the conflicts rules of the *lex fori*. As with jurisdiction clauses in contracts, Articles 21 to 23 will usually provide a solution to the problems which may arise where courts in different

---

[64] Schlosser, para. 178 (para. A1.473 below).
[65] Para. 17.66.
[66] Para. 14.03 above.
[67] Para. 21.06 above.
[68] Paras. 21.25 *et seq.* above.

Contracting States apply different choice of law rules, with the result that different answers are reached as to the validity of the jurisdiction clause in a trust.[69]

2. " . . . a trust instrument . . . "

Choice of jurisdiction provisions relating to resulting or constructive trusts do not seem to fall within the second paragraph of Article 17, and in this respect it is slightly narrower than Article 5(6).[70] It is anyway unlikely that a jurisdiction provision would arise in a resulting or constructive trust. **21.75**

3. " . . . if relations between those persons or their rights or obligations under the trust are involved . . . "

This is equivalent to the "particular legal relationship" provision under the first paragraph of Article 17. It is concerned with the "internal relationships"[71] of the trust which may be subject to a jurisdiction provision in the trust instrument. The "external relationships" of the trust, such as the trustees' rights and obligations as against third parties are governed by the other provisions of the Convention. **21.76**

D. ARTICLE 17, THIRD PARAGRAPH: INSURANCE, CONSUMER AND EXCLUSIVE JURISDICTION CASES

1. "Agreements or provisions of a trust instrument conferring jurisdiction shall have no legal force if they are contrary to the provisions of Article 12 or 15, or if the courts whose jurisdiction they purport to exclude have exclusive jurisdiction by virtue of Article 16"

The effect of this paragraph is to impose extra limitations on the validity of choice of jurisdiction provisions in those areas where the Convention is particularly concerned with the protection of the economically weaker party,[72] or where strong considerations of policy[73] justify the granting of exclusive jurisdiction to the courts of a particular Contracting State. **21.77**

---

[69] *Cf.* para. 21.33 above.
[70] Para. 17.68 above.
[71] So called by the Schlosser Report, at paras. 109–111 (paras. A1.395–A1.397 below).
[72] See paras. 18.02 and 19.02 above.
[73] See para. 20.02 above.

2. Insurance and consumer cases

21.78   Additional limitations on jurisdiction agreements in insurance matters and consumer matters are provided by Articles 12[74] and 15[75] respectively. These Articles do not supplant Article 17, but merely qualify it. So, an agreement falling within Article 17 will still be effective as a choice of jurisdiction, save to the extent that it is invalidated by Articles 12 or 15. For example, a choice of jurisdiction agreement will be valid and effective in either an insurance case or a consumer case if it is entered into after the dispute has arisen,[76] but only if it complies with Article 17.

3. Exclusive jurisdiction cases

21.79   Article 16[77] assigns exclusive jurisdiction over certain matters to the courts of a particular Contracting State, but is silent as to which court has jurisdiction. In the absence of a jurisdiction agreement, it is clear that the allocation of jurisdiction within the Contracting State would be a matter for national law alone.[78] Where there is a choice of jurisdiction provision, though, it is less clear whether Article 17 may continue to apply for the purposes of choosing the particular court which is to be competent. On one hand, the position might be the same as that under Articles 12 and 15, so that a jurisdiction provision complying with Article 17 could apply for the purposes of making a choice of court within the relevant Contracting State both valid and compulsory.

On the other hand, the policy considerations underlying Article 16 could be said to justify an interpretation of that Article such as to give national law an absolute competence to decide which court has jurisdiction over the case.[79] That is probably the better view, but it does not *require* national law to regulate the matter. In the result, therefore, if national law invalidates a particular choice of jurisdiction within the Contracting State, the jurisdiction agreement is without effect. But if national law permits a particular choice of jurisdiction, the jurisdiction agreement will operate effectively, provided that it complies with the requirements of Article 17.[80] In summary, the requirements of Article 17 apply to a choice of juris-

---

[74] Para. 18.49 above.
[75] Para. 19.34 above.
[76] Arts. 12(1) and 15(1).
[77] Chap. 20 above.
[78] A theoretical exception may arise where national law provides no forum: see para. 20.05 above.
[79] Droz, para. 202.
[80] Geimer/Schütze, p. 910.

diction provision, to the extent that that provision is not inconsistent with Article 16 or with national law.[81]

As has been observed,[82] Article 16 does not expressly deal with the situation where the subject matter of the dispute is connected with a non-Contracting State, but the courts of a Contracting State might have to decline jurisdiction in such a case. The question arises whether that conclusion, if it is correct, would be affected by a choice of jurisdiction provision falling within Article 17. Droz raises this question and expresses the view that if in such a case the ordinary rules of jurisdiction in the Convention can be overridden, then the jurisdictional rules in Article 17 can also be overridden.[83]

E. Article 17, Fourth Paragraph: Agreements for the Benefit of Only One Party

"If an agreement conferring jurisdiction was concluded for the benefit of only one of the parties, that party shall retain the right to bring proceedings in any other court which has jurisdiction by virtue of this Convention"[84]

The effect of this paragraph is to enable a party for whose benefit   **21.80**
the jurisdiction agreement was concluded to object to the jurisdiction of any court in which he is sued other than the court chosen; but at the same time to let him take advantage of the fact that the agreement was concluded solely for his benefit. But if he waives the benefit of the jurisdiction agreement by starting an action in another competent court, he cannot then seek to rely on it if he is sued in a counterclaim.[85]

The factors to be taken into account in deciding whether a clause has been concluded for the benefit of only one of the parties were considered by the European Court of Justice in *Anterist* v. *Crédit Lyonnais*,[86] which held that the fact that a clause specified the jurisdiction of a court or the courts of the Contracting State where one of the parties was domiciled was not of itself enough to establish that the clause was concluded for the benefit of that party.[87]

---

[81] Bülow/Böckstiegel/Müller, p. 150.

[82] Paras. 20.06 *et seq.* above.

[83] Droz, para. 204; *Mesch Vermoegensanlage GmbH—Emissions K.G.* v. *Orspan S.A.* Ned.Jur. 1978, No. 621, Digest D I–17.1.2—B1.

[84] See Kohler, "Pathologisches in EuGVÜ: Hinkende Gerichtstandsvereinbarungen nach Art. 17 Abs. 3", I Prax 1986, p. 340.

[85] See para. 17.95 above; *cf. Meeth* v. *Glacetal* [1978] E.C.R. 2133, discussed at para. 21.44 above.

[86] [1986] E.C.R. 1951.

[87] As the U.K. rightly observed in its observations, any other conclusion would have very largely deprived Art. 17 of effect, because jurisdiction clauses usually choose the courts of the state where at least one of the parties is domiciled.

Mr. Anterist, who was domiciled at Saarbrücken in Germany, had entered into a guarantee securing the bank's lending to his company. The company and the bank were both domiciled in France, and the guarantee was arranged through the bank's branch in Forbach, which is in the jurisdictional district of the court at Saareguemines, also in France. The guarantee, which was on the bank's printed form, contained a clause conferring exclusive jurisdiction on the court within whose district the branch was situated, irrespective of the defendant's identity.

The company defaulted on its payments to the bank, which then sued Mr. Anterist on the guarantee in the court for his domicile, the *Landgericht* Saarbrücken. He challenged the jurisdiction, relying on the clause conferring jurisdiction on the court in Saareguemines. The *Landgericht* upheld the objection, but on the bank's appeal, the *Oberlandesgericht* took the view that the clause was concluded for the benefit only of the bank, which was therefore free to bring its action in the court having jurisdiction under Article 2. Mr. Anterist appealed against that decision to the *Bundesgerichtshof*, which referred the following question to the European Court:[88]

> "Is an agreement conferring jurisdiction to be regarded as 'concluded for the benefit of only one of the parties' within the meaning of the third paragraph of Article 17[89] of the Convention, even where all that is established is that the parties had effectively agreed, in accordance with the first paragraph of Article 17, that a court or the courts of the Contracting State in which the party is domiciled are to have international jurisdiction?"

21.81   Although it did not say so expressly, it is apparent from the European Court's judgment that the concept of an agreement "concluded for the benefit of only one of the parties" should be given an independent interpretation. The Court stated:

> "Since Article 17 of the Convention embodies the principle of the parties' autonomy to determine the court or courts with jurisdiction, the third paragraph[89a] of that provision must be interpreted in such a way as to respect the parties' common intention when the contract was concluded. The common intention to confer an advantage on one of the parties must therefore be clear from the terms of the jurisdiction clause or from all the evidence to be found therein or from the circumstances in which the contract was concluded."[90]

The Court pointed out that the choice of a court in the Contracting State where one of the parties was domiciled could be inspired

---

[88] Bundesgerichtshof, decision of December 20, 1984, [1985] E.C.C. 327.
[89] The present paragraph was the third paragraph of Art. 17 in the unamended version of the Convention.
[89a] *Ibid.*
[90] [1986] E.C.R. 1951, 1962 (para. 14).

by a multiplicity of motives[91] and went on to say[92] that such a choice was not of itself sufficient to lead to the conclusion that the agreement was entered into for the benefit of only one of the parties.[93]

It remains to be seen how closely the fourth paragraph of Article 17 is confined to agreements which expressly indicate that they are for the benefit of one party or give one party a wider choice of forum than is available to the other. A wider reading of the words "for the benefit of only one of the parties" raises other problems. While the European Court's decision in *Anterist* v. *Crédit Lyonnais* precludes a purely objective interpretation of these words, in the sense that the parties' intention to confer benefit on one of them must be apparent, it remains to be seen whether there are any principles which classify the type of benefit envisaged.

In principle, the benefit should be one envisaged by the parties at the time of conclusion of the contract, not a benefit which arises by reason of the circumstances of the particular dispute. But what is less clear is whether the court is required, or permitted, to weigh the respective advantages and disadvantages to each of the parties from the point of view of the procedural law, the choice of law rules and the substantive law which apply in the chosen forum. It is also not clear how wide an enquiry the court should or may make into the potential benefits of the agreement, to the extent that they were capable of being envisaged or were actually envisaged when the agreement was made.[94] Too wide an examination of such issues is undesirable at the preliminary stage of deciding whether the court   **21.82**

---

[91] In its decision in *Berghoefer GmbH & Co. KG* v. *A.S.A. SA* [1985] E.C.R. 2699, at p. 2708 (para. 14), the European Court had pointed out the difficulty of determining the party for whose benefit the jurisdiction agreement had been concluded. The case is discussed at para. 21.64 above.

[92] [1986] E.C.R. 1951, 1963 (para. 16).

[93] Earlier decisions whereby parties have escaped the consequences of otherwise valid jurisdiction agreements, on the basis that they were concluded only for their benefit, must now be read in the light of *Anterist* v. *Crédit Lyonnais*: Landgericht Trier, October 30, 1975, case 6 O 74/75, Digest D I–17.3—B1; Landgericht Mainz, February 24, 1978, case HO 5/78; Digest D I–17.3—B2; Oberlandesgericht Bamberg, February 9, 1978, case U 127/77, Ent.OLG Zivilsachen 1978, p. 341, Digest D I–17.3.—B2n.; Landgericht Bonn, April 21, 1982, case 12 O 154/81, I Prax. 1983, p. 243; Digest D I–17.3.—B2 n. 2; Landgericht Giessen, December 10, 1982, case 8 O 57/82, I Prax. 1984, p. 160. But the clauses have been held not to be for the benefit of only one party in other decisions: Oberlandesgericht München, January 29, 1980, case 25 U 3274/79, RIW/AWD 1982, p. 281, Digest D I–17.3—B3; Oberlandesgericht Frankfurt-am-Main, November 22, 1983, case 22 U 4/83, RIW/AWD 1985, p. 71, Digest D I–17.3—B3 n. 1.

[94] Kohler, "Pathologisches im EuGVÜ: Hinkende Gerichtstandsvereinbarungen nach Art. 17 Abs. 3", above.

has jurisdiction, and it is to be hoped that this paragraph of Article 17 will be narrowly interpreted. In view of the fact that the first paragraph of Article 17 gives considerable scope for non-exclusive jurisdiction clauses to be effective,[95] and in the light of the *Anterist* decision, it may be that the fourth paragraph adds little to the other provisions of the Article.

The fourth paragraph of Article 17 seems to envisage only two parties, and appears to leave open the question of what is to occur where there are three or more parties to an agreement, but where a jurisdiction agreement is concluded for the benefit of only one or some of them. It is suggested that, in such a case, any one of those parties should also retain the right to bring proceedings in any other court which has jurisdiction by virtue of the Convention.

Article 18

21.83   Apart from jurisdiction derived from other provisions of this Convention, a court of a Contracting State before whom a defendant enters an appearance shall have jurisdiction. This rule shall not apply where appearance was entered solely to contest the jurisdiction, or where another court has exclusive jurisdiction by virtue of Article 16.*

F. ARTICLE 18: GENERAL NOTE

21.84   *Introduction.* Article 18 provides a means for the parties to confer jurisdiction on a court which would not otherwise be competent,[96] by means of a voluntary submission to that jurisdiction. The Convention treats the entry of an appearance without contesting the jurisdiction as an implied prorogation of jurisdiction,[97] comparable with the express prorogation of jurisdiction envisaged by Article 17.[98] If a defendant puts forward a defence on the merits at the

---

[95] Paras. 21.44 *et seq.* above.

* Jenard, para. A1.171 below. Collins, pp. 91–94; Dashwood/Halcon/White, pp. 32, 130–132; Hartley, p. 76; Kaye, pp. 1116–1128; Maxwell, paras. 5.191–5.196; Anton, para. 7.28; Droz, paras. 170–179, 220–224; Weser, paras. 265.9–265.10; Bülow/Böckstiegel/Müller, pp. 153–157; Geimer/Schütze, pp. 207–209, 947–965; Kropholler, pp. 200–206; Gothot/Holleaux, paras. 188–200; Pocar, pp. 225–232.

[96] If the court would have jurisdiction under the Convention anyway, the question of whether Art. 18 applies will rarely arise: see para. 21.90 below.

[97] The concept of "prorogation" is discussed at para. 21.03 above. It is not quite the same as jurisdiction by agreement, because it may form the basis for jurisdiction against a person who is not a party to the agreement: see para. 18.37 above.

[98] *Spitzley* v. *Sommer Exploitation S.A.* [1985] E.C.R. 787, 797–798. The case is discussed at para. 21.88 below. *Contra,* Geimer/Schütze, p. 948.

same time as objecting to the jurisdiction, he will not be taken to have submitted to the jurisdiction unless his objection is made after his plea on the merits.[99] Although it refers expressly to the entry of an appearance, Article 18 also has the effect in certain circumstances of permitting a prorogation of jurisdiction to be implied from the conduct of the parties.[1]

In order for Article 18 to apply, the subject-matter of the case must fall within the general scope of the Convention[2] and the case must have an international character.[3] If the case is purely internal to the state in which the action is brought, in the sense that the courts of no other state would have jurisdiction under the Convention (including jurisdiction pursuant to a choice of forum agreement), the internal law of that state will alone determine jurisdiction. But if the case has connections with just one Contracting State, except only that the plaintiff has brought his action in the courts of another Contracting State, the entry of an appearance by the defendant in the latter state will itself lend the case an international character as between these two Contracting States sufficient to bring the case within the Convention.[4] In this sense, the entry of an appearance is equivalent to an agreement on the jurisdiction of the courts of the second state.

1. Precedence of Article 18

With only one exception, international jurisdiction can be conferred on a court under this Article by the entry of an appearance without contesting the jurisdiction. That exception is where the courts of another Contracting State have exclusive jurisdiction under Article 16. Article 18 takes precedence over all the other provisions of the Convention, including precedence over Article 3 and over Article 17. The precedence over Article 3 has the effect that if a defendant domiciled in one Contracting State is sued in a court of another Contracting State, which would not otherwise have jurisdiction, that court nonetheless has jurisdiction under Article 18 if

21.85

---

[99] *Elefanten Schuh GmbH* v. *Jacqmain* [1981] E.C.R. 1671, at p. 1689; see para. 21.94 below.

[1] *Spitzley* v. *Sommer Exploitation S.A.*, above, at p. 798 paras. 17–19; see para. 21.88 below.

[2] Chap. 14 above; Collins, p. 91.

[3] *Cf.* Art. 17, para. 21.06 above.

[4] *e.g.*, *Partenreederei m.s. Atlantic Duke* v. *Frenave Agencia Maritima de Fretamentos e Consignacoes S.à.r.l.*, Arrondissementsrechtbank Rotterdam, October 20, 1980, [1982] E.C.C. 348, where the entry of an appearance by a defendant domiciled in Portugal, in proceedings which a plaintiff domiciled in Germany had brought in the Netherlands pursuant to a jurisdiction agreement, was held sufficient to bring the case within the Convention.

the defendant enters an appearance without contesting the jurisdiction.[5] That is so, even if an exorbitant basis of jurisdiction had been used against the defendant, contrary to the first paragraph of Article 3.[6] Similarly, because this Article takes precedence over Article 17, it follows that if the parties have entered into a valid jurisdiction agreement, and the defendant is then sued in a court other than the court chosen, the court seised has jurisdiction if the defendant enters an appearance without contesting the jurisdiction.

The European Court of Justice has ruled on this latter question in *Elefanten Schuh GmbH* v. *Jacqmain*.[7] One of the questions referred by the Belgian *Hof van Cassatie* was:

> "Is Article 18 . . . applicable if parties have agreed to confer jurisdiction on a court within the meaning of Article 17?"[8]

21.86   The European Court ruled that Article 18 was applicable in that case, and commented:

> "The case envisaged in Article 17 is not . . . one of the exceptions which Article 18 allows to the rule which it lays down. Moreoever neither the general scheme nor the objectives of the Convention provide grounds for the view that the parties to an agreement conferring jurisdiction within the meaning of Article 17 are prevented from voluntarily submitting their dispute to a court other than that stipulated in the agreement.
>
> It follows that Article 18 of the Convention applies even where the parties have by agreement designated a court which is to have jurisdiction within the meaning of Article 17."[9]

Accordingly, once the defendant has entered an appearance without contesting the jurisdiction, the court can only decline jurisdiction under Article 19[10] (*i.e.* where the case is principally concerned with a matter falling within Article 16) or under Articles 21 to 23, in the case of *lis pendens* or related actions.[11]

---

[5] Jenard, para. A1.171 below.

[6] Para. 16.09 above: for example, an action brought in the French courts, at the instance of a plaintiff of French nationality, pursuant to Art. 14 of the French Civil Code.

[7] [1981] E.C.R. 1671, discussed at para. 21.27 above, where the facts are set out.

[8] *Ibid.*, p. 1684 (para. 7).

[9] *Ibid.*, pp. 1684–1685 (paras. 10 and 11). This passage was cited by the European Court in *Spitzley* v. *Sommer Exploitation S.A.*, above, at p. 799 (paras. 24–25) which provides a further instance of voluntary submission to the jurisdiction taking precedence over an express choice of a different jurisdiction: see paras. 21.88 *et seq.* below.

[10] Droz, para. 224.

[11] Chap. 23 below.

2. Domicile of the parties

Unlike Article 17, Article 18 makes no mention of the domicile of **21.87** the parties[12] and some controversy surrounds the question whether domicile is relevant for the purposes of this Article.[13] On one view, the defendant must be domiciled in a Contracting State for Article 18 to apply,[14] whereas, on another view, it does not matter where the parties are domiciled.[15] A third view, derived from the express wording of Article 17 and the fact that Article 18 forms part of the same section of the Convention, is that *one* of the parties must be domiciled in a Contracting State.[16] It may be that the view is to be preferred that the entry of an appearance without contesting the jurisdiction will found jurisdiction if the Convention would, but for the entry of the appearance, have conferred jurisdiction on a court or the courts of some other Contracting State.[17]

If that is correct, Article 18 does not apply where the case is purely internal to one Contracting State,[18] in the sense described above,[19] or if the only international connections of the case are with non-Contracting States, so that the only Contracting State involved is the state whose court is seised. In either of those circumstances, national law alone will decide whether the court is competent, and if competent whether it will accept jurisdiction.

3. Set-off and counterclaim, submission implied from conduct

It is clear from the express wording of Article 18 that an implied **21.88** prorogation of jurisdiction occurs when the defendant enters an appearance without contesting the jurisdiction. But the European Court has held in *Spitzley* v. *Sommer Exploitation S.A.*[20] that a voluntary submission to the jurisdiction is also to be implied where a plaintiff has been made a defendant to a counterclaim and has not contested the court's jurisdiction to hear the counterclaim.

Sommer Exploitation S.A., a manufacturer of felt cloth established in France, brought proceedings in the *Landgericht* Koblenz

---

[12] See paras. 21.34 *et seq.* above; *cf.* Droz, para. 221.

[13] Geimer/Schütze, pp. 207–209; Kropholler, pp. 201–202.

[14] This view is implicit in the Jenard Report, para. A1.171 below.

[15] Weser, para. 265.10; Gothot/Holleaux, paras. 189–190.

[16] Kropholler, p. 201. *Cf. Partenreederei m.s. Atlantic Duke* v. *Frenave Agencia Maritima de Fretamentos e Consignacoes S.à.r.l.*, Arrondissementsrechtbank Rotterdam, October 20, 1980, [1982] E.C.C. 348.

[17] Bülow/Böckstiegel/Müller, pp. 154–155 (who also say that the court seised should not otherwise have jurisdiction under the Convention: see para. 21.90 below). *Cf.* the discussion at para. 21.06., at n. 36 above.

[18] This is true also of the Convention generally: paras. 31.10 *et seq.* above.

[19] Para. 21.84.

[20] [1985] E.C.R. 787. The English law relating to submission to the jurisdiction is discussed at para. 1.27 above.

against Mrs. Spitzley, who was domiciled in Germany, claiming payment for cloth sold to her. She did not dispute Sommer's claim, except to claim a right to set-off sums which she alleged Sommer owed her husband by way of commission payments under a contract of commercial agency. Her husband's rights to the sums had been validly assigned to her.

The *Landgericht* considered the case on its merits, allowed the set-off in part and gave judgment to Sommer for the balance. Both parties appealed to the *Oberlandesgericht* Koblenz, which drew attention to a jurisdiction clause in the agency contract, conferring exclusive jurisdiction on the courts of France in respect of disputes arising out of that contract. Sommer had placed no reliance on the clause, but the *Oberlandesgericht* raised the question whether the German courts had jurisdiction to entertain the claim for set-off, in view of the fact that Article 18 referred only to the entry of an appearance by a defendant, and referred the matter to the European Court.

21.89   The European Court drew attention to the fact that Article 18 forms, with Article 17, section 6 of Title II of the Convention, headed "Prorogation of jurisdiction" and pointed out that the Convention allows the parties, subject to certain restrictions, to choose the court to which they intend to submit the settlement of their dispute:

> "Article 18 in particular is based on the idea that, by entering an appearance before the court seised of the proceedings by the plaintiff, without contesting the court's jurisdiction, the defendant is by implication signifying his consent to the hearing of the case by a court other than that designated by the other provisions of the Convention."[21]

In the light of that context and purpose, the European Court concluded that a case such as that referred by the German court fell within the scope of Article 18.[22] The position of a plaintiff disputing the substance of the claim for a set-off without contesting the jurisdiction of the court was similar to that, expressly envisaged by Article 18, of a defendant who enters an appearance without contesting the jurisdiction.[23] The European Court said that that conclusion:

> "is not affected by the fact, emphasised in the order for reference, that the defendant's claim for a set-off is not based on the same contract or subject-matter as the main application. That fact relates to the

---

[21] *Ibid.*, at p. 798 (para. 15).
[22] *Ibid.*, (para. 18).
[23] *Ibid.*, (para. 19).

admissibility of a claim for a set-off which depends on the law of the State in which the court seised of the proceedings is situated."[24]

Similarly, the fact that there was a jurisdiction agreement in favour of the French courts was held to not affect the decision because, on the basis established in the *Elephanten Schuh* decision, Article 17 did not affect the parties' freedom to submit their dispute to a court other than that stipulated in the agreement.[25]

G. ARTICLE 18: JURISDICTION BASED ON APPEARANCE

1. "Apart from jurisdiction derived from other provisions of this Convention . . . "

These words are perhaps ambiguous. They could mean either **21.90** "whether or not jurisdiction may be derived from other provisions of this Convention, . . . " or "except where jurisdiction may be derived from other provisions of this Convention. . . . "[26] In practice, the distinction is likely to be of little relevance, because if the court has jurisdiction anyway, the entry of an appearance adds nothing.[27] Nonetheless, in a case falling within the Convention, a court will normally only have jurisdiction if it is derived from the Convention and it may be necessary (especially in those continental countries where the basis of jurisdiction is regularly set out in a judgment) to decide precisely how jurisdiction is founded in a given case.

For example, if a person applies to be joined in proceedings as defendant or as a third party (assuming that this is permissible under the national procedural law), jurisdiction may only be based on the express wording of Article 18 if the words "enters an appearance" cover such an application.[28] If the person is domiciled in a Contracting State, it could be argued that jurisdiction may be

---

[24] *Ibid.*, at p. 799 (para. 22). *Cf.* the jurisdiction under Art. 6(3) (para. 17.90 above), which is limited to a counterclaim "arising from the same contract or facts on which the original claim was based." The reference to the *lex fori* should, it is suggested, be understood as a reference to that law, including its rules of conflicts of law.
[25] *Ibid.*, (para. 25).
[26] Droz, para. 221 appears to favour the former interpretation, while other language versions tend slightly to favour the latter: *e.g.*, French, *"outre le cas où sa compétence résulte d'autres dispositions de la présente convention . . . "*; German: *"Sofern das Gericht . . . nicht bereits nach anderen Vorschriften dieses Übereinkommens zuständig ist . . . ,"* etc.
[27] Collins, p. 91, n. 1.
[28] Para. 21.92 below.

derived under Article 6.[29] In view of the fact that the domicile of the parties is not mentioned in Article 18,[30] it is suggested that the question whether such an application falls within Article 18 should not depend on the applicant's domicile, but that the interpretation which accords best with the liberal intent of Article 18 and with the European Court's decision in *Spitzley* v. *Sommer*[31] is to read this Article as conferring international jurisdiction[32] over a person on a court of a Contracting State whenever that person voluntarily submits to the jurisdiction without contesting it.

On the other hand, Article 18 probably does not confer on a plaintiff the right to start proceedings in a court which would not otherwise have jurisdiction, in the hope that the defendant will give the court jurisdiction under this Article. Although the first paragraph of Article 20[33] imposes on the court a duty to examine its jurisdiction of its own motion, that duty probably only arises after the defendant has failed to enter an appearance[34] and the question whether the plaintiff has a right at an earlier stage to start proceedings where the court does not otherwise have jurisdiction depends on the procedural law of the court in question.[35]

2. " . . . a court of a Contracting State . . . "

21.91   The reference to "a court" is in the singular and implies that even if national law would not afford jurisdiction to the court before which the defendant appears, that court will have jurisdiction by virtue of Article 18.[36] This is so whether or not the Convention would, but for the unconditional entry of an appearance, regulate the court's local jurisdiction,[37] but it may be that Article 18 will

---

[29] Para. 17.73 above.

[30] Para. 21.87 above.

[31] [1985] E.C.R. 787: see para. 21.88 above.

[32] As to local jurisdiction, see the next paragraph and para. 21.96 below.

[33] Para. 22.11 below.

[34] Para. 22.14 below. Where the case falls within Art. 19 (*i.e.*, it is within the exclusive jurisdiction of the courts of another Contracting State under Art. 16), the obligation arises when the court becomes "seised" of the claim: para. 22.06 below.

[35] For example, English law continues to permit the issue of a writ and its service within the court's territorial jurisdiction where the claim is one which the Convention gives it no power to entertain unless the defendant enters an appearance without contesting the jurisdiction. Only if the writ is for service out of the court's territorial jurisdiction is its issue in any way restricted: R.S.C., Ord. 6, r. 7(1). See chap. 3 above.

[36] The jurisdiction under Art. 18 is compulsory: see para. 21.93 below.

[37] Geimer/Schütze, pp. 957–958. See para. 15.03 above.

only confer local jurisdiction on a court which otherwise would not be locally competent if and to the extent that it is not contrary to national law.[38] The effect of disputing only the local jurisdiction is discussed below.[39]

3. " . . . enters an appearance . . . "

While it will be necessary to refer to national procedural law to determine the precise manner in which and time at which a person enters an appearance and submits to the jurisdiction,[40] these words ought, it is suggested, to be given an independent interpretation to the extent necessary to ensure consistency of application in all the Contracting States. For the reasons suggested above,[41] for example, an application to be joined as a defendant, if it is permissible according to national law, should not constitute the entry of an appearance for the purposes of Article 18 in one country, but not in another.

21.92

4. " . . . shall have jurisdiction . . . "

The jurisdiction contemplated by this Article is the court's international jurisdiction.[42] It probably does not have the effect of conferring on the court jurisdiction of a kind which, as a matter of national law, that court is not competent to exercise. So, if the subject-matter of the case, or its monetary value, is such that the national court does not have jurisdiction, even with the agreement of the parties, to entertain or determine the proceedings, Article 18 does not have the effect of enlarging the court's jurisdiction in those respects.[43]

The international jurisdiction conferred by this Article is compulsory and the court has no discretion not to accept jurisdiction.[44] By contrast with Article 17, the jurisdiction is not expressed to be exclusive, but if the court before which the defendant appears is the

21.93

---

[38] Bülow/Böckstiegel/Müller, p. 157. See, further, para. 21.93 below.
[39] Para. 21.96.
[40] Jenard, para. A1.171 below. The English procedure, which (in the High Court) involves the filing of an acknowledgement of service, is discussed at paras. 4.51 and 4.52 above.
[41] Para. 21.90 above.
[42] The entry of an appearance is usually sufficient as a matter of national law to found local jurisdiction: see chaps. 48 to 58 below, at para. 29.
[43] See para. 21.96 below.
[44] *Cf.* the position under Art. 17, para. 21.15 above. There is a possible exception, where the local jurisdiction is contrary to national law: para. 21.91 above.

first court seised, Articles 21 to 23[45] will normally prevent other courts from exercising jurisdiction.

5. " . . . where appearance was entered solely to contest the jurisdiction . . . "[46]

Contesting the jurisdiction

21.94   If a defendant enters an appearance solely with a view to contesting the jurisdiction, he is not to be taken, in the event of his objection being unsuccessful, to have submitted to the jurisdiction by virtue of having entered the appearance.[47] Equally, if he enters a defence on the merits at the same time as objecting to the jurisdiction, that fact does not necessarily give the court jurisdiction pursuant to Article 18, if his objection fails. This is the effect of two decisions of the European Court of Justice, which it has since reaffirmed.

In *Elefanten Schuh GmbH* v. *Jacqmain*,[48] the defendant company raised a defence on the substance of the plaintiff's claim, and did not seek to place reliance on the parties' jurisdiction agreement until several months later. Among others, the following questions were put by the Belgian *Hof van Cassatie* to the European Court of Justice:

> "Is the rule on jurisdiction contained in Article 18 applicable if the defendant has not only contested jurisdiction but has in addition made submissions on the action itself?
> If it is, must jurisdiction then be contested *in limine litis*?"[49]

The European Court's ruling on these questions was as follows:

> "Article 18 . . . must be interpreted as meaning that the rule on jurisdiction which that provision lays down does not apply where the defendant not only contests the court's jurisdiction but also makes submissions on the substance of the action, provided that, if the challenge to jurisdiction is not preliminary to any defence as to the substance, it does not occur after the making of the submissions which

---

[45] Chap. 23 below.

[46] The French text of this passage (" . . . *si la comparution a pour objet de contester la compétence* . . . ") does not contain an equivalent of the word "solely," but the problem of interpretation raised by this difference has been resolved by the European Court's decision in *Elefanten Schuh GmbH* v. *Jacqmain* (discussed below).

[47] An appearance to contest provisional measures granted under Art. 24 should not be regarded as a submission to the jurisdiction in respect of the substance, at least if the proceedings in respect of the substantive claim have not yet been started: *Société Gola Werke German Gotz K.G.* v. *André Barseqhian*, Sem.jur. Edition Générale 1981, Jurisprudence, No. 19519, Digest D I–5.1.2—B25.

[48] [1981] E.C.R. 1671, discussed at para. 21.27 above.

[49] *Ibid.*, at p. 1684 (para. 7).

under national procedural law are considered to be the first defence addressed to the court seised."[50]

In other words, if the defendant pleads to the merits as well as objecting to the jurisdiction, he will not be taken to have submitted to the jurisdiction unless his objection to the jurisdiction comes after the plea on the merits.

The European Court said that it was more in keeping with the objectives and spirit of the Convention to allow a defendant to contest both the jurisdiction and the substance of the claim, rather than being required to confine himself to contesting the jurisdiction.[51] It stated further:

> "In fact under the law of civil procedure of certain Contracting States a defendant who raises the issue of jurisdiction and no other might be barred from making his submissions as to the substance if the court rejects his plea that it has no jurisdiction. An interpretation of Article 18 which enabled such a result to be arrived at would be contrary to the right of the defendant to defend himself in the original proceedings, which is one of the aims of the Convention.
>
> However, the challenge to jurisdiction may have the result attributed to it by Article 18 only if the plaintiff and the court seised of the matter are able to ascertain from the time of the defendant's first defence that it is intended to contest the jurisdiction of the court."[52]

The interpretation of Article 18 on this point was further developed in *Rohr* v. *Ossberger*.[53] Ossberger was a German manufacturer of water turbines, which Rohr, a French company, bought for onward sale in France under its own name. Proceedings against Rohr for the payment of certain accounts were brought by Ossberger in its local court, the *Landgericht* Ansbach, in reliance on a jurisdiction clause in its general conditions. Rohr unsuccessfully objected to the jurisdiction, but did not plead to the merits, either at first instance or on appeal, for fear of losing its right to object to the jurisdiction. Ossberger accordingly obtained judgment in Germany and sought to enforce it in France. In the enforcement proceedings, Rohr argued that the judgment should not be enforced, because it was contrary to French public policy for a judgment to be enforceable against them without their having an opportunity to defend on the merits.[54] The question submitted to the European Court of Justice by the *Cour d'Appel* Versailles asked, in effect, whether Rohr did have an opportunity to raise a defence on the

21.95

---

[50] *Ibid.*, at p. 1689.
[51] *Ibid.*, at p. 1685 (para. 14).
[52] *Ibid.*, at pp. 1684–1685 (paras. 14–15).
[53] *Etablissements Rohr S.A.* v. *Dina Ossberger* [1981] E.C.R. 2431.
[54] See Art. 27(1), paras. 27.13 *et seq.* below.

merits in the German proceedings. The European Court's ruling was that:

> "Article 18 . . . must be interpreted as meaning that it allows the defendant not only to contest the jurisdiction but to submit at the same time in the alternative a defence on the substance of the action without, however, losing his right to raise an objection of lack of jurisdiction."[55]

The European Court has given rulings in the same terms in two subsequent cases.[56] The procedure to be adopted in contesting the jurisdiction is regulated by the national law of the court in question.[57]

International jurisdiction and national law

21.96   For the purposes of Article 18, if the jurisdiction is contested, the contest must be to the *international* jurisdiction of the court seised. An objection to the jurisdiction on the grounds that the court does not have *local* jurisdiction, or that the subject-matter of the case is not within its jurisdiction, is probably not a contest of the jurisdiction for the purposes of Article 18. Consequently, the entry of an appearance by a defendant for the purpose of contesting the jurisdiction on some basis other than the court's international competence will probably amount to the entry of an appearance for the purposes of Article 18 in the event of the objection being unsuccessful.[58]

What is less clear is whether, in the event of such an objection succeeding, the defendant's initial failure to raise an objection to the international jurisdiction will bar him from subsequently raising an objection to the international jurisdiction of another court in the same Contracting State. The answer will probably depend upon the national procedural law, at least to this extent, that if the result of the successful objection is that the proceedings are dismissed altogether, the procedural rights of the defendant arise *de novo* in any new proceedings; but it would be otherwise if the result of the successful objection is to cause the proceedings to be transferred to another court, without having to be started afresh.[59]

---

[55] [1981] E.C.R. 2413, at p. 2440.

[56] *W.* v. *H.* [1982] E.C.R. 1189, at p. 1205 (discussed at para. 24.14 below); *Gerling Konzern AG* v. *Amministrazione del Tesoro dello Stato* [1983] E.C.R. 2503, at p. 2518 (discussed at para. 21.19 above).

[57] The national procedural law of the Contracting States is summarised in chaps. 48 to 58 below, at para. 42. The procedure under English law is examined in detail in chap. 5 above.

[58] Bülow/Böckstiegel/Müller, p. 156.

[59] In England, the County Court Rules, Ord. 16 rr. 2 and 4, provide for the transfer of proceedings from one court to another. See para. 3.21 above.

6. " . . . where another court has exclusive jurisdiction by virtue of Article 16"

The policy considerations which justify the exclusive jurisdic-   **21.97**
tions under Article 16[60] are sufficiently strong for them not to be
displaced even by the defendant's voluntary submission to the jurisdiction. If a case falls within Article 16, any court which does not
have exclusive jurisdiction under that Article is required by Article
19[61] to decline jurisdiction of its own motion.

As in the case of Article 17 where the subject-matter of the
case falls within Article 16, but is connected only with a non-
Contracting State,[62] it may be that a court of a Contracting State
would be permitted to decline jurisdiction, notwithstanding the fact
that a case falls within the terms of Article 18, and outside those of
Article 16.

Insurance and consumer cases. By contrast with Article 17,[63] this   **21.98**
Article makes no mention of Articles 12 and 15 and the entry of an
appearance will therefore found jurisdiction in insurance and consumer cases. Articles 12(1) and 15(1) each permit jurisdiction to be
founded on an agreement entered into after the dispute has arisen,
and the entry of an appearance without contesting the jurisdiction
is, tacitly, a prorogation which is equivalent to such an agreement.

---

[60] Chap. 20 above, at para. 20.02 and *passim*.
[61] Para. 22.01 below.
[62] See para. 21.79 above.
[63] See paras. 21.77 and 21.78 above.

CHAPTER 22

EXAMINATION AS TO JURISDICTION AND ADMISSIBILITY
(Articles 19–20)

SECTION 7

Article 19

22.01 **Where a court of a Contracting State is seised of a claim which is principally concerned with a matter over which the courts of another Contracting State have exclusive jurisdiction by virtue of Article 16, it shall declare of its own motion that it has no jurisdiction.**[★]

A. ARTICLE 19: GENERAL NOTE

22.02 This Article is complementary to Article 16 and is designed to ensure that courts respect the exclusive jurisdiction of the courts of the other Contracting States. As with Article 16, the domicile of the

---

★ Jenard, para. A1.172 below; Schlosser, para. 22 (paras. A1.311–A1.312 below); Collins, pp. 94–96; Dashwood/Halcon/White, pp. 19, 133; Hartley, pp. 80–81; Kaye, pp. 873–874, 880–883, 1214–1216; Maxwell, para. 5.197; Anton,

parties is not relevant.[1] The court's duty to decline jurisdiction *of its own motion* is unfamiliar to common lawyers, but is of central importance.[2]

1. " . . . principally concerned with a matter . . . "

The duty to decline jurisdiction does not arise if the matter falling within the list of subjects ∴ Article 16 is only preliminary or incidental to the main subject-matter of the claim.[3]   **22.03**

2. " . . . over which the courts of another Contracting State have exclusive jurisdiction . . . "

The possibility has already been noted[4] that a matter may fall within the exclusive jurisdiction of more than one Contracting State. This is especially so in the case of Article 16(2), where the seat of a company is the relevant connecting factor. If this happens, it seems that the plaintiff may choose where to bring his action[5] and a court which, applying the conflicts rules in Article 53, regards itself as being exclusively competent is not required to decline jurisdiction in favour of the courts of another state also having exclusive jurisdiction,[6] unless an action has been started first in the other courts.[7]   **22.04**

3. " . . . by virtue of Article 16 . . . "

A court is only required by this Article to decline jurisdiction if it is Article 16 which gives rise to the exclusive jurisdiction of the courts of another Contracting State. If the exclusive jurisdiction arises by virtue of Article 17, it is still capable of being overridden by the unconditional entry of an appearance under Article 18.[8] If there is no such unconditional appearance, Article 20[9] will require courts to decline jurisdiction unless their jurisdiction has been prorogated by the jurisdiction agreement.[10]   **22.05**

---

paras. 7.04–7.05, 7.39–7.30; Droz, paras. 243–246; Bülow/Böckstiegel/Müller, pp. 157–159; Geimer/Schütze, pp. 324, 329–330; Kropholler, pp. 206–208; Gothot/Holleaux, paras. 207–212; Pocar, pp. 233–234.
[1] Para. 20.02 above.
[2] See para. 22.06 below.
[3] Para. 20.04 above; Jenard, para. A1.172; Bülow/Böckstiegel/Müller, p. 158.
[4] Para. 20.29 above.
[5] *Ibid.*; Schlosser, para. 162 (para. A1.456 below).
[6] Bülow/Böckstiegel/Müller, p. 159.
[7] Art. 23, para. 23.24 below.
[8] Para. 21.85 above.
[9] Para. 22.11 below.
[10] Bülow/Böckstiegel/Müller, p. 158.

4. " . . . it shall declare of its own motion that it has no jurisdiction . . . "

22.06   The obligation on the court to decline jurisdiction is a continuing obligation which is imposed on the court from the time when it becomes "seised" of the claim. The precise determination of that time is a matter for the national law of the court seised.[11] Even if the court initially accepts jurisdiction, but later decides that the case is principally concerned with a matter over which the courts of another Contracting State have exclusive jurisdiction by virtue of Article 16, it must then decline jurisdiction.[12] For example, the principal issues may only become apparent after the defendant has pleaded to the merits.[13] Similarly, the court's duty to decline jurisdiction cannot be waived by the parties, and they may raise an objection at any time.[14]

22.07   In *Duijnstee* v. *Goderbauer*,[15] the question of whether the case fell within Article 16(4) was raised for the first time on appeal in cassation, by the *Hoge Raad* (the Netherlands Supreme Court) itself. According to Dutch procedural law, the court was not permitted to consider the point, it not having been raised by the parties in the grounds of appeal, but the court was concerned to know whether it was required by Article 19 to consider the matter, which involved questions of national law of several other countries. It referred that question to the European Court of Justice.

The European Court drew attention to the need, in the context of the Community legal order, to ensure equality and uniformity of rights and obligations arising from the Convention, regardless of national rules. It therefore concluded that the Convention, which seeks to determine the jurisdiction of the courts of Contracting States in civil matters, must override national provisions which are incompatible with it.[16] The court's ruling on the point was in these terms:

"Article 19 of the Convention requires the national court to declare of its own motion that it has no jurisdiction whenever it finds that a court of another Contracting State has exclusive jurisdiction under Article 16 of the Convention, even in an appeal in cassation where the

---

[11] *Zelger* v. *Salinitri (No. 2)* [1984] E.C.R. 2397, discussed at para. 23.05 below.
[12] Droz, para. 245; Kropholler, p. 206.
[13] Bülow/Böckstiegel/Müller, p. 159; *J. J. Wellen c.s.* v. *W. J. H. G. Wellen*, Ned.Jur. 1980, No. 609, Digest D I–1.2—B11.
[14] Bülow/Böckstiegel/Müller, p. 159; Oberlandesgericht Frankfurt-am-Main, case 13 U 104/83, May 9, 1984, N.J.W. 1984, p. 2045, Digest D I–16.1—B8.
[15] [1983] E.C.R. 3663, discussed at para. 20.34 above.
[16] *Ibid.*, at pp. 3674–3675 (paras. 13 and 14).

national rules of procedure limit the court's reviewal to the grounds raised by the parties."[17]

The Schlosser Report considers in some detail the nature of the **22.08** court's duty to examine its jurisdiction of its own motion. It says that the only essential factor is that uncontested assertions by the parties should not bind the court and that the following proposition is therefore reconcilable with the Convention:

> "A court may assume jurisdiction only if it is completely satisfied of all the facts on which such jurisdiction is based; if it is not so satisfied it can and must request the parties to provide the necessary evidence, in default of which the action will be dismissed as inadmissible. Whether a court is itself obliged to investigate the facts relevant to jurisdiction, or whether it can, or must, place the burden of proof in this respect on the party interested in the jurisdiction of the court concerned, is determined solely by national law."[18]

The court's duty to examine its jurisdiction of its own motion is discussed further in relation to Article 20.[19]

B. ENGLAND AND WALES

As the Schlosser Report observes, English courts have hitherto only **22.09** been able to reach a decision on the basis of submissions of fact or law made by the parties and this long-established practice is incompatible with the court's duty under Articles 19 and 20 to examine its jurisdiction of its own motion.[20]

Under the Rules of the Supreme Court, as amended, if the English Court has jurisdiction under the Convention, a writ may be issued and served out of the jurisdiction without leave on a defendant domiciled in another part of the United Kingdom or in another Contracting State,[21] provided it is duly indorsed.[22]

If and when the plaintiff comes to enter a default judgment against such a defendant, he will need leave to do so,[23] which he will only be able to obtain on the production of an affidavit stating the sources and grounds of the deponent's belief that, *inter alia*, no other court has exclusive jurisdiction.

---

[17] *Ibid.*, at p. 3678.
[18] Schlosser, para. 22 (para. A1.312 below).
[19] Paras. 22.15 *et seq.* below.
[20] Schlosser, para. 22 (para. A1.311 below).
[21] R.S.C., Ord. 6, r. 7(1)(a); Ord. 11, r. 1(2)(a); *cf.* C.C.R., Ord. 3, r. 3(6)(a); Ord. 8, r. 2(2)(a).
[22] R.S.C., Ord. 6, r. 7(1)(b). See paras. 3.23 *et seq.* above.
[23] R.S.C., Ord. 13, r. 7B(1). Leave is also required for the entry of a default judgment against a defendant served within the jurisdiction, but who is domiciled in another part of the U.K. or in another Contracting State: see paras. 4.53 *et seq.* above.

22.10   The Rules do not provide a comprehensive safeguard against the court accepting jurisdiction contrary to Article 19, and the courts will need to remain alert to their duty to decline jurisdiction in such a case. For example, if the writ is served in the jurisdiction on a defendant domiciled in a non-Contracting State and the principal subject-matter of the case is one over which the courts of another Contracting State have exclusive jurisdiction by virtue of Article 16, the court will be obliged to decline jurisdiction, despite the absence of a procedural requirement to bring the infringement of Article 16 to its attention. Similarly, where the writ has been served out of the jurisdiction without leave and either it does not bear the required indorsement, or the indorsement has been wrongly made, and the defendant has entered an appearance without contesting the jurisdiction, the court must still be alert to the possibility that it may have to decline jurisdiction.[24]

Article 20

22.11   **Where a defendant domiciled in one Contracting State is sued in a court of another Contracting State and does not enter an appearance, the court shall declare of its own motion that it has no jurisdiction unless its jurisdiction is derived from the provisions of this Convention.**

   The court shall stay the proceedings so long as it is not shown that the defendant has been able to receive the document instituting the proceedings or an equivalent document in sufficient time to enable him to arrange for his defence, or that all necessary steps have been taken to this end.

   The provisions of the foregoing paragraph shall be replaced by those of Article 15 of the Hague Convention of November 15, 1965 on the service abroad of judicial and extrajudicial documents in civil or commercial matters, if the document instituting the proceedings or notice thereof had to be transmitted abroad in accordance with that Convention.†*

---

[24] The terms of Art. 19 make it plain that the entry of an appearance by a defendant does not confer jurisdiction on the court pursuant to Art. 18, where the case is exclusively within the jurisdiction of the courts of another Contracting State by virtue of Art. 16: see also para. 21.86 above.

† The words "or an equivalent document" in para. 2 were added by Art. 12 of the 1978 Convention to cater for the English practice (since changed), whereby notice of a writ, rather than a writ itself, was served on a defendant out of the jurisdiction—R.S.C., Ord. 11, r. 3, amended by Rules of the Supreme Court (Amendment No. 4) 1980. See Schlosser, para. 182 (para. A1.478 below).

* Jenard, paras. A1.173–A1.179 below; Schlosser, paras. 22, 182 (paras. A1.311–A1.312, A1.478 below); Collins, pp. 94–96; Dashwood/Halcon/White, pp. 133–136;   Hartley,   pp. 81,   90;   Kaye, pp. 1269–1295;   Maxwell,

C. ARTICLE 20: GENERAL NOTE

1. Introduction

This Article affords a defendant a dual protection against the   22.12
consequences of failing to enter an appearance. The first paragraph
should ensure that the court declines jurisdiction if proceedings are
brought against him in breach of the Convention's jurisdictional
rules. But then, having accepted jurisdiction, the court is restrained
by the second and third paragraphs from entering a default judgment against him until it can be reasonably sure that he was aware
of the proceedings in sufficient time to arrange for his defence.

Article 20, described in the Jenard Report[25] as one of the most
important Articles in the Convention, is central to the Convention's
purpose in providing direct rules of jurisdiction applicable throughout the Contracting States. A breach of the second and third paragraphs is one of the very few grounds on which a judgment may be
refused recognition and enforcement.[26]

By their nature, the second and third paragraphs are not apt to be
given effect in the case of an application for provisional measures
under Article 24.[27] The European Court has said of the equivalent
provision in Articles 27(2),[28] that it was:

" . . . clearly not designed in order to be applied to judgments which,
under the national law of a Contracting State, are intended to be
delivered in the absence of the party against whom they are directed
to be enforced without prior service on him . . . "[29]

2. Domicile

The Article refers only to defendants domiciled in other Con-   22.13
tracting States. This is expressly stated in the first paragraph, and it
seems that the second and third paragraphs may be limited in the
same way.[30] Where the defendant is not domiciled in another Con-

---

paras. 5.198–5.222; Anton, paras. 7.29–7.36; Droz, paras. 247–253, 268–286;
Weser, para. 275–6, 301–304; Bülow/Böckstiegel/Müller, pp. 159–168;
Geimer/Schütze, pp. 325–337, 961, 1088; Kropholler, pp. 208–214; Gothot/
Holleaux, paras. 207–215; Pocar, pp. 234–240.

[25] Jenard, para. A1.173 below.
[26] Art. 27(2), para. 27.21 below.
[27] Chap. 24 below.
[28] Para. 27.21 below.
[29] *Denilauler* v. *Couchet Frères* [1980] E.C.R. 1553, at p. 1568 (para. 8).
[30] This appears from the terms of the second para. of Art. 40 (para. 28.63 below),
which extends the effects of Art. 20 for the purposes of that Article to defendants domiciled in non-Contracting States. Also, the French language version of
the second paragraph refers back grammatically to the first paragraph ("*ce défendeur*") and implies that only defendants domiciled in a Contracting State are
envisaged. The reference to Art. 20 in Art. 25(2)(a) of the 1978 Convention

tracting State, even if its international jurisdiction is based on the Convention, the court should apply its internal procedural law if the defendant is domiciled in the same Contracting State as the court. If the defendant is domiciled in a non-Contracting State, the court should apply its internal procedural law as modified, if appropriate, by any relevant international convention, such as the Hague Convention referred to in the third paragraph, or some relevant bilateral convention.[31]

D. Article 20, First Paragraph: Court's Examination of its own Jurisdiction

1. " . . . does not enter an appearance . . . "

22.14   As in the case of Article 18, national procedural law will determine the precise manner in which and time at which a person enters an appearance, although the overall effect of the application of national law should be uniform.[32] By contrast with Article 18, the protection afforded to a defendant by this Article does not require that an exception be made for the entry of an appearance solely for the purpose of contesting the jurisdiction. If a defendant enters an appearance solely for that purpose, the wording of this Article will not affect the position under Article 18, that is to say, he will not be taken to have submitted to the jurisdiction. If he is successful in his objection, the court will have to decline jurisdiction—not of its own motion, but as a result of the objection—and if he is unsuccessful, the question of declining jurisdiction will in any event have been decided against him.

2. " . . . the court shall declare of its own motion that it has no jurisdiction . . . "

22.15   The obligation on the court to decline jurisdiction of its own motion is compulsory and has already been considered in relation to Article 19.[33] Under this Article, by contrast, the duty imposed by the Convention only arises after the defendant has failed to enter an appearance, although such a duty may arise at an earlier stage under the procedural law of the particular court. Again, the court may not

---

(para. 33.07 below) does not detract from this view, because, to the extent that that Article applies to defendants domiciled in non-Contracting States, it too can be seen as extending the scope of the second and third paragraphs of Art. 20 in cases to which it applies.
[31] Bülow/Böckstiegel/Müller, p. 161.
[32] Para. 21.92 above.
[33] Para. 22.06 above.

regard the plaintiff's assertions as decisive on the question of jurisdiction—it must require sufficient evidence to enable it to make an
informed judgment. As the Schlosser Report emphasises,[34] the
unprompted enquiries by the court may be limited, but the court
must not be bound by the uncontested assertions of the parties.

Whereas the subject-matter of the case will be decisive for the
purposes of Article 19, other matters may be decisive for the purposes of this Article and require careful checking by the court. The
point is particularly important in relation to the domicile or seat of a
defendant[35] and in relation to contractual claims, where the terms
of the contract may be highly material—for example, by reason of a
jurisdiction clause[36] or, in the case of an employment contract, for
the purpose of locating the place of performance of the characteristic obligation.[37]

In the context of a contract case under Article 5(1), the European
Court of Justice has emphasised the need for the national court to
consider its jurisdiction in the light of sufficient evidence: *Effer* v.
Kantner.[38] While the court in that case was not primarily concerned
with a question of its duty to decline jurisdiction of its own motion,
the reasoning is directly applicable to the court's duty under the
first paragraph of Article 20, and would apply as much to jurisdiction under one of the Convention's other provisions as to Article
5(1).

"It follows from the provisions of the Convention, and in particular
from . . . [Articles 19 and 20], that, in the cases provided for in
Article 5(1) of the Convention, the national court's jurisdiction to
determine questions relating to a contract includes the power to consider the existence of the constituent parts of the contract itself, since
that is indispensable in order to enable the national court in which
proceedings are brought to examine whether it has jurisdiction under
the Convention. If that were not the case, Article 5(1) of the Convention would be in danger of being deprived of its legal effect, since it
would be accepted that, in order to defeat the rule contained in that
provision it is sufficient for one of the parties to claim that the contract does not exist. On the contrary, respect for the aims and spirit of
the Convention demands that that provision should be construed as
meaning that the court called upon to decide a dispute arising out of a
contract may examine, *of its own motion even*, the essential preconditions for its jurisdiction, *having regard to conclusive and relevant evi-*

---

[34] Schlosser, para. 22 (para. A1.312 below). See para. 22.08 above.
[35] In the U.K., the court is not likely to fall into error, given the very wide definitions in ss.41 and 42 of the 1982 Act: paras. 44.01 *et seq.* below.
[36] Art. 17, paras. 21.01 *et seq.* above.
[37] Art. 5(1), para. 17.26 above.
[38] [1982] E.C.R. 825; discussed at para. 17.08 above.

dence adduced by the party concerned, establishing the existence or inexistence of the contract concerned."[39]

3." . . . unless its jurisdiction is derived from the provisions of this Convention"

22.16 The jurisdictional provisions of the Convention are those in Articles 2 to 24. The case must also fall within the general scope of the Convention as determined by the Preamble and Article 1. If the court has jurisdiction under the Convention, it is to be regarded as being "derived" from the Convention, because the jurisdictional rules are exhaustive for the cases to which it applies.[40]

E. ARTICLE 20, SECOND AND THIRD PARAGRAPHS: STAY OF PROCEEDINGS WHERE INSUFFICIENT TIME FOR PREPARATION OF DEFENCE

1. Court's duty to stay proceedings

22.17 These two paragraphs provide alternative regimes under which a default judgment may only be entered against a defendant domiciled in another Contracting State[41] if the court can be satisfied that the proceedings have, or should have, come to the defendant's notice.[41a] As has already been observed, they do not prevent the making of provisional orders under Article 24.[42]

Where service is undertaken in accordance with the Hague Convention, the third paragraph of this Article has the effect of applying Article 15 of the Hague Convention. Service in a Contracting State other than that in which the proceedings are brought will usually be in accordance with the Hague Convention,[43] but if it is not then the second paragraph of Article 20 applies. The law and

---

[39] *Ibid.*, at p. 834 (para. 7). Emphasis supplied.

[40] There may be an exception where the court has jurisdiction under a specialised convention falling within Art. 57 (para. 33.06 below), in which case its jurisdiction is probably to be regarded as being derived from that convention, but the reference to Art. 20 in Art. 25(2)(a) of the 1978 Convention (para. 33.07 below) leaves the question unclear as to whether a court may avoid examining its jurisdiction of its own motion where the plaintiff asserts a jurisdiction under such a specialised convention.

[41] See para. 22.13 above.

[41a] It is not easy to see how these provisions can sensibly be applied to actions *in rem*, where service is effected on property, rather than on the defendant: Jackson, *Civil Jurisdiction and Judgments—Maritime Claims*, pp. 163–164.

[42] See para. 22.12 above.

[43] The circumstances in which the Hague Convention applies are discussed at paras. 22.21 *et seq.* below.

practice in England and Wales on the service of process outside the jurisdiction has been discussed above.[44]

2. Second paragraph: where the Hague Convention does not apply

The provision applies only to originating process[45] and not to subsequent documents which may need to be served.[46] The means by which service is to be effected is determined by the bilateral arrangements in force between the countries concerned, and by Article IV of the 1968 Protocol.[47]

It is clear from the terms of the second paragraph of Article 20 that the court is under a duty to stay the proceedings unless and until it is shown that the requirements as to service have been fulfilled. It would seem that the court has no discretion in the matter. In practical terms, this means that a default judgment may only be entered upon proof that there has been a valid transmission of the originating process. Any provision of national law, whereby time starts to run against a defendant from a point different from that provided for by this Article, is invalid for cases falling within the Convention.[48]

22.18

The first requirement of the second paragraph of Article 20 is that the defendant should have been able to receive notification of the action. The provision does not require that the defendant should *actually* have been served.[49] While the provision will almost certainly be given a uniform interpretation by the European Court of Justice, details of what constitutes service in the state where the

22.19

---

[44] Chap. 4 above.
[45] As to the meaning of the words, "document instituting the proceedings," which have been considered by the European Court of Justice in *Klomps* v. *Michel* [1981] E.C.R. 1593, see paras. *27.28 et seq.* below.
[46] A court in the Netherlands has held that notice to a tax-payer domiciled in Germany, that a third party's debts to it were to be attached to satisfy the tax assessment, was a document instituting attachment proceedings, and it stayed those proceedings under this paragraph: *Ontvanger der Directe Belastingen* v. *Staat der Nederlanden*, Arrondissementsrechtbank, The Hague, August 31, 1976, Digest D I–20—B1.
[47] Para. 35.17 below.
[48] Bülow/Böckstiegel/Müller, p. 163.
[49] Jenard, para. A1.176 below. In *Ferrero* v. *Curator in het faillisement van Trans-Italia B.V.*, Ned.Jur. 1982, No. 508, Digest D I–20—B2, the Gerechtshof in the Hague dismissed a defendant's application to set aside a default judgment entered against him, where service had been effected in Italy, in error, not in accordance with the second para. of Art. 20, but under the procedure set up under the Hague Convention, but before that Convention came into force there.

service is effected will probably have to be determined by the law of that state.[50] It must be shown (presumably by the plaintiff) that all the necessary steps have been taken, which will usually be steps to be taken by the public authorities in the state of the court seised of the action and in the state where service is to be effected, including such investigations as may be necessary to discover the defendant's address.[51] The words "all necessary steps" should be interpreted strictly, for the protection of the defendant.[52] The best proof that the necessary steps have been taken will be proof that the defendant has actually been served, but this is not strictly necessary. If service has not been effected because of the defendant's attempts to avoid service, or because of his carelessness, or that of his agents, the conditions of the second paragraph of Article 20 may nonetheless have been fulfilled.[53]

22.20   The second requirement is that the necessary steps must have been taken in sufficient time to enable the defendant to arrange his defence. This is a question of fact for the court seised of the matter.[54] It is to be considered by reference to the date when the defendant received, or should have received, the originating process abroad, not by reference to time limits set by national law.[55] Questions which may be relevant include the availability to the defendant of suitably qualified legal advice, his capacity to understand the language of the originating process, and the like. If sufficient time is not allowed, a plaintiff who obtains a default judgment runs the risk that he will not be able to obtain recognition and enforcement of it in other Contracting States, because the sufficiency of the time for the defendant to arrange for his defence may be reviewed under Article 27(2) and the second paragraph of Article 34.[56]

It has been suggested[57] that the second paragraph of Article 20 should be interpreted in the light of the more detailed and precise provisions of Article 15 of the Hague Convention, applied by the third paragraph of Article 20, notably in relation to the need to wait at least six months before proceeding, in the absence of proof of actual service.

---

[50] This is also the position under Art. 15 of the Hague Convention: see below.
[51] Jenard, para. A1.175.
[52] Bülow/Böckstiegel/Müller, p. 164.
[53] Droz, paras. 282 *et seq.*
[54] Jenard, para. A1.176 below; Bülow/Böckstiegel/Müller, p. 165.
[55] In England and Wales, this means that a default judgment may not be entered if, as a matter of fact, the defendant has not had sufficient time to arrange for his defence, even though the time specified in R.S.C., Ord. 11, r. 1(3) has expired. See also para. 4.58 above.
[56] Paras. 27.21 and 28.22 below.
[57] Droz, para. 284.

3. Third paragraph: Hague Convention on Service

The Hague Convention, which is set out in Appendix 2,[58] pro- **22.21** vides a means for the service of proceedings in other countries through a central authority designated for that purpose in each of its contracting states.

The third paragraph of Article 20 of the present Convention gives effect to Article 15 of the Hague Convention, "if the document instituting the proceedings . . . had to be transmitted abroad in accordance with that Convention." It is clear that the Hague Convention provides an optional, and not an exclusive, means of transmission and it envisages that other means of transmission and service will continue to be adopted. It leaves undisturbed the bilateral arrangements between contracting states for the service of process.[59] The words "had to be" in the third paragraph of the present Article, taken from Article 15 of the Hague Convention, do not imply any compulsion on a party to use the mechanism set up under that Convention.

The Jenard Report says that the second paragraph of Article 20 is **22.22** only a transitional measure, to be applied until both Contracting States have ratified the Hague Convention and the more comprehensive provisions of Article 15 have come into effect.[60] That, however, is not a comprehensive statement of the effect of the third paragraph of Article 20. The Hague Convention is concerned only with the service *abroad* of the document instituting the proceedings. Even if that convention is in force, the second paragraph of Article 20 continues to apply to determine whether a default judgment may be entered in circumstances where service on the defendant is effected (or attempted) in the same Contracting State as that in which he is being sued, despite his domicile in another Contracting State.[61]

In addition to setting up a mechanism for the service of docu- **22.23** ments through designated central authorities, the Hague Convention contemplates a wide range of methods by which documents

---

[58] Paras. A2.03 *et seq.* below. The operation of the Convention is discussed in Chap. 4. For more detailed discussion, see *Practical Handbook on the Operation of the Hague Convention of 15th November 1965 on the service abroad of judicial and extrajudicial documents in civil or commercial matters* (Hague Conference on Private International Law, 1983).

[59] The U.K.'s bilateral conventions on the service of process are discussed at paras. 4.34 *et seq.* above.

[60] Jenard, paras. A1.175 and A1.178 below.

[61] This is perhaps most likely to occur in the case of companies. In England, for example, a foreign company may be served at an office designated for that purpose: Companies Act 1985, ss.691 and 725. It may also occur where substituted service has been permitted.

may be served in other states which are parties to that convention.[62] Nonetheless, it is possible that service may be effected in another country by a means, or in circumstances, which are not contemplated by that convention; and in that case also it may be that the court's powers to enter a default judgment will continue to be regulated by the second paragraph of Article 20 of the present Convention, rather than by Article 15 of the Hague Convention.[63]

A notable distinction between Article 15 of the Hague Convention and the second paragraph of Article 20 of the present Convention is that the former leaves intact the national rules as to when time starts to run against a defendant before the originating process is or should have been brought to the defendant's attention.[64]

A nice question arises on the power of the European Court of Justice to interpret Article 15 of the Hague Convention. It is not one of the instruments referred to in Article 1 of the 1971 Protocol on Interpretation[65] and, if that were interpreted strictly, the Court could not give rulings on it. On the other hand, Article 15 of the Hague Convention is so firmly integrated into the Convention's scheme of jurisdiction, that if a dispute should arise on its interpretation, it may well be that the European Court would be willing to rule on the matter, under the guise of ruling on the interpretation of Article 20.

---

[62] The methods by which service may be effected are discussed at paras. 4.04 to 4.15 and 4.40 to 4.50 above, and in chaps. 48 to 58 below, at para. 38.

[63] *e.g.* service by post is not permissible in Germany, but if it can be demonstrated that a defendant domiciled in Germany did in fact receive the document by that means, in sufficient time to enable him to arrange for his defence, a court in another Contracting State may be able to enter a default judgment against him under the second para. of Art. 20 (at least if that is permissible according to its own national law), even though it could not do so under Art. 15 of the Hague Convention.

[64] Bülow/Böckstiegel/Müller, p. 166.

[65] Para. 36.03 below.

CHAPTER 23

LIS PENDENS—RELATED ACTIONS
(Articles 21–23)

SECTION 8

Article 21

Where proceedings involving the same cause of action and   **23.01** **between the same parties are brought in the courts of different Contracting States, any court other than the court first seised shall of its own motion decline jurisdiction in favour of that court.**

A court which would be required to decline jurisdiction may stay its proceedings if the jurisdiction of the other court is contested.*

---

* Jenard, paras. A1.58–A1.180 below; Schlosser, paras. 180–182 (paras. A1.476–A1.478 below); Collins, pp. 96–97; Dashwood/Halcon/White, pp. 32, 136–138; Hartley, pp. 76–77; Kaye, pp. 1216–1233; Maxwell,

629

A. ARTICLE 21: GENERAL NOTE

Introduction

23.02   Article 21 is concerned only with cases of *lis pendens*, where the same parties and the same cause of action are concerned. Where actions are related in some looser way, Article 22 applies, and where an action falls within the exclusive jurisdiction of the courts of more than one state under Article 16, Article 23 applies. Between them, these three Articles are designed to prevent conflicting or incompatible decisions being given by the courts of different Contracting States.[1] They require the courts of each Contracting State to observe and respect the jurisdiction of the courts of each other Contracting State. For Article 21 to apply, it is necessary that the proceedings are brought before courts of different Contracting States.[1a]

B. ARTICLE 21, FIRST PARAGRAPH: MANDATORY DISMISSAL

1. " . . . involving the same cause of action and between the same parties . . . "

23.03   Article 21 only applies where the proceedings brought before the second court involve the same cause of action and the same parties as are involved in the proceedings already pending before the courts in another Contracting State.[2]

The question of what constitutes the "same cause of action" came before the European Court in *Gubisch Maschinenfabrik* v. *Palumbo*.[3] The dispute concerned the sale to Palumbo of a planing machine manufactured by Gubisch. Gubisch brought proceedings in Germany for the price of the machine, and Palumbo then brought proceedings in Italy for a declaration that the contract was

---

paras. 5.223–5.226; Anton, paras. 7.38–7.40; Droz, paras. 287–314; Weser, paras. 277–8, 456–460; Bülow/Böckstiegel/Müller, pp. 168–173; Geimer/Schütze, pp. 41–42, 237, 289–293; Kropholler, pp. 215–220; Gothot/Holleaux, paras. 217–223; Pocar, pp. 240–246.

[1] Jenard, para. A1.58 below; *De Wolf* v. *Cox B.V.* [1976] E.C.R. 1759, discussed at para. 25.36 below; *Gubisch Maschinenfabrik* v. *Palumbo*, case 144/86, decision of December 8, 1987 (para. 8), *The Times*, January 12, 1988.

[1a] Art. 21 may apply even if jurisdiction is founded on a convention having effect under Art. 57, rather than on the 1968 Convention: see para. 33.11 below.

[2] Where one action between two parties who were joint defendants in another action, the French Cour de Cassation has held that the two actions were not "between" the same parties: *Cyanamid Italia* v. *S.A. Gerling Konzern and S.A. Quinoléine*, June 2, 1981, Bull.Cas., Chambres Civiles, 1981, I, No. 186, p. 152, Digest D I–21—B7.

[3] Case 144/86, decision of December 8, 1987, *The Times*, January 12, 1988.

void or should be rescinded. Gubisch objected to the jurisdiction in the Italian proceedings on the basis that its proceedings in Germany created a situation of litispendence which should be resolved in accordance with Article 21 by the Italian court declining jurisdiction. The question of whether such a situation gave rise to a *lis pendens* within the meaning of Article 21 was referred to the European Court by the Italian *Corte Suprema di Cassazione*.

The European Court, having pointed out that the term *"lis pendens"* was used only in the heading of Section 8 and not in Article 21 itself, held that the concepts used in Article 21 to determine a situation of litispendence must be considered as independent concepts. The only conditions are that the parties to the two proceedings should be the same and that the two proceedings should involve the same cause of action. It is significant that the French and Italian texts express the concept of the same cause of action in a double form: *le même object et la même cause*.[4] The Court held that both proceedings had the same *cause*, namely the contractual relationship of the parties. The question was therefore whether the proceedings claiming performance of the contract had the same *objet* as those claiming its annulment or recission.

The judgment of the European Court concentrates particularly on cases involving the international sale of goods. In those cases, proceedings to enforce the contract and proceedings to annul it both involved, in essence, the obligatory nature of the contractual obligations. If the claim for annulment or recission was the later claim, it could be considered as merely a means of defence against the earlier proceedings in the other Contracting State. Accordingly, in the procedural circumstances of the case before it, the European Court held that the same *objet* was involved, and that Article 21 applied. The concept of the same cause of action could not be restricted to cases in which there was a formal identity of the claims.[5]

The Court drew particular attention to the effects which a different decision would have had by reason of Article 27(3), under which a decision given in one Contracting State is to be refused recognition if it is incompatible with a decision given between the same parties in the Contracting State in which recognition is sought.[6]

It would appear from this decision that the term "cause of action" is to be interpreted liberally. Simply because different sub-

---

[4] "The same object and the same basis": Italian, *"il medesimo oggetto e il medesimo titolo."* Neither the German text (*"wegen desselben Anspruchs"*) nor the English text draw this distinction.

[5] Para. 17 of the decision.

[6] See para. 27.43 below.

stantive law is applicable in the different proceedings, it does not follow that different causes of action are necessarily involved.

23.04   *National courts' decisions.* The earlier decisions of national courts in applying Article 21 may still be of assistance, although they must now be read in the light of *Gubisch Maschinenfabrik* v. *Palumbo.* The following are examples of cases where national courts have held that Article 21 did not apply, because the two sets of proceedings did not involve the same cause of action or were not between the same parties: where one action was a seller's claim against a buyer for the price of goods sold, defended on the basis that the goods were defective, and the other action was the buyer's claim for a reduction in purchase price and for damages on the basis of the same defects;[7] where one action was the seller's claim for the price of goods and the other was an application for an interim order appointing an examiner to investigate damage to the goods;[8] where one action was for a declaration that the defendant was obliged to compensate the plaintiff for damage suffered as a result of transactions which the defendant had made the subject of an arrangement with its creditors, and the other action was for damages for breach of that arrangement;[9] where the two actions were, respectively, on bills of exchange in respect of certain consignments of goods, and for payment in respect of other consignments;[10] and where one action was an action *in rem* against a ship and the other was an action *in personam* against the owners of the ship.[10a]

It has been held that the same cause of action was involved, though, where one action was for the payment of a purchase price and the other was for the reduction of that price;[11] and where one action was for damages for misappropriating a stamp collection and for wrongful attachment of assets and the other was for the return of the stamp collection and the lifting of the attachment.[12] In England, it has been held that Article 21 applies where the parties pursue claims for damages against each other arising out of a maritime

---

[7] *Ditta Armet di Giovanni Ferronato* v. *Barth & Pohl K.G. Eletrowerke*, Riv.dir.-int.priv.proc. 1978, p. 74, Digest D I–21—B1.

[8] *Joh. Verhulst & Zn. B.V.* v. *P.V.B.A. Thovadec Plastics*, Ned.Jur. 1980, No. 14, Digest D I–21—B2.

[9] Landgericht Köln, July 28, 1978, case 79 O 394/77, Digest D I–21—B3.

[10] Oberlandesgericht Frankfurt-am-Main, case 5 U 110/80, September 23, 1980, RIW/AWD—1980, p. 799, Digest D I–21—B6.

[10a] *The Nordglimt* [1987] 2 Lloyd's Rep. 470. Such proceedings would be related proceedings for the purposes of Art. 22, *per* Hobhouse J., at p. 482.

[11] *Spa Silpol* v. *Pears Plastics Belgium B.V.*, Riv.dir.int.priv.proc. 1978, p. 834, Digest D I–21—B4.

[12] *Kaptein* v. *Van Haaster*, Arrondissementsrechtbank, The Hague, March 15, 1978, Digest D I–21—B5.

collision, even though the plaintiff in one action was the defendant in the other.[12a]

2. "Where proceedings . . . are brought in the courts of different Contracting States, any court other than the court first seised . . . "

(a) Procedural law applicable

The second Zelger v. Salinitri decision. Because proceedings can   **23.05** only have any existence within the framework of the procedural law of the court in which they are brought, and because that law defines the proceedings, the point at which they become pending must be determined by that law. The European Court of Justice has confirmed that national law is to be applied in determining the point at which a court becomes "seised" for the purposes of Article 21, by its decision in *Zelger v. Salinitri (No. 2).*[13] The plaintiff, Herr Zelger, brought actions in both Munich and Catania in respect of the same debt. In the German action, he lodged the document necessary to commence the proceedings in the *Landgericht* on August 5, 1976 and they were served on the defendant in Italy on January 13, 1977. Meanwhile, he had also commenced proceedings in Italy, having lodged the necessary documents with the *Tribunale Civile* on September 22 or 23, 1976, which were served on the defendant on September 23, 1976. The *Landgericht* dismissed the action, because it held that the Italian court had been seised first, on September 23, whereas the German court did not become seised until January 13. On appeal, the *Oberlandesgericht* in Munich referred the matter to the European Court of Justice, which ruled:

> "Article 21 . . . must be interpreted as meaning that the court 'first seised' is the one before which the requirements for proceedings to become definitively pending are first fulfilled, such requirements to be determined in accordance with the national law of each of the courts concerned."[14]

This means that in borderline cases, a court seised of proceedings will have to apply the procedural law of the foreign court which might have been seised first, in order to decide when the proceedings in the foreign court in fact became pending.[15]

[12a] *The Linda* [1988] 1 Lloyd's Rep. 175.

[13] [1984] E.C.R. 2397. The earlier reference to the European Court in the same proceedings—*Zelger v. Salinitri (No. 1)*, [1980] E.C.R. 89—is discussed at para. 17.15 above.

[14] *Ibid.* at p. 2409.

[15] Jenard, para. A1.180 below; Schlosser, para. 182 (para. A1.478 below); Maxwell, para. 5.226; Droz, paras. 306 *et seq.*

23.06   *English law.* In most Contracting States, the court is said to become seised of proceedings when they are served.[16] In England, proceedings are said to commence when process is issued by the court and the Schlosser Report suggests in the present context that this rule will remain undisturbed.[17] If that is right, it would lead to a substantial lack of uniformity in the application of Articles 21 to 23 as between Contracting States. It is suggested, therefore, that English law should regard a court as being "seised" of proceedings for the purposes of this Article, not when they are commenced, but when they are served. There is authority in the context of Admiralty actions *in rem* to support this view. It is when a writ *in rem* is served, rather than when it is issued, that the action becomes pending[18] and the jurisdiction is said to be invoked.[19] In the context of Articles 21 and 22, moreover, it has been held that the court becomes "seised" of an action *in rem* from the moment, whichever is earlier, when the writ is served or the ship is arrested.[19a]

(b) Courts not in another Contracting State

23.07   By its terms, Article 21 does not apply where the court first seised is not in another Contracting State. If both courts are in the same Contracting State, national law will determine which action, if either, is to have priority. If the court first seised is in a non-Contracting State, national law and, possibly, bilateral conventions will determine whether the second proceedings must, or may, be

---

[16] See chaps. 48 to 58 below, at para. 37. The position is less than clear in Belgium, where service of a summons usually occurs before a case is entered on the court's roll. It is at the latter date, according to one view, that the court is seised: *e.g.*, *B.B.L.* v. *Dubuisson*, Revue régional de droit 1980, p. 253, Tribunal d'Arrondissement, Liège, February 12, 1980. This is the view which the European Court cites as being the law in Belgium (*Zelger* v. *Salinitri (No. 2)*, above, at p. 2407, para. 11); but *cf.* the decision of the Cour d'Appel, Brussels, of November 28, 1979, Journal trib. 1980, p. 511, where the date of service was held to be the relevant date. For a review of the rules on litispendence in the laws of each of the original six Contracting States, and in other Conventions, see Droz, paras. 290–302. The date of service seems to be the relevant date in Scots law: Maxwell, para. 5.226, although the point is not free from doubt: Black, *Civil Jurisdiction: The New Rules*, para. 8.03. *Cf.* Anton, p. 123 n. 95; Anton, *Private International Law*, p. 152.

[17] Schlosser, para. 182 (para. A1.478 below); see also R.S.C., Ord. 5, r. 1. The statement in the Schlosser Report that proceedings become "pending" when the originating document is issued may be misleading, for the reasons discussed below.

[18] *The Helenslea* (1882) 7 P.D. 57, 60.

[19] *The Banco* [1971] P. 137; *The Berny* [1979] Q.B. 80; In *re Avo Co. Ltd.* [1980] Ch. 196. Note, however, that these cases all arose under the Administration of Justice Act 1956, s.3, which has since been replaced by the Supreme Court Act 1981, s.21, the wording of which is materially different.

[19a] *The Freccia Del Nord*, Sheen J., December 14, 1988, not yet reported.

stayed or dismissed. The compulsory nature of the Convention's jurisdictional rules probably does not operate to prevent a court of a Contracting State from staying its proceedings in favour of a court first seised in a non-Contracting State.[20] Support for that view may be derived from Article 27(5),[21] which allows a judgment given in one Contracting State to be refused recognition in another Contracting State if it is irreconcilable with an earlier judgment which was given in a non-Contracting State and which is to be recognised in the Contracting State addressed.

(c) Jurisdiction of foreign court

Generally. It is not necessary for the court to conduct a review of   **23.08**
the jurisdiction of the foreign court (indeed, such an exercise is contrary to the scheme and purpose of the Convention) and it is not necessary that the foreign court should have jurisdiction pursuant to the Convention.[22] Article 20[23] will anyway require the foreign court to review its own jurisdiction, but if it fails to do so, or reaches the wrong conclusion, its judgment will still be entitled to recognition and enforcement in the other Contracting States, except in the limited circumstances allowed by Articles 27 and 28.[24] If the jurisdictional rules of the Convention do not provide for a court in a Contracting State to have jurisdiction, the court first seised may still have jurisdiction under its own rules and under Article 4.

Exclusive jurisdiction. A special and exceptional situation arises where the court second seised has exclusive jurisdiction over the subject-matter of its proceedings, by virtue of Article 16. The situation is not expressly dealt with by Article 21, but it seems that Article 21 should not apply in such a case. If the court first seised had accepted jurisdiction in breach of Article 16, its judgment would be refused recognition and enforcement in the other Contracting States, by reason of the first paragraph of Article 28, and the purpose of avoiding conflicting judgments would not be served by the court second seised declining jurisdiction.[25] If both courts had exclusive jurisdiction under Article 16, Article 23 would apply and the court second seised would have to review the jurisdiction of

---

[20] Droz, paras. 323–330; Bülow/Böckstiegel/Müller, p. 169; Kropholler, p. 215; *cf.* Geimer/Schütze, pp. 292–293.

[21] Para. 27.59 below. See Hartley, p. 77; *contra*, Cheshire and North, p. 328. It is suggested that Hartley's argument for a *general* discretion goes too far: see para. 44.43 below.

[22] Droz, para. 305; Bülow/Böckstiegel/Müller, p. 169. The jurisdiction of the foreign court may be founded on a convention having effect under Art. 57: *The Linda* [1988] 1 Lloyd's Rep. 175.

[23] Para. 22.11 above.

[24] Paras. 27.12 and 27.62 below.

[25] Droz, paras. 311 *et seq.*

the court first seised in order to see whether that Article applied. It would be absurd if, nonetheless, the second court were required to decline jurisdiction under Article 21.[26]

3. " . . . shall of its own motion decline jurisdiction in favour of that court"

23.09   The obligation on the court to decline jurisdiction of its own motion is compulsory[27] and the former practice of the United Kingdom courts, whereby the courts exercised discretion in the matter of litispendence[28] may no longer be followed.[29] It has been suggested[30] that a court need not in every case look into the question of whether proceedings are pending in the courts of another Contracting State, but that such an investigation need only be carried out where the circumstances are such as to put the court on enquiry as to other proceedings[31] or, perhaps, in such wider circumstances as national law may prescribe.[32] Whether or not that is correct, it does not detract from the compulsory nature of the rule in the first paragraph of Article 21.

C. ARTICLE 21, SECOND PARAGRAPH: DISCRETIONARY STAY

"A court which would be required to decline jurisdiction may stay its proceedings if the jurisdiction of the other court is contested."

23.10   The second paragraph should probably be read in conjunction with the first paragraph, so that it only applies if the court is required *by that paragraph* to decline jurisdiction. Only in that way can it make sense. On a strict interpretation of the second paragraph, it would seem that it does not apply where the court first seised is in the process of investigating its jurisdiction of its own motion,[33] but (it is submitted) the provision should be more widely

---

[26] Bülow/Böckstiegel/Müller, p. 171.

[27] *The Linda*, above, at p. 180, Droz, para. 304; see para. 15.02 above. The Bundesgerichtshof has held that later German proceedings must be dismissed even though they were started by the same plaintiff, who had become disenchanted with the pace of his earlier proceedings in Italy: Case III ZR 3/85, November 28, 1985 [1987] E.C.C. 273.

[28] Dicey and Morris, pp. 395–398. See para. 1.43 above.

[29] Schlosser, para. 181 (para. A1.477 below); Dicey and Morris, p. 399. By R.S.C., Ord. 6, r. 7, a writ in a Convention case, which is to be served without leave out of the jurisdiction must be indorsed with a statement that no proceedings relating to the same cause of action are pending in Scotland, Northern Ireland or another "Convention territory": see para. 3.25 above.

[30] Jenard, para. A1.180 below.

[31] *Cf.* Jenard, *loc. cit.*

[32] Bülow/Böckstiegel/Müller, p. 172.

[33] Droz, para. 309.

interpreted, so that a court second seised may stay its proceedings in those circumstances also.

Once the first court has declined jurisdiction, either as a result of a challenge to its jurisdiction by the defendant, or of its own motion, the second court may proceed. The purpose of the second paragraph is to prevent a new action having to be started in such circumstances, which will be of particular importance where the expiry of a limitation period is imminent when the second proceedings are commenced. What the second court should do if the first court decides that it has jurisdiction is not specified, but it is suggested that the second court should then decline jurisdiction and dismiss the action, pursuant to the first paragraph.[34]

Article 22

Where related actions are brought in the courts of different 23.11
Contracting States, any court other than the court first seised
may, while the actions are pending at first instance, stay its pro-
ceedings.

A court other than the court first seised may also, on the appli-
cation of one of the parties, decline jurisdiction if the law of that
court permits the consolidation of related actions and the court
first seised has jurisdiction over both actions.

For the purposes of this Article, actions are deemed to be
related where they are so closely connected that it is expedient to
hear and determine them together to avoid the risk of irreconcil-
able judgments resulting from separate proceedings.*

D. ARTICLE 22: GENERAL NOTE

1. Introduction

The general purpose of Article 22 is clear, namely to avoid the 23.12
risk of conflicting judgments and thus to facilitate the proper administration of justice in the Community.[35] The purpose is achieved by allowing courts other than the court first seised to stay or dismiss their proceedings. The detailed interpretation of Article 22, though, is the subject of some difficulty, notably in relation to

---

[34] Bülow/Böckstiegel/Müller, p. 172.
* Jenard, para. A1.181–A1.183; Collins, pp. 97–98; Dashwood/Halcon/White, pp. 32, 138–139; Hartley, p. 77; Kaye, pp. 1233–1242; Maxwell, paras. 5.227–5.231; Anton, paras. 7.40–7.42; Droz, paras. 315–328; Weser, paras. 278, 462–464; Bülow/Böckstiegel/Müller, pp. 173–177; Geimer/Schütze, pp. 41–42, 237, 292–297; Kropholler, pp. 221–223; Gothot/Holleaux, paras. 224–227; Pocar, pp. 246–253.
[35] Jenard, para. A1.181 below.

the necessity for actions to be pending at first instance[36] and in relation to the words "the law of that court" in the second paragraph.

As with Article 21,[37] Article 22 applies only as between Contracting States.[38] It is not concerned with related actions brought before different courts in the same Contracting State, nor with actions pending before courts in non-Contracting States. Similarly, the domicile of the parties is not normally relevant[39] and questions as to when a court is seised should be treated in the same way as under Article 21.[40] It does not confer jurisdiction. As the European Court has said,

> "Article 22 of the Convention is intended to establish how related actions which have been brought before courts of different Member States are to be dealt with. It does not confer jurisdiction; in particular, it does not accord jurisdiction to a court of a Contracting State to try an action which is related to another action of which that court is seised pursuant to the rules of the Convention."[41]

The principal emphasis of Article 22 is on staying proceedings, not on dismissing them. Proceedings may only be dismissed in limited circumstances envisaged by the second paragraph.[42]

2. Relationship between the first and second paragraphs

23.13   The first two paragraphs should be read together. In particular, the requirement that proceedings be pending at first instance, although expressly stated only in the first paragraph (in relation to staying proceedings), applies equally to the second paragraph (dismissing proceedings).[43] Three reasons may be identified for reading the two paragraphs together. First, there is a textual justification in the word "also" in the second paragraph. This should be read as a reference back to the first paragraph.[44] Secondly, the reasons for referring to the actions being pending at first instance in the case of a stay apply *a fortiori* to the dismissal of the proceedings. Thirdly, there is an historical justification for reading the paragraphs together. Earlier drafts of Article 22 treated staying and dismissing of proceedings in a single paragraph and the two matters were only

---

[36] Para. 23.14 below.
[37] Para. 23.01 above.
[38] *Elefanten Schuh GmbH* v. *Jacqmain* [1981] E.C.R. 1671, 1689. The facts of the case are summarised at para. 21.27 above.
[39] Bülow/Böckstiegel/Müller, p. 174; but see para. 23.22, n. 71 below.
[40] Paras. 23.05 and 23.06 above.
[41] *Elefanten Schuh GmbH* v. *Jacqmain*, above at p. 1687 (para. 19).
[42] Paras. 23.18 *et seq.* below.
[43] Collins, p. 98; Droz, para. 325; Bülow/Böckstiegel/Müller, p. 175.
[44] Some other language versions are clearer in this respect—*e.g.* French: "*Cette juridiction peut également se dessaisir. . . .* "

separated in the final drafting stages. The failure to make a consequential amendment to include a reference to the actions pending at
first instance in relation to the dismissal of proceedings appears to
have been an oversight.[45]

3. Requirement that both actions be pending at first instance

The Jenard Report explains the reason for this requirement as
being that "otherwise the object of the proceedings would be different and one of the parties might be deprived of a step in the hierarchy of the courts."[46] The explanation is more apt to cover
dismissal of the action in the second Contracting State, rather than
a stay. The problem may be illustrated by an example.

23.14

> A brings an action against B in state X and wins at first instance. A
> then brings a related action against B in state Y, in which the issues
> would, *ex hypothesi*, be different from those in the first action.[47]
> Meanwhile, B appeals against the first decision in state X. If the
> courts of state Y had power at that stage to dismiss the second action,
> it would not be easy for A to consolidate the issues in his second
> action with those in the first action, because the first action would
> already have been decided at first instance. But even if he could con-
> solidate them on the appeal in state X, he would have lost the oppor-
> tunity of pursuing B at first instance in either country.
>
> If the proceedings in state Y were stayed, rather than dismissed, A
> would not necessarily lose the opportunity to pursue B at first
> instance, because the action in state Y could be revived after the
> determination of the action in state X. The decision in the action in
> state X would normally be entitled to automatic recognition by the
> courts of state Y, pursuant to Article 26.

E. ARTICLE 22, FIRST PARAGRAPH: DISCRETION TO STAY PROCEEDINGS

The court has a discretion under the first paragraph to stay proceedings at first instance, where a related action[48] is pending[49] also at
first instance in the courts of a different Contracting State. The
court second seised must have jurisdiction to decide the case on its
merits,[50] because otherwise it would be required to decline jurisdic-

23.15

---

[45] Droz, para. 323; Bülow/Böckstiegel/Müller, p. 175.
[46] Jenard, para. A1.181 below. Droz, para. 323, is unconvinced by this explanation, but it seems logical.
[47] If the issues and parties were identical, the *lis pendens* provisions of Art. 21
would apply, not the related actions provisions of Art. 22.
[48] The third para. defines when proceedings are "related" for the purposes of this
Article: para. 23.23 below.
[49] As to what constitutes a "pending" action, see paras. 23.05 and 23.06 above.
[50] Bülow/Böckstiegel/Müller, p. 176.

tion by Articles 19 or 20. By contrast with the second paragraph of Article 22, it is not a condition of the second court's power to grant a stay that the first court should have jurisdiction over both actions. Because the second proceedings are only stayed, they may be revived in the event of the first court having the issues raised in the second action brought before it and deciding that it has no jurisdiction to entertain those issues.[51]

Where these various conditions are fulfilled, and despite the fact that the Jenard Report says that "where actions are related, the first duty of the court is to stay its proceedings,"[52] it is clear from the wording of the first paragraph that a stay lies within the discretion of the second court seised.[53] It is suggested that the court's duty is to consider whether to exercise its discretion, and that it must consider the matter of its own motion.

23.16   The first paragraph of Article 22, unlike the second paragraph, does not require that one of the parties should apply for the stay. It would seem to follow that the court may consider the matter of its own motion, and the passage quoted above from the Jenard Report, together with the general purpose of Article 22, would suggest that it is under a duty to do so. When does that duty arise? Whereas in the case of Article 21, the court is under a duty in certain circumstances to enquire of its own motion into the existence of other proceedings,[54] in order to be in a position to carry out its primary duty to dismiss its proceedings, the position under the first paragraph of Article 22 is probably somewhat different. Here, the court is not under a duty to dismiss the proceedings and it may be that the court need only consider whether to stay its proceedings if it has actual knowledge of the other proceedings. Whether or not it acquires its knowledge of the other proceedings as a result of its own enquiries, though, once it has that knowledge, it should consider whether the actions are related within the meaning of the third paragraph of the Article and, if so, whether to exercise its discretion to order a stay.

23.17   In the exercise of its discretion, the court will, of course, weigh the relative advantages and disadvantages of a stay, and consider the extent to which the two actions are related. What it may probably not do, though, is to consider the likelihood of the first court's

---

[51] *Ditte Mutti* v. *Bald*, Riv.dir.int.priv.proc. 1982, p. 86, Digest D I–22—B4. This case is an excellent illustration of the different features of Art. 22.

[52] Jenard, para. A1.181 below.

[53] Bülow/Böckstiegel/Müller, *loc. cit.*; Oberlandesgericht Frankfurt-am-Main, case 5 U 110/80, September 23, 1980, RIW/AWD—1980, p. 799, Digest D I–21—B6; *Cyanamid Italia* v. *S.A. Gerling Konzern and S.A. Quinoléine* Bull.-Cass., Chambres Civiles, 1981, I, No. 186, p. 152, Digest D I–21—B7; see para. 23.07, n. 20 above.

[54] Para. 23.09 above.

judgment being recognised and capable of enforcement in the second state, although matters which may themselves be a hindrance to recognition (such as public policy in the second state)[55] may, if relevant, be considered.

The reason why the second court should not carry out an assessment of the likelihood of the first court's judgment being recognised and enforced is that the Convention aims to provide clear and precise rules of jurisdiction, which are comprehensive as to the circumstances in which they apply. If the second court were to take into account the question whether the first court's judgment was likely to be recognised and capable of enforcement, it could only do so at that stage on a hypothetical basis, with all its associated uncertainties.[56] Such a question ought properly only to be considered after the decision of the first court has been made.

F. Article 22, Second Paragraph: Discretion to Dismiss Proceedings

Where the conditions are fulfilled for the second court to have discretion to stay its proceedings,[57] and where three further conditions are fulfilled, the court has a discretion under the second paragraph of Article 22 to dismiss its proceedings. The three further conditions are: first, one of the parties must apply for the action to be dismissed; secondly, the consolidation of related actions must be permitted, probably by the law of the court seised second, but possibly of that seised first;[58] and, thirdly, the court first seised must have jurisdiction over both actions.   **23.18**

1. Application by one of the parties

As has been seen,[59] the court is probably under a duty, once it has knowledge of the related action, to consider whether to order a stay. Without an application by one of the parties, it is not under a duty (and it has no power under this paragraph) to consider dismissing its proceedings. It would seem to follow that the court need not consider of its own motion whether the second and third conditions below are fulfilled, nor whether the actions are related, although it will need to be satisfied (presumably by the applicant) on these matters. The means by which, and the time at which, such an application may be made is to be decided by the procedural law of the second court.   **23.19**

---

[55] Art. 27(1): para. 27.13 below.
[56] Bülow/Böckstiegel/Müller, p. 176.
[57] Para. 23.15 above.
[58] See para. 23.20 below.
[59] Para. 23.15 above.

2. Consolidation in the court second seised

23.20   Grammatically, the words, "if the law of that court permits the consolidation of related actions" would seem to refer to the second court, although the English text may be somewhat ambiguous. Other language versions, though, do not bear the same ambiguity.[60] The English language version of the Jenard Report[61] suggests that it is the law of the court first seised which must allow consolidation of related actions. This does appear to be contrary to other language versions of the text, and the views of various commentators.[62]

The purpose of including reference to the power of the court to consolidate related actions was to deal with particular problems under German and Italian law.[63] German law[64] allows consolidation of actions only if they are before the same court, and so does not recognise as a basis of jurisdiction the fact that actions are connected[65] and Italian law contains a similar rule which does not permit Italian courts to decide whether to remit an action to another court.[66] If it is the law of the *second* court which must permit the consolidation of related actions, a German or Italian court second seised would not be able to dismiss an action under the second paragraph of Article 22.[67] On the other hand, if it is the law of the court

---

[60] Maxwell, para. 5.229; Anton, para. 7.41. The French text says: "*Cette juridiction peut également se dessaisir, . . . à condition que sa loi permette la jonction d'affaires connexes. . . .*" The German text is even less ambiguous: "*Das später angerufene Gericht kann sich . . . auch für unzuständig erklären, wenn die Verbindung in Zusammenhang stehender Verfahren nach seinem Recht zulässig ist. . . .*" (Emphasis supplied.)

[61] Jenard, para. A1.182 below. The French and German texts of the relevant passage are ambiguous: "*Ce dessaisissement ne pourra intervenir que sur demande de l'une des parties et si la loi de juge saisi permet la jonction d'affaires connexes qui sont pendantes devant des tribunaux différents.*" "*Eine solche Unzuständigkeitserklärung kann nur auf Antrag einer der Parteien und nur dann erfolgen, wenn das innerstaatliche Recht des angerufenen Gerichts einer Verbindung zusammenhängender Klagen zulässt, die vor verschiedenen Gerichten anhängig sind.*" (Emphasis supplied).

[62] Droz, para. 326; Weser, para. 278; Bülow/Böckstiegel/Müller, p. 177; Geimer/Schütze, p. 294; Kropholler, p. 223; Gothot/Holleaux, para. 226; Schütze, (1975) RIW/AWD, at p. 543. *Contra*, Collins, p. 98, Anton, para. 7.41.

[63] Jenard, *loc. cit.*

[64] German code of civil procedure (ZPO), para. 147.

[65] Droz, *loc. cit.*

[66] *Ditte Mutti* v. *Bald*, above. See the Italian code of civil procedure, Art. 40 of which gives a limited power for jurisdiction to be contested at an early stage on the grounds that there is a related action being pursued, and Art. 274 of which limits the power to consolidate proceedings to those brought before the same court.

[67] Geimer/Schütze, p. 294.

first seised which must permit the consolidation of related actions, it seems that the court second seised must look into the procedural law of the court first seised, to see whether it has the power to consolidate related actions. If it does not, the court second seised will have no power under the second paragraph of Article 22 to dismiss its proceedings.

Logically, it is suggested, it would make more sense for a court **23.21** second seised to have the discretion to dismiss proceedings, and to have no more to do with them, if it was satisfied that the court *first* seised had power to consolidate both actions, even though the second court would have to examine the first court's procedural law in order to reach that conclusion. The power of the second court to consolidate actions would only be relevant if the plaintiff in the first proceedings, as *dominis litis*, were prepared to discontinue those proceedings with a view to starting fresh proceedings in the second state and consolidating them. That seems procedurally wasteful, may frequently not be in the plaintiff's interests, and can hardly have been envisaged by the Convention, in the light of its purposes as expounded by the European Court.[68] Nevertheless, this more sensible interpretation is hard to reconcile with the text of the Convention, and any clear answer must await the decision of the European Court.

On either interpretation, the Convention does not affect the procedure for consolidating actions, which remains solely regulated by the internal law of the relevant state.[69]

3. First court's jurisdiction over both actions

The third condition to be fulfilled before the court second seised **23.22** may dismiss its proceedings is that the court first seised must have jurisdiction over both the related actions. For this purpose, it will need to review the jurisdiction of the first court.[70] Because Article 22 does not itself found jurisdiction, the jurisdiction of the first court must exist independently of the related nature of the two actions, namely under the jurisdictional rules of the Convention or, where this is permissible by virtue of Article 4, under the exorbitant jurisdiction of the first court.[71]

---

[68] See para. 13.15 above.
[69] Jenard, para. A1.183 below.
[70] *Sitra Scheepvaar en Handel B.V.* v. *Raab-Karcher Reederei und Spedition GmbH*, Ned.Jur. 1983, No. 753, Digest D I–22—B5.
[71] As an exception to the general rule under Art. 22, the domicile of the parties is relevant for the purposes of reviewing the first court's jurisdiction.

G. ARTICLE 22, THIRD PARAGRAPH: RELATED NATURE OF THE TWO
PROCEEDINGS

23.23   The third paragraph of Article 22 provides a uniform test for deciding whether actions are related.[72] The test (it is submitted) is not
only uniform, and consequently not subject to interpretation in the
light of national law, but it is also a purely factual one for the court
second seised to decide in the light of all the circumstances.

Nonetheless, a number of comments may be made. First, the
possibility of irreconcilable decisions is central to the test, so that if
there is at least one issue common to the two actions, they are
almost certainly "related."[73] It does not matter if the common issue
plays a different role in the two actions, nor even if the parties to the
two actions are different. It is probably not enough merely that the
respective parties to the two actions should be related.[74]

> For example, in one action, A sues B for damages for breach of con-
> tract and in a second action, A sues C in tort. If the measure of A's
> damages in the second action depends upon the outcome of the first
> action, then there are common questions (namely whether B broke
> his contract and if so what damage A suffered as a result) and the
> actions are related.

Secondly, though, it is not necessary that there should be a common issue between the two actions. It will usually be enough if the
same factual circumstances are involved,[75] although a mere overlap
of factual issues may not be enough.[76]

Thirdly, in order for proceedings to be related, it is not necessary
that one court should have jurisdiction over both actions. In the
above example, the actions are no less related merely because A's
action against B is brought in a court which would not have jurisdiction over his action against C. Just as, under Article 21, the court
may not normally review the jurisdiction of the foreign court[77] for
the purpose of deciding questions of *lis alibi pendens*, so too a review

---

[72] The test is based on Art. 30 of the Belgian Judicial Code: Jenard, para. A1.183
below. *Cf.* the conditions in English law for the consolidation of actions: R.S.C.
Ord. 4, r. 10.

[73] Bülow/Böckstiegel/Müller, p. 174; but *cf. Société Montedison* v. *Départment de la
Haute Corse and others*, Cour d'Appel, Bastia, February 28, 1977, Digest D
I–5.3—B3. An English action *in rem* can be "related" to foreign proceedings *in
personam*: see *The Nordglimt* [1987] 2 Lloyd's Rep. 470, at p. 482.

[74] *Rohstoff-Einfuhr und Handelsgesellschaft* v. *La Continentale Nucléaire*, Cour
Supérieure de Justice, Luxembourg, December 14, 1977, Digest D I–22—B1.

[75] *Sitra Scheepvaart en Handel B.V.* v. *Raab-Karcher Reederei und Spedition
GmbH*, above.

[76] Oberlandesgericht Karlsruhe, case 4 U 187/75, RIW/AWD—1977, p. 718,
Digest D I–5.3—B8.

[77] Para. 23.08 above.

of the foreign court's jurisdiction is not relevant in deciding whether actions are related.[78]

Article 23

Where actions come within the exclusive jurisdiction of several courts, any court other than the court first seised shall decline jurisdiction in favour of that court. * 23.24

H. ARTICLE 23: MULTIPLE EXCLUSIVE JURISDICTIONS

1. Introduction

The circumstances in which a case will fall within the exclusive jurisdiction of more than one court will arise only very rarely,[79] but where it appears that such circumstances arise or may have arisen, the second court seised has to decide whether to decline jurisdiction by reason of Article 23. It has to consider three questions: 23.25

(1) Was the other court seised first?
(2) Do the issues in the second case coincide with the issues in the first case?
(3) Do both courts have exclusive jurisdiction under the Convention over the second case?

The second court must consider these questions, at the latest, when it is put on enquiry as to the existence of other proceedings,[80] and it must do so of its own motion.[81] If the answer to all three questions is in the affirmative, the second court is obliged to decline jurisdiction. It has no discretion[82] in the matter and probably may not even grant a stay of the proceedings. 23.26

---

[78] Bülow/Böckstiegel/Müller, p. 176. But such a review is both permissible and necessary before proceedings may be dismissed under the second para. of Art. 22: para. 23.22 above.
* Jenard, para. A1.184 below; Collins, p. 97, Dashwood/Halcon/White, pp. 32, 139; Hartley, pp. 66–67; Kaye, pp. 883–888; Maxwell, para. 5.232; Anton, para. 7.17; Droz, paras. 312, 314; Weser, paras. 279–281; Bülow/Böckstiegel/Müller, pp. 177–179; Geimer/Schütze, pp. 289–297, 649; Kropholler, p. 224; Gothot/Holleaux, paras. 222, 227; Pocar, p. 253.
[79] Jenard, para. A1.184 below.
[80] Para. 23.09 above.
[81] This follows from the compulsory wording used and the fact that no mention is made of an application by either party: *cf.* para. 23.16 above. It also follows from the compulsory nature of the Convention's rules on jurisdiction.
[82] *Cf.* para. 23.09 above.

(1) Was the other court seised first? To answer this question, the second court must apply the procedural law of the first court, to decide when that court was first seised.[83]

(2) Do the issues in the second case coincide with the issues in the first case? If the issues do not coincide, and the cases are merely related, Article 23 does not apply[84] and the second court has a discretion whether to stay or dismiss the proceedings, under the conditions set out in Article 22.

(3) Do both courts have exclusive jurisdiction under the Convention over the second case? In order to answer this question, the second court will need to review the jurisdiction of the first court.[85] The exclusive jurisdiction of each court must arise under the Convention. Leaving aside cases (discussed below) where exclusive jurisdiction arises by reason of a jurisdiction agreement under Article 17, the most obvious example of exclusive jurisdiction being accorded to the courts of more than one Contracting State is under Article 16(2),[86] which accords exclusive jurisdiction to the courts of the Contracting State where a company or analogous association has its seat. The location of the company's seat may differ, according to the different national laws which, by the operation of Article 53,[87] may be applied.[88]

2. Courts of Contracting States

23.27   Unlike Articles 21 and 22, the present Article does not say expressly that the two courts with exclusive jurisdiction must be in different Contracting States, but this follows from the fact that Article 16 allocates exclusive jurisdiction only on the international level.[89] Where the first court seised is in a non-Contracting State,

---

[83] Paras. 23.05 and 23.06 above.

[84] Bülow/Böckstiegel/Müller, p. 178.

[85] *Cf.* paras. 22.04 and 23.08 above.

[86] Para. 20.26 above.

[87] The problems of conflicting decisions on the location of the seat of a company are discussed at paras. 31.29 *et seq.* below.

[88] A case of conflicting exclusive jurisdictions could theoretically arise under Art. 16(5), where measures of enforcement, intended to take effect in more than one Contracting State, are themselves made the subject of proceedings. For example, if a court in one Contracting State made an order *inter partes* of the type envisaged in *Altertext Inc.* v. *Advanced Data Communications Ltd.* [1985] 1 W.L.R. 457, enabling the plaintiff to enter separate premises of the defendant in two different Contracting States, and the defendant then brought proceedings in both those states to restrain the manner or extent of the plaintiff's execution there, the courts later seised might be required by this Article to decline jurisdiction over those proceedings. Such a situation would be manifestly absurd.

[89] Para. 20.05 above.

national law (including its conflicts rules) applies to determine whether the second court will accept jurisdiction.

3. Exclusive jurisdiction agreements: Article 17

Article 23 (unlike Article 19) does not state that the exclusive **23.28** bases of jurisdiction envisaged are those arising under Article 16. It will be recalled that the Convention also grants exclusive jurisdiction to a court chosen by a valid jurisdiction agreement falling within Article 17, but Article 23 does not necessarily apply to such cases. If the exclusive jurisdiction of one court arises under Article 16, and that of the other arises under Article 17, the former is to have jurisdiction, whether or not it was the first court seised. This is because of the express terms of the third paragraph of Article 17.[90] On the other hand, if the parties have, by their jurisdiction agreement, chosen more than one court to have exclusive jurisdiction,[91] Article 23 will apply[92] to favour the court first seised.

---

[90] Para. 21.77 above.
[91] Para. 21.44 above.
[92] Bülow/Böckstiegel/Müller, p. 179.

CHAPTER 24

PROVISIONAL, INCLUDING PROTECTIVE, MEASURES
(Article 24)

SECTION 9

Article 24

24.01 Application may be made to the courts of a Contracting State for such provisional, including protective, measures as may be available under the law of that State, even if, under this Convention, the courts of another Contracting State have jurisdiction as to the substance of the matter.*

A. GENERAL NOTE

24.02 Article 24 is concerned with what English lawyers call interim relief. It is of substantial practical importance. It enables a court to grant provisional, including protective, measures, whether or not that court has jurisdiction under the Convention over the substance of the dispute.[1] The law of the court granting the interim relief will apply to determine what measures are available and the circumstances in which they will be granted. For Article 24 to apply, the case must have the requisite international element[2] and must also fall within the general scope of the Convention.[3]

---

* Jenard, para. A1.185 below; Schlosser, para. 183 (para. A1.479 below); Collins, pp. 30–31, 98–103; Dashwood/Halcon/White, pp. 32, 140–141; Hartley, pp. 77–78, 95–96, 125–126; Kaye, pp. 1132–1194; Maxwell, paras. 5.233–5.255, 13.191–13.193; Anton, paras. 7.43–7.48; Droz, paras. 331–334; Bülow/Böckstiegel/Müller, pp. 179–183; Geimer/Schütze, pp. 234–236, 264–282; Kropholler, pp. 224–232; Gothot/Holleaux, paras. 201–205; Pocar, pp. 254–264.
[1] See generally, Collins, "Provisional Measures, the Conflict of Laws and the Brussels Convention" (1981) 1 Yb.Eur. Law, 249.
[2] Paras. 13.10 *et seq.* above.
[3] See paras. 24.12 *et seq.* below.

B. THE EFFECT OF NATIONAL LAW

The national law of the state where the application is made deter-   **24.03**
mines the nature of the provisional or protective orders which may
be made.[3a] National law not only regulates the kind of relief which
may be granted and the terms of the order by which the relief is
granted, it also determines such matters as whether the order takes
effect *in personam* or *in rem*, its effect on third parties and the extent
(if at all) to which the order applies outside the territorial jurisdiction of the court which makes it. So, for example, it seems that an
order freezing a bank account in Germany can be obtained from a
French court,[4] although the present practice of the English courts
would normally preclude the granting of a *Mareva* injunction in
respect of the same account.[5]

The first paragraph of Article 3[6] states that persons domiciled in a   **24.04**
Contracting State may only be sued by virtue of the rules set out in
Sections 2 to 6 of Title II; but the other, exorbitant, bases of jurisdiction, some of which are referred to in the second paragraph of
Article 3 remain available as bases of jurisdiction for the purpose of
provisional orders.[7] This is because Article 24 permits the application of national rules governing the making of provisional orders.
It follows that, for this purpose, a national court may rely on a basis
of jurisdiction which is provided by its own law, even if that basis is
not included in the Convention for the purpose of determining jurisdiction over the substance of a dispute.

The availability of exorbitant jurisdictions for the purpose of
making provisional orders is particularly relevant where the
location of goods or other assets forms the jurisdictional basis. So,
for example, paragraph 23 of the German *Zivilprozessordnung*
enables jurisdiction to be based on the presence of a defendant's
assets in Germany. The effect of Article 24 is to sanction the use of
that jurisdiction for the making of a provisional order against a
defendant domiciled in another Contracting State, even if neither
he nor the subject-matter of the dispute have any other connection
with Germany.[8]

[3a] The interim measures available under the laws of each of the Contracting States
are summarised in chaps. 48 to 58 below, at paras. 58 to 60.
[4] See, *e.g. De Cavel* v. *De Cavel* [1979] E.C.R. 1055 and *Denilauler* v. *Couchet
Frères* [1980] E.C.R. 1553, each of which is discussed below.
[5] See para. 7.24 above.
[6] Para. 16.09 above.
[7] Droz, paras. 331 *et seq.*; *Société Nordstern and others* v. *Eon and others*, Cour
d'Appel, Rennes, May 20, 1980, Digest D I–24—B11 n. 1.
[8] On the question of seizure in support of international claims, where enforcement against a third party debtor may be necessary, see Schlosser, para. 207
(para. A1.504 below).

24.05   An example of a different type of exorbitant jurisdiction is afforded by Article 14 of the French Civil Code, which enables the jurisdiction of French courts to be invoked by a person of French nationality. An application for provisional measures may therefore be made to a French court by a French national, whether or not the French courts would have jurisdiction over the substance of the case and whether or not the applicant is domiciled in France. This particular jurisdictional basis may also be relied on by persons of other nationalities if they are domiciled in France, by virtue of the second paragraph of Article 2.[9]

The jurisdiction of the English High Court to grant provisional measures was traditionally limited to those cases where the court had jurisdiction over the substance of the matter.[10] The 1982 Act extended that jurisdiction to cover, in addition, cases which fall within the scope of the Convention, but in respect of which proceedings have been or are to be commenced in another Contracting State.[11] The powers of English courts to grant provisional measures under Article 24 are discussed in greater detail in Chapter 7.[12]

C. LOCATION OF THE MAIN PROCEEDINGS

24.06   The principal effect of Article 24 is to allow a person who is litigating a dispute before the courts of one Contracting State to apply to the courts of another Contracting State for provisional, including protective, measures. The main action need not have been commenced at the time of the application for those measures.[13] However, if the application for provisional measures is made to the court in which the main dispute is being litigated, Article 24 should (it is submitted) allow that court to grant such provisional measures as may be available by its own law.[14] If such measures are granted by

---

[9] Para. 16.01 above.

[10] *The Siskina* [1979] A.C. 210.

[11] s.25, para. 43.03 below. Further extensions may be made by Order in Council to the court's power to grant interim relief in the absence of jurisdiction over the substance of the matter: s.25(3).

[12] Paras. 7.26 *et seq.* above.

[13] Collins, p. 99.

[14] *Bombardieri* v. *Esta Trust Reg.*, Nederlandse Jurisprudentie 1980, No. 512, Digest D I–5.1.2—B24. The question was raised but not decided in *C.H.W.* v. *G.J.H.* [1982] E.C.R. 1189 (discussed at para. 24.14 below), whether the concept of "provisional, including protective, measures" covered interim relief applied for in interlocutory proceedings, and whether it made any difference if the relief sought was in connection with other proceedings pending in the same Contracting State.

that court, they will not be rendered ineffective, even if the court later holds that it has no jurisdiction over the main dispute.[15]

Provided that the case has a sufficient international element and falls within the scope of the Convention, it is clear that Article 24 allows national courts to apply the same criteria in deciding whether to grant provisional measures to a person litigating his dispute in another Contracting State as it would apply if the principal dispute were being litigated in the same court. What is less clear is whether Article 24 obliges the national court to do so.[16]

The scheme and spirit of the Convention, as well as the wording   **24.07**
of Article 24, suggest that a national court may not discriminate against a party applying for provisional measures, merely because the main dispute is being litigated elsewhere, or merely because the court has no jurisdiction over the main subject-matter. National courts have sometimes been willing to grant provisional measures *of a kind* permitted by their law (and to use Article 24 as the jurisdictional basis for doing so) in circumstances where the fact that proceedings over the main issue were not to be brought before the courts of that state would have prevented the grant of such measures pursuant to their national law.[17]

On the other hand, there may be cases where the effectiveness or desirability of the provisional order itself is affected by the fact that the principal dispute is being litigated elsewhere[18] and (it is submitted) in such a case the court can legitimately take into account the actual or potential location of the main litigation.[18a]

---

[15] *Transatlantische Transport- und Rückversicherungsaktiengesellschaft* v. *Von Wulf-fen*, Arrondissementsrechtbank, Leeuwarden, September 22, 1977, Digest D I–24—B5.

[16] Maxwell, paras. 5.234–5.236.

[17] *Société SMAC Acieroid* v. *Thielen*, Pas.lux. 1981, p. 154, Digest D I–24—B9. Where the availability of a protective measure under German law depended on the prospect of a later German judgment needing to be enforced abroad, the measure has been held to be available under this Article in aid of the prospective enforcement of a foreign judgment: Amtsgericht Hamburg-Harburg, case 612 C 257/75, July 9, 1975, Digest D I–24—B2; Oberlandesgericht Düsseldorf, case 3 U 6/77, May 18, 1977, N.J.W. 1977, p. 2034, Digest D I–24—B4. But in at least one reported case, the contrary has been held: Oberlandesgericht Koblenz, case 13 U 9/75, May 2, 1975, N.J.W. 1976, p. 2081, Digest D I–24—B1.

[18] Difficulties created by the fact that the principal dispute is litigated elsewhere may be overcome by the imposition of time-limits or other conditions on the grant of the provisional measure, if the law of the court allows it: *Société Eli Lilly*, Cour d'Appel, Brussels, February 11, 1977, Journal trib. 1977, p. 529, Digest D I–24—B3.

[18a] As regards the U.K., see para. 7.30 above and the 1982 Act, s.25(2), para. 43.07 below.

24.08   *Exclusion of jurisdiction.* It may be, though, that where exclusive jurisdiction over the subject matter of the proceedings is accorded to the courts of one Contracting State by Article 16, the courts of other Contracting States cannot grant interim relief in respect of that subject-matter.[19] The question whether a jurisdiction agreement, valid under Article 17, is effective to exclude jurisdiction[20] for the purposes of this Article, is probably a matter to be determined in accordance with the national law of the court to which application is made for the provisional measures, including its choice of law rules.[21]

D. Enforcement of Provisional Orders; *Ex Parte* Orders

24.09   It is necessary to distinguish clearly between the jurisdiction which arises under this Article to make a provisional order in the absence of jurisdiction over the substance of the dispute, and the enforceability of that order in other Contracting States. An order made pursuant to Article 24 providing for provisional measures is a "judgment" within the meaning of Article 25[22] and, in general, it is susceptible to recognition and enforcement in the other Contracting States, in the same way as any other judgment.[23] But its enforceability is subject to certain steps having been taken to protect the rights of the person against whom the order is made. In particular, an order which has been made *ex parte*, is not enforceable without notice in other Contracting States.[24]

24.10   This is the effect of the decision of the European Court of Justice in *Denilauler* v. *Couchet Frères*,[25] a case concerned with an *ex parte* order made by a French court for the freezing of a bank account in Germany. The case is discussed in more detail in relation to the restrictions it places on the recognition and enforcement of pro-

---

[19] *J. A. Motte* v. *Tecno S.p.A.*, Riv.dir.int.priv.proc. 1981, p. 913, Digest D I–16.4—B3.

[20] See para. 21.03 above.

[21] *Cf.* Collins, "Provisional Measures, the Conflict of Laws and the Brussels Convention" (1981) 1 Yb.Eur. Law 249, at pp. 259–262.

[22] Para. 26.01 below. See also paras. 25.25 to 25.28 below.

[23] *De Cavel* v. *De Cavel (No. 1)* [1979] 1055, at p. 1067 (para. 9); see also, for example, *Calzaturificio Brennero s.a.s.* v. *Wendel GmbH Schuhproduktion International* [1984] E.C.R. 3971: see the Opinion of Advocate General Sir Gordon Slynn, at p. 3973.

[24] There is an argument that an order made *ex parte* is not a judgment within the meaning of Art. 25, but this argument (it is submitted) is ultimately unconvincing: see paras. 25.18 and 25.19 below.

[25] [1980] E.C.R. 1553.

visional orders,[26] but mention should be made here of some fairly extensive comments on the interpretation of Article 24 made by the European Court in the course of its decision. The Court said this:

> "An analysis of the function attributed under the general scheme of the Convention to Article 24, which is specifically devoted to provisional and protective measures, leads . . . to the conclusion that, where these types of measures are concerned, special rules were contemplated. Whilst it is true that procedures of the type in question authorizing provisional and protective measures may be found in the legal system of all the Contracting States[27] and may be regarded, where certain conditions are fulfilled, as not infringing the rights of the defence, it should however be emphasised that the granting of this type of measure requires particular care on the part of the court and detailed knowledge of the actual circumstances in which the measure is to take effect. Depending on each case and commercial practices in particular the court must be able to place a time-limit on its order or, as regards the nature of the assets or goods subject to the measures contemplated, require bank guarantees or nominate a sequestrator and generally make its authorisation subject to all conditions guaranteeing the provisional or protective character of the measure ordered. The courts of the place or, in any event, of the Contracting State, where the assets subject to the measures sought are located, are those best able to assess the circumstances which may lead to the grant or refusal of the measures sought or to the laying down of procedures and conditions which the plaintiff must observe in order to guarantee the provisional and protective character of the measures ordered. The Convention has taken account of these requirements by [the provisions of Article 24] . . . "[28]

E. PROVISIONAL FINDINGS OF FACT

In deciding whether or not to grant provisional measures, a court **24.11** may in some cases have to conduct a fairly extensive investigation into questions of fact, even though it may have no jurisdiction over the main subject-matter, but decisions on such questions of fact can only be regarded as tentative, and cannot be taken to bind the court which decides the main issue. Were it otherwise, the exclusion of exorbitant jurisdictions by Article 3 would be rendered largely ineffective.[29]

A review of questions which will arise on the main issue will be

---

[26] Para. 27.26 below. See also para. 25.19 below.
[27] This is a reference to the original six Contracting States.
[28] [1980] E.C.R. 1553, at pp. 1570–1571 (paras. 15–16).
[29] Droz, para. 334.

particularly important in applications for interim payments, which have been held by national courts to amount to provisional measures within the meaning of Article 24,[30] even where the provisional order is for payment of the whole debt.[31] It has been pointed out, though, that while a provisional or protective measure may be changed or reversed at the trial of the main issue, a provisional order for the payment of damages might prejudice the decision on the substance of the case if it provided partial compensation for the loss. In so far as an injured party might obtain almost full compensation by an order of the court of his own domicile, which would not have jurisdiction over the substance of the matter, it would be possible for the jurisdictional rules of the Convention to be largely evaded.[32] It may be, therefore, that an order for an interim payment which had this effect ought not to be regarded as a provisional order for the purposes of this Article.

F. Cases Falling within the Scope of the Convention

24.12   The question whether a provisional measure falls within the scope of the Convention will depend upon the nature of the rights which the measure serves to protect. It is not necessarily dependent upon whether the subject-matter of the main dispute is itself within the Convention. This appears from the decisions of the European Court of Justice in three matrimonial cases, although none of them is an example of a litigant before the courts of one Contracting State applying for provisional measures to the courts of another Contracting State.

The De Cavel decisions. The first case is *De Cavel* v. *De Cavel (No. 1),*[33] where the husband obtained an interlocutory order in France freezing the couple's assets, which he then applied to

---

[30] *Société Verkor* v. *Roger Tron,* Gaz. Palais 1979, Jurisprudence, p. 453, Digest D I–24—B8; *Sahm* v. *S. A. Maeckler,* Cour d'Appel, Colmar, March 5, 1982, Digest D I–24—B11; *Diehm* v. *Sicre,* Cour d'Appel, Aix-en-Provence, September 27, 1982, Digest D I–24—B11 n. 2.
[31] *Paula Verdonck* v. *N.V. Algemene Bank Nederland,* Arrondissementsrechtbank, Amsterdam, April 15, 1981, Digest D I–24—B10; *Sahm* v. *S. A. Maeckler,* Cour d'Appel, Colmar, March 5, 1982, Digest D I–24—B11. Collins regards such orders as surely contrary to the spirit of the Convention and doubts whether they are really provisional or protective measures within the meaning of the Convention: (1981) 1 Yb.Eur. Law 249, 254.
[32] *Diehm* v. *Sicre, per* the single judge of the Cour d'Appel, Aix-en-Provence, May 4, 1981, Rev. critique 1983, p. 110, Digest D I–24—B11 n. 2; decision confirmed on different grounds by the full court, September 27, 1982.
[33] [1979] E.C.R. 1055, discussed at para. 14.21 above.

enforce in Germany. The principal question referred to the European Court by the *Bundesgerichtshof* turned on the scope of the Convention as defined by Article 1, but in the course of its decision, the
European Court said:

> "As provisional protective measures relating to property—such as
> the affixing of seals or the freezing of assets—can serve to safeguard a
> variety of rights, their inclusion in the scope of the Convention is
> determined not by their own nature but by the nature of the rights
> which they serve to protect.
>
> Furthermore, in relation to the matters covered by the Convention,
> no legal basis is to be found therein for drawing a distinction between
> provisional and definitive measures.
>
> That conclusion is not affected by Article 24 of the Convention . . .
> [which] expressly envisages the case of provisional measures in a Con-
> tracting State where 'under this Convention' the courts of another
> Contracting State have jurisdiction as to the substance of the matter
> and it cannot, therefore, be relied on to bring within the scope of the
> Convention provisional or protective measures relating to matters
> which are excluded therefrom."[34]

The second case was *De Cavel* v. *De Cavel (No. 2)*,[35] between the   **24.13**
same parties. This concerned two interim orders made in favour of
the wife in the divorce proceedings, both of which were held to be
in the nature of maintenance. Maintenance obligations fall within
the Convention, but divorce is outside it.[36] The European Court
therefore had to consider whether the fact that the orders were
made in divorce proceedings meant that they too were outside the
scope of the Convention. The Court concluded that that fact made
no difference and that the maintenance orders were within the
scope of the Convention. The Court stressed that no provision of
the Convention linked the treatment of ancillary claims to the
treatment of principal claims, and cited Articles 42[37] and 5(4)[38] as
supporting that view.[39] The Court continued:

> "Ancillary claims accordingly come within the scope of the Con-
> vention according to the subject-matter with which they are con-
> cerned and not according to the subject-matter involved in the
> principal claim . . . "[40]

---

[34] *Ibid.*, at pp. 1066–1067 (paras. 8 and 9).
[35] [1980] E.C.R. 731, discussed at para. 17.34 above.
[36] See para. 14.19 above.
[37] Para. 28.71 below.
[38] Para. 17.53 above.
[39] [1980] E.C.R. 731, at pp. 740–741 (para. 8).
[40] *Ibid.*, (para. 9).

It went on to say that that was the reason for its decision in *De Cavel (No. 1)*.

24.14   *Orders concerning evidence.* The third case where the scope of the Convention was considered by the European Court of Justice in the context of Article 24 was *C.H.W.* v. *G.J.H.*.[41] Both the husband and wife in that case were of Dutch nationality and domiciled in Belgium. It seems that divorce proceedings were already under way between the parties in the Netherlands,[42] when the wife applied to the *Arrondissementsrechtbank*, Rotterdam, for orders attaching the husband's shares in a private company and for damages to be assessed. The basis of the wife's claim was that the husband had carried out unauthorized and therefore improper management of her separate property. By a counter-summons to the President of the *Arrondissementsrechtbank*, the husband claimed an interlocutory order for the delivery up of a document (referred to as a "codicil") which he said belonged to him alone and which he feared the wife's counsel would seek to use as evidence in support of her claim for damages, and for injunctions restraining its use.

One of the issues was whether the President of the *Arrondissementsrechtbank* had jurisdiction to hear the husband's summons, and this issue went on successive appeals to the Netherlands Supreme Court (*Hoge Raad*), which considered that the answer depended on the applicability of the Convention, and particularly Article 24. The European Court said that, by its very wording, the question which it had been asked related to a case in which the management of the wife's property in question was "closely connected with the proprietary relationship between the spouses flowing directly from their marriage bond,"[43] a subject which falls outside the Convention. The Court continued:

> "Therefore, an application for provisional measures to secure the delivery up of a document in order to prevent the statements which it contains from being used as evidence in an action concerning the management of the wife's property must also be considered to be connected with rights in property arising out of a matrimonial relationship within the meaning of the Convention because of its ancillary nature."[44]

Accordingly, the Convention was held not to apply to the application for provisional measures either. The question asked by the *Hoge Raad* on the interpretation of Article 24[45] therefore arose only

---

[41] [1982] E.C.R. 1189. See also para. 14.22, n. 59 above.
[42] The report is not entirely clear on this point.
[43] [1982] E.C.R. 1189, at p. 1203 (para. 7).
[44] *Ibid.*, (para. 8).
[45] The question is summarised at para. 14.22, n. 59 above.

in a very limited form and was answered by the European Court as follows:

> "Article 24 . . . may not be relied on to bring within the scope of the Convention provisional or protective measures relating to matters which are excluded from it."[46]

---

[46] [1982] E.C.R. 1189, at p. 1205, echoing its decision in *De Cavel* v. *De Cavel (No. 1)*. The decision of the Netherlands court in the light of this decision are noted at Digest D I–1.2—A4n.

CHAPTER 25

RECOGNITION AND ENFORCEMENT—GENERAL INTRODUCTION TO TITLE III

A. PURPOSE OF TITLE III

25.01 Title III (Articles 25 to 49) contains the rules governing the recognition and enforcement of judgments and forms the second substantial part of the 1968 Convention. The rules are far-reaching and compulsory, leaving little scope for judgments given in one Contracting State to be refused recognition and enforcement in the other Contracting States.

It has already been observed that one of the purposes of the 1968 Convention is to simplify the formalities governing the reciprocal recognition and enforcement of judgments[1] and this is what the Jenard Report describes as the Convention's "ultimate objective."[2] As the European Court has pointed out, this purpose is served by the fact that the Convention is based on the direct rules of jurisdiction contained in Title II:

> "It is because of the guarantees given to the defendant in the original proceedings that the Convention, in Title III, is very liberal in regard to recognition and enforcement."[3]

---

[1] EEC Treaty, Art. 220; see para. 13.03 above; Jenard, para. A1.186 below.
[2] Jenard, para. A1.28 below.
[3] *Denilauler* v. *Couchet Frères* [1980] E.C.R. 1553, at p. 1569 (para. 13). The case is discussed briefly at para. 24.10 above, and in more detail at para. 27.26 below, where the facts are summarised.

" . . . Title II of the Brussels Convention contains provisions regulating directly and in detail the jurisdiction of the courts of the State in which judgment was given, and also provisions concerning the verification of that jurisdiction and of admissibility. These provisions, which are binding on the court in which judgment was given, are of such a nature as to protect the interests of defendants. This has made it possible, at the stage of recognition and enforcement which is governed by Title III of the Convention, to facilitate the free movement of judgments within the Community by simplifying the procedure for recognition and by reducing the number of grounds which may operate to prevent the recognition and enforcement of judgments. . . . "[4]

If a judgment or order within the general scope of the Convention[5] is given or made by a court of a Contracting State, it is usually entitled, automatically and compulsorily, to recognition in the other Contracting States. Only in specific and limited circumstances may the judgment be refused recognition or enforcement,[6] and only in specific and limited circumstances may the court of the state where recognition or enforcement is sought (the "state addressed") review the jurisdiction of the court which gave the judgment (the "court of origin").[7]

B. Summary of Provisions in Title III

Article 25 provides a definition of "judgment"[8] and thereafter Title III is divided into three sections. Section 1 (Articles 26 to 30) is concerned with recognition, Section 2 (Articles 31 to 45) is concerned with enforcement and Section 3 (Articles 46 to 49) contains common provision relating mainly to evidence.

25.02

1. Section 1: recognition

Articles 26 to 30 are concerned with the recognition, as distinct from the enforcement, of judgments delivered in other Contracting States. The automatic nature of recognition of a foreign judgment is established by the first paragraph of Article 26.[9] If a question arises as to whether a foreign judgment should be recognised, the issue can be resolved either by proceedings under the second paragraph

---

[4] *Klomps* v. *Michel* [1981] E.C.R. 1593, at p. 1605 (para. 7). The case is considered in more detail at para. 27.29 below.
[5] Chap. 14 above.
[6] Para. 25.11 below.
[7] Para. 27.77 below.
[8] See paras. 25.18 *et seq.* and 26.01 *et seq.* below.
[9] See para. 27.03 below.

of Article 26,[10] specifically directed to that issue, or, if the issue arises incidentally in other proceedings, in those proceedings, pursuant to the third paragraph of Article 26.[11] Recognition *may only* be refused on one of the grounds specified in the Convention. The principal grounds for refusal are set out in Articles 27 and 28,[12] although the Convention does allow various other minor grounds.[13]

If the judgment has been given in proceedings falling within Sections 3, 4 or 5 of Title II (insurance, consumer and exclusive jurisdiction cases), Article 28 permits the *jurisdiction* of the court of origin to be reviewed, but (with certain exceptions[14]) such a review is otherwise prohibited.[15] In no case may the decision of the court of origin be reviewed *as to its substance*: Article 29.[16] If an "ordinary appeal" has been lodged against the judgment in its state of origin, the court of another state where recognition is sought may stay its proceedings: Article 30.[17]

2. Section 2: enforcement

25.03   The enforcement of judgments given in other Contracting States is regulated by Articles 31 to 45 and, in summary, the procedure laid down by the Convention is as follows. The judgment which it is sought to enforce must be enforceable in its state of origin[18] and the application for an order for its enforcement must be made by an interested party.[19] The Convention specifies the court in each Contracting State to which the application is to be made,[20] but the procedure for making the application is left to national law,[21] except that the application is to be made *ex parte* in the first instance[22] and is to be supported by certain specified documents.[23] The applicant must give an address for service within the jurisdiction of the enforcing court, or appoint a representative *ad litem*.[24] The court

---

[10] Paras. 27.04 *et seq.* below.
[11] Paras. 27.10 *et seq.* below.
[12] Paras. 27.12 and 27.62 below.
[13] See para. 25.13 below.
[14] *Ibid.*
[15] See para. 27.73 below.
[16] Para. 27.75 below.
[17] Para. 27.78 below.
[18] Art. 31, first para., para. 28.01 below.
[19] *Ibid.*
[20] Art. 32, para. 28.09 below.
[21] Art. 33, first para., para. 28.16 below.
[22] Art. 34, first para., para. 28.22 below.
[23] Art. 33, third para., para. 28.16 below. See also Arts. 46–49, discussed below.
[24] Art. 33, second para., para. 28.16 below.

must decide the application "without delay"[25] and may only dismiss it for one of the reasons specified in the Convention.[26]

If the court decides to authorise enforcement, the party against whom enforcement is authorised may appeal within one month (or two months if he is domiciled in a different Contracting State) from the date of service of the decision on him.[27] The Convention specifies the courts to which that appeal and any further appeals lie.[28] With the exception of protective measures, no enforcement may be carried out until after the time limited for appealing has expired, or the appeal has been determined.[29] The appellate proceedings may be stayed on the application of the appellant if an ordinary appeal has been lodged against the judgment in its state of origin, or if the time for such an appeal has not expired (in which case, the enforcing court may specify the time within which such an appeal is to be lodged).[30] The court may also make enforcement conditional on the provision of security.[31]

25.04

If the court refuses in the first instance to authorise enforcement, the aggrieved applicant may appeal to the specified court[32] and the Convention also specifies the courts to which any further appeal may be taken.[33] The Convention permits the authorisation of enforcement of part only of a judgment.[34] It also contains certain provisions which relate to penal clauses in judgments[35] and to legal aid[36] and which prohibit the use of foreign nationality or domicile as a ground for ordering security.[37]

3. Section 3: evidential provisions

Articles 46 to 49 supplement the provisions of Article 33 concerning the procedure on an application for a declaration of recognition or an order for enforcement. These Articles contain requirements relating to documentary evidence, but it may be that Article 47(1) goes further and contains a substantive provision, namely that the judgment, to be enforceable, must have been served.[38]

25.05

---

[25] Art. 34, first para., para. 28.22 below.
[26] Art. 34, second para., para. 28.22 below.
[27] Art. 36, para. 28.30 below.
[28] Art. 37, para. 28.38 below.
[29] Art. 39, para. 28.55 below.
[30] Art. 38, para. 28.43 below.
[31] *Ibid.*
[32] Art. 40, para. 28.63 below.
[33] Art. 41, para. 28.69 below.
[34] Art. 42, para. 28.71 below.
[35] Art. 43, para. 28.76 below.
[36] Art. 44, para. 28.81 below.
[37] Art. 45, para. 28.85 below.
[38] See paras. 29.14 *et seq.* below.

Certain documents must be produced on an application for a declaration of recognition or for an order for enforcement,[39] while others are required only on an application for an order for enforcement.[40] The court of the state addressed has power to relax some of the evidential requirements[41] in certain circumstances, and to require translations[42] and Contracting States are prohibited from requiring certain formalities in respect of the various documents.[43]

National law in the state addressed may regulate the way in which the applications are to be made, and provide for matters of detail, such as the number of copies required of various documents, the form of the application and so forth, but may not impose additional requirements or requirements inconsistent with, or in derogation from, the provisions of the Convention.

C. RECOGNITION

25.06 The Convention provides no precise definition of the concept of recognition, but it is a concept which is central to the manner in which the Convention operates. Recognition relates to two different attributes of a foreign judgment. The Jenard Report says:

> "Recognition must have the result of conferring on judgments the authority and effectiveness accorded to them in the State in which they were given."[44]

First, recognition involves equating the authoritative nature of a foreign judgment with a judgment delivered in the state addressed: the *authority* of the judgment. Secondly, it involves an extension of the effects of the foreign judgment into the legal order of the other Contracting States: the *effectiveness* of the judgment. The two characteristics overlap, but it may be helpful to consider them separately.

---

[39] Art. 46, para. 29.01 below. It applies to proceedings under both the second and third paras. of Art. 26.

[40] Art. 47, para. 29.07 below. The document referred to in Art. 47(2) evidencing the applicant's entitlement to legal aid in the state of origin is also required on an application for a declaration of recognition, under the second para. of Art. 26.

[41] Art. 48, first para., para. 29.20 below. The power extends expressly to Arts. 46(2) and 47(2), but it may be that the evidential requirements of Arts. 46(1) and 47(1) may also be relaxed: see paras. 29.22 *et seq.* below.

[42] Art. 48, second para., para. 29.20 below.

[43] Art. 49, para. 29.30 below.

[44] Jenard, para. A1.187 below, a passage cited with approval by the European Court in *Hoffman* v. *Krieg*, case 145/86, decision of February 4, 1988 (para. 10), *The Times*, March 26, 1988, discussed at para. 27.47 below.

1. The authority of the judgment

A judgment is to be regarded as authoritative in determining the   **25.07** rights of the parties if it is a judgment within the meaning of Article 25 and is of a kind susceptible to recognition.[45] If those conditions are fulfilled, the extension of the judgment's authority into the other Contracting States is automatic[46] unless one of a limited number of grounds exists for refusing recognition. These grounds are those contained in Articles 27 and 28 and certain other minor provisions,[47] but even where one or more of these grounds exist, the foreign judgment may in no circumstances be reviewed as to its substance.[48] The requirement that the authority of foreign judgments should be recognised also requires that the legitimacy of the courts and tribunals of the other Contracting States should be respected, whether or not they have jurisdiction over a particular case[49] and whether or not their jurisdiction is subject to review.

The authority of decisions on questions of fact and of substantive law is extended into the legal order of other Contracting States,[50] as is the authority of a court's decisions on its own international jurisdiction.[51] Decisions determining an issue made purely on the ground of the procedural law of the foreign forum are usually not susceptible to recognition.[51a]

If a plaintiff obtains a judgment in the courts of State A, it is con-   **25.08** trary to the Convention for him to litigate the dispute afresh in State B, even if in State B he would be entitled to different or greater relief,[52] provided that the judgment given in State A would be entitled to recognition or enforcement in State B.[53]

Similarly, if an action is dismissed, that judgment is as much to

---

[45] Certain judgments, notably those of a procedural nature, do not impinge on the legal order of other Contracting States and are not susceptible to recognition: see paras. 25.18 *et seq.* below.

[46] Art. 26, first para., para. 27.01 below.

[47] Paras. 25.11 *et seq.* below.

[48] Art. 29, para. 27.75 below.

[49] Presenting a claim to a foreign court without jurisdiction has been held sufficient to stop a German limitation period from running: Oberlandesgericht Düsseldorf, case 16 U 48/77, December 9, 1977, Der Betrieb 1977, p. 584, Digest D I–26—B1.

[50] A foreign decision may raise what an English lawyer would call an issue estoppel or estoppel *per rem judicatem. Cf. Papeteries de la Vesdre Raoul Collin S.p.r.l.* v. *Velourspapiers und Tapeten Ditzel*, Tribunal de Commerce, Liège, March 31, 1983, [1984] E.C.C. 547.

[51] This aspect is discussed in greater detail at para. 25.31 below.

[51a] See para. 25.30 below.

[52] *De Wolf* v. *Cox*, [1976] E.C.R. 1759, discussed at para. 25.36 below.

[53] Even where the entitlement to enforcement is not established, a second action may be inadmissible: see para. 25.36, at n. 55 below.

be recognised as one whereby the plaintiff is granted relief. The basis on which the dismissal was ordered, though, may need to be examined with care, to establish the extent of the judgment's authority, and hence its effect in the Contracting State addressed.[54] So, in the example given by the Schlosser Report,[55] if a German court dismisses an action for want of international jurisdiction, an English court is bound by that decision and cannot itself decline jurisdiction on the ground that the German court has international jurisdiction.[56] But the English court in that case would not be bound by the fact of dismissal itself and would still be entitled to find for the plaintiff on the merits. If, on the other hand, the plaintiff had obtained a default judgment from the German court, the English court would be bound (unless a ground existed for refusing recognition)[57] to recognise it as a valid judgment and to grant it recognition and enforcement. The judgment would be authoritative as to the parties' rights, but not as to the plaintiff's assertions of fact or law.

2. The effectiveness of the judgment

25.09   It does not follow from the fact that the *authority* of a judgment given in one Contracting State attracts recognition in another Contracting State, that the effectiveness of the judgment is to be extended without alteration into the legal order of that state. For example, one aspect of a judgment's effectiveness in its state of origin concerns the manner in which it may be enforced there, but this is not an effect of the judgment which, by virtue of its recognition, is generally extended into the state addressed.[58]

Where a particular decision would have the same legal effect both in its state of origin and in the state addressed, there is not likely to be any problem. But a problem may arise where a judgment has a greater effect in the state in which recognition is sought than in the state where it was given. The Schlosser Report cites as an example the fact that in France a judgment against a principal debtor is also effective as against a surety, whereas in the Netherlands and Germany, it is not. The question is whether such a French judgment is to be recognised in, say, Germany as determining the rights of the

---

[54] The question of the judgment's effectiveness in another Contracting State is discussed in the next paragraph, and the questions of estoppel and *res judicata* are mentioned at para. 25.23 below.

[55] Schlosser, para. 191, (para. A1.487 below).

[56] If the dismissal had been for want merely of local jurisdiction, the position would be different: see para. 25.31 below. The distinction between international and local jurisdiction is discussed at para. 15.03 above.

[57] See paras. 25.11 *et seq.* below. Note that Art. 27(2) relates specifically to default judgments.

[58] See para. 25.15, n. 94 below.

surety.[59] The Schlosser Report suggests no general solution and it may be that these problems of the differences between national legal systems will have to be left to national law to resolve.[60]

In principle, though, a judgment should have as great an effect in other Contracting States as it had in its state of origin.[61] To limit the effects of the judgment by reference to the law of the state addressed would be contrary to the principle of the free movement of judgments which the Convention is designed to secure.[62] This interpretation is confirmed by Article V of the Protocol,[63] which provides that "any effects" which judgments given in Germany have as a result of certain provisions of German law "shall be recognised in the other Contracting States." **25.10**

Only in exceptional cases should a judgment be deprived of its full effect, namely where the effects of the judgment would so contravene the principles of the legal order in the state addressed as to justify a refusal on the grounds of public policy,[64] or, seemingly, where its recognition is precluded because of its incompatibility with a rule of national law on a matter outside the scope of the Convention,[64a] or where the subject-matter of the decision is such as not to impinge on that legal order at all and the decision is not of a kind susceptible to recognition and enforcement.[65] Conversely, a foreign judgment should not be afforded greater effect in the state addressed than it would have in its state of origin.[66] So, in the reverse of the above example, a German judgment against a principal debtor should not be effective against a surety in France.

3. Grounds for refusing recognition or enforcement

Together with certain minor grounds for refusal, Articles 27 and 28 provide an exhaustive list of the grounds on which *recognition* of a judgment given in another Contracting State and falling within the scope of the Convention may be refused. They are also the only **25.11**

---

[59] Schlosser, para. 191 (para. A1.487 below).

[60] Droz, para. 448.

[61] *Hoffman* v. *Krieg*, case 145/86, decision of February 4, 1988, *The Times*, March 26, 1988, discussed at para. 27.47 below. Bülow/Böckstiegel/Linke, pp. 196–197. *Cf.* Droz, para. 448, who suggests a double qualification, namely that a foreign judgment should have no greater effect in the state addressed than in its state of origin, nor any greater effect than an equivalent judgment delivered in the state addressed.

[62] See para. 13.15 above.

[63] Para. 35.20 below.

[64] Art. 27(1): para. 27.13 below.

[64a] This appears to follow from the decision of the European Court in *Hoffman* v. *Krieg*, above: see para. 27.47 below.

[65] See paras. 25.18 to 25.19 and 25.28 to 25.31 below.

[66] Droz, paras. 443–444.

grounds on which *enforcement* of such a judgment may be refused[67] if it is enforceable in its state of origin.[67a] If one of the grounds for refusal of recognition exists, the judgment must be refused recognition.[68] The court has no discretion in the matter.[69] If need be, the court must refuse recognition of its own motion.[70] In considering whether to refuse recognition, the court may neither review the original judgment as to its substance,[71] nor reopen questions of fact.[72]

25.12   *Principal grounds for refusal.*[72a] The principal grounds for refusing recognition to a judgment given by a court of another Contracting State and which falls within Article 25 are those contained in Articles 27 and 28. Each is discussed in more detail below, but in summary they are as follows:

(1) that recognition is contrary to public policy in the state addressed: Article 27(1);[73]

(2) that the court of origin failed to respect certain procedural rights of the defendant: Article 27(2);[74]

(3) where the judgment is irreconcilable with a judgment of the state addressed: Article 27(3);[75]

(4) where irreconcilability arises in the application of private international law rules to a preliminary question of status or legal capacity of natural persons, matrimonial property rights, wills or succession: Article 27(4);[76]

(5) where the judgment is irreconcilable with a judgment of a

---

[67] Art. 34, second para., para. 28.22 below.

[67a] Art. 31, first para. See paras. 28.04 and 28.05 below.

[68] The introductory words of Art. 27 are "A judgment *shall* not be recognised:"

[69] It has however been suggested that a judgment which should be refused recognition under the Convention, may nonetheless be recognised pursuant to the national law of the state addressed if that national legal provision is generally more amenable to recognition than the Convention: Geimer/Schütze, pp. 1005–1006. This view, it is suggested, fails to take sufficient account of the Convention's uniform purpose and would wrongly deprive a party of protection against recognition in circumstances where the Convention provides him with that protection.

[70] See para. 27.04 below.

[71] Art. 29, para. 27.75 below.

[72] Although the Convention does not say so expressly, the prohibition of reviewing questions of fact, provided by the second para. of Art. 28, extends also to reviews of recognisability under Art. 27 and the other minor grounds.

[72a] See also paras. 10.26 to 10.43 above.

[73] Para. 27.13 below.

[74] Para. 27.21 below.

[75] Para. 27.43 below.

[76] Para. 27.52 below.

non-Contracting State which is entitled to recognition in the state addressed: Article 27(5);[77]

(6) where the court of origin accepted jurisdiction in breach of Sections 3 (insurance), 4 (consumer contracts) or 5 (exclusive jurisdiction) of Title II, or in a case provided for in Article 59: Article 28, first paragraph.[78]

The second and sixth of these grounds, under Article 27(2) and the first paragraph of Article 28, involve a review of the first court's jurisdiction.

Additional grounds for refusal. In addition to the grounds set out in **25.13** Articles 27 and 28 recognition may, in certain circumstances, be refused under the following provisions:

(1) Article II(2) of the 1968 Protocol[79] (where the judgment was given in criminal proceedings and the defendant did not appear);

(2) the transitional provisions: Article 54(2),[80] Article 34(3) of the 1978 Convention[81] and Article 12(2) of the 1982 Convention (when it comes into force);[82]

(3) Article 57[83] and Article 25(2) of the 1978 Convention[83a] (where a convention on a particular matter applies and lays down conditions for the recognition and enforcement of judgments);

or on the following grounds:

(4) that the subject matter of the judgment falls outside the scope of the Convention[84]; or

(5) that the procedural formalities of the Convention or of the law of the state addressed have not been complied with.[84a]

With the exception of some of the circumstances arising under Article 57, these grounds also involve a review by the court addressed of the jurisdiction of the court of origin.

In addition, an application for an order for enforcement may be refused in certain circumstances on the following grounds:

---

[77] Para. 27.59 below.
[78] Para. 27.62 below. Art. 59 is at para. 33.24 below.
[79] Para. 35.05 below.
[80] Para. 32.01 below.
[81] Para. 37.06 below.
[82] Para. 38.04 below.
[83] Para. 33.06 below.
[83a] Para. 33.07 below.
[84] See para. 27.65 below.
[84a] Arts. 32, 33 and 46 to 49.

(1) that the judgment is not enforceable in its state of origin;[85]

(2) that the judgment has not been served on the person against whom it is directed;[85a]

(3) that the applicant is not an "interested party;"[86]

(4) that the simplified enforcement procedures in Title III do not apply to the judgment, because it orders the taking of provisional or protective measures and was made without the person against whom it was directed having an opportunity to contest the making of the order;[86a]

(5) that making the order for enforcement would involve the national court ignoring the implications of another judgment given by the courts of the state addressed on a matter outside the scope of the Convention[87] (although it is not clear whether this would apply to cases not already covered by Article 27(3));

(6) that the court to which the application is made does not have local jurisdiction under the second paragraph of Article 32.[87a]

25.14 *Substantive law.* Except in the limited circumstances envisaged in Article 27(4), a court may not refuse to recognise a judgment on the ground that the substantive law applied in deciding the case in its state of origin was not the substantive law which, according to the conflicts rules of the state addressed, would have been the proper law. The choice of substantive law is otherwise wholly irrelevant to the question of recognition. That is so even if the result would have been demonstrably different if the latter law had been applied and even where the foreign judgment would be refused recognition in the state whose law has been applied.[88]

---

[85] Art. 31, first para; see para. 28.04 below.
[85a] Art. 47(1), para. 29.07 below; but service may not be an absolute requirement: see paras. 29.15 to 29.16 below.
[86] Art. 31, first para.; see para. 28.07 below.
[86a] See paras. 25.18 *et seq.*, 25.26 and 27.26 below.
[87] *Hoffman* v. *Krieg*, case 145/86, decision of February 4, 1988: see para. 27.47 below.
[87a] Para. 28.12 below.
[88] Bülow/Böckstiegel/Linke, p. 199. On the other hand, the Convention does not prevent the courts of the state addressed, in the context of the execution of a maintenance order, from drawing the inferences of a divorce decree granted in that same state: *Hoffman* v. *Krieg*, above, para. 17. This may also apply to other judgments on matters falling outside the Convention.

D. Enforcement

The Convention's provisions on enforcement, contained in Articles **25.15** 31 to 45, apply to most "judgments" within the meaning of Article 25.[88a] They are not confined to final judgments, to the judgments of superior courts, to judgments which are no longer subject to appeal,[89] or to judgments ordering the payment of a sum of money. They apply equally to non-money judgments, to interlocutory decisions[90] and to orders for costs.[91]

Procedure for enforcement. Reciprocal enforcement conventions usually leave the procedure for obtaining an order that a foreign judgment should be enforced to the domestic law of the state where the enforcement occurs.[92] By contrast, the 1968 Convention provides a uniform and detailed procedure for the granting of orders for enforcement. The procedure applies in all the Contracting States, to the exclusion of national law, except to the extent that national law is not inconsistent with it (or is specifically invoked).[93] Once the order authorising enforcement has been made, though, the actual means of carrying out the enforcement is left largely to national law and the judgment is thereafter treated for the purposes of its execution as if it were a judgment of that second state.[94] This is not generally a matter where the effects which the foreign judgment had in its state of origin are extended by its recognition into the legal order of the state addressed[95] but the application of national law must not have the effect of impairing the efficacy of the general scheme of the Convention as regards orders for enforce-

---

[88a] Para. 26.01 below. See the discussion below as to the judgments envisaged by Title III.

[89] The point at which a judgment becomes *res judicata*, in the sense understood in the law of most Contracting States, is discussed at para. 25.22 below.

[90] See paras. 25.25 *et seq.* below. The Schlosser Report, para. 207 (para. A1.503 below) mentions the problems which may occur in relation to seizure for international claims, where enforcement against a third party debtor may be necessary.

[91] *Cf.* para. 26.06 below.

[92] Droz, para. 545.

[93] Art. 33, first para. para. 28.16 below.

[94] *Hoffman* v. *Krieg*, case 145/86, decision of February 4, 1988 (para. 27), *The Times*, March 26, 1988; see para. 27.47 below. See also *Deutsche Genossenschaftsbank* v. *Brasserie du Pêcheur S.A.* [1985] E.C.R. 1981, 1992 (para. 18), discussed at para. 28.32 below. The system of enforcement generally adopted in the Contracting States is summarised at para. 25.32 below, and discussed in chaps. 48 to 58 below, at paras. 66 *et seq.* in relation to each Contracting State. On the question of protective measures available as a matter of national law, see also para. 28.59 below.

[95] Droz, para. 439. The recognition of a foreign judgment's effects is discussed at paras. 25.09 *et seq.* above.

ment.[95a] In some cases, though, it may be that the particular means of enforcement chosen should reflect the sort of enforcement which would be ordered in the state of origin.[96]

25.16   *Exclusive nature of Convention's procedures.* Where a plaintiff has obtained a judgment against a defendant from the courts of one Contracting State, he may enforce that judgment in the other Contracting States, but may not start a fresh action in another Contracting State for the same relief.[97] It follows that the procedure under common law, whereby the judgment creditor can bring an action on the original judgment[98] will usually be inconsistent with the Convention.

25.17   *Costs.* The Convention is silent on the question of the costs of enforcement (except, incidentally, in relation to legal aid[99] and security for costs),[1] but, as the European Court pointed out in *De Wolf v. Cox*:

> " . . . it must be observed that the Convention, which, in the words of the preamble thereto, is intended 'to secure the simplification of formalities governing the reciprocal recognition and enforcement of judgments of courts and tribunals', ought to induce the Contracting States to ensure that the costs of the procedure described in the Convention are fixed so as to accord with that concern for simplification."[2]

E. What Judgments are to be Recognised and Enforced?

1. General scope of Title III

25.18   A definition of "judgment" for the purposes of the Convention, drawn in wide terms, is provided by Article 25;[3] but not every judgment which falls within the definition is necessarily susceptible of recognition and enforcement under Title III. For example, it is a condition of enforceability of a foreign judgment that it should be

---

[95a] *Hoffman v. Krieg*, above (para. 29).
[96] Schlosser, para. 212 (para. A1.510 below) and, in relation to penal provisions in default of compliance with the judgment, Art. 43, para. 28.76 below.
[97] *De Wolf v. Cox BV* [1976] E.C.R. 1759, discussed at para. 25.36 below. See also para. 28.06 below.
[98] See paras. 10.30 above and 25.35 below.
[99] Art. 44, para. 28.81 below.
[1] Art. 45, para. 28.85 below.
[2] [1976] E.C.R. 1759, at p. 1768 (para. 15); see also Schlosser, para. 206 (para. A1.503 below).
[3] Para. 26.01 below. Non-money judgments are included, as are judgments of inferior courts.

capable of enforcement in its state of origin[4] but that is not necessarily a condition of recognisability.[5] The concept of "recognition"
and the differences between recognition and enforcement have
already been discussed.

The susceptibility of a judgment to recognition and enforcement
has sometimes been considered in the context of Article 25 and it
has been suggested that those orders which are not susceptible to
recognition or enforcement under Title III do not amount to "judgments" for the purposes of that Article.[6] It is suggested, though,
that it is preferable to consider the question whether a judgment or
order is susceptible to recognition or enforcement under the Convention in two stages: first, whether it falls within the general scope
of the Convention and the wide terms of Article 25; and secondly, if
so, whether it is capable of recognition and enforcement.[7]

This seems to have been the approach adopted by the European **25.19**
Court in *Denilauler* v. *Couchet Frères* in considering whether an
interim order made *ex parte* was capable of recognition and enforcement under Title III.[8] The Court described the question in these
terms:

> "It is necessary to consider whether judicial decisions of this type,
> having regard to the scheme and objects of the Convention, may be
> dealt with under the simplified procedure for recognition and
> enforcement provided by the Convention."[9]

Having pointed out that the liberality of Title III was possible
because of the protection afforded to defendants in the original proceedings, the Court continued:

> "In the light of these considerations it is clear that the Convention
> is fundamentally concerned with judicial decisions which, before the
> recognition and enforcement of them are sought in a State other than
> the State of origin, have been or have been capable of being, the sub-
> ject in that State of origin and under various procedures, of an inquiry
> in adversary proceedings. It cannot therefore be deduced from the
> general scheme of the Convention that a formal expression of inten-

---

[4] See Arts. 31, first para.; see para. 28.04 below
[5] Bülow/Böckstiegel/Linke, p. 197; *cf.* Droz, paras. 497–480.
[6] *e.g.*, Schlosser, para. 187 (para. A1.483 below), quoted below; Collins, p. 106;
Hartley, p. 85; Gothot/Holleaux, para. 238.
[7] So, for example, a writ of execution falls expressly within Art. 25, but is prevented by Art. 16(5) (para. 20.40 above) from being enforced in a Contracting
State other than that in which it was issued.
[8] [1980] E.C.R. 1553, at pp. 1567–1570 (paras. 7 to 14). The case is discussed in
more detail at para. 27.26 below, where the facts are summarised.
[9] *Ibid.*, at p. 1568 (para. 10).

tion was needed in order to exclude judgments of the type in question from recognition and enforcement."[10]

It is suggested that those passages (and the judgment as a whole) show that the Court was concerned with the second stage of the enquiry. The issue principally considered by the Court was whether a judgment of the type in question should be capable of recognition and enforcement under Title III, and not whether the decision was or was not a "judgment" for the purposes of Article 25.

The susceptibility of a judgment to recognition and enforcement is of particular relevance in the context of *ex parte* interlocutory orders and in the context of orders concerning procedure and evidence, each of which is discussed below.

2. Final orders and provisional orders

25.20   Unlike many conventions on the recognition of foreign judgments,[11] the present Convention does not require that the judgment be final and conclusive. A judgment may be recognised even if it is only provisional or interim in nature and the omission of any requirement that the decision be *res judicata* was quite deliberate.[12]

(a) Meaning of "provisional"

25.21   Terminology is important in this field. On one hand, an order (such as an interlocutory injunction or an order for provisional seizure of assets) which is "provisional" in the sense that it does not purport to be a final determination of the rights of the parties, is to be recognised; and, to the extent that it is enforceable in its state of origin, it may be enforced in other Contracting States.[13] On the other hand a judgment may purport to be a final determination of the rights of the parties, but only be "provisionally enforceable," because, for example, it is not yet *"res judicata"* in the sense of that term as understood by continental lawyers.

(b) Res judicata

25.22   The term *"res judicata"* is often used to describe the effects of a judgment and a brief description of it may be helpful in considering the extent (if at all) to which the effects of a judgment given in one

---

[10] *Ibid.*, at p. 1569 (para. 13).
[11] This is also the position at common law, and under the other U.K. statutes regulating the enforcement of foreign judgments: see Dicey and Morris, pp. 428–433, 460 *et seq.*
[12] Jenard, paras. A1.187, A1.189 below.
[13] The enforceability of the judgment is governed by Art. 31: see paras. 28.01 *et seq.* below, where the conditions for enforceability are summarised. The provisional enforceability of judgments in each of the Contracting States is discussed in chaps. 48 to 58 below, at para. 67.

Contracting State are to be extended into the legal order of another Contracting State. The detailed rules as to when a judgment becomes *res judicata* vary from country to country,[14] and this is probably not a matter on which the Convention would apply any uniform rule.[15]

Generally speaking, in continental legal systems, a judgment becomes *res judicata* when it can no longer be altered by an appeal, even though it may well have been at least provisionally enforceable before that moment. In French law, for example, a judgment which has been declared provisionally enforceable may be enforced before it becomes *res judicata*, under the condition that the beneficiary of the judgment should make good any damage suffered by the person against whom the judgment is enforced, if it is later reversed or amended on appeal.[16] On the other hand, even after the judgment has become *res judicata*, it may not become enforceable until after the expiry of a period of grace.[17]

The concept of *res judicata* or "estoppel by record" at common   **25.23**
law involves the judgment having conclusive effect, and being capable of founding an "estoppel *per rem judicatem*," or "claim preclusion." It also involves the separate notion that the cause of action merges in the judgment (*transit in rem judicatem*) and may no longer be relied upon in its own right.[18]

The Convention is not specifically concerned with whether the judgment has or has not become *res judicata*, but the question whether the appeal has been, or may still be, lodged is relevant for the purposes of Articles 30 and 38. If the judgment may still be reversed or amended on appeal, the court of the state addressed has powers under Article 30[19] to stay proceedings in which a declaration of validity is sought, but the judgment is nonetheless entitled to recognition while it subsists. Similar powers arise under Article 38[20] in respect of proceedings for an order of enforcement.

---

[14] See *Industrial Diamond Supplies* v. *Riva* [1977] E.C.R. 2175, discussed at para. 27.83 below, where these differences were canvassed in argument by the U.K. government (at p. 2181) and observed by Advocate General Reischl (at p. 2199). See also chaps. 48 to 58 below, at para. 66, as to the rules in each of the Contracting States.

[15] Geimer/Schütze, pp. 1021–1022.

[16] See para. 50.67 below.

[17] *Ibid.*

[18] See Spencer-Bower and Turner, *Res Judicata* (2nd ed.), paras. 1–6. The former rule of English law, whereby a cause of action did not merge in the judgment of a foreign court, even one which English law regarded as having competent jurisdiction, has been abrogated by the 1982 Act, s.34: see para. 43.36 below.

[19] Para. 27.78 below.

[20] Para. 28.43 below.

(c) Final and conclusive orders

25.24   The question whether a judgment has become *res judicata* is separate from the question whether it is "final" or "conclusive," at least in one sense of those terms. A judgment may be "final" or "conclusive" without being *res judicata* (in the continental sense of that term), if it is a definite determination of the rights of the parties, which is not imperfect, or provisional, or conditional, even if it may still be rescinded, reversed, reopened or set aside.[21]

3. Interlocutory orders generally

25.25   If a judgment is "provisional" in the sense of being an interlocutory order granted by the courts of the state with jurisdiction over the substance of the matter or, under Article 24,[22] by the courts of another Contracting State, the question may arise whether the judgment is susceptible to recognition and enforcement in other Contracting States. Some such orders are capable of enforcement in their state of origin and the Convention's normal rules apply to them, but whether that is so depends on a number of factors.

(a) Ex parte orders

25.26   If an order was made *ex parte*, without the person against whom it was made having had an opportunity to oppose the order, its susceptibility to recognition and enforcement in other Contracting States is restricted. This important proviso arises from the European Court's decision in *Denilauler* v. *Couchet Frères* which is discussed in greater detail below.[23]

(b) Third parties

25.27   Especially where an interim order takes effect *in rem* (such as a *saisie conservatoire*),[24] it may affect third parties, even when it is made under the conditions laid down in *Denilauler* v. *Couchet Frères*.[25] The grounds of opposition to the recognition or enforcement of such an order are those set out in Articles 27 and 28.[26] The Convention provides no means by which a third party affected by the order can oppose its recognition or enforcement in a Contracting State other than that in which it was made. The European Court

---

[21] For a description of the different concepts of finality of a judgment, see Spencer-Bower and Turner, *op. cit.*, para. 164.

[22] Para. 24.01 above.

[23] [1980] E.C.R. 1553. See paras. 27.26 and 27.27 below.

[24] Interlocutory orders available in the different Contracting States are summarised in chaps 48 to 58 below at paras. 58 *et seq.*

[25] See para. 25.26 above.

[26] There are also other minor grounds for refusing recognition or enforcement: see para. 25.13 above.

has held that it is not open to third parties to appeal in the state addressed against an order for the enforcement of the judgment there, but that they may apply, in accordance with the provisions of the national law of that state, for the execution of the judgment to be stayed.[26a]

4. Orders on procedure and evidence

The Convention is primarily concerned with orders which regu- **25.28** late the respective rights and duties of the parties, whether those orders are interlocutory or final.

(a) Enforcement

Generally, orders of a procedural nature are not appropriate to be recognised or enforced under the Convention. Many such orders fall within other civil procedure conventions, such as the Hague Conventions of November 15, 1965 on the service abroad of judicial and extrajudicial documents[27] and of March 18, 1970 on the taking of evidence abroad.[28] These Conventions take precedence over the present convention, by reason of Article 57.[29] Where an order does not fall within such a specialist convention, the question may arise as to whether a procedural order can be enforced under the 1968 Convention.

The Schlosser report considers this matter[30] and, with particular **25.29** reference to the taking of evidence, says:

> "If it were desired that interlocutory decisions by courts on the further conduct of the proceedings, and particularly on the taking of evidence, should be covered by Article 25 of the 1968 Convention, this would also affect decisions with which the parties would be totally unable to comply without the court's co-operation, and the enforcement of which would concern third parties, particularly witnesses. It can only be concluded from the foregoing that interlocutory decisions which are not intended to govern the legal relationships of the parties, but to arrange the further conduct of the proceedings,

---

[26a] *Deutsche Genossenschaftsbank* v. *Brasserie du Pêcheur S.A.* [1985] E.C.R. 1981, discussed at para. 28.32 below.

[27] All the Contracting States except Ireland are parties to that convention. Art. 15 of which is given effect in the context of this Convention by Art. 20: see para. 22.11 above. It is set out in App. 2 (para. A2.03 below) and discussed generally in chap. 4.

[28] All the Contracting States except Belgium, Ireland and Greece are parties to this convention: see App. 2 (para. A2.17 below). It is given effect in the U.K. by the Evidence (Proceedings in Other Jurisdictions) Act 1975. The convention, and questions of judicial assistance generally, are discussed in chap. 8.

[29] Para. 33.06 below.

[30] Schlosser, paras. 184–187 (paras. A1.480–A1.483 below).

should be excluded from the scope of Title III of the 1968 Convention."[31]

For the reasons discussed above, it is suggested that procedural orders of this kind do not need to be excluded from the ambit of Article 25. It is enough to say that the procedural order should not be susceptible of enforcement under Title III if the assistance of the foreign court is required not only for the purpose of ordering its enforcement, but also for the purpose of carrying the order into effect.[31a] Similarly, if the procedural order can only be carried into effect with the co-operation of a third party, it may not be susceptible of enforcement.

(b) Recognition

25.30   The enforcement of a judgment or order necessarily involves its recognition. But if the order is not susceptible of enforcement, it may still be recognised. In principle, it is suggested, the authority of all judgments and orders falling within Article 25 should be respected, even if they are not of a kind which can properly have their effectiveness extended into the state addressed.[32] The bare recognition of the authority of procedural orders is usually of little relevance if their effectiveness does not also extend to the state addressed. Such orders are likely to relate only to matters of procedural law of the court of origin and are not likely to impinge on the legal order of the state addressed. For example, if a court in one Contracting State makes an order that certain evidence is admissible, or that a pleading should be amended, or fixes a date for a stage in the procedure, those decisions are of no relevance in other Contracting States.

On the other hand, if the order relates to a matter of substance, it may well be relevant in other Contracting States. The Convention does not attempt to provide solutions to the difficult questions which may arise in deciding whether a judgment or order relates to matters of substance or of procedure, although those questions may be relevant in deciding the effects of recognising a given judgment. As has been observed, the scheme and purpose of the Convention probably require the authority of all judgments or orders which fall within Article 25 to be respected, but it does not necessarily follow that the judgment's effectiveness is also to be extended into the legal order of other Contracting States.

If the court of one Contracting State dismisses an action for reasons which were of a purely domestic procedural nature (such as

---

[31] *Ibid.*, para. 187 (para. A1.483 below).
[31a] Procedural orders requiring the disclosure of evidence in support of a substantive order may fall within Art. 25: see para. 7.20 above.
[32] See para. 25.09 above.

failure to comply with a procedural time limit, or failure to provide security for costs), that decision should obviously not be taken in another Contracting State as a determination of the parties' rights on the substantive issues.[33] If the dismissal is on a substantive basis, it is a determination of the parties' rights and its recognition in the state addressed becomes a matter of relevance there.

(c) Substance and procedure

Distinguishing between matters of substance and matters of procedure can give rise to notoriously difficult questions.[34] In the context of the Convention, questions of jurisdiction may pose certain difficulties and the distinction between substance and procedure has already been considered in the context of jurisdiction agreements.[35] If a court of one Contracting State concludes that it has international jurisdiction under the Convention, that decision is generally to be recognised in the other Contracting States.[36] Equally, its decision that it is without international jurisdiction must be recognised.[37] But if its decision relates only to its local jurisdiction, that decision, while capable of recognition, relates only to the internal law of the state of origin, and does not preclude the courts of another Contracting State from proceeding on the basis that the courts of the state of origin have international jurisdiction, even if the particular court does not have local jurisdiction.[38]

25.31

5. Judgments on judgments

(a) Execution

The system by which the laws of most Contracting States regulate the enforcement of foreign judgments involves a procedure whereby an application is made to the courts of the state addressed for an order authorising the execution of the judgment.[39] The procedure usually involves a determination that the conditions necessary for the judgment's enforcement in the state addressed are satisfied and that the authorisation (called an "*exequatur*") should

25.32

---

[33] Bülow/Böckstiegel/Linke, p. 198; Geimer/Schütze, p. 986.

[34] The classification of limitation in private international law is a well-known example; but in English law the problem is now eased by the Foreign Limitation Periods Act 1984. (See Law Commission Working Paper No. 75, 1980).

[35] Paras. 21.25 *et seq.* above.

[36] The circumstances in which the international jurisdiction of the court of origin may be reviewed are discussed at paras. 25.12 *et seq.* above.

[37] Schlosser, para. 191 (para. A1.487 below).

[38] The distinction between international and local jurisdiction is discussed at para. 15.03 above.

[39] The system of execution of judgments in each of the Contracting States is discussed in chaps. 48 to 58 below, at paras. 66 *et seq.*

be given. The judgment is then executed by an independent judicial officer whose authority in the particular case is derived from the authorisation. Although the mechanism of execution in the United Kingdom comes more closely under the supervision of the courts, those same propositions apply to the enforcement of judgments under its various statutory systems of registration.[40] In each case, the procedure results in an extension of the authority and effects of the foreign judgment into the territory of the state addressed and the conferring of that state's sovereign authority for the purposes of its enforcement.[41]

(b) Double execution

25.33   A question which sometimes arises is whether an order for enforcement (an *exequatur*) granted in one Contracting State in respect of a judgment given in a third state is itself capable of being enforced in other Contracting States under Title III. The Convention provides no clear answer and the Jenard Report does not deal with the point.[42] It is generally agreed, though, that this is not permissible.[43]

Judgment given in a non-Contracting State. Where the original judgment was given by a court in a non-Contracting State, and an application is made for its enforcement to the court of a Contracting State, the law which that court applies in deciding whether to grant the order for the judgment's enforcement is its own private international law, including any bilateral conventions concluded between it and the state of origin of the judgment. It is clear that Title III of the Convention should not require the decision of that court to be the subject of enforcement in another Contracting State. That court's decision concerns the enforceability of the judgment in the first state, not its enforceability elsewhere,[44] and it is no part of the first court's function to decide what status the original judgment should have in another Contracting State, where a different system of private international law and different conventions apply.

---

[40] See chap. 10, at paras. 10.50 *et seq.* above.

[41] See para. 20.41 above.

[42] Droz (para. 436) points out that the question was never considered in the negotiations.

[43] Collins, p. 106; Droz, paras. 436–437; Bülow/Böckstiegel/Linke, p. 193; Geimer/Schütze, pp. 985–986; Kropholler, p. 176; Gothot/Holleaux, paras. 238–239; *cf.* s.18(7) of the 1982 Act, paras. 41.13 and 41.26 below, which excludes from the intra-U.K. enforcement provisions orders for the enforcement of foreign judgments.

[44] Different considerations apply to an action on a foreign judgment, discussed below.

Judgment given in a Contracting State. On the other hand, where   **25.34**
the state of origin was another Contracting State, the court of the
first state addressed must consider whether the judgment complies
with the requirements of the Convention.[45] If it decides that the
judgment is susceptible of enforcement in its state, it does so on the
basis that the Convention's requirements for enforcement are satisfied. Nonetheless, the authorisation which the court gives should
only be an authorisation for the execution of the judgment in the
territory of that Contracting State, under its sovereignty. It should
not be an authorisation for the execution of the judgment elsewhere. If the decision purports to authorise the execution of the
judgment in another Contracting State, the court of the first state
addressed has probably exceeded its jurisdiction, because Article
16(5)[46] grants exclusive jurisdiction over proceedings concerned
with the enforcement of judgments to the courts of the Contracting
State in which the judgment has been or is to be enforced. The
decision of the court in the first Contracting State must therefore be
refused recognition and enforcement in the other Contracting
States, under the first paragraph of Article 28.[47]

(c) Action on the judgment

The method by which a foreign money judgment is enforced   **25.35**
under English common law, by bringing an action on the judgment, differs in principle from the continental method of enforcement by means of *exequatur*. The action on the judgment[48] is based
on the notion that the foreign judgment gives rise to a substantive
obligation on the judgment debtor to satisfy the judgment and that
this obligation itself forms a cause of action in debt separate from

---

[45] It is difficult to envisage circumstances in which a party would wish to enforce a
judgment given in one Contracting State, not by the direct means of an application to the court of the state where he wished to enforce the judgment, but
indirectly by means of enforcing the decision of a court of a different Contracting State, but the possibility is envisaged by commentators, *e.g.*, Droz,
para. 436; Bülow/Böckstiegel/Linke, p. 193; Geimer/Schütze, pp. 985–986.
[46] Para. 20.40 above.
[47] Para. 27.62 below. Other reasons advanced for refusing recognition are public
policy, under Art. 27(1) (Geimer/Schütze, p. 986, Kropholler, p. 176; Gothot/
Holleaux, para. 238) and the absence of a legitimate interest on the part of the
applicant (Droz, para. 436; Bülow/Böckstiegel/Linke, p. 193).
[48] This is the only means of enforcement of a foreign judgment, other than the
1968 Convention, known to the law of Ireland. In English law, no action may be
brought on a judgment which can be registered under the Foreign Judgments
(Reciprocal Enforcement) Act 1933 (s.6 of that Act). The same is true of judgments given in other parts of the U.K.: s.18 of the 1982 Act (s.18(6): see
para. 41.13 below).

the original cause of action.[49] The original cause of action merges in the foreign judgment.[50] Although it might lead to some inequality of treatment between Contracting States, based on differences in their substantive law, there seems to be no reason in principle why an English judgment, given on the basis of this new cause of action in respect of a judgment given in a non-Contracting State, should not be entitled to recognition and enforcement under the 1968 Convention in the other Contracting States.[51]

25.36   On the other hand, where the original judgment was given in another Contracting State and is one to which Title III of the Convention applies, an action on the judgment is no longer permissible.[52] This is because a plaintiff is precluded by the Convention, where he already has a judgment against a defendant, from pursuing a fresh action in another Contracting State for a judgment in the same terms as that which he has already obtained. That is the effect of the decision of the European Court of Justice in *De Wolf* v. *Cox*,[53] where the plaintiff, having obtained a judgment in Belgium for payment of a debt, pursued a fresh action in the Netherlands for a judgment on the same debt, instead of applying for an order for the enforcement of his Belgian judgment. The European Court ruled that:

> "The provisions of the Convention . . . prevent a party who has obtained a judgment in his favour in a Contracting State, being a judgment for which an order for enforcement under Article 31 of the Convention may issue in another Contracting State, from making an application to a court in that other State for a judgment against the

---

[49] Dicey and Morris, pp. 425 *et seq.* and 462. See para. 10.03 above. For the reasons why an action on a foreign judgment is probably not "proceedings concerned with the enforcement of judgments" within Art. 16(5), see para. 20.43, n. 43 above.

[50] s.34 of the 1982 Act, para. 43.36 below.

[51] See Droz, para. 437, n. 1; *contra*, Collins, p. 106; Dicey and Morris, p. 491, n. 55; Gothot/Holleaux, para. 437. The law of the Netherlands also permits a fresh action to be brought in respect of a matter which has been the subject of a foreign judgment: Art. 431(2) of the Netherlands Code of Civil Procedure. Unlike the action at common law, this procedure involves the retrial of the original issues. It was this procedure which formed the basis of the proceedings in *De Wolf* v. *Cox*, discussed below and in the light of that decision, Netherlands law was amended in respect of cases to which the Convention applies: (1979) 4 Eur.L.Rev. 312.

[52] In the case of judgments given in Belgium, France, Germany, Italy and the Netherlands, an action on the judgment was not possible in England even before the 1968 Convention came into effect, in any case to which the Foreign Judgments (Reciprocal Enforcement) Act 1933 applied: see n. 48 above.

[53] [1976] E.C.R. 1759.

other party in the same terms as the judgment delivered in the first State."[54]

In its reasoning, the European Court said that, "to accept the admissibility of an application concerning the same subject-matter and brought between the same parties as an application upon which judgment has already been delivered by a court in another Contracting State," would be incompatible with the meaning of the first paragraph of Article 26 (automatic recognition) and Article 29 (no review as to the substance) and said that such proceedings were, as the *lis pendens* provisions of Article 21 showed, incompatible with the objectives of the Convention.[55]

That decision seems to be based on the principle that the Convention's procedure should not be abused,[56] rather than on any notion that the cause of action merged in the original judgment.[57] That would have been a matter of substantive law with which the Convention is not concerned. It was the fact that the judgment sought in the new proceedings was the same as that already obtained which raised a bar to those new proceedings, rather than the fact that both proceedings involved the same cause of action.

6. Part of a judgment

Recognition of part only of a judgment is permissible.[58] This may arise either where only part of the judgment falls within the scope of the Convention, or where recognition is refused under Articles 27 or 28 of a severable part of the judgment. Judgments affecting third parties are as subject to recognition as are judgments between the principal parties to an action. This is so as a matter of principle, and is confirmed by Article V of the Protocol,[59] which specifically refers to the recognition of judgments affecting third parties.

25.37

---

[54] *Ibid.*, at pp. 1768–9. On the basis of that decision, the Hoge Raad declared the Netherlands proceedings to be inadmissible: [1979] E.C.C. 80, Ned.Jur. 1978, No. 102; Digest D I–25.0—B1.

[55] *Ibid.*, at p. 1767 (paras. 7 to 11). So, where recognition was sought in Germany of a Netherlands judgment, but it had not yet been established for the purposes of Art. 27(2) that the proceedings had been duly and timeously served on the defendant, a fresh action brought in Germany was still held to be inadmissible: Landgericht Münster, case 14 O 164/78, Juristenzeitung 1978, p. 651, Digest D I–25.0—B2.

[56] See the Opinion of Advocate General Mayras, *ibid.*, at p. 1775.

[57] Where a court settlement was reached in German proceedings, which would have been enforceable in Belgium under Art. 51, Belgian proceedings about the same dispute and between the same parties were held to be barred: *Clausen-Werft K.G. and Clausen* v. *Internationale Stoombootdiensten Flandria N.V.*, Vredegerecht, Amsterdam, February 15, 1977, Digest D I–51—B1. This decision may be misconceived: see para. 30.16, n. 62 below.

[58] Art. 42, para. 28.17 below.

[59] Para. 35.20 below.

JUDGMENTS AND ORDERS
(Article 25)

TITLE III

Article 25

26.01   For the purposes of this Convention, "judgment" means any judgment given by a court or tribunal of a Contracting State, whatever the judgment may be called, including a decree, order, decision or writ of execution, as well as the determination of costs or expenses by an officer of the court.*

A. GENERAL NOTE

26.02   This Article provides a general definition of "judgment" for the purposes of the Convention as a whole, but its principal application is in defining the orders which are capable of recognition and enforcement under the provisions of Title III of the Convention. The term "judgment" is apparently widely defined, but there are a number of respects in which the definition is qualified by the scope and purpose of the Convention as a whole.[1]

In order to fall within the definition, a judgment must fall within the general scope of the Convention, as defined by the Preamble and Article 1,[2] although the domicile of the parties and their nationality is irrelevant.[3] If a judgment falls partly within and partly out-

---

* Jenard, para. A1.186 below; Schlosser, paras. 68, 184–187 (paras. A1.354, A1.480–A1.483; Collins, pp. 105–107; Dashwood/Halcon/White, pp. 36, 145; Hartley, p. 83; Kaye, pp. 1349–1357; Maxwell, paras. 6.1–6.8; Anton, paras. 8.02–8.05; Droz, paras. 429–437; Weser, para. 267; Bülow/Böckstiegel/Linke, pp. 187–194; Geimer/Schütze, pp. 981–987, 1164–1165; Kropholler, pp. 233–244; Gothot/Holleaux, paras. 228–244; Pocar, pp. 265–268.

[1] The question of what types of judgment and order falling within this definition are susceptible to recognition and enforcement under Title III has already been discussed: paras. 25.18 *et seq.* above.

[2] Jenard, para. A1.186 below. See chap. 14 above.

[3] *Ibid.*, Bülow/Böckstiegel/Linke, p. 192.

side the scope of the Convention, it is capable of recognition and enforcement to the extent that it falls within the Convention.[4]

If the court which delivered the judgment has decided that the case falls within the Convention, the court in which the recognition or enforcement is sought will be bound by that decision. If the point has not been decided by the first court, the second court will be free to decide the matter for itself.[5] It would be wise, therefore, in borderline cases, for United Kingdom courts to follow the practice common on the Continent of stating in the judgment the basis upon which jurisdiction is founded.[6] Otherwise, there is a danger that, even though the original court has considered whether it has jurisdiction under the Convention and decided that it has, that decision may not be apparent to the court of another Contracting State in which recognition or enforcement of the judgment is sought. The possibility of the second court having to decide whether the case falls within the Convention is likely to be particularly relevant in cases where proceedings were started before the Convention came into force,[7] but where the decision is capable of recognition and enforcement under the Convention, pursuant to the transitional provisions.[8]

26.03

B. THE DEFINITION

1. "Judgment"

The question whether a particular decision or order is a "judgment" for the purposes of Article 25 has to be decided on the basis of an independent interpretation of the Convention.[9] If the question were to be decided by reference to the law of the state where the judgment was given, it would be possible for each state to determine the extraterritorial effects of its judgments. That is a matter for the Convention itself to determine. On the other hand, the form of the judgment is not material.[10] That may be decided by the law of the court which delivers the judgment, although, in order to

26.04

---

[4] Art. 42, para. 28.71 below.
[5] Bülow/Böckstiegel/Linke, p. 192.
[6] It would also be sensible for the basis of jurisdiction to be set out in the pleadings.
[7] Bülow/Böckstiegel/Linke, p. 192.
[8] Art. 54, para. 32.01 below; 1978 Convention, Arts. 34–36, paras. 37.06 *et seq.* below.
[9] Bülow/Böckstiegel/Linke, p. 188.
[10] Bülow/Böckstiegel/Linke, p. 190; Geimer/Schütze, p. 983.

obtain a declaration of recognition or an order of enforcement, the requirements of Article 46[11] will have to be complied with.

It is plain, both from the examples given in Article 25 itself and from the Jenard Report[12] that the term "judgment" is not confined to final or conclusive orders. Interlocutory and provisional orders are also included, and this aspect has been discussed above.[13] Although the "judgment" must be made by a court or tribunal of a Contracting State, the definition is wide enough to include summary orders made without a judicial consideration, such as default judgments and orders made under the German *Zahlungsbefehl* procedure.[14] The inclusion of writs of execution in Article 25 does not mean that they are susceptible of enforcement in other Contracting States.[15]

2. " . . . a court or tribunal of a Contracting State . . . "

26.05   Just as the term "judgment" must be given an independent interpretation, so too must the words "a court or tribunal," in order to ensure consistency of approach in all the Contracting States. The words may be interpreted broadly, but the court or tribunal must be "of a Contracting State." It is suggested that this means that not only must the court or tribunal be in the territory of a Contracting State, but also that it must in some sense be an organ of the State, exercising the juridical functions of the State.[16] So, the decisions of private tribunals would be outside the definition in Article 25.[17] Arbitration is expressly excluded from the scope of the Convention,[18] but it remains to be seen whether the exclusion extends to the decisions of official arbitral tribunals.[19]

Similarly, the decisions of international courts or tribunals (such as the European Court of Human Rights, or the European Court of Justice itself) would not fall within Article 25.[20] Such decisions are anyway regulated by the treaties or conventions establishing the international forum in question and its jurisdiction, which would accordingly take precedence by reason of Article 57.

---

[11] Para. 29.01 below.
[12] Jenard, para. A1.186 below.
[13] Paras. 25.00 *et seq.* above.
[14] *Klomps* v. *Michel* [1981] E.C.R. 1593, discussed at para. 27.29 below. A *Zahlungsbefehl*, discussed at para. 51.61 below, is now called a *Mahnbescheid*.
[15] See Art. 16(5), para. 20.40 above, and para. 25.18, n. 7 above.
[16] Bülow/Böckstiegel/Linke, p. 193; Geimer/Schütze, pp. 981–982.
[17] Droz, paras. 431–432; Geimer/Schütze, p. 982.
[18] See paras. 14.31 *et seq.* above.
[19] Examples of such tribunals in English law are county court registrars sitting as arbitrators under the County Court Rules and, in the employment field, the Central Arbitration Committee.
[20] Geimer/Schütze, p. 982.

Generally, the decisions of administrative authorities (such as a **26.06**
minister) would not fall within Article 25,[21] although if the administrative authority were performing a clearly judicial function, the
position might be different.[22] It is the judicial function of the court
or tribunal which is probably decisive,[23] or the fact that the decision
is reached by a recognisably judicial procedure.[24] It is necessary
that legal proceedings should have been instituted,[25] but if the
decision was one made by a court in the exercise of administrative,
rather than judicial functions, it is not a "judgment."[26]

Article 25 itself makes it clear that a determination of costs or
expenses by an officer of the court is included in the definition,[27]
but here too judicial procedure is required.[28] An order for costs
relating to proceedings which fall outside the scope of the Convention may itself fall outside the Convention.[29] There seems to be no
reason in principle why other decisions made by an officer of the
court should not also be included, provided that the decision is of a
judicial nature.

---

[21] In matters relating to maintenance the expression "court" includes the Danish
administrative authorities: Art. Va of the Protocol (para. 35.22 below). As the
Schlosser Report observes, Art. 25 must therefore, in this context, be understood as reading: "For the purposes of this Convention, "judgment" means any
judgment given by a court or tribunal of a Contracting State—including in
matters relating to maintenance, the Danish administrative authorities—whatever the judgment may be called. . . . "

[22] Most decisions made by administrative authorities arise in the field of public law
and are outside the scope of the Convention: see paras. 14.08 *et seq.*, 14.17
above. An example of a judicial decision made by a Minister in the field of private law is provided in the case decided by the Oberlandesgericht Hamm, case
20 W 28/77, July 29, 1981, I. P. Rspr. 1981, No. 187, Digest D I–27.3—B3.

[23] Droz, para. 429–430.

[24] Bülow/Böckstiegel/Linke, p. 189.

[25] This appears from the wording of Art. 54, para. 32.01 below.

[26] See also Landgericht Aachen, case 1 O 642/81, February 9, 1982, Digest D
I–25.1—B2.

[27] *Desmazières de Séchelles* v. *M. et Mme. Vloeberghs,* Tribunal de Première
Instance, Brussels, September 17, 1980, Digest D I–25.1—B1. It is irrelevant
that the final sum of costs was not fixed until after the date of the judgment:
Oberlandesgericht Frankfurt-am-Main, December 11, 1984, [1986] E.C.C.
481.

[28] *Cf. Zilken and Weber* v. *Scholl,* Ned.Jur. 1982, No. 466, Digest D I–50—B2;
sub nom., *Re Enforcement of a Bill of Costs,* [1983] E.C.C. 551.

[29] *Groetschel* v. *Smeragliulo,* Riv. dir. int. priv. proc. 1976, p. 559, Digest D
I–31—B3.

CHAPTER 27

RECOGNITION OF JUDGMENTS
(Articles 26–30)

686

SECTION 1

Article 26

A judgment given in a Contracting State shall be recognised in   **27.01**
the other Contracting States without any special procedure being
required.

Any interested party who raises the recognition of a judgment
as the principal issue in a dispute may, in accordance with the
procedures provided for in Sections 2 and 3 of this Title, apply
for a decision that the judgment be recognised.

If the outcome of proceedings in a court of a Contracting State
depends on the determination of an incidental question of recognition that court shall have jurisdiction over that question.*

A. ARTICLE 26: GENERAL NOTE

The concept of recognition generally has already been discussed.[1]   **27.02**
Article 26 provides three means for according recognition to judgments given in other Contracting States. They are not mutually
exclusive, in the sense that a judgment may be recognised pursuant
to the first paragraph of Article 26 without the need for recourse to
the procedure referred to in the second paragraph or the incidental
jurisdiction over the question of recognition provided by the third
paragraph.

B. FIRST PARAGRAPH: AUTOMATIC RECOGNITION

The first paragraph of Article 26 is of central importance to the   **27.03**
Convention, providing the general rule that the judgments of the
courts and tribunals of each Contracting State are automatically
extended into the legal order of every other Contracting State and to
make clear that there is no need for any special procedure or formal
steps before recognition is accorded to such a judgment.

The general rule is not free from qualification. It is not to be read
as laying down any substantive rules on the extent to which a
foreign judgment is entitled to recognition. In other words, a judgment will only be entitled to automatic recognition if it falls within

---

* Jenard, paras. A1.187–A1.189 below; Schlosser, paras. 108, 189–191 (paras.
A1.394, A1.485–A1.487); Collins, pp. 113–114; Dashwood/Halcon/White,
pp. 37, 146–147; Hartley, p. 83; Kaye, pp. 1376–1412; Maxwell,
paras. 6.9–6.21, 6.136–6.142; Anton, paras. 8.07–8.11; Droz, paras. 439–459,
475–481; Weser, paras. 268–272; Bülow/Böckstiegel/Linke, pp. 194–203;
Geimer/Schütze, pp. 1013–1014, 1099–1124; Kropholler, pp. 251–255; Gothot/
Holleaux, paras. 245–253, 387–388, 393–400; Pocar, pp. 268–273.

[1] Paras. 25.06 *et seq.* above.

the scope of the Convention and is not a judgment which should be refused recognition[2] under Articles 27 and 28 or the other minor grounds for refusal.[3] The Jenard Report refers to "a presumption in favour of recognition, which can be rebutted only if one of the grounds for refusal listed in Article 27 is present."[4] It is suggested that that passage is not to be read as meaning that a judgment which should be refused recognition is nonetheless to be recognised unless and until the party opposing recognition establishes a ground for refusal. The first paragraph of Article 26 only raises a presumption in the sense that recognition is automatic, and a party cannot raise an objection to the recognition of the judgment on the ground that it has not been the subject of some formal procedure, even if the relevant national law requires some such step. While the first paragraph of Article 26 may have the effect of shifting the burden of proof where an incidental issue of recognition is to be decided in accordance with the third paragraph,[5] it cannot have that effect where proceedings are taken under the second paragraph for a declaration of recognition, because of the *ex parte* nature of those proceedings.

C. Second Paragraph: Declaratory Proceedings

1. Generally

27.04   An interested party may apply to the court for a declaration that a judgment given in another Contracting State be recognised. The proceedings can only be for declaratory relief, because, if a judgment is entitled to recognition, the recognition is accorded automatically under the first paragraph of Article 26. A decision in proceedings under this paragraph has the status of a final and conclusive decision on the question of recognition in the state addressed[6] and in this respect may differ from a decision made on an incidental issue of recognition under the third paragraph of this Article.[7]

Proceedings under the second paragraph of Article 26 follow the same procedure as those under Articles 31 to 49 for an order for

---

[2] Bülow/Böckstiegel/Linke, p. 200.
[3] See paras. 25.11 to 25.13 above.
[4] Jenard, para. A1.187 below. The presumption is presumably also rebutted if one of other permissible grounds is present.
[5] This depends on national procedural law, see para. 27.10 below.
[6] Kammergericht (Berlin), case 12 U 1600/76, February 16, 1978, Digest D I–26—B2.
[7] See para. 27.11 below.

enforcement, discussed in more detail in the commentary on those Articles.[8] The court which has jurisdiction over the proceedings is determined by Article 32. The procedure is *ex parte* in the first instance. Where an application is made to the court for a declaration of recognition, recognition may only be refused if one of the grounds in Articles 27 and 28 (or other minor provisions)[9] is present.

It is important to note that the court considering the application need not in the first instance carry out a detailed investigation of its own motion as to whether there is any ground for refusing recognition. It is required, though, even if the parties do not raise the matter, to take notice of its own motion of any such ground which appears from the judgment (or the other documents lodged for the purposes of the application) or which is otherwise known to the court.[10]

2. "Any interested party who raises the recognition of a judgment as the principal issue in a dispute . . . "

These words define the person who may apply for a declaration of recognition. Two separate points arise. First, the question may need to be considered as to *what* interest an applicant has in the judgment. Secondly, the question may arise as to whether that interest is sufficient for the purposes of the Convention to make that applicant an "interested party" entitled to make the application. **27.05**

The second question is a matter of interpreting the Convention and is likely to be answered by an independent interpretation. The first question, though, cannot be answered solely by reference to the Convention. This is because the effects of the judgment in its state of origin are a matter for the law of that state, and the Convention is concerned only with the extent to which those effects are extended into the legal order of other Contracting States.[11] As the Jenard Report suggests in the context of enforcement, any person who is entitled to the benefit of a judgment in its state of origin may apply for its enforcement in other Contracting States.[12] The question of *what* interest the applicant has should be answered, it is sug-

---

[8] Chaps. 28 and 29 below. The procedure is summarised at paras. 25.03 and 25.04 above.

[9] Para. 25.13 above.

[10] Schlosser, para. 190 (para. A1.486 below); Maxwell, para. 6.23; Bülow/Böckstiegel/Linke, pp. 211–212; *Wagner* v. *Tettweiler*, Cour de Cassation (France), November 9, 1983, [1985] E.C.C. 258. See also para. 28.25 below.

[11] See paras. 25.09 and 25.10 above.

[12] Jenard, para. A1.211 below. See para. 28.07 below.

gested, by applying whichever system of law is indicated by the choice of law rules of the court to which the application is made.

27.06   *Assignees.* It seems clear as a matter of interpretation of the Convention that the words "any interested party" refer not only to persons who were parties to the original proceedings giving rise to the judgment but also to their assignees. However, the question whether the applicant is the assignee of an original party should be determined by the law of the court of origin.[13] The assignment may be one which arises by operation of law, rather than by any specific act of assignment. For example, the executors or liquidator of an original party are likely, as a matter of national law, to be entitled to the benefit, or subject to the burden, of a judgment.

27.07   *Other persons.* It may be that persons other than the original parties and their assignees are envisaged by the words "any interested party." For example, they may also embrace other persons directly affected by the judgment—such as a surety whose rights are determined by a judgment against a principal debtor.[14] In the light of the Convention's purpose of facilitating the free movement of judgments and their effects, it may be that these words should be liberally interpreted to enable any person to make an application under this paragraph, if their rights are affected by a judgment given in another Contracting State and those rights are in dispute. So, in the example given by Jenard,[15] a bank faced with a negotiable instrument which has been declared void by a judgment given in another Contracting State, might itself be able to apply for a declaration that that judgment is to be recognised, in order to justify a refusal to pay on the instrument.[16]

27.08   *The dispute.* The "dispute" referred to in the second paragraph of Article 26 cannot be a dispute which is already joined in proceedings, because the procedure is *ex parte* in the first instance. The reference to a dispute is perhaps best understood as indicating the extent of the interest needed by a party to apply for relief under this paragraph.

The reference to recognition being the principal issue in the dispute is necessary to distinguish the procedure under Article 26(2) from the case where recognition is an incidental issue, which is covered by Article 26(3).

---

[13] This is one of the instances in which the Convention may require the court addressed to apply foreign law of its own motion.
[14] See para. 25.09 above.
[15] Jenard, para. A1.188 below.
[16] Collins, p. 113.

3. " . . . a decision that the judgment be recognised"

The second paragraph of Article 26 does not specifically permit **27.09** an interested party to apply for a declaration that a judgment be *not* recognised. The Jenard Report justifies this imbalance on the grounds that the simplified procedure "was evolved solely to promote the enforcement of judgments, and hence their recognition." It suggests that a party seeking to oppose recognition, if he wishes to initiate the procedure, may only do so in accordance with the internal law of the state in which recognition is in issue.[17] However, the Convention's silence on the point may not be conclusive.[18]

D. Third Paragraph: Recognition as an Incidental Issue

The purpose of the third paragraph of Article 26 is to prevent other **27.10** courts, trying proceedings principally concerned with some other issue, from having to stay those proceedings while they await the outcome of an application under the second paragraph of this Article. But if an appeal is pending against the judgment in its state of origin, the court may stay its proceedings to await the outcome of that appeal.

The third paragraph is merely a jurisdiction-conferring provision. Jurisdiction only arises under it if the incidental issue of recognition is capable of being decisive in the proceedings with which the court is principally concerned.[19] The provision does not state how the jurisdiction is to be exercised. It seems that the common provisions under Articles 46 to 49[20] would apply, requiring the party whose interests would be benefited by recognition to produce the relevant documents. The burden of proof seems not to be disturbed by this paragraph and is probably to be determined by national procedural law.[21] The court will only be permitted, though, to refuse recognition if one of the grounds of refusal in Articles 27 and 28 is present, and it seems that the court may have to decide of its own motion whether recognition is prohibited.

It may be that a decision on an incidental issue of recognition will **27.11** not be binding on a court before which recognition or enforcement is subsequently the principal issue in proceedings under the second

---

[17] Jenard, para. A1.188 below.

[18] Droz, para. 457.

[19] The French and Italian texts do not contain the requirement that the outcome of the proceedings shall depend on the determination of an incidental issue: "*Si la reconnaissance est invoquée de façon incidente . . .*"; "*si il riconoscimento è richiesto in via incidentale. . . .*"

[20] Chap. 29 below.

[21] Bülow/Böckstiegel/Linke, p. 201. The burden of proof may be shifted by the first para. of Art. 26: see para. 27.03 above.

paragraph of this Article or under Article 32.[22] In those proceedings, the court may only refuse recognition on one of the grounds stipulated in Articles 27 and 28. A court called upon to make a declaration of recognition or to issue an order for enforcement may only refuse recognition on one of the grounds specified in Articles 27 and 28[23] and it will not necessarily be absolved from considering, of its own motion if need be, whether one of those grounds exists, merely because another court has accorded (or denied) incidental recognition to the judgment.[24]

Article 27

27.12   **A judgment shall not be recognised:**

1. **if such recognition is contrary to public policy in the State in which recognition is sought;**
2. **where it was given in default of appearance, if the defendant was not duly served with the document which instituted the proceedings or with an equivalent document in sufficient time to enable him to arrange for his defence;**
3. **if the judgment is irreconcilable with a judgment given in a dispute between the same parties in the State in which recognition is sought;**
4. **if the court of the State in which the judgment was given, in order to arrive at its judgment, has decided a preliminary question concerning the status or legal capacity of natural persons, rights in property arising out of a matrimonial relationship, wills or succession in a way that conflicts with a rule of the private international law of the State in which the recognition is sought, unless the same result would have been reached by the application of the rules of private international law of that State;**
5. **if the judgment is irreconcilable with an earlier judgment given in a non-Contracting State involving the same cause of action and between the same parties, provided that this latter judgment fulfils the conditions necessary for its recognition in the State addressed.**

---

[22] *Ibid., cf.* Droz, para. 452.
[23] See also the minor grounds for refusal listed at para. 25.13 above.
[24] Schlosser, para. 189 (para. A1.485 below). It may not be easy to apply the English doctrine of issue estoppel in considering these questions: *cf.* Collins, p. 114.

Article 27(1)

A judgment shall not be recognised: 27.13

   1. if such recognition is contrary to public policy in the State in which recognition is sought;*

E. ARTICLE 27(1): PUBLIC POLICY

1. General note

A judgment given in another Contracting State should be refused   27.14
recognition on the grounds of public policy only in exceptional
cases.[25] This ground may be seen as a safety valve[26] which may be
resorted to in order to prevent the Convention being ignored.[27]
It is clear, therefore, that the concept of public policy is to be narrowly construed. The overall scope of the concept of public policy
in the context of the Convention must be defined by an independent
interpretation of the Convention and a number of matters can be
identified which either do or do not fall within the concept. These
are considered below. The detailed content of public policy in any
given state, though, must be a matter for the law of that state.[28]

A distinction is to be drawn between the judgment itself being   27.15
contrary to public policy (which is not a legitimate ground for refusing recognition) and the recognition of the judgment being contrary
to public policy (which is).[29] The former would involve the court

---

* Jenard, para. A1.190 below; Schlosser, paras. 188, 192–193; (paras. A1.484,
A1.488 below); Collins, pp. 107–108; Dashwood/Halcon/White, pp. 39–40,
148–149; Hartley, pp. 85–89; Kaye, pp. 1436–1449; Maxwell,
paras. 6.22–6.24, 6.25–6.35; Anton, paras. 8.12–8.16; Droz, paras. 482–499;
Weser, paras. 273–274; Bülow/Böckstiegel/Linke, pp. 204–207; Geimer/
Schütze, pp. 1052–1061; Kropholler, pp. 256–262; Gothot/Holleaux,
paras. 256–260, 271–273; Pocar, pp. 273–295.
[25] *Hoffman* v. *Krieg*, case 145/86, decision of February 4, 1988 (para. 21), *The Times*,
March 26, 1988, citing Jenard, para. A1.190 below; see also Bülow/Böckstiegel/
Linke, p. 205. Droz (para. 553) points out that a strict interpretation of
Art. 27(1) and the second para. of Art. 34 (para. 28.22 below) would mean that
if recognition of the judgment was not contrary to public policy, but its enforcement was, then enforcement should nonetheless be ordered. The point is
unlikely to arise in practice (except, perhaps, in the context of state immunity).
[26] Weser, para. 247.
[27] Droz, para. 488.
[28] For English public policy in the context of foreign judgments, see para. 10.28
above; Dicey and Morris, pp. 472–474 and 494–495; Maxwell, paras. 6.31 *et
seq*. In Ireland, it may be that to recognise a maintenance order ancillary to a
foreign divorce would be contrary to public policy: Schlosser, para. 193,
para. A1.488 below. This particular problem, though, may be adequately
covered by Art. 27(4), para. 27.52 below.
[29] Jenard, para. A1.190 below; Droz, para. 498; Bülow/Böckstiegel/Linke,
p. 205.

seised of the issue of recognition in reviewing the judgment as to its substance, an exercise which is prohibited by Article 29,[30] and to do so by reference to the public policy of the state of origin of the judgment, a matter which the courts of a different state are not competent to judge. The question whether the recognition of the judgment is contrary to public policy, though, is to be examined by reference to the public policy of the state in which recognition is sought[31] and for this purpose, of course, the subject-matter of the decision is relevant.[32] The time at which the public policy test is to be applied is probably the time when recognition is sought,[33] but it may be that national law applies to determine this question.[34] The decision on the public policy point ought not necessarily be conclusive as to the applicability of public policy at any other time.[35]

2. The scope of public policy: particular matters

27.16   The Convention itself states that the public policy test may not be applied to the rules relating to jurisdiction.[36] Equally, it should not be applied where any of the other grounds for refusal specifically mentioned in the Convention is present,[37] nor (it is suggested) should it be used to supplement those grounds. So, for example, the European Court has held that resort may not be had to the public policy ground when the problem is one of compatibility of a foreign judgment with a national judgment, this problem being one which must be resolved by reference to the specific provision in Article 27(3).[37a] Equally, for example, Article 27(2) allows recognition to be refused where certain procedural irregularities have occurred and it would not normally be permissible, therefore, to let public policy bar recognition in the case of other procedural irregularity.[38] On the other hand, a procedural irregularity might be so gross (such as a serious breach of the rules of natural justice)[39] that recognition and enforcement of the judgment could be refused on

---

[30] Para. 27.75 below.
[31] Bülow/Böckstiegel/Linke, p. 206.
[32] Geimer/Schütze, p. 1058.
[33] Bülow/Böckstiegel/Linke, *loc. cit.*; Geimer/Schütze, p. 1061. It may be that the objection must be raised *in limine litis: ibid.*, p. 1057.
[34] Droz, para. 499.
[35] *Ibid.*
[36] Art. 28, third para. See *Rohr S.A.* v. *Ossberger* [1981] E.C.R. 2431, *per* Advocate General Capotorti, at pp. 2441–2442.
[37] Bülow/Böckstiegel/Linke, p. 206.
[37a] *Hoffman* v. *Krieg*, case 145/86, decision of February 4, 1988 (para. 21), *The Times*, March 26, 1988: see para. 27.47 below.
[38] Droz, para. 489; Geimer/Schütze, pp. 1053–1055.
[39] English law treats breach of the rules of natural justice as a separate ground of objection: see Dicey and Morris, pp. 474–476.

the ground of public policy.[40] It may be that, even then, public policy can only be raised if the defendant has exhausted his means of objection to the judgment in the state of origin.[41]

Similarly, public policy should not be used to refuse recognition **27.17** on the ground that the court of origin applied the wrong law, either according to its own conflicts rules or according to those of the court addressed.[42] The former is contrary to Article 29, being a review of the judgment as to its substance, while the only circumstances in which the latter is permitted are those set out in Article 27(4). *A fortiori*, the mere fact that the law applied by the court of origin did not correspond with the law of the state addressed cannot found an objection of public policy.[43]

Again, public policy may not be used to justify a refusal to recognise a civil judgment delivered by a criminal court,[44] because the second paragraph of Article II of the 1968 Protocol[45] allows such a judgment to be refused in limited circumstances. This is so, even where the law of the court addressed would regard such a judgment as being delivered pursuant to the penal laws of the state of origin.[46]

Examples from decided cases

The following are examples of cases where national courts have **27.18** dismissed objections of public policy and recognised judgments given in other Contracting States. It has been held not to be contrary to German public policy to enforce an Italian judgment where the Italian court has overruled a limitation of liability clause,[47] nor where the Italian court has held an arbitration clause to be invalid;[48] and German public policy did not prevent the enforcement of a

---

[40] For this purpose, an irregularity may need to be one which, in the state addressed, cannot be waived: Geimer, "Annerkennung gerichtlicher Entscheidungen nach dem EWG-Übereinkommen von September 27, 1968," (1976) RIW/AWD p. 139.

[41] Geimer/Schütze, p. 1056.

[42] Jenard, para. A1.190 below; Droz, para. 492.

[43] *S.A. Almacoa* v. *S.A. Ets. Moteurs Cérès* Journal dr.int. 1979, p. 623, Digest D I–27.1—B5.

[44] Droz, para. 489.

[45] Para. 35.05 below.

[46] For the circumstances in which English law regards foreign law as penal, see Dicey and Morris, p. 104.

[47] Oberlandesgericht Frankfurt-am-Main, case 20 W 185, December 9, 1975, RIW/AWD—1976, p. 107, Digest D I–5.1.2—B4.

[48] Oberlandesgericht Celle, case 8 W 276/77, December 8, 1977, RIW/AWD— 1979, p. 131, Digest D I–17.1.1—B10; and, on appeal, Bundesgerichtshof, case VIII ZB 1/78, March 28, 1979, RIW/AWD—1979, p. 710, Digest D I–17.1.1— B10.

judgment which awarded the plaintiff more damages than he would have obtained from a German court.[48a] It was not contrary to Italian or German public policy to enforce a French judgment ordering an interim payment of damages,[49] even (in the German case) where the interim judgment was not yet "final" (in the sense that it could still be altered on appeal). French public policy was not held to be a sufficient reason for overriding a jurisdiction clause, despite its being contrary to provisions of French procedural law which themselves were based on public policy.[50] It has been held not to be contrary to French public policy to enforce a maintenance judgment given in Germany on the basis of a finding of paternity, even though that finding had not been based on procedural safeguards which French law would have provided in comparable circumstances;[51] and Netherlands public policy did not prevent the enforcement of a Belgian maintenance order in such a sum that the creditor was driven to claim social assistance payments in the Netherlands.[52] The fact that a Belgian judgment placed a contractual penalty on a defendant who had acted in bad faith was held not to amount to a reason of French public policy for refusing recognition.[53] It was held not to be contrary to French public policy to enforce an Italian judgment where the defendant had been precluded by Italian procedural law from raising on appeal a ground of defence which he failed, by reason of his non-appearance, to raise at first instance.[54] It has been held not to be contrary to French or Italian public policy to enforce a German default judgment which did not state the grounds on which it was given.[55] Similarly, it was held not to be contrary to French public policy to enforce a foreign judgment which did not

---

[48a] Bundesgerichtshof, case VIII 2B 14/82, [1983] RIW 695, [1984] Eur.L.Dig. 51.

[49] *Frigomat S.a.s.* v. *Carpigiani*, Foro pad. 1979, I, Col. 213, Digest D I–16.4—B1; Oberlandesgericht Celle, case 8 W 161/77, June 2, 1977, Digest D I–27.1—B1.

[50] *Mosbacher et Société Uniputz* v. *Banque Nationale de Paris*, Journal dr.int. 1980, p. 252, Digest D I–17.1.1—B12.

[51] *Theillol* v. *Office de la Jeunesse de Fribourg*, Journal dr.int. 1979, p. 383, Digest D I–27.1—B3; and, on appeal, Bull.Cass. 1980, Part I, No. 150, p. 121, Digest D I–27.1—B3n.

[52] *X* v. *Y*, Ned.Jur. 1979, No. 399, Digest D I–27.1—B7.

[53] *S.à.r.l. Ets. Morris* v. *S.A. Oudenaardse Textielfabrieken* Gaz. Palais 1979, Comm. p. 58, Digest D I–27.1—B6; and, on appeal, Bull.Cass., 1980, Part I, No. 74, Digest D I–27.1—B6n.

[54] *Cozzi* v. *Dame Capurro et autres*, Bull.Cass., 1979, Part I, No. 286, p. 233, Digest D I–27.1—B6n.

[55] *Société FIR* v. *Héritiers Baas*, Rev. critique 1980, p. 121, Digest D I–27.2—B12; *Thiesen K.G.* v. *Bertella*, Riv.dir.int.priv.proc. 1976, p. 583, Digest D I–34—B2.

state the grounds on which it was given, if evidence was produced which established what those grounds were.[56]

Cases in which judgments have been refused recognition in other Contracting States on the grounds of public policy include the following: where enforcement in Germany against a shipowner of an Italian judgment given against the shipowner's agent was held to be contrary to German public policy;[57] where French public policy was infringed by a Belgian judgment not stating the grounds on which it was given (in the absence of any documents enabling the court to satisfy itself that the requirements as to public policy had not been infringed);[58] and where Italian public policy was held to have been infringed by a French decision requiring an Italian party to fulfil a distributorship agreement which had not been authorised under Italian exchange control requirements.[59]

27.19

3. Fraud

In principle, fraud can constitute a reason for refusing recognition of a foreign judgment on the ground of public policy,[60] but refusal of recognition will not be automatic,[61] because means of redress are available in most Contracting States—even after the expiry of the normal time for appeal—against a judgment obtained by fraud. The Schlosser Report says:

27.20

> "A court in the State addressed must always, therefore, ask itself whether a breach of its public policy still exists in view of the fact that proceedings for redress can be, or could have been, lodged in the courts of the State of origin against the judgment allegedly obtained by fraud."[62]

---

[56] *Dame Py* v. *Dame Diamedo*, Rev. critique 1981, p. 113, Digest D I–27.1—B9.
[57] Landgericht Hamburg, case 5 O 355/77, December 27, 1977, Riv.dir.int. priv.-proc. 1978, p. 422, Digest D I–27.1—B2.
[58] *Vanclef* v. *Société TTI Trans Traide International*, Bull.Cass., 1978, Part I, No. 191, p. 154, Digest D I–27.1—B4. It is submitted that this decision is arguably too liberal an application of Article 27(1).
[59] *Malanca Motori S.p.A.* v. *Société des Etablissements B. Savoye S.A.*, Guirisprudenzia commerciale 1984, II, p. 76. This case is arguably contrary to Art. 29 and is criticised by Abbatescianni in "Recognition of English Judgments in Italy: The Terruzzi Case," (1985) N.L.J. 179. That article refers to *Wilson, Smithett & Cope Ltd.* v. *Terruzzi* [1976] Q.B. 703, which was refused recognition in Italy on similar grounds, but before the 1968 Convention came into effect: Riv. dir.int.priv.proc. 1982, p. 107.
[60] In English law, fraud is regarded as a separate ground for refusing recognition: Dicey and Morris, pp. 467–471.
[61] Bundesgerichtshof, case VIII ZB 8/79, May 16, 1979, N.J.W. 1980, p. 528, [1979] E.C.C. 321, Digest D I–34—B3; *Sertom s.n.c.* v. *Fecmo s.r.l.* Riv.dir. int.priv.proc. 1982, p. 359, Digest D I–37—B1.
[62] Schlosser, para. 192 (para. A1.488 below).

In such a case, it has been suggested,[63] the court which is seised of the issue of recognition should stay its proceedings and encourage the party complaining of fraud to take the point in the state of origin. Only if no other means of redress against the fraud is available, should public policy be invoked.

Similarly, if the allegation of fraud was, or could have been, made in the original proceedings it ought not to be used as a ground to refuse recognition in the other Contracting States.[64] If it was in fact made, and overruled, in the original proceedings, Article 29 will prevent a review of that decision.

Article 27(2)

27.21   **[A judgment shall not be recognised:]**

2. where it was given in default of appearance, if the defendant was not duly served with the document which instituted the proceedings or with an equivalent document in sufficient time to enable him to arrange for his defence;*†

F. ARTICLE 27(2): DEFAULT JUDGMENTS

1. General note

27.22   The jurisdictional provisions of the Convention contain safeguards protecting defendants from proceedings being decided against them without their knowledge.[65] It is because of this protection that the recognition and enforcement provisions of Title III of

---

[63] Droz, paras. 496–497; Bülow/Böckstiegel/Linke, p. 206.

[64] Droz, paras. 493–495.

* Jenard, para. A1.191–A1.192 below; Schlosser, para. 194 (para. A1.489 below); Collins, pp. 108–110; Dashwood/Halcon/White, pp. 40–41, 149–154; Hartley, pp. 89–92; Kaye, pp. 1449–1482; Maxwell, paras. 6.36–6.38; Anton, paras. 8.17–8.18; Droz, paras. 482, 500–508; Weser, paras. 273, 275–276; Bülow/Böckstiegel/Linke, pp. 204–205, 207–212; Geimer/Schütze, pp. 1071–1095; Kropholler, pp. 262–270; Gothot/Holleaux, paras. 261–273; Pocar, pp. 273–295.

† The words "or with an equivalent document" in this paragraph were added by Art. 13(1) of the 1978 Convention to accommodate the English practice (since changed) of serving notice of the writ outside the jurisdiction, rather than the writ itself.

[65] Art. 20, para. 22.11 above. It is knowledge of the proceedings which is relevant, not their precise content. So, where a defendant in criminal proceedings had a civil order for payment made against him in default of appearance, without his knowing that a civil claim was going to be made, a court in the Netherlands held that that was no bar to the enforcement of the civil order: *Centrale Suikermaatschaappij B.V. and another* v. *M. De Deugd*, Ned.Jur. 1983, No. 308, Digest D I–27.2—B17; but a court in Germany, by contrast, decided that the enforcement of the civil order was precluded in those circumstances: Landgericht Münster, case 11 O 20/82, April 5, 1982. See also the special provisions in Art. II of the 1968 Protocol, para. 35.05 below, concerning civil default judgments given in criminal proceedings.

the Convention are able to be so liberal.[66] That protection is redoubled by Article 27(2), though, where an application is made to the court of another Contracting State for the recognition or enforcement of a default judgment.[67] The court in which recognition or enforcement is sought must be satisfied that the defendant was duly served with the document instituting the proceedings and that, as a matter of fact, he had sufficient time to take the steps necessary to prevent a default judgment being obtained against him. That is so, even where service was duly effected within the territorial jurisdiction of the court which gave the judgment or within the same state as that court.[68]

The European Court of Justice has said of this provision that:

> " . . . for the sole purpose of safeguarding the rights of the defendant, [Article 27(2)] provides for refusal of recognition and, read together with Article 34, for refusal of enforcement, in exceptional cases where the guarantees contained in the law of the State in which the judgment was given and in the Convention itself are insufficient to ensure that the defendant has an opportunity of arranging for his defence before the court in which judgment was given."[69]

As the European Court pointed out, the provision imposes a double requirement namely that, first, the defendant must have been duly served and, secondly, service must have been effected in sufficient time to enable the defendant to arrange for his defence.[70] Each of these requirements is discussed below.

Differences between Articles 20 and 27(2)

There are a number of material differences between the protection afforded by, on one hand, the second and third paragraphs of Article 20[71] and, on the other hand, Article 27(2):   **27.23**

   (1) For the purposes of this provision, unlike Article 20, it is necessary that the defendant should actually have been served;[72]

   (2) Article 20 affords protection only to a defendant domiciled in a Contracting State other than that in which the pro-

---

[66] See chap. 25 above.

[67] Jenard, para. A1.191 below.

[68] *Debaecker and Plouvier* v. *Bouwman*, [1985] E.C.R. 1779. The case is discussed at paras. 27.24 *et seq.* below.

[69] *Klomps* v. *Michel* [1981] E.C.R. 1593, at p. 1605 (para. 7). The facts are summarised at para. 27.29 below.

[70] *Ibid.*, at p. 1607 (para. 15).

[71] The third para. applies Art. 15 of the Hague Convention of November 15, 1965 on the Service Abroad of Judicial and Extrajudicial Documents in Civil and Commercial Matters (para. A2.00 below): see paras. 22.21 *et seq.* above.

[72] *Contra*, Bülow/Böckstiegel/Linke, p. 211: see paras. 27.33 *et seq.* below.

ceedings are brought,[73] whereas Article 27(2) applies wherever the defendant is domiciled;[74]

(3) Whether the document instituting the proceedings has been served is, in the context of the second paragraph of Article 20, probably to be decided by reference to an independent interpretation of the Convention,[75] whereas in the context of Article 27(2), which requires that the process be "duly" served, the national law of the state where the proceedings are brought is to be applied.[76]

2. Substituted service

27.24   *The Debaecker decision.* Article 27(2) is particularly relevant in the case of default judgments entered after the substituted service of the defendant. This aspect was stressed by the European Court in *Debaecker & Plouvier* v. *Bouwman.*[77] The plaintiffs (who were domiciled in Monaco) let industrial premises in Antwerp to the defendant for a term of nine years and the defendant established his residence there. After less than a year, the defendant left the premises, without notice and without leaving a forwarding address. Almost immediately, the plaintiffs brought proceedings and, because the defendant had apparently disappeared, substituted service was effected on him at the local police station.[78] Before the date fixed for the hearing, the defendant wrote to the plaintiff, terminating the tenancy and giving a new postal address in another part of Belgium. The plaintiffs made no attempt to notify the defendant of the hearing and obtained a default judgment against him which they then sought to enforce against his assets in the Netherlands.

27.25   The question whether, in the circumstances, Article 27(2) required that the judgment should be refused recognition in the Netherlands reached the *Hoge Raad*, which referred a number of questions to the European Court, one of which was whether Article 27(2) was inapplicable if service was effected within a period prescribed by the court of the state in which the judgment was given and/or the defendant resided in that state. Having stated that

---

[73] See para. 22.13 above.

[74] *Cf.* Weser, para. 275, who suggests that Art. 27(2) applies *only* if the defendant is domiciled in the state where the proceedings are brought or in a non-Contracting State, and that Art. 27(2) may not be invoked to re-open the question of the protection of the defendant's rights.

[75] Para. 22.19 above.

[76] See para. 27.31 below.

[77] [1985] E.C.R. 1779.

[78] Art. 37 of the Belgian Judicial Code. See para. 48.38 below.

Article 27(2) did not lay down any condition as regards the defendant's place of residence,[79] the European Court continued:

"That provision takes account of the fact that certain Contracting States make provision for the fictitious service of process where the defendant has no known place of residence. The effects that are deemed to follow from such fictitious service vary and the probability of the defendant's actually being informed of service, so as to give him sufficient time to prepare his defence, may vary considerably, depending on the type of fictitious service provided for in each legal system.

For that reason Article 27(2) must be interpreted as being intended to protect the right of a defendant to defend himself when recognition of a judgment given in default in another Contracting State is sought, even if the rules on service laid down in that Contracting State were complied with."[80]

The other questions referred by the European Court concerned the exceptional circumstances in which service would be regarded as not having occurred in sufficient time to enable the defendant to arrange his defence and the effect of the parties' conduct. These questions are considered below.[81]

3. " . . . given in default of appearance . . . "

Article 27(2) applies only to default judgments. If the defendant **27.26**
has actually appeared, even if he did not have enough time to prepare his defence, recognition may not be refused on this ground.[82]

It has been suggested[83] that Article 27(2) applies not only to default judgments but also to other orders made against a party without that party having participated in the proceedings—such as interlocutory orders made *ex parte*. The argument was adopted by the United Kingdom government in its submissions to the European Court of Justice in *Denilauler* v. *Couchet Frères*,[84] but in the event the Court approached the questions raised by that case in a different way.

The Denilauler decision. Couchet Frères were a transport undertaking based in France, who had carried goods for Denilauler, a German undertaking. Couchet sued Denilauler in France for non-

---

[79] [1985] E.C.R. 1779, at p. 1796 (para. 10).
[80] *Ibid.*, at pp. 1796–1797 (paras. 11 and 12).
[81] Paras. 27.36 *et seq.* below.
[82] Droz, para. 501; Bülow/Böckstiegel/Linke, p. 209.
[83] Bülow/Böckstiegel/Linke, p. 208.
[84] [1980] E.C.R. 1553, at p. 1558. The case is also discussed in the context of interlocutory orders in the commentary on Art. 24: para. 24.10 above, and, in the context of the scope of the recognition and enforcement provisions generally, at para. 25.19 above.

payment of invoices and obtained *ex parte* an order authorising them to have Denilauler's bank account in Frankfurt attached as security for the claim. They applied to the German court for an order for enforcement of the French *ex parte* order, arguing successfully that they did not need first to serve Denilauler.[85] The account was duly frozen. Denilauler appealed to the *Oberlandesgericht* in Frankfurt and placed reliance, *inter alia*, on Article 27(2), saying that the application to the French court had not been served on him. That court referred a number of questions to the European Court, including the question whether Article 27(2) applied to proceedings in which provisional protective measures were taken without out the opposite party being heard.

27.27   Referring to Articles 27(2) and 46(2), the Court said that they were clearly not designed to apply,

> "to judgments which, under the national law of a Contracting State, are intended to be delivered in the absence of the party against whom they are directed and to be enforced without prior service on him. It is apparent . . . that these provisions are intended to refer to proceedings in which in principle both parties participate but in which the court is nevertheless empowered to give judgment if the defendant, although duly summoned, does not appear."[86]

The Court went on to consider whether this type of *ex parte* order fell within the scope of Title III and, as has already been observed, concluded that it did not.[87] The enforcement of an interim order in a state other than that in which it was granted is conditional upon the person against whom the order was made having had an opportunity to oppose the order. If it was originally made *ex parte*, it can only be enforced in the other Contracting States if the defendant has since had the chance to apply for the order to be revoked or discharged. It would seem to follow by analogy with Article 27(2) that the notice must have been given in sufficient time to enable the defendant to prepare his opposition.[88]

4. " . . . the document which instituted the proceedings or an equivalent document . . . "

27.28   Article 27(2) applies only to judgments given in default of appearance and not to other default judgments. The requirements of this provision as to service need only have been met in relation to

---

[85] The Landgericht Hamburg had previously granted an order for the enforcement of an *ex parte* Belgian order to the same effect: case 5 O 181/76, March 9, 1977, Digest D I–27.2—B2.

[86] [1980] E.C.R. 1553, at p. 1568 (para. 8).

[87] See para. 25.19 above, where the relevant passage, at p. 1569 (para. 13), is quoted.

[88] As to the effect of such orders on third parties, see para. 25.27 above.

the document which instituted the proceedings "or an equivalent document."[89] The nature of the document is not defined by the Convention, and will take different forms according to the various procedures provided for in the laws of the different Contracting States.[90] The Convention is, however, to be read as imposing some uniform requirements as to the nature of the document.[91]

The Klomps v. *Michel decision.* The European Court of Justice has **27.29** considered these requirements, in the context of the German *Mahn-verfahren* procedure,[92] in the case of *Klomps* v. *Michel*.[93] Under that procedure, if a formal demand (*Zahlungsbefehl*) for a debt or liqui-dated sum is served on a debtor, and the debtor does not raise an objection (*Widerspruch*) within a limited period (in this case, three days), the creditor can obtain an order for payment (*Vollstreckungs-befehl*) which, after it too has been served, can be enforced.[93a] The procedure allowed the debtor a further period in which to object to the order, during which time the order remains provisionally enforceable.

Mr. Michel served a *Zahlungsbefehl* on Mr. Klomps, for payment

---

[89] See para. 27.12, n. † above.
[90] Notification by a lawyer to his client of his intention to have his bill of costs (pay-able by the client) taxed may amount to the document instituting the taxation: *Desmazières de Séchelles* v. *Vloeberghs*, Tribunal de Première Instance, Brussels, September 17, 1980, Digest D I–25.1—B1. But cf. *Arnoux* v. *Van Royen*, Tri-bunal de Première Instance, Tournai, October 6, 1980, Digest D I–25.1—B1n.; *P.W. Kallen GmbH & Co. K.G. and others* v. *Olbertz*, Arrondissementsrecht-bank, Almelo (Netherlands), November 25, 1977, Digest D I–27.2—B7.
[91] Art. 27(2) has been held not to impose a requirement that the document should be in the language of the addressee, or translated into that language: *Theillol* v. *Office de la Jeunesse de Fribourg*, Journal dr.int. 1979, p. 383, Digest D I–27.1—B3; *Vanclef* v. *Société TTI Trans Traide International*, Bull.Cass., 1978, I No. 191, p. 154, Digest D I–27.1—B4; *Calzaturificio LEM di Medori e Giaco-mozzi* v. *Petra Shoe*, Corte d'Appello, Ancona, July 17, 1978, Digest D I–27.2—B9. However, the Oberlandesgericht Düsseldorf has held, on one hand, that a requirement that the document be translated may be deduced from the require-ment that the document be "duly" served (see paras. 27.31 *et seq.* below), coupled with the requirements of the applicable international convention: case 19 W 30/77, April 4, 1978, RIW/AWD—1979, p. 570, Digest D I–27.2—B8; and, on the other hand, that where the document is to be served in the state of the court, there is no such requirement: case 3 W 319/84, October 19, 1984, [1986] E.C.C. 472. A Dutch court has refused to recognise a Belgian civil judg-ment given in criminal proceedings, on the ground that the summons did not indicate that a civil claim might be made: *Gemeente Nemikshem* v. *Holleman* Arrondissementsrechtbank, 's-Hertogenbosch, August 3, 1984, Ned.Jur. 1985, 1463, [1986] Eur.L.Dig. 156.
[92] See para. 51.61 below.
[93] [1981] E.C.R. 1593.
[93a] A *Zahlungsbefehl* is now called a *Mahnbescheid* and a *Vollstreckungsbefehl* is now called a *Vollstreckungsbescheid*.

of agency fees in connection with the purchase of land in Germany. Service was not effected personally, but was in a form which, according to German law, was valid if the defendant was domiciled in Germany. He raised no objection, and the order became final and conclusive between the parties. Klomps later sought to have the order set aside on the ground that he was not domiciled[94] in Germany at the material time, but the German court considered the objection ill-founded and dismissed it as being made out of time. Michel then sought to enforce the order in the Netherlands, and Klomps sought unsuccessfully to oppose the application. He appealed to the *Hoge Raad*, which referred a number of questions to the European Court of Justice.

27.30   One of the questions referred to the European Court concerned the interpretation of the words "the document which instituted the proceedings," and whether either a *Zahlungsbefehl* or a *Vollstreckungsbefehl* fell within those words. The Court held that the former did, while the latter did not:

> " . . . Article 27, point 2, is intended to ensure that a judgment is not recognised or enforced under the Convention if the defendant has not had an opportunity of defending himself before the court first seised. It follows that a measure, such as the order for payment [*Zahlungsbefehl*] in German law, service of which on the defendant enables the plaintiff, where no objection to the order is made, to obtain a decision which is enforceable under the Convention, must be duly served on the defendant in sufficient time to enable him to arrange for his defence and accordingly that such a measure must be understood as being covered by the words 'the document which instituted the proceedings' in Article 27, point 2. On the other hand a decision, such as the enforcement order [*Vollstreckungsbefehl*] in German law, which is issued following service of an order for payment and which is in itself enforceable under the Convention is not covered by those words even though the lodging of an objection against the enforcement order, like the objection to the order for payment, transforms the procedure into adversary proceedings."[95]

The European Court went on to rule that:

> "The words 'the document which instituted the proceedings' cover any document . . . service of which enables the plaintiff, under the law of the State of the court in which the judgment was given to

---

[94] The English language version of the report of the case in the European Court of Justice confusingly uses the term "habitual residence," instead of "domicile."
[95] [1981] E.C.R. 1593, at pp. 1605–1606 (para. 8).

obtain, in default of appropriate action taken by the defendant, a decision capable of being recognised and enforced under the provisions of the Convention."[96]

5. Due service

The defendant must have been "duly" served.[96a] What constitutes due service is to be decided by reference to the national procedural law of the court which delivered the judgment.[97] In this respect, though, the court of another Contracting State, in which recognition or enforcement is sought, is not bound by the findings of fact or law of the court of origin and must itself consider the application of the law of that other court.[98] This applies, even if service takes place outside the territorial jurisdiction of that court.[99] The national law of the court of origin includes any applicable international conventions on service abroad of judicial process (including Art. IV of the 1968 Protocol).[1]

    27.31

For example, it has been held that where service occurred in Germany of the document instituting proceedings in another Contracting State, but the service did not comply with the procedural requirements of the relevant international convention,[2] recognition

    27.32

---

[96] *Ibid.*, at p. 1611.

[96a] See also two cases pending before the European Court at the time of writing: *Carl Schilling, Kirchheimer Muschelkalksteinwerke, Natursteinbetriebe* v. *Merbes Sprimont Travaux*, case 36/88, and *Lancray* v. *Peters and Sickert*, case 305/88.

[97] *Klomps* v. *Michel* [1981] E.C.R. 1593, at p. 1607 (para. 15); see also Oberlandesgericht Düsseldorf, case 3 W 319/84, October 19, 1984, [1986] E.C.C. 472. Jenard, para. A1.191 below; Droz, para. 503; Bülow/Böckstiegel/Linke, p. 202. Droz (para. 504) sees this as a limited departure from the principle that a court should not examine the foreign court's application of its own law, but regards it as permissible because the provision is solely concerned with judgments in default, where the judgment did not result from a procedure *inter partes*.

[98] *Pendy Plastic Products* v. *Pluspunkt* [1982] E.C.R. 2723, discussed at para. 27.42 below. For an example of a court in one Contracting State considering (and applying) the procedural law of another Contracting State, see *Pilny* v. *Vlk*, Arrondissementsrechtbank, Rotterdam, May 7, 1982, Digest D I–27.2—B20; *N.V. Eternit* v. *Kusters*, Gerechtshof, 's-Hertogenbosch, October 16, 1980, Ned.Jur, 1983, p. 958, [1984] Eur.L.Dig. 182; *Trans-Atlantica S.p.A.* v. *Vertom Shipping & Dredging Corp B.V.*, Corte d'Appello, February 20, 1982, [1984] Il Diritto Marittimo 98, [1984] Eur. L.Dig. 393.

[99] Bülow/Böckstiegel/Linke, p. 202.

[1] Para. 35.17 below. The provisions as to service in the national law of each of the Contracting States are summarised in chaps. 48 to 58 below, at para. 38. See the next note.

[2] The Hague Convention on Civil Procedure of March 1, 1954, the provisions of which relating to service have now been replaced, so far as Contracting States to the present Convention are concerned, by the Hague Convention of November 15, 1965 on Service Abroad of Judicial and Extra Judicial Documents: see

of the subsequent default judgment should be refused[3] and the defect could not be overcome merely because the defendant in fact received the document.[4] Similarly, if the decision as to whether service was duly effected depends on a decision as to whether the defendant was domiciled in the state where the proceedings are brought, that question must also be answered by the internal law of that state.[5]

27.33   *Absence of due service.* If the defendant has not been duly served, it is probable that the default judgment must automatically be refused recognition. Two points require consideration.

First, the question arises whether the recognising court can stay its proceedings to give the defendant an opportunity of applying to the court of origin to set aside the default judgment. The first paragraph of Article 48[6] allows the recognising court to stay its proceedings for a limited period, to enable the party applying for recognition to produce evidence of service, but with that exception, it seems that the court may not grant a stay. This is because the first paragraph of Article 34[7] requires the court to give its decision on the application "without delay." Moreover, it can be argued[8] that because the Convention specifically envisages a general stay of the recognition proceedings in the case of an appeal being lodged in the state of origin,[9] a general stay ought not to be granted in other circumstances.

27.34   It might appear that to deny the recognising court an opportunity in these circumstances to grant a general stay, while allowing it in the case of alleged fraud,[10] is contradictory. The two cases are not analogous. Under both Articles 27(1) and 27(2), the court is required to consider whether the ground for refusing recognition

---

paras. 4.30 *et seq.* above and A2.03 *et seq.* below. See also bilateral conventions discussed at paras. 4.34 to 4.36 above and listed at para. A2.01 below.

[3] Oberlandesgericht Stuttgart, Case No. 8 W 196/77, August 16, 1977, Digest D I–27.2—B4; Oberlandesgericht Hamm, Case No. 20 W 29/78, March 7, 1979, MDR 1979, p. 680, Digest D I–27.2—B11; Oberlandesgericht Hamm, Case No. 20 W 14/79, September 10, 1979, Digest D I–27.2—B14. See also *Brähmer* v. *Louer-van Loon*, President of the Arrondissementsrechtbank Breda, [1986] E.C.C. 178; and the cases cited at Digest D I–27.2—B4n.

[4] Oberlandesgericht Hamm, case 20 W 14/79, September 10, 1979, Digest D I–27.2—B14.

[5] Art. 52 first para., para. 31.01 below; *Klomps* v. *Michel* [1981] E.C.R. 1593, at p. 1610 (para. 24).

[6] Para. 29.20 below.

[7] Para. 28.22 below.

[8] Bülow/Böckstiegel/Linke, p. 210.

[9] Art. 30, para. 27.78 below.

[10] Para. 27.20 above.

exists. Here, in the absence of due service, it plainly does. In the case of fraud, on the other hand, the public policy ground will only exist at all if the remedies in the state of origin have been exhausted.

The decision in *Klomps* v. *Michel* does not answer the question of whether the court addressed can grant a stay to enable the defendant to apply to have the default judgment set aside, but it does deal with the similar point which arose in that case.[11] Having emphasised that Article 27(2) is addressed only to the court before which proceedings have been brought for recognition or enforcement of the judgment in another Contracting State, the European Court continued:

> " . . . Article 27, point 2, remains applicable where the defendant has lodged an objection against the decision given in default and a court of the State in which the judgment was given has held the objection to be inadmissible on the ground that the time for lodging an objection has expired."[12]

Article 27(2) probably also applies where the defendant has had the opportunity to apply to the court of origin to set aside the default judgment, but has not availed himself of that opportunity;[13] but the point is not free from doubt.[14]

Secondly, it has been suggested[15] that defective service need not necessarily lead to a refusal of recognition if the defendant had actual knowledge of the proceedings in sufficient time to enable him to prepare his defence. The suggestion is supported by reference to the protective purpose of the provision, but is contrary to the clear words of Article 27(2).[16] It remains to be seen whether the European Court would be prepared to accept it.[16a]

27.35

---

[11] Para. 27.29 above.

[12] [1981] E.C.R. 1593, at p. 1607 (para. 13).

[13] The Oberlandesgericht Karlsruhe, inclined to this view in case 6 W 82/78, October 18, 1978, but referred the following question to the European Court: "In the recognition procedure under Art. 27 . . . is a defendant debarred from objecting that he was not served in sufficient time with the document which initiated the proceedings, if notice of the pending action was served on him later and he failed to take any procedural steps in his defence?". The case was settled, however, and the European Court (case 254/78) deleted it from the register: Digest D I–27.2—B4n.2.

[14] *Société Sheby* v. *Société Canadian Pacific Steamship Ltd.*, Cour d'Appel Paris, February 28, 1978, (1978) European Transport Law, p. 458, Digest D I–27.2–B10.

[15] Bülow/Böckstiegel/Linke, p. 211.

[16] It is also contrary to the decisions of national courts: see the cases cited at para. 27.31, n. 3 above.

[16a] See the cases cited at para. 27.31, n. 96a above.

6. Timely service

27.36   The recognising court must decide, purely as a question of fact, whether due service was effected in sufficient time to enable the defendant to prepare his defence. In the absence of exceptional circumstances, though, the court in which enforcement is sought may usually confine itself to deciding whether the period of time after the date of due service was sufficient to enable the defendant to prepare his defence,[17] but exceptional circumstances arising even after the service has been effected may be taken into account, including circumstances arising by reason of the parties' conduct.[18] As happened in *Klomps* v. *Michel*,[19] a preliminary question may sometimes arise, as to what is it that the defendant must have sufficient time to do—in other words, at what point does the period of time referred to in Article 27(2) come to an end?

27.37   In *Klomps* v. *Michel* the question arose as to whether the Dutch court should look at the time between service and the issue of the (provisionally enforceable) order for payment, or the longer period between the initial service and the last date on which the defendant could object to the order for payment. The European Court ruled that it was the former:

> "In order to determine whether the defendant has been enabled to arrange for his defence as required by Article 27, point 2, the court in which enforcement is sought must take account only of the time, such as that allowed under German law for submitting an objection [*Widerspruch*] to the order for payment, available to the defendant for the purposes of preventing the issue of a judgment in default which is enforceable under the Convention."[20]

27.38   *Timely service is a question of fact.* The question whether due service was effected in sufficient time for the defendant to arrange for his defence is a question of fact for the recognising court[21] and not a question of whether the time limits set by the national law of the state of origin have been complied with[22] (including those appli-

---

[17] *Klomps* v. *Michel* [1981] E.C.R. 1593, at p. 1608 (para. 19), discussed below.

[18] *Debaecker and Plouvier* v. *Bouwman*, [1985] E.C.R. 1779. See para. 27.24 above.

[19] [1981] E.C.R. 1593.

[20] *Ibid.*, p. 1611.

[21] Droz, para. 506. See, for example, *Capezzone* v. *Durull*, Giur.it. 1980, I, 2, col. 17, Digest D I–27.2—B13.

[22] Bülow/Böckstiegel/Linke, p. 211; *Ditta Pollo Guisy S.N.C.* v. *Soc. Rousseau et Vergnaud*, Corte d'Appello, Turin, March 11, 1977, Digest D I–27.2—B3, upheld by the Corte di Cassazione, November 23, 1979, Foro it. 1980, I, col. 2249, Digest D I–27.2—B3n.; *S.p.a. Terraneo* v. *Fernlast Speditionsgesellschaft mbH*, Corte d'Appello, Milan, September 27, 1977, Digest D I–27.2—B6; *Chim-Metal S.n.l.* v. *Anilina S.A.*, Corte d'Appello Milan, March 27, 1981, Riv.dir.int.priv.proc. 1981, p. 951, Digest D I–27.2—B16.

cable under international conventions), nor whether the time limits which its own law would have imposed in comparable circumstances have been complied with.[23] These points were stressed by the European Court in *Debaecker & Plouvier* v. *Bouwman*:

> " . . . the question whether service was effected in sufficient time is a question of fact and therefore cannot be determined on the basis of the domestic law of the adjudicating court or on the basis of the domestic law of the court in which enforcement is sought."[24]

The question of timely service is an entirely separate question from the question of whether service was duly effected. Even if a question has been made in separate proceedings *inter partes* in the state of origin, that service was duly effected, the court in the second state is not absolved from its duty to examine the purely factual question of whether the defendant had sufficient time to arrange for his defence.[25]

The court in which recognition or enforcement is sought must take account of its own motion of such facts as are apparent to it, but need not conduct an investigation into the matter.[26] All the circumstances relevant to the time necessary for the defendant to arrange for his defence should be taken into account.[27] These

---

[23] Bülow/Böskstiegel/Linke, p. 211; also, *S.à.r.l. Ets. Morris* v. *S.A. Oudenaardse Textielfabrieken*, Bull.Cass. 1980, I, No. 74, Digest D I–27.1–B6n.

[24] [1985] E.C.R. 1779, at p. 1800 (para. 27).

[25] *Klomps* v. *Michel* [1981] ECR 1593, at p. 1607 (para. 15); Bundesgerichtshof, case IX 2B 38/85, January 23, 1986, [1987] E.C.C. 276.

[26] See para. 27.04 above. *Wagner* v. *Tettweiler*, Cour de Cassation (France), November 9, 1983, [1985] E.C.C. 258; Oberlandesgericht Düsseldorf, cases 3 W 287 and 290/84, December 13, 1984, [1986] E.C.C. 478. In the latter case it was held that due service of the defendant in sufficient time to enable him to prepare for his defence could be assumed by the court unless he proved otherwise, except that where there was evidence suggesting that service had not been duly and timeously effected, it was for the plaintiff to prove otherwise.

[27] See para. 22.20 above, for some examples of relevant matters. The following are examples of decisions made by national courts on this question:
   (i) Two days notice, by telegram, to a defendant resident in the Netherlands was insufficient for him to present his defence at a site inspection of hunting grounds in Belgium alleged to have been damaged by (wild) rabbits for which he was responsible: *De Jong* v. *Huybrechts*, Ned.Jur. 1978, No. 28, Digest D I–27.2—B1.
   (ii) 35 days was enough time for an Italian company to arrange its defence to French proceedings, where the Italian company's place of business was 600 kilometres away from the court and the company was familiar with the court's practice: *Ditta Pollo Guisy S.N.C.* v. *Soc. Rousseau et Vergnaud*, above (n. 22).
   (iii) A month was enough time where the defendant was based in Milan and the court was in northern Germany (Braunschweig): *S.p.a. Terraneo* v. *Fernlast Speditionsgesellschaft mbH*, above (n. 22).
   (iv) 25 days was insufficient where the defendant was based in Milan and the

points were considered by the European Court in *Klomps* v. *Michel* in these terms:

" . . . it must be stated first of all that Article 27, point 2, does not require proof that the document which instituted the proceedings was actually brought to the knowledge of the defendant. Having regard to the exceptional nature of the grounds for refusing enforcement and to

---

court was in southern Germany (Stuttgart), because the period ran during August, when the machinery of justice was not in normal operation and the defendant's business was closed, but it would have been sufficient at other times of year: *Soc. Ingg. S & Agostino Belotti S.r.l.* v. *Veeder Root GmbH*, Corte d'Appello, Milan, September 28, 1976, Digest D I–27.2—B6n.

(v) 41 days was sufficient for a defendant in Italy to prepare his defence to proceedings in Belgium, even though the proceedings had been served in a foreign language: *Calzaturificio LEM di Medori e Giacomozzi* v. *Petra Shoe*, Corte d'Appello, Ancona, July 17, 1978, Digest D I–27.2—B9. In similar circumstances, though, where the document instituting Belgian proceedings was served in Italy, the Corte d'Appello, Milan, has held that 14 days was insufficient: *Officina Construzioni Meccaniche* v. *Ets. Jean Ivens S.A.*, September 29, 1978, Digest D I–27.2—B9n.1., and, even where no issue arose as to the translation of the document, seven days was also insufficient: *Standers & Zoon* v. *Leguti*, Riv.dir.int.priv.proc. 1980, p. 644, but, in the absence of any special difficulties, the same court held that 22 days was sufficient: *Chim-Metal S.n.l.* v. *Anilina S.A.*, above (n. 22), and, in the case of French proceedings, that 50 days was sufficient: *Ruffini* v. *Fornano*, Riv.dir.int.priv.proc. 1981, p. 758, [1981] E.C.C. 541.

(vi) 13 days was not enough to enable a defendant in Germany to prepare its defence to Belgian proceedings served in Dutch, especially as the language was so archaic that, even in translation, it was not easily intelligible: Oberlandesgericht Hamm, case 20 W 29/78, March 7, 1979, MDR 1979, p. 680, Digest D I–27.2—B11. The Bundesgerichtshof also held 13 days to be insufficient in another case involving the service of Belgian proceedings on a defendant in Germany: case IX ZB 38/85, January 23, 1986, RIW/AWD, 1986, p. 302.

(vii) 19 days was held to be ample time for a defendant to prepare his defence where he was served in the Netherlands with the document instituting proceedings in a Belgian court only 25 kilometres away: *Clemens* v. *van de Laar* Gerechtshof, 's-Hertogenbosch, March 4, 1982, Digest D I–27.2—B18.

(viii) 10 days was enough time for a company in France to prepare its defence to proceedings in the Netherlands: *Société Française de Couvoirs "Sofraco"* v. *Soc. Pluimvee Export Coolen B.V.*, Bull.Cass. 1977, I, no. 401, Digest D I–27.3—B1.

(ix) Where notice was received by a defendant through diplomatic channels on the day after the date stated therein as the date for the hearing, but where the proceedings had in fact been adjourned and heard three months later, it was held that the defendant had had enough time to prepare for his defence, even though he had not sought to take any steps in the proceedings or to have judgment set aside: *Rosco B.V.* v. *S.à.r.l. Fraisgel* Tribunal de Grande Instance, Paris, November 2, 1984, [1986] E.C.C. 175.

the fact that the laws of the Contracting States on the service of court documents, like the international conventions on this subject, have as their objective the safeguarding of the interests of defendants, the court in which enforcement is sought is ordinarily justified in considering that, following due service, the defendant is able to take steps to defend his interests as soon as the document has been served on him at his habitual residence[28] or elsewhere. As a general rule the court in which enforcement is sought may accordingly confine its examination to ascertaining whether the period reckoned from the date on which service was duly effected allowed the defendant sufficient time to arrange for his defence. Nevertheless the court must consider whether, in a particular case, there are exceptional circumstances which warrant the conclusion that, although service was duly effected, it was, however, inadequate for the purposes of enabling the defendant to take steps to arrange for his defence and, accordingly, could not cause the time stipulated by Article 27, point 2, to begin to run.

In considering whether it is confronted with such a case the court in which enforcement is sought may take account of all the circumstances of the case in point, including the means employed for effecting service, the relations between the plaintiff and the defendant or the nature of the steps which had to be taken in order to prevent judgment from being given in default. If, for example, the dispute concerns commercial relations and if the document which instituted the proceedings was served at an address at which the defendant carried on his business activities the mere fact that the defendant was absent at the time of service should not normally prevent him from arranging his defence, above all if the action necessary to avoid a judgment in default may be taken informally and even by a representative.[29],[30]

Matters arising after service. The question of what particular circumstances could be taken into account by the court in which enforcement was sought came before the European Court again in *Debaecker & Plouvier* v. *Bouwman*.[31] In particular, the *Hoge Raad* had raised the question whether the court could take into account only those matters which existed at the time of service and which the plaintiff could take into consideration at that time. The European Court pointed out that,

> "if the circumstances to be taken into account were confined to those which were known at the time of service, there would be a danger of interpreting the requirement of service in sufficient time in such a

27.39

---

[28] See para. 27.29 n. 94 above.
[29] That was the position with the German *Mahnverfahren* procedure employed in that case.
[30] [1981] E.C.R. 1593, at pp. 1608–1609 (paras. 19–20).
[31] [1985] E.C.R. 1779. The facts of the case are summarised at para. 27.24 above.

restrictive and formalistic manner that it would in fact coincide with the requirement of due service."[32]

The Court reiterated that the purpose of Article 27(2) was to ensure that the defendant's rights were effectively protected, and went on to say, therefore, that regard must be had to facts which, although occurring after service was effected, might nonetheless have had the effect that service did not in fact enable the defendant to arrange for his defence.[33] Its ruling on this point, following the terminology used in *Klomps* v. *Michel*, referred to "exceptional circumstances."[34]

27.40   The *Hoge Raad* also referred to the European Court the questions whether Article 27(2) imposed on the plaintiff, by reason of

---

[32] *Ibid.*, at p. 1798 (para. 19).

[33] *Ibid.* at p. 1799 (para. 20).

[34] *Ibid.*, at p. 1802. This also followed the Opinion of Advocate General VerLoren van Themaat, who considered the circumstances which might be "exceptional" for these purposes in rather greater detail. He referred, without endorsing them, to the submissions of the Commission, which had argued that such circumstances might be taken into account, if they were "highly exceptional circumstances for which the defendant cannot be blamed." In a note to his Opinion, at p. 1787, the Advocate General said this:

> "For the benefit of legal practitioners I consider it important to mention in this connexion the detailed, though not exhaustive, list of such highly exceptional circumstances to which the Commission referred at the hearing. The list contains the following examples:
> — Persons having two or more addresses, as was the case in *Klomps* v. *Michel*;
> — Businessmen who are travelling abroad;
> — Persons on holiday;
> — Fishermen on the high seas;
> — A person who unexpectedly has to go to hospital following an accident (which is very exceptional);
> — Persons who move house and register in another area, as was the case in *Pendy Plastic*;
> — Persons who temporarily leave their place of residence;
> — Persons who definitively leave their place of residence without informing the authorities and without sending a letter to the other party: in other words the plaintiff knows only that the defendant has gone away but does not know where he is;
> — A variant of that case, where later on, after service has been effected, the defendant says where he may be found but in so doing takes the responsibility on himself for the fact that process is served on him at his former address;
> — Persons who leave their place of residence, inform the authorities, and write in time to the other party to tell him where they have gone to: in other words, the plaintiff knows in advance where the plaintiff is to be found (in the Commission's view, a very special situation);

circumstances which arose after service, any additional obligations to inform the defendant of the proceedings and, if so, what the effect was of the fact that the defendant was responsible for the failure of the duly served document to reach him. In answering those questions, the European Court did not interpret Article 27(2) as imposing further formal requirements, but ruled that the fact that the plaintiff was apprised of the defendant's new address, after service was effected, and the fact that the defendant was responsible for the failure of the duly served document to reach him, were each matters which the court could take into account in deciding whether service was effected in sufficient time.[35]

Fresh consideration by recognising courts. The recognising court is   **27.41**
bound to consider afresh the question of timely service. It should not be influenced by any decision made by the court of origin, under the second paragraph of Article 20 or under Article 15 of the Hague Service Convention, that the defendant had enough time to arrange for his defence.[36] *A fortiori*, the fact that no stay had been granted under those provisions is not decisive for the purposes of Article 27(2).[37] Moreover, in deciding whether due service was effected in sufficient time for the defendant to arrange for his defence, the recognising court cannot refer merely to the fact of due service, the time limits prescribed by the law of the state of origin and the documents lodged under Article 46.[38]

The Pendy decision. The decision of the European Court in *Pendy*   **27.42**
Plastic Products B.V. v. *Pluspunkt Handelsgesellschaft mbH*[39] illustrates these various points. Pendy, a Dutch enterprise, started pro-

---

      — Private persons who are not businessmen and therefore could perhaps enjoy further protection; (this may, in the Commission's view, represent a highly exceptional circumstance);
and finally
      — Persons who are prevented from entering a defence by extraneous circumstances for which they cannot be held responsible, such as:
        — an accident (caused by somebody else);
        — a general postal strike;
        — a very special reason for leaving the premises (for example to look after a sick member of the family, fire, and so on); these types of facts could be considered to be very unusual."

[35] [1985] E.C.R. 1779 at p. 1803.
[36] Bülow/Böckstiegel/Linke, p. 211, cited with approval by Advocate-General Reischl in *Pendy* v. *Pluspunkt* [1982] E.C.R. 2723, at p. 2744.
[37] Jenard, para. A1.192 below.
[38] Para. 29.01 below. In the comparable case of service in another Contracting State of a notice of a court's decision to grant or refuse an order of enforcement, the Convention itself sets a time limit of two months: Art. 36, second para. (para. 28.30 below).
[39] [1982] E.C.R. 2723.

ceedings in the Dutch courts against Pluspunkt, a German enterprise. The document instituting the proceedings was transmitted to the German authorities for service at a given address, but the German authorities were unable to locate the defendant at that address and issued a certificate to that effect pursuant to Article 6 of the Hague Convention.[40] Pluspunkt did not enter an appearance, and the Dutch court made an interlocutory order under Article 20 of this Convention and Article 15 of the Hague Convention[41] requiring Pendy to prove that Pluspunkt had been able to receive the document instituting the proceedings in sufficient time to enable them to arrange for their defence. This they purported to do by producing an extract from the relevant German commercial register and a communication from the local court in Germany to the effect that its files showed Pluspunkt's address to be that stated in the document which instituted the proceedings. These documents satisfied the Dutch court, which gave Pendy judgment in default of appearance. Pendy then sought to enforce that judgment in Germany, but their application was refused, both at first instance and on appeal. Pendy appealed further to the *Bundesgerichtshof*, which referred the case to the European Court of Justice, asking, in substance, whether the court addressed was bound in reaching a decision under Article 27(2) by the decision under Article 20 and Article 15 of the Hague Convention made by the court of origin. The European Court, in deciding that it was not, said:

> "Although they do not seek to harmonise the different systems of service abroad of legal documents which are in force in the Member States, the provisions of the Brussels Convention are designed to ensure that the defendant's rights are effectively protected. For that reason, jurisdiction to determine whether the document introducing the proceedings was properly served was conferred both on the court of the original State and on the court of the State in which enforcement is sought. Thus, in accordance with the objective of Article 27 of the Convention, the court of the State in which enforcement is sought must examine the question posed by paragraph (2) of that article, notwithstanding the decision given by the court of the original State on the basis of the second and third paragraphs of Article 20. That examination is subject only to the limitation set by the third paragraph of Article 34[42] of the Convention to the effect that the foreign judgment may under no circumstances be reviewed as to its substance."[43]

---

[40] See paras. 4.33 above and A2.06 below.
[41] See paras. 22.17 to 22.23 above.
[42] The third para. of Art. 34 is in the same terms as Art. 29, para. 27.75 below.
[43] [1982] E.C.R. 2723, at p. 2736 (para. 13).

Article 27(3)

[A judgment shall not be recognised:]   **27.43**

3. if the judgment is irreconcilable with a judgment given in a dispute between the same parties in the State in which recognition is sought;*

G. ARTICLE 27(3): CONFLICTING JUDGMENTS

1. General note

Problems of recognition and enforcement may arise where, despite   **27.44**
the safeguards in Articles 21 to 23, conflicting judgments occur.[44] Five types of conflict may occur, but the Convention provides a solution to only two of them. Where recognition of a foreign judgment is sought in Contracting State (State A), the conflict may be any of the following:

(1) between a judgment given in State A and a judgment given in another Contracting State: this is the situation dealt with by Article 27(3);

(2) between a judgment given in Contracting State B and one given in Contracting State C: the Convention is silent on this point, which is considered below;[45]

(3) between a judgment given in another Contracting State and a judgment given in a non-Contracting State: Article 27(5) provides a limited solution to this problem, which is discussed in the commentary on that provision;[46]

(4) between a judgment given in a non-Contracting State and one given in State A: the Convention is not concerned with this conflict, which must be resolved by the national and private international law (including relevant international conventions) of State A;[47]

(5) between judgments given in two different non-Contracting States: again, the Convention is not concerned with this conflict, which must be resolved by the national and private international law of State A.

---

* Jenard, para. A1.193–A1.197 below; Collins, p. 110; Dashwood/Halcon/White, pp. 41, 154; Hartley, pp. 92–93; Kaye, pp. 1482–1492; Maxwell, paras. 6.39–6.41; Anton, paras. 8.19–8.20; Droz, paras. 482, 509–524; Weser, paras. 273, 277; Bülow/Böckstiegel/Linke, pp. 204–205, 212–215; Geimer/ Schütze, pp. 997–999; Kropholler, pp. 271–272; Gothot/Holleaux, paras. 274–281; Pocar, pp. 273–295.

[44] Jenard para. A1.195 below; Collins, p. 110.

[45] Para. 27.50.

[46] Para. 27.60 below.

[47] Geimer/Schütze, p. 999.

2. Irreconcilability

27.45   It is not necessary that the same cause of action be involved,[48] but the irreconcilable judgments must be between the same parties. For example, a judgment in State A ordering the performance of a contract, or awarding damages for its breach would be irreconcilable with a judgment given in proceedings between the same parties in State B in which the contract was declared invalid.[49]

It is the *effect* or *consequences* of the two judgments which must conflict,[50] and differences between them which arise from different provisions of substantive law are not necessarily irreconcilable.[51] So, for example, a judgment given in State A might allow a plaintiff damages for breach of a given statutory duty limited to compensation for physical injury, while a judgment in State B might award him damages for negligence, arising from the same facts, extending also to his economic loss. Those judgments would not be irreconcilable, save to the extent of the duplication of the damages for physical injury. Similarly, judgments will not be irreconcilable merely because they are founded upon different findings of fact.[52] The judgments are irreconcilable, though, if they have *legal implications* which are mutually exclusive.[52a] Where there is partial incompatibility, the court where enforcement is sought can grant partial enforcement, pursuant to Article 42.[53]

In considering whether the consequences of the two judgments conflict, it may be necessary for the court in which recognition and enforcement is sought to consider the relative status of the two judgments. The Jenard Report suggests that it is a matter for the discretion of the court of the state in which recognition and enforce-

---

[48] Jenard, para. A1.194 below. The meaning of "cause of action" is discussed at para. 23.03 above.

[49] *Gubisch Maschinenfabrik* v. *Palumbo*, case 144/87, decision of December 8 1987 (para. 18), *The Times*, January 12, 1988: see para. 23.03 above. Droz, para. 514.

[50] Bülow/Böckstiegel/Linke, p. 214; Oberlandesgericht Hamm, case 20 W 28/77, July 29, 1981, IPRspr. 1981, No. 187, Digest D I–27.3—B3. But, the French Cour de Cassation has held that the fact that the same parties had judgments against each other arising from the same dispute, one for debt and the other for damages, did not give rise to a ground under Art. 27(3) for refusing to enforce the debt judgment, because the two could be set off and were not factually irreconcilable: *Société Française de Couvoirs "Sofraco"* v. *Soc. Pluimvee Export Coolen*, Bull.Cass. 1977, I, no. 401, Digest D I–27.3—B1.

[51] Droz, para. 514; Bundesgerichtshof, case VIII ZB 10/79, September 26, 1979, NJW 1980, p. 527, [1980] E.C.C. 207, Digest D I–27.3—B2.

[52] Bülow/Böckstiegel/Linke, p. 214.

[52a] *Hoffman* v. *Krieg*, case 145/86, decision of February 4, 1988 (para. 22), *The Times*, March 26, 1988: see para. 27.47 below.

[53] Para. 28.71 below.

ment is sought whether the foreign judgment needs to be *res judicata* or merely "final and conclusive."[54]

It is suggested that in order to decide whether a foreign judgment should be refused recognition under this provision, the relative status of the two judgments should be considered according to uniform criteria.[54a] Article 27(3) should differ in its operation between the Contracting States only to the extent that such differences are necessarily caused by differences in national procedural laws.

Provisional orders are clearly included within the definition of **27.46** "judgment" in Article 25,[55] though, and they cannot be considered as excluded from the scope of Article 27(3). But where a decision is of a purely provisional nature, it will not necessarily be irreconcilable with a final decision given by the court of another Contracting State. The consequences of the two decisions may be different in nature.

It may also be that the irreconcilability of the two decisions will depend upon the extent to which either of them is still open to review. For example, if recognition is sought of a decision given in another Contracting State, which is no longer subject to appeal, it can be argued[56] that a later local decision which is apparently irreconcilable with it should not be regarded as irreconcilable for the purposes of Article 27(3), while the possibility remains open that the local decision could be overturned on appeal, and the two decisions be "reconciled." This will be particularly apt where the proceedings giving rise to the foreign decision were started before the proceedings giving rise to the local judgment, because of the likelihood that the latter would have been proceeded with in breach of Articles 21 to 23. Where the foreign judgment is the subject of an appeal, the court in which recognition or enforcement is sought may stay its proceedings pursuant to Article 30.[57]

The Hoffman v. Krieg decision. It is not necessary that the national **27.47** judgment, with which the foreign judgment is irreconcilable, should itself fall within the scope of the Convention. This is one of the matters on which the European Court ruled in *Hoffman* v. *Krieg.*[57a] The parties were married in 1950 and lived in Germany.

---

[54] Jenard, para. A1.194 below; Bülow/Böckstiegel/Linke, p. 214, Droz, para. 514. As to the distinction between a judgment which is *res judicata* and one which is final, see paras. 25.22 to 25.24 above.

[54a] This is implicitly what the European Court did in *Hoffman* v. *Krieg*, para. 23, discussed below.

[55] Paras. 25.20 to 25.21 above.

[56] Bülow/Böckstiegel/Linke, p. 214.

[57] Para. 27–78 below.

[57a] Case 145/86, decision of February 4, 1988, *The Times*, March 26, 1988.

They separated in 1978 and the husband went to live in the Netherlands. The wife obtained an order for maintenance from a German court in 1979 under a provision of German law requiring a husband to maintain his wife. On May 1, 1980, the husband obtained a divorce decree in the Netherlands, which became definitive there in August 1980, but which did not become entitled to recognition in Germany at any material time. In 1981 the wife applied for and was granted an order for the enforcement of the maintenance order in the Netherlands, which the husband took no steps to oppose. The husband applied to the German court for the maintenance order to be set aside, but was unsuccessful because the Dutch divorce decree was not recognised in Germany. The wife then obtained an attachment of earnings order in the Netherlands which the husband sought to oppose. The matter eventually came before the *Hoge Raad*, which referred a number of questions to the European Court of Justice.[57b]

One of these questions was whether the German maintenance order was irreconcilable within the meaning of Article 27(3) with the Dutch divorce decree. In considering whether the two orders had legal implications which were mutually exclusive, the European Court observed that the German maintenance order necessarily presupposed the existence of the matrimonial relationship which the Dutch courts regarded as having been dissolved by the divorce decree.[57c] The two orders were therefore irreconcilable for the purposes of Article 27(3).[57d]

3. Priority

27.48   Article 27(3) gives priority to the judgment given in the Contracting State where the recognition of the foreign judgment is sought. It is not necessary that the judgment given in the state addressed should have been given first (except, perhaps, where the same cause of action is involved),[58] but where that is the case, no problem arises. Where the foreign judgment was delivered first, though, it will have gained automatic recognition in the state addressed, pursuant to the first paragraph of Article 26.[59] At the time when it was given, there will have been no irreconcilable decision in the state addressed and the provisions of Article 27(3) will have not been ful-

---

[57b] In addition to a question of interpretation of Art. 27(3), the questions concerned the interpretation of Arts. 26, 27(1), 31 and 36.
[57c] Para. 24 of the judgment.
[57d] The question whether the husband could object to the attachment of earnings order on this ground, despite his not having opposed the order for enforcement, is considered at para. 28.33 below.
[58] See next para.
[59] Para. 27.01 above.

filled. But when the local judgment is given, the ground for refusal of recognition will become established and the foreign judgment will cease to be entitled to automatic recognition. The question arises whether the ground of refusal of recognition should then operate retrospectively and the foreign judgment be regarded as having been ineffective from the outset. It is suggested that it should not do so, but that the foreign judgment should only be denied recognition from the date of the local judgment.[60] This is because a retrospective denial of recognition would be contrary to the purposes of the Convention generally, and of the first paragraph of Article 26 in particular, namely to promote the free movement of judgments by automatically extending them into the other Contracting States. Furthermore, the protection of third parties would seem to require that the foreign judgment should be accorded recognition unless and until a ground of refusal arises.[61]

4. Same cause of action

Where the same cause of action[62] is involved in the two decisions, though, the position may be different. This is because a plaintiff may not pursue proceedings in one Contracting State for a judgment in the same terms as one which he has already obtained in another Contracting State. That is the effect of the decision of the European Court of Justice in *De Wolf* v. *Cox*.[63] As has been observed,[64] that decision seems to be based on the principle that the procedures in the Convention should not be abused. It may be, therefore, that a later judgment delivered in the state where recognition is sought of the first judgment ought not to be given priority, despite the apparent effect of Article 27(3), because it is a judgment given contrary to the procedural requirements of the Convention.[64a]   **27.49**

While *De Wolf* v. *Cox* does not seem to be based on principles of merger,[65] it should not preclude national law from regarding a foreign judgment as effective to extinguish the cause of action. If

---

[60] Droz, paras. 516–517; Bülow/Böckstiegel/Linke, p. 214; Geimer/Schütze, pp. 999; *cf.* Maxwell, para. 6.40.

[61] Bülow/Böckstiegel/Linke, *loc. cit.*

[62] On the meaning of "the same cause of action" in the context of the Convention, see para. 23.03 above.

[63] [1976] E.C.R. 1759, discussed at para. 25.36 above.

[64] *Ibid.*

[64a] This reasoning would not necessarily apply to all cases in which the two judgments involve the same "cause of action" in the liberal sense ascribed to that term in *Gubisch* v. *Palumbo* (see para. 23.03 above), because the decision in *De Wolf* v. *Cox* involves only the narrower question of whether the later judgment sought is "in the same terms" as the earlier judgment.

[65] Para. 25.36 above.

that is the effect of the national law of the state addressed,[66] it may be that the later national decision would itself be open to attack, even though recognition of an earlier foreign judgment could be refused under Article 27(3).

It remains to be seen how the European Court of Justice will approach these problems.

5. Conflicting judgments from other Contracting States

27.50   The Convention offers no solution to the problem which will be faced by the courts of a Contracting State faced with irreconcilable judgments, each of which is entitled to recognition and enforcement under Title III of the Convention. The Jenard Report suggests[67] that the form of words used covers this situation, but it is by no means clear that this is so.[68] The Convention would appear to require that both decisions be recognised—a clearly impractical proposition—but any solution would appear to involve a breach of that requirement.

The absence of any mention in the Convention of how the problem is to be resolved might suggest that the recognising court should merely apply its own law,[69] but that solution would allow the Convention to be ignored entirely and in a potentially random fashion. Similarly, an examination by the court of the state addressed of the merits of both judgments, to see which of them it considers to accord better with its own ideas, would be wholly contrary to the principle[70] that a judgment of another Contracting State should not be reviewed as to its substance,[71] while to recognise neither judgment would be to defeat the Convention's purpose of promoting the free circulation of judgments.[72]

27.51   Two solutions would seem to comply with the purpose and intention of the Convention and it remains to be seen which (if either) is adopted by the European Court of Justice. The first involves following the rules in Articles 21 to 23, and refusing recognition to the judgment given in the proceedings which were started later. This would provide a clear solution where the same cause of action was

---

[66] That is the case in England, unless the foreign decision is not enforceable or entitled to recognition there: s.34 of the 1982 Act, para. 43.36 below. Whether such a foreign decision is entitled to recognition may depend on the considerations of priority discussed below.

[67] Jenard, para. A1.195 below.

[68] Droz, para. 519; Bülow/Böckstiegel/Linke, p. 215; Maxwell, para. 6.41.

[69] Bülow/Böckstiegel/Linke, *loc. cit.*

[70] Art. 29 and the third para. of Art. 34.

[71] Droz, para. 521.

[72] Droz, para. 520.

involved[73] or where the case came within the exclusive jurisdiction of both courts.[74] Where the two actions were merely related,[75] though, it could be argued that this solution would involve a review of the merits of the decision of the court later seised not to stay its proceedings (or decline jurisdiction).[76] This contrary argument is, it is suggested, ill-founded. If the court of the state addressed were to apply a rule that the judgment given in the proceedings started later should not be recognised, whatever the merits of the decision of the original court not to stay its proceedings or decline jurisdiction (if, indeed, there was a decision to that effect), the recognising court cannot be said to have "reviewed" that decision.

The second solution is to give priority to the decision which was given first. This would have the merit that a judgment which had once obtained automatic recognition under the first paragraph of Article 26 would not lose it,[77] and would avoid any argument, where the same cause of action was involved, as to whether the proceedings giving rise to the later judgment should have been pursued.[78] On the other hand, it might actually encourage a multiplicity of litigation and conflicting decisions, by giving a party, who had already been sued in one state, an incentive to start proceedings in another state, in the hope that he would not be stopped by the terms of Articles 21 to 23 and would be able to press ahead to an earlier judgment in his favour.

Article 27(4)

[A judgment shall not be recognised:]   27.52

    4. if the court of the State in which the judgment was given, in order to arrive at its judgment, has decided a preliminary question concerning the status or legal capacity of natural persons, rights in property arising out of a matrimonial relationship, wills or succession in a way that conflicts with a rule of the private international law of the State in which the recognition is sought, unless the same result would have been reached by the application of the rules of private international law of that State;*

---

[73] Art. 21.
[74] Art. 23.
[75] Art. 22.
[76] Droz, para. 522.
[77] Droz, para. 523.
[78] Para. 27.49 above.
* Jenard, para. A1.196 below; Collins, pp. 110–111; Dashwood/Halcon/White, pp. 41–42, 154; Hartley, p. 88; Kaye, pp. 1492–1497; Maxwell, para. 6.42; Anton, para. 8.21; Droz, paras. 72, 482, 525–533; Weser, paras. 225, 273, 282–283; Bülow/Böckstiegel/Linke, pp. 204–205, 215–217; Geimer/Schütze, pp. 993–995, 1020; Kropholler, pp. 272–274; Gothot/Holleaux, paras. 287–297; Pocar, pp. 273–295.

H. ARTICLE 27(4): CONFLICTS OF PRIVATE INTERNATIONAL LAW ON PRELIMINARY QUESTIONS

1. General note

27.53   The Convention generally prohibits the refusal of recognition of a judgment on the ground that the wrong law was applied,[79] but Article 27(4) provides a limited exception to that principle. Accordingly, its application is to be confined strictly to the topics which it expressly covers.[80] The circumstances in which it permits a foreign judgment to be denied recognition are ones which, according to some systems[81] could be regarded as matters of public policy.

The particular subject-matters of the preliminary question are matters which are themselves excluded from the scope of the Convention by sub-paragraph (1) of the second paragraph of Article 1,[82] but which may be relevant in the context of recognition and enforcement if the principal subject-matter of the judgment falls within the scope of the Convention.

27.54   In applying this provision, the court of the state addressed must ask itself a number of questions, which, it is suggested, may be summarised as follows:

(1) Did the court of origin decide a preliminary question concerning the status or legal capacity of natural persons, rights in property arising out of a matrimonial relationship, wills or succession?[83]

(2) If so, was the answer to that question necessary for the decision which it gave on the main issue?

(3) If so, did the court of origin decide the preliminary question[84] in a way which differed from the recognising court's own private international law—that is to say, is there a conflict between the conflicts rule applied by the court of origin and the conflicts rule of the recognising court?[85]

---

[79] Para. 25.14 above.

[80] Bülow/Böckstiegel/Linke, pp. 215–216.

[81] Collins, p. 111.

[82] Para. 14.03 above. The reason for Art. 27(4) is the same as the reason for excluding those topics from the scope of the Convention generally, namely that the relevant conflicts rules diverge greatly between the various Contracting States: Droz, para. 526. As the European Court observed in *Hoffman* v. *Krieg* (case 145/86, decision of February 4, 1988, para. 16, not yet reported), Art. 27(4) does not derogate from the provisions of national law.

[83] The meaning and scope of each of these concepts is considered at paras. 14.19 to 14.25 above.

[84] Para. 27.58 below.

[85] Detailed treatment of the rules of private international law is beyond the scope of this work. Conflicts between conflicts rules are discussed by Dicey and Morris, pp. 35–36.

(4) If so, was the decision on the preliminary issue different from that which it would have been, if the recognising court had applied its own private international law to the preliminary question?

Recognition is to be refused only if all four questions are answered in the affirmative.

Limited review of the substance. The court addressed could not **27.55** answer the four questions outlined if it was constrained by the strict terms of Article 29 and the third paragraph of Article 34,[86] which prohibit a review of the original judgment as to its substance. To the extent necessary to answer these questions, and to that extent only, it is free to differ on the substance of the matter from the decision of the original court.[87] On the other hand, although it does not say so expressly, Article 27(4) is almost certainly subject to the principle in the second paragraph of Article 28, to the effect that the recognising court is bound, in its examination of those questions, by the findings of fact made by the court of origin.[88]

Nationality and domicile. The application of this ground of refusal **27.56** is not confined to protecting nationals of the state where recognition is sought.[89] The Convention avoids any reliance upon the nationality of the parties[90] and, in the context of recognition and enforcement, the domicile of the parties is also irrelevant for the purposes of the Convention. A person domiciled in a non-Contracting State is as entitled to the benefit of this provision as a person domiciled in a Contracting State.

Maintenance. Article 27(4) may be of particular relevance in **27.57** maintenance cases,[91] where (for example) the entitlement to maintenance may depend upon the question whether a person is the spouse[92] or child of the maintenance creditor.[93] However, a particular problem arises in relation to maintenance proceedings which are ancillary to status proceedings, because of the amended text of Article 5(2), which grants jurisdiction to the court which "according to its own law" has jurisdiction to entertain those proceedings.

---

[86] Paras. 27.75 and 28.22 below.
[87] Bülow/Böckstiegel/Linke, p. 217.
[88] *Ibid.*, Droz, para. 529.
[89] Jenard, para. A1.196 below, where the contrast is noted with a similar provision in the Convention between Belgium and Germany.
[90] See para. 16.08 above.
[91] Collins, p. 111; Weser, para. 225.
[92] For an example of the application of Art. 27(4) to prevent the recognition of a judgment declaring that an ex-husband was not liable to pay maintenance to his ex-wife, see *Onnen v. Nielen*, Ned.Jur. 1977, No. 132, Digest D I–27.4—B1.
[93] In this connection, it will be recalled that "court" includes the Danish administrative authorities: Art. Va of the Protocol para. 35.22 below.

The new jurisdiction provided by the amended text of that Article might be rendered largely ineffective in many cases if an ancillary maintenance order could be denied recognition on the basis of Article 27(4) and it may be that the scope of this ground of refusal is now more limited than formerly.[94]

2. " . . . in order to arrive at its judgment, has decided a preliminary question . . . "

27.58   It is not necessary that the preliminary question should have been in issue before the original court, merely that the decision on the point, even if it was implicit, should have been necessary to the decision on the main issue. The word "decide" should therefore be construed liberally.[95] The interpretation of Article 27(4) affords the opportunity to raise difficult questions as to whether the decision on the preliminary question needs to be strictly "preliminary" and if so, on the interpretation of that word.[96] It is suggested that it is neither desirable nor necessary to consider such questions, and that the requirement that the question be "preliminary" be construed in the context of the words "in order to arrive at its judgment," so that, read as a whole, the provision requires the answer to the preliminary question to be a condition precedent to the answer on the main issue, without itself being the answer to the main issue.

The European Court has referred to Article 27(4) in confirming that the exclusion of the status of natural persons from the scope of the Convention means that the courts of one Contracting State are not required to enforce a maintenance order given in another Contracting State if, by doing so, they would have to ignore the consequences of a divorce decree made in the latter state.[96a] This was so, even though the divorce decree was made later than the maintenance order and the maintenance order was not therefore made on the basis of even an implicit preliminary decision as to the parties' status.

Article 27(5)

27.59   [A judgment shall not be recognised:]

> 5. if the judgment is irreconcilable with an earlier judgment given in a non-Contracting State involving the same cause of action and between the same parties,

---

[94] See para. 17.42 above.
[95] Droz, para. 528.
[96] Droz, paras. 530–532.
[96a] *Hoffman* v. *Krieg*, case 145/86, decision of February 4, 1988 (para. 16), *The Times*, March 26, 1988: see para. 27.47 above.

provided that this latter judgment fulfills the conditions necessary for its recognition in the State addressed.*†

I. ARTICLE 27(5): CONFLICT BETWEEN JUDGMENTS FROM OTHER CONTRACTING AND NON-CONTRACTING STATES

The various different types of conflict which can occur between judgments given in different jurisdictions have been considered above.[97] Article 27(5) provides a solution to one of these types of conflict, namely where the courts of a Contracting State are faced with two irreconcilable judgments, one given in another Contracting State and the other given in a non-Contracting State. **27.60**

Article 27(5) is narrower in its application than Article 27(3), because it imposes additional express requirements before the judgment given in the other Contracting State is to be refused recognition. In addition to the requirements that the two judgments be irreconcilable[98] and be between the same parties, it also requires that the two judgments should involve the same cause of action[99] and that the judgment given in the non-Contracting State should have been given earlier than the judgment given in the other Contracting State.[1]

In order for the judgment given in the other Contracting State to be denied recognition, it is also necessary that the judgment given in the non-Contracting state should fulfil the conditions necessary for it to be recognised in the state addressed. Those conditions need not be imposed on the state addressed by reason of an international convention; it is sufficient if they arise as a matter of that state's national law.[2] **27.61**

---

* Schlosser, paras. 188, 205 (paras. A1.484, A1.501–A1.502 below); Collins, p. 111; Dashwood/Halcon/White, pp. 42, 155; Hartley, p. 93; Kaye, pp. 1498–1501; Maxwell, para. 6.43; Anton, paras. 8.19–8.20; Geimer/Schütze, p. 999; Kropholler, pp. 274–275; Gothot/Holleaux, paras. 283–286.
† Art. 27(5) is new and was added by Art. 13(2) of the 1978 Convention.
[97] Para. 27.44 above.
[98] This requirement is discussed at paras. 27.45 *et seq.* above.
[99] For a discussion of the meaning of "same cause of action" in the context of the Convention, see para. 23.03 above.
[1] By including these requirements, Art. 27(5) does not give rise to the potential problems which can occur under Art. 27(3) in connection with the effect of rules of national law which regard the cause of action as having merged in the earlier foreign judgment: see para. 27.49 above.
[2] Schlosser, para. 205, paras. A1.501–A1.502 below. For the conditions under which English law recognises foreign judgments, otherwise than under this Convention, see Dicey and Morris, pp. 418–489.

Article 28

27.62 Moreover, a judgment shall not be recognised if it conflicts with the provisions of Section 3, 4 or 5 of Title II, or in a case provided for in Article 59.

In its examination of the grounds of jurisdiction referred to in the foregoing paragraph, the court or authority applied to shall be bound by the findings of fact on which the court of the State in which the judgment was given based its jurisdiction.

Subject to the provisions of the first paragraph, the jurisdiction of the court of the State in which the judgment was given may not be reviewed; the test of public policy referred to in Article 27(1) may not be applied to the rules relating to jurisdiction.*

J. ARTICLE 28: GENERAL NOTE

1. Review of original court's jurisdiction

27.63 In order to strengthen the principle that a judgment given in a Contracting State and falling within the scope of the Convention is to be recognised automatically in the other Contracting States,[3] the Convention generally prohibits any review of the jurisdiction of the court of origin. That is the general rule, expressly stated in the third paragraph of Article 28, and it applies even where assumption of jurisdiction by the original court is so offensive to the recognising court as to make its recognition contrary to public policy in the second state. Unless one of the grounds stated in the Convention for refusing recognition applies, the second court is bound to recognise the judgment,[4] without reviewing it. The only grounds upon which recognition may be refused have been listed above;[5] and a major group of grounds is that stated in the first paragraph of Article 28.

27.64 Where a review of jurisdiction is permitted by this Article, the court addressed in the second state may review the original judg-

---

* Jenard, paras. A1.197, A1.245 below; Schlosser, para. 188 (para. A1.484 below); Collins, pp. 107, 111–113; Dashwood/Halcon/White, pp. 42, 155–156; Hartley, pp. 8, 87, 89; Kaye, pp. 888–892, 1501–1510; Maxwell, paras. 6.44–6.46; Anton, paras. 8.22–8.27; Droz, paras. 477, 534–538; Bülow/Böckstiegel/Linke, pp. 218–224; Geimer/Schütze, pp. 331–346, 1033–1051; Kropholler, pp. 275–280; Gothot/Holleaux, paras. 298–303, 311–313; Pocar, pp. 295–300.
[3] Art. 26, first para., para. 27.01 above.
[4] See para. 27.03 above.
[5] Paras. 25.12 and 25.13 above.

ment only to a limited extent. First, it is confined to reviewing questions of jurisdiction and may not go further to review the substance of the judgment.[6] Secondly, even in its review of jurisdiction, it may only re-open the question whether the original court, in accepting jurisdiction, applied the Convention correctly. It may not re-open the findings of fact upon which the original court acted in accepting jurisdiction: Article 28, second paragraph. Although the Convention does not say so expressly, the prohibition of reviewing questions of fact extends also to the other grounds for refusing recognition under Article 27 and the other minor grounds.[7]

2. Does the Convention apply?

It is axiomatic that the Convention only applies to judgments **27.65** which fall within its scope. It cannot therefore prevent the court addressed from considering whether the judgment which it is called upon to recognise falls within the scope of the Convention at all[8] and, to that extent too, the court addressed has power to review the original judgment. It remains to be seen what attitude the European Court of Justice would take to a decision by a court addressed that the court of origin had erred as a matter of fact, rather than law, in deciding that the Convention applied.

It is important to distinguish between a decision by a court addressed that the judgment falls outside the Convention altogether and a decision that the original court wrongly assumed jurisdiction under the Convention. The latter type of decision is prohibited, save in the limited circumstances envisaged by the first paragraph of Article 28. The reasons why the court of origin accepted jurisdiction are irrelevant in any other case (except under the transitional provisions),[9] even if the acceptance of jurisdiction appears to the court addressed to have been blatantly wrong, whether according to the Convention's rules or according to the law of the state of origin. A decision that the Convention did not apply at all could, therefore, normally only be made by a court addressed on the basis that the subject-matter of the judgment fell outside the scope of the Convention.[9a]

---

[6] Art. 29, para. 27.75 below.
[7] Para. 25.13 above; Bülow/Böckstiegel/Linke, p. 223.
[8] Collins, p. 112, who raises the question whether a U.K. court could therefore refuse to recognise a judgment given in breach of an arbitration agreement. See paras. 14.31 *et seq.* above.
[9] See Art. 54, para. 32.01 below; 1978 Convention, Art. 34, para. 37.06 below.
[9a] See para. 28.27 below.

K. First Paragraph: Refusal of Recognition where the Judgment Conflicts with Sections 3, 4 or 5 of Title II or Falls within Article 59

1. Generally

27.66   Section 3 of Title II (Articles 7 to 12A)[10] provides special jurisdictional rules for insurance cases, Section 4 (Articles 13 to 15)[11] does the same for consumer cases, and Section 5 (Article 16)[12] provides for exclusive jurisdiction for cases with certain categories of subject-matter. The rationale of the Convention in providing these special rules of jurisdiction has already been examined.[13] Generally, if those rules have not been complied with, recognition must be refused.[14]

Article 59[15] allows a Contracting State to refuse recognition of a judgment given in another Contracting State against a person domiciled or habitually resident in a third state if the judgment could only have been founded on an exorbitant jurisdiction of that other Contracting State and if it has concluded a convention with the third state requiring it to do so.

27.67   It is noticeable that a conflict with an exclusive jurisdiction agreement falling within Article 17 is not a ground for refusing recognition of a judgment,[16] although, as the Schlosser Report notes in this context, the court of origin is required to take account of any such agreement.[17] If it fails to do so, the defendant's remedy lies in challenging the jurisdiction in the state of origin, rather than in opposing the recognition and enforcement of the judgment in other Contracting States.

As with the grounds under Article 27, the court must review the jurisdiction of the original court of its own motion, but need not conduct an investigation into the matter.[18]

---

[10] Chap. 18 above.

[11] Chap. 19 above.

[12] Chap. 20 above.

[13] Paras. 18.02, 19.02 and 20.02 above.

[14] Bundesgerichtshof, May 2, 1979, case VIII ZB 1/79, NJW 1980, p. 1223; Digest D I–28—B3.

[15] Para. 33.24 below.

[16] Maxwell, para. 6.44; Collins, p. 112.

[17] Schlosser, para. 188, para. A1.484 below. This is not (and is probably not intended to be) a sufficient explanation, because the court of origin is also required, of its own motion, to take account of the exclusive jurisdiction under Art. 16 of the courts of another Contracting State (Art. 19) and, where the defendant does not enter an appearance, to examine its own jurisdiction (Art. 20).

[18] See para. 27.04 above.

2. Insurance and consumer cases

A review of jurisdiction in insurance and consumer cases will **27.68** normally only be necessary where the plaintiff has obtained a default judgment,[19] because if the defendant entered an appearance without contesting the jurisdiction, Article 18[20] will have given the original court jurisdiction.[21] In such circumstances, even if the case was brought in a court which would not have had jurisdiction under Sections 3 or 4 of Title II, the jurisdiction cannot be said to "conflict" with the provisions of those sections. But if the defendant unsuccessfully contested the jurisdiction of the original court, the court addressed will have to review the jurisdiction of the original court.

While the first paragraph of Article 28 appears to make it compulsory for the recognising court to refuse recognition of a judgment which conflicts with the provisions of Sections 3 or 4 of Title II, it seems that there may be an exception to that rule. If the court of origin, although it did not have jurisdiction under Sections 3 or 4 of Title II, is in fact more beneficial to the protected party (the insured, beneficiary, policy-holder or consumer) than a court with jurisdiction under those sections, then it would be illogical to refuse recognition to a judgment given in favour of the protected party.[22] This situation is likely to arise only rarely in practice, because of the extent to which the jurisdictional rules are weighted in favour of the protected party. Even if the recognising court is faced with such a case, it will still be bound by the findings of fact on which the court of origin based its jurisdiction.[23]

3. Cases of exclusive jurisdiction

In considering whether a judgment conflicts with the rules of **27.69** exclusive jurisdiction in Article 16, the recognising court must be aware of the possibility that the case may fall within the exclusive jurisdiction of the courts of more than one Contracting State.[24] This situation is likely to arise rarely, but is most likely in a case where the exclusive jurisdiction is based on the seat of a company or other legal person or association of legal or natural persons, under Article 16(2).[25] Where both the court of origin and the court addressed

---

[19] Art. 20, first para., para. 22.11 above.
[20] Para. 21.83 above.
[21] Bülow/Böckstiegel/Linke, p. 221.
[22] *Ibid.*
[23] Second para. of this Article: see para. 27.71 below.
[24] If an action has been brought in both Contracting States, the court second seised should have declined jurisdiction in favour of the court first seised: Art. 23, para. 23.24 above.
[25] Para. 20.26 above.

claim exclusive jurisdiction and the judgment is given in proceedings which have as their object one of the matters set out in Article 16(2) (*e.g.* the dissolution of a company or the nullity of a decision of its organs), the Jenard Report suggests[26] that the court addressed can refuse recognition of the judgment under the first paragraph of Article 28, if according to its own law, the seat of the company is in that state.[27] This solution accords with Article 53,[28] because, by that Article, each court is to apply its own rules of private international law in determining the seat of a company. It would seem to follow that the courts of a third Contracting State (State C) could claim the same privilege and refuse to recognise such a judgment given in Contracting State A, on the grounds that, according to its (State C's) own conflicts rules, Contracting State B had exclusive jurisdiction over the case. A distinction may need to be drawn, though, between a case where the law of State A provides for the company to have its seat in State A and in no other Contracting State and one where the law of State A recognises a seat in State B as well as in State A.[29]

4. Conventions under Article 59

27.70   Article 59[30] allows a Contracting State to assume, in a convention on the recognition and enforcement of judgments, an obligation towards a third state not to recognise judgments given in other Contracting States against defendants domiciled or habitually resident in the third state where, in cases provided for in Article 4, the judgment could only be founded on a ground of jurisdiction specified in the second paragraph of Article 3, except in certain cases where jurisdiction is founded on the presence of property within the court's territorial jurisdiction. Conventions containing obligations under Article 59 have been concluded by the United Kingdom with Canada, by Germany with Norway, and by Denmark with other Scandinavian countries.[31]

If a court of a Contracting State is asked to recognise a judgment under Title III and that state has assumed an obligation of the kind mentioned in Article 59, the court will need to consider three questions: (i) whether the defendant was domiciled or habitually resident in the particular non-Contracting State with which a convention containing that obligation has been concluded,

---

[26] Jenard, para. A1.245 below; *cf.* Droz, para. 312.
[27] See para. 27.72 below as to the distinction between findings of fact and law in such a case.
[28] Para. 31.23 below.
[29] See para. 44.25 below; Hartley, p. 67.
[30] Para. 33.24 below.
[31] Paras. 33.29 *et seq.* below.

(ii) whether the court of origin could only have founded its jurisdiction on one of the exorbitant jurisdictions in the second paragraph of Article 3 or whether a ground of jurisdiction under the Convention existed as well; and (iii) whether the jurisdiction of the court of origin was based on the presence of property within the jurisdiction in the circumstances specified in Article 59. Strictly, the court is obliged to consider the questions of its own motion,[32] but as with any other case, it need not carry out an investigation into the matter[33] and in the normal course of events the particular matters giving rise to this ground for refusing jurisdiction will only come to the court's notice on an appeal under Articles 36 to 41.

L. Second Paragraph: Court Addressed Bound by Original Court's Findings of Fact

The second paragraph of Article 28 should present little difficulty. **27.71** It applies only to the limited circumstances in which the court addressed is permitted to review the jurisdiction of the court of origin.[34] Where the court addressed is not permitted to review the jurisdiction of the court of origin, no question of the correctness of the findings of fact can arise anyway. Where the court of origin has made findings of fact and accepted jurisdiction on the basis of those findings, they are not open to review. Although the Convention does not say so expressly, logic requires that the same principle should apply to facts which are admitted or agreed and which have been relied upon by the court of origin in accepting jurisdiction. Except where the defendant has unsuccessfully challenged the jurisdiction of the court of origin, the provision will only apply to default judgments, because the unconditional entry of an appearance by a defendant will found jurisdiction under Article 18.

The sort of finding of fact upon which a court might act in found- **27.72** ing jurisdiction is a finding that the defendant was habitually resident, or that a company had its principle establishment, in a particular state, or that a wrongful act had taken place, or damage had been suffered, in a particular place. By contrast, a decision based on such a finding of fact that, say, a person was domiciled in the state where he was habitually resident, or a company had its seat in the state where its principal establishment was situated, or that the damage suffered as a result of the wrongful act was actionable,

---

[32] *Contra*, Droz, paras. 535–536.
[33] Para. 27.04 above.
[34] See paras. 25.12, 25.13 and 27.64 above.

would be a finding of law and would be open to review in the circumstances permitted by the Convention.[35]

M. THIRD PARAGRAPH: REVIEW OF JURISDICTION PROHIBITED

27.73   The reasoning underlying the general prohibition of a review of the original court's jurisdiction is that the court of origin is as well able to judge the applicability of the Convention as the court of the state addressed, and better able than the latter to apply its own law.[36] The decisions of the court of origin on either of these matters is open to review by way of an appeal in the state of origin and it could only impede the principle of the free movement of judgments within the Community if the court addressed were permitted to review the original court's decision as to its own jurisdiction.[37] The effect of generally prohibiting any review of the original court's jurisdiction is to impose on the defendant the choice of either challenging the original court's jurisdiction in the state of origin, or accepting the Community-wide consequences of not doing so.[38]

The exclusion of public policy[39] as a ground for reviewing the jurisdiction of the court of origin emphasises the restricted nature of the concept of public policy in the context of the Convention[40] and limits the possibility of the Convention's integrationist aims being thwarted by national courts.

27.74   The special provisions of Article I of the 1968 Protocol,[41] protecting persons domiciled in Luxembourg from the jurisdiction under Article 5(1), do not involve a departure from the principle that the jurisdiction of the court of origin is not generally open to review by the court addressed.[42]

By way of an exception to the third paragraph of Article 28, the court of the state addressed may be required to examine the jurisdiction of the court of origin under the transitional provisions, where the proceedings were instituted before, but the judgment was delivered after, the Convention came into force.[43]

---

[35] Droz, para. 537; Bülow/Böckstiegel/Linke, p. 223.

[36] Jenard, para. A1.197 below, Droz, para. 477.

[37] The same applies to the substance of the judgment: see Art. 29, para. 27.75 below.

[38] Bülow/Böckstiegel/Linke, p. 220.

[39] Public policy in the context of the Convention is discussed at paras. 10.28 and 27.14 *et seq.* above.

[40] Jenard, para. A1.197 below.

[41] Para. 35.01 below.

[42] *Weinor* v. *S.à.r.l. Wirion Mod'enfants*, Pas.lux. 1976, II p. 230; Digest D I–28—B1.

[43] Art. 54 (para. 32.01 below) and Art. 34 of the 1978 Accession Convention (para. 37.06 below).

Article 29

In no circumstances may a foreign judgment be reviewed as to its substance. *   27.75

N. ARTICLE 29: REVIEW OF THE SUBSTANCE PROHIBITED

It is fundamental to the scheme of the Convention that judgments   27.76
of the courts of Contracting States are to be recognised automatically throughout the Community, and it is an essential and central part of that scheme that such judgments should not be open to review in other Contracting States. There are limited circumstances in which a judgment may be refused recognition and enforcement,[44] but (subject to one exception)[45] none in which a judgment of the court of another Contracting State[46] may be reviewed as to its substance. Any doubt as to whether this rule applies to cases of enforcement as well as to cases of recognition is removed by the fact that the third paragraph of Article 34 is in virtually identical terms.[47]

In other words, the court addressed may not question the correctness of the original decision. Even where a defendant alleges that the judgment against him was obtained by fraud, the substance of the case cannot be reviewed[48] except, to the extent permitted by Article 27(1), for the purpose of deciding whether the judgment should be refused recognition on the grounds of public policy.[49] Equally, where a decision given on appeal upheld a decision given at first instance, the German *Bundesgerichtshof* has held that the judgment debtor could not say at the recognition stage that he had paid the substantial part of the judgment debt before the date of the appellate court's decision.[50]

---

* Jenard, para. A1.198 below; Dashwood/Halcon/White, p. 156; Droz, paras. 463–474; Kaye, pp. 1365; 1441–1442; Hartley, p. 85; Maxwell, para. 6.47; Anton, para. 8.21; Bülow/Böckstiegel/Linke, pp. 224–225; Geimer/Schütze, pp. 1051–1052, 1201–1206; Kropholler, pp. 280–282; Gothot/Holleaux, paras. 315–322; Pocar, pp. 301–303.

[44] See paras. 25.12 and 25.13 above.

[45] The exception relates to the court's power to *entertain* an application for a declaration of recognition, discussed at para. 28.27 below.

[46] The term "foreign judgment" must refer to the judgments of other Contracting States: Maxwell, para. 6.47. See the definition of "judgment" in Art. 25, para. 26.01 above.

[47] See the commentary on that Article, at para. 28.27 below.

[48] *Banque Nationale de Paris* v. *Hochheim*, Bundesgerichtshof, case VIII ZB 8/79, May 16, 1979, [1979] E.C.C. 321, Digest D I–34—B3.

[49] See para. 27.20 above.

[50] Bundesgerichtshof, March 22, 1984, case IZ, ZB 173/83, [1985] E.C.C. 243; Bundesgerichtshof, April 13, 1983, case VIII ZB 38/82, [1984] E.C.C. 128.

27.77   The prohibition against reviewing a judgment as to its substance applies not only to any finding of fact or substantive law and to the exercise of any discretion,[51] but probably also to findings of substance made on the basis of procedural law.[52] So, for example, it is not open to a person against whom a default judgment has been given to raise matters of substance at the recognition and enforcement stage.[53] The dismissal of an action on grounds of limitation,[53a] or for want of prosecution outside the limitation period, would probably be a dismissal on a substantive basis. Similarly, a decision on a point of conflicts of law, whether that is to be regarded as substantive or procedural, would be a decision on the substance and would not be open to review,[54] except to the limited extent permitted by Article 27 and 28.

Provisional findings, whether of fact or law, made for the purposes of provisional measures under Article 24,[55] ought not to be conclusive for the purposes of a trial of the main action, even if the findings are directly in point. This is not a departure from the principle that a foreign judgment is not to be reviewed as to its substance, because the trial of the main action will normally involve a fresh appraisal of the issues, rather than a review of the provisional measure.

Article 30

27.78   **A court of a Contracting State in which recognition is sought of a judgment given in another Contracting State may stay the proceedings if an ordinary appeal against the judgment has been lodged.**

A court of a Contracting State in which recognition is sought

---

[51] Jenard, para. A1.198 below.

[52] *Cf.* Schlosser, para. 191 (para. A1.487 below); Bülow/Böckstiegel/Linke, p. 224.

[53] Objections dismissed as going to the substance of the original judgment include the following: that the judgment was contrary to an earlier judgment which was *res judicata*: *Gronowska* v. *Pfeiffer*, December 18, 1979, Tribunal de Première Instance, Brussels, Digest D I–29—B2 (but see Arts. 27(3) and 27(5)); that the notification of the proceedings was to a person not authorised as the defendant's agent: *Les Assurances Internationales* v. *Elfring*, Jur. Port Anvers 1979–1980, p. 184, Digest D I–29—B3; and that the order was made *ex parte* (although the defendant had been served with the order and given an opportunity to appeal in the state of origin): *Banque Nationale de Paris* v. *Hochheim*, Bundesgerichtshof, case VIII ZB 8/79, May 16, 1979, [1979] E.C.C. 321, Digest D I–34—B3, above.

[53a] In most Contracting States, limitation is a matter of substantive law: see chaps. 48 to 58 below, at para. 32; in England, see Foreign Limitation Periods Act 1984, s.3 (see paras. 9.14 and 9.15 above).

[54] Droz, paras. 472 *et seq.*

[55] Chap. 24 above.

of a judgment given in Ireland or the United Kingdom may stay the proceedings if enforcement is suspended in the State in which the judgment was given by reason of an appeal.*†

O. ARTICLE 30 FIRST PARAGRAPH: STAY OF RECOGNITION PROCEEDINGS PENDING APPEAL

1. General note

This Article gives a discretion to the court in which recognition is sought of a judgment from another Contracting State, to stay its proceedings if an "ordinary appeal"[56] has been lodged against the judgment in the state of origin. The proceedings which may be stayed may either be proceedings under the second paragraph of Article 26[57] for a declaration of recognition, or proceedings under the third paragraph of that Article[58] in which an incidental question of recognition has been raised.[59] In the latter case, a stay would only be appropriate if the outcome of the appeal might affect the outcome of the proceedings in which the incidental issue of recognition is raised.[60]

27.79

The power to grant a stay under this Article apparently applies also where the applicant seeks an order for the enforcement, rather than merely a declaration of recognition, of a judgment given in another Contracting State.[61] In enforcement proceedings, though, there is an additional power to grant a stay at the stage of an appeal against an order authorising enforcement.[62]

The reason for including this provision is as follows. If a party seeks recognition of a judgment which may still be altered or reversed on appeal in its state of origin, it is obviously unsatisfac-

27.80

---

* Jenard, para. A1.199 below; Schlosser, paras. 195–204 (paras. A1.490–A1.500 below); Collins, pp. 120–121; Dashwood/Halcon/White, pp. 43–44, 156–157; Hartley, pp. 93–95; Kaye, pp. 1614–1616, 1645–1654; Maxwell, paras. 6.48–6.49; Anton, paras. 8.28–8.29; Droz, para. 481; Bülow/Böckstiegel/Linke, pp. 225–228; Geimer/Schütze, pp. 1115; Kropholler, pp. 282–285; Gothot/Holleaux, paras. 328–338, 391, 400; Pocar, pp. 303–305.

† The second paragraph was added by Article 14 of the 1978 Convention.

[56] The meaning of "ordinary appeal" is discussed at paras. 27.82 *et seq.* below.

[57] See paras. 27.04 *et seq.* above.

[58] See paras. 27.10 *et seq.* above.

[59] A decision on an incidental issue of recognition may not be binding on a court before which recognition is later a principal issue: see para. 27.11 above.

[60] Bülow/Böckstiegel/Linke, p. 226.

[61] In all enforcement proceedings, recognition can be said to be "sought" for the purposes of this Article. This is so, even if recognition does not become an "issue," for the purposes of the second (and third) paras. of Art. 26, until the party against whom the enforcement is sought lodges an appeal under Art. 36 or the court raises the question of recognition of its own motion.

[62] Art. 38, para. 28.43 below.

tory that the potential effects of the appeal should be pre-empted by the judgment being given immediate recognition in the other Contracting States. If, for example, a party relied on a foreign judgment to found an estoppel in subsequent proceedings in another Contracting State, the recognising court might be bound to give effect to the estoppel if the earlier judgment were entitled to immediate and automatic recognition.[63] If the earlier decision were then to be overturned on appeal, the decisions of the courts in the two countries would conflict, the estoppel would no longer be valid, and an appeal would be necessary in the second proceedings.[64]

On the other hand, to deny altogether the possibility of the original judgment being recognised in the other Contracting States until the appeal process in the state of origin had been completed would be too rigid a rule. First, it might lead to abuse, by causing the judgment debtor to pursue prolonged and hopeless appeals in an attempt to avoid the consequences of the judgment.[65] Secondly, where recognition is raised under the third paragraph of Article 26 as an incidental issue in other proceedings, the second court has jurisdiction to decide the incidental issue of recognition, if the outcome of the other proceedings depends on it. If, for example, those other proceedings were proceedings for provisional measures, the purpose of the proceedings might be altogether defeated if the court were bound to refuse recognition or stay its proceedings.

27.81   The first paragraph of Article 30 is silent as to the point at which the stay may be granted. It may often be sensible for the court addressed to examine the judgment to see whether other grounds for refusing recognition exist, before deciding whether to stay its proceedings; if a stay were granted without the court having examined the question of refusal of recognition of its own motion, it could be said that the discretion had not been properly exercised,[66] although in either case the party seeking recognition would have been frustrated in his attempt to gain immediate recognition for the judgment. For example, if it appears from the judgment or the documents lodged with it[67] that the judgment was given in default of appearance and that the defendant was not duly served with the document in sufficient time to enable him to arrange for his defence, the court addressed should normally refuse recognition of the judgment under Article 27(2) without staying the proceedings.

By contrast with the first paragraph of Article 38,[68] which con-

---

[63] On the questions of *res judicata* and estoppel, see paras. 25.22 and 25.23 above.
[64] Droz, para. 481.
[65] *Cf.* Bülow/Böckstiegel/Linke, p. 227.
[66] Bülow/Böckstiegel/Linke, p. 228.
[67] See para. 27.04 above.
[68] Para. 28.43 below.

tains a similar provision for the case where an order of enforcement is sought, the court may grant the stay of its own motion and may do so even at the initial, *ex parte* stage of the proceedings. Another point of distinction between the two provisions is that, under this Article, the discretion to grant a stay only arises when an appeal "has been lodged" against the original decision, whereas, under Article 38, a stay may be granted, whether or not an appeal has actually been lodged, provided that the time limited for appealing has not yet expired.[69]

2. " . . . ordinary appeal . . . "

This expression is not defined by the Convention, but is to be given a uniform interpretation[70] in all the Contracting States.[71] The concept of an "ordinary appeal" exists to a greater or lesser extent in the legal systems of most of the Contracting States,[72] but is unknown in the United Kingdom and Ireland. The second paragraph of Article 30 (discussed below) was therefore introduced in order to enable the courts of other Contracting States to grant a stay of proceedings in which recognition of a United Kingdom or Irish judgment was in issue in circumstances equivalent to those where an "ordinary appeal" was lodged in a continental Contracting State.   **27.82**

The distinction between ordinary and extraordinary appeals in the context of Article 30 has been the subject of some criticism[73] on the ground that the same provision ought to apply whatever the nature of the appeal, and it has been pointed out[74] that the Italian text of the Convention refers merely to a challenge[75] rather than to an ordinary appeal.

The Industrial Diamond Supplies decision. Much of the point of this criticism, though, is removed by the interpretation actually placed on the words "ordinary appeal" by the European Court of Justice in *Industrial Diamond Supplies* v. *Riva*.[76] Mr. Riva obtained in Turin a judgment against Industrial Diamond Supplies ("IDS") for payment of more than 53 million lire and IDS lodged an appeal against that judgment by way of an appeal in cassation (which did not have the effect of suspending the enforceability of the judgment   **27.83**

---

[69] See para. 28.48 below.
[70] Paras. 13.19 *et seq.* above.
[71] *Industrial Diamond Supplies* v. *Riva* [1977] E.C.R. 2175.
[72] Schlosser, paras. 196–202, paras. A1.491–A1.497 below. See chaps. 48 to 58 below, at para. 64.
[73] Bülow/Böckstiegel/Linke, p. 227.
[74] *Ibid.*
[75] "*se la decisione in questione è stata impugnata*"; see also Schlosser, para. 200, para. A1.495 below.
[76] [1977] E.C.R. 2175.

of the Turin court), but they did not apply for a stay of execution in Italy. Meanwhile, under Article 34 of the Convention, Mr. Riva sought and obtained an order in Belgium for the enforcement of the judgment against IDS, who brought an appeal under Articles 36 and 37 against that order and asked the Belgian court to suspend its proceedings until final judgment had been obtained between the parties in Italy.

The Belgian court referred two questions on the interpretation of Articles 30 and 38 to the European Court of Justice, which ruled first that:

> "The expression 'ordinary appeal' within the meaning of Articles 30 and 38 . . . must be defined solely within the framework of the system of the Convention itself and not according to the law either of the State in which the judgment was given or of the State in which recognition or enforcement of that judgment is sought."[77]

The European Court pointed out that the Convention provided merely a power, rather than a duty, to stay the proceedings and went on to say that,

> "This fact presupposes a sufficiently broad interpretation of the concept of 'ordinary appeal' to enable that court to stay the proceedings whenever reasonable doubt arises with regard to the fate of the decision in the State in which it was given.
>
> It is possible by applying this criterion alone to decide the outcome of a request for recognition or enforcement based on a judgment which, in the State in which the judgment was given, is at present the subject of an appeal which may lead to the annulment or amendment of the judgment in question."[78]

In other words, the European Court seems to have been saying that where an appeal has already been lodged, the recognising court, in deciding how to exercise its discretion, will usually be able to decide that there is a reasonable doubt as to the ultimate fate of the original decision, merely by reason of the fact that an appeal has been lodged.

27.84   The European Court then considered the position (which could arise under Article 38, but not under Article 30) where an appeal had not been lodged in the original state, but the time limited for lodging an appeal had not expired,[79] and went on to rule that,

> "Within the meaning of Articles 30 and 38 of the Convention, any

---

[77] *Ibid.*, at p. 2191.

[78] *Ibid.*, at p. 2189 (paras. 33 and 34). For the subsequent proceedings in Belgium, see Digest D I–38—B4.

[79] This part of the judgment, which forms a necessary part of the European Court's reasoning in interpreting the meaning of the term "ordinary appeal," is discussed in more detail in the commentary on Art. 38, para. 28.49 below.

appeal which is such that it may result in the annulment of the judgment which is the subject-matter of the procedure for recognition or enforcement under the Convention and the lodging of which is bound, in the State in which the judgment was given, to a period which is laid down by the law and starts to run by virtue of that same judgment constitutes an 'ordinary appeal' which has been lodged or which may be lodged against a foreign judgment."[80]

It remains to be seen how this ruling will be applied in the light of the new second paragraph of Article 30, which would seem to treat as an "ordinary appeal" certain procedures, the availability of which is not limited in point of time.[81] As the ruling stands, though, at least when the judgment in question has been given in a continental Contracting State, it would seem that the position is as follows. Where recognition is sought of a judgment given in another Contracting State and against which an appeal has been lodged in that other state, the court in which recognition is sought, in order to decide whether it has jurisdiction under Article 30 to order a stay of its proceedings, will need to look at the procedural law of that other state, to see (i) whether the appeal is one which that law requires should be lodged within a limited time, and (ii) whether that time limit starts to run by virtue of the judgment appealed against.[82]

P. Second Paragraph: United Kingdom and Irish Judgments

As has been observed, the test formulated by the European Court of **27.85** Justice in *Industrial Diamond Supplies* v. *Riva* could not readily apply to the various procedures available under the laws of the different parts of the United Kingdom and of Ireland, which permit review of a judgment without their availability being limited in point of time, or by reference to the date on which the judgment was given. The functions performed by applications to set aside a judgment and various other procedures which a common lawyer would not call an "appeal" are often performed in continental legal systems by various forms of appeal.[83] The Schlosser Report implies that these common law procedures are to be regarded as "ordinary appeals," even though they do not fall easily into the framework of

---

[80] [1977] E.C.R. 2175, at pp. 2191–2192.
[81] For example, an application in England under R.S.C., Ord. 13, r.9, to set aside a default judgment may be brought at any time.
[82] A Belgian court has held that an appeal in cassation is not an "ordinary appeal" as a matter of French procedural law, but is an "ordinary appeal" for the purposes of Arts. 30 and 38 of the Convention: *S.A. Continental Pharma* v. *S.A. Labaz*, Journal trib. 1978, p. 283, Digest D I–38—B3.
[83] These differences in the concept of an "appeal" are discussed in the Schlosser Report at paras. 196–202 (paras. A1.491–A1.497 below); see also chaps. 48 to 58 below, at paras. 63 to 65, where the appeal procedures available in the various Contracting States are described.

the test formulated by the European Court.[84] The differences between the procedures available in the United Kingdom and Ireland, on one hand, and the procedures available in continental legal systems, on the other, are sometimes quite marked, and may perhaps be partly explained by the adversarial nature of common law procedure.

27.86   A further important difference between some continental procedures and English procedural law is that in the latter, the enforceability of a judgment is not suspended automatically by the lodging of an appeal or an equivalent application. A special application for execution to be stayed is required. In continental legal systems, by contrast, ordinary appeals usually have the effect of suspending execution (sometimes unless enforcement is provisionally authorised), whereas extraordinary appeals usually do not.[85]

The new second paragraph of Article 30 provides a simple means whereby a court called upon to recognise a judgment of a United Kingdom or Irish court can decide whether it has jurisdiction to order a stay of its proceedings, although, as the Schlosser Report notes:

> "continental courts will have to use their discretion in such a way that an equal balance in the application of Articles 30 and 38 in all Contracting States will be preserved. To this effect they will have to make only cautious use of their discretionary power to stay proceedings, if the appeal is one which is available in Ireland or the United Kingdom only against special defects in a judgment or which may still be lodged after a long period."[86]

---

[84] Schlosser, para. 240 (paras. A1.499–A1.500 below).
[85] See the submissions of the U.K. government in *Industrial Diamond Supplies* v. *Riva* [1977] E.C.R. 2175, at pp. 2181–2182.
[86] Schlosser, para. 204 (para. A1.500 below).

ENFORCEMENT OF JUDGMENTS
(Articles 31–45)

741

SECTION 2

Article 31

28.01 A judgment given in a Contracting State and enforceable in that State shall be enforced in another Contracting State when, on the application of any interested party, the order for its enforcement has been issued there.

However, in the United Kingdom, such a judgment shall be enforced in England and Wales, in Scotland, or in Northern Ireland when, on the application of any interested party, it has been regis-tered for enforcement in that part of the United Kingdom.*†

A. ARTICLE 31: GENERAL NOTE

28.02 The general scheme of the Convention's enforcement provisions has already been discussed.[1] Provided six conditions are fulfilled, a

---

* Jenard, paras. A1.200–A1.211 below; Schlosser, paras. 206–213 (paras. A1.503–A1.511 below); Collins, pp. 114–115, 124; Dashwood/Halcon/White, pp. 158–159; Hartley, p. 98; Kaye, pp. 1429–1431, 1585–1586; Maxwell, paras. 6.55–6.66, 6.143–6.146; Anton, para. 8.37; Droz, paras. 547–551; Bülow/Böckstiegel/Müller, pp. 228–235; Geimer/Schütze, p. 1125; Kropholler, pp. 286–292; Gothot/Holleaux, paras. 245–253, 339–343; Pocar, pp. 305–312.
† The second para. was added by Art. 15 of the 1978 Convention.
[1] Paras. 25.03 and 25.15 to 25.17 above.

judgment given in a Contracting State may be enforced in each of the other Contracting States. The court to which application is made[2] for an order for enforcement should consider whether each of these conditions are met. The six conditions are:

1. that the case falls within the Convention, both as to its subject-matter[3] and by reference to the transitional provisions;[4]
2. that the judgment is one falling within the definition provided by Article 25;[5]
3. that the judgment is at least provisionally enforceable in its state of origin;[6]
4. that the respondent has been duly served, pursuant to the law of the state of origin (although this condition may not always apply);[7]
5. that the application for an order authorising the enforcement is made by an "interested party";[8]
6. that none of the specified grounds exists for refusing to grant such an order.[9]

The function of the court to which the application is made in the first instance[10] is confined to deciding whether those conditions are met. If they are met, that court has no discretion not to grant an order authorising the enforcement of the judgment. This is implicit in the use of mandatory language in the first paragraph of Article 31 ("*shall* be enforced")[11] and follows from the terms of Article 34,[12] which requires that the court give its decision "without delay" and confines its power to refuse the application to cases where the sixth condition above is not fulfilled. By contrast with the position on an application for a declaration of recognition, the court of first instance may not stay its proceedings where an appeal has been lodged against the judgment in its state of origin.[13]   **28.03**

In considering whether the six conditions are fulfilled, the court must act of its own motion, but, as on an application for a declar-

---

[2] Art. 32, para. 28.09 below.
[3] Art. 1, para. 14.03 above.
[4] Art. 54, para. 32.01 below; Arts. 34–36 of the 1978 Accession Convention, paras. 36.06 *et seq.* below.
[5] Para. 26.01 above.
[6] Art. 31, first para., see para. 28.04 below.
[7] Art. 47(1), paras. 29.07 and 29.14 *et seq.* below.
[8] Art. 31, first para., see para. 28.07 below.
[9] Art. 34, second para., para. 28.22 below. See also paras. 25.11 to 25.13 above.
[10] The particular courts to which the application should be made are those specified by Art. 32, para. 28.09 below.
[11] See para. 28.06 below.
[12] Para. 28.22 below.
[13] *Cf.* Art. 30, para. 27.78 above. Such a power exists only on appeal: Art. 38, see paras. 28.48 *et seq.* below.

ation of recognition, it need not conduct an investigation into the matter.[14] It is, however, required to take notice of any matter relevant to the six conditions which appears from the judgment itself or from the documents lodged for the purpose of the application pursuant to Articles 46 and 47[15] or which is otherwise known to the court. The responsibility for producing the evidence required by those Articles rests with the applicant.

B. Enforcement in Another Contracting State

1. " . . . enforceable in that State . . . "

28.04   One condition (the third of those listed above) for the grant of an order authorising the enforcement of a judgment given in another Contracting State is that the judgment should be enforceable in its state of origin.[16] Although it might appear that this is purely a question to be decided by reference to the law of the state of origin, the Convention does appear to impose at least one extra condition (the fourth of those listed above), namely that the judgment must have been served. A party applying for enforcement of a judgment is required by Article 47(1) to produce documents which establish that, according to the law of the state in which it has been given, the judgment is not only enforceable, but also has been served. The provision seems, on its face, to apply whether or not the national law in question makes service of the judgment a precondition of its enforceability, but for reasons discussed in the commentary on that Article, it is suggested that the Convention does not itself impose a condition that the judgment be served.[17] It merely ensures compliance with the national law of the state of origin in this regard.

28.05   The date at which the judgment must be enforceable in order to meet the requirements of the first paragraph of Article 31 is the date when the enforcing court makes its order.[18] If, at that date, the judgment is not enforceable,[19] or has ceased to be enforceable,[20] or

---

[14] Para. 26.04 above.

[15] Paras. 29.01 *et seq.* below.

[16] This condition does not apply to an application under Art. 26 for a declaration of recognition. The conditions of enforceability in each of the Contracting States are referred to in chaps. 48 to 58 below, at paras. 66 and 67.

[17] See paras. 29.14 *et seq.* below.

[18] Bülow/Böckstiegel/Müller, p. 230.

[19] For example, the internal law of the state of origin may not permit the enforcement of a judgment which is not *res judicata*: Bülow/Böckstiegel/Müller, p. 230.

[20] A judgment may cease to be enforceable by reason of lapse of time: For example, in England, after six years, leave is required for the issue of a writ of execution: R.S.C., O. 46, r. 2.

because it has been satisfied,[21] it may not be enforced in the other Contracting States.[22] If the judgment is only partly enforceable, partial enforcement may be ordered.[23]

It is not necessary for the purposes of Article 31 that the judgment be *res judicata* (in the sense of being no longer subject to appeal),[24] provided that it is enforceable. Equally, the enforceability need not be unconditional and it is sufficient if the judgment is only provisionally enforceable, as for example in the case of an interim order, or one subject to appeal.[24a] But care must be taken in relation to an *ex parte* interim order, because such an order, even if it is enforceable in the state of origin, may not be one to which Title III of the Convention applies.[25]

2. " . . . shall be enforced . . . "

The judgments of each Contracting State are to be accorded full **28.06** faith and credit in the other Contracting States, provided that the conditions for their enforcement are met. The court of the state addressed has no discretion in the matter and (subject to one exception),[25a] once the order for enforcement has been issued there, the foreign judgment is to be treated in all respects (except for the provisions of Articles 38 and 39)[26] as if it were a judgment of the court which authorised its enforcement.[27] The manner of execution of the judgment is a matter for the national law of the state addressed. Where a party has a judgment obtained in one Contracting State, which is capable of enforcement in another Contracting State, he is precluded from starting fresh proceedings for the same relief in that other Contracting State.[28]

It has already been observed that a judgment need not be final or

---

[21] As a German court has held, national law may permit the amendment of an order for enforcement after it has been issued and before it has been executed: Oberlandesgericht München, case 25 W 1937/79, November 30, 1979, RIW/AWD—1980, p. 801, Digest D I–34—B4.

[22] Droz, para. 548; Bülow/Böckstiegel/Müller, pp. 229, 235.

[23] Art. 42, para. 28.71 below.

[24] See para. 25.22 above.

[24a] See, for example, Bundesgerichtshof, case VIII ZB 8/83, May 16, 1983, (1983) RIW 535, [1983] Eur.L.Dig. 501.

[25] See *Denilauler* v. *Couchet Frères* [1980] E.C.R. 1553, discussed at para. 27.26 above.

[25a] This concerns the matters which may be raised in opposing the execution of the judgment: see para. 28.33 below.

[26] Paras. 28.43 and 28.55 below. These Articles relate to a stay of the enforcement proceedings (and the provisional enforceability of the judgment) pending an appeal in the state of origin.

[27] Droz, para. 568.

[28] *De Wolf* v. *Cox B.V.*, [1976] E.C.R. 1759, discussed at para. 25.36 above. *Cf.* s.34 of the 1982 Act, para. 43.36 below.

conclusive before it falls within the scheme of recognition and enforcement.[29] But a judgment may be entitled to automatic recognition under the first paragraph of Article 26 without being enforceable, even if it is final and conclusive. For example, judgments which are merely declaratory may not be susceptible to enforcement[30] and the same applies to the dismissal of an action.[31]

3. " . . . any interested party . . . "

28.07   Another of the conditions (the fifth of those listed above) which must be met before an order for enforcement can be issued is that an application must be made by an "interested party."[32] It is a matter for the national law of the state of origin to decide *what* interest an applicant has in the judgment, but it is a question of interpretation of the Convention to decide *whether* that interest is sufficient to give rise to a right to apply for the enforcement of the judgment in other Contracting States.[33] Generally, as a matter of interpretation of the Convention, any person who is entitled to the benefit of the judgment in its state of origin is an "interested party" and may apply in the other Contracting States for an order for its enforcement.[34] Detailed questions, however, as to who has a right to enforce the judgment,[35] what if any particular conditions must be satisfied before he is entitled to exercise that right,[36] and in what circumstances such a right will be inferred,[37] are matters left to national law.

The date at which the interest must exist is the date at which the enforcing court makes its order for enforcement. It may be that the applicant's interest must be more than merely hypothetical, in the

---

[29] Para. 25.20 above.

[30] Droz (para. 550) gives the example of a judgment declaring that a given person is the rightful owner of, say, a picture, which might be enforceable if the picture were in the possession of someone else, but not if it were already in the possession of the owner. He regards this as an example of lack of a sufficient interest, rather than a lack of enforceability.

[31] See para. 25.08 above.

[32] *Cf.* Art. 36, under which the only person who may appeal against an order for enforcement is the person against whom it has been made: see para. 28.32 below.

[33] See para. 27.05 above.

[34] Jenard, para. A1.211 below.

[35] For example, an assignee of the judgment, or the judgment creditor's executors or liquidator, might be entitled to the benefit of the judgment: see paras. 27.06 and 27.07 above. See also *Société FIR* v. *Héritiers Baas*, Rev. critique 1980, p. 121, Digest D I–27.2—B12.

[36] For example, in English law, an assignee of the judgment will only be entitled to enforce it when he has given notice to the judgment debtor: Law of Property Act 1925, s.136. See also Supreme Court Practice, para. 46/2/6.

[37] Droz, para. 549.

sense that the judgment is capable of enforcement,[38] but the enforcing court's power to investigate the applicant's interest does not grant it a discretion over the issue of the order for enforcement. It must examine the applicant's interest and if it is established (and provided the other conditions for enforcement are met), the order for enforcement must be issued. The documents which the applicant is obliged to lodge in support of the application[39] must show that the judgment is enforceable in the state of origin, but it is not expressly stated that they must show that the applicant is an "interested person." It is suggested, though, that that requirement may be implicit in the wording of Article 47(1).[40]

4. United Kingdom

The inclusion of this new paragraph was necessary to take account of the fact that the United Kingdom contains three separate "law areas" and it requires no special commentary. Sections 4 and 5 of the 1982 Act[41] make provision for the registration of judgments in the different parts of the United Kingdom. **28.08**

Article 32

The application shall be submitted: **28.09**
— in Belgium, to the tribunal de première instance or rechtbank van eerste aanleg,
— in Denmark, to the underret,
— in the Federal Republic of Germany, to the presiding judge of a chamber of the Landgericht,
[— in Greece, to the μονομελές πρωτοδικεῖο,]
— in France, to the presiding judge of the tribunal de grande instance,
— in Ireland, to the High Court,
— in Italy, to the corte d'appello,
— in Luxembourg, to the presiding judge of the tribunal d'arrondissement,
— in the Netherlands, to the presiding judge of the arrondissementsrechtbank,

---

[38] See n. 30 above.
[39] Arts. 46 and 47, paras. 29.01 and 29.07 below.
[40] See para. 29.09 below.
[41] Paras. 40.08 and 40.12 below.

— in the United Kingdom:
1. in England and Wales, to the High Court of Justice, or in the case of a maintenance judgment to the Magistrates' Court on transmission by the Secretary of State;
2. in Scotland, to the Court of Session, or in the case of a maintenance judgment to the Sheriff Court on transmission by the Secretary of State;
3. in Northern Ireland, to the High Court of Justice, or in the case of a maintenance judgment to the Magistrates' Court on transmission by the Secretary of State.

The jurisdiction of local courts shall be determined by reference to the place of domicile of the party against whom enforcement is sought. If he is not domiciled in the State in which enforcement is sought, it shall be determined by reference to the place of enforcement.*†

C. Article 32, First Paragraph: Courts for Initial Application

General note

28.10   Article 32 acts as a compulsory provision on jurisdiction, giving exclusive jurisdiction to each of the courts specified over applications at first instance for orders for enforcement, even where the subject-matter of the judgment would not normally fall within the jurisdiction of that court (in employment cases, for example)[42] or where the judgment is that of a court of a different status.[43] Although the courts specified in the first paragraph of this Article are not necessarily chosen on any uniform basis, the second paragraph provides a uniform rule[44] for determining which of the courts

---

* Jenard, para. A1.212 below; Schlosser, paras. 214–215 (paras. A1.512–A1.513 below); Collins, pp. 116–117; Dashwood/Halcon/White, pp. 38, 159–160; Hartley, p. 99; Kaye, pp. 1590–1593; Maxwell, paras. 6.67–6.68, 6.147–6.149; Droz, paras. 557–561; Bülow/Böckstiegel/Müller, pp. 236–239; Geimer/Schütze, pp. 1122, 1213–1216; Kropholler, pp. 292–294; Gothot/Holleaux, paras. 353–354, 398; Pocar, pp. 312–314.

† The words in square brackets were added by Art. 4 of the 1982 Convention and are not yet in force. See para. 13.05 above. The whole of the rest of the first paragraph was substituted for the 1968 version by Art. 16 of the 1978 Convention.

[42] Bülow/Böckstiegel/Müller, p. 236.

[43] The Convention is not limited to the superior courts of the Contracting States, and all judgments which come within Title III are subject to the same procedure for recognition and enforcement: see para. 25.15 above.

[44] Bülow/Böckstiegel/Müller, *loc. cit.*

of the specified description has local jurisdiction.[45] When an order for enforcement has been made by a court of local jurisdiction, national law will determine the geographical area within which the judgment may be enforced. For the purposes of the recognition and enforcement procedures provided by Title III, England and Wales, Scotland and Northern Ireland are treated as separate states.

Examination of jurisdiction. Where an application for an order for   **28.11** enforcement or for a declaration of recognition is brought before a court, the court must examine its jurisdiction[46] of its own motion,[47] especially in view of the *ex parte* nature of the procedure at this stage.[48] Although there is no express requirement in the Convention for the applicant to provide the information (such as the judgment debtor's address) necessary for the court to establish its local jurisdiction, it is probably implicit in the scheme of Title III that the court can require further information from the applicant in cases of doubt[49] and national law can anyway provide such detailed rules as may be necessary.[50] If the court finds that it has no jurisdiction it may either transfer the application to a court which does have jurisdiction, if that is permitted by the national procedural law, or dismiss the application.[51]

Where the judgment is against several persons, the applicant may bring his application for enforcement against each of them in the court for the place where each is domiciled, in respect of that particular defendant's joint or several liability. What is less clear is whether the applicant may join several defendants to such an application in the court for the place where only one of them is domiciled, by analogy with Article 6(1).[52] If the Convention does permit such an extension of jurisdiction against a co-defendant, it is submitted that it can only apply in the case of joint liability and not in the case of several liability. The same considerations would apply

---

[45] In the U.K., the High Courts of England and Wales and of Northern Ireland and the Court of Session each have local jurisdiction over the whole of their respective areas, so the uniform rule of local jurisdiction will only arise for consideration there in maintenance cases. In Denmark, the *unterret* is now called the *byret*: see para. 49.19

[46] That is, its jurisdiction to entertain the application under this Art.: see paras. 28.12 *et seq.* below.

[47] Droz, para. 560; Bülow/Böckstiegel/Müller, p. 238; *cf.* Art. 20, para. 22.11 above.

[48] Art. 34, first para., para. 28.22 below.

[49] Bülow/Böckstiegel/Müller, p. 238.

[50] See Art. 33, first para., para. 28.16 below. In England, for example, see R.S.C. O. 71, r. 28(1)(c): see para. 10.14 above.

[51] Bülow/Böckstiegel/Müller, p. 239.

[52] Geimer/Schütze, p. 1113.

where jurisdiction was based not on the domicile of the judgment debtor, but on the place of enforcement.[53]

D. ARTICLE 32, SECOND PARAGRAPH: JURISDICTION OF LOCAL COURTS

1. Local jurisdiction

28.12   The uniform rule of local jurisdiction provided by the second paragraph of Article 32 has two limbs. The first limb requires that local jurisdiction be based on the domicile of the person against whom enforcement is sought (the judgment debtor) and is intended to prevent a multiplicity of *ex parte* applications where that person has property within the local jurisdiction of several courts.[54] In deciding whether it has local jurisdiction, the court has first to decide whether the judgment debtor is domiciled in that Contracting State. It is to do so by applying Articles 52 and 53.[55] If the judgment debtor is domiciled in that Contracting State, the court must then apply national law[56] to determine whether he is domiciled within the local jurisdiction of that court.

If the judgment debtor is not domiciled in that Contracting State, the second limb of the rule comes into operation and gives jurisdiction to the court where it is proposed that enforcement should occur. The question arises on the second limb whether it is sufficient for the judgment creditor merely to assert that he proposes to enforce the judgment in the locality of the particular court, or whether there must be some objective link with that court. On one hand, while it would be usual for the judgment debtor to have assets (such as land or chattels or a debt which can be attached) within the local jurisdiction of the court, it seems that this is not strictly necessary.[57] If that were a requirement, the Convention would have said so. On the other hand, there would be little point in the Convention providing a rule of local jurisdiction for the case where the judgment debtor was not domiciled in the Contracting State where enforcement is sought, unless some local link were required. Subject to one qualification, it would seem, therefore, that the judgment creditor must show that he has some prospects of enforcing the judgment in the locality of the court to which he applies.

---

[53] See next para.
[54] Jenard, para. A1.213 below.
[55] Chap. 31 below.
[56] In the U.K., the relevant provisions are ss.41(3), 41(4), 42(4) and 42(5) of the 1982 Act, paras. 44.01 and 44.11 below.
[57] Bülow/Böckstiegel/Müller, p. 237.

Absence of local connecting factor not to exclude applicant. The **28.13**
qualification is this. If an applicant for an order for enforcement
under the second limb of this paragraph must always show some
prospect of enforcing his judgment in the locality of the court to
which he applies, he would be unable to obtain an order for the
enforcement of a judgment which he had (at the time of the application) no prospect of enforcing in that state. But the prospect of
enforcing the judgment goes only to jurisdiction, not to the applicant's entitlement to an order, and to shut out such an applicant
entirely would seem to be contrary to the Convention. For example,
an applicant might wish to seek an order for enforcement in each of
the Contracting States against a judgment debtor domiciled outside
the Community, in order to be able to move quickly to enforce his
judgment as soon as the judgment debtor brought assets into any of
the Contracting States. It is submitted, therefore, for the reasons
discussed below, that an applicant for an order of enforcement
should be free to choose the locality of the court to which he applies
in any given Contracting State, if the person against whom the
order is sought is not domiciled in that Contracting State and the
applicant has no greater prospect of enforcing the judgment in one
locality than in another.

Recognition. Article 32 applies not only to applications for **28.14**
enforcement of judgments, but also to applications for a declaration
of recognition.[58] In the latter case, it may well be that there is no
prospective place for the enforcement of the judgment.[59] The Convention makes no express provision for a court to have local jurisdiction over such an application, if the person against whom the
order is sought is not domiciled in the State where the application is
made. Normally, where the Convention is silent on questions of
local jurisdiction, the matter is determined by national law, and it
may be that this applies also to this situation. On the other hand,
such a solution might lead to a particular local court having jurisdiction if recognition alone were sought, but the applicant having a
large degree of choice over the court where he makes the application if he also applies for an order of enforcement. Such a solution
would be illogical, and it would seem more in keeping with the
Convention's unifying purpose that he should have a choice of
court.[60] It is submitted, therefore, that the Convention should be
interpreted as allowing a choice of local jurisdiction to an applicant
for a declaration of recognition, where the person against whom the

---

[58] Art. 26, second para., para. 27.01 above.
[59] This applies particularly to orders varying earlier maintenance orders: see
Schlosser, para. 108 (para. A1.394 below).
[60] *Cf.* Droz, para. 561.

declaration is sought is not domiciled in the Contracting State where the application is made.

2. Renewal of application

28.15   It has already been noted that the purpose of the rule on local jurisdiction is to prevent a multiplicity of applications to different local courts, without the judgment debtor having an opportunity to be heard. If, therefore, the judgment debtor is domiciled in the Contracting State where enforcement is sought, but a local court dismisses the application, the judgment creditor can probably only appeal against the dismissal under Article 40[61] and is probably precluded from bringing a fresh application before another local court,[62] at least until after the appeal has been disposed of and the judgment debtor has had an opportunity of being heard. This rule would not seem to apply, though, if the application had been dismissed by the local court for want of local jurisdiction. Similarly, if the judgment debtor is not domiciled in the Contracting State where enforcement is sought, a judgment creditor whose application has been dismissed under the second paragraph of Article 34 should be confined in the first instance to his rights of appeal under Article 40. On the other hand, if the application has been dismissed because the judgment creditor failed to show a prospect of enforcing the judgment within the locality of the court applied to, there seems to be no reason why he should not renew his application to another local court.[63] Because England and Wales, Scotland and Northern Ireland are treated as separate states for the purposes of Article 32, there is nothing in the Convention to stop a judgment creditor from applying for an order of enforcement in more than one part of the United Kingdom.

Article 33

28.16   **The procedure for making the application shall be governed by the law of the State in which enforcement is sought.**

The applicant must give an address for service of process within the area of jurisdiction of the court applied to. However, if the law of the State in which enforcement is sought does not provide for the furnishing of such an address, the applicant shall appoint a representative *ad litem*.

The documents referred to in Articles 46 and 47 shall be attached to the application.★

---

[61] Para. 28.63 below.
[62] Droz, para. 560; Bülow/Böckstiegel/Müller, p. 237.
[63] *Cf.* Bülow/Böckstiegel/Müller, *loc. cit.*

E. ARTICLE 33: PROCEDURE FOR APPLICATION

1. General note

Article 33 contains a number of miscellaneous provisions con-   28.17
cerning applications for orders of enforcement or declarations of
recognition of judgments given in other Contracting States, each of
which is discussed in turn.

2. First paragraph: procedure regulated by national law

It is not the aim of the Convention to regulate in detail the pro-   28.18
cedure whereby, in each Contracting State, the application is to be
made for an order of enforcement or declaration of recognition.
Provided that it does not contravene the framework provided by the
Convention, the procedure for making the application is to be
determined by national law. Apart from regulating the general procedure, national law may determine such matters as the particulars
to be contained in the application, the number of copies to be submitted, the language in which documents must be presented[64] and
whether a party must be represented by a lawyer.[65]

3. Second paragraph: address for service; representative *ad litem*

The reason for the requirement that the applicant must give an   28.19
address for service[66] within the jurisdiction of the local court to
which he applies is twofold: first, to enable the court pursuant to
Article 35[67] to communicate to the applicant its decision on the
initial *ex parte* application; and, secondly, in order that the respondent, if he wishes to appeal against the initial decision under Article
36,[68] may comply with any local rules[69] as to the service of a notice

---

* Jenard, paras. A1.214–A1.218 below; Schlosser, para. 218 (para. A1.518
  below); Collins, p. 117; Dashwood/Halcon/White, pp. 160–161; Hartley,
  pp. 97–99; Kaye, pp. 1596–1597; Maxwell, paras. 6.69–6.75, 6.150–6.151;
  Anton, paras. 8.39–8.40; Droz, paras. 562–563; Bülow/Böckstiegel/Müller,
  pp. 239–241; Geimer/Schütze, pp. 1110–1112, 1191–1192; Kropholler,
  pp. 295–297; Gothot/Holleaux, paras. 345–346, 355; Pocar, pp. 314–317.
[64] Art. 48(2) contains a requirement as to translations if they are required by the
  court addressed: para. 29.20 below.
[65] Jenard, para. A1.214 below.
[66] Other language versions refer to the "election" of "domicile." The concept of a
  domicile of election is not to be confused with the concept of domicile envisaged
  by the Convention's jurisdictional provisions: see para. 31.05 below.
[67] Para. 28.28 below.
[68] Para. 28.30 below.
[69] See Art. 37, para. 28.38 below.

of appeal, without having to serve such a notice on the applicant abroad.[70]

28.20   *The Carron decision.* The European Court has considered this paragraph in *Carron v. Federal Republic of Germany.*[71] The Federal Republic had obtained a judgment for over five million Deutschmarks against Mr. Carron in Germany and obtained an order for its enforcement in Belgium from the court in Antwerp. Carron challenged that order on the basis that the German government's application had not stated an address for service within the district of the Antwerp court, but that appeal was dismissed, the court holding that the provision of an address in the document giving notice of the decision to authorise enforcement was sufficient to satisfy the requirements of the second paragraph of Article 33. Carron brought a further appeal to the Belgian *Cour de Cassation*, which in turn referred a number of questions to the European Court of Justice. Those questions, in effect, asked whether the law of the state addressed governed the time at which, and the manner in which, an address for service should be given and, if so, whether that law also governed the sanctions for failure to comply with those requirements. The European Court ruled on those questions as follows:

> "(1) The second paragraph of Article 33 . . . must be interpreted as meaning that the obligation to give an address for service of process laid down in that provision must be fulfilled in conformity with the rules laid down by the law of the State in which enforcement is sought, and if that law is silent as to the time at which that formality must be observed, no later than the date on which the decision authorizing enforcement is served.
>
> (2) The consequences of a failure to comply with the rules on the furnishing of an address for service are, by virtue of Article 33 of the Convention, governed by the law of the State in which enforcement is sought, provided that the aims of the Convention are respected."[72]

If, however, national law makes no provision for furnishing an address for service within the jurisdiction (as, for example, in Germany),[73] the Convention requires that the applicant appoint a representative *ad litem.*[74] The rules governing such appointment may

---

[70] Jenard, para. A1.217 below.

[71] [1986] E.C.R. 2437.

[72] *Ibid.*, at pp. 2446 and 2447.

[73] Jenard, para. A1.217 below; Bülow/Böckstiegel/Müller, p. 240.

[74] In England and Wales, cases other than maintenance cases are covered by R.S.C. Order 71, rule 28(1)(d), which requires the applicant to give an address for service. So far as maintenance cases in the U.K. are concerned, the Schlosser Report, para. 218 (para. A1.518 below), suggests that the clerk of the court to which the application is submitted on transmission by the Secretary of State or Lord Chancellor will act as the representative *ad litem*. However, no express provision has been made to this effect in English law: see para. 11.15 above.

be laid down by national law.[75] Although it might appear anomalous, it seems that there is no reason, so far as the Convention is concerned, why the applicant should not appoint himself as his representative *ad litem*, provided that this is permitted by national law.

4. Third paragraph: documents in support of the application

The documents referred to in Article 46 should be attached to any application, whether it is for an order of enforcement or for a declaration of recognition, whereas those referred to in Article 47 need only be produced on an application for an order of enforcement.[76] Although the third paragraph of Article 33 appears to be compulsory in its terms (*"shall* be attached"), it does not provide a precondition to the grant of the order sought, because the provisions of Articles 46 and 47[77] are themselves qualified by Articles 48 and 49.[78] National law can provide further requirements or qualifications of these rules, provided that it is not inconsistent with the terms of the Convention.[79]

28.21

Article 34

The court applied to shall give its decision without delay; the party against whom enforcement is sought shall not at this stage of the proceedings be entitled to make any submissions on the application.

28.22

The application may be refused only for one of the reasons specified in Articles 27 and 28.

Under no circumstances may the foreign judgment be reviewed as to its substance.*

---

[75] The rule in Germany is that the representative *ad litem* must be domiciled within the local jurisdiction of the court: Bülow/Böckstiegel/Müller, *loc. cit.*

[76] The document required by Art. 47(2), relating to legal aid, may also be produced on an application under the second para. of Art. 26 for a declaration of enforcement: see paras. 29.08 and 29.18 *et seq.* below.

[77] Paras. 29.01 and 29.07 below.

[78] Paras. 29.20 and 29.30 below. The extent to which the third para. of Art. 33 is compulsory is discussed at para. 29.22 below.

[79] Paras. 29.02 and 29.08 below.

* Jenard, para. A1.218–A1.219 below; Schlosser, para. 219 (para. A1.519 below); Collins, pp. 118–119; Dashwood/Halcon/White p. 161; Hartley, p. 98; Kaye, pp. 1365, 1441–1442, 1613–1614; Maxwell, paras. 6.76–6.81; Droz, paras. 552–553, 564; Bülow/Böckstiegel/Müller, pp. 242–245; Geimer/Schütze, pp. 1114–1115, 1126, 1199–1206; Kropholler, pp. 297–301; Gothot/Holleaux, paras. 315–322, 356; Pocar, pp. 317–322. (See also the references under Arts. 27 to 29.)

F. ARTICLE 34: DECISION ON APPLICATION

1. General note

28.23   Article 34 contains a number of further miscellaneous provisions concerning applications for orders of enforcement, or for declarations of recognition, of judgments given in other Contracting States, each of which is discussed in turn.

2. "The court applied to shall give its decision without delay . . ."

28.24   The Convention contains no specific time limit within which the decision on the application must be given.[80] It also contains no sanction to prevent delay at this stage,[81] although such sanction may be provided by national law under the first paragraph of Article 33. Nonetheless, the effect of Article 34(1) should be that an application, if it is properly presented, with the requisite supporting evidence, ought to be decided as swiftly as the business of the court will allow,[82] even if difficult points of law arise on the application.[83]

3. " . . . the party against whom enforcement is sought shall not at this stage of the proceedings be entitled to make any submissions on the application"

28.25   The procedure on the initial application is strictly *ex parte*. Not only does the respondent have no *right* to be heard, it is plain from other language versions[84] that he *may not* be heard.[85] The court has no discretion in the matter[86] and may not even hear him *de bene*

---

[80] Jenard, para. A1.218 below.

[81] Droz, para. 564.

[82] Bülow/Böckstiegel/Müller, p. 242. In the English High Court, an application for an order for enforcement will normally be treated as vacation business. *Cf. Practice Direction* [1983] 1 W.L.R. 432.

[83] Under the 1971 Protocol on Interpretation (chap. 36 below), an application to the European Court for an interpretative ruling is not permitted at this stage.

[84] French: " . . . *sans que la partie contre laquelle l'exécution est demandée puisse . . . présenter d'observation;*" German: " . . . *ohne dass der Schuldner . . . Gelegenheit erhält, eine Erklärung abzugeben;*" Italian: " . . . *senza che la parte contro cui l'esecuzione viene chiesta possa . . . presentare oservazioni;*" Dutch: " . . . *de partij tegen wie de tenuitvoer legging wordt gevraagd, wordt . . . niet gehoord.*"

[85] This applies, it seems, even in the rare case where the respondent is given notice of the application: Schlosser, para. 219 (para. A1.519 below). It makes no difference that the order, being a final order made *ex parte*, was made in the court of origin without his having had an opportunity of being heard: *Banque Nationale de Paris* v. *Hochheim*, Bundesgerichtshof, case VIII ZB 8/79, May 16, 1979, Digest D I–34—B3.

[86] Bülow/Böckstiegel/Müller, p. 243.

esse. Contrasting the procedure under the present provision with that on an appeal under Article 36, the European Court has pointed out that the Convention,

> "provides for a very simple enforcement procedure whilst giving the party against whom the enforcement is sought an opportunity to lodge an appeal. Unlike the initial proceedings concerning the decision authorising enforcement, the proceedings on the appeal are adversary proceedings."[87]

The purpose of the provision is to enable the applicant to take the respondent by surprise,[88] although, by reason of Article 39,[89] enforcement cannot take effect unconditionally until the respondent has had an opportunity to be heard, on an appeal under Article 36. The European Court has described the effect of the provision in these terms:

> "Whilst [a] reason for the unilateral character of the enforcement procedure under Article 34 is to produce the surprise effect which this procedure must have in order to prevent a defendant from having the opportunity to protect his assets against any enforcement measures, the surprise effect is attenuated since the unilateral proceedings are based on the assumption that both parties will have been heard in the State of origin."[90]

If the party against whom enforcement is sought writes to the court informally, drawing attention to matters which would weigh against the grant of an order for enforcement, it seems that the court would be bound to consider these matters in making its decision.[90a]

4. "The application may be refused only for one of the reasons specified in Articles 27 and 28"

Articles 27 and 28 set out the principal grounds on which a judgment may be refused recognition.[91] This paragraph extends the effect of those Articles, so that they apply also to the enforcement

28.26

---

[87] *Calzaturificio Brennero sas* v. *Wendel GmbH Schuhproduktion International*, [1984] E.C.R. 3971, at p. 3982 (para. 10).
[88] Jenard, para. A1.218 below; Schlosser, para. 219 (para. A1.519 below).
[89] Para. 28.55 below.
[90] *Denilauler* v. *Couchet Frères* [1980] E.C.R. 1553, at pp. 1569–1570. The case is discussed at para. 27.26 above. If the defendant has not in fact been heard, he should at least have had the opportunity of presenting his defence. This is the effect of Art. 27(2) (para. 27.21 above).
[90a] See para. 27.04 above; Kaye, pp. 1618 to 1619; Geimer/Schütze, pp. 1200 to 1201; *cf.* Oberlandesgericht Muchen, case 25 W 1937/79, November 30, 1979, RIW/AWD–1980, p. 801, Digest D I–34—B4.
[91] Paras. 27.12 *et seq.* above. The grounds are summarised at paras. 25.11 to 25.13 above.

procedure.[92] Although the second paragraph of Article 34 refers only to Articles 27 and 28, a judgment may also be refused recognition and enforcement on certain other minor grounds.[93] If one of the grounds of refusal exists, the court has no discretion to recognise or enforce the judgment, but must dismiss the application. The Jenard Report[94] points out that the application may also be refused if it fails to comply with Articles 32 and 33, although it may be preferable to regard such a failure as a ground for refusing to entertain the application.[95]

5. "Under no circumstances may the foreign judgment be reviewed as to its substance"

28.27   This provision is the same as Article 29[96] and is based on the requirement that the courts of the Contracting States should accord each other's judgments automatic recognition. Subject to one qualification, no review of the correctness of the original decision may be undertaken by the court of the state addressed. Just how rigorously this rule is to be applied may be illustrated by the case of a set-off. If a defendant objects to the enforcement of a judgment against him, on the grounds that he has a claim against the applicant which he wishes to set off against the applicant's judgment, any submission to that effect will amount to a submission on the substance of the judgment[97] and will not be admissible.

A review as to the substance may, however, be permissible for the purposes of deciding whether the action actually falls within the Convention.[97a] For example, the question may arise whether the subject-matter of the action falls within the general scope of the Convention as defined by Article 1, or within a specialist convention envisaged by Article 57; or the rules applied by the court of origin may need to be reviewed for the purpose of deciding whether the transitional provisions[98] bring the case within the Convention. Although, in the interests of convenience, these matters, which relate to the substance of the decision and the means by which it was arrived at, have been listed as one of the conditions the court has to consider in deciding whether to grant or dismiss an appli-

---

[92] As to the distinction between recognition and enforcement, see paras. 25.06 to 25.10, 25.15 and 25.30 above.

[93] See para. 25.13 above.

[94] Jenard, para. A1.219 below.

[95] *Cf.* Jenard, at para. A1.216 below.

[96] Para. 27.75 above.

[97] See the Opinion of Advocate-General Mayras in *Denilauler* v. *Couchet Frères* [1980] E.C.R. 1553, at p. 1582.

[97a] See also para. 27.65 above.

[98] Art. 54, second para. (para. 32.01 below) and Art. 34 of the 1978 Convention (para. 36.06 below).

cation for an order of enforcement,[99] they are more accurately matters which the court ought to take into account in deciding whether to *entertain* the application. It is for that purpose only that the substance may be reviewed, and once the court has properly entertained the application, it may not review even these matters in deciding whether to grant or dismiss the application for enforcement.

Article 35

The appropriate officer of the court shall without delay bring 28.28 the decision given on the application to the notice of the applicant in accordance with the procedure laid down by the law of the State in which enforcement is sought.*

G. ARTICLE 35: NOTIFICATION TO APPLICANT

The manner in which the applicant is notified of the decision is 28.29 determined by national law,[1] subject to the requirement that the notification should be "without delay."[2] If a representative *ad litem* has been appointed under the second paragraph of Article 33, the notice may be served on that person, rather than on the applicant himself.

Article 35 governs only notification of the decision to the applicant. Unless national law provides otherwise, the court is not responsible for service of notice on the respondent. It is in the applicant's interests that the respondent should be duly served with notice of the decision, because until he has been served and his time for appealing has expired[3] the applicant cannot proceed to enforce the judgment (except by way of protective measures).[4]

If the application for an order of enforcement is dismissed, there is no provision in the Convention for the respondent to be notified, and he will often only find out about the application if and when the applicant appeals against the dismissal[5] under Article 40.[6]

---

[99] Para. 25.13 above.
* Jenard, para. A1.220 below; Dashwood/Halcon/White, p. 162; Maxwell, para. 6.82; Kaye, pp. 1620–1622; Anton, para. 8.49; Droz, para. 565; Bülow/Böckstiegel/Müller, pp. 245–246; Geimer/Schütze, pp. 1216–1220; Kropholler, p. 301; Pocar, p. 322.
[1] Jenard, para. A1.220 below. In England, the relevant provision is R.S.C., Ord. 71, r. 32.
[2] See para. 28.24 above.
[3] Art. 36, para. 28.30 below.
[4] Art. 39, para. 28.55 below.
[5] Bülow/Böckstiegel/Müller, p. 246.
[6] Para. 28.63 below.

Article 36

28.30   **If enforcement is authorised, the party against whom enforcement is sought may appeal against the decision within one month of service thereof.**

If that party is domiciled in a Contracting State other than that in which the decision authorising enforcement was given, the time for appealing shall be two months and shall run from the date of service, either on him in person or at his residence. No extension of time may be granted on account of distance.*

H. Article 36: Service of Decision and Time for Appeals

1. General note

28.31   Articles 36 to 39 regulate appeals against a decision to grant an order for enforcement of a judgment given in another Contracting State.[7] They provide a framework of rules, governing the time for appealing (Article 36), the courts to which appeals are to be brought (Article 37), staying proceedings pending an appeal in the state of origin (Article 38) and the prevention of enforcement pending appeal against the enforcement order (Article 39). These basic provisions are supplemented on matters of detail by national law, provided that the application of national law does not impair the efficacy of the general scheme of the Convention as regards orders for enforcement.[7a]

The matters which can be reviewed on such an appeal are no wider than the matters which the court may take into account on the initial application.[8] The scope of appeals provided for under this paragraph is considered in more detail in the commentary on Article 37.[9]

---

* Jenard, para. A1.221 below; Schlosser, para. 220 (para. A1.520 below); Dashwood/Halcon/White, pp. 44–45, 162–164; Hartley, p. 98; Kaye, pp. 1622–1627; Maxwell, paras. 6.83–6.86; Anton, paras. 8.50–8.51; Droz, paras. 570–574; Bülow/Böckstiegel/Müller, pp. 246–249; Geimer/Schütze, pp. 1115, 1220–1222, 1236–1240, 1249, 1252–1253, 1256, 1259, 1263–1264; Kropholler, pp. 301–307; Gothot/Holleaux, paras. 368, 370, 374, 376; Pocar, pp. 323–7.

[7] Appeals against a decision dismissing an application for an order of enforcement are regulated by Arts. 40 and 41.

[7a] *Hoffman* v. *Krieg*, case 145/86, decision of February 4, 1988 (paras. 28 and 29), *The Times*, March 26, 1988: see paras. 27–47 above and 28.33 below.

[8] Schlosser, para. 220 (para. A1.520 below).

[9] Paras. 28.40 and 28.41 below.

2. " . . . the party against whom enforcement is sought . . . "

It is only the party against whom enforcement is sought who may   **28.32**
appeal. It is not open to other interested parties to object to an order
for enforcement, even if the national law of the state addressed
allows them that opportunity.[10] The wording of the Article does not
appear expressly to exclude an appeal by a person other than the
party against whom enforcement is sought, but the European Court
of Justice has held that it is only that person who may bring an
appeal, although national law may permit other persons to challenge the actual execution of the judgment: *Deutsche Genossenschaftsbank* v. *Brasserie du Pêcheur S.A.*[11]

The applicant was a German bank which was the assignee of an
authentic instrument[12] granting its rights of enforcement against
the assets of one of its creditors, a German company. It sought and
was granted an order for the enforcement of the authentic instrument against the company's assets in France. Brasserie du Pêcheur,
a French company and another of the German company's creditors,
successfully applied to have that order set aside, as it was permitted
to do under French law, but on the bank's appeal, the *Cour d'Appel*
Colmar referred to the European Court the question of whether an
interested third party was prevented by Article 36 from challenging
the order for enforcement.

The European Court reiterated that the objective of the Convention was to provide a simple enforcement procedure in the state
where enforcement was sought[13] and said:

> "In order to attain that objective the Convention established an
> enforcement procedure which constitutes an autonomous and com-
> plete system, including the matter of appeals. It follows that Article
> 36 of the Convention excludes procedures where interested third par-
> ties may challenge an enforcement order under domestic law.
>
> The Convention merely regulates the procedure for obtaining an
> order for the enforcement of foreign enforceable instruments and
> does not deal with execution itself, which continues to be governed by
> the domestic law of the court in which execution is sought, so that
> interested third parties may contest execution by means of the pro-
> cedures available to them under the law of the State in which
> execution is levied."[14]

---

[10] This is in contrast to Art. 31, where persons other than the party in whose
favour the judgment was given may apply for an order for its enforcement in
another Contracting State: see para. 28.07 above.

[11] [1985] E.C.R. 1981.

[12] See Art. 50, para. 30.01 below.

[13] See *Brennero* v. *Wendel* [1984] E.C.R. 3971, at p. 3982 (para. 10, quoted at
para. 28.26 above).

[14] [1985] E.C.R. 1981 at p. 1992 (paras. 17 and 18).

3. Service and time for appealing

28.33   Article 36 contains the Convention's basic provisions on the time for appealing, which runs from the time when the respondent is served with the decision. The detailed computation of time and the detailed rules as to what constitutes service are each to be regulated by national law (and the relevant bilateral conventions), except where the Convention makes specific provision.[14a] Whatever law is applied in deciding whether service has been effected, it seems that time is to run from the date when service is duly effected. If service is not duly effected, time for an appeal does not start to run and the applicant will be unable to enforce the judgment (except by way of protective measures).[15]

The European Court has held in *Hoffman* v. *Krieg*[15a] that if a party has failed to appeal against an enforcement order within the time limits prescribed by this Article, he is precluded thereafter, when the judgment comes to be executed, from relying on a valid reason for opposing the enforcement which he could have raised on such an appeal. That rule is to be applied by national courts, of their own motion if need be. As the Court observed, to allow the re-opening of grounds of appeal at the stage of execution would be to deprive Article 36 of its effect.[15b] The decision in *Hoffman* v. *Krieg* leaves open the possibility of a third party applying to stay the execution of the judgment if he is affected by it. Moreover, the rule formulated by the European Court is subject to the exception that it does not apply when it has the effect of obliging the national court to make the effects of a national judgment lying outside the scope of the Convention conditional on that judgment being recognised in the state of origin of the foreign judgment.[15c]

28.34   Three different situations are to be distinguished, namely where the respondent is domiciled: (1) in the same Contracting State as the court making the decision authorising enforcement; (2) in another Contracting State; and (3) in a non-Contracting State. Each will be discussed in turn. Where the respondent is domiciled is to be decided by the application of whichever national law is indicated by the rules in Articles 52 and 53.[16]

[14a] Under English law, the computation of time is regulated by R.S.C. Ord. 3 and the time for appeal is further regulated by R.S.C. Ord. 71, r.33: see para. 10.25 above.

[15] Art. 39, para. 28.55 below.

[15a] Case 145/86, decision of February 4, 1988, *The Times*, March 26, 1988: see paras. 27.47 above.

[15b] *Ibid.*, para. 30.

[15c] *Ibid.*, paras. 32 and 33.

[16] Chap. 31 below.

(1) Respondent domiciled in the same state. In this case, the first paragraph of Article 36 provides that the time for appealing is one month from the time when the respondent is served. National law alone will apply to determine what constitutes service of the respondent, how the appeal is to be brought and how time is to be computed.[17] An extension of the time is not envisaged in this case,[18] and, although the Convention itself does not expressly exclude such a possibility, the European Court has held that the time limits in Article 36 are compulsory in character and strictly prescribed.[18a] In any event, it may be that a uniform interpretation of the Convention would not permit any more liberal rules for the extension of time in this case than are available under the second paragraph of Article 36, thereby precluding any extension of time on account of distance.

(2) Respondent domiciled in another Contracting State. The period 28.35 within which an appeal may be brought by a respondent domiciled in a Contracting State other than that in which the decision was given is set at two months by the second paragraph of Article 36. While national law alone will apply to determine how the appeal is to be brought, the computation of time and the question of what constitutes service are regulated in part by the Convention itself and will otherwise be determined by any relevant bilateral (or multilateral) conventions as well as national law.

The Convention provides that time is to run from the date of service "either on him" (the respondent) "in person, or at his residence." Service on the respondent "at his residence" means, according to the Jenard Report:

> "delivering the instrument to a person who is present and empowered by law to receive a copy of the instrument or, if there is no such person, to a competent authority."[19]

This explanation would seem to envisage service otherwise than strictly at the respondent's "residence," a concept which is anyway perhaps unsuitable for companies and other legal persons. It is not clear whether, by providing this explanation, the Jenard Report is suggesting that the concept of service, at least in outline, is to be given a uniform interpretation in the context of this paragraph. If

---

[17] Jenard, para. A1.221 below; Droz, para. 573; *Visscher* v. *Gebrüder Bröker K.G.*, Arrondissementsrechtbank, Zwolle, October 19, 1977, Digest D I–36—B1.

[18] Bülow/Böckstiegel/Müller, p. 248.

[18a] *Hoffman* v. *Krieg*, above, paras. 30 and 31. The extension of the time limits, whether on account of distance or otherwise, is not mentioned in the judgment.

[19] Jenard, para. A1.221 below, n. 1.

"service" is to be uniformly interpreted, it would seem that the interpretation should apply not only to service at the respondent's residence, but also to service "on him in person." The explanation leaves unresolved the question of what law is to be applied in deciding who is empowered by law to receive a copy of the "instrument."[20]

28.36   It is submitted that a preferable approach would be to read the second paragraph of Article 36 as requiring that the respondent should actually have been served (as distinct from permitting deemed service), and to leave the enforcing court to decide whether the detailed rules to be applied are the rules of its own law, or the rules of the law of the state where service is effected. On the other hand, this approach may be thought to deviate too far from the actual words of the paragraph, and it remains to be seen how the European Court will interpret this difficult provision.

Where the respondent is domiciled in a Contracting State other than that where the order for enforcement has been made, the time limited for appealing may not be extended on account of distance. The explanation for this rule is said to be that "the time allowed is sufficient to enable the party concerned to contest the decision, if he is so minded."[21]

28.37   *(3) Respondent domiciled in non-Contracting State.* Where the respondent is not domiciled in a Contracting State, the provisions of the second paragraph of Article 36 do not apply, and the case falls within the first paragraph.[22] The primary period allowed to such a respondent to lodge an appeal against an order authorising enforcement of a judgment given in another Contracting State is therefore one month. But, unlike the second paragraph, the first paragraph of Article 36 contains no prohibition on the extension of the period on account of distance and it may be that such an extension is therefore allowed by the Convention, provided that this is

---

[20] Bülow/Böckstiegel/Müller, p. 248, suggest that this will be the law of the state where the order for enforcement was made, but it may be that the enforcing court should itself decide whether its own law or the law of the state where service was effected should decide the point.

[21] Jenard, para. A1.221 below.

[22] There is an alternative explanation, namely that the first paragraph applies only to parties domiciled in the same Contracting State as the court authorising the enforcement (the first situation discussed above) and the Convention is silent as to the time limit for an appeal by a respondent not domiciled in a Contracting State. This explanation is not satisfactory, though, because if Art. 36 did not apply at all to such a party, he would appear to have no right of appeal against an order authorising enforcement against him, which would undoubtedly be contrary to the Convention.

permitted by the appropriate national law.[22a] In this case, what constitutes service and the computation of time are both to be determined by the national law of the enforcing state, including such bilateral conventions as may be applicable.

Article 37

An appeal against the decision authorising enforcement shall be lodged in accordance with the rules governing procedure in contentious matters: 28.38

— in Belgium, with the tribunal de première instance or rechtbank van eerste aanleg,
— in Denmark, with the landsret,
— in the Federal Republic of Germany, with the Oberlandesgericht,
[– in Greece, with the ἐφετεῖο,]
— in France, with the cour d'appel,
— in Ireland, with the High Court,
— in Italy, with the corte d'appello,
— in Luxembourg, with the Cour supérieure de justice sitting as a court of civil appeal,
— in the Netherlands, with the arrondissementsrechtbank,
— in the United Kingdom:

1. in England or Wales, with the High Court of Justice, or in the case of a maintenance judgment with the Magistrates' Court;
2. in Scotland, with the Court of Session, or in the case of a maintenance judgment with the Sheriff Court;
3. in Northern Ireland, with the High Court of Justice, or in the case of a maintenance judgment with the Magistrates' Court.

The judgment given on the appeal may be contested only:

— in Belgium, [Greece,] France, Italy, Luxembourg and the Netherlands, by an appeal in cassation,
— in Denmark, by an appeal to the højesteret, with the leave of the Minister of Justice,
— in the Federal Republic of Germany, by a Rechtsbeschwerde,
— in Ireland, by an appeal on a point of law to the Supreme Court,

---

[22a] The observations of the European Court referred to at para. 28.34 were not made in the context of service in a non-Contracting State.

— **in the United Kingdom, by a single further appeal on a point of law.*†**

I. ARTICLE 37: APPEALS AGAINST ENFORCEMENT ORDERS

1. General note

28.39   Article 37 sets out exhaustively the appeals which may be brought against an order for enforcement or a declaration of recognition in the state where that order has been made. In addition, the 1971 Protocol on Interpretation[23] provides for references to the European Court of Justice on points of interpretation. An appeal under Article 37 is *inter partes* and the first paragraph of Article 37 provides that the first appeal is to be lodged in accordance with the rules governing procedure in contentious matters. The particular rules in question will be a matter for the appropriate national law, but it is inherent in the notion of contentious proceedings that the appellant judgment debtor should summon the original applicant to appear in the appeal proceedings.[24] While the second paragraph of Article 37 is silent on the point, the same must obviously apply to a further appeal under that paragraph.

2. First paragraph: first appeal

28.40   As in the case of Article 32,[25] the first paragraph of Article 37 acts as a compulsory provision on jurisdiction, giving exclusive jurisdiction to each of the courts specified over a first appeal from orders for the enforcement or declarations of recognition[26] of judgments given in other Contracting States. An appeal under this provision, in order to be admissible, must have been brought in compliance with

---

* Jenard, paras. A1.222–A1.223; Schlosser, paras. 216–218, 220 (paras. A1.513–A1.517, A1.520 below); Collins, pp. 119–120; Dashwood/Halcon/White, pp. 45, 46, 164–166; Hartley, p. 98; Kaye, pp. 1639–1642; Maxwell, paras. 6.87–6.92; 6.153–6.154; Anton, paras. 8.51–8.52; Droz, paras. 576–577; Bülow/Böckstiegel/Müller, pp. 249–254; Geimer/Schütze, pp. 1115–1120, 1222, 1240–1241, 1249, 1252–1253, 1256–1257, 1259, 1263–1264; Kropholler, pp. 307–310; Gothot/Holleaux, paras. 367, 369, 378; Pocar, pp. 327–329.

† The words in square brackets were added by Art. 5 of the 1982 Convention and are not yet in force. See para. 13.05 above. The whole of the rest of the Article was substituted for the 1968 version by Art. 17 of the 1978 Convention.

[23] Chap. 26 below.

[24] Jenard, para. A1.222 below.

[25] Para. 28.09 above.

[26] Declarations of recognition are governed by the second para. of Art. 26, para. 27.01 above.

the provisions of Article 36. If an appeal has been lodged against the original judgment (or if the time limited for bringing such an appeal has not yet expired), the appellant may apply for the proceedings to be stayed, pursuant to Article 38.[27]

If the appeal is admissible and within the Convention, the court may examine the same questions as the court of first instance should have examined,[28] but, unlike the court of first instance, it will be able to take account of the appellant's representations. The decision of the European Court of Justice in *Firma P.* v. *Firma K.*,[29] to the effect that both parties are entitled to be heard on an appeal under Article 40, applies equally to an appeal under this Article. It is apparent from the fact that the first opportunity the appellant will have had of making representations is on the appeal, that the appeal is to be by way of rehearing and that the appellate court should examine *de novo* the various questions governing the making of an order for the enforcement of the judgment, at least to the extent that the parties ask it to do so. It would seem, therefore, that the applicant for enforcement (*i.e.*, the respondent to the appeal) should normally be permitted on the appeal to adduce fresh evidence and arguments in support of the application for an order, and not be confined to answering the appellant's case.

If the question arises as to whether the case falls within the Convention at all, it probably ought not to be regarded as affecting the admissibility of the appeal, but as going to the merits.[30]   **28.41**

The most usual grounds on which an appellant may be expected to base an appeal is that one of the conditions for refusing an order of enforcement under Articles 27 and 28 is fulfilled. For example, an appellant may seek to establish, in the case of a judgment given in default, that he was not served with the document instituting the proceedings in sufficient time to enable him to arrange for his defence (Article 27(2)), or, in the case of a consumer contract, that the special rules of jurisdiction in Articles 13 to 15 were not observed (Article 28).

Grounds of substance. While pointing out that it is no part of the duty of the court to review the foreign judgment as to its substance, and that to do so would be contrary to the spirit of the Convention, the Jenard Report suggests that the appellant could adduce grounds

---

[27] Para. 28.43 below.
[28] The six conditions for the grant of an order of enforcement are listed at para. 28.02 above.
[29] [1984] E.C.R. 3033. See para. 28.65 below.
[30] Bülow/Böckstiegel/Müller, p. 251; see para. 28.27 above.

of substance which arose after the original judgment was given.[31] The Schlosser Report appears to take a different view:

> " . . . the substance of the judgment to be enforced or the procedure by which it came into existence can be reviewed only within the limits of Articles 27 and 28."[32]

It is submitted that the view implicit in the Schlosser Report is to be preferred. Questions of substance may on occasions be legitimate areas of enquiry under the Convention itself,[33] but where a review as to the substance of the judgment would be prohibited at first instance by the third paragraph of Article 34, it ought equally to be prohibited on the hearing of an appeal. Except as expressly provided by Articles 27 and 28, the appellant ought to be able to avoid the consequences of the judgment in the other Contracting States only if he could avoid them in the state of origin. Where the judgment is enforceable in the state of origin, his proper recourse is to appeal against the judgment there, and apply under Article 38 for a stay of the enforcement proceedings in the state where enforcement has been ordered.

3. Second paragraph: further appeal

28.42   The second paragraph of Article 37 limits to a single further appeal on a point of law the recourse which may be had against the decision given on an appeal under the first paragraph of the Article.[34] The European Court has ruled that the second paragraph of Article 37 does not permit an appeal against any other order and that it is only the decision made on an appeal under the first paragraph of this Article which may be challenged by way of this further appeal.[35] So, an appeal is not permitted against, for example, an interim order requiring preliminary inquiries.

National procedural law will apply to determine the time within which the appeal is to be brought, as well as other procedural matters.[36] The reason why the right of appeal is limited is to prevent the appellate process being used to delay unduly the enforcement of the judgment in question once the merits on the matter

---

[31] Jenard, para. A1.222 below; Oberlandesgericht Stuttgart, case 5 W 35/77, June 16, 1978, Digest D I–36—B3.

[32] Schlosser, para. 220 (para. A1.520 below).

[33] See para. 28.27 above.

[34] Schlosser, para. 217 (para. A1.514 below).

[35] *Calzaturificio Brennero s.a.s.* v. *Wendel G.m.b.H. Schuhproduktion International*, [1984] E.C.R. 3971, at p. 2983 (para. 15). Brennero had appealed against an interim order made by the Oberlandesgericht Hamm. The case is discussed below at para. 28.52.

[36] The courts to which such a further appeal may be taken in the U.K. are set out in s.6 of the 1982 Act, para. 40.18 below.

have been finally decided.[37] As the Jenard Report points out,[38] the Convention does not interfere at all with rights of appeal on the merits in the state of origin; and if the merits are still subject to appeal there a stay of the enforcement proceedings may be granted under Article 38.[39]

Article 38

The court with which the appeal under the first paragraph of Article 37 is lodged may, on the application of the appellant, stay the proceedings if an ordinary appeal has been lodged against the judgment in the State in which the judgment was given or if the time for such an appeal has not yet expired; in the latter case, the court may specify the time within which such an appeal is to be lodged.   28.43

Where the judgment was given in Ireland or the United Kingdom, any form of appeal available in the State in which it was given shall be treated as an ordinary appeal for the purposes of the first paragraph.

The court may also make enforcement conditional on the provision of such security as it shall determine.*†

J. Article 38: General Note

The purpose of this Article is to protect a judgment debtor from the consequences of enforcement against him of a judgment which may yet be reversed or amended on appeal in the state of origin,[40] either   28.44

---

[37] On an appeal under this paragraph, being an appeal on a point of law, the court may not review the substance of the original judgment, even in the limited circumstances permitted on an appeal under the first para. of Art. 37 (see para. 28.41 above): *Sertom S.N.C.* v. *Fecmo s.r.l.*, Riv.dir.int.priv.proc. 1981, p. 359, Digest D I–37—B1.

[38] Jenard, para. A1.223 below.

[39] The question of a stay of a further appeal under this paragraph is discussed at para. 28.46 below.

* Jenard, para. A1.244–A1.225 below; Schlosser, paras. 195–204 (paras. A1.490–A1.500 below); Collins, pp. 120–121; Dashwood/Halcon/White, pp. 43–44, 166–167; Hartley, pp. 93–95; Kaye, pp. 1642–1657; Maxwell, para. 6.93; Anton, para. 8.52; Droz, para. 579; Bülow/Böckstiegel/Müller, pp. 255–257; Geimer/Schütze, pp. 1128–1132, 1242–1243; Kropholler, pp. 310–313; Gothot/Holleaux, paras. 328–338, 376, 391, 400; Pocar, pp. 329–334; (See also references under Article 30.)

† The second para. was added by Art. 18 of the 1978 Convention.

[40] Jenard, para. A1.224 below; but see next para. below.

by granting a stay of the enforcement proceedings at the appellate stage under the first paragraph of this Article, or by requiring the judgment creditor to provide security under the third paragraph.

Article 38 is very similar, but not identical, to Article 30,[41] which enables the court to which the original *ex parte* application is made under Article 31 to grant a stay pending the outcome of an appeal against the judgment in its state of origin.[42] There are a number of points of distinction between the two provisions, each of which is discussed below, but the more important of which, in summary, are that, under Article 38:

(1) the power to stay may be exercised only on the application of the appellant;

(2) it is not necessary that an ordinary appeal should actually have been lodged in the state of origin, provided that the time limited for appealing has not expired;

(3) if an ordinary appeal has not actually been lodged in the state of origin, the appellate court in the state of enforcement may require the appellant to lodge an appeal within a specified time as a condition of the grant or continuation of a stay;

(4) the treatment of Irish and United Kingdom judgments differs from that under Article 30;

(5) the appellate court may, instead of granting a stay, allow the judgment creditor to enforce his judgment, but on condition that he provide security.

K. ARTICLE 38, FIRST AND SECOND PARAGRAPHS: STAY OF
PROCEEDINGS

1. "The court with which the appeal under the first paragraph of Article 37 is lodged may . . . stay the proceedings . . . "

28.45   The only court with power under Article 38 to stay the proceedings is the court with which an appeal is lodged under the first paragraph of Article 37. It has been held that the appeal under Article 37 needs to be one which itself is based on a permissible ground (principally those in Articles 27 and 28), and that the power to stay under this paragraph can only be exercised where a ground of appeal is advanced other than that an appeal has been lodged in the

---

[41] Para. 27.78 above. See the commentary on that Article.
[42] Art. 30 applies only to proceedings in which, "recognition is sought of a judgment given in another Contracting State," but that condition is fulfilled in the case of enforcement proceedings: see para. 27.79, n. 61 above.

state of origin.[43] It is suggested, though, that this is too harsh a view and that the protective purpose of the provision might be frustrated by such an approach.

If a further appeal is lodged in the enforcement proceedings **28.46** under the second paragraph of Article 37, it might appear that the court seised of the further appeal has no power to grant a similar stay. The Jenard Report, without saying which court has power to grant the stay, seems to suggest that a stay may be granted in these circumstances.[44] A stay of the enforcement procedings would, of course, only be necessary at the stage of a further appeal if the appellant had been unsuccessful on the first appeal. But that decision on the first appeal could only have been given if one of three events had taken place, namely if the appellant had not applied for a stay of the first appeal, if a stay had been refused, or if the stay had been lifted (probably because the appeal in the state of origin had been disposed of). If, in any of those three circumstances, the appellant were to then apply for a stay of the proceedings on his further appeal, it would seem from the wording of the first paragraph of Article 38 that he would have to make his application for the stay to the court referred to in the first paragraph of Article 37, rather than to the court before which he brought his further appeal. The court before which the first appeal had been brought would, perhaps, be unlikely to grant a further stay in any of those circumstances; but, for the rare case where the judgment debtor would be unfairly prejudiced by the judgment creditor being able to proceed with enforcement of the judgment, the court's power to order security under the third paragraph of Article 38 should be sufficient to protect him.

2. " . . . on the application of the appellant . . . "

A stay of the enforcement proceedings may be granted under the **28.47** first paragraph of Article 38 only on the appellant's application. The court is not therefore under an obligation of its own motion to examine the question of whether to grant a stay, but will be able to consider the documents which were before the court of first instance as well as any further evidence and representations made by either party. It must hear the appellant on his application for a stay.[45]

---

[43] Oberlandesgericht Hamburg, case 6 W 82/80, November 21, 1980, Digest D I–38—B5.

[44] Jenard, para. A1.223 below; see also para. 28.42 above.

[45] Bülow/Böckstiegel/Müller, p. 256.

3. "The court . . . may . . . stay the proceedings if an ordinary appeal has been lodged against the judgment in the State in which that judgment was given or if the time for such an appeal has not yet expired; in the latter case, the court may specify the time within which such an appeal is to be lodged"

28.48   The meaning of an "ordinary appeal" is discussed in the commentary to Article 30.[46] It is a necessary condition for the grant of a stay under this paragraph that an ordinary appeal should have been lodged or still be capable of being lodged in the state of origin, but the admissibility of the appeal is probably not a condition precedent to the grant of a stay, although it can be expected to influence the exercise of the court's discretion.[47]

The court has a discretion whether or not to grant the stay and may take all the circumstances of the case into account, including the question whether the ordinary appeal is admissible in the state of origin, the appellant's prospects on the appeal, and the potential prejudice to each party if a stay were to be granted. Different considerations may apply, depending on whether the appeal has actually been lodged in the state of origin.

Equally, if the court does decide to grant a stay, it has a discretion as to how long the stay should be for, but, save perhaps to the extent necessary for the appeal proceedings to be reinstated, it should not normally extend beyond the time limited in the state of origin for the appeal to be lodged, or, if an appeal is lodged, beyond the date of disposal of the appeal.[48] If a stay is granted at a time when the appellant has not lodged his appeal in the state of origin, the court has a discretion to impose a time limit within which that appeal is to be lodged. The time limit operates only as a condition of the stay in the enforcement proceedings and does not affect the appellant's rights in relation to pursuing his ordinary appeal in the state of origin. How long a time limit is imposed is, again, within the discretion of the court which grants the stay and need not be as long as the time available in the state of origin for lodging the ordinary appeal, although it ought not to be longer.

Meaning of "ordinary appeal"

28.49   *The Industrial Diamond Supplies decision.* It has already been observed[49] that the European Court of Justice, commenting on the position where an appeal has already been lodged against the orig-

---

[46] Paras. 27.82 *et seq.* above.

[47] Bülow/Böckstiegel/Müller, pp. 255–256.

[48] It may be that the stay automatically ends when the appeal is disposed of, because the power to grant a stay under this paragraph would then no longer exist: Bülow/Böckstiegel/Müller, p. 256.

[49] Para. 27.83 above.

inal decision, seems to have suggested that that fact will usually be enough for the enforcing court to conclude that there is a reasonable doubt as to the fate of the original decision and, in the exercise of its discretion, to grant a stay of its proceedings.[50] Unlike the position under Article 30, though, under Article 38 the court has power to grant a stay even if the original decision has not yet become the subject of an appeal, provided that the time limited for appealing has not yet expired. The European Court, in construing the meaning of "ordinary appeal," commented on that situation in these terms:

> "A court may be required to make a more difficult appraisal whenever a request for a stay of the proceedings is lodged before it under Article 38 of the Convention when the periods for lodging appeals have not yet expired in the State in which the judgment was given.
>
> In that case, it is also necessary to bear in mind, in addition to the criterion based on the possible effect of an appeal, all the relevant considerations arising from the nature and conditions for the application of the judicial remedies in question.
>
> Considered from this point of view, the expression "ordinary appeal" must be understood as meaning any appeal which forms part of the normal course of action and which, as such, constitutes a procedural development which any party must reasonably expect.
>
> It is necessary to consider that any appeal bound by the law to a specific period of time which starts to run by virtue of the actual decision whose enforcement is sought constitutes such a development.
>
> Consequently, it is impossible to consider as "ordinary appeals" within the meaning of Articles 30 and 38 of the Convention in particular appeals which are dependent either upon events which were unforeseeable at the date of the original judgment or upon the action taken by persons who are extraneous to the case, and who are not bound by the period for entering an appeal which starts to run from the date of the original judgment.
>
> It is for a court before which a request is submitted under Article 36[51] at a date on which the period for entering an appeal in the State in which the judgment was given has not yet expired to exercise its discretion in this respect.
>
> This freedom of discretion is implicit in the actual system of Article 38 which gives the court before which an order for enforcement is sought the power to specify with regard to a party which is opposed to enforcement, although it has not yet taken advantage of the possibility of lodging an appeal in the State in which the judgment was given, a time within which its appeal is to be lodged."[52]

It should be observed that a stay granted under the first para-

---

[50] *Industrial Diamond Supplies* v. *Riva* [1977] E.C.R. 2175, at p. 2189 (paras. 33–34).
[51] This seems to be a misprint for Art. 38.
[52] [1977] E.C.R. 2175, at pp. 2189–2190 (paras. 35–41).

graph of Article 38 is only a stay of the proceedings on the appeal against the order for enforcement. The order itself remains unaffected by the stay, except that, pursuant to Article 39[53] the judgment may not be enforced (save by way of protective measures) until the appeal has been determined.

4. "Where the judgment was given in Ireland or the United Kingdom, any form of appeal available in the State in which it was given shall be treated as an ordinary appeal for the purposes of the first paragraph."

28.50   Whereas in Article 30, in a case where the judgment in question was given by a court in Ireland or the United Kingdom, the power to grant a stay is dependent on the execution of the judgment having been stayed by reason of an appeal, such a solution was less apt in the context of Article 38, because a stay could be granted in this case without an appeal having been lodged. The solution adopted was to treat all appeals in Ireland and the United Kingdom as "ordinary appeals," and to stress in the Schlosser Report that the courts of other states should be careful in exercising their discretion.[54]

L. ARTICLE 38, THIRD PARAGRAPH: SECURITY AS CONDITION OF ENFORCEMENT

"The court may also make enforcement conditional on the provision of such security as it shall determine"

28.51   Despite the use of the word "also," the provision of security by the judgment creditor as a condition of being able to enforce his judgment is an alternative means by which the judgment debtor may be protected, not an additional one. In other words, the court cannot both order a stay and order the judgment creditor to give security. This is because, in order for enforcement to go ahead at all (except by way of protective measures), the appeal must have been determined.[55] The court will only grant security when it has dismissed the appeal; but it may decide to hear arguments on the merits before deciding whether or not to grant a stay, so that it can weigh the relative merits, on one hand, of staying the proceedings and, on the other, of proceeding with them with a view to making

[53] Para. 28.55 below.
[54] Schlosser, para. 204 (para. A1.500 below): see the passage quoted at para. 27.86 above.
[55] Art. 39, para. 28.55 below. See *Calzaturificio Brennero s.a.s.* v. *Wendel G.m.b.H. Schuhproduktion International* [1984] E.C.R. 3971, discussed below.

enforcement conditional on the giving of security if it were to dismiss the appeal.

The Brennero decision. The European Court has had to consider **28.52** the power to order security under this paragraph in *Calzaturificio Brennero s.a.s.* v. *Wendel G.m.b.H. Schuhproduktion International.*[56] Brennero, an Italian shoe manufacturer, obtained an interlocutory order in Italy for the protective seizure of goods belonging to Wendel, a German shoe manufacturer. Brennero then applied for and obtained an order from a German court for the enforcement of the Italian order. In addition, the order authorised Brennero to take protective measures.[57] Wendel appealed to the *Oberlandesgericht* Hamm, and applied under this paragraph for an order making the enforcement of the Italian order conditional upon Brennero providing security. The *Oberlandesgericht* made an interim order under which the enforcement by Brennero of even the protective measures was conditional on security being provided, but did not at the same time determine the appeal.

Brennero lodged a further appeal on a point of law against that decision to the *Bundesgerichtshof* under the second paragraph of Article 37, and that court referred two questions to the European Court. One question concerned the interpretation of the second paragraph of Article 37 and has already been mentioned.[58] The other question was whether the court with which an appeal has been lodged under the first paragraph of Article 37 might issue an order under the third paragraph[59] of Article 38,

> "making enforcement conditional on the provision of security only as part of its final judgment on the appeal or may it also issue the order as an interim measure during the proceedings?"[60]

The European Court pointed out that Article 39 prevented the **28.53** taking of any enforcement procedures other than protective measures until after the decision had been given on the appeal and pointed out that that was the context in which the present provision was set.[61] The Court continued:

> "The whole significance of that provision lies in the fact that as soon as the court gives judgment on the appeal, the restrictions provided for by Article 39 cease to be applicable. Enforcement measures may therefore be taken while that judgment can still be contested by an

---

[56] [1984] E.C.R. 3971.
[57] Art. 39, para. 28.55 below.
[58] Para. 28.42 above.
[59] The question related to the second para. of Art. 38 in the unamended version, which is now the third para.
[60] [1984] E.C.R. 3971 at p. 3980 (para. 6).
[61] *Ibid.*, at p. 3982 (para. 12).

appeal in cassation or by a *Rechtsbeschwerde*,[62] in accordance with the second paragraph of Article 37, and while even the original judgment given in the first State can still be contested by an appeal, which is a possibility expressly provided for by Article 38. That is the time when the protection of the debtor's interests may require enforcement to be made conditional on the provision of security."[63]

The European Court therefore went on to rule that the power given by this paragraph of Article 38 to make enforcement conditional on the provision of security could only be exercised when the court gave judgment on the appeal against the decision authorising enforcement.[64] It follows that this paragraph does not permit the court to order the provision of security as an interim measure pending its own decision. Once the court has reached its decision on the appeal, it may be particularly appropriate to order security after an appeal has been dismissed, if the appellant is going to pursue a further appeal under the second paragraph of Article 37. This is because, as the European Court pointed out, the restriction imposed by Article 39 on a judgment creditor's right to take measures of enforcement only applies until the determination of the first appeal, under the first paragraph of Article 37.[65]

28.54   Although the third paragraph of Article 38 does not say so expressly, it is clear, from the fact that the provision is included in Article 38 and from the Convention's purpose in promoting the free flow of judgments between the Contracting States, that security may be ordered as a condition of enforceability only if an ordinary appeal has been lodged or may still be lodged against the judgment in the state of origin.[66]

As with its power to grant a stay of proceedings, the court's power to order security as a condition of enforceability is discretionary, but the appellant ought usually to show that irreversible consequences would be likely if security were not ordered.[67] It is

---

[62] The equivalent procedure in the U.K. is a single further appeal on a point of law: see Art. 37, second para. (para. 28.38 above) and s.6 of the 1982 Act (para. 40.18 below).

[63] [1984] E.C.R. 3971, at p. 3982 (para. 12).

[64] As a result of that decision, the *Rechtsbeschwerde* to the Bundesgerichtshof was withdrawn, and the Oberlandesgericht revoked its order requiring Brennero to give security. The further outcome of the proceedings is noted at RIW/AWD— 1985, p. 973 and Digest D I–38—A1 n.

[65] See para. 28.56 below.

[66] Oberlandesgericht Koblenz, case 2 W 338/76, September 27, 1976, RIW/ AWD—1977, p. 102, Digest D I–38—B1; Bundesgerichtshof, case VIII ZB 8/83, May 16, 1983, [1983] RIW 535, [1983] Eur.L.Dig. 501.

[67] Oberlandesgericht Köln, case 6 W 15/77, March 2, 1977, Digest D I–38— B2.

suggested that this provision is subject to Article 45[68] and that an order for security may not be made only on the grounds of the applicant's nationality or his lack of domicile or residence in the state addressed. Until an appeal has been disposed of, the judgment creditor is not permitted to take any enforcement measures other than protective measures,[69] but that restriction does not apply if enforcement is authorised under this paragraph, conditional on the grant of security.

The court has a discretion as to the form and amount of security, so far as that is permitted by its own national law. If the enforceability of the judgment in its state of origin is already conditional on the grant of security by the judgment creditor, an order under the third paragraph of Article 38 would be superfluous and, it is suggested, ought not normally to be made.[70]

Article 39

During the time specified for an appeal pursuant to Article 36 and until any such appeal has been determined, no measures of enforcement may be taken other than protective measures taken against the property of the party against whom enforcement is sought.
The decision authorising enforcement shall carry with it the power to proceed to any such protective measures.*

28.55

M. ARTICLE 39: PROTECTIVE MEASURES DURING STAY

1. General note

Article 39 strikes a balance between the competing interests of the parties. On one hand, by the first paragraph, it allows the position of the judgment debtor to be preserved by limiting the judgment creditor's rights of enforcement to protective measures, and preventing the judgment creditor from proceeding to a full-scale enforcement of his judgment until such time as the judgment debtor has had an opportunity to be heard on an appeal under Article 36.[71] Thereafter, the restrictions imposed by this Article

28.56

---

[68] Para. 28.85 below.
[69] Art. 39, para. 28.55 below.
[70] Bülow/Böckstiegel/Müller, p. 257.
* Jenard, paras. A1.226–A1.227 below; Schlosser, para. 221 (paras. A1.521–A1.522 below); Collins, pp. 120, 124; Dashwood/Halcon/White; Hartley, p. 99; Kaye, pp. 1628–1639, 1657–1659; Maxwell, paras. 6.94–6.100; Anton, para. 8.51; Droz, para. 575; Bülow/Böckstiegel/Müller, pp. 257–260; Geimer/Schütze, pp. 1158–1159, 1242–1243; Kropholler, pp. 313–316; Gothot/ Holleaux, paras. 366–368; Pocar, pp. 334–338.
[71] *Capelloni and Aquilini* v. *Pelkmans* [1985] E.C.R. 3147 at p. 3159 (para. 18).

cease to be applicable, even if a further appeal is pursued under the second paragraph of Article 37,[72] although if the appellate court dismisses the appeal, it may make enforcement conditional on the provision of security under the third paragraph of Article 38.[73]

28.57   On the other hand, though, the second paragraph of this Article secures the judgment creditor's right to proceed to protective measures, which, taken together with the *ex parte* nature of the enforcement procedure at first instance, enables the judgment creditor to take the judgment debtor by surprise. He may obtain an order for enforcement of the judgment and take steps to secure the judgment debtor's assets for the purpose of subsequent execution, all without the judgment debtor being aware of the enforcement proceedings.

Once the restriction on taking enforcement measures is lifted, by the expiry of the time limited for appealing or the disposal of the appeal, the judgment creditor may proceed to enforce the judgment in whatever way the relevant national law permits, subject to any order for the provision of security made under the third paragraph of Article 38.[74]

2. Protective measures

28.58   The effect of the second paragraph of Article 39 is to give the party entitled to enforce the judgment the additional right to proceed to protective measures, at least for a period, within certain confines imposed by national law. Each of these aspects was considered by the European Court of Justice in *Capelloni and Aquilini* v. *Pelkmans*.[74a] Mr. Pelkmans obtained judgment in the Netherlands against Messrs. Capelloni and Aquilini for 127,400 Dutch guilders. He obtained an order for its enforcement in Italy and proceeded to take protective measures under the second paragraph of Article 39 against the assets of the judgment debtors. In accordance with Italian procedures, he then sought confirmation of the protective measures from the Italian court. The applicability of national law to those protective measures, and in particular the necessity or otherwise for confirmatory proceedings, were referred by the *Corte di Cassazione* to the European Court.

---

[72] Para. 28.42 above. The suggestion (made by Bülow/Böckstiegel/Müller, at p. 259) that national law may permit enforcement measures to continue to be restricted to protective measures during such further appeal is not compatible with the European Court's approach to Arts. 38 and 39. See the commentary below.

[73] See paras. 28.51 *et seq.* above.

[74] *Ibid.*

[74a] [1985] E.C.R. 3147.

(1) Protective measures envisaged by national law

The concept of "protective measures" is to be given a uniform **28.59** interpretation in all the Contracting States, but the particular measures which may be taken by a judgment creditor will be determined by the national law of the state in which enforcement is being carried out. In considering the relationship between the Convention and national law in this context, the European Court reiterated that the Convention provides a summary and uniform procedure for a party to obtain an order authorising enforcement, but that execution itself remained subject to national law.[75] Referring to Article 39, the Court continued:

> "The obvious purpose of that provision is to offer the party who has obtained authorization for enforcement, but who cannot yet proceed with measures of enforcement, a means of preventing the party against whom enforcement is sought from disposing of his property in the meantime so as to render future enforcement fruitless or indeed impossible.
>
> However, as in the case of enforcement properly so called,[76] the Convention confines itself, with respect to the protective measures referred to in Article 39, to laying down the principle that the party who has applied for enforcement may, during the period indicated in that article, proceed with such measures. By contrast, the Convention leaves the matter of resolving any question not covered by specific provisions of the Treaty[77] to the procedural law of the court hearing the proceedings.
>
> It must nevertheless be made clear that the application of the requirements of the national procedural law of the court hearing the proceedings must not in any circumstances lead to frustration of the principles laid down in that regard, whether expressly or by implication, by the Convention itself and by Article 39 thereof in particular. Accordingly, the question whether any given provision of the national procedural law of the court hearing the proceedings is applicable to protective measures taken pursuant to Article 39 depends upon the scope of each provision of national law and upon the extent to which it is compatible with the principles laid down by Article 39."[78]

It follows that the measures envisaged by "protective measures" are those in the nature of seizure or freezing of the judgment debtor's assets, but not their sale or disposal.[79]

---

[75] *Ibid.*, at pp. 3158 to 3159 (paras. 15 and 16).

[76] This phrase is used earlier in the judgment in a cross-reference to the *Deutsche Genossenschaftsbank* case, which makes clear that it refers to the execution of the judgment (see para. 28.32 above).

[77] This clearly means the 1968 Convention.

[78] [1985] E.C.R. 3147, at pp. 3159 to 3160 (paras. 19 to 21).

[79] *Cf.* Bülow/Böckstiegel/Müller, p. 258.

(2) Automatic right to take protective measures

28.60   The effect of the second paragraph of Article 39 is automatically
to give the judgment creditor a right to take protective measures to
secure the judgment debtor's assets, and the national court is not
left any discretion as to whether measures provided by national law
and falling within the scope of the term "protective measures"
should or should not be granted in any given case.[80] As has been
observed, one of the questions referred to the European Court in
Capelloni v. *Pelkmans* was whether a provision of Italian procedural
law, by which the applicant was required to seek confirmatory
authorisation for his protective measures, was compatible with
Article 39.

28.61   The Court drew attention to the words "shall carry with it" the
power to proceed with protective measures and said that that
expression indicated that the right to proceed with such measures
derives from the decision allowing enforcement, and that a second
decision, which could not in any event undermine that right, would
not be justified.[81] Coupled with the automatic right to take protective measures, is the notion that the measures should not need to be
justified after the event in confirmatory proceedings. Any provisions of national law of a Contracting State which require such
proceedings are not to be applied in the context of Article 39. As the
European Court observed:

> "An examination of that kind is unjustified and even superfluous in
> the case of protective measures adopted under Article 39. Those
> measures are granted not on the basis of a summary procedure for
> authorization but rather on the basis of the legal effect with which a
> decision adopted in another Contracting State is endowed by the Con-
> vention."[82]

The Court's ruling on this point was as follows:

> "By virtue of Article 39 of the Convention, a party who has applied
> for and obtained authorization for enforcement may, within the
> period mentioned in that Article, proceed directly with protective
> measures against the property of the party against whom enforcement
> is sought and is under no obligation to obtain specific authoriza-
> tion."[83]

As the Schlosser Report observes, though, Article 39 must be
seen in the context of the French legal system and systems related

---

[80] *Chim Metal S.n.l.* v. *Anilina S.A.* Riv.dir.int.priv.proc. 1981, p. 951, Digest D
I–27.2—B16; *Commerzbank AG* v. *Giangrande*, Riv.dir.int.priv.proc. 1981,
p. 164, [1982] E.C.C. 207, Digest D I–39—B1.
[81] [1985] E.C.R. 3147, at p. 3160 (para. 25).
[82] *Ibid.*, at p. 3162 (para. 34).
[83] *Ibid.*, at p. 3163.

to it, in which enforcement measures may be taken without reference to the court, by using the services of a *huissier de justice* or his equivalent.[84] In those States (such as the United Kingdom and Ireland) where the court retains control over the means of enforcement, the general right to take protective measures is secured by Article 39, although the court is bound to retain some control over the particular measures adopted. The effect of the European Court's decision appears to be that that control is not one in which the court may exercise a discretion.

(3) Duration of the right to take protective measures

The first paragraph of Article 39 restricts the right of the judg- **28.62** ment creditor to take enforcement measures during the time specified for an appeal pursuant to Article 36 and until any such appeal is determined, limiting them during that period to protective measures. The question arose in *Capelloni* v. *Pelkmans* whether the period during which the judgment creditor could proceed to take protective measures could be further restricted by national law, and the European Court ruled that it could not:

" . . . the right to proceed with the measures in question cannot be restricted in time by the application of national measures prescribing a shorter period.

. . .
. . . a party who has obtained authorization for enforcement may proceed with the protective measures referred to in Article 39 until the expiry of the period for lodging an appeal prescribed in Article 36 and, if such an appeal is lodged, until a decision is given thereon."[85]

Article 40

If the application for enforcement is refused, the applicant **28.63**
may appeal:

— **in Belgium, to the cour d'appel or hof van beroep,**
— **in Denmark, to the landsret,**
— **in the Federal Republic of Germany, to the Oberlandesgericht,**
[— in Greece, to the ἐφετεῖο,]†
— **in France, to the cour d'appel,**
— **in Ireland, to the High Court,**

---

[84] Schlosser, para. 221 (para. A1.521 below). The application of the second para. of Art. 39 in England and Wales is discussed at paras. 10.20 to 10.22 above. For a summary of the means of enforcing a judgment in England and Wales, see paras. 10.55 to 10.62 above, and in each of the other Contracting States, see chaps. 48 to 58 below, at paras. 68 and 69.
[85] [1985] E.C.R. 3147, at p. 3161 (paras. 28 and 30).

— in Italy, to the corte d'appello,
— in Luxembourg, to the Cour supérieure de justice sitting
  as a court of civil appeal,
— in the Netherlands, to the gerechtshof,
— in the United Kingdom:
  1. in England and Wales, to the High Court of Justice, or
     in the case of a maintenance judgment to the Magis-
     trates' Court;
  2. in Scotland, to the Court of Session, or in the case of a
     maintenance judgment to the Sheriff Court;
  3. in Northern Ireland, to the High Court of Justice, or in
     the case of a maintenance judgment to the Magistrates'
     Court.

The party against whom enforcement is sought shall be summoned to appear before the appellate court. If he fails to appear,
the provisions of the second and third paragraphs of Article 20
shall apply even where he is not domiciled in any of the Contracting States.*†

N. Article 40: First Appeals against Refusal of Enforcement Orders

1. General note

28.64   Article 40 is the counterpart of the first paragraph of Article 37[86]
and, like that provision, is a compulsory provision on jurisdiction.[87]
It confers exclusive jurisdiction on each of the courts specified over
a first appeal from the dismissal of an application for an order for
the enforcement, or declaration of recognition, of a judgment given
in another Contracting State;[88] whereas the first paragraph of
Article 37 is concerned with appeals by judgment debtors against
the grant of such an order. Together with Article 41, this Article
sets out exhaustively the appeals which may be brought against the
dismissal of an application against such an order in the state where

---

* Jenard, paras. A1.228–A1.229 below; Schlosser, paras. 216–218 (paras.
  A1.513–A1.518 below); Dashwood/Halcon/White, pp. 45, 169–170; Hartley,
  p. 98; Kaye, pp. 1659–1664; Maxwell, paras. 6.101–6.104, 6.157; Anton,
  para. 8.49; Droz, paras. 580–582; Bülow/Böckstiegel/Schlafen, pp. 260–263;
  Geimer/Schütze, pp. 1115–1118, 1222; Kropholler, pp. 316–317; Gothot/Hol-
  leaux, paras. 367, 369, 379–384; Pocar, pp. 338–339.
† The words in square brackets were added by Art. 6 of the 1982 Convention and
  are not yet in force. See para. 13.05 above. The whole of the rest of the Article
  was substituted for the 1968 version by Art. 19 of the 1978 Convention.
[86] Para. 28.38 above.
[87] The same is true of Art. 32, para. 28.10 above.
[88] Local jurisdiction is determined by national law.

that decision has been made. In addition, the 1971 Protocol on Interpretation[89] provides for references to the European Court of Justice on points of interpretation.

2. Procedure on the appeal

The procedure on an appeal under Article 40 is to be governed by   **28.65**
national law, to the extent that that is compatible with the terms of the Convention. The first of the two provisions in the second paragraph of this Article is a requirement that the respondent be summoned to appear before the appellate court; so, although Article 40 does not expressly state that the appeal is to be regarded as a contentious matter,[90] it would follow that the procedure is intended to be contentious and *inter partes*. The particular means of summoning the respondent will be governed by the appropriate national law.

The Firma P. v. *Firma K. decision.* The interpretation of the first sentence of the second paragraph of Article 40 came before the European Court of Justice in *Firma P.* v. *Firma K.*[91] P had obtained judgment for 687,095 Saudi rials plus interest against K in the Netherlands. Its application for an order for enforcement in Germany was dismissed, for failure to produce the documents required by Articles 46 and 47. P appealed against the order, producing the requisite documents, but wished not to notify K, in order to retain an element of surprise. The *Oberlandesgericht* referred to the European Court the question whether that was permissible. The European Court decided that it was not, observing that the Convention formally requires that both parties should be given a hearing at the appellate level, without regard to the scope of the decision at the lower level.[92]

> "That provision is in accordance with the spirit of the Convention, which seeks to reconcile the necessary surprise effect in proceedings of this nature with respect for the defendant's right to a fair hearing . . . That is why the defendant is not entitled to be heard in the lower court, whereas on appeal he must be given a hearing. There can be no exception to that rule in a situation where, for reasons which may be ascribed to the plaintiff, the lower court has dismissed an application for enforcement on purely formal grounds."[93]

The Court went on to rule in the following terms:

> "The court hearing an appeal by the party seeking enforcement is required to hear the party against whom enforcement is sought, pur-

---

[89] Chap. 36 below.
[90] *Cf.* the first para. of Art. 37.
[91] [1984] E.C.R. 3033.
[92] *Ibid.*, at p. 3042 (para. 11).
[93] *Ibid.*

suant to the first sentence of the second paragraph of Article 40 . . . ,
even though the application for an enforcement order was dismissed
simply because documents were not produced at the appropriate time
and the enforcement order is applied for in a State which is not a State
of residence of the party against whom the enforcement is sought."[94]

28.66   *Time limit regulated by national law.* By contrast with an appeal
brought by a judgment debtor under Article 36, the Convention
sets no time limit within which an appeal is to be brought under
Article 40; but it does not follow that the Contracting States are
obliged to allow an appellant an indefinite time[95] and this, too, may
be regulated by national law.[96]

3. Absence of the respondent

28.67   The second and third paragraphs of Article 20[97] restrict the
entering of a default judgment against a defendant. The second provision contained in the second paragraph of Article 40 extends the
application of those provisions to the jurisdiction under this Article
and applies them also to respondents not domiciled in a Contracting
State. This provision is intended to safeguard the rights of respondents and is of some considerable importance, especially as the only
means of challenging a decision given on an appeal under Article 40
is by way of a single further appeal on a point of law, under Article
41. There is therefore no recourse against the appellate court's
decision on the facts that the appeal should be allowed.

The effect of the provision is that, when the respondent does not
appear in answer to the summons before the appellate court, the
court may only proceed to hear the appeal if it is satisfied that the
respondent's rights have been observed. The precise rights which
have to be observed will depend upon whether or not the Hague
Service Convention applies. If the Hague Service Convention does
not apply, the provisions of the second paragraph of Article 20 will
apply, and the court will only be able to proceed if it is shown that
the respondent has been able to receive the summons in sufficient
time to enable him to arrange for his response to the appeal, or that
all necessary steps have been taken to that end. The requirements
of the Hague Service Convention are similar. The detailed application of these rules is discussed in the commentary on Article 20.[98]

---

[94] *Ibid.*, at p. 3043.
[95] Droz, para. 581.
[96] Time limits applicable in each Contracting State are referred to in chaps. 48 to
58 below, at para. 71. In England and Wales, the time limit is one month:
R.S.C. Ord. 71, r.33(2)(b); see para. 10.24 above.
[97] Para. 22.11 above.
[98] Paras. 22.17 *et seq.* above.

4. Scope of the appeal

As with an appeal against the grant of an order, the court should **28.68** consider first whether the appeal is admissible and within the Convention. If it is, the court may then examine the same questions as the court of first instance should have examined,[99] but, unlike the court of first instance, it will be able to take account of the appellant's representations. The appeal will be by way of rehearing and both parties should be permitted to adduce further evidence and arguments.

Article 41

A judgment given on an appeal provided for in Article 40 may **28.69** be contested only:

— in Belgium, [Greece,] France, Italy, Luxembourg and in the Netherlands, by an appeal in cassation,
— in Denmark, by an appeal to the højesteret, with the leave of the Minister of Justice,
— in the Federal Republic of German, by a Rechtsbeschwerde,
— in Ireland, by an appeal on a point of law to the Supreme Court,
— in the United Kingdom, by a single further appeal on a point of law.*†

O. Article 41: Appeals against Decisions under Article 40

Article 41 is the counterpart of the second paragraph of Article 37 **28.70** (and the commentary on that provision[1] applies equally to this Article). It provides for a single appeal on a point of law against a decision under Article 40, whether that decision allows or disallows an order for enforcement or declaration of recognition. Like the second paragraph of Article 37, it is both a procedural provision limiting the right of appeal to a single further appeal on a point of

---

[99] The six conditions for the grant of an order of enforcement are listed at para. 28.02 above.
* Jenard, paras. A1.228–A1.229 below; Schlosser, paras. 217–218 (paras. A1.514–A1.518 below); Collins, pp. 118–120; Dashwood/Halcon/White, pp. 46, 171; Hartley, p. 98; Kaye, p. 1664; Maxwell, para. 6.105; Anton, para. 8.49; Bülow/Böckstiegel/Schlafen, p. 263; Geimer/Schütze, pp. 1118–1120, 1222–1223; Kropholler, p. 319; Gothot/Holleaux, paras. 385; Pocar, p. 339.
† The word in square brackets was added by Art. 7 of the 1982 Convention and is not yet in force. See para. 13.05 above. The whole of the rest of the Article was substituted for the 1968 version by Art. 20 of the 1978 Convention.
[1] Paras. 28.42 *et seq.* above.

law, and a compulsory provision on jurisdiction, according jurisdiction to those courts which, under national procedural law, have jurisdiction to hear the type of appeal specified. The procedure on an appeal under Article 41, including the time within which the appeal is to be brought, is regulated by national law.[2]

Article 42

28.71   **Where a foreign judgment has been given in respect of several matters and enforcement cannot be authorized for all of them, the court shall authorize enforcement for one or more of them.**
        An applicant may request partial enforcement of a judgment.*

P. ARTICLE 42: PARTIAL ENFORCEMENT

1. General note

28.72   Article 42 governs two different circumstances in which an order for enforcement may be made in respect of part only of a judgment. Different considerations apply to each, and they will be considered separately.

2. First paragraph: court's duty to order partial enforcement

28.73   This provision only applies where the foreign judgment[3] is in respect of several (and severable) matters.[4] In such a case, its effect is probably compulsory[5] in providing that where the conditions are fulfilled for the enforcement in the state addressed in respect of part only of the judgment,[6] enforcement of that part must be ordered. This means that, in examining a foreign judgment pursuant to Article 31,[7] the court of the state addressed must, of its own motion,[8]

---

[2] The courts to which such a further appeal may be taken in the United Kingdom are set out in s.6 of the 1982 Act, para. 40.18 below. See also para. 10.46 above.

* Jenard, paras. A1.230–A1.231 below; Collins, pp. 121–122; Dashwood/Halcon/White, pp. 42, 171; Kaye, pp. 1616–1617; Maxwell, para. 6.106; Anton, para. 8.45; Droz, paras. 583–586; Bülow/Böckstiegel/Schlafen, pp. 263–266; Geimer/Schütze, pp. 1146–1147, 1217–1220; Kropholler, p. 320; Gothot/Holleaux, paras. 359–362, 392; Pocar, pp. 339–340.

[3] A foreign judgment for the purposes of this Article is one given in another Contracting State: see Art. 25, para. 26.01 above.

[4] *Contra*, Geimer/Schütze, p. 1147.

[5] It is suggested that, to the extent that the Jenard Report (at para. A1.230 below) suggests otherwise, by referring to a court being "empowered" to order partial enforcement and having a "discretion" in the matter, it is misleading.

[6] The conditions for enforceability of a judgment under Title III of the Convention are summarised at para. 28.02 above.

[7] The same applies to Arts. 26, 36, 37, 40 and 41.

[8] Bülow/Böckstiegel/Schlafen, p. 264.

(i) consider not only the enforceability of the judgment as a whole, but also of its several parts; and

(ii) refuse enforcement of such parts of the judgment (if any) as do not fulfil the conditions for enforcement.

So, where part of the judgment falls outside the scope of the Convention, that part must be refused enforcement. This may often occur, for example, in the case of judgments given in divorce proceedings which order both the payment of maintenance (which is within the Convention) and the adjustment of property rights (which is outside it).[9] Similarly, if, as to part of the judgment, its enforcement would be contrary to public policy, a refusal to enforce that part should not affect the enforceability of the rest. Equally, where a severable part of the judgment has been satisfied,[10] it will, as to that part, no longer be enforceable in the state of origin, and the conditions for enforcement of that part will not be fulfilled.

Droz suggests[11] that where Article 27(2) applies, the judgment can never be partially enforceable, because a failure to observe the rights of the defendant must affect the whole judgment, but it has been pointed out that that may not be so where the claim has been extended by amendment and it is only the amended claim that has not been duly served, because in such a case the court of the state addressed could order enforcement to the extent only of the unamended claim.[12] The latter is probably the better view, provided that the extension amounts to a severable claim.

3. Second paragraph: application for partial enforcement

While the court's power (and duty) to order partial enforcement **28.74** of its own motion is limited to cases where the foreign judgment is given in respect of several matters and enforcement cannot be authorised for all of them, no such condition applies to a case where the applicant himself applies for partial enforcement. The applicant's right to apply for, and the court's corollary duty to grant,[13] partial enforcement applies even if the judgment is in respect of a single claim such as the payment of a debt. Such a case may arise when the judgment creditor has already been paid in part, or has levied execution in part satisfaction of the judgment in another Contracting State.

The court of the state addressed is not relieved by this provision

---

[9] Paras. 14.20 *et seq.* above. Oberlandesgericht Karlsruhe, case 2 W 7/76, June 4, 1976, Digest D I–1.2—B1; *Bâlon* v. *Mottet*, Tribunal de Première Instance, Arlon, April 20, 1977, Digest D I–1.2—B4.
[10] Para. 28.05 above.
[11] Droz, para. 584.
[12] Bülow/Böckstiegel/Schlafen, p. 265.
[13] Jenard, para. A1.231 below.

of its duty to review the enforceability of the judgment as a whole and, of course, if the conditions for enforcement of all or part of the judgment are not fulfilled, enforcement must be withheld, wholly or in part as the case may be.

4. Recognition

28.75   The reference in the second paragraph of Article 26 to Sections 2 and 3 of Title III means that a declaration of recognition may also be made in respect of part only of a judgment, at least where that part is severable. It has been suggested that recognition of a single claim must either be accorded to the whole of that claim or not at all, and that an applicant cannot therefore rely on the second paragraph of Article 42 to claim recognition of part only of a single, unseverable claim.[14] It is suggested that this approach is too formalistic. If there are grounds for refusal of recognition of the whole claim, recognition is obviously to be refused. On the other hand, the grounds for refusal of recognition might go to only part of the claim (for example, if it is only partly irreconcilable with an earlier judgment given in a non-Contracting State)[15] or the ground of objection might go merely to enforcement of part of the claim (as where part of the claim has already been satisfied). In such a case, the applicant should be allowed to claim a declaration of recognition in respect only of the part of the claim that is enforceable, even if, strictly, he would be entitled to such a declaration in respect of the whole of the judgment. For example, a surety whose rights are determined by the judgment might be interested in obtaining a declaration of recognition of a foreign judgment only to the extent of his guarantee,[16] and would not wish to be concerned with the recognisability or enforceability of the balance of the judgment.

Article 43

28.76   **A foreign judgment which orders a periodic payment by way of a penalty shall be enforceable in the State in which enforcement is sought only if the amount of the payment has been finally determined by the courts of the State in which the judgment was given.***

---

[14] Bülow/Böckstiegel/Schlafen, p. 266.

[15] Art. 27(5), para. 27.59 above.

[16] See para. 27.07 above.

* Jenard, para. A1.232; Schlosser, paras. 213, 222 (paras. A1.511, A1.523 below); Collins, p. 122; Dashwood/Halcon/White, p. 172; Hartley, p. 84; Kaye, pp. 1358, 1363; Maxwell, para. 6.107; Anton, para. 8.36; Droz, para. 587; Bülow/Böckstiegel/Schlafen, pp. 266–268; Geimer/Schütze, pp. 1168–1170; Kropholler, pp. 320–321; Gothot/Holleaux, para. 365; Pocar, p. 341.

Q. ARTICLE 43: PERIODIC PENALTIES

1. General note

Various provisions exist in the laws of different Contracting   **28.77**
States, whereby performance of an obligation ordered by a judgment is enforced by a monetary penalty for default. In some cases,
the penalty is set by the judgment at a daily rate,[17] but, in order to
be enforced, a further order is required in which the penalty is
finally quantified, often at a lower level than the full sum calculated
at the daily rate.[18] It is specifically to deal with this sort of problem
that Article 43 is designed.

2. " . . . periodic payment by way of a penalty . . . "

It is suggested that the provision is not confined to payments   **28.78**
which have to be made on a periodic basis, and that a liability which
is calculated by reference to the length of time it (or some other
obligation) remains unsatisfied falls within the provision. Indeed,
the English text is unusual in referring specifically to the *payment*
being "periodic." While the provisions in the original Contracting
States at which this Article was directed were provisions for payments *calculated* on a periodic basis, and the Jenard Report refers to
payment of a sum of money *for* each day of delay,[19] an obligation to
make payment on a periodic basis does not seem to be a necessary
condition.

It is clear, though, that the payment must be by way of a penalty
if this provision is to apply, and the enforceability of judgments
ordering other periodic payments (such as rent, hire purchase
repayments, or maintenance) or payments calculated by reference
to time (such as interest or some form of mesne profits) is not
necessarily dependent on a final monetary determination by the
courts of the state of origin.[20]

Penalty accruing to the state. There is some doubt as to whether a   **28.79**
penalty can be enforced under the Convention if it accrues not to
the judgment creditor but to the state.[21] As a matter of construction of the Convention, the answer to this question would
seem to lie in the interpretation of "civil and commercial matters"
in Article 1 and it remains to be seen whether the courts will permit

---

[17] For example, in France, an *astreinte*: see para. 50.69 below.
[18] Schlosser, para. 213 (para. A1.511 below); Droz, para. 587. Measures available
under the national laws of other Contracting States are summarised in chaps. 48
to 55 below, at para. 69.
[19] Jenard, para. A1.232 below.
[20] *Cf.* Geimer/Schütze, pp. 1168, 1170–1171.
[21] Schlosser, *loc. cit.*; Bülow/Böckstiegel/Schlafen, p. 266 suggest that it can. As to
the position in England, at common law, see Dicey and Morris, p. 428.

an order for payment of a penalty to the state to be enforced, even if the provision is one properly to be regarded as a provision of private law.

3. " . . . finally determined . . . "

28.80   The judgment need not be final in the sense that it is *res judicata*[22] before it can be enforced.[23] It is necessary merely that the amount of the total sum payable should have been determined,[24] even if the order for payment of that sum is still only provisionally enforceable, or if the order is still susceptible of amendment or discharge on appeal.[25]

Article 44

28.81   **An applicant who, in the State in which the judgment was given, has benefited from complete or partial legal aid or exemption from costs or expenses, shall be entitled, in the procedures provided for in Articles 32 to 35, to benefit from the most favourable legal aid or the most extensive exemption from costs or expenses provided for by the law of the State addressed.**

However, an applicant who requests the enforcement of a decision given by an administrative authority in Denmark in respect of a maintenance order may, in the State addressed, claim the benefits referred to in the first paragraph if he presents a statement from the Danish Ministry of Justice to the effect that he fulfils the economic requirements to qualify for the grant of complete or partial legal aid or exemption from costs or expenses.*†

---

[22] See para. 25.22 above.

[23] Bülow/Böckstiegel/Schlafen, p. 267.

[24] Maxwell, para. 6.107.

[25] A court in the Netherlands has held that, where it had jurisdiction to order a financial penalty in interim proceedings under Art. 24, and had done so, it had jurisdiction to fix the final amount of that penalty: *S. C. Johnson & Son. Inc.* v. *Mobilar Export-Import GmbH*, Arrondissementsrechtbank, Rotterdam, February 4, 1983, [1986] E.C.C. 360.

* Jenard, paras. A1.233–A1.234 below; Schlosser, paras. 223–224 (paras. A1.524–A1.526 below); Collins, p. 122; Dashwood/Halcon/White, pp. 37, 172; Hartley, p. 99; Kaye, pp. 1600–1602, 1607; Maxwell, paras. 6.108–6.116, 6.160–6.164; Anton, paras. 8.69–8.71; Droz, para. 588; Bülow/Böckstiegel/Schlafen, pp. 268–270; Geimer/Schütze, pp. 1152–1153, 1194–1198; Kropholler, pp. 322–324; Gothot/Holleaux, paras. 350–352; Pocar, p. 342.

† This Art. was substituted for the 1968 version by Art. 21 of the 1978 Convention. The second paragraph relating to Danish applicants, is new and the new version of the first paragraph introduces references to partial legal aid and to exemption from costs.

R. Article 44: Legal Aid

1. General note

Article 44 is designed to effect an automatic extension of legal aid **28.82** for the purpose of obtaining the initial issue of an order for enforcement. It does not extend to any of the appellate procedures provided for in the Convention, nor to the actual execution of the judgment. On the other hand, by reason of the second paragraph of Article 26, it does apply also to an application for a declaration of recognition.[26]

The provision applies most frequently in maintenance cases, where its social purpose is most necessary.[27] In such cases it has the added advantage (in its amended version) of corresponding with the terms of Article 15 of the Hague Convention of October 2, 1973 on the recognition and enforcement of maintenance obligations.[28] The entitlement to legal aid in the state addressed is, for the limited purposes envisaged by Artice 44, an entitlement to the most favourable legal aid available in the state addressed, whatever the extent of the applicant's entitlement to legal aid in the state of origin. This generous provision has the effect of making the application of Article 44 uniform in the different Contracting States, whatever the various details of their legal aid schemes.[29]

By granting automatic entitlement to legal aid in the state **28.83** addressed to a party assisted in the state of origin, it avoids the necessity of the applicant having to go through the time-consuming procedure of applying for legal aid in the state addressed. With time often at a premium in the initial stages, if the applicant had to take time in applying for legal aid, he might be placed at a disadvantage compared with the judgment debtor.[30] This is particularly the case where the applicant was in receipt only of partial legal aid in the state of origin.[31] After the initial application for an order of enforcement, the pressure of time is off and the applicant can apply for legal aid in the state addressed. For the purposes of any matter beyond the original application, the entitlement to legal aid and the procedure for applying for it, in the state addressed, is not affected by the Convention.

---

[26] Bülow/Böckstiegel/Schlafen, pp. 268–269.
[27] Jenard, para. A1.233 below.
[28] Schlosser, para. 223 (para. A1.525 below).
[29] *Ibid.* As regards England and Wales, see the commentary on s.40 of the 1982 Act, para. 43.51 below, and see para. 12.13 above.
[30] Jenard, *loc. cit.*
[31] Schlosser, *loc. cit.*

2. Evidential requirements

28.84   A legally aided person applying for an order for enforcement is required by the third paragraph of Article 33[32] and by Article 47(2)[33] to produce with his application a document showing that he was in receipt of legal aid in the state of origin, although the court may waive that requirement under the first paragraph of Article 48[34] if, for example, the fact of the applicant being in receipt of legal aid appears sufficiently from the judgment. The court of the state addressed is not concerned with the correctness of the decision in the state of origin to grant the applicant legal aid, nor with his continued entitlement to it there, but merely with whether the requirements of Article 47(2) are fulfilled.[35]

The reason for the special provision in the second paragraph, relating to an applicant applying to enforce a Danish administrative decision, is because, in Denmark, certain aspects of entitlement to maintenance are a matter for administrative authorities.[36] The provision is further explained in the Schlosser Report.[37]

Article 45

28.85   **No security, bond or deposit, however described, shall be required of a party who in one Contracting State applies for enforcement of a judgment given in another Contracting State on the ground that he is a foreign national or that he is not domiciled or resident in the State in which enforcement is sought.***

S. ARTICLE 45: PROVISION OF SECURITY

28.86   The scope of this Article requires some explanation, not least because the explanation in the Jenard Report appears to be more widely stated than the text.[38] The text of Article 45 suggests that the protection which it affords against an order for security is not a

---

[32] Para. 28.16 above.
[33] Para. 29.07 below.
[34] Para. 29.20 below.
[35] Bülow/Böckstiegel/Schlafen, p. 269.
[36] Para. 35.22 below.
[37] Schlosser, para. 224 (para. A1.526 below).
* Jenard, para. A1.235 below; Collins, pp. 122–123; Dashwood/Halcon/White, pp. 37, 173; Hartley, p. 98, Kaye, pp. 1602–1603, 1610–1612; Maxwell, para. 6.117; Anton, para. 8.70; Droz, paras. 589–592; Bülow/Böckstiegel/Schlafen, pp. 270–271; Geimer/Schütze, pp. 1152, 1192–1194; Kropholler, p. 324; Gothot/Holleaux, paras. 347, 372; Pocar, pp. 342–343.
[38] Jenard, para. A1.235 below: "This Article deals with security for costs . . . Under Article 45, any party, irrespective of nationality or domicile, who seeks enforcement in one Contracting State of a judgment given in another Contracting State may do so without providing security."

general protection, but only prevents an order being made on the ground of the applicant's nationality or his lack of domicile or residence in the state addressed.[39] Indeed, by the third paragraph of Article 38, the Convention expressly envisages security being ordered as a condition of enforcement at the stage of an appeal against an order for enforcement.

Where there are reasons, other than the applicant's nationality or lack of domicile or residence in the state addressed, to suppose that an order for security is or may be necessary, the court may grant such an order in accordance with its own law. The court should always bear in mind that an order made by it for the applicant to pay costs or damages can be enforced in the other Contracting States under the Convention and the fact that such an order might be somewhat more difficult to enforce than a claim against the security ought not, of itself, to be regarded as sufficient to order security to be given. That, it is suggested, would be to place an unwarranted obstacle in the way of the free movement of the original judgment. Where the applicant is not domiciled, or does not have assets, in another Contracting State, though, the extent to which such an order would be difficult to enforce against him may weigh more heavily in the balance.

The provision is not expressly confined to security for the costs of **28.87** the recognition or enforcement proceedings, although that is where it will most often apply.[40] It also provides protection against an order for security in respect of damage caused by the order for enforcement.[41]

It has been suggested[42] that the provision does not apply to security ordered on appeal. If the provision were confined to security for costs, this would make little sense, because the *ex parte* nature of the initial application means that only the applicant is likely to incur any costs at that stage. But, it is suggested, neither the wording of this Article and of Article 33, nor the intention of the Convention, justifies excluding appellate proceedings from its scope. The Convention is concerned to secure the maximum freedom of movement of judgments delivered by the courts of Contracting States and the achievement of that purpose would be hindered by allowing orders to be made for security at any stage of the proceedings, unless such an order were necessary for the proper protection of a judgment debtor. The Convention recognises that a judgment debtor who is

---

[39] In English law, see R.S.C., Ord. 71, r. 29.
[40] English law and practice relating to security for costs is discussed in chap. 6 above.
[41] Bülow/Böckstiegel/Schlafen, p. 271.
[42] Collins, p. 123.

appealing in the state of origin against the judgment needs to be protected if enforcement is permitted to proceed, notwithstanding the appeal on the merits. That is both a necessary and a sufficient explanation for the third paragraph of Article 38. But, it is suggested, there is no reason in those circumstances for security to be ordered solely on the basis of the applicant's nationality or lack of domicile or residence in the state addressed, and, accordingly, the third paragraph of Article 38 is to be read subject to this Article.

CHAPTER 29

PROVISIONS COMMON TO RECOGNITION AND ENFORCEMENT
(Articles 46–49)

SECTION 3

Article 46

A party seeking recognition or applying for enforcement of a   29.01
judgment shall produce:

1. a copy of the judgment which satisfies the conditions necessary to establish its authenticity;
2. in the case of a judgment given in default, the original or a certified true copy of the document which establishes that the party in default was served with the document instituting the proceedings or with an equivalent document.* †

---

* Jenard, paras. A1.236, A1.238 below; Schlosser, paras. 182, 225 (paras. A1.478, A1.527 below); Collins, pp. 117–118, 153; Dashwood/Halcon/White, pp. 38, 173–174; Hartley, p. 98; Kaye, pp. 1597–1598; Maxwell, paras. 6.118–6.122; Droz, paras. 593–597; Bülow/Böckstiegel/Schlafen, pp. 272–277; Geimer/Schütze, pp. 1206–1213; Kropholler, pp. 324–326; Gothot/Holleaux, paras. 269, 324–325, 373; Pocar, pp. 343–347.
† The words "or with an equivalent document" were added by Art. 22 of the 1978 Convention, to cater for the rule of English law (since changed), whereby notice of a writ, rather than a writ itself, was served on a defendant out of the jurisdiction.

A. Article 46: General Note

29.02   The documents referred to in this Article are to be produced on an application for an order for enforcement or for a declaration of recognition, including an application under the third paragraph of Article 26 for a decision on an incidental issue of recognition.[1] That is the effect of the third paragraph of Article 33, although in some cases the requirement may be relaxed under the first paragraph of Article 48.[2] The detailed means by which documents are to be produced, the number of copies required, whether a translation is required[3] and such matters, are to be regulated by the national law of the state addressed, although national law may not impose additional requirements and may not require legalisation or other similar formalities in respect of the documents.[4]

B. Article 46(1): Copy of the Judgment

29.03   The "copy" of the judgment to be produced must be an official copy, as other language versions of the text make clear.[5] The wording of the provision implies that the requirements of authenticity relate only to the authenticity of the copy of the judgment and not to the validity of the judgment itself, an interpretation which is fortified by the need for the copy of the judgment to be an official copy. The conditions necessary to establish the authenticity of the copy are the conditions prescribed by the law of the state of origin.[6]

Article 46(1) does not require that the judgment should include the reasons upon which it is based. Obviously, in the absence of some statement of the reasons on which the judgment is based, the court of the state addressed may find it very difficult to judge whether any of the grounds for refusal of recognition or enforcement are present. Some Contracting States have therefore provided in their internal law for judgments which are to be enforced abroad to include a statement of the reasons upon which they are based.[6a] It is particularly important that a default judgment should be identifiable as such, so that the court addressed can ensure that the requirements of Article 46(2) are fulfilled, in order to decide

---

[1] As to who may make such applications, see para. 29.09 below.

[2] Paras. 29.22 *et seq.* below, where the extent to which this provision is compulsory is considered in more detail.

[3] See Art. 48, second para., para. 29.29 below.

[4] Art. 49, para. 29.30 below.

[5] French: *expédition*; German: *ausfertigung*; Italian: *spedizione*; Dutch: *expeditie*.

[6] Jenard, para. A1.238 below. In England and Wales, see s.12 of the 1982 Act (para. 40.36 below) and R.S.C., Ord. 71, r. 36.

[6a] See chaps. 48 to 58 below, at para. 56 for the practices of Contracting States in this regard.

whether the judgment is to be refused recognition and enforcement pursuant to Article 27(2); but the reasons for the judgment may be just as important in other cases.

C. ARTICLE 46(2): DEFAULT JUDGMENTS, PROOF OF SERVICE

Article 46(2) requires proof, in the case of judgments given in default, that the document instituting the proceedings was served on the party in default. The proof must, in the first instance, be by production of the original or certified true copy[7] of "the document which establishes" the service on the party in default,[7a] although the provisions of this paragraph may be relaxed under the first paragraph of Article 48.[8] It will sometimes be sufficient if the fact that the party in default was served with the document instituting the proceedings appears from the default judgment itself.[9]

While, by its terms, this paragraph would seem to apply only to judgments in default, a wider interpretation may be justified by its purpose, so that it would also apply to judgments in other unilateral proceedings, such as the German *Mahnverfahren*.[10] On the other hand, provisional orders made on an *ex parte* basis, where it is not intended that the defendant should be notified, are not generally susceptible to recognition and enforcement under Title III.[11] Strictly, where national law permits a judgment be entered against a plaintiff in default of his taking some procedural step, Article 46(2) applies also to that judgment, although this will be of little consequence except, perhaps, in matters involving recognition only.

The wording of Article 46(2) gives rise to certain difficulties. First, the Jenard Report says of Article 46(2) that "the court in which recognition or enforcement is sought must, if the foreign judgment was given in default, be in a position to verify that the

29.04

29.05

---

[7] The requirements for certification of copy documents are relaxed by Art. 49: see paras. 29.30 *et seq.* below.
[7a] Where a civil judgment had been given in default of appearance in criminal proceedings, proof in the judgment that the summons to the criminal charge had been served was held by the Landgericht München I to be insufficient to satisfy this requirement: case 32 O 4302/76, October 7, 1976, Digest D I–46—B1.
[8] Para. 29.20 below.
[9] Similarly, if it appears from an interlocutory judgment of the court of origin, dismissing a contest to the jurisdiction: *Christiansen* v. *Fioretti*, Cour d'Appel, Aix-en-Provence, March 16, 1977, Digest D I–46—B2; *cf. Kilger* v. *Hamburger Handelsbank GmbH & Co.*, Cour Supérieure de Justice, Luxembourg, January 16, 1979, Digest D I–46—B3.
[10] Bülow/Böckstiegel/Schlafen, p. 277; see *Klomps* v. *Michel* [1981] E.C.R. 1593, discussed at para. 27.29 above, where the meaning of "document instituting the proceedings" is also discussed.
[11] *Denilauler* v. *Couchet Frères* [1980] E.C.R. 1553. See paras. 25.26 and 27.27 above.

defendant's right to defend himself was safeguarded."[12] Regrettably, while this explanation may help clarify certain anomalies in the wording of the provision, it seems not to be wholly justified by the wording actually adopted.

Secondly, Article 46(2) refers only to proof that the document instituting the proceedings was served and it may not be possible to read it as going as far as Article 27(2) which, by contrast, requires that the document be "duly" served in sufficient time for the defendant to arrange for his defence.[13] There is no requirement in Article 46(2) for the document produced to the court to state *when* service was effected, nor that it was "due" service.[14] As a matter of general construction, "service" ought probably to be tested by the law of the state which governed the service in question—in other words, the law of the state of origin, including its bilateral conventions.[15] If so, any form of service permitted by that law will suffice,[16] but will also be regarded as "due" service. As Article 27(2) demonstrates, though, the fact that service is duly effected does not necessarily mean that it left the defendant sufficient time to arrange for his defence.

Thirdly, Article 46(2) appears to apply to any default judgment, whereas Article 27(2) refers only to judgments given in default of appearance. This is perhaps less of a problem, because if a defendant has entered an appearance, he will have become aware of the proceedings and his rights are less likely to have been infringed in respect of a default judgment entered at a later stage. On the other hand, the problem is not insignificant where the judgment of which enforcement is sought is the judgment of a court, such as the English courts, where the prosecution of the action is left largely in the hands of the plaintiff.

29.06   It is suggested that the potential difficulties to which these anomalies might give rise can largely be resolved by a pragmatic approach. It has already been observed[17] that the court of the state addressed need not carry out an investigation into the question whether the grounds for refusal of recognition exist, but is merely required to take notice of its own motion of such matters as are brought to its attention. The Convention favours a general presumption of validity at the *ex parte* stage, and the court of the state addressed ought therefore only to refuse recognition under Article 27(2) if the grounds for doing so are apparent to it. If the declar-

---

[12] Jenard, para. A1.238 below.
[13] Droz, para. 595.
[14] The meaning of "due service" is discussed at paras. 27.31 *et seq.* above.
[15] Bülow/Böckstiegel/Schlafen, p. 277.
[16] *Cf.* the second para. of Art. 36, para. 28.30 above.
[17] Para. 27.04 above.

ation of recognition or order for enforcement is made, the party against whom it is made will have an opportunity of drawing any further matters to the attention of the court hearing an appeal under Article 36. That court, if the applicant has been less than frank with the court at the *ex parte* stage, may be able to make an appropriate order for costs.

Article 47

A party applying for enforcement shall also produce: 29.07

1. documents which establish that, according to the law of the State in which it has been given, the judgment is enforceable and has been served;
2. where appropriate, a document showing that the applicant is in receipt of legal aid in the State in which the judgment was given.*

D. ARTICLE 47: GENERAL NOTE

Like Article 46, this Article supplements the evidential require-   29.08
ments in the third paragraph of Article 33.[18] Article 47 would seem, on first reading, to require only an applicant for an order for enforcement to produce the documents referred to, but the documents referred to in sub-paragraph (2), relating to legal aid, may also be required where the application is made for a declaration of recognition.[19] The extent to which the requirements of this Article are mandatory is discussed below, but the requirements of Article 47(2), as to evidence of legal aid, are expressly qualified by the first paragraph of Article 48.[20] As with the documents required by Article 46, the detailed means by which they are to be produced, the number of copies required, whether a translation is required,[21] and such matters, are to be regulated by the national law of the state addressed, but national law may not impose additional requirements and may not require legalisation or other similar formalities.[22]

---

* Jenard, paras. A1.236, A1.237, A1.239 below; Schlosser, para. 225 (para. A1.527 below); Collins, pp. 117–118, 153; Dashwood/Halcon/White, pp. 38, 174; Hartley, p. 98; Kaye, pp. 1598–1599, 1602; Maxwell, paras. 6.123–6.132; Anton, paras. 8.39–8.42; Droz, paras. 598–601; Bülow/Böckstiegel/Schlafen, pp. 272–273, 278–288; Geimer/Schütze, pp. 1206–1213; Kropholler, pp. 326–327; Gothot/Holleaux, paras. 324–325, 346, 349; Pocar, pp. 347–350.

[18] Para. 28.16 above.
[19] See para. 29.18 below.
[20] Para. 29.20 below.
[21] See Art. 48, second para., para. 29.29 below.
[22] Art. 49, para. 29.30 below.

1. "A party applying for enforcement . . . "

29.09   Article 31 makes the grant of an order of enforcement conditional not only on the judgment being enforceable in the state of origin[23] and, perhaps, on the judgment having been served,[24] but also on the applicant being an "interested party."[25] Article 47(1) requires the applicant to produce documents which establish the former conditions, but not the latter. It may be, though, that such a requirement is anyway implicit (at least in cases of doubt) in the applicant's obligation to produce documents establishing the enforceability of the judgment in the state of origin.[26]

2. " . . . shall also produce . . . [documents]"

29.10   These words make it clear that the evidence referred to in Article 47 is required in addition to the evidence required by Article 46. The requirement to produce the documents in an appropriate case would appear from the wording of this Article and of the third paragraph of Article 33 to be mandatory, but there is an express qualification in the first paragraph of Article 48 and it may be that the requirement is anyway not compulsory in all cases.[27]

Article 47 does not specify the form which the documents are to take and it is not a requirement of the Convention that the documents should necessarily be distinct from those produced for the purposes of Article 46.[28] For example, if the judgment itself establishes that it is enforceable in the state of origin, the Convention does not require an additional certificate of enforceability, although the national law of the state of origin or of the state addressed may do so. The references to "documents" and "a document" are not references to any particular kind of document, nor do they necessarily refer to public documents; they ought best to be read as meaning "documentary evidence."

E. ARTICLE 47(1): PROOF OF ENFORCEABILITY AND SERVICE

29.11   Article 47(1) requires the applicant to produce evidence both of the enforceability of the judgment in the state of origin and of its service. Each requirement is considered in turn.

---

[23] Para. 29.12 below.
[24] Para. 29.14 below.
[25] Para. 28.07 above. The same applies, by reason of the second para. of Art. 26, to an applicant for a declaration of recognition.
[26] In England, R.S.C., Ord. 71, r. 28(1)(d)(i) requires affidavit evidence of the grounds for the deponent's belief that the party applying to enforce the judgment has a right to do so.
[27] See para. 29.22 below.
[28] Jenard, para. A1.239; Bülow/Böckstiegel/Schlafen, p. 279.

1. Enforceability

In order to qualify for an order of enforcement in another Con- **29.12**
tracting State, the judgment must satisfy the conditions necessary
for its enforceability in the state of origin. These conditions have
already been considered,[29] but it may be reiterated here that it is
sufficient if the judgment is provisionally enforceable,[30] and that
the time at which the judgment is to be enforceable for the purposes
of Article 31 is the time when the order for its enforcement is
issued. Care must be taken before authorising the enforcement of *ex
parte* interim orders, which are not normally susceptible to enforcement in other Contracting States, even if they are enforceable in the
state where they were made.[31]

As observed above, the judgment may contain an express reference to its enforceability. If it does not do so, and if no separate
document establishing enforceability is produced, it is not necessarily the case that the applicant has failed to fulfil the requirements
of Article 47(1).[32] It may be that the judgment is one which is automatically enforceable, if (for example) it is one against which no
appeal lies according to the law of the state of origin. In such a case,
the court of the state addressed may itself be able to deduce from
the copy of the judgment that it is enforceable, although its national
law may require some more specific indication to that effect. On the
other hand, the court of the state addressed may construe the judgment in the light of its knowledge of the law of the state of origin
and conclude that the judgment is not enforceable.[33]

Having discussed those cases where the judgment contains an **29.13**
express reference to its enforceability or where its enforceability
may be deduced as a matter of law, the Jenard Report goes on to
say:

> "But whether other judgments are enforceable can be determined
> only when the date on which they were given has been considered in
> relation to the date on which they were served and the time allowed
> for lodging an appeal."[34]

While in some cases the enforceability of the judgment may be
deduced from those dates, that will not always be the case. For
example, an appeal may be lodged before the expiry of the time

---

[29] The conditions are summarised at para. 28.02 above.
[30] As to the meaning of "provisionally enforceable," see para. 25.21 above.
[31] See *Denilauler* v. *Couchet Frères* [1980] E.C.R. 1553, discussed at para. 27.26
above.
[32] Jenard, para. A1.239 below.
[33] Oberlandesgericht Stuttgart, case 5 W 9/76, May 19, 1976, Digest D I–47—
B1.
[34] Jenard, para. A1.239 below.

limited for appealing, thereby continuing the suspension of enforceability; or the enforceability of the judgment may have been limited in point of time and have now expired.[35]

2. Service

29.14   Although Article 31 does not expressly refer to the judgment having been served as a condition for the grant of an order of enforcement, Article 47(1) contains a requirement that service of the judgment be proved. As with the requirements of service in Articles 20[36] and 27(2),[37] the means and regularity of the service, and precisely what is to be served, are matters to be determined by the law of the state of origin,[38] including its bilateral and multilateral conventions.[39]

The Jenard Report says that the party against whom enforcement is sought "must at least have been informed of the judgment given against him and also have had the opportunity to satisfy the judgment voluntarily."[40] The wording of the Convention does not in fact require evidence that the judgment debtor knew of the judgment, but merely evidence that service has been effected, and while it is open to national law to prescribe the manner in which the documents referred to in Article 47(1) are to be produced, national law cannot impose a requirement of proof of additional matters. It remains to be seen, though, whether the Convention itself requires (as the Jenard Report suggests) that the judgment should have been brought to the knowledge of the judgment debtor. If knowledge is necessary, it may be that constructive knowledge will suffice.

29.15   *An additional requirement?* A question of some difficulty is whether the Convention itself imposes a requirement that the judgment should be served (as distinct from merely requiring proof of

---

[35] Bülow/Böckstiegel/Schlafen, p. 279.
[36] Para. 22.11 above.
[37] Para. 27.21 above.
[38] *A.M.I. s.n.c. and W. Giuliani* v. *Brussels International Trade Mart Ltd. & Co. s.n.c.*, Corte D'Appello, Milan, February 3, 1984, [1984] Foro pad. 103, [1985] Eur.L.Dig. 422. The President of the Arrondissementsrechtbank, Breda (who has jurisdiction under Art. 32) has consistently refused to enforce German judgments which have been served by post, that not being a recognised method of service under German law: *Pohl & Co.* v. *Bullens*, September 21, 1979, Digest D I–47—B4; *Firma Gozze* v. *Vennootschap onder Firma Tegro Textiel Import-Export*, February 14, 1980, Digest D I–47—B5; *Brähmer* v. *Louer-van Loon*, April 11, 1984, [1986] E.C.C. 178; see also three other cases cited at Digest D I–47—B5n.
[39] The Hague Service Convention is particularly relevant in this context. See paras. A2.03 *et seq.* below and chap. 4 above. See also Art. IV of the 1968 Protocol, para. 35.17 below.
[40] Jenard, para. A1.239 below.

service, where service is required by national law), as a prerequisite to the grant of an order for its enforcement.

The starting point for a consideration of whether Article 47(1) contains a substantive requirement that service of the judgment should have been effected before an order for its enforcement can be granted in other Contracting States is to recall that Articles 46 to 49 contain evidential requirements supplementing the provisions of Article 33, and that these requirements are to be given a uniform interpretation in all the Contracting States.

The provision in Article 47(1) requiring an applicant to produce **29.16** documentary evidence that the judgment has been served appears on its face to apply whether or not the national law in question makes service of the judgment a precondition of its enforceability, although the wording is vague.[41] This must be understood in the context of the legal systems of the original Contracting States which usually require that judgments be served before they can be enforced. In some cases, though, the law of the state of origin may not make *prior* service of the judgment a condition of its enforceability and service at the outset of the enforcement may suffice for the purposes of making the enforcement lawful. The decision of the European Court of Justice in *Denilauler* v. *Couchet Frères*[42] makes it clear that, in order to be enforceable, the decision itself must have been reached in adversary proceedings; but an element of surprise may nonetheless sometimes be necessary for the purposes of enforcement.

If prior service is not a condition of enforceability in the state of origin, it would be surprising if, by implication from a provision principally concerned with matters of evidence, the Convention introduced an additional requirement of substance. If, on the other hand, the effect of Article 47(1) is indeed to impose a requirement that the judgment should have been served, then a judgment which could be enforced in its state of origin without service could not be equally enforced in the other Contracting States—an effect which is contrary to the purpose of the Convention in facilitating the free circulation of judgments as between the Contracting States. It is suggested, therefore, that a general substantive requirement of service of the judgment cannot be deduced from the evidential provision in Article 47(1) that proof of service should be produced. Such substantive requirements of service as may obtain, do so as a matter of the national law of the state of origin.

That leaves unanswered the separate question of how Article **29.17** 47(1) is to be applied as a rule of evidence where national law does

---

[41] Droz, para. 598.
[42] [1980] E.C.R. 1553, discussed at para. 27.26 above.

not require service of the judgment before enforcement may be ordered. As an evidential requirement, proof of service would appear to be mandatory, a provision which, if strictly applied, would make nonsense of the absence of a substantive requirement.[43] It is probable, though, that the evidential requirements of Article 47(1) may also be relaxed, for reasons which are discussed below.[44]

F. Article 47(2): Legal Aid

29.18   This paragraph complements the provisions of Article 44.[45] Although the introductory words of Article 47 only refer expressly to applications for enforcement, it is suggested that the requirement to produce a document showing that the applicant is in receipt of legal aid in the state of origin applies equally to applications for a declaration of recognition under the second paragraph of Article 26.[46] This is because this latter Article states that such an application is to be made in accordance with sections 2 and 3 of Title III. As with the documents required by Article 47(1), the documentary evidence need not be in a separate document, if the entitlement to legal aid sufficiently appears from the other documents produced.

The provisions of Article 47(2) may be relaxed in accordance with the first paragraph of Article 48 and, in any event, only apply "where appropriate." In other words, a document evidencing that the party is in receipt of legal aid in the state of origin need only be produced where that is the case. It is probable that a failure to produce such a document (unless the requirement is anyway waived under Article 48) is not fatal to the application for an order for enforcement, but will merely result in the applicant not receiving legal aid for the purposes of the initial application.

29.19   It is no part of the function of the court of the state addressed to review the correctness, or continued correctness, of the decision in the state of origin to grant the applicant legal aid, and there is no need for the documentary evidence to disclose the extent of legal aid provided to the applicant in the state of origin. If he was entitled to any legal aid there, he will be entitled to full legal aid in the state addressed, but only for the initial application. An applicant seeking recognition or enforcement of a Danish maintenance order may produce the document referred to in the second paragraph of Article 44.

---

[43] Bülow/Böckstiegel/Schlafen, p. 287.
[44] Para. 29.23 below.
[45] Para. 28.81 above.
[46] Jenard, para. A1.237 below; Bülow/Böckstiegel/Schlafen, pp. 272, 278, 288.

Article 48

If the documents specified in Articles 46(2) and 47(2) are not **29.20**
produced, the court may specify a time for their production,
accept equivalent documents or, if it considers that it has sufficient information before it, dispense with their production.
    If the court so requires, a translation of the documents shall be
produced; the translation shall be certified by a person qualified
to do so in one of the Contracting States.*

G. Article 48: General Note

Article 48 contains two distinct provisions. The first paragraph per- **29.21**
mits the evidential requirements of the third paragraph of Article
33, and of Articles 46 and 47, to be relaxed in certain circumstances, while the second paragraph enables the court of the state
addressed to require translations.

H. Article 48, First Paragraph: Relaxation of Evidential Requirements

1. Generally

The power provided by the first paragraph of Article 48 for the **29.22**
court of the state addressed to relax the requirements of Articles
46(2) and 47(2) would suggest that the documents required by
Articles 46(1) and 47(1) must be produced as a condition of the
grant of an order for enforcement (or, so far as Article 46(1) alone is
concerned, a declaration of recognition). It would also suggest that
the third paragraph of Article 33[47] is compulsory[48] save only to the
extent that its provisions are relaxed by this Article. That may,
however, not be a correct reading of the Convention. It seems that
the proper interpretation of the Convention on this point may permit the requirements of Articles 46(1) and 47(1) to be relaxed otherwise than within the confines of the first paragraph of Article 48.[49]
    It should be emphasised, though, that if that is the correct inter-

---

* Jenard, para. A1.240 below; Schlosser, para. 225 (para. A1.527 below); Collins,
    p. 117; Dashwood/Halcon/White, pp. 38, 174–175; Hartley, p. 98; Kaye,
    pp. 1599–1602; Maxwell, paras. 6.133–6.134; Anton, para. 8.44; Droz,
    paras. 602, 604; Bülow/Böckstiegel/Schlafen, pp. 272–273, 288–292; Geimer/
    Schütze, pp. 1206–1213; Kropholler, pp. 327–329; Gothot/Holleaux,
    paras. 326–327; Pocar, pp. 350–352.
[47] Para. 28.16 above.
[48] See, *passim, Firma P* v. *Firma K*, [1984] E.C.R. 3033, discussed at para. 28.65
    above.
[49] *Contra*, Droz, para. 604; Oberlandesgericht Frankfurt-am-Main, case 20 W
    994/77, May 29, 1978, RIW/AWD—1978, p. 620, Digest D I–48—B1.

pretation of the Convention, it is the *evidential* requirements of Articles 46(1) and 47(1) which may be relaxed, not the underlying substantive requirements that there should be a judgment and that it should be enforceable in the state of origin (both of which are in any event required by Articles 26 and 31).[50] The fact that the power (if it exists) to relax the requirements of Articles 46(1) and 47(1) in appropriate circumstances is limited to their evidential effects arises as a matter of principle by reason of the scheme and substantive provisions of Title III and by parity of reasoning with the terms of the first paragraph of Article 48.[51]

29.23 The reasoning which supports an interpretation allowing the evidential requirements of Articles 46(1) and 47(1) to be relaxed is, first, that while the terms of the third paragraph of Article 33, and of Articles 46 and 47 might appear to be mandatory, the first paragraph of Article 48 makes it clear that they may in fact be relaxed; secondly, that this provision is not and does not purport to be exhaustive as to the circumstances in which such relaxation may occur;[52] and thirdly, that the purpose of the Convention is to facilitate rather than to hinder the reciprocal enforcement of judgments.[53] Furthermore, a flexible interpretation of the Convention would permit the evidential requirements of Articles 46(1) and 47(1) to be waived by the respondent to the application (at least on appeal under Articles 36 or 40, where he has a right to be heard), and it may also be permissible for the court of the state addressed to relax those evidential requirements if that is permitted by its own law.[54] Indeed, the laws of some Contracting States make specific provision for such an eventuality.[55]

It has already been observed[56] that a strict requirement that service of the judgment should take place before enforcement may be ordered may, by its inflexibility, work injustice,[57] especially in cases where an element of surprise is necessary. If service were not required by the law of the state of origin in such cases, but were imposed as an additional requirement by the Convention, not only would the element of surprise be lost, but the result would also be to render the judgment less effective in the state addressed than it

---

[50] As to whether there is an additional underlying requirement that the judgment should have been served, see paras. 29.15 *et seq.* above.
[51] See para. 29.24 below, n. 61.
[52] Bülow/Böckstiegel/Schlafen, pp. 289–290; Geimer/Schütze, pp. 1209–1210.
[53] Geimer/Schütze, *loc. cit.*
[54] *Ibid.*; see below.
[55] *e.g.*, Art. 2(2) of the Netherlands law enacting the Convention and Arts. 139 and 142 of the German Code of Civil Procedure.
[56] Paras. 29.15 *et seq.* above.
[57] See Droz, paras. 598–600, 604.

would be in the state of origin.[58] If, in any case, service of the judgment is not strictly required as a condition of an order for its enforcement, it must follow that proof of such service cannot be required.

2. Procedure where documents are not produced on the initial application

If the documents required by Articles 46(2)[59] and 47(2)[60] are not **29.24** produced on the initial application, this Article provides a number of choices for the court of the state addressed, each of which is discussed below. It has already been emphasised in relation to the documents required by Articles 46(1) and 47(1) that the court is not free to relax the underlying substantive requirements of those paragraphs. The same reasoning applies to Articles 46(2) and 47(2). In the case of a default judgment, the party in default must still have been served with the document instituting the proceedings, and, if the applicant applies for legal aid, he must still in fact have been legally aided in the state of origin. It is only the *evidential* requirements of Articles 46(2) and 47(2) which the first paragraph of Article 48 permits to be relaxed.[61] Similarly, the exercise by the court of the state addressed of its powers under this paragraph is subject to the general requirement, contained in the first paragraph of Article 34,[62] that it should give its decision without delay.

If the documents required by Articles 46(1)[63] and 47(1)[64] are not produced and if their production is not a prerequisite for the grant of an order of enforcement,[65] the Convention is silent as to the course which may be adopted by the court of the state addressed, which may, subject to two points, apply its own law in deciding whether to relax the requirements that those documents be produced, and if so on what terms.[66] The two constraints on the court of the state addressed in those circumstances are the same as those applying in a case falling within the express terms of the paragraph,

---

[58] Geimer/Schütze, *loc. cit.*

[59] Art. 46(2) relates to documents proving service of the proceedings in the case of default judgments: paras. 29.04 *et seq.* above.

[60] Art. 47(2) relates to documents proving the legally aided status of the applicant: paras. 29.18 *et seq.* above.

[61] This is apparent both as a matter of principle and from the use of the words "if it considers that it has sufficient information before it" as a precondition of a complete waiver of the requirements of Arts. 46(2) and 47(2).

[62] Para. 28.22 above.

[63] Art. 46(1) relates to the judgment or a copy of it: para. 29.03 above.

[64] Art. 47(1) relates to documents proving the enforceability of the judgment in its state of origin and its service: paras. 29.11 *et seq.* above.

[65] Para. 29.10 above.

[66] Bülow/Böckstiegel/Schlafen, p. 290.

namely that it should generally give its decision without delay (which would not necessarily prevent a time being set for the production of the relevant documents) and that it may not depart from the underlying substantive requirements of Articles 46(1) and 47(1).[67]

29.25   *(a) Setting a time limit.* The time set by the court for an applicant to repair his omission in failing to produce the requisite documents is a matter for the discretion of the court concerned; but the court should bear in mind the general requirement of the first paragraph of Article 34 that it should give its decision without delay. That provision is to be read flexibly and should not prevent the court from allowing time in a normal case[68] but it may have the effect that the grant of an unlimited period, or a period substantially in excess of the time reasonably required to repair the omission, would be an improper exercise of the discretion. The first paragraph of Article 48 does not prevent the court from granting successive extensions of time.

29.26   *(b) Accepting equivalent documents.* According to the Jenard Report, the negotiators had in mind the case where the documents had been destroyed;[69] but any documents which sufficiently evidence the underlying substantive requirements may be accepted, whether they are public or private documents[70] and whether or not they are separate documents from those required by the other provisions of Articles 46 and 47. So, for example, in the case of a default judgment, an affidavit of service of the document instituting the proceedings may be accepted in lieu of the original or a certified true copy of the relevant certificate.[71]

29.27   *(c) Dispensing with the production of documents.* As has been observed, the court of the state addressed may not waive the underlying substantive requirements of Articles 46 and 47, but may waive the evidential requirements where evidence of the necessary matters is not necessary—*e.g.* because they are manifest, or known to the court by other means,[72] or appear from the other documents lodged with the application.

29.28   *(d) Dismissing the application.* Although the first paragraph of Article 48 does not expressly say that the court of the state addressed may dismiss the application, it is implicit in the use of the

---

[67] Para. 29.22 above.
[68] Bülow/Böckstiegel/Schlafen, *loc. cit.*
[69] Jenard, para. A1.240 below.
[70] Bülow/Böckstiegel/Schlafen, p. 291.
[71] See also *Société Etoile Cuisine* v. *Firma Tielsa Möbelwerke*, Cour d'Appel, Paris, February 8, 1979, Gaz. Palais 1979, Sommaires, p. 263, Digest D I–48—B2.
[72] Bülow/Böckstiegel/Schlafen, p. 291.

word "may" and in the terms of Articles 46 and 47 that it is not limited to the options specified in this Article and may dismiss the application.[73] Where the documents are first produced on an appeal under Article 36, the appeal may be allowed.[74]

I. ARTICLE 48, SECOND PARAGRAPH: TRANSLATIONS

The second paragraph of Article 48 does not require that a transla- **29.29** tion be produced, but enables the court of the state addressed to require one if it chooses, either generally or in any particular case.[75] Provided that the court's order complies with the requirements of this Article, it may impose conditions (such as a time limit) on the requirement to produce the translation. The translation may be required at any stage of the proceedings, but an applicant would be well-advised to provide a translation at the outset, to avoid later delay.[76] The second paragraph of Article 48 applies only to translations of the documents to be annexed to the application, not to the application itself, although the court of the state addressed may require a translation of that and of any other documents pursuant to its own law.[77]

The provision goes further and provides that if the court requires a translation, it is to be certified by a person qualified to do so in any of the Contracting States. It is apparent from the wording of the text ("the translation shall be certified by a person qualified to do so . . . ")[78] that this is a dual requirement applicable uniformly in all the Contracting States. The requirements are first that, if a translation is required, it must be certified and, secondly, that the person who certifies it must be qualified to do so, for which purpose a qualification in that respect in any of the Contracting States is sufficient.[79] The requirement that the translation be certified cannot be waived by the court of the state addressed.[80] No legalisation or similar formality may be required in respect of the translation.[81]

---

[73] See *Firma P* v. *Firma K*, [1984] E.C.R. 3033, discussed at para. 28.65 above.

[74] Oberlandesgericht Stuttgart, case 8 W 335/77, October 11, 1977, Digest D I–47—B2.

[75] In England, a general requirement has been imposed: R.S.C., Ord. 71, r. 28(1)(a)(iv). See para. 10.14 above.

[76] Bülow/Böckstiegel/Schlafen, p. 291.

[77] Bülow/Böckstiegel/Schlafen, p. 292.

[78] Other language versions provide: French, "*la traduction est cerifiée par une personne habilitée à cet effet* . . . "; German, "*die Übersetzung ist von einer hierzu . . . befugten Person zu beglaubigen*"; Italian, "*la traduzione è autenticata da una persona a tal fine abilitata* . . . "; Dutch, "*de vertaling wordt gewaarmerkt door degene die . . . daartoe gemachtigd is.*"

[79] Jenard, para. A1.240 below. See chaps. 48 to 58 below, at para. 71.

[80] Bülow/Böckstiegel/Schlafen, p. 292; Geimer/Schütze, p. 1211.

[81] Art. 49, see next para.

Article 49

29.30 **No legalisation or other similar formality shall be required in respect of the documents referred to in Article 46 or 47 or the second paragraph of Article 48, or in respect of a document appointing a representative *ad litem*.***

J. ARTICLE 49: GENERAL NOTE

29.31 The effect of this Article is to simplify the procedures necessary for the authentication of foreign documents. It relates only to the documents which the Convention requires to be produced for the purposes of an application for an order of enforcement or a declaration of recognition, or appointing a representative *ad litem* (usually a lawyer) under the second paragraph of Article 33. In respect of those documents, no legalisation or other similar formality is required, although Contracting States can apply their own law as to the evidential requirements in respect of documents to the extent that that is not inconsistent with this Article.

"Legalisation" is the term used to refer to the certification by a public official of certain formal documents for use abroad, required by the laws or practices of certain states. The certification is usually performed by consular officials of the state where the document is going to be used. However, under the Hague Convention for the Abolition of Legalisation of October 5, 1961,[82] consular certification is not usually necessary and instead a certificate (known as an *apostille*) is issued by the appropriate authority in the country of origin of the document. It is principally this certificate which is referred to by the words "other similar formality" in Article 49,[83] and accordingly not even an *apostille* is required in respect of the documents referred to in this Article.[84]

29.32 Neither legalisation nor an *apostille* authenticated the document itself, nor established its evidentiary value, but merely certified the authenticity of the signature of the official who signed the document, the capacity in which he acted and, where appropriate, the

---

* Jenard, para. A1.241 below; Schlosser, para. 225 (para. A1.527 below); Collins, p. 117; Dashwood/Halcon/White, p. 175; Maxwell, para. 6.135; Kaye, p. 1600; Anton, para. 8.42; Droz, para. 603; Bülow/Böckstiegel/Schlafen, pp. 272–273, 292–293; Geimer/Schütze, pp. 1206–1213; Kropholler, p. 329; Gothot/Holleaux, para. 327; Pocar, pp. 352–353.

[82] Cmnd. 2617. The six original Contracting States, Greece and the U.K. have ratified; Denmark and the Republic of Ireland have not signed.

[83] Jenard, para. A1.241 below.

[84] English practice in respect of such documents is referred to at para. 8.62 above.

identity of the stamp or seal on the document.[85] Under the Convention, where these formalities are not required, any doubt as to the authenticity of the document will mean that the burden on the applicant of satisfying the court is increased.[86]

---

[85] *Legalisation of Documents for Use Abroad*, Foreign & Commonwealth Office, London, October 1985.
[86] Bülow/Böckstiegel/Schlafen, p. 293.

CHAPTER 30

AUTHENTIC INSTRUMENTS AND COURT SETTLEMENTS
(Articles 50–51)

TITLE IV

Article 50

30.01   **A document which has been formally drawn up or registered as an authentic instrument and is enforceable in one Contracting State shall, in another Contracting State, have an order for its enforcement issued there, on application made in accordance with the procedures provided for in Article 31 *et seq.* The application may be refused only if enforcement of the instrument is contrary to public policy in the State in which enforcement is sought.**

The instrument produced must satisfy the conditions necessary to establish its authenticity in the State of origin.

The provisions of Section 3 of Title III shall apply as appropriate.*

---

* Jenard, para. A1.242 below; Schlosser, para. 226 (para. A1.528 below); Collins, p. 123; Dashwood/Halcon/White, pp. 36, 179–180; Hartley, p. 100; Kaye, pp. 1680–1686; Maxwell, paras. 7.1–7.7; Anton, paras. 8.57–8.60; Droz,

A. Article 50: Authentic Instruments

1. General note

It is not only judgments which may be compulsorily enforced **30.02** under the Convention. Articles 50 and 51 extend the enforcement provisions to two other classes of enforceable obligations, namely, by this Article, authentic instruments and, by Article 51,[1] court settlements.

2. Meaning of "authentic instrument"

The Convention nowhere defines an "authentic instrument," a **30.03** creature unknown to the common law.[2] It is clear from the wording of Article 50 that only documentary instruments are envisaged. Although there is no express limitation in the Convention on the type of instrument envisaged, it is apparent that this Article is concerned with instruments other than judgments (as defined by Article 25)[3] and court settlements (which are enforceable under Article 51).[3a] A uniform interpretation of the term "authentic instrument," however, would probably not permit all other instruments to be enforceable, on condition only that they were valid and enforceable in the Contracting State where they were registered or drawn up.[4] For example, orders have been refused for the enforcement in one Contracting State of instruments from another Contracting State, on the ground that the party against whom the enforcement was sought was not a party to the creation of the instrument.[5]

In practice, the documents which will most commonly fall within Article 50 are notarially validated documents,[6] but documents auth-

---

paras. 605–624; Bülow/Böckstiegel/Schlafen, pp. 294–303; Geimer/Schütze, pp. 1166–1167, 1271–1278; Kropholler, pp. 330–334; Gothot/Holleaux, paras. 403–410; Pocar, pp. 334–355.

[1] Para. 30.14 below.
[2] Schlosser, para. 226 (para. A1.528 below); Collins, p. 123.
[3] Para. 26.01 above.
[3a] See para. 30.15, n. 61 below.
[4] *Contra*, Bülow/Böckstiegel/Schlafen, p. 296.
[5] Landgericht Aachen, case 1 O 642/81, February 9, 1982, Digest D I–25.1—B2 (statutory determination of liability to pay certain sums under Netherlands social benefits law); *Zilken & Weber* v. *Scholl*, Ned.Jur. 1982, No. 466, Digest D I–50—B2, reported as *Re Enforcement of a Bill of Costs*, [1983] E.C.C. 551 (German notary's bill).
[6] Droz, para. 614. See, for example, *Deutsche Genossenschaftsbank* v. *Brasserie du Pêcheur S.A.* 1985 [1985] E.C.R. 1981, discussed at para. 28.32 above. The notarially attested instrument gave a creditor and its assignees a charge over the debtor's land in respect of a fixed sum and interest at a fixed rate. It also empowered the creditor or its assignees to take immediate enforcement measures, if necessary, against the debtor's other assets. In his Opinion, Advocate

enticated by other public officers or by registration in a special register are also envisaged.[7] The instrument will nearly always contain an express and conclusive statement of a party's indebtedness or other obligation. The obligations enforceable under an authentic instrument are not confined to obligations to pay money.[8] The instrument must, without further formality, be enforceable.

3. Enforceability in the state addressed

30.04   If an authentic instrument is enforceable under Article 50, that fact will not prevent it forming the basis of an action: Article 50 merely extends such automatic enforceability as the instrument may have in its state of origin. No question of recognition of authentic instruments arises under the Convention independently of their enforceability because they do not display the recognisable authoritative effects of a judgment.[9] The Jenard Report identifies three conditions which are to be fulfilled before enforcement of an authentic instrument may be ordered in a Contracting State:[10]

(1) The instrument must have been formally drawn up or registered in another Contracting State and must be enforceable in that state;[11]

(2) It must satisfy the conditions necessary to establish its authenticity in that state;[12]

(3) Its enforcement must not be contrary to public policy in the state addressed.[13]

In the interests of completeness, the following further conditions should be mentioned:

(4) The instrument must fall within the scope of the Conven-

General Lenz summarised some aspects of German law concerning the enforceability of the instrument (at pp. 1983 to 1984). Similarly, *Sunclass Sonnevijver N.V.* v. *B. J. Westerveld q.q.*, Rechtbank van Eerste Aanleg, Tongeren (Belgium), September 26, 1980, Digest D I–50—B1 (An agreement for a lease of land in Belgium, drawn up before a notary in the Netherlands, declared enforceable in Belgium).

[7] Maxwell, para. 7.2. The documents regarded in each of the Contracting States as authentic instruments are summarised in chaps. 48 and 50 below, at para. 70.

[8] *Sunclass Sonnevijver N.V.* v. *B. J. Esterveld q.q.*, above.

[9] Bülow/Böckstiegel, p. 294. The recognisable effects of judgments are discussed at paras. 25.07 *et seq.* above.

[10] Jenard, para. A1.242 below.

[11] First para. of this Art., discussed below.

[12] Second para. of this Art., discussed below.

[13] First para. of this Art., discussed below.

tion, both as to its subject-matter[14] and by reference to the transitional provisions;[15]

(5) The instrument should be of a character falling within Article 50;[16] and

(6) The person against whom enforcement is sought must have been duly served, pursuant to the law of the state of origin (although this condition may not always apply).[17]

If the instrument satisfies these conditions, an order for its enforcement must be issued, provided that the application is correctly made. The wording of the provision is in mandatory terms and the court of the state addressed has no discretion in the matter.

4. Scope of Article 50

The scope of the Convention as a whole is determined by the **30.05** Preamble and Article 1 and authentic instruments will only fall within Article 50 if their subject-matter falls within the Convention's scope.[18] That scope, it will be recalled, is to be determined according to an independent interpretation of the Convention, applicable uniformly in all the Contracting States. This is of some importance in relation to authentic instruments, some of which may, according to some national laws, be wholly or partly creatures of public law and therefore fall outside the scope of the Convention, not being "civil and commercial matters." So long as the *subject-matter* of the instrument falls within the scope of the Convention, it is immaterial that the document itself has public law characteristics in its state of origin.[19]

Arbitration is excluded from the scope of the Convention, although the extent of this exclusion is not settled.[20] If the narrower interpretation of the exclusion is correct, it may be (at least in theory) that in certain circumstances an arbitral award duly drawn up in a Contracting State where (according to the law of that state) it would be enforceable, could thereby be converted into an enforceable instrument and so be enforceable in the other Contracting States.[21] That would require that the subject-matter of the arbi-

---

[14] Art. 1, para. 14.03 above. See also below.

[15] Art. 54, first para. (para. 32.01 below); Art. 34 of the 1978 Convention (para. 37.06 below). The Convention only applies to instruments drawn up or registered after it came into force.

[16] Para. 30.03 above.

[17] Third paragraph of this Article, discussed below. See also Art. 47(1), para. 29.07 above.

[18] *Berufsgenossenschaft* v. *Gerren*, Ned. Jur. 1983, 387, [1984] Eur.L.Drg. 14. The material scope of the Convention is discussed in chap. 14 above.

[19] Geimer/Schütze, p. 1272.

[20] Paras. 14.31 *et seq.* above.

[21] Bülow/Böckstiegel, pp. 29–30.

trated dispute fell within the scope of the Convention. It would usually also require that both parties to the arbitration co-operate in the drawing-up of the authentic instrument, a condition which is perhaps unlikely to be met in practice.[22]

5. "A document which has been formally drawn up or registered as an authentic instrument and is enforceable in one Contracting State . . . "

30.06   The document must *both* have been drawn up or registered in a Contracting State *and* be enforceable in that same state.[23] The national law of that state applies to determine whether the instrument was validly drawn up or registered[24] and whether it is enforceable in that state. The laws of those Contracting States which recognise authentic instruments vary as to the type of instruments which are enforceable, and as to the conditions under which they may be enforced.

The effect of Article 50, therefore, is more complex than merely to extend the effects of authentic instruments from one Contracting State into the others. On the one hand, it does indeed widen the enforceability of such instruments, by enabling them to be enforced in a state which would not otherwise enforce instruments of that type. On the other hand, though, it also extends the limitations of enforceability from the state of origin into the state of proposed enforcement. So, for example, an instrument of a type which would otherwise be enforceable in Contracting State A, but not in Contracting State B, will not be directly enforceable in State A if it was drawn up in State B. Similarly, if the instrument was drawn up or registered in a non-Contracting State, it will not be enforceable under Article 50, even if it is enforceable in another Contracting State under the terms of a bilateral convention between the state of origin and that other Contracting State.[25]

30.07   The requirement that the instrument be drawn up in a Contracting State is independent of any question of the domicile of the parties. It is probable, though, that an instrument drawn up by consular officials of a Contracting State outside the geographical

---

[22] *Ibid.*

[23] The English text is ambiguous as to whether "in one Contracting State" governs the whole phrase, or only the word "enforceable," but the correct interpretation is apparent from the German text: " . . . *die in einem Vertragsstaat aufgenommen und vollstreckbar sind. . . .*" Other language versions provide: French, " . . . *reçus et exécutoires dans un État contractant . . .*"; Italian, " . . . *ricevuti ed aventi efficacia esectiva in uno Stato contraente . . .*"; Dutch, " . . . *verleden en uitvoerbaar in een Verdragsluitende Staat. . . .*"

[24] Para. 30.09 below.

[25] Bülow/Böckstiegel/Schlafen, p. 296.

territory of that state, would be regarded for the purposes of Article 50 as having been drawn up in that state, at least if the consul was empowered in the state in which he was the consul to perform notarial functions.[26]

The requirement that the instrument should be enforceable in the state of origin means that it should have an executory character there.[27] This should be understood in the context of the civil law systems of execution,[28] whereby an order for enforcement is endorsed on the instrument, which may then be enforced without further involvement by the court. In the context of authentic instruments, the requirement that the document should have an executory character means that it should be capable of enforcement without further formality.[29]

6. "The application may be refused only if enforcement of the instrument is contrary to public policy in the State in which enforcement is sought"

The procedure on an application for an order for enforcement of an authentic instrument generally follows the procedure applicable to judgments.[30] Perhaps the most noticeable difference is the grounds upon which enforcement may be opposed. Whereas enforcement of a judgment may be opposed on a number of grounds,[31] Article 50 expressly limits those grounds in the case of authentic instruments to cases in which enforcement is contrary to public policy.   **30.08**

It has already been observed that public policy is to be narrowly construed in the context of Article 27(1)[32] and the same considerations apply in the context of Article 50. Specifically, it is submitted, it would be contrary to the Convention to use public policy to refuse enforcement of an authentic instrument on the grounds that the law of the state addressed does not recognise authentic instruments generally, or the specific kind of instrument in particular. Resorting to public policy as a reason for refusing an order for enforcement should be regarded as an exceptional step, and the court of the state addressed should not normally do so unless the other conditions for enforcement are all fulfilled.[33]

Despite the apparently clear wording of Article 50, though, there

---

[26] Bülow/Böckstiegel/Schlafen, pp. 296–297; Geimer/Schütze, p. 1274.
[27] *Cf.* French text, "*exécutoire*"; Droz, para. 615.
[28] See para. 25.32 above.
[29] Bülow/Böckstiegel/Schlafen, p. 297.
[30] See paras. 30.10 *et seq.* below.
[31] Paras. 25.11 *et seq.* and 28.26 above.
[32] Paras. 27.14 *et seq.* above.
[33] Bülow/Böckstiegel/Schlafen, p. 301.

are other grounds upon which enforcement of an authentic instrument may be refused.[34] The court of the state addressed is expressly prohibited from reviewing a judgment given in another Contracting State as to its substance[35] and this principle applies equally to authentic instruments.[36] On the other hand, the court of the state addressed must satisfy itself that the instrument is valid,[37] that it has been drawn up or registered in another Contracting State and that it is enforceable there. If it is not satisfied of those matters, it may refuse the application.[38] Were it otherwise, the instrument could acquire in the state addressed a greater degree of enforceability than it had in the state of origin.

7. "The instrument produced must satisfy the conditions necessary to establish its authenticity in the State of origin"

30.09   The laws of the different Contracting States vary as to the conditions which apply to establish the validity of an enforceable instrument.[39] The "state of origin" is the state in which the instrument was drawn up or registered and it is the law of that state which has to be applied in determining the validity of the instrument. The validity of the authentic instrument is a condition precedent to the grant in any other Contracting State of an order for its enforcement.[40] The manner in which the court of the state addressed determines the authenticity of the instrument is considered below.[41]

8. Procedure on the application: Articles 31 *et seq.*; Section 3 of Title III

30.10   The procedure for making the application is that which applies to an application for an order for enforcement of a judgment given in another Contracting State, discussed in the commentary on Articles 31 to 45.[42] To the extent that those provisions go beyond matters of procedure, they still apply to an application for an order of enforcement of an authentic instrument. The procedure in the first instance involves an *ex parte* application for an order for enforcement, upon which the court must give its decision without delay.

The third paragraph of Article 50 applies such of the provisions

---

[34] Maxwell, paragraph 7.4.
[35] Art. 29, para. 27.75 above; Art. 34, third para., para. 28.22 above.
[36] Geimer/Schütze, p. 1276; see para. 30.12 below.
[37] Second paragraph of this Article, discussed below.
[38] Third paragraph of this Article, discussed below.
[39] See chaps. 48 to 58 below, at para. 70; see also the commentary on s.13 of the 1982 Act, paras. 40.39 below.
[40] Droz, para. 620.
[41] Para. 30.10 below.
[42] Chap. 28 above.

of Articles 46 to 49 as are appropriate. This means that the applicant must produce a copy of the instrument which satisfies the conditions necessary to establish its authenticity[43] and documents which establish that, according to the law of the state in which the instrument was drawn up or registered, it is enforceable and has been served.[44] The provisions relating to translation[45] and to legalisation or other similar formality[46] are also applicable. It is not easy to conceive of circumstances in which the provisions relating to default judgments[47] would apply *mutatis mutandis* to authentic instruments and this provision probably has no application in this context.

Similarly, a legally aided applicant[48] is rarely likely to apply for the enforcement of an authentic instrument (except, perhaps, in connection with authentic instruments establishing maintenance obligations). On the other hand, an applicant is more likely to be legally aided in the case of a court settlement, to which this provision also applies.[49] The applicability of the express terms of the first paragraph of Article 48 depends upon the applicability of Articles 46(2) and 47(2), but reference should be made to the commentary under that Article concerning the relaxation of the evidential requirements of Articles 46(1) and 47(1).[50] Similarly, the requirement of service inherent in Article 47(1)[51] will apply only in those cases in which the national law of the state of origin requires the instrument to be served before enforcement can take place.

At the initial *ex parte* stage of the procedure, the court will have **30.11** to consider of its own motion whether the conditions are fulfilled for the grant of an order for enforcement. As in the case of judgments, it is not required to carry out an investigation of the matter, but must take notice of any matters appearing from the documents presented to it or which are otherwise known to it.[52] On an appeal under Articles 36 or 40, the same matters may be raised by the parties and argued *inter partes*, but at this stage of the procedure, the person against whom enforcement is sought will have an oppor-

---

[43] Art. 46(1), para. 29.03 above.
[44] Art. 47(1), paras. 29.11 *et seq.* above. *Cf.* Maxwell, para. 7.6, which suggests that the requirement of service has no application; but see below.
[45] Art. 48, second para., para. 29.29 above.
[46] Art. 49, para. 29.30 above.
[47] Art. 46(2), para. 29.04 above.
[48] Art. 47(2), para. 29.18 above.
[49] Art. 51, paras. 30.14 *et seq.* below.
[50] Para. 29.23 above.
[51] Paras. 29.14 *et seq.* above.
[52] Para. 27.04 above.

tunity to raise any matter, whether formal or otherwise, which affects the validity or enforceability of the instrument.[53]

30.12 *Validity of the instrument.* In cases in which enforcement of a foreign judgment is sought, the only questions of validity which can arise are questions of the authenticity of the judgment; other questions of validity are almost certain to be matters of substance, which the court of the state addressed is prohibited from reviewing.[54] In the case of enforceable instruments, on the other hand, the instrument may be apparently authentic, but for some other reason not be valid. While it might be argued that such objections are matters going to the substance of the instrument, the better view[55] is that the person against whom enforcement is sought should be permitted to raise such objections in opposition to an application for an order of enforcement, in order to prevent the instrument having a greater validity in the state addressed than it would have in the state of origin. This is not to say that the court of the state addressed may carry out an untrammelled review of the substance of the instrument, but may consider whether, in truth and whatever the outward appearance, the instrument really is authentic and enforceable.

30.13 *Substance of the obligation.* What the person against whom enforcement is sought may not argue, in objecting to the enforcement of the instrument, and what the court of the state addressed may not consider, is whether as a matter of substance he was not, or should not have been, under the obligation in the first place. In order to raise that objection, the party should bring an action to nullify the instrument (by whatever means may be available) in a court of competent jurisdiction, which, in the context of the Convention, means a court with jurisdiction under Title II. The judgment in such an action would be accorded automatic recognition in the other Contracting States.[56] If he has not done so, or if his action has not yet been concluded, and an application for an order of enforcement is made in a Contracting State other than the state of origin, the person against whom enforcement is sought may find that he is faced with the prospect of enforcement being carried out against him, without his having an opportunity to protest his objections of substance. In those circumstances, the court of the state

---

[53] Droz, paras. 619–620; Bülow/Böckstiegel/Schlafen, p. 302; Geimer/Schütze, p. 1278.
[54] Art. 34, third para., para. 28.22 above.
[55] Droz, paras. 619 *et seq.*; Bülow/Böckstiegel/Schlafen, p. 302; Geimer/Schütze, p. 1278.
[56] Art. 26, first para., para. 27.01 above.

addressed is not competent to consider the objection but, it is sub-mitted, Article 38[57] should be applied to enable the court of the state addressed, as appropriate, to stay its proceedings, to set a time limit within which that person is to bring such proceedings, or to order conditional enforcement. The proceedings to nullify the instrument should be regarded as an "ordinary appeal" for the pur-poses of that Article.[58]

Article 51

A settlement which has been approved by a court in the course   **30.14**
of proceedings and is enforceable in the State in which it was
concluded shall be enforceable in the State in which enforcement
is sought under the same conditions as authentic instruments.*

B. ARTICLE 51: COURT SETTLEMENTS

1. General note

The laws of some Contracting States (notably Germany and the   **30.15**
Netherlands)[59] provide for the enforceability of court settlements.
Such a settlement is not a judgment within the meaning of Article
25[60] and it is to be distinguished from a settlement to which effect is
given by a consent judgment. For the purposes of Article 51 it must
have been approved by a court in the course of proceedings and be
enforceable in its state of origin. Article 51 extends that enforce-ability into the other Contracting States in the same way as Article
50 extends the enforceability of authentic instruments.[61]

---

[57] Para. 28.43 above.
[58] *Cf.* Droz, paras. 621 *et seq.*
* Jenard, para. A1.243 below; Schlosser, para. 226 (para. A1.528 below); Collins, p. 123; Dashwood/Halcon/White, pp. 36–37, 180; Hartley, p. 100; Kaye, pp. 1680–1686; Maxwell, paras. 7.8–7.11; Anton, paras. 8.61–8.65; Droz, paras. 605, 624–628; Bülow/Böckstiegel/Schlafen, pp. 303–307; Geimer/Schütze, pp. 140–141, 1165–1166, 1278–1283; Kropholler, p. 335; Pocar, pp. 355–356.
[59] Jenard, para. A1.243 below. The particular rules under which court settlements may be made in each of the Contracting States are summarised in chaps. 48 to 58 below, at para. 70 below.
[60] Para. 26.01 above.
[61] Para. 30.01 above. See *De Raad vor de Kinderbescherming* v. *A*, Gerechtshof, The Hague, October 18, 1985, Ned.Jur. 1986, 1953, [1987] Eur.L.Dig. 198: a formal document drawn up by a German court to record an agreed order for maintenance was given effect in the Netherlands, although, for reasons which are not clear, Art. 50 rather than Art. 51 was cited as the basis for doing so.

2. Conditions of enforceability in the state addressed

30.16   Article 51 merely extends such automatic enforceability as the settlement may have in its state of origin. As with authentic instruments, no question of recognition of court settlements arises under the Convention independently of their enforceability because they do not display the recognisable authoritative effects of a judgment.[62]

The conditions under which a court settlement may be enforced in another Contracting State are expressly equated by Article 51 with the conditions under which authentic instruments are to be enforced, although, implicity, the conditions will vary slightly to take account of differences between court settlements and authentic instruments. The conditions, discussed in more detail below, are as follows;[63]

(1) The settlement must have been approved by a court in another Contracting State and must be enforceable in that state;

(2) The settlement must satisfy the conditions necessary to establish its authenticity in that state;

(3) The enforcement must not be contrary to public policy in the state addressed;

(4) The settlement must fall within the scope of the Convention, both as to its subject-matter and by reference to the transitional provisions;

(5) The settlement should be of a character falling within Article 51; and

(6) The person against whom enforcement is sought must have been duly served, pursuant to the law of the state of origin (although this condition may not always apply).

As with authentic instruments, if the settlement satisfies these conditions, an order for its enforcement must be issued, provided that the application is correctly made. The wording of the provision is in mandatory terms and the court of the state addressed has no discretion in the matter.

The conditions are discussed in relation to Article 50 and refer-

---

[62] *Cf.* Bülow/Böckstiegel/Schlafen, p. 304. The recognisable effects of judgments are discussed at paras. 25.07 *et seq.* above. A Belgian court was, it is submitted, in error where it refused to permit proceedings on a dispute which had already been compromised by a court settlement in Germany: *Klausen-werft KG and Klausen* v. *Internationale Stoombootdiensten Flandria NV*, Vredegerecht, Antwerp, February 15, 1977, Digest D I–52—B1.

[63] The numbering adopted is the same as that used for authentic instruments at para. 30.04 above.

ence should be made to the commentary on that Article. The following additional points should also be noted.

Condition (1). This condition, that the settlement must have been **30.17** approved by a court in another Contracting State and must be enforceable in that state, imposes a triple requirement. First, the settlement must have been approved, although the form of approval is a matter to be determined by the law of the state of origin. Secondly, the approval must have been made by a court[64] in another Contracting State. Thirdly, the settlement must be enforceable in that state ("the state in which it was concluded"), which means that it must be enforceable there pursuant to the law of that state. A settlement made in a non-Contracting State which is enforceable in the other Contracting State pursuant to a bilateral convention does not fall within Article 51.

Condition (2). So far as this condition is concerned, it has been observed[65] that questions of the validity (as distinct from the substance) of an authentic instrument involve more than just considerations of the authenticity of the instrument itself. The same applies in relation to court settlements. Under the law of some states, the settlement can be challenged if it is invalid in form or substance,[66] although challenges of substance may not be raised in the enforcement proceedings. The authenticity of the settlement itself has to be proved to the satisfaction of the court addressed, and Article 46(1), which applies equally in this context, provides a means of doing so.

Condition (3). This condition, that the enforcement must not be contrary to public policy in the state addressed, is equivalent to the same condition in relation to authentic instruments.[67]

Condition (4). The scope of the Convention, so far as the subject- **30.18** matter of the settlement is concerned is governed by the Article 1.[68] In the case of court settlements, the fact that maintenance obligations fall within the Convention may be of particular relevance. A court settlement made within the scope of the Hague Convention on the Recognition and Enforcement of Maintenance Obligations of October 2, 1973[69] is not necessarily excluded from the scope of the Convention by Article 57.[70] In such a case, the maintenance credi-

---

[64] Para. 26.05 above.
[65] Para. 30.12 above.
[66] Maxwell, para. 7.9.
[67] Para. 30.08 above.
[68] Para. 14.03 above. See also para. 30.05 above.
[69] In England, see Part I of the Maintenance Orders (Reciprocal Enforcement) Act 1972. See also chap. 11 above.
[70] Para. 33.06 below.

tor has a choice whether to enforce the settlement under Article 51 or under the Hague Convention.[71] The settlement must also fall within the Convention in point of time under the transitional provisions.[72]

Condition (5). This condition, that the settlement should be of a character falling within Article 51, involves, in particular, a requirement that it was made in the course of court proceedings, but is not a judgment within Article 25.

Condition (6). The requirement that the person against whom enforcement is sought must have been duly served, pursuant to the law of the state of origin, arises under the third paragraph of Article 50 and the implicit incorporation of Article 47(1). For the reasons discussed under those provisions,[73] the requirement may apply only where service is required by the law of the state of origin as a condition of the settlement's enforceability.

3. Procedure on the application

30.19   The procedure on an application for an order of enforcement is equivalent to that applicable in the case of authentic instruments.[74] The court of the state addressed is prohibited from reviewing the court settlement as to its substance, but other objections to the validity of the settlement may be raised. The court of the state addressed may apply Article 38 as appropriate.

---

[71] Bülow/Böckstiegel/Schlafen, p. 350; Geimer/Schütze, p. 1279. *Cf. Hallais* v. *Kunz*, Cour d'Appel, Paris, November 25, 1977, Digest D I–51—B2; *X* v. *Y*, President of the Arrondissementsrechtbank, The Hague, December 28, 1983, Ned.Jur. 1983, No. 452, Digest D I–51—B3.

[72] Art. 54, para. 32.01 below; Art. 34 of the 1978 Convention, para. 32.01 below.

[73] Paras. 29.14 *et seq.* and 30.10 above.

[74] Paras. 30.10 *et seq.* above.

CHAPTER 31

PROVISIONS RELATING TO DOMICILE AND SEAT
(Articles 52–53)

TITLE

Article 52

In order to determine whether a party is domiciled in the Con-   31.01
tracting State whose courts are seised of the matter, the court
shall apply its internal law.

If a party is not domiciled in the State whose courts are seised
of the matter, then, in order to determine whether the party is
domiciled in another Contracting State, the court shall apply the
law of that State.

The domicile of a party shall, however, be determined in
accordance with his national law if, by that law, his domicile
depends on that of another person or on the seat of an authority.*

---

* Jenard, paras. A1.66–77; A1.244 below; Schlosser, paras. 71–74, 227
(paras. A1.358–A1.361, A1.529 below); Collins, pp. 37–40; Dashwood/Halcon/
White, pp. 19–21, 183–184; Hartley, pp. 24–30; Kaye, pp. 278–319; Maxwell,
paras. 5.1–5.2, 5.14–5.19, 8.6–8.12; Anton, paras. 4.22–4.25, 5.50–5.52; Droz,
paras. 343–382; Weser, paras. 309–317; Bülow/Böckstiegel/Schlafen,
pp. 307–316; Geimer/Schütze, pp. 167–169, 358–377; Kropholler,
pp. 336–341; Gothot/Holleaux, paras. 41–47; Pocar, pp. 357–358.

A. ARTICLE 52: DOMICILE

1. General note

31.02   The concept of domicile is central to the working of the Convention. The jurisdictional rules in Title II nearly all depend either directly or indirectly on the question of where a person is domiciled.[1] Domicile also plays a role in determining which courts have jurisdiction for the purposes of recognition and enforcement of judgments.[2] It follows that a correct determination of domicile is of the greatest importance for the proper application of the Convention.

Articles 52 and 53 provide the rules in the Convention by which a person's domicile is to be determined. Unlike most of the Convention's provisions, though, these are uniform choice-of-law rules, rather than uniform rules of domicile. Article 52 is concerned with the domicile of individuals, while Article 53[3] provides rules for determining the "seat" of a company or other legal person or association of natural or legal persons, which is to be equated with its domicile. It also makes provision in relation to trusts.

The concept of domicile differs as to detail between the national laws of the different Contracting States, although common characteristics can be identified.[4] The authors of the Convention concluded that it would not be wise to provide a uniform definition of domicile and, having considered a number of different solutions, decided to adopt uniform choice-of-law rules.[5]

2. The scheme of the article: summary

31.03   Article 52 provides rules for determining the state in which a party is domiciled, and does so by saying which national law is to be applied. It is silent on the question of how local domicile within a state is to be determined[6] and this matter will have to be decided in accordance with its own law by the court which has international jurisdiction. Where there is a domicile of dependence, though, the Convention does provide a choice-of-law rule in the third paragraph

---

[1] The domicile of the parties is irrelevant for the purposes of the rules in Art. 16 (chap. 20 above), with the possible exception of Art. 16(2) which refers to the seat of a company: see commentary below.
[2] *e.g.* under the second para. of Art. 32, para. 28.09 above.
[3] Para. 31.23 below.
[4] See the discussion below.
[5] Jenard, paras. A1.67 *et seq.* below.
[6] Local domicile is relevant for the purposes of many of the special rules of jurisdiction in Arts. 5 to 15: see para. 15.03 above. The national rules of domicile in each of the Contracting States are summarised in chaps. 48 to 58 below, at para. 25.

of Article 52 which relates to local as well as to international domicile.

In summary, where a court seised of a matter has to decide the domicile of a party for the purposes of the Convention—usually to decide whether it has jurisdiction—it will need to consider some or all of the following questions:

(1) Is the party's domicile, according to his national law, dependent on that of another person or on the seat of an authority? If so, his domicile is to be decided by applying his national law.[7]

(2) If not, is the party, according to the law of the court seised of the matter, domiciled in the state where the matter is pending?[8]

(3) If not, is the party's domicile in any other Contracting State, according to the law of that state?[9]

The answers to these questions will not necessarily provide a definitive answer as to where the party is domiciled, but they will usually enable a court to decide whether it has international jurisdiction over the case. This aspect is considered in more detail below.

Most commonly it is the domicile of the defendant which is relevant, but the domicile of the plaintiff or another party may be relevant for certain purposes.[10] Article 52 applies expressly only to the domicile of the parties,[11] but it may sometimes be necessary to determine the domicile of a stranger to the proceedings[12] and in such a case, it is suggested, the word "party" should be construed widely to include such a person, or Article 52 should be applied by analogy. **31.04**

No reference is made in Article 52 to the time at which a person's domicile is to be judged. In the absence of such a reference, the matter will probably fall to be decided in accordance with national law, but it may be that the uniform application of the jurisdictional rules requires a uniform approach to this question. If so, the applicable time would be the time when proceedings are commenced,[13]

---

[7] Third paragraph of this Article, para. 31.15 *et seq.* below.
[8] First paragraph of this Article, para. 31.13 below.
[9] Second paragraph of this Article, para. 3.14 below.
[10] See Arts. 4 (second para.), 5(2), 8, 12, 14 (first para.), 15 and 17.
[11] Bülow/Böckstiegel/Schlafen, p. 308.
[12] See, for example, sub-para. (2) of the first para. of Art. 8, where an insured person other than the policyholder sues an insurer in the courts for the place of the policyholder's domicile.
[13] *Cf.* Jenard, paras. A1.147, A1.151 below, Schlosser, para. 161 (para. A1.454 below).

in other words, when, as a matter of the applicable procedural law, they become "definitively pending".[14]

B. The Concept of Domicile

31.05   The laws of the different Contracting States each contain a number of different concepts of domicile for different purposes,[15] and Article 52 does not specify which concept of domicile is to apply. The scheme of the Convention requires, though, that the concept of domicile which applies for the purpose of civil proceedings should be the applicable concept.[16] It is important not to confuse that concept with the separate concept, known to the laws of a number of Contracting States, of an elective domicile, or domicile of choice, for the purposes of civil procedure. This, in effect, is an address nominated by a person for the service of process and can amount to an agreement on jurisdiction; but it is not the concept of domicile envisaged by Article 52[17] and has no place in the jurisdictional provisions of the Convention.[18] In Belgian law, and now in the United Kingdom[19] and in Ireland, there is a special domicile provided for the purpose of civil proceedings, but in the other Contracting States the relevant concept is the general concept of civil domicile.[20]

The principal rules of domicile in the laws of each of the Contracting States which are relevant for the purposes of the Convention are summarised in Chapters 48 to 58 below.[20a] Such concepts of domicile are rarely defined in positive terms, but the conditions for a domicile existing are usually drawn fairly precisely. These concepts of domicile in the continental Contracting States are quite different from the traditional common law concept,[21] being more

---

[14] *Zelger* v. *Salinitri (No. 2)* [1984] E.C.R. 2397, discussed at para. 23.05 above.

[15] For example, in addition to a normal civil domicile (see below), a person may have a tax domicile, a domicile for the purposes of social assistance (*domicile de secours*) or a domicile of dependence.

[16] Jenard, para. A1.74 below.

[17] Jenard, para. A1.77 below; Bülow/Böckstiegel/Schlafen, p. 309; Geimer/Schütze, p. 366.

[18] It is relevant, though, for the purposes of the second para. of Art. 33—see para. 28.19, n. 66 above.

[19] s.41 of the 1982 Act, para. 44.01 below.

[20] In each of the Contracting States there are additional fictitious domiciles, which may sometimes be relevant, *e.g.* for diplomats, servants, merchant seamen, members of the armed forces, etc.

[20a] At para. 25.

[21] Droz, para. 213, n. 1 describes the difference in some detail. For the common law concept, see Dicey and Morris, pp. 116 *et seq.*; Cheshire and North, pp. 141 *et seq.*

closely akin to a common lawyer's understanding of habitual residence.[22]

As Droz explains, the Roman law concept of domicile requires **31.06** both a factual element (actual habitual residence or establishment) and an intentional element (an intention to maintain that residence or establishment).[23] In none of the original Contracting States, though, is the intentional element as strong as in the traditional common law concept.[24] Because of the wide divergence between the concepts of domicile in continental legal systems and at common law, the United Kingdom and Ireland were asked to provide a definition of domicile for the purposes of the Convention which more closely reflected the concept as understood in the original Contracting States[25] and they have done so.[26]

Habitual residence. Habitual residence is an imprecise concept **31.07** used in many international conventions[27] and in this Convention it forms an alternative to domicile as a basis for jurisdiction in Articles 5(2),[28] 12(3)[29] and 15(3).[30] Habitual residence is also referred to in Article 59.[31] Neither Article 52 nor any other provision in the Convention provides a definition or uniform conflicts rules for determining where a person's habitual residence is, but in the few instances where it is necessary to make such a determination, the choice-of-law rules in Article 52 should, it is submitted, be applied by analogy.[32]

C. APPLICATION OF NATIONAL LAW OF DOMICILE

Because Article 52 provides only choice-of-law rules, it is the **31.08** national laws of the various Contracting States which are to be applied in determining a person's domicile. This separation of functions between the Convention and national law has a number of consequences.

---

[22] Some English language versions of decisions of the European Court of Justice on the Convention translate "domicile" as "habitual residence": *e.g. Klomps* v. *Michel* [1981] E.C.R. 1593, see para. 27.38, n. 28 above. The concepts are different and should not be confused: see below.
[23] Droz, para. 344.
[24] Dicey and Morris, pp. 130–132, 134–135.
[25] Schlosser, para. 73 (para. A1.360 below).
[26] In the U.K., s.41 of the 1982 Act, para. 44.01 below. The same definition has been adopted for cases outside the Convention in R.S.C. Ord. 11, r. 1(4).
[27] See Dicey and Morris, pp. 166–167; Cheshire and North, pp. 172–173.
[28] Para. 17.31 above.
[29] Para. 18.49 above.
[30] Para. 19.34 above.
[31] Para. 33.24 below.
[32] Bülow/Böckstiegel/Schlafen, pp. 66, 129.

First, the national law's own choice-of-law rules are supplanted by those in Article 52. It is only the normal civil or civil procedure law, and not the private international law, of the particular Contracting State which is to be applied,[33] and this is so whether it is the law of the state where the action is pending which is being applied, or the law of another Contracting State.

31.09   Secondly, the national laws of domicile do not form part of the Convention and their interpretation may not be referred to the European Court of Justice under the 1971 Protocol on Interpretation.[34] What the European Court of Justice may consider on a reference under that Protocol, however, is the correct application of Article 52—in other words it can indicate which national law is to be applied. "Domicile" as a concept is susceptible to an independent interpretation to the extent necessary to ensure the uniform application of Article 52, and to that end the European Court of Justice may also be able to rule which of several concepts of domicile available in any given national law is the correct one for the purposes of the Convention.

Thirdly, detailed matters such as the period of residence necessary to establish domicile and the matters which establish the founding or giving up of a domicile are to be regulated by national law.[35] Moreover, it is open to the Contracting States to amend their law of domicile without the agreement of the other Contracting States, although they may not adopt, as against persons domiciled in the other Contracting States, new exorbitant rules of jurisdiction.[36]

D. Conflicts of Domicile

31.10   *Positive conflicts of domicile.* Application of different national concepts of domicile may result in a party having a domicile for the purposes of the Convention in more than one state (a so-called "positive conflict" of domicile). Indeed, the concept of domicile common to the Contracting States may lead to that result even by the application of just one national set of rules. Article 52 does not provide an express solution to this problem, but an examination of its wording and that of the jurisdictional provisions of the Convention points to the solution.

A court seised of the matter may (or, more usually, must) accept jurisdiction if it is competent to do so, whether or not another court has jurisdiction. Article 52 is logically structured, so that the court

---

[33] Bülow/Böckstiegel/Schlafen, p. 311.
[34] Chap. 36 below; Bülow/Böckstiegel/Schlafen, p. 309.
[35] Bülow/Böckstiegel/Schlafen, p. 308.
[36] Art. 3, first para., para. 16.09 above; Bülow/Böckstiegel/Schlafen, p. 309.

looks first to see whether there is a domicile of dependence,[37] then
to see whether the party is domiciled in the court of the state seised
of the matter[38] and only then to see whether the party is domiciled
in any other Contracting State.[39]

A decision that a party has a domicile in the state where the
action is pending will usually be enough to allow the court to accept
jurisdiction, without it having to go on to consider whether the
party also has a domicile in another Contracting State. If an action
is also pending in another Contracting State, the application of the
rules on *lis pendens* and related actions in Articles 21 to 23[40] may
require a decision as to any other domicile which the party may
have.

If a party is not domiciled in the state whose courts are seised of   **31.11**
the matter, it will usually be sufficient for the purposes of deciding
whether those courts have jurisdiction if the party has a domicile in
any other Contracting State. This is because the special rules on jurisdiction do not normally distinguish between those other Contracting States.[41] In order to decide whether a party is domiciled in
Contracting State A, the law of Contracting State A has to be
applied, but if the party is domiciled there according to that law, it
will not normally be necessary to go on to consider whether, by the
law of Contracting State B, he is also domiciled in that state. It will
only be necessary to do so if he is found not to be domiciled in Contracting State A.

It follows that the absence in Article 52 of a means of resolving a
positive conflict of domicile is not likely to be material.[42] Where
problems of positive conflicts do arise, they will usually be resolved
by applying the rules on *lis pendens* and related actions[43] in Articles
21 to 23.[44]

Negative conflicts of domicile. Difficulties may arise, though, with   **31.12**
"negative" conflicts of domicile—that is where, by the application
of the choice-of-law rules in Article 52 and the national laws determined by those rules—a person is not domiciled in any Contracting
State. In such a case, the court may normally apply its own jurisdic-

---

[37] The third para. of Art. 52 probably qualifies both the first and second paras.:
see para. 31.16 below.
[38] First para. of this Art., para. 31.13 below.
[39] Second para. of this Art., para. 31.14 below.
[40] Chap. 23 above.
[41] The most important example is Art. 5, which provides, "A person domiciled in
a Contracting State may, in *another* Contracting State, be sued. . . . "
[42] The problem is discussed in more detail in the Jenard Report,
paras. A1.72–A1.74 below.
[43] Droz, para. 358; Bülow/Böckstiegel/Schlafen, p. 316.
[44] Chap. 23 above.

tional rules[45] (unless the exclusive jurisdiction rules in Article 16 apply), including its exorbitant rules of jurisdiction;[46] the Convention does not (and does not normally need to) provide any rule for determining in which particular non-Contracting State the party is domiciled.[47] Where a difficulty will arise, though, is in the rare case where, by the application of the court's own law, the party is not domiciled in a non-Contracting State and by the application of the rules in Article 52 he is not domiciled in the state where the action is pending or in any other Contracting State.[48] In such a case, where the party is obviously domiciled in one of the Contracting States, but the rules produce a negative conflict of domiciles, the application of Article 4 would be contrary to the spirit of the Convention and in such a case, it is submitted, resort should be had to subsidiary connecting factors, such as habitual residence.[49] It may be, though, that the court seised of the matter should accept jurisdiction despite the absence of domicile.[50]

E. ARTICLE 52, FIRST PARAGRAPH: DOMICILE IN THE STATE OF THE COURT SEISED OF THE MATTER

31.13   To determine whether a party is domiciled in the same state as the court seised of the matter, the court is to apply its own law (that is, its own domestic law, not its own choice-of-law rules).[51] This choice-of-law rule is subject to the provisions of the third paragraph of Article 52[52] in the case of a domicile of dependence, but otherwise it presents little difficulty. The rule corresponds with the equivalent conflicts rules in the national laws of certain Contracting States.[53]

---

[45] Jenard, para. A1.71 below; Bülow/Böckstiegel/Schlafen, p. 309.

[46] Art. 4, para. 16.15 above.

[47] Art. 59 (para. 33.24 below) provides an exception. The court of a Contracting State may need to determine whether a defendant is domiciled or habitually resident in a third state with which a relevant bilateral convention has been concluded.

[48] *e.g.* if by the law of State A, where the action is pending, and by the law of State B, the party is domiciled only in State C, but by the law of State C he is domiciled only in State B. Such a situation will be rare, but might occur in the case of cross-border workers.

[49] Bülow/Böckstiegel/Schlafen, p. 316; Kropholler, p. 340; Gothot/Holleaux, para. 43. *Cf.* Droz, para. 362, who urges an unspecified pragmatic approach.

[50] Geimer/Schütze, p. 367.

[51] Para. 31.08 above. In the U.K. the relevant provision is s.41 of the 1982 Act, which also contains rules for determining the part of, and the place in, the U.K. where a person is domiciled.

[52] See paras. 31.15 *et seq.* below.

[53] Droz, para. 357; Bülow/Böckstiegel/Schlafen, p. 310.

F. Article 52, Second Paragraph: Domicile in Another Contracting State

If the court decides, by applying its own law under the first para-   **31.14**
graph of Article 52, that the party is not domiciled in its own state,
it may need to decide whether he is domiciled in another Contracting State. The second paragraph of this Article provides that that
question is to be answered in relation to any other given Contracting State by applying the applicable national law of that other state
(again, the domestic law and not the choice-of-law rules of that
other State).[54] It would almost certainly be contrary to the second
paragraph of Article 52 for the court to assume that foreign law is
the same as its own law.[55]

For reasons already explained,[56] it will not normally be necessary
to decide whether the party is domiciled in each of the other Contracting States and it will normally be enough if the party has a
domicile in any one of them; but if the party is found not to be
domiciled in a given Contracting State, the court will need to repeat
the exercise under the second paragraph of Article 52 in relation to
each of the other Contracting States in which the party might be
domiciled.

As with the first paragraph, the second paragraph of Article 52 is
subject to the provisions relating to domicile of dependence in the
third paragraph.

G. Article 52, Third Paragraph: Domicile of Dependence

1. Generally

If a party's domicile is dependent on that of another person or on   **31.15**
the seat of an authority, the third paragraph of Article 52 takes
effect, substituting the dependent person's national law (a concept
discussed below) for the law which would otherwise be applicable
under the first and second paragraphs of the Article.[57] With the
decline in importance of the domicile of dependence of married
women,[58] the provision will be relevant less often than previously,
but will continue to be relevant in the case of minors, mental

---

[54] Para. 31.08 above.
[55] This can be the effect of applying English rules of evidence: see Dicey and Morris, p. 228. The English law and practice relating to proof of foreign law is discussed in chap. 9 above.
[56] Para. 31.11 above.
[57] The precedence of the third para. of this Art. over the first para. is a matter of
some dispute and is discussed below.
[58] In the law of most Contracting States, a married woman's domicile is no longer
dependent on that of her husband. Irish law retains a domicile of dependence
for married women, but this will not apply for the purposes of the Convention.

patients and the like. The provision is most likely to apply in determining jurisdiction over maintenance cases under Article 5(2).[59]

The third paragraph of Article 52 presents a number of difficult questions of interpretation and national courts might hesitate before making definitive rulings on its interpretation and may find it necessary to refer the matter to the European Court of Justice (if it is open to them to do so under the 1971 Protocol on Interpretation).[60] The provision is capable of producing anomalous, even absurd, results,[61] but the absurdity arises from the arbitrary nature of the choice of national law and of the concept of domicile of dependence, rather than from the particular difficulties of interpretation.

2. Scope

31.16   The first difficulty concerns the scope of the third paragraph. The view which most commentators support, expressly or impliedly, is that it qualifies both the first and second paragraphs of Article 52.[62] Other commentators[63] query whether this is the correct interpretation, or whether the third paragraph qualifies only the second, and not the first paragraph, suggesting that the latter would be more practicable. It is submitted that, while the latter narrower interpretation might achieve the desirable result of avoiding some of the anomalous practical consequences inherent in the choice of national law as the law to be applied in determining a domicile of dependence, it is not to be preferred.

There is nothing in the wording of Article 52 to suggest a departure from the principle that the more particular rule (the third paragraph) should take precedence over the more general rules (both the first and second paragraphs). Moreover, the narrower interpretation would mean that the relevance of a person's nationality would depend on where the action was brought, thereby increasing the inconsistencies in the application of the Convention and increasing the potential for forum shopping. Whatever its other deficiencies, the third paragraph of Article 52 at least provides a uniform choice-of-law rule for persons with a domicile of dependence. For the pur-

---

[59] Bülow/Böckstiegel/Schlafen, p. 314.
[60] Only higher courts may refer questions of interpretation to the European Court of Justice: see paras. 36.05 *et seq.* below.
[61] See the illustrations given by Hartley, pp. 27–30 and Droz, paras. 363–375.
[62] Jenard, para. A1.75; Schlosser, para. 74 (para. A1.361 below); Hartley, pp. 27–30; Anton, para. 4.08; Kaye, p. 295; Droz, paras. 353, 363–375; Weser, paras. 309–317; Gothot/Holleaux, para. 44; Bülow/Böckstiegel/Schlafen, p. 314; Kropholler, p. 340; Geimer/Schütze, p. 359.
[63] Maxwell, para. 5.13; Collins, p. 39.

poses of the commentary below, it will be assumed that the wider interpretation is correct.

3. Application of national law

It is suggested that a court should approach the application of the   **31.17**
third paragraph of Article 52 in four stages, as follows:

(1) If the party exhibits potentially relevant characteristics (*e.g.* if the party is a young person, a mental patient or a married woman), it should determine what law is the person's "national law."

(2) Applying that national law, it should then determine *whether* the person's domicile depends on the domicile of another person or on the seat of an authority.[64]

(3) If the party is found at the second stage to have a domicile of dependence, the court should apply that national law to determine the person upon whose domicile the party's domicile is dependent and, if appropriate, the time at which that other person's domicile is to be considered. If the party does not have a domicile of dependence, the court should determine the party's domicile in the normal way, without reference to the third paragraph of Article 52.

(4) In order to determine the party's domicile, the court should determine where (at the time regarded by the national law as relevant) that other party is (or was) domiciled.

Each of these stages requires further elaboration.

(1) Determining the national law

While it is necessary to apply the national law in question to   **31.18**
determine the characteristics which that law treats as relevant for determining whether a person's domicile is one of dependence, it is suggested that the court need only do so if it is put on enquiry as to the dependent status of the party—either by the party himself or another party, or by other matters appearing to it, whether arising in the course of the particular case or known to it from other sources.

The concept of "national law" is not defined by the Convention but, as Droz observes,[65] a person's national law relates to his personal status. It is the law of the state of which the person is a national, an interpretation confirmed by the reference in the Jenard

---

[64] *e.g.* the domicile of certain orphaned children in Germany depends on the seat of the responsible public authority.
[65] Droz, para. 363.

Report to dual nationality.[66] Determining a person's nationality will rarely present a problem, but because nationality is itself a creature of national law, the court of a different state cannot decide a person's nationality by application of its own law[67] and may need to examine the law (the *lex patriae*) of each potentially relevant state, including non-Contracting States.

31.19   *Dual nationality.* The Convention gives no guidance on how problems posed by dual nationality are to be resolved, although the Jenard Report says that "the usual rules relating to dual nationality should be applied."[68] A general solution to the problem (and that to which "the usual rules" is probably intended to refer) is for the court seised to apply its own conflicts rules in determining which nationality is to apply—in other words, the laws of the respective nationalities determine the nationalities of the person, and the conflicts rules of the *lex fori* determine which of them are to have precedence. The Jenard Report gives as an example the case of a woman of German nationality married to a Frenchman[69] who is domiciled in France. A German court would regard her as German[70] and would determine her domicile without reference to that of her husband, whereas a French court would have determined her domicile, pursuant to the French law then applicable,[70a] by reference to her husband's domicile.

That example leaves unresolved the question of which law is to be applied by a court of a state of which the person is not a national.[71] This, too, should be determined by the conflicts rules of the *lex fori* and in the absence of any other rule, the court should, it is submitted, decide which nationality is the one with which the party has the closest real connection,[72] such as that of the state where the person has his habitual residence or, failing that, his residence—an approach which accords with the intention of the third paragraph of Article 52. Similarly, if the person is stateless, in the absence of any other rule in the conflicts provisions of the *lex fori*,

---

[66] Jenard, para. A1.76 below.
[67] Dicey and Morris, p. 31.
[68] Jenard, para. A1.76 below.
[69] *Ibid.* At the date of the Jenard Report, French law, unlike German law, still provided for the domicile of dependence of married women.
[70] The German rule is that if a person has several nationalities, one of which is German, that nationality is to apply: Bülow/Böckstiegel/Schlafen, p. 314, n. 45.
[70a] See para. 50.25 below.
[71] Droz, para. 375.
[72] This is the German conflicts rule: Bülow/Böckstiegel/Schlafen, p. 314, Geimer/Schütze, p. 359. The French rule is less clear: Droz, *loc. cit.* Kaye, p. 306, suggests the application of *both* national laws.

the applicable law should be that of the state with which the person has the closest connection.[73]

Because the United Kingdom has three different systems of law (those of England, Scotland and Northern Ireland), it might appear that a court would have to decide which system applied in the case of a United Kingdom national. In fact, the United Kingdom law on the subject of domicile for the purposes of the Convention[74] contains no provision on domicile of dependence, and is therefore to be read as not making the domicile of anyone dependent on the domicile of another or on the seat of an authority.[75]

(2) Applying the national law to decide whether there is a domicile of dependence

Having determined the nationality of the person in question, the **31.20** court then has to apply the law of that state to determine whether the person's domicile depends on that of another person or on the seat of an authority. This exercise may involve more than merely discovering what classes of person have domiciles of dependence according to that law and applying that law to the facts in order to decide whether the person in question falls into any of those classes. Subsidiary questions of law may arise at this stage, especially as to the person's status. For example, the national law may provide for a married woman's domicile to be dependent on that of her husband, or for a married minor's domicile to be independent of that of his parent. In those circumstances, the validity of the marriage will be a material factor. Again, the domicile of a person under a mental disability may, according to the national law, be dependent on the seat of a public authority, and the question of whether a person is under a mental disability will be a material factor.

In each of those cases, there are subsidiary questions of law. The court will have to decide what law to apply in order to decide those questions. According to the strict wording of the third paragraph of Article 52, such questions ought perhaps also to be answered by the national law of the person in question, or by the law indicated by the choice-of-law rules of the national law, but it is not clear whether that is in fact required by the provision, and it may be that the court could decide these subsidiary questions according to its own conflicts rules.[76] It is not possible to say which solution is cor-

---

[73] *Cf.* Geimer/ Schütze, p. 360.
[74] s.41 of the 1982 Act, para. 44.01 below.
[75] Collins, p. 39; Hartley, p. 32.
[76] Hartley, pp. 27–29. As he notes, the Schlosser Report (para. 74, para. A1.361 below) misrepresents the English choice-of-law rules, which provide that the question whether a dependent person can acquire a domicile of choice is to be

rect, either generally or in any individual case, and each test is capable of giving rise to unsatisfactory or even absurd results, because of the unsatisfactory nature of the choice-of-law rule in the third paragraph of Article 52.

(3) Applying the national law to determine the domicile

31.21   If, according to his national law, a person's domicile is dependent on that of another person or on the seat of an authority, that same law is to be applied to decide the way in which the domicile of dependence is to be determined. This third stage is closely connected with the second stage, but is logically separate. In many cases both stages can be performed as a single exercise. For example, the court may decide at the second stage that the national law provides that an unmarried person under sixteen is to be regarded as having a domicile of dependence, and at the third stage that that domicile is dependent in the case of a legitimate child on the domicile of his father and, in the case of an illegitimate child, on the domicile of his mother.

(4) Determining the domicile from which the party's domicile of dependence derives

31.22   Having decided the rules by which the domicile of dependence is to be determined, and the person whose domicile (or the authority whose seat) is determinative, the court then has to determine where that domicile (or seat) is. The domicile of that other person or the seat of that authority is to be decided according to the first and second paragraphs of Article 52 and Article 53 as appropriate.[77] For example, if the applicable national law provides that a minor's domicile depends upon that of his mother, the minor will be domiciled for the purposes of the Convention in the state where, according to the first and second paragraphs of Article 52, the mother is domiciled.

Article 53

31.23   **For the purposes of this Convention, the seat of a company or other legal person or association of natural or legal persons shall**

---

determined by English law: Dicey and Morris, p. 150. Similarly, for Scotland, see Anton, para. 4.08, n. 14. English law, in the context of the Convention, no longer recognises any domicile of dependence: see para. 44.05 below.

[77] Jenard, para. A1.75 below; Bülow/Böckstiegel/Schlafen, p. 314. Hartley, p. 28, reads the Jenard Report as suggesting that this domicile is also to be determined by the national law, and criticises the result as "clearly absurd." It is submitted, though, that the absurdity does not arise if one separates the third and fourth stages as discussed in the text.

be treated as its domicile. However, in order to determine that seat, the court shall apply its rules of private international law.

In order to determine whether a trust is domiciled in the Contracting State whose courts are seised of the matter, the court shall apply its rules of private international law.* †

H. Article 53: Seat

General note

Article 53 provides the rules for determining the domicile of any party other than a natural person. It contains three distinct provisions. First, so far as a company or other legal person or association of natural or legal persons[78] is concerned, its "seat" is equated by the first paragraph of Article 53 with the domicile of an individual, for all the purposes of the Convention. Secondly, the first paragraph also provides a rule for determining the location of that seat, by ascribing to the private international law of the different Contracting States the function of choosing the law to be applied in determining the seat. Thirdly, by the second paragraph, Article 53 also ascribes to the national choice-of-law rules the determination of whether a trust is domiciled in the state of the forum.

31.24

Article 53 presents less difficulties than the equivalent rules in Article 52, although a number of points require detailed consideration, especially as the provision is based on concepts some of which may be unfamiliar to common lawyers.

I. Article 53, First Paragraph: Parties other than Natural Persons

1. Scope

The first paragraph of Article 53 applies to all parties other than natural persons.[79] The Convention contains no definition of the expression "a company or other legal person or association of natu-

31.25

---

* Jenard, paras. A1.245–A1.246; Schlosser, paras. 75, 114–120, 227 (paras. A1.362, A1.339–A1.403 and A1.529 below; Collins, pp. 37, 40–44; Dashwood/Halcon/White, pp. 20–21, 184–186; Hartley, pp. 30–31; Kaye, pp. 319–339; Maxwell, paras. 5.1–5.2, 5.14–5.19, 8.6–8.12; Anton, paras. 4.22–4.25, 5.50–5.52; Droz, paras. 383–405; Weser, paras. 318–325; Bülow/Böckstiegel/Schlafen, pp. 317–327; Geimer/Schütze, pp. 372–374, 745–746, 768–769; Kropholler, pp. 341–344; Gothot/Holleaux, paras. 48–51; Pocar, pp. 358–360.

† The second para. was added by Art. 23 of the 1978 Convention.
[78] Unless the context otherwise requires, references hereafter to a company are intended as references to a company or other legal person or association of natural or legal persons.
[79] Bülow/Böckstiegel/Schlafen, p. 318; see also para. 20.28 above.

ral or legal persons,"[80] but it is not confined to parties with legal personality, nor merely to associations. The Convention as a whole is intended to cover civil and commercial matters[81] generally and, it may be deduced, its application is not intended to be limited by reference to the nature of the parties.[82] Public bodies may sue and be sued under the Convention, provided that the subject-matter of the action falls within its scope.[83] Between them, therefore, Articles 52 and 53 apply to all persons who have capacity to sue or be sued. Article 52 is apt only to cover natural persons and it follows that Article 53 covers all other possible parties.

The Convention does not provide that a company ceases to fall within its scope merely because it is in liquidation, although proceedings relating to its winding-up are excluded.[84] The circumstances in which, and the conditions under which, a company in liquidation can sue and be sued are to be determined by the *lex fori*, including its own conflicts rules.[85]

2. The concept of "seat"

31.26   The Convention provides no definition of "seat,"[86] but the concept of a "seat" is familiar to continental legal systems, although its detailed scope differs from state to state. Broadly, it covers either or both of two related concepts. First, it covers the place where, as a matter of fact, the company has its central management or control (or, sometimes, its principal centre of activity); while, secondly, it refers to the place where, as a matter of the interpretation of its constitution, the company is founded. The former concept is one of the "actual seat" (*siège réel*) of the company, whereas the latter is the concept of a "statutory seat" (*siège statutaire*). Some legal systems lay more emphasis on the actual seat and some on the statutory seat

---

[80] French: " . . . *des sociétés et des personnes morales* . . . "; German: " . . . *Gesellschaften und juristischen Personen* . . . "; Italian: " . . . *delle società e delle persone guiridiche* . . . "; Dutch: " . . . *vennootschappen en rechtspersonen.* . . . " *Cf.* Art. 58 of the EEC Treaty (second para.), where the expression "companies or firms" is expressly defined, in fairly circumscribed terms, as follows: "companies or firms constituted under civil or commercial law, including co-operative societies, and other legal persons governed by public or private law, save for those which are non-profit-making."

[81] Art. 1, chap. 14 above. Certain matters are expressly excluded.

[82] See, generally, chap. 2 above.

[83] *LTU Lufttransport* v. *Eurocontrol* [1976] E.C.R. 1541, at p. 1551 (para. 4), quoted at para. 14.10 above.

[84] Art. 1, para. 14.03 above.

[85] Bülow/Böckstiegel/Schlafen, p. 327; see para. 2.06 above.

[86] Jenard, para. A1.245 below.

(even, in the case of the Netherlands, to the exclusion of the actual seat).[87]

The location of a company's seat has juridical and jurisdictional consequences in continental law. Under the common law concept of incorporation, the legality of a company and the acts of its organs are determined by the law of the state where the company is incorporated[88] (or, in the case of an unincorporated body, by the law pursuant to which it is constituted). Continental legal systems judge these matters by reference to the "regularity of the constitution" of the company, and that "regularity" is usually to be determined according to the law of the seat.[89]

A consequence of judging the regularity of a company by the law of the seat is that the location of the seat becomes the principal (or sole) determining factor in determining the "nationality" of the company, which is the concept used in some Contracting States as the basis for accepting jurisdiction.[90] In the context of the Convention, the fact that a company's nationality is that of the state where it has its seat means that the second paragraph of Article 2[91] and the reference in the second paragraph of Article 4[92] to a party's nationality are only of any relevance in relation to natural persons.[93] **31.27**

The Convention ascribes exclusive jurisdiction over cases principally concerned with the validity of the constitution, the nullity or dissolution of companies, or the decisions of their organs, to the courts of the Contracting State in which the company has its seat.[94] A given legal system may adopt different rules as to the location of a company's seat for jurisdictional purposes from those adopted for the purposes of deciding the "regularity" of its constitution. So, for example, the law of a given state may regard a company's actual seat as determinative for most legal purposes, but may permit a third

---

[87] The rules for each of the Contracting States are summarised in chaps. 48 to 58 below, at para. 26. For the purposes of the Convention, the U.K. has adopted provisions encompassing both concepts: ss.42 and 43 of the 1982 Act, paras. 44.11 *et seq* below.

[88] *Lazard Bros.* v. *Midland Bank* [1933] A.C. 289, 297.

[89] Droz, para. 386; Rabel, *The Conflict of Laws, a Comparative Study* (2nd ed., 1960), pp. 125–175; Schmitthoff (ed.), *The Harmonisation of European Company Law* (1973), pp. 55–59.

[90] Droz, para. 384.

[91] Para. 16.01 above.

[92] Para. 16.15 above.

[93] Bülow/Böckstiegel/Schlafen, pp. 317–318.

[94] Art. 16(2), para. 20.26 above; see also paras. 31.30–31.31 below. In the law of the U.K., special rules apply to determine a company's seat for the purposes of Art. 16(2): s.43, para. 44.20 below.

party to avail himself of the statutory seat (if different) for the purposes of jurisdiction.[95]

3. Choice of law

31.28   As with the domicile of a natural person, the Convention does not provide a uniform definition of "seat," preferring instead to leave the matter to be determined by national law. But by contrast with Article 52, which provides its own choice-of-law rules, applicable uniformly throughout the Contracting States, the rule in the first paragraph of Article 53 ascribes the choice-of-law function to the rules of private international law of the state of the court seised of the matter, whether the seat is in that state, in another Contracting State, or in a non-Contracting State.[96] The second sentence of the paragraph could be described as a "choice of conflicts rule." It has the distinct practical advantage over the rules in Article 52 that, in this context, national courts are not required by the Convention to apply foreign law, save to the extent that their own conflicts rules require them to do so.

Few of the Contracting States have rules of private international law specifically relating to the seat of a company[97] and it would seem that the choice-of-law rules which it is intended that the courts of Contracting States should apply are those relating to the *concept* of the seat of a company.[98] It has been observed that different concepts of the seat of a company sometimes apply for different purposes even within a given legal system and it may be that one concept applies for the purposes of civil procedure, while a different concept applies for the purposes of private international law.[99] In such a case, the wording of Article 53 makes it clear that it is the latter, private international law, concept which is to be applied.

4. Conflicts of "seat"

31.29   The reason for the Convention employing a reference to the private international law of the Contracting States for the purpose of determining a company's seat was because of the different approaches adopted by their various laws.[1] The approaches of the different legal systems vary as to their concept of the "seat," but in all the Contracting States jurisdiction over companies is based either directly on the seat of the company or indirectly by reference

---

[95] This is the case, *e.g.* in France: para. 50.26 below.
[96] Bülow/Böckstiegel/Schlafen, p. 320.
[97] An exception is the U.K., where s.42(7) of the 1982 Act (para. 44.11 below) may be regarded as such a rule.
[98] Bülow/Böckstiegel/Schlafen, p. 320.
[99] This is the position in Germany: Bülow/Böckstiegel/Schlafen, *loc. cit.*
[1] Jenard, para. A1.245 below.

to the company's nationality. A reference to the private international law of the Contracting States should therefore enable a court to determine in any case whether a company's seat is in any given Contracting State, but problems may arise where the application of the different concepts of "seat" lead to different conclusions as to its location.

These problems are equivalent to the "conflicts of domicile" discussed under Article 52[2] but, because the Convention does not provide a uniform choice-of-law rule, it is not possible to suggest uniform solutions. Nor can problems of conflicting concepts of "seat" be referred to the European Court of Justice under the 1971 Protocol on Interpretation, because the rules of private international law of the Contracting States, although brought within the scheme of the Convention, form no part of it. A number of general observations may nonetheless be made.

Where the law of one Contracting State regards the statutory seat   **31.30**
as definitive[3] and the law of another Contracting State regards the actual seat as definitive,[4] a conflict may arise. For example, a company with its statutory seat in Switzerland, but its actual seat in France, would be regarded by a Belgian court as being domiciled in France, and the Belgian court would have to accept or decline jurisdiction according to Title II of the Convention. If the matter came before a court in the Netherlands, on the other hand, the company would be regarded as being domiciled outside the Contracting States and that court might accept jurisdiction on an exorbitant basis.[5] A company with its statutory seat in the Netherlands and its actual seat in Belgium would be regarded by the courts of both states as domiciled within their own state.

Most such problems of conflict of seat will be resolved by applying the rules on *lis pendens* and related actions in Articles 21 to 23[6] and the judgment of the court first seised will, once delivered, generally be entitled to automatic recognition in the other Contracting States. A problem may arise, though, where more than one state claims exclusive jurisdiction under Article 16(2).[7] In such a case the court first seised should have precedence pursuant to Article 23, but it may be that if the courts of a second state claim exclusive jurisdiction because they apply a different concept of "seat," those

---

[2] Paras. 31.10 *et seq.* above.
[3] This is the case in the Netherlands: see para. 55.26 below.
[4] This is the case, *e.g.*, in Belgium: see para. 48.26 below.
[5] *Dammers & Van der Heide's Scheepvaart en Handelsbedrijff B.V.* v. *Tropical Shipping Company*, Arrondissementsrechtbank Rotterdam, May 25, 1979, Digest D I–53 – B1, upheld on appeal [1982] E.C.C. 353.
[6] Chap. 23 above.
[7] Para. 20.26 above.

latter courts will, exceptionally, be able to review the jurisdiction of the court first seised,[8] refuse to decline jurisdiction in favour of the first court and, under Article 28, refuse recognition to the judgment of the first court.[9]

31.31   If that is right, it would seem to follow, on one view, that the courts of a third Contracting State would also be able to refuse recognition of a judgment given, according to its concept of "seat," in breach of Article 16(2).[10] The point may be illustrated by the example given above of a company with its statutory seat in the Netherlands and its actual seat in Belgium. The courts of each state would accept exclusive jurisdiction under Article 16(2) over an action, say, for a declaration that a particular contract was *ultra vires* the company. Neither would need to cede jurisdiction to the other and each could refuse to recognise the other's judgment. Applying the Convention, the decision as to which of the two judgments (if they are inconsistent) is to be recognised in the other Contracting States will depend upon whether the private international law of the state addressed prefers the Belgian or the Dutch concept of "seat."[11]

An alternative view is that the court of the second state should regard the first court as having properly assumed jurisdiction under Article 16(2), according to its own law, because it has done so in accordance with the Convention.[12] It remains to be seen which view (if either) is correct, and it may be that a distinction is to be drawn between a case where the law of State A provides for a company to have its seat in that state and in no other Contracting State and one where the law of State A recognises a seat in State B as well as in State A.[13]

J. ARTICLE 53, SECOND PARAGRAPH: DOMICILE OF A TRUST

31.32   As with a company, the domicile of a trust is to be determined in accordance with the private international law of the forum.[14] The domicile of a trust cannot be determined by either Article 52 or the first paragraph of Article 53, because a trust cannot sue or be sued

---

[8] Para. 23.26 above.
[9] Jenard, para. A1.245 below.
[10] *Contra*, Droz, para. 397.
[11] See para. 44.26 below.
[12] Weser, para. 252; Bülow/Böckstiegel/Müller, p. 136; Kropholler, p. 279; Geimer/Schütze, pp. 339 (n. 56), 374 (n. 17). *Cf.* Bülow/Böckstiegel/Schlafen, p. 326. As to the effect of a plaintiff starting an action in one state, see para. 20.29 above.
[13] See paras. 27.69 above and 44.26 below; Hartley, p. 67.
[14] Schlosser, para. 119 (para. A1.402 below).

in its own name. The reason why the provision is necessary, and why it applies only to the question whether the trust is domiciled in the state of the forum, is because the domicile of a trust forms the basis for one of the special rules of jurisdiction under Article 5(6).[15] Under that provision, a person domiciled in one Contracting State may be sued in his capacity as settlor, trustee or beneficiary of a trust created by the operation of a statute, or by a written instrument, or created orally and evidenced in writing, in the courts of another Contracting State in which the trust is domiciled.

Where, as in most Contracting States, the concept of a trust is not familiar, there are no rules of private international law for determining the domicile of a trust and these will have to be evolved.[16] The fact that the choice-of-law function has been ascribed to the private international law of the Contracting States leaves open the possibility of conflicting decisions on jurisdiction but, in cases relating to trusts concerned with rights *in rem* in land,[17] the domicile of the trust is not a basis for jurisdiction and problems such as those described above posed by Article 16(2) will not arise. In the common law systems, the concept of the domicile of a trust is not unknown[18] and for the purposes of the Convention a statutory test has been enacted in the 1982 Act,[19] which provides, in effect, a "proper law" test.[20]

---

[15] Para. 17.65 above.

[16] Schlosser, *loc. cit.*

[17] Art. 16(1), para. 20.11 above.

[18] Schlosser, para. 114 (para. A1.399 below); Collins, p. 44; Anton, para. 5.52; Anton, *Private International Law*, p. 470. *Cf.* Geimer/Schütze, pp. 768–769.

[19] s.45, para. 44.30 below.

[20] Hartley, p. 39; Collins, *loc. cit.* As to the "proper law" of a trust, see Dicey and Morris, pp. 1072 *et seq.*

TRANSITIONAL PROVISIONS
(Article 54)

TITLE VI

Article 54

32.01   The provisions of this Convention shall apply only to legal proceedings instituted and to documents formally drawn up or registered as authentic instruments after its entry into force.

However, judgments given after the date of entry into force of this Convention in proceedings instituted before that date shall be recognised and enforced in accordance with the provisions of Title III if jurisdiction was founded upon rules which accorded with those provided for either in Title II of this Convention or in a convention concluded between the State of origin and the State addressed which was in force when the proceedings were instituted.*

A. ARTICLE 54: TRANSITIONAL PROVISIONS

1. General note

32.02   This Article contains the transitional provisions which applied as between the original six Contracting States when the Convention came into force on February 1, 1973.[1] As the 1978 and 1982

---

* Jenard, paras. A1.247–A1.249 below; Schlosser, para. 228 (para. A1.530 below); Collins, pp. 31–32; Dashwood/Halcon/White, pp. 47, 189–190; Hartley, p. 165; Kaye, pp. 192, 227–244; Maxwell, para. 9.1; Anton, paras. 3.49–3.51; Droz, paras. 629–630; Weser, paras. 337–338 bis; Bülow/Böckstiegel/Schlafen, pp. 327–333; Geimer/Schütze, pp. 106, 345–355, 974–975, 1048–1049; Kropholler, pp. 345–349; Gothot/Holleaux, paras. 304–306; Pocar, pp. 361–375; See also references under Art. 34 of the 1978 Convention. See paras. 37.06 *et seq.* below.
[1] Para. 34.12 below.

Accession Conventions contain similar provisions[2] it is instructive to consider the operation of the transitional provisions of the 1968 Convention, although for all other purposes their effect is now likely to be spent.

2. Summary

So far as proceedings are concerned, the effect of Article 54 may be summarised as follows: **32.03**

(1) Proceedings in which the judgment was given before the commencement date: the Convention does not apply;[3]
(2) Proceedings begun before the commencement date, but where judgment was given on or after the commencement date: Title II (the jurisdictional rules) of the Convention does not apply[4] but, subject to a test of recognition (discussed below), Title III does apply to recognition and enforcement of the judgment;
(3) Proceedings begun on or after the commencement date: the Convention applies.[5]

So far as authentic instruments and court settlements are concerned,[6] the Convention applies to them only if they were drawn up or registered (*i.e.* acquired their formal validity) on or after the commencement date.[7]

3. The test of jurisdiction

Where the proceedings were instituted before the commencement date, but judgment was not given until after that date, the judgment will be automatically recognised and enforced under the rules in Title III, provided that the court of origin had jurisdiction over the case. What the second paragraph of Article 54 does is to specify the rules which the court of the state addressed should consider in **32.04**

---

[2] 1978 Convention, Art. 34, para. 37.06 below; 1982 Convention, Art. 12, para. 38.04 below. Arts. 35 and 36 (paras. 37.11 and 37.13 below) of the 1978 Convention also contain transitional provisions.
[3] *Campo* v. *CIBS S.p.A.*, Giur.it. 1980, I, Col. 522, Digest D I–56—B3.
[4] *Firma Michael Weinig* v. *S.A. Rochard and others*, Cour de Cassation, October 15, 1975, Digest D I–54—B2; *S.p.A. Compagnia Allevatori Vitelli* v. *Miscella Macinazione Italo Svizzera Cereali e Lavorazioe Affini S.p.A. and another*, Dir. com. scambi int. 1976, p. 385; Digest D I–54—B3.
[5] This is so, even if the Convention is contrary to a provision of national law governing the legal relationship at an earlier time: see para. 32.10 below.
[6] Arts. 50 and 51, chap. 30 above.
[7] *Deutsche Genossenschaftsbank* v. *Brasserie du Pêcheur S.A.*, European Court [1985] E.C.R. 1981, *per* Advocate General Lenz, at p. 1983.

deciding whether the court of origin had jurisdiction. It provides two alternatives. For these purposes, the court of origin had jurisdiction if it was "founded on rules which accorded with those provided for", *either* (1) in Title II of the Convention; *or* (2) in a bilateral or multilateral convention in force between the state of origin and the state addressed when the proceedings were instituted. These two alternatives will be considered separately.

First alternative: Title II

32.05   Under the first alternative, the direct rules of jurisdiction in Title II of the Convention are treated as indirect rules of jurisdiction. If a court in Contracting State A has assumed jurisdiction over a defendant on a basis which accords with Title II of the Convention, whether or not it also accords with any bilateral rules in force between State A and the state addressed (State B), and whether or not State B would, but for the Convention, have recognised the jurisdiction of the court in State A, the judgment is to be recognised and enforced under Title III. An example will illustrate the point.

A defendant domiciled in State B is involved in a car-accident in State A. He is sued in State A, where the court accepts jurisdiction as the court for the place where the tort was committed. The proceedings are duly served on the defendant at his domicile in State B, in sufficient time for him to arrange for his defence. The defendant ignores the proceedings and judgment is subsequently entered against him in default of appearance. Before the Convention came into force, the court of State B might well have regarded the courts of State A as not having had jurisdiction over the defendant and might not have permitted enforcement against him,[8] but under Article 5(3) of the Convention the court of State A would have had jurisdiction; and the defendant who, at the time when the proceedings were served on him, before the commencement date of the Convention, considered himself safe from having a judgment executed against him, would not be able successfully to challenge the judgment given after the Convention had come into force, because the jurisdiction of the court of origin was based on a rule which accorded with the rules in Title II. If, on the other hand, the defendant had been served with the proceedings, but not in sufficient time for him to arrange his defence, the defendant would be able to rely on that fact in order to show that the court should not have proceeded to judgment against him.[9] He would also be able to

---

[8] This would have been the position under English law: *Société Coopéerative Sidmetal* v. *Titan International Ltd.* [1966] 1 Q.B. 828.

[9] Art. 20, second para. or, under Art. 20, third para., Art. 15 of the Hague Service Convention. See paras. 22.16 *et seq.* above.

rely on Article 27(2)[10] to say that enforcement should not be ordered against him.

The only difference between this case and one to which the Convention applies fully is that in this case the court of the state addressed may review the jurisdiction of the court of origin. In a case to which the transitional provisions did not apply, this exercise would have been prohibited by the third paragraph of Article 28.[11] The reason why the Convention permits a review by the court of the state addressed of the jurisdiction of the state of origin is because the defendant will not have had an opportunity of challenging the international jurisdiction of the court of origin on the basis of the Convention.[12] In carrying out a review of the jurisdiction, the court of the state addressed should comply with the rules in the Convention, rather than with its own procedural law,[13] in order that there should be uniform application of the transitional provisions. It follows that the court of the state addressed is bound by the findings of fact on which the court of origin based its jurisdiction.[14] **32.06**

Second alternative: other convention

Under the second alternative, the court of the state addressed is required to recognise and enforce the judgment pursuant to Title III, if jurisdiction was founded on a basis permitted between the state of origin and the state addressed at the time the proceedings were instituted. The effect of this provision is to preserve for the purposes of the transitional provisions the jurisdictional rules which are otherwise revoked by Article 55.[15] If the court of the state addressed recognises the court of origin's jurisdiction under those conventions, the judgment is to be recognised and enforced under Title III, which involves allowing recognition and enforcement to be refused only on the grounds contained in Articles 27 and 28.[16] **32.07**

If the proceedings were instituted before, and the judgment

---

[10] Para. 27.21 above.
[11] Para. 27.62 above.
[12] Jenard, para. A1.248 below. A German court has held that an Italian court cannot be said to have had jurisdiction under Art. 18 in proceedings commenced before the Convention came into force, despite the defendant's submission to the jurisdiction, because that submission could not be regarded as unconditional where a challenge to the Italian court's jurisdiction, under the law then applying in Italy, could not have succeeded: Oberlandesgericht Frankfurt, case 20 W 185/75, December 9, 1975, RIW/AWD—1976, p. 107, Digest D I–5.1.2—B4.
[13] Bülow/Böckstiegel/Schlafen, p. 331.
[14] Art. 28, second para., para. 27.62 above.
[15] Para. 33.01 below.
[16] Recognition and enforcement may be refused also on certain other minor grounds, see para. 25.13 above.

given after, the commencement date, but the court of origin based its jurisdiction neither on rules which accorded with Title II, nor on rules between the state of origin and the state addressed in force at the time the proceedings were instituted,[17] the judgment is not to be enforced under Title III but only, if at all, under the national rules of the state addressed.[18]

4. Determining relevant times

32.08   *Institution of proceedings.* The date on which proceedings are instituted is the date when, according to the law of the court where the proceedings are commenced, "the requirements for proceedings to become definitively pending are first fulfilled."[19] If a new trial is ordered on appeal, the question whether that involves the "institution" of new proceedings will be a matter for the national law concerned, but usually a new trial would be regarded as part of the same proceedings, with the consequence that the case would not have to be remitted to a court with jurisdiction under the Convention.[20]

Counterclaims. When a counterclaim is brought after the commencement date in proceedings instituted before the Convention came into force, it will not usually be necessary to decide when the counterclaim was "instituted." This is because under Article 6(3), the court where the main action is pending has jurisdiction over the counterclaim (at least if that court had jurisdiction over the main action under the Convention).[21] The test of jurisdiction under the second paragraph of Article 54 is therefore satisfied in relation to the counterclaim, and Title III will apply to the recognition and enforcement of any judgment delivered on it.[22]

32.09   *Judgment.* The date when a judgment is "given" may be a more complex question. A judgment may be delivered before it becomes final and conclusive[23] and may then be reversed or altered on appeal. If a judgment was delivered at first instance before the Convention came into force, but a decision on appeal reversing the original decision was made after the Convention had come into force, it may be that the date of the decision on the appeal would seem to be

---

[17] An example of such a case would be where the court of origin had based its jurisdiction on an exorbitant rule: Jenard, para. A1.249 below.
[18] Bülow/Böckstiegel/Schlafen, p. 333.
[19] *Zelger* v. *Salinitri (No. 2)* [1984] E.C.R. 2397, discussed at para. 23.05 above.
[20] Bülow/Böckstiegel/Schlafen, pp. 328–329; Droz, para. 336.
[21] Para. 17.90 above.
[22] Bülow/Böckstiegel/Schlafen, p. 329.
[23] Para. 25.24 above.

the appropriate date to take into account,[24] at least if the appellate court was able to review the whole of the judgment appealed from.[25] It is not clear, though, whether the same would apply if the decision on appeal upheld the original decision.

If this question is to be decided by a uniform interpretation of the Convention, the correct date to take is probably the date of the latest judicial consideration of the judgment, so that the date when a judgment is given is affected by consideration on appeal, whatever the outcome of the appeal, but not by the expiry of a time for appealing without an appeal having been lodged.[26] If the judgment is varied by consent, that would count as a judicial consideration for these purposes, as would any other changes otherwise than by appeal, such as an assessment of interest to be included in the judgment. The enforceability of the judgment ought to be left out of account for the purpose of deciding the date on which it was given, not least because different systems provide different rules for determining when a judgment is to become enforceable[27] and distinctions drawn between judgments on that basis would be merely artificial in this context.

B. TRANSITIONAL EFFECT OF NATIONAL LAW

It is important to note in the context of the transitional provisions   **32.10**
that the Convention's rules on jurisdiction are compulsory and take precedence over national law. This is starkly illustrated by the case of *Sanicentral* v. *Collin*.[28] In that case, the European Court of Justice ruled that a jurisdiction clause in a contract of employment, unenforceable at the time of the contract as a matter of French law, but valid under Article 17, took precedence over the French law on the matter.

The relevant dates were these: Mr. Collin entered into the contract of employment on October 27, 1971, and it was broken off on December 8, 1971. Proceedings were started by Mr. Collin in the French court in November 1973, after the Convention had come into force. The court accepted jurisdiction on the basis of the French law, which not only gave the court jurisdiction as the court for the employee's residence and by reason of his French nationality, but which also ruled invalid the clause in the contract giving jurisdiction to the local German court.

---

[24] Bülow/Böckstiegel/Schlafen, p. 330.
[25] Bundesgerichtshof, case VIII Z B 1/78, March 28, 1979, RIW/AWD—1979, p. 710, Digest D I–17.1.1—B10.
[26] Bülow/Böckstiegel/Schlafen, p. 330; Geimer/Schütze, pp. 974–975.
[27] *Cf.* Arts. 30 and 38 (second para.), see paras. 27.85 and 28.50 above.
[28] [1979] E.C.R. 3423, discussed at para. 21.29 above.

32.11   The question of jurisdiction went to the *Cour de Cassation*, which referred to the European Court the question (as the European Court rephrased it):

> "whether the clause in the contract of employment conferring jurisdiction, which could have been regarded under French legislation prior to February 1, 1973 as being void, recovers its validity at the date of the entry into force of the Convention."[29]

The Court said this:

> "By its nature a clause in writing conferring jurisdiction and occurring in a contract of employment is a choice of jurisdiction; such a choice has no legal effect for so long as no judicial proceedings have been commenced and only becomes of consequence at the date when judicial proceedings are set in motion. That is therefore the relevant date for the purposes of an appreciation of the scope of such a clause in relation to the legal rules applying at that time."[30]

Having said that, so long as proceedings were started after the Convention came into force, the Convention applied to the legal relationships in question, the Court proceeded to rule that:

> "in judicial proceedings instituted after the coming into force of the Convention, clauses conferring jurisdiction included in contracts of employment[31] concluded prior to that date must be considered valid even in cases in which they would have been regarded as void under the national law in force at the time when the contract was entered into."[32]

---

[29] *Ibid.*, at p. 3429 (para. 4).
[30] *Ibid.*, at pp. 3429–3430 (para. 6).
[31] The reasoning would apply equally to other contracts.
[32] [1979] E.C.R. 3423, at p. 3431.

CHAPTER 33

RELATIONSHIP TO OTHER CONVENTIONS
(Articles 55–59)

TITLE VII

Article 55

Subject to the provisions of the second paragraph of Article   33.01
54, and of Article 56, this Convention shall, for the States which
are parties to it, supersede the following conventions concluded
between two or more of them:

— the Convention between Belgium and France on Jurisdiction and the Validity and Enforcement of Judgments,
  Arbitration Awards and Authentic Instruments, signed
  at Paris on 8 July 1899;
— the Convention between Belgium and the Netherlands
  on Jurisdiction, Bankruptcy, and the Validity and
  Enforcement of Judgments, Arbitration Awards and
  Authentic Instruments, signed at Brussels on 28 March
  1925;
— the Convention between France and Italy on the
  Enforcement of Judgments in Civil and Commercial
  Matters, signed at Rome on 3 June 1930;
— the Convention between the United Kingdom and the
  French Republic providing for the Reciprocal Enforcement of Judgments in Civil and Commercial Matters,
  with Protocol, signed at Paris on 18 January 1934;‡
— the Convention between the United Kingdom and the

Kingdom of Belgium providing for the Reciprocal Enforcement of Judgments in Civil and Commercial Matters, with Protocol, signed at Brussels on 2 May 1934;‡

— the Convention between Germany and Italy on the Recognition and Enforcement of Judgments in Civil and Commercial Matters, signed at Rome on 9 March 1936;

— the Convention between the Federal Republic of Germany and the Kingdom of Belgium on the Mutual Recognition and Enforcement of Judgments, Arbitration Awards and Authentic Instruments in Civil and Commercial Matters, signed at Bonn on 30 June 1958;

— the Convention between the Kingdom of the Netherlands and the Italian Republic on the Recognition and Enforcement of Judgments in Civil and Commercial Matters, signed at Rome on 17 April 1959;

— the Convention between the United Kingdom and the Federal Republic of Germany for the Reciprocal Recognition and Enforcement of Judgments in Civil and Commercial Matters, signed at Bonn on 14 July 1960;‡

[— the Convention between the Kingdom of Greece and the Federal Republic of Germany for the reciprocal recognition and enforcement of judgments, settlements and authentic instruments in civil and commercial matters, signed in Athens on 4 November 1961,]

— the Convention between the Kingdom of Belgium and the Italian Republic on the Recognition and Enforcement of Judgments and other Enforceable Instruments in Civil and Commercial Matters, signed at Rome on 6 April 1962;

— the Convention between the Kingdom of the Netherlands and the Federal Republic of Germany on the Mutual Recognition and Enforcement of Judgments and other Enforceable Instruments in Civil and Commercial Matters, signed at The Hague on 30 August 1962;

— the Convention between the United Kingdom and the Republic of Italy for the Reciprocal Recognition and Enforcement of Judgments in Civil and Commercial Matters, signed at Rome on 7 February 1964, with amending Protocol signed at Rome on 14 July 1970;‡

— the Convention between the United Kingdom and the Kingdom of the Netherlands providing for the Reciprocal Recognition and Enforcement of Judgments in Civil Matters, signed at The Hague on 17 November 1967,‡

and in so far as it is in force:

— **the Treaty between Belgium, the Netherlands and Luxembourg on Jurisdiction, Bankruptcy, and the Validity and Enforcement of Judgments, Arbitration Awards and Authentic Instruments, signed at Brussels on 24 November 1961.*†**

A. ARTICLE 55: GENERAL NOTE

The bilateral (and multilateral) conventions listed in Article 55 are those which are superseded by the present Convention. They are the conventions between the Contracting States covering reciprocal recognition and enforcement of judgments and authentic instruments in general, or in civil and commercial matters generally. No relevant bilateral conventions were concluded by Ireland or Denmark.[1] Conventions dealing with specific matters are covered by Article 57.   **33.02**

The conventions listed in this Article are "superseded" by the 1968 Convention, not abrogated. They continue to have effect in three respects:

(1) In relation to those judgments and authentic instruments which, by reason of their subject-matter,[2] fall outside this Convention: Article 56, first paragraph;[3]
(2) In relation to judgments given (or authentic instruments drawn up or registered) before this Convention came into force: Article 56, second paragraph;[4]
(3) For the purpose of deciding whether Title III of the 1968 Convention applies to judgments delivered after it came

---

* Jenard, paras. A1.250–A1.252 below; Schlosser, para. 237 (para. A1.542 below); Collins, pp. 32–34; Dashwood/Halcon/White, pp. 47–48; Hartley, p. 13; Kaye, pp. 192–195; Maxwell, paras. 10.1–10.3; Anton, para. 3.29; Droz, paras. 634–638; Weser, para. 339, 344–346; Bülow/Böckstiegel/Schlafen, pp. 333–336; Geimer/Schütze, p. 1009; Kropholler, pp. 350–352; Gothot/Holleaux, para. 4; Pocar, pp. 376–379.
† The words in square brackets were added by Article 8 of the 1982 Convention and are not yet in force. See para. 13.05 above. The paragraphs marked with a double dagger (‡) were added by Article 24 of the 1978 Convention: see para. A2–02 below.
[1] Schlosser, para. 237 (para. A1.542 below).
[2] Art. 1, para. 14.03 above.
[3] Para. 33.03 below.
[4] *Ibid.*

into force in proceedings instituted before that date: Article 54, second paragraph.[5]

Article 56

33.03   **The Treaty and the conventions referred to in Article 55 shall continue to have effect in relation to matters to which this Convention does not apply.**

They shall continue to have effect in respect of judgments given and documents formally drawn up or registered as authentic instruments before the entry into force of this Convention. *

B. ARTICLE 56: GENERAL NOTE

33.04   The conventions listed in Article 55 continue to have effect for judgments and authentic instruments which, by reason of their subject-matter,[6] fall outside this Convention.[7] If a case falls partly within the Convention and partly outside it, the order for enforcement under Title III may only extend to that part of the judgment which falls within the Convention.[8] In such a case, it may be necessary to bring separate enforcement proceedings in respect of the different parts of the judgment. This undesirable effect of Article 55 and the first paragraph of this Article seems to be unavoidable and is perhaps most likely to arise in family law cases. For example, a property adjustment order consequent on divorce, coupled with an order for maintenance, might fall both within and outside the Convention.

Articles 55 and 56 were considered by the European Court of Justice in *Bavaria Fluggesellchaft Schwabe & Co. KG and Germanair*

---

[5] Para. 32.01 above.

* Jenard, paras. A1.250–A1.252 below; Schlosser, para. 237 (para. A1.542 below); Collins, pp. 32–34; Dashwood/Halcon/White, pp. 47–48, 194–195; Hartley, p. 13, Kaye, pp. 192–195; Maxwell, para. 10.4, Anton, paras. 3.29–3.30; Droz, paras. 634–638; Weser, paras. 339, 344–346; Bülow/Böckstiegel/Schlafen, pp. 333–334, 336–340; Geimer/Schütze, pp. 1009–1010; Kropholler, pp. 352–353; Pocar, pp. 379–383.

[6] The material scope of the Convention is determined by Art. 1, para. 14.03 above.

[7] *S.A. Jaczon-Frogo* v. *B.V. Rodenburg*, Tribunal de Commerce, Tournai (Belgium), November 24, 1977, Digest D I–1.2—B5; *LTU Lufttransport* v. *Eurocontrol*, Oberlandesgericht Düsseldorf, Case No. 19 W 18/75, January 20, 1978, Digest D I–56—B2: the decision of the European Court in this case is discussed at para. 14.09 above.

[8] Art. 42, para. 28.71 above.

Bedarfsluftfahrt GmbH & Co. KG v. *Eurocontrol.*[9] The Court had already ruled that Eurocontrol's charges were matters of public law and did not fall within this Convention,[10] an autonomous interpretation of which excluded such charges from the expression "civil and commercial matters." The German courts then referred to the European Court the question whether that ruling applied to the expression "civil and commercial matter" in the Convention between Germany and Belgium, a question which the European Court ruled it did not have jurisdiction to answer, because it did not fall within the 1971 Protocol on Interpretation. But the European Court did go on to say that:

> " . . . a national court must not apply the Brussels Convention so as to recognize or enforce judgments which are excluded from its scope as determined by the Court of Justice. On the other hand it is not prevented from applying to the same judgments one of the special agreements referred to in Article 55 of the Brussels Convention, which may contain rules for the recognition and enforcement of such judgments . . ."[11]

and that that was so whether or not the subject-matter of the case fell within one of the specific categories listed in the second paragraph of Article 1.[12]

The second paragraph of Article 56 presents no particular problem. The procedures which existed under the bilateral conventions for the recognition and enforcement of judgments from other Contracting States, before this Convention came into force, continue to operate in respect of judgments delivered before that date. The same applies as between the United Kingdom and the Contracting States with which it had bilateral conventions, by reference to the date when the Convention came into force for the United Kingdom and those other states.[13]   **33.05**

Where there was no applicable bilateral convention before this Convention came into force, the procedures which existed as a matter of the national law of each of the states concerned continue to have effect for the purposes of judgments given before that date.

---

[9] [1977] E.C.R. 1517; see also para. 14.12 above.
[10] *LTU* v. *Eurocontrol* [1976] E.C.R. 1541, considered at para. 14.09 above.
[11] [1977] E.C.R. 1517, at p. 1525 (para. 5).
[12] In the light of that judgment, the Bundesgerichtshof remitted the case for further consideration by the lower courts in the light of the bilateral convention: Bundesgerichtshof, case VIII ZB 44/75, October 10, 1975, Digest D I–56—B1.
[13] January 1, 1987. See Art. 34 of the 1978 Convention, para. 37.06 below. The relevant bilateral conventions are listed at para. A2.02 below.

Article 57

33.06   This Convention shall not affect any conventions to which the Contracting States are or will be parties and which, in relation to particular matters, govern jurisdiction or the recognition or enforcement of judgments.

This Convention shall not affect the application of provisions which, in relation to particular matters, govern jurisdiction or the recognition or enforcement of judgments and which are or will be contained in acts of the Institutions of the European Communities or in national laws harmonised in implementation of such acts.*†

C. ARTICLE 57: INTRODUCTION

1. General note

33.07   Article 57 is concerned with two distinct matters. In the first paragraph, it seeks to regulate the relationship between the 1968 Convention and those specialised conventions which contain provisions either on jurisdiction or on the recognition or enforcement of judgments.[14] In the second paragraph, it regulates the priority of European Community secondary legislation. This second aspect presents few additional problems and is discussed separately below.

2. Article 25(2) of the 1978 Convention

The first paragraph of Article 57 presents particularly difficult problems of interpretation and application, discussed in more detail below. In an attempt to ease these problems, the 1978 Convention contains in Article 25(2) a definitive gloss for the interpretation of that paragraph. Article 25(2) of the 1978 Convention provides:

---

* Jenard, paras. A1.250, A1.253–A1.255 below; Schlosser, paras. 238–248 (paras. A1.543–A1.558 below); Collins, pp. 34–35; Dashwood/Halcon/White, pp. 48–49, 195–196; Hartley, p. 55; Kaye, pp. 197–204; Maxwell, paras. 10.5–10.15; Anton, paras. 3.31–3.36, 3.41; Droz, paras. 639–649; Weser, paras. 339, 344–346; Bülow/Böckstiegel/Schlafen, pp. 333, 340–353; Geimer/Schütze, pp. 105, 1006–1009; Kropholler, pp. 353–361; Gothot/Holleaux, para. 4; Pocar, pp. 383–390.

† This Article was substituted for the 1968 version by Art. 25(1) of the 1978 Convention. In the first paragraph, the only difference is that the former version referred to "jurisdiction *and* the recognition *and* enforcement of judgments." The second paragraph is entirely new.

[14] Some of the more important of these conventions are listed at paras. A2.31 *et seq.* below. See also the list in the Schlosser Report, para. 238, n. 59 (para. A1.543 n. 59 below).

With a view to its uniform interpretation, paragraph 1 of Article 57 shall be applied in the following manner:

(a) The 1968 Convention as amended shall not prevent a court of a Contracting State which is a party to a convention on a particular matter from assuming jurisdiction in accordance with that convention, even where the defendant is domiciled in another Contracting State which is not a party to that convention. The court shall, in any event, apply Article 20 of the 1968 Convention as amended.

(b) A judgment given in a Contracting State in the exercise of jurisdiction provided for in a convention on a particular matter shall be recognised and enforced in the other Contracting States in accordance with the 1968 Convention as amended.

Where a convention on a particular matter to which both the State of origin and the State addressed are parties lays down conditions for the recognition or enforcement of judgments, those conditions shall apply. In any event, the provisions of the 1968 Convention as amended which concern the procedures for recognition and enforcement of judgments may be applied.

D. ARTICLE 57, FIRST PARAGRAPH: SPECIALISED CONVENTIONS

1. Interpretation: summary

The first paragraph of this Article contains a number of difficulties,[15] not all of which are resolved by the new provision in Article 25(2) of the 1978 Convention. It may be helpful to recall the scheme of the 1968 Convention, which contains a comprehensive code of rules for establishing jurisdiction and for recognising and enforcing judgments. The jurisdictional rules are "direct" and apply uniformly in each of the Contracting States, while the recognition and enforcement provisions are largely automatic and generally preclude a review of the jurisdiction of the court of origin.[16]   **33.08**

Under the first paragraph of Article 57, parts of that comprehensive code can be replaced or supplemented by the provisions of a specialised convention. This does, however, give rise to the problem of defining when and how far the provisions of the specialised convention are to be grafted on to the scheme of the 1968 Convention and the consequences of doing so. It is clear that the 1968 Convention is not to have complete priority over the specialised conventions, even if the parties to the particular specialised convention do not include all the Contracting States to the present Conven-

---

[15] Schlosser, paras. 238–239 (paras. A1.543–A1.544 below).
[16] See para. 27.73 above.

tion and even if they include non-Contracting States. As against non-Contracting States, such a convention could not anyway be affected by the 1968 Convention. The problem is one of interpreting the words "shall not affect." It is this which Article 25(2) of the 1978 Convention goes some way towards resolving. The potential problems can conveniently be separated into three categories: (i) the scope of the first paragraph of Article 57; (ii) overlapping rules of jurisdiction; and (iii) recognition and enforcement.

2. Scope of the first paragraph

33.09   A convention dealing with specialised matters does not automatically fall within the first paragraph of Article 57, the purpose of which is to resolve potential conflicts between the provisions of such a convention and the present Convention. If there is no such conflict, the first paragraph of Article 57 would not apply. Two conditions must be fulfilled before such a conflict arises. First, the specialised convention must include provisions on jurisdiction[17] or on the recognition or enforcement of judgments. Secondly, the "particular matters" covered by the specialised convention must be ones which, but for this paragraph, would fall within the scope of the 1968 Convention.

So, for example, the convention on the contract for the international carriage of goods by road[18] governs contracts of carriage by commercial carriers and is concerned with matters which fall within the 1968 Convention,[19] whereas a convention on bankruptcy would

---

[17] The Convention must contain jurisdictional provisions, rather than merely have jurisdictional effects. So, for example, the Hague Convention of July 1, 1964 on the Uniform Law on the Formation of Contracts for the Sale of Goods (Uniform Laws on International Sales Act 1967, Sched. 2), which contains rules on the formation of contracts, but not specifically on jurisdiction, does not displace the jurisdictional rules of the 1968 Convention: *J. Wagner GmbH* v. *Larius Import di Castagna & Co.*, foro it. 1978, I, Col. 2240, Digest D I–57—B5. See now also the U.N. Convention on Contracts for the International Sale of Goods (Vienna, 1980), reproduced in (1980) 19 I.L.M. 668.

[18] "C.M.R.," signed at Geneva on May 19, 1956, enacted in the United Kingdom as the Schedule to the Carriage of Goods by Road Act 1965.

[19] Landgericht Aachen, case 13 O 151/75, January 16, 1976, RIW/AWD—1976, p. 588, Digest D I–57—B2; *Agence Belgo-Danoise N.V.* v. *Rederij Hapag Lloyd A.G.*, Rechtbank van Koophandel, Antwerp, June 25, 1976, European Transport Law 1976, p. 691, Digest D I–57—B3; *L'Etoile-De Ster N.V. and others* v. *Rederij Hapag Lloyd A.G. and others*, Rechtbank van Koophandel, Antwerp, May 21, 1980, Digest D I–57—B9. Similarly in the case of the Convention for the Navigation of the Rhine, *Haeger & Schmidt GmbH* v. *Compagnie Française de Navigation Rhéane S.A.*, Court of Appeal of the Central Commission for the Navigation of the Rhine, Ned.Jur. 1978, No. 62, Digest D I–57—B4.

not be concerned with such matters.[20] The former would fall within the first paragraph of Article 57, while the latter would not. In the latter case, there is no overlap between the Brussels Convention and the specialised convention, and because this Article has nothing to resolve, it does not apply.[21]

Despite the wording ("any conventions to which the Contracting States are or will be parties"), it is clear that this paragraph applies to specialised conventions whether or not all the Contracting States are parties to them. The 1968 Convention does not prevent the Contracting States from entering into specialised conventions, either with each other or with third states, and to include in those conventions provisions which derogate from the 1968 Convention. Whether that freedom would extend to the giving of an undertaking not to recognise judgments given in other Contracting States, though, is an open question.[22]

3. Overlapping jurisdictions

The effect of the first paragraph of Article 57 in the field of juris- **33.10** diction has been to assimilate into the scheme of the 1968 Convention those jurisdictions which courts of Contracting States derive from specialised conventions to which they are parties.[22a] This is so whether or not any or none of the other Contracting States are also parties to the specialised convention in question[23] and irrespective of the domicile of the defendant,[24] who will not be able to place reliance on the exclusive terms of the first paragraph of Article 3 of this Convention.[25]

Specialised convention containing direct rules of jurisdiction. Where a **33.11** specialised convention contains direct rules of jurisdiction, it will be necessary to examine that convention to see whether the jurisdictional rules of the 1968 Convention are displaced. If the specialised convention provides for exclusive jurisdiction, then the provisions

---

[20] Bankruptcy is excluded from the scope of the 1968 Convention by Art. 1, second para., sub-para. (2): see paras. 14.26 *et seq.* above.

[21] Bülow/Böckstiegel/Schlafen, p. 340.

[22] Schlosser, para. 246 (paras. A1.554–A1.556 below); *cf.* Art. 59, paras. 33.24 *et seq.* below.

[22a] Referring to the Brussels Arrest Convention of 1952 in *The Nordglimt* [1987] 2 Lloyd's Rep. 470, 479, Hobhouse J. said, "I consider that it is clear that an English court in applying the terms of . . . the 1968 convention . . . to English proceedings must have regard to the full terms of the jurisdiction which, internationally, has been recognized as being possessed by the United Kingdom courts in the 1952 Convention."

[23] Schlosser, para. 240 (paras. A1.547–A1.548 below); *cf.* Bülow/Böckstiegel/ Schlafen, p. 342.

[24] Geimer/Schütze, p. 69.

[25] Para. 16.09 above.

of that convention take priority over the 1968 Convention in determining jurisdiction,[26] although those Contracting States which have jurisdiction under the 1968 Convention and are not parties to the specialised convention will not be precluded by the specialised convention from accepting jurisdiction over the case. So far as they are concerned, the specialised convention is *res inter alios acta* and does not affect the jurisdiction of their courts.

What is less clear is whether the provisions of the 1968 Convention are entirely displaced in favour of the jurisdictional rules in the specialised convention. In one respect, at least, it is clear that this does not occur. The last sentence of Article 25(2)(a) of the 1978 Convention preserves the application of Article 20.[27] This ensures that if the defendant is domiciled in another Contracting State and does not enter an appearance, the court will only accept jurisdiction over him after it has examined its jurisdiction of its own motion[28] and the defendant is protected against an automatic default judgment. The dual protection thus afforded means that if the judgment is to be recognised and enforced under Title III of the 1968 Convention the defendant is adequately protected. Similarly, it seems that the provisions in Articles 21 to 23 of the 1968 Convention, concerning *lis pendens* and related actions continue to apply to cases in which jurisdiction is founded on a specialised convention which does not itself contain provisions on these matters.[28a]

33.12   *Exclusive jurisdiction under a specialised convention.* Whether any other provisions of Title II remain effective if the specialised convention provides for exclusive jurisdiction, is an open question. The application of each provision will need to be considered in each case. If the rule in the 1968 Convention is consistent with the court exercising its exclusive jurisdiction under the specialised convention, the rule of exclusive jurisdiction will take effect, because the 1968 Convention would not be "affecting" the provisions of the other convention. For example, it may be necessary to decide whether a court is required to decline jurisdiction under Article 21, even though it has exclusive jurisdiction under a specialised convention, because a court with jurisdiction under the 1968 Convention, but in a state which is not a party to the specialised

---

[26] Bülow/Böckstiegel/Schlafen, p. 342; Geimer/Schütze, pp. 62–68.

[27] Para. 22.11 above.

[28] The jurisdiction under the specialised convention would suffice for this purpose: *Pento Cosmetics B.V.* v. *Helena Rubenstein S.A.*, Arrondissementsrechtbank, Amsterdam, August 14, 1975, Digest D I–57—B1.

[28a] *The Nordglimt* [1987] 2 Lloyd's Rep. 470; *The Linda* [1988] 1 Lloyd's Rep. 175; see also Blackburn, "*Lis alibi pendens* and *forum non conveniens* in collision actions after the Civil Jurisdiction and Judgments Act 1982," [1988] L.M.C.L.Q. 91.

convention, was seised of the matter first.[29] Whether it is permissible to apply Article 21 in those circumstances will depend upon the construction of the specialised convention.

Non-exclusive jurisdictional rules. Where the specialised convention contains rules granting jurisdiction to a court or courts in a Contracting State, but those rules, on their true construction, do not provide that the jurisdiction is exclusive, the plaintiff can choose whether to use that jurisdiction or to use any other jurisdiction provided by the present Convention. There is nothing in the wording or purpose of the first paragraph of Article 57 to the effect that the jurisdiction provided by the other convention is to apply to the exclusion of the jurisdiction provided by the 1968 Convention.[30] It should be treated as an additional ground of jurisdiction. In other words, if the court with jurisdiction under the specialised convention would not have had jurisdiction under the 1968 Convention, the first paragraph of Article 57 resolves that conflict by, in effect, recognising the jurisdiction which that court derives from the other convention. In this case, too, if the plaintiff chooses the jurisdiction under the specialised convention, Article 20 will apply and the application of any other rules will depend on whether they are consistent with that choice of jurisdiction. **33.13**

Formal requirements for jurisdiction agreements. One particular application of the principle that the 1968 Convention "shall not affect" the specialised convention should be noted. If the specialised convention expressly or impliedly permits the parties to confer jurisdiction by agreement on a court or courts, whether or not that court or those courts would anyway have jurisdiction under the specialised convention or the 1968 Convention, Article 17 cannot apply to impose additional formal requirements on the validity of such an agreement.[31] Similarly, provisions in a specialised convention preventing the parties from derogating by agreement from jurisdictions expressly envisaged by that convention can continue to apply even if the agreement fulfils the formal requirements of Article 17.[32] **33.14**

---

[29] Schlosser, para. 240 (para. A1.548 below).
[30] Advocate General Warner, in *Netherlands* v. *Rüffer* [1980] E.C.R. 3807, at p. 3837; Collins, p. 35; Bülow/Böckstiegel/Schlafen, pp. 342–343; Geimer/Schütze, pp. 68–69.
[31] Bülow/Böckstiegel/Schlafen, p. 343; Landgericht Aachen, case 13 O 151/75, January 16, 1976, n. 19 above.
[32] *Agence Belgo-Danoise N.V.* v. *Rederij Hapag Lloyd A.G.*, Rechtbank van Koophandel, Antwerp, June 25, 1976, n. 19 above; *L'Etoile-De Ster N.V. and others* v. *Rederij Hapag Lloyd A.G. and others*, Rechtbank van Koophandel, Antwerp, May 21, 1980, n. 19 above.

4. Recognition and enforcement

33.15   Where a specialised convention contains provisions on jurisdiction, but no provisions on recognition or enforcement, a judgment given in one Contracting State on the basis of that jurisdiction is to be recognised and enforced in the other Contracting States in the same way as a judgment given in the exercise of a jurisdiction provided by the 1968 Convention.[33]

If the specialised convention contains provisions on the recognition or enforcement of judgments, the extent to which those provisions displace the provisions of Title III of the 1968 Convention will depend upon a number of factors.

33.16   First, if the Contracting State in which recognition or enforcement is sought is not a party to the specialised convention, the judgment is to be recognised and enforced in accordance with the 1968 Convention.[34] In particular, the court of the state addressed may only review the jurisdiction of the court of origin to the extent which would be permitted in a case falling only within the 1968 Convention. The court of the state addressed need not concern itself with any provisions in the specialised convention concerning recognition and enforcement.

Secondly, if the state of origin is not a party to (and would not therefore have had jurisdiction under) the specialised convention, but did have jurisdiction under the 1968 Convention, the judgment must be recognised and enforced under the 1968 Convention, even in those Contracting States which are parties to the specialised convention.[35]

Thirdly, if the state of origin and the state addressed are both parties to a specialised convention which "lays down conditions" for the recognition and enforcement of judgments, Article 25(2)(b) of the 1978 Convention[36] states that those conditions "shall apply." This presents some difficult problems of interpretation and application. It is apparent from the wording of Article 25(2)(b) that a distinction is to be drawn between "conditions" and "procedures." The party seeking recognition or enforcement can "in any event" make use of the procedures provided by the 1968 Convention—an option apparently open to him even where the specialised convention lays down its own procedures for recognition and enforce-

---

[33] Schlosser, para. 244 (para. A1.552 below).
[34] Schlosser, para. 245 (para. A1.553 below).
[35] *Ibid.*
[36] Para. 33.07 above.

ment.[37] It would seem that Article 25(2)(b) of the 1978 Convention requires national law to make those procedures available to the applicant even though jurisdiction is based on the specialised convention and not on the 1968 Convention.[38]

The conditions laid down by the specialised convention are, it seems, to be applied in the context of the procedures laid down by the 1968 Convention (if that is the procedure chosen); but the extent to which the provisions of the two conventions operate in tandem is not clear.   **33.17**

On the one hand, it may be that the conditions in the specialised convention entirely displace the conditions in the 1968 Convention,[39] so that the judgment is to be recognised if it fulfils the specialised convention's conditions, whether or not it also fulfils the conditions of the 1968 Convention.[40] In such a case, the court of the state addressed might have been entitled (or required)[41] under the 1968 Convention to refuse recognition of a judgment,[42] but might be prevented from doing so because the specialised convention contained no equivalent condition.

On the other hand, the conditions in the specialised convention may be additional to those in the 1968 Convention, so that recognition and enforcement may be refused on a ground provided by the 1968 Convention even if the conditions in the specialised convention are all fulfilled.

It is not possible to say as a general proposition which, if either, of those interpretations of Article 25(2)(b) of the 1978 Convention and of the first paragraph of Article 57 is correct. In approaching   **33.18**

---

[37] Geimer/Schütze, p. 1009. Some earlier decisions, especially in the field of maintenance orders, have given precedence to the procedures under specialised conventions, while others have given precedence to those under this Convention. See *Lorenzetto* v. *Bourada*, Tribunal de Première Instance, Charleroi, June 29, 1978, Digest D I–57—B6 and the cases cited at Digest D I–57—B6n. See also *V.* v. *G.*, President of the Arrondissementsrechtbank, Breda, April 15, 1980, Digest D I–57—B8; *F.* v. *R.*, Cour d'Appel, Paris, July 9, 1981, Digest D I–57—B10; *L.* v. *Office de la Jeunesse de Reutlingen*, Cour d'Appel, Rennes, June 29, 1982, Rev. critique 1983, p. 504, Digest D I—57—B10n.

[38] But, *cf.* Oberlandesgericht Frankfurt-am-Main, cases 131/81 and 132/81, July 14, 1981, IPrax. 1981, p. 213, Digest D I–57—B11. Note, though, that the decision was made before Art. 25(2) of the 1978 Accession Convention came into force.

[39] "Conditions" in this context should be read in the sense of "prerequisites": the German text refers to *Voraussetzungen*.

[40] The conditions for a judgment to be enforced under the present Convention are summarised at para. 28.02 above.

[41] See para. 25.11 above.

[42] The grounds for a judgment to be refused recognition and enforcement under the present Convention are summarised at paras. 25.12–25.13 above.

questions of interpretation, though, it should be recalled that the 1968 Convention is integrationist in purpose and aims to ease rather than hinder the recognition and enforcement of judgments delivered in other Contracting States.[43] The problems involved in grafting a specialised convention on to the scheme the 1968 Convention become particularly acute where the specialised convention permits the court of the state addressed to review the jurisdiction of the state of origin. In the context of the 1968 Convention, the court of origin will have had to review its own jurisdiction pursuant to Article 20[44] and its decision is one which the courts of the other Contracting States are generally required not to question.

5. England and Wales

33.19   As a matter of English law, conventions only have direct legal effect if they have been expressly incorporated into law by an Act of Parliament or delegated legislation.[45] Effect is frequently given to a convention by legislation which does not incorporate the convention directly into law and which often does not even refer to it by name, but which makes such changes to national law as are necessary to give effect to the United Kingdom's obligations as a matter of public international law. In those circumstances, the convention itself cannot normally be applied by national courts. In the context of Article 57, however, the position is probably different. The court's jurisdiction is now probably founded on the jurisdictional provisions of the specialised convention itself, whether or not it also has jurisdiction under the English legislation which gives effect to the specialised convention and whether or not the terms of that legislation are as wide as those of the specialised convention.[45a] This is because Article 57 gives effect to the jurisdictional provisions of the specialised convention as if they were part of the 1968 Convention itself. They are thus given effect in English law by section 2 of the 1982 Act.[45b]

The indirect incorporation into English law of the relevant provisions of the specialised conventions may create practical difficulties, because the courts and the parties may not readily be aware of the conventions which contain such provisions. There is therefore a

---

[43] This principle forms part of the basis for a proposition that conditions laid down in a specialised convention for the recognition and enforcement of judgments are to take precedence over those in the 1968 Convention only if they are more amenable to recognition being granted: Geimer/Schütze, pp. 1005–1007.

[44] Art. 20 is applied in this context by Art. 25(2)(a) of the 1978 Convention: see paras. 33.07 and 33.11 above.

[45] See Mann, *Foreign Affairs in English Courts*, pp. 84 *et seq.*; Higgins, in Jacobs and Roberts (ed.), *The Effect of Treaties in Domestic Law*, pp. 123 *et seq.*

[45a] *e.g.*, see para. 43.13, n. 35 below.

[45b] Para. 40.03 below; *The Nordglimt* [1987] 2 Lloyd's Rep. 470; see n. 22a above.

danger of the courts failing to give effect to a jurisdictional basis which may legitimately be relied upon, despite the contrary terms of the 1968 Convention. A list of some of the conventions to which the United Kingdom is a party appears in Appendix 2.[45c]

If, for example, in a case involving the international carriage of goods by road, jurisdiction may be founded on the C.M.R.,[45d] this is likely to be reasonably apparent, because that convention is given effect as the Schedule to the Carriage of Goods by Road Act 1965. If, on the other hand, the defendant in a maritime claim is domiciled in another Contracting State and none of the bases of jurisdiction in Articles 5 to 18 apply, it may not be immediately apparent whether sections 20 to 22 of the Supreme Court Act 1981 may still be relied on to found jurisdiction. The answer will depend on whether the jurisdiction is based on a ground contemplated by one of the conventions to which, *inter alia*, those sections give effect.[46]

Rhine Navigation Convention. Another example which, because **33.20** its provisions are not even enacted into English law, illustrates the difficulty clearly is the Rhine Navigation Convention.[47] Under that convention, jurisdiction is assigned over certain claims for damages to the court for the district where the damage was caused.[48] If it were not for the 1968 Convention, the High Court would be precluded as a matter of English law from exercising jurisdiction over any case which the Secretary of State certified to be a claim which falls to be determined under the provisions of that convention.[49] Assuming jurisdiction were founded on otherwise valid service of proceedings, the English court, as a matter of purely English law, would not entertain any objection to its jurisdiction on the ground that it did not have jurisdiction under the Rhine Navigation Con-

---

[45c] Paras. A2.31 *et seq.* below.

[45d] See n. 18 above.

[46] The International Convention for the Unification of Certain Rules relating to the Arrest of Sea-going Ships and the International Convention on Certain Rules concerning Civil Jurisdiction in Matters of Collision, both done at Brussels, May 10, 1952, Cmd. 8954, Cmnd. 1128; see Schlosser, para. 121 (para. A1.404 below). See, further, on maritime matters, paras. 1.31 *et seq.* and 7.22 above and 43.12 *et seq.* below.

[47] The Revised Mannheim Convention for the navigation of the Rhine of October 17, 1868, 59 British and Foreign State Papers 470, together with the convention amending the 1868 Convention, signed at Strasbourg, November 20, 1963, Cmnd. 3371, and the Additional Protocol signed at Strasbourg, October 25, 1972, Cmnd. 6175. The U.K. and the states bordering the navigable Rhine are parties. This example is adapted from the Schlosser Report, paras. 241–245 (paras. A1.549–A1.553 below).

[48] *Ibid.*, Art. 35.

[49] Supreme Court Act 1981, s.23.

vention, unless the Secretary of State issued a certificate to that effect.

Under the 1968 Convention, the terms of the Rhine Navigation Convention are themselves capable of review by the courts. The Rhine Navigation Convention allows the parties to assign jurisdiction to a court by agreement[50] and it would seem therefore that, both on that ground directly and because it does not envisage exclusive jurisdiction, the entry of an appearance in the English court would give the court jurisdiction under Article 18, whether or not the Secretary of State granted his certificate. The case is perhaps unlikely to occur, but it illustrates the difficulties which the United Kingdom courts may face in the context of Article 57.

E. ARTICLE 57, SECOND PARAGRAPH: SECONDARY EUROPEAN COMMUNITY LAW

33.21   The second paragraph of Article 57 provides for European Community law to take precedence over the 1968 Convention. The problem of precedence will only arise where European Community law includes provisions on jurisdiction or the recognition or enforcement of judgments, and does so in relation to a "particular matter" which would otherwise be governed by this Convention.[51] In effect, the second paragraph of Article 57 equates secondary European Community law with international conventions on particular matters and gives rise to the same problems of interpretation and application as arise under the first paragraph of this Article. There are not yet any provisions of European Community law which fall within this paragraph.

The provision has a parallel in Article 20 of the EEC Contractual Obligations Convention,[52] and the law covered by both provisions is described in the official report on that Convention:[53]

> "As regards the form which these instruments are to take, the Community provisions contemplated by Article 20[54] are not only the acts of the institutions of the European Communities, that is to say principally the Regulations and the Directives as well as the Conventions

---

[50] Rhine Navigation Convention, Art. 35b.
[51] For example, an EEC Directive or Regulation might contain provisions for jurisdiction in employment disputes (Geimer/Schütze, p. 105) or, as is proposed, in matters relating to trade marks.
[52] EEC Convention on the Law Applicable to Contractual Obligations, Rome, June 19, 1980 (not yet in force), O.J. 1980 L266; para. A2.46 below.
[53] Report by Professors Giuliano and Lagarde, O.J. 1980 C282; reproduced in North (ed.) *Contract Conflicts*, App. B.
[54] The same would apply to the second paragraph of Art. 57 of the present Convention.

concluded by those Communities,[55] but also national laws harmonised in implementation of such acts. A law or regulation adopted by a State in order to make its legislation comply with a Directive borrows, as it were, from the Directive its Community force, thus justifying the precedence accorded to it over this Convention."

Article 58

This Convention shall not affect the rights granted to Swiss nationals by the Convention concluded on 15 June 1869 between France and the Swiss Confederation on Jurisdiction and the Enforcement of Judgments in Civil Matters.*   **33.22**

F. Article 58: Swiss Nationals

The Convention between Switzerland and France is unusual in that   **33.23**
it contains direct rules of jurisdiction. Under this 1869 Convention, a person of Swiss nationality may in certain circumstances invoke the jurisdiction of the French courts against a French national, irrespective of the latter's domicile. This extended exorbitant jurisdiction would be contrary to the present Convention, especially if the French national were domiciled in another Contracting State, but is preserved by Article 58, despite the contrary terms of Articles 2 to 4.[56]

It is important to recognise the limited nature of this exception to the general rules of the present Convention. It is only the privileges of Swiss nationals under the 1869 Convention which are preserved and those privileges extend into the Community only as far as the French courts. The equivalent privileges of French nationals are not preserved so far as the French courts are concerned and their preservation in the Swiss courts is irrelevant for the purposes of the 1968 Convention.[57]

A judgment given by a French court in the exercise of the exorbitant jurisdiction permitted by this Article is to be recognised and enforced in the other Contracting States in the normal way, pursuant to the provisions of Title III. In particular, the courts of the

---

[55] The 1968 Convention was not concluded by the Communities, but by the Member States under Art. 220 of the EEC Treaty: see para. 13.03 above.

* Jenard, para. A1.256 below; Dashwood/Halcon/White, pp. 49–50, 196–197; Maxwell, para. 10.16; Kaye, p. 195; Droz, paras. 650–655; Weser, paras. 339, 347–352; Bülow/Böckstiegel/Schlafen, pp. 353–356; Kropholler, pp. 362–363; Gothot/Holleaux, para. 4; Pocar, p. 391.

[56] Chap. 16 above.

[57] The provision will anyway become redundant when the Lugano Convention O.J. 1988 L319, p. 9 comes into force: see para. 13.07 above.

state addressed may not review the jurisdiction of the French court of origin, save to the extent permitted by Article 28.[58]

Article 59

33.24   **This Convention shall not prevent a Contracting State from assuming, in a convention on the recognition and enforcement of judgments, an obligation towards a third State not to recognise judgments given in other Contracting States against defendants domiciled or habitually resident in the third State where, in cases provided for in Article 4, the judgment could only be founded on a ground of jurisdiction specified in the second paragraph of Article 3.**

However, a Contracting State may not assume an obligation towards a third State not to recognise a judgment given in another Contracting State by a court basing its jurisdiction on the presence within that State of property belonging to the defendant, or the seizure by the plaintiff of property situated there:

1. **if the action is brought to assert or declare proprietary or possessory rights in that property, seeks to obtain authority to dispose of it, or arises from another issue relating to such property, or,**

2. **if the property constitutes the security for a debt which is the subject-matter of the action.*†**

G. ARTICLE 59: SAVING FOR CONVENTIONS WITH THIRD COUNTRIES

1. General note

33.25   The effects of the Convention's scheme of virtually automatic recognition and enforcement of judgments is potentially harsh on defendants domiciled outside the Contracting States. Article 59 permits those effects to be relaxed to a certain extent by conventions with non-Contracting States.

In summary, the effects of the Convention on a defendant domiciled outside the Contracting States are as follows:

---

[58] Para. 27.62 above.

* Jenard,   paras. A1.257–A1.259   below;   Schlosser,   para. 249–250   (paras. A1.559–A1.560 below); Collins, pp. 35–36; Dashwood/Halcon/White, pp. 50, 197; Hartley, pp. 7–8; Kaye, pp. 1524–1538; Maxwell, paras. 10.17–10.21; Anton, paras. 3.37–3.40; Droz, paras. 671–688; Weser, paras. 339, 348–352; Bülow/Böckstiegel/Schlafen,   pp. 356–357;   Geimer/Schütze,   pp. 306–307, 309–310, 346, 1049; Kropholler, pp. 363–365; Gothot/Holleaux, para. 314, Pocar, pp. 391–392.

† The second para. was added by Art. 26 of the 1978 Convention.

(1) Under Article 4[59] the courts of the Contracting States are free (except where the case falls within Article 16) to exercise jurisdiction in accordance with their own law against a defendant not domiciled in a Contracting State. Some of the provisions of national law which a court could rely on against such a defendant are "exorbitant,"[60] notably those listed in the second paragraph of Article 3.[61]

(2) Any judgment delivered by a court of a Contracting State is to be automatically recognised and enforced in the other Contracting States without the jurisdiction of the original court being open to review.[62] This applies equally to a judgment delivered on the basis of an exorbitant jurisdiction against a defendant not domiciled in a Contracting State.[63]

(3) The effect of the Convention is to put at risk of execution assets which a defendant may have in *any* of the Contracting States, not just those assets in the state where he is sued. Where the defendant is not domiciled in a Contracting State, his assets in any of the Contracting States can therefore be put at risk, even where he is sued under an exorbitant jurisdiction.

Such unfairness to the defendant as there may be in his being subjected to an exorbitant jurisdiction is multiplied by the judgment-extending effect of Title III. This unfairness caused some protest when the Convention was first drafted,[64] with the consequence that the negotiators included what is now the first paragraph of Article 59.

2. Scheme of Article 59

Where a judgment is covered by a bilateral convention falling within Article 59, it need not be recognised or enforced in the Contracting State or states which are parties to that convention. This is one of the few instances where the court of the state addressed may review the jurisdiction of the court of origin.[65] For a judgment to be

33.26

---

[59] Para. 16.15 above.
[60] Para. 16.11 above.
[61] Para. 16.09 above.
[62] This is subject to the limited review permitted by Art. 28, discussed at para. 27.71 above.
[63] Landgericht Hamburg, case 5 O 82/77, August 10, 1977, Digest D I–31—B4.
[64] See for example, *e.g.* Collins, p. 50; Hay, (1968) 17 Am.Jo.Comp.L. 160 *et seq.*; Nadelmann, (1967) 67 Columbia Law Review 995, (1968) 5 C.M.L.Rev. 409 *et seq.*, *Conflict of Laws: International and Interstate* (1972), p. 245.
[65] Art. 28, first para., para. 27.62 above.

exempted from recognition and enforcement on this ground, the state addressed must have concluded a convention with a non-Contracting State and a number of further conditions must be fulfilled:

(1) the judgment must have been given by the court of another Contracting State on one of the jurisdictional bases listed in the second paragraph of Article 3;

(2) if the relevant jurisdiction under the second paragraph of Article 3 was based upon the presence of the defendant's property within the state of origin, the property must not have formed the subject-matter of the action, nor security for a debt which it itself the subject-matter of the action;

(3) it must not have been possible to found jurisdiction on any other basis;

(4) the defendant must not be domiciled in any Contracting State;

(5) the defendant must have been domiciled or, depending on the wording of the convention with the third state, habitually resident, in the third state with which that convention has been concluded;

(6) that convention must impose an obligation on the state addressed not to recognise the judgment.

A number of these conditions require further comment.

Condition 2—jurisdiction based on the presence of property

33.27   This condition is the result of the second paragraph of Article 59, which was added, according to the Schlosser Report, "further to limit the possibility of recognition and enforcement,"[66] but the effect of which is just the opposite, namely to circumscribe further the opportunity of *refusing* recognition and enforcement. Exorbitant jurisdictions listed in the second paragraph of Article 3 for Denmark, Germany and the United Kingdom permit jurisdiction to be founded on the location of property,[67] but where that property is connected with the dispute in a way which is not capricious, the policy of Article 59 does not regard the jurisdiction as sufficiently unfair to allow Contracting States to contract out of it by way of a bilateral convention with a third country.

Where the property falls within sub-paragraph (2) of the second paragraph of Article 59 and forms security for a debt which is the subject-matter of the action, it is probably only to the extent that the property forms such security that Contracting States are precluded from undertaking not to recognise the judgment. If so, the

---

[66] Schlosser, para. 249 (para. A1.559 below). This may well be a misprint or slip of the author's pen.

[67] Schlosser, para. 88 (para. A1.376 below).

convention with the third state may exclude enforcement of the judgment to the extent that it exceeds the value of the security.[68]

Conditions 4 and 5—domicile of the defendant

These conditions are derived from the wording of the first para- **33.28** graph of Article 59. Because a person can have more than one domicile it is not enough that the defendant should be domiciled or habitually resident[69] in the non-Contracting State in question. It is also necessary that the defendant should not be domiciled in a Contracting State. This requirement is provided by the reference to Article 4, under which the court of origin can only accept jurisdiction on an exorbitant basis if the defendant is not domiciled in a Contracting State. The relevant time for the purposes of Article 4 is when the court of origin accepts jurisdiction, and it seems therefore that that should also be the relevant time for determining the defendant's domicile in the third state. The seat of a company or other legal person is equated by Article 53 with the domicile of an individual.

3. Conventions falling within Article 59

It is clear that Article 59 will only provide a ground for refusing **33.29** recognition to a judgment given in another Contracting State if the state addressed has undertaken an obligation to that effect in a bilateral convention. What is less clear is the extent to which the terms of the bilateral convention must reflect those of Article 59, but it seems that a state can agree not to recognise judgments based on some of the exorbitant jurisdictions, but not on others, or against certain categories of defendant but not others; moreover, there is nothing in Article 59 which prevents states from limiting the application of their own exorbitant jurisdictions.[70]

So far as the authors are aware, the only conventions falling within Article 59 concluded by Contracting States are that between Germany and Norway, that between the Nordic countries, and that between the United Kingdom and Canada.[71]

---

[68] Collins, p. 36, n. 2. See Art. 42, para. 28.71 below.

[69] Habitual residence was included to accommodate those third countries whose concept of domicile differs from that used for the purposes of the Convention: Jenard, para. A1.259 below.

[70] Jenard, para. A1.257 below. The Federal Republic of Germany has limited the application of para. 23 of the Code of Civil Procedure (*Zivilprozessordnung*) in respect of defendants domiciled in Norway: Art. 20 of the Convention between Germany and Norway, discussed below.

[71] The first two of these will be superseded by the Lugano Convention, when it comes into effect: see para. 13.07 above. Conventions between the U.K. and Australia and between Germany and Canada are thought to be under discussion.

Convention between Germany and Norway dated June 17, 1977[72]

33.30   Under Article 23 of this Convention, Germany and Norway each agrees not to recognise or enforce any judgment given by the court of another state against a person domiciled, habitually resident or, in the case of a legal person, with its seat in the other of those states if jurisdiction was founded only on any of six enumerated bases. Those bases include service of process on the defendant during a temporary presence in the state of origin, the nationality of the plaintiff, and the location of property in the state of origin, except, in the latter case, where the circumstances are those set out in the second paragraph of Article 59, the substance of which is reproduced in the bilateral convention. Each of those states also agrees by Article 20 not to exercise its own exorbitant jurisdiction based on the presence of the defendant's property against domiciliaries of the other state,[73] but this latter provision is expressly limited by reference to the value of the property.

Convention between the Nordic states, dated October 11, 1977

33.31   This convention was entered into between Denmark, Finland, Iceland, Norway and Sweden. It has not come into force for Iceland, but it came into force for the other signatory states on January 1, 1978. Article 2 of the convention follows the provision in Article 59 of the 1968 Convention and enumerates the cases in which the enforcement of judgments given in other Contracting States to the 1968 Convention against persons domiciled or habitually resident in a Nordic country will not be permitted in Denmark, or in the other participating countries.[73a]

Convention between the United Kingdom and Canada dated April 24, 1984[74]

33.32   This Convention, signed at Ottawa, was brought into effect on January 1, 1987.[75] By Article IX, the United Kingdom undertakes, "in the circumstances permitted by Article 59 of the 1968 Convention," not to recognise or enforce under that Convention any judgment given in another Contracting State against a person domiciled

---

[72] BGBl 1981, II, 341, Bülow/Böckstiegel/Schlafen, p. 645–23. See Geimer/Schütze, pp. 1038–1043.

[73] This is the exorbitant jurisdiction under para. 23 of the German Code of Civil Procedure, referred to in the second para. of Art. 3 of the present Convention.

[73a] See Philip, *EF/IP.2 Værneting-Tvangsfuldbyrdelse af fremmede retsafgørelser* (1986), pp. 217–218.

[74] Cmnd. 9337.

[75] The Reciprocal Enforcement of Foreign Judgments (Canada) Order 1987 (S.I. 1987 No. 468) replacing the Reciprocal Enforcement of Foreign Judgments (Canada) Order 1986 (S.I. 1986 No. 2027). The Convention, in both English and French, is set out in the Schedule to the Order.

or habitually resident in Canada.[76] Domicile in Canada is defined in terms equivalent to section 41 of the 1982 Act[77] (in the case of individuals) and section 42(2) of that Act[78] (in the case of corporations and associations).

The bilateral convention does not attempt to explain or define the circumstances in which Article 59 of the 1968 Convention permits recognition or enforcement of a judgment to be refused, nor does it limit the exercise of the United Kingdom's own exorbitant jurisdictions as against persons domiciled in Canada.

Although Article XII of the bilateral convention envisages that it extends only to certain provinces,[79] it is suggested that Article IX probably applies to defendants domiciled or habitually resident in any part of Canada.

---

[76] Para. 7 of the Order constitutes a declaration under s.9(2) of the 1982 Act (para. 40.27 below) that Art. IX of the bilateral convention is a provision to which Art. 59 of the 1968 Convention applies.

[77] Para. 44.01 below.

[78] Para. 44.11 below.

[79] Para. 3 of the Order designates British Columbia, Manitoba, New Brunswick, Nova Scotia and Ontario. The following provinces have since been designated: Yukon (S.I. 1987 No. 2211), Prince Edward Island (S.I. 1988 No. 1304) and Saskatchewan (S.I. 1988 No. 1853). The other provinces and territories are not designated: Alberta, Newfoundland, North West Territories, and Quebec.

FINAL PROVISIONS
(Articles 60–68)

TITLE VIII

Article 60

34.01   This Convention shall apply to the European territories of the Contracting States, including Greenland, to the French overseas departments and territories, and to Mayotte.

The Kingdom of the Netherlands may declare at the time of signing or ratifying this Convention or at any later time, by notifying the Secretary-General of the Council of the European Communities, that this Convention shall be applicable to the Netherlands Antilles. In the absence of such declaration, proceedings taking place in the European territory of the Kingdom as a result of an appeal in cassation from the judgment of a court in the Netherlands Antilles shall be deemed to be proceedings taking place in the latter court.

Notwithstanding the first paragraph, this convention shall not apply to:

1. the Faroe Islands, unless the Kingdom of Denmark makes a declaration to the contrary,
2. any European territory situated outside the United Kingdom for the international relations of which the United Kingdom is responsible, unless the United

Kingdom makes a declaration to the contrary in respect of any such territory.

Such declarations may be made at any time by notifying the Secretary-General of the Council of the European Communities.

Proceedings brought in the United Kingdom on appeal from courts in one of the territories referred to in sub-paragraph (2) of the third paragraph shall be deemed to be proceedings taking place in those courts.

Proceedings which in the Kingdom of Denmark are dealt with under the law on civil procedure for the Faroe Islands (*lov for Faerøerne om rettens pleije*) shall be deemed to be proceedings taking place in the courts of the Faroe Islands.*†

A. ARTICLE 60: TERRITORIAL EXTENT

1. General note

Article 60 defines the territorial scope of the Convention for those **34.02** Contracting States where it is in force.[1] Where territories are referred to generically, the actual extent of the Convention's territorial application is to be determined by the national law of the State in question. If a given territory becomes independent, it ceases to be part of its former Contracting State and it is no longer within the territorial application of the Convention.[2] The Convention is neutral in any dispute as to sovereignty and it is no part of its function to determine whether a given place falls within the territory of a Contracting State. That is to be decided by other means.[3]

By contrast with the EEC Treaty,[4] which (with specified excep-

---

* Schlosser, paras. 251–254 (paras. A1.561–A1.564 below); Hartley, p. 134; Dashwood/Halcon/White, p. 201; Kaye, pp. 211–214; Maxwell, para. 11.2; Anton, paras. 3.42–3.46; Droz, paras. 22–24; Weser, paras. 353–354; Bülow/Böckstiegel/Schlafen, pp. 357–359; Geimer/Schütze, pp. 108–112, 981; Kropholler, pp. 366–368; Pocar, pp. 393–395.

† This Article was substituted for the 1968 version by Art. 27 of the 1978 Convention. In addition to introducing provisions concerning the territories of the new Contracting States or for which those states are responsible, it also takes account of certain changes in the status of territories for which France and the Netherlands were formerly responsible.

[1] The entry into force of the Convention in the different Contracting States is governed by Art. 62 of the 1968 Convention (para. 34.11 below), by Art. 39 of the 1978 Convention (para. 37.18 below) and by Art. 15 of the 1982 Convention (para. 38.08 below).

[2] Schlosser, para. 254 (para. A1.564 below).

[3] *Netherlands* v. *Rüffer* [1980] E.C.R. 3807, *per* Advocate General Warner, at p. 3835. The case is discussed at para. 14.11 above.

[4] EEC Treaty, Art. 227(4). The ECSC Treaty, Art. 79, first para. and the Euratom Treaty, Art. 198, second para., each contains provisions similar to those in the EEC Treaty.

tions) applies to the European territories for whose external relations a Member State is responsible, the 1968 Convention contains no such stipulation.

2. Belgium, Ireland, Luxembourg, Greece

34.03 To the extent that it is force, the Convention extends to the territory of these states, none of which has territories outside Europe.

3. Federal Republic of Germany

34.04 In addition to the territory of the Federal Republic, the Convention also applies to **West Berlin**.[5]

4. Denmark

34.05 The Convention extends to the European territory of Denmark. **Greenland** is referred to expressly in the first paragraph of Article 60, but the operation of the Convention there is now less than clear. With effect from January 1985, its status changed in relation to the European Community, and it acquired the status of an overseas territory. It remains, though, part of the Kingdom of Denmark, which retains responsibility for its international relations. The legislation implementing the Convention into Danish law expressly excludes the operation of the Convention in Greenland and therefore, despite the express wording of Article 60, it is probable that the Convention has no application there. Nonetheless, courts of other Contracting States may not feel able to depart from the clear and express wording of the Convention on this point.

The **Faroe Islands** form part of the European territory of Denmark (although they have an autonomous administration). The Convention does not apply to them unless and until Denmark makes a declaration to that effect.[6] Danish courts may exercise jurisdiction over matters arising in the Faroe Islands, but such proceedings are deemed to be taking place in the courts of the Faroe Islands[7] and the Convention would only apply to them if a declaration were made under the third paragraph of this Article.

---

[5] Art. I(2), 96th Berlin Statute of September 29, 1972, GVBl für Berlin, 1972, p. 1912; Kohler, "Ein Nachtstück: Die Geltung des EuGVÜ in Berlin" (1989) IPrax 75.

[6] Art. 60, third para., sub-para. (1). The matters which would have to be taken into account in extending the application of the Convention to the Faroe Islands are summarised in the Schlosser Report at paras. 252–253 (paras. A1.562–A1.563 below). The legislation implementing the Convention into Danish law expressly excludes the Faroe Islands.

[7] Art. 60, sixth para.

5. France

The Convention applies to the European territory of France. It **34.06**
does not extend to **Monaco**, for whose external relations France is
partly responsible. The same applies to **Andorra**,[8] despite the fact
that French courts treat Andorra as part of France for the purposes
of civil jurisdiction. As it is not mentioned in Article 60, it should
be treated by other Contracting States as being outside the territorial scope of the Convention.[9]

The Convention is expressly applied[10] to French overseas
departments and territories. The former (*départements d'outre mer*)
comprise **Guadeloupe, French Guiana (Guyane), Martinique,
Réunion** and **St. Pierre et Miquelon**; the latter (*territoires d'outre mer*)
comprise **New Caledonia, French Polynesia, the Wassis and
Futuna Islands** and the uninhabited **Austral Islands**. The **Comoro
Islands**, formerly a French overseas territory, are now independent, with the exception of **Mayotte**, to which the Convention is
expressly applied. The **New Hebrides** is a condominium with the
United Kingdom and the Convention does not apply to it. The
former **Afars and Issas Islands** are no longer a *territoire d'outre mer*,
but have become the independent state of **Djibouti** to which the
Convention no longer applies.

6. Italy

The Convention applies to Italian territory. It does not extend to **34.07**
the **Vatican** which is an independent state, nor to **San Marino**,
despite the fact that Italy is responsible for its external relations.

7. Netherlands

The Convention applies to the European territory of the Nether- **34.08**
lands. Unless and until the Netherlands so declares under the
second paragraph of Article 60, it does not apply to the **Netherlands Antilles**, nor to proceedings on cassation in the Netherlands
courts from the courts of the Netherlands Antilles. Formerly, the
Convention applied also to **Surinam**, which was referred to in the
original version of Article 60, and in respect of which a declaration

---

[8] Responsibility for Andorran external relations is shared by the President of
France and the bishop of La Seo de Urgel in Spain.
[9] Bülow/Böckstiegel/Schlafen,p. 358; Geimer/Schütze, p. 110.
[10] Art. 60, first para.

had been made under that paragraph. Surinam is now independent and the Convention no longer applies to it.[11]

8. United Kingdom

34.09   The Convention applies to the territory of England and Wales, Scotland and Northern Ireland. Unless and until the United Kingdom so declares under sub-paragraph (2) of the third paragraph of Article 60, the Convention does not apply to any European territory outside the United Kingdom for the international relations of which the United Kingdom is responsible. The territories in question are each of the **Channel Islands**, the **Isle of Man, Gibraltar** and the sovereign base areas of **Akrotiri** and **Dhekelia** on Cyprus. A declaration may be made in respect of any one or more of those territories.[12]

Proceedings brought in the United Kingdom on appeal from courts in one of the territories referred to in sub-paragraph (2) of the third paragraph of Article 60 are to be regarded as taking place in those courts.[13] In other words, the Convention only applies to appellate proceedings in the United Kingdom on appeal from any of those territories if a declaration under that paragraph has been made in respect of that territory. While the Schlosser Report[14] refers only to Privy Council proceedings, the same applies to proceedings in the specific courts of appeal from the various territories, even if they conduct their proceedings in the United Kingdom.

The Convention does not expressly exclude from its application the proceedings of the Privy Council on appeal from non-European territories, whether they are territories, such as **Hong Kong** or the **Falkland Islands** for whose international relations the United Kingdom is responsible, or independent states, such as certain **Caribbean** states. It would not be safe to conclude that the judicial committee of the Privy Council is not a court for the purposes of the Convention, because of its jurisdiction over certain appeals purely internal to the United Kingdom, but proceedings on appeal from courts to which the Convention does not apply are obviously not apt to be included within its scope, especially where the appeal lies from the courts of an independent state, and a purposive interpretation of the Convention would almost certainly exclude all such proceedings.

---

[11] *D* v. *W*, Arrondissementsrechtbank, 's-Gravenhage, January 18, 1977, Nederlandse Jurisprudentie 1977, No. 578, Digest D I–60—B1.

[12] See s.52(2) of the 1982 Act, para. 44.49 below.

[13] Art. 60, fifth para.

[14] Schlosser, para. 252 (para. A1.562 below).

Article 61

This Convention shall be ratified by the signatory States. The   **34.10**
instruments of ratification shall be deposited with the Secretary-
General of the Council of the European Communities.*

B. ARTICLE 61: RATIFICATION

This Article corresponds with Article 7 of the 1971 Protocol,[15] with
Article 38 of the 1978 Convention[16] and with Article 14 of the 1982
Convention.[17] It is self-explanatory and requires no further com-
mentary.

Article 62

This Convention shall enter into force on the first day of the   **34.11**
third month following the deposit of the instrument of ratifica-
tion by the last signatory State to take this step.*

C. ARTICLE 62: ENTRY INTO FORCE

The 1968 Convention entered into force as between the original six   **34.12**
Contracting States on February 1, 1973 and the 1971 Protocol on
Interpretation came into force between those states on September
1, 1975.[18] Article 39 of the 1978 Convention[18a] regulates the entry
into force of that Convention and hence of the amendments to the
1968 Convention and 1971 Protocol on Interpretation. In their
amended versions, the 1968 Convention and 1971 Protocol came
into force on November 1, 1986 in Belgium, Denmark, France,
Germany, Italy, Luxembourg and the Netherlands; on January 1,
1987 in the United Kingdom; and on June 1, 1988 in Ireland.
   The 1982 Convention, by which Greece accedes to the amended
versions of the 1968 Convention and 1971 Protocol, is to come into
force in accordance with Article 15 of that Convention,[19] which
makes further amendments to both.
   The transitional provisions are discussed under Article 54,[20]

---

* Kropholler, pp. 368–369; Dashwood/Halcon/White, p. 202; Kaye, p. 227.
[15] Para. 36.20 below.
[16] Para. 37.17 below.
[17] Para. 38.07 below.
* Kaye, p. 227; Droz, paras. 13–14; Weser, para. 355; Kropholler, p. 369;
Pocar, pp. 396–397.
[18] Art. 8 of that Protocol regulates its entry into force: para. 36.21 below.
[18a] Para. 37.18 below.
[19] Para. 38.08 below.
[20] Para. 32.01 below.

under Articles 34 to 36 of the 1978 Convention,[21] and under Article 12 of the 1982 Convention.[22]

Article 63

34.13   **The Contracting States recognise that any State which becomes a member of the European Economic Community shall be required to accept this Convention as a basis for the negotiations between the Contracting States and that State necessary to ensure the implementation of the last paragraph of Article 220 of the Treaty establishing the European Economic Community.**

   The necessary adjustments may be the subject of a special convention between the Contracting States of the one part and the new Member State of the other part.*

D. ARTICLE 63: NEW MEMBER STATES

34.14   The negotiations which culminated in the 1978 Convention were carried out pursuant to the terms of Article 220 of the EEC Treaty and Article 3(2) of the Act of Accession, in a manner foreseen by this Article. They are discussed in the Schlosser Report.[23] The 1978 and 1982 Conventions have been concluded as "special" conventions within the meaning of the second paragraph of Article 63.

Article 64

34.15   **The Secretary-General of the Council of the European Communities shall notify the signatory States of:**

   (a) the deposit of each instrument of ratification;
   (b) the date of entry into force of this Convention;
   (c) any declaration received pursuant to Article 60;
   (d) any declaration received pursuant to Article IV of the Protocol;
   (e) any communication made pursuant to Article VI of the Protocol.*†

---

[21] Paras. 37.06 to 37.14 below.
[22] Para. 38.04 below.
 * Jenard, para. A1.261 below; Collins, pp. 1–2; Dashwood/Halcon/White, pp. 202–203; Kaye, pp. 9, 13; Droz, para. 25; Weser, para. 356; Kropholler, pp. 369–370; Pocar, pp. 397–398.
[23] The Schlosser Report is reproduced in App. 1, at paras. A1.287 *et seq.* below.
 † Sub-para. (c) was substituted for the 1968 version by Art. 28 of the 1978 Convention.
 * Kaye, p. 269.

E. ARTICLE 64: NOTIFICATIONS TO CONTRACTING STATES

This Article corresponds with Article 10 of the 1971 Protocol,[24] with Article 40 of the 1978 Convention[25] and with Article 16 of the 1982 Convention.[26] It is self-explanatory and requires no further commentary.

Article 65

The Protocol annexed to this Convention by common   34.16 accord of the Contracting States shall form an integral part thereof.*

F. ARTICLE 65: ANNEXED PROTOCOL

This Article is self-explanatory. The Protocol referred to is the 1968 Protocol.[27]

Article 66

This Convention is concluded for an unlimited period.*   34.17

G. ARTICLE 66: DURATION

This Article corresponds with Article 12 of the 1971 Protocol.[28] It is self-explanatory and requires no particular commentary.

Article 67

Any Contracting State may request the revision of this   34.18 Convention. In this event, a revision conference shall be convened by the President of the Council of the European Communities.*

H. ARTICLE 67: REVISION OF THE CONVENTION

This Article corresponds with Article 13 of the 1971 Protocol.[29] It is self-explanatory and requires no particular commentary.

---

[24] Para. 36.23 below.
[25] Para. 37.20 below.
[26] Para. 38.10 below.
* Kropholler, p. 370.
[27] Chap. 35 below.
* Dashwood/Halcon/White, pp. 203–204.
[28] Para. 36.25 below.
* Pocar, p. 399.
[29] Para. 36.26 below.

Article 68

34.19   This Convention, drawn up in a single original in the Dutch, French, German and Italian languages, all four texts being equally authentic, shall be deposited in the archives of the Secretariat of the Council of the European Communities. The Secretary-General shall transmit a certified copy to the Government of each signatory State.*

I. ARTICLE 68: AUTHENTIC LANGUAGE VERSIONS

34.20   By the second paragraph of Article 37 of the 1978 Convention, the Danish, English and Irish language texts of the 1968 Convention and 1971 Protocol "shall be authentic under the same conditions as the original texts." By Article 41 of the 1978 convention, the Danish, Dutch, English, French, German, Irish and Italian language versions of that Convention are equally authentic. It follows that, now the 1978 Convention is in force, all seven language versions are equally authentic. So, for example, once the amended version of the Convention came into force in the six original Contracting States and Denmark on November 1, 1986, the English and Irish versions became authentic in addition to the other language versions, even though the Convention did not then enter into force in the United Kingdom or Ireland.

Similar provisions are made in relation to the Greek language by Articles 13 and 17 of the 1982 Convention.[30]

The consequences of several language versions of the Convention being equally authentic have already been discussed.[31]

---

* Collins, p. 9; Dashwood/Halcon/White, p. 205; Kaye, pp. 1699–1700; Maxwell, para. 11.3; Kropholler, p. 371; Pocar, pp. 399–400.
[30] Paras. 38.06 and 38.11 below.
[31] Para. 13.29 above.

1968 ANNEXED PROTOCOL AND JOINT DECLARATION

PROTOCOL

The High Contracting Parties have agreed upon the following provisions, which shall be annexed to the Convention: 35.01

Article I

Any person domiciled in Luxembourg who is sued in a court of another Contracting State pursuant to Article 5(1) may refuse to submit to the jurisdiction of that court. If the defendant does not enter an appearance the court shall declare of its own motion that it has no jurisdiction.

An agreement conferring jurisdiction, within the meaning of Article 17, shall be valid with respect to a person domiciled in Luxembourg only if that person has expressly and specifically so agreed.*

---

* Jenard, para. A1.262 below; Collins, pp. 52, 87; Dashwood/Halcon/White, pp. 95, 130; Hartley, pp. 74–75; Kaye, pp. 524–527; Maxwell, para. 12.2; Anton, paras. 5.23, 7.26(13); Droz, para. 219; Weser, paras. 223–223*ter*;

A. ARTICLE I: LUXEMBOURG DOMICILIARIES

1. General note

35.02   This Protocol, referred to in this work as the 1968 Protocol, forms an integral part of the 1968 Convention.[1]

Article I of the Protocol is designed to take account of the fact that, because the preponderance of contractual obligations entered into between domiciliaries of Luxembourg and of Belgium are to be performed in Belgium, the operation of Articles 5(1) and 17 would otherwise weigh unduly in favour of Belgium.[2] If the court of another Contracting State accepts jurisdiction contrary to this Article, the judgment must be recognised and enforced in the other Contracting States,[3] under the compulsory terms of Title III. This is because Article 28[4] admits of no exceptions other than those specified in its prohibition of reviewing the jurisdiction of the court of origin.

2. First paragraph: Rights of persons domiciled in Luxembourg

35.03   Were it not for this provision, a person domiciled in Luxembourg who was sued under Article 5(1)[5] in the courts of another Contracting State for the place of performance of the contractual obligation in question and who failed to enter an appearance in those proceedings would normally be liable to have a default judgment entered against him in accordance with Article 20. This provision protects him from such a judgment if the jurisdiction of the court of the other Contracting State is founded on Article 5(1).[6] It will not protect him if jurisdiction is founded on some other provision of the Convention instead of or in addition to Article 5(1), or if he submits to the jurisdiction,[7] although a submission to the juris-

---

Bülow/Böckstiegel/Linke, p. 63; Bülow/Böckstiegel/Müller, p. 153; Geimer/Schütze, pp. 334, 601–602, 944; Kropholler, p. 74; Gothot/Holleaux, paras. 54, 171; Pocar, pp. 401–405.

[1] Art. 65 of the Convention, para. 34.16 above.
[2] Jenard, para. A1.262 below.
[3] Bülow/Böckstiegel/Linke, p. 63.
[4] Paras. 27.62 above.
[5] Para. 17.02 above.
[6] *AGIP S.p.a.* v. *British Petroleum Company Limited and others*, Riv.dir.int.priv. proc. 1979, p. 96, Digest D I–5.3—B6; *Oving-Diepeveen-Stuycken N.V.* v. *Berliner Frachtschiffahrt Schiller & Köpke, Trauschiffahrt & Co. K.G. and others*, Ned.Jur. 1983, No. 710, Digest D I–17.1.1—B18.
[7] Art. 18, para. 21.83 above.

diction by way of a choice-of-jurisdiction agreement must comply with Article 17 and with the second paragraph of this Article.[8]

3. Second paragraph: Requirement of express agreement

The second paragraph of Article I of the Protocol imposes stricter requirements for a choice-of-jurisdiction clause to be effective under Article 17[9] against a person domiciled in Luxembourg, than against a person domiciled elsewhere. The effect of this provision and the decision of the European Court on its application[10] are discussed under Article 17.[11] **35.04**

Article II

Without prejudice to any more favourable provisions of national laws, persons domiciled in a Contracting State who are being prosecuted in the criminal courts of another Contracting State of which they are not nationals for an offence which was not intentionally committed may be defended by persons qualified to do so, even if they do not appear in person. **35.05**

However, the court seised of the matter may order appearance in person; in the case of failure to appear, a judgment given in the civil action without the person concerned having had the opportunity to arrange for his defence need not be recognised or enforced in the other Contracting States.*

B. Article II: Non-Appearance in Criminal Proceedings

1. General note

If a court has criminal jurisdiction in respect of a particular act over a defendant domiciled in another Contracting State, it also has civil jurisdiction[12] over him in respect of a claim for damages or restitution arising out of the same act, to the extent permitted by its **35.06**

---

[8] A choice of place of performance clause has been held to amount to a submission to the jurisdiction of the court for that place: *Bastin* v. *Cogenal*, Belgische Rechtspraak in Handelszaken 1980, p. 583 Digest D II–1–B1. It is submitted that the correctness of this decision is doubtful.
[9] Para. 21.01 above.
[10] *Porta-Leasing GmbH* v. *Prestige International S.A.* [1980] E.C.R. 1517.
[11] See para. 21.69 above.
* Jenard, paras. A1.38, A1.263 below; Collins, pp. 22, 61; Dashwood/Halcon/White, pp. 97, 210–212; Hartley, p. 53n; Kaye, pp. 1538–1550; Maxwell, paras. 12.3–12.6; Anton, para. 8.25; Droz, paras. 539–541; Geimer/Schütze, pp. 837–843; Kropholler, pp. 94–96; Gothot/Holleaux, paras. 92, 151; Pocar, p. 406.
[12] Art. 5(4), para. 17.53 above.

own law. The subject-matter of the claim must of course fall within the Convention. But it is not only where a single court exercises criminal and civil jurisdiction simultaneously that a defendant's civil interests may be affected by criminal proceedings against him. In some Contracting States, a judgment in the criminal proceedings is regarded as conclusive in subsequent civil proceedings.[13] In others, it may have substantial evidential effect.[14] A defendant may therefore be prejudiced, perhaps irretrievably, in the defence of his civil interests if he is not able to arrange for his defence at his criminal trial.

The purpose of Article II of the 1968 Protocol, therefore, is to enable a person to defend his civil law rights without submitting personally to the criminal jurisdiction of the court.[15] For the protection to apply, the defendant must not be domiciled in, nor a national of, the state of the criminal court, he must be domiciled in another Contracting State, and the offence must not have been "intentionally committed." Also, the defendant's civil interests must be capable of being affected by the decision in the criminal proceedings.[16] In those circumstances, Article II provides a minimum standard[17] of protection for the defendant by allowing him to be represented in his absence.

If the court orders the defendant to appear in person, and he fails to do so, and if he does not have an opportunity to arrange for his defence, the second paragraph of Article II provides that the judgment in the civil action need not be recognised or enforced in other Contracting States. Although the right to be defended without appearing in person, granted by the first paragraph, applies to cases where the defendant's civil law rights are jeopardised in the criminal proceedings, that right does not affect the power of the criminal court to require the personal attendance of the defendant.

2. " . . . an offence which was not intentionally committed . . . "

35.07   These words are qualified by the words "persons . . . who are being prosecuted. . . . " It would seem, therefore, that the application of Article II of the Protocol depends on the offence for which the defendant was being prosecuted, rather than by retrospective reference to the offence (if any) of which he was convicted. The

---

[13] This is the case, for example, under French, Belgian and Luxembourg law.
[14] In England, see, for example, the Civil Evidence Act 1968, s.11; but *cf. McIlkenny and others* v. *Chief Constable of West Midlands* [1980] Q.B. 283, C.A.
[15] Jenard, paras. A1.38, A1.263 below.
[16] *Rinkau*, discussed below.
[17] "Without prejudice to any more favourable provisions of national laws . . . "

interpretation of the words "an offence which was not intentionally committed" arose in the case of *Rinkau*,[18] referred to the European Court by the *Hoge Raad* of the Netherlands.

The Rinkau case. Rinkau, who was domiciled in Germany, had   **35.08**
been summoned before a Dutch court accused of an offence of driving in the Netherlands a vehicle equipped with a radio transmitter, not having the requisite licence. His advocate was given leave to defend him in his absence and he was convicted. He was sentenced to pay a fine or one day's imprisonment in default and the transmitter was ordered to be confiscated. On appeal by the prosecutor, the Regional Court of Appeal ruled that the offence was not one "not intentionally committed" and that Rinkau should not have been defended by his advocate in his absence, but upheld the decision on the substance.

Rinkau appealed to the *Hoge Raad*, which referred two questions to the European Court, the first of which was:

> "Must the expression 'an offence which was not intentionally committed' . . . be understood as including any offence for which the legal definition does not require specific intent in regard to any element of the offence, or should the expression be understood in a narrower sense as relating only to offences in the definition of which there is reference to some element of guilt (*culpa*) on the part of the offender?"[19]

The European Court, having considered what a rule of criminal procedure was doing in the Convention at all, went on to draw attention to the provenance of the provision in the Benelux Treaty and to the reference in the Jenard Report to the inclusion of "road accidents" within the concept of offences not intentionally committed.[20] It decided that the concept should be given a uniform interpretation, especially in view of terminological differences between the different language versions.

The Court noted that offences which were not intentionally com   **35.09**
mitted were generally less serious in nature and that they covered "most offences connected with road accidents which are to be ascribed to carelessness, negligence or the mere actual breach of a legal provision." It went on to rule that:

> "The expression 'an offence which was not intentionally committed' within the meaning of Article II . . . should be understood as meaning any offence the legal definition of which does not require, either expressly or as appears from the nature of the offence defined,

---

[18] *Criminal proceedings against Siegfried Ewald Rinkau* [1981] E.C.R. 1391.
[19] *Ibid.*, at p. 1398.
[20] Jenard, para. A1.263 below.

the existence of intent on the part of the accused to commit the punishable act or omission."[21]

3. Jeopardy of civil law rights

35.10   While Article II of the Protocol is a minimum rule of criminal procedure, it arises in the context of a Convention on civil and commercial matters. The question therefore arises whether it applies to all criminal proceedings. The second question addressed to the European Court of Justice in *Rinkau* concerned this point:

> "If the conditions set out in Article II of the said Protocol are fulfilled, does the right granted to 'the accused' by that article apply without restriction, or does the accused person have that right only where he has to defend himself against a civil claim made in the relevant criminal proceedings, or at any rate where the interests of the accused under civil law are affected by the outcome of the civil proceedings?"[22]

The Court's reasoning leaves the question less than clearly answered:

> "Although it is not expressly provided by the first paragraph of Article II of the Protocol that the right therein granted to the accused applies only during criminal proceedings in which his liability at civil law (arising from the elements of the offence for which he is being prosecuted) is in question or on which such liability might subsequently be based, it should nevertheless not be forgotten that that was the actual intention behind the insertion in the Protocol of the provision in question. That intention precludes the right to be defended without appearing in person from having application in criminal proceedings in which the accused is not open to a civil claim in the circumstances described above.
>
> The answer to the second question . . . should therefore be that the accused's right to be defended without appearing in person, granted by Article II of the Protocol . . . , applies in all criminal proceedings concerning offences which were not intentionally committed, in which the accused's liability at civil law, arising from the elements of the offence for which he is being prosecuted, is in question or on which such liability might subsequently be based."[23]

35.11   It seems, therefore, from the reasoning and the ruling of the European Court on the second question in *Rinkau*, that if some or

---

[21] [1981] E.C.R. 1391, at p. 1403.
[22] *Ibid.*, at p. 1398.
[23] *Ibid.*, at pp. 1402–1403.

all of the elements of the criminal offence are capable of giving rise to civil liability (and provided the other conditions are fulfilled), the first paragraph of Article II applies to afford protection to the defendant. This is almost certainly the case where the elements of the civil liability are entirely encompassed in the criminal liability, even if they are less extensive; but whether the same applies where the elements of the civil liability differ from, but overlap with those of the criminal liability is less clear. If the overlap is substantial the protection probably applies. Taking an example from English law, an offence of driving without due care and attention requires an element of carelessness,[24] but not an element of (legal) proximity to a given victim, nor of damage. It is nonetheless an offence such as the European Court clearly envisaged.

4. Second paragraph: Judgments given in the absence of the defendant

The second paragraph of Article II of the Protocol provides one **35.12** of the instances in which a judgment may be refused recognition on a ground other than those referred to in Articles 27 and 28.[25] The provision is not straightforward. In its reasoning in *Rinkau*, the European Court referred in passing to the provisions in the second paragraph:

> "It is necessary to stress once more that, as Article II expressly provides, the right granted to the accused person to be defended without appearing in person does not prejudice the court's power to order appearance in person. If, notwithstanding such an order, the accused person does not appear, the court may deliver judgment without granting the accused's Counsel leave to defend him. The result of the absence of a defence, according to the second paragraph of Article II of the Protocol, is that a judgment given in the civil action need not be recognized and enforced in the other contracting States."[26]

This passage does not seem to have taken into account the case where a civil action is separate from, and subsequent to, the criminal proceedings. Indeed the words "without the person concerned having had the opportunity to arrange for his defence" do not address the question whether it is the accused person's defence at civil law or at criminal law which is envisaged. Equally, it is not clear whether the provision applies where the civil law judgment

---

[24] Road Traffic Act 1972, s.3.
[25] See paras. 25.12 to 25.13 above. *Cf.* Droz, paras. 540–541.
[26] [1981] E.C.R. 1391, at p. 1400 (para. 9).

has been given by a court other than that which exercised criminal jurisdiction.

35.13   Logically, whenever the defendant has been prejudiced in the defence of his civil law rights by his reluctance to appear personally before a criminal court and the court's refusal to allow him to be defended in his absence by a representative, the civil law judgment delivered then or subsequently, which has or might have resulted wholly or partly by reason of that prejudice, should be capable of being denied recognition and enforcement.[27] It is not clear, though, that that is what is actually provided by the second paragraph, which refers to the accused's opportunity to arrange for his defence, rather than to prejudice. If he had an opportunity to arrange for his defence, but chose to ignore it in the interests of not submitting to the criminal jurisdiction, the case would seem to be within the intention of the provision, but outside its wording. It remains to be seen how these various problems will be resolved.

Article III

35.14   **In proceedings for the issue of an order for enforcement, no charge, duty or fee calculated by reference to the value of the matter in issue may be levied in the State in which enforcement is sought.**[*]

C. ARTICLE III: NO SCALE FEES FOR ENFORCEMENT

35.15   Before the 1968 Convention came into force, the fees payable in some states for the issue of an order of enforcement were fixed, and in others were calculated by reference to the value of the judgment. This difference was regarded by the negotiators as distortive and Article III of the Protocol was accordingly included to prohibit fees calculated by reference to the value of the claim.[28]

The proceedings covered by Article III are those brought in the state addressed under Articles 31 *et seq.* for an order of enforcement. Although it does not do so expressly, the provision almost certainly also applies by analogy to proceedings brought under the second paragraph of Article 26 for a declaration of recognition. Article III applies only to court fees and not to lawyers' fees.[29]

---

[27] Landgericht Berlin, case 24 O 191/73, February 4, 1976, Digest D II–2—B1.
[*] Jenard, para. A1.264 below; Maxwell, para. 12.7; Anton, para. 8.31; Geimer/ Schütze, p. 1151; Gothot/Holleaux, paras. 348, 372; Pocar, p. 406.
[28] Jenard, para. A1.264 below.
[29] *Ibid.*; Geimer/Schütze, p. 1151.

Articles 44 and 45 contain provisions relating, respectively, to **35.16** legal aid and security for costs in enforcement proceedings.[30] The Convention does not contain a requirement that the rules on the costs of proceedings for an order of enforcement should be approximated, but it is one of the Convention's aims that formalities should be simplified in this area. A prohibitive level of court fees for enforcement proceedings would run counter to the Convention's purpose of easing the free movement of judgments. The European Court of Justice has commented on this aspect of the matter in *De Wolf* v. *Cox*.[31] Having discussed the reasons for deciding that a judgment on a given cause of action precluded a fresh action on the same cause of action in another Contracting State, the Court stated:

> "The fact that there may be occasions on which, according to the national law applicable, the procedure set out in Articles 31 *et seq.* of the Convention may be found to be more expensive than bringing fresh proceedings on the substance of the case does not invalidate these considerations.
> In this respect, it must be observed that the Convention, which, in the words of the preamble thereto, is intended 'to secure the simplification of formalities governing the reciprocal recognition and enforcement of judgments of courts or tribunals,' ought to induce the Contracting States to ensure that the costs of the procedure described in the Convention are fixed so as to accord with that concern for simplification."[32]

Article IV

Judicial and extrajudicial documents drawn up in one Contracting State which have to be served on persons in another Contracting State shall be transmitted in accordance with the procedures laid down in the conventions and agreements concluded between the Contracting States.   **35.17**

Unless the State in which service is to take place objects by declaration to the Secretary-General of the Council of the European Communities, such documents may also be sent by the appropriate public officers of the State in which the document has been drawn up directly to the appropriate public officers of the State in which the addressee is to be found. In this case the officer of the State of origin shall send a copy of the document to the officer of the State addressed who is competent to forward it to the addressee. The document shall be forwarded in the manner specified by the law of the State addressed. The forwarding

---

[30] Paras. 28.81 and 28.85 above.
[31] [1976] E.C.R. 1759, discussed at para. 25.36 above.
[32] *Ibid.*, at p. 1468 (paras. 14–15).

shall be recorded by a certificate sent directly to the officer of the State of origin.*

D. ARTICLE IV: SERVICE OF DOCUMENTS

35.18 Article IV of the 1968 Protocol is concerned with the service abroad of judicial and extrajudicial documents.[33] The first paragraph does not affect the methods of service envisaged by the national laws of the Contracting States and by the various bilateral and multilateral conventions on the topic to which the Contracting States are parties.[34] It merely confirms that those conventions are to have effect in the context of the 1968 Convention.[35] On one reading of this paragraph, it might appear to be mandatory in requiring the procedures actually laid down in those conventions to be followed. It is submitted, though, that that reading would be too narrow. Those other conventions themselves permit certain methods of service to be used which are recognised by national laws but which are not set out in detail in the conventions. Service may therefore be effected "in accordance with" those conventions, even if not pursuant to the procedures established by them. This paragraph is certainly not intended to make invalid service which those other conventions would regard as having been validly effected.[36]

---

* Jenard, paras. A1.178–A1.179; Collins, p. 95; Dashwood/Halcon/White, pp. 212–213; Hartley, p. 81; Kaye, pp. 1285–1287; Maxwell, para. 12.8; Anton, para. 7.31; Geimer/Schütze, pp. 1094–1095; Kropholler, pp. 212–214; Gothot/Holleaux, para. 214; Pocar, pp. 407–409.

[33] The question of service generally is discussed in the context of English law in chap. 4 above. Extrajudicial documents are described in the *Practical Handbook on the Operation of the Hague Convention of November 15, 1965 on the Service Abroad of Judicial and Extrajudicial Documents in Civil or Commercial Matters* (Hague Conference on Private International Law, 1983), p. 43: "Extrajudicial documents differ from judicial documents in that they are not directly connected with lawsuits, and they are distinguished from purely private acts by the fact that they require the intervention of an "authority" or of a "judicial officer" under the terms of the [Hague] Convention. Examples given were demands for payment, notices to quit in connection with leaseholds, and protests in connection with bills of exchange, but all on condition that they emanate from an authority or from a process server. There was also mention made of instruments such as objections to marriage, consent to adoption, etc. which required certain formalities." The passage goes on to note that such documents are served in England by private persons.

[34] The United Kingdom has bilateral conventions with all the Contracting States except Ireland and Luxembourg. Its multilateral conventions are referred to below. See further paras. 4.30 to 4.50 above and A2.01 below.

[35] Service of originating process is required by Art. 20 (para. 22.11 above) and proof of service of a judgment is required by Art. 47(1) (para. 29.07 above).

[36] The purpose of this Article, is discussed in the Jenard Report (para. A1.179 below).

The principal multilateral conventions are the Hague Conven-   **35.19**
tions of March 1, 1954 on civil procedure (to which all the Contracting States except the United Kingdom and Ireland are parties) and
of November 15, 1965 on service abroad of judicial and extrajudicial documents in civil or commercial matters[37] (to which all the
Contracting States except Ireland are parties).[38] The 1965 Convention replaces those provisions of the 1954 Convention which deal
with service when Contracting States are parties to both conventions.[39] The 1965 Convention is anyway brought partly within the
scheme of the Convention by Article 20,[40] where its provisions as to
service are applied for the purposes of determining whether a
default judgment may be entered or whether proceedings must be
stayed.

The second paragraph of Article IV provides an additional means
for the transmission abroad of judicial and extrajudicial documents.[41] Contracting States are free to declare that service may not
take place within their territory by this method. Only Germany has
done so, and this paragraph therefore applies in all the other Contracting States. The system permits the direct transmission of documents between the "appropriate public officers" of the state of
origin and their counterparts in the state of service.[42] Who those
officers are and the methods of service permitted by the laws of each
of the Contracting States are summarised in Chapters 48 to 58.[43]

Article V

The jurisdiction specified in Article 6(2) and Article 10 in   **35.20**
actions on a warranty or guarantee or in any other third party
proceedings may not be resorted to in the Federal Republic of
Germany. In that State, any person domiciled in another Con-
tracting State may be sued in the courts in pursuance of Articles
68, 72, 73 and 74 of the code of civil procedure (*Zivilprozessord-*
***nung*) concerning third-party notices.**

Judgments given in the other Contracting States by virtue of
Article 6(2) or Article 10 shall be recognised and enforced in the
Federal Republic of Germany in accordance with Title III. Any

---

[37] Cmnd. 3986. The text is set out at paras. A2.03 *et seq.* below.
[38] This includes Greece.
[39] Art. 22 of the 1965 Convention, para. A2.13 below.
[40] Para. 22.11 above.
[41] As regards Ireland, this is the only method of service regulated by international
agreement, although the national law of the Contracting States may recognise
service in Ireland by other methods.
[42] Jenard, para. A1.179 below.
[43] Official process servers are described in chaps. 48, 50, 54, 55 and 58, below, at
para. 13. Methods of service are described in chaps. 48 to 58, at para. 38.

effects which judgments given in that State may have on third parties by application of Articles 68, 72, 73 and 74 of the code of civil procedure (*Zivilprozessordnung*) shall also be recognised in the other Contracting States.*

E. ARTICLE V: THIRD PARTY PROCEEDINGS IN GERMANY

35.21   The means of making a claim against a third party pursuant to German law differs from that provided by the laws of the other Contracting States. The wording of the second paragraph of Article 6[44] and of Article 10[45] of the 1968 Convention is not apt to cover the German procedure and Article V of the Protocol therefore equates the procedure under the German *Zivilprozessordnung* with the jurisdiction under those Articles. The German procedure is described in the Jenard Report[46] and summarised in Chapter 51.[47]

Article Va

35.22   **In matters relating to maintenance, the expression "court" includes the Danish administrative authorities.***†

F. ARTICLE VA: DANISH MAINTENANCE PROCEEDINGS

35.23   In Denmark, liability to pay maintenance is determined by agreement or by a court order, but the amount of maintenance is determined (and may be varied) by the order of an administrative authority—the *Amtmand*—exercising judicial functions.[48] To exclude such orders from the scope of the Convention would have created an imbalance and Article Va of the Protocol therefore equates the position of the Danish administrative authorities in this context with that of the courts.

Article Va applies in relation to maintenance wherever the

---

* Jenard, paras. A1.118–A1.123 below; Collins, p. 67n; Dashwood/Halcon/White, p. 213; Kaye, pp. 651, 813; Maxwell, para. 12.9; Anton, para. 7.31; Geimer/Schütze, pp. 390–391, 825; Kropholler, pp. 110–111; Gothot/Holleaux, para. 113; Pocar, pp. 409–410.

[44] Art. 6(2), provides for a general jurisdiction over third-party proceedings in the court seised of the original proceedings: para. 17.82 above.

[45] Art. 10 provides jurisdiction over third-party proceedings against liability insurers in the court where the injured party has sued the insured: para. 18.32 above.

[46] Jenard, paras. A1.118–A1.119 below.

[47] Para. 51.35 below.

* Schlosser, paras. 67–68 (paras. A1.353–A1.354 below); Hartley, p. 84n; Kaye, p. 209; Collins, p. 105n; Maxwell, para. 12.10; Anton, para. 8.05(2); Geimer/Schütze, p. 183; Gothot/Holleaux, para. 229.

† Art. Va of the Protocol was added by Art. 29 of the 1978 Convention. In the French, Italian and Dutch texts it is called Article "V bis."

[48] See para. 49.18 below.

expression "court" is used in the Convention. Two provisions require particular mention. First, the consequence of Article Va is that an order made in a matter relating to maintenance by the Danish administrative authorities is a judgment for the purposes of the Convention, because Article Va of the Protocol applies to Article 25 of the Convention.[49] Secondly, as against a defendant not domiciled in a Contracting State, the jurisdiction of the courts of each state is, pursuant to the first paragraph of Article 4,[50] determined by the law of that state. Here, too, Article Va applies, so that the jurisdiction of the Danish administrative authorities in matters relating to maintenance is determined by Danish law. This is so despite the fact that the French, Italian and Dutch texts do not use the expression "court" in the first paragraph of Article 4.[51]

Article Vb

In proceedings involving a dispute between the master and a member of the crew of a sea-going ship registered in Denmark, [in Greece] or in Ireland, concerning remuneration or other conditions of service, a court in a Contracting State shall establish whether the diplomatic or consular officer responsible for the ship has been notified of the dispute. It shall stay the proceedings so long as he has not been notified. It shall of its own motion decline jurisdiction if the officer, having been duly notified, has exercised the powers accorded to him in the matter by a consular convention, or in the absence of such a convention, has, within the time allowed, raised any objection to the exercise of such jurisdiction.* † 35.24

G. ARTICLE VB: MERCHANT MARINERS ON DANISH OR IRISH SHIPS

There is a long-standing Danish practice that a dispute between a crew-member and the master of a Danish ship is to be adjudicated upon only by Danish courts. This is now part of Danish law and is 35.25

---

[49] See para. 26.01 above; Schlosser para. 68 (para. A1.354 below).
[50] Para. 16.15 above.
[51] Schlosser, *loc. cit.*
* Schlosser, para. 132 (para. A1.415 below); Collins, pp. 52–53; Kaye, pp. 1242–1243; Maxwell, paras. 12.11–12.11; Anton, para. 5.24; Geimer/ Schütze, p. 603.
† The words in square brackets were added by Art. 9 of the 1982 Convention and are not yet in force. See para. 13.05 above. Art. Vb of the Protocol was otherwise added by Art. 29 of the 1978 Convention. In the French, Italian and Dutch texts it is called Article "V ter."

recognised in various consular conventions.[52] Article Vb of the Protocol was included to enable Denmark to retain its capacity to claim exclusive jurisdiction in this field, and the provision was also extended to Ireland.[53] The provision is not reciprocal in operation and, in theory, it bound the courts of the Contracting States where the Convention is in force, even before the Convention came into force in Ireland.[54]

The operation of the provision is analogous with Article 20[55] in that the courts in other Contracting States must act of their own motion[56] to determine whether the relevant diplomatic or consular officer has been notified, to stay the proceedings until that has occurred and to decline jurisdiction in the event of that officer either exercising any powers which he may have in that behalf under a consular convention or raising "any objection" to the jurisdiction of the court of the other Contracting State.

35.26 It would seem to follow that the court may examine the question whether the case falls within the Article and, if it does, the court will be required in the absence of a consular convention to decline jurisdiction over the case if any objection is taken by the relevant consular or diplomatic official, without examining whether the objection is well-founded.

If a court accepts jurisdiction in breach of this Article, the courts of the other Contracting States (including, as the case may be, Denmark and Ireland) are required to recognise and enforce the judgment under the compulsory provisions of Title III. This is not one of the jurisdictions which is open to review under the first paragraph of Article 28.[57]

Article Vc

35.27 **Articles 52 and 53 of this Convention shall, when applied by Article 69(5) of the Convention for the European Patent for the Common market, signed at Luxembourg on 15 December 1975, to the provisions relating to "residence" in the English text of**

---

[52] Schlosser, para. 132 (para. A1.415 below). Similar provisions apply as a matter of English law in relation to other countries: see Consular Relations Act 1968, s.4; 10 *Halsbury's Statutes* (4th ed.) 573–574.

[53] It will also apply to Greece when the 1982 Convention comes into force.

[54] The same would have been true of Denmark, but for the fact that the amendment took effect on November 1, 1986, which was also the date on which it came into force in Denmark. It is not true of Greece, though, where the amendment only becomes part of the Protocol upon that country's accession.

[55] Para. 22.11 above.

[56] *Cf.* Paras. 22.06 to 22.08 and 22.15 above.

[57] Para. 27.62 above.

that Convention, operate as if "residence" in that text were the same as "domicile" in Articles 52 and 53.*†

H. ARTICLE Vc: EUROPEAN PATENTS CONVENTION: DOMICILE

This Article does not affect the interpretation or application of the 1968 Convention. It is included because the Convention for the European Patent for the Common Market uses the expression "residence" in its English text and refers to Articles 52 and 53 of the present Convention for the purposes of definition. This Article was therefore necessary for the purpose of removing the anomaly created by the fact that the English text of those Articles uses the expression "domicile," rather than "residence."   35.28

Article Vd

Without prejudice to the jurisdiction of the European Patent Office under the Convention on the Grant of European Patents, signed at Munich on 5 October 1973, the courts of each Contracting State shall have exclusive jurisdiction, regardless of domicile, in proceedings concerned with the registration or validity of any European patent granted for that State which is not a Community patent by virtue of the provisions of Article 86 of the Convention for the European Patent for the Common Market, signed at Luxembourg on 15 December 1975.*†   35.29

I. ARTICLE Vd: JURISDICTION OVER EUROPEAN PATENTS

It will be recalled that Article 16(4) of the 1968 Convention[58] gives exclusive jurisdiction in proceedings concerned with "the registration or validity of patents, trade marks, designs, or other similar rights required to be deposited or registered," to the courts of the Contracting State, "in which the deposit or registration has been applied for, has taken place or is under the terms of an international convention deemed to have taken place." Both the Munich Con-   35.30

---

* Schlosser, para. 73 (para. A1.360 below); Maxwell, para. 12.13; Anton, para. 7.21; Geimer/Schütze, p. 810.

† Art. Vc of the Protocol was added by Art. 29 of the 1978 Convention. In the French, Italian and Dutch texts it is called Art. "V quater."

* Schlosser, para. 173 (paras. A1.467–A1.468 below); Collins, p. 82; Kaye, pp. 199–200; Maxwell, para. 12.14; Anton, para. 7.21; Geimer/Schütze, pp. 802–803; Kropholler, p. 159; Gothot/Holleaux, para. 156.

† Art. Vd of the Protocol was added by Art. 29 of the 1978 Convention. In the French, Italian and Dutch texts it is called Art. "V quinquies."

[58] Para. 20.32 above.

vention on the grant of European patents and the Luxembourg Convention on the European patent for the Common Market contain special jurisdictional provisions which, by reason of Article 57,[59] take precedence over the Convention.

The jurisdictional provisions under those Conventions relate only to specific matters and it is possible that Article 16(4) would be read as requiring that an action in relation to a European patent under the Munich Convention must be brought in the courts of the state where it was applied for, rather than the Contracting State where it was valid or where it was challenged. Article Vd of the Protocol is designed to resolve that potential anomaly by assigning exclusive jurisdiction in such a case to the courts of the state where the patent has its validity.

The same rule would not apply in relation to a European patent under the Luxembourg Convention, because of the Community-wide validity of such a patent, but for an indeterminate transitional period patents under that Convention may be valid in more than one, but not necessarily in all, of the Community countries. For such patents (which are not "Community patents"), Article Vd provides that the state or states in which they are valid shall have exclusive jurisdiction in proceedings concerning their registration or validity. Conflicts of jurisdiction where more than one state has exclusive jurisdiction will normally be resolved by Article 23.[60]

Article VI

35.31 **The Contracting States shall communicate to the Secretary-General of the Council of the European Communities the text of any provisions of their laws which amend either those articles of their laws mentioned in the Convention or the lists of courts specified in Section 2 of Title III of the Convention.***

J. ARTICLE VI: AMENDMENTS TO NATIONAL LAW

Changes in national law referred to in the Convention obviously need to be notified to the other Contracting States. Article VI requires that the changes be notified to the Secretary-General of the Council and sub-paragraph (e) of Article 64 requires him to notify the Contracting States.

---

[59] Para. 33.06 above. These conventions are briefly described at paras. 20.36 and 20.37 above.
[60] Para. 23.24 above.
* Jenard, para. A1.267 below; Kaye, pp. 268–269; Pocar, p. 410.

JOINT DECLARATION

The Governments of the Kingdom of Belgium, the Federal 35.32
Republic of Germany, the French Republic, the Italian Repub-
lic, the Grand Duchy of Luxembourg and the Kingdom of the
Netherlands;
On signing the Convention on jurisdiction and the enforce-
ment of judgments in civil and commercial matters;
Desiring to ensure that the Convention is applied as effectively
as possible;
Anxious to prevent differences on interpretation of the Con-
vention from impairing its unifying effect;
Recognising that claims and disclaimers of jurisdiction may
arise in the application of the Convention;
Declare themselves ready:

1. to study these questions and in particular to examine
   the possibility of conferring jurisdiction in certain
   matters on the Court of Justice of the European Communities and, if necessary, to negotiate an agreement to
   this effect;
2. to arrange meetings at regular intervals between their
   representatives.*

K. Joint Declaration

This Joint Declaration does not form part of the Convention, but it
paved the way for the 1971 Protocol on Interpretation.[61] By acceding to the 1968 Convention, the new Contracting States accede also
to this declaration.[62]

---

* Jenard, *Protocols*, para. 1 (para. A1.270 below); Kaye, p. 1707; Schlosser,
  para. 248 (para. A1.558 below).
[61] Chap. 36 below.
[62] Schlosser, para. 248 (para. A1.558 below).

CHAPTER 36

1971 PROTOCOL ON INTERPRETATION AND JOINT DECLARATION

PROTOCOL

on the interpretation of the Convention of 27th September 1968 on jurisdiction and the enforcement of judgments in civil and commercial matters

36.01 **THE HIGH CONTRACTING PARTIES TO THE TREATY ESTABLISHING THE EUROPEAN ECONOMIC COMMUNITY,**

Having regard to the Declaration annexed to the Convention on jurisdiction and enforcement of judgments in civil and commercial matters, signed at Brussels on September 27, 1968,

Having decided to conclude a Protocol conferring jurisdiction on the Court of Justice of the European Communities to interpret that Convention, and to this end have designated . . . [etc.] . . .

HAVE AGREED AS FOLLOWS*:

---

* Jenard, *Protocols*, paras. 1–4, 8–9 (paras. A1.270–A1.271, A1.273–A1.275 below); Schlosser, para. 255 (para. A1.565 below); Collins, p. 11; Hartley, p. 102–104; Maxwell, paras. 12.16–12.28; Anton, para. 2.04–2.08; Droz, paras. 689–694; Weser, paras. 363–367; Geimer/Schütze, pp. 59–60; Gothot/ Holleaux, para. 5; Pocar, pp. 464–466.

A. 1971 PROTOCOL ON INTERPRETATION: PREAMBLE

The Convention applies to a very large number of cases in the   **36.02**
Contracting States[1] and its purpose of providing a uniform code of
jurisdictional rules and virtually automatic recognition and enforcement of judgments throughout the Community requires, if substantial divergences of application are to be avoided, an authoritative
means of determining the Convention's proper interpretation. This
need was identified in the Joint Declaration annexed to the 1968
Convention, and this Protocol confers on the European Court of
Justice the jurisdiction to rule on the interpretation of the Convention.

As the Jenard Report on the Protocols[2] observes, the most satisfactory way for the European Court of Justice to rule on the Convention's interpretation is by a system of preliminary rulings,
modelled on Article 177 of the EEC Treaty,[3] and accordingly, this
Protocol established such a system by Articles 2 and 3. However,
for reasons mentioned below,[4] it would be neither practical nor
desirable for the scheme to be as liberal as that provided by Article
177, and the courts which can request a preliminary ruling under
the 1971 Protocol are limited to those referred to in Article 2. An
additional means whereby the European Court can rule on the Convention's interpretation is provided by Article 4. Under that
Article, the "competent authority" of a Contracting State can ask
the Court for a consultative ruling.

Article 5 applies the relevant provisions of the EEC Treaty and
associated provisions to this Protocol. In practical terms, this means
that the European Court's case law and practice relating to references under Article 177 of the EEC Treaty apply equally to references under this Protocol, except to such extent as is necessary to ·
take account of the differences between the two sets of provisions.

Article 1

The Court of Justice of the European Communities shall have   **36.03**
jurisdiction to give rulings on the interpretation of the Conven-
tion on jurisdiction and the enforcement of judgments in civil and
commercial matters and of the Protocol annexed to that Conven-

---

[1] See Kohler, "The Case Law of the European Court on the Judgments Convention" (1982) 7 E.L.Rev., 3, at p. 4.
[2] (1979) O.J. C. 59, p. 66, reproduced at paras. A1.269 *et seq.* below.
[3] Jenard, *Protocols*, paras. A1.274–A1.275 below.
[4] Para. 36.06 below.

tion, signed at Brussels on 27 September 1968, and also on the interpretation of the present Protocol.

The Court of Justice of the European Communities shall also have jurisdiction to give rulings on the interpretation of the Convention on the Accession of the Kingdom of Denmark, Ireland and the United Kingdom of Great Britain and Northern Ireland to the Convention of 27 September 1968 and to this Protocol.

[The Court of Justice of the European Communities shall also have jurisdiction to give rulings on the interpretation of the Convention on the accession of the Hellenic Republic to the Convention of 27 September 1968 and to this Protocol, as adjusted by the 1978 Convention.]*†

B. ARTICLE 1: THE CONVENTIONS

36.04   Article 1 of this Protocol gives the European Court jurisdiction to interpret the 1968 Convention and its associated instruments, which it specifies. So far as the 1968 Convention is concerned, the Court has generally no jurisdiction to interpret any conventions other than those specified in this Article. It has said this expressly in the context of bilateral conventions,[5] but it is perhaps an open question whether it may interpret Article 15 of the Hague Convention of November 15, 1965 on the service abroad of judicial and extra-judicial documents in civil or commercial matters,[6] which is brought into the scheme of the 1968 Convention by the third paragraph of Article 20.[7] It seems clear that the European Court of Justice would not have jurisdiction to interpret national law,[8] even where it took the form of legislation derived from the Convention or intended to give effect to it.[9]

---

* Jenard, *Protocols*, para. 10 (para. A1.276 below); Schlosser, para. 255 (para. A1.565 below); Collins, p. 11; Dashwood/Halcon/White, pp. 54, 219–220; Hartley, p. 102; Kaye, pp. 1708–1711; Maxwell, paras. 12.16–12.19; Anton, paras. 2.04–2.08; Droz, paras. 692–694; Kropholler, pp. 24–25; Pocar, pp. 464–466.

† The first para. is the original 1968 version of this Art. The second para. was added by Art. 30 of the 1978 Convention and the third para. (in square brackets), which is not yet in force (see para. 13.05 above), was added by Art. 10 of the 1982 Convention.

[5] *Bavaria Fluggesellchaft Schwabe & Co. K.G. and Germanair Bedarfsluftfahrt GmbH & Co. K.G.* v. *Eurocontrol* [1977] E.C.R. 1517, at p. 1525 (para. 5). The case is discussed at paras. 14.12 and 33.04 above.

[6] Cmnd. 3986. The Hague Convention is set out at para. A2.03 *et seq.* below; Art. 15 is mentioned in the commentary on Art. 20 of the 1968 Convention, at paras. 22.21 *et seq.* above.

[7] Para. 22.11 above.

[8] Jenard, *Protocols*, paras. 6, 13 (paras. A1.272, A1.279 below).

[9] Schlosser, para. 256 (paras. A1.566–A1.567 below). As to the interpretation of Sched. 4 of the 1982 Act, which is modelled on Title II of the Convention, see s.16(3) of that Act, para. 41.01 below.

Article 2

The following courts may request the Court of Justice to give **36.05** preliminary rulings on questions of interpretation:

1.— in Belgium: la Cour de Cassation—het Hof van Cassatie and le Conseil d'Etat—de Raad van State,
— in Denmark: højesteret,
— in the Federal Republic of Germany: die obersten Gerichtshöfe des Bundes,
[— in Greece: the αγωτα τα δικαστήρια,]
— in France: la Cour de Cassation and le Conseil d'Etat,
— in Ireland: the Supreme Court,
— in Italy: la Corte Suprema di Cassazione,
— in Luxembourg: la Cour supérieure de Justice when sitting as Cour de Cassation,
— in the Netherlands: de Hoge Raad,
— in the United Kingdom: the House of Lords and courts to which application has been made under the second paragraph of Article 37 or under Article 41 of the Convention;
2. the courts of the Contracting States when they are sitting in an appellate capacity;
3. in the cases provided for in Article 37 of the Convention, the courts referred to in that Article.*†

C. ARTICLE 2: COURTS WHICH MAY REQUEST RULINGS

Article 2 lists the courts which may refer questions of interpretation **36.06** to the European Court of Justice under this Protocol. The circumstances in which such a court may or must make such a reference are dealt with in Article 3.

Courts of first instance are not included in this list and may not refer questions of interpretation to the European Court. Requests for interpretative rulings made by courts other than those listed in Article 2 have been ruled inadmissible.[10] The reason for their exclu-

---

* Jenard, *Protocols*, para. 11 (para. A1.277 below); Schlosser, para. 255 (para. A1.565 below); Collins, pp. 11–13; Dashwood/Halcon/White, pp. 54–55, 220–222; Hartley, pp. 102–104; Kaye, pp. 1711–1718; Maxwell, paras. 12.20–12.21; Anton, para. 2.07; Droz, paras. 697–702; Geimer/Schütze, p. 60; Kropholler, pp. 25–30; Pocar, pp. 466–467.
† The words in square brackets were added by Art. 11 of the 1982 Convention and are not yet in force. See para. 13.05 above. Art. 2(1) was otherwise substituted for the 1968 version by Art. 31 of the 1978 Convention.
[10] *Habourdin International SA and Banque Nationale de Paris* v. *S.p.A. Italcremona* [1983] E.C.R. 3639; *Von Gallera* v. *Maître*, [1984] E.C.R. 1769.

sion is to prevent frequent and trivial questions of interpretation being referred to the Court, possibly at the instance of a party who wishes to employ a delaying tactic.[11]

Article 37 of the 1968 Convention,[12] it will be recalled, covers appeals against decisions authorising enforcement of a judgment in the state addressed (but not decisions dismissing an application for an order of enforcement, which come within Article 40)[13] and further appeals from the decisions on those first appeals. The reference in the first paragraph of Article 2 in relation to the United Kingdom to the second paragraph of Article 37 and to Article 41 is made because, in those Articles, the United Kingdom courts are not identified by name. They are specified, though, in section 6 of the 1982 Act.[14]

36.07   *England and Wales.* In England and Wales, therefore, the courts which may refer questions of interpretation to the European Court under this Protocol are the House of Lords and the Court of Appeal and, when it is sitting in an appellate capacity, the High Court.[14a] Other courts (for example, the Employment Appeal Tribunal) sitting in an appellate capacity may also make such references.

Article 3

36.08   **1. Where a question of interpretation of the Convention or of one of the other instruments referred to in Article 1 is raised in a case pending before one of the courts listed in Article 2(1), that court shall, if it considers that a decision on the question is necessary to enable it to give judgment, request the Court of Justice to give a ruling thereon.**

2. Where such a question is raised before any court referred to in Article 2(2) or (3), that court may, under the conditions laid down in paragraph 1, request the Court of Justice to give a ruling thereon.*

---

[11] Jenard, *Protocols*, paras. 8(2), 11 (paras. A1.274, A1.277 below).
[12] Para. 28.38 above.
[13] Para. 28.63 above.
[14] Para. 40.18 below.
[14a] References by the Court of Appeal and the High Court are governed by R.S.C., Ord. 114; see *Supreme Court Practice*, paras. 114/1–6/1 *et seq.*, and the works cited at para. 36.09, n. 17 below.
* Jenard, *Protocols*, paras. 12–13 (paras. A1.278–A1.279 below); Schlosser, para. 255 (para. A1.565 below); Collins, p. 11; Dashwood/Halcon/White, pp. 56–57, 222–227; Hartley, pp. 102–104; Kaye, pp. 1718–1748; Maxwell, paras. 12.22–12.25; Anton, para. 2.08; Droz, paras. 703–706; Geimer/Schütze, p. 60, Kropholler, pp. 25–30; Pocar, pp. 467–472.

D. ARTICLE 3: MANDATORY OR DISCRETIONARY REFERENCES

1. General note

Article 3 determines the circumstances in which a national court **36.09**
is permitted to refer a question of interpretation to the European
Court of Justice and the circumstances in which it must do so. By
virtue of Article 5,[15] the European Court's case law and practice on
the application of Article 177 of the EEC Treaty applies to applications under this Protocol. The wording of Article 3 differs
slightly from that of Article 177 of the EEC Treaty, in that, even
where the case is pending before a national court of last instance,
the obligation to refer the question to the European Court is
expressed only to arise where the court considers that a decision on
the question is necessary to enable it to give judgment. The difference is of little or no practical consequence, because that is in any
event the accepted interpretation of Article 177.[16]

The approach adopted by the European Court on references from
national courts has been developed principally in the context of
Article 177 of the EEC Treaty and reference should be made to
standard works on European Community law and the practice of
the European Court of Justice for more detailed guidance on this
topic.[17] The most important points may be summarised briefly.

2. Preconditions for a reference

Certain conditions must be fulfilled before a question may be **36.10**
referred to the European Court of Justice under Article 3 of this
Protocol. If the conditions are fulfilled, only those courts mentioned in Article 2 may refer the question to the European Court.
The courts of last instance, referred to in Article 2(1), are required
to make a reference if the conditions are fulfilled, whereas the
courts referred to in paragraphs (2) and (3) of the Article have a discretion in the matter.[18]

The conditions to be fulfilled are that there must be a question of
"interpretation" raised in the proceedings pending before the
national court and, in the view of that court, a decision on the question is necessary to enable it to give judgment. It is not enough for
one party to assert that there is a question of "interpretation;" the
court must make its own judgment on the matter and the same
applies to the question whether the other conditions are met.

---

[15] Para. 36.16 below.
[16] Jenard, *Protocols*, para. 12 (para. A1.278 below).
[17] 51 *Halsbury's Laws* (4th ed.), para. 2–253; Lasok, *The European Court of Justice,*
Practice and Procedure (1984); Usher, *European Court Practice* (1983).
[18] Landgericht Aachen, case 5 S 339/75, October 24, 1975, N.J.W. 1976, p. 487,
Digest D I–16.1—B1.

As the European Court of Justice has made clear,[19] there is no obligation on a court of last instance to refer a question to the European Court for decision if:

(a) the question is irrelevant; or

(b) the question is substantially identical to a question which has already been the subject of a ruling by the European Court or where the settled case law of that Court resolves the issue; or

(c) the due application of Community law (or, here, the 1968 Convention) is so clear that no reasonable doubt remains as to the answer—the doctrine of *acte clair*;[20]

36.11   It is open to a national court to refer a matter to the European Court even if the second and third of those criteria are not met. The national court must always consider these matters in the light of the specific characteristics of the 1968 Convention, of the particular difficulties of interpretation of the Convention (such as equally authentic versions in different languages and its own particular terminology) and of the risks of divergent case law in different Contracting States.

Article 4

36.12   **1. The competent authority of a Contracting State may request the Court of Justice to give a ruling on a question of interpretation of the Convention or of one of the other instruments referred to in Article 1 if judgments given by courts of that State conflict with the interpretation given either by the Court of Justice or in a judgment of one of the courts of another Contracting State referred to in Article 2(1) or (2). The provisions of this paragraph shall apply only to judgments which have become *res judicata*.**

---

[19] *CILFIT* v. *Italian Minister of Health* [1982] E.C.R. 3415.

[20] National courts have sometimes declined to request a preliminary ruling on interpretation on the grounds that the question raised is one of *application* of the Convention, rather than of its *interpretation*: Bundesgerichtshof, case VIII ZB 10/79, September 26, 1979, Ent.BGH Zivilsachen, vol. 75, p. 167, N.J.W. 1980, p. 527, [1980] E.C.C. 207, Digest D I–27.3—B2; Oberlandesgericht Frankfurt-am-Main, case 21 U 58/79, November 28, 1979, Digest D I–5.1.1—B13; Bundesgerichtshof, case II ZR 198/80, October 26, 1981, Ent.BGH Zivilsachen, vol. 82, p. 110, RIW/AWD—1982, p. 361, Digest D I–5.1.1—B15. Similarly, the Italian Corte di Cassazione has held that for there to be a "question" of interpretation, there must be an "objective doubt and an issue capable of being resolved different ways, rather than mere speculation concerning the meaning of the terms of the question itself, to which there could clearly be only one answer": *Bianco* v. *Andreas Kufferath*, Guist.civ. 1980, I, p. 103, Digest D I–1.1—B6.

2. The interpretation given by the Court of Justice in response to such a request shall not affect the judgments which gave rise to the request for interpretation.

3. The Procurators-General of the Courts of Cassation of the Contracting States, or any other authority designated by a Contracting State, shall be entitled to request the Court of Justice for a ruling on interpretation in accordance with paragraph 1.

4. The Registrar of the Court of Justice shall give notice of the request to the Contracting States, to the Commission and to the Council of the European Communities; they shall be entitled within two months of the notification to submit statements of case or written observations to the Court.

5. No fees shall be levied or any costs or expenses awarded in respect of the proceedings provided for in this Article.*

E. ARTICLE 4: CONSULTATIVE RULINGS

Article 4 provides an additional means whereby questions of inter- **36.13** pretation of the Convention and its associated instruments may be referred to the European Court. Under this procedure, which is modelled on procedures such as the French *pourvoi dans l'intérêt de la loi*, the competent authority in each Contracting State may request the European Court to rule on questions of interpretation. The purpose of the provision is to prevent an erroneous interpretation of the Convention becoming perpetuated.[21] The procedure does not have a parallel in Article 177 of the EEC Treaty, but its inclusion in this Protocol may be explained by the fact that the application of the Convention by national courts will arise far more frequently than most other questions of Community law, and by the fact that not all national courts have a right under this Protocol to refer questions of interpretation to the European Court.

The circumstances in which the competent authority of a given Contracting State may make such a request are if judgments (or, presumably, a single judgment) of the courts of that state conflict with the judgment of the European Court of Justice itself or with the judgment of a court of another Contracting State,[22] provided that that other court is a court of last instance (referred to in Article 2(1)) or a court sitting in an appellate capacity (Article 2(2)).

---

* Jenard, *Protocols*, para. 14 (paras. A1.280–A1.284 below); Schlosser, para. 255 (para. A1.565 below); Collins, p. 12; Dashwood/Halcon/White, pp. 58, 227–229; Hartley, p. 4; Kaye, pp. 1763–1772; Maxwell, para. 12.26, 12.29; Anton, paras. 2.05, 2.07; Droz, paras. 712–718; Geimer/Schütze, p. 60; Kropholler, pp. 24–25; Pocar, pp. 472–474.
[21] Jenard, *Protocols*, para. 14 (para. A1.280 below).
[22] Droz, para. 713.

36.14   The procedure has apparently never been used but a number of observations may be made. Both the judgment given in the state whose competent authority refers the question of interpretation to the European Court of Justice and, where appropriate, the judgment with which it conflicts, of a specified court in the other Contracting State, must be *res judicata*.[23] In this context, "*res judicata*" means final and conclusive.[24] Although judgments containing inconsistent interpretations are necessary before a question may be referred to the European Court, the ruling does not affect the judgments themselves. This is the effect of Article 4(2), which emphasises the consultative nature of the European Court's ruling under this Article.

It does not seem though, that the judgments given by the courts of the referring state need have been the judgments of courts within Articles 2(1) and 2(2). It is to be left to the discretion of the competent authorities of that state not to refer a question of interpretation unless there is a danger of conflicting interpretations of the Convention being perpetrated. The danger of that happening is reduced in the case of decisions of lower courts both by their lesser authority and by the possibility of appeals from their decisions.

The competent authorities are probably not under any obligation to refer questions of interpretation to the European Court, even where the necessary conflicts of interpretation have arisen. The "conflict" need probably only be an inconsistency of interpretation, and it is probably not necessary for the two judgments to conflict in such a way as would have been avoided by the application of Articles 21 to 23—in other words, the parties and factual issues may be quite unrelated. Although Article 4(1) does not say so expressly, it is apparent that the question referred to the European Court must relate to the interpretation of the provision which has been the subject of a conflicting interpretation by the national court of the referring state.

36.15   It seems that the judgment given in the referring state need not post-date the judgment with which it conflicts. If, therefore, the interpretation of a given provision in the Convention has been decided upon by the courts of one Contracting State and a conflicting interpretation is then determined by one of the courts mentioned in Articles 2(1) or 2(2) in another Contracting state, it would be open to the competent authority in either state (and not just the latter state) to refer a question of interpretation to the European Court.

Article 4(3) provides a partial definition of the competent authority. There are Procurators-General of the Courts of Cassation in

---

[23] Art. 4(1).
[24] Para. 25.22 above.

most of the original Contracting States. In Germany, the competent authority is the Federal Advocate-General of the Federal Supreme Court.[25] In the United Kingdom, the Attorney-General and Lord Advocate are the closest equivalents to these officers and may be expected to be designated as the competent authority.[26]

Article 4(4) amends the application of Article 20 of the Protocol on the Statute of the Court of Justice of the EEC, to take account of the fact that there are no private parties to a reference under this Article. That fact also makes it possible to let the costs of the proceedings lie where they fall: Article 4(5).

Article 5

1. Except where this Protocol otherwise provides, the pro- 36.16 visions of the Treaty establishing the European Economic Community and those of the Protocol on the Statute of the Court of Justice annexed thereto, which are applicable when the Court is requested to give a preliminary ruling, shall also apply to any proceedings for the interpretation of the Convention and the other instruments referred to in Article 1.

2. The Rules of Procedure of the Court of Justice shall, if necessary, be adjusted and supplemented in accordance with Article 188 of the Treaty establishing the European Economic Community.*

F. Article 5: European Court of Justice

The effect of Article 5 is to extend the provisions otherwise govern- 36.17 ing the European Court of Justice to cover also references under this Protocol. As has been observed,[27] the case law and practice of the European Court on Article 177 of the EEC Treaty is particularly relevant and reference should be made to specialised works on the subject. The European Court has held that a Member State of the EEC may submit observations on references to the court made under this Protocol, even if the 1968 Convention and this Protocol are not in force in that Member State.[28]

---

[25] *Generalbundesanwalt beim Bundesgerichtshof*: Geimer/Schütze, p. 60.

[26] No designation of a competent authority has in fact been made by the United Kingdom under Art. 4(3).

* Jenard, *Protocols*, para. 15 (para. A1.285 below); Collins, p. 14; Dashwood/Halcon/White, pp. 230–232; Kaye, pp. 1741–1754; Maxwell, para. 12.27; Anton, para. 2.06; Droz, para. 707; Pocar, p. 474.

[27] Para. 36.09 above.

[28] *Industrie Tessili Italiana Como* v. *Dunlop A.G.* [1976] E.C.R. 1473, at p. 1484 (para. 8).

Article 6

36.18   This Protocol shall apply to the European territories of the Contracting States, including Greenland, to the French overseas departments, and to Mayotte.

The Kingdom of the Netherlands may declare at the time of signing or ratifying this Protocol or at any later time, by notifying the Secretary-General of the Council of the European Communities, that this Protocol shall be applicable to the Netherlands Antilles.

Notwithstanding the first paragraph, this Protocol shall not apply to:

1. the Faroe Islands, unless the Kingdom of Denmark makes a declaration to the contrary;
2. any European territory situated outside the United Kingdom for the international relations of which the United Kingdom is responsible, unless the United Kingdom makes a declaration to the contrary in respect of any such territory.

Such declarations may be made at any time by notifying the Secretary-General of the Council of the European Communities.*†

G. Article 6: Territorial Extent

36.19   This Article corresponds with Article 60 of the 1968 Convention, to which reference should be made. No further commentary is necessary.

Article 7

36.20   This Protocol shall be ratified by the signatory States. The instruments of ratification shall be deposited with the Secretary-General of the Council of the European Communities.

H. Article 7: Ratification

This Article corresponds with Article 61 of the 1968 Convention, with Article 38 of the 1978 Convention and with Article 14 of the 1982 Convention. It is self-explanatory and requires no further commentary.

---

* Dashwood/Halcon/White, pp. 233–234; Kropholler, p. 24.
† This Article was substituted for the 1968 version by Art. 32 of the 1978 Convention.

Article 8

This Protocol shall enter into force on the first day of the third   36.21
month following the deposit of the instrument of ratification by
the last signatory State to take this step; provided that it shall at
the earliest enter into force at the same time as the Convention of
27 September 1968 on jurisdiction and the enforcement of judgments in civil and commercial matters.*

I. ARTICLE 8: ENTRY INTO FORCE

This Article corresponds with Article 62 of the 1968 Convention, to
which reference should be made.[29] It corresponds also with Article
39 of the 1978 Convention and Article 15 of the 1982 Convention.
The Protocol entered into force on September 1, 1975 and the first
two references to come before the European Court were registered
on February 13, 1976.[30] No further commentary is necessary.

Article 9

The Contracting States recognize that any State which   36.22
becomes a member of the European Economic Community, and
to which Article 63 of the Convention on jurisdiction and the
enforcement of judgments in civil and commercial matters
applies, must accept the provisions of this Protocol, subject to
such adjustments as may be required.*

J. ARTICLE 9: NEW MEMBER STATES

This Article corresponds with Article 63 of the 1968 Convention, to
which reference should be made, although this Article is somewhat
more coercive in its terms. No further commentary is necessary.

Article 10

The Secretary-General of the Council of the European Com-   36.23
munities shall notify the signatory States of:
  (a) the deposit of each instrument of ratification;
  (b) the date of entry into force of this Protocol;

---

* Kropholler, p. 23.
[29] Para. 34.11 above.
[30] *Industrie Tessili Italiana Como* v. *Dunlop A.G.* [1976] E.C.R. 1473; *Etablissements A. De Bloos S.P.R.L.* v. *Société en commandite par actions Bouyer* [1976]
E.C.R. 1497.
* Kaye, p. 1707.

(c) any designation received pursuant to Article 4(3);
(d) any declaration received pursuant to Article 6.†

K. ARTICLE 10: NOTIFICATIONS TO CONTRACTING STATES

This Article corresponds with Article 64 of the 1968 Convention, but is otherwise self-explanatory and requires no further commentary.

Article 11

36.24   **The Contracting States shall communicate to the Secretary-General of the Council of the European Communities the texts of any provisions of their laws which necessitate an amendment to the lists of courts in Article 2(1).***

L. ARTICLE 11: AMENDMENTS TO NATIONAL LAW

This Article corresponds with Article VI of the 1968 Protocol, to which reference should be made. No further commentary is necessary.

Article 12

36.25   **This Protocol is concluded for an unlimited period.**

M. ARTICLE 12: DURATION

This Article corresponds with Article 66 of the 1968 Convention, is self-explanatory and requires no further commentary.

Article 13

36.26   **Any Contracting State may request the revision of this Protocol. In this event, a revision conference shall be convened by the President of the Council of the European Communities.**

N. ARTICLE 13: REVISION OF THE PROTOCOL

This Article corresponds with Article 67 of the 1968 Convention, is self-explanatory and requires no further commentary.

Article 14

36.27   **This Protocol, drawn up in a single original in the Dutch, French, German and Italian languages, all four texts being equally authentic, shall be deposited in the archives of the Secre-**

---

† Sub-para. (d) was substituted for the 1968 version by Art. 33 of the 1978 Convention.
* Jenard, *Protocols*, para. 16 (para. A1.286 below).

tariat of the Council of the European Communities. The Secretary-General shall transmit a certified copy to the Government of each signatory State.*

O. ARTICLE 14: AUTHENTIC LANGUAGE VERSIONS

This Article corresponds with Article 68 of the 1968 Convention, to which reference should be made.[31] In particular, the English, Danish, Irish and (when the 1982 Convention comes into force)[32] Greek language versions of the 1971 Protocol are authentic "under the same conditions" as the versions in the original four languages. This Article corresponds also with Articles 37(2) and 41 of the 1978 Convention and Articles 13(2) and 17 of the 1982 Convention. No further commentary is necessary.

JOINT DECLARATION

The Governments of the Kingdom of Belgium, the Federal Republic of Germany, the French Republic, the Italian Republic, the Grand Duchy of Luxembourg and the Kingdom of the Netherlands; **36.28**

On signing the Protocol on Interpretation by the Court of Justice of the Convention of September 27, 1968 on jurisdiction and the enforcement of judgments in civil and commercial matters;

Desiring to ensure that the provisions of that Protocol are applied as effectively and as uniformly as possible;

Declare themselves ready to organize, in cooperation with the Court of Justice, an exchange of information on the judgments given by the courts referred to in Article 2(1) of that Protocol in application of the Convention and the Protocol of 27 September 1968.*

P. JOINT DECLARATION: EXCHANGE OF INFORMATION

This Joint Declaration does not form part of the Protocol and its status is equivalent to that of the Joint Declaration annexed to the 1968 Protocol,[33] itself annexed to the Convention. By acceding to the 1968 Convention, the new Contracting States accede also to this declaration.[34] **36.29**

The exchange of information on the case law under the Convention takes place by way of the various Contracting States notifying

---

* Dashwood/Halcon/White, p. 236; Kaye, pp. 1699–1700; Maxwell, para. 12.28.
[31] Para. 34.19 above.
[32] See para. 13.05 above.
* Jenard, *Protocols*, para. 17 (para. A1.286 below).
[33] Para. 35.32 above.
[34] *Cf.* Schlosser, para. 248 (para. A1.558 below).

the Court of Justice of important decisions on the Convention. That information is then used by the Documentation Branch of the Court of Justice to prepare and publish a synopsis. Originally, this took the form of the *Synopsis of Case-Law* on the Convention, published by the Court of Justice in three parts from 1977 to 1979. That publication was then discontinued and the material from it incorporated in the *Digest of Case-Law relating to the European Communities, D Series*, which is published in loose-leaf format by the Court of Justice. In addition to the case law of the national courts referred to in Article 2(1) of the Protocol on Interpretation, the *Digest* includes a synopsis of the decisions of the European Court of Justice and other important decisions of national courts in interpreting the Convention.

CHAPTER 37

1978 ACCESSION CONVENTION [EXTRACTS]

CONVENTION

on the accession of the Kingdom of Denmark, Ireland and the United Kingdom of Great Britain and Northern Ireland to the Convention on jurisdiction and the enforcement of judgments in civil and commercial matters and to the Protocol on its interpretation by the Court of Justice.

PREAMBLE

THE HIGH CONTRACTING PARTIES TO THE TREATY 37.01
ESTBLISHING THE EUROPEAN ECONOMIC COMMUNITY,
CONSIDERING that the Kingdom of Denmark, Ireland and the United Kingdom of Great Britain and Northern Ireland, in becoming members of the Community, undertook to accede to the Convention on jurisdiction and enforcement of judgments in civil and commercial matters and to the Protocol on the interpretation of that Convention by the Court of Justice, and to this end undertook to enter into negotiations with the original Member States of the Community in order to make the necessary adjustments thereto,

917

HAVE DECIDED to conclude this Convention, and to this end have designated as their Plenipotentiaries . . . [etc.] . . . HAVE AGREED AS FOLLOWS:

TITLE I

GENERAL PROVISIONS

Article 1

37.02   **The Kingdom of Denmark, Ireland and the United Kingdom of Great Britain and Northern Ireland hereby accede to the Convention on jurisdiction and enforcement of judgments in civil and commercial matters, signed at Brussels on September 27, 1968 (hereinafter called "the 1968 Convention"), and to the Protocol on its interpretation by the Court of Justice, signed at Luxembourg on June 3, 1971 (hereinafter called "the 1971 Protocol").***

A. Preamble and Article 1: Accession of New Contracting States

37.03   This Convention brought about the accession of the United Kingdom, Ireland and Denmark to the 1968 Convention and to the 1971 Protocol on its interpretation. It was negotiated and signed pursuant to the undertaking given by those three States on their entry into the European Communities, which occurred on January 1, 1973. The juridical and historical background to the negotiations leading to the signature of this Convention has already been discussed.[1] It was signed by all nine Contracting States in Luxembourg on October 9, 1978.[2]

By Article 1, the three new Contracting States acceded to the 1968 Convention and 1971 Protocol.

B. Articles 2 to 33: Amendments

37.04   With the exception of Article 25(2), Articles 2 to 33 are exclusively concerned with amendments to the 1968 Convention, the 1968 Annexed Protocol and the 1971 Protocol on Interpretation. They are not reproduced here, but the amendments have been incorporated in the texts of those instruments reproduced and commented upon above. Article 25(2) is concerned with the uniform interpret-

---

* Schlosser, paras. 1–19 (paras. A1.289–A1.308 below); Kaye, p. 11.
[1] Paras. 13.02 to 13.04 above.
[2] O.J. 1978 L 304; Cmnd. 7395.

ation of Article 57 of the 1968 Convention and it is set out and discussed in the commentary on that Article.[3]

C. ARTICLES 34 TO 41: INTRODUCTION

Articles 34 to 36 contain certain transitional provisions and Articles **37.05** 37 to 41 contain certain final provisions. Articles 34 to 41 are reproduced in Schedule 3 to the 1982 Act and are discussed below.

TITLE V

TRANSITIONAL PROVISIONS

Article 34

1. The 1968 Convention and the 1971 Protocol, with the **37.06** amendments made by this Convention, shall apply only to legal proceedings instituted and to authentic instruments formally drawn up or registered after the entry into force of this Convention in the State of origin and, where recognition or enforcement of a judgment or authentic instrument is sought, in the State addressed.

2. However, as between the six Contracting States to the 1968 Convention, judgments given after the date of entry into force of this Convention in proceedings instituted before that date shall be recognised and enforced in accordance with the provisions of Title III as amended.

3. Moreover, as between the six Contracting States to the 1968 Convention and the three States mentioned in Article 1 of this Convention, and as between those three States, judgments given after the date of entry into force of this Convention between the State of origin and the State addressed in proceedings instituted before that date shall also be recognised and enforced in accordance with the provisions of Title III of the 1968 Convention as amended if jurisdiction was founded upon rules which accorded with the provisions of Title II, as amended, or with provisions of a convention concluded between the State of origin and the State addressed which was in force when the proceedings were instituted.*

---

[3] Para. 33.07 above.
* Schlosser, paras. 228–236 (paras. A1.530–A1.541 below); Collins, pp. 31–32; Dashwood/Halcon/White, pp. 251–252; Hartley, pp. xix, xx; Kaye, pp. 227–244; Maxwell, paras. 9.2–9.4; Geimer/Schütze, pp. 107, 975–980; Kropholler, pp. 345–349; Gothot/Holleaux, paras. 307, 310.

D. ARTICLE 34: GENERAL TRANSITIONAL PROVISIONS

1. General note and accession dates

37.07   Article 34 sets out transitional provisions for the 1978 Convention. It will be recalled that as between the original six Contracting States, the 1968 Convention came into force on February 1, 1973[4] and it contained transitional provisions in Article 54.[5] Entry into force of the 1978 Convention and hence of the amended versions of the 1968 Convention and 1971 Protocol, by contrast, took place on November 1, 1986 for each of the original six Contracting States and Denmark; on January 1, 1987 for the United Kingdom; and on June 1, 1988 for Ireland.[6] Each of those days is referred to in the following commentary as an "accession date."

Because the 1978 Convention has come into force on different days for each of the three new Contracting States, applying the transitional provisions under this Article requires particular attention to be paid in determining those states in which the amended 1968 Convention is in force on any given date.

37.08   The transitional mechanism provided for the original Contracting States by Article 54 of the 1968 Convention has been adopted for the purposes of this Article,

> (a) as between the original six Contracting States on one hand and each of the new Contracting States on the other hand, and
> (b) as between each of the three new Contracting States,

but not as between the original Contracting States. That mechanism, and a number of other matters which are relevant to the interpretation and application of this Article, are discussed in the commentary on Article 54, to which reference should be made.[7] The various different possibilities which can arise are summarised here. Articles 35 and 36 of the 1978 Convention contain further transitional provisions of a specialised nature.

2. Transitional provisions as between the original six Contracting States

37.09   Article 39 of the 1978 Convention has had the effect of bringing the amended version of the 1968 Convention into force in all the original six Contracting States on the day when the Convention

---

[4] Para. 34.12 above.
[5] Chap. 32 above.
[6] Art. 39 of the 1978 Convention, para. 37.18 below.
[7] Chap. 32 above.

came into force in Denmark, which was the first of the new Contracting States to bring it into effect. In other words, it came into force on November 1, 1986, and that is the accession date referred to in the rest of this paragraph.[8]

(1) **Proceedings where judgment was given before November 1, 1986:** the unamended version of the 1968 Convention applies;

(2) **Proceedings instituted before November 1, 1986, where judgment is given on or after the accession date:** the amended version of the Convention applies to the recognition and enforcement of the judgment: Article 34(2). In particular, because the third paragraph of Article 28 of the 1968 Convention[9] prevents the court of the state addressed from reviewing the jurisdiction of the court of origin, a judgment against a defendant who is a domiciliary of one of the new Contracting States would be entitled to automatic recognition and enforcement in the other original Contracting States (but not necessarily the new Contracting States), even if jurisdiction had been founded on an exorbitant basis.[10]

(3) **Proceedings instituted on or after November 1, 1986:** the amended version of the Convention applies both for the purposes of jurisdiction and for the purposes of recognition and enforcement of the judgment;

(4) **Authentic instruments:** the unamended provisions apply to instruments drawn up or registered before November 1, 1986 and the amended provisions apply to instruments drawn up or registered on or after that date.

3. Transitional provisions as between an original Contracting State and a new Contracting State and as between each of the new Contracting States

The accession date is different for each of the three new Contracting States. As between any two Contracting States, the accession date is the date on which the 1978 Convention is first in force in *both* of those countries. The unamended version of the Convention has no application and if the Convention applies at all, it is the amended version which applies.

37.10

---

[8] For the rare case where the proceedings were commenced before February 1, 1973, reference should be made to Art. 54 of the 1968 Convention, para. 32.01 above.

[9] Para. 27.62 above.

[10] Schlosser, para. 232 (para. A1.536 below).

(1) **Proceedings where judgment was given before the accession date:** the Convention does not apply;

(2) **Proceedings instituted before the accession date, where judgment is given on or after the accession date:** Title II of the Convention does not apply to jurisdiction but, subject to a test of jurisdiction (discussed below), Title III applies to recognition and enforcement of the judgment;

(3) **Proceedings instituted on or after the accession date:** the Convention is fully applicable;

(4) **Authentic instruments:** the Convention only applies if the instrument was drawn up or registered on or after the accession date.

These provisions are equivalent to those provided in Article 54 of the 1968 Convention. The test of jurisdiction referred to is the same test as applies under that Article (where it is discussed in more detail),[11] namely, that a judgment is to be recognised and enforced if the court of origin accepted jurisdiction on a basis which accorded with the provisions of Title II of the 1968 Convention (as amended) or on a bilateral convention in force at the time.

Article 35

37.11   **If the parties to a dispute concerning a contract had agreed in writing before the entry into force of this Convention that the contract was to be governed by the law of Ireland or of a part of the United Kingdom, the courts of Ireland or of that part of the United Kingdom shall retain the right to exercise jurisdiction in the dispute.***

E. ARTICLE 35: WRITTEN CHOICE OF LAW

37.12   The courts of England and Wales have, on a discretionary basis, accepted jurisdiction over contractual claims where the parties have agreed that English law applies,[12] and the courts have been pre-

---

[11] Paras. 32.04 *et seq.* above.

* Schlosser, para. 175 (para. A1.470 below); Collins, pp. 32, 52; Dashwood/Halcon/White, p. 252; Hartley, p. xix; Kaye, pp. 235–236; Maxwell, paras. 9.5–9.7; Kropholler, p. 346.

[12] In respect of persons not domiciled in a Contracting State, or for cases falling outside the material scope of the Convention, this rule continues to apply in England: Rules of the Supreme Court, Ord. 11, r. 1(1)(d)(iii). The rule, although it may be regarded as an exorbitant basis of jurisdiction, is not one of the exorbitant bases referred to in the second paragraph of Art. 3 of the 1968 Convention. A person domiciled or habitually resident in a non-Contracting State cannot be protected against the enforcement in other Contracting States of

pared to infer such an agreement,[13] sometimes on a fairly tenuous basis.[14] The 1968 Convention, by contrast, permits jurisdiction to be validly based on agreement only if the requirements of Articles 17 or 18 are fulfilled.

What this Article does is to preserve the discretion of the courts in the United Kingdom and Ireland to accept jurisdiction on the basis of an agreed choice of law, but only if the agreement was in writing, was express, chose the law of that part of the United Kingdom,[15] and was contained in a contract concluded before the 1978 Convention came into force there. This Article is discussed in greater detail in the commentary on Article 17.[15a]

Article 36

For a period of three years from the entry into force of the 1968 Convention for the Kingdom of Denmark and Ireland respectively, jurisdiction in maritime matters shall be determined in these States not only in accordance with the provisions of that Convention but also in accordance with the provisions of paragraphs 1 to 6 following. However, upon the entry into force of the International Convention relating to the arrest of sea-going ships, signed at Brussels on 10 May 1952, for one of these States, these provisions shall cease to have effect for that State.   37.13

1. A person who is domiciled in a Contracting State may be sued in the courts of one of the States mentioned above in respect of a maritime claim if the ship to which the claim relates or any other ship owned by him has been arrested by judicial process within the territory of the latter State to secure the claim, or could have been so arrested there but bail or other security has been given, and either:

   (a) the claimant is domiciled in the latter State; or
   (b) the claim arose in the latter State; or
   (c) the claim concerns the voyage during which the arrest was made or could have been made; or
   (d) the claim arises out of a collision or out of damage caused by a ship to another ship or to goods or persons on board

---

a judgment given in the exercise of this jurisdiction, even if that other Contracting State has concluded a bilateral convention falling within Art. 59 of the 1968 Convention with the non-Contracting State where the defendant is domiciled or habitually resident.

[13] See Dicey and Morris, pp. 1182, *et seq.*
[14] Scottish law does not regard a choice of law as a choice of forum, so this Article will not apply to Scottish courts: Anton, p. 112.
[15] Para. 21.17 above.
[15a] Para. 21.17 above.

either ship, either by the execution or non-execution of a manoeuvre or by the non-observance of regulations; or

(e) the claim is for salvage; or

(f) the claim is in respect of a mortgage or hypothecation of the ship arrested.

2. A claimant may arrest either the particular ship to which the maritime claim relates, or any other ship which is owned by the person who was, at the time when the maritime claim arose, the owner of the particular ship. However, only the particular ship to which the maritime claim relates may be arrested in respect of the maritime claims set out in subparagraphs (o), (p) or (q) of paragraph 5 of this Article.

3. Ships shall be deemed to be in the same ownership when all the shares therein are owned by the same person or persons.

4. When in the case of a charter by demise of a ship the charterer alone is liable in respect of a maritime claim relating to that ship, the claimant may arrest that ship or any other ship owned by the charterer, but no other ship owned by the owner may be arrested in respect of such claim. The same shall apply to any case in which a person other than the owner of a ship is liable in respect of a maritime claim relating to that ship.

5. The expression "maritime claim" means a claim arising out of one or more of the following:

(a) damage caused by any ship either in collision or otherwise;

(b) loss of life or personal injury caused by any ship or occurring in connection with the operation of any ship;

(c) salvage;

(d) agreement relating to the use or hire of any ship whether by charter-party or otherwise;

(e) agreement relating to the carriage of goods in any ship whether by charter-party or otherwise;

(f) loss of or damage to goods including baggage carried in any ship;

(g) general average;

(h) bottomry;

(i) towage;

(j) pilotage;

(k) goods or materials wherever supplied to a ship for her operation or maintenance;

(l) construction, repair or equipment of any ship or dock charges and dues;

(m) wages of masters, officers or crew;

(n) master's disbursements, including disbursements made by shippers, charterers or agents on behalf of a ship or her owner;

(o) dispute as to the title to or ownership of any ship;
(p) disputes between co-owners of any ship as to the owner-ship, possession, employment or earnings of that ship;
(q) the mortgage or hypothecation of any ship.

6. In Denmark, the expression "arrest" shall be deemed as regards the maritime claims referred to in sub-paragraphs (o) and (p) of paragraph 5 of this Article, to include a "forbud," where that is the only procedure allowed in respect of such a claim under Articles 646 and 653 of the law on civil procedure (lov om rettens pleje).*

F. ARTICLE 36: DANISH AND IRISH MARITIME ARREST JURISDICTION

Neither Denmark nor Ireland is a party to the Brussels Convention on the arrest of sea-going ships. Other Contracting States which are parties to that convention can accept jurisdiction under its rules, without having to consider whether jurisdiction also arose under Title II of the 1968 Convention, because of the provisions of Article 57 of the 1968 Convention.[16] The present Article gives Denmark and Ireland the right to accept jurisdiction on the basis of an equivalent series of rules, for a period of up to three years after the 1978 Convention comes into force in each of those countries respectively,[17] in order to give them an adequate opportunity to accede to the Brussels Arrest Convention. The joint declaration annexed to the 1978 Convention[18] urges them to do so.   **37.14**

TITLE VI

FINAL PROVISIONS

Article 37

The Secretary-General of the Council of the European Com-munities shall transmit a certified copy of the 1968 Convention and of the 1971 Protocol in the Dutch, French, German and Ita-lian languages to the Governments of the Kingdom of Denmark, Ireland and the United Kingdom of Great Britain and Northern Ireland.   **37.15**

---

* Schlosser, paras. 121, 131 (paras. A1.404, A1.414 below); Kaye, p. 236; Max-well, paras. 9.8–9.9; Kropholler, p. 104.
[17] See Art. 39 below.
[18] Para. 37.22 below.

The texts of the 1968 Convention and the 1971 Protocol, drawn up in the Danish, Irish and English languages shall be annexed to this Convention. The texts drawn up in the Danish, Irish and English languages shall be authentic under the same conditions as the original texts of the 1968 Convention and the 1971 Protocol.*

G. ARTICLE 37: AUTHENTIC LANGUAGE VERSIONS OF 1968 CONVENTION AND 1971 PROTOCOL

37.16   This is one of two provisions in the 1978 Convention concerned with authenticity of different language versions. By this Article, the English, Irish and Danish language versions of the original, unamended texts of the 1968 Convention and 1971 Protocol are accorded equal authenticity with the original French, German, Italian and Dutch texts. Article 41[19] gives equal authenticity to the various language versions of the present Convention.

Reference should be made to Article 68 of the 1968 Convention and the commentary thereon[20] and to Article 14 of the 1971 Protocol and to Articles 13(2) and 17 of the 1982 Convention. No further commentary is necessary.

Article 38

37.17   This Convention shall be ratified by the signatory States. The instruments of ratification shall be deposited with the Secretary-General of the Council of the European Communities.

H. ARTICLE 38: RATIFICATION

This Article corresponds with Article 61 of the 1968 Convention, with Article 7 of the 1971 Protocol and with Article 14 of the 1982 Convention. It is self-explanatory and requires no further commentary.

Article 39

37.18   This Convention shall enter into force, as between the States which shall have ratified it, on the first day of the third month following the deposit of the last instrument of ratification by the original Member States of the Community and one new Member State.

It shall enter into force for each new Member State which sub-

---

* Kaye, pp. 1699–1700.
[19] Para. 37.21 below.
[20] Paras. 34.19 *et seq.* above.

sequently ratifies it on the first day of the third month following the deposit of its instrument of ratification.*

I. ARTICLE 39: ENTRY INTO FORCE

It has already been observed[21] that in considering the transitional **37.19** provisions it is necessary to pay attention to which states have brought this convention into force at any given date, in view of the fact that different accession dates apply to each of the new Contracting States. This Article has the effect that as between any two Contracting States, the commencement date is the date on which this Convention is first in force in *both* of them. It came into force simultaneously in the six original Contracting States and Denmark on November 1, 1986, in the United Kingdom on January 1, 1987, and, in Ireland on June 1, 1988.

This Article corresponds with Article 62 of the 1968 Convention, to which reference should be made.[22] It corresponds also with Article 8 of the 1971 Protocol and Article 15 of the 1982 Convention.

Article 40

The Secretary-General of the Council of the European Com- **37.20** munities shall notify the signatory States of:

   (a) the deposit of each instrument of ratification,
   (b) the dates of entry into force of this Convention for the Contracting States.*

J. ARTICLE 40: NOTIFICATIONS TO CONTRACTING STATES

This Article corresponds with Article 64 of the 1968 Convention, but is otherwise self-explanatory and requires no further commentary.

Article 41

This Convention, drawn up in a single original in the Danish, **37.21** Dutch, English, French, German, Irish and Italian languages, all seven texts being equally authentic, shall be deposited in the archives of the Secretariat of the Council of the European Communities. The Secretary-General shall transmit a certified copy to the Government of each signatory State.*

---

* Hartley, p. 3; Kaye, p. 227.
[21] Para. 37.07 above.
[22] Para. 34.11 above.
* Hartley, p. 3.
* Dashwood/Halcon/White, p. 258; Kaye, pp. 1699–1700.

K. Article 41: Authentic Language Versions of 1978 Convention

As has already been observed,[23] this Article and Article 37 regulate the authenticity of the various language versions. This Article corresponds with Article 68 of the 1968 Convention, to which reference should be made.[24] This Article corresponds also with Article 14 of the 1971 Protocol and Articles 13(2) and 17 of the 1982 Convention.

JOINT DECLARATION

37.22 THE REPRESENTATIVES OF THE GOVERNMENTS OF THE MEMBER STATES OF THE EUROPEAN ECONOMIC COMMUNITY, MEETING WITHIN THE COUNCIL,
Desiring to ensure that in the spirit of the Convention of 27 September 1968 uniformity of jurisdiction should also be achieved as widely as possible in maritime matters,
Considering that the International Convention relating to the arrest of sea-going ships, signed at Brussels on 10 May, 1952, contains provisions relating to such jurisdiction,
Considering that all of the member States are not parties to the said Convention,
Express the wish that member States which are coastal States and have not already become parties to the Convention of 10th May 1952 should do so as soon as possible.
Done . . . [etc].*

L. Joint Declaration

As with the other Joint Declarations,[25] this Joint Declaration does not form part of the Convention to which it relates, but it was signed at the same time as the 1978 Convention. See, further, Article 36 of that Convention and the commentary thereon.[26]

---

[23] Para. 37.16 above.
[24] Para. 34.19 above.
* Schlosser, para. 121 (para. A1.404 below).
[25] Paras. 35.32 and 36.28 above.
[26] Paras. 37.13 and 37.14 above.

CHAPTER 38

1982 ACCESSION CONVENTION [EXTRACTS]

CONVENTION

on the accession of the Hellenic Republic to the Convention on jurisdiction and enforcement of judgments in civil and commercial matters and to the Protocol on its interpretation by the Court of Justice with the adjustments made to them by the Convention on the accession of the Kingdom of Denmark, of Ireland and of the United Kingdom of Great Britain and Northern Ireland.

PREAMBLE

THE HIGH CONTRACTING PARTIES TO THE TREATY 38.01
ESTABLISHING THE EUROPEAN ECONOMIC COM-
MUNITY,
    CONSIDERING that the Hellenic Republic, in becoming a member of the Community, undertook to accede to the Convention on jurisdiction and enforcement of judgments in civil and commercial matters and to the Protocol on its interpretation by the Court of Justice, with the adjustments made to them by the Convention on the accession of the Kingdom of Denmark, of Ireland and of the United Kingdom of Great Britain and Northern Ireland, and to this end undertook to enter into negotiations with the Member States of the Community in order to make the necessary adjustments thereto,
    HAVE DECIDED to conclude this Convention, and to this end have designated as their Plenipotentiaries . . . [etc.] . . .
HAVE AGREED AS FOLLOWS:

TITLE I

GENERAL PROVISIONS

Article 1

38.02   1. The Hellenic Republic hereby accedes to the Convention on jurisdiction and enforcement of judgments in civil and commercial matters, signed at Brussels on September 27, 1968 (hereinafter called "the 1968 Convention"), and to the Protocol on its interpretation by the Court of Justice, signed at Luxembourg on June 3, 1971 (hereinafter called "the 1971 Protocol"), with the adjustments made to them by the Convention on the accession of the Kingdom of Denmark, of Ireland and of the United Kingdom of Great Britain and Northern Ireland to the Convention on jurisdiction and enforcement of judgments in civil and commercial matters and to the Protocol on its interpretation by the Court of Justice, signed at Luxembourg on October 9, 1978 (hereinafter called "the 1978 Convention").

2. The accession of the Hellenic Republic extends, in particular, to Articles 25(2), 35 and 36 of the 1978 Convention.*

A. Preamble and Articles 1 to 11: Accession of Greece

1. General note

38.03   This Convention will, when it comes into force (in accordance with Article 15), have the effect of bringing Greece within the framework of the 1968 Convention. The adjustments which it makes to the 1968 Convention and 1971 Protocol are limited to those necessary to refer to Greece and Greek law and do not alter the substance of the Convention's scheme.

2. Preamble and Article 1

The Preamble and Article 1 correspond with their counterparts in the 1978 Convention and require no further commentary.

---

* Kaye, p. 228.

3. Articles 2 to 11

Articles 2 to 11 are exclusively concerned with amendments to the 1968 Convention, the 1968 Annexed Protocol and the 1971 Protocol on Interpretation. They are not reproduced here, but the amendments have been incorporated in the texts of those instruments reproduced and commented on above. Article 12 makes certain transitional provisions and Articles 13 to 17 make certain final provisions.

TRANSITIONAL PROVISIONS

Article 12

1. The 1968 Convention and the 1971 Protocol, as amended by the 1978 Convention and this Convention, shall apply only to legal proceedings instituted and to authentic instruments formally drawn up or registered after the entry into force of this Convention in the State of origin and, where recognition or enforcement of a judgment or authentic instrument is sought, in the State addressed.   38.04

2. However, judgments given after the date of entry into force of this Convention between the State of origin and the State addressed in proceedings instituted before that date shall also be recognised and enforced in accordance with the provisions of Title III of the 1968 Convention as amended by the 1978 Convention and this Convention, if jurisdiction was founded upon rules which accorded with the provisions of Title II of the 1968 Convention, as amended, or with provisions of a convention concluded between the State of origin and the State addressed which was in force when the proceedings were instituted.[*]

B. ARTICLE 12: TRANSITIONAL PROVISIONS

This Article corresponds with Article 34 of the 1978 Convention,[1]   38.05
to which reference should be made. Because all the three states added by the 1978 Convention have acceded before Greece acceded,[2] there will be only one accession date for this Convention. See also Article 54 of the 1968 Convention and the commentary thereon.[3] No further commentary on this Article is required.

---

[*] Kaye, p. 243; Geimer/Schütze, pp. 107–108, 980–981; Gothot/Holleaux, paras. 308–310.
[1] Para. 37.06 above.
[2] Art. 15, para. 38.08 below.
[3] Chap. 32 above.

FINAL PROVISIONS

Article 13

38.06   The Secretary-General of the Council of the European Communities shall transmit a certified copy of the 1968 Convention, of the 1971 Protocol and of the 1978 Convention in the Danish, Dutch, English, French, German, Irish and Italian languages to the Government of the Hellenic Republic.

The texts of the 1968 Convention, of the 1971 Protocol and of the 1978 Convention, drawn up in the Greek language shall be annexed to this Convention. The texts drawn up in the Greek language shall be authentic under the same conditions as the other texts of the 1968 Convention, the 1971 Protocol and the 1978 Convention.

C. ARTICLE 13: AUTHENTIC LANGUAGE VERSIONS OF THE OTHER CONVENTIONS

This Article corresponds with Article 37 of the 1978 Convention, to which reference should be made. Together with Article 17, it regulates the authenticity of the different language versions. See also Article 68 of the 1968 Convention and the commentary thereon and Article 14 of the 1971 Protocol. No further commentary is necessary.

Article 14

38.07   This Convention shall be ratified by the signatory States. The instruments of ratification shall be deposited with the Secretary-General of the Council of the European Communities.

D. ARTICLE 14: RATIFICATION

This Article corresponds with Article 61 of the 1968 Convention, with Article 7 of the 1971 Protocol and with Article 38 of the 1978 Convention. It is self-explanatory and requires no further commentary.

Article 15

38.08   This Convention shall enter into force, as between the States which shall have ratified it, on the first day of the third month following the deposit of the last instrument of ratification by the Hellenic Republic and those States which have put into force the 1978 Convention in accordance with Article 39 of that Convention.

It shall enter into force for each Member State which sub-sequently ratifies it on the first day of the third month following the deposit of its instrument of ratification.*

E. ARTICLE 15: ENTRY INTO FORCE

This Article envisaged the possibility that Greece might have **38.09** acceded to the 1968 Convention as amended by the 1978 Convention, before some of the states which were to have acceded under the 1978 Convention. In the event, this has not occurred.

The formula adopted by this Article for bringing this Convention into force is the same as that used in Article 62 of the 1968 Convention,[4] Article 8 of the 1971 Protocol and Article 39 of the 1978 Convention. When this Convention comes into force, it will bring into force the further amendments to the 1968 Convention, Annexed Protocol and 1971 Protocol made by Articles 2 to 11 of this Convention.[5]

Article 16

The Secretary-General of the Council of the European Com- **38.10** munities shall notify the signatory States of:

(a) the deposit of each instrument of ratification,
(b) the dates of entry into force of this Convention for the Contracting States.

F. ARTICLE 16: NOTIFICATIONS TO CONTRACTING STATES

This Article corresponds with Article 64 of the 1968 Convention and Article 40 of the 1978 Convention, but is otherwise self-explanatory and requires no further commentary.

Article 17

This Convention, drawn up in a single original in the Danish, **38.11** Dutch, English, French, German, Greek, Irish and Italian languages, all eight texts being equally authentic, shall be deposited in the archives of the General Secretariat of the Council of the European Communities. The Secretary-General shall transmit a certified copy to the Government of each signatory State.

---

* Kaye, p. 228.
[4] Para. 34.11 above.
[5] When this Convention comes into force, the U.K. legislation will be amended to take account of that fact, by an Order in Council, under s.14 of the 1982 Act: para. 40.40 below.

G. ARTICLE 17: AUTHENTIC LANGUAGE VERSIONS OF 1982 CONVENTION

As has already been observed,[6] this Article and Article 13 regulate the authenticity of the various language versions. This Article corresponds with Article 68 of the 1968 Convention, to which reference should be made.[7] This Article corresponds also with Article 14 of the 1971 Protocol and Articles 37(2) and 41 of the 1978 Convention.

---

[6] Para. 38.06 above.
[7] Para. 34.19 above.

CHAPTER 39

CIVIL JURISDICTION AND JUDGMENTS ACT 1982
GENERAL INTRODUCTION

1. Introduction

The Civil Jurisdiction and Judgments Act 1982 was passed prin- **39.01**
cipally to give effect in the United Kingdom to the 1968 Convention
and its associated Conventions. The 1982 Act also reformed the law
in a number of other respects, not all of which were associated with
the implementation of the Conventions. The text of the Act,
together with commentary on those parts of it which apply in England and Wales, is set out in Chapters 40 to 47 below.

Part I of the Act (Chapter 40) implements the Conventions and **39.02**
enables modifications to be made by Order in Council to take
account of further revisions of the Conventions. As has been seen,
the Conventions provide a uniform code of jurisdictional rules
applicable to civil and commercial matters throughout the Contracting States, and a scheme of recognition and enforcement which
secures a large measure of respect in each Contracting State for the
decisions of the courts of the other Contracting States.

In addition to giving effect to the Conventions in the law of England, Scotland and Northern Ireland,[1] Part I of the Act makes provision for the interpretation of the Conventions by English courts in
accordance with the decisions of the European Court of Justice and
in the light of the official reports prepared by the rapporteurs of the
working parties which negotiated the terms of the Conventions.[2]
Part I also contains supplementary provisions for the effective
implementation of the Conventions.

Hitherto, the jurisdictional rules in England and Wales have **39.03**
generally treated Scotland and Northern Ireland as equivalent to

---

[1] s.4, para. 40.08 below.
[2] s.3, para. 40.05 below.

foreign countries, and leave has been required to serve proceedings in another part of the United Kingdom.[3] If those rules had continued to apply, it would often have been more difficult to bring an action against a person domiciled in another part of the United Kingdom than against a person domiciled in another Contracting State.

Part II of the 1982 Act (Chapter 41) therefore gives effect to a modified version of the Convention as a uniform code of rules which applies for the purpose of determining, for each part of the United Kingdom, whether the courts of law of that part, or any particular court of law in that part, have or has jurisdiction in respect of most civil and commercial proceedings. The effect of this code of rules is principally to allocate jurisdiction between the different parts of the United Kingdom but, as has been explained,[4] it also has the effect in some cases of conferring jurisdiction on the court or courts to which it allocates jurisdiction. Part II also provides a new and simplified procedure for the enforcement in each part of the United Kingdom of judgments given in each other part of the United Kingdom.

39.04   Just as Part II of the Act applies to the United Kingdom as a whole in allocating and conferring jurisdiction in civil and commercial matters, Part III of the 1982 Act (Chapter 42) gives effect to new rules of jurisdiction for Scottish courts. These rules are again largely modelled on the rules in the 1968 Convention.

Part IV of the Act (Chapter 43) contains a number of provisions reforming the previous law on jurisdiction and on recognition and enforcement of judgments. Most importantly, the Act enables English courts to grant interim relief in aid of foreign proceedings, provided that those proceedings are in a Contracting State.[5]

39.05   Part V of the 1982 Act (Chapter 44) contains supplementary and general provisions. Of these, much the most important are the rules in sections 41 to 46 which are concerned with the new definition of domicile and its associated concept of the seat of a corporation or association. These provisions are of such far-reaching importance for the new scheme of jurisdictional rules that they are discussed separately below. Part V contains various further supplementary provisions, including a provision which preserves the courts' dis-

---

[3] The circumstances in which English courts have historically accepted jurisdiction over persons outside the territorial jurisdiction of the courts are described in chap. 1, paras. 1.15–1.16 above.
[4] See para. 1.24 above.
[5] s.25, paras. 43.03 *et seq.* below.

cretionary powers to stay, strike out or dismiss proceedings where to do so is not inconsistent with the 1968 Convention.[6]

2. Domicile: the new rules

The 1968 Convention provides no uniform definition of domicile, **39.06** although the domicile of the parties is of fundamental importance to the scheme of jurisdictional rules provided by the Convention and adopted in a slightly modified form for internal United Kingdom purposes by Schedule 4 to the Act.[7] The definitions of the domicile of an individual and of the seat of a corporation or association (equated with an individual's domicile by Article 53),[8] are left by the Convention to be determined in accordance with the national law of the Contracting States. However, the Convention provides uniform choice-of-law rules in Article 52[9] for determining which national law is to be applied in deciding an individual's domicile, and a uniform rule in Article 53 for determining which national rules of private international law are to be applied in deciding the seat of a corporation or association. These rules, and the concepts of domicile and seat in the Contracting States generally, are discussed in the commentary on those Articles.[10]

Sections 41 to 46 provide United Kingdom law with a self-contained series of rules defining the concepts of "domicile" and "seat" for the purposes of the Convention and this Act and it is important to note that the concept of "domicile" is quite distinct from the traditional common law concept and that the concept of the "seat" of a corporation or association is new to English law, although its constituent elements are not. The concepts are discussed in more detail in the commentary on sections 41 and 42.[11]

As a matter of United Kingdom law, the definitions are compre- **39.07** hensive for the international purposes of the Convention, so that when the application of the relevant choice of law rules results in United Kingdom law being the appropriate system for determining the domicile or seat of a party, it is these sections which are to be applied. Having determined for the purposes of the Convention whether the party is domiciled in the United Kingdom, the court may have to go further and determine for the purposes of the Act whether the party is domiciled in a particular part of, or in a particular place in, the United Kingdom. The same may apply even where the case is purely internal to the United Kingdom and does

---

[6] s.49, para. 44.40 below.
[7] See s.16, para. 41.01 below.
[8] Para. 31.23 above; *cf.* s.42(1), para. 44.11 below.
[9] Para. 31.01 above.
[10] See also paras. 3.05 and 3.07 above.
[11] Paras. 44.01 *et seq.* below.

not therefore fall within the Convention.[12] In these cases, too, sections 41 to 46 provide the rules which are to be applied.[13]

The principal rules are contained in sections 41 (domicile of individuals) and 42 (seat of corporation or association); but there are special rules in the other sections to cater for certain specific types of case. Of these, the most important are probably the provisions in section 44 providing, in certain cases, a deemed domicile in the United Kingdom for insurers and for suppliers of goods, services or credit to consumers.

---

[12] Para. 41.07 below.

[13] The same definitions have also been adopted as a matter of English law for cases not falling within the Convention, where a person's domicile is relevant for the purposes of the service of process outside the jurisdiction: R.S.C., Ord. 11, r. 1(4).

CHAPTER 40

CIVIL JURISDICTION AND JUDGMENTS ACT 1982
PART I—IMPLEMENTATION OF THE CONVENTIONS

A. MAIN IMPLEMENTING PROVISIONS

Section 1

1.—*Interpretation of references to the Conventions and Contracting States*　　　　**40.01**

(1) In this Act—
　　"the 1968 Convention" means the Convention on jurisdic-

tion and the enforcement of judgments in civil and commercial matters (including the Protocol annexed to that Convention), signed at Brussels on 27th September 1968;

"the 1971 Protocol" means the Protocol on the interpretation of the 1968 Convention by the European Court, signed at Luxembourg on 3rd June 1971;

"the Accession Convention" means the Convention on the accession to the 1968 Convention and the 1971 Protocol of Denmark, the Republic of Ireland and the United Kingdom, signed at Luxembourg on 9th October 1978;

"the Conventions" means the 1968 Convention, the 1971 Protocol and the Accession Convention.

(2) In this Act, unless the context otherwise requires—

  (a) references to, or to any provision of, the 1968 Convention or the 1971 Protocol are references to that Convention, Protocol or provision as amended by the Accession Convention; and

  (b) any reference to a numbered Article is a reference to the Article so numbered of the 1968 Convention, and any reference to a subdivision of a numbered Article shall be construed accordingly.

(3) In this Act "Contracting State" means—

  (a) one of the original parties to the 1968 Convention (Belgium, the Federal Republic of Germany, France, Italy, Luxembourg and the Netherlands); or

  (b) one of the parties acceding to that Convention under the Accession Convention (Denmark, the Republic of Ireland and the United Kingdom),

being a state in respect of which the Accession Convention has entered into force in accordance with Article 39 of that Convention.

General note

40.02   This is a definition section, setting out the manner in which the various references in the Act are to be interpreted. The main codes of rules governing jurisdiction and reciprocal enforcement of judgments and orders are contained, as between Contracting States, in the Conventions (which are largely reproduced in Schedules 1 to 3 to the Act)[1] and, as between different parts of the United Kingdom and within Scotland, in Schedules which are modelled on the Con-

---

[1] The status of the Conventions is discussed at para. 40.04 below.

ventions. Some care is therefore necessary in reading references in the Act to the various Articles.

An unamended version of the Conventions has been in force in the original Contracting States for some years,[2] but it is important to note that the amendments made by the Accession Convention are more than merely formal amendments to accommodate the accession of the United Kingdom, Ireland and Denmark. Subsection (2) provides that references in the Act to the Conventions are references to the amended versions.

The English language version[3] of the 1968 Convention and 1971 Protocol and of the Accession Convention are published in (1978) O.J. L304 and in Cmnd. 7395.[4] The Convention of October 25, 1982, providing for the accession of Greece to the Conventions is published in (1982) O.J. L388. That Convention is not yet in force,[5] but this Act may be modified by Order in Council under section 14[6] to take account of its implementation. The texts of the 1968 Convention and the 1971 Protocol as amended by the later Conventions[7] are published in (1983) O.J. C97. Together with the relevant provisions of those Conventions, they are reproduced with commentary in Chapters 14 to 38 above.

Section 2

2.—The Conventions to have the force of law **40.03**

(1) The Conventions shall have the force of law in the United Kingdom, and judicial notice shall be taken of them.

(2) For convenience of reference there are set out in Schedules 1, 2 and 3 respectively the English texts of—

(a) the 1968 Convention as amended by Titles II and III of the Accession Convention;

(b) the 1971 Protocol as amended by Title IV of the Accession Convention; and

(c) Titles V and VI of the Accession Convention (transitional and final provisions),

---

[2] See para. 13.03 above.

[3] Also the Danish and Irish language versions.

[4] The French, German, Dutch and Italian texts of the 1968 Convention appear at O.J. 1972 L299/32 and of the 1971 Protocol at O.J. 1975 L204/28. The texts of the 1968 Convention and 1971 Protocol as amended by the Accession Convention are also reproduced at O.J. 1978 L304, but contain a number of errors, corrected at O.J. 1981 L95, vol. 24.

[5] See para. 13.05 above.

[6] See para. 40.40 below.

[7] The later conventions are hereafter called the "1978 Convention" and "1982 Convention" respectively.

being texts prepared from the authentic English texts referred to in Articles 37 and 41 of the Accession Convention.

General note

40.04   Subsection (1) gives direct effect to the Conventions in the United Kingdom and requires that judicial notice be taken of them. It follows that courts and tribunals in the three parts of the United Kingdom are to apply the Conventions without any need for evidence of their contents, meaning or effect.[8] They have a status equivalent to an Act of Parliament, except that, unlike domestic law, the European Court is the ultimate arbiter in their interpretation.[9]

Subsection (2) gives effect to Schedules 1 to 3 of the Act. These Schedules contain the amended texts of the 1968 Convention, 1971 Protocol and relevant provisions of the 1978 Convention, but for ease of reference only. Although doubtless sufficient for most purposes, the Schedules do not of themselves have the force of law,[10] a privilege reserved to the Conventions. The circumstances in which English courts may refer to foreign language versions have already been discussed;[11] all seven language versions of the Conventions are equally authentic[12] and appear in the Official Journal,[13] of which English courts are required to take judicial notice.[14]

Section 3

40.05   **3.—***Interpretation of the Conventions*

(1) **Any question as to the meaning or effect of any provision of the Conventions shall, if not referred to the European Court in accordance with the 1971 Protocol, be determined in accordance with the principles laid down by and any relevant decision of the European Court.**

(2) **Judicial notice shall be taken of any decision of, or any expression of opinion by, the European Court on any such question.**

(3) **Without prejudice to the generality of subsection (1), the following reports (which are reproduced in the Official Journal of the Communities), namely—**

    (a) **the reports by Mr. P. Jenard on the 1968 Convention and 1971 Protocol; and**

---

[8] *Cross on Evidence* (6th ed.), pp. 66–67.
[9] See the 1971 Protocol, chap. 36 above.
[10] For a practical consequence of this, see para. 44.15 below.
[11] Para. 13.29 above.
[12] 1968 Convention, Art. 68, para. 34.19 above.
[13] See para. 40.02 above.
[14] European Communities Act 1972, s.3(2).

(b) the report by Professor Peter Schlosser on the Accession Convention,

may be considered in ascertaining the meaning or effect of any provision of the Conventions and shall be given such weight as is appropriate in the circumstances.

1. General note

This important section is crucial to the effective incorporation of the Conventions into English law. The interpretation of the Conventions, discussed more fully in Chapter 13, requires English courts to be willing to adopt a purposive approach to a far greater extent than they have been used to in interpreting English statutes.[15] This section not only enables them to do so, it requires them to do so.[16]

40.06

2. Subsection (1)

This subsection requires an English court faced with a question of interpretation to follow the principles laid down by the European Court, as well as any relevant decision of that court. This requirement is compulsory ("*shall* . . . be determined"); it probably follows anyway from the incorporation of the 1971 Protocol into English law, but it is put beyond doubt by this section. The effect of the subsection is to require the English court to have regard not only to those decisions of the European Court which bear directly on the provision in question, but also to such other decisions as are relevant to the meaning and effect of the Convention generally or as lay down principles of interpretation of the Convention. There is already a substantial body of case law on the Convention, and it is considered in some detail in the commentary on the various Articles.[17] Expert evidence would not normally be admissible as to the meaning of the Conventions, but evidence and other material on the law of other Contracting States may be admitted to aid the court in its interpretation of the Convention.[18]

Section 3 refers only to the interpretation of the Conventions. So far as the interpretation of the Act is concerned, though, section 16(3)[19] makes similar provision for the interpretation of Schedule 4,

---

[15] As to the English approach to the interpretation of statutes implementing international conventions generally, see Dicey and Morris, pp. 8–15; Mann, *Foreign Affairs in English Courts*, pp. 97 *et seq.*

[16] Compare s.3 of the European Communities Act 1972 and ss.87 and 91 of the Patents Act 1977, which contain similar provisions in an EEC context.

[17] Chaps. 13 to 38 above.

[18] *Cf. R. v. Goldstein* [1983] 1 W.L.R. 151. As to the proof of foreign law and its citation as an aid to interpretation, see chap. 9 and paras. 13.26 *et seq.* above.

[19] Paras. 41.01 and 41.09 below.

which is modelled on the Convention.[20] Sections 1,[21] 15[22] and 50[23] contain definitions. As to the circumstances in which the English court may, or must, refer a question of interpretation to the European Court under the 1971 Protocol, see Chapter 36.[24]

3. Subsection (2)

40.07   This subsection requires that judicial notice be taken of decisions of, and expressions of opinion by, the European Court. These do not need to be proved and are to be treated in the same way as matters of domestic law. Because the Convention itself requires in some instances that the court act of its own motion,[25] the court must be ready to take judicial notice of the jurisprudence of the European Court, even without citation of authority by the parties.

The provision covers not only the European Court's decisions, but also its expressions of opinion. This would seem to mean that not only are the formal paragraphs constituting the European Court's actual ruling envisaged, but also the rest of its "decision," containing both its *ratio decidendi* and *obiter dicta*. The opinions of the Advocates General probably also fall within the subsection. Certainly it would seem that judicial notice can be taken of them and that they should be given such weight as is appropriate in the circumstances.

4. Subsection (3)

This subsection introduces a novel provision, overcoming the rule of English law that *travaux préparatoires* may be referred to only to see what the "mischief" was with which the Act was designed to deal,[26] or, with caution, in certain other cases.[27] The Jenard and Schlosser Reports,[28] reproduced in full in Appendix 1,[29] are the official reports of the *rapporteurs* of the working parties which negotiated the Conventions.

---

[20] The same applies, in relation to Scotland, to s.20(5) and Sched. 8.
[21] Para. 40.01 above.
[22] Para. 40.42 below.
[23] Para. 44.45 below.
[24] 1971 Protocol, Arts. 2 and 3.
[25] For example, see Arts. 19 to 21, paras. 22.01, 22.11 and 23.01 above.
[26] *Black-Clawson International Ltd.* v. *Papierwerke Waldhof-Aschaffenburg A.G.* [1975] A.C. 591, at pp. 613–615, 629–630, 637–638.
[27] *Fothergill* v. *Monarch Airlines* [1981] A.C. 251, at pp. 277–278, 282–283, 287, 294–295, 302.
[28] O.J. 1979 C59. See para. 13.06 below.
[29] The Jenard Report is a para. A1.001 below, The Jenard Report on the Protocols is at para. A1.269 below and the Schlosser Report is at para. A1.287 below.

While the wording of the subsection makes it clear that it is subject to the compulsory provisions in subsection (1) and that the Reports are to be taken only as subsidiary aids to interpretation, they give much detailed insight into the intention behind the various provisions of the Conventions, and will be a most valuable aid to interpretation, especially to the sort of purposive interpretation favoured by the European Court.[30] Nonetheless, the Reports leave certain points unmentioned and leave others expressly open. Even where they express a view, they are not necessarily definitive and they are referred to only occasionally in the decisions of the European Court.

B. SUPPLEMENTARY PROVISIONS AS TO RECOGNITION AND ENFORCEMENT OF JUDGMENTS

Section 4

4.—*Enforcement of judgments other than maintenance orders*   **40.08**

(1) A judgment, other than a maintenance order, which is the subject of an application under Article 31 for its enforcement in any part of the United Kingdom shall, to the extent that its enforcement is authorised by the appropriate court, be registered in the prescribed manner in that court.

In this subsection "the appropriate court" means the court to which the application is made in pursuance of Article 32 (that is to say, the High Court or the Court of Session).

(2) Where a judgment is registered under this section, the reasonable costs and expenses of and incidental to its registration shall be recoverable as if they were sums recoverable under the judgment.

(3) A judgment registered under this section shall, for the purposes of its enforcement, be of the same force and effect, the registering court shall have in relation to its enforcement the same powers, and proceedings for or with respect to its enforcement may be taken, as if the judgment had originally been given by the registering court and had (where relevant) been entered.

(4) Subsection (3) is subject to Article 39 (restriction on enforcement where appeal pending or time for appeal unexpired), to section 7 and to any provision made by rules of court as to the manner in which and conditions subject to which a judgment registered under this section may be enforced.

---

[30] See paras. 13.22 *et seq.* above.

1. General note

40.09   The 1968 Convention itself provides, in Title III,[31] a code of rules for the recognition and enforcement in one Contracting State of judgments and orders made in another Contracting State. The rules in Title III are supplemented both as to content and as to procedure by the 1982 Act and by rules of court.

Section 4 provides the principal link between the enforcement rules in the Convention and those in the rules of court in the case of judgments other than maintenance orders.[32] The section has the function of providing the legislative basis, as a matter of United Kingdom law, for the procedures governing the issuing of an order for enforcement. It provides for a system of registration[33] and, subject to certain minor matters, equates a registered judgment with the judgment of a United Kingdom court. The procedure, which applies as much to non-money judgments as to money judgments, is discussed in some detail in Chapter 10.[34]

By contrast with measures of enforcement, recognition is automatically to be accorded to judgments and orders without any special procedure being required,[35] although the same procedure may be used to obtain a declaration of recognition in certain circumstances.[36]

2. Subsection (1)

This subsection provides for the registration of judgments (other than maintenance orders) in respect of which an order of enforcement is issued. The registration is to take place in the "prescribed manner" (*i.e.* in the manner prescribed by rules of court[37]) in the "appropriate court" as defined in Article 32.[38] This is the High Court in England and Wales[39] or Northern Ireland, or, in Scotland, the Court of Session. The register for England and Wales is to be kept under the direction of the Senior Master in the Central Office.[40]

The term "judgment" is defined by Article 25 of the 1968 Con-

---

[31] See Chaps. 25 to 29 above.
[32] Maintenance orders are covered by s.5, para. 40.12 below.
[33] It is arguable that, by reason of the wording of Art. 31, second para. (see para. 28.01 above), a system of registration is prescribed for the U.K. by the Convention itself.
[34] Maintenance orders are discussed in chap. 11.
[35] Art. 26, para. 27.01 above.
[36] Art. 26, second para., para. 27.04 above; R.S.C., Ord. 71, r. 35.
[37] s.15(1), para. 40.42 below.
[38] Para. 28.09 above.
[39] Specifically, the Queen's Bench Division: R.S.C., Ord. 71, r. 27.
[40] R.S.C., Ord. 71, r. 31.

vention,[41] in very wide terms. The meaning of "maintenance order," defined by section 15(1), is discussed under section 5.[42] The reference to the registration of a judgment "to the extent that its enforcement is authorised" is a reference not only to the fact that enforcement may be refused in accordance with Articles 27 and 28,[43] but also to the fact that partial enforcement may be authorised under Article 42.[44] Rules of court might also limit the extent of a judgment's enforceability.[45]

3. Subsection (2)

This subsection is concerned with costs.[46] It corresponds with sections 2(6) of the 1933 Act and 9(3)(c) of the 1920 Act. The costs of and incidental to the registration are to be distinguished from the costs of execution, which are governed by the rules relating to the particular process of execution chosen.

40.10

4. Subsection (3)

By this subsection, a judgment registered under this section is equated with a judgment of the registering court. It is subject to the qualifications in subsection (4), but is otherwise comprehensive in its effect. Because a judgment cannot have an order for its enforcement issued under Article 31 until it is enforceable in its state of origin,[47] it cannot ordinarily be registered under this section until that has occurred.[48] Similarly, once its enforceability has expired, it can ordinarily no longer be registered.[49] There is therefore no need for any further restriction in this subsection on the enforceability of such a judgment. All means of enforcement available in England and Wales for a High Court judgment are equally available for a judgment registered under this section.[50]

The assimilation of the registered foreign judgment to a judg-

---

[41] Para. 26.01 above; see s.15(1), para. 40.42 below.
[42] Para. 40.13 below.
[43] Paras. 27.12 *et seq.* An order may also be refused on certain other grounds: see paras. 10.27 and 25.13 above.
[44] Para. 28.71 above.
[45] Para. 40.11 below.
[46] The term "expenses" refers to the Scottish equivalent of "costs."
[47] See para. 28.04 above.
[48] An application may be made for the registration of a judgment for the purposes of its recognition as distinct from its enforcement and, for this purpose, the judgment need not be enforceable in its state of origin.
[49] See para. 28.05, n. 20 above *cf.* the position for intra-U.K. enforcement, para. 46.04 below.
[50] See paras. 10.55 *et seq.* above.

ment of the court where it is registered applies only for the purposes of enforcement. So, while the registering court can order and suspend execution on the same terms as it would in relation to its own judgments,[51] the foreign judgment remains subject to the rules in the Convention, as distinct from those of purely domestic law, for other purposes. For example, an appeal against the registration itself is governed by Articles 37 to 41.[52] Similarly, the enforcement of the foreign judgment in another part of the United Kingdom must be by way of a fresh application to the "appropriate court" in that other part.[53]

5. Subsection (4)

40.11   This subsection qualifies subsection (3) by preventing the registered foreign judgment being entirely assimilated to a judgment of the registering court, even for the purposes of its enforcement, in three specific respects. First, it recognises the effect of Article 39,[54] which is to delay the execution of the foreign judgment (except for protective measures) until after the time for appealing against the enforcement order has expired or such an appeal has been determined. Secondly, it enables the provisions of section 7[55] to have effect, so that the foreign judgment can generally carry interest at the rate, and from the date or time, which would be applicable in the state of origin.

The third qualification is, at present, of no practical effect. The rule-making power in section 48(2)[56] enables rules of court to be made as to the manner in which, and the conditions subject to which, a foreign judgment registered under this section may be enforced and includes power to make provision enabling the court to give directions about those matters. No such rules have been made in England and Wales. If such rules were made, section 4(4) would allow the enforcement of the registered foreign judgment to differ from that of a judgment of the registering court to the extent permitted by such rules. However, the enforceability of the judgment itself ought not, in principle, to be affected by this provision, because the only grounds upon which a judgment may be refused enforcement are those permitted by the Convention.[57]

---

[51] Para. 10.54 above.
[52] Paras. 28.38 *et seq.* above.
[53] See s.18(7), paras. 41.13 and 41.26 below.
[54] Para. 28.55 above.
[55] Para. 40.20 below.
[56] Para. 44.38 below.
[57] See paras. 10.27 and 25.12 *et seq.* above.

Section 5

5.—Recognition and enforcement of maintenance orders **40.12**

(1) The function of transmitting to the appropriate court an application under Article 31 for the recognition or enforcement in the United Kingdom of a maintenance order shall be discharged—

(a) as respects England and Wales and Scotland, by the Secretary of State;

(b) as respects Northern Ireland, by the Lord Chancellor.

In this subsection "the appropriate court" means the magistrates' court or sheriff court having jurisdiction in the matter in accordance with the second paragraph of Article 32.

(2) Such an application shall be determined in the first instance by the prescribed officer of that court.

(3) Where on such an application the enforcement of the order is authorised to any extent, the order shall to that extent be registered in the prescribed manner in that court.

(4) A maintenance order registered under this section shall, for the purposes of its enforcement, be of the same force and effect, the registering court shall have in relation to its enforcement the same powers, and proceedings for or with respect to its enforcement may be taken, as if the order had been originally made by the registering court.

(5) Subsection (4) is subject to Article 39 (restriction on enforcement where appeal pending or time for appeal unexpired), to section 7 and to any provision made by rules of court as to the manner in which and conditions subject to which an order registered under this section may be enforced.

(5A) A maintenance order which by virtue of this section is enforceable by a magistrates' court in England and Wales shall be enforceable in the same manner as a magistrates' court maintenance order made by that court.

In this subsection "magistrates' court maintenance order" has the same meaning as in section 150(1) of the Magistrates' Courts Act 1980.

(6) A maintenance order which by virtue of this section is enforceable by a magistrates' court in Northern Ireland shall be enforceable in the same manner as an affiliation order made by that court.

(7) The payer under a maintenance order registered under this section in a magistrates' court in England and Wales or Northern Ireland shall give notice of any change of address to the clerk of that court.

A person who without reasonable excuse fails to comply with this subsection shall be guilty of an offence and liable on summary conviction to a fine not exceeding level 2 in the standard scale.†

1. General note

40.13   For the purposes of enforcement in the United Kingdom, maintenance orders made in the other Contracting States are subject to a separate regime from that which applies under this Act to other foreign judgments. The reciprocal enforcement of maintenance orders has been a matter for magistrates' courts in England and Wales, and the Convention[58] and Act continue this practice. Maintenance orders are discussed in greater detail in Chapter 11.

Together with Title III of the Convention, this section forms the principal legislative basis for the enforcement in the United Kingdom of maintenance orders made in other Contracting States.[59] The system of enforcement is largely modelled on that adopted in the Maintenance Orders (Reciprocal Enforcement) Act 1972. It provides for a system of registration[60] and, subject to certain minor matters, equates a registered maintenance order with a maintenance order made in a United Kingdom court. The enforcement of maintenance orders under this Act and under other statutory schemes is discussed in Chapter 11 above.

As with judgments other than maintenance orders, the Convention requires that maintenance orders should be automatically recognised (as distinct from enforced) without any special procedure being required.[61] In the rare case in which a declaration of recognition is required, it is suggested that the same procedure may be used.[62]

In a number of respects, section 5 contains provisions similar to those in section 4, and reference may be made to the commentary on that section above.

"Maintenance order." The definition of "maintenance order" presents certain difficulties. It is defined by section 15(1) as "a maintenance judgment within the meaning of the 1968 Convention." Although the Convention uses the term "maintenance judg-

---

† Subs. 5A was added, and a reference to England and Wales in subs. (6) was repealed, by the Family Law Reform Act 1987, s.33(1) and Sched. 2, para. 89, from April 1, 1989. The reference in subs. (7) to level 2 on the standard scale was introduced by the Criminal Justice Act 1982, s.37.
[58] See Art. 32, para. 28.09 above.
[59] The other particularly relevant ss. are 6(3), 7(4), 8, 15 and 48(3).
[60] See n. 33 above.
[61] Art. 26, para. 27.01 above.
[62] This is despite the fact that no specific provision to this effect is included in the Magistrates' Courts (Civil Jurisdiction and Judgments Act 1982) Rules 1986.

ment" in Articles 32 and 37 (in relation only to the United Kingdom), it contains no definition of the expression. Nonetheless, the legislative intention of the Act is reasonably clear from section 15(1), namely that, so far as maintenance orders emanating from other Contracting States are concerned, it should apply only to those orders which fall within the general scope of the Convention.

The term "judgment" is defined in the Convention by Article 25[63] in very wide terms.[64] It is the extent to which "maintenance" falls within the Convention which is more problematic, not least because "rights in property arising out of a matrimonial relationship" are expressly excluded from the scope of the Convention.[65] This question is discussed in some detail in the context of Article 5(2).[66]

2. Subsection (1)

The subsection does not specifically require that an application   **40.14** under Article 31 should be transmitted to the magistrates' court by the Secretary of State, because that requirement is stated in Article 32 itself. Instead, the subsection merely allocates the function and defines the "appropriate court" to which the application is to be transmitted. So far as England and Wales are concerned, it adds little or nothing to the provisions of Article 32.[67] The particular magistrates' court to which the application is to be transmitted is that which has local jurisdiction under the second paragraph of Article 32,[68] usually the court for the place where the maintenance debtor is "domiciled."[69]

3. Subsection (2)

The initial application to the court under Article 31 is to be made *ex parte*.[70] It is this application to which the subsection refers. The rules provide that the "prescribed officer" is to be the justices' clerk.[71] He may refuse the application only on the grounds speci-

---

[63] Para. 26.01 above. The same definition applies for the purposes of this Part of the Act: s.15(1), para. 40.43 below.
[64] In the context of maintenance, a judgment includes an order made by the Danish administrative authorities: paras. 26.06, n. 21 and 35.22 above.
[65] Art. 1, second para., see para. 14.23 above.
[66] Para. 17.31 above.
[67] Para. 28.09 above.
[68] Paras. 28.12 *et seq.* above, see also s.15(3), para. 40.44 below.
[69] For the meaning of "domiciled," see s.41, paras. 44.01 *et seq.* below.
[70] Art. 34, first para., para. 28.22 above.
[71] The Magistrates' Courts (Civil Jurisdiction and Judgments Act 1982) Rules 1986, rule 3.

fied in Articles 27 and 28,[72] or on certain other minor grounds,[73] which include lack of local jurisdiction under the second paragraph of Article 32.[74]

4. Subsection (3)

40.15   This subsection corresponds with part of section 4(1). It requires that the order be registered in the "prescribed manner" (that is, in the manner prescribed by rules of court)[75] in the appropriate court. The manner of registration prescribed by the rules includes provision for the first appeal against the order for registration (or application to set it aside), pursuant to the first paragraph of Article 37.[76] The reference to the "extent" to which the enforcement of the order is authorised is a reference not only to the fact that enforcement may be refused in certain circumstances, but also to the fact that partial enforcement may be authorised under Article 42.[77] In the context of maintenance orders, this may be of particular relevance where a single order contains maintenance provisions falling within the Convention and property adjustment or personal status provisions which fall outside its scope.[78]

5. Subsection (4)

This subsection is equivalent to the provisions in section 4(3) which relate to judgments other than maintenance orders and reference should be made to the commentary on that subsection. Subject to subsection (5), the status of the registered maintenance order is assimilated for the purposes of its enforcement to that of a maintenance order made by the registering court. This probably means that, while the registered foreign order cannot be re-registered in another part of the United Kingdom,[79] it can be re-registered in the High Court under the Maintenance Orders Act 1958 for the purpose of more effective enforcement. Similarly, by equating the registered foreign order with an order of the registering court, the subsection probably has the effect of allowing arrears under the order to be recoverable[80] back to the date when the order was made. These points are discussed more fully in Chapter 11.[81]

---

[72] Art. 34, second para., para. 28.22 above.
[73] Para. 25.13 above.
[74] Para. 28.09 above.
[75] See s.15(1), para. 40.42 below.
[76] See para. 11.17 above.
[77] See para. 28.71 above.
[78] Art. 1, second para., see paras. 14.19 *et seq* above.
[79] See s.18(7), para. 41.13 below.
[80] Interest on arrears is not recoverable unless, in some cases, the order is re-registered in the High Court: s.7(4), para. 40.20 below.
[81] See paras. 11.18–11.20 above.

6. Subsection (5)

40.16

In the same way as section 4(4) qualifies section 4(3), so this subsection restricts the extent to which the registered foreign maintenance order is to be equated with its domestic counterpart. Article 39[82] prevents enforcement measures (other than protective measures) from being taken until after the time for appealing against the decision authorising the registration has expired, or the appeal has been disposed of.[83]

Section 7(4)[84] prevents interest being recovered in the magistrates' court on arrears of sums due under a maintenance order registered under this section. If the order is re-registered in the High Court, it may in certain circumstances be recoverable.

Rules of court may be made under sections 48(2) and 48(3) which cover a number of different matters concerning maintenance orders. To the extent that they prescribe the manner in which, and conditions subject to which, a maintenance order registered under this section may be enforced, or permit directions to be made about those matters, this subsection allows the status of a registered foreign maintenance order to differ from that of a maintenance order made by the registering court. As in the case of section 4(4), the actual enforceability of the order ought not to be affected. The rules of court which give effect to the system of registration in England and Wales require that payments be made through the justices' clerk, leaving the payer no discretion to make payment direct.[85]

7. Subsection (5A)

This subsection supplements subsection (3) by spelling out that a maintenance order registered under this section may be enforced in the same manner as a magistrates' court maintenance order.[86] The particular means by which a magistrates' court maintenance order may be enforced are described in Chapter 11.[87] The subsection was introduced to take account of the abolition of affiliation proceedings in England and Wales.

---

[82] Para. 28.55 above.

[83] The re-registration of the order in the High Court under the 1958 Act probably does not amount to the taking of a "measure of enforcement" for the purposes of Art. 39.

[84] Para. 40.20 below.

[85] Magistrates' Courts (Civil Jurisdiction and Judgments Act 1982) Rules 1986, rule 6.

[86] Magistrates' Courts 1980, s.150(1), as amended.

[87] See para. 11.28 above.

8. Subsection (6)

Affiliation orders, so far as they relate to questions of the status of any person, are outside the scope of the Convention, and therefore of this section. This subsection, though, refers only to the means of enforcement of maintenance orders, and does so in a way that corresponds with other enactments on the same subject.[88] It now applies only to Northern Ireland.[89]

9. Subsection (7)

40.17   This subsection requires the payer under an order registered in a magistrates' court to notify the clerk of the court of any change of address.[90] A failure to comply with the requirements of the subsection will render a payer liable on summary conviction to a fine.[91] The term "payer" is defined by section 15(1) as the person liable to make the payments for which the order provides. Presumably (although this is not clear) it includes a person who is up-to-date with his payments but against whom an order remains registered. Equally, it would seem to include a person who is liable under the original order, even before the expiry of the moratorium on measures of enforcement imposed by Article 39.

The provision is designed to help the justices' clerk in his role as the person charged under the rules with collecting the maintenance and enforcing the order. Where the local jurisdiction of the magistrates' court under the second paragraph of Article 32[92] was derived from the domicile of the maintenance creditor in the district of that court, it is logical to assume that the court will know the address of the payer, even though he is under no obligation to notify the court of his original address. In such a case, there is not likely to be any particular difficulty in practice about this provision. The same applies where the payer has since moved to an address outside the commission district of the registering court, but in the same part of the United Kingdom.

If the payer moves to another part of the United Kingdom, the maintenance order may need to be registered afresh in that other part, because the foreign order is not to be treated as an order of the

---

[88] *e.g.* s.18(2), Maintenance Orders Act 1950; ss.8(4) and 33(3) of the Maintenance Orders (Reciprocal Enforcement) Act 1972.

[89] See, para. 40.12, n. † above.

[90] The provision is equivalent to s.8(3) of the Maintenance Orders (Reciprocal Enforcement) Act 1972.

[91] The maximum fine on level 2 of the standard scale is presently £100: see Criminal Justice Act 1982, s.37(2); Magistrates' Courts Act 1980, s.143; Criminal Penalties etc. (Increase) Order 1984, S.I. 1984 No. 447.

[92] Para. 28.12 above.

registering court for the purposes of its enforcement in other parts of the United Kingdom.[93]

The requirement that the payer should notify the clerk of his change of address becomes rather more problematic when the person against whom enforcement is sought is not domiciled in the United Kingdom, and the jurisdiction of the magistrates' court to register the foreign order is founded under the second paragraph of Article 32 upon the place of enforcement of the maintenance order. In such a case, not only is the payer not under an obligation to notify the clerk of his original address, the court will not necessarily know that address. It may not even be in the United Kingdom.

Section 6

6.—*Appeals under Article 37, second paragraph and Article 41.* 40.18

(1) The single further appeal on a point of law referred to in Article 37, second paragraph and Article 41 in relation to the recognition or enforcement of a judgment other than a maintenance order lies—

    (a) in England and Wales or Northern Ireland, to the Court of Appeal or to the House of Lords in accordance with Part II of the Administration of Justice Act 1969 (appeals direct from the High Court to the House of Lords);

    (b) in Scotland, to the Inner House of the Court of Session.

(2) Paragraph (a) of subsection (1) has effect notwithstanding section 15(2) of the Administration of Justice Act 1969 (exclusion of direct appeal to the House of Lords in cases where no appeal to that House lies from a decision of the Court of Appeal).

(3) The single further appeal on a point of law referred to in Article 37, second paragraph and Article 41 in relation to the recognition or enforcement of a maintenance order lies—

    (a) in England and Wales, to the High Court by way of case stated in accordance with section 111 of the Magistrates' Courts Act 1980;

    (b) in Scotland, to the Inner House of the Court of Session;

    (c) in Northern Ireland, to the Court of Appeal.

General note

The Convention imposes limitations on the rights of appeal 40.19 against the original decision made on the *ex parte* application under Article 31,[94] whether that decision was to grant or to refuse the

---

[93] See para. 40.15 above.
[94] Para. 28.01 above.

order for enforcement. The original application is made to the courts specified in the first paragraph of Article 32.[95] In England and Wales, the relevant courts are the High Court[96] in the case of a judgment other than a maintenance order, and the magistrates' court on transmission by the Secretary of State in the case of a maintenance order.[97]

A first appeal against the *ex parte* order is made under the first paragraph of Article 37[98] (if the order was originally granted) or Article 40[99] (if it was refused) to the courts specified in those Articles. In England and Wales, the first appeals are heard by a judge on appeal from the master[1] and by the magistrates' court on appeal from its clerk.[2] The Convention then permits a further appeal from the order made on the first appeal, and defines the type of appeal permitted. The second paragraph of Article 37[3] and Article 41[4] provide for the United Kingdom that this is "a single further appeal on a point of law." What this section does is to supplement those Articles by defining more precisely the form of appeal envisaged, and the court to which it lies.

By subsections (1) and (2), the further appeal in cases other than those involving a maintenance order lies to the Court of Appeal or, under the "leap-frog" procedure, to the House of Lords. The conditions under which the "leap-frog" procedure is permitted are set out in Part II of the Administration of Justice Act 1969.[5] In summary, the procedure may be invoked if the judge has, with the consent of all the parties, granted a certificate that a point of law of general public importance is involved and that point *either* relates wholly or mainly to the construction of an enactment or statutory instrument and has been fully argued in the proceedings and fully considered in the judge's judgment, *or* is one in respect of which the judge is bound by a decision of the Court of Appeal or the House of Lords in previous proceedings, and was fully considered in the judgments given by the Court of Appeal or House of Lords (as the case may be) in those previous proceedings. Normally, the "leap-frog" procedure is not available where no appeal would be permit-

---

[95] Para. 28.09 above.
[96] The application is made to a Master of the Queen's Bench Division: R.S.C., Ord. 32, r. 11; Ord 71, r. 26; see para. 10.12 above.
[97] See paras. 11.11 *et seq.* and 40.14 above.
[98] Para. 28.38 below.
[99] Para. 28.63 below.
[1] R.S.C., Ord. 71, r. 33(1).
[2] Magistrates' Courts (Civil Jurisdiction and Judgments Act 1982) Rules 1986, rule 5.
[3] Para. 28.42 below.
[4] Para. 28.69 below.
[5] *Supreme Court Practice*, para. [5429].

ted from the Court of Appeal to the House of Lords, but for these purposes subsection (2) removes that restriction.

Subsection (3) is concerned with the single further appeal from the decision of the magistrates' court in the case of a maintenance order. Here, the appeal lies to the High Court by way of case stated under section 111 of the Magistrates' Courts Act 1980.[6]

Section 7

7.—Interest on registered judgments   **40.20**

(1) Subject to subsection (4), where in connection with an application for registration of a judgment under section 4 or 5 the applicant shows—

  (a) that the judgment provides for the payment of a sum of money; and

  (b) that in accordance with the law of the Contracting State in which the judgment was given interest on that sum is recoverable under the judgment from a particular date or time,

the rate of interest and the date or time from which it is so recoverable shall be registered with the judgment and, subject to any provision made under subsection (2), the debt resulting, apart from section 4(2), from the registration of the judgment shall carry interest in accordance with the registered particulars.

(2) Provision may be made by rules of court as to the manner in which and the periods by reference to which any interest payable by virtue of subsection (1) is to be calculated and paid, including provision for such interest to cease to accrue as from a prescribed date.

(3) Costs or expenses recoverable by virtue of section 4(2) shall carry interest as if they were the subject of an order for the payment of costs or expenses made by the registering court on the date of registration.

(4) Interest on arrears of sums payable under a maintenance order registered under section 5 in a magistrates' court in England and Wales or Northern Ireland shall not be recoverable in that court, but without prejudice to the operation in relation to any such order of section 2A of the Maintenance Orders Act 1958 or section 11A of the Maintenance and Affiliation Orders Act (Northern Ireland) 1966 (which enable interest to be recovered if the order is re-registered for enforcement in the High Court).

(5) Except as mentioned in subsection (4), debts under judg-

---

[6] See para. 11.17, n. 80 above.

ments registered under section 4 or 5 shall carry interest only as provided by this section.

1. General note

40.21   The question of interest is not expressly dealt with by the Convention, but this section provides for a judgment given in another Contracting State and registered in the United Kingdom to bear interest. The section applies only to judgments registered under sections 4 or 5. The effect of the section on judgments other than maintenance orders is twofold. First, provided that certain prescribed conditions are fulfilled, it extends to the United Kingdom the provisions under which interest would be recoverable on the judgment debt in the judgment's country of origin. Secondly, by subsection (5), it ensures that the recovery of interest on a judgment registered under the Act takes place only under this section and not, therefore, under section 17 of the Judgments Act 1838 or any other provision. As to maintenance orders, see the commentary below on subsection (4).

2. Subsection (1)

The scheme of the subsection is to enable the judgment to be treated for the purposes of interest as if it were to be enforced in its country of origin. It draws no distinction between the periods before and after registration.[7] The subsection is mandatory in its terms. Provided that the prescribed matters are shown by the applicant,[8] he is entitled to have them registered with the judgment and is entitled to recover interest accordingly, subject to any provision made by rules of court under subsection (2). If no interest is payable in the state of origin, or if the applicant fails to provide the requisite particulars, the judgment debt will carry no interest.

The words in paragraph (b), "in accordance with the law of the Contracting State . . . " are wide enough to encompass an entitlement to interest whether or not it is stated in the judgment itself. Once the particulars are registered, they will continue to determine the rate at which, and the period during which, interest will accrue, even if the law changes in the country of origin, so as to affect the

---

[7] Contrast ss.2(2) and (6) of the Foreign Judgments (Reciprocal Enforcement) Act 1933, which provide for the judgment debt as registered to include such interest as is due under the law of the country of origin as at the date of registration, and for the judgment debt then to bear interest as if it were an English judgment.

[8] The evidence to be adduced by the applicant is prescribed: see R.S.C., Ord. 71, r. 28(1)(b); para. 10.14 above.

entitlement to interest under the judgment in that country. Because the term "judgment"[9] includes an order for costs, this subsection enables interest to be recovered on the sums payable under such an order, provided that the law of the state of origin permits it.

The debt. The section states that interest is recoverable on "the   **40.22** debt resulting, apart from section 4(2), from the registration of the judgment." This gives rise to a problem, at least in theory. The debt under the judgment is recognised by English law independently of the registration, because the judgment is accorded automatic recognition by virtue of Article 26 of the 1968 Convention.[10] An entitlement to interest, if stated in the judgment, is likewise automatically recognised as part of the debt. Strictly, therefore, it is only the costs of registration payable by virtue of section 4(2) which can be said to "result" from the registration. Such an interpretation of the subsection would be absurd. Plainly, it is intended that interest should be payable, in accordance with the registered particulars as to rate and period of interest, on the capital sum of the judgment debt, and that the registration should record the judgment debt without interest, and record the prescribed particulars to enable interest to be recovered on that capital sum in accordance with the law of the country of origin.

Equally, a strict interpretation might in certain circumstances, where an entitlement to interest is stated in the judgment, allow the judgment creditor to recover interest under this subsection not only on the capital sum but also on such further element of interest as is referred to in the judgment. It cannot have been intended that the judgment creditor should become automatically entitled to interest on the interest element of the debt in those circumstances. Such an interpretation would be doubly capricious. First, it would allow the recovery of interest on interest, a substantive effect, merely because the judgment contained a statement of entitlement to interest, potentially a pure matter of form. An entitlement to interest might exist by operation of law even without a statement to that effect in the judgment itself. Secondly, it would enable the judgment creditor to recover interest on interest in this country in circumstances where he could not have done so in the country of origin of the judgment. That would run directly counter to the subsection's designed purpose of equating the interest recoverable under the registered foreign judgment with the interest recoverable in its country of origin.

---

[9] "Judgment" is defined in s.15(1), para. 40.42 below, and Art. 25, para. 26.01 above.
[10] Para. 27.01 below.

3. Subsection (2)

40.23   This subsection adds to the general rule-making powers[11] by allowing rules to be made as to certain aspects of the calculation and recovery of interest. As regards rules made for England and Wales under this Act, the only rule relating specifically to interest on judgments other than maintenance orders is Order 71, rule 28(1)(*b*) of the Rules of the Supreme Court.

4. Subsection (3)

If it were not for subsections (3) and (5), the costs of registration would bear interest as if they were due under an ordinary order for costs[12] at the rate applicable to English High Court judgments generally. The effect of this subsection is to substitute the original court's rules as to rate of (and entitlement to) interest, so that interest on the costs of registration is treated in the same way as interest on the rest of the costs of the foreign judgment, except as to the date from which it runs. This subsection applies only to the costs of and incidental to the registration of a judgment under section 4; it does not apply to the costs of registration of a maintenance order under section 5.

5. Subsection (4)

This subsection specifically provides that interest is not recoverable on arrears payable under foreign maintenance orders registered in a magistrates' court under section 5. There is no provision for the recovery of interest on such arrears if the order originates in this country, and a foreign order is in no better position. Interest is recoverable, though, if the foreign order is re-registered in the High Court under the Maintenance Orders Act 1958.[13]

6. Subsection (5)

Judgments registered under sections 4 or 5 can bear interest in this country only if and to the extent permitted by the combined effect of the law of the country of origin of the judgment, of this section, and, as regards maintenance orders registered in a magistrates' court and re-registered in the High Court, of section 2A of the Maintenance Orders Act 1958.[14]

---

[11] See s.48, para. 44.38 below.
[12] See *Supreme Court Practice*, para. 62/35/8.
[13] Maintenance Orders Act 1958, s. 2A: see para. 11.22 above.
[14] See para. 11.22 above.

Section 8

8.—*Currency of payment under registered maintenance orders*   **40.24**

(1) **Sums payable in the United Kingdom under a maintenance order by virtue of its registration under section 5, including any arrears so payable, shall be paid in the currency of the United Kingdom.**

(2) **Where the order is expressed in any other currency, the amounts shall be converted on the basis of the exchange rate prevailing on the date of registration of the order.**

(3) **For the purposes of this section, a written certificate purporting to be signed by an officer of any bank in the United Kingdom and stating the exchange rate prevailing on a specified date shall be evidence, and in Scotland sufficient evidence, of the facts stated.**

1. General note

A foreign maintenance order registered in this country will nearly   **40.25** always have been expressed in a currency other than sterling. This section aims to provide a simple standard rule for the currency of payments pursuant to an order registered under section 5, requiring them to be in sterling (subsection (1)) converted at the exchange rate prevailing at the date of registration (subsection (2)). This system is equivalent to that provided for orders registered under the Maintenance Orders (Reciprocal Enforcement) Act 1972.[15]

2. Subsection (1)

This subsection is mandatory in requiring that sterling be the currency of payment of the sums to which it refers. The words "Sums payable in the United Kingdom under a maintenance order by virtue of its registration under section 5" give rise to a number of difficulties of interpretation which remain to be resolved. In so far as the maintenance order itself gives rise to obligations to make payments elsewhere than in the United Kingdom, section 8 does not apply to it; and it is hard to see how the registration in the United Kingdom of a maintenance order from another Contracting State could be regarded as itself giving rise to an obligation to make payments outside the United Kingdom. The use of the words "by virtue of" is discussed further below.[16]

---

[15] See ss.16(2) to 16(4) of that Act.
[16] See para. 40.26 below.

3. Subsections (2) and (3)

The actual means of registration is regulated by the rules of court[17] and the bank certificate referred to in subsection (3) will serve as evidence of the prevailing exchange rate. The rate fixed by reference to the date of registration applies not only to arrears but also to future payments as they fall due. It may only be changed by means of a fresh application to register an order; and it remains to be seen whether the same order may be re-registered in the same court merely for the purpose of changing the applicable exchange rate.

4. A possible problem

40.26   It remains to be seen whether this section is inconsistent with the Convention. The difficulty, which may be more than merely theoretical, is illustrated by the wording of subsection (1): "Sums payable in the United Kingdom under a maintenance order *by virtue of* its registration under section 5." On a true analysis of the Convention, it is submitted, the maintenance order is accorded automatic recognition in the United Kingdom pursuant to Article 26 of the Convention, and English law is therefore required to recognise the substantive obligations existing by virtue of that order. It is only the *enforcement* of the payments, rather than their status as "sums payable in the United Kingdom," which can properly be described as being "by virtue of" the registration. The substantive obligations under the order will most probably define the sums due (and becoming due from time to time) in terms of a currency other than sterling. So far from recognising those obligations, English law would be altering them by section 8.

If this were merely a question of the form in which the payments were to be made, it would pose little difficulty, and subsection (1) on its own might well be regarded merely as a matter of procedural law for the law of the state addressed to determine. But the question may be a real one of substance, because subsection (2) fixes the date of registration as the date at which the exchange rate is to be determined, not only for arrears due as at that date (expressly envisaged by subsection (1)), but also for payments falling due thereafter.

If this analysis of section 8 is correct, the rule in subsection (2) will give rise in practice to problems of accounting where the currency of accounting between the parties differs from the currency of payment. As a matter of the law of the country of origin, there might be a balance due to or from one of the parties in the currency of that country which, as a matter of English law, did not exist in

---

[17] The Magistrates' Courts (Civil Jurisdiction and Judgments Act 1982) Rules 1986; see paras. 11.11 *et seq.* above.

sterling. If, for example, an order made in Germany and expressed in Deutschmarks is registered in an English magistrates' court, and payments are duly made to the clerk of that court in sterling in the sums set by reference to the exchange rate at the date of registration, over a period when Deutschmarks are appreciating as against sterling, the total of the sums received by the maintenance creditor in Germany, converted to Deutschmarks at the date of payment to her, would be less than the sums to which she would be entitled under the order as a matter of German law. If the exchange rate moved the other way, the imbalance would be reversed and the maintenance debtor would have been required by section 8 to pay more than the order required.

C. Other Supplementary Provisions

Section 9

9.—Provisions supplementary to Title VII of the 1968 Convention **40.27**

(1) The provisions of Title VII of the 1968 Convention (relationship between that convention and other conventions to which Contracting States are or may become parties) shall have effect in relation to—

> **(a) any statutory provision, whenever passed or made, implementing any such other convention in the United Kingdom; and**

> **(b) any rule of law so far as it has the effect of so implementing any such other convention, as they have in relation to that other convention itself.**

(2) Her Majesty may by Order in Council declare a provision of a convention entered into by the United Kingdom to be a provision whereby the United Kingdom assumed an obligation of a kind provided for in Article 59 (which allows a Contracting State to agree with a third State to withhold recognition in certain cases from a judgment given by a court in another Contracting State which took jurisdiction on one of the grounds mentioned in the second paragraph of Article 3).

1. General note

This section contains provisions clarifying the status in domestic **40.28** law of Title VII of the 1968 Convention. That Title contains Articles 55 to 59,[18] which regulate the relationship between the 1968 Convention and other conventions to which one or more of the Contracting States are or may become parties.

---

[18] Chap. 33 above.

Strictly speaking, this section is probably superfluous, because section 2 gives effect to the 1968 Convention, including Title VII. If in any given case the 1968 Convention conflicted with an existing rule of domestic law implementing a convention affected by Title VII, the courts would almost certainly give effect to the provisions of the 1968 Convention. Nonetheless, the section puts the position in domestic law beyond doubt. The two subsections deal with different aspects of the matter.

2. Subsection (1)

This subsection makes all the various rules of domestic law which have the effect of implementing other international conventions, present or future, subject to the provisions in Title VII. Those provisions are discussed in detail in Chapter 33, but it is important to note that, while Article 55 causes a number of bilateral conventions relating to recognition and enforcement of judgments to be superseded by the 1968 Convention, Article 56 provides for them to continue to have effect in relation to matters to which the 1968 Convention does not apply. The effect in English law is to limit the scope of the Foreign Judgments (Reciprocal Enforcement) Act 1933, and the Orders in Council made under it, to cases falling outside the 1968 Convention.

Article 57 provides that the 1968 Convention "shall not affect any conventions to which the Contracting States are or will be parties and which, in relation to particular matters, govern jurisdiction or the recognition or enforcement of judgments." The interpretation of that provision is far from straightforward,[19] but subsection (1) makes it clear that the provisions of domestic law implementing those conventions are likewise not affected by the 1968 Convention.

English law does not generally give effect to international conventions unless and until they have been given effect in domestic law,[20] but it adopts a number of different methods of implementing conventions. A convention may be incorporated wholesale into domestic law by express reference,[21] or may be re-enacted verbatim as part of English law,[22] or be given effect to by primary legislation which refers to the convention[23] or which does not refer to the con-

---

[19] See paras. 33.07 *et seq.* above.

[20] See Dicey and Morris, pp. 8 *et seq.*; Jacobs and Roberts (ed.), *The Effect of Treaties in Domestic Law*, chap. 7 by Prof. R. Higgins, Q.C.

[21] See, *e.g.* s.2 of this Act.

[22] *e.g.* the Geneva Convention on the Contract for the International Carriage of Goods by Road, of May 19, 1956 (Cmnd. 3455), generally known as CMR, is re-enacted as the Sched. to the Carriage of Goods by Road Act, 1965.

[23] *e.g.* s.25 of the Maintenance Orders (Reciprocal Enforcement) Act 1972 refers to the United Nations Convention on the Recovery Abroad of Maintenance, signed in New York on June 20, 1956 (Cmnd. 4485).

vention.[24] Again, secondary legislation may make provisions implementing international conventions[25] and may make additional provisions adapting domestic law for the purpose.[26] The term "statutory provision" in paragraph (a) is defined by section 50[27] to include any provision in an Act or in subordinate legislation.

In theory, a rule of common law may correspond with a rule in an international convention and have the incidental effect of implementing it, and the purpose of paragraph (b) is to ensure that such a common law rule is as subject to Title VII as a statutory provision implementing a convention.

3. Subsection (2)

The 1968 Convention may have potentially harsh effects on a person domiciled or habitually resident in a third country where jurisdiction has been assumed over him in one Contracting State on an exorbitant basis and recognition and enforcement of the resulting judgment is then sought in another Contracting State. Normally, the judgment would have to be given virtually automatic recognition and enforcement. Article 59[28] permits Contracting States to relax those potentially harsh effects in certain circumstances by undertaking in a convention with that third country not to recognise or enforce such a judgment. **40.29**

The effect of this subsection is to enable such conventions to be easily identified by an Order in Council, although the undertaking not to recognise or enforce such a judgment given against a domiciliary or habitual resident of that third country would have legal effect anyway by reason of its falling within Article 59. The likelihood is that such commitments will arise in bilateral conventions on the recognition and enforcement of judgments, which will then be given effect in domestic law by an Order in Council under section 1 of the Foreign Judgments (Reciprocal Enforcement) Act 1933. No doubt the same Order in Council can serve the purpose of identifying the convention for the purposes of this section. This has already

---

[24] *e.g.* the two maritime conventions signed in Brussels on May 10, 1952 (Cmnd. 1128) were given effect to by the Administration of Justice Act 1956, now replaced by Part II of the Supreme Court Act 1981.

[25] *e.g.* the Hague Convention of 1973 on the Recognition and Enforcement of Decisions relating to Maintenance Obligations (Cmnd. 7939) was implemented by the Reciprocal Enforcement of Maintenance Orders (Hague Convention Countries) Order 1979, (S.I. 1979 No. 1317), made under s.40 of the Maintenance Orders (Reciprocal Enforcement) Act 1972.

[26] *e.g.* the Orders in Council made under s.1 of the Foreign Judgments (Reciprocal Enforcement) Act 1933.

[27] Para. 44.45 below.

[28] See para. 33.24 above.

occurred in respect of the Convention between the United Kingdom and Canada.[29]

Section 10

40.30   **10.**—*Allocation within U.K. of jurisdiction with respect to trusts and
consumer contracts*

(1) **The provisions of this section shall have effect for the purpose of allocating within the United Kingdom jurisdiction in certain proceedings in respect of which the 1968 Convention confers
jurisdiction on the courts of the United Kingdom generally and
to which section 16 does not apply.**

(2) **Any proceedings which by virtue of Article 5(6) (trusts) are
brought within the United Kingdom shall be brought in the
courts of the part of the United Kingdom in which the trust is
domiciled.**

(3) **Any proceedings which by virtue of the first paragraph of
Article 14 (consumer contracts) are brought within the United
Kingdom by a consumer on the ground that he is himself domi-
ciled there shall be brought in the courts of the part of the United
Kingdom in which he is domiciled.**

1. General note and subsection (1)

40.31   In some cases the Convention determines only the international
jurisdiction of the courts (by stipulating that the courts of a given
Contracting State are to be competent), but leaves the question of
local jurisdiction within that state to national law. The allocation of
jurisdiction within the United Kingdom in such cases is determined
almost entirely by section 16 and Schedule 4, but those provisions
apply only where the defendant is domiciled in some part of the
United Kingdom or where the subject-matter falls within the exclusive jurisdiction provisions of Article 16.[30]

Apart from those cases of exclusive jurisdiction, there are two
types of case where the Convention permits a defendant domiciled
in one Contracting State to be sued in another Contracting State,
without allocating local jurisdiction within that latter state. This
section fills that gap for the United Kingdom, by determining the

---

[29] This bilateral convention was signed in Ottawa on April 24, 1984 (Cmnd. 9337),
and it was given effect by The Reciprocal Enforcement of Foreign Judgments
(Canada) Order 1986, (S.I. 1986 No. 2027), which came into force on January
1, 1987; but see now The Reciprocal Enforcement of Foreign Judgments
(Canada) Order 1987, (S.I. 1987 No. 468). This convention is discussed at
para. 33.32 above.

[30] For certain cases where a person is deemed to be domiciled in the U.K., see
s.44, para. 44.27 below.

"part of the United Kingdom"[31] in which the proceedings are to be brought. If the case falls within the Convention and the defendant is domiciled in the United Kingdom, section 16 applies, and this section does not apply.

2. Subsection (2)

Article 5(6) of the 1968 Convention[32] provides that an action against a person domiciled in another Contracting State in his capacity as a settlor, beneficiary or trustee of a trust[33] may be brought in the courts of the state in which the trust is domiciled. This subsection allocates local jurisdiction by providing for such an action to be brought in the part of the United Kingdom where the trust is domiciled. Section 45[34] determines where the trust is domiciled.

3. Subsection (3)

By the first paragraph of Article 14,[35] the Convention gives a consumer[36] the option of bringing proceedings in the State where he is himself domiciled. If he does so in the United Kingdom against a person domiciled in another Contracting State[37] and the case is one to which the Convention applies, he must do so in the part of the United Kingdom in which he is domiciled. Section 41[38] determines the domicile of individuals.

Section 11

11.—*Proof and admissibility of certain judgments and related*   **40.32**
documents

  (1) **For the purposes of the 1968 Convention—**
    (a) **a document, duly authenticated, which purports to be a copy of a judgment given by a court of a Contracting State other than the United Kingdom shall without**

---

[31] England and Wales, Scotland and Northern Ireland: see s.50, para. 44.45 below.
[32] Para. 17.65 above.
[33] This does not include a resulting or constructive trust: see para. 17.68 above.
[34] Para. 44.30 below.
[35] Para. 19.25 above.
[36] A consumer is defined by the first para. of Art. 13, see para. 19.08 above.
[37] If the defendant is domiciled in a non-Contracting State, he may be deemed by the second paragraph of Art. 13 (see paras. 19.19 *et seq.* above) to be domiciled in a Contracting State in which he has a branch, agency or other establishment but, if not, Art. 4 requires that the ordinary rules of national law be applied in determining jurisdiction.
[38] Para. 44.01 below.

> further proof be deemed to be a true copy, unless the
> contrary is shown; and
>
> (b) the original or a copy of any such document as is men-
>   tioned in Article 46(2) or 47 (supporting documents to
>   be produced by a party seeking recognition or enforce-
>   ment of a judgment) shall be evidence, and in Scotland
>   sufficient evidence, of any matter to which it relates.
>
> (2) A document purporting to be a copy of a judgment given by
> any such court as is mentioned in subsection (1)(a) is duly auth-
> enticated for the purposes of this section if it purports—
>
> (a) to bear the seal of that court; or
>
> (b) to be certified by any person in his capacity as a judge or
>   officer of that court to be a true copy of a judgment
>   given by that court.
>
> (3) Nothing in this section shall prejudice the admission in
> evidence of any document which is admissible apart from this
> section.

1. General note

40.33   Articles 46 and 47 of the 1968 Convention[39] require an application for an order of enforcement to be supported by certain documentary evidence[40] (although these requirements may be relaxed to
a certain extent under Article 48)[41] and Article 49[42] provides that
"no legalisation or other similar formality shall be required in
respect of the documents referred to in Articles 46 or 47."

This section provides new and simplified rules of evidence in
relation to those documents which must be produced on such an
application to register a judgment given in another Contracting
State.[43] The effect of the section is to keep to a minimum the formalities necessary to prove these documents, while preserving the
existing rules[44] as to their proof and admissibility under any more
favourable conditions. The proof of foreign judgments and other
documents is discussed in Chapter 8.[45]

The section deals separately with the copy judgments required by
Article 46(1) and with the other documents required by Articles
46(2) and 47. The section applies only to judgments given by courts
in other Contracting States, and the documents which need to be

---

[39] Paras. 29.01 and 29.07 above.
[40] Some of the provisions apply also to an applicant for a declaration of recognition: see para. 25.05 above.
[41] Para. 29.20 above.
[42] Para. 29.30 above.
[43] See also para. 10.14 above.
[44] See subs. (3).
[45] See paras. 8.17 *et seq.* above.

produced to secure their enforcement (or recognition) in this country. It does not apply to judgments given in the United Kingdom.[46]

2. Subsections (1)(a) and (2): **Judgments**

In considering the meaning and effect of these provisions, it is **40.34** necessary to consider them in connection with Article 46(1),[47] which requires the applicant to produce "a copy of the judgment which satisfies the conditions necessary to establish its authenticity." The meaning of that provision has already been considered,[48] but it should be noted that the "copy" judgment which the applicant has to produce must be an official copy, and that the "conditions necessary to establish its authenticity" are conditions laid down by the law of the court of origin, and not by the law of the court addressed.

It follows that the provisions in these subsections relate only to the words "a copy of the judgment" in Article 46(1), and not to the "conditions" referred to in that Article. They do not define the conditions upon which a copy of the foreign judgment is to be considered authentic for the purposes of the 1968 Convention, but provide rules of evidence only, to assist the court in deciding of its own motion[49] whether the document before it, purporting to be an official copy of a judgment of a court in another Contracting State, is a true copy. If either or both of the conditions set out in subsection (2) are satisfied, the copy judgment is deemed to be a true copy, "unless the contrary is shown."

Subsection (2) requires that a document which *purports* to bear the seal of the original court, or *purports* to be certified by a person in his capacity as a judge or officer of the court, should be regarded as "duly authenticated" for the purposes of the section, whether or not the seal or certificate is actually genuine, or the person certifying the document is actually a judge or officer of the court. This ensures that the document is self-proving, and no independent evidence of the truth of the copy judgment is required (or permitted) for the purposes of subsection (2).

On an appeal under Article 37, the party against whom the order for registration has been made may seek to demonstrate that the copy is false. If the appellant adduces evidence impugning the auth-

---

[46] The authenticity of copy judgments given by courts in the U.K. is certified under s.12 (if the judgment is to be recognised or enforced in another Contracting State), or under paras. 2 to 4 of Sched. 6 or Sched. 7 (if the judgment is to be enforced in another part of the U.K.).

[47] Para. 29.01 above.

[48] Para. 29.03 above.

[49] See para. 28.03 above.

enticity of the seal or certificate, or demonstrating that the person certifying the truth of the copy was not a judge or officer of the original court, it might tend to show that the copy judgment was not genuine, but would not of itself prevent the copy judgment from being "duly authenticated" within the meaning of sub-section (2).[50]

3. Subsection (1)(b): Documents referred to in Articles 46(2) and 47

40.35   The documents referred to in Articles 46(2) and 47 are as follows:

  (i) the original or certified true copy of a document which establishes that the party against whom a default judgment has been given was duly served with the document instituting the proceedings: Article 46(2);
 (ii) documents which establish that, according to the law of the state of origin, the judgment is enforceable and has been served: Article 47(1);
(iii) a document showing that the applicant is in receipt of legal aid in the state of origin: Article 47(2).

These documents are referred to in the Rules of the Supreme Court, Order 71, rule 28(1)(a). The meaning and effect of Articles 46(2) and 47 have been discussed above.[51]

The effect of this subsection is to disapply the hearsay rule[52] in relation to those various documents, so that a document falling within its scope is to be taken as evidence (but not conclusive evidence) of the truth of its contents. Like subsection (1)(a), this is merely a rule of evidence, reducing the formalities necessary before a judgment can be the made the subject of an order for its enforcement (or declaration of its recognition) and does not otherwise alter the court's duties in inquiring into the enforceability of the judgment.

This subsection does not include any provision for proving that a copy of a document referred to in Articles 46(2) and 47 is a true copy, and, if in any case such a copy would satisfy the requirements

---

[50] Depending on the law of the country of origin, such evidence might show that the document did not satisfy the conditions necessary to establish its authenticity for the purposes of that law and Art. 46(1). If the appellant shows the copy judgment not to be genuine, there is still a theoretical possibility that his appeal might fail if the court decides to relax the evidential requirements of Art. 46(1): see paras. 29.22–29.23 above.

[51] Paras. 29.04–29.19 above.

[52] As to the effect of the rule against hearsay on documentary evidence, see para. 8.11 above.

of those Articles, its authenticity as a copy will need to be proved under the general law.[53]

4. Subsection (3)

This subsection serves to emphasise that, while the rest of the section provides new and simpler rules in relation to certain documentary evidence, it is not exhaustive and allows the documents (or their contents) to be proved under the other provisions of the law (for example, under the Evidence Act 1851 or the Civil Evidence Act 1968).[54]

Section 12

12.—*Provision for issue of copies of, and certificates in connection with, United Kingdom judgments*   **40.36**

Rules of court may make provision for enabling any interested party wishing to secure under the 1968 Convention the recognition or enforcement in another Contracting State of a judgment given by a court in the United Kingdom to obtain, subject to any conditions specified in the rules—
  (a) a copy of the judgment; and
  (b) a certificate giving particulars relating to the judgment and the proceedings in which it was given.

1. General note

Just as the conditions of authenticity of a copy judgment given by   **40.37**
a court of another Contracting State are to be determined by the law of that state,[55] so the conditions of authenticity of a copy of a judgment given in the United Kingdom are to be determined by United Kingdom law. This section[56] provides for those conditions to be regulated by rules of court in the three "law areas" of the United Kingdom, enabling the interested party to obtain a copy of the judgment and a certificate giving particulars relating to the judgment and the proceedings.

The term "interested party" is not defined in the Act, but it must have the same meaning as in Articles 26 and 31 of the 1968 Convention,[57] and is not therefore confined to persons who were parties to

---

[53] The truth of the copy should be deposed to in the affidavit under R.S.C., Ord. 71, r. 28(1).
[54] See paras. 8.19 and 8.11–8.13 above.
[55] See para. 40.34 above.
[56] s.12 is modelled on s.10 of the Administration of Justice Act 1920 and s.10 of the Foreign Judgments (Reciprocal Enforcement) Act 1933, each of which is substituted by amendments made by this Act: s.35 and Sched. 10, paras. 43.39 and 47.09 below.
[57] Paras. 27.05 *et seq.* and 28.07 above.

the judgment itself. It is not only High Court judgments to which the rule applies. The term "court" includes a tribunal;[58] the term "judgment" is defined by section 15(1)[59] by reference to Article 25 of the 1968 Convention[60] and refers, in effect, to a judgment or order of any court or tribunal, provided that it falls wholly or partly within the scope of the Convention.[61]

2. Rules of court

In England and Wales, the relevant Rule of the Supreme Court is Order 71, rule 36,[62] which provides for the issue of a copy judgment and a certificate[63] on an *ex parte* application[64] supported by an affidavit deposing to certain prescribed matters. The copy judgment is an office copy sealed with the seal of the Supreme Court, which for the purposes of Article 46(1)[65] means that the copy judgment "satisfies the conditions necessary to establish its authenticity," and the certificate prescribed by the rules provides for the information which Articles 46(2) and 47(1) require the interested party to produce in documentary form on his application in another Contracting State for an order of enforcement of the judgment.[66] Similar but less comprehensive provision is made in relation to county court judgments by the County Court Rules, Order 35, rule 3;[67] and in relation to magistrates' courts by the Magistrates' Courts (Civil Jurisdiction and Judgments Act 1982) Rules 1986, rule 12.[68]

Because the Convention covers such a wide range of judgments and courts, cases may arise where an interested party wishes to obtain an official copy of an order made by some tribunal for which

---

[58] s.50, para. 44.45 below.

[59] Para. 40.42 below.

[60] Para. 26.01 above.

[61] Chap. 14 above.

[62] *Cf.* R.S.C., Ord. 71, r. 13, relating to the issue of certificates authenticating judgments for the purposes of Part II of the Administration of Justice Act 1920 and the Foreign Judgments (Reciprocal Enforcement) Act 1933.

[63] The certificate is in Form 110 in R.S.C., Appendix A; *Supreme Court Practice*, para. [111].

[64] The application is made to a Master of the Queen's Bench Division of the High Court: R.S.C., Ord. 71, r. 26; Ord. 32, r. 11. See para. 10.70 above.

[65] Para. 29.01 below.

[66] The certificate should be sufficient in most cases to satisfy Arts. 46 and 47(1), but that is a matter for the enforcing court, which may still require the applicant to provide further information.

[67] This rule apparently applies only to an application by the party entitled to enforce the judgment, and not, for example, to a person who is merely "an interested party" for the purposes of Art. 26 of the Convention (paras. 27.05 *et seq.* below). Such a person would have to apply on an informal basis: see the next para.

[68] See para. 11.29 above.

rules of court[69] have not been made under this section. In such a case, the party has no express right to a copy judgment under this section, but is not precluded from obtaining one on an informal basis, together with such other documentary evidence as he may require for the purposes of his application in another Contracting State.

Section 13

13.—*Modifications to cover authentic instruments and court settlements*   **40.38**

(1) **Her Majesty may by Order in Council provide that—**
  (a) **any provision of this Act relating to the recognition or enforcement in the United Kingdom or elsewhere of judgments to which the 1968 Convention applies; and**
  (b) **any other statutory provision, whenever passed or made, so relating,**
shall apply, with such modifications as may be specified in the Order, in relation to documents and settlements within Title IV of the 1968 Convention (authentic instruments and court settlements enforceable in the same manner as judgments) as if they were judgments to which that Convention applies.

(2) **An Order in Council under this section may make different provisions in relation to different descriptions of documents and settlements.**

(3) **Any Order in Council under this section shall be subject to annulment in pursuance of a resolution of either House of Parliament.**

General note

Title IV (Articles 50 and 51) of the 1968 Convention provide for   **40.39**
the enforceability, under much the same conditions as judgments, of authentic instruments and court settlements. Provided that certain conditions are satisfied, the court of the state addressed is bound to order the enforcement of such instruments and settlements. The meaning of "authentic instruments" and "court settlements," and the conditions under which they will be enforced, are considered in some detail in the commentary on Articles 50 and 51.[70] The types of instrument and settlement which exist in each of the other Contracting States are summarised in Chapters 48 to 58 below.[71]

This section is a widely drawn enabling provision allowing pro-

---

[69] "Rules of court" are widely defined by s.50, para. 44.45 below.
[70] Chap. 30 above; see also paras. 10.47 *et seq.* above.
[71] At para. 70.

visions of this Act or of any other Act or subordinate legislation[72] to be applied to authentic instruments and court settlements, with such modifications[73] as may be specified in the Order, to authentic instruments and court settlements. No order has yet been made under this section.

The absence of any Order in Council under this section, or of the application of any specific statutory provision to authentic instruments or court settlements, does not alter the court's primary obligation under Articles 50 and 51 to issue an order for their enforcement in accordance with the procedures provided for in Articles 31 *et seq.*

Section 14

40.40   **14.—***Modifications consequential on revision of the Conventions*

(1) If at any time it appears to Her Majesty in Council that Her Majesty's Government in the United Kingdom have agreed to a revision of any of the Conventions, including in particular any revision connected with the accession to the 1968 Convention of one or more further states, Her Majesty may by Order in Council make such modifications of this Act or any other statutory provision, whenever passed or made, as Her Majesty considers appropriate in consequence of the revision.

(2) An Order in Council under this section shall not be made unless a draft of the Order has been laid before Parliament and approved by a resolution of each House of Parliament.

(3) In this section "revision" means an omission from, addition to or alteration of any of the Conventions and includes replacement of any of the Conventions to any extent by another Convention, protocol or other description of international agreement.

General note

40.41   This section enables modifications[74] to be made to this Act or to any other statutory provision,[75] in consequence of a revision of any of the Conventions referred to in Article 1. The most likely exercise of this power will be in relation to the accession to the 1968 Convention of further Contracting States, and this example is expressly referred to in the section. Such a revision has already been agreed to by the Government in the form of the Greek Accession Convention

---

[72] See the definition of "statutory provision" in s.50, para. 44.45 below.
[73] These are defined by s.50, *ibid.*
[74] These are defined in s.50, para. 44.45 below.
[75] *Ibid.*

of 1982,[76] but this is not yet in force.[77] A convention providing for the accession of Spain and Portugal will be concluded in due course. It would seem that this section does not enable effect to be given by Order in Council to the Lugano convention with EFTA countries.[78]

Revisions of the Conventions on matters of substance are less likely, although the opportunity may be taken, in conventions providing for the accession of new Contracting States, to resolve points which have proved particularly difficult in practice.

There is a separate power in section 47[79] to make provisions to bring the law of any part of the United Kingdom into accord with the Conventions as interpreted by the European Court.

Section 15

15.—*Interpretation of Part I and consequential amendments*   **40.42**

(1) In this Part, unless the context otherwise requires—
"judgment" has the meaning given by Article 25;
"maintenance order" means a maintenance judgment within the meaning of the 1968 Convention;
"payer," in relation to a maintenance order, means the person liable to make the payments for which the order provides;
"prescribed" means prescribed by rules of court.

(2) References in this Part to a judgment registered under section 4 or 5 include, to the extent of its registration, references to a judgment so registered to a limited extent only.

(3) Anything authorised or required by the 1968 Convention or this Part to be done by, to or before a particular magistrates' court may be done by, to or before any magistrates' court acting for the same petty sessions area (or, in Northern Ireland, petty sessions district) as that court.

(4) The enactments specified in Part I of Schedule 12 shall have effect with the amendments specified there, being amendments consequential on this Part.

1. Subsection (1)

This subsection contains several definitions for the purposes of   **40.43**
Part I (sections 1 to 15) of the Act.

---

[76] This was signed in Luxembourg on October 25, 1982, O.J. 1982 L 388. Relevant extracts are set out and annotated in chap. 38 above.
[77] See para. 13.05 above.
[78] See para. 13.07 above.
[79] Para. 44.36 below.

"Judgment." This term is defined by reference to Article 25 of the 1968 Convention[80] which covers a wide range of final and interlocutory orders, decrees and decisions given by courts and tribunals.[81]

"Maintenance order." This definition is discussed under section 5.[82] It presents certain problems, because the term "maintenance judgment" is not defined by the 1968 Convention.

"Payer." This definition applies in relation to a maintenance order and may be taken as referring to the "maintenance creditor" referred to in Article 5(2).[83]

"Prescribed." The term "rules of court" is itself defined by section 50.[84]

2. Subsection (2)

A judgment may in some circumstances be registered under the Act as to part only: see sections 4(1)[85] and 5(3)[86] and Article 42.[87] This subsection ensures that such judgments are treated, to the extent of their registration, as complete judgments in their own right.

3. Subsection (3)

40.44   Where there is more than one magistrates' court for a petty sessions area, this subsection enables the functions of one to be discharged by another. The civil jurisdiction of magistrates' courts is usually confined to matters arising within the petty sessions area[88] and, for example, the court which has local jurisdiction for the place where a maintenance creditor is domiciled or habitually resident for the purposes of Article 5(2), or which is the "appropriate court" for the purposes of section 5(1) and Article 32, is probably any court for the petty sessions area. The term "petty sessions area" is not defined, but may be taken as having the same meaning as is defined by section 4 of the Justices of the Peace Act 1979.[89]

This subsection is equivalent to provisions in section 148(2) of the Magistrates' Courts Act 1980 and in section 17(4) of the Main-

---

[80] Para. 26.01 above.
[81] See para. 10.07 above.
[82] See para. 40.13 above.
[83] Para. 17.32 above.
[84] See para. 44.45 below.
[85] Para. 40.08 above.
[86] Para. 40.12 above.
[87] Para. 28.71 above.
[88] Magistrates' Courts Act 1980, s.52.
[89] Magistrates' Courts Act 1980, s.150(1) adopts the same definition for the purposes of that Act.

tenance Orders (Reciprocal Enforcement) Act 1972. It has the effect that, where one court is better equipped than another court for the same area to enforce maintenance orders, the former is able to discharge the latter's functions. Equally, an appeal under the first paragraph of Article 37 or under Article 40 against the decision of the justices' clerk at one court respectively to grant or refuse an order for the enforcement of a maintenance order may be lodged with another court for the same area.[90]

4. Subsection (4)

This subsection provides for the consequential amendments set out in Part I of Schedule 12 to have effect.[91] The various Acts affected all relate to maintenance orders or domestic proceedings and are amended to include reference to a maintenance order under Part I of this Act.

---

[90] See para. 11.17 above.
[91] Para. 47.17 below.

CHAPTER 41

CIVIL JURISDICTION AND JUDGMENTS ACT 1982
PART II—JURISDICTION, AND RECOGNITION AND ENFORCEMENT OF JUDGMENTS, WITHIN UNITED KINGDOM

Section 16

41.01 **16.**—*Allocation within United Kingdom of jurisdiction in certain civil proceedings*

(1) The provisions set out in Schedule 4 (which contains a modified version of Title II of the 1968 Convention) shall have effect for determining, for each part of the United Kingdom, whether the courts of law of that part, or any particular court of law in that part, have or has jurisdiction in proceedings where—

(a) the subject-matter of the proceedings is within the scope of the 1968 Convention as determined by Article 1 (whether or not the Convention has effect in relation to the proceedings); and

(b) the defendant or defender is domiciled in the United Kingdom or the proceedings are of a kind mentioned in Article 16 (exclusive jurisdiction regardless of domicile).

(2) In Schedule 4 modifications of Title II of the 1968 Convention are indicated as follows—

(a) modifications by way of omission are indicated by dots; and

(b) **within each Article words resulting from modifications by way of addition or substitution are printed in heavy type.**

(3) **In determining any question as to the meaning or effect of any provision contained in Schedule 4—**

(a) **regard shall be had to any relevant principles laid down by the European Court in connection with Title II of the 1968 Convention and to any relevant decision of that court as to the meaning or effect of any provision of that Title; and**

(b) **without prejudice to the generality of paragraph (a), the reports mentioned in section 3(3) may be considered and shall, so far as relevant, be given such weight as is appropriate in the circumstances.**

(4) **The provisions of this section and Schedule 4 shall have effect subject to the 1968 Convention and to the provisions of section 17.**

(5) **In section 15(1)(a) of the Maintenance Orders Act 1950 (domestic proceedings in which initial process may be served in another part of the United Kingdom), after sub-paragraph (v) there shall be added—**

"(vi) Article 5(2) of Schedule 4 to the Civil Jurisdiction and Judgments Act 1982; or".

1. General note

The 1968 Convention usually regulates only the international jurisdiction of the courts of a given Contracting State in relation to a defendant domiciled in that state, leaving the allocation of jurisdiction within that state to be regulated by national law. In the absence of a code of rules uniformly applicable throughout the United Kingdom, parties (and the courts) might have had difficulty in knowing whether the courts of one part of the United Kingdom, rather than of another, had local jurisdiction over the case.

41.02

The effect of section 16 and Schedule 4 is twofold. First, these provisions allocate jurisdiction between the different parts of the United Kingdom for most cases falling within the scope of the 1968 Convention. Secondly, they also provide the basis for jurisdiction within each part of the United Kingdom for those cases to which they apply. This second effect is a radical innovation in English law and it affects even those cases which are entirely internal to the United Kingdom or to just one part of the United Kingdom.[1] The provisions are subject to section 17[2] and Schedule 5.[3]

---

[1] See paras. 1.23–1.24 above.
[2] Para. 41.11 below.
[3] Para. 45.30 below.

Schedule 4 is closely modelled on the jurisdictional rules in Title II (Articles 2 to 24) of the 1968 Convention itself and, subject to certain modifications, it is an extension of those international rules into the context of the United Kingdom's own different jurisdictions. So, for example, a defendant domiciled[4] in one part of the United Kingdom may generally be sued there and, equally, he may be sued in another part of the United Kingdom in much the same circumstances as if he were domiciled in another Contracting State. Subsection (3) introduces special provisions as to the interpretation of Schedule 4, with a view to keeping its application as closely parallel as possible to the application of the Convention.

Jurisdiction under Schedule 4: summary

41.03   For a court in the United Kingdom to have jurisdiction under the rules in Schedule 4, the following conditions must be satisfied:

1. The court must be a court of law as defined by the Act;[5]
2. The subject-matter of the proceedings must fall within the scope of the 1968 Convention;[6]
3. The defendant must be domiciled in the United Kingdom *or* the case must be of a kind which would fall within Article 16 of the Convention (exclusive jurisdiction);[7]
4. The jurisdiction of the court must not be excluded, either by the Convention or by the terms of section 17 and Schedule 5.[8]

Each of these conditions is discussed in more detail below. If Schedule 4 does not apply and jurisdiction is not allocated by the other provisions of the Act referred to below, the general law on conflicts of jurisdiction will continue to apply to cases not falling within the Convention, and leave will continue to be necessary for the service of process out of England and Wales in most cases.

Other provisions affecting local jurisdiction

There are four types of case where the Convention allocates international jurisdiction to the courts of a particular Contracting State without specifying local jurisdiction, but which do not fall within this section if the defendant is not domiciled in the United Kingdom. Jurisdiction in two of those cases, relating to trusts and consumer contracts, is allocated by section 10.[9] The other two cases are

---

[4] For the special meaning of "domicile" in the context of the Act, see ss.41 to 46, paras. 44.01 *et seq.* below.
[5] s.16(1).
[6] s.16(1)(a).
[7] s.16(1)(b).
[8] s.16(4).
[9] See para. 40.30 above.

where, in certain insurance cases and certain consumer cases,[10] the defendant is not domiciled in a Contracting State, but is nonetheless deemed to be so for the purposes of the Convention. In those cases, where the deemed domicile is in the United Kingdom, section 44 has effect for allocating the domicile within the United Kingdom.

Jurisdiction of United Kingdom courts under Article 17 of the Convention

There is a further category of case where the courts of the United Kingdom may have jurisdiction pursuant to the Convention, without it being clear whether the courts of England and Wales, of Scotland or of Northern Ireland are intended, and where section 16 and Schedule 4 do not provide a solution. This is where there is a valid jurisdiction agreement under Article 17,[11] which falls within the Convention by reason of the plaintiff, rather than the defendant, being domiciled in a Contracting State,[12] and which specifies only the courts of the United Kingdom. Schedule 4 would not apply, unless the defendant were domiciled in the United Kingdom. **41.04**

In such a case, it seems probable that the first court seised would have jurisdiction to the exclusion of the others[13] and this solution, it is submitted, accords best with the Convention. It may be, however, that a discretion which would be available as a matter of general English law will enable an English court first seised to decline jurisdiction in favour of the courts of another part of the United Kingdom, on the ground that it is not the *forum conveniens*.[14] Nonetheless, it is submitted that the English court's inherent and statutory jurisdiction[15] to stay proceedings in such circumstances (if it has survived at all in the light of sections 2 and 16 of this Act), should be very sparingly exercised, in view of the extent to which such discretion is disfavoured by the Convention.[16]

1. Subsection (1): General note

This subsection gives effect to Schedule 4, which contains the code of jurisdictional rules, modelled on Title II of the Convention. The subsection also defines the principal limitations on the application of that code. A number of the more important points of definition should be noted: **41.05**

---

[10] Art. 8, second para. (para. 18.11 above) and Art. 13, second para. (para. 19.01 above), respectively.
[11] See chap. 21 above.
[12] See para. 21.34 above.
[13] See para. 21.40 above.
[14] See para. 21.39 above and 44.44 below; Dicey and Morris, pp. 389 *et seq.*
[15] Supreme Court Act 1981, s.49(3) and *Supreme Court Practice*, paras. [5204] *et seq.*
[16] See paras. 1.37 *et seq.* and 21.15–21.16 above.

(i) "part of the United Kingdom" means England and Wales, Scotland or Northern Ireland;[17]
(ii) "court of law" means only the House of Lords, the Court of Appeal, the High Court, the Crown Court, a county court and a magistrates' court;[18]
(iii) the references to Articles 1 and 16 are to Articles of the 1968 Convention rather than Schedule 4;[19]
(iv) the concept of domicile is the same as that used for the purposes of the Convention, and the defendant's domicile is to be decided by reference to sections 41 to 46.[20]

The principal effect of defining the term "courts of law" exhaustively is to exclude tribunals, which would otherwise fall within the scope of the Schedule in the same way as they fall within the scope of the Convention.[21] The cases which come before tribunals will often fall outside the scope of the Convention,[22] but where that is not the case, the tribunal's jurisdiction will anyway be regulated by statute or by subordinate legislation,[23] often in a manner which applies to the whole of the United Kingdom.

3. Subsection (1)(a): Subject-matter of the proceedings

41.06   For the rules in Schedule 4 to apply, it is first necessary that the subject-matter of the case should fall within the scope of the 1968 Convention as determined by Article 1.[24] The overall scope of the Convention is determined not only by Article 1, but also by a number of other factors,[25] although it seems likely that Article 1 is comprehensive so far as subject-matter is concerned. As with much else in the Convention, Article 1 is to be given an autonomous interpretation,[26] and the precise limits of the material scope of the Convention's application will only be worked out over a period of time, although there is already a small body of case-law in the European Court of Justice, discussed in Chapter 14.

Nevertheless, for most purposes, the Convention's material scope is relatively clear. It extends to civil and commercial matters, a concept which has been held to exclude matters of public law; certain

---

[17] s.50, para. 44.45 below.
[18] *Ibid.* This applies also to Northern Ireland. In Scotland, it means the House of Lords, the Court of Session and a sheriff court: see below.
[19] s.1(2), para. 40.01 above.
[20] Paras. 44.01 *et seq.* below.
[21] Art. 25, para. 26.01 above. See also the definition of "court" in s.50.
[22] *e.g.* social security matters: see para. 14.30 above.
[23] *e.g.* the jurisdiction of industrial tribunals is determined by the Employment Protection (Consolidation) Act 1978, s.128 and rules made thereunder.
[24] See chap. 14 above.
[25] See para. 14.04 above.
[26] See paras. 13.19 *et seq.* above.

other matters are expressly excluded, notably large areas of family law, insolvency and arbitration. Reference should be made to the commentary on Article 1.[27]

4. Subsection (1)(a): Cases to which the Convention does not apply

It is not necessary for the purpose of Schedule 4 that the Convention itself should apply to the proceedings;[28] this is made clear by the words "whether or not the Convention has effect in relation to the proceedings." As has already been observed, the code of rules in the Schedule is not to be read merely as an extension into the United Kingdom of a modified version of Title II, in order to make the Convention workable internationally.[29] While it has that effect, it also has the effect of providing a uniform code of jurisdictional rules for matters which are purely internal to the United Kingdom. For the Convention itself to apply, the proceedings must bear some international character[30] (although this may sometimes appear fairly tenuous),[31] whereas no such element is necessary for the purposes of Schedule 4. The case may not even require connection with more than one part of the United Kingdom.

It is not entirely clear to what extent, if at all, the Convention applies to cases which have international connections with a non-Contracting State, but not with another Contracting State. In some such cases, it seems that the Convention applies, but that the courts have a discretion as to the effect to be given to its rules, whereas in other cases, it may be that the Convention applies without there being any such discretion.[32]

5. Subsection (1)(b): Alternative criteria

There is a further condition which must be satisfied before the rules in Schedule 4 apply. It is in two parts, stated as alternatives, namely that the defendant should be domiciled in the United Kingdom *or* that the proceedings should be of a kind mentioned in Article 16 of the Convention. If neither criterion is satisfied, Schedule 4 does not apply.

Domicile. The concept of domicile used for the purposes of the Act is quite different from that traditionally used in English law, and is more closely akin to habitual residence. So far as individuals

41.07

41.08

---

[27] Paras. 14.04 *et seq.* above.
[28] For cases where the Convention does apply, see para. 41.10 below.
[29] Para. 41.02 above.
[30] See para. 13.10 above.
[31] See para. 21.06 above.
[32] See paras. 1.39–1.40 above and 44.43 below.

are concerned, domicile is comprehensively defined by section 41.[33] Section 42[34] defines the "seat" of a corporation or association for most purposes, and section 42(1) provides that that seat is to be treated as the corporation's or association's domicile for the purposes of the Act.[35] Section 43[36] defines a corporation's or association's seat in narrower terms for certain purposes in relation to its constitution and internal affairs, while section 45[37] defines the domicile of trusts and section 46[38] defines the domicile and seat of the Crown.

Article 16. This Article of the 1968 Convention provides for the exclusive jurisdiction of certain courts over a limited range cases, by reference to their subject-matter. The exclusive jurisdiction is allocated to those courts, irrespective of the domicile of the parties,[39] because the subject-matter of the cases, or the applicable law, is regarded as being closely connected with the particular court or courts. Reference should be made to the commentary on Article 16.[40]

6. Subsection (2)

This subsection, which explains how the typography of Schedule 4 reflects the difference between it and Title II of the Convention, seems to be the first example of the appearance, in addition to the content, of an Act of Parliament having statutory significance![40a]

7. Subsection (3): Interpretation

41.09   This subsection should ensure that the provisions of Schedule 4 are interpreted consistently with the equivalent provisions of Title II of the Convention. The European Court of Justice has the role of giving authoritative rulings on the interpretation of the Convention, and in doing so often expounds principles for its interpretation and makes *obiter* statements of opinion as to its true meaning.[41] A court

---

[33] Para. 44.01 below.

[34] Para. 44.11 below.

[35] Art. 53, para. 31.23 above, makes the same provision for the purposes of the Convention.

[36] Para. 44.20 below.

[37] Para. 44.30 below.

[38] Para. 44.33 below.

[39] The seat of a corporation or association is, however, relevant for the purposes of Art. 16(2).

[40] Chap. 20 above.

[40a] A different typographical convention has been adopted for the purposes of chap. 45: see para. 45.01 below.

[41] The European Court has no jurisdiction to rule on the interpretation of national law and cannot, therefore, rule directly on the interpretation of Sched. 4: see para. 36.04 above.

in the United Kingdom, faced with a question of interpretation of the Convention, is bound by section 3[42] to decide the question in accordance with those rulings and principles and to have regard to those dicta. It may also give such weight as is appropriate to the Jenard and Schlosser Reports.

Similarly, a court in the United Kingdom deciding a question of interpretation of Schedule 4 is required to have regard to the same matters, but in this case would not be actually bound by the rulings of the European Court.[43] The interpretation of the Convention, and consequently of Schedule 4, requires an approach which is different from the literal techniques customarily adopted by English courts in statutory interpretation;[44] the fact that the subsection merely states that "regard shall be had" to the relevant principles and decisions should not mislead English courts into reverting to familiar techniques of interpretation which differ from the purposive approach adopted by the European Court. It will be a rare case where a provision of Schedule 4 bears a materially different meaning from the corresponding provision in Title II of the Convention.

Clearly, the European Court's rulings on the interpretation of specific passages in the Convention cannot be binding with regard to those parts of Schedule 4 which do not correspond with Title II of the Convention and, in such a case, the United Kingdom court would have to refer only to the general principles of interpretation established by the European Court. In theory at least, even where the European Court has ruled on the interpretation of a provision in Title II which is reproduced in Schedule 4, the United Kingdom courts are free, in an appropriate case, to depart from that ruling in interpreting the Schedule. There may be occasional instances, for example, where the differences between Title II and the Schedule materially affect the meaning of even those parts of the Schedule which are directly reproduced from the Convention without modification.[45]

A cursory reading of paragraph (a) suggests that the principles and decisions to which it refers are only those which relate directly to provisions in Title II of the Convention, but such a reading would probably be misleadingly narrow. It is suggested that "rel-

---

[42] Para. 40.05 above.
[43] Binding effect can be given to the decisions of the European Court by an Order in Council under s.47: para. 44.36 below.
[44] The interpretation of the Convention is discussed generally at paras. 13.09 *et seq.* above.
[45] *e.g.* the decisions of the European Court on the interpretation of the words "particular legal relationship" in Art. 17 will have been made in the context of the formal requirements for jurisdiction clauses contained in that Article: see

evant principles laid down by the European Court" are to be considered as having been laid down "in connection with Title II" if
they have any bearing on the interpretation of that Title, whether or
not they were laid down on a reference for the interpretation of a
provision of Title II and whether or not they expressly referred to
that Title. Similarly, a decision of the European Court may be a
"relevant decision . . . as to the meaning or effect" of a provision of
Title II, even if it were a decision as to the interpretation of a different provision of the Convention. For example, principles and
decisions determining the scope of the Convention under Article 1
may well be relevant to the meaning of Title II and of Schedule 4,
and a decision as to the meaning of the words "sufficient time to
enable him to arrange for his defence" in Article 27(2) would clearly
be relevant to the meaning of the same words in Article 20.

8. Subsection (4)

41.10   This subsection ensures that the Convention takes priority over
this section and over the rules in Schedule 4. So, for example, if the
Convention confers exclusive jurisdiction on the Italian courts over
a claim for rent of a holiday cottage in Italy,[46] the court of the part
of the United Kingdom where the defendant is domiciled would not
have jurisdiction, despite Article 2 of Schedule 4. This subsection
also makes section 16 subject to section 17, and so to the list of
exclusions in Schedule 5.

9. Subsection (5)

Under Article 5(2) of Schedule 4,[47] the courts for the place where
a maintenance creditor is domiciled or habitually resident have
jurisdiction in matters relating to maintenance. The effect of the
amendment made by this subsection is to add that basis of jurisdiction to the instances where maintenance proceedings in a competent
court in one part of the United Kingdom may be served on a person
resident in another part of the United Kingdom.

Section 17

41.11   **17.**—*Exclusion of certain proceedings from Schedule 4*
       **(1) Schedule 4 shall not apply to proceedings of any descrip-
tion listed in Schedule 5 or to proceedings in Scotland under any**

---

paras. 21.41 and 21.52–21.70 above. Those formal requirements are omitted in
Sched. 4 and, in that context, the words, "particular legal relationship" may
bear a different meaning: see para. 45.21 below.
[46] *Rösler* v. *Rottwinkel* [1985] E.C.R. 99, discussed at para. 20.18 above.
[47] Para. 45.06 below.

enactment which confers jurisdiction on a Scottish court in respect of a specific subject-matter on specific grounds.

(2) Her Majesty may by Order in Council—

    (a) add to the list in Schedule 5 any description of proceedings in any part of the United Kingdom; and

    (b) remove from that list any description of proceedings in any part of the United Kingdom (whether included in the list as originally enacted or added by virtue of this subsection).

(3) An Order in Council under subsection (2)—

    (a) may make different provisions for different descriptions of proceedings, for the same description of proceedings in different courts or for different parts of the United Kingdom; and

    (b) may contain such transitional and other incidental provisions as appear to Her Majesty to be appropriate.

(4) An Order in Council under subsection (2) shall not be made unless a draft of the Order has been laid before Parliament and approved by a resolution of each House of Parliament.

General note

    Section 17 excludes certain types of proceedings from the general jurisdictional rules in Schedule 4.[48] First, subsection (1) gives effect to Schedule 5, which lists certain specific types of proceedings excluded from Schedule 4, and those exclusions are discussed in more detail in the commentary on that Schedule.[49] Subsections (2) to (4) provide a flexible means of amending the list of excluded matters in Schedule 5, whether because relevant provisions have been overlooked in the drafting of Schedule 5, or because of new specific jurisdictional rules coming into being.[50]   **41.12**

    Secondly, subsection (1) also excludes certain Scottish cases[51] from Schedule 4, namely those cases where a Scottish court has jurisdiction specified under any enactment in respect of a specific subject-matter on specific grounds.[52] The effect of this exclusion is to

---

[48] Proceedings may also fall outside the scope of Sched. 4 for other reasons: see para. 41.05 above.

[49] See paras. 45.30 *et seq.* below.

[50] No Order in Council has been made under this section.

[51] *Cf.* s.21(1)(a), para. 42.02 below.

[52] Courts in England and Wales also have some such specific statutory jurisdictions (*e.g.* s.9(1) of the Mobile Homes Act 1975 confers jurisdiction on the county court for the district where the relevant site is situated) but the jurisdictional rules are often contained in rules of court which may be difficult to distinguish

preserve in Scotland the specific jurisdictional bases provided by statute. The same effect is achieved for the United Kingdom as a whole by Schedule 5 and by any Order in Council made under subsections (2) to (4).

Section 18

41.13   **18.**—*Enforcement of United Kingdom judgments in other parts of the United Kingdom*

(1) **In relation to any judgment to which this section applies—**

(a) **Schedule 6 shall have effect for the purpose of enabling any money provisions contained in the judgment to be enforced in a part of the United Kingdom other than the part in which the judgment was given; and**

(b) **Schedule 7 shall have effect for the purpose of enabling any non-money provisions so contained to be so enforced.**

(2) **In this section "judgment" means any of the following (references to the giving of a judgment being construed accordingly)—**

(a) **any judgment or order (by whatever name called) given or made by a court of law in the United Kingdom;**

(b) **any judgment or order not within paragraph (a) which has been entered in England and Wales or Northern Ireland in the High Court or a county court;**

(c) **any document which in Scotland has been registered for execution in the Books of Council and Session or in the sheriff court books kept for any sheriffdom;**

(d) **any award or order made by a tribunal in any part of the United Kingdom which is enforceable in that part without an order of a court of law;**

(e) **an arbitration award which has become enforceable in the part of the United Kingdom in which it was given in the same manner as a judgment given by a court of law in that part;**

and subject to the following provisions of this section, this section applies to all such judgments.

(3) **Subject to subsection (4), this section does not apply to—**

(a) **a judgment given in proceedings in a magistrates' court in England and Wales or Northern Ireland;**

(b) **a judgment given in proceedings other than civil proceedings;**

---

from rules of court covering general cases falling within Sched. 4. No such blanket exclusion could therefore be enacted for England and Wales: see the Report of the Proceedings of the House of Commons Standing Committee B, April 19, 1982, cols. 6 & 7.

(ba) a judgment given in the exercise of jurisdiction in relation to insolvency law, within the meaning of section
426 of the Insolvency Act 1986;

(c) a judgment given in proceedings relating to—

. . .

(iii) the obtaining of title to administer the estate of a
deceased person.

(4) This section applies, whatever the nature of the proceedings in which it is made, to—

(a) a decree issued under section 13 of the Court of
Exchequer (Scotland) Act 1856 (recovery of certain
rentcharges and penalties by process of the Court of
Session);

(b) an order which is enforceable in the same manner as a
judgment of the High Court in England and Wales by
virtue of section 16 of the Contempt of Court Act 1981
or section 140 of the Supreme Court Act 1981 (which
relates to fines for contempt of court and forfeiture of
recognisances).

(4A) This section does not apply as regards the enforcement in
Scotland of orders made by the High Court in England and
Wales under or for the purposes of the Drug Trafficking
Offences Act 1986 or Part VI of the Criminal Justice Act 1988
(confiscation of the proceeds of offences); or as respects the
enforcement in England and Wales of orders made by the Court
of Session under or for the purposes of Part I of the Criminal Justice (Scotland) Act 1987.

(5) This section does not apply to so much of any judgment
as—

(a) is an order to which section 16 of the Maintenance
Orders Act 1950 applies (and is therefore an order for
whose enforcement in another part of the United Kingdom provision is made by Part II of that Act);

(b) concerns the status or legal capacity of an individual;

(c) relates to the management of the affairs of a person not
capable of managing his own affairs;

(d) is a provisional (including protective) measure other
than an order for the making of an interim payment;

and except where otherwise stated references to a judgment to
which this section applies are to such a judgment exclusive of
any such provisions.

(6) The following are within subsection (5)(b), but without
prejudice to the generality of that provision—

(a) a decree of judicial separation or of separation;

(b) any provision relating to guardianship or custody.

(7) **This section does not apply to a judgment of a court outside the United Kingdom which falls to be treated for the purposes of its enforcement as a judgment of a court of law in the United Kingdom by virtue of registration under Part II of the Administration of Justice Act 1920, Part I of the Foreign Judgments (Reciprocal Enforcement) Act 1933, Part I of the Maintenance Orders (Reciprocal Enforcement) Act 1972 or section 4 or 5 of this Act.**

(8) **A judgment to which this section applies, other than a judgment within paragraph (e) of subsection (2), shall not be enforced in another part of the United Kingdom except by way of registration under Schedule 6 or 7.†**

1. General note

41.14   This section has replaced the century-old machinery, which had existed under the Judgments Extension Act 1868 and the Inferior Courts Judgments Extension Act 1882 (both of which are repealed by this Act)[53] for the reciprocal enforcement of judgments as between the different parts of the United Kingdom. Judgments given in one part of the United Kingdom, in inferior courts as well as in superior courts, may now be registered in the superior courts of the other parts.[54] The function of county courts and sheriff courts in enforcing the judgments of other parts of the United Kingdom has been discontinued.

The section sets out the judgments to which it applies, which include not only most judgments in the strict sense, but also certain other orders, awards and enforceable instruments. The single largest reform effected by this section is the extension of reciprocal enforcement machinery to judgments other than those ordering the payment of money. By subsection (8), the new machinery is made (except in the case of arbitration awards) the sole permissible method of enforcing the judgments to which it applies in other parts of the United Kingdom.

2. Subsection (1)

41.15   This subsection gives effect to Schedule 6,[55] which relates to the enforcement of money provisions, and Schedule 7,[56] which relates to non-money provisions. The two Schedules are in similar terms, defining what is meant by a "money provision" and a "non-money

---

† Para. (ba) of subs. (3) was added by Sched. 8, para. 36 of the Insolvency Act 1985 and amended by s.439 and Sched. 14 of the Insolvency Act 1986. Sub-paras. (i) and (ii) of para. (c) of subs. (3) were repealed by Sched. 10 of the Insolvency Act 1985. All these amendments took effect before this section came into force. Subs.(4A) was inserted and amended by the three Acts referred to therein.

[53] s.54 and Sched. 14, paras. 44.52 and 47.26 below.
[54] For a general description of the new machinery, see paras. 10.63–10.69 above.
[55] Para. 46.01 below.
[56] Para. 46.13 below.

provision,"[57] providing for the issue of a certificate by the court of origin, the registration of the certificate or judgment in the superior court of another part of the United Kingdom and its enforcement as if it were a judgment of the registering court. Each Schedule makes provision as to staying the execution of the judgment, as to the circumstances in which the registration may be set aside, and as to costs. Schedule 6 also contains provisions concerning interest. The procedures are discussed in more detail in the commentary on the Schedules, but the principal difference between the two is that whereas registration of money provisions may occur on application to an officer of the court,[58] the application for registration of non-money provisions must be to the court itself.[59] A non-money provision will not be registered in a part of the United Kingdom if compliance with it would involve a breach of the law of that part.[60]

3. Subsection (2): Scope of the section

This subsection defines the judgments to which the section applies[61] and which may therefore be reciprocally enforced as between the different parts of the United Kingdom, provided that the qualifications in subsections (3) to (7) are satisfied. It differs from the definition of "judgment" in the 1968 Convention,[62] which applies to the recognition and enforcement of judgments as between Contracting States. The subsection divides the various types of judgment into five categories.

41.16

Paragraph (a): Judgments and orders of courts of law

This is the most important category of judgment for the purposes of this section. The words "judgment or order" are not defined, but are a wide expression covering most decisions on questions at issue between the parties.[63] The expression "given or made" would not seem to extend to the mere *entry* of a judgment or order, because that category of case falls within paragraph (b),[64] but it does seem to be wide enough to cover those cases where the order was actually "made" to enforce liabilities arising otherwise than by proceedings

---

[57] The definitions of "money provision" and "non-money provision" are mutually exclusive but, together, they probably cover any provision capable of falling within this section.

[58] Sched. 6, para. 5(1): para. 46.06 below.

[59] Sched. 7, para. 5(1): para. 46.18 below.

[60] Sched. 7, para. 5(5): para. 46.18 below.

[61] The definition of "judgment" in s.50 (para. 44.45 below) is expressly subject to this subsection.

[62] Art. 25 (para. 26.01 above), which is adopted for the purposes of Part I of the Act by s.15(1) (para. 40.42 above).

[63] 26 *Halsbury's Laws* (4th ed.), para. 501.

[64] See para. 41.17 below.

before the court in question.[65] For example, sums payable under an order of an industrial tribunal may be enforced by execution in the county court, if the court so orders.[66]

The paragraph must be read in connection with the definition of "court of law" in section 50,[67] which provides:

> " 'court of law,' in relation to the United Kingdom, means any of the following courts, namely—
> > (a) the House of Lords,
> > (b) in England and Wales or Northern Ireland, the Court of Appeal, the High Court, the Crown Court, a county court and a magistrates' court,
> > (c) in Scotland, the Court of Session and a sheriff court."

It is not all the orders of these courts which fall within the subsection. Orders of the House of Lords are enforced by being made an order of the High Court,[68] and that order itself falls within this provision. Orders made in magistrates' court proceedings are excluded by subsection (3)(a) and most judgments of the Crown Court will be excluded by the limitation to civil proceedings in subsection (3)(b).

Paragraph (b): Other judgments and orders entered in court

41.17   Some judgments and orders may be entered in the High Court or a county court without having strictly been "given or made" by the court and it is these judgments and orders which paragraph (b) covers. The distinction between judgments and orders falling within paragraph (a) and those falling within this paragraph is that the entry of a judgment or order is a purely administrative act performed by officials of the court, rather than by the court itself, and does not involve judicial consideration as to whether the judgment or order should be given or made, even if leave is required to enter the judgment and the decision to grant leave itself involves a judicial decision.

The principle type of judgments which may be entered without having been "given or made" are default judgments, but the paragraph also applies to certain other judgments and orders. For example, a judgment by consent entered pursuant to Order 42, rules 5 and 5A of the Rules of the Supreme Court would fall within the provision, as would a judgment entered in the High Court in the terms of an arbitration award, pursuant to leave given by the court under section 26(1) of the Arbitration Act 1950.[69] Although foreign

---

[65] See County Court Rules, Ord. 25, r. 12.
[66] Employment Protection (Consolidation) Act 1978, Sched. 9, para. 7.
[67] Para. 44.45 below.
[68] R.S.C., Ord. 32, r. 10.
[69] See also para. (3) below.

judgments registered under section 4 of this Act or under the Acts of 1920 or 1933, are treated as having been "entered,"[70] they are expressly excluded from this section by subsection (7).

Paragraph (c): Scottish enforceable instruments

Scottish law permits the enforcement of certain documents regis-   **41.18**
tered for execution in the Books of Council and Session or in sheriff court books.[71] These documents are enforceable in other Contracting States as "authentic instruments" under Article 50 of the 1968 Convention[72] and their inclusion in this subsection enables them to be enforced in other parts of the United Kingdom.

Paragraph (d): Enforceable tribunal awards and orders

This paragraph is framed in general terms, but seems to apply only to the awards of industrial tribunals in Scotland, which may be enforced as if they were an order of the sheriff court.[73] English industrial tribunal awards require an order of the court.[74]

Paragraph (e): Arbitration awards

Arbitration awards may themselves be enforced in certain cir-   **41.19**
cumstances, without a judgment having been entered in terms of the award.[75] Under section 26(1) of the Arbitration Act 1950, the High Court may give leave for an arbitration award to be enforced in the same manner as a judgment or order to the same effect, and if it does so, the award will become enforceable and fall within this paragraph. Even if the court has also given leave to enter judgment in the terms of the award, the award will itself remain enforceable, at least as long as the leave has not been acted upon and judgment has not in fact been entered. Once judgment has been entered, the rights arising under the award probably merge in the judgment and cease to be enforceable in their own right.

Where the sum sought to be recovered under the award falls within the county court limit for the purposes of section 16 of the County Courts Act 1984, the leave of the High Court to enforce the award is still required but, if it is granted, enforcement is carried out in the county court pursuant to an order of that court.[76] It would seem, though, that the effect of paragraph 6 of Schedule 6 to

---

[70] s.4(3), para. 40.08 above; Administration of Justice Act 1920, s.9(3)(a); Foreign Judgments (Reciprocal Enforcement) Act 1933, s.2(2).
[71] See para. 58.70 below.
[72] See para. 30.01 above.
[73] Employment Protection (Consolidation) Act 1978, Sched. 11, para. 21A.
[74] See para. 41.16 above.
[75] If judgment has been entered, it falls under para. (b), para. 41.17 above.
[76] Arbitration Act 1950, s.26(2); County Courts Act 1984, s.105.

this Act[77] is to enable a certificate issued in another part of the United Kingdom for a sum within the county court limit due under an arbitration award within this paragraph, to be registered and enforced in England and Wales as if it were a High Court judgment.

Subsection (8)[78] provides that alone among the judgments referred to in this subsection, an arbitration award within this paragraph may still be enforced otherwise than by use of the new reciprocal enforcement procedure.

The 1968 Convention does not apply to arbitration,[79] but this paragraph is similar in its terms to section 12(1) of the Administration of Justice Act 1920 and to the new section 10A of the Foreign Judgments (Reciprocal Enforcement) Act 1933.[80]

4. Subsection (3): Exclusions

41.20   This subsection excludes certain types of judgment from the operation of section 18, unless they fall within subsection (4).[81] They are discussed in turn.

Paragraph (a): Civil proceedings in magistrates' courts

Judgments[82] given in magistrates courts are excluded by this paragraph. Criminal proceedings are anyway excluded by paragraph (b) and the principal civil judgments excluded by this paragraph are orders made in maintenance proceedings. Maintenance orders are also excluded by subsection (5)(a),[83] but that paragraph does not necessarily apply to the whole of the judgment in which the maintenance provisions are included. This paragraph applies to the whole judgment, including any relevant costs orders.

The wide drafting of this paragraph has the effect of ensuring that no judgment given in civil proceedings in a magistrates' court can fall within the reciprocal enforcement arrangements provided by this section. An example of a money judgment which would, but for this paragraph, fall within those arrangements is an order for payment of a sum recoverable summarily as a civil debt.[84] Non-money judgments given by magistrates' courts are also excluded.

---

[77] Para. 46.07 below.
[78] See para. 41.26 below.
[79] Art. 1, para. 14.03 above.
[80] That section was introduced by para. 4 of Sched. 10 to this Act: para. 47.09 below.
[81] See para. 41.22 below.
[82] Judgments are defined by subs. (2) above.
[83] See para. 41.23 below.
[84] Magistrates' Courts Act 1980, s.58. Sums recoverable under this section include certain arrears of tax or of payments for public services such as gas, water or electricity: see 29 *Halsbury's Laws* (4th ed.), para. 311, n. 1.

Paragraph (b): Non-civil proceedings

It may be assumed that judgments[85] given in criminal proceed- **41.21**
ings are excluded by paragraph (b), unless they fall within subsection (4), which is concerned mainly with fines for contempt of
court. In the absence of any definition of "civil proceedings," it is
not clear what, if any, other judgments are excluded by this paragraph. It follows from subsection (2) that arbitration proceedings
and proceedings before tribunals are not excluded.

Paragraph (ba): Insolvency

The judgments which are excluded by this paragraph are those
which are given in the exercise of jurisdiction in relation to insolvency law, which is defined for these purposes by section 426(10) of
the Insolvency Act 1986. That definition covers provision made by
or under that Act (which governs both personal and company insolvency) or by or under certain sections of the Company Directors
Disqualification Act 1986. It also covers the equivalent legislation
in Scotland, Northern Ireland and certain other territories.

Paragraph (c): Other statutory exceptions

In its amended version, this paragraph excludes only those proceedings which relate to the obtaining of title to administer the
estate of a deceased person. The recognition as between different
parts of the United Kingdom of grants of probate, letters of administration and confirmations is governed by sections 1 to 3 of the
Administration of Estates Act 1971.

5. Subsection (4)

This subsection ensures that, notwithstanding the terms of sub- **41.22**
section (3), certain specific types of judgment remain within the
enforcement arrangements provided by this section. The sections
mentioned in paragraph (b) provide for the enforcement of fines
imposed (or sums due under a recognisance forfeited) by the High
Court and certain other superior courts in the same manner as a
judgment debt due to the Queen's Remembrancer or as a fine
imposed by the Crown Court. They do not generally apply to fines
imposed (or recognisances forfeited) by the Crown Court or by the
Court of Appeal or House of Lords on appeal from the Crown
Court. The terms of this subsection make it clear that it is only an
order for enforcement as a judgment debt to which this section
applies, and not to enforcement as a fine.

6. Subsection (4A): Confiscation and restraint orders

This subsection excludes from the scheme of enforcement within
the United Kingdom certain orders confiscating the proceeds of
crime or restraining dealings with them. Such orders may be

---

[85] "Judgment" is defined for the purposes of this section by subs. (2) above.

enforced in other parts of the United Kingdom under the Acts referred to in the subsection.

7. Subsection (5): Further exclusions

41.23   This subsection excludes certain further provisions from the enforcement arrangements established by this section. Unlike the exclusions provided by subsection (3), the exclusion need not necessarily apply to the whole of a given judgment, but merely to so much of its provisions as fall within paragraphs (a) to (d) of this subsection. For example, a judgment may contain a decree nisi of divorce and a property adjustment order. The former would be excluded from enforcement under this section[86] in another part of the United Kingdom, whereas the latter could be enforced there under this section.

It will generally not be difficult to determine whether or to what extent a judgment falls within paragraphs (a) or (d), but the same cannot be said of paragraphs (b) and (c). The subject-matter of those paragraphs is discussed below, but in each case it will be necessary to determine the extent to which a judgment "concerns" the status or legal capacity of an individual, or "relates to" the management of the affairs of a person not capable of managing his own affairs. It is suggested that it is not every incidental reference to these matters which would bring the judgment (or that part of it) within the exclusion provided by this subsection, but that the relevant part of the judgment must be "concerned directly with legal consequences arising from these matters."[87]

Paragraph (a): Maintenance orders

Section 16 of the Maintenance Orders Act 1950 provides for the enforcement by registration in one part of the United Kingdom of maintenance orders made in another part of the United Kingdom. The provisions under which such orders may be made in each part of the United Kingdom are comprehensively listed in section 16.

Paragraph (b): Status or legal capacity

41.24   The scope of this exclusion is not wholly clear. The meaning of the word "concerns" is discussed above. The meaning of this paragraph is partly defined by subsection (6) and for reasons which are discussed below, the expression "status or legal capacity" probably has the same meaning here as it has in Article 1 of the 1968 Convention.[88] If that is right, it probably covers the following matters:

(i) those mentioned in subsection (6): judicial separation, separation, guardianship and custody; and

---

[86] It would therefore be excluded from recognition under s.19, see para. 41.30 below.
[87] Schlosser Report, para. 51(a), para. A1.338 below. See also, para. 14.18 above.
[88] See para. 14.19 above.

(ii) further matters mentioned in the Schlosser Report[89] as being within the exclusion from Article 1: divorce, nullity of marriage, death, status and legal capacity of a minor, care and control of children, adoption, nationality, domicile, and legal representation of a person who is mentally ill.

It remains to be seen whether the Schlosser Report's interpretation of the phrase is approved, whether generally or in particular cases, by the European Court of Justice, and whether the interpretation of this paragraph by other courts follows the interpretation of Article 1. For example, questions of domicile[90] may yet be held not to fall within the exclusion. Legal representation, or guardianship *ad litem*, of a person who is mentally ill is probably also covered by paragraph (c).

The mutual recognition and enforcement as between different parts of the United Kingdom of some of the matters excluded by this paragraph are dealt with specifically by other statutes.[91]

The term "status or legal capacity" is only partly defined (in subsection (6)) for the purposes of this section and the courts are not expressly required to have regard to the meaning of the same words in Article 1 of the 1968 Convention, nor to the jurisprudence of the European Court in interpreting that Article.[92] Nonetheless, it is probably safe to assume that Parliament's intention was, for purposes internal to the United Kingdom, to exclude the same matters relating to status and legal capacity of individuals both from the enforcement provisions (and thus also from the recognition provisions)[93] and from the jurisdictional provisions. The latter are expressly tied by section 16(1)(a) to the scope of Article 1 of the Convention and it would seem to follow that the same meaning should be given to the words "status and legal capacity" in the context of this section as in Article 1 of the 1968 Convention.

Paragraph (c): Persons under a disability

The matters excluded by this paragraph from the operation of section 18 may well also be excluded by paragraph (b), but this paragraph puts the question beyond doubt. Its principal application is in relation to the management of a mental patient's property in

---

[89] See para. 51(a), para. A1.338 below.
[90] See ss.41 to 46, paras. 44.01 *et seq.* below.
[91] *E.g.* divorce and legal separation are covered by the Family Law Act 1986, s.13, and custody orders are dealt with by s.25 of that Act. Adoption orders made in one part of the U.K. are automatically recognised in the other parts: see the Children Act 1975, Sched. 1, para. 1(2)(a), (b) and (c).
[92] Note the contrast with s.16(3), para. 41.01 above.
[93] See s.19(2), para. 41.27 below.

another part of the United Kingdom, a matter governed by section 110 of the Mental Health Act 1983. It may also extend to the management of a minor's affairs.

The meaning of the word "relates" is discussed at paragraph 41.23 above.

Paragraph (d): Provisional measures

41.25 The expression "provisional (including protective) measures" is used in Article 24 of the 1968 Convention[94] and of Schedule 4 to this Act.[95] For the same reasons as those advanced in relation to the words "status or legal capacity" in paragraph (b),[96] it is suggested that the interpretation of these words for the purposes of the Convention should be followed in interpreting this section, despite the absence of any express provisions to that effect.

The measures envisaged by Article 24 of the 1968 Convention are those available under the law of each Contracting State[97] and, similarly, the measures envisaged by Article 24 of Schedule 4 and by this paragraph are those available under the law of each part of the United Kingdom. The various types of provisional measure available in England and Wales are discussed in greater detail in Chapter 7, but include the powers granted by sections 24 to 27.[98]

The effect of this exclusion is to prevent the enforcement in one part of the United Kingdom of provisional measures (other than orders for interim payment) obtained in another part of the United Kingdom. This is in contrast to the 1968 Convention, under which, subject to certain safeguards,[99] a provisional measure granted in one Contracting State may be enforced in another Contracting State. It follows that a party seeking a provisional or protective order (such as a Mareva injunction) for enforcement in one part of the United Kingdom must apply to the courts of that part, which (it may be supposed) will be better able to police the execution and effects of the order than would the courts of some other part of the United Kingdom.

On the other hand, the jurisdiction of the courts of a particular part of the United Kingdom to entertain an application for provisional measures will not depend upon their having jurisdiction as to the substance of the matter.[1] So, for example, assets in England may be frozen by a Mareva injunction granted by the High Court in

[94] Para. 24.01 above.
[95] Para. 45.29 below.
[96] See para. 41.24 above.
[97] See paras. 24.03 *et seq.* above.
[98] Paras. 43.01 to 43.14 below.
[99] See paras. 24.09–24.10, 25.26 and 27.26–27.27 above.
[1] See ss.25 and 27, paras. 43.03 and 43.14 below; see also Art. 24 of the 1968 Convention, para. 24.01 above and Sched. 4, para. 45.29 below.

London in aid of proceedings commenced, or to be commenced, in the Court of Session, whether or not the High Court would also have had jurisdiction over the main issues.

By contrast with other provisional measures, an order for the making of an interim payment[2] may be enforced in other parts of the United Kingdom.

8. Subsection (6)

The interpretation of subsection (5)(b), which is affected by this subsection, has been discussed above.

9. Subsection (7)

The enactments mentioned in this subsection all provide for the registration of foreign judgments and orders and for those judgments and orders then to be treated for the purposes of their enforcement as judgments of a court of law in the part of the United Kingdom in which they are registered. The section applies not only to judgments from other Contracting States registered under sections 4 or 5 of this Act,[3] but also to any other foreign judgments registered in the United Kingdom.

41.26

The effect of this subsection is to prevent a registered foreign judgment from being completely assimilated to the position of a United Kingdom judgment for the purposes of enforcement, because a registered foreign judgment cannot be re-registered under Schedules 6 or 7 in another part of the United Kingdom. If a foreign judgment is to be registered in a given part of the United Kingdom, it must be registered there directly, rather than by way of re-registration of a judgment already registered in another part of the United Kingdom.[4]

10. Subsection (8)

This subsection prevents a judgment to which this section applies from being enforced in another part of the United Kingdom, save by registration under Schedules 6 or 7. It prevents the judgment from being enforced by an action at common law. In this respect it follows the Foreign Judgments (Reciprocal Enforcement) Act 1933[5] and, probably, also the 1968 Convention.[6] It differs from the previous provisions applying as between different parts of the United

---

[2] R.S.C., Ord. 29, rr. 9–18.
[3] See paras. 40.08 *et seq.* above.
[4] See para. 40.10 above.
[5] See s.6 of that Act.
[6] *De Wolf* v. *Cox BV* [1976] E.C.R. 1759: see para. 25.36 above.

Kingdom, under which a common law action might be brought, but subject to penalties as to costs.[7]

Section 19

41.27 **19.**—*Recognition of United Kingdom judgments in other parts of United Kingdom*

(1) A judgment to which this section applies given in one part of the United Kingdom shall not be refused recognition in another part of the United Kingdom solely on the ground that, in relation to that judgment, the court which gave it was not a court of competent jurisdiction according to the rules of private international law in force in that other part.

(2) Subject to subsection (3), this section applies to any judgment to which section 18 applies.

(3) This section does not apply to—

(a) the documents mentioned in paragraph (c) of the definition of "judgment" in section 18(2);

(b) the awards and orders mentioned in paragraphs (d) and (e) of that definition;

(c) the decrees and orders referred to in section 18(4).

1. General note

41.28   This section is concerned with the recognition, as distinct from the enforcement, of judgments given in other parts of the United Kingdom. The two concepts, the distinction between them, and their practical effects, are discussed more fully elsewhere.[8] Subsection (1) limits the grounds on which recognition of a judgment given in another part of the United Kingdom may be refused, while subsections (2) and (3) define the judgments to which the section applies.

2. Subsection (1)

Whereas the Convention requires that judgments given in one Contracting State should normally be given automatic recognition in the other Contracting States,[9] the Act proceeds on the assumption that judgments given in one part of the United Kingdom will usually be automatically recognised in the other parts.[10] The Act, unlike the Convention,[11] does not set out the grounds upon which

---

[7] Judgments Extension Act 1868, s.6; Inferior Courts Judgments Extension Act 1882, s.8. The same applied to judgments which could be registered under Part II of the Administration of Justice Act 1920: s.1(5).

[8] See paras. 10.01 and 25.06 *et seq.* above.

[9] Art. 26, para. 27.01 above.

[10] Anton, paras. 1.32 and 9.34.

[11] Arts. 27 and 28, paras. 27.12–27.74 above.

recognition may be refused, but by this section it provides that a court in one part of the United Kingdom may not consider whether, according to its own conflicts rules, the court of another part of the United Kingdom had jurisdiction over the case. It is required to respect the assumption of jurisdiction by the court of origin, whether that jurisdiction derives from Schedule 4 or any other provision of this Act or arises independently of this Act. In doing so, it mirrors the provisions of the third paragraph of Article 28 of the 1968 Convention,[12] under which (subject to certain exceptions) the jurisdiction of the court of origin could not be reviewed, even on the grounds of public policy; but unlike the provisions of Article 28, it does not permit any review of the jurisdiction of the court of origin, even where that court has assumed jurisdiction in breach of Sections 4 or 5 of Title II of Schedule 4 (consumer contracts and cases of exclusive jurisdiction).

This subsection does not prevent grounds such as fraud, public policy or absence of natural justice from being raised against the recognition of a judgment given in another part of the United Kingdom, for example, in reply to a defence of estoppel *per rem judicatem.* Similarly, enforcement of a judgment may be opposed on the grounds of a prior judgment between the same parties on the same issues,[13] and the same may apply to prevent the recognition of the judgment.

The effect of this subsection may be best understood in its historical context. At common law, a foreign judgment (at least if it were final and conclusive on the merits)[14] might be refused recognition on a number of grounds, including fraud, public policy and natural justice[15] and, as between the different parts of the United Kingdom, these grounds remain unaffected by the Act.[16] **41.29**

Arguably the most important ground at common law for refusal of recognition of a foreign judgment was that the court of origin did not, according to the private international law rules of the common law, have jurisdiction over the matter. By its silence on the point, the Judgments Extension Act 1868, did not permit lack of jurisdiction in the court of origin to be raised as a ground of opposition to the recognition of a money judgment given by a superior court in

---

[12] Para. 27.62 above.

[13] Sched. 6, para. 10(b) (para. 46.12 below); Sched. 7, para. 9(b) (para. 46.22 below).

[14] Dicey and Morris, pp. 428–430; *Black-Clawson International* v. *Papierwerke Waldhof-Aschaffenburg AG* [1975] A.C. 591; *The Sennar (No. 2)* [1985] 1 W.L.R. 490.

[15] Dicey and Morris, pp. 467–477 and *passim*; Cheshire and North, pp. 370–384.

[16] As between different Contracting States, the grounds of refusal are exclusively regulated by the Convention: para. 25.11 above.

another part of the United Kingdom.[17] By contrast, the Inferior Courts Judgments Extension Act 1882 did prescribe a number of jurisdictional grounds on which the money judgments of inferior courts could be denied recognition in the other parts of the United Kingdom. Both of those Acts are repealed in their entirety by this Act.[18]

The common law rules (under which lack of jurisdiction could prevent the recognition of judgments given in other parts of the United Kingdom) survived those Acts so far as non-money judgments were concerned, because there was no statutory scheme for the enforcement of such judgments in the other parts of the United Kingdom. What this section does is to abrogate these earlier common law and statutory rules for all judgments to which it applies, whether they are money judgments or non-money judgments.

3. Subsections (2) and (3)

41.30   These subsections define the judgments to which the rule in subsection (1) applies, namely those judgments to which section 18 applies, except for:

(i) documents registered for execution in the Books of Council and Session or in the sheriff court books (section 18(2)(c))[19];

(ii) tribunal awards enforceable without an order of the court (section 18(2)(d))[20];

(iii) arbitration awards enforceable as judgments (section 18(2)(e))[21]; and

(iv) certain Scottish decrees for the recovery of rentcharges and penalties and certain fines or sums due for contempt of court or forfeited recognisances (section 18(4))[22].

---

[17] There was one exception, namely Scottish default judgments where jurisdiction was founded on arrestment: s.8 of the 1868 Act.
[18] See s.54 and Sched. 14 below.
[19] Para. 41.18 above.
[20] This probably applies only to Scottish industrial tribunal awards: see para. 41.18 above.
[21] Para. 41.19 above.
[22] Para. 41.22 above.

CHAPTER 42

CIVIL JURISDICTION AND JUDGMENTS ACT 1982
PART III—JURISDICTION IN SCOTLAND

Section 20

20.—*Rules as to jurisdiction in Scotland*

(1) Subject to Parts I and II and to the following provisions of this Part, Schedule 8 has effect to determine in what circumstances a person may be sued in civil proceedings in the Court of Session or in a sheriff court. **42.01**

(2) Nothing in Schedule 8 affects the competence as respects subject-matter or value of the Court of Session or of the sheriff court.

(3) Section 6 of the Sheriff Courts (Scotland) Act 1907 shall cease to have effect to the extent that it determines jurisdiction in relation to any matter to which Schedule 8 applies.

(4) In Schedule 8—

    (a) words resulting from modifications of Title II of the 1968 Convention, by way of addition or substitution, and provisions not derived from that Title are printed in heavy type;

    (b) the marginal notes show, where appropriate, of which provision of Title II a provision of Schedule 8 is a modified version.

(5) In determining any question as to the meaning or effect of any provision contained in Schedule 8 and derived to any extent from Title II of the 1968 Convention—

    (a) regard shall be had to any relevant principles laid down by the European Court in connection with Title II of the 1968 Convention and to any relevant decision of that court as to the meaning or effect of any provision of that Title; and

    (b) without prejudice to the generality of paragraph (a), the reports mentioned in section 3(3) may be considered and shall, so far as relevant, be given such weight as is appropriate in the circumstances.

General note

See the general note on Part III at paragraph 42.05 below.

Section 21

21.—*Continuance of certain jurisdictions*

42.02   (1) Schedule 8 does not affect—
- (a) the operation of any enactment which confers jurisdiction on a Scottish court in respect of a specific subject-matter on specific grounds;
- (b) without prejudice to the foregoing generality, the jurisdiction of any court in respect of any matter mentioned in Schedule 9.

(2) Her Majesty may by Order in Council—
- (a) add to the list in Schedule 9 any description of proceedings; and
- (b) remove from that list any description of proceedings (whether included in the list as originally enacted or added by virtue of this subsection).

(3) An Order in Council under subsection (2) may—
- (a) make different provisions for different descriptions of proceedings or for the same description of proceedings in different courts;
- (b) contain such transitional and other incidental provisions as appear to Her Majesty to be appropriate.

(4) An Order in Council under subsection (2) shall not be made unless a draft of the Order has been laid before Parliament and approved by a resolution of each House of Parliament.

General note

See the general note on Part III at paragraph 42.05 below.

Section 22

22.—*Supplementary provisions*

42.03   (1) Nothing in Schedule 8 shall prevent a court from declining jurisdiction on the ground of *forum non conveniens*.

(2) Nothing in Schedule 8 affects the operation of any enactment or rule of law under which a court may decline to exercise jurisdiction because of the prorogation by parties of the jurisdiction of another court.

(3) For the avoidance of doubt, it is declared that nothing in Schedule 8 affects the *nobile officium* of the Court of Session.

(4) Where a court has jurisdiction in any proceedings by virtue of Schedule 8, that court shall also have jurisdiction to determine any matter which—
  (a) is ancillary or incidental to the proceedings; or
  (b) requires to be determined for the purposes of a decision in the proceedings.

General note

See the general note on Part III at paragraph 42.05 below.

Section 23

23.—*Savings and consequential amendments*

(1) Nothing in Schedule 8 shall affect—   42.04
  (a) the power of any court to vary or recall a maintenance order granted by that court;
  (b) the power of a sheriff court under section 22 of the Maintenance Orders Act 1950 (discharge and variation of maintenance orders registered in sheriff courts) to vary or discharge a maintenance order registered in that court under Part II of that Act; or
  (c) the power of a sheriff court under section 9 of the Maintenance Orders (Reciprocal Enforcement) Act 1972 (variation and revocation of maintenance orders registered in United Kingdom courts) to vary or revoke a registered order within the meaning of Part I of that Act.
(2) The enactments specified in Part II of Schedule 12 shall have effect with the amendments specified there, being amendments consequential on Schedule 8.

General note on Part III

Sections 20 to 23, which form Part III of the Act, together with   42.05
Schedules 8 and 9,[1] provide a new and comprehensive code of jurisdictional rules for the purposes of the Scottish courts. A detailed commentary on Part III is outwith the scope of this work,[2] but the following points may be noted.

The new rules are subject to Parts I and II of the Act[3] and therefore apply only if or to the extent that the 1968 Convention, or the

---

[1] Paras. 47.01 to 47.07 below. Amendments consequential on Sched. 8 are included in Part II of Sched. 12 (para. 47.18 below), which is given effect by s.23(2).
[2] See: A. E. Anton, *Civil Jurisdiction in Scotland*, (Edinburgh, 1984), cited in this work as "Anton," especially Chap. 10, and, for a shorter summary, Robert Black, *Civil Jurisdiction: The New Rules* (Edinburgh, 1983).
[3] s.20(1).

new rules for allocation of jurisdiction as between different parts of the United Kingdom,[4] do not themselves determine the jurisdiction of the Scottish courts. This part applies only to the Court of Session and sheriff courts. Tribunals, which fall within the definition of "court" for other purposes in this Act,[5] do not come within its provisions.[6] The degree of international connection necessary to bring the Convention's rules into play may be fairly tenuous.[7]

Following the recommendations of the Maxwell Committee,[8] the new Scottish rules of jurisdiction are modelled on Title II of the 1968 Convention, although this involves relatively modest departure in practice from the previous Scottish rules.[9] Section 20(5) provides that Schedule 8 is to be interpreted in the light of the European Court's case law under Title II.[10]

---

[4] ss.16 and 17, Scheds. 4 and 5.
[5] s.50, para. 44.45 below.
[6] s.20(1).
[7] See paras. 13.10 *et seq.*, 21.06 and 41.07 above.
[8] Maxwell, paras. 2.13–2.24.
[9] This is demonstrated by Annex II to the Maxwell Report, which compares the previous Scottish rules of jurisdiction with the rules in Title II of the 1968 Convention.
[10] *Cf.* ss.3 and 16(3), paras. 40.05 and 41.01 above.

CHAPTER 43

CIVIL JURISDICTION AND JUDGMENTS ACT 1982
PART IV—MISCELLANEOUS PROVISIONS

A. PROVISIONS RELATING TO JURISDICTION

Section 24

24.—*Interim relief and protective measures in cases of doubtful jurisdiction* **43.01**

(1) Any power of a court in England and Wales or Northern. Ireland to grant interim relief pending trial or pending the determination of an appeal shall extend to a case where—

(a) the issue to be tried, or which is the subject of the appeal, relates to the jurisdiction of the court to entertain the proceedings; or

(b) the proceedings involve the reference of any matter to the European Court under the 1971 Protocol.

(2) Any power of a court in Scotland to grant protective measures pending the decision of any hearing shall apply to a case where—

(a) the subject of the proceedings includes a question as to the jurisdiction of the court to entertain them; or

(b) the proceedings involve the reference of a matter to the European Court under the 1971 Protocol.

(3) Subsections (1) and (2) shall not be construed as restricting any power to grant interim relief or protective measures which a court may have apart from this section.

General note

43.02   This section, by subsection (1), removes doubts as to the powers of the courts in England and Wales and in Northern Ireland to grant interim relief pending the final outcome of proceedings in those cases where the court's jurisdiction is doubtful. It also extends such powers to cases where the proceedings involve a reference to the European Court of Justice under the 1971 Protocol.[1] The powers created (or confirmed) by subsection (1) establish the jurisdiction of the court in those cases to which the subsection applies, but they do not otherwise extend the nature or availability of such relief, nor do they restrict any power which the court may have to grant interim relief.[2] The subsection is not confined to cases where the jurisdictional issue arises under the 1968 Convention or under this Act. Similar provision is made by subsection (2) in relation to Scotland.

The section should be compared with section 25,[3] where the court's power to grant interim relief is extended in cases where the court does not have jurisdiction over the substance of the matter.

The term "interim relief" is not defined for the purposes of this section,[4] but it should be noted that the term "provisional, including protective, measures," used in Article 24 in the 1968 Convention,[5] (and repeated in Schedule 4)[6] has not been adopted, leaving the courts free to decide what provisions fall within the scope of

---

[1] Chap. 36 above.
[2] Subs. (3).
[3] Next para.; *cf.* s.27 in the case of Scotland, para. 43.14 below. Interim relief is discussed in greater detail in chap. 7 above.
[4] This section was added by amendment during the passage of the Bill, and the question of definition may have been overlooked: *cf.* s.25(7). It would be logical for "interim relief" to mean the same in the two sections.
[5] Para. 24.01 above.
[6] Para. 45.29 below.

"interim relief," without being tied by the European Court's case law on Article 24.

Section 25

25.—*Interim relief in England and Wales and Northern Ireland in the* **43.03**
absence of substantive proceedings
(1) The High Court in England and Wales or Northern Ireland shall have power to grant interim relief where—
> (a) proceedings have been or are to be commenced in a Contracting State other than the United Kingdom or in a part of the United Kingdom other than that in which the High Court in question exercises jurisdiction; and
> (b) they are or will be proceedings whose subject-matter is within the scope of the 1968 Convention as determined by Article 1 (whether or not the Convention has effect in relation to the proceedings).

(2) On an application for any interim relief under subsection (1) the court may refuse to grant that relief if, in the opinion of the court, the fact that the court has no jurisdiction apart from this section in relation to the subject-matter of the proceedings in question makes it inexpedient for the court to grant it.

(3) Her Majesty may by Order in Council extend the power to grant interim relief conferred by subsection (1) so as to make it exercisable in relation to proceedings of any of the following descriptions, namely—
> (a) proceedings commenced or to be commenced otherwise than in a Contracting State;
> (b) proceedings whose subject-matter is not within the scope of the 1968 Convention as determined by Article 1;
> (c) arbitration proceedings.

(4) An Order in Council under subsection (3)—
> (a) may confer power to grant only specified descriptions of interim relief;
> (b) may make different provision for different classes of proceedings, for proceedings pending in different countries or courts outside the United Kingdom or in different parts of the United Kingdom, and for different circumstances; and
> (c) may impose conditions or restrictions on the exercise of any power conferred by the Order.

(5) An Order in Council under subsection (3) which confers power to grant interim relief in relation to arbitration proceedings may provide for the repeal of any provision of section 12(6) of the Arbitration Act 1950 or section 21(1) of the Arbitration Act

(Northern Ireland) 1937 to the extent that it is superseded by the provisions of the Order.

(6) Any Order in Council under subsection (3) shall be subject to annulment in pursuance of a resolution of either House of Parliament.

(7) In this section "interim relief," in relation to the High Court in England and Wales or Northern Ireland, means interim relief of any kind which that court has power to grant in proceedings relating to matters within its jurisdiction, other than—

(a) a warrant for the arrest of property; or

(b) provision for obtaining evidence.

1. General note

43.04   This section confers on the High Court a discretionary power to grant interim relief in aid of proceedings in another part of the United Kingdom or in another Contracting State, provided that the subject-matter of the proceedings falls within the scope of the 1968 Convention. As regards those proceedings, it reverses the decision of the House of Lords in *The Siskina*,[7] in which it had been held that the English court might not grant an interlocutory injunction against a defendant who was not amenable to its jurisdiction independently of the injunction.[8] While the court is empowered by Article 24 of the 1968 Convention[9] (and of Schedule 4)[10] to grant "provisional, including protective, measures," even if the courts of another Contracting State (or another part of the United Kingdom) have jurisdiction over the substance of the matter, that power extends only to the grant of such measures as are anyway available under the law of the court applied to.

This section was therefore necessary if the English High Court[11] is to be able to aid proceedings before the courts of other Contracting States or other parts of the United Kingdom by the grant of a Mareva injunction having the effect of freezing a defendant's assets within its territorial jurisdiction, at least in circumstances where it does not have jurisdiction over the main dispute. It is in relation to Mareva injunctions that the section will most often be relevant, but it is drawn in wide terms and will apply to a range of measures which can be described as "interim relief."[12]

---

[7] [1979] A.C. 210.

[8] This was particularly significant, because the presence of a defendant's assets within the court's territorial jurisdiction was not normally sufficient in English law to allow the court to exercise jurisdiction *in personam* over him.

[9] Para. 24.01 above.

[10] Para. 45.29 below.

[11] Or the Northern Ireland High Court.

[12] See chap. 7 above and the commentary on subs. (7), para. 43.10 below.

The section also enables the power to grant interim relief conferred on the High Court by subsection (1) to be extended by Order in Council.[13] Such extensions would enable the English courts to grant interim relief in aid of proceedings outside the Contracting States or outside the scope of the 1968 Convention.

2. Subsection (1)

The power of the High Court to grant interim relief arises under this section if two conditions are fulfilled. **43.05**

First, by paragraph (*a*), there must be actual or imminent proceedings either in another Contracting State or in another part of the United Kingdom. It is not necessary that the English court should itself be without jurisdiction: the fact that the proceedings have been, or are to be, brought elsewhere is sufficient. Similarly, it is not for the English court to decide whether the court in which the proceedings have been, or are to be, brought actually has jurisdiction over those proceedings. That is purely a matter for that other court to decide, although the likelihood of the other court declining jurisdiction is a matter which the English court may take into account in deciding whether to exercise its discretion to grant the interim relief.[14]

The circumstances in which the High Court will grant interim relief pursuant to this section have yet to be worked out in practice. For example, there is no equivalent of Order 29 rule 1(3) of the Rules of the Supreme Court, which provides that only in cases of urgency may the interim relief be granted before the substantive proceedings are commenced. In such cases, it seems likely that the High Court will impose terms as to the commencement of the other proceedings as a condition of the grant of the interim relief. Whether the applicant will need to identify precisely where the proceedings are to be commenced, and how imminent they will need to be, are also matters on which a practice will develop. It would be unfortunate, though, if the wide terms of the section were to become too circumscribed by rules of practice, in view of the potentially large number of different circumstances in which this jurisdiction may be invoked. The range of measures contemplated by the term "interim relief" is considered below under subsection (7).[15]

Secondly, by paragraph (*b*), the subject-matter of the proceedings must fall within the scope of the 1968 Convention as deter- **43.06**

---

[13] Subs. (3) to (6), para. 43.09 below.
[14] *Cf.* para. 43.07 below.
[15] See para. 43.10 below.

mined by Article 1,[16] whether or not the Convention applies to the proceedings. This provision is equivalent to section 16(1)(a) and reference should be made to the commentary on that paragraph.[17] In summary, the case must be civil or commercial in nature and must not be concerned with public law or with certain other matters, notably large areas of family law, insolvency and arbitration.

Because the section is expressed to apply whether or not the Convention applies to the proceedings, the jurisdiction to grant interim relief is not dependent on the proceedings having an international character,[18] nor on the defendant being domiciled in a Contracting State. It applies as much to cases where the defendant is domiciled in a non-Contracting State and the proceedings are brought in another Contracting State pursuant to its domestic law[19] (including its exorbitant jurisdictions) as it does to cases which are wholly internal to the United Kingdom and which have no international connections sufficient to bring them within the Convention. In the latter case, this section applies if the main proceedings are to be brought in another part of the United Kingdom, and this is the case whether or not the jurisdiction of the courts of that other part derives from section 16 and Schedule 4 of this Act.

3. Subsection (2)

43.07   The power created by subsection (1) is discretionary. The effect of subsection (2) is to make clear that the question whether or not the court has jurisdiction over the substance of the case is a material matter for it to take into account in exercising that discretion. This is particularly relevant as regards a case in which, if it had had jurisdiction over the substance, the court would have granted interim relief. In the absence of this provision, subsection (1) might be read as requiring the court to grant interim relief in such a case even though it did not have jurisdiction over the substance.

The subsection is silent on the analogous case where both the High Court and the courts of another Contracting State or another part of the United Kingdom have parallel jurisdiction, but the plaintiff has chosen to invoke the jurisdiction of the latter rather than that of the High Court. This may be regarded as the midway position between the case where the court has jurisdiction over the substance and the case where it does not. The exercise of the power created by subsection (1) remains discretionary in all these cases. It is the expediency of granting the interim relief where the proceed-

---

[16] Para. 14.03 above.
[17] Para. 41.07 above.
[18] *Cf.* paras. 13.10–13.11 above.
[19] Art. 4, para. 16.15 above.

ings are to be conducted elsewhere which affects the *exercise* of the discretion, rather than the question whether the English court does or does not have jurisdiction over the substance. It is suggested, therefore, that the English court need not embark (for the purposes of this section) on a detailed examination of whether it has jurisdiction. It should be sufficient if it knows that the proceedings have been brought or are imminent in another Contracting State or in another part of the United Kingdom.

Matters which are likely to affect the expediency of the court **43.08** granting interim relief include the manner in which the court can exercise control over the conduct of the main action, and the desirability of its doing so in the particular case. If the main proceedings are not taking place in the High Court, but in another Contracting State or in another part of the United Kingdom, the High Court can only influence the conduct of those proceedings indirectly, by imposing terms on the order granting relief.[20]

The English court may not assume its system of justice to be preferable to that of other courts; comparison between the merits of different legal systems is probably contrary to the spirit of the Convention[21] and it has been disapproved by the House of Lords in the context of conflicts of jurisdiction.[22] The discretion of the English court is therefore limited in this respect, especially on an application for interim relief in a case where the English court has jurisdiction as to the substance, but the parallel jurisdiction of a court in another Contracting State or another part of the United Kingdom has been or is to be invoked.

4. Subsections (3) to (6)

The powers to grant interim relief conferred on the High Court **43.09** by subsection (1) may be extended to other categories of case in which that court would not have jurisdiction over the main proceedings, namely to cases where the main proceedings have been (or are to be) commenced in the courts of a non-Contracting State, or where the subject-matter falls outside the scope of the Convention, or where the main proceedings are to be by way of arbitration (including, presumably, foreign arbitration). Different provisions may be made in respect of different classes of case. These subsections make flexible provision for such extensions to be made by Order in Council, but no such Order has yet been made. The flex-

---

[20] See para. 7.30 above.
[21] See paras. 13.09 *et seq.* above.
[22] *Amin Rasheed Shipping Corporation* v. *Kuwait Insurance Co.* [1984] A.C. 50, at p. 67; *The Abadin Daver* [1984] A.C. 398, at p. 410.

ibility of the provisions enables extensions to be made in order to give effect to any future reciprocal agreements with other countries.

5. Subsection (7)

43.10   As with section 24, this section uses the term "interim relief" in preference to the term "provisional, including protective, measures"[23] used in Article 24 of the 1968 Convention and reproduced in Schedule 4. This subsection provides a partial definition of "interim relief" which makes clear that while no new kinds of measure are created by the subsection, it applies to any existing kinds of interim relief (with the two exceptions discussed below) which would be available in the High Court in proceedings relating to matters within its jurisdiction.

At first sight, it would seem that the measures to which the subsection refers are limited to those available after the commencement of proceedings, that is, those measures which the High Court could grant if it were the court seised of the main proceedings. It is suggested, though, that a liberal interpretation of the words "in proceedings" is necessary to make realistic sense of the section, and that it applies also to measures which the High Court has power to grant in contemplation of proceedings relating to matters within its jurisdiction, but before the proceedings have been commenced.[24]

Various types of interim relief which are available in English law are discussed more fully in Chapter 7,[25] to which reference should be made. The most important are injunctions, and in this context particularly Mareva injunctions, but the section is by no means limited to that form of interim relief. For example, because of the wording of Article 5(3) of the 1968 Convention, it has been suggested[26] that that Article applies only to torts already committed, and not to threatened torts, with the consequence that a *quia timet* injunction could only be sought pursuant to Article 2 in the courts of the Contracting States in which the defendant was domiciled.[27] This section suffers from no such limitation and such an injunction would fall within it (and therefore within Article 24 of the 1968 Convention)[28] as much as an injunction to prevent the repetition of a tort already committed.

43.11   The two types of interim relief to which the section does not apply are (a) a warrant for the arrest of property and (b) provision

---

[23] See para. 43.02 above.
[24] For example, an order for detention of property under s.33(1)(*a*) of the Supreme Court Act 1981: see para. 7.17 above.
[25] See paras. 7.05 *et seq.* above.
[26] See, *e.g.*, 426 H.L.Deb. col. 1147, January 21, 1982.
[27] But see para. 17.52 above.
[28] Para. 24.01 above.

for obtaining evidence. The former applies only to warrants for the arrest of property in Admiralty cases,[29] as the High Court has no other jurisdiction to grant that particular form of interim relief. Injunctions restraining a defendant from dealing with his property, or orders requiring him to deliver up goods, for example, do not fall within the scope of this exclusion. The case of the arrest of property in Admiralty proceedings is specifically dealt with by section 26.[30]

Provisions for obtaining evidence fall within the Evidence (Proceedings in Other Jurisdictions) Act 1975 and Order 70 of the Rules of the Supreme Court. This statutory framework is discussed in Chapter 8.[31] Certain conditions are imposed on the obtaining of evidence in aid of proceedings in other jurisdictions;[32] if provisions for obtaining evidence had come within this section, there would have been a risk that those conditions would have been circumvented.[33] An order that a defendant disclose the location of his assets within the jurisdiction, made as part of a Mareva injunction, is not a provision for obtaining evidence for the purposes of this subsection.[33a]

Section 26

26.—*Security in Admiralty proceedings in England and Wales or Northern Ireland in case of stay, etc.*

43.12

(1) **Where in England and Wales or Northern Ireland a court stays or dismisses Admiralty proceedings on the ground that the dispute in question should be submitted to arbitration or to the determination of the courts of another part of the United Kingdom or of an overseas country, the court may, if in those proceedings property has been arrested or bail or other security has been given to prevent or obtain release from arrest—**
    (a) **order that the property arrested be retained as security for the satisfaction of an award or judgment which—**
        (i) **is given in respect of the dispute in the arbitration or legal proceedings in favour of which those proceedings are stayed or dismissed; and**
        (ii) **is enforceable in England and Wales or, as the case may be, in Northern Ireland; or**
    (b) **order that the stay or dismissal of those proceedings be**

---

[29] R.S.C., Ord. 75, r. 5.
[30] Para. 43.12 below.
[31] See paras. 8.63 *et seq.* above.
[32] The Act brings into effect the provision of the Hague Convention of 1970 on the Taking of Evidence Abroad in Civil and Commercial Matters. See paras. 8.26 *et seq.* above. The convention is set out at paras. A2.17 *et seq.* below.
[33] *cf.* Kaye, p. 1152, concerning Anton Piller orders.
[33a] *Republic of Haiti* v. *Duvalier (No. 1), The Independent*, June 13, 1988 (C.A.).

conditional on the provision of equivalent security for the satisfaction of any such award or judgment.

(2) Where a court makes an order under subsection (1), it may attach such conditions to the order as it thinks fit, in particular conditions with respect to the institution or prosecution of the relevant arbitration or legal proceedings.

(3) Subject to any provision made by rules of court and to any necessary modifications, the same law and practice shall apply in relation to property retained in pursuance of an order made by a court under subsection (1) as would apply if it were held for the purposes of proceedings in that court.

General note

43.13　　This section deals with a particular situation which may arise in Admiralty proceedings, where property (normally a ship or cargo) has been arrested for the purposes of security, even if the property has since been released against alternative security.[34] If the proceedings are then stayed or dismissed on the ground that the dispute should be submitted to arbitration, or to a foreign court (including a court in another part of the United Kingdom), this section enables the property to be retained, or alternative security to be given, as security for the satisfaction of the eventual judgment or award.[35] The section applies whether or not the arbitration or foreign proceedings have already been commenced.[35a] If the proceedings have been stayed without an arrest having been effected, application may be made for the stay to be lifted for the limited purpose of effecting an arrest and obtaining an order under this section for the property to be retained.[35b]

It was formerly thought that if Admiralty proceedings *in rem* were stayed, the ability of the English court to order the arrest of property as security, or the retention of any property arrested,

---

[34] The former view that the validity of a writ *in rem* depended on its being issued for the purpose of a determination of the issues on the merits, and not merely for the purpose of obtaining security, was held to be erroneous in *The Vasso* [1984] Q.B. 477.

[35] The section may have been intended to have the effect of completing the implementation of Art. 7 of the International Convention for the Unification of Certain Rules relating to the Arrest of Sea-Going Ships, signed at Brussels, May 10, 1952 (Cmnd. 1128). There is some doubt, however, as to whether it actually does so: *The Nordglimt* [1987] 2 Lloyd's Rep. 470, 478, 484.

[35a] *The Jalamatsya* [1987] 2 Lloyd's Rep. 164. It follows that a writ *in rem* may be issued for the purposes of obtaining security, even if the foreign proceedings or arbitration have commenced.

[35b] *The Silver Athens (No. 2)* 2 Lloyd's Rep. 583.

depended on whether the stay was compulsory or discretionary.[36] It was decided by the Court of Appeal in *The Tuyuti*,[37] however, that a mandatory stay of proceedings in order to give effect to an arbitration clause does not compel the court to discharge the order for arrest. This section is to similar but not identical effect.[38] To take advantage of the decision in *The Tuyuti*, the plaintiff has to show that it is unlikely that he will be able to enforce an arbitration award in his favour if the security is discharged, whereas under this section, the discretion is unfettered. On the other hand, this section applies only to property which has actually been arrested, or in respect of which bail or other security has been given. Under *The Tuyuti*, by contrast, an unserved writ *in rem* could remain in force and available for service on a ship which came within the jurisdiction, for the limited purpose of arresting the property, even if that property had not been arrested before the stay of proceedings had been granted.

Subsection (2) empowers the court to impose conditions on its order and while the subsection refers specifically to conditions with respect to the institution or prosecution of the arbitration or legal proceedings, the conditions which may be imposed are not limited to those matters. Subsection (3) equates orders made under this section, both legally and for the purposes of practice, with orders relating to property retained for the purposes of proceedings in the same court.

The section applies to Admiralty proceedings not only in the High Court, but also in the county court. Its effect is not limited to cases within the 1968 Convention or within section 16 and Schedule 4 to this Act. It applies equally wherever the arbitration is to take place, or whatever the foreign court to which the dispute should be referred.

Section 27

27.—*Provisional and protective measures in Scotland in the absence of substantive proceedings*   **43.14**

(1) **The Court of Session may, in any case to which this subsection applies—**

(a) **subject to subsection (2)(c), grant a warrant for the arrestment of any assets situated in Scotland;**

(b) **subject to subsection (2)(c), grant a warrant of inhibition over any property situated in Scotland; and**

(c) **grant interim interdict.**

---

[36] *The Cap Bon* [1967] 1 Lloyd's Rep. 543; *The Golden Trader* [1975] Q.B. 348; *The Rena K* [1979] Q.B. 377.
[37] [1984] Q.B. 838.
[38] See Jackson, *Civil Jurisdiction and Judgments—Maritime Claims*, pp. 174–175.

(2) Subsection (1) applies to any case in which—
  (a) proceedings have been commenced but not concluded, or, in relation to paragraph (c) of that subsection, are to be commenced, in another Contracting State or in England and Wales or Northern Ireland;
  (b) the subject-matter of the proceedings is within the scope of the 1968 Convention as determined by Article 1; and
  (c) in relation to paragraphs (a) and (b) of subsection (1), such a warrant could competently have been granted in equivalent proceedings before a Scottish court;

but it shall not be necessary, in determining whether proceedings have been commenced for the purpose of paragraph (a) of this subsection, to show that any document has been served on or notice given to the defender.

(3) Her Majesty may by Order in Council confer on the Court of Session power to do anything mentioned in subsection (1) or in section 28 in relation to proceedings of any of the following descriptions, namely—
  (a) proceedings commenced otherwise than in a Contracting State;
  (b) proceedings whose subject-matter is not within the scope of the 1968 Convention as determined by Article 1;
  (c) arbitration proceedings;
  (d) in relation to subsection (1)(c) or section 28, proceedings which are to be commenced otherwise than in a Contracting State.

(4) An Order in Council under subsection (3)—
  (a) may confer power to do only certain of the things mentioned in subsection (1) or in section 28;
  (b) make different provision for different classes of proceedings, for proceedings pending in different countries or courts outside the United Kingdom or in different parts of the United Kingdom, and for other different circumstances; and
  (c) may impose conditions or restrictions on the exercise of any power conferred by the Order.

(5) Any Order in Council under subsection (3) shall be subject to annulment in pursuance of a resolution of either House of Parliament.

General note

See the general note on sections 27–28 at paragraph 43.16 below.

Section 28

28.—*Application of s.1 of Administration of Justice (Scotland) Act 1972.* **43.15**

When any proceedings have been brought, or are likely to be brought, in another Contracting State or in England and Wales or Northern Ireland in respect of any matter which is within the scope of the 1968 Convention as determined in Article 1, the Court of Session shall have the like power to make an order under section 1 of the Administration of Justice (Scotland) Act 1972 as amended by the Law Reform (Miscellaneous Provisions) (Scotland) Act 1985, as if the proceedings in question had been brought, or were likely to be brought, in that court.†

General note on sections 27–28

These sections relate exclusively to Scotland and detailed com- **43.16**
mentary on them is outside the scope of this work,[39] but sections 27 and 28 make provision equivalent to that made for England and Wales by section 25. Section 1 of the Administration of Justice (Scotland) Act 1972 (referred to in section 28) is largely equivalent to section 33(1) of the Supreme Court Act 1981, and relates to such matters as the inspection, preservation and detention of property.

Section 29

29.—*Service of county court process outside Northern Ireland* **43.17**
The County Court Rules Committee established by Article 46 of the County Courts (Northern Ireland) Order 1980 may make county court rules with respect to the service of process outside Northern Ireland and the conditions subject to which process may be so served; and accordingly in Article 48 of that Order (powers of Rules Committee), after paragraph (e) there shall be added—
    "(f) the service of process outside Northern Ireland, and the conditions subject to which process may be so served.".

General note

This section, which enlarges the powers of the County Court Rules Committee in Northern Ireland in relation to rules governing

---

† The section is printed as amended by Sched. 2, para. 24 of the Law Reform (Miscellaneous Provisions) (Scotland) Act 1985.
[39] See the general note to Part III, para. 42.05 above.

the service of process outside Northern Ireland, does not alter the law in England and Wales and detailed commentary on it is therefore beyond the scope of this work.

Section 30

43.18   30.—*Proceedings in England and Wales or Northern Ireland for torts to immovable property*

(1) The jurisdiction of any court in England and Wales or Northern Ireland to entertain proceedings for trespass to, or any other tort affecting, immovable property shall extend to cases in which the property in question is situated outside that part of the United Kingdom unless the proceedings are principally concerned with a question of the title to, or the right to possession of, that property.

(2) Subsection (1) has effect subject to the 1968 Convention and to the provisions set out in Schedule 4.

General note

43.19   Until this section came into force, English courts had no jurisdiction to entertain an action for damages for trespass to foreign land.[40] This restriction on the courts' jurisdiction was confirmed by the House of Lords' decision in *British South Africa Co.* v. *Companhia de Moçambique*[41] and reaffirmed in 1979 by its decision in *Hesperides Hotels Ltd.* v. *Aegean Turkish Holidays Ltd.*,[42] albeit with some criticism.[43] It was not clear to what extent the rule applied to torts other than trespass, nor to claims other than those for damages.

Subject to two qualifications discussed below, the effect of this section is to remove the restriction which the *Moçambique* case placed on the jurisdiction of the English courts. It permits jurisdiction *in personam* to be exercised in cases of torts affecting foreign land, whether in trespass, negligence, or nuisance, or under the rule in *Rylands* v. *Fletcher*,[44] provided that the court would otherwise have jurisdiction over the defendant. It also allows the jurisdiction to be exercised not only in respect of claims for damages but

---

[40] Dicey and Morris, pp. 924 *et seq.*; Cheshire and North, p. 265.
[41] [1893] A.C. 602.
[42] [1979] A.C. 508.
[43] Lord Fraser of Tullybelton doubted whether it was "either logical or satisfactory in its result" (*ibid.*, at p. 544).
[44] (1868) L.R. 3 H.L. 330.

also over claims for other relief, such as an injunction restraining a nuisance or trespass to land outside the territorial jurisdiction of the court.

While the English courts' jurisdiction to entertain proceedings **43.20** concerning immovables is extended by this section to cover immovables situated abroad, the extension is subject to certain qualifications. First, the section does not alter the existing rule that the court cannot normally entertain proceedings concerning title to, or rights to possession of, immovable property situated abroad.[45] The scope of subsection (1) expressly excludes proceedings which "are principally concerned with" such questions, but it would seem that the court is not barred from accepting jurisdiction over an action if questions of title to, or possession of, foreign land are merely incidental to the main issues.

Secondly, though, by reason of subsection (2), where the court's jurisdiction is regulated by the 1968 Convention or by Schedule 4, those provisions take priority. In practice, this will usually affect actions concerned with land falling within the exclusive jurisdiction provisions of Article 16(1),[46] where the courts of the Contracting State (or part of the United Kingdom) where the land is situated have exclusive jurisdiction, irrespective of whether or not the claim is framed in tort. Most often this will occur in relation to tenancies, in view of the wide interpretation given to Article 16(1) by the European Court.[47]

It is likely that the court will often be able to exercise some discretion in deciding whether to entertain proceedings pursuant to the jurisdiction conferred (or extended) by this section,[48] but there is no discretion to accept jurisdiction inconsistently with the 1968 Convention or Schedule 4 and difficult questions may sometimes arise over their precise scope. For example, it is not entirely clear whether the English court would be permitted to refuse jurisdiction against a defendant domiciled in England and Wales in proceedings which are principally concerned with a question of the title to land situated outside the Contracting States, because it would have jurisdiction which is apparently compulsory pursuant to Article 2 of the 1968 Convention and Schedule 4, and Article 16(1) does not apply.[49]

---

[45] Dicey and Morris, pp. 923 *et seq.*; Cheshire and North, pp. 255 *et seq.*
[46] Paras. 20.11 above and 45.19 below.
[47] See paras. 20.16 *et seq.* above.
[48] See s.49, para. 44.40 below.
[49] See paras. 1.39 and 20.06 *et seq.* above.

B. Provisions Relating to Recognition and Enforcement of
Judgments

Section 31

43.21 31.—*Overseas judgments given against states, etc.*

(1) A judgment given by a court of an overseas country against
a state other than the United Kingdom or the state to which that
court belongs shall be recognised and enforced in the United
Kingdom if, and only if—

    (a) it would be so recognised and enforced if it had not been
given against a state; and

    (b) that court would have had jurisdiction in the matter if it
had applied rules corresponding to those applicable to
such matters in the United Kingdom in accordance with
sections 2 to 11 of the State Immunity Act 1978.

(2) References in subsection (1) to a judgment given against a
state include references to judgments of any of the following descriptions given in relation to a state—

    (a) judgments against the government, or a department of
the government, of the state but not (except as mentioned in paragraph (c)) judgments against an entity
which is distinct from the executive organs of government;

    (b) judgments against the sovereign or head of state in his
public capacity;

    (c) judgments against any such separate entity as is men-
tioned in paragraph (a) given in proceedings relating to
anything done by it in the exercise of the sovereign authority of the state.

(3) Nothing in subsection (1) shall affect the recognition or
enforcement in the United Kingdom of a judgment to which
Part I of the Foreign Judgments (Reciprocal Enforcement) Act
1933 applies by virtue of section 4 of the Carriage of Goods by
Road Act 1965, section 17(4) of the Nuclear Installations Act
1965, section 13(3) of the Merchant Shipping (Oil Pollution)
Act 1971, section 6 of the International Transport Conventions
Act 1983 or section 5 of the Carriage of Passengers by Road
Act 1974.

(4) Sections 12, 13 and 14(3) and (4) of the State Immunity Act
1978 (service of process and procedural privileges) shall apply to
proceedings for the recognition or enforcement in the United
Kingdom of a judgment given by a court of an overseas country
(whether or not that judgment is within subsection (1) of this section) as they apply to other proceedings.

(5) **In this section "state," in the case of a federal state, includes any of its constituent territories.†**

1. General note

In cases where a court of one foreign country has given a judg- **43.22** ment against another foreign state, this section determines whether that judgment may be recognised and enforced in the United Kingdom. It gives effect in this field to the restrictive doctrine of sovereign immunity, which does not generally extend immunity to cases where the state's commercial activities are involved. This doctrine has increasingly gained acceptance in recent years[50] and was given effect in United Kingdom law in the jurisdictional field by the State Immunity Act 1978.[51] The effect of this section is to make the rules for the recognition and enforcement of foreign judgments against states generally parallel to those which apply to jurisdiction over such states.

2. Subsection (1)

A double condition is imposed by this subsection on the recognition and enforcement in the United Kingdom of a judgment given in an overseas country[52] against a third state. First, the judgment must be one which, if it had not been given against a state, would have been recognised and enforced in the United Kingdom. Subject to subsection (4), this first limb applies to recognition and enforcement under this Act, under other statutes[53] and at common law.

Secondly, the judgment must have been given by a court which would have had jurisdiction in the matter if it had applied rules corresponding to the rules applicable in the United Kingdom in accordance with sections 2 to 11 of the State Immunity Act 1978. This second limb has the effect of preventing a judgment being recognised or enforced in the United Kingdom if it were given against the third state pursuant to some more liberal rules of jurisdiction than would be applied here, but does not prevent the recognition or enforcement of judgments given in cases where the court of origin applied a narrower jurisdictional test and still accepted jurisdiction in the matter. Sections 2 to 11 of the 1978 Act set out a comprehensive series of tests for jurisdiction against foreign

---

† Subs. (3) is printed as amended by s.11(2) of the International Transport Conventions Act 1983.

[50] *I Congreso del Partido* [1983] 1 A.C. 244.

[51] See paras. 2.14 *et seq.* above; Dicey and Morris, pp. 236 *et seq.*

[52] An overseas country is defined by s.50 (para. 44.45 below) as meaning "any country or territory outside the U.K."

[53] The principal other statutes concerned are the Administration of Justice Act 1920, Part II, and the Foreign Judgments (Reciprocal Enforcement) Act 1933.

states,[54] of which the two most important are where the state has submitted to the jurisdiction of the court[55] and where the proceedings relate to a commercial transaction entered into by the state.[56]

3. Subsection (2)

43.23   This subsection provides a partial definition of the type of judgments which subsection (1) allows to be recognised and enforced, provided its conditions are fulfilled. The subsection deals with circumstances in which it might otherwise be doubtful whether the judgment attracted immunity.[57] It is by no means exhaustive, but the subsection should be read in conjunction with the definition of "judgment" in section 50.[58]

The question, for the purposes of paragraphs (*a*) and (*c*), of whether an entity is distinct from the executive organs of government[59] may be one to be answered by reference to the substantive law of the state concerned as proved by expert evidence, rather than a pure question of fact. Such "entities" will usually include state trading corporations, but not central banks or other monetary authorities.[60]

4. Subsection (3)

The immunity from recognition and enforcement conferred by section 31 does not extend to certain judgments which are enforceable pursuant to multilateral conventions. The relevant statutory provisions of United Kingdom law are referred to in this subsection and give effect to Part I of the 1933 Act, usually in a modified form, for the purpose of enforcing such judgments. If there were otherwise immunity under this section for a judgment which, under the other statutory provisions, ought to be enforced, a conflict between the two sets of provisions would arise. This subsection resolves any such conflict in favour of the specialised statutory provisions.

5. Subsection (4)

43.24   Pursuant to sections 12, 13 and 14(3) and 14(4) of the State Immunity Act 1978 certain procedural privileges, notably immunity from execution on property used otherwise than for com-

---

[54] Dicey and Morris, pp. 236 *et seq.*
[55] State Immunity Act 1978, s.2(1).
[56] *Ibid.*, s.3(1).
[57] The wording of the subsection is similar to that of s.14(1) of the State Immunity Act 1978.
[58] See para. 44.45 below. The definition of "court" in that section means that the decisions of tribunals are also included.
[59] See Dicey and Morris, pp. 238–239 *et seq.*
[60] See s.14(4) of the State Immunity Act 1978.

mercial purposes, are accorded to foreign states in proceedings in the United Kingdom. This subsection extends those privileges to proceedings for the recognition and enforcement of judgments given by courts of an overseas country,[61] whether or not the judgment falls within subsection (1). The term "proceedings" is not defined, but in the context must refer to the process of execution as well as proceedings before an order for execution is made.

6. Subsection (5)

The partial definition of "state" provided by this subsection is drawn from section 14 of the State Immunity Act 1978. Whether a territory constitutes a "constituent territory" of a federal state will usually be straightforward, as in the case of the *Länder* in the Federal Republic of Germany, the states in the United States of America, the provinces in Canada, or the cantons in Switzerland; similarly, municipal authorities will not normally be covered. Nonetheless, questions whether a state is a federal state and whether the territory falls within this definition may occasionally arise and expert evidence on the law of the foreign state in question will then probably be required.

Section 32

32.—*Overseas judgments given in proceedings brought in breach of*   **43.25**
agreement for settlement of disputes
    (1) Subject to the following provisions of this section, a judgment given by a court of an overseas country in any proceedings shall not be recognised or enforced in the United Kingdom if—

    (a) the bringing of those proceedings in that court was contrary to an agreement under which the dispute in question was to be settled otherwise than by proceedings in the courts of that country; and

    (b) those proceedings were not brought in that court by, or with the agreement of, the person against whom the judgment was given; and

    (c) that person did not counterclaim in the proceedings or otherwise submit to the jurisdiction of that court.

    (2) Subsection (1) does not apply where the agreement referred to in paragraph (a) of that subsection was illegal, void or unenforceable or was incapable of being performed for reasons not attributable to the fault of the party bringing the proceedings in which the judgment was given.

    (3) In determining whether a judgment given by a court of an overseas country should be recognised or enforced in the United

---

[61] See n. 52 above.

Kingdom, a court in the United Kingdom shall not be bound by any decision of the overseas court relating to any of the matters mentioned in subsection (1) or (2).

(4) Nothing in subsection (1) shall affect the recognition or enforcement in the United Kingdom of—

    (a) a judgment which is required to be recognised or enforced there under the 1968 Convention;

    (b) a judgment to which Part I of the Foreign Judgments (Reciprocal Enforcement) Act 1933 applies by virtue of section 4 of the Carriage of Goods by Road Act 1965, section 17(4) of the Nuclear Installations Act 1965, section 13(3) of the Merchant Shipping (Oil Pollution) Act 1971, section 6 of the International Transport Conventions Act 1983, section 5 of the Carriage of Passengers by Road Act 1974 or section 6(4) of the Merchant Shipping Act 1974.†

1. General note

43.26   English law grants a very large degree of freedom to contracting parties to choose the forum and means for the resolution of their disputes. The purpose of this section is apparently to preserve the effect of their choice, so far as possible, where the courts of overseas countries have not respected that choice.[62] Subject to certain specific exceptions, it prevents the recognition or enforcement in the United Kingdom of any judgment given by the court of an overseas country, if the judgment was the result of proceedings brought in breach of an agreement that the dispute was to be settled otherwise than by proceedings in the courts of that country.[63] Most commonly, that means judgments in proceedings brought contrary to an arbitration or jurisdiction agreement.

The principal provision, in subsection (1), is modelled on section 4(3)(*b*) of the Foreign Judgments (Reciprocal Enforcement) Act 933,[64] but unlike its predecessor the present provision is of general application. Subject to the exceptions mentioned in subsection (4), it extends the principle in section 4(3)(*b*) of the 1933 Act to the recognition and enforcement of all foreign judgments, whether they are being sought by an action at common law or by an application

---

† Subs. (4)(b) is printed as amended by s.11(2) of the International Transport Conventions Act 1983.

[62] There may be some doubt as to how effective the section will be where the court of origin has correctly applied the proper law of the contract in accepting jurisdiction: see para. 43.28 below.

[63] *Tracomin S.A.* v. *Sudan Oil Seeds Co. Ltd.* [1983] 1 W.L.R. 662, at p. 1026.

[64] That provision is repealed by Sched. 14 of this Act, para. 47.26 below.

for registration under the 1933 Act or under Part II of the Administration of Justice Act 1920 or under any of the various schemes for enforcement of maintenance orders.[65]

The section adopts a quite different approach from that used by the 1968 Convention. The Convention accords virtually automatic recognition and enforcement to judgments of the courts to which it applies[66] and forbids a review of the original court's jurisdiction.[67] This section, by contrast, allows the courts of the United Kingdom to consider afresh the jurisdiction of the original court (subsection (3)) and to do so according to their own rules of private international law, including especially those in subsections (1) and (2). Where the 1968 Convention requires that the judgment be recognised, though, its rules prevail (subsection (4)(*a*)). The same applies to certain other cases where the judgment is enforceable pursuant to statutory provisions giving effect to multilateral conventions.

It is in relation to arbitration agreements that the section is likely to have greatest effect. The extent to which arbitration is excluded from the scope of the 1968 Convention by Article 1 is a matter of some controversy more fully discussed elsewhere,[68] but if the view expressed by the United Kingdom in the accession negotiations is correct[69] and the 1968 Convention does not require a Contracting State to recognise or enforce a judgment given by the courts of another Contracting State in breach of an arbitration agreement, then this section will usually require United Kingdom courts not to do so.

2. Subsection (1)

The effect of this subsection is that a judgment given by a court **43.27** of an overseas country[70] must be refused recognition and enforcement in the United Kingdom if a number of conditions are fulfilled. The provision contains a prohibition only and does not, of course, mean that judgments which fall outside its scope are entitled to recognition and enforcement. It does not itself allow the court discretion in deciding whether to refuse to recognise or enforce the foreign judgment if the relevant conditions are fulfilled, but the provisions of subsection (2)[71] do allow some degree of flexibility in

---

[65] See chap. 11 above.
[66] See especially the first para. of Art. 26, para. 27.01 above.
[67] Third para. of Art. 28, para. 27.62 above.
[68] See paras. 14.31 *et seq.* above.
[69] Schlosser, para. 62 (para. A1.349 below).
[70] "Judgment," "court" and "overseas country" are defined by s.50, para. 44.45 below.
[71] See para. 43.28 below.

its operation. By prohibiting recognition as well as enforcement, the subsection ensures that the foreign judgment will not be regarded as *res judicata* in the United Kingdom, that neither party will be able to use it in aid of an issue estoppel, and that (unless there is some other impediment) the parties may still give effect to their arbitration or jurisdiction agreement.[72]

The first condition which must be fulfilled is set out in paragraph (*a*), which provides that the proceedings must have been brought in the court of the country of origin contrary to an agreement that the dispute in question was to be settled otherwise than by proceedings in the courts of that country. This is the most important of the conditions. In deciding whether there was such an agreement, and if so whether it had the effect contended for, English courts will apply their normal rules of private international law and, in particular, will usually have to decide the proper law of the agreement. They will also have to have regard to the provisions of subsections (2) and (3) of this section.

The second and third conditions which must be fulfilled are set out in paragraphs (*b*) and (*c*). In effect, each ensures that the person against whom the judgment was given should not be estopped from relying on the arbitration or jurisdiction agreement to try to prevent the recognition or enforcement of the foreign judgment in the United Kingdom. So, if that person had waived the agreement, whether expressly, or by instituting the offending proceedings himself, or by counterclaiming or otherwise submitting to the jurisdiction of the foreign court, the resulting judgment against him will not be prevented by the original arbitration or jurisdiction agreement from being accorded recognition and enforcement in the United Kingdom. The question whether that person had submitted to the jurisdiction of the foreign court will have to be determined in the light of section 33.[73]

The recognition and enforcement of the foreign judgment will not be refused pursuant to subsection (1) if, notwithstanding that the conditions in paragraphs (*a*) to (*c*) are fulfilled, subsections (2) or (4) disapply the effects of this subsection.

3. Subsection (2)

43.28   On its own, subsection (1) would prove inflexible in some cases where its conditions were fulfilled but where it would nonetheless be unreasonable to refuse to recognise and enforce the foreign judgment. This subsection refines the prohibition contained in subsection (1), while not going so far as to confer a discretion on the

---

[72] *Tracomin S.A.* v. *Sudan Oil Seeds Co. Ltd.* [1983] 1 W.L.R. 662, at p. 1026.
[73] See para. 43.30 below.

court to allow the recognition and enforcement of a foreign judgment which still contravenes these provisions. In deciding whether there was an agreement of the type mentioned in paragraph (*a*) of subsection (1), and if so whether it had the effect contended for, the court will apply its own law, including its conflicts of law rules,[74] and this will usually mean that most questions will be determined by reference to the proper law of the agreement.

In carrying out that exercise, this subsection requires the court also to consider whether the agreement was illegal, void or unenforceable or was incapable of being performed for reasons not attributable to the fault of the party bringing the proceedings in which the judgment was given. Difficult questions of conflicts of law may arise as to the proper law to be applied in deciding whether the relevant agreement falls within this subsection. Such questions are beyond the scope of this work, but while the United Kingdom court is not bound by any decision of the original court on these questions,[75] it is still quite possible that it may reach the same conclusion by the application of the proper law. Some guidance may be derived from the courts' approach to the similar provisions in section 1 of the Arbitration Act 1975,[76] although a different approach may need to be adopted in the present context. Under the Arbitration Act, the English court is concerned with such matters as the validity or enforceability of an arbitration agreement in the context of an application to stay English proceedings. In the present context, by contrast, the court is concerned with the validity or enforceability of an arbitration or jurisdiction agreement in the context of an allegation that the foreign court should not have accepted jurisdiction.

The reference to an agreement being incapable of being performed applies to such circumstances as the refusal of a named arbitrator to accept the reference[77] or the refusal of a chosen court to accept jurisdiction.

4. Subsection (3)

This subsection provides the English court with a clean slate   **43.29**
when it comes to deciding any of the matters mentioned in subsections (1) and (2). The English court will not be bound by any

---

[74] See subs. (3) below; Collins, p. 142.
[75] See subs. (3) below.
[76] Dicey and Morris, p. 556, suggest that the validity of an arbitration agreement would be a matter for its proper law, but that the other matters would be decided without reference to foreign law. See also Mustill and Boyd, *Commercial Arbitration* (2nd ed.) pp. 61–63.
[77] See Dicey and Morris, pp. 556–557.

decision of the court of origin relating to any of those matters,[78] but it will presumably still be entitled to take any such decision into account and give it such weight as is appropriate, provided that the decision is properly in evidence before it.[79]

5. Subsection (4)

This subsection excludes two categories of judgment from the operation of this section. They are therefore judgments which, even if they were given in breach of an arbitration or jurisdiction agreement, may still be recognised and enforced in the United Kingdom.

The first category, referred to in paragraph (*a*), covers those judgments which the 1968 Convention requires to be recognised or enforced. That is, subject to certain limited exceptions, all judgments given by courts and tribunals[80] in the other Contracting States in matters falling within the Convention.[81] It remains to be seen whether judgments given in proceedings which have been instituted or continued in breach of an arbitration agreement fall within the scope of the 1968 Convention,[82] but if they do, then they cannot be refused recognition or enforcement under the present section.

The grounds on which a judgment may be refused recognition and enforcement under the 1968 Convention are listed in full elsewhere[83] and in virtually all of those cases a judgment falling within those grounds must be refused recognition and enforcement.[84] Where that is so, the question will not arise whether the judgment must also be refused recognition and enforcement under this section. One of the grounds in the Convention for refusing to recognise a foreign judgment is where recognition is contrary to public policy in the state addressed.[85] It is perhaps important to note that the Convention expressly prohibits the application of that public policy test to rules relating to jurisdiction[86] and it is not therefore permissible for the provisions of the present section to be relied on as indi-

---

[78] *Tracomin S.A.* v. *Sudan Oil Seeds Co. Ltd.* [1983] 1 W.L.R. 662, at p. 670.

[79] Where the decision is a decision on a point of foreign law, its correctness may need to be proved by expert evidence: see Civil Evidence Act 1972, s.4 and chap. 9 above.

[80] See Art. 25, para. 26.01 above.

[81] The scope of the Convention is defined by Art. 1, para. 14.03 above; for judgments falling only partly within the Convention, see Art. 42, para. 28.71 above.

[82] See para. 14.32 above.

[83] See paras. 10.27 and 25.11–25.13 above.

[84] An exception is under the second para. of Art. II of the 1968 Protocol (para. 35.05 above), where the judgment was given in criminal proceedings and the defendant did not appear.

[85] See Art. 27(1), para. 27.13 above.

[86] Third para. of Art. 28, para. 27.62 above.

cating matters of United Kingdom public policy for the purposes of Article 27(1).

The second category of judgment excluded from the operation of this section, referred to in paragraph (*b*), covers those judgments to which the 1933 Act applies by virtue of certain statutory provisions listed in the paragraph. They concern particular matters governed by multilateral international conventions (which would fall within Article 57 of the 1968 Convention, and which would not therefore normally be governed by the main provisions of that Convention). The particular conventions in question themselves regulate jurisdiction and enforcement of judgments in a mandatory way, and the provisions of this section would probably be incompatible with their terms.

Section 33

33.—*Certain steps not to amount to submission to jurisdiction of*   **43.30**
overseas court

(1) For the purposes of determining whether a judgment given by a court of an overseas country should be recognised or enforced in England and Wales or Northern Ireland, the person against whom the judgment was given shall not be regarded as having submitted to the jurisdiction of the court by reason only of the fact that he appeared (conditionally or otherwise) in the proceedings for all or any one or more of the following purposes, namely—

 (a) to contest the jurisdiction of the court;
 (b) to ask the court to dismiss or stay the proceedings on the ground that the dispute in question should be submitted to arbitration or to the determination of the courts of another country;
 (c) to protect, or obtain the release of, property seized or threatened with seizure in the proceedings.

(2) Nothing in this section shall affect the recognition or enforcement in England and Wales or Northern Ireland of a judgment which is required to be recognised or enforced there under the 1968 Convention.

1. General note

The effect of this section is to enable a defendant to contest the   **43.31**
jurisdiction of a foreign court without thereby prejudicing his prospects of preventing the judgment of that court from being recognised or enforced in England and Wales or Northern Ireland. Generally, English law provides for the recognition and enforce-

ment of a foreign judgment if it regards the court which gave that judgment as having been a court of competent jurisdiction.[87] One of the principal grounds on which a foreign court may be regarded as competent is if the defendant submitted voluntarily to its jurisdiction.

What the present section does is to specify certain steps which are not to be taken as amounting to voluntary submission to the jurisdiction of the foreign court, notably an appearance before that court to contest its jurisdiction or the exercise of that jurisdiction. In doing so, it replaces and extends the provisions of section 4(2)(*a*)(i) of the Foreign Judgments (Reciprocal Enforcement) Act 1933 and reverses the much-criticised decision of the Court of Appeal in *Henry* v. *Geoprosco International*.[88] The effect of that decision was that an unsuccessful challenge to the foreign court's jurisdiction amounted to a submission to that jurisdiction.[89] If a defendant is unsuccessful in his challenge to the jurisdiction of the foreign court and then takes no further part in the proceedings, the result will usually be that judgment is entered against him, probably in default of appearance or defence.[90] By reason of this section, he will not now be prevented from saying that, as a matter of English law, the foreign court was without jurisdiction and that its judgment should not therefore be recognised or enforced. The English court's decision whether or not to recognise and enforce the foreign judgment may be influenced by the foreign court's decision on its own jurisdiction and this section means that defendants should no longer be discouraged from making submissions on this topic to the foreign court.

In a case to which the 1968 Convention applies, the English court is usually bound by the original court's decision as to its own jurisdiction.[91] In such cases, any challenge to the jurisdiction of the original court should be made to that court. It would be most unwise for a defendant to ignore the foreign proceedings and to let them go by default, intending to challenge the foreign jurisdiction at the enforcement stage. Where there is a conflict between the provisions of this section and those of the 1968 Convention, the latter are to prevail: see the commentary below on subsection (2).

---

[87] The English law regarding the jurisdiction of foreign courts, otherwise than under the 1968 Convention, is detailed: see Dicey and Morris, pp. 436–460; Cheshire and North, pp. 341–354, 356–358.
[88] [1976] Q.B. 726, following *Harris* v. *Taylor* [1915] 2 K.B. 580.
[89] See, further, Dicey and Morris, pp. 441–444; Cheshire and North, pp. 345–346.
[90] See Collins, p. 143.
[91] Art. 28, third para., para. 27.62 above.

2. Subsection (1)

This subsection applies to the recognition or enforcement of a **43.32** judgment given by a court of an overseas country[92] where the question arises as to whether the person against whom the judgment was given voluntarily submitted to the jurisdiction of that court. If he appeared before the foreign court, his appearance will only amount, as a matter of English law, to a submission to its jurisdiction if the purpose of his doing so was for one or more of the enumerated reasons set out in the subsection.

Appearance. What amounts to an appearance will depend to some extent upon the procedural requirements of the foreign court, but it is suggested that the English court will not be bound by the foreign procedural law on the point and will be free to decide as a matter of fact in each case whether any given step or action amounted to "appearing."[93] It is probable that the term "appeared" does not refer to the entry of a memorandum of appearance (or filing of an acknowledgment of service) in any technical sense, and the subsection expressly draws no distinction between conditional and other appearances.[94] Nonetheless, it is suggested that the English courts will wish, in the interests of consistency, to have regard to the meaning of "enters an appearance" in Article 18 of the 1968 Convention.[95]

Multiple purposes. The English court will also be free to decide on **43.33** the facts of each case whether the purpose of the person against whom the judgment was given in appearing before the foreign court was any one or more of the listed reasons. In this connection, it should be noted that the limitation imposed by the word "only" is a limitation not on the purposes for which the defendant appeared in the proceedings, but upon the fact that he appeared for those purposes. In other words, the English court called upon to recognise or enforce the foreign judgment should look to see, not whether the defendant's purposes in appearing before the foreign court were confined to the purposes listed in the subsection, but whether there are facts other than his appearance for those purposes sufficient to conclude that he had submitted to its jurisdiction.

---

[92] "Judgment," "court" and "overseas country" are defined by s.50 (para. 44.45 below).

[93] See Dicey and Morris, pp. 441–444; Patchett, *Recognition of Commercial Judgments and Awards in the Commonwealth*, para. 3.38.

[94] The words "conditionally or otherwise" reverse the ruling in *Henry* v. *Geoprosco International* [1976] Q.B. 726, that even a conditional appearance can amount to a submission to the jurisdiction if it is converted by operation of law into an unconditional appearance in the event of the challenge to the jurisdiction being unsuccessful.

[95] See para. 21.83 above.

It follows that the section would not seem to preclude a defendant who had unsuccessfully contested the jurisdiction of the foreign court, but who had also, subsequently or in the alternative, pleaded to the substance of the case against him, from saying that the judgment against him should not be recognised or enforced by the English courts.[96] Indeed, this is the position under Article 18 of the 1968 Convention,[97] despite the fact that, by contrast with this subsection, the limitation imposed by the word "solely" in that Article[98] would seem to be a limitation upon the reasons for entering an appearance. On the other hand, Article 18 forms part of a framework of rules in the Convention under which the court addressed is required to respect the decision of the court of origin as to its own jurisdiction,[99] whereas such principles of full faith and credit do not necessarily apply in the present context.

43.34   *Paragraph (a): contesting the jurisdiction.* An appearance to contest the jurisdiction is the main case envisaged by the subsection. This paragraph envisages a contest challenging the jurisdiction of the foreign court as a matter of its own law, and it is to be distinguished from an application that that court should refrain from exercising a jurisdiction which it has or which arguably it has, whether by granting a stay of the proceedings or by dismissing them.[1]

Paragraph (b): alternative forum.[2] An application to the foreign court for relief of the type referred to in this paragraph may, but need not necessarily, amount to a dispute of that court's jurisdiction, although if the application is successful, it will probably have much the same effect. The paragraph covers applications both for a stay and for dismissal, in each case irrespective of whether the relief is compulsory or discretionary, and whether the application is based on a contractual term between the parties or merely on the provisions of the law.

---

[96] This is especially so, perhaps, if the law of civil procedure of the foreign court would have barred the defendant from subsequently pleading to the merits in the event of his challenge to the jurisdiction being unsuccessful: *cf. Elefanten Schuh* v. *Jacqumain* [1981] E.C.R. 1671, at p. 1685, discussed at paras. 21.86 and 21.94 above.

[97] See paras. 21.94 *et seq.* above.

[98] Art. 18 states, " . . . where appearance was entered solely to contest the jurisdiction. . . ."

[99] Art. 28, third para., para. 21.62 above.

[1] Some such cases fall under para. (*b*), but not all. As was pointed out in the debates on the Bill, an application for the proceedings to be dismissed on the ground that they are frivolous or vexatious, must usually be taken as an admission that the court has jurisdiction to entertain them: *per* Sir Ian Percival S-G, H.C.Deb., Standing Committee B, April 19, 1982, col. 18.

[2] See *Tracomin S.A.* v. *Sudan Oil Seeds Co. Ltd.* [1983] 1 W.L.R. 662, at p. 671.

Paragraph (c): seized property. This paragraph, like paragraph (*a*), reproduces provisions of section 4(2)(*a*)(i) of the Foreign Judgments (Reciprocal Enforcement) Act 1933.[3] It may apply not only where the property is seized for the purpose of founding jurisdiction,[4] but also where the property has been made the subject of a protective seizure.[5] Similarly, it may apply where the defendant's purpose in appearing is to prevent a default judgment against him in proceedings which are specifically aimed at the seizure of his property. In each case, the court will be concerned to establish the defendant's purpose in appearing; if a defendant appeared and contested such an action on the merits, the English court might well conclude that he had appeared for purposes wider than merely protecting or obtaining the release of his property, and that he had therefore submitted to the jurisdiction of the foreign court.

3. Subsection (2)

The effect of this subsection is to give precedence to the provisions of the 1968 Convention over those of subsection (1), in any case where the two conflict. Whereas English law generally requires that the jurisdiction of the court of origin should be reviewed by the English court where the latter is called upon to recognise or enforce a foreign judgment, and subsection (1) provides some of the tests which are to be conducted on that review, such tests are prohibited by the 1968 Convention in cases which fall within its scope. Because its jurisdictional rules apply throughout the Contracting States, the 1968 Convention generally forbids the court addressed from carrying out a review of the jurisdiction of the court of origin.[6] In a limited range of cases where it does permit such a review,[7] the tests are themselves dictated by the Convention[8] and are not generally concerned with the question of whether the defendant voluntarily submitted to the jurisdiction of the foreign court. Accordingly, they leave no room for the application of tests pursuant to national law, such as those in subsection (1). Nonetheless, the Convention's own jurisdictional rules recognise voluntary submission to the jurisdiction as an important basis of competence, and do not regard an

43.35

---

[3] The 1933 Act was probably wider in this respect than the common law: see Dicey and Morris, pp. 443–444; Cheshire and North, pp. 349–350; Patchett, *op. cit.* para. 3.38.

[4] For example, the jurisdiction of the foreign court may be founded on the arrest of property in an action *in rem*, or (except in cases covered by the 1968 Convention) under Art. 23 of the German code of civil procedure: see para. 51.30 below.

[5] See para. 7.22 above and chaps. 48 to 58 below, at paras. 58–60.

[6] Art. 28, third para., para. 21.62 above.

[7] See paras. 25.12–25.13 above.

[8] *Ibid.*; paras. 27.66 *et seq.* above.

appearance before the court of origin to contest its jurisdiction as being a submission to that jurisdiction.[9]

Section 34

43.36   **34.**—*Certain judgments a bar to further proceedings on the same cause of action*

No proceedings may be brought by a person in England and Wales or Northern Ireland on a cause of action in respect of which a judgment has been given in his favour in proceedings between the same parties, or their privies, in a court in another part of the United Kingdom or in a court of an overseas country, unless that judgment is not enforceable or entitled to recognition in England and Wales or, as the case may be, in Northern Ireland.

General note

43.37   This section largely abrogates the common law rule, known as the "non-merger" rule, whereby a person who had obtained a final judgment before a court other than an English court of record could start a fresh action on the original cause of action.[10] The non-merger rule, which had been much criticised,[11] was an exception to the normal rule of English law, under which a cause of action merged in a final judgment, creating an estoppel by record.[12] While the foreign judgment could itself form the basis of an action at common law,[13] the original cause of action survived (subject to a right of set-off in respect of sums paid under the foreign judgment) and could form the basis of an action in which the foreign judgment was evidence of the debt or right to damages, rather than the foundation of the action itself.[14]

The effect of the section is that a judgment given by a court of competent jurisdiction in another part of the United Kingdom or in

---

[9] Art. 18, para. 21.83 above.

[10] See Cheshire and North, pp. 339–340; Dicey and Morris pp. 1077–1078.

[11] *e.g.*, in *Carl Zeiss Stiftung* v. *Rayner & Keeler Ltd. (No. 2)* [1967] 1 A.C. 853, at p. 966.

[12] This rule is to be distinguished from the question of issue estoppel, which can be created by a foreign judgment: *Carl Zeiss Stiftung* v. *Rayner & Keeler (No. 2)* above; *The Sennar (No. 2)* [1985] 1 W.L.R. 490 (H.L.).

[13] This rule, which is based on the "doctrine of obligation," applied only to a money judgment which was final and conclusive: see Dicey and Morris, pp. 420–421; Cheshire and North, pp. 338–339. It survives unchanged by this section: see paras. 10.03 and 25.35–25.36 above.

[14] s.6 of the Foreign Judgments (Reciprocal Enforcement) Act 1933, which bars the enforcement of judgments to which it applies, otherwise than by registration under the Act, did not preclude the bringing of a fresh action on the original cause of action; Dicey and Morris, p. 1110.

an overseas country[15] bars the bringing of proceedings on the same cause of action, unless the foreign judgment is not enforceable or entitled to recognition in England and Wales.[16] Subject to that proviso, this abrogates the non-merger rule in its entirety. If a judgment is not enforceable under one of the statutory schemes (including the 1968 Convention), it may still be enforceable by means of an action at common law.[17] Until recently, enforcement by this means might have been difficult if the defendant was to be served out of the jurisdiction, but (unless the case is one to which the 1968 Convention applies)[18] such a case is now catered for by Order 11 of the Rules of the Supreme Court, under which a writ may be served out of the jurisdiction (with the court's leave) where the claim is brought for the purposes of enforcing any judgment.[19]

The wording of the section creates a potential difficulty as **43.38** regards a cause of action which has become the subject of a foreign judgment which is entitled to recognition in this country, but which is not enforceable here. For example, a final and conclusive foreign judgment ordering the defendant to perform some act other than the payment of a definite sum of money is not capable of enforcement in England unless it falls within the 1968 Convention or section 18 of this Act.[20] It may nonetheless be entitled to recognition[21] and in such a case it would seem to be impossible to give effect either to the foreign judgment or the original cause of action.[22]

For cases to which the 1968 Convention applies, the necessity for this section is much reduced, because the European Court of Justice has held that if a judgment may be enforced in a given Contracting State under Title III of the Convention, the party entitled to enforce the judgment there is precluded from applying to the courts of that state for a judgment in the same terms as the original

---

[15] "Judgment," "court," "part of the U.K." and "overseas country" are each defined in s.50, para. 44.45 below.
[16] The same applies in Northern Ireland.
[17] See n. 13 above.
[18] It has already been suggested that an action on a judgment does not fall within the exclusive jurisdiction provisions of Art. 16(5) of the 1968 Convention: para. 20.43 above, n. 43. It remains to be seen, however, whether such an action on a judgment can fall under any of the heads of special jurisdiction in Art. 5 of the Convention, or whether a defendant domiciled in a Contracting State can only be sued in that state under Art. 2.
[19] R.S.C., Ord. 11, r. 1(1)(m).
[20] Para. 41.13 above.
[21] Dicey and Morris, pp. 426–427.
[22] Depending on the nature of the judgment, the solution may sometimes be found in regarding the foreign judgment as giving rise to an estoppel, or to an assignment: Dicey and Morris, pp. 431–432, 456–457.

judgment.[23] It remains relevant though, in considering whether a judgment given in another Contracting State is reconcilable with one given by a court in the United Kingdom.[24]

Section 35

43.39   **35.**—*Minor amendments relating to overseas judgments*
    (1) The Foreign Judgments (Reciprocal Enforcement) Act 1933 shall have effect with the amendments specified in Schedule 10, being amendments whose main purpose is to enable Part I of that Act to be applied to judgments of courts other than superior courts, to judgments providing for interim payments and to certain arbitration awards.
    (2) For section 10 of the Administration of Justice Act 1920 (issue of certificates of judgments obtained in the United Kingdom) there shall be substituted—
        "10.—(1) Where—
            (a) a judgment has been obtained in the High Court in England or Northern Ireland, or in the Court of Session in Scotland, against any person; and
            (b) the judgment creditor wishes to secure the enforcement of the judgment in a part of Her Majesty's dominions outside the United Kingdom to which this Part of this Act extends, the court shall, on an application made by the judgment creditor, issue to him a certified copy of the judgment.
        (2) The reference in the preceding subsection to Her Majesty's dominions shall be construed as if that subsection had come into force in its present form at the commencement of this Act."
    (3) In section 14 of the Administration of Justice Act 1920 (extent of Part II of that Act), after subsection (2) there shall be inserted—
        "(3) Her Majesty may by Order in Council under this section consolidate any Orders in Council under this section which are in force when the consolidating Order is made."

General note

43.40   This section, together with Schedule 10,[25] introduces certain amendments to the Foreign Judgments (Reciprocal Enforcement) Act 1933[26] and Part II of the Administration of Justice Act 1920, the two principal statutory schemes (apart from this Act and the

---

[23] *De Wolf* v. *Cox BV* [1976] E.C.R. 1759, discussed at paras. 25.36 above.
[24] Para. 27.49 above.
[25] See para. 47.08 below.
[26] The amendments in paras. 2 and 5(3) of Sched. 10 are also enacted by s.54 and Sched. 14.

1968 Convention) for the international enforcement of judgments. A detailed examination of the amendments is beyond the scope of this work, but their principal effect is to remove certain anomalies and to enable the provisions of the 1933 Act to be extended to a wider range of cases.

Extending the scope of the 1933 Act. The 1933 Act was formerly limited to the final judgments of superior courts. The amendments in paragraph 1 of Schedule 10 mean that it may now be applied (if there is substantial reciprocity) to the judgments of whatever courts or tribunals are designated by Order in Council in respect of the foreign country in question. The judgments to which the Act applies (although they must still be money judgments) need no longer be final judgments, but may include orders for interim payments and may be restricted or extended to such class or classes of judgments as are specified by the relevant Order in Council.[27] The Act does not apply to judgments on appeal from courts which are not themselves recognised for the purposes of the Act, nor to foreign judgments which (or which are intended to) enforce a judgment given in a third country.

The new section 10A of the 1933 Act[28] enables a wider range of arbitral awards to be enforced under that Act than was formerly the case.[29]

Procedural reform. The reciprocal enforcement arrangements usually provide a simple means of authenticating a United Kingdom judgment, for use abroad. Section 10 of the 1920 Act[30] and section 10 of the 1933 Act[31] enable a judgment creditor to obtain a certified copy of the judgment in question.[32] The amendments streamline the procedure, making it parallel to that provided by section 12 of this Act for the purposes of enforcing judgments in other Contracting States under the 1968 Convention.

43.41

Subsection (3) amends section 14 of the 1920 Act to allow consolidation of Orders in Council made under that section. The relevant Orders are those designating the territories to which the

[27] See, *e.g.* the Reciprocal Enforcement of Foreign Judgments (Canada) Order 1987, (S.I. 1987 No. 468), para. 4 and the Orders referred to at para. 33.32 above, n. 75.
[28] The section is inserted by Sched. 10, para. 4 of this Act, para. 47.09 below.
[29] See, formerly, Administration of Justice Act 1956, s.51(*a*), now repealed by this Act.
[30] As substituted by subs. (2) of this section.
[31] As amended by para. 3 of Sched. 10 below.
[32] This is effected pursuant to rules of court: R.S.C., Ord. 71, r. 13; C.C.R., Ord. 35, r. 2.

provisions of Part II apply, and the conditions on which they do so. Orders have been made under the amended provisions.[33]

Section 36

43.42   **36.**—*Registration of maintenance orders in Northern Ireland*
   (1) Where—
      (a) a High Court order or a Court of Session order has been registered in the High Court of Justice in Northern Ireland ("the Northern Ireland High Court") under Part II of the Maintenance Orders Act 1950; or
      (b) a county court order, a magistrates' court order or a sheriff court order has been registered in a court of summary jurisdiction in Northern Ireland under that Part,
   an application may be made to the original court for the registration of the order in, respectively, a court in summary jurisdiction in Northern Ireland or the Northern Ireland High Court.

   (2) In subsection (1) "the original court," in relation to an order, means the court by which the order was made.

   (3) Section 2 (except subsection (6A)) and section 2A of the Maintenance Orders Act 1958 shall have effect for the purposes of an application under subsection (1), and subsections (2), (3), (4) and (4A) of section 5 of that Act shall have effect for the purposes of the cancellation of a registration made on such an application, as if—
      (a) "registration" in those provisions included registration in the appropriate Northern Ireland court ("registered" being construed accordingly);
      (b) any reference in those provisions to a High Court order or a magistrates' court order included, respectively, a Court of Session order or a sheriff court order; and
      (c) any other reference in those provisions to the High Court or a magistrates' court included the Northern Ireland High Court of a court of summary jurisdiction in Northern Ireland.

   (4) Where an order is registered in Northern Ireland under this section, Part II of the Maintenance and Affiliation Orders Act (Northern Ireland) 1966, except sections 11, 11A and 14(2) and (3), shall apply as if the order had been registered in accordance with the provisions of that Part.

   (5) A court of summary jurisdiction in Northern Ireland shall

---

[33] Reciprocal Enforcement of Judgments (Administration of Justice Act 1920, Part II) (Consolidation) Order 1984, (S.I. 1984 No. 129), amended by the Reciprocal Enforcement of Judgments (Administration of Justice Act 1920, Part II) (Amendment) Order 1985, (S.I. 1985 No. 1994).

have jurisdiction to hear a complaint by or against a person residing outside Northern Ireland for the discharge or variation of an
order registered in Northern Ireland under this section; and
where such a complaint is made against a person residing outside
Northern Ireland, then, if he resides in England and Wales or
Scotland, section 15 of the Maintenance Orders Act 1950 (which
relates to the service of process on persons residing in those
countries) shall have effect in relation to the complaint as it has
effect in relation to the proceedings therein mentioned.

(6) The enactments specified in Part III of Schedule 12 shall
have effect with the amendments specified there, being amendments consequential on this section.

General note

This section amends the law of Northern Ireland to increase the **43.43**
flexibility of the arrangements for the registration, for the purposes
of their enforcement, of maintenance orders made in the other parts
of the United Kingdom. It also gives effect to the consequential
amendments in Part III of Schedule 12, but it does not alter the law
in England and Wales and detailed commentary on it is therefore
beyond the scope of this work.

Section 37

37.—*Minor amendments relating to maintenance orders* **43.44**
(1) The enactments specified in Schedule 11 shall have effect
with the amendments specified there, being amendments whose
main purpose is as follows—
   Part I—to extend certain enforcement provisions to lump sum
      maintenance orders;
   Part II—to provide for the recovery of interest according to
      the law of the country of origin in the case of maintenance
      orders made in other jurisdictions and registered in the High
      Court;
   Part III—to extend the Maintenance Orders (Reciprocal
      Enforcement) Act 1972 to cases where the payer under a
      maintenance order is not resident within the jurisdiction but
      has assets there.
(2) In section 27(1) of the Maintenance Orders (Reciprocal
Enforcement) Act 1972 (application by person in convention
country for recovery of maintenance in England and Wales or
Northern Ireland to be treated as a complaint), after "as if it
were a complaint" there shall be inserted "made at the time
when the application was received by the Secretary of State or
the Lord Chancellor."

General note

43.45   Together with Schedule 11, this section makes a number of changes to the law relating to maintenance orders. Whereas the 1968 Convention and section 5 of this Act[34] provide the principal legislative scheme for the enforcement of maintenance orders made in other Contracting States, the legislative schemes for the reciprocal enforcement of maintenance orders made in other countries or in other parts of the United Kingdom remain in place as parallel systems.[35] The amendments effected by this section bring those other systems more closely into line with that provided by the 1968 Convention and section 5 of this Act. Reference may be made to Chapter 11 where the recognition and enforcement of foreign maintenance orders are more fully discussed.

Subsection (2) introduces a minor amendment to the Maintenance Orders (Reciprocal Enforcement) Act 1972, to fix for the purposes of Part II of the Act the point in time when a claim for maintenance is deemed to have been made if it is sent to the Secretary of State by the appropriate authority of another convention country.

Section 38

43.46   **38.**—*Overseas judgments counteracting an award of multiple damages*
(1) Section 7 of the Protection of Trading Interests Act 1980 (which enables provision to be made by Order in Council for the enforcement in the United Kingdom on a reciprocal basis of overseas judgments directed to counteracting a judgment for multiple damages given in a third country) shall be amended as follows.

(2) In subsection (1) for "judgments given under any provision of the law of that country corresponding to that section" there shall be substituted "judgments of any description specified in the Order which are given under any provision of the law of that country relating to the recovery of sums paid or obtained pursuant to a judgment for multiple damages within the meaning of section 5(3) above, whether or not that provision corresponds to section 6 above."

(3) After subsection (1) there shall be inserted—
     "(1A) Such an Order in Council may, as respects judgments to which it relates—
     (a) make different provisions for different descriptions of judgments; and

---

[34] Para. 40.12 above.
[35] See para. 11.07 above.

(b) impose conditions or restrictions on the enforcement of judgments of any description."

General note

This section is exclusively directed at amending one particular   **43.47**
provision in section 7 of the Protection of Trading Interests Act
1980. Section 6 of that Act creates a cause of action whereby a
"qualifying defendant," who has paid sums under a foreign judgment awarding multiple damages (typically in a United States anti-
trust case), can seek to recover part of those damages representing
the penal element. Section 7 of the 1980 Act provides for the
enforcement (on the basis of reciprocity) of foreign judgments
which seek to do the same thing. As unamended, the requirement
of reciprocity was tight, specifying that the provisions of foreign
law under which the judgment was given should "correspond" with
section 6. The amendments made by this section relax that requirement and allow the Order in Council providing for the reciprocal
enforcement of such judgments to specify which descriptions of
judgment counteracting awards of multiple damages may be
enforced in the United Kingdom. The Protection of Trading Interests Act 1980, as amended by this section, has been extended
to Jersey, Guernsey and the Isle of Man.[36]

C. JURISDICTION AND RECOGNITION AND ENFORCEMENT OF
JUDGMENTS, AS BETWEEN UNITED KINGDOM AND CERTAIN
TERRITORIES

Section 39

39.—*Application of provisions corresponding to 1968 Convention in*   **43.48**
relation to certain territories
(1) **Her Majesty may by Order in Council make provision corresponding to the provision made in the 1968 Convention as
between the Contracting States to that Convention, with such
modifications as appear to Her Majesty to be appropriate, for
regulating, as between the United Kingdom and any of the territories mentioned in subsection (2), the jurisdiction of courts and
the recognition and enforcement of judgments.**
(2) **The territories referred to in subsection (1) are—**
   (a) **the Isle of Man;**
   (b) **any of the Channel Islands;**
   (c) **Gibraltar;**
   (d) **the Sovereign Base Areas of Akrotiri and Dhekelia (that**

---

[36] 1983 S.I. Nos. 607, 1703 and 1704.

is to say the areas mentioned in section 2(1) of the Cyprus Act 1960).

(3) An Order in Council under this section may contain such supplementary and incidental provisions as appear to Her Majesty to be necessary or expedient, including in particular provisions corresponding to or applying any of the provisions of Part I with such modifications as may be specified in the Order.

(4) Any Order in Council under this section shall be subject to annulment in pursuance of a resolution of either House of Parliament.

General note

43.49   The United Kingdom is responsible for the external relations of a number of European territories to which the 1968 Convention does not automatically apply, namely the Isle of Man, the Channel Islands, Gibraltar and the sovereign base areas on Cyprus. Under Article 60 of the 1968 Convention,[37] however, the United Kingdom may declare that the provisions of the Convention extend to any of those territories. Such a declaration would have the effect of regulating the relations between other Contracting States and the territory in question, as if it were a part of the United Kingdom.[38] Such a declaration would not of itself regulate the relations between that territory and the other parts of the United Kingdom—a matter which, so far as the other Contracting States are concerned, is purely one of internal United Kingdom law. What this section does, therefore, is to enable the relations between such a territory and the rest of the United Kingdom to be regulated by rules corresponding (with modifications if appropriate) to the 1968 Convention, and by such supplementary provisions as are necessary or expedient. No Orders have yet been made under this section.

D. Legal Aid

Section 40

43.50   **40.**—*Power to modify enactments relating to legal aid, etc.*

(1) . . .

(2) . . .

(3) In Article 22 of the Legal Aid, Advice and Assistance (Northern Ireland) Order 1981 (power of Lord Chancellor to

---

[37] Para. 34.01 above; Art. 6 of the 1971 Protocol, para. 36.18 above, is to the same effect.
[38] An Order in Council under s.52(2) would probably have to be made, to implement the effects of the declaration in the territory in question, although the territory could introduce its own legislation for this purpose.

male regulations), after paragraph (4) there shall be inserted as paragraph (4A)—

"(4A) Without prejudice to the preceding provisions of this Article or any other provision of this Part authorising the making of regulations, regulations may also modify the provisions of, or of any instrument having effect under, this Part (including so much of any of those provisions as specifies a sum of money) for the purposes of the application of those provisions—

(a) in cases where their modification appears to the Lord Chancellor necessary for the purpose of fulfilling any obligation imposed on the United Kingdom or Her Majesty's government therein by any international agreement; or

(b) in relation to proceedings for securing the recognition or enforcement in Northern Ireland of judgments given outside the United Kingdom for whose recognition or enforcement in the United Kingdom provision is made by any international agreement."†

General note

If a person has benefited in proceedings in one Contracting State **43.51** from complete or partial legal aid or exemption from costs or expenses, and he then applies in another Contracting State under Articles 32 to 35 of the 1968 Convention for an order for enforcement of the judgment given in those proceedings, he is entitled under Article 44 of the Convention[39] to the most favourable legal aid or the most extensive exemption from costs or expenses provided for by the law of the state addressed.[40] Article 15 of the Hague Convention of October 2, 1973 on the recognition and enforcement of maintenance obligations contains a provision to the same effect. This section amended the legislation on legal aid in the three parts of the United Kingdom so that the responsible Minister in each case could make rules giving effect to these and similar international obligations and generally to facilitate the recognition and enforcement of foreign judgments. As regards England and Wales, the relevant legislation is now included in the Legal Aid Act 1988.[41] Regulations have been made under these new provisions.[42] Legal aid is discussed further in Chapter 12 above.

---

† Subs. (1) was repealed by the Legal Aid Act 1988, s.45(2) and Sched. 6. Subs. (2) was repealed by the Legal Aid (Scotland) Act 1986, Sched. 5.

[39] Para. 28.81 above.

[40] This also applies to an applicant for a declaration of recognition: see para. 28.82 above.

[41] Legal Aid Act 1988, s.34(4).

[42] As regards England and Wales, the relevant rule is regulation 14 of the Civil Legal Aid (General) Regulations 1989.

CHAPTER 44

CIVIL JURISDICTION AND JUDGMENTS ACT 1982
PART V—SUPPLEMENTARY AND GENERAL
PROVISIONS

1047

A. Domicile

Section 41

44.01 **41.**—*Domicile of individuals*

(1) Subject to Article 52 (which contains provisions for determining whether a party is domiciled in a Contracting State), the following provisions of this section determine, for the purposes of the 1968 Convention and this Act, whether an individual is domiciled in the United Kingdom or in a particular part of, or place in, the United Kingdom or in a state other than a Contracting State.

(2) An individual is domiciled in the United Kingdom if and only if—

    (a) he is resident in the United Kingdom; and

    (b) the nature and circumstances of his residence indicate that he has a substantial connection with the United Kingdom.

(3) Subject to subsection (5), an individual is domiciled in a particular part of the United Kingdom if and only if—

    (a) he is resident in that part; and

    (b) the nature and circumstances of his residence indicate that he has a substantial connection with that part.

(4) An individual is domiciled in a particular place in the United Kingdom if and only if he—

    (a) is domiciled in the part of the United Kingdom in which that place is situated; and

    (b) is resident in that place.

(5) An individual who is domiciled in the United Kingdom but in whose case the requirements of subsection 3(b) are not satisfied in relation to any particular part of the United Kingdom shall be treated as domiciled in the part of the United Kingdom in which he is resident.

(6) In the case of an individual who—

    (a) is resident in the United Kingdom, or in a particular part of the United Kingdom; and

    (b) has been so resident for the last three months or more,

the requirements of subsection (2)(b) or, as the case may be, subsection (3)(b) shall be presumed to be fulfilled unless the contrary is proved.

(7) An individual is domiciled in a state other than a Contracting State if and only if—

(a) **he is resident in that state; and**
(b) **the nature and circumstances of his residence indicate that he has a substantial connection with that state.**

1. General note

This section provides rules for determining the domicile of an **44.02** individual for the purposes of the 1968 Convention and this Act. In doing so it imports into English law a new and distinct concept of domicile, based on residence and substantial connection with the territory in question.

Where a case apparently falling within the Convention is brought before an English court,[1] the court is required to examine its jurisdiction of its own motion,[2] a process which will often involve deciding the domicile of one or other party—usually the defendant. Article 52 of the Convention determines which law the court has to apply in deciding that question and, if that is English law and if the party is an individual, this section provides the rules which the court must apply.

Tests which are similar to each other, but progressively less stringent, apply to determine whether a person is domiciled, respectively, in the United Kingdom, in a particular *part* of the United Kingdom, and in a particular *place* in the United Kingdom. "Part of the United Kingdom" means England and Wales, Scotland or Northern Ireland.[3]

First, for many of the Convention's purposes, it is sufficient to **44.03** determine whether the person is domiciled in the United Kingdom and this is to be done by applying the test contained in subsection (2). Secondly, whether or not the case has the requisite international element so as to fall within the Convention, it will be necessary to decide whether, pursuant to Schedule 4, the courts of a particular *part* of the United Kingdom have jurisdiction over the case and this will often involve a determination of domicile by applying the test in subsection (3). Thirdly, the Convention and Schedule 4 contain a number of provisions where the *place* of a person's domicile is relevant[4] and subsection (4) provides a test for these purposes.

The section contains no test for determining whether a person is domiciled in another Contracting State, because this question is to

---

[1] The same applies in Scotland and Northern Ireland.
[2] Arts. 19 and 20, paras. 20.06–22.07 and 22.15 above.
[3] s.50, para. 44.45 below.
[4] *e.g.* in Art. 5 of the Convention (para. 17.01 above) and Art. 5 of Sched. 4 (para. 45.06 below). Sched. 8, allocating local jurisdiction within Scotland, also contains a number of such provisions: paras. 47.01 *et seq.* below.

be determined not by English law, but by the law of that other state.[5] On the other hand, in subsection (7), it does contain a rule for the few cases where it is necessary to decide whether a person is domiciled in a particular non-Contracting State.

Each of the tests provided by this section is governed by the words "if and only if." It follows that the definitions of domicile are exhaustive[6] for the purposes referred to in subsection (1). While the section contains no express provision as to the point of time at which a person's domicile is to be determined, it is almost certainly at the commencement of the proceedings—*i.e.*, when the jurisdiction of the court is invoked.[7]

44.04   *Concept of "domicile."* The concept of domicile as defined by this section differs substantially from the traditional common law concept[8] and is much more closely allied to the continental concepts of domicile, which require a far smaller degree of permanent attachment to a particular territory and in which the intentional element may be much less important.[9] A person may be resident in more than one place[10] and, by the same token, but by contrast with its common law counterpart, there is nothing in the concept of domicile as defined by this section to prevent a person having more than one domicile.

A person who is domiciled in the United Kingdom by virtue of this section and also in another Contracting State by virtue of its law may be sued in either place under Article 2 of the Convention,[11] although Articles 21 to 23[12] should prevent a multiplicity of proceedings.

Confusing as it may be to common lawyers, the use of the term "domicile" for this new concept is inevitable, given the wording of the English language version of the 1968 Convention. The adjustments made to United Kingdom law by this and the following sections were necessary to ensure that the Convention would be applied with an adequate degree of uniformity in all the Contracting States, and were envisaged by the working party which negotiated the 1978 Convention.[13]

---

[5] Art. 52, second para., para. 31.01 above; see chaps. 48 to 58, at para. 25.

[6] However, s.44, para. 44.27 below, on consumer contracts and insurance may occasionally apply to individuals: Lloyds underwriters, for example.

[7] *Cf.* para. 31.04 above.

[8] See Dicey and Morris, pp. 116 *et seq.*, 278 *et seq.*

[9] Paras. 31.05–31.06 above.

[10] *I.R.C.* v. *Lysaght* [1928] A.C. 234; *Sinclair* v. *Sinclair* [1968] P. 189, at p. 232; *Fox* v. *Stirk* [1970] 3 All E.R. 7; Hartley, pp. 33–34.

[11] Para. 16.01 above. This is subject to Arts. 16 and 17, paras. 20.01 and 21.01 above.

[12] Chap. 23 above.

[13] Schlosser, para. 73, para. A1.360 below.

Domicile of dependence. The provisions in this section contain no **44.05**
reference to a domicile of dependence. Accordingly, where, for the
purposes of the third paragraph of Article 52, a person's "national
law"[14] is the law of England, Scotland or Northern Ireland, his
domicile does not depend on that of another person or the seat of an
authority, and his domicile is to be determined in accordance with
the law applicable pursuant to the first and second paragraphs of
Article 52. Nonetheless, a person's *actual* dependence on another
may be a factor to be taken into account in deciding where his
domicile is as a matter of law. It may be a circumstance of that person's residence, relevant for the purposes of subsection (2), for
example, indicating that he has a substantial connection with the
United Kingdom. The important point is that there is no *legal*
requirement that a person's domicile is dependent on the domicile
of another.

2. Subsection (1)

This subsection defines the purposes for which the definitions in
the rest of the section are to apply and provides that the section is
subject to Article 52. In other words, the tests of domicile contained
in this section do not operate if, pursuant to that Article, some law
other than United Kingdom law is to apply to determine a person's
domicile.

3. Subsection (2): domicile in the United Kingdom

Whether an individual is domiciled in the United Kingdom for **44.06**
the purposes of the 1968 Convention and this Act is to be determined exclusively by whether (a) he is resident in the United Kingdom and (b) the nature and circumstances of his residence indicate
that he has a substantial connection with the United Kingdom.
Neither "residence" nor "substantial connection" is defined by the
Act and both matters appear to be questions of fact, although subsection (6) provides a rebuttable presumption that the latter condition is fulfilled if the person has been resident in the United
Kingdom for the last three months or more.

Residence. The term "residence" has been the subject of judicial
interpretation in many different contexts[15] and it remains to be seen
precisely how the term comes to be interpreted in this context. It is
clear that more is required than mere presence, but whether any,
and if so how great, a degree of permanence is required is less clear.
For example, it seems from subsection (5) that residence in this

---

[14] See paras. 31.15 *et seq.* above.
[15] See Dicey and Morris, pp. 162–167 and *passim.*

context may not require even a fixed abode, at least not for any pro-longed period.[16] The term "residence" is used, otherwise than in conjunction with "ordinary" or "habitual," in comparable contexts in other Acts[17] and some assistance may be derived from a compari-son with such provisions.

4. Subsection (3): domicile in a particular part of the United Kingdom

44.07   A similar test contained in this subsection determines whether an individual is domiciled in a particular part of the United Kingdom. Again, this depends on whether he is resident in that part and whether the circumstances of his residence indicate that he has a substantial connection with that part. As with subsection (2), there is a presumption that a person who has been resident in that part of the United Kingdom for three months has a sufficiently substantial connection for the purposes of this test, unless the contrary is proved.[18]

If a person is domiciled in the United Kingdom but does not have a substantial connection with any particular part of it (*e.g.* because he is itinerant), his domicile is taken for the purposes of this section to be in the part of the United Kingdom in which he is resident. In this respect, therefore, the degree of connection with a particular part of the United Kingdom required for the purposes of this sub-section is weaker than that required by subsection (5) for the United Kingdom as a whole.

5. Subsection (4): domicile in a particular place in the United Kingdom

The test for domicile in a particular place in the United Kingdom is the least stringent, in that it does not require any degree of "substan-tial connection" with that place, but merely residence in that place coupled with domicile in the part of the United Kingdom where that place is situated, determined in accordance with subsection (3).

---

[16] But see *R. v. Barnet London Borough Council, ex p. Nilish Shah* [1983] 2 A.C. 309, where "ordinary residence" in the context of entitlement to educational awards was held to contain an element of "settled purposes." *Quaere* whether residence itself is not a pure question of fact, but one from which intention may be inferred: *cf.* Cheshire and North, p. 146.

[17] *e.g.* Maintenance Orders (Reciprocal Enforcement) Act 1972, ss.2(1), 6(2); Domicile and Matrimonial Proceedings Act 1973, Sched. 1, para. 8(1). For a different context, see Representation of the People Act 1983, ss.1 to 7.

[18] Subs. (6), below.

6. Subsection (5): itinerants

Some individuals may be domiciled in the United Kingdom by **44.08**
virtue of subsection (2)—*i.e.* they are resident in and have a substantial connection with the United Kingdom—while not having a
sufficient connection with any particular part of the United Kingdom to be domiciled in that part. This subsection treats such a person as being domiciled in the part of the United Kingdom in which
he is resident. Because, unless the contrary is shown, three months'
residence in a particular part of the United Kingdom (not necessarily in the same place) will establish the sufficient connection, this
class of people is likely to be limited to itinerants.

The wording of the subsection, and particularly the use of the
word "any," would suggest that a person who is resident in more
than one part of the United Kingdom, but who has a sufficient connection for the purposes of subsection (3)(b) with only one of them,
cannot be treated as domiciled in the other part by virtue of this
subsection.

The subsection does not extend domicile to persons who are resident in the United Kingdom but do not have a substantial connection with the United Kingdom as a whole. Such a rule would have
equated domicile with a pure question of residence, unless a substantial connection with the Contracting States as a whole were to
be required, in which case it is likely that the person in question
would anyway be regarded as domiciled in one of the other Contracting States according to its law.

7. Subsection (6): presumed substantial connection

This subsection is an evidential rule, enabling the courts to **44.09**
avoid, in most cases, too detailed an inquiry into the circumstances
of a person's residence in the United Kingdom or a particular part
of the United Kingdom, as the case may be. For the purposes of
subsection (2), the presumption is that the nature and circumstances of a person's residence indicate that he has a substantial
connection with the United Kingdom if he has been resident anywhere in the United Kingdom for a period of three months or more.
The same presumption applies by reference to residence anywhere
in a particular part of the United Kingdom for the purposes of subsection (3). In each case the presumption applies only unless the
contrary is proved—*i.e.* that despite three months' residence the
nature and circumstances of a person's residence are not such as to
indicate the necessary sufficient connection. The burden of proof
would seem to be on the person who seeks to rebut the presumption. As has been noted,[19] the time at which a person's domicile is

---

[19] Para. 44.03 above.

to be determined is almost certainly when proceedings are commenced. The Act provides no rules for the measurement of the three-month period, nor does it indicate what, if any, break in continuity is permitted.

8. Subsection (7): domicile in a non-Contracting State

44.10   While it is necessary for some purposes to determine whether or not a person is domiciled in a Contracting State—*i.e.* within the territory to which the 1968 Convention applies—it is necessary in the context of the Convention only for one purpose to determine whether a person is domiciled in a *particular* non-Contracting State. This purpose arises under Article 59[20] where a convention concluded between the United Kingdom and that other state contains an undertaking given by the United Kingdom not to recognise or enforce certain judgments given in other Contracting States against a person domiciled or habitually resident in that other non-Contracting State. It is for this limited purpose that the rule in this subsection is necessary and it adopts the same test of residence coupled with a substantial connection as applies under subsection (2) for determining whether a person is domiciled in the United Kingdom, but without the benefit of the rebuttable presumption contained in subsection (6).

Section 42

44.11   **42.**—*Domicile and seat of corporation or association*
(1) For the purposes of this Act the seat of a corporation or association (as determined by this section) shall be treated as its domicile.
(2) The following provisions of this section determine where a corporation or association has its seat—
  (a) **for the purpose of Article 53 (which for the purposes of the 1968 Convention equates the domicile of such a body with its seat); and**
  (b) **for the purposes of this Act other than the provisions mentioned in section 43(1)(b) and (c).**
(3) A corporation or association has its seat in the United Kingdom if and only if—
  (a) **it was incorporated or formed under the law of a part of the United Kingdom and has its registered office or some other official address in the United Kingdom; or**
  (b) **its central management and control is exercised in the United Kingdom.**
(4) A corporation or association has its seat in a particular part

---

[20] Paras. 10.43 and 33.24 above.

of the United Kingdom if and only if it has its seat in the United Kingdom and—

    (a) it has its registered office or some other official address in that part; or

    (b) its central management and control is exercised in that part; or

    (c) it has a place of business in that part.

(5) A corporation or association has its seat in a particular place in the United Kingdom if and only if it has its seat in the part of the United Kingdom in which that place is situated and—

    (a) it has its registered office or some other official address in that place; or

    (b) its central management and control is exercised in that place; or

    (c) it has a place of business in that place.

(6) Subject to subsection (7), a corporation or association has its seat in a state other than the United Kingdom if and only if—

    (a) it was incorporated or formed under the law of that state and has its registered office or some other official address there; or

    (b) its central management and control is exercised in that state.

(7) A corporation or association shall not be regarded as having its seat in a Contracting State other than the United Kingdom if it is shown that the courts or that state would not regard it as having its seat there.

(8) In this section—

    "business" includes any activity carried on by a corporation or association, and "place of business" shall be construed accordingly;

    "official address," in relation to a corporation or association, means an address which it is required by law to register, notify or maintain for the purpose of receiving notices or other communications.

1. General note

This section provides rules for determining the seat[21] of a corporation or association[22] for most of the purposes of the 1968 Convention and this Act.[23]   **44.12**

---

[21] This is equivalent to its domicile: see subsection (1) below.

[22] The domicile of trusts and of the Crown are dealt with by ss.45 and 46 respectively. For the meaning of "corporation or association," see below.

[23] s.43 provides a separate definition for the purposes of Art. 16(2) of the Convention and for provisions related to that Article. s.44 provides supplementary rules for certain cases concerning insurance and consumer contracts.

Article 53 of the 1968 Convention[24] provides that, when the court has to determine the seat of a company or other legal person or association of natural or legal persons, it is to apply its own rules of private international law. This section not only provides a choice of law rule in subsection (7) for that purpose, but it also provides rules of domestic law, applicable in each part of the United Kingdom, for determining whether a seat is located for most of the purposes both of the Convention and of this Act.

The scheme of this section is similar to that of section 41 (which contains rules for determining the domicile of individuals) providing tests for determining, successively, whether a corporation or association has its seat in the United Kingdom,[25] in a particular *part* of the United Kingdom[26] and in a particular *place* in the United Kingdom.[27] It also provides a test for determining whether a corporation or association has its seat in a state other than the United Kingdom.[28] Unlike its counterpart in section 41(7), this test applies not only where the seat is in a non-Contracting State, but also where it is in another Contracting State, unless the courts of that state would hold otherwise.[29]

Like section 41, the tests provided by this section are each governed by the words "if and only if." It again follows that these tests provide a comprehensive and exhaustive code for the purposes of the section (although section 44[30] may apply for allocating jurisdiction within the United Kingdom in a limited range of insurance and consumer cases). The purposes of this section are defined by subsection (2). No express provision is made as to the point of time at which the seat of a corporation or association is to be determined, but here too it is almost certainly at the commencement of proceedings—*i.e.* when the jurisdiction of the court is invoked.

44.13   *The concept of "seat."* The concept of the seat of a corporation or association is drawn from continental law, where it embraces two distinct ideas. First, it covers the place where, according to its constitution and the law applicable to it, the corporation or association is founded (the *siège statuaire*) and, secondly, it covers the place where, as a matter of fact, its central management or control is exercised (the *siège réel*). Some legal systems lay more emphasis on one concept, some on the other. The concepts are discussed in more

---

[24] Para. 31.23 above.
[25] Subs. (3).
[26] Subs. (4).
[27] Subs. (5).
[28] Subs. (6).
[29] Subs. (7).
[30] Para. 44.27 below.

detail in the commentary to Article 53[31] and in relation to individual Contracting States.[32]

Corporation or association. The term "corporation or association" covers all persons and bodies of persons, other than individuals and the Crown, who have a capacity to sue or be sued[33] (whether in their own name or otherwise: see below). Because sections 41 to 46 provide a complete code for determining the domicile of any such person or body, this term must be equivalent in meaning to the phrase "company or other legal person or association of legal or natural persons"[34] used in Article 53 of the 1968 Convention.[35] The capacity of various bodies to sue and be sued is discussed in Chapter 2.

"Corporation" is defined by section 50 as meaning a body corporate and as including a partnership subsisting under the law of Scotland.[36] The most obvious and common example of a corporation is a company formed under the Companies Acts, but the definition extends also to bodies incorporated by charter, to statutory corporations such as local authorities and nationalised industries and to other corporate bodies. The term "corporation" extends also to bodies formed under foreign law having a corporate character as entities separate from their members.[37]

An "association" is defined by section 50 as an unincorporated body of persons, a term which in this context extends beyond its normal meaning of clubs and social organisations[38] to include such bodies as trade unions, friendly societies and industrial and provident societies. Although some doubt has been expressed on the point,[39] it is suggested that partnerships formed under English law almost certainly fall within the term "association," at least if they are formally constituted.[40]

---

[31] Paras. 31.26–31.27 above.

[32] Chaps. 48 to 58, para. 26.

[33] The domicile of individuals is covered by s.41 and that of the Crown by s.46. Trusts, whose domicile is dealt with by s.45, cannot themselves sue or be sued.

[34] The counterpart of this phrase in the other language versions is of interest: see para. 31.52 above.

[35] This interpretation is supported by the wording of s.43(1) (para. 44.20 below), which by the use of the words "such bodies" in para. (a) equates "corporation or association" with the persons and bodies envisaged by Art. 16(2), which itself uses the same wording as Art. 53.

[36] See Partnership Act 1890, s.4(2); see para. 58.73 below.

[37] See Dicey and Morris, pp. 1128 *et seq.* The various types of legal person existing under the laws of the other Contracting States are summarised in chaps. 48 to 58 below, at para. 73.

[38] See 9 *Halsbury's Laws* (4th ed.), para. 344.

[39] Collins, p. 42.

[40] See para. 20.28 above and Schlosser, paras. 55 and 162 (paras. A1.343 and A1.456 below).

44.14   Neither the 1968 Convention nor this Act affects the capacity of a person to sue or be sued, which is a matter for the court to decide according to its own law, including its rules of private international law. It is clear, though, that the fact that a body of persons is not permitted by English law to sue or be sued in its own name does *not* mean that it falls outside the ambit of this section or the 1968 Convention. For example, a body which English law would regard as a foreign firm not carrying on business within the jurisdiction cannot sue or be sued in the firm's name[41] but it may be necessary nonetheless to determine where it has its seat for the purpose of deciding which, if any, of the rules in the 1968 Convention apply to it.

2. Subsection (1)

Article 53 of the 1968 Convention provides that the seat of a company or other legal person or association of legal or natural persons shall be treated as its domicile for the purposes of the Convention. This subsection adopts the same principle for the purposes of this Act, and this applies whether the location of the seat is to be determined under this section or under section 43.

3. Subsection (2): purposes of the section

44.15   This subsection defines the purposes for which the tests in the following subsections are to apply, namely (with one class of exceptions) for all the purposes of the 1968 Convention and the Act. The exceptions are those provisions which refer to the seat of a corporation or association for the purposes of allocating jurisdiction over proceedings which have as their object the validity of the constitution, the nullity or the dissolution of such a body, or the decisions of its organs.

The drafting of this subsection, although logical and consistent, hardly lends itself to an easy understanding of the Act and requires some explanation.

Article 53 refers to the private international law rules of national law for the purpose of determining the location of the seat of a corporation or association. So far as the law of the United Kingdom is concerned, those rules are provided by this Act; by paragraph (b) of this subsection (discussed below), the following provisions of this section apply for most of the purposes of the Act.

Paragraph (a). When a court in the United Kingdom comes to apply the Convention itself, it will need to be able to tell precisely which of the provisions of national law is referred to by the term "seat" in the Convention. The effect of the reference to Article 53

---

[41] *Von Hellfeld* v. *Rechnitzer* [1914] 1 Ch. 748, C.A.; *Supreme Court Practice*, note 81/1/14; but see para. 2.08 above.

of the Convention in paragraph (a) of this subsection is to make clear that the following subsections are to have effect for the purpose of interpreting the term "seat" in that Article—*i.e.* for the purpose of equating the seat of a corporation or association with its domicile.

The reference in paragraph (a) is only to Article 53, rather than to the Convention as a whole, but there are in fact only two references in the Convention outside Article 53 to the seat of a corporation or association. The first is in Article 16(2), and the seat of a corporation or association for the purpose of that Article is defined not by this section but by section 43: see below. The second reference is in Article 52, where the seat of an authority is referred to in relation to a domicile of dependence, but this reference has no application in United Kingdom law[42] and a rule for determining the seat of an authority for the purposes of Article 52 is therefore not necessary.

Paragraph (b). At first sight, it may seem odd that the provisions mentioned in section 43(1)(b) and (c) should be excluded from the scope of this section by paragraph (b), while Article 16(2) of the Convention itself—mentioned in section 43(1)(a)—should not. The reason is that that provision does not, of itself, form part of the Act[43] and the function of determining the seat of a corporation or association is one which the Convention (by Article 53) ascribes exclusively to whichever rules of national law are prescribed by the private international law of the court seised of the matter. The only provision of United Kingdom law which is apt to determine the location of such a seat for the purposes of Article 16(2) of the Convention is section 43, not section 42. Because the determination of the seat of a corporation or association for the purposes of Article 16(2) of the Convention does not fall within section 42 in the first place, therefore, there is no need to exclude it.

4. Subsection (3): seat in the United Kingdom

Whether a corporation or association has its seat in the United Kingdom for the purposes referred to in subsection (2) is to be determined exclusively by whether it meets the requirements of either (or both) of two separate tests. The first test, in paragraph (a), has two limbs, namely (i) whether the corporation or association was incorporated or formed under the law of a part of the United Kingdom, and (ii) whether it has its registered office or some other official address in the United Kingdom. The second test, in paragraph (b), is an alternative to the first and is whether the

44.16

---

[42] See para. 44.05 above.
[43] Although the Convention is set out in Sched. 1, it is the Convention rather than the Schedule which has the force of law: see para. 40.04 above.

central management and control of the corporation or association is exercised in the United Kingdom. The fact that a corporation or association has a place of business in the United Kingdom is not enough to establish its seat there for the purposes of this section unless the other criteria are fulfilled.[44]

Paragraph (a). So far as companies and other corporations and associations having a formal existence are concerned, there is likely to be little difficulty in determining whether they are incorporated or formed under the law of a part of the United Kingdom[45] and this first limb of the test is the traditional common law test of the domicile of a corporation.[46] In the case of partnerships arising incidentally as a matter of law by reason of persons "carrying on business in common with a view to profit"[47] or in the case of informal unincorporated associations, it may sometimes be harder to determine the legal basis of their formation. Such associations are anyway most unlikely to have a registered office or other official address and they would therefore anyway fall outside paragraph (a). The same would probably apply even to formally constituted partnerships under English law, as they are not required to maintain a registered office or other official address.[48]

Companies are required by section 287 of the Companies Act 1985 to have a registered office.[49] Other bodies such as friendly societies, industrial and provident societies, trade unions and so forth are required by law to have a publicly ascertainable address for the service of documents, and this would be an "official address" within the meaning of this subsection, as defined by subsection (8).[50]

Paragraph (b). The alternative test is whether the central management and control of the corporation or association is exercised in

---

[44] Certain insurers and parties to consumer contracts not domiciled in a Contracting State may have a deemed domicile under Art. 8, second para. (para. 18.11 above) or Art. 13, second para. (para. 19.01 above). See also s.44, para. 44.27 below.

[45] "Part of the United Kingdom" is defined by s.50 as meaning England and Wales, Scotland or Northern Ireland. While the legal systems are different in each part, the content of the law may of course be the same—*e.g.* under a statutory provision (such as these sections) applying to the whole of the U.K.

[46] Cheshire and North, p. 177; Dicey and Morris, pp. 1130–1131.

[47] Partnership Act 1890, s.1(1).

[48] See the definition of "official address" in subs. (8), discussed at para. 44.19 below.

[49] Although "oversea companies" with a place of business within the jurisdiction are required to register the addresses of persons resident in Great Britain who are authorised to accept service on the company's behalf (Companies Act 1985, s.691), they do not fall within the first limb of paragraph (a).

[50] See para. 44.19 below.

the United Kingdom. This is the test by which the residence of a corporation is judged at common law and, until recently, especially for the the purposes of taxation.[51] It has not, however, hitherto generally applied for the purposes of jurisdiction.[52] The test is a factual one of where the central management and control of the company is actually exercised (which is usually where the board meetings take place) and it is irrelevant where the company ought to be controlled as a matter of its rules.[53] It seems that a company may have more than one place where its central management and control is exercised,[54] at least, in the context of taxation, where the exercise of that authority is geographically divided. In such a case a company's residence is where "some portion of controlling power and authority can be identified."[55] In the present context there is no difficulty about a company having more than one seat.[56]

5. Subsection (4): seat in a particular part of the United Kingdom

The test contained in this subsection determines whether a cor- **44.17** poration or association has its seat in a particular part of the United Kingdom and is similar to that in subsection (3). The corporation or association must have its seat in the United Kingdom as a whole in accordance with subsection (3), and *either* it must have its registered office or some other official address in that part of the United Kingdom (paragraph (a)), *or* its central management and control must be exercised in that part (paragraph (b)), *or* it must have a place of business in that part (paragraph (c)). Paragraphs (a) and (b) are the counterparts of paragraphs (a) and (b) in subsection (3) and are discussed above, but in allowing a third alternative criterion in paragraph (c) the test is less stringent than that for determining whether the seat of a corporation or association is in the United Kingdom as a whole.

Place of business. Although paragraph (c) provides a fairly wide test for determining the location of the seat of a corporation or

---

[51] Cheshire and North, pp. 174–177; Dicey and Morris, pp. 1132–1134; *cf.* Income & Corporation Taxes Act 1988, s.767(1). This provision has been repealed by the Finance Act 1988, Sched.10, Part IV, and replaced by a test of incorporation: Finance Act 1988, s.64.
[52] Dicey and Morris, pp. 294–297; see para. 4.13 above.
[53] *Unit Construction Co. Ltd.* v. *Bullock (Inspector of Taxes)* [1960] A.C. 351.
[54] *Swedish Central Rail Co. Ltd.* v. *Thompson* [1925] A.C. 495; *Egyptian Delta Land & Investment Co. Ltd.* v. *Todd* [1929] A.C. 1.
[55] *Unit Construction Co. Ltd.* v. *Bullock (Inspector of Taxes)* above, *per* Lord Radcliffe at p. 367.
[56] *Cf.* para. 44.04 above.

association having its seat in the United Kingdom, the concept of "seat" in this context is used only for the allocation of jurisdiction as between different parts of the United Kingdom. The scheme of the Act is therefore similar to the rules which have long applied as a matter of English law—both under statute and at common law. Jurisdiction has been exercised on the basis of service over corporations or associations carrying on business within the territorial jurisdiction of the court, whether the service was on a person nominated by an overseas company[57] or on an officer of a body corporate[58] or at an established place of business[59] or on the principal place of business of a partnership.[60]

The activities carried on at the "place of business" may be entirely incidental to the main business of the corporation or association[61] and "business" is defined for these purposes[62] as including "any activity carried on" by the corporation or association, a definition which certainly goes beyond activities of a commercial nature and which appears very wide indeed. It remains to be seen whether "activity" will be interpreted as meaning only the external activities of the corporation or association or whether activities purely internal to the corporation or association will be regarded as sufficient to establish a place of business.

6. Subsection (5): seat in a particular place in the United Kingdom

44.18   The criteria provided by this subsection for determining whether a corporation or association has its seat in a particular place in the United Kingdom are the same as those for determining whether its seat is in a particular part of the United Kingdom. Its seat must, in accordance with subsection (4), be in the part of the United Kingdom where the particular place is situated and *either* it must have its registered office or some other official address in that place (paragraph (a)), *or* its central management and control must be exercised in that place (paragraph (b)), *or* it must have a place of business in that place (paragraph (c)). The criteria in paragraphs (a) and (b) are discussed under subsection (3) and the criterion in paragraph (c) is discussed under subsection (4).

---

[57] Companies Act 1985, s.691; *South India Shipping Corp.* v. *Bank of Korea* [1985] 1 W.L.R. 586.
[58] R.S.C., Ord. 65, r. 3.
[59] *The Madrid* [1937] P. 40, at p. 47.
[60] R.S.C., Ord. 81, r. 3.
[61] *South India Shipping Corp.* v. *Bank of Korea*, above.
[62] Subs. (8), see para. 44.19 below.

7. Subsection (6): seat in a state other than the United Kingdom

For some purposes it is necessary to determine whether a corporation or association has its seat in another Contracting State—*i.e.* in the territory to which the 1968 Convention applies. In the parallel case of an individual's domicile, the 1968 Convention provides that the question whether a person is domiciled in any given Contracting State is to be answered by the law of that state[63]; but in the case of a corporation or association, it is for the law of the court seised of the matter to determine how the location of the seat is determined.[64] If United Kingdom law had adopted the same solution for corporations and associations as applies to individuals and referred to the law of the state where the seat was said to be located, it would have involved the courts in applying the law of one or more of the other Contracting States.

Instead, by this subsection, it adopts the same criteria for determining whether a corporation or association has its seat in a given state other than the United Kingdom as it does in subsection (3) for determining whether such a seat is in the United Kingdom. Except as provided by subsection (7) (to avoid negative conflicts of jurisdiction), it ignores the law of that other state. These criteria, discussed above under subsection (3), are (a) that the corporation or association was incorporated or formed under the law of the state in question and has its registered office or some other official address[65] there, or (b) that its central management and control are exercised there.

So far as non-Contracting States are concerned, such a test is necessary only for the purposes of a convention, containing a provision falling within Article 59,[66] concluded with such a state.[67]

8. Subsection (7): negative conflicts with other Contracting States

If the application of the rules in subsection (6) leads to the conclusion that a company has its seat in a Contracting State other than the United Kingdom, United Kingdom courts are required to decline jurisdiction unless they have jurisdiction under the Convention.[68] If the courts of that other state, applying whatever rules their private international law[69] requires, decide that the corpor- **44.19**

---

[63] Art. 52, second para., para. 31.01 above.
[64] Art. 53, first para., para. 31.23 above.
[65] "Official address" is defined in subs. (8): see below.
[66] Para. 33.24 above.
[67] See para. 44.10 above.
[68] Art. 20, para. 22.11 above.
[69] Art. 53, para. 31.23 above.

ation or association does not have its seat in that other state,[70] then it would be possible for the courts of no Contracting State to have jurisdiction. This subsection provides, though, that in such a case the courts in the United Kingdom would not regard the corporation or association as having its seat in that other Contracting State and (assuming that it did not have a seat in any other Contracting State) Article 4 of the 1968 Convention[71] would apply, leaving the court free to apply its general law[72] to determine its jurisdiction.

9. Subsection (8): definitions

This subsection contains definitions of "business" and "place of business," discussed under subsection (4) above, and of "official address," referred to under subsection (3) above. An address is only an official address within the meaning of this subsection if it is one which the corporation or association is "required by law" to register, notify or maintain "for the purpose of receiving notices or other communications." It is clear from the reference to "official address" in subsection (6) that the relevant law in a case falling within that subsection would not be the law of a part of the United Kingdom, but of the other state, and in such a case an address which was not strictly equivalent to the United Kingdom concept of a registered office could still meet the requirements of that subsection.

From the wording of the definition, it would seem that, strictly, it does not extend to an address which the relevant law permits to be voluntarily registered, notified or maintained, nor where the purpose for which the law required it to be registered, notified or maintained does not include the receiving of notices or other communications. Neither limitation is likely to prove a problem in practice.

Section 43

44.20 **43.**—*Seat of corporation or association for purposes of Article 16(2) and related provisions*
(1) The following provisions of this section determine where a corporation or association has its seat for the purposes of—
    (a) Article 16(2) (which confers exclusive jurisdiction over proceedings relating to the formation or dissolution of such bodies, or to the decisions of their organs);
    (b) Articles 5A and 16(2) in Schedule 4; and

---

[70] See chaps. 48 to 58 below, at para. 26, for a summary of the law relating to the seat of a corporation or association in each of the Contracting States.
[71] Para. 16.15 above.
[72] *e.g.* R.S.C., Ord. 11, r. 1(1).

(c) Rules 2(12) and 4(1)(b) in Schedule 8.

(2) A corporation or association has its seat in the United Kingdom if and only if—

(a) it was incorporated or formed under the law of a part of the United Kingdom; or

(b) its central management and control is exercised in the United Kingdom.

(3) A corporation or association has its seat in a particular part of the United Kingdom if and only if it has its seat in the United Kingdom and—

(a) subject to subsection (5), it was incorporated or formed under the law of that part; or

(b) being incorporated or formed under the law of a state other than the United Kingdom, its central management and control is exercised in that part.

(4) A corporation or association has its seat in a particular place in Scotland if and only if it has its seat in Scotland and—

(a) it has its registered office or some other official address in that place; or

(b) it has no registered office or other official address in Scotland, but its central management and control is exercised in that place.

(5) A corporation or association formed under—

(a) an enactment forming part of the law of more than one part of the United Kingdom; or

(b) an instrument having effect in the domestic law of more than one part of the United Kingdom,

shall, if it has a registered office, be taken to have its seat in the part of the United Kingdom in which that office is situated, and not in any other part of the United Kingdom.

(6) Subject to subsection (7), a corporation or association has its seat in a Contracting State other than the United Kingdom if and only if—

(a) it was incorporated or formed under the law of that state; or

(b) its central management and control is exercised in that state.

(7) A corporation or association shall not be regarded as having its seat in a Contracting State other than the United Kingdom if—

(a) it has its seat in the United Kingdom by virtue of subsection (2)(a); or

(b) it is shown that the courts of that other state would not regard it for the purposes of Article 16(2) as having its seat there.

(8) In this section "official address" has the same meaning as in section 42.

1. General note

44.21 While section 42 provides definitions of the "seat" of a corporation or association for most of the purposes of the 1968 Convention and of this Act, this section defines that concept for the purposes of allocating jurisdiction over a limited class of proceedings, namely those which have as their object the validity of the constitution, the nullity or the dissolution of a corporation or association or the decisions of its organs. In practice, the most important such proceedings are likely to be those relating to the voluntary winding up of companies.[73]

The seat of a corporation or association is equated with its domicile for the purpose of the 1968 Convention[74] and of this Act.[75] The concept of a seat and the meaning of "corporation or association" are discussed in greater detail above under section 42, as are the exhaustive nature of the tests provided by this section (by the use of the words "if and only if") and the time at which the location of the seat is to be determined.[76]

As with sections 41 and 42, the scheme of this section is to provide rules for determining, successively, whether a corporation or association has its seat in the United Kingdom as a whole,[77] in a particular part of the United Kingdom[78] and in a particular place in Scotland (which is the only part of the United Kingdom where local jurisdiction is relevant for the purposes covered by this section).[79] The section also provides a test for determining whether a corporation or association has its seat in a Contracting State other than the United Kingdom[80] (but not in a non-Contracting State, Article 59 of the 1968 Convention having no relevance here)[81] and rules for resolving conflicts of jurisdiction between different parts of the

---

[73] Winding-up of insolvent companies is excluded from the scope of the 1968 Convention and jurisdictional provisions of this Act: see Art. 1 (para. 14.03 above); s.16(1)(a) (para. 41.01 above); Sched. 5, para. 1 (para. 45.31 below); and Sched. 9, para. 4 (para. 47.06 below: Scotland).
[74] Art. 53, para. 31.23 above.
[75] s.42(1), para. 44.11 above.
[76] See also para. 20.28 above.
[77] Subs. (2).
[78] Subs. (4).
[79] Subs. (5).
[80] Subs. (6).
[81] *Cf.* ss.41(7), para. 44.10 above and 42(6), para. 44.18 above.

United Kingdom[82] and between the United Kingdom and other Contracting States.[83]

2. Subsection (1)

This subsection defines the purposes for which the definitions in the following subsections apply. Article 16(2) of the 1968 Convention grants exclusive jurisdiction in proceedings which have as their object the validity of the constitution, the nullity or dissolution of companies or other legal persons or associations of natural or legal persons or the decisions of their organs, to the courts of the Contracting State where the company, legal person or association has its seat.[84] It does not allocate jurisdiction to specific courts within that Contracting State.

44.22

That function is performed in the United Kingdom by two Articles of Schedule 4, namely Articles 5A and 16(2), which draw a distinction between proceedings which have as their object the decisions of the organs of a company or other legal person or association of legal or natural persons and those which have as their object the validity of the constitution, the nullity or dissolution of such a body. Jurisdiction over the former is allocated by Article 5A on a non-exclusive basis to the courts of the part of the United Kingdom where the body has its seat, while jurisdiction over the latter is allocated by Article 16(2) exclusively to such courts. In each case the proceedings must fall within the scope of Schedule 4: see section 16.[85] In Scotland, local jurisdiction is allocated over such proceedings by rules 2(12) and 4(1)(b) of Schedule 8, which draw the same distinction, to the courts for the place where the body has its seat.

For an explanation of why Article 16(2) of the 1968 Convention needs to be mentioned in this subsection separately from the provisions of the Act, see the commentary on section 42(2).[86]

3. Subsection (2): seat in the United Kingdom

This subsection, which provides a test for the purposes of this section to determine whether the seat of a corporation or association is in the United Kingdom, contains provisions parallel to those in section 42(3).[87] The only difference is that this subsection does not contain the requirement, which forms the second limb of the test in section 42(3)(a), that the corporation or association should have a registered office or other official address in the United Kingdom.

44.23

---

[82] Subs. (5).
[83] Subs. (7).
[84] Para. 20.26 above.
[85] Para. 41.01 above.
[86] Para. 44.15 above.
[87] See para. 44.11 above.

The test in paragraph (a) is therefore less stringent that its counterpart in section 42, but this wider jurisdiction is equivalent to that exercised at present in winding-up proceedings under section 512(1) of the Companies Act 1985.[88] Similarly, the absence of a requirement of a registered office or other official address in the United Kingdom means that a partnership formed under English law does fall within paragraph (a), even if it does not fall within paragraph (b).[89]

The alternative basis on which a corporation or association may have its seat in the United Kingdom is if its central management and control is exercised there: paragraph (b). The problems of conflicts of exclusive jurisdiction to which this provision may give rise are discussed under subsection (7) below.

4. Subsection (3): seat in a particular part of the United Kingdom

The test in this subsection determines whether a corporation or association has its seat in a particular part of the United Kingdom for the purposes set out in subsection (1). The corporation or association must have its seat in the United Kingdom as a whole in accordance with subsection (2), and must then satisfy the requirements of either paragraph (a) or paragraph (b). Those requirements correspond to their counterparts in subsection (2), except that paragraph (a) is subject to subsection (5), which is designed to limit the circumstances where there is a seat in more than one part of the United Kingdom, and paragraph (b) only applies if the corporation or association was formed outside the United Kingdom. So, where a corporation or association was formed under the law of one part of the United Kingdom and has its central management or control in another part, it has its seat for the purposes of this section only in the former.

5. Subsection (4): seat in a particular place in Scotland

44.24 This subsection, which determines the place of a corporation or association's seat for the purposes referred to in subsection (1)(c) above, relates exclusively to Scotland and detailed commentary on it is beyond the scope of this work.[90] It corresponds with section 42(5),[91] except that the seat of the corporation or association must be located in Scotland in accordance with subsection (3) of this section, rather than with section 42(4), and its central management or

---

[88] s.515(1) in Scotland.
[89] *cf.* the position under s.42, para. 44.16 above.
[90] See para. 42.05 above.
[91] See para. 44.18 above.

control is relevant only if it has no registered office or other official address in Scotland. "Official address" is defined by subsection (8) as having the same meaning as in section 42.[92]

6. Subsection (5)

If a corporation or association incorporated or formed under an enactment (such as the Companies Act 1985) forming part of the law of more than one part of the United Kingdom, or under an instrument having effect in the domestic law of more than one part of the United Kingdom, has a registered office, the corporation or association is to be taken as having its seat in the part of the United Kingdom where that office is located. This provision acts as a qualification of subsection (3)(a) and, in the case of companies formed under the Companies Act 1985 or the former Companies Acts, it enables the jurisdiction under sections 512(1) and 515(1) of the 1985 Act to continue in those winding-up cases which anyway fall within this Act.[93]

7. Subsection (6): seat in another Contracting State

This subsection adopts the same criteria for determining whether a corporation or association has its seat in another Contracting State as it does in subsection (2) for determining whether such a seat is in the United Kingdom, but this test is subject to subsection (7), discussed below.

8. Subsection (7): conflicts of seat for the purposes of Article 16(2)

This subsection provides two rules which go some way towards resolving conflicts of jurisdiction arising from different tests for defining the seat of a corporation or association.[94]   **44.25**

The effect of paragraph (a) of this subsection is to make a corporation or association which is incorporated or formed under the law of a part of the United Kingdom have its seat in the United Kingdom in accordance with subsection (2)(a), and not in any other Contracting State, even if it were also formed under the law of that other Contracting State or if its central management and control were exercised there.

Paragraph (b), which is equivalent to section 42(7)[95] is aimed at resolving negative conflicts of jurisdiction in cases falling within

---

[92] Para. 44.11 above.
[93] See para. 44.21 above.
[94] For examples of the way in which this section resolves such conflicts, see Collins, p. 81.
[95] See para. 44.19 above.

Article 16(2) of the 1968 Convention. If, for the purposes of that Article, the courts of another Contracting State, applying whatever rules their private international law require,[96] would decide that a corporation or association did not have its seat in that other state, and if the corporation or association does not have its seat in the United Kingdom under subsection (2), then (assuming that it does not have its seat in any other Contracting State) it would not be regarded as having its seat in any Contracting State. Article 4 of the 1968 Convention[97] would apply, leaving the court free to apply its general law to determine its jurisdiction.

If, on the other hand, a corporation or association not incorporated or formed under the law of a part of the United Kingdom had its seat in the United Kingdom under subsection (2)(b), by virtue of its central management and control being exercised there, *and* had its seat in another Contracting State by virtue either of its being incorporated or formed under the law of another Contracting State[98] or (where the central management and control was divided)[99] by virtue of such management and control also being exercised in another Contracting State, then the corporation or association may be regarded as having more than one seat for the purposes of Article 16(2). In such a situation, the courts of more than one Contracting State would have "exclusive" jurisdiction. This possibility is expressly envisaged by Article 23 of the 1968 Convention[1] which resolves problems of *lis alibi pendens* in such cases by giving precedence to the proceedings started first in point of time.

44.26   Circumstances may arise, though, on the recognition of a judgment given in a case falling within Article 16(2) by a court of another Contracting State, where courts in the United Kingdom would regard the corporation or association as having its seat in the United Kingdom in accordance with this section and therefore regard themselves as having exclusive jurisdiction under Article 16(2). This could occur whether or not the application of the rules in this section also resulted in the corporation or association having its seat in the other Contracting State. In such a case, recognition of the judgment might be refused under the first paragraph of Article 28.[2] It may be, however, that a distinction is to be drawn between those cases where this section envisages an additional seat for the

---

[96] Art. 53, para. 31.23 above.
[97] Para. 16.15 above.
[98] Subs. (6)(a).
[99] Para. 44.16 above.
[1] Para. 23.24 above.
[2] Para. 27.62 above.

corporation or association in the other Contracting State and those where this section provides for the seat to be in the United Kingdom and in no other Contracting State.[3] What this subsection apparently does not do, is to resolve negative conflicts, where conflicting judgments are given by courts in two other Contracting States each of which regards itself as exclusively competent under Article 16(2). These questions are discussed more fully elsewhere.[4]

9. Subsection (8): official address

This subsection extends the definition of "official address" in section 42(8)[5] for the purposes of subsection (4).

Section 44

44.—*Persons deemed to be domiciled in the United Kingdom for certain purposes* **44.27**
 (1) **This section applies to—**
  (a) **proceedings within Section 3 of Title II of the 1968 Convention (insurance contracts), and**
  (b) **proceedings within Section 4 of that Title (consumer contracts).**
 (2) **A person who, for the purposes of proceedings to which this section applies arising out of the operations of a branch, agency or other establishment in the United Kingdom, is deemed for the purposes of the 1968 Convention to be domiciled in the United Kingdom by virtue of—**
  (a) **Article 8, second paragraph (insurers); or**
  (b) **Article 13, second paragraph (suppliers of goods, services or credit to consumers),**
shall, for the purposes of those proceedings, be treated for the purposes of this Act as so domiciled and as domiciled in the part of the United Kingdom in which the branch agency or establishment in question is situated.

1. General note

Under the second paragraph of Article 8 of the 1968 Convention, **44.28**
an insurer domiciled outside the Contracting States but with a branch, agency or other establishment in one of the Contracting States, is deemed to be domiciled in that state for the purposes of disputes arising out of the operations of the branch, agency or other establishment.[6] The second paragraph of Article 13 makes the same

---

[3] *cf.* Hartley, p. 67.
[4] Paras. 27.69 and 31.30–31.31 above.
[5] Para. 44.11 above.
[6] Para. 18.11 above.

provision in relation to a party entering into certain types of contract with a consumer.[7]

Where the branch, agency or other establishment is in the United Kingdom, it is necessary to determine whether the deemed domicile is located in England and Wales, in Scotland or in Northern Ireland, and sections 41 and 42 are not apt for this purpose. What this section does, therefore, is to provide that the deemed domicile of the insurer or party contracting with a consumer is to be treated for the purposes of this Act as being (a) in the United Kingdom as a whole, and (b) in the part of the United Kingdom where the branch, agency or other establishment is situated. By deeming the domicile to be in the United Kingdom as a whole, the section ensures that section 16(1)(b) is satisfied and by determining the part of the United Kingdom where the deemed domicile is located, it enables the rules in Schedule 4 to be applied.

2. Subsection (1)

44.29   This subsection defines the proceedings to which the deemed domicile provision applies, namely those falling within Sections 3 and 4 of Title II of the 1968 Convention—Articles 7 to 12A (insurance contracts) and 13 to 15 (consumer contracts). Because the Convention only applies to proceedings which are international in character[8] (although the international element may sometimes appear fairly tenuous), the section does not apply to proceedings which are purely internal to the United Kingdom. So far as the latter are concerned, Schedule 4 does not contain provisions equivalent to the deemed domicile provisions in Articles 8 and 13 of the Convention[9] and there is accordingly no need for this section to apply to such proceedings. If the insurer or party contracting with a consumer is domiciled outside the United Kingdom in another Contracting State, the Convention applies; and if he is domiciled in a non-Contracting State, he may be sued under the normal extraterritorial jurisdiction provisions.[10]

It remains an open question whether the deemed domicile provisions in Articles 8 and 13 apply to proceedings which fall within the 1968 Convention, but outside Sections 3 and 4. Such an interpretation is perhaps unlikely,[11] but if it is right, the terms of this subsection mean that the Act contains a lacuna in that it does not

---

[7] Para. 19.01 above.

[8] See paras. 13.10–13.11 above.

[9] Arts. 7 to 12A are omitted from Sched. 4 entirely and Art. 13 of Sched. 4 does not adopt the provisions of the second paragraph of its counterpart in the Convention.

[10] *e.g.* R.S.C., Ord. 11, r. 1(1).

[11] See paras. 18.20 and 19.20 above.

allocate to a particular part of the United Kingdom the domicile which the Convention deems to be located in the United Kingdom as a whole.

3. Subsection (2)

This subsection contains the deeming provisions discussed above. The term "arising out of the operations of a branch, agency or other establishment" is not defined by the Act, but should be interpreted to accord with the interpretation of Articles 5(5), 8 and 13 of the Convention,[12] which is not entirely straightforward.

Section 45

45.—*Domicile of trusts*   **44.30**
  (1) The following provisions of this section determine, for the purposes of the 1968 Convention and this Act, where a trust is domiciled.
  (2) A trust is domiciled in the United Kingdom if and only if it is by virtue of subsection (3) domiciled in a part of the United Kingdom.
  (3) A trust is domiciled in a part of the United Kingdom if and only if the system of law of that part is the system of law with which the trust has its closest and most real connection.

1. General note

This section provides rules for determining whether, for the pur-   **44.31** poses of the 1968 Convention and this Act, a trust is domiciled in the United Kingdom and in a particular part of the United Kingdom. The former question is relevant for the purposes of deciding whether a court has jurisdiction under Article 5(6) of the 1968 Convention, while the latter is relevant for the purposes of allocating jurisdiction within the United Kingdom.

Article 5(6) of the 1968 Convention[13] provides that a person domiciled in one Contracting State may be sued in another Contracting State,

> "as settlor, trustee or beneficiary of a trust created by the operation of a statute, or by a written instrument, or created orally and evidenced in writing, in the courts of the Contracting State in which the trust is domiciled."

By the second paragraph of Article 53[14] of the Convention, a court seised of proceedings brought under Article 5(6) is required

---

[12] See paras. 17.61 *et seq.*, 18.21 and 19.22 above.
[13] Para. 17.65 above.
[14] Para. 31.23 above.

to apply its own rules of private international law to determine whether the trust is domiciled in that Contracting State. A court does not need to consider whether a trust is domiciled elsewhere, because the domicile of a trust is relevant for the purposes of the Convention only to establish the court's own jurisdiction under Article 5(6). Subsection (2) contains a rule for the courts of the United Kingdom to apply, whereby a trust is domiciled in the United Kingdom if and only if it is domiciled in a part of the United Kingdom by virtue of subsection (3).

2. Subsection (3)

44.32   This subsection contains the main rule, which locates the domicile of a trust in a particular part of the United Kingdom if and only if the system of law of that part is the system of law with which the trust has its closest and most real connection. The use of the words "if and only if" indicate that the subsection is exhaustive as to the circumstances in which a trust is to be regarded as domiciled in a part of the United Kingdom for the purposes of the Convention and the Act.

The test in this subsection applies in three categories of case. First, it applies in conjunction with section 10(2)[15] and subsection (2) of this section for the purpose of allocating jurisdiction within the United Kingdom over cases which fall within Article 5(6) of the Convention. Secondly, it applies for the purposes of Article 5(6) of Schedule 4 for determining the part of the United Kingdom in which proceedings may be brought under that provision; and thirdly, it applies in Scottish law for determining whether a trust is domiciled in Scotland for the purposes of Rule 2(7) of Schedule 8.

The "closest and most real connection" test is that which English law used traditionally to apply, at least in the absence of an express or implied choice of law by the settlor, to determine the proper law of an *inter vivos* trust of immovables, that is, the law governing the trust's validity, interpretation and effect. It enabled the court to consider a range of matters in deciding which system of law met the test, such as any choice of law by the settlor, the location of the trust assets, the place where the trust was administered and the place where the settlor, trustees and beneficiaries were resident or domiciled.[16] The system of law which applies to a trust is now determined by the Recognition of Trusts Act 1987, which gives effect to the Hague Convention of October 20, 1984 on the Law applicable to Trusts and on their Recognition.[17] Although the Act

---

[15] Para. 40.30 above.

[16] See Dicey and Morris, pp. 1072 *et seq.*

[17] Cmnd. 9494. See Hayton, "The Hague Convention on the Law Applicable to Trusts and on their Recognition" (1987) 36 I.C.L.Q. 260.

does not expressly govern the domicile of the trust, the second paragraph of Article 7 of the Hague Convention, which forms the Schedule to the Act, is relevant. It provides that:

"In ascertaining the law with which a trust is most closely connected reference shall be made in particular to:
(a) the place of administration of the trust designated by the settlor;
(b) the situs of the assets of the trust;
(c) the place of residence or business of the trustee;
(d) the objects of the trust and the places where they are to be fulfilled."

In applying the test provided by the present section, if the court decides that the law of England, Scotland or Northern Ireland is the system of law with which the trust has its closest and most real connection, then the trust is domiciled in the corresponding part of the United Kingdom. If, on the other hand, the court decides that none of those systems is the one with which the trust has its closest and most real connection, it need not go on to decide which system of law does fulfil that criterion, because that question is not relevant for the purposes of the jurisdictional provisions.

Section 46

46.—*Domicile and seat of the Crown* 44.33
(1) **For the purposes of this Act the seat of the Crown (as determined by this section) shall be treated as its domicile.**
(2) **The following provisions of this section determine where the Crown has its seat—**
(a) **for the purposes of the 1968 Convention (in which Article 53 equates the domicile of a legal person with its seat); and**
(b) **for the purposes of this Act.**
(3) **Subject to the provisions of any Order in Council for the time being in force under subsection (4)—**
(a) **the Crown in right of Her Majesty's government in the United Kingdom has its seat in every part of, and every place in, the United Kingdom; and**
(b) **the Crown in right of Her Majesty's government in Northern Ireland has its seat in every part of, and every place in, Northern Ireland.**
(4) **Her Majesty may by Order in Council provide that, in the case of proceedings of any specified description against the Crown in right of Her Majesty's government in the United Kingdom, the Crown shall be treated for the purposes of the 1968 Convention and this Act as having its seat in, and in every place in, a specified part of the United Kingdom and not in any other part of the United Kingdom.**

(5) An Order in Council under subsection (4) may frame a description of proceedings in any way, and in particular may do so by reference to the government department or officer of the Crown against which or against whom they fall to be instituted.

(6) Any Order in Council under this section shall be subject to annulment in pursuance of a resolution of either House of Parliament.

(7) Nothing in this section applies to the Crown otherwise than in right of Her Majesty's government in the United Kingdom or Her Majesty's government in Northern Ireland.

1. General note

44.34   The position of the Crown as a defendant in civil proceedings falling within the 1968 Convention and this Act is generally assimilated by this section to that established by the Crown Proceedings Act 1947, but this section creates a power to modify that position by Order in Council. By specifying that the seat of the Crown in right of Her Majesty's government in the United Kingdom is to be located in every part of, and every place in, the United Kingdom, and by making similar provision for the seat of the Crown in right of Her Majesty's government in Northern Ireland, the section ties the Crown into the jurisdictional provisions of the Convention and this Act.[18]

The Crown (in the sense of government departments) is probably a legal person within the meaning of Article 53 of the 1968 Convention and subsection (1) equates its seat with its domicile, in the same way as section 42(1) does in the case of corporations and associations. The term "company or other legal person or association of legal or natural persons" used in Article 53[19] encompasses both the "corporation or association" referred to in section 42 and the Crown, dealt with by this section.[20] It may be that the Crown is a corporation sole and as such falls within section 42, but the fact that this section is expressly concerned with the Crown suggests that it is not also to be regarded as a corporation for the purposes of the Act. Subsection (7) and section 51 limit the extent to which the Crown is subject to the Act.

The purposes for which the section applies, defined by subsection (2), are those of the 1968 Convention and this Act: the effect of this subsection is equivalent to that of section 42(2). For other purposes, notably proceedings of a public law character, which fall

---

[18] The Crown's seat may also be relevant even where it is not a defendant—*e.g.* where it is a party to a jurisdiction agreement under Art. 17 of the 1968 Convention.

[19] Para. 31.23 above.

[20] See para. 44.13 above.

outside the Convention and the jurisdictional provisions of this Act,[21] the position of the Crown remains unchanged.

2. Subsection (3): seat of the Crown

In order to be sued in the United Kingdom under Article 2 of the **44.35** 1968 Convention, the Crown needs to be domiciled in the United Kingdom as a whole and in order to be sued in a particular part of the United Kingdom under Article 2 of Schedule 4, it needs to be domiciled in that part. The *place* where the Crown is domiciled is also relevant for some purposes, for example Article 6(1) of the Convention and the equivalent Article in Schedule 4 (co-defendants). Paragraph (*a*) of this subsection establishes the seat (and hence the domicile)[22] of the Crown in right of the United Kingdom government in every part of and place in the United Kingdom (and therefore, obviously, in the United Kingdom as a whole). Paragraph (*b*) makes similar provision in Northern Ireland for the Crown in right of the government in Northern Ireland.

The effect of these provisions is to make the government of the United Kingdom susceptible to the jurisdiction of the courts in any part of the United Kingdom and, subject to considerations of state immunity, to the jurisdiction of the courts of other Contracting States under the special rules of jurisdiction, notably those in Article 5 of the Convention. Similarly, the government in Northern Ireland may be sued in Northern Ireland (but not in other parts of the United Kingdom) under Articles 2 of the Convention and Schedule 4, and in the courts of other Contracting States (again, subject to considerations of state immunity) and of other parts of the United Kingdom. The liberal effect of these provisions is tempered, though, by the courts' powers to stay, strike out or dismiss the proceedings on the grounds of *forum non conveniens*[23] or otherwise, where to do so is not inconsistent with the 1968 Convention. These powers are expressly preserved by section 49,[24] but it should be noted that where the court's jurisdiction is founded on the rules of the Convention itself, as distinct from merely those of the Act, the courts' powers to stay the proceedings may well be limited.[25]

3. Subsections (4) to (6): Order in Council

These subsections enable an Order in Council to be made limiting the Crown's seat to a particular part or parts of the United Kingdom for the purposes of any particular description of proceed-

---

[21] See paras. 14.08 *et seq.* and 41.06 above.
[22] See subs. (1).
[23] See para. 1.42 above.
[24] Para. 44.40 below.
[25] Para. 15.02 above.

ings, including (but not limited to) proceedings against particular government departments or officers of the Crown. No such order has yet been made.

4. Subsection (7)

This subsection is self-explanatory in limiting the effect of the section to the Crown in right of the governments of the United Kingdom and Northern Ireland. If the Act is extended to any of the territories mentioned in section 52(2), the Order in Council under that section may extend the provisions of this section to the Crown in relation to that territory. The Crown in right of any other dominion is unlikely to be relevant for the purposes of the Convention and this Act. Section 51[26] imposes further restrictions on the application of the Act to the Crown.

B. Other Supplementary Provisions

Section 47

44.36   **47.**—*Modifications occasioned by decisions of European Court as to meaning or effect of Conventions*
   (1) Her Majesty may by Order in Council—
      (a) make such provision as Her Majesty considers appropriate for the purpose of bringing the law of any part of the United Kingdom into accord with the Conventions as affected by any principle laid down by the European Court in connection with the Conventions or by any decision of that court as to the meaning or effect of any provision of the Conventions; or
      (b) make such modifications of Schedule 4 or Schedule 8, or of any other statutory provision affected by any provision of either of those Schedules, as Her Majesty considers appropriate in view of any principle laid down by the European Court in connection with Title II of the 1968 Convention or of any decision of that court as to the meaning or effect of any provision of that Title.
   (2) The provision which may be made by virtue of paragraph (a) of subsection (1) includes such modifications of this Act or any other statutory provision, whenever passed or made, as Her Majesty considers appropriate for the purpose mentioned in that paragraph.
   (3) The modifications which may be made by virtue of paragraph (b) of subsection (1) include modifications designed to produce divergence between any provision of Schedule 4 or

---

[26] Para. 44.47 below.

Schedule 8 and a corresponding provision of Title II of the 1968 Convention as affected by any such principle or decision as is mentioned in that paragraph.

(4) An Order in Council under this section shall not be made unless a draft of the Order has been laid before Parliament and approved by a resolution of each House of Parliament.

General note

This section enables the law of any part of the United Kingdom **44.37** to be modified[27] by an Order in Council to take account of the effect of decisions of, and principles laid down by, the European Court of Justice interpreting the Conventions. It covers two aspects.

First, under subsections (1)(a) and (2) changes can be made to bring domestic law into line with the Conventions in the event of divergence developing as a result of European Court decisions. The Conventions themselves have the force of law in the United Kingdom[28] and the European Court of Justice can give definitive rulings on their interpretation under the 1971 Protocol. Courts in the United Kingdom are required to apply those rulings and the principles enunciated by the European Court[29] and the occasions on which the power conferred by these subsections will need to be exercised are likely to be rare. It may happen, though, that the European Court will establish uniform rules, applicable in all Contracting States, which cover matters of detail already covered by provisions of domestic law (such as sections 4 to 8 of this Act). In such a case, the potential conflict of rules may be resolved by an Order in Council under this section.

Secondly, under subsections (1)(b) and (3) appropriate changes can be made to Schedule 4 or Schedule 8 (which allocate jurisdiction within the United Kingdom and within Scotland respectively), or any other statutory provision affected by those Schedules, in the light of decisions of, and principles laid down by, the European Court in connection with Title II of the 1968 Convention. In interpreting those Schedules, the courts in the United Kingdom must have regard to those decisions and principles,[30] but they are not bound to follow them. Clearly, divergences in interpretation between Title II of the 1968 Convention and Schedules 4 and 8 would create anomalies which would often be hard to justify, and an Order in Council under this section can remove such anomalies

---

[27] "Modifications" and "statutory provision" are defined by s.50, para. 44.45 below.

[28] s.2(1), para. 40.03 above.

[29] s.3(1), para. 40.05 above.

[30] ss.16(3) and 20(5), paras. 41.01 and 42.01 above.

if and when they occur. Equally, as subsection (3) makes clear, there may be occasions when the interpretation of a particular provision in Title II of the Convention is not appropriate for internal United Kingdom purposes and a divergence between the interpretations of that provision and of its counterpart in Schedules 4 or 8 is necessary. That too can be achieved by an Order under this section.

Section 48

44.38 **48.**—*Matters for which rules of court may provide*

(1) **Rules of court may make provision for regulating the procedure to be followed in any court in connection with any provision of this Act or the Conventions.**

(2) **Rules of court may make provision as to the manner in which and the conditions subject to which a certificate or judgment registered in any court under any provision of this Act may be enforced, including provision for enabling the court or, in Northern Ireland the Enforcement of Judgments Office, subject to any conditions specified in the rules, to give directions about such matters.**

(3) **Without prejudice to the generality of subsections (1) and (2), the power to make rules of court for magistrates' courts, and in Northern Ireland the power to make Judgment Enforcement Rules, shall include power to make such provision as the rule-making authority considers necessary or expedient for the purposes of the provisions of the Conventions and this Act relating to maintenance proceedings and the recognition and enforcement of maintenance orders, and shall in particular include power to make provision as to any of the following matters—**

   (a) **authorising the service in another Contracting State of process issued by or for the purposes of a magistrates' court and the service and execution in England and Wales or Northern Ireland of process issued in another Contracting State;**

   (b) **requesting courts in other parts of the United Kingdom or in other Contracting States to take evidence there for the purposes of proceedings in England and Wales or Northern Ireland;**

   (c) **the taking of evidence in England and Wales or Northern Ireland in response to similar requests received from such courts;**

   (d) **the circumstances in which and the conditions subject to which any powers conferred under paragraphs (a) to (c) are to be exercised;**

   (e) **the admission in evidence, subject to such conditions as** may be prescribed in the rules, of statements contained in documents purporting to be made or authenticated by a court in another part of the United Kingdom or in another Contracting State, or by a judge or official of such a court, which purport—

(i) to set out or summarise evidence given in proceedings in that court or to be documents received in evidence in such proceedings or copies of such documents; or

(ii) to set out or summarise evidence taken for the purposes of proceedings in England and Wales or Northern Ireland, whether or not in response to any such request as is mentioned in paragraph (b); or

(iii) to record information relating to the payments made under an order of that court;

(f) the circumstances and manner in which a magistrates' court may or must vary or revoke a maintenance order registered in that court, cancel the registration of, or refrain from enforcing, such an order or transmit such an order for enforcement in another part of the United Kingdom;

(g) the cases and manner in which courts in other parts of the United Kingdom or in other Contracting States are to be informed of orders made, or other things done, by or for the purposes of a magistrates' court;

(h) the circumstances and manner in which a magistrates' court may communicate for other purposes with such courts;

(i) the giving of notice of such matters as may be prescribed in the rules to such persons as may be so prescribed and the manner in which such notice is to be given.

(4) Nothing in this section shall be taken as derogating from the generality of any power to make rules of court conferred by any other enactment.

General note

This section contains rule-making powers.[31] The definitions of **44.39** "court" and "rules of court" in section 50 mean that these powers extend to rules, orders and regulations regulating the procedure of

---

[31] The following rules have been made under this section in relation to England and Wales: Rules of the Supreme Court (Amendment No. 2) 1983, (S.I. 1983 No. 1181); Rules of the Supreme Court (Amendment) 1984, (S.I. 1984

courts and tribunals. Subsection (1) contains a general rule-making power of this nature.

Subsection (2) extends that power beyond pure matters of procedure and enables provisions to be made as to substantive matters concerning the manner in which, and conditions subject to which, judgments and maintenance orders may be enforced under sections 4 and 5 and Schedules 6 and 7. Sections 4(4) and 5(5) make clear that a judgment's force and effect, when it is to be enforced under those sections, and the powers of the registering court, are subject to provisions of rules of court. That is a reference to rules made under this section. The rule-making power is subject, though, to the requirements of the Convention itself, which makes the granting of full faith and credit to the judgments of other Contracting States a matter which is compulsory, provided that the Convention's conditions are fulfilled.[32] While the manner of enforcement is a matter which is left to national law,[33] any conditions imposed on the right to have a judgment enforced under Article 31 of the Convention must not be inconsistent with that principle. Paragraphs 6 of Schedules 6 and 7 make clear that rules of court may affect the manner of enforcement of a certificate or non-money provisions of a judgment registered under those Schedules, but make no reference to the rules of court imposing further conditions on the enforcement of such certificates or provisions.

Subsection (3) relates to maintenance proceedings and, in addition to rules relating to recognition and enforcement of maintenance orders, contains power to make rules concerning a range of matters which may arise in relation to maintenance proceedings, particularly those brought in magistrates' courts under Article 5(2) of the Convention against a defendant domiciled in another Contracting State.

Section 49

44.40   **49.**—*Saving for powers to stay, sist, strike out or dismiss proceedings*
Nothing in this Act shall prevent any court in the United Kingdom from staying, sisting, striking out or dismissing any proceedings before it, on the ground of *forum non conveniens* or otherwise, where to do so is not inconsistent with the 1968 Convention.

No. 1051); County Court (Amendment No. 2) Rules 1985, (S.I. 1985 No. 1269); The Magistrates' Courts (Civil Jurisdiction and Judgments Act 1982) Rules 1986, (S.I. 1986 No. 1962).
[32] Art. 31, para. 28.01 above.
[33] *Ibid.*

1. General note

By contrast with its continental counterparts, English civil pro- **44.41**
cedure is often characterised by discretionary powers and the High
Court has an inherent jurisdiction to regulate its own process. This
section expressly recognises the courts' powers to stay, strike out or
dismiss proceedings and preserves those powers where they are not
inconsistent with the 1968 Convention.

2. Discretionary powers under English law

The discretionary powers exercised by English courts to regulate
the exercise of their jurisdiction by staying, striking out or dismissing proceedings are discussed more fully in Chapter 1.[34] As will be
seen below, these powers may now only be exercised if and to the
extent that that is not inconsistent with the 1968 Convention. In
summary, the more important of the powers envisaged by this section are as follows[35]:

(1) The court will generally stay its proceedings on the application of the defendant if there is another forum of competent jurisdiction which is the appropriate forum for the
trial of the action, in the sense that the case may be tried
there more suitably for the interests of all the parties and
the ends of justice.[36] The principles applied in staying
proceedings on these grounds have come to be known as
the principles of *forum non conveniens*.

(2) A stay may be granted if there are already other proceedings on foot between the parties covering the same matters
(a *lis alibi pendens*), but a stay is less likely if the other proceedings are before a foreign court.

(3) If the parties have agreed to submit their dispute to arbitration[37] or to the jurisdiction of a foreign court, a stay will
generally (but not inevitably) be granted, at least if the
defendant has not effectively submitted to the jurisdiction
of the court by taking steps in the action.

(4) Pleadings in an action may be struck out if they disclose
no reasonable cause of action and the proceedings may be
dismissed. The same applies if the proceedings are frivolous or vexatious or an abuse of the court's process.[38]

---

[34] Paras. 1.36 *et seq.* above.
[35] See, further, Dicey and Morris, pp. 389 *et seq.*; Supreme Court Act 1981,
s.49(3) and *Supreme Court Practice*, paras. [5215]–[5218].
[36] *Spiliada Maritime Corp.* v. *Cansulex Ltd.* [1987] A.C. 460.
[37] Arbitration Act 1950, s.4; Arbitration Act 1975, s.1.
[38] R.S.C., Ord. 18, r. 19 and *Supreme Court Practice*, paras. 18/19/1 *et seq.*

3. Inconsistency between discretionary powers and the 1968 Convention

44.42   The discretionary powers exercised by English courts are clearly inconsistent with the 1968 Convention to some extent, although the limits of that inconsistency are very far from clear. Where the court's discretionary powers concern the conduct of proceedings rather than the court's jurisdiction, they probably remain unaffected by the Convention. So, for example, proceedings may still be dismissed on the grounds that they are frivolous, vexatious or an abuse of the process of the court, or because they disclose no reasonable cause of action, irrespective of whether or not the court's jurisdiction arises under the 1968 Convention. Similarly, the 1968 Convention does not affect the jurisdiction of the courts as regards the subject-matter of the dispute.[39]

As regards the court's discretionary powers in the matter of its jurisdiction, on the other hand, three separate reasons for the court to consider staying, striking out or dismissing proceedings are to be distinguished: *forum non conveniens, lis alibi pendens* and jurisdiction agreements.[40] These reasons may each arise in any of three separate contexts, as between different Contracting States, and between the United Kingdom and a non-Contracting State, and as between the different parts of the United Kingdom.

As between different Contracting States

The jurisdictional rules of the 1968 Convention undoubtedly apply to cases falling within its scope which have international links between different Contracting States.[41] In this context, it is generally accepted that there is no discretion to decline to exercise jurisdiction on the grounds of *forum non conveniens*.[42] The court either has jurisdiction under the rules or it does not; and it must accept or decline jurisdiction accordingly. As regards *lis alibi pendens* and related actions, Articles 21 to 23 of the 1968 Convention[43] confer some discretion on English courts and it is under these powers, rather than under any other provisions of English law, that the court may decline jurisdiction or stay its proceedings. As regards jurisdiction agreements, if they comply with Article 17 of the 1968 Convention,[44] that Article determines whether the court is to accept

---

[39] Schlosser, para. 81 (para. A1.368 below).
[40] A stay of proceedings on the basis of an arbitration agreement is not considered here, because arbitration falls outside the scope of the 1968 Convention: see paras. 14.31 *et seq.* above.
[41] See para. 15.01 above.
[42] See paras. 1.37 and 15.02 above.
[43] Chap. 23 above.
[44] Para. 21.01 above.

or decline jurisdiction. If the agreement does not comply with Article 17, it is not to be given effect and, if the other jurisdictional rules of the Convention apply, those rules determine whether or not the court may entertain the proceedings.

As between the United Kingdom and non-Contracting States

It has already been suggested that effect may be given to a choice   **44.43** of jurisdiction in favour of a non-Contracting State,[45] provided that that is consistent with those jurisdictional rules of the 1968 Convention which take precedence over Article 17.[46] Similarly, English courts probably retain the power to stay, strike out or dismiss proceedings on the grounds of *lis alibi pendens* if the earlier proceedings are in the court of a non-Contracting State.[47] As has also been suggested above, it may be permissible for a court in a Contracting State to decline to exercise the jurisdiction which it has under the Convention in a further limited class of cases, namely those in which the subject-matter of the proceedings falls within Article 16 and is closely connected only with a non-Contracting State.[48]

On the other hand, in those cases where the parties have not agreed on the jurisdiction of a forum outside the Contracting States, where there is no *lis alibi pendens*, and where the close connections envisaged by Article 16 do not exist with a non-Contracting State, the likelihood is much greater that the compulsory nature of the Convention's jurisdictional rules[49] will be held to predominate. If so, those rules would have the effect of preventing an English court from staying proceedings over which it has jurisdiction under the Convention, even in favour of a more appropriate forum in a non-Contracting State, on the grounds that the English court is a *forum non conveniens*.

As between different parts of the United Kingdom

Within the United Kingdom, jurisdiction over cases which have   **44.44** a subject-matter falling within the scope of the Convention (whether or not the Convention actually applies to them) is allocated by section 16 and Schedule 4.[50] If the jurisdiction of the English court is derived exclusively from the provisions of section 16 and that Schedule, the court will be free to exercise its discretion to stay, strike out or dismiss proceedings in favour of the courts of another part of the United Kingdom. This section expressly preserves the court's powers in this regard; moreover, the wording of

---

[45] Para. 21.13 above.
[46] Para. 21.04 above.
[47] See para. 23.07 above; Dicey and Morris, p. 395.
[48] Paras. 20.06 *et seq.* above.
[49] See para. 15.02 above.
[50] Paras. 41.01 *et seq.* above and 45.01 *et seq.* below.

Schedule 4 differs from the Convention in such a way as apparently to leave the court's discretion intact. As regards *lis alibi pendens*, it is notable that Articles 21 to 23 of the Convention have not been adopted for the purpose of Schedule 4;[51] while Article 17 of Schedule 4 does not confer exclusive jurisdiction on the chosen court.[52] Where the court's jurisdiction does not also arise under the Convention (for example, because the case does not have the requisite international character) the exercise of the court's discretion is not likely to cause a problem.[53]

The position is more complex, though, where the court's jurisdiction is derived both from the Convention and from Schedule 4. In some cases the Convention gives jurisdiction to the courts of a particular Contracting State,[54] leaving the allocation of local jurisdiction to national law. In these cases the court's powers to decline jurisdiction in favour of the courts in another part of the United Kingdom probably remain unimpaired by the Convention, assuming that this section takes priority over the apparently mandatory language of Article 2 of Schedule 4.[55] In other cases, the Convention itself determines local jurisdiction.[56] If the local jurisdiction of an English court arises under the Convention, it is probable that the court normally has no discretion to stay its proceedings on the grounds of *forum non conveniens*.[57]

C. GENERAL

Section 50

44.45   **50.**—*Interpretation: general*
In this Act, unless the context otherwise requires—
"the Accession Convention" has the meaning given by section 1(1);
"Article" and references to sub-divisions of numbered Articles are to be construed in accordance with section 1(2)(b);

---

[51] See para. 45.28 below.
[52] See para. 45.22 below.
[53] Note, however, that s.22(1) expressly saves the application of *forum non conveniens* for the purposes of Sched. 8, but the Act contains no comparable provision for Sched. 4.
[54] *e.g.* under Arts. 2 and 16 and some of the provisions of Arts. 5, 8 and 14.
[55] Para. 45.02 below.
[56] *e.g.* under Arts. 5 (except 5(6)), 6, 9, 10 and some of the provisions of Arts. 8 and 14. As regards jurisdiction agreements, see para. 45.22 below.
[57] The Schlosser Report (para. 80, at para. A1.387 below) discusses the transfer of proceedings from one court to another where both courts have "equivalent jurisdiction." If the effect of the Convention itself in the circumstances of the particular case is to confer *local* jurisdiction on more than one court in the U.K., it may be that the proceedings in one of them may be stayed in favour of the other.

"association" means an unincorporated body of persons;

"Contracting State" has the meaning given by section 1(3);

"the 1968 Convention" has the meaning given by section 1(1), and references to that Convention and to provisions of it are to be construed in accordance with section 1(2)(a);

"the Conventions" has the meaning given by section 1(1);

"corporation" means a body corporate, and includes a partnership subsisting under the law of Scotland;

"court," without more, includes a tribunal;

"court of law," in relation to the United Kingdom, means any of the following courts, namely—

    (a) the House of Lords,

    (b) in England and Wales or Northern Ireland, the Court of Appeal, the High Court, the Crown Court, a county court and a magistrates' court,

    (c) in Scotland, the Court of Session and a sheriff court;

"the Crown" is to be construed in accordance with section 51(2);

"enactment" includes an enactment comprised in Northern Ireland legislation;

"judgment," subject to sections 15(1) and 18(2) and to paragraph 1 of Schedules 6 and 7, means any judgment or order (by whatever name called) given or made by a court in civil proceedings;

"magistrates' court," in relation to Northern Ireland, means a court of summary jurisdiction;

"modifications" includes additions, omissions and alterations;

"overseas country" means any country or territory outside the United Kingdom;

"part of the United Kingdom" means England and Wales, Scotland or Northern Ireland;

"the 1971 Protocol" has the meaning given by section 1(1), and references to that Protocol and to provisions of it are to be construed in accordance with section 1(2)(a);

"rules of court," in relation to any court, means rules, orders or regulations made by the authority having power to make rules, orders or regulations regulating the procedure of that court, and includes—

    (a) in Scotland, Acts of Sederunt;

    (b) in Northern Ireland, Judgment Enforcement Rules;

"statutory provision" means any provision contained in an Act, or in any Northern Ireland legislation, or in—

    (a) subordinate legislation (as defined in section 21(1) of the Interpretation Act 1978); or

    (b) any instrument of a legislative character made under any Northern Ireland legislation;

"tribunal"—
- (a) means a tribunal of any description other than a court of law;
- (b) in relation to an overseas country, includes, as regards matters relating to maintenance within the meaning of the 1968 Convention, any authority having power to give, enforce, vary or revoke a maintenance order.

General note

44.46   This section contains definitions for the purpose of the Act. Reference should be made to the commentary on the sections referred to in this section and the following points should also be noted:

"*Association*" and "*Corporation*": see the commentary on section 42, at paragraph 44.13 above.

"*Court*", without more, includes a tribunal, which is itself defined by this section, and (depending on the context) often extends also to foreign courts.

"*Court of law*" does not include a tribunal. Tribunals therefore fall outside the scope of Schedule 4, because sections 16 and 17 use the expression "court of law": see paragraphs 41.03 and 41.05 above.

"*Rules of court*": the definition of "court" means that these include procedural rules of tribunals.

"*Tribunal*": the definition is not comprehensive, but in the context of the 1968 Convention, although it is undefined, it probably excludes private tribunals.[58] The reference in paragraph (b) to "any authority having power to give, enforce, vary or revoke a maintenance order" is primarily a reference to Danish administrative authorities: see Article Va of the 1968 Protocol.[59]

Section 51

44.47   51.—*Application to Crown*
(1) This Act binds the Crown.
(2) In this section and elsewhere in the Act references to the Crown do not include references to Her Majesty in Her private capacity or to Her Majesty in right of Her Duchy of Lancaster or to the Duke of Cornwall.

---

[58] See para. 26.05 above.
[59] Para. 35.22 above.

General note

The Crown in appropriate cases clearly falls within the ambit of   **44.48**
the 1968 Convention and this Act, and section 46 defines the seat of
the Crown for these purposes. However, many cases will fall outside the scope of the Convention and jurisdictional provisions of
this Act, because the proceedings will be concerned with matters of
a public law nature, such as tax or social security or the decisions of
government departments.[60]
     The Act does not affect other jurisdictional questions affecting
the capacity of the Crown to sue or be sued and this remains a
matter for domestic law. In particular, the Crown Proceedings Act
1947 remains unaffected by this Act, and provisions (including the
restriction on execution against the Crown in section 25(4)) continue to apply. Subsection (2) of this section may be compared with
section 40(1) of the 1947 Act.

Section 52

52.—*Extent*   **44.49**
     (1) This Act extends to Northern Ireland.
     (2) Without prejudice to the power conferred by section 39,
Her Majesty may by Order in Council direct that all or any of the
provisions of this Act apart from that section shall extend, sub-
ject to such modifications as may be specified in the Order, to
any of the following territories, that is to say—
          (a) the Isle of Man;
          (b) any of the Channel Islands;
          (c) Gibraltar;
          (d) the Sovereign Base Areas of Akrotiri and Dhekelia (that
               is to say the areas mentioned in section 2(1) of the
               Cyprus Act 1960).

General note

     This section concerns the territorial extent of the Act. Subsection   **44.50**
(1) extends it to Northern Ireland, while its extension to Scotland is
express in the case of those of its provisions as are directly applicable to Scotland and clearly implicit in all the other provisions not
expressly limited to England and Wales or Northern Ireland.
     Subsection (2) enables the Act to be extended by Order in Coun-
cil to certain other territories, and is the counterpart of section 39,
which enables the relations between those territories and the United
Kingdom to be regulated by an Order in Council corresponding to
the provisions of the 1968 Convention. An Order in Council under

---

[60] Paras. 14.08 *et seq.* above.

this section would enable such a territory to regulate its own civil procedure along the lines of this Act,[61] without having to introduce comprehensive implementing legislation of its own, if and when the Conventions are extended to that territory by a declaration under Article 60.[62]

Section 53

44.51   53.—*Commencement, transitional provisions and savings*
    (1) This Act shall come into force in accordance with the provisions of Part I of Schedule 13.
    (2) The transitional provisions and savings contained in Part II of that Schedule shall have effect in relation to the commencement of the provisions of this Act mentioned in that Part.

General note

Commentary on the commencement and transitional provisions appears under Schedule 13, in Chapter 47 below.

Section 54

44.52   54.—*Repeals*
    The enactments mentioned in Schedule 14 are hereby repealed to the extent specified in the third column of that Schedule.

General note

The most notable repeals in Schedule 14 are the Judgment Extensions Act 1868 and the Inferior Courts Judgments Extension Act 1882, each of which regulated the enforcement of judgments as between the different parts of the United Kingdom and which are replaced by sections 18 and 19 and Schedules 6 and 7. The repeal of sections 1 to 8 of the Crown Debts Act 1801 removes from the statute-book the earliest statutory scheme for the extra-territorial extension of judgments. The repeal of sections 9(1) and 11(1) of the Foreign Judgments (Reciprocal Enforcement) Act 1933 is also effected by paragraphs 2 and 5(3) respectively of Schedule 10.

Section 55

44.53   55.—*Short title*
    This Act may be cited as the Civil Jurisdiction and Judgments Act 1982.

---

[61] The Protection of Trading Interests Act 1980, as amended by this Act, has been extended to Jersey, Guernsey and the Isle of Man: see para. 43.47 above.
[62] Para. 34.01 above.

General note

This section requires no commentary.

D. Schedules to the 1982 Act

Schedules 1 to 3 to the 1982 Act are the English language texts of   **44.54**
the 1968 Convention as amended, of the 1971 Protocol as amended
and of Articles 34 to 41 of the 1978 Accession Convention.[63] These
conventions are reproduced with commentary in Chapters 13 to 37
above. Schedules 4 to 14 are contained with commentary in
Chapters 45 to 47 below.

---

[63] s.2(2), para. 40.03 above.

CHAPTER 45

CIVIL JURISDICTION AND JUDGMENTS ACT 1982—SCHEDULES 4 AND 5 ALLOCATION OF JURISDICTION WITHIN THE UNITED KINGDOM

SCHEDULE 4 Section 16

TITLE II OF 1968 CONVENTION AS MODIFIED FOR ALLOCATION OF
JURISDICTION WITHIN U.K.

TITLE II

JURISDICTION

General note on Schedule 4

This Schedule sets out a code of rules for allocating jurisdiction **45.01**
as between the different parts of the United Kingdom. It is based
on Title II of the 1968 Convention, of which it is a modified version. It is given effect by section 16[1] which, together with section 17
and Schedule 5, defines the proceedings to which it applies and
makes provision for its interpretation.

Title II of the 1968 Convention is discussed in detail in Chapters
15 to 24 above and the following commentary is confined to noting
the principal points of difference between the two sets of rules and
commenting on certain particular features of the intra-United
Kingdom scheme.

The typography of the Schedule indicates the passages which differ from Title II of the 1968 Convention. A row of dots indicates an
omission and a modification by way of addition or substitution is
indicated by underlining.[2] The words "this Title" are substituted
for the words "this Convention" throughout.

Section 1

General Provisions

Article 2

Subject to the provisions of this <u>Title</u>, persons domiciled in a **45.02**
<u>part of the United Kingdom</u> shall . . . be sued in the courts of
that <u>part</u>.[3]

· · · · · · ·

---

[1] Para. 41.01 above.

[2] In the official Queen's Printer's text of the Act, modification by way of addition
or substitution is indicated by the use of heavy type: see s.16(2)(b), para. 41.01
above.

[3] See Art. 2 of the 1968 Convention, discussed at paras. 16.02 *et seq.* above.

General note

45.03   This Article reproduces the Convention's general rule of jurisdiction, whereby defendants may be sued in the courts of their domicile. Where the jurisdiction of the courts of a particular part of the United Kingdom[4] is invoked under this Article, allocation of local jurisdiction within that part is determined by the law of that part. The High Court has jurisdiction over the whole geographical area of England and Wales[5] and the jurisdiction of the county courts, magistrates' courts and other tribunals is determined by their own various Acts and rules.

The words omitted from Article 2 in this version relate to nationality and have no application in a context internal to the United Kingdom.

Article 3

45.04   **Persons domiciled in a <u>part of the United Kingdom</u> may be sued in the Courts of <u>part of the United Kingdom</u> only by virtue of the rules set out in Sections 2, <u>4, 5 and</u> 6 of this Title.**[6]

. . . .

General note

The differences between this version of Article 3 and its counterpart in the 1968 Convention take account of the omission of Section 3 (Articles 7 to 12A), which relates to insurance contracts,[7] and omit the list of exorbitant jurisdictions in the laws of the various Contracting States. That list is necessary only in the context of certain conventions with third states, whereby a Contracting State may undertake not to recognise judgments given in other Contracting States on the basis of a jurisdiction listed in Article 3.[8] It has no relevance in a context internal to the United Kingdom.

[Article 4]

45.05   Article 4, which is omitted from Schedule 4, is concerned with defendants domiciled outside the Contracting States. Except in the case of Article 16 (exclusive jurisdictions),[9] Schedule 4 applies only

---

[4] "Part of the United Kingdom" is defined by s.50 to mean England and Wales, Scotland or Northern Ireland: para. 44.45 above.
[5] See para. 1.03 above; *Supreme Court Practice*, para. 11/1/4.
[6] See Art. 3 of the 1968 Convention, discussed at paras. 16.10 *et seq.* above.
[7] See chap. 18 above.
[8] See para. 33.24 above.
[9] Chap. 20 above.

Schedule 4

to defendants domiciled in the United Kingdom—see section 16(1)(*b*).[10] Article 4 would therefore be superfluous in this context.

Section 2
Special jurisdiction

Article 5

A person domiciled in a <u>part of the United Kingdom</u> may, in   45.06
another <u>part of the United Kingdom</u> be sued:

(1) in matters relating to a contract, in the courts for the place of performance of the obligation in question;

(2) in matters relating to maintenance, in the courts for the place where the maintenance creditor is domiciled or habitually resident or, if the matter is ancillary to proceedings concerning the status of a person, in the court which, according to its own law, has jurisdiction to entertain those proceedings, unless that jurisdiction is based solely on the nationality of one of the parties;

(3) in matters relating to tort, delict or quasi-delict, in the courts for the place where the harmful event occurred <u>or in the case of a threatened wrong is likely to occur</u>;

(4) as regards a civil claim for damages or restitution which is based on an act giving rise to criminal proceedings, in the court seised of those proceedings, to the extent that that court has jurisdiction under its own law to entertain civil proceedings;

(5) as regards a dispute arising out of the operations of a branch, agency or other establishment, in the courts for the place in which the branch, agency or other establishment is situated;

(6) as settlor, trustee or beneficiary of a trust created by the operation of a statute, or by a written instrument, or created orally and evidenced in writing, in the courts of the <u>part of the United Kingdom</u> in which the trust is domiciled;

(7) as regards a dispute concerning the payment of remuneration claimed in respect of the salvage of a cargo or freight, in the court under the authority of which the cargo or freight in question
(a) has been arrested to secure such payment, or
(b) could have been so arrested, but bail or other security has been given;

---

[10] See para. 41.08 above.

provided that this provision shall apply only if it is claimed that the defendant has an interest in the cargo or freight or had such an interest at the time of salvage;
(8) in proceedings—
    (a) concerning a debt secured on immovable property; or
    (b) which are brought to assert, declare or determine proprietary or possessory rights, or rights of security, in or over movable property, or to obtain authority to dispose of movable property,
in the courts of the part of the United Kingdom in which the property is situated.[11]

1. General note

45.07   Article 5 contains most of the special rules which provide alternative and additional jurisdictions to that provided by Article 2. In particular, it should be noted that this Article only applies where a defendant is domiciled in one part of the United Kingdom and is being sued in another part of the United Kingdom. The words added to Article 5(3) make it clear that, in the United Kingdom at least, the jurisdiction over torts extends also to threatened wrongs.[12] As with their counterparts in the 1968 Convention, paragraphs (1) to (5) and (7) allocate jurisdiction to the courts for a particular place or to a particular court.

2. Article 5(8)

45.08   This paragraph, which has no counterpart in the 1968 Convention, enables a defendant domiciled in one part of the United Kingdom to be sued in another part in two additional types of case.

First, by sub-paragraph (*a*), where the proceedings concern a debt secured on immovable property (typically a mortgage debt), an action may be brought in the courts for the part of the United Kingdom where the property is situated. Those courts anyway have exclusive jurisdiction under Article 16(1)[13] over proceedings which have as their object rights *in rem* in, or tenancies of, immovable property and such proceedings may often be coupled with proceedings to recover secured loans. This provision merely enables those courts to deal with such debt proceedings, whether or not there are

---

[11] See the discussion of Arts. 5 to 6A of the 1968 Convention, at paras. 15.05 to 15.08 above and the commentary on Art. 5 at paras. 17.03 *et seq.* above.
[12] The meaning of Art. 5(3) of the 1968 Convention on this aspect is not clear—see para. 17.52 above.
[13] Paras. 20.11 *et seq.* above and 45.19 below.

also proceedings falling under Article 16(1), if the defendant is domiciled in another part of the United Kingdom.

Secondly, by sub-paragraph (*b*), the courts of a part of the United Kingdom where movable property is situated have jurisdiction over a defendant domiciled in another part of the United Kingdom in proceedings which are brought to assert, declare or determine proprietary or possessory rights, or rights of security, in or over the property, or to obtain authority to dispose of the property. This provision applies not only to rights of ownership, but also to liens and other lesser property rights. In England and Wales, it is likely to apply mainly to originating interpleader proceedings.[14] Jurisdiction over actions for wrongful interference with goods is likely to be adequately regulated by Article 5(3), especially in view of its wide interpretation by the European Court of Justice,[15] and applications for interim relief can be brought before the courts of one part of the United Kingdom under Article 24, even where those courts do not have jurisdiction over the substance of the case.[16] Nonetheless, this provision provides an additional basis for jurisdiction in many such cases.

The wording of Article 5(8) appears to be based on the second paragraph of Article 59,[17] which limits the circumstances in which a Contracting State can undertake to a third state not to recognise judgments given on the basis of exorbitant jurisdictions in other Contracting States.

Article 5A

Proceedings which have as their object a decision of an organ of a company or other legal person or an association of natural or legal persons may, without prejudice to the other provisions of this Title, be brought in the courts of the part of the United Kingdom in which that company, legal person or association has its seat.[18]   **45.09**

General note

This Article concerns proceedings which have as their object the   **45.10**
decisions of the organs of companies and certain other bodies. As between the different Contracting States, such proceedings fall within Article 16(2) of the 1968 Convention and exclusive jurisdiction is assigned to the courts of the Contracting State where the

---

[14] R.S.C., Ord. 17, r 3.
[15] Para. 17.46 above.
[16] s.25(1), paras. 43.03 *et seq.* above.
[17] See para. 33.27 above.
[18] See Art. 16(2) of the 1968 Convention, discussed at paras. 20.27 *et seq.* above.

company or other body has its seat. Within the United Kingdom, though, the rule is more relaxed and such proceedings need not be brought in the particular part of the United Kingdom where the seat is located. What this Article does is to provide a rule of jurisdiction additional to the other jurisdictional rules which might apply to such proceedings and enables them to be brought in the part of the United Kingdom where the company or other body has its seat, even if there would be no other basis for jurisdiction over the proceedings in that part of the United Kingdom.

It is important to note that the definition of "seat" for the purposes of this Article is not the general definition in section 42, but the special definition in section 43.[19] The meaning of "company or other legal person or association of natural or legal persons" has been discussed above.[20]

Article 6

45.11   **A person domiciled in a <u>part of the United Kingdom</u> may, <u>in another part of the United Kingdom</u>, also be sued:**

  (1) **where he is one of a number of defendants, in the courts for the place where any one of them is domiciled;**

  (2) **as a third party in an action on a warranty or guarantee or in any other third party proceedings, in the court seised of the original proceedings, unless these were instituted solely with the object of removing him from the jurisdiction of the court which would be competent in his case;**

  (3) **in a counter-claim arising from the same contract or facts on which the original claim was based, in the court in which the original claim is pending.[21]**

General note

45.12   This Article applies where there are multiple defendants, third-party proceedings or a counterclaim. It reproduces as between the different parts of the United Kingdom the provisions which Article 6 of the 1968 Convention applies as between the different Contracting States. It does so without further modification and requires no additional commentary.

---

[19] See paras. 44.21 *et seq.* above.
[20] Para. 44.13 above.
[21] See Art. 6 of the 1968 Convention, discussed at paras. 17.74 *et seq.* above.

Schedule 4

Article 6A

Where by virtue of this <u>Title</u> a court of a <u>part of the United</u> **45.13**
<u>Kingdom</u> has jurisdiction in actions relating to liability arising
from the use or operation of a ship, that court, or any other court
substituted for this purpose by the internal law of that <u>part</u>, shall
also have jurisdiction over claims for limitation of such liability.[22]

. . . .

General note

This Article applies to actions in Admiralty for the limitation of
liability. It reproduces as between the different parts of the United
Kingdom the provisions which Article 6A of the 1968 Convention
applies as between the different Contracting States. It does so without further modification and requires no additional commentary.

[Section 3 (Articles 7 to 12A)]

The 1968 Convention provides special rules of jurisdiction for **45.14**
matters relating to insurance, but these (rather complex) provisions
are not reproduced in Schedule 4. By a modification to Article 13,[23]
insurance is also excluded from the provisions of Articles 13 to 15,
which are concerned with consumer contracts; as between different
parts of the United Kingdom, therefore, jurisdiction over proceedings relating to insurance is governed by the ordinary regime of
rules in this Schedule.

Section 4

Jurisdiction over consumer contracts

Article 13

In proceedings concerning a contract concluded by a person **45.15**
for a purpose which can be regarded as being outside his trade or
profession, hereinafter called "the consumer," jurisdiction shall
be determined by this Section, without prejudice to the provisions of Articles . . . 5(5) <u>and (8)(b)</u>, if it is:

    (1) a contract for the sale of goods on instalment credit
        terms, or
    (2) a contract for a loan repayable by instalments, or for

---

[22] See Art. 6A of the 1968 Convention, discussed at paras. 17.97 *et seq.* above.
[23] Para. 45.15 below.

any other form of credit, made to finance the sale of goods, or

(3) any other contract for the supply of goods or a contract for the supply of services, and . . . the consumer took in <u>the part of the United Kingdom in which he is domiciled</u> the steps necessary for the conclusion of the contract.

. . . .

This Section shall not apply to contracts of transport <u>or insurance</u>.[24]

General note

45.16   This Article, which relates to consumer contracts, defines the proceedings to which Section 4 (Articles 13 to 15) apply. Reference to Article 4 is omitted from this version of Article 13, because Article 4 is itself omitted from this Schedule. Similarly, the second paragraph of the version of Article 13 in the 1968 Convention is omitted. That paragraph creates a deemed domicile in a Contracting State for a defendant domiciled outside the Contracting States, but with a branch, agency or other establishment in that state.[25] An equivalent provision is not necessary in the context of Schedule 4, which only anyway applies to defendants domiciled in the United Kingdom.[26]

The effect of the reference in the first paragraph to Article 5(8)(*b*) is to enable proceedings to be brought under that provision in the part of the United Kingdom where the movable property is situated, even if the proceedings concern a consumer contract falling within this Article. In practical terms, the most important effect of this modification is that an owner or supplier of goods under a consumer contract can bring proceedings for their repossession in the part of the United Kingdom where the goods are located, even if the defendant consumer is domiciled in another part of the United Kingdom.

Sub-paragraph (3) of the first paragraph contains an important difference from its counterpart in the 1968 Convention. In its present version, contracts falling within this sub-paragraph do not need to have been preceded, in the part of the United Kingdom in which the consumer is domiciled, by a specific invitation addressed to him, or by advertising. It is sufficient to bring a contract for the supply of goods or services within this sub-paragraph if it was entered into by a consumer who took, in the part of the United

---

[24] See Art. 13 of the 1968 Convention, discussed at paras. 19.02 *et seq.* above.
[25] Paras. 19.19 *et seq.* above.
[26] s.16(1)(*b*), para. 41.01 above.

Kingdom in which he is domiciled, the steps necessary for the conclusion of the contract.

As noted above,[27] contracts of insurance are excluded from this Section and fall within the general jurisdictional provisions of Schedule 4.

Article 14

A consumer may bring proceedings against the other party to a **45.17** **contract either in the courts of the <u>part of the United Kingdom</u> in which that party is domiciled or in the courts of the <u>part of the United Kingdom</u> in which he is himself domiciled.**

Proceedings may be brought against a consumer by the other party to the contract only in the courts of the <u>part of the United Kingdom</u> in which the consumer is domiciled.

These provisions shall not affect the right to bring a counterclaim in the court in which, in accordance with this Section, the original claim is pending.[28]

General note

This Article contains jurisdictional rules for proceedings concerning consumer contracts (as defined in Article 13). It reproduces as between the different parts of the United Kingdom the provisions which Article 14 of the 1968 Convention applies as between the different Contracting States. It does so without further modification and requires no additional commentary.

Article 15

The provisions of this Section may be departed from only by **45.18** **an agreement:**

(1) **which is entered into after the dispute has arisen, or**
(2) **which allows the consumer to bring proceedings in courts other than those indicated in this Section, or**
(3) **which is entered into by the consumer and the other party to the contract, both of whom are at the time of the conclusion of the contract domiciled or habitually resident in the same <u>part of the United Kingdom</u> and which confers jurisdiction on the courts of that <u>part</u>, provided that such an agreement is not contrary to the law of that <u>part</u>.[29]**

---

[27] Para. 45.14.
[28] See Art. 14 of the 1968 Convention, discussed at paras. 19.26 *et seq.* above.
[29] See Art. 15 of the 1968 Convention, discussed at paras. 19.35 *et seq.* above.

General note

This Article sets out the conditions under which the provisions of this Section may be departed from by agreement. It reproduces for the purposes of Schedule 4 the provisions which Article 15 of the 1968 Convention applies in the context of the Contracting States. It does so without further modification and requires no additional commentary.

Section 5

Exclusive jurisdiction

Article 16

45.19   The following courts shall have exclusive jurisdiction, regardless of domicile:

(1) in proceedings which have as their object rights *in rem* in, or tenancies of, immovable property, the courts of the <u>part of the United Kingdom</u> in which the property is situated;

(2) in proceedings which have as their object the validity of the constitution, the nullity or the dissolution of companies or other legal persons or associations of natural or legal persons . . . the courts of the <u>part of the United Kingdom</u> in which the company, legal person or association has its seat;

(3) in proceedings which have as their object the validity of entries in public registers, the courts of the <u>part of the United Kingdom</u> in which the register is kept;

.   .   .   .

(5) in proceedings concerned with the enforcement of judgments, the courts of the <u>part of the United Kingdom</u> in which the judgment has been or is to be enforced.[30]

General note

45.20   This Article allocates exclusive jurisdiction over certain proceedings to the courts of the part of the United Kingdom with which their subject-matter is (or is likely to be) most closely connected. Unlike the other jurisdictional provisions of Schedule 4, this Article applies whatever the domicile of the parties.[31]

The omission from paragraph (2) of reference to proceedings

---

[30] See Art. 16 of the 1968 Convention, discussed in chap. 20 above.
[31] s.16(1)(*b*), para. 41.01 above.

which have as their object the decisions of the organs of companies or other legal persons or associations of natural or legal persons is discussed above in connection with Article 5A.[32] Article 16(4) of the 1968 Convention is not reproduced in this version because it covers proceedings concerned with the registration or validity of certain intellectual property rights which are excluded from the scope of Schedule 4.[33]

Section 6

Prorogation of jurisdiction

Article 17

If the parties . . . have agreed that a court or the courts of a **part of the United Kingdom** are to have jurisdiction to settle any disputes which have arisen or which may arise in connection with a particular legal relationship, **and, apart from this Schedule, the agreement would be effective to confer jurisdiction under the law of that part**, that court or those courts shall have . . . jurisdiction . . .   45.21

The court or courts of a **part of the United Kingdom** on which a trust instrument has conferred jurisdiction shall have . . . jurisdiction in any proceedings brought against a settlor, trustee or beneficiary, if relations between these persons or their rights or obligations under the trust are involved.

Agreements or provisions of a trust instrument conferring jurisdiction shall have no legal force if they are contrary to the provisions of Article . . . 15, or if the courts whose jurisdiction they purport to exclude have exclusive jurisdiction by virtue of Article 16.[34]

. . . .

1. General note

Article 17 concerns choice of jurisdiction agreements and is of great practical importance. The present version differs from its counterpart in the 1968 Convention in a number of important respects.   45.22

---

[32] Para. 45.10 above.
[33] ss.16(4) and 17(1); Sched. 5, para. 2.
[34] See Art. 17 of the 1968 Convention, discussed in chap. 21 above.

2. Jurisdiction clauses: non-exclusive jurisdiction

In the context of the 1968 Convention, Article 17 generally confers exclusive jurisdiction on the chosen courts,[35] but the omission of the word "exclusive" in the first and second paragraphs of the present version means that, as between the different parts of the United Kingdom, the courts retain their power to decline jurisdiction in appropriate cases.[36] That applies both to contracts, which fall within the first paragraph, and to trust instruments, covered by the second paragraph.

Nonetheless, because the Convention takes precedence over contrary provisions of national law, it is suggested that a court seised of proceedings pursuant to a choice of jurisdiction agreement which complies with the requirements of Article 17 of the 1968 Convention would not be permitted to decline jurisdiction if the effect of doing so would be altogether to deprive the plaintiff of a forum in the United Kingdom. Similarly, if the choice of jurisdiction agreement specified the jurisdiction of the particular court seised of the proceedings, it is probable that Article 17 of the 1968 Convention is effective to confer specific and exclusive jurisdiction on that court and that, even if there were a more convenient forum elsewhere in the United Kingdom, the court could not decline jurisdiction.

3. Domicile of the parties

The version of the first paragraph of Article 17 in the 1968 Convention contains a requirement that one or more of the parties be domiciled in a Contracting State. This version does not itself contain any such requirement, but Schedule 4 as a whole only applies where the defendant is domiciled in the United Kingdom (except where Article 16 applies, which anyway has precedence over Article 17). If, therefore, the plaintiff is domiciled in the United Kingdom, but the defendant is domiciled elsewhere, the court will apply its own law (including, where appropriate, Article 17 of the 1968 Convention) in deciding whether to accept or decline jurisdiction.

The present version of Article 17 does not reproduce the provision in the 1968 Convention which deals with a choice of jurisdiction made by parties neither of whom is domiciled in a Contracting State and which gives priority of jurisdiction to the chosen court or courts without making that jurisdiction exclusive. The omission of such a provision from Schedule 4 means that, as between the different parts of the United Kingdom, the court will apply its own law (again including, where appropriate, Article 17 of the 1968 Convention) in deciding whether to accept or decline jurisdiction under a

---

[35] There are a number of exceptions to the exclusive jurisdiction provisions of Art. 17: see paras. 21.04–21.05, 21.43–21.50, 21.71–21.72 and 21.80–21.82 above.
[36] See also s.49, para. 44.43 above.

jurisdiction agreement which is otherwise valid but where both parties are domiciled outside the United Kingdom.

4. Validity of the choice of jurisdiction

A substantial point of contrast between this version of Article 17   **45.23**
and its counterpart in the 1968 Convention arises from the fact that
the requirement that the choice of jurisdiction agreement should be
made or evidenced in writing is omitted from this version. That
requirement has been interpreted by the European Court of Justice
in a very specific fashion which has given rise to a number of
detailed requirements for the validity of a choice of jurisdiction
agreement.[37] Similarly, the present version of Article 17 omits the
special rules which apply to cases of international trade or commerce and which would be of limited (if any) application in the context of Schedule 4.

Instead, the present version of Article 17 makes it a condition of
the effectiveness of the choice of jurisdiction agreement that it
should, apart from under this Schedule, be effective pursuant to the
lex fori to confer jurisdiction on the chosen court or courts. In doing
so, it provides a uniform conflicts rule applicable in each part of the
United Kingdom and thereby avoids in this context some of the
problems which may arise under Article 17 of the 1968 Convention.[38]

In the case of a clause in a trust instrument purporting to confer
jurisdiction on a court or the courts of a particular part of the
United Kingdom, no similar conflicts rule is included and the court
seised is free to decide according to its own law (including its own
conflicts rules) whether the clause is effective.

5. Insurance contracts

The reference to Article 12 in the third paragraph of Article 17 is
omitted from the present version because that Article, and the other
provisions relating to insurance in Articles 7 to 12A, are omitted
from Schedule 4.

6. Agreements for the benefit of one party only

The fourth paragraph of Article 17 is omitted from the present
version. In the 1968 Convention, it relaxes the allocation of exclusive jurisdiction in cases where the agreement was concluded for the
benefit of only one of the parties. Because this modified version of
Article 17 does not confer exclusive jurisdiction, such a provision
would be unnecessary in the present context.

---

[37] Paras. 21.52 *et seq.* above.
[38] Paras. 21.32–21.33 above.

Article 18

45.24   Apart from jurisdiction derived from other provisions of this Title, a court of a <u>part of the United Kingdom</u> before whom a defendant enters an appearance shall have jurisdiction. This rule shall not apply where appearance was entered solely to contest the jurisdiction, or where another court has exclusive jurisdiction by virtue of Article 16.[39]

General note

    Under Article 18, a defendant confers jurisdiction on the court by entering an appearance without contesting the jurisdiction,[40] except in cases falling within the exclusive jurisdiction provisions of Article 16. This Article reproduces the provisions of Article 18 of the 1968 Convention with only such modifications as are necessary for its application in the internal context of the United Kingdom and requires no additional commentary.

Section 7

Examination as to jurisdiction and admissibility

Article 19

45.25   Where a court of a <u>part of the United Kingdom</u> is seised of a claim which is principally concerned with a matter over which the courts of another <u>part of the United Kingdom</u> have exclusive jurisdiction by virtue of Article 16, it shall declare of its own motion that it has no jurisdiction.[41]

General note

    This Article concerns the court's duty to decline jurisdiction of its own motion over claims falling within the exclusive jurisdiction of the courts of another part of the United Kingdom pursuant to Article 16. The court's duty to examine its jurisdiction of its own motion is discussed elsewhere[42] but it is a feature of the 1968 Convention which is unfamiliar to common law systems and its performance requires some care. The present version of Article 19 reproduces its counterpart in the 1968 Convention with only such

---

[39] See Art. 18 of the 1968 Convention, discussed at paras. 21.84 *et seq.* above.
[40] In certain circumstances, a plaintiff may be able to start proceedings where the court does not have jurisdiction, in the hope that the defendant will submit to the jurisdiction without protest: see para. 21.90 above.
[41] See Art. 19 of the 1968 Convention, discussed at paras. 22.02 *et seq.* above.
[42] Paras. 22.06–22.07 and 22.15 above.

modifications as are necessary for its application in the internal context of the United Kingdom and requires no additional commentary.

Article 20

Where a defendant domiciled in one <u>part of the United Kingdom</u> is sued in a court of another <u>part of the United Kingdom</u> and does not enter an appearance, the court shall declare of its own motion that it has no jurisdiction unless its jurisdiction is derived from the provisions of this <u>Title</u>.
The Court shall stay the proceedings so long as it is not shown that the defendant has been able to receive the document instituting the proceedings or an equivalent document in sufficient time to enable him to arrange for his defence, or that all necessary steps have been taken to this end.[43]

45.26

· · · · · · · ·

General note

Two duties are imposed on the court by this Article, both of which are central to the scheme of jurisdictional rules established by the 1968 Convention and adopted as between the different parts of the United Kingdom by Schedule 4. The first is the court's duty to examine its jurisdiction of its own motion and, unless the defendant enters an appearance, to decline jurisdiction if it does not have jurisdiction under this Schedule. The second is the court's duty to consider whether service of the proceedings on the defendant has taken place in sufficient time to enable him to arrange for his defence, or that all necessary steps have been taken to this end and, if not, to stay its proceedings. As in the case of Article 19, these duties may be unfamiliar to common law courts and care is required in their performance.

45.27

The present version of Article 20 reproduces the first and second paragraphs of its counterpart in the 1968 Convention with only such modification as is necessary for its application in the internal context of the United Kingdom. It does not reproduce the third paragraph of Article 20 in the 1968 Convention, which replaces the provisions of the second paragraph by those of Article 15 of the Hague Service Convention where that Convention applies between the Contracting States in question. That provision could obviously have no application in the internal context of the United Kingdom.

---

[43] See Art. 20 of the 1968 Convention, discussed at paras. 22.12 *et seq.* above.

[Section 8 (Articles 21 to 23)]

45.28   Articles 21 to 23 of the 1968 Convention,[44] covering *lis pendens* and related actions, are omitted from Schedule 4. They provide a scheme of rules for preventing actions being brought in more than one Contracting State on the same causes of action and between the same parties or in circumstances where the proceedings are so closely related as to give rise to the risk of irreconcilable judgments resulting from separate proceedings.

Within the United Kingdom, the courts anyway have powers to stay proceedings,[45] and the adoption of Articles 21 to 23 in Schedule 4 would merely have duplicated those powers in a more circumscribed form.

Section 9

Provisional, including protective, measures

Article 24

45.29   **Application may be made to the courts of a <u>part of the United Kingdom</u> for such provisional, including protective, measures as may be available under the law of that <u>part</u>, even if, under this <u>Title</u>, the courts of another <u>part of the United Kingdom</u> have jurisdiction as to the substance of the matter.**[46]

General note

This Article concerns the powers of the courts in one part of the United Kingdom to grant provisional, including protective, measures where the courts of another part of the United Kingdom have jurisdiction over the substance of the matter. It reproduces its counterpart in the 1968 Convention with only such modifications as are necessary for its application in the internal context of the United Kingdom. Like its counterpart, this version of Article 24 does not itself create the power to grant interim relief in the absence of substantive proceedings, but section 25 (in the cases of England and Wales and Northern Ireland)[47] and section 27 (in the case of Scotland)[48] expressly create such powers.

An order granting provisional or protective measures made in one part of the United Kingdom is not capable of enforcement in

---

[44] Chap. 23 above.
[45] See s.49, para. 44.40 *et seq.* above.
[46] See Art. 24 of the 1968 Convention, discussed in chap. 24 above, and chap. 7, which discusses interim relief available in England and Wales.
[47] Para. 43.03 above.
[48] Para. 43.14 above.

Schedule 4

another part of the United Kingdom under section 18 and Schedules 6 and 7, unless it is an order for the making of an interim payment.[49]

SCHEDULE 5   Section 17

PROCEEDINGS EXCLUDED FROM SCHEDULE 4

General note on Schedule 5

This Schedule is given effect by section 17 and sets out a number **45.30** of types of proceedings excluded from the provisions in Schedule 4 which allocate jurisdiction over most civil and commercial matters as between the different parts of the United Kingdom.

Proceedings under the Companies Acts

1. Proceedings for the winding up of a company under the 45.31 Insolvency Act 1986 or the Companies Act (Northern Ireland) 1960, or proceedings relating to a company as respects which jurisdiction is conferred on the court having winding up jurisdiction under either of those Acts.†

General note

The only winding-up proceedings which would fall within Schedule 4 are those relating to solvent companies. Winding-up on insolvency is excluded from the 1968 Convention by Article 1[50] and, therefore, from Schedule 4 by section 16(1)(a). This paragraph extends that exclusion to all proceedings relating to winding-up under the Companies Acts.

Patents, trade marks, designs and similar rights

2. Proceedings concerned with the registration or validity of 45.32 patents, trade marks, designs or other similar rights required to be deposited or registered.

---

[49] s.18(5)(*d*), paras. 41.13 and 41.15 above.
† The reference to the Insolvency Act 1986 was substituted for a reference to the Companies Act 1985 by s.439 and Sched. 14 of the Insolvency Act 1986. The reference to the Companies Act 1985 had itself been substituted for a reference to the Companies Act 1948 by the Companies Consolidation (Consequential Provisions) Act 1985.
[50] See paras. 14.26 *et seq.* above.

1109

General note

Jurisdiction over these matters is dealt with by provisions in the various statutes concerned with intellectual property, notably the Patents Act 1977 (section 72), the Trade Marks Act 1938 (sections 32 and 66(1)), the Registered Designs Act 1949 (sections 20 and 45) and the Copyright, Designs and Patterns Act 1988 (sections 115, 149 and 287–289). This paragraph preserves the effect of those provisions. The reference in this paragraph to trade marks includes a reference to service marks.[50a]

Protection of Trading Interests Act 1980

45.33   **3. Proceedings under section 6 of the Protection of Trading Interests Act 1980 (recovery of sums paid or obtained pursuant to a judgment for multiple damages).**

General note

Where an award of multiple damages has been given in another country (normally the United States of America) against a person, a court in the United Kingdom can entertain proceedings by that person for recovery of such part of the award as exceeds the part attributable to compensation. The defendant need not be within the jurisdiction of the court,[51] a position which would have been changed if Schedule 4 had applied to such proceedings.

Appeals, etc., from tribunals

45.34   **4. Proceedings on appeal from, or for review of, decisions of tribunals.**

General note

The jurisdiction of tribunals themselves is not governed by Schedule 4[52] and it would therefore be anomalous if jurisdiction over appeal and review proceedings had been allocated by that Schedule.

Maintenance and similar payments to local and other public authorities

45.35   **5. Proceedings for, or otherwise relating to, an order under any of the following provisions—**
    (a) section 47 or 51 of the Child Care Act 1980, section 80

[50a] Patents, Designs and Marks Act 1986, Sched. 2.
[51] s.6(5) of the Protection of Trading Interests Act 1980. See also, R.S.C., Ord. 11, r. 1(2)(*b*).
[52] Para. 41.05 above.

of the Social Work (Scotland) Act 1968 or section 156 of the Children and Young Persons Act (Northern Ireland) 1968 (contributions in respect of children in care, etc.);

(b) section 49 or 50 of the Child Care Act 1980, section 81 of the Social Work (Scotland) Act 1968 or section 159 of the Children and Young Persons Act (Northern Ireland) 1968 (applications for, or for variation of, affiliation orders in respect of children in care, etc.);

(c) section 43 of the National Assistance Act 1948, section 18 of the Supplementary Benefits Act 1976, section 24 of the Social Security Act 1986, or any enactment applying it in Northern Ireland and corresponding to it, Article 101 of the Health and Personal Social Services (Northern Ireland) Order 1972 or Article 23 of the Supplementary Benefits (Northern Ireland) Order 1977 (recovery of cost of assistance or benefit from person liable to maintain the assisted person);

(d) section 44 of the National Assistance Act 1948, section 19 of the Supplementary Benefits Act 1976, section 25 of the Social Security Act 1986, or any enactment applying it in Northern Ireland and corresponding to it, Article 102 of the Health and Personal Social Services (Northern Ireland) Order 1972 or Article 24 of the Supplementary Benefits (Northern Ireland) Order 1977 (applications for, or for variation of, affiliation orders in respect of children for whom assistance or benefit provided).†

General note

Article 5(2) of Schedule 4[53] enables a maintenance creditor to bring proceedings where she is domiciled, but that provision does not apply to local and public authorities. This paragraph preserves the right of those authorities to bring certain proceedings relating to maintenance and such matters in the part of the United Kingdom where the payment is due.

Proceedings under certain conventions, etc.

6. Proceedings brought in any court in pursuance of—
       45.36
   (a) any statutory provision which, in the case of any convention to which Article 57 applies (conventions relating to specific matters which override the general rules in

---

† Paras. 5(c) and 5(d) are printed as amended by the Social Security Act 1986, Sched. 10.
[53] Para. 45.06 above.

the 1968 Convention), implements the convention or makes provision with respect to jurisdiction in any field to which the convention relates; and

(b) any rule of law so far as it has the effect of implementing any such convention.

General note

This paragraph has a similar effect as between the different parts of the United Kingdom as Article 57 of the 1968 Convention has as between the different Contracting States. That Article[54] provides that the 1968 Convention shall not affect any conventions to which the Contracting States are or will be parties and which, in relation to particular matters, govern jurisdiction (or the recognition or enforcement of judgments). While a particular part of the United Kingdom cannot itself be a party to such a convention, certain of the statutes implementing such conventions contain provisions as to jurisdiction which this paragraph has the effect of preserving.[55]

Certain Admiralty proceedings in Scotland

45.37   **7. Proceedings in Scotland in an Admiralty cause where the jurisdiction of the Court of Session or, as the case may be, of the sheriff is based on arrestment *in rem* or *ad fundandam jurisdictionem* of a ship, cargo or freight.**

General note

This paragraph preserves the arrest jurisdiction in an Admiralty cause in Scotland. The equivalent jurisdiction in England and Wales is protected by paragraph 6(*a*) above.

Register of aircraft mortgages

45.38   **8. Proceedings for the rectification of the register of aircraft mortgages kept by the Civil Aviation Authority.**

General note

Proceedings for the rectification of the register of aircraft mortgages would, but for this paragraph, fall within Article 16(3) of Schedule 4 and, because the register is kept in England, would have to be brought in England.

---

[54] Para. 33.06 above.

[55] *e.g.* ss.20 to 24 of the Supreme Court Act 1981 implement for England and Wales the Brussels Convention of May 10, 1952 relating to the Arrest of Seagoing Ships.

Schedule 5

Continental Shelf Act 1964

**9. Proceedings brought in any court in pursuance of an order   45.39
under section 23 of the Oil and Gas (Enterprise) Act 1982.†**

General note

It is not clear whether Article 5, either of the 1968 Convention or
of Schedule 4 would enable proceedings to be brought in the courts
for a particular place if they concerned an act or omission taking
place on an installation on the continental shelf.[56] This paragraph
avoids that anomaly by excluding such proceedings from Schedule
4 and preserving the position under the Oil and Gas Enterprise Act
1982,[57] thereby providing a forum for such proceedings whether
they are purely internal to the United Kingdom or fall within the
1968 Convention.

Proceedings concerning financial services agencies

**10. Such proceedings as are mentioned in Section 188 of the   45.40
Financial Services Act 1986.**

General note

This paragraph refers to proceedings arising out of any act or
omission of the Securities and Investments Board or the Stock
Exchange in the discharge of their duties under the Financial Services Act 1986.

---

† The present wording was substituted for a reference to s.3 of the Continental
   Shelf Act 1964, by Sched. 3, para. 42 of the Oil and Gas (Enterprise) Act 1982.
   The italicised heading has, confusingly, not been changed.
[56] See para. 1.03 n.18.
[57] Jurisdiction is allocated by the Civil Jurisdiction (Offshore Activities) Order
   1987, (S.I. 1987 No. 2197).

CHAPTER 46

CIVIL JURISDICTION AND JUDGMENTS ACT 1982 SCHEDULES 6 AND 7—ENFORCEMENT OF JUDGMENTS BETWEEN DIFFERENT PARTS OF THE UNITED KINGDOM

2

1114

SCHEDULE 6   Section 18

Enforcement of U.K. Judgments (Money Provisions)

General note on Schedule 6

This Schedule is given effect by section 18 and reference should **46.01** be made to the commentary on that section.[1] The enforcement of judgments between different parts of the United Kingdom is discussed in Chapter 10.[2] The Schedule contains a code of rules for the enforcement in each part of the United Kingdom of money provisions in judgments given in either of the other parts (non-money provisions are covered by Schedule 7).

Paragraph 1 contains definitions, paragraphs 2 to 4 concern the issue of certificates in the part of the United Kingdom where the judgment was given, for the purposes of enforcing its money provisions in another part (the "exporting" of the judgment), and paragraphs 5 to 8 cover the registration of the certificate in that other part (the "importing" of the judgment) as well as governing the effect of the registration and making provision for costs and interest. Paragraphs 9 and 10 govern the staying of enforcement and setting aside of the registration.

The provisions of the Schedule are supplemented by rules of court in each part of the United Kingdom. Any judgment which falls within section 18 may be "exported" to another part of the United Kingdom, but the registration of a certificate on its "importation" may only occur in the superior court of that other part. It is only in the superior courts, therefore, that the rules of court govern the registration procedure.

Preliminary

1. In this Schedule— ·   **46.02**
"**judgment**" means any judgment to which section 18 applies and references to the giving of a judgment shall be construed accordingly;
"**money provision**" means a provision for the payment of one or more sums of money;
"**prescribed**" means prescribed by rules of court.

---

[1] Para. 41.13 above.
[2] Paras. 10.63 *et seq.* above.

General note

The judgments to which section 18 applies are defined in sections 18(2) to 18(7).[3] A number of types of civil judgment are excluded, notably most maintenance orders and provisional measures, and judgments in bankruptcy and winding-up as well as the obtaining of title for the administration of an estate.

Although the definition does not say so expressly, the term "money provision" probably only applies to provisions which order the payment of a sum or sums of money which have been precisely ascertained or are capable of ascertainment by calculation. That was the case at common law[4] and it is implicit in the requirement in paragraph 4(1)(*a*) that the certificate should state the sum or aggregate of the sums payable under the money provisions, and particulars sufficient to enable interest on the debt to be precisely calculated.

Certificates in respect of judgments

46.03   2.—(1) Any interested party who wishes to secure the enforcement in another part of the United Kingdom of any money provisions contained in a judgment may apply for a certificate under this Schedule.

(2) The application shall be made in the prescribed manner to the proper officer of the original court, that is to say—

  (a) in relation to a judgment within paragraph (a) of the definition of "judgment" in section 18(2), the court by which the judgment or order was given or made;

  (b) in relation to a judgment within paragraph (b) of that definition, the court in which the judgment or order is entered;

  (c) in relation to a judgment within paragraph (c) of that definition, the court in whose books the document is registered;

  (d) in relation to a judgment within paragraph (d) of that definition, the tribunal by which the award or order was made;

  (e) in relation to a judgment within paragraph (e) of that definition, the court which gave the judgment or made the order by virtue of which the award has become enforceable as mentioned in that paragraph.

---

[3] See paras. 41.16 to 41.26 above.
[4] *Beatty* v. *Beatty* [1924] 1 K.B. 807.

General note

Where a certificate is required in respect of any money provisions in a judgment, the application is made to the "original court"—*i.e.* to the court where the judgment was given or entered in the first place. In the case of judgments entered in the High Court, the application is made to the office where the judgment is entered— *i.e.* the Central Office or appropriate District Registry. The application is made by producing the prescribed form,[5] together with an affidavit, made by the party entitled to enforce the judgment, setting out certain prescribed matters.[6] A similar practice obtains in the county court.[7]

Any "interested party" may apply for a certificate. This expression is not defined, but it is used in Articles 26 and 31 of the 1968 Convention[8] as well as in paragraph 2(1) of Schedule 7.[9] It includes the successors and assigns of the person in whose favour the judgment was originally given.

3. A certificate shall not be issued under this Schedule in respect of a judgment unless under the law of the part of the United Kingdom in which the judgment was given—   **46.04**
    (a) either—
       (i) the time for bringing an appeal against the judgment has expired, no such appeal having been brought within that time; or
      (ii) such an appeal having been brought within that time, that appeal has been finally disposed of; and
    (b) enforcement of the judgment is not for the time being stayed or suspended, and the time available for its enforcement has not expired.

General note

The effect of this paragraph is to ensure that a judgment given in one part of the United Kingdom is not enforceable by registration in another part at a time when it is not enforceable where it was given, or while it could still be reversed on appeal. An applicant has to verify in his affidavit that the requirements of this paragraph are met.[10]

Sub-paragraph (a). The "time for bringing an appeal" probably means the initial period prescribed by the rules during which the

---

[5] R.S.C., Appendix A, Form 111, *Supreme Court Practice*, para. [112].
[6] R.S.C., Ord. 71, r. 37(3).
[7] C.C.R., Ord. 35, r. 5.
[8] See paras. 27.05–27.07 and 28.07 above.
[9] Para. 46.15 below.
[10] R.S.C., Ord. 71, r. 37(3)(*b*); C.C.R., Ord. 35, r. 5(2)(*b*).

applicant may appeal as of right, and any additional period which may have been granted by extension before the application has been made for a certificate to be issued. The detailed application of the provision will need to be developed by the courts, but it should be liberally interpreted, it is suggested, so as to prevent the issue of a certificate at a time when the appeal may be brought without the appellant having to take further preliminary steps. So, for example, if leave to appeal is required and has not been applied for, it would seem that the appellant does not have any "time for bringing an appeal." Similarly, if leave has been applied for to the lower court and refused, the time could be said to have expired. On the other hand, it may be that the time would not be taken to have expired while the appellant still had an opportunity to seek leave to appeal without having to ask for an extension of time.[11] An application for leave in those circumstances might itself count as the bringing of an appeal for the purposes of this paragraph.

Sub-paragraph (b). In England and Wales, enforcement of a judgment is not automatically stayed when an appeal is lodged and a judgment under appeal in respect of which enforcement has not been stayed can be the subject of enforcement in other Contracting States under Title III of the 1968 Convention (although the enforcement proceedings may be stayed under Article 38[12] on the ground that an appeal has been lodged in the country of origin). By contrast with those provisions, though, this paragraph does not permit the enforcement of a judgment in the other parts of the United Kingdom in these circumstances.

As a matter of English law, if a judgment was given or entered more than six years previously, the leave of the court is required before execution may issue upon it.[13] That period, and any extension granted under the rules before the application for a certificate is made, is the "time available" for the execution of the judgment. The position of a certificate issued before, but registered after, the expiry of the time available for the enforcement of the judgment is discussed below under paragraph 6.

46.05　　**4.—(1) Subject to paragraph 3, on an application under paragraph 2 the proper officer shall issue to the applicant a certificate in the prescribed form—**

　　(a) stating the sum or the aggregate of the sums (including

---

[11] *e.g.* on an appeal by leave to the Court of Appeal, an application for leave may be made to the Court of Appeal within seven days of a refusal of leave by the court below: R.S.C., Ord. 59, r. 14(3).

[12] Para. 28.43 above.

[13] R.S.C., Ord. 46, r. 2(1)(*a*); C.C.R., Ord. 26, r. 5(1)(*a*). Also, an action on a judgment becomes statute-barred after six years: Limitation Act 1980, s.24(1).

any costs or expenses) payable under the money provisions contained in the judgment, the rate of interest, if
any, payable thereon and the date or time from which
any such interest began to accrue;

(b) stating that the conditions specified in paragraph 3(a)
and (b) are satisfied in relation to the judgment; and

(c) containing such other particulars as may be prescribed.

(2) More than one certificate may be issued under this Schedule (simultaneously or at different times) in respect of the same
judgment.

General note

The form of certificate in the High Court is prescribed.[14] Sub-
paragraph (2) refers to the issue of more than one certificate: their
simultaneous issue means that registration may occur in both other
parts of the United Kingdom at the same time, their issue at different times takes account of the fact that a certificate can only be
registered within six months of its issue.

Registration of certificates

5.—(1) Where a certificate has been issued under this Sched-   **46.06**
ule in any part of the United Kingdom, any interested party may,
within six months from the date of its issue, apply in the prescribed manner to the proper officer of the superior court in any
other part of the United Kingdom for the certificate to be registered in that court.

(2) In this paragraph "superior court" means, in relation to
England and Wales or Northern Ireland, the High Court and, in
relation to Scotland, the Court of Session.

(3) Where an application is duly made under this paragraph to
the proper officer of a superior court, he shall register the certificate in that court in the prescribed manner.

General note

The application must be made within six months of the issue of
the certificate and it may be made by any "interested party."[15] It
may only be made to the superior court (as defined in sub-
paragraph (2)) in each part of the United Kingdom, and it is primarily in that court, therefore, that judgments given in other parts of the
United Kingdom are to be enforced, whatever the court which gave

---

[14] R.S.C., Appendix A, Form 111; *Supreme Court Practice*, para. [112].
[15] See para. 46.03, n. 8 above.

the original judgment. Nonetheless, a certificate registered in the High Court may be enforced in the county court under section 105(1) of the County Courts Act 1984.

In England and Wales, the application to register the certificate must be made to the Central Office of the High Court[16] by producing the original certificate and a copy of it, certified by the applicant's solicitor to be a true copy.[17]

General effect of registration

46.07   **6.—(1) A certificate registered under this Schedule shall, for the purposes of its enforcement, be of the same force and effect, the registering court shall have in relation to its enforcement the same powers, and proceedings for or with respect to its enforcement may be taken, as if the certificate had been a judgment originally given in the registering court and had (where relevant) been entered.**

(2) Sub-paragraph (1) is subject to the following provisions of this Schedule and to any provision made by rules of court as to the manner in which and the conditions subject to which a certificate registered under this Schedule may be enforced.

General note

This paragraph equates a certificate, once it is registered, with a judgment of the registering court. It is subject to the following provisions of the Schedule (notably the provisions as to interest in paragraph 8) but is otherwise comprehensive. In the context of the enforcement of money provisions as between different parts of the United Kingdom, it mirrors the provisions of section 4(3),[18] which assimilate the position of judgments given in other Contracting States to that of judgments given in the United Kingdom.

An interesting question is whether the certificate takes effect as a judgment of the registering court given or entered on the date when it was given or entered in the original court or as one given or entered on the date of its registration. The wording of the paragraph, if anything, tends to favour the former interpretation and it is noticeable that it differs from the wording of earlier Acts, which

---

[16] R.S.C., Ord. 71, r. 37(2).
[17] R.S.C., Ord. 71, r. 37(1). The Rules are silent as to how a litigant in person should meet this requirement.
[18] See para. 40.10 above.

expressly adopt the latter solution.[19] It is also noticeable that this Schedule itself specifies the date of registration in a different context, namely interest on the costs of registration (paragraph 8(3)).

Treating a certificate as a judgment given in the registering court **46.08** on its original date rather than the date of its registration is also more consistent, it is suggested, with the scheme of the Act. The regime under this Schedule is modelled on that in section 4 for enforcing judgments given in other Contracting States in accordance with the 1968 Convention. Although in that context no order for the enforcement of a foreign judgment may be made unless the judgment is enforceable in its country of origin, when the order for its enforcement is made under Article 31[20] the foreign judgment is automatically entitled to recognition in the other Contracting States without any special procedure being required.[21] A similar rule is implicit in section 19 of this Act.[22] It would be anomalous for a judgment to be *recognised* from the date when it was given, but to be treated as having been given on a different date for the purposes of its enforcement.

If that interpretation is correct, it has a specific and practical effect. It is a condition of the issue of a certificate that the judgment should then be enforceable (paragraph 3(*b*)), but that is not a condition for its registration in another part of the United Kingdom. In the absence of any further conditions imposed by rules of court under section 48(2) and sub-paragraph (2) of this paragraph, there is no provision for setting aside the registration or staying its execution solely on the ground that the time available for the enforcement of the judgment in the part of the United Kingdom where it was originally given has since expired. If the certificate is treated as a judgment which was given in the registering court on the date when it was originally given, the expiry of its enforceability in the part of the United Kingdom in which it is registered will then be regulated by the law of the registering court rather than the court of origin. So, for example, a certificate of money provisions in a Scottish judgment registered in the High Court in England could not be enforced there without leave of the court more than six years after it was given,[23] whether or not its enforceability had expired in Scotland and whenever it had been registered in the High Court.

---

[19] Judgments Extension Act 1868, ss.1, 2 and 3; Administration of Justice Act 1920, s.9(3)(*a*); Foreign Judgments (Reciprocal Enforcement) Act 1933, s.2(2). The exception is the Inferior Courts Judgments Extension Act 1882 (s.5), which is not specific on the point.
[20] Para. 28.01 above.
[21] Art. 26, para. 27.01 above.
[22] See para. 41.28 above.
[23] R.S.C., Ord. 46, r. 2(1)(*a*).

Costs or expenses

46.09   **7. Where a certificate is registered under this Schedule, the reasonable costs or expenses of and incidental to the obtaining of the certificate and its registration shall be recoverable as if they were costs or expenses stated in the certificate to be payable under a money provision contained in the original judgment.**

General note

This paragraph enables the costs of obtaining the certificate in one part of the United Kingdom and its registration in another part to be added to the sum payable under the certificate.[24] Interest on those costs runs as if the order had been made on the date of registration.[25]

Interest

46.10   **8.—(1) Subject to any provision made under sub-paragraph (2), the debt resulting, apart from paragraph 7, from the registration of the certificate shall carry interest at the rate, if any, stated in the certificate from the date or time so stated.**

(2) Provision may be made by rules of court as to the manner in which and the periods by reference to which any interest payable by virtue of sub-paragraph (1) is to be calculated and paid, including provision for such interest to cease to accrue as from a prescribed date.

(3) All such sums as are recoverable by virtue of paragraph 7 carry interest as if they were the subject of an order for costs or expenses made by the registering court on the date of registration of the certificate.

(4) Except as provided by this paragraph sums payable by virtue of the registration of a certificate under this Schedule shall not carry interest.

General note

This paragraph provides the sole means by which money due under a certificate registered under this Schedule carries interest (sub-paragraph (4)). Its provisions (similar to those of section 7)[26] effectively extend to the registered certificate the provisions as to interest which apply under the law of the original court. They

---

[24] See R.S.C., Ord. 62, App. 3, Pt. III, para. 2.
[25] Para. 8(3) below.
[26] Para. 40.20 above.

enable interest to be calculated by reference to the date upon which interest started to accrue in that court, whatever the date of registration. But the interest will only be recoverable if it is stated in the certificate (sub-paragraphs (1) and (4)). It is interest on the judgment debt[27] to which this paragraph applies, not any interest on a principal debt or damages which may have been included in the judgment debt.[28] Interest on the costs added to the judgment debt under paragraph 7, by contrast, runs from the date of registration and is calculated according to the law of the registering court.[29]

Stay or sisting of enforcement in certain cases

9. Where a certificate in respect of a judgment has been regis-   46.11
**tered under this Schedule, the registering court may, if it is satis-
fied that any person against whom it is sought to enforce the
certificate is entitled and intends to apply under the law of the
part of the United Kingdom in which the judgment was given for
any remedy which would result in the setting aside or quashing of
the judgment, stay (or, in Scotland, sist) proceedings for the
enforcement of the certificate, on such terms as it thinks fit, for
such period as appears to the court to be reasonably sufficient to
enable the application to be disposed of.**

General note

In certain circumstances there may be good reason to stay the execution of a certificate which has been validly issued under paragraph 4 and registered under paragraph 5. The registering court may anyway have power to stay execution,[30] which it may exercise in relation to the certificate by reason of paragraph 6(1), but this paragraph gives a specific and additional power to the registering court to stay execution.

The exercise of the power is discretionary and the court may impose terms. The circumstances in which a judgment debtor might apply for a stay under this paragraph are likely to be rare, but they would include cases in which he proposes to apply for leave to appeal out of time on the basis of new evidence (of fraud, for example) which would or might lead to the original judgment being set aside or quashed. The power to stay execution under this para-

---

[27] *e.g.* in England and Wales, under s.17 of the Judgments Act 1838: see *Supreme Court Practice*, para. 42/1/12.
[28] *Cf.* para. 40.22 above.
[29] Contrast s.7(3) (para. 40.20 above) in the case of a judgment registered under s.4. See *Hunt* v. *R. M. Douglas (Roofing) Ltd.* [1988] 3 W.L.R. 975, H.L.
[30] *e.g.* in England and Wales, under R.S.C., Ord. 47, r. 1.

graph should not be confused with the duty or power to set aside registration under paragraph 10.

Cases in which registration of a certificate must or may be set aside

46.12   **10. Where a certificate has been registered under this Schedule, the registering court—**
>   (a) **shall set aside the registration if, on an application made by any interested party, it is satisfied that the registration was contrary to the provisions of this Schedule;**
>   (b) **may set aside the registration if, on an application so made, it is satisfied that the matter in dispute in the proceedings in which the judgment in question was given had previously been the subject of a judgment by another court or tribunal having jurisdiction in the matter.**

General note

This paragraph sets out two grounds for the setting aside of the registration. The Act does not envisage any other circumstances in which the registration, as distinct from the execution of a registered certificate, may be set aside.

The first ground relates to cases in which the registration should not have been granted in the first place, because it was contrary to the provisions of this Schedule, for example, because the application was made more than six months after the certificate was issued. It is not clear whether this paragraph gives the registering court the power to review the original court's decision to grant the certificate, for instance, on the ground that it was in respect of a judgment which did not fall with section 18, or that it was issued before the time for bringing an appeal had expired. If the ground is established, the court is required to set aside the registration.

The second ground enables the registering court to set aside the registration if the issue in the original proceedings had been the subject of a judgment by another court or tribunal which the registering court recognises as having jurisdiction in the matter (whether under this Act, or under the 1968 Convention, or under its other rules of private international law). This ground corresponds with the grounds in Articles 27(3) and (5) of the 1968 Convention for refusing recognition to a judgment given in another Contracting State,[31] although, unlike those provisions, this ground is discretionary.

---

[31] Paras. 27.43 and 27.59 above.

SCHEDULE 7   Section 18

ENFORCEMENT OF U.K. JUDGMENTS (NON-MONEY PROVISIONS)

General note on Schedule 7

Parts of the commentary on this Schedule repeat the commentary   **46.13**
on Schedule 6, but appear again here for ease of reference.

Like Schedule 6, this Schedule is given effect by section 18 and
reference should be made to the commentary on that section.[32] The
enforcement of judgments between different parts of the United
Kingdom is discussed in Chapter 10.[33] The Schedule contains a
code of rules for the enforcement in each part of the United Kingdom of non-money provisions in judgments given in either of the
other parts (money provisions are covered by Schedule 6).

In many respects, the provisions of this Schedule are the same as,
or similar to, those relating to money provisions in Schedule 6, but
there are a number of important differences. Principally, it should
be noted that a certified copy of the judgment itself is registered,
including any provisions in it which fall outside section 18, and the
application for registration is made not to an officer of the court,
but to the court itself.

Where a judgment containing non-money provisions also contains one or more money provisions (which will usually be the case,
even if only an order for costs), and it is wished to enforce both
types of provision, separate applications under the two Schedules
will have to be made.

Paragraph 1 contains definitions, paragraphs 2 to 4 concern the
issue of certificates and certified copies of judgments in the part of
the United Kingdom where the judgment was given, for the purposes of enforcing its non-money provisions in another part (the
"exporting" of the judgment), and paragraphs 5 to 7 cover the
registration of the judgment in that other part (the "importing" of
the judgment) as well as governing the effect of the registration and
making provision for costs. Paragraphs 8 and 9 govern the staying
of enforcement and setting aside of the registration.

The provisions of the Schedule are supplemented by rules of
court in each part of the United Kingdom. Any judgment which
falls within section 18 may be "exported" to another part of the
United Kingdom, but the registration of a certificate on its
"importation" may only occur in the superior court of that other

---

[32] Paras. 41.13 *et seq.* above.
[33] Paras. 10.63 *et seq.* above.

part. It is only in the superior courts, therefore, that the rules of court govern the registration procedure.

Preliminary

46.14   **1. In this Schedule—**
"**judgment**" **means any judgment to which section 18 applies and references to the giving of a judgment shall be construed accordingly;**
"**non-money provision**" **means a provision for any relief not requiring payment of a sum of money;**
"**prescribed**" **means prescribed by rules of court.**

General note

The judgments to which section 18 applies are defined in sections 18(2) to 18(7).[34] A number of types of civil judgment are excluded, notably, in the context of non-money provisions, most provisional measures, and judgments in bankruptcy, winding-up and the obtaining of title for the administration of an estate, as well as provisions concerning the status or legal capacity of an individual or the management of the affairs of a person under a disability.

The term "non-money provision" probably covers all provisions other than money provisions contained in a judgment and falling within section 18.[35] While a non-money provision cannot be one requiring the payment of a sum of money, it may nonetheless concern money or other financial matters—as, for example, an injunction restraining payment or a mandatory order for the delivery up of securities.

Where an order requires the payment of money in a sum which is not ascertained or capable of calculation at the date of the judgment, it is probably not a money provision falling within Schedule 6[36] and it probably is a non-money provision falling within this Schedule. It would be a provision which required the payment of money, but not of "a sum" of money. Examples might be an order for specific performance of a contract to sell goods at auction and to pay the proceeds to the plaintiff, or an order that securities held by trustees be realised and the fund paid to the beneficiaries.

On the other hand, many orders of a financial nature which nonetheless do not require the payment of a sum of money will be excluded from this Schedule because they are provisional measures[37] or otherwise fall outside section 18.

---

[34] Paras. 41.16 to 41.26 above.
[35] See para. 41.15 above.
[36] Para. 46.02 above.
[37] Para. 41.25 above.

Schedule 7

Certified copies of judgments

2.—(1) Any interested party who wishes to secure the enforce- 46.15
ment in another part of the United Kingdom of any non-money
provisions contained in a judgment may apply for a certified copy
of the judgment.

(2) The application shall be made in the prescribed manner to
the proper officer of the original court, that is to say—

(a) in relation to a judgment within paragraph (a) of the
definition of "judgment" in section 18(2), the court by
which the judgment or order was given or made;

(b) in relation to a judgment within paragraph (b) of that
definition, the court in which the judgment or order is
entered;

(c) in relation to a judgment within paragraph (c) of that
definition, the court in whose books the documents is
registered;

(d) in relation to a judgment within paragraph (d) of that
definition, the tribunal by which the award or order was
made;

(e) in relation to a judgment within paragraph (e) of that
definition, the court which gave the judgment or made
the order by virtue of which the award has become
enforceable as mentioned in that paragraph.

General note

Where a certified copy of any judgment is required for the purpose of enforcing any money provisions in it in another part of the
United Kingdom, the application is made to the "original court"—
i.e. to the court where the judgment was given or entered in the first
place. The application is made in the manner prescribed by rules of
court to the "proper officer," but in the case of judgments entered
in the High Court, the rules provide for the application to be made
to the court itself by way of an *ex parte* application on affidavit.[38] In
the High Court, in the normal course of events, the application
should be made to the Practice Master (or District Registrar)[39]
who, provided the application is duly made, must issue the copy
judgment and appropriate certificate.[40] The affidavit must comply
with Order 71, rule 37(3), subject only to such modifications as are
necessary to take account of the fact that the application is in

---

[38] R.S.C., Ord. 71, r. 38(5). This contrasts with the practice under Sched. 6 in
respect of money judgments: para. 46.03 above.
[39] R.S.C., Ord. 32, r. 11 and 23; *cf.* Ord. 71, r. 1.
[40] Para. 4(1).

respect of non-money provisions rather than money provisions.[41] A similar practice obtains in the county court.[42]

Any "interested party" may apply for a certificate. This expression is not defined, but it is used in Articles 26 and 31 of the 1968 Convention[43] as well as in paragraph 2(1) of Schedule 6. It includes the successors and assigns of the person in whose favour the judgment was originally given.

46.16   **3. A certified copy of a judgment shall not be issued under this Schedule in respect of a judgment unless under the law of the part of the United Kingdom in which the judgment was given—**

    (a) either—
        (i) the time for bringing an appeal against the judgment has expired, no such appeal having been brought within that time; or
        (ii) such an appeal having been brought within that time, that appeal has been finally disposed of; and
    (b) enforcement of the judgment is not for the time being stayed or suspended, and the time available for its enforcement has not expired.

General note

Apart from substituting a reference to a certified copy of a judgment for a reference to a certificate, the paragraph is in the same terms as paragraph 3 of Schedule 6 and reference should be made to the commentary on that paragraph.[44]

The effect of this paragraph is to ensure that a judgment given in one part of the United Kingdom is not enforceable by registration in another part at a time when it is not enforceable where it was given, or while it could still be reversed on appeal. An applicant has to verify in his affidavit that the requirements of this paragraph are met.[45]

46.17   **4.—(1) Subject to paragraph 3, on an application under paragraph 2 the proper officer shall issue to the applicant—**

    (a) a certified copy of the judgment (including any money provisions or excepted provisions which it may contain); and
    (b) a certificate stating that the conditions specified in para-

---

[41] R.S.C., Ord. 71, r. 38(6). This sub-rule applies the provisions of Ord. 71, r. 37(3) only to the affidavit, but it would be good practice (although not expressly required by the rules) for the applicant to produce to the Master a form of certificate in Form 112.

[42] C.C.R., Ord. 35, r. 6.

[43] See paras. 27.05–27.07 and 28.07 above.

[44] Para. 46.04 above.

[45] R.S.C., Ord. 71, rr. 37(3)(*b*) and 38(6); C.C.R., Ord. 35, rr. 5(2)(*b*) and 6(2).

graph 3(a) and (b) are satisfied in relation to the judgment.

(2) In sub-paragraph (1)(a) "excepted provision" means any provision of a judgment which is excepted from the application of section 18 by subsection (5) of that section.

(3) There may be issued under this Schedule (simultaneously or at different times)—
   (a) more than one certified copy of the same judgment; and
   (b) more than one certificate in respect of the same judgment.

General note

The court will issue a certified copy of the judgment and a certificate under sub-paragraph (1)(*b*). In the High Court, the copy judgment will be a sealed office copy and the certificate will be in a prescribed form.[46] A similar practice obtains in the county court.[47]

Sub-paragraph (3) refers to the issue of more than one copy judgment and certificate: their simultaneous issue means that registration may occur in both other parts of the United Kingdom at the same time, their issue at different times enables the judgment to be registered in different parts of the United Kingdom at different times and takes account of the fact that the judgment may only be registered within a limited period after the issue of the certificate under sub-paragraph (1)(*b*).[48]

Registration of certificates

5.—(1) Where a certified copy of a judgment has been issued under this Schedule in any part of the United Kingdom, any interested party may apply in the prescribed manner to the superior court in any other part of the United Kingdom for the judgment to be registered in that court. **46.18**

(2) In this paragraph "superior court" means, in relation to England and Wales or Northern Ireland, the High Court and, in relation to Scotland, the Court of Session.

(3) An application under this paragraph for the registration of a judgment must be accompanied by—
   (a) a certified copy of the judgment issued under this Schedule; and
   (b) a certificate issued under paragraph 4(1)(b) in respect of

---

[46] R.S.C., Ord. 71, r. 38(7); R.S.C. Appendix A, Form 112, *Supreme Court Practice*, para. [113].
[47] C.C.R., Ord. 35, r. 6(3).
[48] Para. 5(3)(*b*) below.

the judgment not more than six months before the date of the application.

(4) Subject to sub-paragraph (5), where an application under this paragraph is duly made to a superior court, the court shall order the whole of the judgment as set out in the certified copy to be registered in that court in the prescribed manner.

(5) A judgment shall not be registered under this Schedule by the superior court in any part of the United Kingdom if compliance with the non-money provisions would involve breach of the law of that part of the United Kingdom.

General note

The application for registration of the judgment must be made within six months of the issue of the certificate and may be made by any "interested party."[49] It may only be made to the superior court (as defined in sub-paragraph (2)) in each part of the United Kingdom, and it is primarily in that court, therefore, that judgments given in other parts of the United Kingdom are to be enforced, whatever the court which gave the original judgment. Nonetheless, a judgment registered in the High Court may be enforced in the county court under section 105(1) of the County Courts Act 1984.

The application to register the judgment is made to the court itself, rather than to its proper officer,[50] and in England and Wales this application should normally be made *ex parte* to the Practice Master[51] in the first instance, although he may direct an originating summons to be issued,[52] when the certified copy of the judgment should be produced, together with the certificate issued under paragraph 4(1)(b).[53]

The court will have to consider the judgment in order to satisfy itself that compliance with the non-money provisions would not involve a breach of the law of the part of the United Kingdom in which it is sought to register the judgment: sub-paragraph (5). The fact that a non-money provision orders a person to do or refrain from doing something which the registering court would not have had power to order if the proceedings had originally been brought in that court ought not, it is suggested, to be regarded as bringing the judgment within sub-paragraph (5). It is only if compliance would involve an actual contravention of the law that registration

[49] See para. 46.15, n. 43 above.
[50] *Cf.* para. 2 of this Schedule.
[51] *Cf. Supreme Court Practice*, para. 71/2/1.
[52] R.S.C., Ord. 71, r. 38(1), Ord. 71, rr. 2(2) and 2(3). The summons should be in Form 10 in Appendix A, *Supreme Court Practice*, para. [4].
[53] Para. 5(3)(b); R.S.C., Ord. 71, r. 38(2).

ought to be refused.[54] If the judgment does not fall within sub-paragraph (5), and the application is otherwise duly made, the court is required to order the registration of the whole judgment.[55]

General effect of registration

6.—(1) The non-money provisions in a judgment registered under this Schedule shall, for the purposes of their enforcement, be of the same force and effect, the registering court shall have in relation to their enforcement the same powers, and proceedings for or with respect to their enforcement may be taken, as if the judgment containing them had been originally given in the registering court and had (where relevant) been entered.   **46.19**

(2) Sub-paragraph (1) is subject to the following provisions of this Schedule and to any provision made by rules of court as to the manner in which and the conditions subject to which the non-money provisions contained in the judgment registered under this Schedule may be enforced.

General note

Once a judgment is registered under this Schedule, its non-money provisions are equated by this paragraph with a judgment of the registering court, subject to the following provisions of the Schedule. In the context of the enforcement of non-money provisions as between different parts of the United Kingdom, it mirrors the provisions of section 4(3), which assimilates the position of judgments given in other Contracting States to that of judgments given in the United Kingdom.[56]

Although the whole judgment is registered, it is only in relation to the non-money provisions that the registered judgment is equated with a judgment of the registering court. If there are any money provisions[57] in the judgment, they may be enforced under Schedule 6 and if there are any excepted provisions,[58] they are to be ignored for the purposes of enforcement under these Schedules.

The question of whether the non-money provisions in a registered judgment take effect as if it had been a judgment of the

---

[54] *Cf.* the position under Art. 27(1) of the 1968 Convention, paras. 27.13 *et seq.* above.

[55] Sub-para. (4). Although the money provisions and excepted provisions (if any) of the judgment will be included in the registration, they will not be capable of enforcement under this Schedule: para. 6.

[56] See para. 40.10 above.

[57] "Money provision" is defined in Sched. 6, para. 1: para. 46.02 above; "non-money provision" is defined by para. 1 of this Schedule: para. 46.14 above.

[58] See para. 4(2), para. 46.17 above.

registering court first given or entered on the date of its registration, or whether they take effect as if from some earlier date, is not entirely clear. It is discussed in relation to certificates of money provisions,[59] and the same considerations apply to non-money provisions.

Costs or expenses

46.20   **7.—(1) Where a judgment is registered under this Schedule, the reasonable costs or expenses of and incidental to—**

>   **(a) the obtaining of the certified copy of the judgment and of the necessary certificate under paragraph 4(1)(b) in respect of it; and**
>   **(b) the registration of the judgment,**

shall be recoverable as if on the date of registration there had also been registered in the registering court a certificate under Schedule 6 in respect of the judgment and as if those costs or expenses were costs or expenses stated in that certificate to be payable under a money provision contained in the judgment.

(2) All such sums as are recoverable by virtue of sub-paragraph (1) shall carry interest as if they were the subject of an order for costs or expenses made by the registering court on the date of registration of the judgment.

General note

This paragraph enables the costs of obtaining, in one part of the United Kingdom, the certified copy judgment and certificate under paragraph 4(1)(*b*), and those of its registration in another part, to be recovered without the need for a separate certificate of money provisions. There appears to be no provision for fixed costs in respect of the registration of a judgment containing non-money provisions,[60] and it would seem that the order for registration should therefore contain a provision for the costs of and incidental to the obtaining of the certified copy of the judgment and the certificate; and the costs of and incidental to the application for its registration should be taxed and payable as if they were costs stated in the certificate to be payable under a money provision contained in the judgment.[61]

This paragraph is the only provision whereby money may be recovered by enforcement under this Schedule and sub-paragraph

---

[59] See para. 46.07–46.08 above.

[60] *Cf.* R.S.C., Ord. 62, App. 3, Pt. III, para. 2, which enables fixed costs to be recovered on the registration of a certificate of money provisions.

[61] *Cf.* Sched. 6, para. 7: para. 46.09 above.

(2), which is equivalent to paragraph 8(3) of Schedule 6, is the only provision in this Schedule concerned with interest.

Stay or sisting of enforcement in certain cases

8. Where a judgment has been registered under this Schedule, the registering court may, if it is satisfied that any person against whom it is sought to enforce the judgment is entitled and intends to apply under the law of the part of the United Kingdom in which the judgment was given for any remedy which would result in the setting aside or quashing of the judgment, stay (or, in Scotland, sist) proceedings for the enforcement of the judgment, on such terms as it thinks fit, for such period as appears to the court to be reasonably sufficient to enable the application to be disposed of. 46.21

General note

The power given by this paragraph to stay the execution of a judgment registered under this Schedule is in the same terms as the equivalent power in paragraph 9 of Schedule 6 to stay the execution of a certificate of money provisions.[62] It should not be confused with the duty or power in paragraph 9 to set aside registration.

Cases in which registration of a certificate must or may be set aside

9. Where a judgment has been registered under this Schedule, the registering court— 46.22
  (a) **shall set aside the registration if, on an application made by any interested party, it is satisfied that the registration was contrary to the provisions of this Schedule;**
  (b) **may set aside the registration if, on an application so made, it is satisfied that the matter in dispute in the proceedings in which the judgment was given had previously been the subject of a judgment by another court or tribunal having jurisdiction in the matter.**

General note

This paragraph sets out two grounds for the setting aside of the registration, which are the same as those which apply in the case of a certificate of money provisions registered under Schedule 6 and

---

[62] See para. 46.11 above.

reference should be made to the commentary on paragraph 10 of that Schedule.[63] The Act does not envisage any other circumstances in which the registration, as distinct from the execution of a registered judgment, may be set aside.

---

[63] Para. 46.12 above.

CHAPTER 47

CIVIL JURISDICTION AND JUDGMENTS ACT 1982
SCHEDULES 8 TO 14—MISCELLANEOUS PROVISIONS

SCHEDULE 8† Section 20

RULES AS TO JURISDICTION IN SCOTLAND

General

[Article 2] **47.01**

1. Subject to the <u>following Rules</u>, persons shall . . . be sued in the courts <u>for the place where they are domiciled.</u>

Special jurisdiction

[Article 5]

2. <u>Subject to Rules 3 (jurisdiction over consumer contracts), 4 (exclusive jurisdiction) and 5 (prorogation)</u> a person may <u>also</u> be sued:

---

† The words underlined indicate the passages which result from a modification of Title II of the 1968 Convention or passages not derived from that Title: see s.20(4), para. 42.01 above and para. 45.01, n.2 above.

(1) where he has no fixed residence, in a court within whose jurisdiction he is personally cited;

[Article 5(1)]

(2) in matters relating to a contract, in the courts for the place of performance of the obligation in question;

[Article 5(3)]

(3) in matters relating to tort, delict or quasi-delict, in the courts for the place where the harmful event occurred;

[Article 5(4)]

(4) as regards a civil claim for damages or restitution which is based on an act giving rise to criminal proceedings, the court seised of those proceedings, to the extent that that court has jurisdiction to entertain civil proceedings;

[Article 5(2)]

(5) in matters relating to maintenance, in the courts for the place where the maintenance creditor is domiciled or habitually resident or, if the matter is ancillary to proceedings concerning the status of a person, in the court which has jurisdiction to entertain those proceedings, provided that an action of affiliation and aliment shall be treated as a matter relating to maintenance which is not ancillary to proceedings concerning the status of a person, and provided also that—

(a) where a local authority exercises its power to raise an action under section 44(7)(a) of the National Assistance Act 1948 or under section 81(1) of the Social Work (Scotland) Act 1968; and

(b) where the Secretary of State exercises his power to raise an action under section 19(8)(a) of the Supplementary Benefits Act 1976;

this Rule shall apply as if the reference to the maintenance creditor were a reference to the mother of the child;†

[Article 5(5)]

(6) as regards a dispute arising out of the operations of a branch, agency or other establishment, in the courts for the place in which the branch, agency or other establishment is situated;

[Article 5(6)]

(7) in his capacity as settlor, trustee or beneficiary of a trust domiciled in Scotland created by the operation of a statute, or by a written instrument, or created orally and

---

† Para. 2(5) is printed as amended by the Law Reform (Husband and Wife) (Scotland) Act 1984, Sched. 1.

evidenced in writing, in the <u>Court of Session, or the</u> <u>appropriate sheriff court within the meaning of section</u> <u>24A of the Trusts (Scotland) Act 1921;</u>

(8) <u>where he is not domiciled in the United Kingdom, in the</u> <u>courts for any place where—</u>

    (a) <u>any moveable property belonging to him has been</u> <u>arrested; or</u>

    (b) <u>any immoveable property in which he has any bene-</u> <u>ficial interest is situated;</u>

(9) <u>in proceedings which are brought to assert, declare or</u> <u>determine proprietary or possessory rights, or rights of</u> <u>security, in or over moveable property, or to obtain</u> <u>authority to dispose of moveable property, in the courts</u> <u>for the place where the property is situated;</u>

(10) <u>in proceedings for interdict, in the courts for the place</u> <u>where it is alleged that the wrong is likely to be commit-</u> <u>ted;</u>

(11) <u>in proceedings concerning a debt secured over immove-</u> <u>able property, in the courts for the place where the</u> <u>property is situated;</u>

(12) <u>in proceedings which have as their object a decision of</u> <u>an organ of a company or other legal person or an</u> <u>association of natural or legal persons, in the courts for</u> <u>the place where that company, legal person or associ-</u> <u>ation has its seat;</u>

(13) <u>in proceedings concerning an arbitration which is con-</u> <u>ducted in Scotland or in which the procedure is gov-</u> <u>erned by Scottish law, in the Court of Session;</u>

(14) <u>in proceedings principally concerned with the registra-</u> <u>tion in the United Kingdom or the validity in the United</u> <u>Kingdom of patents, trade marks, designs or other simi-</u> <u>lar rights required to be deposited or registered, in the</u> <u>Court of Session;†</u>

[Article 6]

(15) (a) where he is one of a number of <u>defenders,</u> in the courts for the place where any one of them is domiciled;

    (b) as a third party in an action on a warranty or guaran- tee or in any other third-party proceedings, in the court seised of the original proceedings, unless these were instituted solely with the object of removing him from the jurisdiction of the court which would be competent in his case;

    (c) on a counterclaim arising from the same contract or

---

† See Patents, Designs and Marks Act 1986, Sched. 2.

facts on which the original claim was based, in the court in which the original claim is pending.

Jurisdiction over consumer contracts

47.02   [Article 13]
3.—(1) In proceedings concerning a contract concluded by a person for a purpose which can be regarded as being outside his trade or profession, hereinafter called "the consumer", <u>subject to Rule 4 (exclusive jurisdiction)</u>, jurisdiction shall be determined by this <u>Rule</u> if it is—

   (a) a contract for the sale of goods on instalment credit terms; or
   (b) a contract for a loan repayable by instalments, or for any other form of credit, made to finance the sale of goods; or
   (c) any other contract for the supply of goods or a contract for the supply of services, <u>if—</u>
      (i) the consumer took in <u>Scotland</u> the steps necessary for the conclusion of the contract; <u>or</u>
      (ii) <u>proceedings are brought in Scotland by virtue of section 10(3).</u>

(2) This <u>Rule</u> shall not apply to contracts of transport <u>or contracts of insurance.</u>

[Article 14]
(3) A consumer may bring proceedings against the other party to a contract <u>only</u> in—

   (a) the courts <u>for the place</u> where that party is domiciled;
   (b) the courts <u>for the place</u> in which he is himself domiciled; <u>or</u>
   (c) <u>any court having jurisdiction by virtue of Rule 2(6) or (9).</u>

(4) Proceedings may be brought against a consumer by the other party to the contract only in the courts <u>for the place where the consumer is domiciled or any court having jurisdiction under Rule 2(9).</u>

(5) <u>Nothing in this Rule</u> shall affect the right to bring a counter-claim in the court in which, <u>in accordance with this Rule</u>, the original claim is pending.

[Article 15(1) and (2)]
(6) The provisions of this <u>Rule</u> may be departed from only by an agreement—

   (a) which is entered into after the dispute has arisen; or

(b) which allows the consumer to bring proceedings in a court other than a court indicated in this Rule.

Exclusive jurisdiction

[Article 16] **47.03**

4.—(1) Notwithstanding anything contained in any of Rules 1 to 3 above or 5 to 8 below, the following courts shall have exclusive jurisdiction—

[Article 16(1)]

(a) in proceeding which have as their object rights *in rem* in, or tenancies of, immovable property, the courts for the place where the property is situated;

[Article 16(2)]

(b) in proceedings which have as their object the validity of the constitution, the nullity or the dissolution of companies or other legal persons or associations of natural or legal persons, or the decisions of their organs, the courts for the place where the company, legal person or association has its seat;

[Article 16(3)]

(c) in proceedings (other than proceedings under section 16 of the Abolition of Domestic Rates Etc. (Scotland) Act 1987) which have as their object the validity of entries in public registers, the courts for the place where the register is kept;†

[Article 16(5)]

(d) in proceedings concerned with the enforcement of judgments, the courts for the place where the judgment has been or is to be enforced.

(2) Nothing in paragraph (1)(c) above affects jurisdiction in any proceedings concerning the validity of entries in registers of patents, trade marks, designs, or other similar rights required to be deposited or registered.‡

(3) No court shall exercise jurisdiction in a case where immovable property, the seat of a body mentioned in paragraph (1)(b) above, a public register or the place where a judgment has been or is to be enforced is situated outside Scotland and where paragraph (1) above would apply if the property, seat, register or, as the case may be, place of enforcement were situated in Scotland.

Prorogation of jurisdiction

[Article 17(1)] **47.04**

5.—(1) If the parties have agreed that a court is to have jurisdiction to settle any disputes which have arisen or which may

---

† Para. 4(1)(c) is printed as amended by the Act referred to therein, s. 16.
‡ See Patents, Designs and Marks Act 1986, Sched. 2.

arise in connection with a particular legal relationship, that court shall have exclusive jurisdiction.

[Article 17(1)]

(2) Such an agreement conferring jurisdiction shall be either in writing or evidenced in writing or, in trade or commerce, in a form which accords with practices in that trade or commerce of which the parties are or ought to have been aware.

[Article 17(2)]

(3) The court on which a trust instrument has conferred jurisdiction shall have exclusive jurisdiction in any proceedings brought against a settlor, trustee or beneficiary, if relations between these persons or their rights or obligations under the trust are involved.

(4) Where an agreement or trust instrument confers jurisdiction on the courts of the United Kingdom or of Scotland, proceedings to which paragraph (1) or, as the case may be, (3) above applies may be brought in any court in Scotland.

[Article 17(3)]

(5) Agreements or provisions of a trust instrument conferring jurisdiction shall have no legal force if the courts whose jurisdiction they purport to exclude have exclusive jurisdiction by virtue of Rule 4 or where Rule 4(3) applies.

[Article 18]

6.—(1) Apart from jurisdiction derived from other provisions of this Schedule, a court before whom a defender enters an appearance shall have jurisdiction.

(2) This Rule shall not apply where appearance was entered solely to contest the jurisdiction, or where another court has exclusive jurisdiction by virtue of Rule 4 or where Rule 4(3) applies.

Examination as to jurisdiction and admissibility

47.05

[Article 19]

7. Where a court is seised of a claim which is principally concerned with a matter over which another court has exclusive jurisdiction by virtue of Rule 4, or where it is precluded from exercising jurisdiction by Rule 4(3), it shall declare of its own motion that it has no jurisdiction.

[Article 20]

8. Where in any case a court has no jurisdiction which is compatible with this Act, and the defender does not enter an appearance, the court shall declare of its own motion that it has no jurisdiction.

General note

See the general note on Schedules 8 and 9 at paragraph 47.07 below.

SCHEDULE 9   Section 21

PROCEEDINGS EXCLUDED FROM SCHEDULE 8

1. Proceedings concerning the status or legal capacity of natural persons (including proceedings for separation) other than proceedings which consist solely of proceedings of affiliation and aliment.†   **47.06**

2. Proceedings for regulating the custody of children.

3. Proceedings relating to tutory and curatory and all proceedings relating to the management of the affairs of persons who are incapable of managing their own affairs.

4. Proceedings in respect of sequestration in bankruptcy; or the winding up of a company or other legal person; or proceedings in respect of a judicial arrangement or judicial composition with creditors.

5. Proceedings relating to a company where, by any enactment, jurisdiction in respect of those proceedings is conferred on the court having jurisdiction to wind it up.

6. Admiralty causes in so far as the jurisdiction is based on arrestment *in rem* or *ad fundandam jurisdictionem* of a ship, cargo or freight.

7. Commissary proceedings.

8. Proceedings for the rectification of the register of aircraft mortgages kept by the Civil Aviation Authority.

9. Proceedings under section 7(3) of the Civil Aviation (Eurocontrol) Act 1962 (recovery of charges for air navigation services and proceedings for damages against Eurocontrol).

10. Proceedings brought in pursuance of an order under section 23 of the Oil and Gas (Enterprise) Act 1982.‡

11. Proceedings under section 6 of the Protection of Trading Interests Act 1980 (recovery of sums paid or obtained pursuant to a judgment for multiple damages).

12. Appeals from or review of decisions of tribunals.

---

† Para. 1 is printed as amended by the Family Law (Scotland) Act 1985, Sched. 2.
‡ In para. 10, the present wording was substituted for a reference to s.3 of the Continental Shelf Act 1964, by the Oil and Gas (Enterprise) Act 1982, Sched. 3, para. 43; see para. 45.39 above.

13. Proceedings which are not in substance proceedings in which a decree against any person is sought.
14. Proceedings brought in any court in pursuance of—
    (a) any statutory provision which, in the case of any convention to which Article 57 applies (conventions relating to specific matters which override the general rules in the 1968 Convention), implements the convention; and
    (b) any rule of law so far as it has the effect of implementing any such convention.

General note on Schedules 8 and 9: jurisdiction in Scotland

47.07 Sections 20 to 23 and these two Schedules together govern the civil jurisdiction of the Court of Session and of sheriff courts. Detailed commentary on these provisions is outwith the scope of this work, but they are briefly discussed at paragraph 42.05 above.

SCHEDULE 10   Section 35(1)

AMENDMENTS OF FOREIGN JUDGMENTS (RECIPROCAL ENFORCEMENT) ACT 1933

47.08 1.—(1) Section 1 (power to extend Part I to foreign countries giving reciprocal treatment) is amended as follows.
(2) For subsection (1) and (2) substitute—
"(1) If, in the case of any foreign country, Her Majesty is satisfied that, in the event of the benefits conferred by this Part of this Act being extended to, or to any particular class of, judgments given in the courts of that country or in any particular class of those courts, substantial reciprocity of treatment will be assured as regards the enforcement in that country of similar judgments given in similar courts of the United Kingdom, She may by Order in Council direct—
    (a) that this Part of this Act shall extend to that country;
    (b) that such courts of that country as are specified in the Order shall be recognised courts of that country for the purposes of this Part of this Act; and
    (c) that judgments of any such recognised court, or such judgments of any class so specified, shall, if within subsection (2) of this section, be judgments to which this Part of this Act applies.
(2) Subject to subsection (2A) of this section, a judgment of a recognised court is within this subsection if it satisfies the following conditions, namely—
    (a) it is either final and conclusive as between the judgment debtor and the judgment creditor or requires the former to make an interim payment to the latter; and

1142

   (b) there is payable under it a sum of money, not being a sum payable in respect of taxes or other charges of a like nature or in respect of a fine or other penalty; and

   (c) it is given after the coming into force of the Order in Council which made that court a recognised court.

(2A) The following judgments of a recognised court are not within subsection (2) of this section—

   (a) a judgment given by that court on appeal from a court which is not a recognised court;

   (b) a judgment or other instrument which is regarded for the purposes of its enforcement as a judgment of that court but which was given or made in another country;

   (c) a judgment given by that court in proceedings founded on a judgment of a court in another country and having as their object the enforcement of that judgment.".

(3) After subsection (4) add—

"(5) Any Order in Council made under this section before its amendment by the Civil Jurisdiction and Judgments Act 1982 which deems any court of a foreign country to be a superior court of that country for the purposes of this Part of this Act shall (without prejudice to subsection (4) of this section) have effect from the time of that amendment as if it provided for that court to be a recognised court of that country for those purposes, and for any final and conclusive judgment of that court, if within subsection (2) of this section, to be a judgment to which this Part of this Act applies.".

2. In section 9 (power to make foreign judgments unenforceable in the United Kingdom if no reciprocity), in subsection (1) omit "superior" in both places where it occurs.

47.09

3. For section 10 (issue of certificates of judgments obtained in the United Kingdom) substituted—

"10.—*Provision for issue of copies of, and certificates in connection with, U.K. judgments.*

(1) Rules may make provision for enabling any judgment creditor wishing to secure the enforcement in a foreign country to which Part I of this Act extends of a judgment to which this subsection applies, to obtain, subject to any conditions specified in the rules—

   (a) a copy of the judgment; and

   (b) a certificate giving particulars relating to the judgment and the proceedings in which it was given.

(2) Subsection (1) applies to any judgment given by a court or tribunal in the United Kingdom under which a sum of money is payable, not being a sum payable in respect of taxes or other charges of a like nature or in respect of a fine or other penalty.

(3) In this section "rules"—

   (a) in relation to judgments given by a court, means rules of court;

    (b) in relation to judgments given by any other tribunal, means rules or regulations made by the authority having power to make rules or regulations regulating the procedure of that tribunal.".

4. After section 10 insert—
"**10A.—***Arbitration awards.*
    The provisions of this Act, except section 1(5) and 6, shall apply, as they apply to a judgment, in relation to an award in proceedings on an arbitration which has, in pursuance of the law in force in the place where it was made, become enforceable in the same manner as a judgment given by a court in that place.".

    5.—(1) Section 11(1) (interpretation) is amended as follows.
    (2) After the definition of "Country of the original court" insert—
    " 'Court,' except in section 10 of this Act, includes a tribunal;".
    (3) Omit the definition of "Judgments given in the superior courts of the United Kingdom".

General note on Schedule 10

47.10   This Schedule contains substantial amendments to the Foreign Judgments (Reciprocal Enforcement) Act 1933. It is given effect by section 35(1) and is discussed in the commentary on that section at paragraphs 43.40 to 43.41 above.

SCHEDULE 11   Section 37(1)

MINOR AMENDMENTS RELATING TO MAINTENANCE ORDERS

PART I

ENFORCEMENT OF LUMP SUM ORDERS

Maintenance Orders Act 1950 (c. 37)

47.11   **1. In section 18(3A) of the Maintenance Orders Act 1950 (order not to be enforced by registering court under that Act if re-registered for enforcement in another court), for "whilst it is registered" substitute "to the extent that it is for the time being registered".**

1144

Maintenance Orders Act 1958 (c. 39)

2.—(1) Section 2 of the Maintenance Orders Act 1958 (registration of orders) is amended as follows.

(2) In subsection (3) (registration of magistrates' court order for enforcement in the High Court), for the words from "shall" onwards (which require the court to be satisfied that not less than a certain number of periodical payments are in arrears) substitute "may, if it thinks fit, grant the application".

(3) After subsection (3) insert—

"(3A) Without prejudice to subsection (3) of this section, where a magistrates' court order provides both for the payment of a lump sum and for the making of periodical payments, a person entitled to receive a lump sum under the order who considers that, so far as it relates to that sum, the order could be more effectively enforced if it were registered may apply to the original court for the registration of the order so far as it so relates, and the court may, if it thinks fit, grant the application.

(3B) Where an application under subsection (3A) of this section is granted in the case of a magistrates' court order, the provisions of this Part of this Act shall have effect in relation to that order as if so far as it relates to the payment of a lump sum it were a separate order.".

Maintenance and Affiliation Orders Act (Northern Ireland) 1966 (c. 35) (N.I.)

3.—(1) Section 11 of the Maintenance and Affiliation Orders Act (Northern Ireland) 1966 (registration of orders) is amended as follows.

(2) In subsection (3) (registration of order made by court of summary jurisdiction for enforcement in the High Court), for the words from "shall" onwards (which require the court to be satisfied that not less than a certain number of periodical payments are in arrears) substitute "may, if it thinks fit, grant the application".

(3) After subsection (3) insert—

"(3A) Without prejudice to subsection (3) of this section, where an order made by a court of summary jurisdiction provides both for the payment of a lump sum and for the making of periodical payments, a person entitled to receive a lump sum under the order who considers that, so far as it relates to that sum the order could be more effectively enforced if it were registered may apply to the original court for the registration of the order so far as it so relates, and the court may, if it thinks fit, grant the application.

(3B) Where an application under subsection (3A) of this section is granted in the case of an order made by a court of summary juris-

1145

diction, the provisions of this Part shall have effect in relation to that order as if so far as it relates to the payment of a lump sum it were a separate order.".

Maintenance Orders (Reciprocal Enforcement) Act 1972 (c. 18)

47.12   4.—(1) In section 9 of the Maintenance Orders (Reciprocal Enforcement) Act 1972 (variation and revocation of orders) after subsection (1) insert—
"(1A) The powers conferred by subsection (1) above are not exercisable in relation to so much of a registered order as provides for the payment of a lump sum.".
(2) in section 21 of the Act (interpretation of Part I)—
(a) in paragraph (a) of the definition of "maintenance order" in subsection (1); and
(b) in subsection (2),
for "periodical payment of sums of money" substitute "payment of a lump sum or the making of periodical payments".

PART II

RECOVERY OF INTEREST ON ARREARS

Maintenance Orders Act 1950 (c. 37)

47.13   5. In section 18 of the Maintenance Orders Act 1950 (enforcement of registered orders), after subsection (1) (orders to be enforced in the same manner as orders made by the court of registration), insert—
"(1A) A maintenance order registered under this Part of this Act in a court of summary jurisdiction in England and Wales or Northern Ireland shall not carry interest; but where a maintenance order so registered is registered in the High Court under Part I of the Maintenance Orders Act 1958 or section 36 of the Civil Jurisdiction and Judgments Act 1982, this subsection shall not prevent any sum for whose payment the order provides from carrying interest in accordance with section 2A of the said Act of 1958 or section 11A of the Maintenance and Affiliation Orders Act (Northern Ireland) 1966.
(1B) A maintenance order made in Scotland which is registered under this Part of this Act in the Supreme Court in England or Northern Ireland shall, if interest is by the law of Scotland recover-

able under the order, carry the like interest in accordance with sub-section (1) of this section.".

Maintenance Orders Act 1958 (c. 39)

6.—(1) The Maintenance Orders Act 1958 is amended as fol- 47.14
lows.

(2) After section 2 insert—

"2A.—*Interest on sums recoverable under certain orders regis-tered in the High Court.*

(1) Where in connection with an application under section 2(3) of this Act for the registration of a magistrates' court order, the appli-cant shows in accordance with rules of court—

(a) that the order, though deemed for the purposes of section 1 of this Act to have been made by a magistrates' court in England, was in fact made in another part of the United Kingdom or in a country or territory outside the United Kingdom; and

(b) that, as regards any sum for whose payment the order provides, interest on that sum at a particular rate is, by the law of that part or of that country or territory, recoverable under the order from a particular date or time,

then, if the original court grants the application and causes a certi-fied copy of the order to be sent to the prescribed officer of the High Court under section 2(4)(c) of this Act, it shall also cause to be sent to him a certificate in the prescribed form showing, as regards that sum, the rate of interest so recoverable and the date or time from which it is so recoverable.

(2) The officer of the court who receives a certificate sent to him under the preceding subsection shall cause the certificates to be registered in that court together with the order to which it relates.

(3) Where an order is registered together with a certificate under this section, then, subject to any provision made under the next following subsection, sums payable under the order shall carry interest at the rate specified in the certificate from the date or time so specified.

(4) Provision may be made by rules of court as to the manner in which and the periods by reference to which any interest payable by virtue of subsection (3) is to be calculated and paid, including provision for such interest to cease to accrue as from a prescribed date.

(5) Except as provided by this section sums payable under regis-tered orders shall not carry interest.".

(3) In section 3(1) of that Act (enforcement of registered orders), after "Subject to the provisions of" insert "section 2A of this Act and".

47.15 **7.**—**(1) The Maintenance and Affiliation Orders Act (Northern Ireland) 1966 is amended as follows.**

(2) After section 11 insert—

"**11A.**—*Interest on sums recoverable under certain orders registered in the High Court.*

(1) Where in connection with an application under section 11(3) for the registration of an order made by a court of summary jurisdiction, the applicant shows in accordance with rules of court—

(a) that the order, though deemed for the purposes of this Part to have been made by a court of summary jurisdiction in Northern Ireland, was in fact made in another part of the United Kingdom or in a country or territory outside the United Kingdom; and

(b) that, as regards any sum for whose payment the order provides, interest on that sum at a particular rate is, by the law of that country or territory, recoverable under the order from a particular date or time,

then, if the original court grants the application and causes a certified copy of the order to be sent to the prescribed officer of the High Court under section 11(4)(c) it shall also cause to be sent to him a certificate in the prescribed form showing, as regards that sum, the rate of interest so recoverable and the date or time from which it is so recoverable.

(2) The officer of the court who receives a certificate sent to him under subsection (1) shall cause the certificate to be registered in that court together with the order to which it relates.

(3) Where an order is registered together with a certificate under this section, then, subject to any provision made under subsection (4), sums payable under the order shall carry interest at the rate specified in the certificate from the date or time so specified.

(4) Provision may be made by rules of court as to the manner in which and the periods by reference to which any interest payable by virtue of subsection (3) is to be calculated and paid, including provision for such interest to cease to accrue as from a prescribed date.

(5) Except as provided by this section sums payable under registered orders shall not carry interest.".

(3) In section 12(1) (enforcement of registered orders), after "Subject to the provisions of" insert "section 11A of this Act and".

(4) In section 16(2) of that Act (construction of "rules of court") at the end add "and in section 11A(4) shall be construed as including a reference to Judgment Enforcement Rules made

under Article 141 of the Judgments Enforcement (Northern Ireland) Order 1981".

PART III

RECIPROCAL ENFORCEMENT FOUNDED ON PRESENCE OF ASSETS

Maintenance Orders (Reciprocal Enforcement) Act 1972 (c. 18)

8. The Maintenance Orders (Reciprocal Enforcement) Act 1972 is amended as follows.   **47.16**

9. In section 2 (transmission of United Kingdom order for enforcement in reciprocating country)—
   (a) in subsections (1) and (4), after "residing" insert "or has assets"; and
   (b) in subsection (4), after "whereabouts of the payer," in both places where it occurs, insert "and the nature and location of his assets in that country".

10. In section 6 (registration in the United Kingdom of order made in reciprocating country)—
   (a) in subsection (2), after "residing" insert "or has assets"; and
   (b) in subsection (4)—
      (i) after "is residing" insert "or has assets";
      (ii) for "so residing" substitute "residing and has no assets within the jurisdiction of the court"; and
      (iii) at the end insert "and the nature and location of his assets".

11. In section 8(5) (duty of magistrates' court and its officers to take prescribed steps for enforcing registered orders), after "enforcing" insert "or facilitating the enforcement of".

12. In section 9 (variation and revocation of orders), after the subsection (1A) inserted by paragraph 4(1) of this Schedule, insert—
   "(1B) The registering court shall not vary or revoke a registered order if neither the payer nor the payee under the order is resident in the United Kingdom.".

13.—(1) Section 10 (cancellation of registration and transfer of orders) is amended as follows.
   (2) In subsection (2), for "has ceased to reside within the jurisdiction of that court," substitute "is not residing within the juris-

diction of that court and has no assets within that jurisdiction against which the order can be effectively enforced,".

(3) In subsection (3), after "residing" insert "or has assets".

(4) In subsection (5), for "still residing" substitute "residing or has assets".

(5) In subsection (6)—
  (a) after "is residing" insert "or has assets"; and
  (b) for "so residing" insert "residing and has no assets within the jurisdiction of the court".

(6) In subsection (7)(b), after "payer" insert "and the nature and location of his assets".

14. In section 11(1) (steps to be taken where payer is not residing in the United Kingdom)—
  (a) before "it appears" insert "at any time";
  (b) for the words "in the United Kingdom" to "therein," substitute "and has no assets in the United Kingdom,"; and
  (c) after "payer" in paragraph (c) insert "and the nature and location of his assets".

15. In section 21(1) (interpretation of Part I), in the definition of "the appropriate court"—
  (i) after "residing", in the first and second places where it occurs, insert "or having assets";
  (ii) for "the sheriff court" substitute "a sheriff court"; and
  (iii) after "residing", where it last occurs, insert "or has assets".

16. In section 24 (application of Part I to certain orders and proceedings under Maintenance Orders (Facilities for Enforcement) Act 1920), in paragraph (a)(i) and (ii), after "residing" insert "or having assets".

17. In section 40 (power to apply Act with modifications by Order in Council)—
  (a) in paragraph (a), omit "against persons in that country or territory"; and
  (b) in paragraph (b), omit "against persons in the United Kingdom".

18. In section 47 (interpretation), in subsection (3) (construction of references to a court's jurisdiction), after "the reference is" insert "to assets being located or" and omit the words "or having ceased to reside".

1150

General note on Schedule 11

This Schedule contains minor amendments relating to maintenance orders. It is given effect by section 37(1) and is discussed in the
commentary on that section at paragraph 43.45 above.

SCHEDULE 12　　　Sections 15(4),
23(2) and 36(6)

CONSEQUENTIAL AMENDMENTS

PART I

AMENDMENTS CONSEQUENTIAL ON PART I OF THIS ACT

Army Act 1955 (c. 18) and Air Force Act 1955 (c. 19)

**1. In section 150 of the Army Act 1955 and in section 150 of the
Air Force Act 1955 (enforcement of maintenance and other
orders by deduction from pay), in subsection (5), after "Part I of
the Maintenance Orders (Reciprocal Enforcement) Act 1972"
insert "or Part I of the Civil Jurisdiction and Judgments Act
1982".**　　47.17

Naval Discipline Act 1957 (c. 53)

**2. In section 101 of the Naval Discipline Act 1957 (service of
process in maintenance and other proceedings), in subsection
(5), after "Part I of the Maintenance Orders (Reciprocal
Enforcement) Act 1972" insert "or Part I of the Civil Jurisdiction
and Judgments Act 1982".**

Maintenance Orders Act 1958 (c. 39)

**3. In section 1 of the Maintenance Orders Act 1958 (scope of
application of Part I), in subsection (4), for the words from
"within the meaning" to "the said Part I" substitute "which is
registered in a magistrates' court under Part I of the Maintenance Orders (Reciprocal Enforcement) Act 1972 by Part I of the
Civil Jurisdiction and Judgments Act 1982".**

*Maintenance and Affiliation Orders Act (Northern Ireland) 1966
(c. 35) (N.I.)*

**4. In section 10 of the Maintenance and Affiliation Orders Act
(Northern Ireland) 1966 (orders to which Part II of that Act**

1151

applies), in subsections (2) and (5), after "Part I of the Maintenance Orders (Reciprocal Enforcement) Act 1972" insert "or Part I of the Civil Jurisdiction and Judgments Act 1982".

Administration of Justice Act 1970 (c. 31)

5. In Schedule 8 to the Administration of Justice Act 1970 (orders which are "maintenance orders" for the purposes of Part II of that Act and Part II of the Maintenance Orders Act 1958), after paragraph 12 insert—
   "13. A maintenance order within the meaning of Part I of the Civil Jurisdiction and Judgments Act 1982 which is registered in a magistrates' court under that Part.".

Attachment of Earnings Act 1971 (c. 32)

6. In Schedule 1 to the Attachment of Earnings Act 1971 (orders which are "maintenance orders" for the purposes of that Act), after paragraph 12 insert—
   "13. A maintenance order within the meaning of Part I of the Civil Jurisdiction and Judgments Act 1982 which is registered in a magistrates' court under that Part.".

Magistrates' Courts Act 1980 (c. 43)

7. In section 65 of the Magistrates' Courts Act 1980 (definition of "domestic proceedings for the purposes of that Act)—
   (a) in subsection (1), after paragraph (l) insert—
   "(*m*) Part I of the Civil Jurisdiction and Judgments Act 1982, so far as that Part relates to the recognition or enforcement of maintenance orders;";
   (b) in subsection (2)(a), after "(k)" insert "and (m)".

Magistrates' Courts (Northern Ireland) Order 1981 (S.I. 1981/1675 (N.I. 26))

8.—(1) In Article 88 of the Magistrates' Courts (Northern Ireland) Order 1981 (definition of "domestic proceedings" for the purposes of that Order), in paragraph (a), after "Part I of the Maintenance Orders (Reciprocal Enforcement) Act 1972" insert "or under Part I of the Civil Jurisdiction and Judgments Act 1982 so far as that Part relates to the recognition and enforcement of maintenance orders".

(2) In Article 98 of that Order (enforcement of orders for

periodical payment of money), in sub-paragraph (b) of paragraph (11), after "Part I of the Maintenance Orders (Reciprocal Enforcement) Act 1972" insert "or Part I of the Civil Jurisdiction and Judgments Act 1982".

PART II

AMENDMENTS CONSEQUENTIAL ON SCHEDULE 8

Law Reform (Miscellaneous Provisions) (Scotland) Act 1940 (c. 42)

1. In the Law Reform (Miscellaneous Provisions) (Scotland) 47.18
Act 1940 after section 4(2) there shall be inserted the following subsection—
   "(3) This section does not apply—
   (a) in the case of an agreement entered into after the dispute in respect of which the agreement is intended to have effect has arisen; or
   (b) where the contract is one referred to in Rule 3 of Schedule 8 to the Civil Jurisdiction and Judgments Act 1982.".

Maintenance Orders Act 1950 (c. 37)

2. In section 15(1)(b) of the Maintenance Orders Act 1950 for the words "separation and aliment" there shall be substituted the words "which contains a conclusion for aliment not falling within the scope of paragraph (a)(i) above."

Maintenance Orders (Reciprocal Enforcement) Act 1972 (c. 18)

3.—(1) In section 4 of the Maintenance Orders (Reciprocal Enforcement) Act 1972 (power of the sheriff to make a provisional maintenance order against a person residing in a reciprocating country) the following subsection shall be substituted for subsections (1) and (2)—
   "(1) In any action where the sheriff has jurisdiction by virtue of Rule 2(5) of Schedule 8 to the Civil Jurisdiction and Judgments Act 1982 and the defender resides in a reciprocating country, any maintenance order granted by the sheriff shall be a provisional order.".
(2) In subsections (3), (4) and (5) of that section for the words "in which the sheriff has jurisdiction by virtue of" there shall be substituted in each place where they occur the words "referred to therein".

1153

Consumer Credit Act 1974 (c. 39)

4. In section 141 of the Consumer Credit Act 1974 the follow-ing subsections shall be substituted for subsection (3)—
"(3) In Scotland the sheriff court shall have jurisdiction to hear and determine any action referred to in subsection (1) and such an action shall not be brought in any other court.

(3A) Subject to subsection (3B) an action which is brought in the sheriff court by virtue of subsection (3) shall be brought only in one of the following courts, namely—
  (a) the court for the place where the debtor or hirer is domiciled (within the meaning of section 41 or 42 of the Civil Jurisdiction and Judgments Act 1982);
  (b) the court for the place where the debtor or hirer carries on business; and
  (c) where the purpose of the action is to assert, declare or deter-mine proprietary or possessory rights, or rights of security, in or over moveable property, or to obtain authority to dispose of moveable property, the court for the place where the property is situated.

(3B) Subsection (3A) shall not apply—
  (a) where rule 3 of Schedule 8 to the said Act of 1982 applies; or
  (b) where the jurisdiction of another court has been prorogated by an agreement entered into after the dispute has arisen.".

PART III

AMENDMENTS CONSEQUENTIAL ON SECTION 36

Maintenance Orders Act 1950 (c. 37)

47.19   **1.—(1) the Maintenance Orders Act 1950 is amended as fol-lows.**

(2) In section 18 (enforcement of registered orders), after sub-section (3A) insert—
"(3B) Notwithstanding subsection (1) above, no court in North-ern Ireland in which a maintenance order is registered under this Part of this Act shall enforce that order to the extent that it is for the time being registered in another court in Northern Ireland under section 36 of the Civil Jurisdiction and Judgments Act 1982.".

(3) In section 21(2) (evidence admissible before court where order registered)—
  (a) in paragraph (a) after "1958" insert "or under section 36 of the Civil Jurisdiction and Judgments Act 1982";
  (b) after "that Act" (twice) insert "of 1958";
  (c) after paragraph (b) insert—

"(c) registered in a court in Northern Ireland under section 36 of the Civil Jurisdiction and Judgments Act 1982".

(4) In section 24(3) (notice of cancellation of order to be given to other courts interested), after "Part I of the Maintenance Orders Act 1958" insert "or section 36 of the Civil Jurisdiction and Judgments Act 1982".

Maintenance Orders Act 1958 (c. 39)

2. In section 23(2) of the Maintenance Orders Act 1958 (provisions which extend to Scotland and Northern Ireland) after "section 2" insert "section 2A".

Maintenance and Affiliation Orders Act (Northern Ireland) 1966 (c. 35) (N.I.)

3.—(1) The Maintenance and Affiliation Orders Act (Northern Ireland) 1966 is amended as follows.

(2) At the beginning of section 9 (introductory provisions relating to registration in one court of maintenance order made by another) insert "Without prejudice to section 36 of the Civil Jurisdiction and Judgments Act 1982,".

(3) In section 10 (orders to which Part II applies), after subsection (1) insert—

"(1A) This Part, except sections 11, 11A and 14(2) and (3), also applies in accordance with section 36 of the Civil Jurisdiction and Judgments Act 1982 to maintenance orders made by a court in England and Wales or Scotland and registered in Northern Ireland under Part II of the Maintenance Orders Act 1950.".

(4) In section 13 (variation of orders registered in courts of summary jurisdiction), after subsection (7) insert—

"(7A) No application for any variation in respect of a registered order shall be made to any court in respect of an order made by the High Court of Justice in England or the Court of Session and registered in that court under section 36 of the Civil Jurisdiction and Judgments Act 1982.".

Judgments Enforcement (Northern Ireland) Order 1981 (S.I. 1981/266 (N.I. 6))

4. In Article 98 of the Judgments Enforcement (Northern Ireland) Order 1981, (powers of courts to make attachment of the earnings orders), in sub-paragraph (iv) of paragraph (a) at the end add "but not subsequently registered in a court of summary jurisdiction under section 36 of the Civil Jurisdiction and Judgments Act 1982".

Civil Jurisdiction and Judgments Act 1982

Magistrates' Courts (Northern Ireland) Order 1981 (S.I. 1981/1675 (N.I. 26))

5.—(1) In Article 88 of the Magistrates' Courts (Northern Ireland) Order 1981 (definition of "domestic proceedings" for the purposes of that Order)—
  (a) in paragraph (a), delete the words "or the Maintenance Orders Act 1950";
  (b) after paragraph (a) insert—
    "(aa) in relation to maintenance orders registered in a court of summary jurisdiction under the Maintenance Orders Act 1950 or Part II of the Maintenance and Affiliation Orders Act (Northern Ireland) 1966 or section 36 of the Civil Jurisdiction and Judgments Act 1982, under that Act of 1950 or Part II of that Act of 1966".

(2) In Article 98 of that Order (enforcement of orders for periodical payment of money), in sub-paragraph (d) of paragraph (11), at the end add—

    "or under section 36 of the Civil Jurisdiction and Judgments Act 1982".

General note on Schedule 12

This Schedule contains consequential amendments to a number of enactments concerned with maintenance orders or domestic proceedings in the law of the different parts of the United Kingdom. Its provisions amend the other enactments in order to incorporate references to maintenance orders under this Act.

SCHEDULE 13   Section 53

COMMENCEMENT, TRANSITIONAL PROVISIONS AND SAVINGS

PART I

COMMENCEMENT

Provisions coming into force on Royal Assent

47.20   **1. The following provisions come into force on Royal Assent:**

Provision	*Subject-matter*
section 53(1) and Part I of this Schedule	Commencement.
section 55	Short title.

1156

Provisions coming into force six weeks after Royal Assent

2. The following provisions come into force at the end of the period of six weeks beginning with the day on which this Act is passed: 47.21

Provision	Subject-matter
section 24(1)(a), (2)(a) and (3)	Interim relief and protective measures in cases of doubtful jurisdiction.
section 29	Service of county court process outside Northern Ireland.
section 30	Proceedings in England and Wales or Northern Ireland for torts to immovable property.
section 31	Overseas judgments given against states.
section 32	Overseas judgments given in breach of agreement for settlement of disputes.
section 33	Certain steps not to amount to submission to jurisdiction of overseas court.
section 34	Certain judgments a bar to further proceedings on the same cause of action.
section 35(3)	Consolidation of Orders in Council under section 14 of the Administration of Justice Act 1920.
section 38	Overseas judgments counteracting an award of multiple damages.
section 40	Power to modify enactments relating to legal aid, etc.
section 49	Saving for powers to stay, sist, strike out or dismiss proceedings.
section 50	Interpretation: general.
section 51	Application to Crown.
section 52	Extent.
paragraphs 7 to 10 of Part II of this Schedule and section 53(2) so far as relates to those paragraphs.	Transitional provisions and savings.
section 54 and Schedule 14 so far as relating to the repeal of provisions in section 4 of the Foreign Judgments (Reciprocal Enforcement) Act 1933.	Repeals consequential on sections 32 and 33.

Provisions coming into force on a day to be appointed

3.—(1) The other provisions of this Act come into force on such day as the Lord Chancellor and the Lord Advocate may appoint by order made by statutory instrument.   47.22

(2) Different days may be appointed under this paragraph for different purposes.

General note on Part I

Royal Assent was given, and the Act passed, on July 13, 1982.   47.23
The provisions in paragraph 1 came into force on that day. The provisions in paragraph 2 came into force six weeks later, on August

24, 1982. As regards the other provisions, which are governed by paragraph 3, they came into force on the following dates:

November 1, 1984	Section 26, Schedule 13, Part II, paragraph 6 and section 53(2) so far as it relates to tha paragraph.[1]
November 14, 1986	Section 35(1).[2]
January 1, 1987	The rest of the Act.[3]

The commencement provisions are subject to the transitional provisions in Part II of this Schedule.

The commencement provisions of the various Conventions are: 1968 Convention, Article 62[4]; 1971 Protocol, Article 8[5]; 1978 Convention, Article 39[6]; and 1982 Convention, Article 15.[7]

PART II

TRANSITIONAL PROVISIONS AND SAVINGS

Section 16 and Schedule 4

47.24   **1.—(1) Section 16 and Schedule 4 shall not apply to any proceedings begun before the commencement of that section.**

(2) Nothing in section 16 or Schedule 4 shall preclude the bringing of proceedings in any part of the United Kingdom in connection with a dispute concerning a contract if the parties to the dispute had agreed before the commencement of that section that the contract was to be governed by the law of that part of the United Kingdom.

---

[1] The Civil Jurisdiction and Judgments Act 1982 (Commencement No. 1) Order 1984, (S.I. 1984 No. 1553).

[2] The Civil Jurisdiction and Judgments Act 1982 (Commencement No. 2) Order 1986, (S.I. 1986 No. 1781).

[3] The Civil Jurisdiction and Judgments Act 1982 (Commencement No. 3) Order 1986, (S.I. 1986 No. 2044).

[4] Para. 34.11 above. As between the original six Contracting States, the 1968 Convention came into force on February 1, 1973.

[5] Para. 36.21 above. As between the original six Contracting States, the 1971 Protocol came into force on September 1, 1975.

[6] Para. 37.18 above. The 1978 Accession Convention came into force as between the original six Contracting States, and as between those states and Denmark on November 1, 1986; the accession of the U.K. took place on January 1, 1987, and the accession of Ireland took place on June 1, 1988.

[7] Para. 38.08 above. The 1982 Accession Convention on the accession of Greece has not yet come into force.

Section 18 and Schedule 6 and associated repeals

2.—(1) In relation to a judgment a certificate whereof has been registered under the 1868 Act or the 1882 Act before the repeal of that Act by this Act, the 1868 Act or, as the case may be, the 1882 Act shall continue to have effect notwithstanding its repeal.

(2) Where by virtue of sub-paragraph (1) the 1882 Act continues to have effect in relation to an order to which section 47 of the Fair Employment (Northern Ireland) Act 1976 (damages etc. for unfair discrimination) applies, that section shall continue to have effect in relation to that order notwithstanding the repeal of that section by this Act.

(3) A certificate issued under Schedule 6 shall not be registered under that Schedule in a part of the United Kingdom if the judgment to which that certificate relates is the subject of a certificate registered in that part under the 1868 Act or the 1882 Act.

(4) In this paragraph—

"the 1868 Act" means the Judgments Extension Act 1868;
"the 1882 Act" means the Inferior Courts Judgments Extension Act 1882;
"judgment" has the same meaning as in section 18.

Section 18 and Schedule 7

3. Schedule 7 and, so far as it relates to that Schedule, section 18 shall not apply to judgments given before the coming into force of that section.

Section 19

4. Section 19 shall not apply to judgments given before the commencement of that section.

Section 20 and Schedule 8

5. Section 20 and Schedule 8 shall not apply to any proceedings begun before the commencement of that section.

Section 26

6. The power conferred by section 26 shall not be exercisable in relation to property arrested before the commencement of that section or in relation to bail or other security given—
    (a) before the commencement of that section to prevent the arrest of property; or

(b) to obtain the release of property arrested before the commencement of that section; or

(c) in substitution (whether directly or indirectly) for security given as mentioned in sub-paragraph (a) or (b).

Section 31

7. Section 31 shall not apply to any judgment—
   (a) which has been registered under Part II of the Administration of Justice Act 1920 or Part I of the Foreign Judgments (Reciprocal Enforcement) Act 1933 before the time when that section comes into force; or
   (b) in respect of which proceedings at common law for its enforcement have been finally determined before that time.

Section 32 and associated repeal

8.—(1) Section 32 shall not apply to any judgment—
   (a) which has been registered under Part II of the Administration of Justice Act 1920, Part I of the Foreign Judgments (Reciprocal Enforcement) Act 1933 or Part I of the Maintenance Orders (Reciprocal Enforcement) Act 1972 before the time when that section comes into force; or
   (b) in respect of which proceedings at common law for its enforcement have been finally determined before that time.

(2) Section 4(3)(b) of the Foreign Judgments (Reciprocal Enforcement) Act 1933 shall continue to have effect, notwithstanding its repeal by this Act, in relation to a judgment registered under Part I of that Act before the commencement of section 32.

Section 33 and associated repeal

9.—(1) Section 33 shall not apply to any judgment—
   (a) which has been registered under Part II of the Administration of Justice Act 1920 or Part I of the Foreign Judgments (Reciprocal Enforcement) Act 1933 before the time when that section comes into force; or
   (b) in respect of which proceedings at common law for its

enforcement have been finally determined before that time.

(2) The repeal by this Act of words in section 4(2)(a)(i) of the Foreign Judgments (Reciprocal Enforcement) Act 1933 shall not affect the operation of that provision in relation to a judgment registered under Part I of that Act before the commencement of section 33.

Section 34

10. Section 34 shall not apply to judgments given before the commencement of that section.

General note on Part II

The transitional provisions set out in this Schedule are noted under the various sections to which they apply. There are also transitional provisions in the Conventions themselves, some of which are fairly complex. They are as follows: 1968 Convention, Article 54;[8] 1978 Convention, Articles 34 to 36[9]; and 1982 Convention, Article 12.[10] It should be noted that paragraphs 8(1) and 9(1) have been held to apply to proceedings for enforcement, but not to recognition.[11]

47.25

SCHEDULE 14   Section 54

REPEALS

Chapter	Short Title	Extent of repeal
41 Geo. 3. c.90.	Crown Debts Act 1801	The preamble. Sections 1 to 8.
5 Geo. 4. c.111.	Crown Debts Act 1824	The whole Act.
22 & 23 Vict. c.21	Queen's Remembrancer Act 1859	Section 24.
31 & 32 Vict. c.54	Judgments Extension Act 1868	The whole Act.
31 & 32 Vict. c.96	Ecclesiastical Buildings and Glebes (Scotland) Act 1868	In section 4, the words "of the county in which the parish concerned is situated" and the words from "provided" to the end.
45 & 46 Vict. c.31	Inferior Courts Judgments Extension Act 1882	The whole Act.

47.26

---

[8] Para. 32.01 above.
[9] Paras. 37.06 *et seq* above.
[10] Para. 38.04 above.
[11] *Tracomin S.A.* v. *Sudan Oil Seeds Co. Ltd.* [1983] 1 W.L.R. 1026.

Chapter	Short Title	Extent of repeal
7 Edw. 7. c.51	Sheriff Courts (Scotland) Act 1907	In section 5, the words from "Provided that actions" to "that jurisdiction".†
14 & 15 Geo. 5. c.27	Conveyancing (Scotland) Act 1924	In section 23(6) the words from "of the county" to "is situated".
23 & 24 Geo. 5. c.13	Foreign Judgments (Reciprocal Enforcement) Act 1933	In section 4(2)(a)(i), the words from "otherwise" to "that court". Section 4(3)(b). In section 9(1), the word "superior" in both places where it occurs. In section 11(1), the definition of "Judgments given in the superior courts of the United Kingdom". In section 12, in paragraph (a) the words from "(except" to "this Act)", and paragraph (d). In section 13(b), the words "and section two hundred and thirteen", "respectively" and "and 116".
14 Geo. 6. c.37	Maintenance Orders Act 1950	Section 6. Section 8. Section 9(1)(a). In section 16(2)(b)(v), the words from the beginning to "or".
4 & 5 Eliz. 2. c.46.	Administration of Justice Act 1956	Section 51(a).
1963 c.22	Sheriff Courts (Civil Jurisdiction and Procedure) (Scotland) Act 1963	Section 3(2).
1965 c.2	Administration of Justice Act 1965	In Schedule 1, the entry relating to the Crown Debts Act 1801.
1971 c.55	Law Reform (Jurisdiction in Delict) (Scotland) Act 1971	The whole Act.
1972 c.18	Maintenance Orders (Reciprocal Enforcement) Act 1972	In section 40— (a) in paragraph (a), the words "against persons in that country or territory"; and (b) in paragraph (b), the words "against persons in the United Kingdom". In section 47(3), the words "or having ceased to reside". In the Schedule, paragraph 4.

† The repeal in respect of the Sheriff Courts (Scotland) Act 1907 is printed as amended by the Divorce Jurisdiction, Court Fees and Legal Aid (Scotland) Act 1983, Sched. 1.

Chapter	Short Title	Extent of repeal
1976 c.25	Fair Employment (Northern Ireland) Act 1976	Section 47.
1978 c.23	Judicature (Northern Ireland) Act 1978	In Part II of Schedule 5— (a) the entry relating to the Crown Debts Act 1801; and (b) in the entry relating to the Foreign Judgments (Reciprocal Enforcement) Act 1933, the word "respectively", where last occurring, a d the words "and 116".
1981 c.54	Supreme Court Act 1981	In Schedule 5, paragraph 2 of the entry relating to the Foreign Judgments (Reciprocal Enforcement) Act 1933.

General note on Schedule 14

The repeals in this section are self-explanatory and require no commentary beyond that in section 54.[12]

---

[12] Para. 44.52 above.

PART 3
National Sections

PART 3 contains descriptions of the legal systems, the rules of jurisdiction and the procedure of the civil courts in each of the jurisdictions which are subject to the 1968 Convention. Chapters 48 to 58 are each concerned with a separate jurisdiction, but are written in parallel. Each chapter is arranged according to the same layout, with the same topic being covered under the same paragraph number. The layout of these chapters is generally in accordance with the table set out below.

There are many divergences between the legal systems discussed and while it has been possible to achieve a uniformity of treatment to a great extent, some variations have necessarily occurred. Accordingly, some of the headings mentioned below have been altered as appropriate and if a particular topic does not arise in respect of a given jurisdiction, that paragraph is omitted.

CHAPTER 48

BELGIUM

Written in collaboration with Hugo Callens and Paul Verguts, Advocaten, Antwerp.[1]

[1] Partners in the firm of *Dieryck, van Looveren & Co.*, Antwerp.

A. THE LEGAL SYSTEM

1. Introduction

48.01   *History and territory.* The Kingdom of Belgium was founded in 1830 after the secession of the Belgian provinces from the Netherlands. The Kingdom is divided into nine provinces: Antwerpen, Brabant, Le Hainaut, Liège, Limburg, Luxembourg,[2] Namur, Oost-Vlaanderen, and West-Vlaanderen. The official language in the northern provinces, Antwerpen, Limburg, Oost-Vlaanderen, West-Vlaanderen, and in parts of Brabant, is Flemish. In Brussels and some surrounding areas both Flemish and French must be used as official languages. In the remaining provinces (sometimes called the Walloon provinces) French is the official language, except in the eastern part of Liège, where it is German. In this chapter legal terms are expressed initially in both French and Flemish, and thereafter in French.

Constitution. Belgium is a constitutional monarchy. The constitution, which dates from 1831, establishes the fundamental rights of citizens, the organisation of the state, and the separation of legislative, executive and judicial powers. The constitutional reforms of recent years (1970, 1980 and 1988/89) have brought about the partial decentralisation of government in Belgium. Three regional boards and executives have been set up, to be responsible for regional government in various fields such as planning, housing, and environmental and cultural affairs.

Origins of the legal system. Belgian law is based in part on Roman law, having been codified on the model of the *Code Napoleon*. Wide areas of substantive and procedural law have been codified[3] but there are in addition numerous specific laws on particular subjects. All the codes undergo a continuous process of modification as their provisions are extended, deleted or amended by parliamentary legislation.

---

[2] The Belgian province of Luxembourg should not, of course, be confused with the Grand Duchy of Luxembourg.

[3] The principal civil law codes are listed at para. 48.15 below.

2. The administration of justice

Public and private law. In common with most other continental **48.02**
European countries, Belgium's legal system recognises a clear distinction between public law and private law. The former regulates
acts and decisions of public authorities, while the latter regulates
the relationships of individuals and private legal persons with each
other.

Court system. Matters of private law are subject to the jurisdiction
of the ordinary or judicial courts. There are separate systems of
ordinary courts (or separate chambers of the same court) for civil,
criminal, commercial and employment matters. Courts exercising
criminal jurisdiction may in certain circumstances award civil
damages. Some matters of public law come within the competence
of the *Conseil d'Etat / Raad van State*, or of the newly-established
Cour d'Arbitrage / Arbitragehof, or other specialised administrative
courts, but the ordinary courts have some jurisdiction to entertain
actions by and against the state and other public authorities.

B. LEGAL PRACTITIONERS

1. The *Avocat / Advocaat*

Introduction. There are some 8615 *avocats* in Belgium, who act for **48.03**
their clients not only in the conduct of litigation, but also as general
legal advisers. The separate profession of *avoué / pleitbezorger* was
abolished in 1967, and the procedural functions which they previously performed are now carried out by *avocats*.

Legal education and qualifications. Admission to the profession of
avocat is restricted to Belgian or EEC nationals, who hold the law
degree of *licencié en droit / licentiaat in de rechten*. This takes five
years to obtain. The intending *avocat* is then sworn in as a *stagiaire /
stagiair* and undergoes a three year period of training (*stage*) with an
established *avocat*. An official list of *stagiaires* is kept for each
judicial district (*arrondissement*). A *stagiaire* may use the title of *avocat*, and may appear in any Belgian court, except the *Cour de Cassation* and the *Conseil d'Etat*. He may be obliged to attend lectures on
professional conduct and other professional matters and to participate in the legal aid scheme. Upon conclusion of his *stage* the
stagiaire is admitted to a local bar and his name is added to the
official *tableau* of *avocats* for the *arrondissement*.

Rights of representation and audience. Rights of audience in civil **48.04**
cases before the *Cour de Cassation / Hof van Cassatie* are limited to
some 16 *avocats* specially appointed by the Crown. With that exception, Belgian *avocats* have rights of audience before all courts

in Belgium, and in the higher civil courts these rights are generally exclusive.[4]

Organisation of practice. Partnerships of *avocats* are permitted, but more than half of the *avocats* in Belgium are sole practitioners. Legal work is not generally undertaken by unqualified employees. Partnerships between *avocats* and members of other professions are not permitted at present, although proposals to liberalise this rule are under discussion.

48.05   *Fees.* The fees charged by a Belgian *avocat* are a matter for private agreement with his client. Guidelines are published by the governing bodies of the bar associations, locally and nationally, giving recommended scales of fees according to the amount at stake. If this amount cannot be quantified the factors to be taken into account in arriving at a proper fee are the level of the court, the importance of the case, the time taken by the *avocat*, and the degree of specialist skill required. Larger firms tend to charge their commercial clients on an hourly basis. In the event of a dispute between the *avocat* and the client the bill may be submitted for taxation to the local *Conseil de l'Ordre*. Legal fees in Belgium are exempt from VAT.

Professional organisation and conduct. The profession of *avocat* is organised principally on a local basis with a separate *barreau / balie* (bar) for each of Belgium's 27 judicial districts, known as *arrondissements judiciaires / gerechtelijke arrondissementen*. The governing and disciplinary body of each local bar is the *Conseil de l'Ordre*, which is presided over by an elected *bâtonnier / stafhouder*. The local bars together form the *Ordre National des Avocats de Belgique / Belgische Nationale Orde van Advocaten*.

Although professional indemnity insurance is not compulsory the majority of Belgian *avocats* are insured, either privately or through schemes arranged by the local bars.

[The next paragraph is number 48.09]

2. The *Notaire / Notaris*

48.09   The office of notary is still regulated by legislation dating back to 1803. A notary is a public official, appointed for life by the Crown to practice in a particular district, in which he is required to reside. The extent of the district, and the number of notaries who are permitted to practice there, depends on the size of the local population. The notary authenticates deeds and other instruments which the parties require or are obliged by law to have authenticated. The services of a notary are needed for the sale or mortgage of land, the set-

---

[4] See para. 48.36 below.

ting up of a commercial company, or the making of a marriage settlement. Deeds of gift and wills are usually drawn up by a notary. A notary will also give legal advice in connection with the above types of transaction and in connection with other matters which may overlap with the field of practice of *avocats*.

A notary is not entitled to refuse his services in respect of any transaction which is lawful. He may not engage in any commercial activity nor may he be an officer of a commercial company. A notary is liable for any fault on his part which results in loss to his client or to a third party.

An intending notary must have obtained a general law degree (*licencié en droit*) and a specialised degree for notaries (*licencié au Notariat*) and must have completed a period of training as a *stagiaire* in a notary's office. Most notaries work as sole practitioners, but they will frequently employ a clerk, holding a law degree, and other staff. Professional discipline is regulated by the local chamber of notaries in the area of each *tribunal de première instance*. The organisation of these disciplinary chambers is governed by the law of 1803, as amended. Fees are charged according to a statutory tariff.

[The next paragraph is number 48.11]

3. Foreign lawyers

Lawyers qualified and entitled to practice in other Member **48.11** States of the EEC in the profession equivalent to that of *avocat* may use their own title in Belgium and may, subject to certain restrictions, represent parties in court.[5] In Brussels, the rules of the respective bars provide for foreign lawyers wishing to practice there in association with Belgian lawyers to be listed on the *tableau* of the *Ordre*. The foreign lawyer is subject to Belgian disciplinary rules.

4. Lawyers in business and public employment

Lawyers employed in the legal departments of commercial **48.12** undertakings or of public bodies are not permitted to be members of the bar. Their activities are restricted to the giving of legal advice to their employers.

5. The *Huissier de justice* / *Gerechtsdeurwaarder*

The *huissier de justice* is an officer appointed by the Crown, whose **48.13** principal functions are the service of court documents and the enforcement of judgments. A *huissier* is competent to act only in the particular *arrondissement* to which he has been appointed. He is,

---

[5] See the EEC legal services directive at para. A2.47 below.

however, not attached to a particular court. He maintains an office either as a sole practitioner or in partnership with other *huissiers* and frequently employs staff. His instructions to act in a particular matter usually come not from the court but from the parties or their lawyers.

Huissiers have their own professional organisations at local and at national level and they are subject to certain rules of conduct. They charge their fees according to statutory scales. In addition to serving documents and enforcing judgments they also conduct public auctions of debtors' property. If a party wishes to establish some fact which is likely to be in issue in future litigation, such as the physical condition of goods purchased, he may unilaterally request a *huissier* to draw up a report or *procès verbal* as to the matter in question.

C. Sources of Law

1. Introduction

48.14   The formal sources of Belgian law are legislation (*loi* / *wet*), custom (*coutume* / *gewoonte*), decided cases (*jurisprudence* / *rechtspraak*) and the writings of legal scholars (*doctrine* / *rechtsleer*). *L'équité* / *billijkheid*, in the sense of fair dealing, is also sometimes regarded as a source of law. International treaties only take effect in Belgium after approval by Parliament and formal publication in the state gazette, the *Moniteur Belge* / *Belgisch Staatsblad*. The EEC Treaty has been duly approved in this manner and it takes direct effect together with other provisions of Community law, as part of Belgian internal law.

2. Legislation and custom

48.15   *Legislation.* The term *loi* or *wet* has a wider and a narrower meaning. In its narrower sense it means a statute, but in its wider sense, it means a binding rule promulgated by any competent authority. There are different types of laws in this wider sense, the more important of which, in descending order of priority, are as follows: the constitution (the *constitution* / *grondwet*); parliamentary legislation (a *loi* / *wet* in its narrower sense); a royal decree, (an *arrêté royal* / *koninklijk besluit*) enacted under the authority of parliamentary legislation; a ministerial decree (*arrêté ministériel* / *ministerieel besluit*) also enacted under the authority of parliamentary legislation; and a regulation (*règlement* / *reglement*), subordinate legislation by various bodies. In recent years regional devolution has given rise to various other important types of legislation, notably a regional *décret* / *decreet*. Certain collective employment agreements, which are of contractual origin, become subject to approval by *arrêté royal* and acquire legislative force.

Much of Belgian law is in a codified form. The principal codes of substantive and procedural law should be mentioned. Civil law is largely codified in the *Code Civil / Burgerlijk Wetboek*, but commercial law is separately codified in the *Code de Commerce / Wetboek van Koophandel*. Criminal law is contained to a large extent in the *Code Pénal / Strafwetboek*. Civil procedure is regulated by the *Code Judiciaire / Gerechtelijk Wetboek* and criminal procedure by the *Code d'Instruction Criminelle / Wetboek van Strafvordering*.

Custom. Some legislation makes express reference to custom as a source of law,[6] but it is always subordinate to any express legislative provision.

3. Decided cases and legal writings

Decided cases (*jurisprudence*) and legal writings (*doctrine*) are sources of law of persuasive authority. Decisions of the *Cour de Cassation*, although not of binding authority, are accorded particular respect and they will normally be followed by other courts. **48.16**

4. Publications

The Ministry of Justice is responsible for the daily publication of the *Moniteur Belge / Belgisch Staatsblad* which contains all legislation and official announcements. The bulk of new legislation is also published in private series called *Omnilegie and Pasinomie*. **48.17**

Many practitioners use the privately published annotated legal compendia, such as *les Codes Larcier* and *les Codes belges*, both in French, and the *Story-wetboeken*, which is bilingual Flemish and French. Decided cases are published in a number of different private series, in French or Flemish or in bilingual editions. Judgments of the *Cour de Cassation* are to be found in French in *Pasicrisie Belge* and in Flemish in *Arresten van het Hof van Cassatie*. Reports are also published in legal periodicals in which there may be annotations, commentaries, and longer articles. Those periodicals covering general law are the *Journal des Tribunaux*, *Rechtskundig Weekblad*, the *Revue Critique de Jurisprudence Belge* and *Tijdschrift voor Privaat Recht*. Other publications cover specific fields of law, for instance, the *Revue de Droit Commercial Belge / Tijdschrift voor Belgisch Handelsrecht* (commercial and economic law); the *Journal des Tribunaux du Travail* and the *Revue du Droit Social / Tijdschrift voor Sociaal Recht* (social law), and *L'Entreprise et le Droit / Tijdschrift voor Aannemingsrecht* (construction law).

---

[6] For example, Art. 1135 of the civil code provides that parties to an agreement are bound both by its express provisions and by the requirements of equity, *coutume* and law.

D. Organisation of the Civil and Commercial Courts

1. Introduction

48.18   Belgium is divided into 27 judicial *arrondissements* (districts) and thereafter into 225 judicial *cantons*. The principal division in the court system is between the ordinary judicial courts (the courts of *droit commun*) and the administrative courts,[7] although the former have jurisdiction to entertain certain actions by or against the state or other public authorities. The ordinary or judicial courts are themselves divided into four different types of jurisdiction with civil, commercial, labour and criminal matters being treated separately. In some courts different types of jurisdiction will be exercised in different chambers.[8]

The system of civil and commercial courts. The system of civil and commercial courts is relatively complex in Belgium, but in summary it is as follows. Each of the courts is described in more detail below. Smaller civil and commercial cases are heard at first instance by the *juge de paix / vrederechter*. More important civil cases are heard by the *tribunal de première instance / rechtbank van eerste aanleg* and larger commercial cases by the *tribunal de commerce / rechtbank van koophandel*. These courts also hear appeals from the *juge de paix*. Appeals from the first instance decisions of the *tribunal de première instance* and the *tribunal de commerce* lie to the *cour d'appel / hof van beroep*. Employment cases are heard in the first instance by the *tribunal du travail / arbeidsrechtbank* and on appeal by the *cour du travail / arbeidshof*. Appeals in cassation from decisions which are not otherwise appealable lie to the *Cour du Cassation / Hof van Cassatie*.[9]

Conflicts of jurisdiction. Conflicts of jurisdiction between the administrative courts on one hand and the ordinary or judicial courts on the other hand are resolved by the *Cour de Cassation*. Conflicts of jurisdiction between the different courts in the ordinary court system are resolved by the *tribunal d'arrondissement /arrondis-*

---

[7] There are administrative courts at various levels of national and local government, such as the *Députation Permanente du Conseil Provincial / Bestendige Deputatie van de Provincieraad*. At the head of the system is the *Conseil d'Etat / Raad van State*, located in Brussels, which also carries out important consultative functions in the legislative process.

[8] Minor criminal cases may be heard by the *Juge de Paix* sitting as the *Juge de Police*. Criminal cases of medium gravity are heard by a chamber (the *Chambre Correctionnel*) of the *Tribunal de Première Instance*. Serious criminal cases are heard by a separate criminal court, the *Cour d'Assises*. These courts all have jurisdiction to award civil damages in criminal cases.

[9] The topic of appeals is discussed in greater detail at paras. 48.63 *et seq.* below.

sementsrechtbank.[10] This is a court established for that purpose in each *arrondissement*, consisting of the presidents of the *tribunal de première instance*, the *tribunal de commerce* and the *tribunal du travail* of that *arrondissement*. Its decisions are subject to appeal only by cassation.

2. The *juge de paix / vrederechter*

The lowest civil court is that of the *juge de paix*. It is to be found at the level of the *canton*. The *juge de paix* sits alone and has general jurisdiction over civil and commercial matters in which the amount of the claim does not exceed BEF 50,000 and in respect of which jurisdiction is not allocated by law to some other court. Thus he has no jurisdiction over bankruptcy or maritime matters which are within the exclusive jurisdiction of the *tribunal de commerce*. He himself has exclusive jurisdiction, regardless of amount, over a wide range of matters including leases of property, claims for possession, claims for matrimonial maintenance, other than in connection with divorce proceedings, rights of way and various agricultural disputes. In cases worth more than BEF 15,000, appeal lies to the *tribunal de première instance* or to the *tribunal de commerce*, depending on the nature of the claim.

48.19

3. The *tribunal de première instance / rechtbank van eerste aanleg*

There is a *tribunal de première instance* in each judicial *arrondissement*. It is divided into civil, criminal and juvenile sections. The civil section is commonly referred to as the *tribunal civil / burgerlijke rechtbank*.[11] Each section has several chambers, each of which is composed, when it sits, of either one or three judges.[12]

The *tribunal de première instance* is the normal court with competence in all matters other than those which are directly allocated to the *cour d'appel* and the *Cour de Cassation*. It is also competent to determine matters which are generally allocated to other courts, provided that the defendant does not challenge its competence[13] and it hears appeals from the *juge de paix* in civil cases. It has exclusive jurisdiction, regardless of amount, in respect of a wide range of

48.20

---

[10] See also para. 48.42 below.

[11] The criminal and juvenile chambers are called, respectively, the *tribunal correctionnel / correctionele rechtbank*, and the *tribunal de la jeunesse / jeugdrechtbank*.

[12] In 1986, in order to overcome delays, the practice of judges sitting alone was considerably extended both in the *tribunal de première instance* and in the *cour d'appel*. In important cases, however, the court will always be composed of three judges.

[13] See para. 48.42 below.

matters including the status of individuals, matrimonial disputes, unclaimed inheritances, and the enforcement of judgments (including foreign judgments). At each court one or more of the judges is appointed as the *juge des saisies / beslagrechter* with responsibility for attachments, sitting alone when exercising this jurisdiction.[14] Appeals from the first instance decisions of the *tribunal de première instance* lie to the *cour d'appel*.[15]

4. The *tribunal de commerce / rechtbank van koophandel*

There is a *tribunal de commerce* established in every judicial *arrondissement*.[16] Its procedure is in most respects identical to that of the *tribunal de première instance*. The court is composed of one or more chambers. Each chamber has a president, who is a professional judge, and two *juges consulaires / rechters in handelszaken*, lay judges appointed by the Crown from the local business community for a renewable period of five years. The jurisdiction of the court is generally limited to disputes arising between *commerçants / kooplieden* (businessmen) in respect of acts which are regarded by law as commercial and which fall outside the general competence of the *juge de paix*. For example any transaction in the course of business for the sale of goods, for transportation or carriage, or for building or construction is regarded as commercial. Where the dispute concerns a commercial act and the plaintiff is not a *commerçant* but the defendant is, the plaintiff may, at his option, bring the proceedings either before the *tribunal de commerce* or before the *tribunal de première instance*. The court also has jurisdiction in respect of disputes involving bills of exchange and promissory notes when the amount exceeds BEF 50,000. In addition the court has important jurisdiction in certain further areas, regardless of whether or not the parties are businessmen. These include corporate matters, bankruptcy, winding up, regulation of trade and maritime matters. It also sits as the appellate court from decisions of the *juge de paix* in commercial matters, generally as defined above. Appeals from the first instance decisions of the *tribunal de commerce* lie to the *cour d'appel*.[17]

5. The *tribunal du travail / arbeidsrechtbank*

In every judicial *arrondissement* there is a *tribunal du travail* which deals with disputes between employer and employee, claims in respect of industrial accidents, and social security matters. It is dis-

---

[14] See para. 48.59 below.
[15] See para. 48.21 below.
[16] In larger *arrondissements* there may be a *tribunal de commerce* in more than one town.
[17] See para. 48.21 below.

tinct from the ordinary civil courts. The court consists of one professional judge assisted by two lay judges, appointed from representatives of trade unions and employers' and professional organisations. Appeals from the decisions of the *tribunal du travail* lie to the *cour du travail*.

6. The *cour d'appel* / *hof van beroep*

There are five *cours d'appel*, located at Brussels, Antwerp, Liège, Ghent, and Mons. Each is divided into three sections, one of which hears appeals in civil and commercial cases from the *tribunal de première instance* and the *tribunal de commerce*. The other sections hear appeals in criminal and juvenile matters respectively.[18] The *cours d'appel* also hear appeals from the decisions of the presidents of the *tribunal de première instance* and the *tribunal de commerce* made in the exercise of their special jurisdiction in *référé* / *kort geding* proceedings.[19]

48.21

7. The *cour du travail* / *arbeidshof*

In each area in which there is a *cour d'appel* there is also a *cour du travail*, at the same level as, but distinct from, the *cour d'appel*. It hears appeals from decisions given at first instance by the *tribunal du travail* and by the president of that court. It is composed of a professional appellate judge who sits with lay judges appointed from employers' and employees' organisations.

8. The *Cour de Cassation* / *Hof van Cassatie*

The *Cour de Cassation* is the supreme court of appeal. It is located in Brussels. It has three chambers, each with two sections. The chambers deal respectively with civil or commercial cases, criminal cases, and employment cases. Each section has a president and four judges of appeal (*Conseillers à la Cour de Cassation* / *Raadsheren in het Hof van Cassatie*). The court will occasionally determine an appeal in a plenary session of nine *conseillers*, including the president.[20]

48.22

The *Cour de Cassation* has jurisdiction to entertain appeals which are based on errors of law or non-compliance with essential procedural requirements. It can also consider applications for the annullment of certain acts by judges and public officials performed in excess of their authority. When the *Cour de Cassation* quashes a

---

[18] The *cour d'appel* also has first instance jurisdiction in cases concerning the deprivation of citizenship.

[19] See para. 48.61 below.

[20] There is also provision for the court to sit in its entirety to resolve conflicts of jurisdiction or proceedings against Ministers.

decision it remits the case to another court of the same level as the court from which the appeal in cassation was made. If the second court comes to the same conclusion as the first court and the *Cour de Cassation* then quashes that second decision, the case is remitted to a third court of the same level. This latter court is bound to apply the law as decided by the *Cour de Cassation*.

9. The judiciary

48.23   Judges are appointed by the Crown on the recommendation of the Minister of Justice. An appointee must be of Belgian nationality, be at least 30 years of age, and hold a law degree. He must have practiced law as an *avocat*, notary, or university teacher for at least five years. Once appointed a judge will usually make his career in the judiciary.

10. The *ministère public* / *openbaar ministerie*

The *ministère public* is the general description of the official department, under the Ministry of Justice, which is responsible for the conduct of criminal prosecutions. It also has the right to intervene in civil proceedings in which the issues raised are regarded as being of public concern, for example, bankruptcy, winding up, and matters involving the status of individuals. Its officers, principally the *Procureur du Roi* / *Procureur des Konings*, may appear in court in cases in which it has an interest and may express an opinion, orally or in writing, but the court is not bound by such opinion. In practice the *ministère public* only rarely takes part in civil and commercial cases.

E. JURISDICTION OF THE CIVIL AND COMMERCIAL COURTS

1. Introduction

48.24   When the 1968 Convention confers international jurisdiction on the courts of Belgium, the particular Belgian court in which the claim may be made is determined by the Convention's own provisions on local jurisdiction[21] and by the jurisdictional rules of Belgian law summarised below.

Subject-matter and value. As has been seen above, both the value and the subject-matter of the claim may determine the level and type of court. The subject-matter of the claim may require the proceedings to be brought in a specialised court, such as the *tribunal de commerce* or the *tribunal du travail*.

---

[21] See para. 15.03, nn.10–11 above.

Territorial factors. All courts of first instance have territorial competence which is limited according to detailed rules laid down in the *Code Judiciaire.* These rules, which are summarised in very general terms below, are frequently based on the domicile or seat of the defendant.

2. Domicile and seat

Natural persons. The ordinary definition of domicile in Belgian civil law[22] does not apply for the purposes of jurisdiction in civil proceedings. For these purposes, the domicile of a natural person is separately defined as the place where he is principally registered as resident in the local population register (*régistre de population / bevolkingsregister*). Belgian law requires all persons resident in Belgium to be so registered, although the place where they are registered may not necessarily be the place where they are actually resident. Persons such as minors and mental patients are regarded as domiciled for procedural law purposes at the place where their legal guardian is domiciled. **48.25**

Legal persons. A company is considered for the purposes of jurisdiction and procedural law to be domiciled at the place where, according to its memorandum of association, its seat is located (*siège social / maatschappelijke zetel*). This place does not always coincide with its actual seat (*siège réel*) or principal place of business, that is the place where it has its central administration. **48.26**

Belgian law applies to every company which has its principal establishment in Belgium, even if the memorandum of association was drawn up abroad. Similarly, companies which have their principal establishment abroad are generally regarded as subject to the law of the place where they have that establishment, even if their constitution was drawn up in Belgium.

3. Jurisdiction—general rules

An action must ordinarily be brought in the appropriate local court for the place where the defendant is domiciled. When there are several defendants who are domiciled in different places, the plaintiff may bring the action in the court of the domicile of any one of them. There are no specific rules which give jurisdiction to the courts of a place where a branch is established, but the provisions concerning obligations, summarised below, often achieve this result in practice. A foreign company with a branch in Belgium, at which there is an employee with authority to enter into contracts on the **48.27**

---

[22] Domicile is defined for most purposes as the place where a person has his chief establishment.

company's behalf, may be sued in Belgium at the place where the branch is located.[23]

4. Jurisdiction — specific rules

48.28   As an alternative to domicile forming the territorial basis for jurisdiction, an action which is founded on an obligation may be brought in the courts either for the place in which the obligation in question originated or for the place of its performance. The term "obligation," for the purposes of jurisdiction, includes an obligation in tort as well as one in contract. Belgian law provides as a general rule that, unless the parties otherwise agree, the place of performance of an obligation to pay money is at the domicile of the debtor. Two important exceptions to this rule should be mentioned. First, if payment is due under a contract for the sale of goods, the place of payment, in the absence of agreement to the contrary, is generally at the place of delivery of the goods. Secondly, if the payment obligation relates to a specific and identified object, it is to be performed (again in the absence of agreement to the contrary) at the place where the object was situated at the time the obligation was entered into.

Actions in respect of immovable property must be brought in the courts for the place in which the property is situated. Proceedings for the provisional attachment of property must ordinarily be brought in the *tribunal de première instance* for the place where the property is situated.

5. Choice of court and elective domicile

48.29   The above rules of territorial competence (except that relating to immovable property) may generally be waived by agreement. This agreement may take the form of an election of domicile for the purposes of proceedings. Equally, a defendant who is sued in a territorially inappropriate court and who does not challenge the court's jurisdiction will be taken to have consented to that jurisdiction.

6. Exorbitant grounds of jurisdiction

48.30   There are two jurisdictional rules which, under Article 3 of the 1968 Convention, may not be relied upon against persons domiciled in a Contracting State.[24] First, a Belgian national may not insist, pursuant to Article 15 of the *Code Civil*, on being sued in a Belgian court; and secondly, a plaintiff domiciled or resident in Belgium may not rely on Article 638 of the *Code Judiciaire*, under which he

---

[23] But see para. 17.55 above.
[24] See para. 16.09 above.

would otherwise be able in some circumstances to sue a foreign defendant in the court of the plaintiff's own domicile.

7. Civil claims in criminal proceedings

When a person has a civil claim arising from facts which also give **48.31** rise to a criminal offence for which the defendant is being prosecuted, the plaintiff may bring his civil claim in the criminal proceedings. If, however, he brings a separate civil claim, the civil proceedings are stayed until the criminal proceedings have been finally determined.

F. LIMITATION PERIODS

The law of limitation (*prescription / verjaring*) is complex and the **48.32** following should be taken as only the most general guide.

Limitation periods are regarded as a matter of substantive law, though they cannot be applied by a court of its own motion. Sometimes the time bar is absolute, sometimes it may bar the remedy or shift the burden of proof.

The moment from which time runs is usually when the cause of action arose, but it may be delayed until the plaintiff had (or ought to have had) knowledge of the facts establishing the cause of action. Other factors may also affect the running of a limitation period, and it may be suspended, or may start afresh, in various circumstances.

There is an overall period of limitation of 30 years which applies to **48.33** most claims in contract and tort. There are, however, many shorter periods which are laid down for particular types of claim in the *Code Civil*, the *Code de Commerce*, labour law, and other legislation:

(*a*) an undefined short period (*bref délai*), the length of which depends on the circumstances: actions in respect of latent defects in goods;

(*b*) six months: an action by an indorser of a bill of exchange against another indorser or against the drawer; claims for payment by hoteliers, caterers and manual workers; most actions on a contract of non-international carriage;

(*c*) one year: claims for payment in non-commercial contracts, for example, by doctors, *huissiers*, and businessmen (in respect of sales to non-businessmen); after a year there is a rebuttable presumption that payment has been made;

(*d*) one year: an action by the holder of a bill of exchange against an indorser or the drawer; most actions on a contract of international carriage;

(*e*) three years: actions against the acceptor of a bill of exchange; many claims on contracts of non-marine insurance;

(*f*) five years: actions on debts payable by instalments, including salaries, pensions and (subject to exceptions) rents;

(*g*) five years: claims on debts payable by instalments, such as maintenance, rents of dwelling houses, and interest on loans; civil claims for damages made in criminal proceedings; claims in civil proceedings arising out of a criminal act (or such longer period equal to that during which the particular crime may be the subject of prosecution);

(*h*) ten years: claims against builders or architects for defective work (the time runs from final acceptance of the work);

(*i*) twenty years: a claim by the rightful owner of real property against a purchaser in good faith, unless the plaintiff resides in the same *cour d'appel* district (in which case the period is 10 years). The time runs from the date of purchase by the defendant.

G. CIVIL PROCEDURE—PROCEEDINGS UP TO JUDGMENT

1. General description

48.34   Ordinary civil procedure is regulated by the *Code Judiciaire*. The procedure described below is followed both in the civil courts and in the commercial courts.

Ordinary proceedings are usually started by the service of a summons by the *huissier*.[25] The parties then attend an initial hearing at which, often, the case is adjourned for the exchange of documentary evidence and pleadings. The parties then set the case down for a main hearing at which both sides make opening submissions to the court and deposit their files of documentary evidence. A judgment will then be given, usually after the case has been adjourned for deliberation. This judgment may be an interlocutory judgment (for example, appointing a court expert, or ordering the hearing of witnesses or the attendance of the parties for questioning) or it may be a final judgment. If it is an interlocutory judgment, it will be followed by further pleadings and a further hearing for argument. When the court is satisfied that it has sufficient material before it, it will pronounce a final judgment.

---

[25] Some applications may be made *ex parte* by way of *requête*: see para. 48.59 below.

2. Parties and legal representation

Parties. All natural and legal persons,[26] with a sufficient legal   **48.35**
interest, can sue and be sued, regardless of their nationality. Public
bodies such as the state, provincial and local authorities, and public
utility undertakings can sue and be sued in the ordinary civil or
commercial courts. Minors, and some other natural persons such as
mental patients and bankrupts, can only act through representatives.

The plaintiff and the defendant in proceedings in a Belgian court
are described as the *demandeur / eiser* and the *défendeur / verweerder*
(or *gedaagde*). The defendant may bring a counterclaim against the
plaintiff in respect of any matter which is related to the subject-
matter of the claim. The court does not have to have independent
jurisdiction over the subject-matter of the counterclaim. Further
parties may be added to the proceedings at the request of either of
the main parties. A third party may intervene voluntarily in the
proceedings in order to protect his own interest either by advancing
an independent case or by supporting the case of one or other of the
main parties.

Legal representation. Parties may appear either in person or by an   **48.36**
avocat in all courts except the *Cour de Cassation*. The officers of a
company may appear in person on behalf of the company if so authorised by the articles of association and by the court. Before the *juge
de paix*, the *tribunal de commerce* and the *tribunal du travail* parties
may also, with the permission of the court, be represented by their
spouse or a close relative who must have a written proxy. Trade
union representatives may also appear for employees or independent workers before the employment courts if they have a written
proxy.

3. Commencement of proceedings

There are various methods by which proceedings may be com-   **48.37**
menced. The principal method is by the service of a *citation* (or
assignation / dagvaarding). Some proceedings are commenced by *ex
parte* application or request to the court (*requête / verzoekschrift*).
Some employment cases are, in rare instances, begun by registered
letter to the court. It is also permissible for parties or their representatives to begin proceedings informally by attending the court office
and submitting a joint statement of the matter in dispute. This has
the advantage of saving the time and expense of formal service.

A *citation* must contain specific information required by law.
This includes the name and domicile of the plaintiff, the name and

---

[26] The common forms of legal persons are listed at para. 48.73 below.

domicile or residence of the defendant, a summary of the claim and its supporting grounds, the court before which the claim is brought, and the place, date, and time of the first hearing. The *citation* is normally drafted by an *avocat*, but it may also be drafted by the plaintiff in person. It is, however, in the form of a statement by the *huissier* in which he certifies that he has carried out service on the defendant. The date of the first hearing will normally be selected by the *huissier* from the court calendar, having regard to the date upon which he expects to be able to effect service, and to the time interval that is required by law.[27] Evidential documents are not normally attached to a *citation*.

After service, the original of the *citation* is deposited by the *huissier* (or occasionally by the *avocat* or the plaintiff) at the *greffe* (court office) and the case is entered on the *rôle général* of the court. The *huissier* also sends a copy of the *citation* to the plaintiff or his *avocat*. The entry of the case on the role of the court is considered to be the moment at which the proceedings are definitively pending.[28]

4. Service of proceedings

48.38   In the case of proceedings started by *citation*, service (*signification / betekening*) must be carried out by a *huissier de justice* for the locality in which service is to be effected.[29] If the defendant is a natural person, service is effected by the *huissier* serving a copy of the *citation* on the defendant wherever he can be found; if it is a legal person, service is effected at the company's registered office or at its place of business. Service may also be carried out at any place at which the defendant has an elected domicile.

As regards natural persons, the *huissier* will normally visit the defendant's domicile or residence shown in the local population register, in order to effect personal service on him.[30] If he is not there the *huissier* may leave a copy of the *citation* with a member of his family or with an employee.

When the *citation* cannot be served by the above means the *huissier* will usually leave a copy at the address of the defendant and send notice to him by post. Occasionally the *huissier* will deliver a copy to the local head office of the *huissiers de justice* or at the local police station and leave or send a notice to this effect to the defendant.

---

[27] See para. 48.38 below.

[28] See para. 23.06, n. 16 above.

[29] In proceedings begun by *requête* the proceedings are delivered on behalf of the plaintiff to the court office (*greffe*), or sent by registered letter, whereupon the *greffier* will summon the defendant to attend court on the hearing date.

[30] If his residence is not registered in the population register, he may be served at the address where he is actually residing.

If factual circumstances make it impossible to serve the defendant at his domicile or residence, service may be effected by the *huissier* handing a copy of the *citation* to the *Procureur du Roi* for the district where those circumstances occurred. The *huissier* indorses on the copy of the *citation* a statement of the reasons which made normal service impossible (for example, the defendant may obviously have moved, but without notifying the authorities). It is then the responsibility of the *Procureur* to take such steps as are necessary to bring the *citation* to the defendant's attention as soon as possible. Service on the *Procureur* is not valid if the party requesting service knew of the defendant's elective or actual domicile.

If the defendant is domiciled abroad in a state which is party to the Hague Service Convention[31] then the procedure provided in that Convention is followed. Otherwise the *huissier* simply sends a copy of the *citation* to the defendant at his foreign address. Due service is deemed to have taken place at the moment when the *citation* is delivered to the post office in Belgium against a receipt. If the defendant has no known domicile or residence either in Belgium or abroad the *citation* is served on the *Procureur du Roi*[32] for the district of the competent court.

In the case of a defendant who is domiciled in Belgium there must be at least eight days between the date of service and the date of the first hearing. This period is extended by the following periods if service is to be effected abroad: 15 days in the case of service in an adjoining country or the United Kingdom, 30 days in the case of service in another part of Europe, and 80 days in the case of service in any other part of the world.

If service is effected with too short an interval before the first hearing, it may be declared void.

5. Appearance by the defendant

The defendant must take such steps as may be necessary to ensure that he or his *avocat* appears in person at the first hearing of the case. It is this appearance in person or by an *avocat* which formally constitutes the entry of an appearance in the case.[33] **48.39**

6. Default judgments

If one of the parties does not appear at a hearing the other party may ask for judgment in his favour. The court may give judgment immediately or it may announce that it will give judgment on a **48.40**

---

[31] See paras. 4.30 *et seq.* above and A2.03 below.
[32] See para. 48.23 above.
[33] Appearance may be made instead by the *avocat* writing a letter to the court, if the plaintiff's *avocat* has declared in court that that is acceptable.

specified date. In the latter event the party in default will be warned by letter from the court office. Before deciding in the plaintiff's favour the court should examine its jurisdiction, the admissibility of the claim, and its merits, but in practice any examination of the merits at this stage is minimal. The judgment will not be immediately enforceable unless the court so orders.[34]

48.41 *Setting aside.* A party against whom judgment by default has been given may apply, by a procedure known as *opposition / verzet*, to set the judgment aside, or he may appeal to a higher court. *Opposition* is normally brought by way of a fresh *citation* in the same court, in which the defendant applies for the default judgment to be set aside. The new proceedings automatically suspend the operation of the default judgment which may not then be enforced unless it has been expressly declared to be *"exécutoire par provision"*/*"uitvoerbaar bij voorraad"* (provisionally enforceable despite opposition or appeal). It is not necessary to give any explanation for the default, nor to show that the defaulting party has a meritorious case, but the *citation* should state the grounds for the *opposition*. Thereafter the two sets of proceedings are in effect merged and in the final judgment the court gives its pronouncement as to whether, and if so to what extent, the default judgment should be set aside.

Opposition proceedings must be commenced within one month from the date upon which the default judgment was served on the defaulting party. This period is extended by the following periods if the service of the default judgment takes place in another country: 15 days in the case of a party in an adjoining country or the United Kingdom, 30 days in the case of a party in another part of Europe, and 80 days in the case of a party in any other part of the world.

7. Disputes as to jurisdiction

48.42 If a defendant wishes to dispute the jurisdiction of the court he must do this before advancing any substantive defence to the action, unless his objection is based on public policy. He may do this at the first hearing or at a later stage, provided that in his pleadings he raises the issue at the outset. The plaintiff may apply for the matter to be decided by the *tribunal d'arrondissement*,[35] but normally the court itself will decide the issue. If the court considers the objection to be well founded it will transfer the case to the competent court, or, where a foreign court has jurisdiction, it will dismiss the case, or stay the proceedings in accordance with Article 21 of the 1968 Convention.

---

[34] A default judgment will cease to be enforceable if it is not served on the defendant within one year of its pronouncement: see para. 48.66 below.
[35] See para. 48.18 above.

8. Pleadings

The contents of the *citation* have already been described.[36] Unless **48.43**
a case is disposed of at the initial hearing,[37] the plaintiff's *avocat* will
send copies of the documents upon which he proposes to rely[38] to
the defendant's *avocat* and thereafter the parties will exchange
pleadings known as *conclusions / conclusies*. The purpose of the
plaintiff having to supply his documents is so as to supplement the
allegations made in the *citation* and to enable the defendant to meet
the case against him. The *conclusions* will contain all material allegations of fact and arguments as to law. The original is deposited at
the court office (*greffe*) and a copy is sent to the opposing *avocat*.
The defendant has one month from receipt of the plaintiff's documents within which to deliver his *conclusions* by way of defence.
The plaintiff has one month thereafter within which to reply, and
the defendant then has a further 15 days within which to deliver any
additional *conclusions*. A failure to comply with these time limits
does not result in the nullity of the pleading. However if a party
fails to deliver his first *conclusions* it is open to the other party to
have him summoned to the court under a default procedure.

As the exchange of pleadings proceeds, the parties normally also **48.44**
send each other copies of the documents upon which they propose
to rely, although as an alternative the documents may be lodged at
the court office, where they can be inspected by the parties. On the
application of either party, the registrar of the court (*greffier*) sets a
date for the first hearing. This may happen when the initial
exchange of pleadings is complete, although it frequently happens
that the parties continue an exchange of further additional *conclusions* up to the date of the first main hearing.[39] They may also file
further pleadings at a later stage to take account of an expert's
report or other evidence.

9. The hearings

The initial hearing. The initial hearing takes place at a special sit- **48.45**
ting of the court, called an *audience d'introduction / inleidingszitting*,
at which the cases appointed for first hearing that day will be called
in the order in which they have been entered on the *rôle général*.
The parties, or their *avocats* or other representatives, are normally
obliged to attend this hearing. Straightforward cases, such as
default judgments and judgments by consent, may be dealt with
immediately. In an ordinary contested case the proceedings will be

---

[36] See para. 48.37 above.
[37] See para. 48.45 below.
[38] See para. 48.51 below.
[39] See para. 48.46 below.

"sent to the *rôle*," which means that they will simply be adjourned for the parties to exchange documentary evidence and pleadings. Sometimes the court will make some interlocutory judgment, appointing an expert, for instance, or directing the transfer of the proceedings to another court. Alternatively the court may adjourn the proceedings to a later *audience d'introduction* if the parties or either of them so request. When the parties' *avocats* agree that the case cannot be dealt with immediately, they may notify the *greffier* in writing that they appear for the parties and they are then excused from attending the hearing. Cases which are not disposed of on an initial hearing are allocated by the president of the court to an appropriate chamber and the parties then exchange their pleadings and documentary evidence as described above.

48.46   *The main hearings.* At the request of either of the parties the *greffier* fixes a date for the main hearing, having been given an estimate of time. The purpose of this hearing is to enable the parties to enlarge upon their *conclusions*. The hearing takes place before the full court. The *avocat* for the plaintiff opens the case to the court, and the *avocat* for the defendant replies. However the court at this stage does not normally consider evidence and very frequently it will not even have seen the documentary evidence. At the conclusion of this main hearing the presiding judge formally "closes the debates" and directs the parties to deposit their files of documents with the courts. These files contain all relevant documents such as contracts, invoices, delivery notes and party and party correspondence, together with statements from witnesses, reports from party's experts and police reports.[40]

Once the debates have been closed, the parties may not normally make any further submission or deposit any further evidence. If, however, some new fact or document comes to light a party may, so long as final judgment has not been given, apply to reopen the debates. Depending on the order made by the court at this stage of the proceedings, the parties may have an opportunity to make further submissions.

Written procedure. There is some variation as between different *arrondissements* as to the extent to which main hearings are held. In some areas the parties are encouraged to adopt an alternative procedure which is in writing. In such cases there is no main hearing and the parties deliver written submissions to the court on or before a day fixed for the case to be considered. Depending on its view of the case the court may still require further submissions to be made either orally or in writing.

---

[40] See para. 48.51 below.

Interlocutory and final judgments. On the formal closure of the   **48.47**
debates the judge sets a date on which the court will give its judgment. This is formally required to be given within a month but in
practice the period is frequently extended. In the meantime the
judges will conduct their deliberations in private and the judgment
is then drafted by one of their number. The decision is arrived at by
a majority vote, and dissenting opinions are not stated.[41] It is formally pronounced in open court, although the parties and their lawyers do not ordinarily attend. The *greffier* will send copies to the
lawyers.

The judgment may be interlocutory or final. If the court considers that it has enough material to decide the case, it does so and
gives a final judgment immediately. If it considers that further
investigation is required, it gives an appropriate interlocutory judgment. It might order the examination of witnesses[42] or the disclosure of further documents[43] or the appointment of an expert,[44]
or the examination of the parties.[45] It might direct the reopening of
the oral hearing to permit the giving of further oral argument or
explanation by the *avocats* or the submission of further evidence.

10. Security for costs

A plaintiff who is resident outside Belgium who brings proceed-   **48.48**
ings in a Belgian court against a Belgian defendant, may, if the
latter so requests, be ordered to provide security for the costs of the
defendant (*cautio judicatum solvi*). The request for security must be
made in the defence before any other exception is taken. The court
fixes the amount of the security in its discretion but it will be based
on an estimate of the likely costs of the defendant in defending the
proceedings. Further security can be ordered during the course of
the proceedings. The security will ordinarily be in the form of a
deposit of a sum of money. A plaintiff who has real property in Belgium which is sufficient to satisfy an order for costs will not be
ordered to provide security. Belgium is party to various international conventions under which plaintiffs resident in contracting
states are exempted from the requirement to provide security in
Belgium.[46]

---

[41] The contents of the final judgment are described in more detail at para. 48.56
below.
[42] See para. 48.49 below.
[43] See para. 48.52 below.
[44] See para. 48.53 below.
[45] See para. 48.50 below.
[46] Notably, the Hague Convention on Civil Procedure of March 1, 1954. See also
para. 6.11 above.

11. Witnesses and oral evidence

48.49   The taking of oral evidence in Belgian civil or commercial proceedings is rare, although it more often occurs in divorce or employment cases. The court will ordinarily base its judgment on the documentary evidence, including the written statements of any witnesses. Indeed, it is a rule of substantive law that, except in commercial matters, a contractual liabilty in excess of BEF 3,500 may not be proved by oral evidence. A party will, in his *conclusions*, offer to prove some material allegation by means of a witness and may well include a statement from the witness in the file of documents deposited with the court at the closure of the debates. However the court will, in the majority of cases, consider it unnecessary to have the witness called to give oral evidence. There is no formal prohibition against an *avocat* taking a statement from a witness in interview but generally he does not do so. The witness is simply asked to provide his own statement.

The parties themselves are not competent to be witnesses[47] but, subject to some exceptions, their relatives are. The officers of a company are competent to give evidence in proceedings involving the company. When oral evidence has been given on behalf of one of the parties to the proceedings the other party has the right, if he makes a formal request, to call witnesses to give contrary evidence. In any event the parties may submit further written *conclusions* on the matters arising out of the evidence and a further hearing may take place for argument to be addressed to the court.

The order directing oral evidence. If the court makes an order directing the taking of oral evidence the interlocutory judgment states the date, time and place of the hearing and it specifies the issues upon which oral evidence is to be heard. The party who is directed to produce his witnesses must send a list of those witnesses to the court clerk at least 15 days before the hearing. This list is then sent by the clerk to the other parties. The witnesses are summoned by the *greffier* to the hearing but this formality may be dispensed with. A witness who refuses to attend may be fined and ordered to pay damages if the party can establish resultant loss.

Taking the deposition. The hearing is normally conducted by the trial judge or, in cases before a bench of three judges, before one of their number appointed for the purpose. The hearing takes place in private in the judge's chambers. The witness is questioned by the judge. The *avocats* may only put their questions through the judge. Hearsay evidence is admitted. The evidence is recorded in sum-

---

[47] See para. 48.50 below as to examination of the parties.

mary form by the court clerk,[48] who reads it over afterwards to the witness for any corrections to be made. It is then signed by the witness. The statement is later incorporated into a *procès verbal / proces-verbaal* which constitutes a record of the proceedings at the hearing.

Examination of the parties. Although the parties are not compe- **48.50** tent to give evidence as witnesses in the proceedings, the court may nonetheless, by interlocutory judgment, order their personal attendance for questioning by the court. In the case of a corporate party the officers of the company may be ordered to attend. The judge puts such questions to the party as he considers fit. The party is not on oath and his answers, though not technically "evidence," may be taken into account by the court in deciding the case.

The decisory oath. In some circumstances a party may request that the other party be ordered to swear to the truth of some matter in issue. The sworn answers given are conclusive for the purposes of those proceedings. If it is subsequently discovered that the party has committed perjury then, apart from any criminal sanction, he will be liable in damages to the other party. Refusal to take the oath will lead the court to conclude that the refusing party is not able to substantiate his assertion.

Judicial assistance. Belgium is not a party to the Hague Evidence Convention. It does, however, have a bilateral convention with the United Kingdom which provides for the rendering of judicial assistance in this way.[49]

12. Documentary evidence

All documentary evidence which a party wishes to use during **48.51** proceedings has to be communicated to the other party. In most cases the disclosure of documents is undertaken informally by sending them to the *avocat* on the other side, but the *Code Judiciaire* also provides that they may be lodged at the *greffe*, where they can be inspected by the parties. A party's documents are assembled into a file which is usually handed into the court at the closure of the debates. Documents may not normally be introduced thereafter.

Documentary evidence is not limited to documents such as contracts, invoices, delivery notes or letters, but it may include other material such as unsworn statements from witnesses,[50] or police

---

[48] It is procedurally possible, though rarely done, for a party to insist, by prior notice in writing, that the evidence be recorded verbatim.
[49] See para. 8.49 above.
[50] There is no provision in Belgian law for the making of affidavits and they are not ordinarily used in Belgian proceedings.

reports. Correspondence passing between the respective lawyers is confidential unless it is expressed to be non-confidential. Even then the opposing *avocat* may insist on treating it as confidential, but it loses its character of confidentiality and may be used in court with the permission of the *bâtonnier* (head of the local bar) when, for example, it confirms an agreement between the parties. Strictly speaking correspondence between lawyers may not be disclosed to their respective clients.

48.52 A party is not bound to disclose documents that are adverse to his case. If there are compelling reasons to believe that a party or a third party is in possession of a document which is relevant to the issues of the case, the judge may make an interlocutory order requiring production. This power is rarely exercised. The later discovery of a material document which has been concealed by a party can afford grounds for challenging the judgment given in the absence of the document.[51]

13. Experts

48.53 It is fairly common for the court to appoint an expert in any case in which technical, scientific or other specialist issues are raised as to liability or damages. The appointment of an expert may also be made as a interim protective measure[52] to investigate transient or disputed facts. The expert is chosen by the court usually from a list kept at the court. If the parties agree as to the choice of a suitable expert the court will usually appoint their nominee. A party may challenge the appointment of a particular expert if he has grounds for doing so. A party is at liberty to instruct an expert privately and that expert may participate in the enquiry on behalf of the party.

The court's interlocutory judgment appointing the expert also specifies the terms of his enquiry and fixes a period within which his report is to be presented. The expert will fix the time and place of his enquiry. He may conduct an informal hearing at which he may question the parties and any witnesses, and inspect any documents or other tangible evidence. The *Code Judiciaire* imposes on the expert a positive duty to conciliate, if possible, between the parties.

The expert first prepares a draft report which he submits to the parties for their comments in writing. Then he prepares a final report for the court. Although the court is entirely free to reject the expert's findings if it wishes to do so, it usually accepts them. If the

---

[51] See para. 48.65 below.
[52] See para. 48.58 below.

court is not satisfied with the report it may ask the expert to renew his enquiry and to report further or it may appoint a different expert to report. After the presentation of the report to the court the parties may exchange further *conclusions* and may request a further hearing for oral argument. The fees of an expert may be ordered to be paid by the party who requested the appointment. In practice the fees are frequently paid by the party direct to the expert without the order of the court although in its final judgment the court usually orders the losing party to bear the costs relating to the expert's report.

14. Proof of foreign law

Belgian courts will apply foreign law if it is the *lex causae*. A party will make his submissions on foreign law in his pleadings. The rules as to what constitutes adequate evidence of foreign law are very liberal and foreign statutes, treatises, textbooks and other documentary material, such as the written opinion of a foreign lawyer, may be admitted. Exceptionally, the court may apply foreign law of its own motion, having conducted its own research. **48.54**

15. Compromise

The parties to any litigation are at liberty to settle their differences at any stage. Unless the parties agree to the contrary, the terms of a compromise ordinarily replace the original cause of action, and, if not complied with, may be the subject of a fresh action. If the agreement is noted in the records of the court it has the same effect and will be enforceable by the same methods as a judgment.[52a] The court, however, does not actively promote a compromise, except in employment cases. **48.55**

It is also open to parties to take proceedings with a view to a friendly settlement. A minute of the proceedings is drawn up in which the terms of settlement are noted and of which the parties may obtain enforceable copies.

16. The final judgment

The court's final judgment in a civil or commercial case must identify the court, the judges, the parties, their lawyers, and the subject matter of the claim. It must expressly address and deal with **48.56**

[52a] As to the enforcement of court settlements, see para. 48.70 below.

the arguments raised in the respective written pleadings, giving reasons for its decision. There is no separate requirement in Belgian law that a judgment which is to be enforced outside Belgium should state the basis on which jurisdiction was accepted. This will only appear in practice when the question of jurisdiction has been in issue in the case.

Contractual or compensatory interest on the debt or damages may be included in the sum awarded by the judgment and the judgment itself may state that it carries interest according to law (*les intérêts judiciaires / gerechtelijke interesten*). This runs from the date of service of the proceedings at a set rate which fluctuates with interest rates. The judgment will also make an appropriate order as to costs.

The original of the judgment is signed by the judges. The registrar of the court (the *greffier*) must send a copy of the judgment to the parties within a week of it being given. This copy is not on stamped paper, does not bear the court seal or *greffier's* signature, and may not be used for the purposes of enforcement. For that purpose, it is necessary to obtain an official copy of the judgment, called an *expédition / uitgifte*. This is issued by the *greffier* on payment of the appropriate fee[53] and is certified as an original copy by his signature and the court seal. It bears an indorsement as to its executory character.[54]

17. Costs

48.57   A party's costs (*frais et dépens / uitgaven en kosten*) will be itemised in his pleadings. Recoverable costs include various court fees, the *huissier's* fees, experts' fees, witnesses' expenses and certain expenses incurred by the successful party. They do not include the fees of the successful party's *avocat* for the preparation and conduct of the case, other than a nominal amount fixed by scale. These so-called *indemnités de procédure / rechtsplegingsvergoedingen* are normally much lower than the fees actually payable by a party to his *avocat*. Decisions as to costs are in the discretion of the court. Normally the losing party will be ordered to pay the successful party's costs, but partial success in an action may result in obtaining an order for only part of the costs. The costs of a foreign party's foreign lawyer are usually not recoverable.

---

[53] This is the fee payable for the issue of the copy judgment. In addition, a tax of 2.5 per cent. of the amount awarded by a money judgment is payable by the losing party to the Belgian Ministry of Finance.
[54] See para. 48.67 below.

H. Civil Procedure—Provisional and Protective Measures

1. Introduction

There are two main types of procedure which are employed for ordering provisional or protective measures. First, there is the summary procedure known as *référé / kort geding*, by which an interim order may be obtained in an urgent case. This procedure is discussed in greater detail below.[55] Secondly, there are various forms of attachment which are available as protective measures pending trial or pending the enforcement of a judgment. In addition, certain types of order made by the judge in the course of the proceedings, such as the appointment of an expert, may be made as an interim protective measure. Provisional and protective measures are available in aid of proceedings in a foreign country.

48.58

2. Provisional attachment

Provisional attachment (*saisie conservatoire / bewarend beslag*) of a defendant's assets is available as a protective measure for the purpose of securing those assets in order that they will be available for execution of the judgment if the plaintiff is successful. The plaintiff's claim must be for a sum which is certain or capable of provisional quantification. The attachment of assets situated outside Belgium is not permitted by Belgian law.

48.59

All claims for provisional attachment fall within the competent of the *juge des saisies / beslagrechter*, a judge of the *tribunal de première instance* appointed to undertake this role.[56] He has jurisdiction to entertain applications in respect of commercial as well as civil matters. The proceedings will be dealt with either on an *ex parte* basis (*sur requête*), or *inter partes*, according to the *référé* procedure. Proceedings for the provisional attachment of property must be brought in the courts for the place where the property is situated, or in some other court where related proceedings are pending.

A creditor may apply to the *juge des saisies* either before or during the proceedings for an order permitting him to attach provisionally the assets of the debtor. The application may relate to the debtor's assets generally or to specific assets. The creditor must set out the nature of his claim against the debtor and he must show that he has a good prima facie claim on the merits. He must also show that there is an urgent risk that unless the attachment is made he may be deprived of the fruits of any judgment. The making of the order is in the complete discretion of the judge.

---

[55] See para. 48.61 below.

[56] He also has jurisdiction over matters relating to execution: see para. 48.66 below.

In some circumstances, a creditor may also ask the *huissier* to carry out a *saisie conservatoire* without the intervention of the court, on the basis of a formal document of a private nature such as a bill of exchange, a cheque, a lease, an insurance policy or a will. Similarly, the leave of the *juge des saisies* is not required for the provisional attachment of assets in aid of execution of a judgment, even if the judgment has not been declared provisionally enforceable and is not yet *res judicata*.[57]

48.60 There are different types of *saisie conservatoire*, depending on the type of assets to be attached. The attachment of tangible goods is called *saisie mobilière conservatoire / bewarend beslag op roerend goed* and the attachment of the defendant's assets held by a third party, such as a debt (notably a bank account), is called *saisie-arrêt conservatoire / bewarend beslag onder derden*.[57a] Other forms of provisional attachment are *saisie immobilière conservatoire / bewarend beslag op onroerend goed* (attachment of real property), *saisie-revindication / beslag tot terugvordering* (seizure of property which is the subject of the action in the possession of a third party), *saisie conservatoire sur navires et bateaux / bewarend beslag op zeeschepen en binnenschepen* (attachment of vessels); *saisie en matière de contrefaçon / beslag inzake namaak* (seizure of tangible evidence for use in proceedings relating to patents and other intellectual property); *saisie-gagerie / pandbeslag* (seizure of a tenant's goods for rent).

The order will specify the amount in respect of which seizure is to be made. This may not necessarily be for the full amount claimed by the plaintiff. The provisional attachment of goods is effected by the *huissier* visiting the place where the assets are situated and listing the assets to be attached. The defendant may be left in possession of the assets but he is restrained from disposing of them, under threat of criminal sanctions. The attachment of assets in the hands of a third party by means of *saisie-arrêt conservatoire* may be effected in the same way. Attachment of immovable property is effected by registration of a charge over the land.

The *saisie* will remain in effect for three years unless it is lifted or renewed. Belgian law does not require the plaintiff to bring proceedings for the validation of the attachment. The defendant may obtain the lifting of the attachment by providing alternative security or he may apply to the *juge des saisies* for the order to be discharged or varied. Similarly, a third party whose rights are affected by the order may apply to the court for it to be discharged or varied.

If the plaintiff is eventually unsuccessful in his claim, the defend-

---

[57] See para. 48.66 below.
[57a] Some assets cannot be attached, notably a minimum amount of salary.

ant may apply for the attachment to be discharged, and the plaintiff may be liable in damages to the defendant for any loss which the latter has suffered by reason of the attachment.

I. CIVIL PROCEDURE—SUMMARY PROCEDURES

1. *Référé / Kort geding*

The respective presidents of the *tribunal de première instance*, the 48.61 *tribunal du travail*, and the *tribunal de commerce* have jurisdiction, which they may delegate to other judges of their courts, to grant urgent interim relief in appropriate cases.[58] The court may grant whatever relief is necessary to protect the interest which is being threatened. For example, an order might be made to restrain some harmful act, to enforce the performance of some obligation or to appoint an expert to report on some transient set of facts. Exceptionally an interim award in respect of a claim for debt or damages may be made. The order is always provisional in nature and does not prejudice the ultimate rights of the parties. It is automatically provisionally enforceable,[59] even if it is challenged by *opposition* or appeal.[60]

The party applying for relief must normally commence the proceedings by causing a *citation* to be served on the other party. The *citation* normally gives at least two days notice of the application, but this time is extended in the case of a respondent party domiciled outside Belgium. In cases of urgency the president may authorise a shorter period of notice, even as short as, for example, one hour. At the hearing the judge will consider the evidence and hear argument from both sides before making his order. It is unusual for witnesses to be heard. In maritime cases and in cases of extreme urgency the application may be made by unilateral *requête*, and if necessary the judge will hear the applicant out of normal court hours at his home. The applicant is not normally required to provide security.

The party against whom an order has been made may, if it was made in his absence, challenge it by separate proceedings (*opposition*). An order given following an *inter partes* hearing, can only be the subject of an appeal (*appel*) to the appropriate higher court.

---

[58] The President of the *tribunal de première instance* has a general jurisdiction to do so in respect of any matter brought before him notwithstanding that the particular case might fall within the specific competence of the *tribunal de commerce* or the *tribunal du travail*. The jurisdiction of the presidents of the latter two courts is limited to matters falling within their respective competences.
[59] See para. 48.67 below.
[60] See para. 48.64 below.

2. Summary order for payment

48.62 There is also a simple type of procedure which is used in smaller debt cases. This is the *procédure sommaire d'injonction de payer / summiere rechtspleging om betaling te bevelen.* It is used in the court of the *juge de paix* to claim payment of sums of up to BEF 50,000. The debt must be evidenced in writing. It is only available against a defendant who is resident in Belgium. A formal demand is served on the debtor either by the *huissier* or by recorded postal delivery, calling for payment within 15 days and identifying the judge who will deal with the matter. If payment is not made a request is lodged with the *juge de paix* giving particulars of the claim. The judge then makes an order for payment in chambers. It is equivalent to a default judgment and can be challenged by appeal or by *opposition.*[61]

J. CIVIL PROCEDURE—APPEALS

1. Introduction

48.63 *Types of appeal.* Belgian law distinguishes between ordinary and extraordinary appeals. There are two types of ordinary appeal, namely *opposition / verzet,* which is an application to the court which made an order for the order to be set aside, and *appel / beroep,* which is an appeal in the strict sense to a higher court. Extraordinary appeals comprise an appeal in cassation (*pourvoi de cassation / voorziening in cassatie*), an application to set aside a judgment improperly obtained (*requête civile / herroeping van het gewijsde*) and an application by a third party for the revocation or amendment of a judgment improperly obtained (*tierce opposition / derdenverzet*).

2. Ordinary appeals

48.64 *Opposition / Verzet.* An application by way of *opposition* for a default judgment to be set aside has already been discussed.[62] Applications of a similar type may be made for setting aside various other orders, such as an order for interim measures made in the absence of the applicant (*sur requête / op verzoekschrift*).

Appel / Beroep. Either party may appeal from an interlocutory or final judgment at first instance by taking proceedings by a variety of methods in the appropriate appellate court. In certain circumstances, however, a decision may not be subject to an *appel.* For example, a judgment in a case in which the claim was for less than

---

[61] See para. 48.64 below.
[62] See para. 48.41 above.

BEF 15,000 may not normally be appealed.[62a] Appeals may also not be brought in the absence of an appeal on the substance of a matter, against most interlocutory orders of a procedural nature, such as an order for the production of documents, or ordering a party to attend for the purpose of questioning.

An *appel* is by way of rehearing of the case both as to the facts and as to the law and fresh evidence may be introduced. The appellant and the respondent are called the *appellant / eiser in beroep* and the *intimé / gedaagde in beroep* respectively. An appeal has the effect of suspending the enforcement of the judgment appealed against unless it is provisionally enforceable.[63] In the latter case the appellate court has no power to suspend the enforcement of the judgment.

Time for appealing. An appeal must be brought within one month from the date of service of the judgment, but this period is increased in the case of a party domiciled outside Belgium, by 15 days if he is domiciled in an adjoining country or in the United Kingdom, by 30 days if he is domiciled elsewhere in Europe, and by 80 days if he is domiciled in another part of the world.

3. Extraordinary appeals

Cassation/Cassatie. The organisation and powers of the *Cour de Cassation* have already been described.[64] The ordinary time limit for bringing an appeal in cassation is three months after service of the judgment. The appeal does not suspend the enforceability of the judgment appealed against and the other party may execute the judgment at his own risk. **48.65**

Requête civile / Herroeping van het gewijsde. This is a form of extraordinary appeal which permits the setting aside of a judgment if it was obtained by improper means such as the fraud of a party or the concealment of evidence. Recourse is to the court which gave the judgment in question. The proceedings must be brought within six months of the discovery of the grounds giving rise to the appeal. The appealed judgment is not suspended by the bringing of the proceedings.

Tierce opposition / Derdenverzet. A person whose interests are affected by a judgment given in proceedings in which he has not been a party may challenge the judgment by a special procedure known as *tierce opposition* (third party opposition). This comes before the court which gave the original judgment. The court may

---

[62a] Judgments of the *Tribunal du Travail* may be appealed regardless of amount.
[63] See para. 48.67 below.
[64] See para. 48.22 above.

revoke its decision either to the limited extent to which it affects the third party or, in an appropriate case, generally in respect of all the parties. Judgments of the *Cour de Cassation* cannot be the subject of *tierce opposition*. If the judgment has been served on the third party, *tierce opposition* has to be initiated within three months of the date of service. Otherwise it may be brought within 30 years of the judgment.

K. CIVIL PROCEDURE—ENFORCEMENT

1. Enforcement of Belgian judgments

48.66 A judgment may not be enforced until it has become *res judicata*, unless it is provisionally enforceable (*exécutoire par provision / uitvoerbaar bij voorraad*), and certain further formal requirements must have been complied with. The judgment must be indorsed as to its executory character and it must have been served. There is an ultimate time limit of 30 years on the enforceability of all judgments, except that the execution of a default judgment is further limited by the requirement that it must be served on the defendant within one year of its pronouncement. The commencement of an appeal or of proceedings by way of *opposition* ordinarly operates as an automatic stay of execution. Any dispute concerning the execution of any judgment is heard in the *tribunal de première instance* by the *juge des saisies*.

Res judicata. A normal judgment cannot be enforced (except provisionally) until it has become final, or *res judicata*. That is to say that the judgment must no longer be subject to an ordinary appeal, either because the time limit for such an appeal has expired, or because the appeal has been finally determined. If necessary, the *greffier* will provide a statement confirming that the judgment has not been appealed or challenged by *opposition*. The fact that the judgment may still be challenged by means of an extraordinary appeal does not prevent it from becoming *res judicata*.

48.67 *Provisional enforceability.* A judgment may be expressed to be provisionally enforceable if the court thinks fit. This may happen if the court considers that the chances of a successful appeal being made are remote, and when the plaintiff might be prejudiced by a delay in execution. However, once the creditor has a judgment against the debtor he may, even if it is not provisionally enforceable, instruct the *huissier* to carry out a *saisie conservatoire*[65] in respect of the debtor's assets.

A plaintiff may enforce a provisionally enforceable judgment, but

---

[65] See para. 48.59 above.

he does so at his own risk. If the defendant succeeds in his appeal against the judgment he may recover from the plaintiff not only the amount of the judgment but also damages for any loss which he has suffered by reason of the enforcement. Sometimes the judgment will permit provisional enforcement on condition that the plaintiff provides security. A defendant may prevent the execution of a provisionally enforceable judgment by providing security, known as *cantonnement / kantonnement*, for the amount of the judgment debt. This latter step may sometimes be expressly precluded by the terms of the judgment.

Indorsement as to executory character. Before a judgment can be executed an official copy of it (known as an *expédition / uitgifte*) must be obtained from the *greffier*. This must bear an indorsement as to its executory character (*formule exécutoire / formulier van tenuitvoerlegging*) which is in the following terms:

"*Nous, BAUDOUIN, Roi des Belges: A tous, présents et à venir, faisons savoir: Mandons et ordonnons à tous huissiers, à ce requis, de mettre le présent arrêt, jugement, ordonnance, mandat ou acte à exécution; A Nos procureurs généraux et à Nos procureurs du roi près les tribunaux de première instance, d'y tenir la main, et à tous commandants et officiers de la force publique, d'y prêter main forte lorsqu'ils en seront légalement requis; En foi de quoi le présent arrêt, jugement, ordonnance, mandat ou acte a été signé et scellé du sceau de la cour, du tribunal ou du notaire.*"

and in Flemish as follows:

"*Wij, BOUDEWYN, Koning der Belgen, aan Allen die nu zijn en hierna wezen zullen doen te weten: lasten en bevelen dat alle daartoe gevorderde gerechtsdeurwaarders dit arrest, dit vonnis, deze beschikking, dit bevel of deze akte ten uitvoer zullen leggen; Dat Onze procureurs-generaal en Onze procureurs des Konings bij de rechtbank van eerste aanleg, daaraan de hand zullen houden en dat alle bevelhebbers en officieren van de openbare macht daartoe de sterke hand zullen bieden wanneer dit wettelijk van hen gevorderd wordt; Ten blijke waarvan dit arrest, dit vonnis, deze beschikking, dit bevel, of deze akte is ondertekend en gezegeld met het zegel van het hof, de rechtbank of de notaris.*"

Service. A copy of the *expédition* of the judgment must normally be served on the party against whom it is proposed to execute the judgment. This must be done by a *huissier* for the *arrondissement* in which the party resides. At the same time, he serves a written notice demanding compliance with the judgment. Service of the judgment in this way is normally a necessary precondition to its execution, except that in certain cases, particularly if the matter is urgent, execution may proceed merely by the *huissier* presenting the original *expédition* of the judgment to the person against whom execution is to take place.

48.68   *Execution.* If the judgment is not complied with within one day the *huissier* will execute the judgment by carrying out a *saisie-exécution*. This is a form of attachment by which the *huissier* notionally seizes the assets in question. He prepares a document in which the assets are listed and a date given upon which the assets will be sold. This is served on the debtor who is thereafter prohibited, under criminal sanction, from disposing of the assets. If there has previously been a *saisie conservatoire* it will be converted into a *saisie-exécution* if the debtor does not comply with the judgment and the demand.

In practice the *huissier* may adopt a fairly flexible attitude towards the debtor. Any offer of payment by instalments will be communicated to the judgment creditor for his consideration but unless an acceptable offer is made the assets will be sold on the day fixed. There is no procedure whereby a judgment debtor can be examined by the court as to his means, but the *huissier* will normally give the creditor whatever information he obtains as to the debtor's means.

48.69   *Other methods of enforcement.* Non-money judgments may be enforceable by means of a monetary penalty (*astreinte / dwangsom*) if this is provided for in the judgment. This may be a periodic penalty, calculated as a certain sum for each day or week that the judgment is not complied with, or an incremental penalty payable in a certain sum for each separate infringement of the judgment. The sum payable is subject to review by the court which made the order. It is payable to the person in whose favour the judgment is given, and is enforceable by way of normal execution which must be commenced within six months of the date on which payment was due.

Opposing the execution. A judgment debtor who has grounds for objecting to execution may make complaint to the *juge des saisies* by means of a *citation*. A third party may also challenge the execution by *citation* before the *juge des saisies* if, for example, he claims title to the property seized.

2. Authentic instruments and court settlements

48.70   Under Belgian law the process of execution is available both in respect of judgments and in respect of various forms of enforceable instrument and court settlement. The formal entitlement to carry out execution depends upon the party requesting it having both the legal right to execution (*titre exécutoire / uitvoerbare titel*) and a claim which is quantified and certain.

Authentic instruments. Certain notarial deeds relating to such matters as mortgages, loans, matrimonial gifts, and wills, are regarded by Belgian law as authentic instruments capable of enforcement as such. To be enforceable these documents must have been entered in a register kept by the *receveur des droits d'enregistrement / ontvanger van registratierechten*. For the purposes of enforcement, the notary may be asked to issue an authenticated copy (*expédition*) of the instrument, which he has indorsed with a *formule exécutoire*.[66] He may only place such an indorsement on an instrument once the obligation has become enforceable and, according to some views, if the obligation in question is an obligation to pay money. Various official documents of a public nature, such as decisions by tax authorities, are also enforceable as authentic instruments. Authentic instruments are executed by the *huissier* in the same manner as if they were judgments.

Court settlements. It has already been noted that settlements minuted in the court records may be enforced.[67] On the application of a party, the registrar of the court (*greffier*) issues an official copy (*expédition*) of the relevant part of the records, indorsed with the *formule exécutoire*.[68] It may then be enforced in the same way as a judgment.

3. Enforcement of foreign judgments

Foreign judgments are enforceable in Belgium by all the appro-   **48.71** priate means available in respect of Belgian judgments, once their execution has been authorised by the indorsement of a *formule exécutoire*. The procedure for obtaining this indorsement differs according to whether the 1968 Convention applies, whether some other reciprocal enforcement convention applies, or whether no other convention applies.

Enforcement under the 1968 Convention. The procedure for enforcing a judgment under the 1968 Convention involves an application to the *tribunal de première instance*, regardless of the amount of the judgment. A copy of the foreign judgment must be produced, together with a translation into the language of the court.[69] The judge satisfies himself that the requirements of the Convention have been fulfilled.[70] The order for enforcement is in the form of a judg-

---

[66] See para. 48.67 above.
[67] See para. 48.55 above.
[68] See para. 48.67 above.
[69] The various documents lodged with the application must also be in French or Flemish, or accompanied by a translation in one of those languages, as appropriate. Translations must have been made by a person authorised to do so in one of the Contracting States: see para. 29.29 above. In Belgium, only sworn translators accepted by a *tribunal de première instance* are qualified to translate official documents.
[70] See Title III of the 1968 Convention generally, at Chaps. 25 to 29 above.

ment of the Belgian court. The judgment debtor is not heard on this initial application.

If an order for enforcement is granted by the court, the person against whom the order has been made may file an *opposition* to the enforcement before the *tribunal de première instance*. If the order is refused, the applicant may appeal to the *cour d'appel*. A further appeal may only be by way of cassation.

48.72   *Judgments outside the 1968 Convention*. If the 1968 Convention does not apply, the precise procedure to be followed depends on whether or not another convention applies (and if so what its terms are). If there is no applicable enforcement convention the Belgian court may still authorise the enforcement of the foreign judgment, but it will need to be satisfied that the judgment does not offend Belgian public policy, that the rights of the defence have been respected, and that the judgment is final and conclusive and in proper form according to the law of the state in which it was pronounced. It will also re-examine the merits of the case and refuse to allow enforcement if the trial judge appears to have made any error of fact or law.

L. LEGAL PERSONS

48.73   The common forms of legal entity in Belgium, with their usual abbreviations are:

(*a*) *Société anonyme* (S.A.) / *Naamloze vennootschap* (N.V.), a marketable share company with limited liability;

(*b*) *Société privée à responsabilité limitée* (S.P.R.L.) / *Besloten Vennootschap met beperkte aansprakelijkheid* (B.V.B.A.), a private limited liability company;

(*c*) *Société coopérative* (S.C.) / *Samenwerkende vennootschap* (S.V.), a co-operative company;

(*d*) *Société en commandite simple* (S.C.S.) / *Commanditaire vennootschap* (C.V.), a limited partnership in which the liability of some partners is limited and that of others is unlimited;

(*e*) *Société en commandite par actions* / *Gewone Commanditaire vennootschap op aandelen*, a limited partnership in which the liability of some partners is limited by shares and that of others is unlimited;

(*f*) *Société en nom collectif* (S.N.C.) / *Vennootschap onder firma* (V.O.F.) a partnership with legal personality and unlimited liability;

(*g*) *Société d'une personne à responsabilité limitée* / *Eénpersoonsvennootschap met beperkte aansprakelijkheid*, a sole trader with limited liability;

(*h*) *Association sans but lucratif* (A.S.B.L.) / *Vereniging zonder winstgevend doel* (V.Z.W.), a non-profit making association with limited liability.

M. LEGAL AID

In Belgium, legal aid (*l'aide judiciaire* / *rechtsbijstand*) is available to **48.74** Belgian nationals, foreigners resident in Belgium and, under certain international conventions, to foreigners resident elsewhere. Belgian law also provides that all nationals of member states of the Council of Europe are eligible for legal aid in Belgium.

Legal aid is available in respect of proceedings in court in two forms, first the assistance of an *avocat* in conducting a case free of his charges, and secondly the waiving of court costs, including those for the services of public officials such as *huissiers* and notaries. In both cases the applicant must satisfy certain financial criteria and he must show that he has a prima facie case. In respect of free legal assistance application must be made to the *Bureau de Consultation et de Défense* / *Bureau van Consultatie en Verdediging* set up by the local bar. Applications for legal aid in relation to the court costs must be made to the *Bureau d'Assistance Judiciaire* / *Bureau voor Rechtsbijstand*, set up in each court above the level of the *juge de paix* or *tribunal de police*, who will themselves determine such applications.[71]

If legal aid for an *avocat* is granted, the litigant is assigned an *avocat* (normally a *stagiaire*) who is paid an annual sum based on the number of assisted cases he has undertaken. The money for this purpose is made available by the state and is distributed by the local bars. Legal aid for court costs covers all court fees and other expenses associated with the case. Depending on the legally aided party's means, he may be required to make a contribution towards his costs. If the legally aided party succeeds in the case the other party is usually ordered to pay the costs of the legal aid. If he loses the case he is not ordered to pay the successful party's costs unless his financial circumstances have changed.

Legal aid may also be available in respect of advice unconnected with litigation under schemes administered by the *Bureau de Consultation et de Défense*.

---

[71] In urgent cases the application may be made to the president of the court in question.

CHAPTER 49

DENMARK

Written in collaboration with Advokater Rolf Meurs-Gerken and John Kahlke.[1]

---

[1] Partners, *Advokaterne, Amaliegade No 22*, Copenhagen and Paris. The authors also wish to acknowledge the assistance of Advokat Carsten Iversen, of Copenhagen and London.

Denmark

A. THE LEGAL SYSTEM

1. Introduction

History and territory. Denmark is the oldest kingdom in the world **49.01** and today consists of Denmark, the Faroe Islands and Greenland.[2] At various times in its history it has been linked with various other Scandinavian countries, and was in union with Norway from the fourteenth century until 1813. The country is now governed under a system of parliamentary democracy, with the monarchy playing a constitutional role.

Origins of the legal system. Danish law does not belong to the civil law family originating from Roman law, although it has been influenced first by canon law and later both by the Napoleonic Code and by German legal thinking. In common with other Scandinavian systems, it owes its origins mainly to medieval Nordic law. Although there had been a number of earlier codes, the first codification to cover the whole country was in 1683 under Christian V. The Faroe Islands and Greenland have their own autonomous legal systems, which are outside the scope of this book. Appeals from both these territories lie to the Danish High Court and Supreme Court.

2. Administration of justice

The organisation and administration of the Danish legal system is **49.02** the responsibility of the Ministry of Justice. The principal law which regulates most aspects of court procedure is the *Retsplejelov* (Administration of Justice Act) of 1916, as amended.

Court system. There are two levels of ordinary court of first instance, the *landsret* (high court) and the *byret* (district court) with jurisdiction over both civil and criminal matters. There are no separate systems of administrative courts or labour courts and ordinary civil courts have jurisdiction over the administrative authorities and over disputes between individual employees and their employers.[3]

---

[2] The Faroe Islands have been a self governing region of Denmark since 1948. Having originally opted not to join the EEC with the rest of Denmark, they are expressly excluded from the provisions of the EEC Treaty by Art. 227(5). Greenland, a former colony of Denmark, became a region of Denmark in 1953, and has been self governing since 1979. By a referendum in 1982 Greenlanders voted to leave the Community. This came about with effect from January 1, 1985. The 1968 Convention does not apply in Greenland; but see para. 34.05 above.

[3] The *Arbejdsretten* (literally the labour court) is an arbitration court which hears disputes between unions and employers' associations concerning wage agreements or working conditions, and certain claims brought on behalf of individuals by their respective associations. It is not part of the ordinary court system.

There is no formal distinction between civil and commercial matters. The final appellate court is the *Højesteret*, the Supreme Court.

<h2 style="text-align:center">B. LEGAL PRACTITIONERS</h2>

1. The *Advokat*

49.03   *Introduction.* There is only one legal profession in Denmark, that of the *advokat*. The *advokat* enjoys a monopoly of representing parties in court, and of holding himself out to provide legal services. The *advokat* acts for his clients over a wider range of matters than do his counterparts in most other European legal systems. In addition to his role as advocate in court proceedings, *advokater* act in such matters as the transfer of land, the management of property, the administration of estates of deceased persons, the formation and administration of companies and foundations and the drafting of agreements. They commonly act as liquidators or receivers of property, and sit on the boards of companies, associations and foundations.

Legal education and qualification. The intending *advokat* must first obtain a law degree at the university of Copenhagen or of Århus. This generally takes five years. He must then work for three years as the full-time trainee associate (*fuldmægtig*) of a senior *advokat*. During this period he has no right of audience in his own name, but he may appear on behalf of his principal, initially only in the *byret*, but after two years, and with the permission of the Ministry of Justice, in the *landsret*. Very frequently an experienced *fuldmægtig* is entrusted with the entire conduct of a case. His salary is generally equivalent to the starting salary of a lawyer in public service. After completion of this three year period as a *fuldmægtig* he receives his appointment (*bestalling*) as an *advokat* from the Minister of Justice.

49.04   *Rights of representation and audience.* All *advokater* have the right of audience before any *byret*. To obtain the right of audience before the *landsretter*, an *advokat* must normally have conducted cases there on two occasions to the satisfaction of the court. The *landsret* will indicate beforehand whether it will allow the *advokat* to appear before it for this qualifying purpose. An *advokat* who has appeared regularly before the *landsret* over a period of at least five years may apply for the right to appear before the *Højesteret* (Supreme Court).

Organisation of practice. There are some 3500[3a] *advokater* in Denmark, of whom about half are based in metropolitan Copenhagen. Partnerships are permitted but there are few firms with more than

---

[3a] As at June 1, 1989.

twenty partners. Specialisation is common in the larger partnerships, notably in Copenhagen and Århus. Much routine legal work in a law office is undertaken by the *fuldmægtig* under the general supervision of the *advokat*. Partnerships with other professional persons such as accountants or tax advisers are not permitted. An *advokat* does not normally obtain a written power of attorney from his client but he may sometimes do so when he represents a foreign client.

Fees. The fees of an *advokat* are freely negotiated with the client. **49.05** There is an advisory tariff published by *Det Danske Advokatsamfund* (the Danish Society of Advocates) which is calculated on the amount involved in the transaction or litigation. The tariff is normally followed, except in cases involving an unusual amount of work. It is unusual for a fixed fee to be agreed in advance. Fees are customarily charged on a time basis at anything between Dkr. 600–1800 per hour. Value Added Tax is payable on legal fees, but clients situated abroad may be exempted. The *advokat* may ask for an advance on account of fees and will normally do so if the client is a foreigner or is unknown to him. Contingent fees, whilst not expressly forbidden, are generally not used by the profession. Complaints regarding fees, even those agreed in advance, may be made initially to the board of the regional bar association with a right of appeal to the *advokatnævnet*, a tribunal made up jointly of *advokater* and lay persons.

Professional organisation. The governing body of the *advokater* is *Det Danske Advokatsamfund*, and all *advokater* are members of this body. It has 11 regional sections (*kredse*), which appoint the members of its board of directors or council (*Advokatraadet*) The president of the *Advokatraadet* is elected by a general assembly of all *advokater*. The *Advokatraadet* has statutory responsibility for the maintenance of professional standards, and is generally concerned with the interests of the legal profession.

Professional conduct. Advokater are required to conform with proper professional standards of conduct and ethics laid down by *Det Danske Advokatsamfund*. In addition, they are liable to their clients under the normal law and all *advokater* must be insured against liability for negligence up to a minimum amount of approximately Dkr. 881,000. As additional protection for clients, *Det Danske Advokatsamfund* maintains a trust fund to indemnify them in respect of any fraudulent losses of funds in the hands of an *advokat*. Communications between an *advokat* and his client are confidential and may only be disclosed with the client's permission.

[The next paragraph is number 49.09]

2. The Notary

49.09   There is no obligation under Danish law for any document to be drafted or attested by a notary, and consequently there is no independent profession of notary. For certain purposes, principally the attestation of wills and requirements of international trade and foreign law, the office of notary is vested in the judge of the *byret* who will attest documents if requested. In Copenhagen there is a special office for this purpose attached to the *byret*.

[The next paragraph is number 49.11]

3. Foreign lawyers

49.11   Lawyers from the other Member States of the EEC have the right to establish themselves in Denmark, using their national professional title. They may appear in Danish courts under the EEC Directive on Legal Services,[4] provided that they are accompanied by a Danish *advokat*. They would have to address the court in Danish, or through an interpreter.

A non-EEC lawyer wishing to establish himself in Denmark would have to fulfill the rather restrictive requirements of the *Udlændingelov* (Aliens Act). He would need a work and stay permit which would only be granted if the police were satisfied that he could support himself through the exercise of his profession. He would not be able to advise on Danish law unless he was also qualified as a Danish *advokat*.

4. Lawyers in business and public employment

49.12   *Advokater* are permitted to enter full time employment in commercial enterprises. They may retain their status as *advokater* and carry out legal work, including litigation, on behalf of their employers. If the terms of their employment allow, they may also act on behalf of their own private clients. An *advokat* may not, however, obtain employment with the government or other public body unless he deposits his *bestalling* (practising licence) with the Ministry of Justice for the duration of his public service.

[The next paragraph is number 49.14]

---

[4] See para. A2.47 below.

C. Sources of Law

1. Introduction

Following the advent of the Danish *Folketing*, or Parliament, in **49.14**
1849, the code of 1683[5] was gradually replaced by legislation on
specific subjects so that now only small parts of this original code
remain in force. In consequence legislation, in the form of individual statutes, is the main source of law in Denmark. Case law is of
secondary importance save in certain areas, notably the law relating
to tort and damages. Since the late nineteenth century there has
been considerable harmonisation of substantive law as between the
Scandinavian countries, and there are several Nordic conventions
concerning different aspects of private international law.

International treaties are not internally binding until they have
been incorporated by legislation into Danish law. The question of
the supremacy of EEC law over any subsequently enacted Danish
law has not arisen.

2. Legislation

The Danish legislative system is founded on the constitution **49.15**
(*Grundlov*), which dates in its present form from 1953 and which
has supreme authority over any statute (*lov*), passed by the *Folketing*. A *lov* may confer the power to make subordinate legislation
(*bekendtgørelser*) on a minister, or on a regional or district council.
Ministers may also issue circulars (*circulærer*), which lay down, for
the guidance of their departments, principles of interpretation of
statutes and of subordinate legislation. These are not of binding
force but they are frequently referred to by the courts when interpreting legislation.

3. Decided cases and legal writings

In Denmark case law has a less important role than in common **49.16**
law countries, as courts are not bound by precedent. They will
however normally follow the decisions of higher courts, and there is
a strong element of pragmatism in the development of the law. Certain matters, notably administrative law and tort, are largely
founded on case law.

Legal writings are frequently referred to in court in support of
legal argument. The court's approach to statutory interpretation is
liberal. Much legislation is prepared by commissions composed of
law professors, judges, *advokater* and representatives of interested
parties. Also, when draft legislation is presented to the *Folketing* it

---

[5] See para. 49.01 above.

is accompanied by extensive explanatory notes which may be added to or commented upon during its passage through the legislative process. The commissions' reports and drafts for legislation, together with the explanatory notes and debates may all be relied upon as aids to interpretation.

4. Publications

49.17   All statutes and subordinate legislation are published in the official Law Gazette, *Lovtidende*. The more important circulars are published in the Ministerial Gazette (*Ministerialtidende*). The more important decided cases are published weekly in the *Ugeskrift for Retsvæsen* (UfR). Specialised legal journals also report and comment on cases of particular interest to the specialist practitioner. Civil and commercial cases from all the Scandinavian countries are reported in their original languages in a journal called *Tidskrift for Retsvæsen* (TfR).

D. Organisation of the Civil Courts

1. Introduction

49.18   There are two levels of ordinary court of first instance, the *landsret* (high court) and the *byret* (district court).[6] There are also a number of special courts, of which the most important is the *Sø- og Handelsretten* (Maritime and Commercial Court).[7] Decisions at first instance can generally be appealed only once, from the *byret* to the *landsret*, and from the *landsret* (first instance) and the *Sø- og Handelsretten* in Copenhagen to the *Højesteret*.

Maintenance. It should be noted that the making of orders for the maintenance of spouses and children is not the sole responsibility of the ordinary courts. The order for financial relief for a spouse is made by a court, but the amount of the order is fixed on an application to the *Statsamt* (an office of the Ministry of the Interior). The officials in this office carry out an administrative procedure, investigating the means of the payer, and the *Amtmand* (the public official with jurisdiction to determine the level of maintenance award) then makes an appropriate order according to the payer's means.[8]

2. The *byret*

49.19   There are 83 *byretter* throughout the country. The number of judges, or deputy judges, depends on the size of the jurisdiction. In Copenhagen the *byret* has a president and 33 judges. Similar "presi-

---

[6] Formerly called the underret.
[7] See para. 49.21 below.
[8] See para. 35.23 above.

Denmark

dential" city courts exist in Århus, Odense and Ålborg. Judges in the *byret* sit singly in civil cases.

The *byret* exercises jurisdiction over all cases at first instance except actions against administrative decisions made by a Ministry or an administrative tribunal. Cases may, however, be transferred to the *landsret* if they are of particular importance or complexity or if they involve the application of EEC law or foreign law. Cases with a value exceeding Dkr. 500,000 must be referred to the *landsret* if one of the parties so requests. Landlord and tenant cases come before the *boligret* which consists of a judge of the *byret* sitting with two assessors respectively nominated by landlords' and tenants' associations.

In addition to the trial of ordinary actions at first instance the *byret* has a number of other juridical and administrative responsibilities, notably as a probate court (*skifteret*), land registry (*tinglysningsret*), bailiff's court (*fogedret*),[9] and notarial office (*notarialkontor*). These activities are conducted by one of the judges of the court or, in the smaller courts, by a deputy judge.

3. The *landsret*

There are two *landsretter*, one based in Viborg, (the *Vestre Landsret*), with territorial jurisdiction over Jutland and adjacent islands, the other based in Copenhagen, (the *Østre Landsret*), with territorial jurisdiction over Copenhagen, the rest of Sjælland, Fyn, and the eastern islands. Both these courts sit in other locations on a fairly regular basis. The *Vestre Landsret* has a Chief Justice and 22 judges, and the *Østre Landsret* has a Chief Justice and 45 judges. In civil cases in the *landsret* three judges sit together.[10]

49.20

The jurisdiction of the *landsretter* as courts of first instance is now limited to actions against administrative decisions made by a Ministry or an administrative tribunal. They have subsidiary jurisdiction of first instance over cases referred by the *byret* in the circumstances mentioned above. The procedure of both levels of court is broadly similar.

4. The Maritime and Commercial Court

Jurisdiction in commercial and maritime matters is also exercised by the *Sø- og Handelsretten*, the Maritime and Commercial Court, which sits in Copenhagen. It acts as an alternative to the ordinary courts when its special expertise in maritime or commercial matters

49.21

---

[9] The *fogedret* has important functions concerning protective measures and the enforcement of judgments. See para. 49.58 below.
[10] In commercial and maritime cases the *landsret* or the *byret* may, exceptionally, sit with two lay assessors experienced in commercial or maritime matters, as the case may be. In cases of particular importance the number of assessors may be increased to four. The court determines whether or not to sit with assessors, taking into account the views of the parties on the matter.

may assist in determining the case. It is composed of a presiding judge sitting with expert lay assessors. It normally only hears cases with a value exceeding Dkr. 100,000, but it may assume jurisdiction over smaller cases of particular importance or complexity.

5. The *Højesteret*

49.22   The Supreme Court sits in Copenhagen and comprises a Chief Justice and 14 judges. It hears appeals[11] from the decisions of the *landsret*, given at first instance, and from the *Sø- og Handelsretten*. Appeals from the decisions of the *landsret* given on appeal from the *byret* may also lie in the *Højesteret* if special leave is given by the Ministry of Justice. The *Højesteret* generally sits in two divisions of five judges.

6. The judiciary

49.23   Danish judges are legally qualified and normally serve as judges as part of a career in the Ministry of Justice. In addition to judicial service, such a career may include periods working as a state prosecutor and as a civil servant in the Ministry of Justice, but a judge in the *landsret* would not normally revert to some other occupation. Very few judges are appointed from the ranks of the *advokater*. Judges in the *Højesteret* are selected from the *landsret* or from distinguished lawyers in other walks of public life.

E. JURISDICTION OF THE CIVIL COURTS

1. Introduction

49.24   The civil courts exercise jurisdiction on the basis of the rules contained in the 1968 Convention[12] and the internal Danish rules of jurisdiction. These latter rules, which are summarised below, are based on a defendant's domicile in Denmark or on various other grounds. As has been seen, the particular court which has jurisdiction in any given case is determined in part by the value and subject-matter of the claim. When several courts may have jurisdiction it is for the plaintiff to chose the one in which to sue.

2. Domicile and seat

49.25   *Natural persons.* All persons resident in Denmark are obliged to register their domicile at the local *folkeregister* within five days of

---

[11] See further para. 49.63 below.
[12] The provisions of the Convention which regulate the local jurisdiction of the courts are listed at para. 15.03, nn. 10–11 above. The Danish rules of venue were altered to make them correspond more closely with the 1968 Convention. The Convention came into operation in Denmark on November 1, 1986: see para. 37.19 above.

establishing residence. Danish law does not distinguish between concepts of domicile and residence. Registration is conclusive of domicile, and a person resident in Denmark can have only one domicile there. The domicile of children and of mental patients is dependent on that of their legal guardian.

Legal persons. A limited company or an association has its seat for **49.26** the purposes of civil procedure in the place where it has its principal place of business, even if that place of business is situated outside Denmark, and even if it has its registered office elsewhere.

3. Jurisdiction—general rules

An individual defendant may be sued in the court of the appro- **49.27** priate level for the district where he is domiciled. If he has no domicile, the court in the place of his present abode has jurisdiction. If his whereabouts are unknown the court in the place of his last known domicile has jurisdiction. A limited company or an association may be sued in the courts for the place in which it has its seat.

Branch offices of companies may be sued in the appropriate local court. Companies with their principal place of business outside Denmark may, exceptionally, be sued in the courts for the place in Denmark where a board member is domiciled, if it is not possible to sue them at their principal place of business. In the case of partnerships, which under Danish law have no legal personality, the plaintiff may join all the partners in an action brought in the court for the place where any one of them is domiciled.

4. Jurisdiction—special rules

Jurisdiction based on subject-matter. A court may additionally have **49.28** jurisdiction based on the subject matter of the dispute. In a tort case, for example, the court for the place where a tort has been committed has jurisdiction. In the case of a contract, the claim may generally be brought before the court for the place where the obligation in question was (or was to be) performed. However, the position is different where the claim is one for the payment of money. It is a general rule of Danish law that, in the absence of agreement to the contrary, the place of performance of an obligation to pay money is at the residence of the creditor. Unless the court for that place has jurisdiction by virtue of the 1968 Convention,[13] it only has jurisdiction under internal rules of Danish law if the claim arose while the defendant was within the court's territorial jurisdiction in

---

[13] Art. 5(1): para. 17.02 above. This rules only applies if the defendant is domiciled in a Contracting State other than Denmark.

such circumstances that the obligation should be fulfilled before he leaves that place. In commercial sales of goods, Danish law provides that, in the absence of agreement to the contrary, the place of delivery of the goods is at the business location of the seller.

Cases involving immovable property must be brought in the court for the locality in which the property is situated, irrespective of the domicile of the defendant.

Procedural bases of jurisdiction. A court seised of a claim will normally also have jurisdiction to determine a counterclaim if it arises out of the same contract or relationship as that forming the basis of the plaintiff's claim or if certain other conditions are satisfied. Similarly, co-defendants and third parties[14] may normally be joined into proceedings, provided the courts of Denmark generally would have jurisdiction over those claims, and provided that no objection is raised or the different claims ought properly to be joined together.

Protective measures. It will be seen that applications for protective measures must be made to the *fogedret* for the place where the assets in question are located.[15]

5. Choice of court and entry of appearance

49.29   Except in cases involving immovable property, the parties may agree which court is to have jurisdiction in the event of any dispute between them. They may agree that all disputes, regardless of amount, may be tried by a particular *byret*. If a defendant appears but fails at the first preparatory hearing to challenge the jurisdiction of the court in which he is actually sued, he will be taken to have consented to it.[16]

6. Exorbitant grounds of jurisdiction

49.30   In certain cases sections 246(2) and 276(3) of the *Retsplejeloven* (Administration of Justice Act) provide a form of exorbitant jurisdiction over persons not domiciled in Denmark who cannot be sued there under any of the foregoing rules. In cases of an economic character against such defendants jurisdiction is given to the courts of any place in which any article or asset of that defendant (including an outstanding claim against a third party) is located or at which the defendant is personally present when served with the proceedings. These grounds of jurisdiction may not be relied upon against a

---

[14] See para. 49.35 below.
[15] See para. 49.58 below.
[16] See para. 49.42 below.

defendant domiciled in a Contracting State of the 1968 Convention.[17]

7. Civil claims in criminal proceedings

Criminal courts have jurisdiction to award civil damages to the **49.31** victims of crime and commonly do so, particularly in road traffic cases. The public prosecutor, in the course of his investigation into the facts, will establish the quantum of the victim's loss and will ordinarily include a civil claim for this sum against the defendant. Alternatively, a claimant may himself join in the proceedings by way of an *adhæsionsproces*, and instruct his own *advokat* to appear.

F. LIMITATION PERIODS

The law of limitation is complex and the following should be **49.32** taken as only the most general guide.

Under Danish law periods of limitation are a matter of substantive law. If no limitation period is otherwise prescribed, the overall period of limitation is 20 years. The normal period of limitation for ordinary claims in contract and tort is five years. Time starts to run from the moment when the plaintiff could first have brought his action. If a plaintiff is ignorant, through no fault of his own, of the fact that he has a claim, time runs from when he knew or ought reasonably to have known of that fact, subject, in most cases, to the ultimate limitation period of 20 years from the event which gave rise to the claim. In certain circumstances, the period can be extended, suspended or interrupted; for example, if the defendant resides outside Denmark and his whereabouts are unknown. It is the commencement of proceedings, rather than their service, which has to be achieved to stop the limitation period running.

Under various statutes specific periods of limitation are applied **49.33** to particular types of case. Actions on bills of exchange against the drawer or endorser of the bill must be brought within one year of maturity of the bill. Claims relating to international transport by road must be brought within one year from the date of delivery. Maritime claims must be brought within one year in respect of damage to goods, and two years in respect of salvage. Claims relating to defects in goods sold must be brought within one year of delivery. Apart from statutory periods of limitation a claim may also be barred by the application of a general principle of law which denies the right to claim to a party who has passively acquiesced to

---

[17] Art. 3 of the 1968 Convention. s.246(2) of *Retsplejeloven* was formerly numbered as s.248(2), to which the second para. of Art. 3 of the Convention refers. s.276(3) is not mentioned in the Convention.

another's wrong. For example a purchaser of goods who omits to make a timely complaint about a defect in them may not subsequently bring a claim in respect of such defect.

G. CIVIL PROCEDURE—PROCEEDINGS UP TO JUDGMENT

1. General description

49.34   Court procedures at all levels are governed by the *Retsplejeloven* (Administration of Justice Act).[18] After a series of short formal preparatory hearings, at which the written pleadings are handed to the court and to the opposing party, there is a full trial in open court. In some cases, the judge may order a hearing before the full trial at which the case may be reviewed. The rules governing the preparatory stages lay down set time limits and other requirements, but in practice these are often relaxed. At the trial, the judge plays a passive role, listening to the evidence and only rarely asking questions himself. He will have read the pleadings and documents beforehand but will otherwise have little or no prior knowledge of the case. The *advokat* for the plaintiff opens the case by explaining the facts and issues in an objective fashion, putting forward the contentions of both sides and reading the written evidence. The parties then adduce oral evidence before closing submissions are made by the respective *advokater*. At the conclusion of the evidence and argument the judge will usually give a preliminary indication of his view and urge the parties to settle their dispute. If they do not do so, he may announce his decision and a reasoned judgment will be produced later.

2. Parties and legal representation

49.35   *Parties.* The main parties to an action are the *sagsøger* (plaintiff), and the *sagsøgte* (defendant). All natural and legal persons[19] can sue and be sued. Minors (persons under 18) and others under a disability may sue and be sued through their legal guardian or a representative *ad litem*. Both the plaintiff and the defendant can bring further parties into the proceedings if the court has jurisdiction and in its discretion so allows. A party who has a claim against a third party in the event of his losing the main proceedings may give notice of those proceedings to the third party who may then appear and challenge the evidence at the final hearing of the proceedings.

---

[18] Law No. 90 of 1916, as amended.
[19] The common forms of legal person under Danish law are listed at para. 49.73 below.

The effect of the notice may be to debar the third party from subsequently challenging the facts established in the main proceedings.

A third party who can show good cause may also intervene in proceedings to support of one of the parties or to make his own independent claim against one of the parties.

Legal representation. Any party, who is not under an incapacity, **49.36** may appear in court and conduct proceedings on his own behalf in person. He may also be represented by his spouse, child, brother or sister, or by an employee. Subject to the foregoing a party may not be represented by any person other than an *advokat*. The judge is under a certain obligation to advise a party who is not represented by an *advokat*. He may order a party to be represented by an *advokat* if he considers that the case cannot properly be carried on without such assistance. If a party fails to comply with such an order, judgment in default may be given against him.

3. Commencement of proceedings

Contents of the summons. Proceedings are begun by the delivery to **49.37** the court of a *stævning* (writ of summons). This document must contain the names and addresses of the parties, the name of the competent court, the relief claimed, and a comprehensive statement of grounds for claim (*sagsfremstilling*). The *stævning* is normally drafted by the *advokat*. It must set out the material facts alleged and refer to the documents to be relied upon. It should include a summary of all the legal arguments which will be advanced: for example, that a statute should be interpreted in a particular way, that reference should be made to a *dictum* in a certain judgment, or that damages should be awarded for a particular loss. In practice, the contents of the *stævning* are fairly brief. Accuracy is important and the deliberate inclusion of any false statement may lead to the *advokat* or the party being fined. Claims for damages may be quantified in the *stævning* in a precise amount but this only becomes obligatory eight days before the final hearing.

Procedure. The plaintiff's *advokat* sends the *stævning* to the court office with copies for service. A court fee is payable amounting to about 1 per cent. of the value of the claim. If the claim has no monetary value the fee is Dkr. 500. The court will, according to its practice which varies from court to court, either summon the defendant to a first oral hearing or direct him to file a defence in writing (*svarskrift*). The *stævning* is stamped with the date of the hearing or the date by which a defence must be filed. The period generally given is one of four weeks, but this, and indeed all procedural time limits, may be extended by leave of the court. After service the original writ is returned to the plaintiff's *advokat* and is only submitted by him to the court at the first hearing of the case.

The proceedings become definitively pending when the *stævning* is served on the defendant.

4. Service of proceedings

49.38   The court is normally responsible for serving the *stævning* on the defendant. Service (*forkyndelse*) is carried out by a *stævningsmand* (official process server)[20] who hands the document either to the defendant personally, or to a member of his household or to his employer. In the case of a company or other legal entity, service may be on a manager or any employee at the registered office or place of business. Service by post can, at the request of the plaintiff, be carried out by the court but this method of service is rarely used. When the defendant is already represented by an *advokat*, who has agreed to accept service, the *stævning* may be sent direct to the *advokat* by post, either by the court or by the plaintiff's *advokat*, after it has been stamped with the date by which the defendant must file his defence or the date of the first hearing.

If service is to be effected in a part of Denmark outside the area of the court in which the proceedings are brought, (and in the case of all proceedings in the *landsret*), the *stævning* will be sent for service to the *byret* in the defendant's locality. Service outside Denmark will, where appropriate, be undertaken in accordance with the Hague Service Convention,[21] and otherwise through the Danish consulate.

If the defendant's whereabouts are unknown so that neither personal nor postal service can be achieved, the court will order substituted service by advertisement in the Danish Official Gazette (*Statstidende*).

Service usually must be effected at least two weeks before the hearing of the case, or the date for filing the defence. Sometimes the court will specify a longer minimum period. When service is abroad the period will normally be not less than four weeks. If the defend-

---

[20] The *Stævningsmand* is an official process server. Unlike his counterparts in some other countries, he is not regarded as a member of a separate profession, but is an employee of the Ministry of Justice, attached to a particular court. His function is to carry out the service of writs and other documents which require formal service.

[21] See paras. 4.30 *et seq.* above and A2.03 below. This Convention also governs service in Denmark of documents from other Contracting States.

ant appears and takes part in the hearing any defect in service will be cured.

Service is proved by a certificate to that effect from the *stævnings-mand*, or by production of a recorded delivery receipt.

5. Appearance by the defendant

The *stævning* will be accompanied by instructions from the court **49.39** telling the defendant what action he must take if he wishes to contest the claim. Depending on the procedure directed by the court, the defendant will either have to file a defence (*svarskrift*) within the time specified, or he must attend the first oral hearing of the case and then present his defence. These actions formally constitute the entry of an appearance. If the *stævning* has been served too late to comply with the minimum period of notice fixed by the court, a fresh date for the hearing or for filing the defence will be fixed and the *stævning* will be re-served.[22] The defendant may however waive his objection to short notice and appear at the hearing or file his defence.

6. Default judgments

If the defendant does not appear at the first hearing of the case or **49.40** file his defence as required, the court must itself determine whether or not it has jurisdiction. If it has, and if service has been properly effected, judgment will be given against the defendant. The default judgment will be for the full amount of the claim unless it appears on its face to be excessive, as, for example, where interest is claimed at a rate higher than allowed by statute and no agreement for such a rate of interest has been put in evidence. A defendant who fails to appear at one of the subsequent preparatory hearings of the court may also have judgment given against him.

Setting aside. A judgment in default will be set aside if the **49.41** defaulting party applies within four weeks of the date of the judgment for the case to be re-opened.[23] He does not need to show a reasonable defence or provide any explanation for his default. The court will also entertain an application to set aside a default judgment at any time up to a year after the judgment if the defaulting party has a reasonable excuse for not having applied earlier. In the event of the judgment being set aside the party in default may be ordered to pay the costs thrown away through his default.

---

[22] If the re-service occurs after three months have elapsed, the *stævning* must be re-stamped.

[23] The judgment will become enforceable after 14 days: see para. 49.66 below.

7. Disputes as to jurisdiction

49.42   A challenge as to the jurisdiction or any other formal objection should be made in the *svarskrift* when it is first presented (as to which, see below). If no challenge is made at this stage the defendant may be taken to have waived his right to make objection, unless there is some good reason for the omission. In practice, formal matters other than a contest of the jurisdiction may be raised at any time during the preparatory stages. In an appropriate case, the court may order a challenge to the jurisdiction to be tried as a preliminary issue. If it does so, this ordinarily occurs before the parties complete their exchange of pleadings, and the court's decision on the trial of the preliminary issue may be appealed before the merits are tried.

8. Pleadings

49.43   The written pleadings are called *skriftveksling*. The plaintiff's initial pleadings, the *stævning*, containing a statement of his case (*sagsfremstilling*) have already been described. The defendant's defence, the *svarskrift*, must respond to the allegations in the *sagsfremstilling*. Any matters not challenged then or in any subsequent pleading will be deemed to have been admitted. Like the *stævning*, the *svarskrift* and subsequent pleadings must set out the allegations of facts to be made and refer to the relevant documents and legal arguments; but in practice these matters are covered only briefly in the initial stages. The defendant may make a counterclaim (*modkrav*) if the court has jurisdiction in respect of the matter. If the plaintiff wishes to challenge any assertion in the *svarskrift* he must file a *replik*, and in this he may also enlarge or amend the scope of the allegations in the *stævning* and advance additional evidence and arguments. The defendant may wish to respond by means of a further pleading called a *duplik*. Subsequent pleadings are also permitted.

40.44   The pleadings are handed to the court and to the opposing parties at the preparatory hearings. The defendant should present his *svarskrift* at the first hearing and the plaintiff will then have several weeks within which to submit his *replik* followed by the reply of the defendant, the *duplik*, within another period of several weeks. The time limits are fixed by the court in each case and in practice they are liberally extended by agreement between the parties. Periods of 8 to 12 weeks would be usual where foreign parties are involved. Pleadings can be amended without leave at any time until the closing of the preparatory sessions. Thereafter they may be amended at any time up to eight days before the final hearing if the other party does not object.

9. The hearings

Preparatory hearings

The date of the first oral hearing, save in cases with written prep-   **49.45**
aration,[24] is the return date stated on the summons. The purpose of
the preparatory hearings is to ensure that the case is adequately prepared for the final trial by mutual disclosure of evidence and legal
arguments. Pleadings are exchanged at these hearings which, even
in the *landsret* and in the *Højesteret*, are conducted by a single judge.
Oral evidence from witnesses may not be taken at the preparatory
hearings unless the witness is unavoidably incapable of attending at
the main hearing.

When the exchange of pleadings is complete, the court closes the
preparatory hearings. The date of the final hearing is usually fixed
by agreement between the judge and the parties at the closing hearing of the preparatory stage of the case. Sometimes the judge will
direct an additional extended hearing for the purpose of a comprehensive review of the legal arguments and the evidence to be called.
This hearing is frequently used by the court and the parties to
achieve a settlement of the case.

Strictly speaking, a party is prohibited from calling any witness,
producing any document, or advancing any legal argument to
which reference has not been made in his pleadings; for this reason
the closing by the court of the preparatory hearings at which pleadings are exchanged should be a crucial event. These rules are somewhat relaxed in practice, although it is considered to be
professionally unethical for an *advokat* to put forward new evidence
or new legal arguments shortly before the final hearing of the case.
The court does have a discretion to admit matters not previously
pleaded, but it normally requires at least eight days' notice to have
been given to the other side.

The final hearing

The final hearing is a full oral trial of the action. It has three   **49.46**
elements, the presentation of the case in opening speeches, the taking of evidence and the closing speeches. The role of the judge is
passive. He is not expected to have any prior knowledge of the case
but in practice he will have read the pleadings and the documents
thoroughly. The judgment in the case can only be based on what

---

[24] In certain cases, notably those heard in the *Vestre Landsret*, a procedure may be
followed whereby oral preparatory hearings are dispensed with. The parties
exchange their written pleadings by post within time limits laid down by the
court and the date of the final hearing is notified to the parties in writing.

has taken place at the final hearing. Through their legal advisers, the parties decide which witnesses are to be called and what documentary evidence is to be produced. The witnesses are questioned by the *arvokater* but the judge may ask questions of a witness as he thinks fit.

Opening. The oral presentation of the case is the most important part of a Danish civil trial. The plaintiff's *advokat* makes an opening speech in which he introduces the judge to the facts of the case and the issues in dispute. He does this in an objective way, reading aloud all relevant correspondence and other documents, including any expert's report. The judge may only take account of matters which have been read aloud in court. Consequently the *advokat* for the defendant may draw the attention of the judge to any part of the documentary evidence relevant to the defendant's case which may not have been mentioned.

Evidence. The parties then call their evidence. Unless the *advokater* have for the sake of convenience arranged otherwise, the plaintiff's witnesses are called to give evidence first, followed by the defendant's witnesses.[25] If a party himself is giving evidence, he will normally be called before his witnesses. If a party does not give evidence, the court may draw an adverse inference. The witnesses of fact may be followed by expert witnesses.[26]

Closing speeches. At the conclusion of the evidence, closing speeches are made by the *advokater* for the plaintiff and the defendant respectively. Each *advokat* addresses the court in turn, starting with the plaintiff's *advokat*. In their closing speeches the *advokater* deal at large with all the issues and arguments in the case. Although there are no formal rules or presumptions relating to proof, the burden of proving any matter and of proving the case as a whole is generally on the plaintiff and the court reaches its decision on the balance of probabilities.

49.47   After the closing speeches, if the judge or the panel has formed a clear view of the case, it may give an indication of that view to the parties, either at their request or of its own motion, and may urge a settlement of the disute. Alternatively, the parties may be asked if they wish to hear the decision of the court immediately, with reasons in writing to follow. If the court needs time to deliberate, its decision will be reserved and will be given in open court at a later date.

---

[25] See para. 49.49 below.
[26] See para. 49.53 below.

10. Security for costs

When a plaintiff domiciled abroad brings proceedings in a **49.48** Danish court the defendant may make an application at the first preparatory hearing of the case for an order requiring the plaintiff to deposit with the court an amount to cover any costs which might eventually be awarded to the defendant. Alternatively, the security may be given by a bond or guarantee to the satisfaction of the other side. The court does not investigate the plaintiff's solvency. In practice applications for security for costs are rarely made.

Security for costs will not be ordered against a plaintiff from any country which, by treaty or otherwise, does not require security from Danish plaintiffs bringing proceedings in its courts. Denmark is a party to the Hague Convention on Civil Procedure (1954) which exempts the nationals of the contracting states from any requirement to provide security for costs.

11. Witnesses and oral evidence

The evidence of witnesses is generally given orally at the trial of **49.49** the action. The parties themselves may give evidence but they cannot be forced to appear or to answer questions. The selection of witnesses is a matter for the parties, and the judge may not himself summon a witness. On the application of a party, a witness may be formally summoned by the court to attend the hearing or he may be merely requested to attend by a party or his *advokat*. Any person who is officially summoned to court has a duty to attend and to give evidence, unless he can claim privilege. Privilege can be claimed by any witness who is a civil servant, an officer of the armed forces, a clergyman, a doctor, or an *advokat*, in respect of confidential matters relating to his calling. The authority or person for whose protection the privilege exists may waive objection to the questioning. The court may order a doctor or an *advokat* to give evidence notwithstanding professional privilege if his evidence is of vital importance to the outcome of the case.

In practice witnesses are often interviewed beforehand by the **49.50** *advokat* who is to call them, but this is considered by some *advokater* to be of questionable propriety. The witness does not take the oath but he is directed to tell the truth and is warned of the penalties for committing perjury. He is examined in chief by the *advokat* calling him, then cross-examined by the other *advokat* and if necessary, re-examined again by both *advokater*. When he is examined in chief he is generally asked to give a narrative account of the matters in respect of which he can speak. The judge may ask questions if he wishes. Unlike the common law system there are no rules about what a witness may or may not say. In particular, there is no

1227

rule against hearsay evidence. The judge takes such notes of the evidence as he considers necessary. Written statements from witnesses are rarely used as they are regarded as being of little evidential weight.

A party desiring to obtain the evidence of a witness abroad may apply to the court for letters rogatory to be issued. The procedure will be carried out under the appropriate multilateral or bilateral convention.[27]

12. Documentary evidence

49.51   All documents that are to be relied upon in the proceedings are exhibited to the respective pleadings. The originals are produced to the court and copies are provided for the other party. There is no duty on a party or his *advokat* to produce any document which is adverse to his case. The court may, on the application of one party, order the other party or a third party, to disclose a specified document in his possession, provided that it is not privileged and provided that the party requiring its production specifies the allegations which he says will be substantiated by the disclosure. If a party refuses to comply with such an order the refusal may be construed in the light most favourable to the other party. A third party who refuses to obey the order may be fined or imprisoned and the police may conduct a search for the document.

49.52   Correspondence between opposing *advokater* is not privileged and can be shown to the court unless it is expressly declared to be confidential. Ordinarily the lay client is not entitled to see correspondence thus marked. Communications passing between an *advokat* and his own client are normally privileged from disclosure.

13. Experts

49.53   Some technical or scientific matters can normally only be established by means of expert evidence. Expert witnesses are appointed by the court, usually on the application of the parties. The costs of instructing an expert, which may be substantial, are borne initially by the party who has requested the appointment. The choice of expert will be suggested by the parties who will agree between themselves the terms of reference. There is no panel of court experts. In appropriate circumstances the expert convenes a meeting with the parties and their advisers at which he carries out his inspection of the subject matter in question. He sets out his findings in a written report which is submitted to the court and the parties before the closing of the preparatory stages. At the final hearing

---

[27] Denmark is a party to the Hague Evidence Convention. See paras. 8.26 *et seq.* above and A2.17 below.

it is read out in the expert's presence and he may be questioned upon it by the parties.

Parties are at liberty to call their own experts provided that adequate notice (seven days) has been given to the court and to the other side. Such evidence is regarded as being of less weight than that of the expert appointed by the court but it may nonetheless be necessary to establish some aspect of the case.

14. Proof of foreign law

Foreign law is regarded as a matter of fact which should be set out in the pleadings and adduced in evidence, often in the form of a written statement. The evidence may be given by anyone who can give credible testimony on the subject, not only a lawyer qualified in the legal system in question. If necessary, the court will conduct its own researches and apply its own knowledge of the relevant foreign law.   **49.54**

15. Compromise

There is no procedure for paying money into court in satisfaction of the plaintiff's claim. Any private negotiations with a view to settlement taking place either before or during the proceedings are regarded as confidential and are not disclosed to the judge. A party whose offer has been rejected may repeat the offer in his pleadings and if the other party eventually recovers no more than the offer he may be ordered to pay the offeror's costs.   **49.55**

Although the court is under no duty to do so, it will nearly always encourage a settlement of the case. This may happen during the preparatory hearings, but generally occurs at the conclusion of the final hearing when the judge may ask the parties whether they would like him to put forward proposals for settlement. In practice about a half of all cases which come to trial are resolved by an in-court settlement. The terms of the settlement are entered in the minutes of the court. When this is done the compromise is enforceable as if it were a judgment and it cannot be the subject matter of an appeal.[28] Alternatively, the parties may settle the case out of court and withdraw the proceedings. Settlements for the benefit of children require the approval of the child's legal guardian.

16. The judgment

The judgment must set out the reasons upon which it is based. Where the court consists of more than one judge, they do not give separate reasons for their decision, except that a dissenting opinion   **49.56**

---

[28] See para. 49.66 below.

may be expressed. The judgment is entered in the judgment book of the court. The document required for the purposes of execution is an extract from the judgment book. In addition to the names of the parties, the name of the court and the date the judgment was given, this extract contains a summary of the nature of the claim and the decision. The extracted judgment is certified by the judge's signature and it bears the stamp of the court and the date when the extract was given.

17. Costs

49.57   A single court fee, based on the value of the claim, is payable by the plaintiff at the commencement of the proceedings. If the claim is subsequently increased a supplementary fee may be payable. At the end of the case the losing party is normally ordered to pay costs to the successful party. Costs are awarded by the court as a lump sum specified in the judgment.

The lump sum is calculated according to a scale of fees laid down by *Det Danske Advokatsamfund.*[29] The scale mainly reflects the amount of the claim but the time taken for preparation of the case and at the final hearing is also taken into account, together with any other special factors. For example, the costs could, in an appropriate case, include the fees payable by a foreign party to his foreign lawyer who has instructed the Danish lawyer in the case. Fees paid to a expert will be awarded in addition to the other costs. The costs awarded by the court will normally only cover a proportion of the costs which a party has to pay to his *advokat.* Either side may bring an appeal which is limited to the question of costs. If a litigant considers that his own *advokat's* fees are excessive he may apply for a review by the local *kredsbestyrelse* (the board of the regional bar association).

H. Civil Procedure—Provisional and Protective Measures

1. Introduction

49.58   If the plaintiff fears that the defendant might take steps during the proceedings to frustrate any ultimate judgment of the court by disposing of his assets or by continuing some course of wrongdoing,

---

[29] For examples, scale fees for a case of average complexity might be as follows (as at June 1989):

Value of claim	Fee	
Dkr. 50,000	Dkr. 6,728 + 8%	(+ VAT at 22%)
Dkr. 200,000	Dkr. 16,888 + 6%	(+ VAT at 22%)
Dkr. 300,000	Dkr. 21,988 + 3%	(+ VAT at 22%)

he may apply to the *fogedret*[30] for provisional or protective measures. This will usually be the *fogedret* of the defendant's domicile. The provisional remedies available under Danish law are the *arrest* of assets and the prohibitory injunction (*fogedforbud*). In both cases the plaintiff may have to deposit in court a sufficient sum to compensate the defendant for any loss if it is later found that the measures were not justified.

In addition, these provisional and protective measures are available in aid of proceedings in a foreign court, or in aid of the execution of a Danish or foreign judgment. They are also available to protect the judgment creditor under a foreign judgment whose enforcement proceedings in Denmark have been stayed pending the outcome of an appeal in the country of origin.

Obtaining and validating the order. The application is usually, but not necessarily, made on notice to the defendant. The application is made orally and the applicant may produce documents and, sometimes, oral evidence. If the application has been made before the main proceedings in respect of the claim have been commenced, the plaintiff must commence those proceedings within seven days and claim in addition an order validating the provisional measure. If the main proceedings are already pending the plaintiff must apply for an order validating the provisional remedy also within seven days. The defendant may challenge the order in the proceedings brought by the plaintiff to confirm the validity of the order, or by a separate application to the court. He may also counterclaim for damages if the order should not have been made.

2. Arrest

An order for *arrest* can, as appropriate, result in the attachment of **49.59** personal property or money, the garnishment of debts, or the tentative registration of a judgment lien over real property. It is binding on anyone who has notice of it. The plaintiff has to show either that his claim is due and payable, or that there is some risk that the defendant may obstruct execution of any judgment. If an order is made, the defendant may be allowed to remain in possession of the property in question but he is prohibited from dealing with it in any way. Alternatively he may be ordered to deposit the property with the court or to provide security for the amount of the claim. If he makes an offer to provide appropriate security, that may be accepted in place of an *arrest*. An *arrest* may only be ordered in respect of assets within the territorial jurisdiction of the court.

---

[30] The bailiff's court; see para. 49.19 above.

3. Injunction

49.60 The prohibitory injunction (*fogedforbud*) is used to restrain the defendant from acts which are prejudicial to the plaintiff's presumed rights. An injunction will only be granted if there is evidence that the defendant intends to act in the way complained of, but if this is proved to the court's satisfaction, no offer of security by the defendant will forstall the making of the order.

I. CIVIL PROCEDURE—SUMMARY PROCEDURES

49.61 There is no procedure for obtaining summary judgment; but cheques and other bills of exchange are instruments capable of automatic execution,[31] which can only be contested by the defence of forgery.

[The next paragraph is number 49.63]

J. CIVIL PROCEDURE—APPEALS

49.63 *Introduction.* A decision can generally only be appealed once,[32] from the *byret* to the *landsret* and from the first instance decisions of the *landsret* or from the *Sø- og Handelsretten* in Copenhagen to the *Højesteret*. The procedure for setting aside default judgments, which is not generally regarded as an appeal in Denmark, has already been described.[33] A third party who is adversely affected by a judgment may also appeal against it. Execution of the judgment is stayed automatically if the appeal is lodged within 14 days; and the appellate court may grant a stay of execution if the appeal is lodged thereafter.

Time for appealing. An appeal from a judgment of the *byret* must be brought within four weeks from the date of its pronouncement. Appeals against judgments of the *landsret* and of the *Sø- og Handelsretten* to the *Højesteret* must be commenced within eight weeks of their pronouncement. Appeals against procedural orders (*kendelser*) must be brought within 14 days. An appeal may be brought out of time within a year of its pronouncement, but only if the appellant is able to show good reason for the delay.

Nature of an appeal. The procedure for instituting and prosecuting an appeal is comparable with that for an action at first instance.

---

[31] See para. 49.70 below.
[32] A case which has started at the *byret*, and has been appealed to the *landsret* may be appealed to the *Højesteret* with the leave of the Ministry of Justice. This is granted only in cases which raise questions of fundamental public interest.
[33] See para. 49.41 above.

Appeals are generally by way of complete reconsideration of the merits. However, as the court of first instance does not take notes of evidence, nor is there any transcript, the parties must initially rely on the extensive recital of the evidence contained in the judgment. Witnesses will not normally give evidence at the hearing of an appeal but they may do so when the evidence would cover some new matter or would differ from that recorded in the judgment.

[The next paragraph is number 49.66]

K. Civil Procedure—Enforcement

1. Enforcement of Danish judgments

The enforcement of judgments and authentic instruments is under the direct supervision of the judge in the *fogedret*.[34] **49.66**

A judgment does not expressly state that it is enforceable, but judgments for a sum of money may be enforced after 14 days from their pronouncement, unless their execution has been stayed. In the case of non-money judgments the court will, if necessary, fix an appropriate period for compliance. Service of the judgment is not a condition of its enforceability. A stay of execution pending an appeal occurs automatically if the appeal is lodged within 14 days, but thereafter a stay of execution can only be obtained on application to the appellate court. In such a case a stay will usually only be conditional upon the appellant providing adequate security for the amount in dispute. A judgment becomes time barred and cannot be enforced after 20 years.

Indorsement as to executory character. The copy of the judgment required for the purposes of execution is the relevant extract from the court's book of judgments. It bears the stamp of the court and it is authenticated by the signature of a judge. The operative part of the judgment is that which follows the words *"Thi kendes for ret"* ("This is held to be just"). **49.67**

Execution. If the judgment is to be executed in Denmark, application is made in writing, together with a copy of the judgment, to the *fogedret* for the district where the debtor's place of residence is located, or where the assets themselves are located. A summons is served on the judgment debtor, together with a copy of the judgment, by which he is summoned to the *fogedret*, where he is questioned by the judge (usually assisted by the creditor's *advokat*) as to his property. If the debtor's valuation of his assets is challenged, they are valued by an officer of the court. The judge then makes an **49.68**

---

[34] The bailiff's court: see para. 49.19 above.

order attaching sufficient of the assets to satisfy the debt. These assets may include debts owed by third parties to the judgment debtor. If the judgment debtor does not then pay the debt, the assets may be compulsorily sold to satisfy the debt. Certain of the debtor's goods are exempt from execution. In some circumstances the judge will make an order for payment by instalments. Attachment of earnings orders can only be made in respect of certain claims recovered by public authorities without a judgment, such as alimony claims, taxes and duties.

49.69   *Other methods of enforcement.* Non-money judgments, including mandatory orders to do or refrain from doing something, may be enforced in the *fogedret* by a variety of methods. Normally the judge will try to convert the judgment into a money judgment, including an order for the payment of a periodic penalty for non-compliance.[35] If quantification cannot be easily achieved, it may, ultimately, be enforced by fines or imprisonment. The breach of an injunction is regarded as a criminal offence, to be dealt with by the police.

Opposing the execution. As the procedure for enforcement involves the judgment debtor being summoned before the *fogedret* the only means by which he can challenge any order made by the judge is by way of appeal to the landsret.

2. Authentic instruments and court settlements

49.70   *Authentic instruments.* Despite the absence of notaries in Denmark, certain classes of document are regarded by Danish law as instruments capable of forming the basis of an order for execution in the *fogedret*.[36] Such documents, which can only relate to an obligation to pay money, include cheques, bills of exchange, mortgage deeds and, most importantly, acknowledgments of debt.[37] It is not a pre-condition to enforcement that either the document or any demand for payment should have been served on the debtor.

Court settlements. The minutes of a settlement recorded in court may similarly be made the subject of an order for enforcement in the *fogedret*, the enforcing party having obtained an official extract of the minutes from the court.

---

[35] Such periodic penalties are fines and are paid to the state.
[36] The bailiff's court: see para. 49.19 above. The procedure of enforcement in the *fogedret* is described at para. 49.68 above.
[37] An acknowledgment of debt, also called a "voluntary settlement," can only be enforced if it contains an express provision to the effect that it may be enforced.

3. Enforcement of foreign judgments

Foreign judgments are enforceable in Denmark by all the means **49.71** available in respect of Danish judgments once their execution has been authorised by the judge of the *fogedret*.

Enforcement under the 1968 Convention. If a foreign judgment falls within the 1968 Convention, the judgment creditor applies in the first instance to the *fogedret*. This is part of the *byret*[38] and accordingly such an application satisfies the requirements of Article 32 of the 1968 Convention. The documentation lodged with the application will often be accepted in English.[39] An appeal against the decision made on that application lies to the *landsret*,[40] and from the decision of the *landsret*, with the leave of the Minister of Justice, to the *Højesteret*.

Judgments outside the 1968 Convention. Before the 1968 Conven- **49.72** tion came into force in Denmark,[41] the only foreign judgments that were directly enforceable were those of other Nordic countries.[42] Judgments of the courts of other countries were enforceable only by the means of bringing a fresh action in the Danish courts; and this is still the case for judgments not falling within the 1968 Convention. In such an action the foreign judgment has only an evidential effect. Danish courts would recognise foreign judgments which were declaratory of the status and rights of the parties according to the rules of Danish private international law.

L. LEGAL PERSONS

The principal legal entities which exist under Danish law are as fol- **49.73** lows:

(a) *Aktieselskab* (A/S)—a public limited company;
(b) *Anpartselskab* (ApS)—a private limited company;
(c) *Kommanditselskab* (K/S)—a limited partnership, without legal personality distinct from that of its members, in which the liability of some of the members is limited and of at least one other is unlimited;

---

[38] The byret is referred to in the 1968 Convention as the underret, its former name.
[39] It is a requirement of the Convention that if a translation is required, it must be certified by a person qualified to do so in one of the Contracting States: see para. 29.29 above. In Denmark, the person qualified to act as a translator for these purposes is a chartered interpreter, whose signature must be officially verified.
[40] An appeal against the grant of an order must be lodged within one month from the service of the decision. An appeal against the refusal of an order must be lodged within 14 days of the decision.
[41] November 1, 1986: see para. 37.19 above.
[42] Under a Convention of 1938, judgments given in Germany were afforded recognition, but not automatic enforcement.

(d) *Andelselskab* (A.m.b.a.)—a co-operative, the members of which have limited liability;

(e) *Forening*—an association, the members of which are liable only according to its rules;

(f) *Fond*, or *Stiftelser*—a foundation;

(g) *Interessentskab* (I/S),—a partnership; this has no legal personality under Danish law. Actions must be brought by or against one or more of the partners in person.

M. LEGAL AID

49.74 Any natural person, regardless of his nationality or country of residence, may obtain legal aid (*fri proces*) for proceedings in Denmark if he satisfies certain financial requirements and if he shows reasonable grounds for bringing or defending the proceedings. Legal aid is granted by the *Statsamt*[43] with a right of appeal against refusal to the Ministry of Justice. The legal aid covers court costs, legal fees and witnesses expenses. If the legally aided party is successful, costs may be recovered by the state against the losing party. If the legally aided party is unsuccessful he may be required personally to pay the winning party's costs, but if he has insufficient means the state will pay the winning party's costs with a right of recourse against the legally aided party.

A number of *advokater* in each court district are available to act on behalf of legally aided parties. One such *advokat* will be nominated to act in a particular case, although the party is free to choose his own *advokat* if he wishes. The court assesses the fee payable to the *advokat*, who is not permitted to claim any additional fee from the client.

Legal advice. In addition to state legal aid there are several schemes operated by groups of *advokater* for offering legal advice free of charge or at a reduced rate.

---

[43] An office of the Ministry of the Interior; *cf.* para. 49.18 above.

CHAPTER 50

FRANCE

Written in collaboration with Maître Emmanuel Hayaux du Tilly, Avocat, Paris.[1]

---

[1] Partner, *Serrero, Popineau, Frémy, Hayaux du Tilly*, Paris.

A. THE LEGAL SYSTEM

1. Introduction

50.01   *History.* France had grown by the end of the sixteenth century into a single unified state ruled by a monarchy. The French Revolution of 1789 overthrew the monarchy and established the First Republic, which continued until Napoleon founded the First Empire in 1804. The monarchy was restored in 1814, but it was succeeded in 1848 by the Second Republic and then by the Second Empire, until Napoleon III was deposed in 1870. The Third Republic was then established and survived until the Second World War. The Fourth Republic was established in 1946, and lasted until 1958, when the Fifth Republic was formed under a new constitution. Since then, France has continued to be governed under a mixed system of presidential and parliamentary democracy.

Territory. In addition to mainland France and Corsica, the territory of France includes some 10 overseas departments and territories (*départements d'outre mer* and *territoires d'outre mer*).[2] The administration of the state is organised centrally, but some administrative functions have been devolved to the *régions*, *départements* and *communes*.

Origins of the legal system. French law has its historical origins in customary law (*droit coutumier*, mainly from northern France) and the *droit écrit* derived from Roman law. By the end of the eighteenth century, the law had become relatively uniform and much of it had been committed to writing by jurists. In 1804, the civil code was passed into law. This code, prepared under the authority of Napoleon and with his active participation in its drafting, inspired the civil law of most other European countries and still forms the basis of most of the civil law of France.

2. Administration of justice

50.02   *System of courts.* France has two separate but parallel systems of courts, the administrative courts and the ordinary courts,[3] which apply, respectively, public and private law. This has come about

---

[2] See para. 34.06 above.
[3] The ordinary courts are sometimes called "judicial" courts.

because, after the Revolution, it was desired, in accordance with the principle of the separation of powers, to protect the administration of government from the interference of the ordinary courts.[4] This division of functions is reflected in a fundamental division between matters subject to public law and matters subject to private law.

Public and private law. Generally speaking, public law and the administrative courts are concerned with the relationship of the various organs of the civil administration with each other and with the individual. There is a wide involvement of public authorities in French national life, from the level of the government right down to the *commune*, and public law includes its own distinct rules governing contracts entered into by, and wrongs involving, public officials and institutions. Most claims for damages for breach of contract or tort (except motor accident claims) to which a public authority is party must be brought in an administrative court. The system of administrative courts (*tribunaux administratifs*) consist of 25 regional courts, which are subject to the appellate and cassation jurisdiction of the *Conseil d'Etat*.[5]

Private law governs all matters not subject to public law and it embraces civil, commercial and labour matters. Ordinary courts are also concerned with criminal law and some aspects of tax law. If an administrative issue arises incidentally in the course of proceedings in an ordinary court, the proceedings will be stayed pending the decision of an appropriate administrative court.

Levels of courts. There are two levels of ordinary civil courts of first instance, the *tribunal d'instance* and the *tribunal de grande instance* with separate *tribunaux de commerce* for commercial cases and *conseils de prud'hommes* for employment cases. The regional *Cours d'appel* hear appeals from all these courts. Jurisdiction in cassation is exercised over the whole of France by the *Cour de cassation* in Paris.

B. Legal Practitioners

1. The *Avocat*

The traditional role of the *avocat* is to present oral argument (*plaidoirie*)[6] in court and, except in cases in the *Cour d'appel*, this function is now extended to include formal representation of the client **50.03**

---

[4] It was enacted in Art. 13 of the Law of August 16–24, 1790, that: "Judicial functions are distinct and will always remain separate from administrative functions. Judges in the civil courts may not . . . concern themselves in any manner whatsoever with the operation of the administration, nor shall they call administrators to account before them in respect of the exercise of their official functions."

[5] The *Conseil d'Etat* also has the constitutional function of reviewing the legality of governmental decrees.

[6] The term *plaidoirie* (pleading) has a strictly oral connotation.

and the preparation of his case.[7] In addition, the function of the *avocat* has widened over recent decades to include the role of general legal adviser, although most *avocats* tend to be less involved in the purely business aspects of the matters on which they are advising than are their counterparts in other countries.

Legal education and qualification. The intending *avocat* must first obtain a university law degree. He must next attend law school for one year to qualify for the *Certificat d'Aptitude à la Profession d'Avocat* (CAPA). He may then apply to the *bâtonnier* (head) of a local *Ordre d'Avocats* (a local bar) for admission as a *stagiaire* (trainee). The period of the *stage*, is normally two years. During this time the *stagiaire* works under the supervision of an *avocat* but is able to carry on all activities of the profession. On successful completion of the *stage*, the *stagiaire* applies to the *bâtonnier* for *inscription au Tableau* of the *Ordre* and becomes fully qualified.

50.04   *Rights of representation and audience.* There is no geographical restriction on the rights of audience of an *avocat* although he may only formally represent his client (the function formerly performed by the *avoué*) in the court for the district in which he is enrolled. With the exception of the *Conseil d'Etat* and the *Cour de cassation*, where rights of audience are restricted to some 60 specially appointed *avocats*, he may appear in the ordinary courts at every level. In practice, an *avocat* in one town will instruct an *avocat* in another town to act as his agent (*avocat postulant*) where litigation is to take place there, in order to perform the functions of *avoué*. Alternatively, in smaller cases, it would be normal for the local *avocat* to take over the whole case.

Only an *avocat* may represent a party to ordinary civil proceedings before the *tribunal de grande instance* and before that court he has exclusive rights of representation and audience. However, representation is not compulsory in *référé* proceedings[8] before that court, nor in any proceedings before other courts of first instance. In practice, a party is usually represented by an *avocat* in proceedings before the *tribunal de commerce*. In the *Cour d'appel*, a party must be represented by an *avoué* although the preparation of the case and the presentation of oral argument will continue to be performed by an *avocat*. In cases where legal representation is not com-

---

[7] The function of presenting argument on a client's behalf in court is to be distinguished from the function of formal legal representation. This latter function was formerly performed by members of the separate profession of *avoué*, which, except in respect of proceedings before the *Cour d'appel* (see para. 50.06 below) was abolished in 1971.

[8] See para. 50.61 below.

pulsory, a party may represent himself, or may be represented by any other person.

Organisation of practice. Traditionally the *avocat* was a sole practitioner but for many years there have been expense-sharing arrangements known as *groupements*. In 1956 it became permissible for *avocats* to form partnerships with each other and there are now law firms in all the major towns. Many *avocats* however still prefer to practise individually. Partnership with members of other professions is prohibited. In addition to its partners, a law firm may have one or more *collaborateurs*, *avocats* who are paid a fixed honorarium, equivalent to a salary, although they are not legally employees of the firm. Legal work is not normally undertaken by unqualified employees of a law firm.

There are approximately 18,000 *avocats* in France, of whom about half practise in Paris. Although local bars publish lists of their members, there is no official national law list; there is an unofficial list, however, which gives the names and addresses of most *avocats* in France.[9]

Fees. Fees for advisory work are a matter for negotiation between **50.05** the *avocat* and the client, there being no official fee scales. Scale fees do apply, however, for the representation element of an *avocat's* work in litigation in those courts where representation is compulsory; but fees for other work undertaken in connection with litigation are not regulated. It is usual for an *avocat* to ask for advance payment on account (*provision*). The practice of charging fees on an hourly basis is not yet widespread. VAT is generally chargeable on fees if the *avocat* is registered for VAT, but registration is optional and many *avocats* are not registered. VAT is not generally chargeable on legal services rendered for clients outside France.

If a client disputes the level of fees charged, he may complain to the *bâtonnier* of the local bar who must rule on the matter within three months. His ruling may be appealed by either party to the *tribunal de grande instance* within a further month.

Professional organisation and conduct. The profession of *avocat* is organised on the basis of regional bars (*Ordres des avocats*). Formerly, there was a separate *Ordre des avocats* at each *tribunal de grande instance* but since 1972 it has been permissible for *Ordres* within the area of the same *Cour d'appel* to merge and this has happened in a number of places. Each *Ordre* is governed by an elected council and

---

[9] *Annuaire des Professions judiciaires et juridiques,* published annually by the *Librairie du journal des Notaires et des Avocats* in Paris. It also lists the members of the other legal professions, court experts, and courts.

leader (*bâtonnier*) and its functions are to regulate professional conduct and exercise disciplinary functions, to represent the interests of its members and to arbitrate in disputes between *avocats* and their clients.

The profession of *avocat* is regulated by a law of December 31, 1971 which establishes the principal legal framework for the organisation and conduct of the profession and which is supplemented by a *décret* of June 4, 1972 and by the internal rules adopted by each *Ordre des avocats*.

The *avocat* is bound by the same high standards of professional behaviour as lawyers elsewhere. Thus he may only undertake work which he considers to be lawful. He must devote himself conscientiously to the interests of his client. If he handles his client's money he must do so with scrupulous integrity.[10] He may not advertise or solicit for clients. He may not take salaried employment or be actively involved in the running of a business. He is bound by rules of professional privilege[11] and he is, in addition, subject to a number of rules of etiquette. Meetings with clients must normally take place at the *avocat's* office. Contingency fee agreements are forbidden. He may not communicate directly with an opposing lay client who is represented by an *avocat*. Before proceeding to enforce a judgment he must warn his opponent of his intentions. He is liable at law for negligence and he is required to have a substantial level of professional indemnity insurance.

2. The *Avoué*

50.06   The function of an *avoué* was formally to represent a party before the *tribunal de grande instance* and the *Cour d'appel*, to prepare and file pleadings, and to conduct other procedural formalities.[12] The competence of an *avoué* extended only to the particular court in which he was enrolled. In 1971 the office of *avoué* was abolished in respect of proceedings before the *tribunal de grande instance* and, in respect of that court, the roles of the *avoué* and the *avocat* were merged in the *avocat*.[13] *Avoués* continue to exist as a separate profession with one or more practitioners or firms in each of the cities

---

[10] Clients' moneys are not held by *avocats* themselves but in the joint account maintained by each *Ordre des avocats*, on behalf of all its members. This account is called the "CARPA."
[11] See para. 50.52 below.
[12] The functions of the *avoué* were "*la procédure, l'écriture, et la postulation.*"
[13] Before the *tribunal de commerce* the role of the *avoué* was formerly performed by an official called the "*agrée.*" These too were abolished in 1971 and their functions transferred to the *avocats*.

where there is a *Cour d'appel*, exercising their functions in respect of proceedings before those courts.

[The next paragraph is number 50.09]

3. The *Notaire*

The *notaire* is a publicly appointed official whose function is to draw up all instruments and contracts which the parties either are obliged or wish to have officially authenticated, so as to acquire conclusive probative force. Many formal legal documents, such as deeds of sale and gift, mortgages, marriage contracts, articles of incorporation, partnership agreements and wills may or must be authenticated by a *notaire*. He will usually also draft them. The *notaire* must satisfy himself as to the identity and capacity of the parties. The document will be dated and the original retained permanently in the safe custody of the *notaire*. Certified copies (*expéditions*) are provided for the parties.   **50.09**

In acting for the parties he will if necessary advise them in connection with the matter in hand and frequently the *notaire* performs the wider role of general legal adviser in business and family affairs. His fees for notarial functions are fixed according to a statutory scale, but his fees for advisory and drafting work are not regulated. The number of *notaires* in any given area is limited according to the size of the local population, and a newly appointed *notaire* will purchase the goodwill of his predecessor's practice. *Notaires* are permitted to form firms with each other but not with other lawyers or members of other professions. The profession is regulated by law and is subject to the discipline of its own professional body.[14] There are some 7,500 *notaires* in France.

4. The *Conseil juridique*

The term *conseil juridique* was formerly used to describe an unqualified legal adviser. However the new profession of *conseil juridique* was created by legislation in 1971 and it operates under the supervision of the *ministère public*.[15] The applicant must hold a law degree and be of a certain level of professional experience. His name is then placed on an official register of *conseils juridiques*, kept by the *Procureur de la République*. A *conseil juridique* may not act in proceedings in which legal representation is compulsory,[16] and his work is generally more concerned with non-litigious legal matters,   **50.10**

---

[14] *Le Conseil Supérieur du notariat.*
[15] See para. 50.23 below.
[16] See para. 50.04 above. Many *conseils juridiques* practise before the *tribunaux de commerce*.

especially business matters, and company, tax and employment law. There are approximately 5,000 *conseils juridiques*, of whom about half practise in Paris.[17] They have their own professional body and are subject to standards of professional conduct and discipline comparable with those of *avocats*.

5. Foreign lawyers

50.11   Lawyers from other EEC states have the benefit of the EEC Legal Services Directive.[18] In principle foreign lawyers from non-EEC states who wish to practise in France must, if they were not already established there in 1971, have their names added to the list of *conseils juridiques*. They may then advise only on their own foreign law or on international law. There are over forty firms of foreign lawyers practising in Paris carrying out a substantial proportion of the non-contentious legal activity there.

6. Lawyers in business and public employment

50.12   Lawyers employed in business or the public service[19] may not retain the office of *avocat*. They may give legal advice only to their employer and may represent their employer only in those proceedings in which legal representation is not compulsory.

7. The *Huissier de justice*

50.13   The *huissier* is an official who is publicly appointed to his office after a period of training and a professional examination. His functions are principally to carry out service of court documents and to execute judgments and other enforceable instruments. His competence is limited to the locality to which he is appointed, normally the area of a *tribunal d'instance*. Outside the main urban centres he sometimes also gives legal advice privately and draws up legal documents for clients. In small or straightforward cases he may sometimes appear in court for a party. He may also act at the request of the court as a fact-finding agent, visiting, for example, the scene of an accident, and reporting to the court.[20] His fees for performing his official functions are determined according to a statutory scale.

The *huissiers* in the district of a given *tribunal de grande instance* operate on a rota to perform the functions of the *huissier audiencier* by attending at that court and assisting in the transmission of docu-

---

[17] These include some foreign lawyers: see para. 50.11 below.
[18] See para. A2.47 below.
[19] The role of lawyers in the *ministère public* is described separately at para. 50.23 below.
[20] See para. 50.53 below.

ments between the parties' *avocats* and performing tasks required of them by the court.

Huissiers are permitted to enter into partnerships or office-sharing arrangements and to employ clerks who carry out various of their duties in their name. *Huissiers* have their own national and local professional organisations.

A foreign lawyer wishing to enforce a foreign judgment in France will not normally instruct a *huissier* direct to undertake the necessary formalities, because the judgment may only be executed when a *formule exécutoire* has been obtained from the president of the *tribunal de grande instance* on the application of an *avocat*.[21]

C. SOURCES OF LAW

1. Introduction

The French legal system is founded on the constitution of 1958. **50.14** This provides for an executive, led by the President and the Prime Minister, and for a Parliament, the principal function of which is to legislate. The constitution specifies those matters which are to be the subject of legislation and states that other matters may be regulated by governmental *décret*.

International treaties are ratified by the President of the Republic, although in certain matters, specified by the constitution, he may only do so if the treaty has obtained parliamentary approval. Once a treaty has been promulgated in the *Journal Officiel*,[22] it takes effect in the internal law of France and, in theory at least, takes precedence over the constitution.

In addition to the constitution and treaties, there are three formal sources of law, each of which must be promulgated to take effect. They are, in descending order of precedence, *lois*, *décrets* and *arrêtés*. There are also a number of informal sources.

2. Formal sources

Legislation. Legislation consists of the statutory codes, supple- **50.15** mented by individual statutes (*lois*). The main body of civil law is contained in the *Code Civil* which dates back to the *Code Napoleon* of 1804. Specific areas of law are governed by other codes, for example the *Code de Commerce*,[23] the *Code Pénal*, the *Code Administratif*, the *Code du Travail*, the *Nouveau Code De Procédure Civile*, the *Code de Procédure Pénale*, and the *Code de L'organisation Judiciaire*.

---

[21] See para. 50.71 below.

[22] *Journal Officiel de la République Française*, the official government publication in which all laws are published and other official announcements made.

[23] Civil matters and commercial matters are regarded as distinct in French law.

Décrets. These are decrees made by the President or by the Prime Minister, usually on behalf of a departmental minister.

Arrêtés. These are orders made by ministers, prefects (the local representatives of central government) and mayors.

3. Informal sources

50.16   *Decided cases.* The most important informal source of law is the body of decisions made by the higher courts. This body of case law, called *jurisprudence*, does not formally have the binding authority of precedent but has an important and often decisive influence on the interpretation and application of formal sources of law. The decisions of the *Cour de cassation* are regarded as particularly authoritative.

Legal writings. Academic commentary (*doctrine*) plays a significant role in the interpretation of the law, and courts will often refer to it for guidance, especially in fields where the body of case law is limited in scope.

Other sources. Official statements of the purpose or intended effect of the law may also be referred to by the courts. Such statements may take the form of a governmental *circulaire*, or a minister's opinion (*réponse ministérielle*) stated in Parliament, or preparatory works (*travaux préparatoires*), each of which is published in the *Journal Officiel*.

4. Publications

50.17   Legislation is published in the *Journal Officiel*. The only official law reports are those of the *Cour de cassation*, which, as regards civil cases, is called the *Bulletin des Arrêts de la Cour de cassation rendus en Matières Civiles* (the "*Bulletin Civil*," cited as "*Bull. civ.*").[24] However there are numerous private publications which contain reports of cases, legislation and articles, of which the most important are *Recueil Dalloz* (weekly, cited as "*D*")[25], *Semaine juridique* (also called *Jurisclasseur périodique*, weekly, cited as "*J.C.P.*"), *Gazette du Palais* (cited as "*Gaz. Pal.*," or "*G.P.*"), the *Revue trimestrielle de droit civil* (cited as "*Rev. trim. dr. civ.*"), and the *Revue trimestrielle de droit commercial* (cited as "*Rev. trim. dr. com.*"). The legislative codes are also published in annotated form.

---

[24] It is published in five parts, corresponding with the three civil chambers of the Cour de cassation, and the commercial and social chambers. Commercial and social cases are cited as *Com.* and *Soc.* respectively, in addition to the *Bull. civ.* citation. There is a corresponding series for decisions of the criminal chamber.

[25] The publication *Recueil Sirey* ("*S*") merged with *Dalloz* and for a time was published as *Recueil Dalloz-Sirey* ("*D-S*").

D. Organisation of the Civil and Commercial Courts

1. Introduction

The French court system is divided between the administrative **50.18** courts and the ordinary or judicial courts. It has already been observed[26] that the administrative courts apply public law, which governs the relationships of public authorities and officials with each other and with private persons. The ordinary courts have jurisdiction in all other matters, whether they be civil, commercial or criminal. As regards civil and commercial matters, the ordinary courts are organised on a local and regional basis, and at three levels, *instance*, *appel*, and *cassation*. In addition, there are certain specialised courts and tribunals.[27]

2. The *tribunal d'instance*

At the level of the *arrondissement*, the lowest level, there is the *tri-* **50.19** *bunal d'instance*, of which there are about 450. Here a single judge deals with relatively minor matters of a value of up to F.Fr. 30,000. A *tribunal d'instance* of a country area may have only one judge appointed to it, whereas at an urban court there will be a number of judges. Appeal lies to the local *Cour d'appel*, except in matters of a value less than F.Fr. 13,000 in respect of which there is no right of appeal.

Claims for rent are exclusively allocated to the *tribunal d'instance*, as are certain other summary proceedings for the protection of rights in land (*actions possessoires*) and applications for the enforcement of a judgment by means of an attachment of earnings (*saisie-arrêt sur rémunération*).[28] The *tribunal d'instance* also exercises a criminal jurisdiction as the *tribunal de police*.

3. The *tribunal de grande instance*

At the next level, that of the *département*, there is always at least **50.20** one *tribunal de grande instance*, with more in heavily populated areas. Throughout France there are over 180 *tribunaux de grande instance*. The court has general jurisdiction in all civil matters in which the value of the dispute exceeds F.Fr. 30,000 and it has exclusive jurisdiction in respect of the execution of judgments,[29] trade marks and patents and the status and capacity of natural per-

---

[26] See para. 50.02 above.
[27] The European Court of Human Rights at Strasbourg, established under the European Convention for Human Rights, forms no part of the French domestic legal system.
[28] It is usually referred to as *saisie-arrêt sur salaire*. See para. 50.59 below.
[29] An exception is *saisie sur salaire*: see para. 50.19 above.

sons. Each court consists of one or more civil chambers, one or more criminal chambers[30] and, if there is no separate *tribunal de commerce* in the area, a commercial chamber. In each chamber the bench, when sitting, is composed of three judges.

4. The *tribunal de commerce*

There is a separate system of commercial courts within the judicial court system. The *tribunal de commerce* has jurisdiction over disputes of any value arising out of *"actes de commerce."* These are specific transactions listed in the *code de commerce* and include maritime matters, letters of credit, certain carriage claims and, most importantly, commercial contracts. These are contracts made between *commerçants*, or between *commerçants* and non-*commerçants*, in each case for the purposes of the *commerçant's* business. Any individual engaged in business activity and all limited companies fall within the definition of a *commerçant*. However, a non-*commerçant* may not be sued in the *tribunal de commerce* by a *commerçant*. There are some 250 *tribunaux de commerce* throughout France and they carry a heavy case-load. The judges are businessmen elected by the local *commerçants* to serve on the panel of judges for a number of years. In practice they frequently hold a law degree and may well be employed as lawyers in commercial undertakings. When there is no commercial court in a particular area the commercial jurisdiction is exercised by the local *tribunal de grande instance*. The procedure of the *tribunal de commerce* is somewhat less formal than that of the *tribunal de grande instance*.[31]

5. The *conseil de prud'hommes*

This is a local court with jurisdiction over litigation between employers and their employees. Members of the court, of whom half are employers and half are employees, serve on a part-time basis for a number of years. They sit in panels of four and exercise exclusive jurisdiction over employment matters. Appeals lie to the *Cour d'appel*, except where the value of the case is less than F.Fr. 15,500.

6. The *Cour d'appel*

50.21   The *Cours d'appel*, of which there are 40, are also organised on a regional basis with one *Cour d'appel* for about six or seven *tribunaux de grande instance*. They hear appeals from *tribunaux d'instance* (in cases involving more than F.Fr. 15,500) from *tribunaux de grande instance*, from *tribunaux de commerce* and from *conseils de prud'-

---

[30] This is called the *tribunal correctionel*.
[31] See para. 50.47 below.

hommes. They sit in separate chambers for the purpose of hearing appeals in civil, commercial, social and criminal matters. Each chamber consists of three judges. The decision of the *Cour d'appel* cannot be appealed by an ordinary appeal, but it may be reviewed by the *Cour de cassation* by way of an extraordinary appeal.[32]

7. The *Cour de cassation*

The *Cour de cassation* in Paris is the supreme court of France. It **50.22** sits in six chambers, to which specific types of case are assigned.[33] Each chamber is composed of 15 judges but, as the quorum is only seven, the chambers frequently sit in sub-panels. The *Cour de cassation* reviews the judgments of all courts in cases in which no other appeal lies and where the court is alleged to have exceeded its powers or otherwise to have departed from or misapplied the law. It is accordingly restricted to questions of law.

The *Cour de cassation* does not itself decide the case between the parties. If an appeal succeeds, the decision is annulled and the case is sent back to another court of the same level and kind as the trial court for that court to decide the case, subject to the guidance given by the *Cour de cassation*. That court is not bound to follow the *Cour de cassation*, but if it does not, and if the case is again appealed and the decision quashed, the court to which the case is then remitted is bound by the decision of the *Cour de cassation*.

8. Other civil courts

There are also specialised courts with jurisdiction over agricultural tenancies (*tribunaux paritaires des baux ruraux*) and social security. The *Tribunal des conflits* is a special court which determines conflicts of jurisdiction as between the administrative courts and the ordinary or judicial courts.

9. The judiciary and the *ministère public*

Most judges in France are career judges. Together with the state **50.23** prosecutors (*procureurs de la République*), they make up the *magistrature* and they may serve as judges and as state prosecutors at different stages in their careers. The term *magistrat* applies to all judges and *procureurs de la République*; a *juge* is a judge sitting at first instance. A judge in a *Cour d'appel* is called a *conseiller*.

---

[32] See para. 50.65 below.
[33] Three civil chambers, one commercial and financial chamber, one social chamber and one criminal chamber.

The initial qualification for the *magistrature* is a university law degree followed by a further examination and a three-year training period at the *Ecole Nationale de la Magistrature* in Bordeaux. The appointment of judges is the responsibility of the Minister of Justice. Typically, a judge's first appointment will be as an examining magistrate (*juge d'instruction*) in criminal matters, as a single judge in a *tribunal d'instance* or as a junior judge in a *tribunal de grande instance*. His career thereafter will involve promotion to more senior judicial posts and may well involve one or more periods as a *procureur de la République*. Judges in the administrative courts are separately trained and follow a separate career pattern.

The *ministère public* is the public legal service which represents the interests of the state and whose members are the *procureurs de la République*.[34] One or more of them is attached to each court. Their main function is to prosecute in criminal cases, but they are also entitled to take part in any civil proceedings, either by intervening to represent the public interest in litigation between private parties, or as a principal party in certain cases directly affecting the public interest, such as bankruptcy. In practice, a *procureur de la République* usually only intervenes in cases involving guardianship or status.

E. JURISDICTION OF THE CIVIL AND COMMERCIAL COURTS

1. Introduction

50.24   In cases to which the 1968 Convention applies, the international jurisdiction of the French courts is determined by the rules of competence in the Convention. The rules which determine the part of France in which the proceedings either must or may be brought are known as rules of *compétence territoriale*. Except where the Convention itself regulates local jurisdiction,[35] these are the provisions of French law summarised below. The general rule is that proceedings must be brought in the appropriate court for the locality in which the defendant is domiciled.

The rules which determine the level and type of court are known as rules of *compétence d'attribution*.[36] As has been seen above, both the value and the subject-matter of the litigation may determine the level and type of court. The subject-matter of the litigation may require the proceedings to be brought in a specialised court, of

---

[34] They are also sometimes referred to as *le Parquet*.
[35] See para. 15.03 nn. 10–11 above.
[36] Also called *compétence ratione materiae*, or *compétence absolue*.

which the most important example in the field of civil and commercial law is the *tribunal de commerce*.

2. Domicile and seat

Natural persons. A natural person is generally domiciled under **50.25** French law in the place where he has his principal establishment, and it is this general civil law concept of domicile which applies for the purpose of civil procedure. The location of a person's domicile is a question of fact for the court, although an element of intention is necessary to establish a domicile. Factors which may be relevant are a person's habitual residence, the geographical focus of his family and social life and of his economic and professional interests.

A person may change his domicile by physically moving to another place with the intention of settling there. A person may lose his domicile by manifesting an intention no longer to be domiciled there; but leaving a place without an intention of giving up domicile does not have the effect of removing the domicile. Under French law, a person may not be without a domicile,[37] nor have more than one domicile. In practice, a person is normally domiciled where he is resident. Any person, of any nationality, may register his change of address in the local inhabitants' registers for his old and new places of residence. The registration of a person's residence in that register raises a presumption that the person is domiciled there, but the presumption is rebuttable.

Statutory domiciles. In the case of certain categories of person, domicile is not determined by the general rule, but by special statutory provisions. For example, there are statutory domiciles of dependence for certain minors, adult mental patients under guardianship and adult domestic employees. The domicile of such persons is at the place where the person upon whose domicile they are dependent is himself domiciled. The domicile of a married woman is no longer dependent on that of her husband. There are also statutory domiciles for certain public officials.

Legal persons. For the purposes of civil procedure, a legal person **50.26** is generally regarded as being domiciled at the place where it has its principal establishment. As a general rule of French law, this is the place where, according to its constitution, the company is said to be established and which is registered at the local *tribunal de commerce*. This registered office is called the *siège social* or, sometimes, the

---

[37] Special provisions require persons of no fixed abode to choose a *commune* in which they are deemed to be domiciled.

siège statutaire. If a company has its registered office in France, this general rule applies.[38]

If international elements are involved, the position is more complex. If a company has its actual seat (*siège réel*)[39] in France, third parties may take advantage of that seat, and the company itself cannot in response assert that its registered office is elsewhere.[40] Subject to that rule, under French private international law, it is the formal constitution and the "nationality" of a company that determine which law is to apply in deciding questions of its recognition and the extent of its rights. Much the most important point of reference for determining the nationality of a company is the location of its registered office. In practice, therefore, if a company has neither its registered office nor its actual seat in France, the law to be applied in determining the location of its seat is generally the law of the place where it has its registered office.

3. Jurisdiction—general rules

50.27   As has been observed, a person may generally be sued before the appropriate court for the place where he is domiciled or, in the case of a company or association, where it has its registered office. If there is more than one defendant the plaintiff may select the local court of either defendant. If the defendant has no domicile in France, the court may nonetheless have jurisdiction under one of the provisions of the 1968 Convention or, if that Convention does not apply, under some other jurisdictional rule, including Article 14 of the *Code Civil*.[41]

Which level of court is competent to entertain a case is generally determined by the value of the subject matter in dispute. This depends not on the amount claimed but on the amount in issue between the parties at the close of the *débats*.[42] This amount may include any accrued interest up to the start of the proceedings.

---

[38] Under Art. 3(1) of Law no. 66–537 of July 24, 1966, commercial companies which have their registered office within the territory of France are subject to French law. This is now widely regarded as a universal choice of law applying beyond the scope of commercial companies; and in respect also of associations, partnerships and other non-natural persons, only their registered office will be considered.

[39] The *siège réel* is the place where the company's principal (highest) control and organs of administration are, and not necessarily the place where business is carried on. It must not be a fictional seat, and it must be *sérieux*, not just chosen as a means of avoiding the law.

[40] Art. 3(2) of Law no. 66–537 of July 24, 1966: according to some authors, this provision should also be applied beyond the scope of commercial companies (its strict ambit) in order to provide better protection for the bona fide acts of third parties.

[41] See para. 50.30 below.

[42] See para. 50.46 below.

4. Jurisdiction—special rules

The above general rule is subject to various qualifications and **50.28**
exceptions. Proceedings arising out of the operation of a branch
office may be brought in the appropriate court for the locality of the
branch office. Proceedings relating to real property must be
brought in the court for the place in which the property is situated.
In matters of tort the proceedings may be brought in the court for
the place in which the wrongful act was committed or in which the
damage was suffered.

In disputes arising out of contracts the plaintiff has the choice of
suing the defendant in the local court of the defendant's domicile,
or of the place where goods were, or were to be, delivered or where
services were, or were to be, performed.[43] French law provides as a
general rule that, unless the parties otherwise agree, the place of
performance of an obligation to pay money is at the domicile of the
debtor. Two important exceptions to that rule should be mentioned. First, if payment is due under a contract for the sale of
goods, the place of payment, in the absence of agreement to the
contrary, is generally at the place of delivery of the goods, which
(unless otherwise agreed) is where the goods were at the time of formation of the contract.[44] Secondly, if the payment obligation relates
to a specific and identified object, it is to be performed (again in the
absence of agreement to the contrary) at the place where the object
was situated at the time the obligation was entered into. If the existence of the contract is disputed then the proceedings should preferably be brought in the court of the defendant's domicile.

5. Choice of court and entry of appearance

The above rules of territorial competence may be, in commercial **50.29**
contracts, waived in a number of ways—by a choice of jurisdiction
clause (which may take the form of an election of a domicile[45] for
the purpose of the proceedings) or, by an arbitration clause.
Equally, a defendant who is sued in some territorially inappropriate
court and who does not challenge the court's jurisdiction will be
taken to have consented to that jurisdiction. The rule that proceedings relating to real property must be brought in the court for the
place in which the property is situated cannot be waived.

---

[43] Note that for the purposes of jurisdiction, proceedings instituted by a *commerçant* against a non-*commerçant* may not be brought before the *tribunal de commerce*: see para. 50.20 above.
[44] Different considerations apply to contracts of carriage; but most international
contracts for the carriage of goods by road will be subject to the special rules of
the Geneva Convention of May 19, 1956 ("C.M.R.").
[45] Electing a domicile means nominating an address for the service of proceedings.

6. Exorbitant grounds of jurisdiction

50.30 Articles 14 and 15 of the *Code Civil* are exorbitant rules of jurisdiction which may not be relied on in cases covered by the 1968
Convention. Under Article 14, a person of French nationality may
bring an action in France against a person of foreign nationality.
Under Article 15, a person of French nationality may be sued in
France. In each case, the right may be waived expressly or, in some
circumstances, impliedly; but the jurisdiction of the particular
court under these Articles may normally only be invoked if the
subject-matter of the dispute has a sufficient connection with the
locality of the court.

7. Civil claims in criminal proceedings

50.31 When a criminal offence also gives rise to a claim for civil
damages the plaintiff may choose to pursue his claim as a *"partie
civile"* in the criminal proceedings; but if he does so, he is then precluded from bringing an ordinary civil action in respect of the same
matter. In addition to passing sentence on the defendant, the judge
will also make an award of civil damages. Civil claims are frequently
made in criminal proceedings arising out of traffic accidents. If
criminal proceedings are brought after the commencement of civil
proceedings, the civil case must be stayed pending the result of the
criminal case, the decision in which will bind the civil court. However if the defendant is acquitted in the criminal proceedings the
civil court may still find in the plaintiff's favour if there is some
alternative basis of liability.

F. LIMITATION PERIODS

50.32 The law of limitation is complex and the following should be taken
as only a most general guide.

The limitation periods laid down in the *Code Civil* apply to all
claims, whether civil or commercial, except for commercial claims
especially provided for in the *Code de Commerce*. Most limitation
periods are periods of prescription which extinguish the right, but
some of the shorter periods operate only to bar the remedy.[46]
Periods of limitation generally start to run when the cause of action
accrues, but their commencement may be postponed until the
plaintiff has knowledge of the facts establishing the cause of action,
unless he should reasonably have had that knowledge earlier.

---

[46] Some special periods of limitation of less than five years (particularly in connection with debts) may be lifted, so as to bring the case within the longer general
limitation periods, if the creditor challenges the debtor to swear that he has paid
and the debtor refuses to do so.

The overall period of limitation provided by the *Code Civil* is 30   **50.33**
years; but there are many shorter periods of limitation, particularly
in commercial law, where the general limitation period is 10 years.
The following are examples of some of the more important limitation periods.

(a) an undefined short period (*bref délai*), the length of which
depends on the circumstances; actions in respect of latent
defects in goods;

(b) six months: an action by an indorser of a bill of exchange
against another indorser or against the drawer;

(c) one year: an action by the holder of a bill of exchange
against an indorser or the drawer; most actions on a contract of non-international carriage;

(d) two years: many actions on contracts of services by liberal
professions; most actions on a contract for the sale of
goods to a non-*commerçant* by a *commerçant* who has not
manufactured them but has himself purchased them from
a third party; many claims on contracts of non-marine
insurance;

(e) three years: actions against the acceptor of a bill of
exchange; most claims made by a *partie civile* in criminal
proceedings in respect of *delits*[47];

(f) five years: actions on debts payable by instalments,
including salaries, interest payments, pensions and rents;

(g) ten years: most actions, other than those referred to
above, in respect of commercial matters;

(h) thirty years; actions in tort, including claims for personal
injuries; actions in respect of the sale of land; actions other
than those referred to above, in respect of non-commercial
contracts.

G. CIVIL PROCEDURE—PROCEEDINGS UP TO JUDGMENT

1. General description

Civil procedure in France is now principally governed by the   **50.34**
Nouveau Code de Procédure Civile, adopted in 1975.[48] In common
with other continental systems, French civil litigation is characterised by the dominant role of the judge, although it remains adversarial in theory. The procedure involves both written and oral

---

[47] *Delits* are crimes, but they may often support civil claims for damages by *parties
civiles*. Certain wrongs regarded as civil matters in common law countries are
delits, such as infringements of patents and other intellectual property rights and
defamation. In the case of defamation, the limitation period is two months.
[48] Abbreviated NCPC. The old code of civil procedure of 1806 (ACPC) is still
partly in force and governs, notably, attachments and charging orders.

aspects. Proceedings are commenced by the *huissier* serving a summons (*assignation*) on the defendant, which is then lodged at the
court. The parties or their lawyers attend an initial hearing at which
directions are given for the filing of pleadings and for the further
conduct of the proceedings.

By contrast with common law systems, the normal procedure
involves a series of separate relatively short hearings rather than a
continuous trial of the action. Court experts are commonly engaged
to investigate issues of fact. Hearings may be held, often before a
single judge, for the purpose of determining interlocutory issues
and, occasionally, for the taking of oral evidence. A subsequent
final hearing takes place before the full court at which the oral arguments are presented. After deliberation the court announces its
judgment. Much civil litigation, however, is dealt with by means of
référé proceedings, a summary procedure in which the court may
make an order which in theory is provisional but which in practice
often disposes of the case.

The procedure before the *tribunal de commerce* is similar to that
before the ordinary courts, but differs in detail. Notably, written
pleadings are not compulsory.

2. Parties and legal representation

50.35   Any natural or legal person,[49] may, subject to jurisdictional
rules, bring an action in the French courts, regardless of nationality, domicile or residence. The two principal parties to litigation
are called the *demandeur* and the *défendeur*. Minors and those under
a mental disability may sue and be sued through their legal guard-
ians. Further parties may be added to the proceedings at the
request of one of the existing parties or may intervene to pursue
their own claims or to support one of the existing parties. A party
may also counterclaim in respect of any matter which is sufficiently
connected with the original claim.

Certain public undertakings, such as *Sociétés nationales* or *Etablissements publics* may have to sue and be sued in the administrative
courts.

50.36   *Legal representation.* Except in *référé* proceedings,[50] legal representation by an *avocat* is obligatory before the *tribunal de grande
instance*, and higher courts, but not before the *tribunal de commerce*,
the *tribunal d'instance* or the *conseil de prud'hommes*. However in
these latter courts parties are very frequently represented by *avocats*.
In the *Cour d'appel* the parties must generally be represented by

---

[49] The most common forms of legal persons are listed at para. 50.73 below.
[50] See para. 50.61 below.

an *avoué*,[51] who is normally introduced by the party's *avocat*. In the *Cour de cassation* rights of audience and representation are restricted to some 60 specially appointed *avocats* who also perform the functions there of *avoués*.

3. Commencement of proceedings

The normal method of starting proceedings is by the service of a **50.37** summons, called an *assignation*. Service must be carried out by a *huissier*. The *assignation* is issued by the *huissier* usually in the form drafted by the plaintiff's *avocat*. Once it has been served by the *huissier* a copy is returned to the plaintiff or his *avocat*. It must then be filed at the court within four months from its date of issue, failing which it becomes void. It may be filed by either party, whereupon the registrar of the court enters it on the list of cases for hearing. The proceedings are considered first to become pending when the *assignation* is served on the defendant.

The contents of the *assignation* are as follows: its date; if the plaintiff is a natural person, his name, occupation, domicile, nationality and date and place of birth; if the plaintiff is a legal person, its form, name, registered office and legal representative; the name and address of the *huissier* and his signature; the name and domicile or registered office of the defendant[52]; the court before which the claim is to be brought; a statement of the relief sought with a summary of the factual and legal grounds of the claim[53]; a warning that failure to appear may lead to a default judgment; the number of days within which the defendant must make an appearance by appointing an *avocat*[54]; and, in the case of a foreign plaintiff, an address for service at his *avocat's* office. The *assignation* should also include a list of documents on which the claim is based, but this is often omitted in practice. Once it has been served, the *huissier* will endorse the *assignation* with a statement of the time and place of service.

---

[51] Exceptionally, representation by an *avoué* is not required, notably in employment appeals.

[52] The foregoing requirements are stipulated by Art. 648 NCPC and apply also to other formal acts of a *huissier*.

[53] The grounds of the claim are normally set out fairly briefly and the *avocat* will expect to have the opportunity of enlarging them, if necessary, in the course of the *conclusions* which are normally exchanged later.

[54] In the *tribunal d'instance*, the *tribunal de commerce* and the *conseil de prud'hommes*, where the defendant is summoned to the first hearing of the case, the plaintiff's *avocat* will select a date from the calendar of the court's sittings allowing sufficient time for service to be effected, allowing (in the case of defendants served in France) a minimum of 15 days between the date of service and the date of the hearing.

4. Service of proceedings

50.38   Service (*signification*[55]) must be carried out by a *huissier* for the district in which it is to be effected. For the purposes of service, the *huissier* prepares the necessary number of copies of the *assignation*, one of which he returns after service to the plaintiff or his *avocat* with an indorsement as to service.

The *assignation* must be served personally on the defendant but if this is not possible it may be served on a member of his family, or a servant or neighbour or caretaker at his place of domicile or, if this is not known, at his place of work. If there is no appropriate person there who is able or willing to accept service, the *huissier* delivers the *assignation* at an office at the town hall and sends a registered letter to the defendant informing him of this fact. If the domicile or residence or place of work is not known, the *huissier* records his attempts to effect service in a formal minute. He thereupon sends a copy of the minute by registered post to the defendant's last known address and informs the defendant that a copy of the *assignation* may be collected from his office within the next three months. This procedure amounts to a formal *signification*.

A legal person is served by the *huissier* at its seat[56] or, in actions relating to the activities of a branch, at that branch.

Service on a foreign defendant who is present or resident in France, or on the branch of a foreign company established in France, is effected in accordance with the above procedure. In the absence of any other provision in an international convention,[57] service on a defendant abroad is effected by the *huissier* delivering the *assignation* to the *ministère public*. The *assignation* is then transmitted to the defendant through diplomatic channels or in accordance with the provisions of any relevant convention. Regardless of whether or when it is actually received by the defendant, service is deemed to be complete when the *assignation* is delivered to the *ministère public*. Subject to the provisions of any applicable international conventions, the service of judicial documents from abroad is effected by *signification* by a *huissier*, or by simple delivery.

5. Appearance by the defendant

50.39   *Tribunal de grande instance.* In the *tribunal de grande instance*, if the defendant wishes to appear in the proceedings he must appoint an *avocat* to appear on his behalf. The *avocat* must give written

---

[55] The act of bringing a matter formally to a person's attention is called *notification*; if this is done by a *huissier*, it is called *signification*.
[56] See para. 50.26 above.
[57] France is a party to the Hague Service Convention: see paras. 4.30 *et seq* above and A2.03 below.

notification⁵⁸ of his appointment to the plaintiff's *avocat* and it is the giving of this notification which formally constitutes the entry of an appearance. The *assignation* does not normally state the date of the first hearing⁵⁹ but specifies the period after service within which the defendant must appoint an *avocat* to make such an appearance. This period is 15 days when the defendant is served in France, but it will be extended by two months if he is to be served outside France.⁶⁰ The period for appointing an *avocat* may be reduced in urgent cases at the plaintiff's request if the judge so allows. If the defendant fails to appoint an *avocat*, or if his *avocat* does not give written notice of his appointment, he runs the risk that the plaintiff's *avocat* will have obtained a hearing date of which he will not be notified.

Other courts. In courts other than the *tribunal de grande instance*, the date of the first hearing will be stated in the *assignation* and will normally be fixed for a date late enough to enable service to occur at least 15 days beforehand, although the period may be reduced in urgent cases. The period is extended in the same manner as in the *tribunal de grande instance* if service is to be effected outside France. The appearance is made by the defendant or his *avocat* simply attending the first hearing.

6. Default judgments

If the defendant or his *avocat* does not appear at the first hearing, **50.40** the court may give judgment against him. In practice, however, the court usually fixes a date for a further hearing at which the question of whether the plaintiff is entitled to judgment will be considered. Alternatively, the plaintiff may elect to commence the proceedings again, or he may be directed by the court to do so. If the defendant is domiciled abroad, the court must consider whether the defendant has been notified in sufficient time and, if he has not, the court may direct that he be given further time in which to appear or that further steps be taken to serve him.

There are two types of judgment which may be given in the absence of the defendant. They both involve the court in considering the substance of the claim and they may only be given if and to the extent that the claim is considered to have been validly presented, entertainable by the court and well-founded. Either type of

---

⁵⁸ This notification is called a *constitution*.
⁵⁹ Exceptionally, at the plaintiff's request, the date of the first hearing in the *tribunal de grande instance* may be fixed at the outset and stated in the *assignation*. This practice is always adopted if the *référé* procedure is used (described at para. 50.61 below).
⁶⁰ The period is extended by one month if service is effected in the French *départements d'outre mer*.

judgment will remain valid only for six months from the date it was given, unless it has been served on the defendant within that time.

Jugement réputé contradictoire. The first type of judgment is one deemed to have been given in adversary proceedings (*jugement réputé contradictoire*). It may be given in the absence of the defendant either if the judgment is susceptible to an *appel*,[61] or if the defendant has been personally served, or both. It may be overturned on appeal to a higher court.[62]

Jugement par défaut. The second type of judgment is strictly a default judgment (*jugement par défaut*) and may only be given if, first, the judgment would not be susceptible to an *appel*[61] and, secondly, the defendant has not been personally served. A default judgment rendered against a party domiciled outside France must expressly record the efforts which have been made to inform the defendant of the *assignation*.

50.41   *Setting aside.* A *jugement par défaut* (but not a *jugement réputé contradictoire*) may be challenged by *opposition* before the court which gave it; the plaintiff may therefore seek to save time in such a case by recommencing the proceedings instead of applying for judgment. An application in *opposition* must be made within one month from the service on the defendant of the default judgment; but the period is extended to three months in the case of a defendant domiciled outside France.[63] An application in *opposition* is a fresh procedure for the purpose of objecting to the judgment, and the procedure follows that of normal proceedings, leading eventually to a judgment on the merits. The defendant need not explain his default nor need he, as a condition of proceeding, show that he has a good defence on the merits. However, the lodging of the application in *opposition* does not itself result in the judgment being set aside and the plaintiff may still enforce the default judgment, provided that it has been declared provisionally enforceable.[64] In practice, though, he will often not do so because he may be exposed to a claim for damages if the objection succeeds.

---

[61] A judgment is not susceptible to an *appel* if it falls below a certain financial limit, presently set at F.Fr. 15,500. See para. 50.64 below.

[62] See para. 50.64 below.

[63] The time runs from the date of service, which is normally the date when the *assignation* was served on the *ministère public* for transmission abroad: see para. 50.38 above. The time-limit may be extended on application to the president of the court, provided the application is made within a reasonable period after the defendant acquired knowledge of the judgment and in any event within a year from the date of its notification.

[64] See para. 50.67 below.

7. Disputes as to jurisdiction

A challenge to the jurisdiction must be raised before any other **50.42** defence, and must identify the court which the defendant says has jurisdiction. If the challenge is not made at this stage, the defendant is not entitled to raise it at any later stage, although the court may decline jurisdiction at a later stage if it has no jurisdiction over the subject-matter of the case.

The court may rule on its own jurisdiction. If it decides that an objection is well-founded, it must refer the parties to the court which it considers to be competent to try the dispute. If that court is another ordinary civil court, the latter court and the parties are bound by that ruling, unless it is overturned on appeal. A ruling that the court has or does not have jurisdiction may normally be challenged only by means of a special appeal,[65] unless the issue of jurisdiction has been decided in the same judgment as decides the substance of the dispute. If the court rules that it has jurisdiction, the proceedings are stayed until the expiry of the time limited for appealing, or until any appeal has been disposed of.

8. Pleadings

All matters of fact and law and all the pleas and defences upon **50.43** which the parties intend to rely must be set out, as appropriate, in the *assignation* or in further written pleadings (*conclusions*). In addition, each party must mention appropriate means of proof for the various facts upon which the claim is based, and this will normally involve reference to written material. In proceedings before the *tribunal de commerce*, however, the procedure is theoretically oral and *conclusions* are not required, although they are usually filed and exchanged in practice. Supporting documents (or copies) are not attached to the *assignation* or *conclusions*, but are sent independently to the opposing party. Every *conclusion* must be signed by the party or his *avocat* and, in proceedings before the *tribunal de grande instance*, must be served by a court official (a *huissier audiencier*) on the opposing *avocat*, and a copy delivered to the court. In proceedings before other courts, the *avocats* exchange pleadings directly between themselves and deliver a copy to the court.

The information which must be included in an *assignation* has **50.44** been summarised above.[66] Particulars of the relief claimed and the grounds relied upon must be sufficient to enable the defendant to understand the nature of the claim against him, but the individual items claimed are sometimes left unspecified until the last prepara-

---

[65] A *contredit*: see para. 50.65 below.
[66] See para. 50.37 above.

tory hearing. Additional claims may be added at any stage of the proceedings, provided they are sufficiently related to the original claim. A counterclaim (*demande reconventionelle*) may be included in the *conclusions en défense* and will be decided together with the main action in a single judgment. The plaintiff may answer the defendant's case in a reply and the parties may exchange further pleadings as necessary.

9. The hearings

50.45   If the *assignation* has not been filed in court within four months from the date of service then the service lapses and the *assignation* must be re-served if it is to have effect. When the *assignation* is filed, the case is put on the court list or calendar and it is assigned by the president of the court to a particular chamber. The president of that chamber then fixes a day for the first hearing. In the *tribunal de commerce*, this hearing is before the full chamber, but in the other courts it is either before the president sitting alone, or before a single judge, whom he appoints to conduct the interlocutory stages of the proceedings. In the *tribunal de grande instance*, this judge is called the *juge de la mise en état*.

50.46   *Proceedings in the tribunal de grande instance and the tribunal d'instance.* In these proceedings the president or the single judge gives directions at the first hearing as to the interlocutory stage of the proceedings (known as *instruction*). In practice, the first step will usually be to fix a date for a further hearing and in the *tribunal de grande instance*, the parties' *avocats* may frequently not attend, unless the defendant has failed to appoint an *avocat*. The judge directs the carrying out of such steps as he considers necessary for the investigation of the factual and legal issues in the case, setting time limits. He usually directs the plaintiff's *avocat* to disclose all documents upon which he intends to rely. He directs the defendant's *avocat* to do likewise and, in the *tribunal de grande instance*, to file his *conclusions en défense*.

There will then be a series of further hearings, fixed either by the court or at the request of one of the parties, at which the judge reviews the preparation of the case and makes further orders. The parties may, of their own motion, or at the request of the judge, exchange such further *conclusions* as may be necessary.

In conducting the investigatory stage of the proceedings the judge may make any enquiry he wishes into the facts of the case, by making procedural orders (known as *mesures d'instruction*), although in practice he will usually only make such orders as are requested by the parties. He will frequently direct the appointment of an expert and may, exceptionally, order the taking of oral evidence from witnesses. An important power which the single judge may often exercise is the power to order payment of an interim amount (*provision*), although in such a case the defendant may ask that the order be made conditional on the granting of security by the plaintiff. Decisions ordering any particular means of investigation cannot normally be challenged by appeal or by cassation.

Once the single judge takes the view that the case is ready for a final oral hearing, he announces that at the next hearing he will order the closure of the preparatory stage (*clôture des débats*). Once he has ordered the closure (by an *ordonnance de clôture*), the parties may not exchange further written pleadings or refer to additional documents, unless the court revokes the closure, which it will only do for some serious and legitimate reason. The president of the chamber then fixes a date for the final hearing and the parties or their *avocats* are notified of this date by the court office.

The final hearing, the *audience de plaidoiries*, takes place, normally in public, either before the full chamber, or, if the *avocats* consent, before the single judge who has had charge of the preparatory stages. The parties or their *avocats* present their oral arguments (*plaidoirie*) referring to both facts and law as may be necessary and stressing the important aspects of their cases. They may not adopt arguments or rely on evidence which is not included in their pleadings.[67] The plaintiff's *avocat* addresses the court first, then the defendant's *avocat*. At the conclusion of their submissions the *avocats* hand in their dossiers which contain their pleadings and documentary evidence. No official note of the proceedings is taken.

Proceedings in the tribunal de commerce. The procedure in the *tribunal de commerce* differs from that described above in two main respects. First, as has been noted, written pleadings are not required (although they are often used); and secondly, the procedure does not normally involve a series of preparatory hearings. Once preliminary directions have been given, including, where appropriate, the appointment of an expert, the case is put into the list of cases which are in their preparatory stages (*rôle des parties*). During the period before the case reaches the top of the list, the parties exchange their pleadings (if any) and their documents and, if there is an expert, they assist in his investigations. Once it reaches the top of that list, there is a hearing at which the parties may attend if there is some reason for the final hearing to be delayed or if further directions are required.

50.47

Thereafter one of two procedures is followed. In smaller or less busy courts, the parties or their *avocats* file their dossiers of pleadings (if any) and documents, normally two days before the final

---

[67] They may also refer to the court expert's report and to any court record of oral evidence.

hearing, which then takes place on the appointed day before the full court. The parties address oral argument to the court, which may include arguments which have not been stated in such written pleadings as they may have filed. The court may well address questions to the parties arising from the documents which they have filed. In larger or busier courts, there is a short formal hearing before the full court at which unless the circumstances otherwise dictate, the case is put in the list of cases for a final hearing (*rôle de delibérés*) and the case is referred to a single member of the court (the *juge rapporteur*). If the case is referred to a *juge rapporteur*, he calls the parties to a meeting in his private room and they file their dossiers, normally two days before that meeting. The oral argument is then addressed to him at that meeting and he makes a report to the full court.

Judgment.[68] It is rare for a decision to be announced immediately at the final hearing. Normally the case is adjourned for private deliberation to take place and the president appoints a date, usually some weeks later, upon which judgment will be given. The court comes, by majority vote, to a single judgment. Minority or dissenting views are not expressed. The judgment is announced in open court, but this is usually limited to a recital of the *dispositif* part of the judgment. The full written judgment will then be prepared and the original will be filed in the court.

10. Security for costs

50.48   Plaintiffs domiciled outside France are no longer required to give security for costs.

11. Witnesses and oral evidence

50.49   *Oral evidence.* The taking of oral evidence is very rare in civil and commercial cases. The normal way in which a witness's evidence is made available to the court is by means of a formal written statement (an *attestation*) which is submitted as part of the documentary evidence. In respect of civil matters (as distinct from commercial matters) there are specific and strict rules of evidence limiting the admissibility of evidence which is not in documentary form. For example, in ordinary *civil* proceedings debts over F.Fr. 5000 can only be proved if they are evidenced in writing.

If the taking of oral evidence is ordered, the court makes an order at the preparatory stage, specifying the issues upon which the witness is to be heard. The taking of oral evidence from a witness is called an *enquête* and it usually takes place in private in the judge's room in the presence of the respective *avocats*. It is usually con-

---

[68] The form and contents of judgments are described at para. 50.56 below.

ducted before a single judge. The witness is sworn and is then invited by the judge to give a narrative account of the matters in question, without referring to notes. The respective *avocats* do not themselves question the witness but they may suggest questions to be put to him by the judge. The judge dictates the substance of the evidence to the court clerk (*greffier*), who records it in minutes of evidence. These are then read over to the witness and he is invited to make any alterations or additions. Hearsay evidence is admitted unless it appears to be too remote. The minutes of evidence are subsequently read to the full court by the *greffier* at the final *audience* and added to the court file. The *avocats* may address the court with regard to the evidence. A spouse or a relative of a party in direct line of ascent or descent may decline to give evidence as a witness.

Witness statements. The detailed interviewing of witnesses beforehand by the lawyers would be considered a breach of judicial sovereignty; but a witness may be requested by a party or his lawyer to give a written statement for use as documentary evidence.

Attendance of the parties. The judge, on a request being made by one party in the pleadings, may direct that the other party or both parties shall attend before the full court. The party will be questioned in the same manner as if he were a witness. He cannot be compelled to appear, but if he does not, his non-appearance may be held to constitute evidence of facts alleged against him. The officers of a corporate party are treated for these purposes as if they were individual parties.   **50.50**

12. Documentary evidence

A party who wishes to rely on a document is obliged to send a copy of it to every other party to the proceedings and if this is not done spontaneously it will be ordered by the judge on request. The plaintiff's *avocat* will normally send a bundle of evidential documents to the defendant's *avocat* before the *conclusions en défense* and thereafter documents are usually exchanged in conjunction with the exchange of pleadings.   **50.51**

There is no general rule requiring the disclosure of documents in a party's possession. Any party can ask the judge to order the production or the giving of a copy of a document in the hands of a party or of a third person. Failure to comply may result in the defaulting person being fined. Where such an order is made against a third party, that person may challenge the order before the court which made it.   **50.52**

Legal professional privilege. Correspondence between two opposing *avocats* is, according to the rules of many French bars, confidential to themselves and may not even be disclosed to the lay client. Thus a French *avocat* who is instructed by a foreign lawyer may be reluctant to disclose such correspondence to the foreign lawyer unless he undertakes to be similarly bound by confidentiality. Confidential correspondence between the parties themselves will normally not be admissible in proceedings.

13. Experts

50.53 Experts appointed by the court play an important role in French civil and commercial proceedings and lists of registered experts are kept at all courts. In addition, the parties may appoint their own experts and often do so, especially in cases involving insurance companies. In theory, a court expert should be appointed only in cases in which technical or other specialist issues are raised, but in practice an expert is frequently employed in cases of a more general nature and his investigation (called an *expertise*) is the normal method by which conflicting issues of fact are resolved. For the purpose of determining limited questions of fact, though, the court may direct a *huissier* to conduct the necessary investigation.

A party may request the appointment of an expert in his pleadings or the court may appoint an expert of its own motion. The order appointing the expert will define the issues to be investigated and his powers of investigation are extensive. The expert will carry out whatever inspections may be necessary and he may question witnesses. He will hold one or more hearings, which the parties are required to attend. Statements made by the parties (called *dires*) are submitted to the expert who is required to annex them to his report, to take them into account and to comment on them. In view of the importance of these statements, they are usually drafted by the *avocats*. The expert's report will be filed with the court with copies for the parties. In it, the expert states his findings of fact and his opinion, but he is precluded from expressing any conclusions of law. Thus he may not express his opinion as to liability, but his conclusions carry great weight with the court and are frequently decisive of the case. At the subsequent hearing, the *avocats* may address the court with regard to the report and, in exceptional cases, the expert may be summoned to the court to give explanations.

14. Proof of foreign law

50.54 A party who wishes to rely on foreign law must refer to it in his pleadings and prove it. This is normally done by means of a statement as to the foreign law (*certificat de coutume*), made by a person of suitable qualification or experience, which is included in a party's documentary evidence. The rules as to what constitutes adequate evidence of foreign law are very liberal and foreign statutes, treatises, textbooks and other documentary material may be admitted.

If the parties do not submit evidence of foreign law, the court may apply French law, even if French choice of law rules provide for the applicability of some other law. Exceptionally, the court may nonetheless apply foreign law of its own motion, either by taking judicial notice of it or, in a complex case, by appointing an expert.

15. Compromise

It is open to the parties to settle their dispute at any time during the proceedings, either on their own initiative or at the instigation of the judge. The judge's function includes the reconciliation of the parties, and he may invite them to discuss the merits of the case with him, although in practice this does not often occur in ordinary civil and commercial matters. Such settlements as occur are usually reached without the intervention of the judge. Settlements, including those reached for the benefit of minors, do not ordinarily require the approval of the court. **50.55**

Court settlements. The parties may ask the judge to record their agreement and if this is done, the record of the agreement is signed by the parties and by the judge. An extract of the record containing the agreement may be issued by the court and may then be enforced as if it were a judgment. Alternatively, the parties may request the court to deliver a formal judgment in the terms of their agreement.

Costs. If a case is settled before its conclusion, the settlement will ordinarily dispose of the question of costs. As between the *avocat* and his client, the fees may be reduced if they are calculated on a time-related basis, to take account of the time saved.

16. The judgment[69]

Form of the judgment. The judgment, which is rendered in the name of the French people, states the name of the court, the names of the judges, the date, the names of the parties and their representatives and the parties' domicile or registered office, and certain other formal particulars. It includes a summary of the evidence and the arguments of the respective parties and the reasons upon which the court has based its decision (*les motifs*), and a statement of the decision itself (*le dispositif*). It deals with the question of costs.[70] **50.56**

---

[69] The giving of the judgment is described at para. 50.47 above. A judgment given at first instance is called a *jugement*, unless it is an order of a single judge, which is usually called an *ordonnance*. The judgment given on an appeal is called an *arrêt*.

[70] See para. 50.57 below.

The judgment may state that it is provisionally enforceable,[71] but this may be made conditional on the provision of security by the judgment creditor. The judgment is signed by the president of the court and by the clerk of the court (*greffier*) and it bears the court seal. A single certified copy (a *grosse*), bearing the *formule exécutoire*,[72] is sent to each of the parties or his *avocat*.

Service and appeal. The date of the judgment is the date when it is announced in open court, although time for appeal will usually only start to run against a party when the judgment has been served on him.[73]

Interpretation. A request for interpretation of the decision may be made to the judge who has given it if the matter has not been taken to appeal. In addition, material errors or omissions may be corrected by the court of its own motion or on the application of either party.

17. Costs

50.57   The costs relating to the main proceedings and the execution of the judgment are of two types. The first, known as *dépens*, consists of the formal costs and disbursements incurred by reason of the proceedings. These include the court fees, experts' fees and expenses, the fees of the *huissier* and, in proceedings involving compulsory representation by a lawyer, the lawyer's scale fees. These costs are awarded against the losing party unless, exceptionally, the court otherwise orders in a reasoned decision. The fees and expenses of an expert appointed by the court are usually paid in advance by the party requesting his appointment.

The second type of costs are those not included in the *dépens*. These include the lawyer's fees (except the scale fees for compulsory representation) and such other sums as the party may have spent, including the costs of the party's own time occupied in connection with the litigation. If it appears inequitable to the court that a party should bear the burden of its costs of this type, the court has power to order the other party to pay a sum in respect of these costs. In practice, the sums awarded in the *tribunal de grande instance* and the *tribunal d'instance* in respect of costs other than the *dépens* is often very much less than that claimed, but in the *tribunal de commerce* a greater measure of reimbursement is usually awarded.

A party formulates his claim for each type of costs in detail in his pleadings, giving particulars of his expenditure in respect of the

---

[71] See para. 50.67 below.
[72] See para. 50.67 below.
[73] See further at para. 50.63 below.

dépens. The practice varies as regards the other costs, some lawyers exhibiting their bill as evidence of their fees, others preferring merely to give details of the work undertaken by them. The costs of a party's foreign lawyer do not form part of the *dépens*, but may be included in the claim for other costs. The sums to be awarded in respect of costs are assessed by the court and included in its judgment.

H. CIVIL PROCEDURE—PROVISIONAL AND PROTECTIVE MEASURES

1. Provisional orders obtained summarily

Référé. French law provides a summary procedure by way of **50.58** *référé* proceedings by which a party may obtain protective or other orders from the court. This procedure, which is widely used, is of great importance, and is discussed in detail below.[74] The orders made in such proceedings (*ordonnances de référé*) are always *inter partes* and, in theory at least, they do not finally determine the rights of the parties but are provisional orders.

Requête. Certain protective measures may be obtained on an *ex parte* application (*sur requête*) for the purpose of securing a defendant's assets with a view to the eventual satisfaction of a judgment. Most important of these protective measures is protective attachment (*saisie conservatoire*).

2. Protective attachment

Protective attachment in French law is called *saisie conservatoire*. **50.59** This remedy enables the defendant's assets to be attached and it is available in support of all civil and commercial claims for a money judgment, whether liquidated or not. It is also available in support of proceedings in a foreign country and is not necessarily limited to assets situated in France. The protective attachment of a third party's debt to the defendant (notably that in respect of a bank account) is called a *saisie-arrêt*. If the attachment is of land, it is called a *saisie immobilière* and if it is of goods which are the subject of the action and which are in the possession of a third party, it is called a *saisie revendication*. The provisional arrest of a ship in a maritime claim is called a *saisie-maritime*.

Application is made *ex parte* by *requête* to the presiding judge (or the judge to whom he has delegated this function) of the *tribunal de grande instance*, or the *tribunal d'instance* or, in commercial cases, the *tribunal de commerce* for the area in which the defendant is domiciled or in which the assets are located. The application must set out the grounds for seizure showing a prima facie case on the merits. It

---

[74] Para. 50.61.

must specify the amount for which security is claimed and it may identify the assets to be seized. It must demonstrate some urgent threat to the satisfaction of the claim. In practice the judge usually requires the creditor first to have called on the defendant to pay, usually by means of a *sommation* (a formal demand), served by a *huissier*.

The order will specify the amount in respect of which seizure is to be made. This may not necessarily be for the full amount claimed by the plaintiff. The order is enforced by the *huissier* visiting the place where the assets are situated and listing the assets to be attached. The defendant may be left in possession of the assets but he is restrained from disposing of them under threat of criminal sanctions. Alternatively, if the assets are under the control of a third person, that person (the *tiers saisi*) is similarly required not to dispose of them.

50.60   If proceedings in respect of the main claim have not already been started, the order will also set a time limit within which they must be commenced. The *saisie* must be confirmed by proceedings in the *tribunal de grande instance* for the district where the *saisie* was originally ordered, either by adding a claim in the main proceedings if they are pending before that court, or by bringing a separate validating claim; and in either case this claim must be brought within a time limit set by the original order.

The plaintiff may be ordered to provide security as a condition of the grant of the order, although this is not normally required. He will be liable to the defendant in damages for any loss which the latter may suffer if it is determined in the validating proceedings that the attachment was unjustified.

The defendant may challenge the *saisie* by a number of methods. He may apply for its discharge, normally by a summary application[75] to the same judge who granted the order. The order made on such an application may be appealed by either party. Alternatively, if the discharge of the attachment is not a matter of urgency, he may raise his objections to the attachment in defending the validating proceedings. If the objection is to the formal validity of the *saisie*, the proceedings may be adjourned until after the outcome of the main proceedings.

3. Provisional charges

In addition to the above provisional measures the courts have power to direct the provisional registration of a charge over the debtor's business (*inscription de nantissement de fonds de commerce*) or his real property (*inscription provisoire d'hypothèque judiciaire*). The

---

[75] The application is made by the *référé* procedure: see para. 50.61 below.

effect of registration is to impose certain limitations on disposal of the affected property, and to give the plaintiff priority over other creditors.

I. CIVIL PROCEDURE—SUMMARY PROCEDURES

1. *Référé* proceedings

The principal form of summary procedure available under French law is the *référé* procedure. A substantial proportion of all civil litigation in French courts is conducted by means of this procedure; and a wide range of orders may be obtained. It is available in all the civil and commercial courts of first instance.   **50.61**

The *référé* proceedings are started by an *assignation* served by a *huissier*, in the same way as normal proceedings. The *assignation* states an early date for hearing, which is usually in a list of *référé* cases. In matters of real urgency, the hearing may be fixed for a time only hours ahead, even outside normal court hours. Representation by an *avocat* is not compulsory, even in the *tribunal de grande instance*. The defendant may file pleadings. The hearing is before the *juge des référés*, who is either the president of the court or his nominee. The order made on the application is called an *ordonnance de référé*. It may be appealed by either party within 15 days, and may only be modified or set aside at first instance by the *référé* judge himself if new circumstances have arisen.

The judge has power in cases of urgency to make any order which is not seriously open to challenge or which is justified by the existence of the dispute. Even in cases of serious dispute, such restraining, protective or provisional measures may be ordered as are necessary either to prevent imminent damage or to stop a clearly unlawful disturbance. The court also has power, which it exercises even in cases which are not urgent, to order an interim payment (*provision*) or the carrying out of an obligation.

The *ordonnance de référé* is only provisional and is not binding as to the main issue in dispute. It is automatically provisionally enforceable and security need not be provided by the plaintiff unless the court specifically so orders. An order for interim payment may frequently be made in respect of a substantial part of the claim, or even in respect of the whole claim, and the practical effect of such an order is often to dispose of the case in its entirety.[76]

2. *Injonction de payer*

There is also an abbreviated procedure available in the *tribunal de commerce* and the *tribunal d'instance* (but not in the *tribunal de grande instance*) for the recovery of liquidated sums. The application is   **50.62**

---

[76] See para. 24.11, n.31 above.

made *ex parte* and the order (called an *injonction de payer*) may be enforced after one month (or three months in the case of defendants domiciled outside France[77]) unless, within that time, the defendant makes an application in *opposition* to the court which made the original order.

J. CIVIL PROCEDURE—APPEALS

1. Introduction

50.63   *Types of appeal.* Procedural law distinguishes between two categories of appeals (*voies de recours*): ordinary appeals and extraordinary appeals. Ordinary appeals are an appeal in the strict sense (*appel*) and an *opposition* against a judgment entered in default or against certain other judgments. Extraordinary appeals are third-party opposition (*tierce opposition*), a petition for review (*recours en révision*) and an appeal to the *Cour de cassation* (*pourvoi en cassation*). In addition, there are various special forms of appeal relating to specific matters, notably a *contredit* against a ruling on a question of jurisdiction.

Time for appealing. The time-limit for appealing generally runs from the time when the losing party has been formally served with the judgment.[78] In certain cases, though, such as a *contredit*[79] or a judgment appointing an expert,[80] time runs from the date of the judgment itself.

2. Ordinary appeals

50.64   *Appel.* An *appel* is the normal means of recourse from a judgment made by any court of first instance, and is brought before the *Cour d'appel* for the region in which the court appealed from is located. An *appel* may not be brought against a judgment for less than F.Fr. 15,500. The time-limit for lodging an *appel* is generally one month[81] in the case of a judgment in a contentious matter and 15

---

[77] The period is two months in the case of a defendant in a *département d'outre mer*.
[78] See para. 50.67 above.
[79] See para. 50.65 above.
[80] Judgments of a procedural nature made at the preparatory stage of the proceedings (*jugements avant dire droit*) and those ordering an expert's investigation (*mesures d'instruction*) may only be appealed separately from a judgment on the substance if special leave is given.
[81] If the *appel* is against a *jugement reputé contradictoire* made in the absence of the defendant, the time limited for appealing may be extended on application to the president of the appellate court within a reasonable period after the defendant acquired knowledge of the judgment, and in any event within a year from the date of its notification. Execution is not stayed during this extended period.

days in the case of a summary order[82] or a judgment in a non-contentious matter. The time-limits for appealing do not apply to a cross-appeal, which may be raised at any time in the appellate proceedings. The appellant is called the *appelant*; the respondent, the *intimé*; and a cross-appellant, the *appelant à titre incident*. The appeal is initiated by the appellant's *avoué* filing a *declaration d'appel* with the court. This is then sent by post to the respondent requiring him to appoint an *avoué*. The procedure is then the same as that in the *tribunal de grande instance*.

Unless the judgment is provisionally enforceable,[83] enforcement of the judgment is stayed while the time for lodging of an appeal is running or until the appeal is disposed of. A judgment which is provisionally enforceable may be stayed on summary application[84] to the principal president of the *Cour d'appel*.

An *appel* involves a consideration *de novo* of matters of both fact and law. *The Cour d'appel* will review the whole case and fresh evidence may be submitted, although no new claims may be advanced. It can vary or set aside the judgment of the court below. The respondent may himself raise an incidental cross-appeal, either against the appellant, or against another respondent, or against a person who was a party to the decision at first instance.

Opposition. An application to set aside a judgment which is not subject to *appel* and which is entered in default (a *jugement par défaut*) is called an *opposition* and is made to the court which gave the judgment. It has already been described above.[85] In addition, the procedure for setting aside an *injonction de payer*[86] and some *saisies-arrêts* [87] are also called *opposition*.

3. Extraordinary appeals

The bringing of an extraordinary appeal does not generally have the effect of staying execution; but a stay of execution may sometimes be obtained in an appropriate case. Application is generally made by the *référé* procedure.

50.65

Tierce-opposition. This is an appeal whereby a judgment may be set aside or varied on the application of a person (the third party) who has an interest in the judgment but who was not a party to it. In an appropriate case it may be brought by the creditors or

---

[82] The time for an appeal against a summary order given in *ex parte* proceedings usually runs from the date of the order.
[83] See para. 50.67 below.
[84] The application is made in *référé* proceedings in the *Cour d'appel*: see para. 50.61 above. The appeal must have been lodged before the application is made.
[85] Para. 50.41.
[86] See para. 50.62 above.
[87] See para. 50.59 below.

assignees of a party if the judgment was obtained in fraud of their rights or on other sufficient grounds. As regards the third party, it reopens the matters of fact and law in the judgment challenged in the application. The application is made to the court which gave the judgment and it may generally be made at any time within 30 years from the date of the judgment; but if the third party was served with notice of the judgment, the time limit for making the application is two months from the date of service of the notice, provided that the notice clearly indicated that time limit and the means by which the judgment could be challenged.

Recours en révision. This is a procedure whereby a party may apply to set aside a judgment which has become *res judicata.*[88] It is available only on the ground that the judgment was obtained by fraud or on similar grounds. The application for a stay must be made within two months from the date when the applicant had knowledge of the grounds for review on which he relies and he must not have been able to raise those grounds before the judgment became *res judicata.*

Pourvoi en cassation. An appeal to the *Cour de cassation* may only be brought on a point of law and generally only against a decision which is not appealable by *appel* or *opposition*. The nature of the appeal has been described above.[89] The *pourvoi en cassation* must normally be brought within two months, although this time limit is subject to many exceptions. It does not generally have the effect of preventing the judgment appealed against from becoming *res judicata*, and thus it does not suspend its enforceability.

4. Other appeals

In respect of certain specialised matters, various special forms of appeal may be available, of which only a *contredit* need be mentioned here. This is an appeal against a ruling on a question of jurisdiction, *lis pendens*, or related actions. It is lodged with the court which made the ruling, within 15 days from its date. The court notifies the other party and the parties submit written argument, which is then forwarded to the *Cour d'appel* for decision.

K. Civil Proceedings—Enforcement

1. Enforcement of French judgments

50.66   A judgment may only be executed when it has become enforceable (*"exécutoire"*) and when certain further conditions are fulfilled. As a general rule, a judgment becomes enforceable when it becomes

---

[88] See para. 50.66 below.
[89] Para. 50.22 above.

res judicata (*"il passe en force de chose jugée"*)[90]; but it may be provisionally enforceable at an earlier stage, or its enforceability may be postponed if the debtor has been granted a period of grace. The *tribunal de grande instance* for the place where the judgment debtor is domiciled, or his assets are located, has exclusive jurisdiction over matters concerned with the execution of judgments.[91] Except in the case of default judgments,[92] a judgment remains enforceable for 30 years.

Res judicata. A judgment becomes *res judicata* when it is no longer open to challenge by an ordinary appeal.[93] As has been noted, judgments for less than F.Fr. 15,500 are not open to ordinary appeal and other judgments cease to be appealable at the expiry of the time limited for appealing, which is normally one month from the date of service of the judgment in the case of final judgments and 15 days from the date of the judgment in the case of summary orders.[94] Each party may obtain a certificate from the clerk of the court to which the appeal lies, to the effect that no appeal has been brought.

Provisional enforceability. A judgment may be provisionally 50.67
enforceable before it becomes *res judicata*, that is to say it may be executed, provided the conditions for execution have been satisfied. Some judgements are provisionally enforceable as a matter of law, and need not state on their face that this is so. The three most important categories of judgment which automatically have provisional enforceability are those made on summary application (*ordonnances de référé*), decisions containing provisional orders made during the course of proceedings (such as awards of interim payment), and protective measures, including those granted *ex parte*. Other judgments are provisionally enforceable if it is so stated in the decision.[95] Provisional enforceability may be requested by the parties or ordered of the court's own motion. The *Cour d'appel* has certain powers to vary the decision of a court of first instance as to the provisional enforceability of a judgment, or to stay its execution.

The provisional enforceability of a judgment may be made con-

---

[90] *Res judicata* and provisional enforceability are described at paras. 25.20 *et seq.* above.

[91] Jurisdiction over attachment of earnings (*saisie-arrêt sur rémuneration*) is an exception.

[92] Para. 50.40 above.

[93] Certain appeals to the *Cour de cassation* may also prevent a judgment from becoming *res judicata* (*e.g.* in the case of divorce).

[94] See para. 50.61 above.

[95] The words used to indicate provisional enforceability are *"assortie de l'exécution provisoire"* or *"exécutoire par provision."*

ditional on the judgment creditor furnishing security and he may be liable to pay compensation to the judgment debtor if the judgment is subsequently found not to have been justified, even if it was regularly obtained. If necessary, the court may hold a summary hearing to determine the amount of the security. A party against whom a provisionally enforceable judgment has been given may prevent the execution of the judgment if, with the court's authorisation, he pays into court sufficient cash or securities (such as a bond) to secure the judgment, interest and costs.

Period of grace. A judgment debtor may be given a period of grace within which to satisfy the judgment, but this does not prevent the judgment creditor from obtaining protective measures against him. The period may be granted by the original decision and reasons must be given for the period having been granted. In contentious matters, the period runs from the date of the judgment, if this was given in the presence of the parties, and from the date of its notification to the judgment debtor if it was not. There are restrictions on the grant of a period of grace to an insolvent debtor. As an alternative to a period of grace being granted, the execution of the judgment may be stayed for a maximum period of a year by an order made on a *référé* application by the party against whom the judgment has been given.

Indorsement as to executory character. A judgment is in executory form if it contains an indorsement (a *formule exécutoire*) in the following terms:

République Française

Au nom du peuple français,

. . .

En conséquence, la République française mande et ordonne à tous huissiers de justice, sur ce requis, de mettre ledit arrêt [jugement] à exécution, aux procureurs généraux et aux procureurs de la République près les tribunaux de grande instance d'y tenir la main, à tous commandants et officiers de la force publique de prêter main forte lorsqu'ils en seront légalement requis.

En foi de quoi le présent arrêt [jugement] a été signé par [président/greffier]

Service. Service of the judgment on a party is normally a precondition to its execution against him. Transmission of the certified copy of the judgment to the parties or their *avocats* does not constitute service of the judgment, and service for these purposes is the formal service of the judgment in the above executory form by the *huissier*, on the instructions of the other party (*signification de jugement à parties*). In cases where legal representation is compulsory, it

1276

is a precondition to such service that the judgment should have first been served on the receiving party's *avocat* (*signification de jugement à avocat*), and this is effected by the court official (the *huissier audiencier*) through whom pleadings are exchanged. In certain cases (*ordonnances de référé*), the court has power to order that the judgment may be executed upon the mere showing of the original copy (*minute*) of the judgment to that party.

Before execution can take place, the *huissier* must serve a *commandement* at least one day before he effects execution, usually by attachment.[96] A *commandement* is not required for provisional attachment. In practice, the *commandement* is served with the judgment if it is provisionally enforceable or, if not, when it has become enforceable by becoming *res judicata* or by the expiry of a period of grace.

Execution. The execution is carried out by the *huissier* attaching assets of the judgment debtor (*saisie exécution*). A range of different forms of attachment is available, including the seizure and sale of personal goods, the charging of land (*saisie immobilière*) and the attachment of third-party debts (*saisie arrêt*) such as a bank account or earnings.[97] There is no procedure whereby a debtor can be examined as to his assets or their whereabouts. A stay of execution may be obtained only on an application in *référé* proceedings to the court of first instance. **50.68**

Other methods of enforcement. Non-money judgments are normally enforced by the imposition of a penalty (*astreinte*), which increases periodically until the obligation in question has been performed. The sum finally payable is then usually determined by the court, and the total accumulated sum is often reduced to a more reasonable level than that provided by simple arithmetical calculation. This procedure is also frequently used in the case of money judgments. The court may also order an act required by a non-money judgment to be performed by someone other than the person against whom the judgment was given, and making the latter liable for the costs of such performance. **50.69**

2. Authentic instruments and court settlements

Authentic instruments. French law permits the enforcement of certain authentic instruments (*actes authentiques*) in the same manner as judgments. The principal category of such instruments is **50.70**

---

[96] The *commandement* gives a final warning to the judgment debtor that execution is about to take place and gives him a final opportunity to satisfy the judgment.
[97] Exceptionally, attachment of earnings is within the exclusive jurisdiction of the *tribunal d'instance*. A judgment creditor obtains an order from the court which is then passed to the employer for implementation. The judgment debtor may apply to the court by a procedure of *opposition* to amend or set aside the order.

notarial acts,[98] which may relate to an obligation to pay money or to any other obligation envisaged by civil law. Some matters must be made the subject of notarial acts, notably contracts for the sale of land and marriage contracts. Other acts (especially wills) are frequently notarised in practice.

The instrument is enforceable if it is indorsed with a *formule exécutoire*.[99] Such an indorsement may be made by the notary who authenticated the instrument, but he will only do so if the person against whom enforcement is to be carried out has signified his consent to the instrument being enforceable. A copy of the instrument will be an authentic copy (a *grosse*) if it bears the notary's seal. It must then be served by the *huissier* in the same way as a judgment, normally by showing the debtor the *grosse* and handing him a copy, before execution can proceed.

Court settlements. If the parties to litigation settle their dispute, they may at any time minute the agreement with the court. The minute is signed by the judge and the parties and the minuted settlement is enforceable in the same way as other enforceable orders. The court will issue an authentic copy (a *grosse*) of the minute, which must bear a *formule exécutoire* if it is to be executed.

The various types of consent judgments known to French law (*jugement convenu, jugement d'expédient, jugement de donné acte*) are judgments and therefore do not constitute court settlements for the purposes of the 1968 Convention.

3. Enforcement of foreign judgments

50.71 Foreign judgments are enforceable in France by all means available in respect of French judgments, once their execution has been authorised by the indorsement of a *formule exécutoire*.[1] The means of obtaining this indorsement differs depending upon whether or not the 1968 Convention applies.

Enforcement under the 1968 Convention. The procedure for enforcement under the 1968 Convention of a judgment given in another Contracting State is as follows: The judgment creditor makes an application *sur requête* for an order that a *formule exécutoire* be attached to the judgment. The application is made to the president of the *tribunal de grande instance* for the district in which the defendant is domiciled or, if he is not domiciled in France, the dis-

---

[98] In some circumstances, certain documents which are private instruments, but not strictly notarial instruments, may be treated as notarial instruments if the signature of the party who signed the instrument is recognised before the notary. For the purposes of enforcement, these instruments may be regarded as notarial instruments.

[99] See para. 50.67 above.

[1] Also known as an *exequatur*.

trict in which the assets to be seized are located. The original judgment or an authenticated copy of it must be produced together with proof that the judgment is enforceable in its state of origin and that it has been served on the judgment debtor. If the judgment was given in default of appearance it must be shown that the proceedings were served on the defendant in sufficient time for him to arrange his defence. The judgment and other documents only need to be translated if the judge so requires. If enforcement is authorised, the party against whom it is authorised can only challenge the order by appealing to the *Cour d'appel* within one month, if he is domiciled in France, or two months if he is domiciled elsewhere. If it is refused, the period stipulated by French law for the bringing of an appeal is 15 days.

Judgments outside the 1968 Convention. In the absence of an applicable bilateral or multilateral convention on the recognition and enforcement of judgments, a foreign judgment can only be enforced if an order for its enforcement[2] is obtained from the *tribunal de grande instance*. The appropriate court is that of the judgment debtor's domicile, or, if he has no domicile, the court for the district in which the assets are located. The procedure is commenced by *assignation*. The other documents required are the original judgment, or an authenticated copy, evidence of service, and evidence that the judgment is enforceable in the country of origin. It must also be shown that the foreign court had jurisdiction in respect of the subject matter, that there were no irregularities in the foreign proceedings, that the law applied was that which would have applied under French choice of law rules, that the judgment accords with international public policy (in particular that the defendant was properly notified of the proceedings and was able effectively to present his defence), and that it was obtained and given in the absence of fraud. Provided the above conditions are satisfied there is no examination of the factual or legal merits of the foreign judgment. When the enforcement order is granted, the foreign judgment is enforceable by whatever method is appropriate as if it were a French judgment. This applies both to money judgments and to non-money judgments. **50.72**

L. Legal Persons

The most common French legal persons, with their usual abbreviations, are as follows: **50.73**

  (a) *Société anonyme* (S.A.)—a commercial company with liability limited by shares;

---

[2] *Formule exécutoire* or *executatur.*

(*b*) *Société à responsibilité limitée* (S.A.R.L.)—also a commercial company with liability limited by shares, but in which the shares are not readily marketable;

(*c*) *Société en nom collectif* (S.N.C.)—a general partnership in which the liability of the partners is unlimited;

(*d*) *Société en commandite par actions* (S.P.A.)—a special partnership in which the liability of some of the partners is limited by shares;

(*e*) *Société civile*—a company whose activities are traditionally non-commercial and in which the liability of the members is not limited: the most common forms are the *Société civile immobilière* (S.C.I.—a property company) and the *Société civile professionelle* (S.C.P.—used for the practice of professions);

(*f*) *Association à but non-lucratif* (also known as an *Association de la loi de 1901*)—a non-profit-making association with limited liability.

M. LEGAL AID

50.74   Legal aid (*aide judiciaire*) is available for proceedings in the French courts to any person of any nationality who is resident in France and who has insufficient resources to enforce or protect his rights. It is also available to non-residents when so provided by international convention. It is not available to commercial companies. Legal aid bureaux are attached to most civil and administrative courts. The process of obtaining legal aid normally takes several months, but there is an expedited procedure that can be adopted in urgent cases.

In an ordinary case application is made initially to the local authority for a certificate of means. To receive full legal aid the applicant must have an income of less than F.Fr. 3,465 a month, and for partial legal aid, an income of less than F.Fr. 5,250 a month.[3] These levels are adjusted according to the number of dependants. The application is then passed to the appropriate legal aid bureau for consideration by a panel comprising a judge, an *avocat*, and an honorary *avoué*. The applicant has to show that he has prospects of success in the matter, but in practice few applications are refused. When granted, the application is passed to the *bâtonnier* of the local *Ordre d'avocats* who appoints an *avocat* to act for the legally aided party. This may well be an *avocat* already selected by the party.

Legal aid covers all aspects of the litigation in question including court fees and taxes, experts' fees, the fees of the *huissier* and the costs of enforcement of any judgment. The *avocat* acting for a

---

[3] Levels current at July 1988.

legally aided party receives a fixed fee from the state, the amount of which depends on the nature of the case. This may be considerably less than the fee chargeable to a privately paying client. If the legally aided party recovers an amount which would have disentitled him to legal aid, the *avocat* may, with the consent of the *bâtonnier* charge the client a supplementary fee. If the legally aided party loses the case he is not, by reason of impecuniosity, protected from an order to pay the winning party's costs.

The provision of legal advice, unconnected with court proceedings, does not come within any formal legal aid scheme in France. Free or subsidised legal advice is only available from certain private sources such as information bureaux run by local bars, social welfare offices and trade unions.

CHAPTER 51

FEDERAL REPUBLIC OF GERMANY

Written in collaboration with Dr. Thomas Försterling, Rechtsanwalt, Düsseldorf.

Federal Republic of Germany

A. The Legal System

1. Introduction

History and territory. Until the end of the eighteenth century Ger-   **51.01**
many consisted of a number of separate states, joined as much by a
common language and culture as by political unity. These states
were formed into a loose confederation in 1815 under the domina-
tion of Austria. During the early decades of the nineteenth century,
the political power of Prussia grew until, between 1866 and 1871,
Germany was unified by Bismarck into a single *Reich* which
excluded Austria. After the First World War, Germany was governed successively by the Weimar Republic and by Hitler's Third
Reich. At the conclusion of the Second World War, Germany was
divided up, with eastern territories being incorporated into the
Soviet Union and Poland and with two separate German states
being formed, the German Democratic Republic (East Germany)
and the Federal Republic of Germany (West Germany).

The Federal Republic of Germany is a federation of states
(*Länder*)[1] governed under the federal constitution (*Grundgesetz*) of
1949. The constitution provides for a federal president, parliament
and government and it regulates the respective legislative functions
of the federation and of the *Länder.* Almost all matters of civil and
commercial law are regulated by federal laws and are therefore common to the entire Federal Republic. The laws of the *Länder* are
generally restricted to administrative matters and they rarely have
any application to civil or commercial disputes.

Origins of the legal system. Until Roman law was received into the
German legal system from about the end of the fifteenth century,
German law was of a local and customary nature. The decentralised
nature of political power in Germany, and the consequent lack of a
mature legal system by that time, meant that the reception of
Roman law was relatively far-reaching. Nonetheless, marked
regional differences persisted and, while there had been some codification of the law during the nineteenth century (notably in Austria, Prussia and Bavaria), German private law did not become
unified until the German Civil Code (*Bürgerliches Gesetzbuch*) came
into effect on January 1, 1900.

---

[1] Baden-Württemberg, Bavaria, Bremen, Hamburg, Hessen, Lower Saxony,
Northrhine-Westphalia, Rhineland-Palatinate, Saarland and Schleswig-
Holstein. West Berlin has special status. For the purposes of civil proceedings it
is effectively another *Land.*

2. Administration of justice

51.02   *Public and private law.* As in most other European legal systems there is a distinction between public law and private law. Public law governs the relations of public bodies between each other and with private individuals. Matters of public law are, with the exception of criminal law, generally litigated in the administrative courts. The distinction between public and private law is of less practical importance than in France, because in Germany those transactions between a public law body and a private individual which are of a private character are governed by private law and are thus justiciable in the ordinary courts. However, within the realm of private law the classification of a case as subject either to civil law or to commercial law normally determines by which chamber of the ordinary courts it will be tried.

Systems of courts. There are a number of separate court systems for different types of litigation. The ordinary courts which deal with civil, commercial and criminal matters, are organised into two levels of courts of first instance, with a further level of ordinary appeal court.[2] In addition, there are separate administrative courts, fiscal courts, social insurance courts, and labour courts, all with their separate hierarchies of appeal courts. Each court system has a supreme court at the federal level and there is a federal constitutional court, but with those exceptions, the administration of all courts is the responsibility of the various *Länder*. The same procedure is applied throughout Germany in courts of the same type and level.

B. LEGAL PRACTITIONERS

1. The *Rechtsanwalt*

51.03   The *Rechtsanwalt* acts for his client both as a general legal adviser and as his representative in the conduct of proceedings in court. He has a monopoly in the giving of professional advice on legal matters. It is illegal for any person not so qualified to give legal advice.

Legal education and qualification. The intending lawyer must first read law at a university and pass the first *Staatsexamen*. This generally takes five years. Then he applies to the Ministry of Justice of a *Land* to become a *Referendar* (trainee). The training course lasts two and a half years and during this period he is a civil servant working in different types of courts, in the public prosecutor's department, and in the *Rechtsanwalt*'s office. Then there is a second

---

[2] The ordinary civil courts are discussed in greater detail at paras. 51.18 *et seq.* below.

Staatsexamen. On successful completion of his studies and practical training he is qualified to become a *Rechtsanwalt* or to follow a career as a judge or in the civil service.

Rights of representation and audience. Every *Rechtsanwalt* must be **51.04** admitted to a particular *Landgericht* or *Oberlandesgericht* and he must reside within its district. In civil and commercial matters his rights of audience are, subject to exceptions, limited to that court, but he may appear in any *Amtsgericht*.[3] Rights of audience before the Federal Supreme Court (*Bundesgerichtshof*) are presently limited to some 23 *Rechtsanwälte am Bundesgerichtshof* who are admitted to that court alone. The *Bundesgerichtshof* is in Karlsruhe.

Organisation of practice. There are some 50,000 *Rechtsanwälte* in Germany and their numbers are steadily increasing. Partnerships are permitted and firms comprising up to about ten lawyers are to be found in all the major cities. At the same time there are very many sole practitioners, particularly in smaller towns and rural areas. The letterheading may indicate by the use of the letters LG or OLG against a *Rechtsanwalt's* name the level of court to which he is admitted. It is not permitted, save in respect of fiscal, administrative, labour or social matters, for a *Rechtsanwalt* to indicate publicly any specialisation of practice, nor, as a general rule, can this information be obtained from any professional body. However some *Anwaltsvereine* (lawyers' associations) do maintain lists of practitioners in certain specialist fields of law. These may be obtained on request.

It is permissible for a *Rechtsanwalt* to enter into partnership with a *Steuerberater* (tax consultant) and a *Wirtschaftsprüfer* (certified accountant). A *Rechtsanwalt* also may himself obtain the above qualifications and practise in those additional capacities.

There is no legal requirement for a *Rechtsanwalt* to have a written power of attorney from his client although he will frequently obtain one in case his authority to act is challenged by his opponent. If authority to act cannot be established immediately, the proceedings will be suspended until a power of attorney is produced.

Fees. The fees charged by a *Rechtsanwalt*, both in and out of **51.05** court are rigidly controlled by law. Fees for work connected with litigation are discussed below.[4] In advisory and other non-contentious work he is entitled, in the absence of express agreement in writing, to charge his client an amount calculated according to a

---

[3] A *Rechtsanwalt* in one place may retain a *Rechtsanwalt* in another place to act as a correspondent lawyer (*Korrespondenzanwalt*) on behalf of the client in the conduct of court proceedings there. As to the fees payable in such circumstances, see further para. 51.57 below.
[4] See para. 51.57 below.

sliding scale based on the value of the case. This scale is laid down and published for all categories of work. In the absence of such agreement the *Rechtsanwalt* is rarely permitted to undercut the scale. Application of the scale may sometimes lead to a disproportionately high fee. It is therefore important to make a suitable agreement with the *Rechtsanwalt* as to the fee, which may be a lump sum, or calculated on an hourly basis. Contingent fees are forbidden. The fees of *Rechtsanwälte* are subject to Value Added Tax (*Mehrwertsteuer*) except when they are acting for clients in other EEC countries, who are themselves subject to VAT, in respect of activities abroad. This means in practice that foreign private individuals, but not foreign commercial companies in other EEC countries, must pay VAT on legal fees. Any dispute between a *Rechtsanwalt* and his client regarding fees may be referred to the local *Rechtsanwaltskammer*.

Professional organisation and conduct. The profession of *Rechtsanwalt* is regulated by federal law. The *Rechtsanwälte* admitted to practice in a given territory (usually that covered by an *Oberlandesgericht*) constitute a local bar or chamber of advocates (*Rechtsanwaltskammer*). The *Rechtsanwaltskammer* is administered by an elected committee and is responsible for overseeing professional conduct and resolving disputes between different *Rechtsanwälte* and between them and their clients. Breaches of professional conduct are investigated by disciplinary boards comprising both judges and *Rechtsanwälte*.

The *Rechtsanwalt* has a contractual relationship with his client, and he is bound to exercise proper care in the conduct of his client's affairs. He is liable to compensate the client in damages for loss suffered for breach of that duty. *Rechtsanwälte* are obliged to take out professional liability insurance for a minimum of DM. 50,000.

[The next paragraph is number 51.09]

2. The *Notar*

51.09   Under German law there are many classes of contract which are legally binding only if they have been signed and approved by the parties before a notary (*Notar*). The *Notar* either attests the signatures and approval of the parties or he certifies the identity of the signatory. He retains a copy of the document. *Notare* are concerned in particular with all transactions involving real property and all contracts relating to the setting up and financing of commercial companies. Their professional fees are fixed according to statutory scales.

There are very many *Notare* in the Federal Republic. The rules applicable to their profession are the same in all states, although there is some variation in the method of their appointment and as to whether they may practise concurrently as *Rechtsanwälte*. There are two main types of *Notar*, the *Nur-Notar* and the *Anwaltsnotar*. The former constitute a small separate profession and they are not permitted to practise concurrently as *Rechtsanwälte*. They are found in Hamburg, Bavaria, Rhineland-Palatinate, parts of Northrhine-Westphalia[5] and in Saarland. In Baden-Württemberg the notaries are state officials. Secondly there are the *Anwaltsnotare*. These are *Rechtsanwälte* who, after some years' practice as such are appointed to act in addition as notaries. They are found in Berlin, Bremen, Hesse, parts of Northrhine-Westphalia,[5] Lower Saxony and Schleswig-Holstein.

3. The *Rechtsbeistand* [6]

In some, mainly rural, areas the president of the *landgericht* authorises certain persons who are not qualified as *Rechtsanwälte* to be admitted to appear before an *Amtsgericht* and to represent clients there. They are known as *Rechtsbeistände*. | **51.10**

4. Foreign lawyers

The monopoly of the *Rechtsanwalt* in the giving of legal advice in Germany prevents foreign lawyers from acting as legal consultants there. This rule is, however, subject to the exception provided by the EEC Directive on Legal Services.[7] Under this, lawyers from other Member States may give legal advice on matters relating to their legal systems.[7a] | **51.11**

5. Lawyers in business and public employment

Many lawyers work as full-time employees in the legal departments of commercial companies. They are known as *Syndikusanwälte*. They must register in the local court of appropriate level but they are not permitted to represent their own employers in court. They may undertake work and appear in court for clients other than their employers. Lawyers employed in government and | **51.12**

---

[5] *Nur-Notare* are found in those parts of the Rhineland in which, until 1900, the French civil code applied; *Anwaltsnotare* are found in the rest of the Rhineland and in Westphalia, where the Prussian civil code applied before 1900.

[6] Also known as the *Prozessagent*.

[7] See para. A2.47 below.

[7a] See the judgment of the European Court in *Commission of the European Communities* v. *Federal Republic of Germany*, case 427/85, decision of February 25, 1988, not yet reported. The Court ruled that certain restrictions imposed on foreign lawyers were contrary to EEC law.

other public services, known as *Staatsanwälte* are generally not permitted to act as *Rechtsanwälte*.

[The next paragraph is number 51.14]

C. SOURCES OF LAW

1. Introduction

51.14   Many areas of German law have been codified but there remain numerous statutes which either supplement codified law or which deal with special fields of law. As in other codified systems, legal rules tend to be expressed in general terms and the judge has some latitude in interpreting the intention of the legislature.

2. Legislation

51.15   The various types of legislation, arranged in descending order of precedence are as follows:

(*a*) Fundamental Rights (*Grundrechte*): These fundamental rights are expressed in very general terms in the first part of the federal constitution, known as the *Grundgesetz* (basic law). They take precedence over all other legislation or sources of law.

(*b*) Constitutional law (*Verfassungsrecht*): This is derived from the other provisions of the *Grundgesetz* and takes precedence over all other federal law. It includes a provision that the general principles of public international law take precedence over all national law (except constitutional law) and do not need to be expressly incorporated into German law. International conventions generally require incorporation by enactment into German law.

(*c*) Federal law (*Bundesrecht*): The constitution specifies those matters which are to be the subject of federal law. All other matters are within the competence of state law. The subject-matters of federal law include civil and commercial law, company law, competition law, and most criminal law.

(*d*) Federal ministerial decrees (*Verordnungen*): Certain matters are governed not by statutes passed by Parliament but by subordinate legislation, drafted and brought into effect by the appropriate federal ministries.

(*e*) State constitutional law (*Landesverfassungsrecht*): Each state has its own constitution and *Land* constitutional law takes precedence over other *Land* law.

(*f*) State law (*Landesrecht*): This is the law enacted by the parliaments of the individual states.

(*g*) State ministerial decrees, (*Verordnungen*) These are the provisions of subordinate legislation at the state level.

3. Decided cases and legal writings

Strictly speaking, previous court decisions are not a source of law   **51.16**
nor do they normally establish any binding precedent, although they are of persuasive authority and are frequently referred to. The decisions of the *Bundesgerichtshof* are regarded as particularly authoritative. Legal writings may also be relied on in legal argument, and they may have considerable persuasive authority.[8] A judge may also, as he considers appropriate, refer to preparatory works, previous drafts and parliametary debates, in addition to decided cases and legal commentaries.

4. Publications

Federal laws are published officially in the *Bundesgesetzblatt*   **51.17**
(BGBl), but practitioners normally use any one of a number of private editions with updated texts and commentaries. The decisions of the *Bundesgerichtshof* in civil matters are published officially in the *Entscheidungen des Bundesgerichtshofes in Zivilsachen* (BGHZ).

Decisions of civil courts are reported and commented on in many legal journals, of which the following are the most important:

(*a*) *Neue Juristische Wochenschrift* (NJW), cases mainly from the *Bundesgerichtshof* and the *Oberlandesgerichte*;
(*b*) *Der Betriebsberater* (BB), company, tax, and labour law;
(*c*) *Monatsschrift für Deutsches Recht* (MDR), civil and procedural law;
(*d*) *Der Betrieb* (DB), company and industrial law;
(*e*) *Gewerblicher Rechtsschutz und Urheberrecht* (GRUR), competition law;
(*f*) *Wertpapiermitteilungen* (WPM), banking law;
(*g*) *Recht der Internationalen Wirtschaft* (RIW/AWD), international commercial law.

D. Organisation of the Civil Courts

1. Introduction

Ordinary civil and commercial cases are heard at first instance   **51.18**
either by the *Amtsgericht* or by the *Landgericht*. There are some 613 *Amtsgerichte* and 98 *Landgerichte* in Germany and, as already noted, they are administered by the various *Länder*. The *Amtsgericht* has

---

[8] If legal writers are generally agreed on a point, their opinion is called *herrschende Meinung* (predominant opinion) and is accorded special respect.

jurisdiction over smaller cases (generally, those worth not more than DM 5,000) and certain categories of subject-matter. All other cases are assigned to the *Landgericht*.

Appeals from the *Amtsgericht* in civil and commercial cases are heard by a special division of the *Landgericht*. Appeals from first instance decisions of the *Landgericht*, (and appeals in family cases from the *Amtsgericht*), are heard by the *Oberlandesgericht*. In addition to the ordinary civil courts, there are also separate court systems for labour disputes, and social security, fiscal and administrative matters.

2. The *Amtsgericht* [9]

51.19   The lower tier of ordinary court is the *Amtsgericht*, or local court. Its competence in civil matters is, in general, limited to cases in which the amount in dispute does not exceed DM 5.000, although this figure may be exceeded by agreement. It also has competence regardless of value over certain categories of case, notably matrimonial, maintenance and custody cases and disputes between landlord and tenant. When it is sitting as a civil court, the decisions of the *Amtsgericht* are made by a single professional judge. In addition to its function as a civil court, the *Amtsgericht* also exercises criminal jurisdiction and it has various non-contentious functions, such as the maintenance of the local commercial and land registers.

3. The *Landgericht* [10]

51.20   The higher tier of ordinary civil court is the *Landgericht*, or regional court. It has competence over civil cases which do not fall within the jurisdiction of the *Amtsgericht*. Within many *Landgerichte* there are separate civil and commercial divisions and, although the procedure is the same in both divisions, cases in the commercial division tend to be dealt with rather more expeditiously than in the civil division.

In the civil division (*Zivilkammer*) there are three professional judges[11] and their jurisdiction covers all matters which are not assigned to the commercial divisions. In the commercial division (*Kammer für Handelssachen*) there is one professional judge who is assisted by two "merchant" judges (*Handelsrichter*). These are appointed from the business community on the recommendation of the local chamber of commerce. They serve for a period of three years and they may be reappointed. A case is assigned to the com-

---

[9] Sometimes abbreviated to "AG" (not to be confused with *Aktiengesellschaft*, which is also abbreviated "AG": see para. 51.73 below).
[10] Frequently abbreviated to "LG."
[11] Straightforward cases in the Landgericht are frequently heard by a single judge.

mercial division if it is subject to commercial law and one of the parties requests that it be so assigned.

Commercial law. As a general rule commercial law applies to disputes in which *both* parties are merchants (*Kaufleute*) and the transaction in question can be classed as commercial. For these purposes all limited companies, whether German or foreign, are treated as *Kaufleute*. Private individuals are only treated as *Kaufleute* if they are engaged in some commercial activity and are registered in the local commercial register. A foreign individual will also be treated as a *Kaufmann* if the transaction in question relates to some commercial activity. In the case of a sale, for example, the foreign buyer must have bought the goods for resale and not for his own private purposes. If only *one* of the parties is a *Kaufmann* the case is classified as civil and not commercial.

4. The *Oberlandesgericht* [12]

There are 19 *Oberlandesgerichte*, higher regional courts, in Germany. They exercise appellate jurisdiction over the first-instance decisions of the *Landgericht* and, in family law cases, of the *Amtsgericht*. Appeals are on points of fact and law and are heard by three professional judges.

51.21

5. The *Bundesgerichtshof* [13]

The only appeal from the *Oberlandesgericht* is on a point of federal law to the *Bundesgerichtshof*, the Federal Supreme Court, which sits in Karlsruhe. Appeals are heard by five judges.

51.22

6. The *Bundesverfassungsgericht*

If a court considers that there are valid objections to the constitutionality of a law which applies in a case before it, and if the outcome of the case turns upon that issue, the court must stay the proceedings and refer the issue to the *Bundesverfassungsgericht*, the Federal Constitutional Court. This procedure, which applies to laws enacted since 1949, is called *Vorlageverfahren*. Earlier laws can be declared unconstitutional by any court. If a person considers that his constitutional rights have been infringed by an act of official power, including a court decision, he may complaint to the *Bundesverfassungsgericht* by means of a procedure called *Verfassungsbeschwerde* but only if he has *locus standi* and if he has exhausted all other remedies. Except in the field of family law, the

---

[12] Frequently abbreviated "OLG." In West Berlin the *Oberlandgericht* is known as the *Kammergericht*.

[13] Frequently abbreviated to "BGH."

Bundesverfassungsgericht has rarely been required to rule on questions of civil or commercial law.

7. The judiciary

51.23   The judges of the *Amtsgericht, Landgericht,* and *Oberlandesgericht* are appointed by the *Land.* In the course of his professional career a judge may sit first as the junior judge of three in a *Landgericht,* and then successively as the single judge in an *Amtsgericht,* the presiding judge of a *Landgericht,* and finally as a member of an *Oberlandesgericht.* Federal judges are elected by the federal parliament and appointed to office by the government. At the start of the judicial career there is a probationary period of about three years, but once permanently appointed, a judge cannot be removed from office except on certain statutory grounds.

E. THE JURISDICTION OF THE CIVIL COURTS

1. Introduction

51.24   The international jurisdiction of the German courts is determined, in cases to which the 1968 Convention applies, by the rules contained in the Convention. As has been seen above, under internal rules of German law, both the subject-matter and the value of the claim may determine the type and level of court. Except where the Convention itself regulates local jurisdiction,[14] the rules which determine the part of the Federal Republic in which the proceedings either must or may be brought are the provisions of German law summarised below. The general rule is that proceedings must be brought in the appropriate court for the locality in which the defendant is domiciled or has its seat.

2. Domicile and seat

51.25   *Natural persons.* An individual of full age and capacity is domiciled in the place where he is actually established and intends to reside. It is possible for a person to have more than one domicile. A person may lose his domicile by showing an intention no longer to be domiciled there; but leaving a place without intending to give up domicile does not change the domicile, although it is possible to have no domicile. The domicile of children is dependent on that of their parents or other legal guardian, and that of mental patients on the domicile of their guardian. In practice, a person is normally domiciled where he is resident. Any person, of any nationality, is obliged to register his name and address at the local inhabitants'

---

[14] See para. 15.03 nn. 10–11 above.

registration office. When he moves his residence he must re-register and the office at which he was formerly registered is informed of this fact. The registration of a person's residence is persuasive, but not conclusive, evidence of his domicile; but the system of registration normally provides a means of tracing the whereabouts of a person provided some past address is known.

Legal persons. The statutory seat of a company is the place where, **51.26** according to its constituion, the company has its registered office. The company is registered in the commercial register kept by the local *Amtsgericht* for the district where that registered office is located. The register contains a statement of the company's principal business address, which is where its principal administration is located but which need not be the registered office and may even be in a different district. It is this principal address which is regarded as the company's domicile, or actual seat, for the purposes of civil procedure.[15]

Private international law. There is no rule of German private international law relating specifically to a company's seat, but both the concept of the statutory seat and that of the actual seat are employed for choice of law purposes. The following is a summary of the case law, theory and predominant opinion as to the German private international law rules on the location of a corporation's seat.

First, to determine whether a company has its seat in Germany and, if so, where that seat is located, the court will proceed as follows:

1. If the company is registered in Germany *and* has its principal administration there, the court will apply the rules of German internal law referred to above and treat the place of the principal administration as the seat;
2. If the company is *not* registered in Germany, but has its *de facto* principal administration there, the court will regard the place where the principal administration is located as the company's actual seat;
3. If the company *is* registered in Germany, but does *not* have its principal administration there, the court will treat the company's registered office as its seat: the company cannot rely upon the fact that its administration is abroad to deprive the German court of jurisdiction.

Secondly, to determine whether a company has its seat in another

---

[15] If the company's principal administration is *in fact* in a place other than the principal business address entered in the commercial register, the court is still required to treat the registered business address as the company's domicile.

Contracting State, or in a non-Contracting State, the court will treat the location of the company's principal administration as its seat.

Thirdly, in either case, if the company has more than one place where its principal administration is located, the court will choose the most important administrative place.

3. Jurisdiction—general rules

51.27   Normally all cases are brought before a court of appropriate level for the locality in which the defendant has his domicile. If the defendant has no domicile, the court in the place of his present abode has jurisdiction. If his whereabouts are unknown it will be the court in the place of his last known habitual residence. A corporation may be sued in the courts of the place in which it has its seat according to German law. If a corporation has a branch office (*Niederlassung*) in the district of a particular court, it may be served at that branch office and sued in that court in respect of disputes arising out of the operation of the branch.

4. Jurisdiction—special rules

51.28   There are other rules of jurisdiction which, depending on the subject-matter of the dispute, may provide an additional forum or an exclusive compulsory forum. When several courts may have jurisdiction, it is for the plaintiff to choose in which one to sue. In cases of delict the court for the place where the wrong has been committed may have jurisdiction. In cases of contract the court for the place where the obligation in question was, or was to have been, performed has jurisdiction.

German law provides that when the place of performance has not been determined either by the parties themselves or by the nature of the contract, the obligation is to be performed at the place where the party who is to perform it has his residence or place of business at the date upon which the obligation came into being. However, in the case of an obligation to pay money, the place of performance, in the absence of any provision or agreement to the contrary, is at the residence of the creditor.[16]

Cases involving immovable property must be brought in the court for the locality in which the property is situated. It will be seen below that applications for protective measures may be made to the courts of the place where the asset in question is located.[17] Such applications may be made to the appropriate *Amtsgericht* not-

---

[16] The place of performance of an obligation to pay the price in an international sale of goods may often be governed, in the absence of agreement, by Art. 59 of the Uniform Law of the International Sale of Goods: see para. 17.14 n. 47 above.

[17] Para. 51.59 below.

withstanding that the value of the asset may exceed the normal limit of that court's jurisdiction.

5. Choice of court and entry of an appearance

When both parties are *Kaufleute*[18] they may agree which court is to have jurisdiction in the event of any dispute between them, except in cases involving real property. In commercial sales the conditions of contract (*allgemeine Geschäftsbedingungen*) will frequently attribute jurisdiction to a particular court. They may also specify the place of performance. As a matter of German law it is not necessary that the purchaser should have formally accepted these conditions. If he has notice of them he may be taken to have accepted them.[19] In consumer cases the court specified in general conditions may not be a court other than that of the consumer's domicile. Except where the court's jurisdiction is based on a compulsory rule, as in the case of immovable property, if a defendant does not challenge the territorial jurisdiction of the court in which he is sued and which is otherwise competent over the subject-matter of the case, he will be taken to have assented to it. However, the court must always examine the competence of its own motion. In cases before the *Amtsgericht*, if the defendant need not accept the jurisdiction, the judge is under a duty to point this out to him.

51.29

6. Exorbitant grounds of jurisdiction

Paragraph 23 of the Code of Civil Procedure gives jurisdiction over a defendant not domiciled in Germany to the courts of any place in which that defendant has any article or asset, or where the object of the claim is located. It cannot now be relied upon against a defendant domiciled in a Contracting State.[20]

51.30

7. Civil claims in criminal proceedings

Although criminal courts have the power to award civil damages to compensate the victims of crime, including road traffic infringements, this is rarely done.

51.31

F. Limitation Periods

The law of limitation and prescription is exceptionally complex and the following should be taken as only the most general guide.

Limitation periods are governed not by procedural law but by

51.32

---

[18] See para. 51.20 above.

[19] In a case to which the 1968 Convention applies a choice of jurisdiction clause must satisfy the requirements of Art. 17 of the Convention. See paras. 21.01 *et seq.* above.

[20] Art. 3 of the 1968 Convention; para. 16.09 above.

substantive civil or commercial law. The main limitation periods are set out in the Civil Code. It should be noted that the date or event from which time may run varies as between different classes of case and the period itself may be subject to suspension or renewal.

In most circumstances the date of expiry of a period of limitation may be extended on the first working day after a weekend or public holiday. Only the filing of legal proceedings or an agreement between the parties can interrupt the limitation period. It is the filing of the proceedings in court rather than service upon the defendant which must be accomplished within the limitation period. In cases in which fraud is alleged the time-limits may usually be overridden.

51.33   The general period of limitation is 30 years from the date when the cause of action arose. This applies to most types of action in contract or tort, but it is subject to numerous and important exceptions, both as to the period and as to when time starts to run. Some of the more usual limitation periods are summarised below.

In certain cases, time starts running on December 31 of the year in which the claim arose. Such cases include most claims for payment in respect of commercial sales or payments by instalment, which have a limitation period of four years. They also include claims for payment in respect of non-commercial sales or hire, claims for wages (including lawyers' fees), claims by forwarders and other claims, each of which have a limitation period of two years.

Claims in respect of faults in goods sold must be made within six months of delivery or the discovery of a hidden defect. In a dispute between *Kaufleute* concerning defective goods the defect must be protested without undue delay.

A limitation period of three years applies to claims for damages for personal injuries, with time running from the moment when the plaintiff knows the identity of the wrongdoer.

G. CIVIL PROCEDURE—PROCEEDINGS UP TO JUDGMENT

1. General description

51.34   The procedure of all courts, including the *Bundesgerichtshof*, is regulated by the Code of Civil Procedure (*Zivilprozessordnung*).[21] In common with most other continental systems of law there is, in Germany, no single "trial" of the case in the sense understood by common lawyers. Despite an increased tendency to concentrate the taking of oral evidence into a smaller number of hearings, German procedure still normally involves a succession of relatively short

---

[21] Usually abbreviated as "ZPO."

1296

appearances at which the issues and the evidence are dealt with piecemeal.

Although civil litigation in Germany is adversarial in theory, it is characterised in practice by the dominant role of the judge. It is the judge who controls the progress of the action through its successive preparatory appearances and he is under a positive duty to ascertain the truth to his own satisfaction. If the evidence given in the documents admitted is not sufficient, the judge will direct the attendance of witnesses to give oral evidence. It is he who decides what parts of the evidence tendered by the parties will be given orally in support of the respective cases. If witnesses are called he questions them first before the respective *Rechtsanwälte* are able to put questions. After the last of the hearings at which evidence is given there will be a final hearing at which there will be short argument by the *Rechtsanwälte*, followed, in some instances, by a short oral judgment.

Procedure in the *Oberlandesgericht* is broadly similar to that in the courts of first instance, and appeals may involve a full rehearing.[22]

2. Parties and legal representation

Parties

The main parties to an action are known respectively as the **51.35** *Kläger* (plaintiff) and the *Beklagter* (defendant). All natural and legal persons have capacity to sue and be sued. Special rules provide for minors (under 18), for the mentally ill, and for insolvent companies. Foreign persons and foreign corporations can sue and be sued irrespective of domicile. Further parties may, with leave, be joined in an action as plaintiffs or defendants at any stage of the proceedings.

Third-party proceedings. If a defendant has a claim against a third person which is connected with the plaintiff's claim against him, he may, at any time before judgment, cause a notice to be served on that person informing him of the main proceedings. That person may then intervene in the main proceedings to protect his position; if he does not do so, judgment will not be given against him but he will be precluded in any subsequent proceedings brought against him by the defendant from asserting that the judgment in the main proceedings was incorrectly decided.[23]

---

[22] See para. 51.64 below.

[23] This procedure, called *Streitverkündung*, is regulated by paras. 68, 72, 73 and 74 of the Code of Civil Procedure, which are referred to in Art. V of the 1968 Protocol, para. 35.20 above.

Counterclaims. A defendant may bring a counterclaim (*Widerklage*) against the plaintiff and any party may raise any issue or claim that can conveniently be tried at the same time as the plaintiff's claim. The counterclaim must be related in some way to the subject-matter of the claim, but it is not necessary for the court to have, independently of the claim, jurisdiction over the subject-matter of the counterclaim.[24]

Legal representation

51.36 Parties to proceedings in the *Landgericht* and the *Oberlandesgericht* may only bring or defend proceedings through a *Rechtsanwalt*. They may act for themselves in the *Amtsgericht* except in family cases when they must be represented by a *Rechtsanwalt*. The geographical limitations on the competence of *Rechtsanwälte* have already been described.[25]

3. Commencement of proceedings

51.37 The normal means of initiating civil proceedings is by *Klageschrift* (or, more shortly, *Klage*, meaning claim[26]). In the *Klage* the plaintiff names the parties to the proceedings and the amount and the grounds of the claim. The facts on which he relies are usually set out very extensively, often in 20 or more pages.[27] A precise amount must always be claimed, but in personal injury cases this is frequently stated as a minimum figure. The amount claimed is of great importance as it determines the value of the case, the *Streitwert*, and consequently the level of the fees charged by the court and the *Rechtsanwälte*.[28] If documents form part of the proof of the claim they are attached to the *Klage*.

The plaintiff's *Rechtsanwalt* sends three copies to the court, one for the court itself and two for the defendant and his *Rechtsanwalt*. The case is allocated to a particular section of the court, which may be civil or commercial.[29] This section then continues to deal with the case. It enters the case in the records of the court. At this stage the presiding judge decides whether to have a preliminary hearing

---

[24] If the main proceedings are in the *Amtsgericht* and the counterclaim exceeds DM 5,000 in value, the proceedings may be transferred to the *Landgericht* unless the jurisdiction of the *Amtsgericht* is extended by agreement between the parties.
[25] Para. 51.04 above.
[26] The term *Klage* is used to refer both to the document which institutes the proceedings and to the action itself.
[27] See para. 51.43 below.
[28] See para. 51.57 below.
[29] The sections have different names at different levels of court: *Abteilung* in the *Amtsgericht*, *Kammer* in the *Landgericht*, and *Senat* in the *Oberlandesgericht* and in the *Bundesgerichtshof*.

or to direct preliminary proceedings in writing. The latter course is usually adopted unless the case appears to be straightforward. The court then serves a copy of the *Klage* on the defendant by post. The action is only considered to be pending if and when the proceedings have been served on the defendant.

4. Service of proceedings

Service is ordinarily undertaken by the court's officers. A special form of postal recorded delivery is used. The post office provides the court with documentary evidence of service, usually bearing the signature of the defendant or a member of his household. If service cannot be effected, even through a member of the defendant's household, the document to be served is deposited at the local post office and a notice to that effect is left at the door or in the letter box. In the event that service is refused because the person to whom the document is presented is not willing to accept it, it may be left there and is deemed to have been served.

51.38

When it is known that a *Rechtsanwalt* is already acting for the defendant, the proceedings may be served directly on him if the plaintiff's *Rechtsanwalt* so requests. If the whereabouts of the defendant are unknown the court may make an order for substituted service. In this event the document is displayed on the court's notice board and a notice is published in certain official gazettes. After the lapse of a certain period service is deemed to have been effected and a default judgment can be obtained.

Service may be effected outside Germany under the terms of the Hague Service Convention[30] or of a bilateral convention.

5. Appearance by the defendant

The documents accompanying the *Klage* will specify the action which the defendant is required to take, depending on the procedure selected by the presiding judge.[31] If he ordered a preliminary hearing, the defendant will be required to attend that hearing. If the written preliminary procedure has been adopted, the court will have specified a period of at least two weeks, within which the defendant must declare whether he contests the case, and a further period of at least two weeks within which he must lodge his defence. The judge may also fix a period within which the plaintiff is to file any reply to the defence. These periods may be extended by the court on the application of a party.

51.39

If the defendant fails to take any of these required steps he is

---

[30] See paras. 4.30 *et seq.* above and A2.03 below.
[31] Except in the *Amtsgericht*, these steps will be taken by the defendant's *Rechtsanwalt*: see para. 51.36 above.

deemed to have admitted the allegations contained in the *Klage* and a default judgment may be given in the plaintiff's favour.

In the case of foreign defendants the times allowed for entering an appearance and filing a defence are somewhat extended. The presiding judge is required by law, in any case where a party domiciled outside the Federal Republic is to be served, to determine how long should elapse between service of the proceedings and the hearing. The period will always be longer than the two weeks allowed to parties domiciled in Germany and in practice is likely to be between one and two months.

6. Default judgments

51.40   If the defendant fails to respond within the time limit fixed for him by the court, or if he does not appear at the preliminary hearing (or at any later hearing) of the case, he will be considered to have admitted the facts asserted in support of the claim. If those facts are conclusive the court must give judgment in default for the plaintiff. The judge must, however, satisfy himself that service has been properly effected. In cases to which the Hague Service Convention or a bilateral convention apply, he is to take the terms of the convention into account. A plaintiff who fails to appear at a hearing may also have judgment given against him. If a *Rechtsanwalt* is acting and does not appear at a hearing it is contrary to professional etiquette for his opponent to apply for a default judgment unless he has previously warned him that he may take this step.

51.41   *Setting aside.* Every default judgment specifies a period of two weeks from the date of service within which formal opposition to it (*Einspruch*) can be made. No reason need be given for having failed to appear. The effect of an *Einspruch* is for the judgment to be set aside and the proceedings resumed, although the costs thrown away will have to be paid by the party in default. Foreign parties are normally allowed a longer period, specified in the default judgment, within which to oppose it. Meanwhile, unless the defendant applies for its enforceability to be suspended, the default judgment is immediately enforceable. A default judgment may be appealed by *Berufung*[32] only on a ground which would be sustainable if there had been no default.

7. Disputes as to jurisdiction

51.42   Acknowledging service of the proceedings does not prevent the defendant from disputing the jurisdiction of the court, provided that he does this before making any other response. This means

---

[32] See para. 51.64 below.

that the defendant or his *Rechtsanwalt* must, at the preliminary first hearing (if there is one) or in his defence and again at the first main hearing, clearly state that he is contesting the jurisdiction of the court. He cannot raise the issue for the first time at a later stage. The issue of jurisdiction may be raised without pleading to the merits of the case but, unless there are very strong grounds for challenging jurisdiction, it may be advisable to plead a defence to the merits at the same time. Otherwise there is a risk that, if the court decides that it has jurisdiction, the defendant may be taken to have admitted the matters alleged in the claim. The court may make a ruling on its jurisdiction of its own motion but in practice this is rarely done.

8. Pleadings

Each party must set out his case in written pleadings (*Schrift-* **51.43** *sätze*). As has been seen, the plaintiff's statement of claim is called the *Klageschrift*. The defendant's answer is called a *Klageerwiderung* or a *Klagebeantwortung*. The parties may exchange further *Schrift-sätze*. The purpose of these pleadings is to set out the issues for determination by the court. It is important to note that the parties must include in their pleadings all requisite material at the earliest possible stage of the procedure. If they do not do so they may be precluded from doing so later. If the court considers that a party has not pleaded his case in sufficient detail, it may direct further and better particulars to be given. The party must comply with this request or the court may regard the other party's allegations on the issue to have been admitted.

The pleadings are often very detailed. They set out the facts alleged, identifying witnesses by name and indicating the matters as to which they can speak. Any documents which support the claim or the defence are attached to the appropriate pleadings. Documents in a foreign language must be translated in full. The legal principles underlying the claim are spelt out, citing references and developing legal arguments. The *Klageerwiderung* must either deny or admit every fact alleged in the *Klageschrift* and must state every material fact upon which the defendant intends to rely. Any facts alleged in the *Klageschrift*, which the defendant does not challenge, will be taken to have been admitted. The *Klageerwiderung* must normally be served within the period fixed by the court. A counterclaim, or *Widerklage*, must have some connection with the subject-matter of the claim.

Upon receipt of the *Klageerwiderung* the plaintiff will normally **51.44** plead further facts in a separate *Schriftsatz*, sometimes called a *Replik*. This may contain new arguments or facts. It may also increase or reduce the amount of the claim. As this is normally done before the first hearing the revised amount of the claim may adjust the amount of the *Streitwert*.[33] If the defendant has counterclaimed, the plaintiff must add to his *Replik* a defence to the counterclaim. If a third or subsequent party is to be joined in the proceedings, further pleadings, together with all previous pleadings, are served on the third party.

The pleadings are transmitted by the parties' lawyers to the court, which then transmits copies to the lawyers for the other parties. The lawyers admitted to a particular court each have letter boxes at that court, and the clerk simply puts the copy pleadings into the lawyers' boxes. In practice, though, the lawyers often send copies of their pleadings direct to each other when they send them to the court.

9. The hearings

51.45 *Preliminary hearing.* The presiding judge may order a preliminary hearing or preliminary proceedings in writing. If he orders a hearing, the defendant (or his *Rechtsanwalt*) is required to attend and either he will be required to put forward his defence immediately, or a time-limit will be set for him to file his defence. A simple case may be disposed of at the preliminary hearing. If that does not happen, directions will be given at the preliminary hearing for the further conduct of the proceedings, and the case will be heard by the court in one or more main hearings. The pleadings are normally closed before the first main hearing in court.

51.46 *Main hearings.* As the case proceeds, the court reviews the state of the evidence and considers what further material is necessary for it to reach its decision. The first hearing, whether a preliminary hearing or a main hearing, is a short hearing at which the court announces whether it has sufficient material upon which to give judgment or whether it needs to hear oral evidence or request an expert's opinion. If the court directs the taking of oral evidence or the obtaining of an expert's report, there is another hearing or hearings for the purpose and further pleadings are allowed.

51.47 *Final hearing.* At the conclusion of the last of the hearings at which evidence is given, the judge may be in a position to make his decision or he may permit the parties to submit further pleadings commenting on the evidence and the expert's report, if any. When the evidence has been heard by only one of a panel of three judges there will be a further formal hearing before the full court. At the final hearing, the *Rechtsanwälte* have a last opportunity to address the court or to seek the admission of yet further evidence, but in

---

[33] See para. 51.57 below.

practice this rarely happens. There may be as many as 20 cases fixed for hearing in the same hour. The *Rechtsanwälte* will merely refer to their pleadings and ask for judgment in their clients' favour. The hearing of all the cases will normally take not more than the hour. Once the court decides that it does not require further evidence or comment, it may occasionally announce its decision immediately, especially in an urgent case. More usually it will fix a date on which it will give its decision, normally not more than three weeks after the final hearing. The decision will then be given at a special hearing for the purpose, but the reasoned judgment itself will follow in writing within three weeks.

10. Security for costs

The question of security for costs is normally dealt with at the **51.48** first hearing. Subject to far-reaching exceptions in practice,[34] a foreign plaintiff suing in Germany may, on the application of the defendant, be ordered to provide security within a given time. This may amount to the estimated total of the defendant's costs in defending the proceedings at first instance and on appeal. Security can be provided by the deposit of cash or the obtaining of a guarantee from a bank or insurance company. If security is not provided, the court declares that the action is deemed to have been withdrawn by the plaintiff. However security will not be ordered to be given by a plaintiff from any country which, under treaty or otherwise, does not require security from German plaintiffs bringing proceedings in its courts. As regards plaintiffs resident in the United Kingdom, it has been the practice of German courts to require them to provide security, but the extent to which that practice will survive the accession of the United Kingdom to the 1968 Convention remains to be seen.

11. Witnesses and oral evidence

The *Rechtsanwalt* names in his pleading any witness who, accord- **51.49** ing to his client, can support the facts alleged. The matters as to which the witness can speak will be summarised, but the witness will not normally have been interviewed beforehand by the *Rechtsanwalt*. The witness will only give oral evidence if the court so directs in an order called a *Beweisbeschluss*. When summoned by

---

[34] Germany is a party to the Hague Convention on Civil Procedure of March 1, 1954, under Arts. 17 to 19 of which security for costs is generally prohibited against nationals and domiciliaries of the states which have ratified that Convention, which includes most West European states except the U.K., Ireland and Greece. See para. 6.11 above.

the court the witness is under a duty to appear, but certain close relatives of the parties may refuse to give evidence.

Evidential hearings. The evidence is taken, in private, at a special hearing of the court and the witness does not hear what the other witnesses have said. In courts with a three-judge panel it may sometimes be taken before only one member of the panel. The evidence of the witness is limited to the facts and matters specifed in the *Beweisbeschluss*. He is first invited to give his own account of the matters in question. He is then questioned by the judge and lastly by the respective *Rechtsanwälte*, who in practice do no more than to emphasise particular points or to clear up ambiguities. There is no cross-examination of the kind found in common law systems. The judge dictates a summary of the evidence which is taken down by a clerk or on tape. The respective *Rechtsanwälte* have an important practical function to perform in ensuring that the resultant statement or *Protokoll* accurately summarises the evidence of the witness. If requested the judge will have the *Protokoll* read to the witness at the conclusion of his evidence to check that he agrees with its contents. It is then added to the court's file on the case and copies are later sent to the respective *Rechtsanwälte*. When the witness lives a long distance from the court his evidence may be taken before the judge of the local *Amtsgericht*, with local *Rechtsanwälte* sometimes in attendance.

51.50 *Evidence and burden of proof.* The witness can only speak as to facts that are within his personal knowledge, and may refuse to answer questions if the answers might incriminate or dishonour him, result in financial damage to him, or involve the disclosure of a trade secret. The judge conducts an unfettered evaluation of the evidence, but there are strict rules as to the burden of proof in various factual situations. The court must dismiss the case if a party fails to prove an essential fact, the burden of proving which is on him. Any doubt may be sufficient to allow such a dismissal. The judge may only accept evidence if he holds a personal belief as to its truth. Cases, therefore, are not determined on the balance of probabilities.

The parties. The parties themselves cannot be witnesses on their own behalf. For these purposes, the directors of a corporate party are regarded as being the parties themselves. A party who is not able to call other evidence in support of his case may apply for the opposing party to submit to questions. The opposing party has a right to refuse but adverse inferences may be drawn. However, if he does give evidence, the requesting party runs the risk that the court may be convinced by what his opponent has to say. The court itself may direct one or both of the parties to attend to make statements about the facts of the case. Such evidence derived from the parties themselves is considered to be of less probative value than independent evidence and it must be remembered that the opportunity for rigorous cross-examination by the opposing *Rechtsanwalt* is negligible, although theoretically possible.

12. Documentary evidence

A party who wishes to produce documents which assist his case **51.51** does so by simply attaching copies to his pleadings. Documents in a foreign language must be translated in full. The *Rechtsanwalt* certifies in his professional capacity that any copies are true copies of the originals. The court or the other party may nonetheless ask for the originals to be produced to the court at the hearing. If a *Rechtsanwalt* is unclear as to what documents have been produced he may, with the leave of the court, inspect the file of the court.

The right of one party to insist on the production of a document **51.52** by another party is limited. It may arise only if, according to the rules of civil law, the other party has a legal obligation to produce the document. Such an obligation may arise if the document was written in the "legal interest" of the party demanding its production, if it certifies a legal relationship between that person and another person, or if it records negotiations, to which he was a party, on a proposed legal transaction. The production of such documents may also be required of a third party, by a separate action. A party to proceedings (but not a third party) may also be ordered to produce specific documents of certain further limited kinds if they are known to be in his possession. There is no procedure comparable to the general discovery of documents in common law systems.

13. Experts

If a matter in issue requires to be proved by expert opinion, a **51.53** party will, in his pleading, request the appointment by the court of an independent expert (*Sachverständiger*). If the court considers that it does not have sufficient knowledge of the subject-matter, it will nominate an expert from an official list of approved experts. The court will normally direct the taking of expert evidence in an order (*Beweisbeschluss*) which specifies the questions upon which the expert's opinion is required. The expert will make his own arrangements with the parties for any examination of the subject-matter which may be necessary, and may convene a meeting of the parties at which they may make representations to him. The parties may be accompanied by their own expert advisers if they choose. In due course he will send his report to the court with copies to the parties. They may thereafter file further pleadings commenting on the report and they may request a further hearing so that the expert may be questioned.

14. Proof of foreign law

51.54   The judge has a legal duty to investigate and decide upon questions of foreign law when they arise. In a simple matter he might conduct his own researches in a foreign legal textbook. Frequently the court commissions an expert opinion from an academic comparative laywer but the parties themselves may also submit expert opinions.[34a]

15. Compromise

51.55   Many proceedings in German courts are compromised between the parties, often with the active involvement of the judge who is formally under a duty to encourage a compromise. This usually occurs during or after the first hearing in court and before witnesses have been heard and experts appointed. A compromise (*Vergleich*) in court has the same effect as a judgment of the court.[35] The *Rechtsanwalt* of each party is entitled to charge an additional fee unit in the event of a compromise.[36] There is no equivalent to the English procedure of payment into court. If the defendant recognises that he owes some part of the claim he must pay it to the plaintiff, even though the plaintiff insists on continuing the action for the balance. This payment, of which the judge will be informed, has the effect of reducing the *Streitwert*[36] as from the date of payment. Settlement out of court takes effect as an ordinary contract.

16. The judgment

51.56   The final judgment in an action is called an *Endurteil*. The first part of the judgment, called the *Rubrum*, identifies the court, the parties and the respective *Rechtsanwälte*. There follows the *Tenor* or *Urteilsformel*, which contains the operative part of the decision, including orders as to costs and enforcement. It will state whether the judgment is or is not immediately enforceable and, if it is, whether security is or is not required before enforcement.[37] If the plaintiff has claimed interest it will be awarded according to law at

---

[34a] Germany is a party to the European Convention on Information on Foreign Law (see para. 9.13 above), although it is rarely used in practice.
[35] See para. 51.70 below.
[36] See para. 51.57 below.
[37] As to the enforcement of judgments see para. 51.66 below.

4 per cent. (civil claims) or 5 per cent. (commercial claims), or at a higher rate, if he can show that he has actually paid such higher rate to a bank.

The operative part of the judgment is followed by a summary of the background facts (known as the *Tatbestand*), and a statement of the contested issues, the evidence and the court's reasons (known as the *Endscheidungsgründe*). If the jurisdiction has been disputed, or was doubtful, the *Entscheidungsgründe* will contain a statement of the basis on which the court accepted jurisdiction. In certain circumstances, the facts and reasoning may be omitted, but this is not permitted if the judgment is to be enforced abroad. Dissenting opinions are not stated. The judgment will be signed by the judge or judges.

It is normally only the *Tenor* which is read out in open court when the decision is announced. The full written form of the judgment is lodged at the court office some time later, and the parties may then obtain copies.

Apart from an *Endurteil*, there are also other types of judgment, such as a *Teilurteil*, by which part of a dispute is decided; a *Zwischenurteil* or interlocutory judgment by which incidental procedural matters, such as capacity to act, are decided; a *Grundurteil*, a judgment on liability only; a *Vorbehaltsurteil*, a provisional judgment which is capable of being set aside on proof of further matters.

17. Costs

The costs involved in litigation in Germany can conveniently be divided into two elements, the costs incurred by the court itself and the fees and disbursements of the lawyers. **51.57**

The costs of the court. The court incurs its own administrative costs and in addition it pays the allowances and expenses claimed by witnesses and experts. The court recovers these costs in advance from the party who has nominated the witness or has proposed the step taken by the court. These costs may be considerable, often exceeding the costs payable by a party to his own lawyer. The *Streitwert*, the value of the case, determines, according to a sliding scale, the "fee unit" that the plaintiff has to pay to the court at various stages during the progress of the action: on filing the proceedings, on the hearings (one fee unit covers all hearings), and on judgment. If the plaintiff succeeds in full, the judgment will normally order the defendant to pay him all the court costs together with legal costs (described below). If the plaintiff only recovers a proportion of the sum claimed the defendant will have to pay only that proportion of the costs. If the losing party is insolvent the court costs must be met in full by the winning party.

Lawyers' fees. There is a set fee tariff for *Rechtsanwälte* laid down by law.[38] A fee unit is calculated from the *Streitwert*, and is chargeable in respect of successive stages of the litigation: on taking initial instructions, for appearing at court (regardless of the number of hearings), when the court directs the taking of evidence, and for negotiating a settlement. An amount is also recoverable in respect of disbursements. Thus the size of the fee is not necessarily related to the amount of work involved in the case. The losing party has to pay all the other side's necessary and proper costs including those of his opponent's *Rechtsanwalt*. A *Korrespondenzanwalt*[39] is entitled to a single fee-unit from his client, but this fee may be irrecoverable from a losing party if the court takes the view that the local *Rechtsanwalt* should have been instructed direct. The amount recoverable will be the actual fee or the amount payable to a *Korrespondenzanwalt*, whichever is less. The fees of a foreign lawyer who has instructed a *Rechtsanwalt* on behalf of a lay client are also recoverable as costs in the German proceedings if it can be shown that his intervention was necessary. In proceedings on appeal the fees payable to the *Rechtsanwälte* are calculated on a similar but enhanced basis.

H. CIVIL PROCEDURE—PROVISIONAL AND PROTECTIVE MEASURES

1. Introduction

51.58   German law provides two types of provisional remedy, *Arrest* (an attachment of assets) and *einstweilige Verfügung* (an interim injunction). Both these measures are available before and after the main proceedings have been commenced. The remedies are also available against the assets in Germany of a defendant to proceedings which are contemplated or pending in a foreign court, provided that the

---

[38] The following are representative figures (as at June 1989) in Deutsche Mark for court costs and lawyers' fees for an ordinary trial in Germany with evidence in which judgment is given. The minimum fee for the *Rechtsanwalt* would apply in a case in which no oral evidence was given and in which no *Korrespondenzanwalt* was retained. The maximum figure presumes that oral evidence has been necessary, that a *Korrespondenzanwalt* has been retained and that the issue has been settled with a compromise.

Amount in dispute	Court costs	Rechtsanwalt's fees	
		Minimum	Maximum
10.000,–	222,–	1.078,–	2.695,–
20.000,–	342,–	1.698,–	4.245,–
50.000,–	558,–	2.478,–	6.195,–
100.000,–	918,–	3.778,–	9.445,–
200.000,–	1.548,–	4.828,–	12.070,–

[39] See para. 51.04, n. 3 above.

German court would recognise the eventual judgment of the foreign court.[40]

2. Arrest

In an action in which the plaintiff's claim is for a specific sum of **51.59** money, or is capable of precise evaluation, he may apply to the court for the attachment of the defendant's assets (*Arrest*)[41] up to the value of the claim. The application is made in writing to the court in which the main proceedings are being brought, or to the *Amtsgericht* for the district in which the assets are located (whatever the value of the assets or of the claim). The application is usually made *ex parte* and, in cases of urgency, it may be made outside court hours. In cases of doubt, the court may direct there to be a hearing at which both parties may be heard. An order for *Arrest* (an *Arrestbefehl*) may be addressed not only to the defendant but also to any third party, such as a bank, who may hold the assets in question.

The plaintiff must show that there is a risk that the defendant will so deal with his assets as to obstruct or defeat the enforcement of any ultimate judgment. Evidence as to this is usually given by way of formal written declarations. It is not sufficient to show merely that the defendant is likely to become insolvent. In the case of a foreign defendant there is presumed to be a risk that enforcement of an ultimate judgment may be obstructed. It follows that a plaintiff may always apply for an attachment of assets against a foreign defendant if those assets are located in Germany. The plaintiff may sometimes be ordered to give security for any loss which the defendant may suffer through the attachment. This may be provided in the form of a bank guarantee. A plaintiff who obtains an *Arrest* in circumstances which are later shown to have been unjustified is liable to the defendant in damages for any loss (including consequential loss) which he has suffered thereby.

An *Arrestbefehl* is enforced by the seizure of assets by the *Gerichtsvollzieher* (sheriff), or, if the assets are in the possession of a third party, by an order that they should not be disposed of. Whether the defendant is required to give up actual possession of movable property to the sheriff is a matter which the sheriff decides.

---

[40] This view is however not undisputed. Some authors and courts maintain that these remedies are only available if the dispute between the parties will be heard before a German court. Nevertheless, in any case to which the 1968 Convention applies, Art. 24 gives the German courts jurisdiction to grant these measures in aid of proceedings in other Contracting States: see para. 24.01 above.

[41] More accurately, this type of order is called *dinglicher Arrest*, to distinguish it from *persönlicher Arrest*, referred to below.

Discharge of the order. If the plaintiff obtained an order for *Arrest* before commencing proceedings, a time-limit may be set on the application of the defendant within which the plaintiff must start the proceedings. If he fails to do so within that time, the order becomes automatically discharged. It will also be discharged if the defendant provides satisfactory security. Unless the *Arrest* was made after an oral hearing *inter partes*, the defendant may file an application (*Widerspruch*) with the court for the order to be set aside. A hearing takes place at which both parties may present evidence and the court may then revoke or vary the order as appropriate. The application is made to the court which made the original order, except that where the order was made by an *Amtsgericht* before the proceedings were commenced, the application is made to the court where the main proceedings are pending.

Arrest of persons. A more drastic, though rarely used, procedure is *persönlicher Arrest*, under which a defendant may be committed to prison until he has deposited the sum claimed. It may be used, for example, against a foreign defendant visiting Germany. This procedure is available only in respect of a personal liability and does not extend to the directors or staff of a limited company in respect of the company's liabilities.

3. *Einstweilige Verfügung*

51.60   The remedy of an interlocutory injunction is available, in cases in which an *Arrest* is not appropriate, to safeguard the remedy which the plaintiff may ultimately be granted. Except in cases of urgency, application is made to the court in which the main proceedings have been brought and it is determined after a hearing *inter partes*. In cases of urgency, the application can be made *ex parte* and it may be made to the *Amtsgericht* in which the subject-matter of the application is located. In such cases, the *Amtsgericht* sets a time-limit within which the plaintiff must summon the defendant to an *inter partes* hearing before the court where the main proceedings are pending. If he fails to do so, the order is discharged.

The giving of security will only form a basis for discharging an *einstweilige Verfügung* in exceptional circumstances; but the order may be discharged or varied on a *Widerspruch* filed by the defendant in the same way as an *Arrest*. A plaintiff who obtains an injunction in circumstances which are later shown to have been unjustified is liable to the defendant in damages for any loss (including consequential loss) which he has suffered thereby.

The defendant can sometimes forestall proceedings for an *einstweilige Verfügung* which he suspects may be instituted against him. He can file a protective writ (*Schutzschrift*) in court which sets out the arguments against the granting of the possible injunction. This step is fairly common in unfair competition cases.

I. CIVIL PROCEDURE—SUMMARY PROCEDURES

Two forms of summary procedure are available in Germany for use in straightforward debt cases.   **51.61**

1. *Mahnverfahren*

This procedure is in extremely common use as a means of debt-collecting. It is conducted in the *Amtsgericht* and frequently without the intervention of lawyers. The claimant (*Antragssteller*) may apply to the *Amtsgericht* for the place where he himself is domiciled[42] for a special form of summons called a *Mahnbescheid*[43] to be issued against the respondent (*Antragsgegner*) demanding payment of the debt in a definite sum. The upper financial limits of the *Amtsgericht* do not apply to this procedure. The summons (for which a printed form is normally used) must contain specific information concerning the parties and the claim. It is not necessary for a letter of claim to have been sent beforehand. The court does not examine the merits of the claim but simply sends the *Mahnbescheid* by post, by recorded delivery, to the respondent. The procedure is also available where the *Mahnbescheid* is to be served in another Contracting State to the 1968 Convention, and in this case it must contain notice to the respondent that he should appoint a representative *ad litem* in the district where the court is located.

The respondent may challenge the *Mahnbescheid* by means of a written objection (*Widerspruch*) which must be filed with the court within two weeks from the date of service (or a month, if service took place in another Contracting State to the 1968 Convention). If he does this then an ordinary action follows and the proceedings are transferred, if necessary, to the court of competent jurisdiction under the normal rules. If the respondent does not challenge the *Mahnbescheid* the plaintiff may ask for an enforcement order (*Vollstreckungsbescheid*) to be issued. This has the same effect as a default judgment. The *Vollstreckungsbescheid* is then served on the respondent who can again oppose the order by written protest (*Einspruch*) within two weeks of service. Neither a *Widerspruch* nor an *Einspruch* need specify the grounds of opposition. Although an ordinary action will follow after the *Einspruch*, the *Vollstreckungsbescheid* remains provisionally enforceable[44] in the meantime unless the

---

[42] The *Amtsgericht Schöneberg* in West Berlin is the court which has jurisdiction over all *Mahnverfahren* in which the creditor is not domiciled in Germany.
[43] Formerly called a *Zahlungsbefehl*.
[44] See para. 51.57 below.

respondent successfully applies for the enforceability of the order to be suspended.

2. *Urkundenprozess*

51.62   In certain types of case, such as claims on bills of exchange and promissory notes, another form of summary procedure, the *Urkundenprozess*, is available. This procedure is commenced by a *Klage* in the same way as normal civil proceedings[45] in the court which is competent under the normal rules. The *Klage* must state that the proceedings are by way of *Urkundenprozess*. The judge merely examines the face of the document and if it appears to be regular he gives judgment for the plaintiff. This judgment has the same effect as a default judgment,[46] and can be executed immediately. If the defendant wishes to impugn the document the proceedings may continue, notwithstanding any execution which may have been carried out. If the defendant is ultimately successful, he may recover from the plaintiff the money which he has had to pay, with damages for any losses.

J. CIVIL PROCEDURE—APPEALS

1. Introduction

51.63   *Types of appeal.* German law prescribes a number of methods whereby a court's decision may be challenged, either before the court which made the order or before a higher court. The term *Rechtsmittel* applies to challenges before a higher court. There are three types of *Rechtsmittel*, namely a *Berufung* (a first appeal on fact and law), a *Revision* (a second appeal on a point of law), and a *Beschwerde* (an appeal against an order other than a judgment).

Neither *Berufung* nor *Revision* has the effect of suspending the enforceability of a judgment, but (unless it is provisionally enforceable) the judgment will only become enforceable when it becomes final (*rechtskräftig*).[47]

In addition to these three forms of appeal, German law provides two means of reopening proceedings after a final judgment and certain other specialised forms of challenge, such as applications to oppose or set aside default judgments or various other forms of order. The means by which the constitutionality of a law may be challenged before the Federal Constitutional Court have already been described.[48]

---

[45] See para. 51.37 above.
[46] See para. 51.40 above.
[47] See para. 51.66 below.
[48] Para. 51.22 above.

Time for appealing. An appellant must file a notice of appeal (*Berufungsschrift* or *Revisionsschrift*) at the relevant appellate court within the strict limit of one month of service of the original judgment on him or, if it is not served, within five months of the pronouncement of the judgment. The grounds of appeal (*Berufungsbegründung* or *Revisionsbegründung*), fully argued in writing, must be filed within a further month thereafter, although the court may extend this period on application. There is no general time limit for the lodging of a *Beschwerde*, although various time limits are imposed for specific kinds of *Beschwerde*. An application to reopen proceedings after final judgment must be made within a month from the date when the applicant acquired knowledge of the grounds for the application, and in any event within five years from the date when the decision challenged became final.

2. Appeals

Berufung. With the exception of small cases in which the amount **51.64** at stake is less than DM 700, it is always possible to appeal by way of a *Berufung* from the judgment of a court at first instance. Appeal from the *Amtsgericht* is to an appellate division of the *Landgericht* and from first instance decisions of the *Landgericht* appeal is to the *Oberlandesgericht*. There is no ordinary avenue of appeal against a decision of the *Landgericht* made on appeal from an *Amtsgericht*. A *Berufung* notionally involves a complete rehearing of the case on both fact and law. In most cases, though, the court will not hear the witnesses again unless it appears that fresh points require to be elicited or that a witness may have been unreliable.

Revision. An appeal on a point of law from a decision of the *Oberlandesgericht* lies to the *Bundesgerichtshof*. This type of appeal, called a *Revision*, is generally available only in cases of a value of DM 40,000 or more, but it is also permissible with the leave of the *Oberlandesgericht* in certain other classes of case if important points of law arise. Some points of law will not found a *Revision*, namely questions of purely local law or certain questions of jurisdiction or competence. There is also a rare form of leap-frog appeal on a point of law of general importance from a *Landgericht* to the *Bundesgerichtshof*; this procedure, called *Sprungrevision*, requires the agreement of both parties.

Beschwerde. Certain interlocutory decisions can be challenged by application to the court which made them for a review of the decision. If the court declines to change its decision, the application is passed to the next superior court by way of an appeal. This procedure, called a *Beschwerde*, is used, for example, when legal aid has been refused, or in respect of decisions concerning the *Streitwert* or security for costs. The matter is usually determined without an oral hearing either in the original court or on appeal. No further *Beschwerde* lies against the decision made on appeal, unless it is based on a new and independent ground. If a party brings a *Beschwerde* against a ruling or order made in the course of proceedings, the proceedings may nonetheless continue, but any resulting judgment may be ordered to be provisionally enforceable pending the outcome of the appeal.

There is a specialised form of *Beschwerde* by which a decision of the presiding judge of a chamber of the *Landgericht*, in proceedings under the 1968 Convention for the enforcement of a judgment given in another Contracting State, may be challenged before the *Oberlandesgericht*.[49] The decision of the *Oberlandesgericht* in such proceedings may be challenged before the *Bundesgerichtshof* by a further specialised form of appeal called a *Rechtsbeschwerde*.[50]

3. Other means of challenging a decision

51.65   *Reopening of proceedings.* In certain rare circumstances, a judgment which has become final may be set aside and the proceedings reopened (*Wiederaufnahme des Verfahrens*). This may be done by proceedings for annulment (*Nichtigkeitsklage*) if there was a serious breach of the procedural rules, or by proceedings for restitution (*Restitutionsklage*) on the grounds, for example, that fresh evidence has been discovered.

Applications to set orders aside. There are certain other forms of procedure whereby the decisions of a court may be challenged, the more important of which are discussed elsewhere in this chapter. They include an application (*Widerspruch*) challenging an order for provisional attachment (*Arrest*) or interlocutory injunction (*einstweilige Verfügung*)[51] or against a summary order for payment (*Mahnbescheid*);[52] an application (*Einspruch*) in opposition to a default judgment[53] or to an order for enforcement in summary proceedings;[54] and an application to set aside or vary an order for enforcement of a judgment (*Errinerung*) or proceedings for its annulment (*Vollstreckungsabwehrklage* or *Drittwiderspruchsklage*).[55]

---

[49] Art. 37, first para., and Art. 40: paras. 28.38 and 28.63 above. Unlike a normal *Beschwerde*, this appeal is considered by the higher court from the outset. The procedure is regulated by paras. 11 to 15 AusfG (see para. 51.71, n. 64 below).

[50] Art. 37, second para., and Art. 41: paras. 28.38 and 28.69 above; paras. 17 to 20 AusfG (see para. 51.71, n. 64 below).

[51] Para. 51.60 above.

[52] Para. 51.61 above.

[53] Para. 51.41 above.

[54] Para. 51.61 above.

[55] Para. 51.69 above.

K. CIVIL PROCEDURE—ENFORCEMENT

1. Enforcement of German judgments

The enforceability of a judgment depends upon whether or not it **51.66** is, or has become, a final judgment (*vollstreckbares Endurteil*). A final judgment may be enforced against a party without restriction, once it has been served on him. If it is not final, a judgment may be capable of being enforced provisionally with (or in limited cases without) security. A final judgment remains enforceable for a period of 30 years.

Res judicata. A judgment is said to be final, or *res judicata* (*rechtskräftig*), when it can no longer be appealed. This may be the case if the time for bringing an appeal has expired, or if the amount in dispute is too small to be the subject of an appeal, or if all possible appeals have already been made. In such a case the successful party can obtain from the court of first instance a certificate that the judgment has become *res judicata*. This certificate (*Rechtskraftzeugnis*) is a precondition to enforcement and enables the judgment to be enforced without restriction by whatever means is appropriate.

Provisional enforceability. A judgment which has not become final **51.67** may still be enforced provisionally in the following circumstances:

(a) Certain types of judgment may be enforced provisionally without the executing party having to provide security, and regardless of whether or not the losing party has appealed the original judgment. Such judgments include a default judgment,[56] a judgment given in *Urkundenprozess*,[57] and judgments given on appeal.

(b) All other judgments may be enforced if the executing party has furnished security (*vorläufige Vollstreckbarkeit gegen Sicherheitsleistung*). The amount of this security will be the maximum amount recoverable by the successful party under the judgment, including costs. It must either be deposited in the court or be provided by means of a bank guarantee. Only certain banks are acceptable for this purpose.

Indorsement as to executory character. In order to enforce a judgment, the successful party's *Rechtsanwalt* applies to the court for an enforceable copy of the judgment (*i.e.* one that has been duly certified). The following words, known as a *Vollstreckungsklausel*, are indorsed on the copy:

---

[56] See para. 51.40 above.
[57] See para. 51.62 above.

"Vorstehende Ausfertigung wird der Klägerin zum Zweck der Zwangsvollstreckung erteilt" (This copy has been made for the plaintiff for the purpose of enforcement).

The authenticity of a copy of this document is established by the court's seal and the signature of the official issuing it.

Service. The copy of the judgment duly indorsed as to its executory character is sent by the successful party's *Rechtsanwalt* to the *Obergerichtsvollzieher* (principal sheriff) of the court for the district in which execution is sought. A *Gerichtsvollzieher* (sheriff) in that court is then appointed to proceed with the enforcement. He serves the judgment, usually by post.

51.68   *Execution.* If the judgment debtor does not satisfy the judgment voluntarily, the *Gerichtsvollzieher* visits the debtor and demands payment. If the debtor cannot pay, the *Gerichtsvollzieher* will seize property to the required value by attaching official seals to it. If there is insufficient property at the debtor's premises he will be summoned to court for an examination as to his means. Thereafter, other assets may be seized or an attachment of earnings order may be made. Inability to pay will ultimately lead to bankruptcy. It should be noted that if a company appears to have insufficient assets even to pay for bankruptcy proceedings, the enforcement procedure is closed forthwith and the company is struck from the register.

The plaintiff may also obtain, while the judgment is provisionally enforceable, a form of execution whereby the defendant is required to pay the amount of the judgment and costs to the *Gerichtsvollzieher*. In this latter instance the plaintiff does not put up security, but the money is not paid over to him until the judgment has become final. The protective measure of *Arrest* is also available as an aid to execution.[58]

51.69   *Other methods of enforcement.* If the judgment requires a party to perform acts which only he can carry out,[59] or to refrain from specified acts, it may be enforced by sending him to prison (*Zwangshaft*) or by imposing a fine (*Zwangsgeld*) of a given amount per day until he complies with the order. If the act required to be performed is capable of performance by another person, the court may order such performance and the costs incurred are recoverable from the party in default.

Opposing the execution. If a defendant wishes to object to the grant of the order for enforcement or to the particular method of enforce-

---

[58] See para. 51.59 above.
[59] It is to be noted that German law allows plaintiffs to compel the performance of contractual obligations by action in many circumstances in which English law would regard damages as providing an adequate remedy.

ment he may apply to the court which made the order, by a procedure called *Errinerung*. He may also bring fresh proceedings (*Vollstreckungsabwehrklage*) to annul or reverse the judgment on the basis of fresh evidence arising since the conclusion of the hearings. A third party may also challenge the order for enforcement by making an application to the court (*Drittwiderspruchsklage*), for example if he claims title to the goods the subject of execution. This may often occur where goods are sold under retention of title until fully paid for.

2. Authentic instruments and court settlements

Under German law, certain notarial instruments and court settle-   **51.70** ments are enforceable by the same means of execution as are available in the case of judgments.[60] In each case it is a condition of its enforceability in Germany that the relevant document, known as a *Titel*, should have been certified by the court as enforceable[61] and should have been served.

Notarially authenticated instruments. As regards notarial instruments, it is a condition of their enforceability that they should relate to an obligation to pay a fixed sum of money[62] or to deliver certain types of goods, and that the document should record the debtor's consent to immediate execution. They must have been drawn up by a German notary within the scope of his competence and in the prescribed form.

Court settlements. If the parties have concluded a settlement which has been minuted in the records of a German court,[63] an enforceable copy of the minute may be issued by the court and enforced in the same way as a judgment.

3. Enforcement of foreign judgments

Foreign judgments are enforceable in Germany by the same   **51.71** means as are available in respect of German judgments once their execution has been authorised by the indorsement of a *Vollstreckungsklausel*. The means of obtaining this indorsement differs depending on whether or not the 1968 Convention applies.

---

[60] Arbitration awards are similarly enforceable.
[61] The certification is the same as that required for judgments, namely the attachment of a *Vollstreckungsklausel*: see para. 51.67 above.
[62] Certain variable sums, such as those payable under a mortgage, are deemed to be fixed for this purpose.
[63] See para. 51.55 above.

1317

Enforcement under the 1968 Convention. If the foreign judgment falls within the 1968 Convention,[64] the judgment creditor applies in the first instance to the presiding judge of the relevant chamber of the *Landgericht* for an order authorising the enforcement of the judgment. The application will ordinarily be made in writing and decided without an oral hearing. It is not necessary (although it may be advisable) for the application to be made by a *Rechtsanwalt*; but if a local *Rechtsanwalt* is not instructed, a representative *ad litem* must be appointed who must normally be domiciled within the district for the court. The foreign judgment and supporting documentation required by the Convention must be accompanied by a German translation.[65] If enforcement is authorised, the court office will indorse the judgment with a *Vollstreckungsklausel* in a special form. The decision of the president of the relevant chamber of the *Landgericht* may be appealed by a specialised type of *Beschwerde* to the *Oberlandesgericht* and thence to the *Bundesgerichtshof*.[66]

51.72 *Judgments outside the 1968 Convention.* In cases not covered by the 1968 Convention, a foreign judgment may be enforced after proceedings for an order for its enforcement have been brought in the *Amtsgericht* or the *Landgericht* (depending on the value of the judgment) for the area of the defendant's domicile or where the assets are located. In the absence of any reciprocal enforcement convention with the country in which the judgment was given, the German court will authorise the judgment's enforcement if a German judgment would be enforced in that country and subject to the following conditions. The court will examine the judgment both as to its form and as to its content but it will not reconsider the merits of the case. It will order enforcement if the foreign court had jurisdiction according to German rules of private international law and if the judgment was final. Where the foreign judgment was given in default of appearance the defendant must have been served in accordance with German rules as to service. Enforcement will not be ordered where to do so would be contrary to German public policy.

---

[64] The 1968 Convention is give effect in Germany by a law called the *Gesetz zur Ausführung des Übereinkommens vom 27. September 1968 über die gerichtliche Zuständigkeit und die Vollstreckung gerichtlicher Entscheidungen in Zivil- und Handelssachen*, sometimes abbreviated as AusfG.

[65] The translation must be certified by a person qualified to do so in one of the Contracting States: see para. 29.29 above. In Germany, the persons qualified to act as translators for these purposes are determined by the Ministries of Justice of the various *Länder*.

[66] See para. 51.64 above. The time-limits for an appeal against an order for the enforcement of the judgment are laid down in Art. 36 of the 1968 Convention. There is no time-limit specified for an appeal against the refusal of an order for enforcement; and the only means whereby a judgment debtor can secure the non-enforceability of the foreign judgment in Germany is by bringing his own proceedings (a *negative Feststellungsklage*) before the relevant court.

However, Germany has concluded conventions with a number of countries,[67] according to which certain judgments may be enforced after the simple formal approval of the competent German court.

L. Legal Persons

German law provides for a number of different types of legal entity 51.73
of which the most common are as follows:

(a) *Aktiengesellschaft* (AG)—a public limited company;
(b) *Gesellschaft mit beschränkter Haftung* (GmbH)—a private limited company;
(c) *Kommanditgesellschaft* (KG)—a commercial limited partnership in which the liability of some partners is limited and of others is unlimited. If the partner with unlimited liability is itself a private limited company its abbreviation is shown as "GmbH & Co. KG";
(d) *Kommanditgesellschaft auf Aktien* (KGaA)—a form of limited partnership in which the liability of some partners is limited by shares and of some partners is unlimited;
(e) *Offene Handelsgesellschaft* (OHG)—a form of general partnership under commercial law in which the liability of members is unlimited. Although it is not a legal person, it can sue or be sued in the firm name;
(f) *Eingetragener Verein*—an incorporated association.
(g) *Gesellschaft des bürgerlichen Rechts*[68]—a civil partnership, without legal personality, in which the liability of the members is joint and several. It may not be used for the purpose of pursuing a trade or business, but may be used, for example, for the practice of a profession or for a non-profit-making joint venture. It may only sue or be sued in the names of all its members, although it may practise under a firm name.

M. Legal Aid

Any natural person, regardless of nationality, who can show that he 51.74
has reasonable prospects of success and who satisfies certain financial criteria, can obtain legal aid (*Prozesskostenhilfe*) under the relevant German law. Application is made to the court seised, or to be seised, of the proceedings. The applicant must show that he has reasonable chances of success and that he satisfies the financial criteria. A lawyer is assigned by the court. The legally aided party is

---

[67] In particular, Germany has such conventions with Austria, Switzerland, Greece, Norway and Spain.
[68] This is often referred to as a *BGB-Gesellschaft*.

absolved from paying court costs or, if he loses, the other side's costs, and the fees of his *Rechtsanwalt* are paid by the *Land* in so far as they may not be recoverable from the other party. The giving of legal advice outside judicial proceedings is not part of the national legal aid scheme. Such legal advice is available for persons of limited means, either freely or on payment of a small charge, from public offices established in some *Länder* and from bureaux set up for the purpose by local bars.

CHAPTER 52

IRELAND

Written in collaboration with Petria McDonnell, Solicitor,[1] Dublin.

---

[1] Partner, *McCann Fitzgerald*, Dublin.

A. THE LEGAL SYSTEM

1. Introduction

52.01   *History and territory.* The Republic of Ireland is a unitary republic governed by a national Parliament (*Oireachtas*) consisting of the President, the *Dáil* (lower chamber) and the *Seanad* (upper chamber). It has been independent from the United Kingdom since 1922;[2] but before independence it had been governed for centuries, under a variety of constitutional arrangements, first by England and later as a part of the United Kingdom. The present Irish Constitution dates from 1937.

According to the Constitution, the territory of the Republic extends to all the 32 counties in Ireland; however for practical purposes Irish law applies only to the 26 counties which became independent in 1922. These cover 85 per cent. of the island's area and contain some two-thirds of its population. The other six counties make up the province of Northern Ireland, which remains part of the United Kingdom. The Republic of Ireland has both Irish and English as official languages, although English is the language used predominantly in legal and commercial matters.

Origins of the legal system. Despite its own pre-medieval origins,[3] the Irish legal system has been decisively influenced over the centuries by the English legal system. The common law was first introduced from England towards the end of the twelfth century and was centred in Dublin and its surrounding area, known as the Pale. During the nineteenth century civil law in the United Kingdom, including Ireland, took on its modern shape and the common law still continues to form an important source of Irish law. However, since independence, and particularly with the advent of a written constitution, the Irish and English legal systems have followed separate but parallel paths.

2. Administration of justice

52.02   There is a clear division between the civil and criminal jurisdictions which generally are administered by separate courts. There is no distinction between the courts which deal with civil and commercial cases. There are no administrative courts, but there are

---

[2] The *Dáil* first met in January 1919 and affirmed the Easter Rising Proclamations of 1916. Some regard independence as having occurred then. According to English law, on the other hand, independence did not occur until 1922, when the Irish Free State (Constitution) Act was passed by the United Kingdom Parliament, granting *de jure* independence to the Irish Free State. See also para. 57.01 below.
[3] Early Irish law was known as Brehon law.

tribunals of a judicial or quasi-judicial nature with jurisdiction over certain employment, tax, social welfare and administrative matters. The ordinary courts exercise supervisory and appellate jurisdiction over these tribunals.

B. Legal Practitioners

The legal profession is divided into two branches, solicitors and barristers. **52.03**

1. Solicitors

Introduction. A solicitor acts as a legal adviser to his clients and conducts legal proceedings on their behalf, instructing a barrister when necessary. In addition to acting in litigation, solicitors act for their clients over a wide range of other legal matters such as the drafting of commercial agreements and wills, the transfer of land, and the formation of companies.

Education and legal qualification. After obtaining a university degree,[4] an intending solicitor must pass the entrance examination of the Incorporated Law Society of Ireland and then work for three years as an "apprentice" in the offices of an established solicitor, taking further examinations, including one of competence in the Irish language. Thereafter, he is "admitted" as a solicitor and is free to practice on his own account.

Rights of representation and audience. The solicitor has rights of audience before all courts but this is little exercised in the higher courts. Most cases before the District Court are conducted by solicitors as advocates. **52.04**

Organisation of practice. There are some 3,500 solicitors in practice in Ireland, of whom some 1,800 are established in Dublin. Solicitors frequently form partnerships with each other. Partnerships typically contain two to five partners, but in the cities many larger firms have upwards of 10 partners. Partnerships with members of other professions are not permitted. In the larger firms there is a considerable degree of specialisation. Much day-to-day work in a solicitor's office may be undertaken by clerks who have no formal qualification.

---

[4] Entrants to both branches of the profession will usually have obtained a law degree from the National University or from Trinity College, Dublin, although other degrees are acceptable. The National University has three locations, which may be regarded as distinct universities, University College, Dublin; University College, Cork; and University College, Galway.

52.05   *Fees.* A solicitor's fees are a matter for agreement with the client. In the event of a dispute between the solicitor and the client, the bill may be referred to the Taxing Master[5] for adjudication, provided that this is done within a year from the date of the bill. Save in respect of conveyancing there are no scale fees. Solicitors' fees are subject to VAT at 25 per cent.

Professional organisation and conduct. The governing body of the solicitors' profession is the Incorporated Law Society of Ireland. Professional conduct is controlled by a statutory committee of the Law Society. A solicitor is required to take out a yearly "practising certificate." Professional indemnity insurance is not compulsory although steps are being taken by the Law Society to make it so.

2. Barristers

52.06   *Introduction.* Barristers act both as advocates in court and as legal consultants, drafting pleadings and other legal documents and advising on questions of law and on the conduct of litigation. They have a right of audience before all courts. They can normally accept instructions directly only from Irish solicitors, although in matters which are not the subject of litigation in Ireland they may be instructed by lawyers qualified to practice in other EEC States.

52.07   *Education and qualification.* After obtaining a degree at university,[6] and having become a member of the Honourable Society of King's Inns,[7] an intending barrister must undergo a course of studies provided by the King's Inns and must pass further examinations, including a test of proficiency in the Irish language. He may then be formally called to the Bar by the Chief Justice. If he intends to practise, he must then serve a period of apprenticeship (called "devilling") with an established barrister before he is permitted to practice on his own account.

Organisation of practice. Practising barristers are not permitted to enter into partnership with each other, with solicitors, or members of other professions. Every practising barrister is, therefore, a sole practitioner. There are over 700 barristers in practice in Ireland, of whom about 110 are Senior Counsel. There are many other barristers who, although called to the Bar, do not practise. There is some tendency for barristers to specialise but this is not so pronounced as in England. Irish barristers practise from the Law Library at the

---

[5] See para. 52.57 below.
[6] See para. 52.03, n.4 above.
[7] The King's Inns exercise the same role as the Inns of Court in London, regulating entry into the profession, providing an educational course for Bar students, and maintaining professional discipline.

Four Courts in Dublin, although a small number have professional chambers in addition.

Senior Counsel. Barristers who have been qualified for at least 10 **52.08** years (and usually 15 to 20 years) and who are regarded as being of established capacity and standing may be appointed as "Senior Counsel" and will have the initials S.C. after their name.[8] Applications to become Senior Counsel are addressed to the Chief Justice but the power to appoint is vested in the government. Once appointed, the Senior Counsel may no longer draft the pleadings and consequently they are able to concentrate on advocacy in court and on giving opinions in more important cases. In all cases in which a Senior Counsel is briefed, it is necessary for junior counsel[9] also to be briefed.

Professional organisation and conduct. Discipline over the Bar is exercised by the Benchers, or governing body, of the King's Inns and the interests of the profession are cared for by the General Council of the Bar, the elected representative body of the Bar.

3. Notaries public

There are a limited number of solicitors who are also appointed **52.09** to hold the office of notary public. The role of the notary public is less extensive than that of the continental notary, much of whose work is undertaken in Ireland by solicitors. The Irish notary attests the execution of deeds and other documents and makes certified copies of them for evidential purposes abroad.

[The next paragraph is number 52.11]

4. Foreign lawyers

The Irish legal profession has no monopoly over the giving of **52.11** legal advice and a foreign lawyer is free to act as a legal consultant as long as he does not represent himself to be a solicitor or barrister. Certain activities, such as conveyancing and the administration of the estates of deceased persons, are however reserved by statute to solicitors. EEC lawyers may appear and plead in Irish courts provided they do so in conjunction with a "home" lawyer. A substantial number of British and Northern Ireland barristers have been admitted to practice at the Irish Bar. When they appear in court they must be instructed by an Irish solicitor. To date the qualifi-

---

[8] Appointment to the rank of Senior Counsel is often referred to as "taking silk" because of the silk gown worn by Senior Counsel.
[9] All barristers, other than Senior Counsel, are known as junior counsel, however long they have been in practice.

cations of solicitors admitted in Britain and Northern Ireland do not give entitlement to practice as solicitors in Ireland.

5. Lawyers in business and public employment

52.12   Some solicitors and barristers are not engaged in private practice but are employed in the legal departments of government or of commercial undertakings. Employed solicitors may represent their employers in court, but employed barristers may not normally do so.

[The next paragraph is number 52.14]

C. SOURCES OF LAW

1. Introduction

52.14   Irish law is comprised of legislation passed by or under the authority of Parliament, and the body of case law and custom decided or approved by the courts over many centuries, known as the common law. Legislation comprises the Constitution (which is superior to other legislation), ordinary parliamentary legislation, statutory instruments and other delegated legislation. The law of Ireland as it existed prior to 1922, including United Kingdom statutes which extended to Ireland, forms part of the law of the Republic, except to the extent that it is contrary to the Constitution or has since been amended. International treaties have no effect in Irish domestic law until they are enacted as legislation by Parliament, and only then if the treaty is not repugnant to the Constitution.

2. Legislation

52.15   *The Constitution.* The Constitution (*Bunreacht na hÉireann*) enacted in the name of the Irish people in 1937 is the primary source of law. The power of the *Oireachtas* (Parliament) to legislate is unlimited except that it cannot enact laws which offend any provision of the Constitution. All statutes enacted after the passing of the Constitution are presumed to be constitutional until the contrary is established.

Parliamentary legislation. Statutes are written laws enacted by Parliament, and in some cases those enacted in former times by the English Parliament (1310–1707), the Irish Parliament (1226–1800), the Parliament of Great Britain (1707–1800) and the United Kingdom Parliament (1800–1922). The continued effect of law dating from before 1922 was expressly provided for in the 1922 constitution and subsequently in the 1937 constitution.

Delegated legislation. Statutes often provide for detailed rules to be made by means of delegated legislation, of which much the most important is the statutory instrument. These are generally made by Ministers and are subject to various forms of approval by Parliament. Unless a statutory instrument can be shown to be *ultra vires* it ranks as equivalent to a statute.

3. The common law

Where a matter is not expressly regulated by legislation, it is sub‑ **52.16** ject to the rules of the common law, which are to be found in the decisions of the higher courts. The meaning of legislation as interpreted by the courts also forms part of the common law. Courts are bound by the earlier decisions made by courts of higher status where the same point has arisen for decision. The Supreme Court has since 1964 been able to overrule its previous decisions. Where a point has not previously been decided, it is decided by parity of reasoning with former decisions. The decisions of courts in England and other common law jurisdictions may be cited as persuasive authority.

Although wide areas of civil law are now governed by statute, much of the law of contract and of tort is still determined solely by the common law.

4. Publications

Statutes and statutory instruments are published in an official **52.17** form, but practitioners sometimes refer to editions of annotated legislation published commercially which note amendments to the legislation as they occur. Decisions of Irish courts appear in various series of law reports or law journals, of which the following are the most important:

(*a*) Irish Reports (cited as IR)
(*b*) Irish Law Reports Monthly (cited as ILRM)
(*c*) Irish Law Times.

In addition, the decisions of English courts are often cited and, for this purpose, reference is made to English law reports.

D. ORGANISATION OF THE CIVIL COURTS

1. Introduction

There are three levels of court of first instance, the District **52.18** Court, the Circuit Court and the High Court. There is an appeal from the District Court to the Circuit Court and from the Circuit Court to the High Court. Appeals from the High Court lie to the Supreme Court. The District Court and Circuit Court are commonly known as the inferior courts and the High Court and Supreme Court are known as the superior courts.

2. The District Court

52.19   The District Court has first instance civil jurisdiction over cases with a value up to £2,500, but this limit may be extended by agreement. There are over 200 District Court areas, each with its own court. There are some 40 District Justices who sit alone.

3. The Circuit Court

52.20   The Circuit Court has civil jurisdiction in respect of claims with an upper limit of £15,000, but this may be extended by agreement. It also has exclusive jurisdiction over certain specialised categories of civil claim, notably claims for new leases. The Circuit Court has jurisdiction over appeals from the District Courts. There are nine circuits each with a number of towns in which the Circuit Court sits. The Dublin circuit has seven judges assigned to it (of whom four hear civil matters) and each of the other circuits has one judge who visits courts on his circuit in turn. Circuit judges sit alone when exercising civil jurisdiction.

4. The High Court

52.21   The High Court, which generally sits in Dublin,[9a] has jurisdiction which is not limited financially, although if a claim is brought in the High Court which should have been brought in a lower court, a successful plaintiff may be penalised in costs. It also has jurisdiction over appeals from the Circuit Court. It consists of a President of the High Court and 15 High Court judges. A High Court judge will, when trying a civil case, sit either alone or in some cases (such as those involving defamation) with a jury which decides liability and the amount of the damages. Occasionally the High Court will be constituted as a divisional court of two or more judges when a case of particular importance is to be determined.

5. The Supreme Court

52.22   The Supreme Court is the final court of appeal. It consists of the Chief Justice, who is head of the judiciary, and five other Supreme Court judges. The President of the High Court may act *ex officio* as a Supreme Court judge. Three judges make a quorum in civil cases, unless constitutional or other important issues are involved, in which case five judges will normally sit.

[9a] See also para. 52.45 below.

6. The judiciary

The judges are appointed by the President of Ireland, on the **52.23**
advice of the government, from the practising legal profession. In
the District Court a barrister or solicitor of at least 10 years experience is eligible. In all the other courts only barristers may be
appointed to the bench. The minimum qualification period is 10
years experience for the Circuit Court, and 12 years for the two
superior courts. Almost invariably a barrister or solicitor will have
had at least double the minimum period in practice as a lawyer
before he is appointed to the bench. Some interlocutory stages of
civil proceedings in the High Court are conducted before a judicial
officer called the Master of the High Court.

E. JURISDICTION OF THE CIVIL COURTS

1. Introduction

In cases to which the 1968 Convention applies, the international **52.24**
jurisdiction of the Irish courts is determined by the rules of competence in the Convention. Where the Convention does not itself
regulate territorial jurisdiction within Ireland, this is determined by
the internal rules of Irish law summarised below. For cases to
which the 1968 Convention does not apply, Irish law contains rules
of exorbitant jurisdiction which are also discussed below.

It has already been noted that the competence of different levels
of court in Ireland may depend on the value of the claim or, in some
cases, on its subject matter. The territorial jurisdiction of the Irish
superior courts extends to the 26 counties of the Republic of Ireland. District and Circuit Courts exercise jurisdiction in respect of
the territory which they serve. All courts have an inherent jurisdiction to determine whether they have jurisdiction in any particular
case.

2. Domicile and seat

The common law concept of domicile forms part of Irish law, but **52.25**
it has no application for the purposes of jurisdiction under the 1968
Convention, in respect of which special rules have been adopted.

For the purposes of the 1968 Convention, a person is treated as
being domiciled in the state in which he has his ordinary residence.
He is treated as being domiciled in a particular place within Ireland
if he is ordinarily resident in that place or if he carries on any profession, business or occupation there.

A corporation or association has its seat in Ireland if it was incor- **52.26**
porated or formed under Irish law, or if its central management and
control are exercised there. If its seat is in Ireland, the location of

the seat is at the place in Ireland where it has its registered office, or where its central management or control is exercised, or where it carries on business. Irish private international law specifies that the seat of a corporation or association is located in a state other than Ireland if it was incorporated or formed under the law of that state or if it has its central management and control there; except that such seat is not located in another Contracting State if it is located in Ireland, or if that other Contracting State would not regard it for the purposes of Article 16(2) as having its seat there.

3. Jurisdiction—general rules

52.27   Because the territorial jurisdiction of the High Court extends to the whole of the Republic, the allocation of local jurisdiction in civil cases is only of significance in the District and Circuit Courts. A person domiciled in Ireland may generally be sued in the court for the place where he ordinarily resides or carries on any profession, business or occupation.

4. Jurisdiction—special rules

52.28   In addition to jurisdiction under the above general rule, proceedings in contract may be brought in the court for the place where the contract was made[10] and proceedings in tort may be brought in the court for the place where the tort is alleged to have been committed. Cases relating to the title to land must be brought in the court for the place where the land is situated.

5. Choice of court and entry of appearance

52.29   Except where exclusive jurisdiction is allocated to a particular court, Irish law permits parties to confer jurisdiction on a court by the entry of an appearance or by agreement.

6. Exorbitant grounds of jurisdiction

52.30   In cases to which the 1968 Convention does not apply, jurisdiction is based on the service of originating process on the defendant. Service may be effected as of right in Ireland on a defendant who is present there, even if temporarily. Service may be effected outside Ireland with the leave of the court. Such leave will only be granted if the claim falls within certain specified categories and, addition-

---

[10] The place of performance of the contractual obligation in question is not relevant for the purposes of this rule; but it is relevant if local jurisdiction is to be founded on Art. 5(1) of the 1968 Convention against a defendant domiciled in another Contracting State. The rules of Irish law as to the place of performance of obligations to pay money or deliver goods, in the absence of agreement, are the same as those of English law: see para. 56.28 below.

ally, if the court regards the claim as a "proper" one over which, in its discretion, it should assume jurisdiction. The most important categories of claim in which leave may be granted for service to be effected outside Ireland are those made against a person domiciled or ordinarily resident in Ireland, those concerning land in Ireland, and those concerning a tort committed in Ireland or a contract made in Ireland or subject to Irish law.

7. Civil claims in criminal proceedings

As a general rule, criminal courts do not have the power to order **52.31** defendants to make compensation to the victims of their crimes.

F. LIMITATION PERIODS

The law relating to limitation periods is complex and the following **52.32** should be taken only as a general guide.

The limitation period is the period of time starting from the moment when the plaintiff could first have commenced his action and after which he is normally barred from bringing the proceedings. There are different periods for different types of claim, the majority of which are set out in the Statute of Limitations, 1957.

In general, actions founded on contract or tort (other than claims **52.33** for damages for personal injuries), must be brought within six years from the date on which the cause of action arose. Claims for damages for personal injuries must be brought within three years. Claims for the recovery of land or to enforce an agreement under seal must be brought within 12 years. Irish law does not generally permit the postponement or extension of a limitation period on the grounds that the plaintiff did not know of his damage or cause of action. The moment at which proceedings commence is the issue of the proceedings by the relevant court.

G. CIVIL PROCEDURE—PROCEEDINGS UP TO JUDGMENT

1. General description

Civil litigation in the Irish legal system is adversarial in nature **52.34** with the conduct of the proceedings being mainly in the hands of the parties themselves and with the court playing a relatively passive role. Proceedings are commenced by the issue of a summons or equivalent document. After the exchange of pleadings and, in some cases, the mutual disclosure of documents there is a public trial in court at which the parties and the witnesses give oral evidence and are cross-examined by the opposing lawyer. At the conclusion of evidence and argument the judge gives his judgment orally, either there and then or on a later occasion. In the Supreme Court and High Court procedure is governed by the Rules of the Superior Courts 1986. In the Circuit Court, procedure is governed by the Circuit Court Rules 1950, while the District Court Rules 1948 regulate procedure in that court. Except where otherwise stated, the procedure described in the following paragraphs is that of the High Court.

2. Parties and legal representation

52.35   The two main parties to an action are known respectively as the plaintiff and the defendant. All natural and legal persons can sue and be sued. Special rules provide for minors (under 18), the mentally ill, bankrupts and insolvent companies. Foreign persons may sue irrespective of their domicile.[11] Further parties may be joined in an action as plaintiffs or defendants after its commencement with the consent of the court. In certain circumstances, a person may be permitted to intervene as a party in existing proceedings, but this rarely happens. A person against whom a defendant has a claim, such as for contribution or indemnity, which can be dealt with in connection with the main proceedings, may be added as a third party. A defendant may bring a counterclaim against a plaintiff and any party may raise a claim that can conveniently be tried at the same time as the plaintiff's claim.

52.36   Companies and other legal persons can only bring or defend proceedings through a solicitor. An individual may act for himself but he will normally employ a solicitor to represent him. If a barrister is to be instructed, the solicitor will make the necessary arrangements.

3. Commencement of proceedings

52.37   Actions are commenced in each level of court by the "issue" of proceedings. The document by which proceedings are initiated is known in the High Court as an originating summons, in the Circuit Court as a civil bill, and in the District Court as a civil process. In High Court proceedings the originating summons is prepared by the plaintiff's counsel or his solicitor and is then taken to the court, where it is "issued" by being stamped with the seal of the court, a copy being retained for the court file. The issue of the proceedings takes place in the lower courts when the civil bill or the civil process is handed or sent to a summons server for service, or, if service is by registered post, when it is posted. Unless the court's jurisdiction arises solely under the 1968 Convention, any proceedings which are

---

[11] But see para. 52.48 below.

Ireland

to be served outside Ireland may only be issued with the leave of the court.

In the High Court the originating summons may either be a "plenary summons," a "summary summons," or a "special summons." The plenary summons is used in cases in which facts are likely to be contested, and it is followed by further written pleadings which enable the matters in dispute to be defined before trial. It contains certain formal details, namely the names and addresses of the parties, the plaintiff's occupation and description, and either an address for service of the plaintiff or the name and address of his solicitor. It also contains a short statement, called a "general indorsement of claim," setting out the relief claimed by the plaintiff and, in general terms, the grounds for the claim.

The summary summons is used mainly in debt cases. The special summons is mainly used in proceedings relating to mortgages or trusts, in applications under the provisions of the Companies Act 1963, and in cases in which a declaration is sought from the court as to the construction of a document. A summary summons and a special summons must each contain, in addition to the same formal details as must be included in a plenary summons, a comprehensive statement, called a "special indorsement of claim," which sets out specifically and with all necessary particulars the grounds of the claim and the relief sought.

In proceedings before the Circuit Court, the civil bill will set out the name, description and last known address or place of business of the parties and the main points of the plaintiff's claim, under the heading "indorsement of claim."

4. Service of proceedings

In the High Court, service of the originating summons is normally effected by the plaintiff's solicitor. The document which is served is an official copy stamped by the court at the time of issue. A natural person must, if possible, be served personally. This is done by showing the original of the summons to the defendant and handing him the official copy. If personal service cannot be effected the court will accept service at the defendant's home address on a member of his household, but it must be shown that reasonable efforts have been made to serve him personally. A limited company may be served by posting the copy summons to its registered office. The address of the registered office of all companies is obtainable from the Registrar of Companies. If a company fails to notify the Registrar of the address of its registered office, the summons may be served on the Registrar. Service may also be effected by sending the summons to the defendant's solicitor if the latter has agreed to

52.38

accept service. If personal or postal service cannot be effected, the court will order substituted service by advertisement or some other appropriate means. A summons must be served within 12 months of its issue, unless its validity has been extended for a further period by the court.

The above rules apply equally in the Circuit Court, but here service of the civil bill must be effected by an official summons server[12] or, in places where there is no summons server, by registered post.

5. Appearance by the defendant

52.39   When the defendant is served with a High Court summons or with a Circuit Court civil bill, these documents will contain instructions as to what he should do. In High Court proceedings he must enter an appearance at the Central Office of the High Court within eight days after service (10 days in the Circuit Court), although if service is to be effected outside Ireland, a longer period will be allowed.

In the High Court the defendant enters an appearance by lodging with the court a notice in writing, called a memorandum of appearance, stating an address for service or the name and address of his solicitor. The equivalent documents in the Circuit and District Courts are called a notice of entry of appearance and a notice of intention to defend.

6. Default judgments

52.40   If the defendant fails to enter an appearance within the time limited for doing so, the plaintiff may obtain a default judgment. If the claim is for a liquidated sum[13] he does this by producing to the Central Office an affidavit proving that the defendant was duly served with the originating summons and an affidavit verifying the claim. In such a case judgment will be given automatically. It will be a final one and it may be enforced in the ordinary way. If the claim is for an unliquidated amount (*e.g.* for damages) the plaintiff must apply to the appropriate judge for judgment, on notice to the defendant. The judge will give judgment for damages to be assessed. There will then be a later hearing at which the plaintiff will have to prove the amount of his claim.

---

[12] There used to be a comprehensive network of summons servers throughout Ireland through whom all court proceedings had to be served. They are now only employed in respect of proceedings in the Circuit Court and District Court. Their numbers have diminished considerably over recent years as fresh appointments are no longer made when vacancies occur.

[13] A liquidated sum is a quantified sum due as a debt not as damages.

Setting aside. If a default judgment has been entered against him, **52.41**
the defendant may apply to the court for the judgment to be set
aside. The application must ordinarily be supported by an affidavit
explaining the reason for the failure to enter an appearance and
showing that the defendant has at least an arguable defence to the
claim. There is no time limit within which the defendant must
make such an application. If the application is successful, the court
will usually fix a time within which the defendant must take the
next step or steps in the action.

Default judgments may also be obtained at a later stage in the
proceedings when a party fails to serve a pleading within the appropriate time limits. These may be set aside in a similar fashion.

7. Disputes as to jurisdiction

In the High Court, if the defendant wishes to dispute the juris- **52.42**
diction of the court, he may either apply to set aside service of the
summons or he may enter a conditional appearance. If he enters an
appearance without contesting the jurisdiction, he will be taken to
have submitted to the jurisdiction.

To challenge the jurisdiction, the defendant's solicitor serves a
"notice of motion" on the plaintiff's solicitor, which informs him
that the defendant will make an application to the court, on the date
mentioned in the notice, for an appropriate order. A typical application would be for an order setting aside the service on the defendant and dismissing the action. With the notice of motion, the
defendant serves a copy of the affidavit on which he will rely. This
affidavit, which is filed at the court together with the notice of
motion, is a sworn statement setting out the evidence relevant to the
challenge to the jurisdiction, and exhibiting any documents which
may be relevant to that issue and which support the defendant's
case. The plaintiff in turn may file an affidavit in answer. On the
appointed date the parties' lawyers attend before a judge, the affidavits are read, the lawyers make oral submissions and the judge
announces his decision orally and the reasons for it. In a complicated
case, the judge may announce his decision at a later date. The ruling
on the issue of jurisdiction may be subject to an interlocutory appeal.

8. Pleadings

The purpose of pleadings is to define the issues which the court **52.43**
must decide at the trial of the action. They are formal documents in
which each party sets out the facts upon which he relies, usually in
short numbered paragraphs. The facts are stated in a concise form,
but with sufficient particularity to enable the other party to know
the case which he will have to meet at the trial. The pleadings do
not set out the evidence which the party will adduce to prove those

facts, nor the identity of his witnesses. With certain exceptions (such as a defence based on the expiry of a limitation period), matters of law are not normally pleaded. If a party considers that his opponent's pleading is ambiguous or not sufficiently detailed, he may request further and better particulars. If these are not supplied voluntarily, they may be ordered by the court in an appropriate case. Such a request and the answers to it form part of the formal pleadings.

Pleadings are usually drafted by a barrister, especially in High Court proceedings. They must be delivered to the other party's solicitor within set time limits, although these are often extended by agreement between the solicitors or by leave of the court. Failure to deliver a pleading within the set or agreed time limits may ultimately lead to the court ordering that the action be dismissed or that judgment be ordered against the defaulting party.

Amendment of the pleadings may be made, unless this would unduly prejudice the other party's conduct of the action in a way which could not be remedied by an appropriate order for costs. In certain circumstances, pleadings may be amended once at an early stage without leave (although the amendment may be disallowed on the application of the other party), but otherwise amendment may only occur with the leave of the court.

Statement of claim. In proceedings started by plenary summons, the plaintiff must deliver a statement of claim to the defendant's solicitor, either with the plenary summons or within 21 days from the date when it was served. In addition to setting out the facts upon which the plaintiff will rely, the statement of claim must specify the relief which is claimed. If the plaintiff is claiming special damages,[14] these must be itemised in detail. If the plaintiff is claiming for future loss or for non-pecuniary loss (such as pain and suffering and loss of amenity), his claim is for general damages and no amount need be quantified in the statement of claim. Claims for interest should be specifically pleaded. The judge has a discretion to award pre-judgment interest on the claim. All judgments carry interest from the date of the judgment. The present rate of interest is 8 per cent.

52.44   *Defence (and counterclaim, if any).* The defendant must ordinarily deliver his defence within 28 days from the service of the statement of claim or from the time limited for entry of an appearance, whichever is later. In his defence the defendant must either admit or deny every fact alleged in the statement of claim, and must state every

---

[14] "Special damages" is the term used for quantified pecuniary loss which has occurred before the trial of the action. It covers, for example, loss of income, as well as money which the plaintiff has had to expend, caused by the matters of which he complains.

material fact upon which he intends to rely. If the defendant has a claim against the plaintiff which can conveniently be tried at the same time as the plaintiff's claim then it is added to the defence as a counterclaim. The same rules apply to a counterclaim as to the statement of claim.

Reply (and defence to counterclaim, if any). If the plaintiff wishes to rely on any further facts or matters in response to the defence (or if he wishes to make admissions), he may deliver a reply within 14 days from the date of delivery of the defence. No new cause of action may be pleaded in the reply nor may a plaintiff use the reply to improve his statement of claim. This should be done, if at all, by amending the statement of claim. If the defendant has counter-claimed, the plaintiff must plead a defence to the counterclaim, which will be incorporated into a pleading called a reply and defence to counterclaim. Further pleadings may follow if the court gives leave, but they are exceptional.

Additional parties. When a defendant wishes to bring a third party into the proceedings, he may obtain leave to serve a third party notice on that person, which is comparable with an originating summons. The third party must enter an appearance and the procedure thereafter is comparable with that between plaintiff and defendant, with the issues between the defendant and the third party being defined in pleadings similar to those in the main action. If there are subsequent parties the same procedure applies.

9. The hearings

Interlocutory hearings. At any time before the trial of the action it **52.45** is open to either party to summon the other party to a hearing before the Master or the court and to apply for an interlocutory order concerning some aspect of the case, such as an order for security for costs, or for further and better particulars of a pleading, or for discovery and inspection of documents. Frequently, however, such matters are resolved by agreement between the respective solicitors. There is no routine procedure equivalent to the summons for directions in English proceedings.

Setting down for trial. When all the pleadings have been filed, together with affidavits of discovery, the date and mode of trial are fixed, in the High Court, by the plaintiff giving notice of trial to the defendant and setting the case down for trial at the Central Office. If the plaintiff fails to give such notice within three weeks of the close of pleadings, the defendant may do so, or may apply for the case to be dismissed for want of prosecution. Such an application is not likely to be successful at a first attempt, unless the plaintiff's delay is very prolonged. All High Court trials at first instance take place in Dublin, with the exception that personal injury trials regularly take place also at Cork, Limerick, Galway, Sligo, Dundalk, Kilkenny and other locations.

When a case is set down for trial in the High Court, the plaintiff's solicitor will specify the venue for the trial and the mode of trial (as being trial either by a judge alone or trial by a judge and jury). Defamation cases are the most common class of case in which jury trials take place. In a jury trial, questions of law are decided by the judge and questions of fact by the jury. The jury therefore decides issues of liability and the amount of any damages to be awarded.

52.46 *The trial.* On the day appointed for the trial, the parties, their legal representatives and their witnesses will attend court. Although the judge presides at the trial, he plays a largely passive role while it is in progress. He will have before him initially only the pleadings in the action. It is for the parties, through their legal advisers, to decide what witnesses are to be called and what documentary evidence is to be produced. The judge himself is normally unable to call any witness without the consent of the parties. He will only ask questions of a witness when it is necessary to deal with a point which has been overlooked by counsel or which has been left unclear. The burden of proving any matter and of proving the case as a whole is generally on the plaintiff, and the judge's decision is based on the balance of probabilities.

In the ordinary case, the plaintiff's counsel first makes an opening speech introducing the case to the judge and, if there is one, to the jury. He refers to the pleadings and to the documents in the case, which will usually have been assembled in an agreed bundle. The plaintiff and his witnesses then each give their evidence orally on oath in answer to questions put first by his counsel and then by the defendant's counsel.[15] The defendant and his witnesses will then, in most cases, be called to give their evidence. At the close of the evidence, first the defendant's counsel and finally the plaintiff's counsel, make their closing submissions to the judge or to the judge and jury in support of their respective cases.

52.47 In a case before a judge alone, the judge may, if the case is straightforward, announce his decision immediately, giving a reasoned oral judgment. Sometimes he will take time to consider his judgment and will give judgment orally the next day or some time later. In giving a judgment, the judge summarises the issues,

---

[15] See further as to witnesses at para. 52.49 below.

evidence and arguments which he has heard, makes his findings of fact and rulings on the law, and announces his decision.

In a case before a judge and jury, the judge summarises the issues, and the evidence which has been given on them, and directs the jury as to the questions to be answered. The judge will generally give the jury a list of questions, drawn up in consultation with the respective counsel. The jury then deliberates in private, in the absence of the judge, and announces its decisions on the questions posed and on the amount of the damages, if any, to be awarded. The judge then pronounces judgment in accordance with the jury's findings.

10. Security for costs

When it appears to the court that a plaintiff is ordinarily resident out of the jurisdiction,[16] and that the defendant has a defence on the merits, the judge may, on the application of the defendant, order the plaintiff to provide security for the defendant's costs of defending the claim. The matter is then referred to the Master to determine the quantum of the security. The defendant will usually provide evidence from a costs drawer[16a] as to the likely cost of defending the claim. It used to be the practice to order security equal to only one third of the defendant's probable costs, but this practice has now altered and the court has discretion order full security for such costs. The amount of the security is normally deposited with the court, but a bond may also be accepted. The court may also order security against a plaintiff company, if it appears that the company may not be able to satisfy an order for costs made against it.   **52.48**

11. Witnesses and oral evidence

The evidence is ordinarily given by witnesses, orally, on oath, at the trial of the action. The selection of witnesses is a matter entirely within the discretion of the parties and their advisers and, while the judge has a theoretical right to call witnesses (in the absence of objection of the parties), this is virtually never exercised. It is normal for the parties' lawyers to interview witnesses in advance of the trial and to obtain a detailed statement of their evidence. The attendance of a witness to give evidence or to produce a document at a trial can be enforced by an order issued by the court made on the application of the party who wishes to call the witness to give evidence. The parties themselves are competent to give evidence as   **52.49**

---

[16] This does not apply to plaintiffs resident in Northern Ireland when residence there is the only ground for seeking security. Security will be ordered against plaintiffs resident in Britain.

[16a] A costs drawer is a person engaged by solicitors to draw up a bill of costs; see para 52.57 below.

witnesses on their own behalf and will usually do so before their other witnesses are called.

A witness (including a party) is questioned, first, in examination in chief, by the counsel who has called him. He is then questioned, in cross-examination, by the opposing counsel. Finally he is questioned, in re-examination, by the counsel who called him. The judge will usually only ask questions of a witness when it is necessary to deal with a point which has been overlooked or left unclear by counsel. Witnesses are not normally excluded from court while other witnesses are giving evidence. As a matter of practice, the judge and the parties' lawyers take their own note of evidence given by a witness at trial, although there is no compulsion on them to do so. On the application of any party in the High Court, the judge will order the appointment of a shorthand writer, who then makes a note of the evidence, the judge's rulings to the jury (if there is one), and the judgment.

52.50   A witness may give evidence only of matters of which he has direct personal knowledge. He may not, unless he is an expert, give evidence as to his opinion on any matter. He may not normally report statements made by him or by others out of the presence and hearing of the other party; but this rule against the admission of "hearsay" evidence is subject to limited exceptions.

If a witness will not, for a genuine reason, be able to attend the trial, he may, with the leave of the court, give evidence before a "commissioner" appointed for the purpose, and the parties or their counsel may examine and cross-examine him. The commissioner will cause his evidence to be written down verbatim in a document called a "deposition," which will then be admitted as evidence at the trial.

Ireland is not party to the Hague Evidence Convention. When evidence is required to be taken in a foreign jurisdiction, the procedure laid down in the Foreign Tribunals Evidence Act 1856 is followed.

12. Documentary evidence

52.51   *Discovery of documents.* All documents relevant to a dispute which are or which have been in the possession or control of a party to an action must be disclosed to the other party. This procedure, known as discovery of documents, is intended to enable each side to assess the respective merits of their cases. This disclosure may be carried out by agreement between the parties or following an order for discovery made on application to the Master of the High Court. His decision can be appealed to a judge of the High Court. Usually, however, both parties consent to the granting of reciprocal orders.

The orders will usually require the parties to list on oath all the documents in their actual or former possession or power relating to the issues in the case.

The duty of disclosure extends to all documents including those which are adverse to a party's case. The party against whom an order for discovery has been made is obliged to permit the party obtaining the order to inspect the documents, and to permit him to take copies of them, unless they are privileged. Privileged documents are those which came into existence by reason of the litigation, actual or contemplated. They include correspondence between solicitor and client, counsel's opinions, and correspondence between the opposing parties or their lawyers written with a view to compromising the dispute.[17] The solicitor and counsel acting for a party are professionally required to ensure that proper discovery is made. Non-compliance with an order for discovery will lead to the striking out of the defaulting party's case. Documents to which a party has referred in his pleading are subject to inspection by the other party without a specific order for discovery.

The plaintiff will not normally succeed in obtaining an order for discovery before he has delivered his statement of claim, nor will a defendant until he has delivered his defence. Exceptionally, if a party needs to see documents in the possession of the other party before he can draft his pleading, an order may be made for early discovery.

Proof of documents. Strictly speaking, documents may only be relied upon at a trial if a witness is called to produce the document and to prove its authenticity from his own knowledge. The cumbersome consequences of this rule are avoided in practice by the parties' solicitors agreeing the authenticity of the documents and the copies to be used at the trial. It is usual for the solicitors to agree for the documents to be arranged into one or more bundles for use at the trial, copies of which are then lodged with the court.

52.52

It is not generally permissible for the evidence of a witness to be admitted in written form, except by way of a deposition taken on commission.[18] However, sworn statements (called *affidavits*) may also be admitted as evidence in certain circumstances.

Interrogatories. A party to proceedings may apply to the court for an order compelling the other party to answer questions, called interrogatories, prior to the hearing in a sworn affidavit. The questions must relate to the facts in issue in the case. Interrogatories will

---

[17] Such correspondence is usually marked "without prejudice."
[18] See para. 52.50 above.

be ordered if the court considers that they are necessary for the fair disposal of the case or the saving of costs. They are of particular use to a plaintiff when the facts to be ascertained are fundamental to his case but their proof (unless admitted by the defendant) is difficult or costly.

Discovery against third parties. A person who is not a party to an action may be obliged to disclose documents or to answer interrogatories if the court is satisfied that he has documents or information relevant to the matters in issue. Any party to an action may apply for such an order. The applicant must indemnify any such person in respect of costs reasonably incurred in complying with the order.

13. Experts

52.53 Any party may appoint an expert to consider technical or other specialised aspects of the case and to give evidence on them at trial. The substance of his evidence is usually contained in a report to his client. Such reports are privileged, although they are sometimes disclosed by mutual agreement.

14. Proof of foreign law

52.54 Irish law regards foreign law (including English law) as a question of fact to be proved by the party who wishes to rely on it. Unlike other questions of fact, it is decided by the judge alone and not by the jury. If Irish choice of law rules indicate that foreign law is to be applied, but if neither party adduces evidence of what that law is, the court will usually presume it to be the same as Irish law unless the contrary is proved. Any person who is qualified as a lawyer in the foreign legal system, or who has sufficient experience of that system in practice, may give evidence of the foreign law. The court will not normally conduct its own researches into the foreign law.

15. Compromise

52.55 As the conduct of the proceedings rests with the parties themselves, they may come to a compromise at any time before final judgment is given. There is no duty on the court to promote a compromise although the judge occasionally will do so if he thinks fit. The approval of the court is required for a settlement of any dispute, whether or not proceedings have been commenced, which is entered into on behalf of a minor.

The choice of the precise method of settling proceedings may be of considerable practical importance. If the terms of settlement are made "a rule of court" or are incorporated in an agreed judgment or order of the court, they will be enforceable in the same proceedings. If the action is discontinued on the agreed terms, then those terms constitute a fresh agreement which supercedes the original cause of action. Sometimes the action is not discontinued or dismissed, but merely stayed for all purposes except the enforcement of the agreed terms. In such circumstances, the terms of the settlement may be set out in a schedule to the order staying the proceedings or they may be endorsed on a separate document (such as counsel's brief) retained by the parties. There is no system in Ireland of enforceable court settlements separate from judgments. A party who wishes to impugn a concluded settlement which has not been made a "rule of court" must bring a fresh action for this purpose and must show grounds which invalidate the contract on which the settlement is founded.

Payment into court. The rules of court contain a procedure whereby a defendant may pay money into court in satisfaction of the plaintiff's claim. This procedure, known as "lodgment," is of considerable practical importance, particularly in smaller cases in which the costs are proportionately larger in relation to the size of the claim. The plaintiff may take the money out of court within 14 days, and if he does so that disposes of his claim, although he is entitled in addition to his costs up to the date when he gives notice of his intention to take the money. If, on the other hand, he does not take the money out, but eventually recovers a lesser sum than that paid in by the defendant, then, except in exceptional circumstances, the plaintiff will not recover any of his costs incurred after the date when the payment into court was made and he will be ordered to pay all the defendant's costs incurred after that date. In the High Court, the judge who tries the case knows of the fact of lodgment because reference is made to it in the pleadings, but he will not know the amount of the lodgment until after he has given his judgment. In the Circuit and District Courts the judge is kept in ignorance of both the fact and amount of any lodgment until after judgment.

16. The judgment

When the judgment is pronounced in court by the judge, the orders made by the judge are noted by the registrar of the court who draws up the order in the records of the court. Copies of the order may be obtained from the Central Office, on payment of a fee, about a week later, or sooner if required. Copies of the judge's full reasoned judgment can also be obtained if they were noted by a shorthand writer, or prepared in writing by the judge.   52.56

17. Costs

52.57   When the judge has given his judgment in court, the successful party will normally apply for an order for costs against the unsuccessful party and the judge will consider any argument on the matter. The awarding of costs as between parties to litigation is in the discretion of the court, although normally the successful party will obtain an order for costs against the unsuccessful party. Unless the amount of these costs can be agreed between the parties, the successful party must, after judgment has been given, submit an itemised bill of his costs to the Taxing Master for approval. All the costs of the proceedings, including court fees, witness' expenses, and lawyer's fees may be claimed. Each item must then be justified. In respect of certain items, such as counsel's fees for drafting the pleadings, there is a published scale of costs. In the normal basis for taxation (called "party and party costs"), the recoverable costs are those which are regarded as necessary or proper for the attainment of justice or enforcing or defending the rights of the party whose costs are being taxed. In practice, though, there will be a shortfall of about one third between the costs ordered to be paid by the losing party and those which the successful party will be charged by his solicitor ("solicitor and own client" costs). VAT is chargeable on legal fees at 25 per cent.

When a plaintiff succeeds in an action which should, in view of the amount recovered, have been brought in the Circuit Court, he may be awarded his costs on the less remunerative Circuit Court scale. In the District Court there are a number of scales of costs dependant upon the amount claimed or recovered. If a party considers that he is being charged too much by his own solicitor he can apply to the Taxing Master for the bill to be taxed on a "solicitor and own client" basis. This must be done within one year of presentation of the bill.

H. CIVIL PROCEDURE—PROVISIONAL AND PROTECTIVE MEASURES

52.58   In proceedings in which the plaintiff is seeking an injunction to oblige the defendant to do or to refrain from doing some act, the court will frequently grant an interlocutory (or "interim") injunction. In urgent cases, such an injunction can be obtained even before the issue of a summons, by applying to a High Court judge with appropriate evidence on affidavit. The application may be made without notice to the defendant, in which case the injunction will be of short duration, a few days or a week, so that the defendant can be notified and can attend before the judge to put his side of the case. If the judge decides, on hearing both parties, that the balance of convenience supports the continuance of the original *status quo*, then an interlocutory injunction will be granted until the hearing of the action. The plaintiff seeking an injunction must give an undertaking to compensate the defendant for any loss caused by the injunction if, when the matter is tried on its merits, it is found that the injunction ought not to have been granted.

Mareva and Anton Piller injunctions. Over recent years the Irish   **52.59** courts have developed a jurisdiction to grant an interim injunction to prevent a defendant from disposing of his assets before judgment. In so doing they have followed the decisions of the English High Court, and the remedy is known as a "Mareva" injunction. As under English law, it is necessary for the applicant to show that he has a good arguable case, that the defendant has assets within the jurisdiction, and that there is a real risk that the defendant will remove the assets from the jurisdiction or otherwise deal with them to deprive the plaintiff of the fruits of any judgment.

The Irish courts have also followed the English courts in making   **52.60** orders, called "Anton Piller" orders, which permit the plaintiff's representatives to enter the defendant's premises to inspect and preserve documents or property which are of evidential value in proceedings which have already been commenced or which are contemplated. The plaintiff must satisfy the court that there is a grave risk that the defendant, on being made aware of the proceedings, will remove or destroy such documents or property. Subject to Article 24 of the 1968 Convention, interlocutory injunctions such as the Mareva and Anton Piller injunctions are only available if the Irish court has jurisdiction over the substance of the dispute.

I. CIVIL PROCEDURE—SUMMARY PROCEDURES

The Rules of the Superior Courts make provision for obtaining   **52.61** summary judgment if the defendant has no defence to the action. If an action has been commenced by summary summons and if the defendant has entered an appearance, the plaintiff may set the case down for hearing before the Master on a motion for liberty to enter final judgment for the amount claimed. He must file an affidavit supporting his case in which he (or some other appropriate person) must swear to the truth of facts which show that he is entitled to the amount claimed and that, in his belief, the defendant has no defence to the action. The plaintiff serves the notice of the hearing on the defendant, together with a copy of the affidavit. The defendant may contest the application by filing an affidavit in reply setting out his grounds of defence to all or part of the claim and by attending the hearing to argue his defence.

If the defendant is successful in showing that he has a good defence or that he should be permitted to defend, the Master (or the court, if the matter is referred to it) will give him leave to defend and will give directions for the future conduct of the action, usually by treating it as an action begun by plenary summons. Leave to defend may extend to all or part of the claim, and may be unconditional or subject to conditions, such as the giving of security. If the defendants fails to show that he should have leave to defend, the Master will make an order giving the plaintiff liberty to enter final judgment against the defendant. This order, together with documents prepared by the plaintiff's solicitor, must be lodged in the Central Office in order to obtain final judgment. If an award of discretionary pre-judgment interest is sought, the matter must be referred to the judge, as the Master has no power to make an order in respect of such interest.

[The next paragraph is number 52.63]

J. CIVIL PROCEDURE—APPEALS

52.63 *Introduction.* In most cases an appeal may be made through the hierarchy of the courts: from the District Court to the Circuit Court and from the Circuit Court to the High Court; in the High Court from Master to judge, and from judge to the Supreme Court. Any decision of a court, whether interlocutory or final, may be appealed. The party bringing the appeal is called the "appellant" and the party resisting the appeal is called the "respondent". It is possible for a party to bring a cross-appeal. There is also a procedure whereby a District Court can refer a particular question of law to the High Court by way of "case stated." A default judgment may be challenged by making an application for it to be set aside to the court which granted it, but this is not generally regarded as a form of appeal.[19]

An appeal does not operate as a stay of execution but a stay may be granted on application at the discretion of the court. To bring an appeal, a notice of appeal must, within the specified time limit, be served on the other party and filed in the office of the appropriate court. The time limits may be extended with the leave of the court.

52.64 *Appeal from the District Court to the Circuit Court.* The time for bringing such an appeal is seven days from the day upon which the judgment was given. The appeal takes the form of a complete rehearing and either party may introduce new arguments and

---

[19] The procedure for setting aside a default judgment has already been described at para. 52.40 above.

additional evidence. There is also a direct appeal from the District Court to the High Court by way of case stated on points of law.

Appeal from the Circuit Court to the High Court. The time within which this appeal must be brought is 10 days from the date upon which the decision appealed against was given. It is usually heard by a single judge who hears the case afresh including the oral evidence.

Appeal from the High Court to the Supreme Court. This must be made within 21 days from the perfecting of the judgment or order appealed against. A judgment or order is perfected when it is signed by the Registrar. Although the appeal is formally a re-hearing, the court generally relies entirely on the transcript of the evidence given in the court below and the argument of counsel. The powers of the Supreme Court vary according to whether the action at first instance was tried by a judge and jury or by a judge alone. In the former case, as has already been noted, the jury decides the facts and the judge instructs them as to the law to be applied to those facts. Either one or both of these matters may form the basis of an appeal. A further ground of appeal in such cases is that the damages awarded were insufficient or excessive.

The Supreme Court may set aside the verdict and judgment and either order a re-trial by the High Court or substitute its own decision. A finding of fact by a jury will not be set aside simply because the Supreme Court would have reached a different conclusion. It must be shown that the jury's decision was not reasonably open to them on the evidence. In the case of an appeal against the judgment of a judge sitting alone, the appellant may ask the Supreme Court to reverse the original judgment and to make any order which the trial judge had power to make. Unlike the case of a judge sitting with a jury, the court may reverse a finding of fact if it prefers to substitute its own view of the evidence. In practice, however, the Supreme Court is always reluctant to disturb the trial judge's findings of fact.

[The next paragraph is 52.66]

K. CIVIL PROCEDURE—ENFORCEMENT

1. Enforcement of Irish judgments

Introduction. It is for the successful party to decide whether, and **52.66** if so how, to enforce the judgment. Judgments are enforceable as soon as they have been pronounced and entered in the records of the court. It is not necessary for the judgment to be served or for there to be any other demand for payment or compliance by the person against whom the judgment has been given.[20] The lodging of an appeal does not affect the enforceability of the judgment, but the judgment debtor may apply to the court for a stay of execution. After six years, a judgment may ordinarily only be enforced with the leave of the court.

[The next paragraph is number 52.68]

52.68 *Execution.* The court is involved in the process of execution, in that the orders for particular types of execution are obtained on the winning party's application to the court, and the court retains supervisory jurisdiction over the process of execution.[21]

The principal method of enforcing a money judgment is by means of a writ of *fieri facias*.[22] The successful party's solicitor prepares the writ in the prescribed form. He lodges it in the Central Office where it is checked against the original judgment in the court's records, and it is stamped with the court's seal. The writ is addressed to a public official, called a sheriff, and it directs him to seize the defendant's goods in satisfaction of the judgment. The validity of the writ expires after one year, but it is renewable.

Debts owed to the judgment debtor by a third party, such as a bank, may be attached by means of a "garnishee order." This orders the third party, known as the "garnishee," to show cause why he should not pay to the judgment creditor monies which he owes to the judgment debtor. If the garnishee does not then pay the money into court, the court may order execution to be levied against him. A further means of enforcement of a judgment is a charging order in respect of property, whether land (in which case it is called a judgment mortgage) or securities, owned by the debtor. If the debt is not satisfied, the court may order the sale of the property so as to satisfy the judgment debt. In cases in which it can be shown that the judgment debtor will be in receipt of funds in the future, the court may decide to appoint a "receiver by way of equitable execution." Such a person is then authorised to receive such payments and to hold them to the order of the court. As regards money judgments, the debtor may be summoned to court

---

[20] Service of a copy of the judgment is required before the defendant can be committed to prison for contempt of an order to do or to refrain from doing something. See para. 52.69 below.

[21] The Central Office of the High Court maintains a register of judgments in which money judgments may be registered by judgment creditors. Judgments so registered are published in Stubb's Gazette and other trade journals. This acts as a strong incentive on trading companies to prevent judgments being entered against them.

[22] This is a writ of execution, known as a *fi. fa.*

to be cross-examined as to his assets, and he may be ordered to produce all documents, such as bank statements, which may reveal his assets. The court can then order the debtor to discharge the debt by instalments. A refusal to pay any instalment may result in imprisonment. In addition, an attachment of earnings order may be made directing the debtor's employer to make regular deductions from his wages in satisfaction of the judgment. As a last resort, the debtor can be made bankrupt or, in the case of a company, be made subject to a winding up order.

Other methods of enforcement. Compliance with non-money judg-   **52.69**
ments may be enforced by a fine or imprisonment for contempt of court, provided a copy of the judgment, endorsed with a "penal notice" has been personally served on the defendant. In an appropriate case, the court can make an order for the judgment to be put into effect by the act of a court officer or other appropriate person (*e.g.*, by signing documents).

Opposing the execution. A person against whom execution is being carried out may apply to the court, on an *ex parte* basis in cases of urgency, for the execution to be stayed or for conditions to be attached to it. If ownership of goods against which execution is being levied is disputed by a third party, the sheriff may apply to the court by a procedure called "interpleader" for that issue to be resolved.

2. Authentic instruments and court settlements

Before the implementation of the 1968 Convention, Irish law did   **52.70**
not provide for the direct enforcement of instruments other than court orders and judgments. Similarly, settlements of proceedings were only enforceable by execution if their terms had been incorporated in an order or judgment of the court. Authentic instruments and court settlements originating from other Contracting States are, in principle, enforceable under the Convention, as Irish law equates them with judgments for the purposes of enforcement.

3. Enforcement of foreign judgments

Enforcement under the 1968 Convention. In cases to which the 1968   **52.71**
Convention applies, the foreign judgment is enforced by obtaining an order for its enforcement on an *ex parte* application to the Master of the High Court. The person against whom the judgment is given is then served with notice of enforcement together with a copy of the order. He may appeal to the High Court against it within a month of service, if he is domiciled in Ireland, or two months, if he is domiciled elsewhere. There is a further appeal, on a point of law only, to the Supreme Court. If the application for enforcement is

refused by the Master, the applicant may appeal to a judge of the High Court. A further appeal to the Supreme Court may be brought within 21 days. When an order for enforcement has been granted, the foreign judgment is treated for the purposes of its enforcement as if it were a judgment of the High Court, except that a foreign maintenance order is enforced in the District Court as if it were a maintenance order made under Irish law.

52.72   *Judgments outside the 1968 Convention.* In cases to which the 1968 Convention does not apply, Irish law does not provide any special procedure for the enforcement of foreign judgments, and Ireland is not a party to any other convention providing for the recognition or enforcement of foreign judgments in civil and commercial matters. A foreign money judgment which is final and conclusive and which was given by a court of competent jurisdiction is regarded as a cause of action in its own right, entitling the creditor to the sum for which he has obtained judgment. He can rely on this cause of action in fresh proceedings in the High Court, for which the simplified summary summons procedure is used. The defences to such an action are severely limited, namely that enforcement would be contrary to Irish public policy, that the judgment was obtained by fraud or in breach of the rules of natural justice, that the judgment is for sums due in respect of foreign taxes or penalties, or that the foreign court did not have jurisdiction. The last of these is the most important.

The rules by which Irish law determines whether a foreign court had competent jurisdiction are complicated. Generally, it will regard the foreign court as not having had jurisdiction if the defendant did not submit, or agree to submit, to the jurisdiction of the foreign court. If the defendant contests the proceedings brought on the foreign judgment, they will be heard by the judge. The judgment given in these proceedings is an Irish judgment and enforceable as such.[23] If an appeal is pending in the country of origin, the Irish proceedings will ordinarily be stayed. A plaintiff is not precluded by a foreign judgment from bringing fresh proceedings in Ireland in respect of the original cause of action.

L. LEGAL PERSONS

52.73   The most common form of legal person is a limited liability company, which is a corporate entity with the liability of its members being limited by shares. Such companies may be private companies or companies publicly quoted on the stock exchange (a "public" company or "PLC"). Other forms of legal person include bodies

---

[23] See para 25.35 above.

corporate (state owned), companies limited by guarantee, local authorities and corporations sole.

A partnership, commonly used for the practice of professions, does not have a legal personality distinct from that of its members, but the relationship between its members is regulated within a statutory framework and it may usually sue and be sued in the name of the firm. Its members are usually only natural persons, but legal persons may also enter into partnership with each other or with natural persons. An unincorporated association is an association of persons whose relationship with each other is regulated by the law of contract and which also has no legal personality of its own. It may not sue or be sued in its own name.

M. Legal Aid

Legal aid in civil matters has been available in Ireland since 1979 **52.74** under a scheme which covers both proceedings in court and legal advice. The scheme is administered by an independent Legal Aid Board which operates through a number of "law centres" throughout the country with full time legally qualified staff. All natural persons, including foreigners, are entitled to civil legal aid, subject to satisfying certain criteria. The applicant must not have a disposable income in excess of £5,500 per annum, and where litigation is involved, there must be reasonable grounds for bringing or defending the proceedings. The time taken to process an application for legal aid varies, but there is provision for the granting of immediate assistance in urgent cases. Depending on the applicant's means and the amount of work required to be undertaken, a financial contribution may be required from the legally aided party. If a legally aided party loses the case he is not protected against an order for costs in favour of the successful party. However, in an exceptional case, the Legal Aid Board may make an *ex gratia* payment towards the costs of the successful party. Certain matters are excluded from the scheme, such as disputes concerning land, conveyancing, and defamation.

Legal aid for the first stages of enforcing a foreign judgment is available under the terms of the 1968 Convention.[24]

---

[24] Art. 44, para. 28.81 above.

CHAPTER 53

ITALY

Written in collaboration with Avv. Nicoletta Portalupi, Avvocato, Milan.[1]

[1] Partner, *Gianni*, *Origoni*, *Tonucci*, Milan, Rome and New York.

Italy

A. THE LEGAL SYSTEM

1. Introduction

History and constitution. Italy became a unified kingdom in 1861 **53.01** and Rome was annexed to the Kingdom in 1870. Following a referendum on June 21, 1946, Italy became a republic and a constituent assembly adopted the present Constitution, which came into effect on January 1, 1948. The Constitution establishes the Republic as a parliamentary democracy and it guarantees fundamental civil, economic and political rights; it defines the respective powers and functions of the President of the Republic, the Parliament and the government, it regulates the operation of regions and other local levels of administration and it governs the promulgation of laws. Italy is governed by a central administration, but many administrative and legislative functions are devolved into regions, provinces and municipalities. There are 20 regions, five of which have greater autonomy.

Origins of the legal system. Italian law has its origins in Roman law. It evolved over the centuries until in 1865, following the unification of Italy, a civil code, a commercial code and a code of civil procedure were adopted, modelled to a large extent on their French counterparts. In 1942 the civil code and commercial code were replaced by the current *Codice Civile* and in the same year a new code of civil procedure was introduced.

2. The administration of justice

Public and private law. There is a fundamental division in the Ita- **53.02** lian legal system between public law and private law. Generally speaking, public law governs the organisation and the activities of the state and of all public bodies and it includes such topics as constitutional law, administrative law, tax law and criminal law. Private law governs the relations between private natural or legal persons and it covers such areas as contract law, commercial law, succession and family law. In certain circumstances the activities of public bodies will be subject to private law. There is now no separate body of commercial law nor are there separate commercial courts.

Court system. The court system reflects the division between public and private law. Ordinary civil litigation is dealt with by the civil courts: *conciliatore, pretore, tribunale, corte d'appello,* and *Corte Suprema di Cassazione.*[2] These courts (except the *conciliatore*) also

---

[2] The system of civil courts is described in more detail at paras. 53.18 *et seq.* below.

exercise criminal jurisdiction and some criminal cases may also
come before the *corte d'assise* and the *corte d'assise d'appello*. Disputes governed by administrative law are heard, depending on their
nature, either by the civil courts or by the administrative courts: *tribunale amministrativo regionale*, *Consiglio di Stato*, *corte dei conti*. Tax
matters are determined by the *commissione tributaria*, or by criminal
courts if criminal infringements are involved.

B. LEGAL PRACTITIONERS

1. The *Avvocato*

53.03   The profession of *avvocato* is regulated by law. An *avvocato* acts
as an advocate presenting cases in court and as an adviser to his
clients in all legal matters.

Legal education and qualification. The intending lawyer must first
read law at university and obtain the degree of *Dottore in Giurisprudenza*. He must then seek admission as a *praticante* to the bar of the
tribunale[3] for the locality in which he will practice. Initially he must
work as a *praticante* or apprentice for two years, after which he takes
a bar examination set under the supervision of the local *corte d'appello*. On passing this examination he is admitted as a *procuratore*.
After six years practice as a *procuratore* he is eligible to become an
avvocato. This six year period may be reduced to a minimum of two
years by taking a special examination held yearly in Rome at the
Ministry of Justice.

53.04   *Rights of representation and audience.* A *praticante* may appear
before the two lowest courts, the *conciliatore* and the *pretore*. In civil
cases a *procuratore* may appear in the *corte d'appello* where he is
admitted, and in any other court in the same district.[4] An *avvocato*
may appear before any court in Italy with the exception of the *Corte
di Cassazione*. Rights of audience before this latter court are limited
to those *avvocati* who have been enrolled at the court. Application
for enrollment may be made after eight years' practice as an *avvocato*. *Avvocati* and *procuratori* enjoy a monopoly with regard to
rights of audience. This does not extend to the giving of legal
advice. Any person may give legal advice and charge for his services
provided he does not hold himself out as having a qualification
which he does not possess.

Organisation of practice. Partnerships are permitted and in recent
decades substantial law firms have grown up in the major cities. In
addition to the partners, a law firm will generally have one or more

---

[3] See para. 53.20 below.
[4] There are 23 districts in Italy, each served by a *corte d'appello*.

qualified *avvocati* or *procuratori* as associates. Cost sharing arrangements falling short of full partnerships are also common. Legal work is not undertaken by unqualified staff.

Fees. A tariff of fees is published by the *Consiglio Nazionale* **53.05**
Forense. The fees of a *praticante*, according to the above tariff, are 25 per cent. of the fees of an *avvocato* and the fees of a *procuratore* are 50 per cent. of the fees of an *avvocato*. When a different basis of remuneration is agreed between client and lawyer, as on a time rate, these distinctions will not necessarily be applied; but if the fees have to be assessed by the local *Consiglio dell'Ordine*, any such agreement will be disregarded and the fees will be assessed according to the tariff. Contingent fees are forbidden. Disputes as to fees are referred to the local professional body, the *Consiglio dell'Ordine*.

Professional organisation and conduct. The profession of *avvocato* is organised on the basis of local bars, there being a separate bar for each district served by a *corte d'appello*. Each bar is governed by a council, the *Consiglio dell'Ordine*, the main functions of which are to keep a list of the lawyers entitled to practice in its district, to assess the level of unpaid fees, to settle disputes as between lawyers and between lawyers and their clients, and to exercise disciplinary functions over *avvocati* and *procuratori* in its district. Its decisions are subject to review by the *Consiglio Nazionale Forense*, a body elected by those *avvocati* who are admitted to plead before the *Corte di Cassazione*. Each bar publishes a list in book form of the names and addresses of its members.

Practice as an *avvocato* is incompatible with several specified occupations, such as notary, journalist, broker, and public employee. It is not incompatible with academic employment and many university professors engage in private legal practice. Professional indemnity insurance is not compulsory. *Avvocati* and *procuratori* are bound by a strict rule of professional secrecy and they cannot be compelled to reveal confidential information which they have acquired while acting for their clients.

[The next paragraph is number 53.09]

2. The *Notaio*

The notary (*notaio*) is a publicly appointed, but independent, **53.09**
professional person, whose main functions are to authenticate deeds and wills, to keep them in safe custody, and to release copies, certificates and extracts. Many common legal transactions, such as the transfer and mortgaging of real property, the execution of deeds of gift and the formation of companies, require the assistance of a notary. The notary is obliged to keep a record of all instruments

drawn before and acknowledged by him, and to keep the originals of all deeds drawn by him. His fees are fixed by law. Each notary carries on his profession within a particular district (*Collegio Notarile*). The intending notary must hold a law degree and then serve for two years as a *praticante* in a notary's office, after which he takes a competitive examination. A successful candidate can only be appointed to a district as and when a vacancy occurs.

[The next paragraph is number 53.11]

3. Foreign lawyers

53.11   Lawyers who are nationals of member states of the EEC may become established in Italy either in association with Italian lawyers or independently, under the terms of the EEC Legal Services Directive.[5] They may give legal advice on their own national law and may appear in Italian courts in conjunction with an Italian lawyer. A foreign lawyer from a non-EEC country may only give advice on the law of his own country and may not appear in court or describe himself as "*avvocato.*"

4. Lawyers in business and public employment

53.12   *Avvocati* who become employed in the legal departments of commercial enterprises may no longer retain their membership of the bar, although they are permitted to describe themselves as *avvocati*. Their legal work is restricted to in-house work for their employers and they may not appear in court. *Avvocati* in the employment of certain public entities such as the state, provinces, municipal authorities and state enterprises must be enrolled in a special bar. They may appear in court, but only on behalf of their employers.

[The next paragraph is number 53.14]

C. Sources of Law

1. Introduction

53.14   This section deals not only with the formal sources of Italian law but also with Italian legal material in general. The formal sources of Italian law are set out in Article 1 of the introductory provisions of the *Codice Civile*; but there are also a number of informal sources.

International treaties have binding force only when they have been incorporated into domestic law by legislation.

---

[5] See para. A2.47 below.

2. Formal sources

Statutes. Statutes (*leggi*) are formal legislation and comprise, in   **53.15**
descending order of precedence, the Constitution itself, state laws
and regional laws. State laws include the five main statutory codes,
namely the *Codice Civile, Codice di Procedura Civile, Codice Penale,
Codice di Procedura Penale*, and the *Codice della Navigazione*, which
contain the main provisions of substantive and procedural law. Certain other specific areas of law have been consolidated in unified
texts. All remaining topics of statute law are the subject of individual statutes. Regional laws, passed by regional assemblies (*consigli
regionali*), cover a wide range of topics of regional or local interest.

Regulations. Regulations (*regolamenti*) are made by the government or by the authority to which the power to make the regulation
is delegated in any specific case.

Custom. The term *usi* refers to custom, which is generally defined
as the uniform behaviour of a plurality of citizens, acting in the
belief that that behaviour is required by law.

Priority of sources. A state law may not be contrary to the Constitution, which can only be amended by a constitutional law. A
regional law must be confined within the limits of the fundamental
principles established by state laws. A regulation is invalid if it is
contrary to a state law or a regional law. In matters governed by
laws and regulations, custom is valid as law only if there is express
provision permitting reliance on it.

3. Informal sources

Jurisprudence. Decided cases, known as *giurisprudenza*, are not   **53.16**
formally recognised as a source of law and there is no doctrine of
binding precedent. In practice they may have considerable authority, depending upon the level of the deciding court. Judicial precedents have played an important part in the development of
certain fields of law such as labour law and industrial law.

Doctrine. The writings of legal scholars (*dottrina*) may have considerable persuasive authority in a given case; and *travaux préparatoires* and official reports may occasionally be referred to as an
ancillary aid to interpretation.

4. Publications

Legislation is published officially in the *Gazzetta Ufficiale della*   **53.17**
Repubblica Italiana and in the *Raccolta delle Leggi e Decreti della
Repubblica d'Italia*. The statutory codes are published in various
private editions, with commentaries and case references. There are

no official law reports except in respect of the judgments of the Constitutional Court, which are published in the *Gazzetta Ufficiale della Repubblica Italiana*. There are numerous private series of reports, of which the following are the most authoritative:

(a) *Giurisprudenza Italiana* (Giur.It.), civil law;
(b) *Il Foro Italiano* (Foro It.), civil law;
(c) *Giustizia Civile* (Giust.Civ.), civil law;
(d) *Rivista Trimestrale di Diritto e Procedura Civile* (Riv.Trim. Dir.Proc.Civ.), civil procedure;
(e) *Rivista del Diritto Commerciale* (Riv.Dir.Comm.), commercial law;
(f) *Rivista di Diritto Industriale* (Riv.Dir.Ind.), industrial law;
(g) *Rivista di Diritto Internazionale* (Riv.Dir.Int.), international law;
(h) *Rivista di Diritto Internazionale Privato e Processuale* (Riv. Dir.Int.Priv.Proc.), private international law.

D. ORGANISATION OF THE CIVIL COURTS

1. Introduction

53.18   The ordinary civil courts of first instance are, in ascending order, those of the *conciliatore*, the *pretore*, and the *tribunale*. Above these are the *corte d'appello* and the *Corte di Cassazione*. A single appeal on fact or law can be made from the decision of a court of first instance to the next superior court. Appeals from the *tribunale* lie to the appropriate *corte d'appello*. An appeal on a point of law only can be referred to the *Corte di Cassazione* from a *corte d'appello*, and, in certain instances, from lower courts.

2. The *conciliatore*

53.19   The *conciliatore* exercises limited civil jurisdiction in a court located in each commune. He can decide matters concerning movables up to a value of L. 1,000,000. He may very well have no legal training and he is unpaid. The procedure of his court, though following that of the superior courts, is necessarily fairly informal.

3. The *pretore*

The *pretore* exercises limited jurisdiction over an area known as a *mandamento* comprising several municipalities. There are some 900 *preture* in Italy. The court is staffed by full-time *pretori* who sit singly in separate chambers. The *pretore* can decide all matters which exceed the competence of the *conciliatore* up to a value of L. 5,000,000. He has jurisdiction not limited as to value in various cases including possession actions, labour and social security cases,

provisional remedies and urgent cases under Article 700 of the
Codice di Procedura Civile.[6]

4. The *tribunale*

The *tribunale* is the superior court of first instance for an area **53.20**
known as a *circondario* and is located in the principal town or city in
the area. There are some 160 *tribunali* in Italy. They are staffed by
full-time judges who sit in benches of three, except when one of the
judges is acting, in the course of proceedings, as an examining
judge. The *tribunale* has jurisdiction in all cases which exceed the
competence of the *pretore* and exclusive jurisdiction over, for
example, fiscal matters, and matters of status and capacity.

5. The *corte d'appello*

The *corte d'appello* is the second instance court for an area, called **53.21**
a *distretto*, which normally comprises one Region of the country.
Some Regions, Lombardia, Puglia, and Sicilia, have more than one
corte d'appello. Its judges, called *Consiglieri*, hear appeals from the
tribunali located in its *distretto*. It also has original jurisdiction in
matters concerning the recognition and enforcement of foreign
judgments.

6. The *Corte di Cassazione*

The *Corte di Cassazione*, the highest civil court, is situated in **53.22**
Rome and sits in sections of five judges (simple sections) or nine
judges (united sections) and it hears appeals from inferior courts on
points of law only.

7. The *Corte Costituzionale*

The *Corte Costituzionale*, which also sits in Rome, is not regarded
as part of the system of civil courts. It is concerned with the constitutionality of laws and with conflicts of jurisdiction between the
powers of the state and of the regions.

8. The judiciary and the *pubblico ministero*

The Italian judiciary is made up of career judges. Entry to the **53.23**
judicial service is by competitive examination and is open to Italian
citizens between the ages of 21 and 30 who hold a university law
degree. Successful candidates are appointed *uditori giudiziari* and
their undergo a two year period of training in various courts and
official departments. After this they are appointed judges on the

---

[6] See para. 53.61 below.

recommendation of the *Consiglio Superiore della Magistratura*. A state prosecutor (*pubblico ministero*) is also regarded as a member of the judiciary, and his functions in civil proceedings include the right to intervene, in cases provided for by law, to represent the public interest.

E. Jurisdiction of the Civil Courts

1. Introduction

53.24   *Jurisdiction and competence.* The international jurisdiction (*giurisdizione*) of the Italian courts is established, for disputes falling within the scope of the 1968 Convention, by the relevant Articles of that Convention. For disputes which do not fall within the scope of the 1968 Convention, it is established (subject to the provisions of other international conventions) by Articles 2 and 4 of the *Codice di Procedura Civile*, described below. The adjudicatory jurisdiction, or competence (*competenza*), of Italian courts, which determines the specific Italian court before which proceedings may be brought, is determined according to three factors: subject matter, value and territory.

Subject matter and value. The subject matter and value of a claim will determine the level of court in which proceedings must be brought. The value is taken at the commencement of the proceedings and it includes interest and costs.[7] There are some circumstances in which a court may determine a matter with a value exceeding its jurisdictional limit, for example when no value is given at the outset and the defendant does not challenge the jurisdiction of the court as to value in his first defensive pleading.

Territorial factors. A range of territorial factors, summarised below, determine in which particular court of a given level the proceedings must be brought. The general rule is that a defendant may be sued in the court for the place where he is resident or domiciled or where, being a legal person, it has its seat.

2. Domicile and seat

53.25   *Natural persons.* The concepts of domicile, residence and abode are to be determined according to Italian civil law. A person's residence is where he has his habitual abode and is usually identified by referring to the population register kept by the municipality, although it may be ascertained by other evidence or by presumptions. A person may not rely against a third party on the transfer of

---

[7] Costs are calculated, for this purpose, according to the professional tariff: see para. 53.57 below.

his residence unless that transfer has been completed by registration of the residence in the new locality. There is a legal presumption that a transfer of residence also has effect as a transfer of domicile.

A natural person's domicile is the place where he or she has established the seat of his business or other interests. It is determined by reference not only to the person's economic and ownership interests, but also his or her social and family interests. Except as regards an elective domicile, a person may have only one domicile. There are statutory domiciles for minors (at the residence of the family or guardian) and mental patients (at the guardian's domicile).

A person's abode is where he or she can actually be found when service is to be effected.

Legal persons. The domicile of a legal person is the place where it **53.26**
has its registered office (*sede*). Partnerships and unincorporated bodies are deemed to have their *sede* in the place where they carry on their activities. If the location of a company's registered office is different from the place where it has its effective headquarters (that is, the place where its goods and premises are located and where the managerial, administrative and productive or commercial activities are principally performed), then this latter place may also be considered as the company's seat for the purposes of civil jurisdiction.

Italian law contains no specific provision concerning international conflicts of law on the question of the status (and consequently the seat) of a legal person and various theories have been propounded by legal writers. The most authoritative appears to be that which regards the national law of the company as determining its status. Under this theory, the Italian law described above applies to determine the domicile of a company with Italian "nationality," and a company is regarded as having Italian nationality if it falls within Articles 2505 and 2509 of the *Codice Civile*. Under these Articles a company is regarded as being of Italian nationality *either* if it is formed abroad but has the seat of its administration or principal object of its business in Italy, *or* if it is formed in Italy but has the seat of its administration or principal object of its business abroad.

The *Codice Civile* also provides that foreign legal persons which have a registered branch office in Italy are subject to the provisions of Italian law on the operation of enterprises as regards that branch office. Italian courts have held that that provision, and Article 77 of the *Codice di Procedura Civile*, are the provisions of Italian law to which Article 53 of the 1968 Convention[8] refers where the case con-

---

[8] See para. 31.23 above.

cerns a foreign company with a general representative in Italy, such as a branch office. In the absence of a contrary provision in the terms of his appointment, that representative will be presumed to have been given the power to represent the company in court.

3. Competence—general rule

53.27   It is a general rule of *competenza* that a case must be brought in the court for the locality in which the defendant, being a legal person, has its seat or, being a natural person, has his residence or domicile. If these are unknown, the action may be brought in the court for the place where the defendant has his abode, or, if even this is unknown, it may be brought in the place where the plaintiff resides.

4. Competence—other territorial factors

53.28   There are additional rules of territorial competence which in some cases provide an optional forum and in other cases provide an exclusive compulsory forum. Thus in cases involving obligations, the court for the place in which an obligation arose or has to be performed may be competent in addition to the court of the defendant's domicile.

A contractual obligation is deemed to have arisen in the place where the contract was entered into; an obligation in tort is deemed to have arisen in the place where the harmful event occurred. There are various rules which, depending on the type of obligation involved and in the absence of agreement by the parties, define the place of performance of an obligation. An obligation to pay money is generally to be performed at the domicile of the creditor at the time when the obligation has to be fulfilled, and the obligation to pay the price in a contract of sale is to be performed at the vendor's domicile. An obligation to deliver specific goods is to be performed in the place where the goods were located when the obligation arose.[9]

Mandatory rules. There are certain mandatory rules of competence. For example, cases involving rights in property have to be brought in the court for the place where the property is located; inheritance cases have to be brought in the court for the place where

---

[9] As regards obligations arising in international sales of goods, the place of performance may be determined by the Uniform Law on the International Sale of Goods (Hague Convention of July 1, 1964), or the U.N. Convention on Contracts for the International Sale of Goods (Vienna Convention of April 11, 1980) both of which have been enacted into Italian law: see para. 17.14, n. 47 above Art. 59 of the 1964 convention, for example, determines the place of performance of the obligation to pay the price of the goods.

the deceased was residing at the time of his death; company and partnership disputes must be brought in the court for the place where the registered office or the business is located; and applications for attachment (*sequestro*)[10] must be made in the court having jurisdiction over the main proceedings or in the court for the place in which the goods to be attached are located.

5. Choice of court and entry of appearance

A person may elect a domicile for the purpose of civil proceedings by nominating in writing an address for service, and parties may generally derogate from the territorial competence of the courts by agreeing in writing on an alternative forum. In some cases of mandatory forums, however, the law does not permit a departure from the rules of territorial competence.

53.29

6. Exorbitant grounds of jurisdiction

In cases to which the 1968 Convention does not apply, and subject to the provisions of other conventions, the international jurisdiction of the Italian courts is determined by Articles 2 and 4 of the *Codice di Procedura Civile.*[11] Article 2 provides that the jurisdiction of Italian courts and arbitrators cannot be waived by agreement in favour of foreign jurisdictions except in respect of obligations arising between foreigners, or between foreign and Italian nationals who are neither resident nor domiciled in Italy, except as otherwise provided by international treaties. Article 4 provides that a foreign national may be summoned before an Italian court if, *inter alia,*

53.30

(1) he is resident or domiciled in Italy or has a representative who is specifically authorised to appear in court, or who has a general power of attorney, or who has accepted Italian jurisdiction, unless the claim concerns real property located outside Italy;
(2) the dispute concerns property located in Italy or inheritances of an Italian national or obligations arising or to be performed in Italy;
(3) the dispute is connected with a dispute pending before an Italian court or concerns protective measures to be executed in Italy;
(4) the courts of the foreign national's own country would have jurisdiction over an Italian national in the reciprocal case.

---

[10] See para. 53.59 below.
[11] Reliance on these Articles is expressly excluded by Art. 3 of the 1968 Convention as against persons domiciled in a Contracting State: para. 16.09 above.

7. Civil claims in criminal proceedings

53.31 Any person who has suffered loss as the result of a criminal act has the option of suing the wrongdoer in a civil court or of joining in the criminal proceedings as a civil party (*costituzione di parte civile*), whether or not he is otherwise a party to the criminal proceedings. A party who joins in criminal proceedings as a *parte civile* thereby waives his right to pursue civil proceedings, even if those are already pending. The judge seised of the criminal proceedings decides the claim for restitution or damages and, if assessment of the quantum of the claim would involve an excessively complex investigation, he may determine the party's entitlement to restitution or damages and remit the assessment to the civil judge. If the defendant to the criminal proceedings is acquitted, the judge may not make an order for restitution or damages against him, even if his civil liability is evident, although in some such cases the *parte civile* is not then precluded from pursuing a civil claim. If separate civil proceedings are being pursued in respect of damage caused by a crime, those proceedings are stayed pending the outcome of the criminal proceedings.

F. LIMITATION PERIODS

53.32 The law of limitation is complex and the following should be taken only as a most general guide.

The limitation period starts when the right which is subject to limitation could first have been asserted, but it may thereafter be suspended or interrupted, in the circumstances specified by law. If an event occurs which suspends the limitation period, the running of time resumes when that event ceases to operate,[12] and the time which elapsed before the suspension occurred is taken into account in determining the date on which the limitation period expires. On the other hand, if the limitation period is interrupted by some event (such as a creditor making a written demand for payment from his debtor), the limitation period starts afresh.

53.33 The ordinary limitation period is 10 years. Rights in real property are subject to a limitation period of 20 years. Claims for damages for tort are subject to a five year period, except for claims arising out of road traffic accidents, which are subject to a two year period. Actions by employees and teachers and claims for the payment of fees for professional services are subject to a three year period, as are actions on promissory notes. Actions to recover

---

[12] Grounds of suspension operate as between the parties by reason of their relationship (such as husband and wife, or guardian and minor), for as long as that relationship lasts.

brokers' commission, and actions against forwarders and carriers in respect of carriage within Europe must be brought within one year. If the carriage started or finished outside Europe the period is 18 months. Claims in respect of defects in goods sold must, in the absence of agreement to the contrary, be notified to the seller within eight days of discovery, and proceedings must be brought within one year from delivery.

G. CIVIL PROCEDURE—PROCEEDINGS UP TO JUDGMENT

1. General description

Civil procedure is governed principally by the *Codice di Proce-* **53.34** *dura Civile* and also by certain provisions of the *Codice Civile* and by other legislation.

A civil action in an Italian court has three stages, the introductory stage (*fase introduttiva*), the proof-taking stage (*fase istruttoria*) and the stage leading to the judgment (*fase decisoria*). In the introductory stage the action is commenced by service of the summons, the case is listed in the court calendar, an examining judge is appointed, and the defendant's defence is filed. The proof-taking stage begins, unless certain preliminary defences are raised, after the appearance of the parties before the examining judge. The case then develops before the examining judge during successive hearings at which evidence is given and written pleadings dealing with both fact and law are exchanged between the parties. In the stage leading to the judgment the lawyers present their final arguments, the examining judge reports to the full panel of the court, of which he is also a member, and the court then adjourns to reach its decision, which is published later.

The above description applies to proceedings in the *tribunale* and before the *pretura*, except that in the latter proceedings the *pretore* sits alone. He therefore conducts the proof-taking stage himself as examining judge and the stage leading to judgment is simplified by there being no need for him to report to the full court. A similar procedure is adopted before the *conciliatore*. Proceedings before the *corte d'appello* and the *Corte di Cassazione* are described below.

2. Parties and legal representation

In proceedings at first instance the respective parties are called **53.35** the *attore* (plaintiff) and the *convenuto* (defendant). All natural and legal persons[13] who have an interest to protect or to assert may initiate civil proceedings. Persons under a disability must appear by their legal guardian or other representatives. Legal entities and

---

[13] The various forms of legal person are listed in para. 53.73 below.

unincorporated bodies must be represented as laid down by law and provided by their internal rules. The making of counterclaims and the participation of third parties in proceedings is described below.[14]

53.36 *Legal representation.* Representation in court by a lawyer is compulsory except in proceedings before the *conciliatore* and in some proceedings before the *pretore*. An *avvocato* can conduct proceedings anywhere in Italy, but many procedural steps require to be taken by a *procuratore* enrolled at the bar of the locality in which the proceedings have been brought. If the *avvocato* conducting the case is not so enrolled a local *procuratore* has to be instructed in addition.

3. Commencement of proceedings

53.37 Proceedings are normally started by the service of an *atto di citazione* (*citazione*) or, in the case of certain proceedings, by the filing of a *ricorso* (petition), with the court.

The *citazione* is drafted by the plaintiff's lawyer on stamped paper. It must contain the following information: the name of the court; the names of the parties and of the plaintiff's lawyers; a statement of the facts and law giving rise to the claim; a summary of the evidence by which the facts will be proved (or the reservation that such evidence will be disclosed later); and a formal summons inviting the defendant to enter an appearance within the time set by law and to attend before the examining judge on a given day. The date is chosen by the plaintiff's lawyer from the court calendar, but it may be postponed by the court. The *citazione* must be signed by the plaintiff's lawyer, or by the plaintiff himself in the limited cases in which he is permitted to act in person.

The *citazione*, together with a copy, is taken to the *ufficiale giudiziario* (court process server), for service on the defendant. The moment of service on the defendant is considered to be the moment at which the proceedings are deemed to have commenced.

4. Service of proceedings

53.38 The *Codice di Procedura Civile* contains detailed rules as to the service of the *citazione* and other judicial documents. Service of such documents must be effected by the *ufficiale giudiziario*,[15] who may serve them in a number of ways. First he may do so by per-

---

[14] See para. 53.43.

[15] The *ufficiale giudiziario* is an employee of the Ministry of Justice charged with certain functions concerning, in particular, the service of proceedings and orders and the execution of judgments, orders and decrees. Except in the smaller courts, the *ufficiale giudiziario* will be assisted by an *aiutante ufficiale giudiziario*, to whom the functions of service are delegated.

sonal service directly on the defendant. If the defendant refuses to accept the document there is deemed to have been personal service and the circumstances of the refusal will be referred to in a report to the plaintiff by the *ufficiale giudiziario*. Alternatively the *citazione* may be handed to a member of the defendant's household at his home or to the caretaker or to a neighbour at his home or his place of work. The recipient must sign a receipt and the *ufficiale giudiziario* must send a copy of the document to the defendant by post. If service cannot be effected on any of the above persons the document may be posted to the town hall for the defendant's locality, but an advice of the posting must be fixed to the door of the defendant's home or his place of work, and a further advice must be sent to him by registered post, return receipt requested. When service is to be made outside the *comune* of the *ufficiale giudiziario* he will effect service by sending the *citazione* to the defendant by registered post, return receipt requested. Exceptionally the court may authorise service to be effected by telex or by telegram.

If service is required on a person or body outside Italy the procedure provided for by the Hague Service Convention will be followed in appropriate cases.[16] Otherwise the procedure is that a copy of the document must be sent to the defendant through diplomatic channels, another must be sent by registered post, and a third copy must be fixed to the notice board of the court.

Failure to comply with any of the above requirements will render the service defective, but this will be cured if the defendant appears without challenging the service or if it can be shown that he had actual notice of the proceedings in due time.

A *citazione* must be served on the defendant and received by him a certain length of time before the day fixed for the first hearing. The length of this period will depend on the place at which service is effected. The periods are as follows: in the *circondario* of the *tribunale*, 30 days; in the *distretto* of the *corte d'appello*, 40 days; elsewhere in Italy, 60 days; elsewhere in Europe in the Mediterranean area, 90 days; elsewhere in the world, 180 days.

The document served on the defendant is a copy of the *citazione*. The original is returned by the *ufficiale giudiziario* to the plaintiff with an endorsement stating to whom, when and where service was effected. The plaintiff must then within 10 days of service[17] lodge the *citazione*, together with a file containing any documents which are relevant to the claim, at the appropriate office of the court (*ufficio iscrizioni a ruolo*), for enrolling in the records of the court. The

---

[16] See paras. 4.30 *et seq.* above and A2.03 below.
[17] In proceedings before the *pretore*, this can be done on the day fixed for the hearing.

president of the court then assigns the case to a section of the court, and the president of that section assigns it to an examining judge.

5. Appearance by the defendant

53.39   The defendant must, not later than the day of the first hearing, enter an appearance at the court by lodging a file which contains the copy of the *citazione* which was served on him, the original of his defence (*comparsa di risposta*) with a copy for the plaintiff, any supporting documentary evidence, and his lawyer's power of attorney, unless this is affixed to the *comparsa di risposta*.

6. Default of appearance

53.40   Failure by both parties to appear at the first hearing will result in the adjournment of the hearing to a later date. If neither party appears at the subsequent hearing, the case is struck out from the court list. If the plaintiff fails to appear at the first hearing, unless the defendant requests the court to order the next stage, the proceedings will be adjourned as above. If the defendant, though properly served, fails to appear at the first hearing, he will be declared to be in default. The court will satisfy itself that service has been properly effected by referring to the indorsement (called the *relazione di notifica*) made by the *ufficiale giudiziario* on the *citazione*, or by the relevant certificate under the Hague Service Convention.[18]

The defendant can appear subsequently at any time until the hearing for the final statement of claims but, unless the court otherwise orders, cannot then take procedural steps which he should have taken at any earlier stage. The consequence of this is that he loses the opportunity of raising certain defences which can only be raised at the first hearing, such as lack of jurisdiction and *lis alibi pendens*, and he cannot reopen stages of the procedure which have taken place before he appears.

53.41   The defendant may apply to have some or all of the rights restored to him which he would have had if he had duly appeared at an earlier stage. The court may grant such an application if the defendant shows *either* that the service was a nullity or that there was some impediment which prevented him having knowledge of the proceedings, *or* that his appearance was prevented for some reason without fault on his part. The court has a discretion whether or not to grant the application, but will not take into account the strength or weakness of the defendant's defence on the merits.

---

[18] Art. 6 of the Hague Service Convention: see paras. 4.33 above and A2.06 below.

7. Disputes as to jurisdiction

The defendant may appear for the sole purpose of challenging the **53.42** international jurisdiction of the Italian court, that is, to contend that the dispute is not amenable to the jurisdiction of the Italian courts generally, but he must raise the relevant exception in his first defensive pleading.[19] The judge may either postpone the decision on jurisdiction until the determination of the merits of the case, or refer the issue to the full bench for decision by way of interlocutory judgment. The decision of the bench can be appealed to the next superior court and, thence, in accordance with general rules relating to appeals, to the *Corte di Cassazione*. It is also possible, before the court of first instance has ruled on the case as to its merits, to apply to the *Corte di Cassazione*, (by means of a special procedure known as *regolamento preventivo di giurisdizione*), for a direct ruling on the question of jurisdiction.

As far as the local jurisdiction of the Italian courts is concerned, objections to the court's territorial competence (when this is capable of being agreed by the parties) must be made at the outset of the proceedings. Objections to its competence in respect of the subject matter of the proceedings, or its value, or in respect of territorial matters (when not capable of being agreed by the parties) may be made at any time before the judgment has become *res judicata*.

8. Pleadings

The form and content of the plaintiff's *citazione* have already **53.43** been described. The defendant's *comparsa di risposta* (defence) must contain the same material and it must set out the defendant's case in corresponding fashion. Any counterclaim or claim for a set-off must be included in this document. If the defendant wishes to add a third party he can serve a further pleading on the third party in the form of a *citazione per chiamata in causa* and the same procedure applies to this as to the main proceedings. A third party may also intervene in proceedings of his own volition by serving on the main parties a document in the form of a *comparsa di intervento*. After the appearance in court of each party all subsequent pleadings and notices must be served on the lawyers acting for the respective parties.

As the proceedings progress through the proof-taking stage, des- **53.44** cribed below, the judge may authorise the exchange of further pleadings called *memorie istruttorie* in which the parties comment on the evidence. At the end of the proof-taking stage, parties file their *comparse conclusionali* (closing pleadings) which summarise their

---

[19] This will usually be the *comparsa di costituzione e risposta* which will also include a defence on the merits; if it does not do so, and the challenge to the jurisdiction is not successful, the defendant may *not* subsequently plead to the merits.

submissions in the light of the evidence which has been given. Each party may file replies (*memorie di replica*) to the arguments set out in the *comparsa conclusionale*.

9. The hearings

53.45   The first hearing is held before the *giudice istruttore* (examining judge). The purpose of this hearing is for the defendant to appear and file his *comparsa di risposta* and for the judge to consider whether the *citazione* and the *comparsa di risposta* are in order. In practice, the plaintiff will usually apply for and obtain a period within which to file his reply to the *comparsa di risposta*. At this, or at a subsequent hearing, the court decides whether evidence or further evidence is required and, if so, directs the manner in which it is to be obtained. Challenges in respect of the jurisdiction or competence of the court are dealt with as described above. If the case is ready for final consideration the judge will fix the hearing for the final statement of claims (*udienza di precisazione delle conclusioni*).

53.46   If the taking of evidence is necessary, the proceedings move into the *fase istruttoria*, or proof-taking stage, which begins when the examining judge gives directions as to the taking of the evidence. As has been seen, each party must provide evidence to support and establish his case and will have indicated the relevant evidence in his pleadings. The directions may be given at the first hearing if the parties are ready, but the plaintiff may ask for time for consideration of the defence, in which case the judge will give his directions at the next hearing. There will then follow one or more hearings at which evidence is given,[20] before final pleadings are exchanged and the proceedings move into the *fase decisoria*.

53.47   At the conclusion of the proof-taking stage, or if there is a preliminary procedural or substantive issue which may be decisive, the judge will fix a date for the hearing at which the parties submit their statements of conclusions before him.[21] At this hearing, he will fix a date for the final hearing before the full bench. The bench includes the examining judge, who gives a brief summary of the case and indicates the points that require to be decided. In the majority of cases the parties then will simply request that the case be sent for decision. A full argument at this stage is rare. The judges will then deliberate in closed session to reach their judgment. The judgment is not announced in open court,[22] but it is deposited at the court office.

---

[20] See para. 53.49 below.
[21] This hearing is called the *udienza di precisazione delle conclusioni*.
[22] See para. 53.56 below. In employment cases, the decision, but not the reasons, is announced in open court.

10. Security for costs

There is no provision under Italian law for the ordering of security for costs. **53.48**

11. Witnesses and oral evidence

By contrast with the practice in some other legal systems, civil proceedings in Italy frequently involve the taking of oral evidence. **53.49**

Proof-taking. The witnesses are named in the pleadings as being able to prove specific facts asserted in detailed articles of evidence (*capitoli di prova*). These are drafted by the lawyer in the form of interrogatories. They may either form part of the *citazione* or be contained in a separate document. Neither the lawyers not the parties are supposed to interview the witness beforehand. When either party submits articles of evidence it is for the other party to state, in his next pleading, whether he accepts the evidence tendered, and if not, whether he wishes to call witnesses in rebuttal. In the latter case he must identify the witnesses and submit articles of evidence in respect of their testimony. The judge will evaluate the grounds of non-acceptance raised by the opponent and decide whether a witness is to attend to give evidence and as to the admissibility of the questions formulated in the articles. For instance an article of evidence expressing the personal opinion of a witness will not be admitted.

When the judge orders that the evidence of a witness is to be adduced, the party calling the witness must serve him with a summons at least three days before the hearing. If a witness has been served with a summons to attend the hearing but he does not do so the judge may compel his attendance and may fine him for his non-appearance. A witness-summons is served by the *ufficiale giudiziario*.

The witness is examined on oath by the judge at a special hearing held for the purpose. The examination takes place in the presence of the lawyers but not in the presence of any other witnesses. The lawyers may indicate to the judge additional questions to be put which may be consequential to the answers given by the witness, but they may not ask questions which depart from the issues set out in the articles of evidence. The witness must answer without the help of written notes and his evidence, usually in summary form, is dictated by the judge to the clerk of the court and is recorded by him in the minutes of the proceedings (*processo verbale*), which are signed by the witness. There is no formal rule against the giving of hearsay evidence but it carries little weight.

Restrictions on oral evidence. Oral evidence is not admitted in certain circumstances. It cannot be given as to the contents of any document for which writing is required by law. In addition oral evidence may not be accepted as proof of any contract or payment of a value exceeding L. 5,000, but the judge has a wide discretion to admit such evidence if the nature of the contract or of the other circumstances are such that the existence of documentary evidence is unlikely. Evidence by witnesses is always admitted when there is partial written evidence, or when the party requested to provide evidence is not reasonably able to do so, or when the document has been lost without the negligence of the party on whom the burden of proof lies.

Affidavits. Affidavits are not ordinarily used except in proceedings concerned with personal status and succession. Evidential material from abroad may be in the form of an affidavit and it may be freely evaluated and taken into account by the judge.

53.50 *The parties.* The parties themselves are not regarded as witnesses nor are other persons who may have an interest in the outcome of the case. It is possible, however, for one party to request that the other should be subjected to a formal interrogatory. Specific questions are drawn up, and the answers given may be of probative effect if they are against the interest of the party questioned. The judge may also administer an interrogatory, of his own motion, in which case the answers given by the party are not probative as above, but they may be taken into account in support of other available evidence.

Decisory oath. One party may, if the judge allows, challenge the other to swear to the truth of some matter which is decisive of the case. If the oath is taken it constitutes conclusive proof of the matter sworn. The party challenged may refer the challenge back, but if the party refuses to take the oath the matter is deemed to have been proved against him. A false declaration in such circumstances renders the maker liable to criminal prosecution and to a claim for damages from the other party, but a judgment so obtained is not capable of being set aside.

12. Documentary evidence

53.51 Documents are of considerable importance in Italian civil proceedings. They may be filed at the court with the original pleadings or may be submitted later during the proof-taking stage. Their authenticity can be challenged, depending on the type of document, either by a special procedure, called *querela di falso*, or by disclaiming them in the ordinary course of the action. A party can obtain copies of his adversary's documents from the clerk's office or directly from the other party.

Upon application by a party, the judge has power to order the 53.52
other party or a third person to produce any document which is
alleged to be necessary for the decision. Production may be resisted
on the ground that it would violate a professional or official confidentiality or would cause damage to the person ordered to produce
the document. This question of damage will be evaluated by the
judge by an appraisal of the interests concerned; but if the person
ordered to produce the document is a party to the proceedings, the
likely damage which he must show must be disproportionate in
comparison with advantage to the proceedings of the document
being produced. If a party refuses to comply with an order to produce a document the judge may draw adverse inferences from the
refusal. A third party may resist such an order by intervening in the
proceedings.

13. Experts

An expert (*consulente tecnico*) may be appointed by the judge 53.53
either at the request of the parties or of his own motion. This
usually occurs at the first of the hearings during the *fase istruttoria*,
but may occur later if the need for an expert was not apparent at the
outset. The expert is normally appointed from an official list kept at
the court. The order appointing him will include a list of questions,
drawn up by the judge on the basis of the pleadings and the suggestions of the parties' lawyers, which his report must be directed to
answering. In carrying out his investigation he may inspect persons, places and things and he may question the parties and any
other persons. The expert's report is filed at the court. The parties
are at liberty to instruct their own experts who may accompany the
court expert during his investigation and who may submit their
own reports to the court.

14. Proof of foreign law

Evidence of foreign law must be submitted by the party who 53.54
seeks to rely on it. This is frequently done by means of an affidavit
from a foreign lawyer; but there is no formal requirement that the
deponent must be a qualified legal practitioner of the foreign
country in question. In the absence of such evidence the judge can
either infer the contents of the foreign law from the other available
evidence in the proceedings, or he can rely on his own knowledge,
or he can, as a last resort, apply Italian law.

15. Compromise

Proceedings are frequently compromised either with the involve- 53.55
ment of the judge or by separate agreement of the parties through
their lawyers. In certain types of case, for example in labour law,

the judge is under a statutory duty to explore the possibilities for a settlement at the first hearing. When the compromise is reached with the involvement of the judge, it is minuted in the record of the court (*verbale di conciliazione*) which is signed by the parties, by the judge and by the clerk of the court. It may be enforced in the same way as a judgment.[23]

The lawyers of both parties are entitled to charge a special fee unit in respect of a compromise.[24] Payments under a compromise will be made to the other party direct or to his lawyer as may be agreed. A judicial compromise is subject, as is a judgment, to a registration tax, amounting to 3 per cent. of the value of the matter. There is no procedure comparable to the English payment into court.

16. The judgment

53.56　The court arrives at its judgment by majority vote; dissenting opinions are not disclosed. The reasons for the judgment are drafted by the examining judge and the whole text is filed with the clerk's office, the date of such filing being the date of the publication of the judgment for the purposes of the time limit for appeal.[25] Copies of the operative part of it are sent to the respective lawyers after publication, but they can only obtain full copies when the registration tax[26] has been paid.

A judgment contains the following parts: a heading, which gives the names of the judges; the parties and their lawyers and their respective claims; a summary of the progress of the proceedings; the reasoning on which the judgment is founded both in fact and in law (the *motivazione*); a statement of the relief granted or other order made (the *dispositivo*); the date; and the signature of the judges. It will contain an order as to costs. If it is provisionally enforceable, it will say so.

A judgment is termed *contumaciale* if rendered by default and *parziale* when it is given in the course of the proceedings on an interlocutory matter, without finally determining the merits of the case. Orders made in the course of proceedings, whether they are made of the court's own motion or at the instance of a party, are called *ordinanze* if they are made *inter partes*, or *decreti*, if they are made *ex parte*.

---

[23] See para. 53.70 below.
[24] See para. 53.57 below.
[25] The time for appealing is curtailed if the judgment is served on the other party: see para. 53.66 below.
[26] This tax is set at values which, depending on the type of case, may be fixed or may amount to a percentage (3 per cent.) of the value of the claim.

17. Costs

During the progress of a case each party bears its own costs and **53.57** must pay in advance the court costs for each step required of it by law or which it requests. At the final hearing before judgment is given each party submits an itemised bill of his own costs. This will include court fees, lawyers fees and disbursements. The lawyers fees are calculated according to a tariff which is published periodically by the *Consiglio Nazionale Forense*. The tariff lays down fee units corresponding to each step that the lawyer has taken. Fee units are proportional to the value of the case. Witnesses are entitled to reimbursement of their expenses according to a fixed scale.

Normally the losing party will have to pay the costs of the winning party in addition to his own. In some cases, such as those concerning labour law, each party may be ordered to bear his own costs. This can also happen when the case has involved an uncertain point of law. If it has been agreed with the client that fees should be charged on a time basis, the bill submitted to the court will nonetheless be calculated according to the tariff. Accordingly, there is often a shortfall between the sums which a winning party recovers from the losing part and the sums which he has to pay his own lawyer. The fees of the judicial experts are fixed by the court and they are either equally divided between the parties or charged to the losing party. The costs of a party's foreign lawyer are not generally recoverable, although they may be treated as disbursements in certain cases.

H. Civil Procedure—Provisional and Protective Measures

1. Introduction

The *Codice di Procedura Civile* lists four specific protective rem- **53.58** edies and one general provisional remedy. Each of these remedies is available in aid of proceedings in foreign courts or foreign arbitrations, even outside the scope of Article 24 of the 1968 Convention,[27] provided the evidential criteria are satisfied and provided that the Italian court has jurisdiction over the defendants.

2. Protective remedies

Attachment. The first specific remedy is attachment (*sequestro*). It **53.59** is used to preserve property by ordering that it is kept under custody with a prohibition on its disposal. When attachment is directed at ensuring that a future money judgment can be satisfied

---

[27] See para. 24.01 above.

it is called *sequestro conservativo*. When it relates to the preservation of real or personal property the ownership or possession of which is in dispute, or the preservation of books, ledgers, records, samples or anything else of an evidential value, it is called *sequestro giudiziario*. No lien or preferential lien as against other creditors is created by the attachment.

The application for an order of attachment may be made *ex parte* before proceedings for the merits have begun or while they are in progress. Depending on the value of the claim, the application will be made to the *pretore* or to the president of the *tribunale* either at the place in which the property is situated or in the court which is competent to try the main claim. If proceedings on the main claim are already in progress the application has to be made to the judge of the court already seized of the case.

The applicant must show that he has a *prima facie* case on the merits and that delay in granting the relief could cause prejudice. He may identify the assets which he wishes to have attached or he may request that all the debtor's assets (up to the value of the claim) be made the subject of the attachment. He must indicate whether the attachment is to take effect against the debtor himself or against a third party in respect of assets in the possession of that third party. The applicant may be required to provide security.

In theory, assets located outside Italy may be ordered to be attached, provided the court has jurisdiction over the defendant. The plaintiff may be ordered to provide security either at the outset as a condition of the grant of an order of attachment, or at a later stage as a condition of its continuance. Attachment is also available in support of the execution of a foreign judgment under the 1968 Convention, pending an appeal against an order for enforcement. In this case, attachment is regarded as authorised as of right by the order for enforcement.[28]

Attachments against the defendant himself are effected by the *ufficiale giudiziario*, who visits the defendant's premises and attaches his assets. If the order is in respect of assets in the possession of a third party, on the other hand, there follows a hearing before the *pretore* to which the third party is summoned, to determine the assets against which the order is to take effect, although all the defendant's assets in the possession of the third party are provisionally attached pending this hearing.

Validating proceedings. When an order for *sequestro conservativo*, or for *sequestro giudiziario*, has been obtained, the plaintiff must bring proceedings for the validation of the order (*giudizio di conva-*

---

[28] See paras. 28.60–28.61 above.

lida) and (if these have not already been started) for the main claim, by serving a *citazione* on the defendant within 15 days from the date on which execution of the order has been initiated by the *ufficiale giudiziario*. If the Italian courts have international jurisdiction over the merits, the same court is competent to entertain these proceedings as is competent to determine the issue on the merits; but if the Italian courts do not have jurisdiction over the merits, the court which granted the measure is the court which is competent to entertain the validating proceedings. If it is found that the attachment ought not to have been granted the applicant may be held liable to compensate the other party for any losses which he may have thereby suffered.

Other specific protective measures. The second specific remedy, **53.60** *denuncia di nuova opera*, lies against any person who has undertaken building work in the course of the preceding year provided that the work is still unfinished. If the complainant can show either that he has suffered damage or that there is a risk of damage from the new work, the court will make an order restraining the work or compelling the defendant to provide security to compensate for any damage. The third remedy, *denuncia di danno temuto*, which is related, enables the court to make a restraining order when damage is threatened from the condition of an adjoining property.

The fourth specific measure, preventive proof-taking proceedings (*procedimenti di istruzione preventiva*), are held to obtain and preserve evidence which will be required in later proceedings, but which may then no longer be available, as where a witness is in serious ill health or where a physical location will be materially altered.

3. General provisional orders

In addition to the four above-mentioned specific provisional remedies, the court has power under Article 700 of the *Codice di Procedura Civile* to entertain *provvedimenti di urgenza*, (urgent proceedings). This is a procedure by which a party may be ordered to do or refrain from doing some act so as to prevent irreparable damage being done to the plaintiff's interests pending the bringing or hearing of the main proceedings. An important limitation on the availability of this measure, however, is the fact that it is not available in any case in which recourse may be had to one of the specific protective measures mentioned above. The application must be made to the *pretore* of the place in which, according to the plaintiff's allegation, the harmful event likely to frustrate the decision will take place. Alternatively, in the case of pending proceedings, it must be made to the examining judge.

I. Civil Procedure—Summary Procedure

1. *Procedimento d'ingiunzione*

53.61 This procedure is used in straightforward claims for payment of a debt, and for the delivery of a specific chattel or a specific quantity of fungible goods. It cannot be used if service of the *ricorso* has to be effected outside Italy. The application, called a *ricorso per ingiunzione*,[29] is made *ex parte* to the *conciliatore*, the *pretore* or the president of the *tribunale*, according to the value of the claim. It is in a simplified standard form and is accompanied by supporting documents. Provided the plaintiff can show *prima facie* entitlement to judgment he will obtain an order for payment which he must register with the local registrar's office and serve on the defendant. The defendant then has 20 days in which to apply to have the order set aside by serving on the plaintiff's lawyer a *citazione* in opposition to the judgment. If he fails to do this, the decree will become final and enforceable by execution. If the defendant is out of time he may still apply to have the order set aside if he can show good cause for his delay but he will be required to provide security for the amount of the claim. If the opposition is served the proceedings are converted into an ordinary action. In cases where the plaintiff has a strong *prima facie* case, as where he is suing on a cheque or where the application to set aside is not based on written evidence, the plaintiff can request and obtain provisional execution.[30]

[The next paragraph is number 53.63]

J. Civil Procedure—Appeals

53.63 In common with other civil law systems, Italian procedural law divides appeals (*impugnazioni*) into ordinary and extraordinary appeals, although the division differs from that in, for example, French law.[31]

1. Ordinary appeals

53.64 *Appello.* All judgments given at first instance can be appealed, by an *appello*, to the next superior court in the same locality. The time limit for appealing runs from the date of service of the judgment. The time limits are 10 days for an appeal from the *conciliatore* and 30 days for appeals from the *pretore* and *tribunale*. If neither party

---

[29] This procedure is not related to an "injunction" in the common law understanding of that term.
[30] See para. 53.67 below.
[31] See para. 50.63 above.

serves the judgment it may be appealed at any time within a year from the date upon which it was published.[32] The procedure before the *corte d'appello* is similar to that before the *tribunale*. An appeal involves a fresh consideration of the whole case. It is initiated by a *citazione in appello* which contains a summary of the facts and the grounds of appeal.[33] The appellate court calls for the file on the case from the court below and an examining judge is appointed. He will deal with any application for the granting, suspension or revocation of provisional execution of the appealed judgment.

It is not permissible for the plaintiff to introduce new claims in an appeal, but the defendant may set up new defences. The parties may file fresh documentary evidence and they may apply for the hearing of new witnesses.

Appeal to the Corte di Cassazione. Appeal against a decision of the *corte d'appello* can only be made to the *Corte di Cassazione* for errors of law.[34] Such an appeal is called a *ricorso per cassazione*. Errors of law are classified in two main categories: *errores in procedendo*, which include jurisdictional issues, nullity of the judgment or of the proceedings, deficient or contradictory reasoning in the judgment with regard to one or more items of the claim; and *errores in judicando* which involves violation or misapplication of a provision of law.

The *Corte di Cassazione* also hears applications for a *regolamento preventivo di giurisdizione*.[35]

An appeal before the *Corte di Cassazione* must be conducted by an *avvocato* enrolled in the special list of those entitled to practice in that court.[36] If the appeal is allowed the court either quashes the decision itself, for example when it finds that jurisdiction was lacking, or it remits the case to the court below giving advice as to the principles of law to be applied.

2. Extraordinary appeals

In two cases, a judgment which has become final and binding can be set aside by means of an application, or extraordinary appeal, to the court of trial and the proceedings can be reopened. **53.65**

Revocazione. First, an application may be made by way of *revocazione*, a procedure which is available in any of the following circum-

---

[32] See para. 53.56 above.
[33] The respective parties in an ordinary appeal are called the *appellante* and the *appellato*. In the *Corte di Cassazione* and in certain other special proceedings they are called the *ricorrente* (petitioner) and the *resistente* (respondent).
[34] The time limit for appealing to the *Corte di Cassazione* is 60 days from the date of service of the judgment. If neither party has served the judgment it may be appealed at any time within a year from the date upon which it was given.
[35] See para. 53.42 above.
[36] See para. 53.04 above.

stances: when the judgment has been obtained by the fraud of the other party; when the judgment has been based on false evidence or on an erroneous statement as to fact in a document; when new documentary evidence of a decisive character has been discovered after the judgment which could not have been produced earlier by reason of *force majeure* or the act of the other party; when the judgment is inconsistent with another judgment between the parties; when the judgment is tainted with fraud on the part of the judge. An appeal by way of *revocazione* must be started within 30 days of the discovery of grounds.

Opposizione di terzo. Secondly, an application (called an *opposizione di terzo*) may be made by a third party for the re-opening of a judgment which has become *res judicata*, if it adversely affects his rights and he did not take part in the original proceedings, or if the judgment had been obtained by fraud. There is no time limit within which such an appeal may be brought.

K. CIVIL PROCEDURE—ENFORCEMENT

1. Enforcement of Italian judgments

53.66   This section describes the enforcement of domestic civil judgments. The party who wishes to enforce the judgment will pay the registration tax and cause the judgment to be entered in the court register. He may then obtain an official certified copy of the judgment from the clerk of the court and serve it on the other party. Once a certified copy of the judgment is served on the other party there is a 30 day period in which an appeal may be made. Unless the judgment has been declared provisionally enforceable, execution may not take place until the judgment has become *res judicata*, which occurs on the expiry of the time allowed for appeal, or at the conclusion of any appeal proceedings. Alternatively, if both parties remain inactive and the judgment is not registered or served it will automatically become *res judicata* one year from the date of publication. It remains enforceable for a period of 10 years.

53.67   *Provisional enforceability.* In some cases, a judgment at first instance may be declared to be provisionally enforceable (*sentenza provvisoriamente esecutiva*) at the request of the winning party. This usually happens when the claim appears to be particularly well founded as, for example, when it is based on a public deed or on another final judgment, and also when the winning party may be prejudiced by delay. The ordering of provisional enforceability may be made conditional upon the payment of security by the requesting party. The provisional enforceability of an order made in summary proceedings has already been discussed.[37] If the provisional enforcement of a judgment proves not to have been justified, the defendant may obtain restitution and compensation for consequential damage, either by means of a counterclaim raised in response to the plaintiff's original claim for provisional enforceability, or by means of a separate claim.

Indorsement as to executory character. In order that execution may be effected on a judgment or order, it must bear an indorsement confirming its executory character. This indorsement, called a *formula esecutiva*, is placed by the clerk of the court on the office copy of the judgment issued by him, once the judgment has become enforceable. It is in the following terms:

In Nome della Legge

Comandiamo a tutti gli Ufficiali Giudiziari che ne siano richiesti e a chiunque spetti di mettere a esecuzione il presente titolo, al Pubblico Ministero di darvi assistenza, e a tutti gli ufficiali della forza pubblica di concorrervi, quando ne siano legalmente richiesti.
La presente copia è conforme all'originale e si rilascia a richiesta del Sig . . . [lawyer's name].

The indorsement is completed by the signature of the issuing official. A judgment which bears such an indorsement becomes an executory title (*titolo esecutivo*).

Service of notice to comply with the judgment. The first stage in executing a judgment is for the judgment bearing a *formula esecutiva* to be served on the person against whom execution is to be made. Thereafter, or at the same time, he must be served with a notice, called an *atto di precetto*, requiring him to satisfy the judgment within 10 days on pain of forceable execution against his property. In an urgent case a shorter period for compliance might be fixed by the court, or the period for payment may even be dispensed with entirely. Service of the judgment and *atto di precetto* are carried out by an *ufficiale giudiziario*.

Execution. The normal method for the execution of a judgment **53.68** ordering the payment of money is by seizure (*pignoramento*) of the judgment debtor's property. Subject to certain restrictions the judgment creditor may select the property to be seised. The process of execution is carried out by the *ufficiale giudiziario* who formally attaches the debtor's goods, putting them into the custody of a third party and ordering the debtor not to interfere with them. Ultimately the assets seised may be sold by public judicial auction or

---

[37] See para. 53.61 above.

other form of sale permitted by law, or they may be assigned directly to the creditor. Similarly, land may be made the subject of seizure and sale or transfer. Other creditors having title may intervene in the sale.

Garnishee proceedings can also be brought against a third party who owes money to the debtor or who is in possession of the debtor's property. The third party is summoned before a *pretore* to declare what sums he owes to the debtor or what property of the debtor he has in his possession. If he does not appear, or if he disputes the matter, the *pretore* will make an order within the limit of his own jurisdiction or he will refer the case to the *tribunale*. Meanwhile the garnishee is bound to preserve the money or the property as a judicial custodian.

A judgment for the delivery of specific goods may be executed by the *ufficiale giudiziario* by seizing the goods and handing them to the party entitled to the benefit of the judgment. A judgment for the transfer of specific land is executed by the *ufficiale giudiziario* putting the person entitled to the benefit of the judgment into physical possession of the land and making the necessary changes to the land register.

53.69   *Other methods of enforcement.* Mandatory orders are enforced, if the defendant refuses to perform the act required of him, by appointing some other person to perform the act. Italian law does not employ a system of enforcement by means of periodic penalty payments, nor does it have a system of punishment for contempt of court.

Opposing the execution. The judgment debtor, if he challenges the right of the creditor to proceed to execution, may oppose the *atto di precetto*, by applying to the court by means of an *opposizione all'esecuzione*. He summons the judgment creditor to appear before the court competent under the ordinary rules. Opposition to execution against movable assets must be brought before the *pretore* of the place where the property is located. Opposition to execution against real property must be brought before the *tribunale* for the locality of that property. In each case, the matter is then decided according to the ordinary rules of procedure. In larger courts, the matter is handled by a section specially assigned to deal with matters of execution.

If the judgment debtor challenges the formal regularity of the judgment or of the subsequent *atto di precetto*, the opposition is called *opposizione agli atti esecutivi* and must be made within five days from the service on the debtor of the judgment or *atto di precetto*, as the case may be. The decision made in these proceedings, which otherwise follow the normal rules of procedure, is not subject to appeal.

A third party who claims to have rights in the property against which execution is to be levied may also apply to the judge in charge of execution proceedings. If the parties do not reach agreement at the first hearing, these proceedings are also conducted according to the normal rules of procedure.

2. Authentic instruments and court settlements

In addition to judgments, certain other documents are capable of direct execution. Any such instrument constitutes a *titolo esecutivo*.[38] Their method of execution is the same as that which applies in the case of judgments, and involves the issue of proceedings for the purpose.   **53.70**

Authentic instruments. Certain instruments, notably most negotiable instruments such as bills of exchange, promissory notes and certain cheques, may be executed without the addition of a *formula esecutiva* and after service only of an *atto di precetto* setting out the contents of the instrument. Other instruments are enforceable if a certified copy, bearing a *formula esecutiva*, is issued by the authority which issued the instrument, but in this case a copy of the instrument must be served with or before the *atto di precetto*. Instruments of the latter kind must be in respect of an obligation to pay a specific sum of money, and most important among them are notarial acts. Various instruments may be notarised, and in some cases (such as deeds of gift, or transfers of real property) notarisation is mandatory if the instrument is to have certain effects.

Court settlements. A settlement entered in the court minutes[39] may be enforced in the same way as a judgment. An officially certified copy bearing a *formula esecutiva* is issued by the clerk of the court upon the application of the party who wishes to enforce it and upon payment of the registration tax.

Enforcement of foreign judgments

Foreign judgments are enforceable in Italy by all means available in respect of Italian judgments once their execution has been authorised by the indorsement of a *formula esecutiva*. The means of obtaining this indorsement differs depending upon whether or not the 1968 Convention applies.   **53.71**

Enforcement under the 1968 Convention. Judgments from other Contracting States are recognised and enforced in Italy pursuant to

---

[38] *Cf.* para. 53.67 above.
[39] See para. 53.55 above.

Articles 31 to 49 of the 1968 Convention.[40] A certified copy of the foreign judgment is filed with the *corte d'appello* for the district of the defendant's domicile or, if he is not domiciled in Italy, the *corte d'appello* for the district where execution is to take place, together with certified copies of the documents required by Articles 46 and 47 of the Convention. A translation of the judgment and other documents, made by a sworn translator, must be attached. The documents are accompanied by a petition to the *corte d'appello* for the grant of a *formula esecutiva*. The application must be made by a local lawyer at whose address the applicant has elected domicile for the purposes of these proceedings. The petition and documents are submitted to the public prosecutor for his information, and the court then considers the petition. If the petition is well-founded, the court orders the addition to the judgment of the *formula esecutiva*. Opposition to the grant of a *formula esecutiva* must be made to the *corte d'appello* in accordance with Articles 36 and 37 of the Convention.[41] The decision made on that appeal can only be challenged before the *Corte di Cassazione*.

53.72   *Judgments outside the 1968 Convention.* In the absence of multilateral or bilateral conventions the recognition and enforcement of foreign judgments is governed by the provisions of the *Codice di Procedura Civile*[42] which lay down the following requirements: the foreign judgment must have been given by a court which had jurisdiction over the case according to the principles of the Italian law on jurisdiction; the proceedings must have been served on the defendant in accordance with the law of the state in which the judgment was given and the defendant must have had an adequate opportunity to appear; there must have been either due appearance or default according to the law of the court of trial; the foreign judgment must have been final according to the law of the court of trial; the judgment must not conflict with the judgment of an Italian court; there must be no parallel proceedings between the same parties pending in an Italian court instituted before the foreign judgment became final; the judgment must not be contrary to Italian public policy. If the foreign judgment was given in default or if it is alleged to have been obtained through fraud, forgery or gross mis-

---

[40] The Italian name of the 1968 Convention is *Convenzione concernente la competenza giurisdizionale e l'esecuzione delle decisioni in materia civile e commerciale*.

[41] The time limit for such an opposition is one month if the party against whom enforcement is ordered is domiciled in Italy, and two months if he is domiciled in another Contracting State. See para. 28.30 above. This time limit is also applied by some judges in respect of an appeal against the refusal to grant a *formula esecutiva*, although Italian law does not specifically provide a time limit for such an appeal.

[42] Arts. 796 *et seq.*

take of fact, the Italian court will, on the defendant's application, re-examine the merits of the case and, according to its findings, grant the execution or render an independent judgment.

An application for a *formula esecutiva* must be made by a *citazione* before the *corte d'appello* for the district in which the judgment is to be executed. The proceedings are conducted *inter partes* and result in a judgment ordering or refusing to order the clerk of the court to affix a *formula esecutiva*.

L. LEGAL PERSONS

The following are the various types of legal persons and associations **53.73** under Italian law:

(a) *Societá per Azioni* (S.p.A.), a company limited by shares;
(b) *Societá a responsabilitá limitata* (S.r.l.), a limited company in which the stock is not readily marketable;
(c) *Societá in accomandita semplice* (S.a.s.), a limited company in which the liability of some of the participators is limited and of others is unlimited;
(d) *Societá in accomandita per Azioni* (S.a.p.A.), a limited company in which participation and liability are limited by shares;
(e) *Societá in nome collettivo* (S.n.c.), a partnership;
(f) *Societá semplice*, a partnership;
(g) *Associazione non riconosciuta*, unregistered association.

M. LEGAL AID

At each *tribunale*, *corte d'appello* and at the *Corte di Cassazione* a **53.74** special committee is set up under the supervision of the public prosecutor to consider applications for legal aid. Application is made to the committee at the court where the proceedings are to take place. Legal aid is available for any sort of proceedings, but a legally aided party who was unsuccessful at first instance must make a fresh application in respect of appeal proceedings.

Any person, natural or legal, national or foreign, who satisfies the relevant criteria is eligible for legal aid. The criteria are those of sufficient need, which is proved by a certificate from the municipal authority, and of having a *prima facie* case. The applicant must set out the facts of his case in his application, together with his evidence and his grounds for bringing or defending the case. One member of the committee examines the merits of the application and reports to the committee. If legal aid is refused, the applicant may appeal to the legal aid committee at the *corte d'appello*.

Once legal aid has been granted to the party he is entitled to rep-

1385

resentation without charge. He may have the lawyer of his choice or, if he does not specify a particular lawyer, one will be assigned to him by the committee. The lawyer chosen may only decline to act for the legally aided party for valid reasons, acknowledged as such by the committee.

The lawyer's fees will be paid by the losing party, or by the state, based on a fixed fee depending on the nature of the case. The legally aided party is exempted from the requirement to use the stamped paper, which other litigants must use for pleadings, and from the payment of the registration tax. Costs and official disbursements arising during the course of the proceedings are paid by the state.

CHAPTER 54

LUXEMBOURG

Written in collaboration with Maîtres Guy Harles[1] and Thea Walch.[1a]

---

[1] Avocat-avoué, *Arendt et Medernach*, Luxembourg; Professeur au Centre Universitaire du Luxembourg.
[1a] *Magistrat*.

1387

A. The Legal System

1. Introduction

54.01   *History.* The Grand-Duchy of Luxembourg has existed as an entity for over a thousand years. In 1794 it was overrun by French revolutionary armies and it thereafter remained annexed to the French Republic until 1814. During this period French laws were introduced and a codified system of legislation was adopted largely on the model of the new French codes. In 1815 Luxembourg was ceded to the Dutch Crown by the Congress of Vienna but in 1830 the northern part of the country joined the Belgian provinces in their separation from the Netherlands. The independent national status of Luxembourg was in due course recognised by the Treaty of London in 1839. The present constitution of Luxembourg dates from 1868, with later revisions strongly influenced by the Belgian constitution. It provides for government by means of a constitutional monarchy and an elected parliament.

Territory. Luxembourg is at the heart of western Europe having borders with France, Belgium and the Federal Republic of Germany. The official legislative, administrative and judicial language is French, but German is frequently used in commercial circles. The local language is *Letzeburgesch*, which is of German origins. The Grand-Duchy has a land area of some 2,600 square kilometres and a population numbering about 356,000, of whom about a quarter are in the city of Luxembourg. It has been linked to Belgium by an economic treaty since 1921, and was a founder member of the EEC in 1957.

2. The administration of justice

54.02   *Categories of law.* The three principal divisions of Luxembourg law are public law, private law and social and economic law. Public law includes, principally, constitutional law, administrative law and criminal law. Private law is made up of civil law and certain specialised subjects such as industrial property law.

Court system. The ordinary courts of first instance are the *tribunal de paix* and the *tribunal d'arrondissement*, which exercise jurisdiction in civil, commercial and criminal matters. Appeals lie to the *Cour Supérieure de Justice*. There is a separate system of social courts and matters of public law are dealt with separately by a special committee of the *Conseil d'Etat*.[2]

---

[2] The Court of Justice of the European Communities has its seat at Kirchberg, close to Luxembourg city. It forms no part of the national court system of Luxembourg. But see para. 54.05 below.

B. Legal Practitioners

1. The *Avocat-avoué*

Introduction. The practising lawyer usually combines the func- **54.03**
tions of *avocat* and *avoué*. As an *avocat* he performs the function of
"assistance," the giving of legal advice and the oral presentation of
argument in court (*plaidoiries*). As an *avoué* he performs the function of *"représentation,"* that of formally representing the client in
proceedings in the higher courts and carrying out certain procedural steps which are there reserved to *avoués*, including the signing
of pleadings on behalf of the parties, and lodging them in court.

Legal education and qualification. The intending *avocat* must have
a university law degree which is obtained after a course of studies
lasting at least four years. This degree must necessarily be obtained
in France or in Belgium, which share common principles of law
with Luxembourg, in a university recognised for this purpose by
the Luxembourg Minister of Education. The first year of the course
may be spent, optionally, at the *Centre Universitaire de Luxembourg*.
The Universities of Strasbourg, Brussels, Nancy, Paris, and Aix-
en-Provence are those most commonly attended by law students
from Luxembourg. Having obtained a law degree the intending
avocat must then undergo a six-month course in Luxembourg law
organised by the *Centre Universitaire* in Luxembourg city. This
entitles him to take the oath of the *avocat* and to become an *avocat*
stagiaire. The period of the *stage* is normally three years, during
which he must work under the supervision of an established *avocat*.
As a *stagiaire* he is able to carry out all legal work save that reserved
to the *avoué*. At the conclusion of the *stage* the *stagiaire* takes a
further examination and receives his *Diplome de Fin de Stage Judi-*
ciaire. After this he is entitled to perform the functions of an *avoué*.

Rights of audience and representation. Before the *tribunaux* **54.04**
d'arrondissement (in civil cases) and before the *Cour Supérieure de*
Justice the *avocat* has a monopoly of *plaidoiries* and the *avoué* has a
monopoly of *représentation*. Before the *tribunaux d'arrondissement* (in
commercial cases) and before the *tribunaux de paix* there is no
monopoly as to rights of audience or representation. Parties may
represent themselves or may be represented by an *avocat* or by an
unqualified person.

Organisation of practice. *Avocats* are not permitted to form partnerships in the Grand-Duchy, but expense-sharing arrangements,
called *groupements*, are allowed. However the majority of *avocats* are
sole practitioners. An *avocat* may not be the salaried employee of
another *avocat*.

54.05   *Fees.* Fees are ordinarily agreed with the client according to the amount of work involved in the case and its importance. There are no official tariffs for any class of work. In the event of a dispute the matter may be referred to the *Ordre des Avocats* for taxation. Value Added Tax (TVA) is chargeable in respect of work for residents in the Grand-Duchy but not for residents of other countries.

Professional organisation and conduct. The profession of *avocat* is regulated by a law of February 18, 1885. There are two bars in the Grand-Duchy corresponding to the geographical districts of the two *tribunaux d'arrondissement*, at Luxembourg and at Diekirch. The Luxembourg bar has some 296 members, of whom 204 are *avocats-avoués* and 92 are *avocats-stagiaires*.[3] The Diekirch bar has some 12 members. Members of the respective bars do not appear before each others' courts. All *avocats* are members of the *Ordre des Avocats* which is independent of the state and the judges. Meetings are convened and presided over by the *bâtonnier*. *Avocats* are bound by professional privilege, breach of which is a criminal offence.

The European Court of Justice. The Rules of Procedure of the European Court of Justice require all parties in proceedings before it to elect the domicile of the seat of the Court, that is to say to nominate an address for service in Luxembourg. This necessitates the appointment by each party of a person in Luxembourg who will accept service on his behalf, a task frequently carried out by members of the Luxembourg bar who may then oversee the procedural aspects of the case.

[The next paragraph number is 54.09]

2. The *Notaire*

54.09   The *notaire* is a publicly appointed official whose function is to draw up all instruments and contracts which the parties either are obliged or wish to have officially authenticated, so as to acquire conclusive probative force. Many formal legal documents, such as deeds of sale and gift, mortgages, marriage contracts, articles of incorporation, partnership agreements and wills may or must be authenticated by a *notaire*. The *notaire* must satisfy himself as to the identity and capacity of the parties. The document will be dated and the original retained permanently in the safe custody of the *notaire*. Certified copies (*expéditions*) are provided for the parties. In acting for the parties he will if necessary advise them in connection with the matter in hand and frequently the *notaire* performs the wider role of general legal adviser in business and family affairs.

---

[3] As at 1988/89.

Notaires are appointed by the Grand-Duke to practise in a particular locality. They may only act within the *arrondissement* in which the locality to which they have been appointed is situated. They are forbidden to hold any other public office or any privately salaried appointment which might affect their professional independence. Their fees for notarial functions are fixed according to a statutory scale, but their fees for advisory and drafting work are not regulated. *Notaires* are not permitted to form firms with each other, nor with other lawyers or members of other professions. The profession is regulated by law and is subject to the discipline of its own professional body, the *Chambre de Notaires*.

[The next paragraph is number 54.11]

3. Foreign lawyers

The EEC Legal Services Directive was implemented in Luxembourg in April 1980.[4] This lays down the conditions upon which lawyers from other Member States may appear before Luxembourg courts. There are no foreign law firms established in Luxembourg. **54.11**

4. Lawyers in business and public employment

Lawyers employed by companies, by the state, or by local authorities, may not be admitted to or to remain members of the Bar, as it is considered that they lack the required degree of independence from their client. **54.12**

5. The *Huissier de justice*

The *huissier de justice* is a publicly appointed official whose principal functions are the service of judicial and extra-judicial documents and the enforcement of court orders and judgments. His competence is limited territorially to the *arrondissement* to which he has been appointed. *Huissiers* practise as individuals but employ office staff. They sometimes undertake minor cases on behalf of clients before the *juge de paix*. Unlike *huissiers* in France they do not have a general fact-finding role, nor do they act as ushers in court. **54.13**

C. SOURCES OF LAW

1. Introduction

The Luxembourg Constitution, upon which the state and the legal system are founded, dates from 1868. It has been amended from time to time. Sources of law are formally classified in two main **54.14**

---

[4] See para. A2.47 below.

categories: *sources législatives* (legislation) and *sources interprétatives* (decided cases and legal writings).

2. Legislation

54.15 Although custom was, historically, the major source of law, it now plays only a marginal role. The principal source of law is legislation. This comprises statutes (*lois*), orders (*arrêtés*) and regulations (*réglementations*) passed by the legislature, as well as international treaties. International treaties and European Community law take precedence even over subsequently enacted legislation.

The *Code Napoleon* was introduced in Luxembourg in 1803–1804 and it survives to this day in amended form as the *Code Civil*. Its evolution over the years has followed legislative developments in France and Belgium. The *Code de Procédure Civile* dates from 1806 but is in the course of substantial amendment on the model of the French *Nouveau Code de Procédure Civile*. The *Code de Commerce* of 1807 is largely out of date and unenforced. Substantial areas of commercial law have been the subject of much more recent independent legislation.

3. Decided cases and legal writings

54.16 *Decided cases.* As the courts frequently have to interpret the intention of the legislature and even take decisions in situations not provided for by legislation, court decisions play a significant role as a source of law. Yet the judge is not bound to follow a previous decision in a similar case. This freedom is derived from two fundamental principles enshrined in the *Code Civil*. First it is provided by Article 5 that judges may not make statements of general purport amounting to a regulation when they are ruling on a particular case. Secondly, a judicial decision is considered only to have effect for the purposes of the case in which it is given.

Legal writings. As in many legal systems, legal writings (*la doctrine*) are an indirect source of law. Given the small size of the country there are very few textbooks on specific topics of Luxembourg law.

4. Publications

54.17 All legislative texts are published in the *Mémorial* (Official Gazette), publication being a condition precedent to their coming into force. Practitioners ordinarily use privately published annotated texts of the codes. A summary of the most important laws is published in the *Pasinomie Luxembourgeoise*. Selected judgments are published in the *Pasicrisie Luxembourgeoise*. There are several privately published legal journals. Luxembourg lawyers will generally include Belgian and French legal sources and textbooks in their researches.

D. Organisation of the Civil Courts

1. Introduction

The ordinary courts of Luxembourg exercise concurrent jurisdic- **54.18** tion over civil and commercial matters and over criminal matters. Depending on the value of the claim, civil and commercial matters are heard at first instance either in the *tribunal de paix* or in the *tribunal d'arrondissement*.

Commercial cases. Commercial matters are allocated to the commercial chambers of the respective courts. A transaction is treated as commercial if both parties to it are *commerçants*. If only the plaintiff is a *commerçant* the matter is regarded as civil, but if only the defendant is a *commerçant* the action will be treated as civil or commercial at the choice of the plaintiff. Certain transactions, such as payment by cheque, are classed by law as commercial, and proceedings arising out of them must be treated as commercial regardless of the status of the parties. All limited companies are classed as *commerçants*.

2. The *tribunal de paix*

The lower court of first instance is the *tribunal de paix*. There are **54.19** three *tribunaux de paix*, one in the city of Luxembourg, one at Esch-sur-Alzette, and one at Diekirch. Each court has several chambers in which the *juges de paix* sit singly. The *juge de paix* has civil and commercial jurisdiction (without right of appeal) up to the value of LUF 15,000 and (subject to appeal) up to LUF 100,000. In certain classes of case his jurisdiction is unlimited as to value. These cases include disputes between landlord and tenant, claims for maintenance not connected to divorce proceedings, attachment of goods, and certain agricultural cases.

Employment cases are heard by the *juge de paix* in the *tribunal arbitral*, for salaried employees, and in the *conseil de prud'hommes*, for manual workers. The *juge de paix* sits in both tribunals with two lay assessors representing the employers' associations and the trade unions respectively.

The *juge de paix*, sitting as the *tribunal de police* has criminal jurisdiction over minor offences.

3. The *tribunal d'arrondissement*

The main court of first instance is the *tribunal d'arrondissement*, **54.20** with civil and commercial jurisdiction over cases involving over LUF 100,000. It also hears appeals from decisions of the *tribunal de* *paix* in matters exceeding LUF 15,000. There are two *tribunaux d'arrondissement*, one in the city of Luxembourg and the other at Diekirch. In this court the bench comprises three judges. Its financial jurisdiction is unlimited, and it hears appeals from decisions of the *tribunal de paix*. The *tribunal d'arrondissement* deals with all matters which are not expressly attributed to some other court by reason of the subject-matter or value of the claim. The commercial chamber of the *tribunal d'arrondissement* is known as the *tribunal d'arrondissement siégeant en matière commercial*. Certain other matters, such as the enforcement of foreign judgments, are reserved exclusively to the *tribunal d'arrondissement*.

The *tribunal d'arrondissement* has criminal jurisdiction over serious offences ("*crimes*"), when sitting as the *tribunal correctionel*.

4. The *Cour Supérieure de Justice*

54.21   The highest court is the *Cour Supérieure de Justice* which sits in the city of Luxembourg and has jurisdiction over the whole country. It comprises a *Cour d'Appel* with five chambers each with three judges (*conseillers*), and a *Cour de Cassation* with one chamber of five judges (*magistrats*). The *Cour d'Appel* hears appeals from the two *tribunaux d'arrondissements*. The *Cour de Cassation* hears appeals in cassation[5] from all courts in the country including the *Cour d'Appel*. The sittings are arranged so that no judge sits in cassation on a case which he has himself heard at a lower level.

[The next paragraph is number 54.23]

5. The judiciary and the *ministère public*

54.23   Most judges will have been appointed in their late twenties having passed the *Fin de Stage Judiciaire* examination and they will usually have spent some part of their career as members of the *ministère public*. It is rare for an established practising *avocat* to become a judge. The appointment is for life, subject to retirement at the age of 65 years.

The ministère public. The *ministère public* is the public legal service which represents the interests of the state. It has an office (*parquet*) attached to each of the two *tribunaux d'arrondissement* and to the *Cour Supérieure de Justice*. Its main function is to prosecute in criminal cases, but it is also entitled to take part in any civil proceedings, either by intervening to represent the public interest in litigation between private parties, or as a principal party in certain cases directly affecting the public interest. In practice, it usually only intervene in cases involving guardianship or status.

---

[5] See para. 54.65 below.

E. JURISDICTION OF THE CIVIL COURTS

1. Introduction

Where the 1968 Convention confers international jurisdiction on **54.24**
the courts of Luxembourg, the particular court in which the claim
may be made is determined by the Convention's own provisions on
local jurisdiction[6] and the jurisdictional rules of Luxembourg law
summarised below. Competence based on the subject-matter and
value of the litigation has been described in outline in the preceding
section. This section is concerned with the rules of territorial competence, that is to say, the rules that determine in which particular
court of a given kind and level proceedings may be brought. The
competent court is generally that for the place where the defendant
is domiciled or has its seat.

2. Domicile and seat

Natural persons. The domicile of a natural person is the place of **54.25**
his principal establishment. This is a question of fact. A person can
be domiciled in only one place. The court will have regard to his
habitual residence, and the geographical focus of his family and
his economic and professional interests. A person may change his
domicile if he physically moves to another place with the intention
of settling there. A person may however have an *elective* domicile or
domicile of choice for the purpose of procedural law.

Legal persons. Luxembourg law applies to every company which **54.26**
has its actual seat (*siège réel*) in Luxembourg. The actual seat of a
company is the place of its principal establishment. A company's
principal establishment is where its general meetings and board
meetings take place, and the legal, financial, organisational and
technical administration is established. Thus a company formed
outside Luxembourg, but having its principal establishment there,
will be considered as having its seat there. When a company has
been formed outside Luxembourg, and does not have its principal
establishment there, the court will have regard to the location of its
principal establishment for the purposes of determining whether it
has its seat in another Contracting State or in a non-Contracting
State.

3. Jurisdiction—general rules

In all matters for which a particular territorial jurisdiction is not **54.27**
otherwise specified by law, a defendant domiciled in Luxembourg
may be sued in the court of appropriate level for the district in

---

[6] See para. 15.03, nn. 10–11 above.

which he has his domicile or, in the case of a legal person, in which it has its seat. Subject to the 1968 Convention, if a person has no domicile in Luxembourg, he may be sued in the court for the place where he is actually resident. Proceedings may also be brought in respect of a claim arising out of the operations of a branch or office in the court for the district where that branch or office is located.

4. Jurisdiction—special rules

54.28   In matters of contract the claim may additionally be brought before a court of the appropriate level for the place where the obligation was, or was to be, performed. Luxembourg law has no general provision which determines the place of performance of a contractual obligation. Except in two cases mentioned below the obligation to pay money must, unless otherwise agreed, ordinarily be performed at the domicile of the debtor. First, in cases of sales of goods, payment must be made, unless otherwise agreed, at the place of delivery. This is the place where the goods are located at the time of the sale, unless the parties have otherwise agreed. Secondly, when the obligation relates to a specific object, payment must be made, unless otherwise agreed, at the place where the specific object is situated at the time when payment is to be made. In cases of tort the claim may additionally be brought before the court for the place where the event causing the damage occurred. An insurer may be sued in the court for the domicile of the insured or, if he is joined in proceedings against an insured, in the court before which those proceedings are brought. In proceedings relating to immovable property, the court of the place where the property is situated has jurisdiction.

5. Choice of court and entry of appearance

54.29   The above rules of territorial competence may generally be waived by agreement (which may take the form of an election of domicile for the purpose of the proceedings). Equally, a defendant who is sued in a territorially inappropriate court and who does not challenge the court's jurisdiction, will be taken to have consented to that jurisdiction. The rule that disputes concerning immovable property should be brought in the court for the place where the property is situated cannot be waived.

6. Exceptional rules

54.30   *Exorbitant grounds of jurisdiction.* Articles 14 and 15 of the *Code Civil* contain the provisions of exorbitant jurisdiction which, by Article 3 of the 1968 Convention, are inapplicable as against any person domiciled in a Contracting State. Article 14 provides that any person of foreign nationality, though not resident in Luxembourg, may be sued in Luxembourg in respect of an obligation entered into with a Luxembourg citizen. Article 15 enables a Luxembourg citizen to be sued in Luxembourg in respect of an obligation entered into by him abroad.

Special privileges for Luxembourg domiciliaries. Article 1 of the 1971 Protocol to the 1968 Convention confers special advantages on persons domiciled in Luxembourg in some matters relating to contract and jurisdiction agreements.[7]

7. Civil claims in criminal proceedings

When a criminal offence also gives rise to a claim for civil damages the plaintiff may choose to pursue his claim as a *"partie civile"* in the criminal proceedings; but if he does so, he is then precluded from bringing an ordinary civil action in respect of the same matter. In addition to passing sentence on the defendant, the judge will also make an award of civil damages in respect of loss and damage caused directly by the acts complained of. Civil claims are frequently made in criminal proceedings arising out of traffic accidents. If criminal proceedings are brought after the commencement of civil proceedings, the civil case must be stayed pending the result of the criminal case, the decision in which will bind the civil court. However if the defendant is acquitted in the criminal proceedings the civil court may still find in the plaintiff's favour if there is some alternative basis of liability. **54.31**

F. LIMITATION PERIODS

The law of limitation is exceptionally complex and the following should be taken only as a most general guide. **54.32**

Most limitation periods are periods of prescription which extinguish the right, but certain shorter periods operate only to bar the remedy.[8] Periods of limitation normally start to run when the cause of action arose, but their commencement may be postponed in some cases until the plaintiff had (or ought to have had) knowledge of the facts establishing the cause of action.

It should be noted that the law prescribes certain periods within which a demand for payment should be made (*e.g.* claims for payment by hoteliers, doctors, *huissiers* and artisans). After expiry of

---

[7] See para. 35.01 above; *Porta Leasing GmbH* v. *Prestige International SA* (E.C.J.), [1980] E.C.R. 1517, para. 21.69 above.
[8] Some special periods of limitation of less than five years (particularly in connection with debts) may be lifted, so as to bring the case within the longer general limitation periods, if the creditor challenges the debtor to swear that he has paid and the debtor refuses to do so.

this period there is a rebuttable presumption that payment has been made. The demand for payment during the running of the period renews the liability to pay and the limitation period starts to run again from that moment.

54.33 The general limitation period is 30 years which applies to most claims in contract and tort. There are, however, many shorter limitation periods under Luxembourg law, of which the following are some examples.

(*a*) Six months: an action by an indorser of a bill of exchange against another indorser or against the drawer;

(*b*) One year: an action by the holder of a bill of exchange against an indorser or the drawer;

(*c*) One year: most actions on a contract of non-international carriage; many actions on contracts of services by liberal professions; most actions on a contract for the sale of goods to a non-*commerçant* by a *commerçant* who has not manufactured them but has himself purchased them from a third party; actions in respect of latent defects in goods.

(*d*) Three years: actions against the acceptor of a bill of exchange; most claims made by a *partie civile* in criminal proceedings in respect of *delits*[9]; many claims on contracts of non-marine insurance, including proceedings brought directly against insurers for damage caused by a traffic accident.

(*e*) Five years: actions on debts payable by instalments, including salaries, pensions and rents; actions to nullify or rescind a contractual obligation (from the date of the contract or its breach).

(*f*) 10 years: claims by the purchaser against the vendor of newly constructed premises in respect of defects (the period starts at the date of purchase).

(*g*) 10 years: most actions, other than those referred to above, in respect of commercial matters;

(*h*) 30 years: actions in tort, including claims for personal injuries; actions in respect of the sale of land; actions other than those referred to above, in respect of non-commercial contracts.

---

[9] *Delits* are crimes, but they may often support civil claims for damages by *parties civiles*. Certain wrongs regarded as civil matters in common law countries are *delits*, such as infringements of patents and other intellectual property rights and defamation.

Luxembourg

G. Civil Procedure—Proceedings up to Judgment

1. General description

The civil procedure of the Luxembourg courts is regarded as **54.34** accusatorial. This is because the parties have, by and large, the conduct of the proceedings in their own hands. However the preliminary examination of the case, which a common lawyer would regard as the trial of the action, is to a considerable degree conducted by the judge. The various steps to be taken in the course of proceedings are rigidly prescribed by procedural rules.

Proceedings are begun by the service of a summons by the *huissier*. There then follows an exchange of written pleadings and documents. It is only when the case is fully prepared that oral argument takes place. Hearings may take place for the giving of oral evidence by witnesses or for the intervention of an expert. Final judgment is given in public.

Procedure before the *tribunal de paix* is less formal than in the *tribunal d'arrondissement*. Representation by an *avoué* is not compulsory nor are pleadings exchanged. The procedure in commercial cases differs from that in civil cases, in both courts of first instance, in that it is essentially oral.

2. Parties and legal representation

Parties. The plaintiff in an action is called the *demandeur*. **54.35** The defendant is called the *défendeur*. He may defend the proceedings by way of a *défense* or he may also counterclaim by making a *demande reconventionelle*, provided it has some connection with the subject-matter of the main claim. A third party may be brought into the proceedings by one or other of the main parties or he may apply to join the proceedings of his own motion. Either kind of involvement of a third party is called an *intervention*.

Both natural and legal persons may be parties to proceedings regardless of nationality or domicile. Special rules govern actions by or against persons under a disability and companies which are bankrupt or are being wound up by order of the court.

Legal representation. In all civil cases before the *tribunal* **54.36** *d'arrondissement*, and in all cases before the *Cour Supérieure de Justice*, the parties must be represented by, and the proceedings must be conducted by, an *avocat-avoué*. Any person may represent himself or another person before the *tribunal de paix* or before the *tribunal d'arrondissement* sitting in its commercial jurisdiction.

3. Commencement of proceedings

54.37   Proceedings before the *tribunal d'arrondissement* are begun by the service of an *exploit d'assignation*[10] on the defendant by a *hussier de justice*. The *assignation* is in the form of a statement by the *huissier* certifying that, at the plaintiff's request, he has summoned the defendant to appear at the court on a certain date or within a certain time limit. The *assignation* must contain certain specific information, in particular the names, occupations and addresses of the parties, the name and address of the *avoué* who represents the plaintiff,[11] the name and address of the *huissier*, the relief sought, a summary of the grounds relied upon, the name of the court before which the proceedings are brought, and the time within which an appearance must be made.[12] The proceedings are not regarded as being definitively pending until they are entered on the court's *rôle* and given a number.

Before the *tribunal de paix* proceedings are begun by the service of an *acte de citation* on the defendant by a *huissier de justice*.

Some types of proceedings, notably disputes between employer and employee, can be commenced by means of a simple summons (*requête*), which is deposited at the appropriate court and sent by registered post to the defendant by the court registrar.

4. Service of proceedings

54.38   The service of the *exploit d'assignation* is carried out by the *huissier de justice* attached to the court for the district in which the defendant is domiciled. This is necessary even when both parties are represented by lawyers. Service by the *huissier* must be effected on the defendant in person or on a member of his family or an employee at his registered domicile, or actual residence, by handing such person a copy of the document. If no such person can be found, the *huissier* may serve a copy of the document on a neighbour. The recipient must sign the original which is retained by the *huissier*. If there is no neighbour present who is able or willing to sign for the *assignation*, the *huissier* serves a copy of it on one of a number of competent local officials, such as the mayor, who indorses the original. If the recipient has neither domicile nor any known residence in Luxembourg, service is made by delivering a copy of the *assignation* to the court office (*parquet*) for it to be fixed to the main door of the court-room of the court in which the claim is brought, and by showing the original to the *procureur* for that court

---

[10] A writ of summons, also known as an *assignation*, or *exploit*, or *ajournement*.
[11] As to when representation by an *avoué* is compulsory see para. 54.36 above.
[12] See para. 54.39 below.

and handing him a second copy. At the same time a notice of the proceedings is published in a daily newspaper.

Service on a legal person may be made at its principal establishment or at its domicile as stated in its articles of incorporation, or, in default of both of the above, on such person appointed by the corporation to accept service on its behalf. When the defendant is domiciled abroad two copies of the *assignation* are delivered by the *huissier* to the court office (the *parquet*) for transmission through consular channels. In some instances there are bilateral conventions which provide for the direct transmission of the documents by the *parquet*, or by the *huissier de justice*, to the appropriate authority in the country of the defendant's domicile.

Whatever method of service is employed the *huissier* returns the original of the document to the plaintiff, indorsed with the date and place of service.

Foreign proceedings may be served in Luxembourg by the methods envisaged by the Hague Service Convention.[13]

5. Appearance by the defendant

As has been seen the participation of an *avoué* is obligatory in all **54.39** civil proceedings before the *tribunal d'arrondissement*. In such proceedings the *assignation* requires the defendant to appoint an *avoué* within eight days[14] to act for him. The defendant's *avoué* notifies his opponent *avoué* of his appointment in a formal document called a *constitution d'avoué*. The service of this document constitutes the appearance of the defendant in the proceedings, even though the court does not know of the proceedings until they are later entered on the *rôle*.

Before the *tribunal de paix*, and before the *tribunal d'arrondissement* in commercial matters, the case can be listed at once for hearing (*plaidoiries*), without an *avoué* having been appointed and without the exchange of pleadings. In such a case, an appearance is entered by the defendant or his *avocat* appearing personally at the first hearing.

6. Default judgments

If, in civil proceedings before the *tribunal d'arrondissement*, the **54.40** defendant does not appoint an *avoué* within the period specified in the *assignation*, the plaintiff may deliver a pleading called a *conclu-*

---

[13] See paras. 4.30 *et seq.* above and A2.03 below.
[14] This period is extended in the case of defendants who are to be served abroad, depending on the country involved, as follows: to 15 days for defendants served in Belgium, France, the Netherlands, the Federal Republic of German or Switzerland; one month for other European countries; and two months for the rest of the world.

sions de style par défaut to the court and, at the first hearing, ask for judgment in default in his favour. Similarly, if the defendant does not enter an appearance in commercial proceedings before the *tribunal d'arrondissement* or before the *tribunal de paix*, a default judgment may be given against him. Unless an application is made for the judgment to be set aside, it is enforceable in the same way as a final judgment.[15] In the meantime it may be open to the defendant to have the judgment set aside by means of *opposition*, or he may appeal to a higher court.

54.41 *Setting aside.* A party against whom a decision has been given in default of appearance may apply to the same court, by a procedure called *opposition*, for the judgment to be set aside and for the matter to be considered afresh. *Opposition* is available in respect of all decisions. It may be taken as of right, but the grounds for the *opposition* must be stated in the application. The applicant will not be required to provide security as a condition of being allowed to continue the case. The time limit for bringing an *opposition* is normally 15 days from the service of the judgment on the party or his *avocat-avoué*. These limits are not extended for parties resident abroad. After the expiry of the time limit the decision may still be challenged by an *appel*.[16] *Opposition* suspends enforcement unless the order has been declared to be provisionally enforceable notwithstanding *opposition*.

7. Disputes as to jurisdiction

54.42 If a case is commenced in a jurisdictionally incorrect court the defendant may contest the jurisdiction of the court. Before the *tribunal d'arrondissement* in a civil case the issue must, except as appears below, be raised in the pleadings before any defence on the merits is raised. In a commercial case, or before the *tribunal de paix*, the issue must be raised orally at the first hearing, again before any defence on the merits is advanced. However, an objection that the court does not have jurisdiction over the subject-matter of the claim may be made before all courts at any stage of the proceedings, and the court must examine its subject-matter competence of its own motion.

8. Pleadings

54.43 Each party must set out in his pleadings (*conclusions*) all matters of fact and law, and all the pleas and defences upon which he intends to rely. He must in addition offer appropriate means of

---

[15] There are certain procedural requirements which must be satisfied: see para. 54.67 below.
[16] See para. 54.64 below.

proof for the various facts upon which the claim or the defence is based. For example, he may offer to call a witness, without necessarily naming him at that stage, to prove that some event took place. Supporting documents, or copies, are not attached to the *assignation* or to the *conclusions* but are sent independently to the opposing party. Every pleading and formal notice between the parties must be signed by the *avoué* for the party concerned and must be sent by post to the opposing *avoué*, or served on him by the *huissier*. A copy must also be delivered to the court.

As has been seen above, the *assignation* must contain certain specific information. The particulars of the relief claimed and of the grounds relied upon must be sufficiently set out to enable the defendant to understand the nature of the case which is being brought against him. The plaintiff must specify the overall sum claimed, but individual items may remain unquantified until the last hearing before judgment.

After the defendant's *avoué* has notified his opponent that he is **54.44** acting, the latter has three weeks in which to serve the plaintiff's first pleading, called the *conclusions de style*, in which the contents of the *assignation* are repeated and which also specifies the date for the first hearing.[17] Thereafter, the defendant's *avoué* has three weeks in which to serve his defence (*moyens de replique*). In practice however longer periods are frequently taken by the respective *avoués*

A counterclaim, known as a *demande reconventionelle* may be added to the defence by means of further *conclusions* served between the *avoués*. Claim and counterclaim will normally be dealt with together and will be subject to a single judgment at the end of the case. If the defendant's *avoué* does not serve his defence within the required time the plaintiff's *avoué* may call on him formally to provide a defence and he may restore the case for hearing before the court as a default matter. If the defendant needs more time to prepare his defence he must obtain the consent of the plaintiff.

After receipt of the defendant's defence the plaintiff may, if necessary, serve a reply, called the *conclusions de réponse*, but he is not permitted to introduce any new cause of action or claim. If there has been a counterclaim, the plaintiff will plead to it by way of defence.

The pleadings are considered to be closed after service of the defence to the main claim, or, as the case may be, of the defence to the counterclaim. Only in exceptional cases do further pleadings follow the service of the reply, unless they are required for the purpose of commenting on matters which have arisen during the inves-

---

[17] See para. 54.45 below.

tigatory stage of the proceedings, such as the evidence given by witnesses or the opinion of an expert.

9. The hearings

54.45 *Introduction.* Civil procedure in Luxembourg, unlike that in France, does not provide for the appointment of an examining judge to supervise the interlocutory stages of the case and to ensure that it is brought to a state of readiness for the hearing. The preparation of the case is in the hands of the parties and their lawyers. It is complete when the parties have exchanged their pleadings and no new element on the file requires to be dealt with. It is then for either party to ask the court for a date upon which the first hearing will take place.

The first hearing. In a civil case, as has been seen above,[18] the *assignation* calls upon the defendant to appoint an *avoué* to act for him. When the plaintiff's *avoué* receives notice of this appointment he serves the *conclusions de style* which summon the defendant to appear in court on a given day. At least two days before the day selected for the hearing, another copy of the *conclusions de style* is delivered to the registry of the court for enrolment. This is the first moment at which the court becomes aware of the proceedings. On the day of the first hearing no oral argument takes place. The court either directs that the case be put on the *rôle général* or it specifies the date for the hearing of oral arguments. When the case is put on the *rôle général* the parties will exchange further *conclusions* until one party serves on the other a notice, called an *avenir*, inviting the other to appear in court for the fixing of a date for the hearing of oral arguments. If the other party considers that the case is not sufficiently prepared at this stage, he can file a further pleading asking the court to order additional investigatory steps to be taken.

In a commercial case[19] the *assignation* requires the defendant to appear in court on a given date upon which the case is either put on the *rôle général* for *conclusions* to be exchanged or a date for the oral hearing is specified.

The oral hearing. On the day fixed for the oral hearing of the case the *avocats-avoués* read their *conclusions* aloud to the full court, and enlarge upon their arguments and the evidence in support of the remedies or procedures which they are seeking. If, after the first hearing, the court feels able to give an immediate judgment in

---

[18] See para. 54.37 above.
[19] See para. 54.18 above.

favour of one or other party it will do so. If the court is not able to come to a final decision, the proceedings enter into an investigatory stage.

The investigation. Extensive reforms were introduced into Lux-   **54.46**
embourg civil procedure in 1985. These were modelled on the new French code of civil procedure and were designed to speed up proceedings. The court now has power to direct an investigation (*mesures d'instruction*) at any stage of the proceedings if it considers that it has insufficient material upon which to come to a final decision in the case. The judge may do this of his own motion or at the request of the parties. The investigation will be carried out by the judge who has made the order, or a member of the same bench, and he has a wide discretion as to the method of investigation to be adopted. He may receive evidence from witnesses, which he may direct should be received in the form of a signed statement (*attestation*) or be taken orally at a hearing held for the purpose (*enquête*) under the supervision of a *juge-commissaire*. He may direct the personal attendance of the parties for questioning, he may appoint an expert to report on the matters in issue, or he may conduct a view of the *locus in quo*. At each stage, the court decides whether the evidence before it is legally capable of being received and whether it is sufficient to decide the case.

Evidence. The rules relating to evidence and proof are somewhat formal. There are said to be five types of proof. In addition to documentary evidence (*la preuve litterale*) and oral evidence (*la preuve testimoniale*), each of which is discussed below, the court may take account of a party's admission (*aveu*) and the surrounding circumstances (*les indices*). The fifth form of proof is the decisory oath (*le serment litisdecisoire*), by which one party may require the other to make a solemn oath as to the truth of a material fact, under threat of criminal prosecution. If he does so, it is decisive of the proceedings.

The law provides that certain facts and documents can only be proved by certain types of proof: for example, a claim upon an agreement involving a sum in excess of LUF 100,000 may only be proved by evidence in writing, except as against a *commerçant*.

The final hearing. Once the investigations and evidence-taking is   **54.47**
complete and the parties have had the chance to comment on the investigations in further pleadings, the court appoints a date for a final oral hearing, at which the respective *avocats* make their final addresses to the court. Their submissions are based on the written material contained in their *conclusions*. Generally they will not repeat all the arguments in the case but will merely refer to those points which they feel still need to be emphasised. At the end of this hearing a date is fixed for the judgment to be given. The judges

deliberate on their decision in private before the judgment is announced in open court on the appointed day.

10. Security for costs

54.48   Luxembourg is a party to the Hague Convention on Civil Procedure of March 1, 1954, Article 17 of which abolishes requirements as to security of costs in respect of plaintiffs who are both nationals of, and residents in the Contracting States.[20] Although it is possible to obtain security from plaintiffs from other countries, this is rarely done in practice.

11. Witnesses and oral evidence

54.49   The examination of witnesses is carried out at a special hearing (an *enquête*) held for the purpose, usually before a single judge. The parties must identify the witnesses whom they wish to be called to give evidence, but they may not question them directly. They may only suggest questions for the judge to ask. The witnesses are heard on oath. The judge may question the witness on all facts of which the law permits evidence and he may order any other witness to attend whose hearing seems useful to the discovery of the truth. The judge may recall witnesses, confront them with each other or with the parties, and, in appropriate cases, question them in the presence of any expert. The registrar of the court (the *greffier*) takes a full note of the evidence in the form of a deposition which is entered in a written record (*procès verbal*) of the proceedings. After the enquiry has been held, the proceedings are restored on application of either party and the parties are given an opportunity to exchange further written *conclusions*.

[The next paragraph is number 54.51]

12. Documentary evidence

54.51   All parties are obliged to disclose to each other the documents upon which they intend to rely. The term "documents" is understood in a wide sense and would include, in addition to documentary evidence, correspondence, the statements of witnesses not being called, experts' reports and police reports. This disclosure must be made in due time before the date fixed for the oral hearing of the case. Failure to comply with this requirement may result in the non-admission in the proceedings of the document in question or the granting of an adjournment to the other party.

---

[20] See para. 6.11 above.

There is no general obligation on a party to disclose relevant   **54.52**
documents which would not assist his case, although the judge may
order the production of any document which is known to exist,
against the sanction of a fine. Confidential correspondence passing
between the respective lawyers, as well as correspondence between
a lawyer and his client, is privileged from production.

13. Experts

Any matter which depends upon scientific or expert opinion   **54.53**
may, upon the direction of the court, be investigated by an appropriately qualified expert. The expert is usually selected from an
official list. The court fixes a time limit for the production by the
expert of his report. The *greffier* notifies the expert of his appointment and provides him with all relevant documents. The function
of the expert is to inform the judge as to the technical issues in the
case but not to decide the case itself. The expert may convene a
meeting or question the parties and the witnesses. His report is
made available to the parties who have an opportunity to comment
on or to challenge his findings. The court may, in an appropriate
urgent case, appoint an expert as a provisional measure before the
commencement of the proceedings. After the expert's report has
been obtained, the proceedings are restored on the application of
either party and the parties are given an opportunity to comment on
the report in further written *conclusions*.

14. Proof of foreign law

A party who wishes to rely on foreign law must refer to it in his   **54.54**
pleadings and prove it. This is normally done by means of a statement as to the foreign law (*certificat de coutume*), made by a person
of suitable qualification or experience, which is included in a party's
documentary evidence. The rules as to what constitutes adequate
evidence of foreign law are very liberal and foreign statutes, treatises, textbooks and other documentary material may be admitted.
The court may apply foreign law of its own motion, either by taking
judicial notice of it or, in a complex case, by appointing an expert.

15. Compromise

The parties may settle their dispute at any time before judgment.   **54.55**
Although the court is under no obligation to encourage a compromise, it may do so and become actively involved in the settlement (a
transaction judiciaire). When the court is involved in this way, the
record of the agreement is signed by the parties and the judge. It

will then be capable of being executed as if it were a judgment, provided that it bears the *formule exécutoire*.[21]

Alternatively, the parties to an actual or potential dispute may enter into a written contract to resolve their differences, without the intervention of the court (a *transaction extra-judiciaire*). To be valid, the matters disposed of in the agreement must be legally capable of being so disposed. Thus any special authorisation that may be required must have been obtained. This may arise in settlements involving minors, or other persons under a disability, or public bodies. The effect of a contractual settlement is the same as that of a final judgment in respect of which no appeal may be made.

A debtor may, after the commencement of proceedings, offer to pay his creditor the whole sum owed, together with interest and costs. The debtor may deposit the sum in the *Caisse de Dépôts et Consignations*. This operates to release him from his obligation. To be effective, the deposit must fulfil certain conditions of substance and form. In particular it must be preceded by a notice to the creditor telling him the date, time and place at which the amount offered will be deposited.

16. The judgment

54.56   The judgment, in civil and commercial cases, is announced in open court and a copy, in simple form, may be collected from the court office. A full official copy of the judgment (an *expédition*) may also be obtained on payment of the appropriate fee and after further procedural steps have been taken.[22] In addition to the formal parts of the judgment, setting out such matters as the names of the parties and their representatives, the names of the court, the names of the judges and the date, the judgment also contains a summary of the evidence and arguments of the various parties and the reasons upon which the court has based its decision (*les motifs*), and a statement of the decision itself (*le dispositif*). The judgment will normally contain provisions as to costs and interest and it may state that it is provisionally enforceable.[23]

17. Costs

54.57   The costs of proceedings in court are of three kinds: the *frais judiciaires*, which comprise the court costs, the fees of the *huissier* and of the *greffier*; the *dépens*, which are special scale fees due to each *avocat-avoué* in respect of each step taken by him in the course of

---

[21] As to the enforcement of court settlements, see para. 54.70 below.
[22] See para. 54.67 below.
[23] See para. 54.67 below.

the proceedings; and the *honoraires*, which are the fees of the *avocat-avoué*, additional to the *dépens*, for his assistance and judicial representation during the proceedings.

The *frais-judiciaires* are payable to the court or to the *huissier* by each party as and when a step is taken in the action which requires payment of a fee. The winning party will normally be awarded his costs against the losing party but these will extend only to the *frais-judiciaires* and the *dépens* which he has incurred. Each party is liable to his own lawyer in respect of his *honoraires*. If a party succeeds in part the court may in its discretion order only a part of the recoverable costs to be paid by the losing party. A party who has been ordered to pay his opponent's costs may challenge the amount of those costs by applying to the *Ordre des Avocats* for an official taxation.

H. CIVIL PROCEDURE—PROVISIONAL AND PROTECTIVE MEANS

1. Provisional orders obtained summarily

Luxembourg law provides a summary procedure, called *référé* **54.58** proceedings, by which a party may obtain protective or other provisional orders from the court on an *inter partes* basis. The orders made on this procedure (*ordonnances de référé*) are provisional in nature and are not a final determination of the parties' rights. This procedure is discussed in greater detail below.[24]

2. Provisional attachment

Various forms of protective attachment (*saisie conservatoire*) are **54.59** also available as protective measures in order to obtain security for a claim which is the subject-matter of proceedings. Authorisation for attachment may be obtained initially from the president of the *tribunal d'arrondissement*, or his deputy, on an *ex parte* basis (*sur requête*). The order is then served by the *huissier* on the person in possession of the property to be seized. If that person is a third party, the order is called a *saisie arrêt*. If necessary, some third person may be authorised to take possession of and to safeguard the property concerned.

Within eight days of the original order the applicant must serve an *assignation* on the defendant seeking validation of the order authorising the attachment. The defendant cannot challenge the attachment by *opposition* or appeal against the president's order or by

---

[24] Para. 54.61 below.

seeking an injunction restraining the attachment, but he may secure
the release of the attached property by providing acceptable alternative security. The court which is seized of the validation proceedings will in due course rule upon that issue, and that ruling may be
susceptible to *opposition* or appeal.

3. Interim nature of the order

54.60   In all cases the party who has obtained the provisional measures
must continue to seek a judgment on the merits of the claim or he
will lose the benefit of the measures he has previously been granted.
The order is provisional and only becomes final when a successful
decision on the merits is obtained from the trial judge. If it is found
that provisional measures have been granted in response to an
application which was not justified, or was made in bad faith, the
party against whom they were ordered can claim damages. A provisional order may be varied if a change of circumstances can be
shown.

I. CIVIL PROCEDURE—SUMMARY PROCEDURES

1. *Référé* proceedings

54.61   The president of the *tribunal d'arrondissement* has power, in
appropriate urgent cases, to make an order to restrain some
obviously wrongful activity or to prevent an immediate risk of
harm. This may be done by means of an urgent interim summons,
called an *ordonnance de référé* provided that the substance of the case
will not be prejudiced. Application is made to the president of the
tribunal d'arrondissement, or his deputy, on notice to the respondent.
The applicant has to show good grounds for the making of the
order. A summons has to be served on the respondent but in appropriate cases it may be on very short notice. The president also has
power to make an interlocutory order to prevent the destruction of
evidence.

    Although the *référé* is particularly appropriate for injunctive relief
in non-money claims, it may also be used in money claims. One
type of order which may be obtained by this procedure is a provisional order for payment of all or part of a debt or damages (*référé
provision*). Such an order is available in any case in which the obligation to pay is not seriously contestable. It provides the creditor
with security from the debtor, in order to prevent him from being
prejudiced by the time taken by the proceedings or the delaying tactics of the debtor. When the provisional order is for payment of the
entire claim with interest it often happens that no further proceedings on the merits of the claim take place.

2. Summary order for payment

There is a simple type of procedure which is used in smaller debt **54.62** cases called *ordonnance de paiement*. It is available in the *tribunal de paix* in respect of claims of up to LUF 100,000. The creditor completes a printed form which he files at court with his supporting documents. An order to pay, made by the *juge de paix*, is served on the defendant. The defendant may oppose the proceedings within 14 days, but if he does not judgment will be given against him.

J. CIVIL PROCEDURE—APPEALS

1. Introduction

Types of appeal. A distinction is made between ordinary and **54.63** extraordinary appeals in Luxembourg law. There are two types of ordinary appeal, "*appel*," which is an appeal in the strict sense to a higher court, and "*opposition*," which is an application to the court which made an order in default, for the order to be set aside. Extraordinary appeals comprise an appeal by way of cassation, an application by a third party for an order to be set aside, and an application to reopen a judgment in exceptional circumstances. The lodging of an ordinary appeal generally has the effect of suspending the enforceability of the judgment, unless it has been declared provisionally enforceable,[25] whereas this is not so in the case of extraordinary appeals.

2. Ordinary appeals

Appel. All final judicial decisions in civil and commercial matters **54.64** may be appealed to a superior court, with the exception of decisions of the *tribunal de paix* involving less than LUF 15,000. Interlocutory decisions in respect of investigatory proceedings (*mésures d'instruction*) may normally only be challenged in conjunction with an appeal against the final decision in the proceedings. An *appel* involves a fresh consideration of the case on both fact and law and a decision *de novo*, called an *arrêt*.

Appeal lies from the decisions of the *tribunal de paix* to the *tribunal d'arrondissement*. From the first instance decisions of the *tribunal d'arrondissement* it lies to the *Cour Supérieure de Justice* sitting as an appellate court (*siégeant en matière d'appel*).

Time for appealing. The normal time limit for bringing an appeal is 40 days from the service of the judgment on the defendant, either personally or at his domicile. In the case of default judgments, time runs from the end of the period for bringing an *opposition*. The

---

[25] See para. 54.67 below.

limits are extended for foreign parties by the same periods as apply for responding to an *assignation*.[26]

Opposition. The means by which a party may object to a default judgment by way of *opposition* has already been described.[27] Similar procedures obtain for setting aside various other specialised forms of order.

3. Extraordinary appeals

54.65   *Cassation.* The *Cour Supérieure de Justice* exercises its jurisdiction in cassation as the *Cour de Cassation*. This form of appeal is only available to challenge decisions of last resort, that is to say decisions in respect of which no appeal lies or in respect of which other rights of appeal have been exhausted. The grounds of challenge are restricted to infringements of law and to breaches of substantial formal requirements. The court may reject the appeal on the ground that cassation does not lie. If it accepts the appeal it may either confirm the decision below, or it may quash it. If it quashes an *arrêt* or a judgment of the *tribunal d'arrondissement* or of the *tribunal de paix* it may substitute its own decision or remit the case to a different court. The normal time limit for bringing an appeal by way of cassation is two months. In civil cases appeal in cassation does not normally suspend the enforcement of the decision appealed.

Tierce opposition. This is a procedure whereby a person who is affected by a judgment given in proceedings to which he was not a party may, if appropriate grounds exist, apply to the court for the judgment to be set aside. In practice, the parties to proceedings will forestall this type of application by applying for the judgment to be declared to be *commun*. Enforcement is not automatically suspended by *tierce opposition*.

Requête civile. This is a form of extraordinary appeal which permits the setting aside of a judgment obtained by improper means.

K. Civil Procedure—Enforcement

1. Enforcement of Luxembourg judgments

54.66   *Introduction.* An ordinary judgment cannot be enforced before the expiration of eight days after the date of the judgment, unless it has been declared to be provisionally enforceable. The bringing of an ordinary appeal suspends enforcement unless the judgment has been declared to be provisionally enforceable. In addition certain

---

[26] See para. 54.37 above.
[27] See para. 54.41 above.

formalities have to be complied with before execution can take place, notably the formal service by the *huissier* of a copy of the judgment in executory form.[28] An ordinary judgment remains enforceable for 30 years. A default judgment cannot be enforced until eight days after it has been formally served on the defendant, and remains enforceable only for six months from its date.

Provisional enforceability. Steps may be taken to enforce a judg- **54.67**
ment on a provisional basis if the court has declared it to be pro-
visionally enforceable or if it is of a kind which is anyway only provisional, such as a provisional attachment of assets. If the court orders that a judgment is provisionally enforceable (*exécutoire par provision*) the successful party may proceed directly to execution of the judgment, without taking the other procedural steps which would be necessary in the case of ordinary execution. If he does so, however, he will be liable to the other party for any loss caused if the judgment is eventually reversed.

Period of grace. The court may grant the judgment debtor a period of grace within which to satisfy the judgment. Any such provision must be included in the judgment itself, but if it is made it suspends the execution of the judgment, although not its other legal effects.

Executory form of judgment. A single enforceable copy of the judg-
ment (a *grosse* or *expédition exécutoire*) may be issued on application to the court office (*greffe*) and payment of the appropriate fee. A second or subsequent enforceable copy may be issued only by leave of the president of the court. If the judgment was given in a commercial matter, the copy may be obtained merely by a request to the court. In the case of a civil judgment, as opposed to a commercial judgment, further steps are necessary. The successful party's *avoué* draws up a document known as the "*qualités.*" This sets out the names, occupations, and addresses of the parties, the written pleadings, the issues of fact and of law. A copy is served by the *huissier* on the opposing *avoué* and the original is delivered to the court with a request for the preparation of the "*grosse,*" or "*expédition.*"

The *grosse* or *expédition* is a long form of the judgment, which (in a civil case) sets out the *qualités* as well as the decision of the court, and which bears an indorsement as to its executory character. This indorsement, called a *formule exécutoire*, is in the form of a command by the Grand Duke directing all *huissiers* to carry out execution.[29] The *grosse* must then be served by a *huissier* on the los-
ing party and on his *avoué*.

---

[28] See para. 54.67 below.
[29] *Cf.* the *formule exécutoire* used in France, at para. 50.67 above.

Service. Once the enforceable copy of the judgment has been issued, a number of steps must be carried out before it can be executed. First, in cases in which representation by an *avoué* is compulsory,[30] the judgment must be served by the *huissier* on the *avoué* for the losing party (*signification de jugement à avoué*). If this is not done, subsequent acts of execution are void. Secondly, the *huissier* must serve a copy of the judgment on the person against whom execution is to be carried out and, thirdly, he makes a formal demand to the debtor to pay immediately or within a short period against the threat of execution on his property.

54.68   *Execution.* If the debtor does not comply with the demand to satisfy the judgment, the *huissier* will proceed with one or more of the following methods of execution:

   (*a*) attachment of personal assets (*saisie-exécution*);
   (*b*) attachment of earnings (*saisie-salaires*);
   (*c*) attachment of any sum which a third party owes to the debtor (*saisie-arrêt*);
   (*d*) attachment of immovable property (*saisie-immobilière*).

If the defendant is in a state of bankruptcy the creditor can seek an order to that effect.

54.69   *Other methods of enforcement.* A non-money judgment, such as an injunction ordering a party to perform or to refrain from some act, can be enforced by a financial penalty (an *astreinte*) which may be in a fixed sum or which may accrue on a daily or other periodic basis until the judgment is satisfied. The penalty is payable to the party in whose favour the judgment has been given but, on the application of the party against whom the penalty has been ordered, it may be set aside or reduced before it becomes payable. Unlike the position in France, an *astreinte* may not be imposed to enforce a money judgment.

Opposing the execution. The president of the *tribunal d'arrondissement*, sitting in matters of *référé*, has jurisdiction to determine all questions arising in relation to the execution of judgments.

2. Authentic instruments and court settlements

54.70   *Authentic instruments.* Luxembourg law permits certain authentic instruments (*actes authentiques*) to be enforced in the same manner as judgments. Authentic instruments are used for such matters as contracts for the sale or mortgage of land, marriage contracts, wills, and the articles of association of certain forms of company. Some such documents are required to be in an authenticated form,

---

[30] See para. 54.36 above.

whereas in other cases, this is optional. In order to be authentic, such an instrument must have been drawn up by a notary and entered in his register, and there are additional requirements relating to the registration of certain kinds of authentic instruments, notably certain types of contract for the sale or mortgage of land.

In order for the instrument to be enforceable, the notary must have issued an enforceable copy of it indorsed with a *formule exécutoire*. Such a copy (*la grosse d'acte authentique*) may then be served by the *huissier* and enforced by him in the same way as a judgment.

Court settlements. If the parties have entered into a settlement with the intervention of the court (a *transaction judiciaire*), the terms of the settlement will have been entered in the minutes of the court. An extract from these minutes may be issued by the court indorsed with a *formule exécutoire* in the same manner as a judgment. This document may then be served by the *huissier* and enforced by him as if it were a judgment.

3. Enforcement of foreign judgments

Foreign judgments are enforceable in Luxembourg by the same methods as are available in respect of Luxembourg judgments once their execution has been authorised by the indorsement of a *formule exécutoire*. The procedure for obtaining this indorsement differs depending on whether or not the judgment comes within a convention for the enforcement of judgments, notably the 1968 Convention. **54.71**

Enforcement under the terms of a convention. Under the provisions of the 1968 Convention the enforcement of a judgment given in another Contracting State can be obtained by means of a *requête* to the president of the *tribunal d'arrondissement* of the area in which the debtor is domiciled. An appeal from his decision lies to the *Cour Supérieure de Justice* in its appellate capacity. The judgment which is to be enforced and its accompanying documentation must be in French or German or be accompanied by a translation into one of those languages.[31]

This procedure has been extended to the enforcement of judgments from any country with which Luxembourg has a bilateral convention.

---

[31] The translation must be carried out by a person authorised to do so in one of the Contracting States: see para. 29.29 above. In Luxembourg, translations should be carried out by a sworn translator, but in practice translation (at least between French and German) is carried out by *avocats* and *huissiers*.

54.72   *Judgments not covered by a convention.* In cases to which neither the 1968 Convention nor any other bilateral or multilateral convention applies, proceedings for enforcement of a foreign judgment are brought in the *tribunal d'arrondissement*, for the area in which the defendant is domiciled, by serving an *assignation* on the defendant, as in an ordinary action. The conditions for recognition are: that the foreign judgment is enforceable in the country of origin; that the foreign court had jurisdiction both according to its own rules and according to Luxembourg rules of private international law; that the foreign court applied the same law that would have been applied by a Luxembourg court; that the recognition or enforcement of the foreign judgment does not offend Luxembourg *ordre public*. If the above conditions are satisfied, the court is precluded from considering the merits of the foreign judgment and will authorise enforcement.

L. LEGAL PERSONS

54.73   Luxembourg law provides for a number of different types of legal entity, of which the most common are as follows:

(a) *Société anonyme* (S.A.), a public limited company;

(b) *Société à responsabilité limitée* (S.A.R.L.), a private limited company;

(c) *Société en nom collectif* (S.N.C.), a partnership where the liability of the partners is unlimited;

(d) *Société en commandite simple* (S.C.S.), a partnership in which the liability of some of the partners is limited according to the quantum of their investment;

(e) *Société en commandite par action* (S.C.A.), a partnership in which the liability of some of the partners is limited to the amount of their shares, which are transferable;

(f) *Société co-operative*, a cooperative society, commonly a food producer or a retailer or a bank;

(g) *Association sans but lucratif* (A.S.B.L.), a non-profit-making association;

(h) *Société civile*, a partnership whose activities are traditionally non-commercial and in which the liability of the members is not limited.

M. LEGAL AID

54.74   If a party to a civil case cannot find an *avocat* to act for him, or if he has insufficient means to pay his fees, the *bâtonnier*[32] may, if so requested, nominate an *avocat* to represent him. Also, any resident

---

[32] See para. 54.05 above.

of Luxembourg who is without means may participate in proceedings free of all court costs (*frais judiciaires*) and scale fees of *avocats* (the *dépens*).[33]

To obtain this concession the party must make application to the trial judge, supported by a means test certificate issued by his local authority and a certificate of non-payment of tax. Notice of the application is sent to the *ministère public* who directs the police to investigate the means of the applicant. The judge will grant the application if he is satisfied as to the financial criteria, unless the party's case is devoid of merit. There is no appeal against the decision to grant or to refuse legal aid. A legally aided party is provisionally exempted from stamp duties and registration fees and the *dépens* payable to the *avoué*.

By a Ministerial Regulation of November 16, 1978 a public service was set up to provide individuals with free advice as to the protection or enforcement of their legal rights.

---

[33] See para. 54.57 above.

CHAPTER 55

NETHERLANDS

Written in collaboration with Jhr. mr. Clemens van Nispen tot Sevenaer and mr. Harry Ferment, Advocaten, The Hague.[1]

---

[1] Partners, *Barents, Gasille & Mout*, The Hague.

A. The Legal System

1. Introduction

History and territory. During the period from 1795 to 1813 the   **55.01**
Netherlands were initially linked by treaty to France and were then
annexed by France. Following the defeat of Napoleon the territories comprising the modern Netherlands and Belgium became
united under the Dutch Crown until 1830 when revolution in Belgium brought about its separation as an independent kingdom.[2]
The legacy of French law and French judicial organisation has persisted in both countries.

The origins of the legal system. By the end of the eighteenth century, a system of civil law had developed in the Netherlands based
on Dutch customary law and Roman law,[3] but this was supplanted
in 1809 by the French civil code. In 1838, the Netherlands adopted
its own civil code (the *Burgerlijk Wetboek*) which was closely
modelled on the French civil code and which, although much
amended, still forms the basis of the civil law of the Netherlands.[4]

2. The administration of justice

The ordinary courts deal with both civil and criminal matters.   **55.02**
They are arranged hierarchically on the French model, with two
levels of court of first instance, the *kantongerecht* (local court) and
the *arrondissementsrechtbank* (district court), with regional *gerechtshoven* (courts of appeal) and a single Supreme Court, the *Hoge Raad
der Nederlanden.*

There is no single unified system of administrative courts, but
there are specific administrative courts or tribunals for a number of
areas of administrative activity. The judicial division of the *Raad
van State* (Council of State) has jurisdiction over most administrative decisions which fall outside the scope of the specialised administrative courts.

Public and private law. One of the legacies of the French legal
system is the division between public and private law, although the
distinction between the two is less easy to draw in Dutch law than
in some other systems. The control of the administration and the

---

[2] The Netherlands Antilles form part of the Kingdom of the Netherlands, but do
not presently fall within the scope of the 1968 Convention (see para. 34.08
above). They have their own court system, from which appeal in cassation lies to
the Hoge Raad.
[3] Roman-Dutch law still forms the basis of civil law in South Africa, Sri Lanka
and Zimbabwe.
[4] See para. 55.15 below.

exercise of its functions is governed in part by private law and subject to the jurisdiction of the ordinary civil courts.

B. Legal Practitioners

1. The *Advocaat* and *Procureur*

55.03   The *advocaat* acts for his clients both as a general legal adviser and as an advocate in court. He has exclusive rights to appear for parties in the *arrondissementsrechtbank* and the superior courts. There is however no monopoly in the giving of legal advice, but unqualified persons may not use the title of *advocaat*.

Legal education and qualification. Any person who has obtained the university law degree of *meester in de rechten*[5] is entitled to apply to the president of an *arrondissementsrechtbank* to be enrolled as an *advocaat*. For the first three years after his enrolment he is obliged to practice as a *stagiaire*, under the supervision of a more senior *advocaat*. The period of the *stage* is one of practical training, although from the start the *stagiaire* has full competence as an *advocaat*.

55.04   *Rights of representation and audience.* An *advocaat* must practice from an office in the district in which he is enrolled, but he may appear in all courts throughout the country. However it is a formal requirement that any party in civil proceedings before an *arrondissementsrechtbank* or a *gerechtshof* must be formally represented by a *procureur* who is enrolled in the district in which the court is situated.[6] For practical purposes the profession of *procureur* no longer exists separately from that of *advocaat*, and the vast majority of *advocaten* are also enrolled as a *procureur* in the district in which they have their offices. Accordingly if an *advocaat* has a case in another district he will conduct it in the name of a *procureur* of that district. The *advocaat* will himself prepare the written pleadings but the local *procureur* will sign them and deliver them to the court. Thereafter the *advocaat* will, as necessary, attend and conduct the oral hearings of the case, although the local *procureur* formally represents the client.

Before the *kantonrechter* a party may, if he wishes, represent himself or be represented by any person qualified or not. Often *deurwaarders*[7] will appear on behalf of a party, but in cases of any importance a party will be represented by an *advocaat*.

---

[5] Abbreviated as "mr.". A Doctorate in law also qualifies its holder to become an *advocaat*.

[6] This rule does not apply to the defendant in *kort geding*, (summary procedure), as to which see para. 55.61 below.

[7] See para. 55.13 below.

Before the *Hoge Raad*, which is permanently situated in the Hague, the parties must be represented by an *advocaat* who is enrolled at the *arrondissementsrechtbank* in the Hague. If an appeal comes to the *Hoge Raad* from another part of the Netherlands the respective *advocaten* in the court below will refer it to specialist *advocaten* in the Hague.

Organisation of practice. There are more than 5,000 *advocaten* in the Netherlands. Partnerships are permitted and are very common. Law firms of considerable size are to be found in the four principal cities, Amsterdam, the Hague, Rotterdam and Utrecht. A law firm will generally comprise its partners, associates (salaried), and *stagiaires* (also salaried). The practice according to which in some countries certain categories of legal work are carried out by unqualified clerks is virtually unknown in the Netherlands. Partnerships are permitted with notaries, as are, under certain conditions, association and co-operation with various other free professions. The Dutch lawyers are listed in a general directory of courts, lawyers, and legal services, called the *Gids voor de Rechterlijke Macht.*

Fees. The fees chargeable by an *advocaat* are a matter for agree- **55.05** ment with the client. The fee will usually be calculated on an hourly basis subject to augmentation or reduction by applying a variety of factors recommended by the *Nederlandse Orde van Advocaten*, although these are used only as general guidelines. The recommended basic hourly rate in a civil or commercial matter without particular value is Dfl.240.[8] For a *stagiaire* the rate may fall to Dfl. 140 per hour and, for a senior *advocaat* in an important case in a specialised field, it might rise to Dfl.1000 per hour. VAT is chargeable unless the work can qualify as an export. The ordinary rate is 18.5 per cent., with the reduced rate of 6 per cent. for family and matrimonial cases. An *advocaat* will often ask for some advance payment on account of fees and disbursements.

Professional organisation and conduct. The profession of *advocaat* is regulated by law, the *Advocatenwet*. The combined *advocaten* enrolled in the Netherlands constitute the *Nederlandse Orde van Advocaten*, (the national *Orde*). The combined *advocaten* enrolled at one *arrondissementsrechtbank* constitute the local *Orde*. Each local *Orde* elects representatives for the *College van Afgevaardigden* which in turn elects the members of the *Algemene Raad* (General Council) and the *Deken* (Dean) of the national *Orde*. The *College van Afgevaardigden* has the power to issue regulations on matters concerning the profession. Each local *Orde van Advocaten* has its own governing body, the *Raad van Toezicht*, under the presidency of the local

---

[8] As at June 1989.

Deken, which mainly deals with managerial matters, and the resolving, at an early stage, of disputes relating to fees and professional conduct.

Rules of conduct are laid down by the *Advocatenwet*, the regulations made by the *College van Afgevaardigden*, and rules of conduct by way of general guidelines issued by the *Algemene Raad*. Discipline is enforced by regional *Raden van Discipline* from which there is appeal to the *Hof van Discipline*. Professional indemnity insurance is compulsory.

[The next paragraph is number 55.09]

2. The *Notaris*

55.09   The *notaris* is a public official appointed by the Crown to practice in a particular district (*arrondissement*). Some contracts and other documents, such as those concerned with conveyances of immovable property, mortgages, and the formation of companies, are only valid if they have been drawn up as a *notariële akte*, executed in the presence of a *notaris*. Other transactions are sometimes concluded before a *notaris* at the request of the parties in order to confer on the contractual documents the higher degree of authenticity which attaches to notarial instruments.[9] Thus a debt which is so recorded can generally be enforced without the need for a confirming judicial judgment.[10] The original of each notarial instrument is kept in the safe custody of the *notaris* with certified copies provided for the parties. All instruments drawn up by a notary have to be registered with the Inspector of the Ministry of Finance, and all *akten* have to be listed in a *repertorium* delivered annually to the Inspector. A certified copy of this *repertorium* has to be delivered to the *arrondissementsrechtbank*.

In acting for his clients the *notaris* will often help them in drafting the terms of contractual and other documents and will give them incidental legal advice. However, unlike the *advocaat*, the *notaris* will not represent and take the part of his client in transactions with third parties. The majority of *notarissen* are sole practitioners although they are permitted to form partnerships with each other and with *advocaten*. With the exception of some major firms in Amsterdam and Rotterdam, firms of *notarissen* rarely have more than three partners. Their fees are fixed according to a statutory tariff. They have their own professional organisation called the *Koninklijke Notariële Broederschap*.

[The next paragraph is number 55.11]

---

[9] Notarial instruments are known as *authentieke akte*; see para. 55.70 below.
[10] See para. 55.70 below.

3. Foreign lawyers

There are, as yet, no special rules relating to the establishment of **55.11** foreign lawyers in the Netherlands. A small number of foreign law firms are established in the Netherlands, mostly in partnerships with Dutch law firms. A foreign lawyer is not permitted to describe himself as an *advocaat* unless he is entitled to use the title outside the Netherlands (in the Flemish speaking part of Belgium, for example). The EEC Legal Services Directive[11] permits lawyers qualified in other Member States to appear in the Dutch courts, subject to certain conditions laid down in the *Advocatenwet*. The visiting lawyer must act in conjunction with a local *advocaat*, who must verify whether the visiting lawyer is duly qualified and must introduce him to the presiding judge. He may wear his ordinary legal robes and, if the judge allows, address the court in his own language.

4. Lawyers in business and public employment

The legal departments of the larger business concerns as well as **55.12** several departments of the administration, such as the Departments for Foreign Affairs, for Economic Affairs, and above all the Ministry of Justice,[12] employ highly qualified lawyers, who may formerly have been practising *advocaten*. Although they rarely do so in practice, such lawyers may remain enrolled as *advocaten* but may not act in that capacity for their employers in dealing with third parties or in court proceedings. When the employing organisation becomes involved in litigation an *advocaat* in independent practice must be instructed to represent it.

5. The *Gerechtsdeurwaarder*

The *gerechtsdeurwaarder*, or *deurwaarder*, is a public official com- **55.13** parable to the French *huissier de justice*. He is usually not legally qualified. Every court has one or more *deurwaarders* attached to it, practising either individually or in partnership with other *deurwaarders*. In court, the *deurwaarder* acts as an usher, calling on the cases. His more important functions are out of court. He carries out the service of summonses, judgments and other court documents, and the execution of judgments. In performing these tasks the *deurwaarder* is engaged and instructed not by the court but by the parties, normally through their *advocaten*. Before the *kantongerecht* he often takes part in the conduct of proceedings by representing a party at his, or his *advocaat*'s, request. Thus he may appear before the court on formal hearings to deliver pleadings, sometimes acting

---

[11] Para. A2.47 below.
[12] Note also the *openbaar ministerie* described at para. 55.23 below.

for both parties simultaneously. Many *deurwaarders* have substantial debt collecting practices. Their fees in respect of their official activities are fixed according to a statutory tariff.

C. SOURCES OF LAW

1. Introduction

55.14   The Constitution of the Kingdom of the Netherlands dates from 1815 and it provides for a constitutional monarchy and a parliament and executive. It guarantees certain civil and political rights and freedoms. The principal source of law is legislation, which must conform to the Constitution, although the courts have no power to examine the constitutionality of Acts of Parliament. International treaties are contracted by the Crown but have no force until they have been approved by Parliament. Thereafter they prevail over Acts of Parliament and all subordinate legislation. European Community law prevails over domestic law in its own right.

2. Legislation

55.15   The Netherlands has a codified system of law. Substantive private law is largely set out in the *Burgerlijk Wetboek* (BW, Civil Code), and the *Wetboek van Koophandel* (WvK, Commercial Code). Procedural law is set out in the *Wetboek van Burgerlijke Rechtsvordering*, (WvBRv, or Rv, the Code of Civil Procedure) and the *Wet op de Rechterlijke Organisatie* (Wet RO, the Judicial Organisation Act). In addition to these codes there are numerous statutes of narrower application which deal with substantive and procedural matters in specific fields. There is a strict hierarchy of subordinate legislation. Although for historical reasons a separate Commercial Code is still in existence, there is in fact no practical distinction between civil and commercial law, nor between civil and commercial cases. In the past, important sections of the Commercial Code have been transferred to the Civil Code. A new civil code, which has been in preparation for several decades, will incorporate all the topics currently remaining in the Commercial Code, and the separate Commercial Code will cease to exist. The date of implementation of the new code (NBW) is still uncertain. Current case law sometimes reflects the new civil code by way of anticipatory interpretation.

3. Decided cases and legal writings

55.16   If legislation is silent or deficient on a particular legal point the lawyer will turn to the jurisprudence of the *Hoge Raad* as set out in decided cases. These cases are not binding either on the *Hoge Raad* itself or on lower courts but in practice they will be followed. Some areas of law, in particular those of tort, unfair competition, and industrial disputes, have been mainly formed by case law. In the absence of relevant jurisprudence of the *Hoge Raad* (or to supplement any such jurisprudence) reliance will be placed on the decisions of lower courts, text books and learned articles. The decisions of foreign courts in comparable cases are also sometimes taken into consideration.

4. Publications

National legislation is published officially in the *Staatsblad van het Koninkrijk der Nederlanden*.[13] Other official information, including government departmental announcements, is published in the *Nederlandse Staatscourant*. All important statutes, including the Codes, together with the most important treaties, administrative measures and excerpts from decided cases, are privately published in a commentary known as the "*Editie Schuurman & Jordens*" which runs to some 184 volumes. Statutes, treaties and legislative codes are also published, annotated with references to case law, in the "*Editie Cremers*." Selected judgments and decisions of the European Court of Justice, the Benelux Court of Justice, the *Hoge Raad, gerechtshoven, rechtbanken,* and *kantongerechten,* are published weekly in the *Nederlandse Jurisprudentie* (NJ). Judgments are normally identified by the name of the court and the date of the judgment, and by the year and number in the NJ (*e.g.* Hoge Raad, 29 maart 1985, NJ 1985, 591). This publication often includes scholarly comment but this usually appears after a delay of several months. For recent case law of the *Hoge Raad* the practitioner will refer to the *Rechtspraak van de Week* (RvdW) which is published within a few weeks of the judgments which it contains. There are also specialised series of law reports which deal with fields such as maritime, tax, building, traffic, and environmental law. Legal literature, in the form of text books and journals, is very extensive. Particular mention should be made of two series of textbooks, the *Asser-serie* and the looseleaf Kluwer Editions, which cover many topics of private law and are to be found on most lawyers' shelves.

55.17

D. Organisation of the Civil Courts

1. Introduction

Civil and commercial cases are heard by the ordinary courts. There are two levels of court of first instance (the *kantongerecht* and the *arrondissementsrechtbank*), one intermediate level of court of

55.18

---

[13] Referred to as the "*Staatsblad*," or "S." A particular law may thus be cited as "*Wet van [date], S [number of issue]*."

appeal (the *gerechtshof*) and the Supreme Court (the *Hoge Raad*). The decisions of the courts of first instance may be challenged once by an ordinary appeal to the next higher level of court (except in the smallest cases). If no ordinary appeal is available, a decision may be challenged by an appeal in cassation to the *Hoge Raad*.

There are no separate commercial courts. Some matters of public law, including criminal cases and tax appeals, come before the ordinary courts. Criminal cases are heard by the criminal division of the courts concerned. The International Court of Justice in the Hague forms no part of the Dutch court system.

2. The *kantongerecht*

55.19   The lower court of first instance is the *kantongerecht*. The Netherlands are divided, for jurisdictional purposes, into 62 *kantons*, each with its own court. The *kantonrechter*, the judge of the *kantongerecht*, hears all actions *in personam* in which the amount claimed does not exceed Dfl. 5,000, and, in addition, without upper limit, cases relating to employment, agency, landlord and tenant, hire purchase and agricultural tenancies.[14] If the amount claimed is less than Dfl. 2,500 there is no appeal, except, in limited circumstances, to the *Hoge Raad*. Otherwise there is an ordinary appeal to the *arrondissementsrechtbank*. The *kantonrechter* is appointed to a particular *kantongerecht* and he sits alone. In the *kantongerecht* in a major city there may be a number of *kantonrechters*, but in the smaller towns there may only be one *kantonrechter*. The procedure in the *kantongerecht* was originally intended to be less formal than in the *arrondissementsrechtbank* but it remains broadly similar. Parties may appear in person or may be represented by a non-lawyer. Often they are represented by *advocaten*, *deurwaarders*, or, in employment cases, by trade union officials. The *kantonrechter* also exercises criminal jurisdiction over lesser offences.

3. The *arrondissementsrechtbank*

55.20   The Netherlands are divided into 19 *arrondissementen* (districts), each with an *arrondissementsrechtbank*, often called the *rechtbank*. This is the higher court of first instance with jurisdiction to hear all cases except those specifically assigned to another court. Civil cases, other than *kort gedingen*,[15] are normally[16] heard by a bench of three judges, of whom one presides. As has been seen, the *arrondisse-*

---

[14] Matters related to agricultural tenancies are held before a special chamber called the *pachtkamer*, with a right of direct appeal to the *pachtkamer* of the *gerechtshof* in Arnhem.

[15] See para. 55.61 below.

[16] Some cases, particularly those concerning family matters, are heard by a single judge.

mentsrechtbank also hears ordinary appeals from the *kantongerecht*. Its decision in such appeals is final, subject only to appeal in cassation to the *Hoge Raad*. Ordinary appeal from its decisions at first instance lies to the *gerechtshof*.

4. The *gerechtshof*[17]

There are five *gerechtshoven* in the Netherlands, which sit in   **55.21**
Amsterdam, the Hague, 's Hertogenbosch, Arnhem and Leeuwarden. They hear ordinary appeals from the *arrondismentsrechtbanken* within their respective areas. The judges normally sit in benches of three. The *gerechtshof* in Amsterdam has a special business chamber (*ondernemingskamer*) in which two additional lay members sit as experts to deal with cases concerning the internal affairs of corporations. The *gerechtshof* in Arnhem hears appeals from all *pachtkamers* in the *kantongerechten* in matters relating to agricultural tenancies. All *gerechtshoven* have a special tax chamber in which they act as an administrative court hearing appeals from decisions by tax authorities.

5. The *Hoge Raad*

The Supreme Court of the Netherlands, the *Hoge Raad*, is   **55.22**
located permanently in the Hague. It hears appeals on points of law from all other courts in the country but only in cases in which no ordinary appeal is available. It thus may hear appeals from the *gerechtshoven*, appeals from the appellate decisions of the *arrondissementsrechtbank* on appeal from the *kantongerecht* and, exceptionally, direct appeals from the *kantongerecht* in cases in which less than Dfl. 2,500 has been claimed.

The *Hoge Raad* performs the essential function of ensuring the consistency of judicial decisions throughout the country. As a court of cassation it annuls the decision of the court below if it finds it to be contrary to national law or defective through non-observance of an essential procedural requirement. It is obliged to accept the findings of fact of the court below, but if it regards these findings as incomprehensible it may quash the judgment on the ground of insufficient reasoning. The *Hoge Raad* usually sits in chambers of five judges. In civil matters, with the exception of the *pleidooi*,[18] appearance before it is limited to members of the Bar of the Hague, and in practice to a fairly small number of specialists at that Bar.

---

[17] The *gerechtshof* is also sometimes referred to as the "*Hof*."
[18] See para. 55.46 below.

6. The judiciary and *openbaar ministerie*

55.23　Judges are appointed for life by the Crown, but they retire at the age of 70. Although a considerable number of judges are appointed from the practising legal profession, academic posts and other occupations involving legal work, many judges have spent their whole career in the judicial service. Entry to this is open to persons with a university law degree. There follows a period of training normally lasting six years, part of which is spent as a court clerk and part outside the judicial service, often as a *stagiaire* in a law office. A judge's first appointment is normally as a member of a three judge court in the *rechtbank*. Thereafter he may be promoted to sit as a single judge in the *kantongerecht* or to more senior posts in the *gerechtshof* or the *Hoge Raad*.

The *openbaar ministerie* is part of the administration, sometimes considered to be part of the judiciary, concerned with the maintenance of the law and the prosecution of criminal offences. Its members, all lawyers, are hierarchically organised under the *Procureur Generaal* at the *Hoge Raad*.

E. JURISDICTION OF THE CIVIL COURTS

1. Introduction

55.24　Where the 1968 Convention confers international jurisdiction on the courts of the Netherlands, the particular Dutch court in which the claim may be made is determined by the Convention's own provisions on local jurisdiction[19] and the jurisdictional rules of Dutch law summarised below. These rules determine which particular Dutch court has jurisdiction over a civil or commercial case. This will be the *kantongerecht* or the *arrondissementsrechtbank*, depending on the value or, occasionally, the subject matter of the claim. The locality in which the proceedings may be brought will usually depend upon the place where the defendant is domiciled or has a seat.

2. Domicile and seat

55.25　*Natural persons.* A natural person's domicile is at the place of his principal residence (*woonstede*) or, if he has no principal residence, at the place where he is actually staying. In practice, a person's domicile is normally the place where he has been registered in the local civil register. It is a matter of dispute whether a natural person may have more than one domicile. Minors and mental patients have a statutory domicile of dependence at the domicile of their legal guardian.

---

[19] See para. 15.03, nn. 10–11 above.

Legal persons. The seat of a company, whether incorporated in   **55.26**
the Netherlands or elsewhere,[20] is the place where, according to
statutory provision, or its articles of association or constitution, it is
expressed to have its seat. The statutory seat of a Dutch legal person must be in the Netherlands.

3. Jurisdiction—general rules

As in many other countries the general rule is that a defendant   **55.27**
must be sued in the appropriate court for the locality in which he is
domiciled. If the defendant has no known place of domicile he may
be sued in the courts for the locality in which he is actually residing.
Actions against legal persons may be brought in the appropriate
court for the locality in which the corporation has its seat. Where a
legal person has its central management and control (its actual seat)
in a place other than at its statutory seat, it may be sued in the
courts for that place, in respect of matters arising out of its activities
carried on at that place. Similarly, a company having an office or
branch in the Netherlands may be sued in the place where that
office or branch is located, in respect of claims which relate to that
office or branch.

4. Jurisdiction—special rules

Apart from the provisions of the 1968 Convention which regulate   **55.28**
local jurisdiction,[21] Dutch law does not contain rules which, for
example, give jurisdiction generally to the courts of the place of performance of a contractual obligation or, in cases of tort, where the
harmful event occurred. Special rules do however exist for certain
types of case, such as hire purchase cases, and disputes between
employer and employee. In hire purchase cases the plaintiff can sue
either in the defendant's court or in the court for the place where
the goods were transferred to the hirer. In employment cases the
plaintiff may sue either in the defendant's court or in the court for
the place where the work was normally to be performed. Claims for
the validation of the attachment of a debtor's assets normally have
to be brought in the court which has jurisdiction to hear the main
claim. Claims in respect of immovable property and claims between
landlord and tenant must ordinarily be brought in the appropriate
court for the locality in which the property is situated.

When the 1968 Convention applies to found local jurisdiction
(under Article 5) in the courts of the place in which an obligation is
to be performed, it may be necessary to take account of the relevant

---

[20] Dutch private international law permits parties to choose which law is to apply
for the purposes of determining the location of the seat of a legal person.
[21] See para. 15.03, nn. 10–11 above.

provisions of Netherlands law. These provide that, as a general rule and unless the parties otherwise agree, the place of performance of an obligation to pay money is at the domicile of the creditor, as long as he continues to live in the municipality where he was domiciled when the obligation was created, and otherwise at the domicile of the debtor. However, if payment in cash is due under a contract for the sale of goods, the place of payment, in the absence of agreement to the contrary, is generally at the place of delivery of the goods, which (unless otherwise agreed) is where the goods were at the time of formation of the contract.

5. Choice of court and entry of an appearance

55.29   With regard to cases which are to be heard at first instance by the *arrondissmentsrechtbank*, the parties may by agreement specify in which court their disputes are to be resolved, but, unless the parties have otherwise stipulated, the plaintiff usually retains the right to bring the proceedings in the defendant's court, despite the jurisdiction agreement.[22] Most existing disputes may by agreement between the parties be submitted to a *kantongerecht* within either party's *arrondissement*. Also, territorial jurisdiction may sometimes be conferred on an *arrondissementsrechtbank* which would not otherwise be locally competent, by reason of the defendant entering an appearance without contesting the jurisdiction.[23] A party may also nominate an address as his elective domicile for the purposes of the service of proceedings.

6. Exorbitant grounds of jurisdiction

55.30   A person who has no known domicile or place of residence in the Netherlands (or, being a company, does not have its seat in the Netherlands) may be sued by a plaintiff domiciled in the Netherlands in the court of the plaintiff's domicile.[24] Further, under Article 127 of the Code of Civil Procedure, a person of foreign nationality, even if his residence is not registered in the Netherlands, may be sued in a Dutch court in respect of any obligation, including a liability in tort, owed by him to a Dutch national. All the above rules are subject to the provisions of the 1968 Convention, so these latter two rules of exorbitant jurisdiction may not be relied upon against any person who is domiciled in another Contracting State.[25]

---

[22] Subject to Art. 17 of the 1968 Convention if it applies. See paras. 21–01 *et seq.* above.
[23] Disputes as to jurisdiction are discussed at para. 55.42 below.
[24] Art. 126(3) WvBRv.
[25] Art. 3 of the 1968 Convention. See para. 16.09 above.

7. Civil claims in criminal proceedings

A civil claim for damages can be brought by a victim of crime **55.31** (*beledigde partij*) in the criminal proceedings against the wrongdoer, but the amounts recoverable are severely limited: in the *kantongerecht* the maximum recoverable is Dfl. 600, and in the *arrondissementsrechtbank* it is Dfl. 1500. The claim may be introduced after the commencement of the criminal proceedings. The bringing of a claim in the criminal proceedings prevents the making of a claim for further damages in civil proceedings.

F. LIMITATION PERIODS

The law of limitation and prescription is exceptionally complex and **55.32** the following should be taken as only the most general guide. Distinctions must be made between a limitation period (*verjaringstermijn*), a prescription period (*vervaltermijn*) and a presumption of payment (*vermoeden van betaling*), all of which are regarded as matters of substantive law.

The expiry of a limitation period prevents the bringing of an action, but it does not necessarily extinguish the relevant rights and obligations. For example, performance of an obligation after the expiry of a limitation period is not regarded as having been done voluntarily. Thus money paid under an obligation which has become time-barred by a limitation period cannot be reclaimed. Limitation can be interrupted by certain acts and, in order to be relied on, it must be raised in the proceedings. On the other hand, a prescription period cannot be waived by either party and it extinguishes the relevant rights and obligations. A payment made after the expiry of a prescription period is regarded as having been made voluntarily and may generally be recovered. A period of prescription must be applied by the judge *ex officio*. In practice it is important to determine into which category a particular period falls, although this may not always be clear. The term "time bar" is used below in respect of both categories of period.

The general time bar period is 30 years, which applies to most **55.33** ordinary actions in contract and tort; but shorter periods are provided in respect of many types of claim, and these are set out in the Civil Code and other statutes. The following are some examples:

   (*a*) claims by purchasers in respect of defective goods: an undefined short period, the length of which depends on the nature of the fault and the custom of the place where the sale was concluded; in practice, about six weeks;

   (*b*) claims to set aside termination of contracts of employment without the permission of the Office of Labour: six months;

(c) claims on bills of exchange and promissory notes: various periods depending, for example, on whether it concerns the claim of an indorser or of the holder, or of some other person;

(d) direct claims by the victims of traffic accidents against insurers: three years;

(e) claims relating to most debts payable by annual or shorter instalments, such as annuities or pensions, yearly alimony, rent for houses and other immovable property: five years;

(f) claims for the rescision of agreements on certain grounds: five years;

(g) claims by minors against a guardian in connection with the guardianship: 10 years.

In addition to time bars of the type described above, Dutch law contains rules whereby, after the lapse of a certain period, payment is presumed to have taken place, but the plaintiff may require the defendant to state on oath that that is so. The following are examples of some such periods:

(h) claims for payment by teachers of arts and sciences, by hoteliers and by most workers: one year;

(i) claims for fees by doctors and pharmacists, *deurwaarders*, and boarding school keepers: two years;

(j) claims for payment by builders and shopkeepers: five years;

(k) claims by *advocaten* for fees: in connection with litigation, two years from the date of the judgment or settlement of the case; and for advisory work, 10 years.

G. CIVIL PROCEDURE—PROCEEDINGS UP TO JUDGMENT

1. General description

55.34   The procedure of the ordinary courts in a civil case is governed by the Code of Civil Procedure (*Wetboek van Burgerlijke Rechtsvordering*, usually abbreviated as "WvBRv" or "Rv"). The proceedings are conducted largely in writing. In a simple case the judge or judges will never see the parties, their *advocaten*, or any witnesses, but only the written pleadings, presented to the court at one of its regular special sittings. These sittings, called *rolzittingen*, play an important part in the conduct of Dutch civil proceedings. An *inter partes* hearing takes place only if there is some special reason for it, such as the court wishing to obtain information from the parties in person, or to attempt a settlement. Witnesses will only give evidence if so ordered by the judge. This is not to say that oral hearings are rare. On the contrary, in many cases there may be several oral hearings. A fairly common sequence is for the court to make successive interlocutory orders requiring, first, the attendance of the parties and, next, the hearing of witnesses, before proceeding to give a judgment which finally disposes of the case.

A further feature of Dutch civil procedure is that the role of the court is considered to be a passive one. It is for the parties to present such facts to the court as they, the parties, wish to be taken into account. On the other hand the court is able to intervene actively by ordering the parties to attend court to answer (if they so wish) the court's questions, and to direct the taking of oral evidence from such witnesses as the parties may tender for the purpose.

There are two types of civil proceedings, those commenced by a *dagvaarding* (summons), and those commenced by a *verzoekschrift* (petition).[26] The former is the more common and is that described below, unless the contrary appears.

The following description of civil proceedings applies equally to the *kantongerecht* and the *arrondissementsrechtbank* unless otherwise indicated.

2. Parties and legal representation

Parties. The parties to an ordinary case at first instance are called the *eiser* (plaintiff) and the *gedaagde* (defendant). All persons, natural and legal, regardless of nationality, are able to sue and be sued in the Dutch courts. Minors and persons without full capacity must be appropriately represented. Although it is possible to sue two or more persons jointly from the outset of proceedings, it is not possible for the plaintiff to add a defendant to an action which has already commenced. The same result can however be achieved by starting a separate action against the new defendant and asking the court to consolidate the two actions. A defendant is able, with the leave of the court, to bring a third party into the proceedings. The Code of Civil Procedure contains rules which permit the consolidation of separate proceedings and intervention by third parties.

55.35

Legal representation. It is normally obligatory for a party to be represented by a *procureur* in proceedings in the *arrondissementsrechtbank* and the *gerechtshof*, and by an *advocaat* in proceedings in the *Hoge Raad*. However, *kort geding* proceedings[27] provide an important exception to this rule, as a defendant in them may, if he chooses, represent himself. Although legal representation is not

55.36

---

[26] Proceedings begun by way of *verzoekschrift* are described in para. 55.62 below.
[27] Summary proceedings, see para. 55.61 above.

obligatory in the *kantongerecht* parties there are often represented by an *advocaat*. In the *arrondissementsrechtbank* certain procedural steps have to be undertaken by a *procureur* who is enrolled at that particular court. Thus if an *advocaat* is involved in proceedings outside his own district he will require the formal service of an *advocaat* who is locally enrolled as a *procureur*.[28] In civil matters formal representation before the *Hoge Raad* is limited to members of the Bar of the Hague, although *advocaten* from other districts are allowed to plead the case orally.

3. Commencement of proceedings

55.37   Proceedings are normally begun by the service of a *dagvaarding* (summons) on the defendant.[29] This document combines a summons to the defendant, a certificate of service by the *deurwaarder*, and a statement of the plaintiff's case, including the relief which he is claiming.

The *dagvaarding* is normally drawn up by the plaintiff's *advocaat*. It is in the form of a statement by the *deurwaarder*. It identifies the plaintiff and it calls on the defendant to appear before the court on a set date. The body of the *dagvaarding* sets out the plaintiff's case together with the specific relief which he is seeking. Evidential documents are not normally attached to the *dagvaarding*. The return date, selected by the plaintiff's *advocaat*, is that of a regular *rolzitting*[30] of the court. There must normally be an interval of not less than eight days[31] between the service of the *dagvaarding* and its return date, and the *advocaat* must therefore, in selecting the return date, allow a sufficient interval for service to be effected. The proceedings are regarded as being pending from the moment of service on the defendant.

4. Service of proceedings

55.38   Service of the *dagvaarding* is always carried out by a *deurwaarder* appointed for the locality in which service has to be carried out. The *advocaat* sends the original and a copy to the *deurwaarder* instructing him to carry out service. The *deurwaarder* goes to the defendant's address and hands the copy of the *dagvaarding* to the defendant or to a member of his household. In the case of a business

---

[28] See para. 55.04 above.
[29] Proceedings begun by way of *verzoekschrift* (petition) are described at para. 55.62 below.
[30] See para. 55.45 below.
[31] In the *kantongerecht* the interval is five days. The interval for a defendant with known domicile in the U.K. is one month, but it should be noted that service on a foreign defendant is complete when the *dagvaarding* has been served on the *officier van justitie*: see the next paragraph.

enterprise the copy is served on any office employee at the place of business, or on a director of the company at his private address. In all cases the *deurwaarder* retains the original on which he puts his own stamp and enters the name of the person served and the date of service.

If there is no person at the defendant's domicile, or at the company's place of business, upon whom service can be effected, the *deurwaarder* leaves a copy in a sealed envelope at the defendant's domicile. If this is not possible he may send it by post. When the defendant has no address and cannot be found the *dagvaarding* is served on the *officier van justitie* (public prosecutor) for the court in which the proceedings are to be commenced and notice of the *dagvaarding* is published in a daily national or regional newspaper.

When proceedings are required to be served on a defendant who is resident abroad the *deurwaarder* serves the *dagvaarding* on the *officier van justitie* for the court in which the proceedings are brought, for onward transmission to the Ministry of Foreign Affairs. A second copy is sent by the *deurwaarder* to the defendant by registered post. If applicable the provisions of the Hague Service Convention must be complied with.[32] It should be noted that service is complete when the copy of the *dagvaarding* is delivered to the office of the *officier van justitie*.

Direct service on the defendant's *advocaat* is only carried out when the defendant has chosen the *advocaat's* office as his elective domicile for the purpose of service. In such cases it is still the *deurwaarder* who effects service at the office of the *advocaat*. Detailed rules on the service of *dagvaardingen* and other documents are set out in Article 4 of the Code of Civil Procedure.

If service is in some way defective but the defendant nonetheless appears the defect may be cured, depending on the circumstances.

The original of the *dagvaarding* is returned by the *deurwaarder* to the plaintiff's *advocaat* who delivers it to the registrar of the court (the *griffier*) either directly or, in the case of a court in another district, through the *procureur* whom he engages for the purposes of the proceedings. On receipt of the *dagvaarding*, the *griffier* lists the case for hearing at the *rolzitting* specified in the *dagvaarding*.

5. Appearance by the defendant

The defendant must attend at the *rolzitting* of the court specified 55.39 in the *dagvaarding*. In the *arrondissementsrechtbank* this appearance must be by a *procureur*, whereas in the *kantongerecht* a party may be represented by an *advocaat* or by a *deurwaarder* or he may appear in

---

[32] See paras. 4.30 *et seq.* above and A2.03 below.

person.[33] It is this appearance on behalf of or by the defendant at the *rolzitting*, and the statement that the person so appears, which constitutes the defendant's formal appearance in the proceedings. He may then file his defence or, more usually, ask for an adjournment for that purpose.

6. Default judgments

55.40   If no appearance is made by or on behalf of the defendant on the return date he will be declared to be in default and the plaintiff will, unless the claim appears to the court to be ill-founded, be granted judgment in default. Normally the court does not give judgment in default immediately but announces that it will give judgment at the *rolzitting* on a specific date some weeks later. In the meantime the defendant can rectify his default by appointing his *procureur* (or, in the *kantongerecht*, other representative) who will notify the court that he represents the defendant and will be delivering a defence. The *rolrechter* will then not give judgment but will specify the period for delivery of the defence.

55.41   *Setting aside.* If the defendant does not appear in court and a judgment in default is given against him, he may lodge an objection, called a *verzet*. He must do this within two weeks of the date on which the judgment has been personally served on him or within two weeks of such earlier date upon which it can be proved that he had actual knowledge of it. No longer period for lodging a *verzet* is allowed to a defendant domiciled outside the Netherlands. When the defendant lodges the *verzet* he need give no explanation for his default. The lodging of the *verzet* does not itself set the judgment aside, as it is in effect a new procedure brought for the purpose of challenging the judgment. The plaintiff can still enforce the original default judgment, provided it has been declared to be provisionally enforceable notwithstanding *verzet*, but he will often not do so because he may be liable to the defendant in damages if the *verzet* succeeds. In practice, the court proceeds to determine the original dispute between the parties in the course of the *verzet* proceedings. The *verzet* is the defendant's only remedy against a default judgment, as an appeal against a default judgment cannot be made to a higher court.

7. Disputes as to jurisdiction

55.42   Any challenge to the jurisdiction of the court (*exceptie van onbevoegdheid*) must be made before any arguments are raised on the merits of the claim. This may be done either in the *conclusie van*

---

[33] As to compulsory legal representation, see para. 55.36 above.

antwoord[34] before dealing with the facts and matters pleaded in the *dagvaarding*, or in a separate document limited to the issue of jurisdiction. In the latter event there may be further pleadings on this issue and the court may give a judgment limited to that issue. The challenge may relate both to territorial jurisdiction and to subject matter jurisdiction. The court is in any event obliged to satisfy itself, of its own motion, that it has jurisdiction over the subject matter of the case. Appearance by or on behalf of the defendant does not itself found local jurisdiction if this is contested.

8. Pleadings

The plaintiff's statement of claim, the *conclusie van eis*, is normally a short formal document which refers back to the *dagvaarding*. It is in the *dagvaarding* that the plaintiff must set out his case. The extent to which he will do this depends on the tactical judgment of his *advocaat*, but it must at least contain the grounds upon which the remedies are sought.   **55.43**

The defendant's defence, the *conclusie van antwoord* must contain, first, any challenge to the jurisdiction or other technical defences (*excepties*) and, secondly, any challenge to the facts and matters pleaded in the *dagvaarding* which the defendant deems to be necessary. Reasons must be given and bare denials will normally have no effect. Documents may be attached. If the defendant wishes to pursue a counterclaim against the plaintiff he must raise it at the same time as a *conclusie van eis in reconventie*. The counterclaim need not relate to the subject matter of the claim.

The defence is handed in to the court at a *rolzitting* and the court thereupon nominates the date of a subsequent *rolzitting* for the delivery of the plaintiff's reply and defence to counterclaim (if any). When the reply is duly filed at the nominated *rolzitting*, a day is fixed for the delivery by the defendant of his rejoinder in the main action and his reply to the defence to the counterclaim (if any). If the parties wish to deliver further pleadings, the court may allow them to do so. Copies of all pleadings delivered to the court are also sent by the respective lawyers to each other directly.   **55.44**

9. The hearings

Rolzittingen. The initial stages of the proceedings, at which pleadings are delivered, take place at special sessions of the court called *rolzittingen*. A single judge (the *rolrechter*) deals with dozens of cases in quick succession. A *rolzitting* is held regularly at most courts once a week. Several *procureurs* will normally attend the   **55.45**

---

[34] This is the defence: see the next para.

session to appear in their own cases and as agents for other *procureurs*. It is at these hearings that the parties' pleadings are handed in to the court. If a party is not ready at the appointed date to file any given pleading, one or more applications may be made at the *rolzitting* for extensions of time until the court of its own motion, or on the application of the other party, fixes a final date for its delivery.

55.46 *Pleidooi.* After all the pleadings have been submitted, the respective *advocaten* have an opportunity of addressing oral arguments to the court in a *pleidooi*, a special hearing for the purpose. The date of this will also be fixed at a *rolzitting*. The *pleidooi* is held at the request of either party and its purpose is to clarify or emphasise certain aspects of the case, and not to repeat orally all the matters which have been set out in the pleadings. A *pleidooi* is also sometimes requested in order to be able to reply to statements made or documents submitted in an opposing party's pleading when a written pleading in reply is precluded. A *pleidooi* is used in relatively few cases conducted by the normal procedure, but a similar hearing (which is not strictly a *pleidooi*) is commonly employed in *kort geding* proceedings.[35]

Interlocutory hearings. When the last pleading in the case is delivered, and the *pleidooi*, if any, has been held, the court will fix a date for the announcement of its decision. This is not necessarily the final judgment disposing of the case, and will frequently be an interlocutory order directing some further step in the action to be taken, such as the holding of a hearing at which witnesses may be called, or the parties questioned (at a *comparitie van partijen*), or a compromise sought.[36] It might also order the obtaining of an expert's report or a view by the judge of some place or object. When the further step or steps have been carried out the parties will normally deliver a further pleading to comment on the results of these steps, after which the court will again announce its decision, which again might not be the final judgment.

55.47 *The final judgment.* The progress of the action which has been described above may sometimes take several years. In due course, however, the court will be in a position to reach its decision in the case. The court conducts its deliberations in private in accordance with certain procedural rules. It is not bound by strict rules of evidence and it is free to a large extent to evaluate the evidence as it thinks fit. The judgment is usually announced in short form at a *rolzitting*.[37]

---

[35] See para. 55.61 below.
[36] See paras. 55.50 and 55.55 below.
[37] The form of the judgment is described at para. 55.56 below.

10. Security for costs

In the absence of an applicable international convention, a **55.48** foreign plaintiff in the Dutch courts will, on the application of the defendant, normally be ordered to provide security for costs, known as *cautio judicatum solvi*.[38] The defendant may ask for such an order even before delivering his defence. The amount is fixed by the court on the basis of its estimation of the possible costs of the proceedings. The security can take any suitable form, such as a bank guarantee. A foreign plaintiff with immovable assets in the Netherlands may submit to a charge on those assets as security.

11. Witnesses and oral evidence

Evidential hearings. The court may, of its own motion or at the **55.49** request of a party, make an interlocutory order directing a hearing (called a *getuigenverhoor*) at which oral evidence of witnesses may be called. The court is obliged to order such a hearing if a party offers to prove certain facts by evidence of witnesses, when such proof could be decisive of the case. The order, which is normally directed at one party only, specifies the issues on which evidence is to be called but not the witnesses who are to be called. This is left to the party. A hearing will simply be fixed for the taking of the evidence. In the *arrondissementsrechtbank* only one of the three judges will attend this hearing. He is appointed as examining judge (*rechter commissaris*) for this purpose by the order of the court. In the *kantongerecht*, where there is a single judge, the evidence is taken by that judge. At least seven days before the day of the hearing, the party calling the evidence will inform his opponent and the judge of the names of the witnesses he will be calling. It is for the party to secure their attendance at court, by summons if necessary.

Examination. Witnesses will normally have been interviewed beforehand by the *advocaat* for the party on behalf of whom they are being called, to check that their evidence is helpful. On the day fixed for the taking of evidence the witnesses are called into court one by one and are questioned on oath or affirmation by the judge. Then the *advocaat* for the party on whose behalf the witness has been called, followed by the *advocaat* for the other side, may put further questions to the witness. There are limited grounds, such as professional privilege or family relationship, upon which a witness

---

[38] The Netherlands is a party to the Hague Convention on Civil Procedure of March 1, 1954, which generally prohibits the award of security for costs where the plaintiff is domiciled in another contracting state to that convention: see para. 6.11 above.

may decline to answer questions. The judge will dictate a summary of the witness' evidence to the *griffier*, the clerk of the court, who types it out there and then for signature by the witness. Copies of the witness' statements are sent to the parties later. If there is insufficient time to complete the hearing of witnesses a further date will be fixed for the purpose. At the conclusion of the evidence for the first party the judge asks the other party if he wishes to call evidence. If he does, a day is fixed and the above process is repeated. If he does not wish to call contrary evidence the case is referred to a convenient *rolzitting* for the delivery of further pleadings in which comments and arguments may be advanced on the evidence given.

55.50   *Parties as witnesses.* The parties to civil litigation in the Netherlands are competent to give evidence on their own behalf, but their evidence cannot, by itself, establish matters to their advantage. It may do so only by complementing otherwise incomplete proof. Although a party, unlike other witnesses, cannot be compelled to answer questions, adverse inferences are likely to be drawn from any refusal. The court may also summon parties to attend at a special hearing (a *comparitie van partijen*),[39] in order to give additional information in answer to questions put by the judge and the *advocaten*.

12. Documentary evidence

55.51   If a document supports an allegation contained in a pleading, a copy of that document will normally be submitted as an annex to the pleading. If so desired the *procureur* or *advocaat* signs the copy to certify that it is a true copy. The originals may be inspected by the other party on request. Any document which assists a party's case may be relied upon: correspondence, contractual documents, invoices, delivery notes, statements by the parties, statements by witnesses, police reports, and experts' reports.

55.52   There is no general procedure whereby one party can force the other party to produce a document which assists the first party's case. The fact that a particular document may be in the possession of only one party may lead the court to put on that party the burden of proving the matters to which the document relates. However, any person with a sufficient interest can compel any other person to produce a document concerning a legal relationship to which he is a party; if a party has lost a piece of evidence, he can compel another person to produce documents which can prove the fact to which the

---

[39] Also called a *verschijning van partijen*.

lost evidence related; and notaries can be compelled to produce authentic instruments in their custody.

According to the rules of professional conduct, the contents of a letter from one *advocaat* to another are considered to be confidential (*"confraterneel"*), whether or not the letter is expressly so marked. Ordinary correspondence which has passed between the respective *advocaten* may therefore only be disclosed if the interests of the client specifically so require and only after consultation with the other *advocaat* or, in the event of disagreement, with the *Deken*. The contents of abortive settlement negotiations between *advocaten* may never be disclosed without the consent of the other *advocaat*. An *advocaat* may, however, in making a settlement proposal, expressly reserve the right to disclose it to the court.

13. Experts

The parties themselves are at liberty to adduce the evidence of an expert (*deskundige*). If there remains an issue on a matter of expertise the court may, of its own motion or at the request of a party, appoint one or more experts. There is no official list of experts and the parties are free to suggest the expert to be appointed. The appointment of experts is fairly common.   55.53

The scope of the expert's enquiry will be defined in the order appointing him. He may himself conduct a hearing if he wishes. In his report (*deskundigenbericht*) to the court, which will normally be in writing, he must make reference to the views expressed by the respective parties. Copies are sent by the court to the parties and they may submit further pleadings commenting on its contents.

14. Proof of foreign law

If the court has to apply foreign law it will require information as to the relevant provisions of that law. A party may himself submit such information in some appropriate form, such as an opinion by a foreign lawyer. The court may alternatively obtain such information pursuant to the European Convention on Information on Foreign Law (1968).[40] More frequently the court will consult the *Internationaal Juridisch Instituut* in the Hague for an opinion. It may also conduct its own researches. If foreign law is incorrectly applied an aggrieved party may only bring an ordinary appeal. The *Hoge Raad* may not quash a judgment on the ground of misapplication of foreign law. However, if misapplication of foreign law has rendered   55.54

---

[40] See para. 9.13 above.

the judgment of the lower court incomprehensible, it may quash the judgment on that ground.

15. Compromise

55.55   The court may at any stage of the proceedings, at the request of either part or of its own motion, order a *comparitie van partijen*[41] for the purpose of seeking a compromise. It has become common practice for this to be done in some courts after the *conclusie van antwoord* when it appears to the court from this pleading that a compromise might be possible.

If a compromise is reached, and if the parties so request, its terms will be recorded by the judge in a minute (*proces-verbaal*) and signed by him and by the parties and the *griffier*. This document is made up in an enforceable form and accordingly has the same effect as a judgment. A settlement out of court constitutes an agreement which is not directly enforceable unless it is drawn up by a *notaris* as an authentic instrument (*authentieke acte*).[42]

16. The judgment

55.56   The final judgment is announced by the court in a short form at a *rolzitting*. In a contested case the full judgment, which is in writing, will usually summarise the pleadings and the procedural steps taken. Then there will be a description of the facts found to have been proved, an account of the respective contentions of the parties, and the court's conclusions on the merits of the case with its reasoning. Finally there will be the operative part of the judgment giving the decisions of the court. Dissenting opinions are not expressed. Statutory interest (*wettelijke rente*) may, provided it is claimed, be awarded from the date claimed in the *dagvaarding* until payment.[43] Normally the losing party will be ordered to pay the winning party's costs.[44]

The original of the judgment, the *minuut*, is normally kept at the court. The parties each receive two copies certified by the *griffier* and bearing his signature. The first, called a *grosse* starts with the words "*In naam der Koningin* . . . " ("In the name of the Queen . . . "), and is intended to be used for executing the judgment. The second, called an *expeditie*, is not meant to be so used.

---

[41] See para. 55.50 above.
[42] The enforcement of court settlements and authentic instruments is discussed at para. 55.70 below.
[43] The statutory rate is adjusted periodically. As from April 1987 it was fixed at 8 per cent.
[44] A creditor may charge his debtor statutory interest as when he is in default, upon giving written notice.

17. Costs

The costs of the proceedings are normally made up of the court 55.57
fee, the fees of the *deurwaarder*, and the fees of the *advocaten*. They
may also include witness' expenses and experts' fees. A party who is
ordered to pay costs will have to reimburse the other party in
respect of these. As to the fees of the *advocaten* it is necessary to distinguish between the actual fees to be paid by each party to his own
advocaat and the amount ordered by the court to be paid by the losing party to the winning party. The latter amount is calculated
according to a tariff which takes account both of the number of
steps undertaken at the action, such as pleadings and appearances,
and the amount at stake, and which will normally result in a figure
significantly lower than the actual fees to be paid by the winning
party to his *advocaat*. The amount recoverable from the losing party
may be as little as one third of the amount payable to the *advocaat*.
The fees payable by a foreign party to his own lawyer abroad in connection with the proceedings will not be recoverable.

H. Civil Procedure—Provisional and Protective Measures

1. Provisional orders obtained summarily

Dutch law provides a summary procedure, called *kort geding*, 55.58
whereby a party may obtain a protective or other provisional order
on an *inter partes* basis, if necessary as a matter of urgency. It is discussed in greater detail below.[45]

2. Provisional attachment

Conservatoir beslag. If there are good grounds for supposing that 55.59
the debtor may attempt to dispose of his assets before judgment, a
creditor may, under various articles of the Code of Civil Procedure,
obtain the leave of the court for their provisional attachment (*conservatoir beslag*).[46] The measure is available in respect of any claim
which, if successful, would lead to a money judgment. The leave of
the court may only be obtained on application to the president of
the *arrondissementsrechtbank* who has to be satisfied that there are
sufficient grounds for granting leave. In practice, minimal evidence
is required to obtain leave. The application is usually made *ex parte*
and in an appropriate case it may be made before the main proceedings in respect of the claim have been started.

---

[45] Para. 55.61.
[46] Assets mentioned in the Code of Civil Procedure which may be attached in this
way are the debtor's movable or immovable property, registered shares, ships
and aircraft.

The creditor is not normally required to provide security. The attachment is executed by the *deurwaarder* in whatever manner is appropriate to the case. Once the attachment has been made the creditor must commence special proceedings within eight days to validate it. These proceedings are often combined with the main proceedings before the same court. If the creditor succeeds in the main proceedings the attachment will normally be declared to be valid. If the attachment is not declared valid the creditor will be liable in damages for any loss which the debtor has suffered by reason of the seizure. The debtor can himself take steps to discharge the attachment, either by providing alternative security to cover the claim, such as a bank guarantee, or by attacking the attachment in *kort geding* proceedings.

55.60   *Assets in the hands of a third party.* An alternative kind of provisional attachment (*conservatoir derdenbeslag*) is available against assets of a debtor which are in the hands of a third party, such as a bank or a person owing money to the debtor. The creditor does not in this instance have to show that there is any risk of the assets being concealed or dissipated.

Absence of a Dutch domicile. If a debtor has no known domicile in the Netherlands any assets which he possesses in the Netherlands may be the subject of a conservatory measure known as *saisie foraine*. This is a form of *conservatoir beslag* in which the creditor does not need to prove that there is a danger of disposal of the debtors assets.

Dutch courts do not have jurisdiction to authorise the taking of provisional measures outside the Netherlands.

I. CIVIL PROCEDURE—SUMMARY PROCEDURES

1. Kort geding

55.61   The *kort geding*, meaning literally "short procedure," is a form of summary procedure of great practical importance. It is a somewhat informal and abbreviated procedure which is conducted before the president of the *arrondissementsrechtbank*. Any party who has an "urgent interest" may request the president to order immediate provisional measures. The procedure is initiated by the plaintiff's *procureur* asking the president to appoint a day and a time for a hearing. The plaintiff then summons the defendant to the hearing by means of a *dagvaarding*. The normal eight day minimum period for notice does not apply. The summons sets out the plaintiff's case. Normally there are no other pleadings. At the hearing the plaintiff's *advocaat* explains the applicant's case to the president. The defendant or his *advocaat*[47] then replies. The president puts questions on any matter which may need clarification, and then announces when he will give his judgment. This will usually be one or two weeks later, but in urgent cases it may be given much sooner or even immediately. The judgment constitutes a provisional decision as to the respective rights of the parties, and it is usually declared to be provisionally enforceable (*uitvoerbaar bij voorraad*). It may order a party to perform or to refrain from some act or course of conduct under pain of a periodic fine.[48] The judgment does not bind the court in any subsequent proceedings which may follow (termed the *bodemprocedure*). If an injunction is imposed and the plaintiff fails to substantiate his case in the *bodemprocedure* he may be liable to the defendant in damages for any loss which he may thereby have suffered.

Any appeal from a decision in a *kort geding* must be made within two weeks to the *gerechtshof*. Any further appeal to the *Hoge Raad* must be made within six weeks.

2. Small claims

Another form of summary procedure, the *betalingsbevel* (payment order) procedure, is available in respect of any claim under a contract for a sum of money not exceeding Dfl. 2,500. The plaintiff presents a petition in prescribed form to the *kantongerecht* and a copy is sent by the court to the debtor. The debtor can defend himself by writing to the court. He may also instruct a *deurwaarder* or an *advocaat* to draft and send a statement of defence to the court. If he does this the normal procedure for an action in the *kantongerecht* follows. If he does not defend himself, the court issues a *betalingsbevel*. This has the same effect as a default judgment and it is therefore open to the debtor to seek to set it aside by lodging a *verzet*[49] in respect of it.

55.62

3. Petition proceedings

Some proceedings are commenced by way of petition (*verzoekschrift*). This is a simplified form of procedure which is used particularly in family and matrimonial cases. The petition, which sets out the grounds of the petitioner's request and the relief sought is filed at the court (in cases before the *arrondissementsrechtbank*, by the petitioner's *procureur*). Then, usually, the *griffier* sends a copy to the respondent who may file a defence, but there are no other pleadings. A day is fixed for the hearing at which the court investigates

---

[47] Representation by a *procureur* is not compulsory for the defendant in *kort geding* proceedings.
[48] This is called a *dwangsom*: see para. 55.69 below.
[49] See para. 55.41 above.

the merits of the case, questioning the parties and calling for any evidence from witnesses which it may wish to hear. At the end of the hearing the court will usually fix the date upon which it will give its decision, called a *beschikking*, which is usually provisionally enforceable. An appeal must normally be brought within two months by way of petition to the higher court, or, where appropriate, to the *Hoge Raad*, although in many cases shorter periods are applicable. Some proceedings, such as employment cases, start with a petition but are conducted as though they had been commenced with a *dagvaarding*.

J. CIVIL PROCEDURE—APPEALS

1. Introduction

55.63   *Types of appeal.* The various forms of appeal available under Dutch law may be divided into two categories, ordinary appeals and extraordinary appeals. Ordinary appeals are a normal first appeal (*appel* or *hoger beroep*), an appeal in cassation (*beroep in cassatie*) and (although this is not strictly an appeal) an application to set aside a default judgment (*verzet*).[50] The commencement of an ordinary appeal has the effect of suspending the enforceability of the judgment, unless the judgment has been declared provisionally enforceable (*uitvoerbaar bij voorraad*) or enforceable despite *verzet* (*uitvoerbaar niettegenstaande verzet*).[51] Extraordinary appeals are an application to re-open a case (*rekest civiel*) and a third party's application for a judgment to be set aside or varied (*derdenverzet*).

Time for appealing. The time for commencing an ordinary first appeal or an appeal in cassation is normally three months from the date of the judgment appealed against. However, an appeal to the *gerechtshof* against an order made in *kort geding* proceedings must be commenced within two weeks and any further appeal to the *Hoge Raad* must be made within six weeks.[52] The date of the judgment is the date when it is pronounced.

2. Ordinary appeals

55.64   *First appeal.* An ordinary appeal from a decision at first instance to the next superior court is called *appel* or *hoger beroep*. This type of appeal lies from judgments of the *kantongerecht* to the *arrondissementsrechtbank* in cases in which more than Dfl. 2,500, excluding

---

[50] Additionally, the remedy of revision (*revisie*) is provided as a form of appeal for the rare case of a decision of the *Hoge Raad* given at first instance.
[51] The enforceability of judgments is discussed in greater detail at para. 55.66 below.
[52] The time limits for lodging a *verzet* have been discussed at para. 55.41 above.

interest, has been claimed, and from the first instance judgments of the *arrondissementsrechtbank* to the *gerechtshof*. An appeal of this type may also be made against an interlocutory decision of the court of trial, such as an order concerning the hearing of witnesses, unless the court of trial has declared in its interlocutory decision that such an appeal can only be made in conjunction with an appeal against its final judgment.

The party lodging the appeal is called the *appellant* and the respondent is called the *geintimeerde*. The *deurwaarder*, acting on the instructions of the appellant's *procureur* or *advocaat*, serves an appeal summons (*appeldagvaarding*) on the *geintimeerde* directing him to attend the *rolzitting* of the appellate court on a particular day. On that day, or at a later *rolzitting*, the appellant delivers his *memorie van grieven* (grounds of appeal) to the court, and posts a copy to the *geintimeerde*. The court then fixes a day for the *geintimeerde* to deliver his *memorie van antwoord* (answer). No subsequent pleadings are admitted.

In pursuing and defending the appeal the parties are at liberty to put forward new evidence and to advance new claims and defences. A new defence, however, should not be inconsistent with the case advanced in the court below. The appeal is by way of rehearing and the evidence already recorded is considered afresh, with such new evidence as may have been adduced. If the *advocaten* so request there will be a *pleidooi*.[53] The appeal court will confirm or annul, in whole or in part, the judgment of the court below. If it annuls the judgment below it will substitute its own ruling.

Appeal in cassation. An appeal in cassation to the *Hoge Raad* is called a *beroep in cassatie* or *cassatieberoep* and may only be made against a decision in respect of which no other ordinary appeal is available. It is an appeal on matters of law only.[54] Normally the appellant's *advocaat* will first take the advice of an *advocaat* in the Hague, specialised in *cassatie* proceedings. The procedure is usually conducted entirely in writing. In addition to the written cases presented by the parties, the *Hoge Raad* considers the written opinion on the appeal prepared by the *Procureur Generaal* or one of his deputies, the *Advocaten Generaal*. Oral argument before the *Hoge Raad* used to be common but is now discouraged in the interests of efficiency. If the appeal is successful the *Hoge Raad* will annul the decision of the court below and will substitute its own decision unless it considers that it has insufficient material to do so. If it considers that it has insufficient material the case is remitted to a lower

---

[53] See para. 55.46 above.
[54] The grounds of appeal in cassation are discussed in greater detail at para. 55.22 above.

court for determination in compliance with the decision (*arrest*) of the *Hoge Raad*.

Verzet. An application to set aside a default judgment may be made to the same court as gave the judgment. This procedure has already been described.[55]

3. Extraordinary appeals

55.65   *Rekest civiel.* This is a form of extraordinary appeal which may occasionally be brought if no ordinary appeal is possible. This may occur if all normal appeals have been exhausted, or if no normal appeal is possible (for example, because the amount at issue is less than Dfl. 2,500), or if, in the case of a default judgment, a *verzet* is no longer possible. It is available in only two situations. First, it may be brought on the ground that the judgment was obtained by means of forged or concealed documents or some other fraud. An appeal on this ground must be commenced within three months of the discovery of the fraud. Secondly, it may be brought on the ground that the judgment itself is irregular by reason that, for example, it awards more than has been claimed, or it does not deal with part of the claim, or it is self-contradictory, or it conflicts with an earlier judgment in the same court between the same parties. An appeal on this ground must be brought within three months of the judgment concerned.

Derdenverzet. A form of extraordinary appeal, called a *derdenverzet*, is provided by Dutch law as a means by which a person who was not party to the proceedings but whose rights have been affected by the judgment may apply to have it set aside or varied. For example, a sub-tenant might enter a *derdenverzet* against a judgment which dissolved a tenancy agreement between the superior landlord and the tenant. There is no time limit for entering a *derdenverzet*.

K. CIVIL PROCEDURE—ENFORCEMENT

1. Enforcement of Dutch judgments

55.66   As a general rule, all judgments are immediately enforceable against a party once the enforceable copy of the judgment has been served on that party and he has had a short period of grace within which to satisfy the judgment. Execution against assets in the hands of third parties, though, may not take place until eight days have elapsed after the judgment has been served on the debtor and, unless it has been declared provisionally enforceable, the judgment

---

[55] Para. 55.41 above.

has become *res judicata*. If an ordinary appeal[56] is lodged, enforcement is suspended unless the judgment was declared to be provisionally enforceable. Unless the judgment itself specifies a shorter period, the judgment remains enforceable indefinitely, subject to the overall time bar period of 30 years.

Res judicata. A judgment becomes *res judicata* when it is no longer subject to ordinary appeal, or when any such appeal has been disposed of.

Provisional enforceability. Judgments ordering the payment of a sum of money, judgments in *kort geding* proceedings, and decisions in petition proceedings (*verzoekschrift* procedure) are normally declared to be provisionally enforceable (*uitvoerbaar bij voorraad*). If the judgment is a default judgment, it may be declared provisionally enforceable despite *verzet* (*uitvoerbaar niettegenstaande verzet*). In an appropriate case, a creditor may be ordered to provide security as a condition for the judgment being made provisionally enforceable. If a provisionally enforceable judgment is enforced but is subsequently set aside on appeal or by *verzet*, the enforcing party may have to compensate the other party for consequential losses in addition to reimbursing the amount of the judgment enforced. The winning party may therefore sometimes choose not to enforce such judgments until the losing party's rights of appeal have been exhausted.

55.67

Period of grace. Once a judgment has been served, the person against whom it was given has a period of two days within which to make payment. If the judgment is a default judgment, this period is extended to eight days.

Indorsement as to executory character. One of the two copies of the judgment issued by the court, the *grosse*, is headed by the words "*In naam der Koningin* . . ." ("In the name of the Queen . . ."). This heading, together with the signature of the *griffier*, indicates that the judgment is enforceable.

Service. If a judgment debtor does not pay voluntarily, the creditor's *advocaat* sends the *grosse* of the judgment to a *deurwaarder* in the debtor's locality. The *deurwaarder* then serves the judgment on the debtor, and formally demands payment of the debt within two days. The means of service are the same as those which apply in the case of a *dagvaarding*,[57] namely, in an ordinary case, by the *deurwaarder* showing the debtor the *grosse* and handing him a copy.

---

[56] See para. 55.63 above.
[57] See para. 55.38 above.

55.68   *Execution.* If after two days the judgment has not been complied with, the *deurwaarder* may attach any assets in the possession of the judgment debtor. Thereafter the assets may be sold so as to satisfy the judgment.

Assets of the debtor in the hands of third parties, including debts due to him, such as moneys in bank accounts, may also be subject to execution if the judgment is provisionally enforceable or if the judgment has become *res judicata*. The judgment must first be served on the defendant. The *deurwaarder* then attaches the assets in question, by serving an *exploit* to that effect on the third party, together with a copy of the judgment. The attachment has to be served on the debtor within eight days. Thereafter, the third party may be summoned to court to state what assets of the defendant are in his possession. No execution on assets in the hands of a third party may take place within eight days of service of the judgment on the defendant. If the judgment to be executed is a default judgment, the *griffier* must certify that no application has been made to set the judgment aside.

The debtor's earnings may be attached down to a minimum amount reserved for basic living expenses. There is however no process by which the debtor himself can be examined as to his means or the whereabouts of his assets.

Attachment as a means of execution, as distinct from attachment as a protective measure, is called *executoriaal beslag*. Where there has been an earlier *conservatoir beslag*, this is automatically converted into an *executoriaal beslag* by its validation.[58]

55.69   *Other methods of enforcement.* In the case of non-money judgments, the method of enforcement will depend on the subject matter of the court's ruling. An injunction which orders a party to perform or to refrain from an act may, and generally does, include a clause which provides for the payment of a fine (*dwangsom*) payable to the plaintiff in the event of non-compliance. The fine may take the form of a single amount, or an amount calculated periodically during the continuance of non-compliance, or for each act of non-compliance. It is recoverable as a judgment debt, payable to the judgment creditor. The court that imposed the *dwangsom* can cancel, suspend or reduce it only if compliance with the court order becomes impossible, and then only with effect from the date when performance became impossible.

Imprisonment (*lijfsdwang* or *gijzeling*) on the order of the court is an alternative method of enforcing a judgment which is available in limited circumstances.

---

[58] See para. 55.59 above.

Opposing the execution. A person who wishes to challenge execution which is being levied against him may do so by commencing a *kort geding* before the president of the *arrondissementsrechtbank* seeking an order to restrain the execution.

2. Authentic instruments and court settlements

Dutch law provides for the execution of various instruments in addition to judgments of Dutch courts. These instruments, *authentieke akten*, include orders for the execution of foreign judgments[59] or arbitration awards, authentic instruments drawn up by notaries, court decisions in petition proceedings and judicial minutes of court settlements. An enforceable copy of the instrument is served by the *deurwaarder* and may then be executed, in the same way as a judgment, described above. **55.70**

Notarially authenticated instruments. Instruments drawn up in the prescribed form by notaries in the Netherlands may cover most subjects which could be the subject of a civil judgment.[60] Such instruments may also be drawn up by certain consular officials. The law lays down specific criteria which must be satisfied before a valid authentic instrument may be constituted. The original instrument is kept in the custody of the notary who will issue an enforceable copy (*grosse*) on request. Like a judgment, this will be headed "*In naam der Koningin.*" It will also bear the notary's seal. It is not a necessary condition of an instrument's enforceability that it should be in respect of an obligation to pay money, nor that any money obligations which it establishes should be in a fixed sum. It is sufficient if it is clear from the instrument itself how the sum payable is to be determined.

Court settlements. If a compromise has been reached by the parties and incorporated in a court minute, an enforceable copy (*grosse*) of the minute (*proces-verbaal*) may be issued by the *griffier*.[61] As with judgments and other enforceable instruments, this enforceable copy will bear the words "*In naam der Konignin*" and be signed by the *griffier*. Similarly, judicial minutes of a verification meeting in bankruptcy proceedings may be issued in enforceable form.

3. Enforcement of foreign judgments

Foreign judgments are enforceable in the Netherlands by all the means available in respect of Dutch judgments, once their execution has been authorised by an order of the court (an *exequatur*). **55.71**

---

[59] The enforcement of foreign judgments is discussed at para. 55.71 below.
[60] See, further, para. 55.09 above.
[61] See para. 55.56 above.

The means of obtaining such an order differs according to whether or not the 1968 Convention applies.

Enforcement under the 1968 Convention. When the foreign judgment is covered by the 1968 Convention the judgment creditor must apply for permission to enforce the judgment to the president of the *arrondissementsrechtbank* for the place either of the debtor's domicile or, if the debtor has no domicile in the Netherlands, where the judgment is to be enforced. The application, if the amount involved exceeds Dfl. 5,000, must be filed by a *procureur*. When lesser amounts are involved the creditor can apply in person or through a *deurwaarder*. The supporting documentation is as required by the Convention.[62] The judge authorises execution, endorsing an *exequatur* on a copy of the judgment, and ordering the debtor to pay the costs. The creditor is then given notice of the *exequatur* by means of a letter. The foreign judgment with the *exequatur* has to be served on the judgment debtor. Depending on where he is domiciled, he has one or two months after service in which to lodge opposition with the court. If an order for enforcement is refused the judgment creditor has one month within which to appeal.

55.72   *Judgments outside the 1968 Convention.* A foreign judgment cannot be enforced in the Netherlands unless it is covered by the terms of an appropriate enforcement convention.[63] In the absence of such a convention a fresh action must be brought in respect of the original claim but the foreign judgment may have evidential effect in that action.

The precise procedure to be followed varies, according to whether another convention applies (and if so, what its terms are), or whether a fresh action must be brought.

L. LEGAL PERSONS

55.73   Dutch law provides for a number of different types of legal person, of which the most common are as follows:

(*a*) *Naamloze vennootschap* (N.V.), a public limited company;

---

[62] For the purposes of Dutch proceedings, documents in a foreign language may have to be translated by a sworn translator, *i.e.* a suitably qualified person who is sworn at an arrondissementsrechtbank as an official translator. The signature of such a person certifies the translation as correct. See also para. 29.29 above.

[63] For example, the Netherlands has concluded a bilateral convention with Austria (February 6, 1963) on the recognition and enforcement of judicial decisions and authentic acts, and (with Portugal and Cyprus) is a party to the Hague Convention of February 1, 1971 on the Recognition and Enforcement of Foreign Judgments in Civil and Commercial Matters.

(b) *Besloten vennootschap (met beperkte aansprakelijkheid)* (B.V.), a private limited company;

(c) *Vereniging*, an association;

(d) *Coöperatieve Vereniging*, a cooperative association, often used in agricultural business; and

(e) *Stichting*, a foundation.

There are also several forms of partnership, none of which has legal personality, but which can each sue and be sued in the firm's name:

(f) *maatschap*, a partnership of persons often used in the liberal professions;

(g) *vennootschap onder firma* (v.o.f.), a commercial partnership under common name; and

(h) *commanditaire venootschap*, a limited partnership in which the liability of some partners is limited to the amount of their investment.

M. Legal Aid[64]

Legal aid is available to both natural and legal persons with insuf- **55.74** ficient means. Foreigners residing in the Netherlands may obtain legal aid but those residing elsewhere may not, except under the terms of certain conventions. Applications for legal aid are made to the *Bureau voor Rechtshulp*, located in each town in which there is an *arrondissementsrechtbank*. Each *Bureau* has a permanent staff of lawyers assisted, on a part time basis, by *advocaten* in ordinary practice. The applicant must, if he is resident in the Netherlands, also submit a statement from his local town hall certifying that he is of limited means. If the applicant does not reside in the Netherlands he must, if possible, submit equivalent documents.

The *Bureau* provides legal aid, either by advising the party through its own legal staff or part-time assistants, or by appointing an *advocaat* or a *deurwaarder* to act for the party. It fixes the amount of the contribution, ranging from Dfl. 25 to Dfl. 550, to be paid by the party. The fees of the *advocaat* are then funded by the state at a fixed rate, in most cases substantially lower than the normal level of fees. If the legally aided party loses the case, his potential liability for the costs of the successful party is no different from any other unsuccessful litigant.

---

[64] The Dutch legal aid provisions are presently the subject of proposals for reform which, if adopted, may come into effect in 1989.

CHAPTER 56

UNITED KINGDOM: ENGLAND AND WALES

United Kingdom: England and Wales

A. The Legal System

1. Introduction

History and territory. The United Kingdom of Great Britain and **56.01**
Northern Ireland is a single state, with a single parliament, made
up of historically separate elements.[1] England has been a unified
kingdom since before the Norman conquest in 1066. During the
twelfth century it gained ascendency over Ireland and during the
thirteenth century over Wales. Although the law of Ireland later
diverged from that of England, and both the Republic of Ireland[2]
and the province of Northern Ireland[3] now have their own legal systems, the law of England and that of Wales has been a single system
since at least 1535.[4] Scotland remained a separate kingdom from
England until 1707 and still retains its own separate system of
courts and laws.[5] The constitution of the United Kingdom is not to
be found in any single written document, but in a body of law, custom and practice. In its modern form, it is a constitutional
monarchy with a two-chamber parliament, the lower chamber of
which is elected by direct universal franchise.

2. Administration of justice

There is a clear distinction in the English legal system between **56.02**
the civil and criminal jurisdictions, and, generally, civil cases and
criminal cases are dealt with by separate courts. There is no distinction between civil and commercial cases,[6] nor is there a separate
system of administrative courts. Traditionally, English law has
been reluctant to recognise any distinction between public and private law (at least outside the field of criminal law), holding that the
government and people alike were subject to the same rules. In
recent years, however, there has been a growing recognition that
the procedures appropriate for enforcing private rights and duties
were not always apt for the regulation of public bodies. Disputes
involving the government or public bodies are still determined in
the ordinary courts, but a distinction between public and private
law, based on the means by which each may be enforced in those

---

[1] England, Scotland, Wales and Northern Ireland. The Isle of Man and the Channel Islands are also separate entities, with their own systems of law, but they do
not form part of the United Kingdom. The United Kingdom is responsible for
their international relations, however, and United Kingdom statutes may sometimes be extended to cover one or more of them.
[2] See chap. 52 above.
[3] See chap. 57 below.
[4] The Laws in Wales Act 1535, s.1.
[5] See chap. 58 below.
[6] Certain classes of case, regarded as commercial, may be subject to slightly different procedure in the High Court: see para. 56.20 below.

courts, is now emerging. Specialised tribunals deal with certain types of civil law dispute, such as certain employment or landlord and tenant matters, and with a range of social security and other administrative matters. The magistrates' courts, which normally exercise criminal jurisdiction, also deal with some aspects of maintenance and certain other matters of family law.

Levels of courts. There are two levels of ordinary civil courts of first instance, the High Court of Justice and the county court. The jurisdiction of the High Court is unlimited financially, whereas the upper limit of the county court's jurisdiction is generally £5,000. The procedure of the two courts is broadly similar, although each has its own detailed rules.[7]

B. Legal Practitioners

56.03 The importance of the oral element in English trial procedure has led to the existence of two branches in the legal profession, solicitors and barristers.[7a]

1. Solicitors

Introduction. A solicitor acts as a legal adviser to his clients and conducts legal proceedings on their behalf, instructing a barrister to advise and to conduct cases in court when necessary. The range of work undertaken by English solicitors is wider than that of most of their continental counterparts and includes the transfer of land, the drafting of wills and agreements and the formation of companies. Solicitors have rights of audience before the county court, magistrates' court and certain other courts. Their rights of audience in the High Court are generally limited to appearing in interlocutory proceedings in chambers before a master, district registrar or judge.[8]

Legal education and qualification. The first stage of an intending solicitor's legal education is normally to obtain a law degree at a university or polytechnic, although equivalent academic legal education is available to graduates in other disciplines and mature students. This is followed by a course of vocational training at the College of Law (which is run by the Law Society) lasting at least a year, and by further examinations. A trainee solicitor then becomes an "articled clerk", employed by a firm of solicitors, for two years, before he is admitted as a "solicitor of the Supreme Court" and his name is added to the roll, or list of solicitors kept by the Law Society. Recently qualified solicitors are required to undergo

---

[7] See further at paras. 56.19–56.20 below.

[7a] The government has recently proposed far-reaching changes in the structure and regulation of the legal profession.

[8] See para. 56.23 below.

further training in their early years of practice. In order to appear in court or to hold clients' fund, a solicitor must hold a practising certificate.

Rights of representation and audience. Once he has been admitted **56.04** and has obtained a practising certificate, a solicitor may act for his client in proceedings before any court in England and Wales. As already observed, though, his rights of audience as a trial advocate are limited in the higher courts. Although not required to do so, a solicitor in one place, conducting litigation in a court in another place, will often instruct a local solicitor to act as his agent for the purpose of attending at court, filing documents there and conducting the case in its interlocutory stages.

Organisation of practice. There are some 60,000 solicitors practising throughout England and Wales, normally in partnership with other solicitors, sometimes in firms of considerable size. In the larger firms in paticular there may be a considerable degree of specialisation by individual solicitors. Some of the day-to-day work in a solicitor's office may be undertaken by staff who are qualified as "legal executives" or who have no formal qualification. Solicitors are not permitted to carry on practice in partnership with persons other than solicitors.

Solicitors' fees. A solicitor may fix his fees, or the basis on which **56.05** they are to be charged, by agreement with his client, except that in contentious business his fees may not be on a contingency basis, (that is, they may not depend on the success or failure of the litigation). Normally, a solicitor's fees are based on an hourly rate and do not correlate directly with the value of the claim. It is common practice for a solicitor to ask for a sum of money in advance on account of his fees and disbursements. Value Added Tax at 15 per cent. is payable on solicitors' fees, except, in some instances, where the services are provided to clients based outside the United Kingdom. In the event of a dispute between a solicitor and his client as to the level of fees, the solicitor's bill may be "taxed," that is, subjected to an independent evaluation as to its reasonableness by an officer of the court. Alternatively, in the case of non-contentious business, the Law Society can be asked to assess the bill's reasonableness. Strict time-limits apply if a client is to request a taxation of his bill.

Professional organisation and conduct. The solicitors' professional body is the Law Society, which performs certain statutory functions for the purpose of regulating the practice of all solicitors in England and Wales. It also acts in a non-statutory capacity as a representative body for its members. Membership of the Law Society

1457

is not compulsory, although most solicitors are in fact members of it. In addition, there is a local law society in most counties and major cities, which does not exercise any statutory functions, but which represents the interests of solicitors in its area. Again, membership of local law societies is not compulsory.

A legal directory containing lists of solicitors in practice is published commercially with the sanction of the Law Society.[9] Lists of firms undertaking legal aid work in each locality are published by the Law Society itself. These publications each identify the fields of work in which solicitors' firms hold themselves out as practising.

Solicitors are subject to three forms of regulation. First, they are answerable before the Solicitors' Disciplinary Tribunal for their professional conduct; secondly, as officers of the Supreme Court, they are directly answerable to the court, especially in connection with the conduct of litigation; and thirdly, they are liable to their clients under the ordinary law.[10] A solicitor in private practice is required to carry a substantial level of professional indemnity insurance. Communications between a solicitor and his client and between a solicitor and a barrister on behalf of his client are confidential and, unless the client waives that privilege, their disclosure cannot be ordered.

2. Barristers

56.06 *Introduction.* The role of a barrister (also known as "counsel") is to act as a legal consultant and as an advocate in court. Except in the simplest cases, he will normally draft, or "settle", the written pleadings used in litigation, advise on points of law and on the merits of his client's case and conduct the case in court. Although most work undertaken by barristers involves contentious business, they may also advise and draft documents in non-contentious matters. Barristers have rights of audience in every court in England and Wales and those rights are exclusive in most trials in the High Court, in the Court of Appeal, House of Lords and Privy Council.[11] As a general rule, barristers may only be instructed by a

---

[9] *The Solicitors and Barristers Directory and Diary*, published by Waterlow Ltd. The Law Society also publishes its own Solicitors Regional Directories. In addition, there are various other commercially published directories of solicitors and barristers, notably the annual *Law Directory* published by Butterworths Ltd.

[10] Like barristers, solicitor advocates are immune from actions for negligence in the conduct of proceedings in court or immediately preparatory to a hearing in court.

[11] Rights of audience in the Crown Court, the superior criminal court are also generally confined exclusively to barristers.

solicitor,[12] although in matters which are not the subject of litigation in England and Wales, they may be instructed by a foreign lawyer without the intervention of a solicitor. A foreign lay client may instruct an English barrister direct in respect of matters to be performed outside the United Kingdom.

There are about 5,500 barristers in England and Wales of whom some 550 are Queen's Counsel.[13] About 4,000 barristers practise from about 230 sets of chambers in London and the remainder practise from about 120 sets of chambers in about 35 provincial towns and cities throughout the country. In London, nearly all the chambers are in the four Inns of Court close to the Royal Courts of Justice.

Legal education and qualification. As with solicitors, the first stage **56.07** of an intending barrister's legal education is normally to obtain a law degree at a university or polytechnic, although equivalent academic legal education is available to graduates in other disciplines and mature students. This is followed by a year's course of vocational training at the Inns of Court School of Law and by further examinations. In order to undertake this course of training, an intending barrister must have joined one of the four Inns of Court.[14] He is then "called to the Bar" and becomes a barrister. He may not carry on practice as a barrister until he has completed a year's pupillage under the supervision of a practising barrister, although he may conduct small cases once he has completed the first six months of pupillage.

Organisation of practice. Partnerships between barristers are not permitted and every barrister is, therefore, self-employed. However, barristers customarily join together in sets of chambers, sharing office accommodation and facilities, secretarial staff and the services of one or more barristers' clerks. The barrister's clerk is responsible for the negotiation and collection of the barrister's fees, keeping the diary of his professional engagements and the administration of his practice.

Barristers who have been qualified for at least 10 years (and usually 15 to 20 years) and who are regarded as being of established capacity and standing in the profession may be appointed as

---

[12] Once a barrister is instructed, the client is also, directly, the barrister's client. However, a barrister's relationship with the client is not legally the subject of a contract, but is regulated by the rules of professional conduct and the general law of tort: see para. 56.08 below.
[13] See para. 56.07 below.
[14] See para. 56.08 below. He must also fulfil the traditional requirement of "keeping terms" in his Inn of Court, by dining there on a number of occasions over a period of some two years.

"Queen's Counsel" and will have the initials Q.C. after their name.[15] Once appointed they no longer normally draft written pleadings and usually concentrate on advocacy in court in more complex or difficult cases and on advisory work. All barristers other than Q.C.'s, however long they have been in practice, are called "junior" counsel. In most cases in which a Queen's Counsel is instructed, junior counsel is also instructed.

There is a tendency, especially in London, for individual barristers, and for some chambers, to specialise in particular fields of work. A typical set of chambers specialising in civil and commercial work might have some 25 members, ranging from senior Queen's Counsel to newly qualified barristers.

56.08   *Barristers' fees.* A barrister's fees are negotiated by his clerk with the instructing solicitor. For drafting and advisory work, the fees are usually agreed as a lump sum for each item of work undertaken, while "brief fees" for an appearance in court are agreed as a lump sum for the preparation of the case for trial and first day in court, together with a daily sum in an appropriate case for each day in court thereafter. Fees, particularly for court work, must generally be agreed in advance. Contingency fees are forbidden. Value Added Tax is generally payable on barristers' fees except, in some cases, where the services are rendered to clients outside the United Kingdom. Barristers may not sue for their fees but solicitors are under a professional obligation to pay them.

Professional organisation and conduct. Every barrister is a member of one of the four Inns of Court. These are institutions, medieval in origin, in the nature of a guild. Historically, they provided training for their student members, and they are still responsible for calling them to the Bar and exercising residual disciplinary functions. They own most of the land and buildings in which barristers' chambers in London are housed, and each contain a library, a dining hall and a chapel. The General Council of the Bar is the barristers' professional body which represents the interests of the profession. There is also a system of regional organisation, consisting of six circuits covering England and Wales, each with its own organisation representing the interests of those barristers who practise in that part of the country. Except for some specialised civil practitioners and some barristers practising only in London, most barristers are members of one or other of the circuits.

The professional practices and standards of conduct are regulated by the General Council of the Bar, which co-operates with the Inns of Court in its exercise of disciplinary functions over the profession.

---

[15] Appointment to the rank of Queen's Counsel is often referred to as "taking silk" because of the silk gown worn by Queen's Counsel.

Barristers are also subject to the general law of tort in the conduct of their practice, but they are immune from an action for negligence in the actual conduct of a case in court or in advisory work immediately connected with a court hearing. They are required to carry a substantial level of professional indemnity insurance. Communications between a barrister and his instructing solicitor or his client are confidential and unless the client waives that privilege, their disclosure may not be ordered.

3. Notaries

There are some notaries public in England and Wales. Their role 56.09 is less extensive than that of the continental notary, much of whose work is, in England, undertaken by solicitors. In practice, most notaries are also solicitors. The English notary attests the execution of deeds and other documents and makes certified copies of them for use abroad.

[The next paragraph is number 56.11]

4. Foreign lawyers

The English legal profession has no monopoly in the giving of 56.11 legal advice and a foreign lawyer is free to act as a legal consultant in England and Wales as long as he does not pass himself off as a solicitor or barrister. Certain activities are reserved by statute to solicitors, and a foreign lawyer may not represent a client in court except as provided under the EEC Legal Services Directive.[16] There are numerous firms of foreign lawyers with offices in London.

5. Lawyers in business and public employment

Some solicitors and barristers are not engaged in private practice, 56.12 but are employed in the legal departments of commercial undertakings or in central or local government. Solicitors so employed are permitted to act professionally on behalf of their employers and may represent them in court provided they hold a practising certificate. Barristers who practise in employment remain members of the Bar, but they have no rights of audience before the courts and they may advise only their employers.

[The next paragraph is number 56.14]

---

[16] See para. A2.47 below.

C. SOURCES OF LAW

1. Introduction

56.14   English law is made up of legislation passed by or under the authority of Parliament and the body of case law and custom decided or approved by the courts over many centuries. Strictly, the term "common law" means this body of case law and approved custom, but the term is often used to refer to English law as a whole or to the legal systems of other countries which owe their origins to English law. Although wide areas of the civil law are now governed by statute, most of the law of contract and tort is still determined solely by the common law. There is no formal written constitution.

International treaties are concluded by the executive on behalf of the Crown and they will not be recognised or enforced by English courts unless and until they have been incorporated into English law by Act of Parliament. The provisions of European Community law are expressly stated by the European Communities Act 1972 to take precedence over the provisions of other statutes.

2. Legislation

56.15   The term "legislation" is applied both to statutes and to delegated legislation. Parliament is the supreme legislative authority and Acts of Parliament (statutes) take precedence over all other sources of law. Although English statute law is not codified in the continental sense, there has been a practice over many years to pass specific statutes which have in effect codified limited areas of law.

Statutes often provide for detailed rules to be made by delegated legislation, of which much the most important type is the statutory instrument. These are generally made by Ministers and are subject to various forms of approval by Parliament. Unless a statutory instrument can be shown to be *ultra vires*, or in conflict with some other statute, it ranks as equivalent to a statute.

3. Decided cases and legal writings

56.16   *Decided cases.* Except where a matter is expressly regulated by statute, it will be subject to the rules of the common law, as expounded in the decisions of the higher courts. The meaning of statutes as interpreted by the court also forms part of the common law. When a court has to decide a point of law that has already been decided by a higher court, it is bound to follow the previous decision of the higher court. This rule is applied by the Court of Appeal in respect of its own previous decisions. The House of Lords is not bound by its earlier decisions although it has only rarely contradicted an earlier decision. Where a point of law has not previously been decided, it will be decided by parity of reasoning with previous decisions.

Legal writings. Although the writings of academic commentators are given much less weight in English courts than in continental countries, such writings may be cited to the courts as helpful guides to the interpretation of the law. Textbooks, especially those which have gained a reputation for accuracy and insight, are relied on by the courts from time to time.

4. Publications

Statutes and statutory instruments are published in an official **56.17** form, but practitioners usually refer to compendia of annotated legislation (such as *Halsbury's Statutes*) published commercially, which note amendments to the legislation as it occurs.

Because of the importance of decided cases as a source of law, a large number of series of law reports are published, covering the more important decisions of the higher courts and also, in specialised fields, some of the decisions of lower courts. They are an essential tool for the practitioner. The most authoritative are those called the *Law Reports*, published by the Incorporated Council of Law Reporting for England and Wales, in four separate series: *Appeal Cases* ("A.C."), which contains reports of decisions of the House of Lords and Privy Council; *Queen's Bench Division* ("Q.B."); *Chancery Division* ("Ch."); and *Family Division* ("Fam."),[17] each of which contain mainly reports of decisions of the division of the High Court to which it relates and of the Court of Appeal on appeal from that division.

Two other series of law reports are also frequently cited, each of which contain reports of important decisions from all the courts: the Weekly Law Reports ("W.L.R.") and the All England Law Reports ("All E.R.").

There are numerous other series of specialised law reports, of which the following should be mentioned: *Lloyd's Reports* ("Lloyd's Rep.", containing principally commercial and shipping cases); *European Court Reports* ("E.C.R.," the official reports published by the European Court of Justice); *Common Market Law Reports* ("C.M.L.R.," containing decisions of the European Court of Justice and important decisions of national courts of EEC countries on questions of European Community law); *European Commercial Cases* ("E.C.C.," containing mainly decisions of national courts of EEC countries on questions of commercial importance).

---

[17] Until 1971, the Family Division series was called Probate Divorce and Admiralty ("P."), covering the decisions of the former division of the High Court of that name, and of the Court of Appeal on appeal from that division.

D. Organisation of the Civil Courts

1. Introduction

56.18   There are two levels of ordinary civil courts of first instance, the county courts and the High Court of Justice. Appeals from both levels of court are to the Court of Appeal and thence to the House of Lords. Criminal cases are heard by magistrates' courts at the lower level and by the Crown Court at the higher level. Both these also courts exercise limited civil jurisdiction in the field of administrative law and the magistrates' courts have a significant civil jurisdiction in the field of family law. The ordinary civil courts have jurisdiction over most matters of administrative law, but certain specialised matters are assigned to special tribunals. The Court of Appeal, and the High Court and the Crown Court together constitute the Supreme Court of Judicature.

2. The county court

56.19   There are some 289 county courts in England and Wales, not all of which sit in permanent session. Cases are heard by a circuit judge or, in interlocutory matters and smaller cases, by a registrar. The jurisdiction of the county court is generally concurrent with that of the High Court in civil matters, although some matters are exclusively assigned to the High Court and some to the county court. In general, the jurisdiction of the county court is limited by reference to the value of the claim. In ordinary cases of contract and tort, the upper limit is £5,000. Claims for debt or damages of a lesser sum are nonetheless frequently started in the High Court, because of the perceived advantages of the procedure for summary judgment in that court,[18] but if they are to be contested to trial they are usually transferred to a county court. If the case concerns the ownership of land, trusts, administration of estates or other similar matters, the jurisdictional limit is set by reference to the value of the property at £30,000, except that in some cases relating to land the limit is fixed by reference to its net annual value for rating purposes at £1,000. The jurisdictional limits do not generally apply to counterclaims, and may usually be extended by the agreement of the parties.

3. The High Court

56.20   The jurisdiction of the High Court is not limited by reference to the value of the claim, although costs penalties may result if cases are brought in the High Court which should have been brought in the county court.[18a] Sittings of the High Court are held both in Lon-

---

[18] See para. 56.61 below.
[18a] See para. 56.57 below.

don at the Royal Courts of Justice, its permanent location, and at some 23 towns and cities throughout England and Wales.[19] At first instance, High Court judges sit singly to try cases[20] and, except in commercial cases, they are normally not involved in the interlocutory stages of proceedings, which are conducted by masters and registrars.[21]

The High Court is divided into three divisions, the Queen's Bench Division, the Chancery Division, and the Family Division, to which cases are assigned according to their subject-matter. In some matters a plaintiff may choose the division in which to bring his proceedings.

The largest division of the High Court is the Queen's Bench Division, which hears most ordinary civil and commercial cases. Certain categories of commercial case may be commenced in or transferred to the commercial list[22] and made the subject of a streamlined procedure in the Commercial Court. This is a part of the Queen's Bench Division, but its proceedings are conducted by one of the specially designated commercial judges. Cases of a complex nature, particularly those involving construction and civil engineering, may be heard in the Queen's Bench Division by a circuit judge sitting as an "official referee." Cases involving the exercise of Admiralty jurisdiction are also assigned to the Queen's Bench Division and heard by the specially designated Admiralty judge. In the field of public law, the Queen's Bench Division also exercises supervisory jurisdiction over various inferior tribunals and bodies by means of a procedure known as judicial review.

Cases assigned to the Chancery Division include cases which are principally concerned with the ownership and transfer of land, trusts, the administration of estates, the rectification, setting aside or cancellation of deeds or other instruments in writing, insolvency, partnerships, companies and intellectual property. Specially designated judges hear cases concerned with companies and with intellectual property matters.

The Family Division is concerned with all matters of family law and with non-contentious questions relating to the administration of estates. It hears appeals from magistrates' courts in family law matters.

---

[19] About 45 per cent. of cases in the High Court are started in London.

[20] In a few cases, involving fraud, defamation and similar torts, the judge may sit with a jury.

[21] See para. 56.23 below.

[22] The cases which may be heard in the commercial list are those which arise out of "the ordinary transactions of merchants or traders" including, in particular, cases involving banking, insurance and international trade.

4. The Court of Appeal

56.21   The Court of Appeal sits permanently in London at the Royal Courts of Justice. In civil matters, it hears appeals from the High Court and the county court and it is presided over by the Master of the Rolls. The judges of the Court of Appeal ("Lords Justices of Appeal") sit usually in a court of two or three.

5. The House of Lords

56.22   The House of Lords, in its judicial capacity, is the highest court of appeal, not only for England, but also for Scotland and Northern Ireland. Its judicial functions are exercised in an Appellate Committee by full-time Lords of Appeal in Ordinary (often referred to as "Law Lords") and other members of the House of Lords who have held high judicial office. An appeal to the House of Lords may only be made with the leave of either the Court of Appeal or of the House of Lords. The Appellate Committee of the House of Lords usually sits in divisions of five.

6. Other civil courts

Employment disputes. Employment disputes are usually heard by industrial tribunals. Appeals on points of law lie from their decisions to the Employment Appeals Tribunal and from there to the Court of Appeal. These tribunals consist of a legally qualified chairman (a High Court judge in the Employment Appeals Tribunal) and two lay members.

Maintenance. In addition to their very extensive jurisdiction over criminal cases, magistrates' courts have jurisdiction over certain claims for maintenance and other family law cases. Appeals from magistrates' courts in family law matters lie to the Family Division of the High Court.

The Privy Council. The judicial committee of the Privy Council sits as an appellate court from the highest courts of a number of Commonwealth countries and from the disciplinary tribunals of certain bodies established by Royal Charter.

7. The judiciary

56.23   Judges are appointed by the Queen, on the advice of the Lord Chancellor. The English judicary, unlike many of its continental counterparts, is not a career judiciary but is drawn from the ranks of senior practitioners. High Court judges, of whom there are about 90, are appointed from among the foremost of the practising members of the Bar and of circuit judges who were formerly barristers. Circuit judges, of whom there are about 350 and who sit in the Crown

Court and in the county courts, are appointed from the ranks of the practising Bar and from recorders. Recorders are barristers or solicitors who sit as part-time judges. Masters and registrars, who exercise parts of the jurisdiction of the High Court and county courts are also appointed from among practising barristers and solicitors. Members of the Court of Appeal are appointed by promotion from the High Court judges. Lords of Appeal in Ordinary ("Law Lords") are appointed by promotion from the Court of Appeal and from the judiciary of Scotland, and occasionally, Northern Ireland.

E. Jurisdiction of the Civil Courts

1. Introduction[23]

Before the 1968 Convention came into effect in the United Kingdom, the separate law areas of Scotland and Northern Ireland were regarded by English law as equivalent to foreign countries for the purposes of civil jurisdiction.[24] The 1968 Convention treats the United Kingdom as a single Contracting State, and rules therefore needed to be adopted to cater for the cases in which the 1968 Convention does not itself regulate local jurisdiction. Those rules, which allocate jurisdiction between the three different parts of the United Kingdom, are modelled on the 1968 Convention and, in effect, treat the different parts of the United Kingdom as separate Contracting States.[25] The legislation implementing the 1968 Convention in the United Kingdom also introduced appropriate concepts of domicile and seat for the purposes of the new rules. Where the combined effect of the Convention and these rules is to confer jurisdiction on the English courts, without specifying the particular court which is to have jurisdiction, the question whether a particular English court has jurisdiction over a dispute is determined by the rules summarised below.

56.24

As has been seen above, various specialised types of dispute are assigned to the jurisdiction of special courts and tribunals, but most civil cases fall within the jurisdiction of the High Court and the county courts, depending on the value of the claim.[26] All courts have an inherent jurisdiction to decide whether they are competent in any particular case. Where the 1968 Convention does not apply,

---

[23] The jurisdiction of the English courts is discussed in greater detail in chap. 1.

[24] The territorial jurisdiction of the English Courts includes England and Wales and territorial waters up to a twelve mile limit. It does not include the Isle of Man or the Channel Islands. See further, para. 1.03 above.

[25] 1982 Act, s.16 and Sched. 4; see paras. 41.01 *et seq.* and 45.01 *et seq.* above.

[26] See paras. 56.19–56.20 above.

international jurisdiction is founded on the service of a writ or other process on the defendant according to rules discussed below.[27]

2. Domicile and seat

56.25   *Natural persons.* For jurisdictional purposes in civil and commercial matters, an individual is generally regarded as being domiciled in England at the place where he is actually resident, provided he has a substantial connection with the United Kingdom.[28] A sufficient connection is established in most cases by three months' residence. A person may have more than one domicile for the purposes of civil jurisdiction.

56.26   *Legal persons.* For most jurisdictional purposes, the seat of a corporation or association is treated as its domicile and, in general, it has its seat in the United Kingdom,

    (a) at its registered office or some other official address, or

    (b) where it has its central management and control, or

    (c) at its place of business.[29]

A corporation or association may have more than one seat. For the purposes of private international law, English law regards a corporation or association as having its seat in another country either if it was formed under the law of that country and has its registered office or other official address there, or if it has its central management and control there, unless (in the case of other Contracting States to the 1968 Convention) the courts of that country would not regard the corporation or association as having its seat there.[30]

3. Jurisdiction—general rules

56.27   The High Court has undivided territorial jurisdiction over the whole of England and Wales, although for the purposes of administrative convenience proceedings may be commenced either in London or in any of some 130 district registries. It has jurisdiction in civil and commercial matters[31] over any person domiciled in that territory.[32] The allocation of local jurisdiction in civil cases is therefore only of significance in county courts, magistrates' courts and

---

[27] Para. 56.30.

[28] 1982 Act, s.41: para. 44.01 above.

[29] 1982 Act, s.42: para. 44.11 above.

[30] 1982 Act, s.42(6) and (7): para. 44.11 above.

[31] The precise scope of the subject-matter which falls within the rules allocating jurisdiction between different parts of the U.K. differs slightly from that falling within the Convention: see para. 41.11 above.

[32] This is subject to an exception if the case falls within the exclusive jurisdiction of the courts of another Contracting State or of another part of the U.K.: see para. 41.07 above.

specialised tribunals.[33] In each case, the jurisdiction is invoked by the issue and service of the writ or other originating process.

Each county court has territorial jurisdiction in respect of its own district and, probably, over England and Wales as a whole.[34] Proceedings in the county court are usually commenced in the court for the district where the defendant resides or carries on business, or where the cause of action wholly or in part arose. There are liberal powers to transfer proceedings which have been commenced in the wrong court.

4. Jurisdiction—special rules

As has been observed, a county court usually has local jurisdiction to entertain proceedings in respect of causes of action arising within its district. There are certain rules of local jurisdiction in the county court in hire-purchase matters, actions concerning land and partnership proceedings.

Although local jurisdiction under internal English law in matters relating to contract does not necessarily depend upon the place of performance of the obligation in question, the location of that place is relevant for the purpose of founding jurisdiction under Article 5(1) of the 1968 Convention.[35] Under English law, in the absence of express or implied agreement to the contrary, the place of performance of an obligation to pay money is generally where the creditor is to be found and the place of performance of an obligation to deliver goods is generally at the seller's place of business, if he has one, and if not, at his residence. If, however, the contract is for the sale of specific goods, which the parties know to be in some other place when the contract is made, then that is the place for delivery of the goods, in the absence of contrary agreement.

5. Choice of court and entry of appearance

Except where exclusive jurisdiction is allocated to a particular court, English law permits parties to confer jurisdiction on a court by the entry of an appearance or by agreement.[36]

---

[33] See para. 3.19 above.

[34] It is a difficult question whether the rules concerning venue of proceedings in the county court are strictly rules of territorial jurisdiction, especially in the light of the 1982 Act: see para. 3.21 above.

[35] See paras. 17.12 *et seq.* above. The same applies to Art. 5(1) of Sched. 4 to the 1982 Act: para. 45.06 above.

[36] There are certain restrictions on the validity of jurisdiction agreements in certain types of consumer and other contracts.

6. Exorbitant grounds of jurisdiction

56.30   In cases to which the 1968 Convention does not apply, the English courts will generally exercise jurisdiction over a defendant who can be served with a writ or other originating process. A writ may be served as of right on any person who is in England and Wales (even if only temporarily) or, being a legal person, has a place of business there. Additionally, the writ or other originating process may be served on a defendant outside England and Wales, if the leave of the court is obtained. Such leave will only be granted if the claim falls within certain specified categories and, additionally, if the court regards the claim as a proper one over which, in its discretion, it should assume jurisdiction. The most important categories of claim in which leave may be granted for service to be effected outside England and Wales are those made against a person domiciled or ordinarily resident in England and Wales, those concerning land in England and Wales, and those concerning a tort committed in England and Wales or a contract made in England and Wales or subject to English law. The exercise of the court's discretion includes considering whether it is a *forum non conveniens* and, in some cases, the court may later stay proceedings which have been validly commenced.[37]

7. Civil claims in criminal proceedings

56.31   Criminal courts do not generally exercise concurrent civil jurisdiction, and English law does not provide for civil claims for damages to be joined with criminal proceedings. Nevertheless, there are various circumstances in which a criminal court may make an order against a convicted defendant requiring him to pay compensation to his victim or restore property to its owner. It may be that such orders would be treated as judgments in civil and commercial matters for the purposes of the 1968 Convention.[38]

F. LIMITATION PERIODS

56.32   The English law of limitation is complex and the following should be taken only as the most general guide. Time limits for the bringing of proceedings in English law are generally matters of procedural law (limitation), rather than of substantive law (prescription). There are different periods for different types of claim. In general, actions founded on contract or tort (other than claims for damages arising out of personal injuries or death) must be brought within six years from the date on which the cause of action arose, although

---

[37] See paras. 1.41 *et seq.* above.
[38] See para. 17.54 above.

special provisions allowing longer periods apply to actions for negligence causing latent damage.

Claims for damages for personal injuries or death must be brought within three years, although this period does not necessarily start when the cause of action arose and may be extended in certain circumstances. Actions for damages in respect of defective products are subject to prescription after 10 years, but they may only be brought more than three years after the product was first supplied if the plaintiff's knowledge of relevant facts was postponed. Claims for the recovery of land or to enforce an agreement under seal must be brought within 12 years. There are circumstances in which time may not run or the period may be extended, although these are generally more restricted than in some continental systems. It is the issue of the proceedings at the court, rather than their service, which must be carried out within the limitation period.

Where, under the rules of English private international law, foreign law is to be applied in determining any matter, the provisions of that law relating to limitation are also generally to be applied.[39] This is subject to an exception based on public policy and English law applies to determine when proceedings are commenced. Any provision of the foreign law under which the limitation period is to be suspended or interrupted by reason of the absence of a party from any specified jurisdiction or country is to be disregarded.

56.33

G. Civil Procedure—Proceedings up to Judgment

1. General description

Civil litigation in the English legal system is adversarial in that the conduct of the proceedings is mainly in the hands of the parties themselves and the court plays a passive role. Proceedings are commenced by the issue of a writ or summons. In the High Court, the interlocutory stage of the proceedings, from commencement to the trial, is conducted by the parties under the supervision of the masters.[40] The respective solicitors co-operate in the exchange of pleadings and the disclosure of documents. Application is made to a master if the leave of the court is required for some step or if the solicitors fail to agree on some matter. When the pleadings are closed either party may issue a summons for directions for a hearing

56.34

---

[39] Foreign Limitation Periods Act 1984; see para. 9.14 above.
[40] Where the proceedings are conducted outside London, the interlocutory stages take place in a district registry and the functions of the master are performed by the district registrar.

before a master at which he will give directions as to the further preparation of the proceedings for trial. In practice these directions are often agreed and in personal injury cases they may even be given automatically without a hearing before a master. A particular feature of English civil procedure is the compulsory disclosure by the parties before trial of the relevant documents in their possession.

Except in the Commercial Court and in cases before the Official Referee, where interlocutory hearings are conducted before the judge instead of a master, a judge will usually only become involved at the interlocutory stage if an interim injunction is sought or to hear an appeal from a decision of a master. Most interlocutory hearings take place in private (in "chambers"). When the interlocutory stage has been concluded there is a public trial in court, before a judge sitting alone,[41] at which the parties and their witnesses give oral evidence and are then cross-examined by the opposing advocates. At the conclusion of evidence and argument the judge will give an oral judgment.

In the county court, the procedure is similar to that in the High Court. The interlocutory stages are supervised by a registrar of the county court, who exercises rather more control over the conduct of the proceedings than does a master in the High Court.

2. Parties and legal representation

56.35   The two main parties to an action are known respectively as the plaintiff and the defendant. All natural persons and all legal persons, such as companies and other corporations, can sue and be sued. Special rules provide for minors (under 18), mental patients, and insolvent companies. Foreign persons and corporations may sue or be sued irrespective of domicile.[42] Further parties may be joined in an action as plaintiffs or defendants at its commencement or may be added later, either on their own application or on the application of an existing party.[43] A person against whom a defendant has a claim which can conveniently be dealt with in connection with the main proceedings can be added as a third party. A defendant may bring a counterclaim against the plaintiff and any party may raise any issue or claim that can conveniently be tried at the same time as the plaintiff's claim.

56.36   Any natural person of full age and capacity may bring or defend proceedings in person without the intervention of a lawyer; but

---

[41] In certain rare classes of tort case, such as those involving allegations of fraud, defamation or wrongful imprisonment, the judge will sit with a civil jury.
[42] But see para. 56.48 below on security for costs.
[43] See para. 56.44 below.

companies and other legal persons may only take part in proceedings through a solicitor. In nearly all High Court proceedings and in most county court proceedings of any importance a party normally acts through a solicitor. In the High Court, where only barristers have the right of audience at the trial, the pleadings are customarily drafted by the barrister who is to be briefed at the trial. Interlocutory proceedings before a master or a judge in chambers may be conducted by the barrister, the solicitor or the solicitor's legal executive. In the county court both solicitors and barristers appear as advocates.

3. Commencement of proceedings

In the High Court, the principal methods by which proceedings **56.37** are begun are by the issue of a writ of summons (usually called just a "writ") or of an "originating summons." The writ is the normal method of starting proceedings in the Queen's Bench Division and is appropriate for cases in which the facts are likely to be contested. The procedure by way of originating summons is used for various kinds of application to the court and in cases in which the point at issue is one of law, such as the construction of a statute or a document.

The writ must be in a prescribed form, stating the Division of the High Court in which the proceedings are brought and naming all the parties to the proceedings. It is usually prepared by the plaintiff's solicitor and is taken or sent to the court office where it is "issued" by being stamped with the court seal, a copy being retained for the court file. Certain information must be given on the writ and in particular it must be indorsed with a statement of the plaintiff's claim. This may be a full statement of the plaintiff's claim or it may be in short form. If it is in short form, a further document, called the "statement of claim",[44] must either accompany the writ when it is served or must be served at a later date. An originating summons must also be in the form required by the rules and it must include a statement of the remedy claimed or the questions upon which the determination of the court is required.

If the court has jurisdiction under the 1968 Convention (or the equivalent provisions within the United Kingdom), and the writ or originating summons is to be served outside England and Wales, it must be indorsed with a statement that the court has power to hear and determine the claim and that no other proceedings involving the same cause of action are pending between the parties in another Contracting State or another part of the United Kingdom.[45] In any

---

[44] See para. 56.43 below.
[45] See para. 3.25 above.

other case where the writ is to be served outside England and Wales, the leave of the court is required for the issue of the writ or originating summons.

In the county court an action is commenced by the plaintiff or his solicitor sending written particulars of claim to the registrar of the appropriate court, together with a formal request for a summons to be issued against the defendant. If the summons is to be served outside England and Wales, there are provisions, similar to those which apply in the High Court, requiring the plaintiff to certify that the court has jurisdiction. The court enters the proceedings in the court records, and prepares and issues a summons in the appropriate form. If the case concerns only a claim for money or damages it is called a "default action"; otherwise it is called a "fixed date action."

The moment at which English civil proceedings are considered to commence is when the proceedings are formally issued in the High Court or county court by being stamped with the court's seal.

4. Service of the proceedings

56.38   In the High Court the service of the writ or originating summons is normally arranged by the plaintiff's solicitor. In the county court service of the summons and the particulars of claim is carried out either by officers of the court or by the plaintiff's solicitor. The writ, originating summons, or county court summons, may be served at any time within a year from its date of issue. The proceedings will be served on the defendant either personally or by post or by delivery to his usual or last known address or to his solicitor if he agrees to accept service. A limited company may be served by leaving the document at, or by posting it to, its registered office. There are special provisions for the service of foreign companies carrying on business in England and Wales.[46]

A writ or summons must be served within 12 months of its issue, unless its validity has been extended for a further period by the court. If personal service or postal service cannot be effected, the court will authorise substituted service, that is the taking of such specified steps as are likely to bring the proceedings to the attention of the defendant. These might include service on some person with whom the defendant might be expected to be in communication, such as his bank, or by advertisement in an appropriate newspaper.

Where the defendant is to be served outside England and Wales, whether or not the leave of the court is required, the actual method of service is, in the case of most countries, governed by inter-

---

[46] See paras. 4.12–4.13 above.

national convention.[47] Where there is no convention, service may be through the British consular service or local official channels.

5. Appearance by the defendant

When a defendant is served with a High Court writ or originating **56.39**
summons or with a county court summons, the documents will contain instructions as to what he should do. Once service of the writ or summons has been effected, the defendant has a limited period of time within which to respond to prevent a default judgment being obtained against him. In High Court proceedings he normally has 14 days within which to complete and return to the court a form of "Acknowledgement of Service", which will have been issued by the court and served with the writ. If the writ has been served outside England and Wales, a longer period is allowed.[48] The court then sends a copy of the acknowledgment of service to the plaintiff's solicitor. The defendant must state in the acknowledgment of service whether or not he intends to contest the proceedings, but the filing of such an acknowledgment does not amount to a waiver of any irregularity in the service, nor to a submission to the jurisdiction of the court.

In the county court, a defendant who wishes to contest the plaintiff's claim must file a defence within 14 days, although a longer period is permitted if the summons has been served outside England and Wales.[49]

6. Default judgments

If the defendant does not acknowledge service of a writ or orig- **56.40**
inating summons within the appropriate time-limit, or does not state that he intends to contest the proceedings, the plaintiff may obtain a default judgment against him. If the claim is for a liquidated sum,[50] the judgment will be a final one for that sum, including interest (if it is claimed) to the date of the judgment; if the claim is for unliquidated damages, the judgment will be an interlocutory one for damages to be assessed. Similar provisions apply to other claims, but in some cases a statement of claim must be served. In

---

[47] See paras. 4.30–4.36 above.
[48] See paras. 3.34 and 4.51 above.
[49] See para. 3.34, n.51 above.
[50] A claim is generally said to be "liquidated" if it is for a definite sum, for example the price of goods sold or the return of money lent. It is unliquidated if the amount of the claim is unascertained, for example as where damages for breach of contract or for tort are to be quantified by the judge. Liquidated claims must be expressed in precise money terms whereas unliquidated claims are usually not quantified and the plaintiff merely claims "damages." Any claim for interest must be specifically pleaded.

common with other judgments, a final default judgment is immediately enforceable, unless and until it is set aside or a stay of execution is granted.

The default judgment is obtained by the plaintiff (or his solicitor) applying to the court office and filing an affidavit proving that the writ was duly served on the defendant and giving details of when, where and how the writ was served. If the writ was served outside England and Wales, without the leave of the court, the application must be made to a master and the affidavit must state the basis on which the court has jurisdiction. The default judgment is obtained without consideration of the merits of the plaintiff's claim. Similar provisions apply to enable a default judgment to be entered against a defendant if he fails to serve a defence in time, or against a party who fails to comply with certain orders of the court.

56.41   *Setting aside.* The defendant may apply to set aside a default judgment. He does this by issuing a summons returnable before a master. At the hearing of the summons, if the default judgment was regular, the defendant must not only offer an adequate explanation for having allowed the judgment to be entered against him, but he must also show on affidavit that he has an arguable defence. Whether or not to set aside a default judgment in these circumstances is a matter for the court's discretion, and terms may be imposed if the court thinks fit. For example, the defendant may be required to pay money into court.[51] If the judgment was irregular, the defendant should normally be permitted to have it set aside, but his affidavit should nonetheless disclose the nature of his defence. Although there is no set time-limit within which such an application must be made, it must be made within a reasonable time.

The rules and practice of the county court relating to default judgments are similar to those of the High Court.

7. Disputes as to jurisdiction

56.42   Acknowledging service of a writ or originating summons does not prevent a defendant from disputing the jurisdiction of the court, provided that he gives notice of his intention to defend the proceedings and thereafter makes an application to the court to challenge the jurisdiction.[52] This application must be made within the time limited for serving a defence. This application is made to the master or district registrar, supported by an affidavit verifying the facts relied on. His decision may be subject to an interlocutory appeal. If the application is not successful, the fact that the defendant

---

[51] This should not be confused with a payment into court in satisfaction of the plaintiff's claim: see para. 56.55 below.
[52] See chap. 5 above.

acknowledged service and disputed the jurisdiction will not of itself be treated as a submission to the jurisdiction, but, in order to defend the action, the defendant must file a fresh acknowledgment of service.

In the county court, the defendant must challenge the jurisdiction in his defence or make an appropriate application within the time limited for filing the defence.

8. Pleadings

The pleadings in English civil procedure are the formal written **56.43** documents in which each party must set out his case. Their purpose is to define the issues for the trial of the action and to identify the remedies which are sought, but not to provide the material on which the decision in the case may be made. They do not normally contain references to the law or to witnesses or their evidence. In proceedings begun by writ, the pleadings must state the facts upon which the party will rely and which he needs to prove to obtain the relief sought, so as to enable the other party to know the case which he has to meet. They are normally drafted in short numbered paragraphs, setting out bald assertions of fact or denial. In proceedings begun by originating summons, the summons itself contains a concise statement of the questions to which the plaintiff requires answers or the relief which he seeks, and no further pleadings are required.

The pleadings include the writ or originating summons, statement of claim, defence, counterclaim, reply, defence to counterclaim and any subsequent pleadings. They are normally drafted by the barrister who will be appearing in due course at the trial. If a party has not pleaded his case in sufficient detail, the other party may request "further and better particulars" of the pleading. There is strictly no need for a party to reply to such a request, but if he does not, the requesting party may ask the court for an order that the particulars be given.

Although the rules of court lay down a fairly rigorous timetable for the delivery of pleadings, these time limits are often extended by agreement between the solicitors or by order of the court.

The statement of claim. The statement of claim[53] is the plaintiff's principal pleading, which is either included on the writ itself or served as a separate pleading. If the statement of claim is prepared separately from the writ it must be served on the defendant within 14 days from the time limited for acknowledging service of the writ.

---

[53] In the county court, this is called the "Particulars of Claim", and in the Commercial Court, the "Points of Claim."

56.44   *The defence (and counterclaim, if any).* The defence must, as appropriate, either deny or admit each fact alleged in the statement of claim and must state every material fact upon which the defendant intends to rely. It must be served within 14 days of service of the statement of claim. If the defendant has a claim which can conveniently be tried at the same time as the plaintiff's claim then it is added to the defence as a counterclaim. The same principles apply to counterclaims as apply to statements of claim.

The reply (and defence to counterclaim, if any). If it is necessary for the plaintiff to plead further facts, to deal with any matter raised by the defence, a reply will be pleaded. If the defendant has counterclaimed the plaintiff must, if he contests the counterclaim, add to his reply a defence to counterclaim.

Further pleadings. Only in exceptional circumstances will there be any pleadings after a reply. If there is a need for further pleadings, the leave of the court is required. The pleadings are deemed to be closed 14 days after service of the defence, (or the reply or defence to counterclaim, if any).

Additional parties. If a third or subsequent party is to be joined in the proceedings this is done by serving a third party notice on him. If a third party is to be joined after service of the defence the leave of the court is required. A typical example of third party proceedings would be where a defendant is seeking an indemnity or some other relief against the third party in connection with the plaintiff's claim.

In High Court proceedings the pleadings are served on each other by the respective solicitors and, with the exception of the writ, they are only produced to the court for the purpose of the trial or an interlocutory hearing. In county court proceedings they are filed at court and the court forwards a copy to the other party. A pleading may be amended once without the leave of the court at any time until the exchange of pleadings has been completed. Thereafter any amendments require the leave of the court.

9. The hearings

56.45   *Interlocutory hearings.* In High Court proceedings, except in personal injury cases,[54] the plaintiff's solicitor should take out a "summons for directions" within four weeks from the close of pleadings, for a private hearing before a master.[55] The purpose of this hearing

---

[54] In personal injury cases, automatic directions prescribed by the rules of court take effect unless either party applies to the court for further or different directions.

[55] In cases proceeding outside London in a district registry of the High Court, interlocutory hearings are conducted before the district registrar.

is to review the progress of the action and to deal with as many procedural matters as can be agreed or disposed of. The respective legal representatives, usually the solicitors or their legal executives, attend before the master who deals with any outstanding matters relating to the pleadings and gives directions as to future conduct and main trial of the action. Directions are usually given concerning the disclosure and inspection of documents, the place of trial, time for setting down for trial, exchange of experts' reports and admission of written evidence. The summons for directions is not the only occasion on which interlocutory matters may be dealt with as any interlocutory issue which cannot be agreed between the parties may also be dealt with, at the request of either party, at an interlocutory hearing held for the purpose before the master.

A preliminary hearing in the county court, equivalent to the hearing of a summons for directions, but in which the court plays a more interventionist role, is called a pre-trial review. It takes place before the county court registrar. In a default action, the date for the hearing is fixed by the court of its own motion when the defendant files his defence. In a fixed-date action, depending on the nature of the case, the date either of a pre-trial review or of the final hearing will have been fixed at the commencement of the proceedings. The registrar is required to encourage the parties to make such admissions and agreements as ought reasonably to be made by them in relation to the proceedings.

The trial. In a High Court case, at the time appointed by the 56.46 order on the summons for directions, and even if the interlocutory stages of the action are not yet completed, the plaintiff's solicitor notifies the court and lodges the pleadings, together with the orders made on the summons for directions and certain other documents. This is called "setting down" the action for trial. The case then takes its place in the queue of cases waiting for trial and either party may apply to the court for a fixed date if they wish. In the county court, the court fixes the date for the hearing.

On the day appointed for the trial, the parties, their solicitors and counsel, and their witnesses will attend the court. The judge, sitting alone,[56] presides at the trial, but he plays a largely passive role while it is in progress; and although he may have read the pleadings in advance, he will generally have little or no prior knowledge of the case. It is for the parties, through their legal advisers, to decide what witnesses are to be called and what documentary evidence is to be produced. A trial may well last several days, or sometimes longer.

---

[56] See para. 56.34, n.41 above as to the circumstances in which the judge will sit with a jury.

The plaintiff's counsel first makes an opening speech introducing the judge to the factual and legal issues in dispute, referring him to the pleadings and to any relevant correspondence and other documents. The plaintiff and his witnesses then give their evidence orally in answer to questions put by his own counsel and by the defendant's counsel.[57] The defendant and his witnesses will then, in most cases, be called to give their evidence. At the close of the evidence first the defendant's counsel and then the plaintiff's counsel make their closing speeches to the judge in support of their respective cases.

56.47 The judgment is given at the conclusion of the oral hearing or, if the case is complex or for some other reason the judge wants time to deliberate, a few days or weeks later. The judgment is given orally in the presence of the parties' advocates.[58] The judge recites a summary of the evidence and issues, referring to relevant points of law and decided cases, and stating the reasons for his decision.[59] When the judgment has been given, the judge hears the parties' advocates on the question of costs and any other consequential matters before making an order.

10. Security for costs[60]

56.48 When it appears that the plaintiff is ordinarily resident outside the territorial jurisdiction of the English courts, the defendant may apply for an order that the plaintiff must provide security for the defendant's costs of defending the claim. The application is made by a summons before a master, and is often made early in the proceedings, sometimes before the service of a defence. It is usually supported by an affidavit, setting out the grounds on which the application is made, an estimate of the costs of the action and the sum requested by way of security. Usually the application will not initially be in respect of all the costs of the action up to judgment, but only up to some specified stage in the procedure; if the action proceeds beyond that point a further application may be made. The amount of the security is within the court's discretion, and it is not always the practice to order security on the basis of a full indemnity. The plaintiff is ordinarily ordered to pay the amount of the security into court, but the order may provide for him to give a bond or other adequate security. The court has a wide discretion whether or not to order security and one of the factors which it will

---

[57] In the county court, cases are often conducted by solicitors as advocates.
[58] In some cases, especially in the Court of Appeal, the court may announce its decision and hand down its reasons in writing.
[59] As to the form of the judgment see para. 56.56 below.
[60] This topic is treated more fully in chap. 6.

take into account is the ease with which an order for costs can be enforced against the plaintiff. The former practice, whereby the discretion was normally exercised in favour of ordering security, may therefore be modified where the plaintiff is resident in another Contracting State to the 1968 Convention.

The court may also award security against a plaintiff company, irrespective of where it has its registered office or place of business, if it appears that it may have insufficient assets from which to satisfy an order for costs.

11. Witnesses and oral evidence

The evidence is normally given by witnesses orally, on oath, at the trial of the action.[61] The selection of witnesses is a matter entirely within the discretion of the parties and their advisers and, while the judge has a theoretical right to call witnesses (in the absence of objection by the parties), this is virtually never exercised. It is usual for the parties' solicitors to interview witnesses in advance of the trial to obtain a detailed statement of their evidence.[62] The attendance of a witness to give evidence at the trial, or to produce a document, can be enforced by a "writ of subpoena" or witness summons, issued by the court on the application of a party. The parties themselves are competent to give evidence as witnesses on their own behalf and will usually do so before their other witnesses are called. A witness (including a party) is questioned first, in examination in chief, by the counsel who has called him. He is then questioned, in cross-examination, by the opposing counsel. Finally he is questioned again, in re-examination, by the counsel who called him. The judge will usually only ask questions of a witness when it is necessary to deal with a point which has been overlooked or left unclear by counsel. Witnesses are normally not excluded from court while the parties and the other witnesses are giving their evidence. The evidence given at a civil trial is noted by the judge and, in the High Court, it is recorded in shorthand or electronically, so that a transcript can be prepared for the purposes of any appeal. **56.49**

There are detailed and complex rules governing the evidence which witnesses may give. In general, a person may only give evidence of matters of which he has direct personal knowledge and, unless he is an expert, he may not give evidence of his opinion as to any matter. He may not report statements made by him or by other persons out of the hearing of the other party. This rule against the **56.50**

---

[61] In some circumstances, a witness's evidence may be admitted in a written form: see para. 56.52 below.
[62] In certain High Court actions, the parties will have to disclose their witnesses' statements before the trial.

admission of "hearsay" evidence is subject to various general exceptions and in particular the previous statements of both witnesses
and others may be admitted in evidence when certain conditions
have been satisfied.

Depositions and affidavits. If a witness is unable to attend the hearing on account of infirmity or other serious reason he may give his
evidence before an examiner specially appointed for the purpose.
Similarly, the evidence of a witness who is outside the United Kingdom may be taken under letters of request or otherwise under the
provisions of a bilateral or multilateral convention.[63] In each case, the
evidence is recorded in a deposition which may then be submitted as
evidence at the trial. The court may also permit the evidence of a
witness to be admitted by way of a sworn affidavit, and in some cases
even the unsworn statement of a witness may be admitted.[64]

12. Documentary evidence

56.51   *Discovery of documents.* Within 14 days after the close of the
pleadings each party must, generally, serve on the other a list, setting out all documents which are or have been in his possession,
custody or power and which are relevant to the dispute. This procedure is called "discovery of documents".[65] A document is
regarded as relevant if it contains information which may enable the
party applying for discovery either to advance his own case or to
damage that of his opponent, or if it is a document which may fairly
lead him to a train of enquiry which may have either of these two
consequences. If so required, these documents must then be produced for inspection by the other party. This duty extends to documents which are adverse to a party's case and the solicitor and
counsel acting for a party are professionally required to ensure that
proper discovery is made.

The purpose of discovery of documents is to enable each party to
assess the respective merits of his own and his opponent's cases.
Only privileged documents are exempt from production. These
include principally correspondence between solicitor and client,
counsel's opinions, statements of witnesses or other documents
which have come into existence for the purpose of the litigation and
correspondence between the opposing parties or their lawyers written with a view to settling the dispute and marked "without prejudice." These latter documents may only be referred to in order to
prove a concluded settlement. Any disputes as to whether a particu-

---

[63] See paras. 8.43–8.58 above.
[64] See para. 56.52 below.
[65] It should not be confused with the procedures of pre-trial discovery of witnesses'
evidence known to the American system of civil procedure.

lar document or class of documents is privileged, or should be disclosed, may be resolved on an application to the court.

Proof of documents. Strictly, documents may only be produced at **56.52**
trial if a witness is called to prove from his own knowledge the authenticity of each document or copy. The cumbersome consequences
of this rule are avoided in practice by the parties' solicitors agreeing
the authenticity of the documents and the accuracy of the copies to
be produced at trial. It is usual also for the parties' solicitors to
agree the arrangement of the documents into one or more bundles
for use at the trial, copies of which are then lodged with the court.

Written evidence. If it is inconvenient or impossible to call a witness, or if his evidence is not controversial, the evidence may be
admitted in a written statement in certain circumstances, either by
the agreement of the parties or with the leave of the court. Medical
reports or police reports of traffic accidents are frequently so admitted. Proper notice must be given, but in some cases the evidence
may be admitted as of right. This is the case, for example, if the
witness is overseas.

Sworn affidavits may also be admitted as evidence in proceedings
and this is the normal means for the giving of evidence at interlocutory stages.

Interrogatories. A party to proceedings may apply to the court
for an order compelling the other party before the trial to answer
written questions (called "interrogatories") in a sworn affidavit.
The questions must relate to the facts in issue in the case. Interrogatories will be ordered if the court considers that they are necessary for the fair disposal of the case or the saving of costs. They are
of particular use to a plaintiff when the facts to be ascertained are
fundamental to his case but proving them (unless admitted by the
defendant) would be difficult or costly.

13. Experts

Expert evidence is not normally admissible at the trial of an **56.53**
action except with the leave of the court, although such leave is
given wherever expert opinion is likely to be relevant. The parties
instruct their own experts and bear the costs of doing so as part of
their costs of the action. It is the usual practice to limit the number
of experts who may give evidence in any given field of expertise,
and to require the disclosure of their evidence to the other party
before trial, normally by way of a report prepared by the expert. In
the absence of agreement, the court may order a party to afford the
other side's expert an opportunity to inspect the subject-matter of
the action or other relevant property or to submit himself to a

medical examination by a medical expert instructed on behalf of the opposing party.

The status of an expert witness remains that of a witness called by one of the parties, although it is usual for the expert's report to be handed in at trial and read by (or to) the judge before the expert gives his evidence. He will be examined and cross-examined in the normal way.

The court does have power to appoint a court expert on the application of a party, but this is rarely done.

14. Proof of foreign law[65a]

56.54   Foreign law is a question of fact, and must ordinarily be pleaded. Unlike other questions of fact, though, it is normally to be proved by expert evidence. The evidence may be given by a person who is suitably qualified by reason of his knowledge or experience, whether or not he has practised, or is entitled to practise, as a lawyer in the territory or country of that law. Evidence of a previous finding on the particular point of foreign law by the High Court or Court of Appeal may be admitted if it is in a citable form. The onus of proving the provisions of foreign law is on the party who seeks to rely on it. In the absence of adequate proof of the foreign law, the court will usually assume that it is the same as English law.

15. Compromise

56.55   As the conduct of the proceedings rests with the parties themselves they may come to a compromise at any time before the final judgment is given. The judge is under no duty to promote a compromise although occasionally he will do so, if he thinks fit. Choice of the precise method of settling an action may be important. If the terms of settlement are incorporated in the judgment or order of the court they will be enforceable. If the action is discontinued on terms agreed between the parties, then those terms constitute a fresh agreement which supersedes the original cause of action. Sometimes an action is not discontinued but merely stayed for all purposes save for the enforcement of the agreed terms. A party who wishes to impugn a concluded settlement must bring a fresh action for this purpose and must show grounds which invalidate the contract upon which it is founded. A settlement in favour of a person under 18 years of age requires the approval of the court.

Payment into court. The rules of court contain a means whereby a defendant can put pressure on the plaintiff to compromise the action. They permit a defendant to pay money into court in satisfac-

---

[65a] This topic is discussed in more detail in chap. 9 above.

tion of the plaintiff's claim. This is a procedure of considerable practical importance, particularly in smaller cases in which the costs are proportionately larger in relation to the size of the claim. If the plaintiff declines to settle the case by taking the money out of court but he eventually recovers a smaller sum than that paid in by the defendant, the plaintiff must normally pay all the defendant's costs since the payment in. The judge who tries the case is kept in ignorance of the fact and the amount of the payment in.

16. The judgment

The judgment, which is given in open court, takes effect as soon as it is pronounced, but for the purposes of execution it must first be "perfected" by being entered in the court records. The time for appealing runs from the date on which it is perfected. In the Queen's Bench Division of the High Court, this is done by a party's (usually the plaintiff's) solicitor.[66] He draws up a document setting out the terms of the judge's judgment (but not the reasoned statement leading to it, confusingly also called the judgment) and presents it at the court office together with a certificate recording the terms of the judgment. The certificate is produced by the court official (the "associate") who was present in court when the judgment was pronounced. In addition to the title of the proceedings, which includes the names of the parties, the formal judgment contains the date when it was pronounced, the name of the judge, the place of trial and the final order of the court, together with the order as to costs. A duplicate copy of the judgment, bearing the court seal, is then issued by the court. Any person may obtain a transcript of the full reasoned judgment from the official court shorthand writers, on payment of a fee. A certified copy of a judgment may be obtained for the purpose of enforcement in other countries.

Interest. The judgment may contain an award of interest, if this was claimed in the proceedings. The rate and period of the interest is in the discretion of the court, but on trading debts it usually runs from the date on which the debt was due at about 12 per cent. Interest on the amount of the judgment itself (excluding any element of earlier interest) automatically accrues from the date of the judgment.

17. Costs

The awarding of costs as between parties to litigation is in the discretion of the court, although normally the successful party will obtain an order for costs against the unsuccessful party. Separate

56.56

56.57

---

[66] In the Chancery Division and in the county court the order is usually drawn up by court offcials and entered in the records of the court.

orders for costs are normally made in respect of interlocutory hearings. Certain fees are payable to the court, notably on the issue of proceedings and when the case is set down for trial.

Unless the amount of the costs to be paid by the unsuccessful party is agreed between the respective solicitors, the successful party must submit an itemised bill of his costs to the court's taxing officer for approval. The costs which the losing party will be ordered to pay after taxation include, in addition to the solicitor's fees, disbursements such as counsel's fees, witness's expenses, expert's fees and court expenses.[67] Each item has to be justified against a published scale of costs. In the normal basis for taxation (the "standard basis") the winning party is awarded his reasonable costs reasonably incurred in the proceedings, but in practice there will very probably be some shortfall between those costs, ordered to be paid by the losing party, and the costs which the successful party will be charged by his own solicitor ("solicitor and own client costs"). When a plaintiff succeeds in the High Court in an action which he should have brought in the county court he is normally awarded his costs on the less generous county court scale. In the county court there are four scales of costs dependent on the amount claimed or recovered. The process of taxation of a party's costs need not hold up the execution of any judgment, as the costs can be the subject of a separate execution.

H. CIVIL PROCEDURE—PROVISIONAL AND PROTECTIVE MEASURES

1. Introduction

56.58   The High Court has power to grant a wide range of orders of a provisional or protective nature, usually by way of interlocutory or interim injunctions. In addition, it may make various forms of interim or provisional awards and make protective orders of a procedural nature. The county court has similar but more limited powers. This topic is discussed more fully in Chapter 7.

2. Injunctions

56.59   Either party may apply to a judge, at any time before the trial, for an interlocutory injunction against another party. The grant of such an injunction does not prejudice the court's ultimate decision as to the parties' respective rights and duties. An interlocutory injunction will normally only be granted if the applicant (usually the plaintiff) gives a binding undertaking to compensate the other party

---

[67] The fees of a party's foreign lawyer may sometimes be recoverable as part of the solicitor's costs in connection with the action, if it can be shown that they were necessarily incurred.

in damages for any loss which he may suffer by reason of the injunction if the court in due course finds that an injunction should not have been granted. An injunction will not ordinarily be granted in cases in which an award of damages would be an effective and adequate remedy.

In urgent cases such an injunction may be obtained even before the issue of the writ. Application for an interim injunction must be made to a High Court judge[68] supported by appropriate evidence on affidavit. The application may be made without notice to the defendant (*ex parte*), but in such a case the plaintiff is under a strict duty to make full disclosure to the court of all the relevant facts, not limited to those in his favour. An injunction made *ex parte* will be of short duration, until the defendant can be notified and can attend before the judge (*inter partes*) to put his side of the case. The judge decides, on hearing both parties, whether or not the balance of justice supports the granting or continuance of the injunction.

Mareva injunctions. A particularly important type of interlocutory injunction, called a "Mareva" injunction, restrains a defendant from disposing of or dealing with some or all of his assets before trial, so that they may remain available to satisfy a judgment.[69] It is also granted in aid of execution of a judgment in an appropriate case. Although, in common with other injunctions, it operates only as an order *in personam*, any person (such as a bank) who has notice of it is bound not to assist the defendant in a breach of its terms. It therefore has the effect of a provisional attachment of a defendant's assets. Its availability in respect of assets outside the territorial jurisdiction of the court is limited.[69a]

Anton Piller orders. A further important type of interlocutory injunction, called an "Anton Piller" order, requires the defendant to allow the plaintiff to enter premises to preserve property or documents which are likely to be of evidential value in the proceedings.[70] It has proved particularly useful in intellectual property cases.

Other interlocutory injunctions. Interlocutory injunctions are also available in cases in which the plaintiff is seeking a permanent injunction as part of the substantive relief in the main action. In these cases, it may be right and necessary to oblige the defendant to do some act immediately, or to refrain from some course of conduct, pending the trial of the main action.

---

[68] Except in the field of family law, the power of a county court to grant an interlocutory injunction is limited.

[69] See paras. 7.07–7.11 above.

[69a] See para. 7.23 above.

[70] See paras. 7.12–7.15 above.

3. Other interim and provisional orders

56.60   *Interim payments.* If the defendant has admitted liability, or the court is satisfied that a plaintiff will recover a substantial sum or substantial damages at the trial of an action, it may grant the plaintiff an interim award on account. The fact that such an award has been made will not normally be disclosed to the trial judge until after he has given judgment.

Provisional damages. In certain circumstances, a party may claim and obtain final judgment at trial for provisional damages in a personal injury case. If he does so, and his condition subsequently deteriorates, he may later apply to the court for the assessment of damages to be reopened with a view to his receiving a further award.

Other orders. The court has powers to make orders for the interim detention, custody or preservation of property, or for its inspection or sampling. It may also make an interim order for a party to hand over goods which are the subject of an action.

I. CIVIL PROCEDURE—SUMMARY PROCEDURES

56.61   *Summary judgment.* There is a procedure under Order 14 of the Rules of the Supreme Court, by which the court may give summary judgment in certain cases in which there is no arguable defence. This is usually known as an "Order 14 judgment." In any action commenced by writ in which a statement of claim has been served and the defendant has given notice of intention to defend, the plaintiff may nonetheless apply to the court for a hearing before the master or district registrar at which he will argue that the defendant has no defence and that summary judgment ought to be given against him. The plaintiff must file an affidavit swearing to his belief that the defendant has no defence to the claim. The defendant is summoned to court and is obliged to show by evidence on affidavit that he has an arguble defence to the action. If he fails to do so he may have final or interlocutory judgment entered against him.[71] If his defence appears to be tenuous he may be given leave to defend the action on condition that he pays into court the whole or part of the amount claimed within a specified time. If he shows a good or arguable defence he will be given unconditional leave to defend the action. A similar procedure exists in the county court.

56.62   *Other summary procedures.* There are also similar procedures in the High Court by which the court may make a summary order for the taking of an account between the parties or for summary judg-

---

[71] See para. 56.56 above.

ment in a claim for the performance or rescission of certain agreements.

J. Civil Procedure—Appeals

1. Introduction

In most cases an appeal can be made from every decision successively through the hierarchy of the courts. The parties to an appeal are called, respectively, the "appellant" and the "respondent". An appeal does not operate automatically as a stay of execution. A stay must be applied for whenever it is required. It will only be granted in cases in which it appears that there is no reasonable probability of the appellant recovering the money or other subject-matter of the judgment if the appeal succeeds. **56.63**

2. County Court cases

In the county court the orders of the registrar, whether interlocutory or final, may be appealed to the judge. Appeal lies from the orders of a county court judge to the Court of Appeal and thence to the House of Lords. In some instances, notably where the value of the claim is less than half the limit of the relevant jurisdiction of the county court, appeal only lies with the leave of the county court judge or of the Court of Appeal. **56.64**

3. High Court cases

Decisions of a master or district registrar lie to a judge in chambers and thence to the Court of Appeal and the House of Lords. An appeal to a judge in chambers from an interlocutory order must be made within five days of its pronouncement in the case of a master's order or seven days in the case of a district registrar's order. The appeal involves a reconsideration of the application *de novo*. The application to a master to set aside a judgment which has been given in default of appearance is not regarded as a form of appeal.[72]

An appeal from the judgment or order of a judge in the High Court may generally be made to the Court of Appeal within four weeks of its being signed, entered or otherwise perfected. It is brought by means of a "notice of appeal" which sets out the appellant's grounds of appeal. The respondent may cross-appeal or, if he wishes to argue that the judgment should be supported on grounds other than those relied on by the judge, he must serve a "respondent's notice". An appeal against an interlocutory order may only be brought with the leave of the judge or the Court of Appeal and

---

[72] See para. 56.41 above.

only on a point of law. If the appeal is against a judgment or final order, it may usually be brought as of right, it may be on questions of fact as well as law, and it will be by way of a rehearing on the transcript or notes of evidence of the proceedings in the court below. Only in exceptional cases, where the evidence could not have been adduced at the trial, will new evidence be admitted on an appeal.

4. The House of Lords

56.65   Appeals to the House of Lords may be made only by leave of the House of Lords or of the Court of Appeal. Leave is granted only in cases of public importance and where there is uncertainty as to the law. In the House of Lords the parties file written statements of their case before the oral hearing.

K. CIVIL PROCEDURE—ENFORCEMENT

1. Enforcement of judgments given in England and Wales

56.66   *Introduction.* It is for the successful party to decide whether, and if so how, to enforce the judgment. Money judgments are enforceable as soon as they have been drawn up and entered, or otherwise perfected, and need not be served on the judgment debtor. The bringing of an appeal does not suspend the enforceability of a judgment, although the appellant may obtain an order for a stay of execution from the trial judge or from the appellate court. In certain circumstances, notably after six years from the date of the judgments or when any change has taken place in the identity of the parties entitled to or liable to execution, the leave of the court is required for the issue of measures of execution.

[The next paragraph is number 56.68]

56.68   *Execution.* The principal method of enforcing a money judgment is by means of a writ of *fieri facias*.[73] The successful party's solicitor prepares the writ in the prescribed form. He lodges it in the court office where it is checked against the original judgment in the court's records, and it is stamped with the court's seal. The writ is addressed to the sheriff (a public official) directing him to seize the debtor's goods in satisfaction of the judgment. The writ remains valid for one year, but it is renewable.

---

[73] This is a writ of execution, known as a "fi.fa." The equivalent means of enforcement in the county court is the warrant of execution, issued by the registrar.

Debts owed to the judgment debtor by a third party, such as a bank, may be attached by means of a garnishee order. This orders the third party, known as the garnishee, to show cause why he should not pay to the judgment creditor the moneys which he owes to the judgment debtor. If the garnishee does not then pay the money into court, the court may order execution to be levied against him. A further means of enforcement of a judgment is a charging order against the debtor's land or other assets leading, if necessary, to a sale. Where it can be shown that the judgment debtor will be in receipt of funds in the future the court may decide to appoint a "receiver by way of equitable execution," who is authorised to receive the funds and to hold them to the order of the court. In the case of any money judgment the debtor may be summoned to court to be cross-examined as to his means, and he may be ordered to produce all documents, such as bank statements, which may disclose his assets. In the county court, an attachment of earnings order may be made directing the debtor's employer to make regular deductions from his wages in satisfaction of the judgment. Failure to satisfy a judgment is an act of bankruptcy upon which bankruptcy proceedings, or in the case of a company, winding-up proceedings, can be founded.

Breach of an injunction ordering the defendant to do or to refrain from doing some act is a contempt of court, punishable by a fine or imprisonment or by sequestration of assets. Service of a copy of the judgment or order is a precondition to its enforcement if it orders a person to do or refrain from doing any act.

Opposing the execution. A person against whom execution is being **56.69** carried out may apply to the court, on an *ex parte* basis in case of urgency, for the execution to be stayed or for conditions to be attached to it. If ownership of goods against which execution is being levied is disputed by a third party, the sheriff may apply to the court by a procedure called "interpleader" for that issue to be resolved.

2. Authentic instruments and court settlements

Before the implementation of the 1968 Convention, English law **56.70** did not provide for the direct enforcement of instruments other than court orders or judgments. Similarly, settlements of proceedings were only enforceable by execution if their terms had been incorporated in an order or judgment of the court. Authentic instruments and court settlements from other Contracting States are in principle enforceable under the 1968 Convention as they are now equated to English judgments for the purposes of enforcement.

3. Enforcement of foreign judgments and judgments from other parts of the United Kingdom[74]

56.71   Foreign judgments are enforceable in England and Wales by all the means available in respect of English judgments once their enforcement has been authorised by an order of the High Court.[75] The means of obtaining such an order differs, depending on where the judgment comes from and whether or not the 1968 Convention applies.

Enforcement under the 1968 Convention. Judgments of courts of other Contracting States to the 1968 Convention may be enforced by registration in the High Court (or, in the case of maintenance orders, in a magistrates' court). The application is made in the first instance to a master, and an appeal against his decision to grant or refuse an order for enforcement lies to a judge in chambers. Execution on such a judgment may issue in the same way as on an English judgment.

Enforcement of judgments from Scotland and Northern Ireland. Judgments made by courts in other parts of the United Kingdom are automatically registrable in the High Court and enforceable in the same way as an English judgment. The procedure for that purpose has already been described.[76]

56.72   *Judgments outside the 1968 Convention.* The United Kingdom has entered into bilateral conventions or has reciprocal arrangements with a number of countries for the mutual recognition and enforcement of judgments. The procedure for enforcement is by means of registration and is broadly comparable with that which applies to judgments under the 1968 Convention. Where the foreign judgment is not enforceable under an international convention or reciprocal arrangement, a fresh action "at common law" will have to be started in the English courts in which the cause of action will be the foreign judgment itself.

The grounds on which enforcement will be allowed of a foreign judgment to which the 1968 Convention does not apply, are broadly similar, whether the judgment falls under the statutory schemes of registration or is the subject of an action at common law. In each case, the judgment must be final and must be for the payment of a definite sum of money. It must be given by a court which, according to English private international law, is of competent jurisdiction and the enforcement of the judgment must not be contary to public

---

[74] This topic is discussed in more detail in chaps. 10 and 11 above.
[75] In some cases it is necessary to bring a fresh action on the foreign judgment; see paras. 10.03 and 25.35 above and para. 56.72 below.
[76] See paras. 10.63 *et seq.* and chap. 46 above.

policy and must not involve the direct or indirect enforcement of a foreign penal or tax law.

L. LEGAL PERSONS

56.73
The most common form of legal person is a limited liability company, which is a corporate entity with the liability of its members being limited by shares. The shares may be privately owned (a private company, which usually has the abbreviation "Ltd." after its name) or publicly marketed on the stock exchange (a public company or "p.l.c."). Other forms of legal person include bodies corporate (usually owned by the state), companies limited by guarantee and various other forms of corporate body.

A partnership, commonly used for the practice of professions, does not have a legal personality distinct from that of its members, but the relationship between its members is regulated within a statutory framework and it may usually sue and be sued in the name of the firm. Its members are usually only natural persons, but legal persons may also enter into partnership with each other or with natural persons. An unincorporated association is an association of persons, such as a club, whose relationship with each other is regulated by the law of contract. It has no legal personality of its own and may not sue or be sued in its own name.

M. LEGAL AID[77]

56.74
Any natural person, regardless of nationality, residence or domicile, who satisfies certain financial criteria can obtain legal aid under either or both of two schemes. First it is possible, under what is known as the "green form" scheme, to obtain legal advice and assistance (up to a fairly low cost limit) from a solicitor. Secondly, legal aid is available to bring or defend legal proceedings. The administration of legal aid has been transferred to a new independent authority, the Legal Aid Board. An applicant must demonstrate that he has a *prima facie* case and that his means are inadequate to enable him to pay for legal representation. The financial criteria are strict and it is only persons of very limited means who are eligible for legal aid.

Depending on the applicant's means, the legal aid may be free or it may be subject to his making a contribution assessed on a sliding scale. If the legally aided party loses the case then his liability to the legal aid fund is limited to the amount of his maximum contribution. Costs recoverable from him by the successful party are limited to the amount that the court considers that he can afford. Sometimes he is ordered to pay an amount equivalent to his maximum

---

[77] This topic is discussed in more detail in chap. 12 above.

contribution, but frequently he will pay nothing. Exceptionally, in cases of hardship, a non-legally aided party who wins a case against a legally aided party may recover his costs against the legal aid fund. If a legally aided party wins a case any costs recovered from the losing party will go to the legal aid fund, and any property preserved or recovered by the action will be charged to the fund to satisfy the balance. A party who obtains legal aid to bring or defend proceedings is free to choose solicitor and counsel to conduct the proceedings. The solicitor and counsel are themselves remunerated by the legal aid fund.

CHAPTER 57

UNITED KINGDOM: NORTHERN IRELAND

Written in collaboration with Andrew E. Donaldson Q.C.[1]

THE LEGAL SYSTEM

1. Introduction

History and territory. The province of Northern Ireland was **57.01** formed in 1921 from the six counties in the north-east of Ireland.

---

[1] Member of the Bar of Northern Ireland.

Until then, it had formed part of Ireland which had itself been governed for centuries, under a variety of constitutional arrangements, first by England and later as a part of the United Kingdom. Following civil unrest in the early part of this century, the Government of Ireland Act 1920 was passed to effect a division of Ireland into two separate provinces, Northern Ireland and Southern Ireland. Each province was to have a separate parliament exercising devolved legislative functions within the United Kingdom.

In the event, the Act of 1920 took effect only in Northern Ireland. Articles of agreement for a treaty between Great Britain and Ireland were signed in 1921, under which Ireland, under the style of the Irish Free State, would become a self-governing dominion within the British Empire. The treaty applied equally to Northern Ireland, except that the Northern Ireland parliament could ask to be excluded from the authority of the government and parliament of the Irish Free State and retain its constitutional status as established by the Government of Ireland Act 1920. In 1922 the Northern Ireland parliament exercised this right, thereby severing all Northern Ireland's constitutional links with the Irish Free State. The Irish Free State was replaced by the Republic of Ireland in 1949.[2]

After 1920, the new parliament for Northern Ireland sat at Stormont Castle in Belfast, enjoying a large measure of legislative autonomy over the province. As a result of political unrest in the late 1960's and early 1970's, however, the Northern Ireland parliament was suspended by the United Kingdom government. Subsequent attempts to establish a legislative assembly for Northern Ireland have not proved successful and the province is now governed directly by the government and parliament of the United Kingdom, although the Secretary of State and other ministers exercise most of their functions from their administrative centre in Belfast.

Origins of the legal system. Irish law applied throughout Ireland until 1921 although, as has been seen, this was much influenced by English law over the centuries.[3] Under the Government of Ireland Act 1920, laws in force in Ireland at the commencement of that Act continued in force, subject to that Act and to subsequent legislation of the Northern Ireland and United Kingdom parliaments. The legislative powers of the Northern Ireland parliament extended to all matters except those reserved to the United Kingdom parliament or otherwise excepted. These reserved or excepted matters

---

[2] See, further, para. 52.01 above.
[3] *Ibid.*

included foreign affairs, defence, the armed forces, taxation, postal services and the higher courts.

2. The administration of justice

Legal system. The legal system of Northern Ireland remains separate and distinct both from that of England and Wales and from that of Scotland. The principal legislation relating to the constitution, administration and practice of the judicature in Northern Ireland is the Judicature (Northern Ireland) Act 1978. In most important respects, the legal system is the same as that of England and Wales. It shares both the common law and much of the legislation which is applicable elsewhere in the United Kingdom. The House of Lords is the final appellate court. Northern Ireland judges are appointed by the Queen and the administration of the courts, through the Northern Ireland Court Service, is the ultimate responsibility of the Lord Chancellor.

57.02

Levels of courts. As in England and Wales the superior court of first instance civil jurisdiction is the High Court of Justice. This, together with the Crown Court (with criminal jurisdiction) and the Court of Appeal, forms the Supreme Court of Judicature. The inferior court of first instance jurisdiction, for most types of cases involving amounts up to £5000, is the county court. The procedure of the two courts is broadly similar although each has its own detailed rules.

B. LEGAL PRACTITIONERS

As in England and Wales the practising legal profession is divided into two main branches, barristers and solicitors. Reference should be made to the English section for a fuller description of their respective roles.

57.03

1. Solicitors

Introduction. The solicitor acts as a general legal adviser assisting his clients on all legal aspects of his personal and business transactions. Thus a solicitor will advise on and draft legal documents such as contracts, conveyances of land, leases and wills, he will do the legal work connected with the incorporation of companies and the winding up of deceased persons' estates. He will conduct litigation for his clients, either appearing in court himself or, in appropriate cases, instructing a barrister to do so.

Legal education and qualification. The professional training of both solicitors and barristers is conducted by the Institute of Professional Legal Studies at the Queen's University Belfast under the direction of the Council of Legal Education for Northern Ireland. The intending entrant into the legal profession must first have a law degree which qualifies him for admission to the Institute of Professional Legal Studies. There are different courses, each lasting one year, for intending solicitors and barristers. The intending solicitor then goes on to a further year's pupillage as a trainee solicitor, after which he may be admitted as a solicitor. He may not, however, practice other than as an employee of another solicitor for a period of a further two years.

57.04   *Rights of representation and audience.* As in England, solicitors have rights of audience in the county court and in the magistrates' court and in certain appeals to the Crown Court. There is no geographical limit on the Northern Ireland courts in which they may appear.

Organisation of practice. There are approximately 1500 practising solicitors in Northern Ireland. They are in some 420 law firms, most of which are small; many practices consist of only one solicitor and firms rarely have more than six or seven partners. A person may not practice as a solicitor in Northern Ireland until he has been granted a practising certificate by the Incorporated Law Society of Northern Ireland. This certificate only entitles him to practise in Northern Ireland and not in England or Scotland or (subject to the EEC Legal Services Directive)[4] in the Republic of Ireland or elsewhere. There is some specialization by solicitors' firms, especially in the fields of company law, criminal law and High Court litigation, although most firms do conveyancing and probate work.

57.05   *Solicitors' fees.* In general, fees are a matter for free negotiation. In certain restricted areas, such as county court work, there are statutory scales. In other matters, such as High Court litigation, probate and conveyancing, there are informal guidelines which tend to be observed as regards the upper limits. A client who disputes the solicitor's bill of costs has the right to have the matter considered by a High Court judge, who may refer the bill of costs for taxation by the Taxing Master if he finds that a proper retainer exists.

Professional organisation and conduct. The Incorporated Law Society of Northern Ireland is the governing body for solicitors in Northern Ireland. The powers of the Society are largely contained in the Solicitors (Northern Ireland) Order 1976, under which the

---

[4] Para. A2.47 below. As implemented in the U.K. by the European Communities (Services of Lawyers) Order 1978 (S.I. 1978 No. 1910), the Directive does not permit lawyers qualified in one part of the U.K. to practice in other parts of the U.K.

Society may make regulations as to the professional practice, conduct and discipline of solicitors.[5] All disciplinary matters are dealt with by the Disciplinary Committee, which is appointed by the Lord Chief Justice from among practising solicitors. It has wide powers to deal with professional and other misconduct.

All practising solicitors are required to be covered by professional indemnity insurance, which is organised centrally by the Society. There is also a compensation fund administered by the Society to provide compensation in certain circumstances to those who have suffered loss or hardship as the result of the act or default of a solicitor.

2. Barristers

As in England and Wales barristers act as specialist legal advisers   **57.06**
and as advocates both in the Supreme Court, where they have exclusive rights of audience, and in all other courts and tribunals. The Bar of Northern Ireland grew out of the Irish Bar as it existed until 1921, and the Honourable Society of the Inn of Court of Northern Ireland was established in 1926.

Legal education and qualification. As has been mentioned,[6] the intending barrister, after obtaining a law degree, attends a specialised course at the Institute of Professional Legal Studies for one year. During this period he will seek admission to the Inn of Court of Northern Ireland. On passing his professional examinations he is called to the Bar. He must then serve a pupillage with a more senior barrister for one year, during the first six months of which he may not accept fee earning work.

Organisation of practice. There are approximately 300 practising   **57.07**
barristers in Northern Ireland, of whom about 30 are Queen's Counsel. A barrister may act for a client only on the instructions of a solicitor. If the work is of a contentious nature and related to any proceedings in Northern Ireland then such work may only be accepted from a solicitor who is qualified to act in Northern Ireland.

There is no system of barristers' chambers in Northern Ireland, nor are barristers' clerks employed. All barristers are members of the Bar Library at the Royal Courts of Justice in Belfast, where they are allocated seats and from where they practice. The Library is serviced by an administrative staff funded by the Bar, to which every barrister contributes an annual fee.

Barristers are self employed and may not form partnerships

---

[5] The Solicitors Practice Regulations 1987 regulate, *inter alia*, professional conduct, advertising and restrictions on practice.
[6] See para. 57.03 above.

between themselves or with others. Because of their small numbers there tends to be less specialisation than at the English Bar. A barrister who has reached a certain professional standing may apply to, or be invited by, the Lord Chief Justice to be appointed as Queen's Counsel. Queen's Counsel advise in more important cases and appear in them jointly with junior counsel. Queen's Counsel may appear without a junior but this rarely happens in practice. A Queen's Counsel may not normally settle pleadings in connection with contentious proceedings unless he has agreed to appear as an advocate without a junior. Queen's Counsel are referred to collectively as the Senior Bar.

57.08   *Barristers' fees.* There are statutory scales of fees for certain types of work, notably in the county court and under criminal injury legislation. There are also informal scales affecting such matters as Queen's Bench compensation claims, whereby the amount of the fee is related to the amount of claimed or recovered. If the matter is not covered by any particular scale, the barrister may either charge the fee which he considers appropriate or negotiate the fee with the instructing solicitor.

Professional conduct. The Inn of Court of Northern Ireland is responsible for the admission and education of students, and their call to the Bar, liaison with corresponding bodies in other countries and standards of conduct. The Executive Council of the Inn of Court exercises disciplinary authority over all barristers. The Bar Council deals with matters of professional conduct, the administration of the Bar Library and generally matters of concern and interest to the profession. Professional indemnity insurance is compulsory for barristers.

3. Notaries

57.09   There is no separate profession of notaries in Northern Ireland, although a few solicitors are notaries. They exercise the same functions as notaries in England.[7] All solicitors in Northern Ireland may administer oaths.

[The next paragraph is 57.11]

4. Foreign lawyers

57.11   There are no rules specifically governing the practice of foreign lawyers,[8] and there are no continental or other foreign law firms or practitioners in Northern Ireland. There are reciprocal arrange-

---

[7] See para. 56.09 above.
[8] But see para. 57.04, n. 4 above.

ments under which English or Irish barristers of at least five years' standing may readily be called to the Northern Ireland Bar.

[The next paragraph is 57.14]

C. Sources of Law

1. Introduction

As in England and Wales, there are two principal sources of law **57.14** in Northern Ireland: legislation and the common law. For historical reasons, the statutory and other legislative sources are somewhat diverse. There is no formal written constitution.

International treaties are concluded by the United Kingdom government on behalf of the Crown and they will not be recognised or enforced by Northern Ireland courts unless and until they have been incorporated into Northern Ireland law by Act of Parliament or Order in Council. The provisions of European Community law are expressly stated by the European Communities Act 1972 to take precedence over the provisions of other statutes.

2. Legislation

The territory comprising Northern Ireland has, in the course of **57.15** its history, been subject to a variety of legislative authorities: the English Parliament, the Irish Parliament, the Parliament of Great Britain, the United Kingdom Parliament (since 1800) and, as regards certain devolved legislative powers,[9] the Northern Ireland Parliament (1921–1972). It has already been noted that laws in force in Ireland at the commencement of the Government of Ireland Act 1920 continued in force, subject to that Act and to subsequent legislation of the Northern Ireland and United Kingdom parliaments. Determining the applicability of earlier statute law can cause considerable problems for the practitioner.

Since 1972 the only source of primary legislation has been the United Kingdom Parliament. Some Acts of Parliament, for example, the Judicature (Northern Ireland) Act 1978, are only of application in Northern Ireland; these Acts have the words "(Northern Ireland)" in their title. Other Acts are of general application but they will, for the avoidance of doubt, contain express provision that they extend to Northern Ireland,[10] either wholly or

[9] See para. 57.01 above.
[10] See, for example, the Civil Jurisdiction and Judgments Act 1982, s.52(1), para. 44.49 above.

in part. If any Act of the United Kingdom Parliament extends to Northern Ireland it says so expressly.

Delegated legislation. Since the abolition of the parliament of Northern Ireland in 1972, legislation which principally affects Northern Ireland is passed by means of Parliamentary Order in Council under powers conferred by section 1(3) of the Northern Ireland (Temporary Provisions) Act 1972.[11] What were previously statutes of the Northern Ireland Parliament are now Orders in Council. Just as certain statutes of the parliament of Northern Ireland conferred powers on other persons or bodies to make inferior legislation, known as Statutory Rules and Orders, so the new legislation by Parliamentary Order in Council may confer authority on other persons or bodies to make delegated legislation which are known as the Statutory Rules of Northern Ireland. All such delegated legislation which applies specifically to Northern Ireland, whether made under an Order in Council or under an Act of the United Kingdom Parliament is similarly described.

3. Decided cases and legal writings

57.16   *The common law.* Except where a matter is expressly regulated by statute, it will be subject to the rules of the common law, as expounded in the decisions of the higher Northern Ireland, English and (until 1921) Irish courts over many centuries. The meaning of statutes as interpreted by the courts also forms part of the common law. When a court has to decide a point of law that has already been decided by a higher court, it is bound to follow the previous decision of the higher court. This rule is applied by the Northern Ireland Court of Appeal in respect of its own previous decisions. The House of Lords is not bound by its earlier decisions although it has only rarely contradicted an earlier decision. Where a point of law has not previously been decided, it will be decided by parity of reasoning with previous decisions. The decisions of the higher Irish courts since 1921 are regarded as being of persuasive authority.

Although wide areas of the civil law are now governed by statute, most of the law of contract and tort is still determined solely by the common law.

Legal writings. There are relatively few text books or legal journals devoted specifically to Northern Ireland law and practitioners will generally use the equivalent English law text books and journals. As in England they are of persuasive authority.

---

[11] For example, the first piece of legislation passed in this way was the Prosecution of Offences (Northern Ireland) Order 1972 (S.I. 1972 No. 538) (N.I. 1).

4. Publications

Statutes and statutory instruments are published in an official   **57.17**
form by Her Majesty's Stationery Office called *The Statutes Revised
– Northern Ireland*. An official index of legislation in force is published periodically under the superintendence of the Statute Law
Committee for Northern Ireland. Practitioners also refer to compendia of annotated English legislation such as *Halsbury's Statutes*.
In the field of civil procedure there is no equivalent to the English
Supreme Court Practice or the *County Court Practice*, and practitioners have to rely on the statutory rules themselves.[12]
    The principal law reports for cases decided in Northern Ireland
are the Northern Ireland Law Reports[13] published by the Incorporated Council of Law Reporting for Northern Ireland. Cases are also
reported in the *Northern Ireland Judgments Bulletin*, known also as
the *"Blue Book,"* and in the *Bulletin of Northern Ireland Law*
(*"B.N.I.L."*). Learned articles on legal subjects are published in
the *Northern Ireland Legal Quarterly* (*"N.I.L.Q."*).

D. ORGANISATION OF THE CIVIL COURTS

1. Introduction

The structure of the court system in Northern Ireland is derived   **57.18**
from the former court system of Ireland as a whole. The Supreme
Court of Judicature (Ireland) Act 1877 had established a Supreme
Court for the whole of Ireland, on the model of the Supreme Court
of England and Wales. The Government of Ireland Act 1920 established the Supreme Court of Judicature of Northern Ireland, consisting of a Court of Appeal and a High Court. Following the
restructuring of the criminal courts in England and Wales the
Crown Court, exercising criminal jurisdiction, was created in
Northern Ireland, as part of the Supreme Court, by the Judicature
(Northern Ireland) Act 1978. County courts had been established in
Ireland in the late eighteenth century and these continued in their
more developed form when a separate Northern Ireland came into
being.

2. The County Court

For practical purposes the lower court of first instance is the   **57.19**
county court with jurisdiction limited, in cases of contract and
tort, to claims not exceeding £5,000. There are eight county court

---

[12] The Rules of the Supreme Court (Northern Ireland) S.R. No. 346, 1980, and
    the County Court Rules of Northern Ireland (S.I. No. 225, 1981).
[13] Cases in these reports are cited according to year, followed by the abbreviation
    "N.I." and the page reference.

divisions corresponding very broadly with the six geographical counties of Northern Ireland and the two principal cities, Belfast and Londonderry. There are 11 county court judges, of whom eight are assigned to particular divisions and three are peripatetic. The county courts in the divisions of Belfast and Londonderry are each known as the Recorder's Court and the judges are called recorders. Each county court is administered by a chief clerk. For each county court area there is a circuit registrar who has jurisdiction in interlocutory matters and in small cases up to a general limit of £500. Many cases involving £300 or less are dealt with informally by the registrar in accordance with a simplified small claims procedure. Appeals by way of a full rehearing lie to the High Court, and by way of case stated on a point of law to the Court of Appeal.

3. The High Court

57.20   The High Court is located permanently at the Royal Courts of Justice at Belfast. There are nine High Court judges, including the Lord Chief Justice and three Lord Justices. High Court judges usually sit singly but they may sit with a jury of seven persons in a limited class of actions.[14] Interlocutory decisions in Queen's Bench matters are usually taken by a High Court master, but in Chancery matters they are often taken by a judge.

As in England, the High Court is subdivided into three divisions, the Queen's Bench Division, the Chancery Division and the Family Division to which matters are assigned according to their subject-matter. There is no commercial court. Any case may be transferred from the High Court to the county court by consent, or if it appears that a sum of less than £5,000 is likely to be recovered, or if the case does not raise any important question of law or fact and it is suitable for determination in the county court.

4. The Court of Appeal

57.21   The Court of Appeal sits at the Royal Courts of Justice in Belfast. It consists of the Lord Chief Justice and three other judges called Lord Justices of Appeal. It may comprise two judges but in important cases three will sit.

5. House of Lords

57.22   The House of Lords in London is the final appellate court for Northern Ireland, as well as for England and Scotland. Leave to appeal is required from the Court of Appeal or the House of Lords.

---

[14] In claims for libel, slander, malicious prosecution or false imprisonment any party may have trial by jury if he so requires. The general right to jury trial in civil actions was abolished in 1987. In some cases a High Court judge may sit with assessors.

6. Other civil courts

Magistrates' courts. As in England and Wales, magistrates' courts, in addition to their wide criminal jurisdiction, exercise civil jurisdiction in limited classes of case. Claims for maintenance and other domestic disputes, certain small debt claims, and claims for possession of property, known as claims for ejectment, fall within the jurisdiction of magistrates' courts. Appeals from magistrates' courts in respect both of criminal and civil matters lie to the county court.

Tribunals. As in England and Wales, there are various specialised tribunals in Northern Ireland, with jurisdiction over employment disputes, certain disputes concerning land, and various other matters.

7. The judiciary

Judges of the High Court of Northern Ireland are appointed by the Queen on the recommendation of the Lord Chancellor from the ranks of the county court judges and the practising members of the Senior Bar. County court judges are similarly appointed and it has been the almost invariable practice to make such appointments from among the ranks of practising Senior Counsel. Although there is power to appoint solicitors who have practised as such in Northern Ireland for not less than 10 years as county court judges, no such appointment has been made. 57.23

E. JURISDICTION OF THE CIVIL COURTS

Introduction

The courts of Northern Ireland exercise international jurisdiction in accordance with rules which are identical to those which apply in England and Wales and which have been described in Chapter 56.[15] The High Court of Northern Ireland has territorial jurisdiction over the six counties of the province. The province is divided into county court divisions, with a county court sitting in each division. The choice of division in which proceedings should be brought is governed by the County Court Rules and is determined normally by the residence of the defendant or the place where the cause of action arose. 57.24

[The next paragraph is 57.32]

---

[15] Paras. 56.24 to 56.31 above.

F. Limitation Periods

57.32 The law with regard to limitation of actions is generally the same as in England and Wales. It is contained in the Statute of Limitations (Northern Ireland) 1958 and the Limitation Act (Northern Ireland) 1964, (as amended).

[The next paragraph is 57.34]

G. Civil Procedure—Proceedings up to Judgment

1. General description

57.34   In most respects civil procedure in Northern Ireland is identical to that in England and Wales. In the High Court it is governed by the Rules of the Supreme Court (Northern Ireland) 1980. These Rules follow closely the scheme, and in many cases the wording, of the English Rules of the Supreme Court. However two principal differences should be noted. First, there is no provision for the master to give directions for trial at an interlocutory hearing for this purpose, although Senior Counsel may give certain interlocutory directions. When the pleadings are closed and interlocutory matters, such as discovery and interrogatories have been dealt with, the case is set down for hearing and comes into the warned list for hearing in due course. The preparation and conduct of the proceedings is largely a matter for the parties until the actual time of trial. Secondly, the enforcement of judgments in Northern Ireland is conducted by a special department of the High Court, the Judgments Enforcement Office, which has no counterpart in the English legal system.

In the county court, civil procedure is broadly similar to that in the High Court. It is governed by the County Court Rules (Northern Ireland) 1981.

2. Parties and legal representation

57.35   The rules and practice concerning parties and legal representation are the same as in England and Wales.[16]

[The next paragraph is 57.37]

---

[16] See para. 56.35 above.

3. Commencement of proceedings

In the High Court the procedure is identical to that in England **57.37**
and Wales. In the county court the document which initiates the
proceedings is called a "civil bill." It is taken out by the plaintiff or
his solicitor in the same way as an English county court summons.[17]

4. Service of proceedings

The rules and practice concerning service of proceedings are the **57.38**
same as in England and Wales.[18]

5. Appearance by the defendant

When the defendant is served with a writ or an originating sum- **57.39**
mons from the High Court, or with a civil bill from the county
court, these documents will contain instructions as to what he
should do if he wishes to contest the proceedings. In High Court
proceedings he must enter an appearance on a document known as
a "memorandum of appearance". In the case of proceedings served
in Northern Ireland this must be done within 14 days but a longer
period may be allowed when there has been service out of the jurisdiction. In the memorandum of appearance the defendant merely
acknowledges service of the proceedings but gives no indication of
what his attitude to the trial might be. Failure to enter an appearance may result in judgment being given in favour of the plaintiff.

In county court proceedings the civil bill merely directs the
defendant to appear at a particular county court on a given date. No
acknowledgment of service or entry of appearance is required.
However, in default or summary bills, the situation is different. In
these cases the defendant must within 14 days complete and return
a notice indicating whether he admits or disputes the claim.

6. Default judgments

The rules and practice concerning default judgments and setting **57.40**
them aside are the same as in England and Wales.[19]

[The next paragraph is 57.42]

7. Disputes as to jurisdiction

There is no special procedure for disputing the jurisdiction. It is **57.42**
not clear what the effect is of a defendant entering an appearance to
a writ or originating summons, but it may prejudice his ability to

---

[17] The commencement of proceedings in England and Wales is described at
para. 56.37 above; see also chap. 3 above.

[18] See para. 56.38 above; see also chap. 4 above.

[19] See para. 56.40 above.

dispute the court's jurisdiction. The better view would appear to be that a defendant who wishes to dispute the jurisdiction should enter a conditional appearance, which he may only do with the leave of the court. The jurisdictional dispute could then be dealt with either as an interlocutory matter or as a preliminary issue at the trial. In the county court, as a defendant does not have to enter an appearance to a civil bill, he may raise the jurisdictional issue at the hearing, provided he has pleaded the point at the outset in his defence.

8. Pleadings

57.43   The rules and practice as to pleadings are generally the same in Northern Ireland as in England and Wales. It should be noted that the statement of claim must be served within six weeks after the defendant has entered an appearance to the writ. The time for a defendant to serve his defence is 21 days (as opposed to 14 days in England and Wales) after entry of appearance or service of the statement of claim. Pleadings are deemed to be closed 21 days after service of the defence, or reply (if any). In the county court the defence to a civil bill must be entered at least four days before the next entry day.

[The next paragraph is 57.45]

9. The hearings

57.45   *Interlocutory matters.* There is no procedure in Northern Ireland for a hearing before the master on a summons for directions. As soon as the pleadings have closed the plaintiff's solicitor sends the papers in the case to Senior Counsel for a written direction of proofs. Senior Counsel will decide, *inter alia*, whether or not the case is fit to be set down for trial. It is usual for all interlocutory matters to be dealt with before the case is set down for hearing. Senior Counsel may, for example, consider questions as to further and better particulars of the pleadings, and matters relating to discovery, interrogatories, or the admission of facts. He may give directions as to whether the trial should be by judge alone or by judge and jury. When all such matters have been dealt with, the case is set down by the solicitor and it takes its place in the queue of actions awaiting trial.

57.46   *The trial.* The trial procedure is the same as that which applies in England and Wales.[20]

[The next paragraph is 57.48]

---

[20] Para. 56.46 above.

10. Security for costs

Northern Ireland practice and procedure under this heading is 57.48
the same as in England and Wales,[21] save that courts will not award
security for costs against a limited company on the ground that it
may not be able to pay costs which have been awarded against it.

11. Witnesses and oral evidence

The law of evidence and the manner in which evidence is given 57.49
the courts of Northern Ireland are substantially the same as in England and Wales.[22]

[The next paragraph is 57.51]

12. Documentary evidence

The procedure for discovery and inspection of documents is that 57.51
which operated in England and Wales before the introduction there
of automatic mutual discovery and inspection. After the close of
pleadings, the court may order any party to make and serve on any
other party a list of the documents which are, or have been, in his
possession, custody or power, relating to any matter in question in
the cause or matter. A party may be ordered to make and file an
affidavit verifying such a list. Discovery will only be ordered by the
court if it is considered necessary. A party against whom discovery
has been ordered must allow the other party to inspect the documents referred to in the list. There are special rules requiring the
automatic disclosure of medical evidence in personal injury cases.

Sometimes a party may obtain an order for discovery against a
person who is not a party to the action, for example, against a hospital in respect of medical records relevant to a claim for damages for
personal injuries.

The rules as to privilege are the same as in England and Wales.

[The next paragraph is 57.53]

13. Experts

With the exception of medical experts, there is no requirement 57.53
that expert evidence be disclosed in advance and the expert witness
is treated at trial as any other witness. The rules and practice concerning the use of experts in civil proceedings is otherwise substantially the same as in England and Wales.[23]

---

[21] Para. 56.48 above.

[22] See para. 56.49 to 56.50 above; also chap. 8 above. The Civil Evidence Act
(Northern Ireland) 1971 contains provisions similar to those found in the Civil
Evidence Acts 1968 and 1974.

[23] Para. 56.53 above.

14. Proof of foreign law

57.54   As in England and Wales foreign law is a matter of fact to be proved by evidence.[24] It is for the judge to decide matters of foreign law, even in jury trials. However, in proceedings before a court in Northern Ireland, judicial notice may be taken of the law of England and Wales or of the Republic of Ireland.

15. Compromise

57.55   The rules and practice concerning payments into court and compromise are substantially the same as in England and Wales.[25]

16. The judgment

57.56   The rules and practice concerning the giving of judgments, and their form is substantially the same as in England and Wales.[26]

17. Costs

57.57   The rules and practice concerning costs is substantially the same as in England and Wales.[27]

H. CIVIL PROCEDURE—PROVISIONAL AND PROTECTIVE MEASURES

57.58   The provisional and protective measures which are available in Northern Ireland are the same as those which are available in England and Wales.[28]

[The next paragraph is 57.61]

I. CIVIL PROCEDURE—SUMMARY PROCEDURES

57.61   A creditor who owes a fixed sum of money may be summoned to the Judgments Enforcement Office[29] for examination by the Office as to whether he admits the debt, and, if so, as to his means. It may require him to produce documents relating to the debt and to his means. A debtor who does not comply with the summons may be taken to admit the debt. An admission of debt is treated as a money judgment and all the normal methods of enforcement are available to the creditor through the Office.

[The next paragraph is 57.63]

---

[24] See para. 56.54 above; see also chap. 9 above.
[25] See para. 56.55 above.
[26] See para. 56.56 above.
[27] See para. 56.57 above.
[28] See para. 56.58 above; see also chap. 7 above.
[29] See para. 57.66 below.

J. Civil Procedure—Appeals

In general there is a right of appeal from the decisions of all courts. **57.63**
An appeal usually operates as a stay of execution unless otherwise
ordered.

Decisions of the county court may be appealed to the High Court **57.64**
where there is a full re-hearing of the case. The time for appealing is
21 days from the date of pronouncement of the judgment. Alternatively an appeal may be taken directly to the Court of Appeal by
way of case stated on a point of law. The requisition to state a case
must be lodged within six weeks of the decision complained of, and
the appeal must be entered within 14 days of the receipt of the case
stated.

Decisions of the High Court may be appealed to the Court of
Appeals are either by way of case stated on a point of law, or by way
of a review of the evidence and judgment (but not involving a rehearing). Notice of appeal must be served within three weeks of the
date of pronouncement of the judgment.

Decisions of the Court of Appeal may be appealed to the House
of Lords with the leave of the Court of Appeal or of the House of
Lords. Leave is granted only in cases of public importance and
where there is uncertainty as to the law.

[The next paragraph is 57.66]

K. Civil Procedure—Enforcement

1. Enforcement of judgments given in Northern Ireland

Introduction. The enforcement of most judgments, in particular **57.66**
money judgments and judgments for the possession of goods or
land, is controlled by the Enforcement of Judgments Office, which
is administered by the Northern Ireland Court Service under the
direction of the Lord Chancellor. The Office is administered by the
Master (Enforcement of Judgments), together with a judicial officer. Enforcement is actually carried out by the Chief Enforcement
Officer and other members of the Northern Ireland Courts Service.
The Office has very wide powers as to the manner of execution of a
judgment.[30]

Money judgments are payable as soon as they have been drawn
up and entered. The bringing of an appeal usually suspends the
enforceability of a judgment, unless otherwise ordered.

---

[30] The enforcement of judgments is governed by the Judgments Enforcement
(Northern Ireland) Order 1981, the Judgment Enforcement (Northern Ireland)
Rules 1981, and the Rules of the Supreme Court (Northern Ireland), Orders 45
to 52.

57.67   *Service.* When a judgment is not satisfied, the disappointed party may apply to the Enforcement of Judgments Office for the judgment to be enforced. Initially, the Office causes a copy of the judgment to be served on the defaulting party, together with a formal notice of intention to enforce the judgment, calling on him to satisfy the judgment debt or otherwise comply with the judgment, and warning him of the consequences of his failure to do so. If the defaulting party fails to comply, a custody warrant may be issued and he is then commanded to appear and be examined as to his means.

57.68   *Execution.* The Office has powers to make enforcement orders. These may order the defaulting party to make payment by instalments, or they may order the seizure and sale of goods, enforcement against land, delivery up of goods, enforcement against various funds, stocks or shares, the appointment of a receiver, the attachment of debts or the attachment of earnings.

In some exceptional circumstances, leave to enforce a judgment may have to be obtained in the High Court.[31] An application for an order of sequestration must be made to a judge by motion; and in other cases of difficulty, an application may be made in a similar manner. The High Court has the power ultimately to fine or commit to prison for contempt a person who has wilfully failed to comply with a judgment.

Opposing execution. A person against whom execution is being carried out, or a third party affected by the execution, may apply to the Master (Enforcement of Judgments), on an *ex parte* basis in a case of urgency, for the execution to be stayed or for conditions to be attached to it. If ownership of goods against which execution is being levied is disputed by a third party, the enforcement officer may apply to the court by a procedure called "interpleader" for that issue to be resolved.

[The next paragraph is 57.70]

2. Authentic instruments and court settlements

57.70   Until the implementation of the 1968 Convention, the law of Northern Ireland, like that of England and Wales, did not provide for the enforcement of instruments other than court orders or judgments; but authentic instruments and court settlements from other Contracting States to the 1968 Convention are now, in principle, enforceable in Northern Ireland.

---

[31] R.S.C. (N.I.), Ord. 46.

3. Enforcement of foreign judgments and judgments from other parts of the United Kingdom

The rules and practice for the enforcement in Northern Ireland **57.71** of foreign judgments and judgments from other parts of the United Kingdom are substantially the same as those which apply in England and Wales.[32] The initial application for registration of the foreign judgment is made *ex parte* to the High Court Master. In a case to which the 1968 Convention applies, an appeal against his decision to grant or refuse an order lies to the judge on a summons supported by an affidavit. In a case to which the 1968 Convention does not apply, an application to set aside the registration of a foreign judgment is made by the same procedure.

[The next paragraph is 57.73]

L. LEGAL PERSONS

The different forms of legal person under the law of Northern Ire- **57.73** land are the same as those under English law.[33]

M. LEGAL AID

The law and practice relating to civil legal aid in Northern Ireland is **57.74** substantially the same as in England and Wales.[34] Legal aid in Northern Ireland is administered by the Legal Aid department of the Law Society of Northern Ireland. As in England and Wales, legal advice and assistance is available from all participating solicitors under the "green form" scheme; and legal aid may be obtained to bring or defend proceedings in the civil courts. The assessment of means of an applicant for legal aid may be carried out by the Legal Aid department or by the Department of Social Security.

---

[32] See para. 56.71 to 56.72 above; see also chap. 10 above. R.S.C. (N.I.) Ord. 71 governs the enforcement of foreign judgments and of European Community judgments.

[33] See para. 56.73 above.

[34] See para. 56.74 above; see also chap. 12 above.

CHAPTER 58

UNITED KINGDOM—SCOTLAND

Written in collaboration with Walter G. Semple, solicitor, Edinburgh and Glasgow.[1]

[1] Partner, *Bird Semple Fyfe Ireland WS*, solicitors.

1514

A. THE LEGAL SYSTEM

1. Introduction

History and territory. Scotland remained an independent country **58.01** until 1707 when it was united with England. Although a single parliament was established at that time for the newly-formed United Kingdom, it was a condition of the union that Scotland should retain its own legal system. As a consequence, the law and the administration of justice in Scotland remain markedly different from the other two parts of the United Kingdom. Many of the functions of government in Scotland, while remaining the responsibility of the government of the United Kingdom, are still exercised separately.

2. The administration of justice

Origins of the legal system. Until 1707, the law of Scotland had **58.02** developed quite independently from that of England. As a result of Scotland's political alliances against England, the earlier development of Scottish law was significantly influenced by the civil law systems of continental Europe. Generations of Scottish lawyers received their training in France and, after the Reformation, in the Low Countries. The result is that, although it has never been codified, many elements of Scottish law are derived from the romanistic legal systems. Many areas of substantive law, such as land law, family law, property law, insolvency law, the law of wills, succession and trusts, still differ considerably from English law. Scottish criminal law also differs substantially from English law.

However, in the period since the Act of Union in 1707, the law of Scotland has also been subject to the influence of the common law system of England and Wales. Much of modern commercial law, such as company law, partnership law, insurance law, tax law, employment law and contract law is often either the same as or very similar to English law. Yet because of differences in approach or historic legal principles there can be important differences of principle and detail. For example, in respect of the law of delict, although the law may appear to be the same as the English law of tort, its effect may be different, because of these underlying differences in approach. Scots law has borrowed a number of common law ideas. In particular the concept of a trust is important in Scots law but it has not been developed to the same extent as in England. Scottish law shares with English law a considerable reliance on case law and rules of binding precedent.

Court system. As in England, there is a clear division in the Scottish legal system between civil law and criminal law. Commercial law is part of the civil law. Scottish procedural law in both civil and criminal matters is substantially different from English procedural law. As regards civil matters, the court system consists of two levels of court of first instance, the sheriff courts located throughout Scotland, and the Outer House of the Court of Session, located in Edinburgh.[2] Except in cases exclusively assigned to one or other of those courts, their jurisdiction is concurrent. Appeals are heard by sheriffs principal (from the sheriff courts) and by the Inner House of the Court of Session. Final appeals on points of law lie to the House of Lords in London.

There are also numerous different tribunals exercising jurisdiction over specialised matters, many of them administrative in nature. As in the rest of the United Kingdom, though, there is no separate system of general administrative courts. Claims against the government and public bodies in respect of administrative matters are dealt with in the civil courts by means of a procedure known as judicial review. Claims against the government or public bodies in respect of civil or commercial matters are normally treated no differently from civil claims against private persons or bodies.

B. LEGAL PRACTITIONERS

58.03 The Scottish legal profession is quite separate from that of England and Wales. A lawyer qualified in Scotland has no rights to practise law in England and Wales beyond the rights of a layman, and the situation is the same as regards English lawyers practising in Scotland. The legal profession in Scotland is divided into two branches, solicitors and advocates.[2a]

1. Solicitors

Introduction. Solicitors act as general legal advisers for their clients in connection with a wide range of legal and business matters. They are consulted direct by the public and sometimes by other solicitors. In addition to acting in the conduct of litigation, they draft wills and administer the estates of deceased persons, they advise on and carry out tax planning and they conduct the legal formalities required in connection with the transfer of title and granting security over land and buildings. They transact many different types of commercial work including the purchase and sale of businesses and the formation of companies and the licensing of intellectual property rights.

---

[2] Criminal jurisdiction is exercised by district courts, by sheriff courts and by the High Court of Justiciary.

[2a] The government has recently proposed far-reaching changes in the structure and regulation of the legal profession.

Legal education and qualification. A law degree obtained at one of the five university faculties of law in Scotland is accepted as an initial qualification to be a solicitor. Almost all Scottish solicitors therefore start their legal studies at university. A small number of intending solicitors without a law degree take the Law Society of Scotland's own examination. Thereafter, the intending solicitor must undergo a year's course of practical training at a Scottish university to obtain a Diploma in Legal Practice. Finally he must spend two years in a solicitor's office as a trainee before being admitted by the Law Society of Scotland as a solicitor.

Rights of representation and audience. Solicitors undertake most of the litigation before the sheriff courts and many administrative and other tribunals in any part of Scotland, but they have no rights of audience in the higher civil or criminal courts. As there is no upper financial limit on cases which may be taken in the sheriff court, a considerable amount of litigation takes place there and many solicitors are experienced and skilled in advocacy. They brief advocates in cases in the higher courts. Solicitors practising in Edinburgh have certain special responsibilities and powers in relation to the conduct of litigation before the Court of Session but they do not normally have the right to appear in that court.   **58.04**

Organisation of practice. Solicitors normally practise in partnership. Usually the partnerships are quite small, but in Edinburgh and Glasgow in particular there are a number of larger firms, which are able to specialise to a greater extent than many smaller firms. Solicitors may be employed as full time assistants by other solicitors and some legal work may be undertaken by unqualified staff under the direction of the solicitor. Partnerships with members of other professions are not permitted.

Solicitors' fees. Solicitors' fees are subject to the control of the courts through officers known as "auditors of court." In relation to both civil and criminal litigation the court maintains fee tables which are reviewed periodically. In relation to conveyancing and other non-contentious work there is a fee table maintained by the Law Society of Scotland which, in the event of a dispute, will usually be applied by the court. However, a solicitor may agree with his client the basis on which his fee will be charged, except that, in contentious matters, fees may not be charged on a contingency basis (that is, they may not be calculated by reference to a share in the proceeds of a successful litigation).   **58.05**

Professional organisation and conduct. All practising solicitors must be members of the Law Society of Scotland, the statutory governing body of Scottish solicitors. A legal directory containing lists of solicitors and advocates in practice is published under the authority of the Law Society.[3] It does not identify the fields of work in which individual solicitors or firms hold themselves out as practising.

The Law Society maintains a strict control of solicitors' accounts and of the ethical rules which apply to solicitors, and some of the rules of conduct are matters of law. Solicitors may not share fees with a person not qualified as a Scottish solicitor, nor act in court proceedings or in the preparation of writs for the profit of any person not qualified as a Scottish solicitor. Solicitors have certain exclusive rights to act in legal matters as well as in litigation. Advertising by solicitors is now permitted, within guidelines laid down by the Law Society. There is no rule preventing solicitors from having more than one office or from becoming the director of a trading company.

Solicitors must maintain certain minimum levels of professional indemnity insurance. They must strictly observe rules which require them to keep proper books of account and must keep all clients' funds in special bank accounts. They must contribute to a compensation fund maintained by the Law Society to compensate persons who have suffered loss as the result of any solicitor's dishonesty.

2. Advocates

58.06   *Introduction.* Advocates, of whom there are about 200 in practice, are the equivalent of barristers in England. They act as legal consultants and they perform the oral conduct of cases in court. Especially for the purposes of cases in the Court of Session, an advocate will normally also prepare the written pleadings, advise on points of law and on the merits of his client's case. Advocates have rights of audience in every court in Scotland, and those rights are exclusive in the Court of Session and the High Court of Justiciary. To appear in court they need to be instructed by a solicitor. In addition they give opinions on legal matters referred to them by solicitors. They may not accept direct instructions from members of the public, but may do so from foreign lawyers if litigation is not contemplated.

As in England, the advocates' branch of the profession consists of two tiers, Queen's Counsel (or "seniors") and "juniors." Advocates who are regarded as being of established capacity and standing in the profession may be appointed as "Queen's Counsel" and will have the initials "Q.C." after their name. Once appointed they no longer normally draft written pleadings and usually concentrate on

---

[3] *The Scottish Law Directory*, published annually by William Hodge & Co., Glasgow.

advocacy in court in more complex or difficult cases and on advisory work. In most cases in which a Q.C. is instructed, junior counsel is also instructed. About a third of practising advocates are Q.C.'s.

Legal education and qualification. The first step in an intending **58.07**
advocate's legal education is normally to obtain a law degree at a Scottish university. Thereafter he must obtain a Diploma in Legal Practice from a Scottish university and pass further vocational examinations. This is followed by at least a year's practical training in a solicitor's office and about nine months' pupillage or "devilling" to a practising advocate. Thereafter he is admitted to the Faculty of Advocates and called to the bar, whereupon he is entitled to practice as an advocate.

Organisation of practice. Partnerships between advocates are not permitted. Unlike English barristers, however, advocates do not operate from sets of chambers but practise on their own, usually at the library of the Faculty of Advocates. Each advocate has a box at the Parliament House in Edinburgh, where correspondence and instructions may be left for him. In recent years, administrative and secretarial functions have been centrally organised and are supplied by Faculty Services Limited, a non-profit making company established for that purpose. Advocates' clerks are employed for the purpose of negotiating the advocates' fees and organising their diaries.

Advocates' fees. An advocate's fees are negotiated with the **58.08**
instructing solicitor by the advocate's clerk. The fees are usually agreed as a lump sum for each item of work undertaken, although fees for a long appearance in court may be agreed on a periodic basis. Contingency fees are forbidden. Value Added Tax is generally payable on advocates' fees except, in some cases, where the services are rendered to clients outside the United Kingdom. Advocates may not sue for their fees but solicitors are under a professional obligation to pay them.

Professional organisation and conduct. Advocates are all members of the Faculty of Advocates and they are subject to the disciplinary authority of the Dean of the Faculty. There is no equivalent in Scotland to the Inns of Court in London. Advocates are also subject to the general law of negligence in the conduct of their practice, but they are immune from an action for negligence in the actual conduct of a case in court or in advisory work immediately connected with a court hearing. They are required to carry a substantial level of professional indemnity insurance.

3. Notaries public

58.09 Any solicitor in Scotland is entitled to become a "notary public" and many do so. This confers no additional powers or privileges in connection with the transfer of immovable property, but it does confer certain additional powers in relation to the taking of oaths, dealing with bills of exchange and other special functions. Most notarial functions may also be performed in Scotland by solicitors.

[The next paragraph is number 58.11]

4. Foreign lawyers

58.11 There are no special rules which affect foreign lawyers who may wish to practice as such in Scotland, other than the EEC Legal Services Directive.[4] For most purposes a foreign lawyer is in no different a position from any other member of the public. He may not hold himself out as a solicitor, nor perform, for remuneration, any of the activities reserved to solicitors or advocates. He may not form a partnership with a Scottish solicitor or advocate. Otherwise he is free to carry on practice under his home designation as a lawyer.

5. Lawyers in business and public employment

58.12 Solicitors may retain their membership of the Law Society of Scotland whilst in the full time employment of a commercial organisation or a public body. They will continue to be subject to the rules and discipline of the Law Society. They may represent their employers in court proceedings, provided that they maintain a practising certificate. Advocates who are employed may remain members of the Faculty of Advocates, but they are not permitted to continue in practice as much or to appear in court.

6. Messengers-at-arms and sheriff officers

58.13 The collection of sums due under judgments of Scottish courts and the enforcement of court orders is not a matter for the courts or their officials. After the court has granted its decree[5] the pursuer must instruct a "messenger-at-arms" (for Court of Session decrees) or a "sheriff officer" (for sheriff court decrees) to take the necessary enforcement steps. These officers are also employed whenever personal service of court documents is required as a part of the court procedure. They may practise on their own account or in partnership.

---

[4] See para. A2.47 below.
[5] A final judgment or order of a Scottish court is called a "decree."

C. Sources of Law

1. Introduction

It has already been observed that the constitution of the United   **58.14**
Kingdom is made up of a body of law, custom and practice. Scottish law, in common with the laws of the other parts of the United
Kingdom, recognises the supremacy of the United Kingdom parliament, and Acts of Parliament take priority over all other sources of
law. Delegated legislation is made under powers conferred by Act
of Parliament. Scottish law also recognises previous decisions of the
courts as binding and certain legal writings are considered to be
authoritative. In a limited sense, custom and equity may also be
regarded as sources of Scottish law. International treaties are not
binding as a matter of Scottish internal law unless and until they
have been incorporated into United Kingdom law by or pursuant to
an Act of Parliament. EEC law takes effect in the United Kingdom
by reason of the European Communities Act 1972.

2. Legislation

Scottish legislation consists of Acts of Parliament ("statutes"),   **58.15**
Acts of Sederunt and delegated legislation.

Statutes. There are still in force a substantial number of the Acts
of the former Scottish parliament passed before 1707 and none of
the pre-1707 English Acts has force in Scotland. There being now
no separate Scottish parliament all legislation which affects Scotland is enacted by Parliament in London. The practice is that some
Acts apply exclusively to England and Wales, some apply exclusively to Scotland, and some apply partly to one and partly to the
other or to both. If an act applies exclusively to Scotland, the word
"Scotland" appears in its title.

As in England, statutes are to be construed according to the
intention of Parliament as ascertained from the words of the statute
itself. Reference may not normally be made to parliamentary
debates or to the reports of working parties on which the statute is
based.[6]

Acts of Sederunt. The Court of Session has power to enact formal
resolutions called "Acts of Sederunt" for the purpose of regulating
the powers and procedures of Scottish courts. This power derives in
part from Act of Parliament and in part from the common law.

Delegated legislation. Delegated legislation consists principally of
statutory instruments. These are normally made by government

---

[6] As to the interpretation of statutes enacting international conventions, see also
paras. 13.22 *et seq.* above.

ministers under powers contained in a statute and are subject to parliamentary approval. The power to legislate on certain matters of an administrative nature may be delegated to other bodies, such as regional or district councils.

3. Decided cases and legal writings

58.16 *Case law.* Under the doctrine of binding judicial precedent, adopted from England, the decisions of the House of Lords in a Scottish case, and of any superior Scottish court, will, in general, be binding on a lower court. The decisions of the House of Lords in non-Scottish cases, and of the higher English courts are regarded as being of persuasive authority. Decided cases are therefore a most important source of law in Scotland.

Legal writings. A high degree of authority is attached in the Scottish courts to the writings of certain legal scholars of earlier centuries. They are known as the institutional writers and they were responsible for setting down in writing the principles of Scottish law. The best known are Stair, Craig, Erskine and Bell. The writings of modern authors of standard text books and other legal literature are accorded a degree of respect and authority.

4. Publications

58.17 Statutes and statutory instruments are published in an official form, but practitioners often refer to editions of annotated legislation, which note amendments to the texts as they occur. The decisions of the higher courts, or decisions of particular legal interest, are published in law reports, of which the two most important series are the Session Cases Reports (cited as S.C.) and the Scots Law Times (cited as S.L.T.).

D. Organisation of the Civil Courts

1. Introduction

58.18 There are two levels of civil court of first instance: the sheriff courts and the Outer House of the Court of Session. There are no separate commercial courts. Disputes between employers and employees concerning dismissal and redundancy are, as in England and Wales, allocated to specialised industrial tribunals. Appeals from the sheriff courts lie to a sheriff principal (of whom there are six). Alternatively, an appeal may be brought before the Inner House of the Court of Session which also hears appeals from the Outer House. Further appeal on a point of law lies to the House of Lords (in its judicial capacity) which is the final court of appeal for the whole of the United Kingdom and which includes Scottish as well as English judges.

2. The Sheriff Court

Scotland is divided into six sheriffdoms, and each sheriffdom is   **58.19**
sub-divided into a number of sheriff court districts. There are 49
sheriff court districts in the whole country. In each district there are
a number of judges, called sheriffs, who exercise both civil and
criminal jurisdiction. In the exercise of his civil jurisdiction, each
sheriff sits alone. Each of the six sheriffdoms is presided over by a
sheriff principal who exercises an appellate jurisdiction in civil
cases.

The sheriff courts deal with the main bulk of civil litigation at
first instance. The territorial jurisdiction of each sheriff court is
limited to its own district. The value of the subject matter of the
cases with which the court may deal normally has no upper limit[7]
and a wide range of remedies may be granted. It has exclusive jurisdiction over claims of up to £500. The sheriff will, for example, deal
with actions for debt, contract, reparation, rent restriction, actions
affecting property, leases and tenancies, custody of children and
maintenance ("aliment") of spouses and children.

In recent years there has been a tendency to increase the jurisdiction of the sheriff court and in 1984 it was given jurisdiction to deal
with divorces, which has increased the pressure of its business. The
sheriff court may also wind up smaller limited companies.

Appeals. Appeal lies from the decision of a sheriff on a point of
law to the sheriff principal sitting alone. Many appeals are decided
in this way without having to go to the normal appellate court, the
Inner House of the Court of Session. An appeal may always be
taken direct to the Inner House of the Court of Session if it is so
desired.

3. The Court of Session

The Court of Session is the superior civil court. It always sits in   **58.20**
the Parliament House in Edinburgh and it has territorial jurisdiction over the whole of Scotland. The court hears cases at first
instance before a single judge (known as a Lord Ordinary) in the
"Outer House"[8] and it hears appeals before a bench, usually consisting of three judges,[9] in the "Inner House".[10] The "Inner
House" is divided into the First and Second Divisions, each of
equal authority and importance.

---

[7] There is a summary procedure for claims up to £1,500: see para. 58.62 below.
[8] It has power, rarely exercised, to sit with a jury in a limited range of cases.
[9] In cases of special importance the court can be increased to seven or more
judges.
[10] Although the Inner House is mainly an appellate court there are certain types of
case which it deals with at first instance.

The Court of Session is a collegiate court and all judges have the same rank. The President of the First Division of the Inner House is called the Lord President, and the president of the Second Division is called the Lord Justice Clerk. The judges are not required to specialise in particular categories of business.[11] Various other courts are associated with the Court of Session and the judges of the Court of Session deal with the business of these courts. They include the Court of Exchequer (which deals with tax appeals), the Lands Valuation Appeal Court (for rating appeals), the Restrictive Practices Court, and the Employment Appeal Tribunal (for appeals from industrial tribunals).

The Outer House has a wide-ranging competence, which extends to all kinds of civil claims unless specifically excluded. In respect of the majority of litigation the sheriff court has concurrent jurisdiction with the Court of Session,[12] but certain types of proceedings fall within the exclusive competence of the Court of Session, such as petitions to vary trusts, patent cases, actions to wind up larger companies, and actions to declare as invalid (to "reduce") formal legal documents and judicial decrees. The Court of Session has power to refer cases to a sheriff court if it considers it appropriate to do so.

The Court of Session has an inherent equitable power[13] known as the *"nobile officium"* to provide a remedy where none is available under existing law and to mitigate the effects of the strict application of the law where this would lead to injustice. It may be used, for example, where a procedural lacuna has arisen and may allow a mistake in procedure to be rectified. A number of established remedies depend on the *nobile officium*, but it is normally only used where there is a well-established precedent and its exercise is not readily extended.

[The next paragraph is number 58.22]

4. The House of Lords

58.22   The House of Lords in its judicial capacity is the final appellate court for civil (but not criminal) matters. The appeals are heard by "Lords of Appeal in Ordinary,"[14] usually in a panel of five. Decision is by a majority. Usually there are at least two Scottish

---

[11] All the judges of the Court of Session are also judges of the High Court of Justiciary, the superior criminal court, in which capacity they are called Lords Commissioners of Justiciary.

[12] Certain cases are exclusively assigned to the sheriff courts, such as claims up to £500.

[13] It is exercised by the Inner House: see para. 58.61, n. 46 below.

[14] Legally qualified members of the House of Lords, if they have held high judicial office in England and Wales or in Scotland, may also occasionally sit as judges.

Lords of Appeal, and they normally participate in the hearing of Scottish appeals. The decision of the House of Lords in a Scottish appeal is not an operative judgment but the case must be returned to the Court of Session to be put into effect. Since 1966 the House of Lords has considered itself free to depart from its decisions in previous cases.

5. The judiciary

Scottish judges are appointed from among experienced practising   **58.23** members of the legal profession. Both solicitors and advocates may be appointed as sheriffs, but only advocates (and in practice only Q.C.'s) are appointed as judges of the Court of Session.[15]

E. JURISDICTION OF THE CIVIL COURTS

1. Introduction

Like other aspects of the Scottish legal system, the Scottish rules   **58.24** of jurisdiction have more in common with the rules found in continental countries than with the rules in the other parts of the United Kingdom. This facilitated the implementation of the 1968 Convention in Scotland. In cases to which the 1968 Convention applies, the international jurisdiction of the Scottish courts is determined by the rules in the Convention. As between the three different parts of the United Kingdom, jurisdiction is allocated according to rules which are themselves modelled on the Convention.[16] Where the combined effect of the Convention and these rules is to confer jurisdiction on the courts of Scotland, without specifying the particular court which is to have jurisdiction, the question whether a particular court has jurisdiction over a dispute is determined by the rules of local jurisdiction mentioned below. In respect of most civil and commercial matters, new internal Scottish rules of jurisdiction have been adopted both for the purposes of allocating local jurisdiction within Scotland and for determining the international jurisdiction of the Scottish courts in cases to which the 1968 Convention does not apply.[17] These rules are themselves modelled in large part on the rules in the 1968 Convention and many are based on the defender's domicile or seat. Thus in Scotland jurisdiction in most types of international case will be decided by reference to the rules of the 1968 Convention, or rules modelled on it.

---

[15] Unlike their counterparts in some continental countries, public prosecutors ("procurators fiscal") are not regarded in Scotland as members of the judiciary.

[16] 1982 Act, s.16 and Sched. 4 (paras. 41.01 *et seq.* and 45.01 *et seq.* above). See also paras. 1.23 and 56.24 above.

[17] 1982 Act, ss.20 and 21, Scheds. 8 and 9, paras. 42.01, and 42.02 and 47.01 *et seq.* above. See also para. 58.28 below.

It has already been noted that the jurisdiction of the Court of Session and the sheriff courts is concurrent in respect of most civil matters, but that some specialised matters are assigned exclusively to one of those courts or to specialised tribunals.

2. Domicile and seat

58.25   The rules which determine where a natural or legal person is domiciled or has its seat are common to the whole of the United Kingdom and have already been described.[18]

[The next paragraph is number 58.27]

3. Jurisdiction—general rule

58.27   A defender domiciled or having its seat in Scotland may, as a general rule, be sued in the Court of Session or in the sheriff court for the locality in which that domicile or seat is situated.

4. Jurisdiction—special rules

58.28   In addition to the above general rule as to jurisdiction in Scotland, there is a range of special rules of jurisdiction, modelled on the rules in the 1968 Convention. Where the proceedings are brought in the Court of Session, these rules do not affect jurisdiction as between different places in Scotland, because that court has territorial jurisdiction over the whole of Scotland: but the rules have effect for determining the particular sheriff court in which proceedings may be brought. For example, proceedings in contract may be brought in the sheriff court for the place of performance of the obligation in question and proceedings in delict or tort may be brought in the sheriff court for the place where the harmful event occurred. Scottish law is the same as English law in providing that, in the absence of agreement to the contrary, the place of performance of an obligation to pay money is generally where the creditor is to be found. Proceedings arising out of the operations of a branch, agency or other establishment may also be brought in the appropriate court for the place where that branch, agency or other establishment is situated. Special rules apply in respect of consumer contracts. Certain matters are subject to rules of exclusive jurisdiction; for example proceedings relating to immoveable property must be brought in the court for the place where the property is situated.

---

[18] These rules are summarised at paras. 56.25–56.26 above and discussed in detail at paras. 44.01 *et seq.* above.

5. Choice of court and submission to the jurisdiction

Except where exclusive jurisdiction is allocated to a particular **58.29** court, Scottish law permits the parties to confer jurisdiction on a court by agreement,[19] or by a voluntary submission to the jurisdiction.

6. Exorbitant grounds of jurisdiction

In cases to which the 1968 Convention does not apply, certain **58.30** exorbitant rules of international jurisdiction have been retained as against persons domiciled outside the United Kingdom. Notably, Scottish courts will accept jurisdiction over natural persons temporarily within the territorial jurisdiction of the court (itinerants) who are served with the court's process there particularly when the legal basis of the action is founded in contract. Further, jurisdiction may be founded in certain cases on the presence of immoveable property in Scotland, or on the seizure of assets located there.

7. Civil claims in criminal proceedings

Civil claims may not be made in criminal proceedings in Scot- **58.31** land, although orders for compensation or restitution may be made against a criminal defender in certain circumstances. It is not clear whether such orders constitute civil judgments for the purposes of the 1968 Convention.

F. Limitation Periods

The Scottish law of prescription and limitation is complex and the **58.32** following should be taken as only the most general guide. Most law on this topic is set out in the Prescription and Limitation (Scotland) Act, 1973. In Scottish law, time-bars are generally matters of substantive law, extinguishing an obligation by prescription, although some are procedural rules of limitation, barring the right to pursue legal remedies.

The normal period of prescription for most obligations of a con- **58.33** tractual, quasi-contractual or delictual nature is five years.[20] There are detailed rules providing for when the period begins to run. For example, the obligation to pay money for goods supplied on sale or hire or for services rendered in a single transaction arises when the obligation becomes enforceable. In a series of transactions it arises when payment for the last item became due. Normally an obligation to make reparation for loss, injury or damage arises on the

---

[19] There are certain restrictions on the validity of jurisdiction agreements in consumer contracts.

[20] All the obligations which prescribe in five years are set out in Part I of Sched. 1 to the 1973 Act.

date when the loss injury or damage occurred. If the claimant was ignorant of its occurrence, the five year period runs from the date upon which he discovered, or ought to have discovered, the damage. Prescription is interrupted by the making of a claim in court or in an arbitration. The material date is that of service of the proceedings or notice of arbitration.

Actions for damages for "solatium" (compensation for pain and suffering) for personal injuries or death must be commenced within three years from the date of the injuries. The rule which provides for the limitation is not absolute and the period may in certain cases be extended to take account of delayed knowledge on the part of the pursuer or other causes of potential injustice.

Most other types of obligation become prescribed after 20 years. These include the obligation to comply with a court judgment or an arbitration award or to observe the provisions of a document formally executed or any obligation relating to land.

Some obligations never become prescribed. These include real rights of ownership in land, tenants' rights in land under a formal lease, certain obligations of trustees to beneficiaries and rights to recover stolen property.

If the debtor has indicated, either by performance or a clear admission, that the obligation still exists the prescriptive period comes to an end and a fresh period starts to run.

G. Civil Procedure—Proceedings up to Judgment

1. General description

58.34   By comparison with the main systems of civil procedure elsewhere in Europe, Scottish civil procedure is similar to that in England, but there are many differences both in approach and detail.

As in England, Scottish civil procedure is adversarial. The presentation of evidence is a matter for the parties and not for the court. After the preliminary stages, the final stage of the procedure is a full hearing in court with witnesses personally present to give evidence about the facts in dispute, followed by oral argument by the parties' lawyers. When the matters in dispute are simple, then the hearing, or "proof" will last a relatively short time. If the case raises complex issues of fact or law the hearing may last many days or even weeks.

Great importance is placed on the form of the pleadings. The rules as to pleadings are strict. Each allegation made by a party must be answered by his adversary or it will be held to be admitted. It is improper to make an allegation in pleadings unless the party making the allegation believes that he can prove it by evidence. When the pleadings are closed they are made up into a single document called the "Closed Record", which thus constitutes a reliable summary of the respective cases of the parties with the respective replies to each others' cases. No evidence may be adduced and no argument may be advanced which is not strictly founded on the pleadings. Accordingly, if at any stage of the litigation a new or different case is to be made, the pleadings must be formally amended.

In 1988 a special flexible procedure for commercial cases in the Court of Session was revised and improved.[20a]

Although there are differences in detail between the procedures in the Court of Session and the sheriff courts, the rules are broadly similar in effect. The Court of Session is the senior court where the full range of remedies is available for important litigation and accordingly the rules of procedure in that court are more extensive. But there is no financial limit to the cases which may be taken in the sheriff courts and many important cases are dealt with there. The timetable for cases in the sheriff courts tends to be rather more demanding than the timetable in the Court of Session. In 1985 a special simplified procedure for use in personal injuries cases became available in the Court of Session.

2. Parties and legal representation

Parties. The party who institutes, or "raises," the proceedings is called the "pursuer" and the party defending them is called the "defender." Several persons can pursue an action jointly if they have a common cause of action but not if each has a separate and independent claim against the same defender. Thus "class actions" are not permissible. The rules provide for the joining of additional defenders and the adding of third parties to an action where this is required. A counterclaim may be raised against a pursuer on any matter arising out of the grounds of the principal claim. **58.35**

Persons under some legal incapacity, such as bankrupt persons, persons under age or persons of unsound mind will normally sue or be sued through their legal representative.

Sisting a mandatary. A pursuer who is resident in any country outside the United Kingdom (at least, if he is of foreign nationality) will normally be required to cause an independent person within the jurisdiction to be joined into the proceedings as joint pursuer. It may be that this practice, which is known as "sisting a mandatary," is now of doubtful validity in cases where the pursuer (the "mandant") is domiciled in another Contracting State of the 1968 Convention. The practice is said to have the dual object of guaranteeing the payment of the expenses[21] and having someone in the jurisdic-

---

[20a] See para. 58.61 below.
[21] See para. 58.48 below.

tion who is responsible to the court for the proper conduct of the proceedings. A foreign national resident in Scotland will not normally be required to appoint a mandatary.

58.36   *Representation by a lawyer.* In the Scottish civil courts natural persons who are parties may conduct their own cases personally without legal representation, although it is unusual for them to do so. Except where a party is acting in person, he must be represented by a solicitor in proceedings in a sheriff court or the Court of Session. Solicitors commonly conduct litigation in the sheriff courts at first instance and on appeal; but if the proceedings are in the Court of Session the solicitor must instruct an advocate to represent the client at the hearings. Advocates may not be instructed directly by their lay clients but only by solicitors acting on behalf of the clients. In cases before tribunals, parties may be represented by non-lawyers.

3. Commencement of proceedings

58.37   The pursuer must first prepare a formal document containing a statement of his claim. In normal contentious matters, this is called a "summons" in the Court of Session, or an "initial writ" in the sheriff court.[22] This document must include the names of the parties, a precise description of the remedy sought and a statement of the essential facts and the legal basis of the claim. It does not include a detailed statement of the evidence to be adduced, nor legal argument or references to legal authorities. It is good practice for a pursuer to include all the required items at the outset of the pleadings although in some circumstances actions are started on the basis of facts which are not adequately specified, in the knowledge that, if required, the pleadings can be amended at a later stage.

The summons or initial writ is taken by the pursuer or his solicitor to the court office where, on payment of the appropriate fee, it is validated ("signetted" in the Court of Session, "warranted" in the sheriff court). This involves the court recording the name of the proceedings in the court books, allocating a number to them, and authorising service of the summons or initial writ. The signetting or warranting confers certain rights to take protective measures.[23] The summons or initial writ must be served within a year. The proceedings are regarded as having commenced when service is effected on the defender.

---

[22] Certain matters, usually of a non-contentious nature, are started by a "petition" in the Court of Session or "summary application" in the sheriff court: see paras. 58.61–58.62 below. There are also other procedures for special types of case.
[23] See para. 58.59 below.

4. Service of proceedings

Once the court has authorised service of the summons or initial   **58.38**
writ, it may be served on the defender. This is often called
"citation". It is the responsibility of the pursuer or his solicitor to
effect service, which may normally be done in one of three ways.
First, service may be by post by means of a recorded delivery letter,
including a notice on the envelope that it should be returned to the
court if it cannot be delivered. Secondly, it may be made personally
through a messenger-at-arms or a sheriff officer for the appropriate
location,[24] who must explain its purpose to the defender. Thirdly,
it may be made by a messenger-at-arms or a sheriff officer leaving
the summons or writ at the dwelling place or place of business of
the defender or, in the case of a company, at its registered office.

If the defender is outside the United Kingdom, service may be
effected under the Hague Service Convention or any other applicable international conventions[25] or through appropriate diplomatic
or consular channels. Alternatively, it may be made by post or personally by the pursuer or his agent.

If the defender is outside ("furth of") Scotland and his residence
or place of business is not known or he cannot be successfully
served by other means, substituted ("edictal") service may take
place at the Court of Session. This procedure may also require
advertisement in a newspaper circulating in the area of the
defender's last known address.

Proof of citation. Citation is proved by a certificate to the effect
that citation has been executed. This certificate is made by a solicitor if service was effected by post, or by the messenger-at-arms or
sheriff officer if it was effected by one of the other methods.
Alternatively, service may be accepted by a defender or his solicitor
indicating such acceptance in writing to the court.

5. Appearance by the defender

Once the defender has been served with a summons or initial writ   **58.39**
he must enter an appearance by notifying the court that he intends
to defend the proceedings. An appearance is entered in the Court of
Session by the noting of the details of the defender's solicitor and
counsel on the printed list of cases at the Court. In the sheriff court,
an appearance is entered by lodging at the court of a notice of intention to defend.

When service is effected, a set period, called an *"induciae"*,

---

[24] Certain documents (such as interim interdicts) must be served personally. The
messenger-at-arms or sheriff officer is instructed by the pursuer or his solicitor:
see para. 58.13 above.
[25] See paras. 4.30 *et seq.* above and A2.03 below.

begins to run. The length of this period varies, according to the court involved and depending on the place where citation occurs. In the Court of Session, it is 21 days if citation is effected in the United Kingdom or any other part of Europe,[26] whereas in the sheriff court it is 14 days if citation is effected in the United Kingdom, but 28 days if it is effected in another part of Europe. In both courts, where citation takes place outside Europe, the period is extended to 42 days, except that, where the citation of a Court of Session summons is effected personally, the period remains 21 days. The *induciae* may be shortened by the court in an appropriate case.

In the Court of Session, after the expiry of the *induciae*, a pursuer must have his case listed ("called") for an initial procedure before the court. The defender must enter an appearance within three days after of the date of calling; he then has 14 days from the date of calling within which to lodge his defences. In the sheriff court the defender must lodge his notice of intention to defend before the expiry of the *induciae*. Once it has expired, an initial hearing (a "first calling" or "tabling") will take place on the first court day thereafter, at which the court will order defences to be lodged on the pursuer's motion.[27]

6. Default judgments

58.40   If the defender fails to notify the court of his intention to defend the proceedings, the pursuer may ask the court to grant him a default judgment (called a "decree in absence"[28]). The judge will consider the averments of jurisdiction in the summons or initial writ[29] and if these disclose that the court has jurisdiction, he will grant a decree in absence without considering the merits of the case.

58.41   A decree in absence may be set aside on the application of the defender. In the Court of Session, this may be done by a motion in the proceedings, if the application is made within the first 10 days after the decree is entered in the court books. In such a case, it is not necessary to show a defence on the merits. Otherwise, it must be done by means of new proceedings, namely a petition for the "reduction" of the decree. The defender would normally also apply for execution on the decree to be suspended until the petition has been determined. In the sheriff court, an application to set aside a

---

[26] Europe is not defined for these purposes.

[27] A different procedure is followed for summary cases with a value up to £1,000: see para. 58.62 below.

[28] A "decree in absence" is available in a case where the defender fails to enter an appearance. A "decree by default" may be granted where a defender has entered an appearance but then fails to pursue his defence. This latter type of decree cannot be set aside.

[29] See para. 58.43 below.

default judgment is made by a "reponing note". A petition for reduction of the decree and a reponing note must set out the reasons for the delay in entering an appearance and, in summary form, the defender's defence on the merits.

An application to set aside the decree in absence may be made at any time within 20 years from its date, provided the enforcement procedures have not gone beyond the stage of a formal request for payment (a "charge for payment")[30] being made to the debtor by a messenger-at-arms or sheriff officer, or generally if the decree has not been enforced. If the decree is suspended or reponed, the proceedings continue as if the defender had entered an appearance in the first place.

Unless the decree in absence is set aside, an enforceable copy of the decree (an "extract") must be obtained before it can be enforced, an enforcement may then proceed in the normal way.[31] If the defender is in Scotland, the period of 11 days (in the Court of Session) or 14 days (in the sheriff court) must elapse before the decree may be "extracted". If the defender is outside the United Kingdom, the decree must be served on the defender within seven days from its date. If the defender has no known solicitor in Scotland, the judge will postpone the grant of extract until after a sufficient period has elapsed for the defender to respond by post to the decree in absence which has been sent to him.

7. Disputes as to jurisdiction

A party need not indicate his intention to dispute the jurisdiction **58.42** of the court when he first notifies the court of his intention to defend, but he must indicate this from the outset in his pleaded defences. The defender may plead to the merits as well as to the jurisdiction, without thereby submitting to the jurisdiction of the court, or he may plead solely to the jurisdiction, in which case, if his challenge is unsuccessful, he will be permitted later to amend his pleadings to defend on the merits. The issue may be disposed of if the proceedings go to a debate,[32] but if necessary a preliminary hearing ("proof") may be directed for the purpose of deciding the jurisdictional issue as a preliminary point.

8. Pleadings

The pleadings in Scottish civil procedure perform the function of **58.43** precisely defining the factual and legal issues which the court is to decide, but they do not identify the evidence which will be adduced

---

[30] See para. 58.68 below.
[31] See para. 58.66 below.
[32] See para. 58.46 below.

or the arguments which will be advanced by the parties. They are drafted by the party's solicitor or advocate. The pleadings are lodged in the court, where they go to form part of the "record" (described below), and copies are sent to the other party's solicitor. Documents which form part of a party's case must either be recited in full in the pleadings or incorporated by express reference. In the latter case, copies of the documents referred to must be lodged in court with the pleadings and sent to the other party's solicitor.

Summons or initial writ. The first pleading is the pursuer's summons or initial writ, which, in addition to the name of the court and the names and designations of the parties, is made up of three parts. The first part, which is called the "conclusions" (in a Court of Session summons) or "crave" (in a sheriff court initial writ), sets out details of the remedy sought, including interest and expenses. In a claim for money or damages, the pursuer will always insert a specified sum which he is claiming. The second part is called the "condescendence", which is a series of numbered paragraphs setting out the facts upon which the pursuer relies and also the detailed legal basis of his case. The condescendence must include averments stating the domicile of the defender and other specified matters relevant to jurisdiction. The third part, called the "pleas-in-law", sets out in summary form the legal pleas upon which the pursuer's case is founded. Each separate legal plea is in a separately numbered paragraph.

58.44   *Defences.* The defender's first pleading is called the "defences". In the Court of Session, it must be lodged at the court within 14 days from the initial hearing ("calling"),[33] unless a longer period is allowed by the order of the court or agreement of the parties. In the sheriff court, a time within which the defender must lodge his defences will be fixed at the initial hearing. The defences have two principal parts, the "answers to the condescendence," which answer all the statements of fact alleged by the pursuer in numbered paragraphs, and the "pleas-in-law," which gives a summary of the legal pleas on which the defences are based. A counterclaim can be made in the same manner, requiring answers from the pursuer in the same form as the defences.

Further pleadings. In the Court of Session, after the defences have been lodged at the court, the pursuer's solicitor must draw up a single document called an "Open Record", reproducing the contents of the summons and defences. Six copies of this document are then sent to the defender's solicitor and a further two copies are lodged at the court. There is then a further period, usually lasting

---

[33] See para. 58.39 above.

until some 12 weeks after the initial hearing, during which each party in turn may enlarge his pleaded case against the other by adding to the Open Record. This process is called "adjustment". At the expiry of this period of adjustment, the court orders that the Record be closed, unless either party obtains an extension. When the Record is closed, the pursuer is required to draw up copies of the Closed Record and deliver them to the other parties and to the court. Any interlocutory procedural orders made by the court are also included in the Closed Record.

In the sheriff court, the procedure is similar, except that an Open Record is not normally drawn up as a single document unless the sheriff so orders. The period for adjustment of the pleadings is also not fixed in the sheriff court, but is brought to an end when the sheriff orders the closure of the Record.

Amendment. Each party may, with the consent of the court, amend his pleadings at any time after the Record is closed, provided the other party is given a fair opportunity to consider the amendment and answer it in writing prior to any hearing at which the matters in issue are to be considered. In particular, amendments may occur after a "debate."[34]

9. The hearings

Adjustment roll. When the time limited for entering an appearance (the *induciae*) has expired, the case is listed for an initial hearing and it is then placed on the list of cases in which the Record is still open. This list is called the "adjustment roll." In the Court of Session, unless either party applies in the meantime for procedural orders, the next hearing will normally take place 12 weeks later, at which the court will order the closing of the Record. In the sheriff court, the case will be listed for hearing every two or three weeks, for the sheriff to review its progress. When he considers that the issues have been adequately defined in the pleadings, he orders that the Record be closed. **58.45**

Procedure roll debate. When the court orders that the Record be closed, the case is transferred from the adjustment roll to a separate list of cases, the "procedure roll." At this point, either party may take the other to a preliminary hearing (called a "procedure roll debate"[35]) on the grounds either that the other's pleadings are not sufficiently detailed to give fair notice of the case being made or that the legal basis for the remedy sought does not exist. **58.46**

No evidence is called nor are any documents produced at a

---

[34] See para. 58.46 below.
[35] In the sheriff court it is just called a *debate*.

debate, except in so far as they form part of the pleadings. The object of the hearing is to allow the defender (and sometimes the pursuer) to attack his opponent's case on the basis that the legal remedy sought does not exist, that the case is not specified, or that the defence has no prospect of success. The judge will sometimes decide that there is no legal remedy on the basis of the facts stated and will dismiss the case. More often he will refuse to dismiss the case and will allow proof without making a decision on the law. However the effect of the detailed legal arguments required at the preliminary hearing often allows the parties to recognise better the relative strengths and weaknesses of their cases and may pave the way to a settlement.

If a case is dismissed at debate it may be brought again on a different legal basis, and normally a judge will, on the request of a party who has lost a debate, allow the amendment of pleadings to state a different or better case. The decision following a debate can be appealed right up to the House of Lords. As a result, some cases which decide important matters of principle are dealt with without any examination of the facts taking place.

Other procedural hearings. Either party may bring a motion before the court for an interlocutory order an ("interlocutor"), often of a procedural nature. Orders may be made for the production of documents, appointment of an expert, amendment of the pleadings or for other procedural aspects of the case. The motion may be heard either when the case comes up for a hearing on the adjustment roll, or at a special hearing for the purpose. Notice ("intimation") in writing must be given to the other party's solicitor.

58.47 *The proof.* When the interlocutory stages of the procedure have been completed, a date is fixed for the full hearing of the evidence and legal argument. This hearing is called the proof. It is usually held before a judge alone. In cases of a technical nature and with the consent of the parties, the judge may appoint an expert assessor to sit on the bench to assist him with technical matters.

The judge will have read the record before the hearing and will have acquainted himself with the issues. There are no opening speeches. The witnesses are called to give evidence orally and are questioned in turn by the lawyers for the parties.[36] Their evidence is recorded verbatim by a shorthand writer. The pursuer's witnesses are normally called before those of the defender. As soon as the witnesses have finished giving evidence, the pursuer's lawyer and then the defender's lawyer make their closing speeches to the court, setting out their contentions on the evidence and the law. The pursuer's

---

[36] See para. 58.50 below.

lawyer may be given an opportunity to reply. The burden of proof is normally on the pursuer and the test for proof of facts is the balance of probabilities.

At the conclusion of the evidence and speeches the judge may announce his decision and give his reasons forthwith. If he does not do so he adjourns his decision for deliberation ("avizandum") and, in the sheriff court and in the Court of Session in the court vacation, the decision is issued later in a written form, together with a statement of the reasons on which it is based. In the Court of Session during the court term, the judgment is announced in open court. The question of expenses will then usually be dealt with on a further motion by the winning party.

Referral to a judicial referee. As an alternative to a hearing before a judge, and if both parties agree, they can ask the judge to refer the case to an arbiter or referee for decision (known as a "judicial referee"). This may be done when the subject-matter of the dispute is technically complex. The judicial referee will then decide the case as an arbitrator would. The decision then comes back to court to allow for a formal judgment to be given.

10. Security for costs

In Scotland, security for costs is called "caution for expenses". A   **58.48** foreign pursuer is not obliged to provide security for costs but, as has been seen, he may be required to appoint a "mandatary" who is within the jurisdiction and who may be liable to satisfy any order for costs.[37] Security for costs will however be ordered against a bankrupt pursuer (but not against one who is merely without funds). A limited company which is shown to be without sufficient funds to pay the defender's expenses may be required to find caution or security when pursuing an action.

11. Witnesses and oral evidence

The parties are free to choose whom they wish to call as wit-   **58.49** nesses. Any person having knowledge of the facts is a competent witness. A party is competent as a witness on his own behalf. The evidence that a witness is able to give will be noted in advance of the proof in a statement called a "precognition," by the lawyer of the party proposing to call him to give evidence, but there is no compulsion on a witness to help in this way. Modest expenses may be paid to witnesses of fact. Expert witnesses may also be paid a fee. Witnesses who are reluctant to attend court to be examined at the hearing may be compelled to do so.

---

[37] See para. 58.35 above.

If a witness cannot attend the hearing because of age or illness, or because he is about to leave the country, his evidence may be taken at a suitable time and place by a commissioner specially appointed for the purpose. The evidence will be then taken as if it were at the hearing. If the witness is abroad there are procedures for taking his evidence there.[38]

58.50   *Examination of witnesses at the proof.* Each witness is first examined on oath by the lawyer calling him. Questions must be relevant to matters raised in the pleadings. Leading questions, which suggest the answer, may not be asked in respect of any matter which is in issue. The witness is then cross-examined by the lawyer for the other party. Leading questions and suggestions are permitted in cross-examination. The witness is finally re-examined by the lawyer who called him. Re-examination should strictly be limited to matters which were dealt with in cross-examination. Witnesses are examined separately and not in the hearing of other witnesses. Witnesses may only speak as to facts which are within their personal knowledge. Certain obligations, for example the repayment of most loans, are required to be proved by evidence in writing. Some transactions, for example transfers of rights in land, can only be proved by "formal writings", executed before two witnesses who also countersign the document. Affidavits are rarely used, except in divorce cases.

12. Documentary evidence

58.51   In Scotland there is no compulsory system of disclosure or discovery of documents. The preliminary hearing or debate takes place on the pleadings and only those documents which form part of the pleadings.[39] Where, however, the case depends on disputed questions of fact which have to be resolved at trial, either party may make an application to the judge for an order that the other party must produce documents or items in his possession which are required for resolving the issues in the case, whether or not they are adverse to the interest of the producing party. This usually happens after the Record is closed, but it can take place at any stage of the proceedings.[40]

The scope of an order for the production of documents is limited to documents of class which are relevant to the issues in the case, but within these limits, the terms of such an order may be fairly

---

[38] These procedures are similar to those which apply in England under the various international conventions to which the U.K. is a party: see paras. 8.26 *et seq.* above.

[39] See para. 58.43 above.

[40] Such an order may, exceptionally, be granted before the proceedings have commenced.

wide and specific documents need not be particularised, nor need the applicant demonstrate the existence of specific documents. Certain documents are privileged from production, notably those passing between lawyer and client and those affecting possible or pending litigation.

When the order is made, it is served on all persons ("havers") who are thought to have the relevant documents in their possession. They are required, unless they can certify that they do not have the documents or that the documents are confidential, to bring the documents before the commissioner appointed for the purpose of examining them. Where the documents are in the possession of a non-party haver, he may be required instead to produce them at the proof. **58.52**

13. Experts

Each party may instruct expert witnesses to consider and report on particular matters of a technical or other expert nature. Their evidence may then be led at a proof, without prior disclosure to other parties. **58.53**

If there are particular matters of fact of a technical or specialised nature, the judge may refer these matters to be reported on by an expert (called a judicial reporter, or "person of skill"). Normally this will be done with the consent of the parties, and the resulting written report will be regarded as conclusive.

14. Proof of foreign law

When foreign law forms part of a case, the law in question must be stated in the pleadings. It is then regarded as a matter of fact which must be proved or admitted. If it needs to be proved, this is normally done by means of evidence from a foreign lawyer. Alternatively, the court may remit the questions of foreign law for a report by a suitably qualified expert. **58.54**

15. Compromise

It is open to the parties to settle their dispute at any time. If they do so, the proceedings may be withdrawn or otherwise disposed of by the agreement of the parties. Alternatively, the judge may give formal approval to the terms of settlement, in order that it may be converted into an enforceable judgment. The judge is under no duty to promote a compromise and has no other role to play in the settlement of a dispute. **58.55**

Formal offers of compromise. If a party wishes to offer to settle a case he may formally do so by a "minute of tender," offering a particular compromise settlement inclusive of interest and expenses to date. This minute of tender is lodged in court and a copy sent to the other party. A tender may be withdrawn. If the pursuer is awarded a higher sum than is offered in the tender it has no effect upon the expenses. Normally if he is awarded a lower sum he will be entitled only to expenses to the date of the tender and will be liable for the defender's expenses after the date of the tender.

16. The judgment

58.56   Once the judge's decision has been pronounced, the operative part of it (the "interlocutor") is entered in the court books, whereupon it becomes a formal "decree". After a set period, an official copy of it (an "extract") may be obtained by the parties on application to the court office. In the Court of Session, the decree may be extracted eight days after it was entered in the court books[41]; in the sheriff court, it may be extracted once it is no longer susceptible to appeal,[42] unless the sheriff permits an extract to be made earlier.

The extracted decree will contain the title of the proceedings, the name of the judge, the interlocutor (including an order as to expenses), and the date it was entered in the books, but it will not contain a statement of the reasons on which the judgment was based. The decree may include an award of interest if this has been claimed in the summons or initial writ. Interest rates are fixed from time to time and are intended to be more or less in line with commercial interest rates. Interest usually runs from the date of service of the proceedings unless some other date is fixed by the court by reason of a contract or under statutory powers.

17. Costs

58.57   The costs of Scottish proceedings are called "expenses". The normal rule is that expenses will be recoverable by the successful party. The court does however have a discretion to recognise special circumstances by making a different award. Sometimes a limited award of expenses is made in connection with a particular part of the procedure, often related to amendment of pleadings. Expenses are not awarded in respect of legal work undertaken prior to the commencement of proceedings.

In the absence of agreement, the bill of the winning party's solicitor is submitted to a court official called an "auditor" for determination of the amount payable by the losing party. The amount of expenses awarded in respect of solicitors' work is calculated by reference to the fee tables approved by the court and, for advocates' work, as negotiated for advocates with the advocates' clerks. The solicitors' fee tables set out detailed charges for each piece of work

---

[41] The period is 11 days in the case of a decree in absence: see para. 58.41 above.
[42] See para. 58.64 below.

done. Fees recoverable from the losing party are calculated on a "party and party" basis which is somewhat less generous than the "solicitor and client" basis prescribed for use by the solicitor for charging his own client.

It is common for special charging agreements to be negotiated with clients on, for example, an hourly charging basis. Such agreements do not affect the calculation of the amount which the losing party has to pay to the winning party. Thus there is usually a shortfall of between a half and a third between the amount recoverable from the losing party and the expenses payable by a winning party to his solicitor. Advocates' fees, for which the solicitor is responsible, are normally recovered in full, provided that, in the sheriff court, the employment of counsel was sanctioned by the court.

H. CIVIL PROCEDURE—PROVISIONAL AND PROTECTIVE MEASURES

1. Introduction

Scottish law provides for three principal types of provisional and protective measures: "arrestment", which is a provisional attachment of moveable assets in the hands of a third person, "inhibition", which restrains the party against whom it is ordered from voluntarily disposing of his immoveable property to the prejudice of the applicant, and "interim interdict", which restrains the defender from acting in a particular unlawful manner. These various measures are all available as provisional measures pending the outcome of the proceedings ("on the dependence"), and the Court of Session may grant them in aid of proceedings pending in other Contracting States to the 1968 Convention.[43] Arrestment and inhibition are often put into effect before the proceedings have been served on the defender. Interim interdicts are granted on the basis of the statements made in the pleadings, without the necessity for evidence. **58.58**

Provisional remedies are always granted at the risk of the party seeking them and the court has various powers to award damages against a party who obtains an interim remedy in circumstances which ultimately are found to have been unjustified. A successful defender's prospects of recovering damages in respect of wrongful arrestment or wrongful inhibition, though, are significantly limited by the requirement that he must show malice or want of probable cause on the part of the arrestor or inhibitor.

The Court of Session also has powers to grant interim decrees on

---

[43] Section 27 of the 1982 Act: para. 43.14 above. The power to grant an order in aid of foreign proceedings extends, in the case of interim interdict but not arrestment or inhibition on the dependence, to cases where the foreign proceedings have not yet been commenced.

the substance of a case in pending proceedings, and power to award provisional damages in claims for personal injuries. In addition, the court has power to secure evidence in the hands of a party or a third person if it is needed in pending or contemplated litigation.

2. Arrestment and inhibition

58.59   *Arrestment.* A provisional warrant for attachment (called an "arrest-ment on the dependence" of the action) permits the pursuer to obtain security for a money claim by attaching movable property belonging to the defender which is in the hands of a third party (the "arrestee"). Such property may include debts owed by a third party to the defender, notably a bank account. Its effect is to forbid the holder of the property from parting with possession of it, but it transfers no right of property. It does not attach the defender's movable property in his own possession. The warrant is directed against a named arrestee. It is put into effect by a sheriff officer or messenger-at-arms visiting the premises of the arrestee and ordering him to comply with the order. It may also be effected by post. An arrestment may be put into effect immediately, but if it is to remain effective the proceedings must be served on the defender within 21 days after the arrestment.

The arrestee must himself be subject to the jurisdiction of the Scottish courts. The arrestment is not initially limited in value, but excessive or oppressive arrestments may be restricted by the court on the application of the debtor. Alternatively, an arrestment will normally be lifted ("recalled") or restricted on the provision of security or on the payment ("consignation") of money into the court sufficient to cover the claim and an allowance for interest and expenses. If the person in possession of the fund parts with possession of it he becomes liable for its value to the person making arrestment or he may even have to pay the debt as damages.

Inhibition. A similar warrant (called a "warrant of inhibition on the dependence")[44] may be obtained restraining the defender from dealing with his own immoveable property in Scotland to the prejudice of the pursuer while the action continues. Again, this does not bring about a transfer of ownership, but has the effect of preventing the voluntary disposal of the property by the defender. The measure may be used to secure any type of claim whether or not related to the property in question. It is put into effect by personal service of the warrant on the defender and by registration in the Register of Inhibitions. Notice of the inhibition placed on the register before the warrant is served is effective, provided that service is effected within 21 days thereafter.

---

[44] The inhibition may only be granted by the Court of Session. If it is in aid of proceedings in the sheriff court, the warrant is called "letters of inhibition".

Obtaining the order. The warrant is normally obtained automatically from the Court of Session either upon the signetting of the summons[45] or, if the warrant is required in aid of proceedings in the sheriff court or a foreign court, by a separate application for that purpose. A warrant of arrestment on the dependence may also be issued by the sheriff court.

3. Interim interdicts

The court may grant an interim interdict, ordering the defender   **58.60**
to refrain from doing some act until the final judgment in the case. Interdicts are available where the defender is alleged to be responsible for a wrong being committed or anticipated. Their grant is discretionary. The procedure may be used to obtain a personal order against a defender restraining him from disposing of his assets or removing them from the jurisdiction, pending a resolution of the dispute.

Interim interdicts can be obtained on the application of a pursuer to a Lord Ordinary or a sheriff. Evidence is not adduced and the decision to grant or refuse an order is made on the basis of statements in the pleadings. If an interdict is obtained in the absence of the defender ("without intimation") before the commencement of proceedings, the summons or initial writ must be served immediately on the defender. The defender may then apply for a preliminary hearing to take place within a few days to determine whether the interdict should continue. In an appropriate case, the interdict may be lifted upon the giving of adequate security by the defender. Arguments related to the balance of convenience and the cogency of the pursuer's case will weigh more heavily than those dealing with the overall merits of the case and facts not yet proved.

An interim interdict does not affect the parties' ultimate rights and it is granted at the pursuer's risk in damages. The pursuer may be required to give security as a condition for the grant or continuance of the interdict. The defender can prevent the making of an interim order against him before he is heard by the court by lodging a *caveat* with the court, if he suspects that the pursuer is about to make such an application.

4. Other interim and provisional orders

Interim decree. An interim decree may be granted awarding part of the remedy sought by the pursuer, but not the whole subject of the case. In an action for damages for personal injuries, if the defender has admitted liability or if the court is satisfied that the pursuer would establish liability without substantial contributory

---

[45] See para. 58.37 above.

negligence, a pursuer may obtain a payment of interim damages. The court must be satisfied that the defender has the means to make the payment. In the sheriff court, an interim decree may be made also in cases other than those for personal injuries, on the basis of admissions in the pleadings.

Provisional damages. In certain circumstances, a party may claim and be awarded at the proof, a final decree for provisional damages in a personal injury case. If he does so, and his condition subsequently deteriorates, he may later apply to the court for the assessment of damages to be re-opened with a view to his receiving a further award.

Consignation in court and interim possession. In the sheriff court, the pursuer may ask the court to order the defender to lodge (*consign*) in court a fund or article which is admittedly held by the defender but which is in dispute. The object is to preserve the fund or article pending the outcome of the litigation. The Court of Session has similar but more extensive powers to regulate the interim possession of any property to which the claim relates.

Preservation of documents and other property. The court has power to order the inspection, photographing, preservation, custody and detention of documents and other property (including land) which appear to the court to be property as to which any question may relevantly arise in any existing or likely civil proceedings. This power is exercised in practice, in particular, to order the production of documents before proceedings are commenced.

I. Civil Procedure—Summary Procedures

58.61 There are a number of different procedures which are available in the Court of Session or in the sheriff courts which, to a greater or lesser extent, are summary in nature.

1. Court of Session

Summary trial. A special form of action allows the parties, by consent, to dispose of a case by a summary trial before a single judge in the Court of Session. There is an expedited time table. If there is no dispute on the facts the case is to be heard within six weeks from the order directing a summary trial. Proof may be allowed in the usual way. There is no appeal from the judge's decision.

Defences without substance. The Court of Session rules provide that if at any stage of the proceedings it appears from the pleadings that the defences disclose no defence to the action or part of it, the pursuer may apply to the court, on 14 days' notice, to grant "summary decree" to the pursuer to dispose of the whole or part of the action.

Petition procedure. It has already been observed that the normal procedure for the resolution of civil and commercial disputes in the Court of Session is by way of proceedings commenced by summons. There is an alternative form of procedure available in the Court of Session by way of petition. This procedure, which is summary, is employed in certain types of case, usually when the assistance of the court is required for some administrative or similar purpose, rather than for ordinary contentious disputes. Petition procedure is used for such matters as adoption and guardianship of children, bankruptcy proceedings, regulation of limited companies (particularly in the event of insolvency), and trust administration.[46]

Special case procedure. The Inner House of the Court of Session normally exercises only appellate jurisdiction, but if the parties are agreed as to the facts, they may agree specific questions for decision of the Inner House under an exceptional procedure called the "special case procedure".

Commercial cases. A special procedure exists in order to allow commercial cases to be dealt with in a more flexible and speedy way than under normal procedure. Commercial cases are defined as actions relating to the ordinary transactions of merchants, traders and providers of financial services and include actions relating to the construction of commercial documents, the export and import of goods, carriage of goods, insurance, banking, commercial agency and custom of trade.

Within 14 days after defences have been lodged in court, arrangements are made for a hearing on a specified date. The court has power to regulate procedure in order to achieve a speedy decision of the dispute. Each party is required to provide the other party or parties with a list of relevant documents in his possession. Lists of proposed witnesses are to be exchanged at an early date. Where a preliminary legal debate has been fixed, parties may be required to lodge in court in advance a short note of their legal arguments.

2. Sheriff courts

Summary cause. In the sheriff courts there is a special procedure, **58.62** called the "summary cause" procedure, with applies to cases involving up to £1,500. Its purpose is to simplify and accelerate procedures in the smaller cases. However even this procedure was

---

[46] The Inner House of the Court of Session also exercises by way of petition its general equitable jurisdiction known as the *nobile officium*: see para. 58.20 above.

thought to be too formal for small claims (up to £750) and a new procedure for small claims has been introduced, under which the judge plays a more active role, and the proceedings are conducted less formally and without the need for strict application of the rules of evidence.

Summary application. In the sheriff courts, cases of the type which are dealt with by the petition procedure in the Court of Session are generally dealt with by a procedure called "summary application".

J. CIVIL PROCEDURE—APPEALS

1. Introduction

58.63   Scottish law does not draw formal distinctions between different types of appeal, although in addition to appeals, it does provide several special means for reviewing court decisions. An appeal lies from the sheriff court to the sheriff principal and thence to the Inner House of the Court of Session. Alternatively, an appeal may be taken direct from the sheriff court to the Inner House. Appeals from the Outer House of the Court of Session also lie to the Inner House. The decisions of the Inner House may be appealed to the House of Lords.

The time limit for appeals against a decision of the sheriff or sheriff principal is 14 days from the date of pronouncement of the decision. The time limit for an appeal from the Outer House to the Inner House is 21 days if the decision concerns the whole subject-matter of the case and 14 days if not. Appeals to the House of Lords must generally be lodged within three months. In some cases the time limits may be reduced if the winning party applies for permission to extract the decree earlier than normally permitted.[47] Most interlocutory decisions are appealable.

Normally a final decree of a sheriff court may not be executed until after the time limited for appealing has expired or any appeal has been disposed of. A decree of the Court of Session, on the other hand, may be enforced, despite the fact that the time for appeal has not expired or an appeal has not been disposed of, unless the court has ordered the suspension of execution.

2. Appeals

58.64   *Reclaiming motion.* An appeal, called a "reclaiming motion", lies from a decision of the Outer House of the Court of Session to the Inner House. On the hearing of the appeal, the Inner House may

---

[47] See para. 58.56 above.

re-consider questions of fact and law and has extensive powers of review, including the power to recall and re-examine witnesses.

Appeal from a sheriff. A first appeal may be made from a sheriff to the sheriff principal for the sheriffdom in question. This is the normal method of appeal from a sheriff court, and a further appeal lies from his decision to the Inner House of the Court of Session. Alternatively an appeal may be made directly from the decision of a sheriff to the Inner House. These appeals are on matters both of fact and law.

Appeal to the House of Lords. Appeal to the House of Lords can only be taken from the Inner House of the Court of Session. Findings of fact as well as findings of law may be reviewed, although reviews of findings of fact are unusual. In cases originating in the sheriff court, the House of Lords may not review findings of fact. Appeal may usually be taken without leave. Normally after its decision the House of Lords returns the case to the Court of Session for the judgment to be put into effect.

3. Special forms of review

Suspension or reduction of court decrees. Normally decrees of the Court of Session and sheriff court cannot be challenged except by way of appeal, unless they were granted in the defender's absence, and even then only on strict conditions.[48] However, in certain special circumstances, including extrinsic grounds such as incompetency or irregularity of procedure or fraud, even decrees given after a defence has been stated can be overturned. **58.65**

Rehearing in the Court of Session by a larger court. An unusual procedure is available to the judges of the Court of Session where questions of difficulty or importance make it appropriate. The court may order the case to be reheard by a larger court, usually of seven judges. Where a division of the Inner House is equally divided in opinion it may appoint the case to be reheard before five judges, if no matter of legal principle is involved, or seven judges if such a matter is involved.

K. CIVIL PROCEDURE—ENFORCEMENT

1. Enforcement of Scottish judgments

Introduction. The enforcement of Scottish decrees is effected by a messenger-at-arms or sheriff officer,[49] who is instructed for that purpose by the successful party. The execution of a judgment is **58.66**

---

[48] See para. 58.41 above.
[49] See para. 58.13 above.

called "diligence". The decree becomes enforceable when it is extracted from the books of the court. It is the "extract" which is the enforceable document,[50] and it bears no separate indorsement to evidence its executory character. Decrees generally remain enforceable for a period of 20 years.

There are various different methods whereby a judgment may be enforced. The enforcement may take place against the debtor's moveable property in his own possession ("poinding and sale"), by the arrest of the debtor's moveable property in the hands of a third party ("arrestment and furthcoming") or against the debtor's immovable or heritable property ("inhibition and adjudication"). It may also be enforced by bankruptcy or liquidation proceedings.

[The next paragraph is number 58.68]

58.68   *Poinding*[51] *and sale.* When enforcement is sought against the debtor's moveable property in his own possession, the judgment creditor must first have a "charge for payment" served on the debtor. This must be carried out by a messenger-at-arms or sheriff officer. It takes the form of a personally delivered written demand requiring the debtor within seven days to make payment of the principal debt, interest and expenses. If due payment is not made, the assets may be "poinded". This involves the messenger-at-arms or sheriff officer (who have power to force an entry) inspecting the assets, listing and valuing them. The assets are placed under the authority of the messenger-at-arms or sheriff officer for the benefit of the creditor and the debtor is restrained from disposing of the assets, but may continue to make use of them at this stage. The debtor or any other person who unlawfully deals with or disposes of a poinded asset can be imprisoned until he pays the debt. When the poinding is reported to the judge he may allow sale of the assets at public auction.

Arrestment and furthcoming. Arrestment has already been described in the context of provisional measures.[52] It is also available as a step in the execution of a final judgment. It is carried out by a messenger-at-arms or sheriff officer. As a step in the process of execution, it is often used to attach earnings. Once arrestment has taken place, an entirely separate action of "furth-

---

[50] The extract, and the time at which it may be obtained, are described at para. 58.56 above.
[51] "Poinding" and "poind" are pronounced "pinding" and "pind."
[52] See para. 58.59 above.

coming" must then be commenced by the creditor in order to authorise transfer of the arrested property to him or the sale of the property for his benefit.

Inhibition and adjudication. Inhibition has also been described
above in the context of provisional measures, but it too is available
as a step in the process of execution of a final judgment. The effect
of a warrant of inhibition is that it freezes the defender's immoveable property until the judgment creditor can obtain judgment in a
separate action of "adjudication" in the Court of Session, ordering
the transfer to him of the defender's title in the property. Even if
the creditor obtains a title to the debtor's property, the debtor has
certain rights of redemption within 10 years.

Bankruptcy and liquidation. The normal evidence which is
required to show bankruptcy of a natural person in Scottish law is a
court judgment or decree on which a charge has expired, thus rendering the debtor "apparently insolvent" or liable to "sequestration", which is the term for formal bankruptcy proceedings.
Normally, in making a debtor bankrupt, a creditor would run the
risk of receiving less than full payment and reducing the effect of
payments made in response to other enforcement procedures. In
the case of a limited company the equivalent procedure is liquidation through the winding up of the company by the court. Bankruptcy or liquidation can also be ordered by the court following a
debtor's failure to pay an undisputed debt within 21 days following
a formal demand for payment.

Other methods of enforcement. Non-money judgments may be   **58.69**
enforced by a fine or imprisonment for contempt of court, but the
public prosecutor ("procurator fiscal") must be involved in this
process. If the decree is capable of being performed by some person
other than the person against whom it is directed, the clerk of the
court or some other appropriate person may be required to put the
decree into effect.

2. Authentic instruments and court settlements

Enforceable instruments. Scottish law contains a procedure for the   **58.70**
enforcement of written obligations, which is comparable with the
procedure in many continental legal systems for the enforcement of
authentic instruments.[53] This procedure involves the registration in
the court books of any of a wide range of documents which may
then be enforced as if they were decrees of the court. It is often used
to recover sums due under bills of exchange or promissory notes,

---

[53] See chap. 30 above and para. 70 in chaps. 48 to 55 above.

but it is not limited to obligations to pay money and it may be used in respect of any obligation which could be made the subject of a decree of the court in which it is registered.

Normally the Court of Session is used and registration takes place in the Books of Council and Session.[54] As a general rule, in order for an obligation to be capable of registration, the person against whom it is to be enforced must have expressed his consent in the document to its registration for the purpose of execution, and it must have been signed and witnessed by two witnesses whose occupations and addresses are stated. Registration does not require the leave of the court and once the instrument has been registered, it may be extracted and enforced in the same way as a decree of that court.

3. Enforcement of foreign judgments and judgments from other parts of the United Kingdom

58.71   Judgments from other parts of the United Kingdom, from Contracting States to the 1968 Convention, and from other foreign countries, may be enforced in Scotland by all the means available in respect of Scottish judgments, once their enforcement ("diligence") has been authorised. The means of obtaining such authorisation differ, though, according to where the judgment comes from and whether or not the 1968 Convention applies.

Enforcement of judgments from England, Wales and Northern Ireland. Judgments delivered by courts in other parts of the United Kingdom may be enforced in Scotland when they have been registered for that purpose in the Court of Session. The procedure for that purpose has already been described.[55]

Enforcement of judgments under the 1968 Convention. Judgments to which the 1968 Convention applies may be enforced in Scotland when they have been registered in the Court of Session (or, in the case of a maintenance order, in a sheriff court). The application for registration is made in the first instance to the Lord Ordinary and an appeal against that order also lies to the Lord Ordinary. The time for appealing against an order granting or refusing leave to enforce a judgment is one month from the service of the decision, or two months if the enforcement was to take place against a person domiciled in another Contracting State.

---

[54] Registration may also occur in the books of a sheriff court, for the purpose of execution in the district of that court.

[55] See paras. 10.63 *et seq.* and chap. 46 above.

Judgments outside the 1968 Convention. Money judgments of some **58.72** other countries may be enforced in Scotland under the United Kingdom's bilateral conventions,[56] by a procedure of registration broadly comparable with that which applies in the case of judgments falling within the 1968 Convention. Where the foreign judgment is not enforceable under an international convention, the authority of the Court of Session for its enforcement must be obtained by an action on the foreign judgment for a "decree-conform". If the foreign judgment is regular on its face and was given by a court of competent jurisdiction, it will normally be susceptible to enforcement in Scotland.

L. LEGAL PERSONS

The common forms of legal person under Scottish law are the same **58.73** as under English law,[57] except as regards partnerships. Unlike English partnerships, a partnership in Scotland has legal personality. Accordingly it may litigate in its own name. As a normal partnership implies unlimited liability a judgment against a firm allows enforcement against the partners. An action may also be raised against a firm trading under a descriptive name even though that name is used by one individual only. The judgment will be enforceable against that individual. Incorporated or chartered companies or associations litigate in their registered name. In the case of an unincorporated association, such as a club, a judgment against the club will be enforced against the assets of the club. If it is required to enforce the judgment against any of the office bearers or other members they should be included as defenders.

M. LEGAL AID

In Scotland legal aid is available for civil and criminal litigation and **58.74** for legal advice and assistance in cases not involving litigation. The assisted person has complete freedom in his choice of lawyer.

In civil cases any natural person, irrespective of his nationality, residence or personal status, may apply for legal aid in connection with proceedings in a Scottish court. This will include the sheriff court, the Court of Session and the House of Lords but excludes most employment and administrative tribunals. The applicant must satisfy certain financial criteria relating to his capital and income. He may be required to pay a contribution to the legal costs. He must also obtain from those administering the scheme a certificate that he has a probable cause of action before his action can proceed.

---

[56] See para. 10.04 above.
[57] See para. 56.73 above.

In special circumstances this can be obtained on an emergency basis, but ordinarily it will take two to three months. The other party may object to the grant of the certificate.

If the assisted party wins the case and obtains an order for costs against the other side those costs will be paid to the legal aid fund. The fund may also recoup its costs from property recovered or preserved by the winning party in the litigation. If the assisted party loses he may, depending on his means, be required to pay a limited amount towards the successful party's costs. If a successful party would suffer severe financial hardship through the inability to recover costs from the assisted party, he may apply for his costs to be paid direct by the legal aid fund.

Appendix 1

OFFICIAL REPORTS ON THE CONVENTIONS*

PART I—JENARD REPORT

Report on the Convention

on jurisdiction and the enforcement of judgments in civil and commercial matters

(Signed at Brussels, 27 September 1968)

by Mr P. Jenard

Director in the Belgian Ministry of Foreign Affairs and External Trade.

A committee of experts set up in 1960 by decision of the Committee of **A1.1** Permanent Representatives of the Member States, following a proposal by the Commission, prepared a draft Convention, in pursuance of Article 220 of the EEC Treaty, on jurisdiction and the enforcement of judgments in civil and commercial matters. The committee was composed of governmental experts from the six Member States, representatives of the Commission, and observers. Its rapporteur, Mr P. Jenard, Directeur d'Administration in the Belgian Ministry for Foreign Affairs and External Trade, wrote the explanatory report, which was submitted to the governments at the same time as the draft prepared by the committee of experts. The following is the text of that report. It takes the form of a commentary on the Convention, which was signed in Brussels on 27 September 1968.

CONTENTS   A1.2

Pages

---

* In the text of this Appendix bold numerals in square brackets denote the page numbering of the original texts of the Reports.

CHAPTER I

PRELIMINARY REMARKS

By Article 220 of the Treaty establishing the European Economic Com- **A1.3**
munity, the Member States agreed to enter into negotiations with each
other, so far as necessary, with a view to securing for the benefit of their
nationals the simplification of formalities governing the reciprocal recognition and enforcement of judgments of courts or tribunals and of arbitration awards.

The fact that the Treaty of Rome requires the Member States to resolve **A1.4**
this problem shows that it is important. In a note sent to the Member
States on 22 October 1959 inviting them to commence negotiations, the
Commission of the European Economic Community pointed out that

> "a true internal market between the six States will be achieved only if
> adequate legal protection can be secured. The economic life of the
> Community may be subject to disturbances and difficulties unless it is
> possible, where necessary by judicial means, to ensure the recognition
> and enforcement of the various rights arising from the existence of a
> multiplicity of legal relationships. As jurisdiction in both civil and
> commercial matters is derived from the sovereignty of Member
> States, and since the effect of judicial acts is confined to each national
> territory, legal protection and, hence, legal certainty in the common
> market are essentially dependent on the adoption by the Member
> States of a satisfactory solution to the problem of recognition and
> enforcement of judgments."

On receiving this note the Committee of Permanent Representatives **A1.5**
decided on 18 February 1960 to set up a committee of experts. The committee, consisting of delegates from the six Member countries, observers
from the Benelux Committee on the unification of law and from the Hague
Conference on private international law, and representatives from the
EEC Commission departments concerned, met for the first time from 11
to 13 July 1960 and appointed as its chairman Professor Bülow then Minis-
terialdirigent and later Staatssekretär in the Federal Ministry of Justice in
Bonn, and as its rapporteur Mr Jenard, directeur in the Belgian Ministry
for Foreign Affairs.

At its 15th meeting, held in Brussels from 7 to 11 December 1964, the **A1.6**
committee adopted a "Preliminary Draft Convention on jurisdiction and
the recognition and enforcement of judgments in civil and commercial
matters, and the enforcement of authentic instruments" (document 14371/
IV/64). This preliminary draft, with an explanatory report (document
2449/IV/65), was submitted to the Governments for comment.

The comments of the Governments, and those submitted by the Union **A1.7**
of the Industries of the European Community, the Permanent Conference
of Chambers of Commerce and Industry of the EEC, the Banking Federation of the EEC, the Consultative Committee of the Barristers' and
Lawyers' Associations of the six EEC countries (a committee of the Inter-

national Association of Lawyers), were studied by the Committee at its meeting of 5 to 15 July 1966. The draft Convention was finally adopted by the experts at that meeting.

A1.8   The names of the governmental experts who took part in the work of the committee are set out in the annex to this report.

CHAPTER II

BACKGROUND TO THE CONVENTION

A1.9   It is helpful to consider, first, the rules in each of the six countries governing the recognition and enforcement of foreign judgments.

A. THE LAW IN FORCE IN THE SIX STATES

A1.10   *In Belgium,* until the entry into force of the Judicial Code (Code Judiciaire), the relevant provisions as **[4]** regards enforcement are to be found in Article 10 of the Law of 25 March 1876, which contains Title I of the Introductory Book of the Code of Civil Procedure.[1]

---

[1] Article 10 of the Law of 1876 provides that: They (courts of first instance) shall also have jurisdiction in relation to judgments given by foreign courts in civil and commercial matters. Where there exists a treaty concluded on a basis of reciprocity between Belgium and the country in which the judgment was given, they shall review only the following five points:
  1. whether the judgment contains anything contrary to public policy or to the principles of Belgian public law;
  2. whether, under the law of the country in which the judgment was given, it has become *res judicata*;
  3. whether, under that law, the certified copy of the judgment satisfies the conditions necessary to establish its authenticity;
  4. whether the rights of the defendant have been observed;
  5. whether the jurisdiction of the foreign court is based solely on the nationality of the plaintiff.
Art. 570 of the Judicial Code contained in the Law of 10 October 1967 (supplement to the Moniteur belge of 31 October 1967) reads as follows:
"Courts of first instance shall adjudicate on applictions for orders for the enforcement of judgments given by foreign courts in civil matters, regardless of the amount involved. Except where the provisions of a treaty between Belgium and the country in which judgment was given are to be applied, the court shall examine, in addition to the substance of the matter:
  1. whether the judgment contains anything contrary to public policy or to the principles of Belgian public law;
  2. whether the rights of the defendant have been observed;
  3. whether the jurisdiction of the foreign court is based solely on the nationality of the plaintiff;
  4. whether, under the law of the country in which the judgment was given, it has become *res judicata*;
  5. whether, under that law, the certified copy of the judgment satisfies the

Where there is no reciprocal convention, a court seised of an application **A1.11** for an order for enforcement "has jurisdiction over a foreign judgment as to both form and substance, and can re-examine both the facts and the law. In other words, it has power to review the matter fully."[2,3]

As regards recognition, text-book authorities and case-law draw a dis- **A1.12** tinction between foreign judgments relating to status and legal capacity and those relating to other matters. The position at present is that foreign judgments not relating to the status and legal capacity of persons are not regarded by the courts as having the force of *res judicata*.

However, foreign judgments relating to a person's status or legal **A1.13** capacity may be taken as evidence of the status acquired by that person.[4] Such a foreign judgment thus acts as a bar to any new proceedings for divorce or separation filed before a Belgian court if the five conditions listed in Article 10 of the Law of 1876 are fulfilled, as they "constitute no more than the application to foreign judgments of rules which the legislature considers essential for any judgment to be valid."

In the *Federal Republic of Germany*, foreign judgments are recognized **A1.14** and enforced on the basis of reciprocity.[5] The conditions for recognition of foreign judgments are laid down in paragraph 328 of the Code of Civil Procedure (Zivilprozeßordnung):

"I. A judgment given by a foreign court may not be recognized:
1. where the courts of the State to which the foreign court belongs have no jurisdiction under German law;
2. where the unsuccessful defendant is German and has not entered an appearance, if the document instituting the proceedings was not served on him in person either in the State to which the court belongs, or by a German authority under the system of mutual assistance in judicial matters;
3. where, to the detriment of the German party, the judgment has not complied with the provisions of Article 13(1) and (3) or of Articles 17, 18, and 22 of the Introductory Law to the Civil Code (Einführungsgesetz zum Bürgerlichen Gesetzbuch), or with the provisions of Article 27 of that Law which refer to Article 13(1), nor where, in matters falling within the scope of Article 12(3) of the Law of 4 July 1939 on disappearances, certifications of death, and establishment of the date of decease (RGBl. I, p. 1186), there has been a failure to comply with the provisions of Article 13(2) of the Introductory Law

---

conditions necessary to establish its authenticity." These provisions will enter into force on 31 October 1970 at the latest. Before that date an *arrêté royal* (Royal Decree) will determine the date on which the provisions of the Judicial Code enter into force.

[2] GRAULICH, Principes de droit international privé, No. 248 *et seq.*
[3] RIGAUX, L'efficacité des jugements étrangers en Belgique, Journal des tribunaux, 10.4.1960, p. 287.
[4] Cass. 16.1.1953—Pas.I.335.
[5] Riezler, Internationales Zivilprozeßrecht, 1949, p. 509 *et seq.*

      to the Civil Code, to the [5] detriment of the wife of a foreigner who has been declared dead by judgment of the court[1];

    4. where recognition of the judgment would be contrary to 'good morals' (gegen die guten Sitten) or the objectives of a German law;

    5. where there is no guarantee of reciprocity.

  II. The provision in (5) above shall not prevent recognition of a judgment given in a matter not relating to property rights where no court in Germany has jurisdiction under German law."

A1.15   The procedure for recognising judgments delivered in actions relating to matrimonial matters is governed by a special Law (Familienrechtsänderungsgesetz) of 11 August 1961 (BGBl. I, p. 1221, Article 7).

A1.16   Enforcement is governed by Articles 722 and 723 of the Code of Civil Procedure, which read as follows:

Article 722

"I. A foreign judgment may be enforced only where this is authorized by virtue of an order for enforcement.

II. An application for an order for enforcement shall be heard either by the Amtsgericht or the Landgericht having general jurisdiction in relation to the defendant, or otherwise by the Amtsgericht or the Landgericht before which the defendant may be summoned under Article 23."

Article 723

"I. An order for enforcement shall be granted without re-examination of the substance of the judgment.

II. An order for enforcement shall be granted only if the foreign judgment has become *res judicata* under the law of the court in which it was given. No order for enforcement shall be granted where recognition of the judgment is excluded by Article 328."

A1.17   *In France*, Article 546 of the Code of Civil Procedure (Code de procédure civile) provides that judgments given by foreign courts and instruments recorded by foreign officials can be enforced only after being declared enforceable by a French court (Articles 2123 and 2128 of the Civil Code).

    The courts have held that four conditions must be satisfied for an order for enforcement to be granted: the foreign court must have had jurisdiction; the procedure followed must have been in order; the law applied must have been that which is applicable under the French system of conflict of laws; and due regard must have been paid to public policy.[2]

    The Cour de cassation recently held (Cass. civ. 1ᵉʳ Section, 7 January 1964—Munzer case) that the substance of the original action could not be

---

[1] These Arts. of the Introductory Law to the Civil Code provide for the application of German law in many cases: condition of validity of marriage, form of marriage, divorce, legitimate and illegitimate paternity, adoption, certification of death.

[2] Batiffol, Traité élémentaire de droit international privé, No. 741 *et seq.*

reviewed by the court hearing the application for an order for enforcement. This judgment has since been followed.

In Italy, on the other hand, the Code of Civil Procedure (Codice di procedura civile) in principle allows foreign judgments to be recognized and enforced. **A1.18**

Under Article 796 of the Code of Civil Procedure, any foreign judgment may be declared enforceable in Italy by the Court of Appeal (Corte d'appello) for the place in which enforcement is to take place (Dichiarazione di efficacia).

Under Article 797 of the Code of Civil Procedure, the Court of Appeal examines whether the foreign judgment was given by a judicial authority having jurisdiction under the rules in force in Italy; whether in the proceedings abroad the document instituting the proceedings was properly served and whether sufficient notice was given; whether the parties properly entered an appearance in the proceedings or whether their default was duly recognized; whether the judgment has become *res judicata*; whether the judgment conflicts with a judgment given by an Italian judicial authority; whether proceedings between the same parties and concerning the same claim are pending before an Italian judicial authority; and whether the judgment contains anything contrary to Italian public policy. **A1.19**

However, if the defendant failed to appear in the foreign proceedings, he may request the Italian court to review the substance of the case (Article 798). In such a case, the Court may either order enforcement, or hear the substance of the case and give judgment.

[6]There is also in Italian Law the "delibazione incidentale" (Article 799 of the Code of Civil Procedure) which, however, applies only to proceedings in which it is sought to invoke a foreign judgment.

Luxembourg. Under Article 546 of the Luxembourg Code of Civil Procedure (Code de procédure civile), judgments given by foreign courts and instruments recorded by foreign officials can be enforced in the Grand Duchy only after being declared enforceable by a Luxembourg court (see Articles 2123 and 2128 of the Civil Code). **A1.20**

Luxembourg law requires seven conditions to be satisfied before an order for enforcement can be granted: the judgment must be enforceable in the country in which it was given; the foreign court must have had jurisdiction; the law applied must have been that applicable under the Luxembourg rules of conflict of laws; the rules of procedure of the foreign law must have been observed; the rights of the defendant must have been observed; due regard must have been paid to public policy; the law must not have been contravened (Luxembourg, 5.2.64, Pasicrisie luxembourgeoise XIX, 285).

Luxembourg law no longer permits any review of a foreign judgment as to the merits.

In the *Netherlands*, the Code of Civil Procedure (Wetboek van Burgerlijke Rechtsvordering) lays down the principle that judgments of foreign courts are not enforceable in the Kingdom. Matters settled by foreign **A1.21** courts may be reconsidered by Netherlands courts (see Article 431 of the Code of Civil Procedure).

The national laws of the Member States thus vary considerably.

B. Existing Conventions

A1.22   Apart from conventions dealing with particular matters (see p. 10), various conventions on enforcement exist between the Six; they are listed in Article 55 of the Convention. However, relations between France and the Federal Republic of Germany, France and the Netherlands, France and Luxembourg, Germany and Luxembourg, and Luxembourg and Italy are hampered by the absence of such conventions.[1]

A1.23   There are also striking differences between the various conventions. Some, like those between France and Belgium, and between Belgium and the Netherlands, and the Benelux Treaty, are based on "direct" jurisdiction; but all the others are based on "indirect" jurisdiction. The Convention between France and Italy is based on indirect jurisdiction, but nevertheless contains some rules of direct jurisdiction. Some conventions allow only those judgments which have become *res judicata* to be recognized and enforced, whilst others such as the Benelux Treaty and the Conventions between Belgium and the Netherlands, Germany and Belgium, Italy and Belgium and Germany and the Netherlands apply to judgments which are capable of enforcement.[2] Some cover judgments given in civil matters by criminal courts, whilst others are silent on this point or expressly exclude such judgments from their scope (Conventions between Italy and the Netherlands, Article 10, and between Germany and Italy, Article 12).

There are various other differences between these treaties and conventions which need not be discussed in detail; they relate in particular to the determination of competent courts and to the conditions governing recognition and enforcement. It should moreover be stressed that these conventions either do not lay down the enforcement procedure or give only a summary outline of it.

A1.24   The present unsatisfactory state of affairs as regards the recognition and enforcement of judgments could have been improved by the conclusion of new bilateral conventions between Member States not yet bound by such conventions.

[7] However, the Committee has decided in favour of the conclusion of a multilateral convention between the countries of the European Economic Community, in accordance with the views expressed in the Commission's letter of 22 October 1959. The Committee felt that the differences between

---

[1] It should be noted that at the time of writing this report, the Benelux Treaty has not yet entered into force and there is no agreement existing between Luxembourg on the one hand and Belgium and the Netherlands on the other.

[2] The Franco-Belgian convention, in spite of the provisions of Art. 11(2) which impose the condition of *res judicata*, nevertheless applies to enforceable judgments even if there is still a right of appeal (see Niboyet, Droit international privé français, T.VII 2022).

the bilateral conventions would hinder the "free movement" of judgments and lead to unequal treatment of the various nationals of the Member States, such inequality being contrary to the fundamental EEC principle of non-discrimination, set out, in particular, in Article 7 of the Treaty of Rome.

In addition, the European Economic Community provided the conditions necessary for a modern, liberal law on the recognition and enforcement of judgments, which would satisfy both legal and commercial interests. **A1.25**

C. THE NATURE OF THE CONVENTION

Some of the bilateral conventions concluded between the Member States, such as the Convention between France and Belgium of 8 July 1899, the Convention between Belgium and the Netherlands of 28 March 1925, and the Benelux Treaty of 24 November 1961, are based on rules of direct jurisdiction, whilst in the others the rules of jurisdiction are indirect. Under conventions of the first type, known also as "double treaties," the rules of jurisdiction laid down are applicable in the State of origin, *i.e.* the State in which the proceedings originally took place; they therefore apply independently of any proceedings for recognition and enforcement, and permit a defendant who is summoned before a court which under the convention in question would not have jurisdiction to refuse to accept its jurisdiction. **A1.26**

Rules of jurisdiction in a convention are said to be "indirect" when they do not affect the courts of the State in which the judgment was originally given, and are to be considered only in relation to recognition and enforcement. They apply only in determining cases in which the court of the State in which recognition or enforcement of a judgment is sought (the State addressed) is obliged to recognize the jurisdiction of the court of the State of origin. They can therefore be taken as conditions governing the recognition and enforcement of foreign judgments and, more specifically, governing supervision of the jurisdiction of foreign courts. **A1.27**

The Committee spent a long time considering which of these types of convention the EEC should have. It eventually decided in favour of a new system based on direct jurisdiction but differing in several respects from existing bilateral conventions of that type. **A1.28**

Although the Committee of experts did not underestimate the value and importance of "single" conventions, (*i.e.* conventions based on rules of indirect jurisdiction) it felt that within the EEC a convention based on rules of direct jurisdiction as a result of the adoption of common rules of jurisdiction would allow increased harmonization of laws, provide greater legal certainty, avoid discrimination and facilitate the "free movement" of judgments, which is after all the ultimate objective.

Conventions based on direct jurisdiction lay down common rules of jurisdiction, thus bringing about the harmonization of laws, whereas under those based on indirect jurisdiction, national provisions apply, without restriction, in determining international jurisdiction in each State. **A1.29**

Legal certainty is most effectively secured by conventions based on direct jurisdiction since, under them, judgments are given by courts deriving their jurisdiction from the conventions themselves; however, in the case of conventions based on indirect jurisdiction, certain judgments cannot be recognized and enforced abroad unless national rules of jurisdiction coincide with the rules of the convention.[1]

A1.30 Moreover, since it establishes, on the basis of mutual agreement, an autonomous system of international jurisdiction in relations between the Member States, the Convention makes it easier to abandon certain rules of jurisdiction which are generally regarded as exorbitant.

Finally, by setting out rules of jurisdiction which may be relied upon as soon as proceedings are begun in the State of origin, the Convention regulates the problem of *lis pendens* and also helps to minimize the conditions governing recognition and enforcement.

A1.31 [8] As already stated, the Convention is based on direct jurisdiction, but differs fundamentally from treaties and conventions of the same type previously concluded. This is not the place to undertake a detailed study of the differences, or to justify them; it will suffice merely to list them:

1. the criterion of domicile replaces that of nationality;
2. the principle of equality of treatment is extended to any person domiciled in the Community, whatever his nationality;
3. rules of exclusive jurisdiction are precisely defined;
4. the right of the defendant to defend himself in the original proceedings is safeguarded;
5. the number of grounds for refusal of recognition and enforcement is reduced.

In addition, the Convention is original in that:

1. the procedure for obtaining enforcement is standardized;
2. rules of procedure are laid down for cases in which recognition is at issue;
3. provision is made for cases of conflict with other conventions.

CHAPTER III

SCOPE OF THE CONVENTION

A1.32 The scope of the Convention is determined by the preamble and Article 1.

It governs international legal relationships, applies automatically, and covers all civil and commercial matters, apart from certain exceptions which are exhaustively listed.

I. INTERNATIONAL LEGAL RELATIONSHIPS

A1.33 As is stressed in the fourth paragraph of the preamble, the Convention determines the international jurisdiction of the courts of the Contracting States.

---

[1] WESER, Les conflits de juridictions dans le cadre du Marché Commun, Revue Critique de droit international privé 1960, pp. 161–172.

It alters the rules of jurisdiction in force in each Contracting State only where an international element is involved. It does not define this concept, since the international element in a legal relationship may depend on the particular facts of the proceedings of which the court is seised. Proceedings instituted in the courts of a Contracting State which involves only persons domiciled in that State will not normally be affected by the Convention; Article 2 simply refers matters back to the rules of jurisdiction in force in that State. It is possible, however, that an international element may be involved in proceedings of this type. This would be the case, for example, where the defendant was a foreign national, a situation in which the principle of equality of treatment laid down in the second paragraph of Article 2 would apply, or where the proceedings related to a matter over which the courts of another State had exclusive jurisdiction (Article 16), or where identical or related proceedings had been brought in the courts of another State (Article 21 to 23).

It is clear that at the recognition and enforcement stage, the Convention governs only international legal relationships, since *ex hypothesi* it concerns the recognition and enforcement in one Contracting Stae of judgments given in another Contracting State.[1]

II. The Binding Nature of the Convention

It was decided by the committee of experts that the Convention should apply automatically. This principle is formally laid down in Articles 19 and 20 which deal with the matter of examination by the courts of the Contracting States of their international jurisdiction. The courts must apply the rules of the Convention whether or not they are pleaded by the parties. It follows from this, for example, that if a person domiciled in Belgium is sued in a French court on the basis of Article 14 of the French Civil Code, and contests the jurisdiction of that court but without pleading the provisions of the Convention, the court **[9]** must nevertheless apply Article 3 and declare that it has no jurisdiction.[1]   **A1.34**

III. Civil and Commercial Matters

The Committee did not specify what is meant by "civil and commercial matters," nor did it point to a solution of the problem of classification by determining the law according to which that expression should be interpreted.   **A1.35**

In this respect it followed the practice of existing conventions.[2]

---

[1] A. BÜLOW, Vereinheitlichtes internationales Zivilprozeßrecht in der Europäischen Wirtschaftsgemeinschaft—Rabels Zeitschrift für ausländisches und internationales Privatrecht, 1965, p. 473 *et seq.*

[1] Tribunal civil de Lille, 9.11.1953, Revue critique de droit international privé, 1954, p. 832.

[2] This problem is not dealt with in any treaty on enforcement. See also the report by Professor Fragistas on the Preliminary Draft Convention adopted by the Special Commission of the Hague Conference on private international law, preliminary document No. 4 for the tenth session, p. 11.

A1.36   However, it follows from the text of the Convention that civil and commercial matters are to be classified as such according to their nature, and irrespective of the character of the court or tribunal which is seised of the proceedings or which has given judgment. This emerges from Article 1, which provides that the Convention shall apply in civil and commercial matters "whatever the nature of the court or tribunal." The Convention also applies irrespective of whether the proceedings are contentious or non-contentious. It likewise applies to labour law in so far as this is regarded as a civil or commercial matter (see also under contracts of employment, page 24).

A1.37   The Convention covers civil proceedings brought before criminal courts, both as regards decisions relating to jurisdiction, and also as regards the recognition and enforcement of judgments given by criminal courts in such proceedings. It thereby takes into account certain laws in force in the majority of the Contracting States,[3] tends to rule out any differences of interpretation such as have arisen in applying the Convention between Belgium and the Netherlands[4] and, finally, meets current requirements arising from the increased number of road accidents.

The relevant provisions of the treaty and conventions already concluded between the Member States vary widely, as has already been pointed out in Chapter I(A).

A1.38   The formula adopted by the Committee reflects the current trend in favour of inserting in conventions clauses specifying that they apply to judgments given in civil or commercial matters by criminal courts. This can in particular be seen in the Benelux Treaty of 24 November 1961 and in the work of the Hague Conference on private international law.

It should be noted that the provisions of Article 5(4) of the Convention in no way alter the penal jurisdiction of criminal courts and tribunals as laid down in the various codes of criminal procedure.

As regards both jurisdiction and recognition and enforcement, the Convention affects only civil proceedings of which those courts are seised, and judgments given in such proceedings.

However, in order to counter the objection that a party against whom civil proceedings have been brought might be obstructed in conducting his

---

[3] In *Belgium*, see Art. 4 of the Law of 17 April 1878 containing the Introductory Title of the Code of Criminal Procedure.

In the *Federal Republic of Germany*, see Art. 403 *et seq.* of the Code of Criminal Procedure.

In *France*, see Art. 4 of the Code of Criminal Procedure.

In *Luxembourg*, any person who claims to have suffered loss or injury as a result of a crime or other wrongful act may, under Art. 63 of the Code of Criminal Procedure, be joined as a civil party.

In the *Netherlands*, see Arts. 332 to 337 of the Code of Criminal Procedure, and Arts. 44 and 56 of the Law of Judicial Procedure, which gives jurisdiction to the justices of the peace or to the courts up to Fl 200 and 500 respectively.

[4] In interpreting the 1925 Convention between Belgium and the Netherlands, the Netherlands Court of Cassation held in its judgment of 16.3.1931 (N.J. 1931, p. 689) that Arts. 11 and 12 did not affect orders by criminal courts to pay compensation for injury or loss suffered by a party.

defence if criminal sanctions could be imposed on him in the same proceedings, the Committee decided on a solution identical to that adopted in
the Benelux Treaty. Article II of the Protocol provides that such persons
may be defended or represented in criminal courts. Thus they will not be
obliged to appear in person to defend their civil interests.

The Convention also applies to civil or commercial matters brought **A1.39**
before administrative tribunals.

The formula adopted by the Committee is identical to that envisaged by
the Commission which was given the task at the fourth session of the
Hague Conference on private international law of examining the Convention of 14 November 1896 in order to draw up common rules on a number
of aspects of private international law relating to civil procedure. It
reported as follows:

> "The expression 'civil or commercial matters' is very wide and does
> not include only those matters which fall within the jurisdiction of
> civil tribunals and commercial tribunals in countries where adminis-
> trative tribunals also exist. Otherwise there would be a wholly unjus-
> tifiable inequality between the Contracting States: service abroad of
> judicial **[10]** instruments could take place on a wider scale for coun-
> tries which do not have administrative tribunals than for countries
> which have them. In brief, the Convention is applicable from the
> moment when private interests become involved. . . . "[1]

Thus, for example, decisions of the French Conseil d'État given on such
matters may be recognized and enforced.[2]

IV. MATTERS EXCLUDED FROM THE SCOPE OF THE CONVENTION

The ideal solution would certainly have been to apply the Convention to **A1.40**
all civil and commercial matters. However, the Committee did not feel
able to adopt this approach, and limited the scope of the Convention to
matters relating to property rights for reasons similar to those which pre-
vailed when the Hague Convention on the recognition and enforcement of
foreign judgments in civil and commercial matters was drafted, the main
reason being the difficulties resulting from the absence of any overall solution to the problem of conflict of laws.

The disparity between rules of conflict of laws is particularly apparent in
respect of matters not relating to property rights, since in general the
intention of the parties cannot regulate matters independently of considerations of public policy.

The Committee, like the Hague Conference on private international **A1.41**
law, preferred a formula which excluded certain matters to one which

---

[1] See The Hague Conference on private international law—documents of the
fourth session (May to June 1904), p. 84.
[2] WESER, Traité franco-belge du 8.7.1899, No. 235.

would have involved giving a positive definition of the scope of the Convention. The solution adopted implies that all litigation and all judgments relating to contractual or non-contractual obligations which do not involve the status or legal capacity of natural persons, wills or sucession, rights in property arising out of a matrimonial relationship, bankruptcy or social security must fall within the scope of the Convention, and that in this respect the Convention should be interpreted as widely as possible.

However, matters falling outside the scope of the Convention do so only if they constitute the principal subject-matter of the proceedings. They are thus not excluded when they come before the court as a subsidiary matter either in the main proceedings or in preliminary proceedings.[3]

A. Status, legal capacity, rights in property arising out of a matrimonial relationship, wills, succession

A1.42 Apart from the desirability of bringing the Convention into force as soon as possible, the Committee was influenced by the following considerations. Even assuming that the Committee managed to unify the rules of jurisdiction in this field, and whatever the nature of the rules selected, there was such disparity on these matters between the various systems of law, in particular regarding the rules of conflict of laws, that it would have been difficult not to re-examine the rules of jurisdiction at the enforcement stage. This in turn would have meant changing the nature of the Convention and making it much less effective. In addition, if the Committee had agreed to withdraw from the court of enforcement all powers of examination, even in matters not relating to property rights, that court would surely have been encoraged to abuse the notion of public policy, using it to refuse recognition to foreign judgments referred to it. The members of the Committee chose the lesser of the two evils, retaining the unity and effectiveness of their draft while restricting its scope. The most serious difficulty with regard to status and legal capacity is obviously that of divorce, a problem which is complicated by the extreme divergences between the various systems of law: Italian law prohibits divorce, while Belgian law not only provides for divorce by consent (Articles 223, 275 *et seq.* of the Civil Code), which is unknown under the other legal systems apart from that of Luxembourg, but also, by the Law of 27 June 1960 on the admissibility of divorce when at least one of the spouses is a foreign national, incorporates provisions governing divorces by foreign nationals who ordinarily reside in Belgium.

A1.43 The wording used, "status or legal capacity of natural persons," differs slightly from that adopted in the Hague Convention, which excludes from its scope judgments concerning "the status or capacity of persons or questions of family law, including personal or financial rights and obligations between parents and children or between spouses" (Article 1(1)). The

---

[3] BELLET, "L'élaboration d'une convention sur la reconnaissance des jugements dans le cadre du Marché commun," Clunet, 1965.

reason for this is twofold. Firstly, family law in the six Member States of the Community is not a concept distinct from questions of status or capacity; secondly, the EEC Convention, unlike the Hague Convention, applies to maintenance (Article 5(2)) even where the obligation stems from the status of the persons and irrespective of whether rights [11] and duties between spouses or between parents and children are involved.

Moreover, in order to avoid differences of interpretation, Article 1 specifies that the Convention does not apply to the status or legal capacity of natural persons, thereby constituting a further distinction between this Convention and the Hague Convention, which specifies that it does not apply to judgments dealing principally with "the existence or constitution of legal persons or the powers of their organs" (Article 1(2) third indent).

With regard to matters relating to succession, the Committee concurred **A1.44** in the opinion of the International Union of Latin Notaries.

This body, when consulted by the Committee, considered that it was necessary, and would become increasingly so as the EEC developed in the future, to facilitate the recognition and enforcement of judgments given in matters relating to succession, and that it was therefore desirable for the six Member States to conclude a convention on the subject. However, the Union considered that it was essential first to unify the rules of conflict of laws.

As is pointed out in the Memorandum of the Permanent Bureau of the **A1.45** Hague Conference on private international law,[1] from which this commentary has been taken, there are fairly marked differences between the various States on matters of succession and of rights in property arising out of a matrimonial relationship.

1. As regards succession, some systems of law make provision for a portion of the estate to devolve compulsorily upon the heirs, whereas others do not. The share allocated to the surviving spouse (a question which gives rise to the greatest number of proceedings in matters of succession because of the clash of interests involved) differs enormously from country to country. Some countries place the spouse on the same footing as a surviving child, or grant him or her a certain reserved portion (Italy), while others grant the spouse only a limited life interest (for example, Belgium).

   The disparities as regards rules of conflict of laws are equally marked. Some States (Germany, Italy and the Netherlands) apply to succession the national law of the *de cujus*; others (Belgium and France) refer succession to the law of the domicile as regards movable property and, as regards immovable property, to the law of the place where the property is situated; or (as in Luxembourg) refer to

---

[1] The Hague Conference on private international law, recognition and enforcement of foreign judgments in matters relating to property rights. Memorandum, with Annexes, by the Permanent Bureau. Preliminary document No. 1 of January 1962 for the Special Committee, p. 10.

the law of the place where the property is situated in the case of immovable property, but subject movable property to national law.

A1.46 2. As regards rights in property arising out of a matrimonial relationship, the divergences between the legal systems are even greater, ranging from joint ownership of all property (Netherlands) through joint ownership of movable property and all property acquired during wedlock (France, Belgium and Luxembourg) or joint ownership of the increase in capital value of assets (Federal Republic of Germany) to the complete separation of property (Italy).

There are also very marked divergences between the rules of conflict of laws, and this provokes positive conflicts between the systems. In some States the rules governing matrimonial property, whether laid down by law or agreed between the parties, are subject to the national law of the husband (Germany, Italy and the Netherlands); in the other States (Belgium, France, and Luxembourg) matrimonial property is subject to the rules impliedly chosen by the spouses at the time of their marriage.

A1.47 Unlike the preliminary draft the Convention does not expressly exclude gifts from its scope. In this respect it follows the Hague Convention, though gifts will of course be excluded in so far as they relate to succession.

However, the Committee was of the opinion that there might possibly be grounds for resuming discussion of these problems after the Judgments Convention had entered into force, depending on the results of the work currently being done by the Hague Conference and by the International Commission on Civil Status.

It should be stressed that these matters will still be governed, temporarily at least, by existing bilateral conventions, in so far as these conventions apply (see Article 56).

B. Bankruptcy

A1.48 Bankruptcy is also excluded from the scope of this Convention.

A separate Convention is currently being drafted, since the peculiarities of this branch of law require special rules.

Article 1(2) excludes bankruptcy, proceedings relating to the winding-up of insolvent companies or other legal persons, judicial arrangements, compositions and analogous proceedings, *i.e.* those proceedings which, [12] depending on the system of law involved, are based on the suspension of payments, the insolvency of the debtor or his inability to raise credit, and which involve the judicial authorities for the purpose either of compulsory and collective liquidation of the assets or simply of supervision.

A1.49 Thus the Convention will cover proceedings arising from schemes of arrangement out of court, since the latter depend on the intention of the parties and are of a purely contractual nature. The insolvency of a non-trader (déconfiture civile) under French law, which does not involve organized and collective proceedings, cannot be regarded as falling within the category of "analogous proceedings" within the meaning of Article 1(2).

Proceedings relating to a bankruptcy are not necessarily excluded from the Convention. Only proceedings arising directly from the bankruptcy[1] and hence falling within the scope of the Bankruptcy Convention of the European Economic Community are excluded from the scope of the Convention.[2]

Pending the conclusion of the separate Convention covering bankruptcy, proceedings arising directly from bankruptcy will be governed by the legal rules currently in force, or by the conventions which already exist between certain Contracting States, as provided in Article 56.[3]

C. Social Security

The Committee decided, like the Hague Conference,[4] to exclude social security from the scope of the Convention. The reasons were as follows.   **A1.50**

In some countries, such as the Federal Republic of Germany, social security is a matter of public law, and in others it falls in the borderline area between private law and public law.

In some States, litigation on social security matters falls within the jurisdiction of the ordinary courts, but in others it falls within the jurisdiction of administrative tribunals; sometimes it lies within the jurisdiction of both.[5]

The Committee was moreover anxious to allow current work within the   **A1.51**
EEC pursuant to Articles 51, 117 and 118 of the Treaty of Rome to develop independently, and to prevent any overlapping on matters of social security between the Convention and agreements already concluded, whether bilaterally or under the auspices of other international organizations such as the International Labour Organization or the Council of Europe.

Social security has not in fact hitherto given rise to conflicts of jurisdiction, since judicial jurisdiction has been taken as coinciding with legislative jurisdiction, which is determined by Community regulations adopted

---

[1] Benelux Treaty, Art. 22(4), and the report annexed thereto. The Convention between France and Belgium is interpreted in the same way. See WESER, Convention franco-belge 1899, in the Jurisclasseur de droit international, Vol. 591, Nos. 146 to 148.

[2] A complete list of the proceedings involved will be given in the Bankruptcy Convention of the European Economic Community.

[3] These are the Conventions between Belgium and France, between France and Italy, and between Belgium and the Netherlands, unless the latter convention has been abrogated by the Benelux Treaty on its entry into force.

[4] The Hague Conference on private international law, extraordinary session. Final Act, see Art. 1 of the Convention.

[5] Étude de la physionomie actuelle de la sécurité sociale dans les pays de la CEE. Série politique sociale 3—1962, Services des publications des Communautés européennes. 8058/1/IX/1962/5.

pursuant to Article 51 of the Treaty of Rome; however, the recovery of contributions due to social security bodies still raises problems of enforcement. This matter should therefore be the subject of a special agreement between the Six.

A1.52   What is meant by social security?

Since this is a field which is in a state of constant development, it did not seem desirable to define it expressly in the Convention, nor even to indicate in an annex what this concept covers, especially as Article 117 of the Treaty of Rome states that one of the Community's objectives is the harmonization of social security systems.

Nevertheless, it should be pointed out that in the six countries benefits are paid in the circumstances listed in Convention No. 102 of the International Labour Organization on minimum standards of social security, namely: medical care, sickness benefits, maternity allowances, invalidity benefits, old age and survivors' pensions, benefits for accidents at work and occupational diseases, family allowances and unemployment benefits.[6] It may also be useful to refer [13] to the definition given in Articles 1(c) and 2 of Council Regulation No. 3 on social security for migrant workers which, moreover, corresponds to that laid down in Convention No. 102 of the ILO.

A1.53   However, the litigation on social security which is excluded from the scope of the Convention is confined to disputes arising from relationships between the administrative authorities concerned and employers or employees. On the other hand, the Convention is applicable when the authority concerned relies on a right of direct recourse against a third party responsible for injury or damage, or is subrogated as against a third party to the rights of an injured party insured by it, since, in doing so, it is acting in accordance with the ordinary legal rules.[1]

D. Arbitration

A1.54   There are already many international agreements on arbitration. Arbitration is, of course, referred to in Article 220 of the Treaty of Rome. Moreover, the Council of Europe has prepared a European Convention providing a uniform law on arbitration, and this will probably be accompanied by a Protocol which will facilitate the recognition and enforcement of arbitral awards to an even greater extent than the New York Convention. This is why it seemed preferable to exclude arbitration. The Brussels Convention does not apply to the recognition and enforcement of arbitral awards (see the definition in Article 25); it does not apply for the purpose of determining the jurisdiction of courts and tribunals in respect of litigation relating to arbitration—for example, proceedings to set aside an arbi-

---

[6] Tableaux comparatifs des régimes de sécurité sociale applicables dans les États membres des Communautés européennes. Third edition, Services des publications des Communautés européennes 8122/1/VII/1964/5.

[1] See Michel Voirin, note under Cass. 16.2.1965, Recueil Dalloz 1965, p. 723.

tral award; and, finally, it does not apply to the recognition of judgments given in such proceedings.

CHAPTER IV

JURISDICTION

A. General Considerations

1. Preliminary remarks

Underlying the Convention is the idea that the Member States of the European Economic Community wanted to set up a common market with characteristics similar to those of a vast internal market. Everything possible must therefore be done not only to eliminate any obstacles to the functioning of this market, but also to promote its development. From this point of view, the territory of the Contracting States may be regarded as forming a single entity: it follows, for the purpose of laying down rules on jurisdiction, that a very clear distinction can be drawn between litigants who are domiciled within the Community and those who are not. **A1.55**

Starting from this basic concept, Title II of the Convention makes a fundamental distinction, in particular in section 1, between defendants who are domiciled in a Contracting State and those who are domiciled elsewhere. **A1.56**

1. If a person is domiciled in a Contracting State, he must in general be sued in the courts of that State in accordance with the rules of jurisdiction in force in that State (Article 2).
2. If a person is domiciled in a Contracting State, he may be sued in the courts of another Contracting State only if the courts of that State are competent by virtue of the Convention (Article 3).
3. If a person is not domiciled in a Contracting State, that is, if he is domiciled outside the Community, the rules of jurisdiction in force in each Contracting State, including those regarded as exorbitant, are applicable (Article 4).

The instances in which a person domiciled in a Contracting State may be sued in the courts of another Contracting State—or must be so sued, in cases of exclusive jurisdiction or prorogation of jurisdiction—are set out in sections 2 to 6. Section 7, entitled "Examination as to jurisdiction . . . and admissibility," is mainly concerned with safeguarding the rights of the defendant. **A1.57**

Section 8 concerns *lis pendens* and related actions. The very precise rules of this section are intended to prevent as far as possible conflicting judgments being given in relation to the same dispute in different States. **A1.58**

[14] Section 9 relates to provisional and protective measures and provides that application for these may be made to any competent court of a Contracting State, even if, under the Convention, that court does not have jurisdiction over the substance of the matter. **A1.59**

2. Rationale of the basic principles of Title II

A1.60   The far-reaching nature of the Convention may at first seem surprising. The rules of jurisdiction which it lays down differ fundamentally from those of bilateral conventions which are based on direct jurisdiction (the Conventions between France and Belgium, and between Belgium and the Netherlands, the Benelux Treaty, the Convention between France and Switzerland) and apply not only to nationals of the Contracting States but also to any person, whatever his nationality, who is domiciled in one of those States.

A1.61   The radical nature of the Convention may not only evoke surprise but also give rise to the objection that the Committee has gone beyond its terms of reference, since Article 220 of the Treaty of Rome provides that States should enter into negotiations with a view to securing "for the benefit of their nationals" the simplification of formalities governing the recognition and enforcement of judgments. The obvious answer to this is that the extension of the scope of the Convention certainly does not represent a departure from the Treaty of Rome provided the Convention ensures, for the benefit of nationals, the simplification of formalities governing the recognition and enforcement of judgments. Too strict an interpretation of the Treaty of Rome would, moreover, have led to the Convention providing for the recognition and enforcement only of those judgments given in favour of nationals of the Contracting States. Such a limitation would have considerably reduced the scope of the Convention, which would in this regard have been less effective than existing bilateral conventions.

A1.62   There are several reasons for widening the scope of the Convention by extending in particular the rules of jurisdiction under Title II to all persons, whatever their nationality, who are domiciled in a Contracting State.

First, it would be a retrograde step if common rules of jurisdiction were to be dependent on the nationality of the parties; the connecting factor in international procedure is usually the domicile or residence of the parties (see, for example, Article 3(1) and (2) of the Hague Convention of 15 April 1958 concerning the recognition and enforcement of decisions relating to maintenance obligations towards children; the Hague Convention of 15 April 1958 on the jurisdiction of the contractual forum in matters relating to the international sale of goods; Article 11 of the Benelux Treaty; and Article 10(1) of the Hague Convention on the recognition and enforcement of foreign judgments in civil and commercial matters).

A1.63   Next, the adoption of common rules based on nationality would have caused numerous difficulties in applying the Convention. This method would have necessitated the introduction of different rules of jurisdiction depending on whether the litigation involved nationals of Contracting States, a national of a Contracting State and a foreign national, or two foreign nationals.

In some situations the rules of jurisdiction of the Convention would have had to be applied; in others, national rules of jurisdiction. Under this system the court would, at the commencement of proceedings, automatically have had to carry out an examination of the nationality of the parties, and it is not difficult to imagine the practical problems involved in, for example, establishing the nationality of a defendant who has failed to enter an appearance.

If the Convention had adopted the nationality of the parties as a connecting factor, it might well have been necessary to introduce a special provision to deal with the relatively frequent cases of dual nationality.   **A1.64**

The Convention would thus have had to solve many problems which do not strictly speaking fall within its scope. Using nationality as a criterion would inevitably have led to a considerable increase in the effect of those rules of jurisdiction which may be termed exorbitant. Thus, for example, a judgment given in France or Luxembourg on the basis of Article 14 of the Civil Code in an action between a national of France or Luxembourg and a national of a non-Member State of the Community would have had to be recognized and enforced in Germany even if the foreign national was domiciled in Germany and a generally recognized jurisdiction, that of the defendant's domicile, thus existed.

By ruling out the criterion of nationality, the Committee is anxious not only to simplify the application of the Convention by giving it a unity which allows a uniform interpretation, but also, in fairness, to allow foreign nationals domiciled in the Community, who are established there and who thereby contribute to its [15] economic activity and prosperity, to benefit from the provisions of the Convention.   **A1.65**

Moreover, the purpose of the Convention is also, by establishing common rules of jurisdiction, to achieve, in relations between the Six and in the field which it was required to cover, a genuine legal systematization which will ensure the greatest possible degree of legal certainty. To this end, the rules of jurisdiction codified in Title II determine which State's courts are most appropriate to assume jurisdiction, taking into account all relevant matters; the approach here adopted means that the nationality of the parties is no longer of importance.

3. Determination of domicile

As already shown, the rules of jurisdiction are based on the defendant's domicile. Determining that domicile is therefore a matter of the greatest importance.   **A1.66**

The Committee was faced with numerous questions which proved difficult to resolve. Should the Convention include a common definition of domicile? Should domicile possibly be replaced by the concept of habitual residence? Should both domicile an habitual residence be used? Should the term domicile be qualified?

   1. Should the Convention include a common definition of domicile?   **A1.67**
      The first point to note is that the concept of domicile is not defined in the Conventions between France and Belgium, Belgium and the Netherlands, Germany and Belgium, and Italy and Belgium, nor in the Benelux Treaty.
      It is, however, defined in the Conventions between France and Italy (Article 28), between Italy and the Netherlands (Article 11),

and between Germany and Italy (Article 13); but these Conventions are all based on indirect jurisdiction.

At first, the Committee thought of defining domicile in the Convention itself, but it finally rejected this course of action. Such a definition would have fallen outside the scope of the Convention, and properly belongs in a uniform law.[1] To define the concept of domicile in international conventions might even be dangerous, as this could lead to a multiplicity of definitions and so to inconsistency.

Moreover, such definitions run the risk of being superseded by developments in national law.

A1.68
    2. Should domicile be replaced by habitual residence?

This course was similarly rejected. It was pointed out that the term "habitual" was open to conflicting interpretations, since the laws of some of the Member States provide that an entry in the population registers is conclusive proof of habitual residence.

The adoption of this course would, moreover, represent a divergence from that followed under the laws of the Contracting States, the majority of which use domicile as a basis of jurisdiction.[2]

[16] Adopting habitual residence as the sole criterion would have raised new problems as regards jurisdiction over persons whose

---

[1] The concept of domicile has been specified by the European Committee for Legal Cooperation, set up by the Council of Europe, as one of the basic legal concepts which should be defined.

[2] *Belgium*
Law of 25 March 1876 containing Title I of the Introductory Book of the Code of Civil Procedure.
Art. 39: Except in the case of amendments and exceptions provided for under the law, the court of the defendant's domicile shall be the only court having jurisdiction.
Judicial Code:
Art. 624: Except in cases where the law expressly determines the court having jurisdiction a plaintiff may institute proceedings:
1. in the court of the domicile of the defendant or of one of the defendants.
Federal Republic of Germany
Code of Civil Procedure, Art. 13: A person shall in general be subject to the jurisdiction of the courts of his domicile.
France
Code of Civil Procedure, Art. 59(1): In actions *in personam*, the defendant shall be sued in the court of his domicile or, where he has no domicile, in the court of his place of residence.
Italy
Code of Civil Procedure, Art. 18: Except where the law otherwise provides, the competent court shall be the court for the place where the defendant has his habitual residence or his domicile or, where these are not known, the court for the place where the defendant is resident.
Luxembourg
Art. 59 of the Code of Civil Procedure corresponds to Art. 59 of the French Code of Civil Procedure.

domicile depends or may depend on that of another person or on the location of an authority (*e.g.* minors or married women).

Finally, in a treaty based on direct jurisdiction, it is particularly important that jurisdiction should have a secure legal basis for the court seised of the matter. The concept of domicile, while not without drawbacks, does however introduce the idea of a more fixed and stable place of establishment on the part of the defendant than does the concept of habitual residence.

3. Should both domicile and habitual residence be adopted? A1.69

In a treaty based on direct jurisdiction, the inclusion of both criteria would result in the major disadvantage that the number of competent courts would be increased. If the domicile and the place of habitual residence happened to be in different States, national rules of jurisdiction of both the States concerned would be applicable by virtue of Article 2 of the Convention, thus defeating the object of the Convention. Moreover, the inclusion of both criteria could increase the number of cases of *lis pendens* and related actions. For these reasons, the Committee preferred finally to adopt only the concept of domicile.

4. Should the concept of domicile be qualified? A1.70

In view of the varied interpretations of the concept of domicile, the Committee considered that the implementation of the Convention would be facilitated by the inclusion of a provision specifying the law to be applied in determining domicile. The absence of such a provision might give rise to claims and disclaimers of jurisdiction; the purpose of Article 52 is to avoid this.

Article 52 deals with three different situations:

(i) where the court of a Contracting State must determine whether a person is domiciled in that State;

(ii) where the court must determine whether a person is domiciled in another Contracting State; and finally,

(iii) where the court must determine whether a person's domicile depends on that of another person or on the seat of an authority.

Article 52 does not deal with the case of a person domiciled out- A1.71 side the Community. In this case the court seised of the matter must apply its rules of private international law.

Nor does Article 52 attempt to resolve the conflicts which might arise if a court seised of a matter ruled that a defendant were to be considered as having his domicile in two other Contracting States, or in one Contracting State and a third country. According to the basic principles of Title II the court, having found that a person is domiciled in some other Contracting State, must, in order to determine its own jurisdiction, apply the rules set out in Article 3 and in sections 2 to 6 of the Convention.

Netherlands
Code of Civil Procedure, Art. 126:
1. In actions *in personam* or actions relating to movable property, the defendant shall be sued in the court of his domicile.

In most disputed cases it will be necessary to determine where the defendant is domiciled.

However, when applying certain provisions of the Convention, in particular Article 5(2) and the first paragraph of Article 8, the rules set out will be used to determine the plaintiff's domicile. For this reason Article 52 does not specify either the defendant or the plaintiff since, in the opinion of the Committee, the same provisions for determining domicile must apply to both parties.

A1.72   Under the first paragraph of Article 52, only the internal law of the court seised of the matter can determine whether a domicile exists in that State. It follows that, if there is a conflict between the *lex fori* and the law of another Contracting State when determining the domicile of a party, the *lex fori* prevails. For example, if a defendant sued in a French court is domiciled both in France, because he has his principal place of business there, and in Belgium, because his name is entered there in the official population registers, where the laws conflict the French court must apply only French law. If it is established under that law that the defendant is in fact domiciled in France, the court need take no other law into consideration. This is justified on various grounds. First, to take the example given, a defendant, by establishing his domicile in a given country, subjects himself to the law of that country. Next, only if the *lex fori* prevails can the court examine whether it has jurisdiction; as the Convention requires it to do, in cases where the defendant fails to enter an appearance (Article 20).

Where the courts of different Contracting States are properly seised of a matter—for example, the Belgian court because it is the court for the place where the defendant's name is entered in the population registers, and the French court because it [17] is the court for the place where he has his principal place of business—the conflict may be resolved by applying the rules governing *lis pendens* or related actions.

A1.73   The second paragraph covers the case of a defendant who is not domiciled in the State whose courts are seised of the matter. The court must then determine whether he is domiciled in another Contracting State, and to do this the internal law of that other State must be applied.

This rule will be applied in particular where a defendant is sued in the courts of a Contracting State in which he is not domiciled. If the jurisdiction of the court is contested, then, following the basic principles of Title II, whether or not the court has jurisdiction will vary according to whether the defendant is domiciled in another Contracting State or outside the Community. Thus, for example, a person domiciled outside the Community may properly be sued in Belgium in the court for the place where the contract was concluded[1] while a person domiciled in another Contracting State and sued in the same court may refuse to accept its jurisdiction, since

---

[1] See Art. 634 of the Judicial Code and Art. 4 of the Convention.

Article 5(1) of the Convention provides that only the courts for the place of performance of the obligation in question have jurisdiction. Thus if a defendant wishes to contest the jurisdiction of the Belgian court, he must establish that he is domiciled in a Contracting State.

Under the second paragraph of Article 52 the Belgian court must, in order to determine whether the defendant is domiciled in another Contracting State, apply the internal law of that State. **A1.74**

The Committee considered it both more equitable and more logical to apply the law of the State of the purported domicile rather than the *lex fori*.

If a court, seised of a matter in which the defendant was domiciled in another Contracting State, applied its own law to determine the defendant's domicile, the defendant might under that law not be regarded as being domiciled in the other Contracting State even though under the law of that other State he was in fact domiciled there. This solution becomes all the more untenable when one realises that a person establishing his domicile in a Contracting State can obviously not be expected to consider whether this domicile is regarded as such under a foreign law.[2]

On the other hand, where the law of the State of the purported domicile has two definitions of domicile,[3] that of the Civil Code and that of the Code of Civil Procedure, the latter should obviously be used since the problem is one of jurisdiction.

The third principle laid down by Article 52 concerns persons such as minors or married women whose domicile depends on that of another person or on the seat of an authority. **A1.75**

Under this provision national law is applied twice. For example, the national law of a minor first determines whether his domicile is dependent on that of another person. If it is, the national law of the minor similarly determines where that domicile is situated (*e.g.* where his guardian is domiciled). If, however, the domicile of the dependent person is under his national law not dependent on that of another person or on the seat of an authority, the first or second paragraph of Article 52 may be applied to determine the domicile of the dependent person. These two paragraphs also apply for the purpose of determining the domicile from which that of the dependent person derives.

---

[2] NIBOYET, Traité de droit international privé français, Vol. VI, No. 1723: "It is submitted that domicile is not systematically determined according to the *lex fori*, but according to the law of the country where the domicile is alleged to be. French law alone can therefore determine whether a person is domiciled in France; but whether a person is domiciled in any particular foreign country is a matter, not for French law, but for the law of the country concerned."

[3] Such might for example be the case in Belgium, where Art. 102 of the Civil Code provides that the domicile of a Belgian in so far as the exercise of his civil rights is concerned is where he has his principal establishment, while Art. 36 of the Judicial Code provides that, for the purpose of that Code, a person is deemed to be domiciled in the place where his name is entered in the official population registers.

A1.76   The members of the Committee were alive to the difficulties which may arise in the event of dual nationality, and more especially in determining the domicile of a married woman. For example, where a German woman marries a Frenchman and acquires French nationality while retaining her German [18] nationality, her domicile under French law[1] is that of her husband, whereas under German law she can have a separate domicile, since German law no longer provides that a married woman has the domicile of her husband.[2] In cases of this kind, the Committee considered that the usual rules relating to dual nationality should be applied. Thus, even if she has a separate domicile in Germany, that person may be sued in France in the court for the husband's domicile, since the French court must apply French law. If, however, she is sued in Germany in the court for the place of her own domicile, the German court will apply German law and declare that it has jurisdiction.

A1.77   Finally, it should be made clear that the concept of domicile within the meaning of the Convention does not extend to the legal fiction of an address for service of process.

B. COMMENTARY ON THE SECTIONS OF TITLE II

Section 1

General provisions

A1.78   Section 1 sets out the main principles on which the rules of jurisdiction laid down by the Convention are founded:

1. the rule that a defendant domiciled in a Contracting State is in general to be sued in the courts of that State (Article 2);
2. the rule that a person domiciled in a Contracting State may in certain circumstances be sued in the courts of another Contracting State (Article 3);
3. the rule that a person domiciled outside the Community is subject to all applicable national rules of jurisdiction (Article 4).

A1.79   This section also embodies the widely applied principle of equality of treatment,[3] which is already enshrined in Article 1 of the Convention between France and Belgium of 8 July 1899, Article 1 of the Convention between Belgium and the Netherlands of 28 March 1925 and Article 1 of the Benelux Treaty of 24 November 1961. Whilst this principle thus forms an integral part of treaties based on direct jurisdiction, in this Convention it also ensures implementation of the mandatory rules of the Treaty of

---

[1] French Civil Code, Art. 108: "A married woman has no domicile other than that of her husband."
[2] BGB, Art. 10, repealed by the Gleichberechtigungsgesetz (Law on equal rights of men and women in the field of civil law) of 18 June 1957.
[3] WESER, Revue critique de droit international privé, 1960, pp. 29–35.

Rome. Article 7 of that Treaty lays down the prinicple of non-discrimination between nationals of Member States of the Community.

Specific provisions applying the general principle set out in Article 7 of the Treaty of Rome to the right of establishment are laid down in Article 52 *et seq.* of that Treaty.

During the preparation of the General Programme on establishment, the Economic and Social Committee of the European Communities drew particular attention to this aspect of the problem by requesting that equality of treatment as regards legal protection be achieved in full as quickly as possible.

Article 2

The maxim *"actor sequitur forum rei,"* which expresses the fact that law leans in favour of the defendant, is even more relevant in the international sphere than it is in national law.[4] It is more difficult, generally speaking, to defend oneself in the courts of a foreign country than in those of another town in the country where one is domiciled.   **A1.80**

A defendant domiciled in a Contracting State need not necessarily be sued in the court for the place where he is domiciled or has his seat. He may be sued in any court of the State where he is domiciled which has jurisdiction under the law of that State.

As a result, if a defendant is sued in one of the courts of the State in which he is domiciled, the internal rules of jurisdiction of that State are fully applicable. Here the Convention requires the application of the national law of the court seised of the matter; the Convention determines whether the courts of the State in question have jurisdiction, and the law of that State in turn determines whether a particular court in that State has jurisdiction. This solution seems equitable since it is usual for a defendant domiciled in a State to be subject to the internal law of that State without it being **[19]** necessary for the Convention to provide special rules for his protection. It is, moreover, an extremely practical solution because it means that in most cases the court will not have to take the Convention any further into consideration.

Defendants are usually sued in the courts of the State in which they are domiciled. This is true of proceedings in which there is no international element. It is also true of proceedings with an international element in which, by application of the traditionally accepted maxim *"actor sequitur forum rei,"* the defendant is sued in the courts of the State of his domicile. The Convention does not therefore involve a general reversal of national rules of jurisdiction nor of the practice of judges and lawyers. In fact, judges and lawyers will need to take account of the changes effected by the Convention only in cases where a defendant is sued in a court of a State where he is not domiciled, or in one of the few cases in which the Convention has laid down common rules of exclusive jurisdiction.

The second paragraph of Article 2 embodies the principle of equality of treatment where a foreigner is domiciled in the State of the forum. Such   **A1.81**

---

[4] See report by Professor FRAGISTAS—Hague Conference on private international law—preliminary doc. No. 4, May 1964, for the tenth session.

foreigner, whether he is defendant or plaintiff, is governed in that State by the same rules of jurisdiction as its nationals, or more precisely, as its nationals who are domiciled in that State, where, as in Italy, the law of that State determines the jurisdiction of its courts according to whether the national concerned is domiciled in its territory.

As a result, Article 52 of the Belgian Law of 25 March 1876 will no longer be applicable as such to foreigners domiciled in Belgium.[1]

The positive aspect of equality of treatment is set out in the second paragraph of Article 4.

Article 3

A1.82   Article 3 deals with those cases in which a defendant domiciled in a Contracting State may be sued in another Contracting State. This Article lays down the principle that a defendant may be sued otherwise than in the courts of the State where he is domiciled only in the cases expressly provided for in the Convention. The rule sets aside the rules of exorbitant jurisdiction in force in each of the Contracting States. However, these rules of jurisdiction are not totally excluded; they are excluded only in respect of persons who are domiciled in another Contracting State. Thus they remain in force with respect to persons who are not domiciled within the Community.

The second paragraph of Article 3 prohibits the application of the most important and best known of the rules of exorbitant jurisdiction. While this paragraph is not absolutely essential it will nevertheless facilitate the application of certain provisions of the Convention (see, in particular, Article 59).

A1.83   The following are the rules of exorbitant jurisdiction in question in each of the States concerned.

In Belgium

Articles 52, 52bis and 53 of the Law of 25 March 1876, which govern territorial jurisdiction in actions brought by Belgians[2] or by foreigners against foreigners before Belgian courts, and Article 15 of the Civil Code which corresponds to Article 15 of the French Civil Code.

A1.84   *In Germany*

The nationality of the parties does not in general affect the rules of jurisdiction. Article 23 of the Code of Civil Procedure lays down that, where no other German court has jurisdiction, actions relating to property instituted against a person who is not domiciled in the national territory come under

---

[1] This Article provides, in particular, that foreigners who are domiciled or resident in Belgium may be sued before a court of the Kingdom either by a Belgian or by a foreigner.

[2] Répertoire pratique du droit belge, under "compétence"—No. 17518 *et seq.*—(see Judicial Code, Arts. 635, 637 and 638).

the jurisdiction of the court for the place where the property or subject of the dispute is situated.

German courts have in a number of cases given a very liberal interpretation to this provision, thereby leading some authors to state that Article 23 "can be likened to Article 14 of the French Civil Code."[3]

In France   A1.85

1. Article 14 of the Civil Code provides that any French plaintiff may sue a foreigner or another Frenchman in the French courts, even if there is no [20] connection between the cause of action and those courts.
2. Article 15 of the Civil Code provides that a Frenchman may always be sued in the French courts by a Frenchman or by a foreigner, and can even insist on this.

Despite the fact that Articles 14 and 15 in terms refer only to contractual obligations, case law has extended their scope beyond contractual obligations to all actions whether or not relating to property rights. There are thus only two limitations to the general application of Articles 14 and 15: French courts are never competent to hear either actions *in rem* concerning immovable property situated abroad, or actions concerning proceedings for enforcement which is to take place abroad.[1]

In Italy   A1.86

1. Article 2 of the Code of Civil Procedure provides that an agreement to substitute for the jurisdiction of Italian courts the jurisdiction of a foreign court or arbitral tribunal will be valid only in the case of litigation between foreigners, or between a foreigner and an Italian citizen who is neither resident nor domiciled in Italy, and only if the agreement is evidenced in writing.
2. (a) Under Article 4(1) of the Code of Civil Procedure, a foreigner may be sued in an Italian court if he is resident or domiciled in Italy, or if he has an address for service there or has a representative who is authorized to bring legal proceedings in his name, or if he has accepted Italian jurisdiction, unless the proceedings concern immovable property situated abroad.
   (b) Under Article 4(2) of the Code of Civil Procedure, a foreigner may be sued in the courts of the Italian Republic if the proceedings concern property situated in Italy, or succession to the estate of an Italian national, or an application for probate made in Italy, or obligations which arose in Italy or which must be performed there.
3. The interpretation given to Article 4 by Italian case law means that an Italian defendant may always be sued in the Italian courts.[2]

---

[3] WESER, Revue critique de droit international privé, 1959, p. 636; ROSENBERG, Lehrbuch des deutschen Zivilprozeßrechts, ninth edition, para. 35 I 3.

[1] BATIFFOL, *op. cit.*, No. 684 *et seq.*

[2] MORELLI, Diritto processuale civile internazionale, pp. 108–112.

A1.87   *In Luxembourg*

Articles 14 and 15 of the Civil Code correspond to Articles 14 and 15 of the French Civil Code.

Luxembourg case law applies the same principles of interpretation as French case law.

A1.88   *In the Netherlands*

Article 126(3) of the Code of Civil Procedure provides that, in personal matters or matters concerning movable property, a defendant who has no known domicile or residence in the Kingdom shall be sued in the court for the domicile of the plaintiff. This provision applies whether or not the plaintiff is a Netherlands national.[3]

Article 127 provides that a foreigner, even if he does not reside in the Netherlands, may be sued in a Netherlands court for the performance of obligations contracted towards a Netherlander either in the Netherlands or abroad.

Article 4

A1.89   Article 4 applies to all proceedings in which the defendant is not domiciled in a Contracting State, and provides that the rules of internal law remain in force.

This is justified on two grounds:

First, in order to ensure the free movement of judgments, this Article prevents refusal of recognition or enforcement of a judgment given on the basis of rules of internal law relating to jurisdiction. In the absence of such a provision, a judgment debtor would be able to prevent execution being levied on his property simply by transferring it to a Community country other than that in which judgment was given.

Secondly, this Article may perform a function in the case of *lis pendens*. Thus, for example, if a French court is seised of an action between a Frenchman and a defendant domiciled in America, and a German court is [21] seised of the same matter on the basis of Article 23 of the Code of Civil Procedure, one of the two courts must in the interests of the proper administration of justice decline jurisdiction in favour of the other. This issue cannot be settled unless the jurisdiction of these courts derives from the Convention.

In the absence of an article such as Article 4, there would be no rule in the Convention expressly recognizing the jurisdiction of the French and German courts in a case of this kind.

A1.90   The only exception to the application of the rules of jurisdiction of internal law is the field of exclusive jurisdiction (Article 16).[1] The rules which

---

[3] WESER, Revue critique de droit international privé, 1959, p. 632.

[1] The third paragraph of Art. 8, which concerns jurisdiction in respect of insurers who are not domiciled in the Community but have a branch or agency there, may also be regarded as an exception.

grant exclusive jurisdiction to the courts of a State are applicable whatever the domicile of the defendant.

However, the question arises why the Committee did not extend the scope of the provision limiting the application of rules of exorbitant jurisdiction to include in particular nationals of Member States regardless of their place of domicile.

In other words, and to take another example based on Article 14 of the French Civil Code, why will it still be possible for a French plaintiff to sue in the French courts a foreigner, or even a national of a Member State of the Community, who is domiciled outside the Community?

A1.91 The Committee thought that it would have been unreasonable to prevent the rules of exorbitant jurisdiction from applying to persons, including Community nationals, domiciled outside the Community. Thus, for example, a Belgian national domiciled outside the Community might own assets in the Netherlands. The Netherlands courts have no jurisdiction in the matter since the Convention does not recognize jurisdiction based on the presence of assets within a State. If Article 14 of the French Civil Code could not be applied, a French plaintiff would have to sue the Belgian defendant in a court outside the Community, and the judgment could not be enforced in the Netherlands if there were no enforcement treaty between the Netherlands and the non-member State in which judgment was given.

This, moreover, was the solution adopted in the Conventions between France and Belgium, and between Belgium and the Netherlands, and in the Benelux Treaty, which, however, take nationality as their criterion.[2]

A1.92 The second paragraph of Article 4 of the Convention constitutes a positive statement of the principle of equality of treatment already laid down in the second paragraph of Article 2. An express provision was considered necessary in order to avoid any uncertainty.[3] Under this provision, any person domiciled in a Contracting State has the right, as plaintiff, to avail himself in that State of the same rules of jurisdiction as a national of that State.

This principle had already been expressly laid down in the Convention between France and Belgium of 8 July 1899 (Article 1(2)).

This positive aspect of the principle of equality of treatment was regarded as complementing the right of establishment (Article 52 *et seq.* of the Treaty of Rome), the existence of which implies, as was stated in the General Programme for the abolition of restrictions on freedom of establishment of 18 December 1961,[4] that any natural or legal person estab-

---

[2] The Convention between France and Belgium is interpreted to mean that a Frenchman may not rely on Art. 14 of the Civil Code to sue in France a Belgian domiciled in Belgium, but may do so to sue a Belgian domiciled abroad. BATIFFOL, Traité élémentaire de droit international privé, No. 714.
[3] According to French case law on the Treaty of 9 February 1842 between France and Denmark, a Danish national may not rely on Art. 14 of the French Civil Code.
[4] *Official Journal of the European Communities*, 15.1.1962, p. 36 *et seq.*

lished in a Member State should enjoy the same legal protection as a national of that State.

A1.93   The provision is also justified on economic grounds. Since rules of exorbitant jurisdiction can still be invoked against foreigners domiciled outside the European Economic Community, persons who are domiciled in the Member State concerned and who thus contribute to the economic life of the Community should be able to invoke such rules in the same way as the nationals of that State.

It may be thought surprising that the Convention extends the "privileges of jurisdiction" in this way, since equality of treatment is granted in each of the States to all persons, whatever their nationality, who are domiciled in that State.

[22] It should first be noted that such treatment is already granted to foreigners in Belgium, the Federal Republic of Germany, Italy and the Netherlands, where the rules of exorbitant jurisdiction may be invoked by foreigners as well as by nationals. The second paragraph of Article 4 therefore merely brings into line with these laws the French and Luxembourg concepts, according to which Article 14 of the Civil Code constitutes a privilege of nationality.

A1.94   Secondly, the solution adopted in the Convention follows quite naturally from the fact that, for the reasons already given, the Convention uses domicile as the criterion for determining jurisdiction. In this context it must not be forgotten that it will no longer be possible to invoke the privileges of jurisdiction against persons domiciled in the Community, although it will be possible to invoke them against nationals of the Community countries who have established their domicile outside the territory of the Six.

Section 2

Special jurisdiction

Articles 5 and 6

A1.95   Articles 5 and 6 list the situations in which a defendant may be sued in a Contracting State other than that of his domicile. The forums provided for in these Articles supplement those which apply under Article 2. In the case of proceedings for which a court is specifically recognized as having jurisdiction under these Articles, the plaintiff may, at his option, bring the proceedings either in that court or in the competent courts of the State in which the defendant is domiciled.

One problem which arose here was whether it should always be possible to sue the defendant in one of the courts provided for in these Articles, or whether this should be allowed only if the jurisdiction of that court was also recognized by the internal law of the State concerned.

In other words, in the first case, jurisdiction would derive directly from the Convention and in the second there would need to be dual jurisdiction: that of the Convention and that of the internal law on local jurisdiction. Thus, for example, where Netherlands law on jurisdiction does not recognize the court for the place of performance of the obligation, can the plaintiff nevertheless sue the defendant before that court in the Netherlands? In addition, would there be any obligation on the Netherlands to adapt its national laws in order to give that court jurisdiction?

By adopting "special" rules of jurisdiction, that is by directly designat- **A1.96** ing the competent court without referring to the rules of jurisdiction in force in the State where such a court might be situated, the Committee decided that a plaintiff should always be able to sue a defendant in one of the forums provided for without having to take the internal law of the State concerned into consideration. Further, in laying down these rules, the Committee intended to facilitate implementation of the Convention. By ratifying the Convention, the Contracting States will avoid having to take any other measures to adapt their internal legislation to the criteria laid down in Articles 5 and 6. The Convention itself determines which court has jurisdiction.

Adoption of the "special" rules of jurisdiction is also justified by the fact that there must be a close connecting factor between the dispute and the court with jurisdiction to resolve it. Thus, to take the example of the *forum delicti commissi*, a person domiciled in a Contracting State other than the Netherlands who has caused an accident in The Hague may, under the Convention, be sued in a court in The Hague. This accident cannot give other Netherlands courts jurisdiction over the defendant. On this point there is thus a distinct difference between Article 2 and Articles 5 and 6, due to the fact that in Article 2 domicile is the connecting factor.

Forum contractus (Article 5(1)) including contracts of employment

There are great differences between the laws of the Six in their attitude to **A1.97** the jurisdiction of the *forum contractus*; in some countries this jurisdiction is not recognized (the Netherlands, Luxembourg), while in others it exists in varying degrees. Belgian law recognizes the jurisdiction of the courts for the place where the obligation arose, and also that of the courts for the place where the obligation has been or is to be performed[1]; Italian law recognizes only the jurisdiction of the courts for the place where the obligation arose and where it has been performed[2]; German law in general recognizes only the jurisdiction of the courts for the place where the obligation has been [23] performed[1]; and, finally, French law recognizes the jurisdiction of the *forum contractus* only to a limited extent and subject to certain conditions.[2]

Some of the conventions concluded between the Six reject this forum, **A.98** while others accept it in varying degrees. Article 2(1) of the Convention between *France and Belgium* provides that, where a defendant is neither domiciled nor resident in France or Belgium, a Belgian or French plaintiff

---

[1] Arts. 41 and 52 of the Law of 25 March 1876, Art. 624 of the Judicial Code.
[2] Arts. 4 and 20 of the Code of Civil Procedure.
[1] Art. 29 of the Code of Civil Procedure.
[2] Arts. 59(3) and 420 of the Code of Civil Procedure.

may institute proceedings in the courts for the place where the obligation arose or where it has been or is to be performed.[3]

Article 4 of the Convention between *Belgium and the Netherlands* provides that in civil or commercial matters a plaintiff may bring a personal action concerning movable property in the courts for the place where the obligation arose or where it has been or is to be performed.

In Article 3(5) of the Convention between *Belgium and Germany*, jurisdiction is recognized where, in matters relating to a contract, proceedings are instituted in a court of the State where the obligation has been or is to be performed.

Article 14 of the Convention between *France and Italy* provides that if the action concerns a contract which is considered as a commercial matter by the law of the country in which the action is brought, a French or Italian plaintiff may seise the courts of either of the two countries in which the contract was concluded or is to be performed.

The Convention between *Belgium and Italy* (Article 2(5)) recognizes jurisdiction where, in matters relating to a contract, an action is brought before the courts of the State where the obligation arose, or where it has been or should have been performed.

There are no provisions on this subject in the Conventions between *Italy and the Netherlands*, *Germany and Italy*, and *Germany and the Netherlands*.

Finally, the Benelux Treaty adopts Article 4 of the Convention between Belgium and the Netherlands, but includes a Protocol which in Article 1 lays down that Article 4 shall not apply where Luxembourg is concerned if the defendant is domiciled or resident in the country of which he is a national.[4]

A1.99 Article 5(1) provides a compromise between the various national laws.

The jurisdiction of the forum is, as in German law, limited to matters relating to contract. It could have been restricted to commercial matters, but account must be taken of the fact that European integration will mean an increase in the number of contractual relationships entered into. To have confined it to commercial matters would moreover have raised the problem of classification.

Only the jurisdiction of the *forum solutionis* has been retained, that is to say the jurisdiction of the courts for the place of performance of the obligation on which the claim is based. The reasons for this are as follows.

A1.100 The Committee considered that it would be unwise to give jurisdiction to a number of courts, and thus possibly create conflicts of jurisdiction. A plaintiff already has a choice, in matters relating to a contract, between the competent courts of the State where the defendant is domiciled, or, where there is more than one defendant, the courts for the place where any one of them is domiciled, or finally, the courts for the place of performance of the obligation in question.

If the Committee had adopted as wide-ranging a provision as that of the

---

[3] On the serious controversy to which this Art. has given rise, see WESER, Traité franco-belge du 8 juillet 1899. Étude critique, p. 63 *et seq.*; also Jurisclasseur de droit international, vol. 591, Nos. 42 and 45.

[4] For the reasons for this limitation, see the report on the negotiations.

Benelux Treaty, which recognizes also the jurisdiction of the courts for the place where the obligation arose, this would have involved very considerable changes for those States whose laws do not recognize that forum, or do so only with certain restrictions.

There was also concern that acceptance of the jurisdiction of the courts for the place where the obligation arose might sanction, by indirect means, the jurisdiction of the forum of the plaintiff. To have accepted this forum would have created tremendous problems of classification, in particular in the case of contracts concluded by parties who are absent.

The court for the place of performance of the obligation will be useful in **A1.101** proceedings for the recovery of fees: the creditor will have a choice between the courts of the State where the defendant is domiciled and the courts of another State within whose jurisdiction the services [24] were provided, particularly where, according to the appropriate law, the obligation to pay must be performed where the services were provided. This forum can also be used where expert evidence or inquiries are required. The special position of Luxembourg justified, as in the Benelux Treaty, the inclusion of a special provision in the Protocol (Article I).

Contracts of employment

In matters relating to contracts of employment in the broadest sense of **A1.102** the term, the preliminary draft of the Convention contained a provision attributing exclusive jurisdiction to the courts of the Contracting State either in which the undertaking concerned was situated, or in which the work was to have been or had been performed. After prolonged consideration, the Committee decided not to insert in the Convention any special provisions on jurisdiction in this field. Its reasoning was as follows.

First, work is at present in progress within the Commission of the EEC **A1.103** to harmonize the provisions of labour law in the Member States. It is desirable that disputes over contracts of employment should as far as possible be brought before the courts of the State whose law governs the contract. The Committee therefore did not think that rules of jurisdiction should be laid down which might not coincide with those which may later be adopted for determining the applicable law.

In order to lay down such rules of jurisdiction, the Committee would have had to take into account not only the different ways in which work can be carried out abroad, but also the various categories of worker: wage-earning or salaried workers recruited abroad to work permanently for an undertaking, or those temporarily transferred abroad by an undertaking to work for it there; commercial agents, management, etc. Any attempt by the Committee to draw such distinctions might have provided a further hindrance to the Commission's work.

Next, in most Member States of the Community the principle of free- **A1.104** dom of contract still plays an important part; a rule of exclusive jurisdiction such as that previously provided for in Article 16 would have nullified any agreements conferring jurisdiction.

The general rules of the Convention will therefore apply to contracts of **A1.105** employment. Thus, in litigation between employers and employees, the following courts have jurisdiction: the courts of the State where the defendant is domiciled (Article 2); the courts for the place of performance of the obligation, if that place is in a State other than that of the domicile of the defendant (Article 5(1)); and any court on which the parties have expressly or impliedly agreed (Articles 17 and 18). In the case of proceedings based on a tort committed at work (Article 2, Nos. 2 and 3 of the Arbeitsgerichtsgesetz), Article 5(3), which provides for the jurisdiction of the courts for the place where the harmful event occurred, could also apply. It seems that these rules will, for the time being, prove of greater value to the persons concerned than a provision similar to that of the former Article 16(2), which could not be derogated from because it prohibited any agreement conferring jurisdiction.

A1.106   The rules on the recognition and enforcement of judgments will probably ensure additional protection for employees. If the law of the State addressed had to be applied to a contract of employment, the courts of that State, upon being seised of an application for recognition or enforcement of a foreign judgment, would, on the basis of Article 27(1), which permits refusal of recognition (or enforcement) on grounds of public policy in the State addressed, be able to refuse the application if the court of the State or origin had failed to apply, or had misapplied, an essential provision of the law of the State addressed.

Once the work of the Commission in this field has been completed, it will always be possible to amend the provisions of the Convention, either by means of an additional Protocol, or by the drafting of a convention governing the whole range of problems relating to contracts of employment, which would, under Article 57, prevail over the Convention.

Maintenance obligations (Article 5(2))

A1.107   Matters relating to maintenance are governed by the Convention.

The Convention is in a sense an extension of the Hague Convention of 15 April 1958 concerning the recognition and enforcement of decisions relating to maintenance obligations in respect of children,[1] since **[25]** it ensures the recognition and enforcement of judgments granting maintenance to creditors other than children, and also of the New York Convention of 20 June 1956 on the recovery abroad of maintenance.[1]

A1.108   The Committee decided that jurisdiction should be conferred on the forum of the creditor, for the same reasons as the draftsmen of the Hague Convention.[2] For one thing, a convention which did not recognize the forum of the maintenance creditor would be of only limited value, since the creditor would be obliged to bring the claim before the court having jurisdiction over the defendant.

If the Convention did not confer jurisdiction on the forum of the maintenance creditor, it would apply only in those situations where the

---

[1] In force on 1.9.1966 between Belgium, France, Germany, Italy and the Netherlands.

[1] In force on 1.9.1966 between Belgium, France, Germany, Italy and the Netherlands.

[2] Hague Conference on private international law, documents for the eighth session, p. 315.

defendant against whom an order had been made subsequently changed residence, or where the defendant possessed property in a country other than that in which the order was made.

Moreover the court for the place of domicile of the maintenance creditor is in the best position to know whether the creditor is in need and to determine the extent of such need.

However, in order to align the Convention with the Hague Convention, **A1.109** Article 5(2) also confers jurisdiction on the courts for the place of habitual residence of the maintenance creditor. This alternative is justified in relation to maintenance obligations since it enables in particular a wife deserted by her husband to sue him for payment of maintenance in the courts for the place where she herself is habitually resident, rather than the place of her legal domicile.

The Convention also supplements the New York Convention of 20 June 1956 on the recovery abroad of maintenance. The latter is limited to providing that a forwarding authority will transmit to an intermediate body any judgment already given in favour of a maintenance creditor, and that body will then have to begin proceedings for enforcement or registration of the judgment, or institute new proceedings altogether.

This Convention, by simplifying the formalities governing enforcement, will thus facilitate implementation of the New York Convention.

As regards maintenance payments, the Committee did not overlook the problems which might be raised by preliminary issues (for example, the question of affiliation). However, it considered that these were not properly problems of jurisdiction, and that any difficulties should be considered in the chapter on recognition and enforcement of judgments.

It was suggested that, in order to avoid conflicting judgments, it might **A1.110** be desirable to provide that the court which had fixed the amount of a maintenance payment should be the only court to have jurisdiction to vary it. The Committee did not think it necessary to adopt such a solution. This would have obliged parties, neither of whom had any further connection with the original court, to bring proceedings before courts which could be very far away. Moreover, any judgment by a second court, in order to vary that of the first court, would have to be based on changed facts, and in those circumstances it could not be maintained that the judgments were in conflict.[3]

Forum delicti commissi (Article 5(3) and (4))

This jurisdiction is recognized by the national laws of the Member **A1.111** States with the exception of Luxembourg and the Netherlands, where it exists only in respect of collisions of ships and of road accidents.

The following are applicable in Belgium, Articles 41, and 52(3) of the Law of 1876,[4] in Germany, Article 32 of the Code of Civil Procedure; in

---

[3] For a similar view, see the Hague Conference on private international law, documents for the ninth session. Report on the draft Convention concerning the recognition and enforcement of decisions relating to maintenance obligations in respect of children, p. 321.

[4] Art. 626 of the Judicial Code.

France, Article 59(12) of the Code of Civil Procedure and Article 21 of the Decree of 22 December 1958; and in Italy, Article 20 of the Code of Civil Procedure.

A1.112   This jurisdiction is incorporated in the bilateral conventions by the following provisions: Article 4 of the Convention between Belgium and the Netherlands and Article 4 of the Benelux Treaty, which cover all obligations concerning movable property, whether statutory, contractual or non-contractual,[5] Article 2(b) of the Convention between Belgium and Italy; Article 3(1)(6) of the Convention between Germany **[26]** and Belgium; Article 15 of the Convention between France and Italy; Article 2(4) of the Convention between Germany and Italy; and Article 4(1)(e) of the Convention between Germany and the Netherlands.

The fact that this jurisdiction is recognized under most of the legal systems, and incorporated in the majority of the bilateral conventions, was a ground for including it in the Convention, especially in view of the high number of road accidents.

A1.113   Article 5(3) uses the expression "the place where the harmful event occurred." The Committee did not think it should specify whether that place is the place where the event which resulted in damage or injury occurred, or whether it is the place where the damage or injury was sustained. The Committee preferred to keep to a formula which has already been adopted by a number of legal systems (Germany, France).

A1.114   Article 5(4) provides that a civil claim may be brought before a court seised of criminal proceedings; this is in order to take into account the rules of jurisdiction laid down by the various codes of criminal procedure. A civil claim can thus always be brought, whatever the domicile of the defendant, in the criminal court having jurisdiction to entertain the criminal proceedings even if the place where the court sits (place of arrest, for example) is not the same as that where the harmful event occurred.

Jurisdiction based on a dispute arising out of the operations of a branch, agency or other establishment (Article 5(5))

A1.115   This jurisdiction exists in the bilateral conventions already concluded between the Contracting States: the Conventions between Italy and Belgium (Article 2(3)), between Belgium and Germany (Article 2(1)(4)), between France and Belgium (Article 3(2)), between France and Italy (Article 13), between Italy and the Netherlands (Article 2(3)), and between Belgium and the Netherlands (Article 5(3)); the Benelux Treaty (Article 5(4); and the Conventions between Germany and the Netherlands (Article 4(1)(d)), and between Germany and Italy (Article 2(3)).

This provision concerns only defendants domiciled in a Contracting State (Article 5), that is, companies or firms having their seat in one Contracting State and having a branch, agency or other establishment in another Contracting State. Companies or firms which have their seat outside the Community but have a branch, etc. in a Contracting State are governed by Article 4, even as regards disputes relating to the activities of

---

[5] Report on the negotiations, p. 17.

their branches, but without prejudice to the provisions of Article 8 relating to insurance.

More than one defendant (Article 6(1))

Where there is more than one defendant, the courts for the place where **A1.116** any one of the defendants is domiciled are recognized as having jurisdiction. This jurisdiction is provided for in the internal law of Belgium,[1] France,[2] Italy,[3] Luxembourg[4] and the Netherlands.[5]

It is not in general provided for in German law. Where an action must be brought in Germany against a number of defendants and there is no jurisdiction to which they are all subject, the court having jurisdiction may, subject to certain conditions, be designated by the superior court which is next above it (Article 36(3) of the German Code of Civil Procedure).

This jurisdiction is also provided for in the Conventions between Italy and the Netherlands (Article 2(1)), between Italy and Belgium (Article 2(1)), between France and Italy (Article 11(2)), and between Germany and Italy (Article 2(1)). However, under the latter Convention, jurisdiction depends on the existence of a procedural requirement that the various defendants be joined.

It follows from the text of the Convention that, where there are several **A1.117** defendants domiciled in different Contracting States, the plaintiff can at his option sue them all in the courts for the place where any one of them is domiciled.

In order for this rule to be applicable there must be a connection between the claims made against each of the defendants, as for example in the case of joint debtors.[6] It follows that action cannot be brought solely with the object of ousting the jurisdiction of the courts of the State in which the defendant is domiciled.[7]

[27] Jurisdiction derived from the domicile of one of the defendants was adopted by the Committee because it makes it possible to obviate the handing down in the Contracting States of judgments which are irreconcilable with one another.

Actions on a warranty or guarantee, third party proceedings, counterclaims.

(a) Actions on a warranty or guarantee (Article 6(2)) **A1.118**

An action on a warranty or guarantee brought against a third party by the defendant in an action for the purpose of being indemnified against the

---

[1] Arts. 39 and 52(10) of the Law of 25 March 1876, and Art. 624 of the Judicial Code.
[2] Art. 59(4) of the Code of Civil Procedure.
[3] Art. 33 of the Code of Civil Procedure.
[4] Art. 59(2) of the Code of Civil Procedure.
[5] Art. 126(7) of the Code of Civil Procedure.
[6] MOREL, Traité élémentaire de procédure civile, No. 264.
[7] Cass. française 1924, D.P. 1925, Vol. 13.

consequences of that action, is available in Belgian,[1] French,[2] Italian,[3] Luxembourg,[4] and Netherlands[5] law.

The proceeding which corresponds to an action on a warranty or guarantee in Germany is governed by Articles 72, 73 and 74 and Article 68 of the Code of Civil Procedure.

A party who in any proceedings considers that, if he is unsuccessful, he has a right of recourse on a warranty or guarantee against a third party, may join that third party in the proceedings (Article 72) (Streitverkündung—*litis denunciatio*).

A1.119   The notice joining the third party must be served on that party and a copy must be sent to the other party (Article 73). No judgment can be given as regards the third party, but the judgment given in the original proceedings is binding in the sense that the substance of the judgment cannot be contested in the subsequent action which the defendant may bring against the third party (Article 68). Under the German Code of Civil Procedure the defendant can exercise his right of recourse against the third party only in separate proceedings.

Actions on a warranty or guarantee are governed by the bilateral Conventions between Belgium and Germany (Article 3(10)), between France and Belgium (Article 4(2)), between Belgium and the Netherlands (Article 6(2)), between Italy and the Netherlands (Article 2(4)), between Belgium and Italy (Article 2(10)), and between Germany and the Netherlands (Article 4(1)(c)), and also by the Benelux Treaty (Article 6(3)).

A1.120   This jurisdiction is, in the opinion of the Committee, of considerable importance in commercial dealings, as can be seen from the following example: A German exporter delivers goods to Belgium and the Belgian importer resells them. The purchaser sues the importer for damages in the court for the place of his domicile, for example in Brussels. The Belgian importer has a right of recourse against the German exporter and consequently brings an action for breach of warranty against that exporter in the court in Brussels, since it has jurisdiction over the original action. The jurisdiction over the action on the warranty is allowed by the Convention although the warrantor is domiciled in Germany, since this is in the interests of the proper administration of justice.

A1.121   However, under Article 17, the court seised of the original action will not have jurisdiction over the action on the warranty where the warrantor and the beneficiary of the warranty have agreed to confer jurisdiction on another court, provided that the agreement covers actions on the warranty.

Moreover, the court seised of the original action will not have jurisdiction over an action on the warranty if the original proceedings were insti-

---

[1] Arts. 50 and 52 of the Law of 25 March 1876, Art. 181 of the Code of Civil Procedure.
[2] Arts. 59(10) and 181 to 185 of the Code of Civil Procedure.
[3] Arts. 32 and 36 of the Code of Civil Procedure.
[4] Arts. 59(8) and 181 to 185 of the Code of Civil Procedure.
[5] Art. 126(14) of the Code of Civil Procedure.

tuted solely with the object of ousting the jurisdiction of the courts of the·
State in which the warrantor is domiciled.[6]

The special position of German law is covered by Article V of the
Protocol.

A1.122

Under this provision, the jurisdiction specified in Article 6(2) in actions
on a warranty or guarantee may not be resorted to in the Federal Republic
of Germany, but any person domiciled in another Contracting State may
be summoned before the German courts on the basis of Articles 72 to 74 of
the Code of Civil Procedure.

Judgments given against a guarantor or warrantor in the other Contracting States will be recognized and enforced in Germany.

Judgments given in Germany pursuant to Articles 72 to 74 will have the
same effect in the other Contracting States as in Germany.

Thus, for example, a guarantor or warrantor domiciled in France can be
sued in the German court having jurisdiction over the original action. The
German law [28] judgment given in Germany affects only the parties to the
action, but it can be invoked against the guarantor or warrantor. Where
the beneficiary of the guarantee or warranty proceeds against the guarantor or warrantor in the competent French courts, he will be able to apply
for recognition of the German judgment, and it will no longer be possible
to re-examine that judgment as to the merits.

It is clear that, following the principles which apply to enforcement, a
judgment given in an action on a guarantee or warranty will have no effects
in the State in which enforcement is sought other than those which it had
in the country of origin.

A1.123

This principle, which already applied under the Conventions between
Germany and Belgium (Article 3(10)) and between Germany and the
Netherlands (Article 4(1)(i)), is thus incorporated in the provision govern-
ing relations between the Federal Republic of Germany and the other
Member States of the Community.

(b) Third party proceedings

A1.124

While a third party warranty or guarantee necessarily involves the intervention of an outsider, it seemed preferable to make separate provision for
guarantors or warrantors and for other third parties. The simplest definition of third party proceedings is to be found in Articles 15 and 16 of the
Belgian Judicial Code, which provides that:

> "Third party proceedings are those in which a third party is joined as
> a party to the action.
> They are intended either to safeguard the interests of the third party
> or of one of the parties to the action, or to enable judgment to be
> entered against a party, or to allow an order to be made for the pur-
> pose of giving effect to a guarantee or warranty (Article 15).
> The third party's intervention is voluntary where he appears in order
> to defend his interests.

---

[6] See Art. 181 of the Belgian, French and Luxembourg Code of Civil Procedure,
and Art. 74 of the Netherlands Code of Civil Procedure.

It is not voluntary where the third party is sued in the course of the proceedings by one or more of the parties (Article 16)."

A1.125 (c) Counterclaims (Article 6(3))

The bilateral conventions on enforcement all recognize jurisdiction over counterclaims: see the Convention between Belgium and Germany (Article 3(1)(10)) (counterclaims); the Convention between Italy and Belgium (Article 2(1)(10)) (dependent counterclaims); the Convention between France and Belgium (Article 4(2)) (counterclaims); the Convention between Belgium and the Netherlands (Article 6) (counterclaims, third party proceedings and interlocutory proceedings); the Convention between France and Italy (Article 18) (claims for compensation, interlocutory or dependent proceedings, counterclaims); the Convention between Italy and the Netherlands (Article 2(4)) (dependent proceedings, counterclaims); the Convention between Germany and Italy (Article 2(5)) (counterclaims); the Benelux Treaty (Article 6) (counterclaims, third party proceedings and interlocutory proceedings); and the Convention between Germany and the Netherlands (Article 4(1)(i)) (counterclaims and actions on a warranty or guarantee).

It has been made clear that in order to establish this jurisdiction the counterclaim must be related to the original claim. Since the concept of related actions is not recognized in all the legal systems, the provision in question, following the draft Belgian Judicial Code, states that the counterclaim must arise from the contract or from the facts on which the original claim was based.

Sections 3 to 5

Insurance, instalment sales, exclusive jurisdiction

General remarks

A1.126 In each of the six Contracting States, the rules of territorial jurisdiction are not as a rule part of public policy and it is therefore permissible for the parties to agree on a different jurisdiction.

There are, however, exceptions to this principle: certain rules of jurisdiction are mandatory or form part of public policy, either in order to further the efficient administration of justice by reducing the number of jurisdictions and concentrating certain forms of litigation in a single forum, or else out of social considerations for the protection of certain categories of persons, such as insured persons or buyers of goods on instalment credit terms.

In view of the Convention's structure and objectives, it was necessary to deal with this matter under the Convention. Failure to take account of the problem raised by these rules of jurisdiction might not only have caused recognition and enforcement to be refused in certain cases on grounds of public policy, which would be contrary to the principle of free movement of judgments, but also result, indirectly, in a general re-examination of the jurisdiction of the court of the State of origin.

[29] Several solutions were open to the Committee.　　**A1.127**

The first is found in many bilateral Conventions, and enables the court of the State in which recognition or enforcement is sought to refuse to recognize the jurisdiction of the court of the State or origin where, in the former State, there are "rules attributing exclusive jurisdiction to the courts of that State in the proceedings which led to the judgment."[1]

This system would have been unsatisfactory not only because it gives rise to the objections already set out above, but because it would have introduced into the Convention an element of insecurity incompatible with its basic principles. It is no solution to the problem, and only postpones the difficulties, deferring them until the recognition and enforcement stage.

Another possible solution would have been a general clause like that　**A1.128** contained in the Convention between Belgium and the Netherlands or the Benelux Treaty (Article 5(1)), which takes into consideration the internal law of the Contracting States.[2] Such a clause could however, lead to difficulties of interpretation, since the court of the State of origin must, where its jurisdiction is contested, apply the internal law of the State which claims to have exclusive jurisdiction.

Moreover, while such a solution might be acceptable in a Treaty between three States, it would be much more difficult to incorporate it in a Convention between six States where it is not always possible to determine in advance the State or States in which recognition or enforcement may be sought.

A third solution would have been to draw up a list of the individual jur-　**A1.129** isdictions which would be exclusive and which would thus be binding on all the Contracting States. Such a list would answer the need of the parties for information regarding the legal position, allow the court to give judgment on the basis of a definite common rule, remove any element of uncertainty and ensure a balance between the parties to contractual arrangements.

The considerations underlying the various provisions of the Convention are complex. Sections 3 and 4, for example, concerning insurance and instalment sales and loans, are dictated by social considerations and are aimed in particular at preventing abuses which could result from the terms of contracts in standard form.

Section 5 (Article 16) contains a list of situations in which the courts of a　**A1.130** Contracting State are acknowledged as having exclusive jurisdiction, since the proper administration of justice requires that actions should be brought before the courts of a single State.

---

[1] Convention between Germany and Belgium, Art. 3(2); Convention between Italy and the Netherlands (end of Art. 2); Convention between Italy and Belgium (end of Art. 2).

[2] Art. 5(1) of the Convention between Belgium and the Netherlands reads as follows: "Where a domicile conferring jurisdiction has been chosen in one of the two countries for the enforcement of an instrument, the courts for the place of

The Convention deals with the two categories differently. The first category has been placed in an intermediate position between the general rules of jurisdiction and the rules which are wholly exclusive.

A1.131   The following system adopted:

1. For matters falling within section 3 and 4 there is no single jurisdiction. A choice, albeit a limited one, exists between the courts of different Contracting States where the plaintiff is a protected person, that is, a policy-holder, a buyer or a borrower. In matters falling under exclusive jurisdictions pursuant to section 5, the parties have no choice between the courts of several Contracting States.
2. The parties may, in certain circumstances, derogate from the provisions of sections 3 and 4 (Articles 12, 15, and 18). The provisions of section 5 may not, however, be derogated from, either by an agreement conferring jurisdiction (second paragraph of Article 17) or by an implied submission to the jurisdiction (Article 18).
3. The rules in section 3 and 4 are applicable only where the defendant is domiciled in a Contracting State, whereas those in Section 5 apply regardless of domicile.

A1.132   However, contravention of the provisions of sections 3 and 4, as well as of those of section 5, constitutes a ground for refusing recognition and enforcement (Articles 28 and 34).

[30] Section 3

Jurisdiction in matters relating to insurance

A1.133   Rules of exclusive or special jurisdiction relating to insurance exist in France (Article 3 of the Law of 13 July 1930 concerning contracts of insurance), in Belgium (Law of 20 May 1920, added as Article 43 bis to the Law of 25 March 1876 on jurisdiction), in Germany (§ 48 of the Gesetz über den Versicherungsvertrag (Law on contracts of insurance)), and in Italy (Article 1903(2) of the Civil Code, Article 124 of the Consolidated Law on private insurance). In Luxembourg, the Law of 16 May 1891 on contracts of insurance does not include any provision on jurisdiction. This is due to the small size of the Grand Duchy, which comprises only two judicial arrondissements. However, the Law of 16 May 1891 concerning the supervision of insurance matters governs jurisdiction in regard to foreign insurance companies. This Law requires an insurer resident abroad who is transacting insurance business in the Grand Duchy to appoint a general representative domiciled in Luxembourg who will represent him there judicially and extrajudicially. This representative must give an address for service of process in the judicial arrondissement in which he is not domiciled. Either the domicile of the general representative or his address for service founds jurisdiction in respect of actions arising from contracts of insurance. In the Netherlands, there are no special provisions concerning

---

domicile chosen shall have exclusive jurisdiction over litigation relating to that instrument, save for exceptions and modifications enacted or to be enacted under the national law of one of the two States or by international agreement."

the jurisdiction of the courts in insurance matters. As regards foreign life-assurance companies, the Netherlands Law of 22 December 1922 recognizes rules analogous to those of the Luxembourg Law of 16 May 1891. The rules are approximately the same in Germany.

Section 3 was drawn up in cooperation with the European Insurance **A1.134** Committee.

The provisions of this section may be summarized as follows: in matters relating to insurance, actions against an insurer domiciled in a Contracting State may be brought in the following courts, *i.e.* either:

(i) In the courts of the State where he is domiciled (Article 8), or, subject to certain conditions, in the courts for the place where he has a branch (Articles 7 and 8); or

(ii) (a) in the courts for the place where the policy-holder is domiciled (Article 8);

(b) in the courts of the State where one of the insurers is domiciled, if two or more insurers are the defendants (Article 8);

(c) in the courts for the place where the agent who acted as intermediary in the making of the contract of insurance has his domicile, if there is provision for such jurisdiction under the law of the court seised of the matter (Article 8);

(d) 1. In respect of liability insurance, the insurer may in addition be sued:

(1) in the courts for the place where the harmful event occurred (Articles 9 and 10),

(2) as a third party, in the court seised of the action brought by the injured party against the insured if, under its own law, that court has jurisdiction in the third party proceedings (Article 10);

2. in respect of insurance of immovable property, the insurer may in addition be sued in the courts for the place where the harmful event occurred. The same applies if movable and immovable property are covered by the same insurance policy and both are adversely affected by the same contingency (Article 9).

Where an insurer is the plaintiff, he may in general bring an action only **A1.135** in the courts of the State in which the defendant is domiciled, irrespective of whether the latter is the policy-holder, the insured or a beneficiary.

Agreements conferring jurisdiction which depart from these rules have no legal force if they were entered into before the dispute arose (Article 12).

Article 7

Article 7 specifies that jurisdiction in matters relating to insurance is **A1.136** governed solely by section 3 of Title II.

Specific exceptions are made by the references to Articles 4 and 5(5), which concern respectively defendants domiciled outside the Community and disputes arising out of the operations of a branch, agency or other establishment.

It follows from the first of these exceptions that jurisdiction is determined by the law of the court seised of the matter, including the rules of exorbitant jurisdiction, where the defendant, whether he is the insurer or the policy-holder, is domiciled outside the Community. However, as an exception to the general rules of the Convention, an insurer domiciled outside the Community who has a branch or an agency in a **[31]** Contracting State is, in disputes relating to the operations of the branch or agency, deemed to be domiciled in that State. This exception, which is contained in the last paragraph of Article 8, was adopted because foreign insurance companies can establish branches or agencies in other States only by putting up guarantees which in practice place them in the same position as national companies. However, the exception applies only to branches or agencies, *i.e.* when the foreign company is represented by a person able to conclude contracts with third parties on behalf of the company.

The second exception again relates to branches or agencies, and also to other establishments, which, as appears from the reference back to Article 5(5), depend from a company whose seat is in a Contracting State. The result is that such a company may be sued in the courts for the place in which the branch, agency or establishment is situated, in all disputes arising out of their operations.

Article 8

A1.137   Article 8 lays down general rules of jurisdiction in proceedings instituted against an insurer in matters relating to insurance.

First, the courts of the State where the insurer is domiciled have jurisdiction. This provision determines only general jurisdiction, namely the jurisdiction of the courts of the State where the insurer is domiciled. Each State must then apply its internal law to determine which court has jurisdiction. However, if the insurer is sued outside the State in which he is domiciled, the proceedings must be instituted in a specifically determined court, in accordance with the principles already adopted in Article 5.

A1.138   Secondly, an action may be brought in a State other than that in which the insurer is domiciled, in the courts for the place where the policy-holder is domiciled. "Policy-holder" is to be taken to mean the other party to the contract of insurance. Where the insured or the beneficiary is not the same person as the policy-holder, their place of domicile is not taken into consideration. As was noted in particular by the European Insurance Committee, the insurer, as a supplier of services, enters into a business relationship with the other contracting party (the policy-holder). Because of their direct contact it is right and proper that the insurer can be sued in the courts for the place where the policy-holder is domiciled. But it would be unreasonable to expect the insurer to appear in the court of the insured or of a beneficiary, since he will not necessarily know their exact domicile at the time when the cause of action arises.

The domicile of the policy-holder which is relevant here is the domicile existing at the time when the proceedings are instituted.

Thirdly, if two or more insurers are defendants in the same action, they **A1.139** may be sued in the courts of the State where any one of them is domiciled. This provision is identical to that in Article 6(1), which does not apply here since the Section relating to insurance applies independently of the rest of the Convention.

Furthermore, an insurer may be sued in a State other than that in which **A1.140** he is domiciled, in the courts for the place where the agent who acted as intermediary in the making of the contract of insurance is domiciled, but subject to two conditions: first, that the domicile of the agent who acted as intermediary is mentioned in the insurance policy or proposal, and, secondly, that the law of the court seised of the matter recognizes this jurisdiction. It is not recognized in Belgium or in France, although it is in Germany[1] and in Italy (Article 1903 of the Civil Code). The reference to the insurance proposal takes account of the usual practice in Germany. Insurance companies there in general use data-processing systems, so that the place of the agency often appears in the policy only in the form of a number referring back to the insurance proposal. The insurance proposal, within the meaning of the Convention, means, of course, the final proposal which forms the basis of the contract.

The expression "the agent, who acted as intermediary in the making of the contract of insurance" includes both an agent through whom the contract was directly concluded between the company and the policy-holder, and also an agent who negotiated the contract to conclusion on behalf of the company. The significance [32] of the last paragraph of Article 8 is made clear in the commentary on Article 7.

Article 9

Article 9 allows an insurer to be sued in a State other than that in which **A1.141** he is domiciled in the courts for the place where the harmful event occurred, but without prejudice to the application of Article 12(3). This jurisdiction applies only in respect of liability insurance and insurance of immovable property. It extends to movable property in cases where a building and the movable property it contains are covered by the same insurance policy. This also applies if the movables are covered by an endorsement to the policy covering the immovable property.

Article 10

Article 10 contains rules of special jurisdiction for liability insurance **A1.142** cases. This provision is of particular importance in relation to road accidents.

Under the first paragraph of Article 10, in an action brought by the

---

[1] § 48 of the Gesetz über den Versicherungsvertrag:
   "1. If an insurance agent has acted as intermediary in the making of the contract, or has concluded the contract, then in actions against the insurer arising out of the insurance contract the court for the place where, at the time when the

injured party against the insured, the latter may join the insurer as a third party if the court seised of the matter has jurisdiction in such a case under its own law. This is not possible in the Federal Republic of Germany.[1]

A1.143   The problem arose whether consolidation of the two actions should be allowed even where the insurer and the insured are both domiciled in the same State, which, it must be assumed for the purposes of this argument, is different from the State of the court seised of the matter. For example, where an accident is caused in France by a German domiciled in Germany who is insured with a German company, should third party proceedings, which are recognized under French law, be possible even though the litigation concerns a contract of insurance between a German insured person and a German insurer? As it is subject to German law, should this contract not be litigated in a German court? The contractual relationship between the insurer and the policy-holder would then fall outside the scope of the proceedings relating to personal liability.

While acknowledging the relevance of this question, the Committee was of the opinion that it would be unwise to introduce rules of jurisdiction which would depart from national laws and which could also jeopardize the system in force following the introduction of the green card.[2]

A1.144   The compromise solution adopted by the Committee is to reduce the scope of the first paragraph of Article 10 by inserting, under Article 12(3), a provision that, if the policy-holder and the insurer are both domiciled in the same Contracting State, when the contract is concluded, they may agree to confer jurisdiction on the courts of that State. Such an agreement must not, however, be contrary to the law of that State.

A1.145   Under the second paragraph of Article 10 the insurer may also, in respect of liability insurance, be sued directly by the injured party[3] outside the State in which he is domiciled in any court which, under Articles 7 to 9, has jurisdiction over actions brought by the policy-holder against the insurer.

Where, however, under the first paragraph of Article 8, the court for the place where the policy-holder is domiciled has jurisdiction, there is no provision giving jurisdiction to the court for the place where the injured party

---

contract was negotiated through the agent or concluded, the agent had his agency or, in the absence of an agency, has domicile, shall have jurisdiction.
2. The jurisdiction defined in para. 1 may not be excluded by agreement."
[1] See Art. V of the Protocol.
[2] Insurance against civil liability in respect of motor vehicles is compulsory in all Community countries except Italy.
Belgium: Law of 1 July 1956.
France: Law of 27 February 1958, Decree of 7 January 1959.
Germany: Law of 7 November 1939.
Luxembourg: Law of 10 June 1932, Implementing Regulations of 28 October 1932 and 24 December 1932.
Netherlands: Law of 30 May 1963, Decree of 23 June 1964.
[3] Direct actions are recognized under Belgian, French and Luxembourg law. Under German and Netherlands law they are recognized only with regard to compulsory insurance against civil liability in respect of motor vehicles.

is domiciled. The phrase "where such direct actions are permitted" has been used specifically to include the conflict of laws rules of the court seised of the matter.[4]

Under the last paragraph of Article 10, the insurer may join the policy-holder or the insured as parties to the action brought against him by the injured party. In the interests of the proper administration of justice, it must be possible for the actions to be brought in the same court in order to prevent different courts from giving judgments which are irreconcilable. This procedure will in addition protect the insurer against fraud.[5] **A1.146**

[33] *Article 11*

Article 11 relates to actions brought by the insurer against the policy-holder, the insured or a beneficiary. **A1.147**

The courts of the State in which the defendant is domiciled when the proceedings are instituted have exclusive jurisdiction.

Again, this is a provision dealing with international jurisdiction; local jurisdiction within each State will be determined by the internal law of that State.

Article 11 does not apply where the defendant is domiciled outside a Contracting State, that is to say, outside the Community. In such cases Article 4 applies.

The second paragraph corresponds to the provisions of Article 6(3).

Article 12

Article 12 relates to agreements conferring jurisdiction. Agreements concluded before a dispute arises will have no legal force if they are contrary to the rules of jurisdiction laid down in the Convention. **A1.148**

The purpose of this Article is to prevent the parties from limiting the choice offered by this Convention to the policy-holder, and to prevent the insurer from avoiding the restrictions imposed under Article 11.

A number of exceptions are, however, permitted. After a dispute has arisen, that is to say "as soon as the parties disagree on a specific point and legal proceedings are imminent or contemplated,"[1] the parties completely regain their freedom.

Certain agreements conferring jurisdiction which were concluded before the dispute arose are also permissible. First, there are those made to the advantage of the policy-holder, the insured or a beneficiary, which **A1.149**

---

[4] The rules of conflict must be used to decide whether the law to be applied is the law of the place where the harmful event occurred, the law governing the contract of insurance or the *lex fori*.

[5] J. WAUTIER, L'assurance automobile obligatoire, Brussels 1947.

[1] BRAAS, Précis de procédure civile, Vol. I, No. 795.

allow them to bring proceedings in courts other than those specified in the preceding Articles.

Certain other agreements conferring jurisdiction are allowed under Article 12(3), but only in the strictly defined circumstances therein specified which have been explained in the commentary on Article 10.

Section 4

Jurisdiction in matters relating to instalment sales and loans

A1.150 This section relates to the sale of goods where the price is payable in a series of instalments, and to the sale of goods where the sale is contractually linked to a loan (Abzahlungsgeschäfte). The rules here adopted are similar to those applicable in the national law of several of the Member States and, like them, stem from a desire to protect certain categories of persons. Article 13 provides that this section applies independently of the rest of the Convention and, like Article 7, without prejudice to the provisions of Articles 4 and 5(5).

A1.151 *Article 14* determines the rules of jurisdiction.

In actions against a seller or a lender, proceedings may be instituted by the buyer or borrower either in the courts of the State in which the defendant is domiciled, or in the courts of the State in which the buyer or borrower is domiciled.

Actions by a seller or a lender may in general be brought only in the courts for the place where the buyer or borrower is domiciled when the proceedings are instituted.

The third paragraph, relating to counterclaims, corresponds to Article 6(3).

A1.152 Article 15, which relates to agreements conferring jurisdiction, contains under (3) a provision analogous to that of Article 12(3), but for different reasons. In actions brought by a seller or a lender, it is rather difficult to determine jurisdiction where the buyer or borrower establishes himself abroad after the contract has been concluded. To protect these persons, they should ideally be sued only in the courts of the State where they have established their new domicile. For reasons of equity the Committee has however provided that where a seller and a buyer, or a lender and a borrower, are both domiciled or at least habitually resident in the same State when the contract is concluded, they may confer on the courts of that State jurisdiction over all disputes arising out of the contract, on condition that such agreements are not contrary to the law of that State.

The criterion of habitual residence allows agreements conferring jurisdiction to be concluded even where a buyer or borrower remains domiciled in a Contracting [34] State other than that in which he is resident. It follows, for example, that a seller or lender need not sue the defendant abroad in the courts of the State in which the defendant is domiciled, if, when the proceedings are instituted, the defendant is still resident in the State in which the contract was concluded.

Section 5

Exclusive jurisdiction

Article 16

Article 16 lists the circumstances in which the six States recognize that **A1.153** the courts of one of them have exclusive jurisdiction. The matters referred to in this Article will normally be the subject of exclusive jurisdiction only if they constitute the principal subject-matter of the proceedings of which the court is to be seised.

The provisions of Article 16 on jurisdiction may not be departed from either by an agreement purporting to confer jurisdiction on the courts of another Contracting State, or by an implied submission to the jurisdiction (Articles 17 and 18). Any court of a State other than the State whose courts have exclusive jurisdiction must declare of its own motion that it has no jurisdiction (Article 19). Failure to observe these rules constitutes a ground for refusal of recognition or enforcement (Articles 28 and 34).

These rules, which take as their criterion the subject-matter of the action, are applicable regardless of the domicile or nationality of the parties. In view of the reasons for laying down rules of exclusive jurisdiction, it was necessary to provide for their general application, even in respect of defendants domiciled outside the Community. Thus, for example, a Belgian court will not, on the basis of Article 53 of the Law of 1876 or of Article 637 of the draft Judicial Code, which in actions against foreigners recognize the jurisdiction of the courts of the plaintiff, have jurisdiction in proceedings between a Belgian and a person domiciled, for example, in Argentina, if the proceedings concern immovable property situated in Germany. Only the German courts will have jurisdiction.

Immovable property

Under Article 16(1), only the courts of the Contracting State in which **A1.154** the immovable property is situated have jurisdiction in proceedings concerning rights *in rem* in, or tenancies of, immovable property.

The importance of matters relating to immovable property had already been taken into consideration by the authors of the Treaty of Rome since, under Article 54(3)(c) of that Treaty, the Commission and the Council must enable "a national of one Member State to acquire and use land and buildings situated in the territory of another Member State," in so far as this does not conflict with the principles laid down in Article 39(2) relating to agricultural policy.

The problems which the Committee faced in this connection did not in fact relate to the recognition and enforcement of judgments, since these questions are governed by the provisions of the conventions already concluded between Member States, all of which apply in civil and commercial matters, including immovable property, but rather to the choice of rules of jurisdiction.

The laws of all the Member States include in this respect special rules of jurisdiction[1] which, generally speaking, have been incorporated in the bilateral conventions, whether they are based on direct[2] or indirect[3] jurisdiction.

A1.155   However, the rules laid down in the Convention differ from those in the bilateral agreements in that the Convention lays down rules of exclusive jurisdiction. The Convention follows in this respect the Treaty between France and Germany settling the question of the Saar, Article 49 of which provides that the courts "of the country in which the immovable property is situated shall have exclusive jurisdiction in all disputes regarding the possession or ownership of such property and in all disputes regarding rights *in rem* in such property."

As in that Treaty, the exclusive jurisdiction established by Article 16(1) applies only in international relations; the internal rules of jurisdiction in force in each of the States are thus not affected.

In other words, the Convention prohibits the courts of one Contracting State from assuming jurisdiction in [35] disputes relating to immovable property situated in another Contracting State; it does not, in the State in which the immovable property is situated, prevent courts other than that for the place where the property is situated from having jurisdiction in such disputes if the jurisdiction of those other courts is recognized by the law of that State.

A1.156   A number of considerations led the Committee to provide a rule of exclusive jurisdiction in this matter. In the Federal Republic of Germany and in Italy, the court for the place where the immovable property is situated has exclusive jurisdiction, this being considered a matter of public policy. It follows that, in the absence of a rule of exclusive jurisdiction, judgments given in other States by courts whose jurisdiction might have been derived from other provisions of the Convention (the court of the defendant's domicile, or an agreed forum) could have been neither recognized nor enforced in Germany or Italy.

Such a system would have been contrary to the principle of "free movement of judgments."

A1.157   The Committee was all the more inclined to extend to international relations the rules of jurisdiction in force in the Federal Republic of Germany and in Italy, since it considered that to do so was in the interests of the proper administration of justice. This type of dispute often entails checks, enquiries and expert examinations which have to be made on the spot. Moreover, the matter is often governed in part by customary practices

---

[1] Belgium: Art. 8 of the Law of 25 March 1876, amended by the Arrêté royal of 3 January 1935; Art. 52 of the Law of 1876; Federal Republic of Germany, Art. 24 of the Code of Civil Procedure; France, Art. 59(5) of the Code of Civil Procedure; Italy, Arts. 4 and 21 of the Code of Civil Procedure; Luxembourg, Art. 59(3) and (4) of the Code of Civil Procedure; Netherlands, Art. 126(8) of the Code of Civil Procedure.

[2] Convention between Belgium and the Netherlands (Art. 10).

[3] Conventions between Germany and Belgium (Art. 10); between France and Italy (Art. 16); between Italy and the Netherlands (Art. 2(6)); between Germany and Italy (Art. 2(7)); between Belgium and Italy (Art. 2(8)); and between Germany and the Netherlands (Art. 4(1)(f)).

which are not generally known except in the courts of the place, or possibly of the country, where the immovable property is situated. Finally, the system adopted also takes into account the need to make entries in land registers located where the property is situated.

The wording adopted covers not only all disputes concerning rights *in rem* in immovable property, but also those relating to tenancies of such property. This will include tenancies of dwellings and of premises for professional or commercial use, and agricultural holdings. In providing for the courts of the State in which the property is situated to have jurisdiction as regards tenancies in immovable property, the Committee intended to cover disputes between landlord and tenant over the existence or interpretation of tenancy agreements, compensation for damage caused by the tenant, eviction, etc. The rule was not intended by the Committee to apply to proceedings concerned only with the recovery of rent, since such proceedings can be considered to relate to a subject-matter which is quite distinct from the rented property itself.

The adoption of this provision was dictated by the fact that tenancies of immovable property are usually governed by special legislation which, in view of its complexity, should preferably be applied only by the courts of the country in which it is in force. Moreover, several States provide for exclusive jurisdiciton in such proceedings, which is usually conferred on special tribunals.

Companies and associations of natural or legal persons

Article 16(2) provides that the courts of the State in which a company or **A1.158** other legal person, or an association of natural or legal persons, has its seat, have exclusive jurisdiction in proceedings which are in substance concerned either with the validity of the constitution, the nullity or the dissolution of the company, legal person or association, or with the decisions of its organs.

It is important, in the interests of legal certainty, to avoid conflicting judgments being given as regards the existence of a company or association or as regards the validity of the decisions of its organs. For this reason, it is obviously preferable that all proceedings should take place in the courts of the State in which the company or association has its seat. It is in that State that information about the company or association will have been notified and made public. Moreover, the rule adopted will more often than not result in the application of the traditional maxim *"actor sequitur forum rei."* Such jurisdiction is recognized in particular in German law and, as regards non-profit making organizations, in Luxembourg law.

Public registers

Article 16(3) lays down that the courts of the State in which a public **A1.159** register is kept have exclusive jurisdiction in proceedings relating to the validity or effects of entries in that register.

This provision does not require a lengthy commentary. It corresponds to the provisions which appear in the internal laws of most of the Contracting States; it covers in particular entries in land registers, land charges registers and commercial registers.

[36] *Patents*

A1.160   Article 16(4) applies to proceedings concerned with the registration or validity of patents, trade marks, designs or other similar rights, such as those which protect fruit and vegetable varieties, and which are required to be deposited or registered.

A draft convention has been drawn up by the EEC countries relating to patent law. The draft includes rules of jurisdiction for the Community patent, but it will not apply to national patents, which thus fall within the scope of the Judgments Convention.

Since the grant of a national patent is an exercise of national sovereignty, Article 16(4) of the Judgments Convention provides for exclusive jurisdiction in proceedings concerned with the validity of patents.

Other actions, including those for infringement of patents, are governed by the general rules of the Convention.

A1.161   The expression "the deposit or registration has been applied for" takes into account internal laws which, like German law, make the grant of a patent subject to the results of an examination. Thus, for example, German courts will have exclusive jurisdiction in the case of an application to the competent authorities for a patent to be granted where, during the examination of the application, a dispute arises over the rights relating to the grant of that patent.

The phrase "is under the terms of an international convention deemed to have taken place" refers to the system introduced by the Madrid Agreement of 14 April 1891 concerning international registration of trade marks, revised at Brussels on 14 December 1900, at Washington on 2 June 1911, at The Hague on 6 November 1925 and at London on 2 June 1934, and also to the Hague Arrangement of 6 November 1925 for the international registration of industrial designs, revised at London on 2 June 1934. Under this system, the deposit of a trade mark, design or model at the International Office in Berne through the registry of the country of origin has the same effect in the other Contracting States as if that trade mark, design or model had been directly registered there. Thus where a trade mark is deposited at the International Office at the request of the German authorities, the French courts will have exclusive jurisdiction in disputes relating, for example, to whether the mark should be deemed to have been registered in France.

Enforcement of judgments

A1.162   Article 16(5) provides that the courts of the State in which a judgment has been or is to be enforced have exclusive jurisdiction in proceedings concerned with the enforcement of that judgment.

What meaning is to be given to the expression "proceedings concerned with the enforcement of judgments"?

It means those proceedings which can arise from "recourse to force, constraint or distraint on movable or immovable property in order to

1606

ensure the effective implementation of judgments and authentic instruments."[1]

Problems arising out of such proceedings come within the exclusive jurisdiction of the courts for the place of enforcement.

Provisions of this kind appear in the internal law of many Member States.[2]

Section 6

Prorogation of jurisdiction

This section includes Article 17, on jurisdiction by consent, and Article 18, which concerns jurisdiction implied from submission. **A1.163**

Article 17

Jurisdiction deriving from agreements conferring jurisdiction is already a feature of all the Conventions concluded between Member States of the Community, whether the rules of jurisdiction are direct or indirect: see the Convention between France and Belgium (Article 3), and between Belgium and the Netherlands (Article 5); the Benelux Treaty (Article 5); the [37] Convention between France and Italy (Article 12), between Germany and Italy (Article 2(2)), between Italy and the Netherlands (Article 2(2)), between Italy and Belgium (Article 2(1)(2)), between Germany and Belgium (Article 3(2)), and between Germany and the Netherlands (Article 4(1)(b)). **A1.164**

This jurisdiction is also the subject of international conventions, namely the Hague Convention of 15 April 1958 on the jurisdiction of the contractual forum in matters relating to the international sale of goods, and the Hague Convention of 25 November 1965 on the choice of court.[1]

It is unnecessary to stress the importance of this jurisdiction, particularly in commercial relations.

However, although agreement was readily reached on the basic principle of including such a jurisdiction in the Convention, the Committee spent much time in drafting Article 17. **A1.165**

Like the draftsmen of the Convention between Germany and Belgium, the report of which may usefully be quoted, the Committee's first concern was "not to impede commercial practice, yet at the same time to cancel out the effects of clauses in contracts which might go unread. Such clauses will therefore be taken into consideration only if they are the subject of an

---

[1] BRAAS, Précis de procédure civile, Vol. I, No. 808.

[2] See LEREBOURS-PIGEONNIÉRE, Droit international privé, seventh edition, p. 9; LOUSSOUARN, No. 411: "French courts have exclusive jurisdiction over measures for enforcement which are to take place in France (preventive measures, distress levied on a tenant's chattels, writs of attachment and applications for enforcement of a foreign judgment); over distraint levied on immovable or movable property, and over proceedings concerned with the validity of measures for enforcement."

[1] By September 1, 1966 neither of these Conventions had entered into force.

agreement, and this implies the consent of all the parties. Thus, clauses in printed forms for business correspondence or in invoices will have no legal force if they are not agreed to by the party against whom they operate."

A1.166   The Committee was further of the opinion that, in order to ensure legal certainty, the formal requirements applicable to agreements conferring jurisdiction should be expressly prescribed, but that "excessive formality which is incompatible with commercial practice"[2] should be avoided.

In this respect, the version adopted is similar to that of the Convention between Germany and Belgium, which was itself based on the rules of the Hague Convention of 15 April 1958, in that a clause conferring jurisdiction is valid only if it is in writing, or if at least one of the parties has confirmed in writing an oral agreement.[3]

Since there must be true agreement between the parties to confer jurisdiction, the court cannot necessarily deduce from a document in writing adduced by the party seeking to rely on it that there was an oral agreement. The special position of the Grand Duchy of Luxembourg in this matter necessitated an additional restriction which is contained in the second paragraph of Article I of the Protocol.

The question of how much weight is to be attached to the written document was left open by the Committee. In certain countries, a document in writing will be required only as evidence of the existence of the agreement; in others, however, it will go to the validity of the agreement.

A1.167   Like the Conventions between Belgium and the Netherlands and between France and Belgium, and also the Benelux Treaty and the Hague Convention, the first paragraph of Article 17 provides that the court agreed on by the parties shall have exclusive jurisdiction. This solution is essential to avoid different courts from being properly seised of the matter and giving conflicting or at least differing judgments. In order to meet practical realities, the first paragraph of Article 17 also covers specifically cases of agreement that a particular court in a Contracting State or the courts of a Contracting State are to have jurisdiction, and is similar in this to the 1958 Hague Convention. As Professor Batiffol pointed out in his report on that Convention, an agreement conferring jurisdiction generally on the courts of a Contracting State "may have no legal effect if, in the absence of any connecting factor between the contractual situation and the State whose courts have been agreed on as having jurisdiction, the law of that State provides no way of determining which court can or should be seised of the matter."[4] But as Batiffol remarks, this is a matter which the parties should consider at the appropriate time.

A1.168   The first paragraph of Article 17 applies only if at least one of the parties is domiciled in a Contracting State. It does not apply where two parties

---

[2] Hague Conference on private international law, documents of the eighth session. FRÉDERICQ, Report on the work of the Second Committee, p. 303.

[3] Hague Conference on private international law, Final Act of the tenth session. Convention on the choice of court, Art. 4.

[4] Hague Conference on private international law, documents of the eighth session, p. 305.

who are domiciled in the same Contracting State have agreed that a court of that State shall have jurisdiction, since the Convention, **[38]** under the general principle laid down in the preamble, determines only the international jurisdiction of courts (see Commentary, Chapter III, section 1, International legal relationships).

Article 17 applies where the agreement conferring jurisdiction was made either between a person domiciled in one Contracting State and a person domiciled in another Contracting State, or between a person domiciled in a Contracting State and a person domiciled outside the Community, if the agreement confers jurisdiction on the courts of a Contracting State; it also applies where two persons domiciled in one Contracting State agree that a particular court of another Contracting State shall have jurisdiction.

The second paragraph of Article 17 provides that agreements conferring **A1.169** jurisdiction shall have no legal force if they are contrary to the provisions of Article 12 (insurance) or Article 15 (instalment sales), or if the courts whose jurisdiction they purport to exclude have exclusive jurisdiction by virtue of Article 16.

The intention behind the Convention is to obviate cases of refusal of recognition and enforcement on the basis of Articles 28 and 34, and so, as already stated, to promote the free movement of judgments.

The third paragraph of Article 17 provides that if the agreement confer- **A1.170** ring jurisdiction was concluded for the benefit of only one of the contracting parties, that party shall retain the right to bring proceedings in any other court which has jurisdiction.[1] Agreements conferring jurisdiction cannot of course affect the substantive jurisdiction of the courts.

Article 18

Article 18 governs jurisdiction implied from submission. If a defendant **A1.171** domiciled in a Contracting State is sued in a court of another Contracting State which does not have jurisdiction under the Convention, two situations may arise: the defendant may either, as he is entitled to do, plead that the court has no jurisdiction under the Convention, in which case the court must declare that it does not have jurisdiction; or he may elect not to raise this plea, and enter an appearance. In the latter case, the court will have jurisdiction.

Unlike the case of conventions based on indirect jurisdiction, the defendant may, by virtue of the Convention, rely on its provisions in the court seised of the proceedings and plead lack of jurisdiction. It will be necessary to refer to the rules of procedure in force in the State of the court seised of the proceedings in order to determine the point in time up to which the defendant will be allowed to raise this plea, and to determine the legal meaning of the term "appearance."

Moreover, by conferring jurisdiction on a court in circumstances where the defendant does not contest that court's jurisdiction, the Convention

---

[1] See also the Conventions between France and Belgium, Art. 3, between France and Italy, Art. 2, and between Belgium and the Netherlands, Art. 5 and the Benelux Treaty, Art. 5.

extends the scope of Title II and avoids any uncertainty. The main consequence of this rule is that if a defendant domiciled in a Contracting State is, notwithstanding the provisions of the second paragraph of Article 3, sued in another Contracting State on the basis of a rule of exorbitant jurisdiction, for example in France on the basis of Article 14 of the Civil Code, the court will have jurisdiction if this is not contested. The only cases in which a court must declare that it has no jurisdiction and where jurisdiction by submission will not be allowed are those in which the courts of another State have exclusive jurisdiction by virtue of Article 16.

Section 7

Examination as to jurisdiction and admissibility

Article 19

A1.172   As has already been stated (page 8), a court must of its own motion examine whether it has jurisdiction. Article 19 emphasizes that the court must of its own motion declare that it has no jurisdiction if it is seised of a matter in which the courts of another Contracting State have exclusive jurisdiction by virtue of Article 16.

This rule is essential since the exclusive jurisdictions are conceived to be matters of public policy which cannot be departed from by the free choice of the parties. Moreover, it corresponds to Article 171 of the French Code of Civil Procedure, by virtue of which territorial jurisdiction is automatically examined where the parties are not permitted to reach a settlement.[2]

If this Article deserves particular attention, it is mainly because, in order that the general rules of jurisdiction [39] are observed, it grants wide powers to the court seised of the proceedings, since that court will of its own motion have to examine whether it has jurisdiction.

The words "principally concerned" have the effect that the court is not obliged to declare of its own motion that it has no jurisdiction if an issue which comes within the exclusive jurisdiction of another court is raised only as a preliminary or incidental matter.

Article 20

A1.173   Article 20 is one of the most important Articles in the Convention: it applies where the defendant does not enter an appearance; here the court must of its own motion examine whether it has jurisdiction under the Convention. If it finds no basis for jurisdiction, the court must declare that it has no jurisdiction. It is obvious that the court is under the same obli-

---

[2] The same is true in the Federal Republic of Germany: see ROSENBERG, *op. cit.* para. 38(I)(3).

gation even where there is no basis for exclusive jurisdiction. Failure on
the part of the defendant to enter an appearance is not equivalent to a submission to the jurisdiction. It is not sufficient for the court to accept the
submissions of the plaintiff as regards jurisdiction; the court must itself
ensure that the plaintiff proves that it has international jurisdiction.[1]

The object of this provision is to ensure that in cases of failure to enter
an appearance the court giving judgment does so only if it has jurisdiction,
and so to safeguard the defendant as fully as possible in the original proceedings. The rule adopted is derived from Article 37(2) of the Italian
Code of Civil Procedure, by virtue of which the court must of its own
motion examine whether it has jurisdiction where the defendant is a
foreigner and does not enter an appearance.

The second paragraph of Article 20 is also designed to safeguard the **A1.174**
rights of the defendant, by recognizing the international importance of the
service of judicial documents. The service of judicial documents abroad,
although governed differently in each of the Member States, can broadly
be separated into two main systems. The German system is based on the
cooperation of the public authorities of the place of residence of the
addressee which have jurisdiction to deliver to him a copy of the instrument. A German court cannot in general give judgment in default of
appearance unless it receives conclusive evidence that the instrument has
been delivered to the addressee.[2,3] The system contrasts with those in
force in Belgium, France, Italy, Luxembourg and the Netherlands,[4] all of
which are characterized by the "desire to localize in the territory of the
State of the forum all the formalities connected with the judicial document
whose addressee resides abroad."[5]

Under the laws of these countries, service is properly effected, and
causes time to begin to run, without there being any need to establish that
the document instituting the proceedings has actually been served on its
addressee. It is not impossible in these circumstances that, in some cases, a
defendant may have judgment entered against him in default of appearance without having any knowledge of the action.

The Hague Convention of 1 March 1954 on civil procedure, to which
the six Member States are party, does not solve the difficulties which arise
under such legislation.

---

[1] BÜLOW, *op. cit.*

[2] RIGAUX, La signification des actes judiciaires à l'étranger. Revue critique de
droit international privé, p. 448 *et seq.*

[3] See German Code of Civil Procedure, Art. 335(1)(2) and Art. 202.

[4] Belgium: Code of Civil Procedure, Art. 69bis, and Judgment of the Cour de cas-
sation of 4 March 1954. Revue des huissiers de Belgique, May-June 1954, p. 15.
France: Code of Civil Procedure, Art. 69(10), as interpreted by the French Cour
de cassation. See Revue critique de droit international privé, No. 1, January-
March 1961, p. 174 *et seq.*
Italy: Code of Civil Procedure, Arts. 142 and 143.
Luxembourg: Arrêté-loi of 1 April 1814.
Netherlands: Code of Civil Procedure, Art. 4(8).

[5] RIGAUX, id., p. 454.

A1.175   The Committee also tried to solve the problems arising when service is effected late, bearing in mind that the aim of the Convention is to promote, so far as possible, the free movement of judgments.

The search of a solution was obviously helped by the drafting at the tenth session of the Hague Conference on private international law of the Convention on the service abroad of judicial and extrajudicial documents in civil or commercial matters, which was opened for signature on 15 November 1965. This is the reason why the solution adopted in the second paragraph of Article 20 is only transitional.

This provision summarizes Article 15 of the Hague Convention, which is in fact derived from Article 20 of this present Convention, since the work of the Committee served as a basis for discussion at the meetings of the Special Commission which was established by the Hague Conference and which drew up the preliminary draft which was submitted for discussion at the tenth session.

[40] Under the second paragraph of Article 20, where a defendant domiciled in one Contracting State is sued in the courts of another State and does not enter an appearance, the court must stay the proceedings so long as it is not shown that the defendant has been able to received the document instituting the proceedings in sufficient time to enable him to arrange for his defence, or that all necessary steps have been taken to this end.

This provision is based on the old Article 8 of the Netherlands Law of 12 June 1909, Stb No. 141.[1]

A1.176   The second paragraph of Article 20 requires first that notification of the proceedngs has been given to the party who has not entered an appearance, that is either to him in person or at his domicile, and secondly that it has been delivered in sufficient time to enable the defendant to arrange for his defence. It does not require that the defendant should actually have been notified in sufficient time. The defendant must be responsible for any delay caused by his own negligence or by that of his relations or servants. The critical time is thus the time at which service was properly effected, and not the time at which the defendant received actual knowledge of the institution of proceedings.

The question of "sufficient time" is obviously a question of fact for the discretion of the court seised of the matter.

A1.177   The court may give judgment in default against a defendant if it is shown that "all necessary steps have been taken" for him actually to have received in sufficient time the document instituting the proceedings.

This means that a court will be able to give judgment in default against a defendant even if no affidavit can be produced to confirm service on the defendant of the document instituting the proceedings, provided it is shown that all the necessary approaches have been made to the competent authorities of the State in which the defendant is domiciled in order to

---

[1] This Art. reads as follows: "Where the defendant does not enter an appearance, the court may not give judgment in default if the plaintiff does not show that the defendant received the writ of summons. The plaintiff may ask for a new date to be fixed for the hearing."

reach him in sufficient time. Where necessary, it must also be shown that "all the investigations required by good conscience and good faith have been undertaken to discover the defendant."[2]

As already stated, the second paragraph of Article 20 is only a transitional provision. Under the third paragraph of that Article, where the State of the forum and the State in which the document had to be transmitted have both ratified the new Hague Convention, the court seised of the matter will no longer apply the second paragraph of Article 20 but will be exclusively bound by Article 15 of the Hague Convention. Thus any possibility of conflict between Article 15 of the Hague Convention and the second paragraph of Article 20 of the EEC Judgments Convention is resolved in favour of the Hague Convention. **A1.178**

The Committee also considered it important to ensure certainty and speed in the transmission of judicial documents. In order to achieve this, it considered as a possible solution the transmission of such documents by registered post. However, it did not adopt this system for, although it meets the requirement of speed, it does not offer all the necessary safeguards from the point of view of certainty. In the end the Committee adopted the system which is set out in Article IV of the Protocol.

This Article simply adds a new method of transmission to those already provided for by the Hague Convention of 1 March 1954 on civil procedure, or by the agreements concluded between the Contracting States in application of that Convention. It corresponds, moreover, to the facility provided for by Article 10(b) of the new Hague Convention. **A1.179**

Under the system adopted in the Protocol, documents can be transmitted by public officers in one Contracting State directly to their colleagues in another Contracting State, who will deliver them to the addressee in person or to his domicile.

According to the assurances which were given to the Committee by a representative of the "Union internationale des huissiers de justice et d'officiers judiciaires," it will be easy for a public officer in one country to correspond with the appropriate public officer in another country. In case of difficulty it would moreover be possible for the officer in the State in which judgment was given to invoke the assistance of the national associations of public officers, or of the central office of the "Union" which has its headquarters in Paris.

[41] In the opinion of the Committee these arrangements meet the requirements of speed and certainty. Direct communication between public officers allows a considerable gain in time by avoiding any recourse to intermediary bodies such as Ministries for Foreign Affairs, Ministries of Justice or prosecutors' offices.

Certainty is further guaranteed since if, for example, the address is incomplete or inaccurate, the officer in the State in which service is to be effected may well be able to undertake investigations in order to find the addressee.

---

[2] Cour d'appel de POITIERS, 9.7.1959 (Gazette du Palais, 1959.II.183); cf. GAVALDA, Revue critique de droit international privé, 1960, No. 1, p. 174.

As for the linguistic difficulties which could arise in the context of a grouping of the six countries, these could be overcome by attaching to the instrument a summary in the language of the addressee.

Like Article 10(b) of the Hague Convention, Article IV of the Protocol allows a Contracting State to object to this method of transmission.

Section 8

Lis pendens—related actions

Article 21

A1.180   As there may be several concurrent international jurisdictions, and the courts of different States may properly be seised of a matter (see in particular Articles 2 and 5), it appeared to be necessary to regulate the question of *lis pendens*. By virtue of Article 21, the courts of a Contracting State must decline jurisdiction, if necessary of their own motion, where proceedings involving the same cause of action and between the same parties are already pending in a court of another State. In cases of *lis pendens* the court is therefore obliged to decline jurisdiction, either on the application of one of the parties, or of its own motion, since this will facilitate the proper administration of justice within the Community. A court will not always have to examine of its own motion whether the same proceedings are pending in the courts of another country, but only when the circumstances are such as to lead the court to believe that this may be the case.

Instead of declining jurisdiction, the court which is subsequently seised of a matter may, however, stay its proceedings if the jurisdiction of the court first seised is contested. This rule was introduced so that the parties would not have to institute new proceedings if, for example, the court first seised of the matter were to decline jurisdiction. The risk of unnecessary disclaimers of jurisdiction is thereby avoided.

Jurisdiction is declined in favour of the court first seised of the matter. The Committee decided that there was no need to specify in the text the point in time from which the proceedings should be considered to be pending, and left this question to be settled by the internal law of each Contracting State.

Article 22

A1.181   The solution offered by this Article to the problem of related actions differs in several respects from that adopted to regulate the question of *lis pendens*, although it also serves to avoid the risk of conflicting judgments and thus to facilitate the proper administration of justice in the Community.

Where actions are related, the first duty of the court is to stay its proceedings. The proceedings must, however, be pending at the same level of adjudication, for otherwise the object of the proceedings would be different and one of the parties might be deprived of a step in the hierarchy of the courts.

Furthermore, to avoid disclaimers of jurisdiction, the court may decline **A1.182** jurisdiction only if it appears that the court first seised has jurisdiction over both actions, that is to say, in addition, only if that court has not jurisdiction over the second action. The court may decline jurisdiction only on the application of one of the parties, and only if the law of the court first seised permits the consolidation of related actions which are pending in different courts. This last condition takes into account the specific problems of German and Italian law. In German law, consolidation is in general permitted only if both actions are pending in the same court. In Italian law, the constitution does not permit a court to decide whether it will hear an action itself or refer it to another court. It will, however, always be possible for a German or Italian court which is subsequently seised of a matter to stay its proceedings.

[42] Finally, since the expression "related actions" does not have the **A1.183** same meaning in all the Member States, the third paragraph of Article 22 provides a definition. This is based on the new Belgian Judicial Code (Article 30).

The Convention does not regulate the procedure for the consolidation of related actions. This is a question which is left to the internal laws of the individual States.

Article 23

This Article deals with a situation which will occur only very rarely, **A1.184** namely where an action comes within the exclusive jurisdiction of several courts. To avoid conflicts of jurisdiction, any court other than the court first seised of the action is required under Article 21 or Article 22 to decline jurisdiction in favour of that court.

Section 9

Provisional and protective measures

Article 24

Article 24 provides that application may be made to the courts of a Con- **A1.185** tracting State for such provisional measures, including protective measures, as may be available under the internal law of that State, irrespective of which court has jurisdiction as to the substance of the case. A corresponding provision will be found in nearly all the enforcement conventions.[1]

In each State, application may therefore be made to the competent courts for provisional or protective measures to be imposed or suspended, or for rulings on the validity of such measures, without regard to the rules of jurisdiction laid down in the Convention.

---

[1] Benelux Treaty and Convention between Belgium and the Netherlands (Art. 8); Convention between Germany and Belgium (Art. 15(2)); between France and Belgium (Art. 9); between Italy and Belgium (Art. 14); between Italy and the Netherlands (Art. 10); between France and Italy (Art. 32); and between Germany and the Netherlands (Art. 18(2)).

As regards the measures which may be taken, reference should be made to the internal law of the country concerned.

CHAPTER V

RECOGNITION AND ENFORCEMENT

A. GENERAL CONSIDERATIONS

A1.186 As a result of the safeguards granted to the defendant in the original proceedings, Title III of the Convention is very liberal on the question of recognition and enforcement. As already stated, it seeks to facilitate as far as possible the free movement of judgments, and should be interpreted in this spirit. This liberal approach is evidenced in Title III first by a reduction in the number of grounds which can operate to prevent the recognition and enforcement of judgments and, secondly, by the simplification of the enforcement procedure which will be common to the six countries.

It will be recalled that Article 1, which governs the whole of the Convention, provides that the Convention shall apply in civil and commercial matters whatever the nature of the court or tribunal. It follows that judgments given in a Contracting State in civil or commercial matters by criminal courts or by administrative tribunals must be recognized and enforced in the other Contracting States. Under Article 25, the Convention applies to any judgment, whatever the judgment may be called. It also applies to writs of execution (Vollstreckungsbefehl, Article 699 of the German Code of Civil Procedure)[2] and to the determination of costs (Kostenfestsetzungsbeschluß des Urkundsbeamtean, Article 104 of the German Code of Civil Procedure) which, in the Federal Republic, are decisions of the registrar acting as an officer of the court. In decisions based on Article 104 of the German Code of Civil Procedure, the costs are determined in accordance with a schedule laid down by law and on the basis of the judgment of the court deciding on the substance of the matter.[3] In the event of a dispute as to the registrar's decision, a fully constituted court decides the issue.

[43] It follows from Article 1 that Title III cannot be invoked for the recognition and enforcement of judgments given on matters excluded from the scope of the Convention (status and legal capacity of persons, rules governing rights in property arising out of a matrimonial relationship, wills and succession, bankruptcy and other similar proceedings, social security, and arbitration, including arbitral awards).

On the other hand, Title III applies to any judgment given by a court or tribunal of a Contracting State in those civil and commercial matters which fall within the scope of the Convention, whether or not the parties are domiciled within the Community and whatever their nationality.

---

[2] The Vollstreckungsbefehl is issued by the court registrar.
[3] See also Art. 18(2) of the Hague Convention of 1 March 1954 on Civil Procedure.

B. Commentary on the Sections

Section 1

Recognition

Article 26

Recognition must have the result of conferring on judgments the auth-   **A1.187**
ority and effectiveness accorded to them in the State in which they were
given.

The words *"res judicata"* which appear in a number of conventions have
expressly been omitted, since judgments given in interlocutory proceedings and *ex parte* may be recognized, and these do not always have the
force of *res judicata*. Under the rules laid down in Article 26:

1. judgments are to be recognized automatically;
2. in the event of a dispute, if recognition is itself the principal issue,
   the procedure for enforcement provided for in the Convention may
   be applied;
3. if the outcome of proceedings depends on the determination of an
   incidental question of recognition, the court entertaining those proceedings has jurisdiction on the question of recognition.

The first of these rules lays down the principle that judgments are to be
recognized; recognition is to be accorded without the need for recourse to
any prior special procedure. It is thus automatic, and does not require a
judicial decision in the State in which recognition is sought to enable the
party in whose favour judgment has been given to invoke that judgment
against any party concerned, for example an administrative authority, in
the same way as a judgment given in that State. This provision means that
certain legal provisions which in some countries, such as Italy, make the
recognition of a foreign judgment subject to a special procedure (dichiarazione di efficacia) will be abolished. The Italian delegation stated that it
was able to concur in this solution since the scope of the Convention was
limited to matters relating to property rights.

Furthermore, this system is the opposite of that adopted in numerous
conventions, according to which foreign judgments are recognized only if
they fulfil a certain number of conditions. Under Article 26 there is a presumption in favour of recognition, which can be rebutted only if one of the
grounds for refusal listed in Article 27 is present.

The second rule concerns the case where the recognition of a judgment   **A1.188**
is itself the point at issue, there being no other proceedings involved and
no question of enforcement. For example, a negotiable instrument is
declared invalid in Italy by reason of fraud. The negotiable instrument is
presented to a bank in Belgium. Reliance is placed on the Italian judgment. The bank is faced with two contradictory instruments. The Italian
judgment would normally have to be recognized, but it may be that one of
the grounds for refusal set out in Article 27 applies. In the event of a dispute it is hardly the task of the bank to decide on the grounds for refusal,
and in particular on the scope of Belgian "international public policy."

The second rule of Article 26 offers a solution in cases of this kind. It allows the party seeking recognition to make use of the simplified procedure provided by the Convention for enforcement of the judgment. There is thus unification at the stage of recognition not only of the legal or administrative procedures which govern this matter in a number of States, but also in those countries which, like Belgium, do not allow actions for a declaration that a judgment is not to be recognized. Only the party seeking recognition may make use of this simplified procedure, which was evolved solely to promote the enforcement of judgments, and hence their recognition. It would moreover be difficult to apply the procedure laid down if the party opposing recognition could also avail himself of it; the latter will have to submit his claims in accordance with the ordinary rules of the internal law of the State in which recognition is sought.

[44] The third rule concerns the case where recognition of a judgment is raised as an incidental question in the course of other proceedings. To simplify matters, the Committee provided that the court entertaining the principal proceedings shall also have jurisdiction on the question of recognition.

A1.189 It will immediately be noticed that two conditions which are frequently inserted in enforcement treaties are not referred to in the Convention: it is not necessary that the foreign judgment should have become *res judicata*,[1] and the jurisdiction of the court which gave the original judgment does not have to be verified by the court of the State in which the recognition is sought unless the matter in question falls within the scope of sections 3, 4 or 5 of Title II.

Article 27

A1.190 *Public policy*

Recognition may be refused if it is contrary to public policy in the State in which the recognition is sought. In the opinion of the Committee this clause ought to operate only in exceptional cases. As has already been shown in the commentary on Article 4, public policy is not to be invoked as a ground for refusing to recognize a judgment given by a court of a Contracting State which has based its jurisdiction over a defendant domiciled outside the Community on a provision of its internal law, such as the provisions listed in the second paragraph of Article 3 (Article 14 of the French Civil Code, etc.).

Furthermore, it follows from the last paragraph of Article 27 that public policy is not to be used as a means of justifying refusal of recognition on the grounds that the foreign court applied a law other than that laid down

---

[1] The condition of *res judicata* is required by the Conventions between Germany and Italy, France and Italy, and Italy and the Netherlands. It is not required in the Conventions between Belgium and the Netherlands, Belgium and Italy, Germany and Belgium and Germany and the Netherlands, in the Benelux Treaty, or in the application of the Convention between France and Belgium, in spite of the wording of this last Convention (Art. 11(2)).

by the rules of private international law of the court in which the recognition is sought.

The wording of the public policy provision is similar to that adopted in the most recent conventions,[2] in that it is made clear that there are grounds for refusal, not of the foreign judgment itself, but if recognition of it is contrary to public policy in the State in which the recognition is sought. It is no part of the duty of the court seised of the matter to give an opinion as to whether the foreign judgment is, or is not, compatible with the public policy of its country. Indeed, this might be taken as criticism of the judgment. Its duty is rather to verify whether recognition of the judgment would be contrary to public policy.

Safeguarding the rights of the defendant

A1.191

Where judgment is given in default of appearance, recognition must be refused if the defendant was not duly served with the document which instituted the proceedings in sufficient time to enable him to arrange for his defence. Where judgment is given abroad in default of appearance, the Convention affords the defendant double protection.

First, the document must have been duly served. In this connection reference must be made to the internal law of the State in which the judgment was given, and to the international conventions on the service abroad of judicial instruments. Thus, for example, a German court in which recognition of a Belgian judgment given in default of appearance against a person who is in Germany is sought could, on the basis of the Agreement between Belgium and Germany of 25 April 1959, which was entered into to simplify application of the Hague Convention of 1 March 1954 on civil procedure, refuse recognition if the document instituting the proceedings was sent from Belgium to Germany by registered post, since the Federal Republic of Germany does not permit this method of transmitting documents.

Secondly, even where service has been duly effected, recognition can be refused if the court in which recognition is sought considers that the document was not served in sufficient time to enable the defendant to arrange for his defence.

A1.192

Looking at the second paragraph of Article 20, which lays down that the court of the State in which judgment is given must stay the proceedings if the document instituting the proceedings was not served on the defendant in sufficient time, it might be assumed that Article 27(2) would apply only in exceptional cases. It must not be forgotten, however, that the second [45] paragraph of Article 20 requires the court of the State in which judgment is given to stay proceedings only where the defendant is domiciled in another Contracting State.

---

[2] Conventions between Germany and Belgium, Italy and Belgium; Hague Convention on the recognition and enforcement of foreign judgments in civil and commercial matters.

A1.193 *Incompatibility with a judgment already given in the State in which recognition is sought*

There can be no doubt that the rule of law in a State would be disturbed if it were possible to take advantage of two conflicting judgments.[1]

The case where a foreign judgment is irreconcilable with a judgment given by a national court is, in the existing conventions, either treated as a matter of public policy,[2] as in the Convention between France and Belgium, the Benelux Treaty and the Convention between Belgium and Germany, or is regulated by a special provision.

In the opinion of the Committee, to treat this as a matter of public policy would involve the danger that the concept of public policy would be interpreted too widely. Furthermore, the Italian courts have consistently held that foreign judgments whose recognition is sought in Italy and which conflict with an Italian judgment do not fall within the scope of public policy. This is why the enforcement conventions concluded by Italy always contain two provisions, one referring to public policy, which serves the purpose of providing a safeguard in exceptional cases, and the other whereby the judgment must not conflict with an Italian judgment already given, or be prejudicial to proceedings pending in an Italian court.[3]

A1.194 There are also several other conventions which contain a clause providing for refusal of recognition of a judgment which conflicts with another judgment already given by the courts of the State in which recognition is sought.

In certain conventions, the judgment given in the State in which recognition is sought has to have become *res judicata*,[4] in others it is sufficient for the judgment to be final and conclusive at that stage of procedure,[5] and finally there are some which do not regulate the point.[6]

The Committee preferred a form of wording which does not decide whether the judgment should have become *res judicata* or should merely be

---

[1] NIBOYET, Traité de droit international privé français, Paris 1949, Vol. VI, No. 2028.

[2] BATIFFOL, Traité élémentaire de droit international privé, Paris 1959, No. 761: " . . . any judgment which is irreconcilable with a French judgment previously given is contrary to public policy. This rule holds good even if the judgment is not final" (Civ. 23 March 1936, Sirey 1936.1.175, R.1937–198); Riezler, *op. cit.* pp. 521 and 547.

[3] Conventions between Germany and Italy, Article 4; between France and Italy, Art. 1(5); between Belgium and Italy, Art. 1(4); and between the Netherlands and Italy, Art. 1(3).

[4] Hague Convention on the jurisdiction of the contractual forum in matters relating to the international sales of goods, Art. 5(3).

[5] Conventions between France and the U.K., Art. 3(1)(a); between the U.K. and Belgium, Art. 3(1)(a); between France and Germany on the Saar, Art. 30(I)(d); between Austria and Belgium on maintenance, Art.2(2)(b); between Austria and Belgium (general), Art. 2(2)(b).

[6] Hague Convention of 15 April 1958 concerning the recognition and enforcement of decisions relating to maintenance obligations towards children, Art. 2(4), and the Conventions concluded by Italy. Hague Convention on the recognition and enforcement of foreign judgments in civil and commercial matters (Art. 5).

final and conclusive, and left this question to the discretion of the court in which recognition is sought.

The Committee also considered that, for refusal of recognition, it would be sufficient if the judgment whose recognition was sought were irreconcilable with a judgment given between the same parties in the State in which recognition was sought. It is therefore not necessary for the same cause of action to be involved. Thus, for example, a French court in which recognition of a Belgian judgment awarding damages for failure to perform a contract is sought will be able to refuse recognition if a French court has already given judgment in a dispute between the same parties declaring that the contract was invalid.

The form of words used also covers the situation referred to in Article **A1.195** 5(3)(c) of the Hague Convention on the recognition and enforcement of foreign judgments, under which recognition may be refused if the proceedings which gave rise to the judgment whose recognition is sought have already resulted in a judgment which was given in a third State and which would be entitled to recognition and enforcement under the law of the State in which recognition is sought.

It is to be anticipated that the application of the provisions of Title II regarding *lis pendens* and related actions will greatly reduce the number of irreconcilable judgments.

[46] *PRELIMINARY QUESTIONS*

Recognition is not to be refused on the sole ground that the court which **A1.196** gave the original judgment applied a law other than that which would have been applicable under the rules of private international law of the State in which recognition is sought. However, the Convention makes an exception for preliminary questions regarding the status or legal capacity of natural persons, rules governing rights in property arising out of a matrimonial relationship, wills and succession, unless the same result would have been reached by the application of the rules of private international law of the State in which recognition is sought.

The Convention between Belgium and Germany contains a rule which is similar, but confined to cases where the judgment concerns a national of the State in which it is sought to give effect to that judgment. It is pointed out in the report of the negotiators of that Convention that this exception is justified by the fact that States reserve to themselves the right to regulate the status of their nationals. The wording used is similar to that of Article 7 of the Hague Convention on the recognition and enforcement of foreign judgments in civil and commercial matters.

Article 28

The very strict rules of jurisdiction laid down in Title II, and the safe- **A1.197** guards granted in Article 20 to defendants who do not enter an appearance, make it possible to dispense with any review, by the court in which recognition or enforcement is sought, of the jurisdiction of the court in which the original judgment was given.

The absence of any review of the substance of the case implies complete confidence in the court of the State in which judgment was given; it is similarly to be assumed that that court correctly applied the rules of jurisdiction of the Convention. The absence of any review as to whether the court in which the judgment was given had jurisdiction avoids the possibility that an alleged failure to comply with those rules might again be raised as an issue at the enforcement stage. The only exceptions concern, first, the matters for which Title II lays down special rules of jurisdiction (insurance, instalment sales and loans) or exclusive rules, and which, as has been shown, are in the six countries either of a binding character or matters of public policy, and, secondly, the case provided for in Article 59; reference should be made to the commentary on that Article.

The second paragraph contains a provision which is already included in a number of conventions (Convention between Germany and Belgium; Hague Convention, Article 9) and avoids recourse to time-wasting duplication in the exceptional cases where re-examination of the jurisdiction of the court of origin is permitted.

The last paragraph of Article 28 specifies that the rules of jurisdiction are not matters of public policy within the meaning of Article 27; in other words, public policy is not to be used as a means of justifying a review of the jurisdiction of the court of origin.[1] This again reflects the Committee's desire to limit so far as possible the concept of public policy.

REVIEW AS TO SUBSTANCE

Article 29

A1.198   It is obviously an essential provision of enforcement conventions that foreign judgments must not be reviewed.

The court of a State in which recognition of a foreign judgment is sought is not to examine the correctness of that judgment; "it may not substitute its own discretion for that of the foreign court[2] nor refuse recognition" if it considers that a point of fact or of law has been wrongly decided.[3]

STAY OF PROCEEDINGS

Article 30

A1.199   Article 30 postulates the following situation: a party may, in the course of litigation, wish to plead a judgment which has been given in another Contracting State but has not yet become *res judicata*. In order to remedy the inconvenience which would result if such judgment were reversed, Article 30 allows the court to stay the proceedings upon the principal issue of which it **[47]** is seised, until the foreign judgment whose recognition is sought has become *res judicata* in the State in which it was given.

---

[1] For a similar provision, see Art. 13(2) of the Benelux Treaty.
[2] P. GRAULICH, Principes de droit international privé. Conflits de lois. Conflits de juridictions. No. 254.
[3] BATIFFOL, Traité élémentaire de droit international privé, No. 763.

This power does not prevent the court from examining, before staying the proceedings, whether the foreign judgment fulfils the conditions for recognition laid down in Article 27.

Section 2

Enforcement

(a) Preliminary remarks

As has already been shown, the Committee endeavoured to give the Convention a progressive and pragmatic character by means of rules of jurisdiction which break new ground as compared with the enforcement conventions concluded hitherto. **A1.200**

This means, of course, that at the enforcement stage solutions must be found which follow from the rules of jurisdiction.

The progress achieved by Title II of the Convention would be rendered nugatory if a party seeking enforcement in a Contracting State of a judgment given in his favour were impeded by procedural obstacles.

The aim of Title II of the Convention is to strengthen the role of the court of the State in which the judgment was given. It must not be forgotten that that court must declare that it does not have jurisdiction if there are rules of exclusive jurisdiction which give jurisdiction to the courts of another State (Article 19); the court must also declare that it does not have jurisdiction, in cases where the defendant does not enter an appearance, if its jurisdiction is not derived from the Convention (first paragraph of Article 20). **A1.201**

Moreover, the court must stay the proceedings in the absence of proof that the defendant has been able to arrange for his defence (second paragraph of Article 20).

This role, as set out in Title II, is thus of prime importance.

It follows that the intervention of the court in which enforcement is sought is more limited than is usual under enforcement conventions. That court has in practice only two points to examine: public policy and whether the defendant has had the opportunity of defending himself. The other reasons for refusal—conflicting judgments, preliminary questions, review of jurisdiction in relation to certain specific topics—can, in fact, be regarded as akin to public policy. Since, moreover, the Convention is confined to matters relating to property rights, public policy will only very seldom have any part to perform. **A1.202**

This limitation on the powers of the court in which enforcement is sought led to a simplification of the enforcement procedure. Furthermore, as the position of the defendant in the original proceedings is well protected, it is proper that the applicant for enforcement be enabled to proceed rapidly with all the necessary formalities in the State in which enforcement is sought, that he be free to act without prior warning and that enforcement be obtained without unnecessary complications.

A1.203   The Committee discussed the enforcement procedure at length before adopting it. There were several possibilities open to it: reference back to national laws but subject to certain rules of the Convention, ordinary contentious procedure, summary contentious procedure or *ex parte* application.

Each of these solutions had its advantages and disadvantages. The Committee finally adopted a system for the whole Community based on *ex parte* application. This rapid and simple procedure will apply in all six States.

This uniform solution has the advantage of creating a proper balance as between the various provisions of the Convention: uniform rules of jurisdiction in the six countries and identical procedures for enforcement.

(b) Conditions for enforcement

A1.204   As has been shown, the Convention is based on the principle that a foreign judgment is presumed to be in order. It must, in principle, be possible to enforce it in the State in which enforcement is sought. Enforcement can be refused only if there is a ground for refusing recognition.[1] The foreign judgment must, however, be enforceable in the State in which it was given in order to be enforceable in the State in which enforcement is sought.

[48] If a judgment from which an appeal still lies or against which an appeal has been lodged in the State in which it was given cannot be provisionally enforced in that State, it cannot be enforced in the State in which enforcement is sought. It is an essential requirement of the instrument whose enforcement is sought that it should be enforceable in the State in which it originates. As Niboyet points out, there is no reason for granting to a foreign judgment rights which it does not have in the country in which it was given.[1]

Under no circumstances may a foreign judgment be reviewed as to its substance (Article 34).

(c) Enforcement procedure

A1.205   Before examining the Articles of the section on enforcement it seems appropriate to give an outline of the procedure which will be applicable in the six States.

1. The application, accompanied by the documents required under Articles 46 and 47, must be submitted to the authority specified in Article 32. The procedure for making the application is governed by the law of the State in which enforcement is sought.
    The applicant must give an address for service of process or appoint a representative *ad litem* in the jurisdiction of the court applied to.
2. The court applied to must give its decision without delay, and is not able to summon the other party. At this stage no contentious proceedings are allowed.

---

[1] On the disadvantages resulting from a difference between the conditions for recognition and for enforcement, see RIGAUX, *op. cit.*, p. 207, No. 39.

[1] NIBOYET, Droit international privé français. Vol. VI, No. 1974.

The application may be refused only for one of the reasons specified in Articles 27 and 28.

3. If enforcement is authorized: **A1.206**

   (a) the party against whom enforcement is sought may appeal against the decision within one month of service of the decision (Article 36);

   (b) the appeal must be lodged, in accordance with the rules governing procedure in contentious matters, with the court specified in Article 37;

   (c) if an appeal has been lodged against the foreign judgment in the State in which it was given, or if the time for such an appeal has not yet expired, the court seised of the appeal against the decision authorizing enforcement may stay the proceedings or make enforcement conditional on the provision of security (Article 38);

   (d) the judgment given on the appeal against the decision authorizing enforcement may not be contested by an ordinary appeal. It may be contested only by an appeal in cassation[2] (Article 37);

   (e) during the time specified for an appeal against the decision authorizing enforcement, the applicant may take only protective measures; the decision authorizing enforcement carries with it the power to proceed to such measures (Article 39).

4. If enforcement is refused: **A1.207**

   (a) the applicant may appeal to the court specified in Article 40;

   (b) the procedure before that court is contentious, the other party being summoned to appear (Article 40);

   (c) the judgment given on this appeal may be contested only by an appeal in cassation[2] (Article 41).

Article 31

Under this Article "a judgment given in a Contracting State and   **A1.208**
enforceable in that State shall be enforced in another Contracting State when, on the application of any interested party, the order for its enforcement has been issued there."

As can be seen, this provision is almost identical with that contained in the European Convention providing a uniform law on arbitration.[3] The Committee did, in fact, take the view that judgments given in one **[49]** Contracting State should be enforceable in any other Contracting State as easily as arbitral awards.

---

[2] In the Federal Republic of Germany by a "Rechtsbeschwerde."

[3] European Convention providing a uniform law on arbitration, Strasbourg, 20 January 1966. Art. 29 of Annex I: "An arbitral award may be enforced only when it can no longer be contested before arbitrators and when an enforcement formula has been apposed to it by the competent authority on the application of the interested party."

A1.209   The legal systems of the Member States are already familiar with authorization of enforcement by means of an enforcement order. This is so, for example, in the case of judgments and decisions given by the European Community institutions (Article 92 of the ECSC Treaty, Article 192 of the EEC Treaty, Article 164 of the Euratom Treaty). It is also true of judgments and decisions falling within the scope of the Mannheim Convention.[1]

The Convention of 30 August 1962 between Germany and the Netherlands also provides that judgments given in one of the two States are to be enforced in the other if enforcement is authorized by means of an enforcement order.

A1.210   A rule similar to that in Article 31, that is to say an *ex parte* procedure, was contained in the Franco-German Treaty on the Saar of 27 October 1956. Business circles in the Saar have said that the rule has proved entirely satisfactory.

About 80 per cent. of enforcement proceedings have been successfully completed by means of the first *ex parte* written phase of the procedure. In the majority of cases, judgment debtors have refrained from contesting the proceedings by means of an appeal. This is easily explained by the fact that cases of refusal of enforcement are exceptional, and the risk of having to bear the costs of the proceedings restrains the judgment debtor, unless he feels certain of winning his case.

A1.211   Article 31 does not purport to determine whether it is the judgment given in the State of origin, or the decision authorizing the issue of the enforcement order, which is enforceable in the State in which enforcement is sought.

The expression "on the application of any interested party" implies that any person who is entitled to the benefit of the judgment in the State in which it was given has the right to apply for an order for its enforcement.

Article 32

A1.212   Article 32 specifies the authority in each of the Contracting States to which the application must be submitted and which will have jurisdiction. It was considered to be in the interests of the parties that each relevant authority be indicated in the Convention itself.

The court to which local jurisdiction is given is that for the place of domicile of the party against whom enforcement is sought, or, if that party is not domiciled in the State in which enforcement is sought, the court for the place of enforcement, that is, where the judgment debtor has assets. The jurisdiction of the court for the place of enforcement is thus of minor importance.

A1.213   The provision requiring applications to be submitted to the court for the place where the judgment debtor is domiciled was included for the following reason. It is quite possible that in the State in which enforcement is sought the judgment debtor may possess property situated in the jurisdiction of different courts. If jurisdiction had been given only to the court for

---

[1] Revised Convention for the Navigation of the Rhine signed at Mannheim on 17 October 1868.

the place of enforcement, a choice between several courts would have been open to the applicant. Thus an applicant who was unsuccessful in one court could, instead of availing himself of the methods of appeal provided for in the Convention, have applied to another court which would not necessarily have come to the same decision as the first court, and this without the knowledge of the other party, since the procedure is *ex parte*.

Article 33

Under Article 33, the procedure and formalities for making the application are to be governed by the law of the State in which enforcement is sought. **A1.214**

Reference must therefore be made to the national laws for the particulars which the application must contain, the number of copies which must be submitted to the court, the authority to which the application must be submitted, also, where necessary, the language in which it must be drawn up, and whether a lawyer should be instructed to appear.

The provisions to which reference must be made are the following: **A1.215**

Belgium:

The matter will be governed by the Judicial Code (see Articles 1025 and 1027);

Federal Republic of Germany, Netherlands and Italy:

The question will be governed by the law implementing the Convention;

France:

Code of Civil Procedure, Article 1040;

[50] Luxembourg:

A lawyer must be instructed in accordance with the general law under which no one can officially address the court except through an *avoué*. Article 856 or Article 512 of the Code of Civil Procedure is generally invoked in support of this proposition.

The application must be accompanied by the documents required to be produced under Articles 46 and 47. **A1.216**

In the view of the Committee, if the applicant does not produce the required documents, enforcement should not be refused, but the court may stay the proceedings and allow the applicant time to produce the documents. If the documents produced are not sufficient and the court cannot obtain sufficient information, it may refuse to entertain the application.

Finally, the applicant must, in accordance with the law of the State in which enforcement is sought, either give an address for service of process or appoint a representative *ad litem* within the area of jurisdiction of the court applied to. This provision is important in two respects: first for communicating to the applicant the decision given on the application (Article **A1.217**

35), and secondly in case the party against whom enforcement is sought wishes to appeal, since such an appeal must be lodged "in accordance with the rules governing procedure in contentious matters" (Article 37).

The respondent must therefore summon the applicant to appear; the furnishing of an address for service or the appointment of a representative enables the summons to be served rapidly, in accordance with the law of the country in which enforcement is sought, without risk of error and without all the hazards connected with the service of legal documents abroad. It will in fact usually happen that the applicant is domiciled outside the State in which enforcement is sought.

The appointment of a representative *ad litem* has been provided for because the furnishing of an address for service is unknown in German law.

The two methods will, of course, produce the same result.

Article 34

A1.218   Article 34 provides that the court applied to shall give its decision without delay; "the party against whom enforcement is sought shall not at this stage of the proceedings be entitled to make any submissions on the application."

The Committee considered but rejected the idea of imposing on the court to which application is made a fixed period for giving its decision. Such a time limit is unknown in judicial practice, and there would in any case be no way of enforcing it.

The Convention does not allow the court to which application is made to ask the respondent to make submissions, even in exceptional cases. Such a possibility would have meant that the proceedings were not fully *ex parte*. Certain courts might be inclined to hear the respondent, which would in fact result in the *ex parte* procedure systematically becoming *inter partes*. Moreover, there would be a reduction in the element of surprise which is necessary in an enforcement procedure if the respondent is not to have the opportunity of withdrawing his assets from any measure of enforcement.

The rights of the respondent are safeguarded, since he can institute contentious proceedings by appealing against the decision authorizing enforcement.

A1.219   As has been shown above, the application may be refused only for one of the reasons specified in Articles 27 and 28, and the foreign judgment may not be reviewed as to its substance. Consequently, fresh claims which have not been submitted to the foreign court are inadmissible; the court seised of the application may authorize or refuse enforcement, but it cannot alter the foreign judgment.

The court may, however, refuse the application if it does not satisfy the requirements of Articles 32 and 33.

Article 35

A1.220   Article 35 provides that the appropriate officer of the court shall without delay bring the decision given on the application to the notice of the applicant in accordance with the procedure laid down by the law of the State in which enforcement is sought. It is important that the applicant be informed of the decision taken. This demonstrates the value of an address for service or of the appointment of a representative *ad litem*, particularly where the applicant is domiciled abroad.

The manner in which the decision is communicated to the applicant will be a matter for the national law of the State in which enforcement is sought, irrespective of whether enforcement is authorized or refused.

[51] *Article 36*

If enforcement is authorized, the decision must be notified to the party **A1.221** against whom enforcement has been granted. That party may appeal against the decision from the time it is served on him. As regards the period within which an appeal may be lodged and the moment from which it begins to run, Article 36 makes a distinction between the following situations:

(a) if the party is domiciled in the State in which the decision was given, the period is one month; the moment from which time begins to run is determined by the law of that State, from which there is no reason to derogate;

(b) if the party is domiciled in another Contracting State, the period is two months, and runs from the date when the decision was served, either on him in person or at his residence.[1]

In France and the Netherlands, the day of delivery to the prosecutor's office is not counted for purposes of computation of time. In Belgium, the day of delivery to the postal authorities is not counted (Article 40 of the Judicial Code), nor is the day on which an instrument is dispatched by a Belgian Consul to a foreign authority.[2]

The purpose of this rule, which derogates from some national laws, is to protect the respondent and to prevent his being deprived of a remedy because he had not been informed of the decision in sufficient time to contest it.

No extension of time may be granted on account of distance, as the time allowed is sufficient to enable the party concerned to contest the decision, if he is so minded;

(c) if the party is domiciled outside the Community, the period within which an appeal may be lodged runs from the date when the decision is served or is deemed to have been served according to the law of the State in which the decision was given. In this case the period of one month may be extended on account of distance in accordance with the law of that State.

Computation of time is governed by the internal law of the State in which the decision was given.

---

[1] Service on a party at his residence means delivering the instrument to a person who is present and empowered by law to receive a copy of the instrument or, if there is no such person, to a competent authority.

[2] Belgian Court of Cassation, March 4, 1954; Revue des huissiers de Belgique, May to June 1954, p. 15.

Article 37

A1.222   Article 37 specifies for each country the court with which an appeal can be lodged.

In that court the proceedings are contentious. Accordingly it is incumbent upon the person against whom enforcement has been authorized to summon the other party to appear.

The court seised of the appeal will have to examine whether it was properly lodged and will have to decide upon the merits of the appeal, taking account of the additional information supplied by the appellant. It will therefore be open to the appellant to establish, in the case of a judgment originally given in default of appearance, that the rights of the defendant were disregarded, or that a judgment has already been given in a dispute between the same parties in the State in which enforcement is sought which is irreconcilable with the foreign judgment. The appellant may also plead Article 38 if he has lodged an appeal against the judgment whose enforcement is sought in the State in which it was given.

It is no part of the duty of the court with which the appeal against the decision authorizing enforcement is lodged to review the foreign judgment as to its substance. This would be contrary to the spirit of the Convention. The appellant could, however, effectively adduce grounds which arose after the foreign judgment was given. For example, he may establish that he has since discharged the debt. As Batiffol points out, such grounds are admissible in enforcement proceedings.[3,4]

A1.223   The second paragraph of Article 37 provides that the judgment given on the appeal may be contested only by an appeal in cassation and not by any other form of appeal or review.

This rule was requisite for the following reasons. First, the grounds for refusing enforcement are very limited and involve public policy in the State in which enforcement is sought. No useful purpose is served by further argument on this concept. Next, the situation is different from that in which purely national proceedings are involved. The proceedings on the merits of the case itself have already taken place in the State in which the judgment was given, and the Convention in no way [52] interferes with the rights of appeal. It is true that the Convention applies to judgments which are enforceable only provisionally, but in this case the court with which the appeal is lodged may, as provided in Article 38, stay the proceedings. An excessive number of avenues of appeal might be used by the losing party purely as delaying tactics, and this would constitute an obstacle to the free movement of judgments which is the object of the Convention.

Since appeals in cassation are unknown in the Federal Republic of Germany, it has been provided, in order to establish a certain parity amongst the Contracting States, that an appeal on a point of law

---

[3] BATIFFOL, *op. cit.*, p. 863, n. 57.
[4] For the Federal Republic of Germany, see Art. 767 of the Code of Civil Procedure; see also BAUMBACH-LAUTERBACH, Zivilprozeßordnung, paragraph 723, n. 1.

(Rechtsbeschwerde) shall lie against a judgment of the Court of Appeal (Oberlandesgericht).

Article 38

Article 38 covers cases where an ordinary appeal has been lodged against **A1.224** the judgment in the State in which that judgment was given, and also cases where the period within which such an appeal may be lodged has not yet expired. The court with which the appeal against enforcement under the first paragraph of Article 37 is lodged may either stay the proceedings, authorize enforcement, make enforcement conditional on the provision of such security as it thinks fit, or specify the time within which the defendant must lodge his appeal.

This provision originates in the Convention between Germany and Belgium (Article 10), and its "object is to protect the judgment debtor against any loss which could result from the enforcement of a judgment which has not yet become *res judicata* and may be amended."[1]

Article 38 deals only with judgments which, notwithstanding that they **A1.225** may be appealed against, are enforceable in the State in which they were given.

Only the court seised of the appeal has the power to stay the proceedings, and such a stay can be granted only on the application of the party against whom enforcement is sought. This is because that party does not appear at the first stage of the proceedings and cannot be required to do so.

Article 39

Article 39 contains two very important rules. First it provides that dur- **A1.226** ing the time specified for the lodging of an appeal the applicant for enforcement may take no enforcement measures other than protective measures—namely those available under the law of the State in which enforcement is sought. Similarly, if an appeal has actually been lodged, this rule applies until the appeal has been determined. Secondly it provides that the decision authorizing enforcement carries with it the power to proceed to any such protective measures. Article 39 also allows the judgment creditor in certain States, for example in the Federal Republic of Germany, to initiate the first phase of the enforcement of the foreign instrument. The object of this provision is to ensure at the enforcement stage a balance between the rights and interests of the parties concerned, in order to avoid either of them suffering any loss as a result of the operation of the rules of procedure.

On the one hand, an applicant who, in consequence of a foreign judgment, is in possession of an enforceable instrument, must be able to take quickly all measures necessary to prevent the judgment debtor from removing the assets on which execution is to be levied. This is made possible by the *ex parte* procedure and by the provision in Article 39 that the decision authorizing enforcement carries with it the power to proceed to

---

[1] Convention between Germany and Belgium. See Report of the negotiators.

such protective measures. The power arises automatically. Even in those States whose law requires proof that the case calls for prompt action or that there is any risk in delay the applicant will not have to establish that either of those elements is present; power to proceed to protective measures is not a matter for the discretion of the court.

A1.227 On the other hand, the fact that the enforcement procedure is *ex parte* makes it essential that no irreversible measures of execution can be taken against the defendant. The latter may be in a position to establish that there are grounds for refusal of enforcement; he may, for example, be able to show that the question of public policy was not examined in sufficient detail. To safeguard his rights it accordingly appeared to be necessary to delay enforcement, which is usually carried out by sequestration of the movable and immovable property of the defendant, until the end of the time specified for appeal (see Article 36) or, if an appeal is actually lodged, until it has been determined. In other words, this is a counterbalance to the *ex parte* procedure; the effect of the decision authorizing enforcement given pursuant to Article 31 is limited in that during the time specified for an appeal, or if an appeal has been lodged, no enforcement measures can be taken on the basis of that decision against the assets of the judgment debtor.

[53] *Articles 40 and 41*

A1.228 These Articles relate to the case where an application for enforcement is refused.

Article 40 provides that the applicant may appeal to the appeal court which has jurisdiction in the State in which enforcement is sought.

The Committee did not think it necessary that the Convention should fix the period within which appeals would have to be lodged. If the applicant has had his application refused, it is for him to give notice of appeal within such time as he considers suitable. He will have regard, no doubt, to the length of time it will take him to assemble all the relevant documents.

Upon appeal the proceedings are contentious, since the party against whom enforcement is sought is summoned to appear. The *inter partes* procedure is necessary in order to avoid numerous appeals. If the procedure on appeal had remained *ex parte*, it would have been essential to provide for additional proceedings to enable the defendant to make his submissions if the appellate court were to reverse the decision at first instance and authorize enforcement. The Committee wished to avoid a plethora of appeals. Moreover, the dismissal of the application reverses the presumption of validity of the foreign judgment.

The summoning of the party against whom enforcement is sought is to be effected in manner prescribed by the national laws.

A1.229 The appellate court can give judgment only if the judgment debtor has in fact been given an opportunity to make his submissions. The object of this provision is to protect the rights of the defendant and to mitigate the disadvantages which result from certain systems of serving instruments abroad. These disadvantages are all the more serious in that a party against whom enforcement is sought and who is not notified in time to arrange for his defence no longer has any judicial remedy against the judgment given on the appeal other than by way of an appeal in cassation, and then only to the extent that this is allowed by the law of the State in which enforcement is sought (Article 41).

Because of the safeguards contained in Article 40, Article 41 provides that the judgment given on the appeal may not be contested by an ordinary appeal, but only by an appeal in cassation. The reason why a special form of appeal (Rechtsbeschwerde) is provided for in the Federal Republic of Germany has already been explained (Article 37).

The procedure for the forms of appeal provided for in Articles 40 and 41 is to be determined by the national laws which may, where necessary, prescribe time limits.

Article 42

Article 42 covers two different situations. **A1.230**

The first paragraph of Article 42 empowers the court of the State in which enforcement is sought to authorize enforcement in respect of certain matters dealt with in a judgment and to refuse it in respect of others.[1] As explained in the report annexed to the Benelux Treaty, which contains a similar provision, "this discretion exists in all cases where a judgment deals with the separate and independent heads of claim, and the decision on some of these is contrary to the public policy of the country in whch enforcement is sought, while the decision on others is not."

The second paragraph of Article 42 allows an applicant to request the **A1.231** partial enforcement of a judgment, and *ex hypothesi* allows the court addressed to grant such a request. As mentioned in the report on the Benelux Treaty, "it is possible that the applicant for enforcement himself wants only partial enforcement, *e.g.* where the judgment whose enforcement is sought orders the payment of a sum of money, part of which has been paid since the judgment was given."[2]

As is made clear in the Conventions between Germany and Belgium, and between Belgium and Italy, which contain similar provisions, the applicant may exercise this option whether the judgment covers one or several heads of claim.

Article 43

Article 43 relates to judgments which order a periodic payment by way **A1.232** of a penalty. Some enforcement conventions contain a clause on this subject (see Benelux Treaty, Article 14; Convention between Germany and the Netherlands, Article 7).

---

[1] See Benelux Treaty (Art. 14(4)); the Conventions between France and Italy (Art. 3); between Italy and the Netherlands (Art. 3); between Germany and Belgium (Art. 11); between Belgium and Italy (Art. 10) and between Germany and the Netherlands (Art. 12).

[2] See also the Conventions between Germany and Belgium (Art. 11) and between Belgium and Italy (Art. 10).

[54] It follows from the wording adopted that judgments given in a Contracting State which order the payment of a sum of money for each day of delay, with the intention of getting the judgment debtor to fulfil his obligations, will be enforced in another Contracting State only if the amount of the payment has been finally determined by the courts of the State in which judgment was given.

Article 44

A1.233   Article 44 deals with legal aid.

A number of enforcement conventions deal with this matter.[1]

The provisions adopted by the Committee supplement the Hague Convention of 1 March 1954 on civil procedure, which has been ratified by the six States, so that a party who has been granted legal aid in the State in which judgment was given also qualifies automatically for legal aid in the State in which enforcement is sought, but only as regards the issuing of the order for enforcement. Thus the automatic extension of legal aid achieved by the Convention does not apply in relation to enforcement measures or to proceedings arising from the exercise of rights of appeal.

The reasoning underlying Article 44 is as follows.

First, as maintenance obligations fall within the scope of the Convention, consideration was given to the humanitarian issues which were the basis for a similar provision in the 1958 Hague Convention.

Above all it must not be forgotten that if a needy applicant were obliged, before making his application for enforcement, to institute in the State in which enforcement is sought proceedings for recognition of the decision granting him legal aid in the State in which the judgment was given, he would be in a less favourable position than other applicants. He would in particular not have the advantage of the rapidity of the procedure and the element of surprise which Title III is designed to afford to any party seeking the enforcement of a foreign judgment.

A1.234   It is moreover because of this consideration that the automatic extension of legal aid has been limited to the procedure for issuing the order for enforcement, and has not been extended to the proceedings on appeal. Once these proceedings have been set in motion, the applicant for enforcement, or, in case of appeal, the respondent, may, in accordance with the 1954 Hague Convention, take the necessary steps, in the State in which enforcement is sought, to obtain legal aid, in the same way as nationals of that State.

Under Article 47(2) an applicant must, on making his application, produce documents showing that he is in receipt of legal aid in the State in which judgment was given.

---

[1] Hague Convention of 15 April 1958 concerning the recognition and enforcement of decisions relating to maintenance obligations towards children (Art. 9); Conventions between Italy and the Netherlands (Art. 6) and between Germany and the Netherlands (Art. 15).

Article 45

This Article deals with security for costs. A similar rule is included in **A1.235** the Hague Convention of 1 March 1954 but as regards the obligation to provide security it exempts only nationals of the Contracting States who are also domiciled in one of those States (Article 17). Under Article 45, any party, irrespective of nationality or domicile, who seeks enforcement in one Contracting State of a judgment given in another Contracting State, may do so without providing security. The two conditions—nationality and domicile—prescribed by the 1954 Convention do not apply.

The Committee considered that the provision of security in relation to proceedings for the issuing of an order for enforcement was unnecessary.

As regards the proceedings which take place in the State in which judgment was given, the Committee did not consider it necessary to depart from the rules of the 1954 Convention.

Section 3

Common provisions

This Section deals with the documents which must be produced when **A1.236** application is made for the recognition or enforcement of a judgment.

Article 46 applies to both recognition and enforcement. Article 47 applies only to applications for enforcement. It should be noted that at the recognition stage there is no reason to require production of the documents referred to in Article 47.

[55] Article 47(1) provides for the production of documents which **A1.237** establish that the judgment is enforceable in the State in which it was given. The requirement that the judgment be, in law, enforceable in that State applies only in relation to its enforcement (not to its recognition) abroad. (Article 31).

Article 47(2), which relates to documents showing that the applicant is receiving legal aid in the State in which judgment was given, is also relevant only in enforcement proceedings. The documents are in fact intended to enable a party receiving legal aid in the State in which judgment was given to qualify for it automatically in the proceedings relating to the issue of the order for enforcement (Article 44). However, recognition requires no special procedure (Article 26). If recognition were itself the principal issue in an action, Article 44 and, consequently, Article 47(2) would apply, since Article 26 refers to Sections 2 and 3 of Title III.

Under Article 46(1), a copy of the judgment which satisfies the con- **A1.238** ditions necessary to establish its authenticity must be produced, whether it is recognition or enforcement which is sought.

This provision is found in all enforcement treaties and does not require any special comment. The authenticity of a judgment will be established in accordance with the maxim *locus regit actum*; it is therefore the law of the place where the judgment was given which prescribes the conditions which the copy of the judgment must satisfy in order to be valid.[1]

---

[1] WESER: Traité franco-belge du 8 juillet 1899. Étude critique No. 247.

Under Article 46(2), if the judgment was given in default, a document which establishes that the party in default was served with the document instituting the proceedings must also be produced.

The court in which recognition or enforcement is sought must, if the foreign judgment was given in default, be in a position to verify that the defendant's right to defend himself was safeguarded.

A1.239   Article 47 provides that the following documents must be produced:

(a) documents which establish that the judgment is enforceable according to the law of the State in which it was given. This does not mean that a separate document certifying that the judgment has become enforceable in that State is necessarily required. Thus, in France, "provisional enforceability" would be deduced from an express reference to it in judgments given pursuant to Article 135a of the Code of Civil Procedure. Decisions given in summary proceedings will be provisionally enforceable (Article 809 of the Code of Civil Procedure); and so will decisions in *ex parte* proceedings (Article 54 of the Decree of 30 March 1808). But whether other judgments are enforceable can be determined only when the date on which they were given has been considered in relation to the date on which they were served and the time allowed for lodging an appeal.[2]

Documents which establish that the judgment has been served will also have to be produced, since some judgments may be enforceable and consequently fall within the scope of the Convention even if they have not been served on the other party. However, before enforcement can be applied for, that party must at least have been informed of the judgment given against him and also have had the opportunity to satisfy the judgment voluntarily;

(b) where appropriate, a document showing, in accordance with the law of the State in which the judgment was given, that the applicant is in receipt of legal aid in that State.

Article 48

A1.240   In order to avoid unnecessary formalities, this Article authorizes the court to allow time for the applicant to produce the documentary evidence proving service of the document instituting the proceedings, required under Article 46(2), and the documentary evidence showing that the appli-

---

[2] *Belgium*: Judicial Code: see Art. 1029 for decisions in *ex parte* proceedings, Art. 1039 for decisions in summary proceedings, and Arts. 1398 and 1496 for judgments.

Federal Republic of Germany: "Vollstreckungsklausel"—Under Art. 725 of the Code of Civil Procedure, the order for enforcement is worded as follows:

"This copy of the judgment shall be given to . . . (name of the party) for the purpose of enforcement." This order must be added at the end of the copy of

cant was in receipt of legal aid in the State in which judgment was given (Article 47(2)).

[56] The court may dispense with the production of these documents by the applicant (the Committee had in mind the case where the documents had been destroyed) if it considers that it has sufficient information before it from other evidence.

The second paragraph relates to the translation of the documents to be produced. Again with the object of simplifying the procedure, it is here provided that the translation may be certified by a person qualified to do so in any one of the Contracting States.

Article 49

This Article provides that legalization or other like formality is not necessary as regards the documents to be produced and, in particular, that the certificate provided for in the Hague Convention of 5 October 1961 abolishing the requirement of legalization for foreign public documents is not required. The same applies to the document whereby an applicant appoints a representative, perhaps a lawyer, to act for him in proceedings for the issue of an order for enforcement.

A1.241

CHAPTER VI

AUTHENTIC INSTRUMENTS AND COURT SETTLEMENTS

Article 50

In drawing up rules for the enforcement of authentic instruments, the Committee has broken no new ground. Similar provisions are, in fact, contained in the Conventions already concluded by the six States,[1] with the sole exception of the Convention between Germany and Italy.

A1.242

Since Article 1 governs the whole Convention, Article 50 applies only to authentic instruments which have been drawn up or registered in matters falling within the scope of the Convention.

In order that an authentic instrument which has been drawn up or registered in one Contracting State may be the subject of an order for enforce-

---

the judgment and must be signed by the appropriate officer of the court and sealed with the seal of the court.

Luxembourg: see Arts. 135, 136 and 137 of the Code of Civil Procedure, Art. 164 for judgments in default, Art. 439 for Commercial Courts (tribunaux de commerce) and Art. 5 of the Law of 23 March 1893 on summary jurisdiction.

Netherlands: see Arts. 339, 350, 430 and 433 of the Code of Civil Procedure, also Arts. 82 and 85 of that Code.

[1] Conventions between France and Belgium (Art. 16); between Belgium and the Netherlands (Art. 16); Benelux Treaty (Art. 18); Conventions between Germany and Belgium (Art. 14); between Italy and Belgium (Art. 13); between Germany and the Netherlands (Art. 16); between Italy and the Netherlands (Art. 8); and between France and Italy (Art. 6).

ment issued in another Contracting State, three conditions must be satisfied:

(a) the instrument must be enforceable in the State in which it was drawn up or registered;

(b) it must satisfy the conditions necessary to establish its authenticity in that State;

(c) its enforcement must not be contrary to public policy in the State in which enforcement is sought.

The provisions of section 3 of Title III are applicable as appropriate. It follows in particular that no legalization or similar formality is required.

Article 51

A1.243   A provision covering court settlements was considered necessary on account of the German and Netherlands legal systems,[2] under German and Netherlands law, settlements approved by a court in the course of proceedings are enforceable without further formality (Article 794(1) of the German Code of Civil Procedure, and Article 19 of the Netherlands Code of Civil Procedure).

The Convention, like the Convention between Germany and Belgium, makes court settlements subject to the same rules as authentic instruments, since both are contractual in nature. Enforcement can therefore be refused only if it is contrary to public policy in the State in which it is sought.

[57] CHAPTER VII

GENERAL PROVISIONS

Article 52

A1.244   As regards the determination of domicile (Article 52), reference should be made to Chapter IV (A)(3) which deals with the matter.

Article 53

A1.245   Article 53 provides that, for the purposes of this Convention, the seat of a company or other legal person or association of natural or legal persons shall be treated as its domicile.

The Convention does not define what is meant by the seat of a legal person or of a company or association of natural or legal persons any more than it defines domicile.

In determining the location of the seat, the court will apply its rules of private international law. The Committee did not think it possible to parti-

---

[2] See the Conventions between Germany and Belgium (Art. 14(1)); between Germany and the Netherlands (Art. 16); between Germany and Italy (Art. 9); and the Hague Convention on the choice of court (Art. 10).

cularize the concept of seat in any other way, and considered that it could not be achieved by making a reference to Article 52, in view of the different approaches which the various Member States of the Community adopt in this matter. Moreover, the Committee did not wish to encroach upon the work on company law which is now being carried out within the Community.

It did not escape the attention of the Committee that the application of Article 16(2) of the Convention could raise certain difficulties. This would be the case, for example, where a court in one State ordered the dissolution of a company whose seat was in that State and application was then made for recognition of that order in another State under whose law the location of the company's seat was determined by its statutes, if, when so determined, it was in that other State. In the opinion of the Committee, the court of the State in which recognition were sought would be entitled, under the first paragraph of Article 28, to refuse recognition on the ground that the courts of that State had exclusive jurisdiction.

A1.246 Article 53 does not deal with the preliminary question of the recognition of companies or other legal persons or associations of natural or legal person; this must be resolved either by national law or by the Hague Convention of 1 June 1956 on the recognition of the legal personality of companies, firms, associations and foundations,[1] pending the entry into force of the Convention which is at present being prepared within the EEC on the basis of Article 220 of the Treaty of Rome.

Article 53 refers to companies or other legal persons and to associations of natural or legal persons; to speak only of legal persons would have been insufficient, since this expression would not have covered certain types of company, such as the "offene Handelsgesellschaft" under German law, which are not legal persons. Similarly, it would not have been sufficient to speak only of companies, since certain bodies, such as associations and foundations, would then not have been covered by this Convention.

CHAPTER VIII

TRANSITIONAL PROVISIONS

Article 54

A1.247 As a general rule, enforcement treaties have no retroactive effect,[1] in order "not to alter a state of affairs which has been reached on the basis of legal relations other than those created between the two States as a result of the introduction of the Convention."[2]

---

[1] Ratified on April 20, 1966 by Belgium, France and the Netherlands.
[1] Conventions between France and Belgium (Art. 19); between Belgium and the Netherlands (Art. 27); between Germany and Belgium (Art. 17); between Germany and Italy (Art. 18); between Germany and the Netherlands (Art. 20); between Italy and Belgium (Art. 17); and between Italy and the Netherlands (Art. 16).
[2] See Report of the negotiators of the Convention between Germany and Belgium.

So far as the author is aware only the Benelux Treaty applies to judgments given before its entry into force.

[58] A solution as radical as that of the Benelux Treaty did not seem acceptable. In the first place, the conditions which a judgment must fulfil in order to be recognized and enforced are much stricter under the Benelux Treaty (Article 13) than under the EEC Convention. Secondly, the ease with which recognition and enforcement can be granted under the EEC Convention is balanced by the provisions of Title II which safeguard the interests of the defendant. In particular, those provisions have made it possible, at the stage of recognition or enforcement, to dispense with any review of the jurisdiction of the court of origin (Article 28). But, of course, a defendant in the State in which judgment was originally given will be able to rely on these protective provisions only when the Convention has entered into force. Only then will he be able to invoke the Convention to plead lack of jurisdiction.

Although Article 54 was not modelled on the Benelux Treaty, its effect is not very different.

A1.248   The rules adopted are as follows:

1. The Convention applies to proceedings which are instituted—and in which, therefore, judgment is given—after the entry into force of the Convention.
2. The Convention does not apply if the proceedings were instituted and judgment given before the entry into force of the Convention.
3. The Convention does apply, but subject to certain reservations, to judgments given after its entry into force in proceedings instituted before its entry into force.

In this case, the court of the State addressed may review the jurisdiction of the court of origin, since the defendant originally had no opportunity to contest that jurisdiction in that court on the basis of the Convention.

Enforcement will be authorized if the jurisdiction of the court of origin:

(i) either was based on a rule which accords with one of the rules of jurisdiction in the Convention; for example, if the defendant was domiciled in the State in whch the judgment was given;
(ii) or was based on a multilateral or bilateral convention in force between the State of origin and the State addressed. Thus, if, for example, an action relating to a contract were brought in a German court, the judgment given could be recognized and enforced in Belgium if the obligation had been or was to be performed in the Federal Republic since the jurisdiction of the German court would be founded on Article 3(1)(5) of the Convention between Germany and Belgium.

A1.249   If the jurisdiction of the court of origin is founded on one of those bases, the judgment must be recognized and enforced, provided of course that there is no ground for refusal under Article 27 or 28. Recognition will be accorded without any special procedure being required (Article 26); enforcement will be authorized in accordance with the rules of section 2 of Title III, that is to say, on *ex parte* application.

It follows from Article 54, which provides that the Convention applies only to legal proceedings instituted after its entry into force, that the Convention will have no effect on proceedings in progress at the time of its entry into force. If, for example, before the entry into force of the Convention, proceedings were instituted in France in accordance with Article 14 of the Civil Code against a person domiciled in another Contracting State, that person could not plead the Convention for the purpose of contesting the jurisdiction of the French court.

CHAPTER IX

RELATIONSHIP TO OTHER INTERNATIONAL CONVENTIONS

A1.250 Title VII deals with the relationship between the Convention and other international instruments governing jurisdiction, recognition and the enforcement of judgments. It covers the following matters:

[59]
1. the relationship between the Convention and the bilateral agreements already in force between certain Member States of the Community (Article 55 and 56)[1]
2. the relationship between the Convention and those international agreements which, in relation to particular matters, govern—or will govern—jurisdiction and the recognition or enforcement of judgments (Article 57);
3. the relationship between the Convention and the Convention of 15 June 1869 between France and Switzerland, which is the only enforcement convention concluded between a Member State of the EEC and a non-member State to contain rules of direct jurisdiction (Article 58);
4. the relationship between the Convention and any other instruments, whether bilateral or multilateral, which may in the future govern the recognition and enforcement of judgments (Article 59).

A1.251 It was not thought necessary to regulate the relationship between the Convention and the bilateral conventions already concluded between Member States of the EEC and non-member States since, with the exception of the Convention between France and Switzerland, such conventions all contain rules of indirect jurisdiction. There is, therefore, no conflict between those conventions and the rules of jurisdiction laid down in Title II of the Convention. Recognition and enforcement would seem to raise no problem, since judgments given in those non-member States must be recognized in accordance with the provisions of the bilateral conventions.

---

[1] Mention has been made of the Benelux Treaty although, as it has not been ratified by Luxembourg, it has not yet entered into force; this is to avoid any conflict between the Convention and that Treaty should it enter into force.

Articles 55 and 56

A1.252   Article 55 contains a list of the Conventions which will be superseded on the entry into force of the EEC Convention. This will, however, be subject to:

1. the provisions of the second paragraph of Article 54, as explained in the commentary on that Article;
2. the provisions of the first paragraph of Article 56, the consequence of which is that these conventions will continue to have effect in relation to matters to which the EEC Convention does not apply (status, legal capacity etc.);
3. the provisions of the second paragraph of Article 56 concerning the recognition and enforcement of judgments given before the EEC Convention enters into force. Thus a judgment given in France before the EEC Convention enters into force and to which by virtue of Article 54 this Convention would therefore not apply, could be recognized and enforced in Italy after the entry into force of the EEC Convention under the terms of the Convention of 3 June 1930 between France and Italy. Without such a rule, judgments given before the Convention enters into force could be recognized and enforced only in accordance with the general law, and this would in several Contracting States involve the possibility of a review of the substance of the judgment, which would unquestionably be a retrograde step.

Article 57

A1.253   The Member States of the Community, or some of them, are already parties to numerous international agreements which, in relation to particular matters, govern jurisdiction or the recognition or enforcement of judgments. Those agreements include the following:

1. The revised Convention for the navigation of the Rhine signed at Mannheim on 17 October 1868;[2]
2. The International Convention for the unification of certain rules relating to international carriage by air, and Additional Protocol, signed at Warsaw on 12 October 1929;[3]
3. The International Convention on certain rules concerning civil jurisdiction in matters of collision, signed at Brussels on 10 May 1952[4]
4. The International Convention relating to the arrest of sea-going ships, signed at Brussels on 10 May 1952;[5]

---

[2] These Conventions have been ratified by the following Member States of the European Economic Community (list drawn up on September 15, 1966): Belgium, the Federal Republic of Germany, France and the Netherlands.
[3] Belgium, the Federal Republic of Germany, France, Italy, Luxembourg and the Netherlands.
[4] Belgium and France.
[5] Belgium and France.

5. The Convention on damage caused by foreign aircraft to third parties on the surface, signed at Rome on 7 October 1952;[6]

[60]

6. The International Convention concerning the carriage of goods by rail (CIM), and Annexes, signed at Berne on 25 October 1952;[1]

7. The International Convention concerning the carriage of passengers and luggage by rail (CIV) and Annexes, signed at Berne on 25 October 1952;[2]

8. The Agreement on German external debts, signed at London on 27 February 1953;[2]

9. The Convention on civil procedure concluded at The Hague on 1 March 1954;[3]

10. The Convention on the contract for the International carriage of goods by road (CMR) and Protocol of Signature, signed at Geneva on 19 May 1956;[3]

11. The Convention concerning the recognition and enforcement of decisions relating to maintenance obligations in respect of children, concluded at The Hague on 15 April 1958;[4]

12. The Convention on the jurisdiction of the contractual forum im matters relating to the international sale of goods, concluded at The Hague on 15 April 1958;[5]

13. The Convention on third party liability in the field of nuclear energy, signed at Paris on 29 July 1960,[6a] and the Additional Protocol, signed at Paris on 28 January 1964,[6b] the Supplementary Convention to the Paris Convention of 29 July 1960, and Annex, signed at Brussels on 31 January 1963,[6c] and Additional Protocol to the Supplementary Convention signed at Paris on 28 January 1964.[6d]

14. The Convention on the liability of operators of nuclear ships, and Additional Protocol, signed at Brussels on 25 May 1962;[7]

15. The Convention of 27 October 1956 between the Grand Duchy of Luxembourg, the Federal Republic of Germany and the French Republic on the canalization of the Moselle.[8]

The structure of these agreements varies considerably. Some of them **A1.254** govern only jurisdiction, like the Warsaw Convention of 12 October 1929 for the unification of certain rules relating to international carriage by air, or are based on indirect jurisdiction, like the Hague Convention of 15 April 1958 concerning the recognition and enforcement of decisions relating to maintenance obligations in respect of children, or contain rules of

---

[6] Belgium and Luxembourg.

[1] Belgium, the Federal Republic of Germany, France, Luxembourg and the Netherlands.

[2] Belgium, the Federal Republic of Germany, France, Luxembourg and the Netherlands.

[3] The six States.

[4] Belgium, the Federal Republic of Germany, France, Italy and the Netherlands.

[5] Italy.

[6] (a) and (b) France and Belgium; (c) and (d) France.

[7] Not ratified.

[8] Ratified by the three States concerned.

direct or even exclusive jurisdiction, such as the International Convention of 25 October 1952 concerning the carriage of goods by rail (CIM), which lays down in Article 43(5) that actions arising from the contract of carriage may be brought only in the courts of the State to which the defendant railway belongs.

The approach adopted by the Committee means that agreements relating to particular matters prevail over the Convention. It follows that, where those agreements lay down rules of direct or exclusive jurisdiction, the court of the State of origin will have to apply those rules to the exclusion of any others; where they contain provisions concerning the conditions governing the recognition and enforcement of judgments given in matters to which the agreements apply, only those conditions need be satisfied, so that the enforcement procedure set up by the EEC Convention will not apply to those judgments.

The Committee adopted this approach in view of the fact that the Member States of the Community, when they entered into these agreements, had for the most part contracted obligations towards non-Member States which should not be modified without the consent of those States.

A1.255   Moreover, the following points must be borne in mind:

1. The rules of jurisdiction laid down in these agreements have been dictated by particular considerations relating to the matters of which they treat, *e.g.* the flag or port of registration of a vessel in the maritime conventions; the criterion of domicile is not often used to establish jurisdiction in such agreements.
2. The EEC Convention lays down that judgments are in principle to be recognized, whereas agreements relating to particular matters usually subject the recognition and enforcement of judgments to a certain number of conditions. These conditions may well differ from the grounds for refusal set out in Articles 27 and 28; moreover they usually include a [61] requirement, which the Convention has dropped, that the court of origin had jurisdiction.
3. The simplified enforcement procedure laid down by the Convention is the counterpart of Title II, the provisions of which will not necessarily have to be observed where the court of the State of origin has to apply another convention. Consequently, where agreements relating to particular matters refer for the enforcement procedure back to the ordinary law of the State in which enforcement is sought, it is that law which must be applied. There is, however, nothing to prevent a national legislature from substituting the Convention procedure for its ordinary civil procedure for the enforcement of judgments given in application of agreements governing particular matters.

Article 58

A1.256   This Article deals only with certain problems of jurisdiction raised by the Convention of 15 June 1869 between France and Switzerland.

Under Article 1 of that Convention, a Swiss national domiciled in

France may sue in the French courts a French national domiciled in a third State.

This option, granted by that Convention to Swiss nationals domiciled in France, might, in the absence of Article 58, conflict with the EEC Convention, according to which a defendant domiciled in a Contracting State may be sued in the courts of another Contracting State only in certain defined situations, and in any case not on the basis of rules of exorbitant jurisdiction such as those of Article 14 of the French Civil Code.

Under Article 58, a Swiss national domiciled in France can exercise the option which the Convention between France and Switzerland grants him to sue in France a Frenchman domiciled in another Contracting State, without there being any conflict with the EEC Convention, since the jurisdiction of the French Court will be recognized under the terms of Article 58. As a result of this provision, the rights secured by Swiss nationals domiciled in France are safeguarded, and France can continue to honour the obligations which it has entered into with respect to Switzerland. This is, of course, only an option which is granted to Swiss nationals, and there is nothing to prevent them from making use of the other provisions of the EEC Convention.

Article 59

It will be recalled that under Article 3 of the Convention, what are **A1.257** known as the rules of "exorbitant" jurisdiction are no longer to be applied in cases where the defendant is domiciled in the Community, but that under Article 4 they are still fully applicable where the defendant is domiciled outside the Community, and that, in such cases, judgments given by a court whose jurisdiction derives from those rules are to be recognized and enforced in the other Contracting States.

It must first be stressed that Article 59 does not reduce the effect of Article 4 of the Convention, for the latter Article does not prevent a State, in an agreement with a third State, from renouncing its rules of exorbitant jurisdiction either in whole or only in certain cases, for example, if the defendant is a national of that third State or if he is domiciled in that State. Each State party to the EEC Convention remains quite free to conclude agreements of this type with third States, just as it is free to amend the provisions of its legislation which contain rules of exorbitant jurisdiction; Article 4 of the Convention imposes no common rule, but merely refers back to the internal law of each State.

The only objective of Article 59 is to lessen the effects, within the Com- **A1.258** munity, of judgments given on the basis of rules of exorbitant jurisdiction. Under the combined effect of Articles 59 and 28, recognition or enforcement of a judgment given in a State party to the Convention can be refused in any other Contracting State:

1. where the jurisdiction of the court of origin could only be based on one of the rules of exorbitant jurisdiction specified in the second paragraph of Article 3. It would therefore be no ground for refusal that the court of origin founded its jurisdiction on one of those rules, if it could equally well have founded its jurisdiction on other

provisions of its law. For example, a judgment given in France on the basis of Article 14 of the Civil Code could be recognized and enforced if the litigation related to a contract which was to be performed in France;

A1.259 **[62]**

2. where a convention on the recognition and enforcement of judgments exists between the State addressed and a third State, under the terms of which judgments given in any other State on the basis of a rule of exorbitant jurisdiction will be neither recognized nor enforced where the defendant was domiciled or habitually resident in the third State. Belgium would thus not be obliged to recognize or enforce a judgment given in France against a person domiciled or habitually resident in Norway where the jurisdiction of the French courts over that person could be based only on Article 14 of the Civil Code since a convention between Belgium and Norway exists under which those two countries undertook not to recognize or enforce such judgments. Article 59 includes a reference not only to the defendant's domicile but also to his habitual residence, since in many non-member States this criterion is in practice equivalent to the concept of domicile as this is understood in the Member States of the Community (see also Article 10(1)) of the Hague Convention on the recognition and enforcement of foreign judgments in civil and commercial matters).

As regards the recognition and enforcement of judgments, Article 59 thus opens the way towards regulating the relations between the Member States of the EEC and other States, in particular the increasing number which are members of the Hague Conference. This seemed to justify a slight encroachment on the principle of free movement of judgments.

CHAPTER X

FINAL PROVISIONS

Articles 60 to 62 and 64 to 68

A1.260   These Articles give rise to no particular comment.

Article 63

A1.261   Article 63 deals with the accession of new Member States to the European Economic Community.

It is desirable, in the opinion of the Committee, that, in order to be able to fulfil the obligations laid down in Article 220 of the Treaty establishing the European Economic Community, such States should accede to the Convention. The legal systems of such States might, however, prevent the acceptance of the Convention as it stands, and negotiations might be necessary. If such were the case, any agreement concluded between the

Six and a new Member State should not depart from the basic principles of the Convention. That is why Article 63 provides that the Convention must be taken as a basis for the negotiations, which should be concerned only with such adjustments as are essential for the new Member State to be able to accede to the Convention.

The negotiations with that State would not necessarily have to precede its admission to the Community.

Since the adjustments would be the subject of a special agreement between the Six and the new Member State, it follows from the second paragraph of Article 63 that these negotiations could not be used as an opportunity for the Six to reopen debate on the Convention.

CHAPTER XI

PROTOCOL

Article I

Article I of the Protocol takes account of the special position of the   **A1.262**
Grand Duchy of Luxembourg. It provides that any person domiciled in Luxembourg who is sued in a court of another Contracting State pursuant to Article 5(1) (which provides, in matters relating to a contract, that the courts for the place of performance of **[63]** the obligation shall have jurisdiction), may refuse the jurisdiction of those courts. A similar reservation is included in the Benelux Treaty (Protocol, Article I), and it is justified by the particular nature of the economic relations between Belgium and Luxembourg, in consequence of which the greater part of the contractual obligations between persons resident in the two countries are performed or are to be performed in Belgium. It follows from Article 5(1) that a plaintiff domiciled in Belgium could in most cases bring an action in the Belgian courts.

Another characteristic of Luxembourg economic relations is that a large number of the contracts concluded by persons resident in Luxembourg are international contracts. In view of this, it was clearly necessary that agreements conferring jurisdiction which could be invoked against persons domiciled in Luxembourg should be subject to stricter conditions than those of Article 17. The text adopted is based on that of the Benelux Treaty (Article 5(3)).

Article II

Article II of the Protocol also has its origin in the Benelux Treaty. The   **A1.263**
latter applies *inter alia* to judgments given in civil matters by criminal courts, and thus puts an end of a controversy between Belgium and the Netherlands on the interpretation of the 1925 Convention between Bel-

gium and the Netherlands. As the report annexed to the Treaty explains,[1] the reluctance of the Netherlands authorities to enforce judgments given by foreign criminal courts in civil claims is due to the fact that a Netherlander charged with a punishable offence committed in a foreign country may be obliged to appear in person before the foreign criminal court in order to defend himself even in relation to the civil claim, although the Netherlands does not extradite its nationals. This objection is less pertinent than would appear at first sight under certain systems of law, and in particular in France, Belgium and Luxembourg, the judgment in a criminal case has the force of *res judicata* in any subsequent civil action.

In view of this, the subsequent civil action brought against a Netherlander convicted of a criminal offence will inevitably go against him. It is therefore essential that he should be able to conduct his defence during the criminal stage of the proceedings.

For this reason the Convention, like the Benelux Treaty, provides (see the Protocol) that a person domiciled in a Contracting State may arrange for his defence in the criminal courts of any other Contracting State.

Under Article II of the Protocol, that person will enjoy this right even if he does not appear in person and even if the code of criminal procedure of the State in question does not allow him to be represented. However, if the court seised of the matter should specifically order appearance in person, the judgment given without the person concerned having had the opportunity to arrange for his defence, because he did not appear in person, need not be recognized or enforced in the other Contracting States.

This right is, however, accorded by Article II of the Protocol only to persons who are prosecuted for an offence which was not intentionally committed; this includes road accidents.

Article III

A1.264   This Article is also based on the Benelux Treaty (Article III of the Protocol).

It abolishes the levying, in the State in which enforcement is sought, of any charge, duty or fee which is calculated by reference to the value of the matter in issue, and seeks to remedy the distortion resulting from the fact that enforcement gives rise to the levying of fixed fees in certain countries and proportional fees in others.

This Article is not concerned with lawyers' fees.

In the opinion of the Committee, while it was desirable to abolish proportional fees on enforcement, there was no reason to suppress the fixed charges, duties and fees which are payable, even under the internal laws of the Contracting States, whenever certain procedural acts are performed, and which in some respects can be regarded as fees charged for services rendered to the parties.

---

[1] Benelux Treaty: see the commentary on Article 13 and Article II of the Protocol.

Article IV

(See the commentary on Article 20(2) page 66* *et seq.*)   **A1.265**

[64] *Article V*

(See the commentary on Article 6(2), page 27 *et seq.*)   **A1.266**

Article VI

This Article relates to the case where legislative amendments to national   **A1.267**
laws affect either the provisions of the laws mentioned in the Convention—as might happen in the case of the provisions specified in the second
paragraph of Article 3—or affect the courts listed in section 2 of Title III.
Information on these matters must be passed to the Secretary General of
the Council of the European Communities to enable him, in accordance
with Article 64(e), to notify the other Contracting States.

ANNEX   **A1.268**

**Committee of exports who drafted the Convention on jurisdiction and
the enforcement of judgments in civil and commercial matters.**

[This list is not reproduced]

---

* [Editor's note: this should refer to page 39 *et seq.*, which appear at paras. A1.174
  et seq. above.]

PART II

JENARD REPORT (PROTOCOLS)

[66] Report on the Protocols

A1.269   **on the interpretation by the Court of Justice of the Convention
of 29 February 1968 on the mutual recognition of companies and
legal persons and of the Convention of 27 September 1968 on
jurisdiction and the enforcement of judgments in civil and
commercial matters**

(Signed at Luxembourg, 3 June 1971)

By Mr P. JENARD

*Directeur in the Belgian Ministry of Foreign Affairs
and External Trade*

I. General remarks

A1.270   1. In Joint Declaration No. 3, annexed to the Convention on the mutual
recognition of companies and legal persons, signed at Brussels on 29
February 1968, the Governments of the Member States of the European
Communities expressed their willingness to study means of avoiding differences in the interpretation of the Convention. To this end, they agreed
to examine the possibility of conferring jurisdiction in certain matters on
the Court of Justice of the European Communities and, if necessary, to
negotiate an agreement to that effect.

A similar Joint Declaration was annexed to the Convention on jurisdiction and the enforcement of judgments in civil and commercial matters,
signed at Brussels on 27 September 1968. This Declaration envisages the
possibility of assigning to the Court of Justice jurisdiction both to interpret
the Convention and to settle any conflicting claims and disclaimers of jurisdiction which may arise in applying it.

A1.271   2. In the course of negotiations to give effect to these Declarations, it was
soon agreed to give the Court additional jurisdiction, and to use for the
purpose a system based on Article 177 of the Treaty. The further question
nevertheless arose as to whether it would be appropriate to draft a general
convention applicable to all the conventions which had been or were to be
concluded on the basis of Article 220, or whether it would not be preferable to seek solutions which took into account the individual characteristics of each of these conventions.

This question was approached in an entirely pragmatic manner. A
detailed study was made of the two Conventions already signed, the Convention on the mutual recognition of companies and legal persons, and the
Convention on jurisdiction and the enforcement of judgments in civil and
commercial matters.

3. This study led to the conclusion that these two Conventions have distinct features which justify different arrangements for their interpretation by the Court of Justice. Although it had been suggested that a single convention might determine the jurisdiction of the Court to interpret all the conventions concluded on the basis of Article 220 of the Treaty, in the end it was thought preferable to conclude separate Protocols which would be better adapted to the requirements of each of the Conventions.

4. There was no need to apply the procedure of Article 236 of the Treaty for the purposes of concluding these Protocols since they deal with the interpretation of Conventions drawn up pursuant to Article 220 of the Treaty and in no way aim at revising the Treaty itself.

They merely confer on the Court of Justice further jurisdiction which is additional to, but does not affect, its existing jurisdiction.[1]

II. Protocol on the interpretation of the Convention on the mutual recognition of companies and legal persons

5. As regards the interpretation of the Convention on the mutual recognition of companies and legal persons, [67] there was thought to be no reason for departing from the preliminary ruling system laid down in Article 177 of the Treaty; and this system was therefore adopted in the draft Protocol in question.   **A1.272**

Article 1 of the Protocol confers on the Court jurisdiction to interpret the Convention of 29 February 1968, Joint Declaration No. 1 contained in the Protocol annexed to that Convention, and the Protocol which is the subject of this report. Article 2 repeats, in identical terms, the second and third paragraphs of Article 177, defining the circumstances in which references may be made to the Court by courts which have to decide questions of interpretation.

6. Since the Convention sometimes refers back to national law, the problem arose as to whether it might be necessary expressly to exclude the jurisdiction of the Court to interpret such law. It was thought unnecessary expressly to exclude jurisdiction in this respect, for the cases decided by the Court of Justice have already firmly established that it has no jurisdiction to interpret national law.

7. Article 3 concerns the procedure to be followed before the Court of Justice when, in accordance with the Protocol, the Court is asked to give a ruling.

It was thought appropriate to provide that the Rules of Procedure of the Court should be supplemented to take account of the new jurisdiction.

---

[1] On various occasions, jurisdiction has been conferred on the Court of Justice without reference to the revision procedure set out in Art. 236 (internal agreements under Conventions of Association—see O.J. No. 93, 11.6.1964, p. 1490/64; provisions of Council Regulation No. 17 on appeal to the Court—see O.J. No. 13, 21.2.1962, p. 204/62).

Article 3(2) indicated that Article 188 of the Treaty is to be used for this purpose.

It was considered that, in order to ensure that the Convention would be applied as effectively and as uniformly as possible, an exchange of information should be organized on judgments of national courts against whose decision there is no remedy under national law.

A Joint Declaration to this effect is annexed to the Protocol.

III. Protocol on the interpretation of the Convention on jurisdiction and the enforcement of judgments in civil and commercial matters

A1.273   8. The study of the Convention on jurisdiction and the enforcement of judgments in civil and commercial matters showed that it has features sufficiently distinctive to justify a separate system for its interpretation by the Court of Justice.

There was unanimous agreement on the need to ensure uniform interpretation of the Convention, and hence to confer new jurisdiction on the Court of Justice, using a system based on Article 177. But it was feared that, in view of the number and diversity of the disputes to which the Convention applies, an application for a preliminary ruling on the lines of Article 177 might be made by one of the parties either as a delaying tactic or as a means of putting pressure on an opponent of modest financial means. In short, the application might be made for improper purposes.

A1.274   (1) This Convention will be applicable in a large number of cases. It governs not only recognition and enforcement of judgments, but also the international jurisdiction of the courts, and in particular all cases where a person is sued in the courts of a Contracting State in which he is not domiciled. Moreover, it is not confined to a limited field such as the recognition of companies, but extends to all civil and commercial matters relating to rights in property (litigation over all kinds of contract, non-contractual liability, maintenance, etc.).

   (2) At the stage of recognition and enforcement, Article 34 of the Convention provides that the court to which application is made for the issue of an order for enforcement shall give its decision without delay, and without the party against whom enforcement is sought being entitled at that stage of the proceedings to make any submissions.

   Plainly, an application to the Court of Justice for a preliminary ruling would, if made at this stage, undermine the object of the Convention which, by introducing a new, standardized, *ex parte* procedure for enforcement, aims at eliminating delaying tactics and preventing the respondent from withdrawing his assets from any measure of enforcement.

   (3) Finally it must be stressed that decisions of the Court of Justice on the interpretation of the Convention differ from decisions on the interpretation of other conventions, as regards the consequences for the parties.

   Thus, if the court were to interpret a provision of the Convention so as to rule that the courts seised of a matter had no jurisdiction, the proceedings might well have to be instituted again from the outset, either in a State other than that whose courts were **[68]** originally seised or, perhaps, in other courts in the same State (see, for example, Article 5 of the Convention which lays down special rules of jurisdiction).

9. The Protocol therefore follows the system of Article 177, but subject to such adjustments as were thought necessary to deal with the matters set out above. The system may be summarized as follows: **A1.275**

   (a) the courts which are allowed to refer questions to the court are expressly specified;
   (b) the right to apply to the court for a preliminary ruling is not given to courts of first instance;
   (c) the Protocol provides that the Courts of Cassation and other courts of last instance are required to refer a question of interpretation to the court if they consider that a decision of the Court on that question is necessary to enable them to give judgment;
   (d) in addition to requests for a preliminary ruling, there is a novel provision for interpretation by the Court of Justice, similar to the "pourvoi dans l'intérêt de la loi."

10. Article 1, which is similar to Article 1 of the Protocol on the interpretation of the Convention on the mutual recognition of companies and legal persons, confers on the Court jurisdiction to interpret the Convention of 27 September 1968 and its Protocol, as well as the Protocol which is the subject of this report. **A1.276**

11. Article 2 lists the national courts which may ask the Court to give a preliminary ruling. **A1.277**

   (1) Courts of first instance are not included in this list. Their exclusion is designed mainly to prevent the interpretation of the Court being requested in too many cases, and particularly in trivial matters. Moreover, it was thought that where two courts of first instance, for example a "justice de paix" and an Amtsgericht, gave judgments which became *res judicata* and showed differences of interpretation in the application of the Convention, this should not necessitate further action, any more than would similar differences of interpretation between two inferior courts of the same country. Similarly, it was argued that the Court of Justice should not be required to give rulings unless it was fully informed. In order to achieve this, questions of interpretation should, in the first place, be dealt with by the national courts, especially in view of the fact that in the interests of legal certainty the Court of Justice can only seldom depart from the principles established by its previous judgments.
   (2) Article 2(1) specifies by name the courts which are allowed to refer questions to the Court of Justice, including those which, pursuant to Article 3(1), are required to do so. Such a list seemed to be essential, since the present wording of the third paragraph of Article 177 has given rise to conflicting interpretations as to which are the

courts and tribunals against whose decisions there is no judicial remedy under national law (for example, the theoretical and pragmatic schools of thought in Germany).

It seemed all the more necessary to make this point clear because, under the Protocol, inferior courts have no jurisdiction to refer a question to the Court of Justice.

This list also takes into account the fact that the Convention of 27 September 1968 governs only civil and commercial matters concerning property rights; the list therefore includes only those Courts which have jurisdiction in such cases.

(3) Article 2(2) states that the power to refer a question to the Court is also given to the courts of the Contracting States when they are sitting in an appellate capacity. The Courts in question thus include courts of appeal, save for the exceptional cases when they are sitting at first instance when sitting in an appellate capacity.

In the Federal Republic of Germany the expression "appeal" includes "Beschwerde."

(4) Article 2(3) lays down that in the cases provided for in Article 37 of the Convention of 27 September 1968, the courts referred to in that Article may also refer a question to the Court of Justice. It will be remembered that Article 37 governs appeals against judgments authorizing the enforcement of a foreign judgment.

A1.278   [69] 12. Article 3 lays down that a court of last instance is bound to refer a question to the Court of Justice only "if it considers that a decision on the question is necessary to enable it to give judgment." In Article 177 of the Treaty of Rome this provision appears only in the second paragraph, governing cases in which other courts are entitled to refer a question to the Court of Justice.

The provision contained in Article 3(1) of the Protocol accords with the interpretation now generally given to Article 177: it is generally agreed to be beyond dispute that a court of last instance has discretion to assess the relevance of questions put to it for interpretation.

Nevertheless, this provision seemed necessary to avoid conflicting interpretations; for it will be remembered that, as has already been pointed out in paragraph 8(3) of this report, decisions of the Court of Justice on the interpretation of the Judgments Convention differ, in their consequences, from decisions of the interpretation of other conventions.

Thus if the jurisdiction of a court were challenged on appeal, and the Court of Justice ruled that the Convention had been misinterpreted by the first court, the proceedings might have to be instituted again from the very beginning, either in another State or, perhaps, in another court in the same State.

A party to an action might accordingly be greatly tempted to raise a question of interpretation of the Convention before an appellate court merely in order to gain time, and the temptation would be all the greater if that court were automatically required to refer the question to the Court of Justice.

A1.279   A number of other solutions were considered, including giving the highest courts only a power, rather than a duty, to refer a question to the

Court, or requiring them to refer a question only if they would otherwise give to a provision an interpretation different from the interpretation already given either by the Court of Justice or by other courts. Finally, however, a provision very close to Article 177 was adopted in order to achieve the greatest possible uniformity in Community law.

For the reasons set out above, it was thought necessary to confirm the discretion of courts of last instance by means of a clear and unambiguous text, and above all to make it proof against any possible subsequent tendency automatically to refer questions to the Court.

As regards its form, Article 3 differs from Article 177, in that it sets out first of all the rule for the courts of last instance, and thereafter for the other courts. The object of this modified form was to emphasize that the Protocol was designed solely to provide a specific solution to problems of interpretation of the Convention on jurisdiction and the enforcement of judgments in civil and commercial matters.

13. Since the Convention also refers back to national law, reference should be made to what was said in this connection in the commentary on the protocol on the interpretation of the Convention on the mutual recognition of companies (see paragraph 6).

14. Article 4 lays down a new procedure based in part on the "pourvoi **A1.280** dans l'intérêt de la loi" and in part on the procedure for giving advisory opinions. All the countries of the Community, with the exception of the Federal Republic of Germany, have a form of appeal for the clarification of a point of law which enables the competent judicial authority, in this instance the Procurators-General of the Courts of Cassation, to appeal against a final decision which misunderstands or misapplies either the letter or the spirit of the law. The purpose of this appeal is to avoid perpetuating an erroneous interpretation of the law where the parties have omitted to appeal against the decision which includes that interpretation (see Dalloz, Encyclopédie juridique under Cassation No. 2509).

Article 4 is designed to make for a uniform interpretation of the Convention by introducing a procedure complementary to the request for a preliminary ruling provided for in Article 3. The purpose is to ensure a uniform interpretation for the future wherever existing judgments are in conflict.

In the last analysis, this procedure occupies an intermediate position between the "pourvoi dans l'intérêt de la loi," from which it differs in that it does not entail the setting aside of a judgment which is ultimately shown to have misinterpreted the Convention, and that of an advisory appeal. The procedure is, however, limited to cases in which a court has already given judgment.

Paragraph 1 defines the cases in which the competent authority of a **A1.281** State may apply to the Court of Justice. It will be for that authority to decide whether it is advisable to refer a matter to the Court, and it will presumably not do so unless the national judgment includes reasons which might lead to an interpretation different from that previously given by the Court of Justice or by a foreign court. If there are no factors involved which make it likely that the principles **[70]** established in the decided cases would be changed, the national authority could always seek to clarify the point of law by appealing in its own country in accordance with the procedure there in force.

A1.282 Paragraph 2 lays down that rulings given by the Court shall not affect the decisions submitted to it, in the same way that the setting aside of a judgment following an appeal to clarify a point of law in no way influences the position of the parties.

It follows that the judgments of the Court cannot give rise to any fresh proceedings, even where otherwise an extraordinary avenue of appeal might be appropriate.

A1.283 Paragraph 3 lays down that the Procurators-General of the Courts of Cassation (who, in the countries which know the "pourvoi dans l'intérêt de la loi," are competent) or any other authority designated by a State, are entitled to request the Court of Justice for a ruling. The designation of the Procurators-General is further evidence that the appeal procedure laid down in Article 4 is intended solely to clarify points of law.

The wording of paragraph 3 takes account of the situation obtaining in Germany, where the "pourvoi dans l'intérêt de la loi" is unknown. It furthermore empowers any of the Contracting States to designate any other authority or even to designate two authorities, as for example the Procurator-General for appeals against judgments of civil, commercial or criminal courts in civil matters, and the Minister of Justice for appeals against decisions of administrative tribunals.

A1.284 Paragraph 4 amends Article 20 of the Statute of the Court of Justice to deal with the procedure provided for in Article 4. The amendment takes account of the fact that the parties to the original proceedings will have no interest in intervening at this stage.

It may be wondered what are the implications of a ruling on interpretation given on the basis of Article 4. The ruling certainly is not binding on the parties. It must be acknowledged that such a ruling has no force in law, and that accordingly nobody is bound by it. But clearly it will have the greatest persuasive authority and will for the future constitute the guideline for all Community courts. In this respect it may be compared with the decision on a "pourvoi dans l'intérêt de la loi." Such a decision is binding on nobody, but constitutes a decision of principle of the greatest importance for the future, and on which judges will generally follow.

A1.285 15. Article 5 of the Protocol, like Article 3 of the Protocol on the interpretation of the Convention on the mutual recognition of companies, extends the provisions governing the jurisdiction of the Court of Justice to cover the exercise of the new jurisdiction conferred on it.

However, these provisions are extended only in so far as the Protocol does not otherwise provide; this reservation chiefly concerns Article 177 of the Treaty, whose provisions, even if they should be modified, are not applicable to the Protocol, which has its own separate provisions on this point.

A1.286 16. Article 11 provides for any relevant amendment to the jurisdiction of the courts of the Contracting States.

17. The other Articles of the Protocol, which contain the final provisions, give rise to no particular comment. Again, an exchange of information is to be organized on the decisions of the courts referred to in Article 2(1) in order to ensure that the Convention is applied as effectively and as uniformly as possible. A Joint Declaration to this effect is annexed to the Protocol.

18. The provisions of the Convention on *lis pendens* and related actions should go a long way, if not all the way, towards resolving any problems which may arise from conflicting claims and disclaimers of jurisdiction. Where, however, such problems arise from conflicting interpretations, they will be solved by applying the Protocol.

PART III

SCHLOSSER REPORT

[71] Report on the Convention

A1.287 **on the Association of the Kingdom of Denmark, Ireland and the United Kingdom of Great Britain and Northern Ireland to the Convention on jurisdiction and the enforcement of judgments in civil and commercial matters and to the Protocol on its interpretation by the Court of Justice**

(Signed at Luxembourg, 9 October 1978)

by Professor Dr Peter SCHLOSSER,

of the Chair of German, international and foreign civil procedure, of the general theory of procedure and of civil law at the University of Munich

Pursuant to Article 3(2) of the Act of Accession of 22 January 1972 a Council working party, convened as a result of a decision taken by the Committee of Permanent Representatives of the Member States, prepared a draft Convention on the accession of the Kingdom of Denmark, Ireland and the United Kingdom of Great Britain and Northern Ireland to the Convention of 27 September 1968 on jurisdiction and the enforcement of judgments in civil and commercial matters and to the Protocol of 3 June 1971 on its interpretation by the Court of Justice. This working party was composed of government experts from the nine Member States and representatives from the Commission. The rapporteur, Mr P. Schlosser, Professor of Law at the University of Munich, drafted the explanatory report which was submitted to the governments at the same time as the draft prepared by the experts. The text of this report, which is a commentary on the Convention of Accession signed at Luxembourg on 9 October 1978, is now being published in this issue of the Official Journal.

INDEX

CHAPTER 4

Appendix 1—Official Reports on the Conventions

CHAPTER 5

Recognition and enforcement

CHAPTER 11

Adjustment to the Protocol of 3 June 1971 on the interpretation by the Court of Justice of the European Communities of the 1968 Convention

[77] CHAPTER 1

PRELIMINARY REMARKS

A1.289

1. Under Article 3(2) of the Act of Accession, the new Member States undertook "to accede to the Conventions provided for in Article 220 of the EEC Treaty, and to the Protocols on the interpretation of those Conventions by the Court of Justice, signed by the original Member States and to this end to enter into negotiations with the original Member States in order to make the necessary adjustments thereto." As a first step the Commission of the European Communities made preparations for the impending discussions on the contemplated adjustments. On 29 November 1971, it submitted to the Council an interim report on the additions considered necessary to the two Conventions signed in 1968, namely the Convention on jurisdiction and the enforcement of judgments in civil and commercial matters (hereinafter referred to as "the 1968 Convention") and the Convention on the mutual recognition of companies and legal persons. Following consultations with the new Member States, the Commission on 15 September 1972 drew up a comprehensive report to the Council on the main problems arising from adjusting both Conventions to the legal institutions and systems of the new Member States. On the basis of this report, the Committee of Permanent Representatives decided on 11 October 1972 to set up a Working Party which was to be composed of delegates of the original and the new Member States of the Community and of a representative of the Commission. The Working Party held its inaugural meeting on 16 November 1972 under the chairmanship of the Netherlands delegate in accordance with the rota. On this occasion, it decided to focus its attention initially on negotiations concerning adjustments to the 1968 Convention which had already been ratified by the original Member States of the EEC and to the Protocol of 3 June 1971 on its interpretation ("the Interpretation Protocol of 1971"), and to postpone the work entrusted to it regarding the Convention on the mutual recognition of companies and legal persons. At its second meeting, the Working Party elected the author of this report as its rapporteur. On the basis of a request made by the Working Party at its third meeting in June 1973, the Committee of Permanent Representatives appointed Mr Jenard, the "Directeur d'administration auprès du ministère belge des Affaires Étrangères," as its permanent chairman.

2. The Working Party initially considered proposing the legal form of **A1.290**
a Protocol for the accession of the new Member States to the 1968
Convention, and that the adjustments contemplated should be
annexed thereto. However, this method would have introduced
some confusion into the subject. A distinction would then have had
to be made between three different Protocols, *i.e.* the Protocol
referred to in Article 65 of the 1968 Convention, the Interpretation
Protocol of 1971 and the new Protocol on accession. Furthermore,
there were no grounds for dividing the new provisions required in
consequence of the accession of the new Member States to the 1968
Convention by putting some into a protocol and others into an act of
accession annexed to it. The Working Party therefore presented the
outcome of its discussions in the form of a draft Convention
between the original Member States and the new Member States of
the EEC. This draft Convention makes provision for accession both
to the 1968 Convention and to the Interpretation Protocol of 1971
(Title I) as well as for the necessary changes to them (Titles II and
IV). The accession of Denmark, Ireland and the United Kingdom
to the 1968 Convention extends also to the Protocol referred to in
Article 65 which is an integral part of the 1968 Convention. The
Working Party also proposed adjustments to this Protocol (Title
III).

The decision of the Working Party to adopt the legal form of a **A1.291**
Convention incorporating adjustments instead of replacing the 1968
Convention by a new Convention has the advantage that the
unchanged provisions of the 1968 Convention do not require
renewed ratification.

Accordingly three different "Conventions" will in future have to
be distinguished:

The Convention on jurisdiction and the enforcement of judgments in civil and commercial matters in its original form will be
referred to as "the 1968 Convention."[1]

The expression "Accession Convention" refers to the draft Convention proposed by the Working Party.

After ratification of the Accession Convention certain provisions
of the 1968 Convention will exist in an amended form. References
in this [78] report to the amended form will be indicated by the
addition of that word, *e.g.* "Article 5(2) as amended."

3. The structure of this report does not closely follow the structure of **A1.292**
the proposed new Accession Convention. In many places, this
report can only be understood, or at any rate is easier to understand, if it is read in conjunction with the corresponding parts of the
reports on the 1968 Convention and on the Interpretation Protocol
of 1971 which were drawn up by the present permanent chairman
and erstwhile rapporteur of the Working Party (hereinafter referred

---

[1] When references are given to Arts. without any further mention, reference is to
the 1968 version of the Convention.

to as "the Jenard report"). The structure of this report is based on that of these earlier reports.

CHAPTER 2

REASONS FOR THE CONVENTION

A1.293   4. The second chapter of the Jenard report sets out the reasons for concluding a Convention. They apply with at least as much force to the new Member States as they did to the relationships between the original Member States of the EEC, but they do not call for further close examination here. The obligation on the new Member States to accede to the 1968 Convention is laid down in Article 3(2) of the Act of Accession to the EEC Treaty. However, in order to give a clear view of the legal position, it may be helpful to supplement the references in the Jenard report to the laws in force in the original Member States of the EEC and to the existing Conventions between these States with details concerning the new Member States.

A.

THE LAW IN FORCE IN THE NEW MEMBER STATES

1. UNITED KINGDOM

A1.294   5. The legal position in the United Kingdom is characterized by six significant features.

A1.295   6. (a) In the first place, there is a distinction between recognition and enforcement at common law on the one hand and under the Foreign Judgments (Reciprocal Enforcement) Act 1933 on the other.

At common law, a judgment given in a foreign State may serve as a basis for proceedings before courts in the United Kingdom, if the adjudicating court was competent to assume jurisdiction. This legal consequence follows irrespective of whether or not there is reciprocity. In this connection, recognition and enforceability are not limited to the use of the foreign judgment as evidence. The United Kingdom court dealing with the case may not in general review the substance of the foreign judgment. There are, of course, a limited number of grounds for refusing recognition.

For recognition and enforcement under the Foreign Judgments (Reciprocal Enforcement) Act 1933 on the other hand the successful party does not have to institute fresh proceedings before courts in the United Kingdom on the basis of the foreign judgment. The successful party merely has to have the judgment registered with the appropriate court. However, this simplified recognition and enforcement procedure is available only where the judgment to be recognized was given by a Superior Court, and, more important, where a convention on the reciprocal recognition and enforcement of judgments is in force between the State of origin and the United Kingdom. Once the foreign judgment is registered, it has the same legal force and effect as a judgment given by the court of registration.

7. (b) Both these methods are available in the United Kingdom only **A1.296** for the enforcement of judgments which order payment of a specific sum of money. Consequently maintenance orders made by foreign courts which stipulate periodic payments are not generally enforceable in the United Kingdom. However, the Maintenance Orders (Reciprocal Enforcement) Act which came into force in 1972 makes it possible for international treaty obligations to be concluded in this field.

[79]   **A1.297**
8. (c) Both at common law and under the 1933 Act, it is a requirement for recognition and enforcement that the judgment should be "final and conclusive between the parties." This requirement is clearly satisfied where the adjudicating court can no longer alter its judgment or can only do so in very exceptional circumstances. Similarly, neither the fact that the period during which an appeal may be made is still running nor even a pending appeal prevent this requirement from being satisfied. However, maintenance orders which stipulate periodic payments are excluded from recognition since they may be varied to take account of changed circumstances unless they are covered by the abovementioned Maintenance Orders (Reciprocal Enforcement) Act 1972.

9. (d) It is possible to institute proceedings on the basis of a foreign **A1.298** judgment or to make an application for its registration under the 1933 Act during a period of six years from the date on which the judgment was given.

10. (e) United Kingdom law distinguishes between the recognition and **A1.299** enforcement of foreign judgments in the same way as the other States of the Community. If a foreign judgment fulfils the common law requirements for its recognition or if it is registered with a United Kingdom court, it becomes effective also in fields other than enforcement. A clear distinction is made between recognition and enforcement of foreign judgments in, for example, the bilateral Conventions with France and Germany.

The requirements mentioned in paragraphs 7 and 9 are not set out in those Conventions as requirements for recognition.

A1.300   11. (f) Finally, it should be noted that the United Kingdom although not a federal State, is not a single legal and judicial area. It consists of three areas with different legal systems: England and Wales, Scotland and Northern Ireland. Whilst the common law rules described in paragraph 6 apply uniformly to the whole of the United Kingdom, the different judicial systems in each of the three legal areas of this State have to be taken into consideration when the 1933 Act is applied. Applications for registration have to be made in England and Wales to the High Court of Justice, in Scotland to the Court of Session, and in Northern Ireland to the High Court of Justice of Northern Ireland. If registration is granted, the judgment can be enforced only in the area in which the relevant courts have jurisdiction, which extends to the whole of England and Wales, of Scotland or of Northern Ireland respectively (see paragraph 209; for maintenance orders, see paragraphs 210 and 218). Recognition of a judgment is, nevertheless, independent of its registration.

2. IRELAND

A1.301   12. The common law provisions of Irish law are similar to those which apply in the United Kingdom. The only statutory provisions of Irish law on the recognition and enforcement of foreign judgments are contained in the Maintenance Orders (Reciprocal Enforcement) Act 1974. This Act gives effect to an international agreement between Ireland and the United Kingdom for the reciprocal recognition of maintenance orders made by courts in those States. The agreement is expressed to terminate on the coming into force of the 1968 Convention for both States.

3. DENMARK

A1.302   13. Under paragraph 223a of the Law of 11 April 1916, foreign judgments can be recognized only if a treaty providing reciprocity has been concluded with the State of origin, or if binding effect has been given to judgments of a foreign State by Royal Decree. Denmark has concluded no bilateral conventions on recognition and enforcement. There is only one Royal Decree of the type referred to and it concerns judgments given by German courts.[2]

B.

EXISTING CONVENTIONS

A1.303   14. Apart from Conventions relating to particular matters (see paragraph 238 *et seq.*), the United Kingdom is the only new Member State to be bound to other Member States of the EEC by bilateral

---

[2] The Royal Decree of 13 April 1938, reproduced in "Bundesanzeiger" 1953, No. 105, p. 1 and in Bülow-Arnold, "Internationaler Rechtsverkehr," 925.5.

Conventions on the recognition and enforcement of judgments. These are the Conventions with France, Belgium, the Federal Republic of Germany, Italy and the Netherlands listed in the new version of Article 55 (see **[80]** paragraph 237). These bilateral Conventions serve to implement the Foreign Judgments (Reciprocal Enforcement) Act for the United Kingdom (see paragraph 6) and therefore contain provisions which more or less follow the same pattern. The requirements for recognition and enforcement correspond to the criteria mentioned in paragraphs 6 to 11 above. Rules providing for "direct" jurisdiction[3] are not included.

C.

GENERAL ARRANGEMENT OF THE PROPOSED ADJUSTMENTS

15. Neither Article 3(2) of the Act of Accession nor the terms of reference given to the Working Party provide any clear guide of what is meant by "necessary adjustments." **A1.304**

    The term could be given a very narrow interpretation. The emphasis would then have to be laid above all the requirement of necessity, in the sense of indispensability. At the beginning of the Working Party's discussions it became clear, however, that such a narrow view of the contemplated adjustments was bound to make it more difficult for the 1968 Convention to take root in the legal systems of the new Member States. There are a variety of reasons for this.

1. SPECIAL STRUCTURAL FEATURES OF THE LEGAL SYSTEMS OF THE NEW MEMBER STATES

16. The 1968 Convention implicitly proceeded from a legal background common to the original Member States of the EEC. By contrast the legal systems of the new Member States unmistakably contain certain special structural features. It would hardly have been reasonable to expect these States to adjust their national law to the legal position on which the 1968 Convention is based. **A1.305**

    On the contrary, adjustment of the Convention seemed the more obvious course on occasion. This applies, for example, to the distinction made in Articles 30 and 38 between ordinary and extraordinary appeals (see paragraph 195 *et seq.*), which does not exist in United Kingdom and Irish law, to the system of registering judgments in the United Kingdom instead of the system of granting enforcement orders (see paragraph 208) and to the concept of the trust which is a characteristic feature of the common law[4] (see para-

---

[3] For this concept, see the Jenard report, Chap. II, B and C, and Chap. IV, A and B.

[4] Zweigert-Kötz, "Einführung in die Rechtsvergleichung auf dem Gebiet des Privatrechts," Vol. 1 (1971), p. 78 *et seq.*

graph 109 *et seq.*). The same also applies to the inter-relation existing in Denmark between judicial and administrative competence in
maintenance cases (see paragraph 66 *et seq.*).

2. AMBIGUITIES IN THE EXISTING TEXT

A1.306 17. In certain cases, enquiries about the precise meaning of some provisions of the 1968 Convention by the States obliged to accede to it
clearly showed that their interpretation was often uncertain and
controversial. The Working Party decided therefore to propose that
certain provisions of the 1968 Convention should be given a more
precise wording or an authoritative interpretation. This applies, for
example, to the provisions about granting legal aid in enforcement
proceedings (see paragraph 223). The Working Party also dealt in
this way with the provisions of Article 57 on the relation between
the 1968 Convention and other Conventions, (see paragraph 238 *et
seq.*). In most cases, however, the information requested could be
given in a sufficiently clear and uniform way, so that this report
need do no more than refer to it.

3. FURTHER DEVELOPMENTS IN THE LAW OF THE ORIGINAL MEMBER STATES OF THE EEC

A1.307 18. In yet other cases, enquiries by the new Member States about the
content of some provisions of the 1968 Convention revealed that in
the original Member States of the EEC too the law had in the meantime evolved in such a way that general adjustments rather than
adjustments restricted to relations with the new Member States
seemed advisable. This applies particularly to proceedings in
matters of family law in which ancillary relief, and especially maintenance claims, are now often combined with the main proceedings
concerning status. In family and matrimonial matters, such combined proceedings have replaced the traditional system of separat-
ing status proceedings from subsequent proceedings in many
countries during the years following the signing of the 1968 Convention. This is the reason for the revised Article 5(2) proposed by
the Working Party (see paragraphs 32 and 90). The development of
consumer protection law in the Member States led to a completely
new version of Section 4 of Title II, and in one case the 1968 Convention was amended as a result of judgments of the Court of Justice of the European Communities (see paragraph 179).

[81] 4. SPECIFIC ECONOMIC EFFECTS

A1.308 19. Finally, it became apparent that certain provisions of the 1968 Convention in their application to the new Member States would have
economic repercussions unequalled in the original Member States.
Thus, the worldwide significance of the British insurance market
prompted the Working Party to recommend amendments concerning jurisdiction in insurance matters (see paragraph 136). The new

paragraph (7) of Article 5 (see paragraph 122) is justified by the special position occupied by British maritime jurisdiction.

CHAPTER 3

SCOPE OF THE CONVENTION

20. As already discussed in the Jenard report, the provisions governing the scope of the 1968 Convention contain four significant elements. These required some further explanation in the context of the relationship of the original Member States to each other. They are: **A1.309**

    1. Limitation to proceedings and judgments on matters involving international legal relationships (I).
    2. Duty of the national courts to observe the provisions governing the scope of the 1968 Convention of their own motion (II).
    3. Limitation of the Convention to civil and commercial matters (III).
    4. A list (Article 1, second paragraph) of matters excluded from the scope of the Convention (IV).

    In the relationship of the original Member States to each other there was no problem about a fifth criterion which is much more clearly brought out in the title of the 1968 Convention than in Article 1 which defines its scope. The 1968 Convention only applies where court proceedings and court decisions are involved. Proceedings and decisions of administrative authorities do not come within the scope of the 1968 Convention. This gave rise to a particular problem of adjustment in relation to Denmark (V).

I. Matters Involving International Legal Relationships

21. The accession of the new Member States to the 1968 Convention in no way affects the application of the principle that only proceedings and judgments about matters involving international legal relationships are affected, so that reference need only be made to section I of Chapter III of the Jenard report. **A1.310**

II. Binding Nature of the Convention

22. Under Articles 19 and 20 of the 1968 Convention the provisions concerning "direct jurisdiction" are to be observed by the court of its own motion: in some cases, *i.e.* where exclusive jurisdiction exists, irrespective of whether the defendant takes any steps; in other cases only where the defendant challenges the jurisdiction. **A1.311**

Similarly, a court must also of its own motion consider whether there exists an agreement on jurisdiction which excludes the court's jurisdiction and which is valid in accordance with Article 17.

An obligation to observe the rules of jurisdiction of its own motion is by no means an unusual duty for a court in the original Member States. However, the United Kingdom delegation pointed out that such a provision would mean a fundamental change for its courts. Hitherto United Kingdom courts had been able to reach a decision only on the basis of submissions of fact or law made by the parties. Without infringing this principle, no possibility existed of examining their jurisdiction of their own motion.

A1.312
However, Article 3(2) of the Act of Accession cannot be interpreted as requiring the amendment of any provisions of the Conventions referred to on the ground that introduction of those provisions into the legal system of a new Member State would necessitate certain changes in its long-established legal practices and procedures.

[82] It does not necessarily follow from Articles 19 and 20 of the 1968 Convention that the courts must, of their own motion, investigate the facts relevant to deciding the question of jurisdiction, that they must for example inquire where the defendant is domiciled. The only essential factor is that uncontested assertions by the parties should not bind the court. For this reason the following rule is reconcilable with the 1968 Convention: a court may assume jurisdiction only if it is completely satisfied of all the facts on which such jurisdiction is based; if it is not so satisfied it can and must request the parties to provide the necessary evidence, in default of which the action will be dismissed as inadmissible. In such circumstances the lack of jurisdiction would be declared by the court of its own motion, and not as a result of a challenge by one of the parties. Whether a court is itself obliged to investigate the facts relevant to jurisdiction, or whether it can, or must, place the burden of proof in this respect on the party interested in the jurisdiction of the court concerned, is determined solely by national law. Indeed some of the legal systems of the original Member States, for example Germany, do not require the court itself to undertake factual investigations in a case of exclusive jurisdiction, even though lack of such jurisdiction has to be considered by the court of its own motion.

III. Civil and Commercial Matters

A1.313
23. The scope of the 1968 Convention is limited to legal proceedings and judgments which relate to civil and commercial matters. All such proceedings not expressly excluded fall within its scope.

In particular, it is irrelevant whether an action is brought "against" a named defendant (see paragraphs 124 *et seq.*). It is true that in such a case Article 2 *et seq.* cannot operate; but otherwise the 1968 Convention remains applicable.

The distinction between civil and commercial matters on the one hand and matters of public law on the other is well recognized in the legal systems of the original Member States and is, in spite of some important differences, on the whole arrived at on the basis of similar criteria. Thus the term "civil law" also includes certain important special subjects which are not public law, especially, for example, parts of labour law. For this reason the draftsmen of the original text of the 1968 Convention, and the Jenard report, did not include a definition of civil and commercial matters and merely stated that the 1968 Convention also applies to decisions of criminal and administrative courts, provided they are given in a civil or commercial matter, which occasionally happens. In this last respect, the accession of the three new Member States presents no additional problems. But as regards the main distinction referred to earlier considerable difficulties arise.

In the United Kingdom and Ireland the distinction commonly **A1.314** made in the original EEC States between private law and public law is hardly known. This meant that the problems of adjustment could not be solved simply by a reference to these classifications. In view of the Judgment of the Court of Justice of the European Communities of 14 October 1976,[5] which was delivered during the final stages of the discussions and which decided in favour of an interpretation which made no reference to the "applicable" national law, the Working Party restricted itself to declaring, in Article 1, paragraph 1, that revenue, customs or administrative matters are not civil or commercial matters within the meaning of the Convention. Moreover, the legal practice in the Member States of the Community, including the new Member States, must take account of the above judgment which states that, in interpreting the concept of civil and commercial matters, reference must be made "first, to the objectives and scheme of the Convention and, secondly, to the general principles which stem from the corpus of the national legal systems."

As a result of this all that this report can do is to throw light on the Court's instructions by setting out some details of comparative law.

---

[5] Case No. 29/76 [1976] ECR 1541. The formal part of the Judgment reads as follows:
  1. In the interpretation of the concept "civil and commercial matters" for the purposes of the application of the Convention of 27 September 1968 on jurisdiction and the enforcement of judgments in civil and commercial matters, in particular Title III thereof, reference must not be made to the law of one of the States concerned but, first, to the objectives and scheme of the Convention and, secondly, to the general principles which stem from the corpus of the national legal systems;
  2. A judgment given in an action between a public authority and a person governed by private law, in which the public authority has acted in the exercise of its powers, is excluded from the area of application of the Convention.

A.

ADMINISTRATIVE LAW IN IRELAND AND THE UNITED KINGDOM

A1.315 24. In the United Kingdom and in Ireland the expression "civil law" is not a technical term and has more than one meaning. It is used mainly as **[83]** the opposite of criminal law. Except in this limited sense, no distinction is made between "private" and "public" law which is in any way comparable to that made in the legal systems of the original Member States, where it is of fundamental importance. Constitutional law, administrative law and tax law are all included in "civil law." Admittedly the United Kingdom is already a party to several Conventions which expressly apply only to "civil and commercial matters." These include all the bilateral Conventions on the enforcement of foreign judgments concluded by the United Kingdom. None of these, however, contains any rules which decide the circumstances under which an original court before which an issue is brought may assume jurisdiction. They govern only the recognition and enforcement of judgments and deal with questions of jurisdiction only indirectly as a condition of recognition. Moreover, these Conventions generally only apply to judgments ordering the payment of a specific sum of money (see paragraph 7). In drafting them, a pragmatic approach dispensing with a definition of "civil and commercial matters" proved, therefore, quite adequate.

B.

ADMINISTRATIVE LAW IN THE CONTINENTAL MEMBER STATES

A1.316 25. In the legal systems of the original Member States, the State itself and corporations exercising public functions such as local authorities may become involved in legal transactions in two ways. Having regard to their special functions and the fact that they are formally part of public law they may act outside private law in a "sovereign" capacity. If they do this, their administrative act ("Verwaltungsakt," "décision exécutoire") is of a special nature. The State and some other public corporations may, however, also engage in legal transactions in the same way as private individuals. They can conclude contracts subject to private law, for example with transport undertakings for the carriage of goods or persons in accordance with tariffs generally in force or with a property owner for the lease of premises. The State and public corporations can also incur tortious liability in the same way as private individuals, for example as a result of a traffic accident in which an official car is involved. The real difficulty arises from distinguishing between instances in which the State and its independent organs act in a private law capacity and those in which they act in a public law capacity. A few guidelines on how this difficulty may be overcome are set out below.

The difficulties of finding a dividing line are of three kinds. The field of activities governed by public law differs in the various continental Member States (1). Public authorities frequently have a choice of the form in which they wish to act (2). The position is relatively clear only regarding the legal relations between the State and its independent organs (3).

1. THE VARYING EXTENT OF PUBLIC LAW

26. The most important difference between national administrative **A1.317** laws on the continent consists in the legal rules governing the duties of public authorities to provide supplies for themselves and for public tasks. For this purpose the French legal system has established the separate concept of administrative contracts which are governed independently of the "Code civil" by a special law, the "Code des marchés publics." The administrative contract is used both when public authorities wish to cover their own requirements and when public works, such as surface or underground construction, land development, etc., have to be undertaken. In such situations the French State and public corporations do not act in the capacity of private persons. The characteristic result of this is that, if the other parties to the contract do not perform their obligations the State and public corporations do not have to bring an action before the courts, but may impose unilaterally enforceable sanctions by an administrative act ("décision exécutoire"). The legal situation in Germany is quite different. There the administrative contract plays a completely subordinate role. Supplies to the administrative agencies, and in particular the placing of contracts for public works, are carried out solely on the basis of private law. Even where the State undertakes large projects like the construction of a dam or the channelling of a river, it concludes its contracts with the firms concerned like a private individual.

[84] 2. CHOICE OF TYPE OF LAW

27. However, the borderline between the public law and the private law **A1.318** activities of public agencies is not rigidly prescribed in some of the legal systems. Public authorities have, within certain limits, a right to choose whether in carrying out their functions they wish to use the method of a "sovereign act," *i.e.* an administrative contract, or merely to conclude a private transaction.

In respect of those areas where public authorities may act either under private or public law, it is not always easy to decide whether or not they have acted as private individuals. In practice a clear indication is often lacking.

3. *RELATIONSHIP OF PUBLIC AUTHORITIES TO ONE ANOTHER*

A1.319   28. Relations between public authorities may also be governed either by private or by public law. If governed by public law, such relations are not subject to the 1968 Convention, even if, as in Italy, they are not considered part of administrative law. However, relations of States and public corporations with each other would fall almost without exception within the sphere of private law, if they contain international aspects (and are not subject to public international law). It is hard to imagine how, for example, it would be possible for relations under public law to exist between two local authorities in different States. However, such relations could, of course, be established in future by treaties.

C.

CIVIL AND CRIMINAL LAW

A1.320   29. The Working Party considered it obvious that criminal proceedings and criminal judgments of all kinds are excluded from the scope of the 1968 Convention, and that this matter needed, therefore, no clarification in the revised text (see paragraph 17). This applies not only to criminal proceedings *stricto sensu*. Other proceedings imposing sanctions for breaches of orders or prohibitions intended to safeguard the public interest also fall outside the scope of civil law. Certain difficulties may arise in some cases in classifying private penalties known to some legal systems like contractual penalty clauses, penalties imposed by associations, etc. Since in many legal systems criminal proceedings may be brought by a private plaintiff, a distinction cannot be made by reference to the party which instituted the proceedings. The decisive factor is whether the penalty is for the benefit of the private plaintiff or some other private individual. Thus the decisions of the Danish industrial courts imposing fines, which are for the benefit of the plaintiff or some other aggrieved party, certainly fall within the scope of the 1968 Convention.

IV. MATTERS EXPRESSLY EXCLUDED

A1.321   30. The second paragraph of Article 1 sets out under four points the civil matters excluded from the scope of the 1968 Convention. The accession of the new Member States raises problems in respect of all four points.

A.

STATUS OR LEGAL CAPACITY OF NATURAL PERSONS, RIGHTS IN PROPERTY ARISING OUT OF A MATRIMONIAL RELATIONSHIP, WILLS AND SUCCESSION

31. The Working Party encountered considerable difficulties when **A1.322**
dealing with two problems relating to point (1) of the second paragraph of Article 1. The first problem was that of maintenance proceedings ancillary to status proceedings (1) and the second problem
was the meaning of the term "régimes matrimoniaux" (rights in
property arising out of a matrimonial relationship) (2). Apart from
these two problems, the enquiries directed to the Working Party by
the new Member States in respect of point (1) of the second paragraph of Article 1 were relatively easy to answer (3).

1. MAINTENANCE JUDGMENTS ANCILLARY TO STATUS PROCEEDINGS (ANCILLARY MAINTENANCE JUDGMENTS)

32. When the 1968 Convention was drawn up, the principle still applied in **A1.323**
the original Member States that disputes relating to property could not
be combined with status proceedings, nor could **[85]** maintenance
proceedings be combined with proceedings for the dissolution of a
marriage or paternity proceedings. It was therefore possible, without
running the risk of creating disadvantages caused by artificially separar-
ating proceedings which in reality belonged together, to exclude status
matters, but not maintenance proceedings, from the scope of the 1968
Convention. Once this rule comes up against national legislation
which allows combined proceedings comprising maintenance claims
and status matters, it will perforce give rise to great difficulties. These
difficulties had already become serious in the original Member States,
as soon as the widespread reform of family law had led to an increasing
number of combined proceedings in those countries. Accordingly a
mere adjustment of the 1968 Convention as between the original and
new Member States would have provided only a piecemeal solution.
Time and opportunity were ripe for an adjustment of the 1968 Convention, even as regards the relationships between the original Member States, to take account of the developments in the law which had
taken place (see paragraph 18).

33. (a) The solution proposed by the Working Party is the outcome of a **A1.324**
lengthy and intensive study of the possible alternatives. A distinctive feature of the 1968 Convention is the inter-relation of the application of its rules of jurisdiction at the adjudicating stage and the
prohibition against reopening the question of jurisdiction at the recognition stage. Consequently, on the basis of the original text of the
Convention only two completely clear-cut solutions present themselves as regards the treatment of ancillary maintenance judgments.
The first is that the adjudicating court dealing with a status matter

may give an ancillary maintenance judgment only when it has jurisdiction under the 1968 Convention; the maintenance judgment must then be recognized by the foreign court which may not re-examine whether the original adjudicating court had jurisdiction. The second possible solution is that ancillary maintenance judgments should also be excluded from the scope of the 1968 Convention under point (1) of the second paragraph of Article 1 as being ancillary to status judgments. However, both solutions have practical drawbacks. The second would result in ancillary maintenance judgments being generally excluded from recognition and enforcement under the 1968 Convention, even though the great majority of cases are decided by courts which would have had jurisdiction under its provisions. In an unacceptably high number of cases established maintenance claims would then no longer be able to move freely. The first solution would constitute a retrograde step from the progressive and widely acclaimed achievement of combined proceedings and judgments in status and maintenance matters.

A1.325   34. In view of the above, the simplest solution would have been to include rules of jurisdiction covering status proceedings in the 1968 Convention. However, the reasons given earlier against taking that course are still valid. Therefore, the only way out is to opt for one of the two alternatives outlined above, whilst mitigating its drawbacks as far as possible. In the view of the Working Party, to deprive maintenance judgments ancillary to status proceedings of the guarantee of their enforceability abroad, or to recognize them only to a severely limited extent, would be the greater evil.

35. The Working Party therefore tried first of all to find a solution along the following lines. National courts dealing with status matters should have unrestricted power to decide also on maintenance claims, even when they cannot use their jurisdiction in respect of the maintenance claim on any provision of the 1968 Convention; ancillary maintenance judgments should in principle be recognized and enforced, but the court addressed may, contrary to the principles of the 1968 Convention which would otherwise apply, re-examine whether the court which gave judgment on the maintenance claims had jurisdiction under the provisions of Title II. However, the principle that the jurisdiction of the court of origin should not be re-examined during the recognition and enforcement stages was one of the really decisive achievements of the 1968 Convention. Any further restriction of this principle, even if limited to one area, would be justifiable only if all other conceivable alternatives were even more unacceptable.

A1.326   36. The proposed addition to Article 5 would on the whole have most advantages. It prevents maintenance judgments which are ancillary to status judgments being given on the basis of the rule of exorbitant jurisdiction which generally applies in family law matters, namely the rule which declares the nationality of only one of the two parties as sufficient. One can accept that maintenance proceedings may not be combined with status proceedings where the competence of the court concerned is based solely on such **[86]** exorbitant jurisdiction. For status proceedings, jurisdiction will continue to depend on the nationality of one of the two parties. The maintenance proceedings will have to be brought before another court with jurisdiction under the 1968 Convention.

(b) The significance of the new approach is as follows: **A1.327**

37. It applies uniformly to the original and to the new Member States alike.

38. The jurisdiction of the court of origin may not be re-examined during the recognition and enforcement stages. This still follows from the third paragraph of Article 28 even after the addition made to Article 5. The court of origin has a duty to examine very carefully whether it has jurisdiction under the 1968 Convention, because a wrong decision on the question of jurisdiction cannot be corrected later on.

39. Similar rules apply in respect of *lis pendens*. It was not necessary to amend Articles 21 and 23. As long as the maintenance claim is pending before the court seised of the status proceedings it may not validly be brought before the courts of another State.

40. The question whether the court seised of the status proceedings has indeed jurisdiction also in respect of the maintenance proceedings, without having to rely solely on the nationality of one of the parties to the proceedings, is to be determined solely by the *lex fori*, including of course its private international law and procedural law. Even where the courts of a State may not as a rule combine a status matter with a maintenance claim, but can do so if a foreign legal system applicable under the provisions of their private international law so provides, they have jurisdiction in respect of the maintenance claim under the provisions of Article 5(2) of the 1968 Convention as amended. This is subject to the proviso that the court concerned in fact had jurisdiction in respect of both the status proceedings and the maintenance claim under the current provisions of its own national law.

41. The 1968 Convention prohibits the assumption of a combined juris- **A1.328** diction which may be provided for under the national law to cover both status and maintenance proceedings only where the court's jurisdiction would be based solely on the nationality of one of the two parties. This concerns principally the exorbitant jurisdictions which are referred to in the second paragraph of Article 3, and provided for in Article 15 of the Belgian Civil Code (Code civil), and Articles 14 and 15 of the French and Luxembourg Civil Code (Code

civil), governing proceedings which do not relate only to status and are therefore not excluded pursuant to point (1) of the second paragraph of Article 1. Maintenance actions combined with status proceedings continue to be permitted, even if the jurisdiction of the court is based on grounds other than those which are normally excluded by the 1968 Convention as being exorbitant. Jurisdiction on the basis of both parties having the same nationality is excluded by the 1968 Convention in respect of ordinary civil and commercial matters, (Article 3, second paragraph), but in respect of combined status and maintenance proceedings, it cannot be considered as exorbitant, and consequently should not be inadmissible. The plaintiff's domicile is recognized in any case as a basis for jurisdiction in maintenance actions.

Finally, the proposed addition to Article 5(2) deprives courts of jurisdiction to entertain maintenance claims in combined family law proceedings only where their jurisdiction in respect of the status proceedings is based solely on the nationality of one of the two parties. Where the jurisdiction of a court depends on the fulfilment of several conditions, only one of which is that one of the parties should possess the nationality of the country concerned, jurisdiction does not depend solely on the nationality of the two parties.

Article 606(3) of the German Code of Civil Procedure is intended to ensure, in conjunction with Article 606a, that in matrimonial matters a German court always has jurisdiction, even when only one of the spouses is German. The fact that this provision is only supplementary to other provisions governing jurisdiction does not change the fact that jurisdiction may be based solely on the nationality of one of the parties. Once Article 5(2) of the 1968 Convention comes into force in its amended form maintenance claims can no longer be brought and decided under that particular jurisdiction.

A1.329   42. Article 5(2) does not apply where the defendant is not domiciled in a Contracting State, or where maintenance questions can be decided without the **[87]** procedural requirement of a claim or petition by one spouse against the other (see paragraph 66).

2. RIGHTS IN PROPERTY ARISING OUT OF A MATRIMONIAL RELATIONSHIP

A1.330   43. The exclusion of "rights in property arising out of a matrimonial relationship" from the scope of the Convention (Article 1 second paragraph, point (1)) raises a problem for the United Kingdom and Ireland.

Neither of these countries has an equivalent legal concept, although the expression "matrimonial property" is used in legal literature. In principle, property rights as between spouses are governed by general law. Agreements between spouses regulating their property rights are no different in law from agreements with third parties. Occasionally, however, there are special statutory provisions affecting the rights of spouses. Under English law (Matrimonial Homes Act 1967) and Irish law (Family Home Protection Act 1976), a spouse is entitled to certain rights of occupation of the matrimonial home. Moreover, divorce courts in the United Kingdom have, under the Matrimonial causes Act 1973, considerable powers, though varying in extent in the different parts of the country, to order the payment of capital sums by one former spouse to the other. In England even a general redistribution of property as between former spouses and their children is possible.

The concept of "rights in property arising out of a matrimonial relationship" can also give rise to problems in the legal systems of the original Member States. It does not cover the same legal relations in all the systems concerned.

For a better understanding of the problems involved, they are set out more fully below (a), before the solution proposed by the Working Party is discussed (b).

44. (a) Three observations may give an indication of what is meant by "matrimonial regimes" (rights in property arising out of a matrimonial relationship) in the legal systems of the seven continental Member States. They will deal with the character of the concept which is confined exclusively to relationships between spouses (paragraph 45), with the relationship with the provisions which apply to all marriages irrespective of the particular "matrimonial regime" between the spouses (paragraph 46), and finally with the possibility of third parties becoming involved (paragraph 47). **A1.331**

45. For the purpose of governing the relations between spouses in respect of property, these legal systems do not, or at least not predominantly, employ the legal concepts and institutions otherwise used in their civil law. Instead, they have developed exclusive legal institutions the application of which is limited to relations between spouses, and whose most important feature is a comprehensive set of rules governing property. However, there is not merely one such set of rules in each legal system. Instead, spouses have a choice between several, ranging from general "community of property" to strict "separation of property." Even the latter, when chosen by the spouses, is a special form of "property regime," although special features arising from marriage can then hardly be said to exist any longer. The choice of a "property regime" must take the form of a "marriage contract" which is a special legal concept and should not be confused with the conclusion of the marriage itself. If the spouses do not make a choice, one of the sets of rules governing property rights applies to them by law (known as the "statutory matrimonial regime"). **A1.332**

In some legal systems (France and Belgium) the "matrimonial regime" existing at the beginning of a marriage can subsequently be changed only in exceptional circumstances. In others (Germany) the spouses are free to alter their "matrimonial regime" at any time.

Disputes concerning "matrimonial regimes" can arise in various forms. There may be a dispute about the existence and interpret- **A1.333** ation of a marriage contract. In certain circumstances, a spouse may apply to the court for conversion of one "matrimonial regime" into a different one. Some "matrimonial regimes" provide for different rules in respect of different types of property. A dispute may then arise as to the type of property to which a particular object belongs. Where the "matrimonial regime" in question differentiates between the management of different types of property, there may be disagreement as to which spouse may manage which items of property. The most frequent type of dispute relating to "matrimonial regimes" concerns the winding up of the "matrimonial regime" after termination of the marriage, particularly after divorce. The "statutory matrimonial regime" under German [88] law ("Zugewinngemeinschaft" or community of acquisitions) then results in an equalization claim by the spouse whose property has not increased in value to the same extent as that of his partner.

A1.334 46. Some provisions apply to all marriages, irrespective of the particular "matrimonial régime" under which spouses live, especially in Germany and France. Significantly the German and French texts of the 1968 Convention use the term in the plural ("die Güterstände," "les régimes matrimoniaux").

This can be explained as follows: the Code civil, for instance, deals with property aspects of marriage in two different parts of the code. Title V of the third book (on the acquisition of property) refers in detail to the "contrat de mariage" and then "régimes matrimoniaux," while property aspects of the relations between spouses are also covered by Articles 212 to 226 in Title V of the first book. The new French divorce law of 11 July 1975[6] introduced into the new version of Article 270 *et seq.* of the Code civil equalization payments normally in the form of lump sum compensation (Article 274) which are independent of the particular "regime" applicable between the spouses. German law in the fourth book of the Bürgerliches Gesetzbuch makes a similar distinction between the legal consequences in respect of property rights which generally follow from marriage (Title V, Article 1353 *et seq.*) and those which follow from "matrimonial property law," which varies according to the various "matrimonial regimes." Under both systems (Article 1357(2) of the Bürgerliches Gesetzbuch, Article 220(2) of the French Code civil) it is possible, for example, to prevent a spouse from engaging in certain legal transactions in which he is normally entitled to engage in his capacity as spouse. According to Article 285 of the Code civil[7] the court can, after divorce, make orders concerning the matrimonial home irrespective of the "matrimonial regime" previously applicable. Similar possibilities exist in other States.

A1.335 French legal literature refers to provisions concerning property rights which apply to all marriages as "régime matrimonial pri-

---

[6] Law No. 75–617, JO 1975, 7171.
[7] In the text of Law No. 75–617 (n. 6).

maire." Other legal systems have no such special expression. It is within the spirit of Article 1, second paragraph, point (1) of the 1968 Convention to exclude those provisions concerning property rights affecting all marriages from its scope of application, in so far as they are not covered by the term "maintenance claims" (see paragraph 91 *et seq.*)

In all legal systems of the Community it is possible to conceive of relations affecting rights between spouses which are governed by the general law of contract, law of tort or property law. Some laws contain provisions specifically intended to govern cases where such relations exist between spouses. For example, Article 1595 of the French Code civil contains restrictions on the admissibility of contracts of sale between spouses. Case law has sometimes developed special rules in this field which are designed to take account of the fact that such transactions commonly occur in relations between spouses. All this does not alter the position that legal relations governed by the general law of contract or tort remain subject to the provisions of the 1968 Convention, even if they are between spouses.

47. Finally, legal provisions comprised in the term "matrimonial regimes" are not limited to relations between the spouses themselves. For example, in Italian law, in connection with the liquidation of a "fondo patrimoniale" disputes may arise between parents and children (Article 171(3) of the Codice civile), which under Italian law unequivocally concern relations arising out of "matrimonial property law" ("il regime patrimoniale della famiglia"). German law contains the regime of "continued community of property" ("fortgesetzte Gütergemeinschaft"), which forms a link between a surviving spouse and the issue of the marriage.

48. (b) These findings raise problems similar to those with which the Working Party was faced in connection with the concept "civil and commercial matters." It was, however, possible to define the concept of "matrimonial regimes" not only in a negative manner (paragraph 49), but also positively, albeit rather broadly. This should enable implementing legislation in the United Kingdom and Ireland, in reliance on these statements, to indicate to the courts which legal relations form part of "matrimonial regimes" within the meaning of the 1968 Convention (paragraph 50). Consequently no formal adjustment of the 1968 Convention became necessary. **A1.336**

49. As a negative definition, it can be said with certainty that in no legal system do maintenance claims between spouses derive from rules governing "matrimonial regimes"; nor are **[89]** maintenance claims confined to claims for periodic payments (see paragraph 93).

50. The mutual rights of spouses arising from "matrimonial régimes" correspond largely with what are best described in English as "rights in property arising out of a matrimonial relationship." **A1.337**

Apart from maintenance matters property relations between spouses which are governed by the differing legal systems of the original Member States otherwise than as "matrimonial regimes" only seldom give rise to court proceedings with international aspects.

Thus the following can be said in respect of the scope of point (1) of the second paragraph of Article 1 as far as "matrimonial regimes" are concerned:

The Convention does not apply to the assumption of jurisdiction by United Kingdom and Irish courts, nor to the recognition and enforcement of foreign judgments by those courts, if the subject matter of the proceedings concerns issues which have arisen between spouses, or exceptionally between a spouse and a third party, during or after dissolution of their marriage, and which affect rights in property arising out of the matrimonial relationship. The expression "rights in property" includes all rights of administration and disposal—whether by marriage contract or by statute—of property belonging to the spouses.

3. THE REMAINING CONTENTS OF ARTICLE 1, SECOND PARAGRAPH, POINT (1) OF THE 1968 CONVENTION

A1.338   51. (a) The non-applicability of the 1968 Convention in respect of the status or legal capacity of natural persons concerns in particular proceedings and judgments relating to:

— the voidability and nullity of marriages, and judicial separation,
— the dissolution of marriages,
— the death of a person,
— the status and legal capacity of a minor and the legal representation of a person who is mentally ill; the status and legal capacity of a minor also includes judgments on the right to custody after the divorce or legal separation of the parents; this was the Working Party's unanimous reply to the express question put by the Irish delegation,
— the nationality or domicile (see paragraph 71 *et seq.*) of a person,
— the care, custody and control of children, irrespective of whether these are in issue in divorce, guardianship, or other proceedings,
— the adoption of children.

However, the 1968 Convention is only inapplicable when the proceedings are concerned directly with legal consequences arising from these matters. It is not sufficient if the issues raised are merely of a preliminary nature, even if their preliminary nature is, or has been, of some importance in the main proceedings.

A1.339   52. (b) The expression "wills and succession" covers all claims to testate or intestate succession to an estate. It includes disputes as to the validity or interpretation of the terms of a will setting up a trust, even where the trust takes effect on a date subsequent to the death of the testator. The same applies to proceedings in respect of the application and interpretation of statutory provisions establishing trusts in favour of persons or institutions as a result of a person dying intestate. The 1968 Convention does not, therefore, apply to any disputes concerning the creation, interpretation and administration of trusts arising under the law of succession including wills. On the other hand, disputes concerning the relations of the trustee with persons other than beneficiaries, in other words the "external relations" of the trust, come within the scope of the 1968 Convention (see paragraph 109 *et seq.*)

B.

BANKRUPTCY AND SIMILAR PROCEEDINGS

53. Article 1, second paragraph, point (2), occupies a special position among the provisions concerning the legal matters excluded from the 1968 Convention. It was drafted with reference to a special Convention on bankruptcy which was being discussed at the same time as the 1968 Convention. **A1.340**

[90] Leaving aside special bankruptcy rules for very special types of business undertakings, the two Conventions were intended to dovetail almost completely with each other. Consequently, the preliminary draft Convention on bankruptcy, which was first drawn up in 1970, submitted in an amended form in 1975,[8] deliberately adopted the principal terms "bankruptcy," "compositions" and "analogous proceedings"[9] in the provisions concerning its scope in the same way[10] as they were used in the 1968 Convention. To avoid, as far as possible, leaving lacunae between the scope of the two Conventions, efforts are being made in the discussions on the proposed Convention on bankruptcy to enumerate in detail all the principal and secondary proceedings involved[11] and so to eliminate any problems of interpretation. As long as the proposed Convention on bankruptcy has not yet come into force, the application of Article 1, second paragraph, point (2) of the 1968 Convention remains difficult. The problems, including the matters arising from the accession of the new Member States, are of two kinds. First, it is necessary to define what proceedings are meant by bankruptcy, compositions or analogous proceedings as well as their constituent parts (1). Secondly, the legal position in the United Kingdom poses a special problem as the bankruptcy of "incorporated companies" is not a recognized concept in that country (2).

---

[8] Document of the Commission of the European Communities XI/449/75—F.
[9] The word "analogous" does not appear in Art. 1(1) simply because the proceedings in question are listed in a Protocol.
[10] See the Report on the Convention on bankruptcy, winding-up arrangements, compositions and similar proceedings by Noël-Lemontey (16.775/XIV/70) Chap. 3, s.I.
[11] See preliminary draft Bankruptcy Convention, Art. 17 and Protocol thereto, Arts. 1 and 2 (n. 8).

1. GENERAL AND INDIVIDUAL TYPES OF PROCEEDINGS EXCLUDED FROM THE SCOPE OF THE 1968 CONVENTION

A1.341
54. It is relatively easy to define the basic types of proceedings that are subject to bankruptcy law and therefore fall outside the scope of the 1968 Convention. Such proceedings are defined in almost identical terms in both the Jenard and the Noël-Lemontey reports[12] as those

> "which, depending on the system of law involved, are based on the suspension of payments, the insolvency of the debtor or his inability to raise credit, and which involve the judicial authorities for the purpose either of compulsory and collective liquidation of the assets or simply of supervision by those authorities."

In the legal systems of the original States of the EEC there are only a very few examples of proceedings of this kind, ranging from two (in Germany) to four (Italy and Luxembourg). In its 1975 version[12a] the Protocol to the preliminary draft Convention on bankruptcy emunerates the proceedings according to types of proceedings and States concerned. A list is reproduced in Annex I to this report.* Naturally, the 1968 Convention does not, *a fortiori*, cover global insolvency proceedings which do not take place before a court as, for example, can be the case in France when authorization can be withdrawn from an insurance undertaking for reasons of insolvency.

A1.342
The enumeration in Article 17 of the preliminary draft Convention on bankruptcy cannot, before that Convention has come into force, be used for the interpretation of Article 1, second paragraph, point (2) of the 1968 Convention. Article 17 mentions the kind of proceedings especially closely connected with bankruptcy where the courts of the State where the bankruptcy proceedings are opened are to have exclusive jurisdiction.

It is not desirable at this stage to prescribe this list, or even an amended list, as binding. Further amendments may well have to be made during the discussions on the Convention on bankruptcy. To prescribe a binding list would cause confusion, even though the list to be included in the Protocol to the Convention on bankruptcy will, after the latter's entry into force, prevail over the 1968 Convention pursuant to Article 57, since it is part of a special Convention. Moreover, the list, as already mentioned, does not include all bankruptcies, compositions and analogous proceedings. For instance, it has become clear during the discussions on the Convention on bankruptcy that the list will not cover insurance undertakings which only undertake direct insurance,[13] without thereby bringing the bankruptcy of such undertakings within the scope of

---

[12] *op. cit.*
[12a] See n. 8 above.
 * [Editor's note: see para. A1.568 below.]
[13] 1975 preliminary draft (see n. 8), Art. 1(1), subpara. (3), and Art. II of the Protocol. See Noël-Lemontey report (n. 10) for reasons for exclusion.

the 1968 Convention. Finally the Working Party was not sure whether all the proceedings included in the list as it stood at the beginning of 1976 could properly be regarded as bankruptcies, compositions or analogous proceedings, before the list formally comes into force. This applied particularly to the proceedings mentioned in connection with the liquidation of companies (see paragraph 57).

2. *BANKRUPTCY LAW AND THE DISSOLUTION OF COMPANIES*

55. As far as dissolution, whether or not by decision of a court, and the capacity to be made bankrupt are concerned, the legal treatment of a **[91]** partnership[14] established under United Kingdom or Irish law is comparable in every respect to the treatment of companies established under continental legal systems. Companies[15] within the meaning of United Kingdom or Irish law, however, are dealt with in a fundamentally different way. The Bankruptcy Acts do not apply to them,[16] but instead they are subject to the winding-up procedure of the Companies Acts[17]; even if they are not registered companies. Winding-up is not a special bankruptcy procedure, but a legal concept which can take different forms and serves different purposes. A common feature of all winding-up proceedings is a disposal of assets and the distribution of their proceeds amongst the persons entitled thereto with a view of bringing the company to an end. The start of winding-up proceedings corresponds, therefore, to what is understood by "dissolution" on the continent. The dissolution of a company on the other hand is identical with the final result of a liquidation under continental legal systems.   **A1.343**

A distinction is made between winding-up by the court, voluntary winding-up and winding-up subject to the supervision of the court. The second kind of winding-up takes place basically without the intervention of the court, either at the instance of the members alone or of the members together with the creditors. Only as a subsidiary measure and exceptionally can the court appoint a liquidator. The third kind of winding-up is only a variation on the second. The court has certain supervisory powers. A winding-up of a com-   **A1.344**

---

[14] Although it does not have its own legal personality it corresponds by and large to the "offene Handelsgesellschaft" in German law and the "société en nom collectif" in French law.

[15] In the form of a "private company" it corresponds to the continental "Gesellschaft mit beschränkter Haftung" (company with limited liability) and in the form of a "public company" to the continental "Aktiengesellschaft" (joint stock company).

[16] U.K.: Bankruptcy Act 1914, ss.119 and 126. See Tridmann-Hicks-Johnson, "Bankruptcy Law and Practice" (1970), p. 272.

[17] In respect of Great Britain—Companies Act 1948; in respect of Northern Ireland—Companies Acts 1960 and Companies (Amendment) Act 1963; in respect of Ireland—Company Act 1963, s.213.

pany by the court requires an application either by the company or by a creditor which is possible in a number of circumstances of which insolvency is only one. Other grounds for a winding-up include: the number of members falling below the required minimum, failure to commence, or a lengthy suspension of, business and the general ground "that the court is of the opinion that it is just and equitable that the company should be wound up."

A1.345   56. The legal position outlined has the following consequences for the application of Article 1, second paragraph, point (2), and Article 16(2) of the 1968 Convention in the Continental (b) and other (a) Member States:

57. (a) A voluntary winding-up under United Kingdom or Irish law cannot be equated with court proceedings. The same applies to the non-judicial proceedings under Danish law for the dissolution of a company. Legal disputes incidental to or consequent upon such proceedings are therefore normal civil or commercial disputes and as such are not excluded from the scope of the 1968 Convention. This also applies in the case of a winding-up subject to the supervision of the court. The powers of the court in such a case are not sufficiently clearly defined for the proceedings to be classed as judicial.

A winding-up by the court cannot, of course, be automatically excluded from the scope of the 1968 Convention. For although most proceedings of this kind serve the purpose of the liquidation of an insolvent company, this is not always the case. The Working Party decided to exclude from the scope of the 1968 Convention only those proceedings which are or were based on section 222(e) of the British Companies Act[18] or the equivalent provisions in the legislation of Ireland and Northern Ireland. This would, however, involve too narrow a definition of the proceedings to be excluded, as the liquidation of an insolvent company is frequently based on one of the other grounds referred to in section 222 of the British Companies Act, notably in (a), which states that a special resolution of the members is sufficient to set proceedings in motion. There is no alternative therefore to ascertaining the determining factor in the dissolution in each particular case. The English version of Article 1, second paragraph, point (2), of the 1968 Convention has been worded accordingly. It was not, however, necessary to alter the text of the Convention in the other languages. If a winding-up in the United Kingdom or Ireland is based on a ground other than the insolvency of the company, the court concerned with recognition and enforcement in another Contracting State will have to examine whether the company was not in fact insolvent. Only if it is of the

---

[18] "if . . . the company is unable to pay its debts."

opinion that the company was solvent will the 1968 Convention apply.

58. Only in that event does the problem arise of whether exclusive juris-   **A1.346**
diction exists for the courts at the seat of the company pursuant to
Article 16(2) of the 1968 Convention. In the United Kingdom and
Ireland this is the case for proceedings which involve or have
involved a solvent company.

   The term "dissolution" in Article 16(2) of the 1968 Convention is
not to be understood in the narrow technical sense in which it is
used in legal systems on the Continent. It also covers **[92]** proceedings concerning the liquidation of a company after "dissolution."
These include disputes about the amount to be paid out to a member; such proceedings are nothing more than stages on the way
towards terminating the legal existence of a company.

59. (b) If a company established under a Continental legal system is dis-   **A1.347**
solved, *i.e.* enters the stage of liquidation, because it has become
insolvent, court proceedings relating to the "dissolution of the company" are only conceivable as disputes concerning the admissibility
of, or the mode and manner of conducting, winding-up proceedings. All this is outside the scope of the 1968 Convention. On the
other hand, all other proceedings intended to declare or to bring
about the dissolution of a company are not the concern of the law of
winding-up. It is unnecessary to examine whether the company
concerned is solvent or insolvent. It also makes no difference, if
bankruptcy law questions arise as a preliminary issue. For instance,
when litigation ensues as to whether a company should be dissolved, because a person who allegedly belongs to it has gone bankrupt, the dispute is not about a matter of bankruptcy law, but of a
type which falls within the scope of the 1968 Convention. The Convention also applies if, in connection with the dissolution of a company not involving the courts, third parties contend in legal
proceedings that they are creditors of the company and consequently entitled to satisfaction out of assets of the company.

C.

SOCIAL SECURITY

60. Matters relating to social security were expressly excluded from the   **A1.348**
scope of the 1968 Convention. This was intended to avoid the difficulties which would arise from the fact that in some Member States
this area of law comes under public law, whereas in others it is on
the border-line between public and private law. Legal proceedings
by social security authorities against third parties, for example
against wrongdoers, in exercise of rights of action which they have
acquired by subrogation or by operation of law, do come within the
scope of the 1968 Convention.

D.

ARBITRATION

A1.349 61. The United Kingdom requested information on matters regarding the effect of the exclusion of "arbitration" from the scope of the 1968 Convention, which were not dealt with in the Jenard report. Two divergent basic positions which it was not possible to reconcile emerged from the discussion on the interpretation of the relevant provisions of Article 1, second paragraph, point (4). The point of view expressed principally on behalf of the United Kingdom was that this provision covers all disputes which the parties had effectively agreed should be settled by arbitration, including any secondary disputes connected with the agreed arbitration. The other point of view, defended by the original Member States of the EEC, only regards proceedings before national courts as part of "arbitration" if they refer to arbitration proceedings, whether concluded, in progress or to be started. It was nevertheless that no amendment should be made to the text. The new Member States can deal with this problem of interpretation in their implementing legislation. The Working Party was prepared to accept this conclusion, because all the Member States of the Community, with the exception of Luxembourg and Ireland, had in the meantime become parties to the United Nations Convention of 10 June 1958 on the recognition and enforcement of foreign arbitral awards, and Ireland is willing to give sympathetic consideration to the question of her acceding to it. In any event, the differing basic positions lead to a different result in practice only in one particular instance (see paragraph 62).

1. DECISIONS OF NATIONAL COURTS ON THE SUBJECT MATTER OF A DISPUTE DESPITE THE EXISTENCE OF AN ARBITRATION AGREEMENT

A1.350 62. If a national court adjudicates on the subject matter of a dispute, because it overlooked an arbitration agreement or considered it inapplicable, can recognition and enforcement of that judgment be refused in another State of the Community on the ground that the arbitration agreement was after all valid and that therefore, pursuant to Article 1, second paragraph, point (4), the judgment falls outside the scope of the 1968 Convention? Only if the first interpretation (see paragraph 61) is accepted can an affirmative answer be given to this question.

[93] In support of the view that this would be the correct course, it is argued that since a court in the State addressed is free, contrary to the view of the court in the State of origin, to regard a dispute as affecting the status of an individual, or the law of succession, or as falling outside the scope of civil law, and therefore as being outside the scope of the 1968 Convention, it must in the same way be free to take the opposite view to that taken by the court of origin and to

reject the applicability of the 1968 Convention because arbitration is involved.

Against this, it is contended that the literal meaning of the word "arbitration" itself implies that it cannot extend to every dispute affected by an arbitration agreement; that "arbitration" refers only to arbitration proceedings. Proceedings before national courts would therefore be affected by Article 1, second paragraph, point (4) of the 1968 Convention only if they dealt with arbitration as a main issue and did not have to consider the validity of an arbitration agreement merely as a matter incidental to an examination of the competence of the court of origin to assume jurisdiction. It has been contended that the court in the State addressed can no longer re-open the issue of classification; if the court of the State of origin, in assuming jurisdiction, has taken a certain view as to the applicability of the 1968 Convention, this becomes binding on the court in the State addressed.

2. OTHER PROCEEDINGS CONNECTED WITH ARBITRATION BEFORE NATIONAL COURTS

63. (a) The 1968 Convention as such in no way restricts the freedom of **A1.351** the parties to submit disputes to arbitration. This applies even to proceedings for which the 1968 Convention has established exclusive jurisdiction. Nor, of course, does the Convention prevent national legislation from invalidating arbitration agreements affecting disputes for which exclusive jurisdiction exists under national law or pursuant to the 1968 Convention.

64. (b) The 1968 Convention does not cover court proceedings which are ancillary to arbitration proceedings, for example the appointment or dismissal of arbitrators, the fixing of the place of arbitration, the extension of the time limit for making awards or the obtaining of a preliminary ruling on questions of substance as provided for under English law in the procedure known as "statement of a special case" (section 21 of the Arbitration Act 1950). In the same way a judgment determining whether an arbitration agreement is valid or not, or because it is invalid, ordering the parties not to continue the arbitration proceedings, is not covered by the 1968 Convention.

65. (c) Nor does the 1968 Convention cover proceedings and decisions concerning applications for the revocation, amendment, recognition and enforcement of arbitration awards. This also applies to court decisions incorporating arbitration awards—a common method of recognition under United Kingdom law. If an arbitration award is revoked and the revoking court or another national court itself decides the subject matter in dispute, the 1968 Convention is applicable.

V. JUDICIAL NATURE OF PROCEEDINGS AND JUDGMENTS

A1.352   66. As between the original Member States, and also as between those States and the United Kingdom and Ireland, the 1968 Convention could and can in one particular respect be based on a surprisingly uniform legal tradition. Almost everywhere the same tasks pertaining to the field of private law are assigned to the courts. The authorities which constitute "courts" can everywhere be recognized easily and with certainty. This is also true in cases where proceedings are being conducted in "court" which are not the result of an action by one party "against" another party (see paragraphs 23 and 124 *et seq.*). The accession of Denmark raised new problems.

Although the Working Party had no difficulty in confirming that the Industrial Court under the Danish Industrial Court Act of 21 April 1964 (Bulletin No. 124) was, in spite of its unusual structure, clearly to be considered a court within the meaning of the 1968 Convention, it was more difficult to decide how to classify proceedings in maintenance matters, which, in Denmark, failing an amicable settlement, are almost always held before administrative authorities and terminate with a decision by the latter.

[94] 1. *THE LEGAL POSITION IN DENMARK*

A1.353   67. The legal position may be summed up as follows. Maintenance matters are determined as regards the obligation to pay either by agreement or by a court judgment. The amount of the payment and the scale of any necessary modifications are, however, determined by an authority known as the "Amtmand," which under Danish law is clearly not a court but an administrative authority which in this case plays a judicial role. It is true that decisions given in such proceedings come under The Hague Convention on the recognition and enforcement of decisions relating to maintenance obligations, but this is only because under that Convention the matter does not specifically require a court judgment.

2. *ARTICLE Va OF THE PROTOCOL AND ITS EFFECT*

A1.354   68. There would, however, be an imbalance in the scope of the 1968 Convention, if it excluded maintenance proceedings of the type found in Denmark on the sole ground that they do not take place before courts.

The amendment to the 1968 Convention thus made necessary is contained in the proposal for the adoption of a new Article Va in the Protocol. This method appeared simpler than attempting to amend a large number of separate provisions of the 1968 Convention.

Wherever the 1968 Convention refers to "court" or "judge" it must in the future be taken to include Danish administrative authorities when dealing with maintenance matters (as in Article 2, first paragraph, Article 3, first paragraph, Article 4, first paragraph, Article 5(2), Article 17, Article 18, Articles 20 to 22, Article 27(4),

Article 28, third paragraph and Article 52). This applies in particular to Article 4, first paragraph, even though in the French, Italian and Dutch texts, unlike the German version, the word "court" does not appear.

Similarly, wherever the 1968 Convention refers to "judgments," the decisions arrived at by the Danish administrative authorities in maintenance matters will in future be included in the legal definition of the term "judgment" contained in Article 25. Its content is extended in this respect by the addition of Article Va to the Protocol, so that it is now to be understood as reading:

> "For the purposes of this Convention, 'judgment' means any judgment given by a court or tribunal of a Contracting State—including in matters relating to maintenance, the Danish administrative authorities—whatever the judgment may be called. . . . "

CHAPTER 4

JURISDICTION

A.

GENERAL REMARKS

69. In section A of Chapter 4 of his report, Mr. Jenard sets out the main ideas underlying the rules of jurisdiction of the 1968 Convention. None of this is affected by the accession of the new Member States. The extent to which three features of the law in the United Kingdom and in Ireland are consistent with the application of the 1968 Convention must, however, be clarified. These features are: the far-reaching jurisdiction of the Superior Courts (1), the concept of domicile (2) and, lastly, the discretionary powers enjoyed by the courts to determine territorial jurisdiction (3).   **A1.355**

1. FIRST INSTANCE JURISDICTION OF THE SUPERIOR COURTS

70. The Continental Member States of the Community have geographically defined jurisdictions where courts of first instance are competent to give judgments even in the most important civil disputes. There are many courts of equal status: approximately 50 "Landgerichte" in Germany, and an equal number of "tribunaux de grande instance" in France and "Tribunali" in Italy. Where the 1968 Convention itself lays down both the international and local jurisdiction of the courts, as for example in Articles 5 and 6, jurisdiction is given to only one of the many courts with equal status in a State. There is little room for such a distinction in the judicial systems **[95]** of Ire-   **A1.356**

land and the United Kingdom in so far as a Superior Court has jurisdiction as a court of first instance.

In Ireland, the High Court is the only court of first instance with unlimited jurisdiction. It can, exceptionally, sit outside Dublin. Nothing in the 1968 Convention precludes this. In addition to the High Court, there is a Circuit Court and a District Court. In respect of these courts too, the expression "the Court" is used in the singular and there is only one Court for the whole country, but each of its judges is permanently assigned to a specific circuit or district. The local jurisdiction laid down in the 1968 Convention means, in the case of Ireland, the judge assigned to a certain "circuit" or "district."

A1.357
In the United Kingdom three Superior Courts have jurisdiction at first instance: the High Court of Justice for England and Wales, the Outer House of the Court of Session for Scotland and the High Court for Northern Ireland. Each of these courts has, however, exclusive jurisdiction for the entire territory of the relevant part of the United Kingdom (see paragraph 11). Thus the same comments as those made in connection with the territorial jurisdiction of the Irish High Court apply also to each judicial area. The possibility of transferring a case from London to a district registry of the High Court does not mean transfer to another court. Bearing in mind that foreign judgments have to be registered separately in respect of each of the judicial areas of the United Kingdom in order to become enforceable therein (see paragraph 208), the distinction between international and local jurisdiction becomes largely irrelevant in the United Kingdom. The rules in the 1968 Convention governing local jurisdiction are relevant to the Superior Courts of first instance in the United Kingdom only in so far as a distinction has to be made between the courts of England and Wales, Scotland and Northern Ireland. The competence of the other courts (County Courts, Magistrates' Courts, and, in Scotland, the Sheriff Courts) presents no particular problems.

2. THE CONCEPT OF "DOMICILE" AND THE APPLICATION OF THE CONVENTION

A1.358
71. (a) The concept of domicile is of fundamental importance for the 1968 Convention in determining jurisdiction (*e.g.* Articles 2 to 6, 8, 11, 12(3), 14, 17 and 32). In the legal systems of the original Member States of the EEC, its meaning differs to some extent. In the Federal Republic of Germany, it expresses a person's connection with a local community within the national territory. In France and Luxembourg, it denotes a person's exact address. In Belgium, for purposes of jurisdiction the term denotes the place where a person is entered in the register of population as having his principal residence (Article 36 of the Code judiciaire). These differences explain why, in determining a person's domicile, *e.g.* German law places greater emphasis on the stability of the connection with a specific place than do some of the other legal systems.

Notwithstanding these differences the basic concept of "domicile" is the same in all the legal systems of the original Member States of the EEC, namely the connection of a person with a smaller local unit within the State. This made it possible in Article 52 of the 1968 Convention to leave a more precise definition of the term to the law of the State in which the "domicile" of a person had to be ascertained. It did not lead to an uneven application of the provisions of the 1968 Convention. Clearly, for the purposes of applying them in the original Member States of the Community it is irrelevant whether the concept of domicile refers to a specific address or to a local community.

72. (b) The concept of domicile under the law in Ireland and the United **A1.359** Kingdom differs considerably in several respects from the Continental concept.

First, this concept does not refer to a person's connection with a particular place and even less with a particular residence within a place, but to his having his roots within a territory covered by a particular legal system (see paragraph 11). A person's domicile only indicates whether he comes under the legal system of England and Wales, Scotland, Northern Ireland, or possibly under a foreign legal system. A person's legal connection with a particular place is denoted by the word "residence," not "domicile."

According to United Kingdom law, a person always has one "domicile" and can never have more than one. At birth a legitimate child acquires the domicile of its father, an illegitimate child that of its mother. A child retains the domicile of its parents throughout its minority. [96] After it reaches its majority, it may acquire another domicile but for this there are very strict requirements: the usual place of residence must have been transferred to another country— with the intention of keeping it there permanently or at least for an unlimited period.

73. (c) Article 52 of the 1968 Convention does not expressly provide for **A1.360** the linking of the concept of domicile with a particular place or a particular residence, nor does it expressly prohibit it from being connected with a particular national territory. The United Kingdom and Ireland would, consequently, be free to retain their traditional concept of domicile when the jurisdiction of their courts is invoked. The Working Party came to the conclusion that this would lead to a certain imbalance in the application of the 1968 Convention. In certain cases, the courts of the United Kingdom or Ireland could assume jurisdiction on the basis of their rules on the retention of domicile, although by the law of all the other Member States of the Community, such a person would be domiciled at his actual place of residence within their territory.

The Working Party therefore requested the United Kingdom and Ireland to provide in their legislation implementing the 1968 Convention (see paragraph 256), at any rate for the purposes of that Convention, for a concept of domicile which would depart from their traditional rules and would tend to reflect more the concept of "domicile" as understood in the original States of the EEC.

In Article 69(5) of the Convention for the European patent for the common market which was drawn up concurrently with the Working Party's discussions, the concept of "Wohnsitz" is translated as "residence" and for the meaning of the expression reference is made to Articles 52 and 53 of the 1968 Convention. To prevent confusion, the proposed new Article Vc of the Protocol makes it clear that the concept of "residence" within the meaning of the Community Patent Convention should be ascertained in the same way as the concept of "domicile" in the 1968 Convention.

A1.361   74. (d) It should be noted that the application of the third paragraph of Article 52 raises the problem of different concepts of domicile, when considering which system of law determines whether a person's domicile depends on that of another person. The relevant factor, in such a case, may be where the dependent person is domiciled. Under United Kingdom private international law, the question whether a person has a dependent domicile is not determined by that person's nationality, but by his domicile in the traditional sense of that concept. The re-definition of "domicile" in connection with the first paragraph of Article 52 in no way affects this.

If a foreigner under age who has settled in England is sued in an English court, that court must take account of the different concepts of domicile. As a first step it must establish where the defendant had his "domicile" before settling in England. This is decided in accordance with the traditional meaning of that concept. The law thus found to be applicable will then determine whether the minor was in a position to acquire a "domicile" in England within the meaning of the 1968 Convention. The English court must then ascertain whether the requirements for a "domicile" in the area covered by the English court concerned are satisfied.

A1.362   75. (e) There is no equivalent in the law of the United Kingdom to the concept of the "seat" of a company in Continental law. In order to achieve the results which under private international law are linked on the continent with the "seat" of a company, the United Kingdom looks to the legal system where the company was incorporated ("law of incorporation," section 406 of the Companies Act, 1948). The "domicile" of a company in the traditional sense of the term (see paragraph 72) is taken to be the judicial area in which it was incorporated. The new Member States of the Community are not obliged to introduce a legal concept which corresponds to that of a company's "seat" within the meaning of the continental legal systems, just as in general they are not obliged to adapt their concept of domicile. However, should the United Kingdom and Ireland not change their law on this point, the result would again be an imbalance in the application of the 1968 Convention. It would, therefore, be desirable for the United Kingdom to introduce for the purposes of the Convention an appropriate concept in its national legislation such as "domicile of a company," which would correspond more closely to the Continental concept of the "seat" of a company than the present United Kingdom concept of "law of incorporation."

Such a provision would not preclude a company from having a "domicile" in the United Kingdom **[97]** in accordance with legislation in the United Kingdom and a "seat" in a Continental State in accordance with the legislation of that State. As a result of the second sentence of Article 53, a company is enabled under the laws of several of the original States of the EEC to have a "seat" in more than one State. The problems which might arise from such a situation can be overcome by the provisions in the 1968 Convention on *lis pendens* and related actions (see paragraph 162).

3. DISCRETIONARY POWERS REGARDING JURISDICTION AND TRANSFER OF PROCEEDINGS

76. The idea that a national court has discretion in the exercise of its jurisdiction either territorially or as regards the subject matter of a dispute does not generally exist in Continental legal systems. Even where, in the rules relating to jurisdiction, tests of an exceptionally flexible nature are laid down, no room is left for the exercise of any discretionary latitude. It is true that Continental legal systems recognize the power of a court to transfer proceedings from one court to another. Even then the court has no discretion in determining whether or not this power should be exercised. In contrast, the law in the United Kingdom and in Ireland has evolved judicial discretionary powers in certain fields. In some cases, these correspond in practice to legal provisions regarding jurisdiction which are more detailed in the Continental States, while in others they have no counterpart on the Continent. It is therefore difficult to evaluate such powers within the context of the 1968 Convention. A distinction has to be made between the international and national application of this legal concept.   **A1.363**

77. (a) In relationships with the courts of other States and also, within the United Kingdom, as between the courts of different judicial areas (see paragraph 11) the doctrine of *forum conveniens*—in Scotland, *forum non conveniens*—is of relevance.   **A1.364**

   The courts are allowed, although only in very rare and exceptional cases, to disregard the fact that proceedings may already be pending before foreign courts, or courts of another judicial area.

   Exceptionally, the courts may refuse to hear or decide a case, if they believe it would be better for the case to be heard before a court having equivalent jurisdiction in another State (or another judicial area) because this would increase the likelihood of an efficient and impartial hearing of the particular case.

   There are several special reasons why in practice such discretionary powers are exercised: the strict requirements traditionally imposed by the laws of the United Kingdom and Ireland regarding changes of domicile (see paragraph 72); the rules allowing establishment of jurisdiction by merely serving a writ or originating summons in the territory of the State concerned (see paragraphs 85 and 86); the principles developed particularly strongly in the procedural law of these States requiring directness in the taking of evidence with the consequent restrictions on making use of evidence taken abroad or merely in another judicial area; and finally, the considerable difficulties arising in the application of foreign law by United Kingdom or Irish courts.

A1.365   78. According to the views of the delegations from the Continental Member States of the Community such possibilities are not open to the courts of those States when, under the 1968 Convention, they have jurisdiction and are asked to adjudicate.

Article 21 expressly prohibits a court from disregarding the fact that proceedings are already pending abroad. For the rest the view was expressed that under the 1968 Convention the Contracting States are not only entitled to exercise jurisdiction in accordance with the provisions laid down in Title 2; they are also obliged to do so. A plaintiff must be sure which court has jurisdiction. He should not have to waste his time and money risking that the court concerned may consider itself less competent than another. In particular, in accordance with the general spirit of the 1968 Convention, the fact that foreign law has to be applied, either generally or in a particular case, should not constitute a sufficient reason for a court to decline jurisdiction. Where the courts of several States have jurisdiction, the plaintiff has deliberately been given a right of choice, which should not be weakened by application of the doctrine of *forum conveniens*. The plaintiff may have chosen another apparently "inappropriate" court from among the competent courts in order to obtain a judgment in the State in which he also wishes to enforce it. Furthermore, the risk of a negative conflict of jurisdiction should not be disregarded: despite the United Kingdom court's decision, the judge on the Continent could likewise decline jurisdiction. The practical **[98]** reasons in favour of the doctrine of *forum conveniens* will lose considerably in significance, as soon as the 1968 Convention becomes applicable in the United Kingdom and Ireland. The implementing legislation will necessitate not inconsiderable changes in the laws of those States, both in respect of the definition of the concept of domicile (see paragraph 73) and on account of the abolition of jurisdictional competence based merely on service of a writ within the area of the court (see paragraph 86). To correct rules of jurisdiction in a particular case by means of the concept of *forum conveniens* will then be largely unnecessary. After considering these arguments the United Kingdom and Irish delegations did not press for a formal adjustment of the 1968 Convention on this point.

A1.366   79. (b) A concept similar to the doctrine of *forum conveniens* is also applied within the territory of the State, though the term itself is not used in that context. This may be due to the fact that the same result can be achieved by the device of transferring the case to another court having alternative jurisdiction within the same State or the same legal area (see paragraph 11). The Working Party had to examine to what extent the 1968 Convention restricted such powers of transfer. In this connection certain comments made earlier may be repeated: the powers of the Superior Courts in Ireland or in a judicial area of the United Kingdom (see paragraph 70) to decide as a court of first instance remain unchanged. For the rest, the following applies:

80. (aa) The previous legal position in Ireland and the United Kingdom **A1.367**
    remains essentially the same. Each court can transfer proceedings to another court, if that court has equivalent jurisdiction and can better deal with the matter. For example, if an action is brought before the High Court, the value of which is unlikely to exceed the amount which limits the jurisdiction of the lower court, the High Court has power to transfer the proceedings to such a court, but it is not obliged to do so. A Circuit Court in Ireland, a County Court or Magistrates' Court in England and a Sheriff Court in Scotland—but not an Irish District Court (see paragraph 70)—may transfer proceedings to another court of the same category or exceptionally to a court of another category, if the location of the evidence or the circumstances for a fair hearing should make such a course desirable in the interest of the parties.

    Some Continental legal systems also provide for the possibility, albeit on a much smaller scale, of a judge having discretion to conver jurisdiction on a court which would not otherwise have it. This is the case under, for instance, Article 36 of the German Code of Civil Procedure, if proper proceedings are not possible before the court which originally had jurisdiction. Under section 356 of the new French Code of Civil Procedure[19] proceedings may be transferred to another court of the same type, if a risk of lack of impartiality exists.

81. (bb) The 1968 Convention in no way affects the competence as **A1.368**
    regards subject matter of the courts of a State. The national legal systems are thus free to provide for the possibility of transfer of cases between courts of different categories.

    For the most part, the 1968 Convention does not affect the territorial jurisdiction of the courts within a State, but only their international jurisdiction. This is clearly reflected by the basic rule on jurisdiction contained in Article 2. Unless the jurisdiction of a court where proceedings are instituted against a person domiciled in the United Kingdom or Ireland is derived from a provision of the 1968 Convention which at the same time determines local jurisdiction, as for example Article 5, the 1968 Convention does not prevent a transfer of the proceedings to another court in the same State. Even in respect of exclusive jurisdiction, Article 16 only lays down the

---

[19] Decree No. 75–1123 of 5 December 1975, (JO) 1975, 1251.

international jurisdiction of the courts of a State, and does not prevent a transfer within that State.

Finally, the 1968 Convention does not of course prevent a transfer to the court which actually has local jurisdiction under the Convention. This would occur where both parties agree to the transfer and the requirements for jurisdiction by consent pursuant to Article 17 are satisfied.

The only type of case which remains problematic is where an action is brought before a court in circumstances where the 1968 Convention gives the plaintiff a choice of jurisdiction. An action in tort or a liability insurance claim is brought at the place where the harmful event occurred or a **[99]** maintenance claim at the domicile of the maintenance creditor. It appears obvious that in special exceptional cases a transfer to another court of the same State must be permitted, when proper proceedings are not possible before the court which would otherwise have jurisdiction. However, the Working Party did not feel justified in incorporating these matters expressly in the 1968 Convention. They could be covered by a rule of interpretation to the effect that the court having local jurisdiction may, in exceptional cases, include the court which is designated as having local jurisdiction by the decision of another court. The courts for the place "where the harmful event occurred" could thus be a neighbouring court designated by another court, if the courts for the place of the harmful event should be unable to hear the proceedings.

A1.369   In so far as a court's discretionary powers to confer jurisdiction on other courts and in particular to transfer proceedings to another court are not defined in detail such discretionary powers should, of course, only be used in the spirit of the 1968 Convention, if the latter has determined, not only international but also local jurisdiction. A transfer merely on account of the cost of the proceedings or in order to facilitate the taking of evidence would be possible only with the consent of the plaintiff, who had the choice of jurisdiction.

B.

COMMENTS ON THE SECTIONS OF TITLE II

Section 1

General provisions

A1.370   82. The proposed adjustments to Articles 2[20] to 4 are confined to inserting certain exorbitant jurisdictions in the legal systems of the new Member States into the second paragraph of Article 3. The occasion has been taken to adjust the text of that Article to take account also

---

[20] The adjustment proposed for Art. 57 admittedly has certain repercussions on the scope of Art. 20 (see para. 240).

of an amendment to the law which has been introduced in Belgium. Detailed comments on the proposed alterations (I) precede two more general remarks on the relevance of this provision to the whole structure of the 1968 Convention (II).

I. *Detailed comments*

83. 1. Belgium   **A1.371**

In Belgium, Articles 52, 52 bis and 53 of the law of 25 March 1876 had already been superseded before the coming into force of the 1968 Convention by Articles 635, 637 and 638 of the Judicial Code. Nevertheless only Article 638 of the Judicial Code is mentioned in the second paragraph of Article 3 in its revised version. It corresponds to Article 53 of the law of 25 March 1876 and provides that where Belgian courts do not possess jurisdiction based on other provisions, a plaintiff resident in Belgium may sue any person before the court of his place of residence. The version of Article 3, valid hitherto, erroneously classed the jurisdiction based on Articles 52 and 52 bis of the abovementioned law as exorbitant.

84. 2. Denmark   **A1.372**

The provisions of Danish law included in the second paragraph of Article 3 state that a foreigner may be sued before any Danish court in whose district he is resident or has property when the document instituting the proceedings is served. On this last point the provision corresponds to similar German provisions included in the list of exorbitant jurisdictions. On the first point reference may be made to what follows concerning Ireland (see paragraph 85). There is a separate Code of Civil Procedure for Greenland (see paragraph 253); special reference had therefore to be made to the corresponding provisions affecting that country.

85. 3. Ireland   **A1.373**

According to the principles of common law which are unwritten and apply equally in the United Kingdom and Ireland, a court has jurisdiction in principle if the plaintiff has been properly served with the court process. The jurisdiction of Irish (and United Kingdom) courts is indirectly restricted to the extent of the limits imposed on the service of a writ of summons. Service is available without special leave only within the territory of Ireland (or the United Kingdom). However, every service validly effected there is sufficient to establish jurisdiction; even a short stay by the defendant in **[100]** the territory concerned will suffice. Service abroad will be authorized only where certain specified conditions are satisfied. As regards legal relations within the EEC—especially because of the possibility of free movement of judgments resulting from the 1968 Convention—there is no longer any justification for founding the jurisdiction of a court on the mere temporary presence of a person in the State of the court concerned. This common law jurisdiction, for which of course no statutory enactment can be cited, had therefore to be classed as exorbitant.

A1.374 86. 4. United Kingdom

As regards the United Kingdom it will suffice for point (a) of Article 3, second paragraph, of the 1968 Convention as amended, to refer to what has been said above in the case of Ireland. Points (b) and (c) deal with some characteristic features of Scottish law. To establish jurisdiction merely by service of a writ of summons during the temporary presence of the defendant is a rare, though not totally unknown, practice in Scotland. Scottish courts usually base their jurisdiction in respect of a defendant not permanently resident there on other factors, namely that he has been in Scotland for at least 40 days, or that he owns immovable property in Scotland or that he owns movable property which has been impounded in Scotland. In such cases service on the defendant is also required, but this may be effected by post or, exceptionally, by posting it on the court notice board. In the case of Germany, the 1968 Convention has already classed jurisdiction based solely on the existence of property in Germany as exorbitant. Any jurisdiction based solely on the seizure of property within a country must be treated in the same way.

II. *The relevance of the second paragraph of Article 3
to the whole structure of the 1968 Convention*

1. The special significance of the second paragraph of Article 3

A1.375 87. The rejection as exorbitant of jurisdictional bases hitherto considered to be important in the new Member States should not, any more than the original version of the second paragraph of Article 3, mislead anyone into thinking that the scope of the first paragraph of Article 3 would thereby be more closely circumscribed. Only particularly extravagant claims to international jurisdiction by the courts of a Member State are expressly underlined. Other rules founding jurisdiction in the national laws of the new Member States are compatible with the 1968 Convention also only to the extent that they do not offend against Article 2 and Articles 4 to 18. Thus, for example, the jurisdiction of English courts in respect of persons domiciled in the Community can no longer be based on the ground that the claim concerns a contract which was concluded in England or is governed by English law. On the other hand, the rules on the jurisdiction of English courts in connection with breaches of contract in England or claims connected with the commission or omission of an act in England largely correspond to the provisions in Article 5(1) to (3).

2. Impossibility of founding jurisdiction on the location of property

88. With regard to Germany, Denmark and the United Kingdom the **A1.376**
list in the second paragraph of Article 3 contains provisions reject-
ing jurisdiction derived solely from the existence of property in the
territory of the State in which the court is situated. Such jurisdiction cannot be asserted even if the proceedings concern a dispute
over rights of ownership, or possession, or the capacity to dispose of
the specific property in question. Persons domiciled on the Continent of Europe may not be sued in Scotland, even if the aim of the
action is to recover movable property situated or seized there or to
determine its ownership. Interpleader actions (England and Wales)
and multiple poinding (Scotland) are no longer permissible in the
United Kingdom in respect of persons domiciled in another Member State of the Community, in so far as the international jurisdiction of the English or Scottish courts does not result from other
provisions of the 1968 Convention. This applies, for example, to
actions brought by an auctioneer to establish whether ownership of
an article sent to him for disposal belongs to his customer or a third
party claiming the article.

[101] There is, however, no reason why United Kingdom legislation
should not introduce appropriate measures pursuant to Article 24,
to provide protection to persons (such as auctioneers) faced with
conflicting legal claims. This might, for instance, take the form of a
court order authorizing an article to be temporarily withdrawn from
auction.

As regards persons who are domiciled outside the Community,
the provisions which hitherto governed the jurisdiction of courts in
the new Member States remain unaffected. Even the rules of jurisdiction mentioned in the second paragraph of Article 3 may continue to apply to such persons. Judgments delivered by courts
which thus have jurisdiction must also be recognized and enforced
in other States of the Community unless one of the exceptions in the
new paragraph 5 of Article 27 or in Article 59 as amended applies.

This latter provision in the only one concerning which the list in
Article 3, second paragraph is not only of illustrative significance
but has direct and restrictive importance. (see paragraph 249).

Section 2

Special jurisdictions[21]

89. In the sphere of special, non-exclusive jurisdictions the problems of **A1.377**
adjustment were confined to judicial competence as regards maintenance claims (I), questions raised by trusts in United Kingdom

---

[21] The following cases may be mentioned with regard to difficulties of interpretation which have arisen hitherto in judicial practice in connection with the application of Arts. 5 and 6: Corte Cassazione Italiana of 4 June 1974, "Giur. it."
1974, 18 (with regard to the concept of place of performance); Corte Cassazione

and Irish law (II) and problems in connection with jurisdiction in maritime cases (III). In addition, the Working Party dealt with a few less important individual questions (IV).

Reference should be made here to the Judgments of the Court of Justice of the European Communities of 6 October 1976 (12/76; 14/76) and of 30 November 1976 (21/76) which were delivered shortly before or after the end of the negotiations.[22]

I. *Maintenance claims*

A1.378 90. The need for an adjustment of Article 5(2) arose because the laws of the new Member States—as was also by then the case with the laws of many of the original States of the EEC—allow status proceedings

---

Italiana No. 3397 of 20 October 1975 (place of performance in the case of deliveries via a forwarding agent who has an obligation to install); Tribunal de Grande Instance Paris D 1975, 638 with commentary by Droz (place where the harmful event occurred in cases of illegal publication in the press); Court of Justice of the European Communities, 6 October 1976, Case No. 12/76 [1976] ECR 1473.

[22] In the judgments referred to the formal parts of the judgments read as follows:

The "place of performance of the obligation in question" within the meaning of Art. 5(1) of the Convention of 27 September 1968 on jurisdiction and the enforcement of judgments in civil and commercial matters is to be determined in accordance with the law which governs the obligation in question according to the rules of conflict of laws of the court before which the matter is brought (Case No. 12/76).

In disputes in which the grantee of an exclusive sales concession is charging the grantor with having infringed the exclusive concession, the word "obligation" contained in Art. 5(1) of the Convention of 27 September 1968 on jurisdiction and the enforcement of judgments in civil and commercial matters refers to the contractual obligation forming the basis of the legal proceedings, namely the obligation of the grantor which corresponds to the contractual right relied upon by the grantee in support of the application (Case No. 14/76 [1976] ECR 1497).

In disputes concerning the consequences of the infringement by the grantor of a contract conferring an exclusive concession, such as the payment of damages or the dissolution of the contract, the obligation to which reference must be made for the purposes of applying Art. 5(1) of the Convention is that which the contract imposes on the grantor and the non-performance of which is relied upon by the grantee in support of the application for damages or for the dissolution of the contract (Case No. 14/76)

In the case of actions for payment of compensation by way of damages, it is for the national court to ascertain whether, under the law applicable to the contract, an independent contractual obligation or an obligation replacing the unperformed contractual obligation is involved (Case No. 14/76).

When the grantee of an exclusive sales concession is not subject either to the control or to the direction of the grantor, he cannot be regarded as being at the head of a branch, agency or other establishment of the grantor within the meaning of Art. 5(5) of the Convention of 27 September 1968 (Case No. 14/76).

Where the place of the happening of the event which may give rise to liability in tort, delict or quasi-delict and the place where that event results in damage are not identical, the expression "place where the harmful event occurred" in Art. 5(3) of the Convention of 27 September 1968 on jurisdiction and the

to be combined with proceedings concerning maintenance claims (see paragraphs 32 to 42). As far as other problems were concerned no formal adjustment was required. However, certain special features of United Kingdom and Irish law give rise to questions of interpretation; the views of the Working Party as to their solutions should be recorded. They concern a more precise definition of the term "maintenance" (1) and how maintenance entitlements are to be adjusted to changed circumstances in accordance with the system of jurisdiction and recognition established by the 1968 Convention (2).

1. The term "maintenance"

91. (a) The 1968 Convention refers simply to "maintenance" in Article 5(2), the only Article which uses the expression. Several legal concepts used within one and the same national legal system can be covered by this term. For example, Italian law speaks of "alimenti" (Article 433 *et seq.* of the codice civile) to indicate payments amongst relations and spouses, but payments after divorce are "assegni."[23] The new French divorce law,[24] too, does not speak of "aliments," but of "devoir de secours." In addition French legal terminology uses the expressions "devoir d'entretien" and "contribution aux charges du ménage." All those are "maintenance" within the meaning of Article 5(2) of the 1968 Convention.

A1.379

92. (b) The Article says nothing, however, about the legal basis from which maintenance claims can emanate. The wording differs markedly from that of the Hague Convention of 2 October 1973 on the recognition and enforcement of decisions relating to maintenance obligations. Article 1 of that Convention excludes from its scope maintenance claims arising from tort, contract and the law of succession. However, there is no significant difference regarding the concept of maintenance as used in the two Conventions. The 1968 Convention is in any case not applicable to maintenance claims under the law of succession (second paragraph, point (1) of Article 1). "Maintenance" claims as the legal consequence of a tortious act are, in legal theory, claims for damages, even if the amount of compensation depends on the needs of the injured party. Contracts creating a "maintenance" obligation [102] which previously did not exist are, according to the form employed, gifts, contracts of sale or

A1.380

---

enforcement of judgments in civil and commercial matters must be understood as being intended to cover both the place where the damage occurred and the place of the event giving rise to it (Case No. 21/76 [1976] ECR 1735).

The result is that the defendant may be sued, at the option of the plaintiff, either in the courts for the place where the damage occurred or in the courts for the place of the event which gives rise to and is at the origin of that damage (Case No. 21/76).

[23] Divorce law of 1 December 1970, No. 898, Art. 5.

[24] Law of 11 July 1975, new Art. 281 of the Code civil.

other contracts for a consideration. Obligations arising therefrom, even where they consist in the payment of "maintenance," are to be treated like other contractual obligations. In such cases Article 5(1) rather than 5(2) of the 1968 Convention applies as far as jurisdiction is concerned; the outcome hardly differs from an application of Article 5(2). "Maintenance" obligations created by contract are generally to be fulfilled at the domicile or habitual residence of the maintenance creditor. Thus actions may also be brought there. Article 5(2) is applicable, however, where a maintenance contract merely crystallizes an existing maintenance obligation which originated from a family relationship.

Judicial proceedings concerning "maintenance" claims are still civil and commercial matters even where Article 5(2) is not applicable because the claim arises from a tortious act or a contract.

A1.381 93. (c) The concept of maintenance does not stipulate that the claim must be for periodic payments. Under Article 1613(2) of the German Civil Code, for example, the maintenance creditor may in addition to regular payments, claim payment of a lump sum on the ground of exceptional need. Under Article 1615(e) of the Code a father may agree with his illegitimate child on the payment of a lump sum settlement. Article 5(4), third sentence, of the Italian divorce law of 1 December 1970 allows divorced spouses to agree on the payment of maintenance in the form of a lump sum settlement. Finally, under Article 285 of the French Civil Code, as amended by the divorce law of 11 July 1975, the French courts can order maintenance in the form of a single capital payment even without the agreement of the spouses. The mere fact that the courts in the United Kingdom have power to order not only periodic payments by one spouse to the other after a divorce, but also the payment of a single lump sum of money, does not therefore prevent the proceedings or a judgment from being treated as a maintenance matter. Even the creation of charges on property and the transfer of property as provided on the Continent, for example in Article 8 of the Italian divorce law, can be in the nature of maintenance.

A1.382 94. (d) It is difficult to distinguish between claims for maintenance on the one hand and claims for damages and the division of property on the other.

A1.383 95. (aa) In Continental Europe a motivating factor in assessing the amount of maintenance due to a divorced spouse by his former partner is to compensate an innocent spouse for his loss of matrimonial status. A typical example is contained in Article 301 of the Civil Code in its original form, which still applies in Luxembourg. In its two paragraphs a sharp distinction is drawn in respect of post-matrimonial relations between a claim for maintenance and compensation for material and non-material damages. Yet material damages generally consist in the loss of the provision of maintenance which the divorced party would have enjoyed as a spouse.

Thus the claims deriving from the two paragraphs of Article 301 of the Civil Code overlap in practice, especially since they can both take the form of a pension or a single capital payment. It remains to be seen whether the new French divorce law of 11 July 1975, which makes a clearer distinction between "prestations compensatoires" and "devoir de secours," will change this situation.

Under section 23(1)(c) and (f) and Section 27(6)(c) of the English Matrimonial Causes Act 1973, an English divorce court, too, may order a lump sum to be paid by one divorced spouse to the other or to a child. However, English law, which is characterized by judicial discretionary powers and which does not favour inflexible systematic rules, does not make a distinction as to whether the payments ordered by the Court are intended as damages or as maintenance.

96. (bb) The 1968 Convention is not applicable at all where the payments **A1.384** claimed or ordered are governed by matrimonial property law (see paragraph 45 *et seq*). Where claims for damages are involved, Article 5(2) is not relevant. Whether or not that provision applies depends, in the case of a lump sum payment, solely on whether a payment under family law is in the nature of maintenance.

The maintenance nature of the payment is likely to predominate in relation to children. As **[103]** between spouses, a division of property or damages may well be the underlying factor. Where both spouses are earning well, payment of a lump sum can only serve the purpose of a division of property or compensation for non-material damage. In that case the obligation to pay is not in the nature of maintenance. If payment is in pursuance of a division of property, the 1968 Convention does not apply at all. If it is to compensate for non-material damage, there is no scope for the application of Article 5(2). A divorce court may not adjudicate in the matter in either case, unless it has jurisdiction under Article 2 or Article 5(1).

97. (e) All legal systems have to deal with the problems of how the needs **A1.385** of a person requiring financial support are to be met when the maintenance debtor defaults. Others also liable to provide maintenance, if necessary a public authority, may have to step in temporarily. They, in turn, should be able to obtain a refund of their outlay from the (principal) maintenance debtor. Legal systems have therefore evolved various methods to overcome this problem. Some of them provide for the maintenance claim to be transferred to the payer, thereby giving it a new creditor, but not otherwise changing its nature. Others confer on the payer an independent right to compensation. United Kingdom law makes particular use of the latter method in cases where the Supplementary Benefits Commission has paid maintenance. As already mentioned in the Jenard report[25] claims of this type are covered by the 1968 Convention, even where claims for compensation are based on a payment made by a public

---

[25] Chap. III, end of s.IV. [para. A1.53 above].

authority in accordance with administrative law or under provisions of social security legislation. It is not, however, the purpose of the special rules of jurisdiction in Article 5(2) to confer jurisdiction in respect of compensation claims on the courts of the domicile of the maintenance creditor or even those of the seat of the public authority—whichever of the two abovementioned methods a legal system may have opted for.

2. Adjustment of maintenance orders

1.386 98. Economic circumstances in general and the particular economic position of those obliged to pay and those entitled to receive maintenance are constantly changing. The need for periodical adjustments of maintenance orders arises particularly in times of creeping inflation. Jurisdiction to order adjustments depends on the general provisions of the 1968 Convention. Since this is a problem of great practical importance it may be appropriate to preface its discussion in detail with a brief comparative legal survey.

A1.387 99. (a) Continental legal systems differ according to whether the emphasis of the relevant legal provisions is placed on the concept of an infringement of the principle of finality of a maintenance judgment or more on the concept of an adjustment of the question of the claim (aa). In this respect, as in many others, the provisions of United Kingdom (bb) and Irish (cc) law do not fit into this scheme.

A1.388 100. (aa) The provisions of German law relating to adjustments of maintenance orders are based on the concept of a special procedural remedy in the nature of a review of the proceedings (Wiederaufnahmeklage).

Since there are no special provisions governing jurisdiction, the general provisions governing jurisdiction in maintenance claims are considered applicable. This means that the original court making the maintenance order may have lost its competence to adjust it. Enforcement authorities, even when they are courts, have no power, either in general or in maintenance cases, to adjust a judgment to changed circumstances. Provisions giving protection against enforcement of a judgment for social reasons apply irrespective of whether or not the amount ordered to be paid in the judgment is subject to variation. This is also true regarding the subsidiary provision of Article 765(a) of the Zivilprozessordnung (Code of Civil Procedure),[26] which is of general application and states that enforcement measures may be rescinded or disallowed in very special circumstances, if they constitute an undue hardship for the debtor.

Accordingly legal theory and case law accept that a foreign main-

---

[26] Stein-Jonas (Münzberg) (n. 27), para. 765 a II 3 with reference to case law in n. 28.

tenance order may be adjusted by a German court, if the latter has jurisdiction.[27]

In the legal systems in the other original Member States of the EEC the problem has always been regarded as one of substantive law and not as a **[104]** remedy providing protection against enforcement of judicial decisions. Accordingly jurisdiction depends on the general principles applying to maintenance cases.[28] Indirect adjustments cannot be obtained by invoking, as a defence against measures of enforcement, a change in the circumstances which were taken into account in determining the amount of the maintenance.

In general, the 1968 Convention is based on a similar legal position obtaining in all the original Member States: in the case of proceedings for adjustment of a maintenance order the jurisdiction of the court concerned has to be examined afresh.

A1.389

101. (bb) In the United Kingdom, the most important legal basis for amendment of maintenance orders is section 53 of the Magistrates' Courts Act of 1952 in conjunction with sections 8 to 10 of the Matrimonial proceedings (Magistrates' Courts) Act 1960 which will be suspended in 1979 by the Domestic proceedings and Magistrates' Courts Act 1978. According to these Acts, the Court may revoke or vary maintenance orders, or revive them after they have been revoked or varied. In addition, the court in whose district the applicant is now resident also has jurisdiction in such matters.[29] In principle, the court's discretion is unfettered in such cases, but an application for variation may not be based on facts or evidence which could have been relied on when the original order was made.[30] The same applies under section 31 of the Matrimonial causes Act 1973. A divorce court can vary or discharge an order it has made with regard to maintenance, irrespective of whether the original basis for its jurisdiction still exists or not.

A1.390

102. To these possibilities must be added another characteristic aspect of the British judicial system. Enforcement of judgments is linked much more closely than on the Continent to the jurisdiction of the particular court which gave the judgment (see paragraph 208). Before a judgment can be enforced by the executive organs of another court, it must be registered with that other court. After registration, it is regarded as a judgment of that court. A further consequence is that, after such registration, the court with which it is registered is empowered to amend it. Hitherto, the United Kingdom has also applied this system in cases where foreign mainten-

---

[27] Stein-Jonas (Leipold) "Kommentar zur Zivilprozeßordnung," 19th ed., para. 323 II 2 c and other references.
[28] In the case of France: Cour de Cassation of 21 July 1954 D 1955, 185.
[29] Magistrates' Court Rules 1952, r. 34(2), and Rayden's "Law and Practice in Divorce and Family Matters" (1971), p. 1181.
[30] Bromley, "Family Law," (4th ed.) (1971), p. 451 containing references to case-law.

ance judgments have been registered with a British court to be enforced in the United Kingdom.[31]

A1.391 103. (cc) In Ireland the District Court has jurisdiction to make maintenance orders in respect of spouses and children of a marriage and also in respect of illegitimate children. The Court also has power to vary or revoke its maintenance orders. The jurisdiction of the Court is exercised by the judge for the district where either of the parties to the proceedings is ordinarily resident or carries on any profession or occupation or, in the case of illegitimate children, the judge for the district in which the mother of the child resides. A judge who makes a maintenance order loses jurisdiction to vary it if these requirements as to residence, etc., are no longer fulfilled. Apart from the possibility of having a maintenance order varied there is a right of appeal to the Circuit Court from such orders made by the District Court. The Circuit Court also has jurisdiction to make maintenance orders in proceedings relating to the guardianship of infants. It may also vary or revoke its maintenance orders. Its jurisdiction is exercised by the judge for the circuit in which the defendant is ordinarily resident at the date of application for maintenance or at the date of application for a variation of a maintenance order, as the case may be. An appeal lies to the High Court.

The High Court may order maintenance to be paid, including alimony pending suit and permanent alimony following the granting of divorce *a mensa et thoro*. It has jurisdiction to vary its own maintenance orders and appeals against its orders lie to the Supreme Court.

A1.392 104. (b) Although it nowhere states this expressly, the 1968 Convention is based on the principle that all judgments given in a Member State can be contested in that State by all the legal remedies available under the law of that State, even when the basis on which the competence of the courts of that State was founded no longer exists. In France, a French judgment may be contested by an appeal, appeal in cassation and an application to set aside a conviction, even if the defendant has long since ceased to be domiciled in France. It follows from the obligation of recognition that no Contracting State can claim jurisdiction with regard to appeals against judgments given in another Contracting State. This also covers proceedings similar to an appeal, such as an **[105]** action of reduction in Scotland or a "Wiederaufnahmeklage" in Germany. Conversely, every claim to jurisdiction which is not based on proceedings to pursue a remedy by way of appeal must satisfy the provisions of the 1968 Convention. This has three important consequences (see paragraphs 105 to 107) for decisions concerning jurisdiction for the adjustment of maintenance orders. A fourth concerns recognition and enforcement and is mentioned now as a connected matter. (See paragraph 108).

---

[31] S.9 of the Maintenance Orders (Reciprocal Enforcement) Act 1972.

105. On no account may the court of the State addressed examine whether the amount awarded is still appropriate, without having regard to the jurisdiction provisions of the 1968 Convention. If the proceedings are an appeal, the courts of the State of origin will remain competent. Alternatively the new action may be quite distinct from the original proceedings, in which case the jurisdiction provisions of the 1978 Convention must be observed.

106. (bb) Under the legal systems of all six original EEC States, the **A1.393** adjustment of maintenance orders, at any rate as far as jurisdiction is concerned, is not regarded as a remedy by way of appeal (see paragraph 100). Accordingly the courts of the State of origin lose their competence to adjust maintenance orders within the original scope of the 1968 Convention, if the conditions on which their jurisdiction was based no longer exist. The 1968 Convention could not, however, be applied consistently, if the courts in the United Kingdom were to claim jurisdiction to adjust decisions irrespective of the continued existence of the facts on which jurisdiction was originally based.

107. Applicants for the adjustment of maintenance claims can only be made in courts with jurisdiction under Article 2 or Article 5(2), as amended, of the 1968 Convention. For example, if the maintenance creditor claims adjustment due to increases in the cost of living, he may choose between the international jurisdiction of the domicile of the maintenance debtor and the local jurisdiction of the place where he himself is domiciled or habitually resident. However, if the maintenance debtor seeks adjustment because of a deterioration in his financial circumstances, he can only apply under the international jurisdiction referred to in Article 2, *i.e.* the jurisdiction of the domicile of the maintenance creditor, even where the original judgment (pursuant to Article 2 where it is applicable) was given in the State of his own domicile and the parties have retained their places of residence.

108. If a maintenance debtor wishes effect to be given in another State to **A1.394** an adjusted order, account must be taken of the reversed roles of the parties. Adjustment at the instance of the maintenance debtor can only be aimed at a remission or reduction of the amount of maintenance. Reliance on such a decision in another Contracting State does not therefore involve "enforcement" within the meaning of sections 2 and 3 of Title III, but rather recognition as referred to in section 1 of that Title. It is true that the second paragraph of Article 26 makes provision for a special application to obtain recognition of a judgment, and the provisions of sections 2 and 3 of Title III concerning enforcement are applicable to such an application. If, in these circumstances, recognition is to be granted to a judgment which has been amended on the application of the maintenance debtor, the position is as follows: the applicant within the meaning of Articles 34 and 36 is not the creditor but the debtor, and

therefore, according to Article 34, the creditor is the party who is not entitled to make any submissions. The right of appeal of the party against whom enforcement is sought, provided for in Article 36, lies with the creditor in this case. As applicant, the maintenance debtor has the right laid down in the second paragraph of Article 42, read together with the second paragraph of Article 26, to request recognition of part only of an adjusting order. For the application of Article 44 it has to be determined whether, as plaintiff, he was granted legal aid in the original proceedings.

II. *Trusts*

1. Problems which the Convention in its present form would create with regard to trusts

A1.395 109. A distinguishing feature of United Kingdom and Irish law is the trust. In these two States it provides the solution to many problems which Continental legal systems overcome in an **[106]** altogether different way. The basic structure of a trust may be described as the relationship which arises when a person or persons (the trustees) hold rights of any kind for the benefit of one or more persons (the beneficiaries) or for some object permitted by law, in such a way that the real benefit of the property accrues, not to the trustees, but to the beneficiaries (who may, however, include one or more of the trustees) or other object of the trust. Basically two kinds of legal relationships can be distinguished in a trust; they may be defined as the internal relationships and the external relationships.

A1.396 110. (a) In his external relationships, *i.e.* in legal dealings with persons who are not beneficiaries of the trust, the trustee acts like any other owner of property. He can dispose of and acquire rights, enter into commitments binding on the trust and acquire rights for its benefit. As far as these acts are concerned no adjustments to the 1968 Convention are necessary. Its provisions on jurisdiction are applicable, as in legal dealings between persons who are not acting as trustees. If a Belgian lessee of property situated in Belgium, but belonging to an English trust, sues to be allowed into occupation, Article 16(1) is applicable, irrespective of the fact that the property belongs to a trust.

A1.397 111. (b) Problems arise in connection with the internal relationships of a trust, *i.e.* as between the trustees themselves, between persons claiming the status of trustees and, above all, between trustees on the one hand and the beneficiaries of a trust on the other. Disputes may occur among a number of persons as to who has been properly appointed as a trustee; among a number of trustees doubts may arise as to the extent of their respective rights to one another; there may be disputes between the trustees and the beneficiaries as to the rights of the latter to or in connection with the trust property, as to whether, for example, the trustee is obliged to hand over assets to a child beneficiary of the trust after the child has attained a certain age. Disputes may also arise between the settlor and other parties involved in the trust.

112. The internal relationships of a trust are not necessarily covered by the 1968 Convention. They are excluded from its scope when the trust deals with one of the matters referred to in the second paragraph of Article 1. Thus as a legal institution the trust plays a significant role in connection with the law of succession. If a trust has been established by a will, disputes arising from the internal relationships are outside the scope of the 1968 Convention (see paragraph 52). The same applies when a trustee is appointed in bankruptcy proceedings; he would correspond to a liquidator ("Konkursverwalter") in Continental legal systems.

113. Where the 1968 Convention is applicable to the internal relationships of a trust, its provisions on jurisdiction were in their original form not always well adapted to this legal institution. To base jurisdiction on the domicile of the defendant trustee would not be appropriate in trust matters. A trust has no legal personality as such. If, however, an action is brought against a defendant in his capacity as trustee, his domicile would not necessarily be a suitable basis for determining jurisdiction. If a person leaves the United Kingdom to go to Corsica, it is right and proper that, in the absence of any special jurisdiction, claims directed against him personally should be brought only before Corsican courts. If, however, he is a sole or joint trustee or co-trustee of trust property situated in the United Kingdom and hitherto administered there, the beneficiaries and the other trustees cannot be expected to seek redress in a Corsican court. **A1.398**

Moreover, the legal relationships between trustees *inter se*, and between the trustees and the beneficiaries, are not of a contractual nature; in most cases, the trustees are not even authorized to conclude agreements conferring jurisdiction by consent. Jurisdiction for actions arising from the internal relationships of a trust can be based, therefore, neither on Article 5(1) nor—as a rule—on agreements conferring jurisdiction by consent pursuant to Article 17. To overcome this difficulty simply by amending the 1968 Convention so as to allow a settlor to stipulate which courts are to have jurisdiction would only partly solve the problem. Such an amendment would not include already existing trusts, and the most suitable jurisdiction for possible disputes cannot always be foreseen when creating a trust.

2. The solution proposed

114. (a) The solution proposed in the new paragraph (6) of Article 5 is based on the argument that trusts, [107] even though they have no legal personality, may be said to have a geographical centre of operation. This would fulfil functions similar to those fulfilled by the **A1.399**

"seat" of business associations without legal personality. It is true that United Kingdom and Irish law have so far provided only a tentative definition of such a central point of a trust. However, the concept of the domicile of a trust is not, at present, unknown in legal practice and theory.[32] In his manual on Private International Law the Scottish Professor Anton gives the following definition[33]:

> "The domicile of a trust is thought to be basically a matter depending upon the wishes of a truster and his expressed intentions will usually be conclusive. In their absence the truster's intentions will be inferred from such circumstances as the administrative centre of the trust, the place of residence of the trustees, the situs of the assets of the trust, the nature of the trust purposes and the place where these are to be fulfilled."

No doubt these notions about the domicile of a trust were developed mainly for the purpose of determining the legal system to be applied, usually either English or Scottish law. The principal characteristics of "domicile" so defined and some of the factors on which it is based would also justify making it the basis for founding jurisdiction. The proposed new provision does not, strictly speaking, create a special jurisdiction. It covers only a very limited number of cases and is, therefore, added to Article 5 rather than to Article 2. For the non-exclusive character of the new provision see paragraph 118.

A1.400 115. (b) The following are some detailed comments on the Working Party's proposal (see paragraph 181).

116. The concepts "trust," "trustee" and "domicile" have not been translated into the other Community languages, since they relate to a distinctive feature of United Kingdom and Irish law. However, the Member States can give a more detailed definition of the concept of a trust in their national language in their legislation implementing the Accession Convention.

A1.401 117. The phrase "created by the operation of a statute, or by a written instrument, or created orally and evidenced in writing" is intended to indicate clearly that the new rules on jurisdiction apply only to cases in which under United Kingdom or Irish law a trust has been expressly constituted, or for which provision is made by Statute. This is important, because these legal systems solve many problems with which Continental systems have to deal in a completely different way, by means of so-called "constructive" or "implied" trusts.

---

[32] A. E. Anton, "Private International Law" (1967), p. 470; Graveson, "The Conflict of Laws" (1969), p. 565; Lord President Clyde in Clarks Trustee Petitioners 1966 SLT 249, p. 251.

[33] *op. cit.*

Where the latter are involved, the new Article 5(6) is not applicable, as for instance where, after conclusion of a contract of sale, but prior to the transfer of title, the vendor is treated as holding the property on trust for the purchaser (see paragraph 172). Trusts resulting from the operation of a statutory provision are unlikely to fall within the scope of the 1968 Convention. Since in the United Kingdom, for example, children cannot own real property, a trust in their favour arises by operation of statute, if the circumstances are such that adult persons would have acquired ownership.

118. It should be noted that the new provision is not exclusive. It merely establishes an additional jurisdiction. The trustee who has gone to Corsica (see paragraph 113) can also be sued in the courts there. However, a settlor would be free to stipulate an exclusive jurisdiction (see paragraph 174). **A1.402**

119. If proceedings are brought in a Contracting State, relating to a trust which is subject to a foreign legal system, the question arises as to which law determines the domicile of that trust. The new version of Article 53 proposes the same criterion as that adopted in the 1968 Convention for ascertaining the "seat" of a company. As far as the legal systems of England and Wales, Scotland, Northern Ireland and Ireland are concerned, application of this provision should present no serious difficulty. There are at present no rules of private international law in the legal systems of the Continental Member States of the Community for determining the domicile of a trust. The courts of those States will have to evolve such rules to enable them to apply the trust provisions of the 1968 Convention. Two possibilities exist. It could be contended that the domicile of a trust should be determined by the [108] legal system to which the trust is subject. One could, however, also contend that the court concerned should decide the issue in accordance with its own *lex fori* which would have to evolve its own appropriate criteria.

120. In principle, the exclusive jurisdictions provided for by Article 16 take priority over the new Article 5(6). However, it is not easy to establish the precise extent of that priority. **A1.403**

   In legal disputes arising from internal trust relationships, the legal relations referred to in the provisions in question usually play only an incidental role if any. The trustee requires court approval for certain acts of management. Even where the management of immovable property is concerned, any such applications to the court do not affect the proprietary rights of the trustee, but only his fiduciary obligations under the trust. Article 16(1) does not apply. One could, however, envisage a dispute arising between two people as to which of them was trustee of certain property. If one of them instituted proceedings against the other in a German court claiming the cancellation of the entry in the land register showing the defendant as the owner of the property and the substitution of an entry showing the plaintiff as the true owner, there can be no doubt that, under Article 16(1) or (3), the German court would have exclusive jurisdiction. However, if a declaration is sought that a particular person is a trustee of a particular trust which includes certain property, Article 16(1) does not become applicable merely because that property includes immovable property.

III. *Admiralty jurisdiction*

A1.404   121. The exercise of jurisdiction in maritime matters has traditionally played a far greater role in the United Kingdom than in the Continental States of the Community. The scope of the international competence of the courts, as it has been developed in the United Kingdom, has become of worldwide significance for admiralty jurisdiction. This factor is reflected not least in the Brussels Conventions of 1952 and 1957 (see paragraph 238 *et seq.*). It would have been inappropriate to limit the exercise of admiralty jurisdiction to the basis of jurisdiction included in the 1968 Convention in its original form. If a ship is arrested in a State because of an internationally recognized maritime claim, it would be unreasonable to expect the creditor to seek a decision on his claim before the courts of the shipowner's domicile. For this reason, the Working Party gave lengthy consideration to the possible inclusion of a special section on admiralty jurisdiction in Title II. Article 36 of the Accession Convention is derived from an earlier draft prepared for that purpose (see paragraph 131). Parallel negotiations on Article 57 of the 1968 Convention did, however, lead to a generally acceptable interpretation which will enable States party to a Convention on maritime law to assume jurisdiction on any particular matter dealt with in that Convention, even in respect of persons domiciled in a Community State which is not a party to that Convention (see paragraph 236 *et seq.*). Furthermore, all delegations are in support of a Joint Declaration urging the Community States to accede to the most important of all the Conventions on maritime law, namely the Brussels Convention of 10 May 1952 (see paragraph 238). The Working Party, confident that this Joint Declaration will be adopted and implemented, finally dropped its plans for a section dealing with admiralty jurisdiction. This would also avoid interfering with the general principles of the 1968 Convention, and maintain a clear dividing line between its scope and that of other Conventions.

A1.405   Two issues remain outstanding, however, since they are not fully covered by the Brussels Conventions of 1952 and 1957: jurisdiction in the event of the arrest of salvaged cargo or freight (the new Article 5(7))(1) and actions for limitation of liability in maritime matters (the new Article 6a)(2). Moreover, until Denmark and Ireland accede to the Brussels Arrest Convention of 10 May 1952, transitional provisions had also to be introduced (3). Finally, a particularity affecting only Denmark and Ireland (4) still remained to be settled.

1. Jurisdiction in connection with the arrest of salvaged cargo or freight

122. (a) The Brussels Convention of 1952 allows a claimant, *inter alia*, to **A1.406** invoke the jurisdiction of a State in which a ship had been arrested on account of a salvage claim (Article 7(1)(b)). Implicit in this provision is a rule of substantive law. A claim to remuneration for salvage entitles **[109]** the salvage firm to a maritime lien on the ship. A similar lien in favour of a salvage firm can also exist on the cargo; this can be of some economic importance, if it is the cargo rather than the ship which was salvaged, or if the salvaged ship is so badly damaged that its value is less than the cost of the salvage operation. The value of the cargo of a modern supertanker can amount to a considerable sum. Finally, prior rights can also arise in regard to freight. If freight is payable solely in the event of the safe arrival of the cargo at the place of destination, it is appropriate that the salvage firm should have a prior right to be satisfied out of the claim to freight which was preserved due to the salvage of the cargo.

Accordingly United Kingdom law provides that a salvage firm may apply for the arrest of the salvaged cargo or the freight claim preserved due to its intervention and may also apply to the court concerned for a final decision on its claims to remuneration for salvage. Jurisdiction of this kind is similar in scope to the provisions of Article 7 of the Brussels Convention of 1952. As there is no other Convention on the arrest of salvaged cargo and freight which would remain applicable under Article 57, the United Kingdom would, on acceding to the 1968 Convention, have suffered an unacceptable loss of jurisdiction if a special provision had not been introduced.

123. (b) The proposed solution applies the underlying principle of **A1.407** Article 7 of the Brussels Convention of 1952 to jurisdiction after the arrest of salvaged cargo or freight claims.

Under Article 24 of the 1968 Convention, there is no limitation on national laws with regard to the granting of provisional legal safeguards including arrest. However, they could not provide that arrest, whether authorized or effected, should suffice to found jurisdiction as to the substance of the matter. The exception introduced in Article 5(7)(a) is confined to arrest to safeguard a salvage claim.

Article 5(7)(b) introduces an extension of jurisdiction not expressly modelled on the Brussels Convention of 1952. It is a result of practical experience. After salvage operations—whether involving a ship, cargo or freight—arrest is sometimes ordered, but not actually carried into effect, because bail or other security has been provided. This must be sufficient to confer jurisdiction on the arresting court to decide also on the substance of the matter.

The object of the provision is to confer jurisdiction only with regard to those claims which are secured by a maritime lien. If the owner of a ship in difficulties has concluded a contract for its salvage, as his contract with the cargo owner frequently obliges him to do, any disputes arising from the former contract will not be governed by this provision.

2. Jurisdiction to order a limitation of liability

A1.408 124. It is not easy to say precisely how the application of Article 57 of the 1968 Convention links up with that of the International Convention of 10 October 1957 relating to the limitation of the liability of owners of seagoing ships[34] (see end of paragraph 128) and with relevant national laws. The latter Convention contains no express provisions directly affecting international jurisdiction or the enforcement of judgments. The Working Party did not consider that it was its task to deal systematically with the issues raised by that Convention and to devise proposals for solving them. It would, however, be particularly unfortunate in certain respects if the jurisdictional lacunae of the 1957 Convention on the limitation of liability were carried over into the 1968 Convention and were supplemented in accordance with the general provisions on jurisdiction of that Convention.

A distinction needs to be drawn between three differing aspects arising in connection with the limitation of liability in matters of maritime law. First, a procedure exists for setting up and allocating the liability fund. Secondly, the entitlement to damages against the shipowner must be judicially determined. Finally, and distinct from both, there is the assessment of limitation of liability regarding a given claim.

[110] The procedural details giving effect to these three aspects vary in the different legal systems of the Community.

A1.409 125. Under one system, which is followed in particular in the United Kingdom, limitation of liability necessitates an action against one of the claimants—either by way of originating proceedings or, if an action has already been brought against the shipowner, as a counterclaim. The liability fund is set up at the court dealing with the limitation of liability issue, and other claimants must also lodge their claims with the same court.

126. Under the system obtaining in Germany, for example, proceedings for the limitation of liability are started not by means of an action brought against a claimant, but by a simple application which is not directed "against" any person, and which leads to the setting up of the fund.

If the application is successful, all claimants must lodge their claims with that court. If any disputes arise about the validity of any of the claims lodged, they have to be dealt with by special proceedings taking the form of an action by the claimant against the fund administrator, creditor or shipowner contesting the claim. Under this system an independent action by the shipowner against the claimant in connection with limitation of liability is also possible.

---

[34] The new Convention on limitation of liability for maritime claims, signed in London on 19 November 1976, was not yet in force at the end of the Working Party's discussions.

Such an action leads not to the setting up of a liability fund or to an immediately effective limitation of liability, but merely establishes whether liability is subject to potential limitation, in case of future proceedings to assess the extent of such liability.

127. The new Article 6a does not apply to an action by a claimant against the shipowner, fund administrator or other competing claimants, nor to the collective proceedings for creating and allocating the liability fund, but only to the independent action brought by a shipowner against a claimant (a). Otherwise the present provisions of the 1968 Convention which are relevant to limitation of maritime liability apply (b).　**A1.410**

128. (a) The actual or potential limitation of the liability of a shipowner can, however, in all legal systems of the Community be used otherwise than as a defence. If a shipowner anticipates a liability claim, it may be in his interest to take the initiative by asking for a declaration that he has only limited or potentially limited liability for the claim. In that case he can choose from one of the jurisdictions which are competent by virtue of Articles 2 to 6. According to these provisions, he cannot bring an action in the courts of his domicile. Since, however, he could be sued in those courts, it would be desirable also to allow him to have recourse to this jurisdiction. It is the purpose of Article 6a to provide for this. Moreover, apart from the Brussels Convention of 1952, this is the only jurisdiction where the shipowner could reasonably concentrate all actions affecting limitation of his liability. The result for English law (see paragraph 125) is that the fund can be set up and allocated by that same court. In addition, Article 6a makes it clear that proceedings for limitation of liability can also be brought by the shipowner in any other court which has jurisdiction over the claim. It also enables national legislations to give jurisdiction to a court within their territory other than the court which would normally have jurisdiction.　**A1.411**

129. (b) For proceedings concerning the validity as such of a claim against a shipowner, Articles 2 to 6 are exclusively applicable. In addition, Article 22 is always applicable. If proceedings to limit liability have been brought in one State, a court in another State which has before it an application to establish or to limit liability may stay the proceedings or even decline jurisdiction.　**A1.412**

130. (c) A clear distinction must be drawn between the question of jurisdiction and the question which substantive law on limitation of liability is to be applied. This need not be the law of the State whose courts have jurisdiction for assessing the limitation of liability. The law applicable for the limitation of liability also defines more precisely the type of case in which limitation of liability can be claimed at all.　**A1.413**

[111] 3. Transitional provisions

A1.414   131. All the delegations hope that Denmark and Ireland will accede to the Brussels Convention of 10 May 1952 (see paragraph 121). This will, however, naturally take some time, and it is reasonable to allow a transitional period of three years after the entry into force of the Accession Convention. It would be harsh if, within that period, in the two States concerned jurisdiction in maritime matters were to be limited to what is authorized under the terms of Articles 2 to 6a. Article 36 of the Accession Convention therefore contains transitional provisions in favour of those States. These provisions correspond, apart from variations in the drafting, to the provisions which the Working Party originally proposed to recommend for the special section on maritime law as general rules of jurisdiction regarding the arrest of seagoing ships. In preparing these provisions the Working Party drew heavily, in fact almost exclusively, on the rules of the 1952 Brussels Convention relating to the arrest of seagoing ships (see paragraph 121).

Since they are temporary, the transitional provisions do not merit detailed comments on how they differ from the text of that Convention.

4. Disputes between a shipmaster and crew members

A1.415   132. The new Article Vb of the Protocol annexed to the 1968 Convention is based on a request by Denmark founded on Danish tradition. This has become part of the Danish Seamen's Law No. 420 of 18 June 1973 which states that disputes between a crew member and a shipmaster of a Danish vessel may not be brought before foreign courts. The same principle is also embodied in some consular conventions between Denmark and other States. Following a specific request from the Irish delegation, the scope of this provision has also been extended to Irish ships.

IV. *Other special matters*

1. Jurisdiction based on the place of performance

A1.416   133. In the course of the negotiations it emerged that the French and Dutch texts of Article 5(1) were less specific than the German and Italian texts on the question of the designation of the obligation. The former could be misinterpreted as including other contractual obligations than those which were the subject of the legal proceedings in question. The revised versions of the French and Dutch texts should clear up this misunderstanding.[35]

---

[35] The Court of Justice of the European Communities has already decided in this sense: see judgment of 6 October 1976 (Case No. 14/76).

2. Jurisdiction in matters relating to tort

134. Article 5(3) deals with the special tort jurisdiction. It presupposes **A1.417** that the wrongful act has already been committed and refers to the place where the harmful event has occurred. The legal systems of some States provide for preventive injunctions in matters relating to tort. This applies, for example, in cases where it is desired to prevent the publication of a libel or the sale of goods which have been manufactured or put on the market in breach of the law on patents or industrial property rights. In particular the laws of the United Kingdom and Germany provide for measures of this nature. No doubt Article 24 is applicable when courts have an application for provisional protective measures before them, even if their decision has, in practice, final effect. There is much to be said for the proposition that the courts specified in Article 5(3) should also have jurisdiction in proceedings whose main object is to prevent the imminent commission of a tort.

3. Third party proceedings and claims for redress

135. In Article 6(2), the term "third party proceedings" relates to a legal **A1.418** institution which is common to the legal systems of all the original Member States, with the exception of Germany. However, a jurisdictional basis which rests solely on the capacity of a third party to be joined as such in the proceedings cannot exist by itself. It must necessarily be supplemented by legal criteria which determine which parties may in which capacity and for what purpose be joined in legal proceedings. Thus the provisions already existing in, or which may in future be introduced into, the legal systems of the new Member States with reference to the joining of third parties in legal proceedings, remain unaffected by the 1968 Convention.

[112] Section 3

Jurisdiction in insurance matters

136. The accession of the United Kingdom introduced a totally new **A1.419** dimension to the insurance business as it had been practised hitherto within the European Community. Lloyds of London has a substantial share of the market in the international insurance of large risks.[36]

In view of this situation the United Kingdom requested a number

---

[36] In 1974 the premium income from overseas business amounted to no less than £3,045 million, £520 million of which consisted of business with Member States of the EEC, and 10 per cent. of which was accounted for by re-insurance business. A sizeable proportion of this insurance market consisted of marine and aviation insurance. For these classes alone the overseas premium income amounted to £535 million including £50 million worth of business with other EEC countries.

of adjustments. Its main argument was that the protection afforded by Articles 7 to 12 was unnecessary for policy-holders domiciled outside the Community (I) or of great economic importance (II). The United Kingdom expressed concern that, without an adjustment of the 1968 Convention, insurers within the Community might be forced to demand higher premiums than their competitors in other States.

There were additional reasons for each particular request for an adjustment. As regards contracts of insurance with policy-holders domiciled outside the Community the United Kingdom sought the unrestricted admissibility of agreements conferring jurisdiction to be vouchsafed so that appropriate steps could be taken with regard to the binding provisions contained in the national laws of many policy-holders insuring with English insurers (I). Requests for adjustments also referred, in conjunction with the other requests for adjustments, to the scope of Articles 9 and 10 which seemed to require clarification (III). Finally there were requests for a few minor adjustments (IV).

A1.420   The original request of the United Kingdom in respect of the first two problems, namely that the insurance matters in question should be excluded from the scope of Articles 7 to 12 was too far-reaching in view of the general objectives of the 1968 Convention. In particular a number of features of the mandatory rules of jurisdiction, which differ for the various types of insurance, had to be retained (see paragraphs 138, 139 and 143). However, the special structure of the British insurance market had to be taken into account—not least so that it would not be driven to resort systematically to arbitration. Although the 1968 Convention does not restrict the possibility of settling disputes by arbitration (see paragraph 63), national law should be careful not to encourage arbitration simply by making proceedings before national courts too complicated and uncertain for the parties. The Working Party therefore endeavoured to extend the possibilities of conferring jurisdiction by consent. For the form of such agreements see paragraph 176.

I. *Insurance contracts taken out by policy-holders*
domiciled outside the Community

A1.421   137. As already indicated earlier (see note 36), insurance contracts with policy-holders domiciled outside the Community account for a very large part of the British insurance business. The 1968 Convention does not expressly stipulate to what extent such contracts may provide for jurisdiction by consent. Article 4 applies only to the comparatively rare case where the policy-holder is the defendant in subsequent proceedings. In so far as the jurisdiction of courts outside the Community can be determined by agreement, the general question arises as to what restrictions should be imposed on such agreements having regard to the exclusive jurisdictions provided for by the 1968 Convention (see paragraphs 148, 162 *et seq.*). The main problem in this connection was the jurisdiction under Articles 9 and

10 which, it was thought, could not be excluded. However, this difficulty did not affect insurance contracts only with policy-holders domiciled outside the Community. It also affects, more generally, agreements on jurisdiction which are authorized by Article 12.

In view of the great importance for the United Kingdom of the question of agreements on jurisdiction with policy-holders domiciled outside the Community, it was necessary to incorporate the admissibility in principle of such agreements on jurisdiction expressly in the 1968 Convention. If, therefore, a policy-holder domiciled outside the Community insures a risk in England, exclusive jurisdiction may be conferred by agreement on English courts as well as on the courts of the policy-holder's domicile or others.

[113]   This basic rule had however to be limited again in two ways in the new paragraph (4) of Article 12.

138. 1. Compulsory insurance

Where a statutory obligation exists to take out insurance no departure from the provisions of Articles 8 to 11 on compulsory insurance can be permitted, even if the policy-holder is domiciled outside the Community. If a person domiciled in Switzerland owns a motor car which is normally based in Germany, then the car must, under German law, be insured against liability. Such an insurance contract may not contain provisions for jurisdiction by consent concerning accidents occurring in Germany.   **A1.422**

The possibility of invoking the jurisdiction of German courts (Article 8) cannot be contractually excluded. This is so even although the relevant German law of 5 April 1965 on compulsory insurance (Bundesgesetzblatt I, page 213) does not expressly prohibit agreements on jurisdiction. However, in practice German law prevents the conclusion of agreements on jurisdiction in the area of compulsory insurance because approval of conditions of insurance containing such a provision would be withheld.

Compulsory insurance exists in the following Member States of the Community for the following articles, installations, activities and occupations, although this list does not claim to be complete: **A1.423**

FEDERAL REPUBLIC OF GERMANY[37]

1. Federal

Liability insurance compulsory for owners of motor vehicles, airline companies, hunters, owners of nuclear installations and handling of nuclear combustible materials and other radioactive materials, road haulage, accountants and tax advisers, security firms, those responsible for schools for nursing, infant and child

---

[37] Extract from "Pflichtversicherung in den Europäischen Gemeinschaften," a study by Professor Ernst Steindorff, Munich.

care and midwifery, automobile experts, notaries' professional organizations, those responsible for development aid, exhibitors, pharmaceutical firms;

Life insurance for master chimney sweeps;

Accident insurance for airline companies and usufructuaries;

Fire insurance for owners of buildings which are subject to a charge, usufructuaries, warehouse occupiers, pawnbrokers;

Goods insurance for pawnbrokers;

Pension funds for theatres, cultural orchestras, district master chimney sweeps, supplementary pension funds for the public service.

2. Länder

There is no uniformity as between the Länder of the Federal Republic of Germany, but there is in particular compulsory fire insurance for buildings, compulsory pension funds for agricultural workers, the liberal professions (doctors, chemists, architects, notaries) and (in Bavaria, for example) members of the Honourable Company of Chimney Sweeps and, for example, a supplementary pension fund for workers in the Free and Hanseatic City of Bremen. In Bavaria there is compulsory insurance for livestock intended for slaughter.

BELGIUM:

A1.424 Motor vehicles, hunting, nuclear installations, accidents at work, transport accidents (for paying transport by motor vehicles).

DENMARK:

A1.425 Motor vehicles, dogs, nuclear installations, accountants.

FRANCE:

A1.426 Operators of ships and nuclear installations, sand motor vehicles, operators of cable-cars, chair-lifts and other such mechanical units, hunting, estate agents, managers of property, syndics of co-owners, business managers, operators of sports centres, accountants, agricultural mutual assistance schemes, legal advisers, physical education establishments and pupils, operators of dance halls, managers of pharmacists' shops in the form of a private limited liability company (S.à.r.l.), blood transfusion centres, architects, motor vehicle experts, farmers.

LUXEMBOURG:

A1.427 Motor vehicles, hunting and hunting organizations, hotel establishments, nuclear installations, fire and theft insurance for hotel establishments;

[114] Insurance against the seizure of livestock in slaughterhouses.

NETHERLANDS:

Motor vehicles, nuclear installations, tankers.   **A1.428**

UNITED KINGDOM:

Third party liability in respect of motor vehicles;   **A1.429**

Employers' liability in respect of accidents at work;

Insurance of nuclear installations;

Insurance of British registered ships against oil pollution;

Compulsory insurance scheme for a number of professions, *e.g.* solicitors and insurance brokers.

139. 2. Insurance of immovable property

The second exception referred to at the end of paragraph 137 is   **A1.430**
particularly designed to ensure that Article 9 continues to apply
even when the policy-holder is domiciled outside the Community. However, this exception has further implications. It
prohibits jurisdiction agreements conferring exclusive jurisdiction on the courts mentioned in Article 9. This applies even
where the national law of the State in which the immovable
property is situated allows agreements conferring jurisdiction in
such circumstances.

II. *Insurance of large risks, in particular marine*
and aviation insurance

140. The United Kingdom's request for special rules for the insurance of   **A1.431**
large risks was probably the most difficult problem for the Working
Party. The request was based on the realization that the concept of
social protection underlying a restriction on the admissibility of
provisions conferring jurisdiction in insurance matters is no longer
justified where the policy-holders are powerful undertakings. The
problem was one of finding a suitable demarcation line. Discussions
on the second Directive on insurance had already revealed the
impossibility of taking as criteria abstract, general factors like company capital or turnover. The only solution was to examine which
types of insurance contracts were in general concluded only by
policy-holders who did not require social protection. On this basis,
special treatment could not be conceded to industrial insurance as a
whole.

Accordingly, the Working Party directed its attention to the various classes of insurance connected with the transport industry. In this area there is an additional justification for special treatment for agreements on jurisdiction: the risks insured are highly mobile and insurance policies tend to change hands several times in quick succession. This leads to uncertainty as to which courts will have jurisdiction and the difficulties in calculating risks are thereby greatly increased. On the other hand, there are here, too, certain areas requiring social protection. Particular complications were caused by the fact that there is a well integrated insurance market for the transport industry. The various types of risk for different means of transport are usually covered under one single policy. The British insurance industry in particular has developed standard policies which only require for their completion a notification by the insured that the means of transport (which can be of many different types) have set off.

A1.432
The result of a consideration of all these matters is the solution which figures in the new paragraph (5) of Article 12, as supplemented by Article 12a: agreements on jurisdiction are in principle to be given special treatment in marine insurance and in some sectors of aviation insurance. In the case of insurance of transport by land alone no exceptional rules of any kind appeared justified.

A1.433
In order to avoid difficulties and differences of interpretation, a list had to be drawn up of the types of policy for which the admissibility of agreements on jurisdiction was to be extended. The idea of referring for this purpose to the list of classes of insurance appearing in the Annex to the First Council Directive of 24 July 1973 (73/239/EEC) proved inadequate. The classification used there took account of the requirements of State administration of insurance, and was not directed towards a fair balancing of private insurance interests. There was thus no alternative but to draw up a separate list for the purposes of the 1968 Convention. The following comments apply to the list and the classes of insurance not included in it.

[115] 1. Article 12a(1)(a)

A1.434
141. This provision applies only to hull insurance and not to liability insurance. The term "seagoing ships" means all vessels intended to travel on the sea. This includes not only ships in the traditional sense of the word but also hovercraft, hydrofoils, barges and lighters used at sea. It also covers floating apparatus which cannot move under its own power, *e.g.* oil exploration and extraction installations which are moved about on water. Installations firmly moored or to be moored on the seabed are in any event expressly included in the text of the provision. The provision also covers ships in the course of construction, but only in so far as the damage

is the result of a maritime risk. This is damage caused by the fact that the ship is on the water and not therefore, damage which occurs in dry-dock or in the workshops of shipyards.

2. Article 12a(1)(b)

142. In the same way as (1)(a) covers the value of the hull of a ship or of an aeroplane, (1)(b) covers the value of goods destroyed or lost in transit, but not liability insurance for any loss or damage caused by those goods. The most important single decision taken on the provision was the addition of the words "consists of or includes." The reason for this is that goods in transit are frequently not conveyed by the same means of transport right to their final destination. There may be a sequence of journeys by land, sea and air. There would be unwarranted complications for the insurance industry in drafting policies and settling claims, if a fine distinction had always to be drawn as to the section of transit in which loss or damage had occurred. Moreover it is often impossible to ascertain this. One has only to think of container transport to realize how easily a loss may be discovered only at the destination. Practical considerations therefore required that agreements on jurisdiction be permitted, even where goods are carried by sea or by air for only part of their journey. Even if it can be proved that the loss occurred in the course of transport on land, agreements on jurisdiction permitted by the new paragraph (5) of Article 12 remain effective. The provision applies even if the shipment does not cross any national border. **A1.435**

143. The exception in respect of injury to passengers and loss of or damage to their baggage, which is repeated in Article 12a(2)(a) and (b), is justified by the fact that such persons as a group tend to have a weaker economic position and less bargaining power.

3. Article 12a(2)(a)

144. Whether these provisions also cover all liability arising in connection with the construction, modification and repair of a ship; whether therefore the provision includes all liability which the shipyard incurs towards third parties and which was caused by the ship; or whether the expression "use or operation" has to be construed more narrowly as applying only to liability arising in the course of a trial voyage—all these are questions of interpretation which still await an answer. The exception for compulsory aircraft insurance is intended to leave the Member States free to provide for such protection as they consider necessary for the policy-holder and for the victim. **A1.436**

4. Article 12a(2)(b)

A1.437   145. As there is no reason to treat combined transport any differently for liability insurance than for hull insurance, it is equally irrelevant during which section of the transport the circumstances causing the liability occurred (see paragraphs 142 and 143).

5. Article 12a(3)

A1.438   146. The most important application of this provision is stated in the text itself. In the absence of a provision to the contrary in the charter party, an air crash would cause the carrier to lose his entitlement to freight and the owner his charter-fee from the charterer. Another example might be loss caused by the late arrival of a ship. For the rest the notion is the same as that used in Directive 73/239/EEC.

6. Article 12a(4)

A1.439   147. Insurance against ancillary risks is a familiar practice, especially in United Kingdom insurance [116] contracts. An example would be "shipowner's disbursements" consisting of exceptional operational costs, *e.g.* harbour dues accruing whilst a ship remains disabled. Another example is insurance against "increased value," providing protection against loss arising from the fact that a destroyed or damaged cargo had increased in value during transit.
  The provision does not require an ancillary risk to be insured under the same policy as the main risk to which it relates. The Working Party therefore deliberately opted for a somewhat different wording from that in Directive 73/239/EEC for the "ancillary risks" referred to in that Directive. The definition in that Directive could not be used since it is concerned with a different subject, the authorization of insurance undertakings.

III. *The remaining scope of Articles 9 and 10*

A1.440   148. The revised text of Article 12, like the original text, does not expressly deal with the effect of agreements on jurisdiction or the special jurisdictions for insurance matters set out in section 3. Nevertheless, the legal position is clear from the systematic construction of section 3 of the 1968 Convention, as amended. Agreements on jurisdiction cover all legal proceedings between insurer and policy-holder, even where the latter wishes, pursuant to the first paragraph of Article 10, to join the insurer in the court in which he himself is sued by the injured party. However, jurisdiction clauses in insurance contracts cannot be binding upon third parties. The provisions of the second paragraph of Article 10 concerning a direct action by the injured party are thus not affected by such jurisdiction clauses. The same is true of the third paragraph of Article 10.

IV. *Other problems of adjustment and clarification
in insurance law*

1. Co-insurance

149. The substantive amendment in the first paragraph of Article 8 **A1.441**
covers jurisdiction where several co-insurers are parties to a contract of insurance. What usually happens is that one insurer acts as
leader for the other co-insurers and each of them underwrites a part
of the risk, possibly a very small part. In such cases, however, there
is no justification for permitting all the insurers, including the
leader, to be sued in the courts of each State in which any one of the
many co-insurers is domiciled. The only additional international
jurisdiction which can be justified would be one which relates to the
circumstances of the leading insurer. The Working Party considered at length whether to refer to the leading insurer's domicile,
but the effect of this would have been that the remaining co-
insurers could be sued there even if the leader was sued elsewhere.
An additional jurisdiction based on the leading insurer's circumstances is justifiable only if it leads to a concentration of actions arising out of an insured event. The new version of the first paragraph
of Article 8 therefore refers to the court where proceedings are
brought against the leading insurer. Co-insurers can thus be sued
for their share of the insurance in that court, at the same time as the
leading insurer or subsequently. However, the provision does not
impose an obligation for proceedings to be concentrated in one
court; there is nothing to prevent a policy-holder from suing the
various co-insurers in different courts. If the leading insurer has
settled the claim out of court, the policy-holder must bring any
action against the other co-insurers in one of the courts having jurisdiction under points (1) or (2) of the new version of the first paragraph of Article 8.
The remaining amendments to the first paragraph of Article 8
merely rephrase it for the sake of greater clarity.

2. Insurance agents, the setting up of branches

150. There was discussion on the present text of the second paragraph of **A1.442**
Article 8 of the 1968 Convention because its wording might give rise
to the misunderstanding that jurisdiction could be founded not only
on the intervention of an agent of the insurer, but also on that of an
independent insurance broker of the type common in the United
Kingdom. The discussion revealed that this provision was
unnecessary in view of Article 5(5). The Working Party therefore
changed the present paragraph three into paragraph two. The
addition of the words "or other establishment" is intended merely
to ensure consistency between Article 5(5) and the third paragraph
of the new Article 13. The latter provision is necessary in addition
to the former in order to prevent Article 4 being applicable.

[117] 3. Reinsurance

A1.443 151. Reinsurance contracts cannot be equated with insurance contracts. Accordingly, Articles 7 to 12 do not apply to reinsurance contracts.

4. The term "policy-holder"

A1.444 152. The previous authentic texts of the 1968 Convention use the term "preneur d'assurance" and the equivalent in German, Italian and Dutch; the nearest English equivalent of the term proved to be "the policy-holder." However, this should not give rise to the misunderstanding that the problems arising from a transfer of legal rights are now any different from those existing before the accession of the new Member States to the Convention. The rightful possessor of the policy document is not always the "preneur d'assurance." It is of course conceivable that the whole legal status of the other party to the contract with the insurer might pass to another person by inheritance or some other means, in which case the new party to the contract would become the "preneur d'assurance." However, this case must be clearly distinguished from the transfer of individual rights arising out of the contract of insurance, especially in the form of assignment of the sum assured to a beneficiary. Such an assignment may be made in advance and may be contingent, for instance, upon the occurrence of a claim. In this event it is conceivable that the insurance policy might be passed on to the beneficiary at the same time as the assignment of the right to the sum assured so that he can claim his entitlement from the insurer, if the case arises. The beneficiary would not thereby become the "preneur d'assurance." Hence, where a court's jurisdiction is dependent on individual characteristics of the "preneur d'assurance," the situation remains unchanged as a result of prior assignment of any claim to the sum assured which might arise, even if the policy document is transferred at the same time.

5. Agreements on jurisdiction between parties to a contract from the same State

A1.445 152(a). For the amendment to Article 12(3) ("at the time of conclusion of the contract"), see paragraph 161(a).

Section 4

Jurisdiction over consumer contracts

I. *Principles*

A1.446 153. Leaving aside insurance matters, the 1968 Convention pays heed to consumer protection considerations only in one small section, that dealing with instalment sales and loans. This was consistent with the law as it then stood in the original Member States of the Community since it was in fact at first only in the field of instalment sales and loans that awareness of the need to protect the consumer against unfairly worded contracts became widespread. Since that time legislation in the Member States of the Community has become concerned with much broader-based consumer protection. In particular there has been a general move in consumer protection legislation to ensure appropriate jurisdictions for the consumer. Intolerable tensions would be bound to develop between national legislation and the 1968 Convention in the long run if the Convention did not afford the consumer much the same protection in the case of transfrontier contracts as he received under national legislation. The Working Party therefore decided to propose that the previous section 4 of Title II be extended into a section on jurisdiction over consumer contracts, establishing at the same time for future purposes that only final consumers acting in a private capacity should be given special protection and not those contracting in the course of their business to pay by instalments for goods and services used. The Working Party was influenced on this last point by the proceedings in the Court of Justice of the European Communities in response to a reference from the French Cour de cassation concerning the interpretation of "instalment sales and loans," proceedings which centred on the question of whether the existing section 4 of Title II covered instalment sales contracts concluded by businessmen (Case 150/77: Société Bertrand v. Paul Ott KG).

The basic principle underlying the provisions of the new section is to draw upon ideas emerging from European Community law as it has evolved and is currently evolving. Consequently, most of the existing provisions on instalment sales and loans have been incorporated in the new section which also draws on Article 5 of the preliminary draft Convention on the law applicable to contractual and non-contractual obligations. On points of drafting detail, however, improvements **[118]** were made on the wording of the preliminary draft Convention. One substantive change was necessary, since to accord with the general structure of the 1968 Convention reference had to be made to the place where the parties are domiciled, rather than habitually resident. Details are as follows:

II. *The scope of the new section*

154. Using the device of an introductory provision defining the scope of the section, the proposal follows the practice previously adopted at the beginning of sections 3 and 4 of Title II. **A1.447**

1. Persons covered

155. The only new point of principle is a provision governing the persons covered by the section, including in particular the legal definition of the section's central term, the "consumer." The substances of the **A1.448**

1731

definition is taken from Article 5 of the preliminary draft Convention on the law applicable to contractual and non-contractual obligations the most recent version of which was used by the Working Party. The amendments made were only drafting improvements.

2. Subject matter covered

A1.449   156. As regards the subject matter covered by the new section, a clear distinction is drawn between instalment sales, including the financing of such sales, and other consumer contracts. The consequent effect on the precedence of the provisions of sections 3 and 4 is as follows: section 3 is a more specific provision than section 4 and hence takes precedence over it. A contract of insurance is not a contract for the supply of services within the meaning of the 1968 Convention. Within section 4, the provisions on instalment sales are more specific than the general reference to consumer sales in the first paragraph of Article 13.

A1.450   157. (a) As in the past, instalment sales are subject to the special provisions without any further preconditions. The sole change lies in the stipulation that the special provisions apply only where the purchaser is a private consumer. The rules governing instalment sales also apply automatically to the legal institution of hire purchase, which has developed into the commonest legal form for transacting instalment sales in the United Kingdom and Ireland. For reasons which are not material for jurisdiction purposes, instalment sales in those countries usually take the form in law of a contract of hire with an option to purchase for the hirer. In form the instalments represent the hire fee, whereas in substance they form the purchase price. At the end of the prescribed "hire" period, once all the prescribed instalments of the "hire fee" have been paid, the "hirer" is entitled to purchase the article for a nominal price. As the term "instalment sale" under the continental legal systems by no means implies that ownership of the article must necessarily pass to the purchaser at the same time as physical possession, hire purchase is in practice tantamount to an instalment sale.

Contracts to finance instalment sales to private consumers are also subject to the special provisions without any further preconditions. Contrary to the legal position obtaining hitherto, the Working Party has made actions arising out of a loan contract to finance the purchase of movable property subject to the special provision, even if the loan itself is not repayable by instalments or if the article is purchased with a single payment (normally with the funds lent). Credit contracts are not, moreover, contracts for the supply of services, so that, apart from point (2) of the first paragraph of Article 13, the whole of section 4 does not apply to such contracts. Contracts of sale not falling under point (1) of the first paragraph of Article 13 do not, for instance, come under point (2) of that paragraph, although section 4 may be applicable to them subject to the further conditions contained in point (3) (see paragraph 158).

158. (b) On the other hand, consumer contracts other than those **A1.451** referred to in paragraph 157 are subject to the special provisions only if there is a sufficiently strong connection with the place where the consumer is domiciled. In this, the new provisions once again follow the preliminary draft Convention on the law applicable to contractual and non-contractual obligations. Both the conditions referred to in point (3) of the first paragraph of Article 13—an offer or advertising in the State of the consumer's domicile, and steps necessary for the conclusion of the contract taken by the consumer in that State—must be satisfied. The introductory phrase should, moreover, ensure that Article 4 and 5(5) **[119]** will apply to all consumer contracts, as has until now been the case only for instalment sales and for loans repayable by instalments. One particular consequence of this is that, subject to the second paragraph of Article 13, section 4 does not apply where the defendant is not domiciled in the EEC.

For further details of what is meant by "a specific invitation" or "advertising" in the State of the consumer's domicile and by "the steps necessary for the conclusion of the contract," see the report currently being drawn up by Professor Giuliano on the Convention on the law applicable to contractual and non-contractual obligations.

3. Only a branch, agency or other establishment within the Community

159. The exclusion from the scope of section 4 of contracts between con- **A1.452** sumers and firms domiciled outside the EEC would not be reasonable where such firms have a branch, agency or other establishment within the EEC. Under the national laws upon which jurisdiction is to be founded in such cases pursuant to Article 4, it would often be impossible for the consumer to sue in the courts which would be guaranteed to have jurisdiction for his purposes in the case of contracts with parties domiciled within the EEC. Insurers with branches, agencies or other establishments in the EEC are treated as regards jurisdiction in like manner to those domiciled within the Community (Article 8) and for the same reasons the other parties to contracts with consumers must also be deemed to be domiciled within the EEC if they have a branch, agency or other establishment in the Community. It is, however, only logical that it should not be possible to invoke exorbitant jurisdictions against such parties simply because their head office lies outside the EEC.

4. Contracts of transport

160. The last paragraph of Article 13 is again taken from Article 5 of the **A1.453** preliminary draft Convention on the law applicable to contractual and non-contractual obligations. The reason for leaving contracts of transport out of the scope of the special consumer protection provisions in the 1968 Convention is that such contracts are subject under international agreements to special sets of rules with very

considerable ramifications, and the inclusion of those contracts in the 1968 Convention purely for jurisdictional purposes would merely complicate the legal position. Moreover, the total exclusion of contracts of transport from the scope of section 4 means that sections 1 and 2 and hence in particular Article 5(1) remain applicable.

III. *The substance of the provisions of section 4*

A1.454 161. There are only a few points requiring a brief explanation of the substance of the new provisions.

1. Subsequent change of domicile by the consumer

In substance, the new Article 14 closely follows the existing Article 14, while extending it to actions arising from all consumer contracts. The rearrangement of the text is merely a rewording due to the availability of a convenient description for one party to the contract, the "consumer," which was better placed at the beginning of the text so as to make it more easily comprehensible. The Working Party's decision means in substance that, as in the case with the existing Article 14, the consumer may sue in the courts of his new State of domicile if he moves to another Community State after concluding the contract out of which an action subsequently arises. This only becomes practical, however, in the case of the instalment sales and credit contracts referred to in points (1) and (2) of the first paragraph of Article 13. For actions arising out of other consumer contracts the new section 4 will in virtually all cases cease to be applicable if the consumer transfers his domicile to another State after conclusion of the contract. This is because the steps necessary for the conclusion of the contract will almost always not have been taken in the new State of domicile. The cross-frontier advertising requirement also ensures that the special provisions will in practice not be applicable to contracts between two persons neither of whom is acting in a professional or trading capacity.

2. Agreements on jurisdiction

A1.455 161a. The new version of Article 15, too, is in substance based on the existing version relating to instalment sales and loans. The only addition is intended to make it clear that it is at the time of conclusion of the contract, and not when proceedings are subsequently instituted, that the parties must be domiciled in the same State. It [120] was then necessary to align and clarify Article 12(3) in the same way.

Although Article 13 is not expressed to be subject to Article 17, the Working Party was unanimously of the opinion that agreements on jurisdiction must, in so far as they are permitted at all, comply with the formal requirements of Article 17. Since the form of such agreements is not governed by section 4, it must be governed by Article 17.

Schlosser Report

Section 5

Exclusive jurisdiction

162. The only amendment proposed by the Working Party to the cases of exclusive jurisdiction provided for in Article 16 is a technical amendment in Article Vd of the Protocol annexed to the 1968 Convention, to clarify Article 16(4). The Working Party did, however, spend some time discussing paragraphs (1) and (2) of that Article. Details of the information supplied to the new Member States regarding exclusive jurisdiction in actions relating to the validity of the constitution of companies or to their dissolution have already been given elsewhere (see paragraph 56 *et seq.*). It is only necessary to add that a company may have more than one seat. Where under a legal system it is possible for a company to have two seats, and it is that system which, pursuant to Article 53 of the 1968 Convention, is to determine the seat of the company, the existence of two seats has to be accepted. It is then open to the plaintiff to choose which of the two seats he will use to base the jurisdiction of the court for his action. Finally, it should be pointed out that Article 16(2) also applies to partnerships established under United Kingdom and Irish law (see paragraph 55).   **A1.456**

    Thus essentially the only exclusive jurisdiction left to be dealt with more fully here is that in respect of actions relating to rights *in rem* in, or tenancies of, immovable property. There were five problems with regard to which the new Member States had requested explanations.

163. There was no difficulty in clarifying that actions for damages based on infringement of rights *in rem* or in damage to property in which rights *in rem* exist do not fall within the scope of Article 16(1). In that context the existence and content of such rights *in rem*, usually rights of ownership, are only of marginal significance.

164. The Working Party was unable to agree whether actions concerned only with rent, *i.e.* dealing simply with the recovery of a debt, are excluded from the scope of Article 16(1) as, according to the Jenard report, was the opinion of the Committee which drafted the 1968 Convention.[38] However, the underlying principle of the provision quite clearly does not require its application to short-term agreements for use and occupation such as, for example, holiday accommodation.   **A1.457**

165. Two of the three remaining problems which the Working Party examined relate to the differences between the law of immovable property on the continent and the corresponding law in the United Kingdom and Ireland; they require therefore somewhat more   **A1.458**

---

[38] The Landgericht of Aachen (NJW 76,487) refused to endorse this standpoint.

detailed comments. There is, first, the question what are rights *in rem* (1) within the meaning of Article 16(1), and, secondly, the problem of disputes arising in connection with the transfer of immovable property (2). Certain other problems emerged as a result of developments which have taken place in the meantime in international patent law (3).

1. Rights "in rem" in immovable property in the Member States of the Community

A1.459 166. (a) The concept of a right *in rem*—as distinct from a right *in personam*—is common to the legal systems of the original Member States of the EEC, even though the distinction does not appear everywhere with the same clarity.

A right *in personam* can only be claimed against a particular person; thus only the purchaser is obliged to pay the purchase price and only the lessor of an article is obliged to permit its use.

A right *in rem*, on the other hand, is available against the whole world. The most important legal consequence flowing from the nature of a right *in rem* is that the owner is entitled to **[121]** demand that the thing in which it exists be given up by anyone not enjoying a prior right.

In the legal systems of all the original Member States of the EEC without exception, there are only a restricted number of rights *in rem*, even though they do not rigidly apply the principle. Some rights *in rem* are defined only in outline, with freedom for the parties to agree the details. The typical rights *in rem* are listed under easily identifiable heads of the civil law, which in all six countries is codified.[39] In addition, a few rights *in rem* are included in some special laws, the most important of which are those on the co-ownership of real property. Apart from ownership as the most comprehensive right *in rem*, a distinction can be made between certain rights of enjoyment and certain priority rights to secure liabilities. All the legal systems know the concept of usufruct, which confers extensive rights to enjoyment of a property. More restricted rights of enjoyment can also exist in these legal systems in various ways.

A1.460 167. (b) At first glance there appears to be in United Kingdom and Irish law too a small, strictly circumscribed group of statutory rights corresponding to the Continental rights *in rem*. However, the position is more complicated, because these legal systems distinguish between law and equity.

In this connection it has always to be borne in mind that equity also constitutes law and not something merely akin to fairness lying outside the concept of law. As a consequence of these special concepts of law and equity in the United Kingdom and in Ireland,

---

[39] Germany: Bürgerliches Gesetzbuch, Book 3, ss.3–8; France: Code civil, Book 2, and Book 3, Title XVII, Title XVIII, Chaps. II and III; Codice civile, Book 3, Titles 4–6, Book 6, Title 3, Chap. 2, s.III, and Chap. 4.

equitable interests can exist in immovable property in addition to the legal rights.

In the United Kingdom the system of legal rights has its origin in the idea that all land belongs to the Crown and that the citizen can only have limited rights in immovable property. This is the reason why the term "ownership" does not appear in the law of immovable property. However, the estate in fee simple absolute in possession is equivalent to full ownership under the Continental legal systems. In addition the Law of property Act 1925 provides for full ownership for a limited period of time ("term of years absolute"). The same Act limits restricted rights in immovable property ("interests or charges in or over land") to five. All the others are equitable interests, whose number and content are not limited by the Act. Equitable interests are not, however, merely the equivalent of personal rights on the Continent. Some can be registered and then, like legal rights, have universal effect, even against purchasers in good faith. Even if not registered they operate in principle against all the world; only purchasers in good faith who had no knowledge of them are protected in such a case.[40] If the owner of an estate in fee simple absolute in possession grants another person a right of way over his property for the period of that person's life, this cannot amount to a legal right. It can only be an equitable interest, though capable of registration.[41] Equitable interests can thus fulfil the same functions as rights *in rem* under the Continental legal systems, in which case they must be treated as such under Article 16(1). There is no limit to the number of such interests. The granting of equitable interests is on the contrary the method used for achieving any number of subdivisions of proprietary rights.[42]

168. (c) If an action relating to immovable property is brought in a particular State and the question whether the action is concerned with a right *in rem* within the meaning of Article 16(1) arises, the answer can hardly be derived from any law other than that of the *situs*. **A1.461**

2. Actions in connection with obligations to transfer immovable property

169. The legal systems of the original and the new Member States of the Community also differ as regards the manner in which ownership of immovable property is transferred on sale. Admittedly the legal position even within the original Member States differs in this respect. **A1.462**

170. (a) German law distinguishes most clearly between the transfer itself and the contract of sale (or other contract designed to bring **A1.463**

---

[40] Megarry and Baker, "The Law of Real Property," (5th ed.) (1969), p. 71 *et seq.*, p. 79 *et seq.*

[41] Megarry and Baker, *op. cit.*, p. 546.

[42] R. David, "Les grands systèmes de droit contemporains," (5th ed.) (1973) No. 311.

about a transfer). The legal position in the case of immovable property is no different from that obtaining in the case of movable property. The transfer is a special type of legal transaction which in the case of immovable property is called "Auflassung" (conveyance) and which even between the parties becomes effective only on entry in the land register. Where a purchaser of German immovable property brings proceedings on the basis of a contract for sale of immovable property which is governed by German law, the **[122]** subject matter of such proceedings is never a right *in rem* in the property. The only matter in issue is the defendant's personal obligation to carry out all acts necessary to transfer and hand over the property. If one of the parties fails to fulfil its obligations under a contract for sale of immovable property, the remedy in German law is not a court order for rescission, but a claim for damages and the right to rescind the contract.

Admittedly it is possible with the vendor's consent to protect the contractual claim for a transfer of ownership by means of a caution in the land register. In that case the claim has, as against third parties, effects which normally only attach to a right *in rem*. The consequence for German domestic law is that nowadays rights secured by such a caution may be claimed against third parties in the jurisdiction competent to deal with the property concerned.[43] However, any proceedings for a transfer of ownership against the vendor himself would remain an action based on a personal obligation.

A1.464   171. (b) Under French, Belgian and Luxembourg law, which is largely followed by Italian law, the ownership, at any rate as between the parties, passes to the purchaser as soon as the contract of sale is concluded, just as it does in the case of movable property, unless the parties have agreed a later date (see *e.g.* Article 711 and 1583 of the French Civil Code and Article 1376 of the Italian Civil Code). The purchaser need only enter the transfer of ownership in the land register ("transcription") to acquire a legal title which is also effective against third parties. For the purchaser to bring proceedings for performance of the contract is therefore normally equivalent to a claim that the property be handed over to him. Admittedly this claim is based not only on the obligation which the vendor undertook by the contract of sale, but also on ownership which at that point has already passed to the purchaser. This means that the claim for handing over the property has as its basis both a personal obligation and a right *in rem*. The system of remedies which is available in the event of one party to a contract not complying with its obligations is fully in accordance with this. Accordingly, French domestic law has treated such actions as a "matière mixte" and given the plaintiff the right to choose between the jurisdiction applicable to the right *in rem* and the jurisdiction applicable to the personal obligation arising from the contract, *i.e.* the law of the

---

[43] Stein-Jonas (Pohle) (n. 27), para. 24 III 2.

defendant's domicile or of the place of performance of the contract.[44]

The 1968 Convention does not deal with this problem. It would seem that the personal aspect of such claims predominates and Article 16(1) is inapplicable.

172. (c) In the United Kingdom ownership passes on the conclusion of a contract of sale only in the case of movable property. In the case of a sale of immovable property the transfer of ownership follows the conclusion of the contract of sale and is effected by means of a separate document, the conveyance. If necessary, the purchaser has to bring an action for all necessary acts to be performed by the vendor. However, except in Scotland, in contrast with German law, the purchaser's rights prior to the transfer of ownership are not limited to a personal claim against the vendor. In fact the purchaser has an equitable interest (see paragraph 167) in the property which, provided the contract is protected by a notice on the Land Register, is also effective against third parties. Admittedly the new paragraph (6) of Article 5 does not apply (see paragraph 114 *et seq.*), because a contract of sale does not create a trust within the meaning of Article 5(6), even if it is in writing. It is only in one respect that a purchaser's equitable interest does not place him in as strong a position as the French owner of immovable property prior to "transcription" (see paragraph 171): the vendor's cooperation is still required to make the new owner's legal title fully effective. **A1.465**

This legal position would justify application of the exclusive jurisdiction referred to in Article 16(1) even less than the corresponding position under French law. The common law has developed the concept of equitable interests so as to confer on parties to an agreement which originally gave them nothing more than merely personal rights a certain protection as against third parties not acting in good faith. As against the other party to the contract the claim remains purely a personal one, as does a claim, under German law, to transfer of ownership (see paragraph 170) secured by a caution in the Land Register. In Scotland contracts in favour of a third party are enforceable by that party (*jus quaesitum tertii*). **A1.466**

Actions based on contracts for the transfer of ownership or other rights *in rem* affecting immovable property do not therefore have as their object rights *in rem*. Accordingly they may also be brought before courts outside the United Kingdom. Admittedly, care will have to be exercised in that case to ensure that the plaintiff clearly specifies the acts to be done by the defendant so that the transfer of ownership (governed by United Kingdom law) does indeed become effective.

[44] Code de procédure civile, Art. 46, third indent; Vincent, "Procédure Civile," (16th ed.) (1973) No. 291.

3. Jurisdiction in connection with patent disputes

A1.467   173. Since the 1968 Convention entered into force, two Conventions on patents have been signed which are of the greatest international importance. The Munich Convention on the grant of European patents was signed on 5 October 1973 and the Luxembourg Convention for the European patent for the common market was signed on 15 December 1975. The purpose of the Munich Convention is to introduce a common patent application procedure for the Contracting States, though the patent subsequently granted is national in scale. It is valid for one or more States, its substance in each case being basically that of a corresponding patent granted nationally. The aim of the Luxembourg Convention is to institute in addition a patent granted *ab initio* for all States of the Community in a standard manner and with the same substance, based on Community law; such a patent necessarily remains valid or expires uniformly throughout the EEC.

Both instruments contain specific provisions on jurisdiction which take precedence over the 1968 Convention. However, the special jurisdiction provisions relate only to specific matters, such as applications for the revocation of patents pursuant to the Luxembourg Convention. Article 16(4) of the 1968 Convention remains relevant for actions for which no specific provision is made. In the case of European patents under the Munich Convention it is conceivable that this provision might be construed as meaning that actions must be brought in the State in which the patent was applied for and not in the State for which it is valid and in which it is challenged. The new Article Vd of the Protocol annexed to the 1968 Convention is designed to prevent this interpretation and ensure that only the courts of the State in which the patent is valid have jurisdiction, unless the Munich Convention itself lays down special provisions.

A1.468   Clearly, such a provision cannot cover a Community patent under the Luxembourg Convention, since the governing principle is that the patent is granted, not for a given State, but for all the Member States of the EEC. Hence the exception at the end of the new provision. However, even in the area covered by the Luxembourg Convention patents valid for one or more, but not all, States of the Community are possible. Article 86 of that Convention allows this for a transitional period to which no term has yet been set. Where the applicant for a patent takes up the option available to him under this provision and applies for a patent for one or more, but not all, States of the EEC, the patent is not a Community patent even though it comes under some of the provisions of the Luxembourg Convention but merely a patent granted for one or more States. Accordingly, the courts of that State have exclusive jurisdiction under Article Vd of the Protocol annexed to the 1968 Convention. The same is true for any case in which a national patent is granted in response to an international application, *e.g.* under the

Patent cooperation Treaty opened for signature at Washington on 19 June 1970.

It only remains to be made clear that Article 16(4) of the 1968 Convention and the new Article Vd of the Protocol annexed to the Convention also cover actions which national legislation allows to be brought at the patent application stage, so as to reduce the risk of a patent being granted, and the correctness of the grant being subsequently challenged.

Section 6

Jurisdiction by consent[45]

174. Article 17, applying as it does only if the transaction in question is international in character (see paragraph 21), which the mere fact of choosing a court in a particular State is by no means sufficient to establish, presented the Working Party with four problems. First, account had to be taken of the practice of courts in the United Kingdom (excluding Scotland) and Ireland of deducing from the choice of law to govern the main issue an agreement as to the courts having jurisdiction. Secondly, there was the problem, previously ignored by the 1968 Convention, of agreements conferring jurisdiction upon a court outside the Community or agreements conferring jurisdiction upon courts within the Community by two parties both domiciled outside the Community. Thirdly, special rules had to be made for provisions in trusts. And finally, the Working Party had to consider whether it was reasonable to let Article 17 stand in view of the interpretation which had been placed upon it by the Court of **A1.469**

---

[45] From past case law: Brunswick Landgericht, Recht der internationalen Wirtschaft/Außenwirtschaftsdienst des Betriebsberaters (RIW/AWD) 74, 346 (written confirmation must actually be preceded by oral agreement); Hamburg Oberlandesgericht (RIW/AWD) 1975, 498 (no effective jurisdiction agreement where general terms of business are exchanged which are mutually contradictory); Munich Oberlandesgericht (RIW/AWD) 75, 694; Italian Corte di Cassazione No. 3397 of 20 October 1975 (written confirmation, containing a jurisdiction clause for the first time, is not of itself sufficient); Bundesgerichtshof, MDR 77, p. 1013 (confirmation of an order by the seller not sufficient when the buyer has previously refused the incorporation); Heidelberg Landgericht (RIW/AWD) 76, p. 532 (reference to general conditions of sale not sufficient); Frankfurt Oberlandesgericht (RIW/AWD) 76, p. 532 (reference to general conditions of sale for the first time in the confirmation of the order from the supplier; reminder from the seller does not conclusively incorporate the jurisdiction clause included in the conditions); Düsseldorf Oberlandesgericht (RIW/AWD) 76, p. 297 (jurisdiction clause contained in the condition of a bill of lading of no effect against persons who themselves have given no written declaration); Pretura of Brescia, Foro it. 1976 No. 1, Column I 250 (subsequent national law prevails over Article 17); Tribunal of Aix-en-Provence of 10 May 1974, Dalloz 74, p. 760 (jurisdiction agreements in favour of the courts of the employer's domicile may be entered into even in contracts of employment); Tribunal de commerce of Brussels, Journal des Tribunaux 1976, 210 (Article 17 has precedence over contrary national law).

Justice of the European Communities. It should be repeated (see paragraph 22) that the existence of an agreement conferring jurisdiction on a court other than the court seised of the proceedings is one of the points to be taken into account by the court of its own motion.

[124] 1. Choice-of-law clause and international jurisdiction

A1.470 175. Nowhere in the 1968 Convention is there recognition of a connection between the law applicable to a particular issue and the international jurisdiction of the courts over that issue. However, persons who, relying on the practice of United Kingdom or Irish courts, have agreed on choice-of-law clauses before the entry into force of the Accession Convention, are entitled to expect protection. This explains the transitional provision contained in Article 35 of the proposed Accession Convention. The term "entry into force" within the meaning of this provision refers to the date on which the Accession Convention comes into effect in the State in question. For the various systems of law applying in the United Kingdom, see paragraph 11.

2. Agreements conferring jurisdiction on courts outside the Community

A1.471 176. (a) In cases where parties agree to bring their disputes before the courts of a State which is not a party to the 1968 Convention there is obviously nothing in the 1968 Convention to prevent such courts from declaring themselves competent, if their law recognizes the validity of such an agreement. The only question is whether and, if so, in what form such agreements are capable of depriving Community courts of jurisdiction which is stated by the 1968 Convention to be exclusive or concurrent. There is nothing in the 1968 Convention to support the conclusion that such agreements must be inadmissible in principle.[46] However, the 1968 Convention does not contain any rules as to their validity either. If a court within the Community is applied to despite such an agreement, its decision on the validity of the agreement depriving it of jurisdiction must be taken in accordance with its own *lex fori*. In so far as the local rules of conflict of laws support the authority of provisions of foreign law, the latter will apply. If, when these tests are applied, the agreement is found to be invalid, then the jurisdictional provisions of the 1968 Convention become applicable.

A1.472 177. (b) On the other hand, proceedings can be brought before a court within the Community by parties who, although both domiciled outside the Community, have agreed that that court should have

---

[46] As correctly stated by von Hoffman (RIW/AWD) 1973, 57(63); Droz ("Compétence judiciaire et effets des jugements dans le marché commun") No. 216 *et seq.*, Weser ("Convention communautaire sur la compétence judiciaire et l'exécution des décisions") No. 265.

jurisdiction. There is no reason for the Convention to include rules on the conditions under which the court stipulated by such parties must accept jurisdiction. It is however important for the Community to ensure, by means of more detailed conditions, that the effect of such an agreement on jurisdiction is recognized throughout the EEC. The new third sentence of the first paragraph of Article 17 is designed to cater for this. It covers the situation where, despite the fact that both parties are domiciled outside the Community, a court in a Community State ("X") would, were it not for a jurisdiction agreement, have jurisdiction, *e.g.* on the ground that the place of performance lies within that State. If in such a case the parties agree that the courts of another Community State are to have exclusive jurisdiction, that agreement must be observed by the courts of State X, provided the agreement meets the formal requirements of Article 17. Strictly speaking, it is true, this is not a necessary adjustment. Such situations were possible before, in relations between the original Member States of the Community. However, owing to the frequency with which jurisdiction is conferred upon United Kingdom courts in international trade, the problem takes on considerably greater importance with the United Kingdom's accession to the Convention than hitherto.

3. Jurisdiction clauses in trusts

178. A trust (see paragraph 111) need not be established by contract. A   **A1.473**
unilateral legal instrument is sufficient. As the previous version of Article 17 dealt only with "agreements" on jurisdiction, it needed to be expanded.

4. The form of agreements on jurisdiction in international trade

179. Some of the first judgments given by the Court of Justice of the   **A1.474**
European Communities since it was empowered to interpret the 1968 Convention were concerned with the form of jurisdiction clauses incorporated in standardized general conditions of trade.[47]

---

[47] In the case of an orally concluded contract, the requirements of the first para. of Art. 17 of the Convention of 27 September 1968 on jurisdiction and the enforcement of judgments in civil and commercial matters as to form are satisfied only if the vendor's confirmation in writing accompanied by notification of the general conditions of sale has been accepted in writing by the purchaser (Case No. 25/76, [1976] ECR 1851.

The fact that the purchaser does not raise any objections against a confirmation issued unilaterally by the other party does not amount to acceptance on his part of the clause conferring jurisdiction unless the oral agreement comes within the framework of a continuing trading relationship between the parties which is based on the general conditions of one of them, and those conditions contain a clause conferring jurisdiction (Case No. 25/76).

Where a clause conferring jurisdiction is included among the general conditions of sale of one of the parties, printed on the back of a contract, the requirement of a writing under the first paragraph of Art. 17 of the Convention of 27 September

The Court of Justice's interpretation of Article 17 of the 1968 Convention does protect the other party to a contract with anyone using such general conditions of trade from the danger of inadvertently finding himself bound by standard forms of agreement containing jurisdiction clauses without realizing it. However, the Court's **[125]** interpretation of that Article, which many national courts have also shown a tendency to follow,[45] does not cater adequately for the customs and requirements of international trade. In particular, the requirement that the other party to a contract with anyone employing general conditions of trade has to give written confirmation of their inclusion in the contract before any jurisdiction clause in those conditions can be effective is unacceptable in international trade. International trade is heavily dependent on standard conditions which incorporate jurisdiction clauses. Nor are those conditions in many cases unilaterally dictated by one set of interests in the market; they have frequently been negotiated by representatives of the various interests. Owing to the need for calculations based on constantly fluctuating market prices, it has to be possible to conclude contracts swiftly by means of a confirmation of order incorporating sets of conditions. These are the factors behind the relaxation of the formal provisions for international trade in the amended version of Article 17. This is however, as should be clearly emphasized, only a relaxation of the formal requirements. It must be proved that a consensus existed on the inclusion in the contract of the general conditions of trade and the particular provisions, though this is not the place to pass comment on whether questions of consensus other than the matter of form should be decided according to the national laws applicable or to unified EEC principles. Dealing with the form of jurisdiction agreements in a separate second sentence in the first paragraph of Article 17, rather than in passing in the first sentence as hitherto, is designed merely to obviate rather cumbersome wording.

Section 7

Examination of own motion

A1.475   Adjustments and further clarification were not necessary.

1968 on jurisdiction and the enforcement of judgments in civil and commercial matters is fulfilled only if the contract signed by both parties contains an express reference to those general conditions (Case No. 24/76 [1976] ECR 1831).
In the case of a contract concluded by reference to earlier offers, which were themselves made with reference to the general conditions of one of the parties including a clause conferring jurisdiction, the requirements of a writing under the first para. of Art. 17 of the Convention is satisfied only if the reference is express and can therefore be checked by a party exercising reasonable care (Case No. 24/76).

Schlosser Report

Section 8

"Lis pendens" and related actions[48]

180. As regards *lis pendens*, there are two structural differences between the laws of the United Kingdom and Ireland, on the one hand, and the Continental legal systems on the other. However, neither of them necessitated a technical amendment of the 1968 Convention.   **A1.476**

1. Discretion of the court

181. The rules governing *lis pendens* in England and Wales, and to some extent in Scotland, are more flexible than those on the Continent. Basically, it is a question for the court's discretion whether a stay should be granted. The doctrine of *lis pendens* is therefore less fully developed there than in the Continental States. The practice is in a sense an application of the doctrine of *forum conveniens* (see paragraph 77 *et seq.*). Generally a court will in fact grant an application for a stay of proceedings, where the matter in dispute is already pending before another court. Where proceedings are pending abroad, the courts in England and Wales exercise great caution, and if they grant a stay of proceedings at all, they will do so only if the plaintiff in England or Wales is also the plaintiff in the proceedings abroad. Scottish courts take into account to a considerable extent any conflicting proceedings which a Scottish defendant may have instituted abroad, or which are pending against him abroad.   **A1.477**

After the United Kingdom has acceded to the 1968 Convention, it will no longer be possible for this practice to be maintained in relation to the other Member States of the Community. United Kingdom courts will have to acknowledge the existence of proceedings instituted in the other Member States, and even to take notice of them of their own motion (see paragraph 22).

2. Moment at which proceedings become pending

182. The fact that the moment at which proceedings become pending is determined differently in the United Kingdom and Ireland from the way it is determined on the Continent is due to peculiarities of procedural law in those States. In the original Member States of the Community a claim becomes pending when the document instituting the proceedings is served.[49] Filing with the court is sometimes sufficient. In the United Kingdom, except Scotland, and in Ireland, proceedings become pending as soon as the originating document has been issued. In Scotland, however, proceedings become pending only when service of the summons has been effected on the   **A1.478**

---

[48] For further questions in s.8, see paras. 22 and 240.
[49] Germany: Art. 253(1) of the Zivilprozeßordnung; France: Art. 54 of the Code de procédure civile.

defender. The moment at which proceedings become pending under the national **[126]** procedural law concerned is the deciding factor for the application of Article 21 of the 1968 Convention. The addition to the text of Article 20 does not concern this point. It is justified by the fact that in the United Kingdom and in Ireland foreigners who are abroad do not receive the original writ but only notification of the order of the court authorizing service.

Section 9

Provisional measures

A1.479   183. No particular adjustments had to be made to the provisions of the 1968 Convention concerning provisional measures. The change in emphasis which the accession of further Member States introduced into the 1968 Convention consists in this field entirely in the wide variety of provisional measures available in the law of Ireland and of the United Kingdom. This will involve certain difficulties where provisional judgments given in these States have to be given effect by the enforcement procedures of the original Member States of the Community. However, this problem does not affect only provisional measures. The integration of judgments on the main issue into the respective national enforcement procedures also involves difficulties in the relationship between Ireland and the United Kingdom on the one hand and the original Member States of the Community on the other (see paragraph 221 *et seq.*).

CHAPTER 5

RECOGNITION AND ENFORCEMENT

A.

GENERAL REMARKS—INTERLOCUTORY COURT DECISIONS

A1.480   184. Article 25 emphasizes in terms which could hardly be clearer that every type of judgment given by a court in a Contracting State must be recognized and enforced throughout the rest of the Community. The provision is not limited to a judgment terminating the proceedings before the court, but also applies to provisional court orders. Nor does the wording of the provision indicate that interlocutory court decisions should be excluded from its scope where they do not provisionally regulate the legal relationships between the parties, but are for instance concerned only with the taking of evidence. What is more, the legal systems of the original Member States of the Community describe such interlocutory decisions in a way which corresponds to the terms given, by way of example, in Article 25.

Thus, in France court decisions which order the taking of evidence are also called "jugements (d'avant dire droit)." In Germany they are termed "(Beweis) beschlüsse" of the court. Nevertheless, the provisions of the 1968 Convention governing recognition and enforcement are in general designed to cover only court judgments which either determine or regulate the legal relationships of the parties. An answer to the question whether, and if so which, interlocutory decisions intended to be of procedural assistance fall within the scope of the 1968 Convention cannot be given without further consideration.

1. RELATIONSHIP OF THE CONTINENTAL STATES WITH EACH OTHER

185. This matter is of no great significance as between the original Member States of the EEC, or as between the latter and Denmark. All seven States are parties to the 1954 Hague Convention relating to civil procedure. The latter governs the question of judicial assistance, particularly in the case of evidence to be taken abroad, and its provisions take precedence over the 1968 Convention by virtue of Article 57. In any case, it is always advisable in practice to make use of the machinery of the Hague Convention, which is particularly suited to the processes required for obtaining judicial assistance. See paragraph 238, and note 59(7) on the Hague Convention of 15 November 1965 on the service abroad of judicial and extrajudicial documents in civil or commercial matters and on the Hague Convention of 18 March 1970 on the taking of evidence abroad in civil or commercial matters. **A1.481**

2. RELATIONSHIP OF THE UNITED KINGDOM AND IRELAND WITH THE OTHER MEMBER STATES

186. It is only with the accession of the United Kingdom and Ireland to the 1968 Convention that the problem assumes any degree of [127] importance. Ireland has concluded no convention on judicial assistance of any kind with the other States of the European Community. Agreements on judicial assistance do, however, exist between the United Kingdom and the following States: the Federal Republic of Germany (Agreement of 20 March 1928), the Netherlands (Agreement of 17 November 1967). The United Kingdom is also party to the Hague Conventions of 1965 and 1970 referred to in paragraph 185. It has concluded no other agreements with Member States of the Community. **A1.482**

3. PRECISE SCOPE OF TITLE III OF THE 1968 CONVENTION

187. If it were desired that interlocutory decisions by courts on the further conduct of the proceedings, and particularly on the taking of evidence, should be covered by Article 25 of the 1968 Convention, this would also affect decisions with which the parties would **A1.483**

be totally unable to comply without the court's cooperation, and the enforcement of which would concern third parties, particularly witnesses. It would therefore be impossible to "enforce" such decisions under the 1968 Convention. It can only be concluded from the foregoing that interlocutory decisions which are not intended to govern the legal relationships of the parties, but to arrange the further conduct of the proceedings, should be excluded from the scope of Title III of the 1968 Convention.

B.

COMMENTS ON THE INDIVIDUAL SECTIONS

Section 1

Recognition

A1.484 188. With two exceptions (4), no formal amendments were required to Articles 26 to 30. The Working Party did, however, answer some questions raised by the new Member States regarding the interpretation of these provisions. Basically, these concerned problems arising in connection with the application of the public policy reservation in Article 27(1)—(2), the right to a hearing—Article 27(2)—(3), and the nature of the obligation to confer recognition, as distinct from enforceability (1). The fact that Article 28 makes no reference to the provisions of section 6 of Title II on jurisdiction agreements is intentional and deserves mention. When considering such agreements it must be borne in mind that the court seised of the proceedings in the State of origin must of its own motion take note of any agreement to the contrary (see paragraphs 22 and 174).

1. Article 26

A1.485 189. Article 26, second paragraph, introduces a special simplified procedure for seeking recognition, modelled on the provisions governing the issue of orders for enforcement. However, this is not the only way in which recognition may be sought. Every court and public authority must take account of judgments which qualify for recognition, and must decide whether the conditions for recognition exist in a particular case, unless this question has already been determined under Article 26, second paragraph. In particular, every court must itself decide whether there is an obligation to grant recognition, if the principal issue in a foreign judgment concerns a question which in the fresh proceedings emerges as a preliminary issue. Each of these two recognition procedures involves a problem which the Working Party discussed.

A1.486 190. (a) If proceedings are conducted in accordance with Article 26, second paragraph, the court may of its own motion take into account grounds for refusing recognition if they appear from the judgment or are known to the court. It may not, however, make enquiries to establish whether such grounds exist, as this would not be compatible with the summary nature of the proceedings. Only if further proceedings are instituted by way of an appeal lodged pursuant to Article 36 can the court examine whether the requirements for recognition have been satisfied.

191. (b) The effects of a court decision are not altogether uniform under **A1.487** the legal systems obtaining in the Member States of the Community. A judgment delivered in one State as a decision on a procedural issue may, in another State, be treated as a decision on an issue of substance. The same type of judgment may be of varying scope and effect in different countries. In France, a judgment against the principal debtor is also effective against the surety, whereas in the Netherlands and Germany it is not.[50]

[128] The Working Party did not consider it to be its task to find a general solution to the problems arising from these differences in the national legal systems. However, one fact seemed obvious.

Judgments dismissing an action as unfounded must be recognized. If a German court declares that it has no jurisdiction, an English court cannot disclaim its own jurisdiction on the ground that the German court was in fact competent. Clearly, however, German decisions on procedural matters are not binding, as to the substance, in England. An English court may at any time allow (or, for substantive reasons, disallow) an action, if proceedings are started in England after such a decision has been given by a German court.

2. Article 27(1)—public policy

192. (a) The 1968 Convention does not state in terms whether recog- **A1.488** nition may be refused pursuant to Article 27(1) on the ground that the judgment has been obtained by fraud. Not even in the legal systems of the original Contracting States to the 1968 Convention is it expressly stated that fraud in obtaining a judgment constitutes a ground for refusing recognition. Such conduct is, however, generally considered as an instance for applying the doctrine of public policy.[51] The legal situation in the United Kingdom and Ireland is different inasmuch as fraud constitutes a special ground for refusing recognition in addition to the principle of public policy. In the conventions on enforcement which the United Kingdom concluded with Community States, a middle course was adopted by expressly referring to fraudulent conduct, but treating it as a special case of public policy.[52]

---

[50] For details see Droz (n. 46) No. 448.
[51] Italy: Art. 798(1) together with Art. 395(1) of the Codice di procedura civile; France: Batiffol, "Droit international privé" (5th ed.) (1971), No. 727.
[52] Art. 3(1)(c)(2) of the German-British Treaty of 14 July 1960; Art. 3(1)(c)(ii) of the Franco-British Treaty of 18 January 1934.

As a result there is no doubt that to obtain a judgment by fraud can in principle constitute an offence against the public policy of the State addressed. However, the legal systems of all Member States provide special means of redress by which it can be contended, even after the expiry of the normal period for an appeal, that the judgment was the result of a fraud (see paragraph 197 *et seq.*). A court in the State addressed must always, therefore, ask itself, whether a breach of its public policy still exists in view of the fact that proceedings for redress can be, or could have been, lodged in the courts of the State of origin against the judgment allegedly obtained by fraud.

193. (b) Article 41(3) of the Irish Constitution prohibits divorce and also provides, as regards marriages dissolved abroad:

> "No person whose marriage has been dissolved under the civil law of any other State but is a subsisting valid marriage under the law for the time being in force within the jurisdiction of the Government and Parliament established by this Constitution shall be capable of contracting a valid marriage within that jurisdiction during the lifetime of the other party to the marriage so dissolved."

In so far as the jurisdiction of the 1968 Convention is concerned, this Article of the Constitution is of importance for maintenance orders made upon a divorce. The Irish courts have not yet settled whether the recognition of such maintenance orders would, in view of the constitutional provisions cited, be contrary to Irish public policy.

3. The right to a hearing (Article 27(2))

A1.489 194. Article 27(2) is amended for the same reason as Article 20 (see paragraph 182). The object of the addition to Article 20 was to specify the moment when proceedings became pending before the Irish or British courts; in Article 27(2) it is intended to indicate which documents must have been served for the right to a hearing to be respected.

4. Ordinary and extraordinary appeals

A1.490 195. The 1968 Convention makes a distinction in Articles 30 and 38 between ordinary and extraordinary appeals. No equivalent for this could be found in the Irish and United Kingdom legal systems. Before discussing the reason for this and explaining the implications of the solutions proposed by the Working Party (b), something should be said about the distinction between ordinary and extraordinary appeals in the Continental Member States of the EEC, since judges in the United Kingdom and Ireland will have to come to terms with these concepts which to them are unfamiliar (a).

1750

[129] 196. (a) A clearly defined distinction between ordinary and extra- **A1.491**
ordinary appeals is nowhere to be found.

Legal literature and case law[53] have pointed out two criteria. In
the first place neither an appeal ("Berufung") nor an objection to a
default judgment ("Einspruch") has to be based on specific
grounds; a party may challenge a judgment by alleging any kind of
defect. Secondly execution is postponed during the period allowed
for an appeal or objection, or after an appeal or objection has been
lodged, unless the court otherwise directs or unless, exceptionally,
different legal provisions apply.

Some legal systems contain a list of ordinary appeal procedures.

197. Part 1, Book 4 of the French Code de procédure civile of 1806, **A1.492**
which still applies in Luxembourg, referred to extraordinary forms
of appeal by which a judgment could be contested. It did not say,
however, what was meant by ordinary appeals. Book 3 referred
merely to "courts of appeal." However, in legal literature and case
law appeals ("appel") and objections to default judgments ("opposition") have consistently been classified as ordinary appeals. The
new French Code de procédure civile of 1975 now expressly clari-
fies the position. In future only objections (Article 76) and appeals
(Article 85) are to be classified as ordinary appeals.

198. The Belgian Code judiciaire of 1967 has retained the French system **A1.493**
which previously applied in Belgium. Only appeals and objections
are considered as ordinary appeals (Article 21).

199. There is no distinction in Netherlands law between ordinary and **A1.494**
extraordinary appeals. Academic writers classify the forms of
appeal as follows: objections ("Verzet"—where a judgment is given
in default), appeals ("Hoger beroep"), appeals in cassation ("Beroep in cassatie") and appeals on a point of law ("Revisie") are
classed as ordinary appeals. "Revisie" is a special form of appeal
which lies only against certain judgments of the Hoge Raad sitting
as a court of first instance.

200. The Italian text of Articles 30 and 38 refers to "impugnazione" **A1.495**
without distinguishing between ordinary and extraordinary
appeals. However, Italian legal literature distinguishes very clearly
between ordinary and extraordinary appeals. Article 324 of the
Codice di procedura civile states that a judgment does not become
binding as between the parties until the periods within which the
following forms of appeal may be lodged have expired: appeals on

---

[53] From a comparative law point of view: Walther J. Habscheid, "Introduction à la
procédure judiciaire, les systèmes de procédures civiles," published by the
Association internationale de droit comparé, Barcelona 1968.

grounds of jurisdiction ("regolamento di competenza"), appeals ("appello"), appeals in cassation ("ricorso per cassazione"), or petitions for review ("revocazione"), where these are based on one of the grounds provided for in Article 395(4) and (5). These forms of appeal are classified as ordinary.

A1.496 201. In Denmark, too, the distinction between ordinary and extraordinary appeals is recognized only in legal literature. The deciding factor mentioned there is whether a form of appeal may be lodged within a given period without having to be based on particular grounds, or whether its admissibility depends on special consent by a court or ministry. Accordingly, appeals ("Anke") and objections to default judgments ("Genoptagelse af sager, i hvilke der er afsagt udeblivelsesdom") are classified as ordinary appeals.

A1.497 202. Book 3 of the German Code of Civil Procedure ("Zivilprozeß-ordnung") is headed "Rechtsmittel" ("means of redress") and it governs "Berufung" (appeals) "Beschwerde" (complaints) and "Revision" (appeals on a point of law). These are frequently said to have in common the fact that the decision appealed against does not become binding ("rechtskräftig") until the period within which these means of redress may be lodged has expired. However Article 705 of the Code defines "Rechtskraft" as the stage when these means of redress are no longer available. The material difference between the means of redress and other forms of appeal is that the former need not be based on particular grounds of appeal, that they are addressed to a higher court and that, as long as the decision has not become binding, enforcement is also postponed pursuant to Article 704 unless the court, as is almost invariably the case, allows provisional enforcement. If the expression "ordinary appeal" is used at all, a reference to "Rechtsmittel" (means of redress) is intended.

German legal writers, in accordance with the phraseology used by the law, do not classify objections to default judgments as a means of redress ("Rechtsmittel").[54] It does not involve the competence of a higher court. However, it has the effect of suspending execution and is not tied to specific grounds of appeal, just like an **[130]** objection in the other original Member States of the Community. It must, therefore, be included under "ordinary appeals" within the meaning of Articles 30 and 38 of the 1968 Convention.

A1.498 203. In its judgment of 22 November 1977[55] the European Court held that the concept of an "ordinary appeal" was to be uniformly determined in the original Member States according to whether there

---

[54] Stein-Jonas (Grunsky) (n. 27), introduction to para. 511 I 1; Rosenberg-Schwab, "Zivilprozeßrecht," (11th ed.), para. 135 I 1 b.
[55] Case No. 43/77 (*Industrial Diamond Supplies* v. *Riva*).

was a specific period of time for appealing, which started to run "by virtue of " the judgment.

204. (b) In Ireland and the United Kingdom nothing which would **A1.499** enable a distinction to be drawn between ordinary and extraordinary appeals can be found in either statutes, cases or systematic treatises on procedural law. The basic method of redress is the appeal. Not only is this term used where review of a judgment can be sought within a certain period, without being subject to special grounds for appeal; it is also the name given to other means of redress. Some have special names such as; for default judgments, "reponing" (in Scotland) or "application to set the judgment aside" (in England, Wales and Ireland); or again "motion" (in Scotland) or "application" (in England, Wales and Ireland) "for a new trial," which correspond roughly to a petition for review in Continental legal systems. They are the only forms of redress against a verdict by a jury. A further distinctive feature of the appeal system in these States is the fact that the enforceability of a judgment is not automatically affected by the appeal period or even by the lodging of an appeal. However, the appellate court will usually grant a temporary stay of execution, if security is given. Finally there do exist in the United Kingdom legal procedures whose function corresponds to the ordinary legal procedures of Continental legal systems, but which are not subject to time limits. The judge exercises his discretion in deciding on the admissibility of each particular case. This is the case, for example, with default judgments. The case law of the European Court could therefore not be applied to the new Member States.

The Working Party therefore made prolonged efforts to work out **A1.500** an equivalent for the United Kingdom and Ireland of the Continental distinction between ordinary and extraordinary appeals, but reached no satisfactory result. This failure was due in particular to the fact that the term "appeal" is so many-sided and cannot be regarded, like similar terms in Continental law, as a basis for "ordinary appeals." The Working Party therefore noted that the legal consequences resulting from the distinction drawn in Articles 30 and 38 between ordinary and extraordinary appeals do not have to be applied rigidly, but merely confer a discretion on the court. Accordingly, in the interests of practicality and clarity, a broad definition of appeal seemed justified in connection with judgments of Irish and United Kingdom courts. Continental courts will have to use their discretion in such a way that an equal balance in the application of Articles 30 and 38 in all Contracting States will be preserved. To this effect they will have to make only cautious use of their discretionary power to stay proceedings, if the appeal is one which is available in Ireland or the United Kingdom only against special defects in a judgment or which may still be lodged after a long period. A further argument in favour of this pragmatic solution was that, in accordance with Article 38, a judgment is in any event no longer enforceable if it was subject to appeal in the State of origin and the appellate court suspended execution or granted a temporary stay of execution.

5. Conflicts with judgments given in non-contracting States which qualify for recognition

A1.501   205. In one respect the provisions of the 1968 Convention governing recognition required formal amendment. A certain lack of clarity in some of these provisions can be accepted since the European Court of Justice has jurisdiction to interpret them. However, Member States cannot be expected to accept lack of clarity where this might give rise to diplomatic complications with non-contracting States. The new Article 27(5) is designed to avoid such complications.

This may be explained by way of an example. A decision dismissing an action against a person domiciled in the Community is given in non-contracting State A. A Community State, B, is obliged to recognize the judgment under a bilateral convention. The plaintiff brings fresh proceedings in another Community State, C, which is not obliged to recognize the judgment [131] given in the non-contracting State. If he is successful, the existing text of the 1968 Convention leaves it open to doubt whether the judgment has to be recognized in State B.

A1.502   In future, it is certain that this is not the case. In order to avoid unnecessary discrepancies, the text of the new provision is based on Article 5 of the Hague Convention of 1 February 1971 on the recognition and enforcement of foreign judgments in civil and commercial matters. Its wording is slightly wider in scope than would have been required to avoid diplomatic complications. A judgment given in a non-contracting State takes priority even where it has to be recognized, not by virtue of an international convention but merely under national law. For obligations under conventions not to recognize certain judgments, see paragraph 249 *et seq*.

Section 2

Enforcement

1. Preliminary remarks

A1.503   206. The Working Party's efforts were almost entirely confined to deciding which courts in the new Member States should have jurisdiction in enforcement proceedings, and what appeal procedures should be provided in this context. In this connection four peculiarities of United Kingdom and, to a certain extent, Irish law had to be considered.

The Working Party took no decision on amendments to deal with the costs of the enforcement procedure. On this point, however, reference should be made to the judgment of the Court of Justice to the European Communities of 30 November 1976 (Case 42/76).

According to that decision, Article 31 prohibits a successful plaintiff from bringing fresh proceedings in the State in which enforcement is sought. But the Contracting States are obliged to adopt rules on costs which take into account the desire to simplify the enforcement procedure.

207. The Working Party also abandoned attempts to draft provisions in the Convention on seizure for international claims, although it was clear that problems would occur to a certain extent if debtors and third party debtors were domiciled in different States. If, in one State, the court of the debtor's domicile has jurisdiction over seizure for such claims, then the State of domicile of the third party debtor may regard the making of the order for seizure applicable to the latter as a violation of its sovereignty, and refuse to enforce it. In such a situation the creditor can seek assistance by obtaining a declaration that the judgment is enforceable in the State of domicile of the third party debtor, and enforcing the debtor's claim against the third party in that State, provided that this State assumes international jurisdiction over such a measure. **A1.504**

208. (a) United Kingdom and Irish law does not have the *exequatur* system for foreign judgments. In these countries an action on the basis of the foreign judgment is necessary unless, as in the United Kingdom, a system of registration applies to the judgments of certain States (including the six original Member States with the exception of Luxembourg) (see paragraph 6). In that case the foreign judgments, if they are to be enforced, must be registered with a court in the United Kingdom. They then have the same force as judgments of the registering court itself. The application has to be lodged by the creditor in person or by a solicitor on his behalf. Personal appearance is essential; lodging by post will not suffice. If the application is granted, an order to that effect will be entered in the register kept at the court. **A1.505**

Except in Scotland, however, the United Kingdom has no independent enforcement officer like the French "huissier" or the German "Gerichtsvollzieher" (see paragraph 221). Only the court which gave the judgment or where the judgment was registered can direct enforcement measures. Since this system of registration affords the same protection to a foreign judgment creditor as does the *exequatur* system on the Continent, the United Kingdom registration system could also be accepted for applying the provisions of the 1968 Convention. **A1.506**

[132]

209. (b) A special feature of the constitution of the United Kingdom has already been mentioned in the introductory remarks (see paragraph 11): England and Wales, Scotland and Northern Ireland are independent judicial areas. A new paragraph had to be added to Article 31 to cover this. Similarly the appeal possibilities provided for in Articles 37 and 40 apply separately to each registration. If a judg- **A1.507**

ment has been validly registered with the High Court in London, another appeal is again possible against a subsequent registration with the Court of Session in Edinburgh.

A1.508   210. (c) As far as the enforcement of foreign judgments is concerned the United Kingdom traditionally concedes special treatment to maintenance orders (see paragraph 7). Until now they have been enforced only in respect of a few Commonwealth countries and Ireland, and their enforcement is entrusted to courts different from those responsible for enforcing other judgments. Since the 1968 Convention contains no provisions precluding different recognition procedures for different types of judgment, there is no reason why maintenance orders cannot be covered by a special arrangement within the scope of the 1968 Convention. This will permit the creation of a uniform system for the recognition of maintenance orders from the Community and the Commonwealth and, in view of the type of court having jurisdiction, the setting up of a central agency to receive applications for enforcement (see paragraph 218). For agreements concerning maintenance see paragraph 226.

A1.509   211. (d) Finally there were still problems in connection with judgments ordering performance other than the payment of money. Judgments directing a person to do a particular act are not generally enforceable under United Kingdom and Irish law, but only in pursuance of special legal provisions. These provisions cover judgments ordering the delivery of movable property or the transfer of ownership or possession of immovable property, and injunctions by which the court may in its discretion order an individual to do or refrain from doing a certain act. Enforcement is possible either by the sheriff's officer using direct compulsion or indirectly by means of fines or imprisonment for contempt of court. In Scotland, in addition to judgments for the transfer of possession or ownership of immovable property an preventative injunctions, there are also "decrees *ad factum prestandum*" by means of which the defendant can be ordered to perform certain acts, particularly to hand back movable property.

A1.510   212. (aa) If an application is made in the Federal Republic of Germany for the enforcement of such a judgment given in Ireland or the United Kingdom, the court must apply the same means of compulsion as would be applicable in the case of a corresponding German judgment, *i.e.* a fine or imprisonment. In the reverse situation, the United Kingdom and Irish courts may have to impose penalties for contempt of court in the same way as when their own orders are disregarded.

A1.511   213. (bb) The system for enforcing orders requiring the performance of a specific act is fundamentally different in other States of the Community, *e.g.* Belgium, France and Luxembourg. The defendant is ordered to perform the act and at the same time to pay a sum of money to the plaintiff to cover a possible non-compliance with the order. In France he is initially only threatened with a fine ("astreinte"). In case of non-compliance, a separate judgment is required and is hardly ever as high as the fine originally threatened. In Belgium the amount of the fine is already fixed in the judgment ordering the act to be performed.[56] With a view to overcoming the difficulties which this could cause for the inter-State enforcement of judgments ordering specific acts, Article 43 provides that, if the sanction takes the form of a fine ("astreinte"), the original court should itself fix the amount. Enforcement abroad is then limited to the "astreinte." French, Belgian, Dutch and Luxembourg judgments can be enforced without difficulty in Germany, the United Kingdom and Italy if the original court has proceeded on that basis. However, the 1968 Convention leaves open the question whether such a fine for disregarding a court order can also be enforced when it accrues not to the judgment creditor but to the State. Since this is not a new problem arising out of the accession of the new Member States, the Working Party did not express a view on the matter.

[133] 2. Formal adjustments as regards courts having jurisdiction and authorized appeals

214. Apart from the inclusion of a term equivalent in the Irish and United Kingdom legal systems to ordinary appeal (see paragraph 195), and apart from Article 44 which deals with legal aid (see paragraph 223), the formal adjustments to Articles 32 to 45 relate exclusively to the courts having jurisdiction and the possible types of appeal against their decisions. (See paragraph 108 for adjustments relating to maintenance.) **A1.512**

215. (a) For applications for a declaration of enforceability (see paragraph 208) of judgments other than maintenance orders only one court has been given jurisdiction in each of Ireland, England and Wales, Scotland and Northern Ireland. This is due to the peculiarities of the court systems in these countries (see paragraphs 11, 208 and 209). **A1.513**

216. If the judgment debtor wishes to argue against the authorization of enforcement, he must lodge his application to set the registration aside not with a higher court, as in Germany, France and Italy, but, as in Belgium and the Netherlands, with the court which registered the judgment. The proceedings will take the form of an ordinary contentious civil action.

A corresponding position applies regarding the appeal which the applicant may lodge if his application is refused, although in such a

---

[56] Cour de Cassation, 25 February 1937 Pas. 1937 I 73.

case it is a higher court which has jurisdiction in all seven Continental Member States of the Community.

A1.514 217. The adjustment of the second paragraph of Article 37 and of Article 41 gave rise to difficulties with regard to the solution adopted for Articles 32 and 40.

In the original Member States of the Community an appeal against judgments of courts on which jurisdiction is conferred by Articles 37 and 40 could only be lodged on a point of law and with the highest court in the State. It was therefore sufficient to make the same provision apply to the appeals provided for in the 1968 Convention and, in the case of Belgium, simply to bypass the Cour d'appel. The purpose of this arrangement is to limit the number of appeals, in the interests of rapid enforcement, to a single appeal which may involve a full review of the facts and a second one limited to points of law. It would therefore not have been enough to stipulate for the new Member States that only one further appeal would be permitted against the judgment of the court which had ruled on an appeal made by either the debtor or the creditor. Instead, the second appeal had to be limited to points of law.

A1.515 Ireland and the United Kingdom will have to adapt their appeal system to the requirements of the 1968 Convention. In the case of Ireland, which has only a two-tier superior court system, the Supreme Court is the only possibility. Implementing legislation in the United Kingdom will have to determine whether the further appeals should go direct to the House of Lords or, depending on the judicial area concerned (see paragraph 11), to the Court of Appeal in England an Wales, to the court of the same name in Northern Ireland or to the Inner House of the Court of Session in Scotland. The concept of "appeal on a point of law" is the nearest equivalent as far as United Kingdom law is concerned to the "Rechtsbeschwerde" of German law and the appeal in cassation in the legal systems of the other original Member States of the Community, the common feature of which is a restriction of the grounds of appeal to an incorrect application of the law (as opposed to an incorrect assessment of the facts). Even in relation to appeals in cassation and "Rechtsbeschwerde" the distinction between points of law and matters of fact is no identical; for the United Kingdom and Ireland, too, this will remain a matter for its own legislation and case law to clarify.

A1.516 Traditionally the leave of the Minister for Justice is required for an appeal to the highest Danish court at third instance. The Working Party was initially doubtful whether it should accept this in the context of the 1968 Convention. It emerged, however, that the Convention does not guarantee a third instance in all circumstances. In order to relieve the burden on their highest courts, Member States may limit the admissibility of the appeals provided for in Article 41. The Danish solution is only one manifestation of this idea. There was also no need in the case of Denmark to stipulate that the appeal to the highest court should be limited to a point of law. When granting leave the Ministry of Justice can ensure that the appeal concerns only questions of law requiring further elucidation. Denmark has given **[134]** an assurance that leave will always be granted, if the court of second instance has not made use of its discretion to refer a matter to the European Court of Justice or if enforcement of a foreign judgment has been refused on legal grounds.

218. (b) In Ireland the proposed arrangement also applies to maintenance orders. In the United Kingdom, however, maintenance orders are subject to a special arrangement (see paragraph 210). In England and Wales and in Northern Ireland registration is a matter for the Magistrates' Courts, and in Scotland for the Sheriff Courts. These courts also have jurisdiction in respect of other maintenance matters including the enforcement of foreign maintenance orders. Foreign maintenance creditors cannot, however, have recourse to any of the above courts directly, but must apply to the Secretary of State,[57] who will transmit the order to the appropriate court. This arrangement was made in the interest of the foreign maintenance creditors, because Magistrates' Courts and Sheriff Courts have lay justices and no administrative machinery.

    As regards jurisdiction in respect of appeals which may be brought by either the creditor or the debtor under the 1968 Convention, the usual system will continue to apply, *i.e.* the appeal is decided by the court which registered the order or refused such registration. It is impossible for a maintenance order to be amended during registration proceedings, even if it is claimed that the circumstances have changed (see paragraph 104 *et seq.*).

    The special situation regarding maintenance orders in the United Kingdom offers a series of advantages to the maintenance creditor. After forwarding the order to the Secretary of State, he has virtually no further need to concern himself with the progress of the proceedings or with their enforcement. The rest will be done free of charge. The Secretary of State transmits the order to the appropriate court and, unless the maintenance creditor otherwise requests, the clerk of that court will be regarded as the representative *ad litem* within the meaning of Article 33, second paragraph, second sentence. In England and Wales and in Northern Ireland the clerk in question will also be responsible for taking the necessary enforcement measures and for ensuring that the creditor receives the proceeds obtained. Only in Scotland need the creditor under the order seek the services of a solicitor when applying for enforcement following registration of an order. The Law Society of Scotland undertakes to provide solicitors whose fees are, if necessary, paid in accordance with the principles of legal aid. Should the maintenance debtor

A1.517

A1.518

---

[57] Exact name and address: If the judgment is to be executed in Scotland—Secretary of State for Scotland, Scottish Office, New St. Andrew's House, St. James Centre, Edinburgh EH1 3SX; Otherwise—Secretary of State for the Home Department, Home Office, 50 Queen Anne's Gate, London SW1H 9AT.

move to another judicial area in the United Kingdom (see paragraph 11), a maintenance order will, unlike other judgments, be automatically registered with the court which then has jurisdiction. For agreements concerning maintenance, see paragraph 226.

3. Other adjustment problems

A1.519   219. (a) The United Kingdom asked whether Article 34 excludes the possibility of notifying the debtor that an application for registration of a foreign judgment has been lodged. One of the aims of Article 34 is to secure the element of surprise, which is essential if measures of enforcement are to be effective. Therefore, although this provision does not expressly forbid notifying the debtor in the proceedings of the application for the grant of an enforcement order, such notification should be confined to very exceptional cases. An example might be an application for registration made a long time after the original judgment was given. In any case, the court may not consider submissions from the debtor, whether or not he was notified in advance.

A1.520   220. (b) The appeal provided for in Article 36 can be based, *inter alia*, on the grounds that the judgment does not come within the scope of the 1968 Convention, that it is not yet enforceable, or that the obligation imposed by the judgment has already been complied with. However, the substance of the judgment to be enforced or the procedure by which it came into existence can be reviewed only within the limits of Articles 27 and 28. For the adjustment of maintenance orders, see paragraph 108.

A1.521   221. (c) The Working Party discussed Article 39 at length. The provision in question is modelled on the French legal system and legal systems related to it, to which the institution of "huissier" is familiar. Under these systems, measures of enforcement in respect of movable property or contractual claims belonging to the debtor can be taken, without involving the court, by instructing a "huissier" to deal with their execution. It is for the creditor to choose between the available [135] methods of enforcement. The enforcing agency has no discretion whatsoever in the matter. The legal position obtaining in the United Kingdom (especially in England and Wales and also in Scotland) and Ireland is quite different. In the United Kingdom it is the court which has given or registered the judgment which has jurisdiction over measures of enforcement. In Ireland it is the court which has given or enforced the judgment. The court also has some discretion as to which enforcement measures it will sanction. Protective measures confined to securing enforcement of a claim do not yet exist.

This position will have to be altered by the implementing legislation of these States, which will have to introduce protective measures, in so far as this consequence does not arise as an automatic result of the entry into force of the 1968 Convention for one of these States (see paragraph 256).

The 1968 Convention does not guarantee specific measures of **A1.522** enforcement to the creditor. Neither is it in any way incompatible with the 1968 Convention to leave the measures of enforcement entirely to the court. The 1968 Convention contains no express provision obliging the Member States to employ an institution similar to the French "huissier." Even within its original scope, creditors have to apply directly to the court in the case of certain measures of enforcement; in Germany, for example, they would be required to do so in the case of enforcement against immovable property. It is certain however that in the German text the phrase "in das Vermögen des Schuldners" ("against the property of the party against whom enforcement is sought") does not mean that measures of enforcement are permissible as against third parties. The words quoted above could be omitted without changing the meaning of the provision. The question under what conditions measures of enforcement are possible against persons other than the judgment debtor is to be answered solely on the basis of national law. But the qualifications contained in Article 39 must also be observed.

The court enforcing the judgment need not be the one which grants the order of enforcement or registers the foreign judgment. Therefore, for the purposes of enforcement under the 1968 Convention, Denmark can retain its present system, by which execution is entrusted to a special enforcement judge.

222. (d) For the problems presented by the system of *"astreintes,"* which **A1.523** applies in some Member States, see paragraph 213.

223. (e) In its present form, Article 44 does not provide for the case of a **A1.524** party who had been granted only partial legal aid in the State in which the judgment was given. Although this did not involve an adjustment problem specifically due to the accession of the new Member States, the Working Party decided to propose an amendment. The Working Party's discussions revealed that if the text were to remain in force in its present form, it could result in some undesirable complications. The Working Party's proposal was largely based on the formulation of Article 15 of the Hague Convention of 2 October 1973 on the recognition and enforcement of decisions relating to maintenance obligations which has now come into force. This provision opts for a generous solution: even if only partial legal aid was granted in the State of origin, full aid is to be granted in the enforcement proceedings.

This has a number of further advantages: **A1.525**

As the main application of Article 44 as amended relates to maintenance claims, the amended version contributes to the harmonization of provisions in international conventions.

Moreover, it leads to a general simplification of applications.

Since the rules concerning the granting of partial legal aid are not the same in all the Contracting States, the amended version also ensures a uniform application of the legal aid provisions.

Lastly, it secures the surprise effect of enforcement measures abroad, by avoiding procedural delays caused by difficult calculations concerning the applicant's share in the costs.

The first paragraph of Article 44 does not, however, oblige States which do not at present have a system of legal aid in civil matters to introduce such a system.

A1.526   224. (f) The reason for the new second paragraph of Article 44 relates to the jurisdiction of the Danish administrative authorities (see paragraph 67) whose services are free. No question of legal aid therefore arises. The new provision is designed to ensure that the enforcement of Danish maintenance orders is not, for this reason, at a disadvantage in the other EEC countries by comparison with maintenance orders from EEC countries other than Denmark.

Section 3

Common provisions

A1.527   225. The discussion of Articles 46 to 49 centred on whether the new Member States, in accordance with their legal tradition, could require an affidavit, in particular to the effect that none of the grounds for refusing recognition, specified in Articles 27 and 28, obtain. Affidavit evidence is certainly admissible in appellate proceedings, where the debtor appeals against registration or against a declaration of enforceability, or the creditor against a refusal to register. However, all the other means of giving evidence which are normally admissible must also be available in those proceedings.

The addition to Article 46(2) is proposed for the reasons given in paragraphs 182 and 194.

CHAPTER 6

AUTHENTIC INSTRUMENTS AND COURT SETTLEMENTS

A1.528   226. In England and Ireland there is no equivalent of enforceable instruments. In Scotland, instruments establishing a clearly defined obligation to perform a contract can be entered in a public register. An extract from the public register can then serve as a basis for enforcement in the same way as a court judgment. Such extracts are covered by Article 50.

In the United Kingdom, the courts having jurisdiction for recognition and enforcement of maintenance orders are different from those concerned with other kinds of judgment (see paragraphs 210 and 218). It is for the internal law of the United Kingdom to determine whether foreign court settlements concerning maintenance should be treated as maintenance orders or as other judgments.

CHAPTER 7

GENERAL PROVISIONS

227. The outcome of the discussion of Articles 52 and 53 has already been recorded elsewhere (see paragraphs 73 *et seq.*, and 119). **A1.529**

CHAPTER 8

TRANSITIONAL PROVISIONS

228. Article 54 continues to apply to the relationships between the orig- **A1.530**
inal Member States. For their relationships with the new Member States, and the relationships of the new Member States with each other, an appropriate transitional provision is included in Article 34 of the proposed Accession Convention. It is closely modelled on Article 54 of the 1968 Convention, but takes into [137] account the fact that the latter has already been in force in its present form between the original Member States since 1 February 1973, and also the fact that some amendments are to be made to it. Finally, the Interpretation Protocol of 3 June 1971 also had to be taken into account in the transitional rules. The detailed provisions are as follows[58]:

I. JURISDICTION

229. 1. The provisions on jurisdiction in the 1968 Convention apply in **A1.531**
the new Member States only in their amended version and only to proceedings instituted after the Accession Convention has come into force, and hence after the 1968 Convention has come into force, in the State in question (Article 34(1)).

230. 2. The amended version also applies to proceedings instituted in the **A1.532**
original Member States after that date. Jurisdiction in respect of proceedings instituted in the original Member States before that date but after 1 February 1973 will continue to be determined in accordance with the original text of the 1968 Convention (Article 34(1)). It is to be noted, as regards the relationships of the old Member States with each other, that under Article 39 of the Accession Convention the amended version can only come into force simultaneously for all six of them.

---

[58] Typical case law examples for Art. 54: Hamburg Landgericht (RIW/AWD) 74, 403 *et seq.*; Frankfurt Oberlandesgericht (RIW/AWD) 76, 107.

II. RECOGNITION AND ENFORCEMENT

1. End of the Transitional Period

A1.533 231. The recognition and enforcement of judgments are in all respects governed by the Convention as amended, provided the transitional period had already ended at the time of institution of the proceedings. For this purpose, the Accession Convention must have come into force by that time both in the State of origin and in the State subsequently addressed (Article 34(1)). It is not sufficient for the Accession Convention to be in force in the former State only, since rules of exorbitant jurisdiction may still be invoked under Article 4 of the 1968 Convention against domiciliaries of the State subsequently addressed if that State was not also a party to the Accession Convention at the time of institution of the proceedings. This would render an obligation to recognize and enforce a judgment in that State without any preliminary review unacceptable.

A1.534 If we assume that the Accession Convention comes into force for the original Member States of the Community and Denmark on 1 January 1981 and an action is brought in Germany against a person domiciled in Denmark on 3 January 1981, then a judgment on 1 July 1981 finding in favour of the plaintiff would be enforceable irrespective of transitional provisions, even if, say, the United Kingdom did not become a party to the Convention until 1 December 1981. However, if in this example the action was brought and judgment given against a person domiciled in the United Kingdom, Article 34(1) would not govern recognition and enforcement in the United Kingdom. That would be a true transitional case.

A1.535 Paragraphs (2) and (3) of Article 34 deal with judgments during the transitional period, *i.e.* judgments given after the Accession Convention has come into force in the State addressed, but in proceedings which were instituted at a time when, either in the State of origin or in the State addressed, the Accession Convention was not yet in force. In Article 34(2) and (3) a distinction is drawn between cases involving only the original Member States of the Community and those involving new Member States as well.

2. Among the original Member States of the Community

A1.536 232. Article 34(2) makes the recognition and enforcement of judgments among the original Member States of the Community subject without any restriction to the 1968 Convention as amended, even if the actions were started before the entry into force of the Accession Convention, which will necessarily be simultaneous in those States (see the end of paragraph 230). This amounts indirectly to a statement that the situation as regards the recognition and enforcement of judgments among those States remains that in Article 54 of the 1968 Convention in the case of judgments given before the entry

into force of the Accession Convention. The most important implication of Article 34(2) is that in proceedings for the recognition of
judgments among the original Member States of the Community
there is to be no consideration of whether the court giving the **[138]**
judgment whose recognition is sought would have had jurisdiction
after the entry into force of the Accession Convention. If the action
was started after 1 February 1973 then the jurisdiction of the court
giving the judgment whose recognition is sought may no longer be
examined. The point is of note since that court's jurisdiction could
still have been founded on exorbitant jurisdictional rules where
domiciliaries of the new Member States are concerned.

To illustrate the point with an example, if a Frenchman were in
1978 to bring an action in the French courts pursuant to Article 14 of
the Civil Code against a person domiciled in Ireland, which would be
possible under Article 4 of the 1968 Convention, and judgment was
given in favour of the plaintiff in 1982; then, assuming the Accession
Convention came into force for the original Member States of the
Community and Ireland in 1981, the judgment would have to be
recognized and enforced in Germany, but not in Ireland.

3. Where new Member States are involved

233. The arrangements obtaining under Article 34(3) for the recognition   **A1.537**
and enforcement of judgments between the original Member States
and the new Member States, or as between the new Member States,
differ somewhat from those applying among the original Member
States. Article 34(3) is concerned with the possibility of recognition
and enforcement being sought in one of the new Contracting States
of a judgment from an original Contracting State or from another
new Contracting State. Apart from the cases referred to in paragraph 231, this is possible after the end of the transitional period,
subject to three requirements being met.

234. (a) The judgment must have been given after the Accession Con-   **A1.538**
vention came into force in both States.

235. (b) In addition, the proceedings must have been instituted, in the
words of the Convention, before "the date of entry into force of
this Convention, between the State of origin and the State
addressed." The purport of this is that, at the time when the
proceedings were instituted, the Accession Convention may
have come into force either in the State of the court giving the
judgment for which recognition is sought, or in the State in
which recognition and enforcement are subsequently sought,
but not in both of these States.

236. (c) Finally, the jurisdiction of the court giving the judgment for
which recognition is sought must satisfy certain criteria which
the court in the State addressed must check. These criteria
exactly match what Article 54 of the 1968 Convention laid down

regarding transitional cases which were pending when that Convention came into force between the six original Member States. In proceedings for recognition, the jurisdiction of the court which gave judgment is to be accepted as having been valid, provided one of two requirements is met:

(aa) The judgment must be recognized where the court in the State of origin would have had jurisdiction if the Accession Convention had already been in force as between the two States at the time when the proceedings were instituted.

(bb) The judgment must also be recognized where the court's jurisdiction was covered at the time when the proceedings were instituted by another international convention which was in force between the two States.

A1.539   Reverting to the example in paragraph 232, the position would be as follows: the French judgment would indeed have been given after the Accession Convention had come into force in Ireland and France. The proceedings would have been instituted at a time when the Accession Convention was not yet in force in France (or in Ireland). Had this Convention already been in force as between France and Ireland at that time, the French courts would no longer have been able to found their jurisdiction on Article 14 of the Civil Code and hence, it must further be assumed, would have been unable to assume jurisdiction. Lastly, there is no bilateral convention between France and Ireland concerning the direct or indirect jurisdiction of the courts. Consequently, the judgment would not have had to be recognized in Ireland.

A1.540   If one changes the example so that it now concerns France and the United Kingdom, one has to take into consideration the Convention between those two States of 18 January 1934 providing for the reciprocal enforcement of judgments. However, jurisdiction deriving from **[139]** Article 14 of the Civil Code is not admitted under that Convention; thus the judgment would not have to be recognized in the United Kingdom either.

A1.541   If the example concerned Germany and the United Kingdom, and the defendant resident in the United Kingdom had agreed orally before the commencement of the proceedings that the German courts should have jurisdiction, then under the 1968 Convention the judgment would have to be recognized and enforced in the United Kingdom. Under Article IV(1)(a) of the Convention between the United Kingdom and Germany of 14 July 1960, oral agreement is sufficient to give grounds for jurisdiction for the purposes of recognition ("indirect" jurisdiction). However, the German court would have had to be a "Landgericht," since "Amtsgericht" judgments are not required to be recognized under that Convention (Article I(2)). In the event of a written agreement on jurisdiction, even the judgment of an "Amtsgericht" would have to be recognized, under Article 34(3) of the Accession Convention, as the "Amtsgericht" would in that case have assumed jurisdiction under circumstances in which jurisdiction would also have had to be assumed if the Accession Convention had been in force between Germany and the United Kingdom.

CHAPTER 9

RELATIONSHIP TO OTHER CONVENTIONS

I. ARTICLES 55 AND 56

237. The Working Party included in Article 55 the bilateral conventions **A1.542** between the United Kingdom and other Member States of the Community. No such conventions have been concluded by Ireland and Denmark.

II. ARTICLE 57[59]

1. THE BASIC STRUCTURE OF THE PROPOSED PROVISION

238. Great difficulties arose when an attempt was made to explain to the **A1.543** new Member States the exact scope of Article 57, the main reason being the statement that the Convention "shall not affect" any conventions in relation to particular matters, without stating how the provisions in such conventions could be reconciled with those of the 1968 Convention where they covered only part of the matters governed by the latter, which is usually the case. Special conventions can be divided into three groups. Many of them contain only provisions on direct jurisdiction, as in the case with the Warsaw Convention of 12 October 1929 for the unification of certain rules relating to international carriage by air and the Additional Protocols thereto,* and the Brussels Convention relating to the arrest of seagoing ships which is of great importance for maritime law (Article 7) (see paragraph 121). Most conventions govern only the recognition and enforcement of judgments, and merely refer indirectly to jurisdiction in so far as it constitutes a precondition for recognition. This is the case with the Hague Convention of 15 April 1958 on the recognition and enforcement of decisions relating to maintenance obligations towards children. Finally, there are also Conventions which contain provisions directly regulating jurisdiction as well as recognition and enforcement, as for example the Berne Convention on carriage by rail and the Mannheim Convention for the navigation of the Rhine. It is irrelevant for present purposes whether the con-

---

[59] [Editor's note: footnote 59 is set out at para. A1.569 below.]
* Not to be confused with the Brussels Convention of the same date for the unification of certain rules relating to penal jurisdiction in matters of collision.

ventions contain additional provisions on the applicable law or rules of substantive law.

A1.544   239. (a) It is clear beyond argument that where a special convention contains no provisions directly governing jurisdiction, the jurisdiction provisions of the 1968 Convention apply. It is equally clear that where all the Contracting States are parties to a special convention containing provisions on **[140]** jurisdiction, those provisions prevail. But for situations between these two extremes the solution provided by Article 57 is a great deal less clear. This is particularly the case for a number of questions, which arise where only the State of origin and the State addressed are parties to the special convention. The problems become acute where only one of these two States is a party. If both States are parties to a special convention which governs only direct jurisdiction, will the provisions of the 1968 Convention regarding examination of jurisdiction by the court of its own motion (Article 20), *lis pendens* (Article 21) and enforcement apply? Do the provisions of the 1968 Convention on the procedure for recognition and enforcement apply, if a special convention on the recognition and enforcement of judgments does not deal with procedure? Can a person domiciled in a Contracting State which is not a party to a special convention be sued in the courts of another Contracting State on the basis of jurisdiction provisions in the special conventions, or can the State of domicile which is not a party to the special convention claim that the jurisdiction rules of the 1968 Convention must be observed? Must a judgment given in a court which has jurisdiction only under a special convention be recognized and enforced even in a Contracting State which is not a party to that particular special convention? And, finally, what is the position where the special convention does not claim to be exclusive?

A1.545   240. (b) Tentative and conflicting views were expressed within the Working Party as to how these problems were to be solved in interpreting Article 57 in its original form. It became clear that it would not be practicable to provide a precise solution to all of them, particularly since it is impossible to predict the form of future conventions. It was however appropriate, in the interests of clarifying the obligations about to be assumed by the new Member States, to include in the Accession Convention an authentic interpretation which concerns some problems which are of especial importance. The opportunity was taken to make a drafting improvement to the present Article 57 of the 1968 Convention—the new paragraph 1 of this Article—which will speak of recognition or enforcement. By reason of the purely drafting nature of the amendment to the text, the provision laying down the authentic interpretation of the new Article 57(1) also applies to the present version.

A1.546   The solution arrived at is based on the following principles. The 1968 Convention contains the rules generally applicable in all Member States; provisions in special conventions are special rules which every State may make prevail over the 1968 Convention by becoming a party to such a convention. In so far as a special convention does not contain rules covering a particular matter the 1968 Convention applies. This is also the case where the special convention includes rules of jurisdiction which do not altogether fit the interconnecting provisions of the various parts of the 1968 Convention, especially those governing the relationship between jurisdiction and enforcement. The overriding considerations are simplicity and clarity of the legal position.

The most important consequence of this is that provisions on jurisdiction contained in special conventions are to be regarded as if they were provisions of the 1968 Convention itself, even if only one Member State is a Contracting Party to such a special convention. Even Member States which are not Contracting Parties to the special convention must therefore recognize and enforce decisions given by courts which have jurisdiction only under the special convention. Furthermore, in the context of two States which are parties to a special convention, a person who wishes to obtain the recognition or enforcement of a judgment may rely upon the procedural provisions of the 1968 Convention on recognition and enforcement. **A1.547**

At the same time, the Working Party did not wish to reach a final conclusion on the question whether the general principle outlined above could be consistently applied in all its ramifications. To take a critical example, it was left open whether exclusive jurisdiction under the provisions of a special convention must invariably be applied. The same applies to the question whether a case of *lis pendens* arising from a special convention is covered by Article 21 of the 1968 Convention. The Working Party therefore preferred to provide expressly for the application of Article 20 and to leave the solution of the outstanding problems to legal literature and case law. For the implications of an authentic interpretation of Article 57 for maritime jurisdiction, see paragraph 121. **A1.548**

2. EXAMPLES

241. A river boatman domiciled in the Netherlands is liable for damages arising from an accident which occurred on the upper Rhine. It is however no **[141]** longer possible to determine whether the harmful event occurred on German or French territory or from where the damage emanated. **A1.549**

242. It is not possible in such a case for either German or French courts to assume jurisdiction under Article 5(3) or any other provision of the 1968 Convention. According to Article 34(2)(c) and Article 35a of the revised Rhine navigation Convention of 17 October 1868 in the version of the Protocol of 25 October 1972,[60] jurisdiction in such cases belongs to the court of the State which was the first or **A1.550**

---

[60] See n. 59(1).

only one seised of the matter. That court must, however, take into account Article 20 of the 1968 Convention, even though no equivalent of this Article exists in the Rhine navigation Convention. For example, if the defendant fails to enter an appearance, the court must of its own motion (see paragraph 22) ascertain whether all means have been exhausted of determining exactly where the accident occurred, for only if this cannot be determined does the court have jurisdiction under the abovementioned provisions of the Rhine navigation Convention.

A1.551   243. If the court first seised of the matter was French, then any judgment of that court must be recognized in Germany. The Rhine navigation Convention is even stricter than the 1968 Convention in forbidding any re-examination of the original judgment in the State addressed. According to the correct interpretation of Article 57 of the 1968 Convention the judgment creditor has the choice of availing himself of the enforcement procedure provided by the Rhine navigation Convention or by the 1968 Convention. However, if he proceeds under the 1968 Convention the court may not refuse recognition on any of the grounds given in Article 27 or Article 28 of the 1968 Convention. Unlike the enforcement procedure itself, the conditions for recognition and enforcement are exclusively governed by the special conventions—in this example, the Rhine navigation Convention.

A1.552   244. If, however, a judgment has been given in the court with jurisdiction at the place of destination pursuant to Article 28(1) of the Warsaw Convention of 12 October 1929 for the unification of certain rules relating to international carriage by air, the 1968 Convention applies fully to both recognition and enforcement, because the Warsaw Convention contains no provisions at all on these matters. The same applies where in maritime law the jurisdiction of the court of origin was based on the provisions governing arrest contained in the 1952 Brussels Convention (see paragraph 121).

A1.553   245. If the boatman in the above example on Rhine navigation had been domiciled in Luxembourg, which is not a party to the Rhine navigation Convention, the position would be as follows: any jurisdiction assumed in France or Germany pursuant to the Rhine navigation Convention can no longer be regarded in Luxembourg as an infringement of the 1968 Convention. Under the provisions and procedure of the 1968 Convention, Luxembourg is obliged to recognize and enforce a judgment given by the German or French Rhine navigation courts. If, conversely, the boatman is sued in the court of his Luxembourg domicile, which is also permissible, under the 1968 Convention, Germany and France would have to accept this, even though they are parties to the Rhine navigation Convention which does not recognize jurisdiction based on domicile.

3. UNDERTAKINGS IN CONVENTIONS BETWEEN STATES NOT TO RECOGNIZE JUDGMENTS

246. Whether Article 57 also covers conventions under which one Member State of the Community undertakes not to recognize judgments given in another Member State remains an open question. It could be argued that the admissible scope of such conventions was governed exclusively by Article 59. **A1.554**

International obligations of this sort can result from a special convention which provides for the exclusive jurisdiction of the courts of one of the Contracting Parties. Such an obligation can however also result indirectly from the fact that the exercise of jurisdiction under the special convention is linked to a special regime of liability. For example, the Paris Convention of 1960 on third party liability in the field of nuclear energy, apart from laying down rules of jurisdiction, recognition and enforcement: **A1.555**

1. places the sole liability for damage on the operator of a nuclear installation;
2. makes his liability an absolute one;
3. sets maximum limits to his liability;
[142] 4. requires him to insure against his liability;
5. allows a Contracting State to provide additional compensation from public funds.

The recognition and enforcement of a judgment which is given in a State not party to such a special convention and which is based on legal principles quite different from those outlined above could seriously undermine the operation of that special convention. **A1.556**

The 1968 Convention should always be interpreted in such a way that no limitations of liability contained in international conventions are infringed. The question however remains open whether this result is to be achieved by applying the public policy provision of Article 27(1), by analogy with the new paragraph (5) of Article 27, or by a broad interpretation of Article 57.

For conventions limiting liability in maritime law, see paragraph 124 *et seq.*

4. PRECEDENCE OF SECONDARY COMMUNITY LAW

247. Within the Working Party opinion was divided as to whether secondary Community law, or national laws adopted pursuant to secondary Community law, prevail over international agreements concluded between the Member States, in particular in the case of a convention provided for in Article 220 of the Treaty of Rome. There was, however, agreement that national and Community law referred to above should prevail over the 1968 Convention. This decision is embodied in Article 57; the provision is based on Article 25 of the preliminary draft Convention on the law applicable to contractual and non-contractual obligations. **A1.557**

5. CONSULTATIONS BEFORE THE FUTURE ACCESSION BY MEMBER STATES OF THE COMMUNITY TO FURTHER AGREEMENTS

A1.558   248. By their accession to the Convention, the new Member States are also bound by the Joint Declaration made by the Contracting States at the time of the signing of the 1968 Convention. In the Declaration the States declare that they will arrange for regular periodic contacts between their representatives. The Working Party was unanimously of the opinion that consultations should also take place when a Member State intended to accede to a convention which would prevail over the 1968 Convention by virtue of Article 57.

III. ARTICLE 59

A1.559   249. This provision refers only to judgments given against persons domiciled or habitually resident outside the Community. Such persons may also be sued on the basis of jurisdictional provisions which could not be invoked in the case of persons domiciled within the Community, and which are classed as exorbitant and disallowed pursuant to the second paragraph of Article 3. Nevertheless, any judgment which may have been given is to be recognized and enforced in accordance with the 1968 Convention. As the Jenard report explains, it is intended that the Contracting States should remain free to conclude conventions with third States excluding the recognition and enforcement of judgments based on exorbitant jurisdictions—even though the 1968 Convention permits this in exceptional cases. The aim of the proposed amendment to Article 59 is further to limit the possibility of recognition and enforcement.

A1.560   250. The way this will work may be illustrated by an example. If a creditor has a claim to be satisfied in France against a debtor domiciled in that country, then Danish courts have no jurisdiction under any circumstances to decide this issue, even if the debtor has property in Denmark and even if the claim is secured on immovable property there. Supposing the debtor is domiciled in Norway, then if Danish national law so allows Danish courts may very well claim jurisdiction, *e.g.* on the basis of the presence in Denmark of property owned by the debtor. Normally, the judgment given in such a case would also be enforceable in the United Kingdom. The United Kingdom could however undertake in a convention with Norway an obligation to refuse recognition and enforcement of such a judgment. This kind of treaty obligation may not however extend to a case where the jurisdiction of the Danish courts is based on the ground that immovable property in Denmark constitutes security for the debt. In such circumstances, the judgment would be enforceable even in the United Kingdom.

[143] CHAPTER 10

FINAL PROVISIONS

1. IRELAND

251. Ireland has no territorial possessions outside the integral parts of its territory. **A1.561**

2. UNITED KINGDOM

252. The term "United Kingdom" does not include the Channel Islands, **A1.562**
the Isle of Man, Gibraltar or the Sovereign Base Areas in Cyprus.
There is no obligation on the United Kingdom to extend the scope
of the 1968 Convention to include these territories, even though it is
responsible for their external relations. It might, however, be useful
if the United Kingdom were to extend the 1968 Convention and it
should be authorized to do so. It would have to undertake the
necessary "adjustments" itself, and there was no need to provide
for them in the Accession Convention. The following adjustments
would be required: indication of any exorbitant jurisdictions in the
second paragraph of Article 3; a declaration as to whether in the
newly included territories every appeal should be regarded as an
ordinary appeal for the purposes of Articles 30 and 38; a declaration
as to whether registration in any such territory in accordance with
the second paragraph of Article 31 is effective only within its area;
establishing which courts are competent under Articles 32, 37 and
40, the form in which the application should be made, and whether
the adjustments in respect of the United Kingdom contained in the
second paragraph of Article 37 as amended and in Article 41 as
amended should also apply in the newly included territories. If any
international conventions should apply to any one of the territories
in question, appropriate adjustments would also have to be made to
Article 55.
   The penultimate paragraph of the proposed addition to Article 60
relates to the fact that judgments of courts in these territories which
do not belong to the United Kingdom can be challenged in the last
instance before the Judicial Committee of the Privy Council. It
would be illogical to bring Privy Council decisions within the scope
of the 1968 Convention if they related to disputes arising in territories to which the 1968 Convention does not apply.

3. DENMARK

253. For the purposes of EEC law, Greenland is included in the Euro- **A1.563**
pean territory of Denmark. The special constitutional positions of
the Faroe Islands led to a solution corresponding closely to that proposed for the territories for whose foreign relations the United

Kingdom is responsible. This had to allow for the fact that both appellate and first instance proceedings which relate to the Faroes and are therefore conducted under the Code of Civil Procedure specially enacted for these islands can be brought in Copenhagen.

4. CHANGES IN A STATE'S TERRITORY

A1.564   254. The Working Party was unanimous that any territory which becomes independent of the mother country thereby ceases to be a member of the European Community and, consequently, can no longer be a party to the 1968 Convention. It was unnecessary to provide for this expressly and, in any case, to have drafted such a provision would have gone beyond the Working Party's terms of reference.

CHAPTER 11

ADJUSTMENTS TO THE PROTOCOL OF 3 JUNE 1971 ON THE INTERPRETATION BY THE COURT OF JUSTICE OF THE EUROPEAN COMMUNITIES OF THE 1968 CONVENTION

1. FORMAL ADJUSTMENTS

A1.565   255. Formal adjustments to the Interpretation Protocol were few and fairly obvious. It became necessary to make only one short addition to its provisions: the courts in the new Member States which, in accordance with Article 2(1) and Article 3, are required to request the Court of **[144]** Justice to give preliminary rulings on questions of interpretation, had to be designated.[61] In the United Kingdom, unlike the other Member States, not only the highest court within the country has been included, as it is more difficult to refer a matter to the House of Lords than it is to have recourse to the highest courts on the continent. Therefore, at least the appellate proceedings provided for in the second paragraph of Article 37 and in Article 41 of the 1968 Convention should in the United Kingdom also terminate in a court which is obliged to request a preliminary ruling from the Court of Justice. The expression "appellate capacity" in Article 2(2) should not be construed in a narrow technical sense, but in the sense of any challenge before a higher jurisdiction, so that it might be taken also to include the French "contredit."

The remaining formal adjustments concerned merely the scope

---

[61] The expression "court" should not be taken as meaning the opposite of other jurisdictions (such as tribunals) but means the legal body which is declared competent in each case.

(Article 1) and territorial application of the Protocol. Article 6, which deals with the latter point, is wholly based on Article 60 of the 1968 Convention (see paragraphs 251 to 254). Which authorities are to be designated as competent within the meaning of the third paragraph of Article 4 is a question to be decided entirely by the new Member States.

2. THE SPECIAL NATURE OF IMPLEMENTING LEGISLATION IN THE UNITED KINGDOM AND IRELAND

256. The extension of the Interpretation Protocol to the United Kingdom and Ireland will, however, in all probability also present a procedural problem. A long-standing legal tradition in these States does not allow provisions of international treaties to become directly applicable as national law. In the United Kingdom legislation has to be passed transforming such provisions into national law. In many cases the legislative enactment does not follow precisely the wording of the treaty. The usual form of legislation in this State often calls for a more detailed phraseology than that used in a treaty. The treaty and the corresponding national law are, therefore, to be carefully distinguished. **A1.566**

If the implementing legislation in the United Kingdom follows the usual pattern, courts in that country would only rarely be concerned with the interpretation of the 1968 Convention, but mostly with interpretation of the national implementing legislation. Only when the latter is not clear would it be open to a court, under the existing rules of construction in that country, to refer to the treaty on which the legislation is based, and only when the court is then faced with a problem of interpretation of the treaty may it turn to the European Court of Justice. If the provisions of implementing legislation are clear in themselves, the courts in the United Kingdom may as a rule refer neither to the text of the treaty nor to any decision by an international court on its interpretation.

This would undoubtedly lead to a certain disparity in the application of the Interpretation Protocol of 3 June 1971. The Working Party was of the opinion that this disparity could best be redressed if the United Kingdom could in some way ensure in its implementing legislation that the 1968 Convention will there too be endowed with the status of a source of law, or may at any rate be referred to directly when applying the national implementing legislation. **A1.567**

In the event of a judgment of the European Court of Justice being inconsistent with a provision of the United Kingdom implementing legislation, the latter would have to be amended.

It is also the case in Ireland that international agreements to which that State is a party are not directly applicable as national law. Lately, however, a number of Acts putting international agreements into force in national law have taken the form of an incorporation of the text of the agreement into national law. If the Act putting into force the 1968 Convention as amended by the

Accession Convention were to take this form, the problems described above in relation to the United Kingdom would not arise in the case of Ireland.

ANNEX I

A1.568   **Extract from the Protocol to the preliminary draft Bankruptcy Convention (1975) (see paragraph 54)**

Certain details of this list have been amended by later documents which, however, are not themselves final.

(aa) *Bankruptcy proceedings:*

Belgium:
'faillite' — 'faillissement';

Denmark:
'Konkurs';

Federal Republic of Germany:
'Konkurs';

France:
'liquidation des biens';

Ireland:
'bankruptcy', 'winding-up in bankruptcy of partnerships', 'winding-up by the court under sections 213, 344 and 345 of the Companies Act 1963', 'creditors' voluntary winding-up under section 256 of the Companies Act 1963';

Italy:
'fallimento';

Luxembourg:
'faillite;

Netherlands:
'faillissement';

United Kingdom:
'bankruptcy' (England, Wales and Northern Ireland), 'sequestration' (Scotland), 'administration in bankruptcy of the estates of persons dying insolvent' (England, Wales and Northern Ireland), 'compulsory winding-up of companies', 'winding-up of companies under the supervision of the court'.

(bb) *Other proceedings:*

Belgium:

'concordat judiciaire' — 'gerechtelijk akkoord',
'sursis de paiement' — uitstel van betaling';

Denmark:

'tvangskkord',
'likvidation af insolvente aktieselskaber eller anpartsselskaber',
'likvidation af banker eller sparekasser, der har standset deres betalinger';

Federal Republic of Germany:

'gerichtliches Vergleichsverfahren';

France:

'règlement judiciaire',
'procedure de suspension provisoire des poursuites et d'apurement collectif
du passif de certaines entreprises';

Ireland:

'arrangements under the control of the court,' 'arrangements, reconstructions
and compositions of companies whether or not in the course of liquidation
where sanction of the court is required and creditors' rights are affected';

Italy:

'concordato preventivo',
'amministrazione controllata,'
'liquidazone coatta amministrativa' — in its judicial stage;

Luxenbourg:

'concordat préventif de la faillite',
'sursis de paiement',
'régime spécial de liquidation applicable aux notaires';

Netherlands:

'surséance van betaling',
'regeling, vervat in de wet op de vergadering van hourders van schuldbrieven
aan toonder';

United Kingdom:

'compositions and schemes of arrangement' (England and Wales),
'compositions' (Northern Ireland),
'arrangements under the control of the court' (Northern Ireland),
'judicial compositions' (Scotland),
'arrangements, reconstructions and compositions of companies whether or
not in the course of liquidation where sanction of the court is required and
creditors' rights are involved',
'creditors' voluntary winding-up of companies',
'deeds of arrangement approved by the court' (Northern Ireland).

ANNEX II

A1.569   [This Annex contains the footnotes to the Schlosser report which, with one exception, have been set out in this text below the paragraphs to which they relate. The exception is note 59, which is set out below:]

[59] The original and new Member States of the Community, or some of them, are already parties to numerous international conventions governing jurisdiction and the recognition and enforcement of judgments in particular areas of law. The following should be mentioned, including those already listed in the Jenard report:

1. The revised Mannheim Convention for the navigation of the Rhine of 17 October 1868 together with the Revised Agreement of 20 November 1963 and the Additional Protocol of 25 October 1972 (Belgium, Germany, France, Netherlands, U.K.);

2. The Warsaw Convention of 12 October 1929 for the unification of certain rules relating to international carriage by air and the Amending Protocol of 28 September 1955 and Supplementary Convention of 18 September 1961 (all nine States) with the Additional Protocols of 8 March 1971 and 25 September 1975 (not yet in force);

3. The Brussels International Convention of 10 May 1952 on certain rules concerning civil jurisdiction in matters of collision (Belgium, Germany, France, U.K.);

4. The Brussels International Convention of 10 May 1952 relating to the arrest of seagoing ships (Belgium, Germany, France, U.K.);

5. The Rome Convention of 7 October 1952 relating to damage caused by foreign aircraft to third parties on the surface (Belgium, Luxembourg);

6. The London Agreement of 27 February 1953 on German external debts (all nine States);

7. (a) The Hague Convention of 1 March 1954 on civil procedure (Belgium, Denmark, Germany, France, Italy, Luxembourg, Netherlands),

   (b) The Hague Convention of 15 November 1965 on the service abroad of judicial and extrajudicial documents in civil and commercial matters (Belgium, Denmark, France, Italy, Luxembourg, Netherlands, U.K.),

   (c) The Hague Convention of 18 March 1970 on the taking of evidence abroad in civil or commercial matters (Denmark, France, Italy, Luxembourg, U.K.);

8. The Geneva Convention of 19 May 1956 together with its Protocol of Signature on the contract for the international carriage of goods by road (CMR) (Belgium, Denmark, Germany, France, Italy, Luxembourg, Netherlands, U.K.);

9. The Convention of 27 October 1956 between the Grand Duchy of Luxembourg, the Federal Republic of Germany and the French Republic on the canalization of the Moselle, with the Additional Protocol of 28 November 1976 (the three signatory States);

10. The Hague Convention of 15 April 1958 on the recognition and enforcement of decisions relating to maintenance obligations in respect of children (Belgium, Denmark, Germany, France, Italy, Netherlands);

11. The Hague Convention of 15 April 1958 on the jurisdiction of the contractual forum in matters relating to the international sale of goods (not yet ratified);

12. The Paris Convention of 29 July 1960 on third party liability in the field of nuclear energy (Belgium, France, Germany), together with the Paris

Additional Protocol of 28 January 1964 (Belgium, Denmark, France, Germany, Italy), and the Brussels Convention and Annex thereto of 31 January 1963 supplementary to the Paris Convention of 29 July 1960 and the Paris Additional Protocol to the Supplementary Convention of 28 January 1964 (Denmark, France, Germany, Italy, U.K.);

13. The Supplementary Convention of 26 February 1966 to the International Convention of 25 February 1961 concerning carriage of passengers and luggage by rail (CIV) on the liability of railways for death or injury to passengers, amended by Protocol II of the Diplomatic Conference for the entry into force of the CIM and CIV International Agreements of 7 February 1970 concerning the extension of the period of validity of the Supplementary Convention of 26 February 1966 (all nine States);

14. The Brussels Convention of 25 May 1962 on the liability of operators of nuclear ships and Additional Protocol (Germany);

15. The Brussels International Convention of 27 May 1967 for the unification of rules relating to the carriage of passengers' luggage by sea (not yet in force);

16. The Brussels International Convention of 27 May 1967 for the unification of certain rules relating to maritime liens and mortgages (not yet in force);

17. The Brussels International Convention of 29 November 1969 on civil liability for oil pollution damage (Belgium, Denmark, France, Germany, Netherlands, U.K.) and the International Convention to supplement that Convention of 18 December 1971 on the establishment of an international fund for compensation for oil pollution damage (Denmark, France, Germany, U.K.);

18. The Berne International Conventions of 7 February 1970 on the carriage of goods by rail (CIM) and the carriage of passengers and luggage by rail (CIV), together with the Additional Protocol and Protocol I of 9 November 1973 of the Diplomatic Conference for the implementation of the Conventions (all nine States with the exception of Ireland for Protocol I);

19. The Athens Convention of 13 December 1974 on the carriage by sea of passengers and their luggage (not yet in force);

20. The European Agreement of 30 September 1957 covering the international carriage of dangerous goods by road (ADR) (U.K.) and the Additional Protocol of 21 August 1975 (U.K.) (not yet in force);

21. The Geneva Convention of 1 March 1973 on the contract for the international carriage of passengers and baggage by road (CUR) (not yet in force);

22. The Hague Convention of 2 October 1973 on the recognition and enforcement of decisions relating to maintenance obligations (no Community Member State is a party to this Convention).

APPENDIX 2

BILATERAL AND MULTILATERAL CONVENTIONS

A. THE UNITED KINGDOM'S BILATERAL CONVENTIONS WITH OTHER CONTRACTING STATES

1. Civil procedure conventions

A2.01   The United Kingdom has entered into bilateral civil procedure conventions with the other Contracting States to the 1968 Convention, with the exception of Ireland and Luxembourg. The provisions of these conventions have been described above, so far as they concern the taking of evidence abroad (paras. 8.33 *et seq.*) and the service abroad of judicial and extrajudicial documents (paras. 4.34 *et seq.*).

	signed	ratified		
Belgium	June 21, 1922	February 22, 1924	Cmnd. 2069	117 BSP 237
	November 4, 1932	June 18, 1934	Cmnd. 4639	135 BSP 272
Denmark	November 29, 1932	May 12, 1933	Cmnd. 4334	135 BSP 276
France	February 2, 1922	May 2, 1922	Cmnd. 1661	116 BSP 452
	April 15, 1936	April 4, 1940	Cmnd. 6206	141 BSP 296
Germany	March 20, 1928	February 15, 1929	Cmnd. 3286	128 BSP 302
Greece	February 27, 1936	November 16, 1937	Cmnd. 5643	140 BSP 224
Italy	December 17, 1930	June 17, 1932	Cmnd. 4105	132 BSP 292
Netherlands	May 31, 1932	June 29, 1933	Cmnd. 4381	135 BSP 297
	November 17, 1967	December 16, 1969	Cmnd. 4278	—

2. Recognition and enforcement conventions

A2.02   The United Kingdom has entered into bilateral conventions for the recognition and enforcement of judgments with the other Contracting States to the 1968 Convention, with the exception of Denmark, Greece, Ireland

1780

and Luxembourg. The provisions of these conventions continue to apply in respect of matters which fall outside the scope of the 1968 Convention (see paras. 10.04 and 33.02 above). They are given effect by the Foreign Judgments (Reciprocal Enforcement) Act 1933 and the Orders in Council listed below.

	signed	ratified		
Belgium	May 2, 1934	October 26, 1936	Cmnd. 5321	137 BSP 92

[The Reciprocal Enforcement of Foreign Judgments (Belgium) Order in Council 1936, S.R. & O. 1936 No. 1169]

France	January 18, 1934	May 16, 1936	Cmnd. 5235	137 BSP 123

[The Reciprocal Enforcement of Foreign Judgments (France) Order in Council 1936, S.R. & O. 1936 No. 609]

Germany	July 14, 1960	June 14, 1961	Cmnd. 1525

[The Reciprocal Enforcement of Foreign Judgments (Germany) Order 1961 (S.I. 1961 No. 1199)]

Italy   February 7, 1964 (with Amending Protocol, July 14, 1970)   October 15, 1973   Cmnd. 5512

[The Reciprocal Enforcement of Foreign Judgments (Italy) Order 1973 (S.I. 1973 No. 1894)]

Netherlands   November 17, 1967 June 20, 1969   Cmnd. 4148

[The Reciprocal Enforcement of Foreign Judgments (the Netherlands) Order 1969 (S.I. 1969 No. 1063) as amended by (S.I. 1977 No. 2194)]

B. THE HAGUE CONVENTIONS ON SERVICE AND EVIDENCE

1. The Hague Service Convention of November 15, 1965

The Hague Service Convention is discussed at paras. 4.30 *et seq.* The **A2.03** following states have ratified or acceded to this convention.

Antigua and Barbuda	Japan
Barbados	Luxembourg
Belgium	Malawi
Botswana	Netherlands
Canada	Norway
Cyprus	Portugal
Czechoslovakia	Seychelles
Denmark	Sweden
Egypt	Turkey
Finland	
France	United Kingdom
Germany (Federal Republic)	*extended to:*
Greece	Anguilla
Israel	Bermuda
Italy	Cayman Islands

Falkland Islands and	Dependencies
Dependencies	Turks and Caicos Islands
Gibraltar	Virgin Islands
Guernsey	Saint Christopher and Nevis
Hong Kong	
Isle of Man	United States
Jersey	*extended to:*
Montserrat	Guam
Pitcairn	Puerto Rico
Saint Helena and	Virgin Islands

Convention on the Service Abroad of Judicial and Extrajudicial Documents in Civil or Commercial Matters

A2.04 The States signatory to the present Convention,

Desiring to create appropriate means to ensure that judicial and extra-judicial documents to be served abroad shall be brought to the notice of the addressee in sufficient time,

Desiring to improve the organisation of mutual judicial assistance for that purpose by simplifying and expediting the procedure,

Have resolved to conclude a Convention to this effect and have agreed upon the following provisions:

Article 1

The present Convention shall apply in all cases, in civil or commercial matters, where there is occasion to transmit a judicial or extrajudicial document for service abroad.

This Convention shall not apply where the address of the person to be served with the document is not known.

CHAPTER I—JUDICIAL DOCUMENTS

Article 2

A2.05 Each contracting State shall designate a Central Authority which will undertake to receive requests for service coming from other contracting States and to proceed in conformity with the provisions of articles 3 to 6.

Each State shall organise the Central Authority in conformity with its own law.

Article 3

The authority or judicial officer competent under the law of the State in which the documents originate shall forward to the Central Authority of the State addressed a request conforming to the model annexed to the present Convention, without any requirement of legalisation or other equivalent formality.

The document to be served or a copy thereof shall be annexed to the request. The request and the document shall both be furnished in duplicate.

Article 4

If the Central Authority considers that the request does not comply with the provisions of the present Convention it shall promptly inform the applicant and specify its objections to the request.

Article 5

The Central Authority of the State addressed shall itself serve the document or shall arrange to have it served by an appropriate agency, either— **A2.06**

    (*a*) by a method prescribed by its internal law for the service of documents in domestic actions upon persons who are within its territory, or

    (*b*) by a particular method requested by the applicant, unless such a method is incompatible with the law of the State addressed.

Subject to sub-paragraph (*b*) of the first paragraph of this article, the document may always be served by delivery to an addressee who accepts it voluntarily.

If the document is to be served under the first paragraph above, the Central Authority may require the document to be written in, or translated into, the official language or one of the official languages of the State addressed.

That part of the request, in the form attached to the present Convention, which contains a summary of the document to be served, shall be served with the document.

Article 6

The Central Authority of the State addressed or any authority which it may have designated for that purpose, shall complete a certificate in the form of the model annexed to the present Convention.

The certificate shall state that the document has been served and shall include the method, the place and the date of service and the person to whom the document was delivered. If the document has not been served, the certificate shall set out the reasons which have prevented service.

The applicant may require that a certificate not completed by a Central Authority or by a judicial authority shall be countersigned by one of these authorities.

The certificate shall be forwarded directly to the applicant.

Article 7

The standard terms in the model annexed to the present Convention shall in all cases be written either in French or in English. They may also be written in the official language, or in one of the official languages, of the State in which the documents originate.

The corresponding blanks shall be completed either in the language of the State addressed or in French or in English.

Article 8

A2.07 Each contracting State shall be free to effect service of judicial documents upon persons abroad, without application of any compulsion, directly through its diplomatic or consular agents.

Any State may declare that it is opposed to such service within its territory, unless the document is to be served upon a national of the State in which the documents originate.

Article 9

Each contracting State shall be free, in addition, to use consular channels to forward documents, for the purpose of service, to those authorities of another contracting State which are designated by the latter for this purpose.

Each contracting State may, if exceptional circumstances so require, use diplomatic channels for the same purpose.

Article 10

Provided the State of destination does not object, the present Convention shall not interfere with—

(*a*) the freedom to send judicial documents, by postal channels, directly to persons abroad,

(*b*) the freedom of judicial officers, officials or other competent persons of the State of origin to effect service of judicial documents directly through the judicial officers, officials or other competent persons of the State of destination,

(*c*) the freedom of any person interested in a judicial proceeding to effect service of judicial documents directly through the judicial officers, officials or other competent persons of the State of destination.

Article 11

A2.08 The present Convention shall not prevent two or more contracting States from agreeing to permit, for the purpose of service of judicial documents, channels of transmission other than those provided for in the preceding articles and, in particular, direct communication between their respective authorities.

Article 12

The service of judicial documents coming from a contracting State shall not give rise to any payment or reimbursement of taxes or costs for the services rendered by the State addressed.

The applicant shall pay or reimburse the costs occasioned by—

(*a*) the employment of a judicial officer or of a person competent under the law of the State of destination,

(*b*) the use of a particular method of service.

Article 13

Where a request for service complies with the terms of the present Convention, the State addressed may refuse to comply therewith only if it deems that compliance would infringe its sovereignty or security.

It may not refuse to comply solely on the ground that, under its internal law, it claims exclusive jurisdiction over the subject-matter of the action or that its internal law would not permit the action upon which the application is based.

The Central Authority shall, in case of refusal, promptly inform the applicant and State the reasons for the refusal.

Article 14

Difficulties which may arise in connection with the transmission of judicial documents for service shall be settled through diplomatic channels.

Article 15

Where a writ of summons or an equivalent document had to be transmit- **A2.09**
ted abroad for the purpose of service, under the provisions of the present Convention, and the defendant has not appeared, judgment shall not be given until it is established that—

(*a*) the document was served by a method prescribed by the internal law of the State addressed for the service of documents in domestic actions upon persons who are within its territory, or

(*b*) the document was actually delivered to the defendant or to his residence by another method provided for by this Convention,

and that in either of these cases the service or the delivery was effected in sufficient time to enable the defendant to defend.

Each contracting State shall be free to declare that the judge, notwithstanding the provisions of the first paragraph of this article, may give judgment even if no certificate of service or delivery has been received, if all the following conditions are fulfilled–

(*a*) the document was transmitted by one of the methods provided for in this Convention,

(*b*) a period of time of not less than six months, considered adequate by the judge in the particular case, has elapsed since the date of the transmission of the document,

(*c*) no certificate of any kind has been received, even though every reasonable effort has been made to obtain it through the competent authorities of the State addressed.

Notwithstanding the provisions of the preceding paragraphs the judge may order, in case of urgency, any provisional or protective measures.

Article 16

A2.10 When a writ of summons or an equivalent document had to be transmitted abroad for the purpose of service, under the provisions of the present Convention, and a judgment has been entered against a defendant who has not appeared, the judge shall have the power to relieve the defendant from the effects of the expiration of the time for appeal from the judgment if the following conditions are fulfilled—

    (*a*) the defendant, without any fault on his part, did not have knowledge of the document in sufficient time to defend, or knowledge of the judgment in sufficient time to appeal, and

    (*b*) the defendant has disclosed a prima facie defence to the action on the merits.

An application for relief may be filed only within a reasonable time after the defendant has knowledge of the judgment.

Each contracting State may declare that the application will not be entertained if it is filed after the expiration of a time to be stated in the declaration, but which shall in no case be less than one year following the date of the judgment.

This article shall not apply to judgments concerning status or capacity of persons.

CHAPTER II—EXTRAJUDICIAL DOCUMENTS

Article 17

A2.11 Extrajudicial documents emanating from authorities and judicial officers of a contracting State may be transmitted for the purpose of service in another contracting State by the methods and under the provisions of the present Convention.

CHAPTER III—GENERAL CLAUSES

Article 18

A2.12 Each contracting State may designate other authorities in addition to the Central Authority and shall determine the extent of their competence.

The applicant shall, however, in all cases, have the right to address a request directly to the Central Authority.

Federal States shall be free to designate more than one Central Authority.

Article 19

To the extent that the internal law of a contracting State permits methods of transmission, other than those provided for in the preceding articles, of documents coming from abroad, for service within its territory, the present Convention shall not affect such provisions.

Article 20

The present Convention shall not prevent an agreement between any two or more contracting States to dispense with—
    (*a*) the necessity for duplicate copies of transmitted documents as required by the second paragraph of article 3,
    (*b*) the language requirements of the third paragraph of article 5 and article 7,
    (*c*) the provisions of the fourth paragraph of article 5,
    (*d*) the provisions of the second paragraph of article 12.

Article 21

Each contracting State shall, at the time of the deposit of its instrument of ratification or accession, or at a later date, inform the Ministry of Foreign Affairs of the Netherlands of the following—
    (*a*) the designation of authorities, pursuant to articles 2 and 18,
    (*b*) the designation of the authority competent to complete the certificate pursuant to article 6,
    (*c*) the designation of the authority competent to receive documents transmitted by consular channels, pursuant to article 9.
  Each contracting State shall similarly inform the Ministry, where appropriate, of—
    (*a*) opposition to the use of methods of transmission pursuant to articles 8 and 10,
    (*b*) declarations pursuant to the second paragraph of article 15 and the third paragraph of article 16,
    (*c*) all modifications of the above designations, oppositions and declarations.

Article 22

Where Parties to the present Convention are also Parties to one or both of **A2.13** the Conventions on civil procedure signed at The Hague on July 17, 1905, and on March 1, 1954, this Convention shall replace as between them articles 1 to 7 of the earlier Conventions.

Article 23

The present Convention shall not affect the application of article 23 of the Convention on civil procedure signed at The Hague on July 17, 1905, or of article 24 of the Convention on civil procedure signed at The Hague on March 1, 1954.

These articles shall, however, apply only if methods of communication, identical to those provided for in these Conventions, are used.

Article 24

Supplementary agreements between Parties to the Conventions of 1905 and 1954 shall be considered as equally applicable to the present Convention, unless the Parties have otherwise agreed.

Article 25

Without prejudice to the provisions of articles 22 and 24, the present Convention shall not derogate from Conventions containing provisions on the matters governed by this Convention to which the contracting States are, or shall become, Parties.

Article 26

The present Convention shall be open for signature by the States represented at the Tenth Session of the Hague Conference on Private International Law.

It shall be ratified, and the instruments of ratification shall be deposited with the Ministry of Foreign Affairs of the Netherlands.

Article 27

The present Convention shall enter into force on the sixtieth day after deposit of the third instrument of ratification referred to in the second paragraph of article 26.

The Convention shall enter into force for each signatory State which ratifies subsequently on the sixtieth day after the deposit of its instrument of ratification.

Article 28

A2.14 Any State not represented at the Tenth Session of the Hague Conference on Private International Law may accede to the present Convention after it has entered into force in accordance with the first paragraph of article 27. The instrument of accession shall be deposited with the Ministry of Foreign Affairs of the Netherlands.

The Convention shall enter into force for such a State in the absence of any objection from a State, which has ratified the Convention before such deposit, notified to the Ministry of Foreign Affairs of the Netherlands within a period of six months after the date on which the said Ministry has notified it of such accession.

In the absence of any such objection, the Convention shall enter into force for the acceding State on the first day of the month following the expiration of the last of the periods referred to in the preceding paragraph.

1788

Article 29

Any State may, at the time of signature, ratification or accession, declare that the present Convention shall extend to all the territories for the international relations of which it is responsible, or to one or more of them. Such a declaration shall take effect on the date of entry into force of the Convention for the State concerned.

At any time thereafter, such extensions shall be notified to the Ministry of Foreign Affairs of the Netherlands.

The Convention shall enter into force for the territories mentioned in such an extension on the sixtieth day after the notification referred to in the preceding paragraph.

Article 30

The present Convention shall remain in force for five years from the date of its entry into force in accordance with the first paragraph of article 27, even for States which have ratified it or acceded to it subsequently.

If there has been no denunciation, it shall be renewed tacitly every five years.

Any denunciation shall be notified to the Ministry of Foreign Affairs of the Netherlands at least six months before the end of the five year period.

It may be limited to certain of the territories to which the Convention applies.

The denunciation shall have effect only as regards the State which has notified it. The Convention shall remain in force for the other contracting States.

Article 31

The Ministry of Foreign Affairs of the Netherlands shall give notice to the **A2.15** States referred to in article 26, and to the States which have acceded in accordance with article 28, of the following—
- (*a*) the signatures and ratifications referred to in article 26;
- (*b*) the date on which the present Convention enters into force in accordance with the first paragraph of article 27;
- (*c*) the accessions referred to in article 28 and the dates on which they take effect;
- (*d*) the extensions referred to in article 29 and the dates on which they take effect;
- (*e*) the designations, oppositions and declarations referred to in article 21;
- (*f*) the denunciations referred to in the third paragraph of article 30.

In witness whereof the undersigned, being duly authorised thereto, have signed the present Convention.

Done at The Hague, on the fifteenth day of November, 1965, in the English and French languages, both texts being equally authentic, in a single copy which shall be deposited in the archives of the Government of the Netherlands, and of which a certified copy shall be sent, through the diplomatic channel, to each of the States represented at the Tenth Session of the Hague Conference on Private International Law.

ANNEX

A2.16   [The Annex to the Hague Service Convention contains the following forms in English and French, the English version of which are set out in Appendix 4 below:

Request for Service Abroad of Judicial or Extrajudicial Documents: para. A4.5 below;

Certificate (being the reverse of the Request): para. A4.6 below;

Summary of the Document to be Served: para. A4.7 below.]

2. The Hague Evidence Convention of March 18, 1970

A2.17   The Hague Evidence Convention is discussed at paragraphs 8.26 *et seq.* The following states have ratified or acceded to this convention.

Argentina*	United Kingdom
Barbados*	*extended to:*
Cyprus*	Akrotiri and Dhekelia
Czechoslovakia	Anguilla
Denmark	Cayman Islands
Finland	Falkland Islands and
France	Dependencies
Germany (Federal Republic)	Gibraltar
Israel	Guernsey
Italy	Hong Kong
Luxembourg	Isle of Man
Monaco*	Jersey
Netherlands	
extended to:	United States
Aruba	*extended to:*
Norway	Guam
Portugal	Puerto Rico
Singapore*	Virgin Islands
Spain	
Sweden	

* States marked with an asterisk have acceded to the Convention, rather than ratified it. The Convention only applies as between those states and each of the other contracting states if the latter have declared their acceptance of the acceding state's accession (see Art. 39, fourth paragraph). The United Kingdom has declared its acceptance of all the acceding states' accessions, although the acceptance does not apply in every case to the territories to which the convention has been extended by the United Kingdom.

Convention on the taking of evidence abroad in civil or commercial matters

A2.18   The States signatory to the present Convention,

Desiring to facilitate the transmission and execution of Letters of Request and to further the accommodation of the different methods which they use for this purpose,

1790

Desiring to improve mutual judicial co-operation in civil or commercial matters,

Have resolved to conclude a Convention to this effect and have agreed upon the following provisions—

CHAPTER I—LETTERS OF REQUEST

Article 1

In civil or commercial matters a judicial authority of a Contracting State **A2.19** may, in accordance with the provisions of the law of that State, request the competent authority of another Contracting State, by means of a Letter of Request, to obtain evidence, or to perform some other judicial act.

A Letter shall not be used to obtain evidence which is not intended for use in judicial proceedings, commenced or contemplated.

The expression "other judicial act" does not cover the service of judicial documents or the issuance of any process by which judgments or orders are executed or enforced, or orders for provisional or protective measures.

Article 2

A Contracting State shall designate a Central Authority which will undertake to receive Letters of Request coming from a judicial authority of another Contracting State and to transmit them to the authority competent to execute them. Each State shall organise the Central Authority in accordance with its own law.

Letters shall be sent to the Central Authority of the State of execution without being transmitted through any other authority of that State.

Article 3

A Letter of Request shall specify—
- (a) the authority requesting its execution and the authority requested to execute it, if known to the requesting authority;
- (b) the names and addresses of the parties to the proceedings and their representatives, if any;
- (c) the nature of the proceedings for which the evidence is required, giving all necessary information in regard thereto;
- (d) the evidence to be obtained or other judicial act to be performed.

Where appropriate, the Letter shall specify, *inter alia*—
- (e) the names and addresses of the persons to be examined;
- (f) the questions to be put to the persons to be examined or a statement of the subject-matter about which they are to be examined;
- (g) the documents or other property, real or personal, to be inspected;
- (h) any requirement that the evidence is to be given on oath or affirmation, and any special form to be used;
- (i) any special method or procedure to be followed under Article 9.

A Letter may also mention any information necessary for the application of Article 11.

No legalisation or other like formality may be required.

Article 4

A2.20 A Letter of Request shall be in the language of the authority requested to execute it or be accompanied by a translation into that language.

Nevertheless, a Contracting State shall accept a Letter in either English or French, or a translation into one of these languages, unless it has made the reservation authorised by Article 33.

A Contracting State which has more than one official language and cannot, for reasons of internal law, accept Letters in one of these languages for the whole of its territory, shall, by declaration, specify the language in which the Letter or translation thereof shall be expressed for execution in the specified parts of its territory. In case of failure to comply with this declaration, without justifiable excuse, the costs of translation into the required language shall be borne by the State of origin.

A Contracting State may, by declaration, specify the language or languages other than those referred to in the preceding paragraphs, in which a Letter may be sent to its Central Authority.

Any translation accompanying a Letter shall be certified as correct, either by a diplomatic officer or consular agent or by a sworn translator or by any other person so authorised in either State.

Article 5

If the Central Authority considers that the request does not comply with the provisions of the present Convention, it shall promptly inform the authority of the State of origin which transmitted the Letter of Request, specifying the objections to the Letter.

Article 6

If the authority to whom a Letter of Request has been transmitted is not competent to execute it, the Letter shall be sent forthwith to the authority in the same State which is competent to execute it in accordance with the provisions of its own law.

Article 7

A2.21 The requesting authority shall, if it so desires, be informed of the time when, and the place where, the proceedings will take place, in order that the parties concerned, and their representatives, if any, may be present.

This information shall be sent directly to the parties or their representatives when the authority of the State of origin so requests.

Article 8

A Contracting State may declare that members of the judicial personnel of the requesting authority of another Contracting State may be present at the execution of a Letter of Request. Prior authorisation by the competent authority designated by the declaring State may be required.

Article 9

The judicial authority which executes a Letter of Request shall apply its own law as to the methods and procedures to be followed.

However, it will follow a request of the requesting authority that a special method or procedure be followed, unless this is incompatible with the internal law of the State of execution or is impossible of performance by reason of its internal practice and procedure or by reason of practical difficulties.

A Letter of Request shall be executed expeditiously.

Article 10

In executing a Letter of Request the requested authority shall apply the appropriate measures of compulsion in the instances and to the same extent as are provided by its internal law for the execution of orders issued by the authorities of its own country or of requests made by parties in internal proceedings.

Article 11

In the execution of a Letter of Request the person concerned may refuse to give evidence in so far as he has a privilege or duty to refuse to give the evidence—

(*a*) under the law of the State of execution; or

(*b*) under the law of the State of origin, and the privilege or duty has been specified in the Letter, or, at the instance of the requested authority, has been otherwise confirmed to that authority by the requesting authority.

A Contracting State may declare that, in addition, it will respect privileges and duties existing under the law of States other than the State of origin and the State of execution, to the extent specified in that declaration.

Article 12

The execution of a Letter of Request may be refused only to the extent that— **A2.22**

(*a*) in the State of execution the execution of the Letter does not fall within the functions of the judiciary; or

(*b*) the State addressed considers that its sovereignty or security would be prejudiced thereby.

Execution may not be refused solely on the ground that under its internal law the State of execution claims exclusive jurisdiction over the subject-matter of the action or that its internal law would not admit a right of action on it.

Article 13

The documents establishing the execution of the Letter of Request shall be sent by the requested authority to the requesting authority by the same channel which was used by the latter.

In every instance where the Letter is not executed in whole or in part, the requesting authority shall be informed immediately through the same channel and advised of the reasons.

Article 14

The execution of the Letter of Request shall not give rise to any reimbursement of taxes or costs of any nature.

Nevertheless, the State of execution has the right to require the State of origin to reimburse the fees paid to experts and interpreters and the costs occasioned by the use of a special procedure requested by the State of origin under Article 9, paragraph 2.

The requested authority whose law obliges the parties themselves to secure evidence, and which is not able itself to execute the Letter, may, after having obtained the consent of the requesting authority, appoint a suitable person to do so. When seeking this consent the requesting authority shall indicate the approximate costs which would result from this procedure. If the requesting authority gives its consent it shall reimburse any costs incurred; without such consent the requesting authority shall not be liable for the costs.

CHAPTER II—TAKING OF EVIDENCE BY DIPLOMATIC OFFICERS, CONSULAR AGENTS AND COMMISSIONERS

Article 15

A2.23 In civil or commercial matters, a diplomatic officer or consular agent of a Contracting State may, in the territory of another Contracting State and within the area where he exercises his functions, take the evidence without compulsion of nationals of a State which he represents in aid of proceedings commenced in the courts of a State which he represents.

A Contracting State may declare that evidence may be taken by a diplomatic officer or consular agent only if permission to that effect is given upon application made by him or on his behalf to the appropriate authority designated by the declaring State.

Article 16

A diplomatic officer or consular agent of a Contracting State may, in the territory of another Contracting State and within the areas where he exercises his functions, also take the evidence, without compulsion, of nationals of the State in which he exercises his functions or of a third State, in aid of proceedings commenced in the courts of a State which he represents, if—

    (*a*) a competent authority designated by the State in which he exercises his functions has given its permission either generally or in the particular case, and

    (*b*) he complies with the conditions which the competent authority has specified in the permission.

A Contracting State may declare that evidence may be taken under this Article without its prior permission.

Article 17

In civil or commercial matters, a person duly appointed as a commissioner **A2.24** for the purpose may, without compulsion, take evidence in the territory of a Contracting State in aid of proceedings commenced in the courts of another Contracting State, if—

    (*a*) a competent authority designated by the State where the evidence is to be taken has given its permission either generally or in the particular case; and

    (*b*) he complies with the conditions which the competent authority has specified in the permission.

A Contracting State may declare that evidence may be taken under this Article without its prior permission.

Article 18

A Contracting State may declare that a diplomatic officer, consular agent or commissioner authorised to take evidence under Articles 15, 16 or 17, may apply to the competent authority designated by the declaring State for appropriate assistance to obtain the evidence by compulsion. The declaration may contain such conditions as the declaring State may see fit to impose.

If the authority grants the application it shall apply any measures of compulsion which are appropriate and are prescribed by its law for use in internal proceedings.

Article 19

The competent authority, in giving the permission referred to in Articles 15, 16 or 17, or in granting the application referred to in Article 18, may lay down such conditions as it deems fit, *inter alia*, as to the time and place of the taking of the evidence. Similarly it may require that it be given reasonable advance notice of the time, date and place of the taking of the evidence; in such a case a representative of the authority shall be entitled to be present at the taking of the evidence.

Article 20

In the taking of evidence under any Article of this Chapter persons con- **A2.25** cerned may be legally represented.

Article 21

Where a diplomatic officer, consular agent or commissioner is authorised under Articles 15, 16 or 17 to take evidence—

   (*a*) he may take all kinds of evidence which are not incompatible with the law of the State where the evidence is taken or contrary to any permission granted pursuant to the above Articles, and shall have power within such limits to administer an oath or take an affirmation;

   (*b*) a request to a person to appear or to give evidence shall, unless the recipient is a national of the State where the action is pending, be drawn up in the language of the place where the evidence is taken or be accompanied by a translation into such language;

   (*c*) the request shall inform the person that he may be legally represented and, in any State that has not filed a declaration under Article 18, shall also inform him that he is not compelled to appear or to give evidence;

   (*d*) the evidence may be taken in the manner provided by the law applicable to the court in which the action is pending provided that such manner is not forbidden by the law of the State where the evidence is taken;

   (*e*) a person requested to give evidence may invoke the privileges and duties to refuse to give the evidence contained in Article 11.

Article 22

The fact that an attempt to take evidence under the procedure laid down in this Chapter has failed, owing to the refusal of a person to give evidence, shall not prevent an application being subsequently made to take the evidence in accordance with Chapter I.

CHAPTER III—GENERAL CLAUSES

Article 23

A2.26 A Contracting State may at the time of signature, ratification or accession, declare that it will not execute Letters of Request issued for the purpose of obtaining pre-trial discovery of documents as known in Common Law countries.

Article 24

A Contracting State may designate other authorities in addition to the Central Authority and shall determine the extent of their competence. However, Letters of Request may in all cases be sent to the Central Authority.

Federal States shall be free to designate more than one Central Authority.

Article 25

A Contracting State which has more than one legal system may designate the authorities of one of such systems, which shall have exclusive competence to execute Letters of Request pursuant to this Convention.

Article 26

A Contracting State, if required to do so because of constitutional limitations, may request the reimbursement by the State of origin of fees and costs, in connection with the execution of Letters of Request, for the service of process necessary to compel the appearance of a person to give evidence, the costs of attendance of such persons, and the cost of any transcript of the evidence.

Where a State has made a request pursuant to the above paragraph, any other Contracting State may request from that State the reimbursement of similar fees and costs.

Article 27

The provisions of the present Convention shall not prevent a Contracting State from—
(a) declaring that Letters of Request may be transmitted to its judicial authorities through channels other than those provided for in Article 2;
(b) permitting, by internal law or practice, any act provided for in this Convention to be performed upon less restrictive conditions;
(c) permitting, by internal law or practice, methods of taking evidence other than those provided for in this Convention.

Article 28

The present Convention shall not prevent an agreement between any two   **A2.27**
or more Contracting States to derogate from—
(a) the provisions of Article 2 with respect to methods of transmitting Letters of Request;
(b) the provisions of Article 4 with respect to the languages which may be used;
(c) the provisions of Article 8 with respect to the presence of judicial personnel at the execution of Letters;
(d) the provisions of Article 11 with respect to the privileges and duties of witnesses to refuse to give evidence;
(e) the provisions of Article 13 with respect to the methods of returning executed Letters to the requesting authority;
(f) the provisions of Article 14 with respect to fees and costs;
(g) the provisions of Chapter II.

Article 29

Between Parties to the present Convention who are also Parties to one or both of the Conventions on Civil Procedure signed at The Hague on the

17th of July 1905 and the 1st of March 1954, this Convention shall replace Articles 8 to 16 of the earlier Conventions.

Article 30

The present Convention shall not affect the application of Article 23 of the Convention of 1905, or of Article 24 of the Convention of 1954.

Article 31

Supplementary Agreements between Parties to the Conventions of 1905 and 1954 shall be considered as equally applicable to the present Convention unless the Parties have otherwise agreed.

Article 32

Without prejudice to the provisions of Articles 29 and 31, the present Convention shall not derogate from conventions containing provisions on the matters covered by this Convention to which the Contracting States are, or shall become Parties.

Article 33

A State may, at the time of signature, ratification or accession exclude, in whole or in part, the application of the provisions of paragraph 2 of Article 4 and of Chapter II. No other reservation shall be permitted.

Each Contracting State may at any time withdraw a reservation it has made; the reservation shall cease to have effect on the sixtieth day after notification of the withdrawal.

When a State has made a reservation, any other State affected thereby may apply the same rule against the reserving State.

Article 34

A State may at any time withdraw or modify a declaration.

Article 35

A2.28   A Contracting State shall, at the time of the deposit of its instrument of ratification or accession, or at a later date, inform the Ministry of Foreign Affairs of the Netherlands of the designation of authorities, pursuant to Articles 2, 8, 24 and 25.

A Contracting State shall likewise inform the Ministry, where appropriate, of the following—

   (*a*) the designation of the authorities to whom notice must be given, whose permission may be required, and whose assistance may be invoked in the taking of evidence by diplomatic officers and consular agents, pursuant to Articles 15, 16 and 18 respectively;

   (*b*) the designation of the authorities whose permission may be

1798

required in the taking of evidence by commissioners pursuant to Article 17 and of those who may grant the assistance provided for in Article 18;

(c) declarations pursuant to Articles 4, 8, 11, 15, 16, 17, 18, 23 and 27;

(d) any withdrawal or modification of the above designations and declarations;

(e) the withdrawal of any reservation.

Article 36

Any difficulties which may arise between Contracting States in connection with the operation of this Convention shall be settled through diplomatic channels.

Article 37

The present Convention shall be open for signature by the States represented at the Eleventh Session of the Hague Conference on Private International Law.

It shall be ratified, and the instruments of ratification shall be deposited with the Ministry of Foreign Affairs of the Netherlands.

Article 38

The present Convention shall enter into force on the sixtieth day after the deposit of the third instrument of ratification referred to in the second paragraph of Article 37.

The Convention shall enter into force for each signatory State which ratifies subsequently on the sixtieth day after the deposit of its instrument of ratification.

Article 39

Any State not represented at the Eleventh Session of the Hague Conference on Private International Law which is a Member of this Conference or of the United Nations or of a specialised agency of that Organisation, or a Party to the Statute of the International Court of Justice may accede to the present Convention after it has entered into force in accordance with the first paragraph of Article 38.   **A2.29**

The instrument of accession shall be deposited with the Ministry of Foreign Affairs of the Netherlands.

The Convention shall enter into force for a State acceding to it on the sixtieth day after the deposit of its instrument of accession.

The accession will have effect only as regards the relations between the acceding State and such Contracting States as will have declared their acceptance of the accession. Such declaration shall be deposited at the Ministry of Foreign Affairs of the Netherlands; this Ministry shall forward, through diplomatic channels, a certified copy to each of the Contracting States.

The Convention will enter into force as between the acceding State and the State that has declared its acceptance of the accession on the sixtieth day after the deposit of the declaration of acceptance.

Article 40

Any State may, at the time of signature, ratification or accession, declare that the present Convention shall extend to all the territories for the international relations of which it is responsible, or to one or more of them.

Such a declaration shall take effect on the date of entry into force of the Convention for the State concerned.

At any time thereafter, such extensions shall be notified to the Ministry of Foreign Affairs of the Netherlands.

The Convention shall enter into force for the territories mentioned in such an extension on the sixtieth day after the notification indicated in the preceding paragraph.

Article 41

A2.30 The present Convention shall remain in force for five years from the date of its entry into force in accordance with the first paragraph of Article 38, even for States which have ratified it or acceded to it subsequently.

If there has been no denunciation, it shall be renewed tacitly every five years.

Any denunciation shall be notified to the Ministry of Foreign Affairs of the Netherlands at least six months before the end of the five-year period.

It may be limited to certain of the territories to which the Convention applies.

The denunciation shall have effect only as regards the State which has notified it. The Convention shall remain in force for the other Contracting States.

Article 42

The Ministry of Foreign Affairs of the Netherlands shall give notice to the States referred to in Article 37, and to the States which have acceded in accordance with Article 39, of the following—

(a) the signatures and ratifications referred to in Article 37;

(b) the date on which the present Convention enters into force in accordance with the first paragraph of Article 38;

(c) the accessions referred to in Article 39 and the dates on which they take effect;

(d) the extensions referred to in Article 40 and the dates on which they take effect;

(e) the designations, reservations and declarations referred to in Articles 33 and 35;

(f) the denunciations referred to in the third paragraph of Article 41.

In witness whereof the undersigned, being duly authorised thereto, have signed the present Convention.

Done at The Hague, on the eighteenth day of March, 1970, in the English and French languages, both texts being equally authentic, in a single copy which shall be deposited in the archives of the Government of the Netherlands, and of which a certified copy shall be sent, through the diplomatic channel, to each of the States represented at the Eleventh Session of the Hague Conference on Private International Law.

C. MULTILATERAL CONVENTIONS ON SPECIALISED MATTERS

The United Kingdom is a party to numerous international conventions **A2.31** governing specialised matters, many of which contain provisions relating to jurisdiction or the recognition or enforcement of judgments. The 1968 Convention does not affect these provisions: see Article 57, para. 33.06 above. Some of the more important of these conventions are listed below, with their place and date of signing. This list may be compared with the list set out in note 59 to the Schlosser Report, para. A1.569 above.

Those of the Contracting States to the 1968 Convention which have signed definitively, or signed and ratified/approved or accepted each of these conventions (as at April 1987) are indicated by initial letters as follows:

B — Belgium	IRL — Ireland
DK — Denmark	I — Italy
F — France	L — Luxembourg
G — Germany (Federal Republic)	NL — Netherlands
GR — Greece	UK — United Kingdom

Those Conventions marked with an asterisk were not in force as at April 1987.

1. Conventions on carriage by air

International Convention for the Unification of certain Rules relating to **A2.32** International Carriage by Air.
> Warsaw, October 12, 1929, (1933) T.S. No. 11, Cmnd. 4284
> B, DK, F, G, GR, IRL, I, L, NL, UK

Protocol to amend the Convention for the Unification of Certain Rules relating to International Carriage by Air signed at Warsaw on October 12, 1929.
> The Hague, September 28, 1955, (1967) T.S. No. 62, Cmnd. 3356
> B, DK, F, G, GR, IRL, I, L, NL, UK

Convention supplementary to the Warsaw Convention, for the Unification of Certain Rules Relating to International Carriage by Air Performed by a Person other than the Contracting Carrier.
> Guadalajara, September 18, 1961, (1964) T.S. No. 23, Cmnd. 2354
> B, DK, F, G, GR, IRL, I, L, NL, UK

Protocol to amend the Convention for the Unification of Certain Rules relating to International Carriage by Air signed at Warsaw on October 12,

1929, as amended by the Protocol done at the Hague on September 28, 1955.*
   Guatemala City, March 8, 1971, Cmnd. 4691
   I, NL

Additional Protocol No. 1 to amend the Convention for the Unification of Certain Rules relating to International Carriage by Air signed at Warsaw on October 12, 1929.
   Montreal, September 25, 1975, Cmnd. 6480
   DK, F, NL, UK

Additional Protocol No. 2 to amend the Convention for the Unification of Certain Rules relating to International Carriage by Air signed at Warsaw on October 12, 1929, as amended by the Protocol done at the Hague on September 28, 1955.*
   Montreal, September 25, 1975, Cmnd. 6481
   DK, F, NL, UK

Additional Protocol No. 3 to amend the Convention for the Unification of Certain Rules relating to International Carriage by Air signed at Warsaw on October 12, 1929, as amended by the Protocols done at the Hague on September 28, 1955, and at Guatemala City on March 8, 1971.*
   Montreal, September 25, 1975, Cmnd. 6482
   NL, UK

Additional Protocol No. 4 to amend the Convention for the Unification of Certain Rules relating to International Carriage by Air signed at Warsaw on October 12, 1929, as amended by the Protocol done at the Hague on September 28, 1955.*
   Montreal, September 25, 1975, Cmnd. 6483
   NL, UK

2. Conventions on carriage by rail

A2.33   [Earlier conventions on carriage by rail, including those listed at para. A1.569, n. 59, nos. 13 and 18 above, have been superceded by the COTIF (see below), even in respect of Contracting States which have not ratified, accepted or approved COTIF.]

Convention concerning International Carriage by Rail (COTIF).
   Berne, May 9–December 31, 1980, (1987) T.S. No. 1, Cm. 41
   B, DK, F, G, GR, IRL, I, L, NL, UK

3. Conventions on carriage by road

A2.34   Convention on the Contract for the International Carriage of Goods by Road (CMR).
   Geneva, May 19, 1956, (1967) T.S. No. 90, Cmnd. 3455
   B, DK, F, G, GR, I, L, NL, UK

European Agreement concerning the International Carriage of Dangerous Goods by Road (ADR).
   Geneva, September 30, 1957, (1968) T.S. No. 83, Cmnd. 3769
   B, DK, F, G, I, L, NL, UK

Protocol amending Article 14(3) of the European Agreement of September 30, 1957, concerning the International Carriage of Dangerous Goods by Road (ADR).
> New York, August 21, 1975, (1985) T.S. No. 53, Cmnd. 9650
> B, DK, F, G, I, L, NL, UK

4. Conventions on carriage by sea

Athens Convention relating to the Carriage of Passengers and their Luggage by Sea, 1974.
> Athens, December 13, 1974, (1987) T.S. No. 40, Cmnd. 202
> UK [The convention entered into force on April 28, 1987]

5. Conventions on maintenance obligations

Convention on the Recognition and Enforcement of Decisions relating to   **A2.35**
Maintenance Obligations.
> The Hague, October 2, 1973, (1980) T.S. No. 49, Cmnd. 7939
> F, G, I, L, NL, UK

6. Maritime conventions

International Convention on Certain Rules concerning Civil Jurisdiction in Matters of Collision.
> Brussels, May 10, 1952, (1960) T.S. No. 47, Cmnd. 1128
> B, F, G, GR, I, UK

International Convention for the Unification of Certain Rules relating to the Arrest of Sea-going Ships.
> Brussels, May 10, 1952, (1960) T.S. No. 47, Cmnd. 1128
> B, F, G, GR, I, NL, UK

7. Conventions on nuclear energy

Convention on Third Party Liability in the Field of Nuclear Energy.   **A2.36**
> Paris, July 29, 1960, (1968) T.S. No. 69, Cmnd. 3755
> B, DK, F, G, GR, I, NL, UK

Convention Supplementary to the Paris Convention of July 29, 1960, on Third Party Liability in the Field of Nuclear Energy.
> Brussels, January 31, 1963, (1975) T.S. No. 44, Cmnd. 5948
> B, DK, F, G, I, NL, UK

Additional Protocol to the [Paris] Convention on Third Party Liability in the Field of Nuclear Energy.
> Paris, January 28, 1964, (1968) T.S. No. 69, Cmnd. 3755
> B, DK, F, G, GR, I, NL, UK

Additional Protocol to the [Brussels] Convention of January 31, 1963, Supplementary to the Paris Convention of July 29, 1960, on Third Party Liability in the Field of Nuclear Energy.
Paris, January 28, 1964, (1975) T.S. No. 44, Cmnd. 5948
B, DK, F, G, I, NL, UK

Protocol to amend the Convention on Third Party Liability in the Field of Nuclear Energy of July 29, 1960, as amended by the Additional Protocol of January 28, 1964.★
Paris, November 16, 1982, Cmnd. 9028
B, G, I, UK

Protocol to amend the Convention of January 31, 1963, Supplementary to the Paris Convention of July 29, 1960, on Third Party Liability in the Field of Nuclear Energy, as amended by the Additional Protocol of January 28, 1964.★
Paris, November 16, 1982, Cmnd. 9052
B, G, I, UK

8. Conventions on oil pollution

A2.37　International Convention on Civil Liability for Oil Pollution Damage.
Brussels, November 29, 1969, (1975) T.S. No. 106, Cmnd. 6183
B, DK, F, G, GR, I, NL, UK

International Convention for the Establishment of an International Fund for Compensation for Oil Pollution Damage, 1971.
Brussels, December 18, 1971, (1978) T.S. No. 95, Cmnd. 7383
DK, F, G, GR, I, NL, UK

Protocol to the International Convention for the Establishment of an International Fund for Compensation for Oil Pollution Damage, 1971.★
London, November 19, 1976, Cmnd. 7029
DK, F, G, I, NL, UK

Protocol to the International Convention on Civil Liability for Oil Pollution Damage, 1969.
London, November 19, 1976, (1981) T.S. No. 26, Cmnd. 8238
DK, F, G, I, NL, UK

Protocol of 1984 to amend the International Convention for the Establishment of an International Fund for Compensation for Oil Pollution Damage, 1971.★
Adopted, London, May 25, 1984.
Opened for signature December 1, 1984, Cmnd. 9926

Protocol of 1984 to amend the International Convention on Civil Liability for Oil Pollution Damage.★
Adopted, London May 25, 1984
Opened for signature, December 1, 1984, Cmnd. 9927

9. Conventions on navigation of the Rhine

Convention between France, the Grand Duchy of Baden, Bavaria, the   **A2.38**
Grand Duchy of Hesse, the Netherlands and Prussia for the Navigation of
the Rhine.
   Mannheim, October 17, 1868, 59 B.S.P. 470
   B, F, G, NL, UK

Treaty of Peace with Germany, with Protocol.
   Versailles, June 28, 1919 (1919) T.S. No. 4, Cmnd. 153.
   B, F, G, GR, I, UK

Convention drawn up by the Central Commission of the Rhine to replace
certain Articles of the Convention of October 17, 1868, and the Convention of June 4, 1898, regarding Rhine Navigation certificates.
   Strasbourg, December 14, 1922, (1925) T.S. No. 46, Cmnd. 2521
   B, F, G, I, NL, UK

Additional Protocol to the Convention concerning the Rhine of December
14, 1922.
   Strasbourg, December 22, 1923, (1925) T.S. No. 46, Cmnd. 2521
   B, F, G, I, NL, UK

Convention to amend the Revised Convention for Rhine Navigation
signed at Mannheim, on October 17, 1868.
   Strasbourg, November 20, 1963, (1967) T.S. No. 66, Cmnd. 3371
   B, F, G, NL, UK

Rules of Procedure of the Chamber of Appeals of the Central Commission
for Navigation on the Rhine.
   Strasbourg, October 23, 1969, Cmnd. 4746

Additional Protocol to the Convention as amended for the Navigation of
the Rhine signed at Mannheim on October 17, 1868.
   Strasbourg, October 25, 1972, (1975) T.S. No. 86, Cmnd. 6175
   B, F, G, NL, UK

Additional Protocol No. 2 to the Revised Convention for Rhine Navigation of October 17, 1868, as amended on November 20, 1963, with Protocol of Signature.*
   Strasbourg, October 17, 1979, Cmnd. 8309
   B, F, UK

Additional Protocol No. 3 to the Revised Convention for Rhine Navigation signed at Mannheim on October 17, 1868, as amended on November
20, 1963.
   Strasbourg, October 17, 1979, Cmnd. 8719
   B, F, G, NL, UK

D. VIENNA CONVENTION ON THE LAW OF TREATIES (EXTRACT)

The Vienna Convention on the Law of Treaties was signed on May 23,   **A2.39**
1969. It is published in Command Paper, Cmnd. 7964. Articles 31 to 33,
referred to at paragraph 13.30 above, provide as follows:

Article 31

General Rule of Interpretation

1. A treaty shall be interpreted in good faith in accordance with the ordinary meaning to be given to the terms of the treaty in their context and in the light of its object and purpose.

2. The context for the purpose of the interpretation of a treaty shall comprise, in addition to the text, including its preamble and annexes:
   - (a) any agreement relating to the treaty which was made between all the parties in connection with the conclusion of the treaty;
   - (b) any instrument which was made by one or more parties in connection with the conclusion of the treaty and accepted by the other parties as an instrument related to the treaty.

3. There shall be taken into account, together with the context:
   - (a) any subsequent agreement between the parties regarding the interpretation of the treaty or the application of its provisions;
   - (b) any subsequent practice in the application of the treaty which establishes the agreement of the parties regarding its interpretation;
   - (c) any relevant rules of international law applicable in the relations between the parties.

4. A special meaning shall be given to a term if it is established that the parties so intended.

Article 32

Supplementary Means of Interpretation

A2.40   Recourse may be had to supplementary means of interpretation, including the preparatory work of the treaty and the circumstances of its conclusion, in order to confirm the meaning resulting from the application of article 31, or to determine the meaning when the interpretation according to article 31:
   - (a) leaves the meaning ambiguous or obscure; or
   - (b) leads to a result which is manifestly absurd or unreasonable.

Article 33

Interpretation of Treaties Authenticated in Two or More Languages

1. When a treaty has been authenticated in two or more languages, the text is equally authoritative in each language, unless the treaty provides or the parties agree that, in case of divergence, a particular text shall prevail.

2. A version of the treaty in a language other than one of those in which the text was authenticated shall be considered an authentic text only if the treaty so provides or the parties so agree.

3. The terms of a treaty are presumed to have the same meaning in each authentic text.

4. Except where a particular text prevails in accordance with paragraph 1, when a comparison of the authentic texts discloses a difference of meaning which the application of articles 31 and 32 does not remove, the meaning which best reconciles the texts, having regard to the object and purpose of the treaty, shall be adopted.

E. EEC CONVENTION ON CONTRACTUAL OBLIGATIONS (EXTRACTS)

The EEC Convention on the Law Applicable to Contractual Obligations **A2.41** was opened for signature in Rome on June 19, 1980. It is not yet in force. A Protocol for its interpretation by the European Court of Justice was signed at the end of 1988. The Convention is published in (1980) O.J. No. L266. The Official Report on the Convention, by Professors Mario Giuliano and Paul Lagarde is published in (1980) O.J. No. C 282.

Articles 3 to 6 of the Contractual Obligations Convention, referred to at paragraph 17.27, note 13 above, provide as follows:

Article 3

Freedom of Choice

1. A contract shall be governed by the law chosen by the parties. The **A2.42** choice must be expressed or demonstrated with reasonable certainty by the terms of the contract or the circumstances of the case. By their choice the parties can select the law applicable to the whole or a part only of the contract.

2. The parties may at any time agree to subject the contract to a law other than that which previously governed it, whether as a result of an earlier choice under this Article or of other provisions of this Convention. Any variation by the parties of the law to be applied made after the conclusion of the contract shall not prejudice its formal validity under Article 9 or adversely affect the rights of third parties.

3. The fact that the parties have chosen a foreign law, whether or not accompanied by the choice of a foreign tribunal, shall not, where all the other elements relevant to the situation at the time of the choice are connected with one country only, prejudice the application of rules of the law of that country which cannot be derogated from by contract, hereinafter called mandatory rules.

4. The existence and validity of the consent of the parties as to the choice of the applicable law shall be determined in accordance with the provisions of Articles 8, 9 and 11.

Article 4

Applicable Law in the Absence of Choice

1. To the extent that the law applicable to the contract has not been **A2.43** chosen in accordance with Article 3, the contract shall be governed by the law of the country with which it is most closely connected. Nevertheless, a severable part of the contract which has a closer connection with another

country may by way of exception be governed by the law of that other country.

2. Subject to the provisions of paragraph 5 of this Article it shall be presumed that the contract is most closely connected with the country where the party who is to effect the performance which is characteristic of the contract has, at the time of the conclusion of the contract, his habitual residence, or, in the case of a body corporate or unincorporate, its central administration. However, if the contract is entered into in the course of that party's trade or profession, that country shall be the country in which the principal place of business is situated or, where under the terms of the contract the performance is to be effected through a place of business other than the principal place of business, the country in which that other place of business is situated.

3. Notwithstanding the provisions of paragraph 2 of this Article, to the extent that the subject-matter of the contract is a right in immovable property or a right to use immovable property it shall be presumed that the contract is most closely connected with the country where the immovable property is situated.

4. A contract for the carriage of goods shall not be subject to the presumption in paragraph 2. In such a contract if the country in which, at the time the contract is concluded, the carrier has his principal place of business is also the country in which the place of loading or the place of discharge or the principal place of business of the consignor is situated, it shall be presumed that the contract is most closely connected with that country. In applying this paragraph single voyage charter-parties and other contracts the main purpose of which is the carriage of goods shall be treated as contracts for the carriage of goods.

5. Paragraph 2 shall not apply if the characteristic performance cannot be determined, and the presumptions in paragraphs 2, 3 and 4 shall be disregarded if it appears from the circumstances as a whole that the contract is more closely connected with another country.

Article 5

Certain Consumer Contracts

A2.44 1. This Article applies to a contract the subject of which is the supply of goods or services to a person ("the consumer") for a purpose which can be regarded as being outside his trade or profession, or a contract for the provision of credit for that object.

2. Notwithstanding the provisions of Article 3, a choice of law made by the parties shall not have the result of depriving the consumer of the protection afforded to him by the mandatory rules of the law of the country in which he has his habitual residence:

    —if in that country the conclusion of the contract was preceded by a specific invitation addressed to him or by advertising, and he has taken in that country all the steps necessary on his part for the conclusion of the contract, or

    —if the other party or his agent received the consumer's order in that country, or

—if the contract is for the sale of goods and the consumer travelled from that country to another country and there gave his order, provided that the consumer's journey was arranged by the seller for the purpose of inducing the consumer to buy.

3. Notwithstanding the provisions of Article 4, a contract to which this Article applies shall, in the absence of choice in accordance with Article 3, be governed by the law of the country in which the consumer had his habitual residence if it is entered into in the circumstances described in paragraph 2 of this Article.

4. This Article shall not apply to:

    (a) a contract of carriage;

    (b) a contract for the supply of services where the services are to be supplied to the consumer exclusively in a country other than that in which he has his habitual residence.

5. Notwithstanding the provisions of paragraph 4, this Article shall apply to a contract which, for an inclusive price, provides for a combination of travel and accommodation.

Article 6

Individual Employment Contracts

1. Notwithstanding the provisions of Article 3, in a contract of employ- **A2.45** ment a choice of law clause made by the parties shall not have the result of depriving the employee of the protection afforded to him by the mandatory rules of the law which would be applicable under paragraph 2 in the absence of choice.

2. Notwithstanding the provisions of Article 4, a contract of employment shall, in the absence of choice in accordance with Article 3, be governed:

    (a) by the law of the country in which the employee habitually carries out his work in performance of the contract, even if he is temporarily employed in another country; or

    (b) if the employee does not habitually carry out his work in any one country, by the law of the country in which the place of business through which he was engaged is situated;

unless it appears from the circumstances as a whole that the contract is more closely connected with another country, in which case the contract shall be governed by the law of that country.

Article 20 of the Contractual Obligations Convention, referred to at **A2.46** paragraph 33.21 above, provides as follows:

Article 20

Precedence of Community Law

This Convention shall not affect the application of provisions which, in relation to particular matters, lay down choice of law rules relating to contractual obligations and which are or will be contained in Acts of the institutions of the European Communities or in national laws harmonised in implementation of such Acts.

F. THE EEC LEGAL SERVICES DIRECTIVE AND ORDER IN COUNCIL

1. The EEC Legal Services Directive

A2.47   The following is the text of the EEC Legal Services Directive, which regulates the terms on which lawyers qualified in one EEC country may provide legal services in other EEC countries. The Directive is published in the Official Journal of the European Communities, at O.J. 1977, L.78/17. It is given effect in the United Kingdom by the European Communities (Services of Lawyers) Order 1978, which is set out at paragraph A2.51 below.

Council Directive 77/249 of March 22, 1977
To facilitate the Effective Exercise by Lawyers of Freedom to Provide Services

THE COUNCIL OF THE EUROPEAN COMMUNITIES,

Having regard to the Treaty establishing the European Economic Community, and in particular Articles 57 and 66 thereof,

Having regard to the proposal from the Commission,

Having regard to the opinion of the European Parliament,

Having regard to the opinion of the Economic and Social Committee,

Whereas, pursuant to the Treaty, any restriction on the provision of services which is based on nationality or on conditions of residence has been prohibited since the end of the transitional period;

Whereas this Directive deals only with measures to facilitate the effective pursuit of the activities of lawyers by way of provision of services; whereas more detailed measures will be necessary to facilitate the effective exercise of the right of establishment;

Whereas if lawyers are to exercise effectively the freedom to provide services host Member States must recognise as lawyers those persons practising the profession in the various Member States;

Whereas, since this Directive solely concerns provision of services and does not contain provisions on the mutual recognition of diplomas, a person to whom the Directive applies must adopt the professional title used in the Member State in which he is established, hereinafter referred to as 'the Member State from which he comes,'

HAS ADOPTED THIS DIRECTIVE:

Article 1

A2.48   1. This Directive shall apply, within the limits and under the conditions laid down herein, to the activities of lawyers pursued by way of provision of services.

Notwithstanding anything contained in this Directive, Member States may reserve to prescribed categories of lawyers the preparation of formal documents for obtaining title to administer estates of deceased persons, and the drafting of formal documents creating or transferring interests in land.

2. "Lawyer" means any person entitled to pursue his professional activities under one of the following designations:

Belgium:	Avocat—Advocaat
Denmark:	Advokat
Germany:	Rechtsanwalt
France:	Avocat
Ireland:	Barrister
	Solicitor
Italy:	Avvocato
Luxembourg:	Avocat-avoué
Netherlands:	Advocaat
United Kingdom:	Advocate
	Barrister
	Solicitor

Article 2

Each Member State shall recognise as a lawyer for the purpose of pursuing the activities specified in Article 1(1) any person listed in paragraph (2) of that article.

Article 3

A person referred to in Article 1 shall adopt the professional title used in the Member State from which he comes, expressed in the language or one of the languages, of that State, with an indication of the professional organisation by which he is authorised to practise or the court of law before which he is entitled to practise pursuant to the laws of that State.

Article 4

1. Activities relating to the representation of a client in legal proceedings **A2.49** or before public authorities shall be pursued in each host Member State under the conditions laid down for lawyers established in that State, with the exception of any conditions requiring residence, or registration with a professional organisation, in that State.

2. A lawyer pursuing these activities shall observe the rules of professional conduct of the host Member State, without prejudice to his obligations in the Member State from which he comes.

3. When these activities are pursued in the United Kingdom, "rules of professional conduct of the host Member State" means the rules of professional conduct applicable to solicitors, where such activities are not reserved for barristers and advocates. Otherwise the rules of professional conduct applicable to the latter shall apply. However, barristers from Ireland shall always be subject to the rules of professional conduct applicable in the United Kingdom to barristers and advocates.

When these activities are pursued in Ireland, "rules of professional conduct of the host Member State" means, in so far as they govern the oral presentation of a case in court, the rules of professional conduct applicable to barristers. In all other cases, the rules applicable to solicitors shall apply. However, barristers and advocates from the United Kingdom shall always be subject to the rules of professional conduct applicable in Ireland to barristers.

4. A lawyer pursuing activities other than those referred to in paragraph (1) shall remain subject to the conditions and rules of professional conduct of the Member State from which he comes without prejudice to respect for the rules, whatever their source, which govern the profession in the host Member State, especially those concerning the incompatibility of the exercise of the activities of a lawyer with the exercise of other activities in that State, professional secrecy, relations with other lawyers, the prohibition on the same lawyer acting for parties with mutually conflicting interests, and publicity. The latter rules are applicable only if they are capable of being observed by a lawyer who is not established in the host Member State and to the extent to which their observance is objectively justified to ensure, in that State, the proper exercise of a lawyer's activities, the standing of the profession and respect for the rules concerning incompatibility.

Article 5

A2.50 For the pursuit of activities relating to the representation of a client in legal proceedings, a Member State may require lawyers to whom Article 1 applies:
  —to be introduced in accordance with local rules or customs, to the presiding judge and, where appropriate, to the President of the relevant Bar in the host Member State;
  —to work in conjunction with a lawyer who practises before the judicial authority in question and who would, where necessary, be answerable to that authority, or with an "avoué" or "procuratore" practising before it.

Article 6

Any Member State may exclude lawyers who are in the salaried employment of a public or private undertaking from pursuing activities relating to the representation of that undertaking in legal proceedings in so far as lawyers established in that State are not permitted to pursue those activities.

Article 7

1. The competent authority of the host Member State may request the person providing the services to establish his qualifications as a lawyer.

2. In the event of non-compliance with the obligations referred to in Article 4 and in force in the host Member State, the competent authority of the latter shall determine in accordance with its own rules and procedures the consequences of such non-compliance, and to this end may obtain any appropriate professional information concerning the person

providing services. It shall notify the competent authority of the Member State from which the person comes of any decision taken. Such exchanges shall not affect the confidential nature of the information supplied.

Article 8

1. Member States shall bring into force the measures necessary to comply with this Directive within two years of its notification and shall forthwith inform the Commission thereof.

2. Member States shall communicate to the Commission the texts of the main provisions of national law which they adopt in the field covered by this Directive.

Article 9

This Directive is addressed to the Member States.

Done at Brussels, March 22, 1977.

2. The European Communities (Services of Lawyers) Order 1978

The following is the text of the European Communities (Services of **A2.51** Lawyers) Order 1978 (S.I. 1978 No. 1910), which gives effect to the EEC Legal Services Directive, reproduced above.

Citation and Commencement

1. This Order may be cited as the European Communities (Services of Lawyers) Order 1978 and shall come into operation on March 1, 1979.

Interpretation

2. In this Order, unless the context otherwise requires—
"advocate," "barrister" and "solicitor" mean, in relation to any part of the United Kingdom, a person practising in that part as an advocate, barrister or solicitor as the case may be;
"the Directive" means the European Communities Council Directive No. 77/249/EEC to facilitate the effective exercise by lawyers of freedom to provide services (O.J. 1977, L78/17);
"EEC lawyer" means a person entitled to pursue his professional activities under this designation, in Belgium of an avocat—advocaat, in Denmark of an advokat, in Germany of a Rechtsanwalt, in France of an avocat, *in the Hellenic Republic of a δικηγόρος (dikegoros)*, in the Republic of Ireland of a barrister or solicitor, in Italy of an avvocato, in Luxembourg of an avocat-avoué, or in Netherlands of an advocaat;
"member State of origin," in relation to an EEC lawyer, means the Member State or States in which he is established; and
"own professional authority," in relation to an EEC lawyer, means an authority entitled to exercise disciplinary authority over him in his Member State of origin.

3.—(1) The Interpretation Act 1978 shall apply to this Order as it applies to subordinate legislation made after the commencement of that Act.

(2) Unless the context otherwise requires, any reference in this Order to a numbered Article or to the Schedule is a reference to an article of, or the Schedule to, this Order.

Purpose of order

A2.52   4. The provisions of this Order shall have effect for the purpose of enabling an EEC lawyer to pursue his professional activities in any part of the United Kingdom by providing, under the conditions specified in or permitted by the Directive, services otherwise reserved to advocates, barristers or solicitors; and services which may be so provided are hereafter in this Order referred to as services.

Representation in legal proceedings

5. No enactment or rule of law or practice shall prevent an EEC lawyer from providing any service in relation to any proceedings, whether civil or criminal, before any court, tribunal or public authority (including appearing before and addressing the court, tribunal or public authority) by reason only that he is not an advocate, barrister or solicitor; provided that throughout he is instructed with, and acts in conjunction with, an advocate, barrister or solicitor who is entitled to practice before the court, tribunal or public authority concerned and who could properly provide the service in question.

6. Nothing in this Order shall enable an EEC lawyer:
    (a) if he is established in practice as a barrister in the Republic of Ireland, to provide in the course of any proceedings any service which would not properly be provided by a barrister or advocate;
    (b) if he is instructed with and acts in conjunction with an advocate or barrister in any proceedings, to provide in the course of those proceedings, or of any related proceedings, any service which an advocate or barrister could not properly provide;
    (c) if he is instructed with and acts in conjunction with a solicitor in any proceedings, to provide in the course of those proceedings, or of any related proceedings, any service which a solicitor could not properly provide.

7. An EEC lawyer in salaried employment who is instructed with and acts in conjunction with an advocate or barrister in any proceedings may provide a service on behalf of his employer in those proceedings only in so far as an advocate or barrister in such employment could properly do so.

Drawing of documents, etc., not related to legal proceedings

A2.53   8. No enactment or rule of law or practice shall prevent an EEC lawyer from drawing or preparing for remuneration:
    (i) in England, Wales or Northern Ireland, an instrument relating to personal estate, or

(ii) in Scotland, a writ relating to movable property, by reason only that he is not an advocate, barrister or solicitor.

9. Nothing in this Order shall entitle an EEC lawyer to draw or prepare for remuneration any instrument, or in Scotland any writ:
(i) creating or transferring an interest in land; or
(ii) for obtaining title to administer the estate of a deceased person.

Legal aid

10. Services may be provided by an EEC lawyer by way of legal advice and assistance or legal aid under the enactments specified in Part 1 of the Schedule; and references to counsel and solicitors in those and any other enactments relating to legal advice and assistance or legal aid shall be construed accordingly.

Title and description to be used by EEC lawyers

11. In providing any services, an EEC lawyer shall use the professional title and description applicable to him in his Member State of origin, expressed in the language or one of the languages of that State, together with the name of the professional organisation by which he is authorised to practice or the court of law before which he is entitled to practice in that State. **A2.54**

Power to require an EEC lawyer to verify his status

12. A competent authority may at any time request a person seeking to provide any services to verify his status as an EEC lawyer.

13. Where a request has been made under article 12, the person to whom it is made shall not, except to the extent (if any) allowed by the competent authority making the request, be entitled to provide services in the United Kingdom until he has verified his status as an EEC lawyer to the satisfaction of that authority.

14. For the purposes of articles 12 and 13, a competent authority is:
(a) where the services which the person concerned seeks to provide are reserved to advocates or barristers, or in any case where the person concerned claims to be a barrister established in practice in the Republic of Ireland, the Senate of the Inns of Court and the Bar, the Faculty of Advocates, or the Benchers of the Inn of Court of Northern Ireland, according to the part of the United Kingdom concerned; or
(b) where sub-paragraph (a) does not apply, the Law Society, the Law Society of Scotland, or the Incorporated Law Society of Northern Ireland, according to the part of the United Kingdom concerned;
(c) in any case, any court, tribunal or public authority before which the person concerned seeks to provide services.

Professional misconduct

A2.55   15.—(1) A complaint may be made to a disciplinary authority that an EEC lawyer providing any services has failed to observe a condition or rule of professional conduct referred to in Article 4 of the directive and applicable to him.

(2) Where a complaint is made under paragraph (1), the disciplinary authority concerned shall consider and adjudicate upon it in accordance with the same procedure, and subject to the same rights of appeal, as apply in relation to an advocate, barrister or solicitor (as the case may be) over whom that authority has jurisdiction.

(3) For the purpose of this article and article 16, a disciplinary authority is:

> (a) where the services in question are reserved to advocates or barristers, or in any case where the person whose conduct is in question is established in practice as a barrister in the Republic of Ireland, an authority having disciplinary jurisdiction over advocates or barristers (as the case may be) in the part of the United Kingdom concerned;
>
> (b) where sub-paragraph (a) does not apply, an authority having disciplinary jurisdiction over solicitors in the part of the United Kingdom concerned.

16.—(1) Where a disciplinary authority finds that an EEC lawyer against whom a complaint has been made under article 15(1) has committed a breach of a condition or a rule of professional conduct mentioned in that article, that authority:

> (a) shall report that finding to the EEC lawyer's own professional authority; and
>
> (b) may, if it thinks fit, direct him not to provide services in the United Kingdom, except to such extent and under such conditions (if any) as the disciplinary authority may specify in the direction.

(2) A disciplinary authority may at any time, if it thinks fit, vary, cancel or suspend the operation of a direction given by it under paragraph (1)(b).

17. An EEC lawyer in respect of whom a direction is made under article 16(1)(b) shall not be entitled to provide services in the United Kingdom except as allowed by the direction.

Modification of enactments

A2.56   18.—(1) Without prejudice to the generality of articles 5 and 8, the enactments specified in Part 2 of the Schedule (being enactments which reserve the provision of certain services to advocates, barristers, solicitors and other qualified persons) shall be construed subject to those articles.

(2) Notwithstanding anything in the Solicitors (Scotland) Act 1933 (c. 21), the Solicitors Act 1974 (c. 47) or the Solicitors (Northern Ireland) Order 1976 (S.I. 1976 No. 582), references to unqualified persons, however expressed, in the enactments specified in Part 3 of the Schedule (being enactments relating to unqualified persons acting as solicitors) shall

not include an EEC lawyer providing services within the meaning of this Order.

(3) Nothing in section 42 of the Solicitors (Scotland) Act 1933 shall prevent an EEC lawyer from recovering any remuneration or expenses to which that section applies by reason only that he is not qualified as a solicitor.

SCHEDULE

PART 1   Article 10   **A2.57**

ENACTMENTS RELATING TO THE PROVISION OF LEGAL ADVICE AND ASSISTANCE AND LEGAL AID

Legal Aid, Advice and Assistance (Northern Ireland) Order 1981

Legal Aid (Scotland) Act 1967 (c. 43).
Legal Advice and Assistance Act 1972 (c. 50).
Legal Aid Act 1974 (c. 4).
Legal Aid, Advice and Assistance (Northern Ireland) Order 1977 (S.I. No. 1252 (N.I. 19)).

PART 2   Article 18(1)

ENACTMENTS RESERVING THE PROVISION OF SERVICES TO ADVOCATES, BARRISTERS, SOLICITORS, ETC.

Solicitors (Scotland) Act 1933 (c. 21), s.39.
Magistrates' Courts Act 1952 (c. 55), s.99.
Magistrates' Courts Act (Northern Ireland) 1964 (c. 21) (N.I.)), s.165(1).
County Courts Act 1959 (c. 22), s.89.
County Courts Act (Northern Ireland) 1959 (c. 25 (N.I.)), s.139.
Solicitors Act 1974 (c. 47), ss.20, 22.
Solicitors (Northern Ireland) Order 1976 (S.I. No. 582 (N.I. 12)), arts. 19, 23.

PART 3   Article 18(2)

ENACTMENTS RELATING TO UNQUALIFIED PERSONS ACTING AS SOLICITORS

Solicitors (Scotland) Act 1933 (c. 21), ss.37, 38.
Solicitors Act 1974 (c. 47), ss.25(1), 29(1).
Solicitors (Northern Ireland) Order 1976 (S.I. No. 582 (N.I. 12)), arts.25(1), 27.

Notes:

1. The words in italics in the definition of "EEC lawyer" in paragraph 2   **A2.58**
of the Order were added by the European Communities (Services of Lawyers) (Amendment) Order 1980 (S.I. 1980 No. 1964).

2. The Solicitors (Scotland) Act 1933, the Solicitors Act 1974 and the Solicitors (Northern Ireland) Order 1976, each referred to in paragraph 18 of the Order, have been repealed or amended, but without consequential amendments having been made to this Order.

3. Similarly, a number of the enactments mentioned in the Schedule have since been amended or repealed, but consequential amendments have not always been made to this Order.

4. The reference in the Schedule to the Legal Aid, Advice and Assistance (Northern Ireland) Order 1981 (S.I. 1981 No. 228) is in italics, because that Order substituted those words for a reference to the Legal Aid and Advice Act (Northern Ireland) 1965 (c. 8).

APPENDIX 3

THE 1968 CONVENTION, 1982 ACT AND RELATED TEXTS

1. The 1968 Convention (as amended by the 1978 and 1982 Accession Conventions) A3.01

Convention
on jurisdiction and the enforcement of judgments in civil and commercial matters

Preamble

The High Contracting Parties to the Treaty establishing the European Economic Community,

Desiring to implement the provisions of Article 220 of that Treaty by virtue of which they undertook to secure the simplification of formalities governing the reciprocal recognition and enforcement of judgments of courts or tribunals;

Anxious to strengthen in the Community the legal protection of persons therein established;

Considering that it is necessary for this purpose to determine the international jurisdiction of their courts, to facilitate recognition and to introduce an expeditious procedure for securing the enforcement of judgments, authentic instruments and court settlements;

Have decided to conclude this Convention and to this end have designated as their Plenipotentiaries:

(Designations of Plenipotentiaries of the original six Contracting States)

Have agreed as follows:

TITLE I

SCOPE

ARTICLE 1

A3.02 This Convention shall apply in civil and commercial matters whatever the nature of the court or tribunal. It shall not extend, in particular, to revenue, customs or administrative matters.

The Convention shall not apply to:

1. the status or legal capacity of natural persons, rights in property arising out of a matrimonial relationship, wills and succession;
2. bankruptcy, proceedings relating to the winding-up of insolvent companies or other legal persons, judicial arrangements, compositions and analogous proceedings;
3. social security;
4. arbitration.

TITLE II

JURISDICTION

Section 1

General Provisions

ARTICLE 2

A3.03 Subject to the provisions of this Convention, persons domiciled in a Contracting State shall, whatever their nationality, be sued in the courts of that State.

Persons who are not nationals of the State in which they are domiciled shall be governed by the rules of jurisdiction applicable to nationals of that State.

ARTICLE 3

Persons domiciled in a Contracting State may be sued in the courts of another Contracting State only by virtue of the rules set out in Sections 2 to 6 of this Title.

In particular the following provisions shall not be applicable as against them:

– in Belgium:	Article 15 of the civil code (*Code civil – Burgerlijk Wetboek*) and Article 638 of the judicial code (*Code judiciaire – Gerechtelijk Wetboek*),
– in Denmark:	Article 248(2) of the law on civil procedure (*Lov om rettens pleje*) and Chapter 3. Article 3 of the Greenland law on civil procedure (*Lov for Grønland om rettens pleje*),
– in the Federal Republic of Germany:	Article 23 of the code of civil procedure (*Zivilprozessordnung*),
– in Greece:	Article 40 of the code of civil procedure (Κώδικας Πολιτιμῆς Δικην μίας),[1]
– in France:	Articles 14 and 15 of the civil code (*Code civil*),
– in Ireland:	the rules which enable jurisdiction to be founded on the document instituting the proceedings having been served on the defendant during his temporary presence in Ireland,
– in Italy:	Articles 2 and 4, Nos 1 and 2 of the code of civil procedure (*Codice di procedura civile*),
– in Luxembourg:	Articles 14 and 15 of the civil code (*Code civil*),
– in the Netherlands:	Articles 126(3) and 127 of the code of civil procedure (*Wetboek van Burgerlijke Rechtsvordering*),
– in the United Kingdom:	the rules which enable jurisdiction to be founded on:

(a) the document instituting the proceedings having been served on the defendant during his temporary presence in the United Kingdom: or

(b) the presence within the United Kingdom of property belonging to the defendant: or

(c) the seizure by the plaintiff of property situated in the United Kingdom.

ARTICLE 4

If the defendant is not domiciled in a Contracting State, the jurisdiction of the courts of each Contracting State shall, subject to the provisions of Article 16, be determined by the law of that State.

As against such a defendant, any person domiciled in a Contracting State may, whatever his nationality, avail himself in that State of the rules of jurisdiction there in force, and in particular those specified in the

---

[1] See para. 16.09 above, n. †.

second paragraph of Article 3, in the same way as the nationals of that State.

Section 2

Special jurisdiction

ARTICLE 5

A3.04   A person domiciled in a Contracting State may, in another Contracting State, be sued:
  (1) in matters relating to a contract, in the courts for the place of performance of the obligation in question;
  (2) in matters relating to maintenance, in the courts for the place where the maintenance creditor is domiciled or habitually resident or, if the matter is ancillary to proceedings concerning the status of a person, in the court which, according to its own law, has jurisdiction to entertain those proceedings, unless that jurisdiction is based solely on the nationality of one of the parties;
  (3) in matters relating to tort, delict or quasi-delict, in the courts for the place where the harmful event occurred;
  (4) as regards a civil claim for damages or restitution which is based on an act giving rise to criminal proceedings, in the court seised of those proceedings, to the extent that that court has jurisdiction under its own law to entertain civil proceedings;
  (5) as regards a dispute arising out of the operations of a branch, agency or another establishment, in the courts for the place in which the branch, agency or other establishment is situated;
  (6) as settlor, trustee or beneficiary of a trust created by the operation of a statute, or by a written instrument, or created orally and evidenced in writing, in the courts of the Contracting State in which the trust is domiciled;
  (7) as regards a dispute concerning the payment of remuneration claimed in respect of the salvage of a cargo or freight, in the court under the authority of which the cargo or freight in question:
   (a) has been arrested to secure such payment, or
   (b) could have been so arrested, but bail or other security has been given;
       provided that this provision shall apply only if it is claimed that the defendant has an interest in the cargo or freight or had such an interest at the time of salvage.

ARTICLE 6

A3.05   A person domiciled in a Contracting State may also be sued:
  (1) where he is one of a number of defendants, in the courts for the place where any one of them is domiciled;
  (2) as a third party in an action on a warranty or guarantee or in any other third-party proceedings, in the court seised of the original proceedings, unless these were instituted solely with the object

of removing him from the jurisdiction of the court which would be competent in his case;

(3) a counterclaim arising from the same contract or facts on which the original claim was based, in the court in which the original claim is pending.

ARTICLE 6A

Where by virtue of this Convention a court of a Contracting State has jurisdiction in actions relating to liability arising from the use or operation of a ship, that court, or any other court substituted for this purpose by the internal law of that State, shall also have jurisdiction over claims for limitation of such liability.

Section 3

Jurisdiction in matters relating to insurance

ARTICLE 7

In matters relating to insurance, jurisdiction shall be determined by this **A3.06** section, without prejudice to the provisions of Articles 4 and 5(5).

ARTICLE 8

An insurer domiciled in a Contracting State may be sued:

(1) in the courts of the State where he is domiciled, or

(2) in another Contracting State, in the courts for the place where the policy-holder is domiciled, or

(3) if he is a co-insurer, in the courts of a Contracting State in which proceedings are brought against the leading insurer.

An insurer who is not domiciled in a Contracting State but has a branch, agency or other establishment in one of the Contracting States shall, in disputes arising out of the operations of the branch, agency or establishment, be deemed to be domiciled in that State.

ARTICLE 9

In respect of liability insurance or insurance of immovable property, the insurer may in addition be sued in the courts for the place where the harmful event occurred. The same applies if movable and immovable property are covered by the same insurance policy and both are adversely affected by the same contingency.

ARTICLE 10

In respect of liability insurance, the insurer may also, if the law of the court permits it, be joined in proceedings which the injured party has brought against the insured.

The provisions of Articles 7, 8 and 9 shall apply to actions brought by the injured party directly against the insurer, where such direct actions are permitted.

If the law governing such direct actions provides that the policy-holder or the insured may be joined as a party to the action, the same court shall have jurisdiction over them.

ARTICLE 11

Without prejudice to the provisions of the third paragraph of Article 10, an insurer may bring proceedings only in the courts of the Contracting State in which the defendant is domiciled, irrespective of whether he is the policy-holder, the insured or a beneficiary.

The provisions of this Section shall not affect the right to bring a counterclaim in the court in which, in accordance with this Section, the original claim is pending.

ARTICLE 12

A3.07   The provisions of this Section may be departed from only by an agreement on jurisdiction:

(1) which is entered into after the dispute has arisen, or

(2) which allows the policy-holder, the insured or a beneficiary to bring proceedings in courts other than those indicated in this Section, or

(3) which is concluded between a policy-holder and an insurer, both of whom are at the time of the conclusion of the contract domiciled or habitually resident in the same Contracting State, and which has the effect of conferring jurisdiction on the courts of that State even if the harmful event were to occur abroad, provided that such an agreement is not contrary to the law of that State, or

(4) which is concluded with a policy-holder who is not domiciled in a Contracting State, except in so far as the insurance is compulsory or relates to immovable property in a Contracting State, or

(5) which relates to a contract of insurance in so far as it covers one or more of the risks set out in Article 12A.

ARTICLE 12A

The following are the risks referred to in Article 12(5):

(1) Any loss of or damage to

(a) sea-going ships, installations situated off-shore or on the high seas, or aircraft, arising from perils which relate to their use for commercial purposes,

(b) goods in transit other than passengers' baggage where the transit consists of or includes carriage by such ships or aircraft;

(2) Any liability, other than for bodily injury to passengers or loss of or damage to their baggage,

    (a) arising out of the use or operation of ships, installations or aircraft as referred to in (1)(a) above in so far as the law of the Contracting State in which such aircraft are registered does not prohibit agreements on jurisdiction regarding insurance of such risks,

    (b) for loss or damage caused by goods in transit as described in (1)(b) above;

(3) Any financial loss connected with the use or operation of ships, installations or aircraft as referred to in (1)(a) above, in particular loss of freight or charter-hire;

(4) Any risk or interest connected with any of those referred to in (1) to (3) above.

Section 4

Jurisdiction over consumer contracts

ARTICLE 13

In proceedings concerning a contract concluded by a person for a pur- **A3.08** pose which can be regarded as being outside his trade or profession, hereinafter called "the consumer," jurisdiction shall be determined by this Section, without prejudice to the provisions of Articles 4 and 5(5), if it is:

(1) a contract for the sale of goods on instalment credit terms, or

(2) a contract for a loan repayable by instalments, or for any other form of credit, made to finance the sale of goods, or

(3) any other contract for the supply of goods or a contract for the supply of services, and

    (a) in the State of the consumer's domicile the conclusion of the contract was preceded by a specific invitation addressed to him or by advertising, and

    (b) the consumer took in that State the steps necessary for the conclusion of the contract.

Where a consumer enters into a contract with a party who is not domiciled in a Contracting State but has a branch, agency or other establishment in one of the Contracting States, that party shall, in disputes arising out of the operations of the branch, agency or establishment, be deemed to be domiciled in that State.

This Section shall not apply to contracts of transport.

ARTICLE 14

A consumer may bring proceedings against the other party to a contract either in the courts of the Contracting State in which that party is domiciled or in the courts of the Contracting State in which he is himself domiciled.

Proceedings may be brought against a consumer by the other party to the contract only in the courts of the Contracting State in which the consumer is domiciled.

These provisions shall not affect the right to bring a counterclaim in the court in which, in accordance with this Section, the original claim is pending.

ARTICLE 15

The provisions of this Section may be departed from only by an agreement:

    (1) which is entered into after the dispute has arisen, or

    (2) which allows the consumer to bring proceedings in courts other than those indicated in this Section, or

    (3) which is entered into by the consumer and the other party to the contract, both of whom are at the time of the conclusion of the contract domiciled or habitually resident in the same Contracting State, and which confers jurisdiction on the courts of that State, provided that such an agreement is not contrary to the law of that State.

Section 5

Exclusive jurisdiction

ARTICLE 16

A3.09   The following courts shall have exclusive jurisdiction, regardless of domicile:

    (1) in proceedings which have as their object rights *in rem* in, or tenancies of, immovable property, the courts of the Contracting State in which the property is situated;

    (2) in proceedings which have as their object the validity of the constitution, the nullity or the dissolution of companies or other legal persons or associations of natural or legal persons, or the decisions of their organs, the courts of the Contracting State in which the company, legal person or association has its seat;

    (3) in proceedings which have as their object the validity of entries in public registers, the courts of the Contracting State in which the register is kept;

    (4) in proceedings concerned with the registration or validity of patents, trade marks, designs, or other similar rights required to be deposited or registered, the courts of the Contracting State in which the deposit or registration has been applied for, has taken place or is under the terms of an international convention deemed to have taken place;

    (5) in proceedings concerned with the enforcement of judgments, the courts of the Contracting State in which the judgment has been or is to be enforced.

Section 6

Prorogation of jurisdiction

ARTICLE 17

If the parties, one or more of whom is domiciled in a Contracting State, **A3.10** have agreed that a court or the courts of a Contracting State are to have jurisdiction to settle any disputes which have arisen or which may arise in connection with a particular legal relationship, that court or those courts shall have exclusive jurisdiction. Such an agreement conferring jurisdiction shall either be in writing or evidenced in writing or, in international trade or commerce, in a form which accords with practices in that trade or commerce of which the parties are or ought to have been aware. Where such an agreement is concluded by parties, none of whom is domiciled in a Contracting State, the courts of other Contracting States shall have no jurisdiction over their dispute unless the court or courts chosen have declined jurisdiction.

The court or courts of a Contracting State on which a trust instrument has conferred jurisdiction shall have exclusive jurisdiction in any proceedings brought against a settlor, trustee or beneficiary, if relations between these persons or their rights or obligations under the trust are involved.

Agreements or provisions of a trust instrument conferring jurisdiction shall have no legal force if they are contrary to the provisions of Article 12 or 15, or if the courts whose jurisdiction they purport to exclude have exclusive jurisdiction by virtue of Article 16.

If an agreement conferring jurisdiction was concluded for the benefit of only one of the parties, that party shall retain the right to bring proceedings in any other court which has jurisdiction by virtue of this Convention.

ARTICLE 18

Apart from jurisdiction derived from other provisions of this Convention, a court of a Contracting State before whom a defendant enters an appearance shall have jurisdiction. This rule shall not apply where appearance was entered solely to contest the jurisdiction, or where another court has exclusive jurisdiction by virtue of Article 16.

Section 7

Examination as to jurisdiction and admissibility

ARTICLE 19

Where a court of a Contracting State is seised of a claim which is princi- **A3.11** pally concerned with a matter over which the courts of another Contracting State have exclusive jurisdiction by virtue of Article 16, it shall declare of its own motion that it has no jurisdiction.

ARTICLE 20

Where a defendant domiciled in one Contracting State is sued in a court of another Contracting State and does not enter an appearance, the court shall declare of its own motion that it has no jurisdiction unless its jurisdiction is derived from the provisions of this Convention.

The court shall stay the proceedings so long as it is not shown that the defendant has been able to receive the document instituting the proceedings or an equivalent document in sufficient time to enable him to arrange for his defence, or that all necessary steps have been taken to this end.

The provisions of the foregoing paragraph shall be replaced by those of Article 15 of the Hague Convention of 15th November 1965 on the service abroad of judicial and extrajudicial documents in civil or commercial matters, if the document instituting the proceedings or notice thereof had to be transmitted abroad, in accordance with that Convention.

Section 8

Lis pendens—related actions

ARTICLE 21

A3.12   Where proceedings involving the same cause of action and between the same parties are brought in the courts of different Contracting States, any court other than the court first seised shall of its own motion decline jurisdiction in favour of that court.

A court which would be required to decline jurisdiction may stay its proceedings if the jurisdiction of the other court is contested.

ARTICLE 22

Where related actions are brought in the courts of different Contracting States, any court other than the court first seised may, while the actions are pending at first instance, stay its proceedings.

A court other than the court first seised may also, on the application of one of the parties, decline jurisdiction if the law of that court permits the consolidation of related actions and the court first seised has jurisdiction over both actions.

For the purposes of this Article, actions are deemed to be related where they are so closely connected that it is expedient to hear and determine them together to avoid the risk of irrecocilable judgments resulting from separate proceedings.

ARTICLE 23

Where actions come within the exclusive jurisdiction of several courts, any court other than the court first seised shall decline jurisdiction in favour of that court.

Section 9

Provisional, including protective, measures

ARTICLE 24

Application may be made to the courts of a Contracting State for such **A3.13** provisional, including protective, measures as may be available under the law of that State, even if, under this Convention, the courts of another Contracting State have jurisdiction as to the substance of the matter.

TITLE III

RECOGNITION AND ENFORCEMENT

ARTICLE 25

For the purposes of this Convention, "judgment" means any judgment **A3.14** given by a court or tribunal of a Contracting State, whatever the judgment may be called, including a decree, order, decision or writ of execution, as well as the determination of costs or expenses by an officer of the court.

Section 1

Recognition

ARTICLE 26

A judgment given in a Contracting State shall be recognised in the other Contracting States without any special procedure being required.

Any interested party who raises the recognition of a judgment as the principal issue in a dispute may, in accordance with the procedures provided for in Sections 2 and 3 of this Title, apply for a decision that the judgment be recognised.

If the outcome of proceedings in a court of a Contracting State depends on the determination of an incidental question of recognition that court shall have jurisdiction over that question.

ARTICLE 27

A judgment shall not be recognised;
  (1) if such recognition is contrary to public policy in the State in which recognition is sought;
  (2) where it was given in default of appearance, if the defendant was not duly served with the document which instituted the proceedings or with an equivalent document in sufficient time to enable him to arrange for his defence;
  (3) if the judgment is irreconcilable with a judgment given in a dispute between the same parties in the State in which recognition is sought;
  (4) if the court of the State in which the judgment was given, in

order to arrive at its judgment, has decided a preliminary question concerning the status or legal capacity of natural persons, rights in property arising out of a matrimonial relationship, wills or succession in a way that conflicts with a rule of the private international law of the State in which the recognition is sought, unless the same result would have been reached by the application of the rules of private international law of that State;

(5) if the judgment is irreconcilable with an earlier judgment given in a non-Contracting State involving the same cause of action and between the same parties, provided that this latter judgment fulfils the conditions necessary for its recognition in the State addressed.

ARTICLE 28

Moreover, a judgment shall not be recognised if it conflicts with the provisions of Section 3, 4 or 5 of Title II, or in a case provided for in Article 59.

In its examination of the grounds of jurisdiction referred to in the foregoing paragraph, the court or authority applied to shall be bound by the findings of fact on which the court of the State in which the judgment was given based its jurisdiction.

Subject to the provisions of the first paragraph, the jurisdiction of the court of the State in which the judgment was given may not be reviewed; the test of public policy referred to in Article 27(1) may not be applied to the rules relating to jurisdiction.

ARTICLE 29

In no circumstances may a foreign judgment be reviewed as to its substance.

ARTICLE 30

A court of a Contracting State in which recognition is sought of a judgment given in another Contracting State may stay the proceedings if an ordinary appeal against the judgment has been lodged.

A court of a Contracting State in which recognition is sought of a judgment given in Ireland or the United Kingdom may stay the proceedings if enforcement is suspended in the State in which the judgment was given by reason of an appeal.

Section 2

Enforcement

ARTICLE 31

A3.15 A judgment given in a Contracting State and enforceable in that State shall be enforced in another Contracting State when, on the application of any interested party, the order for its enforcement has been issued there.

However, in the United Kingdom, such a judgment shall be enforced in England and Wales, in Scotland, or in Northern Ireland when, on the application of any interested party, it has been registered for enforcement in that part of the United Kingdom.

ARTICLE 32

The application shall be submitted:
- —in Belgium, to the *tribunal de première instance* or *rechtbank van eerste aanleg*,
- —in Denmark, to the *underret*,
- —in the Federal Republic of Germany, to the presiding judge of a chamber of the *Landgericht*,
- —in Greece, to the μονομελέςπρωτοδικεῖο,[2]
- —in France, to the presiding judge of the *tribunal de grande instance*,
- —in Ireland, to the High Court,
- —in Italy, to the *corte d'appello*,
- —in Luxebourg, to the presiding judge of the *tribunal d'arrondisse-ment*,
- —in the Netherlands, to the presiding judge of the *arrondissements-rechtbank*,
- —in the United Kingdom:
  - (1) in England and Wales, to the High Court of Justice, or in the case of a maintenance judgment to the Magistrates' Court on transmission by the Secretary of State;
  - (2) in Scotland, to the Court of Session, or in the case of a maintenance judgment to the Sheriff Court on transmission by the Secretary of State;
  - (3) in Northern Ireland, to the High Court of Justice, or in the case of a maintenance judgment to the Magistrates' Court on transmission by the Secretary of State.

The jurisdiction of local courts shall be determined by reference to the place of domicile of the party against whom enforcement is sought. If he is not domiciled in the State in which enforcement is sought, it shall be determined by reference to the place of enforcement.

ARTICLE 33

The procedure for making the application shall be governed by the law of the State in which enforcement is sought.

The applicant must give an address for service of process within the area of jurisdiction of the court applied to. However, if the law of the State in which enforcement is sought does not provide for the furnishing of such an address, the applicant shall appoint a representative *ad litem*.

The documents referred to in Articles 46 and 47 shall be attached to the application.

---

[2] See para. 28.09 above, n. †.

ARTICLE 34

The court applied to shall give its decision without delay; the party against whom enforcement is sought shall not at this stage of the proceedings be entitled to make any submissions on the application.

The application may be refused only for one of the reasons specified in Articles 27 and 28.

Under no circumstances may the foreign judgment be reviewed as to its substance.

ARTICLE 35

The appropriate officer of the court shall without delay bring the decision given on the application to the notice of the applicant in accordance with the procedure laid down by the law of the State in which enforcement is sought.

ARTICLE 36

A3.16   If enforcement is authorised, the party against whom enforcement is sought may appeal against the decision within one month of service thereof.

If that party is domiciled in a Contracting State other than that in which the decision authorising enforcement was given, the time for appealing shall be two months and shall run from the date of service, either on him in person or at his residence. No extension of time may be granted on account of distance.

ARTICLE 37

An appeal against the decision authorising enforcement shall be lodged in accordance with the rules governing procedure in contentious matters:
—in Belgium, with the *tribunal de première instance* or *rechtbank van eerste aanleg*,
—in Denmark, with the *landsret*,
—in the Federal Republic of Germany, with the *Oberlandesgericht*,
—in Greece, with the $\varepsilon'\varphi\varepsilon\tau\varepsilon\tilde{\iota}o$,[3]
—in France, with the *cour d'appel*,
—in Ireland, with the High Court,
—in Italy, with the *corte d'appello*,
—in Luxembourg, with the *Cour supérieure de justice* sitting as a court of civil appeal,
—in the Netherlands, with the *arrondissementsrechtbank*,
—in the United Kingdom;
　(1) in England and Wales, with the High Court of Justice, or in the case of a maintenance judgment with the Magistrates' Court;

---

[3] See para. 28.38 above, n. †.

(2) in Scotland, with the Court of Session, or in the case of a maintenance judgment with the Sheriff Court;

(3) in Northern Ireland, with the High Court of Justice, or in the case of a maintenance judgment with the Magistrates' Court.

The judgment given on the appeal may be contested only:

—in Belgium, Greece,[3] France, Italy, Luxembourg and the Netherlands, by an appeal in cassation,

—in Denmark, by an appeal to the højesteret, with the leave of the Minister of Justice,

—in the Federal Republic of Germany, by a Rechtsbeschwerde,

—in Ireland, by an appeal on a point of law to the Supreme Court,

—in the United Kingdom, by a single further appeal on a point of law.

ARTICLE 38

The court with which the appeal under the first paragraph of Article 37 is lodged may, on the application of the appellant, stay the proceedings if an ordinary appeal has been lodged against the judgment in the State in which that judgment was given or if the time for such an appeal has not yet expired; in the latter case, the court may specify the time within which such an appeal is to be lodged.

Where the judgment was given in Ireland or the United Kingdom, any form of appeal available in the State in which it was given shall be treated as an ordinary appeal for the purposes of the first paragraph.

The court may also make enforcement conditional on the provision of such security as it shall determine.

ARTICLE 39

During the time specified for an appeal pursuant to Article 36 and until any such appeal has been determined, no measures of enforcement may be taken other than protective measures taken against the property of the party against whom enforcement is sought.

The decision authorising enforcement shall carry with it the power to proceed to any such protective measures.

ARTICLE 40

If the application for enforcement is refused, the applicant may appeal: **A3.17**
    —in Belgium, to the *cour d'appel* or *hof van beroep*,
    —in Denmark, to the *landsret*,
    —in the Federal Republic of Germany, to the *Oberlandesgericht*,
    —in Greece, to the ε'φετεĩο,[4]
    —in France, to the *cour d'appel*,
    —in Ireland, to the High Court,

---

[4] See para. 28.63 above, n. †.

—in Italy, to the *corte d'appello*,
—in Luxembourg, to the *Cour supèrieure de justice* sitting as a court of civil appeal,
—in the Netherlands, to the *gerechtshof*,
—in the United Kingdom:
  (1) in England and Wales, to the High Court of Justice, or in the case of a maintenance judgment to the Magistrates' Court;
  (2) in Scotland, to the Court of Session, or in the case of a maintenance judgment to the Sheriff Court;
  (3) in Northern Ireland, to the High Court of Justice, or in the case of a maintenance judgment to the Magistrates' Court.

The party against whom enforcement is sought shall be summoned to appear before the appellate court. If he fails to appear, the provisions of the second and third paragraphs of Article 20 shall apply even where he is not domiciled in any of the Contracting States.

ARTICLE 41

A judgment given on an appeal provided for in Article 40 may be contested only:
  —in Belgium, Greece,[5] France, Italy, Luxembourg and in the Netherlands, by an appeal in cassation,
  —in Denmark, by an appeal to the *højesteret*, with the leave of the Minister of Justice,
  —in the Federal Republic of Germany, by a *Rechtsbeschwerde*,
  —in Ireland, by an appeal on a point of law to the Supreme Court,
  —in the United Kingdom, by a single further appeal on a point of law.

ARTICLE 42

A3.18   Where a foreign judgment has been given in respect of several matters and enforcement cannot be authorised for all of them, the court shall authorise enforcement for one or more of them.

An applicant may request partial enforcement of a judgment.

ARTICLE 43

A foreign judgment which orders a periodic payment by way of a penalty shall be enforceable in the State in which enforcement is sought only if the amount of the payment has been finally determined by the courts of the State in which the judgment was given.

ARTICLE 44

An applicant who, in the State in which the judgment was given, has benefited from complete or partial legal aid or exemption from costs or

---

[5] See para. 28.69 above, n. †.

expenses, shall be entitled, in the procedures provided for in Articles 32 to 35, to benefit from the most favourable legal aid or the most extensive exemption from costs or expenses provided for by the law of the State addressed.

However, an applicant who requests the enforcement of a decision given by an administrative authority in Denmark in respect of a maintenance order may, in the State addressed, claim the benefits referred to in the first paragraph if he presents a statement from the Danish Ministry of Justice to the effect that he fulfils the economic requirements to qualify for the grant of complete or partial legal aid or exemption from costs or expenses.

ARTICLE 45

No security, bond or deposit, however described, shall be required of a party who in one Contracting State applies for enforcement of a judgment given in another Contracting State on the ground that he is a foreign national or that he is not domiciled or resident in the State in which enforcement is sought.

Section 3

Common provisions

ARTICLE 46

A party seeking recognition or applying for enforcement of a judgment shall produce: **A3.19**
    (1) a copy of the judgment which satisfies the conditions necessary to establish its authenticity;
    (2) in the case of a judgment given in default, the original or a certified true copy of the document which establishes that the party in default was served with the document instituting the proceedings or with an equivalent document.

ARTICLE 47

A party applying for enforcement shall also produce:
    (1) documents which establish that, according to the law of the State in which it has been given, the judgment is enforceable and has been served;
    (2) where appropriate, a document showing that the applicant is in receipt of legal aid in the State in which the judgment was given.

ARTICLE 48

If the documents specified in Articles 46(2) and 47(2) are not produced, the court may specify a time for their production, accept equivalent documents or, if it considers that it has sufficient information before it, dispense with their production.

If the court so requires, a translation of the documents shall be produced; the translation shall be certified by a person qualified to do so in one of the Contracting States.

ARTICLE 49

No legalisation or other similar formality shall be required in respect of the documents referred to in Article 46 or 47 or the second paragraph of Article 48, or in respect of a document appointing a representative *ad litem*.

TITLE IV

AUTHENTIC INSTRUMENTS AND COURT SETTLEMENTS

ARTICLE 50

A3.20   A document which has been formally drawn up or registered as an authentic instrument and is enforceable in one Contracting State shall, in another Contracting State, have an order for its enforcement issued there, on application made in accordance with the procedures provided for in Articles 31 *et seq.* The application may be refused only if enforcement of the instrument is contrary to public policy in the State in which enforcement is sought.

The instrument produced must satisfy the conditions necessary to establish its authenticity in the State of origin.

The provisions of Section 3 of Title III shall apply as appropriate.

ARTICLE 51

A settlement which has been approved by a court in the course of proceedings and is enforceable in the State in which it was concluded shall be enforceable in the State in which enforcement is sought under the same conditions as authentic instruments.

TITLE V

GENERAL PROVISIONS

ARTICLE 52

A3.21   In order to determine whether a party is domiciled in the Contracting State whose courts are seised of a matter, the court shall apply its internal law.

If a party is not domiciled in the State whose courts are seised of the matter, then, in order to determine whether the party is domiciled in another Contracting State, the court shall apply the law of that State.

The domicile of a party shall, however, be determined in accordance with his national law if, by that law, his domicile depends on that of another person or on the seat of an authority.

ARTICLE 53

For the purposes of this Convention, the seat of a company or other legal person or association of natural or legal persons shall be treated as its domicile. However, in order to determine that seat, the court shall apply its rules of private international law.

In order to determine whether a trust is domiciled in the Contracting State whose courts are seised of the matter, the court shall apply its rules of private international law.

TITLE VI

TRANSITIONAL PROVISIONS

ARTICLE 54

The provisions of this Convention shall apply only to legal proceedings **A3.22** instituted and to documents formally drawn up or registered as authentic instruments after its entry into force.

However, judgments given after the date of entry into force of this Convention in proceedings instituted before that date shall be recognised and enforced in accordance with the provisions of Title III if jurisdiction was founded upon rules which accorded with those provided for either in Title II of this Convention or in a convention concluded between the State of origin and the State addressed which was in force when the proceedings were instituted.

TITLE VII

RELATIONSHIP TO OTHER CONVENTIONS

ARTICLE 55

Subject to the provisions of the second paragraph of Article 54, and of **A3.23** Article 56, this Convention shall, for the States which are parties to it, supersede the following conventions concluded between two or more of them:

—the Convention between Belgium and France on jurisdiction and the validity and enforcement of judgments, arbitration awards and authentic instruments, signed at Paris on 8 July 1899,

—the Convention between Belgium and the Netherlands on jurisdiction, bankruptcy, and the validity and enforcement of judgments, arbitration awards and authentic instruments, signed at Brussels on 28 March 1925,

—the Convention between France and Italy on the enforcement of judgments in civil and commercial matters, signed at Rome on 3 June 1930,

—the Convention between the United Kingdom and the French Republic providing for the reciprocal enforcement of judgments in civil and commercial matters, with Protocol, signed at Paris on 18 January 1934,

—the Convention between the United Kingdom and the Kingdom of Belgium providing for the reciprocal enforcement of judgments in civil and commercial matters, with Protocol, signed at Brussels on 2 May 1934,

—the Convention between Germany and Italy on the recognition and enforcement of judgments in civil and commercial matters, signed at Rome on 9 March 1936,

—the Convention between the Federal Republic of Germany and the Kingdom of Belgium on the mutual recognition and enforcement of judgments, arbitration awards and authentic instruments in civil and commercial matters, signed at Bonn on 30 June 1958,

—the Convention between the Kingdom of the Netherlands and the Italian Republic on the recognition and enforcement of judgments in civil and commercial matters, signed at Rome on 17 April 1959,

—the Convention between the United Kingdom and the Federal Republic of Germany for the reciprocal recognition and enforcement of judgments in civil and commercial matters, signed at Bonn on 14 July 1960,

—the Convention between the Kingdom of Greece and the Federal Republic of Germany for the reciprocal recognition and enforcement of judgments, settlements and authentic instruments in civil and commercial matters, signed in Athens on 4 November 1961,[6]

—the Convention between the Kingdom of Belgium and the Italian Republic on the recognition and enforcement of judgments and other enforceable instruments in civil and commercial matters, signed at Rome on 6 April 1962,

—the Convention between the Kingdom of the Netherlands and the Federal Republic of Germany on the mutual recognition and enforcement of judgments and other enforceable instruments in civil and commercial matters, signed at The Hague on 30 August 1962,

—the Convention between the United Kingdom and the Republic of Italy for the reciprocal recognition and enforcement of judgments in civil and commercial matters, signed at Rome on 7 February 1964, with amending Protocol signed at Rome on 14 July 1970,

—the Convention between the United Kingdom and the Kingdom of

---

[6] See para. 33.01 above, n. †.

the Netherlands providing for the reciprocal recognition and enforcement of judgments in civil matters, signed at The Hague on 17 November 1967,
and, in so far as it is in force:
—the Treaty between Belgium, the Netherlands and Luxembourg on jurisdiction, bankruptcy, and the validity and enforcement of judgments, arbitration awards and authentic instruments, signed at Brussels on 24 November 1961.

ARTICLE 56

The Treaty and the Conventions referred to in Article 55 shall continue to have effect in relation to matters to which this Convention does not apply.

They shall continue to have effect in respect of judgments and documents formally drawn up or registered as authentic instruments before the entry into force of this Convention.

ARTICLE 57

This Convention shall not affect any conventions to which the Contracting States are or will be parties and which, in relation to particular matters, govern jurisdiction or the recognition or enforcement of judgments.

This Convention shall not affect the application of provisions which, in relation or particular matters, govern jurisdiction or the recognition or enforcement of judgments and which are or will be contained in acts of the institutions of the European Communities or in national laws harmonised in implementation of such acts.

ARTICLE 58

This Convention shall not affect the rights granted to Swiss nationals by the Convention concluded on 15 June 1869 between France and the Swiss Confederation on Jurisdiction and the enforcement of judgments in civil matters.

ARTICLE 59

This Convention shall not prevent a Contracting State from assuming, in a convention on the recognition and enforcement of judgments, an obligation towards a third State not to recognise judgments given in other Contracting States against defendants domiciled or habitually resident in the third State where, in cases provided for in Article 4, the judgment could only be founded on a ground of jurisdiction specified in the second paragraph of Article 3.

However, a Contracting State may not assume an obligation towards a third State not to recognise a judgment given in another contracting State by a court basing its jurisdiction on the presence within that State of property belonging to the defendant, or the seizure by the plaintiff of property situated there:

> (1) if the action is brought to assert or declare proprietary or possessory rights in the property, seeks to obtain authority to dispose of it, or arises from another issue relating to such property, or,
>
> (2) if the property constitutes the security for a debt which is the subject-matter of the action.

TITLE VIII

FINAL PROVISIONS

ARTICLE 60

A3.24   This Convention shall apply to the European territories of the Contracting States, including Greenland, to the French overseas departments, and to Mayotte.

The Kingdom of the Netherlands may declare at the time of signing or ratifying this Convention or at any later time, by notifying the Secretary-General of the Council of the European Communities, that this Convention shall be applicable to the Netherlands Antilles. In the absence of such declaration, proceedings taking place in the European territory of the Kingdom as a result of an appeal in cassation from the judgment of a court in the Netherlands Antilles shall be deemed to be proceedings in the latter court.

Notwithstanding the first paragraph, this Convention shall not apply to:

> (1) the Faroe Islands, unless the Kingdom of Denmark makes a declaration to the contrary;
>
> (2) any European territory situated outside the United Kingdom for the international relations of which the United Kingdom is responsible, unless the United Kingdom makes a declaration to the contrary in respect of any such territory.

Such declarations may be made at any time by notifying the Secretary-General of the Council of the European Communities.

Proceedings brought in the United Kingdom on appeal from courts in one of the territories referred to in sub-paragraph 2 of the third paragraph shall be deemed to be proceedings taking place in those courts.

Proceedings which in the Kingdom of Denmark are dealt with under the law on civil procedure for the Faroe Islands (*lov for Faerøerne om rettens pleje*) shall be deemed to be proceedings taking place in the courts of the Faroe Islands.

ARTICLE 61

This Convention shall be ratified by the signatory States. The instruments of ratification shall be deposited with the Secretary-General of the Council of the European Communities.

ARTICLE 62

This Convention shall enter into force on the first day of the third month following the deposit of the instrument of ratification by the last signatory State to take this step.

ARTICLE 63

The Contracting States recognise that any State which becomes a member of the European Economic Community shall be required to accept this Convention as a basis for the negotiations between the Contracting States and that State necessary to ensure the implementation of the last paragraph of Article 220 of the Treaty establishing the European Economic Community.

The necessary adjustments may be the subject of a special convention between the Contracting States of the one part and the new Member States of the other part.

ARTICLE 64

The Secretary-General of the Council of the European Communities shall notify the signatory States of:
  (a) the deposit of each instrument of ratification;
  (b) the date of entry into force of this Convention;
  (c) any declaration received pursuant to Article 60;
  (d) any declaration received pursuant to Article IV of the Protocol;
  (e) any communication made pursuant to Article VI of the Protocol.

ARTICLE 65

The Protocol annexed to this Convention by common accord of the Contracting States shall form an integral part thereof.

ARTICLE 66

This Convention is concluded for an unlimited period.

ARTICLE 67

Any Contracting State may request the revision of this Convention. In this event, a revision conference shall be convened by the President of the Council of the European Communities.

ARTICLE 68

This Convention, drawn up in a single original in the Dutch, French, German and Italian languages, all four texts being equally authentic, shall be deposited in the archives of the Secretariat of the Council of the European Communities. The Secretary-General shall transmit a certified copy to the Government of each signatory State.

In witness whereof . . . [etc.].

2. The 1968 Annexed Protocol

PROTOCOL

A3.25 The High Contracting Parties have agreed upon the following provisions, which shall be annexed to the Convention:

ARTICLE I

Any person domiciled in Luxembourg who is sued in a court of another Contracting State pursuant to Article 5(1) may refuse to submit to the jurisdiction of that court. If the defendant does not enter an appearance the court shall declare of its own motion that it has no jurisdiction.

An agreement conferring jurisdiction, within the meaning of Article 17, shall be valid with respect to a person domiciled in Luxembourg only if that person has expressly and specifically so agreed.

ARTICLE II

Without prejudice to any more favourable provisions of national laws, persons domiciled in a Contracting State who are being prosecuted in the criminal courts of another Contracting State of which they are not nationals for an offence which was not intentionally committed may be defended by persons qualified to do so, even if they do not appear in person.

However, the court seised of the matter may order appearance in person; in the case of failure to appear, a judgment given in the civil action without the person concerned having had the opportunity to arrange for his defence need not be recognised or enforced in the other Contracting States.

ARTICLE III

In proceedings for the issue of an order for enforcement, no charge, duty or fee calculated by reference to the value of the matter in issue may be levied in the State in which enforcement is sought.

ARTICLE IV

Judicial and extrajudicial documents drawn up in one Contracting State which have to be served on persons in another Contracting State shall be transmitted in accordance with the procedures laid down in the Conventions and agreements concluded between the Contracting States.

Unless the State in which service is to take place objects by declaration to the Secretary-General of the Council of the European Communities, such documents may also be sent by the appropriate public officers of the State in which the document has been drawn up directly to the appropriate public officers of the State in which the addressee is to be found. In this

1842

case the officer of the State of origin shall send a copy of the document to the officer of the State applied to who is competent to forward it to the addressee. The document shall be forwarded in the manner specified by the law of the State applied to. The forwarding shall be recorded by a certificate sent directly to the officer of the State of origin.

ARTICLE V

The jurisdiction specified in Articles 6(2) and 10 in actions on a warranty or guarantee or in any other third-party proceedings may not be resorted to in the Federal Republic of Germany. In that State, any person domiciled in another Contracting State may be sued in the courts in pursuance of Articles 68, 72, 73 and 74 of the code of civil procedure (*Zivilprozessordnung*) concerning third-party notices.

Judgments given in the other Contracting States by virtue of Article 6(2) or 10 shall be recognised and enforced in the Federal Republic of Germany in accordance with Title III. Any effects which judgments given in that State may have on third parties by application of Articles 68, 72, 73 and 74 of the code of civil procedure (*Zivilprozessordnung*) shall also be recognised in the other Contracting States.

ARTICLE Va

In matters relating to maintenance, the expression "court" includes the **A3.26** Danish administrative authorities.

ARTICLE Vb

In proceedings involving a dispute between the master and a member of the crew of a sea-going ship registered in Denmark, in Greece or in Ireland, concerning remuneration or other conditions of service, a court in a Contracting State shall establish whether the diplomatic or consular officer responsible for the ship has been notified of the dispute. It shall stay the proceedings so long as he has not been notified. It shall of its own motion decline jurisdiction if the officer, having been duly notified, has exercised the powers accorded to him in the matter by a consular convention, or in the absence of such a convention has, within the time allowed, raised any objection to the exercise of such jurisdiction.[7]

ARTICLE Vc

Articles 52 and 53 of this Convention shall, when applied by Article 69(5) of the Convention for the European patent for the common market, signed at Luxembourg on 15 December 1975, to the provisions relating to

---

[7] See para. 35.24 above, n. †.

"residence" in the English text of the Convention, operate as if "residence" in that text were the same as "domicile" in Articles 52 and 53.

ARTICLE Vd

Without prejudice to the jurisdiction of the European Patent Office under the Convention on the grant of European Patents, signed at Munich on 5 October 1973, the courts of each Contracting State shall have exclusive jurisdiction, regardless of domicile, in proceedings concerned with the registration or validity of any European patent granted for that State which is not a Community patent by virtue of the provisions of Article 86 of the Convention for the European Patent for the Common Market, signed at Luxembourg on 15 December 1975.

ARTICLE VI

The Contracting States shall communicate to the Secretary-General of the Council of the European Communities the text of any provisions of their laws which amend either those articles of their laws mentioned in the Convention or the lists of courts specified in Section 2 of Title III of the Convention.

In witness whereof . . . [etc.].

3. The Joint Declaration annexed to the 1968 Convention

JOINT DECLARATION

A3.27   The Governments of the Kingdom of Belgium, the Federal Republic of Germany, the French Republic, the Italian Republic, the Grand Duchy of Luxembourg and the Kingdom of the Netherlands;

On signing the Convention on jurisdiction and the enforcement of judgments in civil and commercial matters;

Desiring to ensure that the Convention is applied as effectively as possible;

Anxious to prevent differences of interpretation of the Convention from impairing its unifying effect;

Recognising that claims and disclaimers of jurisdiction may arise in the application of the Convention;

Declare themselves ready:

> (1) to study these questions and in particular to examine the possibility of conferring jurisdiction in certain matters on the Court of Justice of the European Communities and, if necessary, to negotiate an agreement to this effect;
> (2) to arrange meetings at regular intervals between their representatives.

4. The 1971 Protocol on Interpretation (as amended by the Accession Conventions)

Protocol
on the interpretation of the Convention of 27th September 1968 on jurisdiction and the enforcement of judgments in civil and commercial matters

The High Contracting Parties to the Treaty establishing the European Economic Community, **A3.28**

Having regard to the Declaration annexed to the Convention on jurisdiction and enforcement of judgments in civil and commercial matters, signed at Brussels on 27 September 1968,

Having decided to conclude a Protocol conferring jurisdiction on the Court of Justice of the European Communities to interpret that Convention, and to this end have designated as their Plenipotentiaries:

(*Designation of the Plenipotentiaries of the original six Contracting States*)

Have agreed as follows:

ARTICLE 1

The Court of Justice of the European Communities shall have jurisdiction to give rulings on the interpretation of the Convention on jurisdiction and the enforcement of judgments in civil and commercial matters and of the Protocol annexed to that Convention, signed at Brussels on 27 September 1968, and also on the interpretation of the present Protocol.

The Court of Justice of the European Communities shall also have jurisdiction to give rulings on the interpretation of the Convention on the Accession of the Kingdom of Denmark, Ireland and the United Kingdom of Great Britain and Northern Ireland to the Convention of 27 September 1968 and to this Protocol.

The Court of Justice of the European Communities shall also have jurisdiction to give rulings on the interpretation of the Convention on the accession of the Hellenic Republic to the Convention of 27 September 1968 and to this Protocol, as adjusted by the 1978 Convention.[8]

ARTICLE 2

The following courts may request the Court of Justice to give preliminary rulings on questions of interpretation: **A3.29**

(1)—in Belgium: la *Cour de Cassation*—het *Hof van Cassatie* and le *Conseil d'Etat*—de *Raad van State*,
  —in Denmark: *højesteret*,
  —in the Federal Republic of Germany: *die obersten Gerichtshöfe des Bundes*,
  —in Greece: the αγωτα τα δικαστήρια,[9]

---

[8] See para. 36.03 above, n. †.
[9] See para. 36.05 above, n. †.

—in France: *la Cour de Cassation* and *le Conseil d'Etat,*
—in Ireland: the Supreme Court,
—in Italy: *la Corte Suprema di Cassazione,*
—in Luxembourg: *la Cour supérieure de Justice* when sitting as Cour de Cassation,
—in the Netherlands: *de Hoge Raad,*
—in the United Kingdom: the House of Lords and courts to which application has been made under the second paragraph of Article 37 or under Article 41 of the Convention;
(2) the courts of the Contracting States when they are sitting in an appellate capacity;
(3) in the cases provided for in Article 37 of the Convention, the courts referred to in that Article.

ARTICLE 3

(1) Where a question of interpretation of the Convention or of one of the other instruments referred to in Article 1 is raised in a case pending before one of the courts listed in Article 2(1), that court shall, if it considers that a decision on the question is necessary to enable it to give judgment, request the Court of Justice to give a ruling thereon.

(2) Where such a question is raised before any court referred to in Article 2(2) or (3), that court may, under the conditions laid down in paragraph 1, request the Court of Justice to give a ruling thereon.

ARTICLE 4

(1) The competent authority of a Contracting State may request the Court of Justice to give a ruling on a question of interpretation of the Convention or of one of the other instruments referred to in Article 1 if judgments given by courts of that State conflict with the interpretation given either by the Court of Justice or in a judgment of one of the courts of another Contracting State referred to in Article 2(1) or (2). The provisions of this paragraph shall apply only to judgments which have become *res judicata*.

(2) The interpretation given by the Court of Justice in response to such a request shall not affect the judgments which gave rise to the request for interpretation.

(3) The Procurators-General of the Courts of Cassation of the Contracting States, or any other authority designated by a Contracting State, shall be entitled to request the Court of Justice for a ruling on interpretation in accordance with paragraph 1.

(4) The Registrar of the Court of Justice shall give notice of the request to the Contracting States, to the Commission and to the Council of the European Communities; they shall be entitled within two months of the notification to submit statements of case or written observations to the Court.

(5) No fees shall be levied or any costs or expenses awarded in respect of the proceedings provided for in this Article.

The 1971 Protocol on Interpretation

ARTICLE 5

(1) Except where this Protocol otherwise provides, the provisions of the **A3.30**
Treaty establishing the European Economic Community and those of the
Protocol on the Statute of the Court of Justice annexed thereto, which are
applicable when the Court is requested to give a preliminary ruling, shall
also apply to any proceedings for the interpretation of the Convention and
the other instruments referred to in Article 1.

(2) The Rules of Procedure of the Court of Justice shall, if necessary, be
adjusted and supplemented in accordance with Article 188 of the Treaty
establishing the European Economic Community.

ARTICLE 6

This Protocol shall apply to the European territories of the Contracting
States, including Greenland, to the French overseas departments, and to
Mayotte.

The Kingdom of the Netherlands may declare at the time of signing or
ratifying this Protocol or at any later time, by notifying the Secretary-
General of the Council of the European Communities, that this Protocol
shall be applicable to the Netherlands Antilles.

Notwithstanding the first paragraph, this Protocol shall not apply to:
  (1) the Faroe Islands, unless the Kingdom of Denmark makes a dec-
      laration to the contrary;
  (2) any European territory situated outside the United Kingdom for
      the international relations of which the United Kingdom is
      responsible, unless the United Kingdom makes a declaration to
      the contrary in respect of any such territory.

Such declarations may be made at any time by notifying the Secretary-
General of the Council of the European Communities.

ARTICLE 7

This Protocol shall be ratified by the signatory States. The instruments
of ratification shall be deposited with the Secretary-General of the Council
of the European Communities.

ARTICLE 8

This Protocol shall enter into force on the first day of the third month
following the deposit of the instrument of ratification by the last signatory
State to take this step; provided that it shall at the earliest enter into force
at the same time as the Convention of 27 September 1968 on the jurisdiction and the enforcement of judgments in civil and commercial matters.

ARTICLE 9

The Contracting States recognise that any State which becomes a member of the European Economic Community, and to which Article 63 of the

Convention on jurisdiction and the enforcement of judgments in civil and commercial matters applies, must accept the provisions of this Protocol, subject to such adjustments as may be required.

ARTICLE 10

The Secretary-General of the Council of the European Communities shall notify the signatory States of:

    (a) the deposit of each instrument of ratification;
    (b) the date of entry into force of this Protocol;
    (c) any designation received pursuant to Article 4(3);
    (d) any declaration received pursuant to Article 6.

ARTICLE 11

The Contracting States shall communicate to the Secretary-General of the Council of the European Communities the texts of any provisions of their laws which necessitate an amendment to the lists of courts in Article 2(1).

ARTICLE 12

This Protocol is concluded for an unlimited period.

ARTICLE 13

Any Contracting State may request the revision of this Protocol. In this event, a revision conference shall be convened by the President of the Council of the European Communities.

ARTICLE 14

This Protocol, drawn up in a single original in the Dutch, French, German and Italian languages, all four texts being equally authentic, shall be deposited in the archives of the Secretariat of the Council of the European Communities. The Secretary-General shall transmit a certified copy to the Government of each signatory State.

In witness whereof . . . [etc.].

5. The Joint Declaration annexed to the 1971 Protocol on Interpretation

JOINT DECLARATION

A3.31   The Governments of the Kingdom of Belgium, the Federal Republic of Germany, the French Republic, the Italian Republic, the Grand Duchy of Luxembourg and the Kingdom of the Netherlands,

On signing the Protocol on Interpretation by the Court of Justice of the Convention of 27 September 1968 on jurisdiction and the enforcement of judgments in civil and commercial matters,

Desiring the ensure that the provisions of that Protocol are applied as effectively and as uniformly as possible;

Declare themselves ready to organise, in co-operation with the Court of Justice, an exchange of information on the judgments given by the courts referred to in Article 2(1) of that Protocol in application of the Convention and the Protocol of 27 September 1968.

6. The 1978 Convention on the Accession of Denmark, Ireland and the United Kingdom (Extracts)

**Convention
on the accession of the Kingdom of Denmark, Ireland and the United Kingdom of Great Britain and Northern Ireland to the Convention on jurisdiction and the enforcement of judgments in civil and commercial matters and to the Protocol on its interpretation by the Court of Justice**

PREAMBLE

The High Contracting Parties to the Treaty Establishing the European **A3.32** Economic Community,

Considering that the Kingdom of Denmark, Ireland and the United Kingdom of Great Britain and Northern Ireland, in becoming members of the Community, undertook to accede to the Convention on jurisdiction and enforcement of judgments in civil and commercial matters and to the Protocol on the interpretation of that Convention by the Court of Justice and to this end undertook to enter into negotiations with the original Member States of the Community in order to make the necessary adjustments thereto,

Have decided to conclude this Convention, and to this end have designated as their Plenipotentiaries:

(*Designation of Plenipotentiaries*)

Have agreed as follows:

TITLE I

GENERAL PROVISIONS

ARTICLE 1

The Kingdom of Denmark, Ireland and the United Kingdom of Great Britain and Northern Ireland hereby accede to the Convention on jurisdiction and enforcement of judgments in civil and commercial matters, signed at Brussels on 27 September 1968 (hereinafter called "the 1968

Convention"), and to the Protocol on its interpretation by the Court of Justice, signed at Luxembourg on 3 June 1971 (hereinafter called "the 1971 Protocol").

ARTICLE 2

The adjustments to the 1968 Convention and to the 1971 Protocol are set out in Titles II to IV of this Convention.

[With the exception of Article 25(2), which is set out below, Articles 3 to 33 provide for amendments to the 1968 Convention and 1971 Protocol, which have been incorporated in the texts reproduced above.]

ARTICLE 25

A3.33 (1). . . .
(2) With a view to its uniform interpretation, paragraph 1 of Article 57 shall be applied in the following manner:

(a) the 1968 Convention as amended shall not prevent a court of a Contracting State which is a party to a Convention on a particular matter from assuming jurisdiction in accordance with that Convention, even where the defendant is domiciled in another Contracting State which is not a party to that Convention. The court shall, in any event, apply Article 20 of the 1968 Convention as amended;

(b) a judgment given in a Contracting State in the exercise of jurisdiction provided for in a convention on a particular matter shall be recognised and enforced in the other Contracting States in accordance with the 1968 Convention as amended.

Where a convention on a particular matter to which both the State of origin and the State addressed are parties lays down conditions for the recognition or enforcement of judgments, those conditions shall apply. In any event, the provisions of the 1968 Convention as amended which concern the procedures for recognition and enforcement of judgments may be applied.

TITLE V

TRANSITIONAL PROVISIONS

ARTICLE 34

A3.34 (1) The 1968 Convention and the 1971 Protocol, with the amendments made by this Convention, shall apply only to legal proceedings instituted and to authentic instruments formally drawn up or registered after the entry into force of this Convention in the State of origin and, where recognition or enforcement of a judgment or authentic instrument is sought, in the State addressed.

(2) However, as between the six Contracting States to the 1968 Convention, judgments given after the date of entry into force of this Convention in proceedings instituted before that date shall be recognised and enforced in accordance with the provisions of Title III as amended.

(3) Moreover, as between the six Contracting States to the 1968 Convention and the three States mentioned in Article 1 of this Convention, and as between those three States, judgments given after the date of entry into force of this Convention between the State of origin and the State addressed in proceedings instituted before that date shall also be recognised and enforced in accordance with the provisions of Title III of the 1968 Convention as amended if jurisdiction was founded upon rules which accorded with the provisions of Title II, as amended, or with provisions of a convention concluded between the State of origin and the State addressed which was in force when the proceedings were instituted.

ARTICLE 35

If the parties to a dispute concerning a contract had agreed in writing before the entry into force of this Convention that the contract was to be governed by the law of Ireland or of a part of the United Kingdom, the courts of Ireland or of that part of the United Kingdom shall retain the right to exercise jurisdiction in the dispute.

ARTICLE 36

For a period of three years from the entry into force of the 1968 Convention for the Kingdom of Denmark and Ireland respectively, jurisdiction in maritime matters shall be determined in these States not only in accordance with the provisions of that Convention but also in accordance with the provisions of paragraphs 1 to 6 following. However, upon the entry into force of the International Convention relating to the arrest of sea-going ships, signed at Brussels on 10 May 1952, for one of these States, these provisions shall cease to have effect for that State.

(1) A person who is domiciled in a Contracting State may be sued in the courts of one of the States mentioned above in respect of a maritime claim if the ship to which the claim relates or any other ship owned by him has been arrested by judicial process within the territory of the latter State to secure the claim, or could have been so arrested there but bail or other security has been given, and either:
  (a) the claimant is domiciled in the latter State; or
  (b) the claim arose in the latter State; or
  (c) the claim concerns the voyage during which the arrest was made or could have been made; or
  (d) the claim arises out of a collision or out of damage caused by a ship to another ship or to goods or persons on board either ship, either by the execution or non-execution of a manoeuvre or by the non-observance of regulations; or
  (e) the claim is for salvage; or

1851

   (f) the claim is in respect of a mortgage or hypothecation of the ship arrested.

(2) A claimant may arrest either the particular ship to which the maritime claim relates, or any other ship which is owned by the person who was, at the time when the maritime claim arose, the owner of the particular ship. However, only the particular ship to which the maritime claim relates may be arrested in respect of the maritime claims set out in sub-paragraphs (o), (p) or (q) of paragraph 5 of this Article.

(3) Ships shall be deemed to be in the same ownership when all the shares therein are owned by the same person or persons.

(4) When in the case of a charter by demise of a ship the charterer alone is liable in respect of a maritime claim relating to that ship, the claimant may arrest that ship or any other ship owned by the charterer, but no other ship owned by the owner may be arrested in respect of such claim. The same shall apply to any case in which a person other than the owner of a ship is liable in respect of a maritime claim relating to that ship.

(5) The expression "maritime claim" means a claim arising out of one or more of the following:
   (a) damage caused by any ship either in collision or otherwise;
   (b) loss of life or personal injury caused by any ship or occurring in connection with the operation of any ship;
   (c) salvage;
   (d) agreement relating to the use or hire of any ship whether by charterparty or otherwise;
   (e) agreement relating to the carriage of goods in any ship whether by charterparty or otherwise;
   (f) loss of or damage to goods including baggage carried in any ship;
   (g) general average;
   (h) bottomry;
   (i) towage;
   (j) pilotage;
   (k) goods or materials wherever supplied to a ship for her operation or maintenance;
   (l) construction, repair or equipment of any ship or dock charges and dues;
   (m) wages of masters, officers or crew;
   (n) master's disbursements, including disbursements made by shippers, charterers or agents on behalf of a ship or her owner;
   (o) dispute as to the title to or ownership of any ship;
   (p) disputes between co-owners of any ship as to the ownership, possession, employment or earnings of that ship;
   (q) the mortgage or hypothecation of any ship.

(6) In Denmark, the expression "arrest" shall be deemed as regards the maritime claims referred to in sub-paragraphs (o) and (p) of paragraph 5 of this Article, to include a "forbud," where that is

the only procedure allowed in respect of such a claim under Articles 646 and 653 of the law on civil procedure (lov om rettens pleje).

TITLE VI

FINAL PROVISIONS

ARTICLE 37

The Secretary-General of the Council of the European Communities **A3.35** shall transmit a certified copy of the 1968 Convention and of the 1971 Protocol in the Dutch, French, German and Italian languages to the Governments of the Kingdom of Denmark, Ireland and the United Kingdom of Great Britain and Northern Ireland.

The texts of the 1968 Convention and the 1971 Protocol, drawn up in the Danish, Irish and English languages shall be annexed to this Convention. The texts drawn up in the Danish, Irish and English languages shall be authentic under the same conditions as the original texts of the 1968 Convention and the 1971 Protocol.

ARTICLE 38

This Convention shall be ratified by the signatory States. The instruments of ratification shall be deposited with the Secretary-General of the Council of the European Communities.

ARTICLE 39

This Convention shall enter into force, as between the States which shall have ratified it, on the first day of the third month following the deposit of the last instrument of ratification by the original Member States of the Community and one new Member State.

It shall enter into force for each new Member State which subsequently ratifies it on the first day of the third month following the deposit of its instrument of ratification.

ARTICLE 40   **A3.36**

4 The Secretary-General of the Council of the European Communities shall notify the signatory States of:
- (a) the deposit of each instrument of ratification,
- (b) the dates of entry into force of this Convention for the Contracting States.

ARTICLE 41

This Convention, drawn up in a single original in the Danish, Dutch, English, French, German, Irish and Italian languages, all seven texts being equally authentic, shall be deposited in the archives of the Secretariat of the Council of the European Communities. The Secretary-General shall transmit a certified copy to the Government of each signatory State.

In witness whereof . . . [etc.].

7. The Joint Declaration annexed to the 1978 Accession Convention

JOINT DECLARATION

A3.37   The Representatives of the Governments of the Member States of the European Economic Community, meeting within the Council,
   Desiring to ensure that in the spirit of the Convention of 27 September 1968 uniformity of jurisdiction should also be achieved as widely as possible in maritime matters,
   Considering that the International Convention relating to the arrest of sea-going ships, signed at Brussels on 10 May 1952, contains provisions relating to such jurisdiction,
   Considering that all of the Member States are not parties to the said Convention,
   Express the wish that Member States which are coastal States and have not already become parties to the Convention of 10th May 1952 should do so as soon as possible.

Done . . . [etc.]

8. The 1982 Convention on the Accession of Greece (Extracts)

Convention
on the accession of the Hellenic Republic to the Convention on
jurisdiction and enforcement of judgments in civil and commercial
matters and to the Protocol on its interpretation by the Court of Justice
with the adjustments made to them by the Convention on the accession
of the Kingdom of Denmark, of Ireland and of the United Kingdom of
Great Britain and Northern Ireland.

PREAMBLE

A3.38   The High Contracting Parties to the Treaty establishing the European Economic Community.
   Considering that the Hellenic Republic, in becoming a member of the Community, undertook to accede to the Convention on jurisdiction and enforcement of judgments in civil and commercial matters and to the Protocol on its interpretation by the Court of Justice, with the adjustments made to them by the Convention on the accession of the Kingdom of Denmark, of Ireland, and of the United Kingdom of Great Britain and Northern Ireland, and to this end undertook to enter into negotiations with the Member States of the Community in order to make the necessary adjustments thereto,
   Have decided to conclude this Convention, and to this end have designated as their Plenipotentiaries:

(*Designation of Plenipotentiaries*)

Have agreed as follows:

TITLE I

GENERAL PROVISIONS

ARTICLE 1

(1) The Hellenic Republic hereby accedes to the Convention on jurisdic- **A3.39**
tion and enforcement of judgments in civil and commercial matters,
signed at Brussels on 27 September 1968 (hereinafter called "the 1968
Convention"), and to the Protocol on its interpretation by the Court of
Justice, signed at Luxembourg on 3 June 1971 (hereinafter called "the
1971 Protocol"), with the adjustments made to them by the Convention on
the accession of the Kingdom of Denmark, of Ireland and of the United
Kingdom of Great Britain and Northern Ireland to the Convention on jurisdiction and enforcement of judgments in civil and commercial matters
and to the Protocol on its interpretation by the Court of Justice, signed at
Luxembourg on 9 October 1978 (hereinafter called "the 1978 Convention").

(2) The accession of the Hellenic Republic extends, in particular, to
Articles 25(2), 35 and 36 of the 1978 Convention.

ARTICLE 2

The adjustments made by this Convention to the 1968 Convention and
to the 1971 Protocol, as adjusted by the 1978 Convention, are set out in
Titles II to IV.

[*Articles 3 to 11 provide for amendments to the 1968 Convention and 1971 Protocol, which have been incorporated in the texts reproduced above.*]

TITLE V

TRANSITIONAL PROVISIONS

ARTICLE 12

(1) The 1968 Convention and the 1971 Protocol, as amended by the **A3.40**
1978 Convention and this Convention, shall apply only to legal proceedings instituted and to authentic instruments formally drawn up or registered after the entry into force of this Convention in the State of origin
and, where recognition or enforcement of a judgment or authentic instrument is sought, in the State addressed.

(2) However, judgments given after the date of entry into force of this

Convention between the State of origin and the State addressed in proceedings instituted before that date shall also be recognised and enforced in accordance with the provisions of Title III of the 1968 Convention as amended by the 1978 Convention and this Convention, if jurisdiction was founded upon rules which accorded with the provisions of Title II of the 1968 Convention, as amended, or with provisions of a convention concluded between the State of origin and the State addressed which was in force when the proceedings were instituted.

TITLE VI

FINAL PROVISIONS

ARTICLE 13

The Secretary-General of the Council of the European Communities shall transmit a certified copy of the 1968 Convention, of the 1971 Protocol and of the 1978 Convention in the Danish, Dutch, English, French, German, Irish and Italian languages to the Government of the Hellenic Republic.

The texts of the 1968 Convention, of the 1971 Protocol and of the 1978 Convention, drawn up in the Greek language shall be annexed to this Convention. The texts drawn up in the Greek language shall be authentic under the same conditions as the other texts of the 1968 Convention, the 1971 Protocol and the 1978 Convention.

ARTICLE 14

This Convention shall be ratified by the signatory States. The instruments of ratification shall be deposited with the Secretary-General of the Council of the European Communities.

ARTICLE 15

This Convention shall enter into force, as between the States which shall have ratified it, on the first day of the third month following the deposit of the last instrument of ratification by the Hellenic Republic and those States which have put into force the 1978 Convention in accordance with Article 39 of that Convention.

It shall enter into force for each Member State which subsequently ratifies it on the first day of the third month following the deposit of its instrument of ratification.

ARTICLE 16

The Secretary-General of the Council of the European Communities shall notify the signatory States of:
    (a) the deposit of each instrument of ratification,

(b) the dates of entry into force of this Convention for the Contracting States.

ARTICLE 17

This Convention, drawn up in a single original in the Danish, Dutch, English, French, German, Greek, Irish and Italian languages, all eight texts being equally authentic, shall be deposited in the archives of the General Secretariat of the Council of the European Communities. The Secretary-General shall transmit a certified copy to the Government of each signatory State.

In witness whereof . . . [etc.].

9. The Civil Jurisdiction and Judgments Act 1982

1982 Chapter 27

An Act to make further provision about the jurisdiction of courts and tribunals in the United Kingdom and certain other territories and about the recognition and enforcement of judgments given in the United Kingdom or elsewhere; to provide for the modification of certain provisions relating to legal aid; and for connected purposes.   [13th July 1982] **A3.41**

BE IT ENACTED by the Queen's most Excellent Majesty, by and with the advice and consent of the Lord Spiritual and Temporal, and Commons, in this present Parliament assembled, and by the authority of the same, as follows:–

PART I

IMPLEMENTATION OF THE CONVENTIONS

Main implementing provisions

1.—*Interpretation of references to the Conventions and Contracting States.*   **A3.42**
(1) In this Act—

"the 1968 Convention" means the Convention on jurisdiction and the enforcement of judgments in civil and commercial matters (including the Protocol annexed to that Convention), signed at Brussels on 27th September 1968;
"the 1971 Protocol" means the Protocol on the interpretation of the 1968 Convention by the European Court, signed at Luxembourg on 3rd June 1971;
"the Accession Convention" means the Convention on the accession to the 1968 Convention and the 1971 Protocol of Denmark, the Republic of Ireland and the United Kingdom, signed at Luxembourg on 9th October 1978;
"the Conventions" means the 1968 Convention, the 1971 Protocol and the Accession Convention.

(2) In this Act, unless the context otherwise requires—
- (a) references to, or to any provision of, the 1968 Convention or the 1971 Protocol are references to that Convention, Protocol or provision as amended by the Accession Convention; and
- (b) any reference to a numbered Article is a reference to the Article so numbered of the 1968 Convention, and any reference to a subdivision of a numbered Article shall be construed accordingly.

(3) In this Act "Contracting State" means—
- (a) one of the original parties to the 1968 Convention (Belgium, the Federal Republic of Germany, France, Italy, Luxembourg and the Netherlands); or
- (b) one of the parties acceding to that Convention under the Accession Convention (Denmark, the Republic of Ireland and the United Kingdom),

being a state in respect of which the Accession Convention has entered into force in accordance with Article 39 of that Convention.

2.—*The Conventions to have the force of law.*

(1) The Conventions shall have the force of law in the United Kingdom, and judicial notice shall be taken of them.

(2) For convenience of reference there are set out in Schedules 1, 2 and 3 respectively the English texts of—
- (a) the 1968 Convention as amended by Titles II and III of the Accession Convention;
- (b) the 1971 Protocol as amended by Title IV of the Accession Convention; and
- (c) Titles V and VI of the Accession Convention (transitional and final provisions),

being texts prepared from the authentic English texts referred to in Articles 37 and 41 of the Accession Convention.

3.—*Interpretation of the Conventions.*

(1) Any question as to the meaning or effect of any provision of the Conventions shall, if not referred to the European Court in accordance with the 1971 Protocol, be determined in accordance with the principles laid down by and any relevant decision of the European Court.

(2) Judicial notice shall be taken of any decision of, or any expression of opinion by, the European Court on any such question.

(3) Without prejudice to the generality of subsection (1), the following reports (which are reproduced in the Official Journal of the Communities), namely—
- (a) the reports by Mr. P. Jenard on the 1968 Convention and 1971 Protocol; and
- (b) the report by Professor Peter Schlosser on the Accession Convention,

may be considered in ascertaining the meaning or effect of any provision of the Conventions and shall be given such weight as is appropriate in the circumstances.

Supplementary provisions as to recognition and enforcement of judgments

4.—*Enforcement of judgments other than maintenance orders.*　　　　**A3.43**

(1) A judgment, other than a maintenance order, which is the subject of an application under Article 31 for its enforcement in any part of the United Kingdom shall, to the extent that its enforcement is authorised by the appropriate court, be registered in the prescribed manner in that court.

In this subsection "the appropriate court" means the court to which the application is made in pursuance of Article 32 (that is to say, the High Court or the Court of Session).

(2) Where a judgment is registered under this section, the reasonable costs and expenses of and incidental to its registration shall be recoverable as if they were sums recoverable under the judgment.

(3) A judgment registered under this section shall, for the purposes of its enforcement, be of the same force and effect, the registering court shall have in relation to its enforcement the same powers, and proceedings for or with respect to its enforcement may be taken, as if the judgment had originally been given by the registering court and had (where relevant) been entered.

(4) Subsection (3) is subject to Article 39 (restriction on enforcement where appeal pending or time for appeal unexpired), to section 7 and to any provision made by rules of court as to the manner in which and conditions subject to which a judgment registered under this section may be enforced.

5.—*Recognition and enforcement of maintenance orders.*[10]

(1) The function of transmitting to the appropriate court an application under Article 31 for the recognition or enforcement in the United Kingdom of a maintenance order shall be discharged—

    (a) as respects England and Wales and Scotland, by the Secretary of State;

    (b) as respects Northern Ireland, by the Lord Chancellor.

In this subsection "the appropriate court" means the magistrates' court or sheriff court having jurisdiction in the matter in accordance with the second paragraph of Article 32.

(2) Such an application shall be determined in the first instance by the prescribed officer of that court.

(3) Where on such an application the enforcement of the order is authorised to any extent, the order shall to that extent be registered in the prescribed manner in that court.

(4) A maintenance order registered under this section shall, for the purposes of its enforcement, be of the same force and effect, the registering court shall have in relation to its enforcement the same powers, and pro-

---

[10] See para. 40.12 above, n. †.

ceedings for or with respect to its enforcement may be taken, as if the order had been originally made by the registering court.

(5) Subsection (4) is subject to Article 39 (restriction on enforcement where appeal pending or time for appeal unexpired), to section 7 and to any provision made by rules of court as to the manner in which and conditions subject to which an order registered under this section may be enforced.

(5A) A maintenance order which by virtue of this section is enforceable by a magistrates' court in England and Wales shall be enforceable in the same manner as a magistrates' court maintenance order made by that court.

In this subsection "magistrates' court maintenance order" has the same meaning as in section 150(1) of the Magistrates' Courts Act 1980.

(6) A maintenance order which by virtue of this section is enforceable by a magistrates' court in Northern Ireland shall be enforceable in the same manner as an affiliation order made by that court.

(7) The payer under a maintenance order registered under this section in a magistrates' court in England and Wales or Northern Ireland shall give notice of any change of address to the clerk of that court.

A person who without reasonable excuse fails to comply with this subsection shall be guilty of an offence and liable on summary conviction to a fine not exceeding level 2 in the standard scale.

A3.44 6.—*Appeals under Article 37, second paragraph and Article 41.*
(1) The single further appeal on a point of law referred to in Article 37, second paragraph and Article 41 in relation to the recognition or enforcement of a judgment other than a maintenance order lies—
    (a) in England and Wales or Northern Ireland, to the Court of Appeal or to the House of Lords in accordance with Part II of the Administration of Justice Act 1969 (appeals direct from the High Court to the House of Lords);
    (b) in Scotland, to the Inner House of the Court of Session.

(2) Paragraph (a) of subsection (1) has effect notwithstanding section 15(2) of the Administration of Justice Act 1969 (exclusion of direct appeal to the House of Lords in cases where no appeal to that House lies from a decision of the Court of Appeal).

(3) The single further appeal on a point of law referred to in Article 37, second paragraph and Article 41 in relation to the recognition or enforcement of a maintenance order lies—
    (a) in England and Wales, to the High Court by way of case stated in accordance with section 111 of the Magistrates' Courts Act 1980;
    (b) in Scotland, to the Inner House of the Court of Session;
    (c) in Northern Ireland, to the Court of Appeal.

7.—*Interest on registered judgments.*
(1) Subject to subsection (4), where in connection with an application for registration of a judgment under section 4 or 5 the applicant shows—

   (a) that the judgment provides for the payment of a sum of money; and
   (b) that in accordance with the law of the Contracting State in which the judgment was given interest on that sum is recoverable under the judgment from a particular date or time,
the rate of interest and the date or time from which it is so recoverable shall be registered with the judgment and, subject to any provision made under subsection (2), the debt resulting, apart from section 4(2), from the registration of the judgment shall carry interest in accordance with the registered particulars.

(2) Provision may be made by rules of court as to the manner in which and the periods by reference to which any interest payable by virtue of subsection (1) is to be calculated and paid, including provision for such interest to cease to accrue as from a prescribed date.

(3) Costs or expenses recoverable by virtue of section 4(2) shall carry interest as if they were the subject of an order for the payment of costs or expenses made by the registering court on the date of registration.

(4) Interest on arrears of sums payable under a maintenance order registered under section 5 in a magistrates' court in England and Wales or Northern Ireland shall not be recoverable in that court, but without prejudice to the operation in relation to any such order of section 2A of the Maintenance Orders Act 1958 or section 11A of the Maintenance and Affiliation Orders Act (Northern Ireland) 1966 (which enable interest to be recovered if the order is reregistered for enforcement in the High Court).

(5) Except as mentioned in subsection (4), debts under judgments registered under section 4 or 5 shall carry interest only as provided by this section.

8.—Currency of payment under registered maintenance orders.
   (1) Sums payable in the United Kingdom under a maintenance order by virtue of its registration under section 5, including any arrears so payable, shall be paid in the currency of the United Kingdom.

(2) Where the order is expressed in any other currency, the amounts shall be converted on the basis of the exchange rate prevailing on the date of registration of the order.

(3) For the purposes of this section, a written certificate purporting to be signed by an officer of any bank in the United Kingdom and stating the exchange rate prevailing on a specified date shall be evidence, and in Scotland sufficient evidence, of the facts stated.

Other supplementary provisions

9.—Provisions supplementary to Title VII of the 1968 Convention   **A3.45**
   (1) The provisions of Title VII of the 1968 Convention (relationship between that convention and other conventions to which Contracting States are or may become parties) shall have effect in relation to—

    (a) any statutory provision, whenever passed or made, implementing any such other convention in the United Kingdom; and

    (b) any rule of law so far as it has the effect of so implementing any such other convention,

as they have in relation to that other convention itself.

(2) Her Majesty may by Order in Council declare a provision of a convention entered into by the United Kingdom to be a provision whereby the United Kingdom assumed an obligation of a kind provided for in Article 59 (which allows a Contracting State to agree with a third State to withhold recognition in certain cases from a judgment given by a court in another Contracting State which took jurisdiction on one of the grounds mentioned in the second paragraph of Article 3).

10.—*Allocation within U.K. of jurisdiction with respect to trusts and consumer contracts.*

(1) The provisions of this section shall have effect for the purpose of allocating within the United Kingdom jurisdiction in certain proceedings in respect of which the 1968 Convention confers jurisdiction on the courts of the United Kingdom generally and to which section 16 does not apply.

(2) Any proceedings which by virtue of Article 5(6) (trusts) are brought within the United Kingdom shall be brought in the courts of the part of the United Kingdom in which the trust is domiciled.

(3) Any proceedings which by virtue of the first paragraph of Article 14 (consumer contracts) are brought within the United Kingdom by a consumer on the ground that he is himself domiciled there shall be brought in the courts of the part of the United Kingdom in which he is domiciled.

11.—*Proof and admissibility of certain judgments and related documents.*

(1) For the purposes of the 1968 Convention—

    (a) a document, duly authenticated, which purports to be a copy of a judgment given by a court of a Contracting State other than the United Kingdom shall without further proof be deemed to be a true copy, unless the contrary is shown; and

    (b) the original or a copy of any such document as is mentioned in Article 46(2) or 47 (supporting documents to be produced by a party seeking recognition or enforcement of a judgment) shall be evidence, and in Scotland sufficient evidence, of any matter to which it relates.

(2) A document purporting to be a copy of a judgment given by any such court as it mentioned in subsection (1)(a) is duly authenticated for the purposes of this section if it purports—

    (a) to bear the seal of that court; or

    (b) to be certified by any person in his capacity as a judge or officer of that court to be a true copy of a judgment given by that court.

(3) Nothing in this section shall prejudice the admission in evidence of any document which is admissible apart from this section.

12.—*Provision for issue of copies of, and certificates in connection with, U.K. judgments.*

Rules of court may make provision for enabling any interested party wishing to secure under the 1968 Convention the recognition or enforcement in another Contracting State of a judgment given by a court in the United Kingdom to obtain, subject to any conditions specified in the rules—

(a) a copy of the judgment; and

(b) a certificate giving particulars relating to the judgment and the proceedings in which it was given.

13.—*Modifications to cover authentic instruments and court settlements.* **A3.46**

(1) Her Majesty may by Order in Council provide that—

(a) any provision of this Act relating to the recognition or enforcement in the United Kingdom or elsewhere of judgments to which the 1968 Convention applies; and

(b) any other statutory provision, whenever passed or made, so relating,

shall apply, with such modifications as may be specified in the Order, in relation to documents and settlements within Title IV of the 1968 Convention (authentic instruments and court settlements enforceable in the same manner as judgments) as if they were judgments to which that Convention applies.

(2) An Order in Council under this section may make different provisions in relation to different descriptions of documents and settlements.

(3) Any Order in Council under this section shall be subject to annulment in pursuance of a resolution of either House of Parliament.

14.—*Modifications consequential on revision of the Conventions.*

(1) If at any time it appears to Her Majesty in Council that Her Majesty's Government in the United Kingdom have agreed to a revision of any of the Conventions, including in particular any revision connected with the accession to the 1968 Convention of one or more further states, Her Majesty may by Order in Council make such modifications of this Act or any other statutory provision, whenever passed or made, as Her Majesty considers appropriate in consequence of the revision.

(2) An Order in Council under this section shall not be made unless a draft of the Order has been laid before Parliament and approved by a resolution of each House of Parliament.

(3) In this section "revision" means an omission from, addition to or alteration of any of the Conventions and includes replacement of any of the Conventions to any extent by another Convention, protocol or other description of international agreement.

15.—*Interpretation of Part I and consequential amendments.*

(1) In this Part, unless the context otherwise requires—

"judgment" has the meaning given by Article 25;

"maintenance order" means a maintenance judgment within the meaning of the 1968 Convention;
"payer," in relation to a maintenance order, means the person liable to
make the payments for which the order provides;
"prescribed" means prescribed by rules of court.

(2) References in this Part to a judgment registered under section 4 or 5
include, to the extent of its registration, references to a judgment so registered to a limited extent only.

(3) Anything authorised or required by the 1968 Convention or this Part
to be done by, to or before a particular magistrates' court may be done by,
to or before any magistrates' court acting for the same petty sessions area
(or, in Northern Ireland, petty sessions district) as that court.

(4) The enactments specified in Part I of Schedule 12 shall have effect
with the amendments specified there, being amendments consequential on
this Part.

PART II

JURISDICTION, AND RECOGNITION AND ENFORCEMENT OF JUDGMENTS, WITHIN THE UNITED KINGDOM

A3.47 16.—*Allocation within U.K. of jurisdiction in certain civil proceedings.*
(1) The provisions set out in Schedule 4 (which contains a modified version of Title II of the 1968 Convention) shall have effect for determining,
for each part of the United Kingdom, whether the courts of law of that
part, or any particular court of law in that part, have or has jurisdiction in
proceedings where—
    (a) the subject-matter of the proceedings is within the scope of the
        1968 Convention as determined by Article 1 (whether or not the
        Convention has effect in relation to the proceedings); and
    (b) the defendant or defender is domiciled in the United Kingdom
        or the proceedings are of a kind mentioned in Article 16 (exclu-
        sive jurisdiction regardless of domicile).

(2) In Schedule 4 modifications of Title II of the 1968 Convention are
indicated as follows—
    (a) modifications by way of omission are indicated by dots; and
    (b) within each Article words resulting from modifications by way of
        addition or substitution are printed in heavy type.

(3) In determining any question as to the meaning or effect of any provision contained in Schedule 4—
    (a) regard shall be had to any relevant principles laid down by the
        European Court in connection with Title II of the 1968 Conven-
        tion and to any relevant decision of that court as to the meaning
        or effect of any provision of that Title; and
    (b) without prejudice to the generality of paragraph (a), the reports
        mentioned in section 3(3) may be considered and shall, so far as

relevant, be given such weight as is appropriate in the circumstances.

(4) The provisions of this section and Schedule 4 shall have effect subject to the 1968 Convention and to the provisions of section 17.

(5) In section 15(1)(a) of the Maintenance Orders Act 1950 (domestic proceedings in which initial process may be served in another part of the United Kingdom), after sub-paragraph (v) there shall be added—

"(vi) Article 5(2) of Schedule 4 to the Civil Jurisdiction and Judgments Act 1982; or".

17.—*Exclusion of certain proceedings from Schedule 4.*
(1) Schedule 4 shall not apply to proceedings of any description listed in Schedule 5 or to proceedings in Scotland under any enactment which confers jurisdiction on a Scottish court in respect of a specific subject-matter on specific grounds.

(2) Her Majesty may by Order in Council—
    (a) add to the list in Schedule 5 any description of proceedings in any part of the United Kingdom; and
    (b) remove from that list any description of proceedings in any part of the United Kingdom (whether included in the list as originally enacted or added by virtue of this subsection).

(3) An Order in Council under subsection (2)—
    (a) may make different provisions for different descriptions of proceedings, for the same description of proceedings in different courts or for different parts of the United Kingdom; and
    (b) may contain such transitional and other incidental provisions as appear to Her Majesty to be appropriate.

(4) An Order in Council under subsection (2) shall not be made unless a draft of the Order has been laid before Parliament and approved by a resolution of each House of Parliament.

18.—*Enforcement of U.K. judgments in other parts of the U.K.*[11]
(1) In relation to any judgment to which this section applies—
    (a) Schedule 6 shall have effect for the purpose of enabling any money provisions contained in the judgment to be enforced in a part of the United Kingdom other than the part in which the judgment was given; and
    (b) Schedule 7 shall have effect for the purpose of enabling any non-money provisions so contained to be so enforced.

A3.48

(2) In this section "judgment" means any of the following (references to the giving of a judgment being construed accordingly)—
    (a) any judgment or order (by whatever name called) given or made by a court of law in the United Kingdom;
    (b) any judgment or order not within paragraph (a) which has been

---

[11] See para. 41.13 above, n. †.

entered in England and Wales or Northern Ireland in the High
Court or a county court;

(c) any document which in Scotland has been registered for
execution in the Books of Council and Session or in the sheriff
court books kept for any sheriffdom;

(d) any award or order made by a tribunal in any part of the United
Kingdom which is enforceable in that part without an order of a
court of law;

(e) an arbitration award which has become enforceable in the part of
the United Kingdom in which it was given in the same manner as
a judgment given by a court of law in that part;

and subject to the following provisions of this section, this section applies
to all such judgments.

(3) Subject to subsection (4), this section does not apply to—
(a) a judgment given in proceedings in a magistrates' court in England and Wales or Northern Ireland;
(b) a judgment given in proceedings other than civil proceedings;
(ba) a judgment given in the exercise of jurisdiction in relation to
insolvency law, within the meaning of section 426 of the Insolvency Act 1986;
(c) a judgment given in proceedings relating to—
. . .
(iii) the obtaining of title to administer the estate of a deceased person.

(4) This section applies, whatever the nature of the proceedings in
which it is made, to—
(a) a decree issued under section 13 of the Court of Exchequer (Scotland) Act 1856 (recovery of certain rentcharges and penalties by
process of the Court of Session);
(b) an order which is enforceable in the same manner as a judgment
of the High Court in England and Wales by virtue of section 16
of the Contempt of Court Act 1981 or section 140 of the Supreme
Court Act 1981 (which relates to fines for contempt of court and
forfeiture of recognisances).

(4A) This section does not apply as regards the enforcement in Scotland
of orders made by the High Court in England and Wales under or for the
purposes of the Drug Trafficking Offences Act 1986 or Part VI of the
Criminal Justice Act 1988 (confiscation of the proceeds of offences); or as
respects the enforcement in England and Wales of orders made by the
Court of Session or for the purposes of Part I of the Criminal Justice (Scotland) Act 1987.

(5) This section does not apply to so much of any judgment as—
(a) is an order to which section 16 of the Maintenance Orders Act
1950 applies (and is therefore an order for whose enforcement in
another part of the United Kingdom provision is made by Part II
of that Act);
(b) concerns the status or legal capacity of an individual;

    (c) relates to the management of the affairs of a person not capable of managing his own affairs;

    (d) is a provisional (including protective) measure other than an order for the making of an interim payment;

and except where otherwise stated references to a judgment to which this section applies are to such a judgment exclusive of any such provisions.

(6) The following are within subsection 5(b), but without prejudice to the generality of that provision—

    (a) a decree of judicial separation or of separation;

    (b) any provision relating to guardianship or custody.

(7) This section does not apply to a judgment of a court outside the United Kingdom which falls to be treated for the purposes of its enforcement as a judgment of a court of law in the United Kingdom by virtue of registration under Part II of the Administration of Justice Act 1920, Part I of the Foreign Judgments (Reciprocal Enforcement) Act 1933, Part I of the Maintenance Orders (Reciprocal Enforcement) Act 1972 or section 4 or 5 of this Act.

(8) A judgment to which this section applies, other than a judgment within paragraph (e) of subsection (2), shall not be enforced in another part of the United Kingdom except by way of registration under Schedule 6 or 7.

19.—*Recognition of U.K. judgments in other parts of the U.K.*

(1) A judgment to which this section applies given in one part of the United Kingdom shall not be refused recognition in another part of the United Kingdom solely on the ground that, in relation to that judgment, the court which gave it was not a court of competent jurisdiction according to the rules of private international law in force in that other part.

(2) Subject to subsection (3), this section applies to any judgment to which section 18 applies.

(3) This section does not apply to—

    (a) the documents mentioned in paragraph (c) of the definition of "judgment" in section 18(2);

    (b) the awards and orders mentioned in paragraphs (d) and (e) of that definition;

    (c) the decrees and orders referred to in section 18(4).

PART III

JURISDICTION IN SCOTLAND

20.—*Rules as to jurisdiction in Scotland*   **A3.49**

(1) Subject to Parts I and II and to the following provisions of this Part, Schedule 8 has effect to determine in what circumstances a person may be sued in civil proceedings in the Court of Session or in a sheriff court.

(2) Nothing in Schedule 8 affects the competence as respects subject-matter or value of the Court of Session or of the sheriff court.

(3) Section 6 of the Sheriff Courts (Scotland) Act 1907 shall cease to have effect to the extent that it determines jurisdiction in relation to any matter to which Schedule 8 applies.

(4) In Schedule 8—
    (a) words resulting from modifications of Title II of the 1968 Convention, by way of addition or substitution, and provisions not derived from that Title are printed in heavy type;
    (b) the marginal notes show, where appropriate, of which provision of Title II a provision of Schedule 8 is a modified version.

(5) In determining any question as to the meaning or effect of any provision contained in Schedule 8 and derived to any extent from Title II of the 1968 Convention—
    (a) regard shall be had to any relevant principles laid down by the European Court in connection with Title II of the 1968 Convention and to any relevant decision of that court as to the meaning or effect of any provision of that Title; and
    (b) without prejudice to the generality of paragraph (a), the reports mentioned in section 3(3) may be considered and shall, so far as relevant, be given such weight as is appropriate in the circumstances.

21.—*Continuance of certain jurisdictions.*
    (1) Schedule 8 does not affect—
    (a) the operation of any enactment which confers jurisdiction on a Scottish court in respect of a specific subject-matter on specific grounds;
    (b) without prejudice to the foregoing generality, the jurisdiction of any court in respect of any matter mentioned in Schedule 9.

(2) Her Majesty may by Order in Council—
    (a) add to the list in Schedule 9 any description of proceedings; and
    (b) remove from that list any description of proceedings (whether included in the list as originally enacted or added by virtue of this subsection).

(3) An Order in Council under subsection (2) may—
    (a) make different provisions for different descriptions of proceedings or for the same description of proceedings in different courts;
    (b) contain such transitional and other incidental provisions as appear to Her Majesty to be appropriate.

(4) An Order in Council under subsection (2) shall not be made unless a draft of the Order has been laid before Parliament and approved by a resolution of each House of Parliament.

22.—*Supplementary provisions.*
    (1) Nothing in Schedule 8 shall prevent a court from declining jurisdiction on the ground of *forum non conveniens.*

    (2) Nothing in Schedule 8 affects the operation of any enactment or rule

of law under which a court may decline to exercise jurisdiction because of the prorogation by parties of the jurisdiction of another court.

(3) For the avoidance of doubt, it is declared that nothing in Schedule 8 affects the *nobile officium* of the Court of Session.

(4) Where a court has jurisdiction in any proceedings by virtue of Schedule 8, that court shall also have jurisdiction to determine any matter which—

    (a) is ancillary or incidental to the proceedings; or

    (b) requires to be determined for the purposes of a decision in the proceedings.

23.—*Savings and consequential amendments.*
    (1) Nothing in Schedule 8 shall affect—

    (a) the power of any court to vary or recall a maintenance order granted by that court;

    (b) the power of a sheriff court under section 22 of the Maintenance Orders Act 1950 (discharge and variation of maintenance orders registered in sheriff courts) to vary or discharge a maintenance order registered in that court under Part II of that Act; or

    (c) the power of a sheriff court under section 9 of the Maintenance Orders (Reciprocal Enforcement) Act 1972 (variation and revocation of maintenance orders registered in United Kingdom courts) to vary or revoke a registered order within the meaning of Part I of that Act.

(2) The enactments specified in Part II of Schedule 12 shall have effect with the amendments specified there, being amendments consequential on Schedule 8.

PART IV

MISCELLANEOUS PROVISIONS

Provisions relating to jurisdiction

24.—*Interim relief and protective measures in cases of doubtful jurisdiction.*   **A3.50**
    (1) Any power of a court in England and Wales or Northern Ireland to grant interim relief pending trial or pending the determination of an appeal shall extend to a case where—

    (a) the issue to be tried, or which is the subject of the appeal, relates to the jurisdiction of the court to entertain the proceedings; or

    (b) the proceedings involve the reference of any matter to the European Court under the 1971 Protocol.

(2) Any power of a court in Scotland to grant protective measures pending the decision of any hearing shall apply to a case where—

    (a) the subject of the proceedings includes a question as to the jurisdiction of the court to entertain them; or

(b) the proceedings involve the reference of a matter to the European Court under the 1971 Protocol.

(3) Subsections (1) and (2) shall not be construed as restricting any power to grant interim relief or protective measures which a court may have apart from this section.

25.—*Interim relief in England and Wales and Northern Ireland in the absence of substantive proceedings.*

(1) The High Court in England and Wales or Northern Ireland shall have power to grant interim relief where—

(a) proceedings have been or are to be commenced in a Contracting State other than the United Kingdom or in a part of the United Kingdom other than that in which the High Court in question exercises jurisdiction; and

(b) they are or will be proceedings whose subject-matter is within the scope of the 1968 Convention as determined by Article 1 (whether or not the Convention has effect in relation to the proceedings).

(2) On an application for any interim relief under subsection (1) the court may refuse to grant that relief if, in the opinion of the court, the fact that the court has no jurisdiction apart from this section in relation to the subject-matter of the proceedings in question makes it inexpedient for the court to grant it.

(3) Her Majesty may by Order in Council extend the power to grant interim relief conferred by subsection (1) so as to make it exercisable in relation to proceedings of any of the following descriptions, namely—

(a) proceedings commenced or to be commenced otherwise than in a Contracting State;

(b) proceedings whose subject-matter is not within the scope of the 1968 Convention as determined by Article 1;

(c) arbitration proceedings.

(4) An Order in Council under subsection (3)—

(a) may confer power to grant only specified descriptions of interim relief;

(b) may make different provision for different classes of proceedings, for proceeding pending in different countries or courts outside the United Kingdom or in different parts of the United Kingdom, and for other different circumstances; and

(c) may impose conditions or restrictions on the exercise of any power conferred by the Order.

(5) An Order in Council under subsection (3) which confers power to grant interim relief in relation to arbitration proceedings may provide for the repeal of any provision of section 12(6) of the Arbitration Act 1950 or section 21(1) of the Arbitration Act (Northern Ireland) 1937 to the extent that it is superseded by the provisions of the Order.

(6) Any Order in Council under subsection (3) shall be subject to annulment in pursuance of a resolution of either House of Parliament.

(7) In this section "interim relief," in relation to the High Court in England and Wales or Northern Ireland, means interim relief of any kind which that court has power to grant in proceedings relating to matters within its jurisdiction, other than—
    (a) a warrant for the arrest of property; or
    (b) provision for obtaining evidence.

26.—*Security in Admiralty proceedings in England and Wales or Northern*   **A3.51**
Ireland in case of stay, etc.
(1) Where in England and Wales or Northern Ireland a court stays or dismisses Admiralty proceedings on the ground that the dispute in question should be submitted to arbitration or to the determination of the courts of another part of the United Kingdom or of an overseas country, the court may, if in those proceedings property has been arrested or bail or other security has been given to prevent or obtain release from arrest—
    (a) order that the property arrested be retained as security for the satisfaction of an award or judgment which—
        (i) is given in respect of the dispute in the arbitration or legal proceedings in favour of which those proceedings are stayed or dismissed; and
        (ii) is enforceable in England and Wales or, as the case may be, in Northern Ireland; or
    (b) order that the stay or dismissal of those proceedings be conditional on the provision of equivalent security for the satisfaction of any such award or judgment.

(2) Where a court makes an order under subsection (1), it may attach such conditions to the order as it thinks fit, in particular conditions with respect to the institution or prosecution of the relevant arbitration or legal proceedings.

(3) Subject to any provision made by rules of court and to any necessary modifications, the same law and practice shall apply in relation to property retained in pursuance of an order made by a court under subsection (1) as would apply if it were held for the purposes of proceedings in that court.

27.—*Provisional and protective measures in Scotland in the absence of*
substantive proceedings.
(1) The Court of Session may, in any case to which this subsection applies—
    (a) subject to subsection (2)(c), grant a warrant for the arrestment of any assets situated in Scotland;
    (b) subject to subsection (2)(c), grant a warrant of inhibition over any property situated in Scotland; and
    (c) grant interim interdict.

(2) Subsection (1) applies to any case in which—
    (a) proceedings have been commenced but not concluded, or, in relation to paragraph (c) of that subsection, are to be commenced, in another Contracting State or in England and Wales or Northern Ireland;

    (b) the subject-matter of the proceeding is within the scope of the 1968 Convention as determined by Article 1; and

    (c) in relation to paragraphs (a) and (b) of subsection (1), such a warrant could competently have been granted in equivalent proceedings before a Scottish court;

but it shall not be necessary, in determining whether proceedings have been commenced for the purpose of paragraph (a) of this subsection, to show that any document has been served on or notice given to the defender.

(3) Her Majesty may by Order in Council confer on the Court of Session power to do anything mentioned in subsection (1) or in section 28 in relation to proceedings of any of the following descriptions, namely—

    (a) proceedings commenced otherwise than in a Contracting State;

    (b) proceedings whose subject-matter is not within the scope of the 1968 Convention as determined by Article 1;

    (c) arbitration proceedings;

    (d) in relation to subsection (1)(c) or section 28, proceedings which are to be commenced otherwise than in a Contracting State.

(4) An Order in Council under subsection (3)—

    (a) may confer power to do only certain of the things mentioned in subsection (1) or in section 28;

    (b) make different provision for different classes of proceedings, for proceedings pending in different countries or courts outside the United Kingdom or in different parts of the United Kingdom, and for other different circumstances; and

    (c) may impose conditions or restrictions on the exercise of any power conferred by the Order.

(5) Any Order in Council under subsection (3) shall be subject to annulment in pursuance of a resolution of either House of Parliament.

A3.52   28.—*Application of section 1 of Administration of Justice (Scotland) Act 1972.*[12]

When any proceedings have been brought, or are likely to be brought, in another Contracting State or in England and Wales or Northern Ireland in respect of any matter which is within the scope of the 1968 Convention as determined in Article 1, the Court of Session shall have the like power to make an order under section 1 of the Administration of Justice (Scotland) Act 1972 as amended by the Law Reform (Miscellaneous Provisions) (Scotland) Act 1985 as if the proceedings in question had been brought, or were likely to be brought, in that court.

29.—*Service of county court process outside Northern Ireland.*

The County Court Rules Committee established by Article 46 of the County Courts (Northern Ireland) Order 1980 may make county court rules with respect to the service of process outside Northern Ireland and the conditions subject to which process may be so served; and accordingly in Article 48 of that Order (powers of Rules Committee), after paragraph (e) there shall be added—

---

[12] See para. 43.15 above, n. †.

"(f) the service of process outside Northern Ireland, and the conditions subject to which process may be so served.".

30.—*Proceedings in England and Wales or Northern Ireland for torts to immovable property.*

(1) The jurisdiction of any court in England and Wales or Northern Ireland to entertain proceedings for trespass to, or any other tort affecting, immovable property shall extend to cases in which the property in question is situated outside that part of the United Kingdom unless the proceedings are principally concerned with a question of the title to, or the right to possession of, that property.

(2) Subsection (1) has effect subject to the 1968 Convention and to the provisions set out in Schedule 4.

Provisions relating to recognition and enforcement of judgments

31.—*Overseas judgments given against states, etc.*[13]   **A3.53**

(1) A judgment given by a court of an overseas country against a state other than the United Kingdom or the state to which that court belongs shall be recognised and enforced in the United Kingdom if, and only if—
  (a) it would be so recognised and enforced if it had not been given against a state; and
  (b) that court would have had jurisdiction in the matter if it had applied rules corresponding to those applicable to such matters in the United Kingdom in accordance with sections 2 to 11 of the State Immunity Act 1978.

(2) References in subsection (1) to a judgment given against a state include references to judgments of any of the following descriptions given in relation to a a state—
  (a) judgments against the government, or a department of the government, of the state but not (except as mentioned in paragraph (c)) judgments against an entity which is distinct from the executive organs of government;
  (b) judgments against the sovereign or head of state in his public capacity;
  (c) judgments against any such separate entity as is mentioned in paragraph (a) given in proceedings relating to anything done by it in the exercise of the sovereign authority of the state.

(3) Nothing in subsection (1) shall affect the recognition or enforcement in the United Kingdom of a judgment to which Part I of the Foreign Judgments (Reciprocal Enforcement) Act 1933 applies by virtue of section 4 of the Carriage of Goods by Road Act 1965, section 17(4) of the Nuclear Installations Act 1965, section 13(3) of the Merchant Shipping (Oil Pollu-

---

[13] See para. 43.21 above, n. †.

tion) Act 1971, section 6 of the International Transport Conventions Act 1983 or section 5 of the Carriage of Passengers by Road Act 1974.

(4) Sections 12, 13 and 14(3) and (4) of the State Immunity Act 1978 (service of process and procedural privileges) shall apply to proceedings for the recognition or enforcement in the United Kingdom of a judgment given by a court of an overseas country (whether or not that judgment is within subsection (1) of this section) as they apply to other proceedings.

(5) In this section "state," in the case of a federal state, includes any of its constituent territories.

32.—*Overseas judgments given in proceedings brought in breach of agreement for settlement of disputes.*[14]
(1) Subject to the following provisions of this section, a judgment given by a court of an overseas country in any proceedings shall not be recognised or enforced in the United Kingdom if—
  (a) the bringing of those proceedings in that court was contrary to an agreement under which the dispute in question was to be settled otherwise than by proceedings in the courts of that country; and
  (b) those proceedings were not brought in that court by, or with the agreement of, the person against whom the judgment was given; and
  (c) that person did not counterclaim in the proceedings or otherwise submit to the jurisdiction of that court.

(2) Subsection (1) does not apply where the agreement referred to in paragraph (a) of that subsection was illegal, void or unenforceable or was incapable of being performed for reasons not attributable to the fault of the party bringing the proceedings in which the judgment was given.

(3) In determining whether a judgment given by a court of an overseas country should be recognised or enforced in the United Kingdom, a court in the United Kingdom shall not be bound by any decision of the overseas court relating to any of the matters mentioned in subsection (1) or (2).

(4) Nothing in subsection (1) shall affect the recognition or enforcement in the United Kingdom of—
  (a) a judgment which is required to be recognised or enforced there under the 1968 Convention;
  (b) a judgment to which Part I of the Foreign Judgments (Reciprocal Enforcement) Act 1933 applies by virtue of section 4 of the Carriage of Goods by Road Act 1965, section 17(4) of the Nuclear Installations Act 1965, section 13(3) of the Merchant Shipping (Oil Pollution) Act 1971, section 6 of the International Transport Conventions Act 1983, section 5 of the Carriage of Passengers by Road Act 1974 or section 6(4) of the Merchant Shipping Act 1974.

---

[14] See para. 43.25 above, n. †.

33.—*Certain steps not to amount to submission to jurisdiction of overseas court.*

(1) For the purposes of determining whether a judgment given by a court of an overseas country should be recognised or enforced in England and Wales or Northern Ireland, the person against whom the judgment was given shall not be regarded as having submitted to the jurisdiction of the court by reason only of the fact that he appeared (conditionally or otherwise) in the proceedings for all or any one or more of the following purposes, namely—

    (a) to contest the jurisdiction of the court;

    (b) to ask the court to dismiss or stay the proceedings on the ground that the dispute in question should be submitted to arbitration or to the determination of the courts of another country;

    (c) to protect, or obtain the release of, property seized or threatened with seizure in the proceedings.

(2) Nothing in this section shall affect the recognition or enforcement in England and Wales or Northern Ireland of a judgment which is required to be recognised or enforced there under the 1968 Convention.

34.—*Certain judgments a bar to further proceedings on the same cause of action.*

No proceedings may be brought by a person in England and Wales or Northern Ireland on a cause of action in respect of which a judgment has been given in his favour in proceedings between the same parties, or their privies, in a court in another part of the United Kingdom or in a court of an overseas country, unless that judgment is not enforceable or entitled to recognition in England and Wales or, as the case may be, in Northern Ireland.

35.—*Minor amendments relating to overseas judgments.* **A3.54**

(1) The Foreign Judgments (Reciprocal Enforcement) Act 1933 shall have effect with the amendments specified in Schedule 10, being amendments whose main purpose is to enable Part I of that Act to be applied to judgments of courts other than superior courts, to judgments providing for interim payments and to certain arbitration awards.

(2) For section 10 of the Administration of Justice Act 1920 (issue of certificates of judgments obtained in the United Kingdom) there shall be substituted—

    "**10.**—(1) Where—

    (a) a judgment has been obtained in the High Court in England or Northern Ireland, or in the Court of Session in Scotland, against any person; and

    (b) the judgment creditor wishes to secure the enforcement of the judgment in a part of Her Majesty's dominions outside the United Kingdom to which this part of this Act extends,

the court shall, on an application made by the judgment creditor, issue to him a certified copy of the judgment.

    (2) The reference in the preceding subsection to Her Majesty's

dominions shall be construed as if that subsection had come into force in its present form at the commencement of this Act."

(3) In section 14 of the Administration of Justice Act 1920 (extent of Part II of that Act), after subsection (2) there shall be inserted—

"(3) Her Majesty may by Order in Council under this section consolidate any Orders in Council under this section which are in force when the consolidating Order is made."

36.—*Registration of maintenance orders in Northern Ireland.*
(1) Where—
    (a) a High Court order or a Court of Session order has been registered in the High Court of Justice in Northern Ireland ("the Northern Ireland High Court") under Part II of the Maintenance Orders Act 1950; or
    (b) a county court order, a magistrates' court order or a sheriff court order has been registered in a court of summary jurisdiction in Northern Ireland under that Part,
an application may be made to the original court for the registration of the order in, respectively, a court of summary jurisdiction in Northern Ireland or the Northern Ireland High Court.

(2) In subsection (1) "the original court," in relation to an order, means the court by which the order was made.

(3) Section 2 (except subsection (6A)) and section 2A of the Maintenance Orders Act 1958 shall have effect for the purposes of an application under subsection (1), and subsections (2), (3), (4) and (4A) of section 5 of that Act shall have effect for the purposes of the cancellation of a registration made on such an application, as if—
    (a) "registration" in those provisions included registration in the appropriate Northern Ireland court ("registered" being construed accordingly);
    (b) any reference in those provisions to a High Court order or a magistrates' court order included, respectively, a Court of Session order or a sheriff court order; and
    (c) any other reference in those provisions to the High Court or a magistrates' court included the Northern Ireland High Court or a court of summary jurisdiction in Northern Ireland.

(4) Where an order is registered in Northern Ireland under this section, Part II of the Maintenance and Affiliation Orders Act (Northern Ireland) 1966, except sections 11, 11A and 14(2) and (3), shall apply as if the order had been registered in accordance with the provisions of that Part.

(5) A court of summary jurisdiction in Northern Ireland shall have jurisdiction to hear a complaint by or against a person residing outside Northern Ireland for the discharge or variation of an order registered in Northern Ireland under this section; and where such a complaint is made against a person residing outside Northern Ireland, then, if he resides in England and Wales or Scotland, section 15 of the Maintenance Orders Act 1950 (which relates to the service of process on persons residing in those

countries) shall have effect in relation to the complaint as it has effect in relation to the proceedings therein mentioned.

(6) The enactments specified in Part III of Schedule 12 shall have effect with the amendments specified there, being amendments consequential on this section.

37.—Minor amendments relating to maintenance orders.
(1) The enactments specified in Schedule 11 shall have effect with the amendments specified there, being amendments whose main purpose is as follows—

Part I—to extend certain enforcement provisions to lump sum maintenance orders;
Part II—to provide for the recovery of interest according to the law of the country of origin in the case of maintenance orders made in other jurisdictions and registered in the High Court;
Part III—to extend the Maintenance Orders (Reciprocal Enforcement) Act 1972 to cases where the payer under a maintenance order is not resident within the jurisdiction but has assets there.

(2) In section 27(1) of the Maintenance Orders (Reciprocal Enforcement) Act 1972 (application by person in convention country for recovery of maintenance in England and Wales or Northern Ireland to be treated as a complaint), after "as if it were a complaint" there shall be inserted "made at the time when the application was received by the Secretary of State or the Lord Chancellor."

38.—Overseas judgments counteracting an award of multiple damages.
(1) Section 7 of the Protection of Trading Interests Act 1980 (which enables provisions to be made by Order in Council for the enforcement in the United Kingdom on a reciprocal basis of overseas judgments directed to counteracting a judgment for multiple damages given in a third country) shall be amended as follows.

(2) In subsection (1) for "judgments given under any provision of the law of that country corresponding to that section" there shall be substituted "judgments of any description specified in the Order which are given under any provision of the law of that country relating to the recovery of sums paid or obtained pursuant to a judgment for multiple damages within the meaning of section 5(3) above, whether or not that provision corresponds to section 6 above."

(3) After subsection (1) there shall be inserted—

"(1A) Such an Order in Council may, as respects judgments to which it relates—
 (a) make different provisions for different descriptions of judgment; and
 (b) impose conditions or restrictions on the enforcement of judgments of any description."

Jurisdiction, and recognition and enforcement of judgments, as between United Kingdom and certain territories

A3.55 39.—*Application of provisions corresponding to 1968 Convention in relation to certain territories.*

(1) Her Majesty may by Order in Council make provision corresponding to the provision made in the 1968 Convention as between the Contracting States to that Convention, with such modifications as appear to Her Majesty to be appropriate, for regulating, as between the United Kingdom and any of the territories mentioned in subsection (2), the jurisdiction of courts and the recognition and enforcement of judgments.

(2) The territories referred to in subsection (1) are—
- (a) the Isle of Man;
- (b) any of the Channel Islands;
- (c) Gibraltar;
- (d) the Sovereign Base Areas of Akrotiri and Dhekelia (that is to say the areas mentioned in section 2(1) of the Cyprus Act 1960).

(3) An Order in Council under this section may contain such supplementary and incidental provisions as appear to Her Majesty to be necessary or expedient, including in particular provisions corresponding to or applying any of the provisions of Part I with such modifications as may be specified in the Order.

(4) Any Order in Council under this section shall be subject to annulment in pursuance of a resolution of either House of Parliament.

Legal aid

A3.56 40.—*Power to modify enactments relating to legal aid, etc.*[15]

(3) In Article 22 of the Legal Aid, Advice and Assistance (Northern Ireland) Order 1981 (power of Lord Chancellor to make regulations), after paragraph (4) there shall be inserted as paragraph (4A)—

> "(4A) Without prejudice to the preceding provisions of this Article or any other provision of this Part authorising the making of regulations, regulations may also modify the provisions of, or of any instrument having effect under, this Part (including so much of any of those provisions as specifies a sum of money) for the purposes of the application of those provisions—
> - (a) in cases where their modification appears to the Lord Chancellor necessary for the purpose of fulfilling any obligation imposed on the United Kingdom or Her Majesty's government therein by any international agreement; or
> - (b) in relation to proceedings for securing the recognition or enforcement in Northern Ireland of judgments given outside the United

---

[15] See para. 43.50 above, n. †.

Kingdom for whose recognition or enforcement in the United Kingdom provision is made by any international agreement."

PART V

SUPPLEMENTARY AND GENERAL PROVISIONS

Domicile

41.—*Domicile of individuals.*　　　　　　　　　　　　　　　**A3.57**

(1) Subject to Article 52 (which contains provisions for determining whether a party is domiciled in a Contracting State), the following provisions of this section determine, for the purposes of the 1968 Convention and this Act, whether an individual is domiciled in the United Kingdom or in a particular part of, or place in, the United Kingdom or in a state other than a Contracting State.

(2) An individual is domiciled in the United Kingdom if and only if—
    (a) he is resident in the United Kingdom; and
    (b) the nature and circumstances of his residence indicate that he has a substantial connection with the United Kingdom.

(3) Subject to subsection (5), an individual is domiciled in a particular part of the Untied Kingdom if and only if—
    (a) he is resident in that part; and
    (b) the nature and circumstances of his residence indicate that he has a substantial connection with that part.

(4) An individual is domiciled in a particular place in the United Kingdom if and only if he—
    (a) is domiciled in the part of the United Kingdom in which that place is situated; and
    (b) is resident in that place.

(5) An individual who is domiciled in the United Kingdom but in whose case the requirements of subsection 3(b) are not satisfied in relation to any particular part of the United Kingdom shall be treated as domiciled in the part of the United Kingdom in which he is resident.

(6) In the case of an individual who—
    (a) is resident in the United Kingdom, or in a particular part of the United Kingdom; and
    (b) has been so resident for the last three months or more,
the requirements of subsection (2)(b) or, as the case may be, subsection (3)(b) shall be presumed to be fulfilled unless the contrary is proved.

(7) An individual is domiciled in a state other than a Contracting State if and only if—
    (a) he is resident in that state; and

    (b) the nature and circumstances of his residence indicate that he has a substantial connection with that state.

42.—*Domicile and seat of corporation and association.*

(1) For the purposes of this Act the seat of a corporation or association (as determined by this section) shall be treated as its domicile.

(2) The following provisions of this section determine where a corporation or association has its seat—

    (a) for the purposes of Article 53 (which for the purposes of the 1968 Convention equates the domicile of such a body with its seat); and

    (b) for the purposes of this Act other than the provisions mentioned in section 43(1)(b) and (c).

(3) A corporation or association has its seat in the United Kingdom if and only if—

    (a) it was incorporated or formed under the law of a part of the United Kingdom and has its registered office or some other official address in the United Kingdom; or

    (b) its central management and control is exercised in the United Kingdom.

(4) A corporation or association has its seat in a particular part of the United Kingdom if and only if it has its seat in the United Kingdom and—

    (a) it has its registered office or some other official address in that part; or

    (b) its central management and control is exercised in that part; or

    (c) it has a place of business in that part.

(5) A corporation or association has its seat in a particular place in the United Kingdom if and only if it has its seat in the part of the United Kingdom in which that place is situated and—

    (a) it has its registered office or some other official address in that place; or

    (b) its central management and control is exercised in that place; or

    (c) it has a place of business in that place.

(6) Subject to subsection (7), a corporation or association has its seat in a state other than the United Kingdom if and only if—

    (a) it was incorporated or formed under the law of that state and has its registered office or some other official address there; or

    (b) its central management and control is exercised in that state.

(7) A corporation or association shall not be regarded as having its seat in a Contracting State other than the United Kingdom if it is shown that the courts of that state would not regard it as having its seat there.

(8) In this section—

"business" includes any activity carried on by a corporation or association, and "place of business" shall be construed accordingly;

"official address," in relation to a corporation or association, means an

address which it is required by law to register, notify or maintain for
the purpose of receiving notices or other communications.

43.—*Seat of corporation or association for purposes of Article 16(2) and*   **A3.58**
related provisions.

(1) The following provisions of this section determine where a corporation or association has its seat for the purposes of—
  (a) Article 16(2) (which confers exclusive jurisdiction over proceed-
      ings relating to the formation or dissolution of such bodies, or to
      the decisions of their organs);
  (b) Articles 5A and 16(2) in Schedule 4; and
  (c) Rules 2(12) and 4(1)(b) in Schedule 8.

(2) A corporation or association has its seat in the United Kingdom if
and only if—
  (a) it was incorporated or formed under the law of a part of the
      United Kingdom; or
  (b) its central management and control is exercised in the United
      Kingdom.

(3) A corporation or association has its seat in a particular part of the
United Kingdom if and only if it has its seat in the United Kingdom and—
  (a) subject to subsection (5), it was incorporated or formed under
      the law of that part; or
  (b) being incorporated or formed under the law of a state other than
      the United Kingdom, its central management and control is
      exercised in that part.

(4) A corporation or association has its seat in a particular place in Scotland if and only if it has its seat in Scotland and—
  (a) it has its registered office or some other official address in that
      place; or
  (b) it has no registered office or other official address in Scotland,
      but its central management and control is exercised in that place.

(5) A corporation or association formed under—
  (a) an enactment forming part of the law of more than one part of
      the United Kingdom; or
  (b) an instrument having effect in the domestic law of more than one
      part of the United Kingdom,
shall, if it has a registered office, be taken to have its seat in the part of the
United Kingdom in which that office is situated, and not in any other part
of the United Kingdom.

(6) Subject to subsection (7), a corporation or association has its seat in a
Contracting State other than the United Kingdom if and only if—
  (a) it was incorporated or formed under the law of that state; or
  (b) it central management and control is exercised in that state.

(7) A corporation or association shall not be regarded as having its seat
in a Contracting State other than the United Kingdom if—
  (a) it has its seat in the United Kingdom by virtue of subsection
      (2)(a); or

(b) it is shown that the courts of that other state would not regard it for the purposes of Article 16(2) as having its seat there.

(8) In this section "official address" has the same meaning as in section 42.

44.—*Persons deemed to be domiciled in the United Kingdom for certain purposes.*
(1) This section applies to—
    (a) proceedings within Section 3 of Title II of the 1968 Convention (insurance contracts), and
    (b) proceedings within Section 4 of that Title (consumer contracts).

(2) A person who, for the purposes of proceedings to which this section applies arising out of the operations of a branch, agency or other establishment in the United Kingdom, is deemed for the purposes of the 1968 Convention to be domiciled in the United Kingdom by virtue of—

    (a) Article 8, second paragraph (insurers); or
    (b) Article 13, second paragraph (suppliers of goods, services or credit to consumers).
shall, for the purposes of those proceedings, be treated for the purposes of this Act as so domiciled and as domiciled in the part of the United Kingdom in which the branch agency or establishment in question is situated.

A3.59 45.—*Domicile of trusts.*
(1) The following provisions of this section determine, for the purposes of the 1968 Convention and this Act, where a trust is domiciled.

(2) A trust is domiciled in the United Kingdom if and only if it is by virtue of subsection (3) domiciled in a part of the United Kingdom.

(3) A trust is domiciled in a part of the United Kingdom if and only if the system of law of that part is the system of law with which the trust has its closest and most real connection.

46.—*Domicile and seat of the Crown.*
(1) For the purposes of this Act the seat of the Crown (as determined by this section) shall be treated as its domicile.

(2) The following provisions of this section determine where the Crown has its seat—
    (a) for the purposes of the 1968 Convention (in which Article 53 equates the domicile of a legal person with its seat); and
    (b) for the purposes of this Act.

(3) Subject to the provisions of any Order in Council for the time being in force under subsection (4)—
    (a) the Crown in right of Her Majesty's government in the United Kingdom has its seat in every part of, and every place in, the United Kingdom; and
    (b) the Crown in right of Her Majesty's government in Northern

Ireland has its seat in every part of, and every place in, Northern Ireland.

(4) Her Majesty may by Order in Council provide that, in the case of proceedings of any specified description against the Crown in right of Her Majesty's government in the United Kingdom, the Crown shall be treated for the purposes of the 1968 Convention and this Act as having its seat in, and in every place in, a specified part of the United Kingdom and not in any other part of the United Kingdom.

(5) An Order in Council under subsection (4) may frame a description of proceedings in any way, and in particular may do so by reference to the government department or officer of the Crown against which or against whom they fall to be instituted.

(6) Any Order in Council under this section shall be subject to annulment in pursuance of a resolution of either House of Parliament.

(7) Nothing in this section applies to the Crown otherwise than in right of Her Majesty's government in the United Kingdom or Her Majesty's government in Northern Ireland.

Other supplementary provisions

47.—*Modifications occasioned by decisions of European Court as to meaning*   **A3.60**
or effect of Conventions.
(1) Her Majesty may by Order in Council—
- (a) make such provision as Her Majesty considers appropriate for the purpose of bringing the law of any part of the United Kingdom into accord with the Conventions as affected by any principle laid down by the European Court in connection with the Conventions or by any decision of that court as to the meaning or effect of any provision of the Conventions; or
- (b) make such modifications of Schedule 4 or Schedule 8, or of any other statutory provision affected by any provision of either of those Schedules, as Her Majesty considers appropriate in view of any principle laid down by the European Court in connection with Title II of the 1968 Convention or of any decision of that court as to the meaning or effect of any provision of that Title.

(2) The provision which may be made by virtue of paragraph (a) of subsection (1) includes such modifications of this Act or any other statutory provision, whenever passed or made, as Her Majesty considers appropriate for the purpose mentioned in that paragraph.

(3) The modifications which may be made by virtue of paragraph (b) of subsection (1) include modifications designed to produce divergence between any provision of Schedule 4 or Schedule 8 and a corresponding provision of Title II of the 1968 Convention as affected by any such principle or decision as is mentioned in that paragraph.

(4) An Order in Council under this section shall not be made unless a

draft of the Order has been laid before Parliament and approved by a resolution of each House of Parliament.

48.—*Matters for which rules of court may provide.*

(1) Rules of court may make provision for regulating the procedure to be followed in any court in connection with any provision of this Act or the Conventions.

(2) Rules of court may make provision as to the manner in which and the conditions subject to which a certificate or judgment registered in any court under any provision of this Act may be enforced, including provision for enabling the court or, in Northern Ireland the Enforcement of Judgments Office, subject to any conditions specified in the rules, to give directions about such matters.

(3) Without prejudice to the generality of subsections (1) and (2), the power to make rules of court for magistrates' courts, and in Northern Ireland the power to make Judgment Enforcement Rules, shall include power to make such provision as the rule-making authority considers necessary or expedient for the purposes of the provisions of the Conventions and this Act relating to maintenance proceedings and the recognition and enforcement of maintenance orders, and shall in particular include power to make provision as to any of the following matters—

(a) authorising the service in another Contracting State of process issued by or for the purposes of a magistrates' court and the service and execution in England and Wales or Northern Ireland or process issued in another Contracting State;

(b) requesting courts in other parts of the United Kingdom or in other Contracting States to take evidence there for the purposes of proceedings in England and Wales or Northern Ireland;

(c) the taking of evidence in England and Wales or Northern Ireland in response to similar requests received from such courts;

(d) the circumstances in which and the conditions subject to which any powers conferred under paragraphs (a) to (c) are to be exercised;

(e) the admission in evidence, subject to such conditions as may be prescribed in the rules, of statements contained in documents purporting to be made or authenticated by a court in another part of the United Kingdom or in another Contracting State, or by a judge or official of such a court, which purport—

(i) to set out or summarise evidence given in proceedings in that court or to be documents received in evidence in such proceedings or copies of such documents; or

(ii) to set out or summarise evidence taken for the purposes of proceedings in England and Wales or Northern Ireland, whether or not in response to any such request as is mentioned in paragraph (b); or

(iii) to record information relating to the payments made under an order of that court;

(f) the circumstances and manner in which a magistrates' court may or must vary or revoke a maintenance order registered in that court, cancel the registration of, or refrain from enforcing, such an order or transmit such an order for enforcement in another part of the United Kingdom;

  (g) the cases and manner in which courts in other parts of the United Kingdom or in other Contracting States are to be informed of orders made, or other things done, by or for the purposes of a magistrates' court;

  (h) the circumstances and manner in which a magistrates' court may communicate for other purposes with such courts;

  (i) the giving of notice of such matters as may be prescribed in the rules to such persons as may be so prescribed and the manner in which such notice is to be given.

(4) Nothing in this section shall be taken as derogating from the generality of any power to make rules of court conferred by any other enactment.

49.—*Saving for powers to stay, sist, strike out or dismiss proceedings.*

Nothing in this Act shall prevent any court in the United Kingdom from staying, sisting, striking out or dismissing any proceedings before it, on the ground of *forum non conveniens* or otherwise, where to do so is not inconsistent with the 1968 Convention.

General

50.—*Interpretation: general.*   **A3.61**

In this Act, unless the contest otherwise requires—

"the Accession Convention" has the meaning given by section 1(1);

"Article" and references to sub-divisions of numbered Articles are to be construed in accordance with section 1(2)(b);

"association" means an unincorporated body of persons;

"Contracting State'" has the meaning given by section 1(3);

"the 1968 Convention" has the meaning given by section 1(1), and references to that Convention and to provisions of it are to be construed in accordance with section 1(2)(a);

"the Conventions" has the meaning given by section 1(1);

"corporation" means a body corporate, and includes a partnership subsisting under the law of Scotland;

"court," without more, includes a tribunal;

"court of law," in relation to the United Kingdom, means any of the following courts, namely—

  (a) the House of Lords,

  (b) in England and Wales or Northern Ireland, the Court of Appeal, the High Court, the Crown Court, a county court and a magistrates' court,

  (c) in Scotland, the Court of Session and a sheriff court;

"the Crown" is to be construed in accordance with section 51(2);

"enactment" includes an enactment comprised in Northern Ireland legislation;

"judgment," subject to section 15(1) and 18(2) and to paragraph 1 of

Schedules 6 and 7, means any judgment or order (by whatever name called) given or made by a court in civil proceedings;

"magistrates' court," in relation to Northern Ireland, means a court of summary jurisdiction;

"modifications" includes additions, omissions and alterations;

"overseas country" means any country or territory outside the United Kingdom;

"part of the United Kingdom" means England and Wales, Scotland or Northern Ireland;

"the 1971 Protocol" has the meaning given by section 1(1), and references to that Protocol and to provisions of it are to be construed in accordance with section 1(2)(a);

"rules of court," in relation to any court, means rules, orders or regulations made by the authority having power to make rules, orders or regulations regulating the procedure of that court, and includes—

    (a) in Scotland, Acts of Sederunt;

    (b) in Northern Ireland, Judgment Enforcement Rules;

"statutory provision" means any provision contained in an Act, or in any Northern Ireland legislation, or in—

    (a) subordinate legislation (as defined in section 21(1) of the Interpretation Act 1978); or

    (b) any instrument of a legislative character made under any Northern Ireland legislation;

"tribunal"—

    (a) means a tribunal of any description other than a court of law;

    (b) in relation to an overseas country, includes, as regards matters relating to maintenance within the meaning of the 1968 Convention, any authority having power to give, enforce, vary or revoke a maintenance order.

A3.62   51.—*Application to Crown.*

(1) This Act binds the Crown.

(2) In this section and elsewhere in this Act references to the Crown do not include references to Her Majesty in Her private capacity or to Her Majesty in right of Her Duchy of Lancaster or to the Duke of Cornwall.

52.—*Extent.*

(1) This Act extends to Northern Ireland.

(2) Without prejudice to the power conferred by section 39, Her Majesty may by Order in Council direct that all or any of the provisions of this Act apart from that section shall extend, subject to such modifications as may be specified in the Order, to any of the following territories, that is to say—

    (a) the Isle of Man;

    (b) any of the Channel Islands;

    (c) Gibraltar;

    (d) the Sovereign Base Areas of Akrotiri and Dhekelia (that is to say the areas mentioned in section 2(1) of the Cyprus Act 1960).

53.—*Commencement, transitional provisions and savings.*

(1) This Act shall come into force in accordance with the provisions of Part I of Schedule 13.

(2) The transitional provisions and savings contained in Part II of that Schedule shall have effect in relation to the commencement of the provisions of this Act mentioned in that Part.

54.—*Repeals.*

The enactments mentioned in Schedule 14 are hereby repealed to the extent specified in the third column of that Schedule.

55.—*Short title.*

This Act may be cited as the Civil Jurisdiction and Judgments Act 1982.

SCHEDULE 1   Section 2(2)

[*Schedule 1 contains the text of the 1968 Convention and Annexed Protocol,* **A3.63** *each as amended by the 1978 Accession Convention: see paras. A3.01 to A3.26 above.*]

SCHEDULE 2   Section 2(2)

[*Schedule 2 contains the text of the 1971 Protocol on Interpretation, as amended by the 1978 Accession Convention: see paras. A3.28 to A3.30 above.*]

SCHEDULE 3   Section 2(2)

[*Schedule 3 contains the text of Titles V and VI (Articles 34 to 41) of the 1978 Accession Convention: see paras. A3.34 to A3.36 above.*]

SCHEDULE 4   Section 16

TITLE II OF 1968 CONVENTION AS MODIFIED FOR ALLOCATION OF JURISDICTION WITHIN U.K.

TITLE II

JURISDICTION

Section 1

General Provisions

ARTICLE 2

Subject to the provisions of this **Title**, persons domiciled in a **part of the**   **A3.64** **United Kingdom** shall . . . be sued in the courts of that **part**.

. . . .

ARTICLE 3

Persons domiciled in a **part of the United Kingdom** may be sued in the Courts of another **part of the United Kingdom** only by virtue of the rules set out in Sections 2, **4, 5 and** 6 of this Title.

. . . .

Section 2

Special jurisdiction

ARTICLE 5

A3.65 A person domiciled in a **part of the United Kingdom** may, in another **part of the United Kingdom** be sued:

(1) in matters relating to a contract, in the courts for the place of performance of the obligation in question;

(2) in matters relating to maintenance, in the courts for the place where the maintenance creditor is domiciled or habitually resident or, if the matter is ancillary to proceedings concerning the status of a person, in the court which, according to its own law, has jurisdiction to entertain those proceedings, unless that jurisdiction is based solely on the nationality of one of the parties;

(3) in matters relating to tort, delict or quasi-delict, in the courts for the place where the harmful event occured **or in the case of a threatened wrong is likely to occur;**

(4) as regards a civil claim for damages or restitution which is based on an act giving rise to criminal proceedings, in the court seised of those proceedings, to the extent that that court has jurisdiction under its own law to entertain civil proceedings;

(5) as regards a dispute arising out of the operations of a branch, agency or other establishment, in the courts for the place in which the branch, agency or other establishment is situated;

(6) as settlor, trustee or beneficiary of a trust created by the operation of a statute, or by a written instrument, or created orally and evidenced in writing, in the courts of the **part of the United Kingdom** in which the trust is domiciled;

(7) as regards a dispute concerning the payment of remuneration claimed in respect of the salvage of a cargo or freight, in the court under the authority of which the cargo or freight in question

(a) has been arrested to secure such payment, or

(b) could have been so arrested, but bail or other security has been given;

provided that this provision shall apply only if it is claimed that the defendant has an interest in the cargo or freight or had such an interest at the time of salvage;

(8) in proceedings—

(a) **concerning a debt secured on immovable property; or**

1888

(b) which are brought to assert, declare or determine proprietary or possessory rights, or rights of security, in or
   over movable property, or to obtain authority to dispose
   of movable property,
in the courts of the part of the United Kingdom in which the property is situated.

ARTICLE 5A

Proceedings which have as their object a decision of an organ of a
company or other legal person or an association of natural or legal persons may, without prejudice to the other provisions of this Title, be
brought in the courts of the part of the United Kingdom in which that
company, legal person or association has its seat.

ARTICLE 6

A person domiciled in a **part of the United Kingdom** may, **in another
part of the United Kingdom**, also be sued:
   (1) where he is one of a number of defendants, in the courts for the
       place where any one of them is domiciled;
   (2) as a third party in an action on a warranty or guarantee or in any
       other third-party proceedings, in the court seised of the original
       proceedings, unless these were instituted solely with the object
       of removing him from the jurisdiction of the court which would
       be competent in his case;
   (3) on a counterclaim arising from the same contract or facts on
       which the original claim was based, in the court in which the
       original claim is pending.

ARTICLE 6A

Where by virtue of this **Title** a court of a **part of the United Kingdom**
has jurisdiction in actions relating to liability arising from the use or operation of a ship, that court, or any other court substituted for this purpose
by the internal law of that **part**, shall also have jurisdiction over claims for
limitation of such liability.

. . . .

Section 4

Jurisdiction over consumer contracts

ARTICLE 13

In proceedings concerning a contract concluded by a person for a pur-   **A3.66**
pose which can be regarded as being outside his trade or profession, hereinafter called "the consumer," jurisdiction shall be determined by this

Section, without prejudice to the provisions of Articles . . . 5(5) **and (8)(b)**, if it is:

    (1) a contract for the sale of goods on instalment credit terms, or

    (2) a contract for a loan repayable by instalments, or for any other form of credit, made to finance the sale of goods, or

    (3) any other contract for the supply of goods or a contract for the supply of services, and . . . the consumer took in **the part of the United Kingdom in which he is domiciled** the steps necessary for the conclusion of the contract.

. . . .

This Section shall not apply to contracts of transport **or insurance**.

ARTICLE 14

A consumer may bring proceedings against the other party to a contract either in the courts of the **part of the United Kingdom** in which that party is domiciled or in the courts of the **part of the United Kingdom** in which he is himself domiciled.

Proceedings may be brought against a consumer by the other party to the contract only in the court of the **part of the United Kingdom** in which the consumer is domiciled.

These provisions shall not affect the right to bring a counterclaim in the court in which, in accordance with this Section, the original claim is pending.

ARTICLE 15

The provisions of this Section may be departed from only by an agreement:

    (1) which is entered into after the dispute has arisen, or

    (2) which allows the consumer to bring proceedings in courts other than those indicated in this Section, or

    (3) which is entered into by the consumer and the other party to the contract, both of whom are at the time of the conclusion of the contract domiciled or habitually resident in the same **part of the United Kingdom** and which confers jurisdiction on the courts of that **part**, provided that such an agreement is not contrary to the law of that **part**.

Section 5

Exclusive jurisdiction

ARTICLE 16

A3.67 The following courts shall have exclusive jurisdiction, regardless of domicile:

    (1) in proceedings which have as their object rights *in rem* in, or ten-

ancies of, immovable property, the courts of the **part of the United Kingdom** in which the property is situated;

(2) in proceedings which have as their object the validity of the constitution, the nullity or the dissolution of companies or other legal persons or associations of natural or legal persons, or the decisions of their organs, the courts of the **part of the United Kingdom** in which the company, legal person or association has its seat;

(3) in proceedings which have as their object the validity of entries in public registers, the courts of the **part of the United Kingdom** in which the register is kept;

. . . .

(5) in proceedings concerned with the enforcement of judgments, the courts of the **part of the United Kingdom** in which the judgment has been or is to be enforced.

Section 6

Prorogation of jurisdiction

ARTICLE 17

If the parties . . . have agreed that a court or the courts of a **part of the United Kingdom** are to have jurisdiction to settle any disputes which have arisen or which may arise in connection with a particular legal relationship, **and, apart from this Schedule, the agreement would be effective to confer jurisdiction under the law of that part,** that court or those courts shall have . . . jurisdiction . . .   **A3.68**

The court or courts of a **part of the United Kingdom** on which a trust instrument has conferred jurisdiction shall have . . . jurisdiction in any proceedings brought against a settlor, trustee or beneficiary, if relations between these persons or their rights or obligations under the trust are involved.

Agreements or provisions of a trust instrument conferring jurisdiction shall have no legal force if they are contrary to the provisions of Article . . . 15, or if the courts whose jurisdiction they purport to exclude have exclusive jurisdiction by virtue of Article 16.

. . . .

ARTICLE 18

Apart from jurisdiction derived from other provisions of this **Title,** a court of a **part of the United Kingdom** before whom a defendant enters an appearance shall have jurisdiction. This rule shall not apply where appearance was entered solely to contest the jurisdiction, or where another court has exclusive jurisdiction by virtue of Article 16.

Section 7

Examination as to jurisdiction and admissibility

ARTICLE 19

A3.69   Where a court of a **part of the United Kingdom** is seised of a claim which is principally concerned with a matter over which the courts of another **part of the United Kingdom** have exclusive jurisdiction by virtue of Article 16, it shall declare of its own motion that it has no jurisdiction.

ARTICLE 20

Where a defendant domiciled in one **part of the United Kingdom** is sued in a court of another **part of the United Kingdom** and does not enter an appearance, the court shall declare of its own motion that it has no jurisdiction unless its jurisdiction is derived from the provisions of this **Title**.

The court shall stay the proceedings so long as it is not shown that the defendant has been able to receive the document instituting the proceedings or an equivalent document in sufficient time to enable him to arrange for his defence, or that all necessary steps have been taken to this end.

. . . .

Section 9

Provisional, including protective measures

ARTICLE 24

A3.70   Application may be made to the courts of a **part of the United Kingdom** for such provisional, including protective, measures as may be available under the law of that **part,** even if, under this **Title,** the courts of another **part of the United Kingdom** have jurisdiction as to the substance of the matter.

SCHEDULE 5   Section 17

PROCEEDINGS EXCLUDED FROM SCHEDULE 4

Proceedings under the Companies Acts

A3.71   1. Proceedings for the winding up of a company under the Insolvency Act 1986 or the Companies Act (Northern Ireland) 1960, or proceedings relating to a company as respects which jurisdiction is conferred on the court having winding-up jurisdiction under either of those Acts.[16]

---

[16] See para. 45.31 above, n. †.

The Civil Jurisdiction and Judgments Act 1982

Patents, trade marks, designs and similar rights

2. Proceedings concerned with the registration or validity of patents, trade marks, designs or other similar rights required to be deposited or registered.

Protection of Trading Interests Act 1980

3. Proceedings under section 6 of the Protection of Trading Interests Act 1980 (recovery of sums paid or obtained pursuant to a judgment for multiple damages).

Appeals, etc. from tribunals

4. Proceedings on appeal from, or for review of, decisions of tribunals.

Maintenance and similar payments to local and other public authorities

5. Proceedings for, or otherwise relating to, an order under any of the following provisions—
   (a) section 47 or 51 of the Child Care Act 1980, section 80 of the Social Work (Scotland) Act 1968 or section 156 of the Children and Young Persons Act (Northern Ireland) 1968 (contributions in respect of children in care, etc.);
   (b) section 49 or 50 of the Child Care Act 1980, section 81 of the Social Work (Scotland) Act 1968 or section 159 of the Children and Young Persons Act (Northern Ireland) 1968 (applications for, or for variation of, affiliation orders in respect of children in care, etc.);
   (c) section 43 of the National Assistance Act 1948, section 18 of the Supplementary Benefits Act 1976, section 24 of the Social Security Act 1986, or any enactment applying it in Northern Ireland and corresponding to it, Article 101 of the Health and Personal Social Services (Northern Ireland) Order 1972 or Article 23 of the Supplementary Benefits (Northern Ireland) Order 1977 (recovery of cost of assistance or benefit from person liable to maintain the assisted person);
   (d) section 44 of the National Assistance Act 1948, section 19 of the Supplementary Benefits Act 1976, section 25 of the Social Security Act 1986, or any enactment applying it in Northern Ireland and corresponding to it, Article 102 of the Health and Personal Social Services (Northern Ireland) Order 1972 or Article 24 of the Supplementary Benefits (Northern Ireland) Order 1977 (applications for, or for variation of, affiliation orders in respect of children for whom assistance or benefit provided).[17]

---

[17] See para. 45.35 above, n. †.

Proceedings under certain conventions, etc.

6. Proceedings brought in any court in pursuance of—
    (a) any statutory provision which, in the case of any convention to
        which Article 57 applies (conventions relating to specific matters
        which override the general rules in the 1968 Convention),
        implements the convention or makes provision with respect to
        jurisdiction in any field to which the convention relates; and
    (b) any rule of law so far as it has the effect of implementing any
        such convention.

Certain admiralty proceedings in Scotland

7. Proceedings in Scotland in an Admiralty cause where the jurisdiction of
the Court of Session or, as the case may be, of the sheriff is based on
arrestment *in rem* or *ad fundandam jurisdictionem* of a ship, cargo or freight.

Register of aircraft mortgages

8. Proceedings for the rectification of the register of aircraft mortgages
kept by the Civil Aviation Authority.

Continental Shelf Act 1964

9. Proceedings brought in any court in pursuance of an order under section 23 of the Oil and Gas (Enterprise) Act 1982.[18]

Proceedings concerning financial services agencies

10. Such proceedings as are mentioned in section 188 of the Financial Services Act 1986.[19]

SCHEDULE 6   Section 18

ENFORCEMENT OF U.K. JUDGMENTS (MONEY PROVISIONS)

Preliminary

A3.72 1. In this Schedule—

"judgment" means any judgment to which section 18 applies and references to the giving of a judgment shall be construed accordingly;
"money provision" means a provision for the payment of one or more
sums of money;
"prescribed" means prescribed by rules of court.

---

[18] See para. 45.39 above, n. †.
[19] See para. 45.40 above, n. †.

Certificates in respect of judgments

2.—(1) Any interested party who wishes to secure the enforcement in another part of the United Kingdom of any money provisions contained in a judgment may apply for a certificate under this Schedule.

(2) The application shall be made in the prescribed manner to the proper officer of the original court, that is to say—

- (a) in relation to a judgment within paragraph (a) of the definition of "judgment" in section 18(2), the court by which the judgment or order was given or made;
- (b) in relation to a judgment within paragraph (b) of that definition, the court in which the judgment or order is entered;
- (c) in relation to a judgment within paragraph (c) of that definition, the court in whose books the document is registered;
- (d) in relation to a judgment within paragraph (d) of that definition, the tribunal by which the award or order was made;
- (e) in relation to a judgment within paragraph (e) of that definition, the court which gave the judgment or made the order by virtue of which the award has become enforceable as mentioned in that paragraph.

3. A certificate shall not be issued under this Schedule in respect of a judgment unless under the law of the part of the United Kingdom in which the judgment was given—

- (a) either—
  - (i) the time for bringing an appeal against the judgment has expired, no such appeal having been brought within that time; or
  - (ii) such an appeal having been brought within that time, that appeal has been finally disposed of; and
- (b) enforcement of the judgment is not for the time being stayed or suspended, and the time available for its enforcement has not expired.

4.—(1) Subject to paragraph 3, on an application under paragraph 2 the proper officer shall issue to the applicant a certificate in the prescribed form—

- (a) stating the sum or the aggregate of the sums (including any costs or expenses) payable under the money provisions contained in the judgment, the rate of interest, if any, payable thereon and the date or time from which any such interest began to accrue;
- (b) stating that the conditions specified in paragraph 3(a) and (b) are satisfied in relation to the judgment; and
- (c) containing such other particulars as may be prescribed.

(2) More than one certificate may be issued under this Schedule (simultaneously or at different times) in respect of the same judgment.

Registration of certificates

5.—(1) Where a certificate has been issued under this Schedule in any part of the United Kingdom, any interested party may, within six months from the date of its issue, apply in the prescribed manner to the proper officer of the superior court in any other part of the United Kingdom for the certificate to be registered in that court.

(2) In this paragraph "superior court" means, in relation to England and Wales or Northern Ireland, the High Court and, in relation to Scotland, the Court of Session.

(3) Where an application is duly made under this paragraph to the proper officer of a superior court, he shall register the certificate in that court in the prescribed manner.

General effect of registration

A3.73 6.—(1) A certificate registered under this Schedule shall, for the purposes of its enforcement, be of the same force and effect, the registering court shall have in relation to its enforcement the same powers, and proceedings for or with respect to its enforcement may be taken, as if the certificate has been a judgment originally given in the registering court and had (where relevant) been entered.

(2) Sub-paragraph (1) is subject to the following provisions of this Schedule and to any provision made by rules of court as to the manner in which and the conditions subject to which a certificate registered under this Schedule may be enforced.

Costs or expenses

7. Where a certificate is registered under this Schedule, the reasonable costs or expenses of and incidental to the obtaining of the certificate and its registration shall be recoverable as if they were costs or expenses stated in the certificate to be payable under a money provision contained in the original judgment.

Interest

8.—(1) Subject to any provision made under sub-paragraph (2), the debt resulting, apart from paragraph 7, from the registration of the certificate shall carry interest at the rate, if any, stated in the certificate from the date or time so stated.

(2) Provision may be made by rules of court as to the manner in which and the periods by reference to which any interest payable by virtue of sub-paragraph (1) is to be calculated and paid, including provision for such interest to cease to accrue as from a prescribed date.

(3) All such sums as are recoverable by virtue of paragraph 7 carry interest as if they were the subject of an order for costs or expenses made by the registering court on the date of registration of the certificate.

(4) Except as provided by this paragraph sums payable by virtue of the registration of a certificate under this Schedule shall not carry interest.

Stay or sisting of enforcement in certain cases

9. Where a certificate in respect of a judgment has been registered under this Schedule, the registering court may, if it is satisfied that any person

against whom it is sought to enforce the certificate is entitled and intends to apply under the law of the part of the United Kingdom in which the judgment was given for any remedy which would result in the setting aside or quashing of the judgment, stay (or, in Scotland, sist) proceedings for the enforcement of the certificate, on such terms as it thinks fit, for such period as appears to the court to be reasonably sufficient to enable the application to be disposed of.

Cases in which registration of a certificate must or may be set aside

10. Where a certificate has been registered under this Schedule, the registering court—
   (a) shall set aside the registration if, on an application made by any interested party, it is satisfied that the registration was contrary to the provisions of this Schedule;
   (b) may set aside the registration if, on an application so made, it is satisfied that the matter in dispute in the proceedings in which the judgment in question was given had previously been the subject of a judgment by another court or tribunal having jurisdiction in the matter.

SCHEDULE 7   Section 18

ENFORCEMENT OF U.K. JUDGMENTS (NON-MONEY PROVISIONS)

Preliminary

1. In this Schedule—   **A3.74**
   "judgment" means any judgment to which section 18 applies and references to the giving of a judgment shall be construed accordingly;
   "non-money provision" means a provision for any relief not requiring payment of a sum of money;
   "prescribed" means prescribed by rules of court.

Certified copies of judgments

2.—(1) Any interested party who wishes to secure the enforcement in another part of the United Kingdom of any non-money provisions contained in a judgment may apply for a certified copy of the judgment.

(2) The application shall be made in the prescribed manner to the proper officer of the original court, that is to say—
   (a) in relation to a judgment within paragraph (a) of the definition of "judgment" in section 18(2), the court of which the judgment or order was given or made;
   (b) in relation to a judgment within paragraph (b) of that definition, the court in which the judgment or order is entered;
   (c) in relation to a judgment within paragraph (c) of that definition, the court in whose books the document is registered;
   (d) in relation to a judgment within paragraph (d) of that definition, the tribunal by which the award or order was made;

1897

(e) in relation to a judgment within paragraph (e) of that definition, the court which gave the judgment or made the order by virtue of which the award has become enforceable as mentioned in that paragraph.

3. A certified copy of a judgment shall not be issued under this Schedule in respect of a judgment unless under the law of the part of the United Kingdom in which the judgment was given—
    (a) either—
        (i) the time for bringing an appeal against the judgment has expired, no such appeal having been brought within that time; or
        (ii) such an appeal having been brought within that time, that appeal has been finally disposed of; and
    (b) enforcement of the judgment is not for the time being stayed or suspended, and the time available for its enforcement has not expired.

4.—(1) Subject to paragraph 3, on an application under paragraph 2 the proper officer shall issue to the applicant—
    (a) a certified copy of the judgment (including any money provisions or excepted provisions which it may contain); and
    (b) a certificate stating that the conditions specified in paragraph 3(a) and (b) are satisfied in relation to the judgment.

(2) In sub-paragraph (1)(a) "excepted provision" means any provision of a judgment which is excepted from the application of section 18 by subsection (5) of that section.

(3) There may be issued under this Schedule (simultaneously or at different times)—
    (a) more than one certified copy of the same judgment; and
    (b) more than one certificate in respect of the same judgment.

Registration of certificates

5.—(1) Where a certified copy of a judgment has been issued under this Schedule in any part of the United Kingdom, any interested party may apply in the prescribed manner to the superior court in any other part of the United Kingdom for the judgment to be registered in that court.

(2) In this paragraph "superior court" means, in relation to England and Wales or Northern Ireland, the High Court and, in relation to Scotland, the Court of Session.

(3) An application under this paragraph for the registration of a judgment must be accompanied by—
    (a) a certified copy of the judgment issued under this Schedule; and
    (b) a certificate issued under paragraph 4(1)(b) in respect of the judgment not more than six months before the date of the application.

(4) Subject to sub-paragraph (5), where an application under this paragraph is duly made to a superior court, the court shall order the whole of the judgment as set out in the certified copy to be registered in that court in the prescribed manner.

(5) A judgment shall not be registered under this Schedule by the superior court in any part of the United Kingdom if compliance with the non-money provisions would involve breach of the law of that part of the United Kingdom.

General effect of registration

6.—(1) The non-money provisions contained in a judgment registered under this Schedule shall, for the purposes of their enforcement, be of the same force and effect, the registering court shall have in relation to their enforcement the same powers, and proceedings for or with respect to their enforcement may be taken, as if the judgment containing them had been originally given in the registering court and had (where relevant) been entered.

A3.75

(2) Sub-paragraph (1) is subject to the following provisions of this Schedule and to any provision made by rules of court as to the manner in which and the conditions subject to which the non-money provisions contained in the judgment registered under this Schedule may be enforced.

Costs or expenses

7.—(1) Where a judgment is registered under this Schedule, the reasonable costs or expenses of and incidental to—
- (a) the obtaining of the certified copy of the judgment and of the necessary certificate under paragraph 4(1)(b) in respect of it; and
- (b) the registration of the judgment,

shall be recoverable as if on the date of registration there had also been registered in the registering court a certificate under Schedule 6 in respect of the judgment and as if those costs or expenses were costs or expenses stated in that certificate to be payable under a money provision contained in the judgment.

(2) All such sums as are recoverable by virtue of sub-paragraph (1) shall carry interest as if they were the subject of an order for costs or expenses made by the registering court on the date of registration of the judgment.

Stay or sisting of enforcement in certain cases

8. Where a judgment has been registered under this Schedule, the registering court may, if it is satisfied that any person against whom it is sought to enforce the judgment is entitled and intends to apply under the law of the part of the United Kingdom in which the judgment was given for any remedy which would result in the setting aside or quashing of the judgment, stay (or, in Scotland, sist) proceedings for the enforcement of the judgment, on such terms as it thinks fit, for such period as appears to the court to be reasonably sufficient to enable the application to be disposed of.

Cases in which registration of a certificate must or may be set aside

10. Where a judgment has been registered under this Schedule, the registering court—

(a) shall set aside the registration if, on an application made by any interested party, it is satisfied that the registration was contrary to the provisions of this Schedule;

(b) may set aside the registration if, on an application so made, it is satisfied that the matter in dispute in the proceedings in which the judgment was given had previously been the subject of a judgment by another court or tribunal having jurisdiction in the matter.

SCHEDULE 8   Section 20

A3.76 [*This Schedule contains rules as to jurisdiction in Scotland. It is set out at paras. 47.01 to 47.05 above and it is not reproduced here.*]

SCHEDULE 9   Section 21

[*This Schedule contains a list of proceedings excluded from Schedule 8. It is set out at para. 47.06 above and it is not reproduced here.*]

SCHEDULE 10   Section 35(1)

[*This Schedule contains amendments to the Foreign Judgments (Reciprocal Enforcement) Act 1933. It is set out at paras. 47.08 and 47.09 above and it is not reproduced here.*]

SCHEDULE 11   Section 37(1)

[*This Schedule contains minor amendments relating to maintenance orders. It is set out at paras. 47.11 to 47.16 above and it is not reproduced here.*]

SCHEDULE 12   Sections 15(4), 23(2) and 36(6)

[*This Schedule contains certain consequential amendments. It is set out at paras. 47.17 to 47.19 above and it is not reproduced here.*]

SCHEDULE 13   Section 53

[*This Schedule contains commencement and transitional provisions and savings. It is set out at paras. 47.20 to 47.24 above and it is not reproduced here.*]

SCHEDULE 14   Section 54

[*This Schedule contains repeals. It is set out at para. 47.26 above and it is not reproduced here.*]

APPENDIX 4

SELECTED FORMS AND PRECEDENTS

Forms and precedents which are not readily available to the practitioner **A4.1** elsewhere are included in this Appendix. In addition, precedents for the two applications most likely to be made in practice on the registration of a judgment given in another Contracting State are included at paragraphs A4.3 and A4.4. Various other forms and precedents appropriate for most purposes connected with the 1968 Convention and 1982 Act may be found in Chitty and Jacob, *Queen's Bench Forms* (21st edition) and in *Atkin's Court Forms*.

A. PROCEEDINGS FOR INTERIM RELIEF IN THE ABSENCE OF SUBSTANTIVE PROCEEDINGS

The power of the High Court, pursuant to section 25 of the 1982 Act, to **A4.2** grant interim relief in the absence of proceedings concerning the substance of the dispute is discussed at paragraphs 7.29 and 43.03 *et seq.* above.

The proceedings must usually be commenced by writ (R.S.C., Ord. 5, r. 2) and it is suggested that the relief claimed and the factual basis for it should be pleaded in a Statement of Claim. The following is a suggested draft in outline:

IN THE HIGH COURT OF JUSTICE   19   No.
QUEEN'S BENCH DIVISION

BETWEEN:

A.B.   Plaintiff

and

C.D.   Defendant

STATEMENT OF CLAIM

1. ⎫
2. ⎬   *Set out briefly the nature of the*
3. ⎭   *substantive claim.*

4. Proceedings have been [*or* are to be] commenced by the Plaintiff against the Defendant in the [*name of court*] in [*name of place and country*] in respect of the said claim. Such proceedings are [*or* will be] proceedings whose subject-matter is within the scope of the 1968 Convention.

> *Set out briefly the factual basis of the claim for interim relief, e.g. in the case of a straightforward Mareva injunction:*

5. The Defendant has assets [*or* There are grounds for believing that the Defendant has assets] within England and Wales from which the judgment likely to be obtained by the Plaintiff may be satisfied.

Particulars

[Brief particulars of the assets]

6. There are grounds for believing that unless restrained by injunction the Defendant will [*or* there is a risk that the Defendant may] remove such assets from England and Wales [*or* from the territory of the Contracting States to the 1968 Convention] or otherwise deal with or dispose of such assets.

Particulars

[Brief particulars of the grounds for belief that the Defendant will remove or deal with assets.]

And the Plaintiff claims:

> *Set out the interim relief claimed, e.g.:*

1. An injunction restraining the Defendant, by himself, his servants or agents or otherwise, from removing from the jurisdiction of this Court or from disposing, transferring, charging or in any way howsoever dealing with any of his assets within the jurisdiction [so as to reduce the value of such assets within the jurisdiction below the sum of £   :   ];

2. Further or other relief.

Served [*etc.*]

1902

An application may then be made by summons for the grant of the interim relief claimed in the action. The application should be made in the normal way on affidavit. In addition to stating details of the dispute and the evidence relied on for the grant of the interim relief, the deponent should state the basis (or bases) on which the foreign court has jurisdiction over the defendant in respect of the substantive dispute. If the relief is granted *ex parte* in the first instance, the resulting order cannot be enforced in the other Contracting States unless and until the defendant has had an opportunity to challenge the order *inter partes*: see paragraph 27.27 above.

B. REGISTRATION IN THE HIGH COURT OF A JUDGMENT GIVEN IN ANOTHER CONTRACTING STATE

1. Affidavit in support of an application for registration

The registration of judgments (other than maintenance orders) in the **A4.3** High Court for the purposes of their enforcement is discussed in Chapter 10 above. The application is made in the first instance *ex parte* on affidavit, usually to the Master. The affidavit should comply with the requirements of the Rules of the Supreme Court, Order 71, rule 28. The following is a suggested draft affidavit in outline:

IN THE HIGH COURT OF JUSTICE   19   No.
QUEEN'S BENCH DIVISION

In the Matter of the Civil Jurisdiction and Judgments Act 1982 (section 4).

And in the Matter of Part III of Order 71 of the Rules of the Supreme Court 1965.

BETWEEN:

A.B.	Plaintiff
and	
C.D.	Defendant

I, [*full name, address and occupation or description of deponent*], make oath and say as follows:

1. I am the Plaintiff's solicitor and the matters to which I depose herein are known to me from the instructions which I have received from the Plaintiff and from [*name and address of foreign lawyer*], who is the Plaintiff's lawyer in [*other Contracting State*] and from a perusal of the documents in my possession. I verily believe them to be true.

2. By a judgment dated [*date*] of the [*name of court*] in [*name of place and country*], the Defendant was ordered to pay the Plaintiff the sum of [*state sum in the currency of the judgment*], together with [*sum*] by way of costs [*or nature of the order*].

3. There is now produced and shown to me marked "XYZ 1" a paginated bundle containing the following documents:

   (1) the said judgment [*or a copy of the said judgment duly authenticated by the seal of the [name of the court of origin]*] [*or a copy of the said judgment duly authenticated by being certified by [name], a judge [or an officer] of the [name of court of origin], to be a true copy of a judgment given by that court*], (pages   to   );

(2) a translation of the said judgment into English certified by a notary public [*or* by [*name*], a [*nature of qualification*], who is qualified in [*Contracting State*] to translate such documents] [*or* authenticated by the affidavit of [*name*]], (pages   to   );

(3) [*specify documents*], which show that according to the law of [*Contracting State of origin*] the said judgment is enforceable and has been served on the Defendant (pages   to   ), together with translations thereof certified as aforesaid (pages   to   );

(4) [*in the case of judgments in default*] the original [*or* a certified true copy] of [*specify documents, e.g. a huissier's* certificate, *or* an affidavit] establishing that the document instituting the proceedings was served on the Defendant on [*date*] (pages   to   ), together with a translation thereof, certified as aforesaid (pages   to   );

(5) [*where the Plaintiff was in receipt of legal aid in the state of origin*] [*specify documents*], which show that the Plaintiff benefited in [*name of Contracting State of origin*] from legal aid [*or* from exemption from costs or expenses] (pages   to   ), together with a translation thereof, certified as aforesaid.

4. Under the laws of [*Contracting State of origin*], interest is payable on the said judgment at the rate of [*x*] per cent. per annum from the date of the said judgment [*or other date from which interest runs*] until payment [*or other date when interest ceases to run*].

[*Or*: The said judgment does not provide for the payment of a sum of money.]

5. The address for service of the Plaintiff within the jurisdiction of this Court is [*address*].

6. To the best of my knowledge, the name of the Defendant is *C.D.* and his usual [*or* last known] address [*or* place of business] is [*full address*].

7. To the best of my information and belief, the Plaintiff is entitled to enforce the said judgment because he is the person in whose favour the said judgment was expressed to be given [*or other grounds on which the Plaintiff is entitled to enforce the judgment*].

8. [*In the case of a judgment under which money is payable:*] To the best of my information and belief, at the date hereof the said judgment remains wholly unsatisfied [*or* the sum of [*amount and currency*] has been paid in part satisfaction of the said judgment and the said judgment remains unsatisfied to the extent of [*amount and currency*]]. [*If appropriate*: There is now due and owing to the Plaintiff from the Defendant the sum of [*amount and currency*], together with interest as aforesaid].

9. The Plaintiff wishes to obtain the registration of the said judgment [*or* of the following parts of the said judgment] in the High Court of Justice, pursuant to section 4 of the Civil Jurisdiction and Judgments Act 1982 and Article 31 of the 1968 Convention referred to therein. [*If appropriate*: The parts of the said judgment which the Plaintiff wishes to have registered are [*set out or identify relevant parts*]. The Plaintiff applies for an order accordingly.

Sworn [etc.]

This Affidavit is filed on behalf of the Plaintiff.

2. Summons on appeal to the judge against the grant of an order for registration of a judgment given in another Contracting State

A4.4   An appeal against the order for registration may be brought by the person against whom it is sought to enforce the judgment, normally within one month from the date of service of the judgment: see paragraph 10.25 above. This is the first *inter partes* hearing. The appeal must be brought by summons to the judge (R.S.C., Ord. 71, r. 33(1)). The following is an outline draft summons which may be used on such an appeal. The potential grounds for such an appeal are discussed at paragraphs 10.27 *et seq.* above.

IN THE HIGH COURT OF JUSTICE   19   No.
QUEEN'S BENCH DIVISION

In the Matter of the Civil Jurisdiction and Judgments Act 1982 (section 4).

And in the Matter of Part III of Order 71 of the Rules of the Supreme Court 1965.

BETWEEN:

A.B.   Plaintiff

and

C.D.   Defendant

Let all parties attend before the Judge in Chambers in Room   at the Central Office, Royal Courts of Justice, Strand, London WC2A 2LL on   day, the   day of   , 19   at   o'clock in the [   ] noon on the hearing of an appeal on the part of the Defendant against the order of Master dated the   day of   19   , whereby he ordered [*set out Master's order, e.g.: that a judgment of the [name of court] in [name of place and country] be registered under section 4 of the Civil Jurisdiction and Judgments Act 1982*].

The grounds of this appeal are:

[*Set out the grounds of appeal in numbered paragaphs*]

The defendant will apply at the hearing of this appeal for an order that the said order of Master   be set aside, that the plaintiff's application for leave to register the said judgment pursuant to section 4 of the Civil Jurisdiction and Judgments Act 1982 be dismissed, and that the plaintiff do pay the defendant the costs of this appeal to be taxed.

Dated the   day of   19 .

This summons was taken out by

[*name and address of Defendant's solicitors*]

solicitors for the Defendant.

To the above-named *A.B.*
and to [*name and address of plaintiff's solicitors*]
his solicitors.

C. Forms for use under the Hague Service Convention

1. Prescribed form of Request

The following is the English language version of the first form annexed   **A4.5** to the Hague Service Convention (see para. A2.16 above).

Appendix 4

REQUEST

FOR SERVICE ABROAD OF JUDICIAL OR EXTRA JUDICIAL DOCUMENTS

Convention on the service abroad of judicial and extrajudicial documents in civil or commercial matters, signed at The Hague, ... 196 .

Identity and address of the applicant	Address of receiving authority

The undersigned applicant has the honour to transmit—in duplicate—the documents listed below and, in conformity with article 5 of the above-mentioned Convention, requests prompt service of one copy thereof on the addressee, i.e.,
(identity and address) ....
....

(a) in accordance with the provisions of sub-paragraph (a) of the first paragraph of article 5 of the Convention*.

(b) in accordance with the following particular method (sub-paragraph (b) of the first paragraph of article 5)*:
....
....
....

(c) by delivery to the addressee, if he accepts it voluntarily (second paragraph of article 5)*.

The authority is requested to return or to have returned to the applicant a copy of the documents—and of the annexes*—with a certificate as provided on the reverse side.

List of documents

....
....
....
....
....
....
....   Done at .... , the ....
....
....   Signature and/or stamp.

* Delete if inappropriate

2. Prescribed form of Certificate

The following is the English language version of the second of the forms **A4.6**
annexed to the Hague Service Convention (see para. A2.16 above). It
forms the reverse of the form of Request set out at para. A4.5 above.

CERTIFICATE

_____

The undersigned authority has the honour to certify, in conformity with article 6 of the
Convention,

1) that the document has been served*
   — the (date) ....
   — at (place, street, number) ....
   ....

   — in one of the following methods authorised by article 5—
      (a) in accordance with the provisions of sub-paragraph (a) of the first paragraph
          of article 5 of the Convention*.
      (b) in accordance with the following particular method*: ....
      ....
      (c) by delivery to the addressee, who accepted it voluntarily*.

   The documents referred to in the request have been delivered to:
   — (identity and description of person) ....
   ....
   — relationship to the addressee (family, business or other): ....
   ....

2) that the document has not been served, by reason of the following facts*:
   ....
   ....

In conformity with the second paragraph of article 12 of the Convention, the applicant is
requested to pay or reimburse the expenses detailed in the attached statement*.

Annexes

Documents returned: ....
....
....
                             Done at ...., the ....
In appropriate cases, documents establish-
ing the service: Signature and/or stamp.
....
....
....

* Delete if inappropriate.

3. Prescribed form of Summary

A4.7   The following is the English language version of the third of the forms annexed to the Hague Service Convention (see para. A2.16 above). Article 5, fourth paragraph, of the Convention requires that this part of the request be served with the judicial or extrajudicial document. A recommended revised version of this form appears at paragraph A4.8 below.

SUMMARY OF THE DOCUMENT TO BE SERVED

Convention on the service abroad of judicial and extrajudicial documents in civil or commercial matters, signed at The Hague, the .... 196 .

(article 5, fourth paragraph)

Name and address of the requesting authority: ....
....
....

Particulars of the parties*: ....
....
....

JUDICIAL DOCUMENT**

Nature and purpose of the document: ....
....

Nature and purpose of the proceedings and, where appropriate, the amount in dispute:
....
....

Date and place for entering appearance**: ....
....

Court which has given judgment**: ....
....

Date of judgment**: ....
Time limits stated in the document**: ....
....

EXTRAJUDICIAL DOCUMENT**

Nature and purpose of the document: ....
....
....

Time limits stated in the document**: ....
....
....

    * If appropriate, identity and address of the person interested in the transmission of the document.
** Delete if inappropriate.

4. Revised form of Summary

The Fourteenth Session of the Hague Conference on Private Inter-   **A4.8**
national Law recommended the following revised bilingual form of summary, which it recommended should be used in all cases where a judicial
or extrajudicial document is to be served abroad. Despite the terms of the
Convention, it seems that this form may be used in place of that set out at
paragraph A4.7 above. Instructions for filling out this form of notice were
established under the authority of the Hague Convention on Private International Law and these are set out at paragraph A4.9 below.

---

identité et adresse du destinataire
identity and address of the addressee

> [ ]

TRÈS IMPORTANT

LE DOCUMENT CI-JOINT EST DE NATURE JURIDIQUE ET PEUT AFFECTER VOS
DROITS ET OBLIGATIONS, LES 'ELÉMENTS ESSENTIELS DE L'ACTE' VOUS
DONNENT QUELQUES INFORMATIONS SUR SA NATURE ET SON OBJET. IL EST
TOUTEFOIS INDISPENSABLE DE LIRE ATTENTIVEMENT LE TEXTE MÊME DU
DOCUMENT. IL PEUT ÊTRE NÉCESSAIRE DE DEMANDER UN AVIS JURIDIQUE.

SI VOS RESSOURCES SONT INSUFFISANTES, RENSEIGNEZ-VOUS SUR LA POSSIBI-
LITÉ D'OBTENIR L'ASSISTANCE JUDICIAIRE ET LA CONSULTATION JURIDIQUE
SOIT DANS VOTRE PAYS SOIT DANS LE PAYS D'ORIGINE DU DOCUMENT.

LES DEMANDES DE RENSEIGNEMENTS SUR LES POSSIBILITÉS D'OBTENIR
L'ASSISTANCE JUDICIAIRE OU LA CONSULTATION JURIDIQUE DANS LE PAYS
D'ORIGINE DU DOCUMENT PEUVENT ÊTRE ADDRESSÉES:......

IMPORTANT

*THE ENCLOSED DOCUMENT IS OF A LEGAL NATURE AND MAY AFFECT
YOUR RIGHTS AND OBLIGATIONS. THE 'SUMMARY OF THE DOCUMENT TO
BE SERVED' WILL GIVE YOU SOME INFORMATION ABOUT ITS NATURE AND
PURPOSE. YOU SHOULD HOWEVER READ THE DOCUMENT ITSELF CARE-
FULLY. IT MAY BE NECESSARY TO SEEK LEGAL ADVICE.*

*IF YOUR FINANCIAL RESOURCES ARE INSUFFICIENT YOU SHOULD SEEK
INFORMATION ON THE POSSIBILITY OF OBTAINING LEGAL AID OR ADVICE
EITHER IN THE COUNTRY WHERE YOU LIVE OR IN THE COUNTRY WHERE
THE DOCUMENT WAS ISSUED.*

*ENQUIRIES ABOUT THE AVAILABILITY OF LEGAL AID OR ADVICE IN THE
COUNTRY WHERE THE DOCUMENT WAS ISSUED MAY BE DIRECTED TO:......*

Il est recommandé que les mentions imprimées dans cette note soient rédigées en langue française et en langue anglaise et le cas échéant, en outre, dans la langue ou une des langues offi-
cielles de l'Etat d'origine de l'acte. Les blancs pourraient être remplis soit dans la langue de
l'Etat où le document doit être adressé, soit en langue française, soit en langue anglaise.

*It is recommended that the standard terms in the notice be written in English and French and where
appropriate also in the official language, or in one of the official languages of the State in which the
document originated. The blanks could be completed either in the language of the State to which the
document is to be sent, or in English or French.*

Appendix 4

ELÉMENTS ESSENTIELS DE L'ACTE/*SUMMARY OF THE DOCUMENT TO BE SERVED*/ – – – – – – – – –

Nom et adresse de l'autorité requérante
Name and address of the requesting authority
– – –
....
....
....

* Identité des parties
Particulars of the parties
– – –
....
....
....

** ACTE JUDICIAIRE/*JUDICIAL DOCUMENT*/ – – – – – – – – – –

Nature et objet de l'acte
Nature and purpose of the document
– – –
....
....
....

Nature et objet de l'instance, le cas échéant, le montant du litige
Nature and purpose of the proceedings and, where appropriate, the amount in dispute
– – –
....
....
....

** Date et lieu de la comparution
Date and place for entering appearance
– – –
....
....
....

** Juridiction qui a rendu la décision
Court which has given judgment
– – –
....
....
....

** Date de la décision/*Date of judgment*/ – – –
....

** Indication des délais figurant dans l'acte
Time-limits stated in the document
– – –
....
....

** ACTE EXTRAJUDICIAIRE/*EXTRAJUDICIAL DOCUMENT*/ – – – – – – – – –

Nature et objet de l'acte
Nature and purpose of the document
– – –
....
....

** Indication des délais figurant dans l'acte
Time-limits stated in the document
– – –
....
....

* S'il y a lieu, identité et adresse de la personne interessée à la transmission de l'acte
If appropriate, identity and address of the person interested in the transmission of the document
– – –

** Rayer les mentions inutiles/*Delete if inappropriate*/ – – – – – – – – – –

1910

Instructions for filling out the notice

a. identity and address of the addressee

The *name* and *address* of the intended recipient should appear clearly on top of the **A4.9** warning.

In addition, where the document is not sent to or served upon the addressee in his private capacity, he should be informed that he is receiving it, *e.g.* in his capacity as director of a company, tutor, representative of an estate, trustee, receiver in bankruptcy, etc.

b. enquiries about the availability of legal aid or advice in the country where the document was issued may be directed to . . .

Here the *name, address* and where appropriate the *telephone number* should be given of the authority or organisation in the country where legal action is to be taken which is most qualified to give the receipient full details on the availability of legal aid or advice (*e.g.* court, legal aid bureau, law society).

c. name and address of the requesting authority (where appropriate the words "*or authority or person who caused the document to be issued*" are to be added)

Besides the *name* and *address*, it is also recommended to insert in the corresponding blank of this item the *telephone number* of the requesting authority or of the authority (or person) who caused the document to be issued, so that the recipient may in a speedy and informal way enquire there for further details.

In the event that further information is only available elsewhere, the name, address and telephone number of the authority or person concerned should be given in addition.

d. particulars of the parties

The corresponding blanks of this item should be completed with the *names* and *addresses* (perhaps sometimes also the *telephone number*) of the parties, *i.e.* the plaintiff and the respondent. Where an extra-judicial document is concerned, the name and address of the person interested in the transmission of the document should be stated. In the case of a judgment it will be the names of the person entitled to the judgment and the person against whom the judgment is given. If the addressee is one of the parties and the corresponding blank to the item "*identity and address of the addressee*" has been properly completed, it is of course unnecessary to complete this item with all the particulars of that party.

e. judicial and extrajudicial documents

The "SUMMARY OF THE DOCUMENT TO BE SERVED" distinguishes between a "JUDICIAL DOCUMENT" and an "EXTRAJUDICIAL DOCUMENT."

Any document relating to litigation, including summary proceedings or uncontested proceedings, *e.g.* summons, judgment, order or application, is regarded as a *judicial document*. Any other legal document is to be classified as an *extrajudicial document*.

If the document to be sent or served is a judicial document, the capitals "EXTRAJUDICIAL DOCUMENT" should be deleted, and *vice versa*.

f. nature and purpose of the document

The nature and purpose of the document means the legal classification of the document, for example, writ of summons, judgment, order, etc. A brief summary of contents of the document (*e.g.* claim or judgment for divorce, alimony or maintenance, or for damages) falls under the "purpose of the document." When the document relates to legal proceedings, the reference to the purpose of the document may be expressed very briefly since the nature and purpose of the proceedings will be described more in detail under the next item (*g*).

1911

g. nature and purpose of the proceedings and where appropriate the amount in dispute

Under this item, which only relates to judicial documents, the remedy or relief sought by the claimant should be mentioned more in detail than under the preceding item. Thus, for instance, when a sum of money is claimed, the exact sum should be mentioned and, where appropriate, briefly the ground for the claim, *e.g.* damages arising out of a traffic accident.

h. date and place for entering appearance

If inappropriate this item, which relates to judicial documents only, should be deleted.

If the recipient who is to take action on the document sent or served abroad is required to enter appearance before a court or an authority, the exact date and place for entering appearance should be mentioned under this item. In order to avoid any misunderstanding, the *month* should be written in *letters*. If possible it may moreover be appropriate to mention the possible qualifications which are required of a representative, *e.g.* a lawyer authorised by the court concerned.

i. court which has given judgment and date of judgment

If inappropriate these items, which relate to judicial documents only, should be deleted.

These two items do not seem to present any problems which have to be dealt with in these instructions. In some cases it may, however, be appropriate to mention the *address* of the court, *e.g.* when the judgment is a default judgment and the person against whom the judgment is given has the possibility to apply to that court for the re-opening of the judgment on the grounds of default.

j. time-limits stated in the document

If inappropriate this item, which may relate to both judicial and extrajudicial documents, should be deleted.

Any time-limit stated in the document for the institution of legal proceedings or review of a judgment or a decision, should be mentioned under this item.

D. FORM FOR USE UNDER THE HAGUE EVIDENCE CONVENTION

A4.10 The Special Commission of the Hague Conference on Private International Law on the working of the Hague Evidence Convention has recommended the following revised model Request for evidence to be taken abroad.

Request for International Judicial Assistance pursuant to
the Hague Convention of 18 March 1970 on the Taking of Evidence Abroad
in Civil or Commercial Matters

N.B. Under the first paragraph of article 4, the Letter of Request shall be in the language of the authority requested to execute it or be accompanied by a translation into that language. However, the provisions of the second and third paragraphs may permit use of English, French or another language.
In order to avoid confusion, please spell out the name of the month in each date.
Please fill out an original and one copy of this form (use additional space if required).
1 Sender .... *(identity and address)* ....
....
....

2 Central Authority of the Requested   .... (*identity and address*) ....
State   ....

3 Person to whom the executed request is   .... (*identity and address*) ....
to be returned   ....

4 Specification of the date by which the requesting authority requires receipt of the
response to the Letter of Request

Date   ....
Reason for urgency*   ....

IN CONFORMITY WITH ARTICLE 3 OF THE CONVENTION, THE
UNDERSIGNED APPLICANT HAS THE HONOUR TO SUBMIT THE
FOLLOWING REQUEST:

5 *a* Requesting judicial authority (article   .... (*identity and address*) ....
3, *a*)   ....

   b To the competent authority of   .... (*the requested State*) ....
(article 3, *a*)   ....

   c Name of the case and any identifying   ....
number   ....

6 Names and addresses of the parties and
their representatives (including representatives in the requested State*)
(article 3, *b*)

   a Plaintiff   ....

     Representatives   ....

   b Defendant   ....

     Representatives   ....

   c Other parties   ....

     Representatives   ....

7 *a* Nature of the proceedings (divorce, ...
paternity, breach of contract, pro-
duct liability, etc.) (article 3, *c*)

b Summary of complaint

....
....
....
....
....

c Summary of defence and counter-claim*

....
....
....
....
....

d Other necessary information or documents*

....
....
....

8 *a* Evidence to be obtained or other judicial act to be performed (article 3, *d*)

....
....
....

a Purpose of the evidence or judicial act sought

....
....

9 Identity and address of any person to be examined (article 3, *e*)*

....
....
....

10 Questions to be put to the persons to be examined or statement of the subject-matter about which they are to be examined (article 3, *f*)*

....
.... (*or see attached list*) ....
....
....

11 Documents or other property to be inspected (article 3, *g*)*

....
....
....

12 Any requirement that the evidence to be given on oath or affirmation and any special form to be used (article 3, *h*)*

....
(*In the event that the evidence cannot be taken in the manner requested, specify whether it is to be taken in such manner as provided by local law for the formal taking of evidence*).

....

13 Special methods or procedure to be followed (*e.g.* oral or in writing, verbatim, transcript or summary, cross-examination, etc.) (articles 3, *i* and 9)*

....
(*In the event that the evidence cannot be taken in the manner requested, specify whether it is to be taken in such manner as provided by local law*).

....

14 Request for notification of the time and place for the execution of the Request and identity and address of any person to be notified (article 7)*

....
....
....
....
....

15 Request for attendance or participation of judicial personnel of the requesting authority at the execution of the Letter of Request (article 8)*

....
....
....
....

16 Specification of privilege or duty to refuse to give evidence under the law of the State of origin (article 11, *b*)*

....
(*attach copies of relevant laws or regulations*) ....
....

17 The fees and costs incurred which are reimbursable under the second paragraph of article 14 or under article 26 of the Convention will be borne by★   .... *(identity and address)* ....

....

....

....

....

DATE OF REQUEST   ....
SIGNATURE AND SEAL OF THE   ....
REQUESTING AUTHORITY   ....

★ Omit if not applicable.

E. Forms for use in Connection with the Taking of Evidence under the Bilateral Conventions with Germany and Italy

1. Order for appointment of British Consul as special examiner to take evidence of a British or other non-German national in Germany and for issue of Letter of Request to German court to cause the attendance of the witnesses

This form is adapted from the prescribed form in the Rules of the Supreme Court, Appendix A, No. 37. It may be used where it is intended to invoke the provisions of Article 12 of the bilateral convention with Germany, in order to secure the attendance of British witnesses before the special examiner. It may be that the compulsory powers of the German courts could also be used, at the discretion of the German authorities, against persons of some other non-German nationality. See paragraph 8.52 above.

A4.11

IN THE HIGH COURT OF JUSTICE   19   , No.
QUEEN'S BENCH DIVISION

Master   , Master in Chambers

BETWEEN:

                A.B.   Plaintiff

                and

                C.D.   Defendant

Upon hearing solicitors for both sides and upon reading the affidavit(s) of
filed the   day of   19 .

It is ordered:

1. that the British Consul or his deputy at [*place*] be appointed as special examiner for the purpose of taking the examination, cross-examination and re-examination, *viva voce*, on oath or affirmation, of [*name of witness*] of [*address of witness*] and of [*name of witness*] of [*address of witness*], witnesses on the part of the plaintiff [*or* defendant], at [*place*] in the Federal Republic of Germany;

2. that such examination shall be taken in accordance with the English procedure;

3. that the plaintiff's [defendant's] solicitors do give to the defendant's [plaintiff's] solicitors [7] days notice in writing of the date on which they propose to send out this order to Germany for execution;

4. that [4] days after the service of such notice the solicitors for the plaintiff and defendant respectively do exchange the names of their agents at [*place*] to whom notice relating to the examination of the said witnesses may be sent;

5. that [2] days (exclusive of Sundays) before the examination of any witness notice of such examination shall be given by the agent of the party on whose behalf such witness is to be examined to the agent of the other party, unless such notice be dispensed with;

6. that the depositions when taken, together with any documents referred to therein, or certified copies of such documents, or of extracts therefrom, be sent by the examiner, under seal, to the Senior Master of the Queen's Bench Division of the High Court of Justice in England and Wales, Royal Courts of Justice, Strand, London WC2A 2LL [*or* the Registrar at the   District Registry of the High Court, at *address*] on or before the [*date*], or such other day as may be ordered, there to be filed in the proper office;

7. that either party be at liberty to read and give such depositions in evidence at the trial of this action, saving all just exceptions;

8. that the trial of this action be stayed until the filing of such depositions;

9. that a Letter of Request do issue directed to the competent court of the Federal Republic of Germany, requesting such court to cause the evidence of the above-named witness to be taken by the said British Consul or his deputy; and

10. that the costs of and incidental to the application for this order and of such examination be costs in the cause.

Dated the   day of   19

2. Letter of Request to German court to cause the attendance of the witnesses

A4.12   To the President of the Landgericht of [*place*] in the Federal Republic of Germany.

I,   Senior Master of the Queen's Bench Division of the Supreme Court of England and Wales respectfully request the assistance of your court with regard to the following matters.

1.   An action is now pending in the   Division of the High Court of Justice in England and Wales, entitled as follows:—

[*full title and action number*]

in which   of   is plaintiff
and   of   is defendant.

2. The names and addresses of the representatives or agents of the parties are as follows:—

3. It is necessary for the purposes of justice and for the due determination of the matters in dispute between the parties that the following witnesses, who are British nationals resident within the jurisdiction of your court, should be examined on oath or affirmation. The name and address of the witnesses are as follows:—

4. This court has appointed the British Consul or his deputy at [*place*] as special examiner for the purpose of taking the examination of the said witness.

5. I request that for the assistance of the High Court of Justice, you will be pleased to summon the said witness to attend at such time and place as the said British Consul or his deputy shall appoint and that you will take the necessary steps to secure the attendance of the said witness, and the giving of evidence and production of documents by him to the said British Consul or his deputy, making use if necessary of the compulsory powers to which you are entitled.

Dated the   day of   19

3. Order for appointment of British Consul or other person as special examiner to take evidence in Italy and for issue of Letter of Request to Italian court to appoint such person and to cause the attendance of the witnesses

This form is adapted from the prescribed form in the Rules of the **A4.13** Supreme Court, Appendix A, No. 37. It may be used where it is intended to invoke the provisions of Article 12 of the bilateral convention with Italy, in order that the compulsory powers of the Italian courts may be used to secure the attendance of witnesses before the special examiner. Those provisions require that the Italian court appoint the examiner on the proposal of the English court, but there seems to be no reason why the English court should not also make an order appointing the examiner. This has the advantage that the English court itself determines the procedure to be adopted on the examination. See paragraph 8.55 above.

IN THE HIGH COURT OF JUSTICE   19   , No.
QUEEN'S BENCH DIVISION

Master   , Master in Chambers

BETWEEN:

	A.B.	Plaintiff
	and	
	C.D.	Defendant

Upon hearing solicitors for both sides and upon reading the affidavit(s) of
filed the   day of   19   .

It is ordered:

1. that the British Consul or his deputy at [*place*] [*or name of examiner*] be appointed as special examiner for the purpose of taking the examination, cross-examination and re-examination, *viva voce*, on oath or affirmation, of [*name of witness*] of [*address of witness*] and of [*name of witness*] of [*address of witness*], witnesses on the part of the plaintiff [*or* defendant], at [*place*] in Italy;

2. that the examiner shall be at liberty to invite the attendance of the witnesses and the production of documents, but that (save in so far as such powers may be conferred on him by the Italian court) he shall not exercise any compulsory powers;

3. that such examination shall otherwise be taken in accordance with the English procedure;

4. that the plaintiff's [defendant's] solicitors do give to the defendant's [plaintiff's] solicitors [7] days notice in writing of the date on which they propose to send out this order to Germany for execution;

5. that [4] days after the service of such notice the solicitors for the plaintiff and defendant respectively do exchange the names of their agents at [*place*] to whom notice relating to the examination of the said witnesses may be sent;

6. that [2] days (exclusive of Sundays) before the examination of any witness notice of such examination shall be given by the agent of the party on whose behalf such witness is to be examined to the agent of the other party, unless such notice be dispensed with;

7. that the depositions when taken, together with any documents referred to therein, or certified copies of such documents, or of extracts therefrom, be sent by the examiner, under seal, to the Senior Master of the Queen's Bench Division of the High Court of Justice in England

and Wales, Royal Courts of Justice, Strand, London WC2A 2LL [*or* the Registrar at the District Registry of the High Court, at *address*] on or before the [*date*], or such other day as may be ordered, there to be filed in the proper office;

8. that either party be at liberty to read and give such depositions in evidence at the trial of this action, saving all just exceptions;

9. that the trial of this action be stayed until the filing of such depositions;

10. that a Letter of Request do issue directed to the competent judicial authority of Italy, requesting such authority to appoint the said British Consul or his deputy [*or name of examiner*] for the purpose of taking the evidence of the said witnesses; and

11. that the costs of and incidental to the application for this order and of such examination be costs in the cause.

Dated the   day of   19 .

4. Letter of request to Italian judicial authorities for the appointment of an examiner and to cause the attendance of the witnesses

A4.14   To the Procuratore Generale presso la Corte d'Appello of [*place*] in Italy.

I,   Senior Master of the Queen's Bench Division of the Supreme Court of England and Wales respectfully request the assistance of your court with regard to the following matters.

1.   An action is now pending in the   Division of the High Court of Justice in England and Wales, entitled as follows:—

[*full title and action number*]

in which   of   is plaintiff
and   of   is defendant.

2. The names and addresses of the representatives or agents of the parties are as follows:—

3. It is necessary for the purposes of justice and for the due determination of the matters in dispute between the parties that the following witnesses, who are resident within the jurisdiction of your court, should be examined on oath or affirmation. The name and address of the witnesses are as follows:—

4. I request that for the assistance of the High Court of Justice you will be pleased to appoint or secure the appointment of the said British Consul or his deputy at [*place*] [*or name of examiner*] as special examiner for the purpose of taking the examination of the said witnesses.

5. I further request that for the assistance of the High Court of Justice, you will be pleased to summon the said witnesses to attend at such time and place as the said British Consul or his deputy [*or name of examiner*] shall appoint and that you will take the necessary steps to secure the attendance of the said witnesses, and the giving of evidence and production of documents by them to the said British Consul or his deputy [*or name of examiner*], making use if necessary of the compulsory powers to which you are entitled.

Dated the   day of   19 .

INDEX

INDEX

[All references are to paragraph numbers]

CONSUMER CONTRACTS—*cont.*
  jurisdiction agreement,
    Brussels Convention 1968, 19.35
    consumer's benefit, 19.40
    court chosen, 19.37, 19.40
    domicile, 19.41–19.42
    existing dispute, 19.39
    formalities, 19.36
    general, 19.35–19.38
    habitual residence, 19.41–19.42
    parties, 19.38
  other establishments, meaning of,
    19.22, 19.23
  overlapping provisions, 19.07
  plaintiff, consumer, 19.27–19.29
  supplier, domicile, 19.25–19.29
  supply of services, 19.14, 19.16
  See also SALE OF GOODS.
CONTRACT,
  associations, members of, 17.07
  Belgium. *See* BELGIUM.
  Brussels Convention 1968, 17.01,
    17.03 *et seq.*, 34.11–37.12
  breach,
    immovable property, 20.13, 20.14
    liability insurance, 18.25
  consumer. *See* CONSUMER
    CONTRACTS.
  credit, 19.14–19.15
  damages, exemplary, 14.14
  Denmark. *See* DENMARK.
  employment. *See* EMPLOYMENT.
  England and Wales. *See* ENGLAND
    AND WALES.
  France. *See* FRANCE.
  general, 17.03–17.04
  Germany. *See* GERMANY.
  Ireland. *See* IRELAND.
  Italy. *See* ITALY.
  jurisdiction, 17.02–17.30
  jurisdiction agreement. *See*
    JURISDICTION AGREEMENTS.
  matters relating to, 17.05–17.10,
    17.45
  national procedural law, application
    of, 17.11
  Netherlands. *See* NETHERLANDS.
  Northern Ireland. *See* NORTHERN
    IRELAND.
  obligation in question,
    characteristic performance,
      17.26–17.30
    general, 17.18
    general rule, 17.20

CONTRACT—*cont.*
  obligation in question—*cont.*
    multiple, 17.24–17.25
    nature of, 17.22–17.23
    original, 17.21
    summary, 17.19
  penalties, 14.14
  performance, place of, 17.12–17.17
  personal rights, immovable property,
    20.13, 20.14
  pre-accession, 37.11–37.12
  quantum meruit, 17.06
  quasi, 17.06
  sale of goods. *See* SALE OF GOODS.
  Scotland. *See* SCOTLAND.
  standard form, 21.33
  supply of services, 19.14, 19.16
  tenancy, of, 20.13, 20.16–20.12
  transport, 19.34
  United Kingdom. *See* UNITED
    KINGDOM.
CONTRACTUAL OBLIGATIONS
    CONVENTION 1980, 17.14, 17.25,
    19.08, 19.16, 19.23, 19.24, 21.33
CORPORATIONS. *See* COMPANIES.
COSTS,
  Belgium. *See* BELGIUM.
  Brussels Convention 1968,
    enforcement of judgments,
    25.17, 35.14–35.16
  Denmark. *See* DENMARK.
  enforcement of judgment, 25.17
  England and Wales. *See* COSTS, legal
    aid; COSTS, letters of request;
    COSTS, security for; COSTS,
    service of process; COSTS, writs.
  France. *See* FRANCE.
  general, 56.57
  Germany. *See* GERMANY.
  Hague Service Convention 1965, 4.32
  Ireland. *See* IRELAND.
  Italy. *See* ITALY.
  legal aid, 56.74
  letters of request, 8.29
  Luxembourg. *See* LUXEMBOURG.
  Netherlands. *See* NETHERLANDS.
  Northern Ireland. *See* NORTHERN
    IRELAND.
  registration of judgments, 40.10,
    40.23, 46.09, 46.20
  Scotland. *See* SCOTLAND.
  security for,
    amount of, 6.15
    application for, 6.14

Index

Index

Index

Index

Index

Index

Index

Index

1966